THE DEPRESSION YEARS

THE DEPRESSION YEARS

As Reported By

The New York Times

Edited By

Arleen Keylin

Introduction By

Sanford L. Chernoff

NYT

ARNO PRESS

NEW YORK • 1976

Distributed by BOOK SALES, INC., 110 Enterprise Avenue, Secaucus, N.J. 07094

A Note to the Reader

Original copies of *The New York Times* were not available to the publisher. This volume, therefore, was created from 35mm microfilm.

Frontispiece photograph courtesy of Wide World Photos

Library of Congress Cataloging in Publication Data
Main entry under title:
The Depression years.
1. Depression—1929—United States. I. Keylin, Arleen. II. New York times.
HB3717.1929.D46 330.9'73'0916 76-23428
ISBN 0-405-09546-5

Assistant to the Editor: Suri Fleischer
Editorial Assistant: Sandra Jones

Manufactured in the United States of America

2 3 4 5 6 7 8 9 10

CONTENTS

INTRODUCTION

The 1920s were exciting years for Americans — a **very** long and **very** frenetic party. Riding high on a wave of economic prosperity, people were blindly optimistic and looked ahead to unlimited progress. Nothing could go wrong. "Every day, in every way, I'm getting better and better," chanted Emile Coue, whose basic "faith cure" philosophy became the litany of the era.

Suddenly everything changed. Almost overnight the nation was faced with disaster. The great economic machine failed and with it failed the fortunes of the super rich and the very lives of the working classes were in danger. The tide of economic well-being crested in 1929 and there were no barriers, private or public, to stem the economic chaos that rapidly affected every aspect of national life.

Millions of men and women were engulfed by the disaster. Some of them had helped to build the economic system and others had been instrumental in directing it. True enough, it had faltered before, but it had never completely stopped. Now people were helpless as their friends, neighbors, and relatives lost their jobs. Community banking and business empires tumbled into financial ruin and dragged down both employer and employee. The bread lines formed, the public dole and the Hooverville became an integral part of the "American way," along with bleak poverty, labor violence and a general feeling of bitterness and despair. Once proud workers lost their livelihood and their pride. Hunger stalked a nation to which millions had emigrated many years before — to escape famine and poverty. Instead of patriotism, there was hopelessness. Anti-establishment figures — including gangsters — were revered as much as they were feared. They took what they wanted by force. The desperate veterans of World War I tried to get what was legitimately theirs — their bonuses — by demonstrating in front of the Capitol. They were met by American troops and driven back with firearms and gas. Survival became more important than virtue.

Suffering under similar economic woes, other countries sought totalitarianism as a remedy. Mussolini wanted to carve out a new Roman Empire and the Japanese elected to secure an economic sphere of influence through force of arms. Franco waged war against his own people in a test case of Fascist aggression. The end of the 1930s brought the most destructive war in history, unleashed by Adolf Hitler and justified by his myth of Aryan supremacy. In a slightly older totalitarian system, Joseph Stalin devoured rivals and former friends and secured an unchallenged position as absolute "Tsar" over the proletarian masses. Would the United States take the same direction? The answer was "no."

One of the chief reasons for the survival of democracy in crisis-torn America was the New Deal. It was radical and innovative, but it was **not** totalitarian. Brought into operation by Franklin Delano Roosevelt, anything but a fiery revolutionary, this new economic program was well within the tradition of American pragmatism and was not wed to a dogmatic or ideological frame of reference. This truly profound transformation in the role of Government in society and economics was based on Keynsian economic thought and justified by a loose interpretation of the responsibilities of the National Government as outlined in the Constitution.

From the 9th of March, 1933, through June 16th of the same year, a special session of Congress succeeded in reversing the downward trend of American life. In only one hundred days, the entire country was given new hope as well as new remedies to resolve its grave problems. The Emergency Banking Act helped to end the money panic. The Volstead Act was repealed and the sale of some alcoholic beverages produced new tax revenues. The first unemployment relief measures were implemented and the Civilian Conservation Corps was created. The United States officially abandoned the gold standard. The purchasing power of agricultural producers was restored through the Agricultural Adjustment Act and the Tennessee Valley Authority was established to provide both work and a new source of energy. Unemployment insurance came into being, the Federal Deposit System was organized, and the National Industrial Recovery Act was designed to revive industrial and business activity and to reduce unemployment. Step by step, the American people were being led out of the crisis by leaders who were determined to bring back economic and social stability and, at the same time, preserve a democratic way of life. The excitement of these times of innovation and the determination of President Roosevelt characterized the entire decade.

But the 1930s also had a lighter side. Americans became fascinated with speed. The airplane, a relatively new invention, was rapidly transformed into a viable means of transporation. Daring pioneers — Lindbergh, Coste, Earhart, Post, Howard Hughes — took their flying machines across oceans and poles. The world became smaller. Short skirts became much longer and the Charleston was replaced by the Big Apple. College kids swallowed goldfish and both tots and adults tapped along behind Shirley Temple. On motion picture screens the world over hundreds of beautiful girls made heavenly music on a forest of harps while Fred Astaire whirled Ginger Rogers around and around. On just as many occasions as time and budget allowed, people rushed to escape their economic and political problems. The world of entertainment came to their rescue.

It would be difficult to capture the 1930s in a more fascinating or vivid way than in this book. The front pages of THE NEW YORK TIMES breathe life into the history of this extremely complicated decade. Such an interesting presentation allows the reader to confront each new event and every important personality in much the same way that they were viewed by contemporary readers of **THE NEW YORK TIMES** — day-by-day, crisis-by-crisis, success-by-success.

Sanford L. Chernoff

July 1976

THE DEPRESSION YEARS

Wall Street on October 29

The mood of Wall Street on October 29 can be seen on the faces in this crowd outside the Stock Exchange.

Crowds gathered outside the Stock Exchange as news of the crash spread. Many rushed to raise more margin; others committed suicide.

"All the News That's Fit to Print."

The New York Times.

Copyright, 1929, by The New York Times Company.

THE WEATHER
Cloudy, probably rain today and tomorrow; warmer tomorrow.
Temperatures yesterday—Max. 49, min. 38.
U. S. Weather Forecast—For details see Page 38.

VOL. LXXIX....No. 26,212. **** NEW YORK, WEDNESDAY, OCTOBER 30, 1929. TWO CENTS in Greater New York | THREE CENTS Within 200 Miles | FOUR CENTS Elsewhere Except 7th and 8th Postal Zones

STOCKS COLLAPSE IN 16,410,030-SHARE DAY, BUT RALLY AT CLOSE CHEERS BROKERS; BANKERS OPTIMISTIC, TO CONTINUE AID

GRUNDY FOR CURBING 'BACKWARD STATES' ON THE TARIFF BILL

Veteran Republican Lobbyist Tells Senate Inquiry the West Needs "Silencing."

PENNSYLVANIA KNOWS BEST

"Unfortunate," He Holds, That the Constitution Gives Equal Voice to States in Senate.

BATTLES INVESTIGATORS

He Assails Borah—Would "Hate to Tell" His Opinion of Wisconsin.

Special to The New York Times.

WASHINGTON, Oct. 29.—Joseph R. Grundy, president of the Pennsylvania Manufacturers' Association, told the Senate Lobby Committee today that certain "backward" States of the West, through their Senators, had been altogether "too vocal" in the consideration of the current tariff bill, and that some method should be found to "silence" them at times when legislation affecting the economic welfare of the United States is under way.

Mr. Grundy declared it "unfortunate" that the framers of the Constitution had seen fit to grant to the States equal rights and representation in the Senate, as the effect of the arrangement was to give sections slow in developing their resources an equal voice in legislation directly involving such great reservoirs of wealth and taxation as Pennsylvania.

Mr. Grundy was recalled today for cross-examination on testimony he gave before the lobby committee on Oct. 24. Last week Mr. Grundy and the Senate investigating committee got along very well, and that session was decorous and orderly in contrast with today, when the witness and his questioners appeared to be antagonistic from the outset.

Criticizes Senator Walsh.

At one stage Mr. Grundy sharply described a series of questions put by Senator Walsh of Montana as "impertinent." There were frequent references to the Vare case, to the party service which Mr. Grundy had performed in the collection of Republican campaign funds, and to the relations of the witness with public men and his activities here as a part of the tariff lobby.

At times the hearing resembled a hot political debate, in which the five members of the committee were arrayed against the witness. Mr. Grundy was once reproved by Senator Blaine of Wisconsin, a member of the committee, for alleged evasion, and Mr. Blaine exclaimed heatedly:

"Look me squarely in the eye and answer my question."

The hearing was marked by frequent spats between Mr. Grundy and Senators Borah, Caraway and Walsh, and in one interchange with the witnesses Mr. Borah denied emphatically a statement that he had opposed the debenture plan at the Kansas City convention.

Chairman Caraway repeatedly indicated that the witness was not frank with the committee and that, while it might be "smart" for him to "sidestep," eventually the investigators would get what they were after.

Hit at "Most Vocal" States.

Mr. Grundy was impelled to enter into a discussion of his belief that "backward Western States" should be silenced on the tariff by questions asked by Senator Walsh. The Senator read from a statement submitted to the committee a week ago, in which Mr. Grundy asserted that if "volume of voice" in the Senate were proportioned to population, productive power or the total contributed toward the national upkeep, some of those States "which are now most vocal would need amplifiers to make their whispers heard."

Mr. Grundy also had declared that "such States as Arizona, South Dakota, Idaho and Mississippi, &c., do not pay enough toward the upkeep of the government to cover the costs of collection." As a result of Mr. Walsh's examination, Mr. Grundy finally included Arkansas and Montana in his list of "backward" States, thus bringing in three of them having representation on the lobby committee.

"You have not mentioned Wisconsin in your list," suggested Senator Walsh. "What do you think about that State?"

"What I think about Wisconsin I'd hate to tell you," replied the witness. This evoked an outburst of laughter in the audience, in which the committee joined.

Favors a Few Concessions.

Mr. Grundy again caused laughter when he said that he would permit the "backward" States, through their Senators, to have their say on questions affecting "Junior Red Cross work and outdoor relief," but that, generally speaking, they should be required to "hold their peace" on

Continued on Page Eighteen.

Von Opel, Rocket Flier, Weds Woman Pilot Who Advised Him

Wireless to THE NEW YORK TIMES.

BERLIN, Oct. 29.—Fritz von Opel, the first to fly a rocket plane, and who intends to sail for New York the beginning of November to study and work at General Motors plants, was married on Saturday to Frau Sellnik, née Loewenstein, the former wife of a Wiesbaden actor. For many months she has been von Opel's professional adviser on aviation and she herself is one of Germany's six woman pilots, flying her Handley Page plane with the greatest skill.

Frau von Opel, who is also a daring automobilist, is handsome, slender and blonde. When the airman landed safely from his rocket flight she was the first to congratulate him, shedding tears of joy. She will accompany him to the United States.

COALITION FIGHTING MOVE TO KILL TARIFF

Will Try to Force Through Bill, While Reed Favors Ending Session Nov. 15.

WATSON QUITTING CAPITAL

Departure for Florida Tomorrow for Health Leaves Jones as Republican Senate Leader.

Special to The New York Times.

WASHINGTON, Oct. 29.—Faced by Old Guard Republican willingness to leave the Smoot-Hawley tariff bill to its fate, the Democratic-Progressive coalition was today more determined than ever to drive the bill through the Senate and force the conservatives to accept it in a completely rewritten form.

Coalition strategy was centred upon fixing on the Old Guard leaders any responsibility for abandonment of the remodeled bill with the Simmons-Norris flexible amendment to the farm debenture plan. To those old-line Republicans who are now ready to desert the measure, the coalition applied the unflattering comparison of "rats and a sinking ship."

The administration Republicans refused to be stirred by such criticism. Senator Reed of Pennsylvania reiterated his conviction that the bill would never emerge from conference. Senator Moses announced that he would vote against the bill in the Senate, before it ever went to conference. The Republicans were so dismayed that they even seriously considered a motion to adjourn the Senate about the middle of November until the regular session starts on Dec. 2.

To add to their disorganization it was revealed that Senator Watson, Republican floor leader, would leave for Florida on Thursday to rebuild his shattered health.

McNary to Act as Aide.

Old Guard lieutenants hurriedly announced that Senator Jones of Washington, assistant leader, would take charge in Mr. Watson's absence, aided by Senator McNary of Oregon, who is popular with all Senate factions, has a fine record as a conciliator and more influence than most regular Republicans with the farming public.

When it was first announced that Senator Watson was going to Florida, reports spread that his illness was so serious that he might never return to the Senate as floor leader. His friends, however, denied this. They admitted that he was an ill man and needed a complete rest for a time, but asserted that he would return to assume his duties.

There was some assumption that Mr. McNary would be made temporary leader, because Senator Jones had not sufficiently recovered from the effects of a recent operation, but Mr. Jones assured Old Guard members that he felt capable of taking over the task.

While pessimistic, Senator Watson, who is dropping work by his physician's orders, would not admit that the outlook for passing the tariff bill by the end of the special session was absolutely hopeless. He did not share the view that the session might as well be adjourned, which Senator Reed may propose for about Nov. 15.

Instead, Mr. Watson will work until his departure to bring about "some sort of agreement for some sort of bill," basing this plea on the idea that the coalition must concede increases on industrial as well as agricultural rates.

Says Action Would Aid Business.

"It would have a quieting effect on business to pass the tariff bill," asserted Senator Watson. "Tariff bills are always the occasion of some unrest, though this bill has caused less agitation than usual because a Republican tariff is to be superimposed on a Republican tariff and everybody knows that if this bill fails the country would continue to be prosperous.

"It is true that there ought to be changes in agricultural rates to meet new conditions, but it is equally true

Continued on Page Fifteen.

KAHN REFUSES POST IN SENATE CAMPAIGN; CALLS CHOICE UNWISE

He Writes to Moses to Withhold His Name for Treasurer Due to 'Divided Reception.'

WAS RELUCTANT, HE SAYS

Recalls He Told Senator of His Stand, but Yielded as a Duty to His Party.

HOLDS VIEWS CONFIRMED

Declares He Is a Wall St. Man but a Liberal in Politics—Friends See Him Put in False Light.

Otto H. Kahn in a letter to Senator George H. Moses of New Hampshire, chairman of the Republican Senatorial Campaign Committee, made public yesterday, declined the post of treasurer of that committee because of the "divided reception" which the announcement of his designation as treasurer had met.

Announcement of the selection of Mr. Kahn was made by Senator Moses at the dinner given last Thursday evening at the University Club here by Jeremiah Milbank for Claudius H. Huston, the new chairman of the Republican National Committee. Publication of this announcement, together with the report that speakers at the dinner attacked the members of the Progressive Republican group in the Senate, brought protests from some of these Senators against the selection of Mr. Kahn.

Mr. Kahn in his letter to Senator Moses declared that, while a Wall Street man, he was a liberal in politics. He said some of the interpretations placed on his designation were erroneous, but added that the way it had been received justified his earlier feeling that he was not the right man for the position. No formal action for the appointment of a treasurer of the Senatorial committee has yet been taken, and Mr. Kahn requested Senator Moses not to present his name to the committee.

Mr. Kahn's Letter.

Mr. Kahn's letter follows:

Oct. 28, 1929.

My dear Senator:

When you did me the honor to ask me to act as treasurer of the Republican Senatorial Campaign Committee I told you that I feared your kindly sentiment toward me, springing from a long friendship, was swaying your judgment, that I felt sure that I was not the right man for the position, that, moreover, I was overwhelmed with demands upon my time and energies and that I hoped very much you would not persist in your request.

You argued to the contrary and, among other things, pointed to the fact that, while a Wall Street man, I was known to be, as indeed I am, a liberal in politics. You repeated your invitation when I had the pleasure of seeing you at Mr. Milbank's dinner last Thursday.

I thereupon stated that, though my views were unchanged, I felt that if we want effective party government, such as our political system requires, every citizen should be willing to make good his professions of party allegiance by submitting to being drafted, within the limits of reason and possibility, and that if the leaders of the party to which I belong demanded of me a service which did not conflict with my other duties and responsibilities I was not at liberty to refuse, however reluctant I was to accept.

You regarded this answer as tantamount to an acceptance in principle, as you were perfectly justified in doing, and at what was supposed and intended to be a strictly private dinner, you made informal reference to that acceptance.

Sees His Doubts Confirmed.

But the divided reception with which the report of the appointment of a separate treasurer for your committee and of my designation as such treasurer has met, however erroneous some of the interpretations placed thereon, appears to have confirmed the validity of the doubts which I ventured to express when you offered that position to me, and to justify me in concluding to abstain from occupying it.

I understand that no formal action has been taken as yet by the National Republican Senatorial committee concerning the appointment of a treasurer, and I am making free to write these lines to request that you will please refrain from bringing my name before the committee for appointment to the treasurership.

Believe me, dear Senator,
Very faithfully yours,
OTTO H. KAHN.

Hon. George H. Moses, The Senate, Washington, D. C.

Influential Republicans expressed regret that Mr. Kahn had decided not to take the post of treasurer of the Republican Senatorial committee. It was recalled that he was re-

Continued on Page Fourteen.

Newark Man, 4 Feet 10, Says He Was Smallest in A. E. F.

WASHINGTON, Oct. 29 (AP).—Nicholas Casale of Newark, N. J., wants to be known as the smallest man who went to France with the American Expeditionary Forces.

He has appealed to Representative Hartley of Kearny to establish that fact. Casale recently secured an affidavit from the Veterans' Bureau certifying that he was 4 feet 10 inches tall and weighed 106 pounds when he enlisted. The bureau has refused to declare him the "smallest man," saying it would require months for clerks to scan the record of every man who served with the A. E. F.

It was not explained how Casale secured enlistment when the minimum requirements are 5 feet and 110 pounds.

MISSING AIRLINER BROUGHT IN SAFELY

Pilot Lands Western Express Ship at Albuquerque After Being Forced Down.

WOULD NOT RISK STORM

Passengers Tell of Cold Night in Deserted Ranch House as Snow Swirled Round.

Special to The New York Times.

ALBUQUERQUE, N. M., Oct. 29.—Lost for more than twenty-four hours while marooned on a bleak New Mexico mesa, Western Air Express tri-motored liner 113 escaped today from the snow-swept stretch where it was forced down Monday and landed here with its crew of three and two passengers, chilled but safe.

Caught in a blinding swirl of snow Monday at 10:15 A. M., the plane was forced down near Crechado, seventy-five miles southeast of Gallup, N. M. The crew and passengers found refuge in an abandoned ranch house.

The passengers are Dr. A. W. Ward of San Francisco and W. E. Merz of Mount Vernon, N. Y. The crew includes James E. Doles, chief pilot, of Los Angeles; Allan C. Barrie, co-pilot, of Burbank, Cal., and R. L. Britton, steward, of Los Angeles.

Employes of the airport and pilots of two planes waiting for the weather to clear to resume the search for the 113 stood amazed as the big craft glided along the runway. They rushed out to the plane and as the group of men who had been given up for dead stepped out they danced around them, clapped them on the back and hugged them in delight.

Wild Night of Intense Cold.

Despite their fatigue, Dr. Ward and Mr. Merz were lighthearted and stepped jauntily from the plane. They regretted only the loss of time but joined in praise of Pilot Doles for his skillful manoeuvring to save the ship in the storm when further progress could not be risked.

They told of a harrowing night which followed the forced landing, of tramping through snow to find shelter, of sleeping on an old bed spring covered with seat cushions from the plane and of shivering in intense cold while they took turns in keeping up a fire.

"A half frozen rabbit and a rabbit's foot brought us good luck," Dr. Ward said.

"The half-frozen rabbit had been captured in the bushes by co-pilot Barrie. The rabbit's foot was worn by steward Britten. He had bought it the day the T. A. T. plane City of San Francisco crashed."

Suddenly Enveloped by Storm.

"We left Holbrook, flying east," Doles said, "and were about one hour out when we had to dodge a storm. I nosed her down towards St. John's. Suddenly the storm seemed to break over us all at once, and a landing became a necessity.

"I found a small spot, and it

Continued on Page Seventeen.

LEADERS SEE FEAR WANING

Point to 'Lifting Spells' in Trading as Sign of Buying Activity.

GROUP MEETS TWICE IN DAY

But Resources Are Unable to Stem Selling Tide—Lamont Reassures Investors.

HOPE SEEN IN MARGIN CUTS

Banks Reduce Requirements to 25 Per Cent—Sentiment in Wall St. More Cheerful.

Resources of the banking group which was organized last Thursday to stabilize conditions in the stock market were utilized yesterday to break the force of the terrific flood of selling which accompanied the biggest day, from the point of view of volume, ever experienced on the New York Stock Exchange.

Despite the drastic decline, sentiment in Wall Street last night was more cheerful than it has been on any day since the torrent of selling got under way. Periodic "lifting spells" which developed between intervals of extreme weakness were cited by bankers at the close of the market, as testifying to the presence of investment buying. The public is in some measure regaining its senses and the unreasoning fear which has prompted the sacrifice of securities for any price they would bring is at length subsiding.

While even the tremendous buying power of the banking group was unable to turn the tide of selling in yesterday's market, the group did not relax its concern over the situation on the Exchange. Two meetings were held during the day, one at noon and one at 4:30 P. M., the latter lasting until 6:30 P. M.

Will Continue Support.

After the evening meeting Thomas W. Lamont of J. P. Morgan & Co. spoke to reporters.

"I want to take occasion," Mr. Lamont said, "to explain again, as heretofore, that the banking group was organized to offer certain support in the market and to act as far as possible as somewhat of a stabilizing factor.

"It was not the intention of the group to attempt to maintain prices, but to maintain a free market; in other words, to correct the condition that prevailed last Thursday.

"The group has continued and will continue in a cooperative way to support the market and has not been a seller of stocks."

The statement was issued at the request of reporters to quiet rumors which had been abroad that the banking group had been selling stocks instead of supporting them.

These rumors were, of course, without foundation, for the group is known to have purchased heavily in directions where the force of its buying power would be most effective in stemming demoralization. It was reliably reported that in many instances when no bids could be obtained on the floor for large blocks of stock forced on the market the group had supplied the necessary bids and in other instances had acted as a stabilizing influence upon the list as a whole.

At the noon meeting of the group Owen D. Young, chairman of the General Electric Company, director of the Federal Reserve Bank of New York and head of the Young committee on reparations which recently developed the Young plan, joined the

Continued on Page Three.

Navy Paymaster Leads Way to $47,000 Loot, Dug Up by Night in Washington Chicken Yard

Special to The New York Times.

WASHINGTON, Oct. 29.—Led by Lieutenant Charles Musil, a navy paymaster accused of embezzling $54,600, naval authorities, in a search late at night, recently uncovered $47,000 of the loot buried in a chicken yard in Southeast Washington on the grounds of the Home of the Aged and Infirm.

When Lieutenant Musil voluntarily surrendered himself, on Oct. 14, to the naval authorities at New York, after having disappeared on Sept. 28 from his post as paymaster for Destroyer Division 40 at Charleston, S. C., he is said to have turned over $1,500 to Captain C. T. Owens, commanding the receiving ship Seattle.

This leaves $6,100 unaccounted for and naval officers, in announcing today the discovery in the chicken yard, said they were trying to locate the rest of the money, although they had scant hope of success.

According to the story told to the officers by Lieutenant Musil, he came here directly from Charleston and buried the money in the yard of his former home. He then left for Chicago, where he bought some stock, and went to Detroit and into Canada. From there he proceeded to New York, where he became conscience-stricken and gave himself up.

He was held at the Brooklyn Navy Yard, but when he told his story of the buried money he was brought here to direct the search for it. He is now awaiting general court-martial on specifications covering embezzlement.

Lieutenant Musil was born in Illinois in 1893, enlisted in the navy twenty years ago and was commissioned in 1921. He has a wife and 9-year-old son in New York City.

240 Issues Lose $15,894,818,894 in Month; Slump in Full Exchange List Vastly Larger

The drastic effects of Wall Street's October bear market is shown by valuation tables prepared last night by THE NEW YORK TIMES, which place the decline in the market value of 240 representative issues on the New York Stock Exchange at $15,894,818,894 during the period from Oct. 1 to yesterday's closing. Since there are 1,279 issues listed on the New York Stock Exchange, the total depreciation for the month is estimated at between two and three times the loss for the 240 issues covered by THE TIMES table.

Among the losses of the various groups comprising the 240 stocks in THE TIMES valuation table were the following:

Group.	Number of Stocks.	Decline in Value.
Railroads	25	$1,128,686,488
Public utilities	29	5,135,734,327
Motors	15	1,689,840,902
Oils	22	1,332,617,778
Coppers	15	824,403,820
Chemicals	9	1,621,697,897

The official figures of the New York Stock Exchange showed that the total market value of its listed securities on Oct. 1 was $87,073,630,423. The decline in the 240 representative issues therefore cut more than one-sixth from the total value of the listed securities. Most of this loss was inflicted by the wholesale liquidation of the last week.

U. S. STEEL TO PAY $1 EXTRA DIVIDEND

American Can Votes the Same and Raises Annual Rate From $3 to $4.

BIG GAIN IN STEEL INCOME

Earnings for Nine Months Are $15.82 a Share, Against $8.17 a Year Ago.

Two leading industrial companies yesterday declared extra dividends of $1 a share on the common stock, as a result of their earnings through the Summer months. The companies were the United States Steel Corporation and the American Can Company, whose interests touch every section of the country. Their action caused the Wall Street district to accept the extra dividends as final proof of the prosperity of the country, despite the breaks which have occurred in the stock market.

While the directors of neither of the companies referred to present conditions in the stock market as a reason for taking the extra dividend action at this time, the opinion was expressed that the directors chose this time to declare the extras as reflecting their belief in the fundamental soundness of industry.

Directors of the American Can Company, in addition to declaring the $1 extra disbursement, also increased the regular dividend rate on the common stock from $3 a year to $4 a year, committing themselves to this payment for the future.

The United States Steel directors contented themselves with announcing that earnings for the first nine months of this year were nearly double those of the same period for 1928, namely, $15.82 a share on the common stock outstanding, compared with $8.17 for the nine months of 1928.

Steel Surplus Up $22,909,447.

Earnings of the United States Steel Corporation for the three months ended on Sept. 30 were reported as $72,009,666, equivalent to $5.57 a share on the common stock outstanding, and the extra dividend makes the disbursements for the quarter less than half of the actual earnings. The operation for the three months, after the preferred and common stock dividends, including the extra dividend, increased the surplus of the company by $22,909,447.

September was the lowest for the three months which enter into the quarterly earnings. The amount reported for this month was $21,794,450, which compares with $25,298,059 in August and $24,917,157 for July. The total earnings for the quarter after deducting all expenses incident to operations, including those for ordinary repairs and maintenance of plants, taxes, including the reserve for Federal income taxes, and the interest on bonds of subsidiary companies, amounted to $70,173,713. Allowances for depreciation, depletion and obsolescence took away another $16,819,393, leaving the net income for the three months at $53,354,320. The interest for the quarter on the bonds of the company outstanding amounted to $1,778,970, and the payment of the 1¾ per cent dividends on the preferred stock amounted to another $6,304,919.

Extra Due to Rise in Earnings.

The official statement issued by the company after the meeting of the directors read as follows:

"The United States Steel Corporation's earnings for the first nine

Continued on Page Six.

RESERVE BOARD FINDS ACTION UNNECESSARY

Six-Hour Session Brings No Change in the New York Rediscount Rate.

OFFICIALS ARE OPTIMISTIC

Mellon Also Attends Cabinet Meeting, but Declines to Discuss Developments.

Special to The New York Times.

WASHINGTON, Oct. 29.—The further decline in stock market prices today passed without expressed apprehension on the part of Federal officials. The situation was watched intently by the Federal Reserve Board, which held a continuous session from 10 A. M. until 4 P. M., with Secretary Mellon in attendance.

Secretary Mellon, as ex-officio chairman of the board, attended the early part of the meeting before going to the White House for the Cabinet meeting. It could not be learned whether the market situation was discussed by the President and the Cabinet.

At 2:30 P. M. Mr. Mellon returned to the Reserve Board meeting, and remained until near its close. During the day he had conferred with Under-Secretary Ogden L. Mills and Roy A. Young, Governor of the Reserve Board. After the board adjourned, neither Secretary Mellon nor Mr. Young would even intimate the nature or scope of the discussions.

The Federal Reserve Board was so absorbed in studying the financial problems facing the country as the result of another violent stock fluctuation that most of its members did not leave the board room for luncheon.

Board Reviews Credit Situation.

Members of the board, while admitting that the market situation was under discussion, declared at the end of the day that there was no change which called upon the board for action relative to credits.

There was a report that the board had reviewed the credit situation to determine whether the time had come to lower the rediscount rate to ease credit for business ventures.

The board has hesitated to act on the rediscount rate during the stock market decline, fearing that lowered rates might be employed to bolster up the market. The board's policy is not to aid in speculation, but it feels that the rediscount rate should be lowered to stimulate credits for business when it is apparent that such action would not be accepted as assistance to speculative loans.

Mr. Young said there was no change in financial conditions which the board thought called for its action.

Cut in Discount Rate Expected.

It is thought the question of lowering rediscount rates may come before the Federal Reserve Board shortly. The Boston Federal Reserve Bank directors will meet tomorrow and the New York directors on Thursday. It is possible that one of these banks may suggest a lowering of the rates.

Some observers believe that a reduction in rediscount rates might have a strong psychological effect not only upon business but the market as well. There was no official indication that such a move was imminent, although some observers thought such action might come if suggested by the New York bank directors, since the rate there is 6 per cent as against 5 per cent in other regions. Some thought the New York rediscount rate might be reduced to 5 per cent soon.

Today's session of the board was the longest since the financial flurry

Continued on Page Six.

CLOSING RALLY VIGOROUS

Leading Issues Regain From 4 to 14 Points in 15 Minutes.

INVESTMENT TRUSTS BUY

Large Blocks Thrown on Market at Opening Start Third Break of Week.

BIG TRADERS HARDEST HIT

Bankers Believe Liquidation Now Has Run Its Course and Advise Purchases.

Stock prices virtually collapsed yesterday, swept downward with gigantic losses in the most disastrous trading day in the stock market's history. Billions of dollars in open market values were wiped out as prices crumbled under the pressure of liquidation of securities which had to be sold at any price.

There was an impressive rally just at the close, which brought many leading stocks back from 4 to 14 points from their lowest points of the day.

Trading on the New York Stock Exchange aggregated 16,410,030 shares; on the Curb, 7,096,300 shares were dealt in. Both totals far exceeded any previous day's dealings.

From every point of view, in the extent of losses sustained, in total turnover, in the number of speculators wiped out, the day was the most disastrous in Wall Street's history. Hysteria swept the country and stocks went overboard for just what they would bring at forced sale.

Efforts to estimate yesterday's market losses in dollars are futile because of the vast number of securities quoted over the counter and on out-of-town exchanges on which no calculations are possible. However, it was estimated that 880 issues, on the New York Stock Exchange, lost between $8,000,000,000 and $9,000,000,000 yesterday. Added to that loss is to be reckoned the depreciation on issues on the Curb Market, in the over the counter market and on other exchanges.

Two Extra Dividends Declared.

There were two cheerful notes, however, which sounded through the pall of gloom which overhung the financial centres of the country. One was the brisk rally of stocks at the close, on tremendous buying by those who believe that prices have sunk too low. The other was that the liquidation has been so violent, as well as widespread, that many bankers, brokers and industrial leaders expressed the belief last night that it now has run its course.

A further note of optimism in the soundness of fundamentals was sounded by the directors of the United States Steel Corporation and the American Can Company, each of which declared an extra dividend of $1 a share at their late afternoon meetings.

Banking support, which would have been impressive and successful under ordinary circumstances, was swept violently aside, as block after block of stock, tremendous in proportions, deluged the market. Bid prices placed by bankers, industrial leaders and brokers trying to halt the decline were crashed through violently, their orders were filled, and quotations plunged downward in a day of disorganization, confusion and financial impotence.

Change Is Expected Today.

That there will be a change today seemed likely from statements made last night by financial and business leaders. Organized support will be accorded to the market from the start, it is believed, but those who are staking their all on the country's leading securities are placing a great deal of confidence, too, in the expectation that there will be an overnight change in sentiment; that the counsel of cool heads will prevail and that the mob psychology which has been so largely responsible for the market's debacle will be broken.

The fact that the leading stocks were able to rally in the final fifteen minutes of trading yesterday was considered a good omen, especially as the weakest period of the day had developed just prior to that time and the minimum prices for the day had then been established. It was a quick run-up which followed the announcement that the American Can directors had declared an extra dividend of $1. The advances in leading stocks in this last fifteen minutes represented a measurable snapback from the lows. American Can gained 10; United States Steel common, 7½; General Electric, 12; New York Central, 14½; Anaconda Copper, 9½; Chrysler Motors, 5½; Montgomery Ward, 4½, and Johns Man-

"All the News That's Fit to Print."

The New York Times.

EXTRA—7 A. M.

THE WEATHER—Colder today, probably snow flurries.

VOL. LXXIX....No. 26,242. ****** NEW YORK, FRIDAY, NOVEMBER 29, 1929. TWO CENTS In Greater New York | THREE CENTS Within 200 Miles | FOUR CENTS Elsewhere Except 7th and 8th Postal Zones

COMMANDER BYRD OFF ON FLIGHT TO THE SOUTH POLE; RADIO REPORTS "ALL IS WELL" AT 6:30 A. M., 8 HOURS OUT; PASSES SLEDGE PARTY ON THE TRAIL AND DROPS MESSAGES

NANKING AND MUKDEN AT ODDS ON POLICY AS HOSTILITIES CEASE

Manchuria's Yielding Ignored by Chiang, Who Offers Reds New Counter-Proposal.

APPEALS SEEN AS GESTURE

Tokio Sees China Completely Beaten and Danger Over as Soviet Withdraws.

POWERS APPROACHED BY US

Envoys to Five Nations Propose Joint Action Under Kellogg Treaty if Situation Warrants.

By HUGH BYAS.

Wireless to THE NEW YORK TIMES.

TOKIO, Nov. 28.—The end of the Chinese resistance in Russia is the important fact emerging from the medley of reports reaching Tokio today. Edwin Lowe Neville, American Charge d'Affaires, called on Baron Shidehara, Foreign Minister, at 6 o'clock last evening, and communicated a dispatch he had received from Washington. The Foreign Office declines to indicate the nature of Secretary Stimson's proposals, or Japan's views on them, but the collapse of Chinese resistance ends the situation which had aroused Secretary Stimson's anxiety.

The ease with which the Russians drove 12,000 Chinese troops from Manchuli in Western Manchuria, added to the financial strain of maintaining armies on a war footing, has forced Mukden to cancel its action of July and consent to the reinstatement of a Russian manager and submanager of the Chinese Eastern Railway. Nanking has been reluctantly compelled to acquiesce in Mukden's surrender, since Mukden had decided to make terms with Moscow anyhow.

Nanking press telegrams announcing that Russia's terms are being conceded add the curious statement that China will ask the United States and Germany to mediate, while the Chinese Minister to Tokio states that China is appealing to the League of Nations. In the Japanese view, direct negotiation with Russia is the better course, since Russia is not a member of the League and the United States has not recognized Russia. These reports appear to be intended to divert the Chinese public's attention from the surrender, although China is doubtless prepared for direct negotiations.

The Japanese are probably relieved that the necessity of international action has been removed. They would have joined the other Kellogg pact powers in issuing a warning, but they have always believed the matter had best be settled by the Chinese and Russians themselves.

The news from Manchuria confirms the Japanese anticipation that the Russians did not intend an invasion. The Russians apparently have not occupied any Chinese towns and are back in their own territory. They have given the Chinese a severe slap, humiliated them by disarming 10,000 troops, and scared Mukden into a settlement all by a relatively small operation which led to no entanglements.

Direct Negotiations Reported.

SHANGHAI, Friday, Nov. 29 (AP).—The North China Daily News, a British newspaper here, published a statement this morning purporting to be from local Russian Tass Agency sources stating that the Chinese commission of Foreign Affairs at Harbin had inaugurated negotiations between Mukden and Moscow seeking settlement of the Chinese Eastern Railway dispute, "on the express authority of both Nanking and Mukden Government officials."

"More War" Forecast.

MUKDEN, Friday, Nov. 29 (AP).—The Russian wireless station at Habarovsk broadcast a statement last night saying conversations between Moscow and Mukden looking to settlement of the Chinese Eastern Railway controversy still were proceeding, but that there would be "more war."

The radio announcer, commenting upon the Manchurian situation, said: "The Chinese Manchurian Army has suffered heavy losses but Russia has no faith in Chang Hsueh-liang's word, as his forces are still fighting. Therefore, Russia must prepare for more war."

Chang Hsueh-liang is Governor of Manchuria.

Nanking Counter-Proposal.

NANKING, Friday, Nov. 29 (AP).—The Nationalist Government has

Continued on Page Four.

Incendiaries Start 19 Fires In Siskiyou National Forest

GRANTS PASS, Ore., Nov. 28 (AP).—Records in the hands of officials of the United States forest office here today revealed that nineteen of the latest fires reported in the Siskiyou National Forest were of incendiary origin.

Several of these blazes were giving rangers serious trouble, but two, located almost directly on the Oregon-California line, were being held back.

A brisk wind from the Pacific last night swept inland various forest fires in Southwestern Oregon. Stands of virgin timber were being devastated.

The Shumate logging camp in the Port Oxford district was reported in danger of destruction, and advices from that front said families were fleeing from their cabins with their personal belongings.

POLLING OF SENATE CHEERS INSURGENTS

They Figure Strength Enough to Dominate Coming Session and Carry Tariff Program.

FOUR BLOCS IN THE PARTY

But Coalition of Progressives and Democrats Is Estimated as Outvoting Old and New Guards.

Special to The New York Times.

WASHINGTON, Nov. 28.—Confident of their ability to retain the balance of power among the Senate Republicans, the insurgents are prepared to continue their drive against the industrial rates of the Smoot-Hawley tariff bill when the measure is again taken up some time next week, a few days after Congress convenes for its regular session.

During the breathing space since the Senate adjourned on Friday, the members of the Republican "New Guard," who are determined to continue their efforts to keep these rates from being cut materially, have made further informal overtures to the insurgents, but without success.

The formation of the Senate's Republican "freshmen" and some Old Guardsmen into a recognized bloc has in no way dismayed the party's insurgents. In fact, the insurgents are positive in predicting success for the program they mapped out before the extra session was begun in April, that is, material benefits for agriculture through increased tariff duties on imported farm products and a reduction of the industrial rates wherever believed to be discriminatory against the farmer.

Time for Reckoning Strength.

This week the insurgents have been counting noses to see if the situation has changed to any extent. Today they said they were able to demonstrate on paper that they were still in command.

They maintained that they still control the Senate through the Democratic-progressive Republican coalition and that they were strong enough numerically to make an important wedge in their own party.

One man who is familiar with the situation and is watching it closely said tonight that the Republican party in the Senate was being "factionalized" through putting all those legally registered as Republicans into their proper groups. So far, it was pointed out, there were four Republican "columns."

First, there are the so-called Old Guardsmen; secondly, the progressives or insurgents; thirdly, the "freshmen," who, with some temporarily shifting Old Guard members, call themselves the "New Guard," and fourthly, the "halfways," as one might call the Old Guardsmen who for the moment have joined with the "freshmen."

How Various Senators Stand.

Continuing his comment, this observer said:

"In their own ranks the Young Guardsmen are counting, for the time being, Senators Cutting of New Mexico and Capper of Kansas, who have been voting with them.

"Senators Couzens of Michigan and Johnson of California, each of whom calls himself 'a one-man bloc,' are being numbered with the Young Guard. Senator Couzens seems to be somewhat sympathetic with the 'New Guard,' but he has not been with them all the time.

"In the Old Guard are listed Senator Baird the successor of Senator Edge of New Jersey, as well as

Continued on Page Twelve.

BUCKNER CENSURES HARVEY FOR PUTTING MOORE BACK ON JOB

Prosecutor of Connolly and Seely Demands Engineer Be Tried as Sewer Grafter.

CITES EVIDENCE IN CASE

Stirred by Failure to Get Reply to Protest Sent Eight Days Ago Urging Action.

QUEENS PRESIDENT RETORTS

Asks Why Charges Were Not Pressed Before and Wants a Formal Complaint.

Emory R. Buckner, special prosecutor in the Queens sewer graft scandals, and George U. Harvey, Borough President of Queens, the two leading figures in the uncovering of the "sewer ring" and the overthrow of the old political régime in that borough, crossed swords yesterday over Mr. Harvey's action in restoring Clifford B. Moore to duty at $8,000 salary as assistant borough engineer.

Indignant at the failure of Mr. Harvey either to acknowledge or act upon a letter of protest delivered eight days before, Mr. Buckner initiated the conflict by making public the letter, which charged that Moore was a co-conspirator in the graft scandals along with former Borough President Maurice E. Connolly, Frederick Seely, former borough engineer in charge of sewer design, and the late John M. Phillips, sewer pipe "czar."

The special prosecutor asserted that Moore escaped indictment as a party to the conspiracy only because the evidence did not appear until the Connolly trial was under way. He insisted that the record of the trial clearly showed Moore's part and pointed to a prevailing opinion of the Brooklyn Appellate Division affirming Connolly's conviction, which held that the engineer acted "in furtherance of the conspiracy" as a "co-conspirator" himself.

"The fact that Mr. Harvey has not acknowledged the letter makes me wonder who is back of Moore," Mr. Buckner said as he gave out copies of his letter.

Invites Action By Buckner.

Stung by the implications of the missive, Mr. Harvey, who has himself won two major campaigns and a primary fight by associating his opponents with the "sewer ring," at once struck back at the special prosecutor. Informed that the letter had been made public, he pointed out that Mr. Buckner had been charged with the duty of bringing all official wrongdoing in Queens before the grand jury.

"Why did Mr. Buckner not bring this matter to the attention of the grand jury at that time?" he demanded, and added an invitation to the special prosecutor to bring formal complaint against Moore "if he is so anxious in this matter."

Mr. Harvey's explanation of the return of Moore to the payroll on Nov. 19 was that his leave of absence had expired and no charges were legally pending against him, former Borough President Bernard M. Patten having failed to take action on accusations for which the engineer was suspended after Connolly had resigned.

The Borough President's statement evoked from Mr. Buckner the response that since the real evidence against Moore appeared after the Connolly trial had started he could not have been made a co-defendant, and the trial of Moore alone on a charge of conspiracy would have been idle. Taking under consideration the matter of preferring formal charges to Mr. Harvey against Moore, but pointing out that the Borough President had ample authority to start the action himself, Mr. Buckner said, "I want to see what Harvey will do. He must answer to the people of Queens, not me."

Moore Indicted Twice.

Although Moore was not indicted as co-conspirator with Connolly and the others, the special grand jury in Queens under Mr. Buckner's direction did indict the engineer for verifying a false State income tax return. He was charged with reporting only his income from the borough in 1926 and omitting additional receipts of over $60,000. Subsequently he pleaded guilty, served thirty days in the workhouse and paid a fine of $1,000. He was also indicted by the Federal grand jury for failing to file Federal

Continued on Page Fourteen.

Byrd, as He Flies, Remembers Those He Left in New Zealand

Wireless to THE NEW YORK TIMES.

LITTLE AMERICA, Antarctica, Nov. 28.—As the moment neared for his start for the Pole, Commander Byrd thought of his men who were turned back from the Barrier last February to winter at Dunedin, N. Z., and by wireless, flashed to THE NEW YORK TIMES station in New York, to be relayed to the Antipodes, this message:

New Zealand Contingent,
Byrd Expedition:

As we take off flying for the Pole, I send the best of good wishes to you and the Tapleys.

I want you all to know that you are playing just as important a part as any one of us down here. BYRD.

(H. L. Tapley, Ltd., are Commander Byrd's representatives in New Zealand.)

FOKKER LAYS CRASH TO HUMAN FAILURE

Says Huge Plane Should Not Have Been Taken Up When in Poor Working Order.

STRESSES SAFETY FACTOR

20,000 Visit Scene of Wreck on Long Island—Two Inquiries by Officials Under Way.

Anthony H. G. Fokker declared yesterday that the crash of his huge thirty-two passenger monoplane, which destroyed two homes in Carle Place, Long Island, on Wednesday afternoon, was due to a failure of the human element in aviation. The disaster should have been avoided, he said as he stepped from the gangplank of the White Star liner Homeric after a tour of the aviation industry of Europe.

"There was no necessity of taking the craft up without having everything in good working order," he said. "The failure of the second engine on the same side as the one which was left idle at the take-off resulted in loss of control before the plane had attained sufficient altitude and speed. There is no doubt that this type plane can be brought to a safe landing regardless of the failure of one or two engines, if flying under normal conditions and at safe altitude.

"Such accidents as this prove that no matter how safe and airworthy a plane may be it can be wrecked at any time by failure of the human element."

Mr. Fokker then declared that he would conduct personally an investigation of the accident. He voiced regret at the loss of his $110,000 plane, and emphasized the additional aggravation of its having been responsible for the destruction of other property which may account for an equal figure.

At Roosevelt Field George Gardner, the local inspector of the Aeronautics Branch of the Department of Commerce, spent the day investigating the crash of the huge Fokker monoplane and that of James Pisani, the private flier who was killed an hour earlier when his plane plunged into a street not more than a mile from the scene of the Fokker disaster. No details of the inspector's findings were revealed. His report will be forwarded to Major Clarence M. Young, his chief in Washington.

District Attorney Edwards of Nassau County also investigated the crash. After a conference with the officials of Roosevelt Field he announced that he would try to have all experimental flights restricted to the air over unsettled country or the landing area. He added, however, that the crash would not be a case for the grand jury, as no criminal negligence was apparent.

Pilot Still in Hospital.

Meanwhile the pilot of the Fokker, Marshall Boggs, also a Department of Commerce inspector who is on leave to compile engineering data on the Fokker plane for commercial interests, remained in the Nassau Hospital. It was said that his injuries were slight. His mechanic, Harry McDonald of the Fokker company, had recovered sufficiently to be removed to his home at Hasbrouck Heights, N. J.

Throughout the day more than 20,000 persons visited the scene of the Fokker crash and fire, accord-

Continued on Page Thirteen.

START IS MADE AT 10:29 P. M. NEW YORK TIME

Climax of Year's Work of the Expedition Comes at 3:29 o'Clock in the Afternoon of Little America's Thanksgiving Day.

BALCHEN IS PILOTING THE BIG PLANE

Two Others With Them, One at the Radio—Airmen Must Climb to 12,000 Feet to Top Mountains on 1,600-Mile Dash to Pole and Back.

By RUSSELL OWEN.

Wireless to THE NEW YORK TIMES.

LITTLE AMERICA, Antarctica, Nov. 28.—A huge gray plane slipped over the dappled Barrier at 3:29 o'clock this afternoon [10:29 P. M. New York time] the sun gleaming on its sides, reflected in bright flashes from its metal wing and whirling propellers. With a smooth lifting movement it rose above the snow in a long, steady glide.

Commander Byrd had started on his 1,600-mile flight to the South Pole and back. With him were Bernt Balchen, flying the plane; Harold I. June at the wireless, and Captain Ashley C. McKinley, photographer, surveyor and general utility man.

Just before the take-off, Dr. Lawrence Gould, head of the geological sledging party now nearing the Queen Maud Mountains, reported by radio that "good flying weather" lay ahead of Commander Byrd at the edge of the Polar Plateau.

Once in the air, as if liberated from the clinging influence of earthly things, the great plane became suddenly light, a true bird of the air. With its three motors roaring their deep song it turned southward and was gone into the wilderness of space over a land of white desolation.

This will be a historic flight over the rolling Barrier, through gaps in towering mountains, where the wind whirls in buffeting eddies, and on over that lonely Polar Plateau, the loneliest spot on earth, where somewhere is a tiny invisible point which, with all his navigator's cunning, Commander Byrd is attempting to reach.

Weather Just Right at the Start.

Byrd's flight came today, as does everything here, with thrilling effect. Here, more than anywhere else, flying depends on the weather, and the genius of the winds brooding over the mysterious heights above us had been idly stirring the conflicting elements into shifting winds and clouds which blocked the way.

Then, as if by magic, a deep hush spread over the rolling plain, shining cream and rose colored under the flowing rays of a sun so bright in this translucent atmosphere that it seemed to fill half the sky. It was as if nature said, "I have done my part now; there is peace before you."

In the glittering silence of such a day, for morning, noon and midnight are all the same, men scurried busily about, intense with excitement. They knew that the moment had come for which they had worked for more than a year, in black isolation and in cold that seared and burned, in winds that shrieked and hid the earth in a shroud of numbing and bewildering drift.

There was elation in their quick movements, confidence and eagerness. If they could have done so, they would have pushed the heavy plane off the ground with their own determination.

Mechanics hurriedly looked with skilled and careful eyes where the huge metal machine rested on the snow like a ponderous, big, confident bird. It looked so strong, so graceful, even in its bulky outlines, so strange in this environment, as if in itself it had the will to conquer.

How different riding this machine from the way men have toiled with aching bodies and troubled minds over the treacherous surface of the snow, above which this great creature soars so easily!

Long Wait That Is Now Over.

It is hard to believe, as it wheels in graceful curves with long sweeping dips of its wings, that it is not a conscious entity. One never tires of watching it. Is it because it is so out of place here or because in this lost land it becomes a prehistoric denizen of the air, this its natural abiding place which by accident we have discovered?

It had come through so many hazards, had been watched with such jealous care. For 10,000 miles it had been transported, through tropics where the sun scorched it and the sea tried vainly to corrode its metal members. It had been lifted and dropped into the holds of ships and to docks, hauled ashore in sections on a crumbling shelf of ice with disaster momentarily ahead and then left to hibernate a long Winter night while the cold closed in around it.

Then the day came when it was brought up into the light, a complete machine, put together with blistered fingers and long hours of toil and, with its engines growling a note of satisfaction, had taken the air to soar in its own element.

Well Prepared for the Flight.

All this some of those watching the big plane made ready for the flight thought of as they stood by. How much it meant to all who have lived here and worked for this day can hardly be imagined by those back home, who can never picture this land as it really is, cold, beautiful, but treacherous and implacable in its resistance. This seemed the way to conquer it.

The plane had been loaded for the flight long before the hour came when the word was given to start. Men had stowed away in its big cabin food and clothing, extra cans of fuel to be poured into the fuselage tank; sleds had been tucked away in the tail for use if, by some mischance, the plane faltered on the way and sought a resting place far inland.

Byrd Watched All Preparations.

Over all the preparations Richard Byrd watched, wrapped in his fur clothing that will keep him warm when taking sights through an open window in temperature far below zero.

The tiny tables on which he will do his navigating were in place, and his instruments, the sextant securely in its case, the compass lashed in a corner where it is free from deviation.

The radio operator, his chunky figure also wrapped in fur, face smiling above the thrust-back hood with its rim of soft brown fur, had tested his instruments, made sure that all the means of keeping camera, with its paraphernalia, over which he will work so rapidly

COMMANDER RICHARD E. BYRD,
Leader of the Antarctic Expedition, Who Is Now in Flight With Three Companions Toward the South Pole.

LATEST MESSAGE FROM BYRD

"All is well with the Byrd plane" was the brief message that Commander Byrd's base at Little America flashed to The New York Times at 6:30 oclock this morning.

As this message was received the radio contact with Little America faded out, and no more was obtainable before this late edition of The New York Times went to press.

From the Commander's airplane, as it sped toward the South Pole, The New York Times radio station last night and early this morning had been receiving frequent messages up to 3:20 A. M. These messages were signed by Harold I. June, the radio operator on the airplane and were routed through Little America, the expedition's base.

Soon after that hour the Byrd plane reached the neighborhood of the Queen Maud range of mountains where an elevation of 10,000 to 12,000 feet was necessary to carry the plane southward. No message came from the plane while this stage of the flight was on, and later daylight coming in the zones northward caused a fading of signals from Little America, as is customary at that hour.

The last clear message that came from Little America before the brief flash telling that all was well, was rceived at 5:15 A. M., New York time. It said that the plane's signals had not then been heard for an hour.

EARLIER MESSAGES FROM PLANE.

Wireless to THE NEW YORK TIMES.

AIRPLANE FLOYD BENNETT, in flight toward the South Pole, 4 P. M. [11 P. M. New York time], Nov. 28.—Flying well over the Geological party's trail. Just passed Forty-five Mile Depot [Depot No. 1 established by the Supporting Party late in October.] Motors fine. JUNE.

4:30 P. M.—We passed the snowmobile [abandoned after an unsuccessful test of Antarctic travel several weeks ago, on the trail southward, some eighty miles from the base] at 4:25 o'clock. JUNE.

5 P. M.—We have made a hundred miles at 4:50 P. M. JUNE.

5:30 P. M.—Flying well. Motors fine. Now at the Crevasses. JUNE.

[The Crevasses are eleven miles beyond Depot No. 3, shown on the map on Page 3.]

7 P. M.—Flying well. Motors fine. About 100 miles from Gould's Geological Party on trail. JUNE.

[Professor Gould's Geological Party was last reported at Depot No. 6 on Nov. 25, and was then making good progress south.]

8:20 P. M.—Reached Gould party 8:15. JUNE.

[The plane carried radio messages for the Geological Party on the trail and it was planned to drop them with a parachute. In the package of messages was also a packet of photographs of the mountains of the Queen Maud Range made by Captain McKinley on Byrd's previous flight a few days ago. These, it is hoped, will help Dr. Gould in his geological work, when he reaches Depot No. 8, shown in the map on Page 3, at the mountains.]

"All the News That's Fit to Print."

The New York Times.

THE WEATHER
Fair and continued cold today; tomorrow cloudy and warmer.
Temperatures yesterday—Max. 30, min. 20.
U. S. Weather Forecast—For details See Page 30.

VOL. LXXIX....No. 26,243. + * * * * NEW YORK, SATURDAY, NOVEMBER 30, 1929. TWO CENTS In Greater New York | THREE CENTS Within 200 Miles | FOUR CENTS Elsewhere Except 7th and 8th Postal Zones

BYRD SAFELY FLIES TO SOUTH POLE AND BACK, LOOKING OVER 'ALMOST LIMITLESS PLATEAU'; DROPS FOOD, LIGHTENS SHIP ON PERILOUS TRIP

FIRST MESSAGE EVER SENT FROM THE SOUTH POLE

By Commander Richard E. Byrd

WIRELESS TO THE NEW YORK TIMES.

ABOARD AIRPLANE FLOYD BENNETT, in flight, 1:55 P. M. Greenwich mean time [8:55 A. M. New York time], Friday, Nov. 29.—My calculations indicate that we have reached the vicinity of the South Pole, flying high for a survey. The airplane is in good shape, crew all well. Will soon turn north. We can see an almost limitless polar plateau. Our departure from the Pole was at 1:25 P. M. BYRD

The difference in the times mentioned in this dispatch, that is between 1:55 P. M. in the date line and 1:25 P. M., given by the Commander as that of his departure from the South Pole, is probably accounted for by the lapse between the writing of the dispatch by the Commander and its coding and sending by the wireless operator, Harold I. June. Greenwich time is five hours ahead of New York time and twelve hours ahead of time at Little America.

The Commander's last sentence was evidently added after he began to fly away from the Pole; the first part written before he left there.

WOMAN HEARD CRASH IN HOTEL AT THE TIME ROTHSTEIN WAS SHOT

Says She Saw Man With Angry or Agonized Look Near McManus's Room.

UNCERTAIN ON HIS IDENTITY

Mrs. M. A. Putnam, "Surprise" Witness for State, Attacked by the Defense.

RAYMOND TELLS OF BIG BET

Testifies He Won $40,000 From Rothstein on One Card—Admits That They Had a Quarrel.

A fragile woman with gray hair, but a schoolgirl complexion, took the stand yesterday in the Criminal Courts Building to aid the State in its effort to convict George A. McManus of the murder of Arnold Rothstein. In clear tones she identified herself as Mrs. Marian A. Putnam of Asheville, N. C., chief of the surprise witnesses for the prosecution.

Loosening the gray squirrel collar of a broadtail fur coat, she said that she had been a guest at the Park Central Hotel on the night of Nov. 4, 1928, when Rothstein received a bullet wound which caused his death two days later. She added that she had registered at the hotel on Oct. 30.

Assistant District Attorney George N. Brothers, urbane in manner and soothing of voice, asked her to tell what she had heard and seen that night. Mrs. Putnam turned her thin face toward the jurymen and folded her hands, asparkle with four diamond rings. Quietly she told how she had heard a "crash" and had seen a man walking down a corridor on the third floor, leading from Room 349, part of a suite hired by McManus.

Saw Agony or Anger in Face.

She had looked at the man's face. It bore the imprint of agony or anger. He had his hands clasped over his abdomen as he followed her down the carpeted passageway. Mrs. Putnam said she locked the door of her room and said nothing about the episode even the following morning when she learned of the shooting.

On through the events of the evening Mr. Brothers led the witness. She told a straightforward story under the prosecutor's questioning and now and then a faint smile curved her tight lips. Mrs. Putnam settled more comfortably in the witness chair and slipped out of the heavy fur coat. As she replied to the questions she smoothed the lace ruffles at the wristbands of her black velvet dress and adjusted the cream-colored lace fichu at her neck.

She completed her story and then James D. C. Murray, attorney for the defense, began his cross-examination. The slow-moving lawyer, his grizzled hair somewhat rumpled, favored the witness with a prolonged stare before he started his questions. Suavely but searchingly he delved into Mrs. Putnam's past. His questions were blunt, but were met with composure by the witness.

Raymond Tells of Winnings.

She made impeaching admissions with a detached calm that almost equaled the perfect poise which had been displayed shortly before by another witness, Nathan (Nigger Nate) Raymond. Raymond, who told how he had won $40,000 from Rothstein when the slain man drew the deuce at high card, admitted that he probably had been guilty of a faux pas—the expression was his own—when he asked Rothstein to give him I. O. U.'s for $200,000 he had won.

During the cross-examination of Raymond the defense developed that he had quarrelled with Rothstein in a taxicab subsequent to the poker game. Raymond said that he had no recollection of any blows having been struck.

When Raymond left the stand the defense sought to have stricken from the record all testimony regarding the poker game. Mr. Murray told the court that the prosecution had failed to carry out its promise to show that the game gave McManus the motive for the murder. Judge Nott refused to grant the motion.

Mrs. Putnam admitted that she had been registered at the Park

Continued on Page Fourteen.

Byrd Lands Radio Amateurs For Help in Message Relays

LOS ANGELES, Nov. 29 (AP).—A congratulatory message sent by Commander Richard E. Byrd just before the start of his flight over the South Pole, was read today at the convention of the Pacific division of the American Radio Relay League.

The message, received by B. E. Sandham, Los Angeles amateur short wave radio operator, read:

"Greetings from Little America to the radio amateurs of the Pacific division. Am glad for this opportunity to acknowledge the big debt our North and South Pole expeditions owe to the amateur radio operators.

"I wish to thank them for their helpfulness and to express my admiration of the high sense of honor they show in handling messages.

"It is radio that has made this expedition possible.

"Cordial good wishes in which all of Little America join.

"RICHARD BYRD."

WINTER GRIPS NATION; MERCURY AT 20 HERE

Icy Blast Sweeping Out of the Northwest Kills 9, Spreads Damage, Blocks Shipping.

BLIZZARDS RAGE IN WEST

One Frozen to Death in New York and No Let-Up in the Frigid Wave Is Seen.

Winter came howling out of the northwest and the Arctic wastes yesterday, bringing blizzards to the Western States and Canada, hampering shipping on the Great Lakes, and holding the West, the Middle West, the East and many Southern States in the grip of sub-freezing temperatures.

It was the frigid season's first general offensive, and it scattered death, suffering and property damage widely. White River, Ontario, which usually claims the distinction of recording low temperatures, shared with Thief River Falls, Minn., first place on the icy list yesterday, both communities recording 26 below zero. At least eight persons died in the North Central States as a result of the sudden zero snap, according to the Associated Press. New York City added one death to the list. ears were felt for the safety of hunters caught unprepared for the severe cold in the Minnesota woods. Near the cradle of Winter, where a 30-mile gale was driving a blizzard over the Saskatchewan Lakes, the fate of fifty fishermen, pushing northward on a 50-mile trip, was in doubt. The fishermen had been gone for three days.

Cold to Continue Here Today.

New York had an uncomfortable sample of Winter, and last night the local Weather Bureau gave practically no hope of a let-up today in the cold temperatures.

This city felt its lowest temperature of the season at 10 o'clock last night when the thermometer registered 20 degrees above zero, 12 below freezing. Even the maximum temperature at 9:30 A. M. was only 30 degrees, or 2 below freezing. The average temperature for the day was 26 degrees, compared with a normal Nov. 29 reading of 39. The coldest Nov. 29 on record occurred in 1872 when the thermometer registered 15 degrees.

The cold here was aggravated by a biting northwest wind, blowing at thirty-eight miles an hour. The city's firemen were put to their first severe test of the season in what was a busy "fire" day in Manhattan, the Bronx and Brooklyn. Up to 9 o'clock last night the number of fires for the day totaled thirty in Manhattan, ten in the Bronx and forty-three in Brooklyn.

Fair Weather Forecast.

Although the barometer in the New York Weather Bureau was rising last night, indicating fair weather for today, the cold snap will continue, according to the official forecaster, and the thousands of football spectators who will swarm into the Yankee Stadium for the Army-Notre Dame game this afternoon will have to wear their warmest clothes and wraps.

"Fresh northeast winds and continued cold" was the prediction for today. At the Weather Bureau it was even considered possible that today might be a little colder than yesterday.

A woman on Staten Island was New York's addition to the list of victims of the cold. She was Mrs. Gladys Todd, 53 years old, who was foun ddead in the back yard of her home, at 4 Schrenkheisen Place, Mar-

Continued on Page Twelve.

CAPITAL DISPLAYS KEENEST INTEREST

President, Waiting News, Is the First in Washington to Hear of Byrd's Success.

OFFICIALS LAUD FLIGHT

Admiral Hughes Says the Commander Is a Worthy Successor to Admiral Wilkes.

Special to The New York Times.

WASHINGTON, Nov. 29.—President Hoover, who had waited anxiously all day for word of the progress of the daring flight to the South Pole, was the first person in Washington, outside of the staff of THE NEW YORK TIMES bureau, to learn of the successful flight of Commander Byrd to the South Pole and back to the base at Little America.

The word was flashed to the White House tonight from the Washington Bureau of THE NEW YORK TIMES. It was transmitted to the President before dinner by Secretary Walter H. Newton.

All day the President had asked for word of the progress of the flight and late in the afternoon had indicated his deep interest. When the news was taken to him, the President expressed his delight over the successful outcome.

Official Washington expressed the most intense relief and the greatest delight at the successful termination of the flight.

Admiral Charles F. Hughes, the Acting Secretary of the Navy, was among the first to be informed.

"We are greatly pleased at the success of Commander Byrd's flight," he said. "He is a worthy successor to Admiral Wilkes, the American naval officer who first discovered the Antarctic Continent."

Earlier in the day Admiral Hughes had said:

"The Navy Department is intensely interested and, knowing Commander Byrd, we are thoroughly confident that he will return successfully."

Davison Congratulates Expedition.

F. Trubee Davison, Assistant Secretary of War for Aeronautics, declared the success of the flight demonstrated again the value of aircraft.

"The flight of Commander Byrd and his brave companions to the South Pole," he said, "is another epic in the annals of the achievements of heavier-than-air craft and proves once again the value of the airplane in exploration of unknown areas where distances can be traveled in hours which under ordinary forms of transportation would require weeks and months. On behalf of the War Department and the Army Air Corps, I wish to congratulate the Byrd Antarctic Expedition. Their achievement will be lauded by Americans the world over."

Major Clarence M. Young, the Assistant Secretary of Commerce for Aeronautics, declared the Byrd flight was simply another demonstration of the "limitless purposes which aviation can serve."

"The flight to the South Pole and back was surely a major accomplish-

Continued on Page Three.

President Sends His Congratulations to Byrd, Saying Spirit of Great Adventure Still Lives

Special to The New York Times.

WASHINGTON, Nov. 29.—After being informed tonight of Commander Byrd's successful flight to the South Pole and back to the base at Little America, President Hoover gave to THE NEW YORK TIMES the following message of congratulations on behalf of himself and the American people, to be transmitted by radio to Commander Byrd:

Commander Richard E. Byrd,
Little America:

I know that I speak for the American people when I express their universal pleasure at your successful flight over the South Pole. We are proud of your courage and your leadership. We are glad of proof that the spirit of great adventure still lives.

Our thoughts of appreciation include also your companions in the flight and your colleagues, whose careful and devoted preparation have contributed to your great success.

HERBERT HOOVER.

BYRD'S FEAT STIRS ENTHUSIASM HERE

Victorious Flight Hailed With Tributes to Commander's Daring and Foresight.

With the reception of news from Little America of the return of Commander Byrd and his companions from their flight over the South Pole, explorers, aviators, aeronautical designers and builders whose names are known throughout the world of aviation and scores of others offered their congratulations to the Commander and expressed their enthusiasm over the success of his efforts.

Some of these comments follow:

Anthony H. G. Fokker, designer of the plane in which Commander Byrd crossed the Atlantic—I didn't expect anything but success from Byrd and Balchen. The Commander is an excellent organizer and Balchen is a fine pilot. With all the qualities fliers need for such an expedition, they have proved the unquestioned value and possibility of the airplane.

Mayor Walker—That's marvelous news. I can sum up the way I feel about it in a single sentence. I knew Dick Byrd would do it. He has made another great contribution to scientific advancement and world knowledge. The American flag will certainly look great down there. I know I speak for the people of this city when I say that we rejoice with him and his intrepid companions in this epoch-making exploit. We will await his return to New York with impatience, so that the city can give him the welcome he so richly deserves. New York City has honored Commander Byrd before. It is glad to honor him again, for it feels that in a very real sense he is one of us.

Lieutenant Governor Herbert H. Lehman—It is glorious news. Commander Byrd's successful flight to the South Pole will go down in history as one of the greatest of human exploits. Its success is all the more noteworthy because achieved in the face of great obstacles after the most painstaking preparation. The nation whose flag he has now carried to the uttermost ends of the globe rejoices with him and his gallant crew for the success they have

Continued on Page Four.

BYRD'S FAMILY GETS NEWS OF FLIGHT

Virginia Governor at Capitol Gets News and Mother Hears It at Winchester.

Special to The New York Times.

RICHMOND, Va., Nov. 29.—Although he knew that his brother, Commander Richard Evelyn Byrd, intended to hop to the South Pole "about this time of the year," Governor Harry F. Byrd said in his office tonight that no one in the family or any one else had known exactly what day the plane Floyd Bennett would leave the base.

Commander Byrd's mother, Mrs. Richard E. Byrd Sr., and Thomas Byrd, his brother, received news of the successful flight at their home in Winchester.

Governor Byrd flew to Richmond late today from Norfolk to get news of his brother. He had been at Chapel Hill for the Virginia-Carolina football game on Thanksgiving Day and stopped in the capital to be the guest of Governor O. Max Gardner of North Carolina. Accompanying Governor Byrd in another plane was Colonel Willard D. Newbill of his staff.

From the Executive Mansion the Governor relayed news of the flight to his mother at Winchester.

When Commander Byrd duplicated his top of the world feat by flying over the South Pole at the very bottom of the world his mother, thought it "glorious" and was "thrilled to death," she said tonight.

"I was in Washington when we heard Dick had hopped off," she said. "My son Tom drove up there to get me when I phoned him and we went back to Winchester to wait for news. THE NEW YORK TIMES called me about 6 o'clock but said they would not release the news generally until later.

"Dick had sent me a Thanksgiving radio message a few hours before they hopped off, 'We are off.' We were very uneasy, but I was never so happy in my life as when we heard he had landed safely back at Little America. We really were quite uneasy because this flight seemed more hazardous than anything he ever tried. Nobody knew anything much about Antarctica.

"When Tom heard Dick had gone over safely he said he was 'tremen-

Continued on Page Two.

BRITISH APPLAUD FLIGHT AS TRIUMPH

Thrill Over Byrd's Feat Puts Polar Land Dispute in the Background.

NEWS EAGERLY AWAITED

German Press and People Followed Commander's Course With Keen Interest.

Special Cable to THE NEW YORK TIMES.

LONDON, Saturday, Nov. 30.—Great Britain watched Commander Byrd's progress over the Antarctic wastes to the South Pole and his return as a magnificent adventure, and what claims he may make to any rich coal or mineral deposits over which he has flown or staked with the American flag is an issue that is exciting no comment here.

Even the publication by New York newspapers of a summary of the State Department's answer to the British Government's year-old note concerning sovereignty over the Antarctic lands, which was read here as clearly indicating that the United States does not intend to abandon its claims based on earlier discoveries by American explorers, was not allowed to distract attention from Commander Byrd's performance or to cause a controversy almost on the eve of the five-power naval parley in London.

Hailed as Byrd Triumph.

The Daily Chronicle outstripped its London rivals this morning by alone printing a full account of Commander Byrd's South Pole flight, as transmitted to it by THE NEW YORK TIMES and associated newspapers. The remainder of the London newspapers were able in their final editions to announce only the bare fact of the aviator's epoch-making flight, with full acknowledgment of the source of their information.

The feat, therefore, was hailed here not only as a personal triumph for Commander Byrd and his three companions, Balchen, June and McKinley, but as an outstanding feat in newspaper organization.

Stupendous as is the accomplishment of a flight of 1,560 miles over the frozen wastes to the South Pole and back in 18 hours and 55 minutes in itself, it has been brought home more vividly to the public mind here by the fact that within a few hours of Commander Byrd's return to his base on the Ross ice shelf, at 10:10 o'clock London time last night, the leading newspapers of the world were able to reproduce the story of the exploit.

It has not escaped notice that scientific development, from the short-wave radio to the finer details of aircraft construction, have been pressed into use on this occasion.

Scientists, aviators and public men on every hand are expressing admiration for Commander Byrd's initiative and courage in carrying out successfully a flight which for scientific results may stand alone.

Commander Byrd had been flying over twelve hours before the British

Continued on Page Four.

CROSSES GLACIER PASS AT 11,500 FEET

Commander Takes Chance and Plane Roars Upward Amid Swirling Drift Out Through Gorge to Tableland

FLYING TIME FOR THE WHOLE CIRCUIT ABOUT 18 HOURS

With Two New Ranges Discovered, the Four Air Argonauts, Guided by Chief, Turn Back to Wild Welcome at Base Camp.

By RUSSELL OWEN.

Wireless to THE NEW YORK TIMES.

LITTLE AMERICA, Antarctica, Nov. 29.—Conqueror of two Poles by air, Commander Richard E. Byrd flew into camp at 10:10 o'clock this morning, having been gone eighteen hours and fifty-nine minutes. An hour of this time was spent at the mountain base refueling.

The first man to fly over the North and South Poles and the only man to fly over the South Pole stepped from his plane and was swept up on the arms of the men in camp who for more than an hour had been anxiously watching the southern horizon for a sight of the plane.

Deaf from the roar of the motors, tired from the continual strain of the flight and the long period of navigation under difficulties, Commander Byrd was still smiling and happy. He had reached the South Pole after as hazardous and as difficult a flight as has ever been made in an airplane, tossed by gusts of wind, climbing desperately up the slopes of glaciers a few hundred feet above the surface.

Radiant Airmen Borne in Triumph.

His companions on the flight tumbled out stiff and weary also, but so happy that they forgot their cramped muscles. They were also tossed aloft, pounded on the back and carried to the entrance of the mess hall.

Bernt Balchen, the calm-eyed pilot who first met Commander Byrd in Spitzbergen and who was with him on the transatlantic flight, came out first. There was a little smudge of soot under the nose, but the infectious smile which has endeared him to those who know him, was radiant.

He was carried away and then came Harold June who, between intervals of helping Balchen and attending to fuel tanks and lines and taking pictures, found time to send the radio bulletins which told of the plane's progress.

And after him Captain Ashley McKinley was lifted from the doorway, beaming like the Cheshire cat because his surveying camera had done its work all the way.

Dumped Food of Forty-five Days, But Not Fuel.

Men crowded about them eager for the story of what they had been through, catching fragments of sentences. It had evidently been a terrific battle to get up through the mountains to the Plateau.

"We had to dump a month and a half of food to do it," said Commander Byrd. "I am glad it wasn't gas. It was nip and tuck all the way."

"Yes," chuckled Balchen. "Do you remember when we were sliding around those knolls picking the wind currents to help us and there wasn't more than 300 feet under us at times? We were just staggering along, with drift and clouds and all sorts of things around us."

When the plane approached the mountains on the way south, Commander Byrd picked out the Livingston Glacier, a large glacier somewhat to the west of the Axel Heiberg Glacier, as the best passageway.

Swooping Upward Through Swirling Drift.

The high mountains shut them in all around as they forced their way upward; Balchen, conserving his fuel to the utmost, coaxing his engines, picking the up-currents of air as best he could to help the plane ride upward.

Clouds swirled about them at times, puff-balls of mist driven down the glacier; drift scurried beneath them; it was a wicked place for an airplane to be, hemmed in by the wall of the towering peaks on either side.

This was the time when they had to lighten ship and Byrd, looking around for what could best be spared, decided to dump some food. There was a dump valve in the fuselage tank, but he had determined to go through and did not know what winds he might face at the top of the glacier. So food was thrown overboard, scattered over the ridged and broken surface of the Livingston Glacier.

"It is an awful looking place," Commander Byrd said.

Over the "Hump" and Vast Panorama Unfolds.

They finally reached the hump at an elevation of 11,500 feet, as indicated by the barograph, although it might have been a little more, because of the difference in pressure inland.

But there was little space under the staggering plane, buffeted by the winds that eddied through the gigantic gorge. Once at the top, Balchen could level off for a time and then gain altitude.

Then there came into view slowly the long sweep of mountains of the Queen Maud Range, stretching to the southeast, and the magnificent panorama of the entire bulwark of mountains along the edge of the Polar Plateau.

Beheld Tinted Slopes of Myriad Mountains.

"It was the most magnificent sight I have ever seen," Commander Byrd said. "I never dreamed there were so many mountains in the world. They shone under the sun, wonderfully tinted with color, and in the southeast a bank of clouds hung over the mountains, making a scene that I shall never forget."

Over the plateau the Commander set his course for the pole. They had had a beam wind all the way in to the mountains which

Marlene Dietrich and Gary Cooper in *Morocco.*

Anna Cristie with Marie Dressler and George F. Marion.

Spencer Tracy appeared with Humphrey Bogart in *Up the River.*

Al Jolson in his starring role in *Mammy.*

The gangster film era began with Edward G. Robinson starring in *Little Caesar.*

Rudy Vallee, one of the first crooners.

"All the News That's Fit to Print."

The New York Times.

THE WEATHER
Cloudy today, with rain tonight; no change in temperature.
Temperatures yesterday—Max., 50; min., 37.
U. S. Weather Forecast—For details see Page 46.

VOL. LXXIX....No. 26,309. **** NEW YORK, TUESDAY, FEBRUARY 4, 1930. TWO CENTS In Greater New York | THREE CENTS Within 200 Miles | FOUR CENTS Elsewhere Except 7th and 8th Postal Zones

BRITISH OFFER NAVAL COUNTER-PROPOSAL, FOR DOWNWARD SHIFTS IN BIG CRUISERS; FULL ANGLO-AMERICAN ACCORD REPORTED

BARS CAPITAL TRANSFERS

Plan Agrees With French on Global Tonnage for Each Nation.

CATEGORIES CUT TO FIVE

Submarines Ignored in Transfer Plans—British Maximum Demands Nearly Ready.

STIMSON SEES MACDONALD

Conversation at House of Commons Said to Have Effected Important Agreement.

By EDWIN L. JAMES.
Special Cable to THE NEW YORK TIMES.

LONDON, Feb. 3.—The British delegation tonight circulated among the other delegations suggestions for modification of the French compromise plan which it will propose to the London naval conference in committee of the whole at 10 o'clock tomorrow morning at St. James's Palace.

The British proposal, which is called a "compromise suggestion," does not attack the major lines of the French scheme, but rather puts forward ideas for making it more specific in essential points. The importance of these suggestions is held to lie in the fact that they represent concrete points which commit Great Britain definitely.

After receipt of the British document Secretary Stimson, head of the American delegation, accompanied by Ambassador Morrow, called on Prime Minister MacDonald at the House of Commons for what is described as an important conversation. It is understood the chiefs of the British and American delegations discussed the possibility that England and America might reach a special accord on the cruiser problem within the frame of the French plan as to the effect of transfer proposals between Washington and London on this class of warship. It is hinted that such an agreement might extend to Japan as well, thus assuring that the proposed transfers, which are regarded as beneficial to smaller navies, would not be allowed in the future to disturb the relative standing of the British, American and Japanese navies in cruisers.

Declare Tonnage Totals Needed.

The British memorandum says it recognizes the ultimate necessity of setting the global tonnage of each fleet as provided in the French plan, this figure being reached by the addition of the totals of the various categories.

Then the British suggest the following categories for warships: First, battleships; second, airplane carriers; third, cruisers, with two subdivisions of them, those with eight-inch guns and those with guns of six inches or less; fourth, destroyers; fifth, submarines.

This differs somewhat from the French suggestion for categories, which are six in number: First, capital ships; second, eight-inch gun cruisers; third, small cruisers and destroyers; fourth, submarines; fifth, airplane carriers; sixth special craft, mine-layers, training ships and so on.

With respect to the much-debated French suggestion for elastic categories arranged so that tonnage might be transferred from one to another on prior notice, the British offer specific suggestions. The French plan left the transfer percentage to be fixed by special arrangements among the powers. The British memorandum asks that there be no transfer from or into the capital ship class. Then it suggests a "slight" transfer from 10,000-ton cruisers downward but not upward. On smaller cruisers and destroyers it suggests a very large transfer right, running to possibly 100 per cent. This amounts to about the same thing as the French proposal to put small cruisers and destroyers in one class.

Suggests No Submarine Transfers.

The British memorandum makes no mention of transfer to or from the submarine class. In principle, the British favor the abolition of submarines, but seeing that this is impracticable at this time they have made it plain they wish no transfer of other tonnage into the submarine class.

The form of the British suggestion

Continued on Page Four.

Effort to Abolish 10,000-Ton Cruisers Hinted As Linked With British Suggestions on Transfers

By P. J. PHILIP.
Special Cable to THE NEW YORK TIMES.

LONDON, Feb. 3.—There seems reason to believe that just as the Washington conference set up the 10,000-ton cruiser as a standard, an effort will be made in the London conference to effect its practical elimination unless the United States insists upon ships of this class.

It will be remembered that the tonnage limit of 10,000 was set at Washington because the British wished to retain in service the Hawkins class of cruisers, which nearly approached that figure. Since that time their experience in building and the use of 10,000-ton cruisers seems to have convinced the British Admiralty that this type should never have been built. Its cost exceeds that of the pre-war dreadnought. Furthermore, the vessels which have been tried out on the China station have failed to give satisfaction either to the Admiralty or their crews.

There is also the disadvantage, from the British point of view, that the Washington type of cruiser carries no side armor. Lastly, the 8-inch gun has never been favorably regarded by the British Navy, which has found that the 7.5-inch gun is more accurate, and the 6-inch even more satisfactory in that it can be man-handled.

Thus it seems, in the light of these experiences, that the British Admiralty is inclined, on the ground of efficiency alone, to take an entirely new position with regard to 10,000-ton cruisers. This is an expert technician's view, and it well accords with the national desire for economy, which is being daily urged by Philip Snowden, Chancellor of the Exchequer.

In this connection, therefore, the British proposal in today's reply to the French memorandum, that a measure of transfers downward from the big-cruiser category, and up to 100 per cent transfer facility be accorded between the light cruiser and destroyer categories, takes on fuller significance.

VITALE ON THE STAND DENOUNCES WHALEN

Declares Hold-Up Was Genuine and Charges Commissioner Is "Most Incompetent."

HE IDENTIFIES BRAVATE

Did Not Know Restaurant Was on Police List—Asks Who Wrote "Murder Contract" Scenario.

Magistrate Albert H. Vitale, testifying in the Bronx County Court yesterday at the trial of Joseph Bravate, alleged bandit in the hold-up of the welcome-home dinner to the magistrate on Dec. 8, denounced Police Commissioner Whalen as "incompetent," called on him to testify at the trial and accused him of "malicious, willful lies" to avoid criticism of the Police Department.

In his detailed description of the hold-up in the Roman Gardens in the Bronx the magistrate was quiet, soft-spoken and deliberate, but at the mention of Mr. Whalen's name he became angry. His bitter attack reasserted itself throughout the day. He sought to control himself, admitting it was an effort, but repeatedly renewed his criticism.

Magistrate Vitale ridiculed Commissioner Whalen's theory that the hold-up was faked and a scheme to get possession of a "murder contract" for the deaths of Frankie Yale and Frank Marlow. He demanded that Mr. Whalen come into court and tell the jury that it was spurious. He positively identified Bravate as the one who "frisked" him, took his watch and chain, "a sentimental" possession; asserted that there was no "make-believe," but that the hold-up was absolutely genuine.

When asked by Lorenzo C. Carlino, Bravate's attorney, if any of the other men alleged to have been accomplices of Bravate had been arrested, the magistrate replied sharply:

"See Whalen about that."

Calls Whalen "Most Incompetent."

Mr. Carlino remarked that Commissioner Whalen was supposed to be "an efficient Police Commissioner," and Magistrate Vitale replied:

"I think he is the most incompetent one we ever had."

Mr. Carlino asked the magistrate why he had not told Detective Arthur Johnson, who was robbed of his pistol at the dinner and later had it returned to him by the magistrate, to take the weapon to the police station and attempt to identify the fingerprints of the bandits on it. The magistrate replied that he had no power to give such orders and that if he had such authority he would "tell Commissioner Whalen to do certain things. And I am serious about that," he added.

"Did you see any one relieved of a murder contract," Mr. Carlino asked.

"Who is the scenario writer of that?" the magistrate replied.

Continued on Page Nineteen.

ROOSEVELT ON RADIO TELLS STATE'S NEEDS

Stresses State Development of Water Power and Its Sale by Contract.

EXPLAINS BUDGET INCREASE

Bond Issue Would Have Saved Taking $30,000,000 From Current Revenue.

Special to The New York Times.

ALBANY, Feb. 3.—Describing the State's needs to its voters, Governor Roosevelt again took up the relations between public utility corporations and the State this evening in a radio speech delivered from the Executive Chamber through Station WGY of the General Electric Company. Early in his talk he devoted attention to water power development and public utility control policies.

He stressed the fact that his plan for water-power development by the State provided for application of the contract principle, as distinguished from the present regulation of rates by the Public Service Commission.

The bill virtually accepted by the Republicans, he said, "also recognizes the principle of selling the electricity when developed by contract rather than allowing it to be distributed by electric light companies, under the old system of mere regulation by the Public Service Commission."

He expressed the hope that the result would be a definite reduction in rates to householders.

Emphasizing that telephones are used primarily for local service, and that therefore regulation of telephone rates could not possibly come within the intent of the Interstate Commerce Commission or within the scope of Federal courts of original jurisdiction, he went on:

"I am making a very strong point with Congress to recognize this and change the Federal court statutes so as to make telephone companies and other utilities present their rate cases to the State courts before they go to the United States Supreme Court."

Explains Budget Increases.

Discussing his annual budget, he explained its large total as the result of neglect on the part of previous State Administrations to make adequate provision for the State's needs. He declared that if the Republican leaders of the Legislature had accepted last year his proposal for a $50,000,000 bond issue, taxpayers would have been saved some $30,000,000 of the $311,000,000 that this year must be raised by taxation to meet the big expense bill for the coming fiscal year.

The Governor expressed the opinion that there would be accord between him and the Republicans in the Legislature on improvements at the prisons and more humane treatment of the inmates of penal institutions.

He expressed his conviction that there would be continued cooperation between the two parties represented in the Legislature in the enactment of measures for rural tax relief.

He regretted that the substantial relief afforded by last year's Legis-

Continued on Page Eighteen.

CITY INQUIRY BILL GOES IN AT ALBANY; COVERS 3 BRANCHES

Magistrates' Courts, Police and Board of Standards and Appeals Are Named.

COULD INCLUDE FIREMEN

Rothstein Murder and Pathe Studio Fire Given as Cause of Move.

DECISION UP TO GOVERNOR

Action After Delay Laid to Maier Pressure—Roosevelt Smiles and Awaits Measure.

Special to The New York Times.

ALBANY, Feb. 3.—Following conversations with William J. Maier, Republican State chairman, the Republican leaders in the Legislature tonight introduced their bill for an executive investigation of New York City.

The bill provides for a commission of five members to be appointed by the Governor with a fund of $50,000 and full power of subpoena over prospective witnesses and records. The commission is directed to delve into the affairs of three departments of the city, the magistrates' courts, the Police Department and the Board of Standards and Appeals, including its rules for protecting people and property against fire.

The unsolved mystery of the murder of Arnold Rothstein, according to a Republican announcement, gives the cue for the inquiry into the Police Department. The Pathé Studio fire, with its loss of life and the subsequent discovery of the storage of an excess quantity of film on the premises, offers the lead for the investigation of the enforcement of fire laws.

The bill gives a grant of general authority in this connection for the investigators to examine any departments or officials performing duties under these laws. The Fire Department would of course be embraced in any such inquiry.

The sponsors of the measure are Senator Knight, leader of the upper house, and Assemblyman Russell Dunmore, Republican floor leader in the lower house. Coming under such auspices the bill will undoubtedly have the solid support of the Republican majority in each house. It will leave upon the Governor the burden of deciding whether to veto the bill or to initiate the investigation.

Measure Had Lain Dormant.

Of what he intends to do, Governor Roosevelt gave no indication tonight. Apprised that the measure had been introduced, he laughed, and said he would await its appearance on his desk before he discussed it.

In Republican circles it is believed that if the Governor acts upon it he will incur some antagonism among New York City Democrats. If he vetoes it, the Republicans argue, he will risk the hostility of non-partisans who want to see revealed the real conditions in the city administration.

The introduction of the bill tonight came after three weeks of inactivity on the part of its sponsors since their announcement of their intentions. For a time it appeared that the measure might never be introduced. Among New York City Republicans there was considerable criticism of the fact that the bill did not provide for a "straight" Republican legislative inquiry. There was also complaint that they had not been consulted by the legislative leaders on the matter.

Speaker McGinnies, who had been one of the sponsors of the announce-

Continued on Page Eleven.

PRESIDENT NAMES HUGHES CHIEF JUSTICE AS TAFT RESIGNS BECAUSE OF ILL HEALTH WHEN TRIP TO ASHEVILLE FAILS TO AID HIM

Times Wide World Photo.
CHARLES EVANS HUGHES.

Times Wide World Photo.
WILLIAM HOWARD TAFT.

SENATE GETS NOMINATION

Speedy Confirmation Is Forecast for New Head of Supreme Court.

OLD OPPOSITION PASSES

Mr. Hoover Acts Quickly as Rumors of Other Choices Circulate at Capital.

TAFT RETIRES ON FULL PAY

Successor's Son, C. E. Hughes Jr., Will Immediately Resign as Solicitor General.

By RICHARD V. OULAHAN.
Special to The New York Times.

WASHINGTON, Feb. 3.—Charles Evans Hughes of New York, who resigned as associate justice of the United States Supreme Court in 1916 to be the Republican candidate for President, was nominated this afternoon by President Hoover to be chief justice of the United States to succeed William Howard Taft of Ohio, whose resignation was tendered and accepted by the President a few hours earlier. Chief Justice Taft was 72 years old on Sept. 15. Mr. Hughes will be 68 on April 11.

Chief Justice Taft, who will continue to draw full pay of $20,500 a year while on the retired list, is on his way to Washington from Asheville, N. C., where he recently went for the benefit of his health. There is reason to believe that the retiring chief justice is seriously ill. His impaired physical condition was the sole reason for his resignation.

Retirement Law Has Changed.

A change made in the judiciary retirement law last March provided that the ten years' service on the Federal bench required to qualify a judge under the retirement rules need not be continuous, as heretofore, and this enabled Chief Justice Taft to go on the retired list. His service on the Supreme bench began in 1921, but he had served as a United States Circuit judge prior to holding certain political offices, including that of President, and this gave him more than the ten years of service which the law stipulated.

Shortly after Mr. Hughes's nomination was sent to the Senate it was announced by the Department of Justice that his son, Charles Evans Hughes Jr., would resign from the office of Solicitor General of the United States, a position which requires frequent appearances before the Supreme Court.

There is no indication of any opposition to the confirmation of Mr. Hughes's nomination. This is surprising to some, who had been aware of a critical attitude toward Mr. Hughes among Senators when there was talk at various times in the past that he might be asked to return to the Supreme bench.

It was contended that a man who left the Supreme Court to run for political office, as Mr. Hughes did in 1916 when he was nominated for President, had impaired his eligibility for further service in the highest court.

An expression used by those who maintained that critical view was that "the Supreme Court should not be used as a stepping stone to political office," and this was reversed to uphold the contention that after a justice of the high court had left it to seek an elective position of a political character, he should not be permitted to return to the court.

Nomination Referred to Committee.

Inquiry among Senators this evening, however, failed to develop any sentiment in favor of contesting Mr. Hughes's nomination on that ground. When the nomination was delivered to the Senate between 4 and 5 o'clock this afternoon by the President's messenger, Senator Watson, the Republican floor leader, moved that it be referred to the Committee on the Judiciary, and the motion was carried without comment of any sort.

Senator Norris of Nebraska, chairman of the Judiciary Committee and leader of the insurgent Republicans, said that he would call a meeting of the committee for Monday.

"There is no objection to Mr. Hughes's appointment," he said. "I think the Judiciary Committee will recommend confirmation by a unanimous vote. I have not heard anything to the contrary."

Senator Johnson of California, with whom Mr. Hughes figured in a famous incident in 1916, when Mr.

DRESS STRIKE TODAY TO CALL OUT 35,000

Police Mobilize to Prevent Clashes as Reds Order Rival Demonstration.

EARLY VICTORY PREDICTED

Workers Will Drop Tools at 10 A. M. and Picket 3,500 Shops for Two Hours.

At 10 o'clock this morning the whirring sewing machines in scores of skyscraper lofts and "hole-in-the-wall" dressmaker shops will be halted and union officials will announce the beginning of what is expected to be the largest general strike in the annals of the International Ladies' Garment Workers Union.

For two hours the strikers, of whom 65 per cent are women, will walk back and forth before the shops in a mass picketing demonstration and then they will march to fifteen meeting halls for instructions and committee assignments and to listen to union officials outline the situation.

The strike appeals will be directed to 35,000 dressmakers. While all are not expected to down tools the first day, the leaders expect a 100 per cent walkout before many days.

A large force of police will be on hand to maintain order in the dress zone. Inspector Patrick S. McCormick will be in command of ten Lieutenants, twenty-six Sergeants and 240 patrolmen. At 3 P. M. an additional 240 patrolmen will be posted.

The union leaders will disregard the Communist element so far as possible, but they said that they would be prepared "for trouble" if the Communist party attempts to mobilize its members in the dress zone this morning. One of the Communist foreign language dailies yesterday called upon all party members of all trades to picket the dress district today. The International Union officials said that perhaps thirty-five shops out of 3,500 were controlled by the Communist organization.

The duration of the strike will depend largely on the workers' response today and tomorrow. A vir-

Continued on Page Fifteen.

Rutledge Preceded Hughes In 2 Appointments to Bench

Special to The New York Times.

WASHINGTON, Feb. 3.—The records of the Supreme Court show that Mr. Hughes is the second member of that tribunal who resigned and was afterward reappointed.

John Rutledge of South Carolina was appointed Associate Justice of the Supreme Court in 1789 and served until 1791. He was elected Chief Justice of South Carolina in 1790 and served on the State bench until 1795. Then he was nominated for Chief Justice of the Federal Supreme Court in place of John Jay, resigned.

Rutledge resigned his State position to become chief justice here and actually presided at the August term of the Federal Supreme Court before the Senate had acted on his nomination.

But on Dec. 15, 1795, the Senate refused to confirm him and his service on the supreme bench ended.

TAFT, ILL, STARTS BACK TO CAPITAL

Marked Change in Chief Justice's Condition Took Place at Asheville, Causing Anxiety.

Special to The New York Times.

ASHEVILLE, N. C., Feb. 3.—With his condition admittedly more serious than when he arrived here three weeks ago for a rest, Chief Justice Taft left here this afternoon for Washington, where earlier in the day it had been announced that he had submitted his resignation.

From those close to the family during their stay here, it was learned that a marked change in Mr. Taft's condition occurred several days ago, causing deep anxiety.

Just before his departure, when newspaper men asked for a statement from Mr. Taft, they were told that his physical condition prevented him from talking to any one and that he was able only to make known his simplest needs.

Chief Justice Taft's return to Washington followed a conference between Dr. Francis Hagner of Washington, his chief physician, and local physicians who had been attending him. The following statement was issued this afternoon prior to the departure:

"Chief Justice Taft improved for the first ten days he was in Asheville. Since then he has not improved, and after a consultation with local physicians, it was decided to send him back to Washington. He will go to his home. His condition is not immediately serious."

Mrs. Taft and Robert A. Taft of Cincinnati, a son, attended the consultation of physicians. Robert Taft departed Sunday for Washington to present the resignation to President Hoover.

The Chief Justice was accompanied on the journey by Dr. Hagner, Mrs. Taft and Miss Gertrude Manifold, a nurse.

Until last Wednesday Mr. Taft had been able to take daily automobile rides about the city and near-by scenic resorts. At that time, however, it was announced that he was weary and preferred to remain in his room at Grove Park Inn. He was not seen in public again until he made the two-mile trip to the railroad station this afternoon. He enjoyed short walks near the inn during the first two weeks of his stay. Mrs. Taft usually accompanying him.

Newspaper men stood outside Grove

Continued on Page Two.

HUGHES GRATEFUL FOR NATION'S HONOR

He Accepts Chief Justiceship as "Greatest Opportunity" to Serve His Country.

LEAVING THE WORLD COURT

It Is Disclosed That He Did Not Desire Re-election—He Pays Warm Tribute to Taft.

Charles Evans Hughes will accept appointment as Chief Justice of the United States Supreme Court and will resign at once from his place on the bench of the World Court.

Displaying a genial, almost beaming urbanity in striking contrast to his reputed sternness and aloofness, the prospective presiding officer of the highest court in the land made this known yesterday afternoon in his law offices at 100 Broadway, following publication of his selection by President Hoover.

Due to the absence of any official notification of the appointment that will crown a notable career in American jurisprudence, Mr. Hughes asked to be excused from making any formal comment other than to say that he regarded it as a high honor and one which afforded the greatest opportunity for service that could be offered by the government.

World Court Calendar Cleared.

Just when he will go to Washington and similar details of the impending change in his status have not been decided, Mr. Hughes said, and intimated that he might have some statement to make today in direct comment on his appointment.

At the same time he made public a statement prepared earlier in the day in which he voiced his deep regret at the retirement of Chief Justice Taft and, lauding Justice Taft's work on the Supreme Court bench, expressed the hope that his health would be improved by freedom from the exactions of his post.

Mr. Hughes's immediate retirement from the World Court, in his opinion, will not disrupt the labors of that body in any way, as it was explained that a number of cases before the court had been disposed of and the calendar had been pretty well cleared up.

The World Court, it was added, would have no business before it until June, while in September an entirely new court would be elected under regulations that would have prevented Mr. Hughes's acceptance of re-election even if he had desired it, and he said that he did not desire it.

Had Not Desired Service Abroad.

The new regulations will require that the judges of the Permanent Court of International Justice hold no public office in their own countries and in addition that they devote the major portion of their energies to World Court work.

Mr. Hughes mentioned the fact that he had been elected to the court last July 30 only to serve out the unexpired term of John Bassett Moore, and that the term would have ended in September. It was made clear when he accepted election at that time that he would be under no obligation to take re-election for the full nine-year term under the new rules.

Acceptance of such a post would have necessitated his spending much of his time abroad for the next nine

Continued on Page Two.

Lindbergh Loses Aileron of His Glider Aloft, But Safely Lands in California Mountains

By The Associated Press.

LEBEC, Cal., Feb. 3.—Colonel Charles A. Lindbergh treated a few flying friends, news-reel camera men and newspaper men to a real thrill today. He disappeared in the heart of the Tehachapi Mountains in a disabled sail plane, causing grave concern for his safety. For an hour or more in this isolated area it was unknown whether the famous flier had cracked up or whether he had mastered a crippled, motorless ship.

Then he came up smiling. Just another experimental flight and no harm done, he revealed.

Colonel Lindbergh came here Sunday with Hawley Bowlus of San Diego, champion American glider pilot, to "play and experiment" with a sail plane—a motorless flying ship. They established a camp ten miles beyond the ridge route, the main highway through the mountains.

It was revealed later that they expected to break the world's record for gliders, eight hours in the air, now held by Germany. For that reason this mountainous area with its diminishing hills leading out into the Mojave Valley to the north was selected for the experiment.

This morning, immediately after the assembly of the sail plane, which was brought here on a motor truck, Mr. Bowlus, who holds the American record of six hours in the air, made two trial flights, hopping in each flight from hill to hill.

Then Colonel Lindbergh took off. As he sailed into the air the right aileron, one of the ship controls, fell off. As warning shouts on the ground sought to apprise him of the mishap, the colonel circled around, gracefully manoeuvring the sail plane on the air current. Then he soared over a distant hill and descended out of view.

Fearing disaster, the little group started from the camp to seek the missing flyer. They had not gone far, however, when they came to a point where it was seen that the sail plane had landed safely. Colonel Lindbergh was found surveying the ship. It was undamaged other than the loss of the aileron.

"I'll try it again tomorrow, if conditions are favorable," Colonel Lindbergh said. "This thing controls as well without wings as it does with them."

The Colonel said he was not alarmed when the aileron dropped off, but just let air currents carry the sailplane. He said he did have "a little trouble" in landing.

"The aileron fell off because the duralumin had become crystalized by hard knocks," Colonel Lindbergh said. "It was an uncomfortable feeling when I saw it fall."

People stood in line for hours to get apples to sell.

An unemployment protest demonstration in St. Louis, Missouri.

Idle Man, a photograph by Lewis W. Hine.

"All the News That's Fit to Print."

The New York Times.

Copyright, 1930, by The New York Times Company.

THE WEATHER
Fair with rising temperature today and tomorrow.
Temperature yesterday—Max., 29; min., 17.
U. S. Weather Forecast—For details see Page 47.

VOL. LXXIX....No. 26,337. **** NEW YORK, TUESDAY, MARCH 4, 1930. TWO CENTS In Greater New York | THREE CENTS Within 200 Miles | FOUR CENTS Elsewhere Except 7th and 8th Postal Zones

UTILITY BODY FAILS TO GUARD PUBLIC, SAYS KNIGHT REPORT; MANY LAW CHANGES URGED

DENY THAT REGULATION FAILS

But Legislators Admit Overemphasis on the Judicial Aspects.

KNIGHT ASSAILS GOVERNOR

Accuses Him and Appointees of Trying to Block Constructive Reforms.

MINORITY FILES DISSENT

Chief Difference Involves Valuation System—Long Battle Predicted in Legislature.

The text of the report of the Special Legislative Commission on the Revision of the Public Service Commission Law will be found on Pages 19, 20 and 21.

By W. A. WARN.

Special to The New York Times.

ALBANY, March 3.—Denial that public utility regulation in this State through the Public Service Commission has been a failure and admission that the commission, by becoming too much wrapped up in what has been termed its quasi-judicial function, has neglected its primary duty of protecting the public against invasion of its rights by public utility corporations are outstanding features of the final report of the commission on revision of the public service commission law filed this evening with Governor Roosevelt and the Legislature.

As had been forecast in previous statements, the three members of the commission appointed by Governor Roosevelt, Frank P. Walsh, Professor James C. Bonbright of Columbia University and David C. Adie of Buffalo, refused to sign the final report. The other members of the commission, whose chairman is Senator Knight, Republican leader of the upper house, are Republican legislators.

Minority Also Files Report.

Mr. Walsh and Professor Bonbright joined in a minority report which also was presented to the Legislature, its contents already having been made public. With the two reports was filed a statement from Senator Warren T. Thayer, chairman of the Senate Committee on Public Service.

Aside from making a charge that the Public Service Commissioners had been lax in the enforcement of the law and showed pronounced leanings toward the public utility corporations, thereby bringing about a breakdown of regulation, the minority report failed to agree with the findings of the majority in only one essential respect, this being the recommendation with regard to the valuation of utility properties for rate-making.

The Governor's appointees urged application of the so-called "prudent investment" principle, under which the prevailing "value of the property" principle is abandoned and the "actual cost" standard substituted. The majority, on the other hand, would enable the Public Service Commission to arrive at agreements with corporations with regard to rate bases, such valuations, with changes to cover additional investments, to be embodied in contracts which would remain in force for periods not to exceed ten years.

Most Differences Minor.

There were minor differences as to methods of meeting situations on which all were agreed. The minority, for example, advocated that the Governor appoint the "people's counsel," while the majority would vest the power in the Attorney General. The minority recommended a minimum increase in salaries for certain positions of the Public Service Commission, while the majority urged a comprehensive survey of existing salary schedules, classification and standardization of the pay of the entire staff.

The minority recommended that grade crossing elimination be allocated in its entirety to the Department of Public Works, while the majority recommended maintenance of the existing system.

The Chief Recommendations.

The chief recommendations of the majority report are:

An immediate valuation, to take three years and cost "several million" dollars, of the properties of all public utility corporations in the State, with the exception of steam railroads and trolley roads.

Establishment and stabilization of rate bases through valuations agreed upon in contracts between

Continued on Page Eighteen.

Byrd, 898 Miles From Port, Speeded by Quartering Wind

By JOE DE GANAHL.

Wireless to THE NEW YORK TIMES.

ON BOARD THE BARK CITY OF NEW YORK, At Sea, Tuesday March 4.—The southerly gale which was sending the City of New York along her course to Dunedin at record speed yesterday had subsided this morning, but strong winds of varying intensity are blowing from the southwest.

According to Captain Melville's dead reckoning, Admiral Byrd's flagship is making seven knots before the quartering wind and sea. This would place us in Lat. 60.42 S., Long. 168.26 E. at noon today, or 898 miles south of Tairoa Head, N. Z.

The day's run was 162 miles, but an observation at noon yesterday showed that the ship had made 179 miles in the previous twenty-four hours, her best run since she left Dunedin on her voyage to the Barrier and return.

Wireless to THE NEW YORK TIMES.

ON BOARD THE STEAMSHIP ELEANOR BOLLING, At Sea, Tuesday, March 4.—With streaks of blue in the clouds overhead, we are sailing into a warmer area, though all the ice has not yet melted off the ship. A west-southwest wind gives a moderate swell to the sea. Our position at noon today was Lat. 62:05 S., Long. 168:12 E.

TARDIEU TO REPEAT HIS NAVAL DEMANDS

Cabinet Shake-Up Leaves Paris Insistent on Security Pact or 724,000 Tons by 1936.

COUNTRY WANTS TAX CUTS

More Anxious About Them Than Defense, So Modification of Stand Is Not Impossible.

By P. J. PHILIP.

Special Cable to THE NEW YORK TIMES.

PARIS, March 3.—There seems little likelihood of any immediate change in French policy at the London naval conference as a result of the political disturbance of the past two weeks in Paris. The French memorandum of Feb. 13 remains the basis of the delegation's position, with its alternative demand for a fleet of some 724,000 tons by 1936, which the English reject, or a treaty of mutual guarantee and security, which the United States and the British dominions reject as likely to embroil them in wars which are not of their making or to their liking.

The treaty the French suggest would, they maintain, transform "the absolute requirements of each power into relative requirements" and would therefore supposedly bring

Continued on Page Four.

HAITIANS ASK RECALL OF GENERAL RUSSELL; CALL HIM DICTATOR

Two Leaders Before Hoover Board Assert Borno Is the Commissioner's Puppet.

WARN OF A "MASSACRE"

They Declare Bloodshed Will Be Sure to Follow if People Are Denied Presidential Vote.

BENEFIT UNDER US DENIED

Dantes Bellegarde, Economist, Says Country Has Gone Backwards Under Americans.

By HAROLD N. DENNY,
Staff Correspondent of THE NEW YORK TIMES.
Special Cable to THE NEW YORK TIMES.

PORT AU PRINCE, March 3.—President Hoover's commission was warned at its hearings today that if the scheduled election of the next President by the Council of State on April 14 is allowed to take place, the populace, though disarmed, would rise in revolt and Haitians again fall before the guns of marines. A demand was also made for the recall of Brig. Gen. John H. Russell.

The warning, uttered calmly and in measured words by some Haitians from among the most prominent intellectual leaders, came as a climax to a day of frank expression of opposition to the American occupation. It served to emphasize a fact which was made evident on the day of the commission's arrival—that the demand for a popular election of the next President presents a crisis of the first magnitude for the very near future.

Opponents of the occupation appear prepared to wait a reasonable time for the actual withdrawal of American control but there is a great body of responsible public opinion which is adamant in the demand that the Council of State, which President Borno appointed, must not elect a successor who, they assert would be a creature of Borno.

The constitutional method for electing a President would be by a Legislative Assembly, elected by the people, corresponding to the American Congress. The difficulties in the way of electing a new Senate and Chamber of Deputies in the brief time now remaining are apparent. Witnesses at the hearing today said several plans for solving the crisis had been evolved. On the request of W. Cameron Forbes they promised to submit soon a unified project for the commission.

"The Council of State does not represent the nation," said Antoin Regal, chairman of the Federated Committee of Patriotic Societies, composed of seven organizations representing, according to M. Regal, "several hundred thousand Haitians." M. Regal, of pure black complexion, courtly and immaculate in morning dress, was outspoken in his demand that the United States recall General Russell.

"The Council of State is only the clerk of the State Department," he said.

"The members are nominated on the recommendation of Russell. It is Russell who is the real ruler of the country. The present President is only a puppet. The Council of State passes without discussion every

Continued on Page Three.

Prince of Wales Improving From Malaria; Queen Mary Sees Slide of the Fever Germ

Special Cable to THE NEW YORK TIMES.

NAIROBI, Kenya Colony, March 3.—The Prince of Wales is better and there is every indication that he will be up in a few days and ready to resume his hunting expedition. The following bulletin was issued today at Government House, where the Prince is staying:

"The condition of the Prince of Wales continues to improve. No complications have occurred and his complete recovery is expected at an early date."

The official announcement indicates that the Prince is making normal progress, common to mild attacks of malaria. Subtertian malaria is not a malignant type, and, although it sometimes brings high temperature, it is quite unlikely there will be any bad after effects. The Prince's temperature is now down to normal and he is making good progress.

The royal patient had a good night and was cheerful during the day today. It is probable that he contracted the trouble in the Voi area of the hinterland, where he went stalking animals with a camera Friday. Voi is a low-lying area too unhealthful for white settlement and is in complete contrast to the healthy highlands. The bracing, cool air of Nairobi should soon restore the Prince to health, although malaria, like a feverish cold, requires several days to pass away.

No change in plans is indicated or suggested at present and there is no reason to believe the Prince will have to abandon his tour.

NAIROBI, Kenya Colony, March 3 (AP).—The Prince of Wales is attended by physicians and nurses who have specialized in this curse of equatorial Africa, and, thanks to their care, with his own strong constitution and optimistic temperament, it is believed that any danger of complications or a relapse is slight.

At the start of his illness the Prince underwent the ordeal of being shaken twenty-four hours in a train ride. His fever developed while the royal hunting party was in a train between Kiu and Voi Friday night, and it was not until early Sunday that the party arrived at Nairobi.

Special Cable to THE NEW YORK TIMES.

LONDON, March 3.—Queen Mary looked into a microscope today and saw the malarial parasite which has attacked her son in Africa. She was visiting the Queen Alexandria Military Hospital at Westminster to see the new wing which the Prince of Wales opened last year and, on going through the laboratory, the Queen asked to have a slide of the malarial parasite shown to her.

Squinting through a microscope, she examined it carefully for some time.

All reports of the Prince's condition reaching the royal family are reassuring. A message from Colonel Piers Legh, the Prince's equerry, said the case was mild, without complications of any kind.

According to Sir Lionel Halsey, controller to the Prince of Wales, there is nothing in the messages from Nairobi to indicate the Prince is abandoning his African tour.

Taft's Condition Again Slightly Improves; Today Is 21st Anniversary of Inauguration

Special to The New York Times.

WASHINGTON, March 3.—Former President Taft, now ill for more than a month, may linger indefinitely on the verge of death unless his heart suddenly fails, his physicians reported today.

Their visit to the former Chief Justice this evening having given them no reason to change that opinion, expressed earlier in the day, it appeared that although hope for the patient's recovery was abandoned the middle of last week, Mr. Taft would live through the twenty-first anniversary, tomorrow, of his inauguration as President of the United States.

On that day in 1909 a blizzard shut off Washington from the outside world for hours.

While it was believed that Mr. Taft probably could not live out the week, it appeared today that he had made such effective resistance that death might be delayed for some days. the attending physicians, Dr. Francis R. Hagner and Dr. Thomas A. Claytor, after their morning visit, issued this bulletin:

The former Chief Justice had a good night. He continues to take some nourishment. A few days ago his condition was very critical, and unless some sudden change occurs, due to arterio sclerosis, his term of life for the present is indeterminate.

Their second bulletin, issued through the White House at 7 P. M., read:

There is no change in the condition of the former Chief Justice since this morning.

Late at night the doctors called again and left their patient sleeping, his condition unchanged.

There were few callers at the Taft home during the day. The police guard maintained in front of the house during the past five critical days was withdrawn in the evening at the suggestion of Robert A. Taft, who departed for his home in Cincinnati. He had been at his father's home since Friday.

Saying that he expected to return in two or three days, he added that there had been a marked improvement in his father's condition and that he might live for some time.

3 LAWYERS INDICTED FOR JURY-FIXING PLOT

Joseph Shalleck, E. H. Reynolds and A. N. Sager Accused in Utah Lead Case.

COURT BAILIFFS IMPLICATED

Attendant and Juror Confessed, Says Tuttle, Who Is Ready to Try Attorneys Today.

Three attorneys were indicted by the Federal grand jury yesterday on charges of bribery, conspiracy and obstructing justice while appearing as counsel for defendants in the Utah Lead Company mail frauds trial. They are:

Joseph Shalleck, brother of Municipal Court Justice Benjamin Shalleck and president of the Monongahela Democratic Club at 292 Manhattan Avenue in the Eleventh District.

Arthur N. Sager, former assistant to the United States Attorney General at Washington and one time Circuit Attorney, or prosecutor, at St. Louis, Mo.

Edward H. Reynolds, formerly an Assistant United States Attorney under Francis G. Caffey.

Mr. Shalleck, whose offices are at 152 West Forty-second Street, and Mr. Sager, whose offices are at 225 Broadway, appeared voluntarily at the Federal Building soon after the indictment had been returned, pleaded not guilty, were released in $2,500 bail and their trial was set down to begin this morning.

It was said that Mr. Reynolds, who lives at Irvington, N. Y., would appear for pleading this morning and that if a Federal judge were available the three would be placed on trial at once if Mr. Reynolds, like the others, announced his readiness.

Eight Counts in Indictment.

The indictment, which contains eight counts, sets forth that John Cruz, the juror who caused the hung jury in the Utah Lead Company trial, and Murray Wechsler, a Federal court bailiff, were conspirators with three attorneys and others unnamed. Wechsler and Cruz were not indicted, however. United States Attorney Tuttle explained that the juror, his wife and the bailiff were "in the care of the government" as material witnesses against the lawyers indicted.

The true bill alleges that Mr. Shalleck, Mr. Sager and Mr. Reynolds "did offer, give and cause to be offered and given various sums of money aggregating over $300 to and for the benefit of John Cruz, to wit, the respective sums of about $15, $10, $50, $50 and $200." It is alleged further that they gave also "promises of money, value and reward" to influence Cruz's decision as a juror in the Utah Lead trial.

The three attorneys are alleged to have conspired with each other, with Cruz, Wechsler and others "to the grand jurors unknown," to cause Cruz to reach a decision unfavorable to the government in the trial. The sixth count of the indictment states that the three attorneys offered, gave and caused to be offered and given, various sums of money to "bailiffs" in attendance at the trial. No bailiff is mentioned by name, however, except Wechsler.

It is charged that not only was the money given to bailiffs to "promote the rendering of a verdict favorable to the defense," but also "to cause the said bailiffs to disclose to the said defendants (naming the attorneys) the opinions and deliberations of the jury with intent to prevent the said bailiffs from assisting the court fairly and impartially in the administration of justice."

"Overt Acts" in True Bill.

The following "overt acts" are set forth:

"1. The defendant, Arthur N. Sager, during the said trial tele-

Continued on Page Twelve.

LIQUOR-BUYER CASE IN SUPREME COURT

Tribunal Will Listen April 14 to Pleas on Reversal of the Norris Conviction.

WETS' INNING AGAIN TODAY

Their Views at House Hearings Will Be Concluded—Drys to Begin Tomorrow.

Special to The New York Times.

WASHINGTON, March 3.—The Supreme Court today announced its determination to review the questions at issue in the Norris case, in which Federal enforcement officials have sought to hold the buyer equally guilty with the seller of liquor in an alleged conspiracy to violate the national prohibition act, where transportation is used to effect the delivery of bootleg liquor.

The court, in an order read by Chief Justice Hughes, granted the government's request for a writ of certiorari to review the judgment of the Circuit Court of Appeals of the Third Circuit (Philadelphia) and set April 14 for hearing arguments in the case.

The suit arose when dry agents proceeded against Alfred N. Norris of 55 East Seventy-third Street, New York, and Joel D. Kerper of Philadelphia for conspiracy based upon the alleged shipment of liquor by Kerper to Norris. It was brought out in evidence that Mr. Norris communicated with Kerper over the telephone and made arrangements for shipments, which were carried under the guise of olive oil, syrup and other articles. Kerper was convicted.

Mr. Norris's contention that the buying of liquor was not a crime under the Volstead act was overruled and he was fined $200 in the District Court. He appealed and the Circuit Court sustained him, holding that "a sale of liquor involving such transportation as is necessary to effect delivery to the purchaser does not subject the purchaser and seller for indictment to transport."

Wets Again to Be Heard Today.

While the Supreme Court's decision to review the liquor-buyer issue attracted chief attention in prohibition developments in the capital during the day, much interest turned toward final presentation tomorrow of the wets' arguments before the House Judiciary Committee, which is holding hearings on several repeal or modification bills.

Representative J. Charles Linthicum of Maryland, leader of the House wet bloc, made public a list of nine witnesses whom he expects to appear. The list included Representative Celler of New York. Breckinridge Long, former Assistant Secretary of State; Noah B. Martin of Lewiston, Idaho; Mrs. W. W. Montgomery Jr. of Philadelphia, Dr. Steward Patton of Baltimore, Mrs. Robert W. Lovett of Boston, Mrs. Courtlandt Nicoll of New York, Mrs. Carroll Miller of Pittsburgh and Henry H. Stroud, former special agent of the Department of Justice.

The prohibition advocates declined to disclose who would be their first witnesses when their day comes Wednesday. Rumors persisted that Henry Ford and John D. Rockefeller Jr. are among the prominent citizens whom they will present to defend the Eighteenth Amendment and the laws enacted under it.

There was a further postponement by the Senate Judiciary Committee of the hearing set for March 10 on the resolution of Senator Norris for an investigation of the Prohibition Bureau. The hearing will be held March 17, in accordance with a request made by Chairman George W. Wickersham of the Hoover Law Enforcement Commission. The commission is scheduled to meet here March 12, and it is understood Mr. Wickersham desires to confer with his associates before expressing any views to the Senate committee.

Hearings on the Williamson bill, already passed by the House, for the transfer of the Prohibition Bureau from the Treasury to the Department of Justice, will also be deferred. The subcommittee in charge

Continued on Page Seventeen.

WALKER WARNS REDS STERN CURB AWAITS LAWLESS OUTBREAKS

City Will Not Tolerate the Use of Its Streets to Exploit Jobless, Mayor Declares.

ASSURES FREE SPEECH

Radicals Will Be Protected as Long as They Keep the Peace, He Promises.

THREE MEETINGS CANCELED

But Communist Leaders Send Out Calls for Big Demonstration in Union Square Thursday.

While Communists continued their preparations yesterday for their "unemployment demonstration" in Union Square on Thursday, Mayor Walker issued last night a statement outlining his policy toward "all future public disturbances." He warned that the City Administration will not permit the unemployment problem to be used "for lawless propaganda" in the streets.

The Mayor's statement will be a guide for the police in their handling of Thursday's demonstrations. The police are awaiting the return from Florida of Commissioner Whalen this morning before deciding their program.

It is expected that, as in previous demonstrations at Union Square, the police will give the Communists full protection, but will be prepared to intervene energetically in the event of any attempt at rioting.

Mayor Assails Rioters.

The Mayor's statement follows:

In common with all thoughtful citizens, I deeply deplore recent demonstrations in our streets which required the intervention of the police to control.

The efficiency, patience and good nature of the New York policeman are recognized by all who have ever come in contact with him. We must, however, recognize that he is human, and surely none of us would expect him to stand supinely by while being spat upon and assaulted by a ruthless mob. The policeman's first duty is to maintain peace and order in our streets.

This leads me to declare what my policy will be toward all future public disturbances, as well as toward the social problems which have been used to excuse such demonstrations.

The serious problem of unemployment demands the sympathetic study of officials and public alike, but this problem shall not be used while I am Mayor for lawless propaganda in our streets by the Communist element.

While I deplore the fact that so many honest and industrious men and women are out of work, the responsibility for this condition by no process of reasoning can be charged to the New York City Administration. Long before the cry of unemployment was heard this administration had inaugurated an unprecedented program of public improvements requiring the services of tens of thousands of workers and the expenditure of approximately one billion dollars.

Communists, as other minority groups, should be protected in their rights of free speech, free assembly and petition when meetings and demonstrations are held in proper places.

I have no fear that the doctrines of communism will gain importance among the American people, whose lives have been built on in-

Continued on Page Sixteen.

Primo's Son Fights Sword Duel With Captain; Both Slightly Wounded in Second Encounter

By The Associated Press.

PAMPLONA, Spain, March 3.—Meeting here secretly yesterday morning, Miguel Primo de Rivera, son of the former Spanish dictator, and Captain Rexach of the Spanish Artillery Corps fought a duel with swords in which each was slightly wounded. Miguel was cut once in the wrist, and Captain Rexach was cut twice.

They separated when the seconds ruled that Captain Rexach's cuts on the wrist were too serious to permit of his continuing the duel, but apparently they were not reconciled. It is rumored that they want to fight again.

Miguel came from Paris, where he has been staying with his father and other members of his family, and slipped over the frontier by automobile through a pass in the Pyrenees. He came by appointment to meet Captain Rexach, a challenge having passed between them in Madrid because of what Miguel considered to be insults to his father made by Captain Rexach.

After the duel Miguel left by automobile, presumably for France, and Captain Rexach, whose present whereabouts are unknown, went off in another.

The two duelists arrived in Pamploma before daylight and went immediately to the hall used for the jai alai games, and after preliminary formalities began to fight at about 8 A. M. In the first round Miguel was wounded in the wrist, but insisted that he could continue fighting. In the second Miguel twice wounded Captain Rexach in the wrist, and the seconds said that he could not go on.

The two parties then went separately to hurried breakfasts of coffee and rolls and departed in different directions. Miguel stopped long enough to send a telegram to his father in Paris, assuring him of his safety.

Every effort was made by the duelists to keep their meeting secret, and it was only discovered today, when the authorities found the telegram sent by Miguel to the former dictator.

Young Miguel was recently sent out of Spain to prevent his fighting duels. He had challenged several officers whom he accused of having insulted his father, slapping a General publicly in one of Madrid's most fashionable cafés. He was escorted to the French frontier at that time by a police guard.

SENATORS DEMAND ACTION TO CHECK UNEMPLOYMENT; HOOVER'S STAND ATTACKED

Normal Business in 2 Months Predicted by Secretary Lamont

By The Associated Press.

WASHINGTON, March 3.—A prediction that American business activity would speed up to a normal rate within two months was made today by Secretary Lamont, who said that a slowing down in the last three months had not been as extensive as had been feared, and that the approach of Spring and warm weather would increase employment.

"My own opinion is that during the forepart of this year American industrial enterprise has had inevitably to slow down," he asserted.

"That slowing down seems to be passing over, and with the usual increase of out-of-door work in the Northern States as weather conditions moderate we are likely to find the country as a whole enjoying its wonted state of prosperity."

HOOVER'S FIRST YEAR ONE OF FACT FINDING

Political Friends and Foes Agree His Is a Definite Economic Regime.

HIS COMMISSIONS A FACTOR

As on Law Enforcement, Aim Is for Basis of Action—Capper Predicts Success on Tariff.

By RICHARD V. OULAHAN.

Special to The New York Times.

WASHINGTON, March 3.—It will be a year tomorrow since Herbert Hoover took up his residence in the White House as President of the United States. The year's period ends with the President under fire from his political enemies, with plenty of evidence at hand that in the coming campaign for control of the Senate and the House of Representatives his policies, acts and tendencies will be severely scrutinized by his critics and as warmly defended by his party friends and supporters.

In a radio address tonight Senator Arthur Capper of Kansas, a strong supporter of the President, but one who has joined on a good many occasions with the Democratic-insurgent Republican coalition in the Senate in its rewriting of the tariff revision schedules, gave his appraisement of Mr. Hoover's first year in the Presidency. In it he made what was intended as an answer to the criticism that there had been little accomplishment by the Hoover Administration.

Explaining that he was speaking as an observer rather than as a Senator, Mr. Capper said:

"It seems to me that this first year of President Hoover has been a year of fact-finding, a year of work on data and blueprints, a year of foundation laying. These are the marks of the engineering mind of President Hoover."

Favors Investigation Method.

The President has not been influenced to change his methods by the contention of his adversaries that he divides responsibility and postpones the exercise of it by appointing com-

Continued on Page Two.

SHARP DEBATE OVER JOBLESS

Wagner Lays to President an Attempt to Divert Nation From Facts.

VACILLATION IS CHARGED

La Follette Discusses 'Red Scare,' Alleging an Effort to Discredit Lack of Work.

JOHNSON PROMISES SPEED

Californian Sets Hearings for Thursday on Wagner's Bill for an Accurate Survey.

Special to The New York Times.

WASHINGTON, March 3.—The existence of widespread unemployment in the nation was portrayed in the Senate today, coupled with an attack on the Administration, which was charged with seeking to "divert" the country's attention from the situation.

The attack came from the Democrats and Insurgent Republicans. Senator Wagner of New York precipitated a long and sharp debate which delayed consideration of the tariff bill for several hours when he appealed for action on his measure for an accurate survey of the labor situation. He characterized President Hoover's reported stand that delay in passing the tariff bill was to blame for industrial idleness as "an unadorned act of tawdry politics."

One response to the New Yorker's speech was a promise by Senator Johnson of California, chairman of the Commerce Committee, that his committee would meet Thursday for prompt action on the Wagner bill.

Attacks Republican Leadership.

The charge that the administration had attempted to divert attention from the real unemployment situation was made by Senator Wagner. Official assurances of an increase in employment, he declared, were at variance with such figures on the subject as the government itself had compiled.

The Republican party, the Senator declared, had shown itself helpless to pass a tariff bill redeeming its pledges which would meet with the approval of its own members. The present situation as to the tariff, he contended, might be laid to the indecision of President Hoover and his refusal to assume leadership.

Charging that the President was "undetermined" and had "vacillated," the New York Democrat asserted that when dissensions arose in the Republican party the President "did not take hold of the reins of party direction and guide a united party back to the performance of its campaign pledges."

Senator La Follette, insurgent Republican of Wisconsin, denounced what he termed attempts to label demonstrations of the unemployed as a movement of "the Reds." For more than an hour he held the attention of the Senate by a speech in which he urged that something constructive be done to relieve the situation. He held the administration and Congress equally responsible for failure to act at a time when the "conditions are growing daily worse."

Johnson Expresses Surprise.

Senator Johnson of California expressed surprise that there should be any unemployment after the statements that had been made recently by "millionaires" and others, who told only of prosperity.

Senator Glass, Democrat, of Virginia, suggested that the problem should be referred to a commission for study and report.

"Why not?" he asked.

Senator Couzens, Republican, of Michigan, said that he had been told by a Federal authority that the known unemployment on Jan. 1 was 3,100,000, "and I suppose that the actual unemployment is twice that amount." He criticized Congress for not permitting a survey of the situation to determine its effect on World War veterans who are unemployed.

Senator Walsh, Democrat, of Massachusetts, charged that the administration was unsympathetic with the unemployed and sought to hide the real situation by diverting the public attention to other questions.

Senator Brookhart, Republican, of Iowa, deprecated what he said was the present desire of some Republicans to becloud the unemployment situation by crying Communism. He declared that Perry Howard, former Republican National Committeeman from Mississippi, had received $4,000 to break up the strike among Pull-

Fight for Work or Wages
Participate in the

Mass Demonstration Against Unemployment

March 6th, 1930, 5:30 P. M.
at 4th Ave. and Broadway, Gary

Comrades, Workers!

[illegible] unemployment and part [illegible] getting so bad that even [illegible] are beginning to TALK [illegible] for the distressed jobless [illegible]. Millions of workers' families [illegible] afford the bare necessities of life. [illegible] of workers are working part [illegible] lead a hand to mouth existence. [illegible] of the capitalists is expending hundreds of millions of dollars for armaments but it won't provide relief for the unemployed. The capitalist corporations made billions of dollars last year by exploiting and speeding up the workers. The workers must force these corporations to provide unemployment insurance from the super-profits.

The Department of Justice and the police are attacking most viciously the leadership of the unemployed workers as represented by the Trade Union Unity League and the Communist Party. Hundreds of working class fighters are arrested, beaten up, and sentenced on inciting to riots and disturbing the peace charges. But in spite of everything the Communist Party and the TUUL will lead the working class in the International Demonstration Against Unemployment.

The oppression in the shops is being intensified. Every worker stands the chance of getting kicked out the next day because of the deepening crisis in the U. S. This should bring to the attention of the employed workers that the struggle against unemployment is of concern to the whole working class.

STRIKE ON MARCH 6th!
FIGHT FOR WORK OR WAGES!
DEMAND FULL WAGES FOR ALL PART TIME WORKERS!
FIGHT FOR THE 7-HOUR DAY!
LONG LIVE THE UNITY OF THE BLACK AND WHITE WORKERS!
DOWN WITH IMPERIALIST WAR!
DEFEND THE SOVIET UNION!

Auspices
Trade Union Unity League
Communist Party
Young Communist League

A Communist party poster urging the unemployed to participate in the demonstrations.

Associated Press Photo

Part of the vast crowd which jammed Union Square in New York City before the disorder began. The Communists and their banners are seen surrounded by Sympathizers and the curious.

Police Commissioner Whalen (L) and Deputy Commissioner Hoyt directing their forces in the drive to prevent a Red march to City Hall.

Times Wide World Photo

Associated Press Photo

Patrolman Arthur Talbot was hit on the head by a brick hurled by a rioter.

Times Wide World Photo

Mounted police riding on the sidewalks and breaking up crowds that refused to disperse.

"All the News That's Fit to Print."

The New York Times.

Copyright, 1930, by The New York Times Company.

THE WEATHER
Cloudy today, followed by showers at night; tomorrow colder.
Temperatures yesterday—Max., 50; min., 28.
U. S. Weather Forecast—For details see Page 42.

VOL. LXXIX....No. 26,340. **** NEW YORK, FRIDAY, MARCH 7, 1930. TWO CENTS In Greater New York | THREE CENTS Within 200 Miles | FOUR CENTS Elsewhere Except 7th and 8th Postal Zones

BRIAND INVITES AMERICANS TO NAVAL MEETING TODAY; AIMS TO MAKE UP FOR DELAY

WILL URGE SECURITY PACT

Would Have Five Powers to Agree to Consultation if War Threatens.

OUR APPROVAL PREDICTED

Italians Also Might Welcome Any Suggestion to Strengthen the Kellogg Pact.

OTHERS' IDEAS UNCERTAIN

French Leader to Meet MacDonald This Morning—His Group to Confer Later.

By EDWIN L. JAMES.
Special Cable to THE NEW YORK TIMES.

LONDON, March 6.—Foreign Minister Briand of France, heading the delegation to the naval conference, arrived in London from Paris late this afternoon, looking well and hearty. Within an hour after reaching the French headquarters, the Carlton Hotel, he had made an appointment with Prime Minister MacDonald for 9 o'clock tomorrow morning, arranged a meeting of the French delegates and experts for 10 o'clock and invited the entire American delegation to lunch. It appears that the veteran diplomat intends to do his best to make up for the delays the conference has had because of the absence of the French during the government crisis at Paris, and he may have an interesting statement to make at the meeting of the heads of the delegations at St. James's Palace tomorrow.

In reply to a question whether France would bring up her desire to have the Kellogg pact implemented, M. Briand replied in the affirmative. It is understood to be his position that the five naval powers should agree to consult in case war is threatened in order to do their best to preserve the peace to which they are devoted. It is further understood that he considers that it is of no importance whether this decision is incorporated in the naval treaty or made a quite separate undertaking.

Time of Action Not Set.

Whether the head of the French delegation will broach this subject in his conversations tomorrow is not known tonight. It may depend on what the other delegates wish to talk about. They may wish to inquire into M. Briand's present position on the figures submitted by Premier Tardieu, which might give M. Briand an opportunity to enlarge on M. Tardieu's declarations in his statement of France's naval needs that some security arrangement might convert France's absolute needs into relative needs.

Considerable interest may attach to M. Briand's reported intention to suggest that the strengthening of the Kellogg pact should suffice for other nations as well as for France to reduce their programs. This would probably be welcomed by the Americans, who now face the prospect of a billion-dollar construction program to achieve parity with Britain, and by Italy as well. The positions of Britain and Japan are not so certain.

In any event there seems tonight some prospect that M. Briand is living up to the expectation that he would enliven what has been a dull conference. It is understood that the American delegation, which has not been approached as yet on any security arrangement, will give careful consideration to any such suggestions which may be made.

New Situation Is Faced.

LONDON, March 6 (AP).—When the French delegation returned to London tonight, Arthur Henderson, Foreign Secretary, and Malcolm MacDonald, son of the Prime Minister, extended the British Government's welcome. After a general greeting like a homecoming party, the veteran Aristide Briand led his party off to re-establish itself at the Carlton Hotel.

An entirely new conference situation faces the French as they return from putting their domestic political house in order.

Considerable technical work has been accomplished, but real progress concerns the larger issues, such as the Anglo-American accord, which, it was authoritatively learned today, is in sight, regarding not only cruisers but all categories of warships.

The American-Japanese naval problem also has changed materially since the French left London. The conversations between Senator Reed and

Continued on Page Thirteen.

Dog's Barking Saves 7 in Fire; They Pray That It May Live

By The Associated Press.

BRISTOL, R. I., March 6.—Seven persons, in the light of their burning home, gathered about the almost lifeless form of a dog on the lawn at 355 Hope Street early this morning and prayed for the little creature, whose barking had sent them fleeing to safety.

Richard J. Simmons, roused by the barking of his pet, Skippy, went to the kitchen to investigate. As he opened the door thick smoke poured out upon him, and the dog, with a last feeble bark, fell at his feet.

Simmons awakened his wife and five other occupants of the house and carried Skippy outdoors. Four fire companies extinguished the blaze. The dog will recover.

COLUMBIA'S NEEDS PUT AT $39,500,000

Six Prominent Citizens Request $9,500,000 for Buildings and $30,000,000 for Endowment.

EXHAUSTIVE STUDY MADE

Their Report Urging Gifts Terms University 'Finest Fruitage of Citizenship' of City.

Upon the invitation of Dr. Nicholas Murray Butler, president of Columbia University, six prominent citizens have made an exhaustive study of the resources and requirements of Columbia University and have united in a report urging contributions for the support of the institution as "the finest fruitage of citizenship" in the city of New York.

The committee's report, made public yesterday by Dr. Butler, fixes Columbia's immediate needs at $39,500,000, of which $9,500,000 is required for buildings and $30,000,000 for endowment.

The members of the committee were:

BERNARD M. BARUCH, financier.
WALTER S. GIFFORD, president of the American Telephone and Telegraph Company.
PHILIP G. GOSSLER, president of the Columbia Gas and Electric Corporation.
DARWIN P. KINGSLEY, president of the New York Life Insurance Company.
MORGAN J. O'BRIEN, former justice of the New York Supreme Court.
HENRY S. PRITCHETT, president of the Carnegie Foundation for the Advancement of Teaching.

In its "appeal to citizenship," the committee pointed out that the fortunes which are built up in New York "come into existence by reason of New York itself" and declares that gifts and bequests to Columbia should arise unasked from the idealism of the people.

Dr. Butler's Letter.

The members of the committee served in response to the following letter from Dr. Butler:

February 16, 1929.

Dear Sirs:

On Oct. 31 next there will be celebrated the 175th anniversary of the granting of the Charter of King's College in the Province of New York, out of which the Columbia University of today has grown. The trustees, after long and most careful consideration of the burdens which they bear and of the varied forms of service which the university is called upon to render, have decided to ask the kindly and generous cooperation of six distinguished representatives of the life of the city of New York in making known to the larger public the university's needs and opportunities.

The trustees have definitely determined neither themselves to undertake nor to authorize any or-

Continued on Page Eighteen.

ASSERT PROHIBITION IS CONSERVING LIFE AND AIDING FARMER

Drys at House Hearing Marshal Statistics—Challenged by Wet Members of Committee.

GRANGE CHIEF BACKS LAW

Two Witnesses Say Catholic Church Favors Liquor Ban—Priest's Letter Read.

SOCIETY WOMEN POLLED

Mrs. R. G. K. Strawbridge Says Half of Philadelphia Matrons Oppose Drinking at Functions.

Special to The New York Times.

WASHINGTON, March 6.—Sharply attacking the wets with charges that their agitation for repeal of the Eighteenth Amendment was creating disregard for law, prohibition supporters testified before the House Judiciary Committee today on the attitude of society matrons toward the dry act, denied that it adversely affected agriculture and asserted that it had added to the span of life.

Mrs. Ruth G. K. Strawbridge of Philadelphia testified as to the results of a secret poll of matrons listed in the Social Register of Philadelpia, which, she said, showed that half of them definitely favor the removal of liquor from social functions.

Mrs. Strawbridge attacked as "utterly unsportsmanlike and unworthy a leader of public opinion" the testimony given for the wets by General W. W. Atterbury. She also criticized the statements of Pierre S. du Pont.

Representative Olger B. Burtness of North Dakota, appearing as a witness, declared conditions in his State were much different than those pictured by a North Dakota farmer, Pearce Bluett who had told the committee that the strained condition of farmers there could be traced directly to the destruction of the market for grains used by brewers.

Taber Says Farmers Gain.

Louis J. Taber of Columbus, Ohio, Master of the National Grange, read figures which, he said, showed that farmers are much better off than before prohibition; that table varieties have replaced the grapes formerly grown for the wine market; that grains have been converted to other uses, particularly cereals, and that rye, once a staple of the alcohol business, now has a greater value than before it ceased to be legally so used.

Two witnesses, Patrick H. Callahan, a paint and varnish manufacturer, of Louisville, Ky., and C. P. Connolly, attorney and former editor and writer of East Orange, N. J., declared that the attitude of the Catholic Church was favorable toward prohibition. Mr. Callahan introduced a letter from the Very Rev. Michael F. Foley, who has headed St. Paul's parish, Baltimore, for fifty years.

Mr. Callahan also cited statistics from the Census Bureau and made deductions based on them, which did not go unchallenged by wet members of the committee. Prohibition, he asserted in this connection, had saved a large number of lives and had materially reduced suffering from disease.

Statements that the country's moral standards have improved under prohibition figured in the testimony throughout the day.

Drys Challenge Chairman.

The hearing was marked by protests of dry members of the committee against the alleged intrusion of arguments into the questioning of witnesses, particularly of Mr. Connolly, by Chairman George S. Graham and Representative La Guardia.

Each statement by a witness contradicting testimony given by the wets was received with applause by an audience including many of the outstanding leaders of prohibition

Continued on Page Seventeen.

Col. Lindbergh Thrown by Pony; Dragged 25 Feet, but Is Unhurt

By The Associated Press.

DEL MONTE, Cal., March 6.—Colonel Lindbergh was thrown from a polo pony here today and dragged for twenty-five feet. He was severely shaken but escaped injury.

Lindbergh was riding a mount owned by J. C. Cowdin of New York at the time of the accident. The aviator was galloping down the Del Monte polo field when the pony suddenly sent its rider sprawling to the turf.

Before he could halt the pony, Lindbergh was dragged along the turf. He laughed off the incident and apparently was not hurt.

The Colonel, here for glider test flights, went for the horse ride when lack of winds prevented him from flying.

CHASE-EQUITABLE TALKING OF MERGER

Discussions Under Way for a Union, Making the World's Biggest Bank.

$2,700,000,000 RESOURCES

Each Bank Now Is the Result of Previous Consolidations—Their Stocks Rise.

Discussions looking toward a merger of the Chase National Bank and the Equitable Trust Company into an institution which would outrank any other bank in the world, by any measure of comparison, are going forward, it was learned yesterday. The combination, if it is made, will create a bank with resources of more than $2,700,000,000, deposits in excess of $2,000,000,000 and capital funds, exclusive of security affiliates, amounting to over $250,000,000.

Officers of the Equitable refused yesterday to discuss the negotiations, but did not deny that these were going on. At the Chase no official qualified to discuss the matter could be reached. From authoritative sources it was learned that, although no decision has yet been reached, the matter has been under discussion for several days.

Both the Chase National Bank and the Equitable Trust Company figured prominently in the merger movement among New York City banks which was an outstanding development of last year's financial history. The Chase Bank absorbed the Garfield National Bank and the National Park Bank in 1929. The Equitable Trust Company combined with the Seaboard National Bank.

Ranking of the Banks.

The Chase has for some time ranked among the first three banks of the country. The Equitable forged into fourth place in the list of New York City's biggest banks by virtue of its merger with the Seaboard. Resources of the Equitable crossed $1,000,000,000 for the first time at the end of last year, its statement as of Dec. 31, 1929, showing total assets of $1,013,970,798.

Should the present discussions result in a merger agreement the combination of these two institutions will constitute the biggest bank merger ever effected. The combined bank will outrank its closest rival by at least half a billion dollars in total resources, and will far exceed in size any of the "big five" joint stock banks of England, which, until their recent displacement by the National City Bank, were the largest banking institutions in the world.

Shares of the two banks were extremely active in the over-the-counter market yesterday and rose to the highest prices touched so far this year. Stock of the Chase National Bank closed at a bid and asked price of $171 to $173, representing a gain of $12 a share on the day. Shares of the Equitable Trust Company closed at $123 bid, $125 asked, which was $8 a share higher than the price quoted at the close of trading on Wednesday. The price of Chase Bank stock has been as low as $154 this year, and that of Equitable as low as $96½.

The Equitable is generally known as a "Rockefeller" bank in Wall Street, a large interest in the institution being held by the Standard Oil family. Winthrop W. Aldrich, president of the Equitable, is a brother-in-law of John D. Rockefeller Jr., and represented the latter in the contest last year to supplant Colonel Robert W. Stewart as head of the Standard Oil Company of Indiana.

Mr. Aldrich became president of the Equitable last December, succeeding Chellis A. Austin, formerly president of the Seaboard National Bank, who had died suddenly. At the time of Mr. Aldrich's election it was believed in some quarters that the step was a prelude to a merger of the Equitable with another bank. Due to the fact that Mr. Aldrich is also a director of the Bankers' Trust Company, on the board of which bank he represents the Rockefeller interests, a combination of the Equi-

Continued on Page Sixteen.

CITY ASKED TO RUSH BUILDING PROJECTS TO AID UNEMPLOYED

Labor Leaders Urge Walker to Speed Subways and Housing—Tell Him Crisis Exists.

FREE AGENCIES ADVOCATED

Illicit Job Bureaus Are Adding to Difficulties of Workers, Petitioners Declare.

FOOD FOR NEEDY SOUGHT

Municipal Relief Stations in All Boroughs Favored—Communist Agitation Disavowed.

A petition urging the speeding of public works, the setting up of a comprehensive system of relief, including stations for the free distribution of food and clothing, and the creation, with the help of the State, of a network of free employment agencies, to relieve the unemployment situation, was submitted yesterday to Mayor Walker by a newly formed Emergency Conference on Unemployment.

The emergency conference said it represented more than 250,000 workers, most of them affiliated with the American Federation of Labor. The petition to Mayor Walker carries the signatures of officials of the International Ladies Garment Workers Union, the Brotherhood of Painters, the Amalgamated Clothing Workers, the Socialist party, the United Hebrew Trades, the Workmen's Circle, a labor fraternal order with 85,000 members, and other organizations in the building, needle and printing industries.

The petition said that "leaders of the conference emphasized that their undertaking has nothing to do with the Communists, from whose antics they emphatically dissociated themselves."

The conference charges that there has been a let-down on subway building and urged the immediate speeding up of this work and also that the city embark on a large-scale program of slum clearance and housing construction.

Says Crisis Exists Here.

The petition read in part:

"The city of New York, in common with the rest of the country, is in the midst of an unemployment crisis of serious proportions. The problem of creating employment for the jobless and of caring for the needs of those already suffering through enforced idleness is one that demands the immediate and energetic attention of the public authorities.

"The reports of the United States Department of Labor, of the American Federation of Labor and of the State Labor Department indicate the unemployment situation is likely to become more serious as the months pass. Because of this and because of the existing widespread suffering, we are submitting for your consideration a series of proposals which we feel will bring an immediate measure of relief.

"The problem of immediately relieving the unemployment situation falls, as we see it, into three principal divisions: (1) the speeding up of public works; (2) the creation of systematic and adequate relief machinery; and (3) the facilitating of the securing of employment without recourse to fee-taking and often dishonest private employment agencies.

"An examination of the contracts recently let for the construction of subways indicates that rather than a speeding up of public works, an actual recession in the letting of contracts has been the case. Since subway construction is by far the largest of the public projects now under way it is important that we consider the actual facts of the situation."

The petition then points out that data on file in the Board of Transportation show that during December, 1928, and January, 1929, the Board of Estimate awarded subway construction contracts totaling $12,862,855, and that during December, 1929, and January, 1930, when the first wave of depression began to be

Continued on Page Three.

REDS BATTLE POLICE IN UNION SQUARE; SCORES INJURED, LEADERS ARE SEIZED; TWO DEAD, MANY HURT IN CLASHES ABROAD

EUROPE ROUTS RED PARADES

German Police Kill Two at Halle—20 Are Hurt, 115 Held in Berlin.

BAYONETS USED IN AUSTRIA

Communists and Gendarmerie Clash in Vienna and Several Provincial Towns.

PARIS AND LONDON QUIET

But Violence Occurs in Spain and Czechoslovakia—Meetings Held in Scandinavia.

Special Cable to THE NEW YORK TIMES.

BERLIN, March 6.—The much-heralded international battle front which the Communists had proclaimed for today failed to materialize so far as Germany was concerned, and the police reports from all metropolitan centres and industrial areas tonight indicate that the day's demonstrations everywhere were of a desultory nature.

The only serious casualties reported were from Halle, where two demonstrators were shot dead after they had opened fire on the police. In Berlin fewer than a dozen Communists and only seven other civilians were hurt in street clashes at various points, while 115 arrests were made. Most of the rioting began with the close of industrial plants, when roving bands of Communists sought downtown centres, where street traffic was halted while the police dispersed the crowds.

Riot at Busy Centre.

At only a few points in Berlin, even in sections where Communists usually congregate, were the police compelled to take recourse to weapons and the free use of nightsticks and "gummi knueppel" (rubber clubs), which served the purpose of restoring order. One of the demonstrators was seriously wounded at the corner of Friedrich and Leipzig Streets, one of the city's busiest centres, when a squad of police found themselves outnumbered by a gang of rowdies. A dozen Berlin policemen were injured in hand-to-hand fighting, in which the Communists used knives and brass knuckles. At midnight order was completely restored in Berlin.

In the Ruhr sector the Communists staged numerous street parades, which moved along peacefully and required no police intervention. Hamburg, which customarily is one of Germany's red storm centres, also failed to provoke the police into taking sharp measures.

Today's developments again proved to be out of all proportion to the noisy advance publicity and the threats with which Communist leaders and the party's organs had sought to intimidate the police and the populace—a performance in which they delight and which invariably yields them undeserved publicity, required for their propoganda.

Sharp Clashes in Austria.

By JOHN MacCORMAC.
Special Cable to THE NEW YORK TIMES.

VIENNA, March 6.—Communist "Hunger March Day" in Central Europe and the Balkans has ended in a complete fiasco.

In Vienna several thousand Communists marched around the Ringstrasse with the permission of the police, who not only formed a strong cordon with alarm contingents concealed in the buildings of Parlia-

Continued on Page Three.

Red Riots in Many Cities in America and Europe

Demonstrations by Communists in the leading cities of this country yesterday resulted in about 100 arrests and injuries to more than three-score persons. In Detroit, mounted police charged 75,000. In Cleveland, twenty persons were hurt in a clash with police. In Pittsburgh, twelve were arrested.

Philadelphia and Chicago saw peaceful demonstrations. In San Francisco, Mayor Ralph received the marchers and addressed them.

Police tear gas bombs routed a Communist demonstration on the sidewalk in front of the White House during which police clashed with a crowd of 100 radicals, and eleven men and two girls are arrested.

Two persons were killed in Germany, both at Halle, and an undetermined number injured, in Berlin and Hamburg, in Communist "unemployment day" demonstrations. Fifteen were hurt in Balboa, Spain, and nine in Gablonz, Czechoslovakia. Demonstrations were held in many other European cities and in London, but were relatively peaceful. The parades scheduled in Paris were effectually prohibited by the presence of 20,000 police and guardsmen.

TEAR GAS ROUTS REDS BEFORE WHITE HOUSE

Police Break Up Demonstration on Sidewalk as One of Radicals Starts Speech.

NINE INJURED, 13 ARRESTED

Band of 100 Parades Half Hour Unmolested, by Hoover's Order, Prior to Disorder.

Special to The New York Times.

WASHINGTON, March 6.—A tear-gas bomb and threatening police blackjacks routed a Communist demonstration on the sidewalk in front of the White House today, during which eleven men and two girls were arrested and a policeman, two elderly women and half a dozen demonstrators were injured.

The tear-gas bomb, tossed by a park policeman, caused a near panic, dispersed the radicals and a hundred followers, both white and colored, and stampeded a luncheon hour crowd of several thousand attracted by the paraders and their banners of protest against unemployment.

Word traveled fast that there was a Red riot under the windows of the President's mansion, and the news brought additional thousands who milled around, adding to the confusion, in which moving picture outfits, which had been strung along the block in front of the White House in anticipation of the heralded demonstration, were jostled about.

The mêlée took place on the White House side of Pennsylvania Avenue, fronting Lafayette Square, during the noon hour, when government clerks were pouring out of buildings on their way to lunch, and the fighting started when William Lawrence, a leader of the demonstration, climbed to the base of the White House fence and attempted to make a speech. Two policemen dragged him down and he struck one of them with his fists.

A riot ensued, with several thousand spectators massed around but not in sympathy with the struggling demonstrators. The police called for reserves. The acrid vapor of the tear-gas bomb which was tossed into the milling crowd at this juncture created a near panic and promptly ended the demonstration.

President Is Not Disturbed.

Quiet prevailed throughout the city after the White House disorder and a parade of demonstrators to the so-called district building at Fourteenth Street and Pennsylvania Avenue, the official home of the municipal commissioners as well as of Police Headquarters, scheduled for this afternoon, in protest against unemployment, failed to materialize.

The White House manifested no alarm over the demonstration and professed not to take the matter seriously. President Hoover, who did not leave his desk during the incident, issued instructions that the demonstrators, who had announced in advance that they were going to the White House, were not to be disturbed unless they became disorderly.

The Communists paraded back and forth in front of the White House

Continued on Page Two.

35,000 JAMMED IN SQUARE

Onlookers Swept Into the Melee as 2,000 Reds Start a Parade.

CHARGED BY MOUNTED MEN

Whalen Defied at the Scene by Foster, Who Orders March Downtown to See Mayor.

PEACEFUL VISIT SPURNED

City Hall Guarded All Day by Big Force—Red Chiefs Taken There Awaiting Followers.

The unemployment demonstration staged by the Communist party in Union Square yesterday broke up in the worst riot New York has seen in recent years when 35,000 persons attending the demonstration were transformed in a few moments from an orderly, and at times bored, crowd into a fighting mob. The outbreak came after Communist leaders, defying the warnings and orders of the police, exhorted their followers to march on City Hall and demand a hearing from Mayor Walker.

Shortly before William Z. Foster, Communist leader of the demonstration, incited the crowd to march on City Hall, Police Commissioner Whalen, who was at the scene directing operations, warned the Communists not to transform a peaceful demonstration into a riot. He offered to send Foster and a Communist committee to City Hall in his own car to present to the Mayor any grievance or petition.

"Do not turn liberty into license," the commissioner told the Communist leaders at a conference in the garden house facing the meeting place. "If you do you will only prove that the demonstration has been all too peaceful for you."

Rejecting Commissioner Whalen's offer, the Communists returned to the speaking platforms, where Foster gave the order to march. The battle soon followed.

Many Hurt in Battle.

More than a score of persons, including four policemen, were injured, and fully 100 suffered minor hurts as an army of 1,000 police, mounted and on foot, supported by scores of detectives, motorcycle men and emergency service crews, barred the advance of the mob and in fifteen minutes of spectacular fighting scattered it in all directions. The police had the unexpected assistance of a group of soldiers in the square, who joined in the battle.

The police prepared for action as soon as it became apparent that all hopes of averting a riot had been shattered by the Communists' defiance. Immediately after Foster's speech some 2,000 Communists forming the heart of the audience, led by special cohorts bearing inflammatory signs, moved in the direction of Broadway and down toward Sixteenth Street and the battle began. Foster himself and his entire staff disappeared from the scene. An hour later Foster and four of his lieutenants were arrested near City Hall, whither they had departed quietly to await the arrival of the rioters.

Leaders Held for Hearing.

Those arrested with Foster were Israel Amter, Robert Minor, editor of The Daily Worker, official Communist organ; Joseph Lester and Harry Raymond. Sam Darcy, another of Foster's lieutenants, who took an active part in the gathering at Union Square, was also arrested later at Communist headquarters on the west side of the square. All were taken to Police Headquarters, where after a conference between Mr. Whalen and District Attorney Crain they were held for arraignment today on a charge of provoking an unlawful assembly. The charge, it was indicated, may be augmented following today's hearing to conspiracy to cause a riot, inciting to riot and assault in the second degree.

Women and Children in Van.

As the riot broke, Commissioner Whalen left the porch of the garden house and entered the heart of the fighting. The mob was led by a group of women and children holding aloft placards and singing the Internationale. A police emergency wagon, parked against the curb for several hours, swung with its siren screaming into the centre of the square, breaking up the huge crowd into a chaotic mass of individuals running for cover as the advancing phalanx

Thousands See 4 Fliers Die in Prague Collision; Masaryk Halts Birthday Celebration Flights

Wireless to THE NEW YORK TIMES.

PRAGUE, March 6.—Four military aviators were killed this afternoon before the eyes of thousands of Czechoslovaks celebrating President Masaryk's eightieth birthday.

While the entire garrison of Prague paraded before the former palace of Bohemia's kings, now the Presidential residence, in honor of the beloved President, forty-two airplanes manoeuvred above them. Suddenly two airplanes which had just left the ground struck each other full force at an altitude of only 150 feet immediately above the Bochnitz Asylum.

The thousands of spectators saw one pilot leap into the air, clear of the machines at the moment of collision, but, to their horror, his parachute failed to open and he dropped to the ground like a stone and was killed instantly.

The military authorities had announced beforehand in a mysterious manner that the manoeuvres would include "complete surprises from the air," and for a moment the intrigued public wondered whether the amazing spectacle was a prearranged sensation. In the next instant all doubts were removed as the two planes burst into flames and fell, interlocked, to the ground.

There was no hope of rescuing the remaining three air officers, whose bodies were recovered later, charred to cinders.

The tragedy cast a gloom over the entire celebrations for the birthday tomorrow. President Masaryk, shocked at the news of the tragedy, issued a personal order that all flying must cease.

London Exchange Cheers and Prices Rise As Bank of England Cuts Rate to 4 Per Cent

Wireless to THE NEW YORK TIMES.

LONDON, March 6.—The directors of the Bank of England at an early meeting today decided to reduce the bank rate from 4½ to 4 per cent. The last change was made on Feb. 6, when the rate was lowered from 5 to 4½ per cent. The present reduction is the fifth since October.

A large crowd of business men and messengers waited in the corridors of the Bank of England. When it was found the meeting was lasting longer than usual, and when no announcement had been made by noon, a reduction was anticipated.

A board, bearing the announcement, "Bank rate, 4 per cent," was displayed, causing a mad scramble to all the exits. Within a few moments the reduction was made known in all quarters.

The large crowds assembled around the electric indicators at the Stock Exchange greeted the decision with cheers.

The rate of 4½ per cent has been ineffective since it came into force, and during the past few days the bill rate in the open market slipped to more than 1 per cent below the bank rate. Another point that made for a reduction is the fact that since the Wall Street slump the Bank of England has been able to build up its gold holdings to the substantial level of £152,290,198.

The present reduction is expected to boost languishing British trade by reducing the rates on temporary loans.

The prices of British stocks which opened strong on the Exchange in anticipation of a reduction of the bank rate, soared sharply when the announcement was made.

"All the News That's Fit to Print."

The New York Times.

THE WEATHER
Rain and slightly colder today; tomorrow fair and warmer.
Temperatures yesterday—Max., 44; min., 30.
U. S. Weather Forecast—For details see Page 36.

Copyright, 1930, by The New York Times Company.

VOL. LXXIX....No. 26,341. NEW YORK, SATURDAY, MARCH 8, 1930. TWO CENTS in Greater New York | THREE CENTS Within 200 Miles | FOUR CENTS Elsewhere Except 7th and 8th Postal Zones

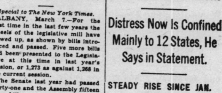

M'DONALD AND STIMSON SEE PARLEY ON WAY TO A TREATY WITH LIMITATION CERTAIN

FULL SESSIONS RESUMED

Demand for Consultation Pact by Briand Won't Bar Accord.

FRENCH MAY DROP PROJECT

British Premier Hopes Task Will Be Completed Before Commons Budget Debate, April 14.

TWO ITEMS ARE DEBATED

Delegates Put Off Till Monday Decisions on Cruiser Limit and Transfer Plans.

By EDWIN L. JAMES.

Special Cable to THE NEW YORK TIMES.

LONDON, March 7.—The naval conference resumed full activity today with an undertone of optimism. The official meetings did not amount to much beyond giving an opportunity for the new French delegates to meet the other conferees, and officially the conference adjourned until Monday, with a number of private conversations scheduled for tomorrow and Sunday.

Both the American and British delegations appear quite determined that a limitation treaty shall be written here. It would appear that these two delegations are much closer together than has been generally known. If the British and French could settle their differences it would require small effort for the Americans and British to reach a complete agreement.

Adjustments Seem Likely.

Indeed, if the British find they have to go a bit higher because of the French figures there would be, it is believed, little trouble for the Americans to adjust their figures to the British. And, furthermore, should the British and Americans find it necessary to raise the tonnage of some categories it is entirely possible they may find compensating reductions in other classes.

Of course, today did not give full opportunity to the British to judge the official French position. The French still are nursing their scheme for a political pact. If Foreign Minister Briand approaches the other delegations on the basis of a simple good-will plan for world peace he is likely to meet discouragement, not only from the Americans but also from the English.

Most of the American delegates doubt the wisdom of any sort of pact, and it appears to be the British feeling that they now have enough commitments. On the other hand, if the French make some sort of pact a condition for the success of the conference the Americans and British may see the affair differently.

It still remains true that no pact has been suggested officially, and, indeed, if M. Briand gets only discouragement he may never openly make a proposal which would be doomed to failure. However, the French leader is to talk over the matter with Premier MacDonald at Chequers on Sunday, and probably with the Americans on Monday.

Although through personal contacts it is easy to obtain the attitude of the various American delegates, the position of the delegation as a whole is that no pact plan is before it and that the subject is like a bridge to be crossed when one gets to it. They may get to it next week or may avoid the bridge by a detour. It probably will depend upon how attractive the French make their proposal or whether M. Briand offers to come down on his figures without any pact.

After seven weeks it remains true that the conference has not really got to grips with basic questions, but observers believe it cannot temporize much longer.

MacDONALD IS "BUOYANT."

By L. C. SPEERS.

Special Cable to THE NEW YORK TIMES.

LONDON, March 7.—In the course of an informal conversation with the correspondents at St. James's Palace this afternoon Premier MacDonald said the naval conference was "now back at work, and from now on it is full speed ahead."

The Prime Minister appeared immediately following the adjournment of the conference of heads of all delegations and, while he admitted he was tired after more than six weeks of hard work seeking an agreement satisfactory to the five powers, he said he never felt more

Continued on Page Five.

Walker Praises Patterson In Adding 17 to Prison Staff

The Board of Estimate yesterday by a unanimous vote granted the request of Commissioner of Correction Richard C. Patterson Jr. for fourteen new prison keepers and three additional prison matrons at $1,769 a year each.

Last year, when there were prison outbreaks throughout the country, Mr. Patterson asked provision in the 1930 budget for 110 new keepers and guards. Under pressure by the budget makers he finally reduced his requisition to fifty-two, which he regarded as an absolute minimum, but the budget director allowed him only thirty-five.

When he started to reiterate those facts yesterday Mayor Walker stopped him.

"Without further inquiry or debate," said the Mayor, "and solely on the splendid record made by the present Commissioner of Correction, the chair is going to move that this petition be granted at once."

The vote was recorded and Mr. Patterson expressed his thanks.

CHURCH JOINS HAITI IN DEMAND WE QUIT

White Bishops and Clergy Grieve With Suffering People, Primate Tells Commission.

MASONS ALSO FOR FREEDOM

Relative of Borno Says Women Will Die With Men if His Faction Elects Successor.

By HAROLD N. DENNY.

Staff Correspondent of The New York Times.
Special Cable to THE NEW YORK TIMES.

PORT AU PRINCE, March 7.—The Catholic Church in Haiti, after a discussion among its five Bishops, officially aligned itself today with opposition to the American occupation.

The attitude of the Church was made known to President Hoover's Commission through a formal statement read by Archbishop Conan to all five American representatives when the latter paid a ceremonial call at the Archbishop's palace. Virtually all the clergy of Haiti, an overwhelmingly Catholic country, are white and of French birth.

The Archbishop in his statement said the clergy were loath to participate in political issues, because they are foreigners, but he declared the people's sufferings were their own, and Haiti, jealous of liberty, had not had true independence since the entry of the American forces in 1915.

Will Rejoice at End of Occupation.

"The clergy will rejoice with all their hearts when the present situation is ended," said Archbishop Conan, "and they will joyfully chant a Te Deum in solemn thanksgiving. As ministers of a church which teaches that the occupation of a free country by another country is an abnormal and sorrowful thing which all should seek to end as soon as possible, and knowing, moreover, as we do, how this beloved people suffers in national dignity by being held in tutelage, with all our hearts we make our own their sufferings, their complaints and their hopes."

The action of the clergy is particularly interesting since President Borno is an active Catholic and the clergy speak very highly of him

Continued on Page Three.

FOUR KILL BEER CHIEF, TURN MACHINE GUNS ON HOBOKEN POLICE

Thug Ends Life When Trapped in Tenement as He Flees After Attack on Dunn.

WAR WAGED IN STREETS

Patrolman Wounded in Hail of Bullets During Battle a Block From City Hall.

THREE OF THE BAND ESCAPE

Two Get Away in Stolen Automobile, Striking Three Children in Wild Flight.

The bold technique of the Chicago underworld was brought to within a block of the City Hall and Police Headquarters in Hoboken yesterday when a band of four men, armed with at least two sub-calibre machine guns, mortally wounded Frankie Dunn, retired leader of North Jersey beer-runners.

Dunn, six-foot flamboyant racketeer, was trapped in the lobby of a seven-story office building he bought when he retired from bootlegging six months ago. He was knocked down by two men and as he sprawled on the tiled floor a machine gunner in the rear of the lobby fired twenty-four shots at him. Only two hit Dunn, who died at 10:50 o'clock last night in St. Mary's Hospital, Hoboken.

Two separate pitched battles between the gunmen and the police followed. In one battle a machine gunner, Frank Dugan of 1,385 Boulevard East, West New York, committed suicide with a revolver. He backed into the doorway of a tenement, firing as he did so, and climbed three flights to the top floor. A stoutly constructed skylight balked his escape, and as he heard the police creaking up the stairs after him he fired a single shot through his temple.

Three of Band Escape.

The man who had joined Dugan in holding off the police got away in an automobile. The second affray between the police and the two other members of the band ended with the gangsters' escape. In the wild flight the gunmen's car brushed against three children, injuring them slightly. The second fight was staged in front of a motion picture theatre, with amazed patrons watching from the lobby a scene as thrilling as any shown inside.

Two men were arrested last night and examined for hours at Hoboken Police Headquarters. They were charged with possessing pistols. They had been arrested because their machine fitted descriptions of one of the gunmen's automobiles. The police were doubtful that the prisoners had participated in the attack on Dunn, which they attributed to a feud between New York and New Jersey beer-runners.

Chief of Police Edward J. McFeeley and Captain Thomas Garrick of the Hoboken police thought the shooting of Dunn was linked in some way with two other murders. They referred to the slaying of James (Bugs) Donovan, a salesman for Dunn, who was shot to death in Manhattan in November, and the slaying of Harry Veasy, Brooklyn bootlegger, whose body was found in an automobile in front of 716 Madison Street, Hoboken, in December. The attack on Dunn and the shooting between the band and the police took place within two blocks of Madison Street.

Police officials in Hoboken did not agree with the prevailing opinion that Dunn's death marked the beginning of a war between beer runners in New York and New Jersey. They were inclined to the belief that he was killed over a personal grudge

Continued on Page Four.

Vare Withdraws From Race for Senator; Will Back Secretary Davis Against Grundy

Special to The New York Times.

PHILADELPHIA, March 7.—William S. Vare, a few hours after returning from his Winter home in Florida, acceded tonight to the pleas of his lieutenants that he withdraw from the race as a candidate for the Republican nomination for Senator. Formal announcement of his decision may be made tomorrow.

At the same time that he makes his retirement plans known, Mr. Vare is expected to announce his support of a ticket headed by James J. Davis, Secretary of Labor, for Senator, and Francis S. Brown for Governor.

Secretary Davis and several others were in conference with Mr. Vare tonight. Agreement was reached for the withdrawal of Mr. Vare as an opponent of Senator Grundy and the entry of Secretary Davis into the Senatorial contest.

Mr. Davis left tonight for Sharon to visit his father and it was indicated that he would announce his candidacy there. He said he wanted it understood that his position was not dependent upon what Mr. Vare might do.

Mr. Vare arrived home at 4:17 o'clock this afternoon, preceded by rumors that he would drop out of the Senatorial race. About 500 friends gave Mr. Vare a warm reception at the West Philadelphia station.

A group of flag-bearing young women sang "Hail, Hail, the Gang's All Here," and Miss Marion L. Pyle, chairman of the Republican Women of Pennsylvania, broke through the ring of photographers and threw her arms about Mr. Vare, who kissed her on the cheek.

His physician, Dr. Elwood R. Kirby, said Mr. Vare was in "fine shape."

Rules Liquor Buying Is Not Violation of Law; Federal Judge Quashes Bay State Indictment

Special to The New York Times.

BOSTON, March 7.—The purchase of liquor is not a violation of the Federal prohibition law, Judge James M. Morton ruled today in quashing an indictment against James E. Farrar of Watertown. Judge Morton upheld the plea of Farrar's counsel that the section of the act under which Farrar was indicted applied only to persons, such as druggists, allowed to handle liquor under government permits.

The opinion recited the fact that the government sought to convict Farrar under Section 6, Title 5, of the national prohibition act, which says, in substance, that no person shall sell, barter, transport or purchase any liquor without first having obtained a permit from the commissioner to do so.

The court added that the enforcement section of the Volstead act is Section 3, and this section clearly eliminates any liability of any kind for the purchase of liquor.

Judge Morton said that had it been the intention of Congress to do otherwise it would have set forth its intention in no uncertain language.

"Not only did Congress carefully exclude the purchaser from the provisions of the act, as originally passed, but has taken no step to extend its provision to the purchaser in the ten years of legislation which have since intervened," he said.

"It is uniformly held that statutes prohibiting the sale of intoxicating liquors are directed against the active selling only, and that the offense is committed only by the vendor or some one who aids him in selling and that the purchaser and those who aid him in the purchase are not guilty of aiding or abetting in the commission of the offense.

"The case is said to be the first of its kind under the present statute, and the question to be new," Judge Morton said. "It is true that there appears to be no direct decision whether the buyer of liquor is guilty of an offense under the national prohibition act. Two circuit courts of appeal, however, have referred to the question, and stated explicitly that in their opinion the purchase of liquor by the general public is not criminal."

MURDER INCITED BY JEALOUS MODEL

Killing of Artist's Wife Is Confessed by Two Indian Women in Weird Story of Witchcraft.

CONSULTED OUIJA BOARD

Her Love for Marchand Led Her to Induce an Aged Friend to Beat Mrs. Marchand to Death.

By The Associated Press.

BUFFALO, N. Y., March 7.—Unrequited affection, spurred by hatred of the wife of the man she professed to love, caused Lillian Jimerson, a 39-year-old Seneca Indian, to invoke the witchcraft of the Iroquois to accomplish through an aged Indian woman ally the slaying yesterday of Mrs. Clothilde Marchand, according to confessions police today said they had obtained from the two Cattaraugus Reservation Indians.

Mrs. Marchand, the 50-year-old wife of Henri Marchand, a distinguished artist-sculptor of the Buffalo Museum of Science, was beaten with a hammer and choked to death with a chloroform-soaked rag by Mrs. Nancy Bowen, a 66-year-old Seneca Indian, according to the confession.

A twelve-year-old son of the dead woman found his mother's body lying on the floor of their home, beneath an overturned radio console and a heavy lamp.

Evidence of the terrific struggle she had fought before repeated hammer blows struck her down were plainly apparent.

Woman Served as Indian Model.

Taken prisoner in her Indian reservation home by police today, Miss Jimerson finally revealed the hiding place of Mrs. Bowen. Both were brought to this city and, after questioning by Police Commissioner Austin J. Roche, Miss Jimerson admitted she had instigated the slaying by playing on the superstitions of her aged confederate, police said.

Mystic warnings from a "Ouija board" that unless the "white woman" were slain she would slay Miss Jimerson were found by police in two letters located in the Jimerson home. Included in them were directions for killing the artist's wife and for burning her body.

Miss Jimerson had served as a model for Mr. Marchand in some of his famous groups portraying the Seneca Indian and had conceived a strong infatuation for the artist, police said.

A pale, gaunt and sickly woman, Miss Jimerson is said to have resented her discharge when the work was completed and began her work of inciting the elderly Mrs. Bowen to carry out her plan of killing Mrs. Marchand.

Artist Said Love Was Not Returned.

Both Miss Jimerson and Mrs. Bowen are now charged with first degree murder. They repeated the confessions they had made to Commissioner Roche and Deputy Commissioner Connolly to Walter F. Hofheins, First Assistant District Attorney, tonight. Then they were lodged in Erie County jail.

Lillian, or Lilac, as she was known on the reservation, loved the artistic and talented Marchand. The artist claims that love was not returned. But that strange love affair of the Indian woman for the nationally known artist is the motive for the murder, so Commissioner Roche and District Attorney Hofheins say.

It was the first part of January that Lilac and the old Indian widow got together over the ouija board in the lamp-lighted cabin of Lilac and her aged father, Anson Jimerson, at which hut Mrs. Bowen had been staying off and on since the death of her husband, Chief Charley.

The conversation turned to the dead Charley and Lilac suggested, so

Continued on Page Four.

A. L. ERLANGER DIES AFTER LONG ILLNESS

Largest Individual Owner of Playhouses and Former 'Czar' of Stage Succumbs at 69.

'WIDOW' RETAINS COUNSEL

Steuer Asserts the Estate Is $75,000,000—Brother Insists Theatre Man Left No Wife.

Abraham Lincoln Erlanger, who, as head of the so-called Theatrical Syndicate and the firm of Klaw & Erlanger, for many years virtually controlled the legitimate theatre in this country, died at 5:30 o'clock yesterday morning at his home, 175 Riverside Drive, after a long illness. He was 69 years old and had been a dominant figure in the theatre for more than half his life.

At the time of his death Mr. Erlanger was still the largest individual owner and operator of legitimate theatres in this country. According to Broadway estimates yesterday, he had amassed a fortune of between $50,000,000 and $75,000,000 in the theatrical field.

Mr. Erlanger had been in failing health for some time. In the past few years he had suffered several paralytic strokes and had made several trips abroad to regain his health. A few weeks ago he went to California to inspect theatre properties and shortly after his return he became ill. The immediate cause of death was given as uremic poisoning, although Mr. Erlanger was said to have suffered from cancer. He had been away from his office about two weeks.

Mr. Erlanger is survived by his brother, Mitchell L. Erlanger, retired Supreme Court Justice, and two sisters, Miss Ray Erlanger and Mrs. Caroline Bergman.

The funeral will be held tomorrow at 2 P. M. at Temple Emanu-El, Fifth Avenue and Sixty-fifth Street, with Rabbis Samuel Schulman and Nathan Krass officiating. Burial will be in Beth-El Cemetery, Brooklyn. Mr. Erlanger's body is now at the home of his brother, 33 East Seventieth Street.

Denies a Widow Survived.

At the Riverside Drive address the superintendent of the building told reporters that "Mrs. Erlanger issued instructions she was not to be disturbed by reporters or any one else." The superintendent said he also had been instructed not to let any one to the Erlanger apartment or to send in any messages.

Former Justice Erlanger when informed of this last night said:

"There is no Mrs. Erlanger. There is no widow. What I am now telling you is 100 per cent the truth."

He said that Mr. Erlanger had been divorced from Mrs. Adelaide Louise Erlanger on Dec. 23, 1911. They had been married July 5, 1891.

Max D. Steuer, attorney, said at his home last night he had been retained as counsel for Mrs Erlanger, "in whose arms Abraham L. Erlanger died in the Riverside Drive apartment." Mr. Steuer said that Mr. Erlanger left an estate which would probably amount to not less than $75,000,000 and that he would protect her interests.

When informed that Mr. Erlanger's brother had declared "there is no Mrs. Erlanger," Mr. Steuer replied:

"Every department store in New York has charge accounts in the name of Mrs. Erlanger with the Riverside Drive address.

"The records at the Ambassador Hotel here and the Shelburne in Atlantic City will show that Mr. and Mrs. Erlanger lived there. Mr. Erlanger was well known to the management of both places.

"Confidential employes of Mr. Erlanger have arranged the transportation and made reservations for Mr. and Mrs. Erlanger here and abroad. There is not the slightest difficulty in proving that there is a

Continued on Page Ten.

LEADERS OF RED RIOT HELD WITHOUT BAIL; FIGHT FOR RELEASE

McAdoo Jails Five for Hearing Monday When Crain Says They Face More Serious Charges.

WHALEN THE COMPLAINANT

Affadavit by Him Tells How Foster and Others Ordered March on City Hall.

DEFENDANTS GET WRIT

Prosecutor Must Show Cause for Opposing Bail—Reds Charge They Were "Railroaded."

Five Communist leaders, headed by William Z. Foster, charged with responsibility for inciting the riot at the unemployment demonstration of the Communist party in Union Square on Thursday, were held without bail for a hearing by Chief Magistrate William McAdoo in Yorkville Court yesterday. Police Commissioner Whalen appeared as the complainant, with District Attorney Crain as the prosecutor. An affidavit made by Commissioner Whalen described the demonstration which resulted when the defendants ordered the march on City Hall. Foster and his lieutenants are to be arraigned on Monday for provoking an unlawful assembly. Technically, they are charged with a misdemeanor.

Reds Get Writ of Habeas Corpus.

Despite the protests of Jacques Buitenkamp and Joseph R. Brodsky, attorneys for the Communist leaders, Chief Magistrate McAdoo refused to admit them to bail, but later the attorneys for the accused obtained a writ of habeas corpus from Justice Alfred H. Townley in the Supreme Court directing District Attorney Crain to show cause why the prisoners should not be released on bail. The writ is returnable at 10:30 o'clock this morning.

Those held with Foster, national leader of the Communists, who returned recently from a conference in Moscow, were Robert Minor, editor of The Daily Worker, official Communist organ; Israel Amter, Communist organizer; Harry Raymond and Joseph Lester.

Raymond and Lester, who gave their addresses as 25 South Street, headquarters of a Communist industrial organization, are not prominent in the Communist party, but are accused of having played a leading part in the preliminaries to Thursday's riot.

Face Assault Charges.

All five, District Attorney Crain said, may yet face the charge of second degree assault, punishable by five years' imprisonment, or of manslaughter, should any of those injured in the riot die. Mr. Crain referred particularly to Patrolman Arthur Talbott, who was hit on the head with a brick. He is in St. Vincent's Hospital. Dr. Daniel Donovan, chief surgeon of the Police Department, visited Talbott yesterday. The policeman's injuries were said to be not as serious as was at first believed.

Foster and his codefendants were arrested near City Hall about an hour after the riot, while awaiting the mob which they had directed to proceed to the City Hall to demand a hearing from Mayor Walker.

Immediately after Foster, in defiance of Mr. Whalen's warning not to parade, had told the crowds to march down Broadway to City Hall, Foster and his codefendants left Union Square in a taxicab.

Mr. Whalen said last night that the Red leaders first turned north into Broadway as the crowd of 2,000 Communists, headed by women and children, swung south along the

Continued on Page Two.

Dr. Cook's Parole Is Approved by Mitchell; His Release Due Tomorrow After Five Years

Special to The New York Times.

WASHINGTON, March 7.—Dr. Frederick A. Cook, Arctic explorer, physician and oil promoter, who has been serving a sentence of fourteen years and nine months in the Federal Penitentiary at Leavenworth, was ordered paroled today by Attorney General Mitchell. The order for his release will be telegraphed to the prison, and it is understood that he will be set at liberty, Sunday.

The explorer's sentence also carried a fine of $12,000, and if this is not settled by March 2, 1935, when the parole expires, Dr. Cook may have to serve another thirty days and take a pauper's oath to escape the fine. The Department of Justice stated today, however, that although Dr. Cook might be temporarily relieved by the pauper's oath, the government could levy upon him if he ever obtains $12,000.

Dr. Cook was sentenced at Fort Worth, Texas, after his conviction on a charge of using the mails to defraud in connection with the sale of oil stock. He has been a prisoner at Leavenworth since April 6, 1925. He sought a Presidential pardon from both President Coolidge and President Hoover, without success.

It is said that Dr. Cook has been a model prisoner.

LEAVENWORTH, Kan., March 7 (AP).—Dr. Frederick A. Cook, whose career as an oil promoter was interrupted by imprisonment at Leavenworth, is prepared to face the world again at the age of 65.

In the early part of his term Dr. Cook assisted in the prison hospital, where his medical knowledge supplemented that of the one regular prison physician.

Later he organized a night school. Released prisoners have told of the scope of his work, and of the good influence exerted over his associates. Two months ago, when a parole board recommended that he be released, it was said that he never had been accused of violating a prison rule.

Plans of the prisoner, who in 1908 contended that he had discovered the North Pole, have not been learned definitely. It is known that he has expressed a desire to continue his writings.

Albany Legislative Mill Lags First Time in Recent Years

Special to The New York Times.

ALBANY, March 7.—For the first time in the last few years the wheels of the legislative mill have slowed up, as shown by bills introduced and passed. Five more bills had been presented to the Legislature at this time in last year's session, or 1,273 as against 1,268 in the current session.

The Senate last year had passed thirty-one and the Assembly fifteen more bills.

Until this year the records at almost any period of a recent session would have shown the legislative mill grinding at a faster pace than in the year previous.

The probability that this session will be longer than usual and difficulties over the executive budget with consequent delay of other legislation are held to be the causes of the present trend.

LABOR SETS MARCH 19 FOR JOBLESS PARLEY

300 Union Bodies Here Called to Consider Situation Now Termed "Acute."

WILL APPEAL TO WALKER

Mayor Expresses Sympathy for Move, but Denies City Has Retarded Subway Work.

A call for a conference on March 19 to consider a program of unemployment was issued yesterday by the Emergency Committee on Unemployment, with headquarters at 7 East Fifteenth Street. The meeting will be held in Beethoven Hall, 210 East Fifth Street. The call, signed by representatives of leading labor unions, most of them affiliated with the American Federation of Labor, and the Socialist Party, was addressed to more than 300 local unions, comprising about 500,000 members of the A. F. of L. in New York and vicinity.

It was said that more than 1,000 delegates representing the labor organizations in question are expected to attend the conference.

The conference call is the second move of the Emergency Committee on Unemployment, of which Abraham I. Sniplacoff, head of the Pocketbook Makers' Union, is chairman, in its efforts to initiate a wide movements of organized labor to ease the existing unemployment situation.

Plans Conference With Mayor.

The committee expects to send representatives to City Hall some time next week, probably Wednesday, to request Mayor Walker to mobilize some relief of the jobless. The emergency committee paved the way for the conference by addressing to the Mayor a petition urging the speeding up of public works, the setting up of a comprehensive system of relief, including stations for the free distribution of food and clothing; the creation, with the help of the State, of a network of free employment agencies, and also that the city embark on a large-scale program of slum clearance and housing construction.

The Mayor took exception yesterday to that part of the petition in which it is charged that there has been a let-down on subway building. The Mayor quoted figures purport-

Continued on Page Two.

MORE WORK, SAYS HOOVER, AND DEPRESSION IS PASSING; 36 STATES ARE NOW NORMAL

PRESIDENT IS OPTIMISTIC

Distress Now Is Confined Mainly to 12 States, He Says in Statement.

STEADY RISE SINCE JAN.

Spring Construction Will Tend Still Further to Create Employment, He Asserts.

RESULTS OF SURVEY GIVEN

Between 600,000 and 1,000,000 Jobless Have Found Work, Lamont and Davis Report.

Special to The New York Times.

WASHINGTON, March 7.—Unemployment "amounting to distress" is mainly concentrated in twelve States, and conditions in the other thirty-six States are either normal or steadily improving, President Hoover stated at the White House this afternoon, after a conference with Secretary Lamont, Secretary Davis, Assistant Secretary of Labor Klein and Francis I. Jones, director general of the Federal employment service.

All evidence in the possession of the President indicates that the worst effects of the stock market slump on employment will have passed within sixty days, he said.

Efforts to learn the names of the twelve States to which the President referred were fruitless. It was indicated that the Administration did not care to "single these out," and that it desired the unemployment problem to be considered as a national rather than a sectional problem.

Mr. Hoover's statement was interpreted in many quarters as being a reply to Senatorial critics, including Senator Wagner of New York, who have asserted that unemployment reaches high figures all over the country, and that the Labor Department has not revealed the actual facts.

President Hoover said that employment had steadily increased since the low point of late December and early January, and that the proportionate number of unemployed is considerably less than one-half—probably one-third—of that resulting from the crashes of 1907-08 and 1920-22.

Along with his own statement, Mr. Hoover made public a joint memorandum by Secretaries Lamont and Davis, which asserted that, although detailed statistics of unemployment were unavailable, there are certainly not more than 1,250,000 more persons out of work than a year ago.

Text of the President's Statement.

The President said in his statement:

"The Departments of Commerce and Labor are engaged in the usual monthly survey of business and unemployment, and especially of the results obtained from the measures which have been in progress since the last of November to reduce unemployment and the hardship following the dislocation from the Stock Exchange crash. The survey is not as yet complete.

"There are, however, certain conclusions that are evident:

1. Unemployment amounting to distress is in the main concentrated in twelve States. The authorities in the remaining thirty-six States indicate only normal seasonal unemployment, or that the minor abnormal unemployment is being rapidly absorbed.
2. The low point of business and employment was the latter part of December and early January. Since that time employment has been slowly increasing, and the situation is much better today than at that time.
3. Nation-wide response to the request for increased construction and improvement work by public authorities, railroads, utilities and industries is having a most material effect. Construction contracts in these categories in January and February were from 40 per cent to 45 per cent higher than ever known in these months. The total construction work for 1930 seems assured to be larger than even 1929.
4. The undertakings to maintain wages have been held.

Unemployment Less Than in 1907.

5. The amount of unemployment is, in proportion to the number of workers, considerably less than one-half (probably only one-third) of that which resulted from the

Section 1

"All the News That's Fit to Print."

The New York Times.

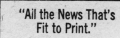

Copyright, 1930, by The New York Times Company.

THE WEATHER
Fair and slightly warmer today and tomorrow.
Temperatures yesterday—Max. 47, min. 30.
U. S. Weather Forecast—Page 10. Section 2.

Section 1

VOL. LXXIX....No. 26,342. NEW YORK, SUNDAY, MARCH 9, 1930. Including Rotogravure Picture Section in three parts—Magazine and Book Sections in Rotogravure. FIVE CENTS In Manhattan, Bronx and Brooklyn | Elsewhere TEN CENTS Except in 7th and 8th Postal Zones

REDS BORING INTO BUSINESS, SCHOOLS AND CITY BUREAUS, WHALEN WARNS, ASKS CURB

HE CALLS A CONFERENCE

Asks Corporation Heads to Fight Underground Drive of Radicals.

SECRET SQUAD GOT DATA

Police, in the Reds' Own Ranks, Compile Index and Note Effect of Propaganda.

PUPILS IN SPECIAL DANGER

Whalen Reveals Campaign in a Brooklyn School—Reds in High Business Posts.

Police Commissioner Whalen has notified some of the largest corporations in New York City that Communist organizers are boring from within their organizations, some as department heads, and he has invited the heads of these corporations to meet him in conference at Police Headquarters this week to discuss what they are doing or ought to do about it. Not only are the Communist organizers secreted and at work within many of the most powerful corporations but they have gained a foothold within New York City departments, and menace the schools especially, he said.

Commissioner Whalen for obvious reasons refused to divulge the names of the corporations whose heads he had warned of the presence of Communists, but he indicated that the Reds were actively at work, especially within the oil industry, the food products industry and the leather goods trades. He would say nothing in regard to the channels through which the workers are supplied with funds.

Mr. Whalen made known some of the discoveries of his secret service squad yesterday when he was asked to elaborate upon what he had said about the work of the secret service among the Reds at the end of an address before the League for Political Education in the Town Hall on Friday night. At that time he said, in answer to questions, that the police secret service had gathered an enormous quantity of information concerning the Communists and knew who they were, how many there were, when they were planning demonstrations of violence and other demonstrations and where they were planning them. In fact, he said, the police had such complete data that they were able to "keep a jump ahead of the Reds."

Card Index File Kept.

The police under-cover men have gathered such a mass of data on the more than 9,700 Communists in New York City, according to the commissioner, that they know each one and have been able to develop a card index system showing very complete records of the thousands under surveillance all the time. As additional information is gathered the card index file is kept up to date.

The police secret service, Mr. Whalen said, is boring from within the Communist organization in New York City as effectively as the Reds are trying to bore from within the institutions of America and the rest of the world.

The secret police are hobnobbing with the Communists in such genuine fashion that the under-cover men are even mistaken for Communists by the police and have to dodge night sticks when occasion requires. These pseudo-Communists, in order to find to what extent the Reds were boring from within a certain department of New York City had to be shifted to that department and placed upon its payroll. They were required to do the work of menials to get their ears close to that part of the ground which proved fallow for the seeds of Communist propaganda. After they had injected themselves into that department they were amazed to find how widespread were the activities of the Communist organizers.

Lists Prepared of Organizers.

In such cases and in the cases involving large business corporations, Commissioner Whalen compiled a list of all the Communist organizers and their converts. He included on the list only those Communists who had been seen and heard at Communists secret meetings, rallies and riots. He then confidentially transmitted to the heads of the private

Continued on Page Two.

Sheriff in Tennessee Quits Over Mill Strike

ELIABETHTON, Tenn., March 8 (AP).—Sheriff J. M. Moreland of Carter County tendered his resignation today, effective March 15, and charged that he was forced to take this action rather than "go out on the highways and shoot down pickets."

The Sheriff's resignation was announced a few hours after union officials had said that a cessation of picketing had been ordered temporarily, and after Moreland had dismissed William Fair, deputy sheriff in charge of officers guarding mill workers.

The Sheriff, in tendering his resignation, said:

"I was forced out by a bunch that wanted me to go out on the highways and shoot down pickets if they didn't do like these people wanted them to do. Politics also had a lot to do with it."

FIVE RED LEADERS FACE FELONY CHARGE

Win Bail at Habeas Corpus Hearing, but Rearrest of One Ends Fight for Release.

CRAIN CRITICIZES COURT

Calls Bond of $2,500 Too Low—Several Magistrates Refuse to Free Riot Instigators.

While the Communist party celebrated International Woman's Day yesterday with several small gatherings and a mass meeting last night at the Irving Plaza, five of their leaders, headed by William Z. Foster, arrested after Thursday's riot in Union Square, remained in jail after efforts to free them failed.

Supreme Court Justice Alfred H. Townley, who gave a hearing on a writ of habeas corpus yesterday morning, had set bail at $2,500 for each of the five prisoners. Not until last night, however, was Jacques Buitenkaut, attorney for the five men, able to obtain a magistrates signature to appplications for bail for three of the men—Harry Raymond, Joseph Lester and Israel Amter, local district organizer. The attorney applied to Magistrate Gottlieb in Night Court on behalf of these three but made no such application in the cases of Foster and Robert Minor, editor of The Daily Worker.

No sooner had Raymond been released from the West Side jail on Fifty-third Street, where he was held with his four companions, than he was rearrested and lodged in the West Forty-seventh Street station, after being booked theer on a charge of felonious assault growing out of the riot in Union Square on Thursday.

Accused of Felony.

Raymond's arrest the moment he emerged from the West Side Jail was viewed as being in line with an announcement made earlier in the day that Police Commissioner Whalen and District Attorney Crain had decided to charge the men whom they held responsible for the fighting in Union Square on Thursday with second degree assault. Second degree assault constitutes a felony punishable by a term in State's prison not to exceed five years or a maximum fine of $1,000 or both.

After obtaining the signature of Magistrate Gottlieb to the applications for bail for Raymond, Lester and Amter, Mr. Bruitenkaut and Philip Treibitz, a representative of the Greater City Surety Corporation, which furnished the bail, went directly from Night Court to the West Side Jail.

The lawyer submitted the bail papers for Raymond first and he was promptly released. As he emerged from the jail three detectives from the Industrial Squad stepped forward and arrested him.

The complainant against him was Detective Robert Quinn, who accused him of felonious assault and acting in concert in the attack on Thursday upon Patrolman Albert Talbott, who was hit on the head by a brick. Talbott's condition was reported as improved at St. Vincent's Hospital last night. Raymond will be held in the West Forty-seventh Street station pending his arraignment tomorrow.

After Raymond's arrest the lawyer and the representative of the surety company made no further efforts to

Continued on Page Two.

BUSINESS DEMANDS FOR TARIFF ACTION AROUSE SENATORS

Complaints at Delay Cause Smoot to Plan Attempt at Lump Votes.

PASSAGE SOUGHT THIS WEEK

But Coalition Will Fight Moves by Old Guard, Now in Control, to Restore Higher Rates.

NYE TO REOPEN SUGAR ROW

Debate on Raising Window-Glass Duty, Pressed by Goff, Takes Up Two-Hour Session.

Special to The New York Times.

WASHINGTON, March 8.—While a battle is in progress in the Senate between the Old Guard combination that has recently gained ascendency and the Democratic-insurgent Republican coalition on the tariff bill, business interests in the East and West are importuning Senators to revise industrial rates upward and to pass the measure at the earliest possible date.

In many messages received by Senators from individuals and organized bodies, the assertion is made that business is halting while uncertainty exists as to action on the tariff and that it is time that Congress disposed of a program that was initiated in January, 1929. The Senate has debated the bill for six months.

The administration has been apprised through various spokesmen that business has taken the position that early enactment of the tariff bill would help to restore "normalcy" in commerce and trade. Whether these representations will impel the Senate to speed up its deliberations is a matter of speculation.

The fight between the Old Guard combination, headed by Senators Smoot, Watson and Grundy, which reversed the Senate action on sugar and cement and which is bent on increasing the duties on aluminum and pig iron and transferring oil and lumber from the free to the dutiable list, will be resumed on Monday.

Nye Presses Sugar Issue.

Senator Nye, one of the Republican coalition leaders, has asked for a reconsideration of the vote by which the Senate increased the sugar rates, and he and his fellows appear to be confident that they can undo the work on this commodity performed so successfully this week by the Old Guard leaders. If, however, they should fail, they are likely to abandon their fight so far as lumber, oil and aluminum are concerned and let the tariff bill go to conference in accordance with the dictates of the Smoot-Grundy-Watson bloc.

The ranks of the original fourteen insurgent Republican members of the coalition have been wavering for several days. Much of their woe they blame on Senator Pine of Oklahoma, who deserted the coalition with a view to putting over an amendment providing for a duty on crude oil and oil derivatives.

"When the coalition votes for the interest of Oklahoma," Senator Pine said today, "I will vote with it. When it goes against Oklahoma's interest I will go the other way. It is to Oklahoma's interest to have a duty on oil."

Several explanations have been offered for the rout of the coalitionists during the closing days of the fight on the tariff. One is the pressure of business conditions and unemployment. The messages received here

Continued on Page Twenty-two.

King of Siam Makes Gift To Cathedral of St. John

William C. Redfield, former Secretary of Commerce, has been informed by Major Gen. Prince Amoradat Kridakara, Siamese Minister to the United States, that the King of Siam has donated two book cabinets to the Cathedral of St. John the Divine. Siam will be the fourteenth foreign government to make a gift to the New York Cathedral.

The work was executed by the Arts and Crafts Department of the Siamese Government in Bangkok. The cabinets are now on their way to the United States. A formal presentation will be made at the Cathedral. The Siamese Minister will attend the ceremony.

While Secretary of Commerce Mr. Redfield aided the Siamese Government in the construction of a model paper mill in Siam and earned the gratitude of that government.

When Bishop William T. Manning was asked about the new gift last evening he said:

"This will be one of the most interesting of the gifts which have been received by the Cathedral from a foreign government."

BOARD WIRES HOOVER PLAN TO FREE HAITI

Neutral Suggested as One-Man Provisional Government, With Elections to Follow.

CRISIS DANGER PASSES

Borno Faction Assures Support in Move—Asks Retention of Some American Aid.

By HAROLD N. DENNY,
Staff Correspondent of The New York Times.
Special Cable to The New York Times.

PORT AU PRINCE, March 8.—The present Haitian crisis, which as recently as forty-eight hours ago threatened to produce a revolt against the Borno Government and the American occupation, appears tonight to be on the verge of an amicable solution.

A tentative plan for an orderly, gradual return of the country to representative government has been sent by wireless by the Hoover investigating commission to President Hoover. No announcement either of the nature of the plan or of the progress of the negotiations was obtainable from the commission tonight, but it is known that the commission has been holding lengthy private conferences with leaders both of the Borno faction and the opposition, and it is generally believed plans have been worked out which in general are acceptable to both sides and at the same time in harmony with the Haitian Constitution and the treaty between Haiti and the United States.

Hoover Move Expected Next.

The next move is expected to come from Washington in a reply from President Hoover.

The communication to President Hoover was sent last night via the naval radio station here. It was a long message, giving a full report of the dramatic events of the last week, stating the nature of the present crisis and proposing a plan for a solution. The present crisis, of which the commission probably was not aware until it landed, just a week ago, grew out of the plan of the Borno Government for the election of President Borno's successor on April 14 by the Council of State, which he controls.

All week the commission has been listening to open warnings from many of the most prominent citizens that the people will rise up if

Continued on Page Twenty-four.

Fog Holds 16 Liners 4 Hours at Piers Here; 5,000 Passengers and Mails Are Delayed

Sixteen ocean-going steamships with fully 5,000 passengers and several thousand sacks of mail were held at the piers yesterday for four hours by a dense fog which rolled into the harbor about 10:30 A. M.

The fog was thick at the Chelsea piers, where the Cunarders Berengaria, Caronia, Ausonia and Antonia. Anchor liner Cameronia, White Star liners Adriatic and Baltic, Panama Pacific liner California, Red Star liner Lapland and the Atlantic Transport liner Minnekahda were ready to leave for European and Southern ports. Ten steamships with a total of more than 3,000 passengers, including the Swedish-American motorship Gripsholm and the Hamburg-American motorship St. Louis, were held at their piers between West Forty-fourth and Fifty-seventh Streets. Smaller passenger steamships were tied up at other piers along the North River on the New York and New Jersey shores and also along both sides of the East River.

Navigators of the big liners feared to leave until the fog lifted because of the danger of collision with coastwise and harbor craft.

When sailing times came bells were rung to warn visitors ashore and friends of passengers left the piers, but no starting whistles were blown until 2:45, when the fog had lifted.

The California was the first to move out into the river. She was followed by the Adriatic, Baltic and Lapland. The Berengaria did not leave until the Caronia, Ausonia, Antonia and Cameronia had started.

The motorship Bermuda and the Hellig Olav of the Scandinavian-American Line were the only two vessels to leave while the fog was still thick. Except for the ferry services there was very little traffic moving in the harbor yesterday morning and no accidents were reported. In the afternoon a fresh wind quickly blew the murky clouds out to sea and shortly after 3 o'clock the visibility at Sandy Hook was four miles and liners were able to steam out at full speed after they cleared Ambrose Channel.

The Royal Mail steamship Araguaya, arriving from the West Indies, left Quarantine at 2 P. M. and went directly to her pier.

The Washington Weather Bureau issued storm warnings at 9:30 A. M. from New Haven, Conn., to Atlantic City, N. J., and to small craft south of Atlantic City to Cape Hatteras.

BRIAND BEGINS TALKS ON POLITICAL TREATY TO BRING NAVAL CUTS

Confers With Stimson, Morrow and Henderson on Mutual Guarantee of Security.

WILL SEE M'DONALD TODAY

French Chief Hopes to Learn This Week Whether Prospect of Arrangement Is Good.

AMERICAN GROUP IS SPLIT

Hoover Must Decide Whether Vote of Stimson Prevails Against 4 Who Oppose the Proposal.

By EDWIN L. JAMES.
Special Cable to The New York Times.

LONDON, March 8.—Foreign Minister Briand said today that he would devote this week-end to inaugurating a detailed discussion of the political proposal made in France's formal statement at the London conference of her naval needs. In that document, it was stated, after France's program of construction was set forth, that she "remains, as she has repeatedly declared herself, ready to consider favorably any form of agreement for mutual guarantee of security the effect of which would be to transform the absolute requirements of each power into relative requirements."

The head of the French delegation entertained at luncheon today Foreign Secretary Henderson, with whom Secretary Stimson and Ambassador Morrow had just conferred. Later M. Briand, accompanied by Mr. Morrow, went to Stanmore to confer with Mr. Stimson on the pact proposal. Tomorrow he will confer with Prime Minister MacDonald and Mr. Henderson at Chequers, where Mr. Stimson may be invited.

M. Briand hopes that next week it can be made clear whether there is any prospect of making here an arrangement for which the French would regard as worth sacrificing some of their naval tonnage. It may be assumed that this week-end he will find no great enthusiasm among the British and Americans.

May Depend on Hoover.

The final British stand in all probability will depend on how much of a cut the French offer in return. As for the American delegation, which is split four to three on the advisability of supplementing the Kellogg pact, it is quite apparent that President Hoover will have to settle whether the Secretary of State's personal approval to the consultative plan shall or shall not prevail against the four members of the delegation who think the Kellogg pact should not be strengthened.

To understand these private negotiations it should be borne in mind that the French attach the greatest importance to the proposed pact of mutual aid among the Mediterranean powers. They do not expect the United States to take part in this, but it appears that England, while not encouraging this plan, takes the position that she could in no case go into it unless some means were found for ascertaining the American point of view in any given crisis; for example, by an American agreement to consult when violation of the peace pact threatens.

The French appear to have some difficulty in understanding the American shyness. They say that if the United States really means what the Kellogg pact says. she ought to be willing to do something if it were violated. Perhaps the French are appearing again too logical, for surely they know about the American Senate. However, manifestations in the United States in favor of some political arrangement have given the French no little encouragement.

Pact Discussed Privately.

There seems among the French some little irritation at the position of the American delegation that no pact proposal has been made. Of course, it has not been made officially and probably never will be unless assured of success, but naturally ever since Premier Tardieu made the suggestion on the opening day of the conference it has been discussed privately. It all comes down to the answer to a question of when a proposal is not a proposal.

That there can be no doubt as to the present situation and the French part in it may be seen from today's London newspapers.

The Daily Herald, which speaks for the government, says, "The plan is that the five powers should sign a new pact of good-will reinforcing those which already exist. Then figures shall be rediscussed under the new situation created by the signature of that pact."

The Daily News, Liberal organ, declares that "political as well as tech-

Continued on Page Twenty.

EX-PRESIDENT TAFT DIES AT CAPITAL, SUCCUMBING TO MANY WEEKS' ILLNESS, FIVE HOURS AFTER JUSTICE SANFORD

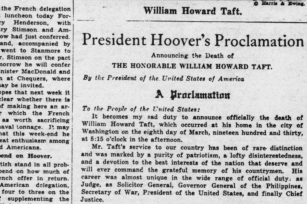

© Harris & Ewing.

William Howard Taft.

President Hoover's Proclamation

Announcing the Death of
THE HONORABLE WILLIAM HOWARD TAFT.

By the President of the United States of America

A Proclamation

To the People of the United States:

It becomes my sad duty to announce officially the death of William Howard Taft, which occurred at his home in the city of Washington on the eighth day of March, nineteen hundred and thirty, at 5:15 o'clock in the afternoon.

Mr. Taft's service to our country has been of rare distinction and was marked by a purity of patriotism, a lofty disinterestedness, and a devotion to the best interests of the nation that deserve and will ever command the grateful memory of his countrymen. His career was almost unique in the wide range of official duty: as Judge, as Solicitor General, Governor General of the Philippines, Secretary of War, President of the United States, and finally Chief Justice.

His private life was characterized by a simplicity of virtue that won for him a place in the affection of his fellow countrymen rarely equalled by any man. In public and in private life he set a shining example, and his death will be mourned throughout the land.

As an expression of the public's sorrow, it is ordered that the flags of the White House and of the several departmental buildings be displayed at half-staff for a period of thirty days, and that suitable military and naval honors, under orders of the Secretary of War and the Secretary of the Navy, may be rendered on the day of the funeral.

Done at the City of Washington this eighth day of March in the year of our Lord nineteen hundred and thirty, and of the Independence of the United States of America the one hundred and fifty-fourth.

HERBERT HOOVER.

By the President:
WILBUR J. CARR, Acting Secretary of State.

SANFORD COLLAPSED IN DENTIST'S OFFICE

Became Unconscious Soon After Tooth Was Pulled—Death Is Laid to Uremic Poisoning.

Special to The New York Times.

WASHINGTON, March 8.—Supreme Court Justice Edward Terry Sanford died at his home here today a short time after he had been carried there from his dentist's office where he had gone to have an ulcerated tooth extracted.

News of the justice's death came with an unexpectedness that startled official Washington, for only yesterday he was on the bench giving the same thorough and industrious attention to business which had characterized his seven years on the country's highest tribunal. The fact that he was even ill became known to friends and associates only a few minutes before the word that the end had come.

Justice Sanford had stopped by the office of his dentist, Dr. Arthur B. Crane, to have the tooth pulled on his way to the Capitol. Dr. Crane said that immediately after the extraction Justice Sanford appeared to be all right, but on arising from the chair he suddenly became dizzy.

The dentist called Dr. J. Lawn Thompson, a physician, who examined the patient's heart and administered a stimulant. He failed to respond to the stimulant, however,

Continued on Page Twenty-eight.

TAFT'S LIFE PRAISED AS TRULY AMERICAN

Public Leaders Acclaim High Character of His Great Services to His Country.

Special to The New York Times.

WASHINGTON, March 8.—Leaders in public life, mourning the death of William Howard Taft, pay high tribute to his character and personality and to the qualities of executive and judicial genius exemplified in his career.

Among them were the following:

CHARLES EVANS HUGHES, Chief Justice—The nation is bereft of the service of a true friend of the people. They recompensed his endeavors in their behalf with a warmth of affection which perhaps has never been so universally felt toward a public officer during his own lifetime. In the varied activities of a long public career, he exhibited unselfish devotion, unwearied industry, and absolute purity of purpose. His service fittingly culminated in his work as Chief Justice. There he could follow his bent. The efficient administration of justice was, after all, the dominant interest of his public life, and his unceasing efforts to that end were irradiated with the charm and helpful influence of a spirit of kindliness and an invincible good-will

Continued on Page Twenty-six.

END COMES AT 5:15 P. M.

Former Executive and Chief Justice Passes in Coma, Wife at Side.

HOOVER HASTENS TO HOME

President Proclaims 30 Days of Mourning for Nation—Military Funeral Planned.

BURIAL TO BE AT ARLINGTON

National Capital Is Saddened by Loss of Man Who Held the Country's Two Highest Honors.

Special to The New York Times.

WASHINGTON, March 8.—William Howard Taft, the only man in the history of this country to have filled both the offices of the President and the Chief Justice of the United States, died at 5:15 o'clock this afternoon. He was in his seventy-third year.

His death, which was caused by cerebro-arteriosclerosis, was preceded by that of Associate Justice Edward Terry Sanford at noon.

Today also was the eighty-ninth birthday anniversary of Justice Oliver Wendell Holmes, oldest member of the Supreme Court.

The deaths of two of the occupants of the highest bench were peculiarly saddening to the capital. During the illness of Mr. Taft Justice Sanford had been an almost daily caller at his home.

The death of Justice Sanford was quite unexpected, occurring after his collapse in a dentist's office where he had had an ulcerated tooth extracted. Taken to his home in an ambulance, he succumbed to uremic poisoning.

President Hoover issued this evening a proclamation authorizing national mourning for thirty days for former President Taft.

Mr. Taft succumbed after a rally a week ago from what his physicians thought was certainly the last phase of his illness and this temporary recovery brought a false hope that he might linger possibly for months.

Hoover Hastens to Taft Home.

President Hoover was on an automobile ride when his intimate friend passed away, and could not be notified until he returned to the White House at the same minute that Mrs. Manning was receiving the unexpected news. He immediately recalled his car and, with Mrs. Hoover, hurried to the Taft home.

During a brief stay, Mr. and Mrs. Hoover consoled Mrs. Taft and Mrs. Manning and repeated their offer of every facility of the White House to lighten the burden of the many arrangements which must be made under the circumstances.

The President also placed at Mrs. Taft's disposal the East Room of the White House for the funeral, but a request by Mr. Taft himself that the services be held from All Souls Unitarian Church on Sixteenth Street, of which the Rev. Ulysses Grant Baker Pierce is pastor, precluded either acceptance of this offer or a funeral in the Capitol, which had been considered a possibility.

The services tentatively have been set for Tuesday, but final arrangements await the arrival of the sons from Cincinnati, when a family conference will be held concerning the details.

Burial will be in Arlington Cemetery, in accordance with the request of the family, Mr. Taft having qualified for this honor both as a former Secretary of War and as former Commander in Chief of the Army and Navy while President.

Lapsed Into Unconsciousness.

In the room with Justice Taft when the peaceful end came were Mrs. Taft, who had entered it about two minutes before, a nurse, and Dr. H. G. Fuller, who had responded to the nurse's hurried summons in the absence of Dr. Francis R. Hagner, Justice Taft's personal physician and friend for a quarter of a century.

Death came quietly, Mr. Taft sinking imperceptibly into unconsciousness, as he had done frequently during the past month, and while in it suffering stoppage of the functioning of his heart.

Immediately after his passing, Dr. Hagner and Dr. Thomas A. Claytor, who has been associated with Dr. Hagner in treating the former Chief Justice, arrived at the house.

They issued the following bulletin,

Continued on Page Twenty-six.

"All the News That's Fit to Print."

The New York Times.

THE WEATHER
Warmer today, probably rain and colder tonight; tomorrow fair.
Temperatures Yesterday—Max. 48; Min. 34.
U. S. Weather Forecast—For details see Page 31.

Copyright, 1930, by The New York Times Company.

VOL. LXXIX....No. 26,346. NEW YORK, THURSDAY, MARCH 13, 1930. TWO CENTS in Greater New York | THREE CENTS Within 200 Miles | FOUR CENTS Elsewhere Except 7th and 8th Postal Zones

PROHIBITION STANDS TEST SAY SCORE OF WOMEN DRYS, 'SPEAKING FOR 12,000,000'

UNANIMOUS FOR THE LAW

Nation More Temperate, Witnesses Assert at House Hearing.

ILLS LAID TO THE LAWLESS

Mrs. A. H. Lippincott Charges Politicians With Non-Enforcement in New Jersey.

GAINS SEEN IN NEW YORK

Representative Dyer Urges 2.75 Beer to Hoover Commission as Aid in Enforcement.

Special to The New York Times.

WASHINGTON, March 12.—More than a score of women, virtually all of them leaders of widely known organizations, unanimously opposed any change in the prohibition laws in testifying today before the House Judiciary Committee.

Pictures of a public becoming debauched and intemperant have not been truly presented by opponents of prohibition, the committee was told, the witnesses maintaining that even in New York and metropolitan centres, where conditions have been pronounced the worst, there has been decided improvement under the dry law.

A New Jersey witness blamed lawlessness in her State on officials who, she said, do not obey their oaths of office to enforce the law. A former Mayoress of Seattle, Wash., ascribed to the same cause conditions in that city.

Contradicting testimony that drinking by students is increasing, the wives of professors at Yale and Harvard said conditions had been greatly improved under the Eighteenth Amendment, though neither denied that there is some drinking. In fact, all of the witnesses agreed there is room for improvement, but it also was contended that a decade is too short a time in which to give prohibition a fair trial.

Mrs. Ford and Mrs. Edison Appeal.

Many women sympathetic with the dry movement, including Mrs. Henry Ford and Mrs. Thomas A. Edison, were represented by statements favoring the present system. Those present forcefully argued their points under cross-examination.

The day's witnesses were marshaled by Mrs. Henry W. Peabody, chairman of the Woman's National Committee for Law Enforcement, which, she told the committee, represents thirty organizations favoring prohibition, with an aggregate membership of 12,000,000 women. Besides her testimony and that of seven others whom she called from among her organization's members, she arranged statements or testimony by four leaders of non-affiliated organizations, introduced thirteen State officers of the women's committee and read several messages from other outstanding personages.

Mrs. Peabody won her request for two hours to present her case without interruptions for cross-examination, but only after protests in the committee, principally by Representatives La Guardia and Emanuel Celler, wets, had forced Chairman Graham to put the question to a vote. Cross-examination of the witnesses had not been completed by Representatives La Guardia and Celler when a late adjournment was taken at 5 P. M.

Mrs. Peabody read into the record a creed of fourteen points which was adopted at a meeting of the delegates of the affiliated organizations yesterday afternoon.

Messages Read to Committee.

Among the messages from prominent women made public by Mrs. Peabody were the following:

MRS. THOMAS A. EDISON—"I stand for the law that has proved a blessing for one station in life and should be an equal blessing to those enjoying greater privileges in this world if they would give the law a fair chance."

MRS. HENRY FORD—"I am heartily in favor of the Eighteenth Amendment without modification. It is a law of the United States and should be observed by all of us. In my opinion it has been of untold benefit to the women as well as men of our country in improved living conditions and a more prosperous nation."

CARRIE CHAPMAN CATT—"I give my testimony that in my own considerable circle of acquaintances and friends, with two exceptions, I have found no man, woman or child who drinks, brews, smuggles, purchases, sells or distributes any form of alco-

Continued on Page Eighteen.

Saturday Is Last Day to File Tax Returns Without Penalty

Frank K. Bowers, Collector of Internal Revenue, called attention yesterday to the fact that Saturday is the last day to file income tax returns without incurring a penalty.

Although Saturday is usually a half holiday, the Collector's office will be open from 9 A. M. until midnight.

A return sent by mail and bearing a postmark up to midnight Saturday will be deemed to have been filed in time.

DRY LAW IS ILLEGAL, LAWYERS VOTE, 6 TO 1

New York County Committee Holds Ratification Method Was Unconstitutional.

TO INFORM SUPREME COURT

Asserts Only the People Had Power to Adopt Amendment, Not States or Congress.

After two years' deliberation, the special committee of the New York County Lawyers' Association has decided by a vote of 6 to 1 that the Eighteenth Amendment was illegally ratified in defiance of the Tenth Amendment to the Constitution, Professor Leslie J. Tompkins, head of the Law Department of New York University, a member of the committee, disclosed last night. He said the committee also moved by the same vote to present its arguments to the United States Supreme Court.

At the same time, a member of the Bar Association revealed that the committee will meet tonight at 8 o'clock to consider the prohibition question and is expected to begin another attack on the legality of the Eighteenth Amendment.

The theory that the Eighteenth Amendment was adopted and ratified in defiance of the Tenth Amendment, which provides that "powers not delegated to the United States by the Constitution nor prohibited by it to the States are reserved to the States respectively or to the people," another member of the committee said, was advanced and developed by Selden Bacon, also a member of the committee. He added that the substance of the committee's findings had been incorporated in a pamphlet, also prepared by Mr. Bacon, and that this pamphlet will be sent out shortly to all members of the New York County Lawyers Association.

Cites Change in Constitution.

"The special committee," Professor Tompkins said, "voted in favor of the proposition that such a matter ought to be taken up with the Supreme Court of the United States at the earliest possible moment on the entirely new ground which is set forth in the report by Mr. Bacon, namely, that the Tenth Amendment to the Constitution modified the Fifth Article of the original Constitution.

"That is, that neither the Congress

Continued on Page Nineteen.

VITALE SAYS HE MADE $165,000 IN 4 YEARS WHILE ON THE BENCH

Attributes Improved Financial Condition to Fortunate Realty Investments.

FORGETFUL ON SALARY RISE

Admits That He Paid $1,500 in Judgments Shortly Before His Appointment in 1924.

HAD DEEDS IN NAMES OF KIN

Court Presses Magistrate to Explain Rothstein Loan—Will Decide Removal Action Today.

Magistrate Albert H. Vitale, testifying yesterday at his trial on removal charges before the Appellate Division of the Supreme Court, disclosed that in four years on the bench he had amassed a fortune of $165,000. Fortunate investments in real estate, he explained, accounted for the improvement in his finances.

When he was appointed to the bench in 1924 he had only recently liquidated debts of $1,500. In June, 1928, when he accepted a loan of $20,000 from Arnold Rothstein, murdered gambler, his assets were $125,000 in real estate, stocks and cash. A month later the total had risen about $40,000. During the first years of the magistrate's incumbency his salary was $8,000 a year, later being increased to $12,000.

The magistrate completed his case against the petition of the Bar Association that he be ousted from the magistracy. Max D. Steuer formally rested, with a renewal of his plea that the two charges against his client be dismissed. Presiding Justice Victor J. Dowling and his four associate justices, who had denied an earlier motion, said that decision would be reserved until this morning. Then, Justice Dowling added, after a half-hour of summing up by each side, the court would recess until this afternoon, when a verdict on Magistrate Vitale would be announced.

In addition to throwing light on his personal finances, the magistrate enlightened the court on his methods in meeting objections from attorneys in his court. He said, in effect, that he had not bothered very much in following testimony from a defendant because no higher court would pass on his work.

Questioned by Justice Finch.

"That is to say," observed Justice Edward R. Finch, "if he had the right of appeal you would have been much more careful?"

"Yes, sir," said the magistrate.

The magistrate himself disclosed that although he had taken Rothstein's check for $19,940 he had actually not entertained a very high opinion of the gambler. He said that he had "hesitated" about cashing the check, because Rothstein was a "notorious" gambler.

"Well," said Justice Dowling, "you knew that when you took the check of his corporation?"

"I did, judge," replied the witness, "and that is why I hesitated in accepting it, but then I felt my conscience was clear about the matter, that I had nothing at all to do with him directly and I felt that I could conscientiously accept it without feeling that I was doing anything unethical."

Mr. Vitale had previously explained

Continued on Page Sixteen.

Woman Broker Convicted of Grand Larceny; Faces 5 to 10 Year Term in $450,000 Failure

Miss Margaret E. McCann, the first woman to enter the brokerage business in Wall Street, was found guilty at 9:35 o'clock last night by a jury in Judge Rosalsky's part of General Sessions on one of five grand larceny indictments returned against her in September, 1928, in the $450,000 failure of her firm. She was remanded to the Harlem Prison for Women, pending sentence on March 19, after the court had denied the motion of her lawyer that she be freed on the $12,000 bail she had furnished at the time of her indictment.

Miss McCann showed no emotion over her conviction on the complaint of one of her patrons, Anthony Traina, a grease manufacturer at 1,412 Broadway, that a few days before the failure of her firm, which had an office at 74 Trinity Place, she had sold $12,800 in Bancitaly stock owned by him, without authorization, and appropriated the money to her own use. Assistant District Attorney Thomas Aurelio brought out during the trial, which lasted two days, that she had paid $12,000 to other customers from the money she had placed in another bank on the day she sold the stock.

Miss McCann, who is 49 years old and gave her address as 101 West Seventy-eighth Street, turned to her lawyer, Hugo Wintner, and smiled when the jury was being polled on her verdict. The penalty for the offense is from five to ten years' imprisonment.

Before she was led from the court she turned to a woman friend and said:

"I think the jury misunderstood the whole thing. I was a victim of circumstances. What I did was to take money from some to pay others. Had my creditors given me an opportunity, I would have gathered enough money in time to pay all of them."

The case was placed in the hands of the jury at 4 o'clock in the afternoon. The only time during the trial that the defendant lost her calm was when, in summing up, the prosecutor told the jury that, "on her own testimony, Miss McCann is a thief."

She jumped to her feet and, glaring at the prosecutor, demanded: "How dare you?"

EXPLORING UNITES NATIONS, BYRD SAYS

Asserts at Dunedin Luncheon Our Claims in the Antarctic Don't Clash With Britain's.

HINT OF NEW EXPEDITION

Plans, if Known, Would Cause a "Sensation," Says Admiral, Who Gives No Details.

By RUSSELL OWEN.

Copyright, 1930, by The New York Times Company and The St. Louis Post-Dispatch. All rights for publication reserved throughout the world.

Special Cable to THE NEW YORK TIMES.

DUNEDIN, New Zealand, Thursday, March 13.—There can be no controversy over the claims to land in Antarctica, said Rear Admiral Byrd yesterday at a Chamber of Commerce luncheon.

He referred to Minister De La Perrelle's talk about trade relations between the United States and New Zealand, adding:

"I have noted that there has been a tendency in some quarters in America and Europe to create a controversy between the British Empire and the United States concerning our claims in Antarctica.

"There is no reason or ground for that. We have considered this expedition a scientific venture and we hope a sporting one, and we went down there with the utmost respect for the Britishers who preceded us.

Controversy Would Be a Pity.

"Our work there should bring us closer together and not further apart, and it would be a pity should any controversy arise. It would go entirely against feeling and things we have held from the first.

"We have from the beginning recognized the Ross Dependency. We asked permission to establish Little America, which was graciously granted. We asked permission to bring back for scientific purposes a few penguins. This also was granted. And we observed the regulations regarding the killing of seal. We killed only enough for food purposes.

"Antarctica is big enough for all of us. Our claim lies entirely outside of the Ross Dependency over to the eastward, and there is nothing in the situation that could cause controversy.

"We are more interested in good-fellowship with you in common investigations down there than we are with any claims in Antarctica. It is another one of those cases where the intangible things of the spirit are more important than the material aspects."

Explains Talk of "Bankruptcy."

Admiral Byrd explained today that his reference to "bankruptcy" made at a dinner the day before was a half-joking rejoinder to a remark by another speaker that the ship might be filled with gold found by Dr. Gould in the mountains. "On the contrary," said Admiral Byrd, "we have several times been on the verge of bankruptcy. We are still in debt, but will be able to meet it eventually."

He did not care to comment further on financial matters.

Today the Admiral was luncheon guest on the British warship Laburnum, and later in the day planned to visit the hospital.

The City of New York went to Port Chalmers this morning to be dry docked. She leaks forward and aft from battering the ice pack but can easily be repaired. The Bolling will follow her in dry dock, and the ships will be ready to sail the latter part of the month.

DUNEDIN, New Zealand, March 12 (AP).—Rear Admiral Richard E. Byrd, who has flown over both the North and South Poles and driven a plane across the Atlantic, is planning another sensational feat.

"If I were to say what I am going to do next," he said today, "my remarks would cause a sensation."

The trend of events here and feel-

Continued on Page Three.

GOVERNOR CENSURES REPUBLICAN POLICY

Blames Leaders for Defeat of Welfare Measure and Blocking the Bond Issue.

PENSIONS BILL "CHARITY"

He Hints at Extra Session in Speech Outlining State's Needs at Schenectady Meeting.

Special to The New York Times.

SCHENECTADY, March 12.—A midsummer session of the Legislature was hinted at by Governor Roosevelt in the course of a radio address he delivered tonight at a dinner of the Democratic organization of Schenectady County, should the Republican majority of the Legislature fail to support his recommendation that an additional large bond issue be authorized for new State hospital construction.

The Governor explained that the first suggestion for consideration of his proposal at an extraordinary session had come from Republican leaders, who appeared to prefer to have action on his recommendation deferred until after the regular session had adjourned. While the Governor did not say so in his address, he attributes the Republican attitude to some political motive which he has not been able to fathom.

Mr. Roosevelt declared that if the Republicans had their way and the taxpayers were burdened with the cost of an extra session the money would be spent for no practical purpose, because the Federal income tax returns at the end of this present week would afford a correct gauge of to what extent the State tax revenue will be reduced as a result of the present depression.

The Governor asserted that failure of the Republican majority last year to heed his recommendation, renewed at the present session, for a $50,000,000 bond issue for permanent improvements had rendered it necessary to spend this year more than $15,000,000 out of current revenues for that purpose and strip the treasury of a surplus.

Another speaker was Controller Morris S. Tremaine, who discussed State home rule and prohibition.

"It may be correct," he said, "that prohibition has brought about certain profitable results, but what does it profit us if we gain the whole world and lose our own soul? To drink or not to drink is not the question. The question is to lie or not to lie—the preservation of the integrity of the Constitution and Bill of Rights in its original spirit."

The Governor's Speech.

After remarking that the Legislature had just adopted a $309,000,000 budget and that the business of the State Government was a growing one which was bound to cost more from year to year as the State's activities were expanded to meet new needs, the Governor went on:

"If we consider government as something more than a necessary evil, if we think of it as an agency first to protect society and then to promote and guide all the people into better ways of living, then we must try to imagine what conditions will be a few years hence, and plan our government to meet those conditions.

"There are some things we can fairly predict, however. For instance, we know that the State must build many hospitals. You have heard a good deal of talk in the past year about the hospital program. Under my predecessor the State began a hospital building program of very large dimensions, but we are finding out that we are still going to be far short of hospital facilities five years from now, even though we continue to build at the present rate.

"The fact is that we are now trying to make up for a couple of generations of neglect. The State in the past has not kept up to date in the manner of caring for our mentally sick and defective."

After describing how plans for more hospitals had been speeded up this year, he continued:

"Today bids were received for the first part of the work, totaling nearly

Continued on Page Four.

Crazed Man Battles Subway Passengers; Crowd in Panic as He Brandishes Pistol

A southbound Seventh Avenue subway express rumbled into the Pennsylvania station just after 10 o'clock last night. Among other passengers who boarded it was a large Negro, wild-eyed and smelling strongly of alcohol. He elbowed his way into an already packed car and started forward through it, hurling passengers left and right and leaving a wake of indignant men and women behind him.

Midway of the car, several men remonstrated with the Negro. He thrust them out of his way. Herman Abramowitz, a Federal prohibition agent, on his way to his home at 850 Lafayette Avenue, Brooklyn, was sitting reading a newspaper. He heard the voices, saw the Negro jostling his way along the aisle, and drew his pistol.

But fearing to use the weapon in the crowded car, Abramowitz first took the precaution to break it open and throw the cartridges out the window. By this time the Negro was using his fists. He knocked down one man who objected to being jostled. At this point Abramowitz interposed.

"That's enough," he said, leveling the empty pistol at the Negro, "keep quiet or I'll have you arrested at the next station."

The Negro lurched toward Abramowitz. With surprising quickness he seized the pistol and wrenched it from the prohibition agent's grasp. Then, pointing it against Abramowitz's abdomen, he announced: "I'm going to kill you," and pulled the trigger. Several women in the car, who had not seen Abramowitz remove the cartridges, screamed and started for the doors. This precipitated a general scramble. By the time the train reached Fourteenth Street the car was a bedlam. Men and women pushed and shoved to get to the doors. Both ends of the cars were jammed tight with struggling humanity, and in the centre, Abramowitz and the Negro, left alone, battled in the aisle.

As the train stopped a guard ran upstairs and called Patrolman Edward Walters of the Charles Street station. The Negro had just backed Abramowitz into a glass window of the car when Walters entered. Seeing the patrolman, the Negro backed off and pointed the pistol at him. But Walters stepped up and with a blow of his nightstick felled the Negro. Then he arrested him. At the Charles Street station, where he was locked up charged with felonious assault, the Negro described himself as James Newkirk, a cook, of 11-21 Garden Street, Maspeth, L. I. The police say he has a record and that he stabbed a man in 1921.

SENATE REPUBLICANS FORCE THROUGH BILL FOR AN INQUIRY HERE

Fearon Voices Suspicion That Murderer of Rothstein Is Known to Politicians.

WHALEN AND CRAIN DERIDED

Majority Refuses to Include Scandals of Up-State Cities in the Investigation.

DEMOCRATS CRY POLITICS

In Storm of Protest They Assert Real Aim Is to Put the Governor in a Hole.

Special to The New York Times.

ALBANY, March 12.—Rejecting a Democratic amendment to make the measure applicable to all municipalities in the State, the Republican majority in the Senate today after two hours of violent debate forced the passage of the Knight bill for an Executive investigation of certain New York City departments.

The Democrats lined up solidly against the measure, their opposition producing the stormiest session of the year. Leaders on both sides displayed more interest in this issue than they did in the prolonged budget controversy of the last two days.

The bill, which will soon be passed by the Assembly also, authorizes the Governor to appoint a commission of five to investigate the administration of the magistrates' courts, of the Police Department with especial relation to the unsolved murder of Arnold Rothstein, the gambler; and the Board of Standards and Appeals and the Fire Department in relation to the Pathé film studio fire catastrophe. An appropriation of $50,000 is provided for the inquiry.

Bring Up Rothstein Case.

Irritated by charges of the Democrats that the measure was framed to embarrass the Governor and supply an issue of "Tammany scandals" for the Fall Gubernatorial campaign, the Republicans countered with a barrage of accusations.

They declared that controlling political circles in the city know the murderer of Rothstein and that Grover Whalen was appointed police commissioner to divert attention from failure to apprehend the murderer. They added that the case killed Joseph Warren, the former Police Commissioner, who was displaced by Mayor Walker. They criticized the abortive prosecution conducted by District Attorney Banton and ridiculed his successor, District Attorney Crain.

"Isn't the present District Attorney, who is now handling the inquiries into magistrates and the Pathé fire, the same man who said he could solve the Rothstein murder within fifteen days after election and whose simple solution was that 'Rothstein was dead,'" taunted Senator George R. Fearon, Republican, of Syracuse.

The Democrats countered by reciting scandals in Monroe and Westchester Counties.

The political ambitions of W. Kingsland Macy, Suffolk County Republican leader, were suggested as the inspiration for the New York City inquiry. Investigations by New York City agencies were recalled to prove that the city is itself competent to handle any derelictions in its departments.

Turn Tables on Fearon.

The minority hammered home their argument by repeating one phrase used by Senator Fearon.

"I have no antagonism against the city of New York. All I want to do

Continued on Page Four.

BRITISH BAR FRENCH PLAN FOR MUTUAL ASSISTANCE; NAVY PARLEY NOW AT CRISIS

Arlington Memorial Bridge Over Potomac Catches Fire

By The Associated Press.

WASHINGTON, March 12.—The Arlington Memorial Bridge, a $14,000,000 structure being built over the Potomac River between the capital and Virginia, was damaged to the extent of about $10,000 today by a fire which started about half an hour after the workmen had gone.

Fire departments from half a dozen surrounding towns, assisted by a fireboat, extinguished the fire after it had destroyed the wooden framework over Columbia Island on the Virginia side, causing a portion of the concrete to cave in. The origin of the blaze was unknown.

REICHSTAG RATIFIES YOUNG PLAN, 265-192

Votes Final Approval, Urgency Resolution Staving Off Bid of Nationalists for Delay.

MUELLER HAILS NEW ERA

Asks Good Faith of Creditors and Warns Republic's Foes —Treaty With Us Carried.

Special Cable to THE NEW YORK TIMES.

BERLIN, March 12.—By a vote of 265 to 192, the Reichstag today set the seal of its definite approval on the Young plan, which commits Germany to reparation annuities until 1988. The plan, which was drafted by international experts at Paris last year and approved by Germany and the various creditor powers at The Hague last January, replaces the Dawes plan, which took effect on Sept. 1, 1924, and is made retroactive beginning Sept. 1.

Today's final adoption of Germany's new reparation commitment was definitely forecast in yesterday's vote on its second reading by the Reichstag, when it was approved by a vote of 263 to 174. The government gained two votes on the final ballot today, while its opponents recruited eighteen more than they rolled up yesterday. As they stand, the final figures make the government's victory in its sturdy fight for the adoption of its reparation bills and liquidation pacts all the more impressive.

Pact With Us Also Passed.

The separate debt refunding agreement between Germany and the United States also received final approval today without recourse to a roll-call.

Transcending the significance of today's vote was a speech by Chancellor Mueller in which he broadly reviewed the genesis of the negotiations leading up to the government's decision to recommend the Young plan for ratification and its implications for Germany. The Socialist Chancellor's speech was of a calibre rarely encountered in governmental utterances and was distinguished by a logic which swiftly disposed of home criticisms, while on the other hand it did not fail to remind the creditor powers that Germany's pledge of good faith embodied in her acceptance of the new plan presupposed a similar demonstration of good faith on their part with respect to obligations mutually assumed.

"Neither the government of the Reich nor any expert, or for that matter any human being in the

Continued on Page Two.

BRIAND IN SECOND FAILURE

MacDonald's Stand, After American Decision, Bars Political Accords.

NEXT MOVE UP TO TARDIEU

Premier Will Arrive Tomorrow to Tell Effect on the Navy Program of France.

TANGLE ON SUBMARINES

Move for Humanization of War Under Sea Meets Difficulty Despite Optimism.

By EDWIN L. JAMES.

Special Cable to THE NEW YORK TIMES.

LONDON, March 12.—Prime Minister MacDonald informed Foreign Minister Briand today that Great Britain found herself unable to take on any new international obligations, and that therefore the British delegation was obliged to give a negative reply to the French proposal that England and France engage in a new mutual assistance pact against aggression modeled on the lines of the Geneva protocol of 1924.

This English decision, following the American decision yesterday to refrain from any political engagement here, ends the political phase of the conference, eliminating all political pacts.

Thus the veteran French Foreign Minister has failed in his effort to bring reinforcement machinery of peace out of the London conference, and especially does he fail to bridge the gap between the League of Nations and the United States.

M. Briand did not make a public statement of France's position today as was expected, but it was said tonight he would do so tomorrow. It is understood the delay was due to a desire to have another conversation with the Italians.

Parley Seen as Grave Crisis.

The London Times says tomorrow: "It can be no secret that the negotiations have now reached a crisis which may easily prove fatal."

This paper says the British had always hoped some security formula could be found midway between the French demand for guarantees and the American determination to avoid any political commitments; "that some formula giving substance to the Kellogg pact might be devised which the American delegates could submit to the Senate and the public of the United States, and which would give France the desired assurances for her security."

"It must be said, however, that the President's subject," it continued, is "entangling military alliance." The London Times concludes there remains some hope, but not a great deal.

Briand Says Rôle Is Ended.

At a meeting of Mr. MacDonald, Secretary of State Stimson and M. Briand this afternoon the French Foreign Minister was asked if, despite the failure of political negotiations, he could not agree to a reduction of the French naval figures. M. Briand replied that so far as he was concerned his rôle at the conference was finished. He had been instructed, he said, by Premier Tardieu and the French Cabinet to negotiate a political pact at London. He had failed, he asserted, and would say no more about it.

As for the French figures, he said he had no authority to reduce them. He said Premier Tardieu would arrive in London Friday evening and that Mr. MacDonald and Secretary Stimson could address their inquiries to the French Premier.

During the discussion it is understood M. Briand informed Mr. MacDonald and Mr. Stimson that his figures would come with better grace if France had undertaken to criticize the British and American naval figures, which she had not done.

Thus the world naval situation is now regarded here as being back where it was on the day when Premier MacDonald and President Hoover sat on a log at the Rapidan River and forgot about France. The next question is whether the British and Americans can get together. If either party of this conference no one seems to know tonight. There still is the possibility of a five-power limitation treaty which will not provide any reductions.

Taking a general view, it is held here that the situation would seem to be up to Washington. Which will President Hoover prefer, no treaty at all or a treaty of limitation without reduction?

The British have said that if the French stand on their figures the British figures must be increased. The increases indicated unofficially are from 339,000 tons to 400,000 tons for cruisers, 150,000 to 200,000 tons for destroyers and from 60,000 to 90,000 tons for submarines, an increase over

Briand Forecasts Parley's End in Two Weeks; Gloomy Over Failure to Get Security Compact

By The Associated Press.

LONDON, March 12.—Aristide Briand, Foreign Minister of France, is gloomy over his failure to get a security compact for his country out of the five-power naval conference. Tonight he gave the parley only another fortnight of life.

The head of the French delegation received French newspaper men, but rigidly excluded reporters of all other nationalities. The French writers came out of the conference convinced that M. Briand was depressed. They quoted him as saying:

"I have finished my rôle and tomorrow the whole thing will be handed over to the delegations."

M. Briand said the delay in reaching conference decisions had not been due to the French attitude in demanding security compacts as a price for reducing their program of naval building, but to the fact that Italy had not produced any tonnage figures at all, but had insisted solely on their right to parity with any Continental European power.

It was understood that the French leader had pressed this point regarding the Italians rather sharply at a meeting today of the British, French and American delegations.

While M. Briand gave the impression of asking for security pacts for a political alliance in connection with naval limitations, other members of the French delegation recalled that the French had consistently maintained that the present conference should only be a prelude to general consideration at Geneva of the whole question of disarmament, covering land and air as well as sea.

The French were quick also to emphasize the importance of the technical work done here. They prophesied that a five-power treaty would be signed, but it would include a further holiday in battleship building. Humanization of submarines and such technical subjects as a general agreement on the category method of measuring navies.

British and American observers agreed that the conference might last three or four weeks.

"All the News That's Fit to Print."

The New York Times.

Copyright, 1930, by The New York Times Company.

THE WEATHER
Cloudy and colder today; probably rain; tomorrow fair and cold.
Temperatures yesterday—Max., 57; min., 44.
U. S. Weather Forecast—For details see Page 55.

VOL. LXXIX....No. 26,359. **** NEW YORK, WEDNESDAY, MARCH 26, 1930. TWO CENTS In Greater New York | THREE CENTS Within 200 Miles | FOUR CENTS Elsewhere Except 7th and 8th Postal Zones

SENATE VOTES $383,000,000 IN BILLS TO AID BUSINESS, PUSHING HOOVER PROGRAM

SWIFT ACTION PROJECTED

Watson Discloses Party Plan for Six Weeks' Drive on Vital Measures.

WOULD AVOID CONTROVERSY

Leader Calls for Disposal of Tariff, Shoals, Prohibition and Supply Bills by June 15.

STABILIZATION CHIEF AIM

$230,000,000 Is Provided for Public Buildings, $153,000,000 for Agriculture Outlays.

Special to The New York Times.

WASHINGTON, March 25.—Plans to stimulate business and bring about stability by prompt passage of the tariff bill and rejection of pending controversial legislation were evolved by Republican Congressional leaders today after the Senate passed two bills aimed to encourage construction and road building.

In less than two hours the Senate passed the agriculture and public buildings bills which carry appropriations of Federal aid in road building and the erection of public buildings throughout the country totaling $383,000,000. These are the first concrete acts by the Senate to carry out the program recommended by President Hoover as the Federal Government's contribution to relieve the business depression by encouraging public works.

After the passage of these measures, following its disposal of the tariff bill yesterday, the Senate took a virtual recess until Tuesday to get a brief rest before tackling the legislation accumulated during the six weary months given over to consideration of the tariff. The Senate will meet on Friday with the understanding that no actual business will be transacted until next week, when the Senate and House will take up the tariff bill and appoint conferees.

Would Centre on Essential Bills.

It is the opinion of leaders of both parties that the long delay in passing the tariff has tended to retard restoration of prosperity and the belief exists that there will be no resort to dilatory tactics in conference to hold up final action by Congress on the tariff bill, which has been before Congress for nearly a year.

Senator Watson, the Republican leader, in outlining the program of his party to expedite tariff legislation and aid business, said today that all controversial legislation would be dropped and the remaining months of the session devoted to passing only such bills as were necessary, including the general supply measures.

"I believe that restoration of prosperity has been retarded greatly by the delay in passing the tariff," Senator Watson said. "This could not be helped because of the Senate situation. But, now that we are through with the political and sectional struggle, I believe that there is a general agreement that Congress should speed up, do nothing to embarrass business and adjourn by June 15 at the latest.

"I feel that business has begun to breathe more freely since the Senate acted on the tariff bill. If the stock market is any symptom of business, it would appear that there is a gradual upward turn in business activity.

"So far as the Republican leaders can control the situation, every effort will now be turned to action aimed to stimulate business and prevent legislation of a disturbing character."

Program for Next Six Weeks.

Senator Watson said that in six weeks Congress should dispose finally of the tariff bill and be headed for early adjournment after passing the annual appropriation bills and some non-controversial matters.

The Senate's program is to pass the Norris Muscle Shoals bill, which provides for government operation of that project. This is scheduled to come up next week, following which the administration prohibition bill and the supply measures, comprising the present legislation program, will be considered.

Senator Watson feels that there should be no other controversial legislation passed in this session and that business should be free to adjust itself to the tariff bill without disturbances and innovations. In his opinion there will be no railroad con-

Continued on Page Twenty-one.

Minister, Wet and a Democrat, Seeks Bay State Senate Seat

BOSTON, March 25 (AP).—State Representative Roland D. Sawyer of Ware, a Congregational minister, announced his candidacy for the United States Senate on an unqualified wet platform today.

He said he would seek the votes of Democrats who "favor a candidate who will at all times be a straight out, uncompromising foe of Federal prohibition."

MAYOR AND THOMAS CLASH ON JOB PLANS

Walker Accuses Socialist of 'Insincerity' in Proposals to Relieve Unemployment.

SCORES 'SOAP BOX' TACTICS

Berry Tells of $2,000,000,000 Improvements Program Under Way by City.

Mayor Walker accused Norman Thomas, leader of the New York Socialists, and a group of associates of "insincerity" in their proposals to relieve unemployment, at a meeting yesterday of the committee of the whole of the Board of Estimate and Apportionment at the City Hall.

Toward the end of a two-hour meeting which was marked by clashes between the Socialists and city officers, the Mayor became indignant over the proposals advanced by Mr. Thomas. The Mayor argued that the laws prevented the city from spending money directly for relief and Mr. Thomas inquired what the Public Welfare Department was planning to do in the present situation.

Mayor Walker interrupted Mr. Thomas to say that he was convinced that the Socialists had entered the meeting room merely for "propaganda and political purposes" and that "the Board of Estimate has wasted two hours listening to political speeches."

Banging his gavel, the Mayor declared: "This is the last time this room will be used as a soap box for political propaganda."

Mr. Thomas insisted that those unemployed and in want must be helped and declared that "if that is political let the public decide."

Mayor Walker admonished Mr. Thomas that under the charter the city was unable to grant outdoor poor relief.

"Why don't you go to the Legislature and amend the charter?" the Mayor asked.

"Why don't you?" retorted Mr. Thomas.

J. P. Ryan Criticizes Socialists.

At this moment Joseph P. Ryan, president of the Central Trades and Labor Council, who had offered organized labor's proposals at the beginning of the hearing, interrupted to assert that last week the Communists had turned the meeting of the board "into a vaudeville show to preach their doctrine and today the Socialists have turned the meeting into a discussion of party principles."

"I want to say that we in the trade unions want the city to formulate plans for relieving the present unemployment situation and we came here on the level," he added.

A few minutes later the meeting recessed for lunch, after which there was a discussion of the proposal of

Continued on Page Twenty-one.

ASSEMBLY PASSES CITY INQUIRY BILL; WHALEN IS ASSAILED

Measure Carries by Strict Party Vote as Republicans Challenge the Governor to Act.

WIDE CORRUPTION CHARGED

Police Commissioner Is Called a 'Broadway Dandy'—Tammany Rule Is Denounced.

MINORITY HOTLY HITS BACK

Capitol Expects a Veto, With Roosevelt Suggesting Legislature Create Own Commission.

By W. A. WARN.
Special to The New York Times.

ALBANY, March 25.—After a debate of three hours, in which Mayor Walker's administration was bitterly assailed by Republicans, who declared that Governor Roosevelt would not dare "go to the bottom of all that is wrong in New York City for fear of jeopardizing his political future," the Assembly, by a strict party vote, today passed the Republican bill authorizing the Governor to appoint a commission to investigate the affairs of New York City.

The bill, which was prompted, according to the Republicans, by the Rothstein murder, the Pathé studio fire and the condition of the magistrates' courts, already had passed the Senate and now goes to the Governor.

The prevailing opinion at the Capitol is that the Governor will veto the measure and issue a statement declaring that if the Legislature wants to investigate conditions in New York City it should create its own commission.

Efforts, however, to induce the Governor to indicate today what action he planned to take on the bill were futile.

"I haven't even read the bill as yet," he said, smiling. "Wait until it reaches my desk."

Whalen Attacked in Debate.

During the course of the debate Police Commissioner Grover Whalen was the target for ridicule on the part of several of the Republicans. At one point Commissioner Whalen was characterized by Assemblyman Edwin H. Wallace, Nassau Republican, as a "glorified floorwalker whose knowledge of nightgowns was transferred to nightsticks."

Democrats returned shot for shot fired at New York City. In many respects the debate was the most bitter of the present session of the Legislature.

Assemblyman Irwin Steingut charged that the measure was a "political fishing expedition," and dared the Republicans to make it Statewide, so that there could be a similar investigation of every up-State city.

"The Republicans are trying to put the Governor in a hole" Assemblyman Steingut said. "Instead, they are putting him into a pretty position, and if he accepts renomination he will be re-elected by one of the greatest majorities in the history of the State."

Instead of spending $50,000, as appropriated in the bill, for the expense of the investigation, Assemblyman Samuel Mandelbaum, Democrat, of New York told the Republicans they might better provide for an investigation of the unemployment situation in New York City.

"To spend $50,000 for a silly investigation like the one that is proposed in this bill, when bread lines are forming in New York City, is nothing less than robbery," Assemblyman Mandelbaum declared. "The Republicans might better investigate the Hoover cry of prosperity. If the Republicans were honest about an investigation of New York City, they would have the Legislature do it."

Assemblyman Russell G. Dunmore, Republican floor leader, said one of

Continued on Page Fourteen.

Jersey Billboards to Be Regulated and Taxed; Law Passed Over Protest, Hits Atlantic City

Special to The New York Times.

TRENTON, N. J., March 25.—The Jones bill to regulate and tax outdoor advertising in New Jersey became law today. Governor Larson signed the measure after the Senate had reconsidered its action of last night when the act was amended to exclude billboards and electric signs on the Atlantic City Boardwalk from the regulatory provisions.

The bill requires a license for billboards and prohibits advertising equipment from being placed on roads where it might endanger traffic or where adjacent property would be damaged. The bill was brought out of committee over protests of advertising interests and occasioned in the Senate today the liveliest debate of this year's session.

The new measure taxes all billboards 3 cents per square foot, prohibits any billboards within 500 feet of a road intersection and places control and regulation of them with the State Motor Vehicle Commissioner.

In the two-hour debate this afternoon the bill was described as a "Morrow pawn" in a political deal by which Republican leaders are bidding for the support of women for Dwight W. Morrow, candidate for the Republican nomination for United States Senator.

This charge was made by Senator Richards of Atlantic County when reconsideration of his amendment last night to exclude Atlantic City billboard signs from the bill's regulation was proposed.

"I am serving notice here and now," he said, "that you can't take away the property of citizens without a protest at the polls. This bill means hundreds of thousands of dollars to Atlantic City."

He declared that the bill was being passed on the promise that 49,000 women's votes would be cast for Mr. Morrow in the Republican Senatorial primary.

Assemblywoman Agnes Jones of Essex introduced the bill. It has had the support of most of the women's clubs of the State and of many civic associations.

To Propose 50-Cent Pieces In Honor of Admiral Byrd

WASHINGTON, March 25 (AP).—Coinage of an issue of fifty-cent pieces in commemoration of Rear Admiral Richard E. Byrd and his Antarctic expedition will be proposed soon in a bill by Representative Cable, Republican, of Ohio.

The original plan for the bill, the Ohioan's office said today, contemplated the sale of the coins to pay off any possible deficit the expedition might face. A radiogram has been received from the Admiral expressing the "deep appreciation" of himself and his companions for the proposed honor, but explaining there would be no deficit.

A similar statement was contained in a letter to Mr. Cable from Captain H. H. Railey, Byrd's personal representative in New York.

FAITHS HERE UNITE TO DECRY RED DRIVE

Mass Meeting Held at Opera House Under Heavy Guard Following Bomb Threats.

CREDIT BOYCOTT PROPOSED

Woll Wants All Nations to Act —Father E. A. Walsh Says Soviet Martyrs Clergy.

Speakers representing Catholicism, Protestantism and Judaism praised the spirit of religious tolerance and lamented its passing in "what once was Holy Russia" last night at a mass meeting in the Metropolitan Opera House to protest against persecution of the church and its followers under the Soviet Government.

The meeting was held under heavy police guard, following the receipt of letters threatening that the old opera house would be "blown to pieces" and that those attending were facing "destruction." Members of the radical and bomb squads mingled with the audience, while seventy-five uniformed policemen under Inspector Patrick S. McCormick stood outside.

The letters were received by the management of the theatre and by Michael Williams, president of the Calvert Associates, a Catholic organization, which arranged the gathering. They were written on ruled paper and were signed only with crude drawings of a sickle and star, emblems of communism and the Union of Socialist Soviet Republics. The threats were regarded as the work of cranks, but because the tickets, which were free, might have fallen into hostile hands, it was decided to notify the police to guard against a possible demonstration.

2,000 Attend Meeting.

Despite the rainy weather and the threatening letters, a gathering of between 2,000 and 2,500 turned out for the meeting.

The police reported minor brushes with two men. One man, who said his name was Bernard Smith, was stopped in the lobby by a member of the police radical squad who said he recognized Smith as a Communist. Smith proffered a reporter's police card which the police took from him on the ground that it had not been issued to him. Smith told them he was a regular reporter on Die Freiheit, whereupon the police allowed him to enter.

Louis Goren of 342 Powell Street, Brooklyn, was stopped after several alleged attempts to enter the lobby without an admission card. He said he was a Russian Jew, interested in all movements. The police told him to move along.

Cardinal and Bishop Absent.

Cardinal Hayes and Bishop Manning, who were among the patrons of the meeting, which commemorated the landing of George Calvert, Lord Baltimore, and the planting of the seeds of religious freedom in this country 296 years ago, were unable to attend. Both were absent from the city.

John W. Davis, Democratic candidate for the Presidency in 1924, was to have been a speaker at the meeting, but was prevented from attending by a severe cold, he informed the committee.

Governor Albert C. Ritchie of Maryland, who also was unable to attend, sent Adjutant General M. A. Reckord to the gathering as his representative. Friendly messages were received from Governor Franklin D. Roosevelt, former Governor Smith, Dr. Nicholas Murray Butler and Colonel Edward M. House, former adviser to the late President Wilson.

Those present in the great auditorium heard the Soviet Government attacked for intolerance and persecution by the Rev. Dr. Nathan Krass of Congregation Emanu-El, the Rev. Edmund A. Walsh, vice president of Georgetown University; District Attorney Thomas C. T. Crain and Mr. Williams.

Matthew Woll, vice president of the American Federation of Labor, who was to have spoken was summoned hurriedly to Washington yesterday and his address was read by William Collins, an A. F. of L. organizer.

His speech declared that religious persecution in Russia "is a world

Continued on Page Sixteen.

EUROPA SETS RECORD; ARRIVES 18 MINUTES UNDER BREMEN TIME

Big German Liner Cuts Through Fog on Last Leg for Mark of 4 Days 17 Hours 6 Minutes.

RAIN DAMPENS RECEPTION

But Crowds Line Brooklyn Shore to Watch New Speed Queen Move Slowly to Her Pier.

CAPTAIN SPEAKS ON RADIO

Tells of Bucking Wind and Sea Over 3,100 Miles—Von Prittwitz Hails Ship as New Tie Between Nations.

The North German Lloyd liner Europa arrived in New York yesterday after a race of 4 days, 17 hours and 6 minutes from Cherbourg to Ambrose Lightship, setting a record for the Atlantic crossing and wresting the crown of queen of the seas from her sister ship, the Bremen. The distance covered by the Europa was 3,100 miles.

Reaching Ambrose Lightship at 5:54 A. M., after breaking through a blanket of fog that threatened to impede her final spurt to victory and after battling head winds and heavy seas nearly all the way, the Europa beat the Bremen's record of last October by 18 minutes, improving by 36 minutes upon the Bremen's maiden voyage last July.

The Bremen's October record was 4 days, 17 hours and 24 minutes, a little better than her first performance last July when she dethroned the long-reigning Mauretania.

Announces Record to Germany.

From Ambrose Lightship Captain Nicolaus Johnsen, commodore of the North German Lloyd line, wirelessed the news of the Europa's achievement to the New York and Bremen offices of the line.

"It was the happiest message I had ever sent," said Captain Johnsen. Later the smiling bearded skipper added:

"We're glad we're here. We did the best we could, with the weather not too favorable."

"It's a good thing for those few extra minutes which make the record," said Captain Paul Koenig, former U-boat commander and now marine superintendent of the North German Lloyd. "Otherwise the Europa would have been just another boat."

The expressions of satisfaction were repeated later when Baron von Prittwitz, German Ambassador, heading a large delegation of German officials and chiefs of the North German Lloyd, boarded the Europa at Quarantine and took part in a special broadcast from Captain Johnsen's cabin, which carried the news of the Europa's triumph to all parts of the United States and across the ocean to Germany.

The voyage of the Europa, which brought 1,608 passengers, of whom 446 were Americans, was made under more difficult conditions than those faced by the Bremen on her record-breaking run. The average speed of the Europa was 27.91 knots, or about thirty-two miles an hour, as compared with 27.86 knots of the Bremen. The top speed achieved by the Europa was 29.1 knots. That of the Bremen was 29.5 knots. The Europa's low speed was 27.6 knots. The low speed of the Bremen was 26 knots.

Slowed in Last 100 Miles.

Because of the fog that came down over the sea during the night as the Europa, straining every ounce of energy, was driving toward her destination, her speed was reduced over the last hundred miles, but even with this handicap she crossed the finish line in time to grasp the "blue pennant" of the ocean.

Passengers aboard the ship said that with the exception of the last 100 miles the last day's run was made at a faster clip than those

Continued on Page Three.

Reds Will Eject Police From Their Meetings, They Warn Whalen, Denouncing Supervision

Policemen who insist upon attending membership meetings of the Communist party without invitations will be "firmly ejected," Police Commissioner Whalen was warned yesterday in a letter from Israel Amter, secretary of the radical party.

Commissioner Whalen said he had not received the letter and would not comment upon it until he had. Amter is one of the four co-defendants with William Z. Foster in the unlawful assembly and felonious assault charges which grew out of the demonstration and riot in Union Square March 6.

The secretary's letter was prompted by the action of police who insisted upon attending a membership meeting of the Communist party at the New Star Casino Sunday, with the result that the meeting was transferred to Communist headquarters. The district representative who capitulated to the police, Amter said, "made a mistake" and "was condemned for it by the district committee of the party." The letter continued:

"The Communist party notifies you as Police Commissioner, agent of Wall Street and of the Tammany Hall machine, that it will hold its next and all future membership meetings without any police or representatives of the city authorities present. Any of these representatives who dare enter the hall at any membership meeting will be firmly ejected.

"The Communist party will not tolerate any interference with its activities. As the fighting party of the working class the Communist party will fight for its rights and the rights of the working class."

The letter declared that police supervision of workers' meetings was a threat against the independence of all working class organizations. As long as such practices continue, the letter said, "Democracy is only an illusion."

STIMSON AGAIN BARS ANY SECURITY PACT; WOULD CONSIDER CONSULTATIVE PLEDGE WITH NO OBLIGATION OF MILITARY AID

Text of American Statement Offers 'Open Mind' Consideration of Parley Problem on New Basis

Special Cable to The New York Times.

LONDON, Wednesday, March 26.—The American delegation to the London Naval Arms Conference gave out the following statement shortly after midnight this morning:

A rumor was current last evening to the effect that the American delegation had made a change in their attitude toward consultative pacts and were willing to enter into such a pact for the purpose of saving the conference. It is authoritatively denied at the headquarters of the American delegation that any change has taken place in the attitude of the American delegation, and its attitude remains as its spokesmen gave it out several weeks ago.

At that time it was made clear that America had no objection to entering into a consultative pact as such. On the contrary, the United States already is a party to a number of treaties involving the obligation of consulting with other powers.

It will not, however, enter into any treaty, whether consultative or otherwise, where there is danger of its obligation being misunderstood as involving a promise to render military assistance or guaranteeing protection by military force to another nation.

Such a misunderstanding might arise if the United States entered into such a treaty as a quid pro quo for the reduction of the naval forces of another power. That danger has hitherto inhered in the present situation, where France has been demanding mutual military security as a condition of naval reduction, as appears from her original statement of her case last December.

If, however, this demand for security could be satisfied in some other way, then the danger of a misunderstanding of a consultative pact would be eliminated, and in such case the question would be approached from an entirely different standpoint. In such case the American delegation would consider the matter with an entirely open mind.

MID-WEST BLIZZARD PARALYZES CHICAGO

12 Inches of Snow, Driven by Gale Into Drifts, Stall Rail, Auto and Air Traffic.

FOUR DEAD, MANY INJURED

Two Train Crashes Take Part of Toll—Rain and Fog Balk Shipping Here—Colder Today.

Special to The New York Times.

CHICAGO, March 25.—A blizzard struck Chicago and Illinois and surrounding States today, the fourth day of Spring, with a sustained fury which piled up twelve inches of snow on a level and drifts up to six feet deep, breaking the previous all-time record for a twenty-four hour snowfall in March.

The blinding snow, driven by a northeast wind of gale proportions, began just after midnight. A freakish low pressure area over Indiana accounted for the protracted violence of the wind and the heavy snow, according to the Weather Bureau. Tonight the storm was blowing itself out.

Daybreak today found the drifts heaped up in town and country. Interstate trains crept cautiously through congested yards to begin their runs, while street cars and buses lumbered with difficulty through the streets carrying the thousands of loop workers to their jobs.

Commuters in Great Difficulty.

By noon the motor and street car traffic was at a standstill in outlying districts, while the Rapid Transit reported trouble on suburban divisions where the tracks run on the surface. How to get home became an acute problem for thousands of suburban commuters this evening.

Buses skidded and stalled on Michigan Avenue, choking the movement of taxis and private cars. Suburban trains on the Illinois Central were running at half speed, while on the steam roads the yards were so congested by drifts and frozen switches that scheduled movement of trains was impossible.

Four persons are known to have lost their lives because of the storm. Edgar Tompkins, a postoffice em-

Continued on Page Eighteen.

WASHINGTON IS FIRM AGAINST AID PLEDGE

Suggestion That Any Form of Security Pact Is Likely Is Termed Groundless.

WOMEN CRITICIZE ATTITUDE

Letter to Hoover Expresses Disappointment—Britten Calls Parley Dead.

By RICHARD V. OULAHAN.
Special to The New York Times.

WASHINGTON, March 25.—With the United States and Great Britain at last convinced that France and Italy will not join in an armament limitation agreement of a competitive character, and with present efforts being directed to bringing Japan into an arrangement with the two English-speaking nations, confidence still exists in official circles here that whatever treaty eventuates from the London conference will be an important step forward in the direction of world peace and the curtailment of fleets.

Hope has not been abandoned that France and Italy will sign a treaty of limited scope, probably confined to a continuation of the battleship building holiday and a declaration that submarines should restrict themselves to humanitarian methods in warfare. But it is evident that in Washington at least there is expectation that even with France and Italy left out, the prospective treaty will be a substantial practical contribution to the cause of naval armament limitation.

Confusion Over Pact Issue.

Much confusion has existed as to what happened in the conference with reference to pacts designed partly to satisfy France's call for additional security as an inducement to modify her claims to high tonnage as a means of national defense.

On March 11, when it was announced authoritatively in London that the United States would not take part in any consultative pact in connection with the projected naval treaty, the natural supposition followed that the French had made some direct proposal for the negotiation of such a pact. If they had done so, however, it must have been within a day or two before the announcement was made, for there was every reason to put confidence in the accuracy of the following opening paragraph in a special Washington dispatch in The New York Times of March 11:

"Up to this time, it is learned in informed quarters here, no proposal concerning a security agreement has been presented, formally or informally, either to the American delegation or to the Washington Government."

The information contained in that statement is now being emphasized. While the whole subject is not entirely clarified, the impression obtained by The New York Times correspondent is that the French had foreknowledge that the American delegation did not see its way clear to enter into a consultative pact and it was quite beyond the question to expect this government, in view of its traditional policy and the course of the Senate with respect to the League of Nations covenant, to con-

Continued on Page Two.

CHANGE OF ATTITUDE DENIED

Americans Suggest Some Other Way May Be Found to Satisfy France.

NAVY CUTS HANG ON MOVE

Possibility of a Mediterranean Accord With British Backing Is Now Renewed.

BRIAND TO RETURN TODAY

French Leader Expected to Ask What English Will Do in New Circumstances.

By EDWIN L. JAMES.
Special Cable to The New York Times.

LONDON, Wednesday, March 26.—The American delegation has reasserted its opposition to the security pact sought by France as the price for reductions in her naval program, but the Americans say they are ready to discuss a consultative pact with open minds if it is understood the United States does not commit itself to promising military security.

Shortly after midnight the American delegation issued a statement to this effect at the Hotel Ritz after early editions of several morning papers had revealed that Secretary of State Stimson in a conversation with Premier MacDonald yesterday had explained the new position of the Americans.

This move by the United States to save the conference represents the first departure from that strict nationalism which has marked the negotiations and has brought them to nothing so far. It may put a new face on the whole proceedings.

Viewed of Great Importance.

The American declaration is looked upon as having great importance. It says the American delegation denies rumors that it has changed its position on consultative pacts. It says the American position is the same as stated by Secretary Stimson on March 11, namely, that the United States had no objection to a consultative pact as such, but that we would not enter into such an arrangement if it could be construed as involving a promise of military aid.

If, however, France's demand for military security could be satisfied otherwise, it is stated, there would be no further danger of such a misunderstanding and then the question could be approached from a different standpoint.

"In such case the American delegation would consider the matter with an entirely open mind," the Americans assert.

The American declaration is believed to mean that in the conversations between Secretary Stimson and Premier MacDonald the possibility was envisaged of England acting as the guarantor for some sort of Mediterranean pact, to do which England has already said would depend in some measure on the assurances which could be obtained from the United States.

Franco-Italian Negotiations.

It is known that for some days an arrangement has been discussed by which France would promise not to maintain in the Mediterranean a greater fleet than Italy had there, while retaining the right to have additional warships in Atlantic and colonial waters. It is proposed that Britain act as guarantor for this arrangement.

Unless Secretary Stimson's new stand was taken on his own initiative, which is not considered probable, it must form part of a new effort to save the conference.

When Secretary Stimson announced on March 11 that America would take no part in a consultative pact here he emphasized that this position had been reached because of fear that France would interpret it as an indirect promise of military aid should she get into trouble. He said America would not purchase French reduction in naval tonnage in return for a treaty which would not carry that measure of security which France had been seeking and which she might be led to suspect.

It was noted at that time that the French did not sympathize with this show of solicitude but pointed out that all that was asked from America was consultation, it being held that in a time of crisis it would be most useful for European powers to know the probable position of the United States.

It is now being understood by France that America promises no

"All the News That's Fit to Print."

The New York Times.

Copyright, 1930, by The New York Times Company.

THE WEATHER
Cloudy today; tomorrow showers, not much change in temperature.
Temperature yesterday—Max., 61; min., 41.
U. S. Weather Forecast—For details see Page 47.

VOL. LXXIX....No. 26,385. **** NEW YORK, MONDAY, APRIL 21, 1930. TWO CENTS in Greater New York | THREE CENTS Within 200 Miles | FOUR CENTS Elsewhere Except 7th and 8th Postal Zones

LINDBERGH SETS A RECORD FROM COAST OF 14¾ HOURS WITH WIFE AS NAVIGATOR; FLIES 180 MILES AN HOUR AT 14,000 FEET

ROBINSON HAILS NAVY PACT AS MARKING ACHIEVEMENTS OF MAGNITUDE AND VALUE

OUTLINES RESULT ON RADIO

Senator Tells Democratic View of the Results of London Parley.

HE ADMITS SHORTCOMINGS

Success Is Not Complete, He Says, but Finds Satisfaction in Most Main Points.

OUR PROGRAM IS EXPLAINED

American Construction to Be Relatively Large Because of Lagging Since War.

By L. C. SPEERS.

Special Cable to THE NEW YORK TIMES.

LONDON, April 20.—That Senator Robinson is slated to be one of the chief supporters of the administration when the treaty of London goes to the Senate for ratification becomes more evident daily. Because of his ability as a debater and his long experience as a member of the Foreign Relations Committee and also in naval affairs, some quarters will not be surprised if the Arkansan assumes command on the floor before the ratification battle ends.

Twice within four days the American naval delegation has emphasized how vitally important is the aid of Senator Robinson by allotting to him two of the most important public announcements concerning the treaty—first the explanation of the contingency clause and tonight the delivery of a farewell radio appeal from London to the people at home to support the pact.

Success Not Complete.

Senator Robinson came to London tonight from Cliveden, the home of the Astors, to read a carefully prepared address in which he frankly admitted the conference had not been the complete success which had been found for, due to the failure to compose the differences of the European signatories to the Washington treaty. The rock on which complete five-power success was wrecked was the French demand for security and the Italian insistence on parity with the French, he pointed out. At no time had the United States delegation even considered subscribing to any pact, consultative or otherwise, which might subsequently be regarded as implying a guarantee of security he said.

For the first time Mr. Robinson disclosed the fact that France refused even to consider such a pact as America was ready to enter into.

"The French said," Senator Robinson asserted, "that a mere consultative pact would not take one ton off their navy."

The agreement to safeguard merchant ships against submarine attack in wartime, while "an achievement of magnitude and value," Senator Robinson frankly admitted may not prevent all abuses which the conferees had in mind. He said he was unable to believe, in the light of past history, that in time of war the belligerents would live up to the strict letter of the treaty. However, he added, it was a great moral move in the right direction, and violation by any power would be an invitation to disaster by the violator.

Defends Contingent Clause.

The Senator again defended the contingent clause and followed with a clarifying argument on the compromises reached in the solution of the cruiser problem. The United States, he concluded, can now proceed in an orderly way to build up her navy to the treaty level. There was a hint of disapproval of the record of Congress in cruiser construction subsequent to 1922 to which is mainly attributable the fact that the United States today is so far behind the other powers in the tonnage of this important class of ships.

Senator Robinson was with Secretary Stimson before delivering the speech and what he said was endorsed by the other American delegates.

SENATOR ROBINSON'S SPEECH.

Senator Robinson's address was heard in New York over a nationwide hook-up.

Senator Robinson, the ranking Democrat in the United States Senate, spoke on the subject of "The Democratic View of the Naval Conference," but he did not speak from a partisan viewpoint. He made his address in the London studios of

Continued on Page Three.

Naval Treaty Preamble Tells Of Hope to End Arms Rivalry

LONDON, Monday, April 21 (AP).—The text of the preamble to the London naval treaty, to be signed by the five powers at the conference, became known here today.

The preamble reads:

"The President of the United States of America, the President of the French Republic, his Majesty the King of Great Britain, Ireland and the British Dominions beyond the seas, his Majesty the King of Italy and his Majesty the Emperor of Japan, desiring to prevent the dangers and reduce the burdens inherent in competitive armaments and desiring to carry forward the work begun in the Washington naval conference and to facilitate the progressive realization of general limitation and reduction of armaments, have resolved, with a view to accelerating these purposes, to conclude a treaty for the limitation of naval armaments and have accordingly appointed as their plenipotentiaries":

The names of the plenipotentiaries and the treaty itself follow.

SKIRMISHES OPEN CHINESE CIVIL WAR

Fighting Between Nanking and Northerners Reported Near Kweiteh, Honan.

YEN HITS FOREIGN TOBACCO

Native Taxpayers in Shanghai Threaten Reprisals in Dispute Over Representation.

Special Cable to THE NEW YORK TIMES.

PEKING, April 20.—Fighting is reported between Nanking forces and Northern detachments which have moved to the southeast from the Kweiteh district on the Lunghai Railroad. It is believed that only small bodies aiming at the interruption of rail communication were involved.

Yen Hsi-shan's tobacco monopoly in Shansi is now in full force, contrary to treaty stipulations and in disregard of the Nanking Government's arrangements with tobacco companies as regards taxation. The products of foreign firms are now admitted only within limited areas of the province and taxation far in excess of that fixed by Nanking is being imposed. Apparently the Shansi authorities are giving preference to the products of Chinese firms. The situation is receiving the attention of the legations concerned.

A demonstration against Chiang Kai-shek was held here yesterday. It was attended by large crowds and fiery speeches were made and resolutions adopted. The city is placarded with notices attacking Chiang.

An agreement for the retrocession of Weihaiwei to China was signed yesterday at Nanking. Since the powers have ceased to maintain rival fleets in Far Eastern waters Weihaiwei has been of value to Britain only as a health station for naval vessels along the Chinese coasts for the protection of shipping and British communities.

In restoring this fine harbor to Nanking it may be presumed that the British arranged with the Chinese to permit British ships to use the harbor in the Summer as heretofore. There is a good deal of Brit-

Continued on Page Ten.

MORROW WILL RESIGN QUICKLY ON RETURN AND BECOME SENATOR

Appointment of Envoy to Place Now Held by Baird Will Be Made Before June Primary.

DEAL HAS LONG EXISTED

Some Republican Leaders in Washington Think He Will State Dry Law Stand.

'FORWARD VIEW' TALKED OF

He Is Scheduled to Speak Before a Women's Republican Club in New Jersey April 30.

Special to The New York Times.

WASHINGTON, April 20.—Dwight W. Morrow, Ambassador to Mexico, will resign soon after his return from the London conference and be named as Senator from New Jersey to succeed Senator Baird, who is expected to resign to enable Governor Larson to make the appointment. This appointment, it was said tonight, would precede the State Senatorial primary on June 17.

According to some Republican leaders, Mr. Morrow will come out in favor of a modification of the Volstead act. Some of those leaders hope that he may present such a view that it may put the party in what they call a forward position on the question. According to New Jersey politicians, Mr. Morrow has not made known his views on the subject, but indicated before he went to London his intention to "take a forward view."

Mr. Morrow's part in the London conference, according to New Jersey friends, will strengthen him not only in the primaries but the general election.

A reference which ex-President Coolidge made to him in a recent article, they say, has added to Mr. Morrow's political strength. Mr. Coolidge in this article, after stating that he could not consent to go to the Senate, said: "So I am going to suggest to those who are discussing the need that they believe there is for me, that he (Mr. Morrow) can provide more talent than I could and exercise it in a more effective way. A sound business man, a scholarly lawyer, a wise statesman, he is eminently qualified to discharge the duties of any public office."

Mr. Morrow and Mr. Coolidge were class-mates at Amherst.

Aside from discussing the attitude of Mr. Morrow on the Eighteenth Amendment, many party leaders are worried over the opposition arising against some dry Republican candidates for Congress. Reports received from nearly all the industrial States show that members of Congress who have supported the party position on the Eighteenth Amendment will be beset by wet candidates.

In Indiana, where the primary to name members of the House will be held on May 6, several districts represented by men of dry tendencies are reported to be full of wet sentiment which seeks candidates for the seats.

Morrow Expected at Luncheon.

Special to The New York Times.

HACKENSACK, N. J., April 20.—Dwight W. Morrow is expected to make his first political speech since he became a candidate for the Senate before the Bergen County Women's Republican Club at a legislative luncheon on April 30. Republican leaders in the county, who said today that they were confident Mr. Morrow would return from London in time to attend the luncheon, added that they expected him to state his platform at that time.

The chief plank of that platform, they believe, will be advocacy of an

Continued on Page Thirteen.

Typhoon Sweeps 14 Towns in the Philippines; Thousands Homeless, Death Toll Unknown

By The Associated Press.

MANILA, April 20.—A destructive typhoon swept fourteen towns on the island of Leyte on Friday, virtually demolishing the communities of Tolosa and Dulag on the East Coast.

Thousands were made homeless and the number of dead and injured was not ascertainable.

First reports of the disaster reached Manila forty-eight hours later, when Governor De La Cruz of Leyte wired the American Red Cross here:

"Please secure immediate aid for thousands homeless people, especially food, clothing and building materials."

The typhoon was of small area but of unusual intensity. It came as a surprise to weather bureau officials, as such storms rarely come at this season of the year in the Philippines.

The Leyte Governor's message described cocoanut trees in the devastated areas as standing like candles with their tops blown off. The entire crop was destroyed.

Many towns in the devastated region have been completely cut off, with telephone and telegraph wires down. The death toll may be large, and official reports of destruction cannot be completed in less than a week or more.

Governor General Dwight F. Davis, who has been making a trip in the Bontoc region with his daughter, Cynthia, had not been informed of the disaster today. He is expected to return to Manila tomorrow.

The Red Cross has taken action toward organizing the provincial forces of Leyte and Samar and has arranged to send doctors, nurses and relief supplies on the first vessel to leave Manila.

Illinois Gives 3½-Ton Bell To Valley Forge Carillon

VALLEY FORGE, Pa., April 20 (AP).—A bell, weighing 3½ tons, the gift of Illinois, was added to the Washington Memorial national carillon at Valley Forge today.

Martin R. Carlson, temporary president of the Illinois Senate, representing the Governor, made the presentation. The bell was accepted by the Rev. Dr. W. Herbert Burk, rector of Washington Memorial Chapel, who offered the prayer of dedication.

The Illinois bell is the 17th in the carillon, the first having been presented by the Daughters of the American Revolution of Massachusetts. When complete, the carillon will have forty-nine bells, one for each State and a National Birthday bell.

SUNNY SKIES GILD CITY'S EASTER FETE

Throngs Stroll in 5th Av. Style Pageant as Park Av. and East Side Mingle With Main St.

CHURCHES ARE JAMMED

Mr. Zero Heads March of the Jobless—Crowds Swarm to All Near-By Resorts.

Fifth Avenue, choked with too much traffic yesterday, paused momentarily. From a belfry, a breeze heavy with the scent of flowers, wafted the silver-clear notes of chimes to a little group at Fifty-third Street near St. Thomas's Church. It was high noon; it was Easter and the sun shone.

In this one little group, an entity in the eddying stream of walkers, a man spoke in the argot of Broadway, a woman expressed ungrammatical appreciation of fair weather and a beautifully dressed girl laughed. A little boy remarked to his father, dignified in a cutaway and a high silk hat, that he would like to be in the country.

They were all part of New York's sidewalk festival of Spring; of the city's pageant of fashion. A few had walked over from Park Avenue after the services at St. Bartholomew's, some had deserted their own neighborhood promenades for a glimpse of the big show on Manhattan's Prado and others were excursionists from Main Street.

Resorts Lure Crowds.

It had taken nearly a week of rainy weather to produce this perfect Sunday, and the crowds which turned out to promenade, not only on Fifth Avenue but on Grand Street, where the east side hails the Spring, and on the boardwalks of nearby resorts, were bigger than in many years.

The police at Coney Island estimated that 400,000 persons visited that place during the day. Another 50,000 promenaded at the Rockaways; Atlantic City's Chamber of Commerce asserted that more than 300,000 marched in its Boardwalk parade, while Asbury Park declared that former records for attendance had been broken. Long Beach entertained about 200,000.

The Holland vehicular tunnel broke all records for the number of automobiles traveling through it. For the twenty-four hours ending last midnight the official count showed that 54,725 cars had passed through the tunnel, going in both directions. The previous record was established last September, when 54,452 cars went through the tubes during twenty-four hours. The traffic yesterday was about evenly divided between eastbound and westbound travel.

Celebrities seemed less numerous on Fifth Avenue than in other years, but perhaps it was because the throng of average folk was so much greater. Still, the city's show street managed to maintain its traditional glory.

The women promenaders there seemed to have abandoned last year's obvious sophistication for subtle femininity in deference to the dicta of the couturières of Paris.

Not all wore the latest fashions, but virtually every one except a Greenwich Villager, who explained that he wore high leather boots, a black collar and a lumberjack shirt to keep his "individuality," made some concession to the occasion, even if it was only to let out the hem of last year's dress.

Mr. Zero's Men Parade.

Even the followers of Urbain Ledoux—Mr. Zero of The Tub—sported once shiny toppers and threadbare cutaways in their traditional parade from St. Patrick's Cathedral to Forty-second Street, a march intended to remind those better off than they that poverty exists in the midst of plenty. A street violinist at Fifty-second Street stopped between selections to polish his shoes with a hand-

Continued on Page Eighteen.

ROOSEVELT GROUP OFFERS WAY TO GIVE YEAR-AROUND JOBS

Says in Preliminary Report 200 Corporations in Country Have Worked Out Plan.

DECRIES "SLUMP BUGABOO"

Urges That Steady Work Be Stressed in Daily Planning of All Business Projects.

GIVES LIST OF REFORMS

Asks That Committee Be Continued Till 1931 to Report on All Phases of Problem.

More than 200 of the largest corporations in the United States have worked out plans for "steady work the year around," according to a preliminary report to Governor Roosevelt being made public today by the committee he appointed on March 30 to consider "a long time program for industrial stabilization and prevention of unemployment."

The committee registered the combined judgment of its membership, comprising representatives of organized labor, organized industry, the State, business and banking, as follows:

"We wish to stress the fact that the present mass production methods of American industry are probably here to stay—at least for many years to come. One of the most important features of such methods is the economic well-being of the individual consumer. The continued success of large-scale production, of quick turnover and of instalment buying hinges upon steady employment for the individual. When some of the largest corporations in the United States have devoted a great amount of time and effort in working out plans for regularization, there must be something in the idea beyond mere words."

Stabilization Plans Studied.

Among the corporations whose stabilization plans were examined by the committee in laying out its own program of inquiry were the International Harvester Company, Columbia Conserve Company, Procter & Gamble Company and the Packard Automobile Company.

The committee announced that it would hold a series of conferences with manufacturers and business men throughout the State, beginning in Buffalo on May 1.

"What we hope to do, and what we are planning to do," the preliminary report says, "is to cooperate with the employers of this State in facing the problem of unemployment, not primarily from the standpoint of immediate relief, but more from the standpoint of discussing practices that will help stabilize employment throughout the year."

The findings of the committee were as follows:

"That steady work the year around be incorporated in business men's thinking, so that it may assume major importance in the employer's daily planning and actions. The slump bugaboo is not necessarily an act of Divine Providence. It is a problem to be faced and worked out like any other business problem.

"That the cooperative efforts of citizens working through their local chambers of commerce, trade unions and other associations to put down unemployment be encouraged.

"That the State, city and town governments direct more attention to the planning of their construction and purchasing activities so that important contracts may be held back in time of prosperity and pushed forward in times of depression. Governmental bodies, by increasing public works and public purchases at the proper time, have it within their

Continued on Page Fourteen.

Chill Winds Give London Most Dismal Easter; Frost Nips France and Even Spain Shivers

Wireless to THE NEW YORK TIMES.

LONDON, April 20.—England was thankful for its fireplaces today in what was everywhere called the most dismal Easter within living memory. For the fourth day a succession of chilling winds blew down the North Sea from the Arctic, while low-lying clouds and fitful torrents of rain did their worst to make it a gloomy holiday.

For London's clerks and office workers it was small consolation that all of Western Europe was shivering in wintry weather and that the somber Easter held Germany, France and even sunny Spain in its grip. Nor did it make the day brighter to learn that brilliant weather shone on the Atlantic, just west of the Irish coast, where it could do no good to any one.

Thousands who had flocked hopefully to the seashore on Thursday returned today after finding little but windswept promenades and deserted beaches. Those who ventured into the countryside were better rewarded, for there were plenty of signs that Spring lay just behind the storm-clouds. Along every country lane primroses and bluebells were braving the chilly Easter weather and everywhere gardens were bright with daffodils.

The King and Queen spent Easter at Windsor Castle with the rest of the royal family and allowed thousands of sightseers to listen to a band concert on the castle grounds. In the course of the concert the crowd caught a glimpse of little Princess Elizabeth, who is 4 tomorrow, and saw the Queen holding her up so she could wave a greeting.

Special Cable to THE NEW YORK TIMES.

PARIS, April 20.—Abnormal cold with several degrees of frost was experienced today in the centre and east of France.

Paris had sunshine and showers, with the wind in the northeast and southeast and a rising barometer.

Lindbergh Says He Plans Further Experiments To Determine Efficiency of High Altitude Flying

Colonel Lindbergh told reporters after he landed at Roosevelt Field last night that the record-breaking flight from Los Angeles to New York did not definitely establish that flying at the greater heights was more efficient for express and passenger plane service. He said he was pleased with the general results, but that further experiments would be necessary and he would undertake the experiments.

"The flight was purely an experimental flight," Colonel Lindbergh said, "a flight testing the theory that greater speed and efficiency can be obtained by taking advantage of better weather conditions in the higher altitudes.

"I encountered no exceptional winds during the flight. At times we had winds that were slightly advantageous and at other times we ran into head winds that impeded us, although only slightly. All in all, we encountered no exceptional weather.

"We were compelled several times to deviate as much as 100 miles from the plotted course in order to get around small areas of cloud and fog. We made the entire flight at altitudes varying from 14,000 feet to 15,500, Mrs. Lindbergh acting as co-pilot and navigator. Throughout the trip she used the aviation sextant to take observations to keep us on our course."

"I suppose," an interviewer ventured, "that you feel rather elated at having broken the speed record."

"I want to make it plain," replied Colonel Lindbergh, "that I really did not break the transcontinental speed record, despite the fact that our elapsed time was less than the time taken by Captain Hawks on his transcontinental flight. The reason for that is that we made one stop while Captain Hawks's flight was non-stop.

"I don't believe that we would have made the same time if we had attempted to come through non-stop. Out of deference to Captain Hawks and his accomplishment I want that made clear."

Captain Hawks did not hold the same view and told the reporters later that there was no doubt of the Lindberghs having set a new record.

"We followed the Transcontinental Airways route all the way from Los Angeles to Wichita," Colonel Lindbergh said, "but after leaving Wichita we were compelled several times to alter our course because of weather conditions. That held true as far as Cleveland. There we hit fog and kept north, following the transcontinental air mail route to New Jersey."

Colonel Lindbergh said he and Mrs. Lindbergh would remain in New York for an indefinite period.

GREEN SAYS COUNT DEFEATS PARKER

A. F. of L. Chief Declares That "Pressure" Cannot Change Indicated Result in Senate.

JUDGE'S FRIENDS ANXIOUS

But They Rely on High Court Nominee's Testimony—Lewis Voices Protest of Miners.

Special to The New York Times.

WASHINGTON, April 20.—William Green, president of the American Federation of Labor, declared tonight that a canvass of the Senate showed "enough votes in opposition to cause rejection" of the nomination of Judge John J. Parker of North Carolina to be Associate Justice of the United States Supreme Court.

"The appointment of Judge John J. Parker to be a member of the Supreme Court of the United States has been definitely rejected," Mr. Green said in a statement. "A canvass of the members of the Senate shows this to be a fact and for that reason a vote on his confirmation by the Senate Judiciary Committee was postponed.

"It remains to be seen whether or not sufficient pressure can be brought to bear upon members of the Senate to cause them to change their attitude. I am confident this cannot be done because the masses of the people have become so thoroughly aroused in their opposition to the appointment of Judge Parker."

From other sources it became

Continued on Page Sixteen.

24 NOTARIES IN BRONX TO BE PROSECUTED

District Attorney's Office Gets Evidence That They Have Posed as Lawyers.

CITY-WIDE INQUIRY LOOMS

Victims Have Lost Money by Badly Drawn Papers, Bar Hears After Secret Investigation.

Evidence of illegal practices by twenty-four notaries public and commissioners of deeds living in the Bronx, some of them with offices in Manhattan, was turned over last night by Owen S. M. Tierney, an Assistant United States Attorney and president of the Bronx County Bar Association, to Assistant District Attorney Israel J. P. Adlerman, who announced that he would begin prosecuting the offenders today or tomorrow, and that he would ask Chief Magistrate McAdoo to hear the cases personally.

The evidence was collected by private investigators who have been working under Mr. Tierney's direction for the last eight weeks, and, according to Mr. Tierney, it shows that the suspected notaries public and commissioners of deeds have posed as licensed attorneys and have drawn up such legal papers as contracts, wills, deeds, bills of sale and chattel mortgages.

Say Papers Were Badly Drawn.

Mr. Tierney explained that while it was not against the law for them to draw up such papers it was a violation of the law for them to represent themselves as attorneys and to collect fees for such work. The worst feature of the situation, he charged, was that such documents were frequently prepared with such woeful lack of knowledge of the law that they involved the persons for whom they had been drawn up in long litigation and caused them heavy financial losses. As an example of this he cited a case in Brooklyn in which a widow and her four children lost $50,000 because her husband's will had been improperly prepared by a notary public.

"The law specifically states," Mr. Tierney said, "that notaries hold office only to acknowledge affidavits and other sworn statements. My investigators, while posing as illiterate immigrants, have gathered enough information to warrant a city-wide investigation. Illegal practices by notaries is not confined to the Bronx and Manhattan, but are common in Brooklyn as well.

The twenty-four notaries living in

Continued on Page Six.

ONLY ONE STOP EN ROUTE

Colonel and Wife Halt for Fuel at Wichita, Then Speed East.

SHE SETS COURSE ALL WAY

Record Made in Test of "Higher Ceilings" as Routes for the Transcontinental Lines.

HAWKS'S TIME IS BEATEN

Lowered by Nearly Three Hours—5,000 Cheer Fliers at Roosevelt Field.

Speeding across country at an average rate of more than 180 miles an hour in an experimental "high altitude" flight, Colonel Charles A. Lindbergh and Mrs. Lindbergh flew a Lockheed Sirius plane from Glendale, Cal., near Los Angeles, to Roosevelt Field, Long Island, yesterday in 14 hours 45 minutes and 32 seconds. Despite a stop at Wichita, Kan., they clipped 2 hours 52 minutes and 44 seconds from the time made last June by Captain Frank M. Hawks in a non-stop flight in another Lockheed monoplane. The actual flying time of the Lindberghs was 14 hours 23 minutes 27 seconds. The distance was approximately 2,700 miles. They landed at Roosevelt Field at 11:11:52 o'clock last night.

The exact distance flown, the altitude and the average speed maintained throughout the flight will not be officially known until the course followed, including variations, has been checked and the barograph, which was placed in the plane at Los Angeles, has been examined.

Flight at High Altitude.

The flight was unusual in that it was made at altitudes ranging from 14,000 to 15,500 feet above the ground. It was a test of the theory that express and passenger plane service can be greatly speeded if the planes fly in the higher reaches where the air is thinner and the resistance correspondingly less than at lower altitudes.

It was a complete triumph in every way and Mrs. Lindbergh shared the honors with her husband because she did not ride merely as a passenger but acted as co-pilot and navigator, guiding her husband in the trackless lane with an aviation sextant. This aid was invaluable since the plane all through the flight was far too high for ground observations. On most of the route thousands watched and listened in vain for an audible or visible sign of the plane's passing. The only time that the ship was observed in its rocket-like dash from coast to coast was at 10:40 P. M., when the thunder of its Wasp motor was heard over Allentown, Pa. By that time the ship had been brought down to normal flying altitudes, since the goal was near.

5,000 Watch at Field.

Five thousand men and women waited in the light-drenched field near Garden City all through the night, many through the day as well, for the chance of seeing Colonel Lindbergh set a new record. They were not disappointed. They cheered wildly and sounded their automobile horns as the pilot set the bullet-shaped, low-winged ship on the field in a neat landing.

Mrs. Lindbergh remained in her mica-covered cockpit while the photographers formed a semicircle and began taking pictures by flashlight, but she shook her head and smiled when asked for an interview. Colonel Lindbergh taxied the ship toward the hangar, lifted his wife out when he got it inside and then told newspapermen that he would be ready to talk with them as soon as he finished inspecting the ship.

He went over every detail, examining the struts, the fuselage and the landing gear, to make certain that all was in order and then issued instructions to the mechanics.

The flight proved again that Colonel Lindbergh is possessed of an uncanny faculty for judging, within the hour, the time it will take him to cover tremendous distances. When the plane was about to take off from Wichita at 3:42:35 P. M. he remarked to officials there that he would reach Roosevelt Field in eight hours, or at 11:42:35 P. M. He landed at 11:11:52 P. M., a variation of about thirty minutes.

Fast Time to Wichita.

When telegraph communications from Wichita, the first stopping place of the Lindberghs, brought the

THE LINDBERGHS IN TEST FLIGHT AND ROUTE OF RECORD DASH.

Times Wide World Photo

The Lockheed Sirius Monoplane which was specially constructed for the test of high altitude flying made by Colonel and Mrs. Lindbergh.

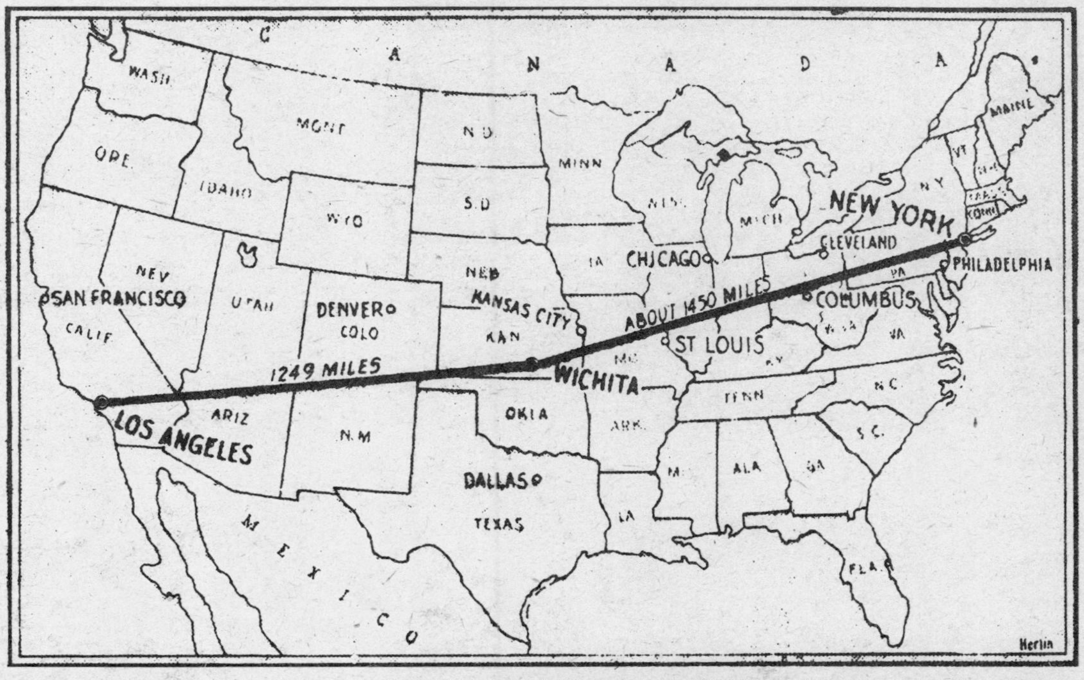

The approximate route of the Lindberghs' record flight in April. They flew at such altitude that they were not sighted until they were over Eastern Pennsylvania. Their only stop on their trip from Los Angeles to New York was at Wichita, Kansas.

Times Wide World Photo

Albert Einstein and his wife arrive in New York enroute to California where Dr. Einstein plans to work in cooperation with scientists at the California Institute of Technology.

Times Wide World Photo

Captain Coste (R) and Bellonte in their plane after their arrival.

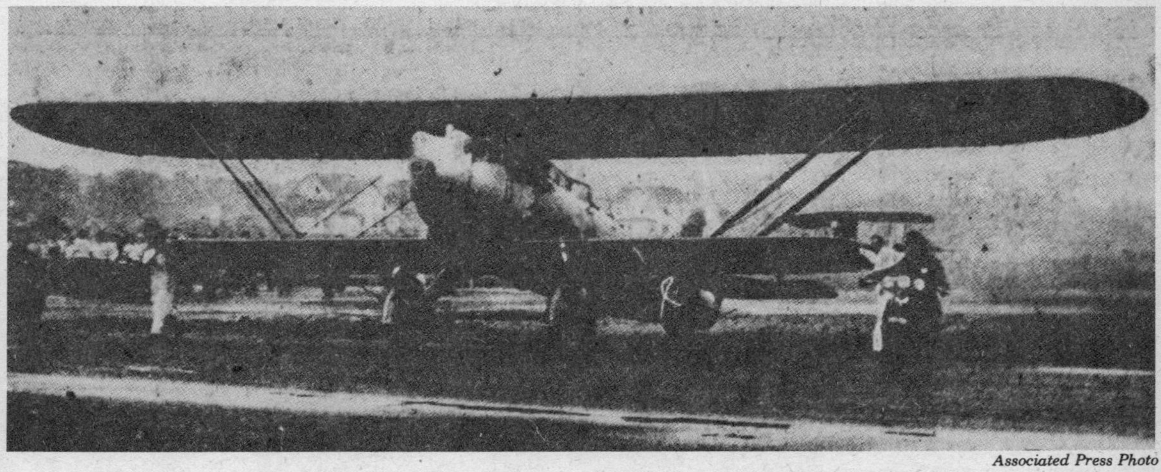

Associated Press Photo

Coste's plan lands safely at Curtiss Field on September 2 after its long flight from Paris.

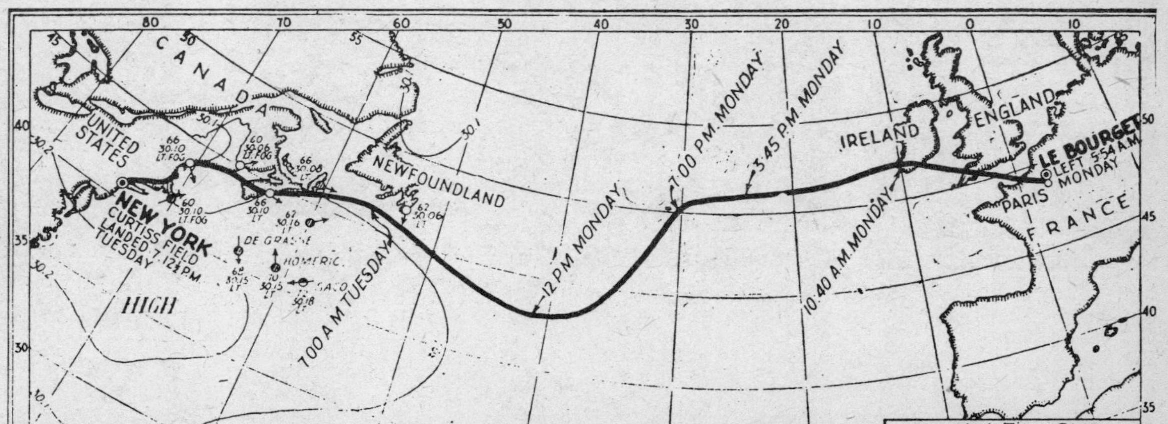

The French fliers' route from Paris to New York.

Another speakeasy is closed by Federal Marshals

Police Commissioner Grover A. Whalen estimated that there were 32,000 speakeasies in New York.

A speakeasy on East 58th Street, New York City, the morning after a raid.

New Jersey Senator Dwight Morrow was an early advocate of prohibition repeal.

"All the News That's Fit to Print."

The New York Times.

Copyright, 1930, by The New York Times Company.

THE WEATHER
Cloudy and continued cool today; tomorrow rain at night.
Temperature yesterday—Max., 52; min., 34.
U. S. Weather Forecast—For details see Page 24.

VOL. LXXIX....No. 26,390. **** NEW YORK, SATURDAY, APRIL 26, 1930. TWO CENTS in Greater New York | THREE CENTS Within 200 Miles | FOUR CENTS Elsewhere Except 7th and 8th Postal Zones

WALKER EXHAUSTED IS ORDERED TO QUIT ALL WORK FOR WEEK

Mayor Completely Worn Out Physically and Nervously by Overwork, Doctor Says.

ALL ACTIVITIES CANCELED

After Relaxation at Home, Dr. Schroeder May Direct Him to Go on Long Vacation.

McKEE TAKES OVER DUTIES

Walker Recently Had Complained of Severe Headaches, but Had Kept Up a Strenuous Program.

Mayor Walker, suffering from what his physician described as "complete physical and nervous exhaustion due to overwork," will be confined to his home and his bed for at least a week. For that period, if not longer, all his public and private engagements will have to be canceled.

The order, which was peremptory in character, was issued yesterday afternoon by the Mayor's personal physician, Dr. William Schroeder Jr., who is also the chairman of the Sanitation Commission by appointment of Mayor Walker. Dr. Schroeder directed that during the week of retirement the Mayor should not receive visitors and that he should be kept entirely free from the cares of office. At the end of a week of complete relaxation, the physician said, he will determine whether or not it may be necessary for the Mayor to leave the city for a longer and more complete rest period.

Cancels Today's Engagements.

Mayor Walker was to have reviewed the annual police parade this afternoon and was expected to preside as toastmaster at the Jefferson Day dinner of the National Democratic Club, to be held tonight in the Hotel Commodore. He has had to cancel both engagements. Joseph V. McKee, President of the Board of Aldermen, consented last night to take the place of the Mayor this afternoon in the reviewing stand. It was said also that he was likely to be invited to act for the Mayor at tonight's dinner.

Under the provisions of the city charter the President of the Board of Aldermen becomes automatically the Acting Mayor whenever the Mayor is unable to discharge his duties in the City Hall. Mr. McKee for brief periods has acted in that capacity on many occasions. Until the Mayor's absence or disability has extended over a period of thirty consecutive days the Acting Mayor lacks power either of appointment or removal, but in virtually all other particulars, including the signing of local laws and ordinances and presiding over the Board of Estimate, Mr. McKee takes over at once the functions of the Mayor.

Surprise to City Hall.

News of Mayor Walker's illness, as disclosed by Dr. Schroeder, surprised the City Hall, where he had been expected to preside over an important session of the Board of Estimate, which had listed on its calendar 450 separate items. Dr. Schroeder, after having ordered the Mayor to bed, communicated with Charles S. Hand, the Mayor's secretary, and Mr. McKee was called upon to preside at the meeting.

Mayor Walker has complained frequently of late of suffering from severe headaches. Dr. Schroeder has been worried about his condition and on several occasions recently has visited him in his professional capacity in the City Hall.

The complimentary dinner to Police Commissioner Whalen is scheduled for the evening of May 6. Fears were expressed in the City Hall yesterday that Mayor Walker might also have to cancel his engagement to be a speaker on that occasion.

Office a Strenuous One.

The condition of Mayor Walker during the last two or three months, although not regarded as serious, has been somewhat alarming to his friends and official associates. The duties of the Mayor impose a heavy toll upon the strength of the incumbent and Mayor Walker is of comparatively frail physique.

The Mayor is called upon to preside at two meetings of the Board of Estimate every week, one the regular open meeting of the board and the other a meeting of the Committee of the Whole. In addition, he has to preside over less frequent meetings of the Sinking Fund Commission, attend special committee meetings and engage in frequent conferences, besides attending the routine of the office. Since his reelection last November, Mayor Walker, it was said at City Hall, has missed very few of these meetings, and he presided at several re-

Continued on Page Two.

Mrs. Hoover Gets Wheel Chair To Use Until Back Is Better

Special to The New York Times.

WASHINGTON, April 25.—Until she has entirely recovered from the effects of a sprained back due to a recent fall Mrs. Herbert Hoover will use a wheel chair, with the assistance of which she will be able to visit the various floors of the White House. She is unable to walk without some pain and her physicians do not think that she will be able to resume her customary activities for several weeks.

Mrs. Hoover, it was ascertained today, wrenched one of her back muscles in the fall and tore several ligaments, but an X-ray examination revealed that she suffered no injury to her spine.

The wheel chair was delivered at the White House yesterday, making it possible for Mrs. Hoover to appear at the dinner table for the first time since the accident. The chair is rolled in and out of the elevator, installed during the illness of President Wilson.

PRINCE IN AIR DASH ENDS RECORD TRIP

British Heir Welcomed Home by King and Queen From Long African Hunt.

FLIES ALL ACROSS FRANCE

Ten French Planes Escort Him to Coast—Prince's Eighth Tour Abroad in 10 Years.

Special Cable to The New York Times.

LONDON, April 25.—After a record air dash across France, the Prince of Wales returned to London today from his four months' hunting expedition in Africa. He landed at his private aerodrome, Smith's Lawn, in Windsor Great Park, at 4 P. M., having completed the 615 miles from Marseilles in six hours and ten minutes of actual flying time.

When he stepped from the plane the Prince was greeted by the Duke of York and Prince George. He then drove to his new country home, Fort Belvedere, near Ascot, where the King and the Queen were waiting to welcome their son home. After a family reunion and dinner at Windsor Castle, the Prince returned tonight to his residence at St. James's Palace, which, during his absence, was the scene of the naval conference.

Wind Adds to Speed.

The Prince traveled in a Royal Air Force machine—a high-speed Wapiti, with slotted wings, piloted by Squadron Leader Davidson. He was escorted for the entire journey by two Royal Air Force machines. Between Marseilles and Paris there was a following wind and the plane averaged about 120 miles an hour. A short halt for refueling was made near Lyons, and at Le Bourget the Prince had luncheon, spending nearly two hours there.

Then he was escorted to the Channel by a number of French fighting planes. When they turned back at Cap Gris Nez, the Prince was greeted by a British flying boat from Calshot, which escorted him during the fifteen-minute Channel crossing. Over Dover, on the Kent coast, the duties of escort were taken up by nine single-seater Siskin fighters. They and other escorting machines swung clear as they approached Windsor Great Park and returned to their bases.

The flight across France is probably one of the fastest ever made. It was known the airplanes allotted to this flight were capable of a speed of 120 miles an hour under favorable conditions, but it was hardly expected they would maintain an average speed of more than 100 miles an hour on so long a journey, made in

Continued on Page Two.

HARBOR BILL PASSED IN STORMY SESSION; HOOVER FOR LIMIT

House Votes $111,500,000 for Waterways and Includes Erie-Oswego Canal Acquisition.

WESTERNERS' DRIVE FAILS

Vehement Charges Made That New Yorkers Plot to Block St. Lawrence Waterway.

LA GUARDIA MAKES ATTACK

Hurls "Bribery" Charge at Dempsey and Blocks Rise in Rank for General Deakyne.

Special to The New York Times.

WASHINGTON, April 25.—An omnibus rivers and harbors bill authorizing more than $111,500,000 for waterways throughout the country was passed by the House today in the stormiest meeting of the session, only to be met with the information that President Hoover will oppose any expenditures for this purpose during the fiscal year 1931 above the $50,000,000 to $60,000,000 proposed in the War Department appropriation bill, now before a Senate committee.

The President, it was learned, is having a study made of the bill just passed and will give his approval for immediate expenditures only to the most urgent projects.

This, it was said, will serve to leave out of early consideration Federal acquisition of the Erie and Oswego canals, provided in the bill along with an authorization of $2,500,000 for maintenance and operation.

These developments were considered in no way a blow to the Erie and Oswego canal projects, however, for it is predicted that it would take three years for the State of New York legally to turn this waterway over to the Federal Government.

La Guardia Makes Bribery Charge.

Passage of the rivers and harbors bill, which now goes to the Senate, came late today. Starting with a few little flurries at the very outset of the day, the "storm" developed into somewhat of a hurricane as the Western Representatives sought to block the Erie-Oswego project, and wound up with one lightning blast when Representative La Guardia of New York hurled the charge of "bribery" at Representative S. Wallace Dempsey of New York, chairman of the Rivers and Harbors Committee.

Mr. La Guardia's charge came during his denunciation of a section of the bill which provided that when Brig. Gen. Herbert Deakyne, assistant to the Chief of Engineers, United States Army, retires, he should be placed on the retired list with the rank and pay of Major General.

When that section was read along toward the end of the bill Mr. La Guardia jumped from his seat.

"I move to strike out that section!" he shouted.

Salary Provision Assailed.

Turning to Mr. Dempsey, standing near the committee table on the Republican side, Mr. La Guardia continued:

"This is the most outrageous provision ever inserted in any bill I ever heard of. I am going to ask the committee chairman why, in the rivers and harbors bill, he is attempting to go over the head of the committee on military affairs; why he is going over the head of the committee on appropriations; why he is going over the head of the

Continued on Page Nine.

Clocks Will Be Put Ahead One Hour Tonight With Daylight Saving Time in Effect at 2 A. M.

Daylight saving time will go into effect at 2 o'clock tomorrow morning. Clocks will be put ahead an hour, thus dropping temporarily from time the hour that would ordinarily tick away between 2 and 3 o'clock. Officially for New York City and for many cities throughout the country, there will be no hour between 2 and 3. Sleepers will be cheated of one hour of sleep, which, however, they will get back in October.

Practically all the other cities in the State, Rochester and Syracuse being notable exceptions, most of New Jersey, all of Massachusetts by State law, and many cities and towns in Connecticut, observance in the latter State being unofficial, will go on the same Summer time tonight. In New York City the use of daylight time will be used in all business establishments and governmental offices.

Both rail and water transportation entering and leaving the city will operate on new schedules tomorrow conforming to the new time. In general, commuter trains will be moved ahead an hour to conform with the general change, while through trains will continue on their present schedules.

All the railroads will have new time tables available today. They will be printed on an Eastern Standard Time basis.

The New York Central announces that several through Chicago trains will be advanced to preserve the present schedule, while the Southwestern Limited from St. Louis will cut an hour from its running time, thus arriving as at present. The Lehigh Valley's New Yorker, to Chicago, will cut four hours from its running time, leaving hereafter at 4:30 P. M. Standard Time. Nearly all the trains of the Jersey Central will be changed to conform with daylight time.

Boat service to Fall River, Boston, Albany and Norfolk, Va., will operate on a Daylight Saving Time schedule beginning tomorrow.

UTILITIES FAVORED, GOVERNOR CHARGES

Accepting 22 More Knight Commission Bills, He Takes Republican Majority to Task.

SAYS MINORITY WOULD CURB

Deletion of Control Over Short Term Loans Assailed as Fostering Evasion.

By W. A. WARN.

Special to The New York Times.

ALBANY, April 25.—Preparing further for an aggressive campaign this Autumn on the public utility regulation issue, Governor Roosevelt today in announcing his approval of twenty-two more bills of the Knight commission series to strengthen the public service law, issued another memorandum in which he condemned as ineffective all the measures involved in his affirmative action, and took the Republican majority in the Legislature to task for the spirit in which it had approached important work of providing a check against extortion by the public utility corporations.

"I am approving this large assortment of relatively unimportant utility bills in the belief that they may prove of some temporary advantage pending the adoption by a far-sighted Legislature of a truly effective program along lines which I have indicated," the memorandum said.

Accuses Republican Leaders.

Governor Roosevelt said the program of legislation proposed by the Knight Revision Commission, following its survey of the public service law and its application, was wholly against the weight of evidence adduced in the course of the inquiry. Without mincing words the Governor accused the Republican legislative leaders of having emasculated some of the measures in response to protests from the public utility corporations against the bills in the form in which they had been drafted and originally introduced.

The Governor praised the minority program proposed by his three appointees on the revision commission as effective, and said that this was obvious from the opposition it had aroused among the utility interests. He summed up the cardinal points of the minority program, which he endorsed as one that would have met the situation, as follows:

Assertion of the State's determination that the return to which owners of privately owned utilities are entitled shall be the original cost of the property used and useful in the public service as shown by their books.

Establishment of a uniform system of accounting which will make available accurate unit cost analysis of all classes of service, such as any modern corporation in competitive industry would insist upon.

Provision for municipal ownership and operation of public services on a referendum vote of the citizens expressing their desire to undertake such enterprises. This provides the keen spur of competition so necessary to induce the privately owned utilities to accept effective regulation.

Simpler Regulation Is Seen.

"I believe that legislation along these lines would make it possible to reduce rather than increase the complexity of the regulatory machinery," the Governor said. "I believe that it would eventually relieve the people of a considerable proportion of the burden of expense incidental to regulation and would permanently lift from the backs of consumers the burden of protracted rate controversies. I believe that it would provide the shortest possible road to reasonable rates readily ascertainable."

The Governor declares in his memorandum that four bills approved today, among those in a group provid-

Continued on Page Five.

EIGHT BYRD MEN BACK; CASUAL ON HARDSHIPS

Returning on the Larsen With 75 Dogs, They Say Silence and Isolation Were Worst.

7 PENGUINS DIED, 2 FREED

"Never Again," Declares Walden—Others Too Happy to Tell Reactions to Antarctic.

Six more men of the Byrd Expedition arrived here yesterday from the Antarctic Continent on the whaler C. A. Larsen, together with two others who helped maintain the sea connection between Little America and New Zealand. The eight brought the sleds and the seventy-five dogs that hauled the food and supplies of the explorers during their fourteen months on the ice.

They reported that seven of the nine penguins which various public zoos had asked the Byrd Expedition by radio to bring back had died shortly after leaving the Ice Barrier, and that the remaining two were dropped overboard while they were still in good condition at Stewart Island, but with very little hope that they could swim back to a climate where they would survive. The tank in the bow of the whaler where these solemn birds paraded and swam while water could be provided with cakes of ice was refilled with water as the ship passed the tropics, so that the returning explorers might have warm baths.

It was not until they came ashore yesterday at Staten Island, however, that the Antarctic expedition really came to an end for the returning group. The six who had previously spent fourteen months in isolation together, including a long polar night of inactivity, had spent forty days more together on the whaler. Their demobilization yesterday seemed to leave them, like men returning from a war, with little to say immediately.

Personal Comments Few.

What they have done as individuals and what the expedition has accomplished was reported by radio from day to day in THE NEW YORK TIMES by Russell Owen, who is now on his way here with Rear Admiral Richard E. Byrd. The men who arrived yesterday could only retell what happened. They found no words to tell how it felt to them as individuals, or how their reasons for going with Byrd appeared to them, in the middle of an Antarctic night.

The only personal comment on the Antarctic was made by Arthur T. Walden, chief dog driver, breeder and veteran of the dog-sled days of the Alaska gold rush of '98.

"There was nothing but snow and ice," he said. "No mountains like Alaska—never again for me." The others laughed, almost automatically, and explained that was what Walden began to say as soon as he arrived at Little America, and that they were used to hearing it.

To clear up the matter for his wife, Mr. Walden told again about the end of Chinook, the leader of the pack of Eskimo huskies which he had organized for the Byrd Expedition, half out of his own kennel breed at Wonalancet, N. H., and half out of Labrador dogs. Mrs. Walden said she had always refused to believe Mr. Owen's story that Chinook had walked off deliberately to die, and that she believed he merely fell into an ice hole, the way the members of the party were always doing.

Tells of Chinook's Death.

"No," said Mr. Walden, "Chinook was downed by three of the other dogs the day before and that means in a pack of husky dogs that he has lost his leadership. He was never off his feet in a dog fight before. As I told Russell, he figured it all out. He was all through. And he came to bid me good-bye, but I didn't realize what he was doing un-

Continued on Page Three.

Ulric Dahlgren, Son of Princeton Professor, Killed in Auto Chasing Wedding Party

Special to The New York Times.

TRENTON, N. J., April 25.—A friendly automobile chase of a newly married couple led to the death here tonight of Ulric Dahlgren Jr. of Princeton and the serious injury of his wife, when their automobile was struck by a passenger train. The newly married couple sped on, unaware of the tragedy. They are John Wallace Thompson Jr. and his wife, the former Miss Susanne Weart Blackwell. Mrs. Thompson is a sister of Mrs. Dahlgren.

The accident occurred at the Willow Street crossing of the Pennsylvania Railroad near the outskirts of Trenton. The only witness was Joseph Reisner, a watchman, who later said that he had lowered the gates.

Dahlgren's car crashed through the thin wood just as a passenger train approached. The automobile was hurled through the air, landing against the side of a garage. When rescuers could reach the spot Mr. Dahlgren, the son of a Princeton University professor and the holder of the Croix de Guerre, was dead. His wife was taken to the Mercer Hospital with a broken arm and other injuries. She will recover.

The victim was 29 years old. He graduated from the Princeton Preparatory School and spent a year at the university. Then, in May, 1917, he joined the Princeton ambulance unit, and in August, after finishing training, went to France. He remained in sevice until the armistice, and was decorated by the French Government for courage in helping wounded men at the front. After the war he returned to college and graduated in 1923. He was a member of the Elm Club while an undergraduate. Recently he has been employed in the production department of the Certain-teed Products Company of Trenton.

He was married a year ago to Miss Katherine M. Blackwell, the daughter of Mr. and Mrs. Henry Clayton Blackwell of West State Street. Miss Susanne Blackwell, who was married today, was maid of honor at the wedding, and today, when the latter was married, Dahlgren was one of the ushers. The marriage took place at St. Michael's Episcopal Church, and was performed by Bishop Paul Matthews and the Rev. Dr. Samuel Steinmetz, the rector. The reception, from which the two cars started out, was at the home of the bride's parents.

Mr. Dahlgren is survived by his widow, his mother and father, and a brother, Joseph Dahlgren, who is a naval officer stationed at the Canal Zone. Professor Dahlgren is an authority of zoology. Recently the young couple have had an apartment in Professor Dahlgren's Princeton home.

SENATORS SUPPRESS DATA ON WET SURVEY OF REPRESENTATIVES

Lobby Committee Bars Field's Report as 'Embarrassing to a Lot of People.'

CURRAN ENDS TESTIMONY

Association No Longer Accepts Money From Distillers and Brewers, He Says.

WADSWORTH LETTERS READ

Ex-Senator Active in Republican Poll Here—Caraway Hints at Vote Buying by Wets.

Special to The New York Times.

WASHINGTON, April 25.—Confidential reports on members of Congress, collected for the Association Against the Prohibition Amendment by Carter Field, a special investigator, were suppressed by the Senate Lobby Committee today.

This was done, according to Senator Walsh, who announced the decision, with the concurrence of Senator Robinson, the committee member who said yesterday that he intended that they should go into the record if he had to read them himself.

The only member of the committee, Senator Walsh added, who voted for the inclusion of the reports was Senator Blaine, who objected to their inclusion yesterday. He explained then, however, that his reason for objecting was that only Senator Robinson and himself were present and he wished a quorum of the committee to pass on the advisability of making public admittedly embarrassing statements about the politicians involved.

Senator Caraway, chairman of the committee, had stated just before Senator Walsh announced the decision that he had not read the reports and that the question was still open, but he then agreed with Senator Walsh, who said:

"We have all agreed that, while these reports would be very interesting to the newspapers, they are so remotely connected with the purposes of this committee that they should not be made public, as they would only cause embarrassment to a lot of people."

Curran Completes Testimony.

Senator Walsh's announcement was made just after the day's hearing, in which Henry H. Curran, president of the Association Against the Prohibition Amendment, completed his testimony after having been questioned through seven sessions. The bulk of the questioning has been based on his files, from which the Field report was taken, and he has repeatedly protested the publication of confidential memoranda which he maintained was not within the jurisdiction of the Lobby Committee.

The readiness with which the committee had given out correspondence of the most confidential nature, a practice which was continued today, had created considerable discussion as to its possible action with the Field reports.

The negative decision caused Senator Walsh to be asked if it might not be construed that the committee is shielding dry Representatives, to which he replied:

"We will have to take the responsibility."

He added that Senator Blaine, after all, had raised the first objection, and although the Wisconsin Senator's reason was repeated to him he reiterated:

"Nevertheless, it was Senator Blaine who first made the objection,

Continued on Page Eight.

SEIZE 11 HIP FLASK PATRONS IN BROADWAY NIGHT CLUB; NEW FEDERAL RAID POLICY

British Artist Tells of Liquor Flooding American Society

Wireless to The New York Times.

LONDON, April 25.—"I never refused so much to drink in my life," was the first comment on America by Frank O. Salisbury, portrait painter, who has just returned here.

"In the big cities, where society demands drink, prohibition simply is not working," he continued. "But in the industrial centres prohibition is one of the secrets of America's success. The workingman has forgotten all about his pint and the banks are full of his money."

America is the happy hunting ground for portrait painters, in his opinion, for, whereas in England the old homes are being given up, American family history is being made and family portrait galleries are being founded.

CAMPBELL ORDERS ARRESTS

First Made for Public Drinking but Not the Last. He Says.

16 EMPLOYES ALSO TAKEN

Police Reserves Are Called as Theatre Crowd Jeers Dry Agents at the Hollywood.

BAIL ARRANGED AT NIGHT

Men and Women at Police Station in Evening Attire—Federal Men Invoke Nuisance Law.

Twenty-seven prisoners, including eleven patrons wearing evening attire, were arrested last night by Prohibition Administrator Maurice E. Campbell and a score of prohibition agents in a midnight raid on the Hollywood Restaurant, one of the most popular night clubs, at Broadway and Forty-eighth Street. Thousands of persons, just out of the theatres, witnessed the raid and jeered and booed the officials.

Explaining the arrest of the patrons, a new practice in New York, the prohibition administrator warned that he had definitely decided to "rid New York of the hip flask toters" who bring their own drinks to night clubs.

"This is the first instance in which persons in possession of intoxicating liquor in public places have been arrested," he said, "but if the practice is not discontinued in New York it will not be last.

Makes Nuisance Charge.

"The action taken tonight is the result of a very careful investigation conducted by my agents over a period of several weeks. This investigation has resulted in the positive fact that, for a very long time, this place has flagrantly violated the law in that practically every patron consumed intoxicating liquor on the premises with the knowledge of the management and that the patrons were further furnished with 'set-ups' to be used in conjunction with the law violations.

"There is no charge of sale against the management. The criminal charge is based entirely on the maintenance of a nuisance. The patrons who have been arrested tonight are charged with the possession of intoxicating liquor and during the evening had been observed by my men in the possession and consumption of liquor on these premises."

The patrons arrested were booked as follows:

HERBERT COOPER, 38 years old, of 280 Hawthorne Street, Brooklyn, cashier; one pint of liquor in his possession.

BENJAMIN ZIMMERMAN, 32, of the Hotel Lincoln, salesman; half pint.

RAYMOND ACKERMAN, 41, of Garden City, L. I., broker; half pint.

WILLIAM S. LEVIN, 47, of 1,551 Fourteenth Street, Brooklyn, insurance broker; bottle of wine.

JOHN ATWATER, 40, of 22 Cedar Avenue, Rockville Centre, L. I., insurance; half pint.

MICHAEL McCASTRO, 39, of 645 Fifth Avenue, Astoria, Queens, bookkeeper; one pint.

THOMAS KANE, 23, of 196 East Seventh Street, Brooklyn, dealer in bonds; one pint.

BENJAMIN McREYNOLDS, 38, of the Astor Hotel, insurance broker; one quart.

JAMES H. CARSON, 27, of 4,537 North Nineteenth Street, Philadelphia, bond business; two quarts.

REGINALD W. O'KIE, 32, of 164 East Seventy-second Street, engineer; one quart.

CHARLES WARREN, 23, of 23-70 Eighteenth Street, Jackson Heights, Queens; one pint.

600 Patrons in Club.

Six hundred men and women, all in evening attire, were in the night club when the prohibition administrator and his men entered. Behind them came a squad of uniformed policemen from the West Forty-seventh Street station. The patrons started out of their chairs but were warned to remain in their places, that there would be no disorder.

The raid was spectacularly staged. The officials broke in at the moment that Nils T. Grantlund was about to stage the revue for which the club is famous. Men and women eating and drinking at the tables were facing the performers, sitting at ease in momentary expectation of the show.

As word of the raid spread in the vicinity thousands of persons congregated in front of the restaurant and began to press forward in an attempt to see what was going on. The few men stationed at the door to turn back late patrons found the crush too much to handle and Mr. Campbell ordered one of his men to telephone to the West Forty-seventh Street station for the reserves.

In a few moments the Prohibition Administrator and his men had singled out the patrons alleged to have

Continued on Page Eight.

DRY TRANSFER BILL APPROVED TO SENATE

Committee Amends Measure to Bar Staff Carry-Over, Aiming to Oust the Inefficient.

INQUIRY WILL BE DROPPED

Shift is Made Effective July 1—Permit System Kept—Tydings Cites School Drinking Data.

Special to The New York Times.

WASHINGTON, April 25.—The administration bill to transfer prohibition enforcement from the Treasury to the Department of Justice was favorably reported to the Senate today by the Judiciary Committee with an amendment giving the Attorney General a free hand in its organization. This, the only important change made in the House measure, eliminated the provision that required the Department of Justice to take over present employes of the prohibition unit who were under civil service status.

The elimination of this section was opposed by some of the drys and by civil service advocates. It is understood that the committee adopted the amendment in the belief that as the responsibility for enforcement would be placed on the Attorney General he should not be hampered by legislation in the organization of the personnel.

Another element that operated in favor of the amendment was the opposition of Senators Norris, Borah and others to the activities of the present enforcement bureau.

Amendment Forestalls Inquiry.

Senator Norris has had pending a resolution to investigate the prohibition bureau. Dry members of the Judiciary Committee objected to this proposal, and Chairman Norris and the others backed the amendment in the hope of ousting enforcement agents charged by them with being inefficient. As a result there will probably be no inquiry made into the bureau.

Following the report of the transfer bill, Senator Norris indicated that he would not press his resolution for an inquiry into the prohibition bureau. This resolution, pending before the committee for nearly a month, has encountered the opposi-

Continued on Page Eight.

Cold Snap Lets Up Slightly on Third Day, But Spring Weather Still Is Not in Sight

Spring remained hidden yesterday in the shadowy region known as "just around the corner," but New Yorkers, still resorting to Winter clothes to protect them against the third day of the unseasonable cold snap, settled down to a long wait for the mild weather season to come to town.

Yesterday's temperature, although still cool, was not as uncomfortable as that of Thursday or of Wednesday, when the cold snap gripped the East. By comparison with the two previous days, Spring, already long overdue, seemed nearer.

The average temperature here was 44 degrees, only nine degrees cooler than normal for the date. However, it was too chilly for the thousands of New Yorkers whose favorite question is, "Will Spring ever come?"

The Weather Bureau forecast was for partly cloudy and continued cool weather today. Tomorrow there will be increasing cloudiness, followed by rain in the late afternoon or evening, it was predicted. Not much change in temperature is promised for tomorrow.

The mercury reached its low point of 36 degrees above zero—four degrees above the freezing point—at 5:15 A. M., and then made a valiant effort to rise to Spring levels, giving up the attempt at 3:45 P. M., with a reading of 52 degrees, the high mark for the day. The coldest April 25 on the records of the Weather Bureau was established in 1919 with a minimum reading of 27 degrees.

An Associated Press dispatch from Harrisburg, Pa., said that the apparent end of the unseasonable cold spell of the last few days found orchardists and county farm agents yesterday surveying the damage to fruit caused by the subfreezing weather. On Thursday night and early yesterday morning there were more chilling temperatures in Pennsylvania, with minimum readings at Pittsburgh at 24. Farm Agent Knode of Franklin County, Pa., reported that apple production probably would be cut by 25 or 30 per cent. On the other hand, orchards in York, Adams and Dauphin Counties were only slightly affected, growers reported.

At Albany, the State Department of Agriculture and Markets said that the unseasonable cold weather would have no serious effect on the commercial apple crop in the State as the buds were not far enough advanced to be injured. But sweet cherries, Japanese plums and possibly peaches in the lower valley districts may have suffered to some extent, it was said.

"All the News That's Fit to Print."

The New York Times.

THE WEATHER
Fair and continued warm today; tomorrow showers and thunderstorms.
Temperatures yesterday—Max. 79, min. 61.
U. S. Weather Forecast—For details see Page 46.

Copyright, 1930, by The New York Times Company.

VOL. LXXIX....No. 26,396. ***** NEW YORK, FRIDAY, MAY 2, 1930. TWO CENTS In Greater New York | THREE CENTS Within 200 Miles | FOUR CENTS Elsewhere Except 7th and 8th Postal Zones

WORST OF DEPRESSION OVER, SAYS HOOVER, WITH COOPERATION LESSENING DISTRESS; PLANS STUDY TO AVERT FUTURE CRISES

CITY'S MAY DAY QUIET; THRONG HEARS REDS AS POLICE STAND IDLE

Communists Mass in Union Square at End of Veterans' Meeting Attended by 30,000.

MARCH THROUGH EAST SIDE

1,000 of Whalen's Men Await Them at Gathering Place—Only 50 Arrests in Day.

MINOR CLASHES IN EUROPE

Police Protect Reds in London—Continental Centres Quiet—Holiday in Moscow.

More than 100,000 persons participated in two May Day demonstrations in Union Square yesterday, one pro-America and the other pro-Soviet Russia. A force of 1,000 policemen looked on, enjoyed the show and had nothing to do, although the Communists and their sympathizers mobilized in greater strength than ever before in the history of the city.

The veterans of Foreign Wars and the Communist leaders had pledged to Police Commissioner Whalen that they would keep to the time allotted to them. Both sides kept the promise and the meetings and the parades which preceded them were orderly to the point of precision. Only one arrest was made during the day in the square, that of a heckler who tried to interrupt a speaker on the veterans' program.

The veterans, with 10,000 in line and with 20,000 spectators, staged a patriotic rally which began at noon and ended at 1:50 P. M., ten minutes ahead of schedule. The square was cleaned and even the paper litter swept away. An hour later the Communists and their adherents, 30,500 strong, according to Commissioner Whalen's figures, appeared. Banked around the northern half of the square were 45,000 onlookers. The Red speakers, hoarse and condemnatory of many things, stopped their speeches on the dot of 4:45 P. M., the time agreed upon. Commissioner Whalen offered them thirty minutes more, but it was like August in Union Square and the audience had marched two miles and the meeting just broke up quietly.

Fifty Arrests Made in City.

Throughout the city only fifty arrests were made. They were chiefly for disorderly conduct. Two of fifty demonstraters who paraded before the British Consulate in behalf of the Indian freedom movement were taken into custody. Most of the minor demonstrations were before schools where Communists tried to keep children from attending classes.

Fully one-third of the marchers in the Red parade were women or children—some as young as five and six years—and they were a very tired lot when they got to Union Square. This proportion of women and children held true at the May Day meeting of the Socialist party, which brought 6,000 persons to the Bronx Coliseum.

Union Square has seldom presented such a study in contrasts. During the morning the veterans, some in uniforms and some in mufti, offering a brilliant and martial spectacle, poured into the square. The sun was reflected on nickeled helmets, it glinted from the medals of the late and earlier wars, and it sparkled from the national colors and the regimental and post flags. Women's auxiliaries of the organization, trim in white duck and sashes, and 4,000 White Russians were cheered as they marched with their colors to reserved seats in the grandstand.

The demonstration, designed to emphasize Americanization, opened with "The Star-Spangled Banner." As the music was played by the massed bands, and as the paraders and spectators joined in the singing, the police preparations for the Red rally unfolded.

Police Forces Mobilized.

Ten sinister looking emergency trucks rolled into the square. A wall of blue crept about the borders of the meeting. Two hundred and fifty mounted men sat astride restive steeds around corners and out of sight. Machine guns appeared on the roof tops of low buildings and their muzzles were tilted downward. Commissioner Whalen and his gold-braided aides, Chief Inspector O'Brien, Assistant Chief Inspector Mulrooney, Inspector Lobdell and First Deputy Commissioner Philip D. Hoyt, took post on the porch of the cottage.

A long list of speakers, each of them strongly assailing Soviet rule and Soviet propaganda here, addressed the rally. Representative Hamilton Fish, in a speech urging Congress to enact legislation for the deportation of alien agitators, took notice of the March 6 clash between the police and the Communists in

Continued on Page Twenty.

40 Brazilian Policemen Killed By Rebels, Argentina Reports

By The Associated Press.

BUENOS AIRES, May 1.—A news agency report from Parahyba, Brazil, today stated that forty provincial policemen had been killed in ambush by rebels near Princeza.

Police casualties in the past few days were said to total fifty dead. The trouble is wholly a State affair, originating locally, and does not affect the Federal Government of Brazil.

CITY SCHOOLS BAR PROF. HAYES' HISTORY

Book Used Here for 7 Years Is Banned on Complaint of Staten Island Rector.

RADICAL PROPAGANDA SEEN

Religious Bias Is Also Charged—Board Acts Without Passing on Facts.

After seven years' use as a textbook in the public schools of this city "Modern History," written by Professor Carlton J. H. Hayes of Columbia University in collaboration with Associate Professor Parker Thomas Moon, has been barred by the Board of School Superintendents "upon complaint that it is objectionable on civic and religious grounds."

Acting Superintendent Harold G. Campbell explained yesterday that the approval of the textbook by the superintendents in 1923 was withdrawn quietly last month after the Rev. Dr. Lefferd M. A. Haughwout, rector of St. Anne's Episcopal Church at Great Kills, S. I., had insisted upon attention to his complaint, which read in part:

"The book is objectionable on two grounds, civic and religious. It is written evidently in the interests of some visionary scheme of internationalism. By direct attack and persistent insinuation it breaks down respect for political democracy, patriotism and everything that pertains to nationalism. It encourages radicalism by continual criticism of the economic basis of modern society under the name of capitalism, contrasting it unfavorably with conditions in the Middle Ages.

Sees Protestantism Injured.

"Where religion is concerned," Dr. Haughwout's complaint continued, "it is difficult to write history without prejudices; but actually these authors transcend all reasonable limits and have produced a work that amounts to out and out propaganda. The Roman Catholic Church is everywhere deliberately defended and both the Church of England and all the branches of Protestantism are persistently criticized."

When this complaint was first received in January the Department of Education set it aside in the express expectation that nothing more would be heard of it. George J. Ryan, President of the Board of Education, said yesterday that his mail is usually filled with complaints from one group or another which feels it is at a disadvantage under the public school system. Dr. Haughwout wrote to the superintendents and to Mr. Ryan again and again, however, and also interested the local Staten Island school board appointed by the Borough President of Richmond.

Mrs. Norman S. Walker, secretary of the local school board at Great Kills, said last night that Dr. Haughwout caused this board to inquire about his complaint and that the local board had simply followed his operations "with gratification but without taking any action of its own."

The effect of the persistent complaint on the Department of Education was described by Acting Superintendent Campbell. He said that Mr. Ryan finally sent the correspondence to him and that the Board of School Superintendents, responsible for the textbooks admitted to use in the public schools of this city, finally decided, "inasmuch as we have an approved list of modern history textbooks from which teachers may choose and which contains fifty other books to which nobody has objected, we should not keep on the list a book which any section of the city objects to."

Ban Surprises Author.

Professor Hayes learned of the decision only when school teachers later told his publisher's salesmen that their requisitions for "Modern History," by Hayes and Moon, had been returned by the supply room of the Department of Education as "unfillable."

Inquiry by the publishing house of Macmillan, which has sold more than 150,000 copies of this history since publication, caused the official city correspondence to be reopened for the following reply by Superintendent Campbell:

"In view of the fact there was this criticism and of the further fact that we had a sufficient number of textbooks on modern European history on our lists, it was decided the best interests of the school would be

Continued on Page Eleven.

COMMISSION CUTS HOME PHONE RATES OF 900,000 USERS

Sweeping Rejection of Company Pleas Puts Charges Slightly Under Present Schedule.

BUSINESS RATE INCREASED

Order Reduces Company Valuation by $35,185,658, Lowers Revenue $900,000.

COMPANY IS CENSURED

Rising Operating Expenses Are Condemned—92 Per Cent of Home Subscribers Here Benefit.

Special to The New York Times.

ALBANY, May 1.—In a sweeping rejection of the claims of the New York Telephone Company, the Public Service Commission today handed down a decision reducing the valuation of the company, denying it the rate increase it had sought and cutting the present temporary schedules which have been in effect since Feb. 1.

Instead of sanctioning the $8,000,000 revenue rise above the present rates for which the telephone company had contended when it closed its case, the commission reduced the present rates so as to lower the yield by almost $1,000,000. It reduced the company's valuation or rate base by $35,185,658.

At the same time the commission, in a belligerent opinion consisting of sixty-six printed pages, censured the telephone company for its rising operating expenses and lashed out at critics who have charged that there is a breakdown in regulation.

The commission also disregarded the company's gloomy outlook on business conditions and its figures which purported to show a slump in business in February and March, and revenues far below what it had anticipated. Instead the commission based its estimate on figures advanced by the company in January and derived largely from experience in 1928 and 1929.

As a final derangement of the company's plan, the commission ordered a change of its rate structure by greatly increasing the differential between residence and business rates. Under an entirely new set of rate schedules prepared by the commission, 900,000 resident telephone subscribers in the State either get their bills reduced below what they are now paying or remain entirely unaffected by changes. In New York City 92 per cent of all residence telephones will enjoy rates decreased slightly below those in effect since Feb. 1, although they will continue to be higher than the schedules of last year.

Business Rates Increased.

Business rates in New York City and throughout the State, however, are ordered increased. The telephone company received almost uniformly the tariffs it proposed in its January schedules for this class of service. With residence rates lowered and business rates increased, the net effect, according to the commission experts, will be to reduce the overall revenue from New York City subscribers by $550,000 and from up-State subscribers by $350,000, as compared with the return from the present temporary rates.

The new rates ordered by the commission will go into effect in New York City on June 1 and in the balance of the State on May 26. They will remain effective until June 1, 1931, or until further order of the commission.

Despite the reductions ordered today on top of the 20 per cent reduction on Feb. 1 in the increases proposed by the company, the commission expects that the net revenue

Continued on Page Fifteen.

How Commission Phone Rates Compare With Others Proposed

Special to The New York Times.

ALBANY, May 1.—This table gives a comparison of the new telephone rates ordered by the Public Service Commission with the rates in effect prior to Feb. 1, the rates proposed in January by the telephone company and the temporary rates now in effect:

Old Rate.	Cos. Pro.	Pres. Rate.	New Rate.
Residence Telephone Monthly Rates in Brooklyn, Manhattan, Western Queens and Most of the Bronx:			
$4.00	$4.50	$4.40	$4.25
Individual Business Phone Rates in Same Areas:			
4.75	6.00	5.75	6.00
Residence Phone Rates in Northern Bronx:			
4.00	4.25	4.20	4.00
Individual Business Rates in Northern Bronx:			
4.75	5.00	4.95	5.00
Residence Phone Rates in Central Queens:			
4.00	4.50	4.40	4.25
Individual Business Phone Rates in Central Queens:			
4.25	6.00	5.65	6.00
Residence Phone Rates Eastern Queens, Far Rockaway and Staten Island:			
4.00	4.25	4.20	4.00
Individual Business Phone Rates for Same Areas:			
4.25	5.00	4.85	5.00

All of these rates are for message rate subscribers.

WALKER, INCOGNITO, SAILS FOR BERMUDA

Only His Valet Accompanies Mayor on Sudden Trip to Regain His Health.

CITY HALL IS SURPRISED

Dr. Schroeder Alone Knew of Plan to Spend Ten Days in Home of H. C. Blackiston.

Mayor Walker, accompanied only by his valet, Robert Abel, sailed for Bermuda yesterday morning aboard the Royal Mail Line steamship Arcadian. He was listed on the vessel as "Mr. Walker," and every possible effort appeared to have been made to protect him and his plans from publicity, at least until after his departure had become an accomplished fact.

Neither Charles S. Hand, his official secretary, nor any member of his Cabinet, with the exception of Dr. William Schroeder Jr., chairman of the Sanitation Commission, who is the Mayor's personal physician, knew that he contemplated leaving New York yesterday. Nor had he intimated to any of them that he had in mind a ten-day vacation to recuperate from his recent illness.

It is said that the Mayor on Wednesday had discussed the matter with Dr. Schroeder and that the physician had then sanctioned the plan. The Mayor suddenly determined to go and his valet was dispatched to reserve staterooms.

Departure Kept Secret.

The Arcadian sailed from her pier at the foot of Morton Street, North River, at 11 o'clock yesterday morning with about 100 passengers. The ship was well on her way before it was learned that Mayor Walker was a passenger. Confirmation of that fact was not easily obtained at the office of the line. It was said there at first that "a Mr. Walker" was among the passengers. Later, when the line officials were confronted with evidence that the "Mr. Walker" was in realty the Mayor, they admitted the fact and said that his passage had been booked only twenty-four hours before sailing time.

Mayor Walker was driven to the pier and arrived there just in time to go aboard before the landing stage was hauled ashore. A small group, including, it is said, his brother, Dr. William H. Walker, waved their adieus from the pierhead.

The Mayor apparently was not recognized by any persons aboard the vessel nor by those who had

Continued on Page Three.

Sudden Storms Follow Summer Heat Here; Lightning Kills Man, Puts Out Liberty's Torch

Summer made a sudden rush on New York and other cities in the East yesterday, bringing uncomfortably warm temperatures that claimed one victim in Jersey City and one in Newark, and winding up the day with two real Summer thunderstorms in which lightning bolts killed an Ozone Park farmhand, injured his companion and struck eight places in the metropolitan area.

One lightning bolt disabled the lighting system on Bedloe's Island, plunging the island into darkness for an hour and extinguishing the light in the torch of the Statue of Liberty. Another bolt hit a power house in Jersey City about 8:30 P. M., putting the city's entire lighting facilities out of commission for fifteen minutes. Bayonne, Union City, Guttenberg and West New York were also dark for brief periods. Four places in Brooklyn and a hospital in Newark also were struck by lightning, which did slight damage.

There were two thunderstorms, both brief, the first beginning about 7 o'clock in the evening and the second about an hour and a half later. The storms were brought on by temperatures that had soared to 79 degrees here at 4:15 P. M., and 81 degrees in Flushing at 3:15 P. M. Officials at the local Weather Bureau were unable to say whether these temperatures marked a record for the date. Continued warm weather was forecast for today, with fresh southwest winds.

When the first thunderstorm broke, Joseph Cenatiento, 26 years old, and Frank Cuomo, 24, were working in one of the fields of Cuomo's father's farm, one of the few remaining farms in Queens County, at Old South Road and Lawn Avenue, Ozone Park. Cenatiento and Cuomo had just started to run for cover from the rain when a lightning bolt flashed in their path, killing Cenatiento. Cuomo suffered a slight shock. A bolt in the same district set fire to a house, doing $2,500 damage.

In Jersey City Felix Ditrich, 38 years old, of 817 Pavonia Avenue, collapsed from the heat at Ocean and Gates Avenues. The heat was blamed also for the illness of Frank Carroll, 35 years old, of East 175th Street, the Bronx, who was stricken while seated in a Newark trolley car. He was taken to the Newark City Hospital.

The minimum temperature recorded in Manhattan was 61 degrees at 6 A. M. The average temperature for the day here was 65 degrees—nine degrees above the normal of 56 degrees.

BANK RATES REDUCED IN WORLD CENTRES; PLACED AT 3% HERE

Cuts in New York, London and Paris Bring Credits to the Lowest Levels in Years.

MOVES TO AID TRADE SEEN

Action, a Surprise, Is Taken as Evidence of International Banking Cooperation.

EXPECTED TO HELP BONDS

Stimulation of Building Also Is Looked For—Renewal of Selling Causes Further Stock Decline.

Discount rates in the leading money markets of the world were simultaneously reduced yesterday, bringing the price of credit to the lowest levels in years and testifying to the world-wide endeavor of central banking authorities to revive business activity through the stimulant of cheap and abundant money.

Following cuts in the discount rates of the Bank of England and the Bank of France, announced yesterday morning, the price at which member banks may borrow from the Federal Reserve Bank of New York was lowered in the afternoon to 3 per cent, the lowest rediscount rate which has been in effect here since Feb. 26, 1925. The reduction was the fifth since last Fall's stock market break and brought the rate to a figure exactly one-half of that which obtained prior to the collapse in security prices.

The spokesman for the Reserve Bank made no announcement concerning the rate at which the bank buys acceptances, but it was believed by leading bankers and bill dealers that this rate would be reduced from 3 per cent, which has been maintained for more than two months, to about 2¾ per cent. On the basis of this assumption, the yield rates on bankers' acceptances were slashed twice for an average reduction of three-eighths of 1 per cent, bringing the price of this important form of credit to 2¾ per cent bid, 2⅝ per cent asked, for most maturities.

Reduction a Surprise.

The general slash in bank rates throughout the world yesterday came as a surprise to the financial community, where it had been generally assumed that the New York rate would not be reduced and that the British rate could therefore not be lowered without serious risk of a loss of gold to this market. In some quarters the unanimity of the reductions was taken as evidence of international banking cooperation. Other observers suggested, however, that the move of the Bank of England had forced the hand of the Reserve Bank here and one prominent banker expressed regret that the New York bank had not anticipated the move.

The 3½ per cent rediscount rate of the Federal Reserve Bank of New York which was displaced yesterday has been in effect since March 14, last, when the price of member bank borrowing was cut from 4 per cent. It had been the opinion of leading bankers that the Reserve authorities would not countenance further reductions in the rate, but would lend their efforts toward a stabilization of credit at the moderate levels which have lately prevailed.

This impression was heightened by the developments of mid-March, when, under the influence of the treasury overdraft, call money rates fell to 2 per cent at the money post of the Stock Exchange, outside funds were available at 1½ per cent, and the yield rate on bankers' bills dropped to the extremely low return of 2½ per cent.

The opportunity was there present, bankers remarked, had the Federal Reserve desired it, to effect another cut in the bank rate. Instead, the Federal Reserve Bank of New York refused to follow the decline in bill rates. It maintained its bill-buying rate at 3 per cent, a full one-half of 1 per cent above the market and so forced bill rates back up again.

Feared Effect on Trading.

It was explained at that time that the price of credit was already sufficiently cheap as to give the business of the country all the encouragement possible in easy money conditions, while a further lowering of money rates would be apt to stimulate a revival of speculation.

From an international point of view, it was remarked by bankers, a further reduction in the rate here might have the effect of setting in motion a movement of gold to Europe. This development was regarded as unwelcome, as an outflow of gold frequently has a depressing effect upon business sentiment.

As money rates weakened in the London market, cable despatches

Continued on Page Seventeen.

Text of the President's Speech

Special to The New York Times.

WASHINGTON, May 1.—President Hoover's speech tonight before the United States Chamber of Commerce was as follows:

Gentlemen of the United States Chamber of Commerce:

We have been passing through one of those great economic storms which periodically bring hardship and suffering upon our people. While the crash only took place six months ago, I am convinced we have now passed the worst and with continued unity of effort we shall rapidly recover.

There is one certainty in the future of a people of the resources, intelligence and character of the people of the United States—that is prosperity.

On the occasion of this great storm we have for the first time attempted a great economic experiment, possibly one of the greatest of our history. By cooperation between government officials and the entire community, business, railways, public utilities, agriculture, labor, the press, our own financial institutions and public authorities, we have undertaken to stabilize economic forces; to mitigate the effects of the crash and to shorten its destructive period.

I believe I can say with assurance that our joint undertaking has succeeded to a remarkable degree and that it furnishes a basis of great tribute to our people for unity of action in time of national emergency. To those many business leaders present here I know that I express the gratitude of our countrymen.

Problems Human and Vital.

It is unfortunate, in a sense, that any useful discussion of the problems behind and before us has to be expressed wholly in the cold language of economics, for I realise as keenly as any one can that individually they are not problems in science, but are the most human questions in the world.

They involve the immediate fears of men and women for their daily bread, the well-being of their children, the security of their homes. They are intensely personal questions, fraught with living significance to everything they hold dear.

The officers of a ship in heavy seas have as deep a consciousness of the human values involved in the passengers and crew whose lives are in their keeping, but they can best serve them by taking counsel of their charts, compass and barometer, and by devotion to navigation and the boilers. In like manner, the individual welfare can best be served by us if we devote ourselves to the amelioration of destructive forces, for thereby we serve millions of our people.

All slumps are the inexorable consequences of the destructive forces of booms. If we inquire into the primary cause of the great boom on the Stock Exchanges last year, we find it rests mainly on certain forces inherent in human minds.

Speculative Trend 'Uncontrollable.'

When our nation has traveled on the high road to prosperity for a considerable term of years, the natural optimism of our people brings into being a spirit of undue speculation against the future. These vast contagions of speculative emotion have hitherto throughout all history proved themselves uncontrollable by any device that the economist, the business man or the government has been able to suggest.

The effect of them is to divert capital and energy from healthy enterprise—the only real sources of prosperity—to stimulate waste, extravagance and unsound enterprise, with the inevitable collapse in panic.

Out of the great crashes hitherto there has always come a long train of destructive forces. A vast number of innocent people are directly involved in losses. Optimism swings to deepest pessimism; fear of the future chokes initiative and enterprise; monetary stringencies, security and commodity panics in our Exchanges, bankruptcies and other losses all contribute to stifle consumption, decrease production, and finally express themselves in unemployment, decreased wages, strikes, lockouts and a long period of stagnation.

Many have looked upon all this rise and fall as a disease which must run its course, and for which nothing could be done either in prevention, or to speed recovery, or to relieve the hardship which wreaks itself especially upon workers, farmers and smaller business people. I do not accept the fatalistic view that the discovery of the means to restrain destructive speculation is beyond the genius of the American people.

First United Effort.

Our immediate problem, however, has been the necessity to mitigate the effect of the recent crash, and to get back onto the road of prosperity as quickly as possible. This is the first time an effort has been made by the united community to this end.

The success of this effort is of paramount importance, not only for our immediate needs but the possibilities it opens for the future. The intensity of the speculative boom on this occasion was, in my view, as great as or greater than any of our major manias before. The intensity of the slump has been greatly diminished by the efforts that have been made.

We—and as we I speak of many men and many institutions—have followed several major lines of action. Our program was one of deliberate purpose to do everything possible to uphold general confidence, which lies at the root of maintained initiative and enterprise, to check monetary, security, and commodity panics in our Exchanges; to assure an abundance of capital at decreasing rates of interest so as to enable the resumption of business; to accelerate construction work so as to absorb as many employes as possible from industries hit by decreased demand; to hold up the level of wages by voluntary agreement, and thus maintain the living standards of the vast majority who remain in employment; to avoid accelerating the depression by the hardship and disarrangement of strikes and lockouts, and by upholding consuming power of the wage earners to in turn support agriculture.

Credit Stringency Avoided.

We may well inquire into our progress thus far. We have succeeded in maintaining confidence and courage. We have avoided monetary panic and credit stringency. These dangers are behind us. From the moment of the crash, interest rates have steadily decreased and capital has become steadily more abundant.

Our investment markets have absorbed two billions of new securities since the crash. There has been no significant bank or industrial failure. That danger, too, is safely behind us.

The acceleration of construction programs has been successful beyond our hopes. The great utilities, the railways and the large manufacturers have responded courageously. The Federal Government has not only expedited its current works, but Congress has authorized further expenditures. The Governors, Mayors and other authorities have everywhere been doing their full part.

The result has been the placing of contracts of this character to the value of about $500,000,000 during the first four months of 1930, or nearly three times the amount brought into being in the corresponding four months of the last great depression of eight years ago. All of which contributes not only to direct employment but also a long train of jobs in the material and transportation industries.

We are suffering from a decrease in residential construction, but despite this we have reason to believe that the total construction will still further expand, and we should during 1930 witness a larger gross volume of improvement work than normal.

No Labor Troubles Resulted.

For the first time in the history of great slumps we have had no substantial reductions in wages and we have had no strikes or lockouts which were in any way connected with this situation.

The accelerated construction has naturally not been able to absorb all the unemployment brought by the injuries of the boom and crash.

Unfortunately we have no adequate statistics upon the volume of unemployment. The maximum point of depression was about the first of the year, when, severe as the shock was the unemployment was much less proportionately than in our two last major depressions.

A telegraphic canvass of the Governors and Mayors, who are cooperating so ably with us in organizing public works, brings with one exception the unanimous report of continuously decreasing unemployment each month and the assurance of further decreases again in May.

All these widespread activities of our business men and our institutions offer sharp contrast with the activities of previous major crashes and our experiences from them. As a consequence we have attained a stage of recovery within this short period greater than that attained during a whole year or more following previous equally great storms.

While we are today chiefly concerned with continuing the meas-

Continued on Page Two.

RECOVERY NEAR, HE STATES

President Tells Chamber of Commerce of Gain in Employment.

LEADERS' EFFORTS PRAISED

National Unity in Facing Situation "Mitigated Effects of Crash," He Says.

NEED OF SURVEY STRESSED

"Wise Planning, Based Upon Accurate Data, Can Prevent a Recurrence," He Asserts.

Special to The New York Times.

WASHINGTON, May 1.—The United States has "passed the worst of the great economic storm," President Hoover said tonight in an address before the Chamber of Commerce of the United States.

Expressing confidence for the future, the President added:

"There is one certainty in the future of a people of the resources, intelligence and character of the people of the United States—that is prosperity."

The unity of action manifest at the outset of the depression last Fall was credited by Mr. Hoover with mitigating its effects and shortening its destructive period.

He voiced the belief that employment was increasing, and commented on the fact that credit for all legitimate purposes was ample.

At the same time the President announced that he would appoint a commission to study the present business depression and devise means of avoiding such slumps in the future.

"While the crash only took place six months ago," he said, "I am convinced that with unity of effort we shall rapidly recover."

He declared that the nation's experience in the financial boom and subsequent slump should be examined with a view to insuring greater stability in the future, both in prevention and remedy.

"If such an exhaustive examination meets with general approval," he said, "I shall, when the situation clears a little, move to organize a body—representative of business, economics, labor and agriculture—to undertake it."

Value of "Wise Planning" Seen.

The President emphatically asserted his belief that voluntary cooperation "in intelligent information and wise planning" by the groups to be represented on the commission would aid the government materially in such crises and produce helpful and wholesome results in the national economic system.

He said that this had been demonstrated by the "great economic experiment," in which so many factors had joined to stabilize economic forces last Winter, and made "our joint undertaking" succeed "to a remarkable degree."

The orgy of stock market speculation was traced by the President to the public state of mind. He said that when the American nation "has traveled on the high road to prosperity for a considerable term of years the natural optimism of our people brings into being a spirit of undue speculation against the future." But the President refused to agree with the idea that such financial disasters are a disease which must run its course.

"I do not accept the fatalistic view," he said, "that the discovery of the means to restrain destructive speculation is beyond the genius of the American people."

Asserting that while the speculative boom was as great or greater than any previous "major manias," he contended that the intensity of the slump has been greatly diminished by the effort made to counteract it. He described in detail the program which was instituted to "uphold general confidence," and told the chamber:

"We have succeeded in maintaining confidence and courage."

Construction Boom Cited.

Construction programs have been accelerated "beyond our hopes," the President said, adding that contracts worth $500,000,000 have been placed during the first four months of 1930, or nearly three times the amount in the comparative period after the depression eight years ago.

"For the first time in the history of great slumps," he said, "we have had no substantial reductions in wages, and we have had no strikes

"All the News That's Fit to Print."

The New York Times.

Copyright, 1930, by The New York Times Company.

THE WEATHER
Fair and warmer today and tomorrow.
Temperatures Yesterday—Max. 66; Min. 44.
U. S. Weather Forecast—For details see Page 37.

VOL. LXXIX....No. 26,421. **** NEW YORK, TUESDAY, MAY 27, 1930. TWO CENTS In Greater New York | THREE CENTS Within 200 Miles | FOUR CENTS Elsewhere Except 7th and 8th Postal Zones

NAVAL TREATY IS PUT OFF UNTIL AN EXTRA SESSION, TO BE CALLED NEXT MONTH

HOOVER APPROVES THE PLAN

Senate Chiefs Act After Caucus on Priority of Legislation.

ONE DAY'S REST FOR SENATE

Treaty Proponents Grow Nervous Over Effect on Japan of Naval Testimony.

BUILDING RACE IS FEARED

Senator Johnson Makes Fiery Speech of Warning to Party as Opponent of Treaty.

By RICHARD V. OULAHAN.
Special to The New York Times.

WASHINGTON, May 26.—As a result of exchanges of views between legislative leaders this afternoon, following a rather inconclusive caucus of Republican Senators this morning, consideration of the London naval armament treaty will be deferred until a special session of the Senate, to be called by President Hoover immediately after the adjournment of Congress, which is expected to take place about the middle of June.

There were oratorical fireworks over the treaty at the Republican caucus, which came to an end with an agreement by general consent, but without adopting any formal resolution, that the Senate should proceed with the pending legislative program before undertaking to determine whether the treaty should be debated at the regular session or at a special session which the President has given notice he will call if it is not acted upon at the regular session.

Longworth Presses for Decision.

Immediately after the caucus Senator Watson, the Republican floor leader, began a series of informal conferences with Senator Robinson of Arkansas, Democratic floor leader, and other Senators. Mr. Robinson, who was one of the American delegates at the London Naval Conference, said he could not see any difference between considering the treaty at the regular session of Congress or at a special meeting of the Senate. The conferences between Senator Watson and his associates were stimulated by Speaker Longworth and leaders of the House, who, when they heard of the inclination of the Senate's Republican caucus to defer decision on when to take up the treaty, took the position that the Senate had no right to keep the House sitting after the legislative program had been acted upon.

Following the argument that the Senate should complete the legislative program before taking up the treaty, Senator Watson informed President Hoover of the decision and was assured by the President that it was agreeable to him.

Senator Watson said afterward that there would be a break of only one day between the adjournment of the regular session and the convening of the Senate's special treaty session.

Various estimates were offered as to when Congress would be able to adjourn, but the rather general opinion was that June 17 would be the outside limit.

Predictions Vary on Extra Session.

There was greater divergence as to the time that would be required for the Senate to dispose of the London treaty. Senator Fess, Republican party whip, thought that the debate would take only a week or ten days, and he put July 1 at the outside as the time when the Senate would be able to take a final vote on ratification. Senator Watson was not so optimistic. In his view, the final vote should come "not later" than July 15.

In the meantime, proponents of the treaty showed signs of nervousness over the outlook for ratification. They are concerned chiefly about the effect of testimony of naval officers before the Committees on Foreign Relations and Naval Affairs which suggest war with Japan as a possibility. Testimony along that line was given today by experts before the Foreign Relations Committee. Such views are being cabled to Japan and published in Japanese newspapers, and information received here is that what diplomatists describe as "a painful impression" is being created in that country.

The fear that exists in the minds of some of the treaty proponents is that if it should be rejected in the Senate, Japanese apprehension would be aroused to such a degree that an

Continued on Page Four.

Dawes Gets Month's Leave To Aid Chicago Fair Plans

Special to The New York Times.

WASHINGTON, May 26.—The State Department has granted a month's leave of absence to General Charles G. Dawes, Ambassador to London, that he may return to the United States to attend duties in connection with the Chicago Exposition planned for 1933. General Dawes will sail on June 7 and spend about two weeks in this country.

Recently Secretary Stimson denied that the Ambassador was being summoned home in connection with the fight in the Senate for ratification of the London naval treaty. The application for his leave of absence was received today and was said to be in accordance with plans he had had for several months to return at this time.

MACDONALD VICTOR IN DEBATE ON INDIA

Benn, Meeting Commons Critics, Says Clashes Are Not Revolt and Order Will Be Kept.

LEFT WING PUSHES ATTACK

Laborite Charges India Is Being Ruled by Bayonet—Sharp Exchange Ends Without Vote.

By EDWIN L. JAMES.
Special Cable to THE NEW YORK TIMES.

LONDON, May 26.—The government came through the India debate in the House of Commons tonight with flying colors. Declaring the disturbances in India represented sporadic anarchy and not any public uprising or revolt, the Cabinet spokesman took the position that it was the duty of the government to preserve order and that the government would perform its duty.

This firm position successfully met most of the Opposition criticism and the difficulties for the government came from the left wing of its own party, members of which accused the socialistic Cabinet of doing imperialistic stuff—"imperialistic dirty work," one Laborite called the government's Indian program.

Says India Needs England.

As a matter of fact, the speech of the Secretary of State for India, Wedgwood Benn, differed but little and that little was in theory, from any statement which might have been made by a Conservative statesman. India needed England and England needed India, he said, and if the newspapers chose to exaggerate the present troubles that constituted no reason why London should not proceed with the plans for the coming Indian conference. That Mahatma Gandhi and some others had been put in jail, it was explained, was not to punish them for their political views but simply to place them where they could not disturb the good order existing in most parts of India and among most of the 300,000,000 population.

In so far as Mr. Benn's Second Internationalist theories may have clashed with the interests of the British Empire, it must be said the British Empire won. This disguisted some members of his own party, but it satisfied a large majority of the House of Commons.

Earl Winterton, Conservative, who began the debate in a very tame

Continued on Page Twelve.

15 Dead, 250 Hurt in Rangoon Strike Riot; Martial Law Likely in Dock Workers' Clash

Wireless to THE NEW YORK TIMES.

RANGOON, Burma, May 26.—The clash between two sections of Burmese and Indian dock laborers culminated today in a riot in which, at a rough estimate, fifteen men were killed and 250 were injured.

The trouble arose out of the shipping strike settled Saturday in favor of the Indian shipping coolies. During the strike Burmans were engaged to load and unload ships, some having been brought from other parts of Burma in expectation that they would be retained. When the Indian Coringsee coolies returned to work this morning some of the stevedores told the Burmans their services were no longer required. This caused friction, which was intensified by a Coringsee abusing the Burmans, telling them to clear out. The Burmans retaliated and a fight followed which spread to many parts of the city despite the efforts of municipal police.

The parading of troops did not check the rioters. Governor Sir Charles Innes was absent at Maymo and the Burma Indian Chamber of Commerce protested that the rioters were attempting to loot and to parade the streets while the military and police were inactive.

Ultimately the police charged the rioters and calm was restored..

RANGOON, May 26 (AP).—Clashes throughout the day between striking dock laborers and imported laborers and police brought a threat of martial law today.

Members of the Cameron Highlanders and the Punjab Regiment stood by tonight, while the streets were patroled by cavalcades of mounted police.

All bazaars were closed.

The injured persons included one European and one Anglo-Indian sergeant. Three of the injured were Andhra coolies, who died later.

Many shops were closed because of the resulting panic. Some houses were stoned during the rioting. A number of rickshaws were smashed and several buses were damaged.

BERRY ACTS TO EASE LOCAL ASSESSMENTS; DRAFTS 16 REFORMS

Report Proposes Putting Part of Cost of Improvements Into City Budget.

WARNS OF MOUNTING TOTAL

Sum, Second Only to Transit Outlay, to Increase Taxes $75,000,000 in 5 Years.

PERIL TO TAXPAYERS SEEN

Spread Between Estimate and Cost Often Menaces Savings, Official Says—Asks Investigating Body.

Drastic recommendations designed to protect property holders against excessive assessments on local improvements and prevent the threatened dislocation of the city's budget arising from the present assessment procedure as related to the improvements in question are proposed in a report to be submitted today by Controller Charles W. Berry to the Board of Estimate.

With a warning that the great number of local improvements already authorized, the costs of which are paid by city and borough assessments, will add between $75,000,000 and $100,000,000 to taxes during the next five years, Controller Berry in his report urges a more rigid and more scientific method of financing.

Mr. Berry presents sixteen suggestions for improving the present procedure, together with the major recommendation that the Board of Estimate authorize the Mayor to appoint a committee, representing the Supreme Court, Corporation Counsel, the Controller and such other interests as may be appropriate, to consider the present assessment procedure and necessary corrective measures. The recommendations of this committee would later be enacted into law by the Municipal Assembly or the Legislature at Albany.

Based on Months of Study.

Mr. Berry's report, based on many months of study, is entitled "The Financing of Local Improvements by Local, Borough or City Assessments," and is believed to be probably the most exhaustive and comprehensive study of the question ever undertaken. The report covers fifty-six pages and is replete with facts, figures and examples showing the successive steps in the progress and financing of various types of local improvements.

A table shows that local improvements in the aggregate are second only in magnitude to the city's vast rapid transit construction program. The table reveals that while the city paid out in actual cash $83,991,753 for rapid transit construction last year $60,959,149 was spent for local improvements.

After discussing some of the evils of the present system of financing local improvements, such as the impossibility of ascertaining the final cost of a project, often resulting in an ultimate cost several times the figure originally set, and the embarrassment arising therefrom to both the city and the taxpayer, Mr. Berry declares that this often imperils the homes and life savings of citizens.

In suggesting changes that will enable both the Board of Estimate and the taxpayer "to know within reasonable limits what an improvement will cost and who is to pay the bill before the improvement is authorized," Controller Berry proposes including in the budget a considerable share of the cost of local improvements that under the present procedure is added to the assessment bills of the property owner.

Mr. Berry says that the expenditures in connection with a local improvement now involving the activi-

Continued on Page Twenty-three.

Miss Ingalls Makes 980 Loops In Plane, Breaking Own Record

By The Associated Press.

MUSKOGEE, Okla., May 26.—Miss Laura Ingalls, 25-year-old New York aviatrix, landed at 7:50 tonight, after making 980 consecutive loops, breaking her own women's record by 636.

She was in the air 3 hours and 40 minutes.

Miss Ingalls at St. Louis recently set a record of 344 loops. Her new mark is within 453 loops of the accomplishment of Charles (Speed) Holman, who looped 1,433 times at St. Paul, March 17, 1928.

By a pre-flight agreement Miss Ingalls is scheduled to receive prize money of $1,036.

Her feat brought to a climax a day of aerial activities dedicating the $200,000 new Hatbox-Municipal airport in which hundreds of army and civilian fliers participated. Taking the air at 4:10, the New York aviatrix averaged about 4⅓ loops a minute.

HUGHES URGES BAR PURGE PROFESSION

Effort Needed Now More Than Ever, He Says in Message to Lawyers Opening Home.

WANTS BENCH IMPROVED

W. N. Cromwell Gives $150,000 to Establish Law Foundation for Research and Reform.

Chief Justice Charles Evans Hughes, in a letter read yesterday at the dedication of the new home of the New York County Lawyers' Association, in Vesey Street, reminded members of the bar that their aid in keeping the profession from disrepute is needed now more than ever. Sharp practice and chicanery have no place in a profession where skill and honor should go hand in hand, he declared.

William Nelson Cromwell, the retiring president of the County Lawyers' Association, announced at the beginning of the ceremonies the establishment of a new Law Foundation. Its chief purposes, he said, will be to aid in law research, law reforms, improvement of standards of bar admissions, cultivation of the highest standards of professional ethics and the establishment in the Vesey Street building of a historical museum of Colonial legal history. He handed to former Judge Samuel Seabury his check for $150,000 as an initial endowment.

The speakers at the dedication formalities in the new building, directly opposite the churchyard of St. Paul's Chapel, included leaders of the local, State and national bar. A message was read from Associate Justice Harlan Fiske Stone of the United States Supreme Court, who was unable to attend. The speakers were:

SAMUEL SEABURY.
BENJAMIN N. CARDOZO, chief judge of the New York State Court of Appeals.
VICTOR J. DOWLING, presiding justice of the Appellate Division.
MARTIN T. MANTON, senior judge of the United States Circuit Court of Appeals.
JOHN W. DAVIS, former president of the American Bar Association.
HENRY W. TAFT, incoming president of the County Lawyers' Association.
MARTIN CONBOY.
CHARLES C. BURLINGHAM, president of the City Bar Association.
BENNO LEWINSON, treasurer of the County Lawyers' Association.

Hughes Urges United Effort.

The message from Chief Justice Hughes expressed his regret in not being able to attend the ceremonies. It then continued:

"On many questions the bar will not have one voice, but many conflicting voices, as those skilled in disputation address themselves to social and political problems which divide opinion. But is it too much to expect a fairly united and therefore effective endeavor to improve the workings of the machinery of justice, an obligation especially laid upon those best fitted to appreciate its defects, and to provide practical remedies? As books and office furniture do not make a lawyer, so a library and reception halls do not make a bar association. The significance of such an association is founded not merely in a common technique, but in the reinforcement of the standards of sound learning, loyalty to the law and fidelity to trust and in the readiness for expert public service, which have given a peculiar dignity to the profession of the law.

"That reinforcement is especially necessary at this time, as vast numbers come to the bar ill-fitted by environment or discipline to withstand the malign influences and increasing temptation of a crowded urban life, where individual delinquencies have become more difficult of detection, and the most important punishment which lies in professional disrepute is more often escaped. The situation would be hopeless were it not for the opportunities of our bar associations to uphold the high aim of the profession, that, while assuring according to our conception of justice that each side of a controversy shall be expertly represented and fully heard, attempts to thwart the administration of justice by delays, sharp practice and chicanery shall be unsparingly condemned. They have no place in a profession where skill and honor should go hand in hand.

"Even when purged, as it should be, of its delinquents, the bar is only at the threshold of its opportunity to devote its technical knowledge to

Continued on Page Twenty-two.

$300,000 IN LOOT, WOMAN AND 4 MEN ARE SEIZED IN HOTEL

Found Seated Around Stolen Jewels as Detectives Break Open the Door of Their Room.

WOMAN SWALLOWS PAPER

Mulrooney Says the Recovered Articles Were Stolen by an International Gang.

HUNT LED OVER COUNTRY

Suspects Are Linked to Park Avenue Robbery and Thefts in Miami Hotels and in C. F. Carson Home.

As a finale to a nine weeks' chase that led to almost every section of the country, the police yesterday afternoon broke into a room of the Hotel Commodore and arrested four men and a woman. When the detectives came upon them the five were seated quietly around a small table on which sparkled a careless heap of jewelry. After checking it over, the captors estimated its total value as upward of $300,000.

Last night, while the prisoners were refusing to tell more than their addresses, the authorities were trying to link the diamonds and sapphires to the robberies in which they had been stolen. The trail started in Miami last February following thefts at the Blackstone and Ambassador Hotels—but there was a thought that the loot might have been included from two New York State robberies. One of these was the $500,000 robbery of George Mauboussin, a jeweler of 330 Park Avenue, the other was the $400,000 hold-up of a dinner at the home of Charles F. Carson Jr. at Snyder, N. Y.

After the five had been arrested Commissioner Mulrooney said that he considered them as part of "an international gang of jewel thieves" who have been responsible for "a million dollars in losses during recent months." They had probably come to New York with the intention of getting rid of their loot, he explained, regarding this city as a good market place for jewels. He said that he hoped to be able to work back from the prisoners and learn from them the identity of others in the gang. It was Commissioner Mulrooney, jubilant at the coup so early in his administration, who told how it had been brought about.

Trail Started in Miami.

On Feb. 2, he said, the Blackstone Hotel at Miami was entered, and a large quantity of jewelry was stolen from the room of David J. Bonwit of Pittsburgh. On Feb. 26 the Ambassador fell a victim and Louis W. Herman of 470 West End Avenue, New York, lost a large sum. Circulars describing the separate pieces were sent out, and nine weeks ago Commissioner Mulrooney—then inspector—received information that the thieves were headed toward New York.

He assigned Lieutenant Richard Oliver to direct command of the case and gave him Detective Daniel J. Ryan and "about a dozen" undercover men. The latter picked up the trail in the South, followed it north to Chicago, Detroit and other places, and then—last Saturday—traced a certain William J. O'Connor to a room on the nineteenth floor of the Commodore. The detectives then stood quietly by, waiting for O'Connor's friends to appear. Yesterday they did so.

At 3:30 in the afternoon the men on watch reported to Oliver that three men and a woman had gone into the room. O'Connor was out—a detective just behind him—but he returned a few minutes later. Waiting only until he had entered the room, the Lieutenant gave the order and he and Ryan opened the door. They rushed in, pistols in their hands. The five jumped up from their chairs, disclosing the jewels on a chamois bag set on the table.

Two of the occupants moved quickly. One of them—a man—stepped to the open window and appeared to

Continued on Page Nineteen.

BUYER OF LIQUOR COMMITS NO CRIME, THE SUPREME COURT RULES IN TEST CASE; MODIFIED JONES LAW REPORTED TO HOUSE

TO DEFINE PETTY OFFENSES

Sale of One Gallon or Less Would Be Called Minor Violation.

JURYLESS TRIALS ENDORSED

But Bill Approved Gives Accused Right to Appeal From Ruling of Commissioner.

WICKERSHAM IDEA IS BASIS

Hoover's Enforcement Program Progresses—La Guardia Opens Fight on Measures.

Special to The New York Times.

WASHINGTON, May 26.—After wrangling since November with its part of President Hoover's prohibition enforcement program, the House Judiciary Committee today reported favorably on a bill modifying the Jones law so as to define minor violations of the dry act, and another providing for the trial of alleged minor violators before United States Commissioners.

These bills are to be added to those providing for seventeen new judges throughout the country and another strengthening the "padlock" law, in making up the House Judiciary's own program for prohibition enforcement.

The committee adopted the original Stobbs bill as the instrument for modifying the Jones law. This provides that sale, manufacture or transportation of liquor in amounts of not more than one gallon, by a person not a habitual violator, shall be considered a minor violation and punishable by fine or a jail sentence of not more than six months or both.

Mitchell Urged Christopherson Bills.

Under another of the measures reported today, known as the Christopherson bill, prosecution of petty offenders defined under the Jones law modification would be by complaint or information before United States Commissioners, who would make a report of the pleas to the district court and a "recommendation" of finding and sentence. The bill would allow the accused to take exception to the commissioner's report and demand trial by jury.

Another Christopherson bill reported provides for a general definition of misdemeanors for the entire criminal code.

This program came from the Judiciary Committee only after Attorney General Mitchell had again urged these particular measures. The committee attempted to have George W. Wickersham, chairman of President Hoover's law enforcement commission, appear again to explain, if not to modify, the things he had proposed.

After a short conference with Attorney General Mitchell and certain "dry" or "conservative" members of the Judiciary body, however, Mr. Wickersham chose not to appear and instead submitted, through Attorney General Mitchell, a communication to the committee, urging a favorable report on the three bills.

La Guardia Deplores Juryless Trials.

Representative La Guardia of New York attacked the whole program. He declared it to be an attempt to do "something to satisfy the clamor of the drys," and predicted that it would not work.

"The mountain labored and brought forth a mouse," Representative La Guardia declared.

"In a desperate attempt to do something, an entire new system

Continued on Page Two.

Alfred E. Smith Is Appointed a Member Of Palisades Interstate Park Commission

Special to The New York Times.

ALBANY, May 26.—Acting Governor Lehman tonight announced the appointment of former Governor Alfred E. Smith as a member of the Palisades Interstate Park Commission, to fill the vacancy caused by the death of Edward L. Partridge.

"It is particularly gratifying that Governor Smith should unselfishly consent to give further of his time on this park board," Mr. Lehman said.

"Because of its adjacency to the great metropolitan area, the needs of which he so thoroughly understands, and because during his incumbency as Governor he contributed so immeasurably to the development of the park and recreational facilities of the State, I am confident that he will lend a further great and lasting contribution in the development of this project that enables so many residents of the States of New York and New Jersey to enjoy the great outdoors as a matter of health as well as pleasure.

"Governor Larson has assured me that the appointment of Governor Smith will be pleasing to the residents of the State of New Jersey, who join with the people of New York State in supporting this park system by contributions and gifts."

First Speakeasy Conviction Here Under Nuisance Law

For the first time in New York County a defendant in a prohibition case was convicted yesterday for violating the State law relating to the maintenance of a nuisance, a statute that Maurice Campbell, Prohibition Administrator, has often called upon the District Attorney to enforce.

The defendant was Bert Roberts, waiter in a speakeasy at 230 West Forty-eighth Street, and tried before Justices Ellsworth J. Healy, Daniel Direnzo and A. V. B. Voorhees, who sentenced him to serve thirty days in the workhouse, with sentence suspended during good behavior. A bench warrant was issued for William Myers, also a defendant in the case, who forfeited his bond of $500 by not appearing in court.

Harry Newman, prohibition agent, the complainant, testified that on March 30 he bought seven drinks of whisky at 75 cents each in the speakeasy after Roberts had admitted him. F. C. Hanford, counsel for Major Campbell said he considered the case one of extreme importance. William Barnes was convicted on a similar charge last July in Mineola, Nassau County, and Harry Berger in Brooklyn, Kings County, a year ago.

SEATTLE DRY CHIEF AND AIDES INDICTED

Grand Jury Charges Conspiracy to Violate Dry Law, Tariff and Revenue Acts.

FOLLOWS ATTACK ON JONES

They Had Charge of Enforcement in Oregon, Washington, Idaho and Montana.

Special to The New York Times.

SEATTLE, Wash., May 26.—The Federal grand jury investigating charges of corruption and bribery in the prohibition unit here returned an indictment this afternoon against Roy C. Lyle, prohibition administrator for Oregon, Washington, Idaho, Montana and Alaska.

Others indicted included William M. Whitney, Mr. Lyle's assistant and legal adviser; Earl Corwin, a prohibition agent; M. L. Fryant, a deputy sheriff who won notoriety as a wire tapper in the famous Olmsted "whispering wires" case; C. T. McKinney, a dynamic young lawyer from Kentucky who led in the prosecution of the Olmsted liquor gang and who has been a favorite speaker before W. C. T. U. gatherings.

Mr. Whitney was charged with "conspiracy to accept a bribe" on one count, and Mr. Lyle, Mr. Whitney and Mr. Corwin were each charged with conspiracy to violate the national prohibition act, the tariff act and the internal revenue act on other counts.

Mr. Lyle and Mr. Whitney surrendered at United States Marshal B. Benn's office an hour after the indictments were returned.

Mr. Lyle was released on his personal recognizance and Mr. Whitney on $5,000 bail. Mr. Corwin arranged for $2,500 bond.

Lyle and Whitney Silent.

Neither Mr. Lyle nor Mr. Whitney would comment tonight on the action of the grand jury. Lyle apparently was surprised by his indictment, but was smiling and showed little concern. Whitney, however, appeared wan and haggard, and carried his arm in a sling as a result of injuries suffered in a recent liquor raid.

"We have nothing to say," Mr. Whitney said. "We will meet the issue at the proper time. We have repeatedly sought admission to the jury room, but it was denied us, so we had no opportunity of laying our side of it before the jury."

Twice today Mr. Whitney sent one of the agents, Leonard Reagan, to the Federal Building with letters supposedly asking that he be permitted to testify, one being delivered to the grand jury foreman, and the second to United States District Attorney Savage after the first had failed to get any result.

Olmstead Aided Prosecutor.

The indictments followed ten days investigation by the grand jury of charges brought by Federal Secret Service operatives, and other witnesses, of purported corruption in the prohibition unit. Mr. Whitney was pictured by these witnesses as the "master mind" of one of the most gigantic rum running conspiracies in the country. The ring's activities were at their height from 1925 to 1928, it was asserted.

Roy Olmstead, so-called "king of the rum-runners," and Chris Curtis, his Gray's Harbor contemporary, were declared to have been mere

Continued on Page Two.

GOVERNMENT LOSES APPEAL

Volstead Act Purposely Ignored the Purchaser, the Opinion States.

UPHOLDS COURT IN BOSTON

But in a New York Case It Declines to Make a Ruling on a Technicality.

PERMIT RULE HELD ILLEGAL

Right Is Denied Treasury to Revoke Industrial Privilege Except for Violation.

Special to The New York Times.

WASHINGTON, May 26.—Purchasers of intoxicating liquor are not guilty of violating the prohibition law, the Supreme Court unanimously decided today, in an opinion handed down by Justice Sutherland.

The opinion, rendered in the case of the government against James E. Farrar of Massachusetts, was regarded of extreme importance, in view of the many attempts now being made to find the buyer equally guilty with the seller.

Taking the ground that Congress had deliberately and designedly omitted to impose any criminal liability upon the purchaser, and that during all the ten years' life of national prohibition the government had never tried to punish the purchaser until now, the Supreme Court upheld the District Court of Massachusetts, which had quashed an indictment against Farrar.

Norris Issue Sidestepped.

In another celebrated case involving the punishment of a purchaser the court, in another unanimous opinion handed down by Mr. Sutherland, declined to rule on the main issue and merely decided that Alfred E. Norris, a New York investment banker, must pay a fine of $200, presumably because he took the wrong legal procedure.

Mr. Norris had bought whisky from Joel D. Kerper of Philadelphia, since convicted as a bootlegger, whereupon the government sought to establish a conspiracy case because the transaction occurred across State borders.

The Supreme Court, however, refused to express itself on the conspiracy issue and sustained the fine on the ground that the plea of nolo contendere was equal to a confession of guilt.

The charge against Farrar was that on Sept. 28, 1929, he "unlawfully and knowingly" purchased liquor from Frank Rotondo in Cambridge. The indictment was quashed by a Federal district court in Massachusetts on the ground that "the ordinary purchaser of intoxicating liquor does not come within the purview of the act."

Opinion in the Farrar Case.

In his opinion in the Farrar case, Justice Sutherland said:

"By indictment returned in the Federal district court of Massachusetts the defendant (appellee) was charged with unlawfully and knowingly having purchased intoxicating liquor fit for use for beverage purpose in violation of the national prohibition act.

"The district court sustained a motion to quash the indictment on the ground that the ordinary purchaser of intoxicating liquor does not come within the purview of the act 38F (2d) 515.

"The government appealed under the criminal appeals act of March 2, 1907 (C2564, 34th Stat., 1246 U. S. C., Title 18, Sec. 682) and Section 238 of the Criminal Code, as amended by the act of Feb. 13, 1925 (C229, 43d Stat., 936, 938, U. S. C., Title 28, Sec. 345).

"Section 3 of the prohibition act (C8541, Stat. 305, 308) makes it unlawful for any person to 'manufacture, sell, barter, transport, import, export, deliver, furnish or possess any intoxicating liquor except as authorized in this act * * *'; but provides that 'liquor for non-beverage purposes and wine for sacramental purposes may be manufactured, purchased, sold * * * but only as herein provided, and the commissioner may, upon application, issue permits therefor * * *.'

Section 6 Covers Permits.

"Section 6 of the act (Stat. 310) provides: 'No one shall manufacture, sell, purchase, transport, or prescribe any liquor without first obtaining a permit from the commissioner so to do, except that a person may, without a permit, purchase and use liquor for medicinal purposes when pre-

Times Wide World Photo.

President Hoover greeted Admiral Byrd and the members of his expedition to the Antarctic on the White House lawn.

Times Wide World Photo.

President Hoover presenting a medal to Admiral Byrd.

Admiral Byrd in his Antarctic clothing.

"All the News That's Fit to Print."

The New York Times.

THE WEATHER
Mostly fair today and tomorrow; little change in temperature.
Temperatures Yesterday—Max. 83, min. 67.
U. S. Weather Forecast—For details see Page 31.

Copyright, 1930, by The New York Times Company.

VOL. LXXIX....No. 26,445. **** NEW YORK, FRIDAY, JUNE 20, 1930. TWO CENTS In Greater New York | THREE CENTS Within 200 Miles | FOUR CENTS Elsewhere Except 7th and 8th Postal Zones

BYRD AND HIS MEN ACCLAIMED BY CITY; WILDLY CHEERED IN BROADWAY PARADE; WALKER BESTOWS MEDALS OF MERIT

MOVE FOR REPRISALS IN FRENCH CHAMBER IF OUR DUTIES STAND

Deputies Favor Ending Most-Favored-Nation Treatment Unless We Heed Protest.

UNANIMOUS BACKING LIKELY

Even Leaders Most Eager to Hold Our Friendship See Drastic Move Justified.

PLEA TO HOOVER EXPECTED

Our State Department Declines to Comment Pending Receipt of Official Representations.

By P. J. PHILIP.

Special Cable to THE NEW YORK TIMES.

PARIS, June 19.—Suppression of most-favored-nation treatment for the United States and wholesale discrimination against American imports into France was urged today on the French Government by the tariff committee of the Chamber of Deputies in the event that all efforts should fail to obtain reductions in the new American import duties on French goods.

The committee met in the morning at the same time that the French Minister of Commerce, Pierre Etienne Flandin, was laying before the Cabinet his report on the effect the Hawley-Smoot act will have on French commerce with the United States. The results of the committee's deliberations were set forth in the following communiqué:

Committee's Statement.

The Committee on Customs of the Chamber, after having attentively examined the consequences of the increase in customs duties decided upon by the United States, notes with regret:

First, that the new American tariffs, imposed on the most active branches of production, will appreciably reduce French exports to this great, friendly country.

Second, that they will seriously aggravate the difficulties which generalized economic nationalism places on international exchange.

Third, that because of the injury done to their commercial balance, those countries which have debts to pay to the United States will incur great risk to the exchange value of their national money.

The committee deems it necessary that the French duties on American goods should be adapted to the same régime as is imposed on French exports to the United States. The committee urges that the government make immediate representations to the President of the United States to obtain such decreases in the American tariffs as may be necessary for the maintenance of French exports.

In the event this intervention fails to yield results, the tariff committee would insist upon the suppression of the clause according most-favored-nation treatment to the United States, believing it illogical to accord beneficial treatment to that country without obtaining any compensation through reciprocal concessions such as are accorded by other nations.

Stand Causes a Stir.

This pronouncement by the tariff committee produced a considerable stir in the Chamber today. It was regarded, however, with general approval. Even those Frenchmen who are most anxious for a continuance of friendly relations with the United States are unwilling to accept any longer a situation in which, they say, the United States lays claim to every commercial advantage and accords none.

All the countries with which France deals, it was pointed out, accord in exchange for most-favored-nation treatment certain specific advantages to certain French products. The recent commercial treaty with Germany was cited, and it was pointed out that immediately on the signing of this treaty the United States demanded equal privileges with Germany.

It is not expected that the United States will depart from its traditional tariff policy, but the recommendation of the tariff committee to the French Government that the highest instead of the lowest scale of French tariffs be imposed on American goods if no concessions are obtained is likely to have almost unanimous support. The legal position, however, will have to be examined by the government, which is expected to act with due deliberation. Undoubtedly, however, official representations to President Hoover will be made within the next few days.

Criticize Embassy Statement.

The Paris press today devotes its attention to the American Embassy's defense of the new law. While the figures in the embassy statement are not challenged, the statement itself is criticized in some quarters for

Continued on Page Seven.

New Manhattan Phone Books Include 285,000 Changes

Delivery of 1,715,000 copies, or about 350 truckloads, of the Summer issue of the Manhattan telephone directory is under way, and 750,000 copies will be in the hands of Manhattan subscribers by tomorrow, the New York Telephone Company announced yesterday.

The new directory contains more than 285,000 changes in names, addresses and telephone numbers. The book comprises approximately 460,000 listings, and includes three new exchanges: Andrews for a part of the financial district, Tompkins Square in the Fourteenth Street district and Tillinghast for a part of Harlem.

BANK RATE TO 2½%; STOCKS RISE AGAIN

New York Reserve Makes Rediscount Charge Lowest in System's History.

MARKET UP 3 TO 15 POINTS

Reactionary Influences Shaken Off After Steady Decline of Three Weeks.

The lowest rediscount rate in the history of the Federal Reserve System was established yesterday by the Federal Reserve Bank of New York when the directors voted to reduce the charge for member bank borrowings to 2½ per cent.

The announcement of the new rate was not made until after the close of the stock market, but in the meantime stocks had made a broad and vigorous rally, shaking off reactionary influences after an uninterrupted decline of three weeks. Stocks that had declined daily from 3 to 15 points went up suddenly, canceling all losses recorded in Wednesday's sweeping break, with a small margin to spare. The market's abrupt about-turn was ascribed in Wall Street, in the absence of a better explanation, to internal technical conditions. Brokers' loans decreased $211,000,000 in the last week, yesterday's report disclosed.

The new rediscount rate, which will go into effect this morning, will replace a charge of 3 per cent established on May 1 when the Bank of England and the Bank of France lowered their rates to 2 per cent and 2½ per cent respectively. The local Reserve Bank now shares with the Bank of France the distinction of having the lowest discount rate in the world. It is a distinction that banks expect to be short-lived, however, for further reductions in rates of leading European central banks are regarded as certain to follow yesterday's action here.

The cut took Wall Street by surprise. Such an action had been discussed a few weeks ago, when open market rates for bankers' bills dropped below 2½ per cent. As the reduction was not made then it was assumed that the banking authorities did not intend to send the rate below the previous low mark.

In the meantime, bill rates had fallen to an asking price of 2⅛ per cent. Following the announcement of the bank rate reduction a further slash was made effective in bill rates, making the open market quotations 2⅛ per cent bid, 2 per cent asked, for all maturities up to 90 days; 2¼ bid, 2⅛ asked for four months' bills, and 2⅜ bid, 2¼ asked for five and six months' paper.

Bill Rates Lowest in Six Years.

These rates are the lowest in six years and offer American business the opportunity to finance its projects at a cost that has been available only at rare intervals.

The reduction of the rediscount rate in New York to 2½ per cent, as in the five previous reductions that carried down the charge from 6 per cent last Fall, was primarily to stimulate business and the bond market, in the understanding of the financial community. But leading bankers said the depressed state of business was already sufficiently well known and had been rather overemphasized than minimized lately. The cut, they said, was amply justified by open market rates for credit and should ultimately have a salutary effect in stimulating trade.

Bankers have for some time held that a strong bond market was the first prerequisite of business improvement. Cheap money, they contend, offers the most powerful stimulant to the bond market available. The New York Reserve Bank's action gives assurance, it is said, that the low price of credit is to continue. Banks, faced with the difficulty of profitably employing their funds elsewhere, must ultimately turn to the bond market for an outlet.

The action was, in a measure, foreshadowed by a reduction from 2¼ to 2⅛ per cent in the rate at which the local Reserve Bank would purchase bankers' acceptances, announced earlier in the week.

One early result of the reduction

Continued on Page Nineteen.

BROOKLYN MAN SHOT IN AUTO AS POLICE HUNT QUEENS SLAYER

Insurance Man Badly Wounded by "Wild-Eyed" Assailant at His Carroll Street Home.

GUNMAN ELUDES SEARCHERS

New Note in Killings, in Writing of Supposed Murderer, Lists Seven for Death.

KILLING RUMOR STIRS BRONX

But Search There Reveals No Body —Several Suspects Freed, Asylum Clues Fail.

While the police were searching Queens and Nassau Counties last night for the mysterious slayer of two men, Morris Horwitz, 50 years old, an insurance man, was shot and seriously wounded by "a wild-eyed, crazy-looking man," as he sat in his sedan in front of his home at 1,267 Carroll Street, Brooklyn, at 10:30 o'clock last night, talking to his wife, who was seated on the porch.

The gunman escaped on the run, disappearing into an automobile driveway between Brooklyn Avenue and Kingston Avenue. Although a strong police guard was thrown around the district, efforts by armed searchers with powerful flashlights failed to discover him.

Horwitz was taken to the Crown Heights Hospital, Lefferts and Brooklyn Avenues, suffering from a gash in the forehead, inflicted by the gunman with the butt of his pistol, and from a bullet which entered his shoulder, penetrated a lung and lodged in his abdomen.

Able to Give Description.

During an interval of consciousness at the hospital Horwitz, who is president of the Municipal Underwriters, Inc., an insurance firm at 26 Court Street, Brooklyn, and also has an insurance office of his own at 186 Joralemon Street, Brooklyn, gave Detectives Edward McNamee and William Riley of the Empire Boulevard station a description of his assailant. He said the man was about 5 feet 4 inches tall, weighed about 130 pounds, wore a dark suit but no hat, had blond hair and was "wild-eyed, as if he were crazy."

Horwitz was leaning out of the right front seat window of his machine, chatting with his wife, Rose, when the man approached. Without warning, he flourished a pistol, and said, "Move over to the steering wheel and start the car and keep going. If you don't, I'll shoot you."

The thug then entered the car and took a front seat beside Mr. Horwitz. Apparently dissatisfied at the slow actions of the insurance man, the stranger struck him on the forehead, then placed the barrel of the pistol against his victim's shoulder and fired.

Second Shot Goes Wild.

While Mrs. Horwitz screamed, the man fled, firing a second shot, which went wild. He ran east on Carroll Street to Brooklyn Avenue, turned north and ran half a block to one of the dark alleys leading to the garages in the rear yards of the neighboring houses and disappeared.

Two acquaintances of the wounded man, Al Zalb, a real estate man, and his brother, Leon, a glassware salesman, both of 377 Montgomery Street, approached in their car as the gunman fired his second shot.

They pursued on foot, but lost the trail at the alley entrance. Then they ran back to the wounded man and rushed him to the hospital.

Horwitz's son, George, 10 years old, was asleep in his bedroom on an upper floor of the three-story house in which they live. A son, Benjamin, 25 years old, a lawyer, and a daughter, Ruth, 14 years old, were away from home at the time of the shooting.

Late last night, while the police were still searching the neighborhood, officials said they had not found any clues to connect the gunman with the supposed madman who is being sought in Queens and Nassau Counties as the slayer of two men in somewhat similar circumstances.

A police alarm brought Deputy Chief Inspector Vincent J. Sweeney, in charge of the Brooklyn detective division, and a score of detectives as well as uniformed policemen and the police emergency squad, from the Empire Boulevard station.

The police sought to get into communication with the wounded man's business partner, Benjamin Herman, to see if he could give any information on whether or not Horwitz had any enemies. They did not know Herman's home address but obtained his telephone number. They were unable, however, to reach him.

New Murder Note Received.

Another letter containing a cabalistic list of seven persons marked for death, in the handwriting of the man who says he murdered two men

Continued on Page Eight.

Lindbergh Congratulates Byrd By Phone, Meets Him Monday

While Rear Admiral Byrd was telling the story of the expedition in an interview with newspaper men at the Biltmore yesterday afternoon an aide whispered to him: "Colonel Lindbergh is on the wire.

Admiral Byrd went to an adjoining room to talk to the flier. It was announced later that Colonel Lindbergh had congratulated Admiral Byrd on the success of his expedition and his scientific achievements. He made an appointment for a private meeting at the Biltmore at 11 o'clock Monday morning.

SAYS G. O. P. GAVE FUNDS CANNON USED

Caraway Tells Senate He Thinks That Jameson Passed on the National Committee's Money.

DEFENDS BISHOP'S RELEASE

Reports of Concessions "Lies," He Declares—Presentation of Report Closes Incident.

Special to the New York Times.

WASHINGTON, June 19.—Chairman Caraway of the lobby committee, in presenting to the Senate today a committee resolution on the case of Bishop James Cannon Jr., said that he thought that when E. C. Jameson, New York insurance man, gave to the Church leader $65,300 to fight the Presidential candidacy of Alfred E. Smith in Virginia, and an almost equal sum to other organizations, "he was passing out the money of the National Republican Committee."

"I may be mistaken," Senator Caraway said, but he emphasized his belief.

The Senator denied any special concessions had been given to Bishop Cannon, who was relieved from testifying about his financial and political affairs when he protested they were no concern of the committee and refused to answer questions. Such reports, the Senator declared, were "lies," adding that "there have been more assertions made that arose from utter ignorance of what did not occur or were prompted by malicious lying than about any other incident I know of."

"It is intimated," said the Senator, "and I am not defending it, or making the charge; I say that it was made in insinuation, at least on the floor of the House, that Bishop Cannon misappropriated the funds. That may be true, but we are not a grand jury. We uncovered several things that we did not pursue."

The reference of the intimations was to a recent speech of Representative Tinkham, who, on the floor of the House, attacked Bishop Cannon.

Walsh's Stand Is Set Forth.

The resolution as adopted at an executive session of the five lobby committee members, was reported as follows:

> Resolved, that it is the sense of the committee that it should not insist upon answers to questions propounded to Bishop James Cannon Jr. Senator Walsh of Montana dissents to this order only because of doubt raised as to the authority of the committee under the resolution pursuant to which it is acting.

Accompanying this resolution was the transcript of the Bishop's testimony, including the questions he declined to answer.

Presentation of the report was believed at the Capitol to have officially closed the incident. Vice President Curtis told newspaper men that he did not intend to present the case to the District Attorney for possible contempt action, adding that if Senator Blaine of Wisconsin, carries out

Continued on Page Seventeen.

50,000 AT CITY HALL FETE

Mayor Lauds Explorer as a Humanitarian and Leader of Men.

N. Y. U. DEGREE CONFERRED

Admiral Dons Cap and Gown—Dr. Brown Cites Him as Poet, Scientist, Man of Learning.

LEADER VOICES GRATITUDE

Acknowledges Roar of Throng as Family Looks On—Salutes Richmond Blues Battalion.

As an old hero whom New York takes repeated pleasure in welcoming because his charm and exploits remain forever new, Rear Admiral Richard E. Byrd was greeted by Mayor Walker at City Hall yesterday in what was the climax of the city's reception program.

About 10,000 persons in the grandstands and in and about City Hall, with another 40,000 in the immediate vicinity, joined in this tribute to the explorer. The platform from which the Mayor extended the welcome in behalf of the people of the city was crowded with distinguished guests, while the entire scene was one of bright color joyous music and warm sentiment, marked repeatedly by tumultuous applause of the spectators and their cheers.

Paying due regard to Admiral Byrd's scientific achievements, it was as a humanitarian, as a great leader of men, as an inspiring example to the youth of the land that the Mayor welcomed the explorer and bestowed the city's medal of merit.

Standing calm and erect before the crowd in his immaculate white uniform, with his face tanned from his sojourn in the Canal Zone en route from the Antarctic, Admiral Byrd heard himself extolled by the Mayor as the man who had brought the North and South Poles together and as one who, by his courage, devotion to his calling and determination to grasp the secrets of the universe, had added glory to his country and enhanced the scope of human knowledge.

Mother and Wife Present.

Proudest of all in the audience which witnessed this eulogy were Mrs. Eleanor Bolling Byrd, the Admiral's mother, and his wife, who, each carrying a bouquet of flowers, stood with faces glowing a short distance from the spot at which the Mayor spoke.

No less proud was a group of Virginians headed by Governor Pollard, who had come to New York to participate in the welcome. They, too, occupied places close to the Mayor.

The first to greet Admiral Byrd on his arrival at City Hall, however, was his son, Richard E. Byrd Jr., and his daughters, Evelyn Bolling Byrd and Katherine Byrd. They were among the early arrivals and were taken to the Mayor's reception room to await the arrival of their father. Here they met the children of Joseph V. McKee, President of the Board of Aldermen, who with Mrs. McKee, were among the guests on the reviewing stand.

With "sincere and very deep gratitude" Admiral Byrd accepted the

Continued on Page Two.

Kingsford-Smith Plans to Refuel in the Air, Allowing Flight Here Against Strong Winds

Wireless to THE NEW YORK TIMES.

BALDONNEL AIRDROME, DUBLIN, June 19.—In order to avoid a possible fuel shortage on his westward transatlantic flight, which was again delayed today by strong westerly winds, Major Charles Kingsford-Smith intends refueling in the air off the American coast, if the necessary preparations are completed in time.

"I had provided for a start only when the adverse winds over the Atlantic averaged less than fifteen miles an hour," said Major Kingsford-Smith. "With any greater wind I should not have enough fuel to reach my destination. By refueling in the air, however, I could start against a headwind averaging as much as twenty miles an hour. Assuming we have to meet such conditions, the petrol would last to within a few hundred miles of Maine, then we could take on more fuel in the air."

To carry out the refueling operation the wireless operator will be provided with a hammer and chisel to punch a hole in the top of the main tank for the insertion of a fuel line.

"My great hope is that preparations can be made in America in time to permit refueling in the air," said the Major, "because in that case the chance of getting away without further delay will be enormously improved."

Officers of the Irish Free State Air Force learned with interest today of the report that former Squadron Leader Wynne-Eyton is contemplating using Baldonnel as the starting point for a solo flight across the Atlantic in a "Puss" Moth plane, but nothing more is known here beyond the indirect news from London.

Representatives here of the Fokker Company, builders of the Southern Cross, and other American representatives of Major Kingsford-Smith, said yesterday that no arrangements for refueling over the ocean had been made. The difficulties of such a plan were pointed out, and pilots here said that, though not impossible, it lacked all probabilities of success.

"It is hard enough to make the contacts over an airport, to say nothing of finding a plane moving at 80 or 100 miles an hour over the open ocean," one pilot said.

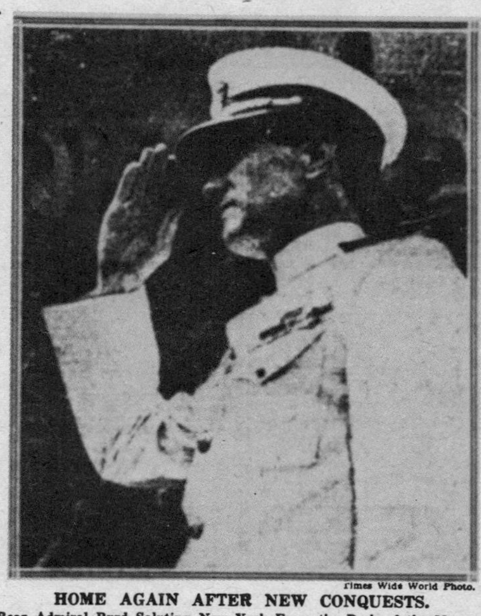

Times Wide World Photo.

HOME AGAIN AFTER NEW CONQUESTS.
Rear Admiral Byrd Saluting New York From the Deck of the Macom.

BYRD IS PROUDEST OF ADVANCING FLAG

In Summing Up Achievements He Puts First the Claiming of Vast New Land.

TELLS SCIENTIFIC FINDINGS

Reveals That 12 of His Men Offered to Stay in Antarctic to Found Weather Station.

As objectively as an outsider, Rear Admiral Richard E. Byrd summed up yesterday the accomplishments and scientific discoveries of the expedition into Antarctica.

The outstanding achievements, to his mind, were the claiming of new land and mountain ranges of more than 125,000 square miles for the United States, and the discovery of carbonaceous material in the Queen Maud Mountains, including the probability of vast deposits of coal and possibly metals. He admitted, however, that these have no immediate value.

Aboard the City of New York, as he discussed the expedition informally while waiting until it was time to dress for the reception committee, the Admiral seemed, at first glance, the same slim and youthful figure. Closer inspection, however, belies the youthful appearance. There are lines of responsibility and worry in the returning Admiral's face today and threads of gray in the dark hair.

On the way up the bay, all informality was gone and he was the naval officer in crisp white uniform taking command of that monstrosity, a mass interview. Again in the afternoon at the Biltmore he submitted to the questioning of newspaper men, and again took command of the interview, steering into the channels he desired.

"A Matter of Providence."

It was the accomplishments of his associates about which he told, and it was the safe return of every man of which he was "glad above all else." Here, too, he declined the honors and said it was "a matter of Providence," although it was "surprising the number of dangerous situations which passed without mishap." This was his story:

"In the field of geology we investigated one of the most important points, geologically speaking, left in the world, the Queen Maud Mountains, about 300 miles from the South Pole. We sent out a dog sled party under Dr. [Lawrence] Gould. They discovered carbonaceous material at 5,000 feet and other material which proved that Antarctica was once tropical or semi-tropical. We investigated the newly discovered Rockefeller Mountains and found them to be granite and some of the oldest in the world.

"In meteorology two men from the United States Weather Bureau, [William C.] Haines and [Henry T.] Harrison, took thousands of observations at temperatures of 60 and 70 below zero. These balloon runs continued all Winter. These are important because this climate affects the

Continued on Page Three.

5 MILES OF CROWDS CHEER EXPLORERS

Half Million Along Parade Route Send Up Din That Dazes Antarctic Veterans.

30,000 MASS AT BATTERY

Many Perch on Ledges of Office Windows—Elevated Station Used as Grandstand.

It was from the packed and sizzling sidewalks of New York that Admiral Byrd and his companions received the ovation yesterday which told them better than could the speeches of the dignitaries of the admiration of the city for their accomplishments and its joy at their safe return.

The acclaim poured out spontaneously from the throats of more than a half-million persons who lined the five-mile route over which they passed through the city. It had been matched only by the welcome to Colonel Lindbergh three years ago on his triumphant return from Paris.

Yesterday's reception was one in which all New York took part. Those who gave it ranged from the Mayor and other high officials to prisoners in the Tombs, who waved and shouted through the barred windows as Byrd sped by, and were rewarded with a cheery wave of the explorer's hand in return.

30,000 at the Battery.

Hours before the landing of Admiral Byrd and his companions the people of the city were getting ready to greet him. Long before noon the crowds were trooping to the Battery for a first glimpse of the polar heroes until some 30,000 finally had gathered there and in the streets leading to it.

The seawall was fringed with a dense mass and the windows and ledges of buildings looking down on the scene, from the Whitehall Building to the custom house, gradually became packed. The crowds had begun coming while the leaden sky showed a threat of rain, and they were still standing patiently when the clouds had melted and the sun was beating down.

The booming of a thirteen-gun salute on Governors Island was the signal which turned the reception from formality to an enthusiastic torrent of public acclaim. The eyes of the thousands along the Battery wall turned in the direction of the Statue of Liberty, and the first ticker-tape floated down from the Whitehall Building.

It was exactly 11:30 A. M. when the salute was fired. In front of the Whitehall Building waited 300 Boy Scouts in their khaki uniforms. They represented all boroughs of the city and five States, and were accompanied by a crack bugle and drum corps from Erie, Pa., home city of Scout Paul Siple, a member of the Byrd Expedition.

Vendors of peanuts and candy, flags, pictures of Rear Admiral Byrd, books describing his career and cigarette cases bearing his likeness,

Continued on Page Three.

HARBOR SHRIEKS WELCOME

Los Angeles Gleams in Sky as Craft Cluster About Polar Ships.

PAPER BLIZZARD LET LOOSE

Crowds Pack Route to City Hall —Admiral Shares Honors With His Aides.

BUSINESS MEN HAIL HIM

He Is Guest at Two Functions —Party to Be Received by Hoover Today.

A page of pictures of Rear Admiral Byrd's homecoming will be found on Page 5.

Rear Admiral Richard E. Byrd came home from the end of the earth yesterday and New York cheered him and honored him and took him to its heart as an old friend returning from new adventures and new conquests.

It was a homecoming that would have quickened the pulse of a Nelson or a Farragut, but he insisted on sharing it with the sunbronzed men who had braved the bleak silences of Antarctica with him while he was preparing for his flight to the South Pole and back.

Nearly two years he had been gone, but New York had not forgotten him. The city's millions remembered the day he rode up Broadway, hailed as the conqueror of the North Pole. They remembered his gallant transatlantic flight, which came so near a tragic end, and they lifted up their voices as they have for no man since Colonel Charles A. Lindbergh captured their imagination by his solo flight from Roosevelt Field to Paris three years ago.

In the wild cacophony of the welcome they accorded Admiral Byrd and his gallant band were blended joy at his return with every member of his expedition safe and well, admiration for his achievement, honor and respect, and, no doubt among the boys that lined his path, more than a little hero worship.

Glorious as was New York's attempt to erase the memory of the long, dreary days and nights in the limitless land of ice 17,000 miles away, it left Admiral Byrd and his followers tired out at the end of the day.

The Byrd party left the Pennsylvania Station on a special train at 2 o'clock this morning for Washington, where they will be received at the White House as the nation's heroes.

Whole Nation Hears Welcome.

Radio carried the speeches of Mayor Walker, Grover A. Whalen and other official greeters to all the country and to foreign lands as well in the greatest hook-up ever arranged for a returning hero's reception. It carried, too, the throaty voice of the city's "Hello," but it could not convey the color and the motion of the pageant on the water, in the air and on the sidewalks of New York.

For the crowds that hailed him Admiral Byrd had a message. He had claimed for his country and theirs, he said, unexplored lands east of the British possessions in Antarctica, rich in carboniferous deposits, indicative of "enormous quantities of coal." He had added 125,000 square miles to the map of the world and added considerably, with the help of the experts with him, to the total of the world's knowledge of biological, geological and meteorological conditions at the bottom of the earth.

From the moment he stepped off the deck of his flagship, the three-masted bark City of New York, to the deck of the city's welcoming tug Macom at Quarantine amid a deafening din of sirens and steam whistles of seventy-odd craft until the day was done, Admiral Byrd was swept along at the will of the crowd with his fellow-explorers excepting one. One man, too modest to face the crowd, remained on the ice-battered old veteran of the Antarctic and smilingly waved adieu as the Macom pulled away. He was George Black, supply officer of the expedition.

Reunions Forced to Wait.

For the rest, separated from their kinsfolk for many long months, reunions had to wait, although some there were aboard who were anxious to see for the first time children born since they started on their

Times Wide World Photos.

Rear Admiral Byrd escorted up Broadway, from the Battery to City Hall, as enthusiastic admirers line the streets.

The reception at City Hall. Admiral Byrd is responding to the warm welcoming speech by Mayor Walker.

The Admiral and his dog, Igloo.

Admiral Byrd and Mayor Walker on their way to the reception at the Advertising Club.

"All the News That's Fit to Print."

The New York Times.

Copyright, 1930, by The New York Times Company.

THE WEATHER
Possibly showers tonight or tomorrow; little change in temperature.
Temperatures yesterday Max. 93, min. 80.
U. S. Weather Forecast—For details see Page 42.

VOL. LXXIX....No. 26,492. ***** NEW YORK, WEDNESDAY, AUGUST 6, 1930. TWO CENTS in Greater New York | THREE CENTS Within 200 Miles | FOUR CENTS Elsewhere Except 7th and 8th Postal Zones

HOOVER TAKES UP DROUGHT RELIEF PLANS; SAYS HE WILL 'LEAVE NO STONE UNTURNED'; TWO DIE HERE AS RECORD HEAT PERSISTS

27 HURT IN RACE RIOT OF 400 PRISONERS ON WELFARE ISLAND

Bats, Chairs and Sharpened Sticks Wielded in Battle Over Use of Baseball Field.

LAUNCHES RUSH POLICE AID

Firemen Stand By With Hoses, but Fight Is Put Down Within 15 Minutes.

BRIDGE AUTOISTS LOOK ON

Patterson, Lauding Keepers, Says No Convicts Tried to Flee—Deputy Warden Slightly Hurt in Melee.

Four hundred white and Negro inmates of the Welfare Island Penitentiary clashed in a race riot on the penitentiary baseball field last night and with bats, sharpened sticks and a chair or two flying in the melée, twenty-seven men were injured, two of them seriously, during the fifteen minutes of conflict.

The battle was sharp while it lasted and was staged in full view of the motorists on the Queensboro Bridge and residents of the Sutton Place district directly across the East River. But with the prisoners intent on their strictly interracial fued, the keepers were able to restore order as soon as they had broken up these fights.

Four police emergency squads and three harbor division launches bearing their crews and police reserves from near-by precincts converged on the island soon after the alarm had been sounded over the new emergency telephone and they aided the keepers in getting the prisoners back into their cells.

No Efforts to Escape.

When it was over and only a few faint calls of derision echoed in the cell blocks, Richard C. Patterson Jr., Commissioner of Correction, announced that there had been no escapes and that there had not even been a single genuine effort to flee the penitentiary.

The battle, he insisted, was purely between the Negroes and the whites over the use of the baseball field and the keepers had the situation in hand when the police arrived. The Island fire squad were summoned when the riot broke out and hoses were rushed into the building for use on the prisoners if they proved balky when the drive to get them to their cells began. The water was not needed, Commissioner Patterson said.

All the twenty-seven injured, most of them suffering from stab wounds and bruises, were inmates, and Commissioner Patterson complimented his force on their handling of the outbreak. Some of the penitentiary force received a few minor hurts, and Deputy Warden Daniel F. Sheehan was knocked down in a scrimmage, but he was hurt only slightly.

The prisoners in the yard at the time were about evenly divided between whites and negroes, and among the white prisoners was former Borough President Maurice Connelly of Queens, who is serving a term for a conviction growing out of the sewer scandal in his borough. Connelly was not injured.

Trouble Brewing Several Days.

The trouble had been brewing for several days, Commissioner Patterson revealed and had centred upon the use of the baseball field at the northwest corner of the jail. It is a comparatively small sandy stretch of ground enclosed by a wire fence, barbed on top, almost under the shadow of the bridge.

The whites, it was said, contended that the Negroes were monopolizing the field and for the past two or three days there had been arguments. On Monday night the trouble became worse. One large Negro seemed to be in the forefront of the feud and a fight developed. A few more scuffles started; but the keepers rushed in and halted the trouble before it made headway.

Last night about 6 o'clock 400 of the 1,596 inmates were taking their regular recreation period when the racial feeling showed itself again. The Negroes, it was said, had the best part of the ball field and the whites objected. Under the stress of the heat, according to prison attachés, the men were at high tension. A blow touched off the rising antagonism.

Abruptly the entire yard became a shouting and angry mob with the large negro—his name was not learned—in the middle of the crowd. The inmates seized whatever object was nearest, a bat, a chair, a stone, and leaped into the fray. From nowhere appeared those unusual implements which inmates are always able to improvise, and sharpened sticks, capable of inflicting painful wounds, constituted the main supply of these.

The groups rushed at each other, howling, and in less than a minute the battle was in full swing with the baseball bats crashing left and right, the sharpened sticks thrashing about

Continued on Page Twelve.

French Mayor a Tourist 'Sight'; Put 10 P. M. Ban on the Radio

By The Associated Press.

VICHY, France, Aug. 5.—Victor Rivet, the "radio dictator," has become one of the sights of this resort region. Thousands of tourists have driven out from here fifteen miles to the hill town of Chateldon this Summer to have a look at M. Rivet, the Mayor who forbade the use of loud-speakers on radio outfits after 10 o'clock at night and before 7 in the morning.

For more than a year M. Rivet has enforced this rule in the interest, he says, of "peaceful sleep" in a town of 1,000 population. Some who opposed the curfew said the Mayor's views were in tune with the twelfth century buildings and towers that make the place picturesque, but the Mayor has quieted that criticism by the installation of machinery to make wooden shoes and the development of a spring which he says has radioactive properties.

Thus he saved one of the town's industries, as hand-made sabots are too expensive, and he offers the hope of eventual wealth and fame for the community as a health resort.

CITY LIKELY TO FIGHT PROPOSED LIGHT RATE

Mayor Will Decide on Course After Consulting Hilly and Utility Officials.

OPPOSED TO METER CHARGE

Maltbie to Begin Hearings Here Tuesday—Aldermen Shelve Motion Against Plan.

With the Public Service Commission's first hearing on the proposed new schedule of rates of the Edison and affiliated companies set for next Tuesday morning, Mayor Walker announced yesterday afternoon that New York City, as one of the largest consumers of electric current, would closely analyze the new schedule offered by the utility companies. He pointed out that the city always had opposed fixed service charges by the Brooklyn gas companies, and he added significantly that the city had won two of tho cases.

Mayor Walker would not commit himself more definitely as to the city's possible course in the matter because he expects to discuss the new schedule with Corporation Counsel Arthur J. W. Hilly when Mr. Hilly returns to the city on Friday. He also expects to confer with John J. Dietz, chairman of the Department of Water Supply, Gas and Electricity.

To See Utility Officials.

In addition, the Mayor will confer with officials of the utility companies and have them elucidate the new schedules for his benefit.

While indicating that the city would oppose the fixed charge of 60 cents a month for meters, Mayor Walker pointed out that the city, through Chairman John H. Delaney of the Board of Transportation, had arranged a contract with the New York Edison Company to supply electric energy for the new Eighth Avenue-Washington Heights subway at a price much lower than the city could undertake to furnish the same current. The contract negotiated by Chairman Delaney provided for 7.99 mills per kilowatt hour.

The city's contract for the Eighth Avenue subway covers a ten-year period, but may be canceled on sixty days' notice. It is estimated that the subways, in part operation, will require 64,405,000 kilowatt hours of energy, costing $514,595, the first year, and that the amount will increase annually to $6,000,000 by the tenth year.

Alderman John C. Hawkins, Republican, from Harlem, introduced a

Continued on Page Eleven.

SAYS GRUNDY GROUP MADE $50,000 OFFER TO SILENCE SCHALL

R. C. Stephens Tells Campaign Funds Body Manufacturer's Tried to Stop Attacks.

VOTING BY MINORS CHARGED

Witnesses Testify Students of Pennsylvania Teachers' College Got $2 Each for Illegal Ballots.

ELECTION BODY ASSAILED

Pittsburgh Man Calls It a "Racket" —Lawyer Says Judge Hid With Ballot Box.

Special to The New York Times.

WASHINGTON, Aug. 5.—Charges that Senator Thomas D. Schall of Minnesota had been offered $50,000 for use in his campaign for reelection, the money to come from funds contributed by the members of the Pennsylvania Manufacturers' Association, if he would cease his attacks on Senator Grundy of Pennsylvania over the tariff act, were made before the Senate Campaign Expenditures Committee here today.

This statement was made by Royal C. Stephens of Philadelphia, who was introduced to Senator Nye of North Dakota, chairman of the committee, through a letter from Senator Wagner of New York. Mr. Stephens told the committee that the story had come from Senator Schall himself, and after the hearing Senator Nye said that "certainly Senator Schall will be called." The witness had asked that each of the 2,700 members of the association tell of his political contributions.

While obviously not attaching much seriousness to the report without further verification, the chairman added that Senator Schall probably would be asked to reply through the filing of a brief with the committee.

Mr. Stephens was one of several witnesses who, through an eight-hour committee session, made charges against the election officials and political machines of Philadelphia, Pittsburgh and Harrisburg.

Students Are Accused.

The testimony included the statement by one witness that students at the West Chester State Teachers College in West Chester, Pa., had received $2 each to vote illegally in the Republican primary election on May 20. Other witnesses described how investigations had shown that ballots were destroyed or changed so as to make them illegal.

Thomas J. Walker of Philadelphia, member of the Committee of Seventy, declared that material was being gathered in preparation for demands that eighty-five election officials in Pennsylvania be arrested for election frauds.

C. C. McGovern, County Commissioner of Allegheny County, in which Pittsburgh is located, and who is in charge of the conduct of elections in the county, said:

"I think that in the matter of election frauds we are the peer of any other county in the State, including Philadelphia."

F. S. Wood, a manufacturer of West Chester, told the committee that he had evidence that tended to show a "conspiracy" through which Dr. Norman Cameron, principal of the school, and State Senator William H. Clark arranged to have students and minors vote in violation of the State laws.

Senate Race Little Discussed.

Most of the testimony had to do with the Gubernatorial campaign though some of it related to the Senatorial race in which Senator Grundy was defeated by James J.

Continued on Page Five.

Heat Locks Engine's Brakes On Way to North Bergen Fire

A fire engine responding to an alarm in North Bergen, N. J., yesterday came to a sudden halt as the result of the expansion of its brakes by the extreme heat. Despite their best efforts the firemen on the truck could not budge it.

By the time fire headquarters had been notified and another engine dispatched, the blazing dairy truck which had caused the alarm was destroyed and the flames had spread to the restaurant of John Lowski at 1,765 Bergen Turnpike, causing damage estimated at $1,500.

DAWES PLANS STUDY OF PREHISTORIC MAN

Ambassador Will Tour Dordogne Region of France and Areas of Spain in Research.

ONE OF LIFELONG HOBBIES

His Interest in Subject Was Aroused by Mounds Near His Boyhood Home.

By CHARLES A. SELDEN.
Special Cable to THE NEW YORK TIMES.

LONDON, Aug. 5.—Ambassador Dawes, who a year ago at this time was up to his eyes in the preliminary work for the naval conference, has enough leisure this Summer to devote a fortnight's holiday to one of his lifelong hobbies—archaeological research.

He will leave London on Aug. 22 for a trip to the Dordogne region in France and to areas in Spain where important neolithic research work is now in progress. His companions will be Professor George Grant MacCurdy of Yale University director of the American School of Prehistoric Research, and Addison L. Green, chairman of the board of trustees of that school.

Mr. Dawes's special interest in the matter is in coordinating the discoveries of the different scientific investigators in the different regions and in putting two and two together as a means of arriving more quickly and accurately at the true story of pre-historic man.

Interest Roused in Boyhood.

Why Mr. Dawes, himself a man of business and of national and international politics, is interested in such research may also be discovered by the simple process of putting two and two together. As a boy at Marietta, Ohio, one of his favorite playgrounds was at the pre-historic mounds in that neighborhood. There was also a family interest in these monuments because Mr. Dawes's great-great-grandfather, Manasseh Cutler, was the first man to make a survey of the mounds and to write a description of them. As a representative of old Revolutionary soldiers, he contracted with Congress for 1,500,000 acres of the public lands northwest of the Ohio as a settlement in the northwest territory. There is a tablet commemorating that event on the Subtreasury Building in Wall Street.

Mr. Dawes himself inherited the early pictures of the Marietta mounds which his ancestor drew and they gave him an interest in the mound builders that is still strong enough to send him to France and Spain on his present archaeological observations.

Wants Coordinated Study.

When asked at the embassy here today what he expected to find in Dordogne, the Ambassador said that so far as he was concerned the trip was merely one of observation in the company of high archaeological authorities.

"As to the expectations," he added, "the trouble with such investigations carried on with a preconceived theory, is that, whether or not it is justified, a feeling is created that the facts revealed have not been impartially weighed.

"I admit I am interested in the study of prehistoric man and his accomplishments in the Mediterranean region, and I feel the work now being done should be encouraged. In my judgment, what is now needed especially is the more detailed and coordinated study which will result from concurrent investigation in the different sections with a specific objective.

"For instance, there are in the museum of Candia, Crete, over 1,000 clay documents written in the script of an unknown language which Sir Arthur Evans, who has been conducting archaeological investigations in Crete since 1893, believes relate to the very beginnings of European civilization. A script differing in detail, but similar in its general nature, has been found in many other sections of the Mediterranean region.

Sees Stone Age Neglected.

"The great megalithic remains of the Maltese Islands of Niebla, in Spain, and of other Mediterranean sections, together with the evidence of the immense extent of prehistoric mining, all indicate we have underrated the age, intelligence and ac-

Continued on Page Five.

Choice of Smith to Nominate Roosevelt Corrects Oversight as to His Campaign Role

Supporters of Governor Roosevelt here were gratified yesterday to receive what they regarded as confirmation of the report that former Governor Alfred E. Smith would place the Governor in nomination at the Democratic State Convention in Syracuse on Sept. 29 and 30.

The selection of Mr. Smith to make the renomination speech was accepted by Democrats here as a happy solution of the difficulty the leaders of the Democratic organization fell into when they picked United States Senator Robert F. Wagner for temporary chairman of the convention to make the "keynote" speech and then realized that Mr. Smith apparently had been left out of the picture. Mr. Smith, it was reported, was somewhat hurt over what appeared to be an attempt to place him in the background and for a time did not expect to attend the convention.

Governor Roosevelt, who twice placed Mr. Smith in nomination for the Presidency, was reported to have been sincerely desirous all along of the support of Mr. Smith and found opportunity to suggest that Mr. Smith might take a leading rôle at the convention by making the nomination speech when he appointed Justice Bernard L. Shientag, a close friend of Mr. Smith, to the Supreme Court bench.

Knowledge that Governor Roosevelt desired him to make the nomination speech was conveyed to Mr. Smith at that time, and it was said to be assured now as the result of recent talks between Governor Roosevelt and his predecessor that Mr. Smith would accede to the Governor's request.

The support of the so-called Smith group in the Democratic party for for Governor Roosevelt has been assured, it was said, by the appointment of Justice Shientag and the Governor's request that Mr. Smith make the speech placing him in nomination.

Governor Roosevelt's plans call for the creation of a Roosevelt and Lehman campaign committee, as in 1928, since Lieut. Gov. Herbert H. Lehman is slated for renomination with him. James A. Farley, secretary of the Democratic State Committee, will be in charge of the organization end of the campaign as State chairman.

122,728,873 IS SET AS THE POPULATION OF UNITED STATES

Increase of 17,018,253 Since 1920 Is Largest Ever Made in a Decade.

14,772,688 IN POSSESSIONS

California, With 64.6% Rise, Tops All States—New York's Numerical Gain Largest.

MONTANA ALONE DECREASES

Result of Count Makes Probable a Change in House Reapportionments in 30 States.

By The Associated Press.

WASHINGTON, Aug. 5.—The population of Continental United States, on the basis of official preliminary census figures, is 122,728,837.

The country had the largest numerical increase in its history in the last ten years. The increase of 17,018,253 compares with a previous record increase for a ten-year period of 15,977,691, made between 1900 and 1910.

The increase was 16.1 per cent, as compared with 14.9 per cent from 1910 to 1920 and 21 per cent from 1900 to 1910.

Only one district in the United States—in Clearfield County, Pa.—was incomplete, but a preliminary estimate by the census supervisor placed its population at 1,319. The total figure for population is subject to revision in the bureau's official announcement, which is not expected for another week.

Territories of the United States and outlying possessions, not included in the continental United States, bring the nation's grand total of population to 137,501,561.

This figure includes an estimate for the Philippine islands, whose census is controlled by the insular government which has not made an enumeration for several years.

The continental United States had 105,710,620 people ten years ago, while the nation with its outlying possessions totaled 117,859,395.

California had the highest rate of growth of any State, but was exceeded by New York in numerical increase. California's rate of growth was 64.6 per cent and her numerical increase was 2,215,421. New York's rate was 21.4 per cent and her numerical increase was 2,224,328.

Florida made a 51.4 per cent growth, with a numerical gain of 497,499. New Jersey added 26.8 per cent, with a numerical gain of 846,668.

Montana was the only State to show a decrease, a 2.8 per cent loss, the numerical decline being 15,370.

In 1920 Arizona had the largest increase in population with 63.5 per cent gain, while Montana was second in line with an increase of 46 per cent.

New York, which for more than a century has been leader of all the States in population, triumphantly held her place in 1930, gaining more than the Census Bureau had expected. Nevada completed a half century in final place.

Means 30 Reapportionment Changes.

As a result of the count thirty States will be required to take legislative action to rearrange their Congressional districts before the election of November, 1932, to conform with the reapportionment of members of the House of Representatives. Twenty-six memberships are involved. Twenty States will lose members. Ten States will gain them.

The increases will probably be California, 9; Michigan, 4; New York, 2; Texas, 3; New Jersey and Ohio, 2 each; Connecticut, Florida, North Carolina and Washington, 1 each. The losses seem likely to be:

Missouri, 3; Georgia, Indiana, Iowa and Kentucky, 2 each; Minne-

Continued Page Fourteen.

Rains Restore Hope to Iowa and Illinois; 100,000,000 Bushels of Wheat to Feed Cattle

By The Associated Press.

CHICAGO, Aug. 5.—A famine of pasture lands and a dwindling crop of corn have combined, to put hogs and cattle of the Ohio and Mississippi Valleys on a wheat diet.

Scattering rains, heavy enough to be of some benefit in parts of the scorched plains, restored hope to grain and live-stock producers of Illinois and Iowa today, but elsewhere, for the most part, the blistering dry heat persisted.

With September wheat at 91⅜ to 91⅝, and September corn selling at 93½ to 93¾, farmers turned more and more to feed their wheat to stock. The Farmers National Grain Corporation estimated that 75,000,000 to 100,000,000 bushels of wheat would be fed this year, thus automatically relieving the overstocked wheat bins that have long weighed wheat prices down.

From the Kansas State Agricultural College came a statement that 25,000,000 to 30,000,000 bushels of hard Winter wheat alone was going to fatten stock, while an estimate from Indiana said 40 per cent of that State's wheat would go for feed. In Colorado wheat was left standing in the field.

Nebraska has suffered a 30 per cent cut in its corn crop prospects since the drought began. An official report today, however, said the subsoil is still in good condition generally and that a rain might bring a fair crop.

Ohio's loss from the drought was estimated at $200,000,000 to date, Missouri's at $100,000,000. Missouri corn has diminished from 50,000,000 to 60,000,000 bushels.

MACARTHUR NAMED CHIEF OF ARMY STAFF

Hoover Calls Him "Brilliant Soldier" and Only General Who Can Fill Full Term.

FULLER TO LEAD MARINES

Commandant Is Promoted by the President Over Smedley Butler and Others.

Special to The New York Times.

WASHINGTON, Aug. 5.—Major Gen. Douglas MacArthur, commanding the forces in the Philippines, was named Chief of Staff of the army with the rank of General by President Hoover today. He is the youngest of all the Major Generals, and also the youngest officer ever appointed Chief of Staff, the highest position in the army. General MacArthur will have but two superiors, the President and the Secretary of War. He succeeds General Charles P. Summerall.

The President also named Brig. Gen. B. H. Fuller as Major General Commandant of the Marine Corps, which post became vacant on the death of Major Gen. Wendell C. Neville. General Fuller was promoted over the heads of the Major Generals of the corps, the senior being Smedley D. Butler.

General MacArthur, who was born in Little Rock, Ark., was 50 years old on Jan. 26 and comes of one of the army's most distinguished families. His father was Lieut. Gen. Arthur MacArthur and a brother was the late Captain Arthur MacArthur of the navy.

General MacArthur was the first honor man of the West Point class of '03 and his army service has been varied and covered a wide field.

Was With Rainbow Division.

At Vera Cruz in 1914, General MacArthur, then a Captain, was an engineer officer, and on his return was promoted to Major. He was with the General Staff in Washington when the United States entered the World War and asked to be transferred to field duty. He was promoted to Colonel and ordered to France as Chief of Staff of the Rainbow Division.

He was promoted to Brigadier General, National Army, in June, 1918.

Continued on Page Three.

King George on Cutter Is Third at Cowes In His First Yacht Race Since His Illness

Wireless to THE NEW YORK TIMES.

COWES, Isle of Wight, Aug. 5.—For the first time since his illness King George took part in a yacht race when he boarded his racing cutter Britannia for the opening of the royal yacht squadron's racing today. There was hardly any wind, but there were constant showers, and the King wore yellow oilskins over his yachting suit. He was accompanied by Earl Jellicoe.

The Britannia in the second race for the 21-24-meter class was the first to get away, and the crowds lining the Cowes green cheered as she slipped past. The sloop Albury was in attendance upon the Britannia, and it was arranged that in the event of bad weather breaking the sloop would convey the King back to the royal yacht, which is the home of the King and Queen at the regatta.

The Britannia finished third, with the Westward first and the Astra second, and the King, while disappointed at the result, heartily enjoyed the day's racing, giving assistance to his crew. The fact that he was able to brave the blustery weather for several hours is regarded as evidence of his complete recovery.

When the Britannia came to her moorings the King disembarked and traveled by pinnace to the royal yacht, from which the Queen had watched the progress of the race through glasses.

The liner Duchess of Atholl passed near by en route to Montreal, with members of the English bar aboard going to the United States and Canada as guests of the American and Canadian Bar Associations. The decks were lined with delegates watching the Britannia's arrival at the moorings and the liner's captain dipped his flag in salute to the royal yacht.

MERCURY GOES TO 93 ON HOTTEST AUG. 5

Showers Likely Today, but No Let-Up in Heat Is Expected—14 Felled in Day.

BROOKLYN COURT CLOSES

Judge Refuses to Trust Case to "Heat Distracted Jury"—4 Drownings Reported.

A relentless sun drove the official thermometer to 93 here yesterday and broke the record for Aug. 5, which had endured since 1881. The average temperature yesterday, the fourth day of the latest heat wave, was 86 degrees, twelve above normal and the second highest of the Summer.

While the local forecaster could offer only the dubiously comforting prediction of possible showers this evening, with not much change in temperature, dispatches to The Associated Press from the Middle West brought the news of scattering rains which drove down temperature and alleviated the drought somewhat in that part of the country.

Crops Still in Peril.

The relief was not sufficient, however, to save the crops, which are still threatened with ruin unless heavier and more general rains sweep over the country. Meanwhile New Jersey was added to the list of States in which the absence of rain is threatening serious harm, particularly to dairy farmers and corn and tomato growers.

The casualty toll of the heat in and near New York yesterday was two dead and fourteen prostrated. Four deaths from drowning were also reported in the metropolitan area.

Not once during the night and early morning hours yesterday did the official thermometer go below 80, the figure recorded at 6 A. M. The high point of the day was registered at 6 P. M. At 4 o'clock the forty-nine-year-old record for the date of 91 had been passed.

The humidity was considerably less than on either Sunday or Monday, which helped to make the day somewhat more bearable in spite of the slightly higher temperature. From a high mark of 56 at 9 A. M. it gradually declined until at 7 P. M. it was only 25.

Temperature by Hours.

The hourly temperature chart follows:

Midnight	84	2 P.M.	89
1 A.M.	83	3 P.M.	89
2 A.M.	[illegible]	4 P.M.	[illegible]
3 A.M.	[illegible]	5 P.M.	[illegible]
4 A.M.	[illegible]	6 P.M.	93
5 A.M.	[illegible]	7 P.M.	92
6 A.M.	80	8 P.M.	90
7 A.M.	[illegible]	9 P.M.	88
8 A.M.	[illegible]	10 P.M.	86
9 A.M.	[illegible]	11 P.M.	*88
10 A.M.	[illegible]	Midnight	*88
11 A.M.	[illegible]	1 A.M.	*85
Noon	87	2 A.M.	*84
1 P.M.	[illegible]		

*Unofficial at Times Square.

Other communities reported even higher temperatures, with Baltimore leading with a mark of 104. Philadelphia experienced the hottest Aug. 5 of its history, with the mercury at 98. In Washington government departments closed at noon because of the great heat. District of Columbia health officials announced that twenty-four deaths had been caused there by the heat this Summer, eight in the last week.

On the other hand, the Central States reported comfortable weather for the first time in weeks. In Chicago the day's maximum temperature was 78, while through Iowa, Kansas and Nebraska temperatures

Continued on Page Two.

SITUATION IS UNDER SURVEY

President Says Report on Affected Areas Is Set for Monday.

MEASURES BEING CANVASSED

Railroads Are Asked to Consider Moving Feed and Stock to Alleviate Situation.

DRY WEATHER TO CONTINUE

No Prospects of General Rain in Afflicted States Are Seen by Forecasters.

Special to The New York Times.

WASHINGTON, Aug. 5.—Declaring in a statement issued at the White House today that "no stone will be left unturned by the Federal Government in giving assistance to local authorities engaged in relief measures in drought-stricken States, President Hoover took steps toward aiding the heat-blighted farm areas.

As reports continued to reach the President from Federal departments of actual and impending ruin to growing crops and suffering of live stock in various sections of the country with no relief in sight he said that information so far indicated a great variation in the effect of the drought, but that such measures of assistance as the Farm Board and other agencies could and should undertake were being determined on. In the meanwhile the eDpartment of Agriculture is making a detailed survey of the situation preparatory to making a report to the President next Monday.

The President's Statement.

The President in his statement said:

"The drought situation has been the subject of several conferences between Secretary Hyde, Chairman Legge and myself. The Department of Agriculture has undertaken a detailed survey of the situation. They will report next Monday upon the condition in each area in the country. The information so far indicates great variation in the effect of the drought, both as between States, between counties in those States, and even between farms in the same counties.

"There can be no doubt as to its most serious character in many localities and that unless relieved there will be real suffering. The maximum intensity seems to lie in a belt roughly following the Potomac, the Ohio and the Mississippi Rivers.

"The measures of assistance that the Farm Board and the other agencies of the Federal Government can and should undertake are being determined. It is evident already that large measures of feed movement to live stock in the drought areas or movement of animals out of the worst areas will need be undertaken later in the Fall.

"It is too early to determine the precise character of relief; much depends upon the further spread of the drought; but no stone will be left unturned by the Federal Government in giving assistance to local authorities. I have asked the railways to investigate the situation from a transportation point of view.

Lower Freight Rates Urged.

While the President did not indicate what specific relief measures are being considered, suggestions have been made to him looking to lower freight rates to move hay and feed into cattle-growing sections and the maximum extension of credit facilities to farmers in the arid regions. He also has been urged to consider spurring road construction work in those areas as a means of employment to the farmers whose source of income the weather is drying up.

Chairman Legge of the Farm Board has asked bankers and business men to extend credit facilities for feed for cattle and dairy herds on the basis of appeals which have come to him for aid.

To those who worked with Mr. Hoover in the national and international relief operations which contributed to his prominence, the statement that he had asked the railways to investigate the situation from a transportation view was taken as significant. The transportation of foodstuffs, animals and even people was a great factor in his success, and his disclosure that he is contemplating the possible movement of food and live stock to or from the stricken areas later in the Fall indicates that he may repeat his former exploits.

While the President was making known his concern over the situation

"All the News That's Fit to Print."

The New York Times.

Copyright, 1930, by The New York Times Company.

THE WEATHER
Showers and cooler today; tomorrow fair.
Temperatures yesterday—Max. 84, min. 70.
U. S. Weather Forecast—For details see Page 46.

VOL. LXXIX....No. 26,520 ****+ NEW YORK, WEDNESDAY, SEPTEMBER 3, 1930. TWO CENTS In Greater New York | THREE CENTS Within 200 Miles | FOUR CENTS Elsewhere Except 7th and 8th Postal Zones

COSTE DOES IT IN 37 HOURS, 18½ MINUTES! FIRST TO MAKE PARIS-NEW YORK FLIGHT; HOOVER, LINDBERGH AND BYRD HAIL FEAT

HEARST IS EXPELLED ON VISIT TO FRANCE FOR 'HOSTILE' ACTION

Government Says Move Was Taken Because of Use of Secret Naval Pact.

NOTE PUBLISHED IN 1928

Tardieu Reported to Have Fixed Ban Aug. 9 After American's Talk to German Press.

ORDER IS OBEYED QUICKLY

Paper Owner Asserts in London He Told French He Would "Save" Nation by Going at Once.

Wireless to THE NEW YORK TIMES.

LONDON, Sept. 2.—Somewhat of a sensation was caused in London today when it was learned that William Randolph Hearst, American newspaper proprietor, who arrived here last night from Paris, had been expelled from France because of the publication of the memorandum on the secret Anglo-French naval pact two years ago in Hearst newspapers.

Mr. Hearst arrived in Paris yesterday morning from the Italian lake district and went to the Hotel Crillon, where he received the expulsion order. He was told the French Cabinet had decided to expel him because his newspapers were "hostile" to France.

Not Molested Month Ago.

Yesterday was not the first time Mr. Hearst had returned to France since the episode of the secret document. He spent some days in Paris a month or so ago on the way to Germany and was not molested then.

When Mr. Hearst reached London last night he told no one here, not even his own representatives who met him at the station, of his expulsion and sudden departure from France. It was learned only this morning when a news agency telephoned to his hotel asking for a statement, after which the American publisher was bombarded by reporters and photographers.

Later today Mr. Hearst, who is remaining in London for a while before going to his 800-year-old castle in Glamorgan, South Wales, issued a statement to the press here in which he defended publication of the secret document because it informed the American people, even though it "upset some international applecarts."

Text of Hearst Statement.

Mr. Hearst's statement follows:

I have no complaint to make. The officials were extremely polite. They said I was an enemy of France and a danger in their midst. They made me feel quite important.

They said I could stay a little while longer if I desired; that they would take a chance on nothing disastrous happening to the republic.

But I told them I did not want to take the responsibility of endangering the great French nation; that America had saved it once during the war and I would save it again by leaving.

Furthermore I was like the man who was told he was going blind and who said he did not mind as he had seen everything anyhow.

Similarly, I had seen everything in [illegible], including some very interesting governmental performances.

Then I asked Mr. Tardieu's emissary to express to Mr. Tardieu my immense admiration at his amazing alertness in protecting France from the peril of invasion, and we parted with quite elaborate politeness.

It was a little bit foolish but extremely French.

The reason for the strained relations—to use the proper diplomatic term—was the publication of the secret Anglo-French treaty two years ago by the Hearst newspapers, which upset some international applecarts but informed the American people, and of course that being the reason, the French Government was entirely right in levelling its attack at me, and quite wrong in its action toward Mr. Horan, who was only my agent.

I think, however, that the general attitude of the Hearst press in opposing the entrance of the United States into the League of Nations

Continued on Page Twenty.

Air and Rail Lines Here Open A Consolidated Ticket Office

Airlines consolidated ticket office was opened yesterday in the lobby of the Hotel Roosevelt by the Airlines Traffic Association. The office will sell tickets for air and air-rail trips on eighteen lines radiating out of the city.

The association opened a similar cooperative ticket bureau in Chicago two years ago with privilege to sell rides on thirty-two lines throughout the country. More such offices will be opened in airplane centres throughout the country soon.

Colonel L. H. Brittin, president of the association, and other officers were present at the formal opening.

HOOVER LAUDS COSTE FOR 'GLORIOUS' FLIGHT

In Cable to Doumergue, the President Calls Exploit of the French Airmen Brilliant.

LINDBERGH HAILS SUCCESS

Own Feat Surpassed, He Says —Byrd, Kimball and Aviation Leaders Add Their Praise.

Special to The New York Times.

WASHINGTON, Sept. 2.—The successful transatlantic flight of Captain Coste and M. Bellonte was a cause of general rejoicing here where interest in the daring Frenchmen had superseded all other interests.

Word that the fliers had landed was the signal for the dispatch of congratulatory messages by ranking officials of the government, while others informally expressed their gratification at the successful crossing of the Atlantic with words of high praise for the French aviators.

President Hoover, in a message to President Doumergue of France, declared that by the flight France "has established a glorious record." His message follows:

Sept. 2, 1930.

His Excellency Gaston Doumergue,
President of the French Republic,
Paris, France.

I join with the people of the American nation in rejoicing over the brilliant exploit of your distinguished aviators, Captain Dieudonné Coste and M. Maurice Bellonte, in successfully completing for the first time in history a non-stop flight from France to the United States.

France has established a glorious record. I hope that in the future many others of your citizens will come to us in this manner.

I extend to your Excellency and to the people of France my heartiest congratulations.

HERBERT HOOVER.

Message to French People.

The State Department at the same time requested Ambassador Edge at Paris to extend to the Minister for Foreign Affairs, and through him to the people of France, the heartiest congratulations of the United States Government on the magnificent flight.

The department's congratulations to the fliers were contained in a message to Captain Coste from Green Hackworth, solicitor of the State Department, and in the absence of higher officials, the acting Secretary of State.

This message read as follows:

Sept. 2, 1930.

Captain Dieudonné Coste,
Curtiss-Wright Airport,
Valley Stream, Long Island.

Personally, and on behalf of the people of this country, I extend to you and Maurice Bellonte our heartiest congratulations upon your magnificent flight and safe arrival. The same splendid courage and undaunted spirit that inspired Nungesser and Coli have at last been rewarded.

[illegible]EEN HACKWORTH.

Among other officials who informally voiced their congratulations was Major Gen. J. E. F[illegible], chief of the Army Air Corps, who said:

"I consider it a very marvelous flight and wish to congratulate them."

Navy Heads Add Greetings.

Secretary of the Navy Adams sent the following message to Captain Coste:

"The American Navy extends its congratulations to you and your companion, Maurice Bellonte, upon the successful completion of the Paris to New York flight in an airplane. Your courageous feat has aroused the admiration of every of-

Continued on Page Three.

COSTE'S OWN STORY TELLS OF FLYING THROUGH MIST

Like Floating Through a Hazy Dream for Hours and Hours—Felt Lucky After Conquering Three Storms Over Atlantic.

ONCE DRIVEN 100 MILES OFF THEIR COURSE

Knew That the Battle Was Over When They Sighted Land at 6 A. M., but Got Into a 'Tight Place' Between Steep Cliffs of a River.

By CAPTAIN DIEUDONNE COSTE.

When we took off from Paris the day before yesterday we knew it was the greatest moment in our lives. It was the culmination of three years of hard effort, not unmixed with many heartbreaking disappointments. If we had not left at that particular minute we might well have faced three more years of delay before accomplishing the first flight from a city of the Old World to the greatest city in the New World.

There were many exciting moments during our trip, and at times I could not be sure from one minute to the next—now that it is all over—which was the greatest thrill. I think, however, that that came after we first sighted the coast of North America. As you know, the coast of Nova Scotia is full of bends and turns, fills and rivers, promontories and little gulfs.

Followed the Winding Coast.

When we reached the coast we were determined not to lose sight of it again. In order to keep it in view we had to follow all these devious turns and that was a job. At the same time we had another problem. The sky was overcast, it was raining and we had to fly below those rain clouds. Sometimes they were extremely low, which made it necessary for us to fly as close to the water as ten meters.

We came to one bend and turned it; we flew on, skirting a precipice. Suddenly there loomed up out of the mist another precipice on our port side. We were caught between the steep banks of a river—what river, I do not know. It was a tight place.

Bellonte was at the controls at that time and he had to think fast. Fortunately, having flown thousands of miles, the ship was light. Bellonte gave her the gas and shot upward.

Decided to Fly by Instrument.

It is not pleasant to think how close we came to those cruel, jagged rocks. We went up fairly high and began to fly steadily by instrument. Some time passed before the clouds and the rain cleared somewhat and then we were over what I believe was the Atlantic off the coast of Maine. We came down a little later through a new bank of fog and headed down the coast until we were over a large city.

We were so interested in trying to determine what city it was that it never occurred to us that this was the first great city we had passed since leaving Paris. Only a few minutes later we passed another city, and now there was no doubt. We identified it as Boston. We continued the flight without further incident before landing at Valley Stream.

The tremendous load of fuel required for this flight, in which we expected to buck prevailing unfavorable winds, gave us the first real thrill of the voyage. Would the ship lift off the ground? That was our great concern. We had 5,200 litres of gasoline on board.

Storms Ahead Cause Concern.

But this great fear passed in a few moments and we found new cause for concern with each passing moment. There were storms ahead. We would have to push our over-weighted ship through them. We ran into the first of these disturbances off the Irish coast. The second gave us some trying moments, not long afterward, over the ocean, but fortunately we were able to escape the worst of it. The third—and probably the worst of all—was the storm we encountered over Nova Scotia.

That it occurred only yesterday morning seems impossible just at this moment. So many things seem to have happened since, that that storm seems remote—something that happened long, long ago.

Driven 100 Miles Off Course.

We had to find the best route to Nova Scotia, and that in short order, if we were to avoid the hazards that faced the Bremen when it ran into fog and storm of a similar nature and was forced down hundreds of miles from its goal.

In seeking to avoid this storm we were obliged to fly 100 miles out of our way to the south. We did not find land, as we had expected, so we turned northward again, flying another 100 miles. Time was swiftly passing. Each minute meant the loss of more of our precious fuel. Again we turned.

It occurred to us that three is a lucky number. We had faced three storms—were we now to be defeated? We were sure that we would not be.

Land Sighted in Early Morning.

After three hours of searching we computed that we must be very near the coast of Nova Scotia. At 3 A. M. (French time)—for we had not changed our clock—we sighted land. At the same moment it became obvious that the winds were abating. Naturally we were very happy—very happy. The only thing that could stop us now, we thought, would be failure of our motor.

It had carried us already from France to North America and we knew that it would not fail us now. We had perfect confidence in its stanch heart and that confidence was justified. The motor was wonderful. It did all that we had hoped it would.

Weather conditions, on the whole, were very favorable—at least the winds were on our side. On the other hand, almost the entire route was clouded over and we went hour after hour over that watery waste through a thick white mist. We could not see what lay ahead, below or above. It was like floating in a dream. There was something unreal about it—unreal and awesome. We were two, but we seemed so all alone.

Up and Down to Find Clear Way.

Most of the time I was at the controls, and there was plenty to keep my mind busy. There was no time for dreaming. Constantly I had to shift my course to find a way out of the haze. Sometimes we dropped the plane down to less than 300 feet from the waves. At other times we were up to 2,500 feet. We seldom went above that mark, and never very much above it.

But we had our reward. Although my mind was taken up with the

Continued on Page Three.

Associated Press Photo.

FRENCH FLIER IN HIS HOUR OF TRIUMPH!

Conqueror of Atlantic Is Carried Off the Field on the Shoulders of His Admirers on His Safe Arrival From Paris.

ALL PARIS ACCLAIMS TRIUMPH BY COSTE

News of Safe Landing Here Shouted Joyfully by Great Throngs in Streets.

FELT CERTAIN OF SUCCESS

Real Demonstration Deferred Until Homecoming of the Two Fliers.

By P. J. PHILIP.

Special Cable to THE NEW YORK TIMES.

PARIS, Sept. 2.—"Vive Coste!" "Vive Bellonte!" "Vive la France!" All over Paris these cries have roused the midnight hours. There is no one in the city who does not know that Coste and Bellonte have crossed safely from Paris to New York by air; crossed between breakfast time on one day and supper time on the next.

"They have done it," has been cried up every street, and every one knew who "they" were and what they had done. And so to bed, with immense, tremendous happiness, contentment and pride.

From Curtiss Field to the Place de la Concorde came the voice of Graham McNamee: "He's taxiing down the field!" The rest was interrupted by the clamor of those who did not understand. Then a French voice broke in: "Coste has landed!"

It was that way that Paris learned that the great adventure of east-to-west crossing of the Atlantic had been accomplished, that Nungesser and Coli and so many others had been avenged, that Lindbergh's great flight had been complemented and that the link between Paris and New York had been forged on both sides by air.

By tremendous handclapping Captain Coste was acclaimed, and there was an immense sigh of relief.

The great historic place, the Place de la Concorde, had been crowded. Even its immense acreage could scarcely hold those who came. It was impossible to count the multitude. For that was a rendezvous of all Paris. It was there that it had been arranged all news should be broadcast from the roof of the automobile club. Only that great space, it was certain, could hold the crowd of those who all day had been asking, "Where are they now; when will they arrive?"

Crowd Sure of Success.

There never was any doubt in any one's mind all day—not in that of Mme. Coste or of Mme. Bellonte; not in that of taxi drivers, who would ask their fares for the latest news; not in that of concierges who exchanged their views with passers-by. It was a day of most extraordinary cama-

Continued on Page Four.

10,000 STORM FIELD TO WELCOME FLIERS

Coste Cuts Whirling Propeller as Police Lines Snap and the Throngs Rush Plane.

WELCOMERS SHOVED ASIDE

Glare of Torches Lights Wild Greeting as Pilots Are Carried in Triumph From Field.

Special to The New York Times.

CURTISS FIELD, L. I., Sept. 2.—As the red biplane of Captain Dieudonné Coste and Maurice Bellonte swung out of the northeast at dusk and circled low over the Curtiss Airport here a cheer of welcome roared from the throats of 10,000 persons massed in rows behind a wire fence and strung out in a long line in front of the field's six hangars.

A large part of the crowd had waited all afternoon through a heavy rainstorm and, though most of the spectators were held behind the fence and got no more than a fleeting glimpe of the red plane, they were as vociferous in their welcome as if they had been a part of the crowd that helped to carry the two fliers off the field in triumph.

Crowd Breaks Police Lines.

As the plane glided to a graceful landing and started to taxi toward the grand stand on the west side of the field, the crowd inside the fence broke through the police lines and ran shouting and dodging policemen toward the craft. Coste, realizing the danger of the whirling propeller, cut the switch, and the metal blade swung slowly to a stop. A score of policemen and mechanics joined hands and, forming a circle about the plane, tried with scant success to hold back the crowd. At least seventy-five persons broke through the cordon and swarmed about the plane. Coste, looking hot and tired, stepped out of the plane into a seething mob, which kissed him, pummeled him, wrung his hands and all but knocked him from his feet.

"Splendid!" "Magnifique!" "Felicitations!" French as well as American voices screamed. French girls embraced the fliers, kissing them time and again, and Frenchmen followed suit. An announcer for the National Broadcasting Company, holding a microphone high above his head, was lost in the struggling throng, and gasped in the microphone:

"We seem to be having a little difficulty here at Valley Stream."

Elinor Smith, girl aviator, was in the midst of the crowd, but did not get a chance to greet the fliers until later.

A delegation of French war veterans, carrying the French tricolor and the American flag, struggled inside the police cordon, but had but

Continued on Page Two.

FLIERS LAND AT 7:12½ P. M. TO WILD CHEERS OF 10,000

Scarlet Plane Alights Smoothly at Goal With Enough Fuel for Three Hours More—Airmen, Speechless, Watch the Mad Scene of Welcome.

LINDBERGH, HIS VISIT RETURNED, HAILS COSTE

'A Great Flight,' He Says, Gripping Hand of Ace Amid Tumult at Curtiss Field—France Hears the Fliers on Radio—They Will Fly On to Texas.

By JOSEPH SHAPLEN.

Special to The New York Times.

CURTISS FIELD, L. I., Sept. 2.—Captain Dieudonné Coste and his co-pilot, Maurice Bellonte, completed tonight the first direct flight from Paris to New York when they landed at the Curtiss airport at 7:12:30 P. M., after a journey of 37 hours 18 minutes 30 seconds. They covered 6,500 kilometers, or about 4,100 miles, and when they landed had 100 gallons of gasoline left, sufficient for nearly three hours more of flight.

Their achievement marked the first non-stop crossing from Europe to the American metropolis. What others have tried to do and failed Captain Coste and M. Bellonte accomplished. In doing so they triumphed magnificently over the elements which sent Nungesser and Coli, the first two Frenchmen to try the westward trip, to death, and took their revenge upon Neptune for the loss of other valiant aviators who sought to achieve the westward flight.

Colonel Charles A. Lindbergh's time for the eastward crossing was better. It took him only thirty-three hours and a half to fly from Roosevelt Field to Le Bourget to pay the visit which Coste and Bellonte repaid tonight. The Spirit of St. Louis rose from earth and started on its historic flight at 7:52 A. M., May 20, 1927. Lindbergh brought it to earth just outside of Paris at 10:24 Continental Time (5:24 P. M., New York Time), on May 21.

Ten thousand throats yelled a wild greeting to the two French masters of the air as their airplane, the scarlet, enigmatic Question Mark, bearing upon her sides the written record of a dozen odysseys of the sky, came down smoothly and gracefully on the east side of the field and taxied rapidly toward the hangars on the west side. Here among the first to greet Captain Coste and M. Bellonte was Colonel Lindbergh, whose visit to Paris had now been returned.

"Great Flight," Colonel Lindbergh Declares.

"It's a great flight," was the enthusiastic comment of Colonel Lindbergh after he had finally managed, with the assistance of policemen, to make his way to the French airmen, following their rescue from the cheering crowds, whose enthusiasm exceeded all bounds. Never before in the history of aviation in this country, according to veterans of the air, have any flying men received the reception accorded tonight to Captain Coste and his companion.

Soon after the Question Mark landed, the fliers were informed that Colonel W. E. Easterwood of Dallas, Texas, had offered $25,000 to Captain Coste and M. Bellonte if they would fly their ship to Dallas. Captain Coste said he would be glad to make the trip because it would give him an opportunity for a cross-country flight, and said he would probably take off Thursday morning, after the plane has been tuned up and tightened.

Asked if he had any plans for the future, which might include a trip around the world via the poles, as one interviewer suggested, Captain Costes replied he had no plans beyond the flight to Dallas.

It was 7:10 P. M. when the Question Mark, easily distinguished by her color and peculiar design, appeared in the sky over the airport, escorted by three Curtiss fledglings from the Naval Reserve aviation field here and flanked by a score of other airplanes which had taken off shortly before to extend a welcome to the French fliers.

After circling the field, the Question Mark came down, making a perfect landing. Veering quickly in the direction of the hangars the French victors of the Atlantic raced toward the hangars, obviously anxious to avoid the onrush of the crowds. But in vain. The moment Captain Coste and M. Bellonte raised their heads out of the cockpit and stepped over the fuselage they were picked up on the shoulders of several of their compatriots and carried to Hangar 2, while a small army of policemen struggled desperately to protect them against what seemed imminent injury from the ever-increasing pressure of the throng of admirers. "Vive la France," "Vive Coste et Bellonte," came the resounding, ever-mounting cries from the hundreds of Frenchmen who formed a prominent part of the surging crowds.

Police Battle Crowds in Great Rush of Welcome.

Above the unrestrained, joyous clamor of voices the boom of a hundred flashlights accompanied the triumphant procession across the field to the hangar, where the police hoped they could isolate the fliers. Here the police had to fight a veritable battle to get Coste and Bellonte to safety, but even in the hangar they found no refuge, for before the police and airport employes could close and bolt the rolling doors hundreds forced their way in, besieging the fliers, eager to shake their hands, uncontrollable in their determination to get as close as possible to the airmen. With their faces dripping perspiration, their backs against a wall, Coste and Bellonte stood speechless for nearly ten minutes, wondering what would be the end of this mad scene which appeared beyond the powers of the police to master, until, in phalanx formation, the guards rushed the crowd back far enough to clear an exit.

With the greatest difficulty, Coste and Bellonte were finally rushed to a room upstairs, to which only a small group of their friends, members of the Nassau County and the Mayor's reception committees and representatives of the French Government made their way in the vain hope of getting a few words with the airmen.

Lindbergh Greets Fliers Returning His Visit.

Here, too, came Colonel Lindbergh, smiling with joy at the success of the flight and rushing forward to congratulate first Coste and then Bellonte.

Captain Coste's eyes flashed as he grasped the hand of the young man who more than any one else had captured the imagination of the world by his solo flight to Le Bourget, the starting point of the Question Mark.

Firmly the two heroes of the air shook hands as thousands outside, standing in the glare of scores of magnesium flares, broke into the wildest outburst of cheering that marked the arrival.

"Comment ca va?" asked Captain Coste.

"I congratulate you, I congratulate you," said Colonel Lindbergh, again pressing the Frenchman's hand and apparently so overcome by

"All the News That's Fit to Print."

The New York Times.

THE WEATHER
Generally fair today and tomorrow; not much change in temperature.
Temperature yesterday—Max., 82; min., 67.
U. S. Weather Forecast—For details see Page 31.

Copyright, 1930, by The New York Times Company.

VOL. LXXX....No. 26,540. **** NEW YORK, TUESDAY, SEPTEMBER 23, 1930. TWO CENTS In Greater New York | THREE CENTS Within 200 Miles | FOUR CENTS Elsewhere Except 7th and 8th Postal Zones.

SOVIET UNDERSELLS OUR WHEAT ABROAD; REPORT OF 10-CENT CUT HALTS EXPORT; CHICAGO PIT ASKS HYDE FOR FULL FACTS

HOOVER TO KEEP OUT OF PARTY FIGHT HERE OVER DRY LAW PLANK

Word From the White House Makes It Plain Leaders Must Work Out State Problems.

CONCERNED OVER SITUATION

President's Attitude Is Made Known After Report He Favored Modification Declaration.

REPEAL PLANK EXPECTED

Leaders Here Predict Tuttle Will Be Nominee and Doubt He Would Run on Moderate Platform.

Special to The New York Times.

WASHINGTON, Sept. 22.—The New York Republicans will have to work out their own problems without any gesture from President Hoover, it was made known today at the White House when reports of various issues developing with the approach of the State Convention were relayed to the executive offices.

It was stated officially that the White House was taking no hand whatever in the New York situation and intended to adhere to that course throughout the remainder of the preconvention period.

This attitude was made to apply to the entire New York situation and the White House sources could not be drawn into a discussion of any of the issues. One of the principal reports relayed there today was to the effect that an already difficult party situation had been further complicated by what purported to be word from Washington that the Hoover Administration would prefer to have "modification" made the basis of the prohibition plank in the party platform to "repeal." From the White House's attitude, whatever is done in this regard is a responsibility [illegible] York party leaders.

Whatever the White House policy, party leaders are said to be considerably concerned over the New York situation. Republican headquarters here is said to have been advised that the convention is virtually certain to approve some kind of wet plank, and the party chieftains do not want to be in the position of having opposed such action.

Tuttle Nomination Held Sure.

In the face of reports yesterday that the Hoover Administration was opposed to the extreme stand in favor of repeal taken by United States Attorney Charles H. Tuttle in his statement, the belief persisted among Republican leaders in this city that Mr. Tuttle would be the party nominee for Governor. It was their opinion that the prohibition plank in the party platform would be consistent with Mr. Tuttle's attitude.

One reason for this belief, it was admitted, was the growing conviction in Republican circles that Mr. Tuttle would, in no circumstances, consent to being "drafted" unless the party platform reflected the stand to which he has publicly committed himself. As friends of Mr. Tuttle who are prepared to stand out to the end for his nomination expressed it yesterday, they would rather see him decline to run if the platform should straddle the wet and dry issue, because under the circumstances the nomination would mean nothing beyond an empty honor to him, while it would spell defeat for their party in the election.

Nor, they believe, would the nomination be of any value to any one whom the convention might substitute as its gubernatorial nominee in the event that Mr. Tuttle should find it necessary to refuse the nomination.

Hoover Pressure Denied.

While Republican leaders who were questioned yesterday denied that any eleventh hour pressure had been brought to bear from Washington to influence the convention on prohibition, reports had been in circulation that President Hoover would much prefer to see the platform in this State "go easy" on prohibition and that Republican State Chairman William J. Maier during his recent tours of the State had been the bearer of a message to that effect to leaders of his party in up-State counties engaged in picking delegates to the convention. Chairman Maier has denied these reports and a statement came from the White House yesterday that President Hoover was maintaining a hands-off policy.

Upon his arrival at Albany yesterday, Mr. Maier said:

"We anticipate no interference from Washington on the wet and dry question." That is all he would say for quotation. Nor would he say a word about what might or might not go into the party's platform.

Former Representative William H. Hill of Broome County, pre-convention leader in the Hoover movement in this State two years ago and viewed by many leaders as the mouthpiece of the President, has taken his stand firmly in favor of a prohibition plank, affirming adherence of the party in this State to the national platform of 1928 which pledged the Republican party in the

Continued on Page Three.

Dean Smith, Back in Air Mail, Sets Record From Cleveland

Dean Smith, who was one of the pilots with the Byrd Antarctic expedition, established a new mail speed record yesterday, one week after resuming his duties in the service, when he landed at the Newark Metropolitan Airport from Cleveland, having completed the flight in 2 hours and 51 minutes.

Smith put his Douglas plane, with its 700-pound mail load, up to 10,000 feet just after leaving Cleveland and came sailing over the Alleghanies on a forty-mile tail wind. The previous record for the 412-mile hop for N. A. T. pilots was established three weeks ago by Charlie Haas, who made the trip in just three hours.

LAMONT DECLARES DECLINE HAS CEASED

Secretary Finds "Distinctly Encouraging Features" in Business Conditions.

RAW MATERIAL GAINS CITED

Retail Trade Is Picking Up—Recent Increase in Exports Is Noted by Him.

Special to The New York Times.

WASHINGTON, Sept. 22.—"It is perfectly clear that business on the whole has crossed a marked decline which was characteristic of a number of earlier months, and there are some distinctly encouraging features," Secretary of Commerce Lamont declared in a statement today.

A "noticeable trend" in business toward buying raw materials far ahead of the current consumption was cited by the Secretary in support of his belief.

This increase, according to the Secretary, was taking place without any government pressure or solicitation.

"Though there have been one or two conferences as to details of raw material buying at the instance of industrialists themselves, the government is not responsible," he said.

Secretary Lamont declared that, although monthly business reports received at the department did not show a constantly upward trend, it was clear that the marked decline which had characterized business as a whole during the early months of the year had come to an end.

Most notable in the improved condition, he said, was a picking up in retail trade for August and an increase in July and August exports of 12½ per cent, as compared with an average increase for the same months from 1922 to 1929 of 5½ per cent.

Export Trade Encouraging.

Secretary Lamont's statement was as follows:

"The various weekly and monthly business indicators which are coming in in a steady stream are more or less mixed in their trends, but it is perfectly clear that business on the whole has ceased the marked decline which was characteristic of a number of earlier months and there are some distinctly encouraging features.

"The most encouraging aspects are the growth of export trade, as revealed by the August statistics and the distinct picking up in retail trade in this country.

"The increase of exports during August was more than is customary at this season. During the years 1922-1929 the increase between these two months averaged 5½ per cent, but in 1930 was more than 12½ per cent. This increase was not confined to one or two commodities but was shared by most of the major groups.

"Metal manufactures other than machinery and vehicles increased 4.4 per cent in value, animal products about 6 per cent, non-metallic min-

Continued on Page Two.

CHILE FOILS A COUP, BUT GROWING REVOLT IS REPORTED THERE

Argentina Hears That the Rebels Have Wider Support Than Santiago Admits.

TWO AMERICANS ARRESTED

Piloted Plane Carrying Two Exiled Officers and Three Civilians to Rendezvous.

RISING NEAR A NAVAL BASE

Three Army Divisions and Many Navy Men Are Said in Buenos Aires to Have Been Involved.

Special Cable to THE NEW YORK TIMES.

SANTIAGO, Chile, Sept. 22.—An attempt yesterday to start a revolution in Chile was revealed today, with the information that it had been suppressed.

Five Chileans and two United States aviators who took them to the city of Concépcion, 300 miles south of Santiago, from Argentina by plane were arrested, according to the government's communiqué. They are believed to have flown non-stop from Buenos Aires. The Chileans, according to the government, are now prisoners aboard a warship at Talcahuano, the port of Concépcion.

The communiqué says that at 5 P. M. the revolutionary party in a tri-motor plane, landed in the vicinity of the army post at Concépcion, after flying over the city, searching for a suitable field. In the plane were General Enrique Bravo, retired; Colonel Mármaduque Grove, also retired, and three civilian political leaders of the old regime, Luis Salas Romo, Carlos Vicuna Fuentes and Pedro León Ugalde.

Soldiers Urged to Revolt.

The Chileans entered the barracks of the Chacabuco regiment, which were almost empty because of Sunday being a national holiday. The five are said to have tried to entice the soldiers to revolt, but that, meeting with no success, eventually were seized by General Victor Figueroa, Governor of the Province, and José Maria Barcelo, the military commander, who sent them in arrest to the Talcahuano naval base, where they were joined by the two American aviators.

The revolutionaries, who were political exiles, have lived for a long time in Buenos Aires. Their sudden appearance at Concépcion has aroused interest, but apparently nothing more.

The Military Council, or General Staff, already has established a court to judge the case, and it is expected that severe measures will be taken, in accordance with a recent statement of the government that it will not tolerate any disturbance and a statement today that it will make examples of the fine Chileans held.

In government circles it is said that perfect order is being maintained throughout the country.

Aviators Will Face Trial.

SANTIAGO, Chile, Sept. 22 (AP).—The Chilean Minister of the Interior, at the request of President Carlos Ibañez, revealed tonight that the names of the two American aviators are Edward Orville de Larin and Reed Smith Doyle.

They were flying a tri-motor Fokker. Although being held by the government, they will not be court-martialed.

The two aviators will be tried on the charge of having violated the laws and regulations of the country regarding forbidden air routes and landing places. If a military inves-

Continued on Page Twelve.

Schwab Indicates Expansion Of Bethlehem Steel Company

Special to The New York Times.

JOHNSTOWN, Pa., Sept. 22.—Within a short time the Bethlehem Steel Company will be far greater than any of its promoters ever dreamed, was the gist of a statement made here today by Charles M. Schwab. The remark, which he refused to amplify, was made during a newspaper publishers' meeting.

Noting that more than $1,000,000,000 is invested in Bethlehem, Mr. Schwab declared "but we are only starting."

USE FOR COSMIC RAY FOUND BY MILLIKAN

Electroscope Detecting It Is a Better Weather Forecaster Than Barometer, He Says.

HIT EARTH AS ETHER WAVES

Physicist Tells Science Academy of Trip to Near North Magnetic Pole to Prove This.

Special to The New York Times.

PASADENA, Cal., Sept. 22.—The cosmic rays that bombard the earth from the depths of space with a penetration 1,000 times that of the hardest X-rays will soon be delivering to scientists information that will aid in predicting meteorological events, Dr. R. A. Millikan, president of the California Institute of Technology and Nobel Prize winner in physics, told the National Academy of Sciences meeting here today.

The perfected electroscope for detecting the cosmic rays is an improvement on the barometer for measuring atmospheric conditions, Dr. Millikan said, thus putting the rays to use in weather forecasting.

Dr. Millikan, the first to measure the cosmic rays, also offered proof of the theory he has held that the rays come to the earth as ether waves of extremely short length. Some scientists have held that they might be high-speed electrons.

Dr. Millikan described his latest researches, which he conducted as near as possible to the north magnetic pole.

Last week he returned from Churchill on the west shore of Hudson Bay, about 700 miles due south of the magnetic Pole. To this remote point he carried instruments and lead shields that weighed 500 pounds, and there he observed night and day for a week to determine the effect of the magnetic currents on the intensity of the cosmic rays.

Found No Magnetic Effect.

Theoretical calculations by Dr. P. S. Epstein, one of Dr. Millikan's colleagues, showed that if the high-speed electron theory of cosmic radiation were correct, there should be a large concentration near the magnetic fields of the earth because of the influence of the earth's field upon the speeding electrons. But Dr. Millikan did not find any difference in the intensity of cosmic rays at Churchill and at Pasadena.

Daily fluctuations observed in the intensity of the rays were found to be concerned with the changes in the earth's atmosphere, and it was found that the constancy of the cosmic rays could be put to work to detect them.

"The barometer," Dr. Millikan said, "is an instrument that responds both to the temperature and to the weight of the superincumbent air, that is, to a mixture of static and kinetic conditions while the cosmic ray electroscope reflects only the mass of the superincumbent air and is quite independent of temperature or kinetic effects of any kind. The cosmic ray electroscope is thus a simpler and a more fundamental instrument than the barometer. I expect it to be an aid in bringing about advances in the as yet little developed science of meteorology and ultimately to find a place in meteorological stations.

"The air is simply an absorbing blanket interposed between us and a constant source of radiation coming into the earth uniformly from all directions. Every eruption or wave, or ripple in that blanket is accurately reflected by the cosmic ray electroscope of the type used in the investigation. The changes that it reveals are considerably larger than the changes revealed by the barometer, because it cares nothing about the temperature, but only about the mass of the interposed layer of air, while with the barometer, a rise in temperature often masks the thinning of the air blanket above. The two instruments between them furnish more information about the condition of the upper air than either one of them alone can do.

"It is desired to point out the utility that this result may have for the future of meteorology, for every new instrument that can furnish us new data about what is happening in the upper air must assist in the important problem of predicting, if not in controlling, meteorological and geophysical events.

"Such an instrument the suitably perfected cosmic ray electroscope

Continued on Page Eleven.

MRS. CRATER BLOCKS MAINE POLICE HUNT; WAGNER HEARD HERE

Deputy Chief Visits Belgrade Lakes Camp, but Is Told Wife of Jurist Is "Too Ill."

THE CHAUFFEUR'S STORY

Says He Came Here Aug. 15 to Seek Employer—Senator Unable to Aid Crain.

GRAFT INQUIRIES TO WIDEN

Todd Names More Aides as Healy and Tommaney Enter Not-Guilty Pleas and Give $2,500 Bail.

While the New York City police continued last night their search for Connie Marcus, said to be a friend of Joseph F. Crater, missing Supreme Court Justice, Maine authorities began their investigation into the Crater mystery, and District Attorney Crain presented the testimony of ten witnesses to the county grand jury in a futile effort to explain the jurist's disappearance.

Captain Joseph F. Young Jr., deputy chief of the Maine State Highway Police, went to the Crater camp at Belgrade Lake yesterday, but was met with the assertion that "Mrs. Crater is seriously ill and can see no one." Captain Young got statements from Henry G. Herbert, brother-in-law of Mrs. Crater; the chauffeur, Fred Kahler, and the maid, Margaret Lynch, which shed no light on the case. Kahler admitted that he and Justice Crater, who has been missing since Aug. 6, had stopped for a meal at an Augusta hotel, but corrected a previous report and said the visit to the hotel was made on July 29, before the jurist's disappearance and not after it.

Kennebec Grand Jury to Act.

After Captain Young's visit County Attorney Frank E. Southard, who commenced the investigation at the request of District Attorney Crain, said that he "probably" would visit the Crater Summer home later in the week if Mrs. Crater's condition was reported improved. It was learned, however, that Mrs. Crater, Mr. Herbert and other members of her household almost certainly would be summoned to appear a week from today before the Kennebec County grand jury for questioning as to their knowledge of the Crater mystery.

Kahler said he last saw his employer on Aug. 2. The jurist was expected back in Maine on Aug. 8 or 9, he said, but when he did not appear "no steps were taken until a week afterward." Then Mrs. Crater told the chauffeur to go to New York, fearing some accident might have befallen her husband. Kahler came here on Aug. 15, he said, and returned to Maine on Aug. 20. While here he visited the Crater apartment at 40 Fifth Avenue and talked to Frederick A. Johnson, the jurist's secretary. According to the statement, Johnson told Kahler that "the judge will be along in a day or so" and advised the chauffeur not to worry about his employer. Acting on this information, Kahler wired "All O. K." to Mrs. Crater and returned to Maine. He told Captain Young that Mrs. Crater had not employed any private detectives on the case.

Verifies Johnson's Statement.

The chauffeur's story differs somewhat from hitherto accepted reports of the events after the disappearance. It had been reported definitely that Kahler came to New York on Aug. 7 to take the jurist back to Maine in his automobile, and that Crater's disappearance first became known then when he failed to keep the appointment. Kahler's description of Johnson's advice verifies reports Johnson is said to have made at the time that "Crater is around town." Mr. Crain questioned the secretary about this last week, and apparently was satisfied with Johnson's explanation that he thought it

Continued on Page Four.

Canada Ready to Aid Soviet Inquiry Here; Bennett Will Stress Wheat Crisis at London

By The Canadian Press.

OTTAWA, Ont., Sept. 22.—Every possible effort will be made by the government to obtain a better price and a wide market for Canadian wheat, Premier Bennett announced in the House of Commons this afternoon.

The government, he said, proposes to offer any assistance it can to the United States in an investigation of the charge that short selling on the Chicago Board of Trade by Russian interests has been responsible for the recent decline in prices.

The Prime Minister spoke of the wheat situation in announcing that representatives of the wheat pool would accompany the government delegation to the Imperial Conference and the Imperial Economic Conference in London.

The government, Mr. Bennett said, proposed to improve the distribution facilities for grain and to lower production costs. This, he said, meant cheaper implements of production. The views of members of the House differed on how this might be achieved, but the government was convinced that the course it had adopted in increasing the tariff would meet the situation.

The matter of cheaper and more efficient means of transportation would also engage the attention of those present at the conference.

But perhaps the greatest problem, he added, was that involving the distribution of products after they were harvested and transported. The bonuses and bounties which other countries had extended to their producers, he said, had stimulated production to a point where conditions had developed hitherto unknown to the people of Canada for many years. The government, however, was endeavoring to find a solution of that problem, and Mr. Bennett expressed the hope that he could report success on his return from London.

He would not rest content merely with an effort to improve the conditions under which the crops were produced, the Prime Minister said, but he would seek to assure to the growers an advantageous return for their work, greater, if possible, than the return to those who risked their capital in other ventures.

ASKS LEAGUE TO END DUMPING BY SOVIET

Rumanian Tells Geneva Group That Agrarian Europe Is Being Crushed.

FOR PREFERENTIAL TARIFF

Inquiry Urged by Swedish Delegate—Frenchman for World Tribunal on Trade Pacts.

By CLARENCE K. STREIT.

Wireless to THE NEW YORK TIMES.

GENEVA, Sept. 22.—Threatened with being "completely crushed" between Russian dumping and overseas competition, Eastern agrarian Europe in the person of Virgile Madgearu, Minister of Commerce of Rumania, renewed in the League Assembly's second commission today its plea for a preferential European tariff for its products—this time as a matter of "life and death."

M. Madgearu spoke in reply to an Australian delegate, whose opposition to a preferential tariff as discrimination was reiterated today by another overseas country, South Africa. They should remember, the Rumanian said, that overseas agricultural exports to Europe have doubled since the war, and whereas they had big home markets, the small agrarian States of Europe had no other market save Europe, and it was "only fair that they should have a chance to live."

Overseas countries talked of a world-wide study for cooperation and of leaving the problem to solve itself by a reduction of acreage, he said. That was all very well, but "we haven't time to wait until that happens," he continued. The positions of four agricultural exporting countries of Europe, M. Madgearu said, were "absolutely tragic."

Overseas countries could produce cheaper and had benefited by the fall in ocean shipping rates, while industrial Europe, to protect her own farmers, had raised her tariffs to a

Continued on Page Two.

LIVERPOOL MARKET UPSET BY RUSSIANS

British Regulations Check Short Selling Tactics, but Dumping of Wheat Continues.

ALL EXPORTERS UNDERSOLD

Exchange Members Assert the Situation Is Demoralizing Trade in World Grain.

Special Cable to THE NEW YORK TIMES.

LONDON, Sept. 22.—The Liverpool wheat market is not suffering from the same affliction of Russian short selling that is reported from Chicago simply because the regulations in the British grain trade make such manoeuvering practically impossible, but vast quantities of Russian wheat are being dumped into this country and the market is upset.

Canadian, Argentine and American shipments are all being undersold by the Soviet Government wheat, and prices, which have been declining for a fortnight, suffered a further drop of 6 cents per quarter (8 bushels) in today's trading. This was followed by a rally which left prices at about 1 pence above Saturday's closing.

Although the Soviet Government's tactics in this country are somewhat different from those said to have been employed to demoralize the Chicago market, the motive is supposed to be the same, primarily to build up for itself credits throughout the world by the means of selling cheap wheat, and perhaps, incidentally, to distress the grain growers of other countries.

Yet the opinion is held here that Russia is distressing its own peasant population as well by compelling the wheat growers to sell their crops to the government at a price far below what could be obtained in open world market if it were not rigged for political purposes. Furthermore, according to expert information here, the Soviet is flooding the rest of the world with its wheat for political purposes when the people of northern Russia are almost starving for it.

Close Firm Despite Russians.

Owing to heavy buying for American account and covering by nervous shorts, the Liverpool wheat market closed firm, with October 3¼ cents per quarter higher on the day and other positions from 1¼ to 1½ cents higher, although at the opening shipment parcels were in very slow demand at a decline of from 6 to 12 cents.

Sellers offered Russian wheat for September and October at $6.90 to $7.32 per quarter. The only sale reported, however, was of No. 2 Manitoba, arrived, at $7.08.

The bottom of the Russian price was 36 cents lower than the seller's offer of White Western Pacific, September and October, at $7.26.

As a result of the fall in wheat prices and consequently cheaper flour, it is stated that the price of

Continued on Page Two.

WORLD BEAR DRIVE IS SEEN

Liverpool and Rotterdam Face Problem of Big Russian Offers.

FORMER MARKET RALLIES

Investigation at Chicago Turns on Names of Brokers Acting for the Soviet.

'HEDGING' IS HELD UNUSUAL

Hyde on Way West Declares More Transactions by Reds Have Been Uncovered.

Special to The New York Times.

CHICAGO, Sept. 22.—Reports that the Russian Government was selling wheat abroad at 10 cents below the world price, resulting in a practical halt to North American export business, were received here today as the Chicago Board of Trade, through its business conduct committee, began its formal investigation of charges made by Secretary Hyde to the effect that the Soviets were selling wheat short in the Chicago pit and causing prices to fall.

That the Soviet Government is seeking to dominate the foreign market in wheat was indicated in cable dispatches. Rotterdam advices reported Russian wheat being offered 10 cents a bushel below the price of similar grades in North America. While no report has been received in Chicago of any considerable purchases of the Russian offerings, some Board of Trade specialists saw in the Soviet action a reason for the almost total absence of any wheat exports, either from American or Winnipeg ports.

The visible supply of United States wheat increased today by 3,947,000 bushels to 202,620,000 bushels, the largest ever recorded.

The Liverpool market was affected only slightly by the Russian grain offerings, rallying strongly to close at ⅝ to 1¾ pence higher after an early decline.

Sales Are Held Unprecedented.

The action of the Russian Government in hedging wheat was called unprecedented in trading annals. Never before, veteran traders declared, has a government been known to hedge wheat. Meanwhile, Chicago grain prices were little affected by the reports of Russia's underselling tactics, pending investigation of its hedging operations on the Board of Trade. Closing prices showed only a fractional decline below Saturday's final levels.

There was a rumor here, wholly unconfirmed, that Russia, or some account representing that nation, had been selling corn on a liberal scale along with wheat. If true, this was regarded as tending to show a motive toward the bearing of prices, while wheat alone might have been sold strictly in hedging operations.

The board of trade's business conduct committee began its investigation into Secretary Hyde's charges in a session lasting a little more than an hour. Then the committee issued a statement informing the public that Secretary Hyde's promised information on the dealings had not been received, but that while awaiting it the "alleged transactions" were being thoroughly investigated.

Chicago Prices Off Slightly.

Meanwhile, Chicago grain prices were little affected by the pending investigation. Closing prices showed only a fractional decline below Saturday's final levels.

The committee chairman, Joseph W. Badenoch, stated that as soon as Secretary Hyde gives the board the names of the brokers who executed the Russian short sales, they will be called on to explain, if they can, what lay behind them.

"It is unprecedented, in my experience," Mr. Badenoch said, "for a foreign government to be accused of manipulating the market. We have always taken the stand here that this is a world market, and that sales could and should be made here so long as the laws are complied with.

"There is nothing unusual in foreigners selling here when they have no intention of actually delivering wheat in Chicago. Canada has done it on several occasions. As for the effect of the sales by Russians, said to be in excess of 7,000,000 bushels, that is a small percentage of the open interest of more than 165,000,000 bushels at present.

"Sales by the Russian Government would have to be covered by pur-

New Princess to Be Margaret Rose of York; Named for Three of Scotland's Queens

Wireless to THE NEW YORK TIMES.

LONDON, Sept. 22.—It was officially announced tonight that the younger daughter of the Duke and Duchess of York, born at Glamis Castle Aug. 21, will be christened as Princess Margaret Rose of York. The christening ceremony will take place in the private chapel of Buckingham Palace next month.

The baby princess is the fourth in line of succession to the British throne, and, should she become queen, it will be the first time there has ever been a Queen Margaret of England. Inasmuch as the Princess was born in Scotland, it was regarded as fitting that she should be christened Margaret, for there have been three Queen Margarets of Scotland.

The first Margaret was the consort of King Malcolm III. Of eminently saintly life, she was canonized several years after her death, and became known as St. Margaret of Scotland.

The second and most noted of the three Margarets, popularly known as the Maid of Norway, was the daughter of King Eric II of that country and his wife, who was the daughter of Alexander III of Scotland. She became titular Queen of Scotland.

But the Margaret of most interest to the British people of today and their royal house was the wife of the Scottish King James IV and daughter of Henry VII of England. It was as descendants of Margaret that Mary Queen of Scots and her son, James VI of Scotland, laid claim to the English throne. James finally was accepted as the successor of Elizabeth in England, then becoming known as James I.

The offices of the Duke of York's controller, equerry and secretaries will be moved soon from his London residence at 145 Piccadilly to 11 Grosvenor Crescent, Belgrave Square, formerly the house of the Duke of Leeds. While this change has been contemplated for some time, the final decision to make it was a consequence of the birth of the new princess, for whose benefit alterations are now being made in her parents' home.

Income Tax Revenue Shows $69,000,000 Drop In Fiscal Year as Compared With 1929 Totals

Special to The New York Times.

WASHINGTON, Sept. 22.—Income tax collections for nineteen days of September, as reported by the Treasury Department today, totaled $432,980,471, or $58,648,210 less than in the same number of business days in September one year ago, indicating that when the quarterly payment, due on Sept. 15, is tabulated it will be about $500,000,000 this year, as compared with $542,000,000 collected in all of September of the previous year.

On the basis of the income tax collections given today for the current fiscal year to date, as comparable with the same days of the fiscal year 1930, income tax payments at $488,846,141 were $69,876,420 behind last year.

All receipts for the fiscal year to date were put at $765,609,465, as compared with $921,237,506 a year ago, a loss of $155,628,401. This coupled with an increase in expenditures, brought the net loss for the fiscal year to date as compared with the last fiscal year to $177,584,400.

The figures, however, are incomplete, especially as to income tax payments, an accurate estimate of which cannot be obtained until the payments cleared within the next few days are tabulated.

"All the News That's Fit to Print."

The New York Times.

THE WEATHER
Light rain this morning; tomorrow fair; little change in temperature.
Temperatures yesterday—Max. 56, min. 37.
U. S. Weather Forecast—For details see page 47.

VOL. LXXX....No. 26,571. **** NEW YORK, FRIDAY, OCTOBER 24, 1930. TWO CENTS in Greater New York | THREE CENTS Within 200 Miles | FOUR CENTS Elsewhere Except 7th and 8th Postal Zones

CUT IN PHONE RATES FOR LONG DISTANCE IN EFFECT ON NOV. 1

Public Service Board Orders a Reduction in State on Calls of Over Forty Miles.

DISCOUNT HOURS EXTENDED

Much Wider Range in Evening Is Provided and Reversal of Charges Permitted.

COMPANY PREDICTS LOSS

Expects $100,000 Drop in Its Annual Revenue—Maltbie Contrasts Different Tariffs.

Special to The New York Times.

ALBANY, Oct. 23.—The long-distance rates of the New York Telephone Company within the State for service beyond forty miles will be generally reduced on Nov. 1 under an order issued today by the Public Service Commission. Substantially, the order accepts the revised schedule submitted by the company after the commission investigated complaints of inconsistencies between the intrastate and interstate rates of the American Telephone and Telegraph Company for similar distances.

A rearrangement in the hours for discounted rates also is included in the new schedule, allowing a much wider range in the evening for reduced rates on toll calls. Regulations imposing additional charges on appointment and messenger calls are eliminated and a new classification permits the reversal of charges.

While the new schedule does not entirely satisfy the commission, Chairman Milo R. Maltbie said the decreases in tolls justified the commission in overlooking minor discrepancies in the structure for the time being, in order to give the public the benefit of lower charges as soon as possible.

The order of the commission brings the toll charges of the company in strict conformity with those of the American Telephone & Telegraph Company, which the commission accepted as a guide. The change, affecting only service between points more than forty miles apart, leaves out of consideration service below forty miles, since the absence of service in the latter zone by the American Telephone and Telegraph Company makes comparison impossible.

5-Cent Increase Under 56 Miles.

While the new schedule provides a five-cent increase in the calls from forty to fifty-six miles, there is no change in the rates from fifty-six to seventy-two miles, and reductions ranging from 5 cents to 80 cents on toll calls covering more than seventy-two miles will be effective Nov. 1.

The new schedule eliminates the appointment and messenger classification for rate purposes and permits such calls at person-to-person rates. The present charge for the former classification is about 20 per cent higher than for person-to-person calls. While the present schedule permits the reversal of charges only at person-to-person rates, the new schedule provides for the reversal of charges on station-to-station calls during day, evening and night periods without additional charges, except that this service is limited to a 25-cent minimum charge.

The reduced evening rates for toll calls will be effective at 7 o'clock instead of at 8:30 o'clock, and the greater reduced rate for the night period of toll calls will be effective at 8:30 o'clock instead of at midnight, to continue until 4:30 A. M. The day period is from 4:30 A. M. to 7 P. M.

The order of the commission, it was said, brings about the largest reduction in toll charges given to telephone users in many months, and considerable reductions in telephone toll bills will result to the large users of long distance service in the State. The company estimates an annual loss in net revenue of $100,000 as a result of the changes.

Maltbie Points Out Inconsistencies.

Chairman Maltbie, in his opinion accompanying the order, pointed out several examples of inconsistencies in the company's rates as compared with those of the American Telephone and Telegraph Company embodied in complaints the commission received, particularly from up-State points. One of the outstanding complaints charged that a station-to-station daytime telephone call from Buffalo to New York City cost $1.90 for three minutes on the New York Telephone Company's schedule, while the rate for the same service from Buffalo to Newark was only $1.30 and from Buffalo to Washington $1.35.

"These inconsistencies were not confined to Buffalo calls," Mr. Maltbie said. "It was pointed out that

Continued on Page Five.

Liberia Ends Slavery There After League Inquiry Charges

Wireless to THE NEW YORK TIMES.

GENEVA, Oct. 23.—All the domestic slaves of the native tribes have been declared free by the Liberian Government, it has officially informed the League of Nations. Liberia also announces it has abolished the system by which a tribesman pledged a member of his family as security for a loan, and has ended forced recruiting for foreign labor contracts.

Liberia explained its action was taken because of the report of the international inquiry commission, which found these forms of slavery still existing there. The report, which the Liberian Government received in September, has not been released here.

The inquiry commission was composed of Dr. Charles Johnson, appointed by the United States; Cuthbert Christy of Great Britain, appointed by the League Council, and Sir Arthur Barclay, named by the President of Liberia.

GEN. SMUTS BACKS ZIONISTS' PROTEST

Cables MacDonald That Powers Which Approved Balfour Plan Must Consent to Change.

BOYCOTT THREAT IS FILED

Grand Mufti Said to Object to Legislative Council, but Other Arabs Welcome Move.

Special Cable to THE NEW YORK TIMES.

LONDON, Oct. 23.—General Jan Christiaan Smuts today placed himself on the side of the Zionists in the controversy over the new British policy on Palestine. The South African statesman, who was one of the originators of the mandates system, sent a cablegram reminding the MacDonald Government that the Balfour declaration of 1917 was an international pronouncement approved beforehand by the allied and associated powers.

The present declaration of policy, in General Smuts's opinion, alters the 1917 pledge and as such cannot become operative without the consent of every nation which consented to the Balfour policy.

Lord Passfield, Colonial Secretary, has refused to comment on the denunciations of the government's new policy by Zionist leaders, including Felix M. Warburg of New York.

At the Colonial Office it was said on Lord Passfield's behalf that he prefers to wait until the question of the Palestine policy is raised in Parliament.

Boycott Resolutions Filed.

Special Cable to THE NEW YORK TIMES.

JERUSALEM, Oct. 23.—Pinchas Rutenberg, chairman of the Jewish National Council, today submitted to High Commissioner Chancellor the resolutions of that body announcing its decision not to participate in the Legislative Council proposed by the British Government. A copy of the resolutions was forwarded to the British Colonial Office.

All branches of the Palestine Jewish Labor Federation are arranging mass meetings throughout the country to protest against the British Government's new declaration.

The sentiment of all Jews in Palestine was characteristically displayed when the extreme orthodox rabbi, Benzion Yadler, at synagogue services opened the Ark of the Covenant and took out the holy scroll. Weeping, he chanted psalms and then said:

"Sad days have come upon Israel, but better days will follow."

There is great diversity of opinion among Palestine Arabs regarding Britain's declaration. It is said the

Continued on Page Eleven.

WINTER DENIES PART IN JUDGESHIP BARTER; HE WILL SIGN WAIVER

Republican Leader to Testify on Story He Put $10,000 Price on a Nomination.

"DOVE" TELLS OF VICE RING

Police Stool Pigeon Examined by Kresel on "Framing" and "Fixing" of Charges.

CONVICT CITES FAKE CASES

Bogus Lawyer Goes Over Records of Actions He Says Were Disposed of Illegally.

Keyes Winter, the first Republican leader to be accused by a witness before the special Ewald grand jury of placing a price upon a nomination for judicial office, met the charge promptly yesterday by denying it and offering to testify under a waiver of immunity.

Hiram C. Todd, Special Assistant Attorney General, accepted the offer of Mr. Winter, who is leader of the Fifteenth Assembly District, a Republican stronghold. In doing so Mr. Todd remarked that it was a "unique experience to have a New York district leader offer to waive immunity."

The case in which Mr. Winter was named centres about the nomination by the county committee of the Fifteenth Assembly District of Jehial Roeder for Municipal Court justice. Herman Hoffman, the unsuccessful aspirant for the place, who since it was denied him has become a member of the Osceola Democratic Club, has charged that an intermediary of the district leader's told him that since the nomination was as "good as election" he ought to be willing to contribute $10,000 to the club's campaign fund.

Winter Aide Denies Charge.

Lester Hofman, secretary of the Republican County Committee for that district, was named by Hoffman as Mr. Winter's spokesman, but Hofman, who appeared before the grand jury, stood by the district leader in denying that money was mentioned at any time in connection with the nomination.

The grand jury's excursion into Republican political practices was not allowed to divert its attention from the inquiry it has been conducting into the nomination and election of Judge Amedeo A. Bertini. Five witnesses, including three bank clerks, a former law partner of the judge and Alderman Joseph R. Smith, a Twenty-third Assembly District Democrat who refused to waive immunity, were examined before the grand jurors adjourned until Monday.

Today the special prosecutor and Supreme Court Justice Philip J. McCook, who granted the former's motion for a special blue-ribbon panel from which juries will be chosen to try former Magistrate George F. Ewald, Martin J. Healy, a Tammany leader, and their co-defendants on an indictment charging office buying, will supervise the drawing of 200 talesmen at the office of the Commissioner of Jurors.

Justice McCook's order called for the drawing of two panels of 100 talesmen each. From one a jury will be drawn to try the former magistrate and his wife, Mrs. Bertha E. Ewald, who is accused of providing the $10,000 he is alleged to have paid for his appointment. From the other a jury will be chosen to try Healy and Thomas T. Tommaney, the alleged intermediary in the transac-

Continued on Page Nineteen.

Chinese President Embraces Christianity; Move Startles China, Which Sees Blow to Reds

Special Cable to THE NEW YORK TIMES.

SHANGHAI, Oct. 23.—An interesting diversion from China's tangled politico-military situation occurred today, taking the country by surprise, when President Chiang Kai-shek, while staying in Shanghai, became a Christian, being baptized as a member of the Methodist Church by the Rev. Z. Kuang, Chinese pastor of the Young Allen Memorial Church.

The ceremony occurred in the home of Mme. K. T. Soong, General Chiang's mother-in-law, in the presence of a few members of the family, President Chiang Kai-shek wearing a simple Chinese gown.

Mei Ling, Mme. Chiang Kai-shek, who is American educated, has long been a Christian, and married General Chiang with a semi-Christian ceremony.

This makes the third member of the Soong family to embrace Christianity, and mission circles are eagerly looking forward to its reaction on the religious education question, which recently resulted in Nanking instituting many restrictions, although declaring freedom of religious belief in the country.

SHANGHAI, Oct. 23 (AP).—The President's baptism was regarded as a blow at the Communists, who are hunting down Christians in Kiangsi Province and elsewhere in the Yangtse Valley, coming after a hard-fought campaign in which he more than once seemed doomed to defeat, only to emerge stronger than ever.

Persons who have studied China's problems expressed the belief that his action was likely to form a striking precedent and have far-reaching effect upon the future of the government of China.

The conversion of President Chiang Kai-shek will once more permit the term "Christian General" to be used in Chinese dispatches. Marshal Feng Yu-hsiang, noted Northern General, once was an adherent of Christianity, but in recent years was reported to have renounced it.

Britain Asks Ban on Unknown Soldier Rites For 'Eradication of Memories of Great War'

Special Cable to THE NEW YORK TIMES.

LONDON, Oct. 23.—The British Government today made a striking gesture toward "eradication of the memories of the Great War" among all nations by suggesting to all governments through the Foreign Office here that during official visits to capitals of the former allies memorial wreaths should not be laid on the tombs of the unknown soldiers or other war memorials. The proposal would apply to foreign visitors to London and to British official guests in other capitals.

Hitherto it has been customary for foreign representatives in London to lay wreaths at the Cenotaph and sometimes on the tomb of the Unknown Warrior as one of their first official acts. Although the proposal will not affect the Armistice Day observance here it will put an end to the practice of paying respect to Britain's 1,000,000 war dead.

"The matter had become perfunctory anyhow," was the comment of Wickham Steed, former editor of The London Times, when he learned the government's decision. "These things, if they have any meaning, are too sacred to degenerate into mere ceremonies."

It was said in government circles that the replies from foreign governments had been favorable. There was an outcry, however, when it was proposed a year ago to omit the military display at the Armistice Day ceremony and there is almost certain to be a stir of protest over the latest suggestion.

SMITH RIDICULES REPUBLICAN WETS

They Illustrate Latest "Duck and Dodge" of Party on Prohibition, He Says.

CITES TUTTLE AND BAUMES

Opening Tour at Troy, He Entertains Crowd With Review of "Dry-Wet Policy."

From a Staff Correspondent of The New York Times.

TROY, N. Y., Oct. 23.—Asserting that the difference in viewpoints on prohibition of Charles H. Tuttle, Republican Gubernatorial candidate, and his running mate, State Senator Caleb H. Baumes, was indicative of the "ducking and dodging" tactics of New York Republicans, former Governor Alfred E. Smith launched a bitter attack on the Republican stand on the wet-dry question, in the opening speech here tonight of his State tour in support of the re-election of his Democratic successor, Franklin D. Roosevelt.

He spoke over a State-wide radio hook-up, facing an audience of more than 3,000 that occupied every square inch of the Troy Music Hall.

Swelled by infusions from a State convention of school teachers, the throng overflowed the hall and many were turned away. The doors were not opened until 7 P. M., but as early as 5:30 o'clock police reserves were called to hold the crowds in check.

The interest in hearing the former Governor was translated into vigorous applause and frequent laughter at his sallies against the Republicans.

At the outset, Mr. Smith announced that he would take his audience by the hand on an inspection of the Republican position as to the Eighteenth Amendment in the last twelve years. If, after he finished, his auditors could show him a greater example of "ducking and dodging," he said, he would like to see it.

Contrasts Candidates' View.

Pointing to Mr. Tuttle's positive declaration for repeal of prohibition, Mr. Smith contrasted with it the long dry record of Senator Baumes. If Mr. Baumes now backed the head of his ticket, the ex-Governor said, Mr. Baumes, running for Lieutenant Governor, had failed to declare himself until after it was too late for the drys to name a candidate against him.

"Duck and dodge No. 1," the ex-Governor asserted, was in 1918, when the Republicans in convention at Saratoga voted down a proposal to submit the Eighteenth Amendment to a State referendum.

Although the amendment was then pending for action by the Legislature, he said, the referendum suggested by William Barnes was voted down in the Committee on Resolutions by 32 to 5.

"That meant the Republican party ducked the issue," he said.

By contrast, he went on, the Democratic party then clearly declared for a prohibition referendum.

First the Republican Legislature had ratified the Eighteenth Amendment as a recognition of dry Republican votes up-State, Mr. Smith remarked. In 1920, because of the ensuing discontent, an almost identical Legislature passed the 2.75 beer bill as a concession to the wets.

"There we have them in 1919 dodging over to the dry side, in 1920 ducking back to the wet side," he said. "This was an attempt to duck away from the whole question; but something else happened in that year.

"The drys were still smarting under the sting of the 2.75 beer bill, and they were far from satisfied, and consequently exacted from the Republican leaders a promise that, in the event of their success in the election of 1920, they would pass a State enforcement act.

"Accordingly, in 1921, we found enacted into law what was known as the Mullan-Gage act. Not one single dollar of public money was appropri-

Continued on Page Thirteen.

TUTTLE SCORES RISES VOTED CITY OFFICIALS

Calls the Increase to Hubbard Especially Unwarranted After Refusal to Testify.

SEES THE GOVERNOR DEFIED

Predicts Roosevelt Will "Take It Lying Down" and Offers to Quit if He Does Not.

Speaking before three audiences on the east side last night, Charles H. Tuttle, Republican nominee for Governor, took up eleventh-hour pay rises aggregating $65,000 to favored city officials in the city budget for the next fiscal year, which were discovered yesterday when it was too late to protest them because the peroid for public hearings on the budget had ended.

"All were inserted," Mr. Tuttle said, "in the interval between the submission of the tentative budget last week and the submission of the proposed budget on Monday. If this method does not indicate intentional secrecy in making these pay rises at this time of unemployment and distress, how are we to account for the manner in which they were slipped into the budget and became known today only through the initiative of the press?"

Denounces Hubbard Increase.

The Republican nominee said that what had been done was a new challenge to Governor Roosevelt as leader of his party in this State, especially as one of the city officials to benefit was H. Warren Hubbard, Commissioner of Public Works for Manhattan, who gets another salary increase of $2,000, following one of $3,000 voted to him in September. Commissioner Hubbard is of the group of Tammany district leaders who are also city officials who refused to waive immunity and testify before the extraordinary grand jury created by the Governor in the Ewald case.

In this connection Mr. Tuttle declared that Governor Roosevelt, as leader of his party, had never called upon public officials who were not in the employ of the city, but who were employes of the State, to withdraw their refusal to testify. He also recalled that although twice indicted, Martin J. Healy still remained in his leadership of the Nineteenth Assembly District. Mr. Healy was indicted as the receiver in connection with the alleged payment of former City Magistrate Ewald of $10,000 for his appointment as city magistrate.

"Is the Governor really content to look to him, to that man who refused to testify lest he incriminate himself, that man indicted; is the Governor content to look to him for the votes of the Nineteenth Assembly District?" the Republican nominee asked amid resounding applause. "It seems to me that that question which has been asked by me requires an answer, or if none will be forthcoming, then the public is entitled to pass upon that refusal, and to answer it with a very just verdict of condemnation."

Reverting to salary rises, Mr. Tuttle said that as leader of his party it was the Governor's concern that one of the recalcitrant group of Tammany leaders, who had refused to testify, had been singled out for special reward at the hands of Tammany Hall.

Sees Tammany Defiant.

"Certainly," he exclaimed, "it would seem as though Tammany Hall felt it entirely safe to snap its fingers in the face not only of public opinion but of the Governor himself."

This was at the first meeting of the evening, at Public School 17, where an audience of from 700 to 800—all the auditorium could hold—listened to Mr. Tuttle's remarks and applauded the shafts he hurled at his Democratic opponent and at Tammany and its practices.

At his second meeting, at the Julia

Continued on Page Sixteen.

SECRET PAY RISES TO TAMMANY MEN FOUND IN BUDGET

Increases of $3,000 Each Given to Five Borough Public Works Heads at Closed Session.

GOT $2,000 LAST MONTH

Five Other Officials and 169 Attendants in Magistrates' Courts Also Included.

KOHLER DISCLAIMS ACTION

Thomas for Reclassification of City Salaries—Taxpayers Want Civic Budget Investigators.

Critics of the 1931 city budget, who for a week have been decrying the magnitude of its figures, apparently have overlooked the fact, uncovered yesterday at City Hall, that, included in the increases voted into the budget, "as proposed for adoption" by the Board of Estimate, in executive session, was about $65,000 for salary increases.

The more important of the beneficiaries are the five borough Commissioners of Public Works, each of whom has his pay raised in the present budget from $12,000 to $15,000 a year, despite the fact that only last September they all received increases from $10,000 to $12,000 annually.

Five other officials come in also for substantial increases, none of which was included in the tentative budget as prepared by Budget Director Charles L. Kohler, but all of which were inserted in "the proposed budget" by vote of the Board of Estimate. In addition, 169 attendants in the magistrates' courts are scheduled to receive average salary increases of $250.

Two Are Tammany Leaders.

Two of the Public Works Commissioners who receive the $3,000 rise on top of last September's advance of $2,000 are Tammany leaders in their boroughs and all are prominent in the affairs of their party. The proposed beneficiaries are as follows:

H. WARREN HUBBARD, Public Works Commissioner of Manhattan; leader in the Tenth Assembly District.

PETER A. CARY, Commissioner of Public Works of Brooklyn; leader in the Tenth District.

DAVID S. RENDT, Commissioner of Public Works for Richmond, recent victor over Borough President John A. Lynch for control of the Staten Island Democratic organization.

JOHN J. HALLERAN, Public Works Commissioner of Queens.

WILLIAM J. FLYNN, Public Works Commissioner of the Bronx.

Commissioner Flynn explained yesterday that, when the increases were voted to take effect last September, the intent was to make them from $10,000 to $15,000 each and that in the action on the present budget was made necessary to correct what had been really "an error or oversight" when the original increases were voted.

It was felt, it was explained, that the pay of the five borough Public Works Commissioners should be equalized with that of the commissioners heading the principal departments coming directly under the Mayor's jurisdiction and appointed by him, especially as the former are not infrequently called upon to sit in the Board of Estimate and vote in the absence of a Borough President.

Other officials receiving increases in the budget as proposed were:

PETER J. McGOWAN, secretary of the Board of Estimate, who received in September a rise from $10,000 to $12,000 and is now slated for an added increase of $1,500 a year, making his salary from Jan. 1 next $13,500.

FRANK SMITH, chief clerk of the Court of Special Sessions, who is increased from $7,500 a year to $10,000. He is said to have been "overlooked" in the September pay-rise schedules.

EDWARD W. COX, county clerk of Queens and leader in the Second Assembly District,

Continued on Page Four.

GOVERNMENT AND INDUSTRY TO CREATE JOBS FOR IDLE; CITY TO FEED 12,000 DAILY

Lehman Greets Trooper Who Ended Auburn Prison Riot

ONEIDA, N. Y., Oct. 23 (AP).—Lieut. Gov. Herbert Lehman's long standing wish to meet the man credited with having turned the tide of battle during the Auburn prison riot of last December and effecting the rescue of the captured warden, Brig. Gen. Edgar S. Jennings, was fulfilled here today.

The Lieutenant Governor left Governor Roosevelt's campaign party and made a special trip to the barracks of Troop D, State police, here to talk with Captain Stephen McGrath.

It was Mr. Lehman, as Acting Governor, who sent the order of "no compromise" to the law officers opposing the rioting prisoners.

Colonel Lehman thus had his first opportunity today of hearing Captain McGrath's account of the riot and how it was ended. McGrath headed the party of troopers who rushed the barricaded rioters and hurled the tear gas bombs that routed them.

FIND BUSINESS READY TO MOVE FORWARD

E. E. Shumaker and Merle Thorpe Say Depression's Causes Have Passed.

PLEAD FOR CONFIDENCE

Merchants' Luncheon Speakers Declare Industry Must Banish Fear of Future.

The membership council of the Merchant's Association of New York was told by speakers at its luncheon yesterday at the Hotel Astor that the causes of our business ills had been removed and that the nation was far from "broke." The speaker who expressed the first view and called upon industry to lead the way to a revival of business was Edward E. Shumaker, president of the R. C. A.-Victor Company, of Camden, N. J. He and Merle Thorpe, editor of "Nation's Business," published by the Chamber of Commerce of the United States of America, agreed that American business now needed confidence.

Mr. Shumaker pointed out that business reacted to prosperity very much like an individual and became sick from over-expansion, over-production and all the attendant evils accumulating in the boom period of 1927 to 1929. He showed that savings accounts had gained $200,000,000 within the past year, and that, after all, business recession was only 10 per cent below normal years.

"It is, therefore, my opinion that to avoid a slow, tedious and expensive convalescence, we must reestablish confidence," said Mr. Shumaker. "No one industry or group of industries can do it alone. Factories must resume normal operations. Merchants must replenish their stocks. Industry and capital must show the way.

Sees Fear as Business Curb.

"I see no sound reason for waiting for better times. In fact, I am convinced that it is a mistake to do so. Let us face this problem as American industry usually faces its other problems. Let us simultaneously do

Continued on Page Two.

Prentiss, Crime Expert, Seizes Thief in Home; Cows Him With Sword Until Police Arrive

Mark O. Prentiss, chief organizer of the National Crime Commission and author of many articles on crime prevention, captured a burglar single handed and without a struggle yesterday afternoon when he found the man robbing his home at 65 Park Avenue.

According to the police, the burglar who said he was Charles Faye, 22 years old, living in a rooming house at 113 West Eighty-second Street, confessed to having committed sixteen burglaries in the mid-town section of Manhattan during the last month.

Mr. Prentiss told the police that he entered his apartment shortly after 3 o'clock and went into his living room to surprise Faye in the act of picking up several pieces of jewelry that lay on a table. The man seemed stunned at the sudden entrance, Mr. Prentiss said, and offered no resistance when he took a Turkish sword which hung on the wall and forced him into a chair.

Telling Faye not to move, Mr. Prentiss called the police. While they were on the way, he said, the thief made no effort to escape, but pleaded with him to "have mercy" and release him. Faye, he said, told him that he had been forced into stealing by unemployment.

Detectives brought Faye to the station, where they questioned him for several hours.

He told them, they said, that his method of working was to enter apartments while the occupants were out, using small, thick pieces of vellum to open the locks.

Mr. Prentiss said last night that the experience was the "most interesting he had ever had."

"It should be a warning," he said, "to New Yorkers to be careful when they enter their homes. The Turkish sword is what saved me."

CAPITAL SPEEDS PROGRAM

Postal Department and Shipping Board Act to Spread Work.

GAIN SHOWN IN INDUSTRY

Ten Fisher Body Plants Will Go on Full Time—1,000 More Jobs Made in Chicago.

POLICE COUNTING NEEDY

City Plans to House 3,000—Salvation Army Opens Free Food Stations Today.

Developments in Employment.

Governmental, civic and industrial organizations attacking the problem of unemployment relief moved forward yesterday on many fronts in various parts of the country.

In Washington, the Postoffice Department took steps to distribute more work among substitute employes, while the Shipping Board abandoned plans to reduce its force. Preliminary organization of President Hoover's relief program was speeded up under Colonel Woods's direction. A gain for September in the construction industry was reported to the President.

From Detroit came the announcement that ten plants of the Fisher Body Corporation located outside of that city will begin operating on full time Monday. A three-day week has been in effect.

From Chicago came word that the Yellow Cab Company will add 1,000 men to its force; officers and employes of the Insull Utilities will contribute to relief funds one day's pay a month for six months, and other organization and enterprises have joined the movement.

The New York police began taking a census of the needy as the city made plans to feed 12,000 to 15,000 persons daily throughout the Winter. The Salvation Army will open eight free food stations in Manhattan and Brooklyn today.

Special to The New York Times.

WASHINGTON, Oct. 23.—With the government setting up the nation's central organization for unemployment relief, the Postoffice Department and the Shipping Board today joined the movement to provide the most work possible for the greatest number of workers.

The Shipping Board, Chairman T. V. O'Connor announced, postponed indefinitely reorganization plans which would have involved the gradual dismissal of about 500 employes. It had not been planned to let out any workers directly, but to cease filling vacancies as resignations or other causes naturally depleted its force.

Postmaster General Brown moved to create an unestimated number of new places in his department, principally for part-time workers, through cancellation of the right of regular employes to increase their earnings by voluntary overtime work.

Postoffice employes will be limited to their regular eight-hour shifts, making it possible for others to obtain work as substitutes at the regular rate or 65 cents an hour. This ruling also applies to carriers on routes, but it is not expected that many openings will be created there in view of the recent action curtailing the number of deliveries in the larger cities.

The War Department already has taken steps to "stagger" employment on Mississippi River work.

Action toward speedily whipping into shape the preliminary organization necessary to set up at once the nationwide machinery for relief of the country's 3,500,000 unemployed was taken today, with the prospect that a definite plan will be ready for announcement tomorrow morning.

Concerned in these activities, all of which revolve around Colonel Arthur Woods of New York, director in chief of the Federal relief forces, were the President, Cabinet members and specialists in government departments, particularly the Department of Commerce, many members of which were associated with Colonel Woods when he took charge of a similar problem in the business depression of 1921 and 1922.

Colonel Woods's conferences continued late into the night, while the

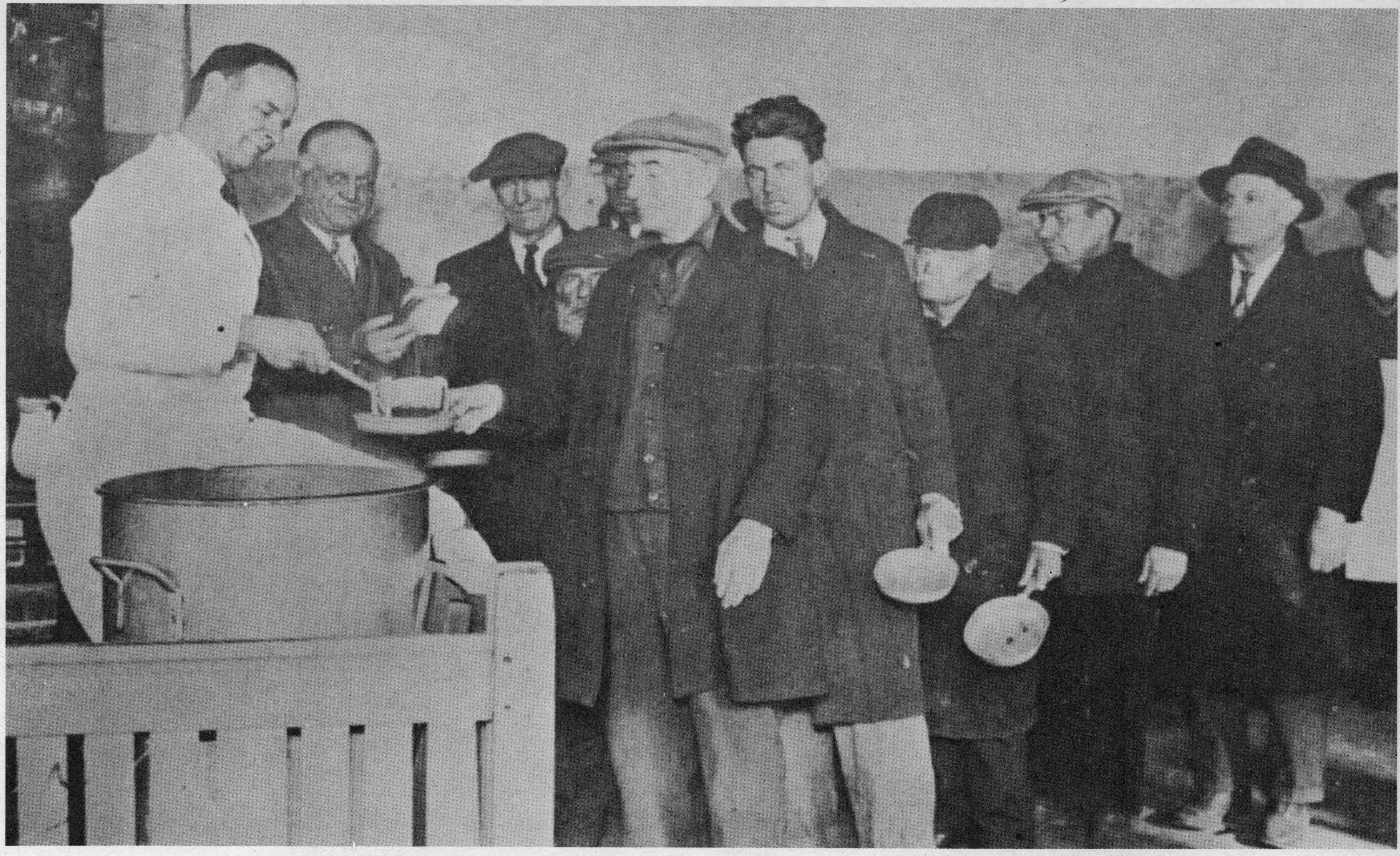

Breadlines and soup kitchens became familiar sights, although President Hoover predicted an end of unemployment by May.

Apple sellers became a familiar sight.

"All the News That's Fit to Print."

The New York Times.

Copyright, 1930, by The New York Times Company.

THE WEATHER
Cloudy, with probably occasional rain today; tomorrow fair, colder.
Temperature Yesterday—Max. 50; Min. 44.
U. S. Weather Forecast—For details see Page 42.

VOL. LXXX....No. 26,583. NEW YORK, WEDNESDAY, NOVEMBER 5, 1930. TWO CENTS In Greater New York | THREE CENTS Within 200 Miles | FOUR CENTS Elsewhere Except 7th and 8th Postal Zones

DEMOCRATIC LANDSLIDE SWEEPS COUNTRY; REPUBLICANS MAY LOSE CONGRESS CONTROL; ROOSEVELT WINNER BY MORE THAN 700,000

WETS GAIN IN HOUSE

Win 32 Seats and Lose None; Hold Senate Places.

AIDED BY ILLINOIS SWEEP

Also Helped by Victory of Bulkley in Ohio—Drys Win in Places.

THREE REFERENDA GO WET

Repeal Proposals Are Carried in Rhode Island, Illinois and Massachusetts.

Forces favoring repeal of the Eighteenth Amendment and liquor laws scored gains in the Congressional elections throughout the country yesterday, adding to these victories substantial majorities in favor of repeal referenda in Illinois, Rhode Island and Massachusetts.

On the basis of returns late last night, the so-called "wet bloc" in the House had picked up thirty new votes to add to the ninety-one which the most optimistic of wets count in the present House.

The Senate wets had picked up several new names, of such imminence as Morrow of New Jersey, Lewis of Illinois and Bulkley of Ohio, but were battling to hold the number of eighteen in the present make-up of the Senate, because of retirements of sitting wet members from States where only dry candidates sought their seats.

Marcus Coolidge of Massachusetts was running well ahead of his dry opponent, William M. Butler, overcoming a substantial lead early in the night.

Results of Referenda.

Wet candidates were carrying with them wet referenda in every State where they were offered. In Illinois the vote went decidedly in favor of repeal of the Eighteenth Amendment. Three proposals, one for repeal of the amendment, another for modification of the Volstead act and the other proposing repeal of the State enforcement act, all carried with good majorities, with the heaviest vote and the heaviest majority recorded on the first question.

Rhode Island registered a vote of more than 2 to 1 in favor of repeal. The vote in Massachusetts was on repeal of the State enforcement act and a majority in favor of the referendum was gaining in size as Marcus Coolidge increased his lead over the dry Butler.

In his landslide in Illinois Mr. Lewis evidently had swept a number of wet Democrats into office, and in Ohio the victory of Mr. Bulkley carried with it an increase in the wet representation of that State in the lower house by at least three. At least two wet gains in the House went with the Morrow victory in New Jersey, and seven apparently had been recorded in Pennsylvania, despite the victories of dry Senate and Gubernatorial candidates.

Many Dry Victories Recorded.

The wets had not actually lost a seat in either house on the face of returns up until early this morning, although dry victories had been scored in a number of States, including three in the South where prohibition figured conspicuously as an issue in the campaign.

The whole delegation in Connecticut, including Representative John Q. Tilson, Hoover spokesman and Republican leader in the House, will be listed among the wets at the next Congress. The only seat in doubt was in the First District, where C. W. Seymour, dry Republican, was pitted with A. Longergan, wet Democrat. Mr. Longergan led on the reports last night.

Four wets evidently had won in Michigan, including S. H. Person, who will occupy the seat held by Grant M. Hudson, former State Superintendent of the Anti-Saloon

Continued on Page Seven.

U. S. SENATORS ELECTED

REPUBLICANS—13.

Delaware	*D. O. Hastings
Idaho	*William E. Borah
Iowa	‡L. J. Dickinson
Kansas	‡Arthur Capper
Maine	¶W. H. White Jr.
Michigan	*James Couzens
Nebraska	*George W. Norris
New Hampshire	*Henry W. Keyes
New Jersey	†Dwight W. Morrow
Oregon	*Charles L. McNary
Pennsylvania	§James J. Davis
Rhode Island	*J. H. Metcalf
Wyoming	†Robert D. Cary

DEMOCRATS—20.

Alabama	‡J. H. Bankhead
Arkansas	*J. T. Robinson
Colorado	‡E. P. Costigan
Georgia	*William J. Harris
Illinois	‡J. H. Lewis
Louisiana	‡Huey P. Long
Massachusetts	‡M. A. Coolidge
Minnesota	‡Einar Hoidale
Mississippi	*Pat Harrison
Montana	*Thomas J. Walsh
New Mexico	*S. G. Bratton
North Carolina	‡Josiah W. Bailey
Ohio	§Robert J. Bulkley
Oklahoma	‡Thomas P. Gore
South Carolina	‡James F. Byrnes
Tennessee	**William E. Brock
Tennessee	‡Cordell Hull
Texas	*Morris Sheppard
Virginia	*Carter Glass
West Virginia	‡M. M. Neely

IN DOUBT—3.

Kansas, South Dakota, Kentucky

*Re-elected for full term ending March 3, 1937. †Elected for both long and short terms. ‡Elected for full term ending March 3, 1937. ¶Elected Sept. 8, 1930 for full term ending March 3, 1937. §Elected for short term ending March 3, 1933. **Elected for short term ending March 3, 1931.

LEWIS, DEMOCRAT, SWEEPS ILLINOIS

Out-and-Out Wet Piles Up 2 to 1 Lead Over Mrs. McCormick, Republican, for Senate.

AHEAD 3 TO 1 IN CHICAGO

Victor Breaks Even or Better in Strong Republican Counties Down-State.

Special to The New York Times.

CHICAGO, Nov. 4.—James Hamilton Lewis, Democrat, and an out-and-out wet, won in a landslide over Representative Ruth Hanna McCormick, Republican and "provisionally wet," in today's election of a Senator from Illinois.

After a campaign in which the Democrats stressed prohibition and prosperity, something of a seismic upheaval struck this rock-ribbed Republican State—the home of Lincoln, the first Republican President—and ex-Senator Lewis's plurality seems likely to approach 700,000. The politicians rate it the greatest blow against national prohibition thus far struck.

Incomplete returns at midnight indicated that the Democrats gained three Congressional seats from Cook County districts, two and possibly three seats down-State, and the two places as members of Congress-at-Large. Correspondingly, the complexion of the Illinois delegation to Washington had been changed by wet gains of eight or nine seats.

Figures from nearly half of the State show Mr. Lewis far in the lead both in Cook County, which includes Chicago, and down-State.

Goes Into Lead Down-State.

In Chicago he was running three to one ahead of Mrs. McCormick, the count indicating that his Chicago plurality will be around 425,000.

Mr. Lewis had 365,982 votes in 1,675 out of 3,009 city precincts; 15,400 in 80 other Cook County precincts, and 256,558 in 1,609 down-State precincts, or a total of 637,940 in 3,394 out of 7,109 precincts in the whole State. His plurality on these returns was 351,676 over Mrs. McCormick, whose vote was 126,724 in Cook County and 286,264 in the 3,394 precincts from all parts of the State. In the same number of districts, Mrs. Lottie Holman O'Neill, Independent Dry, polled 30,448 votes.

Mrs. McCormick seemed likely to

Continued on Page Two.

MORROW WINS EASILY

Majority of 100,000 In Jersey Senate Race Indicated.

PARTY LOSES IN HOUSE

Democrats Leading in Six Districts Nominally Republican.

TWO BOND ISSUES WINNING

Legislature Safely Republican—Anti-Prohibitionists Score Heavily.

Dwight W. Morrow, former Ambassador to Mexico, was leading by a wide margin his two Democratic opponents in his race for both the full and short terms for United States Senator from New Jersey early this morning as the returns were coming in from the 3,321 election districts. Voters in 2,052 districts gave Mr. Morrow 322,014 and Alexander D. Simpson, former State Senator from Hudson County, 227,837.

E. Bertram Mott, chairman of the Republican State Committee, said early this morning a conservative estimate of Mr. Morrow's majority would be 100,000. Republican leaders before the election had predicted a majority of 200,000.

Tabulation of returns from 729 districts showed that Mr. Morrow was leading Miss Thelma Parkinson, Smith College Graduate, in the race for the short term or vacancy caused by the resignation of Walter E. Edge to become Ambassador to France, by a vote of 108,972 to 65,524.

Returns from 1,090 out of 3,321 election districts showed two of the $100,000,000 bond issue proposals winning and one losing as follows: Highways, 83,653 against, 78,740 for; water supply, 78,343 against, 88,442 for, and institutional rehabilitation, 80,105 against and 84.956 for.

Democrats were leading in contests for the House of Representatives in six districts nominally Republican, and that the State Legislature was overwhelmingly Republican.

Mr. Simpson, as candidate for the full term, and Miss Parkinson, as candidate for the short term, polled a surprisingly heavy vote in the early returns although they ran ahead in only three counties, Hudson, Democratic stronghold; Mercer and Middlesex. The Democrats were greatly encouraged by the early returns giving Mr. Simpson and Miss Parkinson leads in half a dozen counties. The leads for the Democratic candidates were accounted for by the fact that they came from industrial centres.

While Mercer, a strongly Republican county, gave Mr. Simpson and Miss Parkinson substantial leads in the early returns, the Republicans expected to see those margins dwindle with the tabulation of returns outside Trenton. The strength of the Democrats in Trenton is said to have been due to the unemployment problem which has been acute there for months.

Representative Mary T. Norton, vice chairman of the Democratic State Committee, conceded the election of Mr. Morrow at 1:25 o'clock this morning.

"Senator Simpson and Miss Thelma Parkinson waged an aggressive and clean battle," said Mrs. Norton. "The opposing forces, wealth and great publicity, supporting fine personality, were hard to overcome and the inevitable resulted. I wish Mr. Morrow every success."

Mrs. Norton Re-elected.

Mrs. Norton was re-elected to the House of Representatives from the Twelfth Congressional District. Fred A. Hartley, Republican, who defeated Paul Moore, Democrat, two years

Continued on Page Five.

Roosevelt Appraises Victory As Expression of Confidence

Governor Franklin D. Roosevelt, speaking over the radio after his re-election had been conceded last night, interpreted the vote he received as one of confidence.

"I want to say a few words to the people of this State tonight," he declared over stations WEAF and WJZ. "I am overwhelmed with gratitude for the vote of confidence you have given to my administration.

"I can only say that in the next two years I will bring all my ability to serve all of the citizens, regardless of party and regardless of locality, in the interest of a program of honest government."

NEW ENGLAND HIT BY DEMOCRATIC WAVE

Massachusetts Elects M. A. Coolidge, Wet, for Senator, and Ely for Governor.

CROSS WINS IN CONNECTICUT

Former Yale Dean Surprises by Victory—Metcalf Rhode Island Winner.

New England Results.

New England Democrats were victorious in two States. Their candidates for United States Senator and Governor, Marcus A. Coolidge and Joseph B. Ely, won in Massachusetts and their nominee for Governor of Connecticut, former Dean Wilbur L. Cross of Yale, was elected. The Republicans carried Rhode Island, New Hampshire and Vermont.

Special to The New York Times.

BOSTON, Nov. 4.—Massachusetts saw a Democratic sweep in today's election which, while not extending throughout the entire State ticket or into the Congressional fight in the sixteen districts, carried a wet Democrat into the United States Senatorship and the Governorship, by decisive margins.

With about two-thirds of the vote counted, it is estimated that former Senator William M. Butler, dry Republican candidate for the Senate, will be defeated by about 75,000 votes by Marcus A. Coolidge, the Democratic candidate. The same returns indicated the defeat of Governor Frank G. Allen, Republican, by 25,000 votes at the hands of Joseph P. Ely, Democrat.

The vote of 1,070 precincts out of the 1,650 in the State gave:

For Governor—Allen, 345,694; Ely, 365,630.

For Senator—Butler, 319,241; Coolidge, 389,432.

State Dry Act Repeal Carried.

At the same time it was indicated that the referendum for repeal of the "baby volstead act," as the State prohibition enforcement law is known, would be carried by more than 200,000.

The vote on the question from 886 precincts, exclusive of Boston, stood: For repeal, 304,951; against repeal, 186,550.

Led by Boston, the cities of the Commonwealth were largely instrumental in piling up the winning Democratic majority. The Boston vote alone, it was estimated, would have

Continued on Page Nine.

Heflin Is Beaten in Alabama by Nearly 2 to 1; Democrats Defeat All Candidates on His Ticket

Special to The New York Times.

BIRMINGHAM, Ala., Nov. 4.—J. Thomas Heflin, senior Senator from Alabama, was defeated by the Democrats of the State today for his defection from the party in the 1928 Presidential election. With three-fourths of the vote counted, John H. Bankhead, his opponent, was leading by 46,007 votes out of a total of 211,627. The vote stood 128,817 for Bankhead and 82,810 for Heflin.

Judge B. M. Miller, for Governor, and Hugh Merrill, for Lieutenant Governor, were holding the same commanding lead over Hugh Locke and Dempsey Powell, "Jeffersonian" candidates running on the same ticket with Senator Heflin.

In a statement to The Montgomery Advertiser tonight Senator Heflin charged "fraud and corruption" in the election and said he would demand an investigation by the Senate Committee on Elections.

"While early returns indicate the vote is going against me, within two hours I will be 100,000 votes ahead."

Boxes which went overwhelmingly for Hoover in the 1928 election went just as strongly for the Democratic nominees today.

No serious political issues were at stake in the election other than whether Alabama would remain in the Democratic column or would become an active two-party State.

TUTTLE IS SWAMPED

Governor's Record Plurality Amazes His Own Party.

CARRIES TICKET WITH HIM

Lehman and Tremaine Re-elected—Bennett Also Victorious.

UP-STATE FOR ROOSEVELT

Sweep Exceeds Smith's Largest Plurality of 385,338—Lieutenant Governor Wins Easily.

Tables of the city and State votes on Pages 10 and 11.

In a Democratic landslide of unprecedented proportions, Governor Franklin D. Roosevelt was re-elected yesterday by a plurality of approximately 730,000 over Charles H. Tuttle, Republican nominee.

In his overwhelming victory, Governor Roosevelt carried with him Lieut. Gov. Herbert H. Lehman, Controller Morris S. Tremaine and John J. Bennett Jr., candidate for Attorney General, who also obtained large pluralities in New York City but ran far behind the Governor up-State.

Professor Robert P. Carroll, Independent dry, running as the candidate of the Law Enforcement party, polled a vote of nearly 170,000, all but about 8,885 of which was outside New York City. Professor Carroll carried Yates County over both Tuttle and Roosevelt and his vote cut heavily into the usual Republican vote in many up-State counties.

556,868 Plurality in City.

New York City gave Governor Roosevelt 556,868 plurality. The vote in the city for Governor was: Roosevelt, 926,665; Tuttle, 369,797; Louis Waldman, Socialist, 88,329, and Carroll, 8,885.

With 168 up-State election districts missing, 4.816 districts out of 4,976 gave Roosevelt, 826.662; Tuttle, 659,163; Carroll, 158,323, an actual plurality for Roosevelt of 167,499 and an indicated up-State plurality of 174,160 and an indicated plurality in the entire State of 730,925. The up-State vote for Roosevelt in these 4,816 districts exceeded the combined vote for Tuttle and Carroll by 10,461.

Carroll's up-State vote was 158,323.

The tremendous vote for Governor Roosevelt was regarded as increasing greatly his chance for the Democratic nomination for President in 1932, for which he is known to be an aspirant. In rolling up his plurality, Governor Roosevelt reached a mark never before attained by any other candidate for State office. His plurality of 556,868 in New York City would have been a record if it had not been exceeded by the city plurality of Lieut. Gov. Lehman, which was 607,087.

The largest plurality ever received in the State by Alfred E. Smith and

Continued on Page Three.

Times Wide World Photo.

OVERWHELMINGLY RE-ELECTED.

Governor Franklin D. Roosevelt, Who, With His Entire Ticket, Is Returned to Office by a Record Plurality.

REPUBLICANS RETAIN CONTROL AT ALBANY

Hold Assembly by a Reduced Margin—Advantage in the Senate Cut to One Seat.

UP-STATE WETS VICTORIOUS

Drys Who Promised to Defeat Them Fail—Hofstadter Elected by 227 Votes.

Despite the landslide which resulted in the re-election of Governor Roosevelt by a towering majority, the Republicans will continue in control of both branches of the Legislature.

Late returns from the legislative elections give the Republicans continued control of both the Senate and Assembly, barring upsets on revised returns in some districts where the vote was close.

Final election returns received early this morning show the Republicans failed to hold their own in the Senate elections. The 1931 Senate, accordingly, will be composed of twenty-six Republicans and twenty-five Democrats.

The Democrats made heavy inroads on the Republicans in the Assembly elections. In the present Assembly the Republicans hold eighty-six seats and the Democrats sixty-four. In the 1931 Assembly the Republicans will have eighty votes and the Democrats seventy, a gain of six votes for the Democrats and a corresponding loss for the Republicans.

The vote necessary to pass a bill in the Senate is twenty-six and in the Assembly seventy-six.

New York City thus will have only one Republican representative in the Senate and only two in the Assembly. In the present Assembly there are four Republican Assemblymen, all from Manhattan. In the 1931 Assembly there will be one from Manhattan, Abbot Lowe Moffat of the Fifteenth, and one from Brooklyn, Robert K. Story Jr. of the Seventeenth Kings District.

Wald Defeated Here.

In the Senate the day was saved to the Republicans through the re-election of Senator Samuel H. Hofstadter of the Seventeenth Senatorial District on the west side of Manhattan. Mr. Hofstadter's victory was won by a slender majority of 227 votes. He defeated Albert Wald, the Democratic nominee, for whom a terrific drive was made by the Democrats in an attempt to gain control of the upper house at Albany

Continued on Page Four.

CITY GIVES GOVERNOR GREATEST PLURALITY

Has Margin of 556,868 as Graft Issue Fails Tuttle—Lehman Leads His Ticket.

MRS. PRATT WINS BY 651

La Guardia Victorious—Miller Elected Judge, Alger Loses—Bond Issue Carries.

Governor Roosevelt carried the city yesterday by the unprecedented plurality of 556,868 votes over his Republican rival, Charles H. Tuttle. His associates on the ticket also piled up huge pluralities over Republican opponents, that of Lieut. Gov. Lehman reaching the mark of 607,087.

The city's vote for Governor was:

Roosevelt	926,665
Tuttle	369,797
Waldman	88,329
Carroll	8,883

Governor Roosevelt's tremendous plurality, although far above the pre-election estimates of John F. Curry and other Democratic leaders, did not arouse the enthusiasm which has greeted the news of large pluralities in the past years. The early estimates were regarded as extremely conservative, the Democratic leaders having somewhat discounted the more optimistic reports which came from the district leaders.

Mrs. Pratt Wins Close Race.

The Democratic landslide carried into office nearly all of the party's local candidates, such strong Republican candidates as Representative Ruth B. Pratt, Representative F. H. La Guardia and State Senator Samuel H. Hofstadter narrowly escaping defeat. The only upset was in Brooklyn where Robert K. Storey Jr., Republican, won against his Democratic rival for an Assembly seat. This was counterbalanced by the victory of D. H. Stephens, Democrat, who was elected to the Assembly in the Nineteenth Manhattan District.

This district, incidentally, is the one in which Martin J. Healy is Democratic leader. Mr. Healy is one of the central figures in the judiciary scandals upon which Mr. Tuttle largely based his fruitless campaign.

The election was one of the quietest in years, there being but few disturbances at the polling places. From the moment that the returns began to come in it was evident that the issue of judicial corruption and alleged bartering of judicial office would have no effect upon the Roosevelt vote. Nor did the driving rain which fell throughout the day keep

Continued on Page Three.

STILL LEAD IN SENATE

But Republican Hold on House Hangs on Belated Returns.

SEE PRESAGE FOR 1932

Democrats Are Victorious in Nearly All the Chief Battles.

PINCHOT BEATS HEMPHILL

Election of Bulkley, a Wet, as Senator in Ohio Seems Indicated.

By RICHARD V. OULAHAN.

A distinct Democratic sweep, suggesting a landslide for that party, extended across the country in yesterday's elections, held in all the forty-eight States except Maine. While the outcome of a number of contests for important public offices is still in doubt, the Democrats were victorious in most of the outstanding battles from which definite returns have been received.

The general trend of these returns up to the time this edition of The New York Times went to press furnished encouraging evidence to Democracy's leaders that the sentiment expressed at the polls throughout a widespread area presaged victory for their Presidential ticket in the elections of 1932.

Democratic Governors were elected in New York, Connecticut, Massacusetts, Rhode Island and Ohio, and in States normally Democratic. In such States as Kansas, Minnesota, Nebraska, Oregan and Wyoming, where the Republicans win more often than not, the result is in doubt on account of the strong trend of Democratic sentiment.

Senate Lead Slender.

Judging by the latest returns, there is a bare chance that the nominal Republican majority in the Senate will be overthrown, although the prospect is that the Republicans may still have a slight excess of members over the Democrats. It is possible, however, that the next Senate will be a tie politically.

Democratic Senators have been elected in place of Republicans in Colorado, Minnesota, Ohio, Oklahoma, West Virginia and Massachusetts, and the chances favor a victory for the Republican Senatorial candidate in South Dakota. Only one Republican Senatorial aspirant has triumphed over a sitting Democratic Senator. This happened in Iowa.

In line with the general Democratic swing, the return showed that candidates of that party have cut heavily into the big Republican majority in the House of Representatives with a fair prospect that the Democrats will get control, though the actual outcome remains in doubt.

Based on the latest returns, the Senate line-up appears to be 45 Democrats, 47 Republicans and 1 Farmer-Laborite, with 3 contests doubtful. This line-up concedes the election of Hoidale, Democrat, over Senator Schall, Republican, in Minnesota. The doubtful contests are in South Dakota, Kansas and Kentucky. Should the Democratic candidates carry all these contests the Senate would stand:

Democrats 48, Republicans 47, Farmer-Laborite 1.

Heavy gains were made by the Democrats in the contest for 431 seats in the House of Representatives, but whether these will be sufficient to wipe out the present Republican majority is uncertain, with returns incomplete from approximately threescore districts.

Results of Latest Figures.

Counting nine vacant seats which had been held by Republicans, the majority of that party in the present House is 103. The latest definite election returns give the Republicans 189 seats, the Democrats 200 and the Farmer-Labor party 1, with 44 in the doubtful column and 1 Independent Republican.

The Democrats have 185 members

"All the News That's Fit to Print."

The New York Times.

THE WEATHER
Fair today; tomorrow fair and slightly warmer.
Temperatures Yesterday—Max. 57; Min. 47.
U. S. Weather Forecast—For details see Page 40.

Copyright, 1930, by The New York Times Company.

VOL. LXXX....No. 26,598. ****+ NEW YORK, THURSDAY, NOVEMBER 20, 1930. TWO CENTS In Greater New York | THREE CENTS Within 200 Miles | FOUR CENTS Elsewhere Except 7th and 8th Postal Zones

MERCHANTS FIGHT SALES TAX AS BLOW TO TRADE RECOVERY

100 Leaders and Groups Make Joint Protest at Meeting of State Commission.

SAY PUBLIC WOULD SUFFER

But Real Estate Interests Tell Inquiry Plan Would Give Them Needed Relief.

MANY SOLUTIONS OFFERED

Grimm Suggests City Might Move to Secede Unless State Cuts Its Tax Burden.

More than 100 representatives of important retail associations, department stores, hardware, furniture, silk, textile, jewelry and other mercantile interests in the city joined forces yesterday in protesting to the State Commission on the Revision of the Tax Laws that their organizations were unalterably opposed to any form of sales tax as iniquitous, burdensome and discouraging to prosperity.

In the commission's first public hearing in the city, throngs filed in and out of the large meeting hall of the bar association on West Forty-fourth Street all day long to express their disagreement with proposed methods of tax revision, to warn against any increase in taxation as unwarranted, or to advocate various methods of redistributing the tax burden to relieve real estate and at the same time maintain the present total revenue.

The forty-four speakers, many of whom represented several groups or organizations, included Samuel W. Reyburn, Grover A. Whalen, Bernard F. Gimbel, Peter Grimm, chairman of the Mayor's committee on taxation and president of the Real Estate Board of New York, and Norman Thomas, Socialist leader.

They advocated solutions of the present problem which were as divergent as their interests. These ranged all the way from the "single tax" to an increased gasoline tax, a different system of distributing tax revenues, a lowering of exemption limitations on income taxes and an increase of rates for incomes exceeding $50,000 annually, an increased inheritance tax and abolition of many of the present tax exemptions.

Despite the coalition of retailers and merchants who opposed any form of sales tax, this form of taxation found its advocates, being approved mostly by representatives of real estate boards.

Norman Thomas opposed single tax or a sales tax, scouted the personal property tax as "farcical and hypocritical," favored an increase in income and inheritance taxes and urged as an eventual solution "a shift in land rates with an emphasis on economic rents."

"Relief Must Come From Albany."

Mr. Grimm, who discussed the part New York City plays in the tax scheme of the State, warned the commission that "unless you can find ways and means of helping the city we can't help ourselves. The greatest relief must come from Albany." Mr. Grimm's premise was that the city faces tremendous but necessary expenditures in the future, and that the present tax system diverts from the city for the benefit of other areas in the State too much of the revenues from the taxes paid by the city.

"From time to time proposals are made that New York and its surrounding metropolitan area be set up as a separate State of the Union," Mr. Grimm said. "If this were done, the city would have few fiscal problems. The burden on real estate could be greatly lightened and the other revenues necessary could be easily secured from personal income, corporation and business taxes. The exchequer could be filled to overflowing and our problems at an end.

"The fact that with great ease New York's metropolitan area could become financially independent is, I trust, a fact which the members of your honorable body will keep in mind as your work proceeds. If the proposal of a separate State ever came on the tapis of political policies it would naturally meet with tremendous opposition from sections of the Commonwealth which are not in the metropolitan area.

"The best way of keeping the question from being mooted is through adequate provision of new sources of revenue for the city, so that in the language of the statute its needs shall 'be adequately cared for in a just manner.' In short, the problem confronting the Mayor's committee

Continued on Page Nineteen.

Borah Ready to Seek Action On World Court if Submitted

Special to The New York Times.

WASHINGTON, Nov. 19.—Senator Borah, chairman of the Committee on Foreign Relations, said today that, if President Hoover sent the World Court protocol to the Senate for ratification at the coming short session, he would see that it was laid before the committee and ample opportunity given for its discussion.

He believed that the protocol would be reported to the Senate by the committee, but said he thought debate on it in the chamber would last a considerable time.

No public intimation has come from the White House as to when the protocol will be laid before the Senate. Some proponents of the court are urging that it be submitted in December, but certain Senators favorable to participation doubt the advisibility of this. They fear a debate so prolonged that the annual supply bills would be jeopardized.

'SCRAMBLED' SPEECH ON RADIOPHONE NEAR

Commercially Practicable Now, Says S. P. Grace, but Company Awaits Further Development.

WILL FOIL EAVESDROPPING

"Singing Flame" Gives Recital for 3,500 at Science Forum on Electrical Wonders.

The scrambling of speech over the transatlantic radio telephone so that listeners-in will hear only a meaningless jumble of words was described last night by Sergius P. Grace, assistant vice president of the Bell Telephone Laboratories, before an audience of 3,500 that filled Mecca Temple, 133 West Fifty-fifth Street.

The singing flame and other recent electrical wonders also were demonstrated at a Science Forum, held under the auspices of the New York Electrical Society, the Museum of the Peaceful Arts and the New York section of the American Institute of Electrical Engineers.

At present transatlantic radio telephony is transmitted by regular short-wave radio on which any one possessing a radio can tune in. Scrambled speech will give privacy, it was said. For example, it was explained, if the individual making the call says "telephone company" any one tuning in will hear the two words come out scrambled as "play-o-fine crink-a-nope." All other conversation will be similarly scrambled so that an outsider listening in will just get a jumble of words.

To protect the transatlantic conversations against eavesdropping, both an electric "transmitting brain" and an electric "translating brain" have been developed, which synthetically manufacture a strange language spoken by no human being.

The electric "translating brain" inverts and distorts the natural speech frequencies or tones so as to make the transmitted speech unintelligible to the ordinary radio listener. So changed are the sounds that the listener-in would hear only unintelligible gibberish.

Then the electric "translating brain" picks up the intentionally intermingled high and low frequencies employed and rearranges the inverted sounds so that they come to the receiver in a proper and intelligible form.

Commercially Practicable Now.

Asked whether scrambled speech had been developed to a point where it could be placed in commercial operation, Mr. Grace said that it could be done commercially right now. However, he added, there are

Continued on Page Two.

TAMMANY LEADERS AT HEALY TRIAL DENY DICTATING ON JOBS

Farley and Hand Admit Trying to Reward Aides but Insist Mayor Made Own Decisions.

EWALD CHECK IN EVIDENCE

$5,000 Draft That His Wife Cashed as Part of Loan to Healy Shown to Jury.

CRAIN TELLS OF INQUIRY

Reads Tommaney Statement Saying He Feared Being Misrepresented if He Explained Deals to Tuttle.

Tammany Hall has a system of rewarding the faithful, but it does not always work because Mayor Walker sometimes disregards the wishes of the organization in appointing men to public office, Charles S. Hand, Commissioner of Sanitation and former secretary to the Mayor, testified yesterday at the trial of Martin J. Healy and Thomas T. Tommaney.

Commissioner Hand and Sheriff Thomas M. Farley were called as witnesses at the third session of the trial before Supreme Court Justice Philip J. McCook and a jury by Hiram C. Todd, special Assistant Attorney General, in an effort to prove that Healy, a Tammany district leader, and Tommaney, his friend and aide, by virtue of their political power could have bartered public office. They are accused of selling former Magistrate George F. Ewald his appointment for $10,000.

After two "expert" witnesses had asserted that the Tammany system was full of loopholes and exceptions, with many a possible slip between a district leader's recommendation of a candidate and his actual appointment, Mr. Todd summoned two officeholders from Healy's district, for whom he got jobs.

Two Job Holders Called.

These two witnesses, Bernard J. Gries, an assistant deputy sheriff, and Frank W. Geraty, a city marshal, however, assured Sydney A. Syme, chief of defense counsel, that Healy had acted on their behalf without asking or receiving remuneration. Geraty explained it thus:

"I said, 'Marty, I'm up for reappointment,' and he said, 'Well, what are you worrying about?' and in a few days I was reappointed. That's all there was to it."

These witnesses completed what Mr. Todd has referred to as "the background" of the State's case. With that disposed of, the special prosecutor began the presentation of evidence more directly concerned with the $10,000 transaction which preceded Ewald's elevation to the bench in April, 1927.

District Attorney Crain, elderly Sachem of Tammany Hall, who was superseded by the Attorney General at Governor Roosevelt's order after his failure to obtain indictments in the case; Peter Eckert, the former magistrate's father-in-law; a bank teller and two stenographers from Mr. Crain's office followed one another on the witness stand in rapid succession.

Crain Asked for Tuttle Letters.

Mr. Crain's appearance as a witness was seized upon by Mr. Syme as an opportunity to bring the name of Charles H. Tuttle, former United States Attorney and defeated Republican candidate for Governor, whom he has accused of engineering a political plot against his clients, once more before the jurors. He called upon the District Attorney to pro-

Continued on Page Twenty-three.

Nation Pays Retail Bills of $20,000,000,000; Average Loss on Bad Debts Is 0.6 Per Cent

Special to The New York Times.

BALTIMORE, Nov. 19.—Despite the nation's retail credit business of $20,000,000,000 annually and avoidable credit losses of $200,000,000, "the American people are paying their bills," Edwin B. George, chief of the Marketing Service Division of the Department of Commerce, told a meeting of retail credit men here this evening. The figures used by Mr. George were based on findings of a national retail credits survey, recently completed by the Bureau of Foreign and Domestic Commerce of the department.

"We can breathe a sigh of relief," said Mr. George, "at the discovery that with all of their open-credit and instalment commitments the American people is not hopelessly mortgaged. Although they are buying from $4,000,000,000 to $5,000,000,000 of instalment goods a year and some $15,000,000,000 more of goods on open credit, the fact remains that the grocer, the butcher and the candlestick maker usually get their money and the last painful instalment is usually paid.

"This survey of retail credit practices is the first nation-wide check on credit made in American history.

"It is really a triumph for business acumen, for throughout all this welter of unregulated growth the average loss from bad debts on open-credit sales has been kept as low as 0.6 per cent. Electrical-appliance stores had the highest credit loss, 1.5 per cent. Radio sets and supply stores were second, with open-credit loss of 1.4 per cent. Department stores kept the tightest griup on their business of all, thereby escaping with a loss of 0.4 per cent.

"The average loss from bad debts on instalment sales was 1.2 per cent. General clothing stores led with 8 per cent, while coal, wood, lumber and building-material dealers brought up the rear with 0.2 per cent."

Tornadoes Kill 23, Injure 124; Half of Oklahoma Town Razed

Twister Buries Victims in Ruins of Buildings in Bethany, a Nazarene Settlement—School Children Among Dead—Two Perish, 12 Missing in Rocky Mountain Blizzard.

Special to The New York Times.

OKLAHOMA CITY, Nov. 19.—Mourning replaced the weekly prayer meeting tonight at Bethany, a suburb of Oklahoma City populated chiefly by members of the Church of the Nazarene. A tornado struck the settlement just before noon, killing 18 persons, injuring 100 and levelling the eastern half of the village.

A few minutes earlier, the same twister demolished the Camel Creek school building three and a half miles north of Bethany, killing four students and injuring a dozen.

The tornado followed a blinding downpour of rain which lasted for more than an hour and flooded the streets of Bethany, greatly impeding rescue work.

Bethany is five miles west of here on Federal Highway Sixty-six and had a population of 1,400. It is the site of Bethany Peniel College, supported by the Nazarenes and drawing students from the western half of the county. None of the church property was destroyed.

The tornado barely missed the municipal airport as it cut a path 200 yards wide across the western half of the county for a distance of more than twelve miles. In places it seemed to rise above the ground and leave the terrain untouched, only to swoop down again and strip the ground of vegetation, fences and telephone lines.

Fully 200 buildings were wrecked in the tornado's path and it is impossible to estimate the damage. Most of the houses demolished were in or near the edge of Bethany.

Martial law was established in the damaged area within an hour, and orders were given to the National Guardsmen to fire on looters. Relief work was under way within a short time and automobiles of all types and interurban cars were commandeered to bring the dead and

Continued on Page Three.

WALL ST. FIRMS GIVE $250,000 FOR JOB AID

Partial Canvass of Financial Houses Swells Drive Fund to Nearly $2,000,000.

GAME SEATS BRING $100,000

Army-Navy Benefit Expected to Net $1,250,000—Queens to Raise $500,000.

Unabated activity marked the campaign against unemployment distress by relief organizations, city and private, yesterday.

The drive of the Emergency Employment Committee for a fund of $6,000,000 to provide jobs for 20,000 idle workers approached the $2,000,000 mark and it was expected that by the end of the week fully half of the amount sought would have been pledged.

The largest single group of new contributions was reported from Wall Street by the Stock Exchange subcommittee headed by John W. Prentiss of Hornblower & Weeks. At the close of the day Mr. Prentiss reported pledges by Stock Exchange houses totaling $250,000.

Mr. Prentiss said his committee had reported a 100 per cent response and expressed confidence that all members of the Stock Exchange would be represented generously in the final tally. Many Stock Exchange houses also assured Mr. Prentiss that they would not cut their payrolls during the unemployment emergency.

Army-Navy Game Seats Go Fast.

That the proceeds of the Army-Navy game, to be played here on Dec. 13 for the benefit of the unemployed, may be as high as $1,250,000 appeared likely when it was announced by Grover A. Whalen, chairman of the general fund committee of the Salvation Army, which brought the game to New York, that applications for seats totaling $100,000 already had been received.

While the Emergency Unemployment Committee was pressing its drive for the $6,000,000 fund final arrangements were under way in Queens by a committee representing both major parties and headed by Borough President Harvey for a campaign for $500,000 to be used for relief purposes in the borough. A similar drive for a like amount is under way in Brooklyn.

The official call for the drive in Queens will be issued today at a meeting of representatives of both parties at the Jamaica office of the Queens Chamber of Commerce. Eighty political leaders, Republicans and Democrats, will attend. Mr. Harvey will preside. "No quarter in the war against poverty and unemployment distress," will be the slogan of the campaign.

The Mayor's Committee on Unemployment continued its preparations to supply all the needy with essentials of life, and charitable organizations in all parts of the city extended still further their relief activities.

Centres of Relief Listed.

For the benefit of those seeking work the emergency employment committee emphasized that its address at 40 Wall Street is that of the fund-raising office only. All who wish to contribute may send their donations to that address. The committee's Emergency Work Bureau is attempting to find jobs for unemployed heads of New York families, but it does not directly receive applicants for jobs. It is the clearing house for unemployed family heads seeking jobs at any of the regular

Continued on Page Twenty-one.

BOB AND BROTHER SURRENDER TO CRAIN

L. P. Jubien Held With Them on Grand Larceny Charges—One Other Is Sought.

ALL PLEAD NOT GUILTY

Bob, Held in $35,000, Promises to Aid Inquiry—Indicates He Has Been Here a Week.

Charles V. Bob, stock promoter who disappeared five weeks ago when the authorities announced that investors in his companies faced a loss of $6,000,000, surrendered to District Attorney Crain shortly before noon yesterday. In the Court of General Sessions later in the day Bob was released in $35,000 bail after pleading not guilty to three counts charging grand larceny in indictments returned Monday against him, his brother and two other business associates.

Two of the others indicted, Beverly W. Bob, the brother, and Louis P. Jubien, also surrendered, the former being released in $5,000 bail and the latter in $2,500. These two were charged with grand larceny, as is the missing business associate of Bob.

When Bob dropped out of sight on Oct. 9 Frederick C. Russell, his aide, also disappeared. The authorities are still looking for Russell. It was intimated yesterday that Russell would appear soon and submit to questioning.

While Bob and the others were being arraigned, Acting United States Attorney Hanley announced that his investigation into the use of the mails by Bob to determine if the postal laws were violated in the sale of stock was being continued.

At the office of Assistant State Attorney General Washburn it was said that a subpoena had been served on Bob requiring him to appear at the State Bureau of Securities, 74 Trinity Place, for questioning this afternoon. It was largely through the efforts of Mr. Washburn and his assistants that the investigations of the Bob case were started.

Banton Accompanies Bob.

Several hours before the surrender Joab H. Banton, former District Attorney and counsel for the Bob brothers, informed Mr. Crain that Charles V. and Beverly W. Bob would give themselves up. The brothers and counsel walked in shortly after Jubien and his attorney appeared in Mr. Crain's office. Mr. Banton, after making a brief statement that Bob would "help the authorities untangle the books and financial affairs," refused to say where Bob had been. It was learned, however, that for several days prior to the return of the indictment on Tuesday Bob had been stopping with friends on Park Avenue near Fifty-ninth Street. Bob gave his age as 42, his address as 1,010 Fifth Avenue. His brother said he was 40 years old and gave his residence as 15 Portmouth Place, Queens. Jubien gave his age as 40 and his address as 72 East Seventy-second Street.

Although Bob was indicted for grand larceny in the theft of $97,000 through fraudulent sales of stock in November last year, it was reported in the District Attorney's office that the amount would be increased to about $1,000,000 before the end of the inquiry. Bob's brother is accused of the theft of $30,000 and Jubien of $35,000. Jubien appeared be-

Continued on Page Three.

MAURETANIA SAVES 28 ON VESSEL SINKING IN GALE IN MID-OCEAN

Capt. Fried Also Speeds to Aid of Swedish Freighter Ovidia, but Arrives an Hour Late.

BRITISH SHIPS IN CRASH

Five Lost When Continental Goes Down Near Holland Coast After Collision.

580 SAVED OFF PORTUGAL

Highland Hope Runs on Rocks and Sinks at Mouth of Tagus, but Passengers Are Taken Off.

The crew of the Swedish freighter Ovidia, consisting of Captain Carlsson, his wife and twenty-six men, were rescued at 1 P. M. yesterday from their sinking ship by the Cunarder Mauretania 1,100 miles east of the Ambrose Lightship in a strong wind and a high sea. The America of the United States Lines, commanded by Captain George Fried, also had steamed at full speed to the aid of the distressed ship, but arrived one hour too late. Captain Fried stood by and made a lee with his ship to shelter the crew of the Ovidia as the two lifeboats made their way to the Cunarder, which was about half a mile from the abandoned vessel.

In the same hour 580 men and women were taken off the British steamship Highland Hope of the Nelson Line in lifeboats after their vessel went on the rocks near the mouth of the Tagus, Portugal.

Five Lost in Ship Crash

About the same time also in the Scheldt off Flushing, Holland, the British steamship Continental and the British freighter Hebble were in collision. The Continental sank with a loss of five of her crew and the remaining five were saved.

Out of the 618 lives in danger of drowning in the three casualties only five were lost.

Captain S. J. S. McNeil of the Maurtania in his first message to the Cunard Line, 25 Broadway, dated at noon said:

S. S. Mauretania, Nov. 19, 1930.
550 miles noon, Tuesday to noon Wednesday. 22.52 average, 2,102 miles total distance, 22-83 total average—standing by disabled ship.
McNEIL.

The second message was dated 1:30 P. M. New York Time, and was as follows:

S. S. Mauretania, Nov. 19, 1930.
Swedish steamer Ovidia abandoned, sinking condition; crew on board Mauretania, now due 11 A. M., Friday.
McNEIL.

The position given by the master of the Swedish freighter in his S O S call was Lat. 42 N. and Long. 50.55 W.

A third message was received at 7:30 P. M. at the Cunard office from the Mauretania in answer to a radio asking for further details of the rescue, but was not signed by Captain McNeil as the two preceding ones were. It read:

S. S. Mauretania, Nov. 19, 1930.
At 2:30 A. M., Wednesday, New York Time, altered course in response to distress signals from Ovidia sinking in Lat. 42 N., Long. 51 W. Arrived alongside at 10 P. M. Ship was abandoned. Total crew of twenty-eight rescued. No loss of life. Proceeded on voyage. Will

Continued on Page Five.

HOOVER CALLS UPON NATION TO GIVE CHILD 'FAIR CHANCE' IN STRESS OF GRUELLING ERA

President Hoover Sums Up Childhood in Five Sentences

By The Associated Press.

WASHINGTON, Nov. 19.—President Hoover drew upon his knowledge of parenthood and a wealth of experience in child relief work for a five-sentence summing-up of childhood.

He expressed it tonight to his child health conference in this way:

"We approach all problems of childhood with affection.

"Theirs is the province of joy and good humor.

"They are the most wholesome part of the race, the sweetest, for they are fresher from the hands of God.

"Whimsical, ingenious, mischievous, we live a life of apprehension as to what their opinion may be of us; a life of defense against their terrifying energy; we put them to bed with a sense of relief and a lingering of devotion.

"We envy them the freshness of adventure and discovery of life; we mourn over the disappointments they will meet."

WINE JUICE MAKERS ASK GANGSTER CURB

Californians Appeal to Government for Protection Against Racketeers in Selling Product.

LEAGUE OPENS NEW DRIVE

Drys Seek Financial Aid of Influential Men in National Educational Movement.

Special to The New York Times.

WASHINGTON, Nov. 19.—An appeal from California grapegrowers for Federal protection against gangsters who are alleged to be menacing the sale of a new grape juice has been made to the Department of Justice and announcement by the Anti-Saloon League of a new campaign in support of the Eighteenth Amendment were developments today in the prohibition situation.

The new drive of the league aims to enlist the financial and moral aid in an educational movement of influential men and industrial leaders.

The letter containing the appeal of the grape growers was laid before Assistant Attorney General John Lord O'Brian.

The disclosures followed an announcement several days ago by Donald D. Conn, managing director of Fruit Industries, Ltd., distributers of the new grape product, that he had appealed to Washington for protection against gangsters who feared that the sale of it might interfere with their "wine rackets."

The California interests today seemed for a time to have suffered a setback when it was revealed that Prohibition Director Woodcock had approved the action of St. Louis agents in raiding a grape juice store. The product seized later developed a real "kick."

Colonel Woodcock said the St.

Continued on Page Twenty-two.

LAYS TASK ON CONFERENCE

President Asks for Program to Meet Changes in Social Structure.

PAYS TRIBUTE TO MOTHERS

But He Emphasizes Country's Responsibility for Children Deficient or Delinquent.

WOULD FULFILL 'FIRST HOPE'

He Tells 1,200 Delegates at the Capital That They Must Carry On Torch of the Founders.

Special to The New York Times.

WASHINGTON, Nov. 19.—Demanding "a fair chance" for every child, President Hoover called tonight for the mobilization of the best thought of the nation to prepare a program to fit the nation's youth for "a complexity of life for which there is no precedent." He spoke in Constitution Hall here before 1,200 delegates to the White House Conference on Child Health and Protection, which opens tomorrow.

"With machines ever enlarging man's power and capacity, with electricity extending over the world its magic, with the air giving us a wholly new realm, our children must be prepared to meet entirely new contacts and new forces," the President warned. "They must be physically strong and mentally placed to stand up under the increasing pressure of life. Their problem is not alone one of physical health, but of mental, emotional, spiritual health."

Meeting Changes in Nation's Life.

To meet the problems arising from the rapid changes in the nation's life, particularly its conversion from a rural, agrarian civilization into an urban, highly industrialized one, new methods of inspiring "creative work and play" and of substituting "love and self-discipline for the rigors of rule" must be developed, Mr. Hoover declared.

Three major phases of the problem challenge the nation, the President asserted. He outlined them as first, the protection and stimulation of the normal child, second, aid to the physically defective and handicapped child, third, the problem of the delinquent child.

Of the 45,000,000 children in the nation, about 1,500,000 were specially gifted, 35,000,000 reasonably normal, at least 10,000,000 deficient in some respect and of the deficient more than 80 per cent were not receiving the proper attention, according to information gathered by a committee of the conference, Mr. Hoover asserted.

Solution of Government Problems.

Declaring that "experience has shown that these deficiencies can be prevented and remedied to a high degree," Mr. Hoover warned that unless the nation carried out its duty to the deficient children they will be left dependent, or "the major recruiting ground for the army of ne'er-do-wells and criminals."

"And we need have great concern over this matter," the President continued. "Let no one believe that these are questions which should not stir a nation; that they are below the dignity of statesmen or governments. If we could have but one generation of properly born, trained, educated and happy children, a thousand other problems of government would vanish."

President Hoover said that for many years he had been hoping for such a gathering of "experts enlisted from every field of those who have given a lifetime of devotion to public measures for care of childhood." Their deliberations, he added, should produce "a series of conclusions and judgments of unprecedented service in behalf of childhood, the benefits of which will be felt for a full generation."

Plea for Parental Cooperation.

A plea for cooperation by the parents of the nation was added by the President in a brief reference to "the unseen millions listening in their homes" to the nation-wide radio hook-up which carried the address. He declared their help essential to "a united and nation-wide effort in behalf of the children."

All the scientific knowledge and public safeguards which could be mustered to meet the problem were "but a tithe of the physical, moral

Crater Reported Seen at Wife's Maine Hotel; She Denies It to Crain Aide, Then Collapses

Special to The New York Times.

PORTLAND, Me., Nov. 19.—Mrs. Stella Crater, wife of Joseph Force Crater, missing New York Supreme Court Justice, collapsed tonight at her hotel after being questioned by Assistant District Attorney John L. McDonnell of New York. Dr. Adam P. Leighton, her physician, was called hastily to attend her.

Throughout the examination Mrs. Crater paced the floor, sobbing and partly hysterical.

Mystery as great as that surrounding the missing jurist himself continued last night to veil the source of new reports here that Crater had been seen at a cottage near Portland, Me. Meanwhile District Attorney Crain received a long-distance telephone report from Mr. MacDonell.

Mrs. Crater, questioned by Portland officials before MacDonnell saw her, asserted that she knew nothing of her husband's disappearance, Mr. Crain was informed. Employes of the hotel insisted that Crater, or a man closely resembling him, had been there in the last few days. Portland officials discounted this.

MacDonnell also said he was convinced that Mrs. Crater knew nothing of her husband's whereabouts and that she had offered to come here to testify before the grand jury if her physician found her health warranted it. Detectives attached to the office of District Attorney Ralph M. Ingalls of Portland were sent out several weeks ago to investigate a story that the missing justice had been seen in a cottage near the city, Mr. MacDonnell said, but were unable to get any verification of the report.

In addition to disclaiming all knowledge of how or why her husband dropped out of sight, Mrs. Crater insisted that she had not seen him nor been in communication with him since he was last seen in New York. She was questioned by Mr. Ingalls from a list of queries mailed to him by Mr. Crain.

Mrs. Crater told Ingalls that after leaving her Summer home at Belgrade Lakes she stopped in Portland instead of returning to her home in New York because it was less expensive and because she wished to avoid the questioning of friends.

Museum of the City of New York

Drawing by Robert C. Wiseman of a "Hooverville" in Central Park.

Museum of the City of New York

Labor Day, a cartoon by Rollin Kirby.

Museum of the City of New York

Unemployed, sketch of a woman selling apples by F. K. Detwiller.

"All the News That's Fit to Print."

The New York Times.

Copyright, 1930, by The New York Times Company.

THE WEATHER
Fair and warmer today; tomorrow increased cloudiness.
Temperatures yesterday—Max. 27, min. 15.
U. S. Weather Forecast—For details see Page 44.

VOL. LXXX....No. 26,611. + * * * * * NEW YORK, WEDNESDAY, DECEMBER 3, 1930. TWO CENTS In Greater New York | THREE CENTS Within 200 Miles | FOUR CENTS Elsewhere Except 7th and 8th Postal Zones

DETERDING CHARGES SOVIET TRIAL CLOAKS 5-YEAR PLAN FAILURE

British Oil Man, "Criminal" in Moscow Case, Sees Move to Shift the Blame.

URGES POWERS' BOYCOTT

Bolsheviki Would Fall in Three Weeks, He Says, Without Credit and World Markets.

WITNESSES' STORIES VAGUE

All Are Glib in Confessions but Fail to Give Details of Deeds in "Vast Conspiracy."

Special Cable to THE NEW YORK TIMES.

LONDON, Dec. 2.—Sir Henri Deterding, one of the "criminals" in the Moscow engineers' trial, is convinced the proceedings are intended to cloak imminent failure of the Soviet's five-year industrialization plan.

With a vacant chair awaiting him in the Moscow court room, Sir Henri regards the trial itself as a "Hollywood show," but considers the conditions underlying it serious for Russia and the outside world. He contends the purpose of the trial is to transfer the blame in the eyes of the Russian people from their dictators in the Kremlin to their foreign "enemies."

The oil man laughed today at the row of empty chairs in which the Bolshevist leaders would like to place Winston Churchill, Colonel Lawrence, Raymond Poincare and himself as the arch conspirators against Russia.

Sees Move to Shift Blame.

"The charge of a foreign plot is ridiculous on the face of it," he said at an interview in his London office today. "Krylenko and the Soviet leaders know those charges are absurd. It is as clear as day that the 'confessions' have been extorted from the engineers and then broadcast by the films and radio throughout the length and breadth of Russia to take the blame from Stalin's shoulders.

"I always have been opposed to military intervention in Russia. It would get us nowhere and could only lead to bloodshed. Just as an example, I remember warning the German General Hoffman against a military expedition into Russia in 1923. Otherwise there has been no hint of foreign intervention—as far as I can remember—since the days of Wrangell and the White armies.

"But I do believe that as long as the present régime exists in Russia there is going to be dislocation of world trade and misery inside and outside Russia's borders. I am certain that Russian underconsumption and lack of buying power is the cause of America's distress today. And if the people in the United States ask me how long the depression will last I will tell them, 'As long as this gang rules Russia.'

"The only thing for foreign powers to do—and I mean the United States, England, France and Germany—is to make an agreement not to buy from Russia or advance a dollar of credit. The further Stalin advances into his five-year plan the more he will need foreign help. And the Bolshevist régime in Russia will collapse in three weeks with joint action by the powers."

Not Worried by Dumping.

Unlike many business leaders of England and the United States, Sir Henri is not worried by Russian dumping. Overproduction, he insisted to this correspondent, is not the cause of the world trade depression. The real cause, he believes, is under-consumption—enforced by the Soviet dictatorship—so Russia's 150,000,000 are consuming only as much as 60,000,000 consumed before the war and China's 400,000,000 are consuming only three-fourths of what they are capable of consuming.

"Nobody can tell me that when you cut off 200,000,000 consumers from the world's export trade you are not affecting it," he continued. "Stalin's very existence depends on under-consumption in Russia. A dictatorship like his cannot exist for a week in a nation of plenty. It can only live by a system of bread cards and by the ruthless cutting off of the people's supplies. Then, if they disobey, you can cut off their bread supply.

"Russian dumping is not intentional. It is the inevitable result of forced under-consumption. Surplus supplies must be rushed outside the country before the people themselves can get them. I don't regard dumping as a deliberate attack on capitalistic nations. It is a result which the Soviet leaders never foresaw and were not prepared for.

"Nobody worries about American overproduction in normal times.

Continued on Page Seventeen.

Barrie 'Can't Abide Children,' He Says, Asking Fund for Them

Special Cable to THE NEW YORK TIMES.

LONDON, Dec. 2.—Sir James Barrie, creator of Peter Pan, Wendy, Mary Rose and the dream child, Margaret, declared whimsically tonight that he "could not abide children."

Presiding at a dinner at the Guildhall to launch an appeal for the London Children's Hospital, he said the marvel to him was that parents could pick out their own.

"Do you really think that when you take them to a party it is always the same ones you bring back?" he asked.

While watching an eclipse on Yorkshire Hill with "thousands of persons reverent and appalled," Sir James recalled, there was the inevitable child.

"What was he doing in one of the most thrilling moments of his life?" he asked. "He was trying to catch earwigs in a soap dish."

After a fervent appeal for money to obtain more hospital beds, Sir James added, tenderly, "The little fools think it's a sort of heaven."

WORLD ARMS PARLEY HELD CERTAIN IN 1932

Preparatory Group Asks the League to Set Date Expected to Be Early in That Year.

TALK OF REICH WITHDRAWAL

Berlin Parliament Will Debate Demand Voted by Committee—Cecil 'Scolds' Bernstorff.

By CLARENCE K. STREIT.
Special Cable to THE NEW YORK TIMES.

GENEVA, Dec. 2.—The date for the long expected world conference to limit land, air and sea armaments was brought sufficiently out of the clouds by the Preparatory Disarmament Commission today for it to be said that it is certain to be held in 1932 and is virtually certain to be convoked early in that year.

This essential development the commission did much to obscure by tortuous manoeuvres to avoid recommending any specific date and by rejecting—after another scolding of Count von Bernstorff by Viscount Cecil of Chelwood—a German proposal to have the commission recommend Nov. 5, 1931, as the date and accepting a British proposal to ask the League of Nations Council at its next session to convoke the conference as soon as advisable.

The discussion, however, made it clear that all thought the commission had virtually finished its draft convention today and agreed that the world conference must be held soon, and a majority favored convoking it in the first part of 1932 at the latest. Conversations in the corridors indicated that February was the date most of the delegates had in mind.

Details Discussed.

Indeed, how near this hitherto far away conference, "which will be unique in the history of the world," as Lord Cecil put it, became today is best shown by the delegates' remarks about practical details—how huge it would be, how long it would last, how small countries such as Greece would need time merely to arrange to send the requisite number of officials to it and how distant countries such as Japan needed weeks merely to assemble the necessary documents. All these reasons, moreover, were advanced with care taken to explain they were not meant to delay the conference indefinitely but only, as Dr. Eduard Benes, Czech Foreign Minister, said, for two or three months at the most beyond the November date the Germans asked, and only because, as Lord Cecil, René Massigli and others said, every precaution ought to be taken to assure the success of the conference, whose failure, Nicolas Politis of Greece said, "would be the greatest catastrophe since the war."

Before this debate the commission finished what yesterday was supposed to be the third, but which is now explained to be the second, reading of its convention. In any case all agree that this amounts to ending the debate on the convention's articles unless unforeseen difficulties arise.

The commission, leaving minor points of the text to be polished by a drafting committee, adjourned until Thursday, when the third reading, which promises to take only a few hours, will begin. The difficulties that remain are outside the text itself and consist of declarations which the various powers want to make, and, above all, in various passages in the commission's report to the League Council.

Naval Transfers Agreed On.

The naval chapter aroused discussion only on the transfer compromise. The British at the last moment got word that the Admiralty was willing to accept this definitely,

Continued on Page Sixteen.

$365,000 IN GRAFT ON THEATRE TICKETS CHARGED TO POLICE

Street Speculators Pay $5 a Day, Kresel Is Told—Seats Traced to Court Aides.

$7,000 BUSHEL FEE UP

Former Magistrate Is Examined on Money Paid Him to Defend Alleged "Fence."

PUBLIC HEARINGS RESUME

New Vice Ring Disclosures Are Promised Today—Police Official Seeks to Quit Under Fire.

A form of police graft in which ticket speculators who hawk their wares outside theatres and places such as the Yankee Stadium before a prize fight are made to give up cash tribute as well as tickets which find their way into the hands of some magistrate's court clerks was described to Isidor J. Kresel yesterday. At the same time the Appellate Division inquiry delved into the circumstances surrounding the payment to Hyman Bushel, a practicing attorney and former Magistrate, of a $7,000 fee by an alleged fence who was subsequently discharged.

In midafternoon Mr. Kresel announced that a public hearing would be held today at 10:30 A. M. and, although he did not reveal its purpose, it was learned that Mapocha Acuna, confessed "stool-pigeon," would make new revelations on the operations of the "women's court vice ring," in which he has implicated policemen, lawyers and bail bondsmen. Acuna would be followed, it was said, by several women who were "framed" by the police, receiving sentences, in some instances, of more than a year in jail.

Early yesterday Lieutenant William Delaney, mentioned by Acuna in his testimony which named twenty-eight policemen, filed an application for retirement, to which he is entitled by reason of twenty-five years' service. The application followed the action of Police Commissioner Mulrooney, who transferred Delaney from the detective division at the West Sixty-eighth Street station to desk duty in five lower Manhattan precincts.

Theatre Ticket Men Questioned.

Revelations of ticket graft followed the examination of Oscar Alexander, a broker, of 200 West Forty-second Street, and representatives of the Adelphia Ticket Agency of 1,504 Broadway and the Broad Street Agency at 25 Broadway, who appeared under subpoena.

They had been told to bring with them their records of the account of James Graff, a bondsman in 315 West Fifty-fourth Street, just across the street from the West Side Court. It was the original supposition that the records might furnish some evidence to show how magistrates, court clerks and attendants obtained choice theatre tickets as favors.

It developed, however, that, unrelated to Graff, investigators had been told how speculators were forced to pay $5 a day to the patrolman on the beat in which they operated to forestall being molested. Occasionally, however, it was said, the speculators were arrested anyway and their tickets confiscated.

Ostensibly these tickets are sent to the property clerk at Police Headquarters, but, it was said, they rarely were. Instead, they go to clerks in the courts where the men are to be arraigned, with the result, it was charged, that convictions rarely follow, although the tickets are never returned.

It was estimated that there were about 200 such speculators in New York, which would fix the amount of money paid patrolmen to let them operate at about $365,000 a year, although no estimate could be obtained on the amount of money which might be involved in the seized tickets.

Bushel Queried on Fee.

The investigation of the Bushel fee of $7,000 came after Carl Ackerman, a second cousin of "Uncle Nathan" Viodinger, who has said that he had cashed the notes of Bushel and General Sessions Judge Max Levine, had been examined privately by Mr. Kresel. Mr. Bushel appeared a few minutes after being called.

He spent fifty-five minutes with Mr. Kresel. On emerging he saw newspaper photographers and darted back into Mr. Kresel's office and left through a rear door. He went, however, to his office, which is on Broadway near the County Courts Building, and there he declared that he had "nothing to say."

Ackerman said he had been questioned concerning a $7,000 fee which was paid to Bushel some seven or eight years ago by an alleged fence.

Continued on Page Seven.

'Money Scarce,' So Rockefeller Gives Nickel Instead of Dime

By The Associated Press.

ORMOND BEACH, Fla., Dec. 2.—John D. Rockfeller hesitated about giving his golfing companion a nickel here today after the latter had executed a good drive.

"If money wasn't so scarce," said Mr. Rockefeller, "I'd give you a nickel for that drive."

The Rev. G. D. Owen, pastor of the Ormond Union Church, who is a tyro at golf, appeared pleased, but to the news photographers it seemed appropriate that the man who has billions of nickels should have given the pastor a nickel, if not the customary dime.

"All right," the philanthropist genially agreed, and the Rev. Mr. Owen now has a shiny new nickel.

$3,004,845 FOR JOBS RAISED IN CITY DRIVE

$25,000 Stock Exchange Gift Helps Carry Fund Beyond Half-Way Mark.

NEW PUBLIC RELIEF VOTED

536 Will Get Work Checking Claims of Needy Aged—$75,000 Goes to Veterans.

With the announcement yesterday that contributions to the Emergency Employment Committee's job-financing fund had passed $3,000,000 and that more than half of the amount sought was in hand, it was revealed that the Emergency Work Bureau had provided jobs three days a week at $5 a day for 12,841 heads of families in the parks or non-profit-making institutions.

Contributions at the close of business Monday totaled $3,004,845.85, an increase of $117,554.91 over the total of last Saturday. Included in the new total was a gift of $25,000 from the New York Stock Exchange, voted by the governors. The central committee of the Emergency Employment Committee will make its second report at 12:30 P. M. today at the Bankers Club.

Park Workers Labor in Cold.

Despite the cold weather, the men sent to work in the parks by the emergency bureau have remained on the job, although exposure to the elements was an unusual hardship for many of them. The lines of applicants were not thinned by the cold yesterday; 1,200 men were waiting when the doors of the bureau were opened in the morning.

Improvised stoves, made of cans or other receptacles, have been set up in many parks so that the men may warm themselves occasionally. Supervisors have been instructed to send thinly-clad men to sheltered jobs. Some of the employed men have been unable to withstand the weather because of privations suffered while seeking employment. A middle-aged man with a family of seven dependent on him and a former white-collar worker with a family of three collapsed while at work. After they had been revived and supplied with food and clothing they were back at work the next day.

A sixteen-year record of the Municipal Lodging House has been broken, Superintendent Joseph Mannix said yesterday. During the first eleven months of this year the house sheltered 375,000 homeless persons, as compared with 333,037 for the record year of 1914. Monday night was the biggest night in the history of the lodging house—2,587 persons, including fifty-six women and eleven children, were cared for. Even this did not tax the capacity of the lodging house and annex, which can accommodate 3,000 persons a night.

While the lodging house accommo-

Continued on Page Two.

HOOVER ASKS $150,000,000 TO AID IDLE; WARNS OF DEFICIT AND END OF TAX CUT; HIS CONTROL OF WORKS FUND OPPOSED

OPPOSE HOOVER METHODS

Democrats and Some Republicans Disagree With His Relief Program.

PARTY REGULARS PRAISE IT

Most of Leaders Are for Putting the Proposals Into Force Without Delay.

WALL STREET IS PLEASED

Holds Ideas for Business Sound—Press Hails Avoidance of Controversial Matters.

Special to The New York Times.

WASHINGTON, Dec. 2.—President Hoover's message, in general, received favorable comment from Republican members of Congress and unfavorable from Democratic members, though some on each side jumped their parties' traces.

Republican members of the House, especially those on the Judiciary Committee, were set to thinking about investigating the administration of the anti-trust laws, while others contented themselves with statements that the message was "good," "timely and sound," or "interesting."

Representative La Guardia, Republican, of New York, expressed disappointment at the message, haying it was "not a fair specimen of Mr. Hoover's great capabilities."

Other comment was as follows:

SPEAKER LONGWORTH of Ohio, Republican—I think the message was a very interesting document. I liked the review of business conditions. It was very encouraging.

REPRESENTATIVE TILSON of Connecticut, Republican—The message was very timely and very sound.

REPRESENTATIVE HAWLEY of Oregon, Republican—It was an excellent presentation of the admirable measures taken by the President for the public good under the conditions prevailing now and in the recent past.

REPRESENTATIVE PURNELL of Indiana, Republican—It impressed me very much.

REPRESENTATIVE GRAHAM of Pennsylvania, Republican—The subject matter of the President's message was ably presented. I agree with him fully in the need of wise legislation covering the administration of the anti-trust laws.

REPRESENTATIVE McDUFFIE of Alabama, Democrat—I was impressed by the conspicuous absence of any specific measures for relief, and also the conspicuous generalities, the President playing safe on every proposition.

SENATOR WATSON of Indiana, Republican—The message is admirable in all respects save one—the World Court, upon which I do not agree with him. Mr. Hoover sets forth the needs of the people and the government at this particular

Continued on Page Nineteen.

Bills Laid Before Congress on Employment Relief And to Deal With Country's Economic Recovery

Special to The New York Times.

WASHINGTON, Dec. 2.—Measures on employment relief and economic recovery introduced in the Senate and House today included the following:

By Senator Glenn—A resolution to carry out President Hoover's recommendation for an emergency fund of $150,000,000 to accelerate public works.

By Senators Robinson of Arkansas, McNary and Caraway—Resolutions to provide $60,000,000 to aid drought-stricken farmers.

By Senator Blaine—Bill for creating a Federal industrial commission to study the stabilization of employment.

By Senator Capper—Resolution to distribute 40,000,000 bushels of the Farm Board's wheat surplus to relief organizations for food.

By Senator Brookhart—Bill increasing appropriations for public roads from $125,000,00 to $500,000,000 for two years.

By Senator Keyes and Representative Elliott—Twin bills to expedite work on Federal buildings.

By Senator Reed—Bill to suspend immigration for two years from all countries on this hemisphere and from Europe.

By Representative Cable—Bill to exclude all immigration of laborers until the Secretary of Labor decides they are needed.

By Senator Oddie—Bill to embargo the importation of all products from Soviet Russia.

By Representative Huddleston—Bill to appropriate $50,000,000 to be used by the President as a "destitution fund."

MACY AGREED UPON AS STATE CHAIRMAN

His Selection Is Unanimously Voted at Meeting of Leaders From All Over State.

TWENTY-EIGHT AT DINNER

Appointment of Tuttle's Successor Expected to Await Suggestion by New Party Head.

The election of W. Kingsland Macy as chairman of the Republican State Committee, to succeed William J. Maier, was assured last night at a dinner conference of twenty-eight party leaders at the Hotel Lexington. The meeting of the committee will be held today at noon at the National Republican Club and Mr. Macy probably will be the only candidate.

The agreement on Mr. Macy was unanimous.

"We took an early poll from one end of the table to the other," Mr. Maier said after the conference. "The vote was unanimous for Mr. Macy."

No opposition to the agreement on Mr. Macy came from any of the so-called Hoover group, which tried vainly to develop a candidate. Mr. Hill, Assistant Secretary of War F. Trubee Davison and Richard W. Lawrence, president of the National Republican Club, each of whom was mentioned for the chairmanship, all refused to become candidates for the post.

Satisfactory to Hilles.

Mr. Macy, although one of the first supporters of President Hoover in this State, is regarded now as allied to the regular organization group. His selection is understood to be highly satisfactory to Mr. Hilles and the other organization leaders.

As the result of Mr. Macy's selection an executive committee of the State Committee will be formed, with one or two members from each of the nine judicial districts. This proposal was made by Mr. Macy more than a year ago. It was discussed at the conference and undoubtedly will be adopted, although no formal approval was voted.

The question of who should represent the Republican party in the State in recommendations for Federal appointments also was discussed. Here again no formal action was taken, but it seemed to be the consensus that Mr. Macy should be the spokesman for the party in patronage matters at Washington, working with Mr. Hilles. Heretofore under the Hoover Administration there has been a lack of recognition of the regular organization, in the opinion of the party leaders.

Maier Called Conference.

The conference was called by Mr. Maier, the retiring chairman, and every part of the State was represented. Those present, in addition to Mr. Maier, were:

CHARLES D. HILLES, National Committeeman.
Miss SARAH SCHUYLER BUTLER, vice chairman of the State Committee.
LAFAYETTE B. GLEASON, secretary.
WILLIAM ZIEGLER Jr., treasurer.
JOHN KNIGHT, Senate leader of Wyoming County.
Senator CHARLES J. HEWITT of Cayuga County.
JOSEPH A. McGINNIES, Speaker of the Assembly, of Chautauqua County.

Continued on Page Three.

SENATE SEATS DAVIS; NYE LOSES CONTEST

Plea for Delay Pending Further Campaign Fund Inquiry Is Defeated, 58 to 27.

DEMOCRATS SPLIT ON VOTE

19 Favor Pennsylvanian After Steering Committee Upholds His Right to Seat.

Special to The New York Times.

WASHINGTON, Dec. 2.—James J. Davis was today sworn as Senator from Pennsylvania over the protest of Senator Nye, whose resolution urging him to step aside until the investigation into campaign expenditures is completed, was defeated by a vote of 58 to 27. This action resulted chiefly from a unanimous decision by the Democratic Steering Committee that Mr. Davis's case differed from those of former Senators-elect Vare of Pennsylvania and Smith of Illinois and that no "justification appears to deny Mr. Davis the right to take office."

The sudden collapse of the opposition to Mr. Davis, which was based upon an expected coalition between the insurgent Republicans and Democrats that failed to materialize, made possible the defeat of the Nye resolution, and the swearing in of Mr. Davis, thirty minutes after the fight in the Senate began and thirty-five minutes after his resignation as Secretary of Labor, became effective.

The decision of the Democrats to abandon the attitude, which most of them had followed in excluding Frank L. Smith and William S. Vare, is accepted as of far-reaching political significance, which Republican leaders interpret as reflecting an intention by the Democrats to co-operate reasonably on legislation in this session to avert an extra session.

Democrats Balk at Committee Rule.

Radical Democrats, who declined to stand with the steering committee, declared that its action also means that the Senate Democrats are veering toward a conservative program as part of a policy to show that radicalism no longer exists in the party, looking to success in the Presidential election in 1932.

Nine Republicans, one Farm-Laborite and seventeen Democrats voted to sustain the Nye resolution, while thirty-nine Republicans and nineteen Democrats opposed it. Immediately after this resolution was defeated Mr. Davis was sworn.

Senator Davis found his way into the Senate after expenditures for the Davis-Brown ticket which Senator Nye said might exceed the $780,000 spent by William S. Vare, whose unexpired term of two years Mr. Davis won in a bitter fight with Joseph R. Grundy.

Introduced by Reed.

Mr. Davis left the Labor Department at 11:02 o'clock this morning and a few minutes before the Senate assembled took his place in the third seat from the aisle on the back row of the Republican side.

The President's measure was next presented to the Senate and then Senator Reed of Pennsylvania an-

Continued on Page Twenty-one.

MESSAGE READ TO CONGRESS

President Asks Speed on Bills to Create Work in Next Six Months.

URGES PUBLIC COOPERATION

He Advocates Federal Loans to Farmers—Hits at Speculation as a Cause of Depression.

TREASURY LOSS $180,000,000

Action on Muscle Shoals and Inquiry for Changing Anti-Trust Law Recommended.

The complete text of the President's message is on Page 18.

By RICHARD V. OULAHAN.
Special to The New York Times.

WASHINGTON, Dec. 2.—Frankly stating that the treasury was confronted with a deficit of $180,000,000 and plainly indicating that this would prevent any continuance of the 1 per cent reduction in income taxes granted last year, President Hoover in his annual message on the state of the Union, which he communicated to both Houses of Congress this afternoon, stressed the need of rigid economy to prevent a tax increase.

At the same time, the President urged the appropriation of from $100,000,000 to $150,000,000 additional for public works in the effort to meet the unemployment situation

It became apparent soon after the President's message had been read in both chambers that there would be determined opposition on the part of many Democrats and some Republicans over the method proposed by the President for utilizing the money he desired appropriated for an extension of the public construction program in order to provide work for those in distress.

The chief point made by those who took this position was that Congress, and not the President, should determine where the money for which he asked should be applied.

Senator Caraway, Democrat, of Arkansas, voiced the main feature of the opposition in commenting on the President's proposal that from $100,000,000 to $150,000,000 should be made available for distribution to the different departments of the Federal Government for further participation in unemployment relief.

Caraway Wants Specific Bill.

"I am in favor of going the limit for relief of unemployment," said Senator Caraway, "but I think I know more about what is needed down home in Arkansas than the President or any other official in Washington.

"Let Congress make whatever distribution is to be made. Let the bill itself specify where the money is to go and not turn it over to a bunch of officials here in Washington to distribute as they please. Congress should seek to aid the whole country and not concentrate the relief in a few places, as could well happen under this proposal."

Other Senators and Representatives expressed the same view, among them Representative Garner, Democratic floor leader in the House. Representative Byrns, chairman of the Democratic Congressional campaign committee, approved the recommendation that $100,000,000 or more should be appropriated, but held that Congress, not the executive departments, should direct its allocation.

Immediately following the reading of the message, bills were offered to carry the recommendations of the President concerning unemployment and other recommendations into effect.

One of these was a bill of Senator Robinson of Arkansas, Democratic leader in the upper chamber, which had been made public, for a $60,000,000 fund for loans to farmers in drought-stricken areas. This had the advance approval of President Hoover. It was similar in purpose resolutions offered by Senators Caraway and McNary, the latter being chairman of the Committee on Agriculture.

Senator Glenn proposed an emergency fund of $150,000,000 for accele-

Continued on Page Eighteen.

Native Australian Named Governor General; Sir Isaac Isaacs, Chief Justice, Son of Tailor

Special Cable to THE NEW YORK TIMES.

LONDON, Dec. 2.—Sir Isaac Alfred Isaacs, a native-born Australian, son of a tailor, who has risen to be a brilliant advocate and now is Chief Justice of Australia, was appointed by King George today to be Governor-General of Australia in succession to Lord Stonehaven.

Under the new status of more complete independence of the British dominions, the appointment was made on the direct application of the Australian Laborite Prime Minister, J. H. Scullin to the King without any reference to the government of the United Kingdom. The King does not even know Sir Isaac by sight.

Sir Isaac, after a distinguished legal and political career, became Chief Justice last March, just a few days before a chance offered itself for the Prime Ministership, he having been actively associated with the political Labor movement since 1904.

The significance of the appointment is emphasized here and The London Times will say editorially tomorrow that the Australians [who are said to have insisted on the change in policy against the advice of the British Cabinet] may, indeed, reflect on the disadvantage of leaving the highest post in the Australian Commonwealth to be the prize of men who will almost inevitably have taken sides in party politics.

"They may also reflect that any step which, however irrelevant, can be quoted as showing a tendency to drift away from other parts of the empire, is hardly calculated to improve their standing and credit in the eyes of the world."

A weaker sovereign, The Times remarks, might have mistaken obstinacy for strength and resisted Mr. Scullin's suggestion but hopes that in the end the powers of the Crown will be all the stronger for his Majesty's consent.

"All the News That's Fit to Print."

The New York Times.

THE WEATHER
Cloudy with rain today; tomorrow cloudy and colder.
Temperatures yesterday—Max. 47, min. 40.
U. S. Weather Forecast—For details see Page 5.

Copyright, 1930, by The New York Times Company.

VOL. LXXX....No. 26,620. **** NEW YORK, FRIDAY, DECEMBER 12, 1930. TWO CENTS In Greater New York | THREE CENTS Within 200 Miles | FOUR CENTS Elsewhere Except 7th and 8th Postal Zones

BANK OF U. S. CLOSES DOORS; STATE TAKES OVER AFFAIRS; AID OFFERED TO DEPOSITORS

ACTION BY CLEARING HOUSE

Twenty-three Members Willing to Lend 50% on Accounts.

$160,000,000 IN DEPOSITS

$1,500,000 of City Money and $164,927 Postal Savings—Garment Funds Tied Up.

CROWDS AT OFFICES CALM

McFadden, Fearing Effect Abroad, Explains Institution Has No Government Connection.

The Bank of United States, a commercial bank with sixty offices in the city, closed its doors yesterday morning and placed its affairs in the hands of the State Banking Department.

While officials of the institution issued a statement expressing hope of an early reopening, leading banks of the city took steps to provide temporary relief for the depositors by offering to lend them 50 per cent of the amount of their deposits.

The institution, despite its name, had no connection with the Federal Government. Deposits at the time of the closing were approximately $160,000,000.

The suspension of the bank followed a night in which representatives of the Federal Reserve Bank of New York and of the principal banking institutions, together with Superintendent of Banks Joseph A. Broderick, had made strenuous efforts to save the institution. On Wednesday evening disturbances had occurred at several branches of the Bank of United States and deposits had been heavily withdrawn. It was recognized that unless relief measures were adopted a run on the bank would have developed yesterday morning.

Ask Broderick to Take Charge.

The meeting of the bankers, which was held at the Federal Reserve Bank, lasted until 4 o'clock yesterday morning, at which time, no practical plan for immediate relief having been agreed upon, directors of the Bank of United States adopted the following resolution:

> Resolved, That, Whereas rumors have been circulated which have caused abnormal withdrawals of deposits and it is feared that if the bank is opened Thursday morning these withdrawals may continue; that there will be in more than one of the branches of the bank large numbers of persons seeking withdrawals of their deposits which may result in disorder, and it is desired that all depositors be treated equally and the assets conserved for their benefit; and
>
> Whereas the directors feel that in view of conditions it would be unwise to continue to receive and pay out moneys, that the officers of the bank be, and they are hereby authorized to advise the Superintendent of Banks of the State of New York that they believe it to be for the best interests of the depositors of the institution that, because of the emergency, he take possession of the assets of the bank in accordance with the banking law of the State of New York, with the hope that a speedy and satisfactory reorganization can be effected, the bank reopened and the moneys due to depositors paid at the earliest possible date.

The resolution was made public at 9 A. M. by Mr. Broderick, who announced at the same time that he had taken possession of the business and property of the bank, pursuant to the provisions of Section 57 of the banking law. Fred W. Piderit, an examiner in the Banking Department, was appointed Special Deputy Superintendent in charge, and the department's corps of examiners set to work immediately to determine the position of the institution.

Mr. Broderick explained the task of examination was a large one as each branch must be examined separately and completely. The last examination of the bank made by the department required three months, it was said, and was completed last September. In recent weeks the department

Continued on Page Two.

23 Clearing House Banks Offer Loans to Depositors

The New York Clearing House Association issued the following statement yesterday:

TO DEPOSITORS OF BANK OF UNITED STATES.

The undersigned, being all of the members of the New York Clearing House Association, will lend to depositors of the Bank of United States, at 5 per cent interest, up to 50 per cent of their net balances properly authenticated.

Bank of New York and Trust Company.
Bank of Manhattan Trust Company.
Bank of America National Association.
National City Bank.
Chemical Bank and Trust Company.
Guaranty Trust Company.
Chatham Phenix National Bank and Trust Company.
Central Hanover Bank and Trust Company.
Corn Exchange Bank Trust Company.
First National Bank.
Irving Trust Company.
Continental Bank and Trust Company.
Chase National Bank.
Fifth Avenue Bank.
Bankers Trust Company.
Title Guarantee and Trust Company.
Marine Midland Trust Company.
Lawyers Trust Company.
New York Trust Company.
Commercial National Bank and Trust Company.
Harriman National Bank and Trust Company.
Public National Bank and Trust Company.
Manufacturers Trust Company.

BIG BANKING HOUSES DECIDE ON MERGER

Brown Brothers & Co., W. A. Harriman & Co. and Harriman Brothers & Co. to Unite.

BUSINESS IS INTERNATIONAL

To Be Brown Brothers, Harriman & Co.—All but One of Old Partners Continue.

Announcement was made last night of the consolidation of Brown Brothers & Co., W. A. Harriman & Co., Inc., and Harriman Brothers & Co., effective on Jan. 1. These are all international banking houses with connections extending throughout the United States and several foreign countries. The new organization will be known as Brown Brothers, Harriman & Co.

The announcement was made last night by the banking groups involved. The combination will bring together three of the most important financial organizations in Wall Street, and under the arrangement that has been agreed upon the Harriman and Brown interests will continue to operate in their respective fields.

The announcement set out that the fusion of interests in the special type of service which private financial houses render will effect a combination of resources and facilities with growing requirements of modern business. Brown Brothers & Co. have been engaged in the private international banking field for nearly 100 years, while the Harriman firm was among the first to see the opportunities in this field following the World

Continued on Page Six.

EINSTEIN ON ARRIVAL BRAVES LIMELIGHT FOR ONLY 15 MINUTES

Submits on Ship to Rapid-Fire Interview by 50 Reporters Flanked by 50 Camera Men.

JESTS, BUT FINALLY FLEES

With Wife Acting as Buffer, He Escapes Reception—Praises America in Statement.

TOURS CHINATOWN IN CAR

Tomorrow German Scientist Will Be Officially Received at City Hall.

Professor Albert Einstein, whose mind works in terms of immeasurable time and space, arrived in New York yesterday and granted a fifteen-minute interview.

Surrounded by a small mob of reporters, publicity men, photographers and movie operators in the drawing room of the liner Belgenland, which brought him here from Antwerp for his second visit to the United States in ten years, he was called upon within the brief quarter of an hour to define the fourth dimension in one word, state his theory of relativity in one sentence, give his views on prohibition, comment on politics and religion, and discuss the virtues of his violin.

He was also requested to answer many other questions, some of which he took seriously but most of which he parried with a jest. He faced the interview bewildered but with good nature.

Taken on deck from the drawing room to pose before the photographers, the shy and retiring scientist tried hard to oblige the camera men but after another fifteen minutes of "torture" finally lost patience, threw up his hands and dashed toward a companionway.

Reminded of Punch and Judy Show.

He said the interview reminded him of a Punch and Judy show and, later, characterized the whole proceeding as "eccentric." Smiling most of the time the whimsical smile of one who knows the difference between eternity and the immediate moment, the scientist submitted to the questions during the allotted fifteen minutes. He then rose, terminated the interview and walked away, followed by Mrs. Einstein and a group of friends.

The worst part of his experience was yet to come, however, as he was led on deck to be photographed. His long gray hair flying in the wind, his brown eyes reflecting resignation, he steeled himself for what to him was obviously unpleasant and he did not conceal his satisfaction when it was over. He then retired to the drawing room for the first of two radio broadcasts from the ship.

In these messages and in a statement prepared for the press Einstein declared he was glad to be in the United States again, paid a warm tribute to the achievements of American science, hailed America as the citadel of democracy and expressed the hope that this country would take the leadership in the solution of the international economic depression and in strengthening the foundations of world peace. In these messages he managed to introduce a serious note to the reception.

Professor and Mrs. Einstein are bound for the California Institute of Technology at Pasadena, where the German scientist will do some work in cooperation with Professor Robert P. Millikan and will also

Continued on Page Sixteen.

Herbert Hoover 3d Sends Word to Santa Via Talkie Camera to Bring Police Uniform

Special to The New York Times.

WASHINGTON, Dec. 11.—President and Mrs. Hoover's grandchildren, Peggy Ann and Herbert Hoover 3d, today settled, at least so far as they are concerned, the momentous questions as to what they want Santa Claus to bring them for Christmas. They conveyed their wishes to Santa Claus by way of the microphones of the sound news reels.

Despite their tender years—Peggy Ann is barely more than 4 years old and Herbert has not yet reached the age of 3—they were forced to bow to public demand and pose for pictures in the south grounds of the White House early today. They lost no opportunity to let it be known what they wanted for Christmas.

Herbert, it was revealed, wants a policeman's uniform, including badge and stick, the same as he has seen since coming to the Executive Mansion last Sunday to join his grandparents. And, too, he wants an engine.

"A big one or a little one?" little Herbert was asked. After eyeing his interrogator somewhat with disdain, little Herbert replied, "A big one."

Peggy Ann asked that Santa Claus bring her a doll, and "a very big one," at that. Then, apparently remembering it might get lonely by itself, she put in a plea for some smaller ones. In addition, she wants a wagon. Herbert opined that he would like a wagon also.

Peggy Ann and Herbert, with their mother, Mrs. Peggy Hoover, and their grandmother, posed at length for the cameramen. The two children made their initial appearance on tricycles.

Their six-month-old sister, Joan, failed to get in the picture. So Santa Claus may have to guess what she wants.

Doak Moves to Deport Alien Gang Leaders; 'All Resources' Put Into War on Underworld

Special to The New York Times.

WASHINGTON, Dec. 11.—In an effort to rid larger populated centres of the United States of gunmen and gangsters the Department of Labor has undertaken a thorough investigation into the history of leading underworld figures with a view to their eventual deportation, William N. Doak, the newly appointed Secretary of Labor, declared today.

"We are going into the gangster problem with all the resources at our command," he said. Many gangsters with millions and millions of dollars behind them, he said, had been able to employ high-class counsel who had been successful in preventing many deportations.

In conducting its investigation, Mr. Doak said, the Department of Labor is planning to ask Congress for increased funds to enable it to enlarge its staff of investigators. The problem of gangsters in American cities is being stressed by the entire department, he said.

To rid cities of "undesirables," he said, a searching investigation is being made of leading gunmen and gang figures in Chicago and elsewhere and a careful check of their careers is being made in an effort to establish grounds for actual deportation.

He emphasized, however, that deportation can only be accomplished when proved warranted through due process of law, and said such proceedings are extremely involved and often very lengthy.

With these difficulties in mind, Mr. Doak said, the department would ask Congress for other funds to set up adequate machinery to hear the cases, so that the procedure might be speeded "all along the line."

Asked to reveal the names of some of those against whom action may be taken, Mr. Doak said he was not at liberty to disclose the names of gang leaders under investigation.

He intimated, however, that the list of Chicago's "public enemies," recently made public, includes several of the names which the department is tracing.

BRODSKY TO TESTIFY ON INCOME TODAY

Magistrate Is Summoned to Public Hearing—Crain Agrees to Defer "Frame-Up" Cases.

TAX FRAUDS ARE HUNTED

Federal Agent Confers With Kresel on Judges' Accounts —Bondsman Is Held.

Magistrate Louis B. Brodsky will be the first witness today at the sixth public hearing in the Appellate Division's investigation of the inferior courts, according to an announcement late yesterday by Isidor Kresel, special counsel to Samuel Seabury, the referee. Mr. Kresel intimated that the day might produce some "surprises."

The magistrate, who as the Democratic standard bearer in the three-cornered Congressional contest in the Seventeenth Congressional District was defeated by Mrs. Ruth Pratt, his Republican opponent in the last election, will be questioned, it was understood, about his finances and the sources of his income.

Frequent withdrawals and deposits of large amounts are shown in his bank records, it was reported. He was questioned privately about the matter early in November, at which time he said that his real estate activities accounted for the frequent turnover of his capital.

Brodsky Is Surprise Witness.

The announcement that Magistrate Brodsky would be the subject of today's hearing came somewhat as a surprise because it had been indicated that Magistrate Henry M. R. Goodman, who was summoned from the bench for questioning Wednesday afternoon, would be the chief witness this morning.

It had been feared in some quarters that the closing of the Bank of United States, of which Mr. Kresel was a director, might demand so much of his time that the present inquiry would be slowed up. The special counsel, however, denied this and declared "nothing will be allowed to interefere with this investigation."

Reports of large incomes enjoyed by magistrates, policemen and court officers have attracted the attention of the Federal authorities, it became known when Hugh McQuillan, chief of the Special Intelligence Bureau of the Internal Revenue Department, and his chief assistant, Arthur Murphy, called at Mr. Kresel's office for a conference on evidence of income tax frauds.

Crain Defers Prosecutions.

District Attorney Crain, at the request of Harland B. Tibbetts, chief assistant to Mr. Kresel, deferred his projected questioning of John C. Weston, the process server, who admitted that while assigned as prosecutor to Women's Court he collected $20,000 in bribes from twenty-odd lawyers practicing there. Mr. Tibbetts explained in a letter that the Appellate Division's investigators were not yet through with Weston.

Other developments of the day included the arraignment of four more policemen on charges of conducting themselves in a manner "unbecoming an officer," the opening of a campaign to maintain public confidence in the Police Department and the holding of John Steiner, a bondsman, for trial in Special Sessions on a charge that he exacted an illegal fee for a bail bond.

Lieutenant Peter J. Pfeiffer, suspended supervisor of the vice squad of the Sixth Division, and owner of a house in the Bronx which produced a comparatively large income for him and his wife, according to his testi-

Continued on Page Eighteen.

ARMY RULE RENEWED AS CUBA RIOTS GROW

Washington and Havana Hear President Will Resign—He Denies It.

NEW BACKING FOR STUDENTS

Business Men Support Foes of Machado—Call for United States Cruisers Rumored.

By The Associated Press.

HAVANA, Dec. 11.—Amid new disorders by students and with rumors buzzing through the city that he soon would resign, President Machado today suspended constitutional guarantees throughout the whole of Cuba.

This is tantamount to martial law and is similar to the suspension decreed in Havana and environs which ended last month. Both were authorized by Congress after much debate, but whereas the first decree was confined to the capital and for only twenty days, the suspension invoked today will run for sixty days over the entire island.

Student activities not only continued but increased meanwhile, and the sound of firing was heard in the streets as police attempted to break up demonstrations. Numbers of business and professional men, graduates of the National University, pledged their support to the rioting undergraduates.

Follows Cabinet Meeting.

The President's action followed a secret meeting of the Cabinet, at which United States Ambassador Harry F. Guggenheim was reported to be present, and it was known that important developments were expected.

Havana at the same time was swimming in a flood of rumors. There were numerous reports that the President would resign, another that he already had placed his resignation in the hands of the Supreme Court and still another that Ambassador Guggenheim had summoned two United States cruisers from the naval base at Guantanamo. All were denied.

Two hundred physicians, representing the Cuban Medical Federation, voted tonight to "strike" if the government makes good its threat to imprison professors of the National University who support the student leaders of recent disturbances. The doctors said they would neither answer sick calls nor issue prescriptions.

Resignation Rumor Flatly Denied.

The President made a direct reply tonight to the rumors which said he would quit.

"I have not resigned," he declared, "and I am not thinking of resigning. I see no reason for giving consideration to such a move on my part."

Concerning the lifting of guarantees, Dr. Ricardo Herrera, President Machado's secretary, explained:

"It is merely a means to insure peace in Cuba during these weeks when trouble seems to have increased. The President is determined that order shall prevail."

Six students were reported injured in the clashes today. As before, the declaration of suspension of guarantees seemed to exercise an immediate pacifying effect and no disorders were reported afterward.

Although the military was not ordered out, some of the most vital rights enjoyed by Cubans under their Constitution were taken away. The privileges of free speech, free press, assembly and habeas corpus are among those which Cuba is destined not to enjoy again until after Feb. 8, 1931. Censorship was not invoked.

The decree ordering the suspension

Continued on Page Seventeen.

DRY CHIEF TO AVOID HOLIDAY RAID FLARE; AIMS AT BIG SELLERS

Woodcock Drops Mobilizing of Agents to Search Drinkers at Resorts in Wet Cities.

BARS "FIRST-PAGE STUNTS"

He Reveals New Policy Centring on "Commercial Violators" as Way to Solve Problem.

DRY STRATEGY SESSION SET

Enlarged Board Will Reconvene to Complete Program—Wets Adopt Dispensary Plan.

Special to The New York Times.

WASHINGTON, Dec. 11.—No "first page" or other "spectacular stunts" will be indulged in by prohibition agents on Christmas or New Year's Eve, Colonel Amos W. Woodcock, Director of the Prohibition Enforcement, declared today.

Abandoning the old practice of mobilizing agents in New York, Chicago, New Orleans and other "wet" spots, garbed in evening clothes to enter hotels, restaurants and other public places and search of patrons for pocket containers of liquor, he said that instead the agents would be ordered to concentrate upon the detection of commercial violators, the large-scale sellers of liquor.

This does not mean that some night clubs and other places where the proprietors are themselves vendors will not be watched. Colonel Woodcock said that there would be no let-up in the effort to arrest and prosecute such offenders, because they were of the "commercial" class.

To Put Pressure on Traffickers.

Colonel Woodcock made it clear that, in his opinion, there was just one way to enforce prohibition and that was to checkmate the traffickers in liquors.

The new policy which the government was putting into effect, he said, was to put an end to the commercial phase and the rest of the problem would take care of itself.

Asserting that using up "government" time chasing the little fellows who "buy" would not go very far in solving the problem, Colonel Woodcock added:

"The policy is a steady pressure all the time against the traffickers and nothing spectacular at any time.

"Aiming at those who sell liquor, I want the prohibition enforcing forces to direct their efforts against the commercial, not the non-commercial, violators."

Colonel Woodcock also announced that he had adopted an "efficiency system" to file a complete history of the activities of all prohibition agents. On the basis of this, he added, "merit" would govern in making promotions. He cited the case of two agents in Oklahoma who subdued a band of armed bootleggers without the firing of a shot. His commendation of the agents has been made a part of their file record.

The system is similar to that of the army and navy. Colonel Woodcock hopes that it will mean weeding out every man who does not measure up to the new standard of merit fixed for the service.

Dry and Wet Programs Evolved.

WASHINGTON, Dec. 11 (AP).—Wet and dry advocates left the capital today after winding up national con-

Continued on Page Twenty-two.

Mellon Asks Corporation Gift Exemption; Bill Advances Plan as Aid to Employment

Special to The New York Times.

WASHINGTON, Dec. 11.—Following a request by Secretary Mellon, Chairman Hawley of the House Ways and Means Committee introduced a joint resolution to authorize corporations to deduct contributions to unemployment relief and other charities in computing their income taxes during the period from July 1, 1930, to June 30, 1931, as a further emergency measure in meeting the present economic situation.

In his recommendation for this legislation, contained in letters to Vice President Curtis and Speaker Longworth, the Secretary of the Treasury pointed out the exemption of gifts by individuals and said:

"A number of inquiries have been made by unemployment relief organizations with a view to ascertaining whether gifts made by corporations to those organizations may be deducted in computing net income for income tax purposes.

"There is no provision in the law which would permit corporations to make such deductions, though courts have held that contributions by corporations to hospitals or to charitable and educational institutions, from which they or their employes derive direct benefit, may be deducted as 'ordinary and necessary business expenses.'

"The Bureau of Internal Revenue feels that while contributions to emergency relief funds or to such organizations as community chests would undoubtedly contribute to the public welfare and as such would be beneficial to the corporations, nevertheless the benefits to be derived by the latter or their employes would not be sufficiently direct as to bring them within the terms of the law as at present interpreted.

"In view of the existing emergency and the fact that corporations as well as individuals should be encouraged to contribute liberally to relief organizations, I believe that it would be advisable, for the time being, to allow corporations the same deductions as are allowed to individuals in respect of gifts made exclusively for charitable or unemployment emergency relief purposes."

HOOVER DEMANDS SUPPORT AND PARTY SENATORS AGREE; EMPLOYMENT BILL PASSED

Smith Urges Gifts for Jobless As Price of Happy Christmas

With a choking voice, former Governor Alfred E. Smith appealed to all New Yorkers yesterday to give aid to the unemployed, so that they may enjoy their Christmas dinner with a clear conscience. He was speaking at a luncheon at the Hotel Astor at which trade groups of the commerce and industry subcommittee reported to the Emergency Employment Committee that additional contributions of $1,215,950.04 had brought the fund's total up to $6,275,000.

"New York has set great standards," said Mr. Smith. "It has always been known for its ability to rise to any situation. The emergency now confronting us will have to be met. Let's put every bit of our energy in it so that when we sit down to our Christmas dinner our inner conscience may say, 'You deserve this—you deserve all the joy and happiness you have'."

PRESIDENT WARNS WATSON

Danger of Treasury Raids Calls for Solid Front, He Declares.

ACTIVE DEFENSE NEEDED

Payne of Red Cross and Woods Will Testify on Relief at the Executive's Suggestion.

SOME SENATORS RESENTFUL

Say White House Should Co-operate, but Agree in Parley to Take the Offensive.

Special to The New York Times.

WASHINGTON, Dec. 11.—President Hoover, aroused over the trend of relief legislation and the failure of the Republican Congress to rally to the defense of the administration, today called upon the Republican leaders to uphold his program.

The President pictured to Senator Watson, the party floor leader, and to Speaker Longworth, the danger of enactment of legislation carrying appropriations that could not be spent for unemployment relief, but which would compel higher taxes.

As the result of the President's attitude, the Republicans in the Senate and House met and decided to stiffen their opposition to what Mr. Hoover termed raids on the treasury made under the guise of aiding employment. In his talk with Senator Watson the President, it is reported, complained not only of the failure of the Republicans of the Senate to hold down excessive appropriations, but of their supine attitude when the administration was attacked in the Senate.

Warns Against Bonus Proposals.

The President's action was the result of the passage by the Senate of the $60,000,000 drought relief bill and the accumulation of proposals which would increase the prospective treasury deficit.

The Republican leaders also were informed, it was said, that unless the Republican opposition was solid, proposals to pay the balance due in adjusted compensation to World War veterans in cash, entailing nearly $3,000,000,000, would be enacted.

The Senate leaders were told that the President, unless the situation becomes more satisfactory, is prepared to issue another statement on the general trend of relief legislation. The statement, it was reported, would be even more positive than his declaration of last Tuesday that Congress was "playing politics at the expense of human misery."

Following the President's complaint, Senator Watson summoned seventeen Republican Senators into a conference, and urged united action by the party to defeat efforts to increase the relief appropriations. He also informed his colleagues, it is said, that the President felt that he had not been supported by his party, in that attacks launched against him in the Senate in the last few days had been met with silence.

The President, it also was reported, not only called upon the Republicans of the House and Senate for cooperation and assistance to oppose "treasury raids," but urged that Colonel Arthur Woods of the President's Emergency Committee on Employment, and John Barton Payne, chairman of the Red Cross, be summoned before Congressional committees to explain that the administration's relief program was adequate, and that additional expenditures would be a waste of money and cause new taxation.

Senators Voice Resentment.

Several Senators participating in the conference resented what they characterized as the President's imputation that he lacked a defense in the Senate. They told Senator Watson that cooperation could not be expected unless the President took the Republicans of the Senate into his confidence.

Senator Watson was asked whether he, as Senate leader, had been informed in advance of the President's recent statement, in which members of Congress seeking greater relief were denounced. Senator Watson replied that his first knowledge of the President's statement was after it had been issued.

Several Senators present declared they did not agree with many things said by Mr. Hoover in his statement,

Continued on Page Three.

HOOVER'S AUTHORITY CUT FROM JOB BILL

Senate Eliminates Executive Power to Shift Money Among Works Projects.

ADDS $8,000,000 TO FUNDS

Amendments to $118,000,000 Measure May Cause Delay—Wagner Urges His Plan.

Special to The New York Times.

WASHINGTON, Dec. 11.—The Senate today passed the $110,000,000 House bill for emergency unemployment relief, but only after adopting several amendments, including an additional $8,000,000 in appropriations, and the deletion of the section giving to the President authority to reallocate the funds provided.

The bill was so changed, particularly through the elimination of the Presidential authority, by an amendment proposed by Senator Robinson, the Democratic floor leader, that uncertainty was aroused as to whether conferees of the Senate and House, who will be appointed to iron out the differences, will be able to reach an immediate agreement.

No other disagreement with the principle of the bill was manifested, and it was adopted without a record vote, only, however, after the conditions which have led to the necessity of such legislation were strongly denounced in a speech by Senator Wagner of New York.

Wagner Criticizes President.

Senator Wagner criticized the administration particularly for putting forward only emergency relief measures, and for the statement in the President's message that "it is as yet too soon to constructively formulate" permanent measures to circumvent unemployment. The President, Senator Wagner added, had previously made repeated recommendations for

Continued on Page Four.

"All the News That's Fit to Print."

The New York Times.

Copyright, 1930, by The New York Times Company.

THE WEATHER
Cloudy and slightly warmer today; tomorrow rain and warmer.
Temperatures yesterday—Max. 29, min. 9.
U. S. Weather Forecast—For details see Page 56.

VOL. LXXX....No. 26,625. **** NEW YORK, WEDNESDAY, DECEMBER 17, 1930. TWO CENTS in Greater New York | THREE CENTS Within 200 Miles | FOUR CENTS Elsewhere Except 7th and 8th Postal Zones

FEDERAL JUDGE HOLDS PROHIBITION VOID; FINDS METHOD OF ITS ADOPTION ILLEGAL; RULING IN NEW JERSEY STIRS WASHINGTON

STRIKES GRIP SPAIN, SUPPORTING REVOLT; REBELS USE PLANES

Government Claims Control, but Frontier Points Report the Insurrection Spreading.

WEALTHY FLEE TO FRANCE

Police Require Passes of All Travelers—Line Waits All Day to Get Them.

BREAD SHORTAGE IN NORTH

Border Hears Insurgents Shot Three Loyal Generals—Censorship Veils Facts.

Special Cable to THE NEW YORK TIMES.

MADRID, Dec. 16.—Innumerable troops and Civil Guardsmen patrolled the streets of Madrid today, but otherwise the capital had returned to normal after yesterday's aerial revolt.

Except for strikes, the rest of the country was quiet. Reliable private sources not in sympathy with the government confirm government assertions that at a late hour this afternoon there had not been any serious rioting or disturbance anywhere in the country.

With the country in the iron grip of martial law, the situation caused by the general strikes, however, is still disquieting. The provinces in the capitals of which there are general strikes, according to an official list, are Coruna, Huelva, Jaen, Logrono, Navarro, Santander, Viscaya and Zaragosela. There are strikes, which are not general, in the Provinces of Cordoba, Granada, Lerida and Seville. On the other hand, workers have returned to their jobs in Leon, Salamanca and Zamora.

There are reports of disturbances at the Rio Tinto mines, where a general strike is in progress.

Passes Required of Travelers.

No one is allowed to leave any city in Spain without police permission, and crowds of Spaniards waited outside the Police Commissioner's office here all day trying to get certificates for departure. Foreigners bearing valid passports experience no difficulty if they leave by train, but secret agents on the cars are keeping a sharp look out for agitators.

Reports exist that the government has not regained control of the situation at Jaca and is out of touch with fifteen States, but these can be discounted.

A court martial has been named at Cuatro Vientos [Four Winds] Air Field, where Major Ramon Franco hid his airplane revolt yesterday. The court will try prisoners who were captured in the attempt and the death penalty will be sought for some.

An icy wind blowing off the peaks of the Sierra Guadarramas is likely to handicap any rebellious activity tonight. Hidden by capes that come over their noses, troops are huddled in doorways or finding shelter behind their horses at street corners.

The government is doing its best to keep all public services going, and tonight nineteen chambers of commerce in various parts of Spain agreed to keep stores open.

At Gijon a mob tore down a marker for Primo de Rivera Street on the façade of a church and then attacked the church itself, smashing windows, images and confessional boxes. The government says one rioter was killed there.

Towns Being Isolated.

The government's policy now is to segregate every town in which there is a strike and prevent concerted Republican action by keeping firm control of all communications.

The Republicans apparently still possess some aircraft, as six machines flew over Barcelona today, dropping subversive leaflets. This city has been subdivided into five sections, each under the command of a General, with forces of cavalry and artillery at his disposal. The procedure is being adopted in other towns, although leaders of the Republican movement are urging peaceful methods and hope to win their cause by a general paralysis of community life.

Quantities of subversive leaflets have fallen into the government's hands and it is officially stated that the government now has no doubt regarding the origin of the communistic revolt, as a number of well-known agitators have signed their names.

King Alfonso and Queen Victoria have suspended all audiences and remained at the palace all day. None of the royal family appeared at a public charitable function at which the King's daughters were to have presided.

Late yesterday afternoon several companies of the Leon Regiment, returning from the capture of Quatro

Continued on Page Twelve.

Mercury Touches 9 Here as Cold Grips Nation; 17 Below Reported Up-State; Relief Due Today

New York experienced yesterday the coldest weather of the rapidly waning Fall. After a night in which the mercury steadily sank at the rate of a degree or more an hour the official thermometer in the Whitehall Building recorded 9 above zero at 7 A. M., only 4 degrees above the record for Dec. 16 established fifty-four years ago.

Rallying as the sun came up, the temperature rose to a high mark of 29 degrees at 2:50 P. M., but the average for the day was only 19, 16 degrees below the normal for the date. Today and tomorrow should be warmer, however, the Weather Bureau promised last night. Rain is looked for tomorrow.

Except for the Pacific Coast and the extreme South the entire nation suffered from the frigid weather, with temperatures as low as 17 below zero reported from Northern New York and New England. Temperatures all the way to the prairie States were generally 15 to 20 degrees lower than on Monday, The Associated Press reported.

One death was attributed to the cold in Boston, where the thermometer dropped to 4 above zero, while overheated stoves led to numerous fires. In South Boston twenty-five persons were made homeless and ten small children had narrow escapes from death or injury when an oil stove used to augment the regular heating plant of a three-family house exploded.

The coldest place in the country yesterday was Owls Head, N. Y., where 17 below zero was registered, but it was closely pressed by many New England points. The cold wave extended to Texas. The Canadian maritime provinces and Newfoundland were blanketed with snow from Monday's blizzard, but fears which had been felt for the Newfoundland fishing fleet were relieved by word of its safety.

The red ball signifying that skating is safe will be raised above all ponds under the jurisdiction of the Long Island State Park Commission today unless the weather modifies, it was announced last night. Tests yesterday showed that the ice on the various ponds averaged almost 2 inches in thickness.

BRODSKY ON STAND FIGHTS TO KEEP POST

Magistrate Disputes Evidence of Financial Difficulties—Defends Wall St. Deals.

BROKER DENIES GUARANTEE

Testifies Former Defendant Curbed Judge's Operations—Byrne Tells of "Savings."

The hearing on Magistrate Louis B. Brodsky's financial and business dealings came to an end as Samuel Seabury, referee for the Appellate Division, yesterday afternoon with the magistrate on the witness stand giving his explanation of a mass of circumstantial evidence.

He was fighting to retain his $12,000-a-year job on the bench, while the investigators tried to make it appear was a more important item in his assets than might have been expected in the case of a man who has been described as "New York's wealthiest magistrate." For Isidor Kresel, special counsel to Mr. Seabury, had sought to establish during the day that Mr. Brodsky's liabilities amounted to about $100,000 and that his financial position was extended, to say the least.

At the conclusion of the hearing Magistrate Brodsky's status was somewhat uncertain. Although he conferred at length with Mr. Seabury in the latter's chambers neither he nor the referee would discuss what was said. It was indicated strongly in other quarters, however, that the referee's report on the case to the Appellate Division would force Magistrate Brodsky to defend himself before that tribunal.

Brodsky Defends Record.

When he received his opportunity to defend himself at the public hearing, the magistrate protested that he was unprepared and then, at the insistence of Mr. Seabury that he speak then or never, he launched into what was in a sense an extemporaneous rebuttal of evidence that was so diffuse that it included a testimony about a mysterious substitution of defendants before Judge Cornelius Collins in General Sessions.

Magistrate Brodsky denied, however, that he was "broke," and said he believed his assets sufficient to meet his obligations. He admitted that he had given Edward J. Byrne, son-in-law of the late James J. Hagan, the Tammany district leader who helped him obtain his judicial office, checks for $6,000 but insisted that it was in a legitimate business transaction.

It was true as Byrne had testified earlier, he said, that the district leader's son-in-law held power of attorney over a brokerage account he had opened for Miss Kitty Carr, Mr. Brodsky's secretary, but, he declared, Byrne had never used it to "buy or sell a share of stock or withdraw a dollar from the account."

Nearly all the indebtedness to which Magistrate Brodsky confessed was in the nature of loans from the doven or more individuals whom he named at the first public hearing. These loans are not secured. In addition, he told of other "collateral loans," amounting to about $30,000, for which he was "partly liable." Chief among his assets he mentioned $81,000 of Class D bonds in the 571 Park Avenue Corporation.

These bonds are secured by a third mortgage upon the property, but three other series have precedence over them in the matter of claims, it was testified. Witnesses said there had been no market for Series D bonds since the failure of the corporation to redeem them last March. It was with bonds of this class that

Continued on Page Two.

PRESIDENT REBUFFS SENATE ON JOB DATA; RECESS PLAN UPSET

Woods Made No Report, but Only Some Notes on Employment, Says the Executive.

DROUGHT VOTE DEMANDED

Democrats Warn That Adjournment Will Be Held Up—Garner Charges Filibuster.

MAJORITY PROMISES SPEED

Secretary Hyde Will Testify Today—Senate Conferees Uphold Public Works Amendments.

Special to The New York Times.

WASHINGTON, Dec. 16.—Democratic leaders in Congress issued a warning to the Republicans today that they will oppose the holiday recess set for Saturday until the drought relief bill has been passed and sent to the White House. At the same time President Hoover informed the Senate that he was unable to comply with its request for Colonel Arthur Woods's report on employment since the head of his emergency committee had submitted only notes and verbal suggestions which had guided the Executive in recommendations already laid before Congress.

Congress had planned to adjourn Saturday until Jan. 5. A statement by Senator Robinson and Representative Garner, floor leaders, that the Democrats would oppose a recess was countered by Senator Watson and Representative Tilson, Republican floor leaders, who said they had no intention of seeking an adjournment until the drought relief bill emerges from its entanglement and is sent to the President.

President Hoover's message to the Senate prompted Senator La Follette to offer a resolution requesting Colonel Woods and John Barton Payne, chairman of the American Red Cross, to appear before the Appropriations Committee and tell it of the actual unemployment situation and the plans the Red Cross has made to care for the hungry and suffering.

Text of the President's Message.

The President's message read:

To the Senate:

I am in receipt of the resolution of the Senate reading as follows:

"Resolved, That the President be, and is hereby, requested to transmit to the Senate, if not incompatible with the public interest, the following: The report of the President's Emergency Commission on Unemployment, Colonel Arthur D. Woods, chairman."

The President's Emergency Committee has made no report on unemployment. I have received notes and verbal suggestions from Colonel Woods from time to time and from the departments in the government on this subject. These were confined to guidance in formulation of the recommendations which I have already laid before Congress. Such notes and discussions are necessarily passing and tentative, and they represent that confidential relation of the President with government officers which should be preserved.

HERBERT HOOVER.

The White House.

Dec. 16, 1930.

Senate Conferees Hold Lines.

Another obstacle to the recess developed when the Senate conferees refused to recede from their position on the Robinson, Couzens and Black amendments to the $118,000,000 emer-

Continued on Page Three.

GERMANS HOLD COURT ON HITLER ROW HERE

Mussolini's Alleged Go-Between Denies He Is Man Who Paid German Fascists.

CHALLENGED TO GO BACK

Italian Agrees to Return to Munich—Affair Is an Echo of Libel Suit.

The hand of German justice was extended to New York yesterday in an effort to clear up the mystery of the relations between Benito Mussolini, Italian dictator, and Adolph Hitler, leader of the German Fascists, who, it has been charged, has been receiving financial support from Italy. The charge is the basis of a perjury suit brought by Hitler and now pending in the District Court of Munich.

In connection with this suit a hearing was held yesterday before William J. Topkens, acting as commissioner for the Munich Court, and a member of the law firm of Schnitzler, Thorn & Dayton, attorneys for the German Consulate. The hearing was in the firm's office, 17 Battery Place, where the consulate also is located.

Participating in the hearing was Werner Abel, a former lieutenant of Hitler and a leader in the Fascist putsch in Munich in 1923, against whom Hitler has brought the perjury action.

Testifying in a previous libel suit brought by Hitler in Munich, Abel declared that Hitler was receiving financial support from Mussolini, in accordance with a political understanding with the Duce, that when the German Fascists attain power they will relinquish all claims to the Southern Tyrol. Armed with authorization from the Munich court, Abel came here from Berlin two days ago to attend yesterday's hearing and to help interrogate Giuseppe Migliorati, said to be a former Italian captain, who, according to Abel, acted for a time as the go-between for Mussolini and Hitler.

Located Here Only Recently.

Migliorati's whereabouts had been unknown for some time and it was only recently that it was learned he was in New York. Abel asked the Munich Court to have him examined here.

The two men faced each other yesterday in Mr. Topkens's office, Abel insisting that Migliorati was the man whom he had introduced to Hitler as Mussolini's envoy and as the one who carried money from Mussolini to Hitler and Migliorati denying Abel's charges. Migliorati admitted, however, that he had met Abel.

The hearing failed to clear up the mystery of the relations between the Italian and German Fascist leaders and was cut short when Abel challenged Migliorati to go to Germany to testify in Hitler's suit. Migliorati accepted the challenge on condition that his expenses be paid. Abel agreed to deposit $1,500 for such expenses in an American bank pending official call upon Migliorati by the Bavarian Ministry of Justice to make good on his promise.

"I do not believe he will come," said Abel last night after the hearing. "He will not dare to face a German court and repeat his denial under oath on German soil."

Abel will sail back for Germany tomorrow to begin preparations for his defense against Hitler's action.

The minutes of yesterday's hearing will be transmitted by Mr. Topkens to the German Consulate and sent as a confidential document through the German Embassy in

Continued on Page Eighteen.

New British Cruisers to Attain Great Speed; Can Raise Long-Range Guns to 70 Degrees

Special Cable to THE NEW YORK TIMES.

LONDON, Dec. 16.—Ever since the new British light cruiser Leander—the first of the new type superseding the 10,000-ton Washington class and designed particularly for the protection of trade routes—was laid down at Devonport last September there has been the widest speculation regarding her speed and armament.

She is still on the Admiralty's "confidential" list and the only official particulars available are that she will displace about 6,700 tons, carry eight 6-inch guns, four 4-inch anti-aircraft weapons and be provided with six 21-inch torpedo tubes.

Her three sister ships, Orion, Achilles and Neptune, will be similarly armed.

It is generally known, however, that all four will be "one-funnel" ships, flues from all her oil-fired boilers being carried to one common smokestack amidships.

What are claimed to be additional details were supplied today by the naval correspondent of The Daily Telegraph, who suggests that the Leander's 6-inch guns will not only be of the new, high-velocity, quick-firing type but will be capable of being elevated to seventy degrees, against the maximum elevation of thirty degrees obtainable by guns of previous cruisers and the battleship Nelson.

This arrangement, it is pointed out, not only gives the guns an enormous range but enables them to be used against aircraft.

Moreover, according to the correspondent, the speed of the new cruiser will be thirty-five knots, or two knots above the speed of any previous British cruiser, and she will be obtainable with all war stores aboard and in full fighting trim.

The Leander, it is added, will have heavily armored decks well above the water line and carry two catapults for launching aircraft.

DRYS PREDICT ITS REVERSAL

They Are Confident the Supreme Court Will Uphold Prohibition.

BECK SEES GRAVE ISSUES

But While He Considers the Decision Interesting, He Doubts Law Will Be Invalidated.

GLASS READY TO FIGHT ON

If Amendment Is Upset He Would Move to Replace It—Borah and Tydings Silent.

Special to The New York Times.

WASHINGTON, Dec. 16.—The decision of United States Judge William Clark of Princeton, who held today, in the Sprague case, that the adoption of the Eighteenth Amendment was invalid and that the ratification of the amendment by State legislatures was not the method prescribed in the Federal Constitution, occasioned the greatest interest in wet and dry, as well as in constitutional law circles, in Washington tonight.

Opinion was divided over the soundness of the decision, and in dry circles the prediction was unanimous that the decision would not survive the test of the Supreme Court.

Senator Borah, an eminent constitutional lawyer, said he was deeply interested, but took the position that, as the question will be in the courts for some time to come, this was not a time for talk by outsiders. The same position was taken by Senator Tydings of Maryland, one of the wet leaders in the Senate. Others were outspoken, among them Senator Brookhart, who said it was "a tomtit" decision.

Glass Fears Long Contest.

Senator Glass of Virginia, talking as a "layman," said he did not know whether the Supreme Court would uphold Judge Clark but that if it did the whole prohibition issue would have to be fought over again, and that if this should be the case it would mean "prolonged combat and bitterness."

Representative James M. Beck of Pennsylvania, former Solicitor General of the United States and leading constitutional lawyer, while hesitating to comment on Judge Clark's decision until he had read the full text, held that, if the New Jersey court had invalidated the Eighteenth Amendment on grounds not heretofore considered by the Supreme Court in prior cases, "then it presents a very interesting decision, for there is no reason why the Supreme Court should not now invalidate the Eighteenth Amendment upon a specific ground simply because it has validated the amendment upon other grounds." He expressed the view, however, that "it is improbable that the court would invalidate the Eighteenth Amendment at this late day."

Detailed Comment of Leaders.

The detailed comment of Washington leaders follows:

Senator Glass of Virginia, Democrat—Not being a constitutional lawyer,

Continued on Page Twenty-one.

Present Contention by Wets Was Held Unsound Ten Years Ago, Anti-Saloon Counsel Asserts

Special to The New York Times.

WASHINGTON, Dec. 16.—The attack on the validity of the Eighteenth Amendment made in the decision of Judge Clark was challenged tonight by Edward B. Dunford, general counsel of the Anti-Saloon League of America.

"The New York lawyers who have announced their intention of launching a new attack upon the Eighteenth Amendment before the United States Supreme Court through cases pending in New York and New Jersey seem to be threshing old straw and in addition face insuperable legal obstacles," said Mr. Dunford.

"The contention which they advance is not new. The same points were made by counsel equally distinguished (among them Elihu Root) in arguments before the United States Supreme Court in 1920, when that court declared the amendment valid.

"The Supreme Court has also said:

"'A long acquiescence in repeated acts of legislation on particular matters is evidence that those matters have been generally considered by the people as properly within legislative control.'

"The present contention was held unsound when first made ten years ago. The Constitution is the same now as it was then. Congress has repeatedly enacted legislation dependent upon the validity of the amendment, all of which have been held constitutional against all attacks. This attempt to restore the legalized liquor traffic through short-circuiting the Eighteenth Amendment by court action will likely prove as futile as have similar efforts in the past."

WETS HAIL DECISION AS DRYS BELITTLE IT

Far-Reaching, Say Advocates of Repeal—Will Not Be Upheld, Contend Antis.

COHALAN PRAISES RULING

Sees Step Toward Return of Respect for Law—"Wet Propaganda," Says Mrs. Colvin.

Leaders in the anti-prohibition movement hailed as an important and far-reaching step the decision in New Jersey yesterday by Federal Judge William Clark that the Eighteenth Amendment never became part of the Constitution, but sharply contrasting statements were issued by dry leaders, who contended that the ruling would have no wide influence, and expressed confidence that it would not be upheld in the higher court.

Daniel F. Cohalan, former Supreme Court justice and a teetotaler, who was a member of the legal staff for the defense in the case, predicted that the effect of the decision would be "extraordinary" and that it would help to restore confidence in "real" government and to re-establish respect for law and order. In his opinion, Judge Clark's decision "is absolutely controlling within the jurisdiction of the Federal Court in New Jersey and persuasive in the rest of the country."

Frederic R. Coudert Jr., Republican candidate for District Attorney of New York County in 1929, and Mrs. Charles H. Sabin, chairman of the Women's Organization for National Prohibition Reform, agreed that Judge Clark had raised a "fundamental" point, which, said Mrs. Sabin, was far more important than the issue involved in the Eighteenth Amendment itself.

Repeal Advocates Are Delighted.

Other advocates of repeal or modification said the decision was "sound," "important," or "very interesting," and expressed delight that such a decision had been handed down.

Dry leaders, however, were unimpressed with the decision, and were in agreement in expressing confidence that it would not be sustained.

Mrs. Ella A. Boole, national president of the W. C. T. U., said the Clark decision was the ruling "of only a lower court" and contended that if the Eighteenth Amendment is unconstitutional, the Sixteenth, Seventeenth and Nineteenth Amendments also are unconstitutional and would be abrogated by this decision of Judge Clark.

Mrs. D. Leigh Colvin, head of the New York State W. C. T. U., denounced the decision as "wet propaganda," while the Rev. James K. Shields, superintendent of the Anti-Saloon League of New Jersey, said the decision would have no far-reaching influence and there was "nothing to worry" over it. Dr. S. E. Nicholson, associate superintendent of the New York State Anti-Saloon League, declared that the United States Supreme Court has settled the question.

Some noted leaders at the bar, such as James W. Davis and Samuel

Continued on Page Twenty-one.

DECISION IS NO BAR TO DRY ENFORCEMENT

Federal Attorney in New Jersey Explains There Will Be No Let-Down in Work.

OTHER JUDGES NOT BOUND

Only 3 of 33 Decisions by Jurist Giving Opinion Reversed Since Appointment in 1925.

Despite Judge Clark's decision declaring the Eighteenth Amendment unconstitutional on the ground that it was not ratified by the States in accordance with terms set down in the Constitution, Federal prohibition authorities announced last night that they would continue their enforcement work as usual in New Jersey.

At the Philadelphia offices of John D. Pennington, Prohibition Administrator for Pennsylvania, New Jersey and Delaware, questioners were referred to United States Attorney Philip Forman at Trenton, who represented the government in the case in which Judge Clark's decision was made. While Pennington was silent, assistants said the law was to be enforced as heretofore.

Mr. Forman explained that he had not obtained a copy of the decision until late in the afternoon and was, therefore, not prepared to discuss its fine points.

"The government will, of course, appeal the decision," he said, "but the course of the appeal will be guided of necessity by the findings in Judge Clark's opinion."

Other Judges Not Bound.

"Meanwhile, as I understand it, no other judge in the United States nor the judges of this district are bound by this opinion, and therefore the enforcement of the Volstead act will continue in New Jersey until the remaining three judges of this bench all decide in agreement with Judge Clark or until a decision of the higher court is reached upon this opinion."

Federal Judge William N. Runyon, senior judge of the New Jersey district, also made it plain that judges in the Federal courts of New Jersey were independent of each other and that Judge Clark's colleagues would not be bound by his opinion until it has been upheld either by the Circuit Court of Appeals or the Supreme Court of the United States.

Judge Clark, himself, admitted that the decision was not binding on other Federal judges in his district and explained that they could make their own decisions as to whether the Eighteenth Amendment is valid or not.

"My decision," Judge Clark said, "will not affect the operation of the prohibition laws in any way nor will it affect other amendments to the Constitution. The Hobart act, the New Jersey enforcement law, is also still in force."

Judge Clark seemed to feel that the question of the validity of his opinion might be decided by the United States Circuit Court without going as far as the Supreme Court.

"Very rarely," he said, "do deci-

Continued on Page Twenty-one.

JUDGE CLARK CITES ARTICLE V

Ratification Should Be by People, Not States, He Maintains.

AN APPEAL TO BE TAKEN

Jurist Believes Ruling Cannot Bring Into Question Passage of Other Amendments.

OPINION CALLS ISSUE NEW

Says Supreme Court Never Has Ruled on Adoption—Others Hold That It Has.

The text of Judge Clark's decision is on pages 22 and 23.

The adoption of the Eighteenth Amendment was held invalid yesterday by United States District Judge William Clark in a decision filed in Newark.

Judge Clark decided that the amendment never had become a part of the United States Constitution. He held that its ratification by the State Legislatures was not the method prescribed by the amending article of the Constitution—Article 5—for amendments which effect a transfer of power from the individual States to the United States. Judge Clark asserted that such amendments must be approved by Constitutional Conventions elected by the people of the various States.

The decision, Judge Clark said, is not binding on other district court judges in the New Jersey district. He, quitting the criminal calender to take up equity cases, will not have to judge cases involving the question which he has ruled upon. Judge Clark also pointed out that an appeal would stay the effect of his decision.

Washington Is Disturbed.

Dry leaders in Washington freely predicted reversal of the Clark decision. They contended that, if the decision should be upheld, it would mean invalidation of all other amendments that have been adopted—the Woman's Suffrage Amendment, and the amendment abolishing slavery among them. Even certain wets seemed doubtful as to the outcome.

High government officials were frankly disturbed by news of the decision. Fear was expressed that district might refuse to issue warrants in prohibition cases and that other authorities might refuse to act against violators. In one part of the Department of Justice, however, it was felt that the decision would have no effect on the national status of enforcement unless it is upheld by the Supreme Court.

Prohibition enforcement authorities in New Jersey declared last night that Judge Clark's decision would in no way affect their course of operation; they intended to continue present routine as if such a decision had never been handed down.

The case on which Judge Clark ruled involved William Sprague, clerk of Wantage Township, who was indicted for transporting beer. The indictment was dismissed by Judge Clark.

There is now before the United States Court of Appeals the case of Louis E. Thibault, which is similar in scope to the Sprague case. Thibault's counsel contend that the Tenth Amendment, counsel for Thibault argued, is applicable in that it limits the powers which may be claimed under Article 5 of the Constitution.

Other Amendments Unaffected.

Judge Clark said, in effect, that his decision on the Eighteenth Amendment would not abrogate previous amendments passed under Article 5. First making it plain that he was considering the adjudication of only the validity of the Eighteenth Amendment, he went on to say that:

"We do not think that legislative ratification of the other amendments of the Constitution need trouble even those who do not agree with us on this point."

He then pointed out that none of the previous amendments involved the same question as the Eighteenth. The Thirteenth Amendment, abolishing slavery, "presents certain points

Continued on Page Twenty-three.

Emperor Haile Selassie I of Ethiopia at his coronation in Addis Ababa.

Mohandas K. Gandhi, champion of Indian independence, leading one of his first meetings.

Section 1

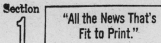

"All the News That's Fit to Print."

The New York Times.

THE WEATHER
Cloudy, rain late today; tomorrow partly cloudy and colder.
Temperatures yesterday--Max. 46, min. 32.
U. S. Weather Forecast--Page 16, Section 2.

Section 1

VOL. LXXX....No. 26,629. * * * * NEW YORK, SUNDAY, DECEMBER 21, 1930. Including Rotogravure Picture Section in two parts—Magazine and Book Sections in Rotogravure. TEN CENTS

HOOVER VICTOR AS CONGRESS ADJOURNS; HIS RELIEF MEASURES PASSED AND SIGNED; ALL POWER BOARD NOMINEES CONFIRMED

RAIL BROTHERHOODS CONSIDER MERGING WITH THE A. F. OF L.

Trainmen Agree to Conference as Result of Negotiations Started by Green.

DOAK IS SAID TO FAVOR IT

Consolidation With "Big Four" Would Swell Federation's Ranks to 3,500,000.

"SOLID LABOR FRONT" GOAL

Parleys With Three Other Brotherhoods to Follow if First Succeeds.

Special to The New York Times.

CLEVELAND, Dec. 20.—Negotiations directed toward affiliating the four major railroad brotherhoods, numbering about 500,000 members, with the American Federation of Labor were revealed here today by Alexander F. Whitney, president of the Brotherhood of Railway Trainmen.

The negotiations, instituted by William Green and conducted by him with officials of the trainmen, are regarded as of great import to organized labor in that the consolidation, if effected, will add much strength to the federation, swell its ranks to 3,500,000 members and enable organized labor to present a "solid front."

Labor leaders, it is said here, hold the belief that "the time is ripe" to unite the "Big Four" with the federation.

The Big Four Brotherhoods consist of the Railroad Trainmen, Locomotive Firemen and Enginemen, Locomotive Engineers and Railroad Conductors. The American Federation of Labor has tried for years to iron out the difficulties that have prevented an amalgamation.

Conference Arranged.

A statement today by Mr. Whitney indicated that the way had been paved for a consolidation.

"I do not think there are any insurmountable obstacles in the way of an agreement," Mr. Whitney said today. "Time has brought about a better feeling and there are possibilities for an affiliation."

Three officials of the Trainmen's Brotherhood, Mr. Whitney, James A. Farquharson, legislative representative, and S. R. Harvey, assistant president, will confer with a committee of American Federation of Labor officials within the next ten days, it was said.

Should the trainmen reach an agreement with the federation, similar parleys will be held with the three other brotherhoods.

Secretary of Labor Doak, former legislative agent for the Brotherhood of Railroad Trainmen, unofficially is reported to favor the step. Both Federation and brotherhood leaders are convince that labor's welfare in the future depends largely on the progress it makes in legislative halls and ranking officials are said to be unanimous in the opinion that the best results will be obtained only when labor presents a united front.

D. B. Robertson, president of the Brotherhood of Locomotive Firemen and Enginemen, said that his organization has taken no part in the consolidation movement.

Jurisdiction Moot Question.

Principal among the disputes between the brotherhoods and the American Federation of Labor has been that over jurisdiction on electrified railroads. The Amalgamated Association of Street Railway Employes, a member of the federation, has contended that its scope should include employes of the electrified roads—a contention the brotherhoods have not agreed with.

There can be no dual organization within the American Federation of Labor. By that is meant that the organizing activities and jurisdiction of bodies affiliated with the federation must not clash. A dozen railroad brotherhoods, already members of the federation, would in some measure be in conflict with the four major brotherhoods on that principle.

It is to attempt to overcome these difficulties that President Green has initiated a new campaign to align a solid labor front.

Should agreement be reached on the most important questions in issue it is probable that the all-important matter will come before the next convention of the American Federation of Labor in October of 1931. It would require action of the conven-

Continued on Page Twenty-one.

24 Woodcock "Baked in a Pie" Ireland's Gift to King George

Wireless to The New York Times.

LONDON, Dec. 20.—King George will receive a Christmas gift of twenty-four woodcock "baked in a pie" from James MacNeill, Governor General of the Irish Free State. This follows a custom begun in 1813, when Lord Talbot, Viceroy of Ireland, presented to George III a pie of twenty-four woodcock, associating with it the old nursery rhyme.

Every Viceroy since has made a similar gift to the reigning king. Tim Healy, first Free State Governor General, continued the practice, but the pie is now made in London instead of in the viceregal kitchen in Dublin.

NOTABLE SPANIARDS 'CONFESS' REBELLION

Thousands Sign Mass Manifesto, Including Publicists and a Leading Army General.

QUIET THROUGHOUT NATION

Troops Off Streets in Chief Cities—Valencia Angered by Legion's Presence.

Special Cable to The New York Times.

MADRID, Dec. 20.—A republican manifesto signed by thousands is going the rounds tonight containing within it much to puzzle the Berenguer Government.

Between 9,000 and 10,000 persons are already within Spanish prison walls in connection with the revolt, 956 in the capital alone, yet the manifesto is a mass "confession" by thousands of others of complicity in the revolutionary conspiracy. The signers are issuing it with full knowledge that a ship is reported waiting off Barcelona to take the ringleaders of last week's uprising to the prison colony on the island of Fernando Po.

The manifesto, addressed to a military judge, declares:

"We, the undersigned, taking cognizance of the charges brought against Alcala Zamora, Miguel Maura, Francisco Largo Caballero, Hernando Rios and others because of the revolutionary manifesto they signed, formally declare that we morally and materially, in the spirit and letter of said manifesto, plotted to obtain through a military and civil uprising the justice and political dignity which today are possible only under a republic."

Signers of Manifesto.

Among the signers are Valle Inclan, noted artist; Sanchez Roman, a Republican, who boasts of having written last week's proclamation, and General Requelme, one of Spain's best-known military men, who was arrested for alleged plotting in Barcelona but later released.

The government today ordered its army on the Franco-Spanish border back to barracks. Interrogations of persons crossing the border will cease and normal conditions will be resumed.

The Spanish Aero Club today voted to drop the name of Major Ramon Franco, the transatlantic flier, from its list, as well as the names of all the other flying officers who fled to Portugal after the recent revolt at the Madrid airdrome. It is believed here that the court-martialing of the

Continued on Page Eighteen.

TREATY NAVY COST RAISED BY PRATT TO $1,100,000,000

Admiral Adds $100,000,000 and Figures Total With Air Program at $1,250,000,000.

HOLDS OUTLAY JUSTIFIED

He Informs House Committee That Pact Stops Arms Rivalry and Creates World Good-Will.

ALSO ENDS 'FEAR' ON PACIFIC

Naval Chief Sees "Confidence" With Japan Restored—Argues "Efficiency" and "Economy."

Special to The New York Times.

WASHINGTON, Dec. 20.—If the United States builds up its combatant units to the strength fixed for the United States in the London naval treaty, the cost will be about $1,100,000,000 and if the air program is added the total will be $1,250,000,000, according to the estimates of Admiral William V. Pratt, the chief of naval operations, transmitted today to the House Committee on Naval Affairs.

The Admiral's nomination for his post in the Navy Department was confirmed today by the Senate.

Estimates for building the navy up to treaty limits in the past have run from $800,000,000 to around $1,000,000,000, dependent upon the time taken to achieve parity and to replace existing ships after they reach treaty age-limits and also have varied according to the number of battleships to be included as replacements. The $1,000,000,000 figure was mentioned when Admiral Pratt testified before the House committee on Dec. 10.

The Navy Department has agreed in a time limit of ten years to reach the treaty limit, or five years in excess of the life of the London treaty, which expires at midnight of Dec. 31, 1935.

When he appeared as a witness before the House Naval Committee recently, Admiral Pratt was asked what the cost would ultimately be if the United States built up to the treaty strength, what would be the ultimate saving to the government in maintenance and replacement costs once parity with Great Britain and the treaty ratio fixed in the case of Japan were attained, and what were his views as to the removal "of a certain amount of friction by elimination of the competitive feature in naval building programs."

In his communication to the committee today Admiral Pratt discussed the treaty situation from three standpoints: first, international good-will; second, efficiency, and third, cost.

From the standpoint of international good-will, he declared that the treaty was almost an immediate guarantee of the elimination of the age-old, trouble-making problem of competition in naval construction, and no less important, he added, was the fact that the treaty had removed the element of "fear" from American-Japanese relations and had substituted an atmosphere of confidence for one of mistrust.

Text of the Admiral's Letter.

The text of Admiral Pratt's communication to the committee, which

Continued on Page Two.

Our Tourists Paid 5 Billions Of World's 1930 Travel Bill

Special to The New York Times.

WASHINGTON, Dec. 20.—The world travel bill for 1930 was approximately $7,500,000,000 and two-thirds of this amount or $5,000,000,000 was spent by Americans at home and abroad and visitors to our shores, according to a survey of the American Automobile Association made public today.

Nearly $325,000,000 was spent in 1930 by Americans entering Canada in more than 5,000,000 automobiles.

More than 300,000 Americans went abroad.

Total expenditures by Americans for travel at home were decreased by shorter tours and a smaller per capita expenditure.

ROB BANK OF $31,633 IN AMSTERDAM AV.

Six Armed Thugs Invade Branch of Seward National—Cow 10 Clerks and Customers.

ROBBERY OVER IN 4 MINUTES

Wall St. Messenger Duped Out of $6,856 Stock—$30,000 Gem Theft Is Reported.

Four minutes after seven shabbily dressed men had driven up to the uptown branch of the Seward National Bank and Trust Company at Ninety-third Street and Amsterdam Avenue yesterday morning, they had disarmed a special policeman, held-up the ten employes and depositors, looted the tellers' cages of $31,633 in currency and escaped. In their haste they overlooked between $5,000 and $6,000 in gold coins within easy reach.

Two other robberies with loot said to be nearly $37,000 were reported here during the day.

Between $30,000 and $40,000 worth of jewelry was reported stolen from the jewelry manufacturing plant of Stein & Koslow, 64 West Forty-eighth Street. Two men, Nathan Koslow, one of the partners, and Ewald Kaelder, an employe, were found bound and handcuffed. They reported that a man had entered the office at about 3:30 P. M. and, after inquiring about a piece of jewelry, had held them, robbed the open safe and ransacked the shop.

In the Wall Street district an 18-year-old messenger boy was robbed of $6,856 worth of stock certificates by a well-dressed stranger who offered to deliver them to "save him the trouble."

It was 9:32 A. M. when the car which brought the robbers stopped at the northeast corner of Ninety-third Street and Amsterdam Avenue, where the branch bank occupies quarters on the ground floor of a sixteen-story apartment house. The engine was still running as six of the men crossed the sidewalk and stepped inside with drawn pistols. Beyond the fact that their leader was more than six feet tall, and that their clothes was shabby, no one was able to describe them.

Take Pistol From Guard.

William Messimer of 2,609 Fifth Avenue, the special bank policeman, was standing near the door as they came in. He carried a revolver in a holster, but saw nothing suspicious as one of the men approached him and asked how to fill out a deposit slip. Messimer walked with him to a desk and had begun to explain when something hard was jammed against his side.

"Don't move or say anything; just give me your gun," the man said in a whisper.

Messimer did as he was told. In the meantime four of the other robbers had stepped forward to the tellers' cages with leveled pistols. Two of them stood in front of the window, behind which Marvin Ayres, the loan clerk, was at work and two others covered Andrew Stuke Jr. and William Kruger, paying tellers. Frank M. Drake, the manager, had not arrived, but Mrs. Sophie Goldberg of 380 Riverside Drive, assistant manager, was seated at her desk inside an enclosure at the left of the front door. She sat speechless, as she raised her eyes and looked into the muzzle of a revolver.

There were three other employes in the bank—Miss Marie Jones, Mr. Drake's stenographer, and Miss Mary McIntyre and Miss Annie Koloski, clerks. The sixth gunman stood over them with a pistol, at the same time holding two unidentified men customers of the bank motionless. One of these men was accompanied by a boy about 7 years old.

"Stick 'em up and keep 'em up!" the tall man called out as he ordered one of the young women clerks to push an electric button that opened

Continued on Page Nineteen.

SENATORS AROUSED BY LUCAS ADMISSION OF FIGHTING NORRIS

Howell and Other Insurgents Demand the Resignation of Republican Director.

NORRIS SEES 'PERJURY' RIFE

Glenn Backs Lucas in Calling Nebraskan a Democrat—Fess Won't Oust His Aide.

HOOVER STATUS ASSAILED

President's Republicanism Defended When Nye and Wagner Raise Issue.

Special to The New York Times.

WASHINGTON, Dec. 20.—Admission by Robert H. Lucas of Kentucky, executive director of the Republican National Committee, before the Nye investigating committee today that he had circulated at his expense cartoons against Senator Norris of Nebraska and opposed his election because he did not consider Mr. Norris a Republican, threw the Senate into a heated discussion late today.

The resignation of Mr. Lucas was demanded by Senator Howell, Mr. Norris's insurgent Republican colleague, while Senator Glenn, Republican, of Illinois, justified opposition to Senator Norris because the Democrats had supported him.

The debate arose in open executive session during consideration of the Federal Power Commission appointments. It continued for more than an hour, with Senator Norris charging that Mr. Lucas's opposition to him was "disreputable, dishonorable and damnable," because it was "not done openly, but like a snake in the grass."

Norris Firm Against Hoover.

Senator Norris alleged that men high in the Republican party had sworn to false expense accounts and predicted that if the investigation was continued there would be "a number of men communicating with their friends behind the bars."

Senator Norris reasserted his opposition to President Hoover, his stand against Mr. Hoover in the 1928 campaign having been given by Mr. Lucas as the basic reason he, Lucas, fought Norris this year. Mr. Hoover, Senator Norris declared on the floor, was "wrong" on the vital issues of the "power trust" and farm relief.

The row in the chamber developed following a remark by Senator Cutting, Republican, of New Mexico, that the nominees for the Power Commission should be carefully examined as to their connections with power interests.

Then, calling attention to Mr. Lucas's testimony before the Nye committee, Mr. Cutting addressed Senator Fess, chairman of the Republican National Committee, and asked him whether the committee would demand Mr. Lucas's resignation. Senator Fess replied that no action had been taken.

When Mr. Cutting pressed the point as to whether Mr. Fess intended to do anything about the situation Mr. Fess replied:

"I do not."

Glenn Turns on Democrats.

Senator Glenn observed that perhaps Mr. Lucas had acted because the Democrats supported Senator Norris in the last election. He insisted that Senator Norris was the "greatest agent of the Democratic party in the Senate."

Senator Tydings, Democrat, of Maryland, said that the Democratic Senatorial Committee, of which he is chairman, had aided Gilbert M. Hitchcock, Democratic opponent of Senator Norris, but expressed the opinion that "some Democrats of Nebraska felt a delicacy in opposing Norris because of the latter's support of Smith in 1928."

"There is not a Senator who would have done as Mr. Lucas did," Senator Howell said. "If the Republican National Committee has any regard for the proprieties, it will immediately ask Mr. Lucas to resign in the interest of honesty and fair play."

Senator Norris sat silent for a while at the back of the Republican side, next to Senator Borah. Finally he began a long speech in which he intimated that Mr. Lucas was only the "man behind the machine," and not solely and personally responsible for the circulation of literature against him.

"At some future day I hope to show that some high officials of nation-wide reputation are guilty of perjury in sworn statements," Senator Norris said. "Senator Glenn may think Mr. Lucas did right in

Continued on Page Twenty-two.

Hoover Will Not Call Extra Session of Senate To Act on Ratifying the World Court Protocol

Special to The New York Times.

WASHINGTON, Dec. 20.—President Hoover does not at this time contemplate calling the Senate into extra session after the adjournment of Congress on March 4 for ratification of the protocol of American adherence to the World Court. This was announced from the White House today as the administration's answer to published reports that the President intended calling such a session for this purpose.

These reports were said to be without foundation in fact and to have been made without any authority.

It is generally understood that about the only contingency which could bring an extra session of the new Congress, urged by some Senators and Representatives, would be the failure of Congress at the present session to pass appropriation bills to meet the expenses of the government for the fiscal year 1932.

The Senate Committee on Foreign Relations by a vote of 10 to 9 on Wednesday decided not to report the World Court protocol at this session, and it was following this action that the reports of a prospective extra session gained circulation. It now appears certain that no action of any kind will be taken on World Court adherence in advance of the convening of the first regular session of the Seventy-second Congress, which will be on the first Monday in December, 1931.

SEABURY PLANS CALL TO 24 MAGISTRATES

Intends to Hear All in Bronx and Manhattan Despite Refusal to Pay Aides.

HE DENOUNCES HILLY STAND

Six Bonding Houses Under Fire—Link to Court Ring Sought—More Women to Testify.

Every one of the twenty-four magistrates in Manhattan and the Bronx will have a chance to testify before the current investigation of the lower courts by the Appellate Division is concluded, it was learned yesterday after Samuel Seabury, the referee, had intimated that the inquiry would continue for another three months.

The hint that the inquiry would run for another ninety days was contained in a formal statement in which Mr. Seabury accused Corporation Counsel Arthur J. W. Hilly of "peculiarly embarrassing" the investigation by holding up the salaries of five members of the staff of Isidor Kresel, special counsel. Mr. Seabury said he was preparing an application to the Appellate Division for a writ of mandamus against the Corporation Counsel, who said he was ready to defend his ruling in court.

As a result of revelations that have been made by witnesses at public and private hearings, it was learned, the activities of half a dozen or more corporate bail bond companies doing business almost exclusively in the magistrates' courts are being scrutinized by members of Mr. Kresel's staff.

Efforts are being made, it was understood, to determine whether any of these companies or individual

Continued on Page Twenty-four.

24 NAMED BY MACY TO LEAD STATE PARTY

Republican Executive Group Represents All Factions and Sectional Policies.

FIRST MEETING THIS MONTH

Chairman Asserts He Acted to Speed Interchange of Ideas and Hasten Cooperation.

Carrying out his own suggestion of more than a year ago, W. Kingsland Macy, the new chairman of the Republican State Committee, appointed yesterday an executive committee of party leaders throughout the State.

This executive committee of twenty-four, on which members of all factions, wet and dry, regular and Hooverite, are represented, is expected to be the ruling body of the party organization in this State. It will establish to some extent sectional leaders in each judicial district of the State and function much as did the old Republican State Committee when its membership was one from each of the State's forty-three Congressional districts, instead of two from each of the 158 Assembly districts, as at present.

A meeting of the executive committee will be held between Christmas and New Year's Day, but the definite date has not yet been selected. At this meeting it will consider the party's legislative program, which will have been put in shape by that time by the legislative leaders. Questions of party policy and patronage will be referred to this committee by the State chairman.

The members of the executive committee follow:

HARRY J. BAREHAM of Rochester, chair-

Continued on Page Twenty-three.

Stricter Curbs on Fraudulent Brokers Urged By Ward Aide in 5 Martin Act Amendments

A draft of five proposed amendments to the Martin act, designed to make it more difficult for fraudulent brokers to operate in New York, has been forwarded to State Attorney General Hamilton Ward in Albany by Watson Washburn, Assistant Attorney General in charge of the Bureau of Securities in the new State Building, 80 Centre Street. Mr. Washburn outlined yesterday the nature of the proposed amendments as follows:

1. To make the "State notice" regarding dealers really effective by requiring considerable additional information to be filed and requiring brokers to file these notices at least fifteen days before they start business. The present law merely requires that a skeleton notice, giving only the title of the firm and its address, be filed when the firm starts to operate. Fraudulent brokers whose past records would arouse suspicion are naturally careful to use firm names which give no inkling of the real personnel.

2. To require some additional information in the "State notice" required regarding each new security issue. The notice provided for in the present law regarding issues of new securities contains no more useful information than the dealer's notice referred to in the preceding paragraph.

3. To authorize the Attorney General to place under bail, pending the result of his investigation, any persons whose testimony is essential to the investigation. Under the present practice, the service of a subpoena often operates merely as a warning to the culprits to disappear.

4. To permit the Attorney General to require an appropriate bond from any brokers whose previous record discloses fraudulent practices.

5. To make plain that violation of a Martin act injunction is not only a contempt of court, but a misdemeanor punishable by a fine of not more than $5,000, or imprisonment for not more than two years, or both.

Mr. Washburn said he also had recommended that a special criminal division be set up in the Bureau of Securities to indict and prosecute stock swindlers directly instead of referring criminal prosecutions to the District Attorneys. He pointed out that stock frauds, especially on a large scale, are extremely technical and require specially trained prosecutors.

SENATE YIELDS ON BIG FUND

Adopts $116,000,000 Bill After 3 Amendments Are Defeated.

ATTACKS ON PLANS FUTILE

McNinch, Smith and Garsaud Win Approval for Places on Power Commission.

FARM BOARD FUND GRANTED

Senators Then Adopt Resolution for Holiday Recess and Session Ends at 12:05 A. M.

Special to The New York Times.

WASHINGTON, Sunday, Dec. 21.—Congress adjourned for the holiday recess at 12:05 o'clock this morning after appropriating $116,000,000 for emergency construction work, $45,000,000 for the relief of needy farmers in the drought area and $150,000,000 for the use of the Farm Board in aiding agricultural interests. President Hoover before adjournment had signed the unemployment and drought relief bills.

As the weary Senators, who had prolonged the final session with their debates, left the Capitol the laurels rested with President Hoover. His program had gone through, even to the confirmation of the last of his nominees for the Power Commission.

The Power Commissioners confirmed were Chairman George Otis Smith of Maine, Frank R. McNinch of North Carolina and Marcel Garsaud of Louisiana. The vote in favor of all three was decisive.

Senate Bows to President.

As sent to the President, the $116,000,000 bill contained none of the three Senate amendments which caused a clash in the conference with the House and for a time seemed to jeopardize the fate of the measure. Without roll-calls, the Senate receded from all these amendments, two of which would have allowed Alabama and Georgia to use about $2,000,000 of formerly appropriated flood relief funds, and the third of which would have forced employment of local labor and the payment of the highest prevailing wages to laborers on government construction work.

The Senate's acceptance of the conference report was preceded by protests from Senators La Follette of Wisconsin and Walsh of Massachusetts, who declared that the appropriation was totally inadequate to cope with the distress throughout the country.

La Follette's Protest.

Senator La Follette's protest against the "smallness" of the appropriation was accompanied by numerous letters, which he read into the record, replying to questionnaires he recently sent out asking for unemployment statistics in various parts of the country. He said these messages constituted "a complete refutation of the statements that the situation is well in hand." His communications came chiefly from points west of the Alleghanies, while Senator Walsh produced similar letters and telegrams from Eastern areas.

"I regard this program," Senator La Follette said, "as sponsored by the administration and insisted upon by the House, as totally inadequate."

The Wisconsin Senator asked Senators who go to their homes for Christmas to study conditions among the unemployed, and added, "I hope that when they return they will be at least as generous as they were to corporations and income taxpayers last year."

Senator Walsh's unemployment statistics included one from Buffalo, N. Y., saying that unemployment there approximated 40,000 persons, or 21.4 per cent of those normally employed.

Unemployment conditions, accompanied by acute distress, are not confined to any one locality, the two Senators reported, Senator La Follette's figures including 9,000 reported unemployed in New Haven, Conn., with "much suffering," and 25,000 unemployed in San Antonio, Texas.

Mr. Walsh said his survey showed generally high percentages of unemployed, and added: "It is rare to find a Mayor who is optimistic as to the near future."

When he stated that Springfield, Mass., had between 7,000 and 8,000 unemployed, Senator Gillett, also of

'American Buddha' Died Heartbroken in India; Feared Healing Power Lost With Spectacles

By The Associated Press.

POONA, India, Dec. 20.—A Coroner's inquest today laid bare the strange story of an American who so steeped himself in the mysteries of occult healing that he died of a broken heart at the loss of a pair of spectacles through which he believed himself capable of seeing and curing the ills of others. He had became known as the "American Buddha."

Beyond that the authorities were unable to go. On his deathbed a week ago James Brandon, described as a former resident of Nashville, Tenn., requested that his body be burned on a pyre of sacred sandalwood and his ashes given to his Hindu friends. He left no other word.

Mr. Brandon was found dead in the squalid cave in which he lived and practiced asceticism, occultism and mystic healing. Since coming to India fifteen years ago he had amassed a fortune by treating the sick, lame, halt and blind with herbs, potions and magic prayers.

It was testified at the inquest today that on his deathbed he complained he had lost his occult power because his "God-given spectacles" had been stolen.

Witnesses revealed that a short time ago some Poona youths, as a practical joke, raided Mr. Brandon's abode, stealing all his property, including the spectacles.

"Through the spectacles I was able to see God," Mr. Brandon was said to have told others as he lay dying, "and through the spectacles God allowed me to see the causes of my patients' diseases and showed me how to cure them. Now, without them, I am helpless even to heal my own malady or to save myself from death."

The Coroner returned a verdict that Mr. Brandon died "from a broken heart, superinduced by a belief that God had deprived him of the divine power of healing."

Although Mr. Brandon had offered a reward of 5,000 rupees (nearly $2,000) for the return of the spectacles, they never came back. Since their loss he had declared he was unsuccessful in his cures, gradually losing his patients and also his own faith in his ability to heal.

One other fact in his strange life was uncovered by police. Every month Mr. Brandon sent a remittance, which ran as high as 5,000 rupees, to a Mrs. Harnup, whose first name and address the authorities were unable to learn.

Section 1

"All the News That's Fit to Print."

The New York Times.

THE WEATHER
Cloudy today; tomorrow occasional rain; little temperature change.
Temperatures yesterday—Max. 46, min. 36.
U. S. Weather Forecast—Page 2, Section 2.

Section 1

VOL. LXXX....No. 26,643. **** NEW YORK, SUNDAY, JANUARY 4, 1931. Including Rotogravure Picture Section in two parts—Magazine and Book Sections in Rotogravure. TEN CENTS

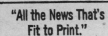

H. D. GIBSON TO HEAD THE MANUFACTURERS IN NEW BANKING DEAL

New York Trust Executive and Associates Buy Goldman Sachs 32 Per Cent Interest.

AND HE BECOMES PRESIDENT

Working Control Passes to a Private Group Identified With Wall Street Leaders.

STOCK ADVANCES SHARPLY

At Present Market Value Purchase Would Have Involved About $12,500,000.

The 32 per cent interest held by the Goldman Sachs Trading Corporation in the Manufacturers' Trust Company has been purchased by Harvey D. Gibson and associates, it was learned last night. Mr. Gibson is now chairman of the executive committee of the New York Trust Company. It is understood that Mr. Gibson will become president of the Manufacturers' Trust Company. An announcement of the details of the purchase probably will be made tomorrow.

Prominent bankers declared last night that purchase of this block of stock should be considered a constructive development, since it placed working control of the Manufacturers' Trust Company in the hands of private interests long identified with leading financial interests in Wall Street.

Mr. Gibson long has been connected with the New York Trust Company, which is one of the group of financial institutions which are prominently associated with the Morgan interests. The Goldman Sachs Trading Corporation is an investment trust formed two years ago by the banking firm of Goldman Sachs & Co. and obtained its holdings in the Manufacturers when it acquired the Financial & Industrial Securities Corporation early in 1929.

Figured in Recent Merger Plan.

Recently the Manufacturers' Trust Company figured prominently in a merger plan which included the Bank of United States, the International Trust Company and the Public National Bank. Following the abandonment of this merger, the Manufacturers' Trust Company was admitted to membership in the New York Clearing House Association. Nathan S. Jonas, chairman of the board of the Manufacturers' Trust Company, said at that time that the bank had total deposits of $295,000,000 and had liquid assets of $180,000,000.

The purchase of the Manufacturers' stock by Mr. Gibson and his associates is understood to be a private transaction. The New York Trust Company, it was explained, did not figure in any way in the transaction.

In view of the fact that Mr. Gibson will become one of the chief executives of the Manufacturers', it is expected that one of the present high officers probably will resign. Nathan S. Jonas is at present chairman of the board of the bank and Henry C. Von Elm is president. Ralph Jonas, brother of Nathan S., is a director.

Stock Advances 4½ Points.

The Manufacturers Trust Company has an authorized and outstanding capital stock of $27,500,000, consisting of shares with a par value of $25 each. The stock was strong yesterday, advancing 4½ points, and closing at 34½ bid, 36½ asked. If the transaction was consummated at the prevailing price for the stock, the amount involved would have been about $12,500,000. The stock was carried on the books of the Goldman Sachs Trading Corporation on Dec. 31, 1929, at its market value of $25,144,505. The book value of the block of stock at that time was $38,989,490.

Stock of the Goldman Sachs Trading Corporation was strong yesterday on the New York Curb Exchange. It advanced 1 point to 6⅞. Less than a week ago the stock sold at 4⅜, which was the low price for 1930. The high price for the stock in 1929 was 120¼.

The Manufacturers Trust Company does a complete banking and trust business with the following departments: commercial, savings, trust, bond, safe deposit and foreign. It is a member of the Federal Reserve System, the American Bankers' Association, and the State Bankers' Association. It owns all the capital stock of the City Safe Deposit Company, the Municipal Safe Deposit Company, and the Colonial Safe Deposit Company.

The bank was organized in 1905 as the Citizens Trust Company of

Continued on Page Three.

R. C. A.-Victor to Reopen Plant, Expecting Trade Gain Soon

Special to The New York Times.

CAMDEN, N. J., Jan. 3.—Operation of the local plant of the R. C. A.-Victor Company, which suspended tamporarily last month, will be resumed on Monday, E. E. Shumaker, the president, said today. Whether all of the 12,000 employes recently laid off will be put to work again will depend on the demand for the plant's products, he said.

Mr. Shumaker declared his company's chief interest was in bringing back to work the largest possible number of employes, and he said he felt this year would show a real business improvement.

"This improvement should be evident by mid-year," he said, "but the degree of improvement will, in my opinion, be entirely dependent upon the re-establishment of confidence and the elimination of fear and doubt as to the future."

MURDERED ON JOB HE HELD 51 YEARS

Confidential Employe of Realty Operator Is Mysteriously Killed at His Desk.

VICTIM'S MONEY IS INTACT

Body of Herman Moench Found by Employer in Obscure Sub-Basement Office.

A life of quiet routine that had been made remarkable only by a record of fifty-one years in one employment was ended by murder yesterday morning in a cramped sub-cellar office deep below sidewalk level on the lower east side.

There was money in the dead man's pockets when the body was found and he had had no known enemies. Twenty-five detectives, homicide squad and pistol bureau experts, worked on the case under Police Commissioner Mulrooney all yesterday afternoon without discovering any motive for the murder or clue to the slayer.

The murdered man was Herman Moench, 60 years old, who had been in the employ of Edward Ridley, once owner of a large dry goods store on the east side and still holder of considerable real estate there, since 1879. He lived with a wife, son and daughter at 137 Moffatt Street, Brooklyn, and his work in recent years had consisted largely of collecting rents and looking after the accounts of Mr. Ridley's realty office at 61 Allen Street.

That office was the scene of the murder. Its location and the means of entrance to it make it, as a place of business, almost unique in New York.

Access to Office Difficult.

At 61 Allen Street, in the shadow of the Second Avenue Elevated, there is a swinging door in a board fence. The door leads down to a wooden ramp that was built for horses in the old days when the garage that is now at 59-61 Allen Street was Moore's livery stable. A small door cut in a larger one at the foot of this ramp opens into a dark automobile storage basement of the garage. A corner staircase descends to a second basement where more automobiles are stored.

Partitioned off from this subbasement is a room about 8 by 15 feet in size, lighted by gas lamps and crowded with the books, files and records of seventy years of business. A large, flat-topped double desk fills the centre of the room.

When Mr. Ridley came in yesterday morning he found his correspondence neatly sorted and laid out on his desk. He noticed his secretary's coat on the rack and decided

Continued on Page Twenty-nine.

JOFFRE TO BE BURIED WITH STATE HONORS; ALL NATIONS MOURN

France Plans Tribute of Pomp Similar to That Accorded to Marshal Foch.

SERVICES TO BE WEDNESDAY

Military Parade Will Follow the Ceremony at Notre Dame—Barthou to Speak.

KING AND PRESIDENT GRIEVE

Messages of Condolence Pour In From Officials and Civil Leaders of the World.

By P. J. PHILIP.
Special Cable to THE NEW YORK TIMES.

PARIS, Jan. 3.—A national funeral for Marshal Joseph Jacques Césaire Joffre, similar in pomp to that which was accorded to Marshal Ferdinand Foch, was decided upon today at a special Cabinet meeting called after the death of the victor of the Marne early this morning.

At the request of Mme. Joffre, however, the Marshal's body will not be laid below the Arc de Triomphe, as was that of Marshal Foch. It will be embalmed tonight and taken tomorrow to the chapel of the Ecole Militaire, and there on Monday and Tuesday it will lie in state, clad in full uniform with the face exposed. When it is taken from there to the Cathedral of Notre Dame, a short halt will be made at the Arc de Triomphe beside the tomb of the Unknown Soldier.

Funeral to Be Wednesday.

The funeral service will be held at Notre Dame at 9 o'clock Wednesday morning and there will be a parade of troops before the gates of the Invalides, as there was at the funeral of Marshal Foch.

Louis Barthou, Minister of War, will make the only speech. Instead of being interred at the Invalides, however, it is believed the body will be taken to the cemetery at Louveciennes, near St. Germain, where Marshal Joffre had his home.

The Marshal's death had been expected for several days, but the news that his long struggle was over produced profound expressions of grief throughout the whole country and abroad. Although he had lived almost in retirement so long, he was held in greater and more universal affection and respect by his own countrymen than any other of the great war leaders, and he had never been forgotten.

To that affection the quiet dignity with which he had always refrained from any controversy contributed greatly. He has left his memoirs, it is stated, but it is certain they will be found to be quite uncontroversial.

Marshal Joffre is said to have had no vanity and no jealousy. He had a deep appreciation of his responsibility and never shirked it. Once when the question was being discussed in his presence as to who or what had most contributed to the victory of the Marne, he remarked:

"My duty was the greatest, for I had to be victorious everywhere. I was victorious because every one else who was in command of a section was victorious in his section." Then he added quietly, "If we had not won I would certainly have got blamed."

Returned to Church.

It was only recently that the Marshal, who had been a Freemason all his life, returned to the Church. He accepted a mass when he became ill, and his "reconciliation" with the

Continued on Page Twenty.

Byrd's Lead Huskie Killed by Hit-Run Auto; Animal Had Been Freed for Exercise in a Park

Special to The New York Times.

MONROE, La., Jan. 3.—Hero of dashes across the frozen wastes of the Antarctic, Unalaska, one of the lead huskies of the dog teams of the Byrd expedition at Little America, died here today a prosaic death under the wheels of a passing automobile.

C. B. Foster, who is in charge of the Byrd South Polar exhibit, now on display here, was exercising Unalaska and his mate, Lady, at the City Park, when the huskie dashed across a crowded thoroughfare and was struck down.

The driver of the light coupé which killed the dog dashed away without stopping after the body of the animal had been dragged about fifty feet. Shamefacedly the driver pulled his slouch hat low enough to cover his face as his car speeded past a group of women and children who had been admiring the magnificent Unalaska as the huskie took his daily exercise. Unalaska was an animal unaccustomed to the warm breezes and the mild temperatures of the Southland. Born of a hardy dog of the North, a Malamute half-wolf, Unalaska first opened his puppy eyes in Lapland five years ago. The animal was selected by Admiral Byrd to lead his team of huskies because Unalaska had shown the courage and qualities of leadership which the top mush dog must possess.

As soon as Foster was able to push his way through the crowd of curiosity seekers who had seen the dog struck down he found that Unalaska had been killed instantly, his spine snapped by the impact of the automobile.

Lady whined piteously and then stoically trotted at Foster's heels as the man gently lifted the body of the dog into his automobile.

The city of Monroe advised Admiral Byrd, who is keeping a speaking engagement at Minneapolis, of the death of the huskie and requested that the pelt of the dog be given to the city for mounting.

500 Farmers Storm Arkansas Town Demanding Food for Their Children

Drought Sufferers, Many Armed, Get Aid for Hungry Families After Pressing Into Stores—Are Appeased by Red Cross Help—Organization Feeds 100,000 in the State.

By The Associated Press.

ENGLAND, Ark., Jan. 3.—Five hundred or more farmers and their wives, half of the men said by City Marshal W. S. Wayne to have been armed, stormed the business section here late today demanding food and threatening to forcibly seize it in event it was not forthcoming. The merchants furnished food to more than 300 before the situation quieted late tonight.

County Red Cross Chairman Albert Walls said the disturbance arose because the supply of questionnaire blanks used by the Red Cross became exhausted. It has been the custom for those requesting aid to sign such blanks.

Marshal Wayne said merchants first told him some of the men had displayed their pistols while in the stores, although not threatening the proprietors. He said while the men were grouped, he strolled through the crowd and in many cases the weapons bulged through clothing and otherwise were apparent. He said knowledge of presence of the guns led the merchants to confer hurriedly over the seriousness of the situation.

George E. Morris, an attorney, spoke to the farmers, practically all of whom were white men, but his speech was interrupted time and again by those in the crowd.

The farmers came from what was a rich agricultural region until it was ravaged by last Summer's drought. Most of them have hitherto been prosperous.

Mr. Morris's address was met with many other interrupting shouts such as: "Our children are crying for food and we are going to get it."

"We are not going to let our children starve."

"We want food and we want it now."

"We are not beggars," another pushed forward to exclaim. "We

Continued on Page Twenty-one.

NICARAGUANS WOUND 2 MARINES IN CLASH

Bandits Try to Ambush Patrol Hunting Them After Killing of Eight Americans.

MIDNIGHT ATTACK IS MADE

Outlaws Are Driven Off and New Detail Goes in Pursuit —Guard Reports Fights.

Special Cable to THE NEW YORK TIMES.

MANAGUA, Nicaragua, Jan. 3.—Two more United States marines were wounded in a clash with bandits early today.

They were shot down in what appears to have been an attempt of 150 outlaws to ambush the marine patrol of fifty men scouring the jungle for the band that killed eight marines Wednesday.

The two men were brought to Managua by plane this morning. One of them, James Robert Earnhardt, was hit in the spine and is seriously injured. His nearest relative is his mother, Mrs. Sarah Earnhardt, of Concord, N. C. The other man is David Monroe Kirkendale, who probably will recover. His nearest relative is Walter Carlson of Chicago.

The patrol, fifty men under command of Captain Ernest L. Russell, established contact with the bandits south of Ocotal, between Totogalpa and Ocotal. The bandits had made a demonstration at the eastern outskirts of Ocotal, Nueva Segovia, about 11 o'clock last night. Several shots were fired into the town and bombs exploded near the outskirts, but the bandits made no effort to enter the town and no casualties were sustained by the inhabitants or the marines.

The commanding officer at Ocotal, Major Dearing, reported by radio at 1:30 A. M. today that everything was quiet.

The marine patrol under Captain Russell, returning to Ocotal from Palacaguina, established contact with the bandits, estimated at 150 men, at about 1 o'clock this morning. The strong marine detachment drove the bandits from their ambuscade and continued to Ocotal.

Second Patrol Goes Out.

Another marine patrol left Ocotal at daybreak today to reconnoitre the scene, try to regain contact with the bandits and ascertain the number of bandit casualties. The identity of the bandit leader is not definitely known, but he is thought to be a Sandino chieftain, Miguel Ortiz.

The commanding officer reported this morning that all telegraph lines leading from Ocotal were down and that communication was being maintained by radio between Managua and Ocotal.

The Nicaragua National Guard reports that the bandit group is thought to be the same that ambushed and killed a party of marines Wednesday and attacked a guard barracks on Jan. 1 at 5 A. M., first with rifle shots, then threw bombs, whereupon the guard and armed civilians returned the fire, and the bandits were driven off in the direction of Palacaguina.

The National Guard also reports a contact yesterday between ten guardsmen under command of Lieutenant Pulver and a bandit force estimated at 150 at Cacao, Northwest Chaquitillo. The bandits were entrenched behind stone walls. The fight had lasted an hour when a patrol of eighteen guardsmen under command of Lieutenant Kerns joined

Continued on Page Three.

2 SHOT DEAD IN FIGHT OVER NOISE IN A HOME

Jobless Man Whose Family Quarrel Annoyed Tenants Is Slain Battling Policeman.

WOMAN NEIGHBOR KILLED

Sergeant and Father-in-Law of Dead Man Wounded in Yonkers.

Two persons were killed and two others wounded in a gun battle before midnight last night in a Yonkers apartment house, at 28 Warburton Avenue, after tenants had called in the police to stop a disturbance in the apartment occupied by Theodore Sasce, 31 years old.

Miss Anna Widner, 28 years old, daughter of a physical director of a philanthropic and athletic association and for several years director of a Yonkers Y. M. C. A., was struck and killed by a stray bullet as she stepped out of her own apartment in the building, directly into the line of fire. Sasce fell dead before pistol fire.

The wounded were Police Sergeant Michael Gilmartin, who is at St. Joseph's Hospital with bullet wounds in his right ear and shoulder, and Bertram Bryant, 50 years old, 22 Warburton Avenue, who is at Yonkers General Hospital, shot in the left arm.

Mr. Bryant, the police disclosed later, was the father of Mrs. Sasce, from whom Sasce had been estranged. Sasce, the police said, had been out of work and had been brooding over his inability to obtain employment.

Tenants of the apartment, which is in the downtown section of Yonkers, complained to the police of a disturbance in Sasce's apartment which prevented them from sleeping. Sergeant Gilmartin was sent to the house to investigate.

Policeman Shot Down.

He entered the apartment and was heard arguing with Sasce. Suddenly the door was flung open and Sasce appeared, waving a revolver and threatening the policeman. As Gilmartin advanced toward him he fired twice and the sergeant fell.

Patrolman William McQuillan, passing the house on his nightly round, heard the shots and dashed into the hallway to see the sergeant fall. Drawing his service revolver he opened fire on Sasce, who turned his weapon on him. During the exchange, Miss Widner stepped into the corridor, was struck by a bullet and slumped back into the apartment which she occupied with her parents.

Suddenly the firing ceased and as the smoke eddied in the murky hallway the body of Sasce was found sprawled on the carpet. Patrolman McQuillan was unharmed. Several of the bullets, however, had whistled past the policeman and imbedded themselves in the walls of the apartment house hallway.

Wounded Rushed to Hospital.

Ambulances were summoned and the two wounded persons were rushed to hospitals, where, it was said, neither was seriously hurt.

The shooting occurred on the second floor of the apartment and aroused tenants of adjoining buildings, who grouped about the door of the house. An emergency squad of policemen arrived shortly after, sent the bystanders home and began an investigation. Up to 1 o'clock this morning they were unable to account for the

Continued on Page Twenty-three.

WOMAN FLIER DOWN AT NORFOLK, PLANS NEW START FOR PARIS

Mrs. Hart and MacLaren Turn Back on Hop to Bermuda After Sextant Breaks.

WILL GO ON TOMORROW

Navigator Tells by Telephone of 16-Hour Flight and Being 75 Miles From First Goal.

UNREPORTED MANY HOURS

Anxiety Was Keen Here, as Friends Feared They Had Overshot the Island or Were Adrift.

The seaplane Tradewind, in which Mrs. Beryl Hart and Lieutenant William S. MacLaren left this city at daybreak in an attempt to fly to Paris with the first "pay load," put into the naval seaplane base at Hampton Roads, Va., at 9:25 o'clock last night.

The fliers had hoped to reach Hamilton, Bermuda, on the first leg of their journey, at 2 o'clock yesterday afternoon. But an accident to their sextant, caused by the "rooking" of the plane at the take-off, left them without the services of this navigating instrument. Uncertain of their course and realizing the hazards of overshooting the island of Bermuda, they put back finally, landing at the naval base after sixteen hours in the air.

With the sextant out of order the plane flew 400 miles after leaving New York. Soon after 10 A. M. it "picked up" the steamships Bermuda and Veendam and with these vessels as bearings held to its course.

MacLaren estimated that he and his companion came within fifty or seventy-five miles of their destination, and then, failing to sight land, decided that their dwindling fuel supply was such that they had "better beat it for the United States." He said he would refuel and resume the flight to Bermuda tomorrow.

MacLaren Tells of Flight.

Speaking over the telephone to THE NEW YORK TIMES from the Naval Air Station at Hampton Roads shortly after landing there last night, MacLaren said:

"When we took off from New York there was virtually no wind to help us climb into the air with our loaded plane. So we had to 'rock' it in order to gain the altitude. In 'rocking' the plane, just above the point of our take-off, our sextant fell to the floor and was damaged. In fact, it was put out of commission, and when a sextant goes out of commission, you can figure on a hard job to navigate, of course.

"Well, we decided to go anyhow, because we figured that rather than turn back, just when our flight had started, we would take a chance on picking up the Bermuda and the Veendam at sea.

"We hit both liners right smack on the nose. Our first guess was right. We sighted the vessels about 400 miles, I should say, from New York.

"Having sighted the Veendam, about 10:15 A. M., I think it was, we decided to guess again and head for Bermuda. We figured on pushing on, and looking around for the island and turning back in the event that we should not sight it.

"Well, for three hours after we left the Veendam we searched and searched. We must have got a change of wind after passing both the Veendam and the Bermuda, because something threw our reckoning out. At any rate, our second guess was

Continued on Page Twenty-six.

Princess Loses Gems at American Legation; Stir Follows at New Year Party in Belgrade

Special Cable to THE NEW YORK TIMES.

BELGRADE, Jan. 3.—A jewelled gold handbag belonging to Princess Olga, a cousin of King Alexander, containing a highly valuable diamond studded cigarette case, which was a gift from the King, mysteriously disappeared at a New Year's ball at the American Legation and has not been found.

The incident is understood to have greatly disturbed the American Minister, John Dyneley Prince.

Nearly the whole of the diplomatic corps and a number of high State officials attended the ball, which was further honored by the presence of Prince Paul, King Alexander's cousin; his wife, Princess Olga, and her sister, Princess Marina. The evening grew very animated and the Princesses, who danced nearly every dance, obviously were enjoying themselves.

At midnight, according to ancient custom, all lights were turned out for a few minutes. After they were switched on again the dancing was resumed. At 1 o'clock the royal party began to prepare for departure. Princess Olga was seen to search, at first casually and then anxiously, for the handbag. Finally she announced its disappearance.

When it was learned that the bag, which was of gold mesh studded with diamonds and other stones, contained, among other valuables, the gold cigarette case inscribed with King Alexander's initials in diamonds, the whole company anxiously began to search the floor, which was covered with confetti and paper spirals. Nothing was found.

Several guests volunteered to be searched and suggested a general personal examination, but in view of the implied reflection on the honor of the foreign diplomats and other distinguished guests this suggestion was rejected except for a search of the servants and orchestra members, which revealed nothing.

Discreet investigations since have proved fruitless.

CITY-WIDE INQUIRY MAPPED BY REPUBLICANS AT ALBANY; GOVERNOR TO GET MEASURE

MACY DOMINATES MEETING

Plan for Inquiry Is Put Through at Executive Committee Session.

AIM AT GENERAL SESSIONS

Proponents Would Also Include Magistrates' Courts in Brooklyn, Queens and Richmond.

MEASURE WILL GO IN LATE

Plan Is to Defer Action by Legislature Until After Budget Is Acted On.

By W. A. WARN.
Special to The New York Times.

ALBANY, Jan. 3.—Making his first appearance in his new role of party pilot at a meeting of the Republican Executive Committee here today, W. Kingsland Macy, the newly elected State chairman, managed to have himself elected executive chairman as well and followed this up by putting through a resolution calling for legislative action to bring about a sweeping investigation of the New York City Administration.

Should the Legislature adopt a bill for this purpose, the Republicans would repeat their tactics of putting up to Governor Roosevelt a far-spreading investigation of the Walker régime and Tammany officeholders.

The inquiry, it is understood, would be broad enough, if Chairman Macy's plan is sanctioned by the Legislature, to include the administration of criminal justice in the Court of General Sessions. It will not, however, intrude upon the domain of the inferior courts of criminal justice, now being investigated by former Judge Samuel Seabury of the Court of Appeals under a mandate from the Appellate Division.

The resolution adopted, in fact, commended the Seabury-Kresel probe and advocated extension of its scope to take in the Magistrates' Courts in the Boroughs of Brooklyn, Queens and Richmond, which have not been touched so far.

Time for Bill Not Set.

The time for legislative action is not set under the tentative decision reached at the meeting today. From what could be gleaned from members of the executive committee after it had adjourned, it is not proposed to bring up the subject in the Legislature until after the executive budget has been acted upon. Under the circumstances, it is regarded as certain that consideration of the inquiry will be deferred until the crowded closing stage of the session.

Under ordinary conditions a legislative investigation such as the one now in contemplation is launched through a concurrent resolution of the Senate and Assembly and financed out of the State fund for contingent expenditures. Unless there is a change in the program, however, the proposed inquiry will be provided for in a bill carrying an appropriation out of the general fund which will require the approval of Governor Roosevelt to become effective.

This was interpreted as reflecting a desire on the part of the Republican leaders either to put up to the Governor a situation affecting an administration controlled by Tammany Hall and its allied organizations or else to eliminate the criticism of partisanship that would attach to any project adopted by a Republican majority recruited almost exclusively from up-State.

Probably both considerations entered into the plan. Chairman Macy has demonstrated to the satisfaction of persons who know him well that proposals for putting a Democratic Governor "in a hole" through action by a Republican Legislature will form no part of his political program, which he proposes to make "constructive." Some of the up-State Republican leaders, however, have not managed to break themselves of a habit that had its inception in the days of Governor Smith's first administration more than ten years ago.

Adoption of the present plan would involve deferring action by the Senate and Assembly on the investigation bill until after the budget bill has been acted on. Under this budget, no bills carrying an appropriation can be taken up and passed until the budget has been balanced.

No Need for Love, Shaw Thinks, Praising Secretaries as Wives

Wireless to THE NEW YORK TIMES.

LONDON, Jan. 3.—The business relationship probably is a much surer basis for married life than love, George Bernard Shaw declared today, commenting upon the assertion by Dr. Edward Lyman in a New York lecture that their secretaries make the best wives for professional men. "I don't say that I ever thought of proposing to one of my secretaries," the dramatist said, "but I happen to be already married.

"There is no need for love to come into the question at all. Taken all around, the doctor's advice seems sound common sense to me. I should think it is a very desirable arrangement. I have known many such marriages to turn out well.

"The question is whether secretaries would have their employers. If they won't, it is a very serious reflection on the employers."

BRODSKY MUST FACE REMOVAL HEARING

Magistrate Ordered to Show Cause on Friday Why He Should Not Be Ousted.

CITY DROPS INQUIRY FIGHT

Berry Assures Seabury That Bills Will Be Paid Promptly—Hilly Won't Appeal.

An order requiring City Magistrate Louis B. Brodsky to show cause next Friday why he should not be removed from office for judicial and other actions complained of by Referee Samuel Seabury in the Appellate Division's inquiry was signed by Presiding Justice Victor J. Dowling yesterday afternoon.

A little earlier, Corporation Counsel Hilly had announced that the city would abandon its fight on salaries paid to legal aides of Isidor J. Kresel, counsel for the investigation.

Mr. Kresel, following a lengthy examination by District Attorney Crain in connection with the affairs of the closed Bank of United States, of which he is a director, said he would continue to serve as counsel for the Appellate Division investigation "just as long as Judge Seabury and the Appellate Division desire me to continue as counsel." Mr. Seabury declined to comment on Mr. Kresel's appearance before District Attorney Crain or its probable consequences.

Must Appear Friday.

The Appellate Division's order compels Magistrate Brodsky to appear at the Appellate Division Court House, Madison Avenue and Twenty-fifth Street, at the opening of court on Friday.

The order was issued on the basis of an affidavit signed by Harland B. Tibbetts, chief assistant counsel to the investigation. The affidavit declared that public interest required a determination of the questions raised in the Seabury report.

Text of Brodsky Order.

The order read as follows:

This court having made and entered an order dated Aug. 25, 1930, and an amended order dated Sept. 23, 1930, directing Honorable Sam-

Continued on Page Two.

"All the News That's Fit to Print."

The New York Times.

Copyright, 1931, by The New York Times Company.

THE WEATHER
Fair today and tomorrow; slowly rising temperature today.
Temperatures Yesterday—Max. 37; min. 26.
U. S. Weather Forecast—For details see Page 31.

VOL. LXXX....No. 26,648. **** NEW YORK, FRIDAY, JANUARY 9, 1931. TWO CENTS In Greater New York | THREE CENTS Within 200 Miles | FOUR CENTS Elsewhere Except 7th and 8th Postal Zones

POPE PIUS XI, IN ENCYCLICAL, CONDEMNS TRIAL MARRIAGE, DIVORCE AND BIRTH CONTROL

CHURCH STAND REAFFIRMED

16,000-Word Document Makes Chaste Wedlock Basis of the Home.

INDISSOLUBILITY IS UPHELD

Companionate Unions, and Other Modern Tendencies Are Denounced as Unchristian.

SACRED CHARACTER URGED

Pope Scores Pagan Propaganda in Novels and Theatres—Calls On State to Help Moral Fight.

The full text of the Pope's encyclical is on Pages 14 and 15.

By ARNALDO CORTESI.

Wireless to THE NEW YORK TIMES.

ROME, Jan. 8.—Pope Pius XI issued his eagerly awaited encyclical on marriage today, his pronouncement bearing the date of Dec. 31, 1930. Its title is "Of Christian Marriage in Relation to Present Conditions, Needs and Disorders of Society," but it will be known from the two opening words of the Latin text as the encyclical "Casti conubii" ["Of chaste wedlock"].

The encyclical is a lengthy document of outstanding importance, as it sums up the Catholic doctrine on the subject of matrimony, combats in very vigorous terms certain modern tendencies, especially birth control, and lists remedies which the Catholic Church suggests for the cure of many ills of modern society.

The Osservatore Romano, the semi-official Vatican organ, today prints only the Latin text, which occupies three full pages.

Divided Into Three Parts.

The encyclical is divided into three parts. The first deals with the sacrament of marriage, pointing out its divine nature and stressing the purposes for which it was instituted. The second speaks of the dangers and pitfalls with which "modern vices and errors" have surrounded marriage. The third contains the remedies which alone, the Pope holds, may again place the institution of matrimony on the high pedestal it once occupied. This last part includes a strong appeal to the civil authorities to collaborate with the Church in defense of morality and the sanctity of marriage.

The first part, after stressing the dignity of the sacrament of marriage, says that modern man derides, spurns and maltreats it, not only on the stage and on the screen, in newspapers and in novels but also in the lives of countless thousands who are either given to vice or forgetful of their matrimonial duties.

The Pope sums up the ends for which the sacrament of marriage was instituted with the famous dictum of St. Augustine, "Offspring, faithfulness, sacrament." Having offspring, the Pontiff says, entails not only the privilege of giving life to children but also the duty of educating them in the Christian way. Faithfulness, he declares, entails the perfect and inviolable faithfulness of man and wife to the duties of their state, to the order of subordination established by God and to mutual love and mutual help, and the sacrament includes the indissolubility of the marriage tie and, since it recalls the mystic union of Christ with the Church, becomes for man and wife a symbol of their particular state of grace for accomplishing their matrimonial duties.

Urges Respect for Church.

The second part of the encyclical deals severely with certain modern tendencies which the Pope declares are contrary to the prime end of matrimony and depopulate families and nations. Such theories, the encyclical asserts, tend to legalize the killing of innocent creatures condemned to death by modern callousness even before they are born.

The Pontiff then lists a long series of "the vices with which human wickedness tends to contaminate the pure spring of life which God opened to man in order that he might perpetuate himself throughout the centuries." All such practices are

Continued on Page Sixteen.

New Daily Planned in London; Edgar Wallace May Be Editor

Wireless to THE NEW YORK TIMES.

LONDON, Jan. 8.—A determined effort is being made to establish a new evening newspaper in London, according to the World's Press News. Edgar Wallace, detective story writer, is said to have been chosen as editor of the new journal, which would compete with Lord Rothermere's Evening News, Lord Beaverbrook's Evening Standard and The Star of the Cadbury group.

The new journal will be published in March, it is said, from the offices of the old Daily Chronicle and aims at 1,000,000 circulation.

PLAN TO END SLUMS IN DECADE PROPOSED

The City, State and Private Capital Would Cooperate in Project of Welfare Council.

REALTY MEN LAUD IDEA

Tenements Are Being Turned Into Lairs for Criminals, Housing Group Is Told.

A plan characterized by its sponsors as "of enormous proportions," whereby the city, the State Housing Board, and private capital would cooperate over a period of ten years in eliminating slums, replacing them with model tenements, parks and thoroughfares, was outlined yesterday by Harold Riegelman, counsel to the Multiple Dwelling Law Committee, at the quarterly meeting of the housing section of the Welfare Council at 130 East Twenty-second Street.

The meeting was attended by Peter Grimm, president of the New York Real Estate Board, who endorsed Mr. Riegelman's proposal; Ira S. Robbins, chairman of the housing committee of the United Neighborhood Houses; Mrs. Joseph M. Proskauer, chairman of the Housing Section, and others interested in the housing problem. The meeting was closed to promote "the greatest frankness" on the part of the speakers.

Quick Action Is Urged.

According to excerpts made public later, Mr. Riegelman declared that, "the time is ripe for the adoption by the city, in conjunction with the State Housing Board, of a ten-year plan of progressive condemnation or purchase by the city of strategically located groups of blocks in slum areas, the use of portions of such land for parks and relocated thoroughfares, and the enlistment of private capital in the development and management of new low-priced housing upon the balance of such land with adequate safeguards to the private investment and to the public.

"The long-term leasing of such balance of the land as is acquired by the city from year to year to limited dividend corporations on a basis not in excess of 4 per cent per annum of its net cost to the city, such rent to include taxes, is socially and economically sound and should result in a substantial supply of decent homes at rents which wage-earners can afford.

"While this task of slum clearance by public action is of enormous proportions, its division into ten progressive units reduces the outlay in any one year to a point where the

Continued on Page Six.

ILLEGAL BANK DEAL INDICATED BY CRAIN; ASKS WIDER POWERS

He Investigates Charge Bank of U. S. Paid Itself $8,000,000 Owed by Affiliates.

CRIMINAL ACTION HINTED

District Attorney Asks Law to Permit Open Inquiry and Special Counsel.

MARCUS IN TEARS ON STAND

Testifies Dividends Were Paid by Subsidiaries From Profits in Previous Year.

Special investigation with a view to possible prosecution, it was revealed yesterday, is being made by District Attorney Crain of alleged juggling of the accounts by the closed Bank of United States and some of its affiliates whereby the bank paid a debt of $8,000,000 to itself with its own money.

Mr. Crain's interest in this transaction was revealed by him after yesterday's session of the grand jury investigating the bank and following a long conference with Max D. Steuer, counsel for the Bank of United States Stockholders and Depositors' Protective Association, said to have been at Mr. Crain's invitation.

The transaction was referred to last week by Saul S. Singer, chairman of the executive committee of the Bank of United States and directing head of its affiliates, in testimony before Referee Robert P. Stephenson in the bankruptcy proceedings on four of the affiliates. Mr. Crain's profession of interest in it raised the possibility of indictments.

Bernard K. Marcus, president of the bank and one of the group of five men said to have dominated the affairs of the bank and its subsidiaries, appeared as a witness before Mr. Stephenson at the latter's office, 32 Broadway, and with tears in his eyes, protested against "imputations" of dishonesty against the bank's officers or directors.

Crain Asks Special Powers.

Dispatches from Albany last night revealed that in a letter to Governor Roosevelt Mr. Crain asked for immediate emergency legislation to enable him to keep the public informed of the progress of his investigation beyond the measure authorized in grand jury proceedings, which are secret, and to appoint special counsel to help him in the investigation.

Replying to Mr. Crain's letter, Governor Roosevelt declared that his suggestion for authorization of wider publicity was so radical that he is seeking the advice of the Bar Association, the County Lawyers' Association and the presiding justice of the Appelate Division before acting upon it. The Governor also informed Mr. Crain that he already had the power to appoint or retain special counsel by making such outside aides special duty assistants.

It was believed that Mr. Crain's suggestion with respect to special counsel was made with the idea of enlisting the services of Mr. Steuer. Mr. Steuer conferred with Mr. Crain for more than an hour and a half. Later he would neither deny or affirm the plan attributed to Mr. Crain. Mr. Crain likewise would not comment upon it.

Mr. Steuer's conference with Mr. Crain, followed by information from Mr. Crain leading to the belief that he might institute criminal proceedings against officers and directors of the bank in the $8,000,000 deal, gave rise to reports that Mr. Steuer might be appointed special prosecutor in any criminal action.

At the office of the State Banking Department it was said that the de-

Continued on Page Four.

Soviet Reported Planning Vast Radio Chain, Costing $45,000,000, to Carry Its Propaganda

Special Cable to THE NEW YORK TIMES.

BERLIN, Jan. 8.—Radio propaganda on a vast scale threatens Western Europe and even overseas countries unless effective counter-measures are taken to offset the chain of high-power broadcasting stations which the Soviets propose to have ready for operation in a year or two, according to reports from the official radio laboratory at Leningrad.

A giant 500-kilowatt station is to be erected in the vicinity of Moscow which is to be linked up with a 60-kilowatt short-wave radio station and a chain of other stations throughout Russia. These various radio undertakings are to constitute part of the Soviet's five-year plan. It is estimated they will cost $45,000,000.

Soviet authorities and the Moscow newspapers, according to the Vossische Zeitung, make no concealment of the Soviet's intention to perfect their net of broadcasting stations into a powerful agency for the dissemination of political and other Communist propaganda for home and foreign consumption.

The German Ministry of Posts has made a formal demand on the Soviet telegraph authorities to put a stop to the Russian "air jamming" which the German radio fans say interferes with the broadcasting of the Königswusterhausen station near Berlin. The official German protest alleges that the Soviet's broadcaster, RAX, interferes with German stations.

Balbo Sends Duce Graphic Report On Hazards His Planes Overcame

Flew for Hours, He Writes, Through Uncharted Darkness by Instruments Without Sight of Sky or Water, Keeping Formation Despite Danger of Collisions.

Special Cable to THE NEW YORK TIMES.

NATAL, Brazil, Jan. 8.—Battling fog and clouds which obscured the full moon of which they had planned to take advantage, ten planes of the Italian air fleet maintained perfect military formation for 1,875 miles of ocean from Bolama, Portuguese Guinea, to Natal, Brazil, according to the official report of General Italo Balbo, the flight commander, cabled today to Premier Mussolini at Rome. The entire flight, he said, was made by dead reckoning.

Careful tests were made, General Balbo pointed out, to ascertain that the Savoia-Marchetti S-55 flying boats could rise from the sea with their gross loads in excess of 10,000 pounds.

At the last moment, the Air Minister declared, he yielded to the earnest pleas of the pilots of the two repair planes and permitted them to accompany the twelve originally scheduled to cross the ocean.

The full text of General Balbo's report follows:

After eighteen hours of flying in formation of threes, which was initiated at Bolama at the moment at the beginning of the flight across, ten hydroplanes reached Natal on the coast of Brazil.

We sketch briefly to your Excellency the phases of the crossing.

On Jan. 1 the planes were ready to depart. They needed a final inspection. On board of all everything that was not strictly indispensable was eliminated from top to bottom. In addition to the navigation instruments and to a full supply of gasoline, an additional life-raft was added to our equipment for the flight across as an extra precaution in case of a forced landing of the fleet. In fact our planes carried sufficient gasoline for another twenty hours of flight.

I had decided to anticipate the taking-off, fixing it for the third hour of the evening, because the moon would not be full until the

Continued on Page Sixteen.

SUGAR ACCORD NEAR AS GERMANS ACCEPT

Chadbourne Wins Them Over by Adding 750,000 Tons to Five-Year Export Quota Offer.

WORLD CARTEL SEEMS SURE

Others Expected to Ratify New Agreement—3,500,000-Ton Surplus to Be Segregated.

Special Cable to THE NEW YORK TIMES.

BERLIN, Jan. 8.—An international sugar cartel became as good as fact today when Thomas L. Chadbourne, on behalf of the Cuban-American interests, offered a reapportioned export quota satisfactory to the German representatives.

With a tentative agreement on the question of quotas reached, there only remains the formal drawing up of the cartel agreement and its signature, unless Poland and Czechoslovakia refuse to accept the new modification of their quotas. This is not thought likely to produce new stumbling blocks.

The basis on which agreement was reached gives the Germans an export quota of 500,000 tons for the fiscal year 1930-1931, the first year of the Chadbourne plan, 350,000 the second year and 300,000 each for the remaining three. In other words, an export quota of 1,750,000 tons was given to Germany for the five years when she had asked for 1,850,000, and as against 1,000,000 foreseen in the original Chadbourne plan.

The extra 750,000 tons is to be made up by reducing the export quotas of the other beet sugar producing countries by 175,000 tons and slicing 575,000 tons from the Cuban quota in the course of the five years. The total amount of sugar to be exported remains the same.

The actual cartel agreement will revolve around the problem of stabilizing the sugar industry and readjusting production to demand. The enormous surplus now on hand, amounting to about 3,500,000 tons, will be segregated and sold over the period of five years, at the same time serving as a safety valve against an unwarranted rise in price, Mr. Chadbourne declared.

The parties to the agreement intend that no rise shall occur in excess of the cost of production plus a fair return on the investment, Mr. Chadbourne added, expressing the conviction that the agreement would provide against the evils of overproduction in at least one commodity.

Opposes Chadbourne Plan.

Wireless to THE NEW YORK TIMES.

THE HAGUE, Jan. 8.—The Netherlands Indian Agricultural Company tonight issued a memorandum against the adherence of Java to the Chadbourne sugar plan.

Emphasizing what it terms the difficulties inherent in production restriction schemes the memorandum says the sugar problem should be treated as agrarian and not industrial and dealt with by a general convention and not by countries separately.

The manifesto holds the European producers would benefit greatly under the Chadbourne plan. In Java, however, it declares, there is no overproduction and restriction is not wanted. Fear is expressed that the permanent control board planned by Mr. Chadbourne might compel Java

Continued on Page Nine.

WARBURG FORESEES FINANCIAL RECOVERY

Banker Calls "Business Cycle" More Matter of Psychology Than of Economics.

DENIES WE STERILIZE' GOLD

Decrying Isolation Theory, He Advises Our Seeking Larger International Cooperation.

An attempt to maintain high prices in the face of constantly accelerated mass production, through the use of tariff barriers and other artificial expedients chiefly was responsible for the present economic depression, according to Paul M. Warburg.

In presenting his annual address as chairman of the Manhattan Company before a joint meeting of the directors of the company and its controlled units, the Bank of Manhattan Trust Company, the International Acceptance Bank, Inc., the International Manhattan Company, Inc., and the New York Title and Mortgage Company, Mr. Warburg said the inventive genius of man had placed behind every visible producer a hundred invisible producers. It had not been able, however, he added, to place any invisible consumers behind the consumer.

Remarking that in a world of free trade and well-governed banking no great harm might have resulted, Mr. Warburg continued:

"Instead of permitting a free and untrammeled flow of goods, customs barriers were erected by nations, old and new, and behind these walls of protection industries were pushed to hothouse growths, based upon high prices exacted from domestic consumers. Valorization schemes, syndicates, cartels, monopolies and all kinds of governmental operations did the rest.

Efforts for High Prices.

"Thus, instead of permitting increased machine production and cheap credit to lead to lower prices, all efforts were bent to rest our economic structure upon a level of high prices. History repeated itself when high prices led to a decreased consumption and a rapid increase in productive capacity, agricultural as well as industrial. When the purchasing power of domestic consumers threatened to become exhausted it was revived by the stimulant of instalment plans, and buyers abroad, at the end of their tether, were assisted by foreign loans. A period of fantastic overbuilding, overproducing and overbuying ensued, largely financed through paper profits or bank credit, freely granted upon inflated securities. When the consumers' credit became exhausted; when new markets failed to open up, while important old markets became impaired (when, in addition, the hydraulic pressure of reparation payments forced Germany to increase her exportable output at all costs); the critical moment came when production overwhelmed manipulation. Prices, overcoming artificial dams, began to seek their own levels."

Mr. Warburg made no attempt to predict the time of the end of the depression, but he said no sane person could doubt that eventually a country as unique in resources and opportunities as the United States ultimately would get back into its stride. Comparatively brief periods of underproduction in a country containing more than 120,000,000 tem-

Continued on Page Four.

REPUBLICANS TO FILE A CITY INQUIRY BILL AT ALBANY MONDAY

Measure to Be Drafted Over Week-End—All the Criminal Courts Will Be Included.

PASSAGE HELD A CERTAINTY

Majority Leaders After Hailing Roosevelt Stand Plan to Play Lone Hand.

LOOK TO 1932 CAMPAIGN

Governor's Cooperation May Be Called for, However, in Getting Funds for the Inquiry

A resolution for a legislative investigation of the New York City Administration, broad enough to cover the criminal courts not now under inquiry, will be introduced in the Legislature Monday night.

This was learned yesterday after the return from Albany of W. Kingsland Macy, Republican State chairman. The drafting of the resolution will be completed over the week-end.

It is not the intention of the Republican leaders to pass the resolution for the investigation at once but to delay its adoption until after enactment of the appropriation bill. It is possible that the resolution first offered may be amended, but its early introduction has been decided upon so that it may be referred to committee, and then taken out and acted upon at any time on short notice.

Macy Certain Measure Will Pass.

Mr. Macy said he had no doubt of the passage of the resolution. The party's majority in the State Senate is only one, but the Republican leaders do not expect defection on the part of their Senators. Senator Cheney of Buffalo, who has gone to Florida for his health, has expressed willingness to return at any time his vote is needed.

Any Republican Senator who refused to vote for the bill might lay himself open to suspicion concerning his motives, and it is not believed that any of them oppose the investigation, or would care to place themselves in opposition, even if doubtful of its advisability.

Speaker McGinnies, whose unwillingness to support an investigation last year caused its abandonment, has promised the State Chairman to support the resolution this year, so the Republican leaders have no doubt of its passage by the Assembly, where there the party has a comfortable working majority.

It is not the intention of the Republicans to interfere in any way with the investigation of the magistrates' courts in Manhattan and the Bronx now being conducted by former Judge Samuel Seabury and Isidor J. Kresel. If legislative action should be needed to strengthen this inquiry, it was said that it will be provided.

The resolution will provide for an investigation of the magistrates' courts in Brooklyn, Queens and Richmond, if the Appellate Division of the Second Department does not order an inquiry there by the time the Legislature is ready to act on the resolution.

The investigation, of course, will give the legislative committee, which probably will be composed of five or six Republicans and two or three Democrats, complete power to investigate any branch of the City Government.

Mr. Macy said that no one had been approached as yet to act as counsel to the proposed investigating committee, but expressed the belief that there would be no difficulty in obtaining counsel of the necessary experience and ability. No definite

Continued on Page Two.

Wickersham Report Goes to Hoover Monday; Congress Likely to Get It Within Two Days

Special to The New York Times.

WASHINGTON, Jan. 8.—The Wickersham commission's report on prohibition, which has been completed and is now being put into shape for transmission to President Hoover, is likely, according to information given to Senate Republican leaders, to be submitted by the commission to the President on Monday and sent to Congress by the latter on Tuesday or Wednesday.

Reports were current today that Congressional leaders had gone to the Wickersham commission in an effort to head off the early submission of the report because it probably would open the floodgates of oratory and delay the passage of appropriation bills, and also invite an extra session.

Officials of the Wickersham commission said tonight they knew of no such visit by members of Congress. Responsible leaders of the Senate also said they knew of no effort to head off the submission of the report.

WASHINGTON, Jan. 8 (AP).—It was made known at the White House yesterday that President Hoover had decided he could not hold up the report of the Law Enforcement Commission and that he was prepared to transmit it to Congress soon after he received it. He is directed by the law creating the commission to submit his recommendations on prohibition along with the report.

The week's recess agreed upon by the commission did not prevent eight of the members from appearing at their desks today. A majority of them, however, were occupied more with other phases of the commission's investigation into crime than with prohibition.

77 MINOR GIRLS IMPRISONED UNLAWFULLY BY 7 JUDGES; CORRIGAN ACTS TO FREE ALL

Boy Patient Gets His Wish; Mrs. Hoover Sends Him Card

Special to The New York Times.

PHILADELPHIA, Jan. 8.—Philip Ratto Jr., a 6-year-old patient at the Eagleville Sanitarium, received a Christmas surprise today from Mrs. Herbert Hoover.

During the holidays the patient wished for a card from the President's wife, and today this letter came:

"My Dear Philip: Santa Claus told me you specially wanted a Christmas card from me—so I sent you one that I thought you would like best of all.

"Alas—there was a mistake in addressing it, and it has come back to me. I am sending it again—and I am so sorry that you have had this long delay.

"I hope you are getting well just as rapidly as possible, and that you had a merry Christmas.

"LOU HENRY HOOVER."

3 RED 'HUNGER' RIOTS STIR ONLY THE POLICE

Crowds Fail to Turn Out for the Demonstrations in Bronx, Brooklyn and Manhattan.

TWO PATROLMEN INJURED

Free Food, Light, Gas and Shelter Demanded for Jobless—Several Reds Arrested.

Communists who organized a "hunger march" of the unemployed to "storm the bread lines" clashed three times with the police yesterday. Mounted patrolmen, wielding riot clubs, dispersed a group of several hundred at Salvation Army headquarters, Tillary Street and Ashland Place, Brooklyn.

The "hunger march," which was carried on simultaneously in Manhattan, the Bronx and Brooklyn, was elaborately executed, but it was the least successful of any of the Communists' unemployment demonstrations in the last year.

Besides the clash at the Brooklyn Salvation Army headquarters, trouble occurred at a Salvation Army bread-line on the Bowery near Fourth Street, around the corner from Manhattan Lyceum, a favorite meeting hall for Communists, and at a branch office of the State Labor Bureau, Lenox Avenue and 132d Street.

In Brooklyn the mounted police rode into the crowd, while a small contingent of patrolmen and detectives beat back men and women with fists and blackjacks. The crowd, exhorted by Communist leaders, pitched in and fought the police, but the timely arrival of the mounted policemen scattered the crowd. In this fracas one detective was cut on the face and mouth. The unemployed Communists took their injured with them.

Policeman's Jaw Broken.

A policeman's jaw was broken at the Salvation Army's bread line at Bowery and Fourth Street, as the result of a battle with the tail-end of a procession on the way to Manhattan Lyceum from a meeting held near the City Free Employment Bureau at 54 Lafayette Street. Two men, picked out of a meeting in Manhattan Lyceum by the injured patrolmen, were arrested.

A Negro policeman, after a tussle in front of the Harlem branch of the State Labor Department, arrest-

Continued on Page Three.

BLANKET PARDON WEIGHED

Habeas Corpus Writs for Fifty Still in Jail Are Also Considered.

NONE OF 77 GOT HEARING

All Were Held on Confessions in Violation of Law, Records at Seabury Hearing Show.

SILBERMANN INQUIRY ON

Magistrate Twice Freed Girl in Theft Despite Strong Evidence, Witness Asserts.

The illegal commitment of seventy-seven girls to Bedford Reformatory as wayward minors was shown yesterday before Samuel Seabury, referee in the Appellate Division inquiry, to be a part of the record of seven magistrates who have sat in Women's Court since 1926, and six of whom are still on the bench.

Of the total, twenty-four were committed by Magistrate H. Stanley Renaud, seventeen by Jesse Silbermann, sixteen by Jean Norris and fourteen by Earl A. Smith. These four were recently transferred from their Women's Court assignments by Chief Magistrate Corrigan, who last night, perturbed by the disclosures, declared that writs should be immediately prepared to obtain the release of the girls still being held.

The remaining six illegal commitments were divided as follows: Three by Magistrate Huion B. Capshaw, who, in the recent transfer, was sent to Women's Court; two by Magistrate Marsh, who is no longer sitting, and one by Magistrate Walsh.

Fifty Still in Jail.

A summary of the records including the present whereabouts of the seventy-seven girls who were unlawfully committed for from one to five years in the reformatory showed that one is now in an insane asylum in Philadelphia, having been discovered to be mentally defective after Magistrate Smith committed her; one is dead; one is in City Hospital on Welfare Island, and three have been discharged. Fifty of the girls are still in the institution, fifteen are on parole and six are being sought by authorities as violators of their paroles.

For the girls who are still in the institution, individual writs of habeas corpus may be obtained in Supreme Court of Westchester County, where the institution is located at Bedford Hills, or they may be pardoned in a blanket action by Governor Roosevelt, officials said. A blanket pardon would free one-seventh of the total registration of the institution, where there are now 351 adults and 38 infants.

Although legally a minor is an infant at any age, Dr. Leo J. Palmer, superintendent of the institution, who sat in the witness chair for two hours yesterday morning listening as Isidor J. Kresel, special counsel, read the seventy-seven names into the record, explained that often women committed to the institution bring their children with them and that the children are those classified as infants.

Illegal Commitment Read.

Preparatory to reading the long list into the record, Mr. Kresel read from the commitment of Margaret Hines, signed July 26, 1927, by Magistrate Norris as follows: "Whereas said charge (that of being a wayward minor) having been duly established by the confession of the defendant in her plea of guilty * * *"

He then read from Section 913B of the Code of Criminal Procedure, which specifically states that a wayward minor may be committed only when the charge is established "by competent evidence upon a hearing." Handing the commitment up to Referee Seabury, he pointed out that on the printed form the phrase "by competent evidence upon a hearing" had been scratched out with a pen and the phrase "by the confession of the defendant in her plea of guilty" substituted.

"That commitment is illegal," the referee interposed.

Out of the seventy-seven commitments, one was prominent because of its nonconformity. It was that of Pauline Keimowitz, now on parole, signed by Magistrate Renaud on Oct. 31, 1927, and the first on the list, which began in May of 1926, to bear his signature.

The record showed that on her appearance before Magistrate Renaud she had entered a plea of guilty to

"All the News That's Fit to Print."

The New York Times.

Copyright, 1931, by The New York Times Company.

THE WEATHER
Generally fair and colder today; tomorrow fair.
U. S. Weather Forecast—For details see Page 43.
Temperatures yesterday—Max. 42, min. 34.

VOL. LXXX....No. 26,660. **** NEW YORK, WEDNESDAY, JANUARY 21, 1931. TWO CENTS in Greater New York | THREE CENTS Within 200 Miles | FOUR CENTS Elsewhere Except 7th and 8th Postal Zones

WICKERSHAM REPORT OPPOSES REPEAL, BUT BOARD MAJORITY FAVORS REVISION; HOOVER IS FIRM FOR DRY ENFORCEMENT

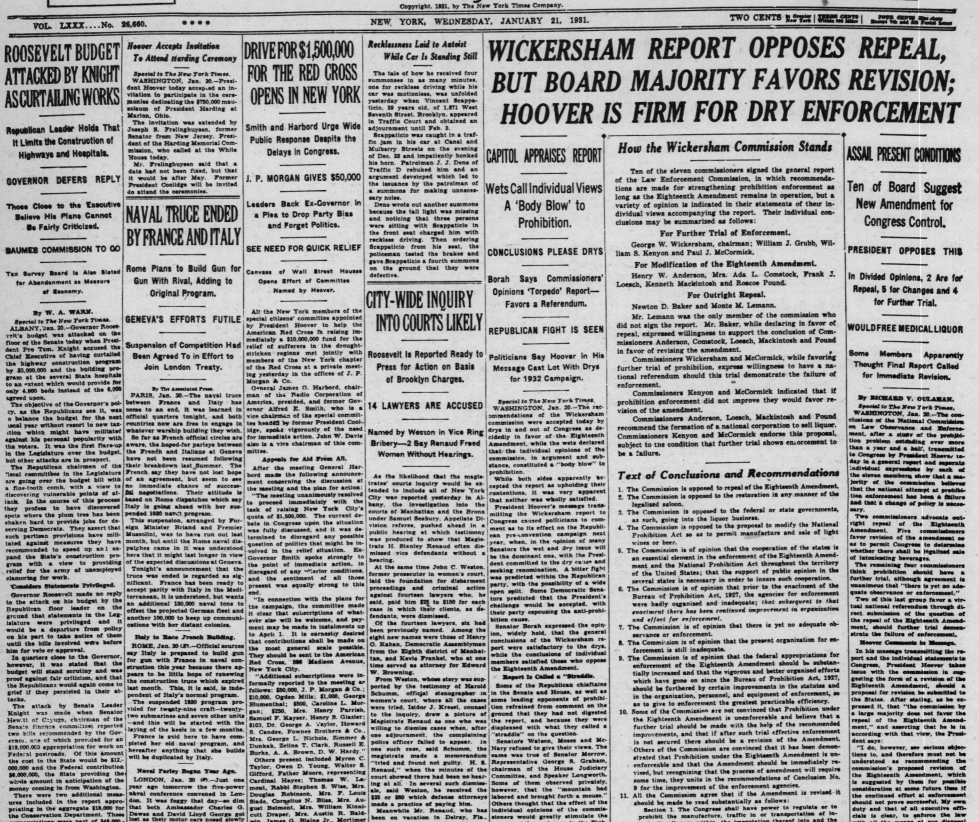

ROOSEVELT BUDGET ATTACKED BY KNIGHT AS CURTAILING WORKS

Republican Leader Holds That It Limits the Construction of Highways and Hospitals.

GOVERNOR DEFERS REPLY

Those Close to the Executive Believe His Plans Cannot Be Fairly Criticized.

BAUMES COMMISSION TO GO

Tax Survey Board Is Also Slated for Abandonment as Measure of Economy.

By W. A. WARN.

Special to The New York Times.

ALBANY, Jan. 20.—Governor Roosevelt's budget was attacked on the floor of the Senate today when President Pro Tem. Knight accused the Chief Executive of having curtailed the highway construction program by $5,000,000 and the building program at the several State hospitals to an extent which would provide for only 4,800 beds instead of the 6,000 agreed upon.

The objective of the Governor's policy, as the Republicans see it, was to balance the budget for the next fiscal year without resort to new taxation which might have militated against his personal popularity with the voters. It was the first flare-up in the Legislature over the budget, but other attacks are in prospect.

The Republican chairmen of the fiscal committees in the Legislature are going over the budget bill with a fine-tooth comb, with a view to discovering vulnerable points of attack. In the course of this process they profess to have discovered spots where the plum tree has been shaken hard to provide jobs for deserving Democrats. They assert that such partisan provisions have militated against measures they have recommended to speed up and expand the State's construction program with a view to providing relief for the army of unemployed clamoring for work.

Considers Statements Privileged.

Governor Roosevelt made no reply to the attack on his budget by the Republican floor leader on the ground that statements in the Legislature were privileged and it would be a departure from policy on his part to take notice of them until the bills involved were before him for veto or approval.

In quarters close to the Governor, however, it was stated that the budget will stand scrutiny and was proof against fair criticism, and that the Republicans would again come to grief if they persisted in their attacks.

The attack by Senate Leader Knight was made when Senator Hewitt of Cayuga, chairman of the Senate finance committee, reported two bills recommended by the Governor, one of which provided for an $18,000,000 appropriation for work on Federal postroads. Of this amount the cost to the State would be $12,000,000 and the Federal contribution $6,000,000, the State providing the whole amount in anticipation of the money coming in from Washington.

There were two additional measures included in the report appropriating in the aggregate $18,000 for the Conservation Department. These appropriations were part of $48,000,000 for public works which Governor Roosevelt had asked the Legislature to approve in advance of the general budget in order to expedite the letting of contracts and the employment of idle labor.

Holds Budget Defeats Federal Action.

Senator Knight said the Republicans had already indicated to the Governor their willingness to cooperate and had pointed a way in which the money might be made quickly available. He expressed a wish that the funds would be put to work promptly.

"But it is a matter of considerable regret to us," he said, "that in examining the Governor's budget we have found that the hospital building program has been curtailed rather than expanded, and that money made available by a Republican Congress to extend the road construction program in the States will be used, if this budget is adopted, actually to reduce the amount to be paid by New York for highway purposes.

"When the Federal Government decided greatly to increase the funds to be paid to the States for highways, it did so with the idea that this money would be added to funds which would be appropriated by the States and that in this way employment

Continued on Page Sixteen.

Hoover Accepts Invitation To Attend Harding Ceremony

Special to The New York Times.

WASHINGTON, Jan. 20.—President Hoover today accepted an invitation to participate in the ceremonies dedicating the $750,000 mausoleum of President Harding at Marion, Ohio.

The invitation was extended by Joseph S. Frelinghuysen, former Senator from New Jersey, President of the Harding Memorial Commission, who called at the White House today.

Mr. Frelinghuysen said that a date had not been fixed, but that it would be after May. Former President Coolidge will be invited to attend the ceremonies.

NAVAL TRUCE ENDED BY FRANCE AND ITALY

Rome Plans to Build Gun for Gun With Rival, Adding to Original Program.

GENEVA'S EFFORTS FUTILE

Suspension of Competition Had Been Agreed To in Effort to Join London Treaty.

By The Associated Press.

PARIS, Jan. 20.—The naval truce between France and Italy has come to an end, it was learned in official quarters tonight, and both countries now are free to engage in whatever warship building they wish.

So far as French official circles are aware, the hoped-for parleys between the French and Italians at Geneva have not been resumed following their breakdown last Summer. The French say they have not lost hope of an agreement, but seem to see no immediate chance of successful negotiations. Their attitude is based on Rome dispatches which say Italy is going ahead with her suspended 1930 naval program.

This suspension, arranged by Foreign Minister Briand and Premier Mussolini, was to have run out last month, but until the Rome naval dispatches came in it was understood here that it might last longer in view of the expected discussions at Geneva.

Tonight's announcement that the truce was ended is regarded as significant. France has been ready to accept parity with Italy in the Mediterranean, it is understood, but wants an additional 150,000 naval tons to offset the projected German fleet and another 100,000 to keep up communications with her distant colonies.

Italy to Race French Building.

ROME, Jan. 20 (AP).—Official sources say Italy is prepared to build gun for gun with France in naval construction this year because there appears to be little hope of renewing the construction truce which expired last month. This, it is said, is independent of Italy's normal program.

The suspended 1930 program provided for twenty-nine craft—twenty-two submarines and seven other units—and this will be started with the laying of the keels in a few months.

France is said here to have completed her old naval program, and hereafter anything that she builds will be duplicated by Italy.

Naval Parley Began Year Ago.

LONDON, Jan. 20 (AP).—Just one year ago tomorrow the five-power naval conference convened in London. It was foggy that day—so dim that both Ambassador Charles G. Dawes and David Lloyd George got lost as their motor cars nosed slowly toward the scene of the opening, the royal gallery of the House of Lords.

King George, speaking into his own

Continued on Page Eleven.

DRIVE FOR $1,500,000 FOR THE RED CROSS OPENS IN NEW YORK

Smith and Harbord Urge Wide Public Response Despite the Delays in Congress.

J. P. MORGAN GIVES $50,000

Leaders Back Ex-Governor in a Plea to Drop Party Bias and Forget Politics.

SEE NEED FOR QUICK RELIEF

Canvass of Wall Street Houses Opens Effort of Committee Named by Hoover.

All the New York members of the special citizens' committee appointed by President Hoover to help the American Red Cross in raising immediately a $10,000,000 fund for the relief of sufferers in the drought-stricken regions met jointly with members of the New York chapter of the Red Cross at a private meeting yesterday in the offices of J. P. Morgan & Co.

General James G. Harbord, chairman of the Radio Corporation of America, presided, and former Governor Alfred E. Smith, who is a vice chairman of the special committee headed by former President Coolidge, spoke vigorously of the need for immediate action. John W. Davis also is a vice chairman of this committee.

Appeals for Aid From All.

After the meeting General Harbord made the following announcement concerning the discussion at the meeting and the plan for action:

"The meeting unanimously resolved to proceed immediately with the task of raising New York City's quota of $1,500,000. The current debate in Congress upon the situation was fully discussed, and it was determined to disregard any possible question of politics that might be involved in the relief situation. Ex-Governor Smith spoke strongly to the point of immediate action, in disregard of any ulterior conditions, and the sentiment of all those present was equally strong to this end.

"In connection with the plans for the campaign, the committee made it clear that subscriptions of whatever size will be welcome, and payment may be made in instalments up to April 1. It is earnestly desired that contributions shall be made on the most general scale possible. They should be sent to the American Red Cross, 596 Madison Avenue, New York City.

"Additional subscriptions were informally reported to the meeting as follows: $50,000, J. P. Morgan & Co.; $10,000, Ogden Mills; $1,000, George Blumenthal; $500, Caroline L. Morgan; $250, Mrs. Henry Parrish, Samuel F. Kayser, Henry S. Glazier; $100, Dr. George A. Taylor, Howard S. Candee, Fownes Brothers & Co., Mrs. George L. Nichols, Zimmer & Dunkak, Zelina T. Clark, Russell E. Burke, A. A. Brown, D. W. Hardy."

Others present included Myron C. Taylor, Owen D. Young, Walter S. Gifford, Father Moore, representing Cardinal Hayes; Thomas W. Lamont, Rabbi Stephen S. Wise, Mrs. Douglas Robinson, Mrs. F. Louis Slade, Cornelius N. Bliss, Mrs. August Belmont, Mrs. William Kinnicutt Draper, Mrs. Austin R. Baldwin, James G. Blaine Jr., Mortimer M. Buckner, H. P. Davison, Douglas Gibbons, Samuel M. Greer, Miss

Continued on Page Fourteen.

Recklessness Laid to Autoist While Car Is Standing Still

The tale of how he received four summonses in as many minutes, one for reckless driving while his car was motionless, was unfolded yesterday when Vincent Scappaticio, 39 years old, of 1,871 West Seventh Street, Brooklyn, appeared in Traffic Court and obtained an adjournment until Feb. 3.

Scappaticio was caught in a traffic jam in his car at Canal and Mulberry Streets on the evening of Dec. 23 and impatiently honked his horn. Patrolman J. J. Dene of Traffic D rebuked him and an argument developed which led to the issuance by the patrolman of a summons for making unnecessary noise.

Dene wrote out another summons because the tail light was missing and noticing that three persons were sitting with Scappaticio in the front seat charged him with reckless driving. Then ordering Scappaticio from his seat, the policeman tested the brakes and gave Scappaticio a fourth summons on the ground that they were defective.

CITY-WIDE INQUIRY INTO COURTS LIKELY

Roosevelt Is Reported Ready to Press for Action on Basis of Brooklyn Charges.

14 LAWYERS ARE ACCUSED

Named by Weston in Vice Ring Bribery—2 Say Renaud Freed Women Without Hearings.

As the likelihood that the magistrates' courts inquiry would be extended to include all of New York City was reported yesterday in Albany, the investigation into the courts of Manhattan and the Bronx under Samuel Seabury, Appellate Division referee, pushed ahead in a public hearing at which testimony was produced to show that Magistrate H. Stanley Renaud often dismissed vice defendants without a hearing.

At the same time John C. Weston, former prosecutor in women's court, laid the foundation for disbarment proceedings and criminal action against fourteen lawyers who, he said, paid him $25 to $150 for each case in which their clients, as defendants, were dismissed.

Of the fourteen lawyers, six had been previously named. Among the eight new names were those of Henry O. Kahan, Democratic Assemblyman from the Eighth district of Manhattan, and Kevie Frankel, who at one time served as attorney for Edward W. Browning.

From Weston, whose story was supported by the testimony of Harold Schumm, official stenographer in women's court, where all the cases were tried, Isidor J. Kresel, counsel to the inquiry, drew a picture of Magistrate Renaud as one who was willing to dismiss cases when, after one adjournment, the complaining police officer failed to appear. In one such case, said Schumm, the magistrate made a memorandum "tried and found not guilty. H. S. Renaud," when the minutes of the court showed there had been no hearing at all. In several such dismissals, said Weston, he received the $25 or $50 which defense attorneys made a practice of paying him.

Meanwhile Mr. Renaud, who has been on vacation in Delray, Fla., yesterday was reported on his way home by motor in response to a telegram from District Attorney Crain. Previously he had written Mr. Seabury, in response to a similar telegram, that he would be home about March 15.

Governor Roosevelt had no comment to make yesterday on the reports emanating from the Capitol in Albany. It was learned from his advisers that, as a result of information reaching the executive office recently, the Governor was inclined toward a city-wide court inquiry.

The extension of the inquiry would necessarily fall under the jurisdiction of the Appellate Division, Second Judicial Department, which takes in Brooklyn, Queens and Staten Island. Last August, when the Governor requested the Appellate Division of the First Department, comprising Manhattan and the Bronx, to instigate such an inquiry, he was informed by Presiding Justice Edward Lazansky of the Second Department that there were no complaints in that district, and no apparent need for such an investigation.

This position was affirmed by the presiding justice as recently as Monday, when, in response to a request made by Mrs. Catherine Park Clivette, the entire court declared the

Continued on Page Seventeen.

Food Rioters Raid Oklahoma City Store; 500 Dispersed by the Police With Tear Gas

OKLAHOMA CITY, Jan. 20 (AP).—A crowd of men and women, shouting that they were hungry and jobless, raided a grocery store near the City Hall today. Twenty-six of the men were arrested. Scores loitered near the city jail following the arrests, but kept well out of range of fire hose made ready for use in case of another disturbance.

The police tonight broke up a second meeting of about one hundred unemployed men and arrested Francis Owens, alleged head of the "Oklahoma City Unemployed Council," who was accused of instigating the raid.

Before the grocery was entered, a delegation of unemployed, led by Owens, had demanded of City Manager E. M. Fry that the authorities furnish immediate relief. Owens rejected a request by Mr. Fry for the names and addresses of the "Unemployed Council," said to number 2,500 men and women, both whites and Negroes.

The raiders disregarded efforts of H. A. Shaw, the store manager, to quiet them.

"It is too late to bargain with us," the leaders shouted, as they stripped the shelves.

The police hastily assembled emergency squads and dispersed the crowd numbering 500, with tear gas. Only those who were trapped in the wrecked store were arrested. Five women among them were released. The windows of the store were smashed as the raiders attempted to flee.

John Simmons was held on a charge of assault after he had leaped on the back of Lee Mullenix, a policeman, when the officer attempted to enter the crowded store.

Floyd Phillips was charged with inciting a riot. The police said he was one of the speakers who harangued the crowd at the City Hall before they began the parade that ended at the store.

CAPITOL APPRAISES REPORT

Wets Call Individual Views A 'Body Blow' to Prohibition.

CONCLUSIONS PLEASE DRYS

Borah Says Commissioners' Opinions 'Torpedo' Report—Favors a Referendum.

REPUBLICAN FIGHT IS SEEN

Politicians Say Hoover in His Message Cast Lot With Drys for 1932 Campaign.

Special to The New York Times.

WASHINGTON, Jan. 20.—The recommendations of the Wickersham commission were accepted today by drys in and out of Congress as decidedly in favor of the Eighteenth Amendment, while the wets declared that the individual opinions of the commission, in argument and substance, constituted a "body blow" to prohibition.

While both sides apparently accepted the report as upholding their contentions, it was very apparent that neither was wholly satisfied.

President Hoover's message transmitting the Wickersham report to Congress caused politicians to comment as to its effect on the Republican pre-convention campaign next year, when, in the opinion of many Senators the wet and dry issue will be the dominant one, with the President committed to the dry cause and seeking renomination. A bitter fight was predicted within the Republican party, with the possibility of a wide open split. Some Democratic Senators predicted that the President's challenge would be accepted, with their party espousing the anti-prohibition cause.

Senator Borah expressed the opinion, widely held, that the general conclusions of the Wickersham report were satisfactory to the drys, while the conclusions of individual members satisfied those who oppose the Eighteenth Amendment.

Report Is Called a "Straddle.

Some of the Republican chieftains in the Senate and House, as well as some leading opponents of prohibition refrained from comment on the ground that they had not digested the report, and because they were displeased with what they called a "straddle" on the question.

Senators Watson, Moses and McNary refused to give their views. The same was true of Senator Morrow, Representative George S. Graham, chairman of the House Judiciary Committee, and Speaker Longworth. Some of them observed privately, however, that the "mountain had labored and brought forth a mouse." Others thought that the effect of the individual opinions of the commissioners would greatly stimulate the movement for a change in the Eighteenth Amendment and the Volstead act.

Borah Says Report Has No Force.

"The general conclusions of the commission will be very satisfactory to the supporters of the Eighteenth Amendment," Senator Borah said. "The conclusions of the individual members of the commission will be very satisfactory to those opposed to the Eighteenth Amendment.

"The personnel of the commission is very high and I have no doubt they worked out the best report possible. But the fact is that the torpedoing of the report of the commission by the individual views of the members of the commission leaves the report without any force or effect in the ultimate solution of the problem.

"This is one of those kind of questions which the people themselves and their duly elected officials will have to settle, and the reports of commissions will not have any very decided effect upon the ultimate solution.

"We have reached the point in the consideration of this question where it is either repeal or no repeal of the Eighteenth Amendment.

"I should like to see those opposed to the Eighteenth Amendment pre-

Continued on [illegible] [illegible] Two.

How the Wickersham Commission Stands

Ten of the eleven commissioners signed the general report of the Law Enforcement Commission, in which recommendations are made for strengthening prohibition enforcement as long as the Eighteenth Amendment remains in operation, but a variety of opinion is indicated in their statements of their individual views accompanying the report. Their individual conclusions may be summarized as follows:

For Further Trial of Enforcement.

George W. Wickersham, chairman; William J. Grubb, William S. Kenyon and Paul J. McCormick.

For Modification of the Eighteenth Amendment.

Henry W. Anderson, Mrs. Ada L. Comstock, Frank J. Loesch, Kenneth Mackintosh and Roscoe Pound.

For Outright Repeal.

Newton D. Baker and Monte M. Lemann.

Mr. Lemann was the only member of the commission who did not sign the report. Mr. Baker, while declaring in favor of repeal, expressed willingness to support the conclusion of Commissioners Anderson, Comstock, Loesch, Mackintosh and Pound in favor of revising the amendment.

Commissioners Wickersham and McCormick, while favoring further trial of prohibition, express willingness to have a national referendum should this trial demonstrate the failure of enforcement.

Commissioners Kenyon and McCormick indicated that if prohibition enforcement did not improve they would favor revision of the amendment.

Commissioners Anderson, Loesch, Mackintosh and Pound recommend the formation of a national corporation to sell liquor. Commissioners Kenyon and McCormick endorse this proposal, subject to the condition that further trial shows enforcement to be a failure.

Text of Conclusions and Recommendations

1. The Commission is opposed to repeal of the Eighteenth Amendment.
2. The Commission is opposed to the restoration in any manner of the legalized saloon.
3. The Commission is opposed to the federal or state governments, as such, going into the liquor business.
4. The Commission is opposed to the proposal to modify the National Prohibition Act so as to permit manufacture and sale of light wines or beer.
5. The Commission is of opinion that the cooperation of the states is an essential element in the enforcement of the Eighteenth Amendment and the National Prohibition Act throughout the territory of the United States; that the support of public opinion in the several states is necessary in order to insure such cooperation.
6. The Commission is of opinion that prior to the enactment of the Bureau of Prohibition Act, 1927, the agencies for enforcement were badly organized and inadequate; *that subsequent to that enactment there has been continued improvement in organization and effort for enforcement.*
7. The Commission is of opinion that there is yet no adequate observance or enforcement.
8. The Commission is of opinion that the present organization for enforcement is still inadequate.
9. The Commission is of opinion that the federal appropriations for enforcement of the Eighteenth Amendment should be substantially increased and that the vigorous and better organized efforts which have gone on since the Bureau of Prohibition Act, 1927, should be furthered by certain improvements in the statutes and in the organization, personnel, and equipment of enforcement, so as to give to enforcement the greatest practicable efficiency.
10. Some of the Commission are not convinced that Prohibition under the Eighteenth Amendment is unenforceable and believe that a further trial should be made with the help of the recommended improvements, and that if after such trial effective enforcement is not secured there should be a revision of the Amendment. Others of the Commission are convinced that it has been demonstrated that Prohibition under the Eighteenth Amendment is unenforceable and that the Amendment should be immediately revised, but recognizing that the process of amendment will require some time, they unite in the recommendations of Conclusion No. 9 for the improvement of the enforcement agencies.
11. All the Commission agree that if the Amendment is revised it should be made to read substantially as follows:

    Section 1. The Congress shall have power to regulate or to prohibit the manufacture, traffic in or transportation of intoxicating liquors within, the importation thereof into and the exportation thereof from the United States and all territory subject to the jurisdiction thereof for beverage purposes.

12. *The recommendations referred to in conclusion No. 9 are:*

    1. Removal of the causes of irritation and resentment on the part of the medical profession by:

    (a) Doing away with the statutory fixing of the amount which may be prescribed and the number of prescriptions;

    (b) Abolition of the requirement of specifying the ailment for which liquor is prescribed upon a blank to go into the public files;

    (c) Leaving as much as possible to regulations rather than fixing details by statute.

    2. Removal of the anomalous provisions in Section 29, National Prohibition Act, as to cider and fruit juices by making some uniform provision for a fixed alcoholic content.

    3. Increase of the number of agents, storekeeper-gaugers, prohibition investigators, and special agents; increase in the personnel of the Customs Bureau and in the equipment of all enforcement organizations.

    4. Enactment of a statute authorizing regulations permitting access to the premises and records of wholesale and retail dealers so as to make it possible to trace products of specially denatured alcohol to the ultimate consumer.

    5. Enactment of legislation to prohibit independent denaturing plants.

    6. The Commission is opposed to legislation allowing more latitude for federal searches and seizures.

    7. The Commission renews the recommendation contained in its previous reports for codification of the National Prohibition Act and the acts supplemental to and in amendment thereof.

    8. The Commission renews its recommendation of legislation for making procedure in the so-called padlock injunction cases more effective.

    9. The Commission recommends legislation providing a mode of prosecuting petty offenses in the federal courts and modifying the Increased Penalties Act of 1929, as set forth in the Chairman's letter to the Attorney General dated May 23, 1^30, H. R. Rep. 1699.

ASSAIL PRESENT CONDITIONS

Ten of Board Suggest New Amendment for Congress Control.

PRESIDENT OPPOSES THIS

In Divided Opinions, 2 Are for Repeal, 5 for Changes and 4 for Further Trial.

WOULD FREE MEDICAL LIQUOR

Some Members Apparently Thought Final Report Called for Immediate Revision.

By RICHARD V. OULAHAN.

Special to The New York Times.

WASHINGTON, Jan. 20.—The conclusions of the National Commission on Law Observance and Enforcement, after a study of the prohibition problem extending over more than a year and a half, transmitted to Congress by President Hoover today in a general report and separate individual expressions by each of the eleven members show that a majority of the commission believes that the national attempt at prohibition enforcement has been a failure and that a change of policy is necessary.

Two commissioners advocate outright repeal of the Eighteenth Amendment. Five commissioners favor revision of the amendment so as to permit Congress to determine whether there shall be legalized sale of intoxicating beverages.

The remaining four commissioners think prohibition should have a further trial, although agreement is unanimous that "there is yet no adequate observance or enforcement."

Two of this last group favor a virtual national referendum through direct submission of the question of the repeal of the Eighteenth Amendment, should further trial demonstrate the failure of enforcement.

Hoover Comments in Message.

In his message transmitting the report and the individual statements to Congress, President Hoover takes issue with the commission in suggesting the form of a revision of the Eighteenth Amendment, should a proposal for revision be submitted to the States. After stating, as he expressed it, that "the commission by a large majority does not favor the repeal of the Eighteenth Amendment," and asserting that he is in according with that view, the President says:

"I do, however, see serious objections to, and therefore must not be understood as recommending the commission's proposed revision of the Eighteenth Amendment, which is suggested by them for possible consideration at some future time if the continued effort at enforcement should not prove successful. My own duty and that of all executive officials is clear, to enforce the law with all the means at our disposal without equivocation or reservation."

This comment of the President has reference to a statement in the report, signed by ten of the members, that "all the commissioners agree" that fi the amendment is revised it should be made to read substantially as follows:

"Section 1. The Congress shall have power to regulate or to prohibit the manufacture, traffic in or transportation of intoxicating liquor within, the importation thereof into and the exportation thereof from the United States and all territories subject to the jurisdiction thereof, for beverage purposes."

Question on Qualified Revision.

The personal views of at least three of the commissioners, appended to the general report of the Wickersham Commission, contained expressions indicating that these members believed that the report itself in final form proposed immediate revision of the Eighteenth Amendment.

The fact that the Conclusions and Recommendations of the report proposed a new wording for the constitutional dry clause with the qualification, "if the amendment is revised," raised the question as to just what these several individual commissioners thought the commission actually had decided on this point.

For example, Colonel Anderson in his individual report said he concurred "in the recommendation of

"All the News That's Fit to Print"

The New York Times.

Copyright, 1931, by The New York Times Company.

VOL. LXXX....No. 26,662. **** NEW YORK, FRIDAY, JANUARY 23, 1931. TWO CENTS In Greater New York | THREE CENTS Within 200 Miles | FOUR CENTS Elsewhere Ex. in 7th and 8th Postal Zones

THE WEATHER
Fair and warmer today; tomorrow fair.
Temperatures yesterday—Max. 27; min. 16.
U. S. Weather Forecast—For details see Page 31.

HOOVER APPEALS TO NATION ON RADIO TO AID RED CROSS; COOLIDGE, SMITH ADD PLEAS

PRESIDENT TELLS URGENCY

Holds There Can Be No Higher Duty Than to Feed the Hungry

COOLIDGE CALLS ON ALL

None Who Can Give Will Be Excused From Aiding Drought Sufferers, He Declares.

REAL DISASTER, SAYS SMITH

Red Cross's Biggest Task, Payne Asserts—Will Rogers and Mary Pickford Appeal.

President Hoover appealed last nigh to "the heart of the nation" for immediate relief for the destitute sufferers of the drought States. The situation there, he said constituted a calamity which called for a common effort to drive suffering and want from the country. His appeal was for the prompt subscription of the $10,000,000 fund that is needed by the Red Cross to carry on its work.

Mr. Hoover's talk was only one of several broadcast for an hour by the National Broadcasting Company over a nation-wide chain of stations. Former President Coolidge made his appeal from his home at Northampton, Mass.; former Governor Smith, Mrs. August Belmont and Mary Pickford spoke from New York. Judge John Barton Payne from Washington, Amos 'n Andy from Chicago, and Will Rogers, who is touring the country with Captain Frank Hawks in the interests of relief, gave his address from Little Rock, Ark.

All the speakers stressed the immediate need for relief. President Hoover's thought that "in the face of calamity let us unite in a common effort to drive suffering and want from our country," was expressed by Mr. Smith as "disaster to any one section of the country should be the concern of us all." This is a time, Miss Pickford said, when "the strong should aid the weak."

Mr. Coolidge felt the time was one when excuses could not take the place of money. "Every one knows trade is depressed, losses have been met and small incomes reduced," he said, but "the suffering for which this appeal is made is such that it comes down to a bare proposal in the name of humanity that those who have something shall share it with those who have nothing."

All the speakers praised the work of the Red Cross. It is to Mr. Hoover "a great voluntary organization * * * on whom the nation places reliance in time of need." Mr. Smith called it an "important arm of our national defense, functioning in time of peace as well as war." Mr. Coolidge referred to it as having a "record for achievement" and as deservedly holding "a high place in the public confidence." But it requires money.

Just before Mr. Rogers started his talk the announcer said that the comedian had just given a check for $5,000—half for the Arkansas quota from Mrs. Rogers; the other half for the Oklahoma quota from himself.

Four orchestras under the direction of Nathaniel Schildkret played selections during the hour and Mme. Freida Hempel sang "The Blue Danube." It was announced that Mme. Schumann-Heink would have been there but for an illness that confined her to her home.

THE PRESIDENT'S ADDRESS.

In his address President Hoover said:

"The American Red Cross is a great, voluntary organization, created by the people themselves, on whom the nation places reliance in time of need. For some months the Red Cross has been providing for those of our fellow-citizens who have suffered from the devastating effects of the long-extended drought.

"The area affected is roughly limited to the States bordering upon the Potomac, Ohio and Mississippi rivers, with limited acute areas in some Southwestern and Northwestern States. The people in this area lost a large part of their crops, and many thousands are even short of food supplies.

"The Red Cross now appeals for

Continued on Page Seventeen.

Legislator's 75-Word Bill Would Repeal Iowa Dry Law

Special to The New York Times.

DES MOINES, Iowa, Jan. 22.—A bill to repeal Iowa's prohibition law was filed today by Representative James N. Hayes, Democrat, of Dubuque County.

The measure contains seventy-five words and would strike out any reference in the Iowa code to the prohibition of intoxicating liquors.

"It is nothing short of ridiculous that Iowa courts must rule under the present laws," Mr. Hayes said, "that the sale of bay rum is illegal. The workings of the law which can interpret bay rum as an intoxicant capable of being used as a beverage are an abuse of individual rights and business privileges."

SALT LAKE CITY, Jan. 22 (AP).—Under the title, "Resolution Relating to Alleged Prohibition," Senator Patterson, Democrat, moved in the Legislature for the repeal of the State prohibition law. The matter was referred to a committee.

RECORD WET DRIVE REPELLED IN HOUSE

Anti-Prohibitionists Muster the Strongest Vote in Years but Lose by 78 to 98.

FAIL TO BAR DRY 'SPYING'

Stormy Debate Turns on Wickersham Report, With Both Sides Quoting It.

Special to The New York Times.

WASHINGTON, Jan. 22.—The anti-prohibition forces in the House mustered their greatest strength in years, in an attempt today to so limit the proposed Prohibition Bureau appropriation of $11,369,500 as to stop some enforcement practices condemned by the Wickersham Commission, but were trodden under foot time after time by the dry forces who refused to countenance any change.

The largest poll of the wets today was 78 votes, against 98 drys, for an amendment to halt tapping of telephone and telegraph wires by prohibition enforcement agents. By proportionate votes the wets also lost in attempts to halt the use of undercover agents and "stool-pigeons," the dissemination of dry publicity by the prohibition bureau and the establishment of government speakeasies to entrap violators and conspirators, purchases of liquor for evidence and obtaining of evidence against home-brew making. They likewise failed to withhold Federal funds from States which have no enforcement laws of their own.

Five of the nine women members of the House were among the seventy-eight that the wets mustered in the vote to prohibit the wire-tapping practices of dry agents. They were Mrs. Kahn of California, Mrs. Pratt of New York, Mrs. Rogers of Massachusetts, Mrs. Langley of Kentucky and Mrs. Norton of New Jersey, all Republicans except Mrs. Norton.

Today's showing in the House was the long-awaited, not to say advertised, performance of the wets who wanted this chance to demonstrate their strength.

Only three drys took part in the

Continued on Page Five.

HOOVER TO CLARIFY STAND ON REVISION, CAPITAL BELIEVES

View That He Rejected Only the Form of Proposed Dry Law Change Stirs Debate.

LONG DELAY HELD UNLIKELY

President Is Not Expected to Wait Until Convention if He Makes a Statement.

STILL LABELED "BONE DRY"

But Other Republican Leaders Join in Movement for a Modification Plank.

By RICHARD V. OULAHAN.

Special to The New York Times.

WASHINGTON, Jan. 22.—Amid heated discussion in the capital on the Wickersham report today the impression was gained that President Hoover might publicly clarify his position with respect to national prohibition.

With this impression went the understanding, however, that no determination had been reached by the President as to issuing a statement to the country, and the possibility existed that he might wait until the Republican National Convention of 1932 before explaining exactly the attitude he takes.

Practically all discussion today concerning the report centred around the President's attitude. The basis for these animated discussions was the overnight assertion that in his short message transmitting the report to Congress the President, contrary to the popular view, did not place himself squarely for the maintenance of our prohibition policy.

Not Likely to Wait Until 1932.

According to representations of the President's position, his message merely rejected the form of the revised amendment submitted by the commission and did not specifically declare opposition to revision in any form. The President, according to one version of his attitude, still has "an open mind" on ways of meeting the wet-dry problem.

That Mr. Hoover, once he has determined that a clarification of his views is necessary, would wait for a year and a half before letting the country know how he feels with respect to the renewed turmoil produced by the report of the Law Enforcement Commission is not accepted as probable.

It was pointed out that if the President is to define his prohibition views, he could not wait until the convention meets in June, 1932, without being subject to the accusation that he changed front on the eve of the convention. For that reason there is a feeling that a statement from the President is likely to appear within a comparatively short time should he once determine that a definition of his position is necessary.

Pending some illuminating declaration from the White House, there appears to be no likelihood that the discussion produced by the report, with its accompanying message from President Hoover, will die down. Developments today showed how keen the interest is in Congress and among politicians generally.

Debate in House and Senate.

There was an outburst of debate in the House and a brief flurry in the Senate, while wherever politicians gathered in groups it was apparent that the report had captured their imagination and had furnished food for discussion for a long time to come.

There was a field day of debate in the House, where the wets attempted to prohibit the use of public funds

Continued on Page Four.

Infantile Paralysis Serum Is Announced; Found by London Lister Institute Doctor

Special Cable to THE NEW YORK TIMES.

LONDON, Jan. 22.—The discovery of an inoculation for the prevention of infantile paralysis has been made in London by Dr. Weston Hurst of the Lister Institute of Preventive Medicine, it was announced today.

Described as an "epoch-making medical discovery," the finding of the inoculation was revealed by Dr. James Collier, lecturer on forensic medicine at St. George's Hospital, London. The virus of the disease was injected into a horse, Dr. Collier explained, and then it was found that by inoculating human beings with blood taken from the horse infantile paralysis could be averted.

"I cannot say how many human beings have been treated," said Dr. Collier. "The crux of the matter is this: Monkeys are more susceptible than humans to the disease and it has been proved conclusively that inoculation with the horse blood invariably protects monkeys, afterward given the disease, from both paralysis and death. The inference, therefore, is that humans will also enjoy this complete immunity."

The original horse upon which the experiments were performed is now receiving the best of pasturage and a profusion of oats at the farm for serum experiments, Dr. Collier added. The experimenters consider it one of the most valuable animals in the world.

Dr. Hurst, to whom the discovery is credited, is the author of several medical books. He took a medical degree at Birmingham University and is now a Fellow of the Royal Society of Medicine.

Port Board Votes to Rename Hudson Bridge; Bows to Protests on 'Washington Memorial'

Taking cognizance of popular objections the Board of Commissioners of the Port of New York Authority voted unanimously yesterday to reconsider its action in naming the new bridge over the Hudson the George Washington Memorial Bridge. Several other names have been suggested, but the commissioners are not committed to any.

The vote to reconsider was taken in executive session, outsiders who had attended the earlier part of the meeting being requested to leave. The name had been advanced two weeks ago by a committee of the commissioners made up of General George R. Dyer, chairman; George Keim and Howard S. Cullman. This committee was asked to reconsider the whole matter. Since General Dyer is now in Florida and probably will remain there a month or more, it was said that early action was unlikely.

"We have no desire to insist on a name that is not satisfactory to the public, or that might cause confusion," John F. Galvin, chairman of the Port Authority, said later. "In giving consideration and approval to the committee's recommendation, the board had been largely influenced, as was the committee, by the fact that the two approaches of the bridge are being erected on ground made historic by events intimately associated with Washington while he was Commander-in-Chief of the Continental Army; also by the further fact that the bridge will be opened to traffic during the bicentennial celebration of the birth of Washington.

"Supplementing the commission's own views, it was supported by the direct request of the George Washington Bicentennial Commission, requesting States, municipalities and other public bodies to take this occasion of naming bridges, highways and other public monuments after George Washington. The entire board as well as the committee believed that it had made a wise suggestion."

Commissioner Cullman said, "It certainly is the desire of the members of the committee that, should they deem it wise and proper to recommend another name in place of the George Washington Memorial Bridge, this name should be one that in every sense will be satisfactory to a majority of the citizens of the respective States and one that will eliminate any possible cause for confusion in the routing of traffic when the bridge is opened."

He invited individuals and organizations to submit more names.

ANNA PAVLOWA DIES AT HEIGHT OF FAME

Succumbs to Pleurisy at The Hague After an Illness of Only Three Days.

WORLD'S PREMIER DANCER

Operation Fails to Aid Her and Vaccine Comes Too Late—Husband at Bedside.

Special Cable to THE NEW YORK TIMES.

THE HAGUE, Friday, Jan. 23.—Mme. Anna Pavlowa, the greatest dancer of her time, died of pleurisy at the Hotel des Indes here at 12:30 this morning.

The end came despite every effort of two Dutch physicians and her own Russian doctor, Professor Valerski, to save her.

Yesterday an operation was performed to withdraw water from one of her lungs. At 10 o'clock last night her condition was extremely serious and as a last resort it was decided to administer Pasteur vaccine. It came too late, however, for she was already sinking and she died soon after midnight.

Ill for Three Days.

THE HAGUE, Friday, Jan. 23 (AP).—Mme. Anna Pavlowa, who died here early this morning after a three-day illness with influenza and pleurisy, was 45 years old and lacked only eight days of being 46, as her birthday was Jan. 31.

The dancer fell ill on Tuesday after she had come here on tour from Paris and at first it was believed that she merely was suffering from grip as the result of a slight cold contracted in Paris. Later the combination of pleurisy and influenza developed, which was complicated by a weakness of the heart.

With the dancer at the end was her husband and accompanist, Victor d'André, whom she married in 1924.

A Favorite for Twenty Years.

Anna Pavlowa was born in St. Petersburg, now Leningrad, Russia, on Jan. 31, 1885. Her rise to fame as one of Russia's leading ballerinas after a struggle against poverty, and later her world-wide triumphs, made her life story one of unusual interest.

During her sensational career as a dancer, dating back more than twenty years, after she had carried her classic art beyond Russia, she is said to have covered 350,000 miles in her tours and was spoken of as the most traveled of all modern artists. Her tours embraced the principal cities of the United States, Canada, Mexico, South America, South Africa, Europe and the Orient.

Proclaimed by her admirers as the greatest of living dancers, her appearance on the stage, whether in New York or Tokyo, was always made the occasion of a demonstration. The passage of time did not seem to dim the luster of her name or the exquisite technique of her dancing. She received ovations of the sort seldom accorded any one in the theatre and she enjoyed high recognition and honors from royalty.

Before the World War she danced before Emperor Franz Josef of Austria and Emperor Wilhelm. King Alfonso of Spain and the King and Queen of the Belgians were among other royal personages who paid her homage. During her first appear-

Continued on Page Sixteen.

STEEG OVERTHROWN BY WHEAT 'SCANDAL'

Loses by 10 Votes in French Chamber Over Leakage Causing Speculation on $2 Grain.

FOUR MENTIONED FOR POST

Laval Believed Most Likely Choice—Briand, Flandin and Maginot Possibilities.

By P. J. PHILIP.

Special Cable to THE NEW YORK TIMES.

PARIS, Jan. 22.—On a question of secondary importance politically, Théodore Steeg's Cabinet was defeated this evening in the Chamber of Deputies by 10 votes and resigned.

Since it was formed on Dec. 13 it always had been regarded as inevitable that the Cabinet would fall on some such minor point. Unfortunately for it, the question at issue was the worst that could have occurred at the present moment.

Victor Boret, Minister of Agriculture, stood accused directly in the press and indirectly in the Chamber of having encouraged speculation in wheat by a public announcement of his policy. It was shown that, while on Dec. 19, when the last Parliamentary session closed, wheat quoted at 166¾ francs a quintal, it rose in price and in the amount of business done each time the Minister of Agriculture gave some new indication of his intentions.

Defeated by 10 Votes.

In a political atmosphere which had been rendered completely abnormal by the Oustric affair, even a breath of scandal such as this was enough to damage any government. It was remarkable that the final vote on which the Cabinet fell was as high as 293 to 283.

Premier Steeg had two courses, either to throw over his Minister of Agriculture or to stand by him with the whole Cabinet. Unity was not obtained until after a severe internal fight. One Under Secretary, Léon Meyer, had already been threatening to resign, and this morning, when it was known that an interpellation on the agricultural policy of the government was planned, a hurried meeting of the Cabinet was summoned. It was apparently somewhat stormy. Premier Steeg, however, succeeded in persuading the Ministers that the Cabinet must stay united and take the risk of a vote.

The afternoon session of the Chamber had been already somewhat nervous, with a duel between Louis Germain-Martin, Minister of Finance, and his predecessor and former colleague, Paul Reynaud, over the manner of financing the project for national equipment. The atmosphere was fully charged with impatience and irritation.

About 7 o'clock Louis Buyat began his interpellation. He told the story which everybody knew of the coincidences between the various public statements and interviews made by Victor Boret in regard to his intentions and the rise in the price of wheat. His argument was that it was only the speculators and not the farmers who had benefited from the rise.

Boret Defends Policy.

M. Boret replied that such speculation as there had been had done no damage to the small growers.

Then Pierre Etienne Flandin, Minister of Commerce in André Tardieu's Cabinet, took the debate on-

Continued on Page Eleven.

EWALD BRIBE CASE ENDS IN DISMISSALS; BERTINI NOT INDICTED

Ex-Magistrate and Wife, Dr. Schirp, Tommaney and Healy Freed by Court.

VERDICT HELD IMPOSSIBLE

Three Disagreements Cited by McCook in Holding Further Trials Would Be Futile.

SPECIAL GRAND JURY QUITS

Finding of "No Bill" Against Bertini Finishes $100,000 Todd Inquiry—Cash Case Also Dropped.

The Ewald job-buying case was ended yesterday when Supreme Court Justice Philip J. McCook quashed all of the indictments which the special grand jury, in session since Sept. 15, had found, and at the same time the investigation into the appointment of General Sessions Judge Amedeo A. Bertini came to a close with a "no bill" from the grand jurors, who were discharged.

The dismissal of the indictments in the Ewald case was asked by Sydney A. Syme, defense counsel, and agreed to by Hiram C. Todd, special prosecutor, and Attorney General John J. Bennett Jr., under whose office the investigation was conducted.

Those named were George F. Ewald and his wife, Mrs. Bertha Ewald, Martin J. Healy, Tammany district leader, Thomas T. Tommaney, sheriff's clerk, and Dr. Francis M. Schirp of the Steuben Society. Ewald and his wife were charged with having paid $10,000 for the magistracy to which he was appointed on April 29, 1927, by Mayor Walker, and Healy and Tommaney were charged with having sold it.

Dr. Francis M. Schirp was charged with having sold the influence of the Steuben Society for $2,000—the Mayor testified that he appointed Ewald on the approval of the society. Another indictment charging Healy with practically the same offense in the case of Jacob Cash, city marshal, was also quashed.

Verdict Is Held Impossible.

In his opinion Justice McCook said that, in view of the circumstances and what had taken place, there probably could not be found in all New York City twelve qualified jurors who could agree on a verdict. Healy and Tommaney were tried twice with a jury disagreement each time, the Ewalds once with the same result. Mr. Syme pointed out in his motion that out of thirty-six jurors who had heard the evidence, substantially the same in each case, sixteen had voted for acquittal and twenty for conviction.

The combined dismissal of the indictments and discharge of the grand jurors brought to an end a four months' investigation which had taken up only one other matter, which was not revealed, and had cost about $100,000.

After the indictments had been dismissed, the grand jury foreman, Robert L. Morris, said: "The jury desires to report that it has completed its investigation of alleged violations of the elective franchise law in regard to Judge Bertini and has found no bill, and therefore requests that it be dismissed."

Justice McCook praised the efforts of the grand jury highly and also lauded the Citizens Union, which provided funds to the extent of about

Continued on Page Eighteen.

Fire Damages Sagamore Hill, Roosevelt Home; President's Widow Gives Alarm as Roof Burns

Special to The New York Times.

OYSTER BAY, L. I., Jan. 22.—Fire which originated in a defective chimney flue and spread rapidly on the roof threatened for a brief time to destroy Sagamore Hill, the famous home of the late President Theodore Roosevelt, three miles from here early this evening. The fire was discovered by a servant, and Mrs. Roosevelt, widow of the former President, telephoned the alarm. The flames were confined to the roof and did damage estimated at about $1,000.

Shortly after 8 o'clock Mrs. Roosevelt had finished her dinner and retired to the north living-room of the house—the famous room in which President Roosevelt conducted many of his important State conferences during his years in office. A fire was burning in the large open fireplace and she had sat down to read when one of the four servants in the house rushed in and told her that the roof was burning at the base of the living-room chimney.

Stepping to the telephone, Mrs. Roosevelt coolly called the Oyster Bay Fire Department. The eight pieces of apparatus of the Atlantic Steamer and Oyster Bay volunteer fire departments responded. Laboring up the long hill which leads to the house overlooking the Sound, the firemen prepared to battle a blaze which appeared to be serious, without any immediate supply of water.

Placing scaling ladders against the house, George Hawxhurst and Townsend Wasner, who were in command, mounted to the roof, and, using chemicals only, extinguished the blaze. Two 40-gallon tanks, the entire chemical supply of the departments, were exhausted.

Meanwhile, hundreds of persons in the vicinity, hearing the fire siren and learning that the house at Sagamore Hill was ablaze, hastened to the scene. Mrs Roosevelt, who never left the house, directed her servants to serve coffee and cakes to the firemen. When questioned about the fire later, she quietly remarked that "just a few shingles were burned off my roof."

DIRECTOR ADMITS HE LOST $250,000 BANK OF U. S. LOAN GAMBLING IN STOCK MARKET

Sunday Blue Law Threat Made Against British Newspapers

By The Associated Press.

MANCHESTER, England, Jan. 22.—England's blue law of 1677, which is under fire by certain elements seeking its repeal by enforcement, now may trouble the British press. Several large newspapers were notified today that the business of getting out their Monday morning editions involves working on Sunday, which is contrary to the provisions of the ancient law, and the editors were asked to answer the notices within a week.

The notifications were circulated by R. H. Cox, secretary of the Sunday Games and Freedom League, who recently had his brother admonished by a court for failing to observe Sunday by going to church, as prescribed by law.

R. H. Cox warned the newspaper publishers that his organization was prepared to order action by attorneys if the notices were answered unfavorably.

FIGHT ON NOMINEES RENEWED IN SENATE

Name of Meyer for Reserve Head Is Recommitted—Walsh Plans Power Board Suit.

WORLD BANK IN CHARGES

Brookhart Also Assails Meyer on Land Deals—Wagner and Glass Defend Him.

Special to The New York Times.

WASHINGTON, Jan. 22.—The struggle between the Senate and President Hoover over Presidential nominations to important Federal offices was renewed today when the Senate re-committed the nomination of Eugene Meyer Jr. as governor of the Federal Reserve Board to the Banking and Currency Committee and Senator Walsh of Montana moved to have the nominations of George Otis Smith, Marcel Garsaud and Claude L. Draper, Federal Power Commissioners, returned to the Interstate Commerce Committee.

The recall of Mr. Meyer's nomination followed charges by Senator Brookhart that although the Senator was a member of the Banking and Currency Committee, he was not permitted to question the nominee. Senator Norbeck, the committee chairman, asserted that Senator Brookhart had never made such a request, but Mr. Meyer's opponents insisted that he should be called for examination by Senator Brookhart, and his friends stated that he would welcome this opportunity.

Walsh Proposes Court Battle.

Offering a motion to re-commit the Power Commission nominations, Senator Walsh announced that if the Senate adopted this he would offer a resolution directing the District Attorney of the District of Columbia to start quo warranto proceedings to ascertain if the three commissioners were illegally holding office and pro-

Continued on Page Two.

KRESEL ASKS HEARING NOW

He Declares He Resents Statements 'Designed' to Reflect on Him.

BROWNSTONE GOT $625,000

Testifies He Borrowed With Only $3,000 in Deposits at Time of Speculations.

STEUER SEES DECEPTION

Charges Marcus Group Hid From Board $2,000,000 Impairment in Bank's Capital.

Isidor J. Kresel, attorney and director of the closed Bank of United States and special counsel in the Appellate Division's inquiry into magistrates' courts, addressed a letter yesterday to Attorney General Bennett requesting that he be examined immediately by Max D. Steuer in the latter's investigation of the affairs of the closed bank.

In his letter to Mr. Bennett Mr. Kresel resented by implication the methods used by Mr. Steuer in his examination of witnesses, saying. "I am not content to remain silent while at hearings conducted by your office through your special deputy in charge of this investigation baseless statements designed to reflect upon me are disseminated." Mr. Kresel rejected the "seeming courtesy" of being permitted to go on undisturbed with his own investigation in the face of these statements.

Mr. Kresel did not mention Mr. Steuer by name but declared that "indeed, I think it would be quite appropriate that he should be my inquisitor."

Mr. Steuer is performing a double rôle in the investigation as Assistant Attorney General and Assistant District Attorney. In the first capacity he is now conducting hearings under the Martin act at the office of the Attorney General, 80 Centre Street.

Kresel's Name Comes Up Again.

Mr. Kresel made public his letter to Mr. Bennett at the close of another day of testimony before Mr. Steuer in which Mr. Kresel was again mentioned several times among a group, including Bernard K. Marcus, president of the bank, who were alleged to have acted as the dictators of the institution while all other directors, according to the testimony and charges by Mr. Steuer, appeared to be mere rubber stamps.

The witnesses were Joseph C. Brownstone and David Tishman, directors of the bank. Mr. Brownstone was also a member of the bank's executive committee. He was the first member of the committee to appear before Mr. Steuer. Although a member of this committee, which, according to witnesses, was in charge of the bank's affairs, Mr. Brownstone, like Mr. Tishman and directors who have testified previously, admitted that he was ignorant of some of the bank's most important transactions, including millions in loans to affiliates of the bank, to corporations, to private individuals, and to directors of the bank.

Bank's Officers Accused.

Backed in large part by yesterday's witnesses Mr. Steuer charged that Mr. Marcus and the other officers of the bank concealed from the board of directors the fact that the bank's capital of $25,000,000 had been impaired to the extent of $2,000,000 at the time the bank made its last report to the State Banking Department, on Sept. 24, 1930. This was the same report in which the bank claimed $17,156,375 in surplus and undivided profits challenged as non-existent by examiners of the State Banking Department.

It was admitted in yesterday's testimony that the special, confidential reports submitted to the bank for its guidance by the banking department had been kept from the board of directors by Mr. Marcus and his fellow-officers for the past three years, that the directors had no knowledge of any security obtained by the bank on loans totaling $12,000,000 to three of its affiliates and were kept in the dark as to the real nature of the transaction by which the bank was alleged to have paid to itself a debt of $8,000,000, part of the $12,000,000, owing to it from two of these affiliates. This transaction was characterized by Mr. Steuer as an effort to deceive the State Banking Department on the eve of an audit

B. K. Marcus, Saul Singer and Herbert Singer (L to R) were charged with misuse of funds in the Bank of the United States case.

Isidor J. Kresel, a director and counsel of the Bank of the United States, was indicted in connection with the bank's failure. He was later exonerated.

Crowds formed outside the Bank of the United States when it closed on December 11, 1930.

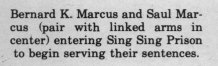

Bernard K. Marcus and Saul Marcus (pair with linked arms in center) entering Sing Sing Prison to begin serving their sentences.

"All the News That's Fit to Print."

The New York Times.

THE WEATHER
Cloudy and warmer today; tomorrow cloudy and slightly colder.
Temperatures yesterday—Max. 29, min. 16.
U. S. Weather Forecast—For details see Page 26.

Copyright, 1931, by The New York Times Company.

VOL. LXXX....No. 26,672. **** NEW YORK, MONDAY, FEBRUARY 2, 1931. TWO CENTS in Greater New York | THREE CENTS Within 200 Miles | FOUR CENTS Elsewhere Except 7th and 8th Postal Zones

GANDHI CHIEFS ORDER CIVIL DISOBEDIENCE TO CONTINUE IN INDIA

Congress Heads Warn People There Must Be No Let-Up During Peace Moves.

BUSINESS MEN SEEK TRUCE

Plan to Have Gandhi Meet London Delegates at Bombay Conference This Week.

MANIFESTO TO BE ISSUED

Party Returning From London to Tell People of India What They Bring From Round-Table Parley.

Special Cable to THE NEW YORK TIMES.

ALLAHABAD, India, Feb. 1.—Mahatma Gandhi and his all-India Congress party are determined that the civil disobedience campaign throughout India shall continue unabated. Regardless of peace talk and plans for a new conference in Bombay, the Congress leaders decreed today that civil disobedience must go on "until explicit instructions are issued to the contrary."

While 50,000 of his followers acclaimed Gandhi tonight in his first public address since his release from prison, the working committee of the Congress published a resolution laying down four terms as conditions for beginning peace negotiations.

The only terms the Congress will consider are: first, the granting of amnesty to all political prisoners; secondly, the withdrawal of all repressive measures; thirdly, permission to continue "peaceful picketing" of foreign cloth, drink and drug shops, and, fourthly, permission to make salt despite the probibitory law during the period of the peace negotiations.

Resolution Held Up.

The resolution including tnese terms was passed by the working committee last week and, although previously withheld at the request of the Round Table delegates, was published today to check rumors that civil disobedience had been called off. Gandhi had intended to make an important political pronouncement tonight at a mass meeting, but was prevented because of the breakdown of the loud speaker system. It was the first time loud speakers had been tried in Allahabad.

Barely able to make himself heard over the vast crowd, Gandhi merely thanked the men and women present for their great sacrifice in the cause of Indian independence. He reminded them of the cosmopolitan nature of their struggle and urged upon them the necessity of observing the strictest non-violence.

The committee reminded the public that the picketing of foreign cloth, liquor and narcotic shops was no part of the civil disobedience campaign but was "an exercise of the ordinary right of a citizen so long as he remains peaceful and causes no obstruction to the public."

The boycott of foreign cloth, the committee stated, was "a vital necessity in the interests of the masses and would remain a permanent feature of Nationalist activity until the nation acquired the power to exclude foreign cloth yarn from India, whether by total prohibition or by a prohibitive tariff.

Boycott of New Parley Likely.

ALLAHABAD, India, Feb. 1 (AP).—Mahatma Gandhi and his colleagues in the working committee of the All-India National Congress, who were released from prison last week to confer on Prime Minister Ramsay MacDonald's constitutional self-government for India, have voted unequivocally for continuance of their civil disobedience program.

It was clear from the decision of the working committee that, under existing conditions, the Congress will have nothing to do with a second round-table conference to be held in India, as envisaged by Premier MacDonald. It is even regarded as doubtful whether Gandhi and his associates will treat with the Indian delegates returning from the London round-table meeting unless the latter recognize the demands formulated by the working committee as a condition precedent to peace.

A number of the wealthy members of Federation of Indian Chambers of Commerce have been financing the Congress campaign out of patriotic motives, but it appears now that they are ready to call a halt. The civil disobedience activities have created such havoc with business throughout India, threatening even large firms with bankruptcy, that these men are said to feel that the time has come to take what England

Continued on Page Nine.

British Liquor Exports Cut By Tightening of Dry Patrol

Special Cable to THE NEW YORK TIMES.

LONDON, Feb. 1.—The tightening grip of American prohibition patrols caused a decline of 21 per cent in British exports of spirits to Canada and the West Indies during 1930, it was disclosed today.

During 1930 a total of 1,070,551 gallons of spirits went from Britain to Canada, as against 1,367,570 in 1929 and 1,749,304 in 1928. Exports to the British West Indies fell to 233,727 gallons, compared with 270,064 in 1929 and 281,865 two years ago. There was a total decline for all countries of 1,552,216 gallons below the 1929 figure.

"Some of this decline was temporary," says a report by George B. Wilson, secretary of the United Kingdom Alliance, "but part of the decline may be due to the strengthening of the prohibition cordon around the United States."

BONUS PLAN FOUGHT BY BANKING LEADERS

14 Bank Officials and Three Insurance Company Heads See Peril in Proposal.

FEAR ABSORPTION OF FUNDS

Investment Chiefs' Meeting Also Warns Public Works Might Be Hampered.

Fourteen prominent bankers and three presidents of life insurance companies, heading institutions scattered throughout the country, have expressed unanimous opposition to the proposal to make cash payments now on war veterans' adjusted compensation certificates in response to a request for their views sent out by the Security Owners Association of 21 East Fortieth Street.

The board of governors of the Investment Bankers of America also went on record yesterday as opposed to the proposal, at its annual midwinter meeting yesterday at the Seaview Country Club at Absecon, N. J.

It was the consensus of the bankers and insurance men that funding of the adjusted compensation certificates now would dry up all funds available for State, municipal and corporate financing for many months to come, and that this other financing bears directly on the employment of labor for public works and expansion of utilities and railroads.

For this reason, the bankers argued, business recovery would be retarded if a bonus were paid to former soldiers, and the depression would be unduly prolonged. At the same time, they asserted that security values would be destroyed by a financing operation of the calibre proposed.

The views of the fourteen bankers, as made public yesterday, were as follows:

Philip Stockton, president, First National Bank of Boston—The statement of Secretary Mellon in opposition to the proposed $3,000,000,000 veterans' bonus financing is so lucid and fundamentally sound that there is nothing to add. No one can read the Secretary's statement without being convinced that the proposed action would produce an economic situation in the country twice as bad as the one it purposes to relieve. It would be even more stupid than the old medical theory of bleeding an already weakened sick patient.

Samuel H. Beach, president, Rome (N. Y.) Savings Bank—If Congress should pass the proposed veterans' bonus financing measure, entailing a huge issue of government bonds, it will not only be a body blow to those who out of sheer patriotism bought Liberty bonds but it will so

Continued on Page Three.

2 FUGITIVE CONVICTS SLAIN BY POLICE HERE AFTER 50-MILE RACE

Sirico and Clark, Who Escaped From Eastview Christmas Eve, Shot in the Bronx.

IN A HOLD-UP IN BEACON

Surprised, They Flee in Auto Across Westchester Into Trap at 242d Street.

HAD $5,000 LOOT WITH THEM

A Confederate in Prison Break and Another Caught After Teletype Spreads the Alarm.

The career of Charles Sirico, to whom housebreaking was a business and jailbreaking a habit, ended abruptly yesterday at Broadway and 242d Street, where he fell at the end of a fifty-mile race for freedom with a bullet in his brain and the loot from his latest crime in his pockets.

In the same encounter with policemen in which Sirico was killed, Charles Clark, who escaped with him last Christmas eve from the Westchester County Penitentiary at Eastview, N. Y., was wounded so badly that he died soon afterward in Fordham Hospital, where he was identified by a picture of a Red Cross nurse tattooed on his back.

The bullets which ended the lives of Sirico and Clark and brought to an end their stolen holiday marked the end also of an automobile race for freedom over Westchester County roads after they had been surprised while helping themselves to the contents of the showcases in a Main Street jewelry shop in Beacon, N. Y.

Peter Reynolds, their confederate in the jail break of a month ago—only the repetition of an old act for Sirico, who had a record of four escapes—was their companion also in the latest robbery but he was caught before the shooting began. He was caught when the robbers, racing to escape the net they knew was spread for them, ditched their car on the Saw Mill River Parkway near Caryl Avenue, in Yonkers.

Engaged in Hi-jacking.

The criminals who had been hi-jacking liquor caravans and robbing stores in Westchester since their escape had enlisted the aid of a recruit whom they had met in a speakeasy behind the gas houses on the lower east side for their "little job" in Beacon. They left him on the sidewalk, where he had been posted as "lookout," and he fell captive to two Beacon policemen without sharing in any of the spectacular events that followed. He gave his name as John Creedon and his address as the Times Square Hotel.

Roaring away from in front of Abraham Caplan's jewelry store at 562 Main Street, Beacon, in a stolen automobile with conflicting license plates fore and aft, Sirico, Clark and Reynolds headed down the Albany Post Road toward New York. With them they took more than $5,000 worth of jewelry. Policemen George Van Pelt and Joseph Dardis, with Creedon, their prisoner, hustled back to headquarters and broadcast the alarm by means of the teletype system to all the towns in Westchester County and to police headquarters in the Bronx.

Sirico had removed his shoes, had not had time to put them on again, and Dardis caught a glimpse of the red socks and light green suit he was wearing. Clark was garbed in a blue suit of rather a striking shade so that despite the misleading license markers the matter of describing the

Continued on Page Five.

Moslem Cooks Beef, Causing Riot in India; Town Set Afire, Sikh Officer Burned Alive

By The Associated Press.

RAWALPINDI, India, Feb. 1.—A Moslem teacher in a boarding house today cooked a tasty meal of beef and thereby started a wild communal riot in a village forty miles from here.

To the Moslems a cow is simply something to be eaten, but to the Hindus it is a sacred animal and one for which they will fight.

When neighboring Hindus and Sikhs learned that the teacher was cooking beef they reprimanded him, whereupon he summoned Moslems from adjoining villages to his aid. His call was answered by several hundred infuriated Moslems, who looted the village, set fire to fifteen shops and threw all the beef they could find into the Hindu temple.

This stirred terrific fighting, which ended with the burning alive of a Sikh jamadar, or native officer, and severe injuries to many others. The trouble was not quelled until a deputy commissioner and a police superintendent took a large force into the village.

The slaughtering of cows always had been a source of trouble between Moslems on one hand and Hindus and Sikhs on the other, and was regarded even by the recent round-table conference as one of the most serious obstacles in solving the delicate communal question.

In some respects today's fight recalled the famous Indian army mutiny of 1857. This occurred after the British had introduced an improved rifle which required the use of greased cartridges. Reports spread among the native soldiers that the cartridges had been greased with beef fat, and for two months numerous regiments mutinied in at least twenty-one garrison points, killing hundreds of Europeans, including women and children.

Bills Drafted at Albany to Bar Judges From Business and Political Activities

Special to The New York Times.

ALBANY, Feb. 1.—Magistrates and judges of inferior criminal courts would be prohibited from serving as officers or directors or engaging in the business of corporations, under the terms of bills prepared by the Citizens Union, which will be introduced in the Legislature tomorrow by Senator Hofstadter and Assemblyman Moffat, both of New York City.

The bills also would extend to such judges the present prohibition against magistrates being members of political committees, through amendments to the judiciary law and the New York City inferior criminal courts act. The prohibition against connection with corporations will not extend to membership in charitable, benevolent, religious or educational corporations.

Declaring that the difficulties in which many judges had become involved could be traced "to attempts to engage in some form of outside business activity," Robert E. McGahen, secretary of the Citizens Union, in explaining the purpose of the bills, added:

"Mancuso was a pitiable figurehead as chairman of the board of the ill-fated City Trust Company. Vause tried to enhance his fortunes through the medium of finance corporations. Magistrate Ewald appears to have specialized in mining stock. Magistrate McQuade tried to mix professional baseball promotion with judicial duties.

"Even if these men had possessed every element of equipment for judicial work, how could they have hoped to 'devote their whole time and capacity' to their public duties while harassed by the worries of their private enterprises?

"Furthermore, some of our most upright and capable judges are besieged constantly with demands that they lend their names and the prestige of their positions to financial and business enterprises, launched under impressive auspices. They dislike to refuse cooperation. But when they consent, embarrassment frequently follows. The insertion in the law of the provisions now proposed, would therefore be of immense benefit to those judges who possess a high sense of duty and public obligation. At the same time it would facilitate the elimination of those defiant of ethical standards."

Mr. McGahen recalled that Governor Roosevelt in his annual message recommended legislation prohibiting judges from serving as officers or directors in any banking or business corporation. He said that the Hofstadter-Moffat bills went a little further but were none the less essential.

FAMILY COURT CASES TO BE INVESTIGATED

Seabury Inquiry Is Said to Be Aimed at the Staff Rather Than at Brodsky.

EILPERIN HEARING TODAY

McQuade Faced Questioning on Former Interest in Havana Gambling Concession.

With at least one public hearing scheduled for this week in the Appellate Division inquiry into the lower courts, it was learned yesterday that Referee Samuel Seabury plans to investigate conditions in Family Court, where Magistrate Louis B. Brodsky often sat.

The evidence to be presented in the next public hearing has already been prepared, and Joseph Wolfman, Sing Sing convict and former unlicensed attorney who practiced in the magistrates' courts, will tell a story of widespread fixing of felony cases for criminals with records.

Meanwhile the conduct of cases in the Family Court will be examined privately. Magistrate Brodsky, who for the past two years devoted practically all of his time to that court, was exonerated last Friday by the Appellate Division on charges made by Mr. Seabury that his business activities while a magistrate warranted his removal.

While the Family Court inquiry was said not to be specifically concerned with Magistrate Brodsky, but rather with the entire court, clerks, attendants and other attachés, it was learned that if any evidence relating to Magistrate Brodsky is found his case may be reopened.

Eilperin Hearing Today.

Magistrate Jacob Eilperin will have a hearing today before official Refcrée James C. Van Sicien in the Brooklyn Municipal Building on charges preferred by Charles Somers, Brooklyn coal dealer, that Eilperin engaged in private commercial ventures while holding a judicial position.

While the evidence concerning Francis X. McQuade, George W. Simpson and Henry M. R. Goodman, the magistrates who resigned rather than face public hearings, will be included in the final report of the inquiry when it is finished, it was learned yesterday that one of the items which Mr. McQuade would have been asked to explain had there been a hearing in his case was his ownership of an interest in a Havana gambling concession.

Mr. McQuade said yesterday that he, with John McGraw, had owned a 10 per cent interest in a Havana race track concession, but said he had disposed of his part in it some seven or eight years ago. He said that he owned no other such interests at present.

Mr. McQuade was first appointed by Mayor Gaynor in 1912 and reappointed by Mayor Hylan in 1921. It was explained that his interest in the concession, due to the fact that gambling in Cuba is legalized, would have constituted no particular breach but would have involved only the question of the propriety of such a holding.

The public hearing which had been tentatively scheduled for Tuesday may be postponed, it was said, by the appearance before Max D. Steuer in the Bank of United States hearings of Isidor J. Kresel, special

Continued on Page Four.

25 BIG EMPLOYERS ASSURE STEADY JOBS

Standard Oil of New Jersey and Bethlehem Steel Join in Pledge to Workers.

AGREE TO MAINTAIN WAGES

Corporation Heads Declare Retaining Employes Leads to Trade Recovery.

Twenty-five additional corporations, with an aggregate of several hundred thousand employes, contemplate no reduction in working forces and have so informed the Welfare Council Coordinating Committee on Unemployment, the committee announced yesterday.

The chief industrial concerns listed were the Standard Oil Company of New Jersey and the Bethlehem Steel Corporation. Similar assurances from the Consolidated Gas Company, the Metropolitan Life Insurance Company and the McCall Publishing Company had been announced previously by the committee.

The committee's announcement yesterday named fifteen of the companies and declared that ten more had given their assurance, but preferred not to be named. The fifteen named are as follows:

Standard Oil Company of New Jersey.
Bethlehem Steel Company.
Travelers Insurance Companies.
Equitable Life Assurance Society.
American Surety Company.
New York Casualty Company.
Guardian Life Insurance Company.
Bank for Savings.
Seamen's Bank for Savings.
Hamlin & Co.
D. Appleton & Co.
Allied Die-Casting Corporation.
New York Life Insurance Company.
Home Life Insurance Company.
American Fence Construction Company.

Give Assurance of Steady Work.

Parts of the letters in which twelve of the companies embodied their pledge to maintain their working forces were made public by the coordinating committee. They read:

Bethlehem Steel Company—An outstanding achievement in industrial history was recorded by Bethlehem in 1930 in the theroughness with which it took care of its employes. The management declared at the beginning of the business recession that it would maintain the wage scale and protect the job of the employe. In a period when unemployment in general was widespread we have maintained our payroll force and through part-time operations given our regular employes an opportunity to work.

Equitable Life Assurance Society of the United States—There has been no reduction in the number or the scale of compensation of the society's employes, nor is such reduction contemplated. On the contrary there have been normal increases in numbers during the past year and further increases in numbers are expected.

American Surety Company and New York Casualty Company—During this period of depression our personnel has not been reduced. In fact we have taken the opportunity to strengthen it. It is difficult to give any definite assurance on this subject as to the future, but as far as possible we intend to adhere to our present policy.

Guardian Life Insurance Company of America—We do not contemplate any reduction in the working

Continued on Page Two.

RELIEF COMPROMISE PROPOSED BY BORAH; DEMOCRATS DEAF

He Suggests $15,000,000 Be Allotted for Use Solely in Drought States.

HOPES FOR PACT DWINDLE

But Leaders, Seeking to Avert Extra Session, Still Try to Adjust Differences.

TILSON WILL NOT RECEDE

Says $25,000,000 Federal "Dole" Would Destroy Red Cross—Debate Goes On Today.

Special to The New York Times.

WASHINGTON, Feb. 1.—Informal discussion over the week-end among leaders of both parties in Congress, anxious to avoid an extra session failed to find a basis for a satisfactory compromise on the $25,000,000 drought and unemployment relief appropriation appended to the Interior Department supply bill by the Senate, where Democrats and insurgent Republicans are demanding its passage by the House under threat of forcing an extra session.

A proposal offered by Senator Borah was that the Democrats abandon their demand for $25,000,000 and agree to an appropriation of $15,000,000 to be used solely in the drought States. Republican leaders in the Senate reported today that this suggestion had not been favorably received by the Democrats but they have not given up hope that it finally may be made the basis of an agreement acceptable to both sides.

While Representative Tilson, Republican leader in the House, insisted today that the administration forces were adamant against a compromise in any form, those who are hoping some Democratic Senators will recede from their ultimatum, while not so confident as they have been, still cling to the belief that because of the force of public sentiment and reported dissension in the Democratic councils over an extra session a common ground of agreement will be found.

Look to Borah for Aid.

Regular Republican Senators are sanguine that Senator Borah will enter the debate in the Senate tomorrow and win over a sufficient number of Democrats to his program to give the administration a majority against the $25,000,000 appropriation. Some Republicans believe the Democrats are more interested in adequate appropriations for the drought areas than in Senator Robinson's proposal, which would include the unemployed in cities among those to receive aid.

Senator Robinson declined tonight to discuss the situation except to say that the Democratic program would be the subject of further party conferences and that he would carry his fight to the Senate floor tomorrow or later in the week.

In his statement Representative Tilson said:

"In all matters of legislation where no question of principle is involved compromise is not only customary, it is oftentimes necessary. But in connection with the proposed $25,000,000 dole there is no proper place for compromise. The amount of money involved in the initial appropriation is of relatively minor importance. Once the door to the Federal Treasury for a dole to aid citizens in distress is opened, the appropriation used as the opening wedge, whatever its magnitude, will soon pale into insignificance in the wake of what will follow.

"Once the Red Cross is destroyed,

Continued on Page Two.

Six Skaters Rescued, One Lost Under Ice; Ladders Used to Save Victims in Jamaica Lake

One man is believed to have been drowned when ice gave way in Baisley Park lake in Jamaica yesterday afternoon, throwing six persons into the water. Firemen and the police were grappling for the body last night, and a cap found floating on the surface was tentatively identified as having been worn by Casper Meyer, 23 years old, a draftsman, living at 25-77 Madison Street, Ridgewood.

The spot where the accident occurred is in the neighborhood of 153d Street and 123d Avenue. The ice there has been thick enough for skating for several days, although danger signs had been posted not far from it. At 5 o'clock, several hundred persons were skating, and when the ice gave way six of them were shot into the water.

The noise of the breaking ice and the victims' cries for help attracted a crowd of skaters, who clustered near the edge until park employes warned them back. The half dozen were trying to clamber back on the crumpling edges of ice, but were dropped back again as other small pieces chipped off. Their number was increased by George Conway, a city fireman living at 115-21 198th Street, who jumped in with his skates on to aid the rescue work.

Park officials brought ladders kept for emergencies, and laid them flat on the ice to enable the victims to climb to safety. Conway, who had been helping Edward Eckard, 21, of 113-10 Ninety-fifth Avenue, Jamaica, was the last out. It was then found that in the plunge he had dislocated his right shoulder, so an ambulance took him and Eckard to the Jamaica Hospital for treatment.

Firemen of Engine Company 302, Jamaica, and the men of the police emergency squad from the Richmond Hill Station began grappling for the body of the drowned man.

$75,000,000 IN BANK OF U. S. LOST, IN DOUBT OR 'FROZEN'; BRODERICK FILES INVENTORY

How Bank's Resources Are Apparently Impaired

Following are principal items of the resources of the Bank of United States regarded as impaired. The round figure has been placed at $75,000,000. It may be slightly more or slightly less.

Loans to affiliates....	$24,726,381.00
Frozen mortgages and building loans......	17,103,945.43
Questionable loans....	13,000,000.00
Surplus and undivided profits, wiped out...	17,000,000.00
Property and prepaid expenses, believed to be affected by liquidation	6,735,810.71
Total	$78,566,587.14

BANK'S OWN FIGURES USED BY BRODERICK

Inventory Fails to Show Official Findings or, What Has Been Done Since He Took Charge.

CONDITION STILL IN DOUBT

State Commissioner Known to Be Making Appraisal of Realty Holdings.

Publication by the State Banking Department of the inventory of assets of the closed Bank of United States, it was declared yesterday, may prove a disappointment to the more than 400,000 depositors of the bank, because of the failure of Joseph A. Broderick, Superintendent of Banking, to include in the inventory a complete statement of the real value of the bank's assets and such other valuations as might cast light upon the actual condition of the institution.

The hundreds of thousands of depositors had been looking forward to a complete report by the Banking Department on what actually happened to the bank, what the present valuation of its resources may be and what the depositors may be expected to get after liquidation.

The inventory made public by the Banking Department is only an accounting based on the bank's books, presenting the bank's own estimate of its resources and giving no idea as to what these resources actually represent. There is no official statement of liabilities accompanying the statement of resources. The statement of liabilities obtained from another source, while pronounced authoritative, remains a doubtful element in the picture and, while balancing with the inventory's total of assets, gives no clue to the actual condition of the bank on the day it was closed or its condition today, after seven weeks of liquidation.

Broderick Absent Two Weeks.

Mr. Broderick has been absent from his office more than a fortnight, due to illness, it is said, and subordinates in the Banking Department have let it be known that because of developments during the last month and the consequent changes in the condition of the bank Mr. Broderick has deemed it advisable to withhold the information desired until his appearance on the stand in the investigation of the bank's affairs now being conducted by Max D. Steuer. What the changes

Continued on Page Ten.

MANY UNSECURED LOANS

Some Were Made to Judges, Other Public Men and to Bank's Directors.

THIRD OF ASSETS INVOLVED

No Official Estimate Is Given of Probable Return to 400,000 Depositors.

NO COMMENT BY BRODERICK

Expected to Reveal Findings in Steuer Inquiry—Marcus and Kresel Called Today.

Loss, impairment or "freezing" of about $75,000,000, or nearly a third of its assets, compelled the closing of the Bank of United States, it was shown yesterday with the publication by the State Banking Department of an inventory of the bank's resources as of Dec. 10, 1930. The bank was closed Dec. 11.

The largest items of loss revealed through the inventory are loans to affiliates totaling $24,726,381, the wiping out of more than $17,000,000 in surplus and undivided profits and some $13,000,000 in weak and questionable loans. With the exception of a small part, the loans to affiliates are regarded as lost. Only the future can tell how many of the bad loans will be collected, bank examiners declared.

The inventory also sets forth that $17,103,945.43 of the bank's resources is tied up in "frozen" and "slow" mortgages and building loans.

Actual Values Uncertain.

Banking Department officials pointed out that only after the liquidation would it be possible to determine accurately the actual values on the bank's books. A factor determining the ultimate return to depositors will be the expenses of the liquidation itself.

According to the inventory, well over 50 per cent of the bank's deposits were thrift accounts.

The inventory, covering 1,000 pages, which is to be filed this morning with the County Clerk's office, gives the resources of the bank as $237,863,937.57. These are listed in detail. No list of liabilities was appended but a detailed statement obtained from another source and confirmed as authoritative showed the total liabilities corresponding with the assets.

The figure of $75,000,000 covering impairment, in one way or another, of the bank's assets was obtained from a study of the inventory and comments thereon by examiners for the State Banking Department.

The difference between the impairment of the bank's assets and its total resources as they appear in the inventory is $162,863,937, or about $3,000,000 in excess of the $160,000,000 of the bank's deposits. This would seem to indicate that the depositors would be able to receive 100 cents on the dollar, it was pointed out, but this apparent conclusion is vitiated by the large expense of liquidation expected, as well as other losses.

The probable loss to the stockholders of the bank, which had a capitalization of $25,000,000, will also be more than the $3,000,000 figure constituting the difference between the amount of resources apparently intact and the amount of the deposits, since costs of liquidation are expected to reduce considerably the assets left for distribution.

The inventory itself was almost entirely devoid of comment or conclusions. These, it is understood, are being reserved by Joseph A. Broderick, State Superintendent of Banks, under whose authority the inventory was made public, for his testimony before Max D. Steuer, who is directing the dual State and county investigation of the bank's affairs. It is not known when Mr. Broderick may be called to testify before Mr. Steuer, who will resume his hearings as Assistant Attorney General this morning.

The witnesses scheduled to appear before Mr. Steuer today are Bernard K. Marcus, president of the bank; Saul Singer, executive vice president; Isidor J. Kresel, counsel and director of the bank and special counsel in the Appellate Division's inquiry into magistrates' courts; C. Stanley Mitchell, chairman of the bank's board of directors, and Jo-

Continued on Page Ten.

"All the News That's Fit to Print."

The New York Times.

THE WEATHER
Fair and slightly warmer today; tomorrow cloudy and warmer.
Temperatures yesterday—Max. 25, min. 25.
U. S. Weather Forecast—For details see Page 24.

VOL. LXXX....No. 26,681. ***** NEW YORK, WEDNESDAY, FEBRUARY 11, 1931. TWO CENTS In Greater New York | THREE CENTS Within 200 Miles | FOUR CENTS Elsewhere Except 7th and 8th Postal Zones

KRESEL, INDICTED WITH 7 IN BANK OF U. S., QUITS AS PROSECUTOR IN COURT INQUIRY; STEUER HALTED; BANK RECORDS BURNED

REICHSTAG FASCISTS WALK OUT AND PLAN WEIMAR PARLIAMENT

Nationalists Join Them, Vowing They Will Return Only to Defend Their Rights.

REFUSE TO HEAR CURTIUS

Foreign Minister Says Nation Has Only Promised to "Try" to Adhere to Young Plan.

OPPOSES QUITTING LEAGUE

Denies German War Guilt and Sees Relations With France About to Improve.

Rump Parliament Planned

By The Associated Press.

BERLIN, Feb. 10.—A threat of an Opposition Parliament was heard in Germany tonight.

After Fascists and Nationalists had walked out of the Reichstag, declaring they would not return until something important demanded their presence, a Fascist spokesman said tonight that his party might call an Opposition sitting at Weimar.

It was at Weimar that the Constitution for the German Republic was written.

Special Cable to THE NEW YORK TIMES.

BERLIN, Feb. 10.—Only a skeleton Parliament was on hand in the Reichstag this afternoon to hear Foreign Minister Curtius deliver his long-awaited address on foreign policy. The Reichstag's decision late last night to reform the House rules and curtail obstructionism bore quick fruit today when the National Socialists (Fascists) and German Nationalists left the hall in closed formation, one after the other, a few minutes after the session opened and before Dr. Curtius could reach the Speaker's platform.

The action of the Right Wing extremists was a protest at what they term "a violation of the rights of the minority." In reality, the changes in the rules were designed to prevent flagrant obstructionism and irresponsibility as practiced for eleven hours yesterday before a weary House could adopt the changes.

Nationalists Define Stand.

The Nationalists confined themselves to declaring that they would not participate in the foreign-policy debate. The Hugenberg newspapers this afternoon promptly supported the party's action by announcing that they would not print a single word about the debate.

The National Socialists, however, went further, saying they would not have anything further to do with this "tribute to the Reichstag" until or unless an opportunity should present itself again to defend the minority against the encroachments of the majority. This may be interpreted to mean that the Hitler cohorts will remain absent for weeks or even months, or it may equally well serve as an excuse for the party's reappearance tomorrow.

However, Franz Stoehr, "Nazi" (Fascist), Vice President of the Chamber, resigned his office, and the two "Nazi" members of the Steering Committee also gave up their offices, which may be taken to indicate that the Hitlerites mean business.

While many are laughing at the Nazi" answer to yesterday's reforms, terming it "sulking," others, recalling the various Hitler declarations that he would try to reach his goal "by legal means," wonder what the "Nazis" will turn to next to get a hearing on their demands. There is some anxiety over this prospect, intermixed with mirth. At present the Communists are the only real opposition party in the House.

Curtius Reports on Geneva.

Dr. Curtius, in a speech lasting more than an hour, opened the floor to a discussion of the policy Germany has been pursuing and intends to continue to pursue in its foreign relations. After reporting fully on the last Council meeting at Geneva, Dr. Curtius took up Franco-German relations, the plan for a European union, the coming disarmament conference, the Polish question, the East Africa question, war guilt, reparations, the "leave-the-League" movement and the economic crisis.

The Franco-German relations he termed the key to most European problems and expressed a willingness to cooperate with France on as many questions as possible.

"I hope the recent aggravated relations with our western neighbor will soon be much better," he said. "The vast majority of Germans are

Continued on Page Thirteen.

Hoover Gives Tenth of Salary To Red Cross Drought Fund

Special to The New York Times.

WASHINGTON, Feb. 10.—A contribution from President Hoover of $7,500, or 10 per cent of his annual salary of $75,000, toward the Red Cross $10,000,000 drought relief fund, was announced by Chairman John Barton Payne today. With the receipt of the President's contribution, total subscriptions to the fund reached $7,313,116.

A registered package containing over 200 individual checks totaling $4,111.50 was received by Judge Payne from Grand Master Charles H. Johnson of the Grand Lodge of Masons of the State of New York, the "first instalment" of contributions from the lodge and officers of the Grand Lodge to the drought fund.

STOCKS GO HIGHER; PUBLIC BUYING AGAIN

Spirited Swing Upward Brings New Advances in Grains, Cotton and Silver.

STEEL HEARTENS WALL ST.

Brokers Expanding Staffs—4,762,725 Shares Dealt In—Wheat Up Sharply at Chicago.

Another runaway market developed yesterday on the New York Stock Exchange, with the public and Wall Street professionals joining hands for the first time in a year in an enthusiastic buying demonstration which lifted the main body of stocks 2 to 6 points and sensitive specialties 7 to 14 points.

The marekt was violent at times, reminding happy brokers of the excited speculation which preceded the collapse in the Autumn of 1929. Yesterday's trading totaled 4,762,725 shares, the heaviest since Dec. 17, but at times the turnover was at a rate of 7,000,000 shares a day. The pace was swiftest between 1 and 2 o'clock, when buying orders came in such volume as to swamp the brokerage personnel.

As on the day before, grains, cotton and bonds advanced with stocks, while silver, which had duplicated its historic low on Monday, rose spiritedly yesterday, adding ¾ cent an ounce to its market value here. Copper also firmed up yesterday, the domestic price advancing ¼ cent, while reports pointed to the possibility of another increase shortly.

Wheat Advances at Chicago.

Wheat advanced to the highest prices in the last two months at Chicago. On heavy buying, ascribed to foreign interests, the new crop deliveries were lifted 3⅝ to 4 cents a bushel, but lost part of the gain later in the day, and closed from 2 to 3⅛ cents higher. The July delivery, after advancing to 72⅝ cents, the highest price since Dec. 12, closed at 71½ cents for a net gain of 2⅛ cents. At Winnipeg, the closing prices were from 2¼ to 2⅝ cents higher for the day. Heavy foreign buying and liberal purchases by Chicago interests were reported in the Canadian market.

The wheat market, as well as the Stock Exchange, was stirred by groundless rumors that a revolution had broken out in Russia. These rumors, which Moscow, London, Berlin and other European capitals later reported to be without foundation, was said to have been one cause of the demoralization which appeared yesterday among the bears.

General List Rises.

The general list on the Stock Exchange went into new high ground for the year. The fifty stocks upon which the combined averages of THE NEW YORK TIMES are based showed a net gain of $3.17, twenty-five industrials a gain of $4.47 and twenty-five rails a gain of $1.86. About 275 issues established new highs for 1931 and the total number of separate issues dealt in was 824.

Sharp gains were scattered throughout the list when trading ended, but the most striking advances were in about twenty-five issues upon which speculative interest centred. United States Steel, after touching a high of 147¼, closed at 146, with a net gain of 3 points. Auburn Auto, which ran up and down the scale sensationally, showed a net gain of 14 points, closing at 188½. Its low for the day was 178¼ and its high 191¼. The short interest in this stock was further embarrassed and there was talk again of a technical corner. It was rumored also that the Business Conduct Committee of the Stock Exchange was inquiring particularly into the market action of this stock.

Among the other wide advances were: J. I. Case, 13⅛ points; Allied Chemical, 2¾; Lackawanna, 4¼; Erie, 3⅛; Industrial Rayon, 7½; International Cement, 4¼; National

Continued on Page Nineteen.

EMBARGO ORDERED ON RUSSIAN LUMBER AND PULP BY MELLON

Secretary Requires Importers to Prove Production by Free Labor Before Entry.

HOUSE PLANS DRASTIC ACT

Committee Approves Tariff Amendment Aimed at All Products of Forced Labor.

REDS INVADE THE CONGRESS

Four Ejected From Gallery of the House After Delegation Leaves Petition for Speaker.

Special to The New York Times.

WASHINGTON, Feb. 10.—Holding that convict labor is used in the production of lumber and pulpwood in four districts of the White Sea in Northern Russia, the Treasury Department placed an embargo on both products today.

Secretary Mellon announced the "finding" on evidence presented to the department.

The treasury decision places the burden of proof on the importer of these products to show that they are not produced by convict labor. In effect, the ruling bars importations of lumber and pulpwood unless the importer is able to prove that only free labor has entered into their production, loading and transportation.

The districts involved in the finding were given as follows:

The Kola peninsula, including the Murman coast, north of the White Sea; the Karelian, Northern and Zyryan autonomous areas. This takes in all of European Russia north of the sixtieth degree of latitude.

Officials anticipated a test of the decision in the Federal courts. Importers of Soviet lumber and pulpwood and consumers in this country are expected to enter an appeal assailing the authority of the Treasury Department to require importers to prove the use of free labor.

The burden of proof would then be transferred back to the treasury to establish the use of convict labor, unless the courts should dismiss the cases on the ground that, under the tariff law, the treasury is empowered to require proof that legal goods are being offered for import.

Proof Shifted to Importer.

The decision, signed by Customs Commissioner F. X. A. Eble and approved by Secretary Mellon, concluded:

"Therefore, on and after the date of the publication of this finding, Collectors of Customs will require compliance with the regulations published as Treasury decision 44385 upon the importation of lumber or pulpwood originating in the localities specified above, or articles manufactured or produced in other localities from such lumber or pulpwood."

Treasury decision 44385 establishes the regulations shifting the burden of proof to the importer to show that imports are not produced by convict labor.

Officials said that no important shipments of lumber or pulpwood from the Russian districts are expected until late in the Spring or early Summer. Throughout the areas named, including the Archangel district at the mouth of the Dvina River on the White Sea, the lumber is cut during the Winter and cannot be moved out by water until the Spring thaw.

The lumber and pulpwood finding ends a fight of over a year by the National Lumber Manufacturers' Association and affiliated industries for an embargo on Soviet lumber and pulpwood.

Against the lumber industry consumers of lumber and paper manufacturers were arrayed, including the International Paper Company. The paper makers asserted that they were dependent for raw material on the Russian woodpulp. They contended that imports of Soviet woodpulp would not diminish the consumption of the American product, but would reduce imports from Canada.

Manganese Case Is Pending.

The treasury decision leaves only the manganese case pending against Russian imports. An anti-dumping order has been sought by the American Manganese Producers Association, but Assistant Secretary Lowman, in a Congressional hearing, indicated that there would be no embargo against manganese.

The Iron and Steel Institute opposed the anti-dumping order on manganese, declaring that the steel manufacturers were dependent upon the Russian ore since the American output was insufficient to meet the demand.

Pennsylvania anthracite operators

Continued on Page Three.

Albany Bill Asks Red Plates On Reckless Drivers' Autos

Special to The New York Times.

ALBANY, Feb. 10.—Motorists convicted of reckless driving would be compelled to carry red plates on their cars containing the letters "R. D." signifying that they are reckless drivers, under the terms of a bill introduced in the Legislature today by Assemblyman Roy Hewitt or Niagara.

These plates would cost reckless drivers $1 each and they would be compelled to carry them on their cars so long as the Motor Vehicle Commissioner or the court might direct.

"I believe that if the State would tag the reckless drivers it would be a step toward reducing deaths by automobiles," Assemblyman Hewitt said. "If the reckless driver was compelled to carry a sign on his car it would give every one an opportunity to watch their step when they came up with such a fellow on the road."

NAVY BILL PASSAGE URGED BY HOOVER

Senators Get Word He Favors Enactment of $74,000,000 Building Measure Now.

"TREATY LIMIT" PLAN HIT

French, in House Debate With Britten, Says Cost in 6 Years May Reach $1,000,000,000.

Special to The New York Times.

WASHINGTON, Feb. 10.—The belief among administration Senators that President Hoover desires passage of the $74,000,000 navy construction bill by this session of Congress, instead of having it sidetracked, increased the determination of certain of them today to push the measure ahead.

At a meeting of the Republican steering committee it was decided immediately to sound out House leaders to see if the bill can be acted upon in that body at this session. If the committee members can be assured that the House leaders can get action in that body there is little doubt that the bill will be shoved ahead in the Senate.

Meanwhile sponsors of the bill in the House were moving for speedy action. Chairman Britten of the naval committee filed application for a special rule giving it prior status, which, according to Chairman Snell of the Rules Committee, probably will be granted. Mr. Britten said he would not push his application for the next few days, however, preferring to await assurances from administration Senators that the bill will not be thrown into the waste basket with several hundred other measures already passed by the House.

House leaders feel that the bill would stand a much better chance of enactment if passed first in the Senate. The Senate is the body with unlimited debate and the one in which the potential controversy in the construction bill might easily force an extra session. Under its rules, the House can act within a few hours, despite any amount of controversy.

The belief that President Hoover would like to see the bill enacted this session arose from information that the State Department had made representations to certain leaders urging its passage as a step toward

Continued on Page Twelve.

SEABURY TO PRESS INQUIRY

He Lauds Kresel Warmly as He Accepts Counsel's Letter of Resignation.

POST WILL BE KEPT VACANT

Investigation of City Court Scandals to Be Carried On With Present Staff.

NO HALT IN PUBLIC HEARING

Tibbetts Assigned to Examine Prosecutor Accused of Bribe and Informers Today.

Isidor J. Kresel resigned yesterday as special counsel in the Appellate Division inquiry into magistrates' courts as a result of the indictment found against him in connection with the affairs of the Bank of United States, of which he was a director and counsel.

"The indictment returned against me today convinces me that I should remove all embarrassment to the important public work you have in hand," he wrote to Referee Samuel Seabury in resigning. Mr. Seabury, after being designated by the appellate division as referee, had appointed Mr. Kresel as his special counsel.

After making public his reply to Mr. Kresel, in which he said that he was sorry to "lose the association," Mr. Seabury said that the inquiry would go on without any one being appointed to Mr. Kresel's post. Harland B. Tibbetts, who has been serving as first assistant to Mr. Kresel, will examine witnesses called at a public hearing set for this afternoon at 2 o'clock.

Mr. Seabury indicated that the interrogation of witnesses at public hearings would probably be divided between Mr. Tibbetts and Jacob Gould Schurman, both of whom have been in the investigation since its beginning and are familiar with most of the ground which has been covered.

"The investigation is going right ahead," Mr. Seabury said in confirming the previously announced public hearing. "I am not going to designate any one to take Mr. Kresel's place. I am going ahead with the staff I now have and in which I have the greatest confidence."

Kresel's Letter of Resignation.

Mr. Kresel's letter, which was written late yesterday and was not made public by Mr. Seabury until early in the evening, read as follows:

Hon. Samuel Seabury, 120 Broadway, New York City.

Dear Judge Seabury:

With keen regret I must request you to relieve me of my position as counsel in the investigation of the magistrates' courts, in which you are acting as referee.

You will recall that shortly after the Bank of United States closed

Continued on Page Sixteen.

City Bar Association Retains Ban on Women; Votes It Is "Inadvisable" to Let Them Join

After two hours of debate and twenty-two speeches at a meeting with four times the usual attendance, the Bar Association of the City of New York decided last night that it was "inadvisable" to admit women lawyers to membership.

The proposal to admit them to the brocaded and marble establishment at 42 West Forty-fourth Street, half a century after the first woman lawyer was admitted to the bar in this State, was in the form of an amendment to the eligibility section of the Bar Association constitution, to provide "there shall be no discrimination on account of sex."

The total vote was 249, of which two-thirds, or 166, were required to adopt the amendment. Those in favor numbered only 136 and the amendment was lost by 30 votes.

The substance of the argument in favor of admitting women was the declared object of the bar association in its constitution, not as a man's club but as "an establishment to cultivate the science of jurisprudence, facilitate the administration of justice, elevate the legal profession and cherish the spirit of brotherhood among lawyers."

The argument against women was not that they were ineligible but that it was "inadvisable" to admit them because the bar association was founded when there were no women lawyers and it could not have been intended for them; moreover, it would be very expensive to remodel the establishment to make it suitable for women; besides, there would be only about fifty women members, and for so few women it was not proper to make so many men disgruntled about their presence; finally, if they wanted a bar association they could start one for themselves.

The amendment was urged by three former presidents of the association, George W. Wickersham, James Byrne and Henry W. Taft, who were its sponsors and who reminded the attendance that women already were received as members by the American Bar Association, the New York State Bar Association and the various county bar associations and that the decision would affect about 500 women lawyers in this city.

The debate threatened to go on all night, until it was closed by motion. Charles C. Burlingham, president of the association was in the chair.

Roosevelt Is Confident Indictment of Kresel Will Not Be Allowed to Hinder City Court Inquiry

Special to The New York Times.

ALBANY, N. Y., Feb. 10.—Governor Roosevelt expressed confidence today that the investigation of magistrates' courts would not be affected by the indictment of Isidor J. Kresel, its counsel, in the Bank of United States failure. The Governor pointed out that the inquiry was under the sole jurisdiction of the Appellate Division and said that it remained for Samuel Seabury, the referee, to take any action regarding the situation resulting from the indictment of Mr. Kresel. He went on to say that he was certain Mr. Seabury would pursue the magistrates' inquiry to its conclusion regardless of what happened.

"Of course, you understand," said the Executive, "it is not my investigation. It is the Appellate Division's inquiry. But I have full confidence that Judge Seabury will carry it through just as far as it can be carried through. I have every confidence in Judge Seabury.

"On the continuance of Mr. Kresel as counsel, that is up to Judge Seabury."

Governor Roosevelt's comment was made before it became known here that Mr. Kresel had resigned from the inquiry. Efforts to reach him for comment on the resignation were unsuccessful.

HIGH COURT ORDERS MANCUSO BE TRIED

Cardozo Ruling Upholds Fraud Indictment of Directors in City Trust Failure.

MAY GUIDE U. S. BANK CASE

Verdict Reversing Lower Judges Validates Statute as to Share in Insolvency.

Special to The New York Times.

ALBANY, Feb. 10.—The Court of Appeals today ruled that former Judge Francis X. Mancuso, chairman of the board of the City Trust Company, and other directors, including Salvatore Soraci, Leonard Rose, Isadore Siegel Tuch and Francis S. Paterno, must stand trial on the indictment charging them with fraudulent participation in the failure of the bank.

The indicted men had attacked the indictments in demurrers alleging Section 297 of the penal law, which makes the acts charged criminal, was invalid and unconstitutional. Judge Tompkins in Supreme Court upheld the demurrers and the Appellate Division unanimously affirmed his ruling.

Reversing the lower courts, Chief Judge Cardozo wrote the majority opinion, which was concurred in by Judges Lehman, Pound, Crane and Hubbs, Judge Lehman also writing a separate opinion. Judge Henry T. Kellogg dissented in an opinion in which Judge John F. O'Brien concurred.

Asserting that "Section 297 of the penal law is descended from Section 604 of the Penal Code enacted in 1881, which in turn derives from the Revised Statutes," Judge Cardozo interpreted the statutes to mean:

"The insolvency of a moneyed corporation is fraudulent unless its affairs have been administered by its directors fairly, legally and with the same care and diligence that agents receiving a compensation for their services are bound by law to observe (of Banking Law, Secs. 123-124), and the burden of proof shall be on a director, when insolvency is proved, to show that it was not fraudulent or that he did not participate in the fraud."

Responsibility of Directors.

He continued:

"We think the statute is not invalid. That objection failing, we think the negligent and illegal acts and omissions enumerated in the indictment are sufficiently stated to have been factors leading to insolvency and ruin. Proof there must be of a causal connection between the wrong and the collapse before negligence will charge it with a penal liability.

"In brief, the insolvency of a moneyed corporation, resulting from the failure to administer its affairs with reasonable care and diligence is a fraudulent insolvency within the definition of the statute, and a director participates in the fraud when he participates in the negligence which ruins as the the consequence."

Judge Lehman wrote that "though I cannot agree in whole with the construction placed in the prevailing opinion upon the statute, my own construction leads in this particular case to the same result.

"Perhaps the Legislature should

Continued on Page Sixteen.

ADMITS DESTROYING VAN LOAD OF RECORDS

Ex-Employe of House in Which Pollock Lives Unable to Say Who Arranged for Burning.

WAS INSTRUCTED BY PHONE

Told That Papers Disposed Of Before Bank Closed Would Be Sent From Main Office.

A van load of Bank of United States records consisting of more than 1,000 bundles was burned last November in the incinerator of the Beresford Apartments, Central Park West near Eighty-second Street, according to testimony yesterday before Special Assistant Deputy Attorney General Harry A. Gordon, assistant to Max D. Steuer in the investigation of the closing of the bank.

The apartment house is owned and operated by the H. R. H. Management Corporation, a subsidiary of the bank, and is the home of Henry W. Pollock, head of the bank's legal department and a vice president, one of the officials indicted yesterday.

At the same hearing, conducted in the State Building, 80 Centre Street, Mr. Gordon suggested to Jacob S. Gluck, a real estate broker of 160 Varick Street, that he return a fee of $100,000 to the York Investing Corporation, an affiliate of the bank, received in connection with the lease of property from the Trinity Church Corporation.

Did Not Know Questioner.

The testimony regarding the burning the bank records came from Saul Ravitch, president of the H. R. H. Management Corporation, who was asked what he knew regarding the destruction of the bank records.

"One day some one whose name I don't know, in the branch of the Bank of United States at Seventy-second Street and First Avenue, called me on the telephone," he testified, "and said they were moving into their temporary offices at Seventy-eighth Street and First Avenue and asked if they could burn some papers in the incinerator.

"I gave my consent and that's the last I heard of it. I know it was done but I didn't see it myself."

The previous witness was Joseph Ravitch, father of Saul, who said he was connected with the H. R. H. Corporation.

"You knew that Henry W. Pollock, vice president of the bank, lived at the Beresford Apartments?" Mr. Gordon asked. "Yes," replied the witness.

"Did you know that on Saturday afternoon early in November a big moving van drove up to the service entrance on Eighty-second Street in charge of two men, that about 1,000 bundles of papers were unloaded and were burned in the building incinerator?" The witness replied he did not know this nor that the bundles contained ledgers, journals, cash books and correspondence.

Mr. Gordon had in his hand an affidavit made by Rudolph Boesch of 384 East 194th Street, a former superintendent of the apartment house. Later in the day Mr. Gordon made public parts of the affidavit.

The affidavit was sworn to and made in the offices of Mr. Gordon last Wednesday. It is in question and answer form, the questions being

Continued on Page Sixteen.

TRIALS TO BE IN OCTOBER

$100,000 Bail Each Will Be Asked Today for Marcus and Singer.

$10,000 FOR THE OTHERS

Mitchell, Pollock, White, Kugel and Singer's Son Accused Also of Misusing Funds.

STEUER HALTED BY STAY

Officials Get Writ to Oust Him—Argument Up Today—Case May Go to Highest Court.

The county grand jury investigating the Bank of United States under the direction of Max D. Steuer as Assistant District Attorney yesterday found indictments against eight officers and directors of the bank, each of the indictments charging a felony.

Among those indicted was Isidor J. Kresel, attorney and director of the bank and special counsel in the Appellate Division's inquiry into magistrates' courts.

Samuel Seabury, referee in the Appellate Division's inquiry, last night announced the resignation of Mr. Kresel from this investigation. Mr. Seabury said that the investigation would continue, Mr. Kresel's assistants taking over the examination of witnesses.

Handing up of the indictments came almost simultaneously with the announcement of a temporary stay obtained by attorneys for the bank officials from Benjamin Cardozo, chief judge of the Court of Appeals, compelling Mr. Steuer to discontinue his public hearings in the investigaton as Assistant Attorney General pending argument today before the Court of Appeals on the legality of these hearings. The appeal is the result of an action brought by bank officials seeking to oust Mr. Steuer from the investigation and may lead to the quashing of the indictments.

Names of Those Indicted.

Following are those indicted:

BERNARD K. MARCUS, president of the bank.

SAUL SINGER, executive vice president of the bank, chairman of its executive committee and directing head of its affiliate corporations.

ISIDOR J. KRESEL, attorney and director of the bank.

HERBERT SINGER, son of Saul Singer, clerk in Mr. Kresel's office, and president of the Bolivar Corporation, a dummy organization which acted as a link in the $8,000,000 transaction.

C. STANLEY MITCHELL, director and chairman of the board of the bank, who has broken with the bank officials and may turn State's evidence.

ALEXANDER S. WHITE, executive head of Bankus Corporation, leading affiliate of the bank, and managing director of the institution's subsidiaries.

HENRY W. POLLOCK, vice president of the bank, head of the bank's law department and member of Governor Roosevelt's State Banking Commission.

SIMON H. KUGEL, director and vice chairman of the bank's board.

Accused in Debt Deal.

The indictments handed up to Judge William Allen in the Court of General Sessions, were based upon the $8,000,000 transaction whereby the Bank of United States is said to have paid to itself a debt to that amount owing it from two of its affiliates.

The defendants are to be tried before a special term of General Sessions in October. They are to be arraigned at 10:30 o'clock this morning before Judge Max S. Levine. Before arraignment they are to present themselves at the District Attorney's office, from where they are to be taken to the Elizabeth Street police station to be booked and to Police Headquarters, where they will be finger-printed.

John W. Davis, attorney for Mr. Kresel, informed Assistant District Attorney Hastings, in charge of the Indictment Bureau, last night, that Mr. Kresel will not be able to appear today because of illness. He is confined to his bed with a severe attack of bronchitis.

There were six indictments each against Mr. Marcus, Saul Singer and Mr. Kresel; four against Herbert Singer and Mr. Pollock; one each against Mr. Mitchell and Mr. White, and two against Mr. Kugel.

Some Named Principals.

The number of counts in each indictment will not be known until the arraignment of the defendants

Continued on Page Sixteen.

"All the News That's Fit to Print."

The New York Times.

Copyright, 1931, by The New York Times Company.

VOL. LXXX....No. 26,687. * * * * NEW YORK, TUESDAY, FEBRUARY 17, 1931. TWO CENTS in Greater New York | THREE CENTS Within 200 Miles | FOUR CENTS Elsewhere Except 7th and 8th Postal Zones

THE WEATHER
Cloudy, rain late today; tomorrow colder, possibly rain in morning.
Temperatures yesterday—Max. 46; min. 32.
U. S. Weather Forecast—For details see Page 46.

$400,000 SPEAKEASY GRAFT FROM 125 RESORTS IS LAID TO 2 POLICE 'COLLECTORS'

OWNERS COERCED BY RAIDS

Arrested if They Failed to Pay Up Monthly, Levey Swears.

DOCTORS TELL OF LEVIES

Two Paid Big Sums When Their Nurses Were 'Framed,' Seabury Witnesses Testify.

HINES SAVED TWO WOMEN

Faked Cases Against Rooming-House Keepers Dismissed After Tammany Leader Intervened.

Harry Levey, who said he served as stool pigeon for Plainclothesmen James J. Quinlivan and William M. O'Connor of the West 100th Street station, testified before Referee Samuel Seabury in the Appellate Division inquiry yesterday that in part of 1927 and throughout 1928 he collected a total of about $7,500 a month from the proprietors of 125 speakeasies on the upper west side, which he turned over to the two policemen.

Irving Ben Cooper, who questioned Levey and the other witnesses yesterday, showed that from 1926 to the end of 1930 Mrs. Sarah Quinlivan had deposited in three banks a total of $57,744, although it was estimated that the two policemen, on the basis of Levey's figures, had in the same period of time collected about $400,000 in speakeasy "shake-downs" alone.

Levey, who was in the witness chair most of the day, also described what he called the "nurse racket," whereby doctors were persuaded to pay large fees for counsel after nurses employed by them had been illegally arrested on vice charges, and the "furnished-room racket," which had as its object the victimization of respectable rooming-house keepers by stool pigeons who posed as married. Two such victims who took the stand to corroborate Levey told, however, how they had escaped without paying anything for a lawyer by appealing to James Hines, the Tammany leader in the Eleventh Assembly District.

Quinlivan Defiant on Stand.

Mr. Cooper prepared the background for the Levey testimony concerning the speakeasy collections early in the day by placing Quinlivan on the witness chair. Through a repetitious refrain of "I refuse to answer on the ground that it may tend to incriminate or degrade me" Quinlivan turned off question after question concerning his wife's banking activities.

By bank records, however, Mr. Cooper showed that on Jan. 1, 1925, the total balance in all of three accounts was nothing—the accounts then being non-existent. Beginning about the middle of 1926, however, when Quinlivan was promoted from a patrolman in uniform to a plainclothes patrolman whose duty was to ferret out vice, gambling and Volstead law violations, and continuing until near the end of 1930, Mrs. Quinlivan made large deposits, Mr. Cooper showed.

He took, as indicative of the activity of the Quinlivan accounts, three months in 1928 from the account record in the First National Bank of Yonkers. There, on April 3, Mrs. Quinlivan deposited $450; April 9, $332; April 15, $197; April 19, $200; April 25, $264; May 2, $417; May 9, $510; May 23, $428; May 29, $579; June 5, $553; June 12, $444, and on June 19, $550. Quinlivan's pay was $2,400 a year.

Quinlivan at a previous hearing had testified that before he became a policeman he had won $10,000 on a horse named Florabelle, had inherited $10,000 and had won, on his honeymoon, $3,000 more. All of the money, he said, he turned over to his wife, and he did not know what she had done with it.

The bank records showed, however, that beginning in 1926, $30,018.20 had been deposited in cash in the Yonkers bank, the New York Savings Bank and the Corn Exchange Bank. Pay checks amounting to $4,859.04 had likewise been deposited, and other checks amounting to $20,163.79 were deposited. Deposits made in an unidentifiable

Continued on Page Fourteen.

Navy Building Bill Is Put Aside In Senate Over Hale's Protest

Special to The New York Times.

WASHINGTON, Feb. 16.—The bill to appropriate $90,000,000 for new naval construction was put aside in the Senate today when the District of Columbia appropriation bill was called up for consideration.

Senator Hale, chairman of the Naval Affairs Committee, had entered a motion to bring in the construction bill, but yielded when Senator Bingham and several others asked for immediate consideration of the District supply bill. Mr. Hale gave notice that he would ask that the naval bill be acted on next.

Senator La Follette argued that the naval bill must take its chance with others, saying that Senator King, opponent of a big navy, should have an opportunity to call up a bill regarding deportation of aliens.

The District supply bill still had the right-of-way when the Senate adjourned.

MORE HUMANE POLICY IS URGED FOR PRISONS

Lewisohn Report, Approved by Governor's Message, Given to Legislature.

FOR BAUMES LAW CHANGE

Restoration of Time Off for Good Conduct Is Recommended With Parole Changes.

By W. A. WARN.
Special to The New York Times.

ALBANY, Feb. 16.—With the report of the Lewisohn Commission, created to investigate prison administration and construction, submitted to the Legislature at its session this evening, Governor Roosevelt sent a special message to the Senate and Assembly in which he warmly praised the document as the most comprehensive and scientific survey of the problem ever prepared in this State.

The State, said the report, should develop a prison system which will protect society from the criminal and his evil deeds by endeavoring to reeducate and retrain the men and women in prison so that they may be fitted upon release to become useful members of the community. This is imperative, because 92 per cent of these prisoners return to society within a comparatively short period of time after their incarceration.

The report recommends, primarily, the classification of all prisoners according to mental and physical standards, and their assignment to particular housing groups throughout the State; the construction of "medium security prisons" for more tractable prisoners and the continuance of road camps.

Would Change Baumes Life Law.

The commission also proposed a reduction of sentence at the rate of five days a month in the minimum sentence for prisoners serving an indeterminate sentence, with the right to earn a similar reduction on the unexpired maximum.

Immediate change is recommended in the Baumes law to provide that a

Continued on Page Seventeen.

CITY INQUIRY LOST, KNIGHT INDICATES AFTER PARTY PARLEY

Republican Senators Make No Decision as to Vote on It Tomorrow.

WARD OPPOSITION IS FIRM

Action on Procedure Deferred Until Appropriations Are Out of Way, Knight Says.

BUDGET ITEM FIGHT TODAY

Macy's Strategy in Forcing Issue Viewed as Bettering Chance for Investigation Later.

Special to The New York Times.

ALBANY, Feb. 16.—Senator John Knight, Republican leader, called party members in the upper house into a conference this evening, following the Senate session, to discuss the proposed New York City investigation. After an hour or more of talk, Mr. Knight decided that it would not be profitable to put the matter to a vote.

After the conference it was thought doubtful whether the Republican strategists would go through with their original plan and bring the resolution for the inquiry before the Senate for debate and final action on Wednesday, as proposed by W. Kingsland Macy, State chairman.

Senators Westall and Mastick, the two Republican members from Westchester, attended the conference and were closeted with their colleagues in the Finance Committee room until the end.

When they emerged Senator Westall told newspaper correspondents that there had been no change in his attitude and that he expected to vote against the resolution. He and Mr. Mastick are opposing the investigation on instructions from William L. Ward, Westchester leader.

Conferees Pledged to Silence.

All who attended the conference were pledged to silence. Reports of up-state defection to the view of Mr. Ward failed of confirmation.

"We discussed the budget and the New York City investigation," said Senator Knight. "It was not a caucus and no vote was taken on any question that came before us."

"In the light of what occurred at the conference, do you think the resolution will go through if brought up in the Senate on Wednesday?" he was asked.

"In view of the fact that no vote was taken at the conference I am unable to say," Mr. Knight said.

"Is it probable that the resolution will be brought up for final action on Wednesday?"

"No decision has been reached with regard to that, nor will there be any decision until the budget is out of the way," he asserted. "I am not actuated by a desire to conceal anything, but I am in no position to say anything more."

Action on Appropriation Today.

There will be a preliminary skirmish on the floor of the Senate tomorrow, in the event that the Assembly, as expected, passes the budget bill, with its appropriation of $250,000 to finance the investigation.

The Democrats are under orders from the leaders in New York City to leave nothing undone to encompass the defeat of the Story-Hofstadter resolution calling for the investigation.

Senator Downing, minority leader, has issued general instructions that every Democratic Senator must be in his seat during the next three days

Continued on Page Twelve.

Assembly by 85 to 62 Passes the Cuvillier Bill For a Convention to Repeal 18th Amendment

Special to The New York Times.

ALBANY, Feb. 16.—The wet forces rode roughshod over their antagonists in the Assembly tonight when by a vote of 85 to 62 they forced the passage of a resolution by Assemblyman Cuvillier of New York, requesting Congress to call a national constitutional convention to repeal the Eighteenth Amendment. It was the third victory in the lower house in this session.

Sixteen Republicans joined the Democrats to pass the Cuvillier measure. Three weeks ago tonight twenty-two Republicans voted with the Democrats for a resolution by Assemblyman Smith, Republican, of Syracuse, asking Congress to submit the question of repeal of the Eighteenth Amendment to conventions in the States. The House earlier in the session adopted a resolution by Assemblyman Steingut, Democratic leader, asking Congress to repeal the Volstead law.

Republicans who voted wet tonight included Assemblymen Marks, McKay, Saunders, Searle and Austin of Monroe, Bernhardt, Marcy, Dickey, Gimbrone and Piper of Erie, Condon, Gamble and Garnjost of Westchester, Taylor of Orange, Story of Brooklyn, and Moffat of New York.

Assemblyman Smith voted against the Cuvillier bill because, he said, it would pave the way for all sorts of amendments to the Constitution.

The high spot of the debate was a speech by Assemblyman Joseph R. Hanley, Republican, of Wyoming, a former Presbyterian minister.

"We are facing the greatest question in prohibition that has come before the American people since slavery," he said, "and we are facing it with prejudices rather than with our brains.

"If the drys have made any mistake it is because they have preceded education with legislation. This is a moral and not a political question. I believe this question has ruined the Republican party in this State."

Passage of all three wet measures in the Senate is expected next week.

Alfonso in Midst of Crisis Prays at His Mother's Tomb

Special Cable to THE NEW YORK TIMES.

MADRID, Feb. 16.—King Alfonso gave an indication of his personal feelings this afternoon when he was driven in one of the royal autos at a high speed to Escurial, the grim monastery built by King Philip II.

There Spain's 45-year-old King alone entered the crypt where the rulers of Spain since the time of the Holy Roman Empire lie buried. Alfonso knelt in prayer before the tomb of his mother, Queen Maria Christina. Then he was driven quickly home, and scarcely any one in Madrid knew he had left the city.

CHASE BANK OFFICER TO HEAD THE CHELSEA

Howell M. Stillman Is Slated to Take Charge of the Reorganized Institution.

REOPENING PLAN SUBMITTED

Personnel Will Not Be Revealed Officially Till Broderick Approves Project.

It was learned in financial circles yesterday that Howell M. Stillman, second vice president of the Chase National Bank, will be the head of the Chelsea Bank and Trust Company, following reorganization and reopening of that institution.

Neither Joseph A. Broderick, State Superintendent of Banks, nor Lamar Hardy, of Hardy & Hardy, attorneys for the Chelsea Bank and Trust Company, would confirm or deny this information.

Mr. Hardy announced yesterday the presentation to Mr. Broderick of the plan for reorganization and reopening of the bank. The announcement was made to newspaper men in the office of Mr. Broderick, 51 Chambers Street.

"The names of officials who are to head the reorganized institution will not be officially revealed until Mr. Broderick approves the plan," Mr. Hardy said. "I am not in a position, therefore, either to confirm or deny the reports that Mr. Stillman is to head the new bank."

Mr. Broderick was even more emphatic in declining to discuss the reports.

It is understood that the list of officials of the reorganized bank, which will not include any of the former officers of the Chelsea Bank and Trust Company, together with the directors of the reorganized institution, will be made public some time this week. A few of the directors of the Chelsea Bank and Trust Company may be retained on the board of the reorganized bank. Execution of the reorganization plan will require Mr. Broderick's approval and that of the Supreme Court.

Plan Submitted to Broderick.

Speaking for the group interested in reopening the bank, which was taken over by the State Banking Department on Dec. 23, 1930, Mr. Hardy, who is a former Corporation Counsel of New York City, said:

"On behalf of the reorganization committee of the Chelsea Bank and Trust Company a proposition has been submitted to Mr. Broderick for his consideration which contemplates the reopening of the bank, and I have given to him today certain names as proposed directors of the new institution, and we are hoping for favorable consideration of the matter. That is all I care to say."

It is understood that no plan has been submitted in writing and that the type of reorganization contemplated by Mr. Hardy's clients as yet is indefinite. The entire plan of reorganization is in process of development. Only the general idea and the formula are before Mr. Broderick, who, it is understood, will have further conference with the group proposing to take over the liabilities of the bank and reopen it subject to the approval of the Supreme Court.

Two Courses Open.

The reorganization may take one of two courses. It may establish an entirely new bank, with a new name, new officers and new directors, or it may continue the business of the bank under its old name, with new officers and a practically new board of directors.

In case of approval by Mr. Broderick it is understood that it would require at least thirty days to reopen the bank, as the banking laws require the banking superintendent to advertise the sale of the effects of the institution.

It is said that hundreds of depositors have written the State Banking Department and officials of the closed bank of their intention to continue their accounts with the bank if it is reopened.

Mr. Broderick said that he had reached no decision on the proposals to reopen the closed Bank of United States, but that he was still considering the matter.

KING CALLS EX-REBEL AS SPANISH PREMIER; TRIES TO SAVE CROWN

Sanchez Guerra Visits Jail to Ask Alfonso's Foes There to Help Him Govern.

MONARCH TO YIELD POWERS

New Cabinet Will Call Assembly With Right to Remove Him if It So Desires.

GENERAL STRIKE LOOMED

Threat of Nation-Wide Walkout Said to Have Forced Move—Santiago Alba Expected to Quit Paris.

By FRANK L. KLUCKHOHN.
Special Cable to THE NEW YORK TIMES.

MADRID, Feb. 16.—With a brave gesture today King Alfonso put his crown in jeopardy in order to save Spain from revolution.

When José Antonio Sanchez Guerra, the gray-bearded and indomitable leader of those who have won their battle against the monarch, presents at noon tomorrow the Cabinet nominees which the King virtually agreed late today to accept, King Alfonso's prerogatives will be suspended and he will be merely an onlooker while the nation's representatives are elected to a constituent cortes, empowered to draft a new Constitution for Spain and decide whether it shall remain a kingdom or become a republic.

Few events in Spanish history have rivaled the colorful drama which came to its climax here today. Few times in the world's history has the ruling monarch of any country agreed to remain passive while his nation decided whether to keep him.

Forced by Strike Threat.

Many times Kings have run from a revolution, such as a general strike ordered last night for today, but King Alfonso, with smiling face, has chosen to stay and face the situation, perhaps because he still thinks he will win. As a result of this decision Spain has received a guarantee of peaceful solution of her nine years' political struggle which began with the disaster in Morocco in 1921, for which he was blamed, was suppressed during the six-year Primo de Rivera dictatorship and which culminated in the December revolution.

It only became definitely established today that orders for a national general strike which would have rocked the country to its foundations had actually been given and that this forced King Alfonso's decision, but it was known early this morning that the King, after three days of struggle to bring about the calling of a constitutional convention under his control, had failed and that he must call some one of his opponents to the helm, abdicate or subject the nation to disorder and hardship.

King's Choice a Surprise.

It was first thought that Melquiades Alvarez would be the King's choice for the Premiership, but José Antonio Sanchez Guerra, whose lifelong record of honesty has endeared him to all factions, was the King's choice.

Señor Sanchez Guerra, dressed in the black coat and tall silk hat customary among Spanish politicians, arrived at the royal palace at 10:15 A. M. and the royal halbardiers, in their picturesque costumes, saluted him as he entered. He was closeted with King Alfonso until noon.

While the blue-coated police, with hats like those of the London bobbies, held back the growing crowd, which realized that history was being

Continued on Page Ten.

Stocks Rise 2 to 8 Points Despite Bonus News As Wall Street Sees Pick-Up in Business

Under the stimulus of aggressive pool operations and helped by a growing public demand, the stock market resumed its advance yesterday in the face of news from Washington that the House of Representatives would adopt the compromise soldiers' bonus bill. The bill was passed late in the afternoon, after the active list on the New York Stock Exchange had scored one of the sharpest advances of the year.

Net gains among the market leaders ranged from 2 to 8 points, but Auburn Auto, which has been a market sensation for ten days, distinguished itself again by crossing 200 for the first time in 1931 and closing at 199 with a net appreciation of 19 points. With yesterday's gain included, this stock has run up more than 60 points since the first of the year. This means that the 173,500 shares outstanding have added more than $10,000,000 to their open market value.

It has been suspected for some time that a condition closely resembling a technical corner has existed in Auburn. The stock was lending flat yesterday and was said to be available in any reasonable quantity. The business conduct committee of the Exchange is watching it.

The total turnover in all issues yesterday was 3,154,090 shares. Fifty selected stocks, according to the combined averages of THE NEW YORK TIMES, showed a net gain of $2.39, while twenty-five industrials advanced $4 and twenty-five rails 78 cents.

United States Steel added 1½ points to its market value yesterday, Allied Chemical was up 3½, American Can 2⅛, American Water Works 2¾, Beatrice Creamery 5⅞, A. M. Byers 3, J. I. Case 8⅝, American Commercial Alcohol 1½, Columbian Carbon 3, Delaware & Hudson 4⅞, Macy & Co. 3¾, New York Central 3¼, Vulcan Detinning 5⅛, Safeway Stores 4½ and Waldorf 1⅞.

Wall Street ascribed yesterday's uniform strength in the stock market to accumulative evidence of an impending pick-up in business and industry.

HOUSE PASSES BONUS LOAN BILL 363 TO 39; SENATE PAVES WAY FOR SPEEDY ACTION; VETO BY THE PRESIDENT IS EXPECTED

Bonus Loan Extension Procedure Is Explained As Applying to All Compensation Certificates

Special to The New York Times.

WASHINGTON, Feb. 16.—The World War veterans' loan bonus bill, as passed by the House today, applies to all holders of adjusted compensation certificates voted to the former service men in 1924 in place of a cash bonus sought at that time.

The bill provides simply that the loan value of these certificates, which are to be paid in full to the veterans in 1945, shall be increased from the present value of 22½ per cent of their face value to a basis of 50 per cent, at 4½ per cent interest compounded annually.

Provision is also made for veterans who are now paying more than 4½ per cent interest on loans already made, to refinance their loans at the lower rate.

If the bill becomes law, application for a new loan under it should be made to the regional manager of the Veterans' Bureau in the area where the veteran resides, and application for extending or refinancing an existing loan should be made to the regional manager where the original loan was negotiated.

Regional managers are located in the District of Columbia and in each of the States except Delaware. There are two each in New York, at New York City and Buffalo, and in Ohio, Texas, Pennsylvania and California. Applications from Delaware should be made to the regional manager in Philadelphia.

The Veterans' Bureau has estimated that it would take about six months to set the necessary new loan machinery in motion. Full details of the procedure remain to be worked out, but will be set forth on forms which it is planned to mail to each applicant in the event the extension is granted.

OPPOSITION OVERWHELMED

Only 39 Republicans Hold Firm in Support of Administration.

SENATE COUNTS 25 FOES

Leaders There Say Report That President Would Accept Bill Upset House Supporters.

MELLON PARLEY RECALLED

But Predictions That Measure May Not Be Vetoed Do Not Stop Filibuster Threats.

Special to The New York Times.

WASHINGTON, Feb. 16.—With none of the excitement and oratorical fireworks usually attending consideration of a controversial matter of major importance, the House of Representatives today passed the veterans' bonus loan bill by the overwhelming vote of 363 to 39.

The Democrats present, 150 of them, voted solidly for the bill. The lone Farmer-Laborite member, Kvale of Minnesota, was for it. Despite the opposition of President Hoover 212 Republicans voted the same way. All the thirty-nine negative votes were cast by Republicans.

Only forty minutes of debate was permitted. Immediately after the bill was passed the House put through, without a roll-call, another measure providing additional hospitalization facilities for veterans, which, it is estimated, will mean a government outlay of $12,500,000. Again without debate and without a roll-call a bill was passed providing $2,850,000 for the erection of additional facilities at branches of the Bureau of National Homes, the new name for the organization which administers the soldiers' homes of the nation.

Other Veterans' Measures Pass.

A few hours before the House Veterans Committee had ordered a favorable report on a bill providing for the payment of pensions to the widows, children and aged parents of deceased World War veterans. It is estimated that this bill would cost $18,000,000 in its first year of operation and $131,000,000 in the first five years. But its passage in the present Congress is not expected.

The bonus bill now goes to the Senate, where opposition has dwindled to a handful as a result of today's decisive vote in the House. Canvasses made late in the afternoon showed that probably not more than twenty-five votes would be recorded in the upper chamber against the measure.

The bill permits World War veterans to borrow immediately up to 50 per cent of the face value of their adjusted compensation certificates, although the certificates will not mature until 1945. According to its sponsors, its chief purpose was to mitigate distress due to depressed economic conditions and unemployment. But, according to some usually loyal followers of President Hoover, one of its designs is to prevent the next Congress from passing a measure which would provide for the immediate cash payment of the full face value of the certificates.

Hold Bill May Not Be Vetoed.

Whether the President has been impressed by the arguments of his followers remains to be seen. All the outward indications point to a Presidential veto when the bill is sent to him from the Senate.

Senator Couzens again served notice on the Senate today that he would object to the consideration of any other measures not only until the Senate passed the bonus bill but until President Hoover had taken action on it. Mr. Couzens took the initiative along that line today by objecting to the consideration of the annual postoffice supply bill.

There is an undercurrent of opinion among prominent Republican Senators and Representatives that President Hoover might approve the bill because of the argument that it would forestall a full-payment measure in the next Congress.

The administration lost support in the House, some Senate leaders said today, because of reports of hesitancy on the part of the administration. According to a report among Republican chiefs, President Hoover had agreed early Friday night to accept the Bacharach bill, as the best possible compromise, after he had been informed that bonus legislation

BALDWIN DEMANDS TARIFF TO SAVE JOBS

British Tory Leader Says Only Protection Can Prevent Vast Wage Reductions.

PLANS TRADE RECIPROCITY

Wheat Would Be Purchased From Nations Dealing Most Fairly With England.

By CHARLES A. SELDEN.
Special Cable to THE NEW YORK TIMES.

LONDON, Feb. 16.—Stanley Baldwin, leader of the Conservative party, gave the last talk tonight in a series of radio addresses on unemployment for the British Broadcasting Association. Restrained by the rules of the corporation against partisan attacks, he said very little about the increase of unemployment during the Laborite administration, but used his twenty minutes at the microphone for the advocacy of a protective tariff for England and assured his listeners that if he was returned to power as Prime Minister he would put such a policy into effect.

He made no reference to the United States, which, since industrial troubles came to that country, has been studiously avoided by the British advocates of protection.

He declared that Liberals and Laborites throughout the country are in sympathy with his tariff program despite their party pronouncements against it, and he defied free trade England's traditional hatred of import taxes on food by declaring he would impose duties on agricultural imports and establish a quota system so England could buy wheat only from countries which admitted her own manufactured products on fair terms.

"When I left office in May, 1929," said Mr. Baldwin, "unemployment was less than when I took office in May, 1924, despite the events of 1926,

Continued on Page Nine.

SOUTHERN SENATORS WARN PARTY WETS

Morrison Calls Raskob Smith's Mistake—Says Democrats Will Name New Candidate in '32.

CONVENTION WAR DECREED

Sheppard Challenges Shouse on Wet Majority—Senate Asks for Wickersham Testimony.

Special to The New York Times.

WASHINGTON, Feb. 16.—Directing their fire at John J. Raskob, chairman of the Democratic National Committee, and Jouett Shouse, head of its executive committee, Southern Democrats, led by Senators Sheppard of Texas and Morrison of North Carolina, in a sharp debate on prohibition in the Senate today served notice on the leaders of their party that they would combat any attempt of the wets to dominate the national convention in 1932.

When the two-hour skirmish was over the Senate, without a roll-call, adopted a resolution by Senator Tydings, wet Democrat, of Maryland, requesting the Wickersham commission to give to the Senate all testimony it had taken concerning prohibition, except that received under the pledge of secrecy and all the reports of its investigators of prohibition. The only comment on the resolution was a statement by Senator Borah that he favored it.

Stating that the testimony supporting recommendations was not included in the Wickersham report, the resolution read:

Resolved, That the commission be requested to send to the Senate, for its information in drafting the legislation recommended, a copy of all the testimony heard by it, and of all the evidence laid before it, except so far as such testimony or evidence may have been received under the pledge of secrecy; and be it further

Resolved, That the commission be requested to send to the Senate, for its information, the reports of its experts, who investigated the various phases of prohibition.

Raskob and Shouse Assailed.

The prohibition debate was started by Senator Sheppard, co-author of the Eighteenth Amendment, who challenged Jouett Shouse to name the States he had in mind when he said in a recent speech in Florida that "they had already taken such action as to indicate that the delegates to the next Democratic national convention" would provide a wet majority.

"I think that such information from Mr. Shouse would be interesting and informing," the Senator said. Then he read a statement he had prepared for The Dallas News in which he declared that the Democratic party was not wet and that he would do everything he could to keep it dry.

Senator Morrison took up the attack on the wet leanings of some of the party leaders, centring upon Chairman Raskob.

"The only political significance Mr. Raskob has ever had, or ever will

Continued on Page Twenty.

"All the News That's Fit to Print."

The New York Times.

THE WEATHER
Rain today and probably tomorrow; not much change in temperature.
Temperatures yesterday—Max. 44, min. 34.
U. S. Weather Forecast—For details see Page 30.

VOL. LXXX....No. 26,690. **** NEW YORK, FRIDAY, FEBRUARY 20, 1931. TWO CENTS In Greater New York | THREE CENTS Within 200 Miles | FOUR CENTS Elsewhere Except 7th and 8th Postal Zones

ROOSEVELT ACTS TO FORCE A CITY-WIDE COURT INQUIRY; GRAFT WITNESS IS DEFIANT

LAZANSKY IS ASKED TO ACT

Governor Reviews Many Recent Charges Against Brooklyn Judges.

REQUESTS PROMPT REPORT

He Presses Plea on Basis of Petition Signed by 1,000 Citing Judicial Scandals.

INVESTIGATION IS EXPECTED

Appellate Justices to Confer Quickly on Naming Referee to Extend Seabury's Work.

Governor Roosevelt took steps in Albany yesterday to extend the Appellate Division inquiry into the lower courts to the entire city.

He wrote to Edward Lazansky, presiding justice of the Appellate Division of the Second Department, asserting that, if reports submitted to him were true, there seemed to be as much reason for delving into conditions in the magistrates' courts of Brooklyn, Queens and Richmond as there was in Manhattan and the Bronx, where Samuel Seabury as referee has uncovered a mass of evidence of graft, corruption and oppression.

Justice Lazansky, upon receiving the letter, which revealed that the Governor was making his second request for an investigation, said he would present the entire matter to his associates on the bench "within a few days" and forward their decision to Governor Roosevelt "at the earliest possible moment."

Governor Acts on Petition.

Governor Roosevelt's letter followed his receipt of a petition from Mrs. Catherine Parker Clivette, president of the Society for Prevention of Unjust Convictions, asking for the initiation of an inquiry in boroughs under the jurisdiction of the Second Department, similar to the one being conducted by Mr. Seabury in the First Department. Mrs. Clivette's communication contained the signatures of 1,000 men and women and named several magistrates recently under fire.

Although the Governor's letter to Justice Lazansky merely called attenton to the complaints he had received, leaving it to the justices of the court to determine what action to take, it was regarded as almost certain that an inquiry would be ordered in the boroughs that thus far have escaped the searching inquiry that has been turned upon Manhattan and Bronx magistrates.

Text of Roosevelt Letter.

Governor Roosevelt's letter follows:

State of New York.
Executive Chamber.
Albany, Feb. 18, 1931.

Hon. Edward Lazansky, Presiding Justice,
Supreme Court, Appellate Division, Second Department,
Brooklyn, N. Y.

Dear Judge:

You are doubtless familiar with the results being produced almost daily by the investigation now being conducted by the Appellate Division of the First Department, which was initiated at my instance, as you know, I have for some time entertained the definite thought that this type of investigation be extended to cover those counties in your jurisdiction which are comprised within the boundaries of the city of New York.

You will recall that in response to my letter to you of Dec. 31, 1930, relative to this subject, you replied on Jan. 2, 1931, as follows:

"Immediately upon receipt of your letter I consulted with all my associates and I find the members of the court to be of the following opinion; Since this court and its members have received no communication and no information which involves city magistrates and magistrates' courts—save in one instances hereinafter mentioned—we believe that no justifiable basis exists for such an investigation. The members of the court are of a mind that if any information comes to the court of any condition of wrongdoing in the magistrates' courts, this court should and would act."

Since then, on Feb. 17, 1931, I received a petition signed by a large

Continued on Page Twelve.

Queen Mary Shuns Long Skirts; 'Difficult to Wear,' She Says

Wireless to THE NEW YORK TIMES.

LONDON, Feb. 19.—Queen Mary has revealed that she does not like long skirts and thinks them "difficult to wear." She said so today when she saw a manikin parade at an exhibition of British artificial silk goods.

"I like frocks of medium length, that come just above the ankle," she declared. "Very long dresses with flared skirts are very difficult to wear, I think. Only an expert like a manikin can really wear them effectively."

Asking why the herald of the manikin parade was dressed as a Persian, the Queen was told that it was because the current exhibition of Persian art here had probably influenced the coming fashions.

POLICEMAN DEFIANT ON $83,057 DEPOSITS

But Fails to Block Seabury by Plea Graft Inquiry Exceeds Referee's Powers.

MRS. NORRIS SHUNS HEARING

Judge Will Be Subpoenaed in Future, Her Attorney Is Warned After Clash.

Two unexpected attempts to block the progress of the Appellate Division inquiry into magistrates courts were turned off yesterday by Referee Samuel Seabury. First, Martin J. Conboy, who appeared as counsel for Magistrate Jean Norris, who failed to attend, demanded that she be informed in advance of the questions to be asked. He was told that when Magistrate Norris was wanted in the future she would be subpoenaed and that he could accompany her as counsel but would not be heard.

Second, Charles A. Wund, a patrolman of the third division, whose bank records turned up deposits of $83,057.27, declined from the stand to answer questions concerning his banking affairs on the ground that the investigation was exceeding its authority and infringing upon his constitutional rights. He was told to take a seat to one side and while he sat there all of the evidence involving him was placed in the record.

At one point in Wund's testimony Referee Seabury halted Jacob Gould Schurman, who was interrogating, to warn Herman L. Falk, Wund's counsel and a former Assistant United States District Attorney, that he must cease making signals to the witness. The attorney apologized.

Four More Frame-Ups Revealed.

Four more instances of "framed" vice arrests were placed in the record. In one of these the woman, Catherine Nolan, told how a policeman, Abe Dicker, since discharged from the department on charges, broke the chain bolt on her door in order to enter her apartment and arrest her.

Wund took the stand late in the afternoon, after his appearance had been partly prepared for during the morning by Harland B. Tibbetts, chief of counsel to the investigation. Mr. Tibbetts placed in the record a list of 733 bail bonds signed by mag-

Continued on Page Twelve.

$100,000,000 IN BONDS TO BE SOLD BY CITY IN RECORD FINANCING

Municipality's Biggest Loan for Long Term to Be Offered March 4 at 4¼ Per Cent.

WALL ST. SHOWS CONCERN

Berry Says Market Will Absorb Issue Rapidly—Talk of Chase-National City Syndicate.

DEBT MARGIN $350,000,000

Total of $247,000,000 Securities to Be Sold to Finance Public Works This Year.

The largest single piece of long-term financing ever scheduled by this city, amounting to $100,000,000 of corporate stock and serial bonds, was announced yesterday by Controller Charles W. Berry, for sale on March 4. This represents the first instalment of the total of $247,000,000 of corporate stocks and bonds which the Controller recently announced would be required for 1931, for rapid transit, schools, docks and other public improvements.

The new financing will consist of $60,000,000 of fifty-year corporate stock for rapid transit purposes; $30,000,000 of bonds, due serially from one to forty years, of which $20,000,000 will be for schools and $10,000,000 for hospital, dock and other improvements; and $10,000,000 of bonds, due from one to fifteen years, of which $5,000,000 will be for schools and $5,000,000 for various other improvements. All of the bonds and corporate stock will bear interest at the rate of 4¼ per cent, and will be dated March 1, 1931.

Debt Margin Still $350,000,000.

The Controller pointed out yesterday that with the sale of this issue, the city will still have a debt limit margin of approximately $350,000,000. Proceeds of the new financing will be used to retire the various blocks of short-term loans contracted during the last few months for improvement purposes.

"The bond market," said the Controller, "is approaching a condition when these obligations can be absorbed very rapidly. In placing the interest rate of 4¼ per cent, the city is assured of a substantial premium which will be utilized in the amortization of the city's debt."

In municipal banking circles yesterday the announcement of the issue, which had been expected for several weeks, was received with great concern because of the magnitude of the task of distributing so large an issue of municipal securities. In this connection it was reported that there was a likelihood that the two major syndicates which have usually furnished the main competition for the city's bonds, headed respectively by the National City Company and the Chase Securities Corporation, might join forces.

It was said yesterday that no plan of consolidation had been worked out, but that a decision one way or the other would be made within a few days. Several times during the last few years the matter of a consolidation of these two syndicates has come up for consideration, but it never has gone beyond the discussion stage. However, it was said that if the matter is ever to receive serious consideration, the present time would be most logical, due to the size of the financing and the somewhat uncertain outlook for the bond market.

The largest single piece of long-term financing done by the city heretofore has been $75,000,000, which

Continued on Page Four.

Canada Raises the Tariff On Our Cars About 15%

By The Canadian Press.

OTTAWA, Ont., Feb. 19.—A fixed discount of 20 per cent from list prices has been placed for duty purposes on all United States automobiles entering Canada for sale, E. B. Ryckman, Minister of National Revenue, announced tonight.

Motor cars now coming into this country enter on a list price, less a discount, and on the reduced amount the duty is assessed. This discount has ranged all the way up to 30 per cent. Canadian automobile manufacturers asked that a maximum discount be set.

Assurances have been received from Canadian manufacturers, Mr. Ryckman stated, that in no event would the price of cars to purchasers be increased by the action taken to protect the home industry.

WINDSOR, Ont., Feb. 19 (Canadian Press).—According to local automobile officials, a car selling for $600 in the United States will be increased in price by about $60 in the Canadian market by the new bill. On a car priced at $1,000 the increase would amount to about $77, while the price of a $2,000 car would be increased $362.

Canada's action amounts to raising the tariff on United States automobiles something like 15 per cent or more.

NEW BABYLON RISES ON VENEZUELAN LAKE

Magnificent Tourist Resort Is Being Built by Dictator Gomez in Tropical Jungle.

VAST PORT IS UNDER WAY

New City of Furiamo Will Have Great Shopping Centre—Work Long Kept Secret.

By GAULT MacGOWAN.

Special Cable to THE NEW YORK TIMES.

PORT OF SPAIN, Trinidad, Feb. 19.—General Juan Vicente Gomez, former President and now dictator of Venezuela, is building a modern Babylon at Maracay on the shore of Lake Valencia to attract visitors from all the Americas to see the fruit of his labors in the cause of progress and reconciliation.

General Gomez's $60,000,000 program of public works is rapidly nearing completion. Since 1924 concrete roads have been pushed from Caracas to La Guayra and Porto Cabello; he is completing a chain of big hotels at key points and is crowning his labors with the construction of a vast port at Furiamo.

A vision from the Arabian Nights greets visitors after a 500-mile air journey from Trinidad across the wilderness of the forests, swamps, plains and mountains of Venezuela to the mystery city of Maracay on the borders of Lake Valencia. There one is amazed to find the world's finest and newest tropical hotel.

Lone Diner in Big Hotel.

I was the lone diner in a pillared tiled hall with tinkling fountains amid 200 empty tables laid with flowers and silver. An orchestra of eight Hungarians played while French, German, Austrian and Swiss English-speaking waiters served a lucullan dinner with rare wines. Afterward I walked alone unchallenged through acres of empty public gardens ablaze with lights.

"Why has no publicity been given to this effort in the outside world?" I inquired of the Minister of State the next morning.

"General Gomez is not ready," was the reply. "He does not believe in advance publicity. When he is ready he will tell the world. The roads and hotels are only partly completed and the ports are yet in the making."

Later, when General Gomez pulls the string, the rising curtain will reveal an amazing scene. Unknown to the outside world, the secret port of Furiamo, which is now being built, will bring Maracay only a few hours away from ocean liners. Work is proceeding night and day, and when it is ready there will be docks and piers large enough to accommodate the world's biggest liners, boulevards lined with glittering department stores designed according to the latest Paris and New York ideas and filled with goods from the East and West.

Concrete Road in Jungle.

Furiamo is half-way between La Guayra and Porto Cabello. A sixty-mile concrete road through the tropical forest, where wild beasts roam amid giant firs and tree ferns, connects Furiamo and Maracay.

That evening I was escorted by the Secretary of State to see General Gomez. He was seated at the base of a giant tree on the shore of Lake Valencia, where he holds open-air conferences with the Cabinet Minis-

Continued on Page Ten.

Painters Threaten to Adopt Half-Size Brush; Employers Say Move Would Double Force

A hallowed tradition of the house-painters' craft has been seriously endangered, it became known yesterday, when Supreme Court Justice Lewis in Brooklyn was informed that the five and six inch paint-brushes, which painters have been wielding since time immemorial, may be supplanted in Brooklyn by a new-fangled thing only three inches wide.

Ernest P. Seelman, counsel for the Boss Painters' Association of Long Island, in telling the court of this attack on an ancient custom, said that if the proposal were carried out it would cause grave economic troubles. The three-inch brush would make it necessary, he said, for just twice as many painters to do the same work compared with men using the standard brushes.

Mr. Seelman asked the court to enjoin the International Painters, Paperhangers and Decorators' Union, Local 102, which he said proposed the three-inch brush, from calling a strike on jobs of the Boss Painters' Association. He said the union had served notice on contractors regarding the new brush and the contractors would not tolerate it. As a result, he said, strikes have been called by the union.

Harry Kopp, counsel for the union, admitted that the subject of brushes had been discussed for some time, but he said the real issue was the employers' reluctance to abide by a wage scale which had been agreed upon some time ago.

"As a matter of fact," he told the court, "we are willing to waive any demand as to the change in the size of the brush and we are willing to go along with the larger brush, but what we insist is that the employers live up to the very agreement they are talking about. We want them to stick to that agreement and pay the scale that agreement provides for."

Justice Lewis reserved decision.

DETECTIVE IS SLAIN, COMRADE KILLS THUG IN HOLD-UP BATTLE

Policemen Trail Two Gunmen to Lexington Avenue Cafe and Surprise Them at Work.

SECOND ROBBER WOUNDED

But Escapes in the Excitement—Mulrooney Hastens to the Scene to Investigate.

PATRONS ARE QUESTIONED

Gunman's Wife Also Taken to the Station—Dead Officer Wore Glove, Was Slow Drawing Pistol.

Detective Christopher W. Schueing of the East Twenty-second Street station was shot and killed last night in a café at 49 Lexington Avenue in a pistol battle with two hold-up men, one of whom was killed and the other wounded by Schueing's partner, Detective Dominick Pape.

The two gunmen, unaware that they had been followed into the establishment by the detectives, were caught in the act of holding up a group of customers, including two women. The wounded gunman, whose identity was not known, escaped in the excitement. A police alarm was broadcast to all hospitals to be on the lookout for him. At least ten shots were fired and in the battle the place was wrecked.

Schueing wore a glove on his right hand which prevented him from drawing his pistol to defend himself. He just had time to yell a warning to Pape when he dropped dead with three bullet wounds.

In the pockets of the dead robber, who was later identified as Albert Checchia, 32 years old, a criminal with records for assault and robbery, the police found a watch that had been taken from one of the women.

On Force Three Years.

Schueing, who was 30 years old, had been on the police force less than three years, having been appointed July 3, 1928. He lived at 62 Lisbon Place, Grant City, S. I. His father is a retired patrolman who received the Congressional Medal of Honor for bravery in performing rescue work when the steamer General Slocum burned in the East River in 1904 with the loss of 1,021 lives.

Inspector Joseph P. Loonam, who took charge of the investigation, learned that Schueing and Pape, who had been working all day yesterday on the Frank Marco killing, were walking east in Twenty-third Street shortly before 9 o'clock when their attention was attracted to two suspicious-looking men turning the corner and walking north on Lexington Avenue.

The detectives followed the pair and saw them enter the ground floor of the three-story red brick building at 49 Lexington Avenue. Hardly had the door closed behind them when the detectives entered.

Pape and Schueing made their way first to the rear room, in which they found a deserted bar. Then they went to a sitting room in the front, where they saw the two men and a small group of customers, including two women.

As Schueing approached the two men one of them whipped a pistol out of his pocket and started to fire, without warning. Schueing dropped with a bullet in the temple and two in the chest.

As Schueing toppled to the floor,

Continued on Page Three.

E. B. McLean Enjoined From Mexican Divorce Prior to Washington Hearing on Wife's Alimony

Special to The New York Times.

WASHINGTON, Feb. 19.—Mrs. Evalyn Lucille Walsh McLean, wife of the publisher, Edward Beale McLean, today asked the District of Columbia Supreme Court to restrain her husband from carrying out an alleged scheme to divorce her in Mexico and to order him lodged in jail for contempt of court.

Told that Mr. McLean thus was attempting to evade a recent court order for payment of $7,500 monthly alimony, Justice Jesse Adkins signed an order restraining the publisher from carrying out the divorce prior to a hearing on March 2. Deputy marshals, armed with writs, were sent to search for Mr. McLean.

This latest chapter in the McLean domestic troubles was the aftermath of a maintenance suit brought by the wife a few months ago. At that time she charged that he had left her marooned without funds at their palatial Washington estate, Friendship, while he vacationed at various expensive resorts.

On Jan. 17 Mr. McLean consented to an order of the court by which he was to pay $7,500 monthly alimony for support of his wife and their three minor children, and $65,000 in settlement of inadequate support for the preceding months.

Since then, Mrs. McLean told the court today, she has received not a penny of the alimony agreed upon.

In her petition, she charged McLean had "resented" the order and has set out to perpetrate a fraud upon the court. She first learned of it Feb. 11 at Palm Beach, she stated, when she was served with papers informing her she was being sued for divorce at Cuernavaca, in the State of Morelos, Mexico.

In the divorce papers, filed Feb. 4, Mr. McLean, she said, told the Mexican court: "I am a resident of the city of Cuernavaca," and that, "notwithstanding the conciliatory efforts I have made, I find that the character of my wife is totally incompatible with mine."

The court here refused to act on any of Mrs. McLean's petitions today.

SENATE VOTES BONUS LOAN BILL, 72 TO 12; PRESIDENT SAYS HE WILL VETO IT AT ONCE; BOTH HOUSES PREPARED TO OVERRIDE HIM

Upholding of Bonus Bill Veto Most Remote; 17 Senators Would Have to Reverse Their Votes

Special to The New York Times.

WASHINGTON, Feb. 19.—As the situation in Congress stands tonight, there appears not the remotest reason to expect that the President's veto of the bonus bill will be sustained in either House or Senate.

Every indication is for an overwhelming rejection of the veto. In the Senate today those voting for the bill numbered seventy-two, four others were paired for it, and of the four unpaired absentees three favored the legislation.

To sustain the veto with all Senators voting, thirty-three votes would be necessary. The record shows there are sixteen Senators against the bill, with the position of one, Senator Deneen of Illinois, not disclosed.

To uphold the President, seventeen Senators would have to reverse themselves, and not even Senator Reed of Pennsylvania, chief opponent of the legislation, has any hopes that such an about-face is in prospect. If the eighty-four Senators who voted today ballot on the motion to sustain the veto, it would require twenty-nine to sustain and fifty-eight to reject. Incidentally, with all Senators voting, the number necessary to override is sixty-six, or six less than the number who voted for the bill today.

In the House the situation is even more overwhelmingly against the President. The number of Representatives necessary to sustain a veto with all members recorded is 146. The number necessary to reject is 290.

On the motion to suspend the rules and pass the bill the House voted against the bill, 363 to 39. Four members were paired for and two against it, with twenty-three absent and not paired. There is one vacancy in the House, due to the death of Charles F. Curry of the Third District of California.

ADMINISTRATION BILL ASKS WORK AGENCIES

Doak Submits Measure for Federal Service in Place of Wagner Cooperative Plan.

SENATOR OPPOSES PROJECT

It Would Hurt Local Initiative and Become Partisan, He Says in Paper Read at Detroit.

Special to The New York Times.

WASHINGTON, Feb. 19.—Secretary Doak has sent to the House Judiciary Committee a bill providing for a national employment system, asking that it be substituted for the second Wagner employment bill, which has been reported to the House and is on the calendar.

The proposal of Secretary Doak would place the national employment system under the jurisdiction of the Department of Labor, whereas the Wagner bill provides for a nationwide Federal and State aid system.

The Doak measure, which has been labeled an "administration substitute," provides for a Third Assistant Secretary of Labor at a salary of $9,000 a year to head this new system, to be known as the United States Employment Service. This would be an enlargement of the duties and personnel of the Employment Service already in existence in the Department of Labor.

The functions of the new service would be to "advance opportunities of employment" by compiling, "furnishing and publishing information as to opportunities for employment, and by establishing and maintaining a system for clearing labor between the several States."

The bill would authorize the estab-

Continued on Page Seventeen.

NAVY BUILDING BILL SHELVED BY HOUSE

Program for Rest of Session Includes Action on Measure to Modernize Battleships.

MUSCLE SHOAL VOTE TODAY

Longworth Issues "Anti-Jam" Edict—$358,150,482 Naval Supply Bill in Senate.

Special to The New York Times.

WASHINGTON, Feb. 19.—Failure in the present Congress of the $74,000,000 naval construction bill, advocated by the administration as an intial step toward enlarging the fleet to the terms of the London treaty, became a virtual certainty today when the legislative slate of the House for the remainder of the session was made known.

Speaker Longworth, in disclosing the program, expressed doubt that the naval building bill would be acted upon. He predicted, however, that the $30,000,000 battleship modernization bill would be acted on next week; and the House Rules Committee during the day voted to have the measure up soon. Another navy bill, to readjust promotions of line officers, also will be brought for action before the end of the session, Mr. Longworth said.

In discussing the probable fate of the $74,000,000 navy construction bill Speaker Longworth asserted that Secretary Adams had asked House leaders to give first consideration to the modernization of the battleships Mississippi, Idaho and New Mexico and the line officers promotion bill.

"I hope to see the $74,000,000 brought up early in the next Congress," the Speaker said.

Supply Bill Reported to Senate.

The Navy Department appropriation bill, carrying $358,150,482, or $10,098,530 more than the House provided, was reported to the Senate during the day by its Naval Affairs Committee. It will be brought up in the chamber tomorrow, if possible.

The committee added provision for ten destroyers, authorized under the 1916 building program, at a cost of $7,500,000 for construction and machinery and $2,500,000 for armor, armament and ammunition. It also added $200,000 for experimental work in connection with a metal-clad airship; while it cut off $226,470 by reducing to seventy the number of reserve aviators with the fleet, from the 140 authorized by the House.

The committee recommended that each Senator and House member should have the privilege of appointing four midshipmen to the Naval Academy annually, instead of three, as voted by the House.

The House meanwhile voted the final supply bill, the second deficiency measure, carrying $59,113,000 for emergency appropriations and allocations for public buildings aggregating $6,994,000. It provides $23,668,-

Continued on Page Two.

ALL AMENDMENTS REJECTED

Reed Leads Fight to Kill Measure, but Against Hopeless Odds.

POCKET VETO TALK ENDED

Hoover Tells Leaders That He Will Act Today if Measure Is Received.

BEGINS DRAFTING MESSAGE

Senate Opponents of Legislation Say House Vote Set the Tide Against Them.

Special to The New York Times.

WASHINGTON, Feb. 19.—The Senate, by a vote of 72 to 12, agreed today to the House bonus loan bill, disregarding President Hoover's warning that it would cause a weakening of the government's financial structure and suggestions by other opponents that it might bring about new taxation next year.

The bill will go to the President tomorrow and he may return it with a veto message to the House late in the afternoon. It is understood that the President began work on the message tonight, so that it might be submitted to Congress without a moment's unnecessary delay.

In the opinion of Republican leaders, Congress will override a veto and the bill may become law before the end of the week.

Under the impetus of the decisive vote cast in the House earlier in the week, the Senate, after five hours of listless debate, went on record by a majority which surprised even the warmest supporters of the measure.

Say House Vote Caused Swing.

The proponents of the bill, according to the few administration leaders who stood by President Hoover, gained strength steadily after the House passed the bill Monday by the overwhelming vote of 363 to 39.

The twelve Senators who voted against the bill were Republicans, including Senator Borah, leader of the insurgent group. Thirty-four Republicans, including Senators Watson and McNary, floor leaders, supported the bill, along with thirty-seven Democrats and one Farmer-Laborite.

The total vote of the House and Senate was 435 for and 51 opposed, representing, it was said, the largest combined vote cast by Congress in twenty years for a bill opposed by a President. Republican Senate leaders said that the sentiment for the bill had been influenced in the last few days by a drive set in motion by the American Legion.

Ten-Day Limit Has Expired.

The House had adjourned today before the Senate acted, and therefore it was impossible to engross the bill and send it to the President tonight. This delay, Senator McNary said, prevented it from reaching the President within the ten days in which he must act before the adjournment of Congress.

Senator McNary explained that authorities had decided the day on which the President received the bill was not included in the computation, and also that March 4, the day of adjournment, was counted as but a half a day. Therefore the plans of the advocates of the bill to get it to the President so he could not kill it by a pocket veto did not work out as they had expected.

President Hoover informed the leaders, however, that he had from the first intended to act promptly, and at no time had given consideration to a pocket veto. His message disapproving the bill, the leaders were assured, would reach the House tomorrow, provided the measure was signed by the presiding officers of Senate and House and was received at the White House in time to make such a program feasible.

In the opinion of the Republican leaders, with the bonus bill out of the way all danger of an extra session will have disappeared.

Senator Reed, Republican, of Pennsylvania, led the fight against the bill. Senator Harrison, Democrat, of Mississippi, led for those favoring adoption. Senator Bingham of Connecticut was the only other Republican who opposed the tidal wave.

An amendment by Senator King, Democrat, who was paired against the measure, was defeated without a roll-call. It would have restricted loans to needy veterans.

Debate on the bonus bill was pre-

Walt Disney entertained the country with his cartoons.

James Cagney in his role as the underworld king in *The Public Enemy.*

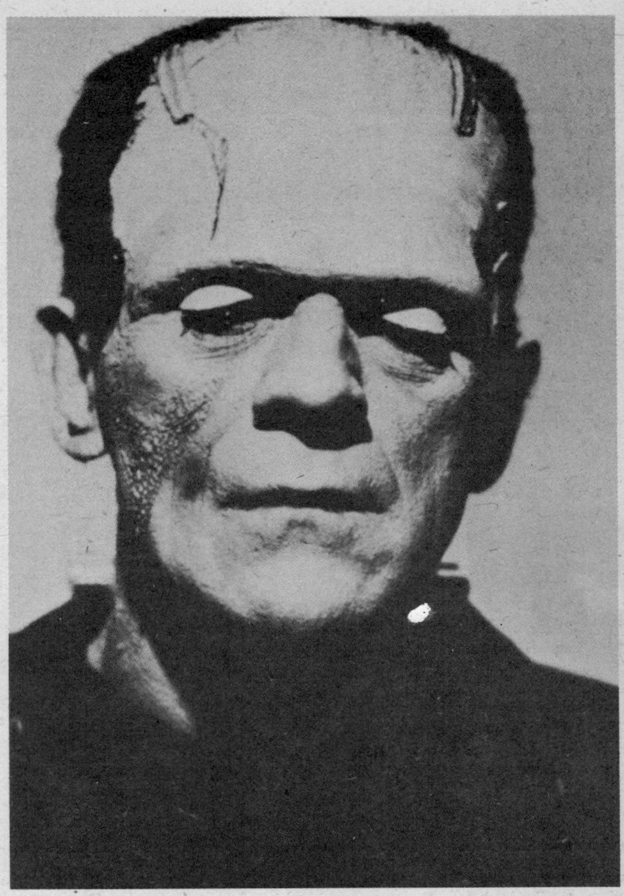

Frankenstein as played by Boris Karloff.

Bela Lugosi starred in *Dracula.*

Cagney with Jean Harlow in a scene from *The Public Enemy.*

Charlie Chaplin, the winsome tramp, in *City Lights.*

New York's Mayor Jimmy Walker. The Gordon case started him on the road to obscurity and disgrace.

SLAIN WOMAN AND HER THREAT OF VICE EXPOSE.

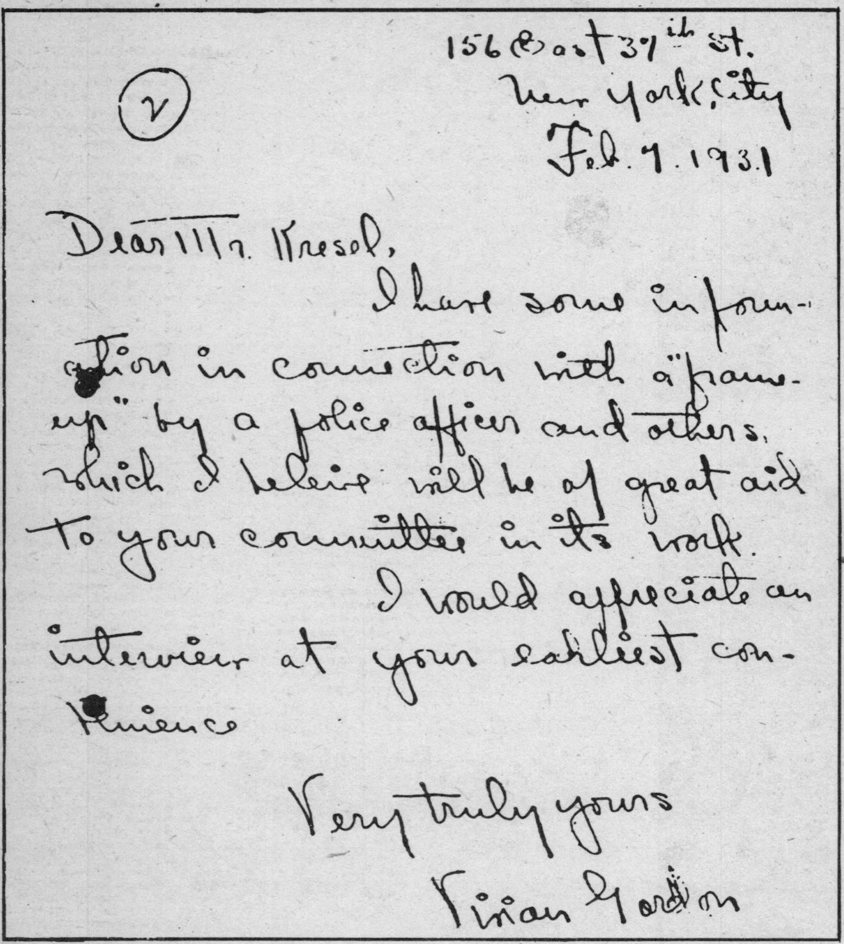

156 East 37th St.
New York City
Feb. 7. 1931

(2)

Dear Mr. Kresel,

I have some information in connection with a "frame-up" by a police officer and others, which I believe will be of great aid to your committee in its work.

I would appreciate an interview at your earliest convenience

Very truly yours
Vivian Gordon

Times Wide World Photo.

Facsimile of the letter written by Vivian Gordon to Isidor J. Kresel, who was then counsel in the Seabury inquiry, offering testimony of having been framed by the police vice squad.

The new cars, for those who could afford them — the La Salle sedan and Ford's Model A.

Times Wide World Photo.

The spot in Van Cortlandt Park where the body was found, near the Moshulu golf course.

Vivian Gordon, also known as Benita Bischoff.

The city room of the New York *World* the day it was sold to the Scripps-Howard syndicate.

"All the News That's Fit to Print."

The New York Times.

Copyright, 1931, by The New York Times Company.

THE WEATHER
Fair today and tomorrow; not much change in temperature.
Temperatures yesterday—Max., [illegible]; min., [illegible].
U. S. Weather Forecast—For details see Page [illegible].

VOL. LXXX....No. 26,697. ***** NEW YORK, FRIDAY, FEBRUARY 27, 1931. TWO CENTS In Greater New York | THREE CENTS Within 200 Miles | FOUR CENTS Elsewhere Except 7th and 8th Postal Zones

WOMAN VICE CASE WITNESS FOUND STRANGLED IN PARK; HER LAWYER IS ARRESTED

SHE WROTE SHE FEARED HIM

He and Another Named in Her Diary Held as Witnesses.

SHE ACCUSED POLICEMAN

Offered to Bare 'Frame-Up'—Vice Squad Man Who Arrested Her Faces Questioning.

TAXI DRIVER SAW STRUGGLE

Followed Cab, in Which Two Men Were Beating Woman, to Van Cortlandt Park.

The body of Vivian Gordon, who had offered to tell the Appellate Division inquiry about a "frame-up by police officers and others," was found at the foot of an embankment off Mosholu Avenue in Van Cortlandt Park, the Bronx, early yesterday. She had a police record which began in 1923 with her arrest on a vice charge under the name of Benita Bishoff.

After many hours of continuous questioning of witnesses, Police Commissioner Mulrooney announced at 1 o'clock this morning that two men had been detained as material witnesses in the case. They are John Radeloff of 66 Court Street, Brooklyn, the woman's attorney, who admitted, according to Mr. Mulrooney, that he had advised her against telling her story to the investigators, and Sam Cohen, alias Charles Harris, a client of Radeloff's and the possessor of a criminal record, according to the Commissioner.

Says She Feared Radeloff.

They were held for further questioning after an entry had been found in one of several diaries kept by the woman, which read, according to the commissioner, as follows:

"The only man I have to fear is Radeloff. He could get Cohen or henchmen to do away with me."

Radeloff told Mr. Mulrooney and Assistant District Attorney Foley of the Bronx that when Mrs. Gordon had told him of her intention of going to the Appellate Division's investigators he had advised her against the step, on the ground that her case was eight years old and that she could gain nothing by reopening it. She replied, according to Radeloff, that she was "going to give McLaughlin the needle just to get even."

The woman's fingerprints revealed that she had been arrested in March of 1923 by Patrolman Andrew J. McLaughlin of the Vice Squad, on a charge of immortality which resulted in her sentence to the Bedford Reformatory. Efforts to locate McLaughlin yesterday developed that he was on a five-day leave of absence and had sailed last Monday on the Cunard liner California for a six-day cruise to Bermuda. The boat is due back Saturday. Mr. Mulrooney said that he wanted to question McLaughlin.

Miss Gordon had been strangled by a clothesline, which had been noosed with a slip-knot, pulled tight with the knot at the back of her neck and then wound thrice around. The rope had apparently been used to drag her along the side of the street before she was tossed off the steep embankment. She had been dead about five hours when the body was found at 7 A. M., according to Louis Lefkowitz, Assistant Medical Examiner.

Taxi Driver Saw Struggle.

Frank Ryan, a taxicab driver of 3,805 Barnes Avenue, the Bronx, last night told the police that at about 2:30 A. M. yesterday morning he had witnessed a struggle in another taxicab between a woman and two men. Ryan said he was parked at a cab stand at Allerton and White Plains Avenues, the Bronx, and that a woman screamed several times in a near-by vehicle.

He could see, said Ryan, that two men were striking her. He followed the taxicab over a long circuitous route through the Bronx until it finally turned into Van Cortlandt Park from 233d Street. There, he said, his machine developed engine trouble and he was forced to drop the chase. The point is about a mile and a half from where the body was found.

McLaughlin is the partner of Rich-

Continued on Page Fourteen.

Legion Men Vote Not to Ask Bonus Loans Except for Needy

An effort will be made to persuade Brooklyn World War veterans not to obtain loans on their adjusted compensation service certificates, except in cases of dire necessity and when aid cannot be obtained elsewhere, under the terms of a resolution adopted by the Kings County committee of the American Legion.

The resolution also asserted "that it be understood that the Legion, in practice, is not interested in the money-grabbing phase of the bonus bill, if enacted."

The resolution was voted unanimously at a meeting Wednesday night at the Cummings Post Clubhouse, 314 Clinton Street, Brooklyn.

CHARGE JEAN NORRIS DEFIED COURT ORDER

Two Seabury Witnesses Swear Magistrate Overrode Decree of Higher Tribunal.

SHE CHALLENGES MINUTES

Is Upheld in Assertion She Did Not See Ruling—Clerk Contradicts Silbermann.

Magistrate Jean Norris appeared yesterday before Samuel Seabury in the magistrates' investigation and heard two witnesses testify under oath that she had ignored a Supreme Court order in a separation case which had a sequel before her in family court. Mrs. Norris, who had appeared under subpoena after having failed to appear by invitation at an earlier hearing, took the stand and denied the accusation.

The stenographer who transcribed the minutes of the separation hearing took the stand and supported Magistrate Norris. The transcript did not show that a certified copy of the court order had been shown to Magistrate Norris as the accusing witnesses had testified.

While the hearing was in progress Justice Edward Lazansky, presiding in the Appellate Division in Brooklyn, mailed to Governor Roosevelt his reply to the Governor's request for a city-wide magistrates' investigation.

Justice Lazansky declined to comment on a report that he had advised against the enlargement of the investigation. Governor Roosevelt in Albany said he had not received Justice Lazansky's reply.

Summary Conviction Told.

Testimony before Mr. Seabury further disclosed that a young woman, living as the wife of a man to whom she was not married, had been convicted before Magistrate Norris within two hours after she was arrested without a warrant on a charge of vagrancy. Two members of the police vice squad took the stand and were questioned about large bank accounts. Chief Magistrate Joseph E. Corrigan testified briefly concerning procedure in the magistrates' courts, and the chief stenographer in the Women's Court contradicted the testimony of Magistrate Jesse Silberman by saying he understood that he was to insert in a steno-

Continued on Page Twelve.

HOUSE OVERRIDES HOOVER BONUS VETO; VOTE IS 328 TO 79

Message Is Acted On in 43 Minutes, Clamor Deterring Speakers Backing President.

HE WARNS OF A TAX RISE

Measure Will Not Benefit Veterans as Much as Believed, the Executive Asserts.

TREASURY MUST BORROW

Senate Will Vote Today, With Slight Chance That Veto Will Be Upheld.

Full text of the President's veto message is printed on page 15.

Special to The New York Times.

WASHINGTON, Feb. 26.—In the swiftest action of recent record in opposing the Executive, the House today rode rough-shod over President Hoover's veto of the Veterans' bonus loan bill, passing it by a vote of 328 to 79, or 56 more than the two-thirds necessary to override the veto.

In forty-three minutes the House had acted and forwarded the message to the Senate, which read it and agreed to consideration at 11 o'clock tomorrow, with indications that enough votes cannot be mustered to uphold the veto and that the bill will become a law before the end of the week.

The message warned of possible increased taxes and injury to the government's financial structure. The House began reading it at 3:20 P. M., with nearly every seat on the Republican side occupied and the galleries crowded.

President Hoover touched on the financial aspects of the legislation and declared that it "was unwise from the standpoint of the veterans themselves and unwise from the standpoint of the welfare of the people."

Benefit Overestimated, He Says.

"The utility of this legislation as relief to those in distress is far less than has been disclosed," the President insisted.

The popular assumption, he added, has been that since the certificates average $1,000, each veteran will be able to obtain $500, the 50 per cent loan permitted in the bill, but the fact is that more than 800,000 men will be able to borrow less than $200, and of these more than 200,000 will be able to borrow only an average of $75.

At the same time, the President said, according to General Hines, the Administrator of Veterans' Affairs, "the probable number who will avail themselves of the privilege under this bill will require approximately $1,000,000,000."

"There not being a penny in the treasury to meet such a demand," the President continued, "the government must borrow this sum through the sale of reserve fund securities, together with further issues, or we must impose further taxation."

In this language the President replied to the statements of members of Congress who insist that the money to make the loans was to be found in the treasury.

The President stated that the measure provided benefits for scores of thousands "in the income-tax paying class" equal to those for veterans in actual need. Most of the for-

Continued on Page Fifteen.

Southern Congressmen Call on Hoover To Urge Him to Sign Muscle Shoals Bill

Special to The New York Times.

WASHINGTON, Feb. 26.—A delegation of Southern members of Congress, most of them from Alabama and Tennessee, called on President Hoover this morning and asked him to approve the resolution passed by Congress for the operation of the Muscle Shoals power plant on the Tennessee River.

Representative Edward B. Almon of Alabama, in whose district the Muscle Shoals plant is located, was spokesman. Other members of the delegation were Senators Brock of Tennessee, Harris of Georgia, Black of Alabama and Williamson of Kentucky, Representatives Taylor and McReynolds of Tennessee and Bankhead and Hill of Alabama. Mr. Taylor was the only Republican present.

Mr. Almon told the President that Congress had made an honest and diligent effort to settle the ten-year-old Muscle Shoals problem and that the resolution passed and now waiting the approval of the President gave him "full and complete authority" to lease the Muscle Shoals properties. He continued:

"The power plant was constructed to generate power to operate the fertilizer plants and not for general distribution. Hence, no one can complain that all of the power should be used for the operation of the plants.

"Chemical and fertilizer interests may not have time to study the provisions of the bill before the 4th of March. I know of one of the largest industrialists in the South who is seriously considering making an offer to lease these properties. When the bill has been approved there will be very sharp competition among the chemical and fertilizer industries and you will experience no difficulty in making a lease that will bring a large income to the government and relieve distressed American agriculture by an increase in fertilizer production and reduction of prices.

"However, in the event you should be unable to make a lease during the next twelve months, there would be operation of the plants for research and experimental purposes which would preserve the plants for national defense, and if the board should at any time recommend to Congress a discontinuance of this operation, Congress would no doubt give favorable consideration to the recommendation of the board."

The President listened attentively to Mr. Almon and his associates. His decision may be announced tomorrow.

MONTGOMERY, Ala., Feb. 26 (AP).—Governor B. M. Miller tonight made public a telegram from President Hoover asking for information as to any one who might lease the nitrate plants at Muscle Shoals "under the conditions imposed."

In reply the Governor said he did know of one Alabama industrialist who was seriously studying the bill with a view of entering negotiations for the lease.

FARM BOARD TO SELL SOME WHEAT ABROAD

Chicago Market Breaks 2½ Cents on Decision to Export 35,000,000 Bushels.

RALLIES ON EXPLANATION

Legge and Milnor Allay Fear of "Dumping"—Move Made to Clear Ports for 1931 Crop.

Special to The New York Times.

CHICAGO, Feb. 26.—A decision to export 35,000,000 bushels of "choice milling wheat" now stored at seaboard, announced today by George S. Milnor, president of the Grain Stabilization Corporation operating under Federal Farm Board supervision, was followed by a break of 2½ cents a bushel in the Board of Trade's wheat pit.

The price recession was due to selling by traders, who interpreted the decision as meaning a price-cutting war with other wheat-surplus producing countries. But both Mr. Milnor and Alexander Legge, chairman of the Farm Board, made it plain that there was no need for under-cutting.

Mr. Milnor, indicating that no dumping policy was contemplated, declared that the wheat, being sold to provide port storage space for the 1931 crop, would not be offered at "lower prices than those of other principal export countries, taking into consideration customary differentials for grades and quality."

The effect of these explanations was felt toward the end of the trading day, the market rallying slightly.

Mr. Milnor's Statement.

In his statement regarding the wheat to be exported, which is estimated to be almost a fourth of the Stabilization Corporation's holdings, Mr. Milnor said:

"There have been persistent rumors, both in this country and abroad, regarding the probable selling policy of the wheat under control of the Federal Farm Board. It is believed that the effect of such rumors upon the grain market creates a feeling of uncertainty that the facts do not justify.

"Therefore, this corporation, which owns all of the so-called Farm Board wheat, is very glad to announce the following policy, which has the full concurrence of the Federal Farm Board.

"The corporation has some stocks of choice milling quality wheat at the Atlantic Seaboard, Gulf, and in the Pacific Northwest, which, on account of position, cannot move into domestic markets advantageously for milling, drought relief or feeding purposes.

"In order that such stocks may be disposed of in ample time to clear the port of facilities for taking care of the new 1931 crop, it is deemed advisable that such wheat be sold in export markets during the next four months. The quantity available will not exceed 35,000,000 bushels, including Pacific Coast wheat, which will move largely to the Orient.

Maximum for Export.

"The wheat will not be offered at lower prices than those of other principal exporting countries, taking into account customary differentials for grades and quality. This enables

Continued on Page Ten.

HOUSE REPUBLICANS RENAME LONGWORTH

But 18 Members Stay Away, Presaging Trouble in Organizing the Next House.

KANSANS SCORE SPEAKERS

Five Denounce Failure to Hear Oil Curb Plea—McGugin Comes Out for Garner.

Special to The New York Times.

WASHINGTON, Feb. 26.—A hard fight for the Republican party in the organization of the House of Representatives in the next Congress was presaged by the refusal of eighteen members and members-elect to attend the Republican conference held tonight to arrange for organization.

The conference renominated Nicholas Longworth for Speaker and John Q. Tilson for floor leader.

Among those who stayed away were several independents who seldom attend a caucus for fear that they will be bound by the action taken. The Kansas regulars, however, stayed out as a protest of the failure of the Longworth leadership to listen to their eleventh-hour plea for an embargo against oil imports as a protection to independent producers in their State.

An effort by Representative Hogg of West Virginia to have the conference go on record in favor of legislation in favor of an oil embargo before the end of the present session was defeated tonight by a point of order against consideration of any legislation.

The eighteen who remained away were McGugin, Sparks, Hoch, Hope, Guyer and Lambertson of Kansas; Frear, Peavy, Schneider, Cooper, Kading, Nelson and Withrow of Wisconsin; Maas, Helvig, Christgau of Minnesota; Campbell and La Guardia.

McGugin Backs Garner.

Word was received in Washington this afternoon that Harold McGugin, Republican, Representative-elect from the Third Kansas District, had announced that he would vote for Representative Garner of Texas, minority leader, who in all probability will be the Democratic candidate for Speaker.

Mr. McGugin is the only Republican who has signified his intention of voting for the Democratic organization of the next House.

The conference referred to the Republican members of the Rules Committee a proposal to revise the rules ad make them more workable for the next Congress.

Speaker Longworth, in a brief speech, said that there had been some misunderstanding of the term used in calling tonight's meeting, that some seemed to think that a "caucus" was to be held, whereas it was only intended to be a "conference," which, unlike a caucus, would not be binding on those attending.

The five Kansas members issued a statement in which they said:

"We are Republicans and believe in party organization and party responsibility and expect to continue that attitude. More than that, we know how hollow are the protesta-

Continued on Page Six.

BANK INDICTMENTS UPHELD BY COURT; EARLY TRIAL LIKELY

Pleas by Marcus and Aides That Jurors Were Biased and Steuer Disqualified Are Denied.

THE DECISION IS FINAL

Bankers to Be Arraigned Today and Are Expected to Ask for Separate Trials.

GRAND JURY HEARS HEDLEY

Steuer to Resume Open Hearings Monday—Two Affiliates of Bank of U. S. File Reports.

The indictments against Bernard K. Marcus, president of the Bank of United States and seven other officers and directors of the bank, were upheld yesterday by Judge William Allen of the Court of General Sessions. The court denied two motions by attorneys for Mr. Marcus and five of his fellow-defendants.

The motions brought by Charles H. Tuttle, counsel for Mr. Marcus, and supported by counsel of five of the indicted bankers, challenged the legality of the indictments on two grounds. These were the alleged disqualification of Max D. Steuer, who as Assistant District Attorney presented the evidence to the grand jury, and of three of the grand jurors because they owned stock in the bank.

Mr. Steuer's disqualification was challenged by the attorneys for the defense on the ground of his dual capacity as Assistant District Attorney and Assistant Attorney General in the bank investigation and of his association with litigations involving the bank.

The decision of Judge Allen is final. The indicted bankers must now prepare for trial. It was learned at the office of District Attorney Crain that an early trial may be expected. While District Attorney Crain would not venture to predict the probable date of the trial, it was believed it would be held before the Summer vacation.

Mr. Marcus and those of the indicted bankers who joined in his motions will again appear for pleading before Judge Allen today. It is considered not unlikely that they may ask separate trials.

The grand jury, which resumed its inquiry on Wednesday into several new aspects of the bank's affairs, met again yesterday and heard Frank Hedley, president and general manager of the Interborough Rapid Transit Company, and Frederick Hobbs, both directors of the bank. Mr. Hobbs will continue his testimony today and will be followed by other directors. No additional indictments are expected for some time, however. The grand jury will adjourn today for about ten days or more to permit Mr. Steuer to resume his open hearings. These will be resumed on Monday.

On the ground of Mr. Steuer's disqualification Judge Allen in his decision pointed out that this contention had already been passed upon by the courts and found wanting. Judge Allen wrote:

"The matters set forth in the moving affidavit in support of the motion to set aside and quash the indictments have been passed upon adversely to the contentions of the moving parties by the Supreme Court at special term, by the Appellate Division and by the Court of Appeals.

"But, irrespective of prior adjudi-

Continued on Page Four.

THE WORLD NEWSPAPERS SOLD TO SCRIPPS-HOWARD AFTER COURT'S SANCTION

LAST EDITIONS ARE PRINTED

Evening to Consolidate Today With Telegram as World-Telegram.

MORNING PAPERS ENDED

Foley, Lifting Ban on Sale, Holds He Has No Jurisdiction as to Purchaser.

EMPLOYES FIGHT TO LAST

They Are to Receive $500,000, Pulitzers Announce—Valedictory to the Readers.

Surrogate James A. Foley, in a decision handed down late last night and made public early this morning, ruled that Ralph, Herbert and Joseph Pulitzer had the right to sell The World newspapers despite a provision in the will of their father, Joseph Pulitzer, to the contrary, and early today the papers became the property of the Scripps-Howard chain.

Although the Surrogate, claiming lack of jurisdiction, refused to rule on the merits of various offers, including that of the employes of The World seeking to purchase the property themselves, he left the way open for consummation of the contract which Roy W. Howard had made with the Pulitzers before the case went to court.

Last Morning Edition.

Announcement that the deal was closed and that this morning's edition of The World, carrying a valedictory to its readers after more than half a century in the Pulitzer family, would be its last, was made at 2 A. M. from the offices of John G. Jackson, attorney for the Pulitzers, at 15 Broad Street, where the principals met. The Evening World will appear in consolidation with The Telegram today as The World-Telegram.

In a statement issued simultaneously with the announcement, the new owner asserted that the transaction meant not the "death of The World but its rebirth."

Workers Get News of Sale.

The sale took place as the "lobster shift," the midnight to dawn workers of The Evening World, were reporting for work. J. M. Bresnahan, circulation manager, had issued orders for distribution of today's edition of the newspaper. H. S. Pollard, the editor, however sent word that the presses would not run. The evening edition had appeared for the last time, he said.

Employes of the defunct newspaper, whose gallant fight to keep it alive and carry on the traditions of its founder attracted nation-wide sympathy and support, were assured by the trustees that their loyalty would not be forgotten. The World in its final edition announced that $500,000—the amount of Mr. Howard's down payment—would be set aside to be distributed among them under the terms of a plan to be announced later.

Further reassuring words for the employes of the scrapped newspapers came from William W. Hawkins, general manager of the Scripps-Howard chain of twenty-five newspapers, who said that provision would be made for employing as many as possible of the men whose jobs have been wiped out.

The actual contract for the transfer of The World's "intangibles," for which Mr. Howard paid what he said was the "largest sum in newspaper history," was executed before the formal handing down of the decree by which the "dead hand" of Joseph Pulitzer was set aside. Although the surrogate's decision made the decree certain, some of the attorneys warned that a sale under the circumstances might be vulnerable to attack. The warning assumed added significance because of rumors of possible injunction and appeals that might be taken by other interested groups.

Upholds the Trustees.

Surrogate Foley's decision was divided into two parts. In holding that the three sons of Joseph Pulitzer might sell the property, which they had testified they could not continue to operate after ninety days on its present resources, the Surrogate

Continued on Page Two.

Park Row's Newspaper Glory Fades Out With The World

The passing the The World and The Evening World marks the end of "Newspaper Row," as Park Row was called when nearly every important newspaper was printed downtown. The World was the last to abandon the old centre. Years ago THE TIMES and The Herald-Tribune, then The Tribune, moved uptown, and The Sun moved to other quarters, but The World remained.

The Pulitzer Building, at 63 Park Row, which it occupied, was not included in the sale to the Scripps-Howard interests nor were the presses and equipment which were the property of The World. They will be sold, it is presumed, as soon as possible, and the proceeds turned over to the heirs.

WORLD'S LAST ISSUE BIDS PUBLIC ADIEU

"Valedictory," an Editorial by Walter Lippmann, Passes on Its "Sword."

SALUTES NEW OWNERS

Pays Tribute to Newspaper Men Who Devoted Themselves to It for Half-Century.

The following is the text of an editorial inserted in the fourth and last edition of The World today marking the last appearance of the publications. It is written by Walter Lippmann, the editor:

VALEDICTORY.

This is the last appearance of The World as its readers have known it. Yesterday the ownership of the newspaper passed from the heirs of Joseph Pulitzer to the publishers of the Scripps-Howard chain of newspapers. With this sale the responsibility of the present editorial direction comes to an end.

On page one of this issue the trustees of the newspaper properties are making the public announcement of the action they have taken. On this page it remains only for us to say a grateful farewell to the readers of The World, to pay tribute to the long line of distinguished newspapermen who over a period of nearly half a century made The World what it has been, and to salute those who now become the owners and directors of the newspaper.

We have striven, subject to the limitations of our own abilities and of ordinary human frailty, to carry out the solemn injunction of the founder that The World should be conducted "as a public institution, from motives higher than mere gain," and at all times "in a spirit of independence." We believe that the readers of The World have shown their faith in the genuineness of this purpose by the loyalty with which they have supported the paper. For such support by its readers The World is deeply grateful.

To the newspaper men who have worked for The World we pay affectionate homage. They include

Continued on Page Three.

Ruin of France's Flax and Linen Industries Feared as Senators Ask Soviet Dumping Curb

Special Cable to THE NEW YORK TIMES.

PARIS, Feb. 26.—Striking figures showing the extent to which Soviet methods have disturbed Continental markets were cited today when the Minister of Agriculture, André Tardieu, was called upon in a Senate interpellation to tell what protection he was prepared to give the French flax and linen industries against disastrous Russian competition.

Senators Cavillon and Yves Le Trocquer, former Minister for the Liberated Regions, declared that French flax growers and linen makers would be driven from the market if the Russian invasion continued. While French flax was worth 1,000 francs [$40] a metric quintal, said the former, Soviet flax was offered in the French market at 500 francs.

"Russian exports of linen to England rose from 31,000 square yards in 1926 to 1,055,000 in 1929," he declared. "Our own market purchased 217,000 quintals of Russian flax in 1930, as compared with 146,000 in 1929."

Senator Cavillon pictured a similar development in Russian wood, wheat, meat and coal exports and predicted a greater effort next year.

Senator Le Trocquer said Russia was able to sell her products cheaply because she did not have to count outlays either for capital or raw materials and used forced labor at negligible wages. The Soviet selling price, he asserted, was 25 per cent under pre-war gold values.

M. Tardieu's reply admitted great danger to the French flax industry from Russian competition, but emphasized the difficulties of the situation. He enumerated measures which the government was preparing to alleviate the situation of the French flax growers, declaring he intended to act quickly.

Repeatedly during his speech the Minister of Agriculture obtained unanimous applause from the house which three months ago defeated his Cabinet.

Stocks Resume Advance in Brisk Trading; Year's Volume Passes 100,000,000-Share Mark

With its technical position repaired by Wednesday's moderate reaction, the stock market resumed its advance in vigorous fashion yesterday, further encouraging the belief in Wall Street that the reviving demand for securities is a harbinger of prosperity.

Yesterday's advance was accompanied by a sizeable expansion in trading interest. Dealings on the New York Stock Exchange involved a total of 4,619,099 shares, against 4,388,942 shares on the day before. The net gains ran from 2 to 7 points in the stocks to which traders devoted most of their attention, but final prices in most instances were substantially below the day's best figures.

The day's turnover brought the total volume of business on the Stock Exchange for 1931 above the 100,000,000-share mark for the first time. Transactions thus far this year have aggregated 101,227,341 shares, as compared with 127,821,990 shares in the corresponding period of 1930 and with 188,772,690 shares in the same period of 1929, in which year the market was swollen to the largest proportions in history.

United States Steel common reasserted its leadership of the market yesterday, touching a new high for the year at 152⅞. The final price was 151, which represented a net gain of 2⅓ points. Trading in Steel was uncommonly heavy. Auburn Auto rose to 217½, also a new high, and closed at 209¾ with a net gain of 6¼ points. American Water Works was up 4 points on the day, Brooklyn Union Gas 2¼, Engineers Public Service preferred 7⅞, Lima Locomotive 3⅞, Norfolk & Western 4, Pierce Oil preferred 3⅝, Pullman 2¾, Standard Gas 2¼, United States Realty 2¾, Wrigley 3 and Western Union 3⅝.

There was another burst of trading enthusiasm on the New York Curb Exchange, where transactions exceeded 1,000,000 shares for the first time this year. Some of the leaders on the Curb rose spectacularly.

"All the News That's Fit to Print."

The New York Times.

Copyright, 1931, by The New York Times Company.

THE WEATHER
Fair and somewhat warmer today; tomorrow rain.
Temperatures yesterday—Max. 42, min. 28.
U. S. Weather Forecast—For details see Page 30.

VOL. LXXX....No. 26,698. ****+ NEW YORK, SATURDAY, FEBRUARY 28, 1931. TWO CENTS In Greater New York | THREE CENTS Within 200 Miles | FOUR CENTS Elsewhere Except 7th and 8th Postal Zones

TWO HELD IN $100,000 BAIL IN GORDON MURDER CASE; SHE CHARGED POLICE PLOT

ACCUSED VICE HUNTERS

Told Seabury Aide They and Her Ex-Husband Framed Her.

POLICE TO BE QUESTIONED

High Bail Asked for Lawyer and Ex-Convict as Hostile Witnesses.

PASTORS CALL FOR ACTION

Wise and Holmes Urge Citizens to Organize Vigilantes in War on Crime.

The murderer of Vivian Gordon, found strangled in Van Cortlandt Park on Thursday, five days after she had become a vice witness in the Appellate Division inquiry, yesterday remained unknown to investigators.

District Attorney McLaughlin of the Bronx assumed charge of the investigation and after a lawyer and a man with a criminal record had been examined at length before a grand jury, he took them into Bronx County Court, where Judge Harry Stackell held each in bail of $50,000 as a material witness. Seven possible motives had been uncovered, said Mr. McLaughlin.

He declared that he would have Andrew J. McLaughlin, the vice squad patrolman who arrested Miss Gordon in 1923, met at the pier when he returns at 2 P. M. tomorrow on the Cunard liner California from Bermuda. Rabbi Stephen S. Wise and John Haynes Holmes, chairman of the New York committee on city affairs, issued a joint statement in which they said:

"This is not so much the murder of a woman as notice by criminals and gangsters inside and outside of the Police Department, on and off the magistrates' bench, that inquiry into and exposure of all organized criminality will meet with swift and awful punishment."

Threatened to Expose Ex-Husband.

While detectives working under Inspector Henry Bruckman of the Bronx and out of the East Thirty-fifth Street Station followed hosts of clues, tips and reports, with Mr. McLaughlin and his assistants examining fifty witnesses, a letter from the woman to her former husband, John E. C. Bischoff, business manager of the Federal reformatory at Lorton, Va., addressed to his home in Audubon, N. J., under date of Jan. 19, was turned up.

"You know," the letter read in part, "that my conviction was caused by a frame-up between you and Detective McLaughlin. You may think that you have had the last laugh, but get this—I am going before the investigation committee this week and intend to tell the whole story of this dirty frame-up.

"When I am through it will be just too bad for you. Little Benita is old enough now to realize that a dirty trick has been played on me. I intend to go the limit, and you know as well as I do that this will mean your finish."

This letter was dated almost three weeks before she wrote first to the Appellate Division inquiry. Irving Ben Cooper, who answered her only letter addressed to the inquiry under date of Feb. 7, yesterday made public an affidavit in which he repeated the substance of the information she had given him in an interview on Feb. 20. Miss Gordon was not under oath at the time of her examination by Cooper.

"She stated to me," the affidavit read, "that she wished me to help her right what she termed a wrong inflicted upon her by reason of the charge of immorality which had been preferred against her in March, 1923.

Charged a Plot Against Her.

"She stated that she was convicted as a result of a plot concocted between arresting officers and her husband, who was anxious to obtain complete custody of their infant daughter.

"Her statement with regard to the events leading up to her arrest in March, 1923, was that she was residing at a hotel in New York City; that she had some mail which she had turned over to some man other than her husband with the understanding that she was to call at his residence later in the day and obtain such mail from him; that while

Continued on Page Three.

Old London Department Store To Be Closed by Younger Rival

Wireless to THE NEW YORK TIMES.

LONDON, Feb. 27.—Shoolbred's the oldest department store in England, which Dickens and Thackeray patronized, will soon pass out of existence. Harrod's purchased the famous store, which had been established more than a century, and announced today that its business would be transferred to Harrod's. It is understood 1,000 persons will join the unemployed.

Shoolbred's suffered a decline in trade because of the change in London's shopping areas. Liquidators were appointed last Summer and have been negotiating for its sale since. At one time it was reported an American syndicate was seeking control.

Shoolbred's was founded in 1817. Harrod's started forty years ago with a capital of about $700,000. The capitalization of the company today is more than $31,000,000.

BROOKLYN INQUIRY OPPOSED BY COURT

Sweeping Investigation of Magistrates Is Not Warranted, Appellate Majority Decides.

PLEA PRACTICES UPHELD

Minority Report to Roosevelt Urges Examination as Vindication of Officials.

Special to The New York Times.

ALBANY, Feb. 27.—The Appellate Division of the Second Department, in a decision made public today, formally opposed extension of the magistrate's court inquiry to Brooklyn, Queens and Richmond.

The court, by a count of four to three, held that, in spite of allegations against specific magistrates dealt with individually, no evidence had been presented to justify any general investigation of the courts in those three boroughs. All seven justices were of the opinion that the facts did not warrant a sweeping inquiry, but the three who took a stand in favor of one expressed the opinion that it would be valuable merely as a means of vindicating the courts in the public mind.

The court forwarded its ruling to Governor Roosevelt in reply to a communication from him last week asking the court to consider a petition demanding the inquiry.

The majority members, composed of Justices Young, Carswell, Scudder and Tompkins, took up in detail the charges made in the petition which Governor Roosevelt sent to them. They examined the complaints against eight magistrates in the department contained in the document prepared by the Society for the Prevention of Unjust Convictions, which forwarded it to Governor Roosevelt.

The majority members cited the investigation conducted by the Appellate Division itself into each of the complaints and pointed out that in only one of these had any basis for action been disclosed. They said that in this case, involving Magistrate Rudich, the court had censured the magistrate and that this disciplinary measure was all that was justified.

At the same time that they as-

Continued on Page Two.

EUROPE IS ANGERED BY FARM BOARD PLAN TO SELL GRAIN THERE

Delegates to Paris Parley Say Our Sales Amount to Dumping on Depressed Market.

SEE BLOW LIKE SOVIET'S

Experts Believe Our Price Will Have to Be Under Russia's to Obtain Buyers.

CONFERENCE ENDS TODAY

Second Agricultural Meeting Has Done Little Toward Solving Central Europe's Troubles.

By CARLISLE MacDONALD.
Special Cable to THE NEW YORK TIMES.

PARIS, Feb. 27.—A feeling closely akin to consternation developed in the second European grain conference late this afternoon when it learned that the United States Farm Board had decided to sell 35,000,000 bushels of wheat in Continental markets at a price considerably below that maintained at home. When the heads of the various delegations had partly recovered from their astonishment, keen interest was the reaction to the move characterized as "American dumping" on a scale comparable with that of Russia.

Some of the delegates hesitated to believe the American Government would consent to a scheme which, according to today's reports, does not differ from the Soviet selling methods which are widely denounced in the United States. Others recalled that Canada and Argentina were conducting intensive selling campaigns throughout Europe, in which the diplomatic representatives of the two nations were actively engaged.

Because of the high prices fixed by the Farm Board, Canada and Argentina have been able to obtain much business which had previously gone to the United States. With the Farm Board apparently determined to overcome this handicap, the question has naturally arisen here as to whether American diplomats will now become wheat salesmen.

Fear Further Depression.

The delegates' resentment was caused by the fact that United States competition would further depress the European wheat market. The only definite thing which the present conference accomplished was recognition of the fact that the European grain crisis could not be solved without the collaboration of the great wheat-producing countries overseas. François Poncet as president of the conference suggested a world grain agreement.

The delegates who accepted the reported decision of the Farm Board as a fact stressed that a world grain accord was imperative now. Unless such an understanding can be reached, these experts believe the European agricultural situation, especially in Rumania, Poland, Yugoslavia, Bulgaria and Hungary, will go from bad to worse with Russia and the United States dumping huge quantities of wheat, further depressing prices and demoralizing markets.

There was much speculation among grain experts as to the price which the Farm Board would fix for its European shipments. Russian high protein wheat is sold for about 10 cents a bushel under the price of the best Canadian product. If the American board desires to compete with the Russians it will have to undersell Canada.

Assuming the figure of 35,000,000 bushels to be accurate, observers here explain, it represents about half of the total amount of wheat which the

Continued on Page Seven.

German Writers Agree to Work for Peace, Appeal to French to Ease Nation's Burdens

Special Cable to THE NEW YORK TIMES.

BERLIN, Feb. 27.—German writers and scholars published a joint manifesto today, addressed to those 186 French men of letters who recently appealed to German intellectuals to join them in working for a Franco-German understanding and a new Europe.

"Our two countries must remain in harmony with the fundamental of humanitarianism: Serve the people, do not sacrifice them," the Germans replied. "But we do not wish to confine ourselves to high-sounding declarations. We invite French intellectuals to join us in considering how best peace may finally be obtained and a genuine settlement of all our problems achieved."

Agreeing with the Frenchmen's prediction that a repetition of the catastrophe of 1914-to-1918 would mean the end of Western culture and that peace could be assured only by free agreements, freely entered into, the Germans nevertheless called attention to the difficult position of German friends of peace. The burdens under which Germany struggles and which she finds unjust and unsupportable were mentioned, not as grievances but to show the point where any attack on the problem must be begun, it was said.

"Help us to create a forum of conscience in a spirit of complete fearlessness. Join hands with us that we may serve together our common cause: the creation of the new Europe," the appeal concluded.

Among the signers were Thomas and Heinrich Mann, Lion Feuchtwanger, Jakob Wasserman, Arnold Zweig, Walter von Molo, Walter Bloem, Elizabeth Bergner, Bernhard Kellermann, Gabriele Reuter, Adele Sternheim, Professor Alois Brandl, Professor Georg Bernhard, Theodor Wolff, editor of the Tageblatt, and Carl Zuckmayer.

London-Cape Town Air Mail to Start Today After Eleven Years Spent Laying Out Route

Wireless to THE NEW YORK TIMES.

LONDON, Saturday, Feb. 28.—Flying over a route that has taken eleven years to prepare, the first African air mail will leave Croydon this morning and on Thursday will pass from Cairo over what is declared to be the worst flying country in the world.

So treacherous are the storms between Khartoum, Anglo-Egyptian Sudan, and Juba, Italian Somaliland, during the rainy season, for instance, that flying is safe only during certain hours of the day. There is a thunderstorm nearly every day, which starts in the morning as a number of small storms, but at about 3 o'clock in the afternoon closes up into one big storm which bars the way for any airplane.

For the first few months the new service, which eventually is to land passengers in Cape Town, 7,000 miles distant, nine days after leaving London, will end at Mwanza, on the southern shore of Lake Victoria Nyansa. During the early stages passengers will not be carried beyond Khartoum. By midsummer the whole route is expected to be in operation.

Airdromes and emergency landing grounds have been hewn from the tropical forest, rest houses and radio stations have been made, airplanes capable of landing and taking off with heavy loads in high altitudes have been tested out on the India route, and many pilots holding special qualifications have been trained. An extensive survey and juggling of time schedules to avoid tropical phenomena will permit the route to be flown every week in the year in either direction.

During the past eleven years Air Ministry officials and officials of the Imperial Airways, Ltd., which is operating the route, have obtained voluminous data on Africa's changing temperatures and tropical rains, on thunderstorms in the desert and on the depth at all seasons of the year of the rivers on which the flying boats employed on certain sections of the route may alight in emergencies. It has been found that for about 800 miles on either side of the Equator the rainy seasons alternate so that at most times of the year a pilot is likely to meet tropical storms somewhere between Khartoum and Johannesburg, Union of South Africa.

The Duchess of Bedford and Captain Barnard, on their return flight from the Cape last year, found rain throughout the whole length of Africa and had to fly for hundreds of miles just above the treetops.

SOVIET TO SHIP WOOD HERE FOR TEST CASE

But Moscow Officials Are Gloomy Over Our Embargo and Question of Proof.

CANADA BANS RED IMPORTS

Coal, Lumber and Furs Among Products Barred on Charge of Forced Labor.

By WALTER DURANTY.
Wireless to THE NEW YORK TIMES.

MOSCOW, Feb. 27.—Complete uncertainty prevails here about the American interpretation of the word "proof" in the United States Treasury Department's embargo on Soviet timber, requiring importers to give "proof" that such timber is the product of free labor. That presumably depends on Washington, but the departments concerned here—doubtless on advices from America—are not optimistic.

As it happens, there have been no lumber shipments to the United States during recent months because of the season, but your correspondent learns a large consignment will leave this country soon, with a test case as the outcome.

To the Soviet public Representative Hamilton Fish Jr. is the villain of the lumber embargo piece. He plays a central rôle in a scurrilous revue that opened yesterday in the Moscow "Music Hall" theatre. Lest that wound his feelings, it may be added that Raymond Poincaré, Winston Churchill and the Archbishop of Canterbury have been similarly caricatured in previous shows.

Canada Linked in Embargo.

Certain circles here do not think Mr. Fish and his committee matter much except as noise and a smoke-screen. They ascribe the embargo to the Washington visit of Premier Bennett of Canada, which sells the United States ten to fifteen times more lumber than the Union of Socialist Soviet Republics. On this account Soviet departments—the Lumber Trust, Amtorg and the Foreign Trade Commissariat—are rather glum about the American embargo and fear that "proof" will be made difficult, though they add plaintively:

"Exile labor is only a small percentage of the total lumber force and export timber is only a small percentage of the total lumber production. So what will be easier than to insure that every foot of lumber exported to the United States is produced by free labor?"

One may illustrate their plight by an anecdote which was current in Moscow last year. Northwestern Poland, the story goes, was suddenly invaded by a flood of Russian rabbits. A soviet of Polish rabbits met to consider the phenomenon and then invited a Russian delegation, saying to the latter:

"Comrades, why do you come here where food is scarce and 40 per cent of our rabbits are unemployed?"

The Russian rabbits replied:

"We know that, and there is plenty of food and no unemployment in Russia, but we have run away from the Ogpu [secret police], which recently decreed that all camels must have their tails cut off to make camel's hair blankets for the northern lumber camps."

"Yes," said the Polish rabbits, "but you are not camels; you are rabbits."

"We know that," said the Soviet rabbits sadly, "but you try to prove it to the Ogpu."

What makes proof difficult where

Continued on Page Eight.

'CLEAN FILM' FRAUD ON CHURCH ALLEGED

Federal Indictments Charge Five Men and Two Women Swindled 400 Priests and 6,000 Laymen.

GOT $2,000,000 IN 2 YEARS

Promoters of "Mary the Virgin" in Pictures Said to Have Sold Stock but Made No Film.

Five men and two women, officers and employes of the bankrupt National Diversified Corporation, which sold stock until last May 30 in an avowed effort to promote clean motion pictures in line with the campaign of the Catholic Church to purify the stage and screen, were indicted yesterday by a Federal grand jury on the charge that they defrauded 400 priests and 6,000 Catholic laymen of $2,000,000 in two years.

The defendants, it is charged, falsely represented themselves as promoters and producers of clean motion pictures, using without authorization the names of Cardinal Hayes, Cardinal O'Connell of Boston, Cardinal Mundelein of Chicago, Archbishop Curley of Baltimore, Bishop Shahan of Washington, Alfred E. Smith, John J. Raskob and other prominent Catholics.

The corporation did not produce a single film, according to George J. Mintzer, Assistant United States Attorney, but took in $3,000,000 in subscriptions, which went partly to the defendants and partly to the Sono-Arts Productions, Inc., which they controlled and which produced "Rainbow Man," starring Eddie Dowling. Of this amount $2,000,000 was received in cash, Mr. Mintzer said.

Obtained Aid of Priests.

The defendants, it is charged, obtained the confidence of priests by false representations. The priests advised their friends to purchase stock in the corporation and, it is alleged, also addressed meetings of church societies and religious groups, where salesmen passed around subscription blanks after talks on "cleaning up the screen."

The stock selling scheme was described by George Z. Medalie, United States Attorney, as "one of the boldest racketeering ventures that ever had been pulled at the expense of persons with religious and moral ideals."

Those named in the indictments, containing fourteen counts of mail fraud, are Otto E. Goebel, voting trustee of the corporation, which had offices at 1,440 Broadway; Frank J. Matre, vice president and sales manager; Thomas A. Lynn, secretary and treasurer; Elizabeth M. Flautt, accountant, bookkeeper and assistant secretary; Irene C. Flautt, contact woman, and James F. Cassidy and Jerome D. Kline, salesmen.

Kline, according to Mr. Medalie, used his own name when addressing German-American Catholics, but became "J. D. Kane" when he attempted to sell stock to Catholics of Irish descent.

The defendants, Mr. Medalie charged, obtained subscriptions for stock in New York, New Jersey, Pennsylvania, Maryland, Massachusetts and Connecticut on the representation that the National Diversified concern would film a motion picture entitled "Mary the Virgin," reverently plotted and staged and approved by the hierarchy of the Catholic Church.

The corporation was organized in Delaware July 16, 1926, with 30,000 shares of preferred stock at $30 par

Continued on Page Four.

THE WORLD PRINTED WITH THE TELEGRAM; EMPLOYES END FIGHT

Purchaser of Pulitzer Papers Uses Combined Names and Associated Press News.

ONE FRANCHISE IS FOR SALE

Howard Says He Has Had Four Bidders for Morning World Rights, but Withholds Names.

OLD STAFF GATHERS AGAIN

Veterans of Park Row Sit in Silent News Room With Presses Stilled and Talk of the Past.

The presses were silent in the old Pulitzer Building at 63 Park Row yesterday, and in the city room the men who once made it hum with the clatter of their typewriters talked of old times to avoid thinking of the future.

The World newspapers, the property of the Pulitzers for nearly fifty years, had passed into the hands of the Scripps-Howard syndicate, not to die but to be "born again," in the words of Roy W. Howard, head of the corporation which bought them.

In the place once occupied on the news stands by The Evening World, which was snuffed out without having a chance to bid farewell to its public, there appeared a new newspaper under the combined masthead of The Evening World, The New York Telegram and The World, with its vignette of the Statue of Liberty between two globes.

For the first time since the Scripps-Howard interests bought The Telegram four years ago, that newspaper published news dispatches of The Associated Press. Mr. Howard made it clear that he intended to retain The Evening World's membership, although three years ago he scrapped one in favor of United Press, which his organization controls.

A. P. Membership for Sale.

The Associated Press membership of The Morning World Mr. Howard said, is for sale to the first person that makes a "suitable bid." He could have sold it "six times over" yesterday, he said, if he had been willing to sell with it the right to use the masthead of the newspaper he scrapped, as soon as Surrogate James A. Foley ruled that the heirs of Joseph Pulitzer had the right, as directors of the Press Publishing Company, which owned it, to sell to any one they chose, despite a prohibition in their father's will.

In order to conform to the technical requirement that an Associated Press membership be used or die, a skeleton staff worked in the offices of The World-Telegram last night getting out a newspaper called The New York Repository, which will be published on a limited scale until Mr. Howard parts with the membership which was valued by experts at the hearings before Surrogate Foley at $500,000.

The last editions of the defunct World, carrying its valedictory by Walter Lippmann, were bought up by collectors, hoping that their value will increase. Mystery, meanwhile, surrounded The New York Repository, which it was understood would be printed this morning and be limited to 250 copies. Employes of the Scripps-Howard chain were secretive about its advent, saying that details of the plan for keeping The Associated Press membership alive had been worked out by offi-

Continued on Page Thirteen.

Whiteman Asks 'Friendly' Divorce in Chicago; Jazz Leader Would Pay Wife $600 a Week

Special to The New York Times.

CHICAGO, Feb. 27.—Paul Whiteman, jazz orchestra leader, today filed a divorce suit in Superior Court against Mrs. Mildred Whiteman of New York.

The formal charge is desertion, but according to Whiteman's counsel, Benjamin J. Kanne, the action is "friendly," with both sides in accord. He said that after a recent conference here with her husband, Mr. Whiteman agreed to the terms, including a substantial sum as a settlement in lieu of alimony.

In his bill Mr. Whiteman sets forth that the couple were married on Nov. 4, 1922, and charges that his wife deserted him on Jan. 15, 1929, "despite the fact that he treated her in a manner well becoming a good and dutiful husband."

"There is no venom in this action whatsoever," Mr. Whiteman said. "I think she's wonderful. We have been practically separated for three years and actually for two. We tried married life on the road for seven years and found it's no go. It certainly was no place to bring up a baby.

"I'll have the boy, Paul Jr., three months out of the year. His mother was very generous about that. He will be with me when I'm not playing one-night stands. Mrs. Whiteman will receive $600 a week."

Whiteman is at present playing an engagement with a South Side cabaret.

Paul Whitman's present wife, the former Miss Mildred Vanderhoff, known on the stage and in the night clubs as Vanda Hoff, the dancer, is his third. They have one child, Paul Whiteman Jr., 6 years old, and Whiteman was reported recently to have settled a $35,000 yearly allowance on his wife and child.

Whiteman, a native of Denver and now about 40 years old, was once a taxicab driver. He was a sailor in the World War and later played in a symphony orchestra, in which his instrument was a viola. As leader of his own orchestra he has made certain jazz tunes popular in this country and Europe. His familiar rotund figure tips the scales at 248 pounds.

SENATE VOTES BONUS LAW, OVERRIDING VETO 76 TO 17; PRESIDENT SPEEDS LOANS

General Pershing's War Story.

"My Experiences in the World War," the memoirs of General John J. Pershing covering the fateful years 1917-1918 and the deeds of the American Armies in France, are published exclusively in New York in THE NEW YORK TIMES daily and Sunday—in this issue on Page 21.

NAVY FUNDS VOTED IN LAST SUPPLY BILL

$358,000,000 Outlay Approved by House and Senate After Hoover Unites Conferees.

EXTRA SESSION TALK ENDS

White House Parley Results in Providing $68,800,000 for Naval Construction.

Special to The New York Times.

WASHINGTON, Feb. 27.—The Navy Department appropriations bill, the last of the departmental supply bills remaining before Congress, was transmitted to the President today after a conference report on the bill carrying about $358,000,000 was adopted by the House and Senate.

Quick action on the measure followed a White House breakfast conference this morning between President Hoover and the Senate and House leaders responsible for the measure. It was reported that the President had asked that nothing be allowed to delay the bill, in view of the fact that its passage would remove the last threat of an extra session.

Pleasing to Big Navy Advocates.

Passage of the bill found the Congressional exponents of a strong navy also fairly well pleased because, despite the failure of the separate bill which sought to authorize $74,000,000 for a naval building program as a step toward attaining the limits authorized by the London treaty, the naval supply bill contains large items for some new construction.

The sums in the bill provided today, plus a carry-over of naval construction funds from last year, added to an item of $10,000,000 contained in the second deficiency bill, which is expected to pass without serious opposition, will leave the Navy Department with $68,000,000 on hand for naval construction activities.

The bill appropriated $23,800,000 for continuance of work on the nine-cruiser program for building the new aircraft carrier Ranger and for three V-type submarines.

In addition to this work, provided for in the original bill, the conferees permitted to remain a $10,000,000 appropriation, inserted by Senate amendment, for the beginning of construction of eleven destroyers.

"Salvage" of $74,000,000 Bill.

This item particularly was considered as "salvage" from the defunct $74,000,000 naval building bill, having been inserted by the Senate when it was certain that the other bill would not pass. The $10,000,000 appropriation for destroyers, in effect, obligates the government to

Continued on Page Twelve.

BILL'S FOES OVERWHELMED

Veterans Fill Corridors and Galleries During 3-Hour Debate.

BINGHAM ASSAILS OUTLAY

Hastings Stirs Ex-Soldiers' Protest—Vandenberg and Glass Call Opposition Baseless.

1,000 LOAN CHECKS MAILED

Hoover, Setting Machinery in Motion, Calls for Aid to the Needy First.

Special to The New York Times.

WASHINGTON, Feb. 27.—The veterans' bonus loan bill became a law soon after 2 o'clock this afternoon when the Senate, by a vote of 76 to 17, passed it over the President's veto.

President Hoover announced at once that the administration would take all measures to provide the veterans with loans promptly, and immediately gave instructions that those in need should have priority.

A statement by the President declared that it was "urgently necessary," moreover, that local relief committees shall continue their services to many veterans.

While today's action was not as summary as that taken in the House, which overrode the veto yesterday in forty-three minutes, the same determination to disregard the objections of the President was apparent in the debate.

Within a few minutes after the bill had become law, there was a rush by veterans to obtain its advantages. Machinery for payment of loans by the Veterans' Bureau already had been set up, and more than 1,000 checks were mailed to applicants today. About 3,397,000 veterans are eligible. The first check went to a needy veteran in Baltimore.

President Hoover has estimated that if all who hold adjusted compensation certificates seek loans up to 50 per cent of the face value, the obligation placed upon the government will reach $1,700,000,000.

Veterans Flock to Capitol.

The galleries were jammed when the debate began at 11 o'clock, and long lines of veterans filled the corridors and gathered in other parts of the building. The scene was not unlike that in 1924, when the original compensation act was passed over the veto of President Coolidge.

The Senate vote followed a three hours' debate, in which Senators Bingham, Republican, of Connecticut, and Hastings, Republican, of Delaware, led those upholding the President's veto message, and Senators Vandenberg, Republican, of Michigan, and Glass, Democrat, of Virginia, headed the forces backing the measure.

Senator Hastings caused a stir in the galleries at one point in his speech. Voicing his opposition, he said he knew of "many ex-soldiers who, if they would get the chance, would steal the certificate from their wives and go out and spend the night with some other woman."

There were cries of protest and such a disturbance that the presiding officer rapped for order. Senators Barkley, Democrat, of Kentucky and Smith, Democrat, of North Carolina, sharply attacked Senator Hastings for his remarks and it was some time before quiet was restored.

Bingham Lauds President.

Senator Bingham pictured President Hoover as the most courageous man who had occupied the White House since Grover Cleveland. On the other hand, Senator Glass, a former Secretary of the Treasury, decried fears expressed by the treasury that the bonus legislation would unduly embarrass government financing and make increased taxation necessary.

Senator Glass, who opposed the original bonus legislation, said he supported the present loan proposal because it did not enlarge the government's obligation, but merely increased the loan facilities.

Senator Vandenberg, opening the debate, held the attention of the galleries with an impassioned defense of the measure. He contended that it would not place a heavy burden on the government.

"Suppose every veteran, contrary

Continued on Page Five.

"All the News That's Fit to Print."

The New York Times.

LATE CITY EDITION

THE WEARTHER—Cloudy, showers late today; tomorrow fair and colder.
Temperatures yesterday—Max. 68; min. 52.
U. S. Weather Forecast—For details see page 52.

VOL. LXXX....No. 26,750. * * * * * NEW YORK, TUESDAY, APRIL 21, 1931. TWO CENTS in Greater New York | THREE CENTS Within 200 Miles | FOUR CENTS Elsewhere Except 7th and 8th Postal Zones

WALKER, IN REPLY, CALLS CHARGES FALSE; CITES HIS REFORMS AND SCORES CRITICS; ROOSEVELT SILENT, DEFERS HIS DECISION

FOREIGNERS BOARD SHIPS OFF HONDURAS TO ESCAPE REBELS

Women and Children Rushed to Safety as Trujillo and Tela Are Menaced.

FEDERALS ARE MOBILIZING

Army of 3,000 Gets Under Way to Crush the Rebellion and Martial Law Is Declared.

CRUISER ARRIVES ON COAST

Plane Carrier Langley Off for Nicaragua—Mexico Hears New Revolt Has Sandino Link.

Copyright, 1931, by The Associated Press.

TEGUCIGALPA, Honduras, April 20.—New threats of rebel attacks at the two Honduran towns of Trujillo and Tela tonight led authorities to hustle foreign women and children in the towns hurriedly aboard ships anchored in the harbors, to insure the foreigners' safety.

A general strike at Tela, said to have reached menacing proportions, was adding to the excitement.

One Leader Declared Captured.

Copyright, 1931, by The Associated Press.

TEGUCIGALPA, April 20.—The Honduran Congress declared a state of martial law throughout the country tonight because of the rebellion. Troops were being called to the colors and civic guards were being organized everywhere.

Guatemalan authorities captured the important Honduran military leader, Filiberto Diaz Zelaya as he was trying to enter Honduras over the Guatemalan border, accompanied by two persons, said to be well-known Sandinista leaders.

Government officials said that Diaz Zelaya was on his way to join the rebels on the north coast.

Government commanders at Tela reported having found six bombs, one Lewis machine gun and several rifles in the munitions left behind among the dead and wounded after Sunday's battle.

Ceiba and Puerto Cortes were quiet tonight but Trujillo was reported to be seriously threatened by a strong rebel force commanded by General Arturo Ordonez, a prominent military leader.

Tela also has been threatened again, it was reported, by another rebel group. Puerto Castilla was quiet.

The cruiser Memphis left Ceiba for Trujillo tonight.

Up to the renewed threat of hostilities at Tela and Trujillo tonight foreigners in the rebel zone have been thought to be not in danger. President Mejia Colindres declared tonight, however, that after the victorious rebel attack upon Progreso yesterday the rebels sacked the properties of all citizens, including those of foreigners.

Martial Law Declared.

Special Cable to THE NEW YORK TIMES.

TEGUCIGALPA, Honduras, April 20.—Martial law was declared today and 3,000 troops have been dispatched to quell the rebellion, which so far is confined to the Caribbean Coast banana zone, where several hundred Americans employed by fruit companies are all reported safe.

The rest of the country is quiet and the government is rapidly organizing its defenses throughout the country. All garrison towns have been reinforced and by taking energetic measures the government is confident it will dominate the situation soon. The governments of Guatemala and Salvador have offered to arrest any rebels crossing the borders to escape.

The cruiser Memphis arrived at Ceiba this morning and the Marblehead and Trenton are expected to arrive on the Honduran coast today for the purpose of protecting, if necessary, American lives and property.

The rebellion began Saturday night when Progreso was captured after a short attack by a force led by Ladislao Santos, which later was forced to retire under a counter-attack by government troops.

Captain Ramon Diaz, a rebel leader, attacked Sonaguera and succeeded in capturing a machine gun and a number of rifles, but later retired under an assault of government troops led by Captain Agapito Sanchez.

Attack on Tela Repulsed.

At 3 P. M. Sunday Diaz joined forces with Mariano Gonzales and with 300 revolutionists launched an attack on the important port of Tela, the centre of the United Fruit Company interests. Tela was well defended by General José Maria Reina, and after two hours of fighting the rebels withdrew to the mountains, leaving five killed and twelve wounded.

Another group of revolutionaries

Continued on Page Two.

Hess Would Give the Marines 'Full Hand in Central America'

By The Associated Press.

SAN FRANCISCO, April 20.—Representative William E. Hess of Cincinnati, member of the House Naval Affairs Committee, who arrived here today from Nicaragua on the army transport Somme, said that "it is high time this country should give the marines a full hand in Central America."

"Tell them to go down there and clean things out," Mr. Hess said. "I disagree with the policy of allowing dangerous bandits to threaten American lives and property, and I know the marines can handle the situation if given the authority.

"Their orders, I understand, are not to fire until fired upon. I don't think they'd need orders for that. Our policy should be to protect the lives of innocent citizens regardless of the lives of the bandits."

LONDON MATCHES US IN NICARAGUA POLICY

Henderson Warns British There Not to Expose Themselves Needlessly to Danger.

REFERS TO U. S. WARSHIPS

Foreign Secretary Says Three of Our Vessels Are There to Give Protection.

By CHARLES A. SELDEN.

Special Cable to THE NEW YORK TIMES.

LONDON, April 20.—Although it is making no formal proclamation of the matter, the present policy of the British Government concerning its nationals in Nicaragua is exactly the same as that recently announced by Secretary of State Stimson for the citizens of the United States who may have the misfortune to be in danger of bandits or insurgents.

There are very few British in Nicaragua as compared with Americans, and it is felt in London that if they use good sense and do not needlessly expose themselves to danger they will have ample protection from the National Guard of the country. So no naval or military protective expedition whatever is contemplated by Great Britain. The British Chargé d'Affaires in Nicaragua has been notified to that effect and has been asked to tell British citizens that if they fail to observe due caution, it will be at their own risk.

When the question arose in the House of Commons today, Arthur Henderson, Foreign Minister, replied: "According to a cablegram received yesterday from his Majesty's Chargé d'Affaires in Nicaragua, bandits have been active on the eastern coast of that country. They have been checked, however, by the National Guard, and are now reported to be retreating inland.

"I regret that in these disturbances two British West Indian subjects from Jamaica, Henry Roper and Walter Manning, are reported to have been killed. Three United States warships have been dispatched to the east coast with the authority, I understand, to disembark armed parties should the necessity arise. Our representative reports that in the view of the officer commanding the National Guard the situation is now under control."

Minister Praises Stimson.

WASHINGTON, April 20 (AP).—Praise for Secretary Stimson's announced policy of protection for Americans in Nicaraguan coastal towns was expressed today by Minister Sacasa of Nicaragua.

The Minister said he believed the American attitude should impress the other Latin-American countries favorably. He added a wish that this course had been followed years ago.

Such a policy, he felt, would bring the United States and Latin-American countries nearer to mutual understanding.

Americans Escape to Safety.

PUERTO CABEZAS, Nicaragua, April 20.—Edwin Fagot, American merchant, who was one of the victims of the looting of Cape Gracias a Dios by outlaws, arrived here today aboard the U. S. S. Asheville, together with four other refugees, two men and two women, not Americans.

He returned to the town early Sunday morning, however, accompanied by a detachment of marines from the U. S. S. Asheville, inspected his station and returned here Sunday night. The outlaws who looted the town numbered about twenty, he said he learned, and they were led by Abraham Rivera.

Dissension among the leaders has existed for some time, he said, because of Rivera's attempts to save the lives of his foreign friends. Rivera, he said, had been previously deprived of military command for his

Continued on Page Two.

FARM BOARD TO SELL ITS STOCK OF WHEAT IN MARKETS ABROAD

Aim Is to Offer Surplus as Rapidly as Possible Without Breaking Domestic Price.

LOSS ON SALES PREDICTED

Stocks Handled by Government Likely to Total 275,000,000 Bushels by July 1.

LEGGE AIDS IN DECISION

Seven Million Bushels Already Sold—Canadians Fear Further Lowering of World Prices.

Special to The New York Times.

WASHINGTON, April 20.—The Farm Board today decided to sell on the European market the huge surplus of wheat acquired under stabilization operations. It has been estimated that the grain controlled by the board will be about 275,000,000 bushels by July 1.

The board appears to be of the opinion that sales can be made abroad without depressing domestic wheat prices. The government purchases were made at an average of about 92 cents a bushel, but estimates have been made that the board might suffer a loss as high as 50 per cent in sales made in Europe at the present time.

Such a policy is contrary to the views of Western Senators and farm leaders, who have been insistent that the board lock up the wheat and throw away the key.

The decision was made at a conference today in which Alexander Legge, former chairman of the board, participated. Other participants included S. R. McKelvie of Nebraska, member of the board in charge of wheat, and Arthur M. Hyde, Secretary of Agriculture.

Storage on Farms to Be Urged.

Farmers are to be urged to store their 1931 wheat at home as far as possible. Mr. Legge will address the National Lumber Manufacturers' Association at Chicago tomorrow with the view of urging them to assist the farmer to construct storage facilities. Aid in this respect is being arranged by the board, probably through the medium of loans to farmers through cooperatives.

The government wheat is to be placed on the European market as rapidly as possible without depressing home prices. Heretofore, it has been contended, wheat could not be "dumped" in Europe without entailing counter legislation abroad, but now, Mr. McKelvie said, market conditions in Europe are the best in eighteen months.

The original statement of the board, announcing abandonment of buying for stabilization purposes, intimated that the surplus would be sold as far as possible without depressing the market.

Market experts contend that to hold the wheat with the prospect that some time or other it might be sold would be a depressing influence on prices. To hold the wheat, moreover, would entail a huge carrying charge, which, in a few years, would exceed the original cost.

Large Crop in Prospect.

Mr. Legge, returning from a tour in the Southwest, reported that a huge wheat crop is in prospect there. Texas farmers, for example, following the advice of the board to abandon cotton, have planted wheat. While decreased acreage is reported

Continued on Page Nine.

S O S Still Heard Over Russia; Now Linked With an Arctic Ship

Wireless to THE NEW YORK TIMES.

MOSCOW, April 20.—The Moscow Radio Centre has reached the conclusion that the mysterious S O S messages which have been heard over Russia for several days emanate from a ship caught in the Arctic ice. Last night an amateur radio operator in Tver Province reported receiving this message:

"S O S—help—we are freezing near land."

Then the message broke off and nobody was certain whether Franz Josef Land or Northland or some other island in the Arctic Ocean or simply the continent was meant.

It is pointed out that the 500 to 600 meter wavelengths of the messages correspond to the waveband of ships. The messages also are said to correspond to the maritime type. In addition, amateurs in the Union of Socialist Soviet Republics are allowed to use only short-wave bands, which, it is held, precludes the possibility of a hoax. It is still believed by some persons that the messages may come from mountain explorers.

STEEL MEN PREDICT GOOD BUSINESS YEAR

Taylor and Farrell Reassure Stockholders on Conditions, Decry Undue Pessimism.

NEW PENSION PLAN PASSED

To Retire All Leaders at 70—2,457 Employes Share in Bonus Distribution.

Stockholders of the United States Steel Corporation, who yesterday at their annual meeting in Hoboken ratified a revised pension plan providing for the compulsory retirement of employes at the age of 70, received assurance from high executives that the corporation faced the future with the utmost confidence and that it did not share the pessimism prevalent in some other quarters.

Myron C. Taylor, chairman of the finance committee, who presided at the meeting, said he entertained no doubt as to the future of American business.

James A. Farrell, president of the Steel Corporation, said the "gloom which seems to be pervading the country has not settled over 71 Broadway," which is the corporation's headquarters. "As a matter of fact," he added, "if we can get a little better tonnage on present prices we are going to have a reasonably good year."

Farrell Commends New Plan.

Mr. Farrell, who is the first of the important executives of the Steel Corporation who will be retired under the revised pension plan, moved its adoption and warmly recommended it as the "greatest thing that the corporation has done with respect to the welfare of its employes." Mr. Farrell would be retired automatically under the plan on Feb. 15, 1933, but he may retire at his own request earlier than that, since there is a provision for retirement at 65 years with the approval of the finance committee or officers delegated by that body to act for it in such matters.

A. F. Banks, president of the Elgin, Joliet & Eastern Railroad, owned by the Steel Corporation, probably will be the first head of a subsidiary to retire under the plan. He is scheduled to retire on May 1. He has been with the railroad thirty-seven years and will be succeeded by S. M. Rogers, now vice president.

Eugene J. Buffington, president of

Continued on Page Seven.

Two Detroit Robbers Invade the City Hall And Take $28,000 From Guarded Treasury

Special to The New York Times.

DETROIT, April 20.—Although the place was guarded by three policemen and tear-gas guns were available to stop them, two bold robbers today took $3,032 in cash and $25,425 in checks, a total of $28,057, from the office of City Treasurer Charles L. Williams late this afternoon. One of them cut through the heavy wire of a cashier's cage to get the booty.

The office is on the second floor of the City Hall. The thieves were chased and a man who said he was Theodore Crowley of Chicago was arrested while running. He denied any knowledge of the robbery and none of the checks or money was found on him.

The robbery was executed after careful study of the treasurer's method of handling tax returns. One of the three policemen assigned to the office usually sits upon a high stool beside the cashier's cage. He was absent for a time and one robber replaced him on the stool. While pretending to read a newspaper, he cut through the heavy wire. George Winchow, the cashier, stepped from the cage and the second robber rushed up, thrust his hand through the opening and grabbed the cash and checks which represented the receipts for the day.

Leo Shiffman, a clerk in the office, saw the robbery and ran after the men, calling to Patrolman Ralph Reynolds, who was stationed on the first floor of the building. They dashed after the thieves and were joined by Patrolman Gill on traffic duty. Reynolds chased Crowley to a store and cornered him in an elevator.

Tear-gas guns were in various cages and employes, by pressing buttons, could throw out gas bombs. The thieves, however, waited until those who could have seen their work had lowered shades in front of their cages while checking up accounts. Mr. Winchow was preparing to balance his books and had piled the money on a shelf within reach of the men.

HOFSTADTER READY TO ACT

Legislative Committee Meets Here for the First Time on Its Task.

SEABURY TOLD TO GO AHEAD

He Entertains Investigators at Old Democratic Club as Answer to Bias Charge.

SILENT ON CHOICE OF AIDES

Declines to Say When Inquiry Will Be Opened—Fortnight's Delay Is Likely.

The Hofstadter committee met yesterday for the first time in the city which is to be its hunting ground for the next year or two and conferred with Samuel Seabury, its counsel, on plans for stalking the Tammany Tiger.

At the close of the meeting, which was held in the grievance committee room of the Bar Association Building at 42 West Forty-fourth Street, Senator Samuel Hofstadter, chairman, announced the committee was "equipped and ready to go ahead as soon as our counsel chooses to do so."

The Senator who sponsored the resolution creating the $500,000 inquiry into the whole City Government added, however, that the committee probably would not hold another meeting before May 4, when it is expected to have taken up its headquarters on the fifth floor of the State Office Building.

Seabury Selecting Staff.

While Mr. Seabury would venture no prophecies, it was believed that the inquiry would not actually get under way for at least a fortnight. It is understood that Mr. Seabury, whose exposure of conditions in the magistrates' courts and the Police Department contributed to the demand for a legislative investigation of the city, has begun selecting his staff of legal assistants. He said, however, that he was not ready yet to announce their names.

His only comment after the meeting was:

"This is the first occasion when I have had the pleasure of meeting the committee as a whole. I shall immediately prepare to discharge the duties which devolve upon me by reason of my destination as counsel to the committee."

In order to get better acquainted with the men with whom he will be associated in what promises to be the most sweeping overhauling of the City Government in more than three decades, Mr. Seabury was host to the entire committee later at dinner at the Manhattan Club.

Senator Hofstadter remarked that Mr. Seabury's selection of the oldest Democratic club in the city for the dinner party ought to end charges that the investigation was inspired by partisan politics. Senator John J. McNaboe and Assemblyman Louis A. Cuvillier, the two Tammany Democrats on the committee of seven, smiled.

Those who attended the meeting in addition to the chairman and the two Democrats were Assemblymen Hamilton F. Potter of Suffolk County, vice chairman; William J. Lamont of Orange County, secretary; Abbot Low Moffat of this city and Senator Leon F. Wheatley of Hornell.

Several Plans Discussed.

Plans were discussed in a most general way, it was said after the meeting. About the only definite action taken so far as could be learned was to authorize Mr. Seabury to proceed with the organization of his staff and to assure him again that the committee would not interfere with him in any way.

So anxious are the Republican members of the committee to live up to the dictum of W. Kingsland Macy, Republican State chairman, that there shall be no interference with the counsel he chose for them before the committee was authorizd, that they have not even asked him whom he is considering for appointment to his staff, it was said.

The meeting of the committee was scheduled for 4:30 P. M. The executive session, however, did not begin until a little after 5 o'clock, for nearly a half hour was consumed in posing for photographers. It was

Continued on Page Nineteen.

Photo New York Times Studio.

MAYOR JAMES J. WALKER.

MACY CENSURES FOX ON WALKER ATTACK

Republican Friction Seen in Reactions to Charges Against Mayor's Private Life.

LATTER TURNS ON CRITICS

Calls Reports Pharisaical and Offers to Meet Accusers "Eye to Eye."

W. Kingsland Macy, Republican State Chairman, disowned yesterday the criticism of Mayor Walker's private life by the City Affairs Committee of the National Republican Club which provoked a stinging statement of rebuke from the Mayor.

With the Mayor turning on his critics in his first extended comment on charges of this nature since his return from California and assailing the committee report as "slanderous" and "pharisaical," Chairman Macy took the lead in the Republican ranks in voicing disapproval of the action of the committee headed by Alan Fox.

In a telephone message to friends from Groton, Mass., where he was visiting his son in school, Mr. Macy expressed regret that Mr. Fox's group had attacked Mayor Walker personally and asserted that he regarded that part of the committee report as in bad taste. Other Republicans, including United States Attorney George Z. Medalie, a member of the committee, and Borough President George U. Harvey announced their strong disapproval of the injection of the Mayor's non-official activities into the current situation.

Mayor's Answer Vitriolic.

The Mayor minced no words in his assault on the committee report, which he characterized as "a shower of sulphurated hydrogen gas," and challenged his assailants to come forward and match their private lives with his.

"As to my private life," he said, "I will match it against all the pharisaical composers of that tirade. My conscience is clear and I would like nothing better than to meet them eye to eye and let them attempt to justify themselves in the sight of God and man."

Despite the stir which the committee report created in Republican circles, where considerable resentment was voiced, Chairman Fox of the City Affairs Committee renewed the attack in a statement replying to the Mayor in which he reiterated, in stronger terms if anything, the same personal charges.

"I am not interested in his private life as such," said Mr. Fox, "and he can make whoopee 'til the cows come home or his night clubs

Continued on Page Fifteen.

TAMMANY IS ELATED AT WALKER'S REPLY

Friends of Mayor Confident the Governor Will Dismiss the Case on Its Merits.

ACCUSERS TO MEET TODAY

Rebuttal Will Go to Albany at Once—Basis for a New Complaint to Be Sought.

Members of Tammany and the City Administration expressed the belief last night that Mayor Walker's answer would result in the dismissal by Governor Roosevelt of the charges brought against him by the City Affairs Committee.

The Mayor's friends held that he had answered the charges fully and that the Governor would be warranted in dismissing the case on its merits.

With a general investigation of the City Government by the Hofstadter legislative committee to begin soon, Tammany would not take kindly to the appointment by the Governor of a commissioner to investigate the charges against the Mayor, as he did in the complaint of the City Club against District Attorney Crain.

The Mayor's conduct of his office will be subject to investigation by the Hofstadter committee. This is believed to be an additional reason why the Governor will not decide on further consideration of the City Affairs Committee's charges.

Mayor's Accusers to Meet.

The City Affairs Committee will meet this morning at 10:15 in Temple Beth-El, Fifth Avenue and Seventy-sixth Street, to read the Mayor's answer, discuss it and frame a counter-reply. When the general structure of this reply is ready it will be turned over to Paul Blanshard, the committee's executive director, who will prepare a final draft. Mr. Blanshard is expected to have the reply on its way to Governor Roosevelt within forty-eight hours.

John Haynes Holmes, chairman of the committee, who, with Rabbi Stephen S. Wise, signed the charges, would not make a detailed comment on the answer without time for further examination of it. Mr. Holmes, who had a general knowledge of its contents, said:

"On the Mayor's answer as a whole I shall not comment tonight. I want time to go over it and to digest it. I shall read it before I go to bed tonight, but I can say at this time that I think that both Dr. Wise and I shall ignore the personal attacks made on us by the Mayor.

"I called Dr. Wise to recommend to him that we adopt that attitude

Continued on Page Fifteen.

MAYOR ASKS EXONERATION

He Asserts Ambition of Repudiated Socialists Dictated Complaint.

DEFENDS ACCUSED AIDES

Holds Kohler Blameless in the Health Bureau Scandals and Denies License Graft.

TELLS OF POLICE CLEAN-UP

Stresses $40,000,000 Hospital Program and Appeals Board Inquiry to Justify His Rule.

The full text of Mayor Walker's reply to the charges of the City Affairs Committee will be found on Pages 16, 17 and 18.

Special to The New York Times.

ALBANY, April 20.—Mayor James J. Walker of New York City filed today with Governor Roosevelt his answer to the charges made against him by John Haynes Holmes and Rabbi Stephen S. Wise as officials of the City Affairs Committee. He asked that the charges be dismissed.

Mayor Walker in his answer of nearly 20,000 words replied in detail to each of the ten specific charges, denying all of them, and also denied the general charges of incompetence and negligence Characterizing the specific charges as false and recklessly made, the Mayor defended the city officials and the departments mentioned.

Charging that the City Affairs Committee is an annex of the Socialist party, the Mayor asserted that its charges were intended to advance the political fortunes of a group repudiated by the voters. Mr. Holmes he declared to be a leader of a group of agitators and Soviet sympathisers. He quoted his predecessor, the late Mayor Gaynor, to describe Dr. Wise as a "rhetorician" and "a man of brilliant mental incapacity and of vast and varied misinformation."

Governor Gets Reply.

Mayor Walker's answer was delivered to Governor Roosevelt by Thomas F. McAndrews, secretary to the Mayor, at 2:15 P. M. Mr. McAndrews and Police Captain Thomas F. O'Connor of the Mayor's staff, who had left New York City on the 11 A. M. train, were met at the station here by Assistant Corporation Counsel Walter B. Caughlan, legal representative of the city at Albany. Mr. Caughlan took Mr. McAndrews and Captain O'Connor by automobile to the Executive Mansion.

Governor Roosevelt received the Mayor's answer without comment and released it for publication in morning newspapers later in the afternoon. It was said authoritatively that any forecast of what the Governor would do regarding the charges would be pure speculation, as he would not reach any decision until he had read the answer and given it careful consideration.

The Governor declined to comment upon the request of the City Affairs Committee for an opportunity to file a rebuttal to the Mayor's answer. It was said that he would make no decision on this request until after he had read the reply.

In maintaining silence on Mayor Walker's reply, Governor Roosevelt assumed the same position as that which he took when the charges of the City Affairs Committee were first presented—namely, that he was in effect donning quasi-judicial robes and could not talk about a case up for adjudication.

"Judge Cardozo of the Court of Appeals," said the Governor, "would not discuss a case pending before him, and neither will I talk about this matter until I have reached a determination."

Attacks Charges as Vague.

Mayor Walker declared in his answer that the accusations consisted almost entirely of generalities without specification or detail, and that an effort had been made, by use of enumerations and headings, to make it appear that the petition consisted of specific items in substantiation of general charges.

"I submit that no elected official, whether he be the President of the United States or the Governor of the State of New York or the Mayor of

Continued on Page Fifteen.

THE HIGHEST STRUCTURE RAISED BY THE HAND OF MAN

NEW YORK TIMES Studio Photo.

The Empire State Building, the 1,250-foot structure on the site of the Old Waldorf-Astoria on Fifth Avenue and 34th Street, which now dominates the New York skyline was formally opened on May 1.

THE FOUR MEN WHO CREATED THE EMPIRE STATE BUILDING.

Kaiden-Keystone Studios.

William F. Lamb, the architect.

Underwood & Underwood.

H. G. Balcom, the engineer.

Kaiden-Keystone Studios.

Col. W. A. Starrett, the builder.

New York Times Studios.

Alfred E. Smith, President of the owning company.

"All the News That's Fit to Print."

The New York Times.

Copyright, 1931, by The New York Times Company.

LATE CITY EDITION
THE WEATHER—Cloudy today, occasional showers; tomorrow clear and colder. Temperature Yesterday—Max. 57, Min. 40. U. S. Weather Forecast—For details see Page 30.

VOL. LXXX....No. 26,761. ***** NEW YORK, SATURDAY, MAY 2, 1931. TWO CENTS In Greater New York | THREE CENTS Within 200 Miles | FOUR CENTS Elsewhere Except 7th and 8th Postal Zones

8 DIE, SCORES HURT IN MAY DAY RIOTS IN FOREIGN CITIES

Killings Result From the Labor Outbursts in Poland, Spain, Portugal and Cuba.

MARCHERS FLY RED FLAGS

1,000,000 Civilians Parade in Moscow With All Branches of the Military.

DAY IS QUIET IN NEW YORK

Heavy Police Guards Insure Order at Radicals' Demonstrations in American Cities.

While a number were killed and wounded in May Day celebrations in Europe, New York observed the day peacefully.

Veterans, Socialists and Communists held mass meetings in Union Square at different hours, guarded by 300 police.

Order prevailed in other American cities holding demonstrations, though some arrests were made in Cleveland. In Boston Representative Fish scored communism.

EUROPE'S MAY DAY RIOTS.

By The Associated Press.

LONDON, May 1.—Serious riots in Barcelona, Bilbao, Oporto, Lisbon and Lubartow, Poland, constituted the principal violence in Europe's observance of International Labor Day.

Three were killed in Poland in fights between the authorities and demonstrators. Two persons lost their lives in a fray in Barcelona and several were gravely wounded in Bilbao. The rioting at Lisbon, in which one was killed, took on the character of a political movement aimed at the overthrow of the dictatorship. One was killed in Oporto.

In general, however, the day passed off more quietly than in some years and with the absence at most places of casualties or serious incidents.

London Demonstration Orderly.

London had the usual Communist demonstration, with the usual absence of anything approaching violence. Paris saw a series of minor skirmishes between the police and Communists, with the former holding the upper hand. Constantinople and Vienna reported that all was quiet. Athens and some of the Balkan capitals had some minor clashes.

Scandinavia was orderly as usual. Geneva was disturbed by a parade of several hundred workers bearing red flags, but their behavior was circumspect. Brussels passed a placid day, although trouble had been expected. Warsaw's police precautions were so effective that the only untoward incident was the smashing of a few shop windows in the Jewish quarter.

At Johannesburg, South Africa, the police had some difficulty with a mob which stormed the Carlton Hotel and the Rand Club, but no one was hurt.

In Spain thousands picnicked in the wooded grounds of the Casa del Campo, formerly a royal estate, which was thrown open to the public.

Berlin Reds Shoot Policeman.

BERLIN, May 1 (AP).—A gang of young Communists today shot and wounded a policeman who attempted to restrict their May Day activities. The policeman was taken to a hospital with a bullet in his lung. His condition is critical.

A few hours later mounted police galloped down Unter den Linden and quelled an outbreak between National Socialist (Hitlerite) students and Social Democrats who were returning from a celebration in the Lustgarten. The Social Democrats found several hundred Nazis gathered in the court of the university, shouting praises to their leader, Adolf Hitler, and singing songs.

Some of the Social Democrats climbed an iron fence and clashed with the Hitlerites. The police had difficulty in intervening because the university gates were locked.

After the courtyard had been cleared, the authorities found that a Communist group had taken advantage of the confusion to hoist a Red flag over the university. The offending banner was removed.

The only serious disorder reported from the provinces was a clash at Mettmann in the Ruhr district, where one workman and one Communist Alderman were seriously wounded by gun-fire.

Wireless to THE NEW YORK TIMES.

WARSAW, May 1.—Two persons were killed in Lubartow in Southern Poland, one was killed at Kutno, near Warsaw, four were wounded in Warsaw and two were injured in Jeziorna, a Warsaw suburb, today in clashes between Communists and the police in International Labor Day celebrations. Nearly 200 Communists

Continued on Page Four.

African Message Gives Hope For Scientist Believed Lost

Wireless to THE NEW YORK TIMES.

BUTA, Belgian Congo, May 1.—Dr. Arthur Torrance, leader of an expedition into the Belgian Congo, arrived here April 24 and proceeded to Banguassou April 29. No one here knows of anything special happening to his party.

Dr. Torrance was believed by his brother, Captain Victor Torrance of Los Angeles, to have been drowned before April 28 after a cloudburst struck his camp in the African wilderness. Captain Torrance said he was so notified by a message carried from the wilderness to Buta by a runner and sent out by Discom Madison, a member of the party.

The explorer, an authority on the tsetse fly, headed a party of ten scientists, ten other white men and sixty natives. The medico-scientific expedition was sponsored by a group of New York business men.

BOMB STARTS MOVE TO END LISBON RULE

Cabinet Takes Refuge After Blast, Seen as Revolutionary Development.

MARTIAL LAW IS EXPECTED

Strong Guards Patrol Deserted Streets—Loyal Troops Advance on Funchal.

Copyright, 1931, by The Associated Press.

LISBON, Portugal, May 1.—Lisbon was a city of unrest tonight. A movement against the dictatorship of President Oscar Carmona obviously was under way, but the populace knew nothing of its scope and could only await developments anxiously.

Following the explosion of a bomb in connection with May Day demonstrations, members of the Cabinet fled to the shelter of the barracks of the Third Artillery Regiment, which has become almost a traditional haven for officials when trouble is brewing.

Heavily armed troops maintained vigil at all strategic points and armored cars patrolled the streets in unceasing watch for a repetition of today's outbreaks. The streets were otherwise deserted and business houses were barred and shuttered.

Declaration of martial law was expected momentarily in view of the government's assertion that the uprising was distinctly different from those of previous years and bore a revolutionary complexion.

Horse the Only Victim.

The explosion occurred in the midst of a great crowd of demonstrators, including many middle-class citizens, which gathered in Rocio Square and raised shouts of "Down with the dictatorship!" The fragments of the bomb flew in all directions, but caused no casualties, the only victim being a horse carrying a Republican Guard. Troops of cavalry rode through the demonstrators and eventually succeeded in clearing the square.

Although the incident occurred in connection with the day's observances, authorities said it was different from May Day outbreaks in previous years and was primarily a political move aimed at the overthrow of the government.

Prior to this several thousand demonstrators had rioted, shouting threats to the Carmona Government and fighting off the police until they were reinforced by soldiers.

Mounted police rode into the crowd laying about with the flat sides of their swords, and after a sharp fight the square was cleared. A score or more were injured and cafés bordering the square were damaged as the crowd fled inside to take shelter.

Today's incidents took one life, that of Antonio Coelho, proprietor of a hotel, who was killed by a stray

Continued on Page Eight.

WASHINGTON IS COOL TO ANY WORLD MOVE ON DEBTS OR TARIFF

Hint Precedes the Discussions Scheduled by International Chamber at the Capital.

HAS DAMPENING TENDENCY

Some Delegations Pinned Hope on Sessions to Start Action, Leading to Changes.

HOOVER WORKS ON SPEECH

He Will Deliver Address to the Business Congress at the Opening Monday Morning.

Special to The New York Times.

WASHINGTON, May 1.—Although the capital will be host to the International Chamber of Commerce next week, the government will not take official cognizance of its deliberations bearing on international relations, or make any commitments to follow policies broached by the chamber, it was learned from an authoritative source today.

This word, coming on the eve of scheduled discussions of such questions as the tariff, debt reduction, the silver problem and other controversial issues, was not expected to limit expressions of opinion, but, admittedly, it tended to dampen the hopes of some delegations which had expected to bring about eventual political changes.

The topics enumerated have definite places on the program in speeches by economists and as topics for group meetings. Likewise, it is generally expected that many criticisms of American policies in regard to these topics will be voiced, either directly or indirectly, as some trade leaders are convinced that lowered tariff rates and reduced or canceled war debts are essential to the world's economic rehabilitation.

President Will Speak.

President Hoover's attitude toward the meeting of the chamber will be voiced immediately after it opens on Monday morning, when he will deliver an address on which he was reported working today.

It is assured that, as an industrial engineer, the President will be intensely interested in the developments of the meeting, but in the light of today's information, coming from a high official who did not wish to be quoted, it was considered that this interest would be more personal than as the head of the government.

As a matter of fact, the entire administration, from the President down, is known to be deeply interested in the work of the chamber and is regarded as feeling that it has accomplished much in smoothing the way in international economic relationships.

In political circles it is considered inevitable that the new tariff act, which has been operative for less than a year, will stand unchanged, except for such revisions as the Tariff Commission may recommend, as long as the Republican party remains in power. It also is conceded that the United States is not willing to reopen the subject of foreign debts, once thought closed with the giving of heavy concessions to the allied debtor nations.

Incidentally, both of these policies find some opposition among American delegates to the international chamber.

The session will last throughout the week. More than 750 foreign and American delegates will exchange views on pending business problems.

A request for the establishment of exceptions to favored-nation treaties will be made by the Austrian delegation.

Austrian representatives heretofore

Continued on Page Six.

Ireland Gives Land to 70,000 Farmers, Ending 50-Year Fight Against Landlords

Wireless to THE NEW YORK TIMES.

DUBLIN, May 1.—The Cosgrave Government has played its trump card in the party game to obtain the agricultural vote in the approaching general elections. Seventy thousand tenant farmers today became absolute owners of their land through the new land act just emerged from the Dail, designed to speed up the process of transfer from landlord to tenant. This measure, the last of a long series of land-purchase acts, finally disposes of the old problems of land tenure and rings down the curtain of a fifty-year-old struggle begun by Michael Davitt to obtain the land for the people.

This is the biggest single transaction in Ireland's land-purchase history. The cost to the government, estimated at $50,000,000, will be met by an issue of land bonds in that amount. Bonds in a sum appropriate to each estate will be placed to the credit of the landlord immediately in the National City Bank of Dublin, from which he will draw dividends.

Thus the landlord is now completely eliminated and the age-old grievance of the Irish farmers is ended. There are 150,000 of these farmer tenants in the Free State—the remaining 80,000 will receive full benefit of the new act in November. It is anticipated that the scheme will be in full operation within twelve months.

A further substantial farm-relief plan is expected from the Minister of Finance, Ernest Blythe, in his budget speech next Wednesday. No hint has been given of the form this relief will take and Mr. Blythe's budget statement is awaited with lively interest in view of the unmistakable signs of an early general election.

Di Robilant's Aide Dies of Jungle Fever; Italian Aviator Is Recovering in Brazil

Wireless to THE NEW YORK TIMES.

SAO PAULO, May 1.—A telegram received at Sao Paulo late today advised the Italian Consul that Mauranta Quarenta, mechanic of Count di Robilant's plane, died at San José this morning from injuries and exhaustion. Count di Robilant, occupying the next bed, when informed of Signor Quarenta's death shortly before noon, at first refused to believe it. Later he developed a high fever, causing considerable alarm. The hospital doctors now fear Count di Robilant may be suffering from a tropical fever contracted during his eighteen days of wandering, after the crash of his plane.

The Italian Consul at Sao Paulo informed Signor Quarenta's family, living at Rio de Janeiro, of his death and the Italian Government will transport the family to Italy.

Count di Robilant is unable to see visitors and the hospital doctors here advised the Vice Consul at Sao Paulo that he will be transported tomorrow morning to Assis, where better medical assistance is obtainable. He is believed to be out of danger, but requires special treatment.

The dispatches are being received here from Porto Presidente Epitacio, which is the nearest town to San José having telegraph connections. It takes half a day even for messages to come through from there.

Signor Quarenta died as the result of yellow fever contracted on the tortuous walk through dense forests, it is reported. Count di Robilant, although also affected, is expected to regain his health soon.

When Count di Robilant left Sao Paulo he followed the wrong route, due to a storm, for two hours. Then he flew three hours without knowing his whereabouts or direction. Aviation experts declare that because of the flier's great skill in landing in the dense forest he saved the plane from destruction.

A cablegram was received by the Italian Vice Consul here today from Count di Robilant's brother, living in New York requesting information about the flier.

AHRENBERG REACHES ICELAND ON FLIGHT

Crosses From Norway and Plans to Go On to Greenland Today to Rescue Courtauld.

ICELANDIC PLANE AT COAST

Ready to Hop Off From Water—British Are Believed Near Missing Man on Ice Cap.

By CAPTAIN ALBIN AHRENBERG.

Wireless to THE NEW YORK TIMES.

REYKJAVIK, Iceland, May 1.—Our flight today went beautifully, the motor functioning like clockwork all the way across the Atlantic [from Bergen, Norway, to Reykjavik, via the Faroe Islands, en route to Greenland to rescue Augustine Courtauld, the British explorer marooned on the ice cap].

Between the Faroe Island and Iceland we encountered rain and mist, accompanied by heavy showers which lasted for more than an hour and a half. This compelled us to fly at a very low altitude. At times over considerable distances we were flying just above the sea.

Immediately after our arrival I had a conference with the commander of the guard ship Hvidebjornen about the steps which should be taken in order to simplify our flight tomorrow across Greenland.

The Hvidebjornen is leaving tonight for a spot right in the middle of Denmark Strait and will remain there on our account for as long as necessary in order to help us with wireless directions and weather reports.

We are starting at daybreak tomorrow provided the weather is not too bad. All the members of the flight are well and prepared with the least possible delay to continue on to Greenland.

Plane Being Refueled.

Wireless to THE NEW YORK TIMES.

REYKJAVIK, Iceland, May 1.—Captain Albin Ahrenberg alighted on the harbor here at 9:05 tonight from the Faroe Islands and his Junkers seaplane is now being refueled for the final dash across Denmark Strait to rescue Augustine Courtauld.

The Swedish flier and his two companions, a mechanic and radio operator, in their heavily-laden monoplane started from Bergen, Norway, at 6:15 this morning, and helped by ideal weather and a following wind, landed at Thorshavn, in the Faroes, at 10:25.

After a brief rest while the gasoline tanks were filled Captain Ahrenberg started again. At 8:19 P. M. he signaled that he was over Ingolishofdi, Iceland, and fifty minutes later he swung over Reykjavik.

Radio Aids Flight.

By SVEND CARSTENSEN.

Special Cable to THE NEW YORK TIMES.

COPENHAGEN, May 1.—Over the most dangerous and difficult stage of his journey today from the Faroes to Iceland, Captain Albin Ahrenberg was aided by a most efficient radio service organized by the Danish Ministry of Marine.

So clear were the signals from his Junkers plane, the Seack, that here in Copenhagen it was possible to follow his progress almost mile by mile. To shore stations he signaled on a wave length of 900 meters, while contact with ships was maintained continuously on 600.

Communication, of course, was conducted in the Morse code, but radio experts believe that if atmospheric conditions are good it should be pos-

Continued on Page Three.

DEMAND CANNON QUIT FOR GOOD OF CHURCH

Petitioners Declare Bishop's Case Is "Doing Untold Harm" to Southern Methodism.

HOLD HIM NOT 'VINDICATED'

College of Bishops May Act on Plea Today—Nye Inquiry Will Refuse Request for Delay.

Special to The New York Times.

RICHMOND, Va., May 1.—Several hundred prominent laymen of the Methodist Episcopal Church, South, have asked that Bishop James M. Cannon Jr. resign his office "for the good and peace of the church" in petitions forwarded to the College of Bishops which met today at Nashville, Tenn.

The text of the petition, expressing the view that the Bishop had not been "vindicated," and that his "case" was "doing untold harm" to the church, was obtained here today. But other more strongly worded personal appeals contained in letters to the individual Bishops asking action to relieve the church of its "embarrassment" were not available.

Letters enclosing copies of the petition were sent to about 500 leading laymen in several States and each one was asked "to get as many of our laymen as possible to sign with you," or, "better still, to draw a petition or letter in your own words and secure the signatures of interested laymen and mail as above directed."

Many of the personal letters to the College of Bishops asked that Bishop Cannon be not allowed to succeed to the presidency of that body. By seniority he was in line for the position last December, but, as he was under duress at the time, Bishop W. B. Beauchamp, second in line, took the post.

Petition for Resignation.

The general petition reads as follows:

"Dear Fathers and Brothers:

"Thousands of laymen throughout our Church are much exercised over the Cannon case, and in the light of reports that are current, do not feel that Bishop Cannon has been vindicated or that the Church has been relieved of a very serious embarrassment.

"The conviction grows that this case is doing the Church untold harm. The injury being done is more far-reaching than any of us know. A great many laymen are refusing to contribute to any of our causes, except the local church expense. Some of our best people who know something of the story have had their confidence in the standards of the Church severely shaken.

"The laymen are the supporters of the Church, but there is no process open to us in our Church law by which we may demand any action in the case of a Bishop except before the Committee on the Episcopacy. The one course open to us at this time is to appeal to our Bishops, to whom is entrusted the leadership of the Church.

"In the light of these facts, which are becoming very generally known, we earnestly pray that our Bishops find some means to restore confidence in the moral integrity of the Church. The least that could be asked of Bishop Cannon under these circumstances is that for the good and peace of the Church he resign his office.

"We regard the situation as very serious for the present and future of the Church. Reports that gravely reflect on the moral character of Bishop Cannon have been published throughout the country. He has made no public statement that would vindicate himself or that would relieve the Church of the embarrass-

Continued on Page Ten.

EMPIRE STATE TOWER, TALLEST IN WORLD, IS OPENED BY HOOVER

President Presses Button in Washington, Lighting Up 1,250-Foot Building.

HE CONGRATULATES SMITH

Governor and Mayor Also Praise Vision and Courage of Leader in Project.

THOUSANDS SEE CEREMONY

Grandchildren of Ex-Governor Cut Ribbons at Entrance—Public to Inspect Structure Today.

The new Empire State Building, the world's tallest structure, which has been erected at a cost of about $52,000,000 on the site of the old Waldorf-Astoria Hotel, Fifth Avenue and Thirty-fourth Street, was opened formally yesterday. The chief executives of the nation, State and city took part in the ceremonies and added their tributes to the greetings that came from all over the world.

President Hoover in Washington pressed a button at 11:30 A. M. that switched on the lights within the building that rears its head 1,250 feet above the sidewalks. He sent a message of congratulation that was read by former Governor Alfred E. Smith, president of Empire State, Inc., at a luncheon and ceremonial on the eighty-sixth floor.

The President paused at the threshold of a Cabinet meeting to play his part in the dedication of the world's loftiest building. Only a few minutes earlier Mary Adams Warner and Arthur Smith Jr., grandchildren of former Governor Smith had cut the ribbon that barred the doors of the Fifth Avenue entrance.

Thousands Witness Ceremony.

Several hundred invited guests, who had waited before the entrance at 350 Fifth Avenue, entered the east lobby while special details of patrolmen and mounted police held back thousands of spectators who tried to rush through the police lines.

The 200 invitations for the luncheon produced 350 guests, because prominent New Yorkers had asked and obtained permission to be accompanied by their wives or other members of their families. Immediately after President Hoover switched on the lights Mr. Smith invited the guests of Empire State, Inc., to go with him to the eighty-sixth floor.

There the guests viewed Manhattan Island and the metropolitan area from a new pinnacle. Few failed to exclaim at the smallness of man and his handiwork as seen from this great distance. They saw men and motor cars creeping like insects through the streets; they saw elevated trains that looked like toys.

"There's Central Park, no bigger than a football gridiron," exclaimed one spectator.

Crowding up to the parapets, the guests gazed long and intently through the blue haze of a cloudless day, as Governor Smith had invited them to look, across the boundaries of three States and over the Atlantic. He had told them that on a clear day they could take a look at Yonkers, Patchogue, L. I., Connecticut, Sandy Hook and Plainfield, N. J.

Following a buffet luncheon the spectators assembled in an enclosure on the east side of the eighty-sixth floor, where the meeting was held. "The Star-Spangled Banner" was played by the Hotel McAlpin Orches-

Continued on Page Seven.

80 Killed at Desert Well As Arabs Battle for Water

By The Associated Press.

LONDON, May 1.—The Daily Herald's Jerusalem correspondent says that more than eighty persons were killed or wounded in a fierce fight between Bedouins and others for water around a desert well, the exact location of which was not determined.

The report came from motorists en route to Damascus from Southern Iraq. It said that the natives, suffering from thirst because of drought, had traveled long distances to the well.

Recent dispatches said that hundreds of shepherds and tribesmen were reported dying of thirst in the deserts of Southern Syria and Central Arabia.

I. R. T. WINS THE RIGHT TO APPEAL FARE CASE

Appellate Division Permits Fight on Five-Cent Rate to Go to Highest State Court.

ARGUMENT BY UNTERMYER

Final Ruling by Mid-June Is Likely—B. M. T. Valuation Up at Unity Conference.

The way for a final decision on the validity of the five-cent fare clause in the city's contracts with the Interborough was cleared yesterday when the Appellate Division gave the company the right to appeal its adverse decision to the Court of Appeals.

The Appellate Division's decision last month against the company was unanimous, and under the rules of the court, its consent was required for an appeal.

The cases that will be argued before the Court of Appeals will be identical with those argued in the Appellate Division, the first being the one brought by the Transit Commission and the city against the company to restrain it from attempting to raise the fare on the combined subway and elevated system from five cents to seven cents, and the other being the result of the application of the company for a writ of certiorari to review the decision of the State Transit Commission denying it a ten-cent fare on the elevated lines alone.

Untermyer Ready This Month.

Samuel Untermyer, special counsel to the Transit Commission, who has devoted a large part of his time to the litigation, since it was begun by the company more than three years ago, will again appear as chief counsel in defense of the five-cent fare before the Court of Appeals. Mr. Untermyer announced yesterday that he was ready to argue the case before the Court of Appeals by the end of this month, and in the event that counsel for the Interborough were not ready, at least before the recess of the Court of Appeals in the middle of June.

After the Interborough's case was thrown out by the United State Supreme Court two years ago, and the State court litigation was started by the city in accordance with the mandate of the highest court, James L. Quackenbush, general counsel to the Interborough, announced that the company did not intend to carry the case again to the Federal Courts if the State court decisions were adverse.

Mr. Untermyer's determination to clear up the fare litigation finally is dictated by a desire, it is understood, to deprive the Interborough of a talking point in the unification negotiations now going on. The point that the company is entitled to a higher fare, and therefore can spurn

Continued on Page Twelve.

SLOT MACHINE PROFIT $20,000,000 A YEAR, COURT INQUIRY FINDS

Gambling Ring Puts Up Bail and Pays Fines of Operators, Witnesses Swear.

LAWYERS PROVIDED FREE

Shopkeepers Tell of Splitting Huge Profits With Group Which Protects Them.

CRAIN CHARTS TO GOVERNOR

Untermyer Gathering Data to Refute Analysis Showing Breakdown in Prosecutor's Office.

A system of organized slot-machine gambling involving receipts estimated at $20,000,000 a year, with the owners of the machines maintaining a staff of lawyers and bondsmen to take care of arrested storekeepers, was revealed in a public hearing of the Appellate Division inquiry into the lower courts yesterday.

A parade of witnesses put the story together for Referee Samuel Seabury under the questioning of Irving Ben Cooper, first assistant counsel. They were, with three exceptions, the keepers of small candy or stationery stores or lunch counters who had had machines in their places of business, had been arrested, and had had all ensuing expenses paid by the concerns renting the machines.

The three exceptions were Hugo Rogers, 109 West 112th Street, a lawyer who had been retained to defend storekeepers by the Automint Vent Company; Vincent Rao, 225 East 107th Street, who had been a bondsman for the same concern, and Aaron Goldenberger, a former agent for the Triangle Mint Company of Brooklyn and for one Samuel Tilton, otherwise unidentified.

Their testimony revealed phases of the business that the small storekeepers could not explain.

Shopkeepers Describe System.

The proprietors of small merchandising establishments who testified were Harry H. McKay, 1,567 Lexington Avenue; Arthur Feller, 1,715 Longfellow Avenue, the Bronx; Leo Rosenthal, 10 Manhattan Avenue; Anthony Calfo, 2,395 Seventh Avenue; Abraham Weintraub, 2,060 Daly Avenue, the Bronx; Harry Lustgarten, 58 Avenue D; Max Spilka, 1,425 Fifty-ninth Street, Brooklyn; Isaac Liebson, 2,120 Tremont Avenue, the Bronx; David Kasmere, 1,797 Bronxville Avenue, the Bronx; John Boland, 4,419 White Plains Avenue, the Bronx, and Nathan Kasten, 1,809 Crotona Avenue, the Bronx.

Their stories were the same, with minor variations. They were approached by representatives of one or another of the companies owning machines, with the result that the machines were placed in the stores. The machines were designed so that a player who put a five-cent piece in the slot, pulled the lever, got a packet of mints and, on occasions, a handful of slugs or coins, sometimes as many as twenty.

Some of the storekeepers said they redeemed the slugs with merchandise. Others said they did not. Rosenthal said the machine in his place returned not slugs but nickels. When the machines were installed the storekeepers were told by the agents, who never went by name but always by number, that in case of "trouble" they were to call an often-changed but always furnished telephone number. McKay told a typical story. "When the detectives arrested me," he testified, "I called the number. I said, 'They are taking the machine out and me with it.' By the time we got to the station house a bondsman was there, and I was out in five minutes."

Next day McKay went to Harlem court. There he met the agent. When his name was called, he stood up, a lawyer he had never seen before appeared for him, and he was discharged by the magistrate. Others of the storekeepers had been held for Special Sessions. The testimony invariably showed that there they had been fined $25. To one witness, Isaac Liebson, this was the principal point of his experience in the courts.

"Do you remember that you were arrested?" Mr. Cooper asked him.

"Yes," he answered.

"What was the charge?"

"Twenty-five dollars," Liebson replied.

Machine Averaged $100 a Week.

William Lubin was one who testified that he had maintained a machine in his place for about two years before being haled into court. The machine took in, he said, from $80 to $120 a week, and this was divided equally with the Triangle Mint Company through its agent, Goldenberger.

Some of the witnesses told of copies of an injunction restraining the police from molesting the ma-

Find Body of Missing Jeweler, Slain, in Sound; A. H. Levy Vanished in February With $20,000

Special to The New York Times.

GLEN COVE, L. I., May 1.—The body of Abraham H. Levy, diamond merchant of 17 John Street, Manhattan, who disappeared mysteriously on Feb. 14 with more than $20,000 of his stock, was found this morning riddled with bullets and with loops of wire knotted about the neck, hands and legs, floating near the Long Island Sound breakwater about 1,000 yards off the shorefront estate of the late Marcus Loew.

Jack Block, a boatman from this village, noticed the body, brought it to the Loew estate and turned it over to the Nassau County police, who made the identification tonight through dental work.

All available Nassau County detectives were immediately assigned to the case. The police believe that the slayers robbed the jeweler, strangled and shot him and then threw the body into the water.

An autopsy performed this afternoon by Dr. Carl Hetteseimer disclosed that the body had been in the water at least a month. Levy had been shot five times with a .32-calibre revolver at close range, Dr. Hetteseimer said.

The identification was established by Detective Sergeant James Farrell, who found that a partial lingual gold plate attached to four teeth in the victim's lower jaw tallied with the description on the alarm sent out by the New York police when Levy's disappearance was reported.

In all other details the descriptions checked, except that a gold wedding band which Levy wore on a finger, was not found. Dr. Clarence Cohen of Hempstead, official police dentist and Levy's family dentist, confirmed the identification.

A reward of $1,000 offered for his recovery, will go to Block, the boatman, Inspector Harold King said. Captain John A. Ayres of the New York Missing Persons Bureau was to confer with Captain Emil Morse of the Nassau Homicide Squad late tonight. Levy lived at 1,510 Ocean Parkway, Brooklyn.

"All the News That's Fit to Print."

The New York Times.

THE WEATHER.
Fair, slightly warmer Thursday; Friday, fair, warmer; moderate winds, becoming south.
For full weather report see Page 22.

VOL. LXXX....No. 26,790. NEW YORK, SUNDAY, MAY 31, 1931. Including Rotogravure Picture Section in two parts—Magazine and Book Sections in Rotogravure. TEN CENTS

HOOVER URGES NATION TO BE STEADFAST IN THIS 'VALLEY FORGE' OF DEPRESSION; WAR DEAD HONORED HERE AND ABROAD

20,000 HEAR THE PRESIDENT

Resist the Lure of 'The Rosy Path to Every Panacea,' He Counsels.

SPEAKS UNDER BLAZING SUN

Sweltering Heat Overcomes Several in Audience, Gathered on Historic Camp Site.

OVATION FOLLOWS SPEECH

Greets Union and Confederate Veterans and Visits Washington's Headquarters.

From a Staff Correspondent of The New York Times.

VALLEY FORGE, Pa., May 30.—President Hoover, surveying the peaceful green slopes of Valley Forge, where Washington's soldiers suffered privation and death in the darkest hours of the War of Independence, told the American people today in his Memorial Day address that they were going through "another Valley Forge" at this time as a consequence of the economic depression. He counseled them to "stand steadfast in our great traditions through this time of stress."

In its efforts to regain the stride of prosperity and progress, the nation was advised to resist the lure of "the rosy path to every panacea" and to depend not upon "any one strategy sprung from the mind of any single genius" but upon "the inventiveness, the resourcefulness, the initiative of every one of us."

Some 20,000 persons stood under a blazing sun to hear the Chief Executive speak at the first Memorial Day observance held on the historic camp ground. The President's message of courage for the present and of hope for the future was carried over the nation-wide chains of two radio broadcasting systems.

Compares Two Crises.

Mr. Hoover delivered his brief address from a platform erected before a natural amphitheatre near the building known as General Huntington's Headquarters. Stretching to the westward were the peaceful acres of the Continental Army's parade ground.

Drawing a parallel between the crisis which faced Washington and his band of hungry patriots and that which now faces the country, Mr. Hoover said:

"Valley Forge met such a challenge to steadfastness in times and terms of war. Our test is to meet this challenge in times and terms of peace. It is the same challenge. It is the same test of steadfastness of will, of clarity of thought, of resolution of character, of fixity of purpose, of loyalty to ideals and of unshaken conviction that they will prevail.

"We are enduring sufferings and we are assailed by temptations. We, too, are writing a new chapter in American history. If we weaken, as Washington did not, we shall be writing the introduction to the decline of American character and the fall of American institutions. If we are firm and far-sighted, as were Washington and his men, we shall be writing the introduction to a yet more glorious epoch in our nation's progress."

"A Triumph of Character."

The President described Valley Forge as "a triumph of character and idealism and high intelligence over the counsels of despair, of prudence and material comfort."

In the present day "for the energies of private initiative, of independence and a high degree of individual freedom of our American system we are offered an alluring substitute in the specious claim that everybody, collectively, owes each of us, individually, a living rather than an opportunity to earn a living, and the equally specious claim that hired representatives of a hundred million people can do better than the people themselves in thinking and planning their daily life."

The Republic was an experiment in securing to a people the maximum of individual freedom. Amazing success has proved it no longer an experiment, and brought America to a greatness unparalleled in the history of the world.

In the growing complexity of our

Continued on Page Twenty-two.

Vice President at Gettysburg Demands Reverence For the Constitution and More Respect for Courts

Special to The New York Times.

GETTYSBURG, Pa., May 30.—On the hallowed ground of the National Cemetery Vice President Curtis pleaded today for the nation's rededication to a reverence for the Constitution and the law and for the substitution of arbitration for arms in the solution of world difficulties.

"What we need now more than ever," the Vice President told the thousands of persons gathered on the battlefield, "is reverence for the Constitution and respect for the courts of our country."

Speaking as a son of a Union Captain, Mr. Curtis paid tribute to the veterans of the Civil War and those of the later conflicts, and made his plea for peace.

"We would like to see the time come when nations will settle their differences by methods other than war," he said.

"As a government and as a people we are doing, and will continue to do, everything possible to bring this about.

"In these days of unrest, of scarcely concealed bitter fear and hatred of many nations of the world, the people of our forty-eight separate and distinct sovereign States, which yet are one nation and one people, present a lesson of mutual trust and confidence, an example of the inestimable value of mutually held and revered aims and ideals, which is a challenge to all other peoples and countries to do likewise.

"Our people and our country present an object lesson for the world to study and to emulate; for other nations and people to equal or to surpass if they can."

Mr. Curtis denounced aliens "whose object is to overthrow our government." "They and racketeers," he said, "should be deported, and the sooner this action is taken the better it will be for our country."

ALL FRANCE HONORS AMERICAN WAR DEAD

Day Almost a National Holiday as Pershing, Mayors and Gold Star Mothers Take Part.

SERVICES AT CEMETERIES

Edge at Suresnes Bids Us Face World Problems Squarely in Spirit of Collaboration.

By LANSING WARREN.

Special Cable to THE NEW YORK TIMES.

PARIS, May 30.—The presence in France of General Pershing, Commander of the American Expeditionary Force, the delegation of American Mayors and groups of Gold Star Mothers gave special importance today to many observances in Paris and at the battlefields and war cemeteries which took place on the occasion of Memorial Day.

The French Government and departmental and local officials, with veterans' associations and large crowds of French people, participated in the services with the Americans everywhere and the day might have almost been a French national holiday.

In Paris all the American monuments, including those of George Washington, the Marquis de Lafayette, Benjamin Franklin and the Volunteers' Monument, were massed with flowers and received visits from individuals and organizations. The special Memorial Day services in the American Church were well attended and several hundred went to Villeneuve l'Etang, where the Lafayette Escadrille Memorial is, and to Suresnes Cemetery near Paris, where Ambassador Edge presided.

Go to Various Cemeteries.

General Pershing went to Romange-sous-Montfaucon, where more than 14,000 Americans are buried. The American Mayors' party went to various cemeteries where dead from their respective States are buried, Mayor Baker of Portland, Ore., heading the delegation to Belleau Wood and Mayor Walmesly of New Orleans that to Bony. Others went with General Pershing to the Meuse-Argonne, to Suresnes with Ambassador Edge and to Saint Mihiel, Thiaucourt or Oise-Aisne.

Ambassador Edge in his address at Suresnes sounded the note of the day, as it was observed in France, when he appealed to Americans to face squarely international problems in a spirit of collaboration that "the blood poured into the maelstrom of the world catastrophe will not have been shed in vain."

"Before these myriad crosses on the soil of France, hallowed by the serried ranks of young Americans who laid down their lives in the World War, it is our solemn duty not only to bring tribute but to measure anew our obligations to the valorous dead," the Ambassador declared.

"We are on the threshold of a period which is momentous in its implications. We are at the crossroads where the foundation is being laid to determine irrevocably what

Continued on Page Twenty-three.

CITY THRONGS CHEER THIN RANKS OF G.A.R.

56 Civil War Veterans Lead 23,000 in Parade Up Drive to Honor Soldier Dead.

MAIMED HEROES IN MARCH

Women Tear Off Flowers to Shower on Cripples Toiling Past to Martial Airs.

The Grand Army of the Republic, with a contingent of fifty-six veterans who wore the blue, almost reached the vanishing point in the annual Memorial Day parade that swung up Riverside Drive yesterday morning with 23,000 in line. In addition to that colorful parade, there were seven parades in Brooklyn and one in the Bronx.

American veterans of three wars, foreign veterans in picturesque uniforms, regular army soldiers, sailors and marines, National Guardsmen, cadet corps, Boy Scouts and Girl Scouts and numerous other patriotic organizations passed in review under a sweltering sun.

The police estimated that more than 100,000 had cheered the paraders along the line of march. The spectators cheered loudest and longest for the aging veterans of the Civil War and for a battalion that hobbled along on crutches under the banner of the United States World War Amputations Association.

The cheering crowds on the sidewalks were supplemented by throngs that filled apartment house windows to greet the aged and bent Civil War veterans with loud applause. Some of Grant's men were too feeble to march, although, out of consideration for them, the parade route had been shortened to start from West End Avenue and Seventy-second Street instead of from Forty-sixth Street. They were carried in automobiles to the reviewing stand just north of the Soldiers' and Sailors' Monument at Riverside Drive and Eighty-ninth Street.

Maimed Veterans Applauded.

Gasps of surprise greeted the maimed veterans of the amputation association, who came toiling along on crutches and wooden legs, with empty trousers legs and coat sleeves flapping. It was the first time that such a contingent had appeared in a Memorial Day parade afoot. Surprise quickly changed to applause, however, which was continuous as the contingent hobbled up the Drive.

The wa[illegible] cripples were determined to make a brave appearance. Passing the reviewing stand, at the command of "Eyes left," they snapped into position as alertly as the able-bodied, while women in the stand stripped their dresses of bouquets which they showered upon them.

The parade started from Seventy-second Street promptly at 9 o'clock and the last of the marchers brought up by a detachment of police, passed the reviewing stand at 11:35. First came a detachment of mounted po-

Continued on Page Twenty-three.

Heat at 89 Sets Memorial Day Record; Shore Resorts Thronged; Many Overcome

Sublimely indifferent to the Weather Bureau's prediction of thunder showers and a cool breeze, the sun focused its blistering rays on New York yesterday and sent the mercury to 89 degrees at 1:30 P. M., establishing a record for May 30. The previous record for the day was 86 degrees, in 1919.

Sweltering in the third day of the hot spell, residents of the city turned to the beaches, parks and river promenades for relief. Traffic in Manhattan, except along the highways leading to suburban resorts, was the lightest in years.

Thousands, unable to join in the holiday exodus, vacated the sidewalks for the much-advertised "Winter" chill in metropolitan theatres and motion picture houses.

Coney Island was crowded with more than 500,000 persons, according to police estimates, and 75,000 of these struggled for room in the surf. There was a stir of excitement along the beach when a twenty-foot motor boat capsized and sank off West Twenty-ninth Street. Four persons who had been aboard were rescued by passing craft. They were treated at a life-saving station for submersion and sent to their homes. They were Henry Gresham, 31 years old, of 157 Herkimer Street, Brooklyn; Miss Katherine Hall, 32, 851 West 177th Street, the Bronx, and Mr. and Mrs. Jack Wells of 2,204 Clarendon Road, Brooklyn.

Patrolmen William J. Riordan and James Rabbit of the Coney Island police were assigned to the beach patrol and ordered to arrest all persons wearing bathing suits that could be considered immodest. Apparently taking their cue from their superior, Captain Henry E. Kelly, who said recently he had no objection to one-

Continued on Page Twenty-one.

ARMY HAS REACHED HIGHEST EFFICIENCY, HURLEY DECLARES

War Secretary Says Progress Under Hoover Puts It on Best Peace-Time Basis.

HARBOR DISPUTES CLOSED

In Radio Speech He Stresses Settlement of Snarl Over Piers on Hudson.

Special to The New York Times.

WASHINGTON, May 30.—The army was said to have achieved its greatest peace-time efficiency during the present administration in a radio address by Secretary of War Hurley tonight broadcast over the Columbia network. He spoke in the Cabinet series of the National Radio Forum conducted by The Washington Evening Star and said "the army is better organized, better trained, better equipped, better housed, and better officered than ever before in peace."

In outlining steps that have been taken, he said:

"We are making steady constructive progress in the development of mechanical equipment for combat purposes. We have now reached the state where we can combine the mechanical equipment into formidable fighting units. Machines are being substituted for animals. These organizational changes keep us abreast or ahead of the current military trend.

New Factors for Defense.

"In the post-war period of intensive study and effort we have secured the following factors for proper defense that we did not possess in 1917:

In proportion to our population we have the smallest standing army in the world, but we now have a carefully detailed plan for mobilization;

A more highly trained staff to execute it;

A decentralized regional machinery for its execution;

A more highly educated and more numerous personnel to employ as commanders and instructors;

A reserve of equipment and munitions for use at the beginning of mobilization;

A strong National Guard;

A leadership reservoir of 100,000 Reserve officers.

"We have succeeded in keeping the part of national income devoted to preparations for defense smaller in proportion to our population than that of any other country. There is room for further economies without injury to proper national defense. In the interest of economy and better business organization, unnecessary forts and reservations to the number of 58 are being abandoned. No fort or reservation that is essential to the training of our soldiers or the defense of the country will be abandoned.

"We are now approaching the completion of the five-year air program. While working toward the attainment of this objective, the army not only has increased the speed, climbing abilities and fighting capacities of its own craft, but its research and developments have contributed greatly to the safety, efficiency and economy of commercial aviation."

New York Dispute Ended.

He devoted most of his address to the non-military activities of the War Department, with river and harbor work emphasized. Declaring that a number of long-standing disputes which had interfered with this program had been adjusted during the Hoover Administration, he mentioned particularly the modification of the established harbor lines along the Hudson River at New York.

"New York and New Jersey," he said, "wanted to build thousand-foot

Continued on Page Five.

PRESBYTERIANS HIT FEDERAL COUNCIL ON BIRTH CONTROL

Assembly Cuts Fund for Church Group From Budget to Rebuke Advocacy.

WITHDRAWAL THREATENED

Question Will Be Decided Later—Floor Debate on Birth Control Is Set for Tomorrow.

From a Staff Correspondent of The New York Times.

PITTSBURGH, May 30.—The Presbyterian General Assembly rebuked the Federal Council of Churches of Christ in America today for its guarded endorsement two months ago of birth control, and made a move which may result in the withdrawal of the Presbyterian Church from this council.

In the mean time, it was learned, the special Presbyterian commission on marriage, divorce and remarriage, which unanimously approved the practice a month ago, has held a third secret session and changed its stand for the third time. It recalled its revised report from the printers, after several copies containing its recommendation that birth control receive "further study" had been run off and again deleted every reference to the subject.

The Assembly's rebuke to the Federal Council was made through the former's committee on bills of overtures. In response to overtures from Presbyteries in various parts of the country demanding severance from the council or repudiation of its expressed views on birth control, this committee submitted to the Assembly for vote the following memorandum:

"1. The General Assembly disapproves ecclesiastical pronouncements on the subject of birth control.

"2. The General Assembly deems it important to remind the Church that the Federal Council cannot and does not assume to represent its constituent denominations in this or any deliverance of opinion not specifically authorized by the denominations.

"The Federal Council has itself recently expressed this view in the following action taken by its administrative committee May 20, 1931: 'The publication of such reports (as that on birth control) is authorized by the administrative committee, as expressing not its own conclusions or the view of the constituent denominations, but rather as the results of

Continued on Page Sixteen.

'Red' Hill Shoots Niagara Rapids in Barrel; Saved by Son When Nearly Lost in Whirlpool

By The Associated Press.

NIAGARA FALLS, N. Y., May 30.—William (Red) Hill for the third time shot the rapids below Niagara Falls safely today, only to mill around for almost three hours in the treacherous whirlpool, from which he was rescued by his 17-year-old son, William Hill Jr.

Four times his big red, white and blue oak barrel went around the huge circle of the whirlpool, and seven times it was carried around a minor eddy far out in the Niagara River. On the last two swings around the whirlpool, Hill opened the manhole, stuck an arm out and yelled:

"Throw me a rope! The barrel is filling up with water."

No boat was handy, and it was impossible for any one to go to his aid for an hour and a half after his cries for help were heard. The barrel bobbed up and down in the rush of white water, every now and then sinking from sight.

Finally, it struck the outer eddy of the whirlpool and was carried to within fifty feet of shore. Young Hill, with a rope around him, swam out into the whirlpool, grabbed a ring tied in one end of the barrel and pulled his father to safety on the Canadian side.

Hill suffered several cuts and bruises in the tumultuous trip down Swift Drift, the rapids from the lower steel arch bridge, to the whirlpool.

When he was pulled out at the whirlpool, Dr. J. H. Davis of Niagara Falls, Ont., tried to persuade him not to complete the journey to Queenstown, but Hill was obdurate until Mrs. Hill arrived and thereupon "Red" decided to postpone the second and more hazardous half of his trip until tomorrow.

Hill entered his barrel from the American side and was towed to midstream above the lower bridge, below the falls themselves, at 2:20 P. M., Eastern Standard Time. It was just before 7 P. M. when he was taken from the water.

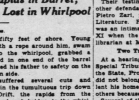

MUSSOLINI SUSPENDS CATHOLIC ACTION; K. OF C. GROUNDS SHUT; VATICAN GUARDED; PIUS XI CANCELS EUCHARISTIC CONGRESS

Koussevitzky Sees Italy's Doors Closed to Him; Links Fascisti and Reds in "Crimes" Against Art

By P. J. PHILIP.

Special Cable to THE NEW YORK TIMES.

PARIS, May 30.—Serge Koussevitzky, conductor of the Boston Symphony Orchestra, declared here today that he had "closed the doors of Italy" on himself by his recent letter refusing to conduct at the Scala Opera House in Milan because of the Fascist treatment of Arturo Toscanini.

"I am sorry, because I love the country," Mr. Koussevitzky said, "but I have suffered too much from the Bolshevists to tolerate what the Fascists are doing to artists. Both these regimes have wrought terrible crimes against culture and the respect which is owing to thought and to art."

Friends of Toscanini here say that his passport has not yet been returned to him.

Mr. Koussevitzky made public the text of his letter to the directors of the Scala Opera House today. It reads:

"Gentlemen: I have learned from newspapers of the unprecedented outrage which has been perpetrated against an artist in your country. I am so shocked and deeply hurt that I am writing to ask you to liberate me from the engagement which I accepted for the month of June.

"Maestro Toscanini does not belong only to Italy, but to the whole world, as does every great artist. We artists of other nationalities cannot remain indifferent to the fate of a colleague who is exposed to blows and prosecution because of his refusal to mix politics with art.

"I resent so keenly the injustice of such an act that I have decided to abandon my engagement, or at least to postpone it until such time as your country shall have effaced the outrage against the man who is one of the most talented of your countrymen."

RELATIONS ARE AT A CRISIS

Pius Meets Challenge by Putting Societies Under Tutelage of Bishops.

ALL ROME'S CLUBS RAIDED

Fascisti Seize Documents of Catholic Groups—Streets to Papal City Barred.

PADUAN LEGATE WITHDRAWN

Pontiff Fears Insult to His Envoy—Says It Is One of Saddest Days of His Life.

By ARNALDO CORTESI.

Wireless to THE NEW YORK TIMES.

ROME, May 30.—The dissolution in all sections throughout Italy of the organization known as the Catholic Action was ordered today by Premier Mussolini. At the same time police closed all Catholic clubs in Rome and three playgrounds financed by American Knights of Columbus, while Pope Pius placed the Catholic Action under the direct tutelage of the Bishops, canceled the Italian Eucharistic Congress scheduled for next week and revoked the appointment of a Papal Legate to the septicentennial celebration of St. Anthony of Padua. Thus relations between the Fascist Government and the Holy See, strained already by the anti-Catholic disorders of the last few days, became increasingly grave.

The order for dissolution of the Catholic Action organizations has been issued, but it has not yet been announced. However, the Vatican has been advised of it and Pope Pius made reference to it this evening in his address to the Salesian graduates. He declared this to be "one of the saddest days of my life."

Earlier in the day he had been advised of the closing of the Catholic clubs. As soon as the news reached him he called a meeting in his private study of all the heads of the Catholic Action. With them he discussed the best course to follow in view of the direct challenge of the Fascist Government.

Result of Papal Parley.

The result of this conference was made public late tonight in a special edition of the Osservatore Romano, the Vatican newspaper. It stated that in view of the continued increasing attacks to which the Catholic Action has been subjected it had been placed under the direct tutelage and management of the Bishops.

Heretofore, while attacking the Catholic Action, the Fascisti have continued to protest their attachment to the Holy See and the sincerity of their Catholic sentiments. Now that the management of that organization has been placed directly under the Bishops, however, the subtle distinction between the Vatican and the organization itself has been removed. The Holy See now assumes entire responsibility for the Catholic Action. Any action against or criticism of the organization automatically becomes action against or criticism of the Holy See itself.

The controversy can no longer be regarded as a journalistic squabble between the Catholic and Fascist press. The Vatican and the Fascist Government now find themselves face to face.

Door Is Left Open.

However, if the Fascist Government does not wish to push matters it has left itself a convenient avenue of escape. It has explained its measures against the Catholic clubs as being justified by the necessity of providing for public order. Should it desire to withdraw from its present position it can, at any time, announce that order has been restored and rescind its order against the Catholic clubs on the ground that conditions no longer render its continued application necessary. In this manner tension between the Vatican and the Fascist Government might be eased without the appearance of a retreat by the Fascists from the position they have assumed.

On the other hand, if the Fascists wish to push matters to a conclusion, there seems to be no escape from an open rupture. The Vatican's move in placing the Catholic Action under the tutelage of the bishops is interpreted as an indication of the Pope's intentions to stand firmly by his guns.

The same issue of the Osservatore that announced the transfer of the

55 AMERICANS WIN IN DUBLIN DRAWING

Fourteen Canadians Also Hold Tickets on Horses in Derby—Sure of $4,000 Apiece.

BOSTONIAN GETS FAVORITE

Stands to Receive $150,000 if Cameronian Takes Race—22 New Yorkers on Lucky List.

Special Cable to THE NEW YORK TIMES.

DUBLIN, May 30.—Fortune smiled today on fifty-five Americans, of whom twenty-two are New Yorkers, who were among the lucky 627 persons in all parts of the world holding tickets on horses in the great Irish sweepstake drawn here.

The Americans hold tickets on all but six out of a total of thirty-three horses. With the exception of the holders of two non-runners, all stand a chance to win large portions of the prize money of $9,502,720 to be distributed.

There will be nineteen first prizes of $150,000 each, nineteen second prizes of $75,000 each and nineteen third prizes of $50,000 each. All other holders of horses will receive $4,165 apiece. Tickets for small consolation prizes will be drawn Monday.

Joseph Kennedy of Boston, Mass., drew the Derby favorite, Cameronian, with ticket FMP-55717. No American holds the second favorite, Pomme d'Api. The third favorite, Doctor Doolittle, went to three Americans.

22 New Yorkers Drawn.

The following New Yorkers drew horses:

Joseph F. Wynne, 319 West Sixty-seventh Street, drew Gallini.

Vincent Cahill, 663 Twentieth Street, Brooklyn, drew Mydas, a non-runner.

Elizabeth Trainor, 616 West 184th

Continued on Page Eighteen.

FIVE INTELLECTUALS SENTENCED IN ROME

Convicted by Fascist Tribunal as Leaders of Association "Justice and Liberty."

FOREIGN GROUPS INVOLVED

Paris and London Societies Said to Back Most Formidable Plot Against Mussolini.

By The Associated Press.

ROME, May 30—A group of five "intellectuals" who admitted they had opposed the Fascist regime and worked to discredit it, but denied that they plotted bombings, were sentenced today to terms of from six to twenty years by a special tribunal.

Two of the seven who faced trial were acquitted.

The testimony showed that the men, who are more accustomed to the usages of invisible ink, fell into a police trap when they harbored incendiary instruments.

They stoutly denied that they intended to use the bombs which were found in their homes, saying they were left there by one of their number who escaped.

The men were members of the "Justice and Liberty" organization, with headquarters at Milan.

The group of seven intellectuals, including university professors and engineers, who were charged with plotting to overthrow the Fascist Government were alleged to be leaders of an organization known as "Justice and Liberty," with headquarters in Milan.

The alleged leaders of the group were Ricardo Bauer, a business man, and Ernesto Rossi, Professor of Political Economy at the University of Bergamo, both of whom, according to dispatches Friday, admitted the formation of the society, but denied charges that they planned the simultaneous discharge of bombs in an attempt to overthrow the Fascisti.

Their testimony was repeated by other defendants, one of whom was Pietro Zari, poet and Professor of Literature. Professor Zari's father was an intimate friend of Pope Pius XI when the Supreme Pontiff was librarian at Milan.

Two Tried in Absentia.

At a hearing on Friday before the Special Tribunal for the Defense of the State, Professor Zari testified he did not belong to the group but had lent his home and his automobile to others because they were his friends.

Several of the defendants admitted communication with anti-Fascist groups in Paris by means of invisible in , but they denied other charges.

Two of the defendants fled the country before the trial began but their cases were heard in their absence.

The special tribunal of six judges who presided at the trial included three jurists who sentenced Michael Schirru, a naturalized American citizen, to death last week.

Recently, Italy was astir following

Continued on Page Two.

"All the News That's Fit to Print."

The New York Times.

LATE CITY EDITION
THE WEATHER—Partly cloudy today and tomorrow; little change in temperature.
Temperatures yesterday—Max. 74, min. 60.
U. S. Weather Forecast—For details see Page 55.

Copyright, 1931, by The New York Times Company.

VOL. LXXX....No. 26,806. ***** NEW YORK, TUESDAY, JUNE 16, 1931. TWO CENTS In New York City | THREE CENTS Within 200 Miles | FOUR CENTS Elsewhere Except 7th and 8th Postal Zones

SOCIALISM FIRST AIM IN SOVIET'S PROGRAM; TRADE GAINS SECOND

Collectivization of the Peasants Ahead of Schedule, Output Is Called Promising.

INDUSTRIES STRESS TEMPO

Factory Products Low in Quality and Quantity, but They Are Improving Slowly.

WASTE IS HELD INEVITABLE

But When They Succeed, Russians Say They Will Demand a Big World Market.

This is the second of a series of articles on Russia today by THE NEW YORK TIMES'S *Moscow correspondent, who is at present in Paris. The first article of the series was published in* THE NEW YORK TIMES *on Sunday.*

By WALTER DURANTY.

Special Cable to THE NEW YORK TIMES.

PARIS, June 15.—To start, as the writer does, from the premise that the five-year plan is not a mere budgetary program or a rigid scale of facts and figures, but a national policy and slogan, and a physical expression of all that is meant by "Stalinism," does not prevent persons outside of Russia from saying. "Whether that is true or not, what we want to know is how the plan is working and what will happen if it works."

The first question is particularly hard to answer because the Soviet Union is the first example in history of a country in which home and foreign policy, home and foreign trade, industry, agriculture, finance and other activities are all gathered, so to speak, in one hand, each of whose fingers is interdependent and mutually affected by each other.

That this is true must be understood from the outset—confusing though it seems at first sight to speak of Maxim Litvinoff's rather unexpectedly successful speech at Geneva as being directly cognate to Soviet oil production or freight-car loadings, or timber export or the Spring catch of fish and the grain-sowing program.

Economic Aspect of Plan.

In an attempt to minimize this confusion the writer will treat Soviet foreign relations and foreign trade in subsequent articles and right now consider the five-year plan's economic side.

First and foremost comes agriculture, which for the next decade at least will count most in Russia. Here, too, something other than economics enters at once—the five-year plan in addition to the economic production of agriculture involves the political socialization of peasant holdings, or collective farming as it is called.

The writer ventures to say that it is far more important to the Kremlin to have 60 per cent of the peasant holdings collectivized this year—which is the case, as compared with the original five-year plan program of 50 per cent collectivization by 1933—than to produce an exportable surplus of 15,000,000 tons over internal needs. Well, collectivization, or the political end, has been done, and it will depend largely on the weather as to how far the production program will be accomplished.

The same applies in general terms to industry. The Kremlin is more concerned over whether the industrial workers are learning their jobs and getting all keyed up for socialism by "shock brigades" and "Socialist competition" than what they actually produce. At least, that is true for the time being. In this respect the political gains are greater than actual production, which varies from fair to middling, as far as raw materials are concerned, down to poor when it comes to finished products.

Oil production is good; manganese, good; coal, iron and steel, middling; transportation, not so good but improving; nonferrous metals, the same, and all manufactured goods, from electric light bulbs to tractors, nothing remarkable but growing in quantity and improving in quality. Detailed figures are confusing and do not matter much as compared with the "tempo," but in any and all cases one may say the supply produced is far inferior to the home demand.

Home Supply Is Growing.

On the other hand, the supply does grow and enables the Soviet Union to export enough to pay for purchases from abroad. What the supply costs and whether or not it is a product of an abominably low living standard simply does not matter to the Kremlin, which dismisses the dumping charge also as nothing

Continued on Page Eight.

Costa Rican Cabinet Resigns; Political Situation Menacing

Special Cable to THE NEW YORK TIMES.

SAN JOSE, Costa Rica, June 15.—The entire Cabinet resigned yesterday. Public opinion indicates that the President will probably be obliged to accept all the resignations except that of Arturo Quiros, Minister of Public Safety, who is the President's son-in-law.

The Cabinet crisis started last week when Manuel Castro Quesada, Minister to Washington, returned to Costa Rica, whereupon the Cabinet threatened to resign unless Señor Castro Quesada resigned. His resignation was not forthcoming, hence the Cabinet action.

The political situation is very unsettled and it is believed there will be important developments soon.

BIG GOLD CREDIT HERE SET UP FOR GERMANY

Shift of $41,680,000 Shown in Metal for Foreign Account—German Bonds Recover.

AID BY FRANCE INTIMATED

Paris Sees Situation Serious, but Not Dangerous—Bruening Warns Tax Opponents.

Movements for assistance to Germany appeared to be under way yesterday in New York and Paris, with a record shift in gold here credited to the Reich.

In Paris it was intimated by government officials that France was prepared to give necessary assistance and that, while the German situation was admitted to be serious, it was not believed any catastrophe was in prospect.

Chancellor Bruening warned leaders of labor unions and political parties that his Cabinet would resign if the Reichstag Committee should decide today to call a special session.

GOLD CREDIT HERE.

A net decline of $41,680,000 in gold earmarked here for foreign account, one of the greatest declines on record, was announced yesterday afternoon by the Federal Reserve Bank of New York in its daily statement on the gold movement. This decline reduced the total gold earmarked here to about $50,000,000.

Although the amount of the decline yesterday was far more than the gold supposed to be earmarked here for the account of Germany, Wall Street concluded that Germany had entered into an agreement with France, whereby French gold here would be released and credited to the account of Germany.

The total decline in the earmarked gold stock here last week amounted to $23,505,000, the previous week, $1,000,000 and from January to May, inclusive, $17,500,000.

Follows Higher Bank Rates.

The change in the gold ownership here yesterday followed closely the increase in the Reichsbank's rediscount rate on Saturday from 5 to 7 per cent, which was followed by the increase in the rates of the central banks of Austria and Hungary from 6 to 7½ and 5½ to 7, respectively.

The German mark moved up a point in the foreign exchange market here yesterday, closing at 23.73¾ cents, compared with 23.72¾ cents on Saturday. French exchange was up 5-16 and London up ⅛ here yesterday. In the London market, however, the German mark was off slightly.

More tangible evidence of the effect sought after by the rise in the German bank rate was to be found in the bond market. To the accom-

Continued on Page Twelve.

TWO 'KEY WITNESSES' NAMED BY FAITHFULL IN DAUGHTER'S DEATH

He Tells Police She Was With Two Men After a Party in Home of Actress.

CALLS INVESTIGATION SLOW

Girl Drugged and Unconscious Before She Died, Toxicologist for City Finds.

HER BROKEN LIFE REVEALED

Had Harrowing Experience in Youth—$20,000 Paid to Family by the Man She Blamed.

The names of two men who, in the belief of Stanley F. Faithfull, stepfather of 25-year-old Starr Faithfull, whose body was washed up off Long Beach a week ago, "could furnish the key to the mystery" of her death, have been given to District Attorney Edwards of Nassau County, Mr. Faithfull revealed last night.

Accounting in detail for his stepdaughter's movements in the three days before her disappearance on June 5—a phase of the case which had hitherto puzzled investigators—Mr. Faithfull asserted as he made public this information that "if the Nassau County police had been a little vigorous in their investigation, this affair would not have lagged so slowly."

On Wednesday, June 3, Miss Faithfull was escorted by a man friend to the apartment of an artist friend of his on West Thirty-seventh Street, Mr. Faithfull said. There she was introduced to the two men who, he believes, could solve the mystery of her death.

Told of "Special Date."

In their company she went that evening to a party in the apartment of a celebrated stage beauty and the next afternoon she again met her two new friends in a club on West Forty-fifth Street, Mr. Faithfull said. Returning home late that afternoon, she told her mother of a "special date" for that evening.

Although she did not specifically name the two new acquaintances as the men with whom she had this engagement, her mother gathered from the conversation that it was with them. She did not return until 1 A. M. Friday, when she announced that she was to meet the two men later that forenoon.

When Mrs. Faithfull awoke on the morning of Friday, June 5, Starr had already left the house, presumably to keep the engagement with her new friends. Her movements since then remain a puzzle, and a report was current, although denied by Police Commissioner Mulrooney, that the New York police had been asked to look for two men and a woman believed to have been with her that day.

Even before Mr. Faithfull's revelations the day had been so crammed with developments in the investigation of the case that Mr. Edwards had determined to drop his plan for continuing the presentation of evidence to the grand jury in a John Doe and Richard Roe proceeding begun last week. It will not be resumed until a week from today, he said.

Analysis Shows Veronal.

Miss Faithfull was under the influence of veronal at the time of her mysterious death, an analysis of her internal organs by Dr. Alexander O. Gettler, New York City toxicologist, developed yesterday. She had taken enough of the drug to induce pro-

Continued on Page Three.

Idle to Work 68-Acre Farm, Lent by Lockport Minister

By The Associated Press.

LOCKPORT, N. Y., June 15.—The Rev. Charles F. Kesting, pastor of St. Peter's Evangelical Church, today turned over to the unemployed of Lockport his 68-acre farm in the town of Newfane, north of here.

A cooperative non-sectarian organization was formed today to operate the farm. The organization meeting was attended by three ministers. A business man was elected treasurer nd John Wendel, hitherto unemployed, was chosen as farm manager.

The entire proceeds from the farm will be turned over to the unemployed, and those who take advantage of Mr. Kesting's offer will be asked to work not only for themselves but to raise vegetables for others who are unemployed.

Several persons have offered farm machinery to aid the project.

WALKER TAKES FLING AT SEABURY INQUIRY

In Welcoming Advertising Men He Indirectly Accuses Counsel of Exaggerating Conditions.

HOOVER SENDS A MESSAGE

Roosevelt Says Government Should Take Leadership in Economic Ills.

Mayor Walker indirectly attacked the Seabury city-wide investigation yesterday in an address before the Advertising Federation of America at a luncheon at the Hotel Pennsylvania. Then turning to the business situation he suggested that the solution would not come from Wall Street, but possibly from government leadership, which so far has been lacking, and he significantly addressed his remarks in that connection to Governor Roosevelt, sitting at the speakers' table.

Preceding Mayor Walker, Governor Roosevelt had appealed to the advertising men to join in the movement to interest people in the functions of government. He asked if the time had not come when government should take "a little leadership" in the search for a cure for our ills.

Message From Hoover Read.

President Hoover in a message to the convention read by Gilbert T. Hodges, president of the federation, said that advertising had played an important part in raising the standard of living. The President's message follows:

> It seems to me most appropriate that at your annual convention you propose to clarify the function of advertising as an economic force, so that its benefits may be better understood not only by those who employ it, but by the public to which in the aggregate it renders its greatest service.
>
> Advertising has played an important part in raising our standard of living, in stimulating invention and in maintaining competition. By promoting production and distribution it has brought within the reach of many the comforts and conveniences previously enjoyed by the few.
>
> The theme of your convention is especially timely, because of the part sound, constructive advertising is bound to play in accelerating the return of normal business activity.

The Mayor and Governor spoke at the luncheon which opened the twenty-seventh annual convention of the Advertising Federation of America. More than 1,500 members and their guests attended the luncheon and more than 3,000 management, sales and advertising executives from the United States, Canada and Europe are expected to attend the sessions continuing through Thursday.

The addresses were broadcast to a radio audience over WJZ, WOR, and WABC, which prompted Mayor Walker to observe, while surveying the big battery of microphones, that they looked "like a full-course dinner," with every important broadcasting station except WNYC represented.

Walker Welcomes Delegates.

After welcoming the advertising men, Mayor Walker asserted that the city's vast program of public improvements always took into consideration "the convenience of business." He said he agreed with the Governor who had preceded him that it might be well for advertising men to take a more active interest in government.

"I agree with that, but that can't be truly said altogether of New York City," continued the Mayor.

"For some time past the eye of the nation has been focused upon the city of New York, and speaking still as the Chief Executive of the city of New York, we solicit study, inquiry, even investigation, but hasn't

Continued on Page Fourteen.

Crippled Nautilus, Under Battleship Tow, To Reach Irish Port in Seven and a Half Days

After wallowing helplessly for more than a day in the rough North Atlantic, nearly 1,000 miles from land, the submarine Nautilus got under way again early yesterday in tow of the battleship Wyoming. Navy officers calculated it would require seven and a half days for the old underseas craft, in which Captain Sir Hubert Wilkins hopes to slide under the ice cap to the North Pole, to reach Cobh, Ireland.

The Wyoming and the Arkansas both of the training squadron of the scouting force, had responded to distress signals and had been standing by since Sunday, waiting for seas to abate sufficiently to permit the crew of the Nautilus to grapple an eight-inch hawser and make it fast; but with its motors crippled and no headway the submarine had tossed and heaved so violently that all attempts had failed.

The feat was accomplished, however, at 6:30 o'clock yesterday morning, according to a radio message received at the Navy Department, Washington, from Rear Admiral Claude C. Bloch, commanding the battleships. He notified the department that the long tow commenced almost immediately, but that a speed of only five knots was being maintained. The distance to Cobh was estimated at nearly 1,000 miles at the time that towing commenced.

Admiral Bloch's message added that the Arkansas would proceed to Copenhagen, where both battleships are due on June 23 with midshipmen of the Naval Academy on their annual foreign cruise. At the instance of the Admiral, according to the Navy Department, those in charge of the Nautilus were persuaded to arrange by radio for a tug to set out from Cobh and relieve the Wyoming of its tow some distance from that port. Just when the transfer would take place was not known.

Later Admiral Bloch sent a second message saying that "the captain of the submarine states that he is trying to get her in shape and that all are well."

NORTHWEST DROUGHT WORSE THAN IN 1930; HUGE LOSS IN CROPS

Federal Agencies Told Serious Dryness Extends From North Dakota to Oregon.

CANADA ALSO IS HARD HIT

Mid-West and Mississippi Valley Lack Normal Moisture and May Also Suffer Loss.

LOAN FUND NOT AVAILABLE

Senators Walsh and Caraway Demand Special Session of Congress to Provide Funds.

Special to The New York Times.

WASHINGTON, June 15.—Drought conditions in the Northwest even more severe than those of last year have been reported to the Weather Bureau and farm agencies of the government. Wheat and other crops in Eastern Montana and North Dakota have already suffered highly and are reported to be threatened with disaster, and crops in sections of Oregon and Washington have also been heavily cut.

The drought also extends to the wheat belt of Canada and threatens great loss there. The Middle Western and Mississippi Valley States have received less than the normal fall of rain this year and unless they get more, the hot Summer months may bring a renewal of last year's troubles.

Senators Walsh of Montana and Caraway of Arkansas, both Democrats, announced today that they will press for a special session of Congress to deal with the emergency.

Centre of the Trouble.

The need is understood to be greatest in Western North Dakota and in the eastern section of Montana, Oregon and Washington. Elsewhere the situation is less serious, though, according to the Weather Bureau, both Winter and Spring wheat has suffered "considerable damage" everywhere in that section except in Western Oregon and Washington.

J. B. Kincer, Weather Bureau meteorologist, explained that no repetition of 1930 drought disaster throughout the country was anticipated, as the rainfall in other sections had afforded moisture sufficient to carry them through safely, although, he said, "the South is getting pretty dry" and in at least six States of the Northwest the rainfall has been less than at the same time last year.

"The Winter wheat crop in Eastern Oregon and Washington has suffered even more heavily than the Spring crop, having been further advanced when the drought set in," he said. "The present condition really is an accumulation of defective rainfalls over a long period in this section of the country. Except in March the rainfall has been deficient everywhere, save for recent rains which gave relief in limited areas in the Red River Valley."

Critical Situation in Canada.

Reports received today by the Weather Bureau from the Canadian Bureau of Statistics says: "The grain crops of practically the entire Western region of Canada, of normally the heaviest production, are in a critical condition as the result of severe and prolonged drought. Combined with greatly reduced precipitation, serious damage also has been caused by high winds, frost and cutworms."

Wisconsin had 59 per cent of normal rainfall this Spring, as compared with 88 last Spring; Minne-

Continued on Page Sixteen.

Henry Ford Raising Cantaloupes for Alcohol To Paint Autos He Hopes to 'Grow' on Farm

Special to The New York Times.

DETROIT, June 15.—Henry Ford has taken up the wholesale growing of cantaloupes, not, however, to compete with truck gardeners but for raw material used in the production of automobiles. On one of the farms near Macon, in Southern Michigan, which forms a part of Ford's 3,000-acre agricultural laboratory in Lenawee County, an extraordinary amount of acreage has been devoted to planting of the cantaloupe seeds. Old dirt farmers, who have sold their land to Ford and gone to work for him on a $5 eight-hour-a-day basis, expressed surprise at the planting of so much.

"We wondered at first who he was going to get to eat so many melons," said John Fisher, one of the Ford's 100 farm laborers.

"But the Ford officials, who have kept everything secret, would give no answer and merely ordered us to go ahead and plant the seeds.

"Then one day when Mr. Ford was on one of his numerous personal inspection trips over the fields I heard him make a remark that gave me the tip. I heard him say, 'I'm going to rush this experiment through with the idea of determining whether every raw material that goes into an automobile can't be raised on a farm.'

"Take these cantaloupes, for instance. His chemists, who have done wonders already in turning farm products into automobile raw materials and fertilizers, plan to get alcohol for auto paint out of the melons.

"With what is left after the alcohol is extracted I understand they intend to make a new cheap substance as serviceable as wood."

Mr. Ford started his $3,000,000 farm venture to determine if automobiles can be "grown" by new processes more efficient and economical than the present ones of mining and smelting.

HOOVER DECRIES DEPRESSION PANACEAS; INDIANAPOLIS SPEECH, HELD BID FOR 1932, PICTURES GLOWING FUTURE FOR NATION

President's Reply to Those Asking for 'Plan' Is Proposal of One for Developing America

Special to The New York Times.

INDIANAPOLIS, Ind., June 15.—President Hoover in his address here had this to say about national "plans":

> We have many citizens insisting that we produce an advance "plan" for the future development of the United States. They demand that we produce it right now. I presume the plan idea is an infection from the slogan of the five-year plan through which Russia is struggling to redeem herself from ten years of starvation and misery.
>
> I am able to propose an American plan to you. We plan to take care of 20,000,000 increase in population in the next twenty years. We plan to build for them 4,000,000 new and better homes, thousands of new and still more beautiful city buildings, thousands of factories; to increase the capacity of our railways; to add thousands of miles of highways and waterways; to install 25,000,000 electrical horsepower; to grow 20 per cent more farm products.
>
> We plan to provide new parks, schools, colleges and churches for this 20,000,000 people. We plan more leisure for men and women and better opportunities for its enjoyment.
>
> We plan not only to provide for all the new generation, but we shall, by scientific research and invention, lift the standard of living and security of life to the whole people. We plan to secure a greater diffusion of wealth, a decrease in poverty, and a great reduction in crime. And this plan will be carried out if we just keep on giving the American people a chance. Its impulsive force is in the character and spirit of our people. They have already done a better job for 120,000,000 people than any other nation in all history.

LINES OF BATTLE DEFINED

President Puts Reliance on Individual Effort for Prosperity.

URGES VOLUNTARY RELIEF

Government Employment Insurance Called a Dole—Capital Gains Tax Assailed.

FARMING FOR EXPORT PAST

Tour Into Middle West, Where Revolt Is Rumored, Becomes a Political Swing.

From a Staff Correspondent of The New York Times.

INDIANAPOLIS, Ind., June 15.—Appearing tonight in a section of the country from which he has heard rumors of revolt against his brand of Republicanism, President Hoover, in a speech before 5,000 of his partisans gathered at a banquet of the Indiana Republican Editorial Association, unmistakably threw in his bid for re-election in 1932 with a redeclaration of the purpose of his administration to see the United States out of its present economic plight by maintaining the doctrine of individualism.

From a platform in the spacious Manufacturers Hall at the State Fair Grounds Mr. Hoover reviewed the activities of his administration in organizing this individualistic effort throughout the country, not in the nature of a defense of his régime but rather as an enunciation of the policy upon which he will stand during the coming months.

An ovation greeted the President when he arose to speak. He already had put the men in a good humor by suggesting, through Paul R. Bausman, master of ceremonies, that they remove their coats because of the oppressive heat. Hundreds of coatless men stood cheering when the President was introduced. After two minutes he waved for silence. There was more vigor and emphasis than noted in any of his speeches within the last two years.

The President fulfilled the highest expectations of his mid-Western followers, who had nursed the hope that he would give them cause to hoist his banner anew in this land of rumored revolt. He gave them platform material aplenty, and his speech left no doubt that Herbert Hoover has cast the die for 1932.

Politics Along the Way.

The President arrived here this afternoon after a trip through West Virginia, Kentucky and Ohio which had all the outward appearances of a regular political swing, with back platform greetings and short talks and consultations with Republican leaders along the way.

Some of Mr. Hoover's party associates had been insisting that he show himself out in the country; particularly that he give them a rallying cry for the coming campaign. Tonight they had practically everything they had asked for. His speech here was interpreted on every side as the laying of the groundwork for 1932, and the promulgation of the issues upon which the President will give fight.

Mr. Hoover made it even more emphatic tonight that his administration would go no further toward outright unemployment relief on the basis of charity. The country is maintaining, he said, and will maintain, systematic voluntary organizations for the care of actual distress. The views of those who think the country can legislate itself out of a "world-wide" depression, he added, "are as accurate as the belief we can exorcise a Caribbean hurricane by statutory law."

He upheld the Smoot-Hawley tariff act and declared against reopening the question in these times of economic distress. He cited the government's activities in speeding up public works, which he termed a reversal of a traditional policy of tightening up on Federal construction during periods of depression. He credited his farm relief program with "giving aid and support to farmers in marketing their crops, by which they have realized hundreds of millions more in prices than farmers of any other country."

Says Economy Shows Results.

The policy of the government in excluding every possible Federal ex-

UNTERMYER'S PLAN REJECTED BY ROADS

I. R. T. and B. M. T. Operating Groups Hold It Is Not Legal Basis for Public Hearings.

DECLINE TO PARTICIPATE

Blow at Counsel Is Seen—Board Experts Fix Price of Lines at $503,540,205.

The $489,678,000 transit unification plan recently submitted to the Transit Commission by Samuel Untermyer, special counsel, was rejected yesterday by the Interborough and the operating companies of the B. M. T. as a legal or proper basis for public hearings. The companies notified the commission that they would not participate in the hearings, which began yesterday, although they were still willing to cooperate in a unification program which they deemed in accordance with the terms of the Downing-Steingut unification law.

The B. M. T. also declined to participate, but on the ground that it was merely a holder of the stocks and bonds of the New York Rapid Transit Corporation and the Williamsburg Power Company and had no physical property which could be incorporated in a unity scheme.

The action of the companies, ordered by unanimous votes of their directorates, was construed in transit circles as a definite demand upon the Transit Commission that it adopt, modify or repudiate the Untermyer plan or prepare one of its own before holding public hearings. It was taken several hours after the opening hearing, which was devoted to the noting of appearances, had been adjourned until next Monday. Counsel for both groups of companies appeared specially at the opening ses-

Continued on Page Nineteen.

POLITICIANS REGARD SPEECH AS 1932 GUN

Hoover Viewed as Putting His Campaign for Re-election on Economic Basis.

SEE TARIFF A MAJOR ISSUE

Stand for Hawley-Smoot Act and Against 'Dole' Likely to Bring Vetoes.

By RICHARD V. OULAHAN.

Special to The New York Times.

WASHINGTON, June 15.—President Hoover's speech before the Indiana Editorial Association at Indianapolis tonight leaves no doubt in the minds of political observers that he has started the next year's battle for the Presidency twelve months ahead of the assembling of the nominating conventions.

The impressive feature of the President's remarks, as these observers see it, is that Mr. Hoover is seeking to have the battle waged on economic issues, rather than upon that of prohibition.

With certainty very generally felt that Mr. Hoover will be renominated by his party, the propositions he set forth appear to forecast the chief fundamentals of the Republican National Platform of 1932 as:

He is unalterably opposed to a Federal dole to the unemployed.

There should be no Federal ownership of public utilities or Federal operation of them.

The Republican protective tariff should be maintained.

"Except in temporary national emergencies," there should be no government-in-business in competition with private enterprise.

"The arm of bureaucracy into a multitude of affairs" should not be extended.

Sees Basis of Welfare.

President Hoover put these party fundamentals, as he sees them, to his immediate audience and to the country in the guise of rhetorical questions, but their meaning was clear. According to the President, the future welfare of the country depends on the answer to these propositions.

One portion of the President's speech attracts particular attention here. Using the Soviet five-year plan as a text, he indicated that he had a plan which embodied the principles enumerated by him as those of the Hoover Administration.

This was obviously a challenge to the Democratic party, which through its spokesmen has been charging that the Republican party had *no* plan, a challenge which brought from authoritative Republican sources the retort that the Democrats had failed to disclose a plan of their own for remedying the conditions of which they complain.

The President, however, did not mention his own or the Democratic party or the Progressive element of the Republicans, but spoke of the divergence of national policy between "some groups" and "other groups."

Continued on Page Two.

The globe-encircling fliers and the *Winnie Mae* are swamped by the rush of an enthusiastic crowd as soon as the wheels touched the ground at Roosevelt Field.

Times Wide World Photo.

Times Wide World Photo.

The exhausted fliers, able to relax at last, in their hotel suite.

Times Wide World Photo.

The *Winnie Mae* circling over Roosevelt Field at the end of her 15,000-mile journey.

Autographed sketches of the airmen made when they landed in Cleveland.

Times Wide World Photo.

May Post, wife of the pilot of the *Winnie Mae*.

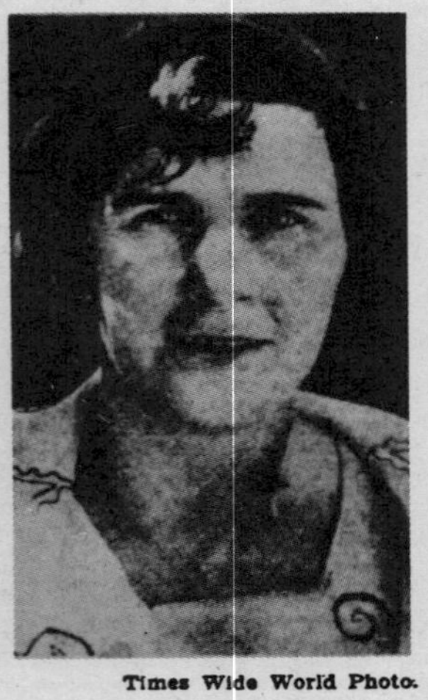

Times Wide World Photo.

Vera Gatty, wife of the navigator.

The *Winnie Mae* on the rain-soaked landing field at Edmonton, Canada.

Times Wide World Photo.

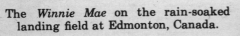

"All the News That's Fit to Print."

The New York Times.

LATE CITY EDITION

Copyright, 1931, by The New York Times Company.

VOL. LXXX....No. 26,822. NEW YORK, THURSDAY, JULY 2, 1931. TWO CENTS In New York City | THREE CENTS Within 200 Miles | FOUR CENTS Elsewhere Except 7th and 8th Postal Zones

POST AND GATTY END THEIR RECORD WORLD FLIGHT; CIRCLED GLOBE IN 8 DAYS, 15 HOURS, 51 MINUTES; 10,000 IN WILD DEMONSTRATION AT FIELD HERE

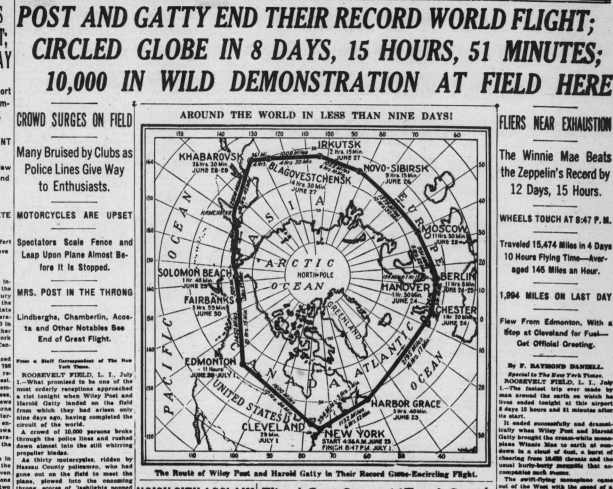

AROUND THE WORLD IN LESS THAN NINE DAYS!

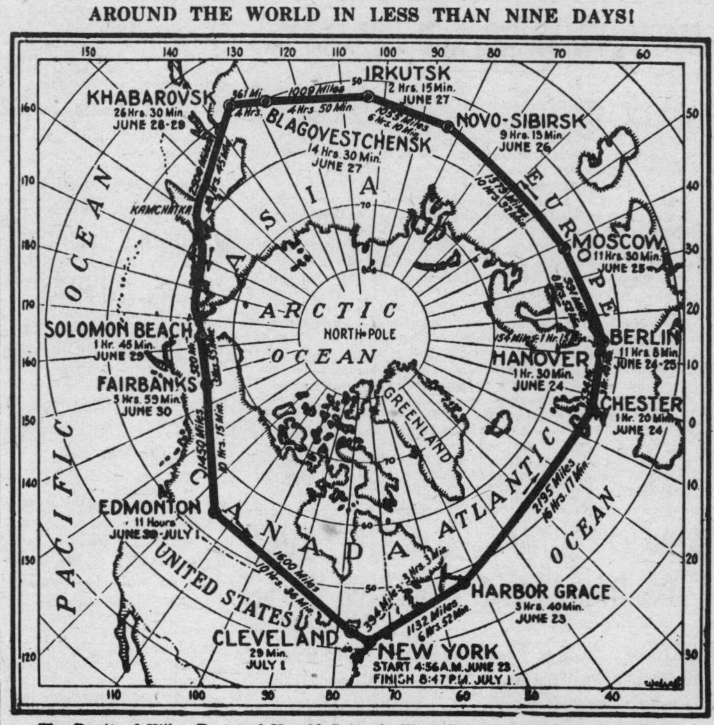

The Route of Wiley Post and Harold Gatty in Their Record Globe-Encircling Flight.

HOOVER DEBT NOTE OFFERS CONCESSIONS TO FRANCE; WARNS OF GERMAN CRASH

STATEMENT SPEEDS PARLEY

Setting Forth Obstacles, It Meets Issue of Time of Repayments.

CITES LOSS IF STEP FAILS

Berlin Call for Young Plan Halt Would Harm French—Alternative Action Studied.

FRENCH CABINET DIVIDED

Mellon Will Continue Parley in Paris Tonight—Hope Grows in Germany for Accord.

A memorandum stating the American Government's position on the Hoover debt relief proposals was presented to France yesterday. It seeks to conciliate France, while offering some concessions, and at the same time warns of the danger of a collapse in Germany's economic structure.

The French Cabinet will consider the memorandum today. Its reception was the chief topic of interest in Paris yesterday.

Germany, worried by new riots precipitated by Communists and Hitlerites, is anxiously watching the negotiations in Paris.

HOOVER'S NOTE TO PARIS.

By RICHARD V. OULAHAN.

Special to The New York Times.

WASHINGTON, July 1.—In a courteously worded memorandum handed to the French Government in Paris today by Ambassador Edge, the United States called upon France to help the world recover its economic and financial balance by harmonizing differences of view and joining with this government to give full effect to President Hoover's proposal for a year's suspension of Germany's reparations and all other intergovernmental debts.

Although at one point the memorandum is sharp and emphatic in its language in contesting the French divergent suggestion, its tone is conciliatory and concessions are offered to bring about an accord with the French position.

The memorandum offers no recession on the part of the United States from its basic principle that Germany shall have the full benefit of a complete suspension of debts between nations and shall have ample time in which to refund the reparation payments which would be suspended during the holiday year proposed by the President.

One of the most interesting features of the memorandum is the pointed hint given by the United States that France would be worse off financially if the President's plan should fail.

It is assumed by the United States, the memorandum says, that on account of the situation in Germany, a failure of the American proposals would cause Germany unquestionably to give notice for the postponement of all conditional reparations, as provided in the Young plan, and therefore, that portion of intergovernmental payments would not be forthcoming.

Berlin Could Use Young Plan.

Explaining just what it means, the United States goes on to say that if the American plan fails and Germany exercises her rights of a Young plan moratorium on the postponable payments, and "even assuming that unconditional payments are maintained," France would receive about $105,000,000 through the unconditional annuity, but at the same time France would be obliged to pay into the Bank for International Settlements the guarantee fund of $106,000,000 required under the Young plan, and about $110,000,000 due to Great Britain and the United States in the year under the terms of the war debt funding settlements.

In other words, France would be out of pocket for the moratorium year to the extent of $111,000,000 if she did not conform to President Hoover's program.

Without adhering to exact figures, the American memorandum puts this suggested situation in the following way:

"Thus, if the American proposal should fail and the suspension pro-

Continued on Page Twenty-one.

Our Envoy's Limousine Is Sign Of Parleys on Debt in Berlin

By The Associated Press.

BERLIN, July 1.—Few persons in Berlin outside of a small circle of political correspondents know what an important utilitarian part in the debt proposal negotiations is being played these days by an American-made limousine bearing the Prussian license plate No. 14.

When No. 14 stands before the official residence of Chancellor Bruening or before the office of Foreign Minister Curtius it means that Ambassador Frederic M. Sackett is conferring about the fate of the Hoover proposal.

Since June 20 this car has been parked more frequently in front of the Bruening residence or the Curtius office than in front of the American Embassy, for Mr. Sackett is keeping in closest touch with the German Government.

FISCAL YEAR DEFICIT TOTALS $903,000,000

Receipts Off $861,000,000 to $3,317,000,000—Expenditures Up $226,000,000.

OUTLAY WAS $4,220,000,000

Mills Charges Increased Spending to Farm and Veterans' Aid and Public Construction.

Special to The New York Times.

WASHINGTON, July 1.—With a deficit of $903,000,000 and an increase in the outstanding public debt of $616,000,000, the Federal Government yesterday ended its most unfavorable fiscal year in recent history.

Acting Secretary Ogden L. Mills issued a detailed statement today showing that treasury receipts were $3,317,000,000, a decline of $861,000,000 from 1930, and expenditures chargeable against ordinary receipts were $4,220,000,000, or $226,000,000 more than last year, when there was a surplus of $184,000,000.

The gross debt yesterday amounted to $16,801,000,000. Money market conditions during the year, however, permitted refunding at unusually low rates, so that there was a reduction of $48,000,000 in interest charges. Revised figures for yesterday on the average rate of interest showed 3.56 per cent, compared with 3.80 per cent the year before.

The decline in the major sources of Federal revenue reflected for the most part the effect of the business depression, Mr. Mills said, while the increase in expenditures was attributed largely to those for agricultural aid and relief, for additional benefits to war veterans and for the accelerated governmental construction activities.

$1,860,000,000 in Income Taxes.

The annual report of Secretary Mellon, submitted to Congress last December, estimated the deficit for 1931 at $180,000,000.

"The discrepancy was due to the difficulty at that time of measuring the severity and duration of the business depression and the extent to which internal revenue and customs receipts would be affected," Mr. Mills declared.

The total income tax collection, including back taxes, was $1,860,000,000, a reduction of $551,000,000 from the 1930 fiscal year. Current corporation taxes amounted to $892,000,000, a reduction of $226,000,000, and current individual taxes $731,000,000, a cut of $330,000,000.

Customs duties fell from $587,000,000 in 1930 to $378,000,000 in 1931.

Text of the Mills Statement.

Mr. Mills's statement was as follows:

"A considerable reduction in Federal revenues during the fiscal year 1931 and an increase in expenditures resulted in a deficit of $903,000,000, as compared with a surplus of $184,000,000 for 1930.

"Retirements of United States obligations to meet sinking fund and other statutory retirements chargeable against ordinary receipts totaled $440,000,000, so that the deficit, exclusive of debt retirement, amounted to $463,000,000. The total gross debt outstanding was increased by $616,000,000. As the general fund balance increased $153,000,000, the net debt increased but $463,000,000.

"The total ordinary receipts amounted to $3,317,000,000, which

Continued on Page Twenty.

RECORD HEAT HOLDS GRIP ON THE EAST; RELIEF IS ON WAY

Chicago and St. Louis Report 18 Fatalities Each—High Temperatures Abate in West.

250 FELLED IN FORD PLANT

Two Killed in Cyclone in New Jersey, Where Entire Fruit and Berry Crop Is Imperiled.

RECORDS BROKEN UP-STATE

High Humidity Adds to Discomfort Here With Mercury at 90—Wave Due to End Tomorrow.

The heat wave concentrated its intensity on the Middle West and the East yesterday, sending the mercury up to record levels in most of the principal cities in New York State and giving this city high temperature readings that varied from 90 in the local United States Weather Bureau, to 134 in the New York Meteorological Observatory in Central Park.

After causing a death toll, placed by The Associated Press at 766 throughout the country, the heat relented in the West and Northwest. Chicago's millions sweltered in temperatures as high as 101.3 degrees, but they were cheered by the news that cool weather was being borne across the great plains by late afternoon, a low pressure area had engulfed the Dakotas, Western Iowa and Minnesota, sending temperatures down twenty points from the century mark.

However, in St. Louis and also in Chicago, eighteen were killed by the heat yesterday. There were seven deaths and twenty-five prostrations in up-State New York. Here, two drownings and several prostrations were reported. In Newark one man dropped dead of the heat and a boy was drowned.

Two Die in Jersey Cyclone.

In Southern New Jersey two farm hands and three horses were killed by lightning when a small cyclone and a terrific electrical storm swept across Cumberland and Cape May Counties. The storm did thousands of dollars of damage to crops, uprooted trees and tore away parts of houses. The dead were William Bradford, 50, of Newport, N. J., and Harrison Parsons, 52, of Cedarville.

As the cyclone swept over Ocean View, in Cape May County, it picked up a roadside stand, with its proprietor, Theodore Hampton, inside it, and carried it forty feet away. Hampton was unhurt.

The Weather Bureau at Albany held no hope of relief for New York State before tomorrow night, when cooling weather is expected to blow in from the Mississippi Valley.

The local Weather Bureau, however, promised a slight improvement today. The forecast was for generally fair weather today and tomorrow, except for probable thundershowers, with gentle to moderate shifting winds and was for somewhat cooler temperatures today.

In Vineland the twister knocked off the steeple of the First Presbyterian Church, ripped away the wires leading from the power plant at the Old Soldiers' Home, cutting off the lights while a funeral was in progress there, and stripped the roof from the home of Dr. John H. Winslow, president of the local board of education. It started two small fires

Continued on Page Twenty-five.

CROWD SURGES ON FIELD

Many Bruised by Clubs as Police Lines Give Way to Enthusiasts.

MOTORCYCLES ARE UPSET

Spectators Scale Fence and Leap Upon Plane Almost Before It Is Stopped.

MRS. POST IN THE THRONG

Lindberghs, Chamberlin, Acosta and Other Notables See End of Great Flight.

From a Staff Correspondent of The New York Times.

ROOSEVELT FIELD, L. I., July 1.—What promised to be one of the most orderly receptions approached a riot tonight when Wiley Post and Harold Gatty landed on the field from which they had arisen only nine days ago, having completed the circuit of the world.

A crowd of 10,000 persons broke through the police lines and rushed down almost into the still whirring propeller blades.

As thirty motorcycles, ridden by Nassau County policemen, who had gone out on the field to meet the plane, plowed into the oncoming throng, scores of flashlights popped and flashed, women screamed, and, in their efforts to protect the two aviators, many of the 300 patrolmen on duty shoved and clubbed those nearest at hand, heightening the confusion.

Many were bruised in the struggle.

Leeds's Pilot Injured.

Edward Connerton, private pilot for William B. Leeds, former husband of Princess Xenia, was severely injured in an altercation with the police. According to eye witnesses, he was trying to extricate his automobile from a jam when he became involved in a dispute with a patrolman.

Connerton, who is vice president of Air Services, Inc., left the automobile, and a scuffle ensued. It was said that he would remain at the Nassau County Hospital until X-ray photos had been developed to determine whether he had received a fractured skull.

It was reported that a photographer had been clubbed to temporary unconsciousness and taken home by a friend in an automobile.

At Nassau County Police Headquarters it was said that Conerton would face a charge of second-degree assault when he recovered.

Throughout the afternoon field officials and police officers had expressed surprise at the small number of persons sufficiently interested in the flight to come to the field.

"They can hear it over the radio," said some. "They're all down at the beach," was another explanation. Others asserted that spectacular flights were "old stuff."

At 6 o'clock in the evening not more than 2,000 had paid the 25

Continued on Page Six.

Astor Estate Wins $16,000,000 Tax Suit; Court Holds Baron Did Not Try to Evade Law

The Federal Government must return $10,000,000 taxes to the estate of the late Baron William Waldorf Astor as well as $6,000,000 in interest accrued since 1922, Federal Judge Francis G. Caffey ruled yesterday, settling the largest tax case ever tried in this district.

The amount in dispute was paid under protest by the estate as an inheritance tax on two trusts created by the Baron on Aug. 15, 1919, two months before he died. The suit was brought by the Farmers' Loan and Trust Company, as trustee.

Judge Caffey ruled that the $10,000,000 collected from the two trusts had been illegally assessed, as Baron Astor had not, as the government contended, created the trust in anticipation of his death to defeat provisions of the inheritance tax laws.

The decision was the second to have been handed down in favor of the trustee, the trust company having won a refund of $4,634,834 plus interest in 1928 for an estate tax upon the trust funds. The government, it was indicated, will appeal.

The case was tried without a jury on the consent of John W. Davis, attorney for the plaintiff, and Samuel C. Coleman, Assistant United States Attorney. Before arriving at his decision Judge Caffey made a thorough study of the correspondence of the late Baron.

In many of his letters the Anglo-American nobleman made it clear that he feared a "capital levy" in England and that he also believed that there was growing prejudice against large accumulations of wealth with a likelihood of tax increases against large property holders.

Judge Caffey decided that the trusts had been created to avoid these levies here and abroad without any thought of death. Baron Astor transferred New York City holdings valued at $46,000,000, and provided that the net income after payment to himself of $300,000 a year should be divided between his sons, William Waldorf Jr. and John Jacob.

Despite the difficulty of finding out what was in the mind of a dead man, Judge Caffey said, it was obvious, in the opinion of the court, that Baron Astor had established the trusts because income taxes alone were preying on his mind. He had an "obsession on the subject of taxation," the court said.

NOISY CITY ACCLAIM AWAITS FLIERS TODAY

Parade to City Hall Welcome to Leave Battery at Noon—Mayor to Give Medals.

DINNER SET FOR TONIGHT

Trophies to Be Presented—City Luncheon Also Will Add to Tributes.

Despite fond hopes of "sleeping for forty-eight hours," expressed by Wiley Post and Harold Gatty at Edmonton yesterday, the globe-circling fliers will face here today one of the busiest periods of their partnership. New York, enthused at their achievement in establishing new records of long-distance piloting and navigation, intends to give them a rousing official welcome.

At 10:30 o'clock this morning they are to be escorted from the Ritz-Carlton, where they and their wives are staying, to Pier 84, North River. There, aboard the municipal steamer Macom, the Mayor's Committee on Reception to Distinguished Guests, of which Dr. John H. Finley is chairman, will meet them and the party will proceed to Pier A.

At this pier, to the west of the Battery, where so many notable visitors and returning heroes have felt the first waves of the city's characteristic boisterous welcomes, the fliers will enter automobiles for the parade up Broadway. Between its canyon walls the air will be white with ticker tape and fluttering paper, which is the financial district's way of saying "Salutamus."

At the head of the parade will be a squadron of mounted police, followed by the Police Department Band. Then will come four battalions of the Sixteenth Infantry, United States Army; next two battalions of sailors and then two battalions of marines, followed by the Fire Department Band. Next in line will be the fliers, their wives, their backer, F. C. Hall of Oklahoma City, members of the Mayor's committee and other distinguished guests.

The parade is scheduled to leave Pier A at noon and to reach City Hall in time for the official welcome at 12:30.

To Receive Medals From Mayor.

At City Hall the military and naval detachments will form in the plaza while the ceremonies are carried out in the Aldermanic chamber. Dr. Finley will introduce the fliers to Mayor Walker, who will give them

Continued on Page Seven.

Fliers' Own Story of 'Tough Spots' Tells of Near-Crashes in Russia

Worried Over Plane When Tractor Yanked It Out of Mudhole in Siberia—Berlin-Moscow Hop Was the Worst—Thrilled by "Generous and Good" Reception Here.

By WILEY POST AND HAROLD GATTY.

Pilot and Navigator of the Monoplane Winnie Mae.

We had a thrill that probably will never come to us again when the New York skyline came into view through the haze and we set our wheels down on Roosevelt Field in the last safe landing of our trip.

Of course we are happy to have finished our trip even in faster time than we had planned—eight days fifteen hours and fifty-one minutes they told us when we landed—and at the same time we are a little bit dazed. Countries, oceans and civilizations have been slipping past us so fast in this journey of a little more than a week that things aren't straight in our minds yet.

And that reception at the field! It was generous and good, even if it was strenuous for a while. To tell the truth we didn't know whether anybody would be out to see us or not until we saw the crowds in the light of the flares as we sailed over the field.

Recall "Four Tough Stretches."

Oh, we had adventures all right! There were four tough stretches that we never will forget. The first was that flight across the North Atlantic which began the night after we left New York and Newfoundland. When we ran into fog on the last part of the ocean crossing, it was just plain hard flying. Flying by instrument, you know, at 12,000 feet. Once in a while it would show just enough of a hole for Gatty to get a sight. We held the course, though. And then we slipped down through a hole and found ourselves over Wales, safely across the Atlantic. We would have patted each other's backs if we hadn't been the length of the plane apart.

The next highlight, so far as tough flying was concerned, was between Berlin and Moscow. The distance was 925 miles, according to our charts. We left early in the morning and pretty soon crossed the border into Poland. There we had absolutely the dirtiest flying of our whole experience on this or any other flight. The ceiling simply closed down on us and forced us right down on the tree tops. We had to fight wind and rain as well as fog. Landmarks slipped by so fast that we had trouble checking the course and, of course, anything like celestial observation was impossible. The drift indicator held out, though, and from it we hit our mark on the nose through dead reckoning.

Another hard hop which gave us no end of concern was the flight between Irkutsk and Blagovestchensk through the wildest country we have ever seen. For hours we flew a bare twenty-five feet above the trees, and in the strange country, which was wholly unknown to us, strange apparitions loomed up in the mist ahead. Two or three times we thought the end had come and pulled the ship up sharply until the angle of climb became dangerous. We got through without "stubbing our toe," however, and wound up the day bogged down on the watersoaked field. Our sleep at Blagovestchensk on the hardest of Soviet beds was somewhat spoiled by the worry of wondering whether the tractor would arrive on time to pull the Winnie Mae to firmer ground, and if it did, whether the Russians could do it without breaking the already taxed landing gear.

In Fog Four Hours on Way to Alaska.

The last really dangerous section of the journey was the water hop from Siberia to Alaska. We flew first across the Okhotsk Sea. It was just getting dark as we started out, and it began to rain. We soon found ourselves enclosed in a fog so thick that we did not see a thing outside the airplane for four hours.

When it began to get light — the nights are short there, you know — we pulled up two large layers of clouds and stayed there. We knew there were mountains ahead on the Kamchatka Peninsula, but we managed that all right. We saw a mountain loom up between the layers and we followed

Continued on Page Two.

FLIERS NEAR EXHAUSTION

The Winnie Mae Beats the Zeppelin's Record by 12 Days, 15 Hours.

WHEELS TOUCH AT 8:47 P. M.

Traveled 15,474 Miles in 4 Days 10 Hours Flying Time—Averaged 145 Miles an Hour.

1,994 MILES ON LAST DAY

Flew From Edmonton, With a Stop at Cleveland for Fuel—Get Official Greeting.

By F. RAYMOND DANIELL.

Special to The New York Times.

ROOSEVELT FIELD, L. I., July 1.—The fastest trip ever made by man around the earth on which he lives ended tonight at this airport 8 days 15 hours and 51 minutes after its start.

It ended successfully and dramatically when Wiley Post and Harold Gatty brought the cream-white monoplane Winnie Mae to earth at sundown in a cloud of dust, a burst of cheering from [illegible] throats and the usual hurly-burly [illegible] that accompanies such events.

The swift-flying monoplane came out of the West with the speed of a meteor as the [illegible] sun turned the cloud-flecked blue of the sky to a brilliant pink back-drop. A white flash in the sky, it tore past slow-flying biplanes, monoplanes and flying boats in the air, banked steeply and circled the field twice.

The third time it swung back, flying low, and swooped down for a perfect three-point landing at break-neck speed against the wind, and headed toward the crowd of 10,000 packing the grand stand, lining the fence and perching on hangar roof tops. Its wheels touched earth at exactly 8:47, two minutes after it first hove into sight, and its arrival was officially recorded at that time by Walter D. Ward, official timer for the National Aeronautics Association.

Crowd Breaks Through Police.

Slowly the bird-like contraption that had crossed the Atlantic and the Pacific, flown high over the Urals, the Northern Rockies and the Alleghanies taxied toward the western end of the field, where the administration building is situated. No sooner had its wheel grounded, however, before the crowd which had shouted until it seemed its members must have exhausted themselves broke through the cordon of Nassau County policemen, and the carefully laid plans for an orderly reception went awry.

Post, his cheeks hollowed by fatigue, his face an ashen gray from the strain he has been under as the pilot of the Winnie Mae, leaped to the ground when the plane roared to a stop, its propeller whirling menacingly at the clustering crowd. His knees sagged under him, and the police had to use their clubs to protect him from the enthusiastic crowd.

His wife, who had sat with her eyes glued on the western sky since her arrival late in the afternoon, became almost hysterical as the airplane rushed earthward, and half crying, half laughing, she was escorted by two six-foot policemen through the crowd to her husband's side. When they met, after six weeks' separation she fought back the tears and managed to greet the hero of the flight with a smile.

Mrs. Gatty missed the show. She flew from California, but was forced to land at Pittsburgh at about the time the Winnie Mae came to earth at Roosevelt Field. She will come on to New York tomorrow and greet her husband at his hotel.

Gatty, whose unerring navigation enabled the expedition to maintain an almost perfect schedule on their 15,474-mile flight around the world, hauled himself up through the cockpit and was sitting, with a grin on his oil-smeared face, on the high wing of the ship when the crowd swarmed around it.

Gatty Also Wabbly in Knees.

He looked it over and waved, and then worked his way through the fuel tanks to the cabin door and jumped out. He too, was wabbly in the knees, and he had the half-dazed expression of a survivor of a ship wreck. Mechanically he answered the perfunctory questions of W. B. Mitchell, the United States Customs Inspector, while the police wrestled

"All the News That's Fit to Print."

The New York Times.

LATE CITY EDITION
THE WEATHER—Fair today and tomorrow; not much change in temperature.
Temperatures yesterday—Max. 80, min. 66.
U. S. Weather Forecast—See next to last page.

VOL. LXXX....No. 26,880. NEW YORK, SATURDAY, AUGUST 29, 1931. TWO CENTS In New York City | THREE CENTS Within 200 Miles | FOUR CENTS Elsewhere Except 7th and 8th Postal Zones

$400,000,000 CREDIT SET UP FOR BRITAIN BY NEW YORK AND PARIS BANKING GROUPS; NEW GOVERNMENT SURE OF MAJORITY OF 50

HUGE LOAN QUICKLY MADE

Paris and New York to Divide It—French Public Gets $100,000,000.

FUND AVAILABLE FOR YEAR

Morgan & Co. Head American Group Which Will Protect Sterling as It Was in 1925.

INTEREST NOT DISCLOSED

Bonds May Be Sold in France at 4¼ Per Cent—Lamont Denies Political Terms.

A one-year credit of $400,000,000 was placed at the disposal of the new British National Government yesterday by private bankers in this country and France, approximately equal portions being advanced by both markets.

The American share of the credit, amounting to $200,000,000, is being extended by a nation-wide group of about 110 banks, headed by J. P. Morgan & Co. The French portion will consist of a $100,000,000 banking credit and a $100,000,000 one-year British Treasury loan to be sold to the French public. None of the American credit will be publicly offered.

Announcement of the arrangement of the credit by American bankers was made late yesterday afternoon by Thomas W. Lamont of J. P. Morgan & Co. Mr. Lamont issued the following statement:

"We have arranged, in association with a group of American banks and banking houses, to extend a one-year credit of $200,000,000 to the British Government. We are informed by the British authorities that they are arranging in the French market for one-year credits and loans in the aggregate amount of approximately $200,000,000."

The credit has been arranged for the purpose of stabilizing sterling exchange, which has recently been weak in the foreign exchange markets of the world. It will not be used for any other purpose, nor will it serve to repay the existing $250,000,000 credit extended on Aug. 1, jointly and equally by the Bank of France and the Federal Reserve Bank of New York to the Bank of England. That credit has been heavily drawn upon during the past four weeks to defend sterling.

Rate Is Kept Secret.

The rate at which the British Government is to secure its funds was not dislosed. Bankers here regard that information as a private detail of the contract between them and the British Government. It is the understanding of American bankers, however, that the $100,000,000 portion of the French credit which is to be sold to the public will carry a rate of 4¼ per cent.

Actually, the rate charged by the American bankers to the British Government will vary during the life of the credit. It is the practice in arranging such credits, bankers stated, to fix a maximum and minimum rate of discount and to permit the fluctuations between these two extremes to be governed by existing money market rates.

The credit was under negotiation approximately thirty-six hours, although tentative inquiries as to whether this market would be disposed to extend such a loan were made early in the week. Announcement of the arrangement had been generally expected in Wall Street since it was recognized that a credit was needed and bankers here expressed their willingness to advance it several days ago.

The amount of the credit, in the opinion of bankers here, is so large as to make certain that no further funds will be needed to assure the stability of sterling. Although Wall Street has guessed between $300,000,000 and $500,000,000, with emphasis on the smaller figure, bankers said yesterday that $400,000,000 was the highest amount discussed at any time in the negotiations.

The readiness with which bankers here agreed to extend the credit was explained as due to "enlightened selfishness." In view of the effects which the German financial crisis had upon our own financial affairs,

Continued on Page Four.

Europe Faces Its Problems "in the Friendliest Way," Says Stimson Returning Home in Optimistic Spirit

Wireless to THE NEW YORK TIMES.

SOUTHAMPTON, England, Aug. 28.—When Secretary of State Henry L. Stimson sailed for home this afternoon on the United States liner Leviathan, he said:

> I am going back encouraged that the countries I have visited and their executive officials are making progress toward the solution of their difficulties. It is not for me to discuss those difficulties now, but there has been very hopeful progress at the conferences that I have attended and witnessed as well as those I have heard about.
>
> The European countries seem to have developed better understanding, and I am sure there is real determination among them to face the position that menaces Europe and to find adequate solution in the friendliest way.
>
> One thing that impressed me is the growth of the spirit of good-will among the European nations, and that is why I am returning home with a spirit of hope and of optimism.
>
> It was my privilege to meet the Foreign Ministers of Great Britain, France, Germany and Italy, as well as high officials and the executive heads, and we had a chance to talk matters over. Better still, we became personally acquainted, and that is a great thing in the present state of the world.
>
> It is my profound view that these personal meetings with the representatives of different countries must lead to an enormous amount of good, and I believe in them thoroughly. I feel better equipped for my own duties, for I have a better knowledge of these European problems.

FRENCH HAIL LOAN TO BRITAIN AS ALLY

$200,000,000 Credit Is Viewed as Evidence That Old Bond Has Been Cemented Anew.

QUICK ACTION SETS RECORD

Paris Financial Market Also Is Sounded on Long-Term Operation by London.

By CARLISLE MacDONALD.
Special Cable to THE NEW YORK TIMES.

PARIS, Aug. 28.—Within the unprecedentedly short period of forty-eight hours France has arranged a new $200,000,000 credit for the account of Great Britain, and the action is being hailed in France as concrete evidence that the old bonds which united France and Great Britain in the dark days of the war have again been forged.

Arriving by air Wednesday evening, Sir Frederick Leith-Ross, Deputy Controller of Finance of the British Treasury, and several assistants were able within the brief space of two days to complete the details of one of the largest outside financial undertakings France has ever assumed. To make the development even more unusual, at least half of the French share of the new Franco-American credit will be offered to the French public, and there is every prospect of its successful absorption.

Approval Nearly Unanimous.

The French credit, which constitutes half of a $400,000,000 operation to which American banks have subscribed the remaining portion, has been received in France with almost unanimous approval. There is also the more practical point of view, expressed in financial and business circles and adequately voiced tonight in L'Information, which remarks:

"The French public, one of the wisest in the world, will understand without difficulty that it is defending itself in contributing its share to the financial rehabilitation of Britain and that it is not only creating in Europe sentiment harmonious and profitable to the revival of business in general but is eliminating the dangers of social upheavals which follow in the wake of financial crises.

"It is not necessary to explain to the French people that in subscribing to the bonds it is defending the capitalistic system and peace and that it is contributing to the return of prosperity, for the nation already understands this."

According to present plans, the initial public offering will begin next week, although actual physical difficulties may delay the operation a few days. Out of a total credit of 5,000,000,000 francs (about $200,000,000), 2,500,000,000 francs will be advanced by a group of leading French banks, and the remaining half will be issued to the public in the form of British Treasury bonds, bearing 4¼ per cent net interest to the investor and running for one year.

A 1 per cent interest stamp and an 18 per cent tax on the coupons, provided for under French fiscal laws, will be borne by the British Government, thus insuring a net yield of 4.25 per cent to purchasers.

While future political developments

Continued on Page Four.

LABOR PARTY NAMES HENDERSON AS CHIEF

Organizes to Battle MacDonald as Liberals and Tories Pledge Aid to Him.

CIVIL SERVICE PAY SLASHED

First Economy Move Besides Dole Cut Proposal Will Save $4,000,000.

By W. F. LEYSMITH.
Special Cable to THE NEW YORK TIMES.

LONDON, Aug. 28.—The new national government under the leadership of Prime Minister MacDonald got three substantial items on the right side of its ledger today.

It got the assurance of a credit of $400,000,000 from the United States and France, to be employed in steadying exchange; it got a unanimous pledge of support from the Conservative and Liberal Parliamentary parties, which assures it of a majority of fifty in the House of Commons, and it received an intimation through the Marquess of Reading that David Lloyd George, now scenting battle from the other side of the fence in his country retreat, was "in complete accord with what is being done."

A vast section of Liberal opinion is hoping to hear something from the Liberal leader himself, but according to the Marquess of Reading he "certainly is not well enough yet to be troubled with much discussion."

On the other hand the government may lose some prestige by the announcement that Chancellor Snowden does not intend to seek re-election to Parliament in the next general election and it also appears certain that Mr. MacDonald will also decide not to stand, although Mr. Snowden today said Mr. MacDonald was "going to carry it through."

May Go to House of Lords.

The critics of the government say these retirements were expected, for neither Mr. Snowden nor Mr. MacDonald, it is alleged, dare face their electorates again after the "backing of capitalists against the working people," especially Mr. MacDonald, who was elected by a majority of 28,000, mostly miners, whose leaders are among the most clamorous of Mr. MacDonald's opponents. The probability is that both statesmen are destined for the House of Lords after their work is done in the present government.

The Opposition further consolidated its strength today when the Parliamentary Labor party met and elected Arthur Henderson as chairman in succession to Mr. MacDonald.

But with its assurance of support, the government got to work and announced its first economy cut, in addition to the proposal to cut the dole 10 per cent. This is to reduce from Sept. 1 the pay of 300,000 civil servants in amounts varying from 25 cents to $1.25 weekly, which means a saving to the treasury of $4,000,000 yearly. This decision, it is noted, has been reached despite the May commission's recommendations against a reduction of pay.

This cutting of salaries has provided the Opposition some heavy-calibre ammunition. It said the low-

Continued on Page Four.

Crowds Strew Flowers in Rain for Gandhi As He Leaves Simla to Sail Today for London

Wireless to THE NEW YORK TIMES.

SIMLA, India, Aug. 28.—Mahatma Gandhi's departure for Bombay last night, following his reaching of an accord with the Viceroy and his decision to sail tomorrow for London to attend the second Indian Round Table Conference, was marked by an exuberant scene such as has been witnessed so often in the last year or so.

Mr. Gandhi, profusely garlanded, beamed from a window of a special train. Pandit Jawaharlal Nehru gesticulated at too importunate admirers and Vallabhai Patel stood with folded arms in the background while a crowd of local Congress adherents swayed, cheered and threw flowers, regardless of the rain sweeping in from the mountains.

The steamship Rajputana is due to sail at noon tomorrow, and certainly every one in Simla will breathe a sigh of relief when the news comes that Mr. Gandhi is actually aboard. All his lieutenants accompanied him yesterday except Abdul Ghaffar Khan, "Red Shirt" leader, who is being received by Mr. Emerson, secretary for the Home Department, and Mr. Howell, secretary of the Foreign Department.

A government communiqué published this morning makes it possible to judge the results of Mr. Gandhi's latest visit to the Viceroy in a more dispassionate atmosphere than hitherto, and scarcely suggests to observers here that his followers have any particular reason to seek a court appeal, for the innumerable cases of alleged breaches of the Delhi pact on the part of the government have

Continued on Page Seven.

MULROONEY ORDERS HARDER CRIME FIGHT BY POLICE OFFICIALS

In Talk to 300 High Officers He Tells Them to Give Time Off to Their Duties.

WARNS ON STREET SAFETY

Says Shooting of Bystanders Must Be Avoided—Widows of Slain Policemen Get Checks.

Police Commissioner Mulrooney gathered 300 high officers of his department about him at Police Headquarters yesterday and gave them a talk on putting down crime.

Chief Inspector John J. O'Brien and Assistant Chief Inspector John J. Sullivan stood on either side of the commissioner as he addressed his audience, which included nine deputy chief inspectors, twenty-eight inspectors, twenty-seven deputy inspectors, 103 captains and nearly as many lieutenants who are acting as captains.

Each officer arrived at headquarters in his automobile. The curbs along Centre Market Place, Centre, Grand, Mulberry and Broome Streets were lined with departmental cars, and it was these that revealed the presence of the officers. The meeting had not been announced.

Newspaper men were not admitted to the conference, but Mr. Mulrooney told them afterward that he had instructed his officers to put forth greater efforts to suppress crime, with especial emphasis on banditry. He expected his commanding officers, he said, to spend most of their time off in their respective station houses and inspection districts supervising patrol and police work.

Drawn Pistols for Payroll Guards.

Policemen guarding payrolls, he said, should have their pistols always in their hands ready to shoot, and not in their holsters. He wanted his men always to have "the drop" on bandits, but he warned against unnecessary and wild shooting of bystanders by policemen chasing bandits.

To make sure that his men shoot straight, he said, the regulation requiring them to practice target shooting at least three times a year in armories in the city would be enforced rigidly. Each man, he said, must attain a certain minimum score at each of the three periods of instruction and practice.

The commissioner directed his officers to see to it that the new regulations applying to dance halls and cabarets are enforced. Already, he said, there were signs of improving conditions and he predicted they would be even better when the roster of dance hall and night club employes was completed.

After the meeting Mr. Mulrooney revealed that he is studying a suggestion that has been made to equip policemen with bullet-proof shields. The suggestion arose from the fact that the bandits who killed Patrolman Walter J. Webb, a week ago yesterday, aimed at his shield, which was punctured and driven into his heart. Bullet-proof vests, the commissioner said, were impractical because of their weight but he had directed Deputy Commissioner James P. Sinnott to confer wth metallurgists at Columbia University on the question of a suitable bullet-resisting metal for shields.

Mulrooney Distributes $1,000 Fund.

Mr. Mulrooney distributed a $1,000 fund collected by taxicab owners and associations among seven persons who helped in the bandit chase of a week ago. Six of the recipients of the award were chauffeurs. They were Herbert E. Gent, 453 East 158th Street, the Bronx; Milton Luhn, 547 Brook Avenue, the Bronx; Rudolph Schnurer, 1,384 Boston Road, the Bronx; Adolph Yeager Jr., 715 Courtlandt Avenue, the Bronx; Harold

Continued on Page Fourteen.

HUSTON GAVE $5,000 TO BISHOP CANNON; SUM NOT REPORTED

Nye Committee Traces Check to Bank of Former Republican Chairman.

TWO WITNESSES DEFIANT

Senator Glass Insists Churchman Diverted Political Funds to His Private Uses.

Special to The New York Times.

WASHINGTON, Aug. 28.—A check for $5,000 sent to the North Carolina Anti-Smith Committee Oct. 24, 1928, was traced by the Senate Campaign Funds Investigating Committee this afternoon to the New York bank account of Claudius H. Huston, former chairman of the Republican National Committee.

W. H. Wood, president of the American Trust Company of Charlotte, N. C., testified that Bishop James Cannon Jr., who was leading the fight against ex-Governor Smith, sent him a check for $5,000 drawn on the International Germanica Trust Company of New York. The actual check was not put in evidence and the name of the signer was not brought out during Mr. Wood's testimony.

A short time later Conrad C. Probst, president of the International Trust Company, successor to the International Germanica Trust Company, testified that the $5,000 check had been received at his bank and charged to the account of Mr. Huston, who had made deposits of $123,356.82 between Oct. 11, 1928, and Nov. 1, 1928. The committee will seek to obtain the actual check.

Mr. Huston did not become chairman of the Republican National Committee until September, 1920. At the time the check was sent to the North Carolina anti-Smith Democrats he was generally credited with working with Colonel Horace Mann to organize the South for Herbert Hoover.

No Report Made by Huston.

In connection with the $5,000 check Mr. Wood said that Bishop Cannon telegraphed him Oct. 19, 1928, that he would send a "sum" he had promised to Mr. Wood. Basil M. Manly, the Nye committee's investigator, testified that on the same day Bishop Cannon obtained $10,000 in cash and an $8,000 check from E. C. Jameson, who furnished $65,300 for the fight against ex-Governor Smith.

Mr. Manly also stated that an examination of the Steiwer investigating committee's records showed that Mr. Huston did not make any report of the $5,000 to that investigating committee.

Miss Ada L. Burroughs, treasurer of the anti-Smith campaign committee, and the Rev. J. Sidney S. Peters,

Continued on Page Seven.

France to Renounce Mandate to Syria; Wants It Independent Nation in League

By The Associated Press.

PARIS, Aug. 28.—The Havas Agency tonight gave out a report from Geneva that the French Government intended to renounce its mandate over Syria.

The announcement would be made at the next meeting of the Council of the League of Nations, the agency reported, and France would make the renunciation after negotiating a treaty of alliance with the authorities of the mandated territory.

Application would be made, it was said, for Syria's admission to the League.

The Supreme Council of the Allied Powers at San Remo on April 25, 1920, gave France the mandate for Syria, which was formerly a province of Turkey-in-Asia, and the action was confirmed by the League of Nations July 24, 1922. The area of the mandate is about 60,000 square miles and the population about 3,000,000.

A constitution was given to Lebanon in 1926, and last year Commissioner Henri Ponsot proclaimed a new set of constitutions, or organic laws for the other regions, which followed closely a document prepared by the Syrian Constituent Assembly. Nationalists have been agitating for full freedom.

France's determination to have an alliance with the country as a condition of its independence has an important international significance. Italy has been agitating for years for transference of the Syrian mandate to her, as part of the Mediterranean settlement to which she believes she is entitled as a great power. But France apparently does not intend to permit Rome to gain any advantage from her action in dropping the mandate.

ROOSEVELT ASKS $20,000,000 FOR JOBLESS, RAISING FUND BY A 50% INCOME TAX RISE; WOULD PROVIDE WORK WITH 5-DAY WEEK

Governor's Unemployment Program

Special to The New York Times.

ALBANY, Aug. 28.—The State program for unemployment relief submitted today by Governor Roosevelt to the Legislature for action would provide:

1. A temporary relief administration of three members appointed by the Governor, with an appropriation of $20,000,000 to be expended wherever possible in employing persons on State public works. The balance is to be apportioned between the various counties and cities to be used in encouraging local efforts in providing work useful to the public or in providing the necessities of life for the unemployed.
2. An additional personal income tax of 50 per cent of the amount of tax payable under the present statute, applicable to all incomes over and above existing exemptions, to provide the $20,000,000. One bill would apply the increase to this year's incomes; an alternative measure would make it retroactive and applicable to the year 1930 on the basis of returns already filed.
3. Authority for cities and counties to issue three-year bonds, over the period of one year, for relief of the unemployed by means of public works. Money so raised is to be spent only on persons resident in the State for two years or more and is to be administered by the usual municipal authority or a special local commission.
4. A five-day week in all contracts for State or municipal public works, except supervisory labor.
5. Payment of $548,000 to veterans who until the business depression set in had failed to apply for their State soldiers' bonuses.

LEGISLATORS ARE CORDIAL

Governor Reads Message Emphasizing Growing Need for Relief.

DECLARES AGAINST 'DOLE'

Federal Government May Act, He Observes, but State Must Lead the Way.

BOARD OF THREE HIS PLAN

Aid for Counties and Cities Authorized as Well as Local Bond Issues.

By W. A. WARN.
Special to The New York Times.

ALBANY, Aug. 28.—Rigidly excluding the use of funds as a "dole," Governor Roosevelt in a special message to the Legislature today recommended a $20,000,000 unemployment relief program for Winter, the revenue to be raised by a 50 per cent increase in the tax rate on personal incomes, general in scope and not confined to the higher brackets.

Under the Governor's proposal, relief would be administered by a non-salaried commission, to be appointed by him without the consent of the Senate, and composed of three members, of whom one probably would be a woman. The Governor said that as yet he had not been assured by the persons under consideration for the posts that they would serve, but hoped to be in a position to announce the personnel within a few days, if, as expected, this part of his program receives legislative sanction.

The message was read by the Governor at a joint session of the Senate and Assembly at 11 o'clock this morning. A great many visitors were on hand, eager to hear the Chief Executive discuss his proposal. When he entered the Assembly chamber, and again when he departed after delivering his message, he was warmly applauded.

Message Warmly Received.

The message was well received by the members, speaking of the Republican majority as well as the Governor's party. Senator George R. Fearon of Onondaga, President pro tem and Republican floor leader, after a conference with Speaker Joseph A. McGinnies, Republican overlord in the Assembly said:

"With the fundamentals of the Governor's plan we are in full accord. If any differences arise it will be over details, and these should be susceptible of adjustment without much delay. It is our aim to put through a relief plan promptly."

Senator Fearon said that the Governor's message and other relief measures which may be presented next week, would have the right of way. Consideration of the Democratic proposal for an investigation of up-State communities will be side-tracked temporarily.

The amount of additional income tax to be paid under the Governor's proposal is shown by the following typical examples:

Net Income.	Single Persons.	Married Persons and Heads of Families (Two Children or Other Dependents).
$2,500	$0.00	$0.00
3,000	2.50	.00
4,000	7.50	.00
5,000	12.50	1.00
10,000	37.50	26.00
20,000	125.00	102.00
50,000	425.00	402.00
100,000	1,162.50	1,126.00

Telling the Legislature that his message was the result of months of study, Governor Roosevelt made it clear that he wanted his State to take a leading part in the efforts to relieve distress without waiting for the Federal Government to act.

"It is idle for us to speculate upon actions which may be taken by the Federal Government," he said, "just as it is idle for the purpose for which we are here gathered to speculate about the causes of national depression.

"It is true that times may get better; it is true that the Federal Government may take action to eradicate some of the basic causes of our present troubles; it is true that the Federal Government may come forward with a definite construction program on a truly large scale; it is true that the Federal Government may adopt a well-thought-out, concrete policy which will start the wheels of industry moving and give to the farmer at least the cost of making his crop. The State of New York cannot wait for that. I face and you face and thirteen million

QUICK NOMINATION SEEN FOR ROOSEVELT

After National Canvass, Aides Count 806 Delegates for Him on First Ballot.

BLOCKING TACTICS VANISH

Ritchie, Robinson and Bryan Held Only Rivals—Break With Tammany Scouted.

As the result of a canvass made by workers in the field and by correspondence with party leaders throughout the country, friends of Governor Roosevelt have become convinced that he has a reasonable chance of getting the nomination for President on the first ballot at the next Democratic National Convention.

A survey covering all the States indicates that, unless conditions change greatly, Governor Roosevelt is likely to go into the convention with a total first-ballot strength of 806, which is 72 more than the 734, or two-thirds, necessary to nominate. A table of Governor Roosevelt's expected strength in the convention, prepared from information furnished by persons active in the Roosevelt camp, shows that 54 delegates are conceded to probable candidates other than Governor Roosevelt and that 240 delegates, many of whom are expected to be for the Governor, are classed as doubtful.

Block Movement Disappears.

The survey, conducted of course by friends of Governor Roosevelt and likely to be questioned for that reason by those not favoring his nomination, indicates the almost complete disappearance of the movement to block the Roosevelt nomination by creating "favorite son" candidates to cause a deadlock.

This movement is believed by friends of the Governor to have been sponsored by John J. Raskob, chairman of the Democratic National Committee, and other friends of former Governor Alfred E. Smith, with the purpose either of bringing about Mr. Smith's nomination, if possible, or of selecting the nominee. Announcement of their support of Governor Roosevelt by Mayor James M. Curley of Boston and Joseph F.

Continued on Page Seven.

ROOSEVELT SIGNS THE IMMUNITY BILLS

Hofstadter Measures to Aid Seabury Inquiry Are Approved Without Comment.

PLAN AN UP-STATE COUP

Republicans Will Seek to Include Democratic Areas in Any Investigation There.

From a Staff Correspondent of The New York Times.

ALBANY, Aug. 28.—Governor Roosevelt signed the two immunity bills passed by the special session of the Legislature today as the Republican leaders made plans to delay action on the Democratic measure for an up-State investigation until the very end of the extraordinary session.

While the Republican chieftains maintained a non-committal stand on the Dunnigan-Steingut measures to conduct inquiries in Republican territory, the general opinion at the Capitol was that the party would support an up-State investigation before the conclusion of the session, but would move to include in the inquiry's scope Democratic as well as Republican up-State areas.

Governor Roosevelt made no comment as he signed the bills introduced by Senator Samuel H. Hofstadter to clothe the inquiry committee bearing his name with full power to grant immunity. The Governor first, signed the measure specifically granting this power to the committee and then the other bill amending Section 584 to give all legislative committees power to grant immunity in conspiracy cases.

Silent on Up-State Bills.

The Governor had nothing to say about the measures introduced by Senator John J. Dunnigan and Assemblyman Irwin Steingut, the Democratic leaders, providing for creation of a legislative commission of seven members to investigate charges of irregularity in a number of up-State counties.

Friends of the Executive asserted, however, that Mr. Roosevelt was convinced he had pursued a consistent course in sending a special message permitting the Democrats to make their move. They declared that, when charges of corruption in government were made by responsible persons, he had called the attention of the Legislature to them and put them up to the legislative branch for whatever action was deemed necessary.

Friends of the Governor denied that Mr. Roosevelt had yielded to threats of Tammany Hall in allowing the Democratic bills to go in.

The Republicans, taken by surprise at the Governor's action at the conclusion of the vote which passed the immunity bills yesterday over Democratic opposition, were better prepared today to shape their position.

The leaders, it was understood, reached an agreement to put aside all consideration of measures affecting an up-State inquiry until the special session had dealt with unemployment and whatever other subjects it might be called to pass upon. Under this arrangement it is probable that action on the Democratic demand for an up-State investigation to match the inquiry being conducted in New York City will be delayed until the week after next.

While some Republican legislators

Continued on Page Fourteen.

"All the News That's Fit to Print."

The New York Times.

LATE CITY EDITION

THE WEATHER—Generally fair and warmer today, tomorrow partly cloudy; showers. Temperatures Yesterday—Max., 74; min., 63. U. S. Weather Forecast—See end to last page.

Copyright, 1931, by The New York Times Company.

VOL. LXXXI....No. 26,903. NEW YORK, MONDAY, SEPTEMBER 21, 1931. TWO CENTS in New York City | THREE CENTS Within 200 Miles | FOUR CENTS Elsewhere Except 7th and 8th Postal Zones

GREAT BRITAIN SUSPENDS GOLD PAYMENTS TODAY; CLOSES STOCK EXCHANGE, DISCOUNT RATE UP TO 6%; GERMAN BOERSES SHUT, STOCK MARKET HERE OPEN

The British Government's Statement

Special Cable to THE NEW YORK TIMES.

LONDON, Sept. 20.—This is the statement issued by the government tonight, announcing suspension of the law requiring that the Bank of England sell gold at a fixed price:

His Majesty's Government have decided after consultation with the Bank of England that it has become necessary to suspend for the time being the operation of Subsection 2, Section 1, of the gold standard act of 1925, which requires the Bank to sell gold at a fixed price.

A bill for this purpose will be introduced immediately, and it is the intention of His Majesty's Government to ask Parliament to pass it through all stages Monday, the 21st of September. In the meantime, the Bank of England has been authorized to proceed accordingly in anticipation of the action of Parliament.

The reasons which led to this decision are as follows:

Since the middle of July, funds amounting to more than £200,000,000 (about $1,000,000,000) have been withdrawn from the London market. The withdrawals have been met partly from gold and foreign currency held by the Bank of England, partly from proceeds of a credit of £50,000,000 (about $250,000,000), which shortly matures, secured by the Bank of England from New York and Paris and partly from proceeds of French and American credits amounting to £80,000,000 (about $400,000,000) recently obtained by the government.

During the last few days withdrawals of foreign balances have accelerated so sharply that His Majesty's Government felt that they were bound to take the above decision.

This decision will, of course, not affect the obligations of His Majesty's Government or of the Bank of England which are payable in foreign currencies.

Gold holdings of the Bank of England amount to some £130,000,000 (about $650,000,000) and, having regard to contingencies which may have to be met, it is inadvisable to allow this reserve to be further reduced.

There will be no interruption of ordinary banking business. Banks will be opened as usual for the convenience of their customers, and there is no reason why sterling transactions should be affected in any way.

It has been arranged that the Stock Exchange shall not be opened on Monday, the day on which Parliament is passing the necessary legislation. This will not, however, interfere with the business of current settlement on the Stock Exchange, which will be carried through as usual.

His Majesty's Government have no reason to believe that the present difficulties are due to any substantial extent to the export of capital by British nationals. Undoubtedly the bulk of withdrawals has been for foreign accounts.

They desire, however, to repeat emphatically the warning given by the Chancellor of the Exchequer that any British citizen who increases the strain on exchanges by purchasing foreign securities himself, or is assisting others to do so, is deliberately adding to the country's difficulties.

The banks have undertaken to cooperate in restricting purchases by British citizens of foreign exchange except those required for the actual needs of trade or for meeting contracts, and should further measures prove to be advisable His Majesty's Government will not hesitate to take them.

His Majesty's Government have arrived at their decision with the greatest reluctance. But during the last few days international financial markets have become demoralized and have been liquidating their sterling assets regardless of their intrinsic worth. In the circumstances there was no alternative but to protect the financial position of this country by the only means at our disposal.

His Majesty's Government are securing a balanced budget and the internal position of the country is sound. This position must be maintained. It is one thing to go off the gold standard with an unbalanced budget and uncontrolled inflation. It is quite another thing to take this measure, not because of internal financial difficulties but because of excessive withdrawals of borrowed capital.

The ultimate resources of this country are enormous and there is no doubt that the present exchange difficulties will prove only temporary.

Gold Standard Subsection to Be Suspended.

Subsection 2 of the British Gold Standard act of 1925, which is to be suspended, reads as follows:

The Bank of England shall be bound to sell to any person who makes demand in that behalf at the head office of the Bank during office hours of the Bank, and pay the purchase price in any legal tender, gold bullion at the price of £3 17s 10½d per ounce troy of gold of the standard of fineness prescribed for gold coin by the coinage act of 1870, but only in the form of bars containing approximately 400 ounces troy of fine gold.

NANKING WILL INVOKE KELLOGG PEACE PACT; NEW FIGHTING FEARED

Foreign Minister of China Says League Also Will Be Told of Japanese Acts.

MANCHURIANS PLAN BATTLE

Kirin Troops Expected to Attack Japanese Garrison—Harbin Reported Tense.

SOVIET TROOPS AT BORDER

Foreign Observers at Mukden Hold Japanese Military Deliberately Caused Incident.

By HALLETT ABEND.

Wireless to THE NEW YORK TIMES.

NANKING, Sept. 20.—"Appropriate steps are being taken to apprise the League of Nations and the powers signatory to the Kellogg pact of the unwarranted actions of Japanese troops," C. T. Wang, Foreign Minister of the Nanking Government, declared in a statement this morning concerning the lodging of vigorous protests by the Nanking Government with the Japanese Government. Mr. Wang continued:

"The National Government is greatly exercised over the situation caused by the unprovoked attack of Japanese troops on Mukden and other cities in three eastern provinces."

Says Chinese Did Not Resist.

Mr. Wang's statement makes no reference to the Japanese charge that Chinese soldiers tried to damage the South Manchuria Railway north of Mukden, but says Japanese troops fired on Chinese soldiers encamped at Peitaying, that the Chinese withdrew without resisting and that the Japanese disarmed the Chinese and set the buildings afire.

Mr. Wang charges that simultaneously the Japanese bombarded the arsenal and the Peitaying camp, but while the arsenal was not damaged the camp's mortar depot was destroyed. The Nanking Foreign Minister also charges the Japanese fired upon and occupied all Chinese police stations inside and immediately outside Mukden and disarmed the policemen, seized the wireless station, forcibly occupied all government offices and interrupted all electrical communications.

The Japanese Consulate at Nanking announces the transmission last night to Tokyo of the formal protest of the Nanking Foreign Office in regard to the occupation of Mukden by Japanese troops and a formal request that they immediately evacuate the city.

It is officially announced that seventy-one Chinese soldiers were killed in the clash incident to the occupation of Mukden. The number of Chinese wounded is not known. No civilians were killed. The total of the Japanese casualties was one soldier killed and two wounded.

Japanese officially stress the assertion that the magnitude of the incident was due to the extreme nervousness and tension existing in the Mukden area as a result of a long series of minor clashes and growing feeling on both sides of uneasiness and hostility, which resulted in minor Japanese commanders taking the bit in their teeth and quickly extending the zone of operations without the knowledge or approval of the higher command.

More Fighting Expected.

Wireless to THE NEW YORK TIMES.

MUKDEN, Sept. 20.—More fighting was expected tonight between Japanese and Chinese between Dairen and the Mukden area at those points where Chinese soldiers are quartered along the South Manchuria Railway zone. Now everything is peaceful everywhere, with the Japanese in control.

Chinese are looting in the international section of Mukden, which area in ordinary times is under Chinese control. The Japanese are taking steps to protect the area. Foreign opinion here is that the Japanese military were angry because the Nakamura affair was about to be closed diplomatically, so, according to all foreign observers here, the outbreak on Friday night was premeditated. A Japanese statement says:

"We were always prepared for an emergency, but we were surprised on the night of Sept. 18, when Chinese tried to blow up the South Manchuria Railway tracks and to attack a Japanese garrison. The occupation in various cities and towns was necessary to protect everybody. The incident is unfortunate."

This morning Frank Sugden, a British subject, an engineer of the Peiping-Mukden Railway workshop, attempted to go to the office, which

Continued on Page Eight.

Byrd's Old Supply Ship Sails To Load Labrador Lime Shells

By The Canadian Press.

ST. JOHN'S, N. F., Sept. 20.—Carrying out plans of a company, financed largely by Newfoundland capital, to develop the natural resources of Labrador, the steamer Eleanor Bolling sailed yesterday with fifty men and necessary machinery to take marine shell from Hamilton Inlet.

The Eleanor Bolling, which was supply ship of the Byrd Antarctic expedition, is one of several vessels chartered to convey cargoes to St. John's, where equipment for screening the product and preparing it for market has been installed.

The sun-bleached shell deposits, which have lain on the foreshore of Hamilton Inlet for ages, are said to be almost 100 per cent lime, valuable for poultry feeding and horticultural purposes. First shipments are expected early in October.

WALKER BACK TODAY, BUT WANTS NO 'FUSS'

Elaborate Reception Vetoed—He Will Stay Aboard Ship Until It Reaches Pier.

HE PHILOSOPHIZES ON LINER

One 'Must Laugh on the Stage of Politics No Matter What the Sadness Within,' He Remarks.

Having been widely fêted, dined and honored in Europe, Mayor Walker will return to New York today on the North German Lloyd liner Bremen, on which he sailed for a month's "rest cure" in Germany on Aug. 4.

His return, in so far as reception plans and organized welcome are concerned, will be quiet, Charles F. Kerrigan, Assistant Mayor, said yesterday. Mr. Kerrigan, Thomas F. McAndrews, the Mayor's secretary, and Police Commissioner Mulrooney will go down the harbor in a revenue cutter and board the Bremen at Quarantine.

The receiving tug Macom, the city's official craft for the reception of distinguished visitors and homecomers, will not be used. Mayor Walker will remain aboard the Bremen until she docks at Pier 4 at the foot of Fifty-eighth Street, Brooklyn, probably between 8 and 9 P. M.

May Speak Over Radio.

There will be met by Mrs. Walker and probably by a group of friends and city officials and he will go from the pier to his home at 6 St. Luke's Place. Mr. Kerrigan said there had been some talk of having the Mayor make a short statement over the radio from the pier. While no definite plans have been made, he felt that if the microphone were installed on the pier the Mayor would make a short speech.

In the Mayor's party and returning with him are Dudley Field Malone, former Collector of the Port of New York, and Dr. William Schroeder Jr., chairman of the Department of Sanitation and the Mayor's personal physician.

It was the Mayor's own wish that his homecoming be without "fuss" or noisy reception. Plans had been made for a demonstration, with a parade, a luncheon or dinner and other details, but the Mayor, by long-distance telephone from London, was understood to have vetoed it.

It is understood that his decision was influenced by the many receptions, dinners and celebrations with which he was met in Germany, creating a spirit more festive than restful, which followed him through Europe.

Feted in Many Cities.

After a short stop in Southampton on Aug. 10 the Mayor landed in Bremen the following day and was the guest at a reception in his honor. The next day he proceeded to Berlin, where he spent several days. While there he visited the Baroness von Huenefeld, mother of the late Baron von Huenefeld, who crossed the Atlantic Ocean in the plane Bremen in 1929.

Among the German watering places he visited were Carlsbad and Marienbad. He went to Pilsen, Budapest, Vienna, Cannes, Monaco and Monte Carlo, everywhere seeking rest and finding that his mere presence prevented it. In Paris he was entertained at luncheon by President Doumer of France and was made a Commander of the Legion of Honor. In London he was the luncheon guest of Premier Ramsay MacDonald.

In Berlin he made a tour of the night resorts within a few hours after his arrival. The next day he was the luncheon guest of the Carl Schurz Association, and the next night, over a radio hook-up by which he was heard in Europe and the United States, he made a speech in praise of the spirit of determination to over-

Continued on Page Five.

PRESIDENT DEPARTS TO ADDRESS LEGION AT DETROIT ON BONUS

He Boards Special Train at Martinsburg, W. Va., After Day at Rapidan Camp.

TO WARN OF HEAVY COST

Washington Thinks He May Touch Also on Economic Situation in Europe.

LEGION COMMANDER FIRM

O'Neil Warns Against Cash-Payment Demands and Hints Danger in Prohibition Stand.

From a Staff Correspondent of The New York Times.

MARTINSBURG, W. Va., Sept. 20.—President Hoover left here on a special train at 8:30 o'clock this evening for Detroit where he will deliver an address tomorrow before the national convention of the American Legion.

The President spent the day at his Rapidan camp in Virginia working on his address, which he will deliver at noon tomorrow, but it was not completed when he left here. There were showers throughout the day, and the President remained indoors most of the time.

The President motored from his Rapidan camp to Martinsburg through Sherryville and Winchester. The last twenty-five miles of the trip were made at the slow speed of twenty-two miles an hour so that the President would arrive just before his train was scheduled to leave. As a result, a long line of automobiles which were not permitted by Secret Service men to pass the President's car trailed after it, and there was a wild blowing of horns.

At Martinsburg about 2,000 people were on hand to greet the President and he was called upon for a speech. He waved his hat, but would not make an address.

Accompanying the President are Captain Train and Colonel Hodges, his naval and military aides, and Secretaries Joslin and Richey. Governor Leslie of Indiana and Mrs. Leslie, who were his guests at the camp, will also accompany the President as far as Indianapolis.

Capital Speculates on Speech.

Special to The New York Times.

WASHINGTON, Sept. 20.—With President Hoover on his way to Detroit tonight to address the national convention of the American Legion tomorrow, speculation continues here as to whether there were several compelling motives for the President's sudden decision to attend the convention, after he had made it plain only a few days previously that he would be unable to do so.

There is unanimity of opinion that the President's chief purpose is to set the great power and authority of the influence which comes from his high office against the movements in the ranks of the Legionnaires for the adoption of a resolution calling on Congress to enact legislation permitting World War veterans to borrow from the government up to the full maturity value of their bonus certificates fourteen years before they mature.

As to Conditions Abroad.

Today's speculative comment had to do with whether the President would give attention in his address to matters of pressing public importance other than the bonus, with a rather widespread inclination to surmise that he would take occasion to sketch economic and financial conditions abroad with their effect on the United States.

Those best informed as to the Ad-

Continued on Page Four.

NEW YORK BANKERS CONFER

See No Need for Drastic Action — Investments in London Moderate.

RECENT LOANS PROTECTED

Federal Reserve Can Demand Gold—Morgan Credit Payable in Dollars.

EFFECT ON PRICES FEARED

Britain's Action Also Expected to Have Repercussions on World Credit Situation.

American security markets will not follow the lead of the London Stock Exchange, but will be open for business as usual today. No emergency has developed here to warrant any action similar to that in the foreign countries, it was stated authoritatively last night.

New York bankers held informal conferences here yesterday, at which the new London crisis was discussed, but no concerted action seemed to them to be called for, it was said. The bankers were in communication with British banking authorities by transatlantic telephone.

According to a competent authority, the short-term balances of American banks in London do not exceed $50,000,000, while Great Britain's external obligations in this country, exclusive of the $125,000,000 credit recently granted by the Federal Reserve banks to the Bank of England and the $200,000,000 private banking credit to the British Treasury, do not exceed $500,000,000.

No further supporting measures will be taken to defend the pound sterling at this time, it was stated. The private banking credit which was opened on Aug. 28 last, while not yet actually used up, will be exhausted shortly with the taking up of forward commitments made by the British banking authorities in their recent attempts to bolster the pound.

Banker Sums Up Situation.

The British financial difficulties, as they are understood here, were summed up last night by an important international banker as follows:

"The emergency measures taken by the British Government to check the heavy outflow of gold from London will undoubtedly occasion widespread surprise here, although the steps to be taken are by no means unprecedented. During the early days of the Great War, it will be recalled, Great Britain suspended the Bank Act temporarily, and in 1920 sterling went as low as an exchange value of $3.20 as against parity of about $4.86⅔. It was not until 1925 that the country returned officially to a gold basis.

"The terms of the announcement by the British authorities make it clear that the suspension of gold payments by the Bank of England is a temporary measure and in no way affects the obligation of the British Government to meet in gold such obligations as it may have outstanding in foreign currencies. Undoubtedly the government had a

Continued on Page Two.

PARLIAMENT TO BACK MOVE

Cabinet Is Unanimous in Decision to End the Drain on Gold.

KING TO SIGN BILL TONIGHT

London Hopes Drastic Measure Will Not Be Necessary More Than Six Months.

MacDONALD EXPLAINS STEP

Government Says Withdrawals of Funds Since July Forced Its Action.

By CHARLES A. SELDEN.

Special Cable to THE NEW YORK TIMES.

LONDON, Sept. 20.—Great Britain will go off the gold standard tomorrow. Legislation amending the existing financial laws to that effect will be rushed through Parliament in the course of the day and will receive the King's royal assent tomorrow night.

To accomplish this, the new National Government, which is responsible for this drastic step, is assured of the necessary majority in the House of Commons to pass the measure through all its Parliamentary stages in one sitting. The House of Lords, which ordinarily does not sit on Mondays, has been summoned for an emergency session to take the required concurrent action.

Bank of England Approves.

A unanimous decision to abandon the gold standard was reached at an emergency session of Premier MacDonald's Cabinet today after consultation with the Bank of England, which agreed it was the only thing to do.

The Bank of England tomorrow will raise the discount rate to 6 per cent from 4½ per cent.

The London Stock Exchange and all provincial exchanges will be closed for the day.

There is no suggestion in the government statement as to how long this state of affairs will continue the official announcement implies it will be only temporary by saying the suspension is "for the time being."

The expectation, or at least the hope, is that it will last only six months if within that period the country manages to balance its international trade as well as its budget.

It was hoped this shock to British government finance would be averted by the change in government a month ago with the subsequent achievement of balancing the budget and cutting down government expenses, but it is evident now that the change was too long delayed.

Blow Was Long Impending.

The present blow has been impending a long time. Now that it has fallen, the situation is explained as due both to international and domestic causes. The foreign factors involved, according to the British appraisal of the situation, have been the hoarding of gold by the United States and France and the recent drain on sterling because of the financial situation of other countries.

Diminished foreign confidence in the stability of the pound was another vital factor which had gone too far to be entirely corrected by the present change in government and by the effect of big loans from New York and Paris. The recent "pay cut mutiny" in the British navy also was one of the various causes of the cumulative effect, which is today's decision to abandon the gold standard.

Also England put a terrific strain on herself six years ago by returning to the gold standard as part of her post-war financial policy and by her whole attitude toward the payment of her war debts. Of all countries on this side of the Atlantic which participated in the war, England is the only one which has not cut the value of its currency. Great Britain alone returned to the pre-war gold parity of its currency while France divided the franc by five.

Plus all this international strain, England has been attempting to carry at the same time a most expensive experiment in socialism, which, with its enormous cost of unemployment insurance, caused the downfall of the Labor Government just a month ago.

Although the British public debt

EVENTUAL BENEFITS SEEN BY WASHINGTON

British Move Is Held Likely to Affect War Debts—Hoover Informed on Friday.

Special to The New York Times.

WASHINGTON, Sept. 20.—While government officials were unwilling to discuss formally the British financial crisis because of the delicacy of the situation, the announcement by the British government did not come as a surprise, as word had been received here as early as Friday that some drastic step was in contemplation.

While informally some experts referred to the present situation as the most serious since the world war, there was also expressed the opinion that as a long range proposition any move by Great Britain to put her financial house in order would have a salutary effect on world economic affairs.

It was reported here tonight that the White House dinner Friday evening attended by President Hoover and Secretaries Stimson, Mellon and Lamont was arranged after the President first obtained definite information of the step that Britain was contemplating.

Situation Thoroughly Discussed.

It is now understood that there was a thorough discussion at the dinner of the situation as it might affect financial interests of this country and that consideration also was given as to whether this government might be able to do anything to aid the British in facing the financial crisis. None of the officials has made known just what conclusions were reached at the dinner.

Whether the course to be followed by Great Britain would result in the ultimate revaluation of the pound sterling was a matter of considerable conjecture. In some quarters the belief was held that Great Britain would be compelled in the end to go on an "adjusted gold basis" which in effect would mean a stabilization of the pound at a lower level. One official also felt that Great Britain would find it difficult to keep her foreign obligations on a gold basis and handle her domestic financial affairs on another basis.

That any adjustments which Great Britain must make would require a

Continued on Page Two.

Canada "Proposes to Maintain" Gold Standard, Premier Says

By The Associated Press.

OTTAWA, Ont., Sept. 20.—R. B. Bennett, Prime Minister and Acting Minister of Finance, said tonight that Canada proposed to maintain the gold standard.

"What Great Britain may do is for the government of Great Britain to determine," said Mr. Bennett. "As for Canada, we propose to maintain the gold standard."

The Prime Minister added that he had nothing further to say on the matter.

GERMANY TO CLOSE ALL BOERSES TODAY

To Keep Them Shut Indefinitely if Need Be — Reichsbank Protected by Credit Truce.

By GUIDO ENDERIS.

Special Cable to THE NEW YORK TIMES.

BERLIN, Sept. 20.—The news that the Bank of England had announced the suspension of gold payments, effective tomorrow, struck Berlin banking and Boerse circles as a bolt from the blue and left leading financiers completely nonplussed as to possible repercussions on the German financial situation.

It was uniformly asserted, however, that the Reichsbank's position was not affected as it was amply protected for the time being through the ratification of the "standstill" agreement on short-term credits.

Pending further developments in London, the German Boerses will remain closed tomorrow and, if necessary, indefinitely thereafter, in keeping with the conclusions reached late today between bank and Boerse leaders and official quarters, as it was commonly feared that the shock resulting from London's procedure would have a devastating reaction upon the German stock markets.

A preponderant number of Berlin bankers incline to the view that the Bank of England's action was an S O S to all capitalistic countries, warning them that the existing currency system was in imminent danger and that the present dislocation

Continued on Page Two.

GENEVA IS SHOCKED BY CRISIS IN LONDON

High French Official There Says Paris and America Must Aid the Pound.

By CLARENCE K. STREIT.

Special Cable to THE NEW YORK TIMES.

GENEVA, Sept. 20.—The news that the Bank of England tomorrow will go off the gold standard and that the London Stock Exchange will not open came as a shock to the few in Geneva who learned of it late tonight.

"If ever there was a time when the United States and France needed to work together it is now," was the instant comment of a high French official. "Together we can and must support the pound sterling."

Told of reports from Basle that the British development probably meant the loss in value of sterling by a third, Frenchmen here expressed surprise bordering on consternation and obviously felt every effort ought to be made to avoid this.

It was stressed in the French delegation to the League of Nations that Minister of Finance Flandin had gone last night to Paris, where he had been conversing with officers of the Bank of England. The results of the conversations here were not known in the delegation, but M. Flandin was expected back here tomorrow. Whether this meant that a move through Geneva was likely none was willing to predict.

In the British delegation the gravity of the situation was indicated by the tone of voices where it was not indicated by the words used. The British stressed that their financial expert, Sir Arthur Salter, did not believe the situation would turn out as tragically as laymen seemed to fear.

Though admitting that in such unprecedented matters incalculable factors may play a deciding role, the British seemed inclined to think that "in view of the nervousness of foreigners, who are withdrawing their money from London," the trouble had come to a head sooner than it would otherwise and might well have come to a head sooner than later. Hope was somewhat wanly expressed that everything would be all right in a few days if every one kept his head.

The reports that Sir Arthur Salter,

Continued on Page Two.

Most Severe Quake Since 1924 Rocks Tokyo; Slipping of Strata Alarms Indiana and Ohio

Special Cable to THE NEW YORK TIMES.

TOKYO, Monday, Sept. 21.—The worst earthquake since January, 1924, rocked Tokyo houses violently at 11:53 A. M. today, causing much alarm but apparently little damage. A second and milder shock occurred at 11:58 A. M.

Special to The New York Times.

CINCINNATI, Ohio, Sept. 20.—Earthquake shocks rocked Cincinnati and the surrounding territory shortly after 6 o'clock last night. The shocks were general, reports coming in from every part of Cincinnati—its suburbs. They were felt extensively on the Kentucky side of the river and in a number of up-State, Indiana and Kentucky cities.

No damage was reported here although large buildings were rocked on their foundations, some as much as three inches.

In Mount Adams some residents became alarmed and rushed into their cellars.

The exact time of the tremors was variously reported from 6:05 to 6:10 o'clock. The shocks, half a dozen or more, lasted less than a minute.

CHICAGO, Sept. 20 (AP).—The earth's surface in parts of Indiana and Ohio did a little readjusting of its own today, but beyond momentarily frightening a few residents, damage was slight.

The disturbance, according to Federal geologists here, was caused by the slipping of strata under the earth's surface.

SIDNEY, Ohio, Sept. 20 (AP).—The Methodist and Lutheran churches, the high school and virtually every house in the village of Anna, Shelby County, were damaged badly by the earthquake today. Authorities said the total damage would exceed $10,000.

Edison's Life and of Some of His Achievements

Thomas Alva Edison at the age of 30, just before he invented the incandescent lamp.

The great inventor at the age of 41, when on June 16, 1888, after five nights of continuous work, he perfected the cylinder type of phonograph.

Times Wide World Photo.

Edison, busy in his laboratory, on his seventy-seventh birthday.

Times Wide World Photo.

Mr. and Mrs. Edison at their winter home in Florida.

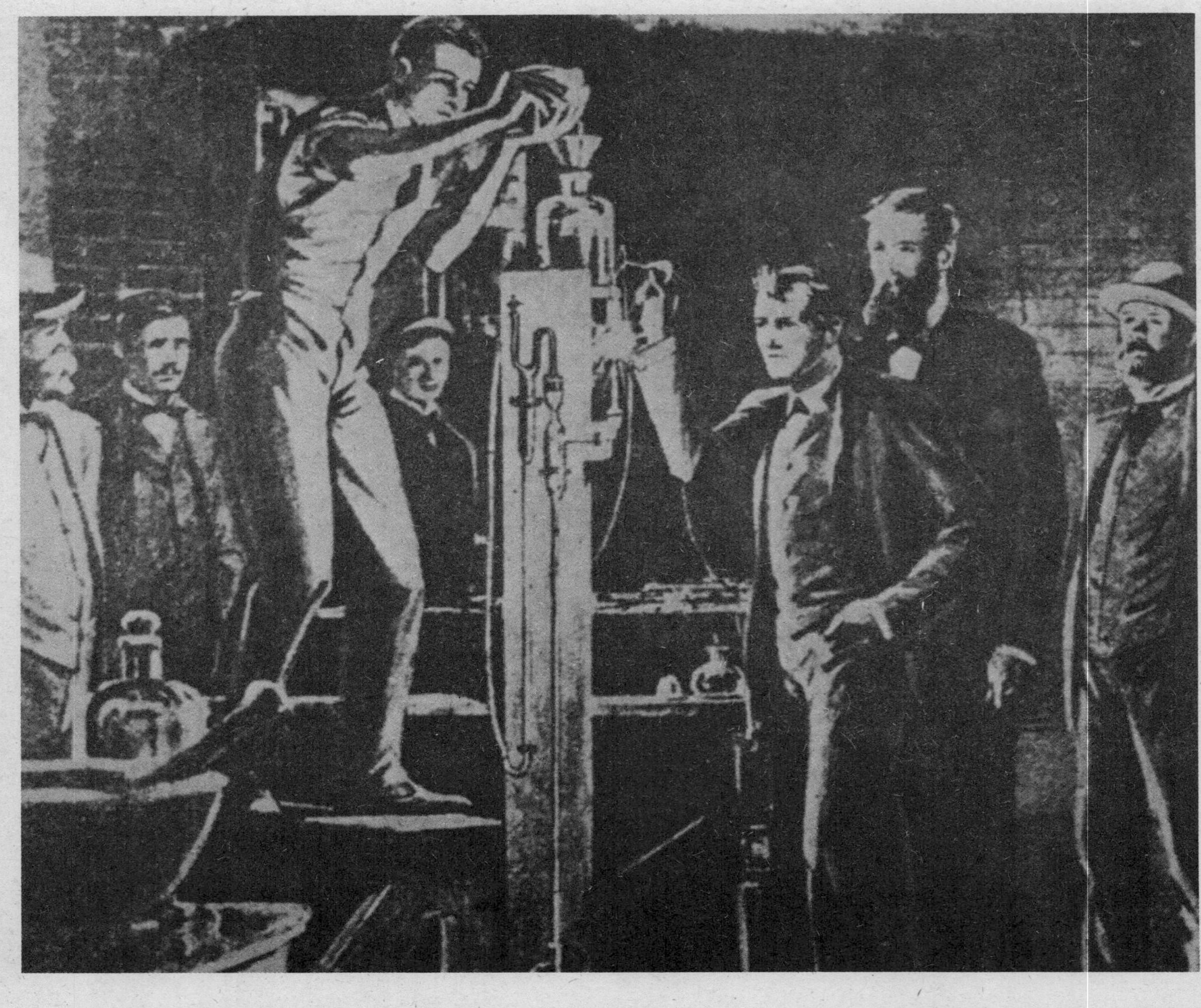

The scene in 1879 in the first Edison laboratory when the young inventor (third from Right) demonstrated the incandescent lamp to skeptics of the day at Menlo Park, New Jersey.

Section 1

"All the News That's Fit to Print."

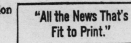

The New York Times.

Copyright, 1931, by The New York Times Company.

LATE CITY EDITION
POSTSCRIPT
THE WEATHER—Fair, continued cool today; tomorrow fair, rising temperature.
Temperatures yesterday—Max. 54, min. 46.
U. S. Weather Forecast—Page 12, Section 10.

Section 1

VOL. LXXXI....No. 26,930. ***** + NEW YORK, SUNDAY, OCTOBER 18, 1931.

Including Rotogravure Picture Section in two parts—Magazine and Book Sections in Rotogravure.

TEN CENTS

BRAZIL SUSPENDS PAYMENTS IN CASH ON $500,000,000 DEBT

To Pay Interest in Scrip for 3 Years Owing to Decline in Exchange Value of Milreis.

$152,800,000 IN BONDS HERE

Bulk of External Obligations Held in England — Service Kept Up on Three Issues.

BANKERS APPROVE TERMS

Brazil Announcement Follows Word From New York and London Financiers.

Cash interest payments on the equivalent of about $500,000,000 of the external debt of the United States of Brazil have been suspended, Sebastiao Sampaio, Brazilian Consul General in New York, announced last night. Sinking fund obligations were suspended on Sept. 1.

Payments on the suspended obligations will be made during a period of three years in special scrip bearing interest at 5 per cent. The service on only three of the twenty-five external issues of the government will be met in cash on the due dates. These are the 5 per cent funding loan of 1898, amounting to £7,065,180; the 5 per cent funding loan of 1914, aggregating £14,278,960, and the 1922 7½ per cent coffee security loan, totaling £8,209,200.

Of the entire external debt affected by Brazil's action $152,800,000 is payable in dollars and most of it presumably is held in this country. All of the interest on such bonds is now to be paid in scrip. The total debt payable in sterling is £106,868,593 ($518,000,000 at the gold parity), but from this is to be deducted £29,094,000 ($141,000,000 at par), covering the three issues on which interest payments in cash are to be continued. The amount payable in French currency is 333,577,000 francs, on all of which the interest payments are to be made in scrip.

Brazil's Explanation of Action.

According to the Consul General's announcement, the action of his government was due to the "impossibility of acquiring foreign exchange for the transfer of funds to the markets where the coupons of the external debt are payable." "The Brazilian Federal Government, after placing before their bankers all facts regarding the position of the country," the statement continued, "is reluctantly obliged to authorize them to communicate to the holders of Brazilian bonds that they are only in a position to pay in full in cash, on the dates stipulated in the contract, the interest and sinking fund" on the three issues described.

"Interest on all other loans," the announcement said, "will be paid on their respective due dates during a period of three years in special scrip, bearing interest at 5 per cent per annum and divided into two series; the first series, redeemable in twenty years, will be in respect of the bonds issued against the following loans: Brazil 1903 5 per cent sterling bonds, Brazil 1909 5 per cent French franc bonds, Brazil 1921 8 per cent gold dollar bonds, Brazil 1922 7 per cent gold dollar bonds, Brazil 1926 6½ per cent gold dollar bonds, Brazil 1927 6½ per cent sterling and gold dollar bonds.

"The second series, redeemable in forty years, will be in respect of all other existing Brazilian Federal Government foreign loans.

"The Brazilian Federal Government undertakes to review the situation at the end of the first and second years with a view to extending cash payments should circumstances permit. The sums in milreis at the rate of exchange last fixed for stabilization, namely, 6 pence, corresponding to the interest not being remitted, will be deposited in an approved bank in the city of Rio de Janeiro and applied in the purchase of bills of exchange, provided that the market can supply them. Such remittances would be sent to the government's bankers and applied to the redemption of the new scrip, either by purchase if below par or by means of drawing if at par. The scrip of the series redeemable in twenty years will be dealt with first. Should the market not supply the necessary foreign exchange, the government will acquire bonds of the internal debt, which will be held in trust until such time as exchange can be obtained.

"The Brazilian Federal Government will pay the interest and the sinking fund on the new scrip in cash on their due dates. The sums in milreis earmarked for the payment of the suspended sinking fund, which are being deposited and which

Continued on Page Twenty-eight.

First German-American Battle In 1917 to Be Marked Saturday

The fourteenth anniversary of the first conflict between American and German troops in the World War will be observed on Saturday, when the First Division will hold its thirteenth annual reunion at Fort Hamilton, Brooklyn, now the division's headquarters. Brig. Gen. Lucius R. Holbrook, commander of the division, announced yesterday that General Charles P. Summerall, retired Chief of Staff, and Lieut-Gen. Robert Lee Bullard, both former battle commanders of the division, would attend.

From all sections of the country veterans of the division will assemble. At least 1,000 officers and men are expected. Major Gen. Hanson E. Ely, who led the Twenty-eighth Infantry of the First Division at Cantigny, will attend, as will Major Gen. Stephen O. Fuqua, one of the division's wartime chiefs of staff.

SHERWOOD DENIES WALKER PHONED HIM

"Disgusted With Entire Affair," His Only Comment on Call From Here to Mexico City.

PUBLIC INQUIRY FOR OLVANY

Legal Fight Expected on Move to Force Ex-Head of Tammany to Reveal His Clients.

Special Cable to THE NEW YORK TIMES.

MEXICO CITY, Oct. 17.—"I'm disgusted with the entire affair," was the only comment Russell T. Sherwood, personal accountant to Mayor Walker, would make today when he was questioned regarding a telephone call he had received from New York. He denied, however, that the call had come from Mayor Walker.

Sherwood is honeymooning in Mexico City with his bride, the former Eleanor Rumpf of Brooklyn, to whom he was married on Oct. 6. The records show that Miss Rumpf was divorced from Eugene Conner of New York in Cuernevaca on Sept. 5.

The Sherwoods spent most of their time today sightseeing with Mr. and Mrs. Burton Wilson of New York. Among other places they visited the Pachuca and the scenic mountain village of El Chico. Efforts to interview Sherwood when he had luncheon at Pachuca were as unsuccessful as on other occasions. He refused to say whether or not he planned to return to New York to tell the Hofstadter committee about his business relations with Mayor Walker, and launched into a long tirade against tabloid newspapers and the reports they had carried regarding him.

MEXICO CITY, Oct. 17 (AP).—Informed that efforts were being made in New York to find a way to bring about his return there, Russell T. Sherwood did not seem greatly concerned. He said he was aware of his legal position while here.

He repeated he had planned to remain in Mexico indefinitely, and that he had hoped to enjoy a honeymoon here, but that since he had been discovered by the press, his stay was anything but pleasant and he might change his plans.

"I detest publicity and I will not consent to have my photograph taken on that account," he said.

Seabury to Question Olvany.

With little prospect of being able to bring Russell T. Sherwood, Mayor Walker's accountant, back from Mexico City in the next few weeks, Samuel Seabury, counsel of the Hof-

Continued on Page Twenty-two.

CAPONE CONVICTED OF DODGING TAXES; MAY GET 17 YEARS

Jury Finds Him Guilty on Two Misdemeanor and Three Felony Counts.

IT IS OUT FOR 8 HOURS

Tuesday Set for Hearing Defense Motion for New Trial, Before Sentence Is Passed.

VERDICT PUZZLES COUNSEL

But Prosecutor Accepts It After Conference—"Not Guilty" on 18 Counts Pleases Gang Chief.

By MEYER BERGER,
Staff Correspondent of The New York Times.

CHICAGO, Oct. 17.—Al Capone was found guilty here tonight on five of the twenty-three counts contained in the two indictments brought against him by the Federal Government for income tax evasion from 1924 to 1929.

Two of the five counts are misdemeanors, failure to file income tax in 1924 and 1928, each carrying possible maximum sentence of one year imprisonment and $10,000 fine. The other counts on which he was found guilty are felonies and each carries a maximum penalty of five years' imprisonment and $10,000 fine for "attempt to evade and defeat" the income tax in 1925, 1926 and 1927.

Judge Wilkerson set Tuesday morning for hearing on motions by defense counsel for arrest of judgment and for a new trial.

The verdict, returned eight hours and ten minutes after the jury filed out at 2:40 P. M., was a puzzling one to all in the court room.

Capone grinned as though he felt he had gotten off easily. His counsel asked that the verdict be re-read that they might grasp it.

Jacob I. Grossman, Assistant United States Attorney, mumbled that he thought the finding "inconsistent" and asked for time to confer with the other members of the prosecutor's staff.

Government Accepts Verdict.

Ten minutes later Mr. Grossman was back in the room. He announced that the government has decided that there was no inconsistency and that it was willing to have the verdict entered. Albert Fink of defense counsel then made a motion for arrest of judgment.

"I will not hold your motion for arrest of judgment," said Judge Wilkerson. "I think you will make another motion."

"You mean a motion for a new trial?" said Mr. Fink. "Do I waive my motion for a new trial if I make a motion for arrest of judgment?"

The court did not answer.

Capone faces a maximum of seventeen years' imprisonment and $50,000 fine. He did not seem to realize that. He kept grinning at all and sundry in the court room, his bulky figure in a screaming green suit (one of the $135 ones) drawing all eyes toward him.

As soon as the verdict was entered, he got out of his seat and virtually ran from the room. He rushed on lumbering feet across the dim corridor, stepped into the elevator and as soon as it touched the rotunda floor he ran out to the street to a waiting automobile. No one interviewed him.

The jury was ready with the verdict at 10:50 P. M., but Capone was not there when the knock on the

Continued on Page Nineteen.

Thomas Edison Dies in Coma at 84; Family With Him as the End Comes

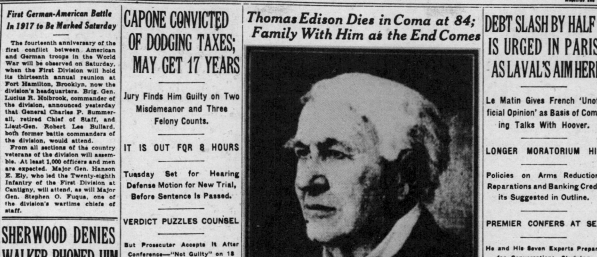

THOMAS ALVA EDISON,
From the Painting by Ellis M. Silvette.

Inventor Succumbs at 3:24 A. M. After Fight for Life Since He Was Stricken on Aug. 1—World-Wide Tribute Is Paid to Him as a Benefactor of Mankind.

From a Staff Correspondent of The New York Times.

WEST ORANGE, N. J., Sunday, Oct. 18.—Thomas Alva Edison died at 3:24 o'clock this morning at his home, Glenmont, in the Llewellyn Park section of this city. The great inventor, the fruits of whose genius so magically transformed the everyday world, was 84 years and 8 months old.

Announcement of Mr. Edison's passing was made at 3:37 A. M. by Arthur L. Walsh, vice president of the Thomas A. Edison Industries, Inc., who had acted as spokesman for the family during the night.

The end came almost imperceptibly as the sick man's ebbing strength, sapped by long months of struggle against a complication of ailments, gradually receded until his heart ceased beating. He had suffered no pain through the later stages of his illness, his attendants said.

With him when death came were his entire immediate family and Dr. Hubert S. Howe of New York, his personal physician. His wife, who was Miss Mina Miller before their marriage in 1886, had been almost constantly at his bedside since his illness became acute early this month.

Their children, Mrs. John Eyre Sloane and Charles and Theodore Edison, all live near by and have been at Glenmont daily through that period, as has Thomas A. Edison Jr., a son of the inventor's first marriage. Mrs. Marion Oser of Norwalk, Conn., and William L. Edison of Wilmington, Del., the other children by the first marriage, had been summoned when it became apparent that the end was near.

Mr. Edison never roused from the coma into which he lapsed last Thursday. Through the last hours of his long and fruitful life he lay in what seemed like deep and restful slumber. He had been unable to take any nourishment since last Sunday or any liquids in almost two weeks.

Through the long days before that when he calmly, cheerfully awaited the inevitable, amazing evidences of the world's affectionate concern for one of its most useful citizens were plentiful. Pope Pius XI, President Hoover, Henry Ford and a host of others kept in daily touch with his condition.

Anxiety for the man whose creative genius gave the world the electric light, the phonograph, the motion picture camera and a thousand of other inventions ranging through all the various fields of science had been general since he collapsed in the living room of his home on Aug. 1.

The obituary of Mr. Edison and a page of pictures of outstanding events in his life in Section II.

PETAIN DECLARES YORKTOWN DEBT PAID

Marshal Praises America's Part in War and Ideals to Maintain Peace.

From a Staff Correspondent of The New York Times.

YORKTOWN, Va., Oct. 17.—The frills and furbelows of an age that is gone graced the ancient streets of this little village today as the second day of the sesquicentennial celebration of the Battle of Yorktown passed into history.

Silks and satins styled in the modes of another era, flounced crinolines and billowing taffetas, powdered wigs and silver buckles, pigtails and perukes flashed against the old brick walls of Yorktown's ancient homes to vie in incongruous but pleasing contrast with the bright uniforms of the soldiers and sailors of today, with the silk hats and frock coats of diplomatic dignitaries, with the neat khaki of General Pershing and the horizon blue of Marshal Petain and with the sombre business suits of political leaders, industrial executives and plain citizens.

It was "Revolutionary Day" in this town that had its birth in 1691, when fifty acres of land for the establishment of "Ye Towne of Yorke" were sold for 10,000 pounds of tobacco. Crisp Fall weather and bright, searching sunshine; pageants of the

Continued on Page Sixteen.

WAGNER TREASURES COMING TO AMERICA

Mrs. Mary Bok Buys the Famous Burrell Collection Throwing New Light on Composer.

Announcement of world-wide importance to music lovers and Wagner students is made in Overtones, the monthly musical magazine of the Curtis Institute of Music, issued yesterday in Philadelphia, that Mrs. Mary Louise Curtis Bok, founder of the institute, is the purchaser and sole owner of the Burrell collection of Wagneriana.

This collection was discovered under highly dramatic circumstances two years ago in England. Very little of its contents has been made public, but enough of its material is known for it to be certain that their publication will necessitate drastic revisions of many chapters in long accepted biographies of the most fascinating and enigmatic characters in history.

The Burrell collection, of which the existence was known only to a few scholars, and of which the whereabouts was completely unknown, was discovered two years ago in an English country house by two Americans, Messrs. Hurn and Root, who were in Europe seeking material for a drama on Wagner. The priceless collection was discovered reposing in

Continued on Page Thirty-one.

Results in Major Sports Yesterday.

FOOTBALL—Local gridirons produced one of the big upsets yesterday when Columbia defeated Dartmouth, 19 to 6, at Baker Field. Fordham tied Holy Cross, 6—6, at the Polo Grounds. The N. Y. U. team beat Rutgers, 27 to 7, at the Yankee Stadium. A determined rally in the second period gave Harvard a victory over Army at West Point, 14 to 13, Army scoring its points in the first period. Celebrating the fortieth anniversary of A. A. Stagg as football coach, Yale on her first trip to the mid-West conquered Chicago, 27 to 0. Cornell downed Princeton, 33 to 0; Pennsylvania vanquished Lehigh, 32 to 0; Navy beat Delaware, 12 to 7, and at Troy, R. P. I. defeated C. C. N. Y., 13 to 8. Other gridiron scores were Colgate 33, Manhattan 0; Brown 38, Tufts 12; Syracuse 33, Florida 12; Villanova 12, Boston College 6; Lafayette 22, St. John's of Annapolis 0; Pittsburgh 32, Western Reserve 0; Ohio State 20, Michigan 7; Notre Dame 63, Drake 0; Wisconsin 21, Purdue 14; Illinois 20, Bradley 0; Northwestern 19, University of California (L. A.) 0; Tennessee 25, Alabama 0; Tulane 19, Vanderbilt 0; Georgia 32, North Carolina 7; Stanford 25, Oregon State 7; Southern California 53, Oregon 0; Washington 39, Idaho 7; California 13, Washington State 7.

RACING—William Woodward's Ormesby won the Pierrepont Handicap, one of the features of the closing day at Jamaica, finishing the mile and a furlong over a slow track a length and a half ahead of A La Carte, the favorite. Mrs. George Harris's Cambal won the Remsen Handicap, for 2-year-olds, by a head from H. C. Phipps's Regula Baddun, with John J. Robinson's Lucky Tom, the favorite, third. At Laurel, the Linton Farms' Flagstone, an outsider, won the Laurel Stakes, with $10,000 added, beating Clock Tower by a head. Mr. Sponge and Curate were among the also ran. At Latonia R. S. Clark's Kakapo won the $15,000 added Kentucky Jockey Club Stakes by three lengths from Pompeius. Air Pilot was third.

Complete Details of These and Other Sports Events in Sports Section.

DEBT SLASH BY HALF IS URGED IN PARIS AS LAVAL'S AIM HERE

Le Matin Gives French 'Unofficial Opinion' as Basis of Coming Talks With Hoover.

LONGER MORATORIUM HIT

Policies on Arms Reduction, Reparations and Banking Credits Suggested in Outline.

PREMIER CONFERS AT SEA

He and His Seven Experts Prepare for Conversations, Studying Our Point of View.

By P. J. PHILIP.
Special Cable to THE NEW YORK TIMES.

PARIS, Oct. 17.—While Premier Laval is taking to Washington no rigid plan and no fixed doctrine as to how calm, credit and confidence can be brought back to the world, he is taking with him what may be called an "official opinion" on all questions which are likely to arise. What that "official opinion" is, is set forth in an article in Le Matin of today, which confirms at every point the outline of the French position as described in a despatch to THE NEW YORK TIMES ten days ago.

While emphasizing that the outline of the French position which it prints does not constitute a definite program, Le Matin says that the suggestions contained in it are those which Premier Laval will contribute in the Washington conversations with President Hoover.

Against Extending Moratorium.

Le Matin's article reads:

"First, the intergovernmental debts:

"While America inclines toward an extension of the moratorium, France believes that this method has grave inconveniences, because it holds the threat of accumulated payments over each debtor country, and might incite some to follow a different road from that of national economy and go even to an appearance of insolvability.

"In place of the moratorium, debt reduction representing inevitable sacrifices and reaching as high as 50 per cent is regarded as the only real help in the world situation. If the United States should consent, it would have to bear a loss, even though only a theoretic loss, of about $200,000,000 yearly.

"Germany's payments would be reduced by that amount, and during a certain period the remaining payments by Germany might be made to the Bank for International Settlements, but instead of being transferred abroad, and finally to the United States, might be reloaned in Germany and other countries which are in financial difficulties.

As to Action in Disarmament.

"Second, disarmament:

"France in compensation for the sacrifice asked from the United States is disposed to embark on a program of progressive disarmament which will be of a kind to help the American budgetary position. This, however, is on two conditions: first, that disarmament shall be sought by a reduction of the present budgets and not by the equalization of armaments; secondly, that the Kellogg pact shall be completed by one or two articles stipulating that in the case of a threat of or the outbreak of a conflict the United States shall act in concert and without delay with the other powers, and once the

Continued on Page Five.

Americans in Japan Suffer As Chinese Cooks Start Home

By The Associated Press.

TOKYO, Oct. 17.—The Sino-Japanese controversy has produced an echo in the kitchens of Americans and others in Japan who employ Chinese cooks. Seventy-two Chinese chefs today decided to inform their employers they would pack their bags and depart for China as a result of the international dispute, and, consequently thirty Chinese restaurants in Tokyo and several in Yokohama, Osaka and Kobe may have to close.

In addition, the kitchens of numerous private families face the loss of their culinary experts, most of whom are from Canton.

JAPAN WILL AWAIT LEAGUE PROPOSALS

Tokyo Accepts Move on China Calmly, Foreseeing Delay, but Continues Protest.

RUSSIAN RIGHTS ARE CITED

Japanese Point Out That Soviet, and 50 Others Also Signed Briand-Kellogg Pact.

By HUGH BYAS.
Special Cable to THE NEW YORK TIMES.

TOKYO, Oct. 17.—The government has accepted the creation of a "united front" at Geneva regarding Manchuria with complete calmness, and displays no intention either of quitting the League or of obstructing the efforts of the enlarged Council.

The attendance of Kenkichi Yoshizawa at the session yesterday at which the American representative, Prentiss Gilbert, was present, is accepted as a matter of course, and he will continue to attend, though his government is still not convinced that the Council acted constitutionally and will press for a decision on the legal points involved.

By instructing Mr. Yoshizawa to repeat its protest regarding the legality of the move, the government is simply marking time until Geneva reaches the stage of practical proposals.

One possibility of obstruction hitherto overlooked, which the League's action opens, is that Russia, as a signatory of the Briand-Kellogg pact also, and with vast interests in Manchuria, might likewise ask to participate. Probably, as Japan is now taking as much care to avoid infringing the Russian sphere as Russia took in 1929 to avoid Japan's sphere, Russia will copy Japan's 1929 attitude of non-interference, but it seems to Japan that by opening the door to America the League also has opened it to Russia, which, conceivably, might seek entirely different results.

Japan Sees Expediency.

In Japan's view, the League was influenced by expediency, and if the covenant is to be interpreted in terms of opportunism at every varying situation, the position of all members is affected. Withdrawal from the League, however, is an unlikely possibility which no responsible persons are as yet considering.

Minister of War Minami gave out a violently worded interview last evening in which he spoke of the League exposing its weakness by inviting America, and America provoking the Japanese people's feelings by attending the League, but his remarks need not be taken too seriously.

The Foreign Office has been furnished with a copy of Prentiss Gilbert's instructions, which empower

Continued on Page Two.

Hitlerites Battle Foes in Brunswick Streets; 10 Sent to Hospital on Eve of 'Nazi' Review

By The Associated Press.

BRUNSWICK, Germany, Oct. 17.—Serious street fights between Hitlerites and anti-Hitlerites occurred here today on the eve of the National Socialist [Nazis] field day, at which Adolf Hitler, the "Nazi" leader, will review forces drawn from all parts of the Reich. Ten persons required hospital treatment and several others received less serious knife wounds.

An automobile containing twenty-seven "Nazis" en route to Brunswick overturned near Wurzen. One of the occupants was killed and all the others were injured.

Thousands of Herr Hitler's followers thundered down the streets here to the accompaniment of martial music as a curtain-raiser to tomorrow's events.

Squad after squad of them, carrying flaming torches, tramped past Herr Hitler, who stood in an automobile and smilingly acknowledged the greeting of "Hoch!" from the legions, responding by raising his arm in the Fascist salute.

"Nazi" headquarters predicted that at least 75,000 of the Hitlerite "storm troops" would be on hand tomorrow, as well as an equal number of civilians. Those arriving on trains tonight already had donned the mustard-colored uniforms which are not permitted in Prussia and some other States. The uniforms were put on as soon as the Brunswick border had been crossed.

Adolf Hitler's "Nazis," Dr. Alfred Hugenberg's Nationalists and the Peasants' League joined forces in a military rally at Bad Harzburg last Sunday and formed the National Opposition, whose immediate aim was the overthrow of the Bruening Government.

Chancellor Bruening, however, succeeded in obtaining a vote of confidence from the Reichstag on Friday by 295 to 270, the Communists and People's party joining the Nationalists in voting against him, with the Socialists, the Centrists and oth. middle parties and smaller groups enabling him to gain the victory. The Reichstag then voted to adjourn until Feb. 23.

LEAGUE INVOKES THE KELLOGG PACT; ASKS NATIONS' AID

Council Drafts Identical Notes Reminding China and Japan of Peace Obligations.

FURTHER ACTION PLANNED

Session Today Will Seek Ways for Japanese Evacuation and Safety in China.

JAPAN TO WIDEN DEMANDS

Tries to Revive Rights Given Up at Washington Parley—Her Delegation Resentful.

By LANSING WARREN.
Special Cable to THE NEW YORK TIMES.

GENEVA, Oct. 17.—As a result of two secret sessions of the League of Nations Council today, at which the American representative, Prentiss B. Gilbert, took part on a basis of full equality, an entirely new force has been brought into play to bring a peaceful settlement of the Manchurian conflict between China and Japan, the only two members of the Council not present at these meetings.

This force, new so far as League action is concerned, is the moral force of the Briand-Kellogg pact, which until America's entry into the League Council sittings had remained inoperative while the League was attempting separate action through the machinery of the League covenants.

The Council decided tonight after long discussions that the Briand-Kellogg pact [known officially as the Pact of Paris] could best be coordinated with the League's action if the countries represented on the League Council would send identical cablegrams to the Nanking and Tokyo Governments reminding them of their obligations under Article 2 of the pact to settle their differences by pacific means.

Some Messages Are Sent.

While all the members of the Council are from countries signatory to the Pact of Paris, only those represented by Foreign Ministers with full powers in the matter were able to dispatch these messages from Geneva tonight. Representatives who were bound to consult their governments notified their Foreign Offices of the action suggested by the Council, with recommendations that like action be taken without delay.

But the decision went further, aiming to include League members outside the Council and even non-members of the League who are signatories to the Briand-Kellogg pact. To all of these, including Russia, the League tonight dispatched telegrams informing them of the Council's decision and urging that they join in putting the pressure of their authority under the treaty into the service of world peace. Mr. Gilbert, as United States representative with the Council, tonight formally sent an identical appeal to Secretary of State Stimson at Washington to join with the other nations in dispatch to China and Japan.

This will be the second time the American Government has had occasion to invoke the Pact of Paris, the first time curiously enough having been also in a conflict in Manchuria, which took place between the Chinese and the Russians. Tonight's action, however, having been initiated through the collaboration of the League, the United States has been relieved of the responsibility for instigating a movement which is shared alike by all nations represented on the Council. In participating, the United States stands exactly in the same position as other non-member States who will decide to take the same action.

Stimson's Action Forecast.

On the basis of a long transatlantic telephone conversation, which is known to have taken place last night between Mr. Stimson and Mr. Gilbert, it is taken for granted that the United States will take part in this move. How many other States will join is not known to the Secretariat. There is particular doubt as to exactly what position will be taken by Russia, which perhaps is the most directly interested non-member in the Manchurian dispute.

Regardless of how the action may be viewed by the governments of Japan and China, it is felt that the receipt of a large number of reminders of obligations from governments in all parts of the world cannot but exert a powerful impression. Not only will they serve to draw the attention of Tokyo and Nanking to world interest in the peaceful settlement of the struggle, but they will bring the problem into prominence in practically every country in the world. Each country thus aroused, it is presumed, will henceforth feel a direct interest in a peaceful settlement, and a moral force not easily neglected will have been set in force.

The Briand-Kellogg pact, without

Section 1

"All the News That's Fit to Print."

The New York Times.

LATE CITY EDITION
THE WEATHER—Fair today and tomorrow, slightly cooler today.
Temperatures yesterday—Max. 66, min. 52.
U. S. Weather Forecast—Page 18, Section 2.

Section 1

Copyright, 1931, by The New York Times Company.

VOL. LXXXI....No. 26,937. ****+ NEW YORK, SUNDAY, OCTOBER 25, 1931. Including Rotogravure Picture Section in two parts—Magazine and Book Sections in Rotogravure. TEN CENTS

LEAGUE SETS NOV. 16 FOR WITHDRAWAL OF THE JAPANESE TROOPS IN MANCHURIA; RUSSIA READY TO PROTECT HER INTERESTS

JAPAN REMAINS UNYIELDING

Yoshizawa Holds to Demand China Negotiate With Tokyo Directly.

COUNCIL QUITS TILL NOV. 16

As Action Was Not Unanimous, It Has Only Moral Validity —Debate Very Frank.

SITUATION IS STILL GRAVE

Fear Is Felt Japanese Will Never Give Way on Recognition of the 1915 Treaty.

By LANSING WARREN.
Wireless to THE NEW YORK TIMES.

GENEVA, Oct. 24.—The League Council by a vote of 13 to 1, with Japan dissenting, passed a resolution today calling upon the Japanese to withdraw their troops within the South Manchuria Railroad zone by Nov. 16. The Council thereupon adjourned until that date.

Due to the fact that action under Article XI of the League Covenant requires unanimity, the resolution only takes the legal form of a recommendation. However, it is hoped that the nations voting for it, supported by the United States, which gave no indication of its attitude today, will make it binding by giving their full moral weight to the resolution during the intervening time.

Japan Is Isolated.

Never was a nation in an international dispute made to feel her isolation and the force of combined disapproval as Japan was in the closing debates of this Council meeting. And seldom has any nation so obstinately resisted, alone, every wile, threat, persuasion and cajolement, as did Japan through Kenkichi Yoshizawa, her delegate, who kept repeating that he could not accept because his government did not agree with the delegate from Spain, from France, from Britain, nor with any of the others. Battered by the shrewd questioning of Viscount Cecil of Chelwood, the caustic clarity of Salvador de Madariaga and the fatherly reasoning appeals of Aristide Briand, Mr. Yoshizawa calmly and tenaciously stood by his guns against every suggestion of concession or compromise.

Importance Is Stressed.

In many respects, as a number of the Council members emphasized in their speeches today, this Far Eastern problem has become the pivotal point of the world political situation at this moment, because its effective solution has become essential to the approach of nearly all the great problems which the Occidental nations are now facing.

Its bearing upon the disarmament problem was repeatedly considered in the debates, and it also involves the whole efficacy of the international machinery for preventing war, of questions of security, boundaries and the sanctity of international treaties themselves. Lord Reading even went so far as to say, before he left Geneva, that the Manchurian problem must be solved before the world can hope to deal successfully with the economic crisis.

That one of the most important matters in connection with the League's action today resides in the future attitude of the United States was made evident by the repeated references to America's participation made by the delegates in the final session today. It is confidently expected here that Secretary Stimson will tomorrow make a formal declaration of the United States support of the Council's recommendations, and that Prentiss Gilbert's silence today represented only his desire to maintain his position as an observer and not to detract from the full effect of a statement by the American Secretary of State.

Eyes Turn to America.

But what most interested the Council members tonight was an answer to a question put by Señor de Madariaga when he expressed the hope that if the Council was obliged to resume its hearing on the conflict, would "the cooperation of the United States also go on?" Mr. Gilbert evaded an answer by merely thank-

Continued on Page Two.

Chang Says Japan Is Mobilizing in Manchuria; Offensive on Capital at Chinchow Is Expected

By HALLETT ABEND.
Special Cable to THE NEW YORK TIMES.

SHANGHAI, Oct. 24.—Marshal Chang Hsueh-liang's headquarters at Peiping issued a statement today asserting that the Japanese army in Manchuria was continuing to mobilize and that Japanese airplane flights indicated Japan's intention of making an early offensive against Chinchow, Marshal Chang's temporary capital in South Manchuria.

Chinese sources also assert that thirty pieces of Japanese heavy artillery have arrived at Mukden and that fifteen more are en route from Korea. These arms, it is said, are being distributed at Changchun, Kirin City, Ssupingkai and Kungchuling, while ten heavy guns and great stores of munitions have already been unloaded at Chuluiro.

A serious clash of crowds of Japanese and Chinese civilians was narrowly averted at Mukden when, during Japanese memorial services in honor of the men who were killed in the Russo-Japanese War, a Japanese airplane got out of control and plunged into a lumber yard, killing the pilot instantly. The Chinese attending the ceremonies laughed or smiled over the disaster, and this enraged Japanese spectators.

A large force of Japanese police intervened in the trouble that followed, preventing a riot.

SOVIET THREATENS TO ACT IN MANCHURIA

Warns Independent General Near Tsitsihar Not to Touch Chinese Eastern Road.

TENSION IN REGION GROWS

Nanking Hears Chiang Kai-shek Has Agreed to Resign to Make Way for Coalition Rule.

By HALLETT ABEND.
Special Cable to THE NEW YORK TIMES.

SHANGHAI, Oct. 24.—For the first time since the beginning of the Sino-Japanese conflict in Manchuria, Russia this afternoon gave formal intimation of possible armed participation when the Soviet Consul at Tsitsihar notified General Chang Hai-peng, who heads the independence faction near Tsitsihar, that if his troops interfered with the Chinese Eastern Railway, Soviet Russia would take action. Russia has 5,000 troops in armored trains across the border from Manchouli.

Tension was increasing tonight through South Manchuria, including the Kirin area, and because of this all South Manchuria Railway civilian officials working outside the railway area have withdrawn into the Japanese zone as an extra precaution.

Chao Hsin-po, the new Chinese Mayor of Mukden, today called a conference of leading Chinese to decide whether to organize a new provincial government independent of Marshal Chang Hsueh-liang. Japanese officials assert that Japan is not interested and is not attempting to influence the decision.

At Shanghai the Nanking-Canton coalition negotiations are proceeding slowly. The Canton opposition to T. V. Soong, Finance Minister of Nanking, is lessening gradually. The Canton group now merely demands that there be open public accounting of all revenues.

Wang Ching Wei, Canton Left-wing leader, announces that General Chiang Kai-shek, under Canton's compulsion, has granted full freedom of the press. Mr. Wang also asserts General Chiang's resignation will not be announced before the establishment of the new coalition government, but advices from Nanking insist that the Nanking leader has finally agreed upon the official text of his resignation.

According to present indications, it is unlikely that the Southern delegates will risk a trip to Nanking until the new government is finally established. Meanwhile all negotiations will be held in the safety of the foreign-controlled area of Shanghai.

Eugene Chen, Canton Foreign Minister, today defined his foreign policy by declaring that "China, having no military force," must depend on diplomatic means to settle the Manchurian affair, and he intimated China must ally herself with nations willing to cope with the "Japanese imperialists."

Among the important questions which the peace delegates discussed today was the early resumption of diplomatic relations with Soviet Russia. Dr. C. C. Wu, former Minister to Washington, says there is no question that China and Soviet Russia will resume friendly relations in the near future.

This week witnessed the arrival in Shanghai of large shipments of Soviet oil and wheat, the latter selling in the local markets below the

Continued on Page Two.

CITY INQUIRY TURNS TO AID OF MOFFAT

Seabury Investigates Charge Tammany Is 'Colonizing' the 15th Assembly District.

TAX BRIBERY BEING HUNTED

One Agent Is Found With Bank Deposits of $100,000—Bench Deal Hearings to Go On.

In an attempt to help in the reelection of one of its own members, Assemblyman Abbot Low Moffat, as well as to perform a public service, the Hofstadter legislative committee started an investigation yesterday into charges of illegal registrations in the Fifteenth Assembly District.

Subpoenas were served on a dozen or more persons believed to have information to support the charge of Keyes Winter, Republican leader of district, that Tammany has colonized "floaters" in the district, and investigators already are reported to have obtained evidence indicating that Mr. Winter's charge may have some basis.

Any evidence obtained probably will be brought out at the public hearings this week by Samuel Seabury, counsel of the committee. The hearings will be resumed on Wednesday, and Mr. Seabury is expected to continue his inquiry into the so-called judicial deal by which seven Democrats and five Republicans were nominated for the twelve new Supreme Court justiceships in the Second Judicial District.

$30,000,000 Piers Under Fire.

Murray Hulbert, former Dock Commissioner and former President of the Board of Aldermen, was questioned by Henry J. A. Collins, associate counsel. The questioning had to do with the Staten Island piers built at Stapleton at a cost of more than $30,000,000 during the administration of Mayor Hylan while Mr. Hulbert was Dock Commissioner.

Mr. Collins is understood to be seeking to establish that the piers owned by the city have been undervalued greatly in the estimates contained in the annual reports of the Dock Department, presumably to make it appear that the rents derived from them are adequate. The piers owned by the city are valued at about $70,000,000. Mr. Collins's information is that with carrying charges added the Staten Island piers alone have cost the city $40,000,000.

John R. Davies, associate counsel in charge of the investigation of the Manhattan Building Bureau, who recently has been engaged on other matters, has returned to his original investigation because of the discovery of a bank account of Charles Brady, former superintendent of the bureau, who is a missing witness.

May Call Party Leaders.

It still is not determined whether Mr. Seabury will call John H. McCooey, Brooklyn Democratic leader; Meier Steinbrink, former Brooklyn Republican leader and one of the judicial nominees, and W. Kingsland Macy, Republican State Chairman. The general belief is that Mr. Seabury will call these witnesses and devote the public hearings during the week before election to their examination and the investigation of reports of registration frauds.

The registration in the Fifteenth

Continued on Page Five.

Results in Major Sports Yesterday

FOOTBALL—A crowd of 45,000 saw N. Y. U. down Colgate yesterday at the Yankee Stadium, 13 to 0. Columbia defeated Williams, 19 to 0, and Fordham vanquished Drake, 46 to 0. At New Haven, Yale and Army battled to a 6-6 tie before 75,000. Harvard beat Texas at Cambridge, 35 to 7, and the Navy invaded Princeton to score a 15-to-0 victory. Pennsylvania won from Wisconsin at Philadelphia, by 27 to 13, and at South Bend, Ind., Notre Dame defeated Pittsburgh, 25 to 12.

Other gridiron scores were: Northwestern 10, Ohio State 0; Syracuse 7, Penn State 0; Drexel 33, C. C. N. Y. 0; Brown 33, Lehigh 0; Amherst 14, Wesleyan 6; Holy Cross 27, Rutgers 0; Lafayette 21, W. and J. 0; Dartmouth 20, Lebanon Valley 6; Tulane 33, Georgia Tech 0; Tennessee 7, North Carolina 0; Georgia 9, Vanderbilt 0; Michigan State 6, Georgetown 0; Minnesota 34, Iowa 0; Nebraska 6, Kansas 0; Michigan 35, Illinois 0; Purdue 13, Carnegie Tech 6; Marquette 7, Boston College 0; Indiana 32, Chicago 6; So. California 6, California 0; Stanford 0, Washington 0.

RACING—Walter J. Salmon's Dr. Freeland beat Reveille Boy by four lengths to win the Yorktown Handicap, the feature event at Empire City. At Laurel, Mate ran third in the $15,000 added Maryland Handicap, which was won by Clock Tower, with Pilate second. The Selima Stake for 2-year-olds, another Laurel feature, was won by Laughing Queen. C. V. Whitney's champion filly Top Flight was scratched.

Complete Details of These and Other Sports Events in Sports Section.

CAPONE SENTENCED TO AN 11-YEAR TERM; JAILED TILL APPEAL

Fine of $50,000 and Payment of Costs Also Ordered—Gang Chief Is Stunned.

SLATED FOR LEAVENWORTH

Judge Wilkerson Sends Him to Cook County Prison Until Tomorrow, Awaiting His Plea.

By MEYER BERGER.
Staff Correspondent of The New York Times.

CHICAGO, Oct. 24.—Federal Judge James H. Wilkerson ended the reign of Scarface Al Capone today.

He sentenced the bulky lord of crime to eleven years' imprisonment, fined him $50,000 and decreed that he pay the cost of his prosecution, which is about $100,000. The fine, the costs and the $137,328 already ascertained as due from Capone for back income taxes, makes his total debt to the government $287,328. Much more in the way of back taxes is expected to be levied before the government is through with Capone.

It was a smashing blow to the massive gang chief. He tried to take it with a smile, but that smile was almost pitiful. His clumsy fingers, tightly locked behind his back, twitched and twisted. He had hoped for a sentence of not more than three years.

Judge Wilkerson, after passing sentence, refused to admit Capone to bail pending appeal. He ordered him at once into the custody of the United States marshal, and for a time it seemed that Capone might start for the United States penitentiary at Leavenworth tonight. Later his attorneys received until Monday to file application for bail with the Circuit Court of Appeals. Capone will spend the week-end in a fifth-tier cell in Cook County Jail.

Dramatic Scene at Sentencing.

The pronouncement of judgment was dramatic. Judge Wilkerson's words, sharply clipped and incisive, rang clear in the hushed court chamber.

When the full import registered on the consciousness of the audience—about 200 persons heard it—a murmur of astonishment broke like surf against the white marble walls. It was the stiffest sentence ever given for income tax evasion.

Capone came in at ten minutes of 10. He looked wide-awake and spruce. A heather-colored, pinch-back suit with a white silk handkerchief in the breast pocket neatly cased his ponderous body. He included reporters and some of the spectators in a wide smile, shook hands with Michael Ahern, one of his lawyers, and sat down at the counsel table.

At 10 o'clock Capone was talking earnestly in a whisper to Ahern, when the door from the judge's chamber opened. The bailiff rapped sharply, every one stood up and Judge Wilkerson, a short, grim-faced man, with iron-gray hair which is almost always slightly tousled, ascended the bench. Capone searched the grim lines of the judge's face as he sat down again.

"The United States versus Capone," the clerk called. "Disposition of motion in arrest of judgment."

A murmur of anticipation swept the chamber. Capone edged forward on his swivel chair, crowding Ahern who sat in front of him. He cupped his hairy right hand over his right ear and his jet-black eyes opened wide under their bushy brows, as if that might help him hear better.

"It was urged here in the argument yesterday," said Judge Wilkerson, "that the counts of the indict-

Continued on Page Twenty-two.

TWO GOVERNORS OPEN GREAT HUDSON BRIDGE AS THRONGS LOOK ON

5,000 Attend Exercises Held in Centre of $60,000,000 Span Linking Palisades to City.

TRIBUTES TO WASHINGTON

Longest Suspension Crossing Dedicated to First President as Planes Soar Overhead.

The new $60,000,000 George Washington Bridge across the Hudson—the world's largest suspension span—was formally opened yesterday afternoon with ceremonies marked by tributes from representatives of the nation, the States of New York and New Jersey and the municipalities which the structure unites.

More than 5,000 guests of the Port of New York Authority, which built the new bridge, opened it eight months ahead of schedule and held the cost down considerably below the original estimates, saw the picturesque ceremonies from a grand stand in the centre of the span.

Altogether, nearly 30,000 citizens of New York and New Jersey were present, according to police estimates. In addition to the 5,000 in the grand stand, 20,000 stood in the Manhattan plaza and 4,000 in the Fort Lee plaza listening to the exercises through amplifiers. Additional thousands lined Riverside Drive and the top of the Palisades.

Those studying the scenic beauty afforded by the new vantage point, the blue waters of the Hudson 250 feet below, Manhattan's towering skyline to the east and the brown Palisades tinged with Autumn colors, were diverted when the head of the parade fro mthe 102d Engineers Armory at 168th Street and Broadway marched onto the bridge at 3 o'clock.

Defying the age-old rule that marching troops break step when

Continued on Page Thirty.

Sheridan, Army End, Breaks Neck in Game; Now Lies Near Death in New Haven Hospital

Special to The New York Times.

NEW HAVEN, Conn., Oct. 24.—While 75,000 spectators in the Yale Bowl were still in a fever of excitement over a brilliant 88-yard run by Dud Parker of Yale at the football game here today between Yale and West Point, Richard B. Sheridan, the Army's stocky right end, was carried off the field with his neck broken.

With the exception of the stretcher bearers and a handful of others, practically all of the assembled thousands were ignorant of the fact that Sheridan lay on the point of death as he was being carried from the field. Sheridan was injured just after Parker had run almost the length of the field for a touchdown that brought the Elis and the cadets to a 6—6 tie.

Dr. Harvey Cushing of Boston, famous brain and nerve specialist who was here attending a surgeons' congress, went to the New Haven Hospital to take charge of the case after Sheridan had been brought there.

Dr. Cushing succeeded in reducing the fracture and with Drs. W. F. De-Witt of West Point and Samuel Harvey of the hospital was making a desperate fight to prolong the player's life. Dr. De Witt said Sheridan had a fracture of the fourth cervical vertebrae and was being kept alive under an artificial respirator. He might live for minutes, for hours or for days, but in the event he survived the accident he would be paralyzed for the rest of his days, the physician said.

Exactly how Sheridan was injured no one seemed to know. After Parker's run for the tying touchdown, Jablonsky of Army kicked off to Lassiter, who ran the ball back twenty yards to his own 22-yard line.

As the members of the two teams picked themselves off the ground following the play, the inert form of Sheridan was seen. Whether he had been knocked down by a Yale blocker or had suffered his injury in making the tackle of Lassiter could not be said with certainty, although he lay near where the Yale back was brought down.

The Army trainer ran out on the field and was followed by the team physician and two cadets. After working over the injured player for several minutes the Army physician called for a stretcher, which was rushed out by two Yale men and Sheridan was carried off. Major Ralph Sasse, the Army head coach, went with him to the hospital.

Sheridan is from Augusta, Ga., and went to West Point from Augusta Junior College. He is a member of the class of '33.

The Army football squad arrived in New York last evening and immediately canceled its engagement to attend a performance of the "Ziegfeld Follies." Captain W. H. Wells said that, in view of the critical injury to Sheridan, the squad would return directly to West Point this morning. Major R. I. Sasse, head coach, and others remained in New Haven.

HOOVER AND LAVAL AGREE TO COOPERATE ON GOLD, DEBTS AND REICH REPARATIONS; NO CONCLUSIONS ON POLITICAL PROBLEMS

Hoover's Statement to Press of Two Nations On Confidence in Outcome of Talks With Laval

Special to The New York Times.

WASHINGTON, Oct. 24.—In a statement read today to the correspondents of French and American newspapers President Hoover said:

The President of the Council of Ministers of France has done us great honor in coming to our country, especially so in these times of grave responsibilities.

I am confident that his visit will be profitable in results for the future.

I need not repeat that the purpose of our conversations has been to find fields from which contributions can be made to enlargement of confidence in the relations between nations and in the economic world.

I have on some occasions stated that the world is suffering more from frozen confidence than from frozen securities.

The press plays a major part in the development of good-will on which such confidence must rest by its search for fields in which cooperation and constructive action can be evolved.

I trust that you of the French press may carry away with you pleasant recollections of your visit and that you will realize the good-will and friendliness of the American people.

JOINT STATEMENT TODAY

President and Premier Will Tell Results of the Conferences.

FRANCE TO END GOLD FLOW

Discount Rate of the Federal Reserve Here Likely to Go to 4 Per Cent.

NO YOUNG PLAN REVISION

Hoover Will Not Propose Further Moratoriums Without Consulting France.

By RICHARD V. OULAHAN.
Special to The New York Times.

WASHINGTON, Oct. 24.—A public statement giving some insight into the conclusions reached by President Hoover and Pierre Laval, Premier of France, will be issued jointly by them tomorrow morning. This will mark the conclusion of the official purpose of the French Premier's brief visit to the United States. He will leave here for New York at 1 A. M. Monday and will sail for France at 12:01 A. M. Tuesday.

While the joint statement is expected to be phrased in general terms, cautiously expressed, the understanding is that the conclusions reached by the President and the Premier were confined entirely to financial questions. Political questions were discussed during the seven hours of conversation between them at the White House yesterday afternoon and last night, but are credited with having been of such a delicate character, both with reference to France and the United States, that if any thought had prevailed that the views of the two governments could be reconciled it was dissipated by the frank interchange of views which marked the dealings of Mr. Hoover and M. Laval.

Security Pact Not Mentioned.

It is understood that the French Premier did not express the well-known sentiments of his government and people in favor of arranging a security pact with the United States and the subject was not even mentioned, according to information obtained tonight.

There was some mention of a consultative pact to implement the Kellogg anti-war treaty, but neither side, it was gathered, pressed this issue.

Disarmament figured in the conversations, but the understanding prevails in informed circles that this subject received no detailed consideration and that no conclusion was reached concerning it.

The joint statement is expected to come nearer a concrete declaration in making known that an understanding has been reached which will emphasize that American and French financial stability is assured, and that no danger exists of either country departing from the gold standard.

Conclusions Reported Reached.

The following conclusions are said to have been reached, although it is not expected that they will be explained in any definite way in the joint statements.

1. There will be no more withdrawals of gold by France from the United States without prior consultation between the central banking interests of both countries.
2. As a result of conferences now in progress, the discount rate of the Federal Reserve Bank of New York may be raised to 4 per cent.
3. No public action affecting the mutual interests of either country will be taken without prior consultation.
4. There will be no proposal of President Hoover to extend the year's suspension of international debt payments without prior consultation with France as well as the other governments concerned.
5. No proposal will be made by the United States for revising the Young Plan of German reparations. The conclusion in this connection is said to carry with it the understanding that if Germany exercises her right under the Young Plan to declare a moratorium on the payment of conditional reparations to the victorious Allies, the legal procedure provided by the Young Plan

Continued on Page Twenty-four.

BORAH'S VIEWS STIR TEMPERS IN FRANCE

He Is Accused of Trying to Upset Treaties While Unwilling to Take Responsibility.

HOPES OF PARIS WANING

No Miracles Are Now Expected From Laval's Visit—Press Gives Rein to Sharp Criticisms.

By P. J. PHILIP.
Special Cable to THE NEW YORK TIMES.

PARIS, Oct. 24.—Much confusion of thought and some disturbance of temper have resulted here from the accounts cabled from Washington about what is being said and done there in the Franco-American conversations. In the first place, the communiqué issued from the White House is taken as an indication that not only are no miracles to be expected but that the mouse which will finally emerge from the mountain may be a very little one.

What has given most hope, and at the same time aroused the most rage, is the pronunciamento of Senator Borah. Even President Wilson's "disposal of peoples" during the Peace Conference is said by some observers here to be nothing compared with the manner in which the Senator from Idaho seems inclined to "tear up half a dozen treaties, redistribute nationalities to a few million people, and generally reconstruct the map of Europe."

"And that," says the Journal des Débats, "while being careful to in-

Continued on Page Twenty-four.

LAVAL AND BORAH TALK AND DISAGREE

They Confer for Hour and a Half at Stimson Home—Premier Asks Meeting Tonight.

TOGETHER ON TWO POINTS

Laval Approves "Without Reserve" All Senator Said on Reparations and Security.

Special to The New York Times.

WASHINGTON, Oct. 24.—Senator Borah and Premier Laval ended a conversation lasting an hour and a half tonight in as complete disagreement as when they began it, Mr. Borah said after attending a dinner in honor of the Premier at the home of Secretary Stimson.

The conversation between the chairman of the Committee on Foreign Relations and M. Laval was arranged by Secretary Stimson so they might try to explain to each other the reasons for their differing opinions.

Despite the disagreement, Premier Laval was so deeply interested in arriving at a mutual understanding that he arranged for a continuance of the conversation tomorrow night at the French Embassy, where Senator Borah will attend a reception honoring M. Laval.

"We talked about one and one-half hours," Senator Borah told a large group of newspaper men who awaited his exit from Woodley, the Stimson estate.

"Dave Reed, Republican Senator from Pennsylvania, was with us all the time. Mr. Stimson was in and out of the room, but left us free to talk. Premier Laval and I did almost all the talking.

"Frank and Pleasant Visit."

"We had a very pleasant visit and a very frank one. I do not think we were any closer together when we parted than when we started. We talked over everything. We were very frank, as I said, and we had a delightful conversation.

"I'm to see him again tomorrow night. He said when we left, 'We'll continue the discussion tomorrow night.'"

Senator Borah talked as he stood, bareheaded, beside his limousine.

No further description of his conversation was offered by Senator Borah, but it is understood that he believed Premier Laval has abandoned any idea he may have had of seeking a security pact with the United States.

Reed Agrees with Borah.

This was one of the points treated by Senator Borah in his long interview with French and American newspaper correspondents yesterday. Occupying a strategic position in the Senate, where such a pact would have to be ratified, he was definitely opposed to it.

Senator Reed, also a member of the Foreign Relations Committee, is understood to have agreed substantially with the stand taken by Senator Borah.

None of the other guests at the dinner submitted to interviews as they left the estate.

Dinner was served at 8 o'clock and concluded by 9:30, but the guests did not emerge until almost 11:30.

Senator Borah was the first to arrive, reaching the estate gates somewhat before 8 o'clock. He evidently realized he was early, as he directed

Continued on Page Twenty-four.

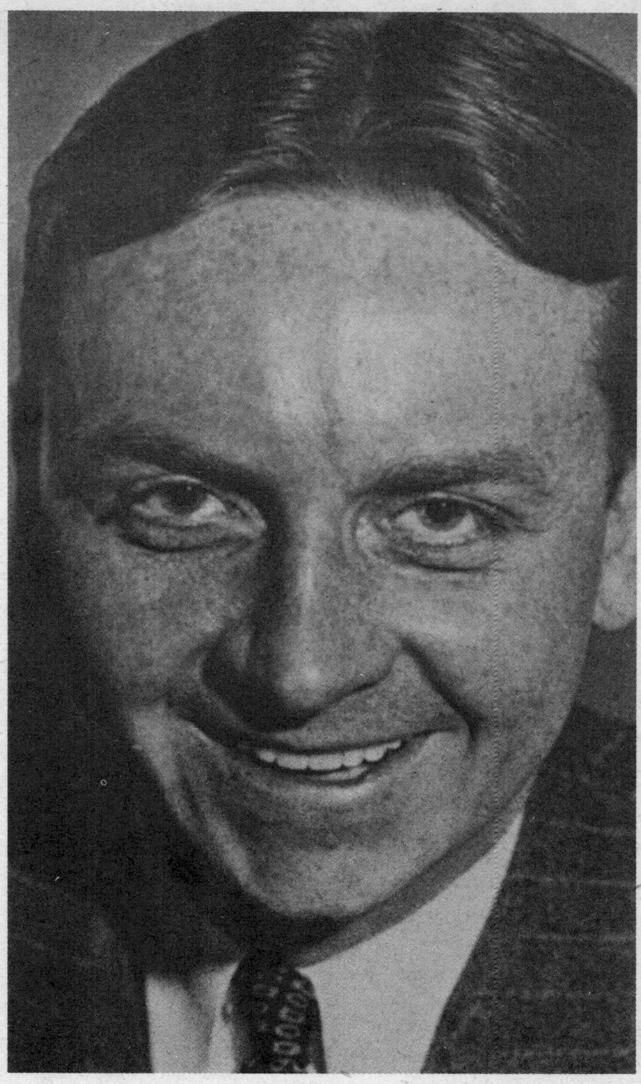

Eliot Ness, the agent who finally crushed Al Capone.

Times Wide World Photo

Jack (Legs) Diamond taking a walk in Albany the day before his death on December 18.

Al Capone was convicted of income tax evasion on October 17 and sentenced to an 11-year term on October 24.

One of the main-span cross-bridges is hoisted into position during the construction of the George Washington Bridge.

56,312 cars and more than 100,000 pedestrians crossed the George Washington Bridge on October 25, the day it opened to the public.

Times Wide World Photo.

"All the News That's Fit to Print."

The New York Times.

LATE CITY EDITION
THE WEATHER—Fair and cooler today; tomorrow fair.
Temperatures Yesterday—Max., 71; min., 54.
U. S. Weather Forecast—See text in last page.

Copyright, 1931, by The New York Times Company.

VOL. LXXXI....No. 26,938. ****+ NEW YORK, MONDAY OCTOBER 26, 1931. TWO CENTS In New York City | THREE CENTS Within 200 Miles | FOUR CENTS Elsewhere Except 7th and 8th Postal Zones

HOOVER AND LAVAL AGREE ON STEPS TO BRING WORLD ECONOMIC STABILITY; GROUNDWORK LAID FOR DEBT REVISION

JAPAN WON'T ACCEPT PROPOSAL OF LEAGUE; PLANS MUKDEN DEAL

Cabinet Decides Not to Alter Policy Against Withdrawing Troops by Nov. 16.

SEEKS DIRECT NEGOTIATION

Settlement With Independent Groups in Manchuria Is Seen as Way Out.

YOSHIZAWA IS CRITICIZED

Geneva Delegate Blamed for Not Clarifying Stand—Shanghai Hears of New Troop Clash.

Manchurian Developments.

Indications that Japan might confront the League of Nations with a fait accompli on Nov. 16 were seen in advices from Tokyo yesterday that she would seek direct negotiations with new administrative bodies now forming in Manchuria.

Tokyo intimated that the League Council's move to bring about troop withdrawal by Nov. 16 would be opposed.

Shanghai heard of new fighting near Changchun between Chinese and Japanese. All shops carrying Japanese goods in Peiping were shut down forcibly.

Peace negotiations between Canton and Nanking reached a deadlock over the control of the military.

Tokyo to Oppose the League.

By HUGH BYAS.

Special Cable to THE NEW YORK TIMES.

TOKYO, Oct. 25.—The government is greatly disappointed with the course of the debate at Geneva. It is realized that the League Council's resolution has no binding force, but it seems to make Japan bear the moral responsibility for the deadlock, which is at least held to be equally due to China's refusal to recognize existing treaties.

Japan is not willing to break with the League of Nations at present, nor to change its attitude regarding Manchuria, but the situation has become distinctly more dangerous. Nothing has been done to expedite direct negotiations. The League has seemed to approve of China's repudiation of treaty obligations which are held vital to Japan's existence and progress.

To the Japanese it seems as if the Chinese have been encouraged in their denial of Japan's right to partnership in the development of Manchuria. As the Japanese believe Manchuria is Chinese now only because they fought Russia for it, there is no shadow of hope that they will surrender their position, and the League's efforts, instead of loosening Japan's grip on Manchuria, may only strengthen those elements which believe China respects nothing but force.

Government to Issue Statement.

The government meantime is preparing a statement, to be issued probably tomorrow evening, which will make their position clear to the world. The Foreign Office is unable to understand how Kenkichi Yoshizawa, Geneva delegate, could have said, as reported, that he was unable to communicate Japan's fundamental principles.

He had received the "five points" regarding direct negotiations and treaty rights on Oct. 20. In the closing stages of the effort to find a formula Japan did not ask China to admit that the terms of security covered those five points, but she expected the League to record in its minutes her claim that security in the full sense meant the enjoyment of treaty rights.

Mr. Yoshizawa did not read the five points, and seems to have been unable to bring the debate to the point where China's refusal to acknowledge the existing treaties would stand out.

The Points at Issue.

It is asserted here with the greatest emphasis that Japan has no cards up her sleeve and asks nothing beyond those five points. In order to make sure that they have been properly reported, their substance was restated by officials this afternoon as follows:

1. Mutual non-aggression.
2. China to suppress boycotts, agitations and anti-Japanese propaganda in schoolbooks.
3. The territorial integrity of China is guaranteed.
4. China will protect the Japanese in Manchuria and permit them to engage in all lawful occupations.
5. China will respect existing treaties concerning Manchuria.

The Cabinet today, as reported in the vernacular press, agreed not to alter the present policy, but to con-

Continued on Page Two.

Chinese Seal Peiping Shops Which Sell Japanese Goods

Wireless to THE NEW YORK TIMES.

SHANGHAI, Oct. 25.—Advices received from Peiping today report extraordinary scenes there when 3,000 pickets, divided into 200 gangs of fifteen men each, made a thorough examination of all shops in the former capital, sealing those places where Japanese goods were found. The search was conducted under the auspices of the Peiping Anti-Japanese Association, aided by the Peiping Public Safety Bureau and the Hopei Kuomintang provincial headquarters.

Japanese sources here have received reports from Changchun in Manchuria indicating that there was a new outbreak at 6 this evening at Kunchuling, where a strong force of Chinese appeared. Fighting is proceeding tonight with the Japanese guards, the initial clash causing two Japanese casualities.

EINSTEIN ANNOUNCES A NEW FIELD THEORY

He Introduces a Vector of 5 Components Into 4-Dimensional Space-Time Continuum.

ABANDONS WORK OF 1929

His New Mathematical Concept Is an Outgrowth of Kaluza's Hypothesis.

A preliminary announcement by Professor Albert Einstein of the completion by him, in collaboration with Dr. Walter Mayer, his assistant, of part of his work on a new unified field theory, supplanting the one announced by him in 1929, upon which he had spent more than ten years of work, was made public yesterday by the Josiah Macy Jr. Foundation of 565 Park Avenue, which last year created a fellowship to provide a competent collaborator to Dr. Einstein in his research work.

Unified field theory is a term widely applied to represent the theory advanced by Einstein, according to which there is but a single background to all material activity—one unified field.

Before Einstein a material object was commonly conceived of as existing in space, time, a gravitational field, and an electromagnetic field, each object thus having four different backgrounds. Einstein's special theory of relativity amalgamated space and time into one, space-time, while the general theory of relativity, with its Riemannian geometry, further absorbed the gravitational field into space-time. Thus Einstein reduced three of the four backgrounds to one. The unified field theory goes a step further by including the electromagnetic field into the synthesis.

Old Unitary Theory Abandoned.

Einstein's new theory will be published in the near future, according to the announcement, probably in Pasadena, in connection with his investigations last Winter while in California. The Einstein statement was submitted in the president's report at the annual meeting of the board of trustees of the Macy Foundation.

Einstein's preliminary announcement does not go into the details of his new theory, confining itself to a general, brief statement of the mathematical lines of procedure followed by him and Dr. Mayer. It contains, however, the frank admission that his older unitary field theory, which was based on the introduction of the theory of distant parallelism in Riemannian geometry, had been abandoned by him when he found, after a year's further work, that it was a "striving in the wrong direction."

Instead of the theory of distant parallelism Einstein, with Dr. Mayer, has worked out a new unitary field theory on new mathematical concepts, based on the theory of Theodore Kaluza, promulgated in 1921, which Einstein had formerly regarded as "not acceptable."

Kaluza's theory rests on the assumption that the physical space-time continuum is five-dimensional instead of four-dimensional, as had been previously considered. By postulating a fifth dimension he was enabled to obtain field laws which agree in first approximation to the known field laws of both electricity and gravitation.

Einstein objected to this theory at first on the grounds that he considered it "anomalous to replace the four-dimensional continuum by a five-dimensional one "only to find it necessary subsequently to tie up artifically one of these dimensions in order to account for the fact that the fifth dimension does not manifest itself in the physical world of space-time. In other words, Einstein found it objectionable to introduce a fifth dimension the reality of which was not on a par with the other four dimensions.

The new theory, Professor Einstein says, "formally approximates Ka-

Continued on Page Two.

56,312 CARS CROSS BRIDGE ON FIRST DAY; FESTIVE AIR REIGNS

George Washington Span Tops Tunnel's Opening Total as Autos Jam Both Plazas.

100,000 GO OVER ON FOOT

Sightseers Use Buses, Cycles and Roller Skates—One Makes Trip on a Horse.

LINES FORM NIGHT BEFORE

Washington Heights Gay With Flags and Lights—Hawkers and Cameras Add to Gala Spirit.

New York and New Jersey met yesterday above the Hudson on the massive steel span of the new George Washington Bridge. The crossing was opened to vehicles for the first time and the public celebrated it. It went across by pleasure car, and service car, on foot, motorcycle and roller skates, and one citizen was on a horse.

Washington Heights was gay with bunting, and Fort Lee with souvenir program salesmen. Nothing like it has been seen locally in years.

After a red sunset had yielded to a clear white moon, that silvered the long span, the authorities became prosaic and issued statistics. These showed that up to midnight 56,312 cars had crossed and 100,000 pedestrians.

During the day elderly men with canes wandered slowly along the walks at the sides, and small boys skated more rapidly than courtesy and the crowd seemed to suggest. There were women with babies and some with carriages as well. There were nautical souls strolling with cameras and opera glasses. Far below were speed boats skipping about like bugs, and high overhead airplanes looked down on the latest massive achievement of man.

Day of Traffic Problems.

It was a day of traffic problems and of harassed police working under the direction of deputy inspectors. Lines of automobiles formed dark snakes for many blocks at each entrance to the bridge, and last night they choked Broadway from 179th Street down as far as 125th and up to the lower Bronx. Wadsworth, St. Nicholas, Audubon and Amsterdam Avenues all had their difficulties, but there were no major accidents. And none whatever was reported on the bridge.

In New Jersey it was the same. Long lines crept along the main roads near Fort Lee. The Bergen County police observed early in the evening that there had been no congestion, but unofficial participants noted that traffic moved slowly. There were no accidents to mar the carnival spirit, and the drivers considered the trip over the bridge worth a little wait.

Some confusion was caused last night at the New Jersey side of the bridge where many motorists were unable to find the approach. The State Highway which will serve as the approach on the New Jersey side has not yet been completed and the county roads now being used, motorists say, are not adequately marked. Many who were unable to find them turned back and came to New York via ferries or the Holland Tunnel.

The carnival spirit perhaps best described the day as a whole. It was a sunlit, and later a moonlit, affair of brightness. Washington Heights celebrated with flags and electric lights that bade "Jerseyites" welcome. On the other side also flags were flying, and the sad, mum-

Continued on Page Three.

Nation's Golf Clubs Get Plea To Raise Funds for Jobless

Through its president, H. H. Ramsay, the United States Golf Association, golf's ruling body in this country, has asked the golf clubs of the country to help swell the unemployment-relief resources. A letter has gone out to State, sectional and district associations requesting that all clubs under their jurisdiction conduct one-day competitions with nominal entry fees, which are to be turned over, to some local relief fund.

"In wartime, golf clubs through competitions of this kind gave substantial amounts to various relief agencies," says the letter. "The emergency is even greater at the present time, and we believe that the golfers of the country are willing to help now as they have in the past."

The letter emphasized that the aim was not to raise a national fund, but to help local agencies.

HIGH TARIFF CALLED CERTAIN IN BRITAIN

Conservatives Expect to Win Big Commons Majority in Election Tomorrow.

LLOYD GEORGE SEES TRAP

Tory Politicians Avoid Talk of Rise in Trade and Drop in Unemployment Figures.

By CHARLES A. SELDEN.

Wireless to THE NEW YORK TIMES.

LONDON, Oct. 25.—After three weeks of recriminations, reiterations of generalities and evasion of what they really have in mind, British politicians will end their parliamentary election campaigning tomorrow. On Tuesday the people will cast the votes which above everything else are going to determine whether Great Britain will join the ranks of the high tariff countries of the world.

In all probability, Britain will get a high tariff, because a victory of the National Government now seems assured by a sufficient majority in the House of Commons to enable it to throw overboard the Liberal free trade adherents and become an undisguised government with power to put into effect a policy of protection.

Premier MacDonald, Socialist ally of the Conservatives in the present situation, hopes nothing of the sort is going to happen. He says that "if there is any party manoeuvring to get a tariff for partisan purposes, I am not their man." But he is relying on the good faith of Stanley Baldwin, Conservative leader, who, it is asserted, will be unable to control his party on the tariff question.

Followers Press Baldwin.

Neville Chamberlain and Lord Beaverbrook are the real leaders of the tariff wing of the Conservative party, and to them and their followers Mr. Baldwin does not move fast enough. Mr. Baldwin needs a vote of confidence from his party so frequently that the existence of that confidence never can be taken for granted.

The evasion of the tariff question by the Conservatives and the almost complete ignoring of the gold standard issue, with the resulting improvement in British industry, by all parties has made the campaign remarkable. The silence on the tariff issue by all advocates except the irrepressibles like Mr. Chamberlain, Lord Beaverbrook and L. S. Amery is understandable, because it is necessary to retain Liberal support until after the election.

The National Government's official appeal to the voters is for "a free hand to impose tariffs for the country's economic rehabilitation." So far as the Conservative element of the coalition, which means 90 per

Continued on Page Seven.

10,000 See Broker Pilot Killed in Stunt; Spectator at Air Show Fatally Injured

More than 10,000 visitors to the closing day's program yesterday of the Jersey City air races for the Emergency Unemployment Relief Fund witnessed two accidents. Harry E. R. Hall, sportsman pilot and broker, crashed into a house in Jersey City and was killed as he was doing stunts in his special racing plane. Samuel Lang, 19 years old, of 560 East 179th Street, was struck by the whirling propeller of a taxiing airplane. He died early this morning in Jersey City Medical Centre.

Hall was not on the regular program, but volunteered to give an exhibition. Officials of the races cautioned him against doing stunts in his tiny and unstable craft. After about ten minutes of screaming dives and zooms he climbed vertically about a half mile from the field, when the plane suddenly dropped off in what is known as an inverted spin. Half over on its back it spun earthward so fast that the pilot had no chance to do more than shut off the fuel and ignition before it struck. The spinning motion wedged him into the cramped cockpit and he could not get clear to use his parachute.

The falling plane struck an unoccupied house at 289 Winfield Street, Jersey City, and caromed off the house next door before it splintered in the rear of the first house. Hall was dead when the first persons arrived. He lived at 444 East Fifty-seventh Street with his wife and two children. He was a partner in the brokerage firm of Stevens & Legg of 25 Broad Street and a member of several clubs.

In the excitement which followed the accident Clyde E. Pangborn prevented a stampede of the 10,000 visitors by rushing to a small biplane, taking it aloft and diverting the attention of the throng with a series of hair-raising stunts until order could be restored by the police.

PARIS SEES MUCH GAINED

Joint Statement Is Taken as Assurance Against Misunderstandings.

ENCOURAGED OVER FINANCE

But Some Circles Are Puzzled by the Reference to 1932 Arms Conference.

STRENGTH IN CHAMBER SEEN

French Observers in Washington Note Three Tangible Results in Premier's Favor.

By P. J. PHILIP.

Special Cable to THE NEW YORK TIMES.

PARIS, Oct. 26.—Everything that could reasonably be hoped for from Premier Laval's short visit to Washington has been accomplished, according to French opinion. What was sought was the establishment of respect by each country for the other's point of view, and it is felt this has been achieved. Beyond that what was sought was an outline of the possibilities of future collaboration, and this also has been obtained.

Although the official statement issued from the White House is very general, it is sufficiently precise on some of the most important points to give reassurance here even to that section of French opinion which always has been excessively sensitive and suspicious.

On the negative side the statement certainly pleases French opinion. The statement that neither government has been in any way engaged in commitments was as essential for M. Laval as it may have been for President Hoover.

See Avoidance of Misunderstandings.

What, however, is by far the most gratifying feature of the statement from the French viewpoint is that it is read as justifying the expectation for the future that there will be an avoidance of such misunderstandings as happened last July when the Hoover moratorium was proposed. At that time it was felt here very strongly that Washington had shown a misconception of and disregard for the deep-rooted French sentiment for preservation of the legal form which augured ill for any possibility of cooperation.

These frank conversations at the White House, it is judged from the tone of the joint explanation and from other circumstances, have changed that situation. It is felt that when France speaks at the other end of the transatlantic telephone she will now be understood in Washington and her preferences will not be treated merely as prejudices.

Of course, it is pointed out here, everything remains yet to be done. It is very well, according to this view, to declare in an official statement after a few hours' conversation that the heads of the two governments seek to restore economic stability, confidence and stable exchange values. It is equally well to declare a firm intention of maintaining the gold standard.

Cite Warnings Not Heeded.

Those here who are most in agreement with the heads of the two governments in hoping for these things are inclined to add that it would be well, perhaps, if both governments, in earnest of their hope, should pay attention to the reports and recommendations of such bodies as the economic conference of the League of Nations, the International Chamber of Commerce and others who for years have been warning and preaching and who for the most part have been treated with little attention.

Some puzzling is being done about just what is meant by the paragraph with the regard to next year's disarmament conference and the great occasion which it offers for the solid and durable organization of peace. In view of the attitude taken by M. Laval in his first speech in New York these sentences are being very variously construed. Perhaps, it is felt by some, they are best viewed rather as a pious wish than as indicating any program.

Le Temps, dealing with the results of the conversations tonight before the contents of the official statement were known on this side, said: "What is of the greatest importance is that the Washington Government now knows clearly what

Continued on Page Fourteen.

Joint Statement on the Conference Issued by President and Premier

World's Economic Situation Canvassed in the Frankest Manner, It Is Stated—"Real Progress" Made Toward Providing Means to Speed Recovery From Depression.

Special to The New York Times.

WASHINGTON, Oct. 25.—The joint statement issued by President Hoover and Premier Laval at the White House this evening reads as follows:

Oct. 25, 1931.

A JOINT STATEMENT BY THE PRESIDENT OF THE UNITED STATES AND THE PRESIDENT OF THE COUNCIL OF MINISTERS OF FRANCE.

The traditional friendship between the United States and France, the absence of all controversy between our two governments, a record of many events in collaboration toward the peace of the world, embracing among its recent phases the adoption of the Kellogg-Briand pact, render it possible and opportune for the representatives of our governments to explore every aspect of the many problems in which we are mutually interested.

Indeed, the duty of statesmen is not to overlook any means of practical cooperation for the common good. This is particularly true at a time when the world looks for leadership in relief from a depression which reaches into countless homes in every land. Relations of mutual confidence between governments have the most important bearing upon speeding the recovery which we seek. We have engaged upon that mission with entire frankness. We have made real progress.

We canvassed the economic situation in the world, the trends in international relations bearing upon it; problems of the forthcoming conference for limitation and reduction of armaments; the effect of the depression on payments under intergovernmental debts; the stabilization of international exchanges and other financial and economic subjects.

An informal and cordial discussion has served to outline with greater precision the nature of the problems. It has not been the purpose of either of us to engage in commitments binding our governments, but rather, through development of fact, to enable each country to act more effectively in its own field.

It is our joint purpose that the conference for limitation of armaments will not fail to take advantage of the great opportunity which presents itself, and that it will be capable of meeting what is in reality its true mission—that is, the organization of firm foundation of permanent peace.

In so far as intergovernmental obligations are concerned, we recognize that prior to the expiration of the Hoover year of postponement some agreement regarding them may be necessary covering the period of business depression, as to the terms and conditions of which the two governments make all reservations. The initiative in this matter should be taken at an early date by the European powers principally concerned within the framework of the agreements existing prior to July 1, 1931.

Our especial emphasis has been upon the more important means through which the efforts of our governments could be exerted toward restoration of economic stability and confidence.

Particularly we are convinced of the importance of monetary stability as an essential factor in the restoration of normal economic life in the world, in which the maintenance of the gold standard in France and the United States will serve as a major influence.

It is our intent to continue to study methods for the maintenance of stability in international exchanges.

While in the short time at our disposal it has not been possible to formulate a definite program, we find that we view the nature of these financial and economic problems in the same light, and that this understanding on our part should serve to pave the way for helpful action by our respective governments.

THRONG HEARS DUCE DEMAND ARMS CUTS

"Tragic Bookkeeping of Debts" Bars World Recovery, He Says at Naples.

Wireless to THE NEW YORK TIMES.

NAPLES, Italy, Oct. 25.—Premier Benito Mussolini today fulfilled his promise to this city to address its population from the balcony of the prefect's palace, closing his two-days' visit amidst the most enthusiastic scenes. The city received him with unusual warmth and spontaneity and he was evidently pleased.

His action marked an epoch in the history of the city because it was the first occasion since the Fascist régime began that Il Duce has addressed the population of any city instead of the Fascists exclusively, also because today was the ninth anniversary of his last visit to Naples when he brought the Fascist army which a week later marched on Rome, thus beginning the revolution.

Long before Il Duce arrived from his yacht Aurora the vast Piazza del Plebiscito began to fill with characteristically gay Neapolitan crowds. The only delegation which was not from Naples city or the province or islands around was from Dalmatia on the Adriatic and it was given a place of honor opposite the damask-decked balcony from which Premier Mussolini spoke.

A colorful scene was made by deputations in black shirts, multi-colored seamen from the warships, airmen in full uniform, the famous Bersaglieri in their picturesque cock-feathered hats, hospital nurses in

Continued on Page Ten.

HOOVER DEPLORES HUGE ARMS SPENDING

War Fears Seem "Incredible" After World's Experience, He Tells Methodists.

Special to The New York Times.

WASHINGTON, Oct. 25.—In a radio address from the White House to the Methodist Ecumenical Congress in Atlanta, President Hoover this afternoon called upon the Methodist religious leaders "to unite with all other lovers of good will and followers of the prince of peace for the making of human brotherhood, in which the peace of God shall prevail in the lives of men."

The President said that it seemed "strange and incredible that after all the centuries of man's experience with war we still have to discuss it and argue against it."

"It seems even more strange that with all the crushing burdens resting upon every nation because of wars we still make progress against them at snail's pace," the President continued. "The nations groan under taxation. People in all lands suffer daily from economic depression. Governments are perplexed—and yet we go on using incalculable sums in evident dread of those that may come upon us."

Mr. Hoover deplored "the kinds of evil now rampant in all lands" not only as "a menace to government," but also as "destructive to all that

Continued on Page Five.

WHITE HOUSE TALKS END

German Capacity to Pay Will Be Re-examined Under Young Plan.

WAR DEBT MOVE BY US NEXT

Premier Reveals That France Acted to Halt Flow of Gold From New York.

CLINGS TO ARMAMENT VIEW

In Farewell Statement at Capital He Sees Renewal of Bonds of Friendship.

By RICHARD V. OULAHAN.

Special to The New York Times.

WASHINGTON, Oct. 25.—The practical outcome of the three days of conversation between President Hoover and Pierre Laval, Premier of France, was an agreement on certain measures designed to assist the world toward its recovery from economic and financial depression.

A joint statement issued by the President and the Premier late this afternoon indicated the character of some of the conclusions reported, but was not illuminating with reference to them and wholly failed to mention other tentative understandings which resulted from the White House conference.

Among the things accomplished were the assurance by Premier Laval that abnormal movements of gold from New York would be stopped and that re-examination of Germany's capacity to pay reparations should be made under the existing provisions of the Young Plan, with the United States deferring action on a survey of European debts to this government to determine the capacity of debtor nations to pay until after a Young Plan committee had reported on Germany's financial position.

Need of Gold Standard Stressed.

In a cautious way, the joint statement made known that President Hoover and Premier Laval had determined that their two governments should stand together in the maintenance of the gold standard.

The statement stressed the necessity of establishing relations of mutual confidence between governments, listed the subjects canvassed, contained a brief and rather colorless expression of hope that next year's armament conference at Geneva would develop a firm foundation of permanent peace, suggested a reexamination of intergovernmental debts prior to the expiration of the Hoover moratorium year on June 30, 1932, stressed the necessity of maintaining the gold standard of France and the United States, and that the two governments should exert their efforts to restore economic stability and confidence. It concluded with an expression that the understandings effected "should serve to pave the way for helpful action by our respective governments."

Understandings Are Far-Reaching.

The understandings reached by the President and the Premier were of a character more far-reaching than the joint communiqué indicates. It was agreed at the outset of the conversations that the cornerstone of the discussions should be the instability, both economic and political, of Central Europe.

Nowhere in the conversation did the United States advance any suggestion for a settlement of political problems. Such problems were discussed at great length on the part of Premier Laval, with President Hoover and Secretary Stimson stressing that we had no concern in the political affairs of Europe.

From the political standpoint it was made clear early in the first day's conference on Friday that a security pact between France and the United States, or even a consultative pact, was out of the question.

Premier Laval recognized that there was no prospect whatsoever that the United States Government would become a party to a security pact, and it was evident that in outlining his idea of a consultative pact he coupled the outline with conditions which obviously were not acceptable to the President and the Secretary of State.

Intimate details disclosed tonight to THE NEW YORK TIMES correspondent show that the following were

Continued on Page Fourteen.

"All the News That's Fit to Print."

The New York Times.

LATE CITY EDITION

THE WEATHER—Cloudy today; tomorrow cloudy, rain in afternoon or at night. Temperatures yesterday—Max. 31, min. 26. U. S. Weather Forecast—See next to last page.

VOL. LXXXI....No. 26,983. ****+ NEW YORK, THURSDAY, DECEMBER 10, 1931. TWO CENTS In New York City | THREE CENTS Within 200 Miles | FOUR CENTS Elsewhere Except 7th and 8th Postal Zones

MELLON ASKS BROAD RISE IN INCOME TAX, ALSO LEVIES ON AUTOS, RADIOS, CHECKS; DEMOCRATS VOICE SHARP OPPOSITION

NOBEL PEACE PRIZE TO GO TO DR. BUTLER AND JANE ADDAMS

Board in Oslo Will Announce Awards Today, Consul Here Reveals.

$40,000 WILL BE SHARED

He Heads Carnegie Foundation and She the Women's League for Peace and Freedom.

MISS ADDAMS IN HOSPITAL

She Enters Johns-Hopkins for Examination Today and for a Possible Operation.

Wilhelm Thorleif von Munthe af Morgenstierne, the Norwegian Consul General in New York, said last night that he had been authorized by his government to announce for this morning's newspapers that Dr. Nicholas Murray Butler, president of Columbia University, and Miss Jane Addams of Chicago would be named the joint winners of the 1931 Nobel Peace Prize today.

Consul General Morgenstierne said the announcement would be made in Oslo at 1 P. M. (8 A. M. New York time).

News Expected in Oslo.

Special Cable to THE NEW YORK TIMES.

OSLO, Norway, Dec. 9.—The belief was expressed here tonight that the Nobel Peace Prize for 1931 would be awarded jointly to Dr. Nicholas Murray Butler and Jane Addams when the committee announces its decision tomorrow afternoon.

For several years past the Women's International League for Peace and Freedom and the League of Nations have submitted the name of Miss Addams for the award and on each occasion the League has been officially forewarned of the committee's rejection. This time, however, the League's suggestion evoked no reply and on the eve of announcing the prize friends of the head of Chicago's Hull House consider this as indicative of her nomination.

Oslo Officials Silent.

OSLO, Norway, Dec. 9 (AP).—The Nobel Peace Prize will be formally awarded tomorrow at the Nobel Institute here.

Miss Jane Addams, Chicago social worker, and Dr. Nicholas Murray Butler, president of Columbia University, New York, have been mentioned as likely recipients of the prize. Officials declined to discuss the matter, however, prior to their formal announcement.

Dr. Butler Active for Peace.

Dr. Nicholas Murray Butler, who already holds many distinctions conferred on him by foreign governments, has been one of the world's active leaders in the advancement of the ideals of peace. He is credited with persuading the late Andrew Carnegie to establish the peace foundation that bears Carnegie's name. Also, he is credited with a large share in arousing public opinion in this country in favor of the Briand proposals that led to the creation of the Kellogg-Briand pact outlawing war.

Dr. Butler's advocacy of world peace through international cooperation long antedated the World War. As far back as 1907 he was chairman of the Lake Mohonk Conference for International Arbitration. At the time of the World War he contributed to THE NEW YORK TIMES a series of anonymous articles, signed "Cosmos," on "The Basis of a Durable Peace," which attracted world-wide attention and were translated into several foreign languages.

He vigorously supported this country's participation in the World War, and took strong measures against unpatriotic tendencies that appeared in certain sections of the Columbia faculty and student body.

Criticized His Own Party.

As president of the Carnegie Endowment for International Peace and president of the American Board of Conciliation Internationale, Dr. Butler took a stand, both in speeches and in written papers on world peace that brought him into conflict with the dominant leadership of the Republican party in post-war days. Moreover, he consistently advocated international cooperation as a substitute for isolation in American foreign policy.

At one time he carried his enthusiasm for world peace into a warm controversy with Whitney Warren, the architect, concerning the inscription on the new library for the University of Louvain, which Whitney designed. Dr. Butler opposed the famous inscription, "Destroyed by Teu-

Continued on Page Three.

French Population 41,835,000; Foreigners Show 400,000 Gain

Special Cable to THE NEW YORK TIMES.

PARIS, Dec. 9.—The first figures from the recent French census show an increase of 400,000 foreigners since 1926 out of a total rise in population of 1,100,000.

The country's total is now 41,835,000, of which 2,891,000 are foreigners.

The world-wide trend from the farms to the cities is repeated here, as there was a sharp drop in the districts where the population is predominantly agricultural. However, as in the United States, the depression is tending to modify the flow.

M'DONALD CALLS FOR AN ECONOMIC PARLEY

International Conference Will Follow Report of Experts at Basle, He Says.

DEFERS STABILIZING POUND

He Tells Commons Such Action Would Be "Madness" Now—Battles Laborite Censure.

By CHARLES A. SELDEN.

Special Cable to THE NEW YORK TIMES.

LONDON, Dec. 9.—Prime Minister MacDonald told the House of Commons tonight it would be sheer madness to attempt to declare a permanent value for sterling before there was a settlement of the international situation which controlled exchange values. He said there would be an international conference after the experts now sitting at Basle had made their report.

"We regret the delay in bringing the nations together at a conference table to settle the question of international debts that lies at the basis of our currency position," the Prime Minister said, "but we are convinced that any move to hasten the matter on our own initiative would be fruitless. But we are sure the able experts now sitting at Basle are fully aware of the urgency of their task and will produce a report with the greatest expedition possible.

"Thereafter a conference of governments will be held, and in the opinion of this government immediate action should be taken after the report of the experts is received. That conference must approach its task in a spirit of realism, examine all the facts and reach an agreement not merely to tide over the difficulties temporarily but to link the whole world in a hopeful effort."

Labor Asks No-Confidence Vote.

This statement by the Premier was the most internationally significant remark in the course of an all-day debate on a motion of lack of confidence in the National Government presented by the Labor Opposition.

Labor leaders were forced to play a very inconspicuous part in supporting their own motion, because the Conservative critics of the government ran away with the debate, using it as an opportunity for expressing their regret that the MacDonald Cabinet had not produced an immediate general tariff program. This group of Conservatives, led by L. S. Amery and Sir Henry Page Croft, of course, will not support the motion of censure when the vote is taken tomorrow, but Mr. Amery warned the government that if a tariff were not forthcoming by February "confidence in the government would be lost beyond recovery."

The Labor motion was as follows: "That, in view of the approaching Winter and the distress prevailing in this country, this House regrets the failure of the government to take any effective steps to deal with the currency exchange situation, the development of international trade and to produce any plan dealing with the position of those for whom normal employment is unavailable or with the problem of high rents now pressing a large proportion of the population."

Labor Leader Demands Action.

Sir Stafford Cripps, who opened the debate for Labor, said the government had been chosen to take quick and decisive action to save the pound, but since the election the pound had gone lower and lower, and unless the government took constructive action soon there would be no financial confidence left. He declared the Labor Opposition believed it would be fatal to return to the gold standard but that there should be currency managed by the government instead of by banks and there should be an international agreement with as many countries as would conform.

Referring to the currency problem, Premier MacDonald said in reply that the government had been continually trying to get advice to discover the best opinion on the subject.

"But," he continued, "our first difficulty is that we can't get two or three men together who hold the same views on the matter. We do

Continued on Page Five.

QUEENS POLICE HEAD UNABLE TO EXPLAIN $35,596 DEPOSITS

Kelly, Mullarkey's Superior, Also Admits Not Being 'Frank' on Brokerage Deals.

URGED HUNTED AIDE TO QUIT

But Denies Knowing of Liquor Ring or Where He Got His Own Cash in 7-Year Period.

FISH WARNS ON INQUIRY

Tells Macy He Will Oppose a New Inquiry if "Higher Ups" Are Not Indicted by Feb. 1.

Deputy Chief Inspector Thomas J. Kelly, in command of the police in the borough of Queens, had bank deposits of $35,596.95 in excess of his salary from Jan. 1, 1925, to Oct. 1, 1931, according to testimony yesterday before the Hofstadter legislative committee. He was unable to explain the source of the money.

Inspector Kelly, described during the preceding day's testimony as one who "could not be touched," proved to be equally hazy regarding his brokerage accounts. The inspector at first could recall only having brokerage accounts with Bamberger & Co., but later admitted transactions with other houses, although he continued to dispute some of the items.

The bank deposits of Inspector Kelly and his wife, Mrs. Ellen M. Kelly, totaled $70,153.59 for the period and of this amount $12,562 was in cash. Inspector Kelly had no recollection of the origin of these cash deposits and could not tell how he happened to deposit $35,596 more than his salary.

"I don't know," he said, when pressed for an explanation by Samuel Seabury, counsel of the committee. I can't figure out where I got $35,000 myself or where it came from.".

Fish Demands Results by Feb. 1.

Republican opposition to the Hofstadter committee inquiry, as conducted by Mr. Seabury, came into the open in Washington when Representative Hamilton Fish Jr. of the Twenty-sixth Congressional District told W. Kingsland Macy, Republican State chairman and sponsor of the investigation, that the inquiry should result in the indictment of some "higher-ups" or be discontinued by Feb. 1. Mr. Fish, who represents Putnam, Dutchess and Orange Counties, declared that the Assemblymen of his district had the same opinion and would not vote for another appropriation for the committee unless results were obtained.

The City Administration struck back at Mr. Seabury's investigation when James A. Higgins, Commissioner of Accounts, issued subpoenas for Oren Herwitz, one of the assistant counsel on Mr. Seabury's staff, and William T. Sterling, an accountant of the committee, to appear before him this afternoon at 2:30 for questioning about the alleged payroll padding in the disbursement of the Richmond unemployment relief fund. A subpoena also was issued for Senator Samuel H. Hofstadter, chairman of the committee, requiring him to produce the records needed for the completion of Commissioner Higgins's investigation which are now in the committee's possession.

Kerrigan and Higgins Confer.

Mr. Higgins's decision to subpoena Messrs. Herwitz and Sterling followed a conference with Charles F. Kerrigan, assistant to the Mayor, who has been assisting Mr. Higgins in investigation of Mr. Seabury's accusation that payees of 123 checks drawn during the first week in June could not be found in the list of registrants for unemployment relief.

"We have discovered that the charges that there were 'phantom' workers on the emergency unemployment payrolls in Richmond County are absolutely without foundation," Mr. Kerrigan said. "Every one of the 123 employes named in Mr. Seabury's list has been checked. Every one of the workers has been accounted for and every one performed work for the money he received."

Mr. Kerrigan said that all but three of the 123 persons on the list has been examined and that of these three two were ill and one at work out of the city.

Mr. Seabury had no comment to make, but it was reported that he was willing to give Commissioner Higgins information to the effect that the 123 names did not appear on the registrants' cards turned over to him by the Department of Public Welfare.

Mr. Seabury was informed that Burton W. Wilson, friend of Russell T. Sherwood, personal accountant of

Continued on Page Eleven.

British Exports Show Decline Despite Gold Basis Suspension

Special Cable to THE NEW YORK TIMES.

LONDON, Dec. 9.—There has been no appreciable gain in the British overseas trade since the suspension of the gold standard, according to preliminary figures on imports and exports for November issued tonight.

The value of imports totaled £83,281,000 [the pound is worth about $3.30 at the present rate of exchange], an increase of £2,546,000 over October, while the value of exports totaled £31,863,000, a decline of about £1,000,000. During August, the last month Britain was on the gold basis, exports were valued at £29,136,000 [when the pound was valued at $4.86⅝].

1,200 IN FIRE PANIC IN SUBWAY; 3 HURT

Fight to Reach Doors, Trampling Women and Children in Smoke-Filled Train.

GUARDS CHECK STRUGGLE

Windows Smashed as Many Try to Leap in Mishap at 110th Street and Lenox Avenue.

Twelve hundred passengers of a Seventh Avenue-Bronx Park subway express became panic-stricken at 7 o'clock last night when a short circuit in the control box filled the ten cars with smoke and extinguished all but the emergency lights on the train. The short circuit occurred as the train was leaving the station at 110th Street and Lenox Avenue.

Fighting, pushing and screaming, the passengers trampled women and children in their attempts to open the doors and windows and reach the station platform. Only prompt action by train guards and station attendants in opening the doors confined the list of those requiring medical treatment to three.

The short circuit ignited the contact shoe extending beneath the first car and flames appeared at the windows and seemed to be feeding on the sides of the car. The coach had passed beyond the platform limits and so the guards were unable to open its doors. Passengers were compelled to make their way to rear cars and thence to the platform.

Choking with the acrid fumes of burning insulation, half-blinded by smoke and fearful of being trapped in the train, passengers broke windows with their umbrellas and many were restrained with difficulty from flinging themselves through the jagged frames. Scarcely an occupant of the first two cars escaped unbruised or with clothing intact. Dozens of hats and scarfs were found in the cars after their owners had escaped.

Several women became hysterical and blows were exchanged by men as the excited crowd milled about on the platform. Patrolmen Necas, Armstrong and Connelly of the West 123d Street station formed a flying wedge which subdued the combatants and cleared the stairs leading to the street.

Dr. Moorehead of Harlem Hospital established a first-aid station in a near-by drug store to treat the injured. Most of the passengers refused medical aid although several

Continued on Page Two.

1924 REVENUE ACT REVIVED

Mellon Program Restores Old Rate Rather Than Trying New Taxes.

'LIMIT' TO DRAIN ON PUBLIC

Income Tax, Starting at 2% and With 40% Top, Would Be Retroactive to This Year.

BURDEN ON ESTATES LARGE

Postal Rate Boost, Recovery of Foreign Debt Sums, Branch Bank Plan in His Proposals.

Special to The New York Times.

WASHINGTON, Dec. 9.—Painting a gloomy picture of official finances and admitting that the limit of diversion of funds from private employment to governmental use is being approached, Secretary Mellon today recommended to Congress far-reaching increases in individual, corporation and other taxes, as well as urging the enactment of legislation providing for new excise assessments on automobiles, radios and other articles.

Among the outstanding recommendations were those for increases in the normal tax rates from 1½, 3 and 5 per cent as contained in the 1928 revenue act, to 2, 4 and 6 per cent; a reduction of the exemption for single individuals from $1,500 to $1,000 and for married individuals or heads of households from $3,500 to $2,500; an increase in the surtax on incomes over $10,000 from 1 to 20 per cent with the maximum on incomes over $100,000 to 1 to 40 per cent, with the maximum on incomes over $500,000; an increase from 12 to 12½ per cent in the corporation tax rate. Income tax rates were applicable to incomes of the calendar year 1931.

Would Extend Admissions Tax.

Secretary Mellon recommended that the 10 per cent admissions tax should apply to tickets costing more than 10 cents as contrasted with $3 under the present law. He advocated an increase of one-sixth on all tobacco products except cigars. There would be a 5, 3 and 2½ per cent tax, respectively, on manufacturers' sales of automobiles, trucks and accessories, and a 5 per cent tax on manufacturers' sales of radio and phonograph equipment and accessories. Other taxes proposed included:

An increase of 1 per cent in the existing stamp tax upon sales or transfers of capital stock; a stamp tax on conveyances of realty of 50 cents for each $500 of value in excess of $100; a stamp tax of 2 cents on each check and draft; and a tax on telephone,

Continued on Page Seventeen.

THE MELLON TAX PROPOSALS

Special to The New York Times.

WASHINGTON, Dec. 9.—Secretary Mellon's proposals for tax increases were as follows:

Miscellaneous Taxes

Tax.	Present.	Proposed.
Amusement admissions (10 per cent)....	Over $3	Over 10 cents
Passenger automobiles	No tax	5 per cent
Automobile trucks	No tax	3 per cent
Tires and accessories	No tax	2½ per cent
Radios and phonographs	No tax	5 per cent
Checks and drafts	No tax	2 cents each
Telephone, telegraph and cable messages (14 to 50 cents)....................	No tax	5 cents each
Telephone, telegraph and cable messages (over 50 cents)	No tax	10 cents each
Realty conveyances	No tax	50 cents per $500 over $100

Tobacco Products—Tax to be increased by 16 2-3 per cent over present.

Transfer Stamp Tax or Capital Stock Sale—Increase of 1 per cent over present rates.

Estate Tax Rates—A super tax up to a maximum of 5 per cent over the present rates.

Corporation Tax Rates

The net incomes will be taxed 12½ per cent instead of the present 12 per cent. Exemptions on incomes of $25,000 will be eliminated and a provision will be made for deducting gifts to the idle, where there are presently no provisions for deductions.

Income Tax

	Taxable Income.	Present.	Proposed.
Married, one dependent.......	$3,000	None	$1.50
Married, one dependent.......	4,000	$1.13	16.50
Married, one dependent.......	5,000	12.38	31.50
Married, one dependent.......	10,000	92.25	153.00
Married, one dependent.......	15,000	336.25	455.75
Married, one dependent.......	20,000	706.25	869.50
Married, one dependent.......	25,000	1,198.75	1,405.75
Married, one dependent.......	50,000	4,573.75	5,549.50
Married, one dependent.......	100,000	15,753.75	22,029.50
Married, one dependent.......	500,000	115,753.75	199,029.50
Single, no dependent..........	2,000	5.63	15.00
Single, no dependent..........	3,000	16.88	30.00
Single, no dependent..........	4,000	28.13	45.00
Single, no dependent..........	5,000	39.38	60.00
Single, no dependent..........	10,000	153.75	225.00
Single, no dependent..........	15,000	426.25	541.25
Single, no dependent..........	20,000	796.25	955.00
Single, no dependent..........	25,000	1,288.75	1,491.25
Single, no dependent..........	50,000	4,663.75	5,635.00
Single, no dependent..........	100,000	15,843.75	22,115.00
Single, no dependent..........	500,000	115,843.75	199,115.00

Personal Exemption

	Present.	Proposed.
Single	$1,500	$1,000
Married	3,500	2,500
Each dependent	400	400

Normal Tax Rates.

	Present.	Proposed.
First $4,000..........................	1½ per cent	2 per cent
Second $4,000.........................	3 per cent	4 per cent
Above $8,000..........................	5 per cent	6 per cent

Surtaxes.

The present rates of 1 per cent on net incomes of $10,000 to $14,000 and 2 per cent plus $40 on net incomes of $14,000 to $16,000 would remain unchanged. Increases would begin with net incomes of $24,000 to $28,000, on which surtax of 7 per cent and $440 would be collected.

SENATE AGAIN FAILS TO BREAK DEADLOCK

Insurgent Lines Hold Against Moses Through Four Ballots for President Pro Tem.

Special to The New York Times.

WASHINGTON, Dec. 9.—The Senate remained deadlocked and unable to organize at the end of the second day of the new session after four roll-calls had failed to end the conflict begun yesterday in attempting to elect a president pro tempore.

The office in itself is of comparatively little importance, but the vote determines control of the Senate, and the insurgent Republicans did not swerve either toward Republicans or Democrats in today's balloting. In fact, they gained one vote through the accession of Senator Brookhart of Iowa, acknowledged member of the insurgent group but supporter in yesterday's balloting of Senator Moses of New Hampshire, the Republican candidate.

The two leading candidates today, as yesterday, were Senator Pittman of Nevada, the Democratic nominee, who polled forty-three votes on each of the four ballots, and Senator Moses, who polled thirty-two votes on each.

The insurgent Republicans had fourteen votes, which they distributed among themselves, refusing either to support Senator Moses, who once termed this group "sons of the wild jackass," or to jeopardize their committee chairmanships and assignments by joining the Democrats in voting for Senator Pittman.

Conferences on the floor by Senator Watson of Indiana, Republican floor leader, and members of the insurgent group apparently availed nothing, for after the fourth ballot, on Senator Watson's motion, the session was adjourned.

The vote for a president pro-tempore will remain the first order of business of each succeeding day

Continued on Page Eighteen.

HOUSE DEMOCRATS ATTACK MESSAGE

Hoover's Record Is Target, but Republicans Cry "Dole" in 4-Hour Battle of Orators.

Special to The New York Times.

WASHINGTON, Dec. 9.—The Democrats opened an attack in the House today on President Hoover's message and his record, but if they expected the Republicans to let the President's deeds stand for themselves, they were disappointed, for the opposition answered their volleys, speech for speech. In the four hours of oratory the Democrats were hard pressed at times.

The first address was delivered by Representative Huddleston of Alabama, an advocate of outright Federal aid for the unemployed.

The Republicans immediately seized upon his "keynote" speech and had about saddled the advocacy of a Federal "dole" upon the Democrats, when Representative Bankhead, also of Alabama, deflecting attention from the message, chided the Republicans over the results of the last election and commented on the fate of those who had followed President Hoover.

But Mr. Bankhead made no attempt to outline a program for the Democrats. Representing that group of so-called "responsible" leaders who must initiate the tax and finance program of the new House, Mr. Bankhead announced that no program had been adopted by the majority.

"Any thoughtful man on that side or on this side," he said, "any man of long and practical political experience in the House, would not expect the Democratic majority, now in control of the House but not in control of the Senate, to hop up here, and, within two or three days after its organization, propose some concrete and definite formula of legislation for the whole session."

Representative Chindblom, Republican, of Illinois, pressed the Ala-

Continued on Page Eighteen.

PROPOSALS FACING A TEST

Democrats Forecast Move to Prepare Own Plan and Push It Through.

SILENCE KEPT ON DETAILS

Senators Robinson and Harrison Denounce Increasing Levy on This Year's Incomes.

LATTER FAVORS BOND ISSUE

Smoot Holds That Increases Will Be Inadequate Unless Business Improves.

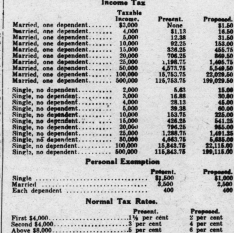

The text of the President's budget message is on Page 16.

By RICHARD V. OULAHAN.

Special to The New York Times.

WASHINGTON, Dec. 9.—The administration's comprehensive temporary tax increase plan for overcoming the deficit by July, 1934, submitted to the House of Representatives today as part of the annual report of the Secretary of the Treasury, is likely to be generally rewritten before it is sanctioned by Congress and sent to President Hoover for his approval.

This appraisal of the plan's ultimate fate at the hands of Congress is made on the basis of developments indicating that the Democrats would prepare one of their own, with the apparent assurance that they will be able to put it through the House, which they now dominate, and stand a fair chance of having it adopted by the Senate through a combination of Democrats and Progressive Republicans.

No inkling was given by Democratic Congressional leaders as to what their plan will provide. In its general outlines it will be left largely to the party's joint advisory committee of the Senate and the House, chosen Monday, whose main function is to preserve a solidarity of action between Democratic members of both branches of Congress. The details of rates and other provisions will be worked out by the Ways and Means Committee, where the legislation must originate.

Objections to Specific Points.

Enough appeared on the surface today, however, to make clear that certain features, at least, of the administration proposals are unacceptable to the Democratic leaders.

For example, both Senator Robinson of Arkansas, the party floor leader in the upper chamber, and Senator Harrison of Mississipi, the senior Democratic member of the Finance Committee, criticized Secretary Mellon's advocacy of applying the new taxes to incomes earned in the calendar year 1931.

Amplifying Senator Robinson's brief and rather cautious expression, Senator Harrison said that not only was the administration tax plan objectionable because of this retroactive feature, but he intimated that it was not acceptable to Democrats in regard to a considerable number of other provisions. He criticized the suggested taxes on bank checks, deeds and telephone and telegraph messages and hinted that the reduction of the exemptions on normal incomes and the taxes proposed for radios and automobiles, increased taxes on cigarettes and a revival of the wartime amusement tax were also objectionable.

Favors Borrowing in Part.

Without indicating that he spoke for his party brethren or merely for himself, Senator Harrison showed that he favored overcoming part of the treasury deficit by a bond issue. His statement was given out in typewritten form, and bore signs of careful preparation. He apparently spoke for his party, however, when he said:

"The Democrats in Congress will present their plan to balance the budget, the details of which will be worked out after thorough investigation and thorough conferences."

But while Senator Harrison may have been reflecting the views of his party in Congress, the party leadership in official capacity was silent as to what its course would be.

Continued on Page Sixteen.

Shot Through Window Kills Bride in Jersey As Prowler Is Sought in Similar Case Near By

Special to The New York Times.

WEST ORANGE, N. J., Dec. 9.—While police were investigating the firing of a .22-calibre bullet through a window of the living room of the home of J. C. Dorn at 9 Colony Drive West, a fashionable residential district of West Orange, tonight, a bullet was fired through the bathroom window of a house two doors away, fatally wounding Mrs. Grace Juliano, a bride of five months.

Mrs. Juliano, who is the wife of Joseph V. Juliano, a Newark furrier, and a daughter of John A. Moffitt, a conciliator of the Federal Department of Labor at Washington, was just preparing to take a bath when the shot was fired. Her husband, who was in the living room downstairs, heard the call, "I've been shot." He telephoned for an ambulance and she was rushed to the Orange Memorial Hospital, but died on the way.

Meanwhile the police at the Dorn home had received word of the shooting. They searched the vicinity, but could find no trace of any prowlers.

Mr. Dorn said that he was in the living room just after 9 o'clock when he heard the sharp report of a rifle, and a bullet crashed through one of the windows and went whistling across the room. He telephoned for the police at once.

They were just answering his call when the shooting at the Juliano home occurred. Mr. Juliano said he did not hear the report of the rifle, and the first warning he had that something was wrong was when his wife called to him. He said he ran first to the bathroom and examined the wound. The bullet had struck his wife in the back just as she was about to step into the tub. Apparently it had been fired from a slight rise of ground directly behind the house.

Mr. Juliano raced down stairs and telephoned for an ambulance. Then he went to the houses next door to summon aid. His calls attracted the attention of police in the Dorn home and they hurried to the Juliano home. They immediately began to search the grounds around the house and the land behind it. Flashlights were brought into play and neighbors joined the search. Although the hunt continued for several hours, no trace was found of the person who had done the shooting.

An inspection of the bathroom by the police disclosed that there was a curtain over the window. Police said that the person who did the shooting could not possibly have seen even a shadow in the bathroom and that he apparently was just firing at lighted windows. They said that the shooting must either have been the work of mischievous boys or a crazy person.

Mr. Juliano said that his wife was a prospective mother.

Andrew W. Mellon, the richest Secretary of the Treasury in American history.

Fiorello La Guardia was labor's spokesman in Congress.

Speaker of the House John Nance Garner who attacked Republican tax schemes and eventually helped remove Mellon from office.

The unemployed line up to register with the State Temporary Employment Relief Administration in New York City.

"All the News That's Fit to Print."

The New York Times.

LATE CITY EDITION

THE WEATHER—Cloudy today, probably rain tomorrow; little change in temperature.
Temperatures yesterday—Max. 44, min. 38.
U. S. Weather Forecast—See next to last page.

VOL. LXXXI....No. 26,992. NEW YORK, SATURDAY, DECEMBER 19, 1931. TWO CENTS In New York City | THREE CENTS Within 200 Miles | FOUR CENTS Elsewhere Except 7th and 8th Postal Zones

HOUSE VOTES MORATORIUM BY 317 TO 100; RECORDS OPPOSITION TO DEBT REVISION; LAMONT BELITTLES FOREIGN LOAN PERIL

'LEGS' DIAMOND SLAIN IN SLEEP AT ALBANY BY TWO ASSASSINS

Landlady, Awakened by Shots, Saw Pair Speed Away in an Automobile.

GANGSTER HAD LEFT PARTY

Deserted His Wife to Call on 'Kiki' Roberts, the Last to See Him.

LONG SOUGHT BY RIVALS

Four Previous Attempts Made on His Life—He Had Long Defeated the Law.

By MEYER BERGER.
Special to The New York Times.

ALBANY, Dec. 18.—Jack (Legs) Diamond, human ammunition dump for the underworld, was killed in a cheap rooming house at 67 Dove Street here this morning, a few minutes after he had dropped off in a drunken sleep, following celebration of his acquittal in Troy last night on a charge of kidnapping.

Three soft-nosed, .38 calibre bullets fired from a pistol held against the back of his head did the job. The gunmen left him lying on the bed with his arms at his side, his white face twisted in a dying leer. The position of the body indicated that one man held him while another did the shooting.

The police are inclined to believe two men were the assassins. Persons in the rooming house and a cobbler who lives next door saw a pair run out of the building after the shots were fired. Down the block a maroon sedan stood with motor purring. The men jumped into it and drove north.

Fifth Attempt Successful.

This was the fifth time that Diamond's enemies had tried to blow him out of the picture and they made certain that this attempt should be successful. The powder marks on his head and remarks overheard by the woman proprietor of the rooming house testified to the particular pains they had taken to complete their task.

One of the killers, as he pounded down the stairs after his companion, said something about being sure that Diamond was dead. He seemed to have some doubt about it. But the other, apparently the man who had fired the shot, four or five of them, retorted:

"Oh, hell! That's enough! Come on!"

Day was just breaking as the front door banged after them. They raced across the street, got into the maroon sedan and sped away with a roar. Not long afterward a patrolman in the main street in Saugerties saw a maroon car with two men in the front seat tear through the town at terrific speed. He took its license number and turned it over to the Albany police.

Many hours elapsed before the police and the District Attorney began to get anything like a clear picture of what had happened. They invaded quiet Dove Street in droves. After them came the crowds and eventually the street was blocked with cabs bringing new loads of curiosity seekers.

Late in the afternoon District Attorney John T. Delaney presented the story as he had assembled it after examining the hytserical Mrs. Diamond, Mrs. Laura Wood, the rooming house owner; Miss Ethel Smith, her sister; Pat Delehanty, who lives next door, and Jack Storey, the taxicab driver who drove Diamond home.

Ten days ago the gangster, his wife, his sister-in-law, Mrs. Edward Diamond, and her son, John, 10 years old, engaged three rooms on the second floor of the Dove Street boarding house. They represented themselves as "Mr. and Mrs. Kelly and relatives." It was not until a few days ago that Mrs. Wood learned who her clients really were.

Constant reference to "the trial at Troy" and a comparison with newspaper photographs betrayed their identity, but there was nothing for Mrs. Wood to do about it. Her lodgers were quiet and she had no real cause for complaint. Diamond, when he wanted to, could play the respectable gentleman in any boarding house. Away from his rackets, he had a pleasing personality.

His trial for the kidnapping of James Duncan ended just before 9 o'clock Thursday night when a jury in the County Court House in Troy returned a verdict of not guilty. The jury was out a little over five hours.

Mrs. Diamond fairly leaped over the rail to fly to her husband's arms. She kissed him, his sister-in-law kissed him and little Johnny Diamond, his nephew, embraced "Uncle Jack" and added his kisses. Accompanied by his relatives, his attorneys

Continued on Page Two.

Selfridge to Build World's Largest Store; £5,000,000 Project Shows Faith in London

Wireless to THE NEW YORK TIMES.

LONDON, Dec. 18.—H. Gordon Selfridge, the Anglo-American merchant who at one time was a member of the firm of Marshall Field & Co., and now is the owner of one of London's biggest stores, announced today that work would start Monday on an extension scheme which is expected to make his store the largest in the world.

The project will take eight years for completion and will involve the expenditure of about £5,000,000 (approximately $25,000,000 at par).

Mr. Selfridge has acquired the principal part of the block adjoining his store, and demolition of the buildings upon it will begin at once. He intends to place on this site two or three basements and a ground floor at the start, adding additional floors as required. It is hoped that the first section will be ready next Autumn.

Outlining his plans today, Mr. Selfridge emphasized that the undertaking was a gesture of confidence.

"At a time when pessimism is in the air, when the building of the great Cunarder has been abandoned, it is an indication of our own confidence in Britain, London and the British Empire to keep on developing," he declared. "London is not lacking in confidence for the future."

The white-haired merchant said more people were crowding his present store now and buying less than they did a year or two ago, but he hoped that the greater space would mean an increase in customers and receipts.

Asked if he were optimistic concerning speedy recovery from the world depression, Mr. Selfridge said:

"Frankly, I see no sign of any sunrise just yet. Germany is in a bad way. In France they are keeping the stores open on Sundays to try to do some business.

"In the United States they are bluer than we are. We are better off than most—better than most of us realize."

The News Chronicle, commenting editorially on Mr. Selfridge's announcement, said: "There is far too pronounced a tendency on the part of some British industrialists to sit down and moan about their difficulties. The courage and enterprise of Mr. Selfridge are in the best traditions of his great firm."

FREE MRS. DONNELLY WITHOUT A RANSOM

Kidnappers Notify Kansas City Police Chief to Pick Her Up With Chauffeur on Street.

"REALIZED THEIR MISTAKE"

Restored to Home Unharmed, She Tells of Seizure and Captivity in Hovel.

Special to The New York Times.

KANSAS CITY, Mo., Dec. 18.—Mrs. Nell Quinlan Donnelly is at home, extremely nervous from her thirty-four-hour ordeal as the hostage of kidnappers, but unharmed.

She was released voluntarily by her captors without the payment of any part of the $75,000 ransom demanded in notes written by her under threat that she would be blinded and that George Blair, her Negro chauffeur, would be killed unless the money was paid.

Mrs. Donnelly and Blair were held blindfolded in a shabby retreat, somewhere in Kansas within an hour's drive of Kansas City, from the time of the kidnapping at 6 o'clock Wednesday evening until they were released on Kansas Avenue, in Kansas City, Kan., at 4 o'clock this morning.

They had been led out of the hiding place into a motor car which bumped over country roads for perhaps forty-five minutes. As they were left on the street the gang leader told them that another car would be along soon to pick them up. They walked to the nearest lighted building, a small restaurant.

At about the same time the telephone in Police Chief Lewis M. Siegfried's office rang. He was told where the woman for whom he had been looking could be found. A hurried trip through the central industrial district into Kansas and Mrs. Donnelly was under the protection of the chief, who took her home to her husband, Paul F. Donnelly, and their adopted baby, David.

Fought Seizure by Gang.

Recounting the abduction today, Mrs. Donnelly said that when Blair drove her from the Donnelly Garment Company's plant to her home at 5,235 Oak Street, they were prevented from entering the driveway by a car parked at the entrance.

A man stepped from this car to Blair's side, placed a revolver against him and told him to move over. Two others then entered the Donnelly automobile, one in the front seat and one in the rear with Mrs. Donnelly.

When an attempt was made to place a sack over Mrs. Donnelly's head she screamed and fought her captor as the car, driven by the apparent leader, sped south to Fifty-fourth Street, west to Brookside Boulevard. Her lips were cut by the rough hand of the man who sought to stifle her screams. That explained the few blood spots found later in the abandoned car.

Mrs. Donelly said she gave up trying to escape when the car left brightly lighted Brookside Boulevard and turned west on Huntington Road. Later she and Blair were transferred to another car and taken to the small and isolated cottage into which filtered sounds of a rural neighborhood.

Mrs. Donnelly believed it was in Kansas, possibly near Bonner Springs. The journey required about an hour.

At the dictation of a "shrewd" man who, she said, "probably would make good in any legitimate business," Mrs. Donnelly wrote the ransom letter to James E. Taylor, her husband's

Continued on Page Eight.

JAPAN WARNED ANEW BY OUR AMBASSADOR

Forbes Acts on Stimson Order to Protest Against Further Invasion of Manchuria.

CHINCHOW DRIVE LIKELY

Tokyo Lifts Ban on Crossing Liao River to Permit Attacks on Bandits.

Special to The New York Times.

WASHINGTON, Dec. 18.—Renewed concern over the course of events in Manchuria has been expressed to the Japanese Foreign Office by W. Cameron Forbes, the American Ambassador in Tokyo. This fact was made known today following the announcement by the Tokyo War Office that it planned army operations west of the Liao River and in the direction of Chinchow.

A week ago, when the Council of the League of Nations had concluded its immediate consideration of the Manchurian question and after Secretary Stimson had expressed approval of what had been done to end the Sino-Japanese controversy and after President Hoover has discussed the Manchurian situation in his message to Congress on foreign affairs, a complete report of the American attitude was sent to Ambassador Forbes. He was authorized to utilize any of it in his discussions at the Foreign Office. No report from him on his conversations was made public by the State Department today.

Treaty Covers Chinchow Issue.

Should Chinchow be captured by Japan, there are excellent grounds for believing that serious consideration would be given by Secretary Stimson to invoking formally the Nine-Power treaty of 1922, which guarantees the territorial and administrative integrity of China.

This pact provides for an exchange of communications among the signatories in an emergency. It has frequently been mentioned during the diplomatic negotiations over Manchuria since September but never has been formally invoked because the League of Nations appealed for peace first in the name of the Kellogg-Briand anti-war treaty and then through applying the conciliation clause of the covenant of the League of Nations, and an international commission of inquiry was agreed upon.

That the United States has never lost sight of the Kellogg-Briand pact or the Nine-Power treaty was made clear when President Hoover in his foreign affairs message to Congress last week declared that the United States as a party to the two treaties had a "responsibility in maintaining the integrity of China and a direct interest with other nations in maintaining peace."

Japanese Conquest Expected.

Officials were of the opinion today that through the appointment as Chief of Staff of Prince Kanin, who was at the front throughout the Russo-Japanese War, and the rumored designation of General Joro Minami, Minister of War in the recent Wakatsuki Cabinet, as administrative chairman of Manchuria, a post which apparently will amount to a military governorship, the military party in Japan has consolidated its position and is prepared to pursue its aims in Manchuria. This situation appears to be evidenced by the announcement in Tokyo that Japanese troops would advance west of the Liao River.

The fall of Chinchow to Japan, in expert opinion here, would mean the definite isolation of Manchuria under

Continued on Page Thirteen.

CITY VOTES $5,000,000 FOR FAMILY RELIEF, FOOD, FUEL AND RENT

Board Circumvents Charter on Welfare Leaders' Pleas for Direct Aid to Homes.

MAYOR SCOFFS AT 'SCANDAL'

Replies to Berry Opposition by Voicing His Faith in Taylor as Fund Administrator.

80 OFFICES TO OPEN SOON

Will Receive Appeals for Orders on Stores—Hodson Says 100,000 of 250,000 in Want Are Aided.

Municipal history was made yesterday when the Board of Estimate appropriated $5,000,000 for home relief to help alleviate the effects of unemployment, which was referred to as "a major social calamity."

The board broke with its policy of refusing appropriations for home relief after hearing the pleas of Frank J. Taylor, Welfare Commissioner, and a group of officers of the leading private welfare agencies, who asserted that public and private relief funds would fall far short of meeting the needs of the army of destitute unemployed.

The board was enabled to circumvent the city charter provision against home relief by the Wicks bill, which permits such public relief in the form of food, shelter, light, fuel, clothing and medical attendance. Approximately 40 per cent of the disbursement made yesterday, or about $2,000,000, will be returned to the city by the State.

Following the board's action, to which only Frank J. Prial, Deputy Controller, dissented, Mr. Taylor announced that the Home Relief Bureau would be ready to function a week from Monday. This bureau, a central organization for the entire city with branches in the various boroughs, will be administered by the Department of Welfare, with the cooperation of a committee of the group on coordination of the Welfare Council. Central headquarters are at 10 East Thirty-fourth Street. An application bureau will be established in each of the eighty police precincts, but not in police stations.

Under the resolution adopted, the bulk of the funds would be made available in January, February and March, when the need is expected to be greatest. The money is to be allocated as follows: December, $300,000; January, $1.200,000; February, $1.-200.000; March, $1.200.000; April, $800,000, and May, $300,000.

Mayor Scouts Fear of "Scandals."

Mr. Prial said he had voted in the negative at the request of Controller Berry and because of "scandals in the past." Mayor Walker, who presided, declared he had no apprehension of scandals, as "most scandals were in the headlines and based on unsupported charges." So long as Mr. Taylor is in charge of this work, "we can have the fullest confidence in the undertaking," the Mayor declared. Mr. Prial then said he had meant no reflection on the Welfare Commissioner.

Joseph V. McKee, president of the Board of Aldermen, in announcing he would vote in the affirmative, said he believed the city was facing "a major social calamity," and declared that those disbursing the funds had the faith and confidence of the administration. He wished, however, to dispel the idea that the city had opened its treasury for unlimited relief funds.

Mr. Taylor explained that the system under which the funds would be distributed would provide that the money be spent locally to assist storekeepers as well as the needy, who would receive food tickets. Agents of the Health, Police and Welfare De-

Continued on Page Twelve.

48,905 Fined for Parking Of 60,389 Arraigned in 1930

Of a total of 60,389 persons arraigned in the traffic courts of Manhattan, Brooklyn and the Bronx in 1930 for violations of the anti-parking regulations, 48,905 were convicted and fined; 10,301 received suspended sentences, while only 1,183 were discharged, Chief Magistrate James C. McDonald revealed yesterday.

The figures were given in a letter to W. J. L. Banham, president of the New York Board of Trade, Inc., who had written to Magistrate McDonald that it had been "freely and publicly intimated" that "laxity on the part of the magistrates" existed in dealing with this offense. Mr. Banham said yesterday that the figures showed that the magistrates actually were doing "excellent work," but asked why more summonses were not served by the police.

STOCKS UP SHARPLY; BONDS JOIN IN RALLY

Market Makes Broad Gains on Lamont Testimony on German Credits and on Rail Wage Move.

BANK SHARES LEAD ADVANCE

Bond Trading Double That of Normal Day—Wheat Rises 2 Cents, Cotton $1 a Bale.

A wave of buying enthusiasm swept over the security markets yesterday, producing the broadest recovery in more than two months. Leading issues on the New York Stock Exchange advanced sensationally, adding from 2 to 15 points to their open-market value, while bond prices rose 1 to 7 points. The gains in bank stocks were spectacular. Wheat improved its position about 2 cents a bushel and cotton $1 a bale.

As soon as the upward movement of stocks became clearly defined buying orders poured into the bond market, with buyers favoring the domestic issues, notably rails. The buying gained great momentum during the late afternoon, with the result that the losses from Monday to Thursday, inclusive, were wiped out, according to THE NEW YORK TIMES compilation of averages. The same was also true of foreign loans, but measured in points the average recovery was far less than in the case of domestic corporation issues.

Concerted support was in evidence in all sections of the domestic list with the exception of the United States Government group, which closed irregularly lower, with six of the eleven active issues making new lows for the year. This was generally attributed to the greater opportunities for large profits in corporation bonds, since government bond prices, at best, are slow moving. Transactions in bonds on the Stock Exchange yesterday exceeded $20,000,000, with $10,000,000 being considered as a normal day.

Rally Starts at Midday.

The rally started at midday after many stocks and bonds had moved into new low ground. Just what touched off the buying demonstration was not clear, but it coincided with the appearance of Thomas W. Lamont of J. P. Morgan & Co. before the Senate Finance Committee and his testimony that "the short-term German credits do not constitute a danger to the American banking system." His reassuring comments on the banking situation had a tonic effect on Wall Street sentiment.

The advance in the markets was also accompanied by reports that powerful financial interests had organized a pool to support the bond market. These reports were not confirmed, but they carried conviction for a time, especially among the speculative element. Traders with short commitments began to bid for stocks to cover their position and this did much to accelerate the ad-

Continued on Page Fifteen.

FINANCIER IS CONFIDENT

No Fear of Repudiation, Morgan Associate Tells Senate Committee.

PROFIT SOMETIMES SMALL

Advance to Austria Was Made as a Duty, He Says—Sees Great Help to Our Trade.

MITCHELL BACKS PRACTICE

National City Head Opposes Debt Cancellation, but Expects Some Scaling Down.

Special to The New York Times.

WASHINGTON, Dec. 18.—Stories that American banks were "loaded up" with foreign securities were denied by Thomas W. Lamont of J. P. Morgan & Co., a witness today before the Senate Finance Committee. Mr. Lamont termed "exaggerated" and "fantastic" such stories and declared especially that German short-term loans were not a danger to American banks.

With Charles E. Mitchell, president of the National City Bank and the National City Company, Mr. Lamont detailed to the committee the methods of floating foreign loans in this country; the "spread" between the sums paid for foreign securities and those received from investors here, by which the expenses and profit of the transaction are paid, and declared that such loans are of direct benefit to American trade.

Mr. Lamont said that in some instances the profit of his company was small and that its work in floating the loans was sometimes done in a spirit of doing a public duty.

Explaining the part the State Department plays in the negotiations for loans, he said that, since the time of President Harding, it had been the custom of a banking house considering a loan to notify the department of its intention. The department's approval always came, he said, in a "negative form."

Lamont for Aid to Railroads.

Mr. Lamont said that the firm of J. P. Morgan & Co. has dealt in foreign securities since 1920 to the extent of almost $2,000,000,000, which was held distinctly contradictory to the alarming reports in the last year.

Mr. Lamont testified that the largest holder of German short-term securities, a bank which he did not name, has $70,000,000 worth, "and there the bank resources are so large that these holdings are not even an occasion for comment."

Citing issues by Morgan & Co. since 1920 for twelve countries, Mr. Lamont testified that none of these had defaulted on interest payments and that out of combined issues of $1,807,578,000, $438,280,100 had been retired, despite provisions under which the bonds might have run for much longer periods.

"While I regard this question of foreign bond issues and its connection with foreign finance as undoubtedly important," Mr. Lamont testified, "we do not regard it as comparable with the domestic situation.

"I think that if we can address ourselves to certain phases of our domestic situation our foreign situation will in due course take care of itself."

In discussing domestic matters with committee members Mr. Lamont said that something must be done soon for the railroads if the "backbone" of domestic industry is to remain unimpaired.

The proposed revival of the War Finance Corporation might aid them, he testified, but such action "would have to come soon."

Allocations Accepted Voluntarily.

The house of Morgan, Mr. Lamont testified, since 1920 has issued securities for Argentina, Austria, Australia, Belgium, Canada, Chile, Cuba, France, Germany, Italy, Japan and Switzerland.

In most of these activities, Mr. Lamont said, Morgan & Co. had other associates. It did not sell the bonds direct to investors, but allocated them among banks which participated voluntarily—without coercion, he emphasized.

Obvious surprise was caused by Mr. Lamont's showing that seldom

Continued on Page Fourteen.

Hoover Holds 'Postponement' Better Word Than 'Moratorium'

Special to The New York Times.

WASHINGTON, Dec. 18.—President Hoover does not like the word "moratorium" as used in connection with the European debt situation.

He prefers the word "postponement," which, he thinks, more accurately describes his proposal before Congress.

The President's preference for "postponement" was disclosed at the White House breakfast conference this morning when he discussed the debt situation with Speaker Garner, Representatives Rainey and Snell, the majority and minority party chiefs, and other House leaders.

DEBT EXPERTS FAVOR LONGER MORATORIUM

Also Find German Railways Cannot Pay Unconditional Reparations Levy.

FRENCH MODERATION ASKED

British Note Shows Part of Loans Made to Germany Were Paid to France.

By LANSING WARREN.
Wireless to THE NEW YORK TIMES.

BASLE, Dec. 18.—Although Germany cannot hope for complete abolition of reparations, the situation demands urgent and permanent relief—these were two general conclusions becoming more substantially confirmed today among the experts of the Bank for International Settlements' advisory committee.

By the stipulations of the Young Plan, this committee cannot go beyond the suspension of the conditional payments and a recommendation for the prolongation of the Hoover moratorium, but statistical evidence which will be passed on to the governmental reparations conference in the report now being drafted would tend to indicate such a course.

The subcommittee under Otto Rydbeck today reported that the German railway earnings next year would fall far below the 660,000,000 reichsmarks [$165,000,000] covering the unconditional annuities they are supposed to guarantee under the Young Plan. As in the reports of the subcommittees on the German budget and foreign indebtedness, the railway subcommittee emphasizes the possibility of the transient nature of the railways' difficulties, but also makes evident a grave uncertainty for the immediate future.

Outline Is Completed.

This report, approved at today's plenary meeting, completed the outline of the Reich's precarious finances after the information supplied by Germany had been examined and checked by testimony and data from other countries. There is only lacking an outside check on the German figures for the balance of trade, but as given it may be concluded they have been found substantially correct.

Dr. Carl Melchior of Germany cited a favorable foreign trade balance averaging 350,000,000 reichsmarks [$87,500,000] for the past six months, bringing the year's favorable total to more than 3,000,000,000 marks [$750,000,000].

This exceptionally good situation in a time of depression is what Germany has to balance against her foreign indebtedness, creating interest and amortization charges of approximately 1,500,000,000 marks [$375,-000,000], a budget balance only through Draconian measures whose efficacy and maintainance are problematical, a large railway deficit fast absorbing reserves and a reichsbank gold cover which has fallen from 30 to 12 per cent. Adding to the complications are psychological conditions of the German people facing the severest measures of economy and the flight of capital from the country, which have made it impossible for the committee to make any estimate of German holdings abroad.

This very flight of capital, which is uncontrollable, becomes a factor to prevent Germany benefiting fully from her favorable trade balance, since a large part of the returns are believed to be never repatriated.

On the other hand, while Germany is credited with having assets amounting to 8,500,000,000 marks [$2,125,000,000] abroad last July and considerably increased since then by the flight of capital, a great deal of these assets can never be brought

Continued on Page Fifteen.

CLASH MARKS THE DEBATE

Free Denounces McFadden, Who Again Attacks Hoover's Purpose.

COLLIER BACKS PRESIDENT

Crisp Joins in Democratic Support, Saying Question Is Not a Partisan One.

HOLDS DISASTER AVERTED

Vote Is Reached Late in Night Session, After a Day of Struggle on the Floor.

Special to The New York Times.

WASHINGTON, Dec. 18.—The joint resolution approving the Hoover moratorium that postpones payments of foreign debts to this country for one year beginning last July 1 was passed in the House at 9:30 P. M. today by a vote of 317 to 100.

The measure was adopted unchanged from the form in which it was reported last night by the Ways and Means Committee; it carries as a provision a declaration of policy of Congress against revision or cancellation of the foreign obligations due the United States.

Administration followers made no attempt on the floor to strike out the declaration of policy inserted by the Democrats. They joined in resisting attempts to amend the measure, and 196 of the 201 present voted for the resolution. One hundred and twenty Democrats voted for the resolution, while ninety-five opposed it.

Amendments offered to the proposals never reached a vote. One provided for a moratorium for American farmers who cannot meet their instalments on Federal farm loan mortgages. Another sought to have Congress protest the heavy armaments of Europe. Both were ruled out by the chair on points of order as not germane to the resolution.

Smoot to Hasten Senate Action.

By its action tonight the House sent the joint resolution to the Senate, which already has a similar measure, offered by Senator Smoot, chairman of the Finance Committee.

That committee has the resolution in charge, and Mr. Smoot said tonight that he would ask for a vote tomorrow. There is little likelihood, however, that it will receive a favorable report immediately, as many members of the committee insist that it be delayed until all witnesses are heard on Senator Johnson's resolution to investigate the floating of foreign loans in this country.

The House tonight prepared the way for consideration of another Hoover proposal, which would authorize $100,000,000 additional capital, to be subscribed by the treasury, for the Federal Land Banks. It was agreed that this would come up tomorrow and remain before the House continuously until acted upon.

Free Defends the President.

Passage of the moratorium resolution in the House followed a tumultuous scene in which Representative Free of California, a personal friend of President Hoover and fellow-alumnus of Leland Stanford University, defended the Chief Executive against the accusation of Representative McFadden, Republican, of Pennsylvania, that he had "sold out" his country in negotiating the debt suspension.

On the heels of punitive action by his Republican colleagues from Pennsylvania, Representative McFadden was a centre of tense interest in the debate. He challenged their attempt to read him from the party so far as patronage is concerned, and declared that he stood ready to submit to the House proof of his charge that President Hoover had "sold out" the country by negotiating the moratorium.

Collier Opens the Debate.

The debate began at 12:35 o'clock this afternoon, with a large number of members constantly in attendance and the public galleries filled most of the time. Until after the dinner hour this evening, there was a scant attendance in the reserved galleries.

Speaking first was Chairman Collier of the Ways and Means Committee, who had reported the joint resolution ratifying the moratorium with a committee amendment putting Congress on record as opposed

Continued on Page Fourteen.

Alfalfa Bill's 'Firebells' Program Losing; Oklahoma Poll Heavily Against Tax Plans

By The Associated Press.

OKLAHOMA CITY, Dec. 18.—Governor W. H. (Alfalfa Bill) Murray's four initiative reform measures, submitted to the voters when the Legislature refused to pass his program, were trailing by 52,000 to 67,000 votes late tonight on returns from 1,967 out of 3,346 precincts.

The vote on each measure was:

Income-tax proposal, which would increase levies on corporation and higher individual incomes—For, 130,631; against, 182,898.

Escheat bill, which would forfeit certain corporation lands to the State—For, 125,914; against, 184,979.

Free text-book proposal—For, 124,661; against, 190,413.

Budget-officer amendment, which would increase authority of the Governor over appropriations—For, 122,891; against, 189,816.

In the cotton country, farmers plowed through seas of mud on horseback to mark "yes" on the ballots of "Falfa Bill" whom some regard as a Moses fitted for the nation's Presidency.

But most of the cities voted heavily against the measures, apparently heeding the warning of Murray's foes that his "firebells" program would drive capital to other States and leave Oklahoma "one of the most backward of Commonwealths." Oklahoma City and Tulsa went four to one against them.

Still confident that the late vote from the "forks of the creeks" would change the picture, Mr. Murray rested in the Executive Mansion.

The unemployed line up every night on Broadway to wait for free sandwiches and coffee.

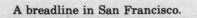

A breadline in San Francisco.

The Depression in Mississippi.

"All the News That's Fit to Print."

The New York Times.

LATE CITY EDITION
WEATHER—Rain today; tomorrow cloudy and colder.
Temperatures Yesterday—Max., 48; Min., 34.

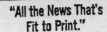

Copyright, 1932, by The New York Times Company.

VOL. LXXXI....No. 27,039. ****+ NEW YORK, THURSDAY, FEBRUARY 4, 1932. TWO CENTS In New York City | THREE CENTS Within 200 Miles | FOUR CENTS Elsewhere Except 7th and 8th Postal Zones

WASHINGTON PLEDGES 100 PER CENT AID FOR SAFETY OF SHANGHAI SETTLEMENT; TOKYO REJECTS PEACE; BATTLE GOES ON

HOOVER ASKS PUBLIC TO CEASE HOARDING AND PUT CASH TO USE

He Estimates $1,300,000,000 Is Hidden Away, Equal to 5 to 10 Times That in Credit.

FOR PATRIOTISM AS IN WAR

Appeal Is Made to Civic Leaders to Further the Campaign Throughout the Nation.

MEETING CALLED SATURDAY

Reconstruction Corporation Already Shows Results in Dissipating Fear, He Says.

The text of the President's statement is printed on page 9.

Special to THE NEW YORK TIMES.

WASHINGTON, Feb. 3.—President Hoover appealed to the country tonight to cease the hoarding of currency, as a patriotic move toward loosening credits and restoring economic stability. Hoarded funds were estimated by the President at $1,300,000,000, every dollar of which, he reasoned, meant the destruction of from $5 to $10 of credit.

"We are engaged," he said, "in a war against depression." With this statement went an announcement that he was summoning the heads of the leading civic organizations of the country to a conference at the White House Saturday to form a national organization to further a campaign against influences which serve to check steps taken to combat the depression.

In warning the country that every dollar hoarded at this time means the destruction of from $5 to $10 of credit, the President pointed out that credit is "the blood stream of our economic life." It is in the interest of the hoarders, and it is their patriotic duty, the President declared, to return this wealth to circulation. Doing so, he said, would put more men to work, would help agriculture and help business generally.

Confers With Finance Chiefs.

The statement, which was issued from the White House early this evening, followed a long conference in the executive offices where the President discussed in detail the work of the new Reconstruction Finance Corporation with Charles G. Dawes, president; Eugene Meyer, chairman of the board, Under-Secretary of the Treasury Mills, a member of the board, and Melvin A. Traylor, the Chicago banker, who was present as an adviser.

Although it still is in the organizing stage, the President said, the Reconstruction Corporation is exerting a definite influence on the American economic situation because the "very act" of its creation shows results "in the dissipation of fear and the restoration of public confidence." This is indicated, he said, by the fact that the balance sheets of the government show no recent increase in the total of hoarded money.

The President's pronouncement is the first move in a definite campaign by the Reconstruction Corporation which the President described as "a patriotic opportunity" for all citizens to enlist in the war against depression.

Recalling that during the World War "our people gave their undivided energies to the national purpose," the President pointed to this "fight we are making on their behalf" and called upon civic organizations "in every State and town" to "make clear the problem and to effect our purpose."

It was in order that "we may have a definite organization for this service" that he summoned the heads of civil organizations to meet with him Saturday "to further the campaign."

Those with whom the President will confer represent all fields of American industry and business. The names of those asked to attend will not be announced before tomorrow.

Senate Confirms McCarthy.

Wilson McCarthy of Salt Lake City, Utah, was confirmed by the Senate today as a member of the board of the Reconstruction Finance Corporation, thus completing approval of the seven directors.

Senator King of Utah gained unanimous consent to have the notice of confirmation sent immediately to President Hoover. Thus Mr. McCarthy may become active on the board tomorrow without waiting for the lapse of two executive sessions of the Senate.

Members of the reconstruction board conferred today with members of Congress and others on the first loans to be made to banks and industries.

The directors discussed methods of perfecting the machinery for loan-

Continued on Page Nine.

Mercy for Envoy's Assailants In Ethiopia Asked by Stimson

Special to THE NEW YORK TIMES.

WASHINGTON, Feb. 3.—Secretary Stimson announced today that he had asked for modification of the punishment of Ethiopian police officers who had been imprisoned for assaulting Addison E. Southard, the American Minister, when he was in an automobile accident recently in Addis Ababa.

"In view of the prompt action taken by the Ethiopian authorities," the State Department said, "in response to the request of this government that suitable punishment be meted out to the Ethiopian police officers guilty of attacking the American Minister at Addis Ababa on Jan. 17, 1932, the Minister has been instructed to express to the Emperor the appreciation of this government and to request at the same time that the fine of 100 Maria Theresa dollars imposed upon the offenders be remitted."

The officers also were sentenced to one year's imprisonment.

MASTICK TAX RISES TO GO OVER A YEAR

Legislature Will Not Consider Proposed Changes at the Present Session.

COMMISSION TO CONTINUE

Republicans Are Confident Their Budget Slash and Gasoline Tax Rate Cut Will Prevail.

By W. A. WARN.

Special to THE NEW YORK TIMES.

ALBANY, Feb. 3.—Republican leaders in the Legislature have virtually decided to postpone consideration of the revolutionary changes in the State tax program recommended by the Mastick commission until next year. An agreement has been reached to continue the life of the commission for another year with an additional appropriation of $25,000 to enable it to continue its survey of taxation.

The decision was reached after a conference among Senator Fearon, Speaker McGinnies and the chairmen of the fiscal committees of the two houses. The conclusion was reached that with the Governor's budget recommendations for emergency taxes conflicting in many respects with the Mastick commission's proposals, which are designed for permanent application, deliberation on both in the closing weeks of what is intended to be one of the shortest legislative sessions on record might bring about confusion, endless delay and possibly endanger both programs. The Mastick commission urged that its recommendations must be enacted as a whole to be practicable.

Republicans are well pleased with the reaction throughout the State to what they regard as their astuteness in cutting the Governor's budget to the bone. A lame defense of his own budget and an ineffective condemnation of their proposals are the most they fear from the Governor.

Republicans Pluming Themselves.

There now appears to be every probability that the slash of $21,000,000 in the budget, as well as the reduction proposed by the Republicans in the tax rate on gasoline from 4 cents a gallon to 3, will become law. The Governor will have no opoprtunity to act on the reductions in the budget bill itself, for these will not go to him for veto or approval. He will pass on the gasoline measure, but the rival party leaders do not believe he will invite unpopularity by exercising his veto power and offending a large class of taxpayers.

The Republicans are pluming themselves on what they term their outmanoeuvring of the Governor, placing him on the defensive and putting him in what they call an awkward position.

The budget bill, with the series of bills providing for collateral changes in taxation, will go before the Senate and Assembly for final passage next Wednesday. In the Senate these bills were moved up to third reading. The Senate session will be held over into the afternoon on Wednesday to allow concurrent action by the Assembly.

While the Republicans assert they have reason to believe the Governor will try to use the huge cut they made in the appropriations for parks and parkways on Long Island as an attack on their budget program, the statement came from one of their number that there was no likelihood that they would recede from the stand, no matter how strong the protests.

There will be a public hearing before the Senate and Assembly fiscal committees on the revenue bills next Tuesday and a storm is ex-

Continued on Page Four.

MELLON ACCEPTS THE POST OF ENVOY TO GREAT BRITAIN

After Nearly 11 Years as Head of Treasury, He Will Become Successor to Dawes.

PRESIDENT ANNOUNCES IT

Says He Is Calling Upon One of Our "Wisest" Public Servants to Take Place.

MILLS LIKELY SUCCESSOR

His Promotion Is Held Certain—Secretary Has Had a Difficult Task in His Long Regime.

Special to THE NEW YORK TIMES.

WASHINGTON, Feb. 3.—President Hoover tonight announced the appointment of Andrew W. Mellon, Secretary of the Treasury to be Ambassador to Great Britain, and Mr. Mellon's acceptance of the post.

The President's announcement was made at the White House, at 10:15, following confirmation by Mr. Mellon in the afternoon of a report that Mr. Hoover had offered him the post made vacant by the recent resignation of General Charles G. Dawes, now president of the Reconstruction Finance Corporation.

In confirming the report, Mr. Mellon said he had not reached a decision as to whether or not he would accept the post.

Later after a conference with the President, he decided to accept the appointment. In announcing this fact the President said:

"The critical situation facing all countries in their international relations, the manifold economic and other problems demanding wise solution in our national interests call for experience and judgment of the highest order. The importance to our country of the sound determination of these world-wide difficulties needs no emphasis.

"I have decided, therefore, to call upon one of our wisest and most experienced public servants to accept a position which will enable him after many years of distinguished public service at home to render equal service to his country in the foreign field.

"I have asked Mr. Mellon to undertake the Ambassadorship to Great Britain. I am happy to say he has now expressed his willingness to serve."

The State Department, it was learned, has not yet asked the British Government if he would be acceptable, a formality which will take place at once.

Mills Held Probable Successor.

The transfer of Mr. Mellon to a post abroad, it is understood, will result in the promotion of Ogden L. Mills, Under-Secretary, to be head of the treasury. Mr. Mills has carried a large part of the work since he succeeded Garrard B. Winston on March 4, 1927.

Mr. Mills has done virtually all the work for the treasury in organizing the Reconstruction Finance Corporation, on the directorate of which he and Mr. Mellon have been alternates.

It also is understood that Arthur A. Ballantine of New York, Assistant Secretary and a member of the old law firm that included Elihu Root, is being considered as "contact man" between the treasury and Congress and may become Under-Secretary to succeed Mr. Mills.

Confirms Report With a Smile.

While Mr. Mellon made no announcement of the President's offer, he confirmed the report with a smile. He told reporters that he had some knowledge of the European situation, but declared that there would be much in the work of an Ambassador with which was not familiar.

News of the appointment of Mr. Mellon to the Ambassadorship was received in the capital with approbation and some surprise, although reports that Mr. Mellon would leave the treasury and be succeeded by Mr. Mills have been recurrent almost from the first of the Hoover Administration.

Members of Congress generally expressed the opinion that Mr. Mellon would make an excellent Ambassador and Mr. Mills a good Secretary of the Treasury.

The indications were that while some of the insurgent Republicans might vote against confirmation of either or both, this opposition would not become formidable.

Although he will be 77 years old on March 24, his next birthday, Mr. Mellon is an active man, both mentally and physically and, because of his dignity, sense of humor and personality, is regarded by the President as particularly well equipped for this important post.

On frequent visits to Europe dur-

Continued on Page Eleven.

Hitler Sends Two Observers To Geneva Arms Conference

Special Cable to THE NEW YORK TIMES.

MUNICH, Feb. 3.—General von Epp and Colonel Haselmayer have been ordered by Adolf Hitler to proceed to Geneva Friday to follow the proceedings of the World Disarmament Conference as "Nazi" observers.

National Socialist papers are continuing their campaign against Chancellor Bruening, asserting that the German delegation at Geneva has not authority to speak for the German people.

They demand that the delegation insist strictly on armament parity for Germany instead of "confining their policy to the Utopic demand for general disarmament after the German model."

FARLEY AND CULKIN INDICTED FOR THEFT

Sheriff and Predecessor Are Accused of Grand Larceny in Keeping Accruals.

BOTH ARE FINGERPRINTED

Officials Freed in $2,500 Bail Each After Not-Guilty Pleas—Public Hearing Put Off.

Two more Tammany district leaders were indicted yesterday, bringing the total to four in little more than a year. They were Sheriff Thomas M. Farley and his predecessor in office, Charles W. Culkin.

Accused of grand larceny in appropriating to their own use the interest on official funds, they pleaded not guilty and were released in $2,500 bail after going through the routine of fingerprinting and photographing for the Rogues' Gallery.

They were indicted, as was James J. McCormick, Deputy City Clerk, and another Tammany district leader about a week ago by the additional January grand jury, on the basis of evidence presented at public hearings of the Hofstadter committee by Samuel Seabury, its chief counsel.

A fourth Tammany leader, Martin J. Healy, was indicted more than a year ago for selling former Magistrate George F. Ewald his appointment to the bench. Healy was tried twice but neither jury was able to agree.

Culkin Charge More Drastic.

Two indictments were handed up to Judge George L. Donnellan in General Sessions against Farley by Arthur G. Stier, the foreman of the grand jury. He was charged in each with grand larceny in the second degree. Culkin was charged in one indictment with grand larceny in the first degree and in another with second degree grand larceny.

The formal charges against Farley and Culkin are the result of Mr. Seabury's revelation that it was the practice of the Sheriff to pocket whatever interest accrued to funds of litigants entrusted to him in his official capacity pending the outcome of litigation. Each indictment contains one count alleging violation of Section 1838 of the penal code, which is a felony. The section provides that:

"The Sheriff, coroner, clerk of the court, constable or other ministerial officer, and every deputy or subordinate of any ministerial officer who fraudulently appropriates to his own use or to the use of another person, or secretes with intent to appropriate to such use any money, evidence of debt or other property entrusted to him in virtue of his office, is guilty of a felony."

The retention of interest on official funds by Sheriff Farley formed part of the charges on which Governor Roosevelt has been asked by Mr. Seabury and several civic organizations to remove him from public office. Culkin's application for re-

Continued on Page Seven.

BARS MANCHURIAN ISSUE

Japan Starts Draft of Her Reply to Be Delivered to Powers Today.

YOSHIZAWA EXPLAINS VIEW

He Draws Clear Distinction Between Manchurian and Shanghai Operations.

REJECTION BEFORE LEAGUE

Reported to Balk at Neutrals in Parleys and Cessation of Military Activity.

By HUGH BYAS.

Special Cable to THE NEW YORK TIMES.

TOKYO, Thursday, Feb. 4.—Some aspects of the four proposals of the powers which Japan substantially accepts require careful examination but they appear to offer a practical framework on which peace in Shanghai can be built, provided always that unpredictable developments do not alter the existing situation.

The fifth point, in so far as it concerns Manchuria, is impossible for Japan. If it was inserted as the price of China's assent to the other four conditions the plan is doomed in advance, for Japan in her present mood will never consent to take the Manchurian subject to a round-table conference.

If the powers mean to insist on that point they must prepare stronger arguments. The other points, always barring unknown contingencies, are negotiable if the Chinese will accept them separately.

Japan's reply will be given to the foreign Ambassadors here this afternoon.

Yoshizawa Explains View.

Kenhichi Yoshizawa, Foreign Minister, last night described Japan's policy and intentions regarding Shanghai in the following statement for THE NEW YORK TIMES:

"The Japanese Government draws a clear distinction between the present disturbances in Shanghai and the dispute in Manchuria and unless the difference is recognized our policy is liable to be misunderstood. In Manchuria Japan's interests are of paramount importance economically and our position there is a matter of life and death.

"In Shanghai, on the other hand, our interests are similar to those of other foreign powers. We only desire to trade peacefully and to secure the safety of our nationals and their legitimate enterprises. We have no territorial or political ambitions.

"The murder of a Japanese priest and an insulting article about the imperial family in the organ of the Kuomintang were only the climax of a long series of anti-Japanese agitations encouraged by the Kuomintang. That phase, however, ended as far as we are concerned when the Mayor accepted our demands.

"The present phase, which began when Chinese troops fired on Japanese marines engaged in the execution of international duty, will enter on its way to settlement as soon as the attacks on Japanese nationals are stopped.

"We are willing to enter into any reasonable proposal for restoring

Continued on Page Thirteen.

NEW NAVAL FIGURES AT SHANGHAI.

Associated Press Photo.

Admiral Kichisaburo Nomura, Who Succeeds Admiral Shiozawa.

Times Wide World Photo.

Captain Robert Alden Dawes, Commander of the U. S. S. Houston.

JAPANESE ATTEMPT TO CAPTURE FORTS

Send a Landing Force Against Woosung Defenses Under Heavy Bombardment.

GUNS OF CHINESE ANSWER

One Japanese Destroyer and Some Airplanes Reported Sunk in Fighting.

Copyright, 1932, by The Associated Press.

SHANGHAI, Thursday, Feb. 4.—Japanese warships bombarded the Chinese Woosung forts at the mouth of the Whangpoo River today in a terrific attack to cover a landing party sent to capture them under Chinese fire.

Three Japanese cruisers and two destroyers joined in the fierce bombardment, started by three destroyers, to which the forts' guns replied.

Japanese naval officials said they were attempting to capture the Woosung forts to "remove the danger of obstructing navigation in and out of Shanghai," as the forts command the entrance to the Whangpoo River, sixteen miles below the city.

The Japanese plans to capture the fortifications indicated that the Chinese still occupied them after the terrific shelling and bombing by Japanese warships and airplanes yesterday.

Chinese authorities said today that their forces shot down a Japanese airplane, killing the pilot, and disabled two Japanese destroyers, in addition to sinking one in the battle of the Woosung forts yesterday. Japanese naval officials, however, continued to deny there had been any losses.

Chinese Accused of Firing First.

Special Cable to THE NEW YORK TIMES.

SHANGHAI, Feb. 3.—Firing by Japanese warships upon the Chinese Woosung forts, at the mouth of the Whangpoo River, twenty miles below Shanghai, began at 11:30 A. M. today, according to the Japanese Consulate, which charges that guns of the forts opened fire first, bombarding passing Japanese warships.

The Japanese asserted the forts were reduced but not occupied because a Chinese ruse was feared. The Chinese deny the forts have been put out of commission and assert that, on the contrary, the guns of the forts were fired upon Japanese warships after the bombing ceased.

The Japanese assertion that the Chinese fired first is not believed by responsible foreign authorities at Shanghai. The Japanese statement says the warships fired upon were "going out from Shanghai," but there is no sign of a voluntary movement to diminish the Japanese naval concentration here.

Repo No Soldiers Visible.

The Japanese Consul General officially notified the Harbor Master, informing him that since the forts had fired upon Japanese warships the situation was considered dangerous for incoming and outgoing vessels and that, therefore, the Japanese intended to occupy the forts.

The Japanese Consulate announced that no Chinese soldiers were visible from a Japanese airplane surveying the forts after 3 o'clock this afternoon.

Bombing of the forts by Japanese

Continued on Page Twelve.

HEAVY GUNS RESUME BATTLE AT SHANGHAI

Japanese Call on Biggest Artillery Yet Used to Break Chinese Defense.

AMERICANS NOT TO GET OUT

They Will Be Defended, Official Announcement Says—Fires Rage in Chapei.

By HALLETT ABEND.

Special Cable to THE NEW YORK TIMES.

SHANGHAI, Thursday, Feb. 4.—The heaviest guns that have been used so far by the Japanese in Shanghai went into action at dawn today while the Chinese replied with smaller pieces. As a drizzling rain was falling no Japanese airplanes had appeared to assist in the battle up to 8:30 A. M.

The fighting was renewed after a night of silence, during which the fires started in the Chapei district yesterday (Wednesday) by bombs from Japanese planes raged unchecked in three areas.

Following the arrival here of Admiral Montgomery M. Taylor aboard the United States cruiser Houston it was officially announced that Americans in the International Settlement would not be evacuated but would be defended because they were entitled to be here legally and to enjoy safety.

Undecided on Command.

Late yesterday evening Admiral Taylor had not decided whether he would assume command of the Shanghai foreign defense forces or waive seniority rights in favor of Brig. Gen. George E. Fleming, British commander.

Probably for the first time in history a throng of civilian Chinese cheered with wild enthusiasm as newly landed foreign troops marched through the streets of a city on Chinese soil. Heralded by the music of Scotch pipers, battalions of the Argyll and Sutherland Highlanders disembarked from a transport from Hongkong and marched along the Bund, thence up Nanking and Bubbling Well Roads to billets.

They were preceded by squads of guides and mounted United States marines, Sikh policemen and Shanghai volunteers. While the music of the bagpipes sounded shrilly along the principal streets of this city, from overhead came the drone of Japanese airplanes bound on their third intensive bombing raid against Chinese.

Chinese Cheer Heartily.

On many sections of the route the Scotsmen were greeted with deafening cheers from Chinese throngs, whereas the Chinese public hitherto had always deeply resented the arrival of fresh foreign forces and had looked upon their parades in sullen silence. Today all the arrivals of foreign defense forces are looked upon by the Chinese as potential saviors of the country from Japanese aggression.

Japanese forces were being withdrawn at midnight (Wednesday) from the border lanes along the northernmost projection of the International Settlement and from the factory district behind these lanes. United States and British forces will

Continued on Page Twelve.

OUR FORCES READY TO ACT

Admiral Taylor Ordered to Assure Other Powers of Military Help.

NEW PROTEST TO JAPAN

State Department Objects to Use of Settlement as Base of Operations.

AMERICANS FLEE NANKING

British Ship Takes 36 Women and Children From Our Colony as the Danger Grows.

Special to THE NEW YORK TIMES.

WASHINGTON, Feb. 3.—Admiral Montgomery M. Taylor, Commander-in-Chief of the United States Asiatic fleet, was directed by the Navy Department this afternoon to assure the other neutral naval and military authorities at Shanghai "one hundred per cent naval and military cooperation" by the United States Navy in maintaining the neutrality and the safety of the International Settlement at Shanghai.

The orders went forward following the receipt of a message from Admiral Taylor which was regarded as of such importance that the Navy Department refused to make it public and rushed it to the State Department for the information of Secretary of State Stimson.

Secretary Stimson subsequently went to the White House. Whether the Taylor report was submitted to the President was a question unanswered at the White House and also the State Department.

The critical situation in the International Settlement resulting from the safety of foreigners being menaced by fighting between Japanese and Chinese occupied the exclusive attention of the administration today simultaneously with the receipt of a reply from China favorable to the peace proposals made by the United States and other powers yesterday. The response of Japan is awaited.

Stimson Confers on Taylor Report.

After Secretary Stimson had conferred with President Hoover, he discussed Admiral Taylor's report at a lengthy conference with Major Gen. Douglas MacArthur, Chief of Staff of the army; Admiral William V. Pratt, Chief of Naval Operations, and State Department officials at Colonel Stimson's home this afternoon.

The result was the dispatch of renewed protests to Japan against the use of the International Settlement as a base of operations and the sending of the orders to Admiral Taylor.

Whether this order points to strong action in support of foreign rights was not disclosed. Although regarding conditions at Shanghai as dangerous, because some incident may develop to affect foreigners, officials were disposed to regard the disturbed situation as being natural under present conditions and thought that Japan would be glad to liquidate her naval venture, if she could do so without loss of international prestige.

China's favorable reply to the five-point peace proposals reached the State Department this morning. A prompt response by Nanking was expected, but there is not so much certainty over the attitude of China should Japan refuse to give complete acceptance, as forecast in press reports from Tokyo.

Capture of Shanghai Feared.

Whether Japan anticipates difficulty in obtaining the assent of China to exclude Manchuria from the negotiations, through the good offices of the other powers, led to speculation today as to whether Japan might want to capture Shanghai and hold it as a trading point in the negotiations.

Ambassador Lindsay of Great Britain conferred with William R. Castle Jr., Under-Secretary of State, this morning and expressed confidence that Japan would agree to the first four points of the peace proposals. These call for cessation of hostilities, no more war-like preparations, separation of the Japanese and Chinese combatants at Shanghai and establishment of neutral zones around

Continued on Page Thirteen.

Bill by Hofstadter Gives New York Voters Power to Move for City Manager Rule

Special to THE NEW YORK TIMES.

ALBANY, Feb. 3.—Elimination of the Board of Estimate and the Board of Aldermen acting as the Municipal Assembly of New York City in amendments to the existing charter or the drafting of a new one under the provisions of the home rule act is the aim of a bill introduced today by Senator Hofstadter, chairman of the New York City investigating committee.

The bill provides that the voters themselves may take the initiative, not only in charter amendments but in the creation of an entire new charter, involving radical structural changes in the City Government, such, for example, as the substitution of a city manager plan of administration. The initiative would be taken through petitions, signed by 15 per cent of the voters and on which would appear the names of the proposed charter commissioners.

When a commission so created had provided the draft for a new charter it would be the duty of the election authorities to refer it for adoption or rejection to a popular referendum. On a majority vote being cast in the affirmative the charter would have the force of law without the usually Tammany-controlled Board of Estimate and Board of Aldermen having any power or function relating to adoption.

The provisions of the measure are already in force as to cities operating under a commission form of government. The Hofstadter bill makes them apply to all cities in the State. It will not require a two-thirds vote in the Legislature or a certificate of necessity from the Governor, but can be passed by the Republican majority in the Senate and Assembly.

"All the News That's Fit to Print."

The New York Times.

LATE CITY EDITION
POSTSCRIPT
WEATHER—Fair today; tomorrow rain; not much temperature change.
Temperatures Yesterday—Max., 44; Min., 37.

VOL. LXXXI....No. 27,066. ***** + NEW YORK, WEDNESDAY, MARCH 2, 1932. TWO CENTS In New York City | THREE CENTS Within 200 Miles | FOUR CENTS Elsewhere Except 7th and 8th Postal Zones

LINDBERGH BABY KIDNAPPED FROM HOME OF PARENTS ON FARM NEAR PRINCETON; TAKEN FROM HIS CRIB; WIDE SEARCH ON

JAPANESE ROUTING CHINESE IN FIERCE SHANGHAI BATTLE; DEATH TOLL EXCEEDS 2,000

WHOLE CHINESE LINE FLEES

Pressure From North of Fresh Japanese Troops Forces Quick Move.

PURSUERS LEFT BEHIND

Tachang, Miaoshin and Chapei Fall Before Advance Made Behind Smoke Screen.

TRUCE EXPECTED AT ONCE

Chinese Are Stunned by Sudden Blow—Say Retreat Meets Terms of Japanese.

By HALLETT ABEND.
Wireless to THE NEW YORK TIMES.

SHANGHAI, Wednesday, March 2.—The Chinese were routed this morning by the Japanese in the most sanguinary battle since the World War.

The Japanese killed and wounded before 10 o'clock admittedly exceeded 250. Yesterday's advance in this region totaled two kilometers (more than a mile) and the Japanese losses up to midnight officially were admitted to be slightly in excess of 300 killed and wounded, while the bodies of 1,800 Chinese soldiers were discovered this morning on the ground won yesterday.

Brief reports from General Kenkichi Ueda's headquarters report that the Chinese retreat is degenerating into an utter, panicky rout and the rapid Japanese advance is finding difficulty in maintaining contact with the fast fleeing Chinese soldiers.

The pall of smoke from burning Chinese villages and towns was thickening over Shanghai. Immense exultation was manifested in Japanese circles and the Chinese were stunned by the suddenness and magnitude of the military disaster.

The Japanese captured Tachang at 12:30 today.

Chinese in Pell Mell Retreat.

Early this afternoon the Japanese forces were rapidly approaching from beyond Taching and the Chinese were in pellmell retreat. There was great confusion at Nantao, where Chinese soldiers were attempting to evacuate in railway trains to Hangchow.

The Nineteenth Route Army has voluntarily withdrawn from Chapei, is abandoning other fronts and concentrating at Chenju, according to official oral notification given at 12:30 by the secretary of Mayor Wu Te-chen to United States Consul General Edwin S. Cunningham in his capacity as senior consul.

This withdrawal, the official notification said, also means the evacuation of all Chinese soldiers from Nantao ad Lunghua, but Mr. Cunningham was assured there was danger of disorders at Nantao because 2,000 regular police and 600 picked volunteers already have taken over the maintenance of law and order. It is understood that Chinese will not attempt to police Chapei, declaring "that is dependent upon the Japanese."

Truce Expected Soon.

Presumably the crumpling of the Nineteenth Route Army will be quickly followed by the signing of a truce and by further retirement of the Chinese forces, since Chenju is inside the twenty-kilometer zone which the Japanese insist must be evacuated.

Between 7:30 and 10 o'clock this morning the Japanese had pushed forward to within two kilometres of Tachang. A vast area was being bombed and shelled with unparalleled intensity and the region was dimmed with smoke from huge conflagrations.

The Chinese began the day's hostilities by using two batteries of big guns, firing from Chapei into the Japanese naval headquarters area in Hongkew Park, where many large fires are now burning. For an hour and a half the Chinese batteries kept the city rocking and the roar of their detonations made sleep impossible.

The Japanese had made exceedingly important gains at 10 o'clock toward Tachang, although the terrain is even more difficult than around Kiangwan, with a multitude of vertical banked creeks and sloughs

Continued on Page Twelve.

Settlement Stores Reopen And Shoppers Flock to Them

Special Cable to THE NEW YORK TIMES.

SHANGHAI, March 1.—Acting upon the request of General Tsai Ting-chai three of the largest Chinese-owned department stores on the Nanking Road of the International Settlement reopened today and many smaller stores and shops followed suit. This action contributed largely to a return to approximate normalcy in general business conditions.

SHANGHAI, March 1 (AP).—Stores and offices in the International Settlement reopened today and bargain hunters turned out in droves.

The three big department stores were crowded with shoppers, but the service staff was considerably depleted. Many of the clerks used to live in Chapei and Hongkew and nobody knows where they are now.

JAPAN WILL OFFER NEW TRUCE TERMS

Accepts League Proposal for Armistice at Shanghai With Reservations.

CHINA AFFIRMS AGREEMENT

Plans for Special Assembly at Geneva Tomorrow Await Outcome of Negotiations.

By CLARENCE K. STREIT.
Special Cable to THE NEW YORK TIMES.

GENEVA, March 1.—Naotake Sato this evening gave Joseph Paul-Boncour, President of the League Council, Tokyo's definite acceptance of the latter's so-called "President's plan" for a Shanghai truce and a round-table discussion. Mr. Sato added that the "details"—which is to say, the truce—were to be worked out in Shanghai. Later he confirmed his oral communication in a brief note.

The note merely said Japan was "happy to accept the plan the President has submitted. It mentioned none of the reservations which Mr. Sato gave M. Paul-Boncour orally regarding the details of the truce to be settled on the spot, apparently because Japan thought the terms of the "President's plan" included such reservations.

At any rate, these reservations not merely still stand, but it is understood Mr. Sato explained to M. Paul-Boncour that Japan, instead of accepting Admiral Kelly's armistice terms, was making a counter-proposal.

The United States delegation preferred to reserve comment on Tokyo's reply.

Diplomatic Move Seen.

There is a suspicion in Chinese and Soviet circles that, if Japan does really accept the truce terms, she will then try to win through diplomacy what she failed to win on the battlefield by seeking to have the boundaries of the International Settlement at Shanghai extended to include some districts largely populated by Japanese. There is nothing, certainly, in either the "President's plan" or Mr. Sato's declaration yesterday to prevent such a manoeuvre, for they bar merely any concession or move which exclusively favors the Japanese.

The wording of the second point of the president's plan" and the whole of Mr. Sato's declaration, especially the third point, appear to some to be designed to facilitate such a plan by their references to strengthening the international character of the Settlement.

The Chinese appear to regard the United States as the only one in the group on which they can count not to take advantage of the present situation to try to block China's old fight on the whole question of extraterritoriality.

New Settlement Status Hinted.

There is also some significant, although still vague, talk of the need of improving the status of the Shanghai International Settlement and possibly of putting it under League jurisdiction, like Danzig.

Although the skepticism here is pointed chiefly toward Japan, some are skeptical too of the Chinese Government being able to keep its troops to the terms of the armistice.

Pending definite developments with regard to the armistice and the

Continued on Page Thirteen.

145 in House Force Vote on Dry Law Test; Texan, Last Signer, Rolls Up in Wheelchair

Special to THE NEW YORK TIMES.

WASHINGTON, March 1.—An outright vote on whether the House shall consider a proposal to return liquor control to the States was assured today when the necessary 145 members had signed a petition to cite the Judiciary Committee for discharge from further study of the measure.

The vote probably will be taken on March 14, the first "discharge" day on the calendar.

The wets hailed it as the greatest day since prohibition when the last signature necessary was obtained soon after noon. The 145th member affixing his signature was Representative Mansfield, Texas Democrat. Mr. Mansfield, who is crippled, rolled up to the desk in his wheel chair, while Representative Blanton, Democrat, of Texas, a militant dry, was on his feet chiding the wets for their "failure" to get the required signatures.

The House was set into an uproar when at that moment it was found that Mr. Mansfield, from Mr. Blanton's own State, had made the "wet failure" a literal "howling success." Some observers were quick to remark that March 2 is the Independence Day of Texas, the anniversary of its Declaration of Independence from Mexico.

Representative La Guardia of New York, a wet, was taking Mr. Blanton to task for his remarks when the news was broadcast that Mr. Mansfield had signed.

"Any time that this House has the experience of seeing the distinguished gentleman from Texas (Mr. Blanton) get unduly excited," Mr. La

Continued on Page Two.

SALES TAX ACCEPTED BY ADMINISTRATION, MILLS ANNOUNCES

Secretary Pledges Cooperation on New Bill Despite Changes in Treasury Plan.

$625,000,000 NOW IS GOAL

Basis for Manufacturers' Levy Is Widened as Subcommittee Completes Draft.

Special to THE NEW YORK TIMES.

WASHINGTON, March 1.—Acceptance by the administration of the new tax measure, including a general sales tax applicable to practically every manufacturing industry in the country, was assured today by Secretary Mills.

Mr. Mills told a Ways and Means subcommittee that, even though the original treasury plan had been changed at nearly every major point, the administration would cooperate to the fullest extent in setting in motion and administering the new tax increases.

The subcommittee completed the new tax bill, excepting one or two minor administrative features, this afternoon.

The manufacturers' tax provisions, as agreed on, exempt only a few articles, chiefly commodities for the "poor man's breakfast table" and his daily paper, and the farmer's products, his magazines and periodicals.

The final meeting of the subcommittee resulted in a decision to recommend an even wider base for the manufacturers' levy. Yesterday the subcommittee tentatively agreed to frame the tax so as to produce around $550,000,000 in additional revenue. Today it decided to extend the scope so as to produce $625,000,000.

The additions to the sales tax base were understood to have been made by adding commodities which were being held "in reserve" for special excises.

Members of the subcommittee declined to discuss details, but it was the prevailing idea that gasoline and industrial alcohol had been included in their definition of "manufactured products."

If this is true, gasoline and industrial alcohol would be subject to the 2 per cent general tax instead of the special excises of one cent a gallon as proposed originally.

Agree on Excess Levies.

Final decision on the special excise levies was reached today. Committeemen likewise declined to discuss these, holding that to mention them would be to let loose an "avalanche" of protests on members of Congress.

Other excises most prominently mentioned in discussions of the measure were a 5 to 10 per cent consumers' levy on electric energy and illuminating gas; a tax on oil, with a differential upward on oil imports, and an increase of 3 cents a share on stock transfers.

The bill probably will be presented to the full Ways and Means Committee tomorrow afternoon and may be offered to the House for action by Saturday night, according to Representative Crisp of Georgia, acting chairman.

Actual passage in the House by the end of next week was the confident hope of authors of the measure.

Representative Crisp, fatigued from his strenuous work on the bill, was buoyed in spirit today with the hope that it might even be introduced in the House tomorrow. He will offer the measure as soon as the Ways and Means Committee has agreed to it. It will then be referred back to the committee, which immediately will go through the routine of making a formal report.

Being a revenue bill, it will have priority in the House and, according to Mr. Crisp, will be called up as soon as possible for action.

He mentioned next Tuesday as a

Continued on Page Four.

SENATE BODY ACTS FOR BROAD INQUIRY ON SHORT SELLING

Banking Committee Will Go Beyond Hoover Idea in Stock Exchange Investigation.

EFFECTS ON TRADE SOUGHT

Subcommittee Named to Go Into Long and Short Sales and Interstate Phase.

Special to THE NEW YORK TIMES.

WASHINGTON, March 1.—An investigation of the New York Stock Exchange was recommended today by the Senate Banking and Currency Committee. A subcommittee, headed by Senator Walcott, Republican, of Connecticut, immediately began drafting a resolution requesting authority for such an investigation from the Senate.

The subcommittee was instructed by the full committee to include in the resolution authorizations covering studies of both long and short selling, the effect of speculation on interstate commerce, the use of interstate communications systems by speculators and the value of a proposed stock transfer tax as a check on speculation.

This decision went far beyond the action believed to have been requested by President Hoover Friday when he called Senator Walcott to the White House for a conference on "bear raiding." No intimation of an investigation of trading other than short selling has come from the White House.

The subcommittee was chosen after an executive session, during which the committee members argued the constitutional right of the Senate to investigate the Stock Exchange.

The full committee finally agreed generally that such authority does exist, and the subcommittee, charged with considering this point in more detail, reached the same conclusion late this afternoon.

Regulation Not Contemplated Now.

Leading members of the full committee, including Senator Walcott, indicated that no regulatory measure affecting the Stock Exchange is contemplated at this time. The committee intends to run to the ground rumors about the Stock Exchange and, if questionable practices are found, to suggest means of correcting them, preferably through the action of the governors of the Stock Exchange itself.

"I hope this will not result in Federal legislation," Senator Walcott told newspaper men. "We have no legislative plans. However, the committee feels that if we can by investigation persuade the Stock Exchange to draw such regulations as will abolish bear raids, bull raids and dangerous pool operations, then we will have done the country good service.

"There is not a man on that committee who wants the Stock Exchange abolished. But we want to see what abuses exist. There is so much talk about the Exchange, and we are just as anxious to clear the Stock Exchange of any unwarranted misrepresentations as we are to uncover abuses in security dealings."

The subcommittee was appointed by Senator Norbeck, Republican, of North Dakota, chairman of the full committee, who named Senators Steiwer, Republican, of Oregon, and Bulkley, Democrat, of Ohio, to serve with Senator Walcott.

What sides were taken by committee members on the question of constitutionality was not revealed, but Senator Norbeck said that eventually "almost every member agreed there is authority under some provision or other." The principal point at issue was whether the Stock Exchange could be considered as engaging in interstate commerce or whether its business should be considered as confined to New York.

The committee's executive session

Continued on Page Thirteen.

FOUR STATES JOIN HUNT

Wire Systems Flash Out Alarm on First Word of Kidnapping.

NEW YORK CAR IS SOUGHT

Roads Are Scoured for Pair Said to Have Inquired Way to the Lindbergh Home.

AUTOS STOPPED ON ROAD

Hunt Here Is Led by Mulrooney—Underworld Haunts Visited in Scores of Cities.

The Baby's Description.

HOPEWELL, N. J., March 2 (AP).—A chubby, golden-haired boy closely resembling his famous father—that is the description given Charles Augustus Lindbergh Jr.

He is 20 months old, has blue eyes, curly hair, fair complexion. He is about normal size for a child his age. He has just begun to toddle and is learning to talk.

At 10:40 o'clock last night Colonel Charles A. Lindbergh telephoned the New Jersey State Police Headquarters at Trenton that his son had been kidnapped from the Lindbergh home in Hopewell, N. J. Within ten minutes every communication method of modern science had been utilized to broadcast the alarm and to mobilize the police systems of four States and scores of communities in the search.

Colonel Lindbergh had scarcely poured out his tale when the vast machinery of cooperating police systems began to function. While one man was calling the State police barracks at Lambertville, N. J., ten miles from Hopewell, on the telephone, another was writing out this message to be flashed over the police teletype system:

"Colonel Lindbergh's baby kidnapped from Lindbergh home at Hopewell between 7:30 and 10 P. M. Boy, 19 months, dressed in sleeping suit. Search all cars."

Pair in Stolen Car Hunted.

Shortly before 1 o'clock this morning the Princeton Police Department sent over the network of wires the first message containing anything approaching a definite clue. It read as follows:

"Information received that two men in blue or black sedan bearing New York license plates stopped a man working on highway and asked to be directed to the Lindbergh home in Hopewell."

Relayed to every outpost, this message gave the searchers their first indication of the possible description of the kidnappers' car. It was so vague, however, that they did not permit it to stop them from questioning the occupants of cars of other descriptions.

As the first alarm was being typed out the telephone connection with the Lambertville barracks had been established and Lieutenant Arthur Keaten, in command of that post, had been informed of the situation. With every man who could be spared, he started at once for Hopewell.

Upon their arrival Corporal Joseph Wolf, at Lieutenant Keaten's direction, telephoned back confirmation of the kidnapping, but he was not at that time able to add further details to the few which had been furnished by Colonel Lindbergh.

Meanwhile picked detectives were sent on the rounds of known underworld haunts to see if they could pick up any clues as to the identity of the kidnappers.

Window Found Open.

An open window in the nursery of the Lindbergh home at Hopewell indicated how the kidnappers had gained entrance to the house. A close watch has been kept on the baby since it was born, but apparently no member of the family dreamed of the possibility of a kidnapping and no one remained in the nursery last night after the nurse had placed the child in his crib and made sure he was asleep.

The small force under Lieutenant Keaten at once began a careful search of the woody areas surrounding the Lindbergh home, on the possibility of uncovering some clue to the

Continued on Page Three.

© The Misses Selby.

The Lindbergh baby photographed a year ago. Left to right are Mrs. Dwight W. Morrow, the baby's grandmother; Mrs. Charles Cutter Long, the great-grandmother; Charles Augustus Lindbergh Jr., and Mrs. Charles A. Lindbergh, his mother.

KIDNAPPING OF BABY SPEEDS FEDERAL LAW

Demand in Capital for Statute Providing Death Penalty Expected to Increase.

OFFICIALS HINDERED NOW

Can Act in Almost Any Other Interstate Crime—Patterson Assails "Filthy Act."

Special to THE NEW YORK TIMES.

WASHINGTON, Wednesday, March 2.—Immediate pressure for early passage of the measure making kidnapping a Federal offense is held certain to be the result of the kidnapping of Colonel Lindbergh's son.

Senator Patterson of Missouri recently introduced a bill to this effect. It provides a death penalty. The measure would give authority to the government when the kidnapped person is removed from one State to another. The bill was approved unanimously two weeks ago by the Senate Judiciary Committee and its supporters are confident that it will be adopted by the Senate.

A companion bill introduced by Representative Cochran of Missouri, chairman of the Committee on Expenditures, has been before the Judiciary Committee in that branch for about ten days. The hearings were scheduled for completion soon and the portents, before this morning's news, were for a favorable report.

Patterson Denounces Crime.

"It is a shock to me to hear of this outrage," said Mr. Patterson this morning when informed by THE NEW YORK TIMES. "I hope the child will soon be returned to its parents. This filthy act will aid us in passing the needed legislation, and I am sorry it will not be retroactive, so that the Lindbergh kidnappers can be dealt with by the Federal Government."

On Jan. 23 a telephone message was received by Senator Patterson from Chicago to the effect that there was a plot to kidnap General Charles G. Dawes, who had just been appointed president of the Reconstruction Finance Corporation. Mr. Patterson then said that this information came from a newspaper correspondent. It created excitement in Washington official circles, although the General refused to take it seriously. However, it spurred the efforts of those behind the legislation.

Action Urged in Chicago.

As a result, when the House Judiciary Committee began hearings, Colonel Isham Randolph of Chicago, head of the "Secret Six" of that city, and former Representative Cleveland A. Newton of St. Louis came to Washington to urge early action. Mr. Newton gave the following list of kidnappings which he said had

Continued on Page Three.

FATHER SEARCHES GROUNDS FOR CHILD

Lindbergh and Troopers Hunt With Flashlights for Clues on Big Estate.

NEWS ROUSES COUNTRYSIDE

Hundreds of Autos Rush to the Home in Lonely Woodland, Clogging Narrow Road.

Copyrighted, 1932, by The Associated Press.

HOPEWELL, N. J., Wednesday, March 2.—Charles Augustus Lindbergh Jr., 20-month-old son of the flying Colonel, was kidnapped last night from his nursery in the Lindbergh country home near here. The child, clad in a blue sleeping robe, was put to bed at the usual hour, 7:30 P. M. At about 10 P. M. someone peered into the nursery. The crib was empty.

Beneath the nursery window, footprints showed in the soft earth. These indicated that the kidnappers, moving with such stealth that the Lindberghs, although in the house, heard no sound, had removed their shoes before climbing a ladder to the window. The trail of the shoeless footprints was followed by The Associated Press reporter to the rutted lane, where police believe a waiting car was parked. Feminine footprints, as well as those of a man, were found.

The first news the Lindberghs had of the crime was when the frightened nurse ran downstairs, screaming that the baby had been kidnapped.

The first newspaper man to reach the home was an Associated Press reporter, who ran a mile over muddy, rut-cut roads to reach a phone to send the first direct news from the residence. This was at 12:40 A. M.

Colonel Lindbergh, bare-headed as usual, was pacing the grounds, while troopers and detectives went over the place with flashlights, seeking clues.

Mrs. Lindbergh, who telephoned the news to her mother, Mrs. Dwight W. Morrow, at the Morrow home in Englewood, N. J., was inside the house. A close friend of Mrs. Lindbergh said she was expecting another child within three months.

The house, glowing with lights from top to bottom, was the only bright spot in the wooded, gloomy district. Wishing to get complete privacy, the Lindberghs picked the site from the air and it is almost inaccessible to the outside world. A winding, muddy lane—their private property—leads to the new house from a country highway, called the Stoutsberg-Worstville Road. The entrance to the Lindbergh road is more than four miles from Hopewell and there are few neighbors near enough to be of any aid in time of

Continued on Page Three.

CHILD STOLEN IN EVENING

At 10 P. M. Nurse Finds Boy, 20 Months Old, Gone, in Nightrobe.

FOOTPRINTS IN THE ROOM

Muddy Trail Leads to Ladder in Wood and Half Mile to Highway, Where Car Waited.

WOMAN BELIEVED INVOLVED

Parents, Distraught, Guarded in Home—Police Deny Report of Ransom Note.

Charles Augustus Lindbergh Jr., 20-month-old son of Colonel and Mrs. Charles A. Lindbergh, was kidnapped between 8:30 and 10 o'clock last night from his crib in the nursery on the second floor of his parents' home at Hopewell, near Princeton, N. J.

Apparently the kidnapping was carried out either while Colonel and Mrs. Lindbergh were at dinner, or soon afterward. The baby's nurse, Miss Betty Gow, visited the nursery about 8:30 o'clock and found everything in order there. When she returned at 10 o'clock, however, the crib was empty.

Muddy footprints that trailed across the floor from the crib to an open window bore mute testimony as to how the baby had disappeared. Miss Gow dashed downstairs. "The baby's been kidnapped!" she shouted. Colonel Lindbergh raced to the nursery, followed closely by his wife. Mrs. Lindbergh recalled that earlier in the day she had tried to fasten a screen on the window that had been opened and had been unable to do so.

Satisfied that there was no mistake and that the baby actually was gone, Colonel Lindbergh telephoned Chief of Police Charles Williamson at Hopewell. Williamson drove to the house accompanied by another officer. Outside the door they met the Colonel. He was bareheaded, and wearing an old black leather jacket such as he frequently wears on his flights.

Footprints Under Window.

Briefly he told Williamson what had occurred. The chief telephoned first to State Police Headquarters at Trenton. Then he, his fellow officer and the Colonel began searching the grounds. Beneath the nursery window were marks where a ladder had stood and the footprints of one person. There were no shoe prints. The kidnapper, apparently, had worn socks or moccasins.

Sixty feet away in rocky ground at the edge of a wood the Colonel and Chief Williamson found a makeshift ladder. Its rungs were caked with mud. Colonel Lindbergh could not say whether it belonged on the premises. He thought it might have been left there by the builders while the house was being constructed during his flight to the Orient last Summer with Mrs. Lindbergh.

The searchers had no difficulty in following the footprints across the muddy ground. A second set of tracks joined them near the edge of the woods. They were much smaller. The two officers thought they might be those of a woman.

The search was interrupted by the arrival of a detachment of State Troopers sent from the barracks at Lambertville and the hunt began anew. The tracks were followed to the main highway, about half a mile from the house, where they disappeared. The kidnappers evidently had entered an automobile at that point.

Lindbergh Aids Search.

Carrying a flashlight, Colonel Lindbergh stayed with the searching party until long after midnight. Once or twice he returned to the house, but he declined to discuss the kidnapping with newspapermen. Instead, he referred them to Major Schoeffel of the State Police, who told the story in detail.

"I hope you boys will excuse me,"

Continued on Page Three.

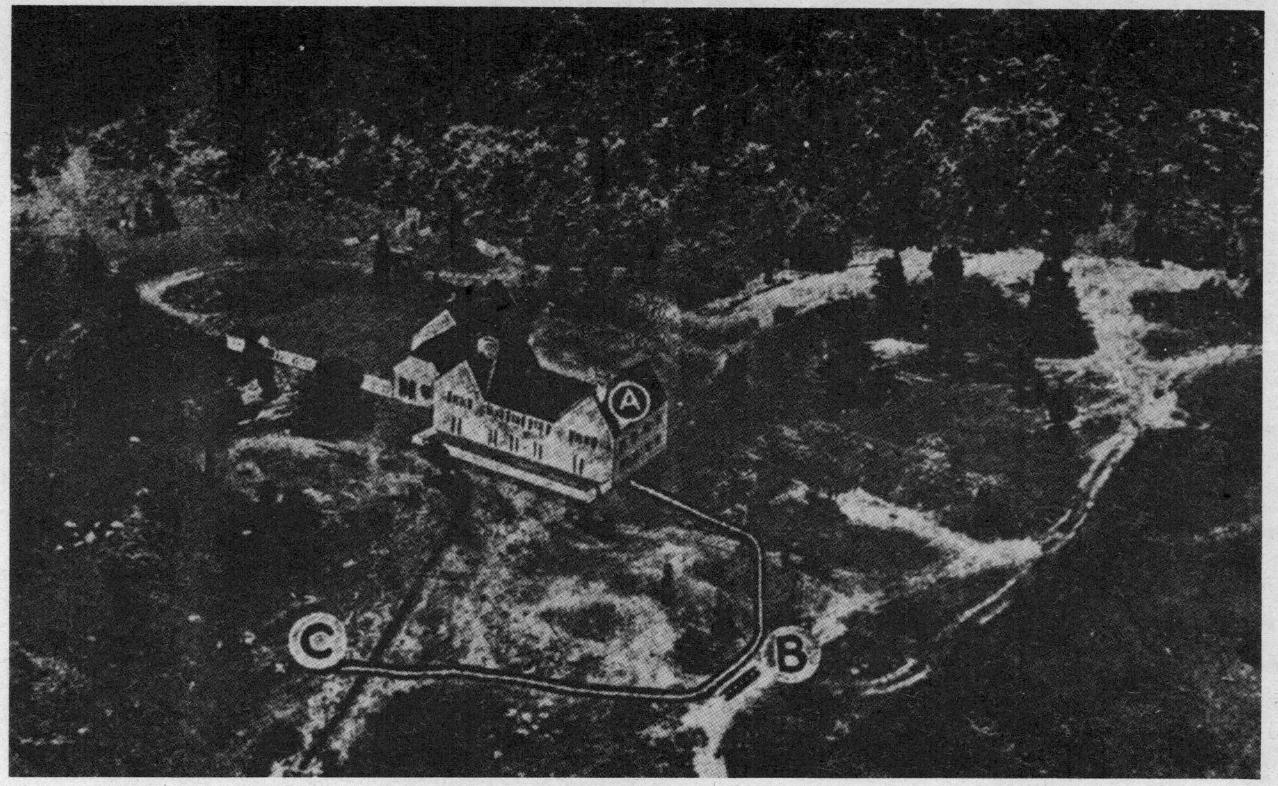

This photo-diagram shows (A) the window of the nursery through which Charles A. Lindbergh Jr. was spirited away, the kidnapper climbing down the ladder with the child and taking the course indicated by the line. The footprints of the abductor, who discarded the ladder at (B), could be traced across the gully to the point marked (C), where in the edge of some shrubbery, they were lost.

Times Wide World Photo.

Colonel and Mrs. Lindbergh after one of their flights.

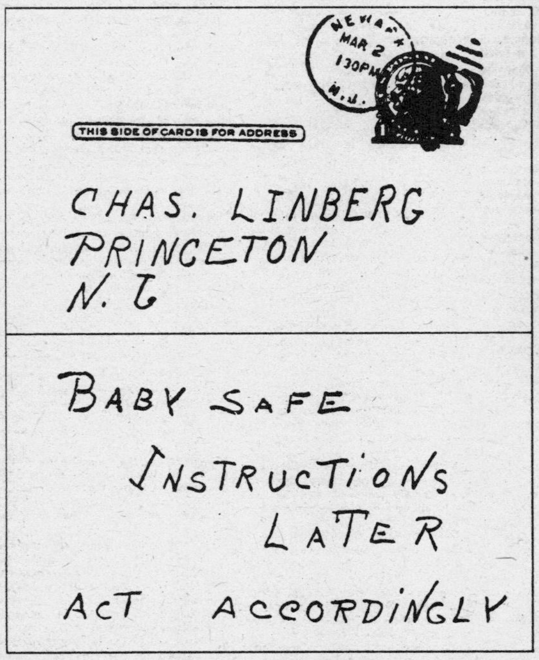

NEWARK MAR 2 1 30 PM N.J.

THIS SIDE OF CARD IS FOR ADDRESS

CHAS. LINBERG
PRINCETON
N. J

BABY SAFE
INSTRUCTIONS
LATER
ACT ACCORDINGLY

This postcard was the first message the Lindberghs received from the kidnapper.

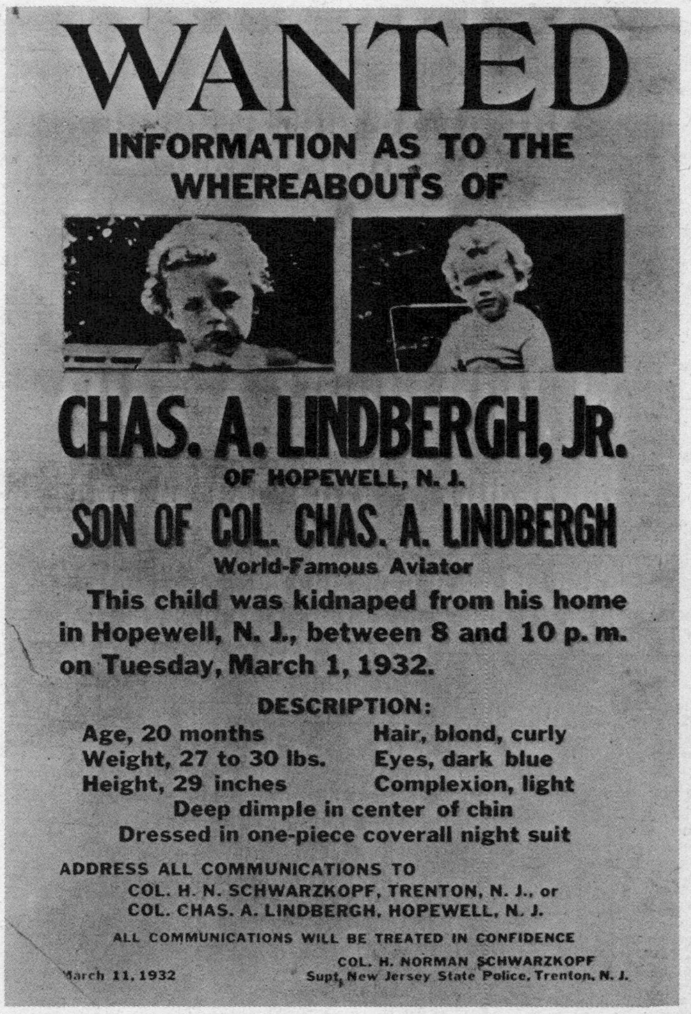

WANTED

INFORMATION AS TO THE WHEREABOUTS OF

CHAS. A. LINDBERGH, JR.

OF HOPEWELL, N. J.

SON OF COL. CHAS. A. LINDBERGH

World-Famous Aviator

This child was kidnaped from his home in Hopewell, N. J., between 8 and 10 p. m. on Tuesday, March 1, 1932.

DESCRIPTION:

Age, 20 months — Hair, blond, curly
Weight, 27 to 30 lbs. — Eyes, dark blue
Height, 29 inches — Complexion, light
Deep dimple in center of chin
Dressed in one-piece coverall night suit

ADDRESS ALL COMMUNICATIONS TO
COL. H. N. SCHWARZKOPF, TRENTON, N. J., or
COL. CHAS. A. LINDBERGH, HOPEWELL, N. J.

ALL COMMUNICATIONS WILL BE TREATED IN CONFIDENCE

March 11, 1932 — COL. H. NORMAN SCHWARZKOPF, Supt. New Jersey State Police, Trenton, N. J.

It was hoped that this widely circulated poster would bring information about the Lindbergh baby and his kidnapper.

Times Wide World Photo.

Photograph of the Lindbergh residence, showing how the baby was kidnapped.

"All the News That's Fit to Print."

The New York Times.

LATE CITY EDITION
WEATHER—Showers today; tomorrow cloudy.
Temperatures Yesterday—Max., 60; min., 40.

VOL. LXXXI....No. 27,120. +**** NEW YORK, MONDAY, APRIL 25, 1932. TWO CENTS In New York City | THREE CENTS Within 200 Miles | FOUR CENTS Elsewhere Except 7th and 8th Postal Zones

NAZIS LEAD IN FOUR STATES; WIN 162 SEATS IN PRUSSIA; LIBERALS NOW IN MINORITY

HITLERITES GAIN HEAVILY

They Poll 8,008,000 in Prussia as Socialists Get 4,675,000.

FINISH SECOND IN BAVARIA

Also Fail to Upset Coalitions in Wuerttemberg and Hamburg but Succeed in Anhalt.

THREE KILLED IN CLASHES

Nazis Likewise Make Big Gains in Elections of Members of Five Austrian Diets.

By GUIDO ENDERIS.
Special Cable to THE NEW YORK TIMES.

BERLIN, April 24.—Liberalism lost Parliamentary control of Prussia today through the defeat at the polls of the Weimar three-party coalition, which had governed the State since 1919. Its slender majority was wiped out by the Hitlerites winning 162 mandates in the new Diet, against six held in the expiring Legislature.

The National Socialists not only increased their vote in Prussia over their Presidential poll on the first ballot March 13 by more than 1,000,000 votes but if backed by Dr. Alfred Hugenberg's Nationalists and scattering groups identified with the so-called National Opposition would definitely control the new Diet provided the Communists abstained from voting.

The parties of the Weimar coalition forfeited sixty-five seats today, the Socialists and Democrats being the chief losers and the Centrists almost holding their own. The Nazis now have the same number of seats as the three coalition parties jointly.

The number of seats won by the parties in the new Prussian Diet and their representation in the outgoing Diet, which was elected May 20, 1928, are as follows:

	Seats in New Diet.	Seats in Old Diet.
National Socialists	162	6
Social Democrats	93	137
Centrists	67	71
Communists	57	56
Nationalists	31	82
People's party	7	40
State's party (Democrats)	2	21
Christian Socialists	2	..
German Hanoverians	1	4

The Economic group, which had twenty-one mandates in the old Diet, failed to win a seat.

Get 30 Per Cent of Total Vote.

Of the 34,500,000 votes cast in today's elections to the Diets of Prussia, Bavaria, Württemberg, Hamburg and Anhalt the Nazis gathered in close to 10,000,000, almost 30 per cent, literally grinding into pulp such Rightist middle parties in Prussia as the People's party and the Economic group.

In Bavaria, Wuerttemberg and Hamburg the Nazis failed to upset the existing middle party coalitions, although they and the Nationalists will control Anhalt, where the present Socialist-Democratic Ministry will disappear.

The new Prussian Diet will not be convoked before the middle of June, and in order to force the election of a new Premier the Nazis and their allies must have a clear majority, which will only be possible if the Communists abstain from voting.

Since the Weimar coalition was unhorsed in today's voting, it may disappear entirely in Prussia and give way to a new line-up wherein the Centrists again will hold the key position.

Socialists Lose Heavily.

It is now viewed as dubious whether the Braun-Severing Ministry will maintain itself in office through the amendment to the Diet's by-laws pushed through in a recent extra session, as the Communists, who cordially hate the Ministry, are believed willing to join the heavily reinforced nationalist line-up in turning it out.

A feature of today's voting in Prussia was the slump in the Socialist vote, which was almost 1,000,000 less than the party polled in the Diet election in 1928.

More than half a dozen nondescript parties on the official ballot failed to win a place and of the 22,000,000 votes cast in Prussia 1,000,000 were wasted through failure to reach the vote prescribed by the election law.

Continued on Page Seven.

16,000 Nazis in Berlin Hall Cheer Returns in Hitler Victory

By The Associated Press.

BERLIN, April 24.—National Socialists to the estimated number of 16,000, including many aged housewives, gathered at the Sportpalast to watch the election returns tonight.

Over their glasses of beer they greeted the mounting figures flashed on a huge screen with frequent shouts of "Hail Hitler!" and wild cheers.

"Despite the taking of our material by the police, we triumphed," said Dr. Joseph Goebbels, a Hitler lieutenant, referring to the recent raids on Nazi storm troops, which the government ordered disbanded.

"Soon we will be able to take it back from police headquarters, well kept," he added.

'LET EUROPE ALONE,' HERRIOT ADVISES US

French Leader Asserts We Take Interest in Affairs Abroad Only When It Is Profitable.

ATTACKS THE MORATORIUM

Young Plan Was to Be Final, He Says in Election Speech—Home Area Heckles Tardieu.

Wireless to THE NEW YORK TIMES

PARIS, April 24.—In an election speech at Avignon today Edouard Herriot, Radical Socialist leader, vigorously attacked the Hoover moratorium and interference by the United States in European affairs.

"If European matters do not interest Americans," M. Herriot demanded, "why don't they let us alone?

"France made important sacrifices in accepting the Young Plan, which was promised as a final settlement of debts and reparations," he said. "Now the whole question is raised again, and France is the only country to protest against the Hoover moratorium."

Referring to the visit of former Premier Pierre Laval to the United States, M. Herriot commented that it had proved wholly unnecessary to send a transatlantic liner to America to bring back the results the Hoover moratorium had yielded.

"Alain Gerbault could have brought them back in his little sailboat," said M. Herriot.

[Alain Gerbault, French sportsman, sailed around the world in a 30-foot sloop, finishing the six-year trip in July, 1929.]

"It hardly seems logical," M. Herriot concluded sarcastically, "that we should be taking orders from the Americans, who disdain our difficulties and only take an interest in them when they think they will prove profitable."

Flandin Attacks Blum Bloc.

PARIS, April 24 (AP).—The leader of the powerful Radical Socialist opposition, Edouard Herriot, brought Franco-American relations into the French election campaign today in a speech at Avignon. The former Premier and long-time Mayor of Lyons protested against the Hoover moratorium and American interference in European affairs.

[The Radical Socialists are next to the straight Socialists in strength in the Chamber of Deputies, with 109 members in their single bloc, and might be described better for the American voter if they were called merely "liberal." France elects a new Chamber next Sunday.]

P. E. Flandin, Republican of the Left and Finance Minister in Premier André Tardieu's Cabinet, in an address at Bordeaux denied that a French loan of $14,000,000 to Hungary had been used for munitions or to pay private Hungarian debts in France.

M. Flandin said definite suspension of reparations would deprive the French budget of an appreciable resource, "which with continued and mounting public charges would create a serious situation."

The Finance Minister's speech was chiefly an attack on Léon Blum's Socialist bloc of 111 members in the Chamber. He said this bloc "unchains appetites it demands that the State satisfy."

PARIS, April 24 (Canadian Press).—Premier André Tardieu, speaking today in his own constituency of Bel-

Continued on Page Five.

450 SEIZED AT DELHI FOR DEFIANCE OF BAN ON INDIAN CONGRESS

Leaders Arrested as Fast as They Arrive for Prohibited All-India Meeting.

ARMORED CARS PATROL CITY

No Violence Reported—Crowd Swarms Streets, Shouting Independence Slogans.

50,000 GANDHISTS IN JAIL.

Detention of Mrs. Naidu and Pandit Malaviya Leaves Party Without an Outstanding Head.

Wireless to THE NEW YORK TIMES.

NEW DELHI, India, April 24.—An attempt by the All-India National Congress to meet here today, despite the government's ban, led to several clashes with the police. More than 450 persons were arrested. Two hundred persons were arrested yesterday, including Pandit Madan Mohan Malaviya, who became president of the Congress when Mrs. Sarojini Naidu was arrested in Bombay Friday.

Until the last moment the Congress kept its plan secret. The illegal session took the form of street demonstrations, which lasted until nightfall. This morning a merchant from Ahmedabad led a crowd of 100 boys, wearing homespun and chanting Congress slogans, to the clock tower in the Chandi Chowk, Delhi's commercial centre, where resolutions were read reaffirming independence as the Congress goal.

A police official, listening with a handful of constables, motioned to the empty police trucks standing near by. The demonstrators marched to the trucks with a serio-comic air, took seats and were driven to the police station, shouting excitedly. As soon as they had gone, 300 Congress supporters rushed from the narrow side streets, shouting aloud the texts of resolutions. Police reinforcements charged with staves and arrested all.

The greatest difficulty was experienced with 100 saffron-shirted Sikhs, who marched from their temple and squatted at the entrance to the police station with their arms linked until removed forcibly. All Moslem shops were open throughout the day, and no Moslems participated in the demonstrations.

Armored Cars Patrol City.

NEW DELHI, April 24 (AP).—Armored cars patrolled Delhi tonight, following the arrest of 369 members of the All-India National Congress who came here for the forty-ninth session of the Congress, in defiance of the government ban. There were no disorders, however.

50,000 Nationalists in Jail.

Approximately 50,000 Indian Nationalists have been jailed since the enactment by the Delhi Government of repressive ordinances prohibiting virtually every form of Nationalist activities. Short-term non-political prisoners have been released in many instances to make way for those guilty of civil disobedience.

Not only thousands of the rank and file, but all of the outstanding leaders of the independence movement are in prison. Mahatma Gandhi is in Yerovda jail at Poona, and his

Continued on Page Eight.

Irish Ministers Quit Ball As Governor General Enters

By The Associated Press.

DUBLIN, April 24.—A sensation was caused in Dublin today by two Ministers of the Irish Free State's new Republican Government having ostentatiously left a social function last night when Governor General James McNeill arrived and the British national anthem was played by a band.

The incident was regarded as an intimation that the Irish Government was determined not to have a Governor General.

The occasion was a ball given by Charles Alphand, the French Minister to the Free State, and Mme. Alphand for a daughter who recently was married.

Many prominent persons attended, including Sean O'Kelly, vice president of the Executive Council, and Frank Aiken, Minister of Defense.

After the guests had assembled Governor General McNeill entered the room and the British anthem was played, whereupon Vice President O'Kelly, Mr. Aiken and their friends left.

PUBLISHERS REPORT BUSINESS IS REVIVING

Associated Press Members Here for Annual Meeting Today Show Optimism.

CITE GAINS IN CIRCULATION

Newspaper Owners of Nation Praise Economic Remedies Adopted by Congress.

Optimistic reports of slowly reviving business in many sections of the country were brought here yesterday by the vanguard of more than 500 publishers or their representatives, who are arriving for the thirty-third annual meeting of The Associated Press, opening today, and the forty-sixth annual convention of the American Newspaper Publishers Association, beginning tomorrow at the Waldorf-Astoria.

Some of the publishers asserted that the slight improvement in business first had been reflected in their circulation. Others said that the upturn, though small, was general. Some expected to see a more marked improvement following the Presidential election. Others held that the election would make no difference. They were practically unanimous in their praise of remedies undertaken by Congress and the administration in Washington and asserted that those remedies had greatly relieved the banking situation and helped to restore confidence.

Major John S. Cohen, publisher of The Atlanta Journal, and Democratic National Committeeman, after expressing the conviction that business conditions would take a turn upward following the Presidential election, said he had no confirmation of newspaper reports from Atlanta that he would be appointed by Governor Richard B. Russell Jr. to fill temporarily the place of the late Senator William J. Harris.

Major Cohen Is Optimistic.

Commenting on the economic situation, Major Cohen said:

"The publishers are doing as well as any other line of business. I really think there are signs of better business. I am optimistic of the whole situation. Atlanta is weathering the storm, and Georgia is

Continued on Page Three.

Slain American Flier Honored by Chinese; Shanghai Throng Acclaims Short as a Hero

Special Cable to THE NEW YORK TIMES.

SHANGHAI, April 24.—The largest crowd ever seen in Shanghai thronged the streets this afternoon to pay honor to Robert Short, American aviator, who was killed in February during an air fight with Japanese planes over Soochow.

Short, who was acclaimed as an American hero and a friend of China, received a State funeral and he was buried at the Hungjao Airdrome near the ruins of the hangars wrecked by Japanese bombs.

Following two memorial services the coffin was escorted through the streets by Chinese soldiers and sailors and representatives of the Nanking Government and of scores of Chinese organizations. Four American and four Chinese aviators acted as pallbearers, while a plane circled overhead during the burial.

Scores of decorated cars bearing laudatory scrolls and banners passed in the procession, in which many Boy Scouts and Girl Guides marched. The streets were so packed during the earlier part of the route to the airdrome that the police had to use batons to clear the thoroughfare when the procession was halted.

The flier's mother and brother, Edmund Short, attended the funeral as guests of the State. They had come here from Seattle, Wash.

SHANGHAI, April 24 (AP).—When Robert Short, American aviator, was shot down over Soochow on Feb. 22 in a Chinese airplane he was "just an aviator." Today he was buried as a Colonel in the Nationalist Government army.

The funeral services were held in a foreign church of the International Settlement with an American clergyman officiating. A Chinese Government spokesman eulogized the flier.

"During the darkest hour of China's desperate defense against a foreign invader," he said, "when the nations of the world were exerting the utmost efforts to check the violence of a country bent upon conquest, Robert Short, a friend from a distant land, flew out of the sky and gave his life that righteousness among nations may be vindicated and upheld.

"To the Chinese people this act of courage and sacrifice was electrifying. It was reassuring evidence of China's faith that in resisting the invasion of those who would foster national aggression she was not fighting alone."

DELANEY TO TESTIFY TODAY AS SEABURY SCANS WALKER ACTS

City Transit Chief Summoned by Wire to First Public Hearing on Mayor.

INQUIRY PLANS SECRET

But Indications Are That Subway Contracts and Bus Franchises Will Be Taken Up.

HASTINGS UNDER SUBPOENA

McNaboe in New Attack on Seabury Says Committee Did Not Pass on Money Paid to Him.

Samuel Seabury, chief counsel to the Hofstadter committee, will begin his attack on Mayor Walker today with a study of the Administration's handling of the transit problem.

John H. Delaney, chairman of the Board of Transportation, was summoned yesterday by telegraph to appear this morning as a witness at the first of a series of public hearings on matters connected with the Mayor's conduct of his office.

These hearings, which Mr. Seabury regards as the most important that he has conducted since he opened his investigation of the city government nearly a year ago, are expected to provide the background and a large part of the material for Mr. Seabury's examination of Mayor Walker.

The Mayor, however, probably will not be summoned as a witness before the end of the month, for it is Mr. Seabury's intention to present all the evidence concerning Mr. Walker before calling upon him to present his side of the story. Ten or twelve hearings will be required for its presentation.

While Mr. Seabury has been secretive regarding the subject matter to be taken up at the coming hearings, his summoning of Mr. Delaney, who has been the director of the city's transit policy since John F. Hylan was Mayor, indicated that subway contracts and bus franchises would be the first matters considered.

Hastings Subpoenaed Today.

Mr. Delaney was not subpoenaed in the usual way but was notified by telegram late in the afternoon that his presence would be required at today's public hearing. State Senator John A. Hastings of Brooklyn, whose name was linked with efforts of the Equitable Coach Company to obtain a franchise for the operation of buses in Manhattan, Brooklyn and Queens, also is under subpoena for today.

The circumstances surrounding the award of a franchise to the Equitable by the Board of Estimate are expected to provide material for a large part of the hearing. Charges of a $500,000 "slush fund" were made in connection with the franchise in 1929 by Cornelius J. Sheehan, who offered to name the "go-between" who handled the money.

The franchise proved valueless when the Transit Commission refused to grant the certificate that would have made it operative, declaring that the company was suffering from "financial paralysis." At Mayor Walker's direction Deputy Controller Frank J. Prial undertook an investigation into the Equitable Company's $500,000 expenses incurred pending approval of its application but the inquiry was dropped when the bus company suddenly withdrew from the field.

Another matter concerning buses may come under the scrutiny of the committee. Mr. Prial and Borough President George U. Harvey of Queens recently have voiced objections to the granting of a franchise to Jamaica Buses, Inc., a subsidiary of the Jamaica Central Railways. Fred C. Harris, an officer in the company, it was revealed some time ago, had power of attorney over a safety deposit box rented to Mayor Walker.

Whether Mr. Seabury intends to take up the questions of cost and the delayed opening of the new Eighth Avenue subway has not been revealed, although it is known that both these matters have been the subject of an intensive inquiry by members of his staff.

Seabury Confers With Aides.

The chief counsel returned to his town house last night after spending the week-end in conference with four assistants in preparation for the hearings opening today. The evening was spent in further study of the evidence to be presented.

On the eve of the opening of the important series of hearings State Senator John J. McNaboe issued a statement repeating what he has often said before, that the investigation was a failure and a needless expense to the taxpayers. He cited the recent criticism of Mr. Seabury's

Continued on Page Ten.

BITTER FIGHT CERTAIN ON ECONOMY BILL OMITTING HOOVER'S 3-POINT PROGRAM; $613,000,000 TOTAL SAVING IS POSSIBLE

Major Items in Economy Measure As Completed by House Committee

Wide Range of Changes Throughout the Government Services Is Provided in Omnibus Bill to Be Introduced in the House Today.

Special to THE NEW YORK TIMES.

WASHINGTON, April 24.—The major items contained in the omnibus bill as finally framed by the House Economy Committee are:

1—Reduce all salaries over $1,000 by 11 per cent.

2—Abolish Saturday half-holidays.

3—Reduce salaries of members of International Joint Commission to $5,000; Shipping Board members reduced from seven to four, with a maximum salary of $10,000, and members of the Board of Mediation reduced to $10,000. (The committee held that in reduction of the Shipping Board's membership it was "reorganizing" that bureau).

4—No increase in pay and no filling of vacancies except by Executive order.

5—Retire about 5,000 superannuated Federal employes.

6—Reduce traveling allowances to $4, $5 and $6 per day, and reduce subsistence for railway mail clerks from $3 to $2 per day.

Overtime Is to Be Eliminated.

7—Eliminate extra overtime and Sunday and holiday compensation.

8—Where a retired officer, who is drawing retirement pay or other compensation, is otherwise employed and the total amount received is more than $3,000, the retired pay shall cease. The individual shall have the privilege of choosing the income he prefers.

9—The Postmaster General is granted authority to convert mail clerk to mail carrier, or vice versa, without additional compensation.

10—The President is directed to disband the Philippine Scouts after July 1, 1932, and after that date the Secretary of War is directed to charge the cost of the Scouts to the Philippine Islands.

11—The Government Printing Office is restricted in certain expenditures.

12—The army and navy transport service is suspended; the Secretary of the Navy is directed to turn over to the Shipping Board the transports Henderson, Chaumont, Kittery, Sirius and Vega.

13—The Panama Railroad Steamship Line is abolished

Government Publications to Yield Profit.

14—The Bureau of Mines and the Bureau of Standards are authorized to charge fees for services; government publications are to be sold at a price 30 per cent above cost of printing, instead of at actual cost, and patent fees are to be raised to $30.

15—Fish cultural stations are to be turned over to such States as are willing to care for them.

16—Agricultural Experiment Stations may be turned over to any State which will continue to operate them.

17—The President receives restricted authority to group, consolidate and coordinate departmental functions.

18—An Administrator of Public Works is created, but is forbidden to use the Corps of Engineers and the Rivers and Harbors Department employed on flood control work.

19—Consolidate the War and Navy Departments into a Department of National Defense.

20—Consolidate the Bureau of Navigation and Steamboat Inspection Service.

21—Transfer the Personnel Classification Board to the Civil Service Commission.

22—Revise Veterans' Bureau legislation.

Three Hoover Measures Omitted.

The bill does not contain three of the measures recommended by the President.

These are the staggered furlough plan for Federal employes, estimated to save $83,000,000 annually; the elimination for a year of the allowance to rural mail carriers for maintenance of vehicles, bringing a reduction of $17,500,000, and the suspension for a year of all leaves of absence and vacation allowances at an estimated saving of $35,000,000.

SPECIAL RULE IS SOUGHT

First Strife Will Hinge on Considering Provisions as a 'Rider.'

FURLOUGH PLAN LEFT OUT

It Will Be Offered Separately—Suspended Leaves and Rural Mail Fee Also Out.

MERGER MIGHT BRING VETO

'Defense Department' Proposal and Public Works Bureau Are Repugnant to President.

Special to THE NEW YORK TIMES.

WASHINGTON, April 24.—Working from early morning until last midnight, the House Economy Committee, created on Feb. 19 to study the methods to reduce Federal expenditures in the fiscal year 1933, completed drafting the huge omnibus bill expected to save the government more than $263,000,000.

Chairman McDuffie was laying plans tonight to introduce the measure tomorrow, to enable all members of the House to complete a thorough study of the bill before Wednesday, when it is to come before the House. The bill came from the government printing presses about noon today.

The measure contains practically every major item discussed during the two recent conferences with President Hoover, with the exception of three important suggestions offered by him and which he continues to believe are superior to comparable items offered by the committee.

These items are his staggered furlough plan, estimated to save $83,000,000 annually by compelling every Federal employe who receives more than $1,200 to take a month's vacation without pay; eliminating for one year the allowance to rural mail carriers for maintenance of vehicles, estimated to save $17,500,000; and suspension for one year of all leave-of-absence and vacation allowances, to save $35,000,000.

The President's furlough plan will be introduced as a separate piece of legislation. The committee added to the bill, over the protests of President Hoover and other administration leaders, two items which he is expected to find so objectionable that some think he might even veto the entire measure, if they remain in it.

These are the Garner-Byrns plan for consolidation of the army and navy into a single Department of National Defense, which Democratic leaders say would save $100,000,000 yearly, and Representative Cochran's plan to establish a Department of Public Works.

Cuts in Veterans' Aid Replaced.

For a time during the last few sessions of the committee it was apparent that tremendous pressure was being brought against the committee's decision to eliminate two World War veterans' sections of the economy bill.

These provided that no veteran paying income tax on $1,500, if single, and $3,500, if married, could receive hospital treatment at government expense, the estimated saving being $20,000,000, and that $20 should be the maximum allowed for hospitalized veterans when single and $75 if married and having dependents, the estimated saving of this item being $8,373,000. Late yesterday the $20,000,000 item was replaced in the bill, and later in the evening the second section was added. The total estimated savings in the Veterans' Bureau was thus brought up to $59,627,000.

The army and navy consolidation plan appeared tonight to be the only one under which the amount of the possible saving was greatly in doubt. Some members of the committee insisted that it would not save more than $25,000,000, while others estimated it in excess of $100,000,000. The latter figure was given by Chairman Byrns of the House Appropriations Committee, and some others said that military experts had estimated that it would be even higher.

To the estimated savings planned by the Economy Committee must be added, Democratic leaders say, the amounts already cut by the House from President Hoover's budget estimates.

So far, and including the Senate's cut of 10 per cent in the Interior De-

Continued on Page Two.

SEEK TO CLEAR WAY FOR TAX BILL TODAY

Senators Press for Decision on Tariffs to Have Measure Ready Next Week.

Special to THE NEW YORK TIMES.

WASHINGTON, April 24.—The Finance Committee will launch a "hurry-up" program tomorrow to have the billion-dollar tax bill ready for action in the Senate by early next week.

With all efforts bent toward speed, Republicans and Democrats alike planned to move for early consideration of the controversial tariff items to decide whether they shall be submitted with the revenue measure.

Senator Hull, Democrat, of Tennessee, will move immediately for the exclusion of all tariffs, including the duties on coal and oil already voted by the House. Senator Smoot, chairman of the committee, said tonight that he would call for early action on this motion.

The tariff question loomed tonight as the greatest obstacle to quick action, both in the committee and on the floor. Various groups insist that copper, lumber, pulpwood, wood pulp and butter be included for protection by special import taxes. The sentiment for additional tariff duties has been a menace to progress on the revenue measure from the start, but

Continued on Page Ten.

PLAN NEW TACTICS IN MARKET INQUIRY

Senators Expect to Decide on Their Course at Executive Meeting Today.

Special to THE NEW YORK TIMES.

WASHINGTON, April 24.—The Stock Exchange "bear hunt" by the Senate Banking and Currency Committee today awaited the formulation of new tactics which the committee expects to develop at an executive session tomorrow morning.

The decision to make new plans, it was learned authoritatively, resulted from a fortnight of investigation in which the committee has taken thousands of words of testimony regarding the operations of the Stock Exchange in general and the activities of a few outstanding speculators, but has not received any evidence supporting the belief that recent market declines were due to "bear raids."

Michael J. Meehan, named yesterday as one of the central figures of the Radio stock pool in 1929, whom the committee is anxious to question, gave notice tonight through a representative that he will be ready to appear at any time convenient. He is motoring here from the South.

At tomorrow's executive session, special counsel for the committee will seek formal approval of a project to send experts to New York to in-

Continued on Page Sixteen.

"All the News That's Fit to Print."

The New York Times.

LATE CITY EDITION

WEATHER—Cloudy, probably rain today; tomorrow fair and warmer. Temperatures Yesterday—Max., 60; Min., 46.

Copyright, 1932, by The New York Times Company.

VOL. LXXXI....No. 27,138. ★★★★+ NEW YORK, FRIDAY, MAY 13, 1932. TWO CENTS In New York City | THREE CENTS Within 200 Miles | FOUR CENTS Elsewhere Except 7th and 8th Postal Zones

WALKER GOT $26,535 BONDS FROM J. A. SISTO AS 'GIFT,' TAXI FINANCIER TESTIFIES

PROFIT IN A STOCK DEAL

Control Board Advocate Bought Shares to Aid Mayor, He Swears.

McKEON WAS INTERMEDIARY

Friend of Walker Says He Took Envelope to City Hall and Handed It Over in Auto.

HASTINGS GOT CAB PROFITS

Terminal Company Hired Him at $18,000 a Year, Seabury Is Told—Unpaid Loans Bared.

J. A. Sisto, who had a hand in financing the Parmelee Transportation Company, gave Mayor Walker bonds worth $26,535.51 before the Municipal Assembly passed the Mayor's bill creating a Board of Taxicab Control, the broker testified yesterday before the Hofstadter committee.

Both Mr. Sisto and John J. McKeon, who delivered the bonds to Mayor Walker in a sealed envelope in the Winter of 1929, demanded that the investigating committee cloak them with immunity before they would say a word about the matter.

Taxi Company Hired Hastings.

Just before Samuel Seabury, chief counsel to the committee, sprang this surprise, B. M. Seymour, vice president and general manager of the Terminal Cab Company, admitted that his company had paid $26,183 in salary to State Senator John A. Hastings, the Mayor's friend.

Colonel George W. Mixter of the firm of Day & Zimmerman testified that it was the Brooklyn Senator who got his company the job of making a traffic survey of New York in 1928. As a result of that survey, the witness said, Mayor Walker appointed a committee, with Frank P. Walsh as chairman, to study the problem of taxicab control.

That committee, of which Colonel Mixter was a member, reported in September, 1930, recommending a board of control, designed eventually to put the city's taxicab industry on a single-franchise basis, which was what the big companies wanted and the independents dreaded. Throughout the entire period of study, Colonel Mixter said, Senator Hastings was in frequent touch with Day & Zimmerman and the taxicab committee. He looked upon the Brooklyn Senator as the "Mayor's messenger or go-between."

More Hastings Loans Bared.

Senator Hastings had been under fire all day as Mr. Seabury sought to show that he had borrowed heavily from companies with which the three backers of the Jamaica Central Railways, an applicant for a Queens bus franchise, were associated, while that company's application was pending in the Board of Estimate.

Park A. Rowley, president of the Manhattan Company, admitted that Hastings had borrowed $7,500 and had not repaid it. William M. Greve, president of New York Investors, was the victim of a $25,000 "touch," which he said he would make good himself. H. P. Williams, chairman of the executive committee of the New York Title and Mortgage Company, admitted that business exigencies had forced him to recommend that Senator Hastings be excused from making good a collateral bond on a $350,000 mortgage because it was cheaper than to resort to litigation.

Throughout the whole proceeding, members of the Democratic minority, especially Assemblyman Louis A. Cuvillier, fought to protect the "dignity of the Senate," as represented in the person of the member from Kings County. Senator Samuel Hofstadter, chairman of the committee, repeatedly overruled their objections to the testimony, and it reached the point where the spectators were laughing every time Assemblyman Cuvillier addressed the chair.

But the court room was gravely sedate and silent, and even the minority dropped their fire of objections, when Mr. Sisto, a slim, gray-haired man, dressed as carefully as the Mayor himself, took the stand and unfolded his story.

He began by refusing to waive im-

Continued on Page Twelve.

Seabury Has a Prior Right To Explanation, Mayor Says

When Mayor Walker was informed at City Hall of the testimony of J. A. Sisto before the Hofstadter committee he broke in and said:

"I received $26,000 in bonds as the profit from that transaction—is that it?"

Informed that his statement was substantially correct, the Mayor parried questions with:

"Well, now, don't you think that Judge Seabury has a prior right to the answer to that question? I have nothing to say about it now, but it will be answered when Judge Seabury asks about it."

METROPOLITAN LISTS NEW AMERICAN OPERA

"Emperor Jones," Gruenberg's Setting of O'Neill Play, to Be Given in Berlin Also.

TIBBETT WILL SING ROLE

14th Native Work Under Gatti Regime Will Be Produced Early in Coming Season.

The Metropolitan Opera Association will present next season a new American opera, "Emperor Jones," based on Eugene O'Neill's play, by the American composer Louis Gruenberg, it became known yesterday.

The libretto has been prepared by Mr. Gruenberg himself. When he sent Mr. O'Neill a copy of his adaptation, the playwright replied that it had been admirably prepared so that the dramatic qualities and flavor of the work were preserved.

Lawrence Tibbett will enact the part of Jones and Tullio Serafin will conduct. No decision has been made by the Metropolitan as to the date of the presentation, but it is believed that it will be early in the season. Erich Kleiber, general music director of the Berlin Staatsoper, one of the largest opera companies in Europe, has already announced that he will produce the opera in Berlin this Fall. It appears, therefore, that Berlin and New York will vie for the right to give the work its world première.

Tom-Tom Used in Score.

Mr. Gruenberg has written the opera in two acts. He has made use, naturally, of the beat of the tom-tom which pursues Jones through the drama. This drum beat, which gradually accelerates in the opera, ceases only in certain brief scenes. These are during the visions and hallucinations which haunt Jones as he flees through the forest.

The work calls for a unique arrangement of the stage. The chorus of pursuing Negroes is grouped out of sight of the audience, below and in front of the stage flooring. At first only crossing hands and arms are seen above it. Then, as the pursuit of Jones draws nearer to its quarry, the bodies of the pursuers gradually emerge as yells of hate and triumph gather in volume.

The hallucinations of Jones—of the murdered crap player, of the sheriff whom Jones has killed, and of the auction block—are shown on small raised stages, to indicate that they are figments of the Negro's imagination.

Finally, Jones is seen, a nearly naked savage, seated on the ground with his fellows, swaying in terror as the medicine man leaps on the stage and indicates him as the tribe's victim. At the end the body of the fugitive, who shoots himself with the silver bullet, is carried by the tribesmen into the forest. Choruses of savage exultation are heard dying away in the distance.

Music Moves Swiftly.

To this drama Gruenberg has written what appears to be swift and pungent music. The principal moment of lyrical expansion is his prayer for the Lord's aid in his plight, which is in the general character, but not in slavish imitation, of a Negro spiritual. The score is also reflective of passing incident and gesture on the stage. Each one of the scenes of hallucination has its special musical counterpart. Toward the end, with an immense crescendo and acceleration, several pairs of drums are employed to intensely stirring effect. The opera takes about one hour to perform.

When Erich Kleiber, who conducted the opening weeks of the recent New

Continued on Page Nine.

Hoover Urges 3-Point Relief Plan Of $1,500,000,000 to Use as Loans

Senate Leaders Are Asked to Put the Proposal Before Colleagues—Finance Corporation Would Help States Handle Jobless and Advance Money for Spurring Business.

By ARTHUR KROCK.

Special to THE NEW YORK TIMES.

WASHINGTON, May 12.—President Hoover today asked Senators Robinson of Arkansas and Watson, the Democratic and Republican leaders of the Senate, to propose to their colleagues a three-point Federal relief program to stimulate private business in reproductive enterprises, to advance money for self-liquidating projects in States and municipalities, to ameliorate agricultural distress and to loan to States—but not municipalities—money for the relief of unemployed citizens.

The President's plan can be achieved simply by extending the powers and financial resources of the Reconstruction Finance Corporation. It involves no new government borrowings; it does not disturb the processes of budget balancing; it contemplates no bond issues for non-reproductive public works, as was proposed by New York financiers. If Congress will pass an amendment to the act establishing the Reconstruction Finance Corporation, the relief measures can be instituted.

The President's plan provides:

1. That the corporation be authorized to issue an additional $1,500,000,000 in debentures, of the proceeds from which $300,000,000 is to be loaned to States for general relief measures; $40,000,000 for export agricultural aid, and the remaining $1,160,000,000 loaned to private business for reproductive enterprises, assured by contracts.

2.—That State bonds and securities which cannot otherwise be floated be purchased by the corporation when the proceeds of these bonds and securities are to be used for unemployment relief.

3.—That the corporation be authorized to loan funds for self-liquidating projects such as toll bridges, tunnels and so forth.

It provides that private business planning reproductive enterprises for which credit cannot be obtained from the banks shall but put on a loaning basis with the corporation, a plan originally proposed by Mr. Hoover when the corporation was created, but rejected by Congress.

Senator Robinson, after a morning conference with the President, called a meeting of Democrats after the Senate adjourned this afternoon and outlined the President's idea. It was favorably received.

Senator Watson talked to a number of Republicans and reported progress with the idea. Speaker Garner and Minority Leader Snell were also consulted, and tonight Republican members of the Senate Committtee on Banking and Currency were called to

Continued on Page Eleven.

TAX BILL'S TARIFFS ASSAILED IN REPORT BY MINORITY GROUP

Their Elimination From Senate Measure Is Demanded and 'Log-rolling' Is Condemned.

GAIN IN REVENUE DOUBTED

Imposts on Oil, Lumber, Copper and Coal Will Mean Embargo, Opponents Assert.

Special to THE NEW YORK TIMES.

WASHINGTON, May 12.—Five Democratic members of the Senate Finance Committee opened a fight on the tariff features of the billion-dollar tax bill today in a minority report demanding elimination of the duties on coal, oil, copper and lumber and condemning the "log-rolling" by which, they said, the items were inserted.

Consideration of the measure, expected today, was delayed by further debate on the Glass banking bill. When it appeared that the Glass measure could not be disposed of, even within another day, Republican leaders asked that it be side-tracked to give right of way to the tax bill.

Senator Glass gave rather reluctant consent, explaining that he long since had found it wise "not to go up against a buzz saw."

Senator Smoot will open discussion of the tax bill tomorrow. He had finished preparation tonight of a 4,000-word speech recommending the compromise measure as the prime step toward business recovery through the guarantee of government credit.

Senate leaders at the same time completed plans for a series of night sessions next week, by which it is hoped to complete the revenue measure well before June 10, the date tentatively set for adjournment.

Minority Questions Efficacy.

The minority tax bill report was signed by Senators Harrison, George, Walsh of Massachusetts, Costigan and Hull. Democratic members of the Finance Committee whose names were not attached were Senators Barkley of Kentucky, who voted in committee for the coal tariff; Connally of Texas and Gore of Oklahoma, who favored the duty on oil, and King of Utah, who stood for the copper tariff.

The report questioned whether the duties would result in additional revenues, cited adverse decisions on some of the items by the Tariff Commission and predicted that in many cases the consumer would be a sufferer.

The "log-rolling" methods, it said, would be odious even in a general tariff measure. But to resort to "trades, exchanges of votes and on-again, off-again" practices, the minority charges, such as were used in writing the tariff items into an emergency revenue measure, was held by the Democrats to be "an exhibition that will raise serious questions in the public mind concerning the capacity of representative government to function promptly

Continued on Page Thirteen.

NEW RELIEF GROUP WITH SMITH AT HEAD NAMED BY WALKER

Merged Bureaus on Jobs and Home Aid Have $5,000,000 to Use Until Aug. 1.

UNITY OF EFFORT IS OBJECT

Leading Lawyers, Bankers and Welfare Officials to Begin Tasks on June 1.

Members of the Emergency Work and Relief Administration, formed by a consolidation of the Home Relief Bureau and the Emergency Work Commission, who will assume their tasks on June 1, were notified of their appointments yesterday by Mayor Walker.

The new committee will consist of the following:

ALFRED E. SMITH, Empire State Building, chairman.

FRANK L. POLK, lawyer, former Under Secretary of State, 15 Broad Street.

LAWSON PURDY, executive director, Charity Organization Society, 105 East Twenty-second Street.

GEORGE V. McLAUGHLIN, president, Brooklyn Trust Company, 177 Montague Street, Brooklyn.

JOHN A. STEPHENS, Thompson Starrett Company, 245 East Twenty-third Street.

SOLOMON LOWENSTEIN, executive director, Federation for Support Jewish Philanthropic Societies 71 West Forty-seventh Street.

FRANK J. TAYLOR, Commissioner of Public Welfare.

MARY L. GIBBONS, Catholic Charities, 10 East Thirty-fourth Street.

WILLIAM EWING, J. P. Morgan & Co., 23 Wall Street.

VICTOR F. RIDDER, president, New York State Board of Social Welfare, 22 North William Street.

WILLIAM J. HODSON, executive director, Welfare Council, 122 East Twenty-second Street.

S. SLOAN COLT, president, Bankers Trust Company, 16 Wall Street.

WILLIAM H. MATTHEWS, Association for Improving the Condition of the Poor; director, work bureau of the Gibson committee, 104 East Twenty-third Street.

JOSEPH J. BAKER, director, Brooklyn Federation of Jewish Charities, 355 First Street.

RALPH WOLF, president, Board of Jewish Social Service, 24 Pine Street.

Coordination of Efforts.

The purpose of the joint committee will be to eliminate the duplication of investigations, obtain a closer cohesion of all public relief under moneys appropriated by the city and to plan for the performance of public work other than by contract. It will also be the task of the committee to select the most beneficial method of assigning those in need to work relief or home relief.

The committee will have $5,000,000 at its disposal from June 1 to Aug. 1.

Mayor Walker announced that he was pleased that so many members of the Emergency Work Commission had agreed to continue with the new organization. Cornelius N. Bliss, chairman of the Emergency Work Commission, whose term began in October, 1931, will relinquish his work on June 1.

Because of the urgent need that still persists among thousands of New York's unemployed for clothing and food the clothing relief and food relief activities of the Emergency Unemployment Relief Committee will continue indefinitely instead of being discontinued as had been planned, it

Continued on Page Eleven.

LINDBERGH BABY FOUND DEAD NEAR HOME; MURDERED SOON AFTER THE KIDNAPPING 72 DAYS AGO AND LEFT LYING IN WOODS

POLICE INTENSIFY HUNT

Curtis, Norfolk Agent, and Condon, Who Paid Ransom, at Hopewell.

TO AID PROSECUTOR TODAY

Schwarzkopf Says Restraints Designed to Safeguard Baby Now Can Be Thrown Off.

A GROUP UNDER SUSPICION

Gov. Moore Pledges Relentless Hunt—Mulrooney Also Promises Full Aid.

Dr. J. F. Condon, the Bronx lecturer who acted as intermediary in the futile payment by Colonel Lindbergh of $50,000 ransom for his son, and John H. Curtis, the Norfolk boat builder, who also has been conducting negotiations, arrived at Hopewell for questioning by the police early this morning. They were scheduled to go to the prosecutor's office in Mercer County later today.

They arrived at the Lindbergh home shortly before 2 o'clock this morning and were at once closeted with the police. A few minutes before their arrival Colonel H. Norman Schwarzkopf, commanding the New Jersey State Police, made this announcement:

"Dr. Condon and Mr. Curtis will be at these headquarters in a few minutes for questioning in connection with this case and they will be turned over by the police authorities at this point to the prosecuting authorities tomorrow morning."

May Have Secret Data.

It is believed that the two intermediaries may have confidential information about the kidnappers which they are now ready to turn over to the authorities.

With this announcement the head of the New Jersey State Police indicated that the hunt for the murderers would be pursued with the aid of State, New York City and Federal authorities, throwing off the restraint that hitherto hampered the police effort. It was disclosed further by the New Jersey authorities that immediate steps are being taken to arrest a group of persons suspected of kidnapping the Lindbergh baby.

The police started their search immediately with a close though apparently unpromising examination of the place where the body was found.

"No footprints were found in the vicinity of where the baby's body was located," said Colonel Schwarzkopf in a statement early this morning. "This whole territory was thoroughly scoured by investigators from this office, even to the extent of scraping the surface of the ground around where the body was found and putting it all in containers and bringing it to these headquarters for the purpose of test and analysis."

Moore Pledges Every Effort.

Governor A. Harry Moore of New Jersey promised that everything possible would be done to "get the murderers" and announced that he expected to confer today with Colonel Schwarzkopf, head of the New Jersey State police. Meanwhile a grand jury investigation of all the Bronx incidents in the case was predicted last night by an aide of the Bronx District Attorney, Charles B. McLaughlin.

President John Grier Hibben of Princeton University called upon the law-enforcement forces of the country to unite in their hunt for the criminals, in a statement issued after he visited the Lindbergh home with Mrs. Hibben last night.

"A national systematic effort must be made right away," he said. "The authorities have been holding off from the beginning in the fear that their actions must cause the death of the child. Now that is over. The forces of law in the country must unite to get the persons who have done this thing."

Schwarzkopf's Statement.

Colonel Schwarzkopf made clear his course in regard to the hunt in an earlier statement, as follows:

"As long as there was a possibility of the baby being alive, the police have been acting with a certain amount of suppressed activity in order not to interfere with any negotiations that might result in the safe return of the baby.

"Now that the body of the baby

Continued on Page Three.

WHERE KIDNAPPERS LEFT SLAIN BABY.

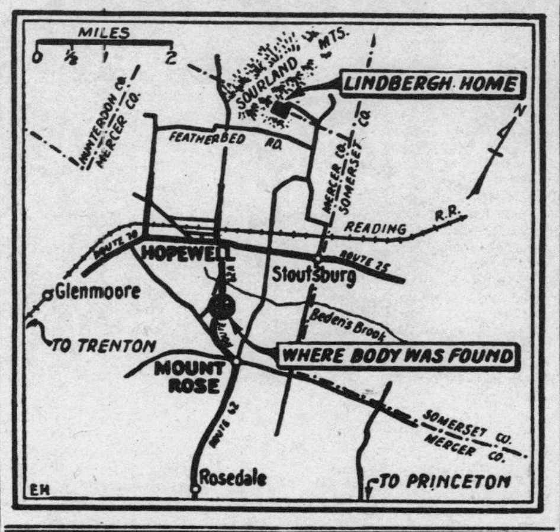

SYMPATHY POURS IN FROM ALL THE WORLD

Grief and Horror Evidenced in Capital Where Hoovers Request Lindbergh News.

ORTIZ RUBIO IS SADDENED

Messages Sent From Mexico City—Inquiries Made From London to Gov. Moore.

Widespread sympathy for the bereaved parents and relatives of Charles A. Lindbergh Jr. and the American people was expressed in messages that poured into the Lindbergh home at Hopewell, N. J., last night from various parts of the world. Officials and civilians who had hastened to join the international search for the kidnappers when the abduction became known sought to assuage the feelings they knew would follow in the wake of the announcement.

The grief and horror with which the nation received the final answer to the question regarding the safety of the child were evidenced at once in Washington, where the report reached the President and Mrs. Hoover among the first. Attachés at the White House, The Associated Press announced, immediately got in touch with the New Jersey authorities to obtain official information.

Deeply moved, Vice President Curtis said, "They have my deepest sympathy, and my most heartfelt condolences go out to the bereaved mother and Colonel Lindbergh and to their families in their sorrow." Mr. Curtis exclaimed with feeling, "It is a most shocking thing."

Unofficial like official Washington was horrified at the news and few persons were able to express their feelings about the tragedy. Captain Emory S. Land, cousin of Colonel Lindbergh, could only declare: "Anything I could say would be futile."

Committee Meeting Halts.

The shocked surprise with which Washington officials, many of them personal friends of the aviator, received the information was exemplified when the meeting of the Democratic steering committee of the Senate broke up on receipt of the barest announcement of the discovery at 6:45 o'clock.

The fifteen Senators present, including Senator Wagner of New York, dropped a momentous question under consideration to express their regrets and seek further details of the development.

"I have never heard more shocking news," Senator Wagner declared.

"It is too awful to talk about," Senator Norris of Nebraska said. Senator Norbeck of South Dakota called the discovery "most tragic," adding "My most heartfelt sympathy goes out to Colonel and Mrs. Lindbergh."

"The world is shocked at the enormity of the crime," Senator Walcott of Connecticut said.

Mrs. Evelyn Walsh McLean, wife of Edward B. McLean, who has put forth great effort and expended upward of $100,000 in an attempt to find the baby, refused to be quoted, but was said by her attorney to be deeply shocked and grieved. He said

Continued on Page Two.

COLONEL BELIEVED ON A YACHT AT SEA

Reported Somewhere Off Block Island on Search for the Kidnappers.

INFORMED OF BABY'S DEATH

Departed May 4 With Norfolk Aides on Mission That Had Seemed Promising.

Colonel Lindbergh was believed to have been on a yacht, somewhere off Block Island, when the body of his son was discovered yesterday. He had been there searching for the kidnappers of his son. There was no question that he had heard of the finding of the body, for Colonel H. Norman Schwarzkopf said that he had been notified, and one of the men with him—telephoning to Norfolk—said that the news had been received.

Colonel Lindbergh set out from Norfolk on May 4, on board the yacht Marcon, owned by Charles H. Consolvo of Baltimore. With him were John H. Curtis, Norfolk boat builder, and one of the trio of negotiators from that city; Edwin A. Bruce of Elmira, N. Y., and Lieutenant George L. Richard, a naval flier. The Marcon cruised up and down the coast near Norfolk until last Saturday, when the men transferred to another boat, which headed out to sea.

Lieutenant Richard Telephones.

The telephone message last night was from Lieutenant Richard to Mrs. Curtis, and was merely "Mr. Curtis is well, and we have heard the news." She could not say from where he had telephoned, nor did he say definitely whether Colonel Lindbergh was still on board. But the Rev. H. Dobson Peacock, one of the other Norfolk negotiators, said that "as far as I know" he was. The second yacht carrying them was generally supposed to have headed directly for Block Island.

When the Marcon sailed from Norfolk it was reported to be going to keep a rendezvous with the kidnappers of Colonel Lindbergh's son, who, according to an unverified rumor at that time, were said be on a foreign ship beyond the twelve-mile limit. Colonel Lindbergh boarded the yacht while in Chesapeake Bay, but bad weather kept the vessel from going out for two days.

The yacht has been running along the Atlantic Coast, it was said, searching for the other ship. Colonel Lindbergh, during the time he was on board, kept watch with the other members of the crew, sleeping in his clothes, always on the lookout for a sign of the second ship. The name of the yacht to which he transferred is not known, nor is its destination. It went straight to sea, however, as soon as he boarded it.

Quest Seemed Promising.

The Norfolk quest had been one of the most promising since the case began. Three prominent citizens of that city were involved, all of them certain that they had been in touch with the kidnappers. They were, besides Mr. Curtis, Rear Admiral Guy H. Burrage, retired, and the Rev. Mr. Peacock. Convinced that they had been in communication with the wanted men, they paid Colonel Lind-

Continued on Page Four.

BODY MILE FROM HOPEWELL

Discovered by Chance Near Centre of Wide Search for Child.

HALF-COVERED BY LEAVES

Skull Fractures Caused Death—Body and Clothing Are Identified by Nurse.

MOTHER IS BRAVE AT NEWS

Neighbors Had Complained That Hunt in Vicinity Had Not Been Thorough.

The baby son of Colonel Charles A. Lindbergh was found dead yesterday afternoon. The child had been murdered.

The body, lying face down in a depression and partly covered with dead leaves and wind-blown débris, was discovered by a Negro truck driver in a patch of woods in the Sourland Mountains less than five miles from the Lindbergh home near Hopewell, N. J.

The discovery was made by accident at 3:15 yesterday afternoon when the driver, walking into the woods from the road, found what he thought was a child's foot sticking out of the ground and notified the police. The identification followed quickly and the official announcement of the Lindbergh baby's fate was made at the Lindbergh home at 6:45 P. M.

The child evidently had been killed soon after he was stolen from his crib in the nursery on the night of March 1. Whether he had been killed with calculating purpose by criminals who found it advantageous to them to get rid of the child, or whether he had been thrown there by kidnappers fleeing in a panic, was not determined last night.

Two Fractures of Skull.

The body showed the marks of two fractures of the skull, one on the left side and the other on the right. The latter was a hole a half-inch in diameter. It was not definitely established whether this was a bullet hole or the result of a blow with a blunt instrument, but since no bullet was found the authorities were inclined to the belief that it was the latter.

The manner in which the baby died was officially stated as follows:

"The diagnosis of the cause of death is a fractured skull due to external violence."

"Unquestionably it was a brutal murder," said Dr. Charles H. Mitchell, County Physician of Mercer County, last night, after he had completed an autopsy.

The condition of the body indicated that the child has been dead at least two months—the kidnapping occurred seventy-two days ago yesterday—and there was a strong possibility that he had been killed on the very night of the kidnapping.

Mother Bearing Up Well.

Mrs. Lindbergh and her mother, Mrs. Dwight W. Morrow, were at home when the body was found, but were in complete seclusion.

Despite the shock of the discovery, Mrs. Lindbergh was bearing up courageously, as she has from the beginning, it was learned last night.

Colonel Lindbergh, who has been away much of the time in recent weeks making fruitless journeys in an attempt to make contact with the kidnappers, was not at home when the discovery was made. Colonel H. Norman Schwarzkopf, commanding the New Jersey State police, said that Colonel Lindbergh had been informed of his baby's death, however, and was on his way home. He did not disclose where the Colonel had been.

Positive identification of the baby's body was furnished last night by Betty Gow, the nursemaid, about whom so much interest in the case

Continued on Page Three.

N.Y. Yankee's stars, Lou Gehrig (L) and Babe Ruth.

Gehrig shakes hands with Ruth as Ruth crosses home plate after hitting a home run in the fifth inning of a World Series game against Chicago.

New York City's Beer Parade, led by Mayor Walker, was among the longest and most colorful. Gene Tunney can be seen waving his hat to the crowd along Fifth Avenue.

Section 1

"All the News That's Fit to Print."

The New York Times.

LATE CITY EDITION
WEATHER—Fair today and tomorrow; temperature unchanged.
Temperatures Yesterday—Max., 76; Min., 59.

Section 1

Copyright, 1932, by The New York Times Company.

VOL. LXXXI....No. 27,140. **** NEW YORK, SUNDAY, MAY 15, 1932. Including Rotogravure Picture Section in two parts—Magazine and Book Sections in Rotogravure. TEN CENTS

ALL-DAY PARADE FOR BEER JAUNTILY LED BY WALKER; CHEERED BY GAY THRONGS

ASK 'TAX FOR PROSPERITY'

BandsPlayDrinkingSongs as Pretzels Are Strewn in Marchers' Path.

BARS APPEAR ON FLOATS

Tin Pails and Pinochle Games Mingle With Banners Urging Remedy for Slump.

NEW START MADE AT NIGHT

Mayor, Cheered by Spectators, Leads That Also—Other Cities Have Similar Parades.

New York went on record yesterday as being in favor of additional taxation. It said so on banners and streamers, on signs painted along the sides of trucks, on small buttons that superseded gardenias in frock-coat lapels. This taxation would balance the budget, put men to work, start moving the rusted wheels of industry and remove the rackets from the social side of life. And, yes, New York likes a glass of good beer now and then.

All day long the city expressed its thought—and hope—in the event that will be known to history as the "Beer Parade." Led by Mayor Walker, an almost endless line of marchers started out long before noon to display their numbers and aspirations. Late last night they were still walking bravely along, the rear guard of one of the metropolitan district's biggest athletic events. Banners that waved against the noonday sun still waved at the midnight moon.

Heralded by all save the drys—and sneered at by them—the parade was indubitably a success. No one was kept out for lack of a horse or a uniform. There were scores of bands to provide music and the better known of the Teutonic drinking songs, and when the musicians ran out there were trucks bearing mechanical devices for playing phonograph records. Overhead circled airplanes, and the route of the event was such that picnic luncheons could be eaten on the grass in Central Park.

Marching Legions Seem Countless.

Just how many took part was an open question. Police and other officials bandied figures about. Mayor Walker said before the event that between 75,000 and 100,000 would march. During the afternoon a policeman reported that "about two million" were participating, either by parading or cheering on the sidelines. A statistician estimated that 2,000 passed a given point on the parade route each hour, and there were a great many hours, indeed.

Last night the numbers were still in dispute. Brig. Gen. John J. Phelan, out of his wisdom of crowds, said 60,000 had taken part in the day parade and 25,000 in the one at night. He estimated that 10,000 persons had gone by each hour. But certain unofficial counters, with mechanical contrivances, declared the total would not go much above 28,000. This was divided into 18,000 marching by day, and the rest in the evening.

Every one seemed interested in beer. Some of the paraders marched past the makeshift reviewing stand at Seventy-second Street and Central Park West proclaiming the future of the balanced budget. They carried statistical banners in red and black. Others passed along, not so much interested in taxation as representation. A few floats carried replicas of old-time bars of happier days, whereat clowns disported. Many men carried tin buckets, and so did a few of the women.

Crowds of marchers went by in uniform, with eyes formally facing left at Mayor Walker and the leaders of the parade. Other units were in everyday dress, just out from shops and offices. The Tammany Society went by, tipping high silk hats with dignity, and a fleet of trucks rolled up the street with hordes of small boys undecided whether they wanted "Beer" or "Jimmie." The choruses of a couple of musical comedies rode by in automobiles.

The marchers came from all parts of the city to take part in the parade. There were district chambers of commerce and veterans' associations from all the boroughs. There were bands from everywhere, many professional ones and some amateur.

Continued on Page Three.

Hoboken Scorns Beer Parade, As Town Suffers No Drought

For one reason or another, principally because it has never seen any reason to carry coals to Newcastle, Hoboken had no beer parade yesterday.

As explained by Mayor Bernard N. McFeely, "people have troubles enough in these times, and nobody seems interested."

As amplified by "Scrappy" McGrath, the riverfront's most notable dry land sailor, as he wiped foam from his lips: "We have plenty of beer. Why beer parades?

"And good beer," added Scrappy. "Of course if you're interested in the 'principle,' a beer parade is all right. Let's have another."

VOTE ON BEER BILLS FORCED ON HOUSE

145th Signer, Bachmann, Completes Petition to Bring Out O'Connor-Hull Plans May 23.

WETS WIN AT TIME LIMIT

77 Democrats, 67 Republicans and 1 Farmer-Laborite Back Tax on 2.75 Per Cent Drink.

Special to THE NEW YORK TIMES.

WASHINGTON, May 14.—A vote in the House on the O'Connor-Hull "beer bills" was assured today when the required 145 signatures were obtained to a petition to discharge the Ways and Means Committee from further consideration. The vote will be taken May 23.

The petition had been on the clerk's desk since April 12, and if it had not been completed today a vote, under the rules, would not have been possible before the national conventions next month. The last signer was Representative Bachmann of West Virginia, the Republican whip.

Recorded on the petition are seventy-seven Democrats, sixty-seven Republicans and one Farmer-Laborite.

Identical in language and introduced to provide "additional revenue," the bills authorize a tax of 3 cents a pint on beer with legal alcoholic content raised from one-half of 1 per cent to 2.75 per cent by weight. The latter percentage would be declared "non-intoxicating in fact."

Plan to Challenge Garner Fails.

In sharp contrast to the final signature on the Beck-Linthicum referendum petition in February, when the invalid Representative Mansfield of Texas was wheeled to the desk to affix the 145th signature, today's final signature was written unnoticed while the House was debating the War Department appropriation bill.

While Representatives Kvale of Minnesota, Lea of California and Bachmann were at the desk ready to sign, members of the wet bloc were seeking a Western Democrat to fill in the 144th blank line. They had intended to have Representative Schafer of Wisconsin, an ardent wet, challenge Speaker Garner to be the 145th signer.

Representative Cullen of New York broke in, shouting to the Speaker: "Sign that! Mr. McAdoo's turned wet!"

But before any reply could be made Mr. Bachman had signed on the last line.

House leaders say they do not ex-

Continued on Page Twenty-eight.

WALKER OUSTER PLEA BY SEABURY IS NEAR; GOVERNOR SET TO ACT

Dilemma Seen for Roosevelt in Move to Force Stand on Tammany Before Convention.

PROMPT RULING EXPECTED

Swift Action on Merits Is Held Most Likely to Win Over National Party.

CURRY IRE IS DISCOUNTED

Accession of McKee to Mayoralty Would Minimize Opposition Here, Observers Hold.

By JAMES A. HAGERTY.

The probability that Governor Franklin D. Roosevelt will face the necessity of deciding before the Democratic National Convention whether he will remove Mayor Walker has become an important factor in the contest for the Democratic nomination for President, as recent developments in the Hofstadter Committee investigation have made it virtually certain that Samuel Seabury, its counsel, will prefer charges against the Mayor within the next three weeks.

Governor Roosevelt, it was disclosed yesterday, is prepared to deal with the charge promptly. While no one is in a position to speak authoritatively for the Governor, and there is no indication that he wishes to prejudge the case, there is reason to believe that the Governor will remove the Mayor if he believes that the evidence to be submitted warrants such action.

Charges Expected Soon.

Whatever the Governor's decision, he will be put in an embarrassing position if, as expected, the charges against the Mayor are filed a few weeks before the national convention, before which he will be a candidate for the Presidential nomination at Chicago on June 27. Mr. Seabury is expected to call Mayor Walker for public questioning next week and to file charges against him not more than a week later. Should Mr. Seabury follow this schedule, Governor Roosevelt will have time to summon the Mayor for a hearing before him and to make his decision on the removal charges before the convention convenes.

The embarrassment to the Governor will be caused largely by the certainty that political motives will be imputed to him, no matter which way he may decide. Should he dismiss the charges, there undoubtedly will be a repetition of the accusation that he seeks to protect Tammany. Should he remove the Mayor, he will be accused of being inspired by a spirit of revenge for the failure of the Mayor and Tammany to support his candidacy.

The political effect of the decision, either way, will be farreaching, but the more important consequences will follow the removal of Mayor Walker if the Governor on the evidence yet to be submitted should decide that way.

Ouster Might Aid Governor.

It is the general opinion among Democratic leaders, among who are those supporting the Governor and those opposing his nomination, that the removal of Mayor Walker would help Governor Roosevelt's candidacy throughout the country by giving tangible evidence that he does not seek to protect Tammany officials in alleged misdoing, and that he has the courage to remove, if the evidence should warrant, Tammany's chief public official.

It was recalled that Grover Cleveland was twice nominated and twice elected in 1884 and 1892 against the strongest sort of opposition from Tammany, and an analogy in the

Continued on Page Twenty.

Woman, Near Death, Pleads for Citizenship; Carried to Long Island Court to Take Oath

Special to THE NEW YORK TIMES.

PATCHOGUE, L. I., May 14.—A woman who had become convinced that she was near death from a lingering illness was carried into the Supreme Court here today for the fulfillment of her desire to die as an American citizen. Against the wishes of her husband she had insisted upon rising from bed to attend the Naturalization Court.

The woman was Mrs. Eva Grassnik, 38 years old, of Third Avenue, Bay Shore. She was accompanied by her husband, Ernest, who also became a citizen. They were among thirty-two aliens who applied for citizenship papers.

Upon learning of the woman's desire, Supreme Court Justice George H. Furman excused her from standing when he administered the Oath of Allegiance. Commending her for her patriotism, he said that any person who went to as much trouble as Mrs. Grassnik to attend court should have a wish to become a citizen fulfilled.

In his address to the new citizens, Justice Furman urged them to study the political parties of this country and to join one. He advised them, however, to beware of political parties committed to revolutionary methods designed to "tear down the greatest form of government and one that gave them more freedom than any other."

Justice Furman said that he did not expect the new citizens to forget their mother countries. To be born under a flag without one's consent was a part of life, he added, but the renunciation of the countries of their birth for citizenship under the "Stars and Stripes" marked the greatest event in their lives.

Kentucky County Bars Civil Liberties Group; Hays and Malone Sue for $100,000 Damages

From a Staff Correspondent of The New York Times.
Special to THE NEW YORK TIMES.

PINEVILLE, Ky., May 14.—Met at the Bell County line by a delegation who informed them that their entrance into Pineville might result in bloodshed, representatives of the American Civil Liberties Union, which had sought to hold a public meeting here, were turned back today and returned to London, Ky.

Arthur Garfield Hays and Dudley Field Malone, heading the Civil Liberties delegation, conferred on the roadway with County Attorney Walter B. Smith and Mayor J. M. Brooks of Pineville and were told that they could not have a permit for any meeting.

The reason assigned was that the situation in Pineville was very tense as a result of injunction proceedings ended yesterday before Federal Judge A. M. J. Cochran at London.

Several hundred persons were on the streets of Pineville as a result of "Trade Day celebration," the officials said, and the temper of the crowd was such that it would be impossible for officers to protect the delegation.

Mr. Malone and Mr. Hays then made formal application for a permit to hold a meeting, and were refused an behalf of the city by Mayor Brooks and on behalf of the county by Mr. Smith.

The delegates, most of whom did not get out of their two automobiles thereupon accepted the decision. Mr. Hays and Mr. Malone shook hands with the officials, and Mr. Malone announced that in view of the decision the delegates could do nothing. There was no disorder.

The delegation in turning back declared that it had tested its right to hold a public meeting in Pineville, and Mr. Malone remarked that the group had "a nice ride through the country anyhow."

About twenty citizens of Pineville accompanied the officials; a Pineville policeman directed traffic past the cars of the delegates, parked by the roadside. Evidence of feeling against the visit was marked in the behavior of some of the citizens, but no violence was threatened. The scene was about six miles from Pineville, on a much-traveled concrete road.

The Civil Liberties group later filed

Continued on Page Twenty-two.

BANK DIRECTOR HELD IN $500,000 THEFTS

Controller of Worcester Salt Company Admits He Gave Bogus Stock as Collateral.

LOST IT ALL IN WALL ST.

Had "Insane Notion" He Could Get Rich—Fled May 4 and Tried Suicide in Baltimore.

Thomas F. Curran, 41 years old, former controller for the Worcester Salt Company at 71 Murray Street and a former director in the National Bank of Queens County, near his home in Flushing, walked into District Attorney Crain's office yesterday and admitted that, since the first crash in the stock market, in October, 1929, he had defrauded six banks and three brokerage concerns in this city of about $500,000 by giving them bogus stock of the salt company as collateral.

Curran, near collapse from having taken poison in a Baltimore hotel last week, where he had been hiding since his disappearance on May 4, was questioned by Joseph P. Martin, Assistant District Attorney. He said he had thought after the first drop in the stock market that he saw an opportunity to become immensely wealthy and had taken blank certificates of the salt company's stock, to which he had signed the names of officials and former employes without any attempt to simulate their signatures and had used them as collateral to get funds to bolster accounts he had conducted in the brokerage firms up to the day he vanished.

Indictments Already Obtained.

Mr. Martin already had a list of the banks and brokerage houses Curran had deceived in this manner, and the grand jury had returned a forgery and a grand larceny indictment against Curran last Friday in connection with one loan of $20,000 Curran had obtained from the Continental Bank and Trust Company at 30 Broad Street, when Curran, accompanied by a lawyer, John T. Clancy of 40-03 National Avenue, Corona, Queens, walked in.

The list showed that the National City Bank also had been victimized to the extent of $265,000 in batches of the bogus stock he had given as collateral at its main office and its branch in Atlantic Avenue, Brooklyn. Other banks defrauded by Curran were the Corn Exchange Bank and Trust Company, $20,000; the Bank of Manhattan Trust Company, $40,000; the National Bank of Queens County, of which Curran was a director, $70,000, and the Bank of America, $30,000. The brokerage houses he had defrauded by placing some of the bogus stock as collateral on accounts were Baar, Cohen & Co., 50 Broad Street, $22,000; Appenzeller, Allen & Hill, 55 Broadway, $23,000, and Phillips & Co., 55 Broadway, $18,000.

Ernest L. King, vice president and cashier of the National Bank of Queens County, said last night that his bank was covered by $50,000 insurance against forgery and that Curran had a balance of $3,000, so that the loss through Curran's fraud would amount to only $17,000.

Says He Had "Insane Notion."

"I don't know what possessed me to do this," Curran told the Assistant District Attorney. "I got the insane notion I could take advantage of the first drop in stock in the crash in October, 1929, and when I lost a small amount I had obtained on the first batch of blank certificates I had taken from the Worcester Salt Company, where I had been employed

Continued on Page Twenty-five.

HOLDS HIGHER SILVER WOULD RAISE PRICES

House Group Report on World Money Parley Stresses Elevating of Commodity Rates.

BIMETALLISM IS AVOIDED

Resolution Asking Hoover to Call Conference Changed to Cover Keeping Gold Standard.

Text of the House committee report on silver is on page 26.

Special to THE NEW YORK TIMES.

WASHINGTON, May 14.—Recommendations made by the House Committee on Coinage, Weights and Measures that President Hoover call, not later than July 1, an international monetary conference, as requested in a joint resolution introduced by Representative Somers of New York, were made public today, together with a preliminary report on the resolution by a subcommittee of which Mr. Somers is chairman.

The resolution was reported to the House by the full committee yesterday.

Under the resolution, the silver problem would be one of the leading topics discussed at the conference. The subcommittee held that plans to restore the value of that metal and revive the purchasing power of countries which use it as the principal medium of exchange was essential to world economic rehabilitation.

The resolution, however, has been altered since its introduction, to broaden the scope of the conference and do away with any impression that the committee is recommending bimetallism or the abandonment of the principle of the gold standard by countries which are now on it or desire to restore their currency to that base.

Proposals of New Provisions.

The change, it was said, was made after Mr. Somers and Representative Perkins of New Jersey visited President Hoover a few days ago in an effort to determine his attitude on the proposal. The new provision included the following subjects to be discussed:

The maintenance or restoration of the gold monetary standard within such countries as are desirous and capable of employing it, and the adjustment of monetary exchanges among such countries and other countries.

At the White House today no word could be obtained as to what the President might do if the resolution was adopted. Acting Secretary Castle of the State Department and Assistant Secretary Rogers saw the President today but silver was not discussed.

Representative Somers and his group, however, are hopeful that the President will look favorably on the resolution, now that the change has been made in it. Copies of it have been sent to the State Department in the expectation that the department will sound out other nations as to their attitude should invitations be issued, or at least make available to the committee such information as it now has.

The understanding is that, pending such information from the State Department, no effort will be made to bring the resolution up for action.

Higher Commodity Prices Urged.

The subcommittee in its report stated that the raising of the level of commodity prices was the most urgent need of the world today and while not mentioning the Goldsborough credit expansion bill by name,

Continued on Page Twenty-six.

NEW HOUSE COALITION ON RELIEF IS BARED; GARNER HITS HOOVER

Bloc Is Formed in Secret by Members Who Call Themselves "Steering Committee."

LED ECONOMY BILL REVOLT

Speaker Says the President's "Double-Barreled" Statements Have "Frozen Confidence."

"HAS TO BE ADVERTISED"

Rainey Comes Out Strongly in Support of Rail Unions' Program of Relief.

Special to THE NEW YORK TIMES.

WASHINGTON, May 14.—Out of the tangled situation over Federal unemployment relief rose today a new House coalition, declared to have sufficient support to hold Congress in session until a non-partisan program, capable of correcting conditions, had been evolved.

The coalition, formed in secret and heretofore unsuspected by the normal House leadership, was announced by three members, who said they had been selected as the "steering committee." They are Representatives Mead, Democrat, of New York; Kelly, Republican, of Pennsylvania, and La Guardia, nominal Republican, of New York, who once before in this session started a revolt against the House leadership that resulted in the death of the manufacturers' sales tax.

While still unaware of the existence of the new coalition, Representative Rainey, the majority leader, issued a statement, praising the seven leading railway brotherhoods, whose presidents asked President Hoover yesterday to take the initiative in working for a twenty-five-year moratorium on war debts and reparations, and said failure of the Government to provide a relief program would force them to back plans for a dole.

Garner Is Outspoken.

The House agitation reached a climax when Speaker Garner in an interview with newspaper men, criticized without stint the President's frequent issuing of statements. While Speaker Garner did not mention unemployment relief, he apparently directed his remarks at the statements on this subject which have come from the Executive Mansion.

Mr. Garner apparently enjoyed his tirade against the President, and frequently asked newspaper men who were in his office whether they thought he was correct.

"If the President will refrain for thirty days from making 'double-barreled statements,' this frozen confidence will naturally melt," he said. "He says himself his messages since 1929 have frozen confidence.

"His statements have done more in the last six months to freeze confidence than all other sources put together. His statements are contrary—they jump from one thing to another—and the people are all upset reading them. He says confidence is frozen. Well, something must have brought it about.

Says Hoover Upsets Country.

"Honestly, I believe his continuous statements in the last two years have done more to keep the minds of the people upset than anything else that has happened.

"I'd suggest now he reverse the process and not give out any statements at all. Hoover's tendency is, 'I've got to be advertised all the time.'

"The Lindbergh incident yesterday was an example. The Attorney General might have issued the statement that all Federal resources had been thrown into action to run down the murderers of the Lindbergh child and have put them into action him-

Continued on Page Twenty-eight.

Mexico Severs Diplomatic Tie With Peru, Which Accuses Her Legation of Aiding Reds

Special Cable to THE NEW YORK TIMES.

MEXICO CITY, May 14.—The Mexican Government severed diplomatic relations with Peru today following a request by the Peruvian Government for the withdrawal of the Mexican Minister and his staff. The Lima Government asserted the Mexican diplomatic officials had intervened in the internal politics of Peru by supporting plans of communistic elements to disturb public order.

Manuel Tellez, Foreign Minister of Mexico, announced the action of the Mexican Government following a visit to him by the Peruvian Minister to Mexico. That envoy, according to Señor Tellez presented a facsimile letter published in the newspaper El Comercio of Lima, according to which Victor Raul Haya de la Torre, Aprista leader in Peru, had been able to send correspondence from Mexico to Lima in a Mexican diplomatic pouch.

The Peruvian Government also charged that the Mexican Minister in Lima had frequently visited Señor de la Torre's house adjoining the Mexican Legation building.

Mexican diplomatic missions, Señor Tellez said, had precise instructions to respect the sovereignty of the States to which they were accredited, and Juan B. Cabral, the Minister to Peru, had never departed from that principle.

Señor Cabral, according to Señor Tellez, once visited the house next door to the Mexican Legation when invited to do so by the owner, and much to the envoy's surprise, he had found Señor de la Torre there.

LIMA, Peru, May 14 (AP).—Juan B. Cabral, Mexican Minister to Peru, and members of his staff left Lima by airplane today.

CONDON KNOWS MAN HE PAID $50,000 IN LINDBERGH CASE; PLANES HUNT GANG AT SEA

Senate Hastily Votes $500,000 To Keep the Record Running

Special to THE NEW YORK TIMES.

WASHINGTON, May 14.—There was no discussion of governmental economy when the Senate today was suddenly faced with the prospect of the discontinuance of the Congressional Record, in which Senatorial speeches are embalmed for posterity.

Without a murmur it voted to appropriate $500,000 to continue the Record and other Congressional printing.

Chairman Jones of the Appropriations Committee read a letter from George H. Carter, the Public Printer, saying that unless measures were taken at once he would be compelled to discontinue all Congressional printing not later than Monday.

AGENT SAYS HE IS CERTAIN

Makes Statement After He Is Questioned Three Hours in Bronx.

FIVE SOUGHT OFF THE COAST

Gangsters, Named by Curtis Traced by 39 Coast Guard Vessels, Three Amphibians.

$100,000 REWARD IS URGED

Finder of Baby's Body Under Inquiry—Federal Power Put Behind Jersey Police.

Dr. John F. Condon, the Bronx lecturer who turned the $50,000 over to the band of extortioners in the Bronx on April 2 in Colonel Lindbergh's desperate and futile effort to regain his kidnapped child, declared flatly last night that he knew the name and appearance of the man with whom he dealt and "could pick him out of a thousand." This description is in the hands of the police.

Dr. Condon made his statement after he had been questioned for three hours by District Attorney Charles B. McLaughlin and the New York police as they began an investigation of the Bronx angles of the case, which turned into a murder mystery last Thursday when the body of the child with its skull fractured was found near the Lindbergh estate at Hopewell, N. J.

While he was declaring his certainty that he could identify the man he is still convinced was a member of the kidnapping gang, a search by land, sea and air was being pushed along the shore of Southern New Jersey and as far north as Cape Cod in an effort to pick up five men whose nicknames and descriptions as well as the description of the fishing schooner they used in their negotiations, had been given by John H. Curtis, the Norfolk boat builder, who tried to bring about the return of the baby.

The investigation revolved actively yesterday around Dr. Condon, Mr. Curtis and Morris Rosner, New York stock promoter who was called into the case soon after the kidnapping as an aide to Colonel Lindbergh, but last evening the inquiry turned into a new channel.

Truck Driver Fingerprinted.

William Allen, the Negro truck driver who found the baby's body Thursday afternoon when he went into a patch of woods near Mount Rose, was taken from his home in Trenton to the State Police Headquarters on the Lindbergh estate and finger printed. His record also is being investigated.

Colonel H. Norman Schwarzkopf commanding the New Jersey State Police, explained last night that this was being done to discover whether there was any possibility that Allen's stumbling upon the body could have been more than a mere coincidence.

"While no suspicion rests upon him," he said, "every possible angle of the case is being investigated."

At the same time it was made known that Rosner had completed a long and detailed statement to the police and had left Hopewell and come to New York. His statement included an account of how he brought one of the ransom notes to New York soon after the kidnapping, which occurred on March 1, and the names of all the persons to whom he gave copies. These, it has been learned, included Salvatore Spitale and Irving Bitz, liaison men with the underworld.

Colonel Schwarzkopf said that in substance Rosner's statement was "to the effect that he did everything possible to cooperate with the Lindbergh family and endeavored to obtain whatever information he could through underworld sources as to the possible whereabouts of the child."

Colonel Schwarzkopf emphasized that Rosner was not under police surveillance. Rosner had not appeared at his apartment, 200 West 16th Street, late last night.

Search for Schooner.

The immediate object of the search off the Jersey coast, based on information supplied by Mr. Curtis, was a schooner of the Gloucester fishing type, and the five men whom Mr. Curtis desribed as constituting the gang. These are the men whom Colo-

Continued on Page Two.

POSTMASTERS TOLD TO SUPPORT HOOVER

Glover Warns Missourians to "Get on Firing Line" or Resign Positions.

"PRESIDENT REAL LEADER"

Convention Is Urged to Stand Behind Him "to Make World Safe Again for Democracy."

Special to THE NEW YORK TIMES.

SPRINGFIELD, Mo., May 14.—Any Missouri postmaster who does not wish to "get out on the firing line" in support of President Hoover was invited today by W. Irving Glover, Second Assistant Postmaster General, to resign.

"I'll be back in Washington Monday," Mr. Glover said, "and I'll be glad at that time to take the resignations of any of you postmasters who don't want to do it."

Mr. Glover, head of the air and railway mail service, praised the President in an address before the biennial convention of the Missouri Postmasters' Association here.

"You are a part of this administration," he reminded the postmasters. "When you hear anybody assailing that man Hoover, remember what I said, or go and read a book, and answer them. As long as you do that you are filling the job of postmaster.

"To make the world safe again for democracy, you must stand behind that man of peerless leadership—of brains, ability and steadfastness. I ask your faith in God, that our country shall not fail."

He suggested that "living beyond our means" was one cause of the "world-wide depression." He warned postal employes that they probably must take some sort of a cut and urged that they accept it graciously.

He especially praised the President's furlough plan of thirty days' vacation without pay. The alternative, if appropriations for the department are cut, will be to cut off 40,000 or 60,000 employes, he said.

He pointed out that postal employes have had "tremendous advances in salaries" in recent years, "sometimes as high as 100 or 200 per cent." appropriated by a "generous Congress."

Mr. Glover explained the Postal Department deficit by saying that appropriation of $30,000,000 for shipyards and the merchant marine, which did not belong in the department, had nevertheless been placed there, and added that the Postmaster General is not permitted to admin-

Continued on Page Eleven.

"All the News That's Fit to Print."

The New York Times.

LATE CITY EDITION
WEATHER—Fair, slightly warmer today; tomorrow showers.
Temperatures Yesterday—Max., 71; Min., 58.

VOL. LXXXI....No. 27,157. ****+ NEW YORK, WEDNESDAY, JUNE 1, 1932. TWO CENTS In New York City | THREE CENTS Within 200 Miles | FOUR CENTS Elsewhere Except 7th and 8th Postal Zones

$75,000 PAYMENTS MADE BY SHERWOOD LINKED TO WALKER

Seabury Accountant Swears Large Sums Went to Person Who Shared Block Profit.

J. A. SMITH BACKS UP MAYOR

Says He Got Cash for $10,000 From Hastings but Was Not Paid in Full for $3,000.

DR. WALKER APPEARS TODAY

Dunnigan Engages in Booing Match With Audience—Cuvillier Says 'Congregation Has Changed Faith.'

Samuel Seabury made a new effort yesterday to demonstrate to the Hofstadter committee that the missing Russell T. Sherwood, whose financial transactions amounted to $961,226.52 in five and a half years, was Mayor Walker's proxy in Wall Street.

The demonstration centred upon the fact that Sherwood had expended more than $75,000 on behalf of a person whose name was not revealed, but to whom the Mayor admitted authorizing a $7,500 payment from the profits of his joint trading account with Paul Block.

In presenting the testimony of James T. Ellis, one of the committee's accountants who analyzed the bank and brokerage accounts of Mr. Walker and the man whom he repudiated as his financial agent after Mr. Seabury had shown that Sherwood drew $264,000 in cash from a secret account just before the Mayor sailed for Europe in 1927, Mr. Seabury said:

"I leave it for you to say, on the inspection of these records, whether there was any reason at all why Russell T. Sherwood should have made, on his own account, that expenditure; and if you determine that you know of no such reason, then there is a fair basis for your conclusion that those securities were paid out for and on behalf of the Mayor of the city, no matter what he may say by way of denial."

J. A. Smith Examined on Credit.

Then Mr. Seabury turned his fire upon the Mayor's denial that the Equitable Coach Company or its backers provided the cash for the $10,000 letter of credit he took with him to Europe in 1927 and his statement that he had neither bought nor caused to be bought any of the stock of the Interstate Trust Company—a statement that has already been contradicted by his friend Park Commissioner Walter R. Herrick.

Mr. Smith, a hostile and belligerent witness, left the stand with no sharply defined discrepancies between his story and the Mayor's, although the accuracy of one of his statements was challenged immediately by Miss Irene Kenney, his former secretary.

Mr. Smith had anything but a friendly audience before which to tell his story. Answers which the crowd took for evasions and quibbling, and the attempts of the minority to straighten out seeming contradictions in his testimony, brought hisses and boos from a crowd as partisan as that which cheered Mr. Walker at intervals in his two days on the witness stand.

"The congregation seems to have changed its faith," remarked Assemblyman Louis Cuvillier after one outburst.

Dunnigan Boos at "Wolves."

A jeering match between the crowd and Senator John J. Dunnigan, the minority leader, wound up the proceedings, when Smith, after charging Mr. Seabury with deliberately destroying evidence, attempted to close his testimony with a verbal attack upon the chief counsel, but was stopped by Senator Samuel H. Hofstadter, the chairman of the committee.

"Boo!" yelled the crowd venomously as the somewhat flustered witness fished hastily for his hat and started for the door.

"Boo! Boo!" retorted Senator Dunnigan from the dais with less volume but more vigor. "Those are the wolves out there—the wolves that are out trying to get in. Boo! Boo!"

Dr. Walker to Testify Today.

Soon afterward Senator Hofstadter declared a recess until this morning, when Dr. William H. Walker, the Mayor's brother, who was reported missing, is expected to take the stand.

Dr. Walker returned to his home at 27 Crestwood Avenue, Tuckahoe, just before 11:30 o'clock last night, and denied that he had been "missing," as reported by Mr. Seabury. He said his wife had been ill, that he had gone away with her on a motor trip, and that they had planned to return yesterday. "And," he added, "here we are."

The doctor said he arrived in the

Continued on Page Ten.

Hitlerites Hail Hindenburg For His Ousting of Bruening

Wireless to THE NEW YORK TIMES.

BERLIN, May 31.—Many thousands of National Socialists, watching the changing of the guards at the Presidential mansion today, acclaimed President von Hindenburg, shouting, "Hail Hindenburg, who ousted Bruening!" The President remained out of sight.

The Nazis accompanied a guard company to the Ministry of Defense across the city, shouting, "Hail Hitler—Germany awake!" They repeatedly clashed with police, who tried to suppress the demonstrations, used clubs freely, and once, when stoned, fired in the air, wounding a woman.

Newsboys sold the Berlin Nazi paper, Der Angriff, as "the new government organ."

JUROR VISITS KRESEL; MISTRIAL DECLARED

Came to Home to Ask Aid in Getting Loan, the Accused Lawyer Reports to Court.

OFFENDER FACES CHARGES

Panel of 200 Talesmen Ordered Friday for the Reopening of Perjury Prosecution.

A mistrial was declared yesterday in the trial of Isidor J. Kresel, former general counsel for the defunct Bank of United States by Justice Samuel J. Harris in the criminal branch of the Supreme Court. Mr. Kresel is accused of perjury in an indictment growing out of his grand jury testimony in February, 1931, in the investigation which led to the indictment of Mr. Kresel and some of the other officers and directors of the bank in an $8,000,000 loan transaction.

The jury was dismissed because of Mr. Kresel's revelation to the court, through his chief counsel, John W. Davis, of a visit one of the jurors, Joseph J. Cohen, made to the defendant's Summer home at Mamaroneck, N. Y., last Sunday, when he asked Mr. Kresel to aid him to obtain a loan from a bank. Cohen, who is a typewriter dealer and lives at 614 West 152d Street, had been ordered taken into custody by the court when the sixth day of the trial was about to begin yesterday.

Held for a Hearing.

As Justice Harris was dismissing the eleven remaining jurors in the afternoon, Cohen was being arraigned before Magistrate Stern in the Tombs Court, on the same floor in the Criminal Courts Building in which the Kresel trial had been in progress, and was released in $5,000 bail, pending a hearing on June 8, on a charge that he violated Section 374 of the penal law.

This law fixes a penalty of ten years' imprisonment or a fine of $5,000 or both for a juror "who asks, receives or agrees to receive any money, property or value of any kind, or any promise or agreement therefore, upon agreement or understanding that his vote * * * shall be influenced thereby."

Mr. Kresel, in a statement which preceded questioning of Cohen in private by Justice Harris in the presence of Mr. Davis and James Garrett Wallace, Assistant District Attorney, in charge of the prosecution, made it clear that Cohen had not stipulated he would be influenced in his verdict through the requested aid. Cohen persisted, he said, in telling him of his financial difficulties after Mr. Kresel had warned him his conduct in coming to him was "highly improper." Subsequently, the indicted lawyer went on, when Cohen had told him he had been unable to pay his bills for six months or his rent for two months and had made mention of his wife and children, Mr. Kresel refused to give any aid "if my life and liberty depended on it."

Cohen denied to Justice Harris he had indicated to Mr. Kresel his part in a verdict would be influenced by possible compliance with his request by Mr. Kresel. When he was before the magistrate he entered a not guilty plea. His lawyer, William Biel, in urging bail be made not more than $2,500, told the magistrate Cohen had been in business for eleven years, and always had borne an excellent reputation.

Doubt as to Action.

The delay of more than five hours in the declaration of the mistrial was said to be based on the uncertainty of the District Attorney's office as to whether any offense, other than possible contempt of court, had been committed by Cohen. At the close of a conference with the prosecutor and the defense lawyers in the forenoon, when Justice Harris informed the remaining eleven jurors the trial would be held up because of Cohen's visit to the defendant, Mr. Wallace joined District Attorney Crain, Assistant District Attorney Harold W. Hastings and Assistant District Attorney Benvenga of the

Continued on Page Ten.

VON PAPEN IS CALLED TO HELM IN GERMANY; OUSTED HERE IN WAR

Hindenburg Asks Ex-Attache, Who Was Linked With Boy-Ed in 1915, to Form a Cabinet.

NATIONAL MINISTRY IS AIM

New Chancellor, Conservative Centrist, Is a Champion of Franco-German Accord.

ELECTION IN FALL LIKELY

Government Expected to Be Merely Transitional—Hitler Reported Withholding Nazi Support.

By GUIDO ENDERIS.

Special Cable to THE NEW YORK TIMES.

BERLIN, May 31.—President Paul von Hindenburg tonight commissioned Lieut. Col. Franz von Papen, former military attaché at Washington and an influential member of the conservative wing of the Centrist party, to form a "national concentration" Cabinet.

The man chosen to succeed Dr. Heinrich Bruening, who resigned as Chancellor yesterday after the President had refused to affirm confidence in him, was compelled to leave the United States with Captain Karl Boy-Ed in December, 1915, for alleged violation of neutrality.

He has been active in promoting Franco-German political and industrial relations.

Colonel von Papen's unconfirmed slate of Ministers as announced tonight indicates that the new government will be non-partisan, with a Rightist orientation, and, incidentally, with a pronounced capitalistic complexion. As a Centrist member of the Prussian Diet Colonel von Papen had been active in national politics for the last ten years, but it was reported tonight he had resigned from the party in view of its decision not to identify itself with the new government by accepting portfolios and unconditionally supporting it in the Reichstag.

Likely to Be Transitional.

President von Hindenburg's tentative selection of Colonel von Papen as the new Chancellor was announced at the conclusion of conferences with leaders of the Reichstag parties which failed to yield a basis for constructing a party coalition government that might command a working majority in the Reichstag. Parliamentary circles predict that the new Ministry, therefore, will be of a wholly transitional nature, designed to carry on until Autumn, when the impasse created by Marshal von Hindenburg's abrupt rupture with Dr. Bruening will necessitate new elections.

Of the two major groups in the Reichstag, the Socialists, who were first called into consultation, told President von Hindenburg they saw no reason for deposing Dr. Bruening, since he was supported by the same majority party line-up that had elected the Field Marshal as President on April 10. They announced they were not interested in forming a new government.

Adolf Hitler, National Socialist (Nazi) leader, who followed the Socialists, made his support of any new government conditional on an early dissolution of the Reichstag and new elections. As no other Reichstag group proposed a workable solution of the crisis, President von Hindenburg began negotiations for a non-partisan government for which he hopes to obtain the tolerance of the Reichstag.

Among the candidates on Colonel

Continued on Page Three.

Prince of Wales Dances Thrice With Mrs. Putnam

Special Cable to THE NEW YORK TIMES.

LONDON, May 31.—Mrs. Amelia Earhart Putnam had three dances with the Prince of Wales tonight at a brilliant Derby charity ball at Grosvenor House.

She was the centre of attraction when she arrived with David Bruce, Ambassador Mellon's son-in-law and was taken straight to the Prince's table. Beneath a short cloak of brown velvet she was wearing a shimmering dress of what may be known soon in London as "Atlantic green."

After only a few moments of animated conversation the Prince led her to the floor for her first dance of the evening. Twice more before the ball was over the two were seen dancing happily together.

BANKER'S SON SLAIN AT PARTY IN LONDON

Cocktail Drinking at Home of Knight's Daughter Ends in Mysterious Shooting.

NEIGHBORS HEAR QUARREL

Hostess Is Divorced Wife of American Singer—Slaying Accidental, Say Police.

By The Associated Press.

LONDON, May 31.—Mayfair society was stirred today by the fatal shooting of Michael Scott Stephen, son of a London banker, after a gay cocktail party in the apartment of Mrs. Elvira Dolores Barney, beautiful golden-haired divorcee and daughter of a knight, whose former husband is John Sterling Barney, an American singer. No charges had been filed tonight against Mrs. Barney.

The story, which it was understood Scotland Yard investigators would tell at an inquest next Friday, is that during discussions about 4 A. M. after the party Stephen brandished a revolver which was accidentally discharged, killing him.

Neighbors Heard Shots.

Many stories were heard of parties which were held in the gayly decorated back-alley flat in William Mews, the London counterpart of Greenwich Village's Macdougal Alley in New York. One room, done in black and white, was especially popular with the guests, who called it "the magpie room."

The attention of neighbors was first drawn to the apartment early this morning by noises usually associated with a cocktail party. Then came sounds of a commotion and unusually loud cries. These were followed by several shots and silence in the fashionable Knightsbridge district, in which the apartment is situated.

In a few moments there came a woman's cry. The neighbors heard her scream, "Come quickly!" Soon the police arrived and found the body of the 35-year-old society man on a sofa. Physicians said his death was due to gunshot wounds.

Police Pathologist Called.

Scotland Yard decided the case was of first importance. It called in Sir Bernard Spillsbury, eminent pathologist, for consultation. The young man's father, T. M. Stephen, manager of the London branch of the North of Scotland Bank, and his mother were called to the morgue where they identified the body.

A groom who lived near Mrs. Barney's apartment said that one night about two weeks ago he saw Stephen leave the apartment, calmly step inside an empty grocer's truck near by and make himself comfortable on the floor to go to sleep.

"He slept soundly for many hours.

Continued on Page Two.

Citizenship Is Restored to Lieutenant Massie; Kentucky Governor Acts to End Doubt of Status

By The Associated Press.

FRANKFORT, Ky., May 31.—Any rights of citizenship Lieutenant Thomas H. Massie may have lost in his native State of Kentucky by his conviction in the Honolulu honor slaying were restored in an executive order from Governor Ruby Laffoon today.

The Governor stated in his order that he did not believe Lieutenant Massie had forfeited any of his rights in this State, but that he issued the order "to put the matter beyond all doubt."

Lieutenant Massie received the order from Governor Laffoon personally in the Executive offices, and a short time later he and his wife, Mrs. Thalia Massie, left Winchester by motor for Charleston, W. Va. They expected to remain there tonight before continuing to Washington and New York. They will visit friends and relatives in the East before he returns to duty on the West Coast.

They have spent several days visiting the naval officer's mother at Winchester.

Coming from the Governor's offices with the order neatly wrapped in his coat pocket, Lieutenant Massie remarked:

"I consider this a package of happiness."

"There are few things more gratifying than to receive a pardon from the Governor of one's own State," he added.

Although he referred to the order as a pardon, it was not issued as such. Asked if he considered whether it had the same effect as a pardon, he exclaimed, "It's splendid" and added he was not acquainted with the legal phases of the order.

E. S. Jouett, vice president and chief counsel of the Louisville & Nashville, who accompanied Lieutenant Massie and helped to draft the order, interposed:

"This is merely to restore citizenship rights which we do not believe were taken away."

SENATE PASSES $1,115,000,000 TAX BILL; BALANCES BUDGET AFTER HOOVER PLEA; $238,000,000 ECONOMY MEASURE REPORTED

FEDERAL SALARIES CUT 10%

Chief Item of Economy Bill Is Expected to Save $121,050,000.

NO SLASH FOR VETERANS

Miscellaneous Items Are Relied Upon to Bring Measure's Total to $250,000,000.

GARNER URGES HIS BILL

Tells Committee Congress Must Relieve Unemployment With "Mercy Money."

Special to THE NEW YORK TIMES.

WASHINGTON, Wednesday, June 1.—An omnibus economy bill, calculated to save more than $238,605,000, was reported favorably to the Senate by the Appropriations Committee at midnight and will be brought up for consideration today.

The principal item of saving in the eighty-page bill, completed in a committee session lasting into the night, was a flat 10 per cent cut in all Federal salaries except those of the active personnel of the army, navy and Marine Corps. This was expected to save $121,050,000 in the fiscal year 1933.

Miscellaneous items, the savings of which have not yet been estimated, were expected to bring the bill's total to about $250,000,000.

The Appropriations Committee eliminated from the Economy Committee's draft a reduction in veterans' allowances which would have saved about $51,500,000.

The Senate bill compares with a bill passed by the House which the latter body contended would save $52,272,740. Other estimates, however, set this total as low as $32,000,000.

Senate and House Bills Compared.

The 10 per cent Federal pay cut compares with the House provision for an 11 per cent reduction on salaries above $2,500, with a saving of $9,000,000. Other points of comparison between the bill passed by the House and the measure reported to the Senate are as follows:

Permanent salary reductions for members of the International Joint Commission, Federal Farm Board and Board of Mediation—House $41,000; Senate $97,500.

Suspension of automatic increases in compensation—$3,090,000 in both bills.

Prohibition of filling vacancies—$16,700,000 in both bills.

Compulsory retirement for age—House $2,672,000; Senate, omitted.

Temporary reduction of travel allowance—$3,056,000 in both bills.

Temporary suspension of overtime compensation—$6,381,000 in both bills.

Limitation on amount of retired pay—Indeterminate in both bills.

Limitation on annual leave with pay—House, none; Senate $22,109,166.

Disbanding of Philippine Scouts—House, indeterminate; Senate, omitted.

Limitation of expenditures for printing and binding—House, $4,000,000; Senate, $3,500,000.

Reorganization of Shipping Board—$2,362,240 in both bills.

Increase in patent fees—$650,000 in both bills.

Restrictions on transfer of army and navy personnel—$3,368,000 in both bills.

Transfer from compensation to pension rolls—House, none; Senate, $3,649,000.

Restriction on the revival of government insurance—House, none; Senate, $9,000,000.

Rate of interest on judgments and overpayments—House, none; Senate, $5,250,000.

General adjustment of veterans' benefits—House, indeterminate; Senate, $13,315,000.

Veterans in institutions—House, none; Senate, $5,370,000.

Emergency officers' retired pay—House, none; Senate, $3,386,000.

Repeal of retroactive benefits—House, none; Senate, $13,694,000.

To Take Up Wagner Bill.

Unemployment relief legislation received considerable attention yesterday in Congress. In the House, Speaker Garner appeared before the Ways and Means Committee to argue for his relief bill, including about $1,000,000,000 for public works,

Continued on Page Thirteen.

Incomes From Violations of Law Taxed 100% Under an Amendment Voted by the Senate

By The Associated Press.

WASHINGTON, May 31.—The Senate tonight voted to put a 100 per cent tax on incomes earned through violations of State or Federal laws.

The action was taken without a record vote in approving an amendment to the revenue bill sponsored by Senator Glenn, Republican, of Illinois, which he said was to take the government out of a "partnership" with crime.

Senator Glenn explained that under existing law the government collected part of the profits as income tax where it could, but under his proposal it could confiscate the earnings of criminals.

He referred to "vice and iniquity, organized gambling syndicates that rob the common laboring men of their wages, beer rings, liquor rings" and other criminal activities as piling up great profits.

"Huge profits runing into millions and millions accrue through the sale of narcotics illegally," Mr. Glenn said. "The proposal changes the position of the government from being a partner in crime to that of confiscating every cent of the profits if they can be reached."

Hoover Supports Britain's Proposal For World Parley to Stabilize Prices

London Will Sound Paris, Rome and Other Capitals on Program Including Currency, Exchange, Gold Standard and Silver—United States Bars Debts, Reparations, Tariffs and Disarmament.

Special to THE NEW YORK TIMES.

WASHINGTON, May 31.—An international conference in London to consider stabilizing world commodity prices appeared assured today when Secretary of State Stimson, after a conference with President Hoover, announced the United States had replied favorably to an inquiry from the British Government as to its attitude toward such a project.

Officials expect that currency, foreign exchange, the gold standard, silver and other questions will be dealt with and that the range of questions to be taken up will be so wide the conference will take on a general economic character.

The United States has barred war debts, reparations and disarmament from discussion, while President Hoover's position in his veto of the Democratic tariff bill May 11 would seem to bar bargaining for tariff reductions.

Secretary Stimson's Statement.

Secretary Stimson made his announcement after he had been informed of newspaper dispatches from London indicating that the plan was becoming publicly known. After a long conference with President Hoover, he issued the following statement:

> The suggestion that there should be called an international conference for the purpose of considering methods to stabilize world commodity prices first came to the attention of this government by an inquiry of the British Ambassador in Washington as to whether we should be interested and would participate in such conference. The suggestion was that it should be called by the British Government in London.
>
> After due consideration, this government has replied, through Mr. Mellon, that it felt that the early convocation of such a conference might be of real value in the present depression. As was stated in the press messages from London, the proposed conference would have nothing to do with war debts, reparations, disarmament, or any other than purely economic subjects.
>
> It is our understanding that the British Government is also approaching, on the same subject, France, Italy and the other powers.

MacDonald Telephoned to Stimson.

The statement was accepted as meaning that the projected conference was the subject of the mysterious transatlantic telephone conversation last Wednesday between Secretary Stimson and Prime Minister MacDonald of Great Britain. It also explained the interview with Mr. MacDonald, published in The London Daily Mail yesterday, in which he declared there was urgent need of a world trade conference.

Although Secretary Stimson favors an early convocation of the conference, no date has been set, nor has an agenda been agreed upon pending the British negotiations with the other powers. For these reasons, officials expressed the opinion that the conference would not meet prior to the Lausanne or Ottawa conferences probably not until November.

No extensive study, it was added, has yet been made here of the agenda requirements, but this question is expected to occupy detailed attention as soon as an international agreement has been reached for the conference.

Primarily, it was said on expert authority today, the conference can be expected to consider in reference to commodity prices the general application of more liberal credit policies, in the belief that this will stop the shrinkage in prices. Once that has occurred there would, in the

Continued on Page Fifteen.

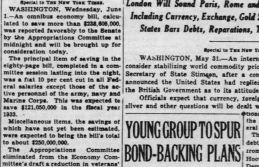

YOUNG GROUP TO SPUR BOND-BACKING PLANS

Encouraged by New Prospect of a Balanced Budget, Leaders Move to Protect Prices.

Greatly encouraged by the action of the Senate Finance Committee yesterday in approving additional taxes sufficient to balance the budget, the Young committee of bankers and industrialists resumed its consideration of financial measures to help to make effective the credit-expansion program of the Federal Reserve.

The fact that the Senate committee rejected President Hoover's suggestion of a sales tax and chose the alternative of a gasoline tax, advanced by Secretary of the Treasury Ogden L. Mills, was considered unimportant by the committee, which has come to regard the balancing of the budget as a prerequisite to any attempts at financial relief.

Owen D. Young, chairman of the committee, who had attended the conference between President Hoover and the Democratic leaders of the Senate on Monday, reported to the group as a whole the results of his Washington inquiries. They evidently were encouraging, for the attitude of the committee was much more hopeful last night than it had been at the close of last week, when the decision to send Mr. Young to Washington was reached.

The view of the committee at the end of last week, as it was interpreted by leading bankers outside the group, was that so long as the budget remained unbalanced and Congress was unable to agree upon an effective tax program, any attempt to organize a bond pool or otherwise mobilize the financial resources of the country in behalf of the stricken markets would be almost futile.

After considering the text of the President's message to the Senate and the subsequent action of the Senate Finance Committee yesterday, the committee's hopes of an early balancing of the budget were so raised that attention was turned once more to specific projects.

The foremost of these was again the plan for a pool in bonds. Among important bankers outside the group it was asserted that, provided continued progress was made in Washington, leading to assurance that the budget actually would be balanced quickly, it might be possible to form a pool for the support of the bond market before the actual tax and economy measures had completed their course through Congress. In some quarters there were hopes that action might be taken this week.

The course of the bond market yesterday emphasized the imperative

Continued on Page Thirteen.

PRESIDENT WARNS OF PERIL

He Appears in Person in the Senate to Urge Swift Action.

$275,000,000 MORE IN TAXES

$70,000,000 Raised by Income Taxes With Normal and Surtax Rates Increased.

1-CENT LEVY ON GASOLINE

3 Per Cent Is Imposed on Gross Receipts of Private Power Companies.

Special to THE NEW YORK TIMES.

WASHINGTON, Wednesday, June 1.—The Senate at 12:25 o'clock this morning passed the $1,115,000,000 tax bill for balancing the Federal budget, by a vote of 72 to 11, thus ending two months of Congressional confusion since the passage of the House revenue measure on April 1.

This sudden termination of the delay and indecision which have marked the Senate's efforts to devise and pass a tax bill in the face of opposition from various interests and sections came after President Hoover had personally appeared on the Senate rostrum and appealed for a demonstration that democracy can act "speedily enough to save itself in an emergency."

Treasury officials agree that the additional revenue of $1,115,000,000, supplemented by $238,000,000 in savings in the proposed economy bill, will meet any requirements on the government for the fiscal year 1933.

As one of the final incidents of the prolonged session the Senate finally rejected the Walsh amendment for a manufacturers' sales levy. The vote was 53 to 27.

President Urges Quick Action.

Viewing the present crisis as calling for the supreme effort of his office, President Hoover decided suddenly yesterday morning that he would visit the Senate in person to urge speed on the budget-balancing program. Accordingly, he went to the Senate, and twelve hours after his visit that body had completed and adopted the tax bill.

The President told the Senate that the natural wealth of the country was "unimpaired" but that the inherent abilities of the people to meet their problems had been restrained largely by the failure of the government to act. He said the Senate held the answer to the question of whether democracy could act to save itself.

"The nation urgently needs unity," he told the divided Senate. "It needs solidarity before the world in demonstrating that America has the courage to look its difficulties in the face and the capacity and resolution to meet them."

Senate Moves Quickly Into Action.

From the moment the Chief Executive ended the slow, hardly audible reading of his message, the Senate went into action. The Finance Committee, which in reality had started action two hours before upon learning of the Presidential visit, went back into session. Before the lunch hour the committee was back at the door of the Senate with amendments sufficient to raise the revenues required of the tax bill.

While the President specifically endorsed the manufacturers' sales tax, the Senate rejected the suggestion.

An alternative plan, suggested by Secretary Mills to raise the funds by which the bill was deficient, was accepted, however, and every faction was apparently satisfied with the compromise tonight.

The Presidential visit came as an absolute surprise to Democratic leaders who had visited the White House Monday night. They had left the Executive Mansion with the understanding that the Senate would go ahead with the tax bill along the lines already laid. They felt that the deficiency in the bill, which Secretary Mills said was growing, could be made up in conference committee from the various provisions passed by the Senate and House.

The surprise of the minority leaders did not affect their cooperation, however. They were in the thick of it all day. The proposal to stay on the job today until the tax bill was completed, "if it takes all night,"

Continued on Page Twelve.

"All the News That's Fit to Print."

The New York Times.

LATE CITY EDITION
WEATHER—Partly cloudy today, tomorrow; slightly cooler today.
Temperatures Yesterday—Max., 87; min., 66.

VOL. LXXXI....No. 27,163. ****+ NEW YORK, TUESDAY, JUNE 7, 1932. TWO CENTS In New York City | THREE CENTS Within 200 Miles | FOUR CENTS Elsewhere Except 7th and 8th Postal Zones

PRESIDENT SIGNS $1,118,500,000 TAX BILL; SEES FINANCES NOW ON A 'SOUND BASIS'; DAWES QUITS THE RECONSTRUCTION BOARD

SENATE VOTE IS 46 TO 35

16 Democrats Join With 30 Republicans to Pass Conference Report.

FIGHT ON ELECTRICITY LEVY

Surrender to Power Trusts Charged by Progressives—Norris Assails Hoover.

PRESIDENT ACTS AT ONCE

Approves Measure a Day Short of 6 Months From Time He Told of Tax Needs.

Special to THE NEW YORK TIMES.

WASHINGTON, June 6.—The new tax bill designed to produce $1,118,500,000 in additional revenue for the fiscal year 1933 became law at 5 P. M. today.

President Hoover signed the measure without ceremony, one and a half hours after the Senate adopted the conference report by a vote of 46 to 35, and one day short of six months from the time he had informed Congress the new revenue would be needed.

The measure had just come from the Capitol when Mr. Hoover added his approval. He had kept in close touch with the provisions as they were voted from time to time, and did not stop to re-read the measure.

The income and gift taxes are retroactive, applicable to the full calendar year of 1932, and permanent thereafter. The additional estate levy went into effect today and is permanent.

The postal increases, a 3 cent letter rate and a rise in second class scale are applicable from July 6, 1932, to July 1, 1934.

The excise levies on lubricating oil, brewers' wort, malt syrups, grape, concentrates, automobiles, trucks, parts, tires and tubes, toilet goods, furs, jewelry, radios, phonographs, firearms and shells, matches, candy, chewing gum, soft drinks, electric energy and gasoline, are effective from June 21, 1932, to July 1, 1934.

Tariffs in Effect June 21.

The tariffs on oil, coal, lumber and copper are in effect from June 21, 1932, to July 1, 1934.

The miscellaneous taxes on telephone, telegraph, radio and cable messages, admissions, bank checks, pipe line transportation, boats and safety deposit box rentals begin June 21, 1932, and run to July 1, 1934.

Stamp taxes on conveyances and bond transfers and the increase on stock transfer, stock and bond issues and futures sales in produce markets run from June 21, 1932, to June 1, 1934.

The last hours of the tax bill in Congress were characterized by both the storm and speed which had alternately marked its career. Progressives tried to defeat the conference report on the grounds that the Senate had "surrendered to the power trust" on the electric energy tax. When this debate was over the bill was caught up in another burst of speed which continued until the measure had become the law of the land.

The officially engrossed copy of the bill had been placed on Speaker Garner's desk before the Senate completed action on the report, so certain was it deemed that the vote at the other end of the Capitol would be favorable. Soon after the Senate had voted, the secretary so informed the House and in a few minutes Speaker Garner signed the bill.

He sent it immediately to Vice President Curtis, who signed in the presence of the Senate and gave the bill to a messenger for delivery to the White House.

Millions of Taxpayers Added.

The President's signature automatically added millions of taxpayers to the nation's rolls. Moreover, it placed additional indirect taxes on almost every man, woman and child in the country through the series of excises and miscellaneous levies. Further, it increased to some extent tariff barriers by the enactment of duties on oil, coal, lumber and copper.

The new tax law is expected to raise for the fiscal year 1933—exclusive of revenue from levies al-

Continued on Page Fourteen.

No Ceremony Marks the Signing of the Tax Bill; Hoover Sees People Courageous in Facing Burden

Special to THE NEW YORK TIMES.

WASHINGTON, June 6.—No ceremony marked the signing of the largest peace-time revenue bill by President Hoover today; no Senator or member of Congress was present. No gold pen was used and no high official sought the one that was employed.

The President did not let the occasion pass, however, without commending the spirit of the people for accepting the new tax burden to safeguard the country's credit. In a statement he said:

"The willingness of our people to accept this added burden in these times in order impregnably to establish the credit of the Federal Government is a great tribute to their wisdom and courage.

"While many of the taxes are not as I desired, the bill will effect the great major purpose of assurance to the country and the world of the determination of the American people to maintain their finances and their currency on a sound basis."

Secretary Mills expressed gratification that a measure had been adopted that would assure a balanced budget, and at once began plans for increasing the force in the Internal Revenue Bureau for handling collections on the various new excises and miscellaneous levies.

DAWES CONSIDERS HIS JOB IS FINISHED

Balancing of Budget and State of Reconstruction Work Cited in Resignation.

PRESIDENT WRITES REGRET

General Emphatically Denies That Differences With Meyer Caused His Retirement.

Special to THE NEW YORK TIMES.

WASHINGTON, June 6.—Charles G. Dawes, president of the Reconstruction Finance Corporation, created to combat the economic depression, resigned this afternoon.

The announcement, which was made by President Hoover immediately after he had signed the tax bill, was a complete surprise to all Washington. Not a word had leaked out that the head of the corporation was ready to quit. Mr. Dawes was at his desk as usual.

In accepting the resignation, the President said he did so with intense regret, at the same time expressing his own as well as the country's gratitude for Mr. Dawes's "great accomplishments" as the head of the corporation.

Called to Chicago, He Says.

Mr. Dawes gave as his reason for resigning his desire to re-enter the banking business in Chicago, where, it is said, many of his former associates have been insisting that he leave public life and "come back home" to help bring about a return of normal conditions.

In tendering his resignation Mr. Dawes referred to the balancing of the budget with the remark that "the turning point toward eventual prosperity in this country seems to have been reached."

Rumors that differences in the board of the Reconstruction Finance Corporation, mainly involving Mr. Dawes and Eugene Meyer, chairman, had hastened the retirement of Mr. Dawes were in circulation within a few minutes after the White House announced the resignation.

Another report was that Mr. Dawes is not so physically robust as when he held the reins over the Senate as Vice President. Also it was suggested that corporate interests in Chicago needed his advice in weathering the economic storm. These were all rumors, and were denied in his own emphatic fashion by Mr. Dawes. His letter to the President, he insisted, told the whole story.

General Dawes's Letter.

In resigning, General Dawes wrote:

Washington, D. C., June 6, 1932.

My Dear Mr. President:

Now that the balancing of the national budget by Congress is assured, the turning point toward eventual prosperity in this country seems to have been reached. The work of the Reconstruction Finance Corporation is now well on its way with loans already authorized for about $700,000,000 and its operations are now properly systematized and effective.

It has been a privilege to participate in the earlier stages of the organization of the Corporation and its work, and to cooperate in your well-considered and constructive plans for the betterment of existing conditions in the country.

In taking my position with the Corporation I interrupted my formerly announced plan to re-enter the banking business in Chicago, which I now desire to do. In accordance with our understanding when I became associated with the

Continued on Page Fourteen.

BOTH HOUSES VOTE ON RELIEF TODAY

Modified Wagner Plan Comes Up in Senate and Garner Measure in Lower Chamber.

RIGID RULE WITH LATTER

Republicans Prepare to Fight It and Bolting by Democrats Foreshadows Close Count.

Special to THE NEW YORK TIMES.

WASHINGTON, June 6.—Under one of the most rigid rules ever accompanying a major bill in the House, Speaker Garner's $2,290,000,000 relief bill will be presented tomorrow noon and its fate will be known in the next few hours.

At the same time, it was indicated tonight, the Senate will vote on the Wagner relief measure, which today was modified to conform largely to President Hoover's program by reducing the amount for State loans from $375,000,000 to $300,000,000.

The Republicans of the House, infuriated at the "tight rule" approved by the Rules Committee for the Garner bill, conferred for two hours and a half late today on plans to defeat the rule, which first requires the approval of a majority of those present before the bill can come up for discussion and a vote.

The rule provides for one hour's discussion before a vote on itself and only three hours for discussion and amendment on the bill. Only the Democratic members of the Ways and Means Committee will be allowed to offer amendments to the bill, but the minority will have one chance to offer a motion to recommit the bill before the final vote.

Hawley Bills as Substitute.

Minority Leader Snell said that he did not expect the Republicans to vote solidly with the leaders against the rule.

"There never was a solid vote, and I cannot predict a solid vote tomorrow," he protested.

If they fail to defeat the special rule, the Republicans plan to offer the Hawley relief bills, which will be incorporated into one measure, as a substitute for the Garner bill, on the motion to recommit.

The Hawley bills, as amended, provide a fund of $1,800,000,000 to be distributed by the Reconstruction Finance Corporation. Of this amount, $300,000,000 would be for loans to States for relief purposes and the remainder would be provided for loans to States, private business and self-liquidating projects.

No funds are provided in the Hawley bill for direct Federal relief as in the Garner measure, and repayment of the loans would be guaranteed to the government by adequate security.

Democratic leaders laughed at the discomfiture of the Republicans. They said the rule might be "tight," but that it was just like the rule under which the Republicans brought in and passed the Smoot-Hawley tariff bill in 1929. The only exception, they said, was that debate was then confined to eight hours instead of three as provided in the Garner bill rule.

Hoover Heartened on 4-Point Plan.

President Hoover's four-point plan for the relief of unemployment, agriculture and business in general was the subject of a conference today between the President and Secretary Mills.

Afterward Secretary Mills said that some of the legislation suggested by the President and the members of

Continued on Page Two.

Davila Pledges Moderation in Chile; Counter-Revolt Starts in the South

By CARLOS DAVILA,
Provisional President of Chile.
Special Cable to THE NEW YORK TIMES.

SANTIAGO, Chile, June 6.—The new administration in Chile has been credited with a fierceness of purpose and violence of action which are entirely groundless in press information and forecasts, with far-reaching effects.

Notwithstanding the socialistic atmosphere, the new government has not contemplated drastic measures far removed from the past practices of most affairs of state. In this respect, international relations will be maintained as hitherto, with an endeavor to improve without exception the spirit of good-will and understanding. No changes of importance are considered, except to foster international understanding between countries. It is probable that Soviet Russia will be recognized.

In regard to the foreign debt service, which was suspended by the previous administration when the economic depression made payments difficult, there is no reason whatsoever to supposethat the new government considers breaking away from the usual line of procedure in these matters. There are not contemplated any changes of any nature in international and national financial problems which might be considered a departure from recognized and accepted principles governing international monetary problems.

As to the difficult question of whether the new government intends

Continued on Page Four.

IRISH SUDDENLY CALL PARLEY WITH BRITAIN TO BREAK DEADLOCK

Thomas and Hailsham Confer in Dublin Today and de Valera Will Visit London Friday.

OTTAWA IS FORMAL ISSUE

But Discussion of Oath Is Held Inevitable—Talks Viewed as Face-Saving on Both Sides.

By FERDINAND KUHN JR.
Wireless to THE NEW YORK TIMES.

LONDON, June 6.—On a sudden invitation from Eamon de Valera, President of the Irish Free State Council, J. H. Thomas, British Secretary for Dominions, and Viscount Hailsham, Secretary for War, left for Dublin tonight to discuss with him the existing deadlock between the British and Free State governments.

Mr. de Valera himself is coming here to go over the problem with Prime Minister MacDonald and it is understood tomorrow's conference in Dublin will be only a preliminary to the more crucial meeting here at the end of the week. It will be Mr. de Valera's first visit to London since the fateful days of 1921.

The beginning of direct discussions between the two governments took both nations completely by surprise today. It is regarded in London and Dublin as an event of the first importance in a determination of the future relations of the Free State and the British Empire, although the atmosphere tonight was not exactly optimistic. The overture from Mr. de Valera was made through J. W. Dulanty, Irish High Commissioner here, and led to a hurriedly summoned Cabinet meeting. After a telephone call to Mr. MacDonald at Lossiemouth it was decided that the two British Ministers should go to Dublin as quickly as possible and the Prime Minister would cut short his vacation for the conference on Friday.

De Valera Accused of Yielding.

Naturally the air is thick with talk of a "comedown" by each side in the long and bitter controversy. Mr. de Valera is being accused of yielding because the original invitation came from him and because two months ago he announced he would not visit London "under any circumstances."

Similarly the British Ministers are being taunted by some of their Tory supporters for backing down and an indignant meeting of Tory backbenchers in Parliament was held tonight at which a protest against Mr. Thomas's trip was sent to Acting Prime Minister Stanley Baldwin. Labor leaders in Parliament, however, congratulated Mr. Thomas in the warmest terms on his decision to go to Dublin.

As is usual in such situations each side loudly insists there has been no comedown except by the other side. The Irish assert they will discuss only the prospects for the Ottawa imperial conference and will refuse even to talk about the oath of allegiance—although the British see the two as indissoluble. Mr. Thomas himself told the House of Commons today that the British attitude was not changed in the slightest.

"The British Government has never refused to discuss," he exclaimed. "It never received an invitation to discuss prior to this."

Face-Saving on Both Sides.

It is nearer to the truth to say that both sides are engaged in face-saving—with Mr. de Valera genuinely alarmed over the prospect of British tariff retaliation and the British equally alarmed lest the Free State be lost to the empire. Members of the British Cabinet do not look for any immediate or spectacular results from the conversations, but they are glad of an opportunity for a full and frank discussion. They realize it would have been difficult to begin

Continued on Page Seven.

RETORT BY SHOUSE ACCUSES ROOSEVELT OF BREAKING FAITH

He Says Governor Approved Action 'Commending' Him for Convention Post.

PLANS HOT FIGHT FOR PLACE

Roosevelt Backers Here Deny Any Knowledge of Commitment—Press Campaign for Walsh.

By ARTHUR KROCK.
Special to THE NEW YORK TIMES.

WASHINGTON, June 6.—In reply to the announcement of James A. Farley yesterday that the Roosevelt leaders will support Senator Thomas J. Walsh of Montana for Permanent Chairman of the Democratic National Convention, Executive Chairman Jouett Shouse of the party's national committee today made a charge of broken faith against Governor Franklin D. Roosevelt personally.

This charge Mr. Shouse supported with the statement that Mr. Roosevelt's dictated assent to the April 4 agreement at Chicago, whereby the Democratic committee on arrangements "recommended" Senator A. W. Barkley for temporary chairman and "commended" Mr. Shouse for permanent chairman, is in his possession.

It is, said Mr. Shouse, in the handwriting of National Committeeman Robert H. Jackson of New Hampshire, a Roosevelt captain, who, he explained, had set down the Governor's approval of the "Chicago compromise" during a long-distance telephone conversation with Albany from Chicago, undertaken at Mr. Shouse's request.

Regardless of Mr. Farley's announcement as to Senator Walsh, said Mr. Shouse, he will be a candidate for permanent chairman at Chicago. He said, moreover, that if chosen no candidate or faction shall be permitted to "censor" or "inspire" what he proposes to say in his speech.

This attitude, fortified by the reported intention of Mr. Shouse to deliver as permanent chairman a full-length, unauthorized keynote, was described in a Washington dispatch to THE NEW YORK TIMES of Sunday, and was quickly followed by Mr. Farley's announcement that Senator Walsh will be the Roosevelt candidate for permanent chairman.

Stand Assures Hot Fight.

The charge of bad faith, made against the leading candidate for the Presidential nomination by the party spokesman at national headquarters, came just three weeks before the Democrats assemble at Chicago. It enlivened the prospect for a fight over every important convention detail between the Roosevelt forces on the one hand and the anti-Rooseveltians, augmented by some favorite-son delegations, on the other.

If the supporters of New York's Governor are as numerous as Mr. Farley asserts, and if his organization will be solid on convention details as well as on the Presidential nominee, then Senator Barkley will be temporary chairman, Senator Walsh will be permanent chairman and Mr. Shouse will have to obtain the platform as a mere delegate to deliver any views he may have in his system.

That he and others will utter notes—though unofficial—discordant in the ears of the Roosevelt group hardly admits of doubt. Some of these will deal with the tariff questions, which the designation of Senator Walsh has made even more embarrassing in the Governor's camp.

Mr. Barkley voted for all four tariff increases in the tax bill, and Mr. Walsh voted or was paired for three. He would not add to the protection of coal, but he was kindly to oil, lumber and copper. The hope, therefore, of Senators Hull and Harrison—ardent Roosevelt men—that

Continued on Page Thirteen.

JOHN D. ROCKEFELLER JR. OUT FOR REPEAL; SAYS DRY LAW EVILS OUTWEIGH BENEFITS; URGES WET PLANKS IN BOTH PLATFORMS

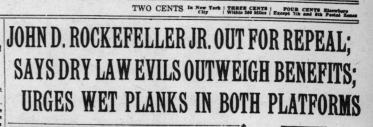

Underwood & Underwood Photo.

JOHN D. ROCKEFELLER JR.

BACKS BUTLER REPEAL PLAN

Holds 18th Amendment Must Go to Restore Respect for Law.

FOR 'GENUINE TEMPERANCE'

A Lifelong Teetotaler, He Was a Chief Supporter of the Anti-Saloon League.

FAVORS STATE CONTROL

Dr. Butler Predicts Repeal in Two Years if Both Parties Declare For It.

The text of Mr. Rockefeller's statement is printed on page 12.

John D. Rockefeller Jr., regarded as the most prominent individual in the ranks of prohibition supporters, one of the largest contributors to the Anti-Saloon League, and who together with his father subscribed $350,000 to make possible adoption of prohibition legislation, declared himself yesterday in favor of repeal of the Eighteenth Amendment.

Mr. Rockefeller pronounced prohibition a failure. He said that its evils have more than outweighed its benefits, and that these evils "unless promptly checked are likely to lead to conditions unspeakably worse than those which prevailed before." Urging that the prohibition question be taken out of partisan politics, Mr. Rockefeller expressed the hope that both the Republican and Democratic parties would adopt planks for its repeal.

Mr. Rockefeller expressed his new stand on prohibition in a letter to Dr. Nicholas Murray Butler, president of Columbia University, in which he endorsed Dr. Butler's proposal that Congress submit the question of repeal to the people. Dr. Butler's proposal calls for ratification of repeal by conventions of the people of the several States, in accordance with the provisions of Article V of the Constitution of the United States. He has made known his intention to submit his repeal proposal for incorporation in the platform of the Republican party at the national convention in Chicago.

Dr. Butler expressed gratification at "Mr. Rockefeller's kind support" of his repeal proposal and said it would have great influence in swinging public opinion in the direction of repeal.

"If both national conventions now have the intelligence and the courage to declare for unqualified repeal, that question will be taken out of the coming campaign, and repeal will be assured within two years," Dr. Butler said.

Dr. Butler's aim is to return the whole liquor question to the States, to be dealt with by them in a manner as best suits their individual ideas and requirements. The proposal also pledges the Republican party to bring the liquor traffic, when not prohibited, under public supervision and control through the instrumentality of the several States, as the most effective method to promote temperance.

In Accord With Dr. Butler.

"With this resolution I am in complete sympathy," Mr. Rockefeller wrote, "and earnestly hope not only that it will be incorporated in the Republican platform, but that a similar resolution will be incorporated in the Democratic platform, thus taking the question of repeal out of the field of partisan politics."

Mr. Rockefeller said he had revised his views on prohibition "slowly and reluctantly" but that he was now convinced, contrary to his hopes when the Eighteenth Amendment was adopted, that prohibition has increased drinking, that it has substituted the speakeasy for the saloon, "not only unit for unit but probably two-fold if not three-fold," that it has stimulated the spirit of lawbreaking, and increased crime "to an unprecedented degree."

Admitting that prohibition has not been without its benefits, such as the abolition of the saloon, Mr. Rockefeller declared that it is now his conviction "that these benefits, important and far reaching as they are, are more than outweighed by the evils." Repeal of the Eighteenth Amendment is an essential prere-

Continued on Page Twelve.

WET PLANK MOVES GAIN IN BOTH PARTIES

Proposal That Conventions Take Identical Stands Is Spurred by Rockefeller Letter.

REPUBLICANS ALTER PLANK

Submission to Legislatures Is Decided On—Tydings, Borah Attack It as Hypocritical.

Special to THE NEW YORK TIMES.

WASHINGTON, June 6.—The declaration of John D. Rockefeller Jr. in favor of repeal of the Eighteenth Amendment and adoption of similar planks by both parties to remove the question from partisan politics caused the greatest political sensation in the capital in years. His conviction that the cause of temperance could be strengthened by repeal of the twelve-year-old amendment brought depression to the dry forces, facing hostile action in the coming political conventions.

The wet forces generally accepted the conversion of Mr. Rockefeller as the greatest support that had been given to the repeal movement. Its effect politically was to strengthen the intentions of both parties to adopt liberal planks on prohibition. But perhaps the most significant and far-reaching effect of the unexpected statement by Mr. Rockefeller, whose family had loyally promoted the campaign for adoption of the Eighteenth Amendment, was the impetus given to plans for identical prohibition planks in the platforms of the major parties. This, supporters of this proposal assert, would take a non-political question out of the 1932 campaign, and cause it to turn on the great economic issues of the day. Senators Reed and Robinson (Arkansas) renewed their efforts in this direction with some hope of success.

Weakens the Drys.

The entrance of Mr. Rockefeller into the political arena in behalf of repeal not only weakened the dry cause generally but brought hope to the Republican leaders that the wet resubmission plank tentatively agreed on could not be successfully attacked by the drys in the Republican convention. The same group of Senate leaders who yesterday had agreed upon the tenor of the plank met Postmaster General Brown and James R. Garfield today and perfected its language.

The plank printed in THE NEW YORK TIMES today was altered slightly to provide that resubmission should be made to State Legislatures rather than to State conventions. This plank will have an alternative plan to protect dry States. The language was not definitely agreed upon today, but its effect is to amend the Constitution so as to prevent shipments in interstate commerce into dry territories. In other words,

Continued on Page Fourteen.

DRYS ARE RESENTFUL; WET CHIEFS JUBILANT

Rockefeller's Statements on the Evils of Prohibition Termed "Wild" by Some.

PRAISED FOR HIS COURAGE

His Conversion to the Cause Will Help Drive for Repeal, Dr. Butler Declares.

The stand of John D. Rockefeller Jr. against the prohibition amendment was greeted with surprise, criticism and some resentment yesterday by dry leaders and Mr. Rockefeller was accused of "wild" statements, impossible of proof.

Several dry leaders insisted that repeal of the Eighteenth Amendment would not only "hurt humanity" but would increase crime. Others objected to the plan that Dr. Nicholas Murray Butler advanced and which Mr. Rockefeller endorsed, on the grounds that it offered no substitute for prohibition and that it would reverse the stand of the conventions of the two major parties in 1928 and would put prohibition into politics. Mrs. Ella Boole, president of the Woman's Christian Temperance Union, questioned whether "people who have refused to obey the prohibition law" would obey any other law restricting liquor sales.

Jubilation Among the Wets.

In the wet camp, however, the note was mainly one of jubilation and gratification that Mr. Rockefeller, for so long a supporter of the dry cause, had been convinced, at last, of the evils of prohibition. Wet leaders from every walk of life, men and women representing business, labor, finance, society, the professions, the schools and the churches, expressed satisfaction that such a notable recruit as Mr. Rockefeller had joined the wet ranks.

Dr. D. Leigh Colvin, chairman of the Prohibition National Committee, and the Rev. James K. Shields, New Jersey State Superintendent of the Anti-Saloon League, took exception to the facts expressed in Mr. Rockefeller's résumé of the evils wrought by prohibition.

Dr. Colvin, who a few weeks ago described women wets as "Bacchantian maidens parching for wine," characterized Mr. Rockefeller's letter as "amazing" and said it showed the financier's "lack of specialized knowledge" of prohibition. Both he and the Rev. Mr. Shields denied, as Mr. Rockefeller said he believed, that "drinking generally has increased" since prohibition, and that lawlessness and crime have flourished. Both the dry leaders contended that accurate statistics showed that both crime and the consumption of liquor had decreased rather than increased under prohibition.

Henry Ford, regarded as one of the

Continued on Page Twelve.

Museum of the City of New York

Bread Line, etching by Reginald Marsh.

Hard Luck Town, drawing by Robert C. Wiseman of a "Hooverville" at the foot of East 10th Street in New York City.

Museum of the City of New York

Pencil drawing by Robert C. Wiseman of the "Hooverville" in the Erie Basin in Brooklyn. A man and his son lived in the remains of this automobile.

Museum of the City of New York

"All the News That's Fit to Print."

The New York Times.

LATE CITY EDITION
POSTSCRIPT
WEATHER—Possibly showers today; tomorrow fair and warmer.
Temperatures Yesterday—Max., 85; Min., 64.

VOL. LXXXI....No. 27,173. ****+ NEW YORK, FRIDAY, JUNE 17, 1932. TWO CENTS In New York City | THREE CENTS Within 200 Miles | FOUR CENTS Elsewhere Except 7th and 8th Postal Zones

HOOVER, CURTIS RENAMED ON FIRST BALLOTS; DRY-WET PLANK IS DEFENDED BY STIMSON

LAUSANNE TO OFFER REPARATIONS TRUCE TILL FINAL SOLUTION

Britain and France Agree on Plan to Be Put to Reich at Closed Session Today.

IDEA IS TO SATISFY PAPEN

Proposal Can Be Interpreted Fairly in Germany as Virtual End to War Debts.

M'DONALD ASKS BOLDNESS

In Opening Speech He Holds Out Hope That We May Cooperate in Solving Economic Problems.

By FREDERICK T. BIRCHALL.
Wireless to THE NEW YORK TIMES.

LAUSANNE, June 16.—To a private plenary meeting of the Lausanne conference tomorrow will be presented a memorandum, to which Great Britain and France have already agreed, extending the suspension of all reparations payments, including the French unconditional annuities under the Young Plan, until a final settlement can be worked out.

The idea behind this move is that it will give Chancellor von Papen of Germany something to take home that can be fairly interpreted as a practical ending of reparation payments and therefore something to talk about in the German elections. A second advantage of the step is that it removes from the Lausanne conference the curse of having to work in a hurry before payments by Germany should begin again on July 2.

Third, it is believed it will satisfy French opinion as preparing the way for a larger consideration of the entire economic problem, for which Prime Minister MacDonald appealed in his opening speech today.

Not Moratorium Extension.

It is to be noted that this proposal is not for an "extension of the moratorium," which would bring in the matter of United States debts. It is rather for a continuation of the European status quo and therefore in full accord with the purpose of this conference. Germany, however, would not be obligated to pay indemnities to the Bank for International Settlements on the next instalments, due July 2, of non-postponable reparations she owes France, which under the present arrangement are returned to Germany in the form of railway bonds redeemable in ten years. Thereby will be removed the metaphorical sword overhanging Chancellor von Papen's head. Yet, at the same time, the end of reparations is not formally acknowledged, which satisfies Premier Herriot of France.

Should the proposal prove acceptable tomorrow it will be in fact a success for the method of temporizing as against the clean-cut method of cancellation which Germany came here to demand. On that point Lieut. Col. von Papen is still to be heard from, but the friendliness toward him manifested by frequent visits from M. Herriot and Mr. MacDonald may not be without reward.

Pending the complete economic discussion and final settlement that Mr. MacDonald envisages, the work of exploration and liquidation, if the proposal carries, will be continued by technicians and experts. Thus the conference will in truth have fulfilled some of the expectations based on it as a preparatory movement toward a real world adjustment.

MacDonald Sounds Keynote.

By P. J. PHILIP.
Wireless to THE NEW YORK TIMES.

LAUSANNE, June 16. — Elected unanimously as president of the Lausanne conference, Prime Minister Ramsay MacDonald in a speech that strongly set forth the principles that must be established began the work of trying to get Europe to put its financial house in order.

He mentioned the United States twice, both times to emphasize her unity with the rest of the world. But there was no mention, and from the British delegation there will be no mention, of Europe's debts to the United States. That is another problem to be settled at some other time

Continued on Page Four.

12-Year Sentence on American In Assault Protested to Spain

Special to THE NEW YORK TIMES.

WASHINGTON, June 16.—United States Consular officers at Malaga and Seville, Spain, have intervened with the military authorities in behalf of John C. Wiley of Inglewood, Cal., who has been sentenced by a military tribunal to twelve years' imprisonment, with recommendation for commutation, on charges of assaulting a carabinero in Malaga on March 10.

The carabinero is said to have suffered a broken nose and to have been incapacitated for duty for nineteen days.

The State Department said today that the case would come up for review soon and the American officials had been promised that it would be submitted to the Premier. The consuls contend that the sentence was out of all proportion to the offense and have urged commutation or deportation.

CHILE OVERTHROWS REGIME AS TOO RED

Army Storms Palace and Captures General Grove as His Guards Quit Him.

DAVILA'S FRIENDS IN POWER

Mobs Fight in Streets as Planes Circle Overhead, Dropping Flares.

Special Cable to THE NEW YORK TIMES.

SANTIAGO, Chile, Friday, June 17.—Colonel Marmaduque Grove was overthrown early today as provisional head of the Chilean Government, according to a manifesto by army leaders who launched a counter-revolt against him last night.

Troops opposed to communism surrounded the government palace and demanded Colonel Grove's surrender by midnight. An earlier manifesto signed by General Agustin Moreno on behalf of all garrisons of the army said if he did not yield by that time, planes and troops would bombard the palace if necessary to obtain control of the government.

Colonel Grove replied that he would die rather than surrender. Shortly after midnight troops began attacking the palace and soon afterward it was announced by the counter-revolutionists that their drive had been successful.

At an early hour the army leaders had not yet named the new junta to take over the government, but it was assumed that Carlos G. Dávila, who, because of his moderate views, was driven out of the junta dominated by Colonel Grove, would be a member.

Coup a Blow at Communism.

Both manifestos declared the counter-revolt was intended to prevent the establishment of communistic practices and to carry forward the socialistic principles enunciated by the junta which seized power from former President Juan Esteban Montero on June 4.

Early last evening rebellious troops began marching on the palace and surrounded it, facing a loyal guard of carabineers. Soon after the midnight attack began, it was observed that the members of the Presidential guard were quietly abandoning their arms and slipping out of the courtyard and palace. When the surrender of the men was practically complete General Moreno announced the success of the counter-revolt.

Earlier there had been considerable disorder in the city, with mobs parading and shouting for and against Colonel Grove.

The rising was made necessary, according to the counter-revolutionists, by the failure of Colonel Grove to keep promises made before the revolution of June 4 and by his encouragement of Communism. The new régime, it was declared, has the support of the entire army, will put down Communism with a firm hand and will maintain order throughout the country.

Colonel Grove Captured.

SANTIAGO, Chile, Friday, June 17 (AP).—Colonel Marmaduque Grove, leading member of the new Socialist junta that deposed President Montero twelve days ago, was captured early today in a counter-revolutionary overthrow of his régime.

When the troops first approached the palace several officers got past the guards and demanded the surrender of General Grove, who re-

Continued on Page Three.

BONUS BILL REPORTED ADVERSELY, 14 TO 2; CAMP MORALE SAGS

Break-Up Starts After Senate Delays Action Till Today and Defeat Appears Likely.

CRUCIAL PERIOD AT HAND

Officials Believe Jobless Men Will Roam Nation in Bands, Hungry and Penniless.

TEMPER OF MEN ON EDGE

Former Leader Flares at the Police, Saying Veterans Are Going to Quit "Soft-Pedaling."

From a Staff Correspondent.
Special to THE NEW YORK TIMES.

WASHINGTON, June 16.—The Senate vote on the Patman bill for the payment of $2,400,000,000 to World War veterans, which was passed by the House yesterday and was scheduled for action by the upper body today, was deferred until tomorrow after the Finance Committee had reported it adversely following a swift consideration this morning.

Late this afternoon Senator Smoot, chairman of the Finance Committee, gave formal notice that the bonus bill would be taken up as soon as the Senate met tomorrow morning. Opponents of the measure say that it will be defeated in the Senate, and even should it unexpectedly succeed, its veto by President Hoover is assured. Its friends admit that it could not possibly be passed over his veto.

Just before the Senate recessed tonight Senator Watson obtained unanimous consent to have the bonus made unfinished business. He remarked that he hoped for a final vote tomorrow, and said that if this did not materialize there would be ample time for discussion anyway.

With today's developments the morale of the bonus expeditionary force, which has remained high in the face of amazing difficulties, began almost visibly to sag. The unexpected delay, the adverse report of the committee and the growing expectation of defeat began to weigh heavily on the thousands of destitute ex-service men encamped here, and the movement of the veterans homeward, only a trickle thus far, was notably increased.

Officials believed that the beginning of the long-expected break-up of the camp was at hand, and would begin in earnest after the Senate vote.

Officials Plan Evacuation.

Hence they began planning for what they concede is the most dangerous period of the bonus army's existence—the period in which the men will start roving about the country as isolated bands of unemployed, without funds, without food and without the discipline to which they submitted voluntarily when they thought there was a chance of achieving their objective.

The bill was opposed in the Finance Committee by fourteen of the sixteen members present. Those voting for the adverse report were Senators Watson, Reed, Shortridge, Couzens, Keyes, Thomas of Idaho, Metcalf and Smoot, all Republicans, and King, George, Walsh of Massachusetts, Connally, Gore and Harrison, Democrats. Those voting favorably were Senators La Follette and Jones of Washington, both Republicans.

Senator La Follette later explained on the floor that he felt that a measure so important should not have had an adverse report, but should have been reported without recommendation.

A motion by Senator Connally to pay the present value of the adjusted compensation certificates, giving the veterans the option of cashing and surrendering them now or of holding them until 1945, was defeated by vote of 11 to 4.

Senator Connally then proposed an amendment to change the interest rate on loans on the certificates from 4 per cent to 3, but this also was voted down. A similar fate met a proposal of Senator Thomas of Oklahoma, principal proponent of the bonus payment in the Senate, that the certificates be cashed when the holders presented proof of absolute want.

When the bill was reported to the

Continued on Page Two.

DENIES IT IS A 'STRADDLE'

Secretary, Over Radio, Says Liquor Plan Is 'Definite and Logical.'

'FAITH' WITH PEOPLE KEPT

'Real Gains' Under Dry Law Must Be 'Disentangled From Evils Incurred,' He Holds.

THE ADMINISTRATION REPLY

Mr. Stimson's Address Is First Move to Justify the Party's Stand to Country.

Special to THE NEW YORK TIMES.

CHICAGO, June 16.—Defending the prohibition plank in the Republican platform, Secretary of State Stimson declared over the radio tonight that instead of being a "straddle," the proposed method of dealing with the prohibition problem was "consistent, definite, logical and well-founded in law and fact."

Secretary Stimson was speaking over a nation-wide radio hook-up of the National Broadcasting Company and his was the first move on the part of the administration to justify the party's stand before the country.

Asserting that the Eighteenth Amendment represented in its adoption the hopes of millions of American wives and mothers, he added:

"To ruthlessly destroy such a faith by indiscriminately condemning an effort like the Eighteenth Amendment, instead of taking the trouble to disentangle the real gains that have been accomplished from the evils which have been incurred, would be an act of social folly and national wrong."

MR. STIMSON'S ADDRESS.

Secretary Stimson's address was as follows:

"My friends of the radio audience:

"At their meeting last night the members of the Republican National Convention took a momentous step in the direction of American constitutional history. By a vote of 1,153 they have unanimously recommended to submit to the voters of this country a proposal to change the Eighteenth Amendment.

"They divided by a vote of 681 to 472 as to the form of the proposed change which should be submitted. But they were unanimous in recommending the submission of a proposal to change. Should the Democratic party in its approaching convention take similar action, the constitutional steps toward this momentous change will be well under way.

"There has been so much misunderstanding on the subject that it is well to analyze carefully the nature of what has been done. In the first place, both parties, in the convention last evening, advocated a new amendment to the Constitution. Even those who seek solely the repeal of the Eighteenth Amendment require a new amendment to accomplish such a repeal.

"The two proposals which were before the Republican National Convention last evening differed only as to the form which the new amendment should take.

Basis of the Majority Plank.

"In the second place, both propositions were clear and explicit, and the difference between them was fundamental and easily understood. The newspaper criticism that the majority plank was a straddle is quite unfounded. It is perfectly consistent, perfectly definite and perfectly logical. It is well founded in law and fact.

"Let us see what this fundamental difference between the two proposals was, and the reason for that difference. One proposal was an impatient demand to abrogate the entire work of the past thirteen years under the prohibition amendment, and to confess it to be an entire failure; to do away with all direct power on the part of the Federal Government in regard to the liquor traffic, and to leave the situation in respect to liquor as it was before 1919.

"This proposal was tantamount to asserting that everything which we have done during those years was useless or evil, that we should confess it to be a great and complete failure and go back and start over again.

"Right here it is well to remind you of what is frequently forgotten, namely, that the Eighteenth Amendment did not come out of thin air

Continued on Page Seventeen.

AGAIN THE REPUBLICAN STANDARD BEARERS

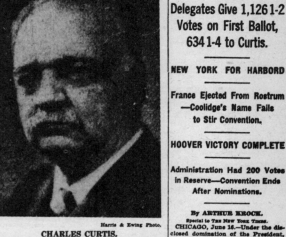

Harris & Ewing Photo. Harris & Ewing Photo.

HERBERT HOOVER. CHARLES CURTIS.

HOOVER LAYS PLANS FOR COMING FIGHT

His First Move Is Selection of Everett Sanders to Be Head of Committee.

SPEAKING TOURS UNLIKELY

Friends of Executive Expect Him to Direct Much of Fight From His Camp on the Rapidan.

Special to THE NEW YORK TIMES.

WASHINGTON, June 16.—Gratified by the outcome of the Republican convention, President Hoover began preparations this afternoon for the campaign for his re-election.

His first move, after sending a message of appreciation for his nomination to Chairman Snell of the convention, was to let the national committee know that he preferred the election of Everett Sanders of Indiana as chairman of the committee.

Mr. Sanders is a former Representative, was secretary to President Coolidge and is experienced in national politics and national campaigns. Since 1929 he has been practicing law here and in Chicago.

The new chairman and the executive committee of the national committee are expected to come here shortly and map out campaign plans with the President. No definite word escaped from the White House on the question today, but it was predicted by Mr. Hoover's close political advisers that he would conduct the campaign from here and make relatively few speeches. It was pointed out that this would be in accordance with past custom when Presidents standing for re-election have attended to the duties of their high office and not engaged in far-flung campaign trips or many speeches.

Trip to California Suggested.

There is some talk among friends of the President of his going to California by warship through the Panama Canal to keep an engagement tentatively set for him to open the Olympic Games at Los Angeles late in July. This would permit a campaign trip back across the country.

Close friends of the President, however, declared that practically all chance of his going to California for notification ceremonies at his Palo Alto home had disappeared, due to the pressure of public business and the efforts he is making to combat the economic depression.

The ceremonies notifying him of the nomination and his acceptance speech, it was predicted, would be held either here or at his Rapidan camp in about six weeks. The chances were said to favor Washington and there were suggestions by his advisers that his acceptance speech might be delivered from the south portico of the White House. President Coolidge, it was recalled, delivered his acceptance speech here in 1924 at a night meeting in Memorial Continental Hall.

In any event the Rapidan camp will be the scene of important campaign activities, since the President intends to spend week-ends there during the Summer as often as pos-

Continued on Page Fourteen.

Ballot for President

Special to THE NEW YORK TIMES.

CHICAGO, June 16.—The vote of the Republican National Convention by which President Hoover was renominated here today was as follows:

State.	Delegates.	France.	Coolidge.	Dawes.	Blaine.	Wadsworth.	Hoover.
Alabama	19	..	..	..	..	..	19
Arizona	9	..	..	..	..	..	9
Arkansas	15	..	..	..	..	..	15
California	47	..	..	..	..	..	47
Colorado	15	..	..	..	..	..	15
Connecticut	19	..	..	..	..	..	19
Delaware	9	..	..	..	..	..	9
Florida	16	..	..	..	..	..	16
Georgia	16	..	..	..	..	..	16
Idaho	11	..	..	..	..	..	11
*Illinois	61	..	3½	..	..	..	54½
Indiana	31	..	..	..	..	..	31
Iowa	25	..	..	..	..	..	25
Kansas	21	..	..	..	..	..	21
Kentucky	25	..	..	..	..	..	25
Louisiana	12	..	..	..	..	..	12
Maine	13	..	..	..	..	..	13
Maryland	19	..	..	..	..	..	19
Massachusetts	34	..	..	..	..	..	34
Michigan	41	..	..	..	..	..	41
Minnesota	25	..	..	..	..	..	25
Mississippi	11	..	..	..	..	..	11
Missouri	33	..	..	..	..	..	33
Montana	11	..	..	..	..	..	11
Nebraska	17	..	..	..	..	..	17
Nevada	9	..	..	..	..	..	9
N. Hampshire	11	..	..	..	..	..	11
New Jersey	35	..	..	..	..	..	35
New Mexico	9	..	..	1	..	..	8
New York	97	..	..	..	..	..	97
No. Carolina	28	..	..	..	..	..	28
No. Dakota	11	..	..	..	2	..	9
Ohio	55	..	..	..	..	..	55
Oklahoma	25	..	..	..	..	..	25
†Oregon	13	3	..	..	..	..	9
Pennsylvania	75	1	..	..	..	1	73
Rhode Island	8	..	..	..	..	..	8
So. Carolina	10	..	..	..	..	..	10
So. Dakota	11	..	..	..	..	..	11
Tennessee	24	..	..	..	..	..	24
Texas	49	..	..	..	..	..	49
Utah	11	..	..	..	..	..	11
Vermont	9	..	..	..	..	..	9
Virginia	25	..	..	..	..	..	25
Washington	19	..	..	..	..	..	19
W. Virginia	19	..	..	..	..	..	19
Wisconsin	27	..	1	..	11	..	15
Wyoming	9	..	..	..	..	..	9
Alaska	2	..	..	..	..	..	2
Dist. of Col.	2	..	..	..	..	..	2
Hawaii	2	..	..	..	..	..	2
Philippines	2	..	..	..	..	..	2
Puerto Rico	2	..	..	..	..	..	2
Total	1,154	4	4½	1	13	1	1,126½

*Three not voting.
†One absent.

REPUBLICAN PRESS SPLIT ON 'WET' PLANK

Many Papers Hold That It Is a 'Meaningless Evasion'—Others See Notable Step.

Editorial comment of Republican and independent newspapers over the nation differs on the merits of the prohibition plank in the Republican platform, telegraphed excerpts of editorials to THE NEW YORK TIMES indicated last night, with the wet papers bitter at what they called a "straddle."

In New York, The Sun declared that out of the "mountain of minds at Chicago comes a ridiculous mouse." The evident purpose of its authors "was to be obscure, and they have succeeded."

The Post, also Republican, headed its editorial "A moral failure at Chicago," and The World-Telegram, wet and independent, agreed with numerous other newspapers in calling the plank a "meaningless evasion."

The Herald Tribune, wet and Republican, declared that "in some paradise for politicians may yet be devised a compromise more inclusive and vague than the wet-moist-dry plank. * * * To date it has no rival." It added that the "great compromisers of Chicago can retire for a long rest, assured of the hearty disapproval of every one with an honest conviction on the subject."

The Chicago Tribune, Republican,

Continued on Page Fifteen.

CURTIS VICTORY WON AGAINST FIELD OF 12

Snell, Harbord, Alvin Fuller, Replogle and MacNider Were Put in Nomination.

PENNSYLVANIA TURNS TIDE

Suddenly Gives 75 to Kansan—Foes Unable to Muster Behind One Candidate.

By L. C. SPEERS.
Special to THE NEW YORK TIMES.

CHICAGO, June 16.—Charles Curtis of Kansas won renomination as the Republican Vice Presidential candidate, but it was not an easy victory, and save for the fact that Pennsylvania swung its seventy-five votes to him after the roll-call of the States was concluded, he would have been 19¼ ballots short of the majority necessary for nomination.

The anti-Curtis elements in the convention fought to the last, but were unable to concentrate on any one candidate. With General Charles G. Dawes standing as their candidate, there was apparently every justification for their boast they had Mr. Curtis stopped, but with the Illinoisan out of the picture the backbone of the opposition was broken.

Six nominations were made for Vice President, and thirteen names, all told, were on the tally sheet when the roll-call was completed. One of them was that of Senator Couzens of Michigan, who received two of the eleven "Progressive" votes in the Wisconsin delegation. The fact that Mr. Couzens was born in Canada, and therefore ineligible, did not deter the La Follettites from allotting him a share of their honorary vote.

Three ex-soldiers constituted the main opposition to the renomination of Mr. Curtis—Hanford MacNider of Iowa, former National Commander of the American Legion; Major Gen. James G. Harbord of New York, chief of staff of the A. E. F., and General Edward Martin, chairman of the Republican State Committee of Pennsylvania.

Six Placed in Nomination.

Mrs. Edward Everett Gann, sister of the Vice President, was on the firing line to the end. She was tired and smiling when Pennsylvania withdrew the name of General Martin and cast its seventy-five votes for her brother, which assured his renomination on the first ballot.

The six nominations placed before the convention were those of Mr. Curtis, former Governor Alvin E. Fuller of Massachusetts, Mr. MacNider, J. Leonard Replogle of Florida, Representative Bertrand Snell of New York, the permanent chairman of the convention, and General Harbord.

Those who in addition to these were named in the voting that followed were Mr. Dawes, Judge William S. Kenyon of the United States Circuit Court of Appeals, Senator Couzens, Secretary Hurley of Oklahoma, David Ingalls, Republican

Continued on Page Thirteen.

CHEER HOOVER 27 MINUTES

Delegates Give 1,126 1-2 Votes on First Ballot, 634 1-4 to Curtis.

NEW YORK FOR HARBORD

France Ejected From Rostrum—Coolidge's Name Fails to Stir Convention.

HOOVER VICTORY COMPLETE

Administration Had 200 Votes in Reserve—Convention Ends After Nominations.

By ARTHUR KROCK.
Special to THE NEW YORK TIMES.

CHICAGO, June 16.—Under the disclosed domination of the President, the Republican national convention at its closing session today renominated Herbert Hoover and gave a grudging but safe majority to Charles Curtis of Kansas, renominated as the party candidate for Vice President.

Mr. Hoover received 1,126½ votes on the first ballot, his nomination immediately thereafter being made unanimous. Mr. Curtis, the beneficiary of a last-minute switch of Pennsylvania's 75 votes from its Republican State Chairman, General Edward Martin, to the Vice President, had a first ballot majority of 55¾, with a total of 634¼. His nomination also was made unanimous. Until Pennsylvania responded to the Administration goad, Mr. Curtis lacked 19¼ votes of the sum required for his renomination.

It has been twenty years since the obvious will of a Republican National Committee has been so completely and publicly subordinated to a President's program. In 1912, as today, both President and Vice President were renominated, the only time in its history that the Republican party has repeated its ticket.

But then Theodore Roosevelt bolted the convention and formed the Bull Moose party, badly defeating the regular Republicans under William H. Taft in the election and assuring the victory of the Democratic ticket headed by Woodrow Wilson.

No Prospect of a Bolt.

So far as the political elements of the Republican party are concerned, there were no prospects of a bolt as the result of the defeat of the repeal plank last night and the renomination of Mr. Curtis today. The only menacing element was the insurgency of the New York delegation. Today its members cast ninety-five of their ninety-seven votes for General J. G. Harbord for Vice President, ignoring the plain warning which lay in the fact that the two New Yorkers who voted for Mr. Curtis were the Secretary of State, Henry L. Stimson, and the Secretary of the Treasury, Ogden L. Mills.

Last night the New Yorkers cast seventy-six of their votes for the Bingham repeal plank. The administration, which made that struggle the test of its control, had only twenty-one. Had not Charles D. Hilles, the national committeeman, declined to aid the State chairman, W. Kingsland Macy, in his effort to supplant Representative Ruth B. Pratt as national committee woman, this steadfast friend of the President would have been defeated.

The church drys, and those who are dry before they are Republican or Democratic, will not be heard from until they meet in national conclave in August, after they have examined the prohibition plank which the Democrats will adopt in Chicago the week after next.

It may be that then, as they did against James W. Wadsworth Jr. and Charles H. Tuttle, they will put independent New York State and national tickets in the field. Should this happen, the effect of that action, joined to the demonstrated dissatisfaction with Mr. Hoover's program of New York's regular Republicans, may be as disastrous to the national Republican candidates as was Colonel Roosevelt's third-party movement twenty years ago.

For days before this convention opened, and for the first day of the session, administration leaders maintained the strategic fiction that the delegates were to "work their will" on all points. In every respect save

Continued on Page Thirteen.

"All the News That's Fit to Print."

The New York Times.

LATE CITY EDITION

WEATHER—Partly cloudy today; possibly showers tomorrow.
Temperatures Yesterday—Max., 75; Min., 64.

VOL. LXXXI....No. 27,174. ⁊ **** NEW YORK, SATURDAY, JUNE 18, 1932. TWO CENTS In New York City | THREE CENTS Within 200 Miles | FOUR CENTS Elsewhere Except 7th and 8th Postal Zones

PRESIDENT TAKES UP PLANS FOR CAMPAIGN WITH AIDES; ECONOMIC ISSUE PUT FIRST

CABINET MEMBERS REPORT

Executive Does Not Want the Liquor Question to Submerge Others.

CONGRATULATIONS POUR IN

Some of the Telegrams, It Is Admitted, Criticize the Prohibition Plank.

BISHOP McDOWELL CALLS

Dry Leader Says He Does Not See 'Any Occasion for a Third Party at Present.'

Special to THE NEW YORK TIMES.

WASHINGTON, June 17.—Plans for the political campaign occupied much of the attention of President Hoover today and practically all of the discussion at the regular Friday Cabinet meeting, which was attended by Secretaries Mills, Wilbur and Lamont, Attorney General Mitchell and Vice President Curtis. Other Cabinet officers had not arrived from Chicago in time for the meeting.

Pending conferences which the President will have with Everett Sanders, the new chairman of the national committee and the executive committee of that organization, it was said that only general consideration was being given to the political prospects, while announcements of policies will await a more detailed shaping of plans.

Messages of congratulation continue to be received at the White House from all sections of the country, but some telegrams, it was tacitly admitted, contained criticisms of the prohibition plank. In general, however, it was said, the messages were commendatory.

To Stress Economic Issues.

Whether the stand of the party on the liquor question will cause internal troubles is not yet apparent, but it is clear that President Hoover intends to stress his record in the White House and the economic problems of the country during the campaign. According to those who have conferred with him, he does not want the wet and dry issue to submerge other questions which he considers of outstanding importance to the country at this time.

For the time being, at least, prominent drys who call at the White House are making no outright criticism of the Republican platform. They evidently are reserving formal comment until after the Democratic party has taken its position on the liquor issue.

The Rev. William F. McDowell of this city, retired Methodist bishop and former president of the Board of Temperance, Prohibition and Public Morals of that church, was among the callers on President Hoover today. He said afterward that he had called to pay his respects and offer his congratulations, and did not discuss the prohibition plank with the President.

Bishop McDowell sought to forestall comment on the topic of prohibition by explaining that a statement would more properly be made by his successor, Bishop Edwin H. Hughes. But when pressed for his views he said:

"I do not see any occasion for a third party at present."

Bishop McDowell is a close personal friend of the President and is understood to have been consulted by Mr. Hoover when the prohibition plank was under consideration prior to the convention.

President Obviously Happy.

President Hoover was said by Secretary Wilbur to feel that the convention did "a prompt and effective job." He obviously was in a happy frame of mind when he received newspaper men for their regular Friday afternoon press conference.

The correspondents congratulated the President on his renomination and he said he "felt very proud of the tribute." He also declared that he appreciated the attitude of the press which, he added, had been very friendly and cordial.

President Hoover and Vice President Curtis met just before the Cabinet meeting for the first time since they were nominated. They shook hands heartily and then, talking in low tones, walked to the south lawn of the White House grounds and posed for pictures before a platoon of motion-picture camera men. They

Continued on Page Two.

Huey Long and Coxey Picked To Head Farmer-Labor Ticket

Special to THE NEW YORK TIMES.

COUNCIL BLUFFS, Iowa, June 17.—Roy M. Harrop, chairman of the national executive committee of the Farmer-Labor party, said today that Senator Huey P. Long of Louisiana had been asked to become the party's Presidential candidate.

The credentials of Frank E. Webb of San Francisco, who was named Presidential nominee in the convention held at Omaha, have been withheld by Harrop and Thomas R. Poundstone, secretary of the committee. Webb, according to Harrop, refused to abide by the party's platform.

General Coxey of Ohio has been asked to be the Vice Presidential nominee and, according to Harrop, has accepted.

SHOUSE PREDICTS SUBMISSION PLANK

He Says on Arrival at Chicago That the Democratic Stand on Liquor Will Be Clear-Cut.

LOOKS FOR TEST ON FLOOR

Says Party Is Not Likely to Pledge Repeal, but Will Ask a Vote by People.

By JAMES A. HAGERTY.
Special to THE NEW YORK TIMES.

CHICAGO, June 17.—A clear-cut prohibition plank will be adopted by the Democratic National Convention, according to party leaders who are beginning to arrive.

They assert that the plank will declare for the submission of a resolution calling for outright repeal of the Eighteenth Amendment, or for an amendment to the amendment to restore to each State desiring it complete control over the liquor traffic without any Federal control except for Federal protection against liquor imports into States that wish to remain dry.

It is their opinion also that the plank will not pledge the party to support ratification.

Jouett Shouse, executive chairman of the Democratic National Committee, said on his arrival that the committee had received more than fifty suggested planks, and that, while these varied from outright repeal to moderate resubmission, the trend was toward a definite declaration to give the American people a chance to vote on whether the Eighteenth Amendment should be repealed and whether the problem of liquor regulation should be returned to the States with power to deal with it without Federal interference.

"My guess is that this is about as far as the Democratic party will go," Mr. Shouse said. "I doubt that the party will go on record to pledge itself for repeal, but it will declare for submission."

The submission of a repeal amendment was the minority proposal submitted by Senator Bingham, but the Republican convention turned it down in favor of the administration plank, which the Democrats and many Republicans say is without definite meaning.

The Democrats intend to get a

Continued on Page Three.

GOVERNOR AND CURRY CONFER, BAR WAGNER IN CONVENTION ROLE

Roosevelt Defers to Wishes of Leader and McCooey to Drop Senator as Nominator.

CHOICE IS KEPT SECRET

Chiefs, to Leave for Chicago Tuesday, Withhold Decision on Support Till After Arrival.

WALKER COURSE DEBATED

Propriety of Voting at Chicago Is Questioned—Slated for Part in Fight to Check Roosevelt.

John F. Curry, leader of Tammany, and John H. McCooey, Democratic leader in Brooklyn, conferred with Governor Roosevelt at the home of George Foster Peabody in Saratoga on Thursday, it was disclosed yesterday. National politics in general and the name of the man who is to place Governor Roosevelt in nomination at the Democratic National Convention were discussed at length.

The Governor, it was revealed, advanced the name of United States Senator Robert F. Wagner as the one to nominate him, but deferred to Mr. Curry's request that some one else be selected. The reports of the meeting coincided with the announcement yesterday from Roosevelt headquarters that the name of the man to nominate the Governor would be announced today or tomorrow, instead of yesterday, as had been planned.

Senator Wagner is not a member of the New York State delegation to the convention, but the Roosevelt forces had planned to have Thomas F. Conway of Clinton County, former Lieutenant Governor, resign one of the two places he holds in the delegation and then have the delegation elect to the vacancy the man who is to place the Governor in nomination. Mr. Conway was elected a district delegate before he was chosen one of the sixteen delegates at large.

Mr. Curry, Mr. McCooey and their up-State allies, the O'Connell brothers of Albany and Joseph Murphy of Troy, control a majority of the delegation, and the veto power over the Roosevelt nominating speaker thus rested in their hands.

Wagner Out of Tammany Favor.

Ordinarily the request would have been granted without question, but Mr. Wagner incurred the enmity of Tammany some time ago, the charge of Tammany being that he had "run out" on them when the legislative investigation of the City Government was started. He has also lost favor in the Smith camp, where it is charged that he has favored Governor Roosevelt for the Presidency, despite the fact that he is a Smith "protégé."

The incident strengthened the belief that there is a well-defined plan in Tammany to shelve Mr. Wagner when he comes up for renomination this Fall, if that can be done without endangering the rest of the ticket.

If, as contended in the Roosevelt camp, some one to place the Governor in nomination has been agreed upon, his name was kept secret yesterday. It had been known that one of those under discussion was Claude C. Bowers, keynoter of the 1928 convention at Houston and now an editorial writer on The New York Evening Journal. Mr. Bowers's connection with a newspaper of William R. Hearst, who is supporting Speaker John N. Garner for the Presidential

Continued on Page Three.

House Calls for a World Economic Parley, Adopting Somers Resolution, 235 to 24

Special to THE NEW YORK TIMES.

WASHINGTON, June 17.—Despite the opposition of Representative McFadden of Pennsylvania, the House today adopted, 235 to 24, the Somers resolution approving an international conference to discuss the world economic situation.

The resolution adopted today, after Mr. McFadden had played his last trump with a challenge of no quorum following a division vote of 83 to 5, did not mention silver or monetary troubles, but it was a committee revision of the original Somers resolution authorizing the President to call an international conference to adjust the gold standard and standardize silver.

It read:

"Resolved, That the House of Representatives of the Congress of the United States does hereby approve and encourage the efforts which have been made to hold an international economic conference to be participated in by as many countries as may be willing to send representatives for the purpose of considering methods for the improvement of general economic and monetary conditions."

The substitute resolution, the Foreign Affairs Committee reported, "was decided upon after the government of Great Britain had issued an invitation to the United States Government to attend a conference for the discussion of the economic and financial difficulties that are responsible for and which may prolong the world crisis."

Mr. McFadden based his opposition on a letter he said he had received from a correspondent in Paris. It was dated June 3, he said, and the writer declared that "gold is the only thing of importance here in France." It also asserted that gold was being withdrawn from the United States to force down the American dollar.

"At the Lausanne conference today plans are being laid for a recess of reparations and debts," Mr. McFadden declared. "They will not be taken up again until after the Fall elections in the United States. Europe knew what was going to happen here long before we did."

Senate action will not be necessary, as it was a House resolution and will be sent tomorrow to the White House for President Hoover's attention.

ONE FOX POOL PROFIT IS PUT AT $1,937,762

Raskob, Chrysler, Kenny and Brady Shared in It, Gray Tells Senate Committee.

LOEW DEAL IS DESCRIBED

Stockholders Lost $3,314,724, Counsel Says—Committee Would Lengthen Inquiry.

Special to THE NEW YORK TIMES.

WASHINGTON, July 17.—Allegations that William Fox, creator and for five years the dictator of the vast motion-picture enterprises bearing his name, participated in pool operations while issuing hundreds of thousands of shares of non-voting stock entered into the Senate stock market inquiry today. Mr. Fox again was absent, confined to his bed by illness.

William A. Gray, counsel for the Banking and Currency Committee, in a presentation of the investigation he intends to pursue into the Fox interests, charged again that Mr. Fox "manipulated his stock as he saw fit."

According to Mr. Gray, others who shared in the $1,937,762 profits of the pool in 1929 were John J. Raskob, Nicholas F. Brady, William F. Kenny, Walter P. Chrysler, Joseph E. Higgins, Bradford Ellsworth and Mrs. Elizabeth Meehan.

Mr. Gray told the committee that Mr. Fox's daughter, Mrs. Caroline Leah Taussig, received $441,000 as a share of the brokerage commission in the issuance of Fox stock in 1925, although her name was not signed to a contract providing, it was alleged, for division of the commissions.

He charged further that Mr. Fox's trading accounts had been traced through twenty-two brokerage offices, being found in his own name and the names of various relatives, associates and brokers.

He also presented what he termed evidence to show that Mr. Fox had violated income tax laws through deducting stock losses on his personal return after charging the same losses against his companies.

To Urge Inquiry's Extension.

Following the hearing, the committee, behind locked doors, voted five to three to ask extension of its authority until the end of this Congress on March 3, 1933, instead of to the end of the current session, and to request another $50,000 for expenses.

Chairman Norbeck revealed that the committee has taken up a serious study of alleged income tax violations by stock market operators. He said that no one voted against continuance, the only difference being on whether the committee should request $50,000 or $25,000.

"I maintain that this investigation will not cost the Treasury one cent," said Senator Norbeck.

"The recovery of evaded income tax will offset the expense 100 times. A new system of apparently legal tax evasion has been uncovered, and we are just getting into it."

No hearings will be held during the Summer, Mr. Norbeck said, but investigations will be pursued.

Senator Couzens announced that he planned to introduce a motion requesting the Treasury to deliver income tax reports by persons involved in this and previous hearings.

Tells of $95,000,000 Purchase.

According to records produced by Mr. Gray, the Fox Film and Fox Theatre Corporations prospered greatly until the stock market crash in 1929.

In April, 1930, Mr. Fox sold his controlling shares to a syndicate for

Continued on Page Eight.

DE VALERA DEMANDS REPUBLIC OF IRELAND

But British Ministers Refuse to Discuss Project, Thomas Reveals in Commons.

ARBITRATION PLAN BANNED

Lloyd George Supports Stand of Government—Ottawa Tariff Agreement Ruled Out.

By FERDINAND KUHN Jr.
Wireless to THE NEW YORK TIMES.

LONDON, June 17.—A republic of United Ireland, associated "in some circumstances and for some reasons" with the British Empire and with the King as the head of the association, was the proposal Eamon de Valera submitted to the British Ministers in last week's conferences.

This disclosure was made in the House of Commons today by J. H. Thomas, Secretary of State for the Dominions, who explained that the plan was Mr. de Valera's "ultimate aim" for securing the lasting peace and good-will of Ireland. Union of the Free State and Ulster was the first part of the scheme, and when that had been accomplished, recognition of the Irish Republic by Great Britain would follow, he said.

Mr. de Valera admitted to the British Ministers he had no electoral mandate for a republic immediately, but he assumed he would get such a mandate ultimately. At the same time, he urged them to end the present difficulty by accepting abolition of the oath of allegiance to the Crown and the withholding of the land annuities, together with the reopening of certain other financial questions involved in the Anglo-Irish treaty.

The scheme was flatly rejected by the British Ministers when Mr. de Valera was in London a week ago.

"We told him straightaway," said Mr. Thomas, "that in our judgment no useful purpose would be served by a discussion along these lines and that quite clearly and definitely not only the present British Government but no British Government would ever agree to such suggestions."

Arbitration Rejected.

Mr. Thomas also read a new note from Mr. de Valera expressing willingness "in principle" to arbitrate the question of land annuities but naming such conditions that the British indignantly rejected them as "impossible."

The first condition was that the arbitral tribunal should include citizens of countries outside the British Commonwealth. In Mr. de Valera's opinion, "the dice would always be loaded against Ireland" in a purely British Empire court. The second was a judicial review not only of the land annuities but of all financial agreements existing between the two governments.

"In my view," Mr. Thomas told the Commons, "the new note leaves matters even worse than before."

Then, with the emphatic approval of David Lloyd George and Winston Churchill, who signed the Anglo-Irish treaty, Mr. Thomas asserted that Britain would uphold her rights and would "take steps" to deal with the situation. He repeated what has been told to Mr. de Valera many times—that Britain would make no tariff agreement with the Free State at Ottawa—and also hinted that speedy tariff retaliation would be taken to recover the £3,000,000 annually that Mr. de Valera is refusing to pay.

"We have had experience with Mr. de Valera as a negotiator," said Mr. Lloyd George, speaking for the first time in the present Parliament. "Quite frankly, I have never found

Continued on Page Three.

Study of Gold Standard by Brown University Gets Aid of the Rockefeller Foundation

Special to THE NEW YORK TIMES.

PROVIDENCE, R. I., June 17.—Brown University has received a grant from the Rockefeller Foundation to finance a research project involving a comprehensive study of the gold standard, it was announced tonight by the president's office.

The study, to be carried out by Professor William A. Brown Jr. and Carel Jan Smit of the Department of Economics, aims at a reinterpretation of the international gold standard in the light of its history.

A statement issued here in behalf of Dr. Albert D. Mead, acting president of the university, said the decision to undertake the research was "based upon the view that the present breakdown of the gold standard in several countries cannot fully be understood by an examination of the present conditions alone." He declared the difficulties the gold standard had encountered since 1925 could not be explained except by an analysis of the history of world credit.

"This approach," continued Dr. Mead, "will throw light upon the fundamental problem of the present—whether there are any reasonable grounds for hope that the gold standard can develop, under the conditions which may be expected to prevail during the next decades, the same efficient international clearing and stabilizing services as it did before the war.

"The study in these ways is intended to go behind but not to neglect the tremendously disturbing questions of the day and to examine the international gold standard as an economic institution, and to consider whether the environment in which it must now function is or is not so changed from that of the pre-war period in which it flourished most successfully as to require any really fundamental changes in the nature of the international gold standard itself, its management and the service which it is expected to render to the world."

CREDITORS WIPE OUT $45,000,000 IN DEBTS AT LAUSANNE PARLEY

Five Powers "Reserve" Sums Due to Them During Period of the Conference.

NONE EXPECTS PAYMENT

Great Britain Again Expresses Willingness to Clear Slate if Others Also Agree.

REICH STRESSES POVERTY

Von Papen Asserts Moratorium on $355,500,000 Private Debts May Be Needed.

By FREDERICK T. BIRCHALL.
Wireless to THE NEW YORK TIMES.

LAUSANNE, Switzerland, June 17.—The conference for the consideration of German reparations and European war debts took a notable step forward today. As a preliminary to taking up the general problems with which it will try to deal it wiped out some $45,000,000, comprising payments due in July from various European governments, including those due from Germany to other European governments, by "reserving" them "during the period of the conference."

Wiped out is the correct expression, because none here expects for a moment that these sums will ever be paid. When the question of reparations and debts is taken up again it will be from a fresh start, dating back to the period of the conference.

Britain Urges Cancellation.

But once again today Germany frankly and officially stated her position that she cannot pay this debt, and through Franz von Papen, her new Chancellor told why. And once again Neville Chamberlain, British Chancellor of the Exchequer, reiterated Britain's willingness to cancel the entire obligations due to her provided the other European governments would do likewise.

It was a gesture which today evoked no echo of acquiescence from the other governments represented, but that acquiescence can only be delayed. Privately it is universally admitted that German reparations and inter-European war debts have alike passed into the limbo of things that are dead. Only the ceremony of burial remains.

Meantime, it was no small step toward the inevitable denoument that the conference took today's "indefinitely deferred" as meaning "renounced." Here the items are:

German reparations payments, excluding service of Young and Dawes loans, payable July 15, 132,000,000 reichsmarks	$35,000,000
Czechoslovak liberation debts, payable July 1, 5,000,000 gold marks	1,000,000
Hague annuity instalment payable to France and Britain July 1, 8,325,000 reichsmarks	2,000,000
Hague annuity instalment payable to Belgium and Britain July 1, 1,575,000 reichsmarks	400,000
War debt of France to Britain due July 15, £1,041,666	4,000,000
Hague annuity instalment payable by Italy to Britain July 1, 4,500,000 reichsmarks	1,100,000
War debt payment by Italy to Britain due July 15, £343,168	1,500,000
Total	$45,000,000

Clears Way for Progress.

Thus does the conference move toward the goal to which Prime Minister MacDonald in his opening address directed it, of so clearing the ground of entanglements which hinder economic progress that a real beginning may be made toward that economic and financial reconstruction which shall herald the opening of a new era of prosperity.

It is undoubtedly progress as far

Continued on Page Four.

SENATE DEFEATS BONUS, DESPITE 10,000 VETERANS MASSED AROUND CAPITOL

Herriot Says Debt Settlement Hinges on Understanding Here

Special Cable to THE NEW YORK TIMES.

PARIS, June 17.—"The declaration of the six powers at Lausanne makes an ultimate European settlement conditional upon eventual understanding with the United States," said Premier Edouard Herriot in a statement given out at Lausanne and reproduced tonight in the Paris press.

M. Herriot added that he considered that the declaration itself constituted appreciable progress in the European situation.

"My relations not only with my old friend Mr. MacDonald, but also with Chancellor von Papen, are excellent, and I believe we have made a step along the route toward peace," he declared.

PRESIDENT ATTACKS ECONOMY DEADLOCK

Furlough Employment Bill in Reality Means 5-Day Week, He Says.

SYMBOL FOR JOBLESS AID

Senate Conferees Indicate That They Will Ask to Be Freed From Binding Instructions.

Special to THE NEW YORK TIMES.

WASHINGTON, June 17.—With the fiscal year rapidly drawing to a close and drastic reductions in Federal expenditures due to be placed in effect July 1, President Hoover moved today to break the deadlock between the Senate and House conferees on the special economy bill by appealing to them to accept the furlough plan for dealing with Federal employes.

In reality the furlough plan is the five-day week applied to government, the President said; an application of a "symbol for indicating the shortening of hours of labor for the purpose of giving some employement to a maximum number of people."

The economy bill is designed to save about $131,000,000 during the next fiscal year.

President Hoover also urged that the conferees agree to give to him unlimited authority to make departmental changes instead of the restricted authority the House and Senate approved in the economy bill.

Hoover's Statement on Furlough.

The President's statement was as follows:

I am in hopes that the conferees and the Congress will find it possible to accept the so-called furlough plan for dealing with Federal employes. It is in reality the five-day week applied to the government. It will produce a larger saving in expenditures in Federal employment than any other plan which is likely to pass Congress.

The objection that it permits of discrimination has been met by the proposal that the few employes receiving over $1,200 a year to whom it might not be applied shall take an 8 1-3 per cent reduction in pay, thus giving the equivalent reduction in government expenses.

It avoids discharges and enables some increases in the number of

Continued on Page Two.

VOTE ON THE BILL IS 62-18

City at High Tension as Hundreds Camp in the Plaza.

LEADERS MAINTAIN ORDER

But Metropolitan Police and Marines Are Held in Readiness for an Emergency.

SENATE GALLERIES PACKED

Crowd Takes Defeat in Silence and Returns to Quarters—Will Hang On, Leaders Say.

From a Staff Correspondent.
Special to THE NEW YORK TIMES.

WASHINGTON, June 17.—The bonus bill to issue $2,400,000,000 in new currency to pay World War veterans their certificates in cash was defeated in the Senate by a vote of 62 to 18 at 8:20 o'clock tonight.

Immediately afterward Senators Bankhead and Thomas of Oklahoma made efforts to have the vote reconsidered and change the bill so as to pay the former soldiers the amount of their bonus certificates on their present surrender value. These steps were looked upon as hopeless, even though Senators Bankhead and Thomas went so far as to change their original votes for the bonus bill to "no" in order to seek such a reconsideration.

The vote came at the close of the tensest day Washington has known since the war and in the midst of a scene never before enacted in the Capitol grounds. There had been no situation resembling it since the siege of Congress by the unpaid Continental soldiers in Philadelphia at the close of the Revolution.

The Bankhead motion for reconsideration was beaten by a vote of 44 to 26. When the bonus forces seemed unwilling to push the reconsideration vote immediately, Senator Reed, a bonus enemy, made the necessary motion. Senator Moses, another opponent, moved to table the Reed motion. The Moses motion was carried, 44 to 26.

The motion to reconsider is now lying on the table, but it will require a majority vote to take it up. This is unlikely in view of the overwhelming ballot against the bonus.

Leaders Keep Control.

Washington in general and the Capitol in particular never has been as nervous as today. When the vote was announced to the thousands of veterans in front of the Capitol, the bonus army seemed for the first time about to get out of hand. Commander Waters and other leaders appealed to them to return to their encampments in military formation and bugles sounded appealingly to the men to rally.

The veterans were silent for a second after they heard the news of their defeat and then showed their disappointment in a murmur which 10,000 voices multiplied almost into a shout. They seemed reluctant to move.

This was due partly to the belief of some of them that they were being told to go back to their homes.

"We are not telling you to go home," Commander Waters shouted to them and a resonant cheer arose. "Go back to your camps. We are going to stay in Washington until we get the bonus, no matter how long it takes. And we are 100 times as good Americans as those men who voted against it. We are just asking you to obey the law and not antagonize the authorities. There is no more to be done tonight."

Then the veterans began marching back to their quarters in individual units, though hundreds still tarried on the Capitol steps. A few collapsed and were taken away in ambulances.

Determined To Stay On.

The veterans immediately began planning their next steps, which will include bringing pressure on the Democratic National Convention to declare for the bonus payment and campaigning actively in each State and Congressional district against the Congressmen who voted against the bonus.

Leaders and rank and file alike declared that the army would not return home now, as officials have been hoping, but that it would stay.

Continued on Page Seven.

Belgian Calls Civil Flying Military Menace; Says at Geneva War Aims Divert Its Progress

By CLARENCE K. STREIT.
Wireless to THE NEW YORK TIMES.

GENEVA, June 17.—"Commercial aviation so far has progressed on a basis of purely military considerations," Senator de Brouckère of Belgium, chairman of the League of Nations standing committee on air transit, told the disarmament conference air commission today when it began discussing the Spanish proposal to internationalize civil flying as a part of air disarmament.

"If the development of commercial aviation had been free," the Belgian Senator continued, "comfort, economy and security would have been the principal factors sought, but if the present apparatus is examined it is clear that its development has followed non-business lines that aim at a posible use of these aircraft for military purposes."

Asserting that plans for a national and efficient international air mail service had failed, M. de Brouckère said this was because only national organizations were able to obtain the necessary subsidiaries. Stressing how generous the governments had been to their national civil air lines, he said:

"Since the advantages they gain are not commercial, economic or social, they must be military."

He reported his committee favored internationalizing civil aviation if the standpoint of business interest was adopted, and said it was certainly vain to try to keep the question of civil aviation out of the disarmament conference.

The Germans, British and French spoke non-committally.

Wireless to THE NEW YORK TIMES.

TOKYO, June 17.—In view of the lack of progress at Geneva and the advisability of curtailing expenses, the government is contemplating the recall of Admiral Nagano and General Matsui, together with about half the delegation from Geneva, leaving Mr. Komaki and Mr. Tatekawa as naval and military representatives, respectively, instead. A suggestion to this effect from the delegation is approved by the government.

The Bonus Army's main camp at Anacostia.

Times Wide World Photo.

Thousands of Marchers Cluster About Capitol Steps, Threatening to Make an Extended Stay.

These bonus marchers settled down to sleep on the lawn surrounding the Capitol despite police efforts to disperse them.

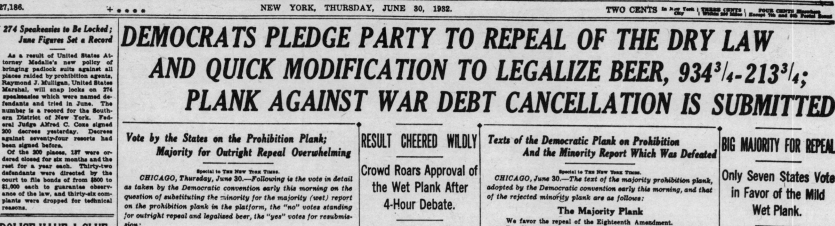

"All the News That's Fit to Print."

The New York Times.

LATE CITY EDITION
WEATHER—Fair today and tomorrow, temperature unchanged.
Temperatures Yesterday—Max., [illegible]; Min., [illegible].

VOL. LXXXI....No. 27,186. + * * * * NEW YORK, THURSDAY, JUNE 30, 1932. TWO CENTS In New York City | THREE CENTS Within 200 Miles | FOUR CENTS Elsewhere Except 7th and 8th Postal Zones

DEMOCRATS PLEDGE PARTY TO REPEAL OF THE DRY LAW AND QUICK MODIFICATION TO LEGALIZE BEER, 934¾-213¾; PLANK AGAINST WAR DEBT CANCELLATION IS SUBMITTED

BRITAIN TO DELIVER SWIFT TARIFF BLOW IF IRISH DO NOT PAY

Parliament Will Rush Taxes if £1,500,000 Annuities Are Not Met by Midnight.

TREASURY TO PAY DIVIDENDS

Funds Will Be Given to the Bank of England to Protect the Holders of Irish Stock.

OTHER SUMS ALSO SOON DUE

Levies Will Be Devised, Effective Before July 14, to Raise Total of £5,000,000 a Year.

Special Cable to THE NEW YORK TIMES.

LONDON, June 29.—As reprisal for the refusal of the Free State to pay the half-yearly land annuities amounting to £1,500,000 (the pound was quoted at $3.60 yesterday) which are now due, Britain proposes to impose a sweeping tax on Free State goods entering Britain. Unless the money is in the hands of the British National Debt Commissioners by midnight tomorrow, machinery will be put in motion for rushing a tax bill through all stages of Parliament next week to become law before the Summer recess on July 14.

The Irish land stock is guaranteed by the British Treasury and the holders will receive their dividends as usual on Friday. The Treasury will provide the money to enable the Bank of England to make the payments, but the Cabinet is determined that the burden shall not be borne by the British taxpayer.

To this end it has now been arranged that taxes shall be imposed even on Irish live stock and dairy produce, notwithstanding a provision in the import duties act that all goods imported from the dominions shall enter Britain free of duty until Nov. 15.

The British Cabinet is agreed that President de Valera's attitude has left it no choice but to insist on the recovery of sums due to Britain by an alternative method.

Britain's Last Note Ignored.

Thus far no reply has been received from the Free State to the last note of Britain, which made it clear that the United Kingdom could not agree to arbitration by a tribunal the personnel of which was not confined to citizens of the British Commonwealth of Nations. Mr. de Valera suggested in his last note that other financial matters should be referred to arbitration, and Britain assumes that other moneys due will not be handed over. The moneys payable amount altogether to about £5,000,000 in a full year, including the land annuities of £3,000,000, the Royal Irish Constabulary pensions of £1,000,000, local loan annuities of £600,000, compensation for damage to property in the Free State in 1919 and 1921 of £250,000 and small amounts for pensions and allowances to judges and civil servants.

As the value of imports from the Free State during the present financial year are estimated at about £30,000,000, it is realized that it will not be an easy matter to levy duties amounting to £5,000,000, and one of the principal tasks of the government framing any new proposals will be to see that the duties do not cease to be revenue duties and become protective duties.

Payment Stoppage Campaign Pledge

In the campaign leading to his recent election as President of the Irish Free State Council, Eamon de Valera announced his intention of withholding the £3,000,000 of annual land payments due to the British Treasury under the treaty of 1920. These annuities, payable for some fifty years or more, are collected from Irish Free State farmers in repayment of the amount borrowed on their behalf to buy out their landlords.

The British Treasury acts as an intermediary between the tenants and those from whom the money was borrowed. Mr. de Valera contends that this is neither morally nor legally correct and that Britain must prove her right to these monies before a court acceptable to both parties.

Great Britain threatened several months ago that if Mr. de Valera should ever succeed in abolishing the oath of allegiance to the King—another of the Free State Council President's objectives—and repudiating the payment of the land annuities that it would resort to tariff weapons instead of troops and guns.

Economic Strangulation Possible.

Under these conditions, the Free State would be regarded simply as a seceder from the empire and be cut off automatically from the tariff privileges she now enjoys with the other British dominions. The British market absorbs 90 per cent of the Free State's products. Britain

Continued on Page Three.

274 Speakeasies to Be Locked; June Figures Set a Record

As a result of United States Attorney Medalie's new policy of bringing padlock suits against all places raided by prohibition agents, Raymond J. Mulligan, United States Marshal, will snap locks on 274 speakeasies which were named defendants and tried in June. The number is a record for the Southern District of New York. Federal Judge Alfred C. Coxe signed 200 decrees yesterday. Decrees against seventy-four resorts had been signed before.

Of the 200 places, 137 were ordered closed for six months and the rest for a year each. Thirty-two defendants were directed by the court to file bonds of from $500 to $1,000 each to guarantee observance of the law, and thirty-six complaints were dropped for technical reasons.

POLICE HAVE A CLUE, CURTIS TRIAL SHOWS

Federal Investigator Says Definite Group Is Suspected in Lindbergh Case.

SWEARS HOAX BALKED HUNT

Norfolk Man Said He Signed Confession "to Get Some Sleep," Another Testifies.

From a Staff Correspondent.
Special to THE NEW YORK TIMES.

FLEMINGTON, N. J., June 29.—The New Jersey State police, who for nearly four months have been vainly trying to find the kidnappers of the Lindbergh baby, have a definite group of men under suspicion. This much and no more about the hunt was revealed here today, the third of the trial of John H. Curtis, Norfolk boat builder, on a charge of willfully misleading the police in their efforts to arrest the kidnappers and murderers of Charles A. Lindbergh Jr.

The revelation came while Lloyd Fisher, the young Flemington lawyer who is heading the defense, was cross-examining Frank J. Wilson of Baltimore, investigator for the Department of Internal Revenue, who has been associated for many weeks with the hunt. Wilson, a bland and obviously experienced court witness, is one of the government's expert investigators who spent two years accumulating under-cover evidence on which the government finally sent Al Capone to jail.

Insists Hoax Aided Kidnappers.

Wilson had testified for more than an hour and had told of meeting Curtis for the first time on the night of May 12 at the Lindbergh home after the body of the child had been discovered. Mr. Fisher was seeking to break down the assertion of the witness that Curtis had caused attention to be taken from important clues and diverted to checking up his tales of Gloucester fishing boats, kidnappers with hide-outs in Cape May, with the witness sticking stoutly to his opinion.

Finally Wilson admitted that in one case he questioned some one at the instigation of Curtis, and that but for Curtis he would have let this unnamed person alone for the time being.

Wilson, under questioning, declared further that on May 13 he was convinced that Curtis did not have actual knowledge of the kidnappers. The defense lawyer picked him up quickly and reached for a copy of Colonel Lindbergh's testimony yesterday morning.

"Then you disagreed with Colonel Lindbergh's testimony?" he asked sharply as he prepared to read it. Harry Stout, associate prosecutor, interrupted and Judge Robbins ruled that the Lindbergh testimony should not be read.

The cross-examination continued as follows:

Q.—What other things did you do or not do as a result of Curtis's information? A.—It is possible that interviewing a certain man at a certain time interfered with the apprehension of the kidnappers.

Refuses to Detail Suspicion.

Q.—Who was the man you normally would not have interviewed that you did interview because of Curtis? A.—I can't answer that question.

Here Mr. Stout interceded again and over Mr. Fischer's protest obtained permission from the court to ask the witness why he could not tell the story of this mysterious man.

"We have a right to know who that man is," protested the defense counsel.

Mr. Stout continued:

Q.—Mr. Wilson, is the person in question suspected of being implicated in the crime? A.—No, not he, but he is in touch with others who we strongly suspect.

Q.—If you disclose this man's name, would it affect the people with whom he is in touch? A.—I think it would.

Q.—The exposure of the person to whom you refer might prevent the

Continued on Page Two.

Vote by the States on the Prohibition Plank; Majority for Outright Repeal Overwhelming

Special to THE NEW YORK TIMES.

CHICAGO, Thursday, June 30.—Following is the vote in detail as taken by the Democratic convention early this morning on the question of substituting the minority for the majority (wet) report on the prohibition plank in the platform, the "no" votes standing for outright repeal and legalized beer, the "yes" votes for resubmission:

State or Territory.	Votes.	Yes.	No.
Alabama	24	21	3
Arizona	6	..	6
Arkansas	18	13	5
California	44	11	33
Colorado	12	1	11
Connecticut	16	¼	15¾
Delaware	6	4	2
Florida	14	1	13
Georgia	28	28	..
Idaho	8	..	8
Illinois	58	..	58
Indiana	30	..	30
Iowa	26	..	26
Kansas	20	12	8
Kentucky	26	..	26
Louisiana	20	3	17
Maine	12	2	10
Maryland	16	..	16
Massachusetts	36	..	36
Michigan	38	..	38
xMinnesota	24	4	18
Mississippi	20	20	..
Missouri	36	7½	28½
Montana	8	..	8
†‡Nebraska	16	5	9
Nevada	6	..	6
New Hampshire	8	..	8
New Jersey	32	..	32
New Mexico	6	1	5
New York	94	..	94
North Carolina	26	18	8
North Dakota	10	..	10
‡Ohio	52	2	49
Oklahoma	22	22	..
Oregon	10	3	7
Pennsylvania	76	..	76
Rhode Island	10	..	10
South Carolina	18	..	18
South Dakota	10	6	4
Tennessee	24	6	18
Texas	46	..	46
Utah	8	..	8
Vermont	8	..	8
Virginia	24	13	11
Washington	16	1½	14½
*West Virginia	16	8½	7
Wisconsin	26	..	26
Wyoming	6	..	6
Alaska	6	..	6
Dist. of Columbia	6	..	6
Hawaii	6	..	6
Philippines	6	..	6
Porto Rico	6	..	6
Canal Zone	6	..	6
Virgin Islands	2	..	2
Totals	1,154	213¾	934¾

†One refused to vote.
‡One absent.
*One-half absent.
xTwo absent.

RIVAL MANOEUVRES KEEP LEADERS BUSY

Reports of Gains and Losses in Various Delegations Bring Rumors of Trading.

BOTH SIDES TELL OF BREAKS

Roosevelt Managers Concentrate on Winning 6 States and Opposition Centres on 5.

By L. C. SPEERS.
Special to THE NEW YORK TIMES.

CHICAGO, June 29.—With political eyes turning to all points of the compass, with rumblings heard in at least four of the Roosevelt delegations and with echoes audible in four or five others in the same column, the strategy of the Roosevelt managers is centred tonight in a last-minute drive to win the nomination for Governor Roosevelt on the first two ballots.

The friends of Governor Roosevelt are bringing their heavy artillery into action in an effort to break the opposition strength in the New York, Illinois, Texas, California, Missouri and Oklahoma delegations. Of these, Missouri is considered the best bet from the Roosevelt standpoint. Under the instructions the unit rule binding the forty-six votes of Texas can be broken only with the consent of Speaker Garner.

Senator Jim Reed is still in control of a majority of the Missourians, while California is linked to Texas with instructions almost as binding as those voted by the Texans in their State convention. Oklahoma must stand by Governor Murray as long as he cares to hold them.

Tammany Support in Demand.

The Tammany element in the New York delegation and the Illinois delegation are therefore the "mystery" of the situation. They are under fire from both sides of the controversy, the anti-Roosevelt forces seeking to hold them in line for any candidate just so long as it isn't Roosevelt, while the Roosevelt organization is hammering away day and night to bring them into the Roosevelt camp, believing that success in that direction probably would start a band-wagon movement and bring about the nomination of Governor Roosevelt.

The Roosevelt opposition is concentrating on the Indiana, Mississippi, Iowa, Minnesota and Alabama delegations, in all of which there is a strong anti-Roosevelt movement under way. The situation in these five States is tonight the most serious menace facing the Roosevelt management.

[illegible] votes involved total 124, every one of them figuring in the original forecasts made by Chairman Farley

Continued on Page Sixteen.

ROOSEVELT RANKS FIRM, FARLEY SAYS

Defections Denied as Manager Predicts 690 on First Ballot and Possibly Two-thirds.

LIQUOR FIGHT DISCOUNTED

Chairman Holds It Will Not Affect Candidate—Declares No Pact Made on Second Place.

By JAMES A. HAGERTY.
Special to THE NEW YORK TIMES.

CHICAGO, June 29.—Reports of defections in the Roosevelt ranks were denied today by James A. Farley, campaign manager for the Governor. Mr. Farley declared that the contrary was the case and that Mr. Roosevelt would pick up votes when the test comes on the first ballot.

"Governor Roosevelt will have between 690 and 700 votes on the first ballot," Mr. Farley said, sticking to his original prediction. "We hope there will be a sufficient number of shifts to give him two-thirds and bring about his nomination on the first ballot."

Mr. Farley's optimistic statement followed a day of pulling and hauling by the campaign managers of the various candidates.

Taking the vote of 626 for Senator Walsh in the permanent chairmanship fight as the low point of Roosevelt strength so far revealed, the supporters of the Governor asserted that they would have at least fifty or sixty more votes for Governor Roosevelt on the first ballot.

The Roosevelt men admitted that on the first ballot they would lose the 6½ votes which Senator Walsh received from Connecticut and the 19½ from Missouri, a total of 26.

They claimed as prospective gains on the first ballot 4½ cast for Jouett Shouse in Alabama, 1 in Delaware, 10 in Iowa, 6½ in Kansas, 7 in Maine, 1 in Nebraska, 3 in New Mexico and 4 in North Carolina, a total of 37.

The Roosevelt managers also expect 22 or 25 votes from Indiana and to gain 5 or 6 in New York.

Mr. Farley declined in his interview to give any details of his first-ballot expectations.

"How is New York going to vote?" he was asked.

"I don't know about New York," he replied, "but I hope for the best."

"How about reports that Governor Roosevelt is losing votes in Mississippi, Iowa, West Virginia, Minnesota and Alabama?" he was asked.

"There is no danger there," he said.

"Do you think the coming fight over the prohibition plank will affect Roosevelt adversely?" was the next question.

"I see no reason why it should,"

Continued on Page Eighteen.

RESULT CHEERED WILDLY

Crowd Roars Approval of the Wet Plank After 4-Hour Debate.

LONG OVATION FOR SMITH

Gets 10-Minute Demonstration on Making First Appearance on Convention Platform.

RITCHIE JOINS IN APPEAL

David I. Walsh Also Takes Part—Hull Booed When He Champions the Prohibition Cause.

By W. A. WARN.
Special to THE NEW YORK TIMES.

CHICAGO, Thursday, June 30.—A tumultuous night session of almost five hours in which the repeal champions of the Democratic party debated with the advocates of moderation, while packed galleries cheered or jeered or laughed and delegates broke into two impromptu parades, led up to the convention's rejection of the minority report on its prohibition plank early today.

The decision was greeted with a thunder of applause by the throng which had listened to former Governor Alfred E. Smith of New York, Senator David I. Walsh of Massachusetts and Governor Albert C. Ritchie of Maryland demanding the end of prohibition by outright repeal and to Senator Cordell Hull of Tennessee pleading for submission of the Eighteenth Amendment without making acceptance of repeal a test of party loyalty.

Roar of Welcome for Smith.

When Mr. Smith's turn came and he appeared on the rostrum the convention rose to acclaim him with a roar of welcome.

The delegates, alternates and visitors, as he made his way to the front of the platform, let loose a tumult of cheering and for nearly ten minutes he was compelled to wait for it to subside before he could begin to speak.

The former Governor of New York, a pioneer in the movement for the repeal, stood smiling, but it was very evident that as wave after wave of cheers swept through the stadium a lump was rising in his throat.

It was not long before the giant organ started out to fill the stadium with the east side melodies that signalize public appearances of Mr. Smith. The organist took the audience on a prolonged tour of "The Sidewalks of New York." After a while delegations pledged to Smith took the cue and began marching behind their standards.

New York Aloof in Parade.

The New York banner remained anchored to its moorings where the delegation sat. The standards of Connecticut, Massachusetts, Rhode Island and New Jersey had been bobbing up and down for a while and then they began to move through the aisles in the most spontaneous of all the demonstrations that have marked the convention.

Ohio was followed by Pennsylvania's standard as the demonstration was drawing to a close.

The Smith demonstration followed the reading of the minority plank by Senator Hull, who proceeded to defend its refraining from pledging the party to repeal on the ground that politics should be eliminated from the elections for conventions in the several States set up to act on the question of repeal following submission from Congress.

The convention did not seem to take kindly to the discourse, and even when he mentioned the name of Woodrow Wilson, whom he quoted in support of his own contention, it failed to stir the delegates.

Mr. Smith in his address declared that the failure of the Republican National Convention to write into its platform a clear-cut, forthright declaration on prohibition had provoked country-wide distrust. He was applauded vigorously and cheered when at the close of his short address he called upon the convention to adopt the majority plank presented by the resolutions committee.

"I ask that for the sake of the party, for the sake of the country and for the sake of the taxpayers," he said.

Maury Hughes of Texas, scheduled to speak for the minority report,

Continued on Page Fourteen.

Texts of the Democratic Plank on Prohibition And the Minority Report Which Was Defeated

Special to THE NEW YORK TIMES.

CHICAGO, June 30.—The text of the majority prohibition plank, adopted by the Democratic convention early this morning, and that of the rejected minority plank are as follows:

The Majority Plank

We favor the repeal of the Eighteenth Amendment.

To effect such repeal, we demand that the Congress immediately propose a constitutional amendment to truly representative conventions in the States called to act solely on that proposal.

We urge the enactment of such measures by the several States as will actually promote temperance, effectively prevent the return of the saloon and bring the liquor traffic into the open under complete supervision and control by the States.

We demand that the Federal Government effectively exercise its power to enable the States to protect themselves against importation of intoxicating liquors in violation of their laws.

Pending repeal, we favor immediate modification of the Volstead act to legalize the manufacture and sale of beer and other beverages of such alcoholic content as is permissible under the Constitution and to provide therefrom a proper and needed revenue.

The Minority Plank

We advocate that the Congress immediately propose to truly representative conventions in the States, called to meet solely on the proposal, a repeal of the Eighteenth Amendment.

In the event of repeal, we urge that the Democratic party cooperate in the enactment of such measures in the several States as will actually promote temperance, effectively prevent the return of the saloon and bring the liquor traffic under complete supervision and control by the States and that the Federal Government effectively exercise its power to protect States against importation of intoxicating liquors in violation of their laws.

The text of the majority prohibition plank which was adopted by the Republican National Convention and that of the minority report for repeal, which was rejected by a vote of 681 to 422, will be found on page 17.

ROOSEVELT IS READY FOR CHICAGO FLIGHT

Plane Waiting at Albany Would Also Carry Mrs. Roosevelt and Their Sons.

TRIP WOULD TAKE 7 HOURS

Governor's Friends Say Presence at Convention Would End Physical Incapacity Rumor.

From a Staff Correspondent.
Special to THE NEW YORK TIMES.

ALBANY, June 29.—With an airplane poised for a flight to Chicago if he is nominated, Governor Roosevelt gathered the members of his family about him in the Executive Mansion tonight to listen to the session of the Democratic National Convention over the radio.

The Governor maintained his usual silence about flying to the convention to address the delegates if chosen as their standard bearer, and, if anything, was more uncommunicative than on other convention developments of the past few days. If he does make the air trip, his wife and sons will probably accompany him.

It has been known for some days that the Governor would probably hurry to the convention if selected in the hope of reaching Chicago before the final adjournment. A trimortored passenger plane has been sent to the Albany airport from Cleveland by the American Airways, Inc., and is ready to depart on short notice.

The Governor turned aside all questions concerning the flying trip, but did not deny that he would choose that spectacular method of going to the convention city.

"I may go in a submarine," he bantered.

He was in excellent spirits and continued to exchange badinage with the correspondents about the Chicago trip while steadfastly refusing to commit himself.

Trip Would Take Seven Hours.

The plane, according to an announcement of the Airways Company, was brought to Albany after Guernsey Cross, secretary to the Governor, had intimated that the Executive might want to use it.

In the face of the Governor's silence concerning the plane, Walter Pollock, manager of the Airways station here, declined to permit the taking of photographs in the hangar, on orders from Mr. Cross.

If the Governor should use the plane, it is estimated that the trip would take about seven hours. If a nomination were made tomorrow night he could leave early Friday morning and arrive in Chicago just

Continued on Page Eighteen.

PLATFORM DEMANDS TARIFF FOR REVENUE

Lays Depression to Disastrous Policies Pursued "Since the World War."

FOR ECONOMIC PARLEY

Party's Declaration of Policies Set Forth With Record-Breaking Brevity.

By CHARLES R. MICHAEL.
Special to THE NEW YORK TIMES.

CHICAGO, June 29.—The extreme wets crushed the moderate submissionist group and the chief spokesmen for Governor Roosevelt in the Democratic convention's resolutions committee late today, and by a vote of 35 to 17 forced the insertion of a wringing wet and modification plank into the platform, which was submitted to the convention tonight.

This step, representing chiefly a victory for the opponents of Governor Roosevelt, was taken under the leadership of Senator David I. Walsh of Massachusetts, a Smith adherent, who, however, received support from Senator Wheeler of Montana, one of the Roosevelt leaders. Senators Glass and Hull, William G. McAdoo and A. Mitchell Palmer fought the ultra-wets, who commanded nearly two-thirds of the membership of the resolutions committee.

The platform, of about 1,400 words, is concise in its definition of party principles and is regarded as the shortest one ever produced by the Democratic party.

The platform does not mention the names of President Hoover or of the Republican party. It has a preamble charging present economic conditions to "the disastrous policies pursued by our government since the World War," and urges a complete change in government as a cure.

Points of the Platform.

With the introductory words "we advocate," the platform favors a 25 per cent cut in the costs of government; a balanced budget; non-confiscatory taxation; a sound currency; an international silver conference; a tariff for revenue with a tariff commission "free from executive interferences"; an international economic conference; the form of unemployment relief passed by the Senate; State unemployment and old-age insurance; broad farm relief; a frugal armed service but one qualified for national defense; strict enforcement of the Sherman law; divorce of the government from private business connection; greater regulation of utility and holding companies and stock exchanges; detailed advertising of flotation costs in stock offerings; quicker liquidation of deposits in closed banks; separation of affiliates from commer-

Continued on Page Sixteen.

BIG MAJORITY FOR REPEAL

Only Seven States Vote in Favor of the Mild Wet Plank.

THREE CANDIDATES DEBATE

All the Contenders Release Their Delegates to Vote Their Own Opinions.

ARENA IN WILD ACCLAIM

Southern and Western States Which Helped Adopt Prohibition Reverse Former Stand.

Text of Democratic platform as submitted to convention, Page 15.

By ARTHUR KROCK.
Special to THE NEW YORK TIMES.

CHICAGO, Thursday, June 30.—Early this morning the Democratic party went as wet as the seven seas at the fourth session of its national convention in the Stadium. By an overwhelming majority the delegates sustained the majority plank in the platform which puts the party on record as favoring outright repeal of the Eighteenth Amendment and immediate modification of the Volstead act to permit the manufacture and sale of beer.

The vote was 934¾ against substitution of the minority report and 213¾ for.

The minority proposal was that the party merely pledge prompt submission of repeal to State conventions and guarantee Federal protection to those which desire to remain dry.

Although Senator Cordell Hull of Tennessee pleaded with the convention not to make prohibition a party question, and W. A. Fitts of Alabama said that the committee action would make doubtful the vote of five States in the election, the majority proposal carried overwhelmingly.

Only from Alabama, Arkansas, Georgia, Kansas, Mississippi, North Carolina and Oklahoma did the minority plank command the support of a majority.

Kentucky was the first State to vote for the dripping wet plank, followed by Louisiana, South Carolina and Texas.

The once dry South and West deserted the amendment which they put in the Constitution in 1919 after fifty years of agitation. California, Florida, Indiana (which had the driest of bone-dry enforcement acts), Iowa, Kentucky, Louisiana, Maine (the first dry State), Michigan, Minnesota, Missouri, Montana, Nebraska, Nevada, North Dakota, Ohio, Oregon, South Carolina, Tennessee, Texas, Utah, Washington—all these gave majorities of their total strength to the party advocacy of repeal.

Debate Thrills Hearers.

The convention action was preceded by a thrilling debate in which three Presidential candidates made their first appearances on the platform, Alfred E. Smith, Governor Ritchie and Governor Murray. The first two were for the majority plank. Mr. Murray was on the other side.

Not since the convention began has there been such a demonstration as was given to Mr. Smith. Galleries and delegates joined in the storm of applause which greeted the candidate of 1928 and roared out approval of a statement by a delegate from Texas who followed him with the statement that it was not prohibition but religious prejudice which lost Texas for Mr. Smith in 1928.

Every seat in the galleries and on the floor was filled and during the four-hour debate few left the hall. The galleries were almost always turbulent, their wet sentiments leading them to give the minority plank orators indifferent attention.

Other dissents to the platform planks on the veterans' bonus, farm relief, guarantee of bank deposits and home rule for Hawaii were noted in other minority reports made by Governor Murray, W. G. McAdoo and others. These will be voted on tomorrow when the platform as a whole is considered.

But tonight's vote demonstrated that the platform as written by the full committee will be overwhelmingly

Continued on Page Fifteen.

Sections 1 AND 4

"All the News That's Fit to Print"

The New York Times.

LATE CITY EDITION
WEATHER—Fair, moderate temperature; Monday fair and warmer.
Temperatures Yesterday—Max., 75; Min., 66.

Sections 1 AND 4

VOL. LXXXI....No. 27,189. **** NEW YORK, SUNDAY, JULY 3, 1932. Including Rotogravure Picture Section in one part—Magazine and Book Sections in Rotogravure TEN CENTS

ROOSEVELT PUTS ECONOMIC RECOVERY FIRST IN HIS ACCEPTANCE SPEECH AT CONVENTION; GARNER FOR VICE PRESIDENT BY ACCLAMATION

CURTIS IS CONVICTED; JURY FINDS HE KNEW ACTUAL KIDNAPPERS

Lindbergh "Negotiator" Faces a 3-Year Term for Story He "Confessed" Was Hoax.

LENIENCY IS RECOMMENDED

Judge Had Ordered Acquittal Unless Accused Was Held to Have Dealt With Gang.

PROMPT APPEAL IS PLANNED

Verdict Reached in Four Hours With Six Ballots Taken—Majority for Conviction From First.

From a Staff Correspondent.
Special to THE NEW YORK TIMES.

FLEMINGTON, N. J., July 2.—John Hughes Curtis, the Norfolk boat builder and self-styled "intermediary" for the return of the Lindbergh baby, was found guilty here today of deliberately giving false information for the purpose of preventing the arrest of the kidnappers.

The tall, rugged Norfolk manufacturer, who for many years had been a man of high repute in his own community, now stands convicted, under the indictment and the charge, as Judge Robbins gave it to the jury, not only of lying but of having actually known who the kidnappers were. Curtis had "confessed" that his entire story was a hoax.

Sentence was deferred until July 11. The maximum penalty is three years in prison and a fine of $1,000.

The jury was out four hours and five minutes. As is the Hunterdon County custom, the court house bell was tolled when it was ready to return.

From store and hotel porch spectators came on the run. Curtis, who had been in the jail, entered the court room head erect, facing the eyes of the curious who have been watching him throughout the five days of the trial. Until today he has been smiling, confident and affable. When he entered the room this afternoon the smile was gone, his normally ruddy face was white and the blue eyes stared straight ahead.

He took his seat behind his counsel table. The jury filed in, and Judge Adam O. Robbins, dressed in a linen suit and without his robe, ascended the bench.

Woman Announces Verdict.

"Have you reached a verdict?" asked C. Leon Fells, clerk of the court.

"We have," the five women and seven men answered in chorus.

"What is your verdict?" demanded Mr. Fells.

Miss Leila Alpaugh, forewoman, then read from a slip of paper:

"We, the jurors in the State of New Jersey, in the County of Hunterdon, find the defendant guilty with recommendation of mercy by the court."

Instantly the defendant's brothers, Sandusky and George, jumped to his side and put their arms about him. He held himself erect, staring straight ahead.

Lloyd Fisher for the defense asked that the jury be polled and each of the twelve pronounced the word "guilty."

There was a moment of silence and Mr. Fisher bent over Curtis, with his brothers. Suddenly the defendant jumped to his feet, hurled his great bulk through the little group of brothers and friends and ran to the door leading to the jail.

Photographers snapped him as he went out and bailiffs hurried after him. In the home of Warden George Anderson, which is in the jail building, his 11-year-old daughter, Constance, who has been at his side all through the trial, was awaiting him. The little girl remained with him until evening.

The twenty-four-hour guard which has watched Curtis since his arrest on March 18 resumed its duties tonight to avoid any risk of suicide.

Immediate Appeal Planned.

The convicted man's counsel went to work preparing their appeal to be presented Tuesday. Lloyd Fisher, who has led the defense forces, declared that he would carry the case to the highest court of the State, the Court of Errors and Appeals, if he could not get a reversal in the State Supreme Court.

Colonel Charles A. Lindbergh, who has sat through all the sessions of the trial itself at the State counsel's table, did not appear today, nor did Colonel Schwarzkopf. Colonel Lindbergh learned of the verdict by telephone at his home. He had no comment to make. Staying with him through the trial has been Edwin Bruce, the Elmira business man who accompanied Colonel Lindbergh and Curtis on many of their boat trips. He will stay at the Hopewell home over the week-end. Colonel Lindbergh, it is understood, feels that Mr. Bruce has been most self-

Continued on Page Six.

Major Sports Results.

Track—William Carr of Penn broke the accepted world's record for the 440-yard run in defeating Ben Eastman of Stanford in the Intercollegiate A. A. A. A. meet at Berkeley, Cal.

Tennis—Ellsworth Vines Jr., American tennis champion, overwhelmed H. W. (Bunny) Austin of England, 6—4, 6—2, 6—0, to win the Wimbledon tennis championship.

Rowing—The Penn A. C. four and Bachelors Barge Club double won national rowing championships and will represent the United States in the Olympics. The Leander Rowing Club captured the Grand Challenge Cup in the Royal Henley Regatta.

Racing—Faireno defeated Gusto in the Dwyer stakes at Aqueduct. Top Flight annexed the Arlington Oaks at Chicago, while Stepenfetchit won the Latonia Derby.

Complete details in Sports Section.

PRIEST DEFIES CITY ON QUITTING RECTORY

Mgr. Cashin of St. Andrew's Will Stay "Until Marshal Puts Us on Street."

HOLDS PLEDGE NOT KEPT

Property of Historic Church in Federal Deal—Land for New Buildings Not Provided.

Faced with a city order to vacate the rectory of St. Andrew's Roman Catholic Church, at Duane Street and City Hall Place, by Aug. 1, Mgr. William E. Cashin, pastor of the church, declared yesterday that he and his staff would remain until the "marshal puts us on the street," because the city had failed to carry out its share of an agreement to exchange other land for the rectory site.

The small red brick church in the old part of New York has been known for years as the home of the printers' mass. Mass has been celebrated there at 2:30 every Sunday morning since the time when most of the daily newspapers had their plants along Park Row.

The first church there was built about 1796 and was used by Methodists. After the Methodists abandoned it with the drift of population uptown, the church building was used as a wine warehouse for a time. In 1840 it became a Catholic club and was used as a rallying place for Catholics in the city. Two years later it became a Catholic church and is now the ninth oldest Catholic church in the city.

The church's difficulties with the city arise from the city's sale of a new site for a court house to the Federal Government. The court-house site lies to the north and east of the church property, forming a triangular plot just south of the State Courts Building. In assembling the site the city agreed to give the church additional land on the south of the church building in exchange for an equal acreage in the bed of City Hall Place owned by the church.

Says City Failed to Keep Bargain.

"The city promptly took over the land in the bed of City Hall Place and opened a street there," Mgr. Cashin said yesterday. "The city, however, has failed to give us the land promised in exchange in the rear of our church. Under those conditions we have not been able to go ahead with plans for a new church and rectory which were drawn three years ago, because we do not know exactly what the site for these buildings will be. If we vacate the parish house on the first of August we will have no rectory. I think we are entitled to stay, and we will stay until the city marshal puts us on the street."

Cardinal Hayes was born at 17 City Hall Place and was baptized in St. Andrew's, where he later served as an altar boy. The site of his birthplace has been cleared, but the church was anxious to obtain it for sentimental reasons. Under its agreement with the city, the church agreed to cede its rectory, at 20 City Hall Place. The city agreed to give the church title to 15, 17 and 19 City Hall Place, in the rear of the church building. The city further agreed to give additional land on the south side of the church in return for the rights to land in the bed of City Hall Place, but this part of the bargain has not been fulfilled.

Plans for the new church and rectory involve an expenditure of about $500,000. It will require about a year to complete the new buildings. The same type of structure as now exists will be built, to preserve the character of the old church. In addition to the attendance at the printers' mass, now in its thirty-second year, the church has an average daily congregation of 600 worshipers while it is overcrowded on Easter, Christmas and other holy days.

The church was remodeled about 1860 after the widening of Duane

Continued on Page Two.

REICH BALKS AT PLAN FOR FINAL PAYMENT THROUGH BOND ISSUE

Berlin Is Expected to Announce at Lausanne Today Its Refusal to Meet Creditors' Terms.

SOME REMAIN OPTIMISTIC

British Delegation Still Believes Settlement Will Be Reached at Powers' Parley.

DEBTS NOT NOW INVOLVED

Other Nations Owing Reparations Meet at Lausanne to Follow Course Set for Germany.

By P. J. PHILIP.
Wireless to THE NEW YORK TIMES.

LAUSANNE, July 2.—Final agreement was reached today among Germany's governmental creditors on the terms of a reparations settlement. The plan will be officially communicated to the German delegation tomorrow.

The capital amount to be paid by Germany has been fixed, as anticipated at 4,000,000,000 marks [$952,000,000]. Germany will, according to the plan, hand over bonds to that amount which will be put on the market when conditions are favorable but not before three years. The interest rate will be 5 per cent on the marketed bonds.

No Mention of War Debts.

In the scheme no mention is made of the creditor powers' indebtedness to the United States. Prime Minister MacDonald from the first insisted and today obtained Premier Herriot's consent that this should be so and that this settlement should be exclusively a European concern and not have the appearance of being conditional on United States action on debts. At the same time Germany's creditors will retain this juridical right, that they can defer ratification for at least three years, that is to say, until after they and others have reached a new settlement with the United States.

Furthermore, the French are satisfied with having obtained from the British Government a promise that there will be no separate settlement with the United States without consultation and agreement with the other debtors. This formula provides for a united front.

The whole future, however, still remains dependent on Germany's attitude toward the capital payment plan. Under the pressure and persuasion of Prime Minister MacDonald the Reich delegation here seems perfectly willing to consent in the belief that this proposed bond issue will never be made but will join the bonds handed over many years ago to the Reparation Commission.

Many Expect Rejection Today.

Berlin still is unconvinced, and tonight it is anticipated by many that tomorrow Chancellor von Papen, in the name of his government, will reject this carefully prepared proposal. During the day telephonic communication with Berlin has been almost continuous and the capital's resistance to the proposal has not lessened.

Louis Germain-Martin, French Finance Minister, summarized the situation this morning when he said everything was going well in Lausanne and that it was a pity that all the people in Berlin had not been able to come to Lausanne.

The German opposition is partly political and partly based on the argument that it will be impossible for Germany at the end of three or even five years to add to her present burdens the service on this debt. The interests of private creditors and holders of Dawes and Young Plan bonds are being urged as a reason why the plan should not be accepted.

Continued on Page Four.

Women Speakers to Front In Democratic Campaign

By The Associated Press.

CHICAGO, July 2.—This campaign is going to be a big opportunity and bring a lot of hard work for women. Among those likely to be prominent as campaign speakers for the Democratic nominee are:

Miss Frances Perkins, Industrial Commissioner of New York State, a close friend of Governor Roosevelt.

Mrs. Caspar Whitney and Mrs. H. Goddard Leach of New York, both former presidents of the State's League of Women Voters.

Mrs. John C. Greenway of Arizona, a family friend to whom was given her State's complimentary vote for the Vice Presidency.

Mrs. R. F. Lindsay of Texas, president of her State's Federation of Women's Clubs.

Mrs. Harrison Parkman of Kansas, a magazine editor, who asserted today "this is a non-political fight for the good of the country."

Mary W. Dewson, leader of the Roosevelt women's headquarters.

DEMOCRATS NAME FARLEY CHAIRMAN

Roosevelt Manager Assumes Charge at Once to Launch Pre-Election Campaign.

CHEERS GREET ROOSEVELT

Governor Praises Raskob and Shouse for Building Up the Party Nationally.

From a Staff Correspondent.
Special to THE NEW YORK TIMES.

CHICAGO, July 2.—Governor Roosevelt and his supporters lost no time in taking control of the new Democratic National Committee, which met tonight in the Gold Room of the Congress Hotel and elected as chairman James A. Farley, who successfully conducted Governor Roosevelt's campaign for the nomination. He succeeds John J. Raskob, selected by Alfred E. Smith, the Presidential nominee in 1928.

By the election of Mr. Farley, the Roosevelt supporters wrested control of the national party organization from the friends of Governor Smith. The call for the meeting immediately after the adjournment of the convention was issued at the suggestion of Governor Roosevelt, who expressed himself as desiring immediate organization of the committee and an early start of the campaign.

Mr. Farley was placed in nomination by John H. McCooey, the new committeeman from New York, and seconded by Mrs. Bernice S. Pyke of Ohio.

Mr. Raskob appointed Mr. McCooey, Governor White of Ohio and Arthur F. Mullen of Nebraska to escort Mr. Farley to the chair. Mr. Farley was appauded as he stepped onto the platform.

Cheers Greet Roosevelt.

The committee re-elected Robert Jackson, another Roosevelt supporter, as secretary. A moment later Governor Roosevelt entered the room, to be received with cheers.

"Ladies and gentlemen, and fellow-Democrats," Governor Roosevelt said when the cheering died down, "this is the second time I have been

Continued on Page Ten.

Reynolds, a Wet, Wins in North Carolina Over Morrison, a Dry, in Senatorship Race

Special to THE NEW YORK TIMES.

RALEIGH, N. C., July 2.—Robert Rice Reynolds, a militant wet, won an overwhelming victory in today's Democratic primary, when he was nominated over Senator Cameron Morrison upholder of the dry cause by a majority far in excess of the 50,000 plurality Mr. Reynolds received in the first primary on June 4.

John C. B. Ehringhaus, administration candidate for Governor, ran behind Mr. Reynolds, but was leading Lieut. Gov. Richard T. Fountain, who based his campaign largely upon an attack upon the administration of Governor Max Gardner and "machine" rule. Mr. Ehringhaus had a plurality of 47,000 in the first primary.

In the Senatorship contest returns from 1,292 of the 1,829 precincts in the State gave: Reynolds, 167,710; Morrison, 115,868.

For the governorship nomination the same precincts gave: Ehringhaus 129,317, Fountain 124,736.

Reynolds and Fountain had a common cause in that both attacked the "machine."

Captain A. L. Fletcher, high man for Commissioner of Labor in the first primary, had an easy victory over Clarence E. Mitchell today.

The Reynolds campaign was undoubtedly helped by the wet position taken by the Democratic National Convention, political observers say, since Senator Morrison had expressed disapproval of the party's repeal plank.

From the earliest precincts to be reported the overwhelming nature of Mr. Reynolds's victory was apparent. He swept county after county regardless of whether Ehringhaus or Fountain was the victor in the Gubernatorial contest.

CONVENTION HAILS GARNER

Delegations Rush to Line Up Behind Candidate of Roosevelt Leaders.

McDUFFIE OFFERS HIS NAME

Alabamian, an Intimate Friend, Calls Speaker "the Man America Needs."

LONE CONTESTANT YIELDS

General Tinley, Nominated by Iowa, Moves Convention Make Action Unanimous.

By L. C. SPEERS.
Special to THE NEW YORK TIMES.

CHICAGO, July 2.—John Nance Garner of Texas, Speaker of the House of Representatives, of which he has been a member nearly thirty years, was nominated at 3:40 P. M. today as the Democratic candidate for Vice President of the United States.

The convention, tired but still noisy, for once during the week was in complete agreement. Only one other nomination was made—that of General Matthew A. Tinley of Iowa. When the roll-call of the States was concluded General Tinley moved the nomination be made unanimous.

There was no excitement attending the placing in nomination, the seconding and the final action of the convention to make the man from Uvalde, Texas, the running mate of Governor Roosevelt, who was speeding by airplane to Chicago to accept the nomination for the Presidency.

It was 2 o'clock when Senator Walsh, the chairman, called the convention to order. The hall, already comfortably crowded, was gradually assuming a "standing room only" status. The big pipe organ pealed forth "The Eyes of Texas," and the final business of the convention was under way.

Close Friend Names Garner.

Alabama yielded to Texas, and Texas in return called on a son of Alabama, Representative John W. McDuffie of Monroeville, an intimate friend of Mr. Garner and Democratic whip of the House, to place the name of "the gentleman from the cactus country" before the convention.

It was a task Mr. McDuffie relished, for Mr. Garner in his eyes is the biggest man in public life. Mr. McDuffie, who was the leader in the fight for his own and the Garner relief plans, went at his task with a will. Others may have doubts, but he is certain a landslide is coming and that it will sweep Roosevelt and Garner into office next November.

"A few days ago," he said, "the Republicans everywhere were predicting dissension in the ranks of the Democratic party. On that prediction they based their hopes of victory. Then we named Franklin D. Roosevelt for President and in doing so chilled the heart of every Republican in the United States."

This hit a responsive chord on the floor. Texas whooped back in true cowboy style, and the others just yelled. Everywhere in the land, declared Mr. McDuffie, Democrats are happy because the people are swarming into the Democratic camp as the place where real progressive leadership awaits them.

"In any crisis," said the Alabamian, "the American people, when they are thinking, call on the Democratic party for leadership."

Naming Mr. Garner for the second place on the ticket, he lauded the Speaker as a man of "sturdy and rugged character," as the "outstanding leader in Congress," and as a "real, red-blooded he-man." "Just the kind," he exclaimed, "America needs for Vice President at this time."

Predicts "Greatest Victory."

"Roosevelt and Garner," concluded Mr. McDuffie, "will lead the Democratic party to the greatest victory it has ever achieved."

The Texans jumped up, waved the Lone Star flag and gave a few war whoops. California waved its own flag with its big grizzly bear, and the other delegations indicated their approval in ways less demonstrative. The demonstration was quickly over with, and then came the long roll call and its short seconding speeches and announcements.

Tammany caused a burst of real

Continued on Page Eight.

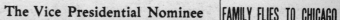

The Vice Presidential Nominee

© Harris & Ewing Photo.
JOHN NANCE GARNER.

SMITH-HEARST FEUD AIDED ROOSEVELT

Break to the Governor Is Looked Upon as Furnishing Revenge for the Publisher.

GARNER SHIFT TURNED TIDE

Ten-Year Conflict Goes Back to Smith's Ban on Hearst's Ambitions in This State.

By JAMES A. HAGERTY.
Special to THE NEW YORK TIMES.

CHICAGO, July 2.—Last night's sensational break in the balloting for President by the delegates to the Democratic National Convention, by which Texas and California furnished ninety votes and started the stampede which resulted in the nomination of Roosevelt, furnished revenge on Alfred E. Smith for William Randolph Hearst as well as for William G. McAdoo.

Mr. Smith's feud with Mr. AcAdoo, which resulted from the defeat of the latter in the 1924 convention, was recalled immediately by most of the delegates when Mr. McAdoo took the platform to announce that California and Texas had decided to vote for Roosevelt. The part of Mr. Hearst, or his friends, in the arrangement by which Roosevelt obtained the nomination for President and Speaker John N. Garner the nomination for Vice President became known today.

The Smith-Hearst feud, although not active recently, has existed for more than ten years. It reached its highest point in the New York State convention of 1922, when Mr. Smith, a candidate for the Democratic nomination for Governor, resisted all attempts to get him to accept Mr. Hearst as a running mate as a candidate for United States Senator. Mr. Smith, it was said at the time, even disregarded the advice of the late Charles F. Murphy, leader of Tammany, who believed that the nomination of Hearst was advisable to prevent a break in the party that might bring about Mr. Smith's defeat.

Four years earlier, in 1918, when Mr. Smith was first nominated and elected to the Governorship of New York State, he clashed with Mr. Hearst at the New York State convention. Mr. Hearst also was a candidate for the nomination, and a large force of his supporters went to Saratoga Springs in an unsuccessful attempt to bring about his nomination. This clash resulted in bitterness, but later in the campaign Mr. Hearst in his newspapers supported Mr. Smith against Governor Charles S. Whitman, who had been renominated for a third term by the Republicans.

Mr. Hearst always asserted—and the assertion was not denied—that

Continued on Page Ten.

ROOSEVELT URGES EARLY CAMPAIGN

He Declares in Interview That Object of Plane Trip Was to Spur Vote Drive.

DISAPPOINTED OVER SMITH

He Had Hoped to See His Rival Soon—Plans to Take Train Home From Chicago Tonight.

From a Staff Correspondent.
Special to THE NEW YORK TIMES.

CHICAGO, July 2.—An early and vigorous Democratic campaign throughout the country was urged by Governor Roosevelt tonight as he established himself in the Presidential suite at the Congress Hotel for a brief stay in the convention city.

Holding his first "levee," for a large group of correspondents, Mr. Roosevelt set forth a supplementary reason for making an airplane trip to the convention.

"The whole idea of flying here," he said, "was to bring forward the idea of getting the campaign started. You know that August is usually the month to get stirring. But I believe that some votes can be made in July.

"I do not know just what my own plans will be for the next few months. I am starting back for Albany tomorrow night if the present schedule holds. But, of course, these plans are tentative."

The Governor was asked if he planned to speak in every State during the campaign. He smiled and replied:

"No, I hardly think so. You know, those coast-to-coast trips are all right for a young man such as I was when I was a candidate for Vice President and I was only 38, but it is a bit different now."

The Governor seemed in fine spirits, although the rush of convention congratulations was a bit overwhelming.

On one score the Governor indicated some disappointment. When asked if he expected to see Alfred E. Smith, his chief convention rival, he replied:

"I am afraid not for a few days."

Before Mr. Roosevelt left Albany he had expressed a desire to see Mr. Smith as soon as possible, but the ex-Governor had already left Chicago when the Roosevelt plane arrived.

Governor Roosevelt's comment on the nomination of Speaker Garner for the Vice Presidency was:

"I am very happy at the selection of Jack Garner. There are two reasons for that. One is his possession of splendid ability. The other is that we are very old friends, for I have known him ever since my own Washington days."

The Governor said he had no definite schedule for tomorrow and that he planned to take a train for home about 10 o'clock in the evening.

FAMILY FLIES TO CHICAGO

Thundering Cheers Greet the Governor at Airport and in Stadium.

'100%' FOR THE PLATFORM

"Eighteenth Amendment Is Doomed From This Day," He Declares in Speech.

PLEDGES SELF TO 'NEW DEAL'

He Calls for Enlightened International Outlook and Shorter Work Day and Week.

The text of Gov. Roosevelt's acceptance speech is on page 8.

By ARTHUR KROCK.
Special to THE NEW YORK TIMES.

CHICAGO, July 2.—Before it adjourned tonight, after unanimously nominating Speaker John N. Garner of Texas for Vice President, the Democratic National Convention saw and heard its Presidential choice of yesterday, Governor Franklin D. Roosevelt of New York.

Mr. Roosevelt confessed that in coming here he was breaking a tradition.

"Let it be from now on," he said, "the task of our party to break foolish traditions. We will break foolish traditions and leave it to the Republican leadership * * * to break promises."

Pledges Aid to "Forgotten Man."

His speech was aggressive. He pledged his aid, "not only to the forgotten man, but to the forgotten woman, to help them realize their hope for a return to the old standards of living and thought in the United States." He would, he said, "Restore America to its own people."

Mr. Roosevelt began with a tribute to Woodrow Wilson. He then described the economic situation from his own viewpoint, saying that swollen surpluses went into the building of "unnecessary plants and Wall Street call money." The government should be "made solvent" again, said Mr. Roosevelt.

The galleries warmed to him when he firmly endorsed the platform plank advocating repeal of the Eighteenth Amendment and modification of the Volstead act, and the Southern delegations noted his pledge to protect the dry States in their wish to keep out intoxicating liquors and to prevent the return of the saloon.

Work and Security the Need.

He suggested as one means of decreasing unemployment, putting men at work on reforesting waste areas. As to agriculture, he would aid that by production planning, by the adoption of a tariff equalizing world prices and by lowering interest rates of farm loans. He expressed it as his firm conviction that the popular welfare depends on the granting of what the great mass of the people want and need.

Their demand is for work and reasonable security, he declared, and he pledged his efforts to effect them.

In concluding, he told his hearers that he intended to make a number of short visits during the campaign to various parts of the country.

Jefferson, the father of the Democratic party, rode to his inaugural on horseback, but the nominee of 1932 flew to the scene of his triumph by airplane from Albany and covered the ninefold greater distance in less time. The convention rose enthusiastically to the voyager of the skies, and accepted his method of travel and the fact that he endured its rigors so well as a proof of his venturesome spirit and fine physical equipment for the office of President of the United States.

Animosities Are Forgotten.

Governor Roosevelt, when he had reached the platform, faced a hall almost as crowded and as emotional as at any time during the convention period. Except in small groups among the galleries and the delegates the disappointment and animosity of the preceding days were buried, and it was evident that the thousands of people believed they were in the presence, not only of the nominee of the Democratic party, but of the next President of the United States.

Before Mr. Roosevelt appeared, and his appearance was delayed by

Continued on Page Nine.

Al Smith was a contender for the Democratic nomination.

Roosevelt arrived in Chicago on July 2 to accept his party's nomination. It was the first plane trip ever taken by a Presidential nominee.

As this sign shows, Roosevelt was in favor of legalizing beer.

James A. Farley of New York was one of Roosevelt's biggest supporters for the Democratic nomination for President.

Although Garner had the support of Texas and California, he did not get the nomination for President. He became Roosevelt's running mate.

"All the News That's Fit to Print"

The New York Times

LATE CITY EDITION

Weather: Fair, very cold today and tonight. Chance of snow tomorrow. Temp. range: today 24-14; Sunday 33-26. Full U.S. report on Page 30.

VOL. LXXXI....No. 27,195. *****+ NEW YORK, SATURDAY, JULY 9, 1932. TWO CENTS In New York City | [illegible] | [illegible]

LAUSANNE ACCORD ENDS REPARATIONS; BERLIN TO ISSUE $714,000,000 IN BONDS; WASHINGTON OPEN TO DEBT OVERTURES

GARNER HOLDING OUT ON RELIEF, TAKES UP TREASURY INQUIRY

Speaker Rejects Senate Democrats' Plea to Accept Hoover Plan on Relief Loans.

REPUBLICANS WANT A VETO

Meanwhile, Garner Calls for Treasury Investigation When McFadden Challenges Him.

FAVORED DELAY AT PRESENT

Reserve System to Be Included—Committee Is Urged to Report a Resolution Today.

Special to THE NEW YORK TIMES.

WASHINGTON, July 8.—Speaker Garner held the centre of the stage in the Capitol today. He stood adamant against his fellow party members in the Senate who favor acceding to President Hoover's wishes in the unemployment relief bill controversy. Then, making a surprise speech in the House, he accepted for the majority there what he termed a Republican challenge to press a Congressional investigation into the Treasury, the office of the Controller of the Currency and the Federal Reserve System.

The Democratic candidate for the Vice Presidency flatly refused to consent to alteration of the $2,100,000,000 relief bill during a two-hour conference with Senate Democratic leaders. His insistence speeded the measure toward an apparently inevitable Presidential veto.

The Speaker remained firm in his stand, approved by the House yesterday, that the base of the Reconstruction Finance Corporation be broadened to permit loans "to any person" with adequate security from the proposed $1,500,000,000 additional capital for the corporation. This in face of the fact that he was informed that a conference of Democratic members of the Senate this morning had shown many of them desiring compromise with the administration.

Garner Presses Inquiry.

For a while it appeared that the Senate Democrats opposing the bill, estimated at between fifteen and twenty, would be able to send it back to the House and Senate conferees, but Republican leaders checkmated this possibility, preferring to let the Democrats proceed head on into a Presidential veto.

Goaded by the Republicans, Speaker Garner took the floor this afternoon and moved for immediate authorization of the investigation into the Government's fiscal affairs. The resolution, an expanded version of one offered some time ago by Representative McFadden of Pennsylvania, will be taken up by the House Rules Committee tomorrow morning and is expected to be brought immediately before the House.

The Speaker's outburst followed a personal defense and explanation of his previous opposition to the resolution. He told the House, in response to accusations by Mr. McFadden, that he opposed the resolution because of the effect it would have on the Nation at this time. He added that about all the American people now possess is faith in the government, and expressed fear that revelations of an investigation of the Treasury would unsettle this faith.

Representative Michener, of Michigan, acting minority floor leader in the absence of Representative Snell, was challenged by the Speaker in a warm interchange.

Democrats Tight-Lipped.

The first hint of Democratic dissension in the Senate over the Wagner-Garner relief bill was manifested by the tight-lipped silence of many Democrats who had responded to the call by Senator Robinson of Arkansas to meet behind locked doors in the minority caucus room at 10 A. M.

The meeting adjourned after two hours. Senator Robinson's announcement was brief:

"The subjects considered were unemployment relief and adjournment, and discussions were had. There is a desire to speed up the session to a conclusion. No definite decision was reached as to the action to be taken on the conference report. The Democratic conference will resume its session tomorrow morning at 10 o'clock."

It soon was learned that considerable dissension had broken out in the conference, particularly on the part of Eastern Senators, who felt that Speaker Garner, through his insistence on his point, backed by the House, would give the President a political advantage.

It then developed that Senators Robinson, Wagner, Bulkley and Pittman had been delegated to lay this

Continued on Page Two.

Missing Yacht Curlew Found Off Nantucket; Crew of Six Hunted 5 Days by Sea and Air

Fears for the safety of the forty-nine-foot ketch Curlew and her crew of six New York yachtsmen, long overdue in the 628-mile race from Montauk Point to Bermuda, which started June 25, were dissipated last night when the Coast Guard cutter Marion reported sighting the tiny craft off Nantucket.

Beyond saying that the yacht was proceeding toward New York under her own sail, the message wirelessed by the Marion to Coast Guard headquarters here gave no details. It was assumed, however, that the crew of the yacht had suffered no serious hardship or they would have been taken aboard the cutter.

The first announcement of the sighting of the Curlew, made by Coast Guard headquarters here, gave the position of the ketch as off the North Carolina coast, but subsequent advices received by the Coast Guard and the Radiomarine Corporation of America established the correct position, far north of the yacht's course for Bermuda.

The Marion, which was one of more than 100 Coast Guard and naval vessels which, with the navy dirigible Akron, have been searching the seas for the ketch since alarm for her safety was first felt early this week, reported that she sighted the Curlew 100 miles southeast by east of Nantucket.

The news of the Curlew's safety did not reach here until 9:45 o'clock last night, at the close of a day in which hopes for her safety had dwindled almost to the vanishing point. David Rosenstein, owner of the missing craft, had announced his intention to charter a monoplane to aid in the search and plans had been made at the naval air station at Lakehurst, N. J. to send the Akron out on another scouting flight, but these moves were regarded as offering only slight hope.

The Curlew was one of twenty-seven yachts that cleared the Great Eastern Rock Buoy off Montauk on June 25. Her skipper was Nat Blum, 33 years old, of 734 Noble Avenue, the Bronx; her navigator was A. S. Rosenberg, 24, of 555 Gates Avenue, Brooklyn.

Carl Parnes, head of the unit control department of Gimbel's department store; Benjamin Theeman, an attorney with offices at 245 Fifth Avenue, and Frank Riger and Larry Weiss, both of New York, were also on board.

Her crew had estimated that even

Continued on Page Two.

NEIGHBORS TURN OUT TO GREET ROOSEVELT

Mother Also Welcomes Him as He Reaches Hyde Park for a Rest Before His Cruise.

WALKER'S REPLY AWAITED

Governor Says That He Cannot Make Campaign Plans Until the Ouster Case Is Settled.

From a Staff Correspondent.
Special to THE NEW YORK TIMES.

HYDE PARK, N. Y., July 8.—Governor Roosevelt came here to his birthplace tonight to greet his mother for the first time since his nomination and to receive an impromptu reception from his neighbors in a rural setting.

Back at the house above the Hudson River for a busy week-end before starting a cruise of New England waters with his four sons, the Governor revealed that his plans for the following weeks would depend on developments in the case of Mayor Walker. The charges against the Mayor must be disposed of before any definite program can be arranged.

The Governor's mother was at the door of her home when the Governor arrived by motor from Albany, where he held a series of conferences with leaders. She had not seen her son since the all-night session of the convention, when she sat by him at the radio in Albany. She left that night before the nomination was achieved.

Home Club Welcomes Him.

It was a small but exuberant throng that gave the Governor his reception at the Moses Smith farm on a back road in Hyde Park, composed of members of the Roosevelt Home Club of Hyde Park, which was formed several years ago to support him.

The Governor drove across his acres to the back road to meet his admirers, many of them known to him personally for some years. Out under the sky, with the last of the sunset still glowing in the west, the Home Club members stormed around the Governor to shake his hand, and he acknowledged the tribute.

The club, one of the earliest to back the Roosevelt Presidential candidacy, was holding a regular meeting on the Smith lawn, which was decorated with colored lanterns. The Governor alighted from the automobile in which he had ridden with his mother.

While a kitten chased fireflies on the edge of the little group the Governor talked informally about his plans for his cruise and expressed his gratification at the work done by the club.

"I am very happy that my neighbors have shown their feeling in this way," he said.

Afterward Mrs. Caroline O'Day vice chairman of the State committee, spoke.

Former Governor Smith is an honorary member of the club.

Old District Plans Welcome.

Tomorrow Dutchess, Putnam and Columbia Counties, comprising the old Senate district from which the youthful Franklin D. Roosevelt, just out of Harvard, was elected to the upper house at Albany in 1910, will give a more elaborate celebration at the Governor's home. Several thousand persons are expected to attend.

On Sunday the Governor will give a victory party for the members of his headquarters staff in New York and the office staff from Albany. Then he will motor to New York Sunday night to be ready for an

Continued on Page Three.

WORLD FLIERS CRASH IN A BOG IN RUSSIA

Mattern and Griffin Receive Slight Injuries in Forced Descent at Borisov.

TO CARRY ON, AIRMAN SAYS

Mrs. Griffin Gets Message Explaining Plane Hit Something in Dark After Landing.

Wireless to THE NEW YORK TIMES.

MOSCOW, July 8.—Moscow officials learned at 11 A. M. today, after a thirty-one-hour vigil at the Moscow airport, that James Mattern and Bennett Griffin, American round-the-world fliers, had crashed in a forced landing at Borisov, near Minsk, in White Russia, at 4 A. M. yesterday. Both fliers were injured, but their injuries are slight.

They were able to work on their damaged plane to make it ready for shipment. For the present they are staying at the only hotel in Borisov, but they are expected to come to Moscow soon.

[Mrs. Bennett Griffin, according to The Associated Press, received a cable message from her husband last night saying the plane had made a "perfect landing but struck something in the dark after landing," and he added, "Will carry on."]

Minsk, the capital of White Russia [which is one of the republics of the Union of Socialist Soviet Republics], is 400 miles from Moscow and is on the railway that links Moscow, Warsaw and Berlin. Borisov is about fifty miles east of Minsk and is on the same railway.

Farm Workers Aid Them.

The fliers landed in a bog near a State farm, the workers of which rushed to them, extended first-aid and gave them food. The farm workers are now helping them to dismantle their plane. The telephone connections between Moscow and Borisov are so indistinct that no further details of the aviators could be made out tonight.

It is assumed that the airmen had been lost for some time and decided to land near a settlement on what appeared to be a smooth field but which proved to be a bog. The length of time it took the news of their landing to reach Moscow gives some idea of the disorganized state of communcations in Russia.

Not even Soviet aviation officials could get any news of the fliers sooner. No border stations reported the passage of the plane. Before the fliers had reached Berlin Russian aviation bodies, such as Osoaviakhim and the civil aviation fleet, called on foreign correspondents for news as to whether the plane had started, whether it was coming through Russia and, if so, what route it planned to take.

Russia is an excellent land for aviation, with broad flat steppes for landings, but as yet the facilities here are undeveloped, making flying here a pioneering work. At that Mattern and Griffin would have had an easier time crossing Siberia than Wiley Post and Harold Gatty because a beacon system installed this Spring is operating part of the way across the continent.

Damage to Plane Reported.

MOSCOW, July 8 (AP).—The globe-circling adventure of James Mattern and Bennett Griffin has come to an abrupt end in Western Russia with only one-third of the flight behind them.

The world learned today that the American pair had crashed in their racy monoplane just over the Polish-

Continued on Page Six.

BORAH FIGHTS BEER BY INFLATION MOVE; BINGHAM COUNTERS

Dry Leader Displaces Brew Rider to Home-Loan Plan in Senate Manoeuvre.

IDAHOAN BACKS GLASS BILL

He Says Gold Supply Suffices for Expansion to Billions—Urges a Money Parley.

BINGHAM TAUNTS THE DRYS

Derides Them on Aiding Democrats to Avoid Vote—77 Republicans in House Ask Ballot.

Special to THE NEW YORK TIMES.

WASHINGTON, July 8.—The contest for a Senate vote on beer resolved itself into a battle of parliamentary strategy today, with Senator Bingham, champion of the beer forces, matching wits with Senator Borah.

The issue was the Bingham amendment to legalize beer, and Mr. Borah tonight had sidetracked it for the time being at least by offering as a substitute for the beer amendment to the home loan bill the Glass temporary inflation measure which would give all government bonds a five-year circulation privilege and permit currency expansion up to $995,000,000. Mr. Borah in his move had the support of some Democrats who do not want a beer vote now.

Debate proceeded on the Glass substitute, but suddenly Senator Bingham withdrew his amendment, which had the effect of shelving the Borah plan. Mr. Borah immediately offered it as an out-and-out amendment, however, and Mr. Bingham plans to re-offer his proposal later. Thus, both schemes would have to be voted upon independently unless some new strategy develops.

Borah Move Pleases Democrats.

The effect of today's manoeuvring was to make the Glass bill embodied in the Borah amendment the pending business of the Senate, with a preferred status over other amendments, relegating to the future—possibly next week—consideration of the Bingham beer bill.

Senator Bingham had a partial victory, since, if the Glass bill in the Borah substitute been adopted, a vote on beer would have been forestalled. Now a vote can be obtained regardless of the fate of the Glass bill.

At any rate, it seems probable that the beer discussion will be postponed until next week, because the conference report on the relief bill will be brought into the Senate tomorrow with a privileged status.

Many Democrats were manifestly pleased when Senator Borah came forward with his substitute. Their platform calls for immediate modification of the Volstead act, and those doubtful about supporting it now did not wish to be placed in the position of voting for beer or repudiating the plank. Further, many of them saw in Mr. Bingham's drive a Republican program to take away from the Democrats the glory of prohibition modification, which they desire to make a campaign issue.

Senator Bingham was chagrined and taunted the Democrats with leaving their own ship.

"I want to congratulate the Senator," he said to Senator Robinson, the Democratic leader, "with having drawn a red herring across the trail."

"The Senator," he said to Mr. Borah, "has established himself as

Continued on Page Two.

PLEAS AWAIT OUR ELECTION

White House Will Take No Initiative Toward Cuts in Obligations.

CONGRESS IS COOL TO IDEA

Senators and Representatives Hostile Toward Any Effort at Cancellation.

POLITICAL REVISIONS SEEN

State Department Thinks Road to Disarmament May Be Made Much Easier.

Special to THE NEW YORK TIMES.

WASHINGTON, July 8.—The way is now open for the foreign governments indebted to the United States to approach this country for revision of their debt-funding agreements as a result of the reparations settlement made at Lausanne, it was said at the State Department today.

As the situation stands, it was said no government has made any suggestion looking to a revision of its debt agreement. The United States, it was added, has consistently stated that Europe should first solve the reparations problem before turning to the United States in any hope of debt relief.

Now that Europe has accomplished a reparations settlement, which appears to be final, it was asserted, the way naturally would be open for the various governments separately to approach this country for debt revision on the basis of their various capacities to pay.

No Immediate Request Expected.

Officials expressed the personal opinion, however, that such approaches might not be made before the Presidential election because of the possibility that by such a course sentiment in Congress and the country might be crystallized against any modification of the debt arrangements.

That this view has some justification was apparent from the attitude of Congress today toward the announcement from Lausanne that a final reparations agreement had been reached in which German payments would be reduced to $714,000,000.

As in administration circles, Senators and Representatives generally expressed pleasure that Europe had been able to dispose of a problem that had been troubling her relations since the war. Unlike the silence maintained at the State Department and in administration circles concerning the possible effects of the Lausanne agreement on the United States, Senators and Representatives were vocal and generally expressed hostility toward any effort at canceling the debts owed the United States. Some voiced suspicion that the Lausanne settlement was made in an effort to hammer down the American debt.

The view of State Department officials was that the European situation had been appeased at Lausanne and high hopes were expressed that the way was now open for general

Continued on Page Four.

Fluttering Army of Moths Invades the City; Mysterious Swarms Beset Autoists and Shops

Fluttering so thickly that they resembled a snow storm, enormous swarms of moths swept down over the Bronx in the middle of last evening and by 1 o'clock this morning had beset many of the more brightly lighted sections of Manhattan, Queens and Brooklyn. No explanation of where the pests had emerged from so unexpectedly was immediately available.

Motorists along many thoroughfares complained that the insects made driving very difficult. So numerous were they along Riverside Drive, West End Avenue, Jerome Avenue, Fordham Road, and Pelham Parkway that traffic was considerably delayed as drivers found their windshields continually obscured with the moths.

Complaints began coming into the police about 10:30 o'clock from motorists and pedestrians in the Fordham section of the Bronx. Just what the police were expected to do remained unanswered, but they were deluged with telephone calls about the prevalence of the insects.

Storekeepers open late last evening soon began to add their voices to the indignation. They reported that the moths were swarming into their shops, apparently attracted by the bright lights, and were clustering in the shop windows in such numbers as to be a decided nuisance.

Persons emerging from their homes or from theatres late last night asserted that the insects filled the air so thickly that they had actually believed for a moment that it was snowing in mid-July. The insects gathered on the hats and clothing of pedestrians annoyingly, some observers reported.

The insects were small white bugs and were described by many observers as gypsy moths. One veteran policeman said that he recalled a similar visitation which swept over Harlem more than twenty years ago, but many other long-time residents of the sections affected said they did not recall anything like the present plague.

Herriot Calls Settlement a Victory for None; Says France Gives Hand to World in Friendship

By FREDERICK T. BIRCHALL.
Special Cable to THE NEW YORK TIMES.

LAUSANNE, July 8.—The new spirit that is animating France in this Lausanne agreement was eloquently expressed by Premier Herriot in a brief address in his workroom in the Palace Hotel tonight to representatives of the international press just after the announcement of the settlement. He spoke in a tone of deep emotion.

"Prime Minister MacDonald pleaded with me to come to the middle of the road," he said in substance. "I went further and we have reached, I believe, the best conclusion that could be reached for world peace, especially European peace.

"In this settlement there are no victors and no vanquished. It is an agreement equitable to all, and none can say that it was a victory one over the other.

"I feel that France has shown great moderation. We have given up thirty-seven annuities, totaling 32,000,000,000 marks, for a sum scarcely sufficient to pay the one year's Hoover-postponed annuity and one Young Plan annuity.

"My government at this moment is in grave danger on account of financial difficulties and the budgetary deficit. I am obliged now to go before Parliament to ask the French citizens to provide money to make up the 1,800,000,000 francs that were due this year.

"But we came here not to reach a solution for profit, but for justice. I believe that we have succeeded. And here for France I hold out my hand in friendship to the world."

PARIS HOLDS HERRIOT HAS SAVED CABINET

Lausanne Settlement Brings an Overnight Reversal of His Political Fortunes.

SATISFACTION IS GENERAL

Right Press Reminds Hoover That "Everything Depends on the United States."

Special Cable to THE NEW YORK TIMES.

PARIS, July 8.—The general satisfaction with the Lausanne settlement is reflected in the press comment here.

Premier Herriot is credited with having saved his government and greatly enhanced his political prestige. This change in his political fortunes has taken place overnight, for his fall had been predicted by many keen observers last night.

Now he is expected to get an ovation in the Chamber of Deputies Monday when he returns to tackle the grave budgetary problems that are menacing his government's financial program.

The Right press, notably Pertinax in L'Echo de Paris, is losing no time in reminding President Hoover that "everything now depends upon the United States." It is recalled that he said last year that Europe must settle the reparations problem before the United States would talk about the war debts.

All Factions Appear Placated.

M. Herriot seems to have succeeded in placating almost all shades of political opinion in France with the course that he steered at Lausanne. By not asking too much from Germany he has conciliated the Socialists, who have been advocating the complete cancellation of reparations.

By at least getting something from Germany he has avoided the wrathful denunciation of the parties of the Right and probably has pleased them more than they will admit. The Right press indicates its moderate satisfaction with the agreement although making the reservation that Germany's final payment should be larger than the amount stipulated.

As regards Article 231 of the Treaty of Versailles and the question of German war guilt, French opinion is generally still united in its refusal to whitewash the Reich or admit Germany was altogether blameless.

The Right press insists as stoutly as ever upon Germany's guilt. The Left press, notably Leon Blum in Le Populaire, believes the war guilt to have been rather generally shared by everybody, but disapproves the raising of the question at Lausanne "because it is too irrelevant to be a factor influencing the settlement of the reparations problem."

American Partisanship Seen.

"Practical semi-official approval by the United States Government of the thesis championed by France at Lausanne," says the Agence Economique et Financiere editorially, "is a great political event."

Senator Henry Berenger, who concluded the Franco-American debt settlement in 1926, wrote in the same newspaper:

"The Americans did not in the least desire the annulment of reparations. They let it be known in time

Continued on Page Five.

PAPEN ON AIR TELLS REICH LOAD IS LIFTED

In Dramatic Recital He Serves Notice That Nation Will Now Fight for Political Equality.

HIS FOES BACK SETTLEMENT

Reichstag Approval Foreseen Despite Paradox That His Supporters Are Critical.

By GUIDO ENDERIS.
Special Cable to THE NEW YORK TIMES.

BERLIN, July 8.—The Young Plan is extinct—the burden of 34,000,000,000 marks in reparations annuities that was to be carried until 1988 has been lifted from the shoulders of the German people—that was the message that all Germany received over the radio from Chancellor Franz von Papen in Lausanne early this evening.

In a dramatic recital of the German delegation's battle for the end of reparations, the head of President von Hindenburg's Cabinet of "national concentration" recounted with considerable emotion how the broken threads had been retied when crisis after crisis threatened the breakdown of the negotiations.

He told how the ever-present realization that such a failure would destroy the last shreds of world confidence and lead the Western world to the brink of economic and political chaos had kept the statesmen's faith alive.

The German delegation, he stressed, had steadfastly opposed any attempt to establish an inter-relationship between reparations and the Allied debts to the United States, and if it had failed in its endeavor to have political concessions embodied in the treaty he was convinced that these, by virtue of the emphasis given them in the course of the parleys, had now formally been brought before the world forum.

Demands Equality.

"Here and now," Chancellor von Papen declared in a voice charged with strong feeling, "I give renewed notice that Germany has a right to equality of treatment and that she is entitled to assume equal duties with the other peoples in the community of nations."

This statement followed the Chancellor's declaration that with her economic freedom won Germany would now wage a sturdy battle for her political rights.

The reparations settlement reached at Lausanne will in all likelihood be accepted by Germany through the Reichstag to be elected July 31. This was fairly well indicated in advance comment in political circles and party organs, which are now refraining from discussing the highly anomalous Parliamentary position of the von Papen Government, which is not yet the recipient of a Reichstag mandate.

The so-called Weimar group, comprising the Socialists, Centrists and Democrats, who accepted the Dawes and Young Plans, will not only approve today's definitive settlement on the ground of its economic advantages, but because it represents a consistent sequel to the policy of fulfillment championed by them for the past eight years.

Dr. Hugenberg's Nationalists and

Continued on Page Five.

WAR GUILT ISSUE AVOIDED

Deadlock Is Broken When Germans Agree to Later Action on Charge.

NO BONDS FOR THREE YEARS

European Debtors to the United States Agree Ratification May Depend on Our Stand.

ECONOMIC PARLEY CALLED

Conference Adopts Resolutions on Non-German Reparations and on Danubian Aid.

The text of the Lausanne Accord is printed on Page 4.

By P. J. PHILIP.
Special Cable to THE NEW YORK TIMES.

LAUSANNE, July 8.—What Prime Minister Ramsay MacDonald described today as the most difficult task of his life has been brought to success. After thirteen years of effort and failure and suffering, payment by Germany to the victorious allies of that tribute that was to serve for restoration and reparation has been brought to an end.

A new start has been made today at Lausanne and the spirit of Lausanne has been brought to aid the spirit of Locarno to make that new start, the beginning of a new era, a fresh achievement in the way of peace and reconciliation.

In earnest of that new beginning, this long day of gradual realization at the end of three weeks of fervent negotiation came to an end with a hearty handshake between Edouard Herriot, the French Premier, and Lieut. Col. Franz von Papen, the Chancellor of the German Reich. It was past eleven o'clock in the evening of a working day which had begun fourteen hours before and had seen success pulled out of last night's failure.

War Guilt Issue Avoided.

During these last forty-eight hours the whole battle had been over the question of whether the wiping out of reparations should carry with it or only imply the wiping out of that accusation of German war guilt on which the claim for reparations was founded. In some sense in the final act the issue was avoided and left for future decision if any country cares to raise it. Almost any meaning can be read into this formula in the preamble of the treaty: "The signatory powers do not claim that the task accomplished at Lausanne, which will completely put an end to reparations, can alone assure that peace which all nations desire, but they hope that an achievement of such significance and so arduously attained will be understood and appreciated by all pacific elements in Europe and the world and that it will be followed by fresh achievements."

By this treaty, which was approved tonight by all the principal countries of Europe and will be signed tomorrow morning, Germany agrees in the final settlement to deliver to the Bank for International Settlements five per cent redeemable bonds to the amount of 3,000,000,000 gold marks ($714,000,000). These bonds will not be negotiated for at least three years, and if they are not negotiated within fifteen years will be canceled.

If the bonds are negotiated they will be issued at a rate not below 90 per cent. In reality, therefore, this final German payment amounts to 2,700,000,000 marks, or only slightly more than the past year's suspended Hoover moratorium payment under the Young Plan.

America's Reaction Awaited.

Alongside today's agreement there was another which will not be published. It is an agreement among the creditors of Germany who are debtors to the United States that ratification may be made dependent on circumstances outside the control of this conference. That point was raised publicly by Chancellor von Papen at tonight's [illegible] public meeting. If this agreement were not ratified he asked if [illegible] conference would be held. [illegible] MacDonald formally [illegible] it would.

There was no little [illegible] to-day's events. At 3 o'clock this morning there still was a [illegible] the question of war guilt. [illegible]

Continued on Page Four.

"All the News That's Fit to Print."

The New York Times.

LATE CITY EDITION
WEATHER—Showers today, probably tomorrow; cooler tomorrow night.
Temperatures Yesterday—Max. 87, Min. 72.

VOL. LXXXI....No. 27,208. **** NEW YORK, FRIDAY, JULY 22, 1932. TWO CENTS In New York City | THREE CENTS Within 200 Miles | FOUR CENTS Elsewhere Except 7th and 8th Postal Zones

EMPIRE NATIONS SEEK NEW TRADE DEAL AS ECONOMIC PARLEY OPENS IN OTTAWA; CANADA READY TO BARGAIN WITH BRITAIN

BENNETT OPENS MEETING

Dominion Premier Offers to Increase Preference to British Products.

OUR EXPORTS FACE CURBS

But Baldwin and Others Warn Not to Attempt to Antagonize Rest of the World.

SOUND MONEY BASIS URGED

Delegates Requested to Pave Way for World Monetary and Economic Conference.

Addresses at Ottawa Conference are printed on Pages 8 and 9.

By CHARLES A. SELDEN.
Special to THE NEW YORK TIMES.

OTTAWA, July 21.—R. B. Bennett, Prime Minister of Canada, today was elected president of the Imperial Economic Conference of the nine States within the British Empire whose delegates have assembled at Ottawa to devise some system of trading among themselves with greater mutual benefit than they now enjoy.

Mr. Bennett's statement of policy at the outset did not meet expectations of frankness. It was dramatic, however, when he declared with specifications that Canada's program was to increase the preferences now given to England under the present Dominion tariff laws, to put more commodities on the preferential list, and to remove the tariff altogether from many of the imports from Great Britain on which duties are now imposed. He also said this program would be applied to the Canadian trade with her dominions wherever it would prove mutually advantageous.

Furthermore, Mr. Bennett gave a very definite warning to the protected manufacturing interests of his own country that they must accept and support his proposals.

From England in return he demanded greater preferences in the British market for the exports from Canada. In that demand was a very definite implication that Great Britain must in future prevent the flooding of her markets with lumber and other primary products from Russia and the Scandinavian countries to the detriment of the natural exports from Canada.

Baldwin for Lower Barriers.

Stanley Baldwin, who presented the case for Great Britain, was somewhat less definite than the Canadian Premier and his speech was more after the old manner of conference oratory. But he met Mr. Bennett half way when he said that there were two ways by which the countries of the empire could give each other increased trade preferences, either by lowering the existing barriers among themselves or by increasing the tariffs against foreign countries.

He definitely preferred the first method and stressed that no matter what the empire countries might do for each other none of them could dispense with its foreign trade and he had in mind what effect this conference might have on the future fiscal policies of the United States and other high tariff countries.

"Let us therefore aim at the lowering rather than the raising of barriers, even if we cannot fully achieve our purpose now, and let us remember that any action we take here is bound to have its reaction elsewhere."

The chiefs of the other delegations also placed themselves on record as ready to try new ways of getting on together. So this conference, unlike previous empire assemblies that have tried in vain to find an economic policy, has begun its work not only with a definite objective upon which all agree but with a set of tangible concrete proposals for reaching that objective. The task of the next four or five weeks is to agree upon these means to an end. The situation is not regarded as hopeless.

Peace Tower Marks Opening.

The emotional and decorative aspects of the opening of the conference were in harmony with its ultimate

Continued on Page Eight.

King Sees 'New Page of History' Opened at Ottawa; Conference in Reply Presents 'Respectful Duty'

Special to THE NEW YORK TIMES.

OTTAWA, July 21.—The texts of King George's message to the Imperial Economic Conference, which opened here today, and the resolution of the conference in response appear below.

Message From the King.

My thoughts and prayers are with the delegates of my governments who are gathered in conference today to explore the means by which they may promote the prosperity of the peoples of this great empire. At this conference you are opening a new page of history, on which, within a few weeks, will be written the record of a determined effort to solve the difficulties weighing so heavily not only on us, but upon the whole world. It is my earnest hope that when this conference rises there will be a record of results worthily reflecting the frankness, the sincerity and the spirit of helpfulness with which, I feel confident, your deliberations will be conducted.

The British Empire is based on the principle of cooperation, and it is now your common purpose to give the fullest possible effect to that principle in the economic sphere. By so doing you will set in motion beneficial forces within the British Commonwealth, which may well extend their impulse also to the world at large. I pray that you may be given clear insight and strength of purpose for these ends. GEORGE R. I.

Reply of the Conference.

The representatives of the governments of the British Commonwealth assembled in conference at Ottawa at their first meeting and as their first official act desire to present their respectful duty to the King and to thank him for his gracious message, which has just been read by his Excellency the Governor General. They join in thanksgiving for your Majesty's continued health, and earnestly hope that your Majesty and her Majesty, the Queen, may long be spared to strengthen the feelings of love and devotion shared by all the peoples of the British Commonwealth of Nations.

LEHMAN CANDIDACY HELD PATH TO PEACE

Endorsed by Roosevelt for Governor, He Returns to Albany After Talk With Smith.

WILL ENTER RACE ACTIVELY

With Both Rival Leaders Supporting Mutual Friend, Healing of the Breach Is Predicted.

Special to THE NEW YORK TIMES.

ALBANY, July 21.—Arriving here fresh from a long conference with former Governor Smith, Lieut. Gov. Lehman was looked upon today at the Capitol as the man who might reunite the political interests of Governor Smith and Governor Roosevelt.

Colonel Lehman merely said that he and the former Governor met in New York and went over the political situation. Soon afterward it became known that Mr. Lehman plans within a short time to announce formally that he is a candidate for Governor.

The decision to enter the race actively, coming so soon after Colonel Lehman's conference with former Governor Smith, gave rise to the supposition that the former Governor would "go to the front" for him in any contest over the nomination.

Governor Roosevelt has already plainly indicated his desire that Colonel Lehman lead the State fight for the party.

Lehman a Friend of Both.

The Lieutenant Governor and former Governor Smith have remained the warmest of personal friends despite their differing political stands. The Lieutenant Governor as a member of the Albany Administration voted for Governor Roosevelt at Chicago.

At the same time the Lieutenant Governor has proved in the past that he was willing to go to great limits to aid the fortunes of Mr. Smith.

Colonel Lehman was asked if Governor Smith would support him for the nomination and if Mr. Smith had given any intimation as to the part he expected to play in the national campaign.

"I do not want to speak for Governor Smith, you know," was the reply. "I think you had better ask him."

The Lieutenant Governor's declaration of his candidacy for the Governorship is believed to be likely next week, although the exact date, it is understood, has not been fixed. Governor Roosevelt is expected to follow it up with an open avowal that he would like to see his running mate in two elections named to head the State ticket.

If former Governor Smith and Governor Roosevelt should get together back of a man who is personally and politically close to both the situation would provide a con-

Continued on Page Two.

RESTAURANT RAIDED IN HOTEL MARGUERY

Dry Agents Seize Two Bottles and Arrest Three Employes on Park Avenue.

30 DINERS NOT MOLESTED

Leader of Foray Sponsored by 5th Av. Photographer—Place Not Operated by Hotel.

The Restaurant Marguery, one of the centres of Park Avenue social life, in the Hotel Marguery, at 270 Park Avenue, was raided shortly after 7 o'clock last night by five Federal agents, who made three arrests and confiscated two bottles purporting to contain gin and whisky. The raiders did not disturb the diners or the restaurant's routine.

One of the raiders, believed by the police to be Agent Krisel, who pressed the charge of selling liquor, had posed as a man of affluence, the headwaiter said later. He had obtained an introduction in accordance with the establishment's rules and had received an identification card for purposes of credit, the employe, who refused to give his name, explained.

His sponsor was a responsible resident of the section, a photographer with studios on Fifth Avenue, the headwaiter said ruefully. The sponsor himself had been vouched for by "a prominent man of unimpeachable integrity." The agent was introduced two weeks ago and had dined four of five times at the restaurant. He did not take advantage of his card to charge his meals, but paid for each one, and liquor had never been served to him, the headwaiter insisted.

Poured Drink Into Vial.

While dining at the restaurant last night, however, the agent obtained a drink. He poured it into a vial and signaled four fellow-officers loitering in the lobby outside. They searched the restaurant without permitting their presence to be observed by more than a few of the twenty-five or thirty customers and took the three prisoners to the East Fifty-first Street police station.

Agent Krisel booked Ercole Marchisio, who said he was 47 years old and lived at Swartswood, N. J., as the "restaurant keeper," a title that amused employes of the fashionable resort. The other prisoners were waiters and said they were Vincent Sota, 39, of 1,160 Colgate Avenue, the Bronx, and Bert Bertolini, 27, of 316 East Fiftieth Street.

The three were charged with the sale of liquor in violation of the Volstead act. A charge of possession was not made, although the headwaiter said they had taken two bottles the ownership of which the restaurant disclaimed. The agents declined particulars of the arrests to the

Continued on Page Sixteen.

Bank Hands $56,325 to Robber in Disguise; "Armored Truck Guard" Just Asked for It

Wearing the uniform of a guard of an armored car crew, a man bustled into the main offices of the Chemical Bank and Trust Company at 165 Broadway last Saturday forenoon, asked for "the money for the United States Trucking Corporation," received $56,325 in cash and disappeared, giving the police one of the most brazen robberies in the history of the financial district to work upon.

Details of the theft have been closely guarded by the police since they were notified of the robbery on Monday afternoon, when officials of the bank learned for the first time that they had been hoodwinked of the small fortune in ready money.

The man entered the bank at 11:15 A. M. Saturday, three-quarters of an hour before the offices were to be closed for the week-end. He was dressed in the uniform of a United States Trucking Company guard and appeared to be thoroughly familiar with the work of asking the bank for money assigned to one of its customers.

The "guard" marched up to a cage in which a teller, Louis Scala, was working, and announced calmly, "I was sent here to get the money for the United States Trucking Corporation."

Scala, noting the dark uniform and the belt with a holster for a pistol, promptly passed the money through the grillwork of his cage and received a receipt. It was learned yesterday that the receipt was signed with a bogus name.

The police declined to divulge any further details yesterday. Whether the man had any accomplices in the theft, whether he had an automobile or an armored car waiting outside the bank, or whether he merely walked through the scurrying crowds of the financial district to the nearest subway station was not known.

Soon afterward, the bank closed for the week-end. On Monday officials of the institution got into communication with the trucking corporation's main offices at 372 South Street to inquire if the $56,325 had been delivered to the customer to

Continued on Page Two.

ARMS ACCORD 'VAIN,' MUSSOLINI ASSERTS; HE WITHHOLDS VOTE

As Foreign Minister, He Says Geneva Resolution Falls Short of World's Hopes.

ATTACKS NAVAL CLAUSE

Soviet Move to Insert Hoover Plan Into Agreement Fails—Discontent Crops Up.

By CLARENCE K. STREIT.
Wireless to THE NEW YORK TIMES.

GENEVA, July 21.—Premier Mussolini, as Italy's new Foreign Minister, was behind the most significant of several significant moves by the various powers in a sharp debate in the general commission today over the resolution registering the agreements reached in the first phase of the disarmament conference.

It was understood yesterday that Great Britain, France, the United States and Italy supported this resolution. Today a seaplane alighted on Lake Leman near the conference building with a message inspired by Mussolini which General Italo Balbo, Air Minister, read to the commission saying that Italy would abstain from voting on the measure. The message called the resolution a "vain" effort, "entirely inadequate when compared to the wishes and hopes of the world." It said "it is not enough to lay down principles" when "no marked progress is made toward effective attainment of disarmament."

One of the sorest spots was hidden in these words:

"As far as the naval problem is concerned the draft report merely indicates a mode of procedure and does not even state definite and positive principles for reduction."

It came out then that the three other powers had had a hint that this was coming when at yesterday's secret four-power meeting Italy made a general reservation. It had not been taken too seriously as under Foreign Minister Dino Grandi the Italians had given a strong impression that they would vote for the resolution.

Reversals Indicate Ferment.

Hard on this reversal, it is understood, came two others, both behind the scenes. The reversals indicate the present ferment under the surface in all the big capitals.

Yesterday the British apparently renounced their idea of a meeting of naval experts of the five naval powers in London in September because of French and Italian opposition and accepted the idea of a meeting in Geneva during the September League Assembly. Today, it is understood, the British, switching back, pushed for a meeting of naval experts in London early in August. It seems that they believe Premier Mussolini dropped Signor Grandi because he was left out of the Anglo-French accord which Rome suspects contains much under the surface, particularly of a naval character, and that Premier Mussolini, having hastily adhered to the accord as a precaution, now is taking an abstentionist stand not merely here, but all along the European line.

Thus, at the moment when things are tense in Berlin he is giving the British and French a taste of the uncertainty their accord is still giving him.

Discontent Is Evidenced.

Meanwhile, the long debate in the general commission revealed much wider and more open discontent with the weakness of the resolution than

Continued on Page Three.

DICTATOR TO REMOVE PRUSSIAN SOCIALISTS; NO NEW CABINET NOW

Bracht Will Dismiss "Political" Officials—Ministry Not to Be Named Till Election.

PAPEN TO SEE STATE HEADS

Three Cabinets Appeal to the Supreme Court—Police to Shoot to Kill Rioters.

By FREDERICK T. BIRCHALL.
Special Cable to THE NEW YORK TIMES.

BERLIN, July 21.—There will be for the present no new Prussian Cabinet succeeding the ousted Ministers to whom Adolf Hitler objected and whom Chancellor Franz von Papen's government held guilty of carelessness and negligence in having permitted the Hitlerites and Communists to shoot each other and innocent bystanders in political riots in the Prussian streets.

It was decided today to defer all steps in that direction until after the elections a week from Sunday, when the political complexion of the next Reichstag will be determined and, therewith, the continuation or replacement of Colonel von Papen and his fellow Ministers.

Possession of the Prussian Ministry of the Interior formally passed to Dr. Franz Bracht, former Mayor of Essen and dictator as Deputy Commissioner for the Chancellor. Dr. Bracht will remove from the State government all "political"—meaning Socialist—secretaries and under-secretaries who can be spared, carrying on with the remainder.

At the same time Dr. Kurt Melcher took charge of the Berlin police as their new chief.

Orders Police to Shoot to Kill.

General Gerd von Rundstedt, Reichswehr commander in charge of Berlin and the province of Brandenburg under the state of emergency decreed yesterday, ordered that hereafter policemen should shoot to kill when threatened by rioters.

The comparative political quiet following yesterday's upheaval afforded opportunity for men of all parties to appraise the significance of recent developments and their probable effect on the great contest between democracy and autocracy at the polls ten days hence.

That contest is being described here as the last chance for democracy in Germany, and there are many who believe it will be just that.

In no other country anywhere just now could there be found a parallel for the present state of affairs in the Reich. Democracy has been more or less thrust upon the Germans. In principle the mass of the people undoubtedly favor it, but they are unversed in its practice and bedeviled and bewildered by the strange situations it has produced and the economic and financial chaos wherein it has come to them.

Hence the score or more of political parties in existence—twenty-eight actually applied for places on the ballot for the coming election—parties that are constantly changing both in membership and principles, in everything but leadership.

Opportunity for Extremists.

Hence also the unrivaled opportunity afforded to both communism and fascism to keep things stirred up in the hope that out of the turmoil they may seize power to exercise their individual theories of government.

Fascism in the shape of the Hitler movement is the particular danger at present. Communism is more or less in the discard. It dropped 1,000,000 votes in the last election and will probably lose more in the coming

Continued on Page Three.

I.C.C. APPROVES 4 EASTERN RAIL SYSTEMS; NEW ENGLAND CONSOLIDATION DEFERRED; WABASH-SEABOARD PROJECT IS CANCELED

How Some Outstanding Railways Are Shifted By the I. C. C. in Its Four-System Decision

Special to THE NEW YORK TIMES.

WASHINGTON, July 21.—The consolidation plan announced by the Interstate Commerce Commission calls for assembling the Eastern railroads into four groups, based, respectively, on the New York Central, Pennsylvania, Baltimore & Ohio and Chesapeake & Ohio-Nickel Plate systems. Some lines allocated to each of the four trunk lines have been in their possession for many years. The most important new additions proposed by the commission for the four systems are as follows:

New York Central—Delaware, Lackawanna & Western, except the Chenango Forks-Oswego branch; Virginian Railway; one-fourth interests each in the Lehigh & New England, Monongahela Railroad, Montour Railroad, Pittsburgh, Chartiers & Youghiogheny and in the Pittsburgh & West Virginia east of Gould's Tunnel; full control of the Rutland (now shared with the New York, New Haven & Hartford), except the Ogdensburg & Lake Champlain Division.

Pennsylvania—Wabash Railway; Detroit, Toledo & Ironton; one-half interest in the Raritan River Railroad; one-fourth interests each in the Lehigh & New England, Monongahela Railroad, Montour Railroad, Pittsburgh, Chartiers & Youghiogheny and the Pittsburgh & West Virginia east of Gould's Tunnel.

Baltimore & Ohio—Reading Company, Central of New Jersey, Western Maryland, Ann Arbor, Detroit & Toledo Shore Line, Lehigh & Hudson; one-half interest in the Raritan River Railroad; one-fourth interests in the Lehigh & New England, Monongahela Railroad, Montour Railroad, Pittsburgh, Chartiers & Youghiogheny and the Pittsburgh & West Virginia east of Gould's Tunnel; the Alton Railroad, Buffalo, Rochester & Pittsburgh and Buffalo & Susquehanna (recently merged with the Baltimore & Ohio system).

Chesapeake & Ohio-Nickel Plate—Lehigh Valley; Chenango Forks-Oswego branch of the Lackawanna Railroad; Bessemer & Lake Erie; Wheeling & Lake Erie; Pittsburgh & West Virginia west of Gould's Tunnel and also one-fourth interest in line east of Gould's Tunnel; Pittsburgh, Shawmut & Northern; one-fourth interest each in the Lehigh & New England, Monongahela Railroad, Montour Railroad, Pittsburgh, Chartiers & Youghiogheny; Pere Marquette (now controlled by the Chesapeake & Ohio); Chicago & Eastern Illinois and Erie (controlled by the Van Sweringen interests, who control the Chesapeake & Ohio-Nickel Plate system).

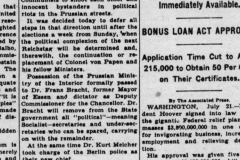

LINES' PETITION GRANTED

Groups Centre in P. R. R., the Central, B. & O. and C. & O.-Nickel Plate.

P. R. R. STOCK HOLDING HIT

Road Must Divest Itself of New Haven Interest if the Plan Is to Be Approved.

VAN SWERINGENS TAP CITY

D. & H. Left Independent Pending New England Ruling—Two Commissioners Dissent.

Text of I. C. C. decision on Pages 4 and 5.

Special to THE NEW YORK TIMES.

WASHINGTON, July 21.—Consolidation of all Eastern railroads, except those of New England, into four great systems was approved by the Interstate Commerce Commission today in the most far-reaching decision ever handed down by the commission. The lines involved number about 300.

Commissioner Joseph B. Eastman dissented from the decision and was joined by Commissioner McManamy. They based their dissent on two reasons in particular: First, that the four dominant lines already have allegedly put much of the plan into effect illegally, and, second, that present changing conditions form an improper background for radical revision of railway systems.

The four systems to be created, if the railroads agree to the commission plan, will be known as the New York Central, the Pennsylvania, the Baltimore & Ohio and the Chesapeake & Ohio-Nickel Plate.

The commission's ruling caused an immediate reaction approaching jubilation in railroad circles, which hailed the plan as the most helpful factor in that industry in twelve years. In fact, as both the majority report and Commissioner Eastman's dissent pointed out, the leading railroads have received virtually all that they have asked for to work out a new plan of economies.

Expense Problem Tackled.

As for the expense involved in the consolidations, a point that Commissioner Eastman also raised, it was stated here that plans already are afoot to utilize in many cases an exchange of securities, thus avoiding transfer of cash at a time when railroads are particularly short of money.

The commission altered its plan promulgated in 1929 by eliminating a proposed fifth system to be built around the Wabash-Seaboard, leaving unallocated the Seaboard Air Line Railway Company. It also left out of its plan the Delaware & Hudson Railroad Corporation, controlled by Leonor F. Loree, who has bitterly fought the four-system plan.

Terming the Delaware & Hudson "the most important of the New England bridge carriers," the commission's statement said that disposition of it would await a decision on whether one or two New England systems are to be recommended.

Under the commission's plan the systems will be known as Nos. 3 to 6 inclusive, as follows:

SYSTEM No. 3—New York Central: Including seventy-five long and short roads and trackage rights over six roads.

SYSTEM No. 4—Pennsylvania: Including eighty-two long and short roads and trackage rights over four roads.

SYSTEM No. 5—Baltimore & Ohio: Including sixty-eight long and short roads and trackage rights over eight roads.

SYSTEM No. 6—Chesapeake & Ohio-Nickel Plate: Including seventy long and short roads and trackage rights over seven roads.

Ban on P. R. R.'s New Haven Stock.

While the commission deferred for the time being its decision on consolidation of the New England roads, it discussed the penetration of the Pennsylvania into that territory and its possible effect on consolidation. It stated that no application of the Pennsylvania designed to carry out the formation of its system would be approved unless that company first divested itself of its stock in the New England roads.

The commission said:

"If the New Haven, with its 2,122

Continued on Page Five.

RELIEF BILL SIGNED BY THE PRESIDENT

He Acts Without Comment—$3,800,000,000 Is Made Immediately Available.

BONUS LOAN ACT APPROVED

Application Time Cut to Allow 215,000 to Obtain 50 Per Cent on Their Certificates.

By The Associated Press.

WASHINGTON, July 21.—President Hoover signed into law today the gigantic Federal relief plan that masses $3,800,000,000 in one coffer for invigorating business, increasing employment and relieving destitution.

His approval was given five days after the $2,122,000,000 bill that nearly doubles resources of the Reconstruction Finance Corporation and opens its purse to needy States, emerged from a final Congressional snarl.

The President's signature, attached without ceremony or public comment, makes the relief act immediately effective. This means:

Operating funds of the Reconstruction Corporation increased from $2,000,000,000 to $3,800,000,000.

Funds made available for advances to States for unemployment relief, $300,000,000.

Provision of $1,500,000,000 for public construction and self-liquidating private loans, and the financing of agriculture through credit corporations.

Money available for advances to States under the Federal-aid highway law, $120,000,000.

For roads and trails in the national parks and forests, $16,000,000.

Provision of $186,224,000 for public building and waterway improvement when the condition of the Treasury permits.

Federal Reserve banks may discount eligible paper for individuals and corporations.

Within ten days, Eugene Meyer, Governor of the Federal Reserve System, and Paul Bestor, Farm Loan Commissioner, are automatically removed from the Reconstruction Board.

Reports of all reconstruction loans must be filed with Congress monthly.

Under terms of another act signed today by Mr. Hoover about 215,000 World War veterans will be able to borrow half the value of their bonus certificates from the veterans administration offices after Monday, July 25.

The new law extends the borrowing privilege to those excluded from benefits of previous legislation, and Frank T. Hines, administrator of veterans' affairs, immediately an-

Continued on Page Six.

WASHINGTON ORDERS B. E. F. TO EVACUATE

Board Tells Gen. Glassford to Give Veterans Until Aug. 4 to Quit Sites They Occupy.

LEADERS PREDICT DANGER

Say Few of the Men Will Leave Voluntarily — Police Report More Than 11,000 Remain.

Special to THE NEW YORK TIMES.

WASHINGTON, July 21.—The Bonus Expeditionary Force faced enforced disbandment late today when General Pelham D. Glassford, the Superintendent of Police, made public a letter from the District of Columbia Board of Commissioners ordering him to evacuate the marchers completely by noon of Aug. 4.

At the same time the Board of Commissioners, acting upon authority of the Treasury Department, ordered the evacuation of several thousand men who have made their home in downtown Washington on sites being demolished by the Treasury in connection with the new Federal building construction along Pennsylvania Avenue. Wreckers stopped demolition work when the bonus army first reached Washington on Decoration Day and a number of the partly torn down structures have since been occupied by groups of veterans.

The downtown area, the order said, must be cleared of all bonus marchers by midnight next Sunday, the same time that the law providing for government transportation for those who wish to return home expires.

Order Is Widely Distributed.

Copies of the commission's order to General Glassford were widely distributed among the twenty-four "cantonments" officially listed by the police and thousands of others were scattered about the city by police officers.

While the order was being sent out several hundred men were at work in the downtown area erecting wooden huts which they said they expected to occupy "until the bonus is paid."

"You will instruct all precinct commanders," the order read, "to see that private buildings are not occupied by bonus marchers without previous consent by the owners, and then only after they are pronounced to be in sanitary condition and structurally safe and free of fire hazards by the board previously appointed."

This section of the order, the surprised leaders of the B. E. F. de-

Continued on Page Two.

"All the News That's Fit to Print."

The New York Times.

LATE CITY EDITION
POSTSCRIPT
WEATHER—Showers today, cooler tonight; tomorrow fair.
Temperatures Yesterday—Max., 78; Min., 70.

Copyright, 1932, by The New York Times Company.

VOL. LXXXI....No. 27,209. ***** NEW YORK, SATURDAY, JULY 23, 1932. TWO CENTS In New York City | THREE CENTS Within 200 Miles | FOUR CENTS Elsewhere Except 7th and 8th Postal Zones

WALKER CALLS ON 147,000 CITY EMPLOYES TO GIVE UP MONTH'S PAY, SAVING $26,000,000; WARNS ALBANY WILL ACT IF THEY DON'T

HOOVER APPROVES HOME LOANS BILL; PREDICTS JOB RISE

He Holds Glass Rider, in Its "Practical Working," Will Not Cause Inflation.

HAILS STEP TO RECOVERY

President Lays Unemployment Partly to "Stagnation in Construction."

LARGE DEMAND REPORTED

"Huddling" Conceals a Shortage, He Says, Putting Building Needs at Over $300,000,000.

Special to THE NEW YORK TIMES.

WASHINGTON, July 22.—President Hoover today signed the home loan bank bill, the last of his reconstruction measures aimed to stimulate industry and expand credit facilities.

The measure not only provides for a system of financing home-building but also carries the Glass rider for temporary inflation of the currency. The rider permits national banks to use government bonds bearing interest up to 3⅜ per cent as security for temporary currency expansion which, it is estimated, may reach about $1,000,000,000. This provision is limited to three years.

In signing the bill the President issued a statement summarizing the advantages to the banks. He held that the government was not placed in business by the act, but that the banks' entire resources would be obtained by debentures and through financing raised by the regional banks.

He hailed the operation of the measure as another step toward economic recovery and as a means of lifting the burdens from the shoulders of taxpayers who have been facing mortgage foreclosures and great hardships because of their inability to renew mortgages expiring in the period of restricted credit.

The President expressed the opinion that extensive home-building would result through the financing of the home loan banks and that this would relieve unemployment considerably, which, he declared, was due in part to "stagnation in residential construction."

Reports Demand for Homes.

Home construction, he said, had outstepped the demands in some of the larger cities, but had not kept pace with population increases in the smaller communities.

The survey of the Department of Commerce, he asserted, shows that there was "an immediate demand for homes amounting to from $300,000,000 to $500,000,000, which could be undertaken at once if financing were available."

To this extent the President foresaw home building activity and an immediate increase in employment.

The President said he had been advised by the Treasury that the expansion provision would not lead in its practical workings to inflation.

The Controller of the Currency also informed him that while this section ran counter to the Federal Reserve act, which was intended to do away with inflexible bond-secured currency and represented a "step-back" in currency and banking legislation, he did not feel justified in recommending that the bill be vetoed, since the currency expansion section was a rider to an important and constructive piece of legislation.

"I do not, therefore, feel," the President said, "that the amendment is such as would warrant refusal to approve the measure, which means so much to hundreds of thousands of home owners, is such a contribution to their relief; such a contribution to establishment of home-ownership and such an aid to immediate increase of employment."

THE PRESIDENT'S STATEMENT.

The President's statement is as follows:

I have today signed the home loan bank bill. This institution has been created on the general lines advocated by me in a statement to the press on Nov. 13 last. It is the outcome of the national conference on home ownership which represented every part of the country.

Its purpose is to establish a series of discount banks for home mortgages, performing a function for home owners somewhat similar to that performed in the commercial field by the Federal Reserve banks through their discount facilities.

There are to be eight to twelve such banks established in different parts of the country with a total capital of $125,000,000 to be initially subscribed by the Reconstruction Finance Corporation.

Building and loan associations, savings banks, insurance com-

Continued on Page Two.

Hoover Tells Newspaper Men He Has Been "Fairly Busy"

By The Associated Press.

WASHINGTON, July 22.—Holding his first press conference in three weeks, President Hoover smilingly recalled to newspaper men today that his last seven talks with them had been canceled.

But, added Mr. Hoover, he had been "fairly busy."

Just before turning to a long mimeographed statement he held in his hand, the President observed that he did not believe the cancellation of conferences had hindered the press from being "well supplied with news."

ROOSEVELT WILL SEE O. D. YOUNG TODAY

They Will Discuss International Affairs and Party Plan for Economic Recovery.

RAIL CHIEF AT HYDE PARK

Carl Gray of Union Pacific Explains Railroad Problems —Mrs. Ross Visits Governor.

Special to THE NEW YORK TIMES.

HYDE PARK, July 22.—Governor Roosevelt arrived here tonight prepared to discuss international affairs tomorrow with Owen D. Young, who will stop for several hours at the Governor's home on a motor trip to Van Hornesville.

Governor Roosevelt is anxious to obtain the attitude of Mr. Young on several phases of international developments in order to crystalize his own program for the coming campaign.

"We will talk about the foreign situation," said the Governor tonight.

"Will you take up debt cancellation and German reparations?" he was asked.

The Governor, who is already on record as opposed to cancellation, replied:

"Our conference will be on general international relations."

Mr. Young is generally looked upon as a "conservative" in the Democratic party and Governor Roosevelt has avowed that he is calling upon all elements in the party for aid and information which will help him to develop a program of economic rehabilitation for presentation to the country.

Before he left for Albany, Governor Roosevelt discussed women's part in the campaign with Mrs. Nellie Tayloe Ross, former Governor of Wyoming, head of the women's division of the party.

Mrs. Ross said Mr. Roosevelt would have a wide popular appeal to the women voters of the nation.

Pleased That Gov. Ely Is Coming.

The Governor received the news of the forthcoming visit of Governor Ely next week without any comment, but it was apparent that he was pleased with the prospect of ironing out the difficulties that loomed in the Bay State.

The recent trip of the Governor in Massachusetts saw the beginning of a drive to end the post-convention feeling which the ardent supporters of former Governor Smith still seemed to hold in that State. It was recognized that steps were needed to bring about harmony and the conferences Governor Roosevelt held with the more moderate leaders of the opposition paved the way from the meeting with the Massachusetts Governor next week.

Governor Ely has refrained from saying anything to indicate that he feels the convention struggle should be forgotten and that the party

Continued on Page Six.

FLORENZ ZIEGFELD DIES IN HOLLYWOOD AFTER LONG ILLNESS

Leading Figure in New York Theatre World Succumbs to Attack of Pleurisy.

BILLIE BURKE NEAR HIM

Noted Producer of 'The Follies' and Gorgeous Musical Shows Was in 63d Year.

BEGAN CAREER IN CHICAGO

Known as "Glorifier of the American Girl," He Reaped Millions From Big Hits.

By The Associated Press.

HOLLYWOOD, July 22.—Florenz Ziegfeld, musical comedy producer, died tonight at a hospital here.

Death came at 10:31 P. M., after an unexpected setback that developed only tonight. Only Dr. Marcus Radwin, attending physician, and a nurse were in the room when the producer died.

His wife, Billie Burke, the actress, reached the bedside two minutes after his death.

The noted "glorifier of the American girl" had been here only a few days, having been brought from a New Mexico sanitarium. He never had recovered from an attack of pneumonia last Winter. A hard season after his illness caused a relapse and complications, although in the last few days he had appeared to be improving.

Florenz Ziegfeld had been ill intermittently since February. He suffered a relapse in June, and was confined to his home at Hastings-on-the-Hudson.

His physician said at that time that Mr. Ziegfeld had never fully recovered from a severe attack of influenza dating back to the try-out of "Hot-Cha!" in Pittsburgh during the Winter.

On July 19 a dispatch from Hollywood had reported Dr. E. C. Fishbaugh as saying that he was "hopeful" of Mr. Ziegfeld's recovery. He said Mr. Ziegfeld had suffered an attack of pleurisy and that, although both lungs had become affected, the producer's heart was improved.

His Career as "Glorifier."

Mr. Ziegfeld, known as the "glorifier of the American girl," began his career in professional theatrics with the profitable exploitation of the strong man, Eugene Sandow, as the "perfect man."

A number of years elapsed between the time of his rising popularity at the Chicago World's Fair in 1893 to the production of the first of the Ziegfeld "Follies" that ran through twenty-two editions with more and more beautiful choruses. Perhaps, beneath the surface, the same idea underlay the two; that of exhibiting something so nearly perfect that people were attracted by their own desire to admire.

Mr. Ziegfeld was the son of Dr. Florenz Ziegfeld, who organized the Chicago Musical College, and recruited the symphony orchestra for Theodore Thomas. He was born on March 21, 1869, and grew up against a background of Beethoven, Schumann and Bach.

The younger Ziegfeld had a flair for the theatre, and was constantly active in amateur promotions. His father seized the World's Fair as an excellent excuse to give him a chance at the business in a professional way,

Continued on Page Six.

Britain Succeeding in Big Loan Conversion; 'Wartime' Propaganda Stirs Patriotic Spirit

Wireless to THE NEW YORK TIMES.

LONDON, July 22.—From all available indications, Britain's £2,000,000,000 war-loan conversion operation is assured of success.

With only a week more before the bonus offer of £1 a share expires, it was announced officially today that 1,500,000 of the 2,500,000 holdings had been converted from a rate of 5 per cent to one of 3½ per cent.

The treasury is confident that the demand for cash repayment instead of conversion will be so small that it can be met by easy short-term borrowing.

Nothing is being left to chance, however, in this daring effort to save the national budget £23,000,000 a year in interest charges. All the devices of wartime propaganda are being enlisted in the campaign. Subway trains and billboards bear posters saying: "Convert your war loan now and help your country to better times."

The last part of the slogan is said to have been written by the Prince of Wales, who was dissatisfied with the original poster when it was submitted to him.

It is known that the big banks and commission houses have converted most of their war-loan holdings, although it is rumored that some of them were subjected to great pressure before they agreed to do so.

Next week that pressure is bound to be intensified by the publicity and argument in the newspapers and over the radio.

While all important figures are still lacking, it is possible to note which way the wind is blowing. The Bank of England announced this week that only 3 per cent of the 728,000 applications made to it had refused conversion. Similarly, the Bank of Ireland reported yesterday that to 11,000 applications for conversion in the Irish Free State there were only 400 for cash redemption, while in Northern Ireland the proportion is 11,200 to 300. Reliable estimates on the basis of these figures are difficult, however, because the amounts are not stated. Thousands of persons may choose to sacrifice their £1 bonus and wait until the end of September before deciding.

Greenland Dispute Intensified As Rival Ships Reach the Scene

Wireless to THE NEW YORK TIMES.

COPENHAGEN, July 22.—Ships carrying several small Danish and Norwegian expeditions have arrived in disputed Greenland waters, and no one knows what may happen if they meet.

The Norwegian polar ship Polarbjorn, with a Norwegian expedition, has arrived at Cape Borlace Warren, north of Tyrolerfjord, in the area occupied by Norway last Summer. Following this strategic move, the motorship Sea King, Captain Einar Mikkelsen, reached Cape Dalton. One of Dr. Lauge Koch's ships, the Gustav Holm, has arrived at Esquimauxnaes, and Dr. Koch's main ship, the Godthaab, is off Cape Hold With Hope.

ROADS TO ACT SOON ON CONSOLIDATIONS

Heads of Four Proposed Eastern Systems Likely to Meet Here Tuesday.

MARKET HAILS THE PLAN

Wall Street Looks on Exchange of Stocks as Key to Problem of Financing.

The railroads gave every indication yesterday of considering the problem of consolidation in the East with the promptness shown by the Interstate Commerce Commission in announcing its four-system plan on Thursday.

It was thought likely that the heads of the New York Central, Pennsylvania, Baltimore & Ohio and Chesapeake & Ohio-Nickel Plate system—the four properties around which the Eastern railroads are grouped in the commission's plan—would meet here next Tuesday to resume their deliberations on the problem.

While refraining from committing themselves on the points taken up in the plan, railroad officials praised the commission for issuing at this time a reply to the consolidation plan they filed at Washington last October. The railroads' plan called for four systems instead of five, as was proposed in a plan of the commission issued in 1929, and the commission in its most recent pronouncement approved the four-system principle.

The reaction of the markets to the announcement of the consolidation plan was favorable. Railroad stocks and bonds led other issues in advances.

Central Official Praises Promptness.

"The Interstate Commerce Commission was faced with an enormous problem which it disposed of with great expeditiousness," said C. C. Paulding, vice president of the New York Central.

This was the only statement to be issued from the New York Central offices on the subject, F. E. Williamson, president of the line, announcing that he could make no statement until after a thorough study of the commission's decision.

Praise for the commission was forthcoming from an unexpected quarter in a statement by L. F. Loree, president of the Delaware & Hudson Company, who has frequently been at odds with the commission.

The point in the commission decision which it was thought would most likely offer the greatest problem for the railroad presidents to surmount was the condition that the Pennsylvania divest itself of its direct and indirect control in the New York, New Haven & Hartford and Boston & Maine before going ahead with its main consolidation plan. W. W. Atterbury, president of the Pennsylvania, declined to discuss the plan, but it was conjectured that the Pennsylvania would give deep consideration to the New England situation before acting.

Akin to the Trunk Lines' Plans.

If the Pennsylvania declined the commission's condition, the other three railroads would be free to go ahead with their consolidations. However, until now they have acted in unison in presenting their plans to Washington, although in some cases they have shown great industry in capturing shorter railroads from one another.

It was said in railroad circles that the general plan of the commission was in remarkable harmony with the ideas put forward by the trunk lines. Thus, while the commission allocated the Virginian Railway to the New York Central, instead of jointly to the Pennsylvania and the C. & O., as the railroads proposed, it is not thought that the latter two companies will offer serious objection to this change.

The New York Central had asked for all the Delaware, Lackawanna & Western, but, in deference to sentiment at Oswego, the commission awarded the Oswego branch to the C. & O. Such a disposition of the Lackawanna had been con-

Continued on Page Twelve.

GERMANY DEMANDS ARMS PARLEY PARITY ON THREAT OF BOLT

Says She Will Reject Resolution Today and Not Return in 1933 Unless Equality Is Admitted.

HERRIOT IS CONCILIATORY

Declares That France Wants Security for All, Former Enemies Included.

ROW AT MEETING ON PEACE

French and Italian Deputies Clash as Former Shouts About the "Assassins of Matteotti."

By CLARENCE K. STREIT.

Wireless to THE NEW YORK TIMES.

GENEVA, July 22.—Germany bluntly told the disarmament conference today that she would no longer undertake to continue to participate in it unless before its second session opened in January she got her demand for "equality with regard to national security and the application of all the provisions of the treaty."

Her spokesman, Count Rudolf Nadolny, declaring that he must otherwise reject the resolution with which the conference plans to adjourn tomorrow, insisted repeatedly on "prompt and cleancut" recognition "without delay" of his principle of equality, which would be equivalent to scrapping the disarmament section of the Treaty of Versailles.

His formal statement concluded with this hint of practical concessions if recognition of the principle were obtained:

"In so far as different questions arising from the application of the principle of equality required clarification, the German Government was ready immediately to enter negotiations with the interested States."

Simon Prevents Clash.

Sir John Simon, the British Foreign Secretary, then stepped into the tense situation and in a brilliantly argued impromptu speech successfully sought to prevent the conference from blowing up in a Franco-German outbreak as the Interparliamentary Union's peace debate in an adjoining chamber had blown up a few hours before in a Franco-Italian tempest.

Sir John's method was to heap coals of fire suavely upon Germany's head by showing how much there was to be said in favor of the substance of her demand and how little in favor of her ultimatum method of trying to get it suddenly by leveling a pistol at the conference. His views were very similar to those heard in the corridor from the American delegates, who were clearly incensed by Germany's tactics.

Then the bulky figure of Premier Edouard Herriot of France filled the rostrum and the packed hall listened anxiously. For an hour eyes had been centred upon him, the only man in the room with the responsibility of a Premier carrying on a private meeting on the floor of the conference with the French delegation huddled around him.

Would he "shoot the works," people asked. Would he pull out the famous speech on Germany's secret arming that André Tardieu never delivered? Would he give the speech he had prepared before Count Nadolny spoke? Would he, in Sir John Simon's words, follow Count Nadolny's example and demand that the

Continued on Page Five.

Mayor to Give Views on Debt Service Next Week; $207,000,000 Item Is Second Largest in Budget

Before leaving City Hall last night, Mayor Walker said that he intended to speak next week on the subject of the city's debt service, which, next to the amount spent for salaries, is the largest item in the budget. It amounted to $207,000,000 of the $631,000,000 budget for 1932.

This was interpreted as direct confirmation of the statement printed in THE NEW YORK TIMES last Monday that the administration had under consideration modification of the Delaney plan for short-term bond financing of the city's subway construction work. The budget appropriations for the Delaney plan have run up to between $50,000,000 and $60,000,000.

Critics of the short-term financing policy have consistently held that elimination of the plan and conversion of the notes to long-term bonds would save some $25,000,000 in the succeeding tax budget. Were the plan to be suspended for one year, with the revolving fund of short-term notes lessened by $52,000,000 for that period, the reduction in the budget would be approximately $13,000,000 for the coming year, according to unofficial calculations last night.

While the administration has defended the plan as the sole means of saving the five-cent fare, the Mayor, in his forthcoming address, may, if the plan under contemplation calls merely for suspension of the plan for one year, point out that the fare is not endangered.

TWO DOMINIONS SEEK CURB ON ARGENTINA

South Africa and Australia Ask at Ottawa for Greater Trade Preferences From Britain.

COMMITTEES BEGIN WORK

Plan General Treaty for Empire and Group of Supplementary Pacts for Special Cases.

By CHARLES A. SELDEN.

Special to THE NEW YORK TIMES.

OTTAWA, July 22.—South Africa and Australia startled the Imperial Economic Conference here today with suggestions for greater preferences from Great Britain which would give them a large part of the meat trade now held by Argentina.

The suggestions were made immediately after the conference had split itself up into groups and committees and settled down to the work of considering the various proposals offered yesterday at the opening plenary session. There will be many other proposals next week, out of which the conference hopes to build a new economic system for the whole empire.

If they agree upon such a system there is no doubt about its being adopted, because the delegations of the nine British countries represented here are virtually the governments of those countries. They are all Ministers of Cabinets in political control of their Parliaments at home and they have plenary powers to negotiate and agree. It is not likely that whatever they agree on will be upset by legislative failure to ratify.

General Trade Pact Sought.

The program now is to formulate some general sort of trade treaty including all the self-governing countries of the empire. Also there probably will be a group of supplementary treaties within the general organic act. Some of these lesser treaties will be bilateral or include only three or four States and apply to trading

Continued on Page Four.

INDICTMENTS FOUND IN '3D DEGREE' DEATH

Grand Jurors Accuse Nassau Policemen of Murder and Assault in Stark Death.

SPECIAL COURT IS ORDERED

More Charges Expected When Hearings Resume on Tuesday —3 Tell of Being Beaten.

From a Staff Correspondent.

Special to THE NEW YORK TIMES.

MINEOLA, L. I., July 22.—The Nassau County grand jury, after two days' investigation into the death of Hyman Stark, an east side thug arrested last Friday on suspicion of beating and robbing a Nassau County detective's mother, handed up indictments tonight against a number of members of the Nassau County Police Department. These indictments contained charges ranging from second-degree murder to assault.

The indictments were handed up to County Judge Cortland A. Johnson and were immediately impounded. No inkling was given out as to the identity of the defendants but it was stipulated that all the accused men would be notified in time to appear and plead on Monday morning.

Rumors about the court house had it that the indictments were ratification of the charges levelled against county policemen by Supreme Court Justice Meier Steinbrink at the conclusion of a John Doe inquiry into the fatal beating of Stark.

Thirteen Had Been Accused.

Justice Steinbrink had ordered four of the suspected policemen held for second-degree murder. He issued warrants for one as an accessory and for seven other policemen on charges of second-degree assault. One other man was held on his order, together with all the others, for conspiracy to obstruct justice.

The grand jury has not completed its investigation. It is to meet again on Tuesday to consider charges of perjury against various members of the Police Department who testified before Justice Steinbrink. In rendering his decision, the Justice said that the policemen who testified before him had concealed the truth about Stark's death by means of "a conspiracy of silence" and "perjury."

All the indicted policemen are already under bail on warrants issued by Justice Steinbrink, who sat as a committing magistrate at John Doe proceedings instituted immediately after Stark's death. Because of this, no bench warrants were issued.

The indictments handed up tonight came after three of Stark's companions, survivors of the third degree which resulted fatally for him, had told their stories.

They were Alex Drangel, Alexander Feldman and Philip Cacala.

Special Term of Court Called.

While the grand jury was deliberating over these charges District Attorney Elvin N. Edwards made preparations to bring the accused men to trial at an early date. Defense attorneys at the same time made it clear that they would not be rushed to trial.

At the request of Mr. Edwards, however, the Appellate Division in Brooklyn assigned Supreme Court Justice John B. Johnston to preside over a special term of Supreme Court at Mineola, convening Aug. 8.

That the defense intends to block

Continued on Page Two.

Officer Survives Poison as Police of 2 States Hunt for Him to Warn of Drug-Store Error

Special to THE NEW YORK TIMES.

SEA GIRT, N. J., July 22.—After swallowing two tablets containing the wrong amount of strychnine Major George R. Koehler, a regular army instructor attached to the National Guard quarters at Camp Moore, arrived unworried in his quarters at 9:15 o'clock tonight unaware of the fact that New Jersey and New York State police had made a widespread search to warn him against taking the tablets.

Major Koehler received the tablets by mistake about 5 P. M. in a Paterson (N. J.) drug store, where he went with a physician's prescription calling for capsules for a nervous complaint. The New Jersey State police explained that the prescription called for a certain amount of strychnine, but that the content of this poison in the tablets was stronger than it would have been in the capsules.

When the Major left the drug store and started to drive back to camp with Sergeant Gerald Van Blaicom at the wheel of his machine the drug clerk discovered his error and notified Camp Moore authorities by telephone.

The word was flashed to State Police Headquarters at Trenton and from there a warning was flashed over the teletype system calling on all State troopers to be on the lookout for the Major's car with the license number S. G. 80.

About 8:30 P. M., when the Major's whereabouts were still unknown, the State police received a report that he was en route to the United States Military Academy at West Point, N. Y., where he had been in the habit of consulting medical officers. Accordingly, the teletype alarm was flashed to New York State police. Meanwhile West Point authorities took elaborate precautions, even halting a motion picture show to inquire if the Major were in the audience.

Three-quarters of an hour afterward the Major's car whisked into the grounds of Camp Moore. Major Koehler was astonished to learn that there had been "all this hullabaloo" about him. He said he had stopped for dinner in Keyport, N. J., between 7 and 8 P. M. and had taken two of the tablets after dinner without feeling any ill effects.

PERIL TO THE CITY IS SEEN

'No Taxes, No Municipal Government, No Civil Employes,' Says Mayor.

HINTS AT BANKERS' DEMAND

Declares Taxpayers Must Be Relieved in 1933 and That Levies Must Be Slashed.

URGES VOLUNTARY ACTION

Order in Radio Speech to Aides to Ascertain Workers' Sentiment Contains Threat.

The text of Mayor Walker's plea for city pay cuts is on Page 3.

Mayor Walker told the city's 147,000 employes in a radio address last night that their next year's pay must be cut 8 1-3 per cent or the city would face "embarrassment, if not a defunct condition." The pay cut, which he asked them to accept voluntarily, would be in the form a deduction of a month's pay from their 1933 salaries, and would amount to $26,000,000.

It would be better to have a reduced pay check than no pay check at all, he told them. He painted a picture of the plight of the city's taxpayers, who in some cases, he said, were unable to realize from their property enough to meet the taxes that keep the city's government going.

"No taxes, no government, no city employes," was the way the Mayor phrased it.

Warns of Legislative Action.

The pay cut will be voluntary in theory. The Mayor explained at length that no power rested in the Board of Estimate to change the salaries of about 60 per cent of those on the city payroll. But, he threatened repeatedly in the course of his forty-five-minute speech, that if the city employes did not agree, they would find their salaries cut by action of the Legislature.

If the reduction is made by the Legislature, it will be years before it is restored, and the pension status of employes will have suffered as well, Mr. Walker said. However, he added, if the cut is voluntary, the higher level of pay can be restored in a year or two when the depression is over.

Were the Board of Estimate to impose a pay cut on the employes whose salaries are not fixed by law, only 39 per cent, or 56,000 employes, would be affected. These, the Mayor declared, would be in the high payroll brackets of employes exempt from civil service, and in the lowest brackets, affecting nurses, hospital attendants and employes whose salaries run down from $3,000 a year to $450 a year.

The Mayor indicated that per diem employes, mostly laborers, would have the 8 1-3 per cent deducted directly from their pay checks, as the easiest way of collecting the cut.

Of the $631,000,000 city budget for 1932, $312,000,000, or 49.9 per cent, was for personal service, "the payroll," the Mayor declared.

Orders Poll of Workers.

The Mayor ordered the heads of the city's departments, assembled before him in the Board of Estimate Chamber at City Hall, to poll their employes to find out whether they will accept the cut, or whether they wanted it forced on them by the Legislature. He added, with another implied threat, that he wanted them also to report to him who would accept the cut, and who would not.

Assembled in the Board of Estimate chamber to hear the address was an imposing array of the city's higher-paid officials. Conspicuously absent, however, was Controller Berry, the city's fiscal officer, who, earlier in the day, said he saw no reason why he should be present, his advice on economy having been disregarded by the Mayor. Aldermanic President McKee also was absent, due to a prior engagement.

City commissioners, their deputies, judges and magistrates, all were there. Outside the hall, however, there was no such imposing array of expensive automobiles as there was earlier this year, when the Mayor told the department heads the budget for 1933 must be reduced. The cars were sent away from

Continued on Page Three.

"All the News That's Fit to Print."

The New York Times.

LATE CITY EDITION
WEATHER—Thunder showers and cooler today; tomorrow fair.
Temperatures Yesterday—Max., 86; Min., 69.

VOL. LXXXI....No. 27,215. Entered as Second-Class Matter, Postoffice, New York, N. Y. NEW YORK, FRIDAY, JULY 29, 1932. ****+ TWO CENTS In New York City | THREE CENTS Within 200 Miles | FOUR CENTS Elsewhere Except in 7th and 8th Postal Zones

WALKER REPLY A DENIAL OF ALL SEABURY CHARGES; CALLS 10 OF 15 OUTLAWED

GOVERNOR TO ACT QUICKLY

Turns Answer Over to His Advisers—New Move Expected in Week.

POLITICAL PLOT IS CHARGED

Mayor Says He Is the Victim of a Campaign of Calumny to Aid Hoover Regime.

DEFENDS EQUITABLE DEALS

Declares Men Who Gave Him Cash Got No Favors—Denies Sherwood Was Agent.

The text of Mayor's reply to Gov. Roosevelt, Pages 6, 7 and 8.

Terming himself the victim of political misrepresentation, and insisting that his entire official life would bear the closest scrutiny, Mayor Walker filed with Governor Roosevelt yesterday his answer to the removal charges pending against him as the result of allegations first made by Samuel Seabury, counsel to the Hofstadter committee.

The Mayor's answer, a 27,000-word document, contained specific denials of wrongdoing in connection with the Equitable Bus franchise, the receipt of securities from brokerage firms interested in taxicab legislation, the "benificences" of Paul Block, publisher, or the huge bank accounts of Russell T. Sherwood, missing accountant. The document came from the printers yesterday forenoon, and was given at once to Thomas F. McAndrews, the Mayor's secretary, who carried it by train to the Governor at Albany.

Mr. Roosevelt, after scrutinizing it briefly, released the reply for publication. A conference between the Governor and his two legal advisers, Martin Conboy of New York and John E. Mack of Poughkeepsie, will probably be held in the near future, it was indicated, to determine the next step in the removal case that, it is held, cannot but affect the political fortunes of Mr. Roosevelt as the Democratic Presidential nominee.

Seabury Is Denounced.

In form the Mayor's answer consisted of an attack upon Mr. Seabury and the Hofstadter committee, before which the evidence against the Mayor was developed, followed by a point-by-point reply to the allegations made by Mr. Seabury and subsequently embodied in charges filed with the Governor by William Jay Schieffelin, head of the New York Committee of One Thousand.

Two appendices contained an answer to the separate and supplementary charges filed by James E. Finegan, Brooklyn Democrat, and legal citations and details on financial transactions covered in the main body of the answer.

Most of the legal citations were to support the Mayor's assertion that ten of the fifteen allegations advanced by Mr. Seabury related to a previous term in office, and therefore could not be made the basis of action at present by the Governor. The answer, however, also replied in detail to these allegations.

Mayor Walker did not mention Mr. Seabury's statement that the Mayor had a "metallic receptacle" in his home, where he put cash received in stock and bond deals, nor did he mention the "unnamed person" said to have received payments from both the Mayor and from Sherwood.

The payments to the unnamed person were stressed at committee hearings as tending to prove a connection between the bank accounts of Sherwood and the Mayor. Mr. Walker in his reply denied Sherwood was his financial agent.

Calls Inquiry Political Plot.

The Mayor declared that the Hofstadter committee was organized and Mr. Seabury retained as counsel "to carry out a deliberate plan of calumny" in the hope of discrediting the Democratic administration of New York City. He accused Mr. Seabury of conducting a "manhunt," and declared the counsel would have fixed upon any Democratic Mayor of New York as a victim, in order to divert attention from the shortcom-

Continued on Page Eight.

Walker Hastens to Saranac; Gets Word Brother Is Worse

Mayor Walker left on a midnight train for Saranac Lake last night, after he had received a call at City Hall informing him that the condition of his brother, George F. Walker, had taken a sudden turn for the worse.

The brother, the youngest of the three Walker brothers, has been a patient at a Saranac sanitarium for several months, and in the past few days his condition has been a source of worry to the Mayor. A request had been made at City Hall, however, that no publicity be given to the illness of the Mayor's brother, until developments forced it.

George Walker is 48 years old, is married, and has two children. He is in the insurance business, being a member of the firm of Hughes & Walker of 27 William Street.

COOLIDGE EXPECTED TO AID HOOVER DRIVE

Sanders to Spend Week-End at Former President's Vermont Home for Political Talk.

NO EASTERN MANAGER YET

Senator Hebert Is Likely to Be Named to Run Campaign in This Section.

The probability that former President Calvin Coolidge will aid President Hoover in his campaign for re-election was indicated yesterday when Everett Sanders, chairman of the Republican National Committee, said that he would visit Mr. Coolidge Saturday and Sunday at the Coolidge homestead at Plymouth Notch, Vt., and expected to discuss the political situation with him.

Mr. Sanders, who was secretary to Mr. Coolidge when he was President, declined to be definite, because the invitation to visit his former chief came before he had been elected national chairman.

"I have no doubt he will take some part in the campaign," Mr. Sanders said, when asked if he expected Mr. Coolidge to make some campaign speeches for the President.

Mr. Sanders said that there had been no selection yet of an Eastern campaign manager and indicated that the choice was between Senator Felix Hebert of Rhode Island and Earl S. Kinsley, national committeeman from Vermont. From other sources it was learned that Senator Hebert probably would be named. Should Senator Hebert not be named for this post he will be the Eastern campaign manager for the Republican Senatorial Committee, Mr. Sanders said.

Mr. Sanders also indicated that General Edward Martin, who was under consideration for Eastern campaign manager, had found his duties in Pennsylvania too exacting to take on additional responsibility. General Martin, besides being active in military affairs, is the Pennsylvania State treasurer and chairman of the Republican State Committee.

Mr. Sanders had a luncheon conference with W. Kingsland Macy, New York State Republican chairman, and earlier in the day conferred with Charles D. Hilles, national committeeman, and former Governor Henry J. Allen of Kansas, publicity director of the national committee.

Asked to make a prediction on New York State, Mr. Sanders said:

"I am very confident that the President will be re-elected, but I do not wish to discuss his chance of carrying the different States."

One point of difficulty in the Republican campaign situation in this State has been cleared up by the recent visit to Washington of Mr. Macy and conferences here with Mr. Sanders, as a result of which it has been decided that the Republican State Committee will be in complete charge of the campaign in this State and that there will be no Hoover campaign committee as there was in 1928.

Sought to Supersede Macy.

Members of the so-called Hooverite group in this State suggested the re-establishment of the Hoover campaign committee and some members of the group went so far as to make suggestions which, if adopted, virtually would have put the officers of the proposed Hoover campaign committee in charge of the campaign and

Continued on Page Thirteen.

Thousands Crowding Into Los Angeles For Opening of Olympic Games Tomorrow

By ALLISON DANZIG.
Special to THE NEW YORK TIMES.

LOS ANGELES, July 28.—The biggest migration to California since the Forty-niners wrote an imperishable story of man's courage in braving the perils of the unknown has made Los Angeles the cosmopolitan capital of the world.

Not for a pot of gold at the end of the covered wagon trail has this world exodus to the jewel city of Southern California taken place, but for the tenth revival of the Olympic Games, which begin here on Saturday, with approximately 2,000 representatives of thirty-eight countries competing in an athletic plant that dwarfs the imagination, along with the coliseums and stadiums of the ancient Greeks and Romans.

Already, with the spectacular grand opening parade forty-eight hours away, there are thousands of visitors encamped in Los Angeles and its environs.

By railroad, plane, ship and motor car they continue to pour into the city and no one knows what sagas of enterprise and fortitude are being written on the national highways by athletic zealots who have seized upon the most desperately dilapidated means of conveyance to bring them to the games.

Los Angeles, festooned and bedecked with flags, streamers and banners of welcome to all within its domain, is assimilating this tremendous influx of people in the same ample fashion that it has prepared, over a period of nine years, to stage this tremendous athletic carnival, the first Olympiad to be held in this country since 1904.

With its enormous hotel capacity, it is well prepared to accommodate the great burden of humanity resting within its confines and thus far there is no overcrowding or dearth of reservations.

So far as it has been possible to ascertain, there has been no mark-up in the rates for rooms, nor have prices in the restaurants or else-

Continued on Page Nineteen.

BRITAIN ASKS EMPIRE FOR MORE PURCHASES TO BALANCE HER AID

Baldwin Says United Kingdom Imports Exceeded Exports by £95,700,000 in 1930.

RHODESIA FILES DEMAND

British In Drive at Ottawa to Capture United States Sales of Machinery in Canada.

The text of Britain's trade statement is on Page 10.

By CHARLES A. SELDEN.
Special to THE NEW YORK TIMES.

OTTAWA, July 28.—Two more cards were placed face up on the Imperial Economic Conference table today when Stanley Baldwin, leader of the British delegation, presented a statement plainly intimating to the dominions that in his opinion they were lagging behind the United Kingdom in the mutual exchange of trade benefits and H. W. Moffatt, spokesman for Southern Rhodesia, filed a request that Britain help his country by buying more of its cattle.

The statement of the United Kingdom contained neither threat nor promise of what Great Britain would or would not do after the dominions have agreed upon what they can or cannot do for the mother country. It confined itself to what the United Kingdom already had done for the rest of the empire and showed by figures that she was buying from them annually £100,000,000 worth of goods in excess of what they were buying from her.

Advantages Are Contrasted.

Mr. Baldwin called attention to the fact that practically all of the dominion products were admitted to the ports of Great Britain free of duty, whereas British exports to the dominions had only the benefit of preferences. Although the preferences are much better than nothing, Mr. Baldwin considers them far less of a boon than free entry. He spoke particularly of the fact that even preferences may be based on tariffs so high that they restrict imports.

He did not refer to the fact, fully and painfully realized at Ottawa by all the dominion delegations, that after Nov. 15 the United Kingdom may deprive them of all the benefits of free entry which the empire countries now enjoy by simply applying to them the new British tariff act. That is England's trump card at this conference, which she may play to get from the dominions the trade concessions and preferences she thinks are just and fair.

Although no threats were made today nor even hinted, the British statement added nothing to the harmony of the conference and no doubt the dominions considered it as a rebuke, which they all think undeserved in spite of the figures that support it.

Denies Witholding Assistance.

Perhaps Stanley M. Bruce, leader of the Australian delegation, felt personally rebuked. He told the conference the other day that Great Britain had been tardy in recognition of all the preferences the dominions had given her. No doubt Mr. Baldwin had that remark definitely in mind today when he said:

"Any suggestion that the United Kingdom has been backward in developing or assisting dominion trade or that the concessions on the side of the dominions have not been fully reciprocated, both in the letter and

Continued on Page Ten.

HERRIOT PROTESTS SCHLEICHER SPEECH; EDITORS ATTACK IT

Premier Summons Germany's Envoy to Tell Him Arms Talk Disturbs France.

CITES HIS FRIENDLY POLICY

Description of French Stand as "Hypocritical" Results in Bitter Resentment.

By P. J. PHILIP.
Wireless to THE NEW YORK TIMES.

PARIS, July 28.—Premier Edouard Herriot summoned the German Ambassador, Dr. Leopold von Hoesch, to the Quai d'Orsay today to explain to him vigorously that the French people are considerably disturbed by the terms of Lieut. Gen. Kurt von Schleicher's radio speech Tuesday evening, in which he gave notice that Germany would arm, if necessary, contrary to the provisions of the Versailles treaty, and also attacked France.

M. Herriot's protest was the second the Reich Government has received in two days, for Ambassador André François-Poncet called at the Wilhelmstrasse in Berlin yesterday to make formal denial of some statements made by the German Defense Minister.

In the Paris press the substance of General von Schleicher's statement is the subject of strong comment today, but all that either Premier Herriot or the French Ambassador could do was to point out that its form was distinctly impolitic, not to say impolite.

Says He Went Too Far.

Even in the midst of the German electoral period, M. Herriot is believed to have told Dr. von Hoesch that it was going too far for a Minister of the Reich to make such a speech only a few weeks after the conclusion of the Lausanne agreement, in which France showed the utmost generosity to Germany and had abandoned all claim to further reparations payments.

It was even less opportune, it was pointed out, for the German Defense Minister to speak as he did within twenty-four hours of the time when

Continued on Page Eleven.

Stocks Rise Again in Year's Heaviest Trading; 2,735,635 Shares Sold, Leaders Up 1 to 4 Points

Invigorated by fresh optimism, the security markets made another broad advance yesterday. The day's transactions in stocks on the New York Stock Exchange totaled 2,735,635 shares, which represented the heaviest trading since Dec. 18 of last year. The net gains in market leaders ranged from 1 to 4 points, while there were scattered advances of 6 points or more.

In the bond market the net gains were widest among domestic corporation issues, running from 3 to 10 points in the conspicuously strong favorites. The extreme gain of 10 points occurred in Schulco 6½s, due in 1946, Series B. United Biscuit 6s, due 1942, were up 6½ points, Purity Bakeries 5s, due 1948, were up 6 points; Allis Chalmers 6s, due 1937, gained 4½; Atchison, Topeka & Santa Fe bonds showed a maximum gain of 6 points; Atlantic Coast Line issues advanced as much as 7 points and Bethlehem Steel 5s of 1936 rose 4⅝ points. Dealings in bonds were the heaviest in a month.

Aside from a further demonstration of strength in commodities, the development which contributed most to the cheerfulness in Wall Street was a spectacular rise of the dollar in terms of foreign currencies which reflected the further reinforcement of the gold position of the United States. Sterling fell 2¾ cents, while the French franc was off 7-16 point. All the other Continental currencies except the mark, which was unchanged, lost ground.

The upswing in stock prices was most striking in the forenoon. Profit-taking at midday and in the last hour reduced the early gains to some extent, but final prices showed substantial net appreciation in the average. For instance, Allied Chemical was up 3 points on the day; American Telephone, the market leader, closed with a net gain of 4⅜ points after falling more than a point from its high; Santa Fe preferred was up 4⅛ points and the common 2¾, Bangor & Aroostock 7½, Detroit Edison 10, du Pont 2¼, Norfolk & Western 3¼ and Eastman 1⅝. United States Steel common touched a high of 28½, but closed at 27⅝ with a small fractional gain. Steel preferred was up ¾ point after falling 2 points from its high.

Bank stocks again advanced vigorously, the bid price of First National showing a gain of 25 points and that of the Fifth Avenue 40 points.

TROOPS DRIVE VETERANS FROM CAPITAL; FIRE CAMPS THERE AND AT ANACOSTIA; 1 KILLED, SCORES HURT IN DAY OF STRIFE

ANACOSTIA CAMP NO MORE

Troops Move Into Last Bonus Army Refuge as Flames Start.

AND FINISH DESTRUCTION

Marchers Stream Away, Some in Broken-Down Autos, Some Trudging Afoot.

FEW KNEW WHITHER TO GO

At Midnight the Former Home of 20,000 of Bonus Army Is Held by the Military.

Special to THE NEW YORK TIMES.

WASHINGTON, July 28.—Flames rose high over the desolate Anacostia flats at midnight tonight and a pitiful stream of refugee veterans of the World War walked out of their home of the past two months, going they knew not where.

Cavalry stood guard at all the bridges leading across the river to the camp and thousands of onlookers gazed across the river at what had been the teeming residence of 20,000 persons.

The veterans were leaving at the behest of the military forces of the government, summoned by the President after collisions between the bonus marchers and the police. Some were departing in broken-down automobiles; some, on foot, dragged listlessly in search of new quarters.

Flames were raging in the camp. Many of the tents, numbering 2,100 and mostly belonging to the army, were ablaze and the infantry was busy trying to salvage as many as possible.

A heavy barrage of tear gas, laid down by the troops, penetrated to the houses for blocks around, and residents were forced to close their doors and windows in spite of the sweltering heat.

Had Thirty Minutes to Evacuate.

It was soon after 9 o'clock tonight that the troops, headed by General MacArthur, surrounded the main camp of the Bonus Expeditionary Force at Anacostia, wheeled their tanks into position, unlimbered their gas bombs and gave the thousands of veterans massed there thirty minutes in which to evacuate. They then sat down waiting for the order to be obeyed.

The spirit of the veterans seemed broken. Leaderless and aghast at the failure of their confident prediction that no soldier would go into action against them, they moved their women and children out of the camp and prepared to leave themselves.

General MacArthur and his staff followed the first troop of cavalry into the field at Anacostia through a road leading off from the bridge.

Several veterans, as they heard the troops approach, set fire to improvised huts. The glow from the

Continued on Page Three.

Text of Hoover's Statement on Call for Troops To Put an End to Bonus Rioting in the Capital

Special to THE NEW YORK TIMES.

WASHINGTON, July 28.—The text of President Hoover's statement explaining his action in calling out troops to combat the bonus rioters is as follows:

For some days police authorities and Treasury officials have been endeavoring to persuade the so-called bonus marchers to evacuate certain buildings which they were occupying without permission.

These buildings are on sites where government construction is in progress and their demolition was necessary in order to extend employment in the district and to carry forward the government's construction program.

This morning the occupants of these buildings were notified to evacuate and at the request of the police did evacuate the buildings concerned. Thereafter, however, several thousand men from different camps marched in and attacked the police with brickbats and otherwise injuring several policemen, one probably fatally.

I have received the attached letter from the Commissioners of the District of Columbia, stating that they can no longer preserve law and order in the district.

In order to put an end to this rioting and defiance of civil authority, I have asked the army to assist the District authorities to restore order.

Congress made provision for the return home of the so-called bonus marchers, who have for many weeks been given every opportunity of free assembly, free speech and free petition to the Congress. Some 5,000 took advantage of this arrangement and have returned to their homes. An examination of a large number of names discloses the fact that a considerable part of those remaining are not veterans; many are Communists and persons with criminal records.

The veterans amongst these numbers are no doubt unaware of the character of their companions and are being led into violence which no government can tolerate.

I have asked the Attorney General to investigate the whole incident and to cooperate with the District civil authorities in such measures against leaders and rioters as may be necessary.

[The text of the letter from the District Commissioners to the President is printed elsewhere.]

BOMBS AND SABRES WIN CAPITAL BATTLE

Cavalry, Infantry and Tanks, Advancing as Gas Spreads, Swiftly Drive Veterans.

SHACKS BURN BEHIND THEM

Bayonets Clear the Section of Squatters, Who Are Ringed Finally by 1,500 Soldiers.

Special to THE NEW YORK TIMES.

WASHINGTON, July 28.—The Federal troops came out today and cleared Washington proper of the members of the Bonus Expeditionary Force. The cantonments, the "forts" in the unused Federal buildings, the huts that the men themselves had built, were evacuated by the veterans when they found themselves faced with tear-gas bombs, bayonets and tanks.

The regulars had the equipment to do the job, the equipment that the Capitol Police had lacked and they had the orders to do it. The irregulars of the bonus army had only their stubborn sullenness in most cases and bricks, rocks and epithets in others and the fight did not last long.

Down Pennsylvania Avenue at 4:30 this afternoon the regulars came, cavalry leading the way, and after them the tanks, the machine-gunners and the infantry. For them the objective was the "fort" of the B. E. F., in the skeletonized building at Third Street.

There was a wait for maybe half an hour while the army officers talked it over with the police and the bonus marchers shouted defiance. They wanted action, and they got it.

Steady Sweep Down Avenue.

Twenty steel-helmeted soldiers led the way, with revolvers in their hands, and others advanced until about 200 were in position in front of the "bonus fort." Then the mounted men joined. They rode down street, clearing the path with their sabers, striking those within reach with the flat of the blades.

The action was precise, well executed from a military standpoint, but not pretty to the thoughtful in the crowd. There were those who resisted the troops, fought back, cursed and kicked at the horses; there were those who scrambled for safety and those who tried to rescue their meager belongings from the fort.

Inch by inch, foot by foot, they were forced down Pennsylvania Avenue as the soldiers headed them toward Anacostia camp. They left in their path those who had been knocked over, and one passive resister, who sat down and waited unscathed while the storm blew over his head.

The success of the movement, the

Continued on Page Three.

B.E.F. TO CARRY ON, WATERS DECLARES

Men Will Organize Elsewhere if Driven From Capital, Commander Says.

WHITE HOUSE IS ASSAILED

'Political Interests' Cost a Life, He Charges, Admitting He Has Lost Control.

By The Associated Press.

WASHINGTON, July 28.—Walter W. Waters, titular commander of the "Bonus Expeditionary Force," declared tonight that "no matter what may happen from now on, the B. E. F. will carry on."

"If driven from Washington, it will organize elsewhere and continue the fight for justice for the veterans and the common people of the United States" he said in a statement. "We have gone too far now to quit."

The Waters declaration, telephoned to newspaper offices, included the assertion that a life was sacrificed "to serve the political interests of the administration."

The one-time dictator of the bonus army watched from the sidelines while the men who formerly paid him allegiance swept completely out of his control.

Before Federal troops arrived to push former service men off their encampments in front of a cloud of tear gas, "Commander" Waters threw up his hands in a gesture of defeat. He said frankly that he no longer had any control over the men.

Accompanied by a handful of his aides, Waters viewed from the sidewalks about the trouble-ridden area the swiftly breaking developments, which resulted in the death of a war veteran.

Just before arrival of the troops, he went to a small restaurant on Pennsylvania Avenue for a cup of coffee.

Asked about the day's happenings he replied:

"The men got completely out of control. There was nothing and is nothing I can do to control them."

In his statement later he said:

"Every drop of blood shed today or that may be shed in days to come as the result of today's events can be laid directly on the threshold of the White House.

"The B. E. F. had been organized on strictly American lines of respect for law and order and is pledged to uphold American institutions.

"They were under strictest orders to conduct themselves in orderly manner in the event of attempted

Continued on Page Two.

HOOVER ORDERS EVICTION

Blaming Reds, He Asserts Bonus Camps Included Many Criminals.

QUICK ACTION BY SOLDIERS

Eject Squatters After Police Fail and Then Burn Camps In and Near Capital.

BONUS ARMY SCATTERED

Demoralized by Soldiers' Gas Attack, Remnants Are Left Leaderless and Helpless.

Special to THE NEW YORK TIMES.

WASHINGTON, July 28.—Amidst scenes reminiscent of the mopping-up of a town in the World War, Federal troops late today drove the army of bonus seekers from the shanty village near Pennsylvania Avenue in which the veterans had been entrenched for months. Earlier in the day the police had fought and lost a battle there which resulted in the death of one veteran, possibly fatal injuries to a policeman and a long list of other casualties, many of them serious.

Ordered to the scene by President Hoover after the District of Columbia authorities confessed defeat, detachments of infantry, cavalry, machine-gun and tank crews laid down an effective tear-gas barrage which disorganized the bonus-seekers, and then set fire to the shacks and tents left behind by the veterans on the government land near Third and Pennsylvania Avenues, scene of the earlier clash with the police.

Begin to Clear Anacostia.

After the disputed area near the Capitol had been cleared, the troops moved late in the evening on Camp Marks, on the Anacostia River, the bonus army's principal encampment. At 10 o'clock this evening infantrymen with drawn bayonets advanced into the camp, driving the crowd before them with tear gas bombs. Then they applied the torch to the shacks in which the veterans lived.

Troops shortly afterward halted at the main bonus camp in response to what General Perry L. Miles, commanding the soldiers, said was a Presidential order. Theodore G. Joslin, the President's secretary, later denied positively that the President had issued any such order, and word came from the camp that the troops would resume operations within an hour.

At 11:15 P. M. the first troop of cavalry had moved into the disordered camp, now a mass of flames as the bonus-seeking veterans set fire to their own miserable shacks. At midnight practically all the veterans had left the place.

Warr[illegible] that the soldiers would use tear gas the veterans had arranged to evacuate the 600 women and children earlier.

The normal population of Camp Marks was augmented by more than 2,000 veterans who had been evicted from other camps, bringing the total male population to 7,000.

Troops Avoid Bloodshed.

Soon after the khaki-clad regulars descended on the various camps along Pennsylvania Avenue this afternoon the bonus seekers were straggling sullenly away from the ominous blue mist of the tear gas, leaderless and apparently demoralized, seeking shelter in other open places scattered afar through the city. A few of them were sore from minor bruises, but on the whole the Federal troops had conducted their offensive without bloodshed. The veteran who was killed in the earlier clash with the police was identified tonight as William Hashka of Chicago.

The day's disturbances were blamed on the radical element among the bonus-seekers. Walter W. Waters, the young veteran from Oregon who led the unsuccessful bonus march to Washington, disclaimed responsibility for his followers' part in resisting the first eviction order of the police. Waters announced tonight that he was "through."

"The men got out of control. There was nothing and there is nothing that I can do to control them," he said.

With the bonus army in the city

Continued on Page Two.

The New York City contingent of the Bonus Army left for Washington, D.C., on June 4.

MAP OF THE BONUS FIGHT IN THE NATIONAL CAPITAL.

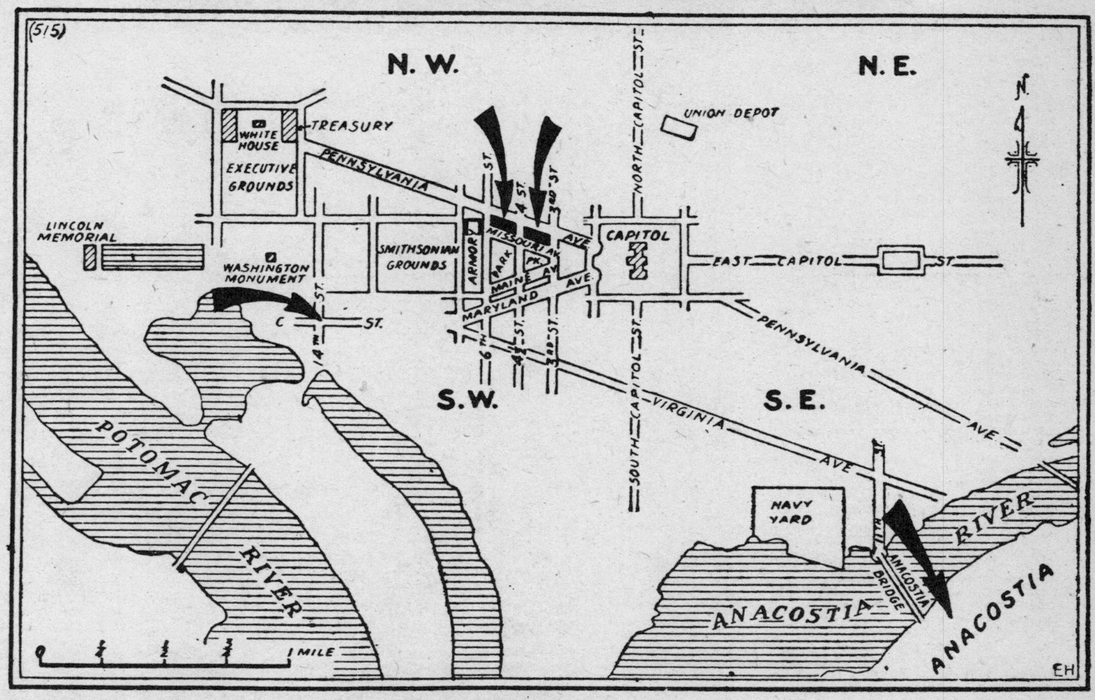

Showing the Streets of Washington Through Which the Police and the Troops Fought the Veterans. Arrows Mark Sites of the Veterans' Camps.

Veterans marching toward the White House to demand their bonus.

Camp Marks, which had housed 20,000 bonus marchers, was set afire by the Army and burned through the night.

These bonus marchers were driven from their shacks by soldiers wearing gas masks.

General Douglas MacArthur, Chief of Staff of the Army, was under President Hoover's orders to get rid of the bonus marchers who had remained in Washington.

"All the News That's Fit to Print."

The New York Times.

LATE CITY EDITION
WEATHER—Fair today; tomorrow fair and slightly warmer.
Temperatures Yesterday—Max., 84; Min., 68.

Copyright, 1932, by The New York Times Company.

VOL. LXXXI....No. 27,216. Entered as Second-Class Matter, Postoffice, New York, N. Y. NEW YORK, SATURDAY, JULY 30, 1932. **** TWO CENTS In New York City | THREE CENTS Within 200 Miles | FOUR CENTS Elsewhere Except 7th and 8th Postal Zones

CURTIS TODAY OPENS THE OLYMPIC GAMES IN COLORFUL SCENE

100,000 Expected to See the Vice President Officiate in Place of Hoover.

PRESIDENT SENDS MESSAGE

Los Angeles Seethes With Excitement as Athletes of 39 Nations Await Start.

ANCIENT RITES REVIVED

2,000 Young Men and Women to Parade in Costume Before Oath-Taking Ritual.

By ALLISON DANZIG.
Special to THE NEW YORK TIMES.

LOS ANGELES, July 29.—At 3:30 o'clock tomorrow afternoon [7:30 New York Daylight Saving Time] Vice President Charles Curtis, representing President Hoover and the nation, will formally open the tenth revival of the Olympic Games.

Arriving by train from Washington this morning, Mr. Curtis was acclaimed by a cheering throng at the station. A parade through the gayly bedecked streets, which are now fairly seething with excitement on the eve of the biggest day in Los Angeles history, followed.

Mr. Curtis tendered a formal statement from the President in which Mr. Hoover expressed his regret that he would be unable to attend the games, extended his cordial greetings to all those gathered here and sent his encouragement and best wishes to the athletes of this country.

Message From President.

The message from President Hoover follows:

"Will you please extend my cordial greetings to all those gathered at Los Angeles for the opening of the Olympic Games, and also my hearty welcome to our visitors from abroad. I deeply regret that I am unable to be present, for I had looked forward with eagerness to the pleasure of seeing those wonderful sports and also to visiting my home State.

"In the years since the Olympics were held in America for the first time at St. Louis, they have grown steadily in the interest of all the nations, until today they occupy at least as great a significance in our world as the original Olympic Games occupied in the ancient world, when Greece was at the height of its glory. They have become a positive force for international acquaintance and understanding and good-will.

"They teach that the hardest competition may be accompanied by good humor and that rivalry may be expressed with good sportsmanship. I warmly hope that the games may be in every way successful. Especially do I send my encouragements and best wishes to our American athletes."

More than a hundred thousand spectators are expected to fill the huge coliseum in Exposition Park tomorrow when the Vice President assists in the stirring inaugural ceremonies of the biggest athletic festival ever promoted in this country, an undertaking staged on so colossal a scale as to make the ancient forerunners of these world championship games dwindle by comparison into rustic assemblages of the scope of the democratic Greek agora.

Mr. Curtis will speak these words in behalf of President Hoover:

"I proclaim open the Olympic Games of Los Angeles, celebrating the tenth Olympiad of the modern era."

To Parade in Costume.

Two thousand young men and women athletes, a group such as would rejoice the hearts of Phidias and Praxiteles, representing the survivors of the Nietzschean ordeals of the fittest held in thirty-nine countries, will parade in costume on the greensward of the stadium in the time-honored ritual of the grand march on the administration of the Olympic oath.

The opening of the games having been proclaimed to the fanfare of trumpets and the roar of cannon, Lieutenant George C. Calnan of the United States Navy, a member of the Olympic fencing team for the fourth time, will step up before the Vice President and the tribune of honor.

Holding the corner of the Stars and Stripes, carried by F. Morgan Taylor of Quincy, Ill., the American flagbearer, and with the flagbearers of the other competing nations standing in a semicircle behind him, Lieutenant Calnan will take the oath voicing the creed of true sportsmanship on behalf of the entire army of athletes, drawn up in deep columns on the green oval within the running track.

Such will be the exalted prologue to the raising of the curtain on Sunday on the most kaleidoscopic sporting canvas painted by man. In spite of the tremendous burden which the

Continued on Page Ten.

Spain Sees League Weakened By New Anglo-French Accord

Wireless to THE NEW YORK TIMES.

MADRID, July 29.—Leaders of the Spanish Government believe that with the adhesion of other European nations to the Anglo-French consultative pact the importance of the League of Nations as a place for the heads of States to talk things over has been greatly diminished.

Luis de Zulueta, Minister of State, said today the consultative pact offered a good means to get together to talk over affairs, but added that Spain would not have entered anything she thought would weaken the League, of which she is a member. Other officials said the pact upsets the old European way of doing things and that if nations like Spain talk things over outside Geneva they cannot fail to weaken the League.

Señor de Zulueta said Spanish adhesion to the pact was merely "a graceful gesture" and denied it implied a union of Europe against the United States.

REICH CABINET FIRM ON THREAT TO ARM

French Envoy Is Told That the Great Majority of Germans Also Back von Schleicher.

PAPEN BARS A DICTATORSHIP

Speaks to America on Radio—Bruening Acclaimed—Post-Election Truce Decreed.

By FREDERICK T. BIRCHALL.
Special Cable to THE NEW YORK TIMES.

BERLIN, July 29.—André François-Poncet, the French Ambassador, who called on Foreign Minister von Neurath after the address on the radio by Lieut. Gen. von Schleicher Tuesday night, departed in no doubt that the German Government was squarely behind the utterances of its Defense Minister, a semi-official bulletin today revealed.

In his talk General von Schleicher assailed the "hypocrisy" of the French attitude on arms and asserted that the German Government was absolutely determined to reorganize the army so as to obtain a certain degree of security if the other nations did not disarm.

Today's bulletin also made it known that M. François-Poncet was told that General von Schleicher's declaration of Germany's determination to help herself to such privileges in connection with her defensive resources as treaties did not positively forbid also reflected the views of the overwhelming majority of the German people.

Police Mobilized for Election.

The entire Berlin police force has been ordered mobilized for forty-eight-hour service beginning at noon tomorrow to insure an orderly Reichstag election Sunday. Parades and all outdoor demonstrations for election day have been banned and the sale of hard liquor has been stopped. This is the answer of the authorities to rumors that the National Socialists, if disappointed may start disturbances, which would appear highly improbable.

In view of the probable failure of either the Right or the Left to obtain a clear majority, a ten-day post-election truce was decreed tonight by President von Hindenburg to enable the parties to sift the returns calmly and occupy themselves with negotiation for the formation of a coalition.

All political meetings and outdoor demonstrations have been banned for the duration of this armistice, effective Monday, which the President hopes will allow the passions aroused in the furious campaign of the past six weeks to subside.

Similar truces have been proclaimed

Continued on Page Two.

CITY FIREMEN FIGHT 'VOLUNTARY' PAY CUT; DORMAN ORDERS POLL

1,500 at Meeting Demand That Complete Economy Program Be Submitted First.

CHARGE OF GAGGING LEADER

Secretary of Uniformed Group Says President Was Told He Must Not Address Men.

BALLOTS ARE DISTRIBUTED

Commissioners, After Opposition Arises, Instructs Slips Be Signed and Returned by Wednesday.

Mayor Walker's proposal of a voluntary cut in the salaries of city employes received its first serious setback yesterday. It became known that the sentiment among the members of the Uniformed Firemen's Association was against the plan. The association includes in its ranks virtually the entire personnel of the Fire Department.

The fact became known yesterday after a conference between heads of the association and Fire Commissioner John J. Dorman. James F. Chambers, business secretary of the association, issued a statement revealing that at a meeting attended by 1,500 members, last Tuesday, sentiment was clearly against the cut, and that "hasty action" was averted only when the matter was deferred for thirty days by the officers of the association.

Dorman Acts Quickly.

However, when Commissioner Dorman left his office early in the afternoon he gave orders that distribution of ballots to the fire houses was to begin last night and that the ballots must be signed, marked and returned to headquarters by next Wednesday. A subordinate made this announcement on behalf of the Commissioner.

When asked what would happen if the uniformed men insisted on the full period of thirty days for consideration of the pay cut plan, the subordinate said:

"They can't do that. If they fail to comply with this order, signed by the commissioner, it would amount to insubordination."

The city's firemen and policemen received substantial pay increases as a result of a referendum held at the same time as the 1929 Mayoralty election. Refusal to take the pay cut would force the administration to do what the Mayor has tried to avoid—request the Legislature to make the reductions possible.

The president of the Uniformed Firemen's Association is Vincent J. Kane. Reporters went to his office in the Pulitzer Building, after getting Mr. Chambers's statement, and were met by Mr. Chambers.

"Mr. ane can't see you," Mr. Chambers said. "He has been gagged. He is not allowed to talk to reporters and he has even been ordered not to address the firemen or discuss the cut."

Asks Economy Program First.

Mr. Chambers is not a member of the Fire Department, being a civilian employe of the association. In his statement he declared that the cutting of salaries should be requested only as a last resort, and that in justice to the city's employes a complete program of economies planned by the administration first should be presented to them.

His statement follows:

"On last Tuesday, July 26, at a special meeting of the Uniformed Firemen's Association, at which I was present as business secretary, and which was attended by approxi-

Continued on Page Fourteen.

'Buy Now' Campaign Planned Through Philadelphia Movies

Special to THE NEW YORK TIMES.

PHILADELPHIA, July 29.—"Buy now for future security" was announced today as the slogan of a campaign starting here next week to stimulate buying, put money into circulation and relieve unemployment.

Patrons of the 800 movie theatres in the Philadelphia district, having a weekly attendance estimated at 5,000,000, will be bombarded with the idea on the screen and by speakers at every performance.

"This, I believe, will prove to be the first step toward the provision of employment for thousands and better times for every one," said Mayor J. Hampton Moore. Early next week he will appoint a committee to direct the campaign.

HEARING ON WALKER BY GOVERNOR LIKELY

Public Examination of Mayor Expected to Be Next Step in Removal Case.

FINEGAN DENOUNCES REPLY

He Denies His Charges Were Frivolous—Seabury and Schieffelin Silent.

As Governor Roosevelt plunged yesterday into a detailed study of the reply of Mayor Walker to the removal charges started by Samuel Seabury, the belief grew in informed quarters here and at Albany that the next important move in the case would be the fixing of a date for a public hearing.

Associates of the Governor held that, despite the 27,000 words of explanation presented by Mr. Walker, the Governor would require more information before taking action. This was interpreted as meaning that the charges in all probability would not be dismissed without a hearing, as were the previous accusations of Rabbi Stephen S. Wise and John Haynes Holmes.

At the same time, no one close to the Governor would venture to predict the ultimate decision regarding Mr. Walker, and Mr. Roosevelt himself refused all information.

"There is no use asking questions about it," he told newspaper men who made inquiries concerning the Walker answer. "The study is going on and as soon as something happens, I will let you know."

Two-Week Delay Likely.

It was suggested further that action by the Governor might not come for two weeks or more. That much time, it was understood, would be allowed to John E. Mack of Poughkeepsie and Martin Conboy of New York, attorneys who are acting as special advisers to Mr. Roosevelt, to study the Mayor's answer and to compare it with the original allegations made by Mr. Seabury.

Mayor Walker, in his answer, made use in the main of the same testimony before the Hofstadter legislative committee cited by Mr. Seabury, but stressed different portions of it and drew different inferences from the facts established. A public hearing would give Mr. Roosevelt an opportunity to ask any additional questions he might desire concerning the opposing inferences, and then make his own decision on the basis of the information obtained.

If this course is followed, it may be several weeks before it is possible to dispose of the Walker case, since Mr. Roosevelt has numerous engagements, many of them connected with his campaign as the Democratic nominee for President.

Mr. Walker was at Saranac Lake, where his brother, George F. Walker, is critically ill. In his absence no statement concerning the answer was made at City Hall.

Mr. Seabury, as has been his habit since the charges were placed in the hands of Governor Roosevelt, refused to discuss any phase of the matter. William Jay Schieffelin, who embodied the Seabury charges in a formal request for the removal of Mr. Walker, was quoted as saying at Ashland, Me., where he is on vacation, that he did not feel that he should comment on a matter that was before the Governor for adjudication.

Finegan Denounces Reply.

The only local comment came from James E. Finegan, one of the sponsors of supplemental charges against Mr. Walker. The Mayor had answered these only briefly in his formal reply, holding that the allegations of malfeasance and nonfeasance advanced by Mr. Finegan were general and not deserving of a detailed reply. Mr. Finegan said, in part:

"Fortunately, Governor Roosevelt has our charges before him. He cannot fail to see that they refer to specified laws violated, specified evidence of gross waste, specified iniquities of assessing, specified methods that make iniquities inevitable, specified acts that constantly foster

Continued on Page Three.

League Invites Us to Economic Parley; Acceptance Depends on Agenda Subjects

Special to THE NEW YORK TIMES.

WASHINGTON, July 29.—The State Department received today the official invitation to the United States to be represented at the International Monetary and Economic Conference called under the auspices of the League of Nations.

The invitation was taken under consideration, but its text was withheld and comment refused pending the framing of a reply. It is assumed by officials that Washington will accept, particularly if debts, reparations and tariff rates are not to be listed formally for discussion.

Should there be no such reservation, the attitude of the government is considered in doubt, since it has not indicated its attitude toward the proposal of Senator Borah for a world conference at which all such questions, disarmament and other issues should be discussed.

In informed circles here the belief has been expressed that Europe might not raise the debt question formally at this time because of a possibility that an adverse reaction in this country might prejudice the whole conference. Were debts not listed on the agenda, however, there are many who believe ways would be found to discuss them informally. In any event, it has been maintained consistently by officials that the administration lacks the power to negotiate new debt settlements without authorization from Congress.

The invitation is understood to contemplate American representation on a committee of experts to assist in the formulation of the agenda for the conference. The time and place of the meeting was said today not to be stipulated in the invitation, but the general assumption has been that it would probably be held in London in October.

Congress voted an appropriation of $40,000 for American representation at a monetary conference and it is expected that this will provide for the expenses of the American delegation at the London meeting.

HOOVER OUTLINES 9-POINT PROGRAM TO SPUR REVIVAL

He Tells Purpose of Recent Talks in Capital to Clear 'Erroneous Speculation.'

RELIEF WORKS HASTENED

Board of Engineers to Direct Self-Liquidating Projects—Slum Razing Speeded.

FARM MARKETING STUDIED

Increase of Rail Jobs Is Sought—Business Leaders to Be Called for 'Concerted Action.'

Special to THE NEW YORK TIMES.

WASHINGTON, July 29.—A nine-point program looking to business recovery along a broad front was submitted to the nation today by President Hoover in making known what he is doing to make immediately operative the far-reaching relief program of the Reconstruction Finance Corporation.

In a statement issued to correct "some erroneous speculation," the President said conferences during the last two weeks in the capital had looked toward "concerted action" to help business. He went on to say what these activities included.

He told for the first time of plans to create a board of engineers to supervise loans by the Reconstruction Corporation for self-liquidating public works.

"Immediate examination" of proposals for stimulating slum demolition and replacement was being given, pointing to increased employment, Mr. Hoover said in outlining his program.

To provide adequately for livestock and feeder loans, a coordinated program to solve these and other farm problems was being worked out with the Farm Board. Restoration of orderly marketing of agricultural commodities was also being studied.

More Credit Expansion Studied.

The President and his advisers had taken up the further expansion of credit facilities to business and industries, he said, "particularly for the purpose of supplying full credit for production where consumption of goods is assured, and thus materially expand employment, which has been hampered by dislocation of the credit machinery."

Directors of the Home Loan Bank Board were being selected as quickly as possible.

Mr. Hoover was still considering means of spreading existing employment through the shorter working-week and working-day.

"When this program is more fully developed I shall confer with the 'business and industrial' committees created in each Federal Reserve District and other groups in the country that are primarily interested, with a view to establishing united and concerted action on a broad front throughout the country," Mr. Hoover said.

The President's statement explained the recent appearance in Washington of Daniel Willard, president of the Baltimore & Ohio Railroad; W. W. Atterbury, president of the Pennsylvania, and Hale Holden, head of the Burlington. "Preliminary conferences" with some railroad leaders had been held with a view to increasing employment by railways.

Army Engineer to Head Board.

No details as to the proposed board of engineers for self-liquidating projects were offered, except that the President said "an engineer of standing" would be designated by the army engineers corps to act as chief.

From unofficial sources it is

Continued on Page Six.

BONUS STRAGGLERS 'MOPPED UP' BY TROOPS; 36 REDS SEIZED; GRAND JURY INQUIRY ON; HOOVER DENOUNCES ATTEMPT AT MOB RULE

Challenge to Government Authority Has Been Met, Says Hoover, Defying Coercion by 'Mob Rule'

Special to THE NEW YORK TIMES.

WASHINGTON, July 29.—President Hoover officially closed the "bonus war" today with this statement:

A challenge to the authority of the United States Government has been met, swiftly and firmly.

After months of patient indulgence the government met overt lawlessness as it always must be met if the cherished processes of self-government are to be preserved. We cannot tolerate the abuse of constitutional rights by those who would destroy all government, no matter who they may be. Government cannot be coerced by mob rule.

The Department of Justice is pressing its investigation into the violence which forced the call for army detachments, and it is my sincere hope that those agitators who inspired yesterday's attack upon the Federal authority may be brought speedily to trial in the civil courts. There can be no safe harbor in the United States of America for violence.

Order and civil tranquillity are the first requisites in the great task of economic reconstruction to which our whole people are now devoting their heroic and noble energies. This national effort must not be retarded in even the slightest degree by organized lawlessness. The first obligation of my office is to uphold and defend the Constitution and the authority of the law. This I propose always to do.

WATERS URGES ALL TO JOIN NEW FORCE

"Khaki Shirts," He Says, Will Help Him to Bring Government Back to "Common People."

'MONEYED POWER' A TARGET

"Wall Street's Servant Sits in White House," He States—Bars Revolutionary Talk.

Special to THE NEW YORK TIMES.

WASHINGTON, July 29.—While the ragged horde of veterans began straggling today toward a proffered haven at Johnstown, Pa., W. W. Waters, their commander-in-chief, issued a national call for volunteers to join a "khaki shirt" movement to "clean out the high places of government."

Although he was not in evidence during the fracas yesterday, and although he informed the police he was powerless to control his men, Waters today assumed the rôle of an American Hitler.

He first set up headquarters in a three-story brick house at 1,841 North Capital Street and sent out "staff members" to make preparations to receive his "army" at Johnstown. Then he issued his call to every citizen to join a movement to take "the United States Government away from the moneyed powers, by legal means, and return it to the common people, whose government it should be."

In his call Waters described the army of veterans as the nucleus of a great force which will have ideals transcending the mere thought of a bonus. But he invited all to rally around the bonus army, now "tried by fire," for the primary purpose of "turning out all whose interests are not the interests of the masses."

"B. E. F. to Be Torch Bearer."

"The B. E. F. will carry on," Waters announced, "no longer as merely a bonus army, but as torch bearers for the inarticulate masses of the country."

He invited every citizen, veteran or

Continued on Page Six.

GRAND JURY INQUIRY ORDERED BY HOOVER

Agents Posing as Veterans in "Red" Camp Expected to Be Chief Witnesses.

JUSTICE BLAMES THE MOB

Luhring in Charging the Jurors Says He Hopes Non-Soldiers Will Be Found Instigators.

Special to THE NEW YORK TIMES.

WASHINGTON, July 29.—A sweeping investigation by a District of Columbia grand jury was ordered today by President Hoover into charges that ringleaders in the bonus army riots were not ex-service men but Communists and other radicals.

A short time after Attorney General Mitchell announced that the grand jury investigation would proceed President Hoover wrote to Dr. Luther H. Reichelderfer, chairman of the District Commissioners, stating that "subversive influences" got control "of the men remaining in the District, a large part of whom were not veterans."

The grand jury inquiry will begin promptly at 10 A. M. Monday, and it is understood that the chief witnesses will be Secret Service agents who have been posing as veterans in some of the bonus army camps, notably that headed by John Pace, Communist agitator.

Hopes are expressed that the grand jury will report by the end of next week. The prediction is uttered in some quarters that nearly twenty indictments will be handed down. Representatives of the Department of Justice seem convinced that Red agents stirred up discontent among the ex-service men and incited yesterday's violence.

Hurley Confers With Hoover.

Secretary Hurley, who is expected to appear before the grand jury, conferred with the President today for almost an hour. Later he said that the instigators of the assaults on police were not ex-soldiers and that bona fide veterans implored others not to engage in violence.

In his charge to the grand jury this afternoon, Oscar Luhring, Supreme Court Justice, declared that the mob attacked the police, and expressed a hope that the grand jury would find it was composed "mainly of Communists and other disorderly elements" and not of former soldiers.

President Hoover's letter to Dr. Reichelderfer placed responsibility for order directly upon the District Commissioners.

He declared bonus marchers "undoubtedly were led to believe that the civil authorities could be intimidated with impunity because of attempts to conciliate by lax enforcement of city ordinances and laws in many directions."

This sentence was instantly construed in many quarters as a reflection upon the three District Commissioners, upon Brig. Gen. Pelham D. Glassford, Metropolitan Police Superintendent, or upon all four.

The commissioners are said to have replied to the President, but the answer has not been made public.

Dr. Reichelderfer conferred with General Glassford but later denied reports that the Police Superintendent had resigned or contemplated doing so.

General Glassford, who has received

Continued on Page Four.

CAMPS NOW CHARRED RUINS

Unkempt and Hungry Veterans Take Roads to Johnstown, Pa.

'KHAKI SHIRTS' NEXT MOVE

Commander Waters Urges Public to Take Government Away From "Moneyed Powers."

SOME TROOPS STAND BY

Red Cross to Care for Women and Children—States Press Marchers Onward.

A page of pictures of the veterans' eviction, page 5.

Special to THE NEW YORK TIMES.

WASHINGTON, July 29.—Soldiers patrolled the charred ruins of camps occupied until yesterday by the "bonus expeditionary force" in silent contrast tonight to the intensive fighting of twenty-four hours ago when with tear gas and the threat of fixed bayonets they routed more than 10,000 bonus seekers from their makeshift hovels.

Most of the bonus army, unshaved and hungry, were en route to Johnstown, Pa., where they had been invited by Mayor Eddie McCloskey, and the "war" was ended which had brought a military expedition into the capital for the first time since the War of 1812.

President Hoover signaled the end of the incident that brought 1,500 soldiers completely equipped for battle, escorted by cavalry and tanks, into action on Pennsylvania Avenue—famed "avenue of the Presidents"—with a brief statement in which he said:

"Government cannot be coerced by mob rule."

The troops had been called out, he explained, in keeping with "the first obligation of my office" to uphold the Constitution and "the authority of the law."

"This I propose always to do," he added.

Soldiers Continue 'Mopping Up.'

Thus an end was written to two months of vacillation, during which thousands of World War veterans were endeavoring to make the government, by the sheer force of their presence, pay the balance of their adjusted service compensation certificates.

Police, directing a drive against radicals, arrested thirty-six of them at a meeting in an abandoned church. Among those rounded up were James Ford, Negro, who is the Communist party's candidate for Vice President, and Emmanuel Levin of New York City, leader of the Communist group in the bonus army.

Meanwhile, upon the orders of President Hoover, a grand jury was charged with the task of an inquiry into the riots to bring action against agitators held responsible.

The 500 soldiers who were brought into action near the Capitol itself were not inactive today as they "mopped up" numerous small encampments in scattered parts of the city, but there was no necessity for a repetition of charges with tear bombs and fixed bayonets, such as yesterday and last night sent the veterans scurrying from encampments on Pennsylvania Avenue, on C Street and at Anacostia.

The veterans had received sufficient notice of the fact they were unwelcome.

However, W. W. Waters, their commander-in-chief, gave notice that they have not "surrendered," but had only changed tactics. After directing the march to Johnstown, toward which the men straggled in groups, Waters took a dramatic step by issuing a public statement calling on all citizens to join his "khaki shirts," an organization with which he purposes to take government out of the hands of the "moneyed powers" and turn it over to "the common people."

Waters issued the appeal from his headquarters in a red brick house on North Capital Street, where he established himself and a staff after sending emissaries to Johnstown to prepare to receive his "army" as well as to provide for them en route.

A final count of casualties in yesterday's engagements revealed one

Continued on Page Four.

Belgium to Modernize Fortifications on East With Chain of Sunken Batteries and Dugouts

Special Cable to THE NEW YORK TIMES.

BRUSSELS, July 29.—Ultra-modern fortifications for Belgium's eastern frontier, patterned after the strong fortifications that France has built up since the World War in Alsace and Lorraine, are called for in the program outlined today by the Minister of National Defense in an interview with a writer for the newspaper La Libre Belgique.

"In case of invasion the right bank of the River Meuse will be defended to the extreme limit of our strength," the Minister declared.

The first line of defense, as he described it will consist in a chain of concrete dugouts along the frontier linking the towns of Maesyck, Arlon, Saint Vith, Houffalize, Bastogne and Martelauge. These dugouts, commanding all the international highways, will not be guarded in peace time by permanent garrisons, but will be either occupied or looked after by the rural gendarmerie.

In the event surprise automobile raids by invaders force the defenders out of these dugouts, it will be possible hastily to destroy them so they will be useless to the enemy.

Hombourg, which the first German Uhlans passed through on Aug. 4, 1914, will be the centre of the frontier fortifications. Behind the outer ring of dugouts will be established a second line of defense, consisting of a system of the latest improved types of concealed sunken batteries. Each of these subterranean batteries will be spread out over about thirty to forty acres and will be almost invisible on the surface.

It is planned to place strong forts at Eben-Emael, Battich and Pepinster, which will be of the same type that France has adopted for defense on the Rhine at Longyon.

For the defense of the Meuse, Belgium plans to build a chain of nine forts around Liege and seven more at Namur.

"All the News That's Fit to Print."

The New York Times.

LATE CITY EDITION
WEATHER—Fair and continued cool today; tomorrow fair.
Temperatures Yesterday—Max., [illegible]; Min., [illegible].

VOL. LXXXI....No. 27,229. Entered as Second-Class Matter, Postoffice, New York, N. Y. NEW YORK, FRIDAY, AUGUST 12, 1932. * * * * TWO CENTS In New York City | THREE CENTS Within 200 Miles | FOUR CENTS Elsewhere Except in 7th and 8th Postal Zones

GOVERNOR QUERIES MAYOR ON SISTO BONDS; CURBS ORATORY BUT ALLOWS WITNESSES; WALKER PLEADS FOR HIS OFFICIAL LIFE

GOVERNOR KEEPS FIRM GRIP

Promises 'Fair Deal,' but Refuses to Let Mayor Dictate Program.

REJECTS LIMIT ON CHARGES

Decides Walker Must Answer for Acts in First Term Over Protests of Curtin.

EXAMINATION IS SEARCHING

Accused City Executive Hotly Defends Pool Profits After Denouncing Accusers.

Transcript of the hearing on Mayor Walker, pages 8, 9, 10.

By F. RAYMOND DANIELL.
Special to THE NEW YORK TIMES.

ALBANY, N. Y., Aug. 11.—A subdued and earnest "Jimmy" Walker opened his fight against removal as Mayor of the city of New York with an impassioned plea to Governor Roosevelt to allow him to face his accusers and cross-examine them.

Flippancy and witticisms were laid aside. They had no place in the quiet dignity of the executive chamber, presided over by the grave but kindly Governor and kept free of the atmosphere of politics. A dozen towering State troopers guarded the hearing room.

No Charge Held 'Outlawed.'

The Governor, at the opening of the hearing, ruled that the Mayor must answer for the acts of his first administration as well as for those of his second, and promised that any witnesses whose testimony was needed would be called. But the Mayor wanted more. He wanted Samuel Seabury, gray-haired and silent chief counsel to the Hofstadter committee, to present his case all over again, and, irked by a victory that was not a victory, he interrupted his counsel to plead his own case.

Angrily charging his accusers with a plot to destroy him with "hand-picked" evidence, the Mayor cried: "I can't be unlike every other human being in the world. I can't be driven this way, without an opportunity to look into the faces of my accusers. I can't be so different than the rest of the human family. I haven't been transported back to Russia. I haven't been taken into other kingdoms and empires in Dark Ages and never to return again."

At another point he spoke with biting sarcasm saying:

"Maybe I am wrong, maybe countless others are wrong, that there was a disposition to railroad me by these men who made the complaint. Maybe, after all, they would like to have the comfort, the conscientious relief, maybe they would like to have the moral satisfaction of bringing to you and pouring into your own ear the testimony upon which they relied, which I never heard, which you never heard, and which was adduced in an ex parte proceeding."

Examined on Sisto Deal.

Cutting off further argument with a final pledge of fairness, the Governor personally administered the oath to the Mayor and examined him for more than an hour upon his receipt of $26,500 in bonds from J. A. Sisto, broker and taxicab financier, and upon the Mayor's possession of convertible bonds in the Reliance Bronze Company.

Taking the Mayor over his testimony before the Hofstadter committee, the Governor insisted upon a more detailed explanation of the meeting in Atlantic City, at which the Mayor was "declared in" on a "pool" in Cosden Oil stock, of which the bonds were said to represent the Mayor's profit. Mayor Walker, repeating in substance his story of "meeting a crowd of people at a moving picture convention," at first denied that he knew until he received the money months later that Sisto was connected with the transaction. A moment later he corrected himself, saying that he had known from the first that Sisto was the operator and "banker" of the pool.

The Reliance bonds, which were received in the Sisto transactions, were accepted, the Mayor insisted, without any knowledge on his part of the nature of the company's business or that it would be in a position

Continued on Page Ten.

Court Fight to Stop Walker Hearing Collapses; Bronx Man Also Is Rebuffed by the Governor

From a Staff Correspondent.
Special to THE NEW YORK TIMES.

ALBANY, Aug. 11.—Defeated in a court fight to block the hearing on the charges against Mayor Walker, George Donnelly, secretary of the Bronx Chamber of Commerce, tried to carry his battle directly to Governor Roosevelt tonight, but failed to get any satisfaction.

With Supreme Court Justice McGeehan of the Bronx already on record as requiring application for a writ of prohibition to be made in the local jurisdiction, Mr. Donnelly went before Supreme Court Justice Bliss at Schoharie this morning to renew his motion.

Sidney Levine, attorney for the Bronx man, made a spirited attempt to substantiate his contention that the ouster proceedings were unconstitutional. Justice Bliss, however, ruled that he, too, had no jurisdiction. He held that an application of the kind sought should be made to the special term of the court in the district meeting in Albany on Aug. 19.

Previously, Supreme Court Justice Hinman, a member of the Appellate Division of the district, had turned down a similar plea on the same grounds. But despite the two setbacks Mr. Donnelly and Mr. Levine came to the Capitol just as today's hearing closed to battle for their cause.

They attempted to serve on the Governor a notice that they intended to renew the motion for the prohibition writ before Justice Staley on Aug. 19. Meanwhile Mr. Donnelly urged that Governor Roosevelt withhold any final decision until the issue could be threshed out in the courts.

Even the attempt to serve the notice of motion failed as far as Governor Roosevelt was concerned. M. Maldwin Fertig, his counsel, told the attorney and the Bronx Chamber of Commerce representative that the document did not have official standing and for that reason there was no occasion for the Governor to receive it.

Governor Roosevelt received newspaper correspondents just after the hearing concluded. He was asked about Mr. Donnelly's suggestion for a delay. The Governor said he was making no comment on any phase of the Walker case against the Mayor during the progress of the Gubernatorial inquiry, but it was made plain that the Bronx man's proposal would not be considered seriously.

WALKER IS MAGNET TO ALBANY CROWDS

On Way to and From Capitol Mayor Is Acclaimed by the Sidewalk Groups.

MANY FRIENDS AT HEARING

Ahead of Time for "Big Show" to Which John F. Curry Jr. Has Trouble Gaining Admittance.

From a Staff Correspondent.
Special to THE NEW YORK TIMES.

ALBANY, N. Y., Aug. 11.—Amid the scenes of his youthful induction into a public career, Mayor Walker was an attraction for crowds today while Governor Roosevelt and Samuel Seabury, his chief accuser, went their ways, quietly and unobtrusively.

When he left his hotel to ride to the Capitol, where he rose to become Senate leader of his party, and when he returned after an arduous day of questioning, the Mayor was cheered.

Mr. Seabury, as did also Governor Roosevelt throughout the day, preserved an air of purely objective interest in the merits of the charges against the Mayor. There were no crowds for them as they traveled to and from the Capitol. And in the big executive chamber the proceedings were of such a dignified character that there was no possibility of a display of feeling for any of the principals.

Walker Appears Early.

The Mayor was ahead of time for his appointment at 1:30 o'clock when the hearing was scheduled to open. He rode up from the Ten Eyck to the acclaim of sidewalk groups. With Mrs. Walker by his side he came into the Capitol well in advance of the time set, while the Governor sat in the inner chamber holding a final conference with his legal aides.

In fact, it was Governor Roosevelt who was late today, but he was only a few minutes tardy in coming into the chamber, and that was because no one had told him of the deadline. Mr. Seabury and his corps of young aides were at their counsel table well before the curtain was rung up on the drama.

In an effort to prevent any untoward disturbances in the neighborhood of the executive chamber the State police, more than twenty-five strong, kept close watch on that entire wing of the Capitol. None but those accredited could come into the corridor opening into the chamber.

But a small group did gather at the head of the stairs leading to the Governor's office and it was plain to see and hear that most of them were backers of the Mayor. When he came in with his wife and his party the cheers sounded through the Capitol. When he left handclaps echoed through the halls.

Governor Roosevelt came as usual

Continued on Page Ten.

SEABURY VOTE COSTS LOVE RENOMINATION

Senator Scored as 'Traitor,' McCooey Machine Designates Esquirol in His Place.

MAY RUN AS INDEPENDENT

Legislator, Backed by Citizens Union Head, Says Ouster Shows Kings Leader Is 'Slipping.'

State Senator William Lathrop Love of Brooklyn, the only Democratic Senator who voted for granting additional funds to continue the Seabury investigation of New York City affairs, was denied last night re designation for the nomination to succeed himself.

The Democratic organization in the Seventeenth, Eighteenth and Twenty-first Brooklyn Assembly Districts, which Senator Love has represented at Albany for ten years, unanimously decided upon Assemblyman Joseph A. Esquirol as the candidate for State Senator. John H. McCooey, the Kings County Democratic leader, is a resident of this Senatorial district.

At none of three meetings, one in each Assembly District, was Senator Love mentioned by name, but at the gathering in the Seventeenth, Edward F. Cadley, assistant to Dr. William Schroeder Jr., Sanitation Commissioner, denounced the Senator as "a traitor" and a "political faker."

McCooey's Comment Brief.

Mr. McCooey's only comment on last night's action was that Mr. Esquirol, who has served five terms in the Assembly, had served "faithfully" and was "eligible for promotion."

The Brooklyn leader headed a nominating subcommittee of the Madison Democratic Club that put forward the name of Assemblyman Esquirol. Mr. McCooey is the executive member of this club, whose membership is made up of Democratic followers in the Eighteenth Assembly District, and as such he was chairman of its meeting in the club's headquarters at Kingston and St. Marks Avenues.

The Democratic machine functioned at this meeting, as at the two others in the Eighth Brooklyn Senatorial District, with its accustomed smoothness, and when Mr. McCooey's subcommittee of the nominating committee put forward its list of designations for candidates there was no dissenting voice.

"Not True to Party."

The meeting of the Seventeenth Assembly District Democratic Club, held at 590 Gates Avenue, was enlivened by the denunciation of Dr. Love by Mr. Cadley, who followed the course of his co-leaders by refraining from mention of Dr. Love's name.

"He is not true to his own party," Mr. Cadley told the 200 or more persons present. "He can have the rest

Continued on Page Ten.

Miss Holm of Brooklyn Wins Olympic Swim; Crowd of 10,000 Sees Two Records Broken

By ARTHUR J. DALEY.
Special to THE NEW YORK TIMES.

LOS ANGELES, Aug. 11.—Churning the pale blue waters of the Olympic pool into a white froth, 19-year-old Miss Eleanor Holm of the Women's Swimming Association of New York won the Olympic 100-meter back-stroke championship today to give the United States its third successive women's crown.

Although she was clocked in 1:19.4, figures better than the listed games record of 1:21.3, the pretty little Brooklynite was well above the new Olympic and world's standard of 1:18.3 that she set two days ago.

Today Miss Holm cast record-breaking ideas to the four winds and merely raced to win. This she did by almost two yards, Miss Phyllis Mealing of Australia taking runner-up honors, while a crowd of 10,000 looked on.

Not once did Miss Holm pay any attention to the guiding line of red flags strung overhead. She stroked rhythmically and perfectly, but her black-capped head was ever turned toward Miss Mealing's lane. It was not until she was ten meters from the end and well ahead that the Brooklyn girl paid strict attention to her own race. Then she flailed away at the water in a sprint finish that insured her triumph beyond any doubt.

But while Miss Holm failed to better her own record, Olympic marks fell in two other tests. Miss Lenore Kight of Homestead, Pa., smashed Miss Martha Norelius's standard of 5:42.8 for 400 meters with a dazzling 5:40.9 performance, while two of the amphibious Japanese, Yoshiyuki Tsuruta, the defending 200-meter breast-stroke champion, and his 14-year-old team-mate, Reizo Koike, each won his heat in the identical clocking of 2:46.2, time far better than Tsuruta's own record of 2:48.8.

The lone final event on the day's long program saw Miss Holm fight off the challenge of Miss Mealing for 75 meters before breaking away from her completely. The other starters never even figured in the race. The Australian was timed in 1:21.3 in second place.

After her came Miss Valerie Davies of Great Britain, third in 1:22.5; Miss Phyllis Harding of Great Britain, fourth in 1:22.6; Miss Joan McSheehy of the United States, fifth in

Continued on Page Nineteen.

SEVILLE MOBS BURN ROYALIST CENTRES: REVOLT LEADER HELD

Churches Saved From Torch as Crowds Take Revenge for Blow at Republic.

SANJURJO IN MADRID JAIL

Regime Rounds Up His Aides Trying to Flee Spain—He Says He Was Betrayed.

By FRANK L. KLUCKHOHN.
Special Cable to THE NEW YORK TIMES.

MADRID, Aug. 11.—An infuriated republican mob at Seville burned today the building of La Union, a newspaper which served as the mouthpiece, perhaps involuntarily, of General José Sanjurjo in his royalist revolt yesterday.

The crowd later demolished the houses of the Marquess of Esquivel, where General Sanjurjo made his headquarters; Señor Luca de Tena, the wealthy owner of Spain's chief monarchist newspaper, A B C, and the Seville branch plant of that newspaper, and four clubs owned by a membership of wealthy landholders.

There was also a demonstration at Granada today, in which a rioter was killed by the police in suppressing it.

Churches were burned or attempts made to burn them in a number of small Spanish towns tonight. In Aznalcollar the churches were burned to the ground. In Granada Las Tonasen Church was fired, as was the Church of Santa Tomas. The first was destroyed, according to reports, and Civil Guards were called out to quell rioters.

A mob burned down the Agrarian Casino in the historic town of Santa Fé, near Granada, where Isabella's forces launched their attack on the Moors. The Mayor addressed the crowd, asking them to disperse, but they misunderstood and opened fire on him. One man was killed and three were wounded. The Mayor was unhurt.

Revolt Leader in Madrid Jail.

General Sanjurjo, his customary smile no longer gracing his usually jovial face, was under arrest in Madrid tonight waiting to hear whether he and his fellow-Monarchist generals would face a firing squad or life imprisonment for their part in yesterday's revolt. He was arrested early today by a single policemen, armed with a rifle, in Huelva, when he stopped his automobile to inquire the way to the Portuguese border after a sixty-mile dash from Seville.

The policeman instantly recognized his former chief and, although all of General Sanjurjo's party were armed, he took them to the local jail. Later General Sanjurjo was brought under a strong escort to Madrid.

"I was deceived," General Sanjurjo is quoted as having said to the Colonel of the Civil Guard who escorted him to Madrid. 'I was abed at Escorial, near Madrid, Tuesday night when my son, Colonel Sanjurjo, came to me and said 'I want you to accompany me. It is a matter of life and death.'

"Half way to Seville my son told me I must head a national revolt. He cited the names of regiments throughout Spain adhering to the movement, also general and political leaders. That morning I took Seville. I was betrayed."

Tonight leading jurists discussed with administrative officials whether the leaders of a revolt could be sen-

Continued on Page Three.

REPUBLIC IS IGNORED ON REICH FETE DAY; HITLER STRIKES SNAG

Von Papen and Von Gayl Call for Changes in Constitution at Cabinet "Celebration."

NAZI CHANCELLOR UNLIKELY

Von Hindenburg Bars Leader of Largest Party Because He Can't Run Reichstag.

By FREDERICK T. BIRCHALL.
Special Cable to THE NEW YORK TIMES.

BERLIN, Aug. 11.—Today is Constitution Day in Germany. On this day, thirteen years ago, the Constitution under which the Reich now rules itself was promulgated at Weimar and the republic, as it is at present, was proclaimed. So today the black, red and gold republican banner flies everywhere in Berlin, sometimes side by side with the defiant black, white and red flag of the old monarchy.

As customary, the heads of the government assembled in the Reichstag to do honor to the republic they serve. How many went there to pay it mere lip service, only they who know in their own hearts could tell, but the impression left on observers inside the chamber was that of a funeral rather than a birthday.

Meanwhile the plan to make Adolf Hitler Chancellor was checked because President von Hindenburg objected to giving the place to a party leader who could not obtain a majority in the Reichstag.

Unlike Gay French Fête.

In Paris on Bastile Day recently, blue battalions under the flags that saved France paraded through cheering crowds, the people danced in Paris streets through half the night and every one made holiday. Democracy was triumphant and joyful. The French Republic is half a century old and the French are proud of it and resolved to keep it. It was different today here, where democracy is new and very much on trial.

At noon a fair-sized assemblage gathered outside the Reichstag to see the various notables as they arrived for the celebration. It was a moderately interested crowd which gave no sign of enthusiasm over the high officials beyond thin applause for President von Hindenburg when he appeared.

Inside the chamber there also was no great throng. The seats on the floor, where the Reichstag members normally sit, were occupied by invited guests, mostly government officeholders, bureaucrats of various degrees, and their wives.

The diplomatic gallery was filled. Ambassador Sackett of the United States was in the front row with the British, French, Italian and other Ambassadors, and there was a fair attendance of distinguished strangers in the gallery on the other side of the Presidential box. Behind the chairman's vacant desk were banked mournful purple hydrangeas and twice through the open door a concealed orchestra played solemn music—Beethoven's "Egmont" overture and the slow third movement from Brahms's Fourth Symphony.

But in the whole attendance there was visible not a single face known to represent any of the three great parties comprising four-fifths of the voting population of Germany. Nobody expected to see Communists there, and they were not, but neither was a known Socialist nor a lead-

Continued on Page Two.

HOOVER ADMITS FAILURE OF PROHIBITION, DECLARING FOR STATE CONTROL OF LIQUOR; WOULD BARTER WAR DEBTS IN TRADE DEAL

Points of Policy Set Forth by the President On Issues That Figure in National Campaign

Special to THE NEW YORK TIMES.

WASHINGTON, Aug. 11.—The position taken by President Hoover on the issues in the Presidential campaign were set forth in his speech of acceptance tonight as follows:

Prohibition—Favors change in the Eighteenth Amendment to give each State the right to deal with the liquor problem as it may determine, subject to constitutional guarantees protecting each State from interference by its neighbor and avoidance of the return of the saloon.

War Debts—Opposes cancellation, but is inclined to some arrangement by which "some other tangible form of compensation such as the expansion of markets for American agriculture and labor and the restoration and maintenance of our prosperity" may be substituted for any particular annual payment.

Unemployment Relief—Re-emphasizes advocacy of State and local responsibility in meeting the needs for relief, and opposes "distortion" of needed works into "pork barrel non-productive works which impoverish the nation."

Foreign Relations—Again urges joining the World Court "under proper reservations." Proposes to consult with other nations in times of emergency to promote world peace. Opposes entering any agreements "committing us to any future course of action, or which call for use of force to preserve world peace." Stands upon his "new doctrine" of refusing to recognize title and territory gained in violation of peace pacts.

Government Finances—Insists upon balanced budget and rigid economy. Favors revision of recent tax increases "if they tend to sap the vitality of industry and thus retard employment."

Tariff—Stands "squarely for a protective tariff." Challenges Democrats to "descend from vague generalizations to any particular schedule."

Farm Relief—Calls for readjustment and coordination of national, State and local taxation. Favors continuance of Federal Farm Board.

Power—Opposes the Federal Government undertaking operation of power business.

THRONG SEES NOTIFICATION

President Goes Beyond His Platform by Urging Dry Law Change.

AGAINST SALOON'S RETURN

Federal Check Demanded to Protect Dry States—Democratic Stand Attacked.

BAN ON DEBT CANCELLATION

Panic Repelled, He Says, Resting Claim for Re-election on Economic Measures.

The text of President Hoover's acceptance speech is on page 4.

Special to THE NEW YORK TIMES.

WASHINGTON, Aug. 11.—In a speech accepting the renomination of the Republican party for the Presidency, President Hoover tonight turned his back on what four years ago he termed "a noble experiment" and declared virtually for an end of national prohibition.

Addressing a crowd of more than 4,000 persons in Constitution Hall and millions more throughout the United States and the world over the radio, Mr. Hoover went one step further than the platform on which he will run for re-election when he said:

"The Republican platform recommends submission of the question to the States that the people themselves may determine whether they desire a change, but insists that this submission shall propose a constructive and not a destructive change. It does not dictate to the conscience of any member of the party. * * *

"It is my belief that in order to remedy present evils, a change is necessary. * * *"

Plank for Submission Only.

Thus Mr. Hoover gave force to the Republican prohibition plank over which controversy has raged since it was first made public. That plank at no point recommends a change, but simply advocates submission of the question to the people without committing the party one way or the other. Mr. Hoover came out flatly for change, prefacing his profession of faith by saying:

"The Constitution gives the President no power or authority with respect to changes in the Constitution itself; nevertheless, my countrymen have a right to know my conclusions upon this matter. They are clear and need not be misunderstood."

The President's recommendation was that liquor control be turned back to the States, with the right to deal with the problem as each may decide, but with constitutional safeguards to protect them against each other and a guarantee against the return of the open saloon. He insisted that it was a "constructive and not destructive change," and not "a blind leap back to old evils."

While uncluttered with the mechanics of putting the proposed constitutional change into effect, a point which was blamed by party leaders for the contradictory interpretations of the platform, Mr. Hoover's proposal was for a less drastic change than that of the Democrats, whose national platform calls for outright repeal of the Eighteenth Amendment and immediate modification of the Volstead act. It was not the less sensational, however, as it was the first time that Mr. Hoover has openly acknowledged failure of the prohibition experiment.

Had Hoped Law Would Succeed.

The nominee treated the liquor question as one that had cut across the path of the nation's consideration of "vast problems of economic and social order," but admitted its importance largely because of the abuses growing from the failure of enforcement.

He refused to admit that the doctrine embodied in the Eighteenth Amendment had been a complete failure. If it had done nothing else, he said, it had smashed the old saloon régime "as by a stroke of lightning."

He had hoped that it would succeed completely, and had used every power at his command to make it work, he said, but he could not con-

Continued on Page Five.

BOND PRICES SOAR IN HEAVY TRADING

Gain 1 to 12 Points on Most Active Demand of 1932—Stocks Slightly Lower.

4,402,000 SHARES TRADED

Market Drops After Excited Buying at Opening but Rallies Before the Close.

With the stock market pausing to catch its breath after a fresh display of speculative enthusiasm in the morning, the financial focus shifted yesterday to bonds, in which the trading was the heaviest since Dec. 18 of last year, and in which the net gains ran from 1 to 12 points.

Trading in stocks continued at high speed in the morning. About 900,000 shares were turned over in the first half-hour, and at this pace, if continued for the full five hours, the volume would have involved something like 9,000,000 shares. In that first tumultuous thirty minutes the brokerage houses and the floor of the Stock Exchange presented scenes of excitement such as had not been witnessed since the end of the bull market in the Autumn of 1929.

The total volume was 4,402,000 shares, as compared with 4,430,290 shares on Wednesday. Before the advance was checked at mid-day the general list of stocks was driven to a new high level for the movement. The upswing was led by such stocks as American Telephone, United States Steel, Santa Fé, Union Pacific, Westinghouse Electric, Consolidated Gas, Eastman, and New York Central.

Stocks React With Wheat.

The reaction coincided with a fall in wheat, but was believed to have been due mainly to profit-taking and to the retirement of professionals who wished to be out of the market until after President Hoover's acceptance address had been digested. Brokers reported that many of their largest speculative customers preferred to be free of commitments over-night. Some selling resulted from Wall Street's appraisal of unfavorable industrial developments which were largely overlooked the afternoon before.

Whatever the inspiration for the reversal may have been, the advance was halted abruptly, and for a time in the early afternoon the market was under rather heavy pressure. There was a mild rally shortly before the close, which left the main body of stocks only moderately lower, in the average, than at the end of the previous day. There were only a few wide declines and these were balanced by gains of about equal scope in scattered issues. The price changes generally were negligible. The composite averages, based upon

Continued on Page Sixteen.

NOTIFICATION MADE A SOCIAL OCCASION

Hoovers Give Garden Party for 500 on South Grounds of the White House.

MANY NOTABLES ATTEND

Theodore Roosevelt's Widow and Daughters Are the Centre of Interest.

Special to THE NEW YORK TIMES.

WASHINGTON, Aug. 11.—Under cheerful skies and in the gracefully historic setting afforded by the White House and the gardens and green lawns of the south grounds, President and Mrs. Hoover this afternoon entertained Republican leaders gathered here for the party's notification ceremonies.

The entertainment combined features of a reception, luncheon and garden party, the President and Mrs. Hoover receiving at 1 o'clock in the Blue Room and afterward joining their guests in the open, where a buffet luncheon was served from tables set under gayly striped marquees on the south lawn.

The Marine Band, in the brilliant scarlet of their full dress uniforms, played from a platform under the oak trees at the right, near the house, leaving the lawns sloping away to the fountain free and unobstructed for the guests, most of whom chose, however, the shade of the trees on the right of the grounds. The day was quite warm.

Among the guests were Mrs. Theodore Roosevelt Sr. and her son-in-law and daughter, Dr. and Mrs. Richard Derby. They arrived by plane this morning to be overnight guests at the White House, Mrs. Roosevelt for the second time and Mrs. Derby for the first time since their own seven-year residence there.

The Roosevelt Administration was represented also by Mrs. Nicholas Longworth, who came from New York with Representative and Mrs. Robert L. Bacon, and will leave tomorrow with Secretary and Mrs. Mills on their yacht Avalon.

Mrs. Roosevelt received with President and Mrs. Hoover in the Blue Room, while Mrs. Longworth and Mrs. Derby held an informal reception of their own on the portico, many guests after "going down the line" pausing to greet them before descending the steps to the garden.

Snell Welcomes Mrs. Roosevelt.

Mrs. Roosevelt's airplane trip had been "perfectly wonderful," she said, but when asked by newspaper men for "a statement," she remarked:

"I haven't talked for the press, not in seventy-one years, and it's too late to begin now."

Mrs. Roosevelt had urged Republican women in New York to "roll

Continued on Page Five.

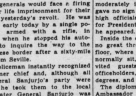

"All the News That's Fit to Print."

The New York Times.

LATE CITY EDITION
WEATHER—Partly cloudy today, tomorrow; temperature unchanged.
Temperatures Yesterday—Max., [illegible]; Min., [illegible].

VOL. LXXXI....No. 27,244. Entered as Second-Class Matter, Postoffice, New York, N. Y. NEW YORK, SATURDAY, AUGUST 27, 1932. * * * * TWO CENTS In New York City | THREE CENTS Within 200 Miles | FOUR CENTS Elsewhere Except in 7th and 8th Postal Zones

SHERWOOD'S FUNDS KEPT FROM SHERIFF BY WALKER WITNESS

Employe in Law Firm Admits Putting Checks in Her Own Account in New Jersey.

STANTON DISPUTES HERRICK

Denies Any Part in Purchase of Stock Linked to Mayor and Equitable Backers.

STORY STIRS THE GOVERNOR

Curtin Rebuked for Trying to Curb Roosevelt's Questions—Walker Home for Week-End Rest.

Summary of the testimony in the Walker hearing, Page 9.

By F. RAYMOND DANIELL.

Special to THE NEW YORK TIMES.

ALBANY, N. Y., Aug. 26.—The woman who has been looking after Mayor Walker's personal business affairs since Russell T. Sherwood dropped from sight a year ago admitted before Governor Roosevelt today that she had kept her predecessor's income from the Sheriff by sequestering it in New Jersey.

She was Miss Mildred T. Day, who with her employer, Francis MacIntyre, former law associate of Mr. Walker, was called in the Mayor's defense to testify that Sherwood handled funds and gave advice on such diverse matters as finance and dairy farming to many persons besides the Mayor.

They named the Dolly sisters, Beatrice Lillie, Johnny Dundee and Mike McTigue, together with several corporations, as among the missing Sherwood's clients. They credited him with being an expert on income tax matters, passports, pedigreed cattle and sound investments.

Seabury's Examination Sharp.

All this was part of an attempt by John J. Curtin, attorney for Mr. Walker, to puncture Samuel Seabury's conclusion that Sherwood acted solely for the Mayor in Wall Street operations totaling $1,000,000. But the gray-haired chief counsel to the Hofstadter committee had another turn.

Under his disarmingly gentle cross-examination Miss Day, who has worked as a stenographer for the law firm of Warren and MacIntyre since 1910, admitted that, since the disappearance of Sherwood, she had deposited his dividend checks in her own account and safe deposit box in a New Jersey bank. Among the dividend checks thus sequestered were those paid on some $10,000 worth of stock in the Century Circuit Company, which Abe Schwartz says he gave the Mayor as a fee for special legal services, and which the Mayor said he supposed were given by Sherwood to his former associates in his law practice.

All together, Miss Day estimated, she had banked between $2,000 and $2,500 for the absent Sherwood, and she insisted she had done it all on her own initiative without a suggestion from anybody, and for that matter without a power of attorney from Sherwood.

Miss Day, who was a phlegmatic witness in a blue silk dress and gray straw hat, said it had never occurred to her that she might deposit Sherwood's income in his own accounts in Rockland or New York counties. Nor had she thought of putting it in one of the accounts the law firm had in New York banks.

That was fortunate for Sherwood for, had the money been deposited in a New York bank, it might have been seized by the sheriff who is still trying to get hold of enough of the missing man's property to satisfy a $50,000 fine imposed upon him for disobeying a subpoena served upon him in Mexico City last Fall. But, Miss Day explained, the sheriff had never approached her.

Stanton Contradicts Herrick.

Mr. Walker's defense again encountered rough going when Edward G. Stanton, the Mayor's former secretary, who took the stand to deny any part in the purchase of a block of Interstate Trust Company stock, ran afoul of a passage in Park Commissioner Walter R. Herrick's testimony which he was unable to reconcile with his own.

Mr. Stanton insisted that he knew nothing about the transaction by which Mr. Herrick picked up 300 shares of the trust company stock which former Governor Silzer of New Jersey had set aside for Mayor Walker. This stock later fell into the hands of Frank R. Fageol and J. Allan Smith, who were interested in the Equitable Coach Company's application for a franchise.

When Mr. Herrick first told his story at a private examination he did not mention Mr. Stanton's name, but said he had bought the stock in

Continued on Page Nine.

Bretons Cheer "Death Song," Calling for Break With France

By The Associated Press.

RENNES, France, Aug. 26.—Breton autonomists, who have kept alive their antipathy toward union with France for 400 years, gave vent to their feelings again today.

Early this month a bas-relief at the City Hall symbolic of the union between France and Brittany was bombed. Today the remaining fragments were carried away and as the motor trucks left City Hall a hunting horn sounded the "Hallali," the hunting air which signifies that the stag is near death.

A group of autonomists massed in cafés opposite the City Hall applauded. Gendarmes arrested the trumpeter.

OSLO FLIERS MISSING; GASOLINE EXHAUSTED

But Hopeful Crowd Still Waits at Airdrome for Clyde A. Lee and John Bochkon.

UNSIGHTED SINCE TAKE-OFF

Low Clouds and Fog Over England—Backers in Vermont Begin to Grow Anxious.

Special Cable to THE NEW YORK TIMES.

OSLO, Saturday, Aug. 27.—Watchers for Clyde Allen Lee and John Bochkon, who are now more than ten hours overdue on their transatlantic flight from Harbor Grace, Nfld., have almost given up hope.

Airdromes at Oslo and in the surrounding country have been lighted all night long and flares have been placed at prominent positions and Coast Guard stations. At one time the passage of an airplane with bright navigation lights aroused the hopes of the expectant people, but it proved to be a military craft on a reconnaissance flight.

Meteorological reports indicate bad weather conditions on the eastern side of the Atlantic.

Fuel Supply Exhausted.

OSLO, Saturday, Aug. 27 (AP).—Airdrome officials here calculated this morning that if Clyde A. Lee and John Bochkon had remained aloft their gasoline supply must by this time have been exhausted. But lights were kept burning for them and great projectors swept the darkened sky.

Their plane, the Green Mountain Boy, had not been sighted once since the take-off, and weather conditions over the Eastern Atlantic were bad.

The fliers had planned to make the non-stop flight in thirty hours. At 12:02 o'clock yesterday, Eastern Daylight Time, the thirty hours had elapsed. There were low-lying clouds and some fog over the water to Great Britain from noon on, and because of these conditions it was possible Lee and Bochkon had flown over England without being seen.

Earlier, large crowds had gathered in the hope of witnessing the termination of the first transatlantic flight to Oslo. Weather conditions in the immediate vicinity of the city were good, with a westerly wind blowing.

Flying a Great Circle course, the red monoplane, according to its plotted course and estimated speed, should have hit the Irish coast near Galway at about 11 o'clock last night. The airmen planned to fly over Dublin, Southern England, and Cuxhaven, Germany, before coming down at Kjeller Field, Oslo. Galway is on the west coast of Ireland and about 1,800 miles from Harbor Grace.

Backers Grow Anxious.

BARRE, Vt., Aug. 26 (AP).—As hours passed with no word from Clyde Allen Lee and John Bochkon, overdue at Oslo, Norway, on their flight from Barre and Harbor Grace, anxiety grew among the 100 or more business men in Barre and Montpelier who backed the venture.

Meanwhile Hubert Huntington, navigator for the flight, stoutly reaffirmed his confidence in the plane and its pilots and insisted he would not at present become "greatly worried."

Between calls Huntington scanned maps of the route he had charted for the flight of the Green Mountain Boy, in which Lee and Bochkon flew out from the Barre-Montpelier Airport on Tuesday into treacherous fog and rain over Newfoundland.

"Naturally we are all concerned," he said. "Weather reports indicate they probably hit storms and headwinds over England that would retard their speed. Moreover, they were flying so high it is unlikely that they would be sighted on the way."

Ship Calls for Solberg Plane.

ST. JOHN'S, Nfld., Aug. 26 (Canadian Press). — The Newfoundland Government steamer Argyle today called at Merasheen Island in Placentia Bay to pick up Thor Solberg and Carl Petersen, who have dismantled their ill-fated sesquiplane and

Continued on Page Three.

I.R.T. IN RECEIVERSHIP; MOVE HAILED AS AID TO UNIFICATION PLAN

Action Is Agreed To by Company Due to Inability to Refund $41,500,000 Securities.

CITY'S STAKE $184,170,000

Speculation as to Whether Road Will Seek to Rid Itself of the Burden of Elevateds.

PUBLIC OFFICIALS ALOOF

But City Is Likely to Step In Later—Untermyer Sees Chance for Unity at "Fair Price."

The Interborough Rapid Transit Company consented yesterday to an equity receivership, and appointment of two receivers, Victor J. Dowling and Thomas E. Murray, was immediately made by Presiding Judge Martin T. Manton of the Circuit Court of Appeals.

The receivership, staved off several times during the history of the company, notably in 1922, immediately raised the question whether the action would free the subway division, which has always made money, from the burden of supporting the elevated lines of the Manhattan Railway Company, leased in 1903 to the Interborough for a term of 999 years.

Such an action probably would be resisted by the Rockefeller interests, who in the past have been successful in avoiding the step taken yesterday. The Rockefeller interests donated large Manhattan Railway holdings to various philanthropic institutions.

City's Stake $184,170,000.

The capitalization of the Interborough is $248,585,900, with a company investment of $216,143,000, and a city investment of $184,170,000. The city, under the terms of its contract with the company, becomes the eventual owner of the property, when the contract expires in 1968.

The move for an equity receivership was received with mixed feelings yesterday. Bonds of the company went up, principally because the move had been so sharply discounted in the market in advance, but also because of the belief that the company might rid itself of the Manhattan burden.

City officials were disposed to sit back and wait, to see also whether the Manhattan lease was planned to be terminated. Samuel Untermyer, special counsel to the Transit Commission in unification negotiations for a long time, hailed it as a golden opportunity for the city to put through a unification deal at a "fair price," namely, the $400,000,000 for the combined properties of the Interborough, Manhattan and B. M. T. that he offered in his last transit unification plan. He hinted that the receivership was not necessary and he is understood to be of the belief that shedding of the Manhattan is the real aim.

$831,709 Deficit in Year.

Figures available at the Transit Commission yesterday, showing the revenues of the company for the fiscal year ending June 30, 1932, disclosed a net corporate income for the subway division, after all fixed charges had been paid, of $3,586,640.97. On the elevated division the deficit was $4,418,183.90, leaving a system deficit of $831,709.17.

Should the two systems be separated, the Interborough's sole obligation to the Manhattan would be to pay the interest and sinking fund charges on the $44,000,000 of Interborough bonds issued to finance the third tracking of the elevated lines. Last year the Manhattan earned $951,000 above operating expenses toward its fixed charges, and the Interborough paid the Manhattan $1,808,240 as interest on the Manhattan bonds, $304,000 as dividends on a small part of Manhattan stock that never consented, in 1922, when the rest did, to abrogation of the guarantee of 7 per cent, and $51,000 in cash for running expenses of the company's offices.

Unofficial computation showed the Interborough to have earned a profit for the fiscal year ending June 30 of some $400,000, were its earnings to be calculated on the basis of having lost the Manhattan revenues, together with the Manhattan burden.

Crisis Averted in 1922.

In 1922, when the Interborough narrowly avoided receivership, the 7 per cent guarantee on the stock of the elevated roads was cut to 5 per cent, if and when earned, with the consent of all but a small group of the Manhattan stockholders. The latter are still receiving the 7 per cent every quarter while the majority have received occasional dividend payments, whenever the Interboroughh could spare the money.

Construction of the Brooklyn, Queens, and Bronx extensions, the lower half of the west side line, the

Continued on Page Eight.

March of Jobless Thousands Halted by Mexican Troops

Special Cable to THE NEW YORK TIMES.

MEXICO CITY, Aug. 26.—Thousands of hungry and jobless men and women began a march on Mexico City, it was learned today, but have been halted by troops on the way.

A large number, it is said, started in Tampico, and others joined them at every town and village they passed. At first the government was disinclined to intervene, but as the throng swelled and reports spread that they were dominated by Communists it was decided to take steps to avert incidents such as occurred in Washington in the dispersal of the bonus expeditionary force.

Troops barred the way of the marchers and persuaded them to abandon their plans.

GARNER PUTS BLAME ON HOOVER IN SLUMP

In Acceptance Letter He Lays Distress to Lack of Courage, Tariff and Delay on Relief.

OPPOSES CANCELING DEBTS

Holds Fair Duties Will Go Far to Solve Problem—Backs Platform on Repeal.

Accepting the Democratic nomination for Vice President in a letter to Senator Alben W. Barkley, made public yesterday, Speaker John N. Garner charged President Hoover and the Republican leaders in Washington with failure to meet the depression courageously or to take adequate relief measures.

He also assailed the Hoover Administration for the enactment of the Hawley-Smoot tariff, which he said had caused a tremendous decline in our trade, and declared that the Federal Government's $3,000,000,000 deficit lay entirely "on the doorstep of the Republican party."

Mr. Garner's letter, which was dated at his home in Uvalde, Tex., on Aug. 23, was made public here by the Democratic National Committee, along with the notification letter of the Kentucky Senator, who was temporary chairman of the Democratic National Convention.

Release of the letters for publication completed the first mail notification ceremony of a national candidate of a major party, which Mr. Garner had estimated would not cost more than 6 cents, but which caused a trifle more expense because of the postage required to mail copies of the letter to the national committee.

Attacks Federal Encroachment.

In his letter Mr. Garner asserted that nearly all the civic troubles of the American people were the consequence of the government's departure from its legitimate functions, and he attacked the steady encroachment of the Federal Government on the rights and duties of the States. Mr. Garner added that it was not the business of government to make individuals rich, although too often bent to that purpose, and characterized attempts to enforce morals by law as unjustifiable.

Mr. Garner criticized the Hoover Administration for failure to enact remedial action when it became obvious that the decline of international commerce and the bursting of

Continued on Page Four.

HOOVER SEES MAJOR CRISIS OVERCOME; CONFERENCE ADOPTS REVIVAL PROGRAM; BANK FORECLOSURES ON HOMES HALTED

HOUSE OWNERS GET RESPITE

Controller Pole Orders a 60-Day Suspension by All Receivers.

STATES ARE ASKED TO JOIN

Chairman Fort of Home Loan Board Cites "Portia's" Plea in an Appeal for Cooperation.

WIDE RELIEF IS EXPECTED

Industrial Conference Delegates Are Told That Move May Extend to All Foreclosures.

Special to THE NEW YORK TIMES.

WASHINGTON, Aug. 26.—A moratorium on foreclosures on first mortgages by receivers of closed national banks until the various Home Loan Banks are set in operation has been ordered by J. W. Pole, Controller of the Currency, at the request of Franklin Fort, chairman of the Home Loan Bank Board, who sent a similar request today to all State banking superintendents.

This was disclosed by Mr. Fort today in his address before the National Conference of Business and Industrial Committees. The Home Loan Banks are to begin operation by Oct. 15, and Mr. Fort, in addressing the leaders from the twelve Federal Reserve Districts, appealed to them to see to it on their return "not only that receivers generally grant this sixty days' respite but that other leaders do likewise."

A wave of enthusiasm which greeted Mr. Fort's direct appeal to the industrialists and business men composing his audience rivaled that which greeted the appearance at the opening of the session by President Hoover and his words of confidence in the future.

"It would be shameful," Mr. Fort declared with reference to owners of mortgaged homes, "if with relief in sight so soon, their courage and hope should be extinguished by taking away their homes and their life savings."

"There are times when forced liquidation of indebtedness is indefensible—certainly if other means of procuring funds exists.

"Payment may be nominated in bond, but, as Portia proved, it may not rightfully be exacted when payment drains the life-blood. And these days, the courage and hope of men and women are the life-blood of our recovery."

Proceedings Are Held Up.

The instructions of Controller Pole, sent yesterday to all receivers of insolvent national banks, said foreclosure proceedings already instituted in connection with first mortgages on homes of debtors are to be discontinued and none others instituted

Continued on Page Seven.

OPENING THE CONFERENCE.

Associated Press Photo.

President Hoover on the speaker's stand yesterday at the meeting of the nation's financial and industrial leaders to solve unemployment and other problems arising from the depression.

RENEW FARM SIEGE OF COUNCIL BLUFFS

Pickets, Reassembling, Clamp Down Truck Embargo and Sheriff Warns Marketers.

SIX MACHINE GUNS READY

Terming Situation 'Dangerous,' Embattled Officer Says That 'Anything May Happen.'

Special to THE NEW YORK TIMES.

COUNCIL BLUFFS, Iowa, Aug. 26.—All five highways converging here in this gateway to the great produce market of Omaha were blocked this evening by Farmers' Holiday pickets, reorganized from the scattered forces dispersed yesterday by Sheriff P. A. Lainson, and the Sheriff described the situation as "dangerous and acute."

As the picket posts were reinforced hourly in anticipation of the night movement of live stock, the Sheriff sat surrounded by 100 special deputies armed with six machine guns, 100 baseball bats and 100 pick handles.

"Anything may happen," he said.

Farmers, who bring their live stock into town at night to be ready for the early morning market opening and to avoid shrinkage, were warned by the Sheriff in a radio address of the chance of trouble and asked to cooperate by keeping their hogs and cream at home "until we work this thing out."

The pickets, striking farmers who are waging a non-selling campaign for higher prices, were "working it out" with telephone poles stretched across the roads to bar the progress of market-bound trucks.

Return of Pickets to Highways.

Most of the picket force, claiming a strength of 1,200, withdrew today, having accomplished its objective of releasing from jail a barber and piccolo player from Pierson, and the possibility of sending National Guard troops here was at least temporarily forestalled.

About 1,000 of the pickets went to their homes in the northwestern part of the State, Sioux City and Pierson being the principal cities, but 100 went by truck to Shenandoah to heckle Secretary Arthur M. Hyde of the Department of Agriculture and to picket the roads leading to the produce concentration centre of Henry Field, Republican candidate for the Senate. Others rejoined pickets already stationed on the various highways a mile or so out of town.

Sheriff Lainson, a captain in the Rainbow Division, who says his machine guns are there to "kill people if we must, but we don't want to," was credited by the citizenry with one defeat last night and another today. He had threatened to meet all attempts to deliver sixty-three

Continued on Page Eight.

CHALLENGES CRITICS OF LOANS BY R. F. C.

Pomerene Directs Fire at Those Who Have Alleged Favoritism to "Big Business."

SAYS FIGURES DISPROVE IT

69.3% of Loans Made to Small Banks, 37% of Nation's Depositors Aided.

Special to THE NEW YORK TIMES.

WASHINGTON, Aug. 26.—Critics of the Reconstruction Finance Corporation, particularly those who have contended that it is being operated for the sole benefit of "big business," were challenged by Atlee Pomerene, a Democrat and chairman of the corporation's board, in a speech he made today before the national conference of Business and Industrial Committees.

He quoted figures showing that 69.8 per cent of the total number of loans made by the corporation have been to banks in towns of under 5,000 population with only 2.1 per cent in cities above 1,000,000.

"It is estimated," he said, "that 37 per cent of the depositors in the United States have been benefited by the loans that have thus been made. Why, then, should anybody take the position that it is the bank that is favored and not the individual?"

Cites Reduced Bank Failures.

Mr. Pomerene's statements were construed in some quarters as a direct reply to some of the members of his own party, who have alleged favoritism to "big business" by the Reconstruction Finance Corporation. He had hardly begun his speech, in which he proposed to outline the place of the Reconstruction Finance Corporation in the new program for recovery, when he lashed out at the critics. He had started to quote figures.

"But before giving these figures," he said, "let me advert to a criticism that is being made by some people who are always ready and willing to criticize, no matter what the government may do. It is said that we are providing finances for the banks and for the railroads, but we are doing nothing for the individual.

"How strange that any thinking man should make a declaration of that kind! It is true we are financing banks, but let me tell you of the number of banks that have been financed both before and since the Reconstruction Finance Corporation was adopted.

"In the six months before this act was adopted the total bank failures were 1,860. During those six months the smallest number of failures in any one month was 158, the largest number 522.

"During the months which have intervened since the passage of this law only 604 have closed their doors. The largest number, 149; the smallest

Continued on Page Eight.

CENTRAL COUNCIL SET UP

H. M. Robinson to Head Drive for Spreading Credit and Jobs.

6-FOLD CAMPAIGN MAPPED

Committees Named to Study Needs on Specific Problems as Outlined by Mills.

CONFIDENT SPIRIT IS SHOWN

Industrialists at National Parley Echo the President's Belief That Upturn Is on Way.

Texts of all speeches at the conference on Pages 6 and 7.

Special to THE NEW YORK TIMES.

WASHINGTON, Aug. 26.—Spurred by a declaration from President Hoover that the "major financial crisis" had been successfully overcome, business and industrial leaders called together from over the nation set up a central council of war today for a vigorous new attack on what remains of the depression.

The drive of the forces of economic destruction had been stopped, the President told the National Conference of Business and Industrial Committees, but there had been casualties. "Château Thierry" had been won, he went on to say, and then he added:

"But I warn you that the war is not over; we must now reform our forces for the battle of Soissons."

Taking up this challenge, the 250 business and industrial leaders voted unanimously to create a central committee to bring Federal agencies and private business into an immediate six-point campaign to expand credit and spread employment.

H. M. Robinson Heads Drive.

The conference, scheduled for one day, was called together in the auditorium of the new Commerce Department Building at 10 A. M. and adjourned shortly after 4:30 this afternoon, an hour having been taken for lunch. Two subcommittees will meet tomorrow morning for a more detailed discussion of their plans and it is expected that by tomorrow night most of the delegates will be on their way home.

The central committee, organized along lines recommended by Secretary Mills, Governor Meyer of the Federal Reserve Board, Owen D. Young and others, was placed under the chairmanship of Henry M. Robinson, Los Angeles banker and close friend of President Hoover.

To its membership were named the chairmen of the banking and industrial committees of the Federal Reserve districts: Jackson E. Reynolds, president of the First National Bank of New York; A. W. Robertson, chairman of the board of the Westinghouse Electric and Manufacturing Company; George L. Harrison, governor of the Federal Reserve Bank of New York; Atlee Pomerene, chairman, and Charles A. Miller, president of the Reconstruction Finance Corporation; Robert P. Lamont, former Secretary of Commerce; Mr. Meyer and Secretaries Mills and Chapin.

Six Subcommittees Named.

The conference named six subcommittees as follows to begin immediate study of specific proposals in the sixfold program outlined by Secretary Mills, pointing to recovery:

1. The problem of making available credit affimatively useful to business—Chairman, Mr. Young.
2. Increased employment on railroads and stimulation of industry through expansion or maintenance of equipment and purchase of new equipment in cooperation with the Interstate Commerce Commission and the Reconstruction Finance Corportion—Committee, Daniel Willard, president of the Baltimore & Ohio Railroad, and George H. Houston, president of the Baldwin Locomotive Works.
3. Expansion of capital expenditures b industry in the way of replacement of obsolete and worn-out equipment and otherwise—Chairman, Mr. Robertson.
4. Increased employment through the sharing-work movement—Chairman, Walter C. Teagle, president of the Standard Oil Company of New Jersey.
5. Stimulation of repair and improve-

Continued on Page Eight.

Textile Industries Report a Wave of Buying; Trade Is Heaviest Since the Depression Began

Sharp gains in cotton this week, coupled with price advance in other basic textile commodities, have caused the most widespread buying movement the textile industries have witnessed since the depression began, flooding the selling houses with orders, a survey of these markets revealed yesterday. Commitments were so heavy that numerous cotton and woolen mills were compelled to withdraw quotations on finished goods and place them on an "at value" basis.

The one-cent rise in cotton, lifting it to $8\frac{1}{2}$ cents a pound for middling, or nearly 3 cents higher than levels prevailing a month ago, brought about a tremendous demand for gray cloth, the unfinished material used for cotton fabrics, which advanced $\frac{1}{4}$ to $\frac{1}{2}$ cent a yard, with many mills reporting a sold-up condition.

At yesterday's close of $1.75 a pound for the key style, raw silk has shown a rise of almost 60 per cent since the low point of $1.10 reached on June 2.

During the week rayon mills experienced a demand for yarn which was estimated to be the largest on record, causing a price advance of 5 to 10 cents a pound. Wool gains, ranging as high as 2 cents in some types, spurred a wide buying movement, which was said to have taken about 90,000,000 pounds off the market in the last ten days.

Cotton, silk and woolen fabrics all reflected the strength apparent in the basic commodities. Virtually every important cotton goods line was advanced in price. Leading bedsheet and pillow-case lines were advanced 10 per cent and towel prices were marked up a similar amount. Bedspread quotations were raised 5 per cent, while advances were registered in denims, outing flannels, muslins, shirting fabrics, wash goods and other lines.

Huge orders were placed by leading operators such as chain and department stores, mail-order houses, large wholesale organizations and apparel manufacturers.

Silk fabric prices continued to forge ahead and advances of 4 to 10 per cent were marked up. Completion of the showings of new dress models within the next ten days is expected to exert a fresh stimulus of buying, and a shortage of goods is considered likely.

During the week woolen cloth prices showed an upward tendency for the first time in five years. Important suiting lines were advanced $2\frac{1}{4}$ to $12\frac{1}{2}$ cents a yard and the largest producer withdrew quotations on its men's wear lines. Orders for fabrics and men's clothing were heavy and a scarcity of desirable goods was predicted in the market.

"All the News That's Fit to Print."

The New York Times.

LATE CITY EDITION
WEATHER—Showers today; rain and cooler tomorrow.
Temperatures Yesterday—Max., [illegible]; Min., 66.

VOL. LXXXI....No. 27,263. Entered as Second-Class Matter, Postoffice, New York, N. Y. NEW YORK, THURSDAY, SEPTEMBER 15, 1932. TWO CENTS In New York City | THREE CENTS Within 200 Miles | FOUR CENTS Elsewhere Except in 7th and 8th Postal Zones

ROOSEVELT MAPS FARM RELIEF PROGRAM, PLEDGES TARIFF AID IN TOPEKA SPEECH; HOOVER POLICIES DECLARED A FAILURE

10,000 CHEER THE NOMINEE

He Offers a Six-Point Outline, Including Aid on Mortgages.

STABILIZATION IS ASSAILED

Governor Attacks Farm Board Policy as Costly to Taxpayers and Ineffective.

HE IS HAILED AS VICTOR

Garner, Woodring and Others Predict Candidate's Triumph in the Middle West.

The text of Governor Roosevelt's speech is printed on Page 14.

By JAMES A. HAGERTY.

Special to THE NEW YORK TIMES.

TOPEKA, Kan., Sept. 14.—Speaking from the steps of the Kansas State Capitol, Governor Roosevelt presented today to an immediate audience of about 10,000 persons and a vastly larger radio audience his program of farm relief, on which he expects to carry all or most of the disaffected agricultural States of the Middle West.

Criticising President Hoover and the Republican national administration for complete failure to realize the desperate position of the farmers or to do anything useful to relieve their distress and prevent the foreclosure of thousands of farm mortgages in the corn and wheat belt, Governor Roosevelt made three definite proposals for immediate remedies.

He also presented a six-point program of principles, which, while not offering any very concrete plan, formed a basis for something more definite to be worked out after advice from those best fitted to suggest remedies.

The Governor did not suggest any particular method to make effective his program of principles, but both the phraseology of the principles and information from his advisers indicated that he had in mind the so-called domestic allotment plan.

Mid-West Victory Predicted.

During his stay here Governor Roosevelt, as the guest of Governor Woodring at the Executive Mansion, conferred with party leaders from Missouri, Iowa, Oklahoma, Texas and Nebraska as well as from Kansas, and was informed that the present indications were that he would carry all these States.

"Ninety per cent of the farmers in Kansas will vote for Governor Roosevelt," Governor Woodring said. "This means that he will carry the State by between 60,000 and 70,000. President Hoover in 1928 carried Kansas by more than 300,000. My predecessor won by more than 250,000. I was elected by 251 votes."

R. M. McCool, Oklahoma State chairman, sent a telegram predicting 200,000 plurality for Governor Roosevelt in that State.

Senator Thomas P. Gore telegraphed that Mr. Roosevelt would carry Iowa, native State of President Hoover, and added congratulations on the result of the Maine election.

Governor Roosevelt in his speech broke away from the panaceas which have been offered for the ills of agriculture in the past. He denounced the stabilization attempted by the Farm Board as useless and costly to the taxpayers; ridiculed crop control, as a hardship on the farmers; urged cooperative marketing and stressed "tariff adjustment" as the chief hope of immediate improvement.

Urges "Planned Use of Land."

Sharply separating the steps he declared should be taken for permanent remedies and immediate relief, Governor Roosevelt proposed as permanent measures reorganization of the Department of Agriculture, planned use of farm land, with elimination of relatively poor or marginal land for the raising of farm products, and the lightening of the tax burden on farm property.

For immediate relief he suggested the refinancing of farm mortgages to relieve the burden of excessive interest charges and the threat of fore-

Continued on Page Fourteen.

Roosevelt's Farm Program

Special to THE NEW YORK TIMES.

TOPEKA, Sept. 14.—Following are the "six points" Governor Roosevelt offered for the relief of the farmers in his address here today:

First—The plan must provide for the producer of staple surplus commodities such as wheat, cotton, corn (in the form of hogs) and tobacco, a tariff benefit over world prices which is equivalent to the benefit given by the tariff to industrial products. This differential benefit must be so applied that the increase in farm income, purchasing and debt-paying power will not stimulate further production.

Second—The plan must finance itself. Agriculture has at no time sought and does not now seek any such access to the public treasury as was provided by the futile and costly attempts at price stabilization by the Federal Farm Board. It seeks only equality of opportunity with tariff-protected industry.

Third—It must not make use of any mechanism which would cause our European customers to retaliate on the ground of dumping. It must be based upon making the tariff effective and direct in its operation.

Fourth—It must make use of existing agencies and so far as possible be decentralized in its administration so that the chief responsibility for its operation will rest with the locality rather than with newly created bureaucratic machinery in Washington.

Fifth—It must operate as nearly as possible on a cooperative basis and its effect must be to enhance and strengthen the cooperative movement. It should, moreover, be constituted so that it can be withdrawn whenever the emergency has passed and normal foreign markets have been re-established.

Sixth—The plan must be, in so far as possible, voluntary. I like the idea that the plan should not be put into operation unless it has the support of a reasonable proportion of the producers of the exportable commodity to which it is to apply. It must be so organized that the benefit will go to the man who participates.

PRESIDENT DECIDES TO TAKE THE STUMP

Roosevelt Farm Speech Spurs His Determination to Make Reply in the West.

LEADERS' URGINGS HEEDED

Five Addresses Planned, With That on Agriculture at His Iowa Birthplace.

Special to THE NEW YORK TIMES.

WASHINGTON, Sept. 14.—President Hoover has definitely decided to take the stump and personally carry the "issues at stake" to the electorate, it was learned today after Governor Roosevelt's Topeka speech on the farm problem had been analyzed by administration advisers.

Mr. Hoover and his advisers immediately decided that the views expressed by Governor Roosevelt on farm relief presented a vulnerable spot in the Democratic offense, and that the President was the only person who could adequately reply to the suggestions advanced by his rival.

The reply to Mr. Roosevelt probably will be made early in October in an address at West Branch, Iowa, Mr. Hoover's birthplace.

In the discussion of the President's plan, which took place after Senator Dickinson of Iowa and Secretary Hyde had discussed with the President what they termed the "fallacies" of Governor Roosevelt's farm program, it was intimated that the President probably would make five speeches.

Party Leaders See a Crisis.

In revamping his campaign plans, the President, it is said, was influenced not only by the Topeka speech, but by telegrams that poured in on the White House today from worried party leaders. Some of these counseled him to go on the hustings as the only hope of successfully carrying his economic policies to the country. They urged him to face a situation which they described as critical.

Some leaders who have been watching the progress of the campaign were severe in criticizing the Republican National Committee. They said the committee had been slow in getting under way.

The Maine election had a decided effect on Republican concern over the way the campaign was progressing. Some party workers suggested a conference of chieftains here to discuss ways to combat the electorate's discontent. It is understood that such a conference may be held within a few days, and that the President will see several party war horses this week-end.

The Maine election undoubtedly is responsible in part for the decision of the President to conduct his campaign more aggressively in the next two months. Senator Dickinson, who,

Continued on Page Thirteen.

LEON KRAEMER FLEES FROM GREAT MEADOW

'Brains' of Whittemore Gang Escaped Aug. 23 Hidden in Auto Driven by Trusty.

CAR FOUND, NO OTHER TRACE

Dangerous International Crook Was Serving a 40-Year Term —Plotted Break in 1927.

Leon Miller, who escaped from the Great Meadow prison at Comstock, N. Y., on Aug. 23, was Leon Kraemer, notorious safe-blower and hold-up man who was serving a sentence of forty years for his part in the activities of the Richard Reese Whittemore gang, it became known yesterday.

Kraemer's getaway was made with the connivance of a trusty named Thomas Burke who, as the driver of the warden's car and other prison automobiles, had a pass permitting him to go in and out of the gates. Kraemer hid himself in the rumble seat of a convertible coupe owned by the adopted son of Warden Joseph H. Wilson while it was in the prison garage. Burke drove him past the guards without arousing their suspicion.

Although the precise time they left the prison has not been determined, it was some time between 1 and 4 o'clock in the afternoon. Their disappearance was not noted until several hours later. The car in which they passed the gates was found that evening abandoned near Saratoga.

Announcement of the escape of the two men was made that night over the State police teletype system and also over Radio Station WGY, Warden Wilson said last night. Kraemer, however, was named in the alarm as Leon Miller, the name by which he was listed in the prison records, with the result that the news of the escape did not attract widespread attention.

"Brains" of the Gang.

There is no doubt, however, that Miller and Leon Kraemer, who, with his half-brother Jacob, was considered the "brains" of the Whittemore gang, are identical, Mr. Wilson said. Jacob Kraemer, who was also serving a forty-year sentence, died about two months ago of tuberculosis in Dannemora.

No trace of either Kraemer or Burke has been found since the discovery of their car, Warden Wilson said. The police alarms which have been sent out have contained warnings that Kraemer, or Miller, is an exceptionally dangerous man who is likely to shoot on sight any one attempting to recapture him.

Warden Wilson is the man who was severely rebuked last June by Commissioner of Correction Dr. Walter N. Thayer Jr. for his "thoughtlessness" in acting as host to the late Charles (Vannie) Higgins only

Continued on Page Three.

Algerian Wreck Kills 120 in French Legion; 150 Others Hurt as Train Plunges 250 Feet

By The Associated Press.

ORAN, Algeria, Sept. 14.—A troop train carrying 500 officers and members of the famous French Foreign Legion plunged into a ravine near Tlemcen today and the Havas News agency said probably 120 Legionaires had been killed and 150 more seriously injured.

The train left the track in the mountainous district between Zelboun and Turenne and plunged 250 feet to the bottom of the ravine.

The wreck was believed to have been caused by a mushy roadbed which had been affected by heavy rains recently.

The 500 soldiers were en route from Sidi-bel-Abbès, Algeria, to Oujda, Morocco, the territory made famous by Abd-el-Krim a few years ago during his stubborn resistance against French and Spanish troops in this area.

Thirty-one cars made the plunge down the ravine with the locomotive. From the wreckage came the cries and groans of the buried soldiers.

One of the two officers commanding the detachment was killed and most of the train crew were among the dead.

Rescue work was made most difficult by the limited means of communication but the whole population of the town of Turenne turned out to help.

These people were headed by General Paul Rollet, inspector of the Foreign Legion, and local authorities, who arrived in a special train late today.

The train turned about and took the first of the injured who had been extricated from débris to Tlemcen.

The territory in which the wreck occurred is in the foothills of the Atlas Mountains, which stretch from the Atlantic Ocean across Northwestern Africa to Tunis on the Mediterranean Sea.

The French Army authorities use the coastal line for transportation of troops very frequently, and it is the principal public conveyance medium along the Northern African coast.

The Foreign Legion maintains headquarters in both Sidi-bel-Abbès and Oujda, and it is presumed this was one of the regular troop movements.

Tlemcen is seventy miles southwest of Oran and is at an altitude of 2,703 feet.

M'KEE TENURE URGED FOR THE PUBLIC GOOD IN SUIT ON ELECTION

Tammany Counsel Ridicules Miller's Plea—Holds Citizens Best Served by Vote in Fall.

BOTH CITE THE SAME LAWS

Prompt Decision Is Expected—Newly Formed Departments Overmanned, Says Mayor.

Tammany went into court yesterday and laughed down as a "jury plea" the argument that the city's welfare required the retention of Joseph V. McKee as Mayor until the end of James J. Walker's unexpired term. The argument was made by former Governor Nathan L. Miller, appearing as counsel in Mr. McKee's suit to bar an election this Fall. It was contested by John Godfrey Saxe, chairman of the law committee of the Democratic State Committee, who appeared in behalf of the New York County Democratic organization.

Mr. Saxe declared that public policy demanded an election, rather than the contrary as contended by Mr. Miller. Basing their arguments on the same sections of the city charter and the State Constitution, Mr. Miller drew the conclusion that there could be no election for Mayor this Fall, and Mr. Saxe and Morris Hillquit, for the Socialist party, the conclusion that an election must be held.

The argument, which ended with decision reserved, was before Supreme Court Justice John E. McGeehan, in the new County Court House, and while it held the spotlight most of the day in the city's tangled political drama, other happenings served to emphasize the drawing of the battles lines between Mayor McKee and Tammany, in a fight that may last until the end of the year.

Hits at Predecessor.

Mayor McKee, in an interview at City Hall, made his first direct criticism of the administration of his predecessor by declaring that every time a new city department had been created it had been overloaded with manpower "until it sank of its own weight," and he announced his intention of keeping departmental forces down to the size necessary for the functioning of the particular department. Four new departments, Sanitation, Hospitals, City Planning and Taxicab Control, were created during the Walker Administration.

John H. McCooey, Brooklyn Democratic leader, revealed in an interview that his visit to City Hall on Tuesday, which had been interpreted as a friendly gesture to the Mayor, was at Mr. McKee's request. The statement left Mr. McCooey, in the eyes of political observers, pursuing his usual middle course.

Former Mayor John F. Hylan received a committee of the Hylan-for-Mayor League, and despite his previous assertions to the direct contrary, said he would run for Mayor this Fall, if an election is held, if there is sufficient demand for him.

Controller Berry asked Corporation Counsel Hilly a series of questions concerning the status, as far as the city payroll is concerned, of Mayor McKee, and also of Dennis J. Mahon, acting president of the Board of Aldermen. The Controller said he wanted a legal ruling on the point, or he might be responsible for any overpayment to either of the two officials.

Justice McGeehan reserved decision

Continued on Page Two.

ROME AWAITS PLANE OF AMERICAN NURSE OVERDUE FROM HERE

Machine With Three Aboard Fails to Arrive, Though It Is Sighted Over Ocean.

GASOLINE RUNNING LOW

With Fuel for 43 Hours, Ship Had Been Up 41—Italian Air Fields Lighted.

By The Associated Press.

ROME, Thursday, Sept. 15.—Italian air officials expressed apprehension early today in the absence of any reports of the transatlantic plane American Nurse after it had been out of New York for forty-one hours.

The information at Ciampino Airport was that the ship had gasoline for about forty-three hours and should arrive in Rome within that time. The air distance between Rome and New York is 4,200 miles and previous reports on the American Nurse indicated that it was making less than 100 miles an hour.

As the forty-first hour passed, a tired and sleepy group became tense at the airport. It was realized that, at the most, only an hour or two of gas remained in the craft.

There was no anxiety on the score of missing reports of progress, since the American Nurse would, in any event, have touched Europe in hours of darkness. The anxiety was over the possibility the ship had given out of gas in the Mediterranean area.

At 5:30 A. M. (12:30 A. M., Eastern Daylight Time) daylight had come and the airport lights were extinguished at Ciampino, and welcoming authorities went to Littorio Air Field north of Rome, where most fliers usually land in daylight hours.

Eclipse of Moon an Obstacle.

An eclipse of the moon occurred early last evening, making the route of the fliers over the Mediterranean extremely dark for a time, and it was believed possible they may have lost their way. Sighting of the plane would be extremely difficult in this darkness, and the plane's lack of radio eliminated any method of contact.

The latest report that could have involved the American Nurse was the sighting of an airplane over Sardinia flying low in the direction of Florence, Italy. This was at 9 P. M. (4 P. M., Eastern Daylight Time). The identification was not positive.

The report that the American Nurse had been sighted over Sardinia was discredited last night, however, by information from Carabinieri headquarters on three of the island's provinces which said nothing had been seen or heard of the plane.

Plane Seen by Liner France.

This meant that the last sighting of the plane probably was that of the liner France, which reported she had sighted a plane at 4:50 P. M., Greenwich Time (12:50 P. M., Eastern Daylight Time), flying eastward at Lat. 49.36 degrees N. and Long. 17.38 degrees W., or 400 miles southwest of Cape Fastnest, Ireland.

This would indicate that the American Nurse had flown 2,800 miles of the 4,200 between New York and Rome in 29 hours 34 minutes, or a little less than 100 miles an hour.

If she kept her course she should have struck the French coast in the vicinity of Bordeaux about nightfall.

This would also mean that the plane could not reach Rome in less than forty-four hours. The take-off was at 8:15 A. M. Tuesday. This allowed the American Nurse until 8:16 A. M., Eastern Daylight Time, or

Continued on Page Three.

HOOVER WARNS LEGION HE OPPOSES BONUS AS FATAL THREAT TO RECOVERY PROGRAM; CONVENTION COMMITTEE ASKS PAYMENT

The President's Statement

Special to THE NEW YORK TIMES.

WASHINGTON, Sept. 14.—Following is the text of President Hoover's statement concerning the proposed payment of a soldiers' bonus:

It is due to the country and to the veterans that there should be no misunderstanding of my position upon payment of the face value of the adjusted service certificates prior to maturity, as recommended in the resolution pending before the convention at Portland. I have consistently opposed it. In public interest I must continue to oppose it.

I have the duty not alone to see that justice and a sympathetic attitude is taken by this nation toward the 4,000,000 veterans and their families but also to exert myself for justice to the other 21,000,000 families to whom consummation of this proposal at this time would be a calamity. Cash payment of face value of certificates today would require an appropriation from the Treasury of about $2,300,000,000.

No matter how or in what form the payment to the veterans is imposed it will come out of all these families, but of more importance it will indefinitely set back any hope of recovery for employment, agriculture or business and will impose infinite distress upon the whole country. We owe justice and generosity to the men who have served under our flag. Our people have tried to discharge that obligation. Regular expenditures on account of the veterans already constitute nearly a billion a year or almost one-fourth of our whole Federal budget.

Every right-thinking man has the deepest sympathy for the veteran suffering from disability, for those out of work or for veterans on farms struggling with the adversities of the depression. No one who began life in the humble circumstances that I did, and who at the earliest and most impressionable age learned the meaning of poverty from actual experience, can be lacking in feeling and understanding of the problems and sufferings of these men and their families. I have seen war at first hand. I know the courage, the sacrifice of our soldiers.

But there are many million others in the same circumstances. They, too, must be entitled to consideration. Their employment and their farm recovery, as well as that of the veterans, can be secured only by the restoration of the normal economic life of the nation. To that end we have been and are devoting our best efforts. Anything that stands in the way must be opposed. The welfare of the nation as a whole must take precedence over the demands of any particular group.

I do not believe that the veterans generally really understand the adjusted service certificate law (so-

Continued on Page Four.

ASK 2 YEARS' GRACE IN DEBT PAYMENTS

Poland, Estonia and Latvia Take Advantage of Option in Funding Agreements.

NO OTHER NATIONS APPLY

State Department Announces Mellon and Reed Have Not Discussed Debts in London.

Special to THE NEW YORK TIMES.

WASHINGTON, Sept. 14.—Three foreign debtors, Estonia, Latvia and Poland, have notified the Treasury Department that they will take advantage of the option granted in the debt-funding agreements by postponing for two years the payment of principal on their debts to the United States due Dec. 15.

These governments owe $1,252,000 in postponable principal payments, as follows: Poland $1,125,000, Estonia $90,000 and Latvia $37,000. These represent the principal due in December on the bonds first issued under the funding agreement.

"In accordance with the terms of the agreement, the amount of the principal so postponed will bear interest at the rate of 3½ per cent per annum, payable semiannually," Secretary Mills said.

The payments postponed are somewhat less than the principal due. Treasury officials explained that under the agreements with these countries they were permitted to pay slightly less than payments provided for in the early years of the liquidation of their obligations and that therefore the entire principal is not postponable, since they took advantage of that option.

Poland Owes $4,427,980.

Poland owes $1,357,000 principal and $3,070,980 interest Dec. 15, or a total of $4,427,980. The payment due thus will be $3,302,980.

Estonia's total obligation Dec. 15 is $256,370, including $245,370 interest and $111,000 principal, while that of Latvia is $148,852, including $102,652 interest and $46,200 principal.

The interest payments are not postponable under the agreements and must be made or the debtor nations will be considered in default.

No reference was made by the Treasury to the other countries owing principal payments in December as no notice of postponement has been received. Under the debt pacts a ninety-day notice of postponement must be given, although the Secretary of the Treasury, within his discretion, may waive the ninety-day notice.

The substantial interest payment due Dec. 15 is $30,000,000 from Great Britain. Czechoslovakia owes $1,500,000 in principal at that time, while

Continued on Page Eight.

LEGION COMMITTEE DEMANDS THE BONUS

Votes 21 to 9 for Immediate Payment Following a Bitter Battle.

MINORITY REPORT UNLIKELY

Other Committees Reject Proposal to Censure the President and Approve Wet Measure.

By HAROLD N. DENNY.

Special to THE NEW YORK TIMES.

PORTLAND, Ore., Sept. 14.—The legislative committee of the American Legion ended a long battle on the bonus question tonight and wrote its report, embodying a demand for immediate and unqualified payment. The vote was 21 to 9, and it was said that there would be no minority report.

The text of the resolution was as follows:

Be it Resolved, That the American Legion endorses and urges the full and immediate payment of the adjusted compensation certificates.

Opponents of the proposal said tonight that the battle would certainly be carried to the floor tomorrow morning.

The legislative committee also approved a wringing-wet resolution calling for the immediate repeal of the Volstead act and the Eighteenth Amendment.

The proposal to censure the President was overwhelmingly defeated in the resolutions committee. After all the argument was over, only one vote, that of George Brown of Pennsylvania, was cast for the censure resolution. Mr. Brown sought to make a minority report but was informed that three members of a committee were needed for such a report. He was uncertain tonight what course the Pennsylvania delegation would take, but said it was determined to bring the matter to the floor in some way.

Opposition Fought Hard.

The decisions made tonight followed fights of unexpected intensity over the bonus and over censure of President Hoover for eviction of the bonus marchers from Washington. These were carried on behind the scenes here today and forced the national convention to defer final action on them until tomorrow.

The two chief committees of the convention, the committee on resolutions and legislation, struggled with these two explosive questions in locked chambers throughout the day, after trying unsuccessfully all last night to reach unanimity of opinion.

After the convention had ground away for hours today at routine business, hope of hearing from the committees was abandoned and the convention adjourned in midafternoon.

A resolution demanding immediate

Continued on Page Four.

PRESIDENT CITES HIS DUTY

Says Taxpayers Cannot Pay and Loan Would Impair Credit.

FIAT MONEY 'UNTHINKABLE'

Thus He Thrusts at the Bill Passed by House 'Under the Leadership' of Garner.

RECALLS POVERTY AS BOY

Welfare of 21,000,000 Families Besides the Veterans Is at Stake, He Declares.

Special to THE NEW YORK TIMES.

WASHINGTON, Sept. 14.—Formal notice was given by President Hoover tonight to the nation and the American Legion that he would continue to oppose veterans' bonus legislation. Such a proposal, he said, constitutes a "fatal threat to the entire program of recovery."

Coming on the eve of a probable demand by the Legion convention in Portland, Ore., for immediate payment of the bonus, and within a day of a challenge by Alfred E. Smith to both Presidential candidates to make known their position on the bonus, Mr. Hoover's statement emphasized that he not only had a duty to see that justice was done to the 4,000,000 veterans and their families, "but also to exert myself for justice to the other 21,000,000 families to whom consummation of this proposal at this time would be a calamity."

He said the $2,300,000,000 required to pay the bonus now was not available, and could not be raised by adding to the "crushing burden of taxes which drains every family budget in our country today, and weighs heavily upon business struggling in the midst of depression."

Calls Garner Idea "Unthinkable."

The money could not be borrowed, the President said, without impairment of the national credit, and he termed it "unthinkable" that the government would resort to the issuance of fiat money, "as provided in the bill which passed the House at the last session of Congress under the leadership of the Democratic Vice Presidential candidate."

The President's statement was accepted clearly as a challenge to the Legion convention. He had been informed that the service organization already had lying before it a resolution calling for immediate cash payment of the bonus, and that it probably would be adopted by a substantial majority.

Mr. Hoover reiterated his sympathy for the ex-service men. He recognized, he said, that "we owe justice and generosity" to the men who served under the flag. Sympathy had been deepened for those suffering from disabilities and for those out of employment. He made a brief reference to his own early life in expressing feeling for those who might be struggling with adversities at this time.

Refers to Poverty in Youth.

"No one who began life in the humble circumstances that I did," he said, "and who at the earliest and most impressionable age learned the meaning of poverty from actual experience, can be lacking in feeling and understanding of the problems and sufferings of these men and their families. I have seen war at first hand. I know the courage, the sacrifice of our soldiers."

The President added, however, that there were many million others in the same condition.

"They, too," he said, "must be entitled to consideration. Their employment and their farm recovery, as well as that of the veterans, can be secured only by the restoration of the normal economic life of the nation."

He declared that anything that stood in the way of this recovery "must be opposed." "The welfare of the nation as a whole must take precedence over the demands of any particular group."

The President said that, no matter in what form the payment was made, money for cashing the veterans' certificates at this time would have to come out of the resources of all families; from a people who in trying to discharge its obligations to its ex-soldiers was already spending nearly a billion dollars a year—"al-

Continued on Page Four.

Roosevelt, on the campaign trail, telling farmers in Topeka, Kansas, how the New Deal could help them.

F.D.R. aboard the Roosevelt Special.

Roosevelt brought his message to the miners in Wheeling, West Virginia.

President Herbert Hoover looked tired as he campaigned for re-election.

A campaign photograph of the Democratic candidates, Franklin Delano Roosevelt and John Nance Garner, at Hyde Park.

"All the News That's Fit to Print."

The New York Times.

LATE CITY EDITION
WEATHER—Rain today; tomorrow partly cloudy, much colder.
Temperature Yesterday—Max., 50; Min., 42.

VOL. LXXXII....No. 27,346. Entered as Second-Class Matter, Postoffice, New York, N. Y. NEW YORK, WEDNESDAY, DECEMBER 7, 1932. TWO CENTS In New York City | THREE CENTS Within 200 Miles | FOUR CENTS Elsewhere Except in 7th and 8th Postal Zones

CITY FACES DEFAULT TODAY; $25,000,000 FURTHER SAVING NEEDED TO GET NEW LOAN

$40,000,000 PAYMENT DUE

$55,000,000 Additional Must Be Met Before the End of the Week.

$20,000,000 CASH ON HAND

Board Approves $20,000,000 Cut in Salaries, but Bankers See Need for More Economy.

McKEE AND MAHON IN CLASH

Acting Mayor Charges Plot as Tammany Bloc Seeks to Shift Responsibility for Slashes.

Facing an inescapable default on the city's obligations today, the Board of Estimate voted unanimously yesterday at a special meeting for a resolution declaring that city salaries should be cut $20,000,000 next year in all grades down to $2,000 a year, with full protection of the pension rights of civil servants.

Members of the Patrolmen's Benevolent Society launched a campaign at the same time to enlist the public's support in their fight aginst pay cuts. Through newspaper advertising the patrolmen reminded the public that they had borne extra duty resulting from unemployment without complaint and that they had given generously to the needy on many occasions. They took the position that having received their first-grade increases by referendum, it would be a "gross injustice" to cut their salaries without another referendum giving the people of the city a full voice in the matter. By their action the policemen lined up with the teachers and firemen in fighting pay cuts.

The city's financial affairs reach a crisis today when, unless the bankers agree to advance funds, the city will be unable to meet the maturity of $40,000,000 of revenue bills drawn against the $151,000,000 revolving credit. On Monday and yesterday the city met maturities of $15,000,000 each, thereby eating heavily into its $50,000,000 in available cash. Today's maturity will be beyond its means, in the opinion of the financiers, while, without help, tomorrow's maturity of $25,000,000 and Friday's maturity of $30,000,000 are hopelessly beyond the ability of the city to meet.

Bankers Are Watching.

There was no formal meeting of the bankers yesterday, but individually they watched the progress of the Board of Estimate meeting with keen interest. It was the prevailing view among them late last night that the resolution providing for salary reductions of $20,000,000 had fallen considerably short of the economies needed to rehabilitate the city's credit. The bankers indicated that additional savings of about $25,000,000 through the elimination of unnecessary appropriations and useless city departments would probably restore the city's credit sufficiently to permit aid to be extended.

Charles E. Mitchell, chairman of the National City Bank, kept in touch last night with the situation by telephone. Members of the banking group, including Winthrop W. Aldrich, president of the Chase National Bank and representatives of J. P. Morgan & Co., the Bankers Trust, the Bank of the Manhattan Company, the New York Trust and other leading institutions, said that no further conferences were necessary before action on a loan to the city could be taken. If the city took the required steps Mr. Mitchell and Mr. Aldrich could approve a credit on behalf of the group, it was said.

The Salary Resolution.

The resolution adopted yesterday after a heated clash between Acting Mayor Joseph V. McKee and Dennis J. Mahon, acting president of the Board of Aldermen, read as follows:

> Resolved, by the Board of Estimate and Apportionment, that, in the event that the Legislature grants to the city authorities full power to fix all salaries paid out of the city treasury, it is the sense of the board that there be a reduction in payment of salaries for 1933 of $20,000,000 below the budget for 1933 adopted by the Board of Estimate and Apportionment, without impairment of pension rights; no reduction however to affect those

Continued on Page Nineteen.

Creditors Study Repurchasing By Germans of Own Securities

Wireless to THE NEW YORK TIMES.

LONDON, Dec. 6.—The reported large-scale repurchasing by Germans of their own securities in New York was among the subjects coming before the study commission of the German standstill committee when it met in London today.

It is understood the delegates had before them the memorandum from the Reichsbank giving the first exact figures on this buying movement, which had been reported in some quarters as being of extraordinary proportions.

The first day's session was mostly preliminary, however, and no announcement of any decision was issued. The meeting will be resumed tomorrow.

CITY HIDES DEFICIT, M'GOLDRICK CHARGES

Overestimates of Revenue Unbalance Budget More Each Year, He Testifies.

BONDS SOUND, BERRY HOLDS

Admits They Won't Sell, but Tells Seabury They Are Best Possible Investment.

The most dismal picture of the city's finances to date was drawn before the Hofstadter legislative committee yesterday. As a climax, Controller Charles W. Berry appeared with assurances that the city was solvent, a condition entirely dependent, he admitted, upon its ability to sell bonds and collect taxes.

"Our present trouble," he told Samuel Seabury, counsel to the committee, "is that it is impossible to sell a New York City security anywhere. There is a feeling that there is something wrong with the city, or, anyway, they are not salable."

Mr. Berry was affable, willing and not at all gloomy. He did not share the opinion of other witnesses, including Professor Joseph McGoldrick of Columbia University, that the sinking funds were a "bookkeeping fiction," that the city's budget was about $150,000,000 out of balance due to accumulated tax deficiencies, or that the reduction of real estate assessments to the level of current sale values would cut down the city's margin under its debt limit to less than $200,000,000.

Freeing of Policeman Sifted.

With an abrupt change in the nature of the testimony, the committee held a night session in an effort to finish by tomorrow. The work of the Parole Commission was taken up.

John C. Maher, chairman of the commission, after being unable to explain clearly why the commission had shortened the prison terms of several convicts, including Canice Neary, who was later convicted of first degree murder in the Elizabeth mail robbery, said that what his department needed was more men and more money.

He was followed on the witness stand by Irving Halpern, chief probation officer of the Court of General Sessions. Mr. Halpern, asked if his department could absorb the Parole Commission and do its work, said he thought it could.

At the earlier session Mr. Berry proposed as at least one remedy for the present situation the adoption of a capital outlay budget, the operation of which, he thought, would reduce the city's annual interest charges and other corollary items by between $30,000,000 and $40,000,000, and said the proposal would be placed before the Legislature at the special session.

On the theory that, regardless of the value in the open market, the city's short-term securities sold to the sinking funds must be redeemed by the city at par—giving the sinking funds, he said, the best possible investment at the present time—Mr. Berry defended the operations of those funds as sound. He could not agree with Mr. Seabury that the selling of city bonds to the sinking funds might be a mere bookkeeping operation.

Senator John J. McNaboe of the Democratic minority on the committee insisted upon being assured that the city was solvent. "I can tell you that it is, yes, sir," the Controller said.

"In answering the question of Senator McNaboe," Mr. Seabury asked, "you based your answer, did you

Continued on Page Eighteen.

Tammany Labor Chief Paid by Contractors, Medalie Charges, to Protect Non-Union Men

Patrick J. Commerford, vice president of the New York State Federation of Labor and a powerful figure in a group of Tammany labor leaders, received $75 a week from the payroll of a hoisting concern which employed non-union labor, it was testified yesterday in Federal court.

The testimony followed a charge made by George Z. Medalie, United States Attorney, that Commerford had collected from at least two hoisting concerns while he was drawing a salary of $200 a week as supervisor of Local 125 of the International Union of Operating and Hoisting Engineers.

Mr. Medalie also charged before Federal Judge Robert P. Patterson that Commerford, who is vice president of the Building Trades Council, had accepted sums ranging from $2,500 to $7,000 from four building contractors as his price for settling labor disputes.

The charges were made at the opening of Commerford's trial on three indictments charging perjury and evasion of the Federal income tax law for 1929, 1930 and 1931. The court room was crowded and many of the spectators were members of New York labor organizations.

The witness who testified to carrying Commerford on his company's payroll was Edward A. White, treasurer of the United Hoisting Company, who admitted that his concern had employed non-union labor on a union job.

He pointed out that union men had complained of this practice and in reply to Mr. Medalie's question as to why Commerford had been carried on the company's payroll, he said:

"It was necessary to have some one to straighten out these difficulties."

"Do you mean," Mr. Medalie

Continued on Page Thirteen.

SMALL POWERS ASK FOR CHECK ON JAPAN AT LEAGUE MEETING

Four Nations, Including Irish Free State, Say Action on Manchuria Is Essential.

STAND ON LYTTON REPORT

Big Five, Including Americans, Halt Disarmament Talk to Heed Far East Problem.

By CLARENCE K. STREIT.
By Cable to THE NEW YORK TIMES.

GENEVA, Dec. 6.—The members of the League of Nations gathered here in special assembly began today finally to pass judgment on the Chino-Japanese conflict, which W. W. Yen, spokesman for China, reminded them began fifteen months ago.

Representatives of four governments, the Irish Free State, Czechoslovakia, Sweden and Norway, successively gave their verdict. All explained that they were judging now only of the methods the disputants used to advance their case, not the substance of the dispute itself.

All then strongly urged the adoption of the Lytton report. They condemned Japan specifically, rejecting flatly her plea that she acted in self-defense and that Manchukuo was not a puppet State and roundly declaring her methods "infringed" the vital principles of the League, which must be maintained "at any cost."

All said their governments would not recognize Manchukuo.

All Plead for Reconciliation.

All pleaded for the reconciliation of China and Japan. All urged Japan not to force the League to execute the compulsory provisions of the covenant, which they warned it must do, failing conciliation, if it were to survive "this supreme test."

This was the minimum of their four solemn statements this afternoon. Some went further. Edouard Benes for Czechoslovakia made the strongest speech. He was most applauded.

Tomorrow other small powers will give their verdicts.

The delegates of the great powers all sat silent and none is yet listed to speak. Their Premiers and Foreign Ministers did make a point of showing the importance they attached to the Assembly's problem by breaking up the Five-Power disarmament talks, for which they obviously needed every hour today, when the Assembly began at 11 A. M., and sitting through its morning session.

Ramsay MacDonald, Sir John Simon, Premier Herriot, Joseph Paul Boncour, Foreign Minister von Neurath and Baron Pompeo Aloisi all were in the Assembly, while Norman H. Davis and Minister Hugh Wilson sat with the Russian observer, Stein, in the non-Leaguers box. The Big Five leaders resumed their disarmament work while the others were passing on their verdict in the afternoon.

Condemns Chinese Boycott.

Declaring that the Chinese boycott and anti-foreign propaganda in China should be condemned, M. Bencs told the assembly.

"But if the League condemns them, it must with equal firmness proceed with regard to a member of the League which decides to be its own judge and carries out military operations on a great scale, which result in detaching several provinces from another member of the League."

He called the establishment of Manchukuo a "flagrant anomaly in relationship to members of the League," and "contrary to Article X of the Covenant."

Joseph Connolly, for the Irish Free State, referring to the multilateral treaty, said the Lytton Report "makes it clear that actual infringements have taken place, and it is due to those infringements and to

Continued on Page Four.

SHAH DEFIES BRITAIN IN 'OFFENSIVE' NOTE; BREACH IS WIDENING

Sending of a Single Soldier to Guard the Oil Fields Would Be Resisted, Persian Ruler Says.

HINTS AT BOMBING OF PLANT

Company Blames Cancellation of Lease to Disappointment at Slump in Royalties.

Wireless to THE NEW YORK TIMES.

LONDON, Dec. 6.—The British Foreign Office today received a note from the Persian government which was "so offensive" to officials here that it will not be published.

In it the Shah warns the British government that, if a single soldier or marine is sent to guard the Anglo-Persian Oil Company's oil fields, he will regard it as a direct provocation. He reminds the British in effect that it needs only a couple of Persian shells or a single well-aimed bomb dropped into the vast refinery at Abadanto to send millions of barrels of British oil up in smoke.

The cancellation of the Anglo-Persian Oil Company's concession is "final," the Persian government declares, and it is up to that company to request a new concession based on terms fairer to the Persian people.

Persia's note is a retort to recent communications from the British government refusing to recognize the annulment of the concession and threatening to take "all legitimate measures" necessary to protect British interests. The Anglo-Persian Oil Company is leaving the conduct of the case entirely to the British government, which owns more than half its shares.

Situation Appears Precarious.

So far the Persians have not confiscated any British property or interfered with operations in the Anglo-Persian oil fields. With bitterness blazing up on both sides, however, the future of the company's properties is hanging by a thread, and the slightest impulsive act on either side might have serious consequences. Unless there is to be an open rupture, either the British or the Persians must back down, but so far neither is yielding an inch.

The British denounce Persia's action as a repudiation of a solemn contract and demand that the cancellation be rescinded. The Persians claim complete authority to annul any concession in their own territories but add that they are willing to lay the whole case before the World Court or any other interna-

Continued on Page Five.

HOOVER MESSAGE CALLS FOR SALES TAX, PAY CUTS, ECONOMY AND BANK REFORM; HOUSE IS WORKING ON 2.75% BEER BILL

BEER HEARINGS ON TODAY

42 Witnesses Called for Collier Measure, Also Legalizing Wines.

DRY STATES PROTECTED

Interstate Shipment Would Be Restricted—Tax of $5 a Barrel Is Tentatively Urged.

REPEAL MOVE IN SENATE

Glass Resolution, Banning the Saloon, Sent to Committee—Numerous Bills Proposed.

Special to THE NEW YORK TIMES.

WASHINGTON, Dec. 6.—Recovering from the defeat of their first attempt at prohibition reform in the "lame-duck" session, the Democratic leadership of the House today started machinery seeking to legalize beer and wine for purposes of revenue.

The Democratic modification bill, proposing beer of 2.75 per cent alcohol by weight and wine described only as "non-intoxicating vinous liquors made by the natural fermentation of grape juice without the addition of distilled spirits," was introduced by Representative Collier, chairman of the Ways and Means Committee, with the announcement that hearings on the measure would begin before that committee tomorrow.

But while the House leaders placed repeal legislation for this session into the discard, the Senate gave signs of action.

The Glass resolution, proposing repeal along the lines of the Republican platform plank, was referred to the Judiciary Committee for study on the request of its author, Senator Glass. Senator Robinson of Arkansas, the Democratic leader, indicated that it would be the general model for the Democratic program in the Senate.

Beer also drew attention, with Senator Tydings introducing a modification bill, proposing to eliminate all figures with reference to alcoholic content from the Volstead act and levying a tax of 16 cents a gallon on such beverages as would be allowed.

His bill also proposes that the revenues thus accruing should, after three years, be segregated in an "unemployment reserve fund" until they should reach $5,000,000,000, the fund to be used for relief purposes.

Blaine Proposes Repeal.

Senator Blaine proposed a repeal resolution with little deviation from the measure defeated in the House yesterday.

Senator Bingham offered an amendment to the Volstead act, exempting beer and wine of not more than 3.2 per cent by volume from the classification of intoxicants.

The House measure, entitled "A bill to provide revenue by taxation of certain non-intoxicating liquor, and for other purposes," proposed a tax of $5 a barrel on the beer and 20 cents a gallon on the naturally fermented wine.

Mr. Collier explained that the figures were strictly "arbitrary," and might be changed one way or the other after a study by the committee.

The House Democrats went at the

Continued on Page Seventeen.

Points Stressed by the President

Special to THE NEW YORK TIMES.

WASHINGTON, Dec. 6.—The principal objectives which President Hoover urged upon Congress in his message today were:

Immediate and complete reorganization of the banking system, which the President said, "has failed to meet this great emergency."

Imposition of a special excise tax to cover practically all manufactures at a uniform rate, except necessary food and, possibly, some grades of clothing.

Continuance of the "furlough" system among Federal employes, amounting to an 8 1/3 per cent pay-cut, and adding to this an 11 per cent reduction on that part of all government salaries above $1,000 a year, making an average reduction of about 14.8 per cent on pay in excess of $1,000.

Reorganization of the government through grouping and consolidation of more than fifty executive and independent agencies.

A reduction in appropriations below those of the last Congressional session by more than $830,000,000, the reduction to be offset in part, however, by an increase of about $250,000,000 in "uncontrollable items, such as increased debt services."

A scaling of expenditures for public works down to $442,769,000 as compared to $717,262,000 for the present year.

Elimination of payments to veterans where "abuses have grown up from ill-considered legislation."

Cooperation in a vigorous and whole-hearted way with other governments in the economic field, and a strengthening of commodity prices by expansion in consumption of goods through the return of stability and confidence in the world at large.

A reduction of all governmental expenditures, national, State or local, and the balancing of the Federal budget.

The President said this government had informed foreign nations it disapproved of suspending the Dec. 15 payments. He added: "I have stated that I would recommend to the Congress methods to overcome temporary exchange difficulties in connection with this payment from nations where it may be necessary."

FRANCE IN DEBT TALK WITH BRITAIN TODAY

May Arrange to Let London Use Her Credits Here for Payment to Shield Pound.

WAY OUT FOR HERRIOT SEEN

London Abandons Hopes for Delay of Instalment and Studies Ways to Pay.

By P. J. PHILIP.
By Wireless to THE NEW YORK TIMES.

PARIS, Dec. 6.—A debtors' conference of great importance will be held in Paris tomorrow and Thursday.

Although tonight only the most fragmentary hints were allowed to trickle out, it is believed that at the meeting France and Great Britain may make a common front not as debtors but as to debt payments to the United States.

France, who is a debtor to Britain, may arrange to put her credits in New York at the disposal of Britain to help in the payment of the Dec. 15 instalment to the United States. By such action the ill effects to sterling that might result from payment in gold or otherwise may be avoided. By coming to the help of her British creditor in time of need, France would discharge the moral obligation she is under for the great reduction of her debt to Britain in the past and would be in a position to earn the most favorable consideration for the future. She would fulfill the rôle that Premier Herriot claimed for her in the last note to Washington of a bulwark against further financial collapse in Europe, and will so complete the contribution she made to world stability by wiping out reparations at Lausanne and beginning constructive work at Stresa.

Such, at least, is the belief—it is not more than a belief—that is entertained here tonight about the objects and probable results of the forthcoming conference of Prime Minister MacDonald, Premier Herriot and Neville Chamberlain, British Chancellor of the Exchequer.

Mr. MacDonald and M. Herriot are traveling tonight from Geneva. Mr. Chamberlain, who will be accompanied by British Treasury experts, will arrive tomorrow evening by a late train.

Premier Herriot's day will be a whirlwind of events. He will reach Paris about 8 o'clock tomorrow morning. At 9 he will attend a Cabinet meeting which will be followed by a Ministerial Council meeting at 11. He has asked that the Finance Commission of the Chamber of Deputies be summoned in the morning so that he may be free for conversations with Mr. MacDonald, and doubtless also with experts of the Finance Ministry, in the afternoon. He has informed Louis Jean Malvy, president of the Finance Commission, that he will furnish the precise intention of the government with regard to the Dec. 15 payment.

The Premier's position is difficult.

Continued on Page Ten.

DEMOCRATS PROPOSE TO BROADEN RELIEF

Main Suggestion Is to Take From R. F. C. Power Over Loans to States.

RESTRICTIONS CRITICIZED

Senators Complain That Relief Measures Used Thus Far Are Inadequate.

Special to THE NEW YORK TIMES.

WASHINGTON, Dec. 6.—Senate Democrats who at the last session of Congress were forced to restrict their unemployment relief demands to a program that President Hoover would approve are planning an immediate fight for a greatly broadened program.

As described today in an authoritative quarter, the Democratic program is aimed principally at removing Federal loans to States from under the auspices of the Reconstruction Finance Corporation.

This revolt against the corporation was ascribed by one Democratic spokesman to the "strangulation" of State relief work by the strictures placed on relief loans by the corporation, as well as the general attitude that States should not be held accountable to a semi-public corporation.

The tentative plan now regarding this phase of relief is either to set up a separate agency to administer loans primarily for the relief of destitution or to authorize these loans under definite conditions by the Treasury itself.

The new Democratic relief activity served to recall the fact, shown by reports of the Reconstruction Finance Corporation, that while Congress at the last session authorized a fund of $300,000,000 from which loans for direct relief were to be made to States, only about $60,000,000 of such loans have been authorized and less than $50,000,000 actually granted.

Senators to Sound Out Opinion.

Sponsors of the new program will not discuss their plans until they have been placed in concrete form, which is expected within a fortnight. In the meantime, Senators plan to make speeches regarding relief to sound out the opinion of the Senate as a whole and gauge, if possible, the disposition of the House.

Democratic leaders, it is understood, are resentful of the attitude expressed in administration quarters that the relief program is an accomplished fact. This feeling, expressed privately, has been intensified recently, particularly among those who come from urban centres, by visits to their home States incident to the political campaigns.

It is said that virtually no results have been shown thus far by the comparatively small Federal relief loans, and even less by public building programs and the loans for self-

Continued on Page Two.

DEBT ISSUE IS KEPT OPEN

President Promises New Message on Economic Cooperation Abroad.

FOR CUT IN VETERAN FUNDS

Pay Reduction of 11 Per Cent Urged, With $830,000,000 Slash in Appropriations.

LESS FOR PUBLIC BUILDINGS

Banking Recommendations Are Construed as Endorsement of Branch System.

The text of President Hoover's Message to Congress, Page 16.

By ARTHUR KROCK.

WASHINGTON, Dec. 6.—As provided in the Constitution, the President sent an annual message (his last) to Congress today, and it was read to the members by clerks in each chamber.

The message, save in a few particulars, was general in its recommendations. The President restated firmly his doctrine of American "individualism." Notable among his specific proposals for legislation during the short session were the imposition of a general manufacturers' sales levy, except on some of the necessaries of life; a one-year reduction of 11 per cent in all government salaries over $1,000; the elimination of allowances for able-bodied war veterans, and a reform in the banking system.

He did not mention prohibition reform, one aspect of which (with relation to legalizing and taxing "real beer") is about to engage the concentrated attention of Congress in its efforts to balance the budget.

His reference to the war debts included the statement that the administration does not favor suspension of the payments due Dec. 15, and contained a promise that in a special message he will soon make recommendations looking to economic cooperation with the rest of the world through disarmament and the leveling of destructive trade barriers.

Keeps the Debt Question Open.

Obviously, with a full knowledge of the unwillingness of Congress to reopen the debt question at this time, the President is moving to keep it open. He reiterated that the world is interdependent; that no part of it can refuse to consider the economic difficulties of another part. Civilization, he said, depends upon the wise and friendly solution of these questions.

But, looking straight toward Europe, Mr. Hoover added that these friendly solutions depend in part upon "adherence to agreements entered upon until mutually revised," thereby giving his own adverse opinion of default.

Comment from the Senators and Representatives to whom the message was addressed was prompt and plentiful, but not illuminating as to what fruit the document will bear in legislative enactments.

Branch Banking Suggestion Seen.

With the exception of Representative McDuffie of Alabama, no member interviewed by THE NEW YORK TIMES referred to the proposed cut in the cost of Veterans' Bureau administration. Many Democrats and some Republicans construed the President's call for banking reform as an endorsement of branch banking, since he pointed to the absence of depression bank failures in Great Britain and Canada. Most of them oppose the Canadian plan.

Republicans who discussed the message for publication were generally restrained in their praise, although Senator Smoot thought it "wonderful." Democrats chided the Chief Executive for "generalities" and demanded specifications for his proposed cures, although they admitted "off the record" that they would probably not vote for them anyhow.

The net effect on Congress was about that which usually follows the submission of such a State paper by a defeated President—partisan criticism, tempered by the reflection that the critics will soon be in power themselves and do not intend to do

Continued on Page Seventeen.

Market Up 1 to 6 Points on Hoover Message; Sales Tax, Economy and Aid Abroad Hailed

President Hoover's message to Congress, particularly those sections touching the need of a manufacturers' sales tax, rigid governmental economy and cooperation with other governments, evoked such enthusiasm in Wall Street yesterday that leading issues on the New York Stock Exchange engaged in one of the broadest advances in several weeks.

Net gains ran from 1 to 6 points, with the sharpest movement occurring in the last hour after the financial community had had time to take it in hurriedly.

The point which impressed Wall Street most, judging by the comment, was Mr. Hoover's strong advocacy of a sales tax with its promise of "an adequate basis of revenue." Approval of other recommendations, including that of a broad reorganization of various departments of the Federal administration, was also expressed.

Comment on the suggested reforms in the banking system was guarded.

The pace of trading on the Stock Exchange was accelerated sharply in the last hour and the total turnover, 1,108,000 shares, was nearly 400,000 shares greater than on the day before.

American Telephone and Telegraph, one of the leaders of the upswing, closed with a net gain of 4⅝ points; Auburn Auto was up 5, Santa Fé 3¼, Allied Chemical 4⅛, American Can 3⅛, Atlantic Coast Line 3¼, J. I. Case 3½, International Business Machines 4¾, Eastman 2¼, du Pont 2¼, Louisville & Nashville 3⅛, National Biscuit 3½, New York Central 2¼, Norfolk & Western 4, United States Steel 2¾, United States Steel preferred 3¼, Union Pacific 5⅜ and Delaware & Hudson 6.

The improvement in bond prices was pronounced in the railway group, some of them registering substantial net gains. United States Government obligations advanced in anticipation of the Treasury's financing plans for Dec. 15.

Increased optimism in Wall Street was ascribed to the more hopeful attitude adopted toward the present session of Congress with respect to matters of major economic importance.

Times Wide World Photo

This photograph was taken 11 days before the assassination attempt on a fishing trip from Jacksonville, Florida on Vincent Astor's yacht, the *Nourmahal.* Left to right, Dr. Leslie Heiter of Mobile, George St. George of New York, Justice Frederic Kernochan of New York, Kermit Roosevelt, President-elect Roosevelt and Mr. Astor.

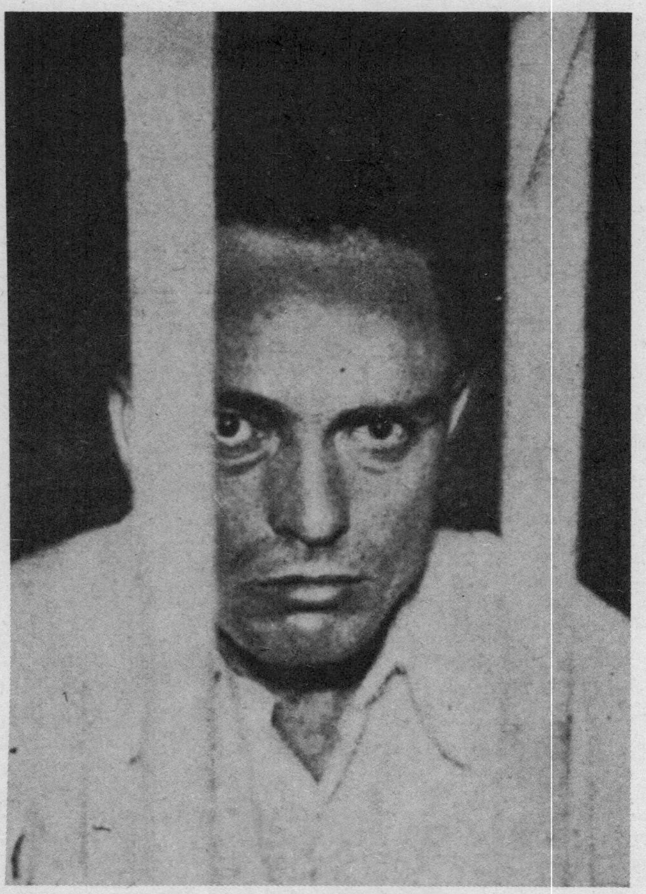

The alleged anarchist looks out through the bars in his cell in the jail at Miami City Hall. Zangara just missed killing FDR, but killed Chicago's Mayor Anton J. Cermak. He was executed on March 21.

Time Wide World Photo

The policemen who arrested Zangara, and the revolver from which he fired at the President-elect. Officer Leaston Crews is holding the gun at left. In center is Arthur Clark at right is Raymond Jackson.

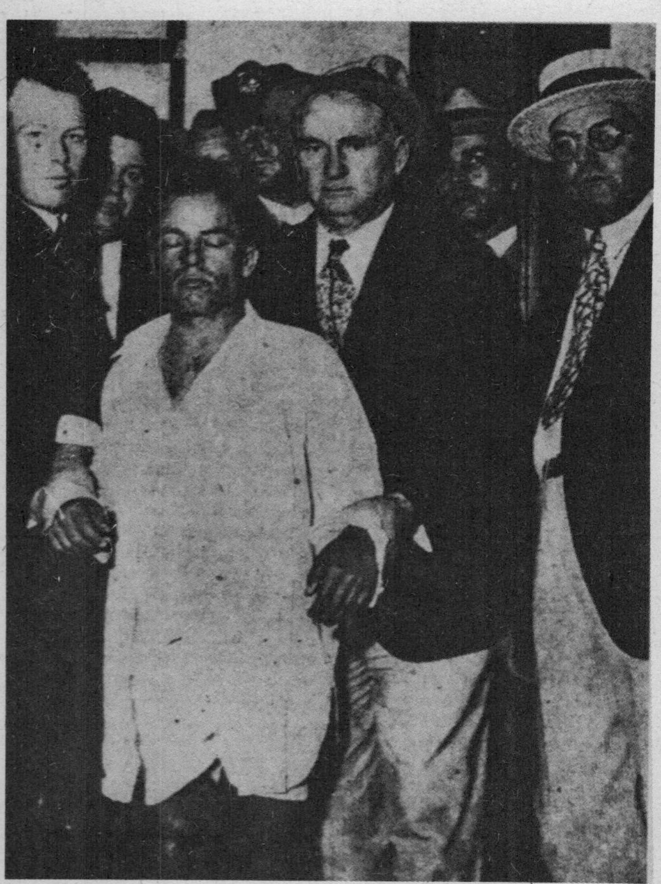

Times Wide World Photo

Joseph Zangara at Police Headquarters after attempting to assassinate President-elect Roosevelt. Part of his clothing had been removed in a search of his effects.

Roosevelt in the motorcade that took him to address a huge Miami crowd.

"All the News That's Fit to Print."

The New York Times.

LATE CITY EDITION
POSTSCRIPT
WEATHER—Fair today; tomorrow cloudy, warmer, probably rain
Temperature Yesterday—Max., 42; Min., 27.

Copyright, 1933, by The New York Times Company.

VOL. LXXXII....No. 27,417. Entered as Second-Class Matter. Postoffice, New York, N. Y. NEW YORK, THURSDAY, FEBRUARY 16, 1933. TWO CENTS In New York City. | THREE CENTS Within 200 Miles | FOUR CENTS Elsewhere Except in 7th and 8th Postal Zones

ASSASSIN FIRES INTO ROOSEVELT PARTY AT MIAMI; PRESIDENT-ELECT UNINJURED; MAYOR CERMAK AND 4 OTHERS WOUNDED

REPEAL VOTE TODAY SET IN THE SENATE; FILIBUSTER BROKEN

Wets Win in Test Ballots as Blaine Plan Is Stripped of Protective Clauses.

ROBINSON LEADS FIGHT

Borah Backs Him on Removing the Anti-Saloon Section, Voted Out 33-32.

STATE LIQUOR PLAN OUT

Commission Proposes to Bar the Saloon—Limit on Places to Sell Beer.

Report of the State Liquor Control Commission is on Page 15.

Special to THE NEW YORK TIMES.

WASHINGTON, Feb. 15.—The Senate today stripped the Blaine prohibition resolution to practically "naked" repeal and agreed to vote on the measure at 3 P. M. tomorrow.

Senator Robinson, the Democratic leader, who led the fight to simplify the resolution, predicted that the Senate would furnish the necessary two-thirds majority for adoption on the morrow.

He expressed confidence, too, that the resolution as amended tonight would be acceptable to Speaker Garner and other House leaders, who announced at the outset that the House would be allowed to vote only on the Democratic repeal plan as advocated in the last campaign.

Every prediction was that the vote tomorrow would be extremely close. Senator McNary, assistant Republican leader, described the resolution as "teetering," with the possibility of going one way or the other. He would make no forecast.

Wet leaders, scanning the votes of today, were very hopeful as to the outcome tomorrow. They had succeeded in breaking the filibuster started by the drys to prevent a vote.

Coincidental with the agreement to vote tomorrow, the Senate, by a vote of 33 to 32, struck the so-called anti-saloon provisions from the Blaine resolution and, on a ballot of 45 to 15, decreed that ratification should be by conventions in the several States instead of Legislatures.

Passage in House Predicted.

A deciding vote on the amendment, proposed by Senator Robinson, to strike out the anti-saloon section, was cast by Senator Borah, long a dry stalwart. He held it was impossible for the government properly to exercise any supervision over saloons once the Eighteenth Amendment was repealed.

As the resolution stood tonight, its proposal was only one degree removed from outright repeal. It carried a clause directing Federal protection of dry States which the Garner repeal resolution, submitted at the outset of the session, did not contain but which Senate leaders said tonight was not sufficiently controversial to bring a deadlock between the two branches.

The resolution as it emerged was believed to have a better chance of passage in the House than the proposal submitted by Speaker Garner the first day of Congress. The Speaker's resolution failed by only six votes of obtaining the necessary two-thirds majority, and it was pointed out tonight that the six votes from Senator Robinson's own State, which were cast in the negative at that time, were sufficient to change the tide should repeal be proposed anew to the House.

It was recalled, too, that Senator Robinson was opposed to the Garner resolution, whereas his espousal at this time of the Democratic platform plan was responsible for much of the weight given the revival of the repeal movement.

The dry filibuster against the Blaine resolution broke up in the Senate today when wets announced

Continued on Page Fourteen.

Illinois Senate Passes Bills For Repeal of Prohibition Laws

By The Associated Press.

SPRINGFIELD, Ill., Feb. 15.—The State Senate today passed two prohibition repeal measures and sent them to the House for further action.

The vote on the repeal measures, which had been delayed because of Governor Henry Horner's insistence that regulatory acts should be provided first, was preceded by promises in the debate that they would not be signed until the regulatory bills also had been adopted.

The two bills would remove from the statute books State prohibition, and the search and seizure acts.

A measure designed to authorize banking holidays was introduced in the House. Under its terms, the Governor would be empowered to declare a holiday for the State and Mayors authorized to do so for municipalities.

BOY GANG CHIEF, 15, ADMITS KILLING 'FOE'

Says He Stabbed Queens Lad, 12, for "Lying" About Him and Vowed to "Get" Him.

VICTIM MISSING 2 WEEKS

Found Bound in Closet of a Vacant House to Which Killer Had Lured Him by Ruse.

Bound, gagged and stabbed through the heart, the body of 12-year-old William Bender, who disappeared Jan. 31, was found yesterday in a closet in one of a row of partly-built dwellings, less than two blocks from his home at 43 Bergen Landing Road, Richmond Hill Circle, Queens. He had been dead for at least two weeks.

Nine hours after the body was found, Harry Murch, 15-year-old leader of a juvenile gang, confessed he had murdered the Bender boy. Murch and his chum, John Miller, 10, who was with him when the crime was committed, were picked up by the police yesterday afternoon. For more than five hours, despite persistent questioning by officials of the Police Department and the District Attorney's office, they calmly denied all knowledge of the crime. Then finally they broke down.

"I did it," Murch is said to have declared. "Bender lied about me. He told the whole neighborhood that I had hit Mrs. Peterson on the head with a monkey wrench. I said I'd get him and I did."

He is to be arraigned today in children's court, Jamaica, on a charge of homicide.

Tells of Meeting Victim.

Murch said that on the afternoon of Jan. 31 he and Miller had met Bender outside the latter's home.

"I told him," Murch said, "that I was going to stick up a peanut peddler and that if he'd come over to the houses in Mauretania Avenue with me I'd show him how I was going to do it. He came along all right. But he seemed a bit suspicious.

"So I tied up Miller first. Then I untied Miller and tied up Bender. As soon as I had him where I wanted him I took out my knife and stabbed him in the heart."

Miller corroborated Murch's story. Afterward, the boys said, they fled from the house and agreed to say nothing to any one. The knife which Murch used for the crime, they said, was taken from the kitchen of his home.

The clue that broke the case was a small piece of gingham cloth that had been used to gag the dead boy. The fact that Murch had threatened to "get Bender" was well known in the neighborhood and soon after the body was discovered detectives went to the home of Murch's parents, Mr. and Mrs. Charles Murch, in Philbert Avenue, just a short distance from the home of the Bender boy.

In the Murch garage the detectives found other pieces of gingham of exactly the same quality and pattern as that which had been used for the gag. Young Murch and Miller were immediately taken into custody.

The body of the missing boy was

Continued on Page Ten.

TAX RATE OF $2.40 SEEN AS VALUATIONS DROP $1,195,006,742

Sexton Estimates a 19-Point Reduction to the Lowest Basic Levy Since 1920.

REALTY BURDEN EASED

Assessment Totals Cut in All Boroughs—Personalty Less, Franchise Values Rise.

ALDERMEN VOTE BUDGET

Adopt $518,427,972 Document Without Change—Mayor Denies Plea on Sergeant-at-Arms.

Final adoption of the revised 1933 budget at a total of 18 per cent below that of the 1932 budget and announcement of a cut of $1,195,006,742 in assessed valuations of city real estate, personal property and franchises provided yesterday a substantial basis for belief that the basic tax rate this year will be appreciably lower than the 1932 rate of $2.59 per $100 of assessed valuation.

For the first time in the city's history the total of assessed valuations is lower than in a preceding year. Valuations placed upon franchises for tax purposes were increased in every borough this year. Valuations on real estate showed decreases in every borough, while in the Bronx alone the valuations on personal estate showed a rise. The total valuations for all boroughs in 1932 was $19,977,077,315. For 1933 the final valuations aggregate $18,782,070,573.

The Board of Aldermen adopted a final budget of $518,427,972.16, the same total recently approved by the Board of Estimate. This figure shows a decrease of $112,933,325.81 from the total budget for 1932, which was $631,366,297.97. The budget now goes to Mayor O'Brien for his signature. It must be filed with Controller Berry by Feb. 25.

Nineteen-Point Tax Drop Seen.

James J. Sexton, president of the Department of Taxes and Assessments, said that he was certain the basic tax rate would show a decided drop. He expressed the belief that the rate would not exceed $2.40, a drop of nineteen points.

Deputy Controller Frank J. Prial, in the absence of the Controller, said that no accurate estimate of the rate could be made before the amount of the city's general fund for reduction of taxation is known. The general fund, the budget and the final total of assessed valuation, are the three factors used in computing the basic rate. Borough tax rates are added to the basic rate to pay for local improvements.

Mr. Prial said that the amount of the general fund would depend

Continued on Page Nine.

SERIOUSLY WOUNDED.

Times Wide World Photo.
Mayor Anton J. Cermak of Chicago

WOMAN DIVERTED AIM OF ASSASSIN

100-Pound Wife of Miami Doctor Tells How She Forced Up Man's Arm.

HELD ON DURING SHOOTING

Gun Had Been Pointed "Right at Mr. Roosevelt" 15 Feet Away, She Relates.

By Telephone to THE NEW YORK TIMES.

MIAMI, Fla., Feb. 15.—Mrs. Lillian Cross, 48 years old, and weighing only 100 pounds, probably saved the life of the President-elect tonight when she forced the would-be assassin's shooting arm upward and caused the bullets to go high.

"He was aiming right at the President," said Mrs. Cross. "I saw him. That's why I caught his arm and forced the gun up. I said to myself, all in a flash, 'Oh! He's going to kill the President!'"

Mrs. Cross said that she was not frightened when she saw the weapon. Her only thought was for Mr. Roosevelt.

"I didn't begin to get nervous at all until it was all over," she related after she reached her home at 1,069 Northwest Second Street.

"I drove to the park tonight with my husband, Dr. W. F. Cross (he's a physician and surgeon here) and with my friend, Mrs. Willis McCrary of Atlanta, Ga. My husband got a seat somewhere in the back of the crowd, but Mrs. McCrary and I found seats right up front, by the guard rail they'd put up.

"President Roosevelt" was only about fifteen feet away from us. He finished his speech and got down from the back of the automobile—an open car it was—and had settled in the back seat. I stood up on the bench on which I'd been sit-

Continued on Page Three.

Cermak in Critical Condition at Hospital; "Glad It Was I, Not You," He Tells Roosevelt

Special to THE NEW YORK TIMES.

MIAMI, Thursday, Feb. 16.—Mayor Cermak was shot in the right side, just below the ribs, and was in a critical condition at Jackson Memorial Hospital. An X-ray showed the bullet lodged in the back of the abdomen.

An emergency operation was considered at 12:30 A. M. and plans were made to undertake it at once. A short time later physicians put off the operation.

When President-elect Roosevelt called to see Mayor Cermak at the hospital the Mayor turned his head and smiled faintly, saying:

"I'm glad it was I, instead of you. I wish you would be very careful. The country needs you badly. You should not take any more such chances as you took tonight."

The President-elect replied:

"The country needs a man like you, too. I can only express my deepest regrets. I have decided not to leave tonight and will return to see you in the morning."

James B. Bowler, Chicago City Councilman, who told of the conversation, said Mr. Roosevelt was expected to call again at the hospital about 8 A. M.

Mr. Bowler was with Mayor Cermak in the emergency room and took from the front of the Mayor's shirt a .32 calibre bullet, which was believed to be a spent shot that had hit one of the other victims.

A bulletin on Mayor Cermak's condition, issued at 2 A. M., said:

"Pulse, 88; temperature, 98.6; respiration, 24. His condition is regarded as dangerous, but not immediately critical. The bullet evidently traversed the diaphragm and margin of the liver and lodged in the body of the eleventh dorsal vertebra. Surgical intervention is deemed unwise unless his condition becomes worse."

The bulletin was signed by Dr. John W. Snyder, Dr. Thomas H. Hutson and Dr. T. S. Nichol. Dr. Snyder is in charge, and at the hospital this morning he said:

"Mrs. Gill and Mayor Cermak have more than a fifty-fifty chance to recover."

WASHINGTON IS STUNNED

Hoover Wires Roosevelt, Rejoicing That He Was Not Wounded.

ASKS NEWS OF CERMAK

Senators Express Gratitude President-Elect Escaped Madman's Shots.

RISK TO PRESIDENT SEEN

Determination is Voiced That Life of His Successor Be Safeguarded by All Means.

Special to THE NEW YORK TIMES.

WASHINGTON, Feb. 15.—The nation's capital was deeply shocked tonight on hearing of the attempt on the life of President-elect Roosevelt.

From President Hoover to the lowliest citizen the reaction was instant that the country cast every safeguard around the President-elect.

President Hoover himself struck the keynote when he said:

"I am deeply shocked at the news. It is a dastardly act."

Hoover's Message to Roosevelt.

At the same time the President sent a telegram to Mr. Roosevelt which read:

"Together with every citizen I rejoice that you have not been injured. I shall be grateful to you for news of Mayor Cermak's condition."

Official and unofficial Washington was stunned at the first reports of what appeared to be an attempt on the life of the man who within less than three weeks will become Chief Executive. Newspaper extras were on the street almost immediately, and citizens sat close to their radios, receiving the latest news flashes. General relief was expressed that Mr. Roosevelt escaped injury.

Comment of Leaders.

Speaker Garner said:

"I am gratified beyond words that the President-elect is uninjured and that he will assume the administration of the Government of the United States, which is desired by the American people as expressed in the overwhelming result of the November elections."

Secretary Mills said:

"I am thankful that our next President escaped injury and that the act of a misguided or crazy individual will not deprive the American people of their chosen leader."

"Of course, I am overjoyed that the President-elect escaped," said Senator Byrnes, one of Mr. Roosevelt's closest advisers, "but I deplore profoundly that such a thing could happen. It's awful!"

Senator Robinson of Arkansas, Senate minority leader, said:

"Assuming that the shots were fired at Mr. Roosevelt, it should be understood that this is the United States, not Russia. No fanatic, crank or revolutionist, or any number of them will be permitted to prevent the orderly transfer of power in the government of the United States."

Thinks Assailant Deranged.

"How dreadful, and how fortunate he did not hit!" said Senator Lewis of Illinois. "I do not know what to say except that it was a deplorable thing. I do hope it was not attempted out of ill will. It must have been the result of a deranged mind; certainly no one in his right mind would attempt such a thing. If, as appears possible, the shots were actually fired at Mayor Cermak, it undoubtedly was some member of the old lawless element in Chicago with a fancied grievance against the Mayor."

Chief Moran of the Secret Service, ill at his home here, received a report late this evening from Joseph E. Murphy, Assistant Chief, from the hospital in Miami where Mayor Cermak had been taken.

Commenting on the shooting, Senator Shipstead said:

"This unfortunate incident shows the risk the President and the President-elect of the United States are subject to. There are always cranks in the country. Every citi-

Continued on Page Three.

ESCAPES ASSASSIN'S BULLETS.

New York Times Studio Photo.
President-Elect Franklin D. Roosevelt.

GUNMAN LAYS ACT TO BODY 'TORMENT'

Joe Zingara, Hackensack Bricklayer, Says Pain Made Him 'Hate All Presidents.'

DESCRIBED AS ANARCHIST

Man Who Fired at Roosevelt Says He Once Tried in Italy to Kill King Victor Emmanuel.

By Telephone to THE NEW YORK TIMES.

MIAMI, Feb. 15.—Surrounded by detectives and high police officials, the man who shot at President-elect Roosevelt tonight gave his name as Joe Zingara of New York and related, in spasms of words during questioning at Police Headquarters, how "constant torment from a stomach operation" had impelled him to attempt the life of the President-elect.

Zingara, a short, stocky man of about 35, a brick mason who came to Miami two months ago from Hackensack, N. J., betrayed by his manner even in the rational portions of his statement the warped mentality which resulted in his deed tonight.

In an almost boastful tone, he declared that he had attempted the life of King Victor Emmanuel of Italy ten years ago. That failed, he said, for the same reason as his attempt tonight—"there was too big a crowd."

He admitted he had no personal grievance against Mr. Roosevelt. Saying "No, I had none," he swept away questions of that nature.

Nor could the police discover that he had any personal grievance against the King of Italy. But he hated "rich and powerful persons," he said with a hiss, and they were figures, he indicated, for his wrath.

"I Don't Like Presidents."

"I like Roosevelt personally, but I don't like Presidents," he replied when asked if he didn't like the President-elect. He intended to kill him, he said, "and I would be glad if I had killed the President-elect." He did not like Presidents because of "rich men send their children to schools."

He said this was because "when I was a young man, rich men's sons went to school while I worked in a brick factory in Italy and burned myself."

Zingara indicated a scar on his stomach which he said was the result of the burn.

He was seized with the idea of trying to kill the President-elect only two days ago, he declared.

"About two days ago I bought a paper for 5 cents and saw that the President-elect was coming to Miami," he related.

"So yesterday I went to a place

Continued on Page Two.

MRS. ROOSEVELT TAKES NEWS CALMLY

She Telephones Immediately to Husband and Is Relieved to Find Him Unhurt.

KEEPS SPEAKING PROGRAM

Assured That "He Is Not Even Excited," She Takes Train Later for Ithaca.

Mrs. Franklin D. Roosevelt returned to her home at 49 East Sixty-fifth Street about 10:30 o'clock last night and found the household upset. The Negro butler's face betrayed his agitation as he admitted her.

"What's it all about?" she demanded.

Stammering, the butler told her that her husband, the President-elect, had been fired upon in Miami. He had only the meager information gleaned from newspapers, which called the house when the first brief reports were received.

Mrs. Roosevelt was met at her home by her daughter, Mrs. Anna Roosevelt Dall, and received the news calmly and without apparent emotion.

"Those things are to be expected," she remarked.

With a calm and steady voice she placed a long distance telephone call which reached the President-elect at the bedside of Mayor Cermak. There followed a few minutes of conversation and then Mrs. Roosevelt turned to the group in the room and said:

"He's all right. He's not the least bit excited."

Leaves for Ithaca.

A few minutes later Mrs. Roosevelt, accompanied only by her maid, was on a railroad train bound for Ithaca, N. Y., to fill a speaking engagement on the program of Cornell University's Home and Farm Week. The train left at 11:35.

Mrs. Roosevelt was speaking at the Warner Club at 321 West Forty-fourth Street when the first of the dramatic incident in Miami was received in New York newspaper offices. She left there without knowledge of what had happened.

In his telephone conversation with Mrs. Roosevelt, members of the household said, the President-elect informed her that it was his belief that the would-be assassin's bullets were aimed at Mayor Cermak, and not at him.

They quoted him as saying that five persons were in the hospital as a result of the shooting, and that he wasn't even scratched. Instead of starting back for New York last night, as he had planned, however,

Continued on Page Two.

ASSASSIN SHOOTS 5 TIMES

Police and Bystanders Leap for Him and Take Him Prisoner.

ACCOMPLICE TAKEN LATER

Cermak and New York Officer Rushed to Hospital—Now in Serious Condition.

ROOSEVELT DELAYS TRIP

Had Been Warmly Welcomed and Intended to Start for North at Once.

By JAMES A. HAGERTY.
Special to THE NEW YORK TIMES.

MIAMI, Feb. 15.—An unsuccessful attempt was made to assassinate President-elect Franklin D. Roosevelt just after he ended a speech in Bay Front Park here at 9:35 o'clock tonight, two hours after his return from an eleven-day fishing cruise on Vincent Astor's yacht Nourmahal.

Although the gunman missed the target at which he was aiming, he probably fatally wounded Mayor Anton Cermak of Chicago and four other persons were hit by five shots from his pistol before a woman destroyed his aim on the last shot by seizing his wrist and a Miami policeman felled him to the ground with a blow of his night stick.

List of the Wounded.

The wounded are:

Mayor Anton Cermak of Chicago, shot through the chest; condition critical.

Miss Margaret Kruis of the Henry Clay Hotel, Miami Beach, a visitor from Newark, N. J., shot through the hand.

Mrs. Joe H. Gill, wife of the president of the Florida Power and Light Company, shot in the abdomen; condition critical.

William Sinnott, a New York policeman, living at 612 West 178th Street, shot in the head; condition critical.

Russell Caldwell, 22, of Miami, shot in the head.

Roosevelt Was Target.

The would-be assassin, who was arrested immediately and lodged in the city prison on the nineteenth floor of Miami's skyscraper City Hall, is Giuseppe Zingara of Hackensack, N. J.

Although early reports were that he intended to kill Mayor Cermak rather than the President-elect, due to his remark, "Well, I got Cermak," it appeared later that Mr. Roosevelt was his target.

"I'd kill every President," he was reported by the police to have said after his arrest.

"I'd kill them all; I'd kill all the officers," he also is reported to have said, indicating that he may be an Anarchist.

Evidence that the attempted assassination of Roosevelt was premeditated was obtained by the police late tonight and Andrea Valemti, who lived with Zingara, was arrested on suspicion of being an accomplice.

A search of Zingara's clothing disclosed several newspaper clippings, mostly from local newspapers announcing Mr. Roosevelt's intended visit to this city.

Clipping on McKinley.

One clipping, however, contained an account of the assassination of President McKinley by the anarchist Czolgosz. This strengthened the police belief that Zingara might belong to some anarchist group, although no direct evidence has been obtained showing such a connection.

Detectives, deputy sheriffs and policemen were working on several clues, obtained by the questioning of Zingara and Valemti.

Zingara is charged with assault with intent to kill, pending the preferring of the more serious

Section 1

"All the News That's Fit to Print."

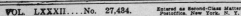

The New York Times.

LATE CITY EDITION
WEATHER—Fair today and tomorrow; temperature unchanged.
Temperature Yesterday—Max., 42; Min., 34

Section 1

VOL. LXXXII....No. 27,484. Entered as Second-Class Matter. Postoffice, New York, N. Y. NEW YORK, SUNDAY, MARCH 5, 1933. F Including Rotogravure Picture Magazine and Book Sections. TEN CENTS | TWELVE CENTS Beyond 200 Miles. Except in 7th and 8th Postal Zones.

ROOSEVELT INAUGURATED, ACTS TO END THE NATIONAL BANKING CRISIS QUICKLY; WILL ASK WAR-TIME POWERS IF NEEDED

PLAN TO USE SCRIP HERE

Bankers Ready to Issue Clearing House Paper at End of Holiday.

WILL MEET WOODIN TODAY

Eastern Financiers to Join Parley at Capital on Plans to Permit Reopenings.

STOCK EXCHANGES CLOSED

Drain on the Gold Reserve Is Halted—Cash Being Set Aside to Meet Payrolls.

The Banking Situation.

The New York Clearing House Association prepared to print and issue certificates to be used by the public as substitute money.

In every State of the nation, including the District of Columbia, banking was wholly or partly suspended.

In London, Paris and other European capitals, dollar transactions were suspended.

Bankers from New York and other financial centres will confer with Secretary of the Treasury Woodin on remedial plans for presentation by the President to this afternoon's legislative conference.

Scrip Being Rushed.

Clearing house certificates will be used instead of currency in New York when the banks reopen on Tuesday after the two-day holiday proclaimed by Governor Herbert H. Lehman, according to present plans of the New York Clearing House Association, it was learned last night.

This was confirmed by Mortimer N. Buckner, president of the New York Clearing House Association and chairman of the board of the New York Trust Company, following a meeting of the clearing house committee at the clearing house, 77 Cedar Street.

Bankers from New York and other centres have been called to Washington to confer with William H. Woodin, Secretary of the Treasury, at 10 o'clock this morning on plans for meeting the emergency. George W. Davison, chairman of the Central Hanover Bank and Trust Company and head of the Clearing House Committee, left for Washington yesterday afternoon; and George L. Harrison, governor of the Federal Reserve Bank of New York was scheduled to go last night. Charles S. McCain, chairman of the board of the Chase National Bank, was in Washington yesterday and it was thought likely that he would remain for the conference.

In the event that the discussions of the bankers with Mr. Woodin develop a plan which can be put into effect through Congressional action, the proposals will be laid before President Roosevelt this afternoon and presented by him to a conference of legislators. It is expected that the results of the conference may have a bearing upon how quickly the new Congress is called into session.

In addition to the New York bankers, representatives from the banking communities of Philadelphia, Chicago, Baltimore and Richmond are expected to attend the conference

Act to Meet Payrolls.

It was indicated last night that arrangements would be made whereby payrolls due yesterday or tomorrow would be met by the withdrawal from the banks of sufficient amounts of currency to pay all or part in cash. Concerns accustomed to paying by check would be permitted to withdraw cash, it was predicted, or the banks would make special provision for cashing pay checks. Governor Lehman is expected to give his approval to a payroll plan being worked out by the banks and business houses.

The banking holiday ordered by Governor Lehman in a proclamation issued at his apartment, 820 Park Avenue, at 4:20 o'clock yesterday morning, was effective yesterday, and will expire at the

Continued on Page Twenty-five.

Checks Still Accepted Here For Federal Income Taxes

Collectors of Internal Revenue in New York City were still accepting checks yesterday in payment of Federal income taxes, and it was said that checks would continue to be accepted during the bank holiday.

No consideration was yet being given to possible postponement of payments, due on March 15. This could only be granted by the Secretary of the Treasury or Commissioner of Internal Revenue in Washington, although the law allows individual applications for extension of time.

Walter E. Corwin, Collector in Brooklyn, said clearing-house certificates would not be accepted, if issued as a medium of exchange. The law permits payment in cash, checks, Treasury notes or Liberty bonds.

VICTORY FOR HITLER IS EXPECTED TODAY

Repression of Opponents Held to Make Election Triumph for Regime Inevitable.

FIRES BLAZE ON BORDERS

Nazis Light Them as Sign of "Reawakening"—Imperial Flag to Be Restored.

By FREDERICK T. BIRCHALL.
Special Cable to THE NEW YORK TIMES.

BERLIN, March 4.—In a countrywide blaze of bonfires and torchlight parades the allied National Socialist and Nationalist parties tonight closed the electoral campaign, which tomorrow is expected to entrench them securely in power not only throughout Germany as a result of the Reichstag elections but throughout Prussia, where the electorate will vote simultaneously for a separate State ticket.

Tonight, on every eminence along Germany's borders, not excluding the Polish Corridor, a bonfire flamed to signalize the Nazi ideal of an awakening nation. In Köenigsberg, East Prussia, Chancellor Adolf Hitler himself made his closing appeal to aroused patriotic fervor.

In every city and every town of considerable size uniformed Nazis marched to some centre, where amid the blare of brass bands playing partiotic songs, in which the whole assemblage joined, Nazi orators proclaimed the dawning of a new day.

In Berlin alone there were twenty-four parades to an equal number of meeting places, where through loud-speakers the voice of Herr Hitler was heard and acclaimed.

No Counter-Demonstrations.

There were no counter-demonstrations from the opposition. They were "verboten," for this is a one-way election Nor, late tonight, despite the dire predictions sent to the outside world, had any serious disturbance been reported. All that is over, for what is the use of inviting inevitable and overwhelming reprisals when all the authority and all the weapons are monopolized by the other side?

In Thuringia, the only State in which a few Socialist newspapers remain unsuspended, they were all compelled by the Nazi State government today to reprint Chancellor Hitler's recent speech against "Marxism" on the front page.

The utmost left for those opposed to an all-Nazi régime is to vote against it silently and secretly tomorrow—if they dare—and to hope for the best.

So confident today are the government leaders of a verdict in their favor that even before the polls are open they are already announcing the first act of the new Reichstag. It will be to retire the Republican flag of black, red and gold under which Germany has fought her way out of the difficulties in which the World War left her and to replace it with the black-white-red banner of the former imperialism.

"We shall be happy to get rid of that emblem of 'Marxism,'" declared Captain Hermann Wilhelm Goering, Minister Without Portfolio and the spokesman of militant na-

Continued on Page Twenty.

READY TO CALL CONGRESS

President Probably Will Summon Extra Session for Wednesday.

WORKS ON LEGISLATION

Cabinet Ordered to Meet With Him Today to Draft Banking Reform Measures.

AID LIKELY IN A WEEK

Steps Considered Include Deposit Guarantee, Use of Scrip and Tax on Hoarded Gold.

Special to THE NEW YORK TIMES.

WASHINGTON, March 4.—President Roosevelt plunged immediately into the banking situation tonight by summoning members of his Cabinet and leaders of Congress to meet tomorrow afternoon to decide upon a program to deal with it.

As soon as the program is agreed upon, Congress will be called into special session, probably on Wednesday, and it is the expectation of administration advisers that legislation will be enacted within another week.

The White House issued the following statement at 7:20 P. M.:

"Respecting the date for the extra session of Congress, no decision has been reached tonight, but probably will be by tomorrow night.

"The Secretary of the Treasury will begin tomorrow a series of discussions called at the request of President Roosevelt, looking to prompt action in the banking situation. He is calling a number of individuals and Reserve Bank officials to Washington. Some have already been invited and more will be called tonight."

Bankers from New York, Philadelphia, Chicago, Baltimore and Richmond were invited to the conference with Secretary Woodin at 10 o'clock tomorrow morning.

After they have discussed the banking situation, whatever plan may be adopted will be transmitted to President Roosevelt for presentation to the legislative conference in the afternoon.

Four Proposals Advanced.

While President Roosevelt was reviewing the parade from the stand in front of the White House this afternoon, members of his Cabinet and two former Secretaries of the Treasury, David F. Houston and William G. McAdoo, were engaged in discussion of a program which will be laid before the conference tomorrow.

The main points advanced but not finally decided upon at this informal conference, in which Secretary Woodin participated for a few minutes, were:

1. The organization of a corporation to which banks must subscribe to guarantee bank deposits.

2. The issue of scrip, as was resorted to in the banking emergency in 1907, to be put out by the banks to the amount of frozen deposits.

3. A tax on hoarded gold, as high as 15 per cent.

4. Other measures to protect our gold holdings.

Secretary of State Hull said, however, that a tax on hoarded gold did not seem practicable, and probably would not be resorted to in the hope of raising any considerable amount of money, but merely as a move to force hoarders to put gold into circulation and restore confidence in the banks.

These suggestions with others will come before the conference tomorrow and the new administration leaders were confident tonight that a program could be agreed upon for submission to and prompt action by Congress by the middle of next week.

Problem Is to Allay Fear.

"The main thing right now," said Secretary Hull, "is to allay the unreasonable and unreasoning fear in the public mind. That in itself would be a long step in the direction toward restoration of confidence. Nothing right now is more unjustifiable than attempts to hoard money."

Former Secretary of the Treasury

Continued on Page Twenty-four.

THE NEW PRESIDENT TAKING THE OATH OF OFFICE.

Associated Press Photo.

Franklin D. Roosevelt, With Hand Raised, Being Sworn by Chief Justice Charles Evans Hughes on the Rostrum in Front of the Capitol at 1:08 P. M. Yesterday. At the Right Are His Son, James Roosevelt, and Former President Hoover.

HOOVER, AS CITIZEN, HERE ON WAY HOME

Spends Evening in Seclusion in Hotel After Seeing His Successor Take Office.

SEEMS GLAD TO GET AWAY

Bids Genial Farewell to Old Friends in Capital After Morning of Heavy Cares.

By RUSSELL OWEN.

Herbert Hoover entered private life yesterday after a day of foreboding, in which his successor addressed the nation as though it were entering upon a war. With downcast eyes and a diffident manner, Mr. Hoover went to the Capitol to see Mr. Roosevelt inaugurated as President, and left hurriedly, as if glad to throw from his shoulders the mantle of responsibility for the affairs of a country desperately distressed.

Immediately after the ceremony he left the Capitol and drove to the railroad station to take a train for New York, where he arrived at 5:50 o'clock last night. He went to the Waldorf-Astoria and spent the evening in seclusion, avoiding visitors.

Until half an hour before he stepped into the automobile that was to bear him and President Roosevelt to the inaugural ceremonies in Washington, he was busy with affairs of state. As no other man who has stepped from the office of Chief Executive, he was beset with complex problems until the end of his term. The last bills he signed were those to aid the country through the present crisis. He signed them grimly, with a grave face, realizing to the full the difficulties which he was bequeathing.

Raises Hat Only Once.

The drive from the White House to the Capitol was through lines of people who watched with serious, rather than enthusiastic faces. A sense of depression had settled over the capital so that it could be felt. The two men, side by side, were looked upon as symbols of a government trying to cope with dangers which were as subtle as they were treacherous. The few cheers were for Roosevelt rather than Hoover. He realized that, and only raised his hat once during the trip, although the new President smiled and doffed his hat frequently in response to the faint cheers from the stands and sidewalk.

But once in the railroad station to take the train to New York after the inauguration, Mr. Hoover came into his own again. There were people who firmly believed in him,

Continued on Page Four.

Text of the Inaugural Address; President for Vigorous Action

"This Is Pre-eminently the Time to Speak the Truth," He Says, in Demand That "the Temple of Our Civilization Be Restored to the Ancient Truths."

Special to THE NEW YORK TIMES.

WASHINGTON, March 4.—President Roosevelt's inaugural address, delivered immediately after he took the oath, was as follows:

President Hoover, Mr. Chief Justice, my friends:

This is a day of national consecration, and I am certain that my fellow-Americans expect that on my induction into the Presidency I will address them with a candor and a decision which the present situation of our nation impels.

This is pre-eminently the time to speak the truth, the whole truth, frankly and boldly. Nor need we shrink from honestly facing conditions in our country today. This great nation will endure as it has endured, will revive and will prosper.

So first of all let me assert my firm belief that the only thing we have to fear is fear itself—nameless, unreasoning, unjustified terror which paralyzes needed efforts to convert retreat into advance.

In every dark hour of our national life a leadership of frankness and vigor has met with that understanding and support of the people themselves which is essential to victory. I am convinced that you will again give that support to leadership in these critical days.

In such a spirit on my part and on yours we face our common difficulties. They concern, thank God, only material things. Values have shrunken to fantastic levels; taxes have risen; our ability to pay has fallen; government of all kinds is faced by serious curtailment of income; the means of exchange are frozen in the currents of trade; the withered leaves of industrial enterprise lie on every side; farmers find no markets for their produee; the savings of many years in thousands of families are gone.

More important, a host of unemployed citizens face the grim problem of existence, and an equally great number toil with little return. Only a foolish optimist can deny the dark realities of the moment.

Yet our distress comes from no failure of substance. We are stricken by no plague of locusts. Compared with the perils which our forefathers conquered because they believed and were not afraid, we have still much to be thankful for. Nature still offers her bounty and human efforts have multiplied it. Plenty is at our doorstep, but a generous use of it languishes in the very sight of the supply.

Charges "Money Changers" Lack Vision.

Primarily, this is because the rulers of the exchange of mankind's goods have failed through their own stubbornness and their own incompetence, have admitted their failure and abdicated. Practices of the unscrupulous money changers stand indicted in the court of public opinion, rejected by the hearts and minds of men.

True, they have tried, but their efforts have been cast in the pattern of an outworn tradition. Faced by failure of credit, they have proposed only the lending of more money.

Stripped of the lure of profit by which to induce our people to follow their false leadership, they have resorted to exhortations, pleading tearfully for restored confidence. They know only the rules of a generation of self-seekers.

They have no vision, and when there is no vision the people perish.

The money changers have fled from their high seats in the temple of our civilization. We may now restore that temple to the ancient truths.

The measure of the restoration lies in the extent to which we apply social values more noble than mere monetary profit.

Happiness lies not in the mere possession of money; it lies in the joy of achievement, in the thrill of creative effort.

The joy and moral stimulation of work no longer must be forgotten in the mad chase of evanescent profits. These dark days will be worth all they cost us if they teach us that our true

Continued on Page Three.

500,000 IN STREETS CHEER ROOSEVELT

Their Spirits Are Lifted by His Smile of Confidence as They Watch Parade.

MANY ON ROOFS, IN TREES

Throng Waiting for Ceremony Is Solemnly Silent Until New President Appears.

Special to THE NEW YORK TIMES.

WASHINGTON, March 4.—The quadrennial pageant which traditionally accompanies the inauguration of a new President was enacted here today with all the pomp and panoply of more prosperous years and with all solemnity.

Before the august Capitol, in an inadequate and windswept forty acres, 100,000 of his countrymen saw Franklin D. Roosevelt swear on the ancient Bible of his Dutch fathers to cherish and defend the Constitution of his country.

Five hundred thousand others saw his reassuringly confident smile as he rode from Capitol to White House at the head of a parade of 18,000 marching men and women, among whom were such of his formidable rivals for the nomination as Alfred E. Smith and Governor Albert C. Ritchie of Maryland.

Mr. Roosevelt became the thirty-second President of the United States on a day that was cloudy and chill, with an occasional ray of sunlight piercing the clouds below which rode majestically the navy airship Akron and ninety-six military airplanes from Bolling and Langley Fields.

Flags flew at half-taff on the Senate and House Office Buildings in memory of Senator Walsh, who was to have been Attorney General in the new Cabinet.

Over the vast throngs there hung a cloud of worry, because of the economic and business outlook. The new President's recurrent smile of confidence, his uplifted chin and the challenge of his voice did much to help the national sense of humor to assert itself.

Reviews Parade for Three Hours.

Again, standing throughout the afternoon while legions of men of all degrees and colors marched past his glass-enclosed reviewing stand in the Court of Honor, the new President, advocate of a new deal, set an example of resolute fortitude and cheerfulness as he doffed his hat in deference to the colors and in greeting to old friends and supporters.

He stood between Admiral William V. Pratt, Chief of Naval Operations, and General Douglas Mac-

Continued on Page Two.

100,000 AT INAUGURATION

President, Grim, Terse, Pledges 'Adequate but Sound Currency.'

SCORES 'MONEY-CHANGERS'

In Fighting Speech He Demands Supervision of Credits and Investments.

STICKS TO CONSTITUTION

Calls on People and Congress to Follow Him as Leader in War on Depression.

By ARTHUR KROCK.
Special to THE NEW YORK TIMES.

WASHINGTON, March 4.—With solemn mien, Franklin D. Roosevelt of New York took the oath of office and became the thirty-second President of the United States on the main steps of the Capitol at eight minutes after 1 o'clock this afternoon.

A deep consciousness of the task before him was patent in his unusual demeanor as, his face stern, his voice grave, he repeated after Chief Justice Hughes the historic words of the oath. This realization animated also the inaugural address which Mr. Roosevelt then delivered in the presence of at least a hundred thousand persons who gathered in the Capitol grounds.

The sense of the administration's burden was apparent, too, in the manner and speech of Vice President Garner, who, an hour before the President took the oath, laid down his gavel as Speaker of the House of Representatives and was inducted into his new office in the Senate chamber, where he will henceforth preside.

Keeps Pledge of Action.

"Action" was the promise of Mr. Roosevelt's speech, and action was immediately forthcoming. The first moment after the ceremonies were over, the President swore in his Cabinet, summoned the party leaders to a Sunday conference to work out the plan for banking relief and arranged to call an extra session of the Seventy-third Congress, probably on Wednesday, to legislate the plan into law.

"This nation asks for action, and action now," he said on the steps of the Capitol. Within a few hours, he acted.

The President had consistently maintained his attitude that he would not accept responsibility without power in the period between his election and his inauguration. Powerful and subtle suasions could not move him. But when authority came he moved at once as he had said he would.

Atmosphere Is Grim.

Though the city was gay with flags and lively with the music of bands and cheers for the marchers in the inaugural parade which followed the oath taking, the atmosphere which surrounded the change of government in the United States was comparable to that which might be found in a beleaguered capital in war time.

The President in his address told the people that they were at war with the forces of depression and offered them leadership and action in the new campaign to be raged against these forces.

In words that burned and scourged he denounced the financial leaders of the nation, declared that these "money changers" should be driven from the temple and that they should not be allowed to return to their high places. No more, he declared, should those entrusted with other people's money be permitted to misuse it.

The inaugural address was a Jacksonian speech, a fighting speech, implicit with criticism of the lack of leadership and the philosophy of government which the President imputed to his predecessor, who sat there, listening. He would lead, he said, as the people expect, within the confines of the Constitution, and he will demand that Congress follow this leadership.

But if his present powers prove insufficient to win the war to which he pledged his full mind and

Continued on Page Three.

"All the News That's Fit to Print."

The New York Times.

LATE CITY EDITION
WEATHER—Fair today; tomorrow cloudy, warmer, rain following
Temperatures Yesterday—Max., 40; min., 26.

VOL. LXXXII....No. 27,435. Entered as Second-Class Matter. Postoffice, New York, N. Y. NEW YORK, MONDAY, MARCH 6, 1933. P TWO CENTS In New York City. | THREE CENTS Within 200 Miles | FOUR CENTS Elsewhere Except in 7th and 8th Postal Zones

ROOSEVELT ORDERS 4-DAY BANK HOLIDAY, PUTS EMBARGO ON GOLD, CALLS CONGRESS

HITLER BLOC WINS A REICH MAJORITY; RULES IN PRUSSIA

Stay-at-Homes Turn Out and Give Government 52% of 39,000,000 Record Vote.

NAZIS ROLL UP 17,300,000

Get 44% of Total Poll and Even Wrest the Control of Bavaria From Catholics.

ELECTION IS PEACEFUL

Berlin Is Closely Guarded—The Stahlheim Holds Parade Under Sunny Skies.

By FREDERICK T. BIRCHALL.

Special Cable to THE NEW YORK TIMES.

BERLIN, Monday, March 6.—With almost mathematical precision the results in yesterday's German elections for the Reichstag and the Prussian Diet bear out the predictions based on the pre-election campaign. Just as two and two make four, so suppression and intimidation have produced a Nazi-Nationalist triumph. The rest of the world may now accept the fact of ultra-Nationalist domination of the Reich and Prussia for a prolonged period with whatever results this may entail.

At 2 o'clock this morning, when 39,000,000 out of the Reich's eligible vote of 44,000,000 counted and with every indication of a probable total vote of 90 per cent, exceeding all precedents Nazi-Nationalist control of the Reichstag was assured. The Nazis will have at least 288 seats and the Nationalists 53 more, giving them together 341 seats, or a clear 52 per cent in a total of 648.

The tabulated vote follows:

	Vote.	Seats.
National Socialists	17,300,000	288
Nationalists	3,100,000	53
Socialists	7,000,000	118
Communists	4,800,000	81
Centrists and Bavarian People's Party	5,500,000	91
People's Party and Allied Groups	1,014,000	12
State (Democratic)	333,000	5
Total	39,047,000	648

The Nazis have increased their vote to 44 per cent of the adult population, or 11 per cent over that of last November and 6½ per cent over their previous high-water total of last July. The Nationalist increase is barely 1 per cent over their vote of last November. This, therefore, is a Nazi rather than a Nationalist triumph.

Nazis Control Bavaria.

Apart from the size of the vote—the 90 per cent of the eligible voters being as nearly unanimous as any election in any large country has ever shown—the sensation of the election is that the Nazis have wrested control of Bavaria from the Catholics. They have wiped out the deficit in their November vote compared with that of July and have beaten the Bavarian People's party by approximately 600,000. This is likely to dispose of any dream of restoring the Wittelsbach monarchy in Bavaria, as it will of the idea of a possible secession of Bavaria from the Reich.

More than this, in the city of Cologne, the Catholic capital of Germany, under the influence of an unexpected 25 per cent increase in the total vote—three-fourths of which has gone into the Nazi column—Herr Hitler's party has come within an ace of seizing control there.

The so-called stay-at-home vote came out with a vengeance and almost the whole of it went to the Nazis; while, in addition, the Hitlerites gained a full 10 per cent from the other parties.

Gain 4,000,000 Votes.

The Nazis have increased their own vote by more than 4,000,000, or almost 30 per cent over the November total. The Centrists and Socialists throughout the country have almost held their own. The Communists lost more than 20 per cent, but their lost votes did not go to the Socialists, as had been expected. While a few may have gone

Continued on Page Eight.

Mob Attacked Stalin's Home In Wide Revolt, Tokyo Hears

Wireless to THE NEW YORK TIMES.

TOKYO, Monday, March 6.—Private information reaching Tokyo states that discontent due to famine conditions is so acute in Soviet Russia that a mob attacked Joseph Stalin's house in Moscow on Jan. 20 and was driven off by troops after 400 persons had been killed. Other reports from Siberia, partly corroborated by information reaching military circles here, indicate the farmers are in widespread revolt. Serious disturbances occurred at Irkutsk, and 80,000 men are said to have joined the revolt, including Communists and Red soldiers.

The Japanese discount a good part of these rumors, but they come from too many sources to be entirely ignored. It is believed these disturbances are much more serious than the Soviet Government has admitted.

CERMAK NEAR END; LAPSES INTO COMA

Death Is Imminent From Shot Aimed by Zangara at Roosevelt.

FAMILY AT HIS BEDSIDE

Third Transfusion Futile in 19-Day Fight to Save Chicago Mayor in Miami Hospital.

By The Associated Press.

MIAMI, Fla., Monday, March 6.—Physicians of Mayor Anton Cermak early this morning relinquished hope for his life.

In a bulletin issued at 12:30 A. M., the physicians said that Mayor Cermak was in a condition of coma and that he probably would live only a few hours. The bulletin said Mr. Cermak was "failing rapidly."

It was issued after a third blood transfusion had been administered yesterday in an attempt to save his life.

The Mayor's right lung, punctured on the night of Feb. 15 by a bullet from the pistol of the assassin, Joseph Zangara, in an attempt to kill Franklin D. Roosevelt, was aspirated yesterday and physicians found a gangrenous condition.

Father Morrison of St. Bartholomew's Church in Chicago entered the sun parlor room at 1:15 A. M. Mayor Cermak's wife was a Roman Catholic and his children are of that faith.

Dr. Frederick Tice of Chicago told newspaper men at 1:25 A. M. that the Mayor probably would live an hour. He said Cermak's breathing was very labored. He called members of the family and said Mr. Cermak's life was "a matter of another hour."

Members of Family Weep.

Members of the family, summoned to the bedside, emerged weeping.

Joseph Cermak, a brother, his wife and Mrs. John Kallal, a sister, came from the sun porch at 12:35 A. M. Mrs. Cermak and Mrs. Kallal took their seats on the lawn before the sun porch door and wept.

Vivian Graham, a granddaughter, emerged soon and joined the group. Daughters of the Mayor had been at his side a short time before.

At midnight newspapermen were allowed to go into the sun porch where the Mayor lies in an oxygen room and see the patient through the glass window of the oxygen apparatus.

The Mayor lay back on his pillow, hands folded over his chest, breathing heavily. Dr. Frank Jirka and Dr. E. S. Nichol were attending him.

Dr. Jirka, who is Mr. Cermak's son-in-law, said the Mayor recognized members of the family. "My wife asked him if he knew her. He told her, 'Yes, kiss me.'"

The greatest air of concern prevailed in the little sun porch, where a heavy guard of police and detectives was maintained.

"Reaction" After Transfusion.

After the blood transfusion yesterday afternoon Mr. Cermak suffered a "slight reaction," causing a weakening of the pulse and irregular respiration, the doctors said.

Reports immediately upon conclusion of the transfusion were that the operation apparently was successful. One pint of blood given by Thomas Pendray Jr. of Miami was

Continued on Page Fourteen.

JAPANESE PUSH ON IN FIERCE FIGHTING; CHINA CLOSES WALL

Jehol Forces Offer Stoutest Resistance of Campaign as They Are Cornered.

BUT LOSE ANOTHER PASS

Chang's Troops at Kupei Bar Retreat Southward to the Peiping Area.

NANKING ADMITS DEFEAT

Asserts 'What Will Happen Next Depends on Military'—Tientsin Fears Clashes.

By The Associated Press.

TOKYO, March 5.—Rengo (Japanese) news agency dispatches from Chengteh (Jehol City) today said the final phase of the Japanese campaign in Jehol Province, a move to seize passes in the Great Wall north and northeast of Peiping, was producing some of the most bitter fighting of the whole drive. Cornered Chinese units were resisting desperately.

The Sixteenth Infantry Brigade of Major Gen. Tadashi Kawahara, en route to Koupei Pass through the wall, fought fiercely with remnants of the troops of Tang Yu-lin, Governor of Jehol Province, ten miles west of the provincial capital, Chengteh. Thereafter the detachment advanced to Changshanku, which is sixteen miles northeast of the pass.

Marshal Chang Hsiao-liang, military commander of North China, was reported to have sealed the pass against Governor Tang and his followers. Governor Tang himself was reported to have fled to Fengning, which is about forty miles northwest of Chengteh.

Pass in Wall Taken.

Fighting in the shadow of the Great Wall preceded the occupation by the Fourteenth Infantry Brigade of Major Gen. Heijiro Hattori of Fanchia Pass, which is one of three important Great Wall passes south of Chengteh. General Hattori faced a large Chinese force south of the wall.

Major Gen. Kaoru Nakamura, commanding the Thirty-third Infantry Brigade, en route from Lingyau to Chiehliing Pass, summoned an air squadron to aid him before he succeeded in routing remnants of Marshal Chang's Sixteenth Brigade.

The Fourth Cavalry Brigade of Major Gen. Kennosuke Mogi, pushing on from Chihfeng, 100 miles northeast of Chengteh, captured Weichang, fifty-five miles to the southwest, the centre of the Jehol opium-producing region, after stiff fighting.

Thousands of Chinese Dead.

Special Cable to THE NEW YORK TIMES.

SHANGHAI, Monday, March 6.—While members of the Nanking Government are expected to discuss a unified policy at Peiping this week, Jehol reports today tell of indescribable confusion among the Chinese forces there, with thousands killed, wounded and missing among the troops in Marshal Chang Hsiao-liang's best brigades, which originally totaled 20,000.

War Minister Ho Yin-ching arrived by airplane at Peiping at noon, and Acting Premier T. V. Soong and others are expected to follow him there for a belated stocktaking of the present situation. The Chinese troops in Jehol appear to be scrambling for the passes out through the Great Wall, with the Japanese bombing Chinese concentrations near Kupei and Hsifeng passes and at Dolonnor, in Northern Jehol.

The Japanese artillery is in action at Sanshihchiatze, between Pingchuan and Lingyuan.

The Japanese brigade led by General Hattori is expected to attack the main Chinese force tomorrow at Paishihlatzushan Hill, twenty miles south of Pingchuan and thirty-three miles from Hsifeng Pass.

The Charhar Provincial Government is reported to be negotiating with the Japanese for inclusion of that province in Manchukuo, but the Chinese military deny this.

The Nanking Foreign Office yesterday made this terse and incisive statement:

"Jehol is lost. What will happen

Continued on Page Eight.

Relief Wages Will Be Paid Despite Holiday, Gibson Says

Harvey D. Gibson, chairman of the Emergency Unemployment Relief Committee, declared yesterday that the bank holiday would not interfere with the payment of wages to unemployed men and women holding emergency jobs through the committee's work and relief bureau.

"Emergency wages must be paid and some way must be found to pay them," Mr. Gibson said. "I have no doubt that we will find a way to do it. We are not worried about it at all. Arrangements can certainly be made to meet the emergency relief payroll."

The weekly payroll of the committee exceeds $1,000,000.

BEWILDERED CITY STILL PAYS IN CASH

Faces Use of Scrip Calmly and Continues to Patronize the Theatres and Stores.

HOPEFUL MOOD PREVAILS

Merchants and Travel Lines Uncertain on Use of Tender—Many Extending Credit.

Bewildered but still cheerful, the city followed its usual routine yesterday, talked of the possibility of using scrip instead of cash, but still patronized the movie theatres, restaurants and concert halls.

Railroads reported, generally, that there had been no appreciable decrease in week-end travel, that there had been "no embarrassment" and that they were carrying on as usual, on an all-cash basis.

A spokesman for the Pennsylvania Railroad reported that the outward movement yesterday was good and an official of the New York Central reported everything going smoothly with enough cash on hand to meet all the road's needs for the present, including payrolls.

One form of nuisance cropped up at Pennsylvania Station. It started Saturday night, when persons with banknotes of large denominations demanded change. There was a tremendous number of $100 notes, quite a few $500 notes and even a few $1,000 notes were presented for change. One or two of the more timid persons tried to cover up their real purpose by buying Newark tickets.

Railroads Accept Only Cash.

None of the railroads is accepting anything but cash for transportation. This is in accord with general practice, an official pointed out, and up to yesterday no change in that plan had been proposed. Officers of the New York Central Railroad held a special meeting yesterday apparently to arrange for eventualities that might arise from the banking situation, but no decision was reached so far as could be learned.

Airplane lines and steamship lines, on the other hand, were accepting checks from old clients and were following a policy of being "reasonable" about accepting checks from other customers.

"We will maintain a sensible and reasonable attitude during this crisis," said John Gammie, assistant manager of the Cunard Line. "We will try to carry on much as we did in ordinary times. We haven't taken up the matter of scrip, but it is likely that a meeting of steamship line officials may be called to decide on a policy with regard to it."

Rise in Grocery Store Sales.

Increased sales were reported in most of the chain grocery stores in the poorer districts on Saturday, owners reported yesterday. They believed it might have been caused by a desire to stock up before an inflation policy might be decided upon by the government.

The Grand Union Grocery Stores, an official said last night, are planning to issue coupon books redeemable for food at their stores. The books would be sold to industrial and commercial concerns that would use them as part payment to employes. The same official considered it likely that guaranteed Clearing House scrip might be acceptable at the Grand Union stores.

A spokesman for the Great Atlantic and Pacific Tea Company, which maintains chains of grocery stores in several States, said his concern had not yet formulated any

Continued on Page Three.

BANKS HERE ACT AT ONCE

City Scrip to Be Ready Today or Tomorrow to Replace Currency.

EMERGENCY STEP PRAISED

Financiers Look for Little Interruption in Business Under Federal Program.

'TRUST DEPOSITS' TO AID

Cash Now Can Be Placed in New Accounts and Drawn Upon Without Limitation.

Clearing House certificates will be issued in New York, if needed, just as soon as they are printed, possibly today and probably not later than tomorrow, as a result of President Roosevelt's proclamation of last night.

The President's emergency decree not only made the banking holiday national and extended it through Thursday when Congress meets in special session, but it also gave the banks permission to issue scrip in the form of Clearing House certificates to take the place of regular currency.

Thus there will be little or no interruption in the ordinary routine of New York's business affairs, which can be carried on with scrip as a substitute medium of exchange just as well as with other currency. Paychecks, for instance, would be converted into scrip by the banks, which would be open for that purpose and for receiving new deposits.

Leading bankers indicated their approval of the President's proclamation last night and signified their belief that the use of scrip would be just as successful in New York as it was in the 1907 panic.

May Pay in Currency.

There is a possibility, some bankers said, that the New York banks might pay out currency when they reopen in place of, or in addition to, clearing house certificates. Such action would be possible only with the express permission of the Secretary of the Treasury under the President's order. These bankers said that the local banks have large amounts of till money on hand and that they could, if permitted, meet substantial demands from their depositors out of these cash holdings. From the standpoint of the central banking system the paying out of this till money to the public would have no effect upon the position of the national currency, since it is already a part of total money in circulation.

Subject always to the sanction of the Secretary of the Treasury, the banks will be able, under the President's proclamation, to operate along nearly normal lines. Under the provision for creation of special trust accounts, business men, merchants and wage earners will be able to find a safe depository for any cash they receive instead of having to face the dangers of carrying large amounts of currency. Those who withdrew money from the banks just before the shutdown and who have since been worrying about its safety will be able to redeposit the funds in special trust accounts and be assured of getting it back again without limitation.

Lehman Defers State Action.

When informed of the President's proclamation late last night, Governor Lehman withheld comment for the present as to whether he would issue a new decree extending the New York State holiday. Although such an action probably would be regarded as a mere formality, it was thought likely that the Governor would take it. Before President Roosevelt's proclamation was made public, Governor A. Harry Moore of New Jersey issued a decree last night extending the banking holiday in New Jersey indefinitely.

In both New York and New Jersey the banking holiday was proclaimed first for two days—Saturday and today—and was to have ended with the close of business this afternoon. Under the original proclamations by Governors Lehman and Moore the New York and New Jersey banks were to have been reopened tomorrow morning.

All security and commodity exchanges will remain closed, barring unexpected changes in present

Continued on Page Three.

The President's Bank Proclamation

Special to THE NEW YORK TIMES.

WASHINGTON, March 5.—The text of President Roosevelt's proclamation on the banking situation, issued at the White House at 11 o'clock tonight, was as follows:

BY THE PRESIDENT OF THE UNITED STATES OF AMERICA.

A Proclamation

WHEREAS there have been heavy and unwarranted withdrawals of gold and currency from our banking institutions for the purpose of hoarding; and

WHEREAS continuous and increasingly extensive speculative activity abroad in foreign exchange has resulted in severe drains on the nation's stocks of gold; and

WHEREAS these conditions have created a national emergency; and

WHEREAS it is in the best interests of all bank depositors that a period of respite be provided with a view to preventing further hoarding of coin, bullion or currency or speculation in foreign exchange and permitting the application of appropriate measures to protect the interests of our people; and

WHEREAS it is provided in Section 5 (b) of the act of October 6, 1917 (40 stat. L. 411) as amended, "that the President may investigate, regulate or prohibit, under such rules and regulations as he may prescribe, by means of licenses or otherwise, any transactions in foreign exchange and the export, hoarding, melting or earmarkings of gold or silver coin or bullion or currency * * *";

WHEREAS it is provided in Section 16 of the said act "that whoever shall wilfully violate any of the provisions of this act or of any license, rule or regulation issued thereunder, and whoever shall wilfully violate, neglect or refuse to comply with any order of the President issued in compliance with the provisions of this act, shall, upon conviction, be fined not more than $10,000 or, if a natural person, imprisoned for not more than ten years or both * * *";

NOW, THEREFORE, I, FRANKLIN D. ROOSEVELT, PRESIDENT OF THE UNITED STATES OF AMERICA, IN VIEW OF SUCH NATIONAL EMERGENCY AND BY VIRTUE of the authority vested in me by said act and in order to prevent the export, hoarding or earmarking of gold or silver coin or bullion or currency, do hereby proclaim, order, direct and declare that from Monday, the sixth day of March, to Thursday, the ninth day of March, nineteen hundred and thirty-three, both dates inclusive, there shall be maintained and observed by all banking institutions and all branches thereof located in the United States of America, including the Territories and Insular Possessions, a bank holiday, and that during said period all banking transactions shall be suspended.

During such holiday, excepting as hereinafter provided, no such banking institution or branch shall pay out, export, earmark or permit the withdrawal or transfer in any manner or by any device whatsoever of any gold or silver coin or bullion or currency or take any other action which might facilitate the hoarding thereof; nor shall any such banking institution or branch pay out deposits, make loans or discounts, deal in foreign exchange, transfer credits from the United States to any place abroad, or transact any other banking business whatsoever.

During such holiday, the Secretary of the Treasury, with the approval of the President and under such regulations as he may prescribe, is authorized and empowered (a) to permit any or all of such banking institutions to perform any or all of the usual banking functions, (b) to direct, require or permit the issuance of clearing house certificates, or other evidences of claims of assets of banking institutions, and (c) to authorize and direct the creation in such banking institutions of special trust accounts for the receipt of new deposits which shall be subject to withdrawal on demand without any restriction or limitation and shall be kept separately in cash or on deposit in Federal Reserve Banks or invested in obligations of the United States.

As used in this order the term "banking institutions" shall include all Federal Reserve Banks, national banking associations, banks, trust companies, savings banks, building and loan associations, credit unions, or other corporations, partnerships, associations or persons, engaged in the business of receiving deposits, making loans, discounting business paper, or transacting any other form of banking business.

IN WITNESS WHEREOF I have hereunto set my hand and caused the seal of the United States to be affixed.

Done in the City of Washington this 6th day of March, 1 A M., in the year of Our Lord One Thousand Nine Hundred and Thirty-three, and of the Independence of the United States the one hundred and fifty-seventh.

(SEAL) FRANKLIN D. ROOSEVELT.

By the President:
CORDELL HULL,
Secretary of State.

ROOSEVELT MEETS GOVERNORS TODAY

Conference Will Centre on Bank Problem—Confidence in President Apparent.

Special to THE NEW YORK TIMES.

WASHINGTON, March 5.—The Governors conference which President Roosevelt called nearly a month ago to discuss with him interlocking governmental problems will meet with him tomorrow morning in the White House at 11 o'clock. But its discussion will be largely directed toward the more immediate issue of banking moratoriums, with the possibility that what is done may indicate the eventual Federal action to be suggested by President Roosevelt.

The present situation so far overshadows the issues which Mr. Roosevelt stressed in originally calling the conference that they have become entirely secondary. It was his first intention to confine the discussion to a limitation on overlapping Federal and State

Continued on Page Two.

ON GOLD STANDARD, WOODIN DECLARES

Other High Officials Concur in His View of Suspending Payments for Period.

Special to THE NEW YORK TIMES.

WASHINGTON, March 5.—Secretary of the Treasury William H. Woodin declared tonight emphatically that the United States had not gone off the gold standard on account of the proclamation of the President. He was supported in this view by other high officials of the administration, both in the executive and legislative branches, among them Senator Key Pittman, chairman of the Committee on Foreign Relations.

Secretary Woodin said:

"It is ridiculous and misleading to say that we have gone off the gold standard, any more than we have gone off the currency standard.

"We are definitely on the gold standard. Gold merely cannot be obtained for several days. In other

Continued on Page Six.

USE OF SCRIP AUTHORIZED

President Takes Steps Under Sweeping Law of War Time.

PRISON FOR GOLD HOARDER

The Proclamation Provides for Withdrawals From Banks Against New Deposits.

CONGRESS SITS THURSDAY

Day of Conference With the Cabinet and Financial Men Precedes the Decree.

Special to THE NEW YORK TIMES.

WASHINGTON, March 5.—To prevent the export, hoarding or earmarking of gold or silver, coin or bullion or currency, President Roosevelt issued a proclamation at 11 o'clock tonight, in which he ordered a bank holiday from tomorrow through Thursday, March 9. Earlier in the day he had summoned a special session of Congress to meet on Thursday.

This sweeping action was taken after a day of conferences, among officials and bankers, the President taking recourse to war powers granted under the trading-with-the-enemy act.

As a result of the proclamation all banking activities will be suspended during the holiday, except as permitted by regulations of the Secretary of the Treasury, thus taking this country technically off the gold standard until the four-day period expires.

In order that there may not be a complete suspension of all banking and exchange operations, the proclamation authorizes the issuance of Clearing House certificates, which may be used as currency until the banks return to more normal functioning.

Points of the Proclamation.

The main points in the proclamation are:

1. A national banking holiday from March 6 to March 9 inclusive.

An embargo on the withdrawal of gold and silver for export or domestic use during that period, except with permission of the Secretary of the Treasury.

3. The issuance of Clearing House certificates or other evidence of claims against the assets of banking institutions to permit business to carry on.

4. Authorization to banking institutions under regulations of the Secretary of the Treasury to receive new deposits and make them subject to withdrawal on demand without any restrictions or limitations.

Friends of the President said he had a definite three-point program for the solution of the banking problem and that tonight's action included two of them. The first, they said, was a protection of the currency against unreasonable withdrawal. The second was to furnish a temporary currency. The third is permanent reorganization of the whole banking system, which, they predicted would be proposed to the special session of Congress meeting here Thursday.

Officials Act Quickly.

The Federal Reserve Board and Secretary Woodin, with the advice of former Secretary Ogden L. Mills acted immediately after the issuance of the proclamation to make it effective.

The proclamation was issued at 11 o'clock, bringing to an end a series of conferences held by Treasury officials and the new Cabinet throughout the day.

The proclamation affects all Federal Reserve Banks and national banks, trust companies, savings banks, building and loan associations, credit unions or other institutions engaged in any form of banking business.

The proclamation provides for a fine of $10,000 or imprisonment of not more than ten years or both for any violation of its provisions by gold hoarding or otherwise.

The President acted under Section 5 (b) and Section 16 of the trading with the enemy act to place these extraordinary restrictions on the nation's banking structure. The courts have interpreted the act as giving the President authority to bring about a complete suspension of gold and silver payments as well as an embargo on their export.

Section 5 (b) of the trading-with-

"All the News That's Fit to Print."

The New York Times.

LATE CITY EDITION
WEATHER—Mostly cloudy and colder today; tomorrow fair.
Temperatures Yesterday—Max. 46; Min. 35.

VOL. LXXXII....No. 27,439. Entered as Second-Class Matter. Postoffice, New York, N. Y. NEW YORK, FRIDAY, MARCH 10, 1933. P TWO CENTS In New York City. | THREE CENTS Within 200 Miles | FOUR CENTS Elsewhere Except in 7th and 8th Postal Zones

ROOSEVELT EXTENDS THE NATIONAL BANKING HOLIDAY; CONGRESS EMPOWERS HIM TO REOPEN SOUND INSTITUTIONS; HALF BILLION BUDGET CUT NEXT, CHIEFLY VETERANS' FUND

3 MORE AMERICANS ATTACKED IN BERLIN AS RAIDING GOES ON

Anti-Semites Compel Shops to Close and Invade the Boerse Demanding Directors Quit.

EMBASSIES FILE PROTESTS

Sackett Reports Government Voiced Regret, Pledging No Repetition of Assaults.

NAZIS TAKE OVER BAVARIA

Name Von Epp State Police Head as Held Cabinet Gives Way—Army to Guard Vienna.

By FREDERICK T. BIRCHALL.
Special Cable to THE NEW YORK TIMES.

BERLIN, March 9.—Three more specific cases of molestation of American citizens by men wearing National Socialist uniforms were presented to the Berlin authorities today by George S. Messersmith, the United States Consul General, who in the name of the victims made a formal complaint and asked action on it.

Altogether six cases, including three previously brought to the attention of the Foreign Office by the American Embassy, have now been carried direct to Rear Admiral Magnus von Levetzow, the new Nazi police president, affidavits accompanying each case. Five of the complainants are of the Jewish faith.

Admiral von Levetzow expressed regret for the occurrences outlined to him and promised Mr. Messersmith that he would immediately initiate investigations.

[Washington got reports that the United States and other embassies had protested attacks on foreigners. Ambassador Sackett was assured that attacks would not be repeated.]

The worst of the new incidents concerned a midnight attack on Max Schussler and his wife in their private apartment on the Olivaerplatz off the Kurfuerstendamm. The affidavit presented by Mr. Messersmith sets forth that Mr. Schussler owns the apartment house in which he lives.

Nazi Refused to Pay Rent.

One of his tenants, who operates a beer house on the ground floor, is a Nazi. Months ago, it is alleged, he announced throughout the neighborhood that he no longer intended to pay rent to the "American Jew" after Adolf Hitler took office. Last month he kept his word and refused to pay, and Mr. Schussler thereupon obtained a decree of eviction.

At 2 o'clock Tuesday morning Mr. Schussler's bedroom was invaded by four men, two of whom wore Nazi uniforms, and who were armed with revolvers. Mr. Schussler and his wife were forced at the point of pistols to rise and dress, the invaders refusing to leave the room during this process.

They then compelled Mr. Schussler to sign an order recalling the eviction decree, informing him that he was marked for death if he disavowed it later.

As evidence indicates that the invaders gained access to the house through the connivance of the recalcitrant tenant, it is charged that he is directly implicated and a clue to their identity is thus directly available.

In the two other cases Leon Jaffe, who resides at 414 Howe Avenue, the Bronx, and Solomon Friedman, temporarily residing in Berlin, charge that they were attacked without provocation by men wearing Nazi uniforms.

Other Cases of Extremism.

The attacks on Americans were accompanied by other instances of Nazi extremism today, although police reports, which are virtually the sole source of information, have it that the greater part of Germany remains quiescent and peaceful.

Groups of men wearing Nazi uniforms gathered in front of several of the large department stores in Berlin, Magdeburg and Kassel, especially German and American chain stores, and organized shouting choruses urging the populace to buy "in German, not Jewish, stores!" Several of these stores

Continued on Page Thirteen.

Japanese Says Metal Imports Are for Earthquakes, Not War

By The Canadian Press.

ST. JOHN, N. B., March 9.—Earthquakes, not war, have been responsible for large shipments of scrap metal to Japan, according to Captain Mayeda of the Japanese steamer England Maru, now loading 6,500 tons of scrap metal purchased from the Canadian National Railways. This will bring the volume of steel and iron shipped from here to Japan this year to more than 18,000 tons.

Earthquakes in recent years, the captain said, had resulted in a number of Japanese cities in the "danger zone" enacting laws that all buildings must be constructed of steel and concrete, with the result that Japan, short in ore, must import great quantities of metal.

CITY GETS $3,995,696 FOR MARCH JOB AID

State Relief Bureau Includes $106,000 for School Lunches in Donation for Month.

ALL PAYROLLS TO BE MET

Gibson Committee Will Give Out $325,000 by Week-End in Maintenance Wages.

The State Temporary Emergency Relief Administration will contribute $3,995,696 to New York City for unemployment relief this month, according to an announcement yesterday by Harry L. Hopkins, chairman of the State Temporary Emergency Relief Administration.

The funds will be allocated as follows:

The sum of $1,550,000 will go to the city besides the statutory 40 per cent reimbursement of $2,000,000 for approved home and (or) work relief expenditures of the city; $106,000 for school lunches; $50,000 for medical and nursing care of relief recipients, and $290,696 for work of unemployed men and women of New York City on work relief projects of various State departments.

"It is expressly understood that this sum is to be expended in addition to the appropriation by the Board of Estimate to be made available for work and home relief," said Mr. Hopkins in his notification to Lawson Purdy, chairman of the City of New York Emergency Work and Relief Administration. "Upon this latter appropriation the administration will reimburse the City of New York 40 per cent of approved expenditures for home or work relief. In the immediate future we shall make arrangements for the advance to you of the items."

Palisades Work to Go On.

The allocation for State Department work relief projects includes $152,000 for continuation of the improvements at the Palisades Interstate Park, upon which unemployed men of New York City are being put to work, and $7,650 for the wages of homeless New York City men who are working on these improvements and are being maintained at the State work camp at Blauvelt, N. Y.

The Emergency Unemployment Relief Committee hopes to be able to pay the 20,000 unemployed men and women receiving maintenance wages their full weekly pay of $325,000 by the end of the week, it was announced yesterday. Approximately 6,500 workers received part of their wages due yesterday and Wednesday. Most of these workers received one day's pay, which varies from $4 to $5.

The Emergency Work and Relief Bureau doubled the staff of its paymaster's department last night in order to complete payrolls for 4,200 emergency workers today, according to William H. Matthews, the director.

"Although those who were paid today received only one day's pay of what was owed them, enough currency has been released to us so that those who are due to be paid tomorrow, Friday, will get every cent of their money," said Mr. Matthews. "I have assurances from Harvey D. Gibson, chairman of the Emergency Unemployment Relief Committee, that we will have enough cash made available to us so that all emergency workers can be paid in full by Saturday.

"In order to facilitate the pay-

Continued on Page Nine.

SAVINGS BANKS FREE CASH

All in State to Permit Depositors to Obtain Small Sums Today.

SOME CHECKS CLEARED

Commercial Units Clean Up Last Friday's Business to Be Ready for Holiday's End.

SERVICE IS ALSO WIDENED

Greater Latitude on Payrolls, Food Movement Financed—State Holiday Extended.

Savings banks will be open today for small withdrawals to meet urgent needs of depositors, it was announced last night by Henry R. Kinsey, president of the Savings Banks Association of the State of New York. Several savings banks did this yesterday, permitting withdrawals up to $10.

The commercial banks and trust companies will be open today for the same limited facilities as yesterday—that is, financing food supplies for the city, advancing funds to meet payrolls at least in part, cashing small personal checks for essentials, receiving new deposits, and other specified functions permitted by Secretary of the Treasury Woodin.

President Roosevelt's new proclamation last night extending the national banking holiday until further notice, continued in effect Secretary Woodin's regulations providing for restricted operation of such banks as choose to take advantage of the exceptions to the moratorium permitted by the Treasury Department.

Announces Savings Bank Move.

Mr. Kinsey's statement follows on the withdrawals permitted by the savings banks:

"With the permission of the State Banking Board, the savings banks of this State, pending the end of the holiday, will pay out to their depositors small sums vitally necessary for their living expenses. This is in accord with Secretary Woodin's authorization allowing small withdrawals for 'immediate needs.'"

Mr. Kinsey also issued a statement last night expressing gratification that for the first time the savings banks have been brought into direct contact with the Federal Reserve Board. He said:

"Under the bill adopted today we have been given direct contact with the Federal Reserve Board for the first time. We are now placed in position to rediscount our government bonds directly with the Federal Reserve Banks. That means that that portion of our portfolios consisting of government bonds is to all practical purposes cashed. That's about the only tie-up we have in this picture."

All of the 139 savings institutions in the State would come under the classification of "sound," Mr. Kinsey said. He added he could see no restrictions to their opening when the bank holiday had been declared at an end.

New York banks of all types are all ready to reopen on a normal basis as soon as the moratorium ends and they receive permission from the Treasury Department. They made all plans yesterday to reopen on a normal basis this morning, expecting that they would receive orders last night to do so, but the issuance of the President's new proclamation forced them to hold their plans in abeyance.

State Holiday Extended.

Shortly before 1 o'clock this morning Governor Lehman issued a proclamation coinciding with that of President Roosevelt and continuing the banking holiday in the State until further order.

The proclamation was as follows:

Whereas a proclamation has been issued by the President of the United States continuing in full force and effect until further proclamation by him all of the terms and provisions of his proclamation of March 6, and regulations and orders issued thereunder,

Now, therefore, I, Herbert H. Lehman, Governor of the State of New York, do hereby declare that the bank holiday heretofore ordered by me in the State of

Continued on Page Five.

Hull Asks Treasury to Aid Envoys Whose Funds Are Held

Special to THE NEW YORK TIMES.

WASHINGTON, March 9.—Secretary Hull has referred to the Treasury Department the appeal for relief of foreign envoys whose funds are tied up in closed banks.

He has expressed the hope that steps can be taken for the diplomats to obtain some of their funds. He has made the suggestion broad enough to cover officials of foreign consulates throughout the country.

The appeal for aid was made, it was said by the State Department today, concerning funds in banks closed by the legal holiday but not banks that closed prior to the general holiday. Names of the appealing diplomats and the amount of the funds have not been disclosed.

HOARDERS IN FRIGHT TURN IN $30,000,000

Gold Pours Into Banks and the Federal Reserve as Owners Act to Avoid Penalty.

NAMES TAKEN OFF LIST

Even Christmas Coins Help to Swell Week's Recovery of Metal to $65,000,000.

Spurred by fear of public exposure and the threat of fines and imprisonment, gold hoarders scurried back to the Federal Reserve Bank and its member institutions yesterday to redeposit the yellow coins that they had lately stampeded to withdraw. Including the little piles of gold pieces brought in by frightened individuals and the boxes of gold and gold certificates turned in by member banks in response to the orders of the Secretary of the Treasury, a total of $30,000,000 in gold was poured into the central bank, swelling the total recovery of gold since the start of the week to about $65,000,000.

Officials of the Reserve Bank and of commercial banks all over the city were deluged with inquiries as to how gold could be returned. All who asked were informed that they could bring the gold in, if they acted promptly, without incurring any penalty and could obtain in exchange Federal Reserve notes. Those with gold were advised to return the metal to the banks from which they got it and to leave their names and addresses.

Steady Stream of Depositors.

At the Reserve Bank a steady stream of hoarders flowed in and out the gates. They were admitted quickly to the receiving windows, where they were asked to fill out deposit slips, similar in form to the withdrawal slips that they had filed upon taking the gold out. On the slips was a place for the name and address of the depositor and the amount of gold he was returning. Tellers at two windows rapidly counted out the gold pieces and set aside the deposit slips, so that the names could be crossed off the list of those who previously had made withdrawals before it was forwarded to Washington.

Much of the gold returned by individuals yesterday came back intact in the bags and paper-rolled stacks in which it had been withdrawn, but nevertheless each coin was counted before the deposit slip was approved. The repentant hoarders displayed a good deal of agitation, but they were received courteously by the guards of the Reserve Bank and came out with an evident air of relief when they had disposed of their dangerous treasure.

Christmas Coins Turned In.

They came with little bags and brief cases, paper bundles, boxes or bulging pockets. Many had only a few coins, while others had bags of thousands of dollars of double-eagles. The drastic character of the proposed law against gold hoarding frightened even those who had not thought of themselves as hoarders, but who suddenly recalled a few odd coins left over from Christmas presents which had not been spent because they were too "pretty." One important banker, informed of the proposed law, reflectively drew from his pocket a gold piece received at the last

Continued on Page Six.

LEADERS AGREE ON SLASH

White House Parley Shapes Economy Proposal for Today.

PAY REDUCTION UP TO 15%

Bill as Drafted Also Gives Executive Power to Reduce Non-War Disability Aid.

$500,000,000 FOR WORKS

President Will Offer Vast Employment Relief Plan in Message Tomorrow.

Special to THE NEW YORK TIMES.

WASHINGTON, March 9.—President Roosevelt will submit to Congress tomorrow recommendations for reduction in the expenditures for war veterans and the civil list amounting to $500,000,000.

Agreement to support this proposal was reached tonight by a conference of Democratic and Republican Senate leaders, who estimated that through further reductions, to be effected later in reorganizations and liminations, annual expenditures would be reduced $1,000,000,000, carrying out the pre-election pledges of Mr. Roosevelt.

In his message tomorrow the President will deal with the budget and suggest further government economies. He will submit another message to Congress on Saturday proposing a $500,000,000 appropriation for internal construction to relieve unemployment and further the Muscle Shoals and related "work relief" plans employing at least 500,000 persons.

Convinced that the emergency measures will deal adequately with the present banking situation and open the banks, the President is said to believe that the best way to overcome the banking difficulties is to embark upon a constructive program to solve the political and economic problems which have been prolonging the depression.

Bills to Empower President.

The administration has prepared bills to carry out its proposals. Speaker Rainey, who was at the White House conference tonight at which the plan was revealed, said that the legislation that would be offered would authorize the President to make arbitrary cuts in the appropriation for the Veterans Administration and permit him to make reductions in all salaries not to exceed 15 per cent.

Senator Robinson, upon leaving the conference, said:

"It is expected that the President will send a message to Congress tomorrow bearing on the budget and looking to important and substantial reductions in expenditures for pensions, veterans' compensation, disability allowances and emergency officers' retired pay. Coupled with the proposition will be a plan for salary reductions. The total amount of reductions will be in the neighborhood of $500,000,000."

Snell Doubts Swift Action.

Representative Snell, who was the only regular Republican at the conference, said it evolved a very comprehensive program which undoubtedly would encounter some opposition.

He, as well as Speaker Rainey, was of the opinion that the reductions could not be made hastily and therefore would have to go over until after the recess which, it is planned will be taken Monday for a few weeks.

Senator Glass, another conferee, said he approved the general idea and hoped that Congress would adopt it. Senator Robinson, who as majority leader will introduce the legislation in the Senate, was confident that the administration's program would succeed. He said that the people were demanding reductions in taxes and that it was absolutely necessary for the administration to begin at once to balance the budget.

Other Congress leaders at the conference were Senators Wagner, Costigan, Byrnes and La Follette and Representatives Connery, Rankin, McDuffie, Rayburn and Buchanan. Also present were Secretaries Ickes, Dern and Wallace of the Interior, War and Agriculture Departments, respectively, and Lewis Douglas, Director of the

Continued on Page Ten.

The President's Proclamation

Special to THE NEW YORK TIMES.

WASHINGTON, March 9.—The text of the proclamation issued by President Roosevelt tonight was as follows:

BY THE PRESIDENT OF THE UNITED STATES OF AMERICA.

A Proclamation

WHEREAS, on March 6, 1933, I, Franklin D. Roosevelt, President of the United States of America, by proclamation declared the existence of a national emergency and proclaimed a bank holiday extending from Monday, the 6th day of March, to Thursday, the 9th day of March, 1933, both days inclusive, in order to prevent the export, hoarding or embarking of gold or silver coin, or bullion or currency, or speculation in foreign exchange; and

WHEREAS, under the act of March 9, 1933, all proclamations heretofore or hereafter issued by the President pursuant to the authority conferred by Section 5 (b) of the act of Oct. 6, 1917, as amended, are approved and confirmed; and

WHEREAS said national emergency still continues, and it is necessary to take further measures extending beyond March 9, 1933, in order to accomplish such purposes;

NOW, THEREFORE, I, FRANKLIN D. ROOSEVELT, President of the United States of America, in view of such continuing national emergency and by virtue of the authority vested in me by Section 5 (b) of the act of Oct. 6, 1917 (40 Stat. L., 411), as amended by the act of March 9, 1933, do hereby proclaim, order, direct and declare that all the terms and provisions of said proclamation of March 6, 1933, and the regulations and orders issued thereunder, are hereby continued in full force and effect until further proclamation by the President.

In witness whereof I have hereunto set my hand and have caused the seal of the United States to be affixed.

Done in the District of Columbia, this 9th day of March, in the year of Our Lord one thousand nine hundred and thirty-three, and of the independence of the United States the one hundred and fifty-seventh.

[Seal.] FRANKLIN D. ROOSEVELT.

By the President:
CORDELL HULL,
Secretary of State.

WOODIN PREPARES STEPS FOR OPENINGS

Invites Banks to Apply for Authority—List Drawn Up of Sound Institutions.

REGULATIONS ARE DRAFTED

Treasury Head Permits Issue of Scrip Where Local Conditions Make It Necessary.

Special to THE NEW YORK TIMES.

WASHINGTON, March 9.—Working far into the night, Treasury and Federal Reserve officials were rapidly whipping into shape details of regulations pertaining to the operation of banks of the country.

Declaring it to be the policy of the Treasury to permit the opening of "sound" banks as soon as possible, Secretary Woodin late tonight invited banks to make application for reopening.

No reopenings would be authorized before Saturday, Mr. Woodin said.

Secretary Woodin's Statement.

Secretary Woodin, expressing his general satisfaction with the emergency legislation and the work of the Treasury Department, issued the following statement:

"The emergency banking legislation passed by the Congress today is a most constructive step toward the solution of the financial and banking difficulties which have confronted the country. The extraordinary rapidity with which this legislation was enacted by the Congress heartens and encourages the country.

"This legislation makes possible the opening of banks upon a sound basis, backed by an adequate supply of currency. Through this law the banks which will open will be placed in a position to meet all demands. This assurance should restore confidence and create the foundation for a forward movement in business activities.

"It will be the policy of the Treasury to permit as rapidly as possible the opening of the sound banks. There are, of course, many thousands of such banks which will promptly be restored to the performance of their normal functions.

"The Treasury has already taken steps to secure information through proper authorities as to the condition of the various banks of the country and immediately invites from the banks applications for reopening.

"While much information has already been assembled, the comple-

Continued on Page Four.

SPIRIT OF CONGRESS GRIM IN BANK TASK

Prayerfully Takes Up Bill of Which It Knew but Little, Relying on President.

GALLERIES ARE SERIOUS

Large, Intent Crowds Fill the Capital — Mrs. Roosevelt Knits in House Gallery.

Special to THE NEW YORK TIMES.

WASHINGTON, March 9.—It was a grim Congress which met today, the most momentous gathering of the country's legislators since war was declared in 1917.

It is trite to say that they declared war, but it is nevertheless true that they hurled against the enemy of depression and despondency a weapon which they hoped would penetrate the subtle armor of an allegorical or Bunyan-like antagonist.

Congress hardly knew what was in the bill it passed today. In the House there were no copies of the measure, and it was read and explained on the floor by Representative Steagall. There was no time to study the implications and ramifications.

In the Senate copies had been printed by the time consideration began, and members followed the clerk's reading with an attention seldom devoted to a measure offered for their action.

In both chambers, with slight differences, the members gave the impression of men, who, like poker players, throw in some of their last chips in the belief that they will win.

They were glad to place the responsibility for action in the hands of one man, happy that a man had offered to assume that burden, and showed in their demeanor their hope that the revolutionary means they were adopting would bring to the country some surcease from growing economic casualties.

Representative Steagall voiced this feeling when, with arms widespread and voice ringing through the large chamber of the House, he said:

"We rely on leadership whose face is lifted to the skies."

It was a declaration of faith, almost a prayer, and in it there was an unmistakable note of optimism. Whatever the outcome of today's action may be, it was taken with the belief that by that way, and no other, could confidence and economic peace return, even though

Continued on Page Four.

BANK BILL IS ENACTED

Emergency Program Put Through in Record Time of 7 1-2 Hours.

NEW CURRENCY PROVIDED

Tax Is Imposed to Assure Retirement of the Issue When It Is No Longer Needed.

DICTATORSHIP OVER GOLD

President Empowered to Retrieve Hoardings and Continue the Embargo.

Text of the new bank act signed by President, Page 2.

Special to THE NEW YORK TIMES.

WASHINGTON, March 9.—A record for Executive and legislative action was written today in the effort of the nation to end its banking difficulties, but progress was partly checked tonight by the inability of an administrative arm of the government to keep pace.

After Congress had passed emergency legislation designed to effect a wholesale resumption of banking activities throughout the United States and the measure had been signed by the Executive, all within eight hours and thirty-seven minutes, President Roosevelt was forced to issue a proclamation at 10:10 o'clock tonight, extending the bank holiday and gold embargo indefinitely until the Treasury Department could make regulations to meet the new conditions. This may be as late as Monday.

The President last night had said that a large number of banks could open tomorrow.

Keen disappointment at the outcome was apparent at the White House, where President Roosevelt and his associates had worked almost incessantly since his inauguration last Saturday to bring about the reopening of the banks of the country.

Sense of Disappointment Felt.

The President's sense of disappointment was radiated to leaders of Congress.

The President had told them that enactment of the emergency banking law would bring about the opening of a large number of banks tomorrow and they had held out this statement to their colleagues as the reason for haste, resulting in such action as the House passing the bill unanimously after forty minutes' debate and the Senate following within three hours.

Undismayed by the turn of affairs, the President and his Congressional advisers went into conference tonight to work out the task for the remainder of the present extraordinary session.

It was expected that the President would send up a message urging two other legislative enactments, one to provide for unemployment relief and the other carrying out the economy program which the President's party has promised.

After the White House conference ended Senator Glass said that the bank holiday had been continued, first, to permit the State banks to come under the shelter of the Federal Reserve System, and second, to give the Federal Reserve and regional banks opportunity to ascertain more accurately than the Controller of the Currency had been able to do, what banks should be opened when the holiday ended.

Congress Moves With Speed.

The new Congress moved with a speed that dazzled the veteran members of that assembly. Within less than seven hours and a half the Congress convened in special session, organized, received the message from President Roosevelt asking a measure to "reopen all sound banks," passed that measure and sent it to the White House.

Barely an hour and fifteen minutes after the Senate passed the act by a vote of 73 to 7, the House having adopted it unanimously, it became law by the signature of Franklin D. Roosevelt.

This deferment of the reopening of banks already rated as sound by tests which national bank examiners have been making during the last two days was made necessary by the fact that there was no time

On Sunday evening, March 12, President Roosevelt spoke to the nation on the radio about the banking crisis. This was the first of his "fireside chats."

Associated Press Photo.

With the Secretary of the Treasury looking on, Roosevelt affixes his signature to the Emergency Banking Relief Act passed by Congress.

Crowds appear on Wall Street again after the Bank Holiday ended on March 13.

"All the News That's Fit to Print."

The New York Times.

LATE CITY EDITION
WEATHER—Occasional light rain, warmer today and tomorrow.
Temperature Yesterday—Max., 48; Min., 38.

Copyright, 1933, by The New York Times Company.

VOL. LXXXII....No. 27,442. Entered as Second-Class Matter. Postoffice, New York, N. Y. NEW YORK, MONDAY, MARCH 13, 1933. P TWO CENTS In New York City. | THREE CENTS Within 200 Miles | FOUR CENTS Elsewhere Except in 7th and 8th Postal Zones

MANY BANKS IN THE CITY AND NATION REOPEN TODAY FOR NORMAL OPERATIONS, BUT WITH HOARDING BARRED; ROOSEVELT APPEALS ON THE RADIO FOR FULL CONFIDENCE

HINDENBURG DROPS FLAG OF REPUBLIC; NAZIS CARRY CITIES

President Orders Black-White-Red of Empire and Swastika Banner Flown Side by Side.

FASCISTS WIN IN PRUSSIA

Capture Majorities Alone or With Allies in Local Polls, Sweeping 'Red Berlin.'

HITLER CURBS FOLLOWERS

Commands Them to Cease Petty Persecutions—All Germany Marches on Memorial Day.

By FREDERICK T. BIRCHALL.

Special Cable to THE NEW YORK TIMES.

BERLIN, March 12.—This was the German Memorial Day, the day on which all Germany, mourning her war dead, might theoretically be expected to meditate upon the past and take warning therefrom. And on this day the whole Reich took formal farewell of the Weimar republic and the régime built upon it.

No other interpretation can be placed on the outstanding incident of the day, which was the promulgation of a President's decree providing that henceforth the colors that shall fly upon all public buildings in Germany shall be the black, white and red of the former imperialism and the Nazi swastika—the hooked cross—side by side.

The red, black and gold ensign of free republican Germany has thus waved its last, for a time at least, and the new era has begun in earnest.

The National Socialists further consolidated their position in today's municipal and communal elections throughout Prussia, polling the largest vote in most of the important cities and generally obtaining majorities with their Nationalist allies.

Nazis and Allies Win Berlin.

Greater Berlin returned the Nazis and Nationalists with an absolute majority, leaving the Socialists, Communists and Centrists combined in a minority. This ends "Red Berlin" and terminates fourteen years of domination by the parties of the Left.

Exactly what the new era symbolized by the flag ruling will bring forth and whither it will lead belong in the realm of prophecy. The day's news is that the fourteen-year-old structure of the republic is now being dismantled and left to the wreckers, and upon its foundation something quite new is being begun.

President von Hindenburg's decree was read to the whole nation over the government radio by Chancellor Hitler, who in so doing announced himself for the first time as the authorized mouthpiece of the President.

The decree says:

"On this day, when throughout Germany the old black-white-red flag is floating at half-staff in honor of our war dead, I decree that beginning tomorrow and until the definitive regulation of the national colors the black-white-red and the hooked cross flags are to be displayed together.

"These flags unite the glorious past of the German Reich and the puissant rebirth of the German nation. Unitedly they shall embody the power of the State and the imminent interconnection of all the national sections of the German people. Military establishments will display only the Reich war flag."

"Until the definitive regulation of the national colors" may be taken as foreshadowing a constitutional provision for a new flag altogether. In all probability it will be made by incorporating the swastika in the old black-white-red stripes. In the meantime it is ordered that the two flags shall be flown alongside each other for three days continuously.

Hitler Curbs Followers.

Another highly important incident of the day was the issuance by Chancellor Hitler to his followers of a direct command to end imme-

Continued on Page Six.

Two More Americans Beaten By Bands of Nazis in Berlin

By The Associated Press.

BERLIN, March 12.—Two more Americans were the victims of assaults here yesterday. Julian Fuhs, a New York musician, was beaten by men in Nazi uniforms who demanded money. A storm troop leader interfered, calling the police

Herman Roseman of Brooklyn, a medical student in the University of Berlin, was attacked as he was coming out of a department store with a package. He showed his passport, but a policeman refused to intervene. At the police station the police told him they could not interfere with the Nazis.

Both Mr. Fuhs and Mr. Roseman made affidavits at the United States Consulate.

QUAKE ZONE BEGINS TASKS OF RECOVERY

Central Agency Created—Use of R. F. C. Funds Sought for California Relief.

TREMORS STILL GO ON

Long Beach Under Rehabilitation Dictator—Check-Up Cuts Death List to 110.

Special to THE NEW YORK TIMES.

LOS ANGELES, March 12.—The count of human lives lost in the earthquake disaster in Southern California beginning Friday evening was reduced today, following an official check by Coroner Nance of Los Angeles County and deputy sheriffs.

The known loss of life from the earthquake is now put at 110 persons, of whom ninety-eight died of injuries and twelve of shock.

In Long Beach, where the check-up revealed duplicated reports, the dead numbered fifty-one with the death of a hospital patient today. The bodies of three, a woman and two men, were unidentified at Long Beach.

With the estimate of damage remaining at nearly $50,000,000, the tasks of recovery through local, State and Federal effort were begun under centralized direction.

Minor shocks occurred through the day and this evening, continuing to shake down weakened structures.

New Direction of Shocks.

Last night the more pronounced shocks changed to the opposite direction in stress from those of the previous twenty-four hours, residents of Long Beach reported.

Friday night's tremors rocked the surface of the earth from north to south, but last night the direction changed from west to east. What the change in direction of the shocks may signify is problematical.

One arrest for looting at Long Beach was reported by the police. The authorities locked up a man who gave the name of Terence Morgan, after he had been discovered, they asserted, in a wrecked residence with various articles of value in his pockets.

Public schools throughout Los Angeles will remain closed all this week to check all buildings for damage, the Board of Education has ordered. In the county outside of Los Angeles only those schools in the heavy earthquake area will be closed until further notice, County Superintendent of Schools Clifton announced. About 50,000 children will be out of school because of the orders.

Three cities have formally requested Reconstruction Finance Corporation aid through Rolland A. Vandegrift, State Director of Finance, to start rehabilitation. Santa Ana requested $750,000 for reconstruction and unemployment, its estimated property loss being $1,250,000, with only 10 per cent of buildings insured against earthquake.

Compton, with estimated property damage of $5,000,000, asked for $125,000 to start immediate reconstruction of business houses and private residences. Mayor Pomeroy of South Gate stated that $25,000 would see the city through the preliminary period and $125,000 more would restore its original status.

Mr. Vandegrift sought information from Washington as to how far the State may use R. F. C.

Continued on Page Ten.

ECONOMY VICTORY LOOMS

Measure Up in Senate Today, With Passage Predicted This Week.

VETERANS FIGHTING CUTS

8 or 10 Democrats Champion Cause, but Republicans Will Offset Defections.

EMPLOYMENT PLANS NEXT

Roosevelt Also May Submit Emergency Farm Relief Bill Before Congress Recesses.

Special to THE NEW YORK TIMES.

WASHINGTON, March 12.—Passage by the Senate of the $500,000,000 economy bill voted by the House yesterday was predicted today by Senate leaders. They told President Roosevelt that vigorous opposition to the reduction of veterans' benefits was indicated but that they expected the measure to be accepted by a substantial majority after three or four days' debate. The bill will come up in the Senate tomorrow.

The President was informed that eight or ten Democratic Senators were opposed to the proposed reductions in the veterans' budget. The opposition of some Senators has become so pronounced against the scaling down of Federal aid to veterans that Senator Robinson of Arkansas, majority floor leader, has decided to abandon any attempt to bind Democratic members by a caucus, although a conference may be held tomorrow to exchange views before the Senate begins consideration of the economy bill.

Senator Pittman of Nevada, who, with Senator Robinson of Arkansas, was expected to lead the administration battle for the bill, which would empower the President to effect the economies, said tonight that before the end of the present week the measure would be passed by the Senate and put into legal effect.

Pittman Predicts 2-to-1 Vote.

"As far as I can learn, there are from eight to ten Senators who will vote against the veterans' cut and may finally oppose the bill if there is not some modification of the reduction to the veterans," Senator Pittman said. "Because of this situation there will be a full discussion in the Senate, lasting three or four days. Despite the opposition it is my belief that the measure will be passed by the Senate by a 2-to-1 majority."

President Roosevelt has refused compromises suggested by some Senators to make a cut of 10 per cent in appropriations for veterans not disabled in the service. He has insisted that there is no justice in such expenditures in the face of increasing deficit and that the only way to balance the budget is through the drastic reductions he proposes.

Messages received at the White House today from Governors, business leaders and others strongly commended the President for his prompt action looking to balancing the budget. Some of the Governors offered to submit resolutions to their Legislatures urging their State representatives in the Senate to stand solidly behind the administration. While the telegrams and letters were chiefly of a congratulatory nature there were plenty of protests from American Legionnaires. On the other hand, many veterans of the World War, among them men who have been prominent in Legion affairs, strongly endorsed the President's stand.

Republican Help Expected.

Opposition to the reductions on veterans has been strengthened over the week-end by the activities of lobbies and the flood of protests received by Senators from the veterans in their States. Latest surveys of the Senate, however, indicate that the administration's program will be accepted by the Senate without substantial change.

It is expected that the administration may lose some Democratic support but that the losses will be more than made up by the promised Republican accessions. Senator McNary, minority Senate leader, believes that fully two-thirds of the Republicans will go along with the administration. He has called a

Continued on Page Five.

Opening of Stock Exchange Awaits More Bank Facilities

The New York Stock Exchange, the New York Curb Exchange and the various commodity markets of New York will remain closed today, according to latest advices, in order to await a resumption of fuller banking operations.

In the absence of definite knowledge as to the number of banks that will be open on Wednesday under the schedule for reopening sound institutions on three successive days this week, it is not expected that transactions in securities or in commodities will be resumed until then.

A meeting of Stock Exchange executives held last night considered a series of additional regulations governing the conduct of affairs by members. The rules will be made public today after they have been communicated to the members.

M'COOEY DISAVOWS SLAP AT ROOSEVELT

Repudiates Action of Kings Delegation in Not Backing Federal Economy Bill.

HE WIRES THE PRESIDENT

Curry Plans No Similar Step—Says He Did Not Know How Tammany Men Would Vote.

John H. McCooey, veteran Kings County Democratic leader, last night took the unprecedented step of repudiating the action of the Brooklyn delegation in Congress which voted on Saturday against the Roosevelt economy bill. Mr. McCooey sent a personal telegram to President Roosevelt, informing him of his action, and made public the statement here, at the same time.

Tammany Leader John F. Curry, asked last night if he intended to take the same step as Mr. McCooey did, said he had no such plans at present. He said that he, and Mr. Cooey as well, were on their way home from the Cermak funeral in Chicago when the House voted on the bill, and he did not know how the New York delegation voted until he returned late Saturday night.

Mr. McCooey's telegram to President Roosevelt said that he repudiated the action of Brooklyn Representatives in voting against the economy bill and that a statement in the press this morning explained his stand.

Expects Fairness on Pensions.

The statement itself follows:

"The action of the members of the House of Representatives from this county in voting against legislation proposed by the President does not meet with my personal approval and I am confident it is likewise displeasing to the people of Brooklyn.

"I know that the President will deal in a fair and impartial manner in the matter of veterans' pensions and I am firmly convinced that those who are not of this opinion are unduly alarmed.

"Never has our country been in the sad plight which has enveloped it for over three years and the President is entitled to and must receive the support of every American citizen and their representatives in Congress in his efforts to end the depression and restore the country to its former prosperous condition."

The line-up of the Representatives from New York City on the economy program had been the topic of conversation in political circles from the time the roll-call was printed in newspapers here, and Mr. McCooey's statement last night added fresh fuel to the flames.

Seen as Political Move.

It was construed generally as a bid by Mr. McCooey to keep "in" with the Roosevelt camp, now in control of the State and Federal Governments, and it renewed the talk of the possibility of Mr. McCooey being won over to join forces with Edward J. Flynn, the Bronx leader, instead of sticking to Tammany Leader Curry.

In quarters close to the Roosevelt camp, however, it was said that resentment over the vote of the New York Representatives is strong. It was pointed out that Mr. Curry

Continued on Page Two.

NEAR NORMAL HERE TODAY

52 Members of Reserve and All State Banks in This City to Open.

SAVINGS GROUP INCLUDED

They Waive 60-Day Clause, but Are Ordered to Limit Withdrawals at Present.

NEW CURRENCY IS AMPLE

Federal Reserve to Function as Usual Except for Rules Safeguarding Gold.

New York City banks which on first examination by the Federal and State authorities have been found to be completely sound will reopen in full today. Authorization to resume full banking functions were issued at 12:30 o'clock this morning by the Federal Reserve Bank of New York to its member banks and a half hour later by Superintendent of Banks Joseph A. Broderick to institutions under his jurisdiction which are not members of the Federal Reserve System.

The licenses to Federal Reserve member banks were sent out immediately after President Roosevelt's radio address to the people explaining the banking situation and the Administration's program of gradual re-openings. The list of those licensed, as made public by the Reserve Bank, comprises fifty-two institutions. All of the important member banks are included.

As soon as the Federal Reserve list was issued, Superintendent Broderick began notifying institutions under his jurisdiction in Greater New York, but not members of the Federal Reserve, that they had been licensed "to perform the usual banking functions, except as restricted by executive order of the President and regulations of the Secretary of the Treasury."

Banks Licensed by Broderick.

The list of banks licensed by the Superintendent of Banks included all twenty-four of the State-chartered non-member banks in the five boroughs. The fifty-nine savings banks in the city were authorized to open without invoking the protection of the sixty-day clause, but they will limit withdrawals for the time being to $25 weekly for each depositor, under a ruling of the State Banking Board.

Simultaneously with the licensing of banks here to reopen, Federal Reserve and State banking authorities in the eleven other Federal Reserve Bank cities throughout the country issued permits to banks in their respective cities which had been examined and found in good order. In this way the first step in President Roosevelt's program for a staggered reopening of banks will bring about the resumption of normal business today by all the principal banks in the leading cities of the country.

In succeeding steps, banks in the 250 cities of the country having recognized clearing house associations and which have been examined and found sound will be opened tomorrow and banks in other sections of the country will be licensed to resume business on Wednesday.

Lehman Issues Proclamation.

Earlier, Governor Lehman had issued a proclamation authorizing the State banking authorities to make regulations for the resumption of business by State-chartered institutions. His proclamation follows:

Whereas the President of the United States issued on the tenth day of March, nineteen hundred and thirty-three, an executive order prescribing methods whereby banking institutions could commence the performance of their functions:

Now, therefore, I, Herbert H. Lehman, Governor of the State of New York, by virtue of the authority vested in me by chapter forty-two of the laws of nineteen hundred thirty-three, and by virtue of all other authority vested in me, hereby proclaim, order and direct that each of the appropriate authorities of the State of New York having immediate supervision of institu-

Continued on Page Four.

Banks Opening Today

The Federal Reserve Bank of New York at 12:30 o'clock this morning made public a list of the New York City member banks which it had authorized to open for business at the usual banking hours today.

This list was as follows:

FEDERAL RESERVE MEMBERS.

Manhattan.

Amalgamated Bank of New York.
Bankers Trust Company.
Bank of the Manhattan Company.
Bank of New York & Trust Company.
Bank of Yorktown.
Central Hanover Bank & Trust Company.
Chase National Bank.
Chemical Bank & Trust Company.
Clinton Trust Company.
Colonial Trust Company.
Commercial National Bank & Trust Company.
Continental Bank & Trust Company.
Corn Exchange Bank Trust Company.
Dunbar National Bank.
Federation Bank & Trust Company of New York.
Fifth Avenue Bank of New York.
First National Bank of New York.
Fulton Trust Company of New York.
Grace National Bank.
Guaranty Trust Company
Harbor State Bank.
Irving Trust Company.
Manufacturers Trust Company.
Marine Midland Trust Company.
Merchants Bank.
National Bank of Yorkville.
National City Bank.
National Safety Bank and Trust Company.
New York Trust Company.
Public National Bank and Trust Company.
J. Henry Schroder Trust Company.
Sterling National Bank and Trust Company.
Trade Bank of New York.
United States Trust Company.

Brooklyn.

Bensonhurst National Bank of Brooklyn.
Brooklyn Trust Company.
Flatbush National Bank of Brooklyn.
Fort Greene National Bank of New York.
Kingsboro National Bank of Brooklyn.
National Exchange Bank and Trust Company.
Peoples National Bank of Brooklyn.

Queens.

Bayside National Bank of New York.
College Point National Bank of New York.
National Bank of Far Rockaway.
National Bank of Queens County in New York.
Forest Hills National Bank of New York.
Springfield Gardens National Bank of New York.
Woodside National Bank of New York.

Bronx.

National Bronx Bank.

Richmond.

Mariner Harbor National Bank.
Staten Island National Bank & Trust Company of New York.
Tottenville National Bank.

NON-MEMBERS OF FEDERAL RESERVE.

State commercial banks in New York City authorized by State Bank Superintendent Broderick to open today:

Manhattan.

Anglo-South America Trust Company.
Banca Commerciale Italiana Trust Company.
Banco di Napoli Trust Company.
Bank of Athens Trust Company.
Bank of Sicily Trust Company.
City Bank Farmers Trust Company.
Corporation Trust Company.
County Trust Company.
Empire Trust Company.
Equitable Trust Company.
Fiduciary Trust Company.
Hellenic Bank Trust Company.
Hias Immigrant Bank.
Lawyers Trust Company.
Pennsylvania Exchange Bank.
Title Guarantee and Trust Company.
Trust Company of North America.
Underwriters Trust Company.

Brooklyn.

Citizens Bank.
Kings County Trust Company.

Queens.

Boulevard Bank, Forest Hills.

Bronx.

Bronx County Trust Company.

Richmond.

South Shore Bank.
West New Brighton Bank.

SAVINGS BANKS.

All savings banks throughout the city will be open for business today. Under an order by the State Banking Department, however, depositors will not be permitted to withdraw more than $25 a week. The savings banks have decided not to invoke the sixty-day clause against withdrawals.

News of the opening of banks throughout the country will be found on Page 2.

The President's Speech

Special to THE NEW YORK TIMES.

WASHINGTON, March 12.—The text of President Roosevelt's radio address on the banking situation, delivered at 10 o'clock tonight from his study in the White House, was as follows:

My friends, I want to talk for a few minutes with the people of the United States about banking—with the comparatively few who understand the mechanics of banking, but more particularly with the overwhelming majority of you who use banks for the making of deposits and the drawing of checks. I want to tell you what has been done in the last few days, and why it was done, and what the next steps are going to be.

I recognize that the many proclamations from State Capitols and from Washington, the legislation, the Treasury regulations, &c., couched for the most part in banking and legal terms, ought to be explained for the benefit of the average citizen. I owe this in particular because of the fortitude and the good temper with which everybody has accepted the inconvenience and the hardships of the banking holiday.

I know that when you understand what we in Washington have been about, I shall continue to have your cooperation as fully as I have had your sympathy and your help during the past week.

First of all, let me state the simple fact that when you deposit money in a bank, the bank does not put the money into a safe deposit vault. It invests your money in many different forms of credit—in bonds, commercial paper, mortgages, and many other kinds of loans.

In other words, the bank puts your money to work to keep the wheels of industry and of agriculture turning around. A comparatively small part of the money you put into the bank is kept

Continued on Page Three.

SOUND BANKS CLASSIFIED

Reserve Board Flooded by Applications to Enter System.

R. F. C. ALSO WILL RESUME

President Declares That Ample Currency Will Be Provided for Needs of All.

STATE BANKS WILL GET AID

His Address Emphasizes This Point After Governors Lehman and Ritchie Protest.

Special to THE NEW YORK TIMES.

WASHINGTON, March 12.—President Roosevelt explained the banking situation to the people of the United States in a fifteen-minute radio address tonight. The President's appeal for confidence in the government's program was made after preparations had been completed for the progressive reopening, beginning tomorrow morning, of banks classified as sound by Federal and State officials.

The banks to open tomorrow are member banks of the Federal Reserve System in the twelve Federal Reserve Bank cities, licensed by the Treasury, and non-member State banks which have received the approval of the State banking superintendents.

On Tuesday licensed banks will reopen in cities having recognized clearing house associations, and on Wednesday will come the reopenings in other communities of banks in other categories.

Officials, headed by Secretary Woodin, labored all day and all night at the Treasury to make the necessary arrangements and several new regulations were issued. The Executive Offices at the White House remained open also.

Woodin Defines Banks' First Duty.

Secretary Woodin shortly before 11 o'clock tonight issued the following statement:

"The first duty of the banks reopening under license of the Secretary of the Treasury for the performance of their usual functions is to see that the primary needs of the people for funds for necessaries of life and for normal business undertakings are met.

"Accordingly, withdrawals for hoarding have been prohibited, and the Secretary of the Treasury suggests that until more normal conditions have been established, transfer of funds by banks or their customers be limited to necessary purposes."

Instructions went forth from the Federal Reserve Board to the Reserve Banks to release locally the names of member banks and State banks licensed to open tomorrow. When it was reported that the Cleveland Federal Reserve Bank had declined to give out the list the Reserve Board sent peremptory instructions that this should be done in Cleveland as elsewhere.

A flood of applications by State banks not members of the Federal Reserve System for membership were being received by the Federal Reserve Board by mail and telegraph. They came from almost every section of the country, where they had first been passed upon by the Federal Reserve Banks.

The rush of applications began almost immediately after the emergency banking legislation was adopted, and the Federal Reserve Board will pass upon them as rapidly as possible. There is every prospect that one result of the national banking holiday will be a very considerable increase in the membership and resources of the Reserve System.

Among Treasury Department regulations issued today was one granting permission to private banking houses and other financial institutions which do not come under Federal or State supervision, to resume normal operation, with restrictions, however, as to the release of gold or gold certificates and transactions in foreign exchange.

Another regulation of major importance permitted the Reconstruction Finance Corporation to renew its operations tomorrow. An effort will be made to have the corpora-

Continued on Page Three.

"All the News That's Fit to Print."

The New York Times.

LATE CITY EDITION
WEATHER—Fair today; tomorrow cloudy, warmer, probably rain
Temperatures Yesterday—Max., 44; Min., 31.

Copyright, 1933, by The New York Times Company.

VOL. LXXXII....No. 27,445. Entered as Second-Class Matter. Postoffice, New York, N. Y. NEW YORK, THURSDAY, MARCH 16, 1933. TWO CENTS In New York City. | THREE CENTS Within 200 Miles | FOUR CENTS Elsewhere Except in 7th and 8th Postal Zones

SENATE PASSES ECONOMY BILL, 62-13, BARRING ALL BUT MINOR AMENDMENTS; STOCKS SOAR AS TRADING IS RESUMED

M'DONALD WILL SEE MUSSOLINI IN PLAN TO END WIDE UNREST

Expected to Travel to Rome This Week-End in Move to Salvage Arms Parley.

TO MEET DALADIER FIRST

French Premier Leaves for Geneva—Effort to Get Paris-Rome Navy Accord Likely.

BRITISH DRAFT ARMS PACT

Agreement to Be Offered Today Covers Points Already Settled and Provides Compromises.

By ARNALDO CORTESI.
Wireless to THE NEW YORK TIMES.

ROME, March 15.—Prime Minister MacDonald of Great Britain and Premier Mussolini of Italy will meet to discuss disarmament some time over the week-end, it became known here tonight.

Arrangements for the meeting were still being discussed by telephone between Rome and Geneva this evening, but all details will be settled before tomorrow, when an official announcement is probable. It is expected that the conference will be held in Rome.

A report that Chancellor Hitler of Germany might participate in the meeting was said to be entirely groundless, as no desire to invite him had been expressed on either the British or the Italian side.

Initiative Taken by MacDonald.

That a direct exchange of views between the British and Italian Premiers on disarmament would occur in the near future was considered certain here as soon as it became known that Mr. MacDonald, on his way through Paris to Geneva, had discussed the situation with leading French politicians. It was said here, however, that the MacDonald-Mussolini conference had not been sought by Italy but that the initiative had been taken by Mr. MacDonald.

The British Prime Minister's suggestion was welcomed by Premier Mussolini, who sees the only hope of saving the disarmament conference in common action by all the powers that truly believe in reduction of armaments.

The prospect of the forthcoming meeting has somewhat revived hopes for the disarmament conference, but even so they are not particularly sanguine here. The results so far achieved have been so disappointing that an attitude of resigned gloom has gradually replaced the optimism that prevailed when the conference began. The chief reason for the lack of results, according to the Italian view, lies in the fact that the United States, Britain and Italy, which may be considered the chief champions of disarmament, are not agreed on a common policy. The United States and Italy are virtually in agreement both because the proposals submitted by them are similar and because the American proposal was immediately and unreservedly accepted by the Italian Government. Britain, however, has hitherto followed a somewhat divergent course. It is hoped something more closely resembling a united Anglo-Italian front may be established as a result of Mr. MacDonald's meeting with Signor Mussolini.

Stir Created in Geneva.

Special Cable to THE NEW YORK TIMES.

GENEVA, March 15.—Prime Minister MacDonald and Foreign Secretary Simon will leave here for Rome Friday or Saturday for a "bilateral general talk" with Premier Mussolini. Although none of the details is yet fixed, the present probabilities are that they will leave here Saturday and remain in Rome two days, possibly traveling by air, and returning home by way of Geneva. The British arms delegation gave out this information tonight, and it created no small stir.

It is officially explained that although Mr. MacDonald has traveled to Paris and talked with French Premiers a dozen times, he has never met Signor Mussolini, and wishes to "shake his hand and talk things over very generally." To the British press it has been further explained that Mr. MacDonald hopes to form "a nucleus of Premiers and Foreign Ministers of good-will to dissipate the fears and settle the grievances now upsetting Europe." In this connection, the British give every evidence of being greatly worried over how the French will take this trip to Italy.

The reference to a "nucleus" per-

Continued on Page Twelve.

Glasgow Students Join Oxford In Voting Not to Bear Arms

By The Canadian Press.

GLASGOW, March 15.—Glasgow University students have followed those of the Oxford Union and Manchester University in voting not to bear arms for King or country.

Male students of Glasgow University today defeated a motion that they would be prepared to fight for the King by a vote of 634 to 568.

When the Oxford Union went on record against bearing arms, a considerable fuss was stirred up. Unperturbed commentators, however, point out that similar motions have been passed for many decades, but as soon as the need was urgent the students were among the first to "rally round."

EINSTEIN HONORED AT A DINNER HERE

Attack Upon Nationalism as a Menace to Civilization Marks Address to 1,000.

HE WILL SHUN GERMANY

Scientist Going to Belgium Instead—Urges Support for Palestine University.

Albert Einstein, explorer of the cosmos and champion of humanity, arrived in New York yesterday from California, where he had been engaged in scientific work at the California Institute of Technology. Last night he received the enthusiastic greeting of nearly 1,000 admirers at a dinner given in his honor at the Hotel Commodore under the honorary chairmanship of Governor Lehman and Felix M. Warburg.

Mayor O'Brien greeted Dr. Einstein in behalf of the city, welcoming him as an honored guest and an illustrious representative of the world's science and culture.

In a message from Albany, Governor Lehman greeted him in behalf of the State of New York as "a brilliant scientist and friend of mankind."

The dinner was under the joint auspices of the American Friends of the Hebrew University in Palestine and the Jewish Telegraphic Agency. Dr. Einstein appealed for the support of both these institutions.

Noted scientists, diplomats and representatives of the world of art, literature, jurisprudence, finance and philanthropy joined with the audience in paying homage to Dr. Einstein. Representing the German Ambassador, Baron von Prittwitz und Gaffron, was Dr. Otto C. Kiep, German Consul General in this city and former Counselor of the German Embassy.

Escorted by Consul.

Dr. Einstein was met at Albany by Dr. Paul Schwarz, German Consul, who escorted him to this city. There was no official reception at the Grand Central Terminal, however, in deference to Dr. Einstein's request that this be omitted.

Dr. Kiep spoke warmly of Dr. Einstein's contributions to science and extolled his services to humanity.

He expressed gratitude for the hospitality shown by the United States to German science and scientists and especially to Dr. Einstein. This was after Mayor O'Brien had invited Dr. Einstein to make this country his permanent home.

Bringing a message of greeting from President Masaryk, Ferdinand Veverka, Czechoslovakian Minister to the United States, hailed Dr. Einstein not only as a great scientist but as a prophet. "You do not belong to any one," he said. "You belong to the whole of thinking mankind." Dr. Einstein, said Mr. Veverka, has shown the way to a solution of the problems of the universe, society and man's relationship to both.

Dr. Karl T. Compton, president of the Massachusetts Institute of Technology, discussed at length the revolutionary significance of Dr. Einstein's labors in the field of science, while Dr. Harlow Shapley of the Harvard Observatory delivered a scientific address on problems of astronomy.

Other speakers were Dr. Nathan Ratnoff, chairman of the American Jewish Physicians' Committee; Dr. A. S. W. Rosenbach, president of the American Friends of the Hebrew University; James Marshall, a vice president of the organization, Dr. Solomon Lowenstein, executive director of the Federation for the Support of Jewish Philanthropic Societies, and Dr. Emanuel Libman.

Dr. Einstein was to have sailed for Germany immediately after last night's dinner, but changed his plans because of the disturbing situation arising from the accession of Hitler to the Chancellorship. Dr.

Continued on Page Ten.

WINE OF 3.2% ADDED TO HOUSE BEER BILL IN SENATE REPORT

Measure Is Approved by Committee After Amending It at McAdoo's Request.

PASSAGE SLATED TODAY

Harrison Predicts Victory, Which Will Send It to Conference for Action on Change.

STATE BEER BILLS READY

Commission and Dunnigan Plans Go to Legislature Today—Lehman Demands Speed.

Special to THE NEW YORK TIMES.

WASHINGTON, March 15.—The beer bill was favorably reported out of the Senate Finance Committee today, but action was not taken upon it in the Senate because discussion of the economy bill had not been completed. Senator Harrison, chairman of the committee, said he felt sure the bill would be taken up by the Senate tomorrow and that it would be passed.

The bill was amended in the committee to provide for the making of wine of the same alcoholic content as beer, 3.2 per cent of alcohol by weight.

It was recognized by members of the committee that wine of such low alcoholic content would be neither palatable nor salable, but as Senator McAdoo wished the provision included it was agreed to.

This action, of course, will result in the bill's being sent to conference, although it is not believed this will delay its final passage by the House.

There was no report on the amendment of the bill, but it was said that the inclusion of wine would be by merely writing the words "and vinous liquors" after every reference to "beer, ale, porter or other similar fermented liquor." The actual amendment embodying this simple formula will be long and technical, providing for the proper insertion of the words in the bill.

New Test on Senate Stand.

Senator Harrison, in voicing his opinion that the bill would pass the Senate, said: "Look at the majority in the House," but he would not predict how long the debate on it would last.

The expected vote on beer tomorrow will bring the first show-down on this topic in the Senate since a serious effort was begun in December to amend the Volstead act by legalizing a light type of beer through pronouncing it non-intoxicating.

As almost its first important act, the House, in the lame-duck session, passed in December a beer bill very similar to the one now before the Senate, pronouncing beer of 3.2 per cent alcohol by weight non-intoxicating.

Hopes raised among wets by that action, which gave rise to the slogan "beer by Christmas," quickly faded, however, when Senate leaders and Senate drys particularly—many of whom now are gone from that body—began a game of legislative juggling which resulted in no vote being taken.

The most important moves in this admitted vote-avoiding game consisted of a double committee reference of the beer bill. It was sent first to the Finance Committee to determine the amount of revenue

Continued on Page Three.

Chemical Company Restores Wage Cuts as Profits Rise

Wireless to THE NEW YORK TIMES.

LONDON, March 15.—The Imperial Chemical Industries, one of the world's biggest concerns and Britain's largest manufacturers of chemical and war materials, is restoring all wage cuts.

It was announced today that the past year's profits amounted to £6,415,423, compared with £4,668,685 the previous year. A final dividend of 3½ per cent, making 6 per cent for the year, was announced.

The company's capital is £76,000,000 and it employs about 45,000 persons. The wage cuts were estimated at 5 per cent of the total payroll.

GEM THIEF TRAPPED WITH $500,000 LOOT

Sidmore, Known the World Over, Is Found in Bungalow at Miami Beach, Fla.

NEW YORK LED IN CAPTURE

Mulrooney's Men Find $81,000 Loot for Grace Moore and $60,000 for Mrs. Keller.

Special to THE NEW YORK TIMES.

MIAMI BEACH, Fla., March 15.—An arm of the law which reached out 1,500 miles from Police Headquarters, New York, to an obscure bungalow near the northern limits of this resort city today trapped Harry Sidmore, 38-year-old "Raffles" of Miami Beach, and better known as Harry Sitamore, international jewel thief.

In the comfortable dwelling in which Sitamore, a man of many aliases, lived quietly with his wife and 5-year-old son when he was not preying upon fashionable visitors of this city, the long-sought fugitive yielded up from hiding places $500,000 of stolen jewelry to his captors. The loot accounted for all but one important jewel robbery here this Winter.

Police Force an Entrance.

Led by Lieutenants Michael McNamara and Thomas Fitzgerald of the New York detective force, who knowing Sitamore of old, were imported here a few days ago, the local police ferreted out Sitamore's hideaway. Four detectives surrounded the bungalow at dawn and uniformed patrolmen helped form a cordon.

A patrolman rapped on the door, calling for Sitamore. He remained inside, refusing to answer, so several patrolmen hurled their bulks against the entrance and it gave way.

The raiders were greeted by Sitamore's wife, who, with her child crying by her side, attacked the policemen, attempting to hold them at bay. Sitamore, meanwhile, was hastily destroying papers.

Reveals Loot After Seven Hours.

For seven hours during questioning at the police station Sitamore maintained that his loot was in a safe deposit box. Finally, toward noon, he agreed to lead the police to it if they would take him home for a change of clothes. Mayor A. Frank Katzentine went along, and, as the prisoner finished dressing demanded the jewelry. Sitamore smiled and replied:

"We don't have to move out of the house to get them." Rummaging through closets, trunks and furniture, he now produced half a dozen bags, each containing a small fortune in precious stones. Taking

Continued on Page Eighteen.

Farley Agrees to Consult Senators on Jobs; Modifies Plan After Visit to Roosevelt

Special to THE NEW YORK TIMES.

WASHINGTON, March 15.—The first patronage conference of this administration, delayed because of the bank situation, was held tonight at the White House. President Roosevelt summoned Postmaster General Farley, Frank C. Walker, treasurer of the Democratic National Committee, and Edward H. Flynn of New York to discuss the major appointments, and especially jobs to be apportioned to New York.

It was agreed that the patronage distribution program conceived early by Mr. Farley would have to be modified. Mr. Farley had announced that he would recognize State chairmen and the Roosevelt leaders in the respective States.

In carrying out this scheme in a minor way, Mr. Farley at once aroused the animosity of Senators.

Hereafter he will consult the Senators before making selections. Mr. Farley found that unless this plan was followed the administration would run the danger of the Senators banding together and preventing appointments.

As to New York patronage, the program of deferring to the State committee will be changed. Senators Wagner and Copeland will be consulted in Federal appointments for New York State.

Ambrose O'Connell of New York was appointed today special assistant to Postmaster General Farley, in place of Ed M. Martin, who recently resigned.

Mr. O'Connell is a native of Iowa but has lived in New York City a number of years. He served as assistant chairman of the Democratic National Convention in 1932 and as secretary to its chairman, the late Senator Thomas J. Walsh of Montana.

He is assistant treasurer of the Democratic National Committee, was office manager and personnel director of the finance division of the Democratic National Campaign Committee, is a member of the New York and Federal bars, and was law secretary and private secretary to Justices Francis B. Delehanty and Edward B. Amend for ten years.

RECORD RISE IN SHARES

$3,000,000,000 Added to Values in Day by Advance of 15%.

SELLING ORDERS CANCELED

Trading Delayed at Opening as Brokers Are Unable to Buy—'Wet' Stocks Strong.

BONDS SHARE IN UPSWING

Governments Lead in General Rally—Commodities Also Go Forward Rapidly.

Led by the New York Stock Exchange, most of the security and commodity markets in the country reopened yesterday, and investors and traders promptly showed their approval of the reconstruction program of President Roosevelt by starting one of the most emphatic buying movements in many years.

The average gain of stocks was approximately 15 per cent, the largest one-day advance in terms of percentage within Wall Street's memory. In market value stocks showed an appreciation of $3,000,000,000. Representative issues advanced from 2 to 12 points. All groups participated in the upswing.

Trading on the Stock Exchange totaled 3,065,000 shares, the heaviest turnover since Sept. 22, 1932. Buying orders poured in over the wires from all parts of the country, and on several occasions the stock ticker fell two or three minutes behind.

Bonds Share in Upswing.

The bond market participated in the advance under the leadership of United States Government issues, which scored gains of 1 to 3 points. Domestic bonds advanced 1 to 7 points, and foreign issues 1 to 6.

Brokers declared that just as bank depositors had shown their confidence in financial institutions by redepositing their money, so investors were demonstrating their faith in the recovery program of President Roosevelt by buying stocks and bonds. Some brokers immediately termed the advance a "Roosevelt market," as it was the first session since the administration took office.

Among the gains of representative stocks yesterday were Allied Chemical, 10 points; United States Steel common, 5⅞; J. I. Case, 10⅞; Union Pacific, 11⅜; American Telephone, 7⅜; American Can, 6¼; Consolidated Gas, 4¾; du Pont, 6⅜; General Motors, 3, and General Electric 3.

In the commodity markets, sugar, hides, rubber, silk and silver all moved sharply higher on heavy trading.

The New York Cotton Exchange and the Chicago Board of Trade, which delayed their reopening until many banks in the interior of the country had been restored to a normal basis, will resume today. With a view to preventing a runaway advance in grain futures, the Board of Trade announced that the largest daily fluctuation for wheat would be 5 cents a bushel, and for other grains smaller amounts. Broad advances in wheat and cotton, compared with the quotations of March 3, are expected by brokers today.

No Curb on Shorts.

The Stock Exchange opened without any special restrictions on short selling, indicating the confidence of Exchange officials that the market would receive good support. Early in the morning there was an unusually heavy influx of brokers, traders and clerks into Wall Street, all prepared for a busy day. Board rooms were crowded with customers.

At 9 o'clock, an hour before the Exchange opened, specialists and clerks took up the task of matching orders that had already been received, and it was at once apparent that buying orders were heavily preponderant. In many issues there was a complete absence of selling orders except at prices from 10 to 40 per cent higher than the final quotations of March 3.

The floor was jammed when the

Continued on Page Six.

Senate Vote on Economy

Special to THE NEW YORK TIMES.

WASHINGTON, March 15.—The Senate vote in detail on passage of the economy bill tonight was as follows:

For the Bill—62

DEMOCRATS—43.

Adams	Connally	Reynolds
Ashurst	Copeland	Robinson (Ark.)
Bachman	Dieterich	Russell
Bailey	Dill	Sheppard
Bankhead	Duffy	Smith
Barkley	George	Stephens
Black	Gore	Thomas (Okla.)
Bone	Harrison	Thomas (Utah)
Bratton	Lewis	Trammell
Brown	Lonergan	Tydings
Bulkley	McKellar	Van Nuys
Bulow	Murphy	Wagner
Byrd	Neely	Walsh
Byrnes	Pittman	
Caraway	Pope	

REPUBLICANS—19.

Austin	Hastings	Reed
Barbour	Hebert	Townsend
Capper	Johnson	Vandenberg
Dale	Kean	Walcott
Fess	Keyes	White
Goldsborough	McNary	
Hale	Metcalf	

Against the Bill—13

DEMOCRATS—4.

Clark	McCarran	McGill
Long		

REPUBLICANS—9.

Borah	Frazier	Patterson
Couzens	Hatfield	Robinson (Ind.)
Dickinson	Nye	Steiwer

Pairs.

FOR THE BILL—Coolidge, Glass, Kendrick and McAdoo, Democrats.

AGAINST THE BILL—Cutting and La Follette, Republicans; Overton, Democrat, and Shipstead, Farmer-Labor.

It was announced that Senators King, Costigan and Logan Democrats, would have supported the bill had they been present.

BUSINESS RESUMES IN MORTGAGE LOANS

Restricted Activity Permitted In Companies Supervised by Insurance Department.

ASSETS ARE SAFEGUARDED

Van Schaick Issues List of Regulations Pending Return of Normal Conditions.

Mortgage loan companies under State Insurance Department supervision which came within the scope of the President's proclamation declaring a bank holiday are permitted to resume business with restrictions under regulations made public last night by Superintendent of Insurance George S. Van Schaick.

The regulations, according to Mr. Van Schaick, will tend to conserve the assets of the companies for the benefit of those holding their guarantees, creditors and the public at large, and insure the resumption of business by such corporations with the greatest amount of safety to all who have invested in such guarantees.

The most important of the regulations insures to the clients of the companies the collection of principal and interest received by the companies pending negotiations with the holders of their guarantees for modification of the guarantee contracts. The regulations are deemed necessary by the Insurance Department to maintain sound methods of insurance and to safeguard the interest of the public generally during the present emergency.

There are about forty mortgage loan companies under the supervision of the Insurance Department and seven subject to the rules and regulations of the State Banking Department. Not all of the companies under the supervision of the Insurance Department came within the provisions of the President's banking holiday proclamation, because of the type of business they handle.

It was said at the Banking Department last night that a statement would probably be issued today regarding the mortgage loan companies under its supervision. All of the companies under Banking Department supervision are doing business subject to such limitations as are contained in the President's proclamation.

The statement issued last night by Mr. Van Schaick follows:

"In preparing regulations under which mortgage guarantee companies closed by the President's

Continued on Page Seven.

FARM AND JOB BILLS TO GO TO CONGRESS

President Expected to Send Emergency Message on One or Both Today.

WORLD CUT IN FARM PLAN

Domestic Features to Be Basis for Later Legislation—Work Aid for 200,000 at Once.

Special to THE NEW YORK TIMES.

WASHINGTON, March 15.—President Roosevelt will send messages to Congress within twenty-four hours on unemployment relief and a bill to deal with the farm situation for one year, it was indicated today.

Conferences were held at the White House during the day by the leaders engaged on both of these features of the administration's emergency program. The message on unemployment has been completed and may be submitted tomorrow, followed closely by a recommendation for temporary farm legislation.

The unemployment relief proposal involves putting about 200.000 men in jobs by the use of unexpended balances in the Treasury, deferring for a time the plan for a $500,000,000 bond issue.

The farm-aid project includes a provision for the President to seek an international agreement to reduce wheat acreage. The domestic features of the bill would be effective at once, and would be the basis, after a year's trial, of more permanent farm legislation.

To Wind Up Congress Action Now.

President Roosevelt informed the Congressional leaders that he desired to have the two measures enacted in the present session, after which a recess of two or three weeks might be taken, during which he would prepare his formal legislative program.

The President desires to get some legislation to put people to work and to aid the farmers without delay. The measures, he believes, are necessary and constructive and would greatly aid in the restoration of prosperity.

Regarding the plans to deal with unemployment, President Roosevelt feels that enough money can be obtained from unexpended balances to place probably 200,000 men at work on reforestation in national preserves in States near the large centres of population.

The floating of a $500,000,000 unemployment bond issue for vast Federal improvements, Mr. Roosevelt holds, would tend to defeat

Continued on Page Two.

MEASURE LITTLE ALTERED

It Will Go Quickly to Conference for Final Revision.

FOUR DEMOCRATS VOTE NO

Result Comes Suddenly After Lively Discussion Lasting Nine Hours.

LEGION PROPOSALS LOST

Other Amendments, Which Would Limit the President's Power, Are Defeated.

Special to THE NEW YORK TIMES.

WASHINGTON, March 15.—By a vote of 62 to 13 the Senate at 9:23 o'clock tonight passed the $500,000,000 economy bill, which gives the President practically dictatorial powers in reducing veterans' benefits and Federal salaries.

The bill as adopted was substantially in the form in which it passed the House Saturday, but a few minor amendments written into the measure must run the gauntlet of conference.

The bill is likely to be reported back to the House early tomorrow and the lower body will probably ask an immediate conference to adjust the amendments written in by the Senate. The measure, it is expected, will be in the President's hands before the end of the week.

Find Victory Amazing.

Official Washington was amazed at the completeness of Mr. Roosevelt's victory. Within four legislative days from his sending a message to Congress both houses had passed the legislation requested, which is likely to slash $400,000,000 from the payments to veterans.

Eight amendments in all were adopted, the most far-reaching of these was the one of yesterday, offered by Senator Black, allowing veterans who now have insurance claims pending in the courts to pursue them to ultimate judgment. This is expected to reduce the gross savings by about $5,000,000.

Another, offered by Senator Black to allow veterans of non-service-connected disabilities free hospital treatment as under the present law, was calculated to involve only $3,000,000 more.

More than a score of amendments were offered today by Senators seeking to change its provisions or limit the powers granted to the President, but only those which received the approval of Senator Harrison, leader of the Roosevelt forces, were accepted by the Senate.

Eighty-six Senators were recorded on the final vote. Besides the sixty-two who voted for it and the thirteen who voted in opposition, eight Senators were recorded through pairs and the support of the bill by three absentees was announced.

Of the thirteen opponents, four were Democrats—Clark, Long, McCarran and McGill.

Move for Bank Legislation.

One Democrat, Senator Overton, was paired against the bill. Senator Hayden did not vote because of prior pledges to his constituents. Senator Wheeler, known to be against the bill, was not recorded.

An attempt at banking legislation was made just before the recess when Senator Bulkley vainly sought consideration for a bill affecting the double liability of stockholders in certain States. His bill, which was reported from the Banking and Currency Committee yesterday, would empower the Reconstruction Finance Corporation to allow State banks and trust companies to sell capital notes or debentures to the corporation instead of preferred stock. This is intended to offset State laws which impose double liability on preferred stock.

Senator McNary, the Republican leader, said the matter was of such importance that it must go over until tomorrow.

Just before the Senate recessed, at 9:28 o'clock, Senator Harrison announced that he would call up the beer bill as soon as the Senate meets tomorrow.

The first real test on the economy bill during today's long debate

Continued on Page Two.

"All the News That's Fit to Print."

The New York Times.

LATE CITY EDITION
WEATHER—Cloudy today and tomorrow; temperature unchanged.
Temperatures Yesterday—Max., 42; Min., 34.

Copyright, 1933, by The New York Times Company.

VOL. LXXXII....No. 27,452. Entered as Second-Class Matter, Postoffice, New York, N. Y. NEW YORK, THURSDAY, MARCH 23, 1933. P TWO CENTS In New York City. | THREE CENTS Within 200 Miles | FOUR CENTS Elsewhere Except in 7th and 8th Postal Zones

PRESIDENT SIGNS BILL FOR LEGAL BEER; EFFECTIVE HERE AT 12:01 A. M. APRIL 7; HOUSE APPROVES FARM RELIEF 315-98

REICH REGIME SPLIT ON PRUSSIAN RULE; PAPEN HOLDS POWER

Choice of Premier Put Off Till May 2 at Latest as He and Goering Vie for Post.

DIET HOLDS FIRST SESSION

Nationalist Counters Eulogy of Hitler With Appeal for Return of Hohenzollerns.

NO MORE RAIDS REPORTED

Hope That Persecution of Jews Has Ended Rises in Paris as Exodus Declines.

German Developments.

BERLIN—The meeting of the Prussian Diet yesterday was marked by a decision to postpone the choice of a Premier. Vice Chancellor von Papen and Minister Goering, Nazi chieftain, are rivals for the post.

Under an amnesty decree, Nazis escape punishment for outrages against Americans committed before March 21.

PARIS—Information from Germany indicated that racial persecutions were abating. The exodus of Jews was reported falling off.

WASHINGTON—Three resolutions were introduced in the House to authorize the State Department to protest to Germany against attacks on American Jews.

NEW YORK—The protest against anti-Semitic attacks in Germany became nation-wide and the American Federation of Labor joined in the movement. Rabbinical associations proclaimed next Monday a day of fasting and prayer for Jews. Jewish war veterans will parade today as a protest.

Meeting of Prussian Diet.

Special Cable to THE NEW YORK TIMES.

BERLIN, March 22.—The opening session of the recently elected Prussian Diet today passed off just as quickly and quietly as yesterday's initial meeting of the Reichstag.

Within less than an hour the Diet had constituted itself and adjourned, after having adopted a National Socialist motion sanctioning the ousting of the former Prussian Cabinet by President von Hindenburg and approving government by the Reich's commissioners, headed by Vice Chancellor Franz von Papen, for the time being pending the election of a new Prussian Premier.

The election of the Premier was postponed with the explanation that the choice would be made by May 2 at the latest. Supporters of Captain Hermann Wilhelm Goering, Nazi Minister without portfolio, acting Prussian Interior Minister and president of the Reichstag, believe the post will be given to him and not to Colonel von Papen, as had been reported, nor to Chancellor Adolf Hitler himself.

[Failure of the controlling parties in Prussia to elect a Premier indicates that no solution has yet been found for a sharp rivalry between the Nazis and President von Hindenburg's chief representatives in the present federal government. Colonel von Papen was made Federal Commissioner for Prussia by Presidential appointment and has insisted on obtaining the Premiership. Captain Goering, however, has demanded that the Nazis have it and has pressed his claims to it.]

Hopes for Monarchy's Return.

Dr. Friedrich von Winterfeld, leader of the Nationalist delegation in the Diet, concluded a brief address thus:

"On today's anniversary of the birth of Emperor William I, I may express the hope, in accordance with the traditional platform of the Nationalist party, that the time will return when Prussia and Germany will be ruled again by the Hohenzollern crown."

When Dr. von Winterfeld returned to his seat Wilhelm Kube, the Nazi floor leader, stepped up to him and shook his hand.

Hans Kerrl, a National Socialist, was re-elected speaker of the Diet. He will be assisted by a Centrist, a Nationalist and another Nazi, but Herr Kube made it clear in a speech that the election of a Centrist Deputy was not to be taken as an indication that there would be any compromise with the Catholic party in political or cultural matters.

Nevertheless, the Centrists voted consistently with the National Socialists and Nationalists, and prob-

Continued on Page Eleven.

First Post-War Silver Coins Soon to Be Issued by France

Wireless to THE NEW YORK TIMES.

PARIS, March 22.—Silver coins will reappear in France toward the end of this month for the first time since the war. One and a half billion francs worth of ten and twenty franc pieces have been minted and now repose in the vaults of the Bank of France. That institution's regents will decide tomorrow the date on which the new money will be put into circulation.

A law voted by the French Parliament in June, 1928, authorized the minting of 100-franc coins in gold at the same time the silver pieces were cast, but the date for issuance of the gold money has not yet been decided.

The new ten-franc coins, worth roughly forty cents, measure twenty millimeters in diameter—about the size of American quarter dollars.

OUR GAIN A MIRACLE, SAYS CHAMBERLAIN

Chancellor of Exchequer Tells Commons Roosevelt Has Restored Confidence.

SEES EUROPE BETTER OFF

Refuting Gloominess Charge, He Predicts World Economic Parley in a Few Months.

By CHARLES A. SELDEN.

Wireless to THE NEW YORK TIMES.

LONDON, March 22.—Neville Chamberlain, described in the House of Commons tonight by a Labor member as "the gloomiest Chancellor of the Exchequer England ever had," immediately undertook to disprove the charge by saying that the world situation was likely to improve in the next few months. As evidence on which he based his new optimism Mr. Chamberlain cited the case of the United States since the inauguration of President Roosevelt.

"Only a few weeks ago," he said, "anybody looking at the situation in the United States could only have done so with feelings of gravest anxiety. Today, thanks to the initiative, courage and wisdom of the new President, a change has taken place which might almost be called miraculous.

"Confidence has been largely restored and people who had withdrawn their deposits from banks are bringing their holdings back. Now a sense of hope and anticipation of the future is coming back to the American people and that confidence is being reflected over here in the City of London and the stock and financial markets."

Sees Gain on Continent.

Concerning the European situation, Mr. Chamberlain said he must not anticipate what Prime Minister MacDonald was going to tell Parliament tomorrow about his trip to Geneva, Rome and Paris, but added that it was evident matters on the Continent had undergone a remarkable and beneficial change.

"Then there is the World Economic Conference," he continued. "It may be the fashion to sneer at international conferences. Some members of the house genuinely wonder whether it was ever intended to hold that conference at all. I see no reason except some entirely unforeseen occurrence arising why the conference should not take place in the course of the next few months.

"Meantime preparations for the conference are going on everywhere. It was always best when going to a conference to agree as much as possible before getting there. Conversations between the parties principally interested save an indefinite amount of time and trouble when they come to a round table. I had the pleasure last week of a conversation with the French Minister of Finance, and I hope shortly to have a similar conversation with the Italian Minister. After the French conversation I didn't think that at any time since the war had there been closer cooperation between the views of the British and French Governments upon the economic subjects which have to be discussed by the conference.

Finds Pessimism Wrong.

"When one saw so many hopeful signs, when one saw that the very severity of the crisis through which the countries have been passing had made them feel that something must be done, that we cannot be satisfied with pious resolutions but must take joint and wise action to get an actual mitigation of the evils from which all are suffering, it was an altogether mistaken pessimism to think there was no chance of making progress at the world conference."

Mr. Chamberlain's hopeful remarks were received with cheers

Continued on Page Eight.

O'BRIEN PUTS HOPE OF UNIFYING TRANSIT IN SECURITY OWNERS

Mayor Announces He Will Deal Directly With Them to Fix Fair Price for Lines.

HOLDS TO 5-CENT FARE

Finding Efforts at Valuation Plan Fruitless, He Looks for Buyer-Seller Deal.

PLEDGES FULL PUBLICITY

Mayor Seeks to Halt Speculation in Stocks—His Move Seen as Blocking McKee Activity.

Mayor O'Brien yesterday invited all classes of security holders of the B. M. T. and Interborough to organize committees with which he could immediately begin direct negotiations for early unification of rapid transit lines on a five-cent fare basis.

These negotiations, he declared in a long statement issued at City Hall, would form the basis for agreement between the city and the various classes of security holders on the prices to be paid for their holdings. Payment, he said, would be in "some form of bond.

Declaring that the time had come to cut red tape and get down to the practical tactics generally adopted by prospective buyers and sellers, Mayor O'Brien announced that John H. Delaney, chairman of the Board of Transportation, and William G. Fullen, chairman of the Transit Commission, would be called upon to aid in the necessary and complicated negotiations.

In some political circles Mayor O'Brien's proposal for a "new deal" in unification procedure was viewed as an effort to shunt into an inconspicuous place in the proceedings Aldermanic President McKee, who has recently been insistent upon early resumption of the unification conferences between the Transit Commission and the Board of Estimate, which were dropped last September.

Other Members Excluded.

Under the new procedure, as outlined by Mayor O'Brien, he would be the only member of the Board of Estimate to take an active part in the negotiations, while Chairman Fullen's two associates on the Transit Commission would also be excluded. Mayor O'Brien's statement said, however, that the negotiators would welcome the "advice" of their associates and would keep them fully advised regarding developments.

Preservation of the five-cent fare, Mayor O'Brien declared, would be the primary object of the proposed negotiations. The city, he said, would insist upon paying no more than a fair price for company properties, but would recognize the right of the security holders to obtain a fair price. There would be no desire to "confiscate" private property or assail the integrity of private contracts.

This was construed as an indirect criticism of Mr. McKee's recent suggestion that the company properties might be acquired by condemnation should it appear that unification by agreement was not possible.

The direct negotiations proposed by Mayor O'Brien, he conceded,

Continued on Page Twelve.

Roosevelt to Lunch Daily In His Executive Offices

By The Associated Press.

WASHINGTON, March 22.—President Roosevelt expects to continue having luncheon in the Executive offices throughout his administration.

He favors the plan because it enables him to continue his work without a break. There will be occasions, however, when there are White House guests for formal luncheons.

Barring these, however, he expects to keep his problems before him while he eats the noonday meal.

Thus far, he has arrived at his office around 10 o'clock. Mr. Hoover was almost always at his desk before 9, but he returned to the Executive Mansion at noon to lunch.

The former President left about 6 o'clock. President Roosevelt has been leaving about the same time.

MITCHELL EVIDENCE GOES TO GRAND JURY

Income Tax Return and Bank Records Submitted—Three Witnesses Are Examined.

FRIENDS DEFEND FINANCIER

Say Real Story of Deals Has Not Been Told—Mortgage on Home Filed by Morgan's Son.

The case of the United States Government against Charles E. Mitchell, former chairman of the National City Bank, on the charge of income-tax evasion was presented to the Federal grand jury yesterday.

United States Attorney George Z. Medalie, Thomas E. Dewey, Chief Assistant United States Attorney, and Murray Gurfein, Assistant United States Attorney, placed the evidence before the grand jury. Three witnesses were examined, and exhibits, including Mr. Mitchell's income-tax return for 1929 and his bank records, placed in evidence.

Mr. Medalie refused to identify the witnesses who appeared before the grand jury or to comment upon the proceedings. His promptness in presenting the evidence was in line with the statement issued in Washington on Tuesday night to the effect that President Roosevelt knew of and approved the prosecution, and that the case was to be presented to the grand jury and brought to trial, in case of an indictment, at the earliest possible moment.

Decision on Arrest Sudden.

Mr. Mitchell was arrested at 9 o'clock Tuesday night in his home at 934 Fifth Avenue on a warrant issued by Federal Judge Alfred C. Coxe, based on an affidavit by Mr. Dewey, charging that the banker had evaded payment of $657,152.40 due as income tax on an income of $2,823,405.85 in 1929.

It was revealed yesterday that Attorney General Cummings decided about 6 o'clock Tuesday night to have Mr. Mitchell arrested immediately. According to information received here from Washington, it is understood that the Federal authorities wanted quick action.

Friends of Mr. Mitchell said that only part of the story dealing with Mr. Mitchell's 1929 income tax had become public. When the whole story was known, they asserted, it would put an entirely different light on the case and will prove an

Continued on Page Four.

Mrs. Nellie Ross to Be Federal Treasurer; State Department Post for Ruth Bryan Owen

Special to THE NEW YORK TIMES.

WASHINGTON, March 22.—Mrs. Nellie Tayloe Ross, vice chairman of the Democratic National Committee and a former Governor of Wyoming, is slated to be made United States Treasurer and Mrs. Ruth Bryan Owen is thought likely to get a position in the State Department.

Mrs. Owen, it is reported, told the President that she was happy that she was to enter the State Department of which her father, William J. Bryan, was head in the Wilson administration.

Mrs. Ross has been considered for several other positions including the Federal Power Commission and Assistant Secretary of the Interior, while Mrs. Owen was suggested for Minister to Denmark, Civil Service Commissioner, and a place in the Labor Department.

As treasurer, Mrs. Ross's name would appear on all paper money.

With the naming of these two women to office President Roosevelt will have given three honors to the women voters, the other being the appointment of Miss Frances Perkins as Secretary of Labor.

Former Representative Collier of Mississippi will be appointed a member of the Tariff Commission and James H. Hawley, vice chairman of the Democratic Committee of Nebraska, is to go on the Radio Commission.

Mrs. Ross is the widow of William Bradford Ross, Governor of Wyoming at the time of his death, Oct. 2, 1924. She was chosen to fill his unexpired term, which ran until January, 1927, and has since been active as a lecturer and writer of magazine articles. Mrs. Ross was born in 1880.

Mrs. Owen, who is 47 years old, is the widow of Major Reginald Owen, a British Army officer, who died of war wounds a few years after the armistice. Although they had four children, Mrs. Owen volunteered for active service during the struggle and was an army nurse in the campaigns in Egypt and Palestine. After the war she studied law in Florida and was elected to the Seventy-first and Seventy-second Congresses.

She was defeated for renomination in the Democratic primary because, she said later, her opponent was wetter than she was. As a "lame duck" she voted for beer and for repeal of the Eighteenth Amendment.

FARM TEST IN THE SENATE

House Leaders Drive the Measure Through, but Expect Revision.

SENATOR SMITH IS A FOE

Agriculture Committee Chairman Moves to Redraft All Except Cotton Provisions.

CONSTITUTION SNAG SEEN

Representative Beck Challenges the Plan in Debate—Wadsworth Denounces It.

Special to THE NEW YORK TIMES.

WASHINGTON, March 22.—The administration farm relief bill, which seems likely to be rewritten in large part in the Senate, was passed by the House this afternoon by a vote of 315 to 98.

The bill went through under a suspension of the rules without amendment of any kind, 38 Republicans and 4 Farmer-Laborites joining 273 Democrats in favor of the bill, while 24 Democrats and 1 Farmer-Laborite voted with 73 Republicans against the measure.

That the bill will be radically amended in the Senate was fully realized by the Democratic House leaders, and the prospect brought continual chiding from the minority side of the aisle.

While the debate was in full swing, word came from the Senate that Senator Smith, chairman of the Agriculture Committee, had announced that he will not support the bill as submitted by the White House and will move to strike out everything following Section 1, which is the cotton clause sponsored by himself.

McNary Favors Limitation.

Senator Smith will urge the redrafting of all the clauses applying to commodities other than cotton. Senator McNary, the ranking Republican on the committee, announced about the same time that he will work to limit the proposed relief to cotton and wheat.

The House debate was one of the liveliest of the extra session and there were few dull moments in the three hours of speeches. The Democrats were continually under fire from the Republican side.

Representative Beck of Pennsylvania declared that the bill was of doubtful constitutionality. In his view, it would make the Secretary of Agriculture the dictator of the farming population. The men who wrote the Constitution were for the most part farmers, he said, but they would not have endorsed a proposal such as the one the House was about to pass.

"The only argument in favor of this bill," said Mr. Beck, "is that it is an emergency proposition. That is a most damnable thing, and in Germany, with the same excuse, they are voting power today to Hitler."

The bill, he declared, was just a matter of "robbing Peter to pay Paul," while the provisions in the Constitution to hold the Federal Government within certain well-defined limits are in their "death agony."

Jones Replies to Beck.

Representative Jones of Texas, in charge of the bill, retorted that he seriously doubted the accuracy of Mr. Beck's views as to the constitutionality of the bill. The bill, he declared, was drafted to meet an acute economic emergency through the establishment and maintenance of such balances between production and consumption of agricultural commodities as will re-establish prices at a level equivalent to the purchasing power of the farmers in the five-year pre-war period.

Representative Sumners, also of Texas, remarked that in his opinion the action the House was about to take should have been taken several years ago.

"Every section of this bill," said Representative Treadway of Massachusetts, "can be analyzed to show its absurdity, impossiblity and impracticability.

"But of greater importance, perhaps, than any other section is Section 17, by which an exporter of an article that has paid the processing tax is to have the amount

Continued on Page Three.

Roosevelt Will Press for Mortgage Relief As Benefit to Farmers and Home Owners

By the Associated Press.

WASHINGTON, March 22.—President Roosevelt's next message to Congress will recommend a program of farm mortgage and small home mortgage relief, including methods of refinancing. It will be ready for presentation in a few days.

The President will follow this measure with propositions for Federal control of the stock exchanges and reorganization of the railroads.

Reduction of interest rates is one of the essentials in the mortgage refinancing contemplated by the President. He wants the program to extend to all paper, government and private.

Mr. Roosevelt also contemplates reorganization of eight Federal farm credit agencies into one organization, to be headed by Henry Morgenthau Jr., chairman of the Farm Board. Aides are working out details of the banking and railroad bills which he wants enacted at this session.

Legislation putting stock exchanges under Federal license and requiring full publicity of transactions, including the amounts of bonus and commission paid on security flotations is contemplated.

Supplementary bills along the lines proposed by Senator Glass to prevent the use of Federal funds in speculation and to divorce security affiliates from the banks are also in preparation.

According to one administration authority the farm mortgage bill will propose to scale down the mortgage interest rate to 3 per cent, and the farmer, who obtains its benefits, will be required to pay the government 3½ per cent instead of 7 and 8 per cent interest as now.

ROOSEVELT TO ASK RIGHT TO FIX DUTY

Seeks the Advance Support of Congress for Negotiation of Tariff Concessions.

LEWIS WILL OFFER BILL

Plan Aims to Lend Authority to Our Delegates—Wide Application Is Sought.

Special to THE NEW YORK TIMES.

WASHINGTON, March 22.—The first illustration of how the administration planned to obtain the support of and powers from Congress in advance of negotiations with other nations, particularly in respect to economic questions, was given by the State Department today in the announcement that when emergency domestic legislation had been disposed of President Roosevelt would ask Congress to set out certain limits within which he could effectively negotiate reciprocal commercial treaties based on mutual tariff concessions.

Reports were current that Representative Lewis of Maryland, a recognized tariff expert, planned to introduce a bill carrying out the desires of the President. Mr. Lewis is known to believe that adequate tariff schedules cannot be maintained through legislation alone.

That the President was preparing to follow this general method of obtaining advice and consent of Congress in advance instead of the method by which the Versailles Treaty failed, was reported in THE NEW YORK TIMES Tuesday morning.

The immediate negotiating authority which the President is expected to seek is with respect to commercial agreements which will not require the ratifying process if Congress gives the power and fixes the limits in advance. Treaties, however, and agreements affecting revenue will require ratification, and the method which will be followed in those instances will be to get "advance advice," which will constitute a pledge of Congress to ratify after these treaties and agreements have been made.

Prestige Is Expected.

It is believed by the administration that a first grant of authority to make commercial agreements will arm the President with prestige for negotiations in the proposed world monetary and economic conference and for revision of the war debts in return for concessions to this country. The authority will constitute valid evidence that he can make tariff reductions in return for reductions by others.

The plan has developed out of considerations that have been given to the economic conference and the war-debt problem, including exploratory conversations that Secretary Hull has carried on since entering office with foreign envoys of the important countries looking to debt revision and a readjustment of the world's economic machinery and methods.

Specifically, the first grant of authority now contemplated is that the President be empowered to negotiate reciprocal tariff arrange-

Continued on Page Eight.

SALES TAX PRESSED IN ALBANY PARLEY

Democratic Leaders in Talk With Governor Incline Toward 2% Levy.

TO CONSULT REPUBLICANS

Decision Likely Today on Plan for $60,000,000 Revenue, Eliminating Other Taxes.

Special to THE NEW YORK TIMES.

ALBANY, March 22.—Governor Lehman and the Democratic legislative leaders conferred tonight on proposals for new and additional taxes to balance the budget. The Governor found the leaders favorable toward a 2 per cent retail sales tax, but not completely committed to it.

The Governor's own attitude was not learned. It was announced that early tomorrow afternoon he would confer with both the Democratic and Republican leaders in an attempt to reach an accord on a tax program.

During the past week or more growing sentiment for a 2 per cent sales tax to replace several proposed by Governor Lehman has been evident among the members of both parties. The Governor suggested in his budget message a sales tax of three-fourths of 1 per cent.

At the evening conference the Governor and the Democratic leaders reviewed the entire tax picture. John J. Dunnigan, President pro tem of the Senate, said that the Governor had not indicated any definite decision on the 2 per cent sales tax.

Senator Jeremiah F. Twomey, chairman of the Finance Committee; Senator John L. Buckley, chairman of the Taxation Committee, and Irwin Steingut, minority leader of the Assembly, also were at the tax parley with the Governor. In the general discussion the same group will have tomorrow with the Republicans, it is expected a final decision will be reached.

Assembly Majority for 2%.

The Republicans in the Assembly have already displayed a desire to rally around Assemblyman Horace S. Stone of Onondaga, who has introduced a bill for a retail sales tax at the 2 per cent rate. Mr. Stone's bill would include a tax on food, but he has said that he would be agreeable to having that stricken out if there were real protests.

The Democratic fiscal leaders of the Senate, it has been learned, have been accumulating data for the past week with a view to going before Governor Lehman to support their proposal for the 2 per cent sales tax. The Democratic plan at present would be to exempt food from the provisions of the tax.

A poll of the Democratic members of the Senate revealed striking unanimity of sentiment concerning the wisdom of enacting the 2 per cent tax. None of the members queried desired to express an opinion for publication, but they all appeared to favor the higher rate.

Senator George R. Fearon, Republican leader in the upper house,

Continued on Page Four.

BOTTLING TO START NOW

Regulations Are Issued for Permits and Posting of Brewery Inspectors.

RACKETEERS ARE BARRED

Licenses Will Be Issued Only to Those Who Can Show a Reputable Past.

DRYS MAP AN EARLY FIGHT

Six Grounds for Attack Are Outlined—Small Violators Likely to Be Pardoned.

Special to THE NEW YORK TIMES.

WASHINGTON, March 22.—The beer bill was signed today by President Roosevelt and lawful 3.2 per cent brew, after thirteen years of proscription, will be sold in States variously estimated at fourteen to twenty-three when the act becomes operative at 12:01 A. M. on April 7.

Wet organizations here estimate that the new beer can probably be sold in twenty-three States immediately. Fifteen States have repealed their enforcement acts, although the Supreme Court of Louisiana has held that the State had no power to repeal its enforcement act by popular referendum, as was done in November.

To the fourteen States which have acted to permit the sale of beer have been added States like Maryland, which never enacted enforcement laws. Others have enforcement laws, predicated on the national law, the alcoholic content permitted varying with Congressional action.

Still others, including Massachusetts, have laws permitting the sale of wine and beer of 2.75 or 3 per cent alcoholic content. These States, it is held, would be able to legalize beer with slight dilution, even under State legislation.

Licenses Made Ready.

As soon as the bill was signed the government issued regulations to permit 158 breweries and bottlers to bottle 3.2 per cent beer so that it can be put on the market on April 7. Under the law beer can be served in restaurants and clubs and be sold by grocery and drug stores. Since it is classed as non-intoxicating, sale to minors is permissible.

The bill to legalize 3.2 per cent beer in the District of Columbia will be considered by the House tomorrow, with indications of enactment before the national act becomes operative so that the capital may have real beer the first week in April.

The beer bill reached the White House today before 2 o'clock. Seated at the head of the Cabinet table, President Roosevelt began slowly to scan the bill, page by page, as sound pictures were taken.

He used four pens in signing, which were later given to Senator Harrison, Representative Cullen, the American Federation of Labor and the American Legion. When he had proceeded to the point of signing one of his secretaries called to the movie men, "cut for the signature," and slowly the President wrote his name.

As he did so the members of Congress who had brought the enrolled bill to the White House—Representatives Cullen and O'Connor of New York, Sabath of Illinois, McCormick of Massachusetts and Parsons of Illinois—came into the picture.

"It's Off," Says Roosevelt.

The President again posed as in the act of actually affixing his signature.

"Well, it's off," he said to Representative Cullen, adding:

"I notice that the Vice President blotted his signature. He must have been excited."

Before the President approved this measure, carrying out one of his pre-election promises, he called the attention of the Department of Justice to Representative Sabath's bill, authorizing the granting of pardons to the small violators of the prohibition law, especially those who had been convicted of making and selling beer on a small scale.

Indications are that these pardons will be granted. More than 12,000 persons are serving terms in Federal and State prisons for violations of the prohibition law, but Department of Justice statistics do

President Roosevelt at home with his wife, Eleanor, and his sons, John and Elliott.

As First Lady, Mrs. Roosevelt played an active role. Here she is seen wearing a miner's cap on a visit to a coal mine.

President Roosevelt's first Cabinet: (left to right, front row) Secretary of War, George F. Dern; Secretary of State, Cordell Hull; President Roosevelt; Secretary of the Treasury, William H. Woodin; Attorney General, Homer Cummings. (Left to right, rear) Secretary of Agriculture, Henry Wallace; Secretary of the Interior, Harold Ickes; Secretary of the Navy, Claude Swanson; Postmaster General, James A. Farley; Secretary of Commerce, Daniel Roper; Secretary of Labor, Frances Perkins.

Secretary of Labor Frances Perkins, the first woman Cabinet member, tried in vain to get a minimum wage law passed in 1933.

President Hoover and President-elect Roosevelt enroute to the inauguration ceremonies, March 4.

In Germany, Adolph Hitler (right of center) was on the march. President Von Hindenburg made him Chancellor on January 30 after twice before refusing to do so.

"All the News That's Fit to Print."

The New York Times.

LATE CITY EDITION
WEATHER—Fair today; tomorrow cloudy, warmer, followed by rain.
Temperatures Yesterday—Max., 46; Min., 3o.

Copyright, 1933, by The New York Times Company.

VOL. LXXXII....No. 27,453. | Entered as Second-Class Matter, Postoffice, New York, N. Y. | NEW YORK, FRIDAY, MARCH 24, 1933. | P | TWO CENTS In New York City. | THREE CENTS Within 200 Miles | FOUR CENTS Elsewhere Except in 7th and 8th Postal Zones

HITLER CABINET GETS POWER TO RULE AS A DICTATORSHIP; REICHSTAG QUITS SINE DIE

NEW YORK UNLIKELY TO GET BEER APRIL 7 DUE TO ALBANY ROW

Measure to Prevent Its Sale Until After State Perfects License Plan Predicted.

MAY MEAN A WEEK'S DELAY

Lehman and Aides Discuss Plans Until After Midnight, but Fail to Agree.

DRYS AT CAPITOL HEARING

Governor Announces His Own Views Will Prevail—Many States Are Ready.

The Outlook on Beer.

Beer delay beyond April 7 faced in New York due to difficulties in effecting State control at Albany.

Governor and Democratic and Republican legislative leaders fail to agree on bill in night conference, to be resumed this noon. Lehman is drafting own measure. Drys and wets give views at State Senate Committee hearing.

Commissioner Doran at Washington predicted beer would sell at 5 cents a glass.

Attorney General Cummings ruled that the new 3.2 per cent beer should go on sale at 12:01 A. M., April 7, local time. Advertisements of the new brew, meanwhile, will be legal if no intent to violate the law is involved.

The House passed a bill to legalize the sale of beer in the District of Columbia.

Meanwhile, more States were taking or beginning legislative action looking toward beer. Massachusetts made brewing legal, but sale is not yet provided.

Moves for repeal-ratification conventions went forward in Iowa, New Mexico, South Carolina and Ohio.

Conferees Balked on Bill.

By W. A. WARN.

Special to THE NEW YORK TIMES.

ALBANY, Friday, March 24.—Governor Lehman and the Democratic and Republican leaders of the Legislature, after a conference which came to a close just before 2 o'clock this morning, failed to reach an agreement on legislation for control and regulation of the prospective traffic in beer, which will be inaugurated as a result of the new statute enacted by Congress legalizing 3.2 brew.

Senator John J. Dunnigan, Democratic leader, returning from the conversation at the Executive Mansion, which had been in progress since early last evening, said that there had been a very frank exchange of views on points at issue in connection with the proposed regulatory measures pending and that some progress had been made.

It was admitted by one of the conferees that no definite agreement had been reached on any detail of the proposed legislation, but it was asserted that both the legislative chiefs of the two major parties and the Governor were hopeful that a bill mutually acceptable to him and them could be evolved, possibly in time for introduction later today.

Machinery to Cause Delay.

In the meantime it was predicted in an official quarter at the Capitol that in all probability the State would not be in a position to provide prospective consumers with the new beverage legalized by Congress by April 7, when the Federal statute giving sanction to 3.2 per cent beer becomes effective.

In connection with the predicted delay, it was remarked in official quarters that, with a beer-control bill passed prohibiting the sale of beer in this State without a license, traffic in the new beverage would have to await the setting up of proper machinery for licensing and regulation of the traffic.

There is no doubt that such legislation will be passed within a couple of days. In any event such a law will be on the statute books before April 7, when the Federal law liberalizing the Volstead act will become operative.

One point over which conflict arose in the course of the discussion at the Executive Mansion was the proposal contained in the Lehman Liquor Commission bill for creation of county boards, as well as a central board of control to regulate the traffic in beer.

Governor Against County Boards.

Governor Lehman, it is understood, voiced his opposition to the county boards as unnecessary and involving too complex regulatory machinery. The two Republican leaders of the Legislature, Senator

Continued on Page Eight.

Sacasa Ends State of Siege In Nicaragua After 2 Months

Special Cable to THE NEW YORK TIMES.

MANAGUA, Nicaragua, March 23.—The state of siege [modified martial law], which has been in effect here since Jan. 19, was abolished by President Sacasa today.

The President's proclamation invites foreign capital to Nicaragua, guaranteeing protection and encouragement to gold mining and other enterprises. Gold mines closed on account of disturbances in Segovia probably will be reopened soon.

By a decree of the Nicaraguan Senate, the entire republic, with the exception of the southwestern provinces of Rivas, Granada, Masaya and Carazo, was placed under a state of siege late in January.

TRANSIT SPOKESMEN BACK MAYOR'S PLAN

Groups of Security Holders Hasten to Accept Bid to Discuss Unification.

B. M. T. BOARD WILL ACT

Morgan Committee in I. R. T., Amster and Loasby Also Approve Proposal.

Representatives of security holders' groups of the Interborough, the B. M. T. and the Manhattan elevated lines responded yesterday to Mayor O'Brien's invitation to discuss transit unification with an alacrity that indicated that they were not unprepared for his invitation.

Mayor O'Brien made public a letter from Arthur M. Anderson, vice chairman of the J. P. Morgan committee of Interborough security holders, saying that he would start negotiations whenever the Mayor wished.

The executive committee of the B. M. T. met yesterday afternoon and adopted a resolution requesting the board of directors, at a special meeting next Monday, to appoint a committee to deal directly with the Mayor.

Nathan L. Amster, president of the Manhattan Railway Company, expressed approval of Mayor O'Brien's plan and offered to work toward a fair agreement between the city and the company. He said that any agreement reached would have to be submitted to the stockholders for approval. A similar statement came from Arthur W. Loasby, head of an Interborough stockholders' protective committee.

Speed Held Essential.

The city administration, it was learned, thinks that speed is essential in the negotiations with the security-holders, if stock market speculation is to be held to a minimum. While the city has no expectation of getting the securities at their present low market prices, there is a definite limit to what it can and will pay.

Owing to the city's restricted financial condition, the question was raised in political and financial circles whether it might not be faced with the problem of deciding between a higher fare, under unification, or being seriously crippled financially.

Mayor O'Brien, in his statement Wednesday announcing the decision to seek unification by dealing directly with the security-holders, emphasized that the five-cent fare would be retained. However, ever since the Board of Estimate scrapped the Delaney plan of subway financing last Fall in order to cut the current budget so that loans might be obtained from Wall Street, transit circles have regarded the five-cent fare as dead, either under municipal operation or under unification.

There has been considerable discussion of the possibility of an increased fare, on a unified system, for a limited period of years. But it was not thought likely that this solution would be formally suggested to Mayor O'Brien in any of the conferences with security holders.

B. M. T. to Name Committee.

Among those present at the meeting of the B. M. T. executive committee were William Menden, president; Charles Hayden of Hayden, Stone & Co., Matthew C. Brush, Herbert Bayard Swope and Arthur Bunker. The B. M. T. statement follows:

"In compliance with the request of the Mayor that committees of security holders of the various transit companies be organized to deal with the city in bringing about city-wide unification, members of the executive committee of the B. M. T. will ask the board of directors of the corporation at a special meeting called for Monday next to name a special committee charged with this duty. The gentlemen to

Continued on Page Seven.

ROOSEVELT PUSHES $2,000,000,000 PLAN TO CUT FARM DEBTS

President Outlines Program of Refinancing by Government to Congress Chiefs.

LINKS IT TO RELIEF BILL

Reduction of Mortgage Principal as Well as Interest Slash Is Contemplated.

TREASURY STUDIES TERMS

Joint Stock Land Banks Would Be Eliminated, With Their Holdings Underwritten.

Special to THE NEW YORK TIMES.

WASHINGTON, March 23.—A program for lightening the farm mortgage burden which would involve from $1,000,000,000 to $2,000,000,000 of refinancing by the government, according to some estimates, was approved today by President Roosevelt at a conference with Democratic Congressional leaders.

The Senate Committee on Agriculture today postponed consideration of the farm relief bill passed by the House yesterday, in the expectation that a farm mortgage refinancing measure approved in principle at the White House conference would be completed and made a part of the House bill.

The administration is reported to have decided that after action on the farm mortgage plan a similar bill for refinancing the mortgages on city and village homes will be presented.

Major Points in the Plan.

Outstanding points in the farm mortgage plan are reported to be:

Voluntary reduction of principal by mortgagees in consideration of each settlement made possible by an advance of funds by the government.

Reduction of interest to a figure not exceeding 5 per cent in consideration of arrangements for eventual liquidation.

Amortization over a long period of years.

Suspension of foreclosures for two years.

Advance of funds by the government to farmers to pay taxes and past-due instalments of mortgage loans.

Immediate liquidation of the joint stock land banks.

Continuation of the Federal land banks on modified lines.

Reduction of interest rates by the Federal Land Bank System to 5 per cent.

As to Joint Stock Financing.

For the purpose of liquidating the Joint Stock Land Banks, the plan provides that these institutions shall issue no more obligations and shall proceed to buy in their outstanding bonds. To procure funds for the operation the Joint Stock Banks would be authorized to borrow not to exceed $500,000,000 from the United States Treasury.

Inasmuch as a mortgagee cannot be compelled to scale down principal and interest, the intent of the proposed legislation is to make it to his interest to do so. To that end, Federal financing would be designed to bring about settlements with mortgagees who are willing to accept a reduced amount of principal in cash, or to continue the loan at a lower interest rate in consideration of cash payments. The amount of Federal financing that would be involved in this scaling down is conjectural, but estimates ran from $500,000,000 to $1,000,000,000.

The proposed act would be administered by the Federal Farm

Continued on Page Thirteen.

France to Shun Chicago Fair; Holds It of Slight Interest

Wireless to THE NEW YORK TIMES.

PARIS, March 23.—Chicago's Century of Progress Exposition is insufficiently interesting for France to participate, Lucien Lamoureux, the Minister of the Budget, declared today in response to a question in the Chamber of Deputies.

Deputy Charles Pomaret complained of the government's failure to take part in the fair, declaring that it presented an excellent opportunity to display French products abroad.

The Budget Minister answered that a former government had proposed credits for French representation but that these credits had not been voted for the reason that the Chicago exhibition was of such slight interest that the United States Government itself was showing little interest in it and numerous European countries would not be represented.

HARRIMAN INQUIRY BY PECORA ORDERED

Senators Act on Medalie's Statement That Washington Held Up Prosecution.

PUBLIC HEARING PLANNED

Cummings Seeks to Excuse Preceding Administration Because of Banking Crisis.

Ferdinand Pecora, special counsel for the Senate Committee on Banking and Currency in the recent hearings at Washington, announced yesterday that he would begin an investigation of the affairs of the Harriman National Bank and Trust Company, as requested by the committee.

He said that first he would determine whether the case came within the scope of the resolution under which the committee is acting and that if it did he would present the evidence at a public hearing.

This followed the disclosure by George Z. Medalie, United States Attorney, that he had withheld prosecution of Joseph W. Harriman, former chairman of the bank, last December at the direction of the Department of Justice in Washington after counsel for the New York Clearing House Association and the Controller of the Currency had requested that action be withheld until the bank's affairs could be straightened out.

Statement by Pecora.

Mr. Pecora's statement follows:

It has been suggested to me by Senator Duncan U. Fletcher, chairman of the Senate Committee on Banking and Currency, that I give my attention to the situation which has been disclosed with respect to the Harriman National Bank and Trust Company.

I shall do so as soon as I am able to detach myself from certain other matters which I am investigating for the committee.

The first question to be determined is whether the Harriman National Bank and Trust Company matter comes within the scope of the resolution under which the Senate Committee on Banking and Currency is conducting its present stock-market inquiry. To that end I shall seek to ascertain all the basic circumstances as speedily as possible; then, in the event that the subject comes within the purview of the existing resolution, I shall gather all the available facts and present them to the committee at a public hearing.

It was understood at the Federal Building yesterday that the Department of Justice restrained Mr. Medalie from taking action on the ground that the arrest of a prominent New York banker would have

Continued on Page Twelve.

Cunard and White Star Discuss Merger; Lines Agree Drastic Economy Is Urgent

Wireless to THE NEW YORK TIMES.

LONDON, March 23.—Negotiations between the Cunard and White Star lines, which Neville Chamberlain made known yesterday, may result in a closer working agreement if not actual amalgamation.

The two companies were reported tonight to have agreed that drastic economy must be achieved by common consent. It has been suggested that one of four Atlantic giants, the Aquitania, Berengaria, Olympic and Majestic, be laid up until prosperity returns, leaving the other three to maintain weekly service.

The Mauretania and Homeric will be cruising extensively in the coming year and will not be important factors in competition for Atlantic traffic.

No headway is being made, however, toward the actual fusing of the two companies. Cunard's annual report at the coming week-end is expected to show heavy losses and its officials seem unable to offer much hope of acquiring the White Star, with several antiquated ships and a debt of millions of pounds. The White Star is suffering as much as Cunard, but has put its finances in order with the help of a two-year moratorium and regards a reported Cunard offer as wholly unacceptable.

Efforts by an impartial third party may be necessary if the two are ever amalgamated. In the meantime the government is anxious for the two lines to economize, but also anxious over the unemployment which the withdrawal of a single big liner would cause.

BIG GAIN BY BANKS THROUGHOUT NATION, RESERVE REPORTS

Gold Holdings for Week Up $181,545,000, the Gain Here Totaling $56,535,000.

CIRCULATION HEAVILY CUT

Decline Totals $661,000,000 —Ratio of Reserves Jumps From 49.1% to 55.5%.

NOTE PRINTING IS HALTED

Emergency Issue of Currency No Longer Needed, as Money Comes Out of Hoarding.

Details of Federal Reserve report are printed on Page 31.

A sweeping recovery in the strength of the Federal Reserve System and its member banks was revealed in the report for the week ended Wednesday, published last night.

The gains included a rise of $181,545,000 in the gold holdings of the system, a reduction of $661,000,000 in the volume of money in circulation in the country and a recovery in the ratio of the system's reserves to its deposits and note liabilities from 49.1 per cent a week ago to 55.5 per cent. Member banks of the system were able to reduce their borrowings from the Reserve Banks by $561,447,000 and there was a net retirement of $638,000,000 in the amount of Federal Reserve Bank credit in use.

These changes, unparalleled in size save for the losses suffered just before the national bank holiday, reflected a liquidation of the bank crisis at an extraordinary speed. They indicated that the position of the Reserve System and its members has been restored to better than the condition shown in the statement of March 1, the last before the general closing of banks.

Rise in Excess Reserves.

The extent of the improvement may be judged from the fact that the excess reserves of the system, on the basis of the current statement, amount to $1,050,000,000, against $687,000,000 a week ago and $440,000,000 two weeks ago.

The reduction of $661,000,000 in the volume of all kinds of money in circulation in the country brought the total outstanding as of Wednesday to $6,608,000,000, against $7,538,000,000 on March 8 when the record high was reached. Of this week's reduction, $376,360,000 was accomplished through the retirement of Federal Reserve notes, bringing the total of this currency in use to $3,916,342,000, compared with the record high of $4,292,702,000 reached last week. The amount of the new Federal Reserve Bank notes in use increased during the week to $9,269,000, against $3,301,000 last week, when they first appeared in the reserve's report.

The sharp rise in the reserve ratio of the system was accounted for by this drop in note circulation, combined with the gain of $181,545,000 in gold holdings reported. The current total of gold reserves, $3,192,322,000, compares with the recent low of $2,684,000,000 reached on March 8.

Big Cut in Bank Borrowings.

In managing to pay off $561,447,000 of their borrowings from the Reserve Banks during the week member banks of the system cut their indebtedness to the central banks to $670,869,000, or less than half of the peak of $1,414,000,000 to which they rose on March 8 when the banks of the country in order to meet the demands of their depositors, were compelled to go deeply into debt. Despite this large reduction of their discounts, the member banks managed to maintain their reserve balances at a level only $46,000,000 below where they stood a week ago.

The Federal Reserve Bank of New York, which, owing to the drain placed upon local member banks in meeting withdrawals by all sections of the country, had been driven to the limit of its legal reserves just before the holiday, showed a strong recovery. The bank was able to wipe out its borrowings from other Federal Reserve Banks, which amounted a week ago to $143,800,000 and two weeks ago to $210,000,000.

The local bank of issue showed a gain of $56,535,000 in its gold holdings, a reduction of $96,975,000 in the amount of its Federal Reserve notes outstanding and a decline of $15,640,000 in its deposits. The ratio of its reserves to its note and deposit liabilities rose to 50.4 per cent, from 43.6 per cent last week.

In addition to paying of its borrowings from other Reserve Banks, the New York institution took over $70,175,000 of United States Govern-

Continued on Page Eleven.

Text of Dictatorship Act

Special Cable to THE NEW YORK TIMES.

BERLIN, March 23.—The text of the enabling act by which the Hitler Cabinet becomes a dictatorship follows:

Article I—Federal laws may be enacted by the government [the Cabinet] outside of the procedure provided in the Constitution, including Article LXXXV, Paragraph 2—providing that the budget must be adopted by legislative act—and Article LXXXVII of the Constitution—providing for legislative action to authorize the government to make loans and credits.

Article II—The laws decreed by the government may deviate from the Constitution so far as they do not deal with the institutions of the Reichstag and the Federal Council as such. The prerogatives of the President remain untouched.

Article III—The laws decreed by the government are to be drafted by the Chancellor and announced in the Reichsgesetzblatt [the organ in which laws are published]. If not otherwise ordered they shall become effective the day following the announcement. Articles LXVIII to LXXVII of the Constitution—regulating the procedure of the announcement and publication of laws—do not apply to laws decreed by the government.

Article IV—For treaties of the Reich with foreign nations regarding matters of the Reich's legislative authority the consent of legislative bodies is not needed so long as this act is in force. The government shall issue decrees necessary for the enforcing of these treaties.

Article V—This law shall become effective on the day it is announced. It shall remain in effect until April 1, 1937. It shall expire when the present government is replaced by another one.

The German Cabinet of eleven members contains three Nazis: Chancellor Hitler, Dr. Wilhelm F. Frick and Hermann Wilhelm Georing. The others are Nationalists and personal appointees of President von Hindenburg. The leaders of the majority element are Vice Chancellor von Papen and Dr. Alfred Hugenberg. The Cabinet includes Franz Seldte, leader of the Stahlhelm, the organization of war veterans, and General Werner von Blomberg, the Minister of Defense, who has charge of the Reichswehr, the standing army.

The powers of the President include the right to appoint and dismiss the Chancellor.

EXPERTS PERFECT RECIPROCITY PLANS

"Plurilateral" Pacts to Share Trade Advantage Urged by Roosevelt Aides.

EARLY ACTION EXPECTED

Adoption of Modus Vivendi at World Economic Parley Is Viewed as Possible.

Special to THE NEW YORK TIMES.

WASHINGTON, March 23.—Technicians engaged here in investigating the possibilities of a change in American tariff policy have decided that the "most-favored-nation" and reciprocity systems can be reconciled, inquiry today brought out.

The problem involved, while intricate, can be solved, they think. The problem was presented today by one authority as that of "securing the advantages of reciprocity without sacrificing the security of the most-favored-nation method."

The procedure most often mentioned for arriving at the reconciliation of these two opposing ideals was the "plurilateral" treaties which are much advocated among European countries. Such treaties presuppose the adherence of a large number of countries, so trade advantages can be shared among them in such logical fashion as to permit their generalizaton without injuring the trade of the contracting parties.

It is generally thought here that progress toward the reduction of trade barriers, if made at the World Economic Conference, must hang on whatever suggestion the American Government will bring forward.

It is felt that the other countries of the world will wait on the United States as the arch protectionist, to reverse its traditional policy and to show signs of sincere conversion before taking any active steps in remedying the paralysis of world commerce. For this reason, careful preparatory work is going forward in many quarters.

It is a foregone conclusion among the experts who were consulted today that the Roosevelt administration will not advocate sudden or radical departure from the protectionism which has prevailed in this country for so long. It is thought that, not only in the United States, but in other protectionist countries, the general tendency will be to treat protectionism like the drug habit, "curing it by tapering off the doses," as a tariff technician called it today.

From the practical point of view, the experts now at work are trying to find a group of countries, each

Continued on Page Ten.

M'DONALD DEFENDS REVISION IN EUROPE

'Every Treaty Holy, but None Eternal,' He Tells Commons, In Urging 4-Power Plan.

ASKS EQUALITY FOR REICH

But Says It Must Be Granted Gradually—Assures Small Nations of Part in Scheme.

By CHARLES A. SELDEN.

Wireless to THE NEW YORK TIMES.

LONDON, March 23.—Prime Minister MacDonald told Parliament today of his mission with Sir John Simon, the Foreign Secretary, to Geneva to save the disarmament conference and to Rome to reconstruct the political situation in Europe by revision of treaties as an indispensable preliminary to peace.

"The last word in this whole matter," he exclaimed, "is the political word."

It was evident he considered the four-power movement set on foot by Premier Mussolini in Rome of more immediate importance than his own disarmament scheme, which he presented in Geneva a week ago.

The first part of today's speech in the House of Commons was merely a summarized repetition of what he had said at Geneva when offering his arms-reduction program. In this part of the speech he again said Germany must have equality. But he emphasized that such equality must come by stages and said that recent events in Germany made gradualness more important than ever.

Stresses Treaty Revision.

The most important part of the Rome section of the Prime Minister's speech was the declaration that "the big and almost only purpose of the Rome plan was revision of treaties." By which he meant the Versailles Treaty and the others that followed the war. Everything was to be done within the framework of the League of Nations. He agreed with Premier Mussolini that Article XIX of the covenant which says that treaties that become inapplicable and endanger the peace of the world should be reconsidered and must not remain dormant.

Mr. MacDonald's sole reference to the United States came in his peroration, in which he said:

"Cooperation may be in the nucleus of the four-power plan, but it is by no means confined to that. Cooperation may begin in Europe, but there is no intention to have it end there, for it must be in such form and spirit as will draw to it

Continued on Page Four.

HINDENBURG LESS ACTIVE

Hitler to Issue Decrees, With More Authority Than Predecessors.

BARS A MONARCHY NOW

Says He Wants Disarmament and Peace, but Will Crush Treason With Barbarity.

SOCIALISTS OVERRIDDEN

Vote for Dictatorial Rule 441 to 94—Goering Denies Reports of Atrocities.

Chancellor Hitler's speech on his policies appears on Page 2.

German Developments.

BERLIN—The Reichstag passed by a vote of 441 to 94 yesterday the enabling act that permits the Cabinet to make laws without consulting that body and without action by the President. The prerogatives of the President, including dismissal of the Chancellor, were preserved. Chancellor Hitler, in asking for the law, said Germany had no desire to increase her armed forces if other nations disarmed and that a monarchy was "not discussable" at this time.

WASHINGTON — Representative Dickstein invited leaders of all faiths to give their views at a hearing next Wednesday on the House resolution to facilitate immigration passports from Germany.

LONDON—Archbishop Downey of Liverpool said he would do all in his power "to protest against such pseudo-nationalism." James Maxton in the House of Commons told of reports that 1,400 persons had been killed in Hamburg.

NEW YORK—Four thousand persons participated in a protest parade, called by the Jewish War Veterans, to City Hall where their leaders were received by Mayor O'Brien. Meanwhile, city action was forecast in a resolution by Alderman James F. Kiernan, denouncing Nazi anti-Semitism, which he will introduce next Tuesday.

Quick Action in the Reichstag.

Special Cable to THE NEW YORK TIMES.

BERLIN, March 23.—The Reichstag quickly completed today the work for which it had been elected and had been called together by adopting in three readings the government's enabling act which gives to the Cabinet authority to make laws by decree for four years if it is not meanwhile displaced. The vote was 441 to 94.

Following this action, which was preceded by a speech by Chancellor Adolf Hitler and an objection from the Socialists, the Reichstag adjourned indefinitely.

Under the enabling act the Cabinet will have power to promulgate laws without reference to the Reichstag. In its deeper implications the law will enable the Hitler-Papen government to override the Federal Constitution even to the extent of eliminating President von Hindenburg from further promulgating laws and decrees, as this power is given to the Cabinet.

The law says that the prerogatives of the President remain untouched, but it is felt that the old Field Marshal has now retired from daily politics.

Held to Be Master of Reich.

Thus Herr Hitler today achieved the great triumph for which he has been fighting for fourteen years, and it is considered that he is now the master of Germany with power greater than that of any of his predecessors in the Chancellery.

The enabling act means that the Weimar Constitution has ceased to exist for a long period, probably for good, and that an important part of the authority of President von Hindenburg has passed to Herr Hitler. It will be the Chancellor who wields the power conveyed by Article XLVIII of the Constitution, which is now superseded by the enabling act.

The President's right to dismiss the Chancellor, under the present

Continued on Page Two.

"All the News That's Fit to Print."

The New York Times.

LATE CITY EDITION
WEATHER—Cloudy today; tomorrow cloudy, slightly warmer.
Temperatures Yesterday—Max., 56; Min., 44.

VOL. LXXXII....No. 27,480. Entered as Second-Class Matter, Postoffice, New York, N. Y. NEW YORK, THURSDAY, APRIL 20, 1933. TWO CENTS In New York City. | THREE CENTS Within 200 Miles | FOUR CENTS Elsewhere Except In 7th and 8th Postal Zones

GOLD STANDARD DROPPED FOR THE PRESENT TO LIFT PRICES AND AID OUR TRADE POSITION; PLANS FOR CONTROLLED INFLATION DRAFTED

REICH MASONS PUT ON NATIONAL BASIS AS CHRISTIAN BODY

Take the Name of Frederick the Great to Separate Order From Others Abroad.

FETE FOR HITLER TODAY

New German Flags Ordered Flown on 44th Birthday as Heartfelt Tribute Is Urged.

NEURATH MAY BE SHIFTED

Talk of His Becoming Governor of Wuerttemberg, With Bruening Taking Foreign Portfolio.

Wireless to THE NEW YORK TIMES.

BERLIN, April 19.—Another important step in the reorganization of Germany was taken today when the national Masonic mother lodge—the Three Globes—announced that German Masonry would be reformed on a strictly national and Christian basis. It will be transformed into the National Christian Order of Frederick the Great.

It is explained that the measure will be taken in order to prevent the organization from being mistaken for an affiliate of the lodges of Free Masons in other countries.

Two other old Prussian lodges, which also have no connection with the Free Masons abroad, will be dissolved and reorganized.

The Reich's new flags have been officially ordered out in honor of Chancellor Adolf Hitler's forty-fourth birthday tomorrow and the day has been decreed a national fête. President von Hindenburg today dedicated an autographed photograph, silver-framed, to the Chancellor.

Hopes for Heartfelt Tribute.

The government, through Dr. Paul Joseph Goebbels, its Minister of Popular Enlightenment and Propaganda, expresses the hope that the observance of Herr Hitler's birthday will bear the stamp of a genuine expression of national homage.

The official flag decree specifies that the old black, white and red colors shall fly alongside the Nazi standard, while official buildings in Prussia will be allowed to hoist the Prussian black and white colors.

The Cabinet meeting scheduled for today was called off because of Chancellor Hitler's absence. He is still conferring with party leaders in Munich and will not return to the chancellery until Saturday, since he will spend his birthday in complete retirement at his country home in Bavaria.

As Vice Chancellor Franz von Papen and Captain Hermann Wilhelm Goering, Minister Without Portfolio and Prussian Premier, are also still absent from Berlin, and Dr. Goebbels is on an official visit to the Rhineland, it is probable that the government will not proceed with its post-Easter business until Monday, although it was announced earlier in the week that the Cabinet would immediately proceed to take up a number of important measures dealing with economic, social and agricultural matters.

Meanwhile reliable official information concerning the nature of the conversations carried on in Rome by Colonel von Papen and Captain Goering remains unavailable, except for a brief denial of a report that the question of the Polish Corridor was discussed with Premier Mussolini. Neither it nor Prime Minister MacDonald's compromise solution of a German corridor within the corridor was up for discussion, it was declared.

Foreign Section Organized.

That the National Socialist party intends to have an active voice in the Reich's foreign affairs was indicated today by the formal announcement of the organization of the party's foreign political section under the direction of Alfred Rosenberg as Chancellor Hitler's "private Foreign Minister."

The section will comprise three departments: Organization, under the subdirection of Arthur Schumann; personnel, under the subdirection of Arno Schickeganz, and foreign trade, under the subdirection of Werner Daitz.

All three men are active members of the Nazi party, Herr Schickeganz being Berlin correspondent of the Voelkische Beobachter.

The Nazi foreign political section will be located in Berlin.

In connection with the impending appointment by Chancellor Hitler of more Federal Governors, it is rumored that Baron Constantin von Neurath, the Foreign Minister, will probably receive the Governorship of Wuerttemberg. The report lends color to another rumor that the

Continued on Page Eleven.

Farms Lure 1,000,000 Back; Population Breaks Record

By The Associated Press.

WASHINGTON, April 19.—The back-to-the-land movement was credited today with boosting the American farm population by more than 1,000,000 in the past year, giving the nation its largest agricultural population in history.

The Bureau of Agricultural Economics estimated the farm population on Jan. 1 as 32,242,000, compared with 31,241,000 on the same date in 1932.

This is the largest increase for a single year since 1920 and completes a net gain of more than 2,000,000 people on American farms since 1930. The previous high mark in estimated farm population was in 1910 when the Census Bureau credited farms with 32,076,960 people.

CHINESE IN CHAOS AS FOES SWEEP ON

Soldiers Lose Discipline and Many Flee to Peiping Area, Causing Wide Confusion.

AMERICAN MISSION RAZED

Is Struck by Japanese Bombs as Planes Attack Towns Over 100-Mile Region.

By HALLETT ABEND.
Special Cable to THE NEW YORK TIMES.

SHANGHAI, Thursday, April 20.—While Japanese bombing planes extended their operations in North China today to a huge arc, its furthest point reaching within ten miles of Peiping, and Japanese and Manchukuo troops continued to smash their way southward, chaos appeared to be spreading among the Chinese forces.

The general disorganization was growing apparently because the heterogeneous elements lacked personal leadership around which to rally, as General Ho Ying-ching, the War Minister, who recently took control in the north, is not proving popular. Thus many cases are arising of disobedience to orders from Peiping headquarters and many troops commanded to hold the front lines against the Japanese are retiring into the immediate vicinity of Peiping and Tientsin, where confusion prevails.

It is feared that the Japanese will allege that this disorganization, danger of disorders on a large scale and looting justify carrying the invasion to Peiping and Tientsin.

Despite the conditions in North China, Premier Wang Ching-wei announced yesterday at Nanking that a strong counter-offensive against the Japanese would be launched within a few days, although if this is done it will afford to the Japanese an excuse for further incursions.

High Chinese officials, after being telegraphically informed of the results of a Peiping conference of North China leaders, are convinced that if the pro-Manchukuo coup de force fails in the North China area, the early arrival of a conquering Japanese army in Peiping and Tientsin will become inevitable.

Yu Hsueh-chung, Governor of Hopei, whose headquarters are at Tientsin, visited Peiping today and conferred with the War Minister. A telegram from Peiping quotes him as saying he plans an immediate protest to authorities in the Japanese concession in Tientsin for harboring a Manchukuo bureau which is "widely distributing anti-Chinese and pro-Manchukuo propaganda."

Mission Property Is Damaged.

Special Cable to THE NEW YORK TIMES.

PEIPING, Thursday, April 20.—The Rev. Mark Brown, secretary of the North China Conference of the Methodist Episcopal Church, announced today that as a result of Japanese bombing at Miyun, fifty miles north of Peiping, American mission property was struck repeatedly and many buildings were destroyed. The Chinese pastor, who was hiding in Miyun in a dugout during the bombing, arrived at Peiping today. He declared the United States flag had been flying when the mission was bombed by twelve Japanese planes and believed the American property was a total loss.

General Ho, in a communiqué, reported that an American missionary had been killed when Japanese airplanes bombed Miyun. The United States Legation has investigated, but has been unable to confirm the report. It believes no United States missionaries were at Miyun, although possibly Americans were aiding Chinese Y. M. C. A. war workers near by.

Rail Line May Be Cut.

The Japanese bombing operations, if enlarged, could easily cut the Peiping-Tientsin Railway as well as threaten Paoting, the principal Chinese military base in Hopei Province.

The bombing began yesterday at

Continued on Page Thirteen.

BRITAIN ORDERS BAN ON CHIEF IMPORTS FROM SOVIET UNION

Embargo, Effective in a Week, Would Bar 80 Per Cent of Goods From Russia.

AIM IS TO AID 2 PRISONERS

The Action May Be Revoked if Russia Commutes Their Sentences to Exile.

PLEA IS MADE IN MOSCOW

One of Four Britons Preparing to Leave Asks Permission for Russian Wife to Accompany Him.

Special Cable to THE NEW YORK TIMES.

LONDON, April 19.—Great Britain's answer today to the Moscow verdict in the trial of the engineers of the Metropolitan-Vickers Electrical Company was the imposition of an embargo, effective next Wednesday, on about 80 per cent of the Russian goods imported by the United Kingdom.

King George signed the proclamation ordering the embargo at a special meeting of the Privy Council in Windsor Castle at 9:30 A. M., only nine hours after the Moscow court had passed the sentence on the Britons accused of spying and wrecking.

[Two of the Britons convicted were sentenced to three and two years, respectively, in prison. Three were ordered banished from the Soviet Union. One, A. W. Gregory, was acquitted.]

The fact that Britain has given Russia a week's grace is viewed by some persons here as indicating that Britain may cancel the embargo order before it becomes effective if the Soviet Government commutes the prison sentences of the two Britons to banishment from the country. The British Government, however, is not willing to give such an impression.

The news of the Soviet court's verdict was not received here until just before last midnight. A meeting of the Privy Council was immediately summoned for this morning, and the session lasted less than a half hour. By 2 o'clock this afternoon a special edition of The London Gazette had been published giving the details of the proclamation.

Products to Be Banned.

It explains that the embargo will not be put into effect until a week from today in order that shipments in transit, the property of British purchasers, shall not be affected. The banned commodities are to include petroleum, timber, butter, grain and raw cotton, Russia's chief exports to Britain. The reason for the choice of specific imports of an important nature, it was stated, is that an embargo on these would be simpler to operate than a complete embargo on Russian imports.

British imports from Russia in 1932 were valued at £19,679,013 [about $66,908,644]. British exports to Russia were valued at £9,274,534. While the Soviet Union has been

Continued on Page Thirteen.

Morgan Praises Gold Embargo As the 'Best Possible Course'

The embargo on gold exports was praised yesterday by J. P. Morgan, head of J. P. Morgan & Co., in the following statement:

"I welcome the reported action of the President and the Secretary of the Treasury in placing an embargo on gold exports. It has become evident that the effort to maintain the exchange value of the dollar at a premium as against depreciated foreign currencies was having a deflationary effect upon already severely deflated American prices and wages and employment.

"It seems to me clear that the way out of the depression is to combat and overcome the deflationary forces. Therefore, I regard the action now taken as being the best possible course under existing circumstances."

SPECIAL TAX URGED TO FINANCE RELIEF

Mrs. Belmont Holds System of Volunteer Gifts Unfair as Well as Unscientific.

WANTS CHARITY DICTATOR

Mrs. Roosevelt, at Meeting of Jewish Federation, Replies to Reforestation Critics.

After Mrs. Franklin D. Roosevelt had outlined efforts of the Federal Government to combat unemployment, Mrs. August Belmont, for three years head of the women's division of the emergency unemployment relief drive, yesterday urged sweeping changes in emergency relief administration in this city.

With Mrs. Rebekah Kohut, they took part in a symposium at the annual luncheon meeting of the women's division of the Federation for the Support of Jewish Philanthropic Societies at the Hotel Commodore. More than 3,000 guests filled the main ballroom and two adjoining halls, while two broadcasting systems carried the program throughout the nation.

Mrs. Belmont was introduced by Mrs. Herbert H. Lehman after the President's wife had opened the discussion of "Social Service in a Changing World" by declaring that "all government—good government—should be social service."

"It is certainly time to go forward with social service," Mrs. Belmont said, "for our present haphazard method of handling the multitudinous and varied philanthropic enterprises in this great city is wasteful of money and energy and

Continued on Page Eight.

Prince Wilhelm to Wed German Commoner; Ex-Crown Prince's Son Breaks Family Rule

Wireless to THE NEW YORK TIMES.

BERLIN, April 19.—Germany, especially its monarchists, was surprised today by an announcement that Prince Wilhelm, eldest son of the former Crown Prince, was engaged to marry a commoner. His fiancée is Fraulein Dorothea von Salviati of Bonn, whose father was a court marshal to the late Princess Victoria of Schaumberg-Lippe, sister of the former Kaiser.

The Prince would be in direct succession to the throne, following the former Kaiser and former Crown Prince, in event of a restoration of the Hohenzollerns, and he has been regarded by many as the logical candidate for such a restoration. Should he marry he would still be eligible under the old Prussian law, but his children would have no right of succession. Moreover, under the monarchical law, the marriage would be valid only if sanctioned by the head of the family.

The former Crown Prince is said to have known little if anything of the engagement. Prince Wilhelm and the former Crown Princess are now traveling in Italy. Representatives of the royal house in Berlin and Potsdam, who learned the news only from the newspapers, tried frantically tonight to establish connection with them.

The bride's family does not belong to old German nobility. Her ancestors came to Prussia from Italy less than 200 years ago. The family was knighted in 1830. The bride's mother was the former Fraulein Crasemann of an old Hamburg family.

The Prince met her six years ago during student days at Bonn, where she was living. Her brother, one of Germany's best-known horsemen, was a member of the celebrated Borussia fraternity, as was Prince Wilhelm.

After his graduation the Prince, who was born in 1906, studied law and economics. He is at present engaged in the management of one of his father's large estates in Upper Silesia. Since 1923 he has been a member of the Stahlhelm and today is leader of a detachment. One of his future brothers-in-law is a leader of the National Socialist party in Baden.

There is talk of the Prince having disregarded purposely the Hohenzollern family tradition, since he feels it is no longer in accord with the spirit of the times. His decision is expected to be opposed by the royal house, especially by the former Kaiser.

By The Associated Press.

AMSTERDAM, Holland, April 19.—The reported engagement of Prince Wilhelm to Dorothea von Salviati was understood today to grieve the former Kaiser deeply.

Wilhelm has always been the former Kaiser's favorite grandchild and the aged Wilhelm is said to have had a secret hope that one day he might see this grandson restore the "glory of the Hohenzollerns."

ALL MARKETS BOOSTED

Stocks Rise 1 to 9½ and Commodities Spurt as Bonds Move Lower.

DOLLAR DROPS ABROAD

Value Sinks to 88.54 as the Pound Climbs Highest Since 1931 and Others Rise.

MONEY DEALINGS CHAOTIC

Up to $4 Bid for Sterling Here —Control Is Predicted to Check Rise of Dollar.

Officially cut adrift from the gold-standard anchor by President Roosevelt's announcement prohibiting exports of gold to support exchange, the dollar fell yesterday to a discount of 11½ per cent in terms of the gold-standard currencies of the world.

Embracing the belief that inflation was at hand, the stock and commodity markets soared, while United States Government bonds and other high grade fixed-interest securities broke sharply.

The imposition of an air-tight embargo upon gold exports, coupled with intimations from Washington of plans for expanding credit and, if necessary, enlarging the basis of the currency unleashed in Wall Street yesterday a stampede for "equities."

Although there was confusion of opinion in the banking community, the rank and file of the financial district embraced with enthusiasm the prospects of inflation after the hungry years of grinding deflation. In this rejoicing the Street received, late in the day, the blessing of J. P. Morgan, head of the great private banking house which bears his name.

Confusion in Lack of Details.

Mr. Morgan's statement had a profound effect upon the financial community. With the exception of a similar statement made in London in September, 1931, describing the British suspension of gold payments at that time as constructive under the circumstances, yesterday's comment by the financier was the first formal expression of his opinion upon financial developments in many years.

Elsewhere in the Wall Street section opinion was confused by the lack of details as to the administration plans. The banking community was uncertain whether to conclude that President Roosevelt had definitely adopted a program of inflation or whether the imposition of the embargo had been designed to head off more radical schemes in Congress and to give this country a bargaining point in the forthcoming conversations with Prime Minister MacDonald and Premier Herriot.

Pending further disclosure of the full policy of the administration, the financial markets took their cue from the course of the dollar in foreign exchange. Here the response to the news was spectacular as the dollar was forced down in chaotic trading to a record post-war low.

Pound Rises 32 Cents.

The pound sterling rose 32 cents to $3.85, the highest price since Oct. 31, 1931; the French franc went to 4.50 cents, up 47 points on the day and 58 points above par, a record high for the present currency and the highest price for French exchange since 1925; Dutch guilders rose 3.84 cents to 45 cents, a record price, 4.80 cents above par; Belgian belgas were up 1.28 cents to 15.40 cents, also a record high for the present currency and 1.50 cents above par; the Swiss franc rose 2.30 cents up to 22 cents, another record for all time, and 2.70 cents above par.

At their highs for the day the four gold-standard exchanges showed the following percentage gain over their dollar gold parities: Francs, up 15.11 per cent; Swiss francs, up 14.02 per cent; belgas, up 10.76 per cent; guilders, up 11.95 per cent. The pound sterling, while still $1 below par, showed an appreciation of 11.35 per cent over its quotation for March 3, just before the suspension of domestic specie payments here.

Measured in terms of the fall in the power of the dollar to purchase

Continued on Page Two.

Dollar Developments

Official abandonment of the gold standard by the United States yesterday produced a violent reaction in the foreign exchange markets of the world and a broad upward movement in stocks and commodities here. Repercussions were felt, as follows:

NEW YORK—The dollar fell to a discount of 11½ per cent in terms of European gold currencies. In expectation of inflation, stocks rose 1 to 9½ points in the most active trading since last September. Total volume on the New York Stock Exchange was 5,088,000 shares. United States Government and other high-grade bonds were sharply depressed, while speculative issues were in demand at higher prices. Cotton advanced $2 a bale. Silver bullion rose 3½ cents, to 32⅜ cents an ounce, and silver futures advanced the maximum of 300 points in all active positions. Minor commodities were correspondingly strong. J. P. Morgan endorsed President Roosevelt's anti-deflation policy.

CHICAGO—Wheat showed an extreme gain of 4 cents a bushel and closed 1⅝ to 2¼ cents higher on the day.

WASHINGTON—The signal for the broad movement in the markets was given by President Roosevelt in announcing a rigid embargo against gold shipments to support the dollar in the foreign exchange markets. Positive moves in the direction of controlled inflation were indicated.

LONDON—Following a wild uprush in the pound sterling against the dollar, directors of the Bank of England were reported to be planning measures for restraining the British monetary unit, including a proposal to raise the Exchange Equalization Fund to £500,000,000. Possibilities of a great trade war between the United States and Great Britain are seen.

PARIS—Francs rose sharply against the dollar. Fluctuations in the American unit were characterized as "scarcely dignified for a money that pretends to be based on gold" and actions of the United States Government were criticized.

PRESIDENT'S ACTION FORCED BY EVENTS

Advisers Point to Domestic Deflation and Devalued Foreign Currency Competition.

FEARED RADICAL MEASURES

Roosevelt Preferred Power for Guiding Inflation to Possibly Dangerous Legislation.

Special to THE NEW YORK TIMES.

WASHINGTON, April 19.—Forced by events, President Roosevelt will accept dictatorial powers from Congress for entering upon an emergency currency inflation program in the hope of increasing commodity prices and reducing unemployment.

This is the view of his advisers, who say that he began his duties in March determined to maintain a "sound national currency" and uphold, technically, the present gold standard. But the deflation that has taken place in the last month, including the reducing of government and State expenditures by at least $2,000,000,000, and the frozen assets in closed banks, amounting to $5,000,000,000, have produced a situation where, with competition from foreign countries off the gold standard, it appeared necessary to meet the situation with a modified currency, according to these confidants of the President.

The measures suggested by the administration to overcome deflation, such as loans to States for self-liquidating projects and a public works program of enormous proportions, apparently have failed to stimulate industry sufficiently and revive confidence that the country was on the road to recovery.

In the opinion of the President and his advisers, these emergency measures were not enough to prime the prosperity pump, and unemployment, instead of decreasing or standing still, has increased. The last reports of the American Federation of Labor estimated that unemployment was now 13,000,000, as against 12,000,000 before the November election.

Inflation Clamor Grows.

The administration had hoped that emergency measures such as reforestation, farm relief and refinancing of farm and home mortgages, together with the public works program, would stimulate industry and check the demands of the inflationary group in Congress. But nevertheless, the clamor for inflation grew louder and more insistent. The vote last Saturday on Senator Wheeler's amendment to remonetize silver at 16 to 1 showed that the strength of the inflationists was increasing.

President Roosevelt has steadily refused to define what he meant by an "adequate but sound currency," which he advocated in his inaugural address. Those who seek to interpret the President's mind say that he favored "a technical gold stand-

Continued on Page Two.

MONEY CHIEF ISSUE FOR WORLD PARLEY

Washington Believes Topic May Dominate Talks as a Result of Our Embargo.

SOME ADVANTAGES SEEN

Easing of Disparity in World Currencies Expected to Act as Stimulus to Trade.

Special to THE NEW YORK TIMES.

WASHINGTON, April 19.—The domination of the international currency problem in the economic discussions which President Roosevelt will conduct with foreign representatives in the next few weeks became assured today as a result of the President's embargo on gold shipments and movements in the direction of devaluating the dollar.

The monetary question was already assured of a prominent place in the talks to be held with Prime Minister MacDonald of Great Britain, former Premier Herriot of France and Premier Bennett of Canada. The events of today, in official opinion, make it certain that the issue will occupy first place in these conversations. Moreover, it is predicted that the question is bound to extend with equal force over into the World Monetary and Economic Conference.

Officials would not talk for publication on the domestic currency situation in its relation to the conferences to begin Friday with the representatives of foreign powers, but it was regarded as settled that, through the developments of today, the position of the United States for negotiating had been materially strengthened.

Britain Drawn Closer to Us.

Particularly by bringing the United States and Great Britain closer to the same monetary plane, it was believed by the authorities, agreements as to common objectives between them would be made less difficult of accomplishment.

By the same token, the part to be played by France in the discussions is made more important, inasmuch as France remains on the gold standard. Having passed previously through a period of deflation and having attained relative stability as to domestic values, France, it was believed, might look with less favor than either the United States or Great Britain on commodity-price increases.

Nevertheless the French position, according to the views of officials today, is not expected to present insurmountable difficulties to international action looking to world economic rehabilitation.

Much less certainty prevailed with respect to the position of Canada. Yet with huge obligations to be met in gold at New York and with revaluation of the dollar at a lower figure than at present virtually assured, the arrangement would seem to be entirely to the benefit of Canada. On the assumption that less Canadian gold would be required to

Continued on Page Three.

PRESIDENT TAKES ACTION

Moves to Bring Dollar Closer to the Pound and Raise Prices.

CURRENCY STEP CHARTED

Farm Bill Amendment Drafted to Give Roosevelt the Broadest Powers.

THOMAS TO SPONSOR IT.

Note Issue, Gold Devaluation or Limited Silver Authority to Be Sought.

Special to THE NEW YORK TIMES.

WASHINGTON, April 19.—President Roosevelt today ordered an embargo on all exports of gold except that earmarked for foreign countries, thus taking the United States definitely off the international gold standard.

His action was deemed by his advisers to be a constructive step, from both a domestic and an international viewpoint, in that it would tend to raise commodity prices in this country and, by putting the United States on an equal monetary footing with most of the other countries of the world, increase the chances of all governments getting together on a more stable monetary basis following the world economic conference.

It is understood to be the hope of this country's financial leaders that that basis will be gold.

Secretary Woodin for the first time publicly admitted that the United States was off the gold standard, adding that it was "for the time being." How long the "time being" will be depends on domestic and world conditions and the results of the world economic conference.

Congressional Action Mapped.

Simultaneously with this bold step, which was frankly welcomed by many Congressional leaders, the administration sought broad powers to dictate a policy of controlled inflation and, if it so desires, to lower the gold content of the dollar. Such authority would be given in an amendment to the pending farm-relief bill.

This amendment, fathered by Senator Thomas of Oklahoma and withdrawn yesterday, was being revised by Senator Thomas in collaboration with the President, Secretary Woodin, Under-Secretary of State Phillips, Raymond Moley, Assistant Secretary of State; Lewis Douglas, Director of the Budget, and Senators Byrnes and Pittman.

After a two-hour conference Senator Thomas said tonight he would reintroduce his amendment probably tomorrow, and in view of his frank statement that he would offer nothing opposed by the administration it was taken for granted that the administration wants authority to inflate the currency.

This was taken in informed quarters to mean, not that the administration desired currency inflation, but that it did wish to have such authority in its hands and out of the hands of Congress when and if such a step became necessary. It would be an authorization only and not a mandate.

The only restriction to the Thomas amendment set up by the administration spokesman, according to reports, was that there should be a definite limitation on the use of silver as a monetary basis.

The original Thomas amendment was withdrawn from consideration at the request of the administration.

Three Courses in View.

It was indicated that the revised measure will contain three provisions, relating respectively to the volume of the currency, to the gold content of the dollar and to silver, the last provision being along lines advocated by Senator Pittman, a leader of the silver forces in Congress.

The President would be authorized, in his discretion, to issue Treasury certificates, to be legal tender for all debts, including interest and principal payments on the public debt. They would be backed solely by the credit of the United States Government.

A reduction in the gold content of the dollar at the discretion of the President would be authorized, a

"All the News That's Fit to Print."

The New York Times.

LATE CITY EDITION

WEATHER—Fair and warmer today; tomorrow fair.

Temperature Yesterday—Max., 55; min., 41.

VOL. LXXXII....No. 27,489. Entered as Second-Class Matter, Postoffice, New York, N. Y. NEW YORK, SATURDAY, APRIL 29, 1933. TWO CENTS In New York City. | THREE CENTS Within 200 Miles | FOUR CENTS Elsewhere Except in 7th and 8th Postal Zones

SENATE PASSES INFLATION-FARM BILL BY 64-20; INDUSTRY CONTROL BILL PERMITS PRICE FIXING; THREE NATIONS TO ACT TO STABILIZE EXCHANGE

CENTRAL PARK PLAN PRESSED AS SHEEHY REBUFFS ITS CRITICS

He Tells Them at Hearing He Cannot Promise Sport Field Will Not Be Permanent.

BUT CALLS IT 'TEMPORARY'

School Officials and Others Back Reservoir Project as Meeting Needs of Youth.

CIVIC GROUPS OPPOSE IT

Urge "Beauty and Tranquillity" Be Not Marred—Issue Not Yet Closed, Litchfield Warns.

Disregarding growing protests by organizations and individuals who have been fighting for years to save the city's parks from encroachments, John E. Sheehy, newly appointed Park Commissioner, announced yesterday that he would proceed at once with his plans to convert the thirty-four-acre site of the abandoned lower reservoir in Central Park into a series of baseball diamonds and athletic fields. He would "give no guarantee" against the permanency of those features.

Commissioner Sheehy arrived at his decision immediately following a public hearing on his plans at Park Department headquarters in the Central Park Arsenal, Sixty-fifth Street and Fifth Avenue. He had listened to more than a score of spokesmen arguing for or against his plans.

Advocates of the plan, largely from the public schools and neighborhood and church organizations, frequently insisted that the Park Commissioner give definite assurance of the permanency of the athletic and playground features he is introducing into Central Park. They demanded all the accessories that go with athletic fields.

"We want showers and lockers," was the demand of the spokesmen.

Civic, art, landscape and other organizations opposed the athletic fields contemplated by the new commissioner on the ground that they had no place in the park, and that they would certainly become permanent despite Mr. Sheehy's announcement that they were intended to be only temporary.

Says 40,000 Will Watch.

When it was pointed out that the ten contemplated baseball diamonds would furnish recreation for only 200 players to the exclusion of every one else, and especially small children and their mothers for whom a sunken meadow had been planned by a committee of the New York Chapter, American Society of Landscape Architects, Commissioner Sheehy shot back this rejoinder:

"After all, there will be baseball leagues in the park with 40,000 to 50,000 watching them."

"How many?" asked William Bradford Roulstone, more incredulous than he had ever been in the course of his bitter fight that forestalled Mayor Hylan's effort to place an art centre in the park.

"Forty to fifty thousand," repeated Commissioner Sheehy.

"Saints save us, if that's what we're planning to do," said Mr. Roulstone.

At that point Nathan Straus Jr., president of the Park Association of New York City, intervened to suggest that the Park Commissioner did not mean to say that he would erect grand stands in Central Park to accommodate 40,000 to 50,000 spectators. Mr. Sheehy explained that he had not meant to convey the impression that he contemplated building stadia.

At the end of the hearing, held from 10 o'clock till noon, Commissioner Sheehy was asked whether he would disclose his next step.

"I intend to proceed with my original plan for utilizing the park reservoir site immediately," he replied.

Can't Guarantee for Future.

Asked whether he favored development of the reservoir tract ultimately in accordance with the plans designed by the landscape architects' committee headed by A. F. Brinckerhoff, Mr. Sheehy explained that so far as he personally was concerned he favored those plans.

When asked whether the baseball fields and athletic facilities would be temporary, he said: "They will be temporary as far as I myself personally am concerned, but I can't guarantee for the future."

Mr. Sheehy reiterated his statement, in opening the hearing, that by temporary use he meant until such time as funds become available for the more comprehensive architects' plan for the reservoir.

The first of the ten baseball diamonds contemplated will resound to the crack of ball and bat and the shouts of players and [illegible] with-

Continued on Page Six.

Clocks Should Be Set Ahead For Daylight Time Tonight

Before retiring tonight millions of Americans and Canadians will advance their clocks one hour, for Daylight Saving Time will become effective at 2 A. M. tomorrow. The lost hour will be recovered Sept. 25, when the daylight saving period will end.

More persons than ever before will use daylight time this year in the United States and Canada, according to the Merchants' Association of New York, although the time will be observed in only thirteen States this year, as compared with fifteen last year. However, large gains in Maine, where the area of observance virtually will be doubled, and gains in Canada have more than offset the population loss caused by the defection of Florida, last year represented by Pensacola, and of Minnesota, where last year business men belonging to the chambers of commerce in St. Paul and Minneapolis observed the time.

In New York State, Rochester, Syracuse and Binghamton are the only large cities not in line.

MILKY WAY STARS FOUND IN FLIGHT

Dr. Ross Gunn Tells Physicists His Tests Back Theory of an "Exploding" Universe.

PROOF OF ETHER CLAIMED

Prof. D. C. Miller Asserts He Has Traced Drift—Transparency of Alkali Metals Told.

By WILLIAM L. LAURENCE.

Special to THE NEW YORK TIMES.

WASHINGTON, April 28.—Evidence that the stars and constellations in our own Milky Way galaxy, of which our solar system is a relatively insignificant part, are running away from each other at a uniform speed of three miles a second from the centre of gravity of the galaxy was presented today before the meeting of the American Physical Society by Dr. Ross Gunn of the Naval Research Laboratory.

His data, Dr. Gunn added, agreed with the observational data made by Dr. Edwin P. Hubble and others at Mount Wilson Observatory, showing that the nebulae are receding from us and from each other at the explosive speed of 15,000 miles a second, and thus offered independent proof that the universe as a whole is "exploding."

Basing his calculations on previously observed velocities of recession of the hot stars in our galaxy known as B-type stars, Dr. Gunn said he found that not only did these hot stars recede, but that all the other stars and constellations in the galaxy did likewise.

Applying the figures for our galaxy to the figures previously obtained by other observations of Dr. Hubble, Dr. Gunn found that they corresponded to within a very small percentage of error.

Uniform Recession Shown.

Both sets of calculations showed, Dr. Gunn said, that the rate of recession was uniform throughout the universe, increasing with distance by uniform steps of 100 miles a second for each million light years, so that the furthest galaxies so far observed, at a distance of 150,000,000 light years, should recede at the rate of 15,000 miles a second.

This figure checks exactly with that obtained by Dr. Hubble by measuring the observed shift of spectrum lines toward the red, a shift known to increase at a definite rate when an object is receding.

From his data Dr. Gunn evolved a new hypothesis, reconstructing the beginnings of the universe. Some time about 5,000,000,000 years ago, he held, the universe was but one immense supernebula, in a very gaseous state, revolving at terrific speed. As it kept whirling around it broke up into smaller fragments in the course of about 100,000,000 years.

These fragments, which made up the galaxies, island universes, constellations, suns and stars, were asymmetrical in the distribution of their heat energy; that is, one side was necessarily much hotter than the other side, just as a piece from a hot baked potato is much hotter on the side that came from inside the potato than on the surface of the skin.

Star Heat Divided.

For this reason each star, Dr. Gunn reasoned, had one half which was about twice as hot as the other half.

Now, this extra heat, by the known laws of radiant energy, would be radiated away in two directions. Part of it, by far the largest part, would be radiated away in the surrounding space, while the other part would keep going toward the cooler part of the

Continued on Page Six.

IOWA TROOPS RULE FARM RIOT AREAS; MOB BLOCKS A SALE

Martial Law Is Declared In Plymouth County, Where Judge Was Abducted and Beaten.

CROWD ROUTS DEPUTIES

Officers Are Forced to Stop Denison Foreclosure and Governor Sends Militia There.

COURTS SPLIT ON NEW LAW

State Act Aimed to Help Debtors Is Upheld and Held Unconstitutional in Decisions.

Special to THE NEW YORK TIMES.

LEMARS, Iowa, April 28.—Martial law was established here today under a proclamation by Governor Clyde Herring and the arrival of 250 National Guardsmen as a result of the attack yesterday on District Court Judge C. C. Bradley by farmers who demanded that he refuse to sign foreclosure papers.

Other State troopers were ordered to Denison, Iowa, sixty miles from Sioux City, after 800 farmers had attacked six State agents, a Sheriff and forty special deputies when they attempted to conduct a foreclosure sale on J. F. Field's farm.

The crowd stopped the sale after a fight in which many were slightly injured.

Governor Herring's martial-law order covered all Plymouth County.

Terming the attack on Judge Bradley "a vicious and criminal conspiracy and assault upon a judge while in discharge of his official duties, endangering his life and threatening a complete breakdown of all law and order," he authorized the troops to work beyond the borders of the county if necessary.

"The public peace and good order will be preserved upon all occasions and throughout the county, and no interference will be permitted with officers and men in the discharge of the duties under this order," the proclamation read.

Doubts Crowd All Farmers.

The Governor declared he believed Sioux City hoodlums were in the crowd that attacked the judge. He urged the newspapers not to be too quick in describing the assailants as all farmers. Talk of "Red" agitators was also heard.

In Lemars rumors of outside help for the farmers was not taken seriously. Persons who saw a hundred or more men sweep into the court room of Judge Bradley while court was in session, who saw the jurist slapped and choked and otherwise maltreated before a noose was placed around his neck, asserted that many in the crowd were recognized as farmers from O'Brien, Primrose and Sioux Counties.

"It seemed to be a crowd without direction," said one observer, "moving under the impulses of mob psychology. The members had gone into the court to demand that Judge Bradley refuse to sign any more foreclosure actions. When he declined to promise that on oath they seemed to move mechanically about seizing him."

This observer said that the plague of drought and grasshoppers had well nigh ruined farmers in this section before the low prices of farm products in the last year or two added to their troubles.

Meanwhile Judge Bradley, suffering only slight effects of the manhandling by the mob, presided over a routine court session. He said he had not recognized any of those who seized him, although he had been on the district bench for many years.

The troops are under command of Colonel Golden C. Hollar. The men carried full field equipment and are quartered for the time being in the armory.

Courts Differ on Law.

By The Associated Press.

DES MOINES, April 28.—Constitutionality of Iowa's emergency debtor's relief law was both upheld and denied by district courts today.

District Judge A. P. Barker, in a ruling at Muscatine, upheld the constitutionality of the law passed by the recent Iowa General Assembly, but earlier in the day Judge W. E. Dingwell, at Winterset, had held the same law unconstitutional in several mortgage foreclosure actions brought before the Madison County District Court.

The law provides for continuance of all mortgage foreclosure actions until March 1, 1935, on request to the court and also gives the court custody of the property during the period of continuance with authority to direct the application of rents, profits and income.

Continued on Page Five.

State Income Tax Receipts To Equal Those of Last Year

Special to THE NEW YORK TIMES.

ALBANY, April 28.—For the first time since 1920 State income tax collections this year will not show a drop from the preceding year.

Mark Graves, president of the State Tax Commission, announced today that the present returns will equal the $30,858,000 mark of last year. To date the State has collected $29,198,591. In the boom period income tax collections totaled $78,000,000.

"The number of paid tax returns received in the calendar year 1932 was 238,834," the Tax Commission statement said. "The number of returns filed this year to date is 150,294. It is estimated that 25,000 additional returns will be filed during the year, making a total for this year of 175,294 returns."

Governor Lehman in his executive budget estimated the income tax for this year at $31,000,000.

LABOR PROTECTION ASKED IN RAIL BILL

Union Chiefs Demand Provision for Men Losing Jobs by Operation Economies.

TO FIGHT IN COMMITTEES

Meantime, Eastman Conditions Taking Coordinator's Post on Final Shaping of Measure.

Special to THE NEW YORK TIMES.

WASHINGTON, April 28.—The administration's railroad legislation, providing for a Federal coordinator of transportation to direct and if necessary to force more economical operation, is not acceptable to organized railway labor, George M. Harrison, acting chairman of the Railway Labor Executives' Association, said today in demanding adequate protection of the union workers.

In his statement, issued after a meeting of the association called to consider the legislation, Mr. Harrison assailed the proposed setting aside of the anti-trust laws and other Federal and State statutes, which he said was "merely to permit monopolized railroads to gather unjust and unearned profits."

The labor executives plan to carry their fight to Senate and House committees with a demand that provision be made for railroad workers thrown out of employment by elimination of services and facilities in the interests of economical operation.

Eastman Approached on Post.

Publication today of the text of the administration measure again brought to the fore the name of Interstate Commerce Commissioner Joseph B. Eastman as the outstanding candidate for the office of Federal Coordinator.

He has been "sounded out" on the proposition by some of President Roosevelt's economic advisers and is understood to regard the bill as satisfactory as it now stands but to condition his acceptance of the post on the final form of the measure.

He is said to feel that he could accept the responsibilities only if he received a "free hand" to work out the complicated railroad problem according to his own judgment, subject to the limitations which include judicial review of the coordinator's decisions by the full commissions.

Objections Made by Unions.

In stating the position of organized railway labor on the bill, Mr. Harrison said:

"We are thoroughly opposed to the prospective railroad legislation. We see no justification for drastic reductions of essential transportation service in order that unearned interest may be paid on idle capital.

"Communities deprived of adequate and competitive rail transportation will be further depressed. Thousands of railway workers will be added to the breadlines. Economic recovery will be retarded by this further deflation of business and labor.

"Communities, shippers and employes threatened with irreparable losses, should be able to prevent the passage of such a law as now proposed. But, at least, the organized railway employes will do all within their power to have written

Continued on Page Five.

RECOVERY ACT DRAFTED

National Board Would Rule Output, Hours and Markets.

TRUST LAWS TO BE WAIVED

Trade Associations Would Seek to Correlate Production and Demand in Each Line.

SPUR TO BUYING AN AIM

Proponents Admit Idea Is Daring—Moley and Warburg Are Said to Endorse It.

By LOUIS STARK.

WASHINGTON, April 28.—The "national industry recovery act," a bill that envisages complete control of industry through a national board modeled after the War Industries Board, is being hurried for submission to the President next week, it was reported today.

The tentative draft of the act, which has just been completed, sets aside the anti-trust laws and the Federal Trade Commission act, empowers the national board to designate any industry as one affected with a public interest, permits price fixing under government supervision for the period of the emergency, and agrees to a plan of self-organization of industry through trade associations.

Designed to stabilize industry, and to bring about increased employment and an enlarged purchasing power, the tentative bill follows out in detailed form the first outline of the plan set forth in a Washington dispatch to THE NEW YORK TIMES on April 14.

The general outlines of the measure have been submitted to Raymond Moley, Assistant Secretary of State, who early endorsed the idea behind it, and to James P. Warburg, New York banker, who is active in plans concerning economic recovery. Mr. Moley and Mr. Warburg, according to those in charge of the proposal, expressed enthusiasm when the plan to stimulate manufactures and increase employment were placed before them.

Backers Admit Plan Is "Daring."

Admitted by its proponents to be a "daring" and "audacious" plan to further industrial recovery, the scheme sets up a board consisting of seven members, headed by the Secretaries of Commerce and Labor. The others are to be spokesmen for commerce, finance, labor, agriculture and the public.

The plan sanctions the formation of industrial and trade associations which shall work with the national board to correlate production with demand, establish prices of commodities at fair levels and stabilize markets.

Each trade association will have on its governing board a representative of the supreme body of seven. Before the government, through the national board, can approve prices and trade arrangements set up by the trade associations the national body must be in complete possession of the facts, which will be obtained through its own agents and through the data submitted by the trade association.

The government's agent on the Trade Commission body will be the liaison officer, while the national board will be the umpire or the court of last resort in making effective or revising the decisions arrived at by the trade association.

Loans, Not Subsidies Provided.

Loans but no subsidies are provided for private industry, according to the revised plan. The national board will be empowered to certify to the Reconstruction Finance Corporation any plant that may require a loan.

It is expected that such loans would be repaid quickly, once the plan achieves its result of the stimulation of purchasing power and the opening of factories, mines, mills and workshops to idle employes.

A higher price level which will be caused by the act, it was said, will encourage banks to pour into industry the credit now frozen in their vaults because of the continuing downward spiral of commodity prices.

Under the Fred I. Kent plan, the

Continued on Page Five.

Points in the Farm-Inflation Bill

Special to THE NEW YORK TIMES.

WASHINGTON, April 28.—The farm relief bill, as passed by the Senate, clothes President Roosevelt and his assistants with virtually dictatorial powers in his discretion for the regulation of currency and agriculture.

The bill is divided into three parts, providing:

DIRECT AGRICULTURE RELIEF.

The President and the Secretary of Agriculture are authorized to use one or all of three methods to raise farm values as follows:

1. Domestic Allotment—To determine the consumption of wheat, cotton, corn, hogs, dairy products, tobacco, rice and beet and cane sugar; to license producers and processors so that only domestic consumption requirements shall be sold in the domestic market at prices equal generally to the average in 1909-1914, and to collect a tax from processors to pay the cost.

2. To lease marginal lands and withdraw from production sufficient acreage to cut production of agricultural commodities to domestic needs.

3. To guarantee cost of production to farmers.

An amendment providing that the 2,500,000 or more bales of cotton held by farm credit agencies as collateral for crop production and other purposes should be withheld from the market until the Spring of 1934 was adopted.

FARM MORTGAGE RELIEF

To refinance through voluntary arrangements with mortgagors farm mortgages at interest rates of 4½ per cent through the issuance of bonds, the interest of which would be guaranteed by the government.

INFLATION.

Authorizing the President to use three methods of raising the dollar values of commodities.

1. By increasing Federal Reserve credits by a maximum of $3,000,000,000.

2. By issuing up to $3,000,000,000 of Treasury notes, secured not by gold, but solely by the credit of the United States. This money would be used to buy back government securities.

3. Devaluing the gold content of the dollar by as much as 50 per cent, with additional authorization for the President to establish, at his discretion, a fixed ratio of silver to gold and to provide for the unlimited coinage of silver at that ratio.

HERRIOT SAYS TALKS SAVE TRADE PARLEY

In Final Messages Here, He Holds Roosevelt Avoided a "Tower of Babel."

PLEADS FOR COOPERATION

Former Premier Is Honored at French Chamber Dinner—Sails at Noon Today.

The text of M. Herriot's speech here last night is on Page 2.

Edouard Herriot, former premier of France, returned to New York yesterday after conversations with President Roosevelt on world economic problems had been closed and, in a farewell address at the Waldorf last night, declared that important progress had been made toward their solution. He will sail for France at noon today on the Ile de France.

M. Herriot spoke before an audience of distinguished French and Americans under the auspices of the French Chamber of Commerce in the United States and French American societies.

Denies France Is "Egoist."

He denied that France was "an international egoist," pledged that France would join with England and the United States in efforts for world peace and hailed a movement to restore a suffering world in which politics and morality would never be separated.

Political agreements were not enough, he declared, but a sense of security and stability must be passed down to the family and to the individual before political tranquillity could be restored.

"We must reconstruct the world on a new moral basis," he said. "We must rebuild it upon a basis of justice, law and liberty."

Finally, he brought the whole assemblage to its feet with a toast to Mr. Roosevelt as "a great President directing a great people."

Sees World Parley Saved.

It was the last of a series of statements and interviews, which he gave yesterday in Washington and New York and in which he declared that the conversations in Washington had gone far to forward the objects of the economic and monetary conference to begin in London June 12, and declared that the London conference might well have degenerated into a "Tower of Babel" had not President Roosevelt taken this step.

He further declared that the conversations had made the London

Continued on Page Two.

PLAN TO STABILIZE CURRENCY, TARIFFS

Great Britain, France and United States Will Seek Action Before London Parley.

JOINT STATEMENT ISSUED

Roosevelt and Herriot Refer to Understanding 'of the Realities of the Situation.'

Special to THE NEW YORK TIMES.

WASHINGTON, April 28.—Edouard Herriot, envoy of France, left Washington today after his conferences with President Roosevelt bearing an olive branch but leaving behind him a few significant words on the French idea of what constitutes political security. Prime Minister Bennett of Canada continues here for another day, and the Italians and Argentines are due here next week.

What possible differences of opinion there may be between Mr. Roosevelt and M. Herriot revolve around their point of view as to how far this country can commit itself through diplomatic channels to consultative pacts, and to the definition of what is an aggressor nation.

It is believed that Mr. Roosevelt must have told M. Herriot that both of these subjects were extremely delicate flags to wave before the Congress of the United States. As to an embargo, the President would have power under pending legislation to join in such an action.

Joint Statement Encouraging.

The well-known American practice of refusing to commit this country to foreign decisions may have been reflected in a statement issued by M. Herriot just before leaving when he said that the solidarity of nations must "find its expression" and when he referred to the desire for freedom "and the organization of France."

A joint statement issued by the President and M. Herriot, however, carried the encouragement that both governments "are looking with like purpose at the main problems of the world and the objectives of the World Economic Conference." The disarmament conference was not mentioned.

In a second joint statement on war debts an understanding "of the realities of the situation" was referred to, and it was said that further conversations will be continued in Paris and Washington, which carries out the avowed intention of the President to discuss these debts separately with each

Continued on Page Two.

SWEEP FOR THE FARM BILL

Authority for Inflation Voted in Measure to Raise Prices.

BONUS PAYMENT IS BEATEN

Amendment Is Adopted to Accept $200,000,000 in Silver on War Debts.

NEW CURRENCY FOR BONDS

Thus Treasury Will Meet Maturities—Farm Mortgage Refinancing Is Approved.

Special to THE NEW YORK TIMES.

WASHINGTON, April 28.—In an overwhelming response to the administration's recommendations, the Senate today adopted the Thomas inflation amendment to the farm relief bill and then quickly passed the farm relief measure itself, after voting down the resurrected proposal for immediate payment of the veterans' bonus.

Meanwhile, the Senate adopted an amendment to the Thomas amendment, sponsored by Senator Hayden and approved by the administration, permitting the acceptance of as much as $200,000,000 of silver, at a maximum rate of 50 cents an ounce, in payments on the war debts.

Four decisive roll calls were taken with the following results:

The Thomas amendment, adopted—64 to 21.

The bonus amendment, defeated—60 to 28.

The Hayden amendment, adopted—53 to 32.

The farm bill, passed—64 to 20.

Measure Goes to the House.

The bill will go before the House Monday. That body has passed the farm relief bill proper and the farm mortgage relief sections as separate bills. It has not yet considered the inflation measure, which originated in the Senate. In anticipation of the House's asking a conference on the bill, Vice President Garner tonight named Senators Smith, Fletcher, Thomas of Oklahoma, Wagner, McNary and Walcott as conferees.

The bill now incorporates three alternative plans for giving direct relief to agriculture, a program of refinancing farm mortgages at interest rates of 4½ per cent, and the inflation amendment.

In addition, the measure authorizes the withholding from the market until the Spring of 1934 of all stocks of government-owned cotton and includes a plan to permit cotton growers to take options on these stocks at present low prices in return for a reduction of acreage. Under the latter plan, the grower would be compensated on an advance in price by selling the optioned cotton.

In the inflation amendment are four major authorizations under which the President could, although he has not indicated he will use all the authority, inflate the currency by many billions of dollars.

Inflation Authorizations.

The inflation amendment authorizes:

(1) Expansion of Federal Reserve credits by $3,000,000,000.

(2) The issuance of Treasury notes to a maximum of $3,000,000,000.

(3) Reduction of the gold content of the dollar by as much as 50 per cent, with discretionary authority to fix a definite ratio between silver and gold and provide for the unlimited coinage of silver.

(4) Acceptance of payments on the war debts in silver.

Some of these sections of the bill were added after the original draft was approved, particularly the silver monetization authorization, but it has been emphasized that no amendment was adopted without the administration's approval.

On the three major roll calls an average of only 23 votes was cast against the stand taken by administration leaders.

Only in the last hours of debate today did Senator Robinson of Arkansas, the Democratic floor leader, make an announcement on a question which has been the basis of much speculation, namely, that the inflation amendment is primarily a plan for refinancing obliga-

Continued on Page Four.

"All the News That's Fit to Print."

The New York Times.

LATE CITY EDITION
WEATHER—Fair today and tomorrow; little temperature change
Temperatures Yesterday—Max., 75; Min., 62

VOL. LXXXII....No. 27,509. Entered as Second-Class Matter, Postoffice, New York, N. Y. NEW YORK, FRIDAY, MAY 19, 1933. P TWO CENTS In New York City. | THREE CENTS Within 200 Miles | FOUR CENTS Elsewhere Except in 7th and 8th Postal Zones

GENEVA LOOKS TO REICH TO COOPERATE ON ARMS AS PARLEY MEETS TODAY

OUTLOOK HELD HOPEFUL

But Delegates Await Concrete Statement by Germany.

HITLER IS STRENGTHENED

Even Foes at Home Praise His Address as the Reaction Abroad Is Hailed.

PARIS PUT ON DEFENSIVE

Fears Mildness of the Berlin Address May Compel a Cut in Military Power.

By CLARENCE K. STREIT.

Wireless to THE NEW YORK TIMES.

GENEVA, May 18.—President Roosevelt's message and Chancellor Hitler's statement have changed the character of the much-postponed disarmament conference meeting, which is now scheduled for tomorrow afternoon.

When it was originally called for Monday the idea was to end the deadlock on effectives, materials and procedure by isolating Germany in public debate on the whole disarmament problem at the risk, if this failed, of a breakdown of the conference. Now that corner has been turned, and instead of a fighting type of debate, what looms is an explanatory, negotiating type.

In Another "Final Phase."

All sides are waiting for further views on the Roosevelt and Hitler declarations and for the French and British reactions to judge better what they mean and to measure exactly how the deadlocked situation has been affected. This conference, which moves by crisis and gains ground only when it seems to be breaking down, has lurched, in short, out of another mire into another new "final phase." Credit for this is being given more and more to President Roosevelt, who, one conference official said, "gave Hitler a way out."

The plans for tomorrow's program were still very indefinite late tonight. Arthur Henderson, president of the conference, wants first to consult both Norman H. Davis of the United States and Rudolf Nadolny of Germany, who are expected to arrive here in the morning, to ascertain whether they wish him to lay before the conference the two statements or whether they prefer to speak, each for his own chief.

Indications point to Herr Nadolny's taking the floor first, and to Mr. Davis's making a short declaration, but postponing until late next week detailed announcements regarding the consultation, neutrality and non-aggression pact, about which every one is waiting to hear from him.

Many delegations are anxious to ascertain whether Chancellor Hitler's speech represents a genuine change of policy or merely a time-gaining manoeuvre. One of the first tests will be to see whether his statements on the Reichswehr, Brown Shirts and materials are really as negotiable as they appear to be.

The Reichswehr reference seems to fit in with a compromise that has been talked of here behind the scenes for synchronizing better the change of the professional army into militia with a reduction of materials. Similarly, possibilities are seen for trading Brown Shirts against trained reserves, as Chancellor Hitler seems to desire.

French and Others Skeptical.

The French and other interested delegations remain very skeptical that the German change is more than skin deep, and some talk of the need of "grilling" Herr Nadolny. More impartial circles admit it is hard to believe in Herr Hitler's pacifist denunciation of war while Colonel von Papen remains Vice Chancellor of Germany, and while all German pacifists remain in jail or exile.

But they balance this with the assertion that Herr Hitler is the first German Chancellor who has dared to speak of the Poles in the conciliatory terms he has used and that he is the only man likely to succeed in swinging Germany to these and the other peaceful conceptions he has expressed.

These neutrals desire more proof that Germany really wants to negotiate a disarmament treaty, but

Continued on Page Two.

United Reich Church Joins All Evangelical Lutherans

By The Associated Press.

BERLIN, May 18.—An important step toward unification of German churches was accomplished today by the fusion of all Evangelical Lutheran churches of the Reich, which hitherto were conducted separately in the different German States.

A Federal board was established under the presidency of the Bavarian Bishop, Hans Meiser of Munich. On the board will sit representatives of the church unions of the States.

The object of the fusion, according to the new Nazi statute, is to form a homogeneous Lutheran bloc within the coming Reich's Evangelical Church.

CUBAN TROOPS MASS AS REVOLT WIDENS

Regime Draws In Outposts, Concentrating 600 Men at Sancti Spiritu.

REBEL FORCE PUT AT 2,000

Federals Reported Deserting —Field Commander Asks for Reinforcements.

Wireless to THE NEW YORK TIMES.

HAVANA, May 18.—The revolt now in progress in Santa Clara and Camaguey Provinces spread southward today when fighting broke out in the small village of Omeja, east of Victoria de las Tunas, in Oriente Province, where rebels seized and ransacked a small Rural Guard post, carrying off arms and ammunition.

While military headquarters in Havana asserted no important engagement had taken place today, sniping on government troops now attempting to rout insurgents firmly entrenched in the mountainous districts of the provinces and harassing of small army posts continued.

A request by H. J. Schreber, the American manager of a sugar mill at Jatibonico, Camaguey Province, for replacement of a Rural Guard detachment of about fifteen men at the mill who had disappeared gave color to reports that soldiers were deserting various sections of the turbulent district and joining the insurrectionists.

A traveler returning from Sancti Spiritus who refused to allow his name to be used said this afternoon that government troops being concentrated at that point were estimated at about 600 and all personnel of military outposts were being ordered in with all supplies and equipment to avoid capture by the rebels.

This informant, who has been in the disturbed area in Santa Clara and Camaguey Provinces during the past two weeks, said residents of that region were becoming impatient over the apparent inactivity of the United States Government, which they hoped would solve the distressing political situation. He asserts the strength of the anti-administration element is steadily

Continued on Page Three.

JAPANESE CLOSE IN ON PEIPING SUBURB; CHINESE JOIN FOES

One Force Is Within 6 Miles of Tungchow—Another Is 30 Miles From Tientsin.

MIYUN YIELDS AT LAST

Invaders Sweep Into the City the Chinese Had Defended for More Than a Week.

COMPROMISE HOPE ENDS

Time for Such Action Has Passed, Says Japan — British Guard in Peiping Strengthened.

By HALLETT ABEND.

Wireless to THE NEW YORK TIMES.

TIENTSIN, May 18.—"No one can do anything; the time for compromise has passed," declared a Japanese Army spokesman here today, in announcing the arrival of the vanguard of the central Japanese columns in North China at a village six miles from Tungchow, which is a suburb of Peiping, only thirteen miles from that city.

At the same time the Japanese eastern force, after a rapid advance westward along the Mandarin Highway, reached today a point only thirty miles by airline from Tientsin and was nearing Lutai, which yesterday was the headquarters of the Chinese retreat.

"Unless responsible Chinese agree to our terms without equivocation, without further delay and without new major attacks we will occupy Peiping and Tientsin at once," the highest Japanese official circles in North China notified foreign diplomats today.

Occupation Believed Near.

The greatest significance is attached to the fact that the Japanese Emperor's personal aide de camp, who has been distributing the Emperor's gifts to the Japanese garrison in Tientsin canceled today his reservations for a personal private car and a second-class car for his military guard for a trip to Peiping tomorrow, notifying the railway authorities that the trip had been abandoned in view of the situation.

The British garrison in Peiping sent an additional 150 men of the Queen's regiment to Peiping today, nominally as "replacements" for the legation guard, though actually to reinforce the guard, which is of only 300 men, in contrast with more than 500 marines guarding the United States Legation.

Populace Is Indifferent.

In the face of the fact that the tide of Japanese invasion is rolling southward hourly, marking a momentous period in the history of the Far East, the attitude of indifference of most foreigners and many Chinese is amazing. Japanese Generals and other army men and Japanese consular officials continue to employ Chinese cooks, chauffeurs and other servants and to traverse this city unguarded. Japanese civilians are unmolested in the streets and bargain cheerfully with the Chinese shopkeepers.

Chinese passengers on trains between Tientsin and Peiping were robbed today by disorganized soldiery between the towns of Yangtsun and Peitsang.

By The Associated Press.

TOKYO, May 18.—The city of Miyun, forty miles north of Peiping, which has been the objective of a Japanese drive for the last week, was occupied this afternoon by the attacking army, the Rengo (Japanese) News Agency reported.

$230,000,000 Navy Building Begins Aug. 1 Under Administration's Public Works Plan

Special to THE NEW YORK TIMES.

WASHINGTON, May 18.—A $230,000,000 naval building program, to begin Aug. 1 and continue for three years, is being planned by the administration under authority of the public works section of the national Industrial Recovery bill.

The estimated expenditure during the fiscal year 1934 would be $46,000,000, it was learned today, and not $100,000,000 as previously reported.

Chairman Vinson of the House Naval Committee said today that there would be thirty-four vessels in the program: Twenty destroyers, six cruisers, four submarines, two gunboats and two aircraft carriers.

The present intention was to start their construction as soon as possible after enactment of the proposed legislation, he added.

As introduced yesterday the industrial recovery bill provided that "if in the opinion of the President it seems desirable," the Federal emergency administration of public works should include in its "comprehensive program of public works" the construction of naval vessels within the terms and limits established by the London Naval Treaty of 1930.

Representative Vinson expressed the view today that this language should be broadened to include construction of naval vessels within the terms and limits established by the treaty signed at the Washington arms conference. He has proposed to the administration such an amendment.

Mr. Vinson said the proposed building program was in full harmony with President Roosevelt's message to the heads of fifty-four nations, advocating disarmament and complete elimination of weapons of offensive warfare.

He pointed out that the President, in his parallel disarmament message to Congress, specifically said that "while these steps are being taken no nation shall increase existing armaments over and above the limitations of treaty obligations."

State Beer Board Favors Bars; 20,000 Places to Lose Licenses

Sales at Road Stands, Lunch Wagons and Filling Stations Will Cease on June 1 When the New Regulations Take Effect.

Special to THE NEW YORK TIMES.

ALBANY, May 18.—About 20,000 places now selling beer will go out of business when the new licenses go into effect on June 1. The State Alcohol Beverage Control Board is prepared to make a careful check on the applications which have been filed thus far and all that arrive in the next few days.

Chairman Mulrooney is planning for a meeting of the board in New York City tomorrow, when final details for the selling of beer will be discussed. It is believed that when the license applications are checked up it will be found that about 10,000 places in New York City will be closed and an equal number up-State. Chairman Mulrooney said that gasoline stations, news rooms, road stands, lunch wagons and other similar places will be forced to stop selling beer.

At present about 60,000 places in the State are selling beer. This number will probably be cut down to 40,000.

"We have checked the number of liquor licenses that were issued by the State before prohibition," Chairman Mulrooney said, "and we find that the highest number was 22,000 and that the number had shrunk to about 14,000 in 1919, the year when prohibition went into effect."

The question of bars will be one of the most important to be determined at tomorrow's meeting. Chairman Mulrooney believes that bars had little to do with the complaints against the saloon of other days.

"The old saloon abuses were conducted in the back room," he said. "It was there that gambling, drunkenness and other abuses were carried on."

He pointed out that the new State law prohibits any alliance between brewery and saloon such as formerly existed.

Mr. Mulrooney said a strong sentiment for bars has been indicated at meetings of the board. Workingmen would not like to be compelled to sit at a table and tip a waiter after being served with beer, he declared.

Mr. Mulrooney made it plain that gangsters, racketeers and other offenders against the dry laws will not receive licenses to sell beer.

UNTERMYER ASSAILS TAMMANY MISRULE

Long a Defender, Now Scores Extravagance, Incompetence and Padded Payroll.

ATTACKS BAR'S INACTIVITY

He Sees City Near Bankruptcy —Judge Knox Denounces Party's Frauds at Polls.

Samuel Untermyer, who for years has been a stanch defender of Tammany Hall, joined the ranks of its critics last night. He declared that New York had been driven to the verge of bankruptcy by the "extravagance and incompetence of the management of the city, with its padded payrolls."

Mr. Untermyer addressed himself to a large group of lawyers and judges attending the Bronx County Bar Association's testimonial dinner to Supreme Court Justices Charles B. McLaughlin and Edward R. Koch and City Court Justice I. J. P. Adlerman at the Hotel Astor. In a broad plea to members of his profession to take a more active and effective part in public affairs, Mr. Untermyer called for reform in methods of selecting the judiciary.

Tammany Hall was attacked from another quarter earlier in the day and by another Democrat, Federal Judge John C. Knox, who has been presiding over the election fraud cases. Addressing a luncheon of the New York Young Democratic Club, he declared that the people of the city had lost confidence in the party locally. Although he was a Democrat Judge Knox asserted he had not reached the "stage of partisanship which will condone repeaters, strong-arm men, terrorism of voters and false returns of a canvass."

"Neither do I believe," he added, "that any decent Democrat can lend approval to such conduct."

1,500 At the Dinner.

J. Philip Van Kirk, president of the Bronx County Bar Association, presided at the dinner, which was attended by about 1,500 guests. Other speakers besides Mr. Untermyer were James W. Gerard, former Ambassador to Germany, and Edward P. Mulrooney, chairman of the New York State Alcoholic Beverage Control Board, who praised each of the three new members of the judiciary.

Mr. Gerard warned of the dangers of uncontrolled inflation and declared that the danger point of inflation was reached when governments met their obligations in fiat money. He urged members of the bar to use their influence to prevent its reaching that stage in this country. Referring to the disbarment of Jewish lawyers in Germany under the Hitler régime, Mr. Gerard declared members of the profession here had been remiss in not organizing a mass meeting to make formal protest.

"In all history," he said, "there is nothing more cruel than the treatment of the Jews in Germany today."

Judiciary Reforms Asked.

After denouncing the anti-trust laws as uneconomic and unenforceable, and calling for stricter regulation of the New York Stock Exchange, the operations of which he said were "subject to no law," Mr. Untermyer, who helped shape

Continued on Page Six.

MRS. BELMONT NAMED TO BOARD OF OPERA

She Is One of 5 New Directors, First Woman So Honored—Headed $300,000 Drive.

JUILLIARD AIDE CHOSEN

Wardwell, Trustee of Fund, Added With C. N. Bliss, R. S. Brewster and M. C. Taylor.

Mrs. August Belmont is the first woman to serve on the board of directors of the Metropolitan Opera Company. She was one of the five new members elected at the annual stockholders' meeting at the Metropolitan Opera House yesterday afternoon. The other new members are Cornelius N. Bliss, Robert S. Brewster, Myron C. Taylor and Allen Wardwell.

The resignations of two members who have been on the board for many years, R. Fulton Cutting and Edward T. Stotesbury, were accepted. Mr. Cutting resides in Buffalo and as his business is there he is unable to attend all the meetings of the board, it was said, and Mr. Stotesbury, whose home is in Philadelphia, finds it inconvenient to get to New York for the regular meetings of the board.

17 Are Re-elected.

The five new directors were elected for a term of one year, as were the seventeen directors who were re-elected. Those who remain on the directorate are Paul D. Cravath, chairman; Vincent Astor, Robert Low Bacon, Rawlins L. Cottenet, Clarence Dillon, Louis Eckstein, Marshall Field, Frank Gray Griswold, E. Roland Harriman, Charles Hayden, Frederic A. Juilliard, Otto H. Kahn, Ivy L. Lee, Clarence H. Mackay, Frederic Potts Moore, Cornelius Vanderbilt Whitney and Henry Rogers Winthrop.

Yesterday's election brought the list of directors up to the number stipulated in the by-laws of the company. The Metropolitan Opera Company is the stock corporation which was the operating company of the Opera House until the Spring of 1932. At that time the Metropolitan Opera Association, a membership corporation, was organized and is the present operating company. The company leases its sets, scores and other properties to the association. The same board of directors serves both companies.

Mrs. Belmont's interest in the Metropolitan goes back more than three decades. As the famous actress, Eleanor Robson, she used to slip out after performances at the Empire Theatre, just across Broadway, and buy admission at the Metropolitan to hear Calvé, Ternina or Caruso. Her interest in the first lyric stage of the country has never lapsed, and during the recent drive to save the Metropolitan by raising a fund of $300,000 Mrs. Belmont took an active part. She appeared on the stage of the Metropolitan two months ago to speak in behalf of this drive. At the Opera Ball, which was the culminating event of the drive and which had as its setting the court of the Empress Eugénie in Paris in 1860, Mrs. Belmont took the rôle of the Empress in the pageant.

Mrs. Belmont's interests, however, have been far-flung and varied. Ever since her marriage to August Belmont in 1910, when she retired from an active career on the stage, she has occupied her-

Continued on Page Ten.

POWER MEN ACCUSED AT MUSCLE SHOALS; NORRIS BILL SIGNED

Alabama and Tennessee Companies Charged With Cheating and Damaging Plant.

CONGRESS INQUIRY LOOMS

Cummings Is Investigating Complaint — Companies' Heads Deny Charges.

PRESIDENT ACTS ON BILL

Warns Investors to Beware of Land Speculators After Approving Long Fought Bill.

Special to THE NEW YORK TIMES.

WASHINGTON, May 18.—An investigation by Congress of alleged misuse of government property at Muscle Shoals by two private power companies with the acquiescence of plant authorities was in prospect today, following disclosures made by Secretary Ickes as President Roosevelt signed the Norris bill providing direct government operation and control of the huge Federal development.

After a conference with Secretary Ickes this afternoon, the President called in Huston Thompson, former counsel for the Federal Trade Commission and special assistant to the Attorney General, who is understood to have been selected to investigate the charges.

Involved in the case, which took Washington by surprise, are charges that the Alabama Power Company and the Tennessee Power Company, which lease power from the government plant under a contract with the War Department, have been using its facilities to effect an interchange of surplus energy. In this way the two affiliates of the Commonwealth and Southern Corporation are alleged not only to have reduced the cost of their contract with the government, but also damaged government property and placed the policy of government operation in a bad light.

Charges Contained in Report.

These alleged irregularities are stated in a report made by Louis R. Glavis, special investigator for the Interior Department, which for a month has been in the hands of officials of the Department of Justice, who have extended the inquiry with a view to possible future prosecutions.

Secretary Ickes said the case was now in the hands of the Department of Justice, which was to decide whether any civil or criminal violations were involved.

"The practice complained of was first noticed," said Secretary Ickes, "by an electrical engineer who was in the party of President Roosevelt and Senator Norris when they went on an inspection trip of the Muscle Shoals plant last January. Nothing was done about it at the time, but the engineer subsequently wrote to the Senator about it, and his letter was turned over by Senator Norris to the President, who ordered me to make an investigation. I called in Mr. Glavis, who was formerly connected with the Federal Power Commission, to investigate.

The wartime power plant, costing $140,000,000 has been under the jurisdiction of the War Department, with army engineers directly in charge. Under an arrangement with this department, the Alabama Power Company was authorized to purchase government-produced

Continued on Page Three.

O'Brien Asks Crews to Quit Tax Board; Reprisal Is Seen for Defeat of Hastings

Without any explanation, Mayor O'Brien has asked for the resignation of John R. Crews, one of the two Republicans on the Board of Taxes and Assessments, it was disclosed last night. The mysterious move had leaders in both the Brooklyn Republican and Democratic organizations guessing as to the cause.

With the aid of John F. Curry, Tammany leader, Mayor O'Brien recently brought about the retirement of George Henry Payne, the other Republican member of the tax board, to make way for the appointment of Thomas W. Whittle, Bronx district leader, thus causing a bitter controversy between the Bronx Republican organization and W. Kingsland Macy, Republican State leader.

But if this strategy had any connection with Mayor O'Brien's request to Commissioner Crews, both John H. McCooey, Brooklyn Democratic leader, and Frederick J. H. Kracke, Brooklyn Republican leader, declined to throw any light on it. Mr. McCooey professed ignorance of the move; Mr. Kracke grew angry when asked if he sought the post. The Brooklyn Republican leader will shortly resign as Federal Port Appraiser to make way for a Democrat.

Mr. Crews, a Republican district leader, would not discuss the Mayor's action other than to admit he had not sent the resignation. Friends of Mr. Crews said the basis for the demand was in the defeat of John A. Hastings for the State Senate in the Seventh Brooklyn District last year.

The city charter provides that two members of the Tax Board of seven members shall be affiliated with the minority party. The salary is $10,800 annually. The term of office is "at the pleasure of the Mayor."

Mr. Crews, who had been in Trinity Hospital with arthritis for a month, hobbled to his office from the hospital for the first time on Wednesday. He had hardly greeted his subordinates when Thomas F. McAndrews, secretary to the Mayor, called on the telephone to say that Mr. O'Brien would like to have the commissioner's resignation. Mr. Crews, dumfounded, asked for an explanation but Mr. McAndrews merely expressed his sympathy.

HUGH S. JOHNSON CHOSEN 'DICTATOR' OF INDUSTRY; FOUR TAX PLANS OFFERED

Lord Ashfield, Transit Head, Was Detroit Messenger Boy

Wireless to THE NEW YORK TIMES.

LONDON, May 18.—Lord Ashfield, who started work in life as a messenger boy for a Detroit trolley company, was today appointed chief controller of all London's subways, tramways and omnibuses at a salary of about £12,500 ($48,750 at current exchange).

As chairman of London's new Passenger Transport Board, he will control local transit systems in an area occupied by 10,000,000 persons.

Frank Pick, managing director of the underground group, which Lord Ashfield has revolutionized, joins the new board as a full-time member at a salary of £10,000 ($39,000).

DOUGLAS SUBMITS LEVIES FOR WORKS

Sales Tax, Suggested by the Budget Chief to House Committee, Is Held Favored.

OTHER CHOICES ADVANCED

They Include Higher Income Rates and Putting Dividends Under Increased Normal Levy.

Special to THE NEW YORK TIMES.

WASHINGTON, May 18.—Passage by the House of President Roosevelt's industrial recovery bill by the end of next week was predicted today by Democratic Leader Byrns and Chairman Doughton, as the Ways and Means Committee began a study of four tax programs, submitted by Director of the Budget Douglas, with which to finance the $3,300,000,000 public works program contemplated in the measure. Mr. Doughton expressed the hope that House action would be obtained as early as Tuesday or Wednesday.

Mr. Douglas's four-way tax plan included:

1—A general manufacturers' sales tax of 1½ per cent without exemption, to raise $214,000,000, or a 1 1-5 per cent tax to raise $224,000,000.

2—Sharp increases in normal income tax rates.

3—Application of normal income tax levies to corporation dividends.

4—Other miscellaneous levies, such as a tax on coffee, tea and cocoa, increases in admission taxes, telephone toll and gasoline taxes.

It was generally believed, however, that the general sales tax was favored by the administration and would be adopted.

At least $220,000,000 in new taxes will be required to furnish the sinking fund and interest for borrowings which the Treasury will have to make, and the Budget Director insisted that this be amply provided before the goverment embarked upon such an extensive program.

Mr. Douglas reiterated the suggestion made by President Roosevelt in his message yesterday that

Continued on Page Four.

NEW LAW IS ANTICIPATED

President Telephones Associate of Baruch of His Selection.

ANSWER AWAITS PASSAGE

As Administrator, He Would Have Under Roosevelt Vast Powers Over Business.

LEADER IN DRAFTING BILL

Plans Made to Put Measure in Operation Within Week After It Is Enacted.

WASHINGTON, May 18.—To administer the almost unlimited powers over industry which would be conferred upon the government by the pending Industrial Regulation Bill, President Roosevelt has chosen Hugh S. Johnson, soldier, lawyer and manufacturer.

The post was offered to General Johnson by the Chief Executive over the telephone and he immediately set about whipping together a tentative organization, although the bill had been laid before Congress only twenty-four hours before. He has not given his answer to President Roosevelt as yet, however.

In view of the fact that General Johnson was one of those foremost in drafting the bill, the administration expected him to accept the appointment when the post is formally created by passage of the sweeping public works-industrial control measure.

Headed First Draft Board.

A close associate of Bernard Baruch, Democratic leader and New York financier, General Johnson was a member of the old War Industries Board. He also was head of the first draft board during the World War and since then has had extensive experience in manufacturing.

As administrator of industry with the authority created by the momentous bill which President Roosevelt sent to Congress yesterday, General Johnson would have the most extensive powers ever wielded by one man over the private business enterprises of the nation.

The legislation, which declares the existence of a national emergency, is designed to present to the President broad powers to approve agreements within industry for the purpose of stabilizing production, regulating working hours and setting minimum wages.

It also authorizes a rigid system of licensed industry, if necessary, to enforce the agreements. It empowers the Chief Executive to transfer this authority to an administrator.

As a leader among those who drafted the bill, the former Brigadier General was asked by the Chief Executive to undertake the difficult task of administering it.

Seated tonight in his apartment, he declined to say that he would accept the post, but admitted in answer to questions that it would not be easy to refuse.

Confers With Baruch.

Soon afterward he went into conference with Mr. Baruch, with whom he has been associated since before the war, and Lewis W. Douglas, Director of the Budget, who worked with him far into the night for many nights in completing the legislation.

Called to Washington to lend his wide experience in the drafting of a bill to bring industry together as a cooperative instrument for combating the depression. General Johnson had no idea that he was writing legislation which he would be called upon to administer.

"My major thought is that I may not be the most competent to handle this bill," he said when confronted with the assertion that it was known he was to be the administrator.

He was born in Kansas in 1882 and was graduated from Oklahoma Northwestern Normal School in 1901. He turned to the army for a career and was graduated from West Point in 1903. When he retired in 1919 he was a Brigadier General.

Since leaving the army he has been vice president and general counsel of the Moline Plow Company, and since 1925 has been

Continued on Page Four.

"All the News That's Fit to Print."

The New York Times.

LATE CITY EDITION
WEATHER—Fair today; tomorrow local thunder showers.
Temperatures Yesterday—Max., 76; Min., 57

Copyright, 1933, by The New York Times Company.

VOL. LXXXII....No. 27,514. Entered as Second-Class Matter, Postoffice, New York, N. Y. NEW YORK, WEDNESDAY, MAY 24, 1933. P TWO CENTS In New York City. | THREE CENTS Within 200 Miles | FOUR CENTS Elsewhere Except in 7th and 8th Postal Zones

REPEAL BY 20 TO 1 IS VOTED IN STATE; 6TH WET VICTORY

41-TO-1 LEAD IN THE CITY

Wet Majority Exceeds All Estimates, Rising to Above a Million.

VOTE LIGHT IN RURAL AREAS

Lack of Interest May Put All but One Prohibition County in the Repeal Column.

BIG UPSET IN DRY NASSAU

It Goes 51,594 for Repeal to 3,651 Against—Roosevelt District Heavily Wet.

New York State voted yesterday by a tremendous majority to ratify the Congressional resolution to repeal the Eighteenth Amendment.

New York, home of President Roosevelt, thus became the sixth State to vote to ratify the repeal amendment, the others being Michigan, Wisconsin, Wyoming, Rhode Island and New Jersey. The magnitude of the wet victory by a vote which may be 20 to 1 in the entire State, double the most optimistic estimates of the repeal advocates, is expected to have great influence in other States, thirty more of which are necessary for ratification.

The wet victory at yesterday's special election far exceeded the last test on prohibition in this State, which was held in 1926. At that time a referendum to memorialize Congress to modify the Volstead Act to permit each State to determine whether a beverage was intoxicating in fact was carried by a vote of three to one and a majority of about 1,200,000.

Lead 41 to 1 in the City.

The vote against prohibition in New York City was about forty-one to one. The majority for repeal was more than a million. Up-State, with incomplete returns from about half the counties and one-quarter of the election districts, the vote for repeal was about four to one, which ratio will be cut down by later returns from rural counties, where the dry strength is centred.

With the leaders of the three official parties, Democratic, Republican and Socialist, united in support of the 150 repeal candidates for delegates to the ratification convention at Albany on June 27, there was little effective dry organization in the cities. Up to 2 o'clock this morning the dry candidates were leading only in incomplete returns from Yates County, and the anti-prohibition leaders estimated that the drys would carry only this county and possibly Schoharie and Allegany.

The vote in New York City, complete, was 1,047,068 for repeal and 25,506 against it, a majority for repeal of 1,021,562.

The Vote by Boroughs.

The vote by boroughs in New York City follows:

Boroughs.	For.	Against.	Elec. Dists. Miss'g.
Manhattan ...	269,420	5,216	0
Bronx	186,572	2,867	0
Brooklyn	360,688	10,262	0
Queens	201,195	5,520	0
Richmond	29,193	1,641	0
Total	1,047,068	25,506	0

Incomplete returns from up-State with approximately half the counties and a fifth of the election districts represented gave an actual majority for repeal of 190,143 and a vote of about 4 to 1, which ratio will be cut down by later returns from the rural counties. The actual up-State vote with 4,002 out of 5,043 election districts missing was 217 for repeal and 27,013 against it.

The result of the votes tabulated is shown by the following table:

Majority for repeal 1,331,393, with 3,006 election districts missing out of 8,837.

	For Repeal.	Against Repeal.	Elec. Dists. Miss'g.
New York City..	1,047,068	25,506	0
Up-State	403,608	93,778	3,006
Totals	1,450,677	119,284	

Surprise in Nassau.

Nassau County, originally regarded as dry, furnished a surprise in the extent of the repeal victory. With only two election districts missing the vote in that county was 51,594 for repeal and 3,651 against repeal.

The home election district of

Continued on Page Two.

Not a Vote Cast by Drys In 16 Districts in the City

The overwhelming vote for repeal in New York City yesterday manifested itself by a clean sweep for the ratification slate of delegates in a number of election districts.

As the returns were compiled four districts in Queens, three in Brooklyn, eight in the Bronx and one in Richmond showed as many as 300 votes for repeal, with not a ballot against it.

The zero for the drys was not confined to New York City. Montauk, L. I., known as the rum port of New York during the years of prohibition, went solidly for repeal, 124 to 0.

GENEVA ADVANCES CURB ON BIG GUNS

First Reading of Chapter of Draft Convention Results From Davis's Pledges.

FRANCE BALKS AT TERMS

Paul-Boncour Insits That the Banned Weapons Be Given to League Police Force.

By CLARENCE K. STREIT.

Wireless to THE NEW YORK TIMES.

GENEVA, May 23.—The disarmament conference today ended the first reading of the chapter in the draft convention abolishing the most formidable army weapons, big cannons and big tanks.

One week ago few here believed it possible even to discuss this chapter. The improvement in the atmosphere was not the most astonishing development. Disarmament made notable, concrete progress today in every article discussed.

Reaction to Davis Pledges.

That was the first reaction to yesterday's promise by Norman H. Davis of the United States that if a disarmament treaty were reached the United States would join in supervising it, would pass neutral judgment on every threat to peace and refrain from interfering with the collective enforcement of peace against aggression. The day's most eloquent individual commentaries on that promise were these:

The French, who insisted yesterday that the European mutual assistance pact be discussed before touching on weapons, agreed this morning to take up weapons first. The Germans and the Italians then agreed to talk on security tomorrow. It was decided thus to alternate in the future.

The Germans opened the afternoon meeting by withdrawing all their amendments to the chapter on army weapons which, with the amendment barring the immediate standardizing of European armies, which they withdrew yesterday, had helped to bring the conference to its recent deadlock. They still ask that all cannon above 4½ inches be destroyed within five years.

Their tone was very conciliatory and, instead of defeating their disarmament claims by making the question appear a Franco-German issue and arousing animosity and suspicion, they kept in the background.

That step appealed to the disinterested Dutch, Swedish and Norwegian delegates. The Germans thus allowed the full force of neutral opinion to be brought to bear on the British and French. The British, by conceding several points, left the French sufficiently isolated for the Japanese to cease stressing that this conference will fail.

Britain to Meet Objections.

The British, under pressure of Dutch, Swedish and Chinese delegates, who stressed the ease with which mobile guns could be saved by removing the wheels and calling them coast-defense cannon, conceded "there is force in the contention that coast-defense guns should be limited." The British spoke rather receptively on limiting also the number of small cannon and agreed their draft had "loopholes" which they said they would be glad to fill before the second reading.

Arthur Henderson, chairman of the conference, quickly arranged for that to be pushed in private

Continued on Page Four.

NORTH CHINA TRUCE REPORTED REACHED; JAPANESE ADVANCE

Agreement Is Said to Bar Occupation of Peiping by Invading Forces.

HEAVY FIGHTING OBSERVED

Tokyo Foreign Office States Armistice Is Ready for Signing Tomorrow.

FOREIGN ENVOYS CONFER

American, British and French Ministers Meet as Japanese Set Up Patrolling Forces.

By HALLETT ABEND.

Special Cable to THE NEW YORK TIMES.

TIENTSIN, China, Wednesday, May 24.—It is taken for granted here that the Japanese forces will occupy Peiping today, for while official and unofficial Chinese sources asserted that some form of truce had been signed which would obviate Japanese occupation of the city, Japanese here officially made a flat denial of the statements.

[The Tokyo Foreign Office announced an armistice would be signed by the Chinese tomorrow, in contradiction to the Tientsin denials.]

Moreover, the facts appeared to confirm the Japanese denial because fighting went on along the Tungchow front at a point ten miles from Peiping, as well as along the front north of Tientsin, and Japanese cavalry were only five miles from Peiping yesterday (Tuesday) and were continuing to converge rapidly upon the ancient capital.

The evacuation of Nanking troops from Peiping continued throughout the day, but it was noticeable that the troops of most of the North China Generals were not participating in the retreat southward along the Peiping-Hankow Railway. Those leaders were tenuously holding their positions, watching hopefully for a new political alignment.

Bombing Planes Fly Over City.

Three big Japanese bombing monoplanes flew over Peiping, and while soaring over the city they were joined by three biplanes. The Japanese fliers did no bombing, but merely observed the progress of the evacuation. The big planes each carried three men, three machine guns and a full load of bombs.

The Japanese sent 600 reinforcements from Tientsin to the legation guard at Peiping during the day.

In connection with the reports of a truce, Sei-ichiro Nakayama, the Japanese Chargé d'Affaires at Peiping, said:

"Japan is not negotiating with any Chinese. Instead Japanese operations are proceeding along the entire front."

And his declaration was supported by assertions at the headquarters of Lieut. Gen. Kotaro Nakamura, commander of the Japanese concession garrison here.

A spokesman for General Nakamura went so far as to say that after the Japanese forces had entered Peiping an "independent North China" would be founded, but he would not reveal the name of the proposed new government of North China.

Apparently the evacuation of Peiping by the Nanking troops astounded Chinese military leaders here. At any rate, Yu Hsueh-chung, Governor of Hopei Province, continued to hold this city for the Chinese. Fighting took place near Lutai, thirty miles to the north on the Shanhaikwan-Tientsin Railway,

Continued on Page Seven.

R. F. C. Has Only $1,468 Left Of $300,000,000 Relief Fund

By The Associated Press.

WASHINGTON, May 23.—The Reconstruction Finance Corporation today allotted $78,560 of its emergency relief fund to assist five States over the rest of May.

This leaves $1,468 of the $300,000,000 appropriated last Summer by Congress to be allocated in the next nine days, after which the corporation relief activities will cease and will be taken over by the Emergency Relief Administration, headed by Harry L. Hopkins.

Money was allocated today as follows: Maine, $42,255 for use in nine political subdivisions from May 20 to May 31; Indiana, $24,599 for seven counties; North Dakota, $3,203 for use in three political subdivisions; Virginia, $5,060 for one undesignated political subdivision, and Michigan, $3,443 for use in Wayne County outside the city of Detroit.

ELECTRICAL GROUP FOR INDUSTRY ACT

Manufacturers Vote to Cooperate With Roosevelt in Regulation Program

AS THE WAY TO RECOVERY

First Big Industry to Declare Intention to Try Partnership With Government.

By LOUIS STARK.

Special to THE NEW YORK TIMES.

HOT SPRINGS, Va., May 23.—Aware of the "wholly and utterly revolutionary" nature of the proposed National Industrial Recovery Act, the electrical manufacturing industry, by vote of its members tonight, became the first large industry to signify its intention of embarking on the new experiment of partnership between government and industry.

Acting for companies which employed 250,000 men and women in 1929 and which did a business of $2,500,000,000 that year in making everything electrical "from doorbells to 400,000-horsepower turbines," the 269 members of the National Electrical Manufacturers Association conveyed blanket authority to the thirty members of the board of governors. They authorized the board of governors to do anything that may be required under the Recovery Act or any law having similar purposes.

In order to obtain sufficient power to cooperate promptly and effectively with President Roosevelt or his authorized agent in carrying out the terms of the pending act, the board of governors met this morning and asked the members to amend the constitution and confer on them more sweeping power than had hitherto resided in the board. At the same time the governors formulated a resolution declaring that the association should act promptly and effectively in view of the imminence of legislation for the regulation of industry. The resolution was adopted tonight, after considerable discussion.

J. S. Tritle, president of the association and vice president and general manager of Westinghouse Electric and Manufacturing Company, declared that "the action taken today is in line with the desire of the National Electrical Manufacturers Association to offer its hearty and loyal support and sincere cooperation to the President and the agency delegated by him so that through the joint effort of government and industry employment and purchasing power may be increased and the well-being of

Continued on Page Thirteen.

Women's Forest Work Camps May Be Set Up If Enough Ask Them, Says Mrs. Roosevelt

Special to THE NEW YORK TIMES.

WASHINGTON, May 23.—Reforestation camps for women, where they can be employed on emergency conservation work under the same conditions as men, though in different lines of work, may be established if women in sufficient numbers desire them, Mrs. Roosevelt said at her press conference today.

Several letters addressed to her on the subject, she said, had been turned over to Miss Frances Perkins, Secretary of Labor, with a request for investigation and an expression of opinion as to the feasibility of such a project.

Mrs. Roosevelt said that she agreed with suggestions which had been advanced as to the practicability of the employment of women on work in plant and tree nurseries, and their instruction in horticulture to fit them for undertaking that line of work on their own account when the present emergency was a thing of the past.

There was, she said, no obstacle to the use of funds provided for emergency conservation work for the establishment of camps for women, provided the applicants for admission justified such an addition to the original plan.

Mrs. Roosevelt returned from New York this morning by air line and held her press conference within an hour of her arrival. She made the trip in an army plane with the Secretary of War and Mrs. Dern.

This afternoon she entertained at tea on the south portico the men and women who worked with Admiral Grayson on the inauguration committee. Tomorrow afternoon she will be the honor guest at a garden bridge party to be given at the home of Admiral and Mrs. Grayson by the Women's National Democratic Club.

CREDIT EXPANSION BEGUN BY WOODIN AS RECOVERY STEP

Reserve Banks Authorized to Buy $25,000,000 in Federal Bonds in Open Market.

MOVE WILL RELEASE CASH

Expectation Is That It Will Be Used for Industrial and Commercial Loans.

SPRAGUE BECOMES ADVISER

Harvard Professor, Hitherto Aide of Bank of England, Accepts Treasury Post.

Special to THE NEW YORK TIMES.

WASHINGTON, May 23.—Secretary Woodin started the government on its credit expansion program today with authorization to the Federal Reserve Banks to buy $25,000,000 in government securities in the open market and thus release commercial credit. This is one of the chief steps in President Roosevelt's national recovery program.

Coincidentally Mr. Woodin announced the appointment of Professor O. M. W. Sprague of Harvard University, hitherto an adviser to the Bank of England, as financial and economic adviser to the United States Government with the rank of executive assistant to the Secretary of the Treasury.

The effect of the open-market operations will be to release $25,000,000 in cash, which will be added to the excess reserve balances of Federal Reserve Banks available for industrial and commercial purposes. There is said to be a demand for commercial and industrial loans and the expectation is that **commercial banks will now be more liberal in granting credit.**

Announcement Follows Conference.

Secretary Woodin declined to indicate what volume of government obligations would be added to the investment portfolios of the Reserve banks. Purchases will be made from time to time as conditions justify, he said.

The open-market operations will not be on the gigantic scale started in April, 1932, when for a substantial period the Reserve banks averaged purchases of $100,000,000 a week, according to Mr. Woodin.

Governor Black of the Federal Reserve System conferred with Governor Harrison of the New York bank, Governor Roy A. Young of the Boston bank and other officials prior to the announcement.

Officials believed that further acquisition of government securities from time to time would have a stimulating influence on the general situation and would prove an aid to the June financing by the Treasury. On June 14, $373,856,500 in 1½ per cent certificates mature and will be retired. A bond issue for a larger amount may be authorized at that time. Federal Reserve and Treasury officials, including Professor Sprague, will confer soon to work out details of the new offering.

The Federal Reserve banks, prior to today's operations, held $1,837,000,000 in government securities, there having been no change since April 5. On Jan. 4 the holdings were $1,851,000,000, a level of $1,085,000,000 greater than a year earlier. The present level is about $371,000,000 greater than on May 18, 1932.

In addition to purchases in the open market, the Federal Reserve Banks are authorized to acquire government securities directly from the Treasury. While it is the intent of the Treasury to market the new construction bonds and other securities in the regular way, by sale to the investing public, should it not be possible to obtain the funds desired in that way the government could fall back on the Reserve Banks.

One belief is held that the government may float more than $4,000,000,000 in bonds in the next two years, although the general business situation and the rate of business recovery will determine definitely what course is to be pursued. The Treasury will borrow at one time only funds which can be employed promptly.

The Federal Reserve Banks have also adopted the policy of substituting Federal Reserve Bank notes for Federal Reserve notes. The bank notes may be backed by the government securities and eligible paper, while reserve notes must have at least forty per cent gold backing, the remainder eligible paper and government securities.

By substitution of the bank notes a considerable quantity of gold is freed for any domestic or international purpose which may be

Continued on Page Three.

MORGAN PAID NO INCOME TAX FOR THE YEARS 1931 AND 1932; NEITHER DID HIS PARTNERS

Morgan Inquiry Highlights

Special to THE NEW YORK TIMES.

WASHINGTON, May 23.—Following are the more important points in today's investigation of J. P. Morgan & Co. by the Senate committee on banking and currency:

Admission by J. P. Morgan that he paid no income taxes for 1931 or 1932, it being inferred but not explained that this was due to business losses.

Statement by Leonard Keyes, office manager, who prepared income tax returns for the firm, that none of the Morgan partners paid an income tax for 1931 or 1932.

Attempt to show that the admission of S. Parker Gilbert as a partner on Jan. 2, 1931, two days after the close of the taxable year, was for the purpose of revaluing securities on a cost basis, and permitting the firm to show a loss of $21,000,000, which could have been charged against profits for the next year.

Demand by J. P. Morgan that Mr. Keyes be permitted to clear up this point by showing that the revaluation always occurred when a partner left the firm or joined, and at no other time, and that on some previous occasions such revaluations had resulted in larger sums being paid to the government in taxes.

Objection to presenting in the record the names of bank officials to whom the Morgan company had made loans, and the names of subscribers to securities issued by the firm at prices below public offerings. This was voted down in executive session, permitting Ferdinand Pecora, counsel, to continue with his planned investigation, by which he hopes to show a "peculiar relationship" between Morgan & Co. and other banking officials.

Mr. Morgan's statement that he can see no inconsistency in a member of his firm being a director of a corporation, and that the interests of the firm and the corporation in a financial matter may be identical.

Disagreement among Senators, bickering, and the unusual spectacle of some of them, including Senator Glass, rushing to Mr. Morgan's assistance when the latter was pressed for an answer.

Statement of firm's assets showing great losses between 1927 and 1931, in both deposits and capital.

SENATORS QUESTION HIM

Banking Firm Revalued Securities and Showed $21,000,000 Loss.

$48,000 TAX PAID IN 1930

Pecora Challenges Statement That Write Off Dated With Gilbert's Partnership.

HUGE DECREASE IN ASSETS

Counsel and Senators Clash Over Listing Loans Made to Other Bankers.

Special to THE NEW YORK TIMES.

WASHINGTON, May 23.—J. P. Morgan, head of the international banking firm which bears his name, paid no income tax in 1931 and 1932, nor did any of his partners.

This fact was established today through questioning of Mr. Morgan by members of the Senate Banking and Currency Committee and by Ferdinand Pecora, committee counsel for the investigation. In 1930, it was indicated but not confirmed, the aggregate income tax payments of Mr. Morgan and his partners was about $48,000.

An attempt also was made to show that the reorganization of the firm, made Jan. 2, 1931, when a new partner, S. Parker Gilbert, was admitted, was for the purpose of permitting the revaluation of securities to show a loss of $21,000,000.

Mr. Pecora read into the record the report of an Internal Revenue agent that the Morgan firm changed its estimates of losses and gains through the sale of assets at market values, to carrying them at cost after July 1, 1930. A witness for the firm denied this, however, by saying that the firm was not qualified under the tax laws as a dealer who can inventory the cost or market value, according to which is lowest.

The admission of Mr. Gilbert at that time rather than before the end of the previous year merely happened naturally, however, Mr. Morgan maintained. At the time the revaluation was made, the loss could have been applied to profits for the years 1932 and 1933, but the law was revised and there were no profits in 1932.

In a Senatorial Cross Fire.

These were the chief developments during a long, hot day of bickering, in which Mr. Morgan, mild and genial, sat between the fire of two groups of Senators on the committee and was generally uncomfortable. Not the least interesting aspect of the hearing was Senatorial dissension, which frequently brought Senator Glass to grips with Mr. Pecora and also with the pugnacious Senator Couzens.

At one time during the afternoon it seemed that the rather muddled picture of how $21,000,000 was written-off for income-tax purposes might be left overnight without an explanation other than Mr. Morgan's statement that he did not know anything about the details. But when the committee was about to go into executive session, Mr. Morgan turned to Mr. Pecora and in a firm voice demanded that this be cleared up at once so that the country would not get a wrong impression of what had occurred.

After some hesitation Mr. Pecora yielded and Leonard Keyes, office manager of the firm, who handles income-tax matters, took the stand. He said that although it was known before Dec. 31, 1930, the close of the tax year, that Mr. Gilbert was to join the firm, there was no intent to defer his joining it. In the fact that he joined on Jan. 2, 1931, and that the revaluation at cost instead of current market value then took place.

Although revaluation had taken place at the end of the taxable year, he said, there were other years when, by death or retirement of partners or other reasons, such revaluation had taken place at other times, and during several of those years the firm had paid a greater income tax than would have been paid had such procedure not been followed.

Crowd Packs the Room.

There has been no hearing like this since Teapot Dome. The fact that Mr. Morgan, whose name has been a magic one in American finance since the house of Morgan

Continued on Page Sixteen.

INDUSTRY BILL VOTE EXPECTED FRIDAY

Rule Limiting Debate and Allowing Only Committee Changes Scheduled.

INCOME TAX PROTESTED

Ballot on Sales Levy May Be Allowed Through Motion to Recommit.

Special to THE NEW YORK TIMES.

WASHINGTON, May 23.—President Roosevelt's Industrial Recovery Bill, combining a far-reaching plan for Federal control of industry with a $3,300,000,000 public works authorization and a $700,000,000 tax program, was today all set to go through the House before the end of the week.

A special rule is expected to be reported by the Rules Committee when the House meets tomorrow, limiting debate to not more than five hours, precluding all but committee amendments and providing for a vote not later than Friday.

The rule, in all probability, will permit a vote on the sales tax through a motion to recommit the whole bill to the Ways and Means Committee with instructions to write in this levy. Otherwise, it will be "air tight" as to amendments, according to House leaders.

Fail to Force Vote Today.

A plan of the handlers of the measure to force a vote tomorrow, formulated suddenly as pressure was brought to bear for the inclusion in it of the Mariand oil regulation plan, was thwarted with the development of opposition in the Rules Committee to the industrial-control features, resulting in a five-to-five deadlock.

Another meeting of the committee was called for tomorrow by Chairman Pou, and Representatives Bankhead of Alabama and O'Connor of New York, Democrats, will then be on hand to help put over the administration plan. Representative Cox of Georgia, a Democrat, joined with the Republicans today in making the tie vote.

Every disposition was shown to rush the bill, both to get ahead of the oil regulation lobby and opposition to the income tax increase which the Ways and Means Committee adopted yesterday as the means for furnishing the sinking fund and interest for the $3,300,000,000 public works bond issue.

Members of Congress, particularly of the committee, received hundreds of telegrams today protesting against the increases in lower-bracket income taxes, the corporate dividend levy and the additional gasoline impost. Opposition has

Continued on Page Three.

MITCHELL'S WIFE MISSED BIG PROFIT

Could Have Made $800,000 if Stock Had Really Been Hers, Prosecution Insists.

TAX-LOSS SALES ADVISED

Defense Brings Out Letter of Trust Official Explaining One of Her Deals.

If Charles E. Mitchell's sale of 18,300 shares of National City Bank stock to his wife in 1929 had been a genuine sale, Mrs. Mitchell could have resold the stock early in 1930 at a profit of more than $800,000 and thus nearly doubled her personal estate, the prosecution emphasized yesterday at Mr. Mitchell's income tax evasion trial.

Evidence on this point was developed by Assistant United States Attorney Thomas E. Dewey to offset the defense contention that the sale was a bona fide transaction for the purpose not merely of enabling the banker, then chairman of the National City Bank, to establish a loss for tax purposes but also of giving his wife an opportunity to enhance her fortune.

Mr. Dewey produced copies of THE NEW YORK TIMES, The Wall Street Journal and publications of the National Quotation Bureau, Inc., with closing bid and asked prices for National City Bank stock on Dec. 20, 1929, when Mr. Mitchell sold the stock to his wife; on March 24, 1932, when he repurchased it, and on intervening dates.

Price Range 43 to 256.

The quotations for Dec. 20, 1929, were 212 bid, 214 asked; for March 24, 1932, 43½ bid, 45½ asked, and for Feb. 14, 1930, 256 bid, 258 asked, the highest point reached by the stock after Dec. 20, 1929. It had previously been shown that the stock was purchased by Mr. Mitchell at the end of October, 1929, at an average of $367 a share.

Mr. Dewey emphasized the point that if Mr. and Mrs. Mitchell had actually regarded the stock as the wife's property between the sale dates in 1929 and 1932, and if one purpose of the transaction had been to increase her estate, she might have sold it on Feb. 14, 1930, at a maximum profit of 44 points a share, or a total profit of $805,200. Instead she waited to dispose of it until March 24, 1932, when the bid price was 43½, and she would have had to take a loss of 168½ points a share, or a total loss of $3,083,550, had not Mr. Mitchell taken it off her hands at $212 a

Continued on Page Twelve.

"All the News That's Fit to Print."

The New York Times.

LATE CITY EDITION
WEATHER—Possibly showers today, tomorrow; temperature same.
Temperatures Yesterday—Max., 66; Min., 56

VOL. LXXXII....No. 27,538. Entered as Second-Class Matter, Postoffice, New York, N. Y. NEW YORK, SATURDAY, JUNE 17, 1933. TWO CENTS In New York City. | THREE CENTS Within 200 Miles | FOUR CENTS Elsewhere Except in 7th and 8th Postal Zones

PRESIDENT STARTS RECOVERY PROGRAM, SIGNS BANK, RAIL AND INDUSTRY BILLS; WHEAT GROWERS WILL GET $150,000,000

CITY TO SELL BONDS DIRECT TO PUBLIC; $50,000 FOR STAFF

Interest Up to 5½% Provided in Scheme to Get Money and Reduce Bank Loans.

CANVASSERS TO BE HIRED

All Kinds of Securities Will Be Offered—Outstanding Issues Drop Sharply.

BERRY PROGRAM ADOPTED

He Foresees Wide Market for Offerings—Long-Term Issue Is Likely—No Action on Taxes.

Direct sale of city securities to the public at interest rates not exceeding 5½ per cent was authorized by the Board of Estimate yesterday. The action was taken upon the recommendation of Controller Charles W. Berry.

The Board appropriated $50,000 for a corps of trained bond salesmen to sell the securities. At the same time it raised the interest rate on baby bonds sold recently from 4¾ per cent to 5½ per cent. The baby bonds were issued in multiples of $10. Their use was restricted solely to payment of taxes. The plan adopted yesterday extends this sale to other forms of city securities without restrictions.

City Securities Decline.

Prices of New York City bonds dropped 1 to 3 points in the over-the-counter market yesterday. The movement was held to reflect the uncertainty regarding the city's ability to raise new revenues rather than its move to sell its obligations direct to the public. The ground lost canceled only part of the gains built up earlier in the week. The long-term 4¼s closed at 82 bid, 84 asked, and the 6s due 1935 to 1937, at 93½ bid, 95 asked.

New York City banks are already large holders of the city's short-term securities and current market conditions do not permit the sale to investors. Thus, bankers who have been identified with the city's financing in the past appeared to be pleased that the city was about to make an effort to place the new short-term securities direct with the public instead of calling on them to underwrite the new issues.

As far as the city's plan to sell fifty-year bonds to the public is concerned, it was pointed out in banking circles that the current yield on long-term bonds of the city was 5.60 per cent and that new bonds would necessarily have to meet the competition of outstanding issues. It was further stated that any new long-term financing was out of the question at present, in so far as the bankers were concerned, because of the heavy discounts ruling on old issues.

Controller Berry declared his belief that a wide market existed for city securities. In addition he announced a plan to float a fifty-year issue of corporate stock or serial bonds by selling them directly to the public. He said frankly that direct selling was undertaken to cut down the 5¾ interest rate charged by the city's bankers on loans.

Bids to Be Asked First.

Corporate stock, under the City Charter, may be offered for sale only upon public letting when sealed bids are received. The charter also provides, however, that the Controller may sell at private sale the unsold portion of stock remaining after public sale. Taking advantage of this provision, the Controller said he would first advertise the public sale, with notice that any portion not bid in would be sold over the counter at par.

By authorizing an interest rate of not more than 5½ per cent, the Board of Estimate eliminated one large difficulty in the public sale of city securities. It had been pointed out that if the securities bore a 4¾ per cent rate, they would be in disadvantageous competition with other issues bearing 5¾ per cent. Securities sold only a quarter-point below the current rate will be readily absorbed, the Controller believes.

Without any salesmanship, Mr. Berry said, the Finance Department had marketed more than $24,000,000 of the baby bonds carrying a 4¾ per cent rate. Of that total he said $15,000,000 was bought by taxpayers in liquidation of their taxes for the first half of this year. Raising the interest rate to 5½ per cent, in Mr. Berry's opinion, will bring substantial sums into the city treasury now in prepayment of the second half year's taxes. Purchasers will have the advantage of the interest between now and Nov. 30.

Many property owners, the Controller reported, were not aware of the opportunity for profitable investment presented to them in the city's securities. The city's

Continued on Page Seven.

Harvard Defeats Yale Crew For Third Successive Year

For the third successive year Harvard won its annual crew race with Yale on the Thames River at New London, Conn., last evening. The Crimson captured the seventy-first varsity four-mile contest by a length and three-quarters, coming from behind in the last mile to triumph before a crowd of 35,000.

Harvard started the race in front, but at the half-mile mark Yale had gained the lead. The Eli oarsmen maintained their advantage until the three and a half-mile mark was reached when the Crimson went ahead by an eighth of a length. Harvard gained steadily to the finish line.

Harvard also took the junior varsity race, after trailing the Eli boat up to the last quarter-mile. Its late spurt gave the Crimson the victory by the scant margin of half a length. Yale won by a wide margin in the freshman race, also at two miles, scoring by five lengths. The two minor contests were held yesterday morning.

Complete Details on Page 9.

COMMON COLD LAID TO 2 AGENTS UNITED

Vaccination Against Virus Instead of Bacteria Is Urged at Doctors' Meeting.

NERVES CUT TO EASE PAIN

Whooping Cough Vaccine Is Upheld—Type 1 Pneumonia Serum Found Effective.

By WILLIAM L. LAURENCE.
Special to THE NEW YORK TIMES.

MILWAUKEE, June 16.—Evidence leading to a new theory on the origin and prevention of the common cold and epidemic influenza was presented here today before the closing sessions of the convention of the American Medical Association.

The findings on the two ailments, which so far have baffled all the efforts of medical science to combat them, were reported before the section on pharmacology and therapeutics by Dr. Alphonse R. Dochez, Dr. Yale Kneeland Jr. and Kathryne C. Mills of the College of Physicians and Surgeons, Columbia University.

There are two schools of thought on the origin of colds and influenza. One contends the diseases are due to the type of micro-organisms known as filterable viruses, which are invisible under the most powerful microscope and pass through any porcelain filter employed by bacteriologists.

The other school holds the two ailments are due to the various kinds of bacteria generally present in the upper respiratory tracts.

Studies of Dr. Dochez and his coworkers lead them to conclude that colds and influenza are due neither to a virus alone nor solely to the action of the bacteria, but rather to a combination of the two agents.

The virus, according to this hypothesis, acts as the "preparer of the soil," the "initiating agent" for the bacteria.

The investigators said they believed the way for prevention of colds and influenza lay in vaccination against the virus and not against the bacteria.

Dog Distemper Is Cited.

"From observations," the paper states, "the inference has been drawn that there may exist in respiratory disease a complex etiology (causality), comprising an initiating agent which can give rise to a mild disturbance like the common cold, and in certain instances one or another pathogenic bacteria which are by it empowered to invade the host and give rise to more severe secondary manifestations.

"There are two diseases in animals which immediately come to mind in this connection—in dog distemper and particularly in swine influenza it has been shown that more than one etiological agent is required to produce the typical disease.

"It has been demonstrated that in swine influenza there exists a filterable virus which by itself produces only the mildest of diseases; if administered together with a culture of certain bacterium it gives rise to typical, highly contagious swine influenza.

"But the culture of the organism alone, even if given in large doses, produces absolutely no effect at all.

"Here we have what might possibly be an analogue to human pandemic influenza, reconciling the divided views as to the rôle of a filterable virus on the one hand and of the influenza bacterium on the other.

"There is evidence that both colds and influenza are due to a complex etiology—a filterable virus acting in

Continued on Page Seven.

REICH ASKS RETURN OF AFRICAN LANDS AT LONDON PARLEY

Also Seeks Other Territory, Presumably in Europe, for 'Works of Peace.'

LINKS PLAN AND DEBTS

Hugenberg Statement Is Held to Confirm Nazi Hints of Eastward Expansion Aim.

MONEY RATIO PACT READY

Stabilization Plan Is Likely to Go to Conference Next Week—Two Boards Start Work.

By FREDERICK T. BIRCHALL.
Special Cable to THE NEW YORK TIMES.

LONDON, June 16.—The World Economic Conference went to work in two sections today—monetary and economic, respectively. The monetary commission, as it is called, made the most progress.

It divided itself into two committees, one to consider temporary, the other permanent, remedies for the distressful monetary conditions. Each of these quickly laid out a program of work. One of the subcommittees, under the chairmanship of Senator Key Pittman of the United States, will consider the advisability of remonetizing and extending the use of silver.

The chief feat of the economic commission was to draw out the Germans. Through the medium of Dr. Alfred Hugenberg, German Minister of Economy and Agriculture, it is now determined what Germany wants at the conference. She wants to recover her colonies in Africa. Also, apparently, she wants some further territory, presumably in Europe, for the "settlement of her active race and for the construction of great works of peace."

Revelation to Conference.

This was somewhat of a revelation to a conference called to deal with economic questions, not with territorial questions. This did not, however, cause much of a sensation. Germany being what she is under her present control and Dr. Hugenberg being hardly a person whom Chancellor Hitler would select as his chosen mouthpiece.

Nevertheless, there it is on record in plain words, at the close of a long statement by the head of the German delegation, dealing with the economic hardships of a "noncolonial" country and the responsibility of Germany's "international indebtedness" for the present parlous state of national economies.

The latter is taken as rather an expression of Dr. Hugenberg's personal fear—shared by few others—of a future demand for the issuance of that 3,000,000,000 marks' worth of "if and when" bonds to which Germany agreed in lieu of reparations at the Lausanne conference. The attitude is also believed to be due to the German Minister's personal dislike, which he has frequently expressed, of the interest rates and the capital extent of Germany's private debt.

The official English translation of his actual declaration of Germany's colonial and territorial aspirations follows:

"From the German viewpoint wise and peaceful cooperation between debtor and creditor countries might include two large-minded measures whereby Germany's

Continued on Page Four.

Wiley Requested Sea Duty; Policy on Air Officers to Go On

By The Associated Press.

WASHINGTON, June 16.—The navy disclosed today that Lieut. Commander Herbert V. Wiley, sole surviving officer of the airship Akron, was ordered to sea "at his own request."

Rear Admiral Ernest King, Chief of Naval Aeronautics, made the explanation in relation to orders for the officer to report to the cruiser Cincinnati as navigating officer.

Secretary Swanson has said he foresaw no change in the navy's policy of ordering fliers to sea duty.

"Lieut. Commander Wiley testified before the joint Congressional committee that he believed in the navy's system of occasional sea duty for airship officers," Admiral King said.

This system was termed a "mistaken policy" by the Congressional committee in reporting on its investigation of the Akron disaster. Since then Lieut. Commander Wiley has been serving on the trial board of the new airship Macon, which has successfully passed trial flights.

KIDNAPPERS SEIZE ST. PAUL BREWER

Hold William Hamm, 39, for $100,000 Ransom—Death Threat Made in Note.

SANKEY LINKED TO GANG

Fugitive in Bohn and Boettcher Abductions Is Identified as Sender of Missive.

By The Associated Press.

ST. PAUL, June 16.—William Hamm, aged 39, St. Paul millionaire, was kidnapped yesterday and is being held for $100,000 ransom, it was announced tonight.

News of the kidnapping was withheld by the police in an effort to discover the identity of the abductors and bring about their arrest. When officials became convinced this was impossible immediately they decided to make the abduction known and enlist the aid of the public in apprehending the kidnappers.

Mr. Hamm is president and treasurer of the Hamm Brewing Company of St. Paul and son of the late William Hamm, a local capitalist.

The first news of the kidnapping was received yesterday by William W. Dunn, manager of the company, through a telephone call.

"We have kidnapped Mr. Hamm," said a voice. "You will hear from us later."

Cabman Names Verne Sankey.

Today Mr. Dunn received a note which stated Mr. Hamm was being held for $100,000 ransom and that unless the money was paid Mr. Hamm would be killed. Attached to the bottom of the note was postscript signed by Mr. Hamm, in which he urged immediate payment of the money.

The note was delivered by a taxi driver who told the police that he was approached by a man Thursday night.

"This man told me," the driver stated, "that he would give me $2 if I would take a note to Mr. Dunn. He said that his name was Gordon and that he lived in the Lowry Hotel. I took the note and delivered it."

Police said that the taxi driver later identified a picture of Verne Sankey, sought for two kidnappings already, as the man who gave him

Continued on Page Three.

Roosevelt Takes Special Train for Boston To Embark on Vacation Voyage 'Down East'

Special to THE NEW YORK TIMES.

WASHINGTON, June 16.—President Roosevelt left on his vacation tonight after working hard all day and signing all the important bills passed in the final days of Congress. Following a driving four months, filled with great responsibilities, the President boarded his train soon after 8:30, saying that he felt "tired but happy that Congress has ended its important legislative program so successfully."

The last visitor appeared at the Executive Offices just before 7. Then, closing his desk, the President took a plunge in his swimming pool. He had his secretaries and office staff with him at dinner and gave final instructions for work to be done during his vacation, which will last until the first week in July.

Hundreds of friends were at the station to say good-bye. The special train on the Pennsylvania Railroad, which followed the Federal Express to Boston, carried the President's party, including Stephen Early, his assistant secretary, and Miss Marguerite Le Hand, his personal stenographer, in addition to correspondents and photographers.

From Boston the President will go to Groton to see his sons Franklin Jr. and John. The former was graduated there yesterday. After luncheon with his family, the President will motor to Marion, on Cape Cod, where he will set sail on the Amberjack II with his son James and several of the latter's companions. The President will navigate the schooner to Portland, Me., stopping at convenient places for watering and revictualing.

Franklin Jr. and John will join him at Portland and continue the trip by water to Campobello Island, N. B., arriving about June 28. Joined there by Mrs. Roosevelt, the President will return on the cruiser Indianapolis on its speed trial from Eastport to the mouth of the Potomac.

On this trip he will not be accompanied by newspaper men or photographers.

AIDS FARMERS THIS YEAR

Wheat Processing Tax, 30 Cents, to Take Effect Soon After July 1.

ACREAGE CUTS IN 1934-35

Payments to Growers on Production Allotments Will Also Include This Year's Crop.

WILL PROTECT CONSUMERS

Wallace Promises No Undue Price Rises—Will Give Decision on Cotton Today.

Special to THE NEW YORK TIMES.

WASHINGTON, June 16.—Soon after July 1, Secretary Wallace announced today, the farm relief plan under which wheat growers agreeing to curtail their crops will receive approximately $150,000,000 will become operative.

The acreage reduction and allotment provisions of the Farm Relief Act will be applied to the wheat crops of 1934 and 1935, and the fund of $150,000,000 will be raised by a processing tax of around 30 cents a bushel levied against milling. By Sept. 15 two-thirds of the $150,000,000 will have been distributed among wheat growers who have complied with the government's terms.

Eligibility to share in this distribution requires that growers agree to reduce planting up to a maximum of 20 per cent next year. The exact reduction called for will depend on the outcome of the negotiations at the economic and monetary conference for joint international action to reduce world wheat production. It is possible that no reduction actually will be required.

No attempt will be made to reduce the already planted and growing 1933 crop, although the bonuses embrace this year.

Decision on Cotton Today.

Secretary Wallace will announce, probably tomorrow, the decision on what course will be followed with respect to cotton. The belief is that a 25 per cent destruction of the present cotton crop by leasing agreements, to be paid for out of a fund built up by a processing tax of 4 cents a pound, will be required. Cotton growers probably will have the opportunity to rent their land to the government for around $10 an acre and acquire the right to take options on cheap government-owned cotton.

The government reserved the right to establish the amount of reduction of the domestic wheat crop of 1934 at a later date so that the United States might retain a free hand in negotiating for world reduction at the London conference.

The Adjustment Administration will not know until actual operations are begun what the exact amount of the processing tax will be. On the basis of prices paid for wheat on farms for the first half of June, the tax would be about 30 cents because that amount represents the difference between the current farm price and the established average price of 1909-14, which is the base period on which the parity plan is based.

Basis for Payment.

The amounts to be paid to each individual wheat grower will be determined on the basis of his average production for the past three years and the percentage of that production which went into domestic consumption.

The average annual output for the country as a whole in that period was about 800,000,000 bushels, and of this amount about 500,000,000 bushels went into domestic consumption. With these totals the administration has produced a formula under which the individual grower will receive 30 cents on five-eighths of his production for the last three years.

If a grower's average production from 1930 to 1933 was 1,000 bushels, he would be entitled to benefit payments this year aggregating $187.50.

Secretary Wallace, in announcing the decision, stated that, contrary to the popular impression, the processing tax was not to be superimposed on the current market price for wheat. The farmer would continue to sell his wheat for what-

Continued on Page Two.

Powers Granted to the President

Special to THE NEW YORK TIMES.

WASHINGTON, June 16.—Extraordinary powers granted in the first session of the Seventy-third Congress to President Roosevelt are:

To establish control over all industry with the view to fixing minimum wages and maximum hours of work, regulating production and otherwise to promote, encourage and require fair competition.

To set up a system of government licenses for business if necessary to require conformance to the above.

To initiate and direct, through a Federal director of public works, a $3,300,000,000 public works program as a further government contribution to re-employment.

To direct, through a Federal director of relief, expenditure of $500,000,000, supplied by the Reconstruction Finance Corporation, for relief of destitution.

To invoke the Presidential powers of the World War to regulate transactions in credit, currency, gold and silver, even to embargo gold or foreign exchange; to fix restrictions on the banking business of the Federal Reserve System irrespective of the Federal Reserve Board.

To eliminate the old system for compensation and allowances for veterans and set up an entirely new pension system, with himself at the head.

To reduce by executive order the salaries of government employes by an amount not to exceed 15 per cent upon the finding of commensurate reduction in cost of living.

To transfer, eliminate, consolidate or rearrange bureaus in the executive branch of the government in the interest of public economy.

To repeal by executive proclamation certain new taxes voted in Industrial Recovery Act upon showing of restoration of business or in event of repeal of the Eighteenth Amendment.

To publish heretofore secret income tax returns to the extent he may deem in the public interest, and under such rules and regulations as he may prescribe.

To inflate the currency either by requiring open market operations in Federal securities, devaluing the gold dollar by not more than 50 per cent, issuing United States notes up to $3,000,000,000 or accepting up to $200,000,000 in silver in payment of the allied war debts.

To employ more than 250,000 unemployed young men in reforestation operations as still further government contribution to re-employment.

To appoint a coordinator of railroads to effect economies among the carriers and increase service to the public.

To appoint a Tennessee Valley Authority to develop natural resources of Tennessee River basin, including completion of Muscle Shoals project.

WIDE WORK SPREAD ASKED BY JOHNSON

Recovery Chairman Urges Industry to Unite for Shorter Week, More Employes,

AND PAY TO MEET PRICES

Forced Down in Plane at Pittsburgh, He Addresses Coal Men by Radio.

Special to THE NEW YORK TIMES.

CHICAGO, June 16.—General Hugh S. Johnson, chairman of the Industrial Administrative Board, warned industry tonight that a critical economic stage had been reached at which there was danger of relapse from recent improvement because prices had risen faster and further than wages.

Such a relapse will be prevented, he told delegates to the annual convention of the National Coal Association in an address over the National Broadcasting Company's network from Pittsburgh, where he was forced down while flying here, by an immediate movement on a broad front for spreading work on a living-wage basis.

"The President has pointed out the way to start our business on a strong, sound, upward spiral," General Johnson said in his first public utterance as administrator.

"The idea," said he today, "is simply for employers to hire more men to do the existing work by reducing the work hours of each man's week and at the same time paying a living wage for the shorter week."

Such a program cannot be undertaken unless all competing companies and industries adopt it at about the same time, he pointed out, hailing the approval of a simple, basic code in line with the President's policy at the convention here as an expression of industry's willingness to cooperate.

Suggests Industry's Course.

"The simplest and most direct course for each industry," he said, "is now to submit as an industry entirely what it would like to do, first, to carry out our primary purpose, which is to put men back to work at decent living wages in the shortest possible time, and second, those provisions which you find it absolutely necessary to include to protect the willing and forward-

Continued on Page Three.

TREASURY TO ORDER $25,000,000 WORK

Roberts and Farley Decide to Ask Bids at Once on More Federal Buildings.

PROJECTS HERE INCLUDED

Vesey Street Plans Already Prepared—22 Sites Have Been Selected in This State.

Special to THE NEW YORK TIMES.

WASHINGTON, June 16.—Bids will be asked at once by the Treasury Department on Federal buildings to cost $25,000,000, it was announced today after a conference between Postmaster General Farley and L. W. Robert, Assistant Secretary of the Treasury.

Already bids have been asked on twenty-two projects to cost about the same and bids will be sought within the next ninety days on sixty-two additional projects calling for expenditures of $50,000,000.

This will put $100,000,000 of the $3,300,000,000 construction appropriation under the National Industrial Recovery Act to work by Oct. 1 through Treasury-Postoffice building alone.

It is the hope of General Hugh S. Johnson, Federal Industrial Control Administrator, to get $1,000,000,000 of the $3,300,000,000 allotted to various kinds by Oct. 1. He estimates that for every $1,000,000,000 in construction awarded, 1,000,000 men can be put to work.

Mr. Robert has been in conference with Mr. Johnson relative to the general program. Both wish to get the money at work quickly, rather than to spread it out over a long period and the Treasury's policy will be directed to that end.

$494,604,187 Authorized.

Treasury figures showed that, under the regular $700,000,000 building program, projects with a limit of cost of $494,604,187 have been authorized, while under the so-called relief program, $85,865,900 was authorized.

The government, under the $700,000,000 regular Treasury-Postoffice program has completed 355 projects with a limit cost of $121,387,119. There are 280 projects with a limit of cost of $321,254,310 under contract, while eighty-one projects were

Continued on Page Two.

ROOSEVELT HAILS GOAL

He Calls Recovery Act Most Sweeping Law in Nation's History.

JOHNSON ADMINISTRATOR

Col. Sawyer Is Named to Direct Public Works, Eastman as Railway Coordinator.

'MILLION JOBS BY OCT. 1'

Employers Urged to Hire More Men With Government Stopping Unfair Competition.

Text of President's statement on recovery policies, Page 2.

Special to THE NEW YORK TIMES.

WASHINGTON, June 16.—Assuming unprecedented peacetime control over the nation's economic life, President Roosevelt placed in operation today his sweeping program for recovery from the depression.

Within two hours he signed acts of Congress giving him control over industry, power to coordinate the railroads, and authority to start work on a $3,300,000,000 public works program, and then began the active administration of these and other major measures.

In signing the National Industrial Recovery Act the President declared that it was "the most important and far-reaching legislation ever enacted by the American Congress," and said that it "represents a supreme effort to stabilize for all time the many factors which make for the prosperity of the nation and the preservation of American standards."

The Glass-Steagall Banking Reform Act, which the President described as "the second most important banking legislation enacted in the history of the country"; the long-disputed Independent Offices Act, including the veterans legislation; the Deficiency Act, the Taxation Act, and the Farm Credits Act received the President's signature during the day.

Administrators Are Named.

Turning to the administrative side of the industrial recovery program, President appointed General Hugh S. Johnson, former soldier and manufacturer, as administrator of industry; made available $400,000,000 under the public works title for State roads, and allotted $238,000,000 to the Navy Department for laying down thirty-two new war vessels under the terms of the London treaty.

A special recovery board was named by Mr. Roosevelt to work with General Johnson. It consists of Secretary of Commerce Roper, chairman; Attorney General Cummings, Secretaries Wallace, Perkins and Ickes, Budget Director Douglas and Chairman March of the Federal Trade Commission.

General Johnson also will have an advisory council of business and labor leaders, the personnel of which has not yet been announced. Among those reported under consideration, however, are Myron C. Taylor, Alfred P. Sloan, Walter C. Teagle, Gerard Swope and Will Vereen.

Colonel Donald H. Sawyer was named temporary administrator of public works and was directed, with a special Cabinet board consisting of Secretary Ickes, chairman; Secretaries Wallace, Roper and Perkins, Assistant Secretary of the Treasury Robert, Colonel George R. Spaulding, and Budget Director Douglas, to submit to the President without delay the works on which construction can be undertaken promptly and to outline a program for future work.

Eastman Rail Coordinator.

Joseph B. Eastman, a member of the Interstate Commerce Commission, was appointed coordinator of railroads and was directed to begin his work at once. His most important immediate concern will be the railway wage scale negotiations, following which, savings by the production of duplicating facilities will be undertaken.

General Johnson conferred with the President late today and then left by airplane for Chicago to meet with leaders of the bituminous coal industry. He said that he would return late tomorrow night, and that he hoped to name a large group of men to aid him in perfect-

President Roosevelt signing the bill giving the Treasury title to the gold in the Federal Reserve banks.

FDR signing the Railroad Reorganization bill on June 16. Senator Dill (L) and Representative Rayburn look on.

Secretary of Agriculture Henry A. Wallace led the New Deal's drive for higher farm prices.

The President signs the Farm Measure. Secretary of Agriculture Henry Wallace is at right.

"All the News That's Fit to Print."

The New York Times.

LATE CITY EDITION
WEATHER—Probably showers, cooler today; tomorrow fair.
Temperatures Yesterday—Max., 78; Min., 60

VOL. LXXXII....No. 27,543. Entered as Second-Class Matter, Postoffice, New York, N. Y. NEW YORK, THURSDAY, JUNE 22, 1933. TWO CENTS In New York City. | THREE CENTS Within 200 Miles | FOUR CENTS Elsewhere Except In 7th and 8th Postal Zones

1,629,000 NEW JOBS CREATED IN NATION IN PAST 2 MONTHS

SHARPER RISE FORECAST

Labor Federation's Data Indicate Steady Gains in Rest of June.

UP 1,000,000 SINCE MAY 1

Specialty Groups, Especially Those Supplying Forest Corps, Show Marked Advance.

STATISTICS TASK SPEEDED

Secretary Perkins Orders Her Department to Keep Pace With Changes.

Special to THE NEW YORK TIMES.

WASHINGTON, June 21.—Employment in the United States has increased about 1,629,000 since the end of March, and a comparable increase during the rest of June is expected, according to estimates of the American Federation of Labor.

Statisticians at the office of William Green, president of the Federation of Labor, said 629,000 more persons were employed in April than in March. Their estimate was that about 1,000,000 had been re-employed since April 30. It was thought probable that completion of the official tabulations would increase these totals.

These indications of recovery greatly cheered government officials. It was noted that the reduction in unemployment amounted to about 12 per cent. Under normal circumstances there would be several million unemployed, so that all the jobless would not have to be eliminated in order to restore normal prosperity.

It would not take a very long time to make a startling change in the situation, in the opinion of observers here. Evidences of increased employment in establishments all over the country have been noted.

Labor Department Notes Change.

At the Department of Labor it was said that Secretary Perkins had ordered more prompt and accurate reports by the government.

"Miss Perkins has a special committee working out a plan whereby we will be able to keep up with the rapidly changing situation, especially now when employment is increasing at such a favorable pace," said one official.

Over the last two years until recently the increase in unemployment was steady, reaching a peak of 13,359,000 in March. The April figure of 12,730,000 compared with 10,496,000 in April, 1932.

The monthly tabulations by the American Federation of Labor from April, 1932, to April this year were as follows:

Month. 1932.	Unemployment.
April	10,496,000
May	10,818,000
June	11,023,000
July	11,420,000
August	11,460,000
September	10,880,000
October	10,875,000
November	11,589,000
December	11,969,000
1933.	
January	12,821,000
February	12,988,000
March	13,359,000
April	12,730,000

Increases in various specialty groups, it was said today, have been marked, but the number of newly employed will not be known until the complete reports are received. The specialty groups producing clothing, shoes and food preparations have benefited from activities of the Civilian Conservation Corps, shipping supplies on rush orders.

Some of Forest Army Counted.

Some of the reforestation army were included in the Federation of Labor statistics on employment. To that number, however, can be added 51,000 recruits enlisted since June 1. New naval construction is expected to give work to 52,000 men, and the Home Owners Loan Corporation, one of the new Federal agencies, will employ between 5,000 and 7,000 others.

Several thousand more persons will be engaged by the various new Federal agencies throughout the country. Many of those slated for early retirement in keeping with the administration's departmental economy steps will be shifted to the new agencies.

Political Jobs Ruled Out In Tennessee Valley Work

Special to THE NEW YORK TIMES.

WASHINGTON, June 21.—The man fits the job for the Tennessee Valley Authority or he does not get it, regardless of his political affiliations and backing.

In substance, this was the pronouncement today of officials who are setting up the administrative force.

Several Democratic Senators and Representatives who telephoned to ask that so-and-so receive a job were told that it was not how the applicant voted but what he could do that counted.

"Political affiliations mean nothing," one was told. "We want people who are qualified. The best qualified gets the job."

Officials were not able to estimate the force needed in the administrative section, but it was expected to be several hundred.

RAIL WAGE SLASH PUT OFF 8 MONTHS

Agreement of Roads and Labor Is Announced by Eastman After 2-Day Parleys.

PRESENT CUT IS CONTINUED

Management Moved by Appeal to Await the Results of Recovery Program.

Special to THE NEW YORK TIMES.

WASHINGTON, June 21.—An agreement between railroads and railway labor suspending their wage reduction controversy until June 30, 1934, out of deference to President Roosevelt's recovery program, was announced tonight by Joseph B. Eastman, the new coordinator of transportation.

Under the terms of the "armistice," which Mr. Eastman said was arrived at through a commendable spirit of cooperation between the disputants, the existing temporary 10 per cent pay cut was extended eight months from Nov. 1 and the rail managements' notice of a further 12½ per cent reduction effective Nov. 1 was canceled.

Mr. Eastman emphasized in his announcement that neither side had relinquished its views regarding what railway wages should be.

But both appreciated, he said, that it would be difficult to deal wisely now with the matter "and that the active prosecution of such a controversy at the present time might have a most disturbing and unsettling effect."

Statement by Eastman.

Mr. Eastman's announcement read as follows:

"Under this agreement the railroads will surrender for a period of eight months their right to seek a further reduction in employes' compensation and the employes will surrender for an equal period of time their opportunity to secure an elimination of the present 10 per cent reduction.

"The notice given by the railroads on June 15 of an intention to seek a 22½ per cent reduction in the basic rate of pay will be canceled.

"This agreement has been reached because both the railroads and the employes wish to do nothing which would in any way embarrass or threaten the present policy of the administration.

"They realize that the government has now embarked upon a wholly new policy to promote business and industrial activity and to further the general welfare.

Wait for Recovery Results.

"They appreciate that until the results of this policy can be more clearly determined, it will be difficult to deal wisely with this wage controversy and that the active prosecution of such a controversy at the present time might have a most disturbing and unsettling effect.

"Neither side relinquishes in any way its views as to what the wages should be, but they have agreed to a postponement of the controversy out of deference to what they believe to be the desire and policy of the administration and in the general public interest.

"The railroad managers and the railroad labor executives have entered into an agreement under which the arrangement by which 10 per cent is being deducted from the pay checks of employes will be extended from Oct. 31, 1933, until June

Continued on Page Five.

MITCHELL TAX JURY DEBATES 10 HOURS, THEN IS LOCKED UP

Banker, Facing 10-Year Term if Guilty, Waits Anxiously as Deliberations Drag On.

PART OF CHARGE RE-READ

Jurors Ask Light on $666,666 Item—Intent in Sales Is Stressed by Court.

The judge's charge to the jury in Mitchell case, Pages 12 and 13.

The case of the United States against Charles E. Mitchell, former chairman of the National City Bank, on charges of evading payment of his 1929 and 1930 income taxes, went to the jury at 12:30 o'clock yesterday afternoon.

At 10:30 o'clock last night, the jurors having deliberated ten hours except for luncheon and dinner intervals without reaching a verdict, Federal Judge Henry W. Goddard ordered them locked up for the night. Deputy marshals escorted them to the McAlpin Hotel, with instructions to return them to the jury room in the Federal Building at 10:30 o'clock this morning.

Before ordering the jury locked up, Judge Goddard called George Z. Medalie, United States Attorney, and Max D. Steuer, counsel for the defense, into conference.

During their deliberations yesterday afternoon and last night, the jury were locked in a room on the third floor of the Federal Building, guarded by deputy marshals.

Mitchell Paces Room.

Across the corridor, in an anteroom of the courtroom in which he had been on trial for six weeks, the banker paced nervously, smoking one cigarette after another, and discussing the evidence with Mr. Steuer. Sharing his suspense were some of his close friends and business associates, including Hugh B. Baker, who resigned as president of the National City Company at the time Mr. Mitchell resigned as chairman.

Mr. Medalie and his aides waited in the crowded court room, along with newspaper men with telephone and telegraph wires near at hand, ready to flash the news of the verdict which would send the once powerful financial leader forth a free man, or would subject him to the possibility of a maximum ten-year prison sentence or $20,000 fine.

Part of Charge Reread.

At 6:05 o'clock the jury sent a note to Judge Goddard asking for another reading of that section of the judge's charge dealing with Mr. Mitchell's failure to report as income $666,666.67 he received from the management fund of the National City Company in July, 1929. With the jurors, defendant and counsel all in their places, Judge Goddard read from this part of his charge for fifteen minutes. James K. Campbell, the foreman, then interrupted him, saying that he had covered the section about which the jurors wished further enlightenment. The jurors then returned to their room. This was the only request for instructions.

Judge Goddard delivered his charge to the jury yesterday morning, beginning at 10:30 o'clock, and speaking for an hour and three-quarters. When he finished, he dis-

Continued on Page Thirteen.

9 Polish Peasants Slain By Police in Tax Riots

Wireless to THE NEW YORK TIMES.

WARSAW, June 21.—Nine peasants and one policeman were killed and twenty-three peasants and five policemen were injured in riots at Grabina and two other villages near Cracow, Southern Poland.

The peasants, incited by anti-State elements, refused to pay taxes and were attacking and robbing Jewish shops and breaking into private woods and stealing timber. Policemen who tried to establish order were attacked by the villagers.

The whole affair was kept secret by the authorities until today, when an official statement said the riots were due to anti-State and Communist activity. About 100 peasants have been arrested and more are being arrested, although order prevails now.

ATOM STUDY BACKS CREATION THEORY

Millikan Declares Elements Are Constantly Forming in Interstellar Space.

COSMIC RAY PROOF CITED

Einstein Energy-Mass Thesis Upheld, Scientists Are Told —Positron Is Weighed.

By WILLIAM L. LAURENCE.
Special to THE NEW YORK TIMES.

CHICAGO, June 21.—New evidence garnered in the dark interior of the atom to prove that creation is still going on in the cosmic vastness of interstellar space was presented here tonight by Dr. Robert A. Millikan.

His address on "New Light on Nuclear Physics" was made before the Summer meeting of the American Association for the Advancement of Science. The audience of internationally known scientists included six Nobel Prize winners.

In presenting the new findings, which he offered as proof that "the Creator is still on the job," Dr. Millikan made a dramatic announcement of great importance to science.

He revealed for the first time that he and his associates at California Tech had succeeded in weighing the positron, or the positive electron, recently discovered by Dr. Anderson in Professor Millikan's laboratory.

They have determined within a small percentage of error that the positron has the same mass as the negative electron.

This discovery is used by Dr. Millikan as one of the links in the new chain of evidence of the continuous process of creation. Dr. Millikan won the Nobel Prize in 1923 for being the first accurately to measure the charge of the negative electron and to determine its mass.

Dr. Millikan also presented data that would indicate the creation in interstellar space of elements even heavier than uranium, the last on the chemicable table of ninety-two elements and the heaviest element known on earth.

This beyond-uranium element is so unstable that it breaks up into lower elements in the manner of radium, however.

One of the cornerstones of his formidable scientific structure is the assumption of the correctness

Continued on Page Ten.

Baruch Is Called 'Unofficial President'; Goes to Washington to Take Up New Task

By The Associated Press.

WASHINGTON, June 21.—The State Department today received a telegram addressed to "Bernard M. Baruch, unofficial President of the United States." It said:

"Congratulations. I know of no better man for the job," and was signed by a citizen of Tulsa, Okla.

Receipt of the telegram followed an announcement that Mr. Baruch, at the request of President Roosevelt, would assist government heads in the President's absence.

Bernard M. Baruch left New York for Washington yesterday after conferring here briefly with Raymond Moley, Assistant Secretary of State, who sailed with instructions from President Roosevelt for the London conference delegates. Mr. Baruch will fill the position which Mr. Moley has held as contact man between the President and the government administrators.

It is expected that Mr. Baruch will devote a good part of his time to keeping in touch with the National Industrial Recovery Act and the new Farm Control and Financial Bills. He has been interested in all these important instruments of economic recovery since the first days of the administration.

General Hugh Johnson, who is putting the industrial recovery machinery into motion, with Mr. Baruch drew up a tentative outline of coordination between the government and industry in the latter days of the War Industries Board in 1918 and 1919. Its members were impressed with the plan's possibilities in peace time for controlling production and consumption, and when President Roosevelt and his advisers formulated the Industrial Recovery Act Mr. Baruch was one of the most important contributors to that legislation. It was said yesterday that as a result of these preliminary studies General Johnson had a concrete plan of action ready to his hand when he took over the task of administrator.

Although Mr. Baruch has been more or less in the background in recent months despite his frequent visits to Washington, it was said that this year for the first time in years he has given up his Summer trip abroad and will probably devote some time to active public, although unofficial, duties in the capital.

HITLER DISSOLVES HUGENBERG 'ARMY'; CATHOLICS JAILED

'Battle Ring,' Uniformed Guard of Young Nationalists, Is Raided Throughout Reich.

DRIVE ON BAVARIAN PARTY

Homes Searched Because of Austrian 'Link'—Stahlhelm Men Must Join Nazis.

By GUIDO ENDERIS.
Wireless to THE NEW YORK TIMES.

BERLIN, June 21.—The National Socialist claim to exclusive control in all matters of organization found reinforced expression today in the summary suppression throughout the Reich of Dr. Alfred Hugenberg's private green-shirted army, the German National Battle Ring, in which about 10,000 young Nationalists were enrolled.

The dispersal of Dr. Hugenberg's uniformed guards, organized in the image of the Nazi brown shirts and as an offset to them, represents the breaking of the long-accumulating strain between the Nazis and their numerically vastly inferior partners in the "national resurgence."

Simultaneously with the suppression of the "Battle Ring," the Stahlhelm League of Veterans was definitely incorporated in the National Socialist party, and its members, most of whom have been Nationalists, were forbidden to belong to any party except the Nazis.

In addition, the Bavarian political police today invaded the offices of the Catholic Bavarian People's party in Munich and also searched the homes of its leaders.

Link With Austria Seen.

An official communiqué explained that this step was the result of suspicion that "leading personalities of the Bavarian People's party were connected with recent events in Austria, and especially with the suppression of the National Socialist party." A number of party leaders were arrested and documents were seized.

The suppression of Dr. Hugenberg's "Battle Ring" was ordered by Chancellor Hitler and Premier Goering of Prussia and its execution saw the new governmental machinery established by the Nazis in smooth and precise action for the first time.

In Prussia the dissolution, including a series of arrests of Nationalist leaders in raids on headquarters of the party and its auxiliaries was under the direction of the secret political police, and in the other States it was carried out by the Reich Governors instead of by the respective State administrations.

The immediate reasons advanced by the government for the action were that Dr. Hugenberg's "Battle Ring" had become honeycombed with subversive Marxist and Communist elements; that its management had failed to take any remedial action, despite information placed at the party's disposal by the political police, and that, therefore, the government found itself forced to resort to summary suppression. This, it is declared, is not to be regarded as involving any hostility to the so-called National German Front, the revamped Nationalist party.

Hugenberg Sees Hitler.

Chancellor Hitler and Dr. Hugenberg conferred tonight with no others present. No statement on their conference was forthcoming from Dr. Hugenberg or his party, but a government communiqué—significant in its brevity—stated that the Minister of Economics and Agriculture had called on the Chancellor to report on the London conference and to confer with respect to the government's procedure against his organizations. It said that the Chancellor "explained to him the reasons that had led up to their suppression."

While the dissolution of Dr. Hugenberg's fighting units—they were ostensibly organized to protect his political meetings—was foreshadowed yesterday, it was carried out in Berlin with the precision of the old-time German army mobilization. Storm Troopers and Nazi auxiliary police with revolvers strapped to their sides cooperated with the regular police.

Dr. Hugenberg's Green Shirts numbered about 3,000 in Berlin. About 100 of the leaders here were arrested. They included a nephew of Dr. Hugenberg. The arrests were made after the Green Shirts' barracks had been raided and searched.

Action throughout the Reich was conducted on similar lines. The Green Shirt organization in the provinces was small and numerically altogether inferior to the brown-shirted raiding squads, who swooped down upon the Green

Continued on Page Eight.

AMERICANS SET WIDE ACCORD AS PRICE OF STABILIZATION; SMALL NATIONS ASK ACTION

Huge Inflation in Britain Charged

Special Cable to THE NEW YORK TIMES.

LONDON, June 21.—A charge that the British Government had been indulging in inflation to the extent of £200,000,000 in connection with the financing of its exchange equalization fund caused a furor in Parliamentary quarters tonight.

According to some critics, the government's action thus far has not been completely explained. The government's secretly operated fund that was created to control exchange rates by buying and selling currency was increased to £200,000,000 on May 15 from the previous level of £175,000,000.

A suggestion that the government had been taking the public's savings from the postal banks brought Leslie Hore-Belisha, Financial Secretary, to his feet in the House of Commons tonight with a denial that any Treasury bills created in connection with the advance to the fund had been taken up by the postal savings bank or any other government department.

Amid roars of laughter he said: "The Exchequer made an advance of £200,000,000 to the exchange fund. The same day the fund lent back the money to the Exchequer for ninety days. That same moment the Exchequer gave the fund ninety-day Treasury bills as acknowledgment of the loan."

Laborites were not satisfied that the transaction was "merely in the nature of a bookkeeping transaction," and afterward, in the lobbies, argued that if the money was not being borrowed it was simply being created.

Late tonight Treasury officials were rushed to the Commons lobbies to explain that the government's procedure was not inflation, although it was said to have been admitted that new money had been created.

According to the Treasury's explanation, the bills were issued "for the immediate purchase of gold"; therefore, it could not be said they had been issued without gold backing.

The financial editor of The Laborite Daily Herald, commenting on the situation tonight, says:

"However much the transaction may be disguised, it seems clear that in effect the government is inflating to an enormous extent with finance exchange operations on which a huge loss may eventually be made."

41 LEADERS CALLED FOR TRADE PLANNING

Roper Names Group of Industrialists to Map Our Economic Course.

SNARL ON JOHNSON CODE

Complaints Arise Over Proposed Deletion of All Elements of Price Fixing.

Special to THE NEW YORK TIMES.

WASHINGTON, June 21.—Secretary Roper of the Commerce Department today set up an advisory committee of forty-one business men to help chart the course of the country toward economic recovery.

Meanwhile, the Industrial Recovery Administration apparently found itself headed for difficulties with industry over the enforced deletion from present codes of fair competition of any element of price fixing or regulation of productive capacity.

Complaints were heard from industrial representatives in Washington that the recovery administration officials were demanding that codes at this time contain only such provisions as will spread employment and raise wages, with no compensation in the way of price or production increases.

At the same time the recovery administration was applying the maximum of pressure for formulation of the fair competition codes in order that domestic re-employment might start on a large scale at once and that results from the internal program might give some indication as to whether our foreign policies should be recast.

Administration officials regarded the protests as "growing pains." They had apparently little doubt as to the eventual outcome of the difficulties. So feeling, they went ahead with their plans.

Members of the Committee.

In announcing the membership of the Advisory and Long Range Planning Committee, Secretary Roper called a meeting for next Monday to organize.

The personnel of the committee follows:

Robert G. Elbert, chairman of board Aeolian Company and International Holding Company.
Ralph E. Flanders, manager Jones & Lamson Machine Company.
Alexander Legge, president International Harvester Company.
Alfred P. Sloan Jr., president General Motors Corporation.
Edward N. Hurley, Chicago.
William A. Julian, Treasurer of the United States.
Robert L. Lund, vice president and general manager Lambert Pharmacal Company.
Pierre du Pont, chairman E. I. du Pont de Nemours & Co.

Continued on Page Four.

CONFERENCE GROUPS BLAME AMERICANS

Increasing Pessimism Felt as Committees Meet and 'Talk in Vacuum.'

WARNING GIVEN ON RUMORS

Talk of Setting Dollar Rate, Heard as Moley Sails, Is Linked to Speculation.

From a Staff Correspondent.
Special Cable to THE NEW YORK TIMES.

LONDON, June 21.—There is a deeper feeling of pessimism among many of the delegations tonight regarding the results that can be extracted from the World Economic Conference than there has been since it assembled.

The conference continued its work today, the monetary commission discussing price levels publicly without making perceptible progress and the subcommittees of the economic commission dealing with commercial policies, silver and wheat in private sessions. But in large part they were merely going through the motions of continuance—"talking in a vacuum," as one delegate put it—while vital questions before the conference waited.

Renewed rumors of adjournment arose, failed to awake a response and subsided, without, however, producing any satisfactory determination to tackle underlying difficulties.

Of course, blame for much of the overclouding pessimism was laid on the American delegation; along with the general European tendency to blame America for most of the world's evils. In the eyes of others, the American delegation continues to give a public impression of disunity and inability to produce any concrete proposals or to agree with proposals advanced by anybody else.

Americans Under Scrutiny.

The delegates of the United States held their first daily conference late in the afternoon. The purpose was rumored to be to send a message to Washington putting forward certain views and seeking instructions upon them. No message was sent, because, according to a general report, the delegation had adopted a rule of unanimity to govern its actions and could not obtain unanimity.

Other delegations watched the Americans, for every such conference as this is one big whispering gallery.

The American leadership is criticised among these other delegations as insufficiently firm. They inquire if the Americans have no program; or, if they have one, are they afraid to put it forward and fight for it; or, if they have none, why they came at all.

All this, while probably natural

Continued on Page Two.

MONEY IS SUBORDINATED

Roosevelt Seen Holding a Trump Card in His Power to Inflate.

PLEA MADE TO BIG POWERS

Ten Delegates Ask Them to Take Lead on Currencies to Avoid 'Grave' Perils.

OUR DELEGATES CONFER

Take No Part in Debate on Freer Credit, but Are Said to Have a Price Plan.

By CLARENCE K. STREIT.
Wireless to THE NEW YORK TIMES.

LONDON, June 21.—There was reason to believe today that the United States delegation, in part at least, was swinging toward the British view of recent years that currency stabilization is a good thing, but possible only as part of a general program. Because of the domestic price situation it is swinging away from the present British and French view that stabilization must come ahead of everything else.

It is noteworthy that in this the delegation has the support of many expert international officials who think the British and French are making too much political capital of the question of immediate stabilization. So long as President Roosevelt is adhering fundamentally to sound financial policy, these experts, who are familiar with international negotiations and who are interested only in obtaining international agreement, seem to hope he will keep the threat of American inflation dangling over the Europeans until he forces them into agreements on tariffs, quotas, public works and other things.

Find We Hold Big Card.

Regardless of nationality, they agree that tariffs in Europe will be the conference's most difficult problem and, since President Roosevelt did not obtain from Congress the power to lower tariffs, they think the world's only hope of breaking down trade barriers is the wise use by Mr. Roosevelt of the big card he has left—his power to inflate, something the Europeans have been taught by their own recent experience to fear deeply.

These questions of strategy were discussed by the United States delegation at a meeting tonight.

Rumors repeated here from the United States that the delegation had received new instructions were authoritatively denied by the delegation's spokesman, despite a statement from New York saying that Raymond C. Moley, Assistant Secretary of State, who sailed from there today as emissary for President Roosevelt, had telephoned to the delegation advising that stabilization be ignored until he arrived here.

The denial possibly was intended to put emphasis on the adjective "new," it having been understood here for several days that it was the administration's view that stabilization proposals should rest until the latest intelligence that Professor Moley was bringing could be communicated to the delegation.

What the United States wants in general in return apparently for stabilization is understood to be freer access to European markets by the lowering of tariffs and elimination of other trade barriers. What is wanted specifically the conference is still waiting to learn from the American delegation.

Big Powers Asked to Lead.

The big powers heard today the plea that they give a lead in stabilizing currencies if the world was to avoid "grave dangers." This plea ran like a refrain through most of the speeches of the delegates of ten small countries who addressed the monetary commission's committee on immediate recovery measures. They spoke on the resolution of Neville Chamberlain of Great Britain in favor of raising prices by monetary and credit policies.

Delegates of four big powers, France, Italy, Germany and Japan, spoke, too. The first three nations opposed the British views and wanted prices raised by stabilizing and by a "more prudent" monetary and credit policy. Even the only one

Continued on Page Two.

"All the News That's Fit to Print."

The New York Times.

LATE CITY EDITION
WEATHER—Generally fair today, tomorrow; same temperature.
Temperatures Yesterday—Max., 80; Min., 66.

Copyright, 1933, by The New York Times Company.

VOL. LXXXII....No 27,569. Entered as Second-Class Matter, Postoffice, New York, N. Y. NEW YORK, TUESDAY, JULY 18, 1933. P TWO CENTS In New York City. | THREE CENTS Within 200 Miles | FOUR CENTS Elsewhere Except in 7th and 8th Postal Zones

1,000,000 BEGIN SHORT WEEK, OR RECEIVE HIGHER WAGES, AS 'NEW DEAL' FUNCTIONS

POST ON LAST HALF OF FLIGHT, 17 HOURS AHEAD OF OLD TIME

Flies On From Novosibirsk After 1,800-Mile Hop From Moscow in 13¼ Hours.

DOWN 3 HOURS IN CAPITAL

Takes City by Surprise as He Halts for Repair to Oil Line Feeding Robot Pilot.

DOCTORS FIND HIM FIT

Aviator Eats Lightly and Freshens Up While Soviet Mechanics Work on the Machine.

Wiley Post's own story of his flight is on Page 3.

By The Associated Press.

NOVOSIBIRSK, Siberia, Tuesday, July 18.—Wiley Post, the American round-the-world flier, took off toward Irkutsk, Siberia, at 9:02 A. M. today, Moscow time [2:02 A. M. Eastern Daylight Time] just two hours and thirty-five minutes after completing an 1,800-mile jump from Moscow.

He said he planned to stay overnight at Irkutsk before continuing, perhaps to Kharbarovsk, Siberia, whence he is scheduled to take off for Nome, Alaska.

By cutting short his stay here he gained six hours and thirty-eight minutes more on the time he made with Harold Gatty on a round-the-world hop in 1931. At that time the pair stayed here nine hours thirteen minutes.

He left Moscow at 5:12 P. M. Monday [10:12 A. M. Eastern Daylight Time] and arrived here at 6:27 A. M., 11:27 P. M. Monday, Eastern Daylight Time, thirteen hours and fifteen minutes later, and sixty-six hours seventeen minutes after leaving New York last Saturday.

On his departure he was sixteen hours fifty-seven minutes ahead of the time he and Gatty took for a like distance.

Post has completed a little more than half the distance of his world flight, calculated on the basis of his plotted course.

He asserted that at his average flying time so far he "will be back in New York in less than three full days."

As soon as Post's plane touched the ground, Fay Gillis, an American girl flier who made refuelling arrangements for him, and Ivan Roncharoff, chief of the Novosibirsk airport, rushed out on the field to greet him.

A doctor joined them and started an examination of the Oklahoman. Miss Gillis acted as interpreter.

Makes Stop in Moscow.

By WALTER DURANTY.
Special Cable to THE NEW YORK TIMES.

MOSCOW, July 17.—Wiley Post took Moscow by surprise today when he made a short stop-over here on his journey in quest of the round-the-world flight record. He alighted at the Moscow airport at 2:20 P. M. [7:20 A. M. Eastern Daylight Time] and was off again for Novosibirsk at 5:12 P. M. [10:12 A. M. Eastern Daylight Time].

[When Post arrived at Moscow he was 4 hours and 24 minutes ahead of the time he and Harold Gatty had made on their record flight in 1931. But he gained additional time by making the stop a brief one, and when he took off from the Soviet capital he was 13 hours and 2 minutes ahead of the record time.]

As Post had not been expected to stop at Moscow but to fly on to Novosibirsk, barely a hundred persons were at the airport here when his white and purple monoplane flashed across the field from the southwest, circled and swooped down, then with a big bump touched the ground and taxied to within a few yards of the fence around the airport buildings. Greeted by Airport Commander Miko, officials and foreign correspondents, Post said that the pipe supplying oil to the automatic pilot on his plane needed fixing. The Russians promised to repair it, and then M. Miko rushed him off to a rest room.

Before any questions were asked, a doctor felt Post's pulse and examined his eyes, appearing disappointed that the flier showed no signs of fatigue. Altogether he was examined by three doctors, all of whom found his condition good.

The flier looked fresh enough after he had washed, shaved and eaten a light lunch. He sat on a sofa answering the eager questions of the Russians. The flight from Koenigsberg to Moscow was quite uneventful, Post said, and he would have taken the risk of pushing on to Novosibirsk but he was not sure about the length of the night and

Continued on Page Three.

Bowers Demands Release of 5 Americans; Warns Spain Dispute May Become Serious

Wireless to THE NEW YORK TIMES.

MADRID, July 17.—Ambassador Claude G. Bowers of the United States called on Foreign Minister Fernando de Los Rios today and demanded immediate action in the case of the five Americans arrested after a fight with the Guardia Civil in Palma, Island of Majorca, more than a month ago.

The Ambassador told the Minister that Mrs. Clinton B. Lockwood, the American woman who was arrested, was on the point of a complete collapse and that it seemed expedient in view of the friendly relations now prevailing between Spain and the United States to avert a serious dispute which would undoubtedly ensue if Mrs. Lockwood collapsed.

Ever since her arrest she has been confined in a cell next to a demented woman, whose raving Mrs. Lockwood has endured day and night until she herself has been made very nervous. The jailer is not brutal, but merely says he has no other cell for her.

Indication is given that the United States might feel the case had a decided similarity to the recent Russo-British incident if Mrs. Lockwood should suffer a breakdown.

The American Ambassador has also addressed a written note to the Foreign Minister. Authoritative reports from Majorca say that the Spanish military judge in charge of the case is highly prejudiced against Americans, has made strong open remarks about them and for that reason will not admit the accused to bail.

Spanish civil authorities have acted in complete accord with legal formalities, and since the striking of a member of the Guardia Civil is one of the worst offenses in Spain the case is complicated. It is hoped that Premier and Minister of War Azana, the strong man of the revolutionary Spanish régime, will see

Continued on Page Six.

KAUNAS FLIERS DIE IN CRASH IN REICH

Bodies of Darius and Girenas Found With Wrecked Plane Near Soldin, Pomerania.

GASOLINE TANKS EMPTY

Airmen Believed to Have Lost Way in Storm, Crashing 400 Miles From Goal.

By OTTO D. TOLISCHUS.
Wireless to THE NEW YORK TIMES.

BERLIN, July 17.—The transatlantic flight of the Lithuanian pilots Captain Stephen Darius and Stanley Girenas came to a tragic end when, after conquering the Atlantic Ocean, both died as their plane crashed in a forest outside Soldin, Pomerania. Peasant women found the wreckage and the bodies this morning.

Apparently the aviators had flown as far as Koenigsberg, East Prussia, which is only about 400 miles by air from Kaunas, their goal, where thousands of their countrymen, headed by Premier Juozas Tubelis, were waiting to cheer them as heroes of the nation.

The same thunderstorm which put out of commission the instruments of Wiley Post's plane and forced him to land at Koenigsberg last night apparently caused the Lithuanian fliers to lose their direction They doubled back on their track and were killed while attempting to land when their fuel ran out, in the opinion of the German authorities

"Lost" Plane Seen Last Night.

At about 10 o'clock last night, the Koenigberg police saw the lights of a plane, flying in a southerly direction. It was assumed this was the Lithuanica, and signal rockets were sent up to guide her. The plane disappeared in a westerly direction.

At about midnight a plane appeared over the town of Berlinchen, approximately 120 miles northeast of Berlin, circled the town at a height of only about 200 feet and appeared twice over the voluntary labor camp near by. The second time it lit two flares and one of its occupants was seen leaning far out of the cockpit.

As this was close to the Polish frontier, labor camp guards assumed it was a "hostile" plane and making a photographic record of the camp. The plane disappeared in a southwesterly direction.

At about 1:30 A. M. a farmer near the village of Kuhdamm on the edge of the Soldin forest, approximately thirty miles west of Berlinchen, heard a plane which came out of the northeast, turned around in a sweeping curve and flew off in southeasterly direction. Soon afterward he heard a violent crash, but, since the weather was bad, he did not investigate.

It was 5 o'clock this morning when a group of women gathering mushrooms found the shattered plane. It had hit the edge of the forest, slid along the treetops for more than 200 feet, then smashed into the ground. The motor and propeller were deeply buried in the soil. The rest of the machine was a tangled mass of wood and wire.

Soldin forest is on a slight eminence and the trees are exceptionally high. A few hundred feet beyond where the plane crashed is a meadow, which apparently the pilots had attempted to reach.

Darius's Body in Pilot's Seat.

Darius's body was in the pilot's seat. Girenas lay beside the machine, with one foot still in it. Apparently he had tried to save himself by a last-minute jump. The skulls of both were fractured. Presumably they were killed instantly.

The plane's gasoline tanks were dry, and the reserve fuel supply

Continued on Page Five.

ARGENTINA IN CRISIS ON BRITISH TREATY

Finance Minister Offers to Quit After Dispute Over Pending Trade Pact.

OTHERS REPORTED IN RIFT

New Offer for Commercial Treaty Made Recently by President Roosevelt.

By JOHN W. WHITE.
Special Cable to THE NEW YORK TIMES.

BUENOS AIRES, July 17—A governmental crisis involving the pending trade treaty with Great Britain and continued payments on foreign debts resulted tonight in an offer of the resignation of Finance Minister Alberto Hueyo. President Justo is trying to get him to withdraw the resignation.

There were reports also that Foreign Minister Saavedra Lamas had resigned and that two other Ministers were ready to follow him as the result of their opposition to ratification of the treaty with Britain. The Foreign Minister, however, denied that he had resigned and he added that he had no differences with Señor Hueyo.

Opposition Also in Congress.

The treaty, which was negotiated by Vice President Julio A. Roca on his visit to London, has also been meeting with considerable opposition in Congress. It is on the order of the day for debate in the Chamber of Deputies tomorrow and it is stated in Congressional circles tonight that the opposition to it will be led by Deputy Federico Pinedo, leader of the government majority in the Chamber. Such action by him would create an embarrassing political situation in addition to the crisis in the Cabinet.

There has been so much delay over action on the treaty that the British Government last week lodged a formal complaint. On the same day it was said unofficially in London that because of this delay there would be further reductions in British imports of Argentine chilled meats.

Roland Fraser, special British commissioner, and a committee of advisers have been trying since the middle of June to complete the trade deal by negotiating the protocol on tariffs and quotas which is to be an integral part of the pact. The Argentine negotiations have been under the supervision of Señor Hueyo.

He opposes ratification on the ground that tariff concessions to Britain will seriously curtail Argentina's customs revenues. His delay and the British protest are believed to have precipitated the present Cabinet crisis, although in government circles it is said that his resignation was directly due to the opposition of several Ministers to his financial program. They have especially objected to his proposed curtailment of budget expenses in order to meet obligations to foreigners.

Insists on Payments.

Señor Hueyo has steadfastly insisted upon Argentina's continuing to make prompt payment of her foreign obligations, despite the opposition of several other Ministers and also Congressional opposition. The Congress at the last session passed a law suspending sinking fund payments on the foreign debt, but Señor Hueyo refused to be guided by the law.

The heavy decline in the dollar has decreased Argentina's foreign obligations about 25 per cent, and Señor Hueyo insisted that the country's finances were such that

Continued on Page Two.

HARRIMAN MISSING AGAIN; POLICE HEAR OF SUICIDE EFFORTS

Deckhands on 2 Boats Stop Man of His Description From Leaping Into Hudson.

HE SLIPS OUT OF HOSPITAL

Searchers Lose Trail at River, Keep Watch for Banker Near Grave of Son.

Joseph W. Harriman disappeared yesterday from the Regent Nursing Home for the second time since he was indicted for falsifying the books of the Harriman National Bank.

His disappearance forced Federal Judge Francis G. Caffey to adjourn the hearing into the banker's sanity and led United States Attorney George Z. Medalie to move for forfeiture of his $25,000 bond.

Federal agents joined the police of this and half a dozen neighboring cities in a general search for the ailing banker, who two months ago ran away and tried to commit suicide. They traced him to the Liberty Street ferry, but from that point on become snarled in a maze of conflicting reports.

Suicide Efforts Reported.

What appeared to be the most plausible report came from Captain John W. Johnston of the railroad police at the Communipaw Terminal of the Jersey Central, who said that deckhands had prevented an elderly man answering Mr. Harriman's description from jumping off two ferryboats.

This man, according to Johnston, was seen pacing about the ferry waiting room about 11 A. M. At 11:13 he boarded the ferryboat Wilkes-Barre for Liberty Street and in midstream was hauled back by a deckhand after he had thrown one leg over the rail of the upper deck.

"I just wanted to see how the understructure of the boat was made," the stranger told his rescuer, according to Captain Johnston.

After wandering around the Liberty Street waiting room, Captain Johnston said, the man returned to Jersey City, where he immediately boarded the Cranford, bound for West Twenty-third Street. He returned on the same boat to Jersey City and then boarded the Somerville for West Twenty-third Street. In midstream, a deckhand restrained him from climbing over the rail and at the terminal saw the elderly man debark and board a taxicab.

Heard Testimony on Suicide.

During the hearing into his mental condition, Mr. Harriman had heard physicians testify that his failure to carry out his suicidal intent at Roslyn indicated an unsound mind. One doctor testified that a more certain method of self-destruction than the stabbing he attempted would be to jump in the river or in the path of a subway train.

Detectives of the East Sixty-seventh Street station, after learning the results of Captain Johnston's investigations, visited Mr. Harriman's former town house at 2 East Seventieth Street in the belief that he might have gone there after

Continued on Page Eight.

Morgenthau Forbids Loans in Puerto Rico

Wireless to THE NEW YORK TIMES.

SAN JUAN, P. R., July 17.—Henry Morgenthau Jr., Governor of the Farm Credit Administration, has instructed all Federal agencies that have been lending money secured by mortgages in Puerto Rico to cease doing so.

His action is taken on the ground that mortgage investments are insecure, due to the insular law giving income tax and workmen's compensation assessments prior rights over mortgages, along with property taxes.

This interpretation of the law, long held by the insular Treasurer, has been sustained by the Circuit Court of Appeals at Boston. Mr. Morgenthau has requested Governor Gore to investigate the situation and, if possible, correct it.

MAYOR STILL CLINGS TO STATE TAX PLAN

Confers With Dunnigan and Steingut on Special Session to Finance Relief.

SILENT ON LEHMAN LETTER

Budget Commission Lists 7 Economy Measures—Needy Begin Getting Pay.

Mayor O'Brien conferred yesterday with Assemblyman Irwin Steingut and State Senator John J. Dunnigan on the special session of the Legislature through which the city hopes to raise $41,000,000 a year in new revenue.

The Mayor was extremely reticent on Governor Lehman's statement taking the city to task for its attitude in asking the extraordinary session. He refused to comment on the statement, grew angry when questions on it were pressed and finally cut off his interviewers abruptly.

While the city was going ahead with plans for the session Governor Lehman dropped his Summer vacation program. He canceled an engagement to address a conference of Governors in California at the end of the month and dropped his usual Summer inspection of prisons and hospitals. He intends to give the legislators at least one week's notice before the session opens. If the session begins toward the end of this month it is expected to last through August.

To See Other Leaders.

Yesterday's conference between the Mayor and the legislative leaders was preliminary to a later session at which all leaders of the Legislature will be present. The Mayor made that statement as he was leaving City Hall. Despite the Governor's declared opposition to increasing State taxes as the city recommended, the city administration is still advocating a 1 per cent increase on the sales tax and a like increase on the State stock transfer tax.

The Mayor was silent on the possibility that new city taxes would be proposed to replace those opposed by the Governor. Both recommendations were contained in a financial report written by Controller Charles W. Berry. Governor Lehman takes the position that

Continued on Page Two.

Massachusetts Maps Drive Against Crime With the Attorney General as a Dictator

By The Associated Press.

BOSTON, July 17.—Attorney General Joseph E. Warner told a legislative committee today that what the State needed was a fearless, capable and relentless leader to cope with crime conditions.

The committee felt that he measured up to such specifications and suggested he draw up legislation to enable him to carry out his ideas.

Within three hours the Attorney General was back in the committee room with a resolution, which, if enacted, would make him the generalissimo of an anti-crime crusade in the Bay State. His resolution would give him almost unlimited powers.

Among the actions it would authorize were:

Formation of special agencies to fight crime.

Selection by Mr. Warner of any persons he saw fit to use, regardless of civil service law provisions, and utilization of any members of the established police organizations of the State.

Drafting of any State, county or municipal officials for work in prosecuting cases.

Marshaling of all law enforcement and prosecuting agencies in a unit for concerted action for suppression and extermination of crime.

Search by a police officer without a warrant of any boat, vehicle, car, box, locker or package, and any building other than a dwelling house where an officer had reason to believe gambling apparatus, pool or lottery tickets or dangerous weapons existed.

Seizure by an officer of such implements or articles and arrest of the possessor without a warrant.

The resolution would provide also for a general investigation to ascertain to what extent persons charged with and convicted of crime obtained advantages, legal or otherwise, as against the right of the people.

Toward this end Mr. Warner would be permitted to hold public hearings with the witnesses testifying under oath and could require the production of books and papers pertinent to his investigation. He would receive $25,000 to carry out his plan.

The powers conferred on the Attorney General and the special agencies established would cease to exist one year from the date of passage of the resolution or earlier if the General Court declared the resolve void.

The committee to which Mr. Warner presented his resolution held a hearing on Governor Ely's message criticizing law enforcement in Boston and asking appointment of a committee to study the situation.

BLANKET CODE NEXT STEP

Voluntary Agreement by All Industries and Trades Is Aim.

JOHNSON WORKS ON DRAFT

Plans Are Shaped for National Campaign Comparable to Liberty Loan Drives.

RAYON HEARING ON JULY 25

Indiana Limestone Men Ask President to Apply Licensing Powers to Their Trade.

Special to THE NEW YORK TIMES.

WASHINGTON, July 17.—The entire staff of the National Recovery Administration was pressed into action today by General Hugh S. Johnson to frame a blanket code for all business without waiting for approval of the various fair-competition agreements.

The goal of the administration is to have in effect in a few days a scale of shorter work hours with compensatory higher wages throughout the country. It is the present plan that the new scale shall be established by industries and trades voluntarily. The most intensive publicity campaign indulged in by the government since the Liberty Loan drives of the World War is contemplated.

General Johnson revealed this afternoon that he is proceeding with formulation of the blanket code with the sanction of both President Roosevelt and the Cabinet Recovery Board. The whole program, he said, awaits a detailed document which is nearing completion. He expressed the hope that it would be in such shape as could be taken up tomorrow at the meeting of the President's Executive Council.

Urges Speed on the Staff.

The Recovery Administrator called his staff into session this morning for a discussion of the proposal. He urged the greatest possible speed in preparing for promulgation of the blanket code.

A fair practice code was received today from the National Rayon Weaving Industry and it was docketed for public hearing on July 25. This agreement proposes the same wages and hour arrangement as in the cotton textile industry, which went under its new constitution today—a minimum $12 in the South and $13 in the North for a 40-hour week.

Should the blanket code as originally proposed by the combined Industry, Labor and Consumers Advisory Boards of the Industrial Recovery Administration be successfully negotiated, a 40-hour maximum week for mercantile establishments and thirty-five hours for industry would become general, with minimum wage scales of $15 and $14 respectively.

This blanket code would not affect the cotton textile industry, as it would apply only to those industries that have not obtained approval of their agreements. As fast as these single codes should be approved, they would in each case supersede the general code.

The publicity program under contemplation is understood to include every idea and device known in the Liberty Loan drives. Under the suggestions which General Johnson is studying, President Roosevelt would be the leader of the campaign and probably would start it off with a radio appeal to the nation to help the movement for industrial recovery.

The publicity suggestions include the establishment of speakers bureaus throughout the country and motion picture campaigns. Individuals and firms entering into the proposed voluntary arrangement to shorten work hours and increase wages would be supplied with official insignia for stationery, window plaques, smokestack adornments and the like.

The insignia tentatively agreed upon is a blue eagle, poised above a legend "We Do Our Part," with the inscription "N. R. A." above his head.

Seek Quick Rise in Buying Power.

The self-imposition by industry and trade of the blanket code would in no wise abrogate the necessity of

Continued on Page Nine.

President Fit After Cold Caught on River Cruise

By The Associated Press.

WASHINGTON, July 17.—President Roosevelt was pronounced physically fit tonight after a day spent away from his desk because of a slight cold contracted on his week-end cruise on the Potomac.

"The President is perfectly all right," said Captain Ross T. McIntyre of the Naval Hospital as he left the White House. "There certainly is nothing wrong with him now."

Mr. Roosevelt transacted business today in the oval room on the second floor of the White House.

STOCKS RISE 1 TO 9½; WHEAT UP TO $1.26

Average of 50 Leading Issues Reaches 109% Above March 2 Level in Heavy Trading.

ALL COMMODITIES JUMP

Cotton Gains 85c to $1.25—Dollar Continues Decline—Bond Market Strong.

Stocks and commodities continued to rise yesterday in extraordinarily heavy trading. Many new highs for the year were established. The markets were apparently stimulated by the approval of codes by the steel and woolen industries, reports of rapid improvement in general business and corporate earnings, the expectation of the repeal of the Eighteenth Amendment, and by a further moderate weakness in the dollar.

Active stock issues rose from 1 to 9½ points. The largest gains were in the so-called alcohol stocks. Hopes that the three Southern States voting this week would not upset the progress of repeal stimulated heavy speculative activity in the shares of companies which are planning, or believed to be planning, the manufacture of hard liquors once repeal is accomplished.

New Codes a Factor.

The new code for the steel industry and those for the woolen and other important lines, as made public over the week-end created a favorable impression in the financial community. Week-end summaries showing a continuation of the progress in leading industries such as steel and cotton were also encouraging, as was the improvement shown in the first of the semi-annual earnings reports.

The turnover on the Exchange was 6,386,000 shares. In THE NEW YORK TIMES average of fifty stocks the rise amounted to 1.31 points. The index touched a new high for the year at 97.97. At this level it had recorded a rise of 109 per cent since March 2.

Although the foreign exchange market was relatively quiet, the dollar continued to depreciate. Sterling advanced 2 cents to $4.80, while the franc closed 3½ points higher at 5.64½ cents.

The most sensational movements of the day were in the commodities. Wheat, which has been moving ahead steadily, was 5 cents a bushel higher at one time and closed up from 3⅛ to 3¾ cents, with the May delivery at $1.26. Veteran grain traders who predicted "dollar wheat" several months ago were reported to be forecasting $1.50 or $2 for the grain if speculation continued on the present huge scale.

Barley Up 11¾ Cents.

Barley rose 11¾ cents a bushel on heavy buying linked to the beer trade. Other grains showed smaller advances.

In the New York commodity markets cotton futures gained 85 cents to $1.25 a bale. Record trading occurred in crude rubber and cocoa futures. The spot price of crude rubber advanced above 10 cents for the first time since August, 1930. Coffee and sugar futures also were strong.

An increase of 50 per cent in memberships in the new Commodity Exchange, Inc., was reported, the price advancing from $5,000 to $7,500. The seats were issued at $900 when the Exchange was formed in May through the consolidation of several smaller exchanges.

Stocks in the alcohol and allied

Continued on Page Two.

RECOVERY PLANS IN FORCE

Textile Mills in North and South Spread Work Under Code.

STEEL PAY IS UP 15%

Bethlehem Declares Increase for 50,000—Others in Line in Advance of Trade Order.

AUTO INDUSTRY PICKS UP

Business Gains Are Shown in Year's High Figure for Car Loadings.

As the textile code went into effect and many steel mills anticipated the 15 per cent wage increase promised by that industry's code, nearly a million Americans benefited yesterday by pay rises or increased employment through shorter working hours.

Under the stimulus of the general pick-up in business, other lines of industry which have not yet made ready their codes, announced voluntary wage rises or placed more workers back in jobs, dispatches to THE NEW YORK TIMES and by The Associated Press revealed.

Long lines of eager job-seekers waited hopefully at the gates of Southern cotton mills, while in New England an actual shortage of experienced weavers and spinners was reported in several textile centres.

In addition to the 700,000 or more workers who went on a forty-hour week basis in the cotton textile, rayon, silk and thread industries, George A. Sloan, president of the Cotton Textile Institute, estimated that 100,000 new jobs would be created in that field under the code.

Big Steel Companies in Line.

The Bethlehem Steel Company announced a 15 per cent pay rise for about 50,000 workers, while the Jones & Laughlin Steel Corporation, one of the largest independents in the industry, fell into line with a similar announcement in Pittsburgh.

It was estimated that more than 125,000 steel mill workers in the Pittsburgh area alone would receive the increase, which lifted the pay of common labor from 33 to 40 cents an hour. This brings their wages to the level which prevailed before the 15 per cent reduction of May, 1932.

The United States Steel Corporation was leaving announcement of the increase to its various subsidiary companies. The Carnegie Steel Company announced the rise Saturday, the American Steel and Wire Company and the National Tube Company of McKeesport yesterday.

Employment in the steel industry has jumped 233 per cent in July, as compared with the first quarter of the year, officials of steel companies estimated. They calculated that the increased purchasing power of the workers amounted to 283 per cent.

The American Window Glass Company announced an 11 per cent wage rise, effective at once, for its 750 employes.

Detroit Auto Industry Gains.

In Detroit, Roy D. Chapin, president of the Hudson Motor Car Company, announced wage increases of from 5 to 10 per cent for 5,000 of the company's 7,000 employes. The annual increase, it was said, amounts to more than $750,000.

"These increases are effective as of July 17 and are in line with the constructive spirit of American industry to rebuild the buying power of the nation," Mr. Chapin said.

Irving J. Reuter, president of the Buick Motor Company, said that more than 1,000 former employes would be put back to work there because the company was continuing production of its present models until Sept. 15. Last year production of new models began at the end of July.

Tabin Picker & Co., Chicago wash frock makers, announced a pay rise of 20 per cent for its 2,800 employes, most of whom are women. The new scale was to go into effect immediately.

The Phelps Dodge Corporation reported at its headquarters here that it had decided to step up its monthly production to 6,000,000 pounds of copper, an increase to

Continued on Page Ten.

Section 1

"All the News That's Fit to Print."

The New York Times.

LATE CITY EDITION
WEATHER—Probably local thunder showers today and tomorrow.
Temperatures Yesterday—Max., 88; min., 69.

Section 1

VOL. LXXXII....No. 27,574. Entered as Second-Class Matter, Postoffice, New York, N. Y. NEW YORK, SUNDAY, JULY 23, 1933. P Including Rotogravure Picture, Magazine and Book Sections. TEN CENTS | TWELVE CENTS Beyond 200 Miles. Except in 7th and 8th Postal Zones.

POST ARRIVES SAFELY IN NEW YORK, CIRCLING WORLD IN 7 DAYS, 19 HOURS; MOLLISONS ARE FLYING THE ATLANTIC

GOVERNMENT FIXES FLUCTUATION LIMIT FOR GRAIN TRADING

MINIMUM PRICES ARE SET

Must Not Go Below Closing Quotations on Thursday.

DAILY LIMIT IS ALSO SET

Suggested by the Chicago Board of Trade, but Affects Others Also.

LASTING REFORM SOUGHT

Talk Renewed in Washington of Restriction on the Stock Exchange.

Special to THE NEW YORK TIMES.

WASHINGTON, July 22.—Minimum prices for trading in wheat, corn and other grains until further notice were announced tonight by Secretary Wallace, who approved a program suggested by the Chicago Board of Trade to avert further collapse of commodities.

No trading below the closing prices of Thursday will be permitted.

The closing prices of grains on the Chicago Board of Trade on Thursday were as follows:

Wheat—July, 90 cents; September, 91 cents; December, 95¼ cents; May, $1.

Corn—July, 46 cents; September, 53 cents; December, 56½ cents; May, 64 cents.

Oats—July, 35 cents; September, 34½ cents; December, 37 cents; May, 41 cents.

Rye—July, 69 cents; September, 67 cents; December, 73 cents; May, 81½ cents.

Barley—September, 85⅞ cents; December, 80¾ cents.

Fluctuations in any single day's movement in wheat would be limited to 5 cents and other grains in proportion, a formal statement said. This was at variance with a version given out in Chicago where Board of Trade officials insisted the limit of fluctuation on wheat was eight cents.

This drastic action to control grain prices was taken by the government when it became known to adjustment officials that several large speculators had been caught on the long side by the decline of the last few days and were unable with their large commitments to cover the increased margins that were being demanded. The only alternative would have been to sell out these large accounts with the opening of the market Monday, with the result of a further break in prices.

Statement of the Agreement.

The department's announcement of the agreement with the Chicago Board of Trade read:

"An astounding illustration of the result of individual unrestrained speculation as it affects commodity prices has been brought to the attention of the President and his Secretary of Agriculture.

"During the last administration a regulation requiring the reporting of all large grain holdings on the Chicago Board of Trade was rescinded and the regulation was not revived by this administration because it was believed that individual speculators had learned that it was contrary to public policy for individuals to gamble so heavily in wheat, corn and other grains that the prices to the farmers producing the grain could be thrown wholly out of line with the broad economic situation.

"Early this week the Department of Agriculture came to the conclusion that the old order calling for information should be reinstated, and this was done on July 20. Today it turns out that one man who had been 'long' on corn by roughly 13,000,000 bushels and was probably also long on other grains to the extent of several million bushels was caught in the decline of prices during the past few days, was unable to put up any more margin and would have to be sold out.

Results of Selling Out.

"This selling-out process would mean in effect that by Monday morning, his brokers, seventeen in number, would be compelled to dump 13,000,000 bushels of corn and several million bushels of other grain on the market, and this dumping would naturally cause a severe break in grain prices—all the result of the selfish speculation of one individual.

"This speculator is only one of several who have traded wildly in large volume on both sides of the market.

"In order to protect the farmers

Continued on Page Twelve.

Trotsky, in Naples, Denies Making Up With Stalin

By The Associated Press.

NAPLES, July 22.—Leon Trotsky denied reports of a possible reconciliation with Joseph Stalin as he arrived here today aboard the steamer Bulgaria.

Mr. Trotsky said he would proceed with his five aides to Genoa tonight en route to Marseilles or Corsica in order to take a health cure for his ailing heart. He declined the privilege of debarking here, but Mrs. Trotsky enjoyed a shopping tour.

The former Russian leader's secretary was described to port authorities as a Pole traveling on an American passport.

TRADING HOURS CUT BY STOCK EXCHANGE

Business Will Start at Noon to Aid Hard-Pressed Brokers—Holiday Saturday Likely.

STOCKS FIRMER FOR DAY

Heavy Selling Absorbed With Small Decline—Short Session Is Orderly.

As a relief measure for the army of Wall Street brokerage clerks, the New York Stock Exchange ordered yesterday that, beginning at noon tomorrow, trading hours should be shortened from five to three. This action, taken before the market opened at 10 o'clock, was followed by an orderly two-hour market.

Stocks and commodities developed a firm tone after three days of heavy, uncontrolled selling. There were indications at the same time that a new feeling of confidence was developing in Washington and elsewhere. The share market was quieter and more composed than it had been in some days.

Reports from Washington that the administration was not alarmed by the sharp decline of Wednesday, Thursday and Friday contributed to the improvement in sentiment. Brokers continued to view the slump merely as a correction of the speculative excesses of the last month or two. Many expressed the opinion that the selling movement seemed slowly to be exhausting itself.

In reducing the trading hours from five to three, under which program the Stock Exchange will open at 12 o'clock noon instead of 10 o'clock as usual, the governors have gone back to the practice of 1929 when in uncommonly heavy trading, the market hours were shortened. If the trading pace continues to increase, the Exchange may be closed all day on next Saturday. That market will open tomorrow and thereafter at noon until further notice and will close at 3 P. M. as usual. The change did not affect yesterday's trading hours. The purpose solely is to relieve the strain upon clerical workers in the commission houses.

Pecora to Meet Officers.

After the Exchange had made its announcement, Ferdinand Pecora, counsel for the Banking and Currency Committee of the United States Senate, which has been investigating Wall Street practices, announced that "in view of conditions prevailing on the Stock Exchange, and on similar markets throughout the country," he would confer tomorrow with officers of the Stock Exchange.

At Mr. Pecora's offices it was said that he was out of town, and that no information was available as to what he would discuss with representatives of the Exchange.

Trading on the Stock Exchange yesterday totaled 4,224,070 shares, the second heaviest turnover for a Saturday this year, and the third heaviest in the history of the Exchange. The record, 4,867,530 shares, was established May 3, 1930. Despite heavy necessitous selling by traders whose margins had been impaired, the losses in leading stocks were not larger than 2 or 3 points, and many prominent railroad and industrial issues closed with net gains of 1 to 2 points. THE NEW YORK TIMES average of fifty stocks declined .42 of a point.

Wheat Drops in Winnipeg.

The grain markets of the country, which were closed Friday, following wheat's drop of 15 cents a bushel on Thursday, did not open yesterday. Reports from Chicago declared that a proposal to limit

Continued on Page Twenty.

PRESIDENT CALLS WARTIME FORCES TO SPEED RECOVERY

About 500 Lieutenants Will Be Leaders of the Liberty Loan Drives.

AGREEMENTS ARE MAILED

Goal Is Signature of 5,000,000 Employers—Patriotism, Publicity and Pressure the Plan.

Special to THE NEW YORK TIMES.

WASHINGTON, July 22.—A wartime organization was being whipped into shape today by President Roosevelt and his Recovery Administration for the greatest peace-time assault on a national enemy this country has ever seen.

The task was begun of selecting more than 500 lieutenants who are to bear the brunt of the nation-wide drive for acceptance by employers of the voluntary minimum wage and maximum hour agreement that will, the President hopes, return 6,000,000 men to work soon after Labor Day.

As the chief officials studied the question of personnel, half a dozen government plants were printing at top speed tons of literature which is to be distributed throughout the country next Thursday.

This literature was to start leaving Washington literally by the carload tonight, bound for post-offices in all parts of the nation, whence it will be distributed to employers and consumers.

Like Liberty Loan Drive.

The chief items in the first batch of literature were copies of the President's blanket agreement providing for a 35-hour week among industrial employes and forty hours for white-collar workers, with minimum weekly wage scales of $14 in the former and $12 to $15 in the latter.

The expectation of the administration is that these will be returned signed by a large majority of 5,000,000 employers, impelled by either business or patriotic motives or the heat of the publicity campaign which President Roosevelt officially will open on Monday night.

The organization being perfected is similar to that which put the Liberty loans over the top. The plan is to use the wartime methods, Four-Minute Men and all, augmented by the radio and talking picture.

The same leaders who carried the Liberty Loan drives to success have been recalled for the peacetime job. The campaign is to be directly under the supervision of Charles Francis Horner of Kansas City, director of the speakers' bureau of the Treasury during the Liberty Loan drives.

At the head of the organization division is Frank R. Wilson, former Sioux City (Iowa) newspaper publisher, who was director of publicity in all three war loan campaigns. The speakers' bureau this time will be in charge of Louis J. Alber of Cleveland, who was Mr. Horner's assistant. The newspaper division is to be headed by Labert St. Clair, who held the same place in the Liberty Loan appeals.

Recovery officials make no secret that the intent of the campaign is to build up such a public psychology that employers cannot afford not to "sign up" for the President's mass attack on unemployment. They purpose to encourage patriotic citizens to trade with and favor those individuals and business firms who agree "voluntarily" to the President's proposal.

They propose to make no defense

Continued on Page Eighteen.

Ban on 'Marxist Pictures' In Essen, Even in Homes

Wireless to THE NEW YORK TIMES.

ESSEN, Germany, July 22.—The local police president has forbidden "Marxist pictures," even in private homes. Such "offensive" pictures, his order states, "are still found in the dwellings of former members of the Socialist party."

"To have the minds of the young poisoned thereby cannot be tolerated," the order adds. "The continued display or possession of such pictures will be construed as a challenge to the national resurgence and as propaganda for Marxism."

Those offending may, therefore, be taken into custody, the order concludes, but the term "Marxist pictures" is left undefined.

M'ANENY SHIFTS 59 IN BIGGEST SHAKE-UP

Every District Head in the Sanitation Department Sent to a New Area Today.

MORE 'ELASTICITY' IS AIM

Commissioner Also Wants More Efficiency Among His Chief Aides and Cleaner Streets.

Every one of the fifty-nine district superintendents of the Sanitation Department was transferred last midnight in the largest shake-up in the department's history.

The superintendents go to their new posts today with added responsibility for keeping the streets of the city clean. Each district superintendent is responsible to his borough superintendent. The borough superintendents are responsible to George McAneny, Sanitation Commissioner appointed by Mayor O'Brien a few months ago.

In announcing the changes Commissioner McAneny said:

"Since assuming office as head of the Department of Sanitation I have spent much time in examining the condition of the streets, garages and other plants under the care of the department. I have noted that many of the district superintendents have been in their present assignments for many years. I am convinced that a greater flexibility and elasticity of the supervising force would be of great benefit both to the efficiency of the department and to the supervising officers themselves."

Tells Department's Problems.

Turning to the department's problems in various parts of the city, Mr. McAneny said:

"In some districts there are peculiar traffic problems, such as in Fifth Avenue, Park Avenue, Broadway, Queens Boulevard, the "Hub" in the Bronx, the downtown section of Brooklyn, all of which have their relationship to street cleaning and the collection of ashes, garbage and rubbish. Then, too, we have the various pushcart market districts presenting separate and distinct problems. In the downtown section of Manhattan we have in the Winter time a specialized work in the matter of speedy snow removal.

"It is my desire that all of our superintendents know as much about all the districts as possible, and that they be prepared through experience to assume any detail in the course of departmental reorganization that may be given to them."

Mr. McAneny was appointed by Mayor O'Brien after the Board of Estimate had changed the department's set-up, reducing it from a body of three commissioners to one.

Continued on Page Twelve.

Lindberghs Arrive Safely in Greenland After a Perilous Flight From Labrador

Special Cable to THE NEW YORK TIMES.

GODTHAAB, West Greenland, July 22.—Colonel and Mrs. Charles A. Lindbergh completed safely one of the most perilous stages of their Atlantic flight tonight when their seaplane floated gently down to the water at Godthaab Harbor at 7:30 o'clock tonight Greenland time.

A crowd of Greenlanders and Eskimos clustering on cliffs above this little settlement first sighted the plane flying out of the southwest at 6:15. The Eskimos shouted with excitement as the machine roared inland, circled high over the town and then vanished in the distance. An hour later it reappeared. This time Colonel Lindbergh flew so low he could almost see Danish and American flags fluttering in the gayly decorated streets.

The plane came down just outside the entrance of the bay, but the crowd of natives who had been hoping to paddle Lindbergh ashore in their kayaks met disappointment. Instead of leaving the plane where seas might batter it, the Lindberghs taxied it into the harbor opposite the town and went ashore in a motorboat.

Officials of the Danish colony and leading Eskimos then welcomed them to Greenland, expressing the hope they would stay for a time before proceeding on their flight to Iceland and Europe.

The first persons to greet the Lindberghs in the outer harbor were native boys in two tiny rowboats. Not knowing English, they tried to welcome the fliers by frantically waving their arms. Soon afterward Governor Svane of West Greenland arrived in a motor launch and towed the plane to its mooring place near the town.

The following radiogram from the Lindberghs was received here by the Radiomarine Corporation:

"Flew from Hebron, Labrador, to Godthaab, Greenland. Landed at 5:14, Eastern Standard Time." The message was received here at 7:13, Eastern Daylight Time.

BRITONS START IN WALES

Mollison and Wife Due at Bennett Field Here This Evening.

OCEAN WEATHER IMPROVES

Fliers Speed From London for Pendine Beach on Receiving Air Ministry's Report.

NEXT JUMP TO BAGDAD

Holders of Air Records Plan to Retire to Cottage After 6,000-Mile Non-Stop Flight.

Wireless to THE NEW YORK TIMES.

PENDINE, Wales, July 22.—After weeks of waiting, Captain James A. Mollison and his wife, Amy Johnson, started their flight for New York at noon today (7 A. M. Eastern Daylight Time) in their big black bi-plane, Seafarer.

They hope to reach their destination by 5 o'clock tomorrow afternoon, New York time, and after a brief stay fly back non-stop 6,000 miles to Bagdad and so break the distance record. Then they plan to return to London, covering altogether 12,000 miles.

After their return, Captain Mollison said they would retire to a country cottage and "look twice before crossing the road."

The Mollisons started in a whirlwind rush, even missing breakfast in their excitement after receiving the Air Ministry's weather report. The weather was not considered perfect, but was thought good enough for them to take a chance.

Rush Away from London.

They tore out to the Staglane airdrome, near London, finishing dressing in their car. Ten minutes after reaching the airdrome and an hour after getting the weather report they were in the air, crossing England to the broad sandy South Wales beach chosen for the take-off.

After landing at Pendine, where fuel and oil were ready, the fueling began. The Mollisons were so busy superintending the final arrangements they had time only to snatch a few mouthfuls of food. As they took along only barley sugar, raisins and coffee, they are likely to be very hungry on the flight.

In spite of the heavy load of 400 gallons of fuel, giving a range of 3,800 miles, the Seafarer made a perfect take-off, with Captain Mollison at the controls, in a little more than 900 yards. Then it slowly rose, passed once over the crowds on the beach and headed out to sea for Ireland and the Atlantic.

Half a minute before the take-off a last-minute weather forecast promising somewhat better Atlantic weather was handed to them. Both had the greatest confidence in their plane.

Bad Weather Only At Start.

"The weather is not perfect, but is good enough for us," said Captain Mollison. "The weather for the first 800 miles is reported bad—low clouds and headwinds—but by nightfall we should be running into better weather. We are glad the worst will be at the beginning."

Both will take turns at the controls.

On June 8, when conditions were ideal, the Mollisons crashed in an attempt to take off at Croydon. To avoid further risk they decided to make their second attempt from Pendine.

The Seafarer was flown there early in July and remained pegged down on the sands for some days, but when an Atlantic gale swept in July 13 the Mollisons returned to London, where they remained since, impatiently scanning the Air Ministry's weather reports. Today for the first time the strong winds over the Atlantic were reported to be calming down.

Lipstick Is Only Baggage.

By The Associated Press.

PENDINE, Wales, July 22.—Carrying a lipstick for Amy and no baggage at all for Jim, the flying Mollisons took to the air today to make their long-delayed flight to New York.

For Amy it was "the greatest adventure of my life"; for Jim, "this may be my last spectacular flight."

At 1:20 P. M., Greenwich Time (9:20 A. M., Eastern Daylight Time) the Mollisons were sighted

Continued on Page Five.

HOME WITH A NEW GLOBE-CIRCLING RECORD.

Times Wide World Photo.

Wiley Post Leaving His Plane at Floyd Bennett Field Last Midnight After Having Completed His Second Trip Around the World in the Winnie Mae.

Post 'Disgusted' by Flight; Hoped for a Better Record

Thinks He Could Cover Route Again in Four Days With Good Weather—Ice on Wings Over Rockies Added to His Perils.

By WILEY POST.

Now that it's over, and I am back where I started from, the chief idea in my mind is that I am disgusted with my flight. I realize, of course, that I have broken the record of eight days, fifteen hours and fifty-one minutes which Harold Gatty and I made together two years ago, but I had expected to break it by a much wider margin, and I am disappointed.

I should have made this flight a month earlier. Then I would have escaped some of the fogs and stormy weather which I have had almost ever since I left New York. As a matter of fact, until well along on the last leg of the flight today, I had had only three hours of good weather all the way around the world.

That was one hour going into Moscow, and two hours going out of Moscow. The bad weather began five minutes after I left Floyd Bennett Field and it dogged me all the way. Today it started out as bad as ever. Half way from Fairbanks to Edmonton, where I was flying the Canadian Rockies, I had to fly blind for three hours at 20,000 feet. The mountains there have an elevation of 15,000 feet.

While I was up at that extreme height, ice began to form on my wings. It got heavy enough so that I mushed down some. It cleared up the last half of the way into Edmonton, and then it was plain sailing until between Toronto and New York. There I encountered considerable smoky haze, and I also had to fly around two thunderstorms.

No Thrill in Final Hop.

There was a kick in getting back to the old field and meeting my wife and friends, but there was no thrill to the flight coming in. I was so disappointed with my record that I actually thought today of sitting down and coming on in tomorrow.

I couldn't realize then that I was coming home. After I had got out of the bad weather today the going was so smooth that I flew mechanically and I kept going to sleep all along. I have no idea how many times I dozed off, but I slept a great deal of the way in. I had my hand on the extension of my control stick and every time I went clear to sleep my hand would fall off and that would cause me to wake up with a jump.

Don't think from this, though, that I am dead for sleep. I am not. I am not much fresher than I was when I finished the trip with Gatty two years ago. As a matter of fact, I had too much sleep. I could have done without nearly as much as I had. I say too much sleep because it was due to delays caused by weather, &c., or to having the plane tuned up.

Another disappointment is that I had hoped to see a little of the world while I was flying around it. When Harold and I flew the route before, I was too busy with the controls to enjoy the scenery. This time, I thought, with the automatic pilot to take over most of the actual work, I would be able to sit back and look the countries over.

But the weather was so bad most of the way that all the scenery I saw was an occasional mountain jumping at me out of the fog.

Thinks Four-Day Flight Possible.

After two flights around the world in the Winnie Mae, I know just about what the flight could be done in. It can be done in a lot better time than I made it. I am convinced that with the equipment I used on this flight, with the Winnie Mae's cruising speed stepped up, and the robot pilot to take off a lot of the strain, I could fly the same route in four and a half days or better with ordinarily good weather.

I'd like to try it again, but, of course, I can't say at this time whether I ever will. There are too many things to be considered.

I have said a lot about the dirty weather I had on this flight, but don't get the idea that I am kicking about bad luck. There is bound to be a lot of luck on a flight of this length, both bad luck and good luck. The weather was bad luck, all right, but I had such good luck also at critical points that I can almost forget about the weather.

It was just plain good luck that when I was forced down in Alaska after flying blind from Khabarovsk, Siberia, and being lost seven hours while trying to find the Yukon River, I came down in a place where there was a good machine shop and good mechanics who could repair my damaged ship.

When I landed at Flat, Alaska, and my ship nosed over, bending

Continued on Page Two.

RECORD IS CUT 21 HOURS

75,000 at City Airport Greet Flier After a 15,596-Mile Trip.

LAST LAP IN FAST TIME

Winnie Mae Took Off From Edmonton at 10:41 A. M. for 2,004-Mile Hop.

FLEW HIGH, AIDED BY WIND

First Man to Circle the World in Solo Flight Brings Back Many Records.

Wiley Post landed safely in his fleet monoplane, the Winnie Mae, on Floyd Bennett Field, Brooklyn, at 11:59½ o'clock last night, completing a record flight around the world.

The aviator, who used to be a farmer in Texas and an oil driller in Oklahoma, thus became the first person in history to fly alone around the world. He also established a new speed record in circumnavigating the globe in 7 days, 18 hours, 49½ minutes.

Post beat the record of 8 days, 15 hours, 51 minutes, established by himself and Harold Gatty, then his navigator, two years ago, by 21 hours, 1½ minutes.

The 34-year-old flier, who has only one eye, is the first person to fly around the world twice. His purple-and-white Winnie Mae, which is three years old, now has the distinction of being the first airplane ever to circle the globe twice as well as being the fastest thing on wings when it comes to flying around the world. The Winnie Mae carried Post and Gatty around the world in 1931, and was rebuilt for the flight just ended.

On Time to the Minute.

Post's arrival just half a minute before midnight more than bore out the prediction he made at Edmonton, Canada, yesterday morning that he would arrive at Floyd Bennett Field "about midnight" and beat the Post-Gatty record by nearly a full day.

Speeding through the dark, moonless night, with no lights on his plane, Post was almost on top of the airport before the crowd of 75,000 caught sight of him. He had his motor throttled down, so that it was even more of a surprise when the crowd saw a dark spot approaching the field from the north, about 800 feet up.

"There's a plane!" shouted some one near the automobile in which Mrs. Post, the flier's wife, sat.

"It has no lights!" cried Lee Trenholm, Post's manager, sitting in the car with Mrs. Post and Harold Gatty. "It must be Wiley!"

The cry then spread like wildfire throughout the crowd: "It's Post! He's made it!"

Even the airport managers were caught napping by the terrific speed Post made in the last few hours of his journey through the black night, with only the stars, the transatlantic air mail beacons and the illumination of cities and towns below him to light his way.

Just before he landed an erroneous report was received that he had been sighted in Pittston, Pa., 155 miles away, at 11:50 o'clock, which would have meant another hour or more before he could have reached Floyd Bennett Field. The last previous report of the Winnie Mae had been at Corning, N. Y., at 10:50.

Accordingly, the airport did not expect him for some time after midnight, and did not have the floodlights on when he was first seen. The amber boundary lines all around the field, the red obstruction lights on gas tanks and buildings and the green and white beacon atop the administration building, were all on, and Post had no difficulty in finding his way.

Floodlights Turned On.

As soon as his plane was identified aloft, the floodlights were thrown on, bathing the whole landing field in brilliant light and overcoming the adverse effect of the slight ground fog that had hung over the field all night. Post's luck was with him to the last, for a shift of the wind from south southwest to southeast would have thrown a dangerous pall of fog over the field—but the wind did not shift.

Post flew the Winnie May in from the north as if he had flown over

Continued on Page Two.

Britain's flying couple, Amy Johnson Mollison and Captain James A. Mollison, in their flying uniforms at the Croyden air field. They failed to complete their flight as planned, crashing in Bridgeport rather than landing in New York.

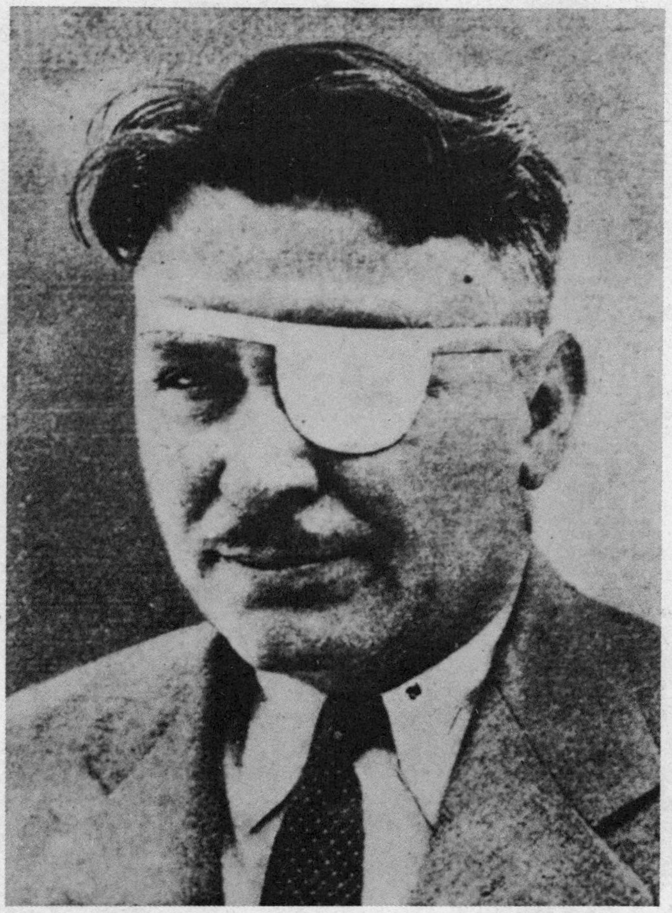

Wiley Post, the first aviator to circle the globe alone.

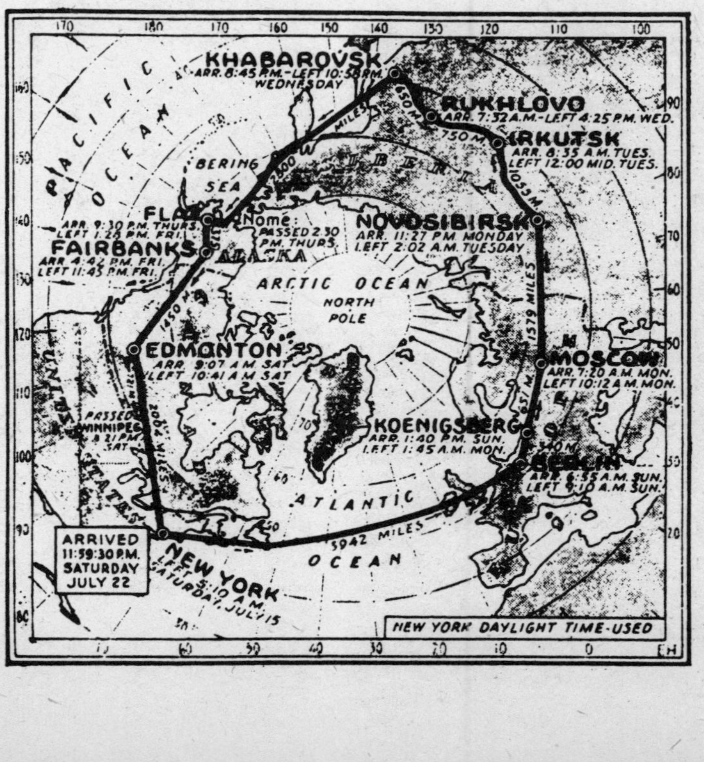

Map shows Wiley's record-breaking route. On the last leg of his journey he landed at Edmonton at 9:07 A. M. and took off for New York at 10:41 A. M. He was reported over United States soil again at 5:33 P. M., thirty miles west of Grand Marais, Minn. At 9:47 P. M. he was over Toronto and at 11:59 he landed at New York.

Comparison of Post's Present World Flight With the One Made by Him and Gatty in 1931

New York Daylight Time.

POST.

Saturday, July 15, 1933.

5:10 A. M.—Took off from Floyd Bennett Field, New York.

Second Day.

6:55 A. M.—Landed at Berlin.

9:10 A. M.—Took off for Novosibirsk, 2,600 miles.

1:40 P. M.—Landed at Koenigsberg.

Third Day.

1:45 A. M.—Took off from Koenigsberg.

7:20 A. M.—Landed at Moscow, 670 miles away.

10:12 A. M.—Took off from Moscow for Novosibirsk.

11:27 P. M.—Landed at Novosibirsk.

Fourth Day.

2:02 A. M.—Took off from Novosibirsk.

8:35 A. M.—Landed at Irkutsk.

Fifth Day.

12:00 Midnight—Took off from Irkutsk.

7:32 A. M.—Landed at Rukhlovo.

4:25 P. M. — Took off from Rukhlovo.

8:45 P. M.—Landed at Khabarovsk.

10:58 P. M.—Took off from Khabarovsk.

Sixth Day.

2:30 P. M.—Passed over Nome, Alaska.

9:30 P. M. — Landed at Flat, Alaska. 360 miles from Fairbanks.

Seventh Day.

1:28 P. M.—Took off at Flat for Fairbanks.

4:42 P. M. — Landed at Fairbanks.

11:45 P. M.—Took off from Fairbanks.

Eighth Day.

9:07 A. M.—Landed at Edmonton.

10:41 A. M.—Took off from Edmonton for New York.

11:59½ P. M.—Landed at Floyd Bennett Field. Total distance, 15.596 miles. Total elapsed time. 7 days, 18 hours, 49½ minutes.

POST—GATTY.

Tuesday, June 23, 1931.

4:56 A. M. — Took off from Roosevelt Field, New York.

11:48 A. M.—Landed at Harbor Grace.

3:28 P. M.—Took off for Berlin.

Second Day.

7:45 A. M.—Landed at Sealand Airdrome, near Chester, England.

8:05 A. M.—Took off for Germany.

12:45 P. M.—Landed at Hanover.

2:15 P. M.—Took off from Hanover.

3:30 P.M.—Landed at Berlin.

Third Day.

2:38 A. M.—Took off from Berlin.

11:30 A. M.—Landed at Moscow.

11:00 P.M.—Took off from Moscow.

Fourth Day.

9:32 A. M.—Landed at Novosibirsk.

6:45 P.M.—Took off from Novosibirsk.

Fifth Day.

12:56 A. M.—Landed at Irkutsk.

3:10 A. M.—Took off from Irkutsk.

8:00 A. M.—Landed at Blagoveshchensk. Elapsed time from New York, 90 hours 4 minutes.

10:30 P. M.—Took off from Blagoveshchensk.

Sixth Day.

2:30 A. M.—Landed at Khabarovsk.

Seventh Day.

5:00 A. M.—Took off from Khabarovsk.

9:45 P. M.—Landed at Solomon, Alaska, 30 miles from Nome.

11:30 P. M.—Took off at Solomon for Fairbanks.

Eighth Day.

3:25 A. M. — Landed at Fairbanks.

9:24 A. M.—Took off from Fairbanks for Edmonton, Canada.

7:30 P. M.—Landed at Edmonton.

Ninth Day.

6:30 A. M.—Took off from Edmonton.

5:15 P. M.—Landed at Cleveland, Ohio.

5:44 P. M.—Took off from Cleveland.

8:47 P. M.—Landed at Roosevelt Field, N. Y. Total distance, 15,474 miles. Average speed 145.8 miles an hour. Total elapsed time, 8 days 15 hours 51 minutes.

Post Made Record Flight Around the World In 11 Hops at Speeds Up to 161.7 Miles an Hour

A summary of Wiley Post's eleven hops in his around-the-world solo flight, their distances, the flying time and the average speed follows:

Distance.	From	To	Time.	Aver. Speed. M. P. Hr.
B.942	New York	Berlin	25:45	153.5
340	Berlin	Koenigsberg	4:30	77.77
651	Koenigsberg	Moscow	5:15	119.68
1.579	Moscow	Novosibirsk	13:15	111.58
1.055	Novosibirsk	Irkutsk	6:33	161.7
750	Irkutsk	Rukhlovo	7:32	99.55
650	Rukhlovo	Khabarovsk	4:20	150.
2.800	Khabarovsk	Flat	22:32	124.2
375	Flat	Fairbanks	3:14	115.98
1.450	Fairbanks	Edmonton	9:22	154.8
2,004	Edmonton	New York	13:18¼	150.5
15,596	New York	New York	115:36:30	127.43

Fay Wray (in tree), the star of *King Kong*.

King Kong in his famous pose, atop the Empire State Building.

George Burns and Gracie Allen, the famous comedy team.

Marie Dressler and Wallace Beery starred in *Tugboat Annie*.

A publicity photograph of Mae West.

"All the News That's Fit to Print."

The New York Times.

LATE CITY EDITION
WEATHER—Cooler, possibly showers today; tomorrow fair.
Temperatures Yesterday—Max., 95; Min., 73.

Copyright, 1933, by The New York Times Company.

VOL. LXXXII....No. 27,576. Entered as Second-Class Matter, Postoffice, New York, N. Y. NEW YORK, TUESDAY, JULY 25, 1933. P TWO CENTS In New York City. | THREE CENTS Within 200 Miles | FOUR CENTS Elsewhere Except in 7th and 8th Postal Zones

ROOSEVELT APPEALS TO THE NATION FOR UNIFIED ACTION TO SPUR RECOVERY; PEEK DEMANDS GRAIN TRADING REFORM

MOLLISONS ARRIVE AS AIR PASSENGERS; LIFTED FROM PLANE

Doctors Fly With Them From Bridgeport and They Are Put to Bed Again Here.

FUTURE PLANS ARE VAGUE

Captain and Wife Fear They Cannot Get New Craft for Flight to Bagdad.

BALBO DELAYED BY FOG

Italian Armada Prepares for an Early Hop This Morning if the Mist Lifts at Shediac.

Day's News in Aviation.

Mollison and wife reach New York as air passengers.

Balbo postpones flight until today because of fog at Shediac.

Post hopes to raise funds for tests to aid aviation progress.

Lindberghs plan six-week series of flights over the inland ice of Greenland to seek emergency landing fields.

Mollisons Arrive by Air.

The flying Mollisons came to New York yesterday, not as they had hoped to come, but they flew. Lying back wearily on white hospital pillows, with a nurse and two physicians beside them, Captain James A. Mollison and his wife, Amy, made the flight from Bridgeport, Conn., where they had crashed the night before, as passengers in a roomy amphibian plane.

Four other planes flew in formation with them, Commander Frank Hawks piloting one.

At Floyd Bennett Field a thousand persons were gathered to meet them and as the five planes landed together a great shout went up from the crowd. The noise was silenced in a hush of quick sympathy a few minutes later when the onlookers saw policemen gently lift the flying couple from the plane, carry them to an automobile and carefully place them on more pillows.

"We feel fit," both the Mollisons said yesterday morning in the Bridgeport Hospital. Last night at Floyd Bennett Field they appeared far from fit, and many who saw them wondered why they had not remained in the hospital a day or two longer. The Mollisons, however, were not content until they had reached their objective.

Put to Bed Again.

They were met at the field by Richard F. Hoyt of Hayden, Stone & Co., a director of the Curtiss-Wright Corporation. It was the first time in many years that the Mayor's official representative to greet famous fliers had been a flying man himself. E. H. Gerald Shepherd, Acting British Consul General, and Mrs. Floyd Bennett were also there.

Quickly the procession got under way and went directly to the Plaza Hotel, where the Mollisons were examined again by physicians and put to bed. Wheel chairs met the car at the hotel and police protected the visitors.

From the crowd a woman with the burr of the Highlands in her voice cried, "Scotland forever, Jimmie!" as Captain Mollison was lifted from the car to a wheel chair. Captain Mollison looked up and smiled, too weary to raise his hands. His wife was obviously in better condition, although she did not attempt to walk from the car to the elevator.

In their suite on the fourth floor the fliers took tea and went directly to bed. Dr. Isaac Harschbarger and Dr. L. C. Heldger, who accompanied them from Bridgeport, then turned their patients over to Dr. Joseph Nash. All three physicians declared that the fliers should have absolute rest and quiet for several days. Ten minutes later the Captain and his wife were fast asleep.

Lack of Fuel to Blame.

It had been a hard day for them, harder perhaps on their nerves than the long perilous hours over the Atlantic and the wearisome time after night fell, bringing the realization that they did not have enough fuel left to dare the last forty miles of their 3,000-mile flight.

"That is why we decided to land at Bridgeport," Mrs. Mollison said yesterday morning. "We knew our petrol was low. We had never flown to Floyd Bennett Field before and the idea of flying over New York City hunting for the airport and running out of petrol just couldn't be contemplated."

As she reviewed again the story of the landing Mrs. Mollison turned to her husband, lying in the hospi-

Continued on Page Three.

Police Begin Tagging Illegally Parked Cars

The police began yesterday to attach cardboard tags to automobiles parked in violation of traffic regulations. The new procedure is a time and labor saving substitute for the former practice of waiting to serve a summons on the driver.

The new tags call upon the registered owner of the car, regardless of who was driving it when it was parked, to appear in the Traffic Court of the district and answer the charge of illegal parking. The police have been instructed to fasten the tags to the steering wheel, or, when the automobile is locked, to the handle of the door next the curb.

The authorities said that a number of tags were served yesterday but that it was too early to tell how the new system would work. They were apprehensive that many motorists would maintain that the tag had disappeared before they returned to their cars.

SPAIN ARRESTS 500 IN REPORTED PLOT

Government Speeds Jailing of Reactionaries to Insure Its Power in Country.

EIGHT PRIESTS ARE SEIZED

Purported Anarchist Uprising Is Linked to Monarchists—De Rivera Aides Sentenced.

By FRANK L. KLUCKHOHN.

Special Cable to THE NEW YORK TIMES.

MADRID, Tuesday, July 25.—Arrests on a wholesale scale have been made throughout Spain during the night and are continuing early this morning. Leaders of both the extreme Right and Left parties have been gathered in by hundreds in a movement to repress what the government asserts was a plot for a conservative coup d'état. The Syndicalist leaders also were rounded up, however.

The police dragnet took aristocrats, priests, doctors, lawyers, engineers and various other "bourgeois reactionaries." The arrests were started Sunday at the direction of the Socialist-dominated coalition government and now number about 500.

In Madrid alone 125 were arrested yesterday. At least eight priests have been jailed, of whom four are Jesuits. Their order was dissolved by the Spanish Republic, but no curb was placed on their residence. Three of the Jesuits were arrested in Granada, one in Malaga and one in Madrid.

The wholesale arrests came on the eve of the government's attempt to muster an absolute majority in the Cortes Wednesday. La Nación, the Opposition organ, protests at the action, saying:

"The government has saved Spain. It has arrested the sleeping priest, the lawyer drinking lemonade in a cafe and the dynamic journalist who was on a party."

Government Claims Provocation.

In government quarters, however, it is asserted the conservatives were ready to launch a "dangerous avalanche" of revolt to coincide with the sentencing of the leaders of the military rebellion of August 1932.

The sentences were made public late yesterday, making convicted

Continued on Page Ten.

GANG CHIEF JAILED IN HAMM ABDUCTION; THREE AIDES HELD

Roger Touhy of Chicago Taken to Milwaukee Under the Lindbergh Law.

IDENTIFIED, SAYS OFFICER

Federal Agents Lay Factor Kidnapping as Well as St. Paul Case to Prisoners.

The Drive on Crime.

The intensified drive by Federal agents, police and other peace officers against kidnappers and gangsters in general brought telling results yesterday. Outstanding achievements in the campaign for law and order were:

At Milwaukee four prisoners, members of the Roger Touhy gang of Chicago, were under arrest, charged with kidnapping William Hamm Jr., St. Paul brewer, on June 15.

At Cold Spring, N. Y., an ex-convict was captured after attempting to kidnap Miss Edis Neumoegen of Lake Mahopac. She was rescued unharmed.

At Dexter, Iowa, members of the Clyde Barrow gang of Oklahoma outlaws fought a machine gun battle with police. A brother of Barrow was wounded and captured. Clyde Barrow and two wounded companions escaped but their capture is imminent.

Touhy Gangsters Accused.

Special to THE NEW YORK TIMES.

MILWAUKEE, Wis., July 24.—Roger Touhy, Chicago gang leader, and three of his henchmen were locked in the county jail here this afternoon on Federal warrants charging them with the kidnapping of William Hamm Jr., St. Paul brewer. Touhy's lieutenants are Willie Sharkey, Edward (Father Tom) McFadden and Gustave (Gloomy Gus) Schaefer.

Not until his prisoners were jailed under the machine guns and pistols of a score of Chicago and Milwaukee detectives and Federal agents did Melvin H. Purvis, agent in charge of the Chicago Bureau of Investigation of the Department of Justice, disclose that he was certain of their identity as the Hamm kidnappers.

The gangsters were taken from Chicago to Elkhorn, Wis., upon the excuse that they were to be charged there with carrying concealed weapons. When a rookie policeman arrested them in Elkhorn last Wednesday after an automobile accident he found a rifle and seven pistols, the latter concealed in a golf bag, in their automobile. After the arrest last week they were returned to Chicago.

Mr. Purvis and Chief of Detectives Schoemaker of Chicago took elaborate precautions to prevent the Touhy gang, said to number eighty gunmen, from rescuing their leader. They had in mind the recent incident in Kansas City, where gangsters machine-gunned four officers and their prisoner to death.

Two squads of Chicago detectives and two cars of Federal agents guarded the prisoners' cars on their trip to Elkhorn. The detectives carried machine guns and the automobiles were routed 35 miles off the direct route to Elkhorn to avoid

Continued on Page Four.

Frau Goebbels Quits German Fashion Office

Special Cable to THE NEW YORK TIMES.

BERLIN, July 24. Frau Magda Goebbels, wife of the Minister of Propaganda, resigned today as honorary president of the German Fashion Office, which was recently created to promote the German fashion industry.

Of the two doctors and one professor on the executive board of the Fashion Office one of the doctors and the professor also resigned. The announcement was made by the three in a joint notice to the press.

The Prussian Ministry of Culture is making preparations to add another year to the elementary school term, bringing the total to nine years. The additional time is to be a "country year."

Pupils from the cities are to be lodged in rural communities to experience "unity of blood and soil" and learn the needs of the German peasant.

WORLD BANK SPLIT ON CURRENCY PLAN

Three Blocs Develop at Basle, but All Fear Disorder Until Dollar Returns to Gold.

UNITY PLEDGE RENEWED

But Central Banks Fail to Draft Rules to Curb Speculation in Foreign Exchange.

Wireless to THE NEW YORK TIMES.

BASLE, July 24.—Governors of European central banks, after a meeting of the board of the Bank for International Settlements here today, returned to their countries to prepare to entrench themselves in the status quo until after the United States monetary experiment has been completed.

Their conversations at Basle over the week-end resulted in no agreement for concerted European action to combat currency fluctuations while the dollar and the British pound remain detached from gold.

The American experiment, in the estimation of experts here, can last anywhere from two to six months more. Meanwhile only nations having similar interests can hope to cooperate.

Three European Blocs Forming.

Three separate blocs are apparently forming among European nations. There is the gold bloc headed by France, including Italy, Switzerland, Holland and Poland. There is the sterling bloc with Great Britain and the Scandinavian countries. The third includes Germany and some Central European countries.

The members of the gold bloc, all represented on the World Bank board, will have an opportunity to consult again here. After examining developments since their meeting here at the Bank of France recently, they again pledged common assistance in restraining speculation affecting their currencies, but without making rules as to the nature of the action to be taken except for keeping close contact through the central banks.

In view of the improvement in the florin, Swiss franc and belga since the Paris meeting, they decided there was no need to put in order their plan for mutual action at this time, but agreed they would confer again whenever the situation requires consultation.

Although it is believed representatives of small countries belonging to the sterling group evinced irritation at the long delay in fixing the pound, it is understood Montagu Norman, governor of the Bank of England, was unwilling to make any engagement until the United States policy had been more clearly defined. Though sterling has been almost stable in its relation to the French franc, no assurances could be obtained that this stabilization would be continued.

Third Group Awaits Help.

The third group has adopted a policy of tranquil waiting. Depending upon gold embargoes and other restrictions, they are awaiting the decision of solvent countries to aid them in reorganization, and particularly to relieve them from the pressure of their heavy indebtedness.

The World Bank Board protested to Germany and Austria against their making interest payments in the currency of lending countries instead of giving gold value, as was stipulated when these obligations were contracted. The German attitude, however, was that everywhere—in the United States regarding bond issues and recently in Great Britain regarding the war loan issue—the gold clause was being disregarded.

It was also maintained that any payments in gold to the United States and Great Britain would

Continued on Page Five.

Unions Call Strike of 6,000 at Hollywood When the Studios Employ Non-Union Men

Special to THE NEW YORK TIMES.

LOS ANGELES, July 24.—Retaliating against employment of non-union sound technicians to replace strikers, 6,000 union workers were called out today from Hollywood motion-picture studios on a sympathetic strike.

The strike order was issued by Richard Green, international representative of the International Alliance of Theatrical Stage Employes. It is to be effective at midnight.

Affected by the order are camera men, laboratory technicians, motion-picture projectionists, one group of electricians, "grips," property men, set dressers, property makers, special-effect makers and miniature makers.

Studios affected are Educational, Fox, Metro-Goldwyn-Mayer, Paramount, RKO-Radio, Hal Roach, United Artists, Universal, Warner Brothers-First National, Columbia, Harold Lloyd Corporation and Bryan Foy. About forty independent companies will not be affected.

A complete cessation of production was predicted in some quarters, but producers declared the plants will be kept open despite the strikes. Advertisements signed by the major studios will appear in tomorrow's newspapers here, seeking workers to replace the sympathetic strikers.

Louis B. Mayer, president of the Association of Motion Picture Producers, said tonight:

"There is a very small percentage of the working forces involved and we expect to keep on the job every man and woman who wants to work. Our wage scales are the highest in any industry on the Pacific Coast, and will continue to be."

If the walkout does effect a complete shut-down of the major studios, 30,000 workers, with a weekly payroll of $1,500,000, will be thrown out of employment.

With strike-breakers and other studio employes replacing absent sound technicians, practically every major studio resumed production today where it left off Saturday, though with difficulty.

The Hal Roach studio shut down. Columbia has been shut down for two weeks following the original walkout there of sound technicians. The Harold Lloyd company and Educational are inactive.

MEETING ON MARKET CODE

Farm Adjustment Chief Warns Exchanges of Licensing Powers.

URGES VOLUNTARY ACTION

Meanwhile, Agreement Is Reached to Retain Curb on Sharp Price Fluctuations.

BIG TRADER IS SUSPENDED

E. A. Crawford, Long for Millions of Bushels, Held Unable to Meet Obligations.

Special to THE NEW YORK TIMES.

WASHINGTON, July 24.—Continuation of the emergency restrictions on grain trading already in effect until the submission and approval of codes of fair competition for grain exchanges was agreed upon today at a conference of representatives of the grain trades with the Agricultural Adjustment Administration.

In addition, it was decided to abolish the practice of indemnity trading, under which traders may buy the privilege of purchasing or selling grain below or above the market level at a future date. It was felt by the conferees that this privilege had been an important factor in the rapid rise and fall of the grain market, and that its elimination would contribute much toward its stabilization.

Restrictive regulations which will be continued pending the approval of a code of fair competition include the prohibition against purchase or sale of grain at less than the closing prices of last Thursday, and the ranges of maximum fluctuation above or below which transactions will not be permitted in a day's trading. Thus, until further notice, July wheat may not be bought for less than 90 cents, September at less than 91, December at less than 95½, nor May at less than $1. The corresponding Thursday closings for other grains will likewise prevail as minimums.

Peek Uses Blunt Terms.

Frankness and the use of the bluntest terms characterized the meeting between the Farm Adjustment officials and the grain trade representatives called for the express purpose of putting an end to the sharp fluctuations in grain prices such as that which carried wheat down 26 cents in two days of trading last week.

Scarcely was the conference under way when George N. Peek, administrator for the Farm Adjustment Act, told the delegates that they had "any divine right to handle the farmer's products." He left no doubt that the government mean business and warned that "the institutions engaged in marketing exist and will continue to exist only so long as they perform a useful service."

If the abuses connected with grain exchange operation were not eliminated, Mr. Peek added, then the farmer would find other methods for marketing his products. And lest the impression be gained that this was just another warning, he called particular attention to the authority under the Adjustment Act to license the exchanges and all other handlers of farm commodities.

Calls for Prompt Action.

"I want to emphasize to every one concerned with the grain trades the necessity that you put your own house in order where it needs to be put in order," said Mr. Peek.

"We are not going to undertake to superimpose something on the grain trades until after they have had an opportunity to work out their problem themselves.

"If this is not done promptly, however, I will make no promises. An attempt will be made to meet that situation. Abuses exist in the grain trades and in the marketing medium of the farmers, should correct these abuses.

"If they do not succeed then the government will act. We conceive it to be the government's function to protect any group which is unable to protect itself. I know of no industry other than farming which has nothing to say about the price received for its product. I under-

Continued on Page Eleven.

The President's Speech

Special to THE NEW YORK TIMES.

WASHINGTON, July 24.—President Roosevelt's radio address to the nation, appealing for support of the National Recovery program, was, in full:

After the adjournment of the historical special session of the Congress five weeks ago, I purposely refrained from addressing you for two very good reasons.

First, I think that we all wanted the opportunity of a little quiet thought to examine and assimilate in a mental picture the crowding events of the hundred days which have been devoted to the starting of the wheels of the New Deal.

Secondly, I wanted a few weeks in which to set up the new administrative organization and to see the first fruits of our careful planning.

I think it will interest you if I set forth the fundamentals of this planning for national recovery; and this I am very certain will make it abundantly clear to you that all of the proposals and all of the legislation since the Fourth Day of March have not been just a collection of haphazard schemes, but rather the orderly component parts of a connected logical whole.

Long before Inauguration Day I became convinced that individual effort and local effort and even disjointed Federal effort had failed and of necessity would fail and, therefore, that a rounded leadership by the Federal Government had become a necessity both of theory and of fact. Such leadership, however, had its beginning in preserving and strengthening the credit of the United States Government, because, without that, no leadership was a possibility. For years the government had not lived within its income. The immediate task was to bring our regular expenses within our revenues. That has been done.

'Granite Foundation' of Credit Built.

It may seem inconsistent for a government to cut down its regular expenses and at the same time to borrow and to spend billions for an emergency. But it is not inconsistent because a large portion of the emergency money has been paid out in the form of sound loans which will be repaid to the Treasury over a period of years, and to cover the rest of the emergency money we have imposed taxes to pay the interest and the instalments on that part of the debt.

So you will see that we have kept our credit good. We have built a granite foundation in a period of confusion. That foundation of the Federal credit stands there broad and sure. It is the base of the whole recovery plan.

Then came the part of the problem that concerned the credit of the individual citizens themselves. You and I know of the banking crisis and of the great danger to the savings of our people. On March 6 every national bank was closed. One month later 90 per cent of the deposits in the national banks had been made available to the depositors. Today only about 5 per cent of the deposits in national banks are still tied up.

The condition relating to State banks, while not quite so good on a percentage basis, is showing a steady reduction in the total of frozen deposits—a result much better than we had expected three months ago.

The problem of the credit of the individual was made more difficult because of another fact. The dollar was a different dollar from the one with which the average debt had been incurred. For this reason large numbers of people were actually losing possession of and title to their farms and homes. All of you know the financial steps which have been taken to correct this inequality. In addition, the Home Loan Act, the Farm Loan Act and the Bankruptcy Act were passed.

Vital to Restore Buying Power.

It was a vital necessity to restore purchasing power by reducing the debt and interest charges upon our people; but while we were helping people to save their credit, it was at the same time absolutely essential to do something about the physical needs of hundreds of thousands who were in dire straits at that very moment. Municipal and State aid were being stretched to the limit.

We appropriated half a billion dollars to supplement their efforts and in addition, as you know, we have put 300,000 young men into practical and useful work in our forests and to prevent flood and soil erosion. The wages they earn are going in greater part to the support of the nearly 1,000,000 people who constitute their families.

In this same classification we can properly place the great public works program running to a total of over $3,000,000,000, to be used for highways and ships and flood prevention and inland navigation and thousands of self-sustaining State and municipal improvements.

Two points should be made clear in the allotting and administration of these projects: First, we are using the utmost care to choose labor-creating, quick-acting, useful projects, avoiding the smell of the pork barrel; and secondly, we are hoping that at least half of the money will come back to the government from projects which will pay for themselves over a period of years.

Links to Lasting Prosperity Forged.

Thus far I have spoken primarily of the foundation stones—the measures that were necessary to re-establish credit and to head people in the opposite direction by preventing distress and providing as much work as possible through governmental agencies. Now I come to the links which will build us a more lasting prosperity.

I have said that we cannot attain that in a nation half boom and half broke. If all of our people have work and fair wages and fair profits, they can buy the products of their neighbors and business is good. But if you take away the wages and the profits of half of them, business is only half as good.

It doesn't help much if the fortunate half is very prosperous—the best way is for everybody to be reasonably prosperous.

For many years the two great barriers to a normal prosperity have been low farm prices and the creeping paralysis of unemployment. These factors have cut the purchasing power of the country in half. I promised action.

Congress did its part when it passed the Farm and the Industrial Recovery Acts. Today we are putting these two acts to work, and they will work if people understand their plain objectives.

First, the Farm Act: It is based on the fact that the purchasing power of nearly half our population depends on adequate prices for farm products.

We have been producing more of some crops than we consume or can sell in a depressed world market. The cure is not to produce so much. Without our help the farmers cannot get together and cut production, and the Farm Bill gives them a method of bringing their production down to a reasonable level and of obtaining reasonable prices for their crops.

I have clearly stated that this method is in a sense experi-

Continued on Page Two.

PRESIDENT EXPLAINS PLAN

Asks Every Employer to Write His Acceptance of Blanket Code.

WON'T USE PENALTIES 'NOW'

To Employ Only 'the Cooperation That Comes From Opinion and Conscience.'

URGES WORKERS' SUPPORT

Lays 'Economic Hell' of Last Four Years to a Few Selfish Men.

Special to THE NEW YORK TIMES.

WASHINGTON, July 24.—President Roosevelt opened his national re-employment drive tonight in a frank, vigorous appeal to his countrymen to subscribe to the emergency industrial code and thereby put millions back to work by Autumn.

Hardly had he finished before telegrams and long-distance telephone calls came pouring into the White House acclaiming his speech and pledging cooperation.

The "testimonials" came from all branches of industry and all walks of life, from the big employer of labor to the day worker and the "white-collar slave." One and all pledged utmost cooperation with the President in his organized campaign against the forces of depression.

A half hour after the President had finished speaking he was notified that 350 telegrams were awaiting his pleasure, all pledging support of his program.

Response of the Nation.

By 11 o'clock, an hour after Mr. Roosevelt had finished speaking, more than 5,000 telegrams had arrived at the White House and at the offices of the two principal broadcasting systems to be relayed to the President. Attachés were swamped sorting and receiving a multitude of local and long-distance telephone calls.

One local woman, saying she was unable to send a telegram because the telegraph offices were swamped, telephoned Marvin McIntyre, the president's secretary, to read him the telegram she had intended to send. It read:

"The women of the country constitute 80 per cent of the purchasing power. In the war we had a star in our window to show that one of our men was entered in the American cause. In this emergency, in response to your appeal, we will carry an emblem in our windows that we will do our part."

A telegram signed "Voter" came to Mr. Roosevelt from Great Neck, L. I., indicating that one enthusiastic woman had voluntarily applied the blanket code to her domestic help. It read:

"After listening to the President's appeal, I am raising my maid's wages 10 per cent."

"All for Common Good."

The President discussed the several links in his new economic policy for the American people, a policy, he said, designed to accomplish a "reasonable prosperity" for everybody instead of great prosperity for a few and poverty for the rest.

Prosperity, he said, cannot be attained in a nation "half boom and half broke," and in this he launched into a direct appeal for support by capital and labor alike of his recovery program. There must be cooperation by all, he said, by the employers that they must work in harmony for the common good.

"While we are making this great common effort there should be no discord and dispute," he said. "This is no time to cavil or to question the standard set by this universal agreement. It is time for patience and understanding and cooperation.

"The workers of this country have rights under this law which cannot be taken from them, and nobody will be permitted to whittle them away but, on the other hand, no aggression is now necessary to attain those rights. The whole country will be united to get them for you. The principle that applies to the employers applies to the workers as well and I ask you workers to cooperate in the same spirit."

After picturing conditions of un-

NRA U.S. WE DO OUR PART

"All the News That's Fit to Print."

The New York Times.

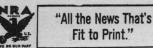

LATE CITY EDITION
WEATHER—Showers today and probably tomorrow.
Temperatures Yesterday—Max., 71; Min., 56

VOL. LXXXII....No. 27,627. Entered as Second-Class Matter, Postoffice, New York, N. Y. NEW YORK, THURSDAY, SEPTEMBER 14, 1933. P TWO CENTS In New York City. THREE CENTS Within 200 Miles | FOUR CENTS Elsewhere Except In 7th and 8th Postal Zones

1,500,000 CHEER VAST NRA PARADE; MARCH OF 250,000 CITY'S GREATEST; DEMONSTRATION LASTS TILL MIDNIGHT

Times Wide World Photo.

NEW YORK MARCHES UNDER BLUE EAGLE.
A Section of the Parade up Fifth Avenue Yesterday Which Started at 1:30 P. M. and Lasted Until Midnight.

BROKERS PUSH PLAN TO MOVE EXCHANGE IN CITY TAX FIGHT

Counsel Acts to Organize a New Market in Northern New Jersey.

UNTERMYER ASSAILS MOVE

Scores Offer as 'Contemptible' and Predicts New Board Here if Carried Out.

TAXPAYERS SPEED TEST

Savings Banks Pick Committee —Ratification by Aldermen Is Expected Today.

With approval of the city's new tax program by the Board of Aldermen scheduled for this afternoon, plans for establishing a branch of the New York Stock Exchange in New Jersey to avoid the impending stock transfer tax of four cents a share were receiving serious consideration last night.

Although Samuel Untermyer, financial adviser to the city administration and proponent of the new program, discounted the move as an idle threat, the law firm of Cadwalader, Wickersham & Taft let it be known that it was studying the legal details involved, at the direction of a leading brokerage firm.

Officials of the Stock Exchange were publicly non-committal about the proposal, but privately indicated that they regarded it sympathetically. One of them declared that it might be necessary for the Exchange to adopt some such drastic move as a measure of self-protection.

Approval Is Likely.

Despite the bitter feeling which prevailed throughout the financial district, passage of the four new tax measures approved on Tuesday by the Board of Estimate is expected this afternoon by the Board of Aldermen, acting as the lower branch of the Municipal Assembly.

The measures are the stock transfer tax, the 5 per cent tax on stock brokers, the levy of ¼ of 1 per cent on the investments of savings banks and insurance companies having their principal offices here, and the tax of 1½ per cent on the gross income of public utility companies within the city.

After ratifying these measures, the Board of Aldermen will probably convene again to pass the five-cent tax on taxicabs and the 50 per cent increase in water rates, both of which fall exclusively within their jurisdiction.

Bitterly scornful of the threat, Mr. Untermyer attacked as "contemptible" the offer of a tax-free refuge in New Jersey to the Stock Exchange by Governor A. Harry Moore. Mr. Untermyer also predicted that if the Stock Exchange should move from New York another exchange would develop here in its place.

Would Transfer Active Stocks.

The plan under consideration, however, would avert any such occurrence by continuing the present exchange, but shifting the bulk of the trading in the more active stocks to an associated floor in Northern New Jersey, according to a statement issued by De Coursey Fales, a partner in Cadwalader, Wickersham & Taft.

His outline of the proposal follows:

"We have received instructions from a client who is a partner in one of the large firms registered on the New York Stock Exchange to take the necessary steps to organize a Stock Exchange in New Jersey.

"It is contemplated that the new exchange will rent quarters in some city in Northern New Jersey which will be easily accessible to persons doing business in New York City, and which will have banking facilities and telephone and telegraphic communications adequate to supply the needs of a large stock market.

"The plan contemplates the organization of an exchange with 1,375 members, and membership in the New York Stock Exchange will be one of the conditions of membership in the new corporation. The new exchange will offer to elect the existing members of the New York Stock Exchange.

"While complete plans have not as yet been developed, it is anticipated that trading in the most prominent and active stocks now dealt in on the New York Stock Exchange will be commenced as soon as the new city taxes become effective."

Legal Fight Promised.

Mr. Untermyer's program met with another threat yesterday when the Greater New York Taxpayers Association, the largest association of real estate owners in the city, promised a court fight against his

Continued on Page Sixteen.

American Educator Is Barred by Turkey

By The Associated Press.

ISTANBUL, Sept. 13.—The Turkish Government today forbade the return to Turkey of Dr. Edgar J. Fisher, for many years dean of the faculty of arts and sciences and Professor of History and Political Science in Robert College.

Dr. Fisher was returning to the Istanbul institution from a vacation in the United States and was told in a telegram that he could not enter Turkey. The government declared an article in an American educational magazine discussed Turkey's new official history textbook in a manner displeasing to Turkish authorities and cited Dr. Fisher as the source of the information.

The article objected to by the Turkish authorities appeared in the July 12 number of School and Society and was written by Professor Walter W. Hyde of Pennsylvania University.

A footnote acknowledged indebtedness to Dr. Fisher for having translated the text.

WORKERS BESIEGE AMERICANS IN CUBA

Sugar and Mining Officials Held in Homes as Hostages for Labor's Demands.

ARMY IS REORGANIZED

Officers Appointed From Among Enlisted, Ignoring Former Leaders in Hotel Refuge.

By J. D. PHILLIPS.
Special Cable to THE NEW YORK TIMES.

HAVANA, Sept. 13.—While the Cuban public maintained its attitude of watchful waiting, the government of President Grau San Martin, ignoring the rebellious army officers who have taken refuge in the National Hotel, set about reorganizing the armed forces and accumulating funds to meet the immediate obligations of the administration.

Rumors of dissension in the army ranks spread through Havana today, causing considerable uneasiness, but the rumors proved unfounded. Officials of the government stated that the entire armed forces of the republic were in complete accord with the revolutionary régime. Colonel Fulgencio Batista, chief of staff, said: "The army and the public are with the government, and between them is the heroic legion of students, acting as a safeguard."

Denies Dissension in Army.

At Camp Columbia this afternoon Major Pablo Rodriguez Silverio, a former sergeant recently commissioned as chief of the Sixth Military District, told your correspondent: "There is much propaganda at present concerning rifts among the enlisted men, but I can assure you no such condition exists. The soldiers and all the noncommissioned officers, as well as the recently commissioned personnel, are absolutely supporting the revolutionary government, both in the interior and in Havana."

Colonel Batista was busily engaged today making promotions among the enlisted personnel to officer the army. Despite his assurance that more than 100 officers had returned to their commands and more were expected, sergeants and corporals were rapidly being promoted to become Lieutenants, Captains and Majors.

Major Enrique Rivera Fernandez, retired, this afternoon was appointed chief of the naval staff. Major Rivera served two years in the United States Navy.

Ordered to Guard Foreigners.

Orders have been given to the soldiers to protect the lives and property of foreigners above all else. Every effort is being made to convince the public that no disorders exist. However, the continuance of labor troubles in the interior is far from conducive to peace and order.

Twelve hundred Americans living in the interior provinces, of whom at least 700 are employed in sugar mills, mines and other industries, now are the objects of attempts by Cuban laborers to force a betterment of wages and living conditions and are in potential danger.

At the Baguanos sugar mill in Oriente Province, it is reported the manager and office personnel are imprisoned in their homes by workers.

A similar condition prevails in central Tacajo. There striking laborers have broken into warehouses and are distributing sacked sugar among the populace.

At Antilla, at the extreme eastern end of the island, banana workers have given the plantation owners until Saturday to accept their demands. Trouble is expected, as it is understood the employers refuse to accede to the workers' terms,

Continued on Page Thirteen.

GERMANS TO SKIMP ON A MEAL A MONTH AND FEED JOBLESS

Nation Is Asked to Go on Short Rations Every First Sunday as Basis of Winter Relief.

NAZIS WILL KEEP CHECK

Jail Threatened for Evaders—Workers Must Contribute Part of Their Wages.

By GUIDO ENDERIS.
Wireless to THE NEW YORK TIMES.

BERLIN, Sept. 13.—Shortened rations once a month for every man, woman and child in the Reich, as well as for the strangers within its gates, are to constitute the nucleus of the government's program for social relief this Winter. What is saved through voluntary curtailment of a regular Sunday meal is to help feed the jobless and hungry.

The Nazi government's plan for combating hunger and cold was unfolded by Dr. Paul Joseph Goebbels, the Minister of Popular Enlightenment and Propaganda, at a press conference convoked in the "throne room" of his ministry in former Prince Leopold's palace today.

It was staged in a setting not lacking in pomp, and the presence of Chancellor Hitler, Vice Chancellor von Papen, Foreign Minister von Neurath and other Cabinet members lent it additional authority. Full contingents of storm troop leaders, Governors of the federated States and representatives of big business and industry also were present.

For First Sunday of Month.

All of Dr. Goebbels's program for keeping the jobless and their dependents fed and warmed during the Winter, the advent of which the government is obviously viewing with some apprehension, was embodied in a fervent appeal to more fortunate folk to go on short rations the first Sunday of each month, the money thus saved to go into a general relief fund for the benefit of the needy.

Chancellor Hitler, it was said by Dr. Goebbels in his elucidation of the project, demands that the plan shall be put into execution without distinction of class or person, and that it shall be a clear demonstration to the poor and suffering that their more prosperous fellow-citizens are prepared to share their fate, at least one day a month. It must be a demonstration of national solidarity, the Chancellor demands.

The plan, Dr. Goebbels said, is the fruition of months of preparation and calculation. It is proposed that on the first Sunday of each month every family or individual shall curtail his habitual bill of fare by restricting it to a simple dish, the cost not to exceed 50 pfennigs [currently about 17 cents] per capita. It will then be up to the housewife to calculate the amount saved on the family meal and this saving will be donated to the general relief fund.

This restricted Sunday bill of fare is not to be confined to householders, but will extend to hotels, restaurants and railway dining cars. Gourmands who selfishly insist on an extra dish or two will have an opportunity to repent by contributing a fine to the general fund.

It is a fine-meshed dragnet that the Nazi Government proposes to cast and since it commands the

Continued on Page Eleven

Two Rothschilds Cede Big Estates to Austria

Wireless to THE NEW YORK TIMES.

VIENNA, Sept. 13.—Barons Alphonse and Louis Rothschild, the heads of the Austrian branch of the famous banking family, ceded two estates in Gaming and Ybbsitz to the Austrian Government today.

This was done in connection with the liquidation of the Credit-Anstalt, of which Baron Louis Rothschild was president and the other Baron a large shareholder. The estates cover 35,000 acres and consist of valuable woods and agricultural land.

The Austrian public has demanded that the Rothschilds be forced to make partial compensation for losses of the Credit-Anstalt. The two bankers sacrificed their stock in that institution.

This additional concession will enable the Austrian Government to use the land for the colonization of several hundred settlers. The Gaming estate was one of the most famous hunting preserves in Austria.

R. P. LAMONT QUITS AS STEEL DICTATOR

Lack of Sympathy With NRA Seen—Schwab to Return as President of Institute.

NEW REGULATION FEARED

Hoover Cabinet Member Says 'No One Knows How Far' Federal Policy May Go.

Robert P. Lamont has resigned as president of the American Iron and Steel Institute, it was announced yesterday at the institute's offices in the Empire State Building. Mr. Lamont, it was learned, will be succeeded by Charles M. Schwab, who stepped out of the post a year ago to make room for Mr. Lamont.

Mr. Lamont's letter of resignation was dated Sept. 1 and apparently had been submitted at the meeting of more than 200 steel company executives at the institute on that date. Copies of the letter were made public, without comment, at the institute's offices.

Mr. Lamont had been Secretary of Commerce in the Hoover administration. He resigned on Aug. 3, 1932, and the following day his selection as "dictator" of the steel industry, with the title of president of the American Iron and Steel Institute, was announced.

Sees Government Regulation.

The tone of his letter of resignation clearly indicated a lack of sympathy with the NRA. He referred to the attendance of three government representatives at the meeting of the board of directors of the Steel Institute on Aug. 29 as "the beginning of government regulation of business" and added, "no one knows how far it may go."

"From now on," Mr. Lamont said, "for an indefinite period, the principal activities of the Iron and Steel Institute will be in seeing that the obligations of the industry under the code are properly carried out and reported to the government.

"The opportunity for constructive, forward-looking studies and plans for the industry as a whole, that seemed possible a year ago, must give way to the present prac-

Continued on Page Sixteen.

Uchida Quits as Japan's Foreign Minister; Hirota, Successor, Even More Nationalistic

By HUGH BYAS.
Wireless to THE NEW YORK TIMES.

TOKYO, Thursday, Sept. 14.—Count Yasuya Uchida resigned as Foreign Minister today for reasons of health and Koki Hirota, former Ambassador to Moscow, accepted the post. The change was unexpected.

Mr. Hirota's appointment is acceptable to the nationalists, with whose ideals he sympathizes. Much younger than Count Uchida, he is an experienced diplomat who knows foreign affairs thoroughly and may be expected to conduct his policies with vigorous regard to Japan's interests. Several of his seniors were passed over in making the appointment.

A complete change of Cabinet is probable before the end of the year.

The work of Japanese Cabinet Ministers is arduous and the pillars of the present Ministry are septuagenarians who would gladly avoid the labors involved in another session of the Diet.

It is universally admitted that in the circumstances the only effective government for Japan is one that the army trusts. It may be expected the new government will be a reversion to the type with which Japan is familiar—a super-party Cabinet headed by a non-party statesman commanding the confidence of the Emperor and the innermost circle of imperial advisers.

Broadly speaking, the change will mean a further step away from party government toward one resembling the German pre-war system, which the Chancellor, responsible to the Emperor, governed without dependence on parties.

The functions of the Diet will be interpreted strictly in the terms of the Constitution, which gives Parliament power to veto financial measures.

By The Associated Press.

TOKYO, Thursday, Sept. 14.—While failing health was given as the reason for Count Uchida's resignation as Foreign Minister today, reactionary pressure in favor of Koki Hirota's succession was regarded as an important factor in the change.

Mr. Hirota is known as a stanch nationalist, closely connected with reactionary patriotic organizations in the army clique. His accession is interpreted as presaging a Japanese foreign policy even more nationalistic and uncompromising than at present.

JOHNSON PLEDGES CREDIT

Government Will Act to Assure Ample Funds to Industry, He Says.

CHIDES BANKERS AS TIMID

NRA Has Not Surrendered to Labor, He Tells Merchants —Asks Moderate Prices.

LEHMAN HAILS PROGRESS

Governor Declares Millions in New Wages Are Reviving the Buying Spirit.

Prompt action by the Federal Government to release the springs of credit, so that the march of the national recovery program might continue unchecked, was forecast last night by General Hugh S. Johnson, NRA Administrator. He addressed the NRA Day dinner of the Merchants Association of New York at the Hotel Pennsylvania.

Speaking before 1,000 merchants, industrial leaders and public officials while the city's parade in celebration of progress under President Roosevelt's program still was pouring up Fifth Avenue, General Johnson challenged them to accept the new deal in industry as the greatest opportunity ever presented to industry and trade. He evoked a tumult of applause.

Pledges Rigid Impartiality.

He stirred his audience to cheers when he denied that labor had had undue influence in the framing of the codes, and declared:

"Wholly apart from the abstract consideration of rectitude, complete impartiality is the only salvation I have in the hot spot on which I stand."

More applause greeted his emotional tribute to the parade he had reviewed for hours as marvelous beyond anything he had ever seen, and the high spot in his life.

General Johnson's declaration of confidence that the American people would continue their triumphant march was reinforced by Governor Lehman. In an address after the General's, Governor Lehman quoted new figures showing that 39,765 persons had been put back to work in 813 up-State communities, pouring $698,178 of new purchasing power into the channels of trade every week.

The recovery program is actually working, the Governor declared.

"Men and women have been put back at work," he declared.

The restoration of credit cannot be accomplished by haranguing the bankers, General Johnson said.

Predicts Action on Credit.

"It can be done by creating confidence," he declared, "by releasing restrictions requiring a too great liquidity of banks, and, if necessary, by direct governmental interposition (through the powers of the Federal Reserve and the Emergency Banking Act), to extend credit on capital loans and on good commercial risks in cases where the existing banking system has been unable or unwilling, through timidity or otherwise, to perform its normal function. This problem is under consideration, and we can, I think, expect prompt action along this line.

"We must have sympathy with the argument about the banks' trustee relationship to depositors' money, as set forth in a recent report to the bankers' association, but it is a little curious to hear about this now when the need for normal banking assistance is so acute, and in cases where liquidity is almost at a peak, and when every economic index points upward—and then to think of what was happening when every condition was in reverse of this, when speculative loans were being made at the peak of a stock market hysteria, and when—if ever—extreme liquidity was indicated.

"Then these same custodians of the public savings were getting themselves into a condition which required the closing of every bank in the country, and all that I recall hearing from the particular authority that made that report at that time was that we were in a 'creeping bear market.'

"There is no use in haranguing our banker friends about extending commercial loans where they do not think it wise. They move in a spe-

Continued on Page Two.

NEW RETAIL CODE CONTROLS PRICES

NRA Master Plan Embracing Drug Stores Also Bars 'Inaccurate Advertising.'

RETAILERS AT ODDS ON IT

Wage and Hour Scales Adjusted to Varying Length of Business Day in Stores.

Special to THE NEW YORK TIMES.

WASHINGTON, Sept. 13.—A master code for retail stores, including drug stores and pharmacies, which is expected to bring a sharp clash between certain prominent New York department stores, has been drawn by Deputy Administrator Whiteside of the NRA, and was reviewed by a number of well-known retailers this afternoon.

The code, which supplants the charter presented on Aug. 24 by the retail trade, exclusive of drug stores, includes the principle of price control by providing that all goods must be sold at the invoice price, plus 7½ per cent for food and food products, and 10 per cent for other goods.

Druggists, however, have succeeded in inserting a provision that nationally advertised drugs must not be sold at more than 21 per cent below the manufacturers' retail price on the package. The retailers present today objected to this latter proviso.

The language regarding unfair trade practices, which has been a bone of contention, has been changed to bar advertising "inaccurate in any material particular," and to forbid advertising referring "inaccurately in any material particular" to a competitor. The revision also prohibits advertising which "inaccurately" lays claims to a policy of underselling competitors.

Strenuous objection is lodged by a certain group of retailers to the insertion of the words "inaccurately" and "in any material particular." The charge is made that this gives far too great latitude.

Wage and Hour Scales Adjusted.

The minimum wage and hour scales have been adjusted in order to cover establishments remaining open for shorter or longer periods. Drug stores which are open seven days weekly may work their employes up to fifty-six hours, but they must pay them a minimum of $16 weekly in cities of more than 500,000 population. Exceptions in the wage and hour scales are made in certain cases.

The portions of the proposed code relating to price cutting follow:

"Section 1—'Stop Loss Provisions' In order to check extreme forms of

Continued on Page Seven.

PRESIDENT WEIGHS PAYROLL LENDING

Considers Direct Loans to Aid NRA Industries if Bank Credit Lags.

FIRST WILL ASSIST BANKS

Further Increase of $3,000,000,000 in Farm Income Also Held Essential.

Special to THE NEW YORK TIMES.

WASHINGTON, Sept. 13.—President Roosevelt revealed today that the administration has under consideration direct Federal loans to industries for payrolls should banks fail to furnish sufficient credit for business operating under the NRA codes.

Conferences held by the President with Treasury and other officials in the last few days have further developed plans to put the full power of the government behind the banks in the drive for additional credit in the NRA campaign.

Banks will be assisted through the Reconstruction Finance Corporation to strengthen their resources to meet the requirements of deposits insurance under the new Banking Act and such further NRA credits as may be needed.

In his semi-weekly conference with newspaper correspondents today the President not only commented upon the plans to work with the banks and, perhaps, forestall radical inflation of the currency but pictured the plight of the farmers, whose purchasing power, he pointed out, must be increased to bring it into accord with the index of 1914. The President would not comment upon currency inflation, but indicated that every effort was being made by the government toward credit expansion.

Banking Survey Under Way.

The credit situation is expected to be eased soon, when a survey in connection with the insurance of deposits will be completed. The survey is being made by the Reconstruction Finance Corporation, the Treasury and the new Deposit Insurance Corporation. Just as soon as the information comes in as to the financial condition of the banks, national as well as State, the three agencies will decide which institutions have need of additional capital.

In determining the position of the banks in connection with the insurance of deposits, each one will be considered as a special case. The general rule, however, will be that they must at least have sufficient assets to pay off all deposits, as distinct from meeting other liabilities.

Those banks which require greater

Continued on Page Five.

FERVOR SWEEPS THRONGS

The Great Outpouring to Show Faith in NRA Recalls Armistice.

NIGHT SCENE IS BRILLIANT

Notables and Humble From All Occupations March Under Avenue's Golden Lights.

BROKERS JEER AT O'BRIEN

Johnson Is Unable to Halt 18-Minute Tax Protest at Reviewing Stand.

Under the golden glow of Fifth Avenue's festive arc lights the legions of the Blue Eagle marched until midnight last night before hundreds of thousands of spectators whom weariness could not drive away from a demonstration of confidence and enthusiasm such as had not been seen for half a generation.

More than a quarter of a million strong—employers and employes side by side—the President's NRA Day parade took the evening as well as the afternoon in which to manifest its faith in President Roosevelt's recovery program.

Governor Lehman, Mayor O'Brien and other officials were still in the stand in front of the main building of the New York Public Library at Forty-first Street when the last detachment—fifteen makers of artificial flowers—marched by at 11:22 P. M.

It was the greatest march in New York City's history, the reviewing officials agreed. That note of superlative was echoed along the dim-lit canyon of Fifth Avenue throughout the evening by the man in the street and his wife, too, and the children for whom the day was an important page in a new chapter of history.

Cigar Makers Last in Line.

The flower makers had to yield to the cigar makers the distinction of having marched to the last. At 11:45 P. M., after the flower makers had fallen out, the cigar makers broke ranks at Sixty-fifth Street, bedraggled physically but jubilant still.

Only then did the last of the spectators, estimated at 1,500,000 before their ranks ebbed with the passing of the hours, start for home. They taxed transportation in the midtown area as they had the police while the parade was on.

At frequent intervals during the day they were so enthusiastic that they swept aside the police—and there were 2,100 of them on parade duty—and bottled up the marchers at numerous points along the line. Storming the police lines, they proved too much even for the mounted men, in one instance throwing both mount and rider to the ground. The determined throngs refused to give way until motorcycle policemen were ordered to charge them.

Police Tired But Exuberant.

When the midtown area was cleared at last after midnight, long rows of worn policemen were sitting on the Central Park fence from the Plaza north, recovering their strength for the journey to their station houses.

But tired or not, they too were exuberant—the spirit was contagious.

Back at the reviewing stand, with the parade over, Governor Lehman dallied to appraise the event. He had left the stand to address the dinner of the Merchants' Association, but had returned a half hour before its close.

"The demonstration was the greatest New York has ever seen," the Governor declared. "It was an inspiration and a proof that the NRA is going over. Nothing of its kind has ever been seen before. New York State can well be proud."

Mayor O'Brien, ignoring the tax upon his good humor occasioned when a contingent from Wall Street booed him and his new levies, was equally enthusiastic on leaving the stand. "It was a great triumph," he said.

Red Flares Light Way.

Except for the brewers' unit, resplendent under red flares sobered to a mellow tone by the golden arcs, and communications workers

Continued on Page Three.

The great NRA parade moving up Fifth Avenue at 49th Street in New York City, cheered by throngs lining the thoroughfare.

The National Recovery Administration Board: (left to right) Walton Hamilton, Chairman of the Advisory Council; Leon Henderson, Director of the Division of Research and Planning; Blackwell Smith, Assistant General Counsel; S. Clay Williams, Chairman; Arthur Whiteside, Divisional Administrator; Leon C. Marshall, Assistant Administrator for Policy; Sidney Hillman, Labor Advisory Board.

The NRA symbol and its creator, C. T. Coiner of Philadelphia.

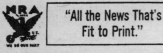

"All the News That's Fit to Print."

The New York Times.

LATE CITY EDITION
WEATHER—Showers late today; cooler tonight; tomorrow fair.
Temperatures Yesterday—Max., 74; Min., 61

Section 1

VOL. LXXXIII....No. 27,644. Entered as Second-Class Matter, Postoffice, New York, N. Y. NEW YORK, SUNDAY, OCTOBER 1, 1933. F Including Rotogravure Picture, Magazine and Book Sections. TEN CENTS | TWELVE CENTS Beyond 200 Miles, Except in 7th and 8th Postal Zones.

ROOSEVELT DECIDES TO BUY COAL, FOOD AND CLOTHING FOR THE NEEDY THIS WINTER

Farm Administration Plans to Demand Modification of Retail Code Price Fixing

By The Associated Press.

WASHINGTON, Sept. 30.—Modification of the price-fixing provisions of the retail code will be demanded of the NRA by the Agricultural Adjustment Administration unless they are eliminated or changed substantially by Hugh S. Johnson.

This was disclosed tonight by a high authority in the farm organization, which already has slated for rejection minimum mark-up provisions of a code for the food and grocery branch of the retail industry.

The basis for the farm administration's protest will be the tendency of prices the farmer pays to outdistance the prices he receives for his products. Government figures show farm purchasing power has decreased rather than increased in the last thirty days compared with the pre-war period, 1909-1914.

The retail code now before the NRA, affecting distribution fields outside of food and groceries, is designed to stabilize prices by prohibiting retailers from selling at less than wholesale cost plus 10 per cent.

Agricultural administration economists are convinced that this would stimulate the rise in prices paid by farmers and would contribute to offsetting increases in the prices for farm products.

Informal representations have been made by farm administration officials to the NRA that the 10 per cent mark-up would increase their difficulties in getting parity prices for farm products, based on pre-war relationships.

A spokesman for the farm administration said "these representations will be followed up as far as necessary, but of course, they will be on a friendly and informal basis—there is no conflict and probably no difference of opinion."

RELIEF FUND $700,000,000

All Will Be Needed, Says Hopkins After Talk With President.

START PLANNED IN WEEK

Roosevelt Approves Plan Extending Federal Aid 'Shorn of Red Tape.'

STATES' HELP COUNTED ON

Program Is Expected to Help Credit Expansion and Commodity Price Rise.

From a Staff Correspondent.

HYDE PARK, N. Y., Sept. 30.—A Federal relief program, shorn of red tape, in the interest of feeding, clothing and providing coal for the needy during the coming Winter will be started within a week under plans approved today by President Roosevelt in a three-hour conference with Harry L. Hopkins, Administrator of Federal Relief.

"We'll be going in a week," he informed newspaper correspondents immediately after his talk with Mr. Roosevelt.

The program was approved a few hours after the President had signed, in the early morning hours, an agreement he hopes will end the strike involving 100,000 workers in the "captive" coal mines operated by steel companies in the bituminous fields of Western Pennsylvania.

Aims of Relief Program.

The relief program is counted on to accomplish four basic results:

1. Succor the needy.
2. Contribute materially to credit expansion through the expenditure of more than $330,000,000 of Federal relief funds and an equal amount of other public funds for coal, food and clothing for distribution to the needy.
3. Assist in raising commodity prices by the placement of surpluses through channels that otherwise could not purchase them.
4. Assure harmonious cooperation in the Federal program through providing for the destitute until they can again be absorbed in gainful occupation through the gradual operation of the NRA.

Mr. Hopkins declined to go into statistical discussions, but in talking with newspaper men emphasized rather the determination of the administration to protect the unemployed against hardship.

State cooperation was being urged and effected daily, he said, and there was a total, estimated at almost $700,000,000, in the coffers of the Federal Government, of States, counties and municipalities available for the relief program.

"Will you need it all?" he was asked.

"Yes, we will need it all," he replied.

"Are the States and cities doing their share?"

"Most of them are, but not all."

May Relax Restrictions.

While it was not definitely so stated, the impression prevails among those close to the President that the ironclad restrictions heretofore surrounding Federal relief grants, such as the requirement that States match Federal grants, will be relaxed if necessary to provide for those in desperate need.

President Roosevelt insists that the States take every possible step to assist their own needy, and the Federal Government is prepared to use every persuasive force to bring this about. But the administration hopes that State cooperation will be as spontaneous in all cases as it has been in Missouri and Montana, which Mr. Hopkins cited today as excellent examples.

Both these States, he said, had agreed to call special sessions of their Legislatures to enact the necessary measures for cooperation with the Federal Government in relief work. Montana has pledged a State expenditure of $100,000, a large sum in comparison with its population.

Mr. Hopkins said he had given the President a general outline of the probable needs of his division, adding:

"We need food of all kinds, coal

Continued on Page Three.

13 ARE CONVICTED IN 2 KIDNAPPINGS; LIFE TERMS TO 3

Seven of Them in the Urschel Case—3 'Money-Changer' Defendants Freed.

ALL GUILTY IN LUER PLOT

Woman Is One of the Three Facing Life in Prison—Victims Hail Results.

WASHINGTON IS ELATED

Ex-Governor La Follette Says Two Masked Men Tried to Ambush Him in Wisconsin.

Progress of Kidnap War.

Seven defendants were convicted at Oklahoma City in kidnapping of Charles F. Urschel. Three were acquitted.

All six charged with Luer abduction were convicted at Edwardsville, Ill. Three of them, one a woman, were sentenced to life terms.

At Washington officials hailed successful termination of two cases and will turn next to solution of Kansas City Union Station massacre.

Former Governor Philip La Follette said that two masked men tried to ambush him Friday night outside a friend's cottage in Wisconsin. Mr. La Follette believed that the pair intended to kill him for the economic beliefs he has expounded.

Seven Guilty in Urschel Plot.

By The Associated Press.

OKLAHOMA CITY, Sept. 30.—Seven defendants in the Charles F. Urschel kidnapping conspiracy case were convicted by a Federal Court jury here today and held for sentence next Saturday to terms which may range up to life imprisonment.

Three others were freed and left for their homes in St. Paul and Minneapolis. They were Sam Kronick, Sam Kozberg and Isadore Blumfeld.

The first Federal Court jury to act under the "Lindbergh" Federal Kidnapping Law convicted not only the actual gunmen who abducted Mr. Urschel, but also persons who participated in guarding him during his nine days' imprisonment, and two of those who took part in attempts to change the $200,000 of ransom money paid for his return.

Those who were convicted were:

Alfred Bates, gunman, identified as one of the two men who broke up a bridge game on the sunporch of Mr. Urschel's home on July 22, and, with machine guns, forced Mr. Urschel and Walter Jarrett, a guest, to accompany them. Mr. Jarrett was released an hour later, and robbed of $51.

Harvey Bailey, gunman and escaped convict, who was found asleep, machine gun at his side and Urschel ransom money in his pockets, on the Shannon farm near Paradise, Texas, where Mr. Urschel was held.

R. G. (Boss) Shannon, his wife and their son, Armon, who entertained at their farm home both Bates and Bailey, guarded Mr. Urschel there while he was being held for ransom and attempted to mislead investigators after the farm hide-out was discovered.

Barney Berman and Clifford Skelly, brought to Oklahoma City for trial from Minneapolis and St. Paul, where, it was charged, they aided in the kidnapping conspiracy by attempting knowingly to dispose of part of the ransom money.

Two More to Be Tried.

Two alleged principals in the plot were not yet on trial, but were frequently mentioned in the testimony which led to today's convictions. They are George (Machine Gun) Kelly and his wife, Kathryn, daughter of Mrs. R. G. Shannon. Both are under arrest in Memphis.

The jury's verdict was reached after only an hour and a half of deliberation last night, but could not be announced until today because of orders of Judge Edgar S. Vaught. It left the penalties to the court.

Judge Vaught said he would grant three days to attorneys for the convicted defendants to prepare motions for new trials, and lawyers for all except Bates said they would have these motions ready Monday. Bates's attorney, Ben Laska of Denver, was not present.

The result of this major test of the "Lindbergh" law, passed by Congress in June, 1932, was hailed jubilantly by Herbert K. Hyde, District Attorney, and Joseph B. Keenan, assistant to the Attorney General, who were in charge of the prosecution.

"The verdict means the government is on top in this fight against

Continued on Page Thirty-four.

Major Sports Results

POLO—Seymour Knox's Aurora four won the national open championship by defeating Greentree in the final at Meadow Brook, 14 to 11. Boeseke of the victors captured individual scoring honors with seven goals.

FOOTBALL—Fordham opened its season with a triumph over Albright, 52 to 0. Army started with a 19-6 victory over Mercer and Navy stopped William and Mary, 12—0. Other scores were: Cornell 48, St. Lawrence 7, Manhattan 13, Clarkson Tech 6, Rutgers 10, Franklin and Marshall 0, Iowa 7, Northwestern 0.

RACING—William R. Coe's Osculator won the Havre de Grace Handicap, defeating C. V. Whitney's Equipoise by one length. The race had been announced as the last for Equipoise.

Complete details in sports section.

DAVIS BALKED PLAN FOR SHIFT ON ARMS

Refusal to Attend Any Talks Under 4-Power Pact Hailed as Saving Geneva Parley.

MINORITY RIGHTS PRESSED

Haiti Offers Resolution in the League Asking Equality for All Regardless of Race.

By CLARENCE K. STREIT.

Wireless to THE NEW YORK TIMES.

GENEVA, Sept. 30.—A decisive rôle in recent disarmament developments was attributed to Norman H. Davis, United States Ambassador at Large, today in the local Journal des Nations, which usually is extremely well informed on this subject. It says:

"If the disarmament conference is meeting on Oct. 16, this is very largely due to Mr. Davis. It was the flat refusal of the American delegate to attend as an observer or in any other capacity disarmament conversations within the framework of the Four-Power pact which led to British rejection of this proposal.

"Moreover, if the proposal that Germany be allowed samples of arms banned at Versailles has been buried, it is also largely due to American refusal to consider this."

This reflects widespread satisfaction with the American attitude among the secondary and smaller European powers, which hold in suspicion anything savoring of a practical restoration of the old European concert of great powers and want everything kept in the hands of the League or its conferences.

Among those most pleased with the American position are the Poles, the visit of whose Foreign Minister, Dr. Beck, to Mr. Davis was returned today, and the Foreign Ministers of the Little Entente who have just arrived from their conference in Rumania.

"Competition" Is Seen.

The action of the latter in holding their meeting there, ostentatiously competing with the first week of the League of Nations Assembly to some extent, however, has defeated their purpose. It has given Italy an opportunity to say that if Foreign Minister Titulescu of Rumania, as vice president of the Assembly, and Foreign Minister Benes of Czechoslovakia, who has always played a prominent rôle in it, can ignore its opinion in this way, they can no longer seriously object to having the four great League powers follow their example.

Pending Berlin's decision on its stand, disarmament negotiations have lagged here, but Mr. Davis and Sir John Simon, British Foreign Secretary, spent most of the day together. When they parted,

Continued on Page Twenty-five.

SOVIET AERONAUTS ASCEND 11.8 MILES FOR WORLD RECORD

Stratosphere Balloon Lands 62 Miles From Moscow—Up 8 Hours 19 Minutes.

89 BELOW ZERO RECORDED

But Crew of Three Sweltered at 86 Above in Gondola—Important Data Gleaned.

By WALTER DURANTY.

Special Cable to THE NEW YORK TIMES.

MOSCOW, Sept. 30.—The Red Army balloon Stratostat, U. S. S. R., beat Professor Auguste Piccard's record today by nearly 9,000 feet with an ascent of 19,000 meters (about 11.8 miles). The balloon landed at 5 P. M., two miles beyond Kolomna, a town about sixty miles southeast of Moscow, after eight hours, nineteen minutes in the air.

It was a fine, windless Autumn day and the balloon made a successful landing near a former monastery. Half of Kolomna's 80,000 population rushed across the river to welcome the three aeronauts.

The commander of the flight, Georgi Prokofief, said their instruments had registered a temperature of 67 degrees below zero Centigrade (about 89 below zero Fahrenheit), but they had suffered from the heat in their hermetically sealed gondola in which the temperature reached 30 Centigrade (about 86 Fahrenheit) from the effect of the sun.

None of the balloon's instruments was hurt in the landing. They are expected to give interesting data about the cosmic rays and other scientific information.

Flight "A Great Experience."

By The Associated Press.

MOSCOW, Sept. 30.—Three men in an aluminum sphere hooked to a balloon ascended 11.8 miles today, the greatest height ever reached by man. They enjoyed themselves so much that when they landed the first thing they said was they would do it again as soon as they could.

"None of us seems to be any worse for the experience, and we could go up again tomorrow," said Ernest Birnbaum. He was accompanied on the record-breaking flight by two other air service veterans, Georgi Prokofief and Konstantin Gudenoff.

"It was a great experience," said Mr. Prokofief. "The temperature outside the gondola was 67 below (Centigrade), but inside it was 30 above and we were almost stifled, particularly in view of our heavy clothing."

"All the scientific instruments which we carried functioned splendidly and every calculation proved to be correct. Our landing was so perfect that the Stratostat was not injured and we could very well ascend again tomorrow.

"After resting and correlating our scientific data, we intend to make another attempt, and perhaps we shall be able to reach a still greater height. We want not only to confirm our present data, but also obtain more information regarding the cosmic rays. I am convinced that such attempts will be possible throughout the entire Winter."

Gondola Sealed at 2,000 Meters.

M. Birnbaum was immensely pleased with the success of the flight. He said:

"We sealed ourselves in at a height of 2,000 meters (6,564 feet) and did not open up again until we

Continued on Page Thirty-six.

Vote Registration Here To Be From Oct. 9 to 14

Registration of voters in New York City will begin on Monday, Oct. 9, and continue through Saturday, Oct. 14. Only those who register will be allowed to vote at the general election on Nov. 7.

The registration places will be open from 5 P. M. to 10:30 P. M. from Monday to Friday and on Saturday from 7 A. M. to 10:30 P. M. The qualification for voting includes residence of one year in the State, six months in the county and thirty days in the election district. First voters must take a literacy test.

GERMANS TO FAST FOR CHARITY TODAY

Decree Orders Frugal Meal for All—Price of Big Dinner Will Go to Unemployed.

ALSO DAY OF THANKSGIVING

Chancellor Hitler Is Expected to Address Over 1,000,000 Near Hamlin.

By FREDERICK T. BIRCHALL.

Wireless to THE NEW YORK TIMES.

BERLIN, Sept. 30.—Tomorrow, which in America will be just another Sunday, is the official Thanksgiving Day in Germany, but it is a Thanksgiving Day of another kind. It is not to be a feast day, but a fast day inaugurating a series of monthly self-denial Sabbaths for the benefit of the government fund for the unemployed and destitute.

With voices and legs Germany through the length and breadth of the land will celebrate in endless parades and innumerable mass meetings—all under official auspices—this year's bountiful harvests, the triumph of the National Socialist régime and the German unity its measures have brought.

Under the same auspices Germans at the same time will go on short commons between the hours of 11 and 5, eating only a single modest dish instead of the usual elaborate Sunday dinner, but putting the price of a full meal into relief fund contribution boxes which Nazi patrols will collect.

Foreigners Must Contribute.

All will do this because they have to, but all Germans will do it gladly because the German loves to obey when he cannot command. Foreigners will have no choice because hotels, restaurants and pensions will serve only one dish while charging the full price of a meal. But they, too, will be cheerful about it because they also will be contributing toward ameliorating German unemployment hardships.

Anyway, the official restriction does not apply to liquids taken with the meal. Anybody can drink all the wine and beer he can pay for without contributing any of that payment to the official chest. And after 5 P. M. the lid will be off.

The only persons who do not seem to share in equal measure the general enthusiasm about this are the butchers and grocers, who are not doing their usual Saturday's thriving business today, and restaurateurs, who, however well filled their establishments may be tomorrow, will not reap their customary profits. They are somewhat disposed to feel that their contribution to self-sacrifice is somewhat inordinate. But the general public is completely satisfied.

Will Add to Large Fund.

The total sum collected in this way to remove, or at least to soften, the widespread distress which Germany faces in the coming Winter will be comparatively trivial compared with the needs. It will not be the mainstay of the fund, for big industrial concerns already have been assessed and are generously responding. Jewish firms are conspicuously in the foreground.

But the large receipts from the foregone Sunday dinners once a month are not the main objective. The aim is rather to focus public attention on the unemployment problem and to demonstrate picturesquely the determination and efficiency with which the new régime is meeting it. And in this respect the unrivaled Nazi propaganda machine is again achieving great success. Memories of the restricted German dinner will certainly last one month until the next restricted dinner comes due.

Putting this into effect has been quite simple. It has been decreed that the Sunday noon meal shall comprise one dish only and that its cost must not exceed 50 pfennigs, which is about 12 cents computed on the basis of the old United States dollar. For the trained hausfrau the task of confining the meal within the modest limits is easy. It has been somewhat more intricate for high class hotels and

Continued on Page Thirty-nine.

TAMMANY FACES A BOLT TO M'KEE OF DISTRICT CHIEFS

12 to 14 Desertions Likely, but Curry Moves to Win Away His Support in the Bronx.

GIBSON SUPPORTS McKEE

Vincent Astor Also Backs Him—LaGuardia Says Roosevelt Will Not Give Aid.

By JAMES A. HAGERTY.

Joseph V. McKee's campaign for the Mayoralty as an independent candidate will start tomorrow with a conference at his headquarters in the Biltmore Hotel. A campaign manager will be announced and plans for nominating a full ticket for places on the Board of Estimate will be considered.

With the political picture completely changed by the injection of the former Aldermanic President into the Mayoralty race, the outcome will depend entirely on the strength his candidacy develops and how he draws from his two major opponents, Mayor John P. O'Brien, Tammany nominee for re-election, and Fiorello H. LaGuardia, the Fusion candidate.

It was learned yesterday that Mr. McKee in addition to the support of the Roosevelt administration, though the President will not participate personally, will have powerful backing. Harvey D. Gibson, chairman of the Emergency Unemployment Relief Committee, and Vincent Astor, personal friend of President Roosevelt, were said to be among his influential backers. It also was reported that former Police Commissioner George V. McLaughlin and former State Senator Thomas I. Sheridan, turned down for renomination by Tammany, would support him and that one of the latter might be his campaign manager.

Bolts to McKee Probable.

Mr. McKee's sponsors expect the support of a number of Assembly district leaders in both Manhattan and Brooklyn but the number cannot yet be determined definitely. It is probable that six or seven district leaders in each of these boroughs will give Mr. McKee either open or secret support, led by Edward J. Ahearn of Manhattan and Kenneth S. Sutherland of Brooklyn. Assemblyman Jerome G. Ambro, who ran for the Democratic nomination for Mayor, is a Brooklyn district leader and is expected to support Mr. McKee.

Tammany was said to be trying to build a back-fire against the McKee candidacy by efforts to get some of the Bronx district leaders away from him and Secretary of State Edward J. Flynn, Bronx Democratic leader. These efforts were said to be directed mainly against Park Commissioner Thomas J. Dolen, License Commissioner James F. Geraghty and Charles F. Griffin, Deputy Commissioner of Sanitation. These leaders with several others hold city jobs at the pleasure of the Mayor.

How far Tammany intends to go in reprisals because of Mr. McKee's candidacy may be indicated at the convention to nominate Supreme Court justices for the First Judicial District to be held at Tammany Hall Tuesday night. Justice Samuel I. Rosenman, friend of President Roosevelt, and Justices Charles B. McLaughlin and Edward R. Koch, Bronx Democrats, are sitting on the bench by appointment and are up for nomination. Tammany, which refused last year to nominate Justice Rosenman, after his appointment by Mr. Roosevelt, then Governor, to make possible the nomination of Aron Steuer, Democrat, and Samuel H. Hofstadter, Republican, might decide to take similar action this year, it was said. This, however, is believed to be unlikely because of the possibility of the endorsement of these judges by the Fusionists.

To Build Up an Organization.

The present plans of Mr. McKee's sponsors call for the beginning of his speaking campaign on Oct. 16 and a three weeks' intensive drive for his election. The entervening two weeks will be used to build up an organization.

Tammany also will delay the opening of its campaign for the re-election of Mayor O'Brien until the world's series is out of the way, experience having shown the leaders of Tammany that it is difficult to interest the New York public in politics when a New York team is battling for the baseball championship.

The Tammany strategy calls for the stressing of what its orators will call Mayor O'Brien's achievements in office. An attempt will be made to claim credit for him in averting financial catastrophe for the city and the suspension of payroll payments and unemployment relief payments by the recent agreement with the bankers. The out-

Continued on Page Three.

TAX-FREE REALTY NOW FACES A LEVY

Untermyer Seeks Law to End Exemption for Much of Land Valued at $268,827,000.

MANY HOSPITALS ON LIST

Cemeteries, Private Schools, Bar Buildings and Clubs Would Be Affected.

Tax exempt property carrying a total assessed valuation of $268,827,000 was studied yesterday by the city administration with a view to placing most of it on the 1934 tax rolls.

Samuel Untermyer, financial adviser to the city, said in a letter to Mayor O'Brien that tax exemption should be abandoned on all enterprises engaged in commercial activity. In this category he listed hospitals, club hotels, cemeteries, schools and colleges and bar associations. Mr. Untermyer complained that the Department of Taxes and Assessments had given him a jumbled list of these properties to work on. Despite that he asked for immediate instruction on the Board of Estimate attitude on removing the tax exemptions.

Cemeteries Valued at $67,117,630.

In listing the assessed valuations of tax-exempt properties, Mr. Untermyer found that cemeteries represented $67,117,630 of the total. Schools and colleges carry a valuation of $98,250,000, while the two bar associations in Manhattan and the one in Brooklyn are valued at $1,975,000. Three Masonic club hotels and three Knights of Columbus club hotels are appraised at $6,485,000. Hospitals with "very limited charity wards" are rated at $95,000,000.

Mr. Untermyer's letter made no

Continued on Page Three.

RFC PUTS MILLIONS INTO TRADE DRIVE

New Policy Makes Capital Available at Once to Industries Under NRA.

TWO LOAN TYPES READY

Plan Is Said to Be Quickest Way to Utilize All Banks to Diffuse Credit.

The text of the RFC rules for loans to industry is on Page 28.

Special to THE NEW YORK TIMES.

WASHINGTON, Sept. 30.—The Reconstruction Finance Corporation today ordered full speed ahead in the administration's plan to assist in the financing of the NRA industries.

While the capital continues to buzz with speculation as to the prospect of inflation or stabilization, this credit arm of the government announced the policy and procedure under which hundreds of millions of dollars may be rushed to the aid of industry until better inducements can be offered to private capital.

In Circular No. 11, the corporation outlined how applicants may proceed at once to obtain financial assistance from the government through mortgage-loan companies and banks and trust companies.

This circular, it was understood, is to be followed within twenty-four hours by a move by the RFC to effect fairly universal acceptance of its preferred stock plan for going financial institutions. Under this plan it is contemplated that lending institutions be supplied with new capital dollars for relending to industry by offering their preferred

Continued on Page Twenty-eight.

Swanson, in Hawaii, Defends Naval Policy; Holds No Nation Can Object to Treaty Fleet

Wireless to THE NEW YORK TIMES.

HONOLULU, Sept. 30.—Secretary of the Navy Swanson said today that he still stood by his policy of a navy built up to the treaty limit for the United States, and he indicated his conviction that America's building program was no concern of any other world power.

The Secretary arrived here today for a week's inspection of naval installations in the Territory. He was met by high civil, navy and army officials when the cruiser Indianapolis docked at 7:30 A. M.

"The Navy Department's shipbuilding program to bring the sea forces to treaty strength," he said, "is not aimed at any other power but is merely a treaty measure. Japan is entirely within her rights in her plans for a larger navy, but an American navy second to none is the best assurance of continued world peace.

"No other nation can object to our plans. We haven't objected to others building, provided they do not exceed their ratio as signatories to the [London] treaty. They can't object to our program."

Mr. Swanson emphasized that there was no talk of war in Washington, and he added, "As has been said many times before, the keeping of our fleet in the Pacific is merely an economy measure since it is cheaper to keep the vessels concentrated."

The development of Pearl Harbor, the Secretary said, will depend largely on the result of an investigation he is to make while here. It is his belief, he added, that the base is destined to become, perhaps, the most important of the United States.

He denied that he was here as an agent of President Roosevelt to investigate the Hawaii political situation, and said his visit to Hawaii had no unusual significance. The cruiser Indianapolis was met off Diamond Head by twenty-five naval seaplanes, which escorted the cruiser to the harbor entrance.

Blast on City Ferryboat Kills One, Hurts 2, After 1,000 Richmond Commuters Debark

One man was fatally burned and two others were seriously scalded early yesterday when a steam pipe in the boiler room of the municipal ferryboat Brooklyn exploded shortly after she had landed 1,000 commuters and forty vehicles from Staten Island.

The Brooklyn had left St. George, S. I., at 8:10 and was preparing to return when the explosion occurred just before 8:45 o'clock. The blast shook the vessel violently and threw the crowded terminal into confusion until police and firemen arrived.

Andrew Murray, 61 years old, who lived at 1,185 Bay Street, Rosebank, S. I., an employe of the vessel, was so badly injured that he died later in the day at Broad Street Hospital. The two other injured employes were rushed to the hospital after first-aid treatment. They were Joseph Santorell, 125 Brighton Avenue, New Brighton, S. I., and Max Kellwert, 77 Beach Street, Stapleton, S. I. In the afternoon Santorell was sent to his home. Kellwert will remain at the hospital. Last night his condition was described as "satisfactory."

The muffled explosion of the steam pipe was heard outside the Barge Office, and policemen on traffic duty there sent calls for an ambulance, firemen and a police emergency squad.

Scalding steam filled the engine room, and the three men standing nearest the fourteen-inch main pipe were drenched. Patrolmen Frederick J. Franklin and Peter McDowell of the Greenwich Street station descended into the room to bring the injured men to the deck level where Dr. Weinstein of Broad Street Hospital treated them.

Captain J. P. Robinson, master of the boat, took his ship later to St. George, where repairs were started immediately, and last night an engineer of the Department of Plant and Structures said it was likely that the ferry would be placed back in operation last night.

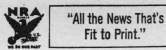

"All the News That's Fit to Print."

The New York Times.

Copyright, 1933, by The New York Times Company.

LATE CITY EDITION
WEATHER—Cloudy, rain tonight or tomorrow; same temperature.
Temperatures Yesterday—Max., 60, min., 45.

VOL. LXXXIII....No. 27,667. Entered as Second-Class Matter. Postoffice, New York, N. Y. NEW YORK, TUESDAY, OCTOBER 24, 1933. P TWO CENTS In New York City. | THREE CENTS Within 200 Miles | FOUR CENTS Elsewhere Except In 7th and 8th Postal Zones

ROOSEVELT WILL BUY GOLD AT ONCE ABOVE WORLD PRICE; STOCKS RISE; CODE FOR RETAIL STORES IS SIGNED

LAGUARDIA SAYS M'KEE AND FLYNN CONNIVE IN GRAFT

City Contractors Underpaid Workers and 'Split' With Bosses, He Declares.

CITES WILLARD'S SUICIDE

Says He Was Hounded to Death—But It Was W. J. Flynn Whom Willard Accused.

McKEE REBUKES CRITICS

Recalls That Opposition Press Once Praised Him—O'Brien Says He Is 'Unbossed.'

The City Campaign.

F. H. LaGuardia charged that Joseph V. McKee and Edward J. Flynn had connived with contractors in grafting on labor.

Joseph V. McKee quoted from newspapers now opposing him to show they praised his régime as Acting Mayor.

Mayor O'Brien declared at the City Club that he was "unbossed"; that no political power ever had interfered with his official duties.

John H. McCooey, Tammany leader of Brooklyn, blocked the expected revolt of his district leaders.

Election Board decided that voting machines will be used.

LaGuardia Charges Graft.

F. H. LaGuardia, Fusion candidate for Mayor, bitterly attacked Joseph V. McKee, his Recovery Party opponent and Edward J. Flynn, Democratic leader of the Bronx, last night as protectors of graft, racketeering and exploitation.

He accused them of conniving with unscrupulous contractors to cheat labor on city jobs of its just wages; he charged them with responsibility for the suicide of Louis H. Willard, a Hofstadter Committee witness, and he said that the former Aldermanic President was a candidate in this campaign "becaue Ed Flynn had the goods on him."

This series of attacks was delivered before large audiences at the Yorkville Lyceum, Eighty-sixth Street and Third Avenue; at the Madison Avenue Presbyterian Church, 921 Madison Avenue, and at the Powhatan Democratic Club, 183d Street and St. Nicholas Avenue.

In between his appearances at these rallies, the Fusion candidate found time to deliver a brief radio address over Station WABC urging voters not to entrust the problem of charter revision to "a lame duck commission," to be appointed by a Tammany Mayor, but reiterated his own promises of charter reform, under a Fusion administration.

Mr. LaGuardia's most vitriolic attack upon the Recovery party candidate and its principal political backer came at the end of the evening before 2,800 men and women crowded into the Powhatan Club, an organization which broke away from Tammany Hall last year and affiliated itself with the Knickerbocker Democrats, who are backing Fusion.

Recalls Willard Suicide.

There he reviewed for his audience the testimony of Willard, who declared before the Hofstadter Committee that William J. Flynn, Bronx Commissioner of Public Works, was responsible for his financial ruin and finally drove Mrs. Willard to suicide. Willard subsequently was indicted for perjury, tried and acquitted. Later he committed suicide.

[Editor's Note—The Bronx Commissioner of Public Works, although he bears the same surname as the Democratic leader of that borough, is not related to Edward J. Flynn, and at the present time is campaigning against Mr. McKee on behalf of Mayor O'Brien.]

"With the assistance and the knowledge and connivance of politicians of the Bronx who now pretend to purity," said Mr. LaGuardia, "they indicted Willard for perjury."

Telling of Willard's suicide after Irving Ben Cooper, now a Fusion candidate for City Court Justice, successfully defended him at his trial, Mr. LaGuardia said:

"The tragic end of Willard remains on the soul of Ed Flynn and Joe McKee. Let them, if they can, although resorting to the lowest kind of politics, abandoned in this country fifty years ago—the resort to lies and falsehoods—let Joe McKee, who is invited by some silly grandma to tea on Park Avenue, let him, when he looks in the mirror in the morning and Ed Flynn, when he gets up—there must arise before them the spirits of Willard

Continued on Page Four.

New Orleans Women Try To Boycott Long's Book

By The Associated Press.

NEW ORLEANS, La., Oct. 23.—Women opposed to the politics of Senator Huey P. Long today called for individual boycotts against stores selling Long's book, "Every Man a King."

A score of women, some wealthy, called department stores and drug stores where the book was advertised for sale and canceled their charge accounts and said they would do no further business there unless the sale was stopped.

The managers refused to withdraw the book. It was a business proposition with them, they said, and politics was not involved, but the women countered with assertions that it was spreading political propaganda and abuse against some of the stores' best customers.

STERN NAZI ORDERS PROTECT AMERICANS

Berlin Decree Says Attacks Hurt Reich Policy of Friendly World Relations.

STORM TROOPS WARNED

In Line With Hitler's Promise to Ambassador Dodd, Edict Is Expected to End Incidents.

By FREDERICK T. BIRCHALL.
Wireless to THE NEW YORK TIMES.

BERLIN, Oct. 23.—The recent direct representations by Ambassador William E. Dodd and the constant pressure from the American Consulate General in Berlin regarding assaults upon Americans and other foreigners who did not salute the Nazi flag in Nazi fashion have resulted in the sending of a new circular on the subject to the authorities throughout Prussia. It is in Prussia that most of these fanatical attacks have occurred.

The circular has not been published in Germany, nor is it probable it will be, for this is a matter of confidential instruction. But the American Consulate General has been informed there is no objection to its transmission abroad, as indicating the intention of the German authorities to put an end to these attacks, as Chancellor Hitler promised Ambassador Dodd would be done.

George S. Messersmith, the American Consul General, and his assistants, morever, see in the issuance of the circular, combined with other steps already taken and brought to their notice, a sincere effort to end the situation, which has given them great concern for many months.

Two persons, one of them a Nazi storm trooper, have been sentenced to six months each in jail for the latest unprovoked assault upon Roland Velz, an American, in Duesseldorf, and are already serving their sentences. A Nazi who struck Dr Daniel Mulvihill in Unter den Linden for failing to take off his hat for a Nazi parade is in a concentration camp. For other attacks apologies have been tendered.

The American officials are hopeful, therefore, that this latest circular will finally end the outrages.

TEXT OF THE CIRCULAR.

It was issued by Hermann Wilhelm Goering as Prussian Minister of the Interior and was immediately wired to every Governor and Police Chief in the Prussian provinces. A copy obtained for THE NEW YORK TIMES reads textually as follows:

To all provincial and district Governors: to the Police President, Berlin; to Secret State Police; to all State Police Inspectors:

Complaints to the Reich authorities by foreign diplomatic representatives regarding unpermissible interference of organs of the State, as well as members of national organizations, with the freedom and property of foreign nationals in Germany have increased lately.

It has been noticed that in numerous cases the homes and business offices of foreign nationals who were known to the authorities and had been placed under their protection have been subjected to police interference, despite all warnings and references to the desirability of treating foreigners in a friendly manner in the interests of the international relations of the Reich, although under the circumstances it might have been expected that instructions should be obtained first from a superior authority.

The central authorities have been able so far to avert official steps on the part of foreign powers; nevertheless, it cannot be denied that maltreatment, especially of American, British and other citizens of foreign States, because of neglect to salute the national banner with a German greeting, has considerably im-

Continued on Page Ten.

DALADIER FALLS ON BUDGET ISSUE; CHAMBER GUARDED

French Premier Defeated, 329 to 241, Despite Warning of Inflation in Six Weeks.

SOCIALIST PARTY SPLITS

Taxi Drivers Protesting Tax Blockade Square—Police Arrest Demonstrators.

By P. J. PHILIP.
Wireless to THE NEW YORK TIMES.

PARIS, Tuesday, Oct. 24.—Premier Edouard Daladier's government has been beaten. By 329 votes to 241 the Chamber of Deputies at nearly 3 o'clock this morning rejected an amended version of an article of the financial bill reducing the salaries of civil servants on which the Premier had asked a vote of confidence.

For a time it seemed possible that the Cabinet might be saved because the Socialist party for the first time in history split in two, one part under Pierre Renaudel voting with the government and the simon purists under Leon Blum voting against it.

While the debate was going on in the Chamber policemen and municipal Guards took extraordinary precautions to guard against rioting by taxpayers. Traffic was detoured from the vicinity of the Chamber and streets leading to it were barricaded by police trucks. Attempts at demonstrations were put down with the arrests of the leaders and the taxpayers were forced to retire to other parts of the city.

Just before midnight, however, taxi drivers blockaded the Place de l'Opéra as a protest against the proposed new tax on gasoline. The blockade was broken up after half an hour.

Moderate Centre in Opposition.

The votes of the two Socialist blocs this morning nearly neutralized each other. What was more serious was that only the Radical Socialists followed the Premier. The Moderate Centre to a man voted against the government's proposal.

It is that phase of the situation that will dominate the choice of a new Premier. The names of Albert Sarraut, Minister of Marine, and former Premier Joseph Caillaux are already being mentioned with those of François Pietri and others of the Centre. But that is for the next day or so.

Today was in itself historical enough. Premier Daladier went as far toward the Left as he could go. He went so far that he broke the Socialist party and brought barely half to his support. But he could not move M. Blum.

Between them and between M. Blum and M. Renaudel there were dramatic passages. For a moment the Premier did a thing rare in French politics. He threw a veiled personal reference at the Socialist leader. The latter had spoken of influences that had been brought to bear in the Finance Commission. Later he explained that he had meant the influence of certain Senators. But M. Daladier had understood him to mean financial interests.

"I have neither capital nor capitalists to defend," he cried from the tribune, and every one knew what he meant. For M. Daladier is a peasant's son and a schoolmaster by profession. M. Blum is among

Continued on Page Fourteen.

Briton to Fly 50,000 Miles On Business Trip to Orient

Wireless to THE NEW YORK TIMES.

LONDON, Oct. 23.—A London business man named Shaw left Croydon today in a light plane on the longest business journey ever undertaken by air, nearly 50,000 miles.

Representing the Asiatic Petroleum Company, Mr. Shaw will inspect business houses in the Orient, Australia and South Africa in which his company is interested. His only companion is a mechanic.

Their route will take them to Shanghai, Hongkong, Australia and Durban, returning by the West Coast of Africa. They expect to be back in London by February.

Mr. Shaw was one of the pilots who inaugurated the London and Paris air service in 1919.

AL SMITH STRIKES AT 'BUREAUCRACY'

Its 'Cold, Clammy Hand' Hinders Industry, He Asserts in Address at Chicago Fair.

HE EXTOLS INDIVIDUALISM

Private Initiative Is 'Vastly Superior' to Federal Control of Business, He Says.

Special to THE NEW YORK TIMES.

CHICAGO, Oct. 23.—Alfred E. Smith in an address at A Century of Progress Exposition today declared that "the heavy, cold, clammy hand of bureaucracy" had done much to hinder industry. Although there may be times when private industry needs "the curb and bit of government regulation," he said, "still it is vastly superior to government planning and government control of business and of all human effort."

The former New York Governor's remarks, which were broadcast, came in the midst of his laudation of the World's Fair as a monument to the accomplishments of individual initiative. His address was delivered before a shivering crowd of 5,000 "Al Smith Day" celebrants.

"As I went through the fair," Mr. Smith said with a generous wave of his hand that included a dirigible overhead and the miles of exhibits north and south, "I thought to myself that there is still another great lesson for the people of this country to learn from this great exposition. Aside from the assistance of Divine Providence, what has made this century of progress?

"Triumph Without Dictatorship."

"If you will study this fair, you will be obliged to come to the conclusion that this century of progress was brought about by individual initiative; by the strength, the power, the courage, the brains and the ability of the men and women of the Republic of North America. Whether you point to progress in industry, science, invention, transportation, or the arts, what you see here is the triumph of the mind and the hand of free men, without dictatorship.

"Ninety per cent of the exhibits here mark advances in our civilization due entirely to individuals, private individuals, working without inspiration, compulsion, control, or even suggestion, from the government itself. In fact, it is noteworthy that the government has done very little to contribute to this century of progress, while,

Continued on Page Fifteen.

Cummings Rules Volstead Law Applies In Federal Zones Until Congress Acts

Special to THE NEW YORK TIMES.

WASHINGTON, Oct. 23.—Attorney General Cummings tonight ruled that after repeal of the Eighteenth Amendment the Volstead Act "will be in full force and effect in the District of Columbia, Alaska, Hawaii, Puerto Rico, the Virgin Islands and the Canal Zone."

The ruling ended months of uncertainty as to the post-repeal status of these Federal areas under the jurisdiction of Congress and, in effect, it applied to continuance of the Volstead Act in them pending legislation by Congress at the session which meets in January. Enactment of a model liquor control law is then expected.

The Attorney General's brief opinion, telephoned to the newspapers at 10 o'clock night, gave no reasons or legal precedents and did not confirm previous reports that, while the provisions of the dry enforcement law would apply in the District and the Federal Territories and possessions, a policy of leniency would be followed. The ruling does not affect the States.

Opinion had been divided as to the liquor status of the national capital after repeal, one group contending that all restrictions would cease pending new legislation and the other that either the Volstead Act or the Sheppard Act, its local predecessor, would apply.

The first group argued that the Sheppard Act was repealed by the Volstead Act and that the latter, as the enforcement vehicle for the Eighteenth Amendment, would cease to apply anywhere after the repeal of its parent.

Some persons have maintained that if the Volstead Act continues to have effect in Federal areas it also could apply with equal legal force in States failing to adopt their own laws restricting liquor trade. But this opinion has not been general.

Howard Lee McBain, Ruggles Professor of Constitutional Law and Dean of the Faculty of Political Science at Columbia University, said last night that the Volstead Act "would not apply for one second in the States beyond repeal of the Eighteenth Amendment."

'LOSS LEADERS' BARRED

Retailers Must Charge Invoice Cost Plus an Allowance for Wages.

FARM AREAS WIN POINT

Dealers Hiring Fewer Than 5 in Towns Under 2,500 Are Exempt From the Code.

DRUGGISTS ARE INCLUDED

'Inaccurate' and 'Underselling' Advertising Banned—War on Profiteers Is Pledged.

Text of the retail code signed by the President, Page 17.

Special to THE NEW YORK TIMES.

WASHINGTON, Oct. 23.—The master code for more than 1,000,000 retailers prohibits selling below invoice cost plus an allowance for store wages, and exempts from its provisions employers hiring fewer than five persons in towns of less than 2,500 population, it was revealed today with announcement that President Roosevelt signed the code last night.

The code, which goes into effect next Monday, bore an appendix covering drug stores, thus obviating the need for a separate compact for druggists.

The barrier against selling below cost is a compromise suggested by General Johnson, NRA administrator, replacing an orginal plan banning sales at less than cost plus 10 per cent. The compromise was offered after the Agricultural Adjustment Administration and farming interests had strongly opposed the first plan.

According to a statement by General Johnson, it is aimed directly at the vicious practice of "loss leaders," or articles sold below cost to persuade customers that the store's entire price level is equally low.

Exemption of the small-town merchants was effected through an Executive order by President Roosevelt relieving them of the necessity of complying with the code or with Presidential re-employment agreements. Both the Executive order and General Johnson's statement assert that the exemption will lift hardships from the shoulders of farmers and rural merchants. It does not apply to chain stores in small towns.

Advertising Claims Curbed.

The long controversy over unfair trade practices is settled, with the code prohibiting "inaccurate" advertising references to competitors and "inaccurate" claims of underselling. Insertion of this qualification was fought by the great majority of the retailers, who termed "inaccurate" a "weasel" word.

According to general sentiment here, the compromise on selling below cost is a victory for the farmers and some of the urban consumers and a defeat for the great body of retailers, mitigated perhaps by the exemption of so many small merchants from the code's terms.

Recently the National Dry Goods Association told President Roosevelt that without the 10 per cent mark-up hundreds of retailers would go to the wall in three or four months. Farmers, on the other hand, defiantly said the mark-up would mean rising prices.

The new program is "frankly" experimental, according to General Johnson, pending the ultimate decision of a "distinguished" committee which will make a report Feb. 1.

In the provision against the "loss leader" the code said this did not prohibit a storekeeper from selling an article without any profit to himself, adding:

"But the selling price of articles to the consumer should include an allowance for actual wages of store labor, to be fixed and published from time to time by the Trade Authority hereinafter established."

Can Meet Competition.

Explaining then that this labor cost clause need not apply in communities of less than 2,500 population, the code went on:

"Provided, however, that any re-

Continued on Page Sixteen.

Dollar Takes Drop Under Pressure Abroad; Foreign Reception of New Policy Divided

The dollar fell on the Paris, London and Berlin Exchanges yesterday in reaction to President Roosevelt's announcement of his plan to continue in the direction of a managed currency by setting up a government market for gold.

In relation to the dollar the pound on exchange here rose 9⅞ cents, the French franc 6 points, the Dutch guilder 95 points, the belga 30 points, the Swiss franc 40 points and the Canadian dollar ½ cent. The best price for the pound, $4.64¾, was the highest since Oct. 11, but the price fell to $4.62⅛ at the close.

Sentiment among financial and editorial spokesmen in Paris ranged from skepticism to hostility.

The Journal des Débats contended that the effort to control prices through directing the gold value of the dollar was doomed to failure, but suggested that the President could limit fluctuations of the dollar against gold and gold currencies through the Reconstruction Finance Corporation's playing the same rôle toward United States currency as the British stabilization fund plays toward the pound.

The London Times, through its financial editor and its editorial columns, expressed doubt about the wisdom of the President's move. The financial editor said dollars were offered from all quarters on the London market yesterday largely "because bankers and business men in the United States and elsewhere regard his currency policy, in so far as they understand it, as impracticable and likely to result in a loss of confidence in American currency and thereby to hinder rather than assist the process of recovery."

German financial commentators were not unfriendly to the plan, but they did not venture specific predictions as to its effect.

The point which recurred in comments both abroad and in the United States was that the Reconstruction Finance Corporation would probably function in regard to the policy in the same manner as the stabilization fund functioned in Britain. This was the view taken in Geneva.

MARKETS SPURT; DOLLAR DECLINES

Speculative Buying, Induced by Inflation View, Sends Up Stocks and Commodities.

RISE IS CHECKED LATER

Partial Recovery of Dollar Is Reflected—Gold Issues Close 3½ to 40 Points Up.

Interpreting President Roosevelt's new gold policy as inflationary, speculators bought stocks and commodities heavily yesterday, causing one of the sharpest rises in several months. This movement was accompanied by a rapid decline in the dollar in terms of foreign currencies.

Virtually all of the gains in stocks and commodities were scored when the markets opened. In the afternoon the dollar recovered part of its early losses, thus abruptly ending the rise on the security and commodity exchanges.

Wheat closed within a fraction of a cent of the highest prices of the day, but other commodities lost about half of the morning's gains.

Strength of Mining Issues.

The feature of the rise in stocks was the strength in the gold mining issues, which advanced 4 to 25 points at the outset on the Stock Exchange. The buying in this group was based on a belief that further devaluation of the dollar, in terms of gold, was likely to result from the administration's plan to enter the gold market.

The gold stocks closed from 3½ to 40 points higher slightly below the day's highest prices.

Other stock groups did not hold their gains so well, however. As measured by THE NEW YORK TIMES index of fifty stocks, the net gain for the session averaged $3.36, the largest advance for any day since Oct. 4.

The index closed at $76.33, against a high of $78.09, and a low of $75.06. The advance brought the index back to last Wednesday's price range.

Volume and Trend of Trading.

Trading was active during the morning, but gradually decreased during the afternoon reaction. The turnover on the Stock Exchange was 2,128,000 shares, as compared with 2,697,000 shares on Friday. More than half of the day's business was transacted between 10 A. M. and noon.

Gains of representative stocks were United States Steel, 1½; General Motors, 1⅝; Union Pacific, 7½; Homestake Mining, 40; Dome Mining, 4⅝; McIntyre Porcupine, 6⅛, and Alaska Juneau, 3½. The four latter issues are gold-mine stocks.

Wheat futures closed 4 to 4½ cents a bushel higher at Chicago, after opening about 3 cents higher. The gains brought wheat prices 19 cents above the lows of last Tues-

Continued on Page Three.

ROOSEVELT CALLED 'FARMERS' FRIEND'

Peek Declares His Assurance of Price Rise for Them Is Answer to Strike Talk.

THOMAS GROUP WON OVER

Senator's Farm-Money Conference Is Expected to Endorse President's Step.

Special to THE NEW YORK TIMES.

WASHINGTON, Oct. 23.—The agricultural arm of the government was particularly gratified today by President Roosevelt's authorization to the Reconstruction Finance Corporation to purchase newly mined gold in the United States, ostensibly to increase commodity prices, and by his pledge to increase the return to farmers for their products.

Speaking for the Agricultural Adjustment Administration, of which he is chief administrator, George N. Peek construed the President's program as a direct reply to the sponsors of the farm strike. Referring to recent activities of the Farmers Holiday Association, he said:

"These farmers should fight with their enemies rather than with their friends, and the President has shown himself to be their friend by providing banking facilities where they have not existed for years and by assuring an improvement in prices."

Thomas Group Satisfied.

Senator Thomas of Oklahoma, leader in the Senate inflationist group, not only expressed satisfaction wtih the President's action but also said he would recommend to a conference of farm leaders and the committee for the nation tomorrow the adoption of resolutions supporting the administration on the money question.

This conference, which Senator Thomas summoned about two weeks ago to arrange a farm and monetary program for the consideration of Congress, will consist of twenty-five persons representing farm and money policy groups. Its original purpose was to spur the administration to define its monetary stand and to advance new plans for raising farm prices.

Senator Thomas now believes that the conference will content itself with an endorsement of the President's latest stand on money and the advancement of several far-reaching suggestions for helping the farmer.

Peek Sees Farmers Reassured.

Mr. Peek's reaction to the monetary policy set forth by the President and its effect on the farmers' dissatisfaction with the recovery program was in striking contrast to his remarks on the farm strike situation last Friday, when he said that "these people are only fighting to save their homes," and added

Continued on Page Two.

DOLLAR PLAN IS SPEEDED

Way Is Cleared Without Further Formalities for RFC to Act.

NO FREE SELLING LIKELY

Treasury Also Probably Will End World Market Agency for Our Mine Output.

EXCHANGE FACTOR TO FORE

Views Differ on Prospect of Adopting the Commodity Dollar Scheme.

Special to THE NEW YORK TIMES.

WASHINGTON, Oct. 23.—The administration moved today to put into immediate operation its plan for the Reconstruction Finance Corporation to purchase gold, as announced by President Roosevelt in a radio speech last night.

The first step probably will be the offering of prices higher than the world market quotations for newly mined gold produced in the United States.

Through these purchases, affecting 20,000 to 30,000 ounces each week, the President hopes to raise the price of gold in relation to foreign currencies, and to break the control over the dollar said to be exerted by banks in London and Paris and by foreign speculators. These actions in turn would operate further to cheapen the dollar in this country.

No Executive order or additional machinery of government is required to take this step, as the President's advisers have ruled that the RFC may proceed without additional authorization so long as its gold dealings have the approval of the President and the Secretary of the Treasury.

RFC Policy on Selling Defined.

There appeared to be considerable confusion in official circles here today as to many of the details of the operations set in motion by the President. Some of the details were cleared up unofficially, however, among them that the RFC will not freely sell the gold it purchases in the domestic market.

It also was believed probable that the present policy of permitting the Treasury to obtain the world price for newly mined production would be rescinded, and that all such sales would thereafter be made to the Reconstruction Finance Corporation at the prices quoted by the administration. Thus any element of competition between the RFC and the world markets for this gold would be eliminated and the stocks retained in this country.

The statement of the President that prices for such transactions would be quoted "from time to time" was interpreted to mean that, while quotations would not be made daily, they would be announced at frequent intervals.

The speed with which it is intended that the President's plan shall be carried out was exemplified today by a special meeting of the RFC to study procedure and conferences at the White House between the President, Mr. Jones, Harvey C. Couch, a director of the RFC, and Under-Secretary Acheson of the Treasury.

Immediate Action Forecast.

Messrs. Jones and Couch were uncommunicative concerning their talks with the President, in each instance referring all inquiries to the President. The President made no statement beyond that contained in last night's speech, but an official close to him stated that the first purchase of newly mined gold will be made "almost immediately."

The reaction of the Department of Agriculture to the President's program was favorable. George N. Peek, Agricultural Adjustment Administrator, expressed the belief that it would result in advancing farm prices. He also saw in it an answer to the farm strike movement.

The inflation group in Congress, headed by Senator Thomas of Oklahoma, expressed satisfaction and planned to submit to the conference of farmers and the Committee of the Nation to be held here tomorrow—a resolution endorsing the President's monetary policy. He hoped that the farmers who had

Continued on Page Two.

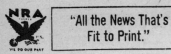

"All the News That's Fit to Print."

The New York Times.

4:30 A. M. EDITION
WEATHER—Cloudy, colder today; tomorrow fair, slightly warmer.
Temperatures Yesterday—Max., 46; min., 35.

VOL. LXXXIII....No. 27,682. Entered as Second-Class Matter, Postoffice, New York, N. Y. NEW YORK, WEDNESDAY, NOVEMBER 8, 1933. F TWO CENTS in New York City | THREE CENTS Within 200 Miles | FOUR CENTS Elsewhere Except in 7th and 8th Postal Zones

LAGUARDIA ELECTED MAYOR OF NEW YORK; FUSION CONTROLS BOARD OF ESTIMATE; REPEAL OF 18TH AMENDMENT IS ASSURED

3 STATES VOTE WET

Utah Is the 36th, Insuring End of the Dry Law

OHIO, PENNSYLVANIA WON

Repealist Forces Never in Danger in Heavy Balloting.

NORTH CAROLINA IS DRY

Anti-Repealists Hold the Lead in Incomplete South Carolina Figures.

LARGE VOTE IN KENTUCKY

But Result Will Not Be Known Until Today, When Ballots Are Counted.

The Salt Lake City (Utah) Tribune announced early this morning that on the basis of more than three-eighths of the total vote in that State, Utah had voted for the Twenty-first Amendment to the Constitution of the United States, repealing the Eighteenth or prohibition amendment, by a safe majority of more than five to three.

Utah thus made the thirty-sixth State, completing the necessary three-fourths of the forty-eight States, to vote for ratification of the repeal amendment. Its vote means that repeal will become effective on Dec. 5 or 6.

Over the telephone early this morning THE NEW YORK TIMES learned from The Salt Lake City Tribune that 337 out of the 804 precincts in Utah had voted as follows:

For repeal, 42,475.
Against, 24,567.

Later returns from 399 precincts gave a total vote of 46,760 for repeal and 34,810 against.

Repeals State Dry Law.

Utah also voted to repeal her State constitutional prohibition amendment, on the basis of returns from the same precincts, which were 29,821 for repeal and 21,754 against repeal of State-wide prohibition.

The Salt Lake City Tribune explained that there was no likelihood of the trend of the vote on repeal being upset by later returns. comparatively few of the 197 precincts in Salt Lake City County, which is known to be predominantly wet, are included in the precincts already reported. The rest of the Salt Lake City vote to be recorded is counted on to hold the repeal majority safe.

Before the result in Utah became known, definite repeal victories had been recorded in Ohio and Pennsylvania. On the basis of about three-fourths of the total vote, Ohio went more than two to one for repeal. Ohio also voted for repeal of her State prohibition amendment, according to results from more than one-fourth of her precincts.

Pennsylvania's vote was more than ten to one for repeal in one-sixth of her precincts.

Before yesterday thirty-three States had voted for repeal.

Kentucky Wets Confident.

Of the other three States which voted on repeal yesterday, North Carolina rejected repeal by a large majority. The race in South Carolina was very close, with the drys leading by a small margin. Late last night the repeal leaders conceded defeat on the basis of two-thirds of the count.

No returns were received from Kentucky, where the ballots will not be counted until today. Wet leaders said they were confident that Kentucky had voted for repeal.

A[illegible] that Utah remains in

Continued on Page Thirty.

LaGuardia Promises A 'New Era' for City

At 9:55 o'clock last night, when his victory was assured, F. H. LaGuardia, the Mayor-elect, issued the following statement:

"Returns up to this moment indicate the election of the majority of the Fusion ticket. The results are indeed gratifying. This opens the way to a new era in municipal government.

"I fully realize the responsibility I shall assume on Jan. 1. I need and ask for the cooperation of all interested in good city government. I promise and now pledge a real non-partisan administration. I shall take no active part in politics for the next four years.

"I am anxiously awaiting complete returns on my running-mates on the ticket, and naturally cannot be fully happy until I hear definitely of their success.

"To all my associates and workers of the campaign thanks. To the people of the City of New York I say that I appreciate the confidence placed in me and shall strive to be worthy of it."

LITVINOFF GREETED AT WHITE HOUSE

Roosevelt Officially Renews Link With Russia After 15 Years.

PARLEYS TO BEGIN TODAY

Commissar, Hopeful of Recognition, Will Confer With Hull and His Aides.

Special to THE NEW YORK TIMES.

WASHINGTON, Nov. 7.—The official silence which has separated the United States and Russia for more than fifteen years was ended at the White House this afternoon when President Roosevelt and Maxim Litvinoff, Soviet Commissar for Foreign Affairs, clasped hands cordially and extended greetings on behalf of their respective governments.

This first meeting of the two executives who expect to work out a formula for recognition of the Soviet by this government was scheduled as a formal call. It was attended only by aides of the President.

But M. Litvinoff's broad smile and evident happiness as he posed for photographers on the portico of the White House after the conference were held an indication of a happy beginning for the negotiations.

As an added touch of hospitality, Mrs. Roosevelt greeted M. Litvinoff after he had held a brief conversation with the President.

Prior to the White House call the Soviet envoy was greeted on arriving at Union Station by Secretary Hull and an official party. He had been escorted from New York by a State Department official.

By a coincidence, M. Litvinoff's arrival at President Roosevelt's invitation fell on the date counted the sixteenth anniversary of the Soviet.

The business that brought M. Litvinoff to the United States for his first visit will be taken up at the State Department tomorrow morning, when he confers with Secretary Hull and a staff of selected American experts on Russo-American relations.

Hull Welcomes Visitor.

The Russian emissary arrived here at 3:45 P. M. on a special train of five cars which brought him from Jersey City, where he had been landed by the Coast Guard cutter Manhattan, chartered by the State Department to remove him from the Berengaria in New York Harbor.

M. Litvinoff was the first to descend from the private car of the special train, and close behind him came Mr. Dunn, who introduced the Soviet envoy to Secretary Hull and others in the official welcoming party.

These included William Phillips, Under-Secretary of State; Marvin H. McIntyre, assistant secretary to the President, and State Department experts who will be in close contact with M. Litvinoff throughout his visit.

"I am very glad to see you!" was Secretary Hull's greeting.

The reception, while as formal and complete as that accorded of

Continued on Page Twenty-four.

RELIEF BONDS VOTED

$60,000,000 Is Approved by a Huge Majority

CHARTER PLAN IS LOSING

'Lame Duck' Measure Appears Doomed—Count Is Slow.

THREE AMENDMENTS SAFE

But Veterans' Preference Act Is in Doubt After Getting Lead Up-State.

The voters of the entire State piled up a huge majority for the $60,000,000 relief bond issue, and approved at least three of four proposed amendments to the Constitution. In the city the Tammany plan for charter reform apparently was defeated. The amendment which was still in doubt early today would extend the preference now given to veterans under the Civil Service Law.

Figures from twenty-one up-State counties, with only one county, Erie, complete, gave 243,589 votes in favor and 52,469 against the relief bond issue, known as Proposition 1. In the city 1,703 of the 3,842 election districts recorded 137,623 ayes and 11,368 nayes.

Three Amendments Safe.

Amendment 1, calling for reform in condemnation proceedings by permitting the setting up of a special term of court to handle such cases, was leading in the city, 90,053 to 18,438, in returns from 703 election districts, and it had a comfortable lead up-State, from the twenty-odd counties which sent in incomplete returns.

Amendment 2 was in doubt. It would permit the extension of civil service preferences to disabled veterans who have become citizens since the World War. The city was vetoing it, with 97,060 nayes and 85,651 ayes, in returns from 713 districts, but the up-State margin in favor of the extension, with returns slow, were balancing the city vote.

Amendment 3, permitting the construction of a State highway between Indian Lake and the Village of Speculator in the Adirondacks, led in the city 96,690 to 35,978 on returns from 704 election districts. It was running well ahead up-State.

City to Get Barge Terminal.

Amendment 4, permitting the State to cede to the city the Barge Canal terminal at Fifty-seventh

Continued on Page Three.

OFFICIALS ELECTED

CITY TICKET	
Mayor	F. H. LaGuardia, R.-F.
Controller	W. A. Cunningham, R.-F.
Pres. of Aldermen	B. S. Deutsch, R.-F.
BOROUGH PRESIDENTS	
Manhattan	Samuel Levy, D.-J.*
Bronx	James J. Lyons, D.-Rec.
Brooklyn	R. W. Ingersoll, R.-F.
Queens	George U. Harvey, R.-F.*
Richmond	Joseph A. Palma, R.-F.
NEW YORK COUNTY	
Sheriff	Daniel E. Finn, D.-J.
Dist. Attorney	William C. Dodge, D.-J.
Register	Martha Byrne, D.-J.*
BRONX COUNTY	
Sheriff	John J. Hanley, D.-Rec.
County Clerk	N. J. Eberhard, D.-Rec.
Dist. Attorney	Samuel J. Foley, D.-Rec.*
Register	Herman M. Albert, D.-Rec.
KINGS COUNTY	
Sheriff	F. J. Quayle, Jr., D.-Rec.
Register	Aaron Jacoby, D.-Rec.*
QUEENS COUNTY	
County Clerk	Jenkins R. Hockert, R.-F.
RICHMOND COUNTY	
Sheriff	John Timlin, R.-F.
COURT OF APPEALS	
Associate Judge	Leonard C. Crouch, D.-R.-F
SUPREME COURT JUSTICES	
First District	S. I. Rosenman, D.-Rec.*
First District	C. B. McLaughlin, D.-R.-F.*
First District	Edward R. Koch, D.-Rec.*
First District	Philip J. McCook, D.-R.-F.*
First District	Denis O'L. Cohalan, D.-J.
Second District	Peter P. Smith, D.-Rec.*
CITY COURT JUSTICES	
Manhattan	James C. Madigan, D.-J.*
Bronx	I. J. P. [illegible]dlerman, D.-Rec.*
Bronx	H. G. Shackno, D.-Rec.
Queens	Peter M. Daly, D.-Rec.
GENERAL SESSIONS JUDGE	
Manhattan	Owen W. Bohan, D.-J.
SURROGATES	
New York	James A. Foley, D.-R.-F.
New York	J. A. Delehanty, D.-R.-F.*
COUNTY JUDGE	
Bronx	L. W. Patterson, D.-Rec.

*Reelected

BEAT VARE MACHINE IN PHILADELPHIA

Democrats and Allies Capture Local Offices—Democrat Ahead in Pittsburgh.

Special to THE NEW YORK TIMES.

PHILADELPHIA, Nov. 7.—In a city-wide political revolution without parallel here for more than two decades, a surprisingly strong coalition of Democrats and Republicans today swept to defeat the powerful Republican machine of William S. Vare, long dictator of Philadelphia politics.

The organization's downfall all along the line in the city-county election was admitted at the headquarters of the Republican city committee, where Chairman James M. Hazlett had said a few hours before that he saw "no decided swing away from the Republican party."

Not only were the four Democratic candidates for City Controller, Treasurer, Register of Wills and Coroner carried into office, but three sitting judges opposed by the Vare machine for re-election came through successfully.

It was the first city-wide defeat for the Republican machine, known

Continued on Page Fifteen

New ABC Revolt in Cuba; Planes Bomb Army Camp

By J. D. PHILLIPS.

By Telephone to THE NEW YORK TIMES.

HAVANA, Wednesday, Nov. 8.—Revolt flared up anew in Havana this morning when the ABC uprising, which was reported to have been scheduled for midnight, began just two hours and thirty minutes behind schedule.

At that time three airplanes circled the city and loosed a number of bombs upon Camp Columbia, the headquarters of Colonel Fulgencio Batista, the army's chief of staff. It was reported that the Presidential Palace was to be bombed next, although President Grau San Martin was not there but at his home in Seventeenth Street.

The revolutionists are said to have at their disposal a force of from 6,000 to 8,000 men in and around Havana. In addition to this force, armed with rifles landed recently in Santiago and sent overland to Havana, they are reported to have several units of the Air Corps.

Behind the revolt move are said to be a number of former army sergeants who are bent upon returning former President Carlos Manuel de Cespedes to office.

As the correspondent is writing this dispatch, bombs dropped from the airplanes overhead are exploding in the city and two batteries of government anti-aircraft guns have just opened fire upon the planes.

A general atmosphere of anxiety was noticeable in Havana yesterday, and it was evident that something was in the wind. Returning from Cienfuegos to Havana late in the day, the writer was stopped and searched six or eight times by government troops, indicating that the government was not wholly ignorant of the threatened revolt.

Tonight's outbreak marks the third revolt in the last two months. On Aug. 12 President Gerardo Machado was ousted by a revolt of the army, climaxing long-continued revolutionary activities.

VOTING DISORDERLY

Thugs Invade Polls, Slug Watchers, Defy Police

85 ARRESTED IN THE CITY

East Side and Harlem Gangs Terrorize Tammany Foes.

LAGUARDIA ROUTS TOUGHS

Drives Them From School—His Manager Arrested in Row Over Fraud.

Blackjacks, brass knuckles, lead pipe, bricks, stones and hob-nailed boots played an important part in the elections yesterday.

The lower East Side, part of Greenwich Village and parts of Harlem were overrun with roving groups of thugs and strong-arm men who intimidated, slugged and booted voters. Bricks were hurled through windows of various political headquarters in Harlem.

Several officials engaged in encounters with election workers. F. H. LaGuardia tore the badges from Tammany election workers and directed the clearing-out of hangers-on in Harlem polling places.

William Chadbourne, Fusion campaign manager, was arrested after a fracas on the East Side and Robert Minor, Communist candidate for Mayor, was thrust out of a polling place as thugs booted one of his workers.

The police were harried all day with calls for additional men to put down disturbances in storm centres.

Commissioner Bolan announced after 7 o'clock that there had been eighty-five arrests in the city from 6 A. M. to 5:30 P. M. on charges of illegal voting, false registration and disorderly conduct, sixty-six of them in Manhattan.

"In view of the fact that there was a major three-cornered fight, with nine candidates for Mayor, it was an unusually peaceful election," Mr. Bolan said.

LaGuardia Routs "Thugs."

Major LaGuardia, the Fusionist Mayoralty candidate, became a storm centre in his home district early in the day when he found certain practices of election workers objectionable.

He walked into a public school on 113th Street between First and Second Avenues with Mrs. LaGuardia and a party of reporters and photographers, shouldering his way through a crowd of more than 100 men and women who were blocking the sidewalk. At the threshold he came face to face with a burly man wearing a Tammany badge.

"You're a thug," the Fusion candidate snapped. He ripped the badge from the man's coat. "Now get out of here and keep away," he said. Then he swung toward a group of men in the front ranks of the crowd who seemed ready to surge in upon him.

"I know you," he shouted. "You're thugs. You get out of here and keep moving." As they drew back he said to the newspaper men: "I recognize them. They are Harlem hoodlums."

Snatches Tammany Badge.

Thirty men loitering around the voting machines inside the school rekindled the flame of Mr. LaGuardia's anger. He strode toward the spot, bearing down on a Tammany captain who wore a forbidden badge in his lapel. His hand shot out and the button came away in his hand.

"Get out!" he commanded.

The Tammany man took a step toward him, but changed his mind and stopped. A policeman stepped between the two as they glared at each other. At that point a newspaper photographer leveled his camera for a snapshot of the scene.

"Oh, that's what you want—publicity!" the Tammany captain shouted.

From behind him three men reached out, seized the photog

Continued on Page Four.

THE MAYOR-ELECT.

New York Times Studio.

Fiorello H. LaGuardia.

REPUBLICANS GAIN 8 ASSEMBLY SEATS

Party Will Have 85 Members in Lower House, 13 From City Districts.

CHARTER FIGHT AIDED

Democrats Regain Districts in Monroe, Erie, Chemung and Westchester Counties.

The next Assembly will be composed of eighty-five Republicans and sixty-five Democrats, a net gain of eight seats for the Republicans, who in the present Assembly have seventy-seven seats while the Democrats have seventy-three.

The Republican gains were due to almost revolutionary changes in the representation from New York City districts in the next Assembly. The party suffered a net loss of three seats, but to offset this gained eleven districts in this city. Thus the City of New York will have a larger Republican representation in the lower house at Albany next year than the city has had in more than a decade.

In some of the New York City districts won by the Republicans the margins for the winning candidates are pretty narrow and the same is true about some of the districts where the Democrats continue in control. Consequently there may be recounts and perhaps shifts in some cases.

The results in the city on the face of final figures last night show Republican victories in the Ninth, Eighteenth, Twentieth and Twenty-third in Manhattan; the Sixth, the Sixteenth and the Nineteenth in Brooklyn; the Seventh in the Bronx; the Fourth in Queens, and both districts in Richmond. This last result was the most startling change effected in the Assembly elections.

13 Members from City.

With the two districts in the city in which the Republicans retain control, the Fifteenth in Manhattan, where Abbot Low Moffat, the incumbent, won, and in the Tenth, also in Manhattan, where Herbert Brownell Jr. was re-elected, the Republicans will have thirteen members from the city to make a fight for the radical New York City charter changes which the victorious Fusion officials have in contemplation.

The first woman to sit in the Assembly in many years will be Miss Doris I. Byrne, the Democratic representative from the Second Assembly District in the Bronx. She won by a substantial plurality over

Continued on Page Three.

TENSITY PERVADES TIMES SQ. THRONGS

200,000 Grimly Await News—Shouting and Cheering of Other Years Is Lacking.

SURGE ON TO POLICE LINES

Mounted Patrolmen Posted at Ten-Foot Intervals Along Mid-Broadway.

The tenseness with which New York had waited for the results of the city election was evident last night in the attitude of the crowds which filled Times Square. Generally there is a blaring of horns and the rasping of other noise-making devices early in the evening, but last night New York's watching thousands stood silently, their eyes intent on THE NEW YORK TIMES bulletins flashed on the screen or the electric board around the Times Building.

Until their desire to know what had happened in the hurly-burly of yesterday's election was gratified they were willing to let their propensities for celebration remain under strict control. They were too interested to be noisy, too anxious to cheer a single bulletin until well on into the evening.

Tammany Gives the Word.

Then there was the clanging of a bell on the marquee of the Criterion Theatre, from which Mayor O'Brien and his running mates had talked to Times Square crowds for many days, and the announcement that Tammany conceded the election of F. H. LaGuardia.

There was an instant relaxation, a few handclaps were heard, and although there were no cheers, it was as if the bars of restraint were suddenly dropped by all the tens of thousands in the square. Even the policemen, on foot and on horseback, who had been shepherding in good-humored spirit a patient throng for hours, seemed to give in to the general feeling of "Thank God, that's over."

The crowds moved in and out of the police lines unchecked for a time, and the minds of the police were apparently more on problems of the future than their duties. Then they snapped out of inattention, their lines formed again and order was restored to the square.

There was no untoward disturbance during this brief interval; it was merely that for a time all minor rules went by the board and the crowd relied upon its own sense of orderliness to keep from stampeding all over the place. But there was no wild enthusiasm, no blaring of horns, no cheering, ex-

Continued on Page Three.

M'KEE RUNS SECOND

Loses Even Bronx, Smashing Blow To Farley

LAGUARDIA BY 254,506

Carries Every Borough, Sweeping In His Chief Running-Mates.

TAMMANY FORCES ROUTED

O'Brien Loses Manhattan by 5,895—Levy Victor, Dodge Wins, Prial Loses.

PECORA, STRAUS DEFEATED

Fusion Victory Is First in 20 Years—Vote Biggest Ever Cast in City Election.

By JAMES A. HAGERTY.

For the first time in twenty years, Fusion yesterday wrested control of the city government from Tammany and elected former Representative F. H. LaGuardia Mayor and a majority of the Board of Estimate. The last Fusion victory was in 1913 when the late John Purroy Mitchel was elected Mayor.

It took an outpouring of men and women from the apartment houses and the one and two family houses in the outlying sections of the city to drive the Tiger from City Hall with the largest vote ever cast in a city election.

Vote Totals 2,112,146.

The tremendous vote, which ran to 2,112,146 for the three major Mayoralty candidates and Charles Solomon, Socialist, developed into what amounted to a landslide for Mr. LaGuardia.

He defeated Joseph V. McKee, Recovery party candidate, who ran second, by a plurality of 254,506 and a plurality of 272,451 over Mayor John P. O'Brien, Tammany candidate for re-election.

The vote for Mayor follows:

O'Brien, 586,100; LaGuardia, 858,551; Solomon, 63,450; McKee, 604,045.

Mr. LaGuardia carried every borough. He led Mayor O'Brien in Manhattan, former stronghold of Tammany, by 5,895. He carried the Bronx, home borough of Mr. McKee, by a margin of 21,126 over the Recovery party candidate. He had the very large plurality of 135,210 in Brooklyn over Mayor O'Brien, who in turn led Mr. McKee in that borough by 862. Mr. LaGuardia carried Queens, another borough in which Mr. McKee was believed to be strong, by 13,446 over McKee, and Richmond by 8,645 over the same candidate.

At the request of two candidates, Frank J. Prial, Tammany candidate for Controller, and Frederic Kernochan, Fusion candidate for Judge of General Sessions, Chief Inspector of Police John O'Brien early this morning instructed the police to continue to guard the voting machines in view of the possibility of contests.

Sweeps Running Mates In.

With Mr. LaGuardia went to victory a majority of the other important Fusion candidates. These were W. Arthur Cunningham, nominee for Controller; Bernard S. Deutsch, nominee for President of the Board of Aldermen; Raymond V. Ingersoll, nominee for Borough President of Brooklyn; Borough President George U. Harvey of Queens, candidate for re-election, and Joseph A. Palma, nominee for Borough President of Richmond.

This is sufficient to give Fusion not only a majority on the board, but the thirteen out of sixteen votes necessary to grant a franchise and for certain other purposes.

The Fusionists, however, failed

Continued on Page Two.

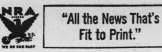

"All the News That's Fit to Print."

The New York Times.

LATE CITY EDITION
WEATHER—Rain and warmer today; tomorrow fair and colder.
Temperatures Yesterday—Max., 57; Min., 15

Copyright, 1933, by The New York Times Company.

VOL. LXXXIII....No. 27,692. Entered as Second-Class Matter, Postoffice, New York, N. Y. NEW YORK, SATURDAY, NOVEMBER 18, 1933. TWO CENTS In New York City. | THREE CENTS Within 200 Miles | FOUR CENTS Elsewhere Except in 7th and 8th Postal Zones

UNITED STATES RECOGNIZES SOVIET, EXACTING PLEDGE ON PROPAGANDA; BULLITT NAMED FIRST AMBASSADOR

WRIT BARS TAX AID FOR CITY SUBWAY; 5-CENT FARE HIT

Appellate Division Finds That 3 Years of Trial Operation Began Sept. 10, 1932.

$12,000,000 SAVING SEEN

Huge Service Charge Must Be Taken From Budget if Decision Is Upheld.

LAGUARDIA TO ACT AT ONCE

Will Speed Negotiations as Unity Is Seen as Sole Hope of Averting Fare Rise.

The Appellate Division ruled yesterday, in a 4 to 1 decision, that the city no longer has any right to use tax funds to pay interest and amortization on bonds issued to finance construction of the Eighth Avenue subway. Reversing a ruling made in June by Supreme Court Justice John J. Walsh, the court granted a taxpayers' application for a temporary injunction against such payments.

If the decision is upheld, it will mean that approximately $12,000,000 must be stricken from the debt service appropriation in the 1934 budget, which is $24,000,000 out of balance. City officials, including George McAneny, Controller, and John H. Delaney, chairman of the Board of Transportation, indicated that an immediate appeal would be taken, which would automatically stay the temporary injunction.

Five-Cent Fare Imperiled.

In transit and financial circles the decision was regarded as of vital importance to the future of the five-cent fare. Responsible city officials, although declining to be quoted, indicated their belief that affirmation of the ruling by the Court of Appeals would mean that the nickel fare could be preserved, if at all, only by speedy unification of all rapid transit lines under city ownership and control.

In effect the decision fixed Sept. 10, 1932, the date of the opening of the Eighth Avenue line, as the beginning of the three-year trial period allowed the city if it elected to operate its own subways on a 5-cent fare. At the end of that period, under the State laws, the fare must be sufficient to pay all expenses, including fixed charges of every nature. It has always been the city's contention that the three-year period would not begin to run until after the entire system, including the Sixth Avenue line, for which no contracts have yet been let, was completed and in operation.

City Faces Dilemma.

Affirmation of the decision by the Court of Appeals, it was also said in financial circles, would leave the city in a serious dilemma, so far as the fare question was concerned. The consensus was that while it would make speedy unification highly desirable from the city's point of view, the prevailing economic conditions, together with the strictures placed upon the city's fiscal freedom by the four-year financing compact with its bankers, might well force a general upward revision of all traction fares, without unification.

In any event, it was said, consummation of a unity plan which would preserve the five-cent fare and still be workable would be quite difficult under existing conditions. City officials made light of this viewpoint, declaring that the pressure of economic conditions was such that the traction companies would be glad to "get out from under" at prices which would permit the city to engage in unified ownership and control of rapid transit lines and still continue the five-cent fare. None of these officials, however, would be quoted, preferring to leave the problem to the incoming Fusion administration.

LaGuardia to Act at Once.

Coincident with the handing down of the Appellate Division's ruling was the receipt of word from the Canal Zone that Mayor-elect F. H. LaGuardia planned to begin unification negotiations immediately upon his return to the city next week, instead of waiting until he assumed office on Jan. 1. Mr. LaGuardia and his advisers, it was understood, reached the conclusion some time ago that the unification problem must be settled speedily if the five-cent fare was to be preserved.

The issue upon which the Appellate Division ruled was raised last February in a taxpayers' action brought by William Church Osborn and the Anahma Realty Corporation, under the sponsorship of the Citizens Budget Commission. The decision upheld their contention that the beginning of operation of the Eighth Avenue subway on

Continued on Page Nine.

Bolan and Aide Quell Fire in Car on 5th Av.

Police Commissioner Bolan usurped the duties of fire chief yesterday and directed a one-man fire company in the extinguishing of a blaze.

As the commissioner was being driven up Fifth Avenue, he noticed smoke coming from beneath an expensive limousine. Signaling his chauffeur to stop at Fifty-eighth Street, the commissioner and the driver, Detective Bernard Shanley, went into action with a hand extinguisher. Shanley did the pumping and the commissioner "kibitzed."

Meanwhile a pedestrian had turned in an alarm, but when a fire truck rolled up its work had been done. The limousine was owned by former Governor R. L. Beeckman of Rhode Island, whose home is at Newport. The fire was under its floorboards, and was caused by a short circuit.

BREWERS WIN FIGHT ON ALCOHOL LABEL

State Board Rules They Need Not Show Strength of Beer After Repeal.

RUSH FOR LIQUOR PERMITS

10,000 Seek Applications for Licenses for Restaurants, Hotels and Clubs.

Edward P. Mulrooney, chairman of the State Alcoholic Control Board, announced yesterday that after Dec. 5, the day repeal goes into effect, brewers would not be required to state the alcoholic content of their brew on beer bottle labels.

He explained that this was ordered by the board at the request of the brewers to eliminate unfair competition. Mr. Mulrooney said the board would test the beer on sale in this State from time to time to see that it was palatable and had at least the present alcoholic content.

Representatives of about 10,000 restaurants, hotels and clubs appeared during the day at the temporary offices of the City Alcoholic Beverage Control Board for applications for licenses to sell liquor and wine for consumption on the premises.

Wait Nine Hours in Cold.

Many of the applicants waited for more than nine hours in the cold. Hundreds were turned away because the supply of blanks had been depleted. Applications for club licenses had not arrived and will not be available until this morning.

When the offices of the board were closed for the day, more than 6,000 application blanks for permission to sell liquor in restaurants and hotels had been distributed. At closing time fifty-six restaurant liquor license applications and one hotel liquor application, one drug store application and one restaurant wine application had been filed.

The restaurant applications were the first to be distributed. The hotel license applications were not received from the printer until 11 o'clock in the morning. The supply ran out about 4 in the afternoon as did the restaurant application forms.

There was no disorder attendant on the passing out of the applications. The blanks were handed out rapidly as soon as they were received at the Reade Street premises. Applicants as well as officials of the State and city boards were disappointed that there were not enough to take care of all applicants during the entire day.

State Regulations Clarified.

Mr. Mulrooney clarified some of the regulations of the State board governing the sale of wine and liquor for off-premise consumption. He ruled that the 1,500-foot distance could not apply to stores that sell only wine at retail. The board will waive the 1,500-foot rule in these cases whenever it deems such action necessary and every case will be passed on by the board.

The 1,500 foot rule was explained in more detail by Mr. Mulrooney. He said the measurement to separate liquor retail stores is not to be made by the board "as the crow flies," but such distances will be measured as the street and block runs. "The measurement guide will be as one walks or rides on a bicycle," Mr. Mulrooney said.

Long after those in line had been told to return today or Monday for restaurant and other licenses, word was received from the State Board that additional restaurant licenses were available and would be sent over immediately to the City Board. Those who wanted this form of application received the blanks until the board offices closed. Applicants for hotel and club licenses were told to return today or Monday.

The regulation requiring restau-

Continued on Page Nine.

FLIGHT OF DOLLAR SET AT ONE BILLION BY LONDON EXPERTS

Americans' Investments in Britain in Past 3 Months Put at $375,000,000.

BAN IS DISPUTED HERE

Washington Opinion on Volume Is Divided—Dollar Rises Again in World Markets.

By CHARLES A. SELDEN.
Special Cable to THE NEW YORK TIMES.

LONDON, Nov. 17.—A tangible estimate in a reliable quarter of American capital which has "flown" to Great Britain in the last three months is only £75,000,000 roughly $375,000,000.

That figure was obtained today from a source whose periodical estimates of foreign investments in this country and British investments abroad are accepted as authentic by the British Board of Trade. Its figures are often used in compiling Board of Trade documents and statements to Parliament.

The financial expert and his advisers who reach the conclusion that £75,000,000 will amply cover the American flight of capital to England also venture the suggestion that such flight from the United States to all countries in the last three months would not exceed £200,000,000, or roughly $1,000,000,000. But they feel much surer of their estimate for this country than of the aggregate figure, although they regard the latter as reasonable for all countries to which the dollar has been going.

"Loose Talk" of Billion Loss.

There has been much loose talk in London about the flight of $1,000,000,000 to Great Britain alone. That is regarded as absurd, but there is a simple explanation for such an exaggeration. It is that $1,000,000,000 is a rough estimate of the total American capital invested in this country, chiefly in industrial and mercantile concerns which have their parent houses in the United States and branch or subsidiary concerns in England, like Ford, General Motors, Woolworth, &c. These investments, of course, are permanent and long antedated the Roosevelt administration. When the flight of American capital did begin and attempts were made to measure it by the amount of American capital in this country, it was sensational but easy to garble the figure on permanent investments as a part of the money which had left the United States.

The wonder in financial circles in London is not that the flight is not larger because of President Roosevelt's policy, but that it has been even £75,000,000, despite the reluctance to buy dollars. There is not much eagerness to purchase American currency today if there is a virtual assurance that it is going to be cheaper tomorrow, and there is no assurance whatever when President Roosevelt is going to end the depreciation.

So, under existing circumstances, the British market for the dollar is confined to those who need American currency to pay bills or buy goods in the United States. Even they are inclined to postpone purchases of dollars on the chance that they are going to go even lower.

American currency bought here for discharging obligations or buy-

Continued on Page Ten.

Australia Plans to Cut Curbs on Immigration

Wireless to THE NEW YORK TIMES.

CANBERRA, Australia, Nov. 17.—Suggestions for relaxing the restrictions on immigration will be placed before the Commonwealth Cabinet by J. A. Perkins, Minister of the Interior.

Mr. Perkins told the House of Representatives today there was a growing feeling that it was time to modify the restrictions.

"No sweeping change is contemplated," he said, "but the Ministry is well aware of Australia's need for population. However, the economic position, although it is improved, is still sufficiently acute to justify the continuance of some restrictions on the entry of immigrants."

SEEK A WOMAN AIDE IN HART ABDUCTION

Police on Coast Think She Helped in Ransom Notes to Dead Boy's Father.

NEW WITNESSES FOUND

Seller of 22-Pound Bricks for Murder Identifies Thurmond—Victim's Body Still in Sea.

Special to THE NEW YORK TIMES.

SAN JOSE, Calif., Nov. 17.—Waters of San Francisco's lower bay still held the body tonight of Brooke L. Hart, but authorities moved swiftly in perfecting a case against his confessed kidnappers and slayers, John Holmes and Thomas H. Thurmond.

Bit by bit they put together the many clues which, by their very unpremeditated simplicity, had for almost a week served to confuse investigators and aid in the kidnappers in escaping detection.

Motive for the crime has apparently been established. Ransom of $40,000 was demanded, according to the confession of Thurmond, to enable Holmes to satisfy the insatiable demand of a woman for finery and a "good time."

In this connection, authorities disclosed information indicating that a woman helped prepare one of the ransom notes sent to Alexander J. Hart, wealthy San Jose merchant and father of the slain 22-year-old youth.

The woman's name is known, Sheriff Emig announced, and she is sought for questioning.

Sheriff Emig said that Wesley Shaves of Campbell, home town of Holmes, reported seeing a woman and a man helping another man write a note last Monday. This preceded by some hours the mailing of the first ransom letter in the case. Shaves will be asked to view the prisoners.

Friend Chosen for Go-Between.

One more vital point in identification was established during the day, coincidentally with disclosure that Charles O'Brien Jr., friend of the slain youth and proprietor of a confectionery, had been selected by the kidnappers as the intermediary in the ransom negotiations.

O'Brien identified Thurmond, it was announced, as the man who leaped on the running board of his automobile at dusk last Tuesday, put his hand on the door handle, looked inquiringly at O'Brien and then dropped off and disappeared.

Less than an hour later O'Brien received a telephone call, supposedly from Thurmond. The person instructed him to have Mr. Hart drive south on the coast highway "toward Los Angeles" the fol-

Continued on Page Seven.

Roosevelt Leaves for Warm Springs; Will Speak at Savannah This Morning

Special to THE NEW YORK TIMES.

WASHINGTON, Nov. 17.—President Roosevelt left Washington late this afternoon for Warm Springs, Ga., where he plans to spend the Thanksgiving holidays.

He is going on a special train by a circuitous route in order to visit Savannah and make a speech tomorrow morning as part of the ceremonies celebrating the bicentennial of that city.

The stop there will be brief, however, and the President will take all his meals tomorrow aboard the special train, which is due at Warm Springs late tomorrow evening.

At Warm Springs the President will divide his time between official duties and the children at Warm Springs Foundation, which he helped to establish as a place for special treatment for victims of infantile paralysis.

He is expected to have an active official schedule, beginning on Sunday, when he will receive Sumner Welles, Ambassador to Cuba. Events in the island republic reached a stage a few days ago where Ambassador Welles believed they required a personal conversation between himself and the President, so the President invited Mr. Welles to come from Havana for a conference.

Mr. Roosevelt was accompanied on the train by only one member of his family, Mrs. James Roosevelt, his mother. Other engagements detained his wife here, but she will join the President in time to spend Thanksgiving Day with him.

His party included a large staff from the White House offices which will handle the business of the Chief Executive, with the assistance of telephone and telegraph, much the same as if he were in Washington.

This staff is under the direction of Stephen T. Early, assistant White House secretary, and Miss Marguerite A. Le Hand, the President's personal secretary. It includes six others, stenographers and telephone operators, in addition to the White House Secret Service detail.

Fifteen newspaper correspondents and twelve news picture men completed the party.

TRADE AWAITS CREDITS

Russians Ready to Buy $520,000,000 Goods, Says Brookhart.

ARRANGEMENT EXPECTED

Deal for $50,000,000 Cotton Likely at Start—Soviet Declared 'Good Risk.'

EXPORT GUARANTEE SEEN

Government Will Underwrite Sales, Iowan Holds—Predicts Work for 300,000.

Special to THE NEW YORK TIMES.

WASHINGTON, Nov. 17.—Russian orders for American goods worth $520,000,000 are immediately available to the United States if the government will extend the credit necessary for financing such exports, it was stated today by Smith W. Brookhart, special adviser to the Agricultural Adjustment Administration. He thought the needed credit would be provided.

On the same condition, he said, a continuing annual market would exist in Russia for a similar amount of American products for many years to come. The former Iowa Senator said he had discussed trade possibilities with M. Litvinoff since the latter's arrival in the United States and added:

"We will be able to sell them two or three times as much as they expect to sell us, if the proper credits are extended."

A long-time advocate of Russian recognition, Mr. Brookhart has been negotiating with the Amtorg Trading Corporation on behalf of the Adjustment Administration for the sale of surplus farm products to Russia. He said today that the first deals with the Russian Government would be in shipments of cotton and cotton textiles, live stock and heavy machinery.

Demand for $50,000,000 Cotton.

He thought the cotton deals would come first with government-financed exports of raw cotton worth from $50,000,000 to $60,000,000. An additional $30,000,000 is expected by Mr. Brookhart in orders for cotton textiles, and to this he added another $30,000,000 in live stock.

Other items included in the $520,000,000 of orders which Mr. Brookhart said awaited only the extension of credits were about $400,000,000 of so-called heavy equipment, such as rolling mill apparatus and machine tools. In this total $400,000,000 of heavy equipment would be about $100,000,000 of railroad equipment, including rolling stock and other materials.

Such orders as were described by Mr. Brookhart as being immediately available would, he said, provide direct employment for 300,000 to 400,000 presently idle workers, and additional work indirectly for several thousands more.

These orders are definitely provided for in the present Five-Year Plan, according to Mr. Brookhart. He said that large orders outside the plan were being contemplated, and recalled that M. Litvinoff at the recent London Economic Conference expressed the intention of his government to buy $1,000,000,000 of products, apart from such plans.

Calls Russians "Good Risk."

"There's no reason why we shouldn't be able to get more than half of those orders if we go after them," he said.

Mr. Brookhart placed much weight in "the utmost scrupulousness of the Russian Government about paying its debts."

"It's far better credit risk than Wall Street," he said, "and the best credit risk in the world, other than the United States Government itself."

Characterizing the Soviet Government as "the most stable one in Europe," Mr. Brookhart continued:

"They conduct all their operations on a five-year plan and the second one started last January. They won't buy any more than they see themselves able to pay for, and in that way they never get in over their head.

"They will buy beyond those periods only if credit is extended enabling them to buy abroad, and it is a fact worth noting that they

Continued on Page Four.

Points Conceded by Russia

Special to THE NEW YORK TIMES.

WASHINGTON, Nov. 17.—The exchange of agreements and concessions made public at the White House today in connection with the resumption of diplomatic relations with Russia was said in informed quarters to include virtually every concession the Soviet Government has ever made to any country. These points, the basis of recognition, are:

1. The Soviet Government promises "to respect scrupulously the indisputable right of the United States to order its own life within its own jurisdiction in its own way," pledging itself not to disseminate Communist propaganda in this country nor to attempt in any way to overthrow American institutions.

2. The Soviet Government expressly agrees to permit complete freedom of worship to Americans resident in Russia, including rites in the English or any other language, and leasing, erecting or maintaining buildings for the purpose.

3. A consular convention will be negotiated immediately, in which United States citizens will have rights of legal protection "not less favorable" than those enjoyed by "nationals of the nation most favored in this respect."

4. Preparatory to a final settlement of claims and counterclaims, the Soviet will not prosecute any claims against Americans as the successor of prior governments of Russia, or otherwise.

5. The Soviet Government waives all claim to damages arising from the American military expedition to Siberia in 1918.

In addition to the agreements signed, there took place an exchange of views regarding methods of settling all outstanding questions of indebtedness and claims.

'TRIUMPH' HAILED BY SOVIET PEOPLE

Recognition Is Likened to the Tale of the Ugly Duckling Which Became Swan.

NEWS TOO LATE FOR FETES

Mezhlauk and Sokolnikoff Are Regarded as Candidates for Envoy to Washington.

Special Cable to THE NEW YORK TIMES.

MOSCOW, Saturday, Nov. 18.—Word of the recognition of the Soviet by the United States came to Moscow in the dead of night because of the difference in time, but not too late for a communiqué to appear in every morning newspaper. Trusts, restaurants and trams will be buzzing with the news later in the morning.

Official comment is not available at this hour, but to the Soviet leaders recognition by the greatest of capitalistic powers brings the same degree of elation felt by the "ugly duckling" of Hans Christian Andersen when it was recognized as a beautiful swan.

"It hid its head under its wing," said the old fairy tale, "and felt too happy—but had no thought of pride. It remembered how it had been mocked and persecuted, and now every one said it was lovelier than all."

Soviet leaders have been living all their lives as "ugly ducklings." They are almost afraid to believe the fairy tale has reached its traditional ending.

Youth Hails Event.

But to the komsomols (young revolutionaries and future Soviet leaders) recognition comes as part of their birthright, somewhat unexpectedly delayed. It is almost impossible to explain to them why the United States has not recognized the U. S. S. R. before. From their point of view, purely Marxian, the economic and political situation has been demanding su.. action for three years.

To Soviet economists, engineers and scientists it brings a hope of easier budgeting, with new equipment to realize their plans for projects which are necessary to development of Russia's natural resources.

To artists, writers and actors come greater possibilities of travel to that strange land where movie stars receive unbelievable salaries, and where no party line shapes the theme of plays or poems or guides the painter's brush.

To the Red Army it probably is interpreted as meaning one less enemy in the next war.

Peasants Are Pleased.

To the peasant in the fields it shows that "Uncle Kalinin was right, right again. Now perhaps he will manage to get some more of those American chickens for me."

To the workers it is one more triumph for the policies of Joseph Stalin and Maxim Litvinoff.

To the American specialist it means a consulate which will un-

Continued on Page Six.

LITVINOFF PLEDGES SOVIET FRIENDSHIP

Looks to Cooperation With America for Peace Under Economic and Cultural Ties.

ASSURANCE ON NATIONALS

Roosevelt Got This First, He Says in Speech—Disavows Moscow Link to Reds Here.

Special to THE NEW YORK TIMES.

WASHINGTON, Nov. 17.—Foreign Commissar Litvinoff disclosed in a statement before the National Press Club tonight that the first commitment sought by President Roosevelt as a requisite to a recognition of Russia was an assurance of the Soviet policy toward nationals of other countries.

M. Litvinoff, in answer to a question, also took occasion to disavow the Communist party of America so far as it claims to represent the governing group in Russia.

"The Communist party of America is not concerned with the Communist party of Russia and the Communist party of Russia is not concerned with the Communist party of America," he said.

Creation of Understanding.

M. Litvinoff said that he gladly supplied President Roosevelt with all the information he desired concerning the Soviet policy toward nationals of other governments. He put his answers as convincingly as possible, he said, to cut away a sixteen-year accumulation of false ideas concerning Russia which had sprung up here in the absence of normal diplomatic relations.

The obviously happy diplomat traced the history of recognition as it came to a full realization today.

He added that his government would seek to make the new relations with the United States not merely a conventional or technical diplomatic intercourse, but such an understanding between two countries which have never had a conflict as would produce a common ground for cooperation in economics, culture and international peace.

Address by M. Litvinoff.

M. Litvinoff's speech was as follows:

"I am happy today because the hopes which I have cherished for sixteen years have been realized. Ever since the beginning of my diplomatic activities I have been striving to obtain a good understanding between the Soviet Union and the United States.

"Toward that end I proposed to my government in 1918, during the war, that it send me to Washington. I was sent, but I did not reach my destination. Many things might have happened, and many historical events might have taken different shape, if we could then have entered into relations with this country.

"At the end of 1918 I made another attempt in the same direction by sending a long telegram and making certain proposals to President Wilson on his arrival in Europe. I failed again, but I con-

Continued on Page Five.

PRESIDENT REVEALS PACT

Reads to Press Letters in Which He and Litvinoff Bind Nations.

FREE WORSHIP CONCEDED

Russia Also Agrees to Allow Americans Own Counsel if Brought to Trial.

WORLD PEACE IS STRESSED

Russo-American Claims Will Be Adjusted Through Regular Diplomatic Channels.

The notes of the President and Maxim Litvinoff, Page 3.

By WALTER DURANTY.
Special to THE NEW YORK TIMES.

WASHINGTON, Nov. 17.—Official relations between the United States and the Soviet were established at ten minutes before midnight yesterday. Or, to express it more simply, the United States recognized the U. S. S. R. at that hour after sixteen years and nine days of the Soviet Government's existence. The fact of the establishment of relations was announced this afternoon by President Roosevelt, but historically speaking the date was 11:50 P. M., Nov. 16.

The undertakings of the two governments were set forth in eleven letters and a memorandum exchanged between the President and Maxim Litvinoff, Soviet Commissar for Foreign Affairs, covering agreements and concessions completed in ten days of negotiation.

Subject to the approval of the Soviet Government, William C. Bullitt of Philadelphia, special assistant to the Secretary of State, was designated to be the first American Ambassador to the U. S. S. R.

The pact, read to the press by Mr. Roosevelt at his press conference this afternoon, covers propaganda, freedom of worship, protection of nationals and debts and claims.

Anti-Propaganda Pledge.

The United States receives the most complete pledge against Bolshevist propaganda that has ever been made by the Soviet Government, and includes "organizations in receipt of any financial assistance from it" as well as persons or organizations under the jurisdiction or control of the government. Complete freedom of worship is assured Americans, as well as assurance against discrimination because of "ecclesiastical status."

To Americans is accorded "the right to be represented by counsel of their choice" if brought to trial in the U. S. S. R., which represented perhaps the most definite concession that M. Litvinoff made. The President made reciprocal pledges except regarding religion, which the Soviet did not desire.

Debts and claims were left to be thrashed out later for "a final settlement of the claims and counterclaims" between the governments "and the claims of their nationals." Claims arising out of the military occupation of Siberia by American forces, or assistance to military forces in Siberia after 1917, were waived, but the Murmansk occupation was not mentioned.

One may surmise that the article relating to propaganda was drawn up after the most careful consideration by the Americans of the propaganda treaties or clauses between the Soviet and Latvia and the Soviet and Afghanistan, or both, but it goes further than either of these two, and might almost be termed a diplomatic victory of high order.

The question of religious freedom has great political importance and is treated with corresponding detail. Americans are allowed everything they can want in this respect, but it is worth noting that M. Litvinoff takes the opportunity of "slipping something over" in a quiet way by quoting the laws of the Soviet Union to show that many of the reports upon the restriction of religious liberty in that country have been exaggerated.

The American side, however, scores a tactical success in M. Litvinoff's admission that "no persons having ecclesiastical status"

Continued on Page Two.

United Press International

Each customer in Sloppy Joe's Bar in downtown Chicago got a free drink as the news flashed that Utah had voted for repeal, thus ending Prohibition.

Rudy Vallee (Center) is joined by other revellers in a toast to the end of Prohibition at the repeal celebration at the Hollywood Restaurant in New York on December 5th.

United Press International

United Press International

A view of the joyous crowd that gathered in front of the Hotel Astor, at 45th Street and Broadway in New York City, on the evening of December 5th, to celebrate the repeal of Prohibition.

NRA MEMBER U.S. WE DO OUR PART

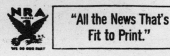

"All the News That's Fit to Print."

The New York Times.

LATE CITY EDITION
WEATHER—Rain and warmer today; tomorrow fair and colder.
Temperatures Yesterday—Max., 44; min., 34.

VOL. LXXXIII....No. 27,710. Entered as Second-Class Matter, Postoffice, New York, N. Y. NEW YORK, WEDNESDAY, DECEMBER 6, 1933. MP TWO CENTS In New York City. | THREE CENTS Within 200 Miles | FOUR CENTS Elsewhere Except in 7th and 8th Postal Zones

PROHIBITION REPEAL IS RATIFIED AT 5:32 P. M.; ROOSEVELT ASKS NATION TO BAR THE SALOON; NEW YORK CELEBRATES WITH QUIET RESTRAINT

LINDBERGHS AT SEA ON BRAZIL FLIGHT; 'O.K.' SHE REPORTS

630 MILES FROM AFRICA

Breeze Starts Fliers After Twenty Attempts in Dead Calm.

MOON LIGHTS THEIR WAY

10,000 Natives See Take-Off as Motor's Roar Stirs Them From Slumber.

RIDE THROUGH SQUALLS

Wife Radios Every Fifteen Minutes of Progress on 1,800-Mile Flight.

Colonel and Mrs. Charles A. Lindbergh were flying across the South Atlantic from Africa to Brazil this morning, reporting their progress by radio every fifteen minutes and their location every half hour.

At 2:20 A. M., New York time, five hours and twenty minutes after taking off from Bathurst, Gambia, in bright moonlight, they were 630 miles on their way across the Southern Ocean.

The first message from the plane was picked up by the Miami, Fla., station of Pan American Airways soon after 9:02 P. M. last night, New York time. It reported that the plane had taken off from Bathurst at that time. At 10 P. M., New York time, another message picked up by the Bahia, Brazil, station of Pan American Airways advised that the plane was flying Course 224 true, and gave its position, which Pan American officials estimated to be about 115 miles southwest of Bathurst. At 10:40 P. M. another message, also picked up by the Bahia station, reported "everything O. K.," and said the plane's position would be given every half hour and a progress O. K. sent out every fifteen minutes. The first progress O. K. was received by the Pan American station at Miami at 11 P. M., New York time.

Made 240 Miles in Two Hours.

At 11 P. M., the Bahia station also picked up a message. It gave for the plane a position approximately 240 miles southwest of Bathurst and right on her course. The operators at Bahia said that in her first message, Mrs. Lindbergh reported considerable static. But her messages, they said, were coming into Bahia strong, fast and clear, as if they were being sent by an experienced wireless operator.

The next message was received by the Pan-American station at Para, Brazil, at 11:50 P. M., New York time. It reported that the plane was flying at an altitude of 2,000 feet and making about 100 knots. There was unlimited visibility, the message said, with the sky about one-tenth overcast, and a quartering ten-knot tail wind.

At 12:30 this morning, the Pan American radio station at Miami and the Chatham, Mass., station of the Radiomarine Corporation each picked up a message from the plane giving a position approximately 446 miles southeast of Bathurst. The message said the plane was flying at an altitude of 1,200 feet, that there was visibility of about ten miles, that the sky was nine-tenths overcast, and that there was a quartering tail wind of 10 knots.

Squalls Met at Daybreak.

A message was received at 1:27 this morning at Pará, Brazil, reporting "skies eight-tenths overcast, scattered squalls, visibility three miles, daybreak; all's well."

At 1:50 A. M. the Bahia station picked up a message, "All's well."

At 2:20 A. M. a message was received at the Pará station reporting the plane's position as 630 miles southwest of Bathurst, flying at 1,000 feet, the skies nine-tenths overcast, frequent squalls, calm seas and no wind. That position indicated the Lindberghs had covered about one-third of the distance to Natal.

Natives Awaken for Start.

Special Cable to THE NEW YORK TIMES.

BATHURST, Gambia, Wednesday, Dec. 6.—With bright moonlight turning the waters around the little island of St. Mary, on which

Continued on Page Twenty-six.

Lindbergh Flight to Fame Twice as Long as New Hop

On the morning of May 20, 1927, six years and six months ago, Captain Charles A. Lindbergh, a mail pilot, left Roosevelt Field for Paris.

He flew alone, and veteran pilots shook their heads when they saw him take off. His silver plane, dripping with rain, lumbered slowly—too slowly—down the muddy runway. It gathered speed, bounced from the ground and settled back again. It barely cleared a tractor at the end of the runway and just climbed over low telephone wires at the end of the field.

Thirty-three and a half hours later the young mail pilot brought his gray plane down at Le Bourget. That famous flight covered 3,610 miles. The present flight, also in a single-engined plane, is about 1,875 miles.

PWA READY TO BAR CITY SUBWAY LOAN

Security for $25,000,000 Advance to Finish System Is Held Inadequate.

BANKERS' PACTS A FACTOR

Officials Here Say Attitude of Washington Is Based on a Misunderstanding.

Special to THE NEW YORK TIMES.

WASHINGTON, Dec. 5.—Inability of New York City to furnish security satisfactory to the Public Works Administration has caused the latter to abandon the allotment of $25,000,000 for completion of the Eighth Avenue subway.

New York officials have not been notified, but it was learned from reliable sources that the application for the loan would be refused.

At his press conference today Secretary Ickes said there was "nothing new" to report on the loan. He added, however, that the matter was held up by the question of security.

Senator Wagner announced virtual assurance of the loan more than two weeks ago. Since then the matter has been before the Special Board of Public Works, while PWA engineers and lawyers were investigating.

Application Signed by Mayor.

The application, for $25,000,000, signed by Mayor O'Brien, was on a loan and grant basis, 30 per cent of the cost of materials and structure to be an outright grant and the rest a loan on security furnished by the city.

The amount of money which completion of the subway would require is indefinite. Public Works Administration officials have scaled the sum down to some $22,500,000 under one estimate.

The money would be applied to equipping, tracking and finishing some eighteen miles of subway already dug, mainly in Brooklyn and Queens, and to the building of stations. Seven thousand men would obtain work through the Winter, it was estimated, and large supplies of capital goods would be purchased.

The allotment was discussed at the recent conference between Secretary Ickes and Mayor-elect La Guardia, but it was not gone into in any detail.

The attitude of the PWA, it was learned, is that the city has tied up the revenues of the subway by its financing agreements with the banks, and would be operating on a margin too slender to enable it to guarantee any return on the investment, even if the PWA funds allowed the subway to open miles of route and thus tap new sources of revenue.

Unification Another Problem.

The PWA feels that the situation is further complicated by the competition of the other New York subway lines. If the other lines were taken over by the city under the unification plan, a campaign premise of the Mayor-elect, the PWA feels that there would be a general scaling down of the demands of creditors and a consequent loss to the government on its investment. The question of the 5-cent fare is not worrying the administration, Secretary Ickes has said.

While Mr. Ickes has already ex-

Continued on Page Twenty-seven.

TAX PLAN OFFERED TO CURB EVASIONS, RAISE $237,000,000

House Subcommittee Urges a Check on Personal Holding Concerns by 35% Levy.

WOULD INCREASE SURTAX

Normal Income Tax of 4% and Revision of Capital Gains Are Also Proposed.

Special to THE NEW YORK TIMES.

WASHINGTON, Dec. 5.—Broad tax reforms designed to increase the Federal revenue $237,000,000 a year and prevent "the avoidance and evasion of the internal revenue laws" were recommended today in a report submitted to the House Ways and Means Committee by a subcommittee.

The full committee immediately began study of the suggestions, and Representative Doughton, the chairman, said a completed bill would probably be ready for presentation soon after Congress meets next month.

Changes sought are aimed principally at persons whose incomes are in the higher brackets, as well as at corporations now legally permitted to take advantage of what committee members said were "unfair but legal" provisions of the revenue laws.

Some discord was apparent within the committee, but no member would publicly express his feelings.

"It isn't law yet, and it is not even past the committee," said one member. "It must go to the House and Senate."

Nine Changes are Urged.

Nine phases of the present law were recommended for modification as follows:

1. Establishment of a normal income tax rate of 4 per cent, instead of the present 4 per cent on the first $4,000 and 8 per cent on the remainder of net income, and revision of the surtax rate on a graduated scale, with the brackets reduced from 53 to 27; estimated to increase revenue $36,000,000 annually.

2. Change for three years in the depreciation and depletion section of the 1932 Revenue Act by reducing allowances by 25 per cent; estimated to add $85,000,000 for each of the three years.

3. Revision of the capital gains and losses section by revising the method of adjustment and prescribing a scale-length of ownership; estimated to add $30,000,000.

4. Amendment of the personal holding companies' section to prevent persons with large incomes from forming companies to evade taxes; estimated to add $25,000,000.

5. Abolition of certain sections of the "exchanges and reorganization" provisions to "close the door to one of the most prevalent methods of tax avoidance"; estimated to add $18,000,000.

6. Imposition of a tax on dividends paid out of corporation earnings accumulated before March 1, 1913; estimated to add $6,000,000.

7. Amendment of the foreign tax credit sections of the 1932 act; estimated to add $10,000,000.

8. Withdrawal of permission for corporations which are affiliated through 95 per cent stock ownership to file consolidated returns; estimated to add $20,000,000.

9. Revision of the partnership losses section of the 1932 Revenue Act; estimated to add $7,000,000.

Eager to expedite the "major problems," the subcommittee passed over a group of minor matters, according to the chairman, Representative Sam B. Hill of Washington. He said the subcommittee would continue study of these problems,

Continued on Page Fourteen.

State House Bootlegger Is Barred in Maryland

Special to THE NEW YORK TIMES.

ANNAPOLIS, Md., Dec. 5.—Wet legislators here will patriotically support legal liquor. The State House bootlegger received formal notice today to discontinue his trade. The notice was served by a policeman on duty at the Capitol.

Throughout this session, the bootlegger has conducted a thriving business; a business which, he says, has been especially arduous because of the sudden demands made on him by legislators and their desire for prompt service.

While his services were cut off eight hours before post-prohibition stuff could be bought, the bootlegger thought the legislators had obtained a sufficient reserve to carry them through until evening and legal liquor.

RATIFYING BY UTAH ENDS PROHIBITION

With Impressive Ceremony, the 36th State Follows Ohio and Pennsylvania in Day.

CONVENTIONS ALL SOLEMN

Moderation Pleas Are Made at Columbus—Hush Greets Vote at Harrisburg.

Special to THE NEW YORK TIMES.

SALT LAKE CITY, Dec. 5—The Eighteenth Amendment to the Constitution of the United States passed out of existence officially at 3:32½ o'clock this afternoon, Mountain standard time (5:32½ New York time) with the ratification of repeal by the convention of Utah, the thirty-sixth required State.

The passing of national prohibition was marked by impressive ceremony in the hall of the House of Representatives in the State Capitol here.

To Delegate S. R. Thurman, a repeal leader of Salt Lake City, whose father was a member of the State's constitutional convention in 1895 before Utah was admitted to the Union, fell the honor of being the last to record his vote, the roll being called in alphabetical order.

His "Yea," placing the Twenty-first Amendment to the Constitution in effect, was greeted by enthusiastic applause from the audience of a few hundred persons.

About ninety seconds later Ray L. Olson of Ogden, president of the convention, who had been manager of the repealists' campaign, brought down his gavel and announced that the repeal amendment had been ratified. Notification was transmitted immediately to the White House by a special wire from the Capitol.

At the same time Delegate A. S. Brown, former president of the Salt Lake Chamber of Commerce, sent out word to President Roosevelt over the Columbia Broadcasting System. He congratulated the President on the successful culmination of the repeal movement.

The whole proceedings were in keeping with the historic aspect of the occasion. Besides high officials

Continued on Page Five.

Italy to Quit League Unless It Is Reformed; Demands Altered Aims and Set-Up at Once

By ARNALDO CORTESI.

Wireless to THE NEW YORK TIMES.

ROME, Wednesday, Dec. 6.—At the end of a long sitting lasting far into the night, the Fascist Grand Council, which had been convoked to decide on Italy's relations with the League of Nations, passed a suspended sentence on Geneva.

After having discussed every aspect of the probable effect of Italy's withdrawal, the Grand Council decided "to render Italy's further participation in the League dependent on radical changes in that organization to be brought about within the shortest possible time, which changes must affect the League in its constitution, in its methods and in its objectives."

At the same time the Grand Council reached a temporizing decision also in the matter of payment to the United States of the debt instalment due on Dec. 15. In view of the impossibility of conducting negotiations on the debt problem, the Grand Council decided "to effect on Dec. 15 a token payment of $1,000,000 as renewed proof of Italy's good-will, while awaiting a final settlement of this whole question."

Since the breakdown in the disarmament negotiations Premier Mussolini has been advocating efforts outside Geneva and the League of Nations. He has favored action under the Four-Power Pact initiated by Great Britain, France, Italy and Germany, or at any rate negotiations by the leading powers, including the United States.

As to reforms in the League, the press has suggested that the League be divorced from the Versailles Treaty, and that its constitution be revised to give the larger powers a freer hand in directing its affairs.

CITY TOASTS NEW ERA

Crowds Swamp Licensed Resorts, but the Legal Liquor Is Scarce.

CELEBRATION IN STREETS

Marked by Absence of Undue Hilarity and Only Normal Number of Arrests.

MANY SPEAKEASIES CLOSE

Machine Guns Guard Some Liquor Trucks—Supplies to Be Rushed Out Today.

Slowly gathering momentum from the time when the news began to spread just at nightfall that national prohibition was no more, the public rejoicing at the end of the long dry reign was carried on last night with restraint and absence of undue hilarity.

Throngs of New Yorkers ventured into Times Square and other centres of the metropolis and many of the thousand restaurants, hotels and clubs fortunate enough to have received their licenses for the sale of alcoholic beverages were swamped.

But gay as were their spirits, they were well-behaved. With the city's entire police force of 19,000 men mobilized to guard against overexuberant celebrants, arrests did not exceed the normal number for any day of the last five years. Incidentally, official word that repeal was a fact did not go out to the police until 9:20 P. M., just about four hours after Utah acted.

Stores Fail to Get Stocks.

The thronging to places of public entertainment was enhanced by the fact that only a handful of New Yorkers was able to drink a toast to the occasion with lawful liquor in their own homes. Because Utah did not make repeal effective until 5:32½ P. M., retail liquor stores with only two exceptions were unable to obtain wines and whiskies from the warehouses in the brief time left.

Indeed, the supply of lawful liquor even in the licensed places was woefully scant. Only fifty-four truckloads of bonded liquor were released from the warehouses before they closed last night, and the two largest warehouses shut their doors before the Twenty-first Amendment displaced the Eighteenth.

With 3,000 places licensed to dispense the newly legalized beverages in the metropolitan area and 2,000 more up-State, hardly one in a hundred was able to move in a stock in the few hours available. Some of the others, of course, had had the foresight to lay in supplies under medicinal permits during the dying days of prohibition.

Bootleggers and speakeasies came to the rescue, however, despite a stern warning from Police Commissioner Bolan that his men would not tolerate any such activity. They operated with a little more caution than usual, but nevertheless they took advantage of the occasion to dispose of a large part of their unlawful stocks. The raids threatened by Mr. Bolan proved few and on little known places.

Many Cordial Shops Close.

Cordial shops and other neighborhood dispensaries during the long drought showed fear of police activity last night for the first time in years. Hundreds of them closed their doors, others dealt only with long-known and trusted customers, and only a scattering number, principally in downtown Manhattan, carried on business as usual. Some of them carried signs promising to open as licensed liquor stores in a few days.

There was every indication, however, that New York's long reliance on contraband cheer was near its end. The warehousemen promised deliveries on a large scale would begin today, with 400 trucks licensed to speed legal liquors throughout the city and its suburbs.

A cargo of 6,200 cases of assorted wines and spirits worth about $170,000 arrived on the White Star liner Majestic from France and England late in the afternoon, but the ship was delayed five hours by

Continued on Page Two.

The Repeal Proclamation

Special to THE NEW YORK TIMES.

WASHINGTON, Dec. 5.—The text of the proclamation by William Phillips, Acting Secretary of State, certifying to the adoption of the Twenty-first Amendment repealing prohibition, follows:

WILLIAM PHILLIPS,
Acting Secretary of State of the United States of America.

To all whom these presents shall come, greeting:

KNOW YE, That the Congress of the United States, at the second session, Seventy-second Congress, begun and held at the city of Washington on Monday, the fifth day of December, in the year one thousand nine hundred and thirty-two, passed a joint Resolution in the words and figures as follows:

To wit—

JOINT RESOLUTION.

Proposing an amendment to the Constitution of the United States.

Resolved by the Senate and House of Representatives of the United States of America in Congress assembled (two-thirds of each House concurring therein), That the following article is hereby proposed as an amendment to the Constitution of the United States, which shall be valid to all intents and purposes as part of the Constitution when ratified by conventions in three-fourths of the several States:

ARTICLE.

Section 1. The Eighteenth Article of Amendment to the Constitution of the United States is hereby repealed.

Section 2. The transportation or importation into any State, Territory, or Possession of the United States for delivery or use therein of intoxicating liquors, in violation of the laws thereof, is hereby prohibited.

Section 3. This article shall be inoperative unless it shall have been ratified as an amendment to the Constitution by conventions in the several States, as provided in the Constitution, within seven years from the date of the submission hereof to the States by the Congress.

And, further, that it appears from official notices received at the Department of State that the amendment to the Constitution of the United States proposed as aforesaid has been ratified by conventions in the States of Arizona, Alabama, Arkansas, California, Colorado, Connecticut, Delaware, Florida, Idaho, Illinois, Indiana, Iowa, Kentucky, Maryland, Massachusetts, Michigan, Minnesota, Missouri, Nevada, New Hampshire, New Jersey, New Mexico, New York, Ohio, Oregon, Pennsylvania, Rhode Island, Tennessee, Texas, Utah, Vermont, Virginia, Washington, West Virginia, Wisconsin and Wyoming.

And, further, that the States wherein conventions have so ratified the said proposed amendment constitute the requisite three-fourths of the whole number of States in the United States.

NOW, therefore, be it known that I, William Phillips, Acting Secretary of State of the United States, by virtue and in pursuance of Section 160, Title 5, of the United States Code, do hereby certify that the amendment aforesaid has become valid to all intents and purposes as a part of the Constitution of the United States.

In testimony whereof, I have hereunto set my hand and caused the seal of the Department of State to be affixed.

Done at the city of Washington this fifth day of December in the year of our Lord one thousand nine hundred and thirty-three.

WILLIAM PHILLIPS.

Roosevelt Proclaims Repeal; Urges Temperance in Nation

President's Announcement Is in Accordance With the Instruction of Congress Contained in the Recovery Act—Declares Social Evils of Liquor Shall Not Be Revived.

Special to THE NEW YORK TIMES.

WASHINGTON, Dec. 5.—President Roosevelt's proclamation of the repeal of the Eighteenth Amendment was as follows:

By the President of the United States of America.

A Proclamation.

Whereas the Congress of the United States in the second session of the Seventy-second Congress, begun at Washington on the fifth day of December in the year one thousand nine hundred and thirty-two adopted a resolution in the words and figures following: to wit—

JOINT RESOLUTION.

Proposing an amendment to the Constitution of the United States.

Resolved by the Senate and House of Representatives of the United States of America in Congress assembled (two-thirds of each House concurring therein), That the following article is hereby proposed as an amendment to the Constitution of the United States, which shall be valid to all intents and purposes as part of the Constitution when ratified by conventions in three-fourths of the several States:

ARTICLE.

Section 1. The Eighteenth Article of amendment to the Constitution of the United States is hereby repealed.

Section 2. The transportation or importation into any State, Territory or possession of the United States for delivery or use therein of intoxicating liquors, in violation of the laws thereof, is hereby prohibited.

Section 3. This article shall be inoperative unless it shall have been ratified as an amendment to the Constitution by conventions in the several States, as provided in the Constitution, within seven years from the date of the submission hereof to the States by the Congress.

Declares Amendment Repealed.

Whereas, Section 217 (a) of the Act of Congress entitled "An act to encourage national industrial recovery, to foster competition and to provide for the construction of certain useful public works, and for other purposes," approved June 16, 1933, provides as follows:

Section 217 (a) The President shall proclaim the date of ——
(1) the close of the first fiscal year ending June 30 of any year after the year 1933, during which the total receipts of the

Continued on Page Two.

FINAL ACTION AT CAPITAL

President Proclaims the Nation's New Policy as Utah Ratifies.

PHILLIPS SIGNS DECREE

Orders 21st Amendment in Effect on Receiving Votes of Three Final States.

RECOVERY TAXES TO END

$227,000,000 a Year Automatically Dropped—Canadian Whisky Quota Is Raised.

Special to THE NEW YORK TIMES.

WASHINGTON, Dec. 5.—Legal liquor today was returned to the United States, with President Roosevelt calling on the people to see that "this return of individual freedom shall not be accompanied by the repugnant conditions that obtained prior to the adoption of the Eighteenth Amendment and those that have existed since its adoption."

Prohibition of alcoholic beverages as a national policy ended at 5:32½ P. M., Eastern Standard Time, when Utah, the last of the thirty-six States, furnished by vote of its convention the constitutional majority for ratification of the Twenty-first Amendment. The new amendment repealed the Eighteenth, and with the demise of the latter went the Volstead Act which for more than a decade held legal drinks in America to less than one-half of 1 per cent of alcohol and the enforcement of which cost more than 150 lives and billions in money.

Earlier in the day Pennsylvania had ratified as the thirty-fourth State and Ohio as the thirty-fifth.

Proclamation by President.

President Roosevelt at 6:55 P. M. signed an official proclamation in keeping with terms of the National Industrial Recovery Act, under which prohibition ended and four taxes levied to raise $227,000,000 annually for amortization of the $3,300,000,000 public works fund were repealed.

But the President went further. Accepting certification from Acting Secretary of State Phillips that thirty-six States had ratified the repealing amendment, he improved the occasion to address a plea to the American people to employ their regained liberty first of all for national manliness.

Mr. Roosevelt asked personally for what he and his party had declined to make the subject of Federal mandate—that saloons be barred from the country.

"I ask especially," he said, "that no State shall, by law or otherwise, authorize the return of the saloon, either in its old form or in some modern guise."

Makes Personal Plea.

He enjoined all citizens to cooperate with the government in its endeavor to restore a greater respect for law and order, especially by confining their purchases of liquor to duly licensed agencies. This practice, which he personally requested every individual and every family in the nation to follow, would result, he said, in a better product for consumption, in addition to the "break-up and eventual destruction of the notoriously evil illicit liquor traffic" and in tax benefits to the government.

The President thus announced the policy of his administration—to see that the social and political evils of the preprohibition era shall not be revived or permitted again to exist. Failure of citizens to use their new freedom in helping to advance this policy, he said, would be "a living reproach to us all."

He expressed faith, too, in the "good sense of the American people" in preventing excessive personal use of relegalized liquor. "The objective we seek through a national policy," he said, "is the education of every citizen toward a greater temperance throughout the nation."

As a means of enforcing his policy, the President has the Federal Alcohol Control Administration ready to take control of the liquor traffic and regulate it at the source of supply.

In its first major step today, the

Continued on Page Two.

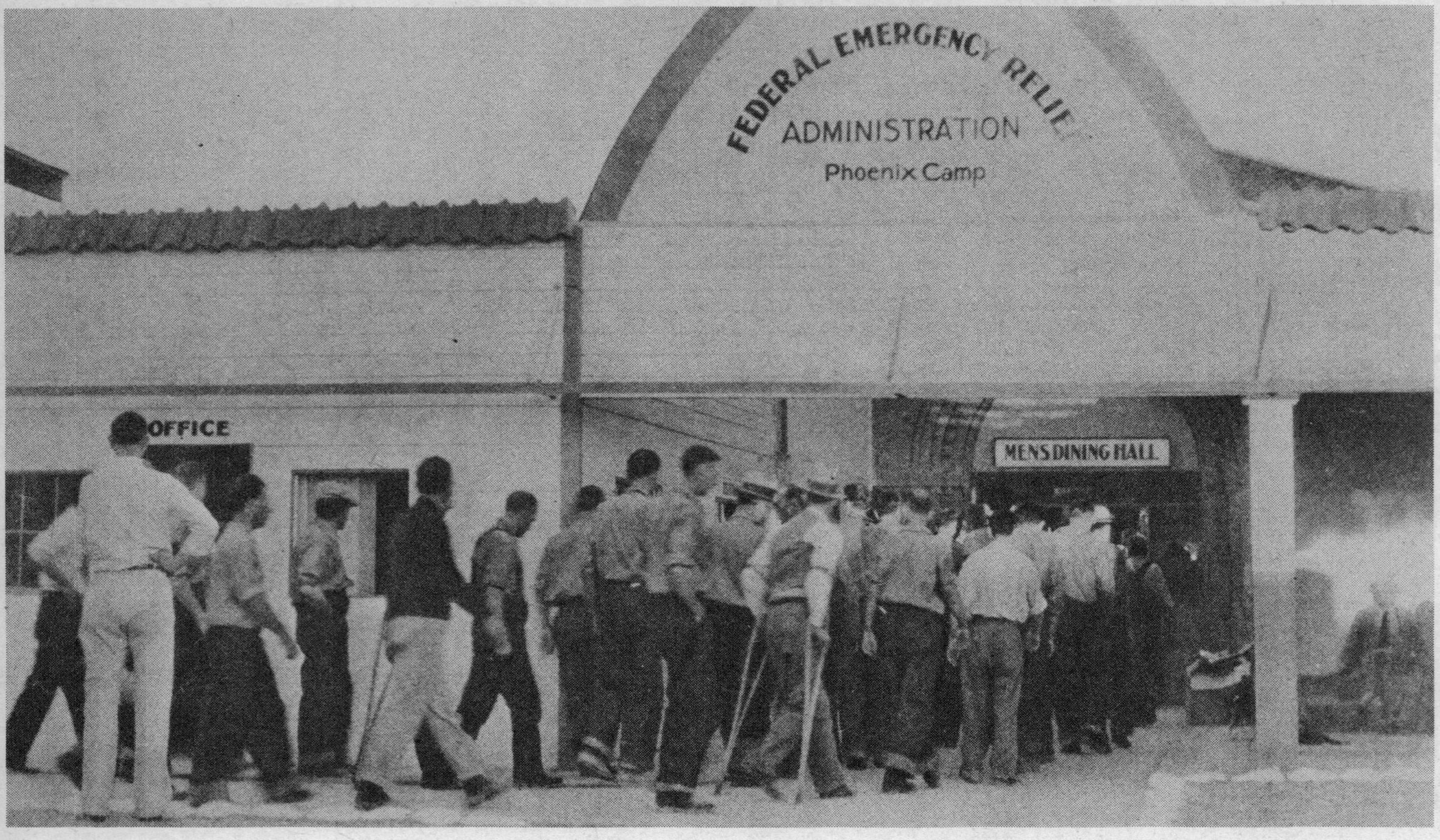

The Federal Emergency Relief Administration camp at Phoenix, Arizona provided food and shelter for the unemployed.

At South Ferry in New York City, the Army fed CCC recruits.

CCC recruits on line outside the Army building in New York City.

These unemployed men waited through the night to register for the CWA.

NRA U.S. WE DO OUR PART

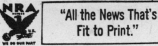

"All the News That's Fit to Print."

The New York Times.

LATE CITY EDITION
WEATHER—Cloudy today and tomorrow; slightly colder tonight.
Temperatures yesterday—Max., 47; Min., 38.

VOL. LXXXIII....No. 27,726. Entered as Second-Class Matter, Postoffice, New York, N. Y. NEW YORK, FRIDAY, DECEMBER 22, 1933. M P P TWO CENTS In New York City. | THREE CENTS Within 200 Miles | FOUR CENTS Elsewhere Except in 7th and 8th Postal Zones

PARIS YIELDS TO US IN LIQUOR DEADLOCK; RAISES FRUIT QUOTA

France to Quadruple Apple and Pear Imports as We Double Wine Allowance.

$2 LIQUOR TAX EXPECTED

Meanwhile, the Alcohol Control Board Plans Drive to Bar All Profiteering.

RACKET IN IMPORTS FOUND

Choate Asks Mulrooney's Aid in Halting Traffic in Permits Under Quota Rules.

Repeal Developments

France agreed to quadruple the quota on our fruit imports and will get double her wine quota.

A basic Federal tax of $2 a gallon on spirits was forecast in Washington.

Profiteering in all branches of the alcoholic beverage business will be prosecuted.

Federal Alcohol Control Administration asked the State board to help to close a loophole in the liquor import quota regulations which racketeers were believed to be exploiting.

France Ends Deadlock.

Special to THE NEW YORK TIMES.

WASHINGTON, Dec. 21.—The protracted deadlock over a reciprocal agreement by which France would buy more American fruit in exchange for an increased wine quota was broken tonight, with France agreeing to quadruple her import quota on American apples and pears in exchange for double the present wine quota.

The agreement came late tonight after a deadlock lasting a week. The French Government gave written assurances to the State Department that the quota on apples and pears would be fixed at 20,000 long tons, about four times the present amount. In return, the wine quota will be doubled.

The differences over the reciprocal agreement arose after this government had already decided to increase the quota on verbal assurances of similar action by France in relation to fruit. When the matter had appeared to be settled, it became known that France proposed to increase her tariff on apples and pears, thus partially at least offsetting the gain to this country by the more liberal quota.

A week of negotiation followed, with the United States refusing to permit an additional amount of French wines to be imported without adequate reciprocal assurances from the French.

Wine Values Small.

While the actual value of the French wine imports is relatively small, estimated semi-officially as less than a million dollars, yet the contest over this agreement assumed greater importance as a test on the basis of which reciprocal agreements with some twenty other countries would be negotiated.

These negotiations, held in abeyance for some time, now can proceed.

Until late tonight the situation was reported at the State Department and the FACA to be "stalemated." Then information of the agreement leaked out.

It was assumed that M. Maurice Garreau-Dombasle, commercial attaché of the embassy here, who has been conducting the negotiations with Dr. Frederick Livesey, economic adviser to the State Department, had received the long-awaited instructions from his government, on the basis of which an agreement could be concluded.

The original French quota was fixed at 784,000 gallons, so that with the doubled quota the imports permitted will amount to more than a million and a half gallons. It was pointed out that since this comprises largely wines, its value would be considerably less than the British quota of 607,000 gallons, largely whisky and gin. The Italian quota was set originally at 1,100,000 gallons, also principally wines. This has not been changed so far.

Hint $2 Basic Liquor Tax.

A basic Federal liquor tax of $2 a gallon on spirits without regard to State levies was forecast tonight on the eve of a meeting tomorrow morning of the House Ways and Means Committee called for the express purpose of casting a liquor tax bill.

An understanding was said to have been reached today among majority members of the Ways and Means body that the proposal of

Continued on Page Four.

Lindberghs Make Surprise Gift Of Their Plane to Museum Here

Flier Presents Craft by Phone to Natural History Institution and Includes All Equipment Carried on Survey Flight—Will Be Exhibited in a Few Days.

The plane and all the equipment used by Colonel and Mrs. Charles A. Lindbergh on their recent 30,000-mile survey flight, in which they spanned both the North and South Atlantic and visited twenty-one countries, has been presented by them to the American Museum of Natural History. The plane is the same in which the Lindberghs established a new transcontinental record in April, 1930, and in which they flew to the Far East the following year.

Up to yesterday, no one at the museum had an inkling that the Lindberghs intended to dispose of the plane. F. Trubee Davison, president of the museum, was seated in his office in the morning when the phone rang and he was apprised that Colonel Lindbergh wished to talk to him. The Colonel lost no time explaining the object of his call. He said that if the museum authorities were willing, he and Mrs. Lindbergh would like to make a present of the ship and all its equipment.

Mr. Davison was delighted. He invited the Colonel and Mrs. Lindbergh to the museum to discuss plans for the disposal of the plane. They accepted and made an appointment for later in the day. Then it was agreed that the plane should be delivered some time between Christmas and New Year, and placed on exhibition in the new Hall of Ocean Life.

When it came to parting with the engine in the plane, which has only flown about 250 hours and is good for 4,000, and with his aerial photographic apparatus, which is practically brand new, the Colonel showed signs of hesitancy. But Mr. Davison reminded him jokingly that he had promised "all the equipment" and Colonel Lindbergh assented.

Included as equipment is an assortment of several hundred items. There are electrically heated flying clothes for Arctic weather, tropical sun helmets, rifles, pistols, ammunition, two radio sets, a thirty-day emergency food supply, an eleven-foot sledge, an eight-foot rubber boat, a sextant, chronometers, maps, charts, parachutes, landing flares, sea anchors, pumps, mosquito netting, goggles, a tent, stove, cooking utensils, fur flying boots and the ship's log book.

"These gifts, as unexpected as they are welcome," said Mr. Davison afterward, "will form a valuable nucleus for the collections of the geographic hall, which is one of

Continued on Page Twelve.

O'DUFFY RELEASED; BLOW TO DE VALERA

High Court's Decision Freeing Blue-Shirt Leader Hurts the Government's Prestige.

OPPOSITION IS JUBILANT

Bishop of Killaloe Scores the Present Free State Regime as Tyrannical.

By FREDERICK T. BIRCHALL.

Special Cable to THE NEW YORK TIMES.

DUBLIN, Dec. 21.—After an all-day hearing in which counsel for the de Valera government attempted to justify and continue the detention of General Owen O'Duffy, militant leader of the Opposition, and his companion, Captain John Sullivan, the High Court in Dublin peremptorily ended the proceedings this evening by ordering the immediate release of both men.

The court's action is regarded throughout the Free State as the worst blow the government has received since it assumed office. The Opposition is jubilant.

General O'Duffy, on emerging tonight from Arbour Hill military prison after the court's order had been served upon the prison governor, was met by a throng of cheering supporters, who carried him in triumph to the headquarters of the United Ireland party in Merrion Square.

Sees Victory for Blue Shirts.

When interviewed, General O'Duffy, who looked fit and none the worse for his prison experience, said to this correspondent:

"The Blue Shirt movement is perfectly lawful and constitutional, and we will go on to victory. I do not anticipate that there will be any more interference with the Blue Shirts after the High Court's vindication.

"If there is, we are prepared to meet it. We will carry on until the objects which we have established are achieved and until eventually, as I hope and believe, the Irish people entrust us with the government of the country.

"The High Court decision has taught the government a lesson in law which I trust has not been lost upon them. So far as we are concerned, we always have stood for the upholding of the law."

At the hearing of the two men, who were arrested in Western Ireland Sunday for wearing blue shirts, Dublin enjoyed the satisfaction of hearing a veritable cause celebre, for which as many of the population as possibly could jammed into the small court room. Leaders of the Irish bar had been retained by both sides.

Justice O'Byrne, who heard the argument, is not only a former Attorney General but one of the drafters of the Free State Constitution, on which the applicants relied.

Throughout the long afternoon Gavan Duffy, James Geoghegan and Patrick Lynch, King's Counsel, all contended by affidavit and argument that the police had stopped General O'Duffy, on his way to a political meeting in Westport, because he was wearing a blue shirt and that they had arrested him when he began to speak while he was still wearing the blue shirt,

Continued on Page Fourteen.

TRUCK STRIKE ON IN PHILADELPHIA

Unions Call Walkout of 27,000, Saying Transit Company Defies NRA.

FEDERAL APPEAL FAILS

Action Is Outcome of Taxicab Drivers' Fight for Independent Labor Group.

Special to THE NEW YORK TIMES.

PHILADELPHIA, Friday, Dec. 22.—Representatives of 27,000 truckmen and drivers, defying a last-minute plea of the National Labor Board, voted a city-wide walkout at 11:30 o'clock last night, threatening a tie-up of general delivery and transportation facilities. The street car and subway lines, while not yet involved, may be drawn into the shutdown.

Strike Order Forbids Violence.

The formal order announcing the strike issued at 1 A. M., said in part:

"The committee asks that no violence or illegal actions take place, and has issued definite orders to that effect. Arrangements have been made to serve hospitals and welfare agencies with milk, meat and bread.

"This strike is in defense of the NRA."

"As things now stand, as a result of the Budd and P. R. T. actions in defying the National Labor Board, organized labor has no alternative to the strike method."

The strike order immediately affected nine local unions of the International Brotherhood of Teamsters, Chauffeurs, Stable Men and Helpers of America. The order was announced to crowds gathered outside union headquarters by Albert J. Barandt, chairman of the strike committee.

After the announcement the joint council went into executive session to perfect strike plans.

Not only taxicab drivers but thousands of men who deliver such family necessities as milk, bread and coal to Philadelphia's homes are involved in the general strike.

The strike is a protest against the assumed refusal of the Philadelphia Rapid Transit Company to comply with the demands of the National Labor Board for termination and subsequent arbitration of the taxicab strike.

In a letter addressed to Senator Wagner, chairman of the National Labor Board, the Philadelphia Rapid Transit Company's president, Ralph T. Senter, in effect, stood pat on the company's terms.

At a special meeting on Wednesday, the joint council of the brotherhood voted to call a general strike at 10 o'clock tonight, unless the P. R. T. accepted the terms of the Labor Board's ultimatum, which the Taxicab Drivers' Union had accepted previously.

Mr. Senter's statement wrecked these hopes to avoid a walk-out so far as the union leaders were concerned.

General orders issued by Acting Superintendent of Police Joseph Lestrange held all police, including patrolmen, foot traffic, detectives and motor-bandit men, on duty.

The National Labor Board had

Continued on Page Eight.

$7,000 FOR LICENSE TO RUN NEWS STAND BARED BY VETERAN

Lost Permit When He Failed to Pay $2,000 More, He Swears at Hearing.

3 OTHERS TELL OF DEALS

Second Disabled Service Man Testifies He Was Ousted for Lack of $1,000.

Four stories of extortion or irregularity in the issuance of news-stand licenses were told to License Commissioner Sidney S. Levine yesterday as he continued an inquiry into his department as run by former Commissioner James F. Geraghty, Bronx district leader. One man testified that he paid $7,000 only to lose his stand when he could not raise $2,000 more.

When Mr. Levine had finished examining his witnesses for the day, a parade of widows, war veterans and cripples, he charged that Mr. Geraghty should have been eliminated from the department long before he was, but that "he was kept there by Edward J. Flynn, the Bronx leader, for political reasons."

Geraghty Denies Blame.

Mr. Flynn was reported out of the city, but Mr. Geraghty, who was dropped on Oct. 9 as commissioner because he supported Joseph V. McKee in the Mayoralty race, disclaimed any connection with any irregularity in his department and replied that conditions under Mr. Levine had been even worse.

Except for the aspect of official responsibility, Mr. Levine declared that there had been no evidence to connect Mr. Geraghty with the charges of extortion.

The $7,000 extortion story was told by Irving Abrams, 86 Ludlow Street, a wounded war veteran. Although Abrams said he had previously served six months in jail because he had refused to name the man to whom he paid the money, he testified yesterday that the recipient was Assemblyman Henry O. Kahan, who died in February, 1932.

Kahan was one of fourteen lawyers implicated by John C. Weston in the operations of the "vice ring" of Women's Court. Disbarment proceedings against him were later dismissed by Referee Clarence J. Shearn.

Abrams said that late in 1930 he decided to get a license to run a news stand at 30 Broadway, and learned that he would have to pay $7,000. He said he borrowed $3,000 from a man named Joe Herman of Brooklyn on condition that he would give Herman half interest in the stand.

Tells of New Demand.

Finally, he testified, he raised the $7,000, and gave $3,800 at one time to Kahan in Haan's Restaurant at Broadway and Reade Street. He got his license and began business. Within two months, he said, he was approached by a "big-shot politician" whose name he did not know, and told to pay $2,000 more.

He could not raise the money, and several days later received a letter bearing the name of Commissioner Geraghty instructing him to turn in his license. The letter was identified by Samuel H. Martin, chief inspector of the department, as bearing Geraghty's name in the handwriting of Inspector Joseph O'Connor, who is at present on leave of absence.

The license was then revoked and

Continued on Page Seventeen.

MACY NOW FACES LEGISLATIVE CALL IN INQUIRY BATTLE

Foes Move to Block Plan for Seabury Investigation of His Accusations.

'WHITEWASH' AIM DENIED

Leaders Say Charges Must Be Sifted Before They Can Organize Assembly.

By W. A. WARN.

Special to THE NEW YORK TIMES.

ALBANY, Dec. 21.—Investigation by a committee of Republican Assemblymen into charges by Chairman Macy will be no "whitewash," according to a statement issued today by the committee as it sent a formal request to the chairman to appear Wednesday to substantiate his accusation that power interests, through H. Edmund Machold and Fred W. Hammond, clerk, had exerted improper pressure on the Assembly in connection with utility legislation.

It was said that if Mr. Macy declines to appear voluntarily before the Republican caucus committee he may be haled before the bar of the Senate and Assembly to supply such proof. This proposal was taken up by the committee of seven after word had reached the Capitol that Mr. Macy had challenged the powers and purposes of the committee. It will be considered again next Tuesday.

A motive for calling the chairman before the Legislature was found, it was said, in the threat of Mr. Macy to force an investigation of his charges through a duly constituted Legislative committee, with Samuel Seabury as counsel.

While some profess to view Chairman Macy's advocacy of such an inquiry as a confession that he is not in a position to prove his accusations, other Republican members admit opposition to an investigation along the lines he proposed.

Would Avoid Seabury Inquiry.

Many of the Republicans are anxious to avert a Seabury investigation and hope to do so by having Mr. Macy appear before the Legislature, where they would attempt to riddle his accusations.

There is no doubt here regarding the power of the Legislature to issue the summons for Mr. Macy and, in the event of his refusal to comply or his failure to substantiate the charges, to hold him in contempt.

Men in similar positions in the past have been reduced to the unpleasant necessity of lingering in the Albany County penitentiary at the pleasure of the Legislature or until purged of the contempt charges.

The general belief among members of the committee of seven is that Mr. Macy will not appear at the Wednesday hearing. Following is the text of the request sent to Chairman Macy:

Dec. 21, 1933.

Mr. W. Kingsland Macy,
State Republican Committee, 100 East 42d Street, New York City.

My Dear Mr. Macy:

On Dec. 5 at Utica you addressed a meeting of the county chairmen of the party called by you. In that address you made definite charge that H. Edmund Machold, representing special interests, exercises control over the

Continued on Page Three.

Chicago Police Kill Three in Gang Battle; Picked Marksmen Rake Arsenal Hideout

Special to THE NEW YORK TIMES.

CHICAGO, Dec. 21.—Three gunmen, two of them fugitive bank robber suspects, were shot and killed by police tonight in a sensational raid on an apartment at 1,428 Farwell Avenue, which was believed to be the hideout of John Dillinger and members of his band of escaped Indiana convicts.

Fingerprint comparisons established their identities as follows:

GINSBURG, SAM, 33 years old.
KATZWITZ, LOUIS, 28.
TATTLEBAUM, CHARLES, 30

Katzwitz and Tattlebaum had been sought since June 15, 1932, as two of the three prisoners freed in a delivery from the La Salle County Jail, where they were being held for a $52,000 hold-up of the Union National Bank of Ottawa.

Acting on information that the quarries were Dillinger and his "mob," the police came prepared for a last-ditch battle.

The raid was executed by Captain John Stege, veteran "strong-arm" squad leader, and a picked detail of twenty expert police marksmen. By a miracle all of them escaped injury, although targets for six hostile guns. When they entered the apartment, the bullet-torn bodies of the gangsters lay on the floor.

The gun battle took place soon after 9 o'clock. But hours before that time Captain Stege's men had surrounded the gang's hideout.

When it was time to strike, the street was practically deserted. Captain Stege ordered the attack.

The men all raced toward the apartment. Doors and windows were smashed in. A charge from a shotgun passed over Sergeant Frank Reynolds.

Reynolds, standing inside the front door, was in the thick of it. He let go four times with a submachine gun. The gangster nearest him dropped with a groan. Reynolds fired blindly at the others.

Meantime, his brother-policemen were inside fighting. In the mêlée lights went out. Men fired at will with pistols. There was an occasional shotgun blast.

Suddenly all firing ceased. On the floor lay three men, dead. Near each were two pistols. All around them were other weapons. The room resembled an arsenal. There were three machine guns, six shotguns. Twenty bullet-proof vests were on a wall.

PRESIDENT ORDERS PURCHASE OF 24,421,410 SILVER OUNCES YEARLY, HALF TO BE COINED

21½c ABOVE DAY'S MARKET

Statutory $1.29 Will Be Paid on Half, With Rest Kept as Seigniorage

FOR ALL NEW MINE OUTPUT

President Acts in Ratifying Agreement Reached at the London Conference.

INDIA TO CARRY OUT PACT

Step Is Expected to Satisfy 'Silver Group' Inflationists at Washington.

Text of the President's Silver Proclamation is on Page 2.

Special to THE NEW YORK TIMES.

WASHINGTON, Dec. 21.—With one Executive order, President Roosevelt tonight ratified the silver agreement negotiated at the London Economic Conference, and provided for the purchase of virtually all newly mined domestic silver, half to be coined and half to be deposited in the Treasury.

The net price to be paid under an order effective until Dec. 31, 1937, will be 64½ cents an ounce. The old statutory price for silver is $1.29 an ounce, put under the order miners will be paid that rate for one-half of their production, "surrendering to the government one-half of it as seigniorage and to cover all usual charges and expenses."

The price set is thus about 21½ cents above today's market price for silver. The President's proclamation said the amount to be absorbed annually by the United States will be "at least 24,412,410 ounces of the silver produced in the United States during such period of time."

Move Against World Dumping.

In its international aspect, the order carries out an agreement designed to prevent the dumping of silver on the world market and the debasing of silver coinage, under an arrangement perfected at London by Senator Pittman.

The President's order, announced at 6 P. M., came a few hours after the Reconstruction Finance Corporation had set aside another $25,000,000 for its gold-purchase fund, raising to $100,000,000 the sum available for such operations.

The new Executive order is expected to satisfy the advocates of silver monetization, looked upon as one of the more powerful groups of inflation proponents.

This action by the United States, with that of other governments under the London agreement, which was adopted unanimously by sixty-six nations, is expected by silver advocates to appreciate the price of the metal to a notable degree. Senator Pittman and others have contended for years that such an appreciation in price would automatically raise the purchasing power of China and other countries using silver money, and thus create large new markets for export products of the United States.

Ratification of the London agreement was withheld by President Roosevelt until he was assured that India, the central point of contention over silver "dumping," would carry out her part of the London agreement.

India Limits Annual Sales.

India, with hundreds of millions of ounces of silver coins available for sale on the world markets, agreed to market annually not more than 35,000,000 ounces of silver reclaimed from coins between Jan. 1, 1934, and Jan. 1, 1938. Spain agreed to limit her sales in the same period to not more than 5,000,000 ounces annually. China agreed to withhold all sales of such de-

Continued on Page Two.

RFC Adds $25,000,000 to Gold Fund; $60,000,000 Used of $100,000,000 Total

Special to THE NEW YORK TIMES.

WASHINGTON, Dec. 21.—The Reconstruction Finance Corporation announced today that it had allocated another $25,000,000 for gold purchase at home and abroad, bringing the total set aside for this purpose to $100,000,000. Of this it was indicated that over $60,000,000 had been used, $16,976,000 for 507,485 ounces of newly mined domestic gold and about $45,000,000 for foreign purchases.

The original allocation, made on Oct. 26, was $50,000,000; another $25,000,000 was set aside two weeks ago, and the most recent authorization of $25,000,000 was made on Tuesday. Chairman Jones of the RFC said that a "substantial" amount of the first $25,000,000 allocation still remained and that the second $25,000,000 was set aside after a survey of available funds for various purposes of the RFC.

It was intimated, however, that no limits had been placed upon future expenditures for gold and that further authorizations might be made from time to time as funds became available. The high level of the gold-purchase fund is one of the fighting points of Congress opponents of the President's monetary policy.

There was no indication today of any immediate change in the gold-purchase policy, the RFC price for newly mined domestic gold standing for the fourth successive day at $34.06 in the face of a very small drop in commodity prices and a further strengthening of the dollar on the foreign exchanges.

In some responsible quarters the President was pictured as harassed in his efforts to reach a decision on future policy by pressure of inflationists, who would have him immediately devalue the dollar and take over the profit on gold held by the Federal Reserve Banks, and by equally insistent counsel by other advisers to maintain the present status and work out the devaluation question over a long range.

Governor George L. Harrison of the Federal Reserve Bank of New York remained here today for conferences with Federal Reserve and Treasury officials, but he would make no comment.

PITTMAN PREDICTS SHARP EXPORT RISE

Nevadan Sees Buying Power of 'Silver Nations' Raised 50% by President's Move.

A CURB ON INFLATIONISTS

Some of Radicals Held Muzzled—Roosevelt Message Expected to Seek No New Steps.

Special to THE NEW YORK TIMES.

WASHINGTON, Dec. 21.—President Roosevelt's decision to buy and coin silver will greatly increase our exports to the Orient and other countries with a silver coinage, and prove a powerful stimulus to recovery, Senator Pittman, author of the silver resolution adopted at the World Economic Conference, declared today.

"The action of the United States will be followed by Canada, Australia, Mexico and Peru, which constitute the great silver-producing countries of the world," the Nevadan said. "This action undoubtedly will stabilize the price of silver throughout the world at 64½ cents an ounce until some further action is taken to raise it to a higher price.

Increased Buying Power.

"This price will increase the exchange value of the money of China, India, Mexico and South American countries 60 per cent in relation to our currency. It will increase the buying power in the United States 50 per cent. There is no doubt it will enormously increase our export trade to those countries on a silver currency. This, of course, will tend greatly to hasten our recovery and will hasten the return to normal conditions.

"Locally it will greatly relieve the mining situation and will bring happiness to millions depending on mining."

Senator Pittman described the new move as the most constructive in the monetary situation yet made by the President.

Western Senators who were prepared to offer bills to remonetize silver on a basis of 16 to 1, and other bills dealing with the question, believed that the President's action would tend to weaken the silver advocates in their promotion of legislation in the coming session.

They thought that the tendency would be to delay the presentation of silver legislation until the effect of the international treaty had been felt.

See Radicals Muzzled.

Other Senators who have been demanding inflation legislation agreed frankly that this move would partially muzzle the radical inflationists. It was generally accepted by Senators as the administration's answer for the present to the inflation faction in the Democratic party.

Others who thought they inter-

Continued on Page Two.

MARKET SURPRISED BY SILVER COINAGE

Friends and Opponents of Monetization See Sweeping Possibilities in Move.

EFFECT IN ORIENT DEBATED

At RFC's Gold Price of $34.06 an Ounce, the Ratio of the Metals Is 53 to 1.

President Roosevelt's action, extending the provision of the International Silver Agreement to provide for the monetization by the government of virtually all newly mined silver in this country came as a distinct surprise to the financial community. Even the silver futures and bar silver markets had displayed a heavy tone during the day.

Several features of the plan seemed highly significant both to those who have favored the monetization of the metal and to those who have opposed such a program. Among them were:

1. The announced price of 64½ cents an ounce is 21½ cents above yesterday's New York quotation for bar silver.

2. The revelation by the President that this country's share of the 35,000,000 ounces to be bought by five producing countries each year, amounting to 24,421,410 ounces, represents approximately the total production of this country this year.

3. At yesterday's RFC gold purchase price of $34.06 an ounce, the new price for silver indicates a remonetization on a basis of approximately 53 to 1.

4. The new high price for silver is expected to result in a sharp increase in all mining operations, inasmuch as 75 per cent of the silver produced in this country is a by-product of the production of other metals.

5. The effect of the new step on Far Eastern economic conditions and this country's trade with that part of the world is being closely studied.

Effect on World Price Doubted.

There was a general feeling in Wall Street that the action of the President represents another step in his program to raise the general price level of the country. Inasmuch, however, as this country produces on an average at present only about one-sixth of the total amount of silver produced in the world, there were some expressions of doubt as to whether or not the move will have any very great effect on the world price of silver for some time.

In this respect it was pointed out that India might well be expected to sell a large portion of its 35,000,000-ounce annual quota under the international agreement in this market, and thus tend to offset any rise in prices which might result from the purchases by the mints.

The fact that the proclamation

Continued on Page Two.

"Problems of Recovery"

The eighth of the series of ten articles on sound money and recovery by Dr. O. M. W. Sprague appears today on the Editorial Page of The Times.

The ninth article will be printed next Tuesday.

Crowds gather at a construction site hoping more men will be needed for the job.

A soup kitchen in New York City.

The ever-present long lines of people waiting to register for employment in New York City.

President Roosevelt spoke to a joint session of Congress and the nation calling upon the legislators to work with him in the rebuilding of the nation. Behind him are Vice President Garner and Speaker of the House Rainey. At the President's right is his son, James Roosevelt.

"All the News That's Fit to Print."

The New York Times.

LATE CITY EDITION

WEATHER—Rain, warmer today; colder tonight; tomorrow colder. Temperatures Yesterday—Max., 28; min., 8.

VOL. LXXXIII....No. 27,767. Entered as Second-Class Matter, Postoffice, New York, N. Y. NEW YORK, THURSDAY, FEBRUARY 1, 1934. P TWO CENTS In New York City. | THREE CENTS Within 200 Miles | FOUR CENTS Elsewhere Except in 7th and 8th Postal Zones

BRITAIN AND ITALY OFFER TWO PLANS TO REARM REICH

BOTH URGE GENEVA ACTION

Demand That Germany Return to the League and to Parley.

LONDON FAVORS BIG GUNS

Rome Would Grant Hitler Plea for an Increase in Army to 300,000 Men.

WE MAY PROPOSE TALKS

Conference With Japan at an Early Date Is Favored by Our State Department.

Official summary of the British arms proposals is on Page 5.

Arms Developments.

LONDON—Great Britain, in a memorandum, published yesterday, called for an arms agreement based on equality and granting "some measure of rearmament" to Germany, along with disarmament in other quarters.

ROME—Premier Mussolini issued an eight-point program, favoring an army of 300,000 men for Germany, asking in return that she rejoin the disarmament conference and the League of Nations.

WASHINGTON—The State Department is considering the possibility of a naval parley with Japan to try to prevent the threatened break-down of the 1935 conference.

TOKYO—The Navy Minister said Japan would exceed us in naval auxiliaries by 1937. The Diet was informed the American and Japanese naval programs made a rupture of the 1935 conference likely.

British Issue Proposals.

By CHARLES A. SELDEN.

Special Cable to THE NEW YORK TIMES.

LONDON, Jan. 31.—Great Britain and Italy issued new disarmament suggestions today, but Rome apparently stole a march on London by getting its memorandum before the world first.

The British memorandum on the subject, which was sent to Berlin, Paris, Rome and Washington on Monday, was withheld from publication by the British Foreign Office to give the governments time to study it. This consideration was chiefly for Premier Mussolini who had told Foreign Secretary Simon at Rome early this month that he had a new disarmament scheme of his own.

Sir John Simon asked the Italian Premier to withhold his project until the British Government had a chance to decide what they could do. Signor Mussolini agreed to that, so after the British had decided on their plan Sir John wanted the Italian Premier to have ample opportunity to examine and approve it before making it public.

Italians Issue Plan First.

Perhaps Signor Mussolini did not think much of it. At any rate, at 7 P. M., two hours before the British Foreign Office finally decided to publish its own proposals by distributing them to Members of Parliament, the news of the Italian proposals had reached London and all European capitals.

However, the incident is not likely to damage the cause of disarmament because it does not seem probable to observers in London that either the Italian or the British memorandum, taken separately or together, will succeed in saving the Geneva conference.

Both London and Rome agree that Germany must return to the League of Nations and the Disarmament Conference. Premier Mussolini adds that his Four-Power pact should function in the situation. The pact is not mentioned by Sir John Simon.

The Italian Premier declares that Germany's demand for an army of 300,000 must be accepted, but Sir John hedges on that point. While expressing his own opinion that 200,000 would be better, he rather airily suggests that an agreement

Continued on Page Five.

French Building Airplane For Stratosphere Sea Hop

Wireless to THE NEW YORK TIMES.

PARIS, Jan. 31.—René Cousinet, French airplane designer, has just started the construction of a plane which he hopes will cross the Atlantic to America in July or August, traveling in the stratosphere.

At M. Cousinet's factory today it was admitted the studies had all been completed, and high hopes were held for the venture. It was stated the plane would embody no revolutionary principles but that the design of the cabin would be different from that of an ordinary plane and the engine would be exceptionally strong.

SANKEY, KIDNAPPER, CAUGHT IN CHICAGO

Suspect in Lindbergh Case Is Seized by Federal Agents After National Search.

HEADED MINNESOTA GANG

Admits Boettcher and Bohn Abductions—Planned Once to Kidnap Babe Ruth.

Special to THE NEW YORK TIMES.

CHICAGO, Jan. 31.—Verne Sankey, a suspect in the kidnapping of the Lindbergh baby and long hunted for crimes in the Middle West, was arrested here today by Federal agents as he sat in a barber's chair.

Word soon came from M. F. Kinkead, County Attorney at St. Paul, Minn., that evidence had been unearthed on Sankey's ranch, presumably at Kimball, S. D., connecting Sankey with the Lindbergh baby kidnapping and murder.

Sankey denied any part in the Lindbergh case, but confessed to taking part in the kidnapping of Charles Boettcher 2d of Denver, for whom $60,000 ransom was paid, and of Haskell Bohn of St. Paul, for whose release $12,000 was paid.

Three Federal agents and three Chicago detectives overpowered Sankey as he awaited a haircut in a barber shop at 4,823 North Damen Avenue. He was unarmed, but put up a fight. When he was subdued he admitted his identity.

The agents hurried to Sankey's apartment and arrested Helen Matern, 28 years old, with whom he had been living. In a tin box in a trunk $3,450 was found, in $100, $20 and $1 bills.

Government agents are checking the serial numbers of these bills with those paid in the Lindbergh and other kidnapping cases.

A shotgun, two revolvers and several boxes of cartridges were found in the apartment.

Several suspects were arrested in the Boettcher kidnapping, but only Mrs. Sankey was indicted. She was released on bond when her trial was postponed. She was tried and acquitted in the Bohn kidnapping and Ray Robinson was sentenced to twenty-five years in prison. He named Sankey as the leader of the gang.

Handwriting experts found a marked similarity between the writing on the ransom notes in the Boettcher and Lindbergh kidnappings.

Sankey will be taken to Denver and tried in the Federal court as Boettcher was transported from Colorado into South Dakota by his kidnappers.

Had Moles Removed.

Melvin H. Purvis, chief of the Federal Bureau of Investigation here, notified the police a month ago that he had information Sankey was believed to be hiding in Chicago. Last week Sankey appeared at the barber shop and had three moles removed from his face with an electric needle. For five days he was unable to shave, and when he appeared today, his captors said, he "looked like a bum." He wore a baggy brown suit, gray dirty hat, and his shirt was soiled.

When Sankey's participation in the Boettcher kidnapping was established it was then learned that he had also engineered the kidnapping of Haskell Bohn on June 30, 1932.

Besides the similarity of the handwriting in the ransom demands in these cases and the Lindbergh case, it was said the manner in which telephone messages were

Continued on Page Three.

GERMANY WILL PAY 77% TO CREDITORS; TO END FAVORITISM

Accord Is Reached Which Will Add $3,200,000 to Annual Payments Here.

NEW CONFERENCE IN APRIL

Final Pact to Be Sought Then—Dutch and Swiss Lose Preference on June 30.

By OTTO D. TOLISCHUS.

Wireless to THE NEW YORK TIMES.

BERLIN, Jan. 31.—The conference between Germany and her long-term creditors ended today with a compromise agreement, which, as far as the holders of German bonds are concerned, not only wipes out Dr. Hjalmar Schacht's recent cut in Germany's interest payments, but even increases them above what they were before Jan. 1.

The agreement provides:

1. Germany continues to remit 30 per cent of her interest payments in cash and 70 per cent in scrip, but scrip issued after Jan. 1 is to be redeemed, not at 50 per cent as heretofore, but at 67 per cent of its face value. This raises Germany's total interest payments on her obligations falling under the partial transfer moratorium to a net of 76.9 per cent of the contractual amount, as against 75 per cent before Jan. 1, and only 65 per cent under the recent reduction ordered by the president of the Reichsbank. It means German 6 per cent bonds will now pay 4.6 per cent instead of 3.9 per cent as provided under Dr. Schacht's previous moratorium terms, while the rate on German 7 per cent bonds is raised from 4.6 to 5.4 per cent.

Special Treatment to End.

2. The bilateral agreements which Germany concluded with Switzerland and Holland, granting to these countries payment in full in return for "supplementary imports" from Germany, and against which Britain and America protested as discriminatory, remain intact, but are to end definitely on June 30. Germany obligates herself not to renew them, and after that period to treat all her creditors alike. In consideration of their special agreements the Dutch and Swiss do not receive the benefit of the increased price for the scrip, but this increase applies to all other creditors.

3. Germany and the creditors' representatives agree to meet in a new and more general conference in April, which is to be prepared by previous negotiations and at which an effort will be made to put the German debt on a new contractual basis which Germany can and must observe.

A German communiqué announcing the accord stresses that the revision of the interest payments does

Continued on Page Six.

Rail Business Is Gaining, Gray Says at White House

Special to THE NEW YORK TIMES.

WASHINGTON, Jan. 31.—Carl R. Gray, president of the Union Pacific Railroad Company, said after a call at the White House today that there had been considerable increase in the railroad business.

"Railroad business has shown considerable improvement recently," he stated. "During the second and third weeks of this month there was an increase in every commodity we handled."

Asked to what he attributed this increase, Mr. Gray said:

"I think it is an accumulation of all that is being done."

Mr. Gray said that he had called at the White House to congratulate the President on his birthday.

LOAFERS LOSE JOBS IN CWA PARK DRIVE

66 Dismissed in Brooklyn for Loitering—Others Go as They Defy Superior.

BOOTLEGGERS PLY TRADE

Gambling and Racketeering Also Investigated by Moses and De Lamater.

A clean-up of CWA projects employing nearly 60,000 men in the city's parks was launched yesterday by Robert Moses, Park Commissioner, in cooperation with the local Civil Works Administration, with a view to weeding out loafers and straightening irregularities.

Both Mr. Moses and Colonel Walter A. De Lamater, local civil works administrator, announced "loafers must go." Colonel De-Lamater said that he would back up fully the program of Mr. Moses to improve the efficiency of the personnel at work in city parks.

As the first disciplinary action in the clean-up campaign, sixty-six men from a group of 2,720 employed in Marine Park, Brooklyn, were dismissed yesterday when Percy H. Kenah, a new superintendent on the park project, found them loitering on the job. Some of the men left the park quietly. Others refused to go, showing signs of belligerency.

Ordered Out by Police.

Several police radio cars were dispatched to the park from the Vanderveer Park station and the discharged laborers were sent from the park precincts at once.

It was learned also that bootleggers had been doing brisk business among the men at work in the park, selling drinks at 25 cents each, and that quantities of material had been stolen from the park and sold. Suspected groups of the men have been watched closely

Continued on Page Ten.

Austrian Trade Mission Is Coming Here; Seeks More Sales as Aid in Fighting Nazis

By FREDERICK T. BIRCHALL.

Wireless to THE NEW YORK TIMES.

VIENNA, Jan. 31.—An Austrian trade commission will leave Vienna for the United States next Tuesday. On it are pinned high hopes for closer relations between the two countries for the benefit of both.

The commission's first job will be to discover further outlets for Austrian goods, samples of which it will take along, and to study concurrently what American products can be profitably sold in Austria, thereby promoting reciprocal trade.

This is necessary because Austria is poor in cash. She needs raw materials, machinery and some American specialties, but she must pay for them mostly with goods.

The foreign currency she needs for payment has hitherto been largely collected from American tourists, and it is not enough. She hopes to enhance this contribution also, but her chief reliance must be placed on the sale of Austrian products in America.

The opportunity for achieving this seems to be particularly good just now because a great wave of sympathy for Austria as the last barrier against the spread of Naziism throughout Southeastern Europe has swept through the world. That is the political situation.

But the conditions that have produced the Nazi peril to Austria are largely economic. An Austria economically strong could afford to flout the Hitler pretensions. This commission will therefore sail with the slogan "Help Austria by buying Austrian."

The commission is composed of four leading Austrian industrialists—Dr. Otto Boehler, president of the Boehler Steel Corporation, the largest of the Austrian heavy industry concerns; Arthur Kuffler, president of the Mautler Textile Corporation; Hans Gogenhofer of the exporting house of Henri Kuehn and Kommerzialrat Robert Granichstaedten, head of the Kanitz export house.

The secretary who will accompany the commission and arrange its activities is Count Seegfried, a great-grandson of the late Emperor Francis Joseph. Like most of the members of the commission, he speaks English fluently and is familiar with American business tradition and practice.

The commission will sail from Havre on the President Harding, arriving in New York about Feb. 16. There it will pay its respects to George H. Earle, the American Minister to Austria, who is now on leave at home. Then it will go to Washington, Chicago, St. Louis and possibly other cities. It will be gone for a month.

The visit is really Mr. Earle's idea, and one of the reasons for his trip home was to pave the way for it. Since his appointment as Minister he has been much impressed by the gallantry of Austria's struggle to maintain her independence and the heavy economic handicap under which she is making it.

The commission desires to have it known that it is going to the United States to ask no favors and seek no gifts. Particularly, it does not intend to request the lowering of American tariffs, believing it the business of the United States to set the proper level for these. What it wants to do is to promote larger trade on a reciprocal basis.

It is in objects of luxury produced at low prices that Austria particularly excels, and to make known the possibilities of these is one of the commission's chief aims. Another is to see why Austrian wines and liqueurs should have so poor a representation in the United States.

LEGISLATORS WANT PROOF MAYOR'S BILL WOULD RESCUE CITY

Senators Ask LaGuardia to Revisit Albany—He Sends Berle With Data.

A COMPROMISE IS SOUGHT

Democrats Blame Republicans for Assembly Action, Seek to Forestall Radio Appeal.

By W. A. WARN.

Special to THE NEW YORK TIMES.

ALBANY, Jan. 31.—Republicans in the Legislature are strangely unsympathetic and aloof in the face of the defeat yesterday in the Assembly of the New York City Economy Bill, which has been pronounced by Mayor LaGuardia the only measure that can help to restore the credit of the city.

In the meantime the Democrats today were engaged in an effort to shift responsibility to the Republicans for the failure of the bill. John J. Dunnigan, Senate leader, declared in a statement made public this evening that the uncompromising opposition of Republican members of the Assembly committee on the affairs of New York City toward amendments offered by Democratic members was responsible for defeat of the measure.

Mayor Asked to Return.

Senator Dunnigan is credited with initiating a proposal to have Mayor LaGuardia, Controller Cunningham, former Controller George McAneny and former Acting Controller Frank J. Prial make another trip to the Capitol to reconcile differences among their respective estimates of the amount of savings necessary to balance the city budget.

Ostensibly the demand for the reappearance of Mayor LaGuardia and the others emanated from the Senate Cities Committee, of which Senator Samuel Mandelbaum, a Tammany Democrat, is chairman. Mr. Dunnigan said tonight that the invitation to the Mayor to appear before the committee had been subscribed to by the Republican as well as the Democratic members of that body. The Senate leader is holding all the members of the Cities Committee at the capital in the hope that the Mayor will come.

The efforts to make an immediate start on a compromise bill are ascribed at the Capitol to a decidedly nervous feeling on the part of the Democratic members of the Legislature. There is a widespread belief that in trying to get Mayor LaGuardia to come here at once and afford them an opportunity to agree on a bill, they are inspired by a desire to forestall his radio appeal for support of his economy measure, announced for tomorrow night.

Governor Lehman made no attempt to disguise the fact that he felt not only chagrined, but incensed over the repudiation of his leadership by members of his own party.

"My views have not changed in any respect from what was defined by me in the message I transmitted to the Legislature," the Governor said today. In that message the Governor unequivocally declared that he favored passage of the LaGuardia bill with all its essential features, as agreed upon by him with the Mayor.

The Governor did not betray any feeling except one of keen disappointment that the Democrats in the Assembly had not taken advantage of the opening he provided them to retire from an untenable position of opposition to a measure that he believes essential to the financial rehabilitation of the city in the present emergency. There is a feeling at the Capitol, however, that Governor Lehman cannot afford under the circumstances to submit to the recalcitrant lawmakers of his own party without a serious loss of prestige and that there is still much that he can do, both as Chief Executive and party leader.

Republicans Hold Aloof.

Republicans in both branches of the Legislature apparently are quite willing to let the Democrats have the right of way in relation to the legislation asked by the Mayor. In the Senate the Republicans have a convenient excuse in the nominal Democratic control, and have been doing nothing to push the LaGuardia bill. In the Assembly, where the Republicans are in control by a substantial majority, there is pronounced lukewarmness toward the measure.

Mayor LaGuardia is regarded at the Capitol as only nominally a Republican, and the fact that W. Kingsland Macy, Republican State chairman, is behind the bill has not helped it with the legislators of his party.

According to friends of Speaker McGinnies, he feels that the bill is

Continued on Page Two.

DOLLAR REVALUED AT 59.06, GOLD PUT AT $35 AN OUNCE; STABILIZATION FUND SET UP

Stocks Leap to New Highs in San Francisco; Eastern Buying a Factor in Huge Turnover

Special to THE NEW YORK TIMES.

SAN FRANCISCO, Jan. 31.—In the most spectacular advance in many a day, security prices on the exchanges went into new high ground on a great wave of late buying today. Turnover on the Stock Exchange reached the highest peak since July, 1933, as 80,694 shares changed hands.

The bullish speculation was apparently set off by announcement from Washington of the gold price, which came too late to affect trading on Eastern exchanges. Much of the buying here was reported to be in response to Eastern orders.

The advance started in the gold shares as Natomas rose to an all-time high at 83½, up 2½; Alaska Juneau scored a new high at 23½, up ¼. On the Curb, Argonaut Mining led advances as it soared to a new high at 6⅞, and Idaho Maryland climbed 45 cents to $3.70.

Industrial issues followed closely as Caterpillar gained 1⅝, California Packing 1 and Paraffine 1, while many recorded smaller gains. Coast Counties Gas preferred jumped 5 points to 70 to lead utilities, while Wells Fargo Bank added 6½ points to reach 200.

Advances on the Curb Exchange were slightly less spectacular, as net changes for the day were smaller, but recoveries from early morning lows were large.

Closing prices on conspicuous stocks traded on Eastern exchanges were: American Telephone and Telegraph, 119; American Smelting, 46; Chrysler, 57; General Motors, 40⅝; General Electric, 23¼; International Telephone and Telegraph, 16⅜; Montgomery Ward, 28; Pacific Gas, 19⅝; Radio Corporation, 8¼; Southern Pacific, 30⅞; Standard Oil of California, 42¾; United Aircraft, 37, and United States Steel, 57¼.

By The Associated Press.

LOS ANGELES, Jan. 31.—The Los Angeles Stock Exchange experienced its most active day in several months following the devaluation of the dollar today.

Stocks on the Los Angeles Exchange were one to three points higher than the closing quotations on the New York Exchange in competitive issues, Exchange officials said.

DOLLAR DROPS FAST IN DRAMATIC SHIFT

However, Decline Stops Short 2 Cents Above the Level Fixed by President.

BUT ABOVE NOVEMBER LOW

Foreign Funds Sent to Buy Stocks Aid Resistance and Close Is 61.01, Off 1.32.

The President's announcement stabilizing the dollar on a modified gold bullion standard at 59.06 per cent of its former parity brought a swift decline in the dollar in foreign exchange late yesterday.

Reflecting the uncertainty and skepticism of the market, however, the reaction stopped short nearly 2 cents above the level fixed by the President as the dollar's new value, leaving the currency worth 61.01 per cent of its old parity in terms of the gold franc, down 1.32 cents on the day.

The movement involved a dramatic reversal of the day's trend. During most of the trading day the dollar had been obstinately buoyant. Sterling fell to $4.97¼ and the franc to 6.25½ cents, at which level the dollar was worth 62.63 per cent of parity. The news of the President's action found the exchanges at about these levels.

At once the foreign currencies began to rise. Sterling rushed up to $5.03¾ and closed near the high at $5.03½, up 3½ cents net. The franc advanced to 6.42 cents, up 13½ points net.

Still Over Its Low Point.

This was the highest price for French exchange since Nov. 23, and the dollar, correspondingly, stood at the lowest level since that date.

At its lowest price, however, the dollar was still well above its recent record low which was 58.34 per cent of the old parity, reached on Nov. 16.

The resistance of the dollar in foreign exchange to the Roosevelt announcement was due to the continued heavy influx from abroad of funds sent here to participate in the rising stock market.

This movement had dominated the market up to the time of the President's announcement. It had carried forward the dollar in the face of very general expectancy of action by the administration along the lines taken.

The wave of liquidation of dollar holdings which followed the actual declaration of stabilization was too strong to be resisted, although not strong enough to bring the exchange down to its newly-proclaimed parity.

Among foreign exchange dealers it was generally taken for granted that the existing premium on the dollar would be rapidly reduced

Continued on Page Twelve.

GOLD STANDARD BACK, SAY BANKERS

Modified Gold Bullion Basis Seen in Buying and Selling Metal at a Fixed Price.

BANKS MAY NOW PROFIT

Tendency of the Dollar to Rise Can Be Checked by Their Purchases Abroad.

By ELLIOTT V. BELL.

The United States has returned to a gold standard, according to the interpretation of the President's proclamation by leading monetary authorities in Wall Street. It will not be like the old gold standard and, at present, at any rate, can only be looked upon as temporary—but it has the essential feature of a monetary gold basis, the purchase and sale of gold at a fixed price.

By providing for the purchase of gold from abroad at $35 an ounce, less charges, the Treasury will be able, according to bankers, to make the United States mint price for gold the effective world price. This may take time but in the end it must come.

The other important new provision in the gold regulations, sale of gold to foreign central banks for export, does not appear of immediate practical significance, according to the bankers, but it is vital to the establishment of a gold standard.

The importance of bringing the world market into the scope of the Treasury's gold buying and selling activities has been demonstrated in recent months when the dollar has consistently sold in foreign exchange at a price higher than that indicated for it by the Treasury's buying price for newly mined domestic gold. It is the purchase and sale of gold to the world which makes the gold value of a currency effective in the world market.

Banks May Sell to Treasury.

Under the new rulings commercial banks here will be able to buy gold abroad, ship it to this country and sell it to the Treasury whenever the movements of the foreign exchange market make such operations profitable. In this way any tendency of the dollar to rise more than a few points above its new parity will be checked instantly by the gold-importations of commercial banks.

While the provision restricting sales of gold for export to foreign central banks will not operate so promptly to check a fall in the dollar, due to the probable reluctance of foreign banks of issue to initiate gold movements as quickly as commercial banks do, it would be bound to take effect if the dollar fell far below its new parity.

The gold standard to which the United States returns is described

Continued on Page Thirteen.

GOLD BULLION STANDARD

Metal to Be Sold at $35 as Well as Bought to Steady the Dollar.

$2,792,859,126 THE PROFIT

The President in Proclamation Reserves Right of Further Changes Under Law.

BASES ACT ON EMERGENCY

Gold Dollar Cut From 25.8 to 15 5/21 Grains 9/10 Fine—Silver Dollar Unchanged.

Text of gold proclamation and President's statement, Page 12.

Gold regulations text, Page 13.

By ARTHUR KROCK.

Special to THE NEW YORK TIMES.

WASHINGTON, Jan. 31.—At 3:10 o'clock today the President, acting under powers conferred on him by Congress in the Thomas amendment of 1933 and the Monetary Bill passed this week, put his signature to a proclamation and, by so doing, automatically effected these momentous changes:

1. Reduced the dollar's gold weight from 25.8 grains to 15 5/21 grains, 9/10 fine, making its gold value 59.06+ per cent of the par fixed by the act of 1900. In other words, the American dollar is now worth 59.06 cents plus in gold.

2. Fixed $35 (less a ¼ of 1 per cent mint charge) as the price this government will pay per fine troy ounce for gold mined in or delivered to the United States, authorizing the Secretary of the Treasury, through the New York Federal Reserve Bank, to begin purchasing at that price tomorrow morning. It was announced at the Treasury that the government will also sell gold at $35 an ounce if that method appears necessary to keep the dollar at 59.06 cents plus, or any later value that may be set.

3. Took title for the government on all the gold held by the Federal Reserve Banks, for which new gold certificates will be given to these banks.

4. Created a dollar profit on this gold, estimated at $2,792,876,058, and credited to the United States Treasury.

5. Set up $2,000,000,000 of this sum to be used as a fund, operated exclusively by the Secretary of the Treasury, to stabilize the dollar on international exchange at as near 59.06 cents as can be done; and to be used also to support the government bond market when necessary.

6. Put the United States on an international gold bullion standard as a substitute for the old gold standard.

Right to Changes Reserved.

In his proclamation and in an accompanying statement to the press the President specifically reserved the right, granted to him by the monetary legislation, to move the dollar's gold weight up and down the percentage scale between the equivalent of 50 and 60 cents, the range fixed by Congress. gress.

The President gave as his official reason for the act of devaluation today the fact of his conclusion that it was necessary to protect our foreign trade from the effects of depreciated currencies in competing nations, and that domestic conditions call for an expansion of credit. These are two of the bases laid down by Congress on which he may, from time to time, alter the gold content of the dollar.

Once more the President chose the occasion of a press conference to announce a super-important act of administration. Today's was scheduled to be held as usual at 10 o'clock in the morning, but the President changed the hour to 4 P. M. in order to be able to report that devaluation had been effected.

Round Figure for Gold Ounce.

In answer to a question why he had valued the gold dollar at 59.06 per cent plus instead of 60 per cent of the 1900 fixation of par, the President explained that it was desired to set a round figure purchase price for the gold ounce, and

Continued on Page Twelve.

NRA — We Do Our Part

"All the News That's Fit to Print."

The New York Times.

LATE CITY EDITION

WEATHER—Fair, not so cold today; tomorrow cloudy and warmer. Temperatures yesterday—Max., 8; min., —14.

VOL. LXXXIII....No. 27,776. Entered as Second-Class Matter, Postoffice, New York, N. Y. NEW YORK, SATURDAY, FEBRUARY 10, 1934. P TWO CENTS In New York City. | THREE CENTS Within 200 Miles | FOUR CENTS Elsewhere Except in 7th and 8th Postal Zones

DRASTIC STOCK MARKET BILL PROVIDES FEDERAL CONTROL; OUTLAWS 9 TYPES OF DEALS

INTRODUCED IN CONGRESS

President, in Special Message, Urges Curb on 'Naked Speculation.'

BILL SETS MARGIN AT 60%

But Buyer Has Alternative of Credit of 80% of Lowest Price in Three Years.

TRADE BOARD TO CONTROL

Short Selling, Wash Sales, Proxies and Option Trading Regulated.

Stock Exchange Bill, Pages 6, 7. President's message Page 6 and Fletcher's speech, Page 7.

Special to THE NEW YORK TIMES.

WASHINGTON, Feb. 9.—President Roosevelt in a special message today asked for legislation to regulate stock exchanges and immediately the long-awaited bill was introduced in Senate and House. It proved to be one of the most drastic regulatory measures ever submitted to Congress.

Subsequently the White House announced that the bill was strictly a Congressional measure and had neither the approval nor the disapproval of the President. The message to Congress recommended Federal regulation of stock and commodity exchanges "for the protection of investors, for the safeguarding of values and so far as it may be possible for the elimination of unnecessary, unwise and destructive speculation."

Chairman Fletcher of the Senate Banking and Currency Committee, and Chairman Rayburn of the House Interstate Commerce Committee introduced the measure.

Commodity Exchanges Next.

While the President asked for regulation of commodity as well as stock exchanges, the Fletcher-Rayburn bill relates only to the operations of stock exchanges. A measure applying to commodity exchanges, which, it is said, will be directed principally at the operations of the New York and New Orleans cotton exchanges and the Chicago Board of Trade, probably will be introduced next week.

Hearings on the Fletcher-Rayburn bill will begin before the Senate Banking and Currency Committee next week. The measure, Senator Fletcher said, strikes "the first blow at a system that has given a small and willful group of men control over the properties and savings of the great mass of investors."

Mr. Rayburn, in the House, described the bill as designed to protect not only investors but the public generally from "evils of manipulation of prices on stock exchanges."

Nine specific devices or practices are outlawed and made criminal offenses. They are:

Wash sales.

Matched orders.

Combinations or pools formed for the purpose of raising or depressing prices of securities.

The spreading of rumors involving price changes on Exchanges.

The disseminating of misleading information regarding any security.

Payments by manipulators for the dissemination of information favorable to their operation.

The pegging of security prices when the Federal Trade Commission is not given complete advance information as to all details of the transaction.

The cornering of the supply of a security.

The use of options and trading against options.

Punishment for Violators.

Violations of any provision would be punishable in the case of an individual by a fine of not more than $25,000 or imprisonment for not more than ten years, or both.

Where the violator is an Exchange, a maximum fine of $500,000 could be imposed.

While the White House expressly disclaims responsibility of the Fletcher-Rayburn bill, administration members of Congress are convinced the measure harmonizes in its major aspects with the views of the President. The action of the White House in disclaiming spon-

Continued on Page Seven.

Chief Points of Stock Exchange Bill

Special to THE NEW YORK TIMES.

WASHINGTON, Feb. 9.—The principal provisions of the Fletcher-Rayburn Stock Exchange Regulation Bill, introduced in Congress today, are as follows:

Requires registration of stock exchanges as "national securities exchanges" with the Federal Trade Commission, the agency administering the proposed law.

Makes it a criminal offense to manipulate security prices on exchanges, the devices outlawed including pools, wash sales, spreading of rumors of impending price changes, cornering the supply of a security and pegging prices without informing the Trade Commission of all details of the transaction.

Stipulates 60 per cent of current prices as a margin requirement, but gives to a trader the option of covering his share purchase with credit up to 80 per cent of the lowest quotation on the security within the three preceding years.

Authorizes the Trade Commission to require annual, quarterly and monthly reports on financial condition from corporations whose stocks are registered on exchanges.

Prohibits short selling or stop loss orders and "over-the-counter" market transactions unless authorized by and in compliance with regulations of the Trade Commission.

Imposes a fine not to exceed $25,000 or imprisonment for not more than ten years for violation of any provision of the law by an individual and a fine not to exceed $500,000 for violation by an exchange.

STOCKS OFF 1 TO 3 ON NEWS OF BILL

Then They Rally When President Fails to Endorse the Fletcher Measure.

CURBS HELD TOO SEVERE

Wall Street Now Expects to Be Regulated, but Will Wage Fight for Moderation.

Wall Street received with something like alarm yesterday news of the proposed bill to regulate the security markets. Although the text of the measure was not available in the financial district until after the Stock Exchange had closed, advance reports of its nature seeped through from Washington and caused a decline of 1 to 3 points in leading stocks.

During the last half hour, prices rallied moderately on rumors that President Roosevelt's message, which was issued after the market closed, would omit endorsement of the bill introduced by Senator Fletcher.

When the President's message appeared, brokers expressed satisfaction that the administration was not committed to the passage of the Fletcher measure. The message was regarded as moderate in tone, and was held to indicate that the administration recognized the economic value of stock exchanges and would not allow them to be crippled.

Determination to carry a fight to Congress against some provisions of the Fletcher bill was expressed by brokers. Since the administration is not sponsoring the measure, brokers felt that it was open to amendment and that at hearings they would be permitted to present their case.

Modification Is Sought.

But all hope that regulatory legislation would not be enacted at this session of Congress disappeared with the President's message, and the aim of bankers and brokers now is to obtain passage of a bill that will cause as little unsettlement as possible in Wall Street.

The scope of Senator Fletcher's measure caught brokers, bankers and corporation executives by surprise. Virtually every phase of financial and business activity was affected by the bill, brokers declared.

Some described the measure as a long step toward nationalization of the security markets; others said it was an effort to obtain, by statute, assurance of honest and fair dealings in securities.

Surprise over the nature of the bill was caused by the fact that in many respects it went further than the legislation outlined by the President's interdepartmental committee, headed by John Dickinson, which submitted a report two weeks ago.

Not all of the comment with regard to the Fletcher bill was hostile, however. Brokers praised many passages, particularly those dealing with corporation accounting and financial reports, as measures which would protect the public.

Points in the bill which were attacked in many quarters were the

Continued on Page Seven.

VIENNA FOES UNITE AGAINST HEIMWEHR

Clerical Deputies Join With the Socialists in Diet to Fight Demands for Dictatorship.

GOVERNOR BALKS FASCISTS

Lower Austrian Head Turns Away Their Delegation—Dollfuss Back in Capital.

By G. E. R. GEDYE.

Wireless to THE NEW YORK TIMES.

VIENNA, Feb. 9.—The clerical Christian Social party, to which Chancellor Dollfuss belongs, joined forces with the Socialists in the Vienna Diet tonight against the dictatorial demands of the Heimwehr, which is calling for the dissolution of the political parties.

Deputy Kunschak, one of the leading Christian Social members of the Diet and a lifelong opponent of the Socialists, declared that all broadminded Viennese must now stand together in the hour of trial to prevent the triumph of those who demand dictatorial coordination.

"The political parties will exist peacefully long after this present madness has been written down as an age of the decay of cultural institutions under extremist pressure," he said.

"Only such an emergency could ever have brought me to stand side by side with those [the Socialists] from whom a world of political difference otherwise separates me."

Both Parties Cheer Him.

Both the Socialists and clericals loudly cheered him, and Mayor Seitz of Vienna, who is the head of the Socialist party, concluded the sitting by calling for cheers for a free and autonomous Vienna.

The Finance Bill that was before the Diet was unanimously voted by both the Christian Social and Socialist deputies.

Another sign of opposition to the Heimwehr demands in non-Socialist quarters was manifested tonight when Governor Reither of Lower Austria, a leading figure in the clerical party, declined even to receive a deputation of local Heimwehr leaders in Vienna who had come to make the usual demand for the dissolution of parties. The Vienna newspapers were forbidden to mention this rebuff.

The importance of this revolt of the Christian Social leaders in Vienna and Lower Austria against the Heimwehr demands lies in the fact that about half the population and most of the wealth of the country is in Vienna and Lower Austria.

Even in the thinly populated Alpine provinces the Governor of Tyrol has strongly opposed and the Governor of Salzburg is unfriendly to the Heimwehr demands. Both are local leaders of the Christian Social party.

As for Carinthia, its Governor is a strong anti-Heimwehr man of Nazi sympathies.

Chancellor Dollfuss returned to Vienna tonight from Budapest and immediately presided over a Cabinet meeting. A conference with the Governors of the provinces to consider the Heimwehr demands was postponed until Monday, but the Chancellor received the Heim-

Continued on Page Four.

Mercury 14.3 Below Zero On New York's Coldest Day

Six Dead and Hundreds Treated for Frost-bitten Ears and Noses—8 to 10 Below Due Here Today.

The average New Yorker shivered and complained yesterday in the city's coldest day on record, but he did not suffer.

To some—the destitute, the homeless and the unemployed—however, the day brought misery and death, not only in the city but throughout the East.

With below-zero weather recorded, schools were closed, traffic was snarled and hospital attendants were kept busy attending cases of frostbite and exposure. In New York the worst sufferers were policemen, firemen and school children.

Relief agencies, already sorely pressed, were on their mettle, and William Hodson, Welfare Commissioner, declared that whatever the cost might be, no man or woman need freeze for lack of shelter.

"With the municipal lodging houses, private charities and the commercial lodging houses," he said, "we are more than able to care for every homeless man and woman in the city.

"Our policy with the homeless unemployed is to care for them and then pay for it."

The record-breaking low temperature was set at 7:25 A. M. yesterday, the sixty-fourth birthday anniversary of the Weather Bureau, when the thermometer registered 14.3 degrees below zero.

From that time on the temperature rose until at 4 P. M. it was 7 degrees above, but by 10 P. M. it had fallen to 4 above.

Weather Bureau officials said that today would be fair and "not quite so cold." They expected, however, that the mercury would sink to 8 or 10 degrees below zero between 6 A. M. and 8 A. M. today. The forecast for tomorrow was increased cloudiness and warmer weather.

The high pressure area which brought the cold wave from Canada is moving eastward to the sea and the probability is that tomorrow the mercury will rise higher than the maximum of 20 degrees that is expected today.

Although the local Weather Bureau records go back only sixty-four years, the likelihood th- yesterday was the coldest day in the

Continued on Page Three.

Yesterday's Temperatures.

Midnight	—7	2 P. M.	4
1 A. M.	—8	3 P. M.	5
2 A. M.	—9	4 P. M.	7
3 A. M.	—10	5 P. M.	7
4 A. M.	—11	6 P. M.	6
5 A. M.	—12	7 P. M.	5
6 A. M.	—13	8 P. M.	5
7 A. M.	—13	9 P. M.	4
7:25 A. M.	—14.3	10 P. M.	4
8 A. M.	—13	11 P. M.	2
9 A. M.	—10	Midnight	2
10 A. M.	—8	1 A. M.	*1
11 A. M.	—2	2 A. M.	*1
Noon	2	3 A. M.	*—1
1 P. M.	3		

*Unofficial street temperature in Times Square.

PARIS RIOTS FLARE AFTER DOUMERGUE FORMS A CABINET

Two Churches Fired and Shops Are Looted as Police Fight Gangs in Hail of Shots.

PREMIER ASKS FOR ORDER

National Ministry Includes Herriot, Tardieu, Barthou, Sarraut and Laval.

By P. J. PHILIP.

Wireless to THE NEW YORK TIMES.

PARIS, Feb. 9.—Former President Gaston Doumergue has formed the government of national union and national safety that the country demanded, and tonight on public billboards throughout France the following declaration signed by him is being posted:

To the French People.

Dear Citizens:

I have been called to form a government of truce, of appeasement and of justice.

This government is constituted.

In its name I invite you to accomplish in turn your duty by renouncing all agitation and placing above all other interests France and the republic.

Stiff Fighting in Streets.

Tonight gangs acting in the name of communism engaged in some stiff street fighting with the police in the Place de la Republique and in the neighborhood of the Gare de l'Est.

The fighting at several points reached perhaps a higher pitch than any thus far and squads of police were forced time and again to charge under a rain of bullets to break down barricades in the Rue de Forillon, Fauborg du Temple and in the narrow passages of the Rue Saint Maur.

When the fighting ceased twelve policemen had been wounded by bullets, all seriously, and twenty-five had been admitted to hospitals for treatment.

The casualties among the demonstrators were not known, but they must have been high, for great numbers were severely clubbed in police assaults within the iron fenced approaches of the Gare de l'Est. More than 800 manifestants were arrested.

Among the demonstrators, according to police bulletins, were many whose purposes were not political, because many acts of depredation showed they were bent on looting.

A committee of the General Labor Federation has called a complete strike "against fascism and dictatorship in any form" for Monday, but has asked the strikers to refrain from demonstrations. Its leaders, like Leon Jouhaux, secretary of the federation, want the strike to be dignified and have real political significance.

During the afternoon the new Premier called in M. Jouhaux and, according to a statement made later by the labor leader, urged that the country needed calm for both internal and external reasons and that

Continued on Page Sixteen.

FAVORITISM IS LAID TO E. J. FLYNN IN USE OF CITY TRUST FUND

As Chamberlain He Invested Largely in Title Concern for Which He Was Counsel.

PARTNER LINKED TO IT

Goldwater Denies the Leader Handled Money—Data Given in Report by Berle.

Trust funds in custody of the City Chamberlain were consistently invested in securities of the State Title and Mortgage Company for more than four years, according to a report by Professor A. A. Berle Jr., the present City Chamberlain. Professor Berle has submitted his report to Mayor LaGuardia, who ordered a copy sent to George W. Algar, Moreland Act Commissioner, who is investigating the State Insurance Department.

The period during which the State Title Company was favored was from 1928 to and including part of 1932. During part of this time Secretary of State Edward J. Flynn was City Chamberlain. His law firm, Goldwater & Flynn, was counsel to the State Title and Mortgage Company, and Monroe Goldwater, the other member of the firm, was a director of National American Company, Inc., listed in Poor's Directory as the company that controls State Title and Mortgage.

Goldwater Defends Company.

The Berle report did not link the State Title and Mortgage Company to Mr. Flynn's firm, but persons familiar with the situation said yesterday that Mr. Flynn's firm had acted as counsel. Mr. Flynn was not reached for comment. Mr. Goldwater was quoted as saying:

"Mr. Flynn had nothing personally to do with the funds. They were invested by employes of his office. The mortgages were in good standing at the time. The majority of all of the mortgages issued by title companies are in default now. I understand that there is a smaller percentage of State Title certificates in default than of any other company."

In the Berle report, members of the permanent office staff of the Chamberlain's office were quoted as saying that when money was available for investment, a check was sent to the company and securities not otherwise examined were sent by the company, in the amount of the check, to the Chamberlain's office.

It was conceded yesterday that the percentage of defaults on the State Title and Mortgage Company was no greater than the percentage of other companies in which the Chamberlain's funds were invested. Considerable sums were invested in the New York Title and Mortgage Company and the Prudence Company.

The percentage of default under the State Title Company has been reduced somewhat in the last few weeks on the guaranteed mortgages, as the Chamberlain's office has ac-

Continued on Page Eight.

AIR CONTRACTS CANCELED; ARMY TO CARRY THE MAILS; M'CRACKEN EVADES ARREST

Order to Army to Carry Mails

Special to THE NEW YORK TIMES.

WASHINGTON, Feb. 9.—The text of the executive order concerning the air mail issued by President Roosevelt follows:

EXECUTIVE ORDER.

WHEREAS by an order of the Postmaster General of the United States all domestic air-mail contracts for carrying the mails have been annulled; and

WHEREAS the public interest requires that air-mail service continue to be afforded and the cancellation of said contracts has created an emergency in this respect;

NOW, THEREFORE, I, FRANKLIN D. ROOSEVELT, President of the United States, under and by virtue of the authority in me vested, do hereby order and direct that the Postmaster General, Secretary of War and Secretary of Commerce, together with other officers of their respective departments, cooperate to the end that necessary air-mail service be afforded.

It is further ordered and directed that the Secretary of War place at the disposal of the Postmaster General such airplanes, landing fields, pilots and other employes and equipment of the army of the United States needed or required for the transportation of mail, during the present emergency, by air over routes and schedules prescribed by the Postmaster General.

THE WHITE HOUSE, Feb. 9, 1934. FRANKLIN D. ROOSEVELT.

AIRLINE HEADS ASK FAIR PLAY ON MAIL

Executives Here Defend Their Contracts and Insist Upon Right to a Hearing.

PROTEST SENT PRESIDENT

One Company Offers to Fly Mail 30 Days and Waive Pay if Fraud Is Found.

Officials of the nation's leading air-mail systems gathered in their offices last night in New York to plan a fight to the end against what they consider is an unfair decision by the government in canceling the air-mail contracts.

Richard W. Robbins, president of the Transcontinental and Western Air Corporation, which flies mail, passengers and express between New York and Los Angeles, sent a telegram of protest to President Roosevelt stating that he felt the company was entitled to be heard "as a matter of fair play."

At the same time Mr. Robbins offered to continue carrying the air mail for the next thirty days, pending further hearings, with the understanding that if any evidence of fraud were found the company would waive payments for the mileage flown.

Defense of United Lines Contracts.

Philip G. Johnson, president of the United Aircraft and Transport Corporation and also of United Air Lines, which is made up of National Air Transport, Boeing Air Transport and Pacific Air Transport, had this to say:

"We have received no official communication from the government informing us that our contracts have been canceled. However, all of our contracts, which are held by Boeing Air Transport, National Air Transport and Pacific Air Transport, all divisions of our system, are the result of competitive bidding and were received in the years 1926 and 1927 because we were the lowest responsible bidder.

"We have never at any time been party to any collusive arrangement with any other contractor for the carriage of air mail.

"Any meetings which our representatives attended at which other contractors were present were at the express invitation of the Post Office Department."

United Air Lines, in addition to its New York-Chicago-San Francisco services, operates through National Air Transport a line from Chicago to Dallas, through Boeing a line from Salt Lake City to Pasco, Wash., and Portland, Ore., and through Pacific Air Transport from San Diego to Seattle.

Eastern Transport Confident.

Captain Thomas B. Doe, president of Eastern Air Transport, which flies mail, express and passengers between New York, Washington, Atlanta and Miami, said:

"Eastern Air Transport received its air mail contract under open bidding during the Coolidge administration. No charges have been made against this company, and, so far as known, no charges are contemplated.

"No official of this company has been called before the Senate investigating committee. I think I have a right to assume that I will be given a chance to answer spe-

Continued on Page Two.

M'CRACKEN DEFIES SENATE SUMMONS

Sends Note Denying Body's Power to Call Him—Hunt by Officer Is Futile.

CO-DEFENDANTS APPEAR

Brittin Admits Torn Letters Touched Airway Matters—Hanshue and Givvin Heard.

Text of W. P. MacCracken's letter to the Senate, Page 2.

Special to THE NEW YORK TIMES.

WASHINGTON, Feb. 9.—William P. MacCracken Jr., cited to appear before the Senate today to show cause why he should not be punished for contempt for allowing correspondence under Senate subpoena to be removed from his law office, defied that body by refusing to appear.

The Assistant Secretary of Commerce in the Hoover administration did this by sending a statement to the Senate, and hardly had Vice President Garner called the session to order when the message was read. It said, in part:

"I have the greatest respect for the Senate of the United States and would not knowingly or intentionally commit any act in contempt of its constitutional rights and powers.

"I am constrained, however, to deny the constitutional right of your honorable body to compel the attendance before its bar of a private citizen of the United States to there show cause why he should not be punished for an alleged past and completed act."

The letter also contended that while the Senate had the power to deal with contempt so far as it was necessary to preserve and exercise the legislative authority expressly granted it, the power did not extend to the infliction of punishment.

Senator Black immediately read a resolution asking for the rearrest of Mr. McCracken, who had previously been arrested and released for appearance today. This was adopted by acclamation.

MacCracken Is Not Found.

Up to a late hour tonight no arrest had been made. When ordered to find Mr. MacCracken, Chesley W. Jurney, Senate sergeant-at-arms, immediately set out, garbed in a Western sheriff's black hat and a morning coat with a red carnation and gray striped trousers.

He returned in two and a half hours to announce his quest had been unsuccessful.

Frank J. Hogan, Mr. MacCracken's attorney, who also was attorney for Edward L. Doheny, Albert B. Fall and Colonel Robert M. Stewart in their disputes with the government, declined to disclose where his client could be found.

He offered to escort Mr. Jurney to Mr. MacCracken's presence, however, indicating that he would immediately sue for a writ of habeas corpus as a means of taking the matter out of the hands of the Senate and placing it in the courts. The sergeant-at-arms, therefore, declined to accept the attorney's offer.

Senator Black suggested that Mr. Jurney have more time to find Mr. MacCracken. He indicated that

Continued on Page Two.

PRESIDENT ACTS QUICKLY

Citing Evidence of Fraud, He Bars All Companies, Effective Feb. 19.

ARMY READY TO PROCEED

800 Observation and Cargo Planes Are Serviceable and About 100 Fast Bombers.

MAY DROP SOME ROUTES

Ousted Pilots to Be Cared For—Black Sees Senate Inquiry Justified, and Will Proceed.

Special to THE NEW YORK TIMES.

WASHINGTON, Feb. 9.—President Roosevelt took the troublesome air mail situation into his own hands today, ordered annulment of all existing domestic air-mail contracts and directed the army to fly the mail during the emergency created by his act.

The annulment order, issued by Postmaster General Farley, came as the climax of a day packed with developments involving the air mail, a day which witnessed, among other things, a continuance of defiance by William P. MacCracken of the Senate's attempt to try him for contempt.

The Hoover Assistant Secretary of Commerce deliberately stayed away from the Senate, where he had been scheduled to answer to charges of allowing some of his air-mail-carrying clients to withdraw from his files and destroy evidence sought by a special Senate committee investigating air-mail and ocean-mail contracts.

Twenty-six Routes Are Affected.

The decision to cancel all domestic air-mail contracts, effective at midnight Feb. 19, and have the Army Air Corps transport the mail after that date was reached at a conference of the President, Postmaster General Farley and Attorney General Cummings, following the regular Cabinet meeting this afternoon.

At his usual press conference a few minutes later, Mr. Roosevelt quietly announced the steps to be taken.

An executive order directed the Postmaster General, the Secretary of War and the Secretary of Commerce, together with the officials of their departments, to cooperate in maintaining air-mail service, in the public interest, during the emergency situation created by the annulment of contracts.

An announcement by Mr. Farley showed that twenty-six air mail routes, flown by twelve companies, were affected. The companies whose contracts were annulled are American Airways, National Air Transport, Western Air Express, Boeing Air Transport, Pacific Air Transport, Northwest Airways, Kohler Aviation Corporation, Pennsylvania Air Lines, Eastern Air Transport, National Parks Airways, United States Airways and Transcontinental and Western Air.

Ground for annulment, the President said, was what is believed to be sufficient evidence of collusion or fraud. No indication was given of what further action, if any, the government intended to take against any offending companies.

Five-Year Bar Against Bids.

President Roosevelt, in making his announcement, said it was his understanding that the companies whose contracts were annulled could not bid for five years on any government contract.

Section 3950 of the United States Statutes provides:

"No contract for carrying the mail shall be made with any person who has entered or proposed to enter into any combination to prevent the making of any bid for carrying the mail, or who has made any agreement or given or performed or promised to give or perform any consideration whatever to induce any other person not to bid for any such contract; and if any person so offending is a contractor for carrying the mail, his contract may be annulled and for the first offense the person so offending shall be disqualified for carrying the mail for five years; and for the second offense shall forever be disqualified."

It was emphasized that only domestic routes had been affected. Pan American Airways flies mail

Continued on Page Two.

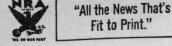

"All the News That's Fit to Print."

The New York Times.

Copyright, 1934, by The New York Times Company.

LATE CITY EDITION

WEATHER—Fair and somewhat colder today; tomorrow fair.
Temperatures Yesterday—Max., 58; min., 47.

VOL. LXXXIII....No. 27,800. Entered as Second-Class Matter, Postoffice, New York, N. Y. NEW YORK, TUESDAY, MARCH 6, 1934. P TWO CENTS In New York City. | THREE CENTS Within 200 Miles | FOUR CENTS Elsewhere Except in 7th and 8th Postal Zones

NEW DEAL PERMANENT, PRESIDENT SAYS; ASKS HIGHER PAY, SHORTER HOURS, NOW; SUPREME COURT UPHOLDS PRICE FIXING

LEHMAN MESSAGE URGES EXEMPTIONS IN GROSS TAX LEVY

He Also Attacks Republican Effort to Impose 2 Per Cent Sales Impost.

CONDEMNS MONEY BILLS

Governor Denounces Effort to Unbalance Budget as Means of Forcing Sales Plan.

30 GROUPS JOIN IN FIGHT

Grange and Doctors Aid Foes of Measure—Whalen Sees Recovery Hampered.

Special to THE NEW YORK TIMES.

ALBANY, March 5.—Governor Lehman came out strongly tonight against efforts of the Republicans to impose a 2 per cent sales tax.

In two messages to the Legislature the Governor condemned the rejection of his $81,000,000 reduction program and substitution of the Fearon-Wadsworth bill for a sales tax.

The Chief Executive insisted upon prompt passage of the bill, containing his recommendations for including normal exemptions in the emergency income tax so that taxpayers would be saved $14,000,000 this year.

In the other message he criticized the Republican plan to add considerably to the appropriations already voted, so that the budget would be unbalanced and a better argument provided for the sales tax.

The Republicans who passed the Governor's budget bill, in which appropriations were balanced against his own estimates of much lower taxes, have already offered bills for added appropriations totaling almost $15,000,000.

The manoeuvring of the Republicans on all tax and appropriation measures had been predicated on the stand that if the budget is thrown out of line as a gesture, the sales tax will have a better chance. Up-State municipalities are clamoring for it in the belief that a State refund of 90 per cent of the tax will go far to solve their fiscal problems. For this reason the Republican leaders have held up bills in the tax-reduction program urged by the Governor and offered the measures for extra appropriations.

Urges Normal Exemptions.

In his message the Governor took formal notice of the sales tax campaign, reiterated that he was against continuance of the present 1 per cent sales tax and wanted quick action to provide the normal exemptions in the "gross" income tax to give taxpayers $14,000,000 relief at once.

"Regardless of any other consideration," he said in one message, "there hardly can be valid objection to the prompt adoption of an amendment which will save $14,000,000 for the taxpayers of the State and relieve thousands of men and women of small or moderate incomes."

The Governor pointed out once more than he was opposed to the continuance of a sales tax, the guiding point of the Republican fiscal policy as set forth by Senator Fearon. He demanded action on his general revenue measures.

In his second message, the one dealing with the extra appropriations provided for in bills introduced by Republican leaders, the Governor declared that the policy was out of line with what should be correct procedure in giving him an opportunity to consider appropriation bills at one time so that he could have a complete picture of the fiscal prospects for the coming year.

"On Jan. 15 I transmitted to your honorable bodies," the Governor said, "my executive budget containing, in accordance with the Constitution, 'a complete plan of proposed expenditures and estimated revenues.' Some days ago you enacted into law, without one single change, all of the proposed expenditures.

"Now I note that many new bills carrying very substantial appropriations have been introduced and I am informed that many others are about to be introduced. In the aggregate these bills, if passed, will result in additional expenditures of many millions of dollars.

"If your honorable bodies disagreed with the appropriations I recommended in the Executive budget, the procedure intended by the Constitution would seem to me to require your amendments or additions to those proposed recommendations before they were enacted into law. In my opinion, the Constitution did not contemplate that the Legislature should enact into law the appropriations recommended in the Executive budget without a single change, and then immediately thereafter have the

Continued on Page Twenty.

Aversion to Jury Duty Called Sign of Recovery

Frederick O'Byrne, Commissioner of Jurors for New York County, said yesterday that "the barometer of business," judging from activities of his office, registers "clear and fair for the future." He said that out of 700 jurors summoned for the March term in the Supreme Court, which began yesterday, only 300 were willing to serve.

Mr. O'Byrne, who has been in the office since 1883 and commissioner for eighteen years, said:

"In normal times we almost have to draft jurors, and even then we can count on only about a third of those called to serve. Things have been different in the last three or four years. Thousands of unemployed men have called at my office and asked to have their names put on the list."

DILLINGER'S AUTO FOUND IN CHICAGO

Disclosure Spurs the Hunt for Him There—Fugitive Twice Encountered in the City.

WOMAN LINKED TO BREAK

Jail Visitor Known as 'Wife' Is Identified as Sweetheart of a Confederate.

Special to THE NEW YORK TIMES.

CHICAGO, March 5.—John Dillinger was believed tonight to be in Chicago following a disclosure by the police that the sheriff's automobile in which he escaped from the jail at Crown Point, Ind., on Saturday morning was found that same evening in front of a northwest side apartment building.

The information had been kept secret so that no interference might hamper the work of police squads searching every possible hideaway of the fugitive in the city.

The police also disclosed that Dillinger was encountered Saturday afternoon by Detective Lorimer Hyde of the State's Attorney's office, who, off duty, was driving north on Broadway when he recognized the desperado in a car with an Indiana license.

Dillinger parked his car. Hyde halted 100 feet to the rear and was advancing with a drawn pistol when Dillinger turned and saw him. Dillinger sped away before Hyde had time to re-enter his own car.

Several hours later Hyde again saw Dillinger with a woman, driving on Halsted Street. The fugitive eluded pursuit by driving around the left side of a street car.

Hand of Hamilton Seen.

Meantime, in the inquiry into the jail break, Mrs. Lillian Holley, the sheriff, identified a picture of Elaine Burton, sweetheart of John Hamilton, a Dillinger gangster still at large, as the woman who visited Dillinger in his cell just before he got away.

Hamilton is believed responsible for his chief's success in eluding pursuit and in slipping through the tight cordon of police thrown about Chicago.

With Dillinger was Herbert Youngblood, a Negro awaiting trial for murder. When they fled in Sheriff Holley's car they were armed with two machine guns, seized at the jail after Dillinger had locked up thirty guards and inmates at the point of a wooden pistol.

"Signals" in Talk With Woman.

Crown Point officials were convinced that "Mrs. Burton," Dillinger's visitor, laid the groundwork for his escape. She first went to the jail about ten days ago with Louis Piquett of Chicago, Dillinger's lawyer, who vouched for her as his client's wife in obtaining Judge William Murray's permission for her to visit the prisoner.

Sheriff Holley asserted that the woman was Elaine De Kant Dent Burton, previously known as Mary Kinder and also linked with Harry Pierpont, another member of the Dillinger gang who is now in jail at Lima, Ohio, with two others awaiting trial for murder.

Guards at the jail recalled that when the woman came in to see Dillinger she attempted to get close to him, but was told to stand back. She then talked to him in a jargon which sounded like football signals, but which was probably a code. The guards said she interspersed her words with a series of numbers until ordered to desist.

She gave her name as Ann Martin when she sought the interview, but said she was actually Dillinger's wife. Mr. Piquett said he knew her as "Billy" and that she also represented herself to him as Mrs. Dillinger. He was using her, he said, to build up a defense.

"She was in my office Saturday morning when we got news that Dillinger had broken jail," Mr.

Continued on Page Sixteen.

LAGUARDIA ACTS TO FORCE REPAIRS IN FIRETRAP FLATS

Mayor Tells Post to Condemn Tenements if Unsafe or if Owners Defy Law.

SCORNS WALKOUT THREAT

Landlords Deny Challenge, but Assert Many Need Loans to Make Improvements.

Mayor LaGuardia disclosed last night an eight-point program he had prepared to combat the threat of a wholesale abandonment of tenement houses, which was made on Sunday by Joseph Goldsmith, president of the Council of Real Estate Associations.

As the Mayor was ordering Tenement House Commissioner Langdon W. Post to put his program into effect, Mr. Goldsmith said his earlier statement had been misconstrued. Speaking as a representative of real estate owners, he had said that if the city enforced safety and sanitation laws in tenement houses, their owners would be compelled to abandon them. He said on Sunday that 670,000 families occupying 67,000 dwellings thus would be made homeless.

After conferring with Mr. Post yesterday, Mr. Goldsmith issued another statement to clarify his position. He said landlords were eager to eliminate unsafe and insanitary tenements and welcomed the Mayor's suggestion that Federal funds might be available for that purpose.

Denies Owners Defy Law.

Increased taxes, increasing water rates and reduced income, he declared, made it impossible for them to finance the repairs themselves. Instead of tearing old houses down, he suggested that they be repaired and rehabilitated.

"The policy of the council is not defiance of law, but to endeavor to formulate a plan which will enable owners of property to obtain sufficient funds from the Federal or State Government to eliminate fire hazards to the end that several hundred thousand occupants of tenements will be given sanitary and safe housind at moderate rentals," Mr. Goldsmith said.

"This will inure to the benefit of the city by reducing the amount of delinquent taxes, which now amounts to over $250,000,000, and will create employment for many thousands of mechanics now unemployed in the building trades."

Commenting on the threatened walk-out of tenement-house owners, the Mayor said:

"We are ready—we will see what happens. We can invoke the tremendous health and police powers of the State in this matter and I am sure that the courts will sustain us. The city has the power in conflagrations to blow up buildings to prevent the spread of fire and, in case of disease, to quarantine a building.

"It can also condemn a building which is structurally weak. Most of the buildings are beyond repair, anyhow. Federal funds to replace them have been available for a long time from the Federal Government."

The Mayor's directions to Mr. Post in the event of a wholesale abandonment of dwellings follow:

"In the event of any organized movement on the part of owners of

Continued on Page Seven.

Fake Dollfuss Account Saved Socialists' Funds

Wireless to THE NEW YORK TIMES.

VIENNA, March 5.—In the efforts they have made since March, 1931, to remove part of their property out of the reach of the Fascists in the event of such a victory as the latter have just won, the Socialists appear to have been highly ingenious.

Finance Minister Buresch revealed with indignation tonight that one of the many accounts through which they removed trade union funds beyond Fascist reach stood in the name of "Dr. Dollfuss, Federal Chancellor." Dr. Buresch said 6,000,000 schillings escaped the victors' grasp.

He somewhat naively called on the Socialist leaders, who are in government prisons or in exile, to cause the immediate return of these funds to Austria.

PLANE RESCUES 12 STRANDED IN ARCTIC

Ten Women and Two Infants of Chelyuskin Group Flown to Siberian Mainland.

ICE LANDING HAZARDOUS

Runway Cleared for Aircraft by Marooned Party—Fishermen Saved in Caspian Sea.

Special Cable to THE NEW YORK TIMES.

MOSCOW, March 5.—Ten women and two children were rescued today from the camp of the marooned Chelyuskin survivors on the ice of the Arctic Ocean near the Bering Strait by Pilot Lapidevsky with Mechanic Petroff, flying the big plane ANT-9 from Cape Wellen and back.

Lapidevsky alighted on a 200-yard runway prepared on the ice three miles from the camp. The women made two miles of the journey from the camp in boats across open water and then they traveled over the ice hummocks.

Eight of the women were original passengers on the Chelyuskin, which sank Feb. 13. Another is the wife of the commander of Wrangel Island. She had been taken aboard the ship with her year-old baby. The tenth is the wife of the Wrangel Island radio operator and also had been taken aboard from the island. She gave birth to a child a few days before the vessel sank.

All are reported to be in good health, and the rest of the Chelyuskin group are vastly encouraged now that some of their number have been rescued.

Big Floe Is Landing Place.

By The Associated Press.

MOSCOW, March 5.—Pilot Lapidevsky and Mechanic Petroff, who flew from Cape Wellen to the camp of the 101 persons marooned on Arctic Ocean ice, landed under extreme difficulties. The flight was made in a temperature of 40 degrees below zero, and the fliers swooped down on a landing space which the marooned party had cleared on the cracking ice field. Descending on this space, the airmen found themselves surrounded by open water. The landing space had separated from the main ice.

Now that the ice has begun to crack, the government considers an early rescue imperative, regardless of weather and difficulties. Other planes, several ships, and a large

Continued on Page Eight.

Livermore, Plunger, Bankrupt Fourth Time; $2,259,212 Debts, $184,900 Assets Listed

Jesse L. Livermore, celebrated stock market plunger, is bankrupt for the fourth time in his spectacular career. He filed a petition in Federal court yesterday listing liabilities of $2,259,212.48 and assets of only $184,900, which includes the face value of insurance policies totaling $150,000.

Samuel P. Gilman, the trader's attorney, said that on each of the three previous occasions on which his client had failed he had ultimately paid 100 cents on the dollar to all his creditors. He expressed the belief that Mr. Livermore would "once more triumph over present difficulties."

His petition revealed that Mr. Livermore still owes $406,528 plus interest for his Federal income taxes for the years 1930 and 1931; and $154,675 plus interest for his New York State income taxes in the same year. The schedule also disclosed that on June 1, 1933, Mr. Livermore agreed to pay $150 a month for five years to Lucille Ballantine of the Montclair Hotel.

Another liability is a disputed claim for $250,000 demanded by Naida L. Krasnova of 68 West Fifty-eighth Street, plaintiff against the stock operator in a breach of promise suit. The Harriman National Bank and Trust Company is listed as last holder of a note for $142,525 given to Joseph W. Harriman, former president of that institution, who has been indicted for misapplication of the bank's funds. The note fell due on Feb. 15.

Livermore owes $125,000 to Harriman & Co. of 111 Broadway under a guarantee of a debit balance of Dorothea F. Livermore, his second wife, from whom he was divorced in 1932. The balance was secured by a deed to property in Great Neck, L. I. He also owes, according to the petition, $100,000 to his present wife, the former Harriet Metz Noble of Omaha, whom he married last March. It is secured by an assignment of interest in annuity policies.

His known assets, it was said, consist of a seat on the Chicago Board of Trade valued at $7,000; a seat on the Commodity Exchange, Inc., valued at $3,500; $20,000 worth of jewelry pledged as security for loans, and other assets, the value of which he was unable to state.

After recovering from bankruptcy in 1915, when his debts were reputed to have totaled $2,000,000, Livermore established a $1,000,000 trust fund which was so ironclad that he never could touch its principal.

SUSTAINS STATE MILK ACT

Court Division of 5 to 4 Is Same as on Previous Emergency Ruling.

PUBLIC GOOD PARAMOUNT

Opinion, Written by Roberts, Finds Price-Fixing Illegal 'Only if Discriminatory.'

SHARP DISSENT IS VOICED

Wisdom of Legislation Is Attacked by McReynolds, Van Devanter, Sutherland, Butler.

Text of majority and minority opinions on milk prices, Page 18.

Special to THE NEW YORK TIMES.

WASHINGTON, March 5.—In an opinion which is regarded as of great significance in relation to the emergency powers of the New Deal, the Supreme Court by a 5-to-4 decision upheld today New York State's right to fix milk prices.

The decision of the court was identical with that in the Minnesota moratorium case, which also sustained emergency legislation.

Justice Roberts, who wrote the majority opinion, was joined by Chief Justice Hughes and Justices Brandeis, Stone and Cardozo.

The dissent, written by Justice McReynolds, was concurred in by Justices Van Devanter, Sutherland and Butler.

For months the government and the public have been awaiting the decision, which was given less than an hour after President Roosevelt's voice went out over the air to millions of Americans in support of the New Deal.

Adherents of the Presidential recovery program hailed the opinion enthusiastically and declared that it exceeded the moratorium opinion in its importance. It proved, they asserted, that the high court was sympathetic with the New Deal, even though by a narrow margin.

"Due Process" Clause Clarified.

Jerome Frank, general counsel of the Agricultural Adjustment Administration, after remarking that the decision removed all doubt "from the point of view of the due process clause, as to our power to fix milk prices," said:

"This opinion clarifies the true meaning of 'due process.' The Supreme Court lays down, once and for all, that a legislative body may, when economic conditions warrant it, regulate any business, and that the only test is whether the public need outweighs the private interests involved in that business, provided only that the regulation be not unreasonable or discriminatory."

Seldom has such a sharp clash of ideas and arguments occurred among the nine justices of the Supreme Court. Justice Roberts's opinion insisted that government could not exist if the citizen might at will use his property to the detriment of his fellows, but Justice McReynolds held that legislative power to fix prices in an emergency meant ultimate "anarchy and despotism."

Case Involved Fine of $5.

This vital decision arose from a case involving a $5 fine, the facts being, said John J. Bennett Jr., New York Attorney General, "trivial and even frivolous." Leo Nebbia, a small Rochester grocer, had sold Jedo Del Signore, on April 19, 1933, two quarts of milk and a loaf of bread for 18 cents, when the New York Milk Control Board had fixed the minimum price of milk at 9 cents a quart—without any bread.

Nebbia thus violated a law which, Mr. Bennett said, the New York State Legislature had enacted "in the supposed interest of the dairy business and public welfare generally." The $5 fine was imposed by the Rochester City Court and subsequently upheld by the Monroe County Court and the New York Court of Appeals, which the Supreme Court sustained today.

Nebbia, puzzled, had said:

"I sell a bottle of milk at what the law says; at that price I make a good profit—so good that to my best customers, my friends and

Continued on Page Nineteen.

Points Made by President

By The Associated Press.

WASHINGTON, March 5.—Striking statements by President Roosevelt today in his address to NRA Code Authorities were:

It is the immediate task of industry to re-employ more people at purchasing wages and to do it now.

With millions still unemployed, the power of our people to purchase and use the products of industry is still greatly curtailed. It can be increased and sustained only by striving for the lowest schedule of prices on which higher wages and increasing employment can be obtained.

We must consider immediate cooperation to secure increase in wages and shortening of hours.

The government cannot forever continue to absorb the whole burden of unemployment.

The National Recovery Act was drawn with the greatest good of the greatest number in mind.

We have arrived at the time for taking stock for correcting manifest [code] errors, for rooting out demonstrated evils.

The reorganization must be permanent for all the rest of our lives in that never again will we permit the social conditions which allowed vast sections of our population to exist in an un-American way, which allowed a maldistribution of wealth and of power.

The essential provisions of the codes should check or reverse the competitive methods by which the small business man was or is being squeezed out.

Anti-trust laws must continue in their purpose of retaining competition and preventing monopoly; it is only where these laws have prevented the cooperation to eliminate things like child labor and sweat-shops, starvation wages and other unfair practices that there is justification in modifying them.

WALLACE OUTLINES 4 PLANS FOR NATION

Real Inflation or a Return to 1932 Status Is Due Unless We Choose, He Says.

HE FAVORS DUAL COURSE

Raise Imports by Tariff Cut and Reduce Acreage, He Tells National Policy Group.

A warning that "warring class interests" may drive the United States to "genuinely uncontrolled inflation" unless the nation chooses a definite course and sticks to it was sounded here yesterday by Henry A. Wallace, Secretary of Agriculture, in a symposium on national destiny at the Bar Association.

Mr. Wallace, who wrote the pamphlet "America Must Choose," appeared at the first hearing of the Commission of Inquiry on National Policy in International Economic Relations. The commission is financed by the Rockefeller Foundation and was appointed by the Social Science Research Council. President Roosevelt has approved it.

Robert M. Hutchins, president of the University of Chicago, presided at the hearing as chairman of the commission. After hearings throughout the country during the Summer, the commission is to make a report on the trends and indicated economic policy of the United States.

In addition to Mr. Wallace, the commission heard the views of Lionel D. Edie, chairman of Edie-Davidson, Inc., and Dr. Benjamin M. Anderson Jr., economic adviser to the Chase National Bank on the tariff and foreign trade. The hearing will be resumed this morning at 10 o'clock.

Wallace Outlines Four Courses.

Mr. Wallace outlined four possible courses for the United States, with a return to conditions of 1932 as the only alternative. These were: Complete isolation, "an international approach to the problem," a combination of nationalism and internationalism, or a "return to the simple life" through taxing modern machinery out of existence—a solution which he said he regarded as a "manifestation of infantilism."

While he said he favored the lowering of trade barriers to stimulate the interchange of farm products and manufactured articles between this and other nations, Mr. Wallace conceded that the United States could make itself self-sustaining, even producing its own rubber, coffee, tea and silk, and at the same time "maintaining a very high standard of living."

In reply to a question, he asserted, however, that he believed the standard of living would be much higher if we adopted an internationalist approach to our problems. He believed the country would be forced to resort to some phases of both theories of national

Continued on Page Three.

HINTS AT SHELVING OF EXCHANGE CURB

Senator Robinson Asserts There Is No Assurance of Passage at Present Session.

AIR STOCK SALES LISTED

Morgans Disposed of 4,500 Shares—Many Went Short Before Mail Cancellation.

Special to THE NEW YORK TIMES.

WASHINGTON, March 5.—While the Senate Banking and Currency Committee was studying today a list of all trading in aviation stocks, short and long, for the two weeks preceding cancellation of air-mail contracts, Senator Robinson, Democratic leader of the Senate, expressed doubt that Congress at its present session would authorize Federal regulation of security exchanges.

In the course of a speech on the Senate floor reviewing the first year of the Roosevelt administration, the Democratic leader said:

"As to whether the Stock Exchange Regulation Bill may be ready for disposition during this session of Congress, no assurance at this time can be given. Pendency of the measure has two important effects. First, it arouses those who control exchanges to act to set their house in order. It is the neglect of this duty and obligation by those who operate the exchanges that has created the necessity and demand for this legislation.

"In the second place, the fact that the subject is being carefully studied by committees of Congress will deter those racketeers who have prospered by plundering the uninformed and unsuspecting investors. The spotlight will shine on their malignant practices and motives."

Senator Robinson, in further comment after the day's session, said the bill must be ready for action well in advance of May 15 if it was to be acted on, since May 15 would be the date for final adjournment of Congress.

Fletcher Does Not Agree.

On the other hand, Senator Fletcher, one of the authors of the bill and its principal proponent in the Senate, insisted that the bill would be called up and passed. He admitted that amendatory action might be taken in the committee and said that the objections and criticisms of the New York Stock Exchange and other opponents of the legislation would receive careful consideration.

J. P. Morgan & Co. sold long 4,500 shares of United Aircraft just before the airmail contracts were canceled, according to a complete list of all trading in aviation stocks for the two weeks preceding the cancellation, handed today by Richard Whitney, president of the New York Stock Exchange, to Senator

Continued on Page Ten.

NRA 'THE AMERICAN WAY'

Program Not Communist or Fascist, Roosevelt Tells Code Leaders.

A CHALLENGE TO INDUSTRY

More People Must Be Employed at Purchasing Wages at Once, He Declares.

JOHNSON ASKS HOURS CUT

10 Per Cent Reduction, Offset by 10% Pay Rise, Outlined by Administrator.

Text of President's address at the conference on codes, Page 2.

Special to THE NEW YORK TIMES.

WASHINGTON, March 5.—President Roosevelt today told a large audience of business and industrial leaders that the recovery program as represented by the NRA and other government agencies was here to stay; that the reorganization of a "disintegrating system of production and exchange" undertaken last Spring must be "permanent for all the rest of our lives."

"Never again," said the President, speaking directly to the leaders gathered here for the NRA Code Authority conference, "will we permit the social conditions which permitted the vast sections of our population to exist in an un-American way, which permitted a maldistribution of wealth and of power."

This direct challenge and promise came at the close of an address in which Mr. Roosevelt, at the beginning of his second year in office, emphatically justified the processes of the New Deal and the formulation of codes of fair competition under the NRA as democratic procedure in the "American way," committing the nation neither to communism nor to fascism.

Says Industry Will Aid.

With this sentiment as the keynote of his address this morning before 4,000 members of nearly 600 code authorities gathered in Constitution Hall, the President challenged industry to what he considered its immediate task, "to re-employ more people at purchasing wages and to do it now," and pleaded for a better "balance in our economic system."

In calling for the employment of more workers and for wage increases so that purchasing power may be expanded further, the President said that the great bulk of industry would act. As for the reluctant portion, he called on the public to make it "play the game" by refusing to patronize nonconformers. The progress of the New Deal demands, he declared, that business temporarily put "humanity first and profits afterward."

To Make Democracy Function.

The NRA, the President maintained, has given industry a protected form of self-government.

"I am always a little amused and perhaps at times a little saddened," he said, "and I think the American people feel the same way—by those few writers and speakers who proclaim tearfully either that we are now committed to communism and collectivism or that we have adopted fascism and a dictatorship.

"The real truth of the matter is that for a number of years in our country the machinery of democracy had failed to function."

The nation's leaders in industry, labor and agriculture heard the President's dramatic portrayal of the near collapse of the country on the eve of his inaguration and his description of the "crazy decade" of 1919-29. On the platform were members of the Cabinet, leaders of the House and Senate, government officials and, headed by Recovery Administrator Hugh S. Johnson, the leading figures of the recovery administration.

In the blue-draped boxes surmounted by the seals of the forty-eight States, sat the Ambassadors and Ministers of foreign nations, with their wives and families, while more than 2,500 men and women gathered in two halls at overflow meetings to which the President's words were carried by amplifiers. The nation listened in on a national radio-hookup. The scarlet tunics of

Continued on Page Two.

Minneapolis police clash with striking truckdrivers during their July strike which crippled the city.

Police battle with strikers during the general strike in July which paralyzed San Francisco life.

This scene typifies the violence of the taxi strike in New York City. Here a taxi is hauled out of the East River with the dead driver still at the wheel.

Strikers force an independent cab driver off the streets during the taxi strike in March.

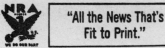

NRA — WE DO OUR PART

"All the News That's Fit to Print."

The New York Times.

LATE CITY EDITION
WEATHER—Cloudy today; snow or rain tonight and tomorrow.
Temperatures Yesterday—Max., 46; min., 27.

VOL. LXXXIII....No. 27,820. Entered as Second-Class Matter, Postoffice, New York, N. Y. NEW YORK, MONDAY, MARCH 26, 1934. P TWO CENTS in New York City. | THREE CENTS Within 200 Miles | FOUR CENTS Elsewhere Except in 7th and 8th Postal Zones

VIOLENCE RENEWED BY TAXI STRIKERS WHO REJECT POLL

MANY DRIVERS ARE BEATEN

Cabs Wrecked and Riders Menaced as Bands Hurl Stones.

POLICE MASS IN MIDTOWN

Strikers Resort to Guerrilla Tactics to Evade Open Clashes With Them.

MAYOR SUMMONS LEADERS

Will Demand Explanation of Their Repudiation of Peace Plan They Had Ratified.

Resuming the violence of last week after a lull of three days, taxicab strikers last night again invaded the Times Square and midtown sections of the city, assaulted cab drivers, wrecked a dozen cabs and shouted defiance of the police. Sporadic acts of violence occurred also in other sections of the city.

The violence was resumed after a meeting of 7,000 strikers, members of the Taxicab Drivers Union, in St. Nicholas Arena, Columbus Avenue and Sixty-sixth Street, late in the afternoon, had rejected the peace program worked out Saturday at the City Hall in conferences with representatives of the union and the large fleet operators.

This program, calling for a plebiscite of the 12,000 drivers employed by the Parmelee, Terminal and Radio cab companies, against whom the strike is principally directed, was rejected by the strikers on recommendation of the same leaders who on Saturday had agreed to accept it in their conferences with Mayor LaGuardia, Aldermanic President Deutsch and Ben Golden, executive secretary of the Regional Labor Board. The strikers demanded an immediate vote of all the 40,000 drivers in the city.

Leaders Called to City Hall.

When told of the action of the strike meeting Mr. Golden immediately communicated with the Mayor and announced that the strike leaders would be summoned to City Hall at 9:30 A. M. today to explain their conduct. Mayor LaGuardia was reported as incensed at the action of the strikers and the behavior of the strike leaders, who now have placed themselves in the position of violating their pledge to the Mayor.

Although warned by Deputy Chief Inspector David J. McAuliffe, who attended yesterday's strike meeting, that no parades of strikers would be permitted and that the police were prepared to suppress all violence, groups of strikers in numbers of seventy-five and more came down Broadway and Eighth Avenue and, mingling with the theatre crowds on the sidewalks, made frequent sorties into the street to carry out their attacks.

Showing more of the fighting spirit which marked their actions last Wednesday night, when they invaded Broadway, the strikers were ready last night to do battle with the police.

"Let's give it to the cops" and "Chase the rats" were cries raised as the groups attempted to stand their ground after changing their method of attack from mass formation to group sorties.

Police Concentrate Forces.

The police were ready for them, however. Their forces, including detectives, uniformed men, emergency squads, radio cars and motorcycles with side cars carrying riot guns, were assembled in Times Square and adjacent areas to the north and south. Nearly 400 detectives, or about one-fourth of the entire detective force, were on strike duty. It was this concentration which prevented the guerrilla warfare from developing into a general battle. Four arrests were made. Seven other alleged rioters were arrested later in the Bronx.

Although the police appeared to be well in control of the situation, the atmosphere in the streets affected was electric.

The large Sunday crowds, among which the striker groups sought to lose themselves before and after they made their attacks, witnessed the repeated spectacles of violence. With the assistance of mounted men, the detectives and police managed finally to restore order.

A bullet was reported fired at a taxicab containing two passengers at Broadway and Fifty-fifth Street,

Continued on Page Four.

President Plans to Start On Fishing Trip Tuesday

Special to THE NEW YORK TIMES.

WASHINGTON, March 25.—President Roosevelt's fishing trip in Florida waters scheduled for this week became a virtual certainty tonight with settlement of the threatened automobile strike.

He plans to leave Tuesday for Jacksonville to board the Nourmahal, Vincent Astor's yacht, for a week's fishing, principally off Miami. Miami will be "White House headquarters."

SOLID VOTE IN ITALY CAST FOR FASCISTI

90 Per Cent of Those Eligible Go to Polls to Pass Upon 400 Party Candidates.

MUSSOLINI IS CHEERED

Settlers of Redeemed Pontine Marshes, Though Unable to Ballot, Endorse Regime.

By ARNALDO CORTESI.
Wireless to THE NEW YORK TIMES.

ROME, March 25.—The election for the approval of a list of 400 candidates for Parliament prepared by the Fascist Grand Council was held today and gave the result that had been universally expected.

The final official figures will not be known until tomorrow, but from information available at the time of writing it may be said that about 90 per cent of the registered voters went to the polls, a proportion about equal to or slightly greater than that in the last general election in 1929. The vote was almost solidly Fascist, the number of negative votes being insignificant.

No incidents worthy of note were reported. The result, indeed, was such a foregone conclusion that there was little excitement. In some rural districts voters marched to the polls in military formation with bands playing. Some smaller centres are able to report proudly a 100 per cent Fascist vote.

Torchlight Parades Held.

In the larger cities large crowds cheered when the results of the elections were posted in the principal squares. Torchlight parades passed through the main thoroughfares in Rome and other cities in the evening, while the streets were artistically illuminated and flags appeared at almost all windows. Apart from these manifestations the day was much like any other Sunday.

Among the first to register his vote in Rome was Premier Mussolini. He appeared in the early morning in his motor car at the central electoral station, which at that time was still almost deserted. He wore a black shirt and replied with the Fascist salute to the greetings of the Prefect of Rome, the Secretary General of the Fascist party and the Rome Provincial Sec-

Continued on Page Eleven.

EXTREMISTS FIGHT IN 2 FRENCH CITIES; MORE RIOTS FEARED

Fifty Are Injured at Toulon—800 Leftists Raid Meeting of Nationalists in Tours.

SHOTS ARE FIRED IN FIGHT

Veterans Vote to Back Premier in Efforts to Avert Civil War and Threat of Invasion.

Wireless to THE NEW YORK TIMES.

PARIS, March 25.—Right and Left forces fought in the streets of Toulon and Tours tonight at the end of political meetings. Strong forces of police restored order.

At Tours 800 Left supporters broke up a Nationalist meeting and fought the police for three hours. Paving stones were used as missiles and several shots were fired.

At Toulon, following a meeting addressed by Jean Ybarnegaray, a Nationalist Deputy, there was a similar Left demonstration. The local police had to send for reinforcements, so 250 Mobile Guards from Marseilles rushed there to help restore order. There was considerable fighting and many demonstrators and policemen were injured. Three naval officers also were hurt. Traffic was held up in the centre of the city for several hours.

At Sete, where Colonel de la Rocque, president of the Croix de Feu, addressed a meeting of his followers, Communists had announced their intention to make trouble, but failed to carry out their threat.

The hunt for illegal arms brought three arrests in the Paris Flea Market, where junk of all kinds is sold Sunday mornings. Two schoolboys were seized after having purchased four revolvers and 200 cartridges. They were later sent home. A man who was arrested for purchasing a revolver said he bought it to commit suicide because his wife had been unfaithful.

Premier's Plea Ignored.

By The Associated Press.

PARIS, March 25.—Political extremists, ignoring the plea of Premier Gaston Doumergue to guard against civil war, battled each other today in provincial France. Fifty persons were injured in a clash at Toulon between Nationalists and Socialists outside a meeting hall. A score of others received bruises in street fights between Rightist and Leftist groups at Tours.

Precautions were being taken at Tours to prevent further violence tomorrow night at a demonstration called by the Anti-Fascist Front in protest against a manifestation of Solidaritie Française, a Rightist organization formed by François Coty, perfume manufacturer.

Premier Doumergue, who in a national broadcast told France yesterday that foreign invasion was to be feared as a result of threatening internal unrest, obtained today the support of 3,000,000 war veterans pledged to "save France from civil war and the risk of foreign invasion."

The council of the Veterans' National Federation unanimously voted to launch a campaign to reform French politics, which a delegation immediately carried to M. Doumergue. Terms of the program will be drafted by a committee later, but it is expected to propose dissolution

Continued on Page Eight.

Throngs Bask in Tardy Spring Sunshine; Fifth Av. Gets Preview of Easter Styles

A bright, warm sun in an azure sky proclaimed the arrival of Spring weather yesterday.

City apartments and suburban homes were left empty as men and women went out into the sun for a dress rehearsal of Easter. The bright reds, blues and greens of the women's new costumes provided relief from the vanishing grayness of Winter and hinted at the trend of the Spring styles.

The parks, boardwalks and beaches in and near the city were thronged with the first large crowds this year, and highways leading from the city were jammed with traffic. Many persons who remained in town strolled leisurely on Fifth Avenue, as though preparing for next Sunday's Easter parade.

Despite the bright sun and clear sky, the average temperature was several degrees below normal. However, warming breezes from the south brought a promise of real Spring. The highest temperature was reached at 4:30 P. M., when it was 48 degrees. A low of 27 was set at 5:15 A. M., establishing a mean temperature of 36.

Burton Salisbury, night forecaster of the Weather Bureau, said cloudy weather was expected today, with a possibility of light snow flurries late this afternoon. Although it was impossible to look as far ahead as next Sunday, he said general indications pointed to fair weather for the latter part of the week.

Shortly after noon the walks of Central Park were dotted with pedestrians out for their first Spring Sunday stroll. Overcoats were thrown open and in some instances discarded as the warmth of the sun increased. Men and boys gathered on the park athletic fields to watch baseball practice. Nursemaids and mothers pushed baby carriages. Amateur naturalists ventured into the park groves to study the reaction of nature to Spring. On the bridle paths there was a veritable procession of riders.

The main highways leading to the beaches were thick with traffic. Ocean Parkway, through Brooklyn, carried a stream of automobiles toward Coney Island, and similar lines of traffic moved to the Rockaways, Long Beach, Jones Beach and other resorts.

De Valera Is Accused Of Aiming to Be Dictator

By The Associated Press.

DUBLIN, March 25.—President Eamon de Valera, who charges his Blue Shirt opponents are attempting to establish a dictatorship, was accused by General Owen O'Duffy, leader of the United Ireland party, of seeking to be dictator.

Speaking at Ennis today, General O'Duffy said:

"Let there be no mistake in the minds of the people that President de Valera is heading for a dictatorship. With the Senate removed, the independence of the judiciary can be attacked."

By Canadian Press.

DUBLIN, March 25.—Conspirators tonight removed rail joints from the track over which General Owen O'Duffy traveled to Ennis, but his train passed over the route without accident.

AUSTRIA PROJECTS AUTOCRATIC STATE

New Constitution to Put Full Power in Ruler—Laws to 'Emanate From God.'

FIVE COUNCILS WILL ACT

Plebiscites to Be Held at the Discretion of Government—Plan Effective in Week.

By G. E. R. GEDYE.
Wireless to THE NEW YORK TIMES.

VIENNA, March 25.—The details of the new Austrian Constitution, which is to come into force by Easter, were published today and they indicated the new Austria would become the most autocratic State in Europe.

Anything that could recall the democratic era is to be done away with, and those safeguards that are to be erected are against any possibility of the voice of the people being heard, so that the democratic form of government will be impossible as long as the projected Constitution stands. The new Austria is to be an anti-democratic, Clerical-Fascist State.

New Concordat With Vatican.

Instead of the first article of the present Constitution, which declares that Austria is a democratic republic and that its laws emanate from the people, the first article of the new Constitution says Austria is a Federal State and that its laws "emanate from God the Almighty." The Roman Catholic Church will be made a privileged, established church. A new concordat with the Vatican will govern the religious and educational paragraphs of the Constitution.

All educational institutions will be placed under direct control of the government. As previously indicated, there will be no freedom of the press, the stage, the movies or the radio.

Five chambers will be set up. The Council of State will be composed of forty to fifty members, all nominated by the head of the State, who is at present the President of the defunct republic but tomorrow may be a Hapsburg monarch. The Council of Culture will consist chiefly of priests and representatives of the Catholic Church.

The Economic Council will be composed of representatives of industrialists, bankers, members of the learned professions and government servants. The Council of the Provinces will consist of nominated Governors of the provinces and their financial experts.

Meetings to Be Closed to Public.

All these bodies will sit in secret, so that if any of their members should venture to criticize any matters of government such criticism cannot become known.

Only the government may initiate legislation, and these advisory bodies will be expected to present commentary upon any measures submitted to them. The commentary may be required to be delivered within a specified period.

The fifth body, called the Federal Chamber, will be composed of delegates from the first four. Its only powers will be to accept or reject measures submitted to it. No interpellations, criticisms or amendments will be allowed. Its sittings will, therefore, be public.

What will happen if that body ventures to reject any government measures seems not to have been decided, or, at any rate, it is not desired to make it public yet. It is announced that the general right of plebiscite will be withdrawn. Plebiscites will be held only when the government desires them.

None of the new bodies will have the least power over the new government. The government will be appointed or dismissed only by the ruler of the State, who is today President Miklas, who swore loyalty to the republic's Constitution. The ruler will receive wide powers of legislating by decree, which go so far that he will have the right

Continued on Page Nine.

NAZIS PUT INDUSTRY ON WARTIME BASIS IN FINANCIAL CRISIS

Import Curbs Show Strain the Hitler Program Inflicts on Country's Reserves.

LIVING STANDARD MENACED

Experts Wonder Whether Mark Can Be Held Stable—But Budget Is Increased.

By FREDERICK T. BIRCHALL.
Wireless to THE NEW YORK TIMES.

BERLIN, March 25.—The economic decrees issued in the last few days embargoing or restricting purchases of foreign raw materials show plainly that Germany is going on a wartime basis for industry to meet a crisis as serious as any that the war brought upon her.

The object of the decrees seems to be threefold: To warn the world to buy more German manufactured goods and reduce or at least postpone payments on German debts; to fortify the Reichsbank's gold reserves, and to give the government a tighter grip upon home industry.

The recent speech of Dr. Hjalmar Schacht, president of the Reichsbank, was a prelude to this new and sensational development. It means a Nazi determination to carry through the labor placement program at all costs, even that of forcing down the standard of living of the German people, which, in the lower classes especially, is already low. The slogan of "Work and Bread" is to mean exactly that—plenty of work, especially for the government; pittance wages, and the plainest fare including domestic substitutes for some important necessaries.

Coffee May Be Rationed.

It is said coffee is soon to be among the rationed imports. If that means, as seems probable, that coffee is to be adulterated to maintain the national supply it will be a real hardship. The acorn coffee of wartime still is remembered unpleasantly by the mature.

In other words Germany is stripping to the belt to meet the emergency. The nation has to face an unemployment situation still more serious than that of any nation except perhaps the United States. It wants to be rid of its foreign debts so as to be strong to meet what the future may bring.

Germany is in a better situation to do this than she was even under war conditions. Although this régime has been in office only a year it has already coordinated and regimented industry to a degree unachieved under the empire, when industry was still independent and patriotism and good-will had to be depended upon for the whole-hearted enforcement of government measures. The Nazis now have industry—employers and employed—virtually at their mercy.

Strain on Financial Reserves.

These drastic measures, however, clearly illustrate the strain that the Nazi program and Nazi policies are putting on Germany's financial reserves. In part the strain is counteracted by the reduction in Germany's foreign debt. The same measures and policies compel Germany's creditors to finance that program, in part at least, with the money due them.

Nevertheless, the tightened control of foreign exchange, the slashing of exchange allotments for for-

Continued on Page Nine.

RFC Cuts Interest Rate to 4 Per Cent; Action to Release Capital for Recovery

Special to THE NEW YORK TIMES

WASHINGTON, March 25.—The Reconstruction Finance Corporation will reduce its dividend and interest rates on preferred stock and capital notes in banks and in insurance companies to 4 per cent for five years beginning April 1, Jesse H. Jones, chairman, announced today. After that period the rate will be raised to 5 per cent, Mr. Jones said. The new rate will also apply to loans for self-liquidating projects.

The 4 per cent rate also applies to preferred stock and capital notes which may be retired within three years.

Mr. Jones said that this action was taken to remove the incentive to quick payments by the banks, and thus release capital for the recovery program.

"In keeping with the President's views as to lower interest rates and with his approval," Mr. Jones said, "the RFC will reduce the dividend and interest rates on preferred stock and capital notes in banks and insurance companies to 4 per cent for five years from April 1, 1934. The rate after five years will be 5 per cent. At present a 4 per cent rate applies for three years to such preferred stock and capital notes as may be retired within that period.

"Believing that this added capital will serve a better purpose and be more helpful in the recovery program if employed by the banks without too great an incentive to repay within so short a period and the government being now able to borrow at such low rates, these dividend and interest rates are definitely fixed at 4 per cent for five years.

"Adjustments may be effected by the banks refunding their present capital notes with notes drawing the new rate, or in interest settlements. In the case of preferred stock, banks and insurance companies may, if they prefer to do so, amend their charters so as to conform to the new rates, or agreements may be entered into between the corporation and the issuing bank or insurance company, covering the reduction.

"The corporation will also give self-liquidating borrowers, the equivalent of a 4 per cent interest rate for five years from April 1, 1934, upon conditions to be approved by it, provided it owns the securities during that period. While the securities carry a greater rate than 4 per cent, adjustments will be made on a basis of 4 per cent net to the corporation."

ROOSEVELT AVERTS STRIKE; AUTO WORKERS AND MAKERS HAIL WAGE BARGAINING PLAN

White House Statement

Special to THE NEW YORK TIMES.

WASHINGTON, D. C., March 25.—The White House statement on the settlement of the threatened automobile strike follows:

After many days of conferring in regard to the principles of employment in the automobile industry the following statement covers the fundamentals:

1. Reduced to plain language Section 7a of NIRA means:

(a) Employes have the right to organize into a group or groups;

(b) When such group or groups are organized they can choose representatives by free choice and such representatives must be received collectively and thereby seek to straighten out disputes and improve conditions of employment;

(c) Discrimination against employes because of their labor affiliations or for any other unfair or unjust reason is barred.

A settlement and statement of procedure and principles is appended hereto.

It has been offered by me to and has been accepted by the representatives of the employes and the employers. It lives up to the principles of collective bargaining. I hope and believe that it opens up a chance for a square deal and fair treatment. It gives promise of sound industrial relations. It provides further for a board of three of which the chairman will as a neutral represent the government.

In actual practice details and machinery will of course have to be worked out on the basis of common sense and justice; but the big point is that this broad purpose can develop with a tribunal which can handle practically every problem in an equitable way.

Settlement of the threatened automobile strike is based on the following principles:

1. The employers agree to bargain collectively with the freely chosen representatives of groups and not to discriminate in any way against any employe on the ground of his union labor affiliations.

2. If there be more than one group each bargaining committee shall have total membership pro rata to the number of men each member represents.

3. NRA to set up within twenty-four hours a board, responsible to the President of the United States, to sit in Detroit to pass on all questions of representation, discharge and discrimination. Decision of the board shall be final and binding on employer and employes. Such a board to have access to all payrolls and to all

Continued on Page Two.

COMPROMISE IS REACHED

Workers May Organize—Impartial Board Will Settle Grievances.

MACAULEY IS PLEASED

Terms Reached in Long Dispute Held in Accord With Chamber Principles.

GREEN SEES A 'NEW DEAL'

'Great Step Forward' for Labor—He Says President's Hand 'Led All the Way.'

By LOUIS STARK.
Special to THE NEW YORK TIMES.

WASHINGTON, March 25.—An automobile strike scheduled for tomorrow morning in Detroit, Flint, Pontiac, St. Louis and Cleveland was averted today by President Roosevelt.

The President in announcing the settlement declared that it provided "a framework for a new structure of industrial relations."

The terms guarantee the right of collective bargaining, state that employes have the right to organize into a group or groups, and provide an impartial board to be set up by the NRA within twenty-four hours to settle cases of alleged discrimination. The board would consist of one employer, one labor representative and an impartial chairman.

General Johnson is considering his son, Lieutenant J. Kilborne Johnson, for the impartial member.

Union Men Ratify Terms.

Late this evening the union delegates ratified the agreement. At that time they were advised by telephone from Flint that the automobile union in that city, in the absence of a message from Washington, had issued a strike call for tomorrow. Assurance was given that the strike order would be canceled.

Within five days of his first conference with automotive leaders the President brought peace into an industry which was on the verge of an industrial war that might have imperiled the entire recovery program.

Only a few persons in the confidence of the White House were aware of the crucial situation which menaced the nation due to the bitter dissension within the automobile industry. Had the strike begun it was regarded as likely that it would spread to scores of accessories plants and to the steel industry.

It would have affected the railroads, lumber, glass and textile industries particularly, for these furnish a large part of the automobile industry with raw materials.

Pleased by the Results.

Both sides expressed gratification at the outcome. They united in praising the President and General Johnson for their handling of the situation.

Alvan Macauley, chairman of the board of the National Automobile Chamber of Commerce, said:

"We are very grateful to the President and to General Johnson that they have been able to find a settlement in accord with the principles in which we believe."

William Green, president of the American Federation of Labor, said:

"Let us hope this means continued peace, the establishment of a better relationship between employers and employes and the recognition on the part of the automobile manufacturers that the old order is passing and a New Deal which provides for the proper recognition of the rights of labor is here and fully recognized."

Sees "Great Step Forward."

Mr. Green regarded the settlement as "a great step forward for the automobile workers."

"For the first time in the history of the automobile industry the right to organize has been conceded, and collective bargaining is assured through representatives chosen by the employes."

He said that the method of comparing union rolls and payrolls was selected as means of determining representatives for collective bar-

Continued on Page Two.

ROMANOFF SWORD STOLEN ON PARK AV.

Art Gallery Window Smashed by Thief Who Leaves Other Czarist Items Untouched.

SENTIMENT HELD MOTIVE

Blade, With a Jeweled Gold Hilt, Was Regiment's Gift to Grand Duke Vladimir.

A discriminating thief shattered a display window of the Hammer Galleries at Park Avenue and Fiftieth Street before daybreak yesterday and got away with the gold-hilted, jewel-crusted sword of the late Grand Duke Vladimir, uncle of the last Czar of Russia.

Other valuable items, all associated with the last of the royal Russian families, were within reach of the thief, but he left them. The plain black leather scabbard of the Grand Duke's sword, which lay at the base of the display stand, was untouched.

Miss Alva Lowrey of the Hammer Galleries, an expert on the Russian Imperial treasures, said she was inclined to believe the thief might have been some Russian refugee of noble birth who, for some sentimental reason, wanted the sword and

Continued on Page Three.

GIANT 'EYE' MOLDED IN CORNING FACTORY

Four Thousand Watch Glass Pouring for Reflector of Greatest Telescope.

35 MEN LABOR TEN HOURS

Job Is Held Successful Despite Mishaps—3 More Years' Work Remains.

By JAMES STOKLEY,
Associate Director of the Franklin Institute Museum.
Special to THE NEW YORK TIMES.

CORNING, N. Y., March 25.—Twenty tons of molten white hot borosilicate glass, at a temperature of 2,400 degrees Fahrenheit, resting here tonight under a fire brick "beehive," seventeen feet in diameter, will some day form the world's largest telescope mirror.

If all goes well, it will be in operation a few years from now in the 200-inch reflecting telescope of the Department of Astrophysics of the California Institute of Technology.

Twice the diameter of the Mount Wilson observatory's telescope, now the world's largest, the new instrument is expected to have about ten times the light-gathering power.

A group of distinguished scientists saw the glass, about the consistency of taffy, being taken from the furnace at the Corning Glass Works. Into one end was fed the raw material, while the molten glass was taken from the other in huge ladles, each with a capacity of a fifth of a ton, manned by half a dozen workmen.

Three ladles were used, each from its own door of the furnace, and by overhead trolleys they were carried thirty feet to the beehive covering the mold. This also had three doors, and the glass was poured through each one successively in order that the bottom might be uniformly covered.

Mishaps in Pouring.

During the pouring a series of mishaps occurred, but Dr. John C. Hostetter, director of research of the glass works, did not believe they would harm the mirror, and he considered that the work, which was completed at 7:30 P. M., had been successful.

The bottom of the mold is covered with a number of hemispherical cores so that it looked, before the pouring, like a miniature Eskimo village. The purpose of these cores is to produce a series of cylindrical holes in the back surface of the mirror. This will lighten the mass considerably, and also it is planned to support the mirror by the ridges between the holes.

After about half of the glass had been poured several of these cores worked loose from the bottom and could be seen floating on the sur-

Continued on Page Three.

"All the News That's Fit to Print."

The New York Times.

LATE CITY EDITION
WEATHER—Fair and warmer today; fair tomorrow.
Temperatures Yesterday—Max., 74; min., 56.

VOL. LXXXIII....No. 27,876. Entered as Second-Class Matter, Postoffice, New York, N. Y. NEW YORK, MONDAY, MAY 21, 1934. P TWO CENTS In New York City. | THREE CENTS Within 200 Miles | FOUR CENTS Elsewhere Except in 7th and 8th Postal Zones

DARROW BOARD FINDS NRA TENDS TOWARD MONOPOLY; JOHNSON CONDEMNS REPORT

ROOSEVELT EXTOLS LAFAYETTE'S DEEDS BEFORE CONGRESS

'We Cherish His Memory Above That of Any Foreigner,' Declares President.

PACKED GALLERIES LISTEN

Cabinet, Supreme Court and Diplomatic Corps Take Part in Centenary Exercises.

GREETINGS FROM LEBRUN

Laboulaye Conveys Gratitude of France—Pershing Lays Wreath at Marquis's Statue.

Text of President Roosevelt's address, Page 4.

Special to THE NEW YORK TIMES.

WASHINGTON, May 20.—At a special joint session of Congress today, held to observe the centenary of the Marquis de Lafayette's death, President Roosevelt paid tribute to the French nobleman whose memory, the President said, "we cherish above that of any citizen of a foreign country."

Virtually every chief of a diplomatic mission here, justices of the Supreme Court and Cabinet members joined the Senate and the House of Representatives in the exercises in the Capitol, while packed galleries witnessed the scene.

André de Laboulaye, the French Ambassador, conveyed to the gathering a message from Albert Lebrun, President of the French Republic, expressing the "grateful and fraternal greetings of the French people," and speaking of the Revolutionary War hero as "a citizen of France and a citizen of the United States."

Mrs. Roosevelt sat in the Presidential gallery, and Mrs. Woodrow Wilson was seated on the floor of the House, next to Representative Bulwinkle of North Carolina, at the committee table. Wives of diplomats filled the diplomatic gallery. Count René de Chambrun, a descendant of Lafayette, occupied a seat of honor on the floor.

Visit of Marquis Recalled.

President Roosevelt devoted his address principally to an account of Lafayette's visit to the United States in 1824, when he and Andrew Jackson became firm friends. Lafayette's relationship with Washington, the President said, was that of father and son, but with Jackson, a man nearer his own age, the French patriot achieved an intimate friendship.

He recalled their first meeting in Washington, and the welcome which Jackson accorded to his newly found friend at The Hermitage, Jackson's home near Nashville. Mr. Roosevelt described how the United States Senate was adjourned as soon as the distinguished visitor made his appearence, in order that the Senators might crowd around his chair and welcome him.

The President related how Lafayette stayed at an inn during the Winter he spent in Washington, because it was felt by the citizens of Washington that he must be the guest of the people and should not stay at the White House.

Ambassador de Laboulaye recalled the celebration in Paris, two years ago, of the bicentennial anniversary of the birth of Washington, when President Lebrun took part in the ceremonies as President Roosevelt participated today. Speaking of the friendship between the youthful and impetuous Lafayette and the mature and self-possessed Washington, the Ambassador said:

"This friendship between these two champions of liberty, based on complete devotion to the same ideals, must continue, as in the past, to inspire the American and French nations, not only in the present but in the days to come."

Friendship Stressed by Lebrun.

The message from President Lebrun, which the Ambassador read, mentioned the Franco-American friendship during the Revolutionary War and during the World War.

"The ideals of liberty which bound us together in those heroic days continue to inspire us in the task of building peace," the message said. "Our two peoples are seeking progress and prosperity through orderly processes and through respect for the individual.

"Their common endeavor is the strongest safeguard for these ideals. Their mutual understanding continues to be one of the basic conditions for the maintenance of world peace.

"In this spirit the French people understand the full meaning and implication of the impressive homage rendered to Lafayette by the

Continued on Page Four.

Pope Condemns Nazis' Paganism As a German Saint Is Canonized

Tells 5,000 Pilgrims That Life of Humble Capuchin Doorman Is 'Admonition to All Who Have Wandered Far From Truth' and Seek to Restore Pagan Customs.

By The Associated Press.

VATICAN CITY, May 20.—Pope Pius XI, speaking to 5,000 German pilgrims today, vigorously condemned what he termed a pagan movement in Germany.

The remarks were made in the course of a colorful ceremony which elevated to sainthood a humble lay brother who for forty years had been doorman at a German Capuchin monastery. The canonization of the doorman, Conrad of Parzham, took place at St. Peter's in the presence of nineteen Cardinals and a number of German Bishops. The Pope said:

"The life of Conrad of Parzham is an admonition to all those who have wandered far from the truth and seek to restore and magnify with phrases the practices and customs of paganism, and who repudiate Christian doctrine which alone can recall them to virtue, civilization and the true processes."

The bells of Rome's 500 churches rang out as the name of the simple doorman, whose earthly name was Johann Birndorfer, was added to the calendar of saints.

The throng of pilgrims drew inspiration from his life, which he devoted to assisting afflicted persons who came to the monastery at Altoetting for assistance. Four miracles were attributed to his intercessions. Born in 1818, he died in 1894.

It was the fourth time since the Reformation that a German has been canonized.

Among American church authorities who participated in the ceremony were Bishops Joseph F. McGrath of Baker City, Ore., and Philip G. Scher of the Monterey-Fresno Diocese, California.

The Pope's remarks were rendered even more significant in their relation to Germany by the presence of Cardinal Faulhaber of Munich, who led the Catholic opposition to many of Chancellor Hitler's religious experiments.

Among those who heard the Pope's brief speech were also Prince Conrad of Bavaria, Prince Frederick Leopold of Prussia and Princesses Anna and Louise of Bavaria.

The Pope commented on the fact that the canonization of Conrad of Parzham fell on the Pentecost, and held that Conrad was an example to be followed by every one.

PARAGUAY REPELS A COUNTER-ATTACK

Repulses Bolivians Who Try Offensive to Ease Pressure Along Ballivian Front.

PUSHES BACK LEFT WING

Asuncion Forces Report They Counted 150 Dead and Took Over 100 Prisoners.

By JOHN W. WHITE.

Special Cable to THE NEW YORK TIMES.

BUENOS AIRES, May 20.—Paraguay repulsed a strong Bolivian counter-offensive on the Fort Ballivian front yesterday and pushed back the Bolivian left wing along a front of several miles at Fort Canada, according to today's communiqué from Asuncion.

The counter-offensive had been designed to break up the heavy pressure the Paraguayans were exerting all week against the Bolivian centre, accompanied by heavy artillery fire. The communiqué says the Bolivian attack was preceded by a heavy artillery barrage along the entire front.

It is reported that the Bolivians paid a heavy price in killed, wounded and men taken prisoner. The communiqué says more than 150 Bolivian dead were counted yesterday afternoon, including several officers, two of whom were identified. The prisoners included two officers, several non-commissioned officers and more than 100 privates.

Franco Leads Assault.

Colonel Franco, commanding the Paraguayan right wing with some of the army's most famous regiments, took advantage of the Bolivian defeat to make a new assault against Bolivia's left wing. The communiqué says he pushed back several miles of the Bolivian front and forced one regiment to retreat in disorder.

Colonel Franco has become famous for his enveloping flank operations. He is now trying to push back the northern end of the Bolivian line to enable the Paraguayans to surround Fort Ballivian as they surrounded Fort Boqueron at the beginning of the war.

Yesterday's fighting occurred along Bolivia's front line trenches ten miles from Fort Ballivian, which is Paraguay's objective. Two Paraguayan divisions have been strongly pressing the centre of this line while Colonel Franco is trying to push back or get around the left wing.

Reorganize Left Wing.

Paraguay's left wing is being reorganized after the disastrous defeat at Fort Conchitas in April and the pressure of the rest of the Paraguayan front is preventing the Bolivians from concentrating against this weak point.

Bolivia is reported to have only 7,000 veterans at Fort Ballivian and the remainder of her estimated 20,000 soldiers are recruits who are receiving their baptism of fire.

During the two months the Paraguayans were laboriously advancing to the present line the Bolivian Engineers Corps built a fine new road for auto trucks from Fort Ballivian to Villa Montes and Tupiza. This runs on high ground, permitting abandonment of the old road paralleling the Pilcomayo River and enables Bolivia to bring up fresh troops and supplies rapidly and efficiently.

TOKYO TAKES STEPS TO CURB OUTBREAKS

Watch Put on All Patriotic Groups to Halt Agitation Over Treasury Scandal.

EXTRA GUARDS FOR SAITO

Unrest Grows Through Nation With Five Officials Among 15 Now Under Arrest.

By HUGH BYAS.

Wireless to THE NEW YORK TIMES.

TOKYO, Monday, May 21.—Fearing a recrudescence of Right Wing agitations over the Treasury scandal, the Home Office has instructed all prefectural governors to exercise vigilance over members of patriotic societies. Arrangements have been made whereby the prefectural police will immediately warn the central authorities of any suspicious movements.

[Some of the patriotic societies of the Right Wing in Japanese politics have not only been responsible for assassinations of high officials in recent years, but they have been agitating for a strong central government under military domination. The patriotic societies have a strong hold on men and younger officers in the army and navy. They have powerful followings among the farmers, who have suffered greatly from the depression.]

Police activity continued today in the scandal, which centres on the sale at cheap prices of rayon and other stock put up as collateral in the Bank of Taiwan, a semi-official institution.

Teiji Okubo, chief of the banking section of the Treasury, was taken to the Department of Justice for examination this morning. It is expected that he will be committed to prison before evening. According to the press, he is suspected of accepting 10,000 yen for giving facilities for disposal of rayon shares to favored interests. When the scandal was mentioned in the Diet at the last session Mr. Okubo made himself responsible for the statement that an investigation had shown that no officials were involved in the criticized transactions.

A general belief that Premier Saito will not resign is keeping public opinion remarkably calm, but the arrest of so many Treasury officials is making Finance Minister Takahashi's position extremely difficult.

Premier Saito Guarded.

By The Associated Press.

TOKYO, Monday, May 21.—Fearing that the Cabinet's difficulties following upon the arrest of Kideo Kuroda, Vice Minister of Finance, will encourage ultra-patriotic organizations to attempt acts of terrorism, the Home Ministry began to take extraordinary precautions today. Extra guards were assigned to protect Premier Saito and other Cabinet members. Thus far, however, the country has reported no disorders.

The total in detention in connection with the Kuroda scandal reached fifteen today. Five officials of the Finance Ministry are included.

The consensus among the newspapers is that the Cabinet will wait until judicial processes indicate

Continued on Page Six.

GUNMEN ON PAROLE TRAPPED BY A BOY AS POLICE KILLERS

2 Held in Rassmusen Murder After Child Reveals Where Hunted Men Live.

PRISON RELEASES SCORED

Suspects Traced by Detectives Whom Old Regime Demoted—Two More Sought.

A 10-year-old boy aided in the capture of two men charged with the murder of Patrolman Arthur P. Rassmusen after a robbery on the lower East Side on May 4, and in the arrest of a third man linked to the gang, who was accused of receiving stolen property. The men were held without bail yesterday.

All three are former convicts. Two were out on parole after serving time for crimes of violence. One of these two, according to the police, made a complete confession, admitting that he had killed Rassmusen with a shot in the back while the policeman was firing at the other robbers.

He also identified one of the other prisoners as a participant in the affray. Rassmusen shot this second man in the leg, according to his companion. Three civilians were wounded in the battle.

The police said the confession named two other ex-convicts as members of the robber gang who took part in the fight with the policeman. These men are being sought. The third man arrested was charged with illegal possession of firearms and receiving property stolen by the gang.

Magistrate Denounces Paroles.

Magistrate Thomas A. Aurelio in Tombs Court criticized the working of the parole system when he held two of the prisoners without bail on murder charges. These two are Ralph (Whitey) DeLillio, 26 years old, of 238 East 112th Street and Eugene Giovanni, 27, who gave his address as 3,434 Irwin Avenue, the Bronx.

DeLillio was the one who confessed, according to the police. Giovanni had an infected gunshot wound in his right leg. He is known as Gene Gianinni, a small-time boxer, according to the police.

Magistrate Aurelio made the following comment on the parole system:

"According to the record, Giovanni was given one to five years for robbery on March 27, 1928, and five to ten years for possession of a gun at the same time. That is about six years ago. He is one of the men who spoil the parole system. Had he been kept where he belonged for the full time, Officer Rassmusen might be walking our streets today doing his duty as a policeman.

"In my opinion, the Mayor of the City of New York is to be congratulated for spurring on the Police Department, 18,000 strong, to hunt down these men who, in cold blood, murdered this young policeman who was doing his duty.

"The detectives in this case, who made the arrests, are likewise to be congratulated, and I am quite certain that the Mayor will remember them because they have made marvelous arrests under very trying

Continued on Page Three.

M'GOLDRICK TO ASK BANKERS TO MODIFY CITY AGREEMENT

Looks for Terms to Be Eased as Fast 'as We Are Permitted to Carry Out Program.'

HE ISSUES BALANCE SHEET

Value of City's Property Put at $4,054,600,000—Cut in Tax Borrowings Hailed.

Controller Joseph D. McGoldrick, in making public yesterday the city's first financial balance sheet, indicated that he hoped soon to effect substantial modifications of the bankers' agreement under which the city is at present being financed.

The balance sheet listed the city's assets as $2,774,420,333, the major portion of which represents public improvements against which bonds are outstanding. The report gave the value of city-owned land, buildings, subways, &c., at $4,054,600,000, but these are listed in the balance sheet only to the extent that they are not yet paid for.

Tax Borrowings Cut.

The balance sheet reflected the city's financial condition as of Dec. 31, 1933, but supplemental figures as late as the middle of this month are given. These show a sharp reduction in the tax-anticipation borrowings as a result of collections of taxes in arrears.

The idea of a city balance sheet instead of the annual report of the Finance Department was conceived by the late Controller W. Arthur Cunningham, and was carried into execution by Mr. McGoldrick. The balance sheet will be followed by weekly statements of the current financial transactions, with a new balance sheet showing the city's position as of June 30 as soon after that date as possible.

Agreement Already Relaxed.

Discussing the bankers' agreement, Mr. McGoldrick said:

"It was the intention of my predecessor, Mr. Cunningham, to seek equitable modification of that agreement after he could demonstrate to the banking community and the investing public that this administration could be entrusted to handle the city's affairs outside the limitations that the lenders had seen fit to impose; limitations for their own protection and for the protection of those whose money they were lending to the city as well as limitations for the benefit of the city whose credit is at stake.

"Already our efforts have borne fruit. Within the last few days I have had the pleasure of announcing a 25 per cent saving in interest on the current funds we borrow from this banking syndicate for our day-to-day operations. From the conversations I have already had, I have reason to believe that modification of various terms of the agreement will be forthcoming as rapidly as we are permitted to carry out our program.

"I must say that this reduction in interest undoubtedly could have been obtained several months ago had not our administration encountered the hostility of the Legislature, which prevented us from car-

Continued on Page Two.

4-Cent Fare on City Subway Considered As Move to Add Revenue and Spur Unity

Mayor LaGuardia's principal advisers in transit matters are seriously considering the advisability of reducing the fare on the city's independent subway lines to 4 cents. They are prepared to advocate such a reduction, it was reliably reported yesterday, if a study now in progress convinces them that two major benefits would result.

The first of these is a substantial rise in operating revenues. The second is a definite improvement in the city's bargaining position in negotiating with the B. M. T. and Interborough for unification of all rapid transit lines.

The power to lower the fare now reposes in the Board of Transportation and can be exercised at any time between now and Sept. 10, 1936. After that date, under a decision of the Court of Appeals and the terms of the Rice law recently approved by Governor Lehman, the fare must be "self-sustaining."

Before the Rice bill was enacted a "self-sustaining" fare was obligatory after Sept. 10, 1935. Until that date the present five-cent fare was mandatory. The Rice bill provides that the fare, up to Sept. 10, 1936, shall be "not more than 5 cents."

Although only partly completed, and operating on a five-cent fare, the city's new system already has diverted considerable business from the Interborough subway and elevated lines in Manhattan and the Bronx.

Mayor LaGuardia's advisers are confident that reduction of the fare to four cents would divert more than enough additional traffic to offset the loss of one cent for each passenger now being carried by the city lines. A careful check is being made, however, to ascertain whether this confidence is well grounded.

Completion of the city system, now made possible by the Federal Government's loan and grant of $23,160,000, is counted on by the LaGuardia administration to make possible the diversion of a great deal of traffic from other lines of the Interborough as well as from Brooklyn units of the B. M. T.

Although it will take about eighteen months to complete the city system, exclusive of the proposed Sixth Avenue subway, short units may be added to the existing lines at relatively early dates.

Mayor LaGuardia's advisers are attempting to reach a decision on the four-cent fare policy before beginning definite unification negotiations with the B. M. T. and Interborough. The groundwork for the actual negotiations, it is said, has already been laid.

The first negotiations, it is reported, will be with the B. M. T., leaving those with representatives of the Interborough and the Manhattan Railway Company to await further developments in the pending Federal receiverships of those two companies.

General Johnson's Letter to the President Prefacing NRA Reply to the Darrow Report

Special to THE NEW YORK TIMES.

WASHINGTON, May 20.—The 155-page reply of NRA officials to the Darrow report was prefaced by the following letter to the President from General Johnson:

May 15, 1934.

Hon. Franklin D. Roosevelt,
President of the United States,
The White House,
Washington, D. C.
Dear Mr. President:

Attached hereto are the reports of each divisional administrator replying to the strictures of the Darrow report, and a summary of the latter by our general counsel, Donald Richberg—all of which I have carefully read and with all of which I agree. A more superficial, intemperate and inaccurate document than the report, I have never seen.

In the hope of an impartial forum to which "little fellows" might complain, I agreed with Senator Nye on the creation of the board and, as the record demonstrates, nobody could have shown more good faith than I in its composition.

But this board is not in good faith. It assumes, after a few hours of cavalier inquiry and prejudiced and one-sided testimony, to pass on codes upon which we have spent days and weeks of inquiry and negotiation.

It impugns the motives of the divisional administrator in the Motion Picture Code because he formerly worked for an attorney who has clients in that field, and it asks his removal. Nobody here has rendered more public-spirited, disinterested and intelligent service than this divisional administrator.

In my judgment, this board has missed a great opportunty for a real public service. As it is now acting, it is of no service to anybody—it is a political sounding board.

In view of its fixed prejudices and partisanship and its unfair methods of taking and reporting on testimony, the conclusion is inescapable that the board is not proceeding in good faith to fulfill its public obligations.

Its continuance as an agency of government would enable it to promote private purposes at the public expense, and in my judgment would impair seriously the usefulness of the National Recovery Administration.

The board was established at my suggestion to supply fair and constructive criticism. It is clearly incapable of fulfilling this function and, therefore, I recommend that it be abolished forthwith.

Sincerely,
HUGH S. JOHNSON, Administrator.

BRANCH BANK BILL SIGNED BY LEHMAN

He Holds It Offers Only Way to Provide Facilities in 182 Communities.

SAFEGUARDS POINTED OUT

Governor Notes Manhattan Institutions Are Barred From Operations Outside City.

Special to THE NEW YORK TIMES.

ALBANY, May 20.—Governor Lehman announced today that he had approved the D. M. Stephens bill to permit branch banking within specified districts in the State.

The new law creates nine districts within which branch banking may be conducted, but provides that no new branches may be opened in communities already possessing banking facilities except through acquisition or merger.

The Governor in a memorandum said that the bill was a worthy measure in that it paved the way for supplying banking facilities to many of the 182 communities of the State which are now without any banks at all. The measure was opposed by George V. McLaughlin, president of the State Bankers Association, but supported by Joseph A. Broderick, Superintendent of Banks.

The Governor's memorandum follows:

"This bill divides the State into nine banking districts and permits a bank to engage in branch banking within its own district.

"Under existing law any bank or trust company in a city which has a population of more than fifty thousand may open branch offices within the city upon approval of the Superintendent of Banks. The bill before me retains that provision, but implements it with the additional safeguard that no branch can be opened without the approval of the banking board by a two-thirds vote of all of its members.

State-Wide Branches Barred.

"The main feature of the bill authorizes a bank or trust company to open a branch office in any city or village located in the banking district in which it has its principal office, provided, however, that in no event shall a branch be opened and occupied in a city or village in which are already located one or more banks, trust companies or na-

Continued on Page Eleven.

PRESIDENT SHAPES A LASTING NEW DEAL

Full Outline Is Expected in Time to Permit Fall Campaign to Pass Upon It.

IT HAS 3 MAIN PHASES

Permanent Social, Business and Economic Legislation Will Be Sought.

Special to THE NEW YORK TIMES.

WASHINGTON, May 20.—With all emergency relief and recovery legislation in the hands of Congress, President Roosevelt and his aides are concentrating on developing before adjournment the general outlines of a permanent economic and social program.

This program involves a consolidation and smoothing out of emergency measures and their development into proposals for permanent legislation at the next session of Congress.

Some observers have remarked that this early defining of a broad permanent and constructive program will supply ample campaign ammunition for members of the House and for Senators up for reelection in November.

However, whether the framing of the program was timed or not, it is understood that it could not have been framed before more pressing measures were disposed of.

The permanent program, as differentiated from the expedients, contains three main aspects, aside from war debts, tariffs and similar questions which are ordinarily a part of the political picture. These are divided roughly as follows:

1. The social program—expected to be outlined in a message to Congress on the eve of adjournment and embracing adjudication of labor disputes, Federal unemployment insurance, national old-age pensions, nation-wide insurance of workers against sickness, a Federal housing program, establishment of a permanent public relief system, and amendment of NRA provisions to bring minimum wages into line with costs of living.

Program for Codes.

2. The business program—involving anticipated changes in the National Recovery Administration which would result in the dropping of minor codes, possible exemption of the "service" industries from the general code scheme and other

Continued on Page Eight

CODES SHARPLY ASSAILED

Committee Centres Its Main Fire on Steel and Movie Industries.

'LITTLE FELLOW' STIFLED

Administrator's Reply Charges Darrow Aims at Choice of Fascism or Communism.

RICHBERG HELPS DEFENSE

'More Superficial, Intemperate Document' Never Written, Says Gen. Johnson.

Summaries Darrow Report and Johnson Reply, Pages 8 and 9.

By LOUIS STARK.

Special to THE NEW YORK TIMES.

WASHINGTON, May 20.—Irreconcilable differences of opinion on the workings of NRA Codes and on the social, economic and political philosophy underlying the Recovery Act were disclosed today when the long-awaited Darrow report to President Roosevelt was made public together with its "antidote" in the form of a reply by General Johnson and his associates.

As a result of the examination of eight codes, Chairman Clarence Darrow and four of his five associates on the National Recovery Review Board united in condemnation of the trend of the codes, which were alleged to be in the direction of monopoly and oppression of the small business man by the larger units.

A minority report by John F. Sinclair, financial writer, asserted that the majority of the board failed to approach the investigation from the viewpoint of careful research and analysis, and as a result the conclusion "must necessarily be inconclusive, incomplete and at times misleading and unreliable."

Using Mr. Sinclair's repudiation of the majority members—who include Fred P. Mann Sr., W. W. Neal, Samuel C. Henry and William O. Thompson—as a starting point, General Johnson, General Counsel Donald R. Richberg of the NRA, and a group of NRA divisional administrators attempted to demolish the Darrow report point by point, replying specifically to every case adduced by the Darrow board in support of their conclusions.

The Steel Code Is Attacked.

The Darrow report concentrated much of its fire on the Steel Code, in which one of the particular targets was the Code Authority, made up of the board of directors of the Iron and Steel Institute. It was the contention of the report that these directors were financially interested in questions they were called upon to decide as members of the Authority, and that the code was administered for the benefit of the "big fellows" in the steel industry.

Another issue of which much was made by the review board was the question of freight rates calculated on "basing points." The report pointed out one case in particular—that of a Duluth manufacturer who was forced to pay $6.60 a ton freight on steel bars, although those bars were made in Duluth.

This amount of freight was called for because Chicago is the "basing point" for that area, although, as the report pointed out, the bars never had seen Chicago.

The system of "basing points" was made part of the code, with the result, the Darrow investigators reported, that industries were enabled to live in localities where they could not if economic forces were allowed free play, and that industries in other places were starved. The Duluth manufacturer testified that he no longer could continue business if the $6.60 rate remained in force.

Moving Picture Industry Hit.

Another great section of the report was given over to the moving picture industry. Here the NRA critics found that monopolistic practices were common, and they held that there was no proper chance for the independent producer, distributor and exhibitor.

One of the recommendations was that Sol A. Rosenblatt, who is in

Continued on Page Eight

NRA MEMBER U.S. WE DO OUR PART

"All the News That's Fit to Print."

The New York Times.

Copyright, 1934, by The New York Times Company.

LATE CITY EDITION

WEATHER—Fair today and tomorrow; temperature unchanged.

Temperatures Yesterday—Max., 70; Min., 54

VOL. LXXXIII....No. 27,879. Entered as Second-Class Matter, Postoffice, New York, N. Y. NEW YORK, THURSDAY, MAY 24, 1934. PP TWO CENTS In New York City. | THREE CENTS Within 200 Miles | FOUR CENTS Elsewhere Except in 7th and 8th Postal Zones

BARROW AND WOMAN ARE SLAIN BY POLICE IN LOUISIANA TRAP

Bandit Pair Are Riddled With Bullets as Car Speeds at 85 Miles an Hour.

BOTH HAD GUNS IN HANDS

Ambuscade on the Highway Ends Long Criminal Career of the Pair.

DILLINGER DOCTOR JAILED

Outlaw's Woman Aide Also Convicted—Moley Submits Crime Report.

The War on Crime.

Clyde Barrow and a woman companion were killed by police as they drove along a Louisiana highway.

Dillinger's sweetheart and a Minneapolis doctor were convicted of aiding the bandit.

Professor Moley in a report to the President outlined broad plans for law enforcement. (Text on page two).

Barrow's End Is Sudden

Special to THE NEW YORK TIMES

SHREVEPORT, La., May 23.—Clyde Barrow, notorious Texas "bad man" and murderer, and his cigar-smoking, quick-shooting woman accomplice, Bonnie Parker, were ambushed and shot to death today in an encounter with Texas Rangers and Sheriff's deputies.

The 24-year-old desperado, who was accused of twelve murders in the last two years, and his companion whizzed along a little-traveled, paved road near Gibsland, about fifty miles east of here, at eighty-five miles an hour in a high-speed gray automobile, rushing into a carefully-laid death trap.

Before they could use any of the weapons in the small arsenal they had with them, the Rangers and others in the posse riddled them and their car with a deadly hail of bullets.

The onrushing machine, with the dead man at the wheel, careened crazily for an instant and then catapulted into an embankment. While the wheels of the wrecked machine still whirled, the officers, taking no chances with the gunman who had tricked them so often, poured another volley of bullets into the machine.

Both Died Holding Guns.

A moment later the uproar in the otherwise peaceful countryside spot had subsided and the officers swarmed over to the car. They found that Barrow and Bonnie had died with weapons in their hands, prepared to kill at the slightest alarm. The woman was crumpled up on the seat, her head between her knees and a machine gun in her lap. Barrow, a smear of red, wet rags, had been clutching a sawed-off shotgun in one hand as he drove.

The car proved to be a traveling arsenal. In it the officers found three submachine guns, six automatic pistols, one revolver, two sawed-off automatic shotguns and enough ammunition for a siege.

Governor O. K. Allen of Louisiana congratulated Sheriff Anderson Jordan of Bienville Parish, where Barrow and the Parker woman were killed, when he was informed of the details today.

The so-called "Public Enemy No. 1 of the Southwest," a mere hoodlum in Dallas up to 1930, met his end in an ambush that had been planned carefully by Frank Hamer, a former captain in the Texas Rangers, who had clung to Barrow's trail for years.

Hamer, who was recently commissioned as a highway patrolman for the special purpose of getting his man, as well as his gunwoman, trailed Barrow into Bossier Parish, where the criminal was said to have relatives.

It was reported that Hamer had received a tip as to Barrow's whereabouts from the father of a convict who recently escaped from a Texas penitentiary. The father, a resident of Louisiana, whispered the word to the authorities in the hope of winning clemency for his son.

Several weeks ago Hamer and his fellow officers barely missed the couple at a hide-out at Black Lake. Since then, the Rangers and Sheriff's deputies charted the highways that had been frequented by the pair and then quietly adopted a scheme of watchful waiting.

Once again Hamer picked up a "red-hot" clue to Barrow's trail, this time in Bossier Parish. He anticipated that the outlaw and his woman friend would head west toward Texas. Hamer, a Ranger associate, Sheriff Jordan and his

Continued on Page Three.

British Navy Work Shown In Reich as School Drill

Wireless to THE NEW YORK TIMES.

BERLIN, May 23 (London Times Dispatch).—A curious example of misleading propaganda is contained in a news film now being shown in Berlin.

The German newsreels regularly contain one or two pictures designed to illustrate the "armaments of others" and to drive home the lesson of Germany's military inferiority. In the present case the text announced pictures showing the "training of youth in England—English schoolboys exercising with light artillery."

The pictures actually show men of the royal navy rehearsing "Gun Across the River," a display that has been for many years a favorite item of the royal tournament.

MONARCHIST 'PLOT' BARED IN HANOVER

Nazis Make 'Great Conspiracy' Excuse for New Whirlwind Drive on 'Reactionaries.'

CRITICS ALSO ITS TARGETS

Der Angriff Denounces the Ex-Kaiser—Austrian Hitlerite Chief Flees to Munich.

By FREDERICK T. BIRCHALL.

Wireless to THE NEW YORK TIMES.

BERLIN, May 23.—The energies of the National Socialist party have recently been concentrated upon two campaigns. One was against "carpers, critics and killjoys"; the other was against "reactionaries," meaning Monarchists and such. These energies are now to be combined in one great drive.

All the party speakers are scheduled for a whirlwind campaign that like some famous American newspaper mergers will combine the best features of both previous efforts. I. will be started by Gustav Staebe, the press chief of the Hitler Youth organization, who will speak over a national radio hookup in a joint denunciation of all the targets of those campaigns—reactionaries, grumblers, critics and "killjoys."

Herr Staebe is the official who is engaged in a violent quarrel with the remnants of the Stahlhelm over the latter's suggestion that the revolutionary sentiments of the Hitler Youth are merely a "symptom of adolescence." This is resented as an aspersion on the sacred character of the national revolution.

The excuse for the new belaboring of the Monarchists is the discovery of a "great conspiracy of the Guelphs." Guelph is the family name of the house of Hanover, from which the royal strain that now rules Britain originally came.

Two monarchists, members of the former Hanoverian party, were arrested some time ago on suspicion of harboring disloyal sentiments toward the Nazi régime. It is now announced that these arrests have led to the discovery of a widespread political conspiracy against the State, "promoted by agitation and secret meetings," and that more conspirators are to be arrested and the full penalty of the law is to be imposed upon them.

The new treason law provides decapitation as the extreme penalty for conspiracy against the State, but whether this régime will go to the length of chopping off any notable heads is presently open to some doubt.

Concurrently postcards that combine a picture of Chancellor Hitler

Continued on Page Twelve.

TROOPS IN TOLEDO TO CHECK RIOTING; WORKERS BESIEGED

Battle Rages at Auto-Lite Plant as 3,000 Strikers Batter Factory Gate.

MINNEAPOLIS GUARD READY

Mobilized as Employers Accept, Unions Reject, Labor Board Terms—Truce Renewed.

By The Associated Press.

TOLEDO, Ohio, May 23.—Adjt. Gen. Frank D. Henderson ordered 700 Ohio National Guardsmen into Toledo tonight to patrol the area around the Electric Auto-Lite Company plant, where 1,500 workers are held prisoners by 3,000 strikers and sympathizers.

Just before General Henderson's order was given, company guards set up machine guns and trained them on a steel gate which the rioting strikers had torn from its hinges.

Fire started at the main gate of the plant here at 11:20 P. M. as the crowd of workers and their sympathizers continued to besiege the 1,500 employes. The crowd scattered as the fire apparatus screeched up to the gates. The firemen found that a blaze in the shipping room had been put out by employes.

Wreck Workers' Automobiles.

Soon after 10:30 the rioters broke into a parking lot at the plant and wrecked workers' automobiles. Deputies dispersed them with tear gas. At that hour J. Arthur MacMinch, vice president of the company, estimated the damage to the plant property at $75,000.

The company officials asked that fire apparatus be stationed at the plant after two automobiles had been overturned, saturated with gasoline and fired.

The automotive workers have been on strike for five weeks, demanding a 10 per cent wage increase, recognition of their union and priority rights. Officials of the company tonight offered to submit all the questions involved to the Detroit Auto Labor Board for mediation.

In the most serious skirmish tonight rioters broke into the plant at three places and engaged in hand-to-hand fighting with employes and guards. After a brisk battle the rioters were driven from the building. Guards were ordered to shoot at the legs of any others who attempted to enter the building through broken windows.

Tear Gas Bombs Used.

A new shipment of tear gas bombs was received at 9 o'clock tonight and police and deputies immediately began firing the bombs into the crowd of sympathizers. Several shots were heard.

The 1,500 workers in the plant prepared to sleep in the factory building, as the strikers showed no signs of moving away or letting up on the rock barrage which they had put down for more than seven hours.

Eight rifle companies, three machine gun companies and a medical unit were included in the groups ordered to muster. The 107th Cavalry, at Toledo, was not ordered out, as the Sheriff's office had asked that no local units be mobilized.

At 9:30 o'clock E. H. Dunnugan, Labor Board conciliator, was taken into the plant in a police car, tears streaming down his face from the effects of the gas bombs. He said he had discussed a truce with labor

Continued on Page Seven.

U. S. to 'Consider' More Pacific Fortifying If Japan Builds in Excess of Naval Ratios

Special to THE NEW YORK TIMES.

WASHINGTON, May 23.—The United States will "consider" extending its naval bases in the Pacific if the Japanese carry out their reputed intention to build in excess of existing naval treaty ratios, Secretary Swanson said today.

He favored continuation of the present 5—5—3 treaty ratio as among the United States, Great Britain and Japan, and saw no reason for its modification so as to grant parity to the Japanese Navy.

The Secretary was asked at his Wednesday press conference whether he desired to comment on repeated reports from Tokyo that Japan wanted naval parity and would insist on the point at the naval limitation conference of 1935.

"I believe in maintaining the present ratios," he replied. "The naval powers met at London and distributed the naval power in the way they thought safe to each nation and for their best interests. I see no reason to change that at this time."

"If Japan should build in excess of existing ratios," he was asked, "do you think there would be need of additional fortifications in the Pacific?"

"That question has not been settled yet," he replied. "No conclusion has been reached."

Mr. Swanson was then asked whether the question was being considered.

"It will be," was his answer.

By Article XIX of the Washington naval treaty, signed Feb. 6, 1922, the United States, the British Empire and Japan agreed "that the status quo at the time of the signing of the present treaty with regard to fortifications and naval bases shall be maintained in their respective territories and possessions specified hereunder." The Hawaiian Islands were excepted.

Speculation is developing on the place for the 1935 naval conference. The latest suggestion is that the conference be held in Canada. The United States is understood to oppose having the conference in Washington or Tokyo, and there are intimations that the British are not altogether desirous of staging it in London.

Doctors in Planes Reach Galapagos And Find Explorer Critically Ill

After 1,000-Mile Dash From Canal Zone in Two Navy Craft, They Decide to Rush W. A. Robinson to Balboa on Destroyer for Appendicitis Operation.

Special Cable to THE NEW YORK TIMES.

BALBOA, C. Z., May 23.—Two navy seaplanes speeding medical officers to the aid of William Albert Robinson, Cambridge (Mass.) textile engineer and explorer, stricken with appendicitis on board his ketch, Svaap, at the Galapagos Islands, landed at Tagus Cove, Albemarle Island, in the archipelago at 6:40 this evening, eastern standard time, after a 1,000-mile flight from the Canal Zone.

The medical officers boarded the Svaap immediately and examined Mr. Robinson, deciding not to operate tonight. A report from them at 8:15 P. M. said that his condition was critical and that his appendix was probably ruptured, with general peritonitis. It added that an immediate operation was not advisable.

Upon the arrival of the destroyer Hale tomorrow morning Mr. Robinson and the medical officers will be transferred to the warship and will be rushed here at forced speed. The Hale will refuel the planes for the return flight to Balboa.

Mrs. Robinson, the former Florence Crane, Chicago heiress, will return on the Hale with her husband. Daniel West, an artist and cousin of Mr. Robinson, is also on the Svaap, but it is not reported whether he is returning here.

The arrival of the planes ended a trying vigil for Mrs. Robinson in desolate islands isolated from the world, with her only contact through an amateur radio operator on the tuna fisher Santa Cruz, which sent out the first call for help.

A message last night sent by Mrs. Robinson from the Santa Cruz had urged the utmost haste, as her husband was suffering severe pain. The reply instructed that he be kept packed in ice, which was believed to be available on the fishing vessel.

The two naval planes made the flight in exactly twelve hours. They took off from the fleet air base at Coco Solo, crossed the Isthmus of Panama and swung across Panama Bay for the islands. The planes reported flying over the Hale at 11 A. M.

HOUSE AUTHORIZES LOANS TO INDUSTRY

Passes, 178 to 6, a $440,000,000 Measure for Action by RFC and Reserve Banks.

$75,000,000 IN SCHOOL AID

Differences With the Senate Go to Conference—Bank Pay-Off Fight Begins.

Special to THE NEW YORK TIMES.

WASHINGTON, May 23.—With but six members dissenting, the House passed today and sent to the Senate the $440,000,000 Direct Loans to Industry Bill. The count was 178—6 on a rising vote.

Under the bill the Reconstruction Finance Corporation is authorized to lend $300,000,000 to small industry, including $75,000,000 to public school systems upon "adequate" security. The Federal Reserve Banks are authorized to lend to small industry an amount not to exceed their surplus as of July 1, 1934. This was estimated at about $140,000,000.

The measure was a substitute for one recently passed by the Senate, but leaders believed that an early agreement would be reached in conference.

The Senate bill fixed five-year loans by the RFC at a maximum of $250,000,000, and the maximum for the reserve banks at $280,000,000.

Deposit Guarantee Next.

The House immediately went into Committee of the Whole for three hours of discussion of the Bank Deposit-Guarantee Bill, to which has been attached a rider providing for liquidation of closed banks at a cost of about $1,000,000,000.

Representative Byrns, the Democratic leader, after conferring with Speaker Rainey and the minority leader, Mr. Snell, said that he hoped to conclude debate early tomorrow on the bank bill, so that it could be passed and sent to the Senate.

Although the offering of many amendments prolonged passage of the industrial loans measure until the House leadership had to exert strenuous pressure, only two major ones were accepted.

On a motion by Representative Brown of Michigan, after more than an hour's debate, an amendment to permit the fishing industry to borrow from the RFC upon adequate security was adopted.

The provision for $75,000,000 in loans to school systems, which would permit the use of the funds to meet arrears in teachers' salaries, was offered by Representative Meeks of Illinois.

"Close the doors of schools of the country—and they will be if Federal aid is not extended—and you open the doors of the jails to the children of the nation," said Representative Douglas of Massachusetts.

Says Chicago Alone Qualifies.

The draft read that debts incurred prior to Jan. 1, 1934, could be repaid through government aid, but loans could not be applied for after Jan. 31, 1935. The first date was changed to June 1, 1934, and the amendment passed by 113 votes to 80.

"Not a single school district in the country outside of Chicago can meet the requirements of this amendment for full and adequate security," said Representative Luce of Massachustets. "You are just

Continued on Page Four.

'ICKES'S OGPU' SPURS PWA INDICTMENTS

Federal Grand Juries Have Returned 13 Writs So Far Out of 88 Cases Presented.

350 AGENTS KEPT ON TRAIL

Group of 130 Hunts Down Oil Code Violators—Secretary Holds No One Immune.

Special to THE NEW YORK TIMES.

WASHINGTON, May 23.—Information was made available today that the Division of Investigations of the Interior Department, headed by Louis R. Glavis, and sometimes called "Ickes's Ogpu" on Capitol Hill, has presented eighty-eight cases to United States attorneys as a result of its inquiries into public works projects.

Out of this number thirteen indictments have been returned to date. It is possible that more indictments will be returned when grand juries can give consideration to all of the eighty-eight cases.

According to figures obtained today, 2,515 investigations have been conducted by the public works section of the division. These have resulted in 757 adverse reports and 1,758 favorable reports. The cases presented to Federal attorneys for grand jury proceedings were developed from the adverse reports.

The division was set up by Secretary Ickes to check all possible instances of corruption and other violations of law in the conduct of the business of the department. One section of 143 agents is concerned with public works affairs, one of about 130 agents with the Oil Code, and one of seventy-five agents with general Interior Department affairs, such as supervision of Indians, reclamation and other matters.

Expense Held Justified.

The cost of the division of about 350 agents will run to around $700,000 for the next year, but the expense is regarded as relatively small in view of the huge outlays, or $3,300,000,000 for public works alone, on which tab is being kept.

The division in effect is a bureau of investigation similar to that of the Department of Justice, or a special secret service of the Interior Department, but it undertakes the constant surveillance of manifold activities which would burden heavily the Justice Department with its other duties, and has meant prompt court proceedings when circumstances have warranted.

As head of the division, Mr. Glavis has been directed by Secretary Ickes to follow trails wherever they may lead and not to stop at Congress, the White House or the Secretary himself. However, according to Mr. Glavis, no occasion has been found for investigating activities of Representatives, Senators, or other officials.

Just how the division operates in detail is not being disclosed. The explanation is given that each case is a separate one and is handled as circumstances justify. The country has been divided into ten regions and offices have been established in each. A force of eighteen agents is maintained in New York No headquarters staff is main-

Continued on Page Nine.

NRA ADVISERS ASK ROOSEVELT TO END THE DARROW BOARD

Action Is Voted After Hillman Says He Was Not Allowed to Elicit Facts at Hearing.

'SWEATSHOP HAVEN' HIT

Row Splits Review Group, One Member Assailing Its Counsel as 'Insull Attorney.'

Special to THE NEW YORK TIMES.

WASHINGTON, May 23.—The NRA Advisory Board condemned the Darrow Recovery Review Board today and declared it "should have its unhappy existence promptly terminated by Executive Order of the President."

This action was taken in a resolution adopted unanimously after Sidney Hillman, a member of the advsory board and president of the Amalgamated Clothing Workers of America, had related an experience at a meeting this morning of the Darrow board.

He repeated to the advisory board charges he had made before the Darrow group, alleging that it had, "in the most shameful manner, made itself the haven of the sweat shoppers."

In its resolution the advisory group charged the Darrow board with failing to invite accredited labor representatives before it on any of the subjects upon which the board had rendered judgment.

Mr. Hillman, in a clash today with W. W. Neal, member of the Darrow board and a North Carolina hosiery manufacturer, was prevented from further cross-examination of a witness who had admitted benefiting from the fair trade provisions of the cotton garment code, but wished to be freed from paying minimum wages and from the maximum hour provisions of the code.

The witness had also admitted paying wages of $3 or less a week in pre-code days but objected to paying the present $12 minimum.

Darrow Board Is Divided.

The row split the Darrow board. W. O. Thompson supported Mr. Hillman and demanded that Lowell Mason, counsel to the board, referred to by him as "a former Insull attorney," cease his attempts to shut off the union official.

Clarence Darrow, the chairman, who was not present at the clash but presided at the next session, when an adjournment was taken to allow both sides to cool off, sided with Mr. Neal. Mr. Hillman returned to the attack, however, and amplified his charges against the board and particularly Mr. Neal.

The hearing at which Mr. Neal presided was on complaints made against the provisions of the cotton garment code. The witness was John W. Moore, a cotton shirt manufacturer of Washington, N. C., who said he wished to have the right to determine labor and hour questions for himself. He was unable, he said, to afford 30 cents an hour, or $12 for a forty-hour week.

Under examination by Mr. Hillman, the manufacturer admitted that he had formerly paid wages of $3 a week and lower, that he was now receiving $4.35 a dozen for work-shirts which he formerly sold at $1.98, and that his business had greatly increased since the code went into effect.

When Mr. Neal interrupted this line of questioning Mr. Hillman persisted for a time, and the witness said he was opposed to the NRA labor provisions. Then Mr. Mason, the board's attorney, object-

Continued on Page Eight

Blue Eagle Flies Till '35; Roosevelt Stands by NRA

Copyright, 1934, by The Associated Press.

WASHINGTON, May 23.—President Roosevelt will stand by the Blue Eagle of NRA for the second year of its emergency flight.

This was ascertained today amid the whirl of controversy over the Darrow report, coupled with word that the Chief Executive is eager to hear from the country as to the permanent future of NRA after June, 1935.

The President has told inquirers he is keeping an open mind on just how far the government should go a year hence in seeking a permanent arrangement between the government, industry and labor.

He plans to survey the results in his tour across the country this Summer. In the meantime, he intends to stand pat on the general principles of the National Recovery Administration.

MOSES BIDS CASINO QUIT CENTRAL PARK

Cancels Dieppe Corporation's 10-Year Lease and Orders It Out by June 15.

LEGAL FIGHT IS INDICATED

Commissioner Holds It Illegal for 'Exclusive Night Club' to Use City Property.

Park Commissioner Robert Moses announced yesterday that he had notified the management of the Central Park Casino that it must vacate the premises by June 15. He said that the restaurant and night club, which opened in June, 1929, with the unofficial blessing of former Mayor James J. Walker, were not being conducted to his satisfaction and constituted "an improper and illegal use of the premises in a public park."

He added that he had canceled the ten-year agreement for its operation.

The notification was in the form of a letter drafted by the Corporation Counsel's office and signed by the Park Commissioner. It was addressed to the Dieppe Corporation, of which Sidney Solomon, who was active in Mayor Walker's campaign in 1925, is president.

Members of the board of governors of the Casino include Anthony J. Drexel Biddle Jr., Joseph N. Schenck, Winfield R. Sheehan, Adolph Zukor, Sam H. Harris, Jules S. Bache and William Rhinelander Stewart.

Tuttle Defends Casino.

Charles H. Tuttle, former United States Attorney and counsel for the restaurant, accused Mr. Moses last night of breaking off without notice negotiations to reach a satisfactory compromise.

In reply to the letter of May 21 notifying the corporation that its agreement with the city had been canceled, Mr. Tuttle wrote:

"Last Monday (May 21), and before your letter of May 21, I communicated with you by telephone and expressed the willingness and desire to explore further the possibility of a mutual understanding in the matter of prices, and I stated that the Dieppe Corporation was making certain investigations into the economic possibilities which I would be prepared to lay before you on Thursday of this week. You stated that you would let me know later. Your aforesaid letter arrived on the following day."

Noting that the letter did not re-

Continued on Page Ten.

$8,000,000 of B. M. T. Bonds to Be Sold Orally in State, Avoiding Registration

A group of bankers arranged yesterday to sell $8,000,000 of bonds of the Brooklyn-Manhattan Transit Corporation in such a manner that the financing will not come within the provisions of the National Securities Law. The transaction will be entirely intrastate and the mails will not be used, even to the limited extent which would be possible without invoking the provisions of the law.

The offering, the first of its kind to be made since the law was enacted last year, consists of fifteen-year secured sinking fund 6 per cent bonds due on June 1, 1949. The bonds are secured by $9,600,000 of New York Rapid Transit Corporation refunding 6 per cent bonds due in 1968, which are now pledged for bank loans. The sale of the new bonds will therefore transfer to the public a debt until now owed to bankers.

The vendors of the new issue are Hayden, Stone & Co., J. & W. Seligman & Co., Lehman Brothers and Kuhn, Loeb & Co. They are not acting as a syndicate, which would have been the procedure immediately before the passage of the law, but as individual firms. They will sell the securities privately without recourse to printed statements.

The new law requires the utmost accuracy in statements used in the sale of securities and attaches penalties for misstatements which Wall Street considers onerous. Under the law, securities offerings must be registered with the Federal Trade Commission. Lacking this registration, the use of interstate communication or transportation is unlawful in their sale. However, intrastate use of the mails is permissible for unregistered securities.

The B. M. T. vending group will not avail itself of this exemption as to local use of the mails. The group will sell its bonds within the State by oral representation only.

The New York Central and Pennsylvania Railroads have sold some $75,000,000 of bonds interstate since passage of the law. Railroad bonds are exempt from the clauses of the law calling for registration of securities with the Federal Trade Commission because plans for railroad financing must be filed with the Interstate Commerce Commission.

MACY SNUBS MILLS ON NEW DEAL FIGHT AS A STATE ISSUE

Republican Chairman Resists Move to Use Fall Campaign as Presidential Prelude.

PUTS GOVERNORSHIP FIRST

Would Stress Utilities Stand in Drive to Add to Party's Strength in Congress.

TUTTLE TAKES UP BATTLE

Warns Old Guard Program in Defense of 'Vested Rights' Courts New Defeat.

W. Kingsland Macy, Republican State chairman, intends to insist that the State campaign this Fall be fought on State issues and not be turned into a test of the popularity of the Roosevelt New Deal, it developed yesterday.

Mr. Macy was absent when former Secretary of the Treasury Ogden L. Mills and Representative James W. Wadsworth, the latter a leading member of the Old Guard, attacked the New Deal before the Republican Builders on Tuesday night. Yesterday it was revealed that Mr. Macy's reason for not attending was that he had been informed of the nature of the speeches and was out of sympathy with them.

Mr. Macy, it was disclosed, feels that the Old Guard is determined to emphasize national issues in the campaign this Fall for two purposes—as a sort of test of strength for the 1936 Presidential campaign and to subordinate the utilities issue, which Mr. Macy feels he has developed and which he believes must be continued to rid the party of control by the power interests.

Warns of Costly Losses.

Mr. Macy takes the stand that the Congressional seats that the party now holds in the State represent its rock-bottom minimum, and that not one of these seats is in danger in the Fall campaign. To win additional seats, the strength of the ticket must be at the top, in the Gubernatorial candidate, Mr. Macy has told friends, and the issue must be on State-wide lines.

No ground can be gained for the party by making the fight at the bottom, on Congressional issues, and trusting to those issues to poll votes for a Gubernatorial candidate, he has argued.

Mr. Mills and Mr. Wadsworth both have been considered leading candidates for the Republican Presidential nomination in 1936, and both are regarded as conservatives within the party.

Mr. Macy's attitude was expressed last night to an audience in the Fifteenth Assembly District by Charles H. Tuttle, former Republican candidate for Governor and a close ally of Mr. Macy. He spoke at the monthly meeting of the district Republican club on East Eighty-third Street.

Mr. Tuttle declared that, in his belief, the American people "have definitely turned their backs upon a social and economic order dominated and exploited by ever-augmenting aggregations of wealth and inspired by an insatiable thirst for profits."

"I do not believe," he added, "that the great body of our party or the mass of the people would accept a program or welcome a leadership which would proceed as if nothing had happened and nothing had been revealed between the years 1929 and 1932.

"Nor do I believe that any issue can be isolated and carried to success which is empty of any constructive program for the betterment of the working man, the farmer and the average citizen; or which, in the name of a defense of liberty, implies restoration of the chaotic individualism which spiraled down to the greatest economic smash in our history."

Attacks Stand of Mills.

Mr. Tuttle struck out squarely at Mr. Mills by declaring that it was all right to speak of the Bill of Rights, but that "the Bill of Rights was never intended to be a mere legalistic formula." In the initial leadership of the Republican party, there was no dignified Toryism, Mr. Tuttle declared.

Reviewing the Republican alliance with Fusion to obtain good government for New York City, and the fight on the power interests, Mr. Tuttle said:

"These considerations make it vital that the coming State election this Fall be fought on State and not on national lines. Unfortunately, there seems to be a desire by some Republicans to use this State election as a preliminary test of the President and his policies with an eye to the national election of 1936.

"Such personal equations and issues have a proper place in the Congressional campaign, but their in-

Continued on Page Four.

"All the News That's Fit to Print."

The New York Times.

5 A. M. EDITION
WEATHER—Fair, warmer today and tomorrow.
Temperatures Yesterday—Max., [illegible] min., [illegible]

Copyright, 1934, by The New York Times Company.

VOL. LXXXIII....No. 27,883. Entered as Second-Class Matter, Postoffice, New York, N. Y. NEW YORK, MONDAY, MAY 28, 1934. TWO CENTS In New York City. | THREE CENTS Within 200 Miles | FOUR CENTS Elsewhere Except in 7th and 8th Postal Zones

ROSSI AND CODOS FIGHT FOG OFF COAST OF NOVA SCOTIA; DUE OVER NEW YORK AT NOON

FRENCH FLIERS CONFIDENT

Said at Midnight All Was Well Despite Thick Weather.

HAD TAIL WINDS AT SEA

Kept in Touch With Ships and Land by Wireless for Many Hours.

FRENCH WATCH EXCITEDLY

All Paris Keeps Eyes on the Airmen, Whose Goal Is San Diego, Calif.

GLACE BAY, N. S., May 28 (AP).—Signals from the transatlantic airplane Joseph Le Brix were picked up at 2:50 A. M., Eastern Standard Time, today by the Canadian Government wireless station.

The plane's position was not learned. The aviators were sending to a station in France and no messages were exchanged with the Glace Bay station.

It was believed, however, that the big silver ship was speeding along the south shore of Nova Scotia, heading toward New York.

The giant French monoplane Joseph Le Brix, with Lieutenant Maurice Rossi and Paul Codos at the controls, on their way from Paris to San Diego, Calif., was plowing through thick fog off Nova Scotia early today.

Radio messages received direct from the plane shortly before 11 o'clock last night by the Radio Marine Corporation's Chatham (Mass.) station told of the fog and the failure of attempts by the fliers to get definite bearings from Cape Race, Nfld. At midnight the Mackay Radio and Telegraph Company picked up a message which, translated from the French, read:

"We are laying course for Nova Scotia. Navigation difficult, piloting laborious with no outside visibility. All goes well.

"Rossi and Codos."

May Be Here at Noon.

If all continues to go well the Joseph Le Brix should be flying through the skies over New York by noon today, unless the pilots elect to take a shorter and more northerly route to California.

At 10:48 last night, New York daylight time, the Chatham station received a message from the plane which said in part:

"Tried to get bearings from Cape Race, but intense fog prevented. Wind light, visibility poor."

Another part of the message was not clear.

The huge Bleriot plane, weighing more than nine tons, lumbered off the runway at Le Bourget, France, at 12:10 A. M. yesterday, and throughout the day and last night, riding tail winds most of the way, it averaged more than 100 miles an hour.

Eighteen hours lacking six minutes after the plane left Le Bourget the fliers were within 630 miles of Cape Race, according to a radio message from the plane picked up by the Chatham station. The message, sent at 6:04 P. M., daylight time, said:

"Position: 44.18 North, 40.54 West. All well on board."

The steamship Washington, according to a message received by Mackay Radio, was in touch with the fliers at 7:30 last night and gave them a radio bearing. At that hour officers on the steamer figured that the Joseph Le Brix was about 400 miles from Cape Race. The message, however, did not contain an exact position.

Report Perfect Weather.

At 3:50 P. M. the Chatham station picked up the following message from the plane:

"Position, 45 North, 35 West, at 19:50 Greenwich mean time [3:50 P. M. daylight time]. Expect to arrive over Newfoundland at 4 G. M. T. tomorrow morning [12 P. M. Sunday, daylight time]. Perfect weather since departure."

The fliers had been in touch with other ships during the day. At 10 o'clock yesterday morning they flew over the Europa about 700 miles out from Southampton. Their signals were heard coming in with great strength by the steamship Washington and again by the steamship Albert Ballin.

Weather conditions as plotted at the New York branch of the

Continued on Page Three.

Few Have Succeeded in Westward Flight From Europe Across the North Atlantic

If Rossi and Codos reach the shores of the United States theirs will be the second of many attempted expeditions westward across the North Atlantic to make the flight from Continental Europe non-stop by airplane. The prevailing winds are from west to east, and it is only rarely that a combination of weather conditions is found and charted correctly enough to give fliers even a possible chance of completing their journey.

Four years ago Dieudonne Coste and Maurice Bellonte, in a Breguet plane, flew non-stop from Paris to Curtiss Field at Valley Stream, L. I. They zigzagged their way between storms across the ocean, taking advantage of the favoring winds and shifting their course abruptly when radioed weather reports showed them changing conditions. Even more favorable conditions made for the success of Rossi and Codos.

Others have met with failure and death or have been close to failure in the westward North Atlantic test.

The first to reach land in the Western Hemisphere was the German-Irish team in the Junkers monoplane Bremen, but they did not fly from the Continent of Europe. Captain Herman Koehl, Major James Fitzmaurice and Baron Gunther von Heunefeld left Dublin in April, 1928, and landed at Greeneley Island, off the Labrador Coast, after having wandered for hours over inland Labrador.

Two years later Air Commodore Sir Charles Kingsford-Smith in his Southern Cross, with a crew of three, flew from Dublin to Harbor Grace, Nfld., and thence to Roosevelt Field, N. Y. Although they made one stop, they were the first to fly the ocean non-stop and then reach New York with their plane intact.

In 1932 Captain James Mollison, flying alone in a tiny Puss Moth monoplane, flew from Portmarnock, Ireland, to Pennfield Ridge, N. B., near St. John. The following year Captain Mollison and his wife, Amy Johnson Mollison, made the attempt again and reached Bridgeport, Conn., only to crash in attempting a night landing.

WEST SIDE PROJECT READY TO HIRE 4,000

Signing of Buckley Bill Will Permit Immediate Starting of Work, Moses Announces.

NEEDY TO GET THE JOBS

Diggings From 30-Block Track Depression to Be Used as Riverside Park Fill.

Work on the $20,500,000 West Side improvement, involving the roofing of the New York Central tracks in Riverside Park and depression of the railroad tracks between Thirtieth and Sixtieth Streets, will be started immediately, it was announced yesterday by Park Commissioner Robert Moses. The project has been virtually at a standstill for two years.

More than 4,000 relief workers can be engaged without delay on the project, made possible by Governor Lehman on Saturday when he signed the bill sponsored by Senator John L. Buckley under which the State is authorized to advance to the New York Central Railroad $7,000,000 out of grade-crossing elimination funds.

The New York Central Railroad has spent to date $32,000,000 to elevate its tracks south of Thirtieth Street and $52,000,000 to eliminate its tracks north of Thirtieth Street on Eleventh Avenue.

The $84,000,000 expended by the railroad is in addition to the $20,500,000 about to be spent and the $25,000,000 which will have been spent by the city on the West Side elevated express motor highway below Seventy-second Street.

Much of Work Completed.

In announcing that work would begin at once with the funds made available by legislative action, the Park Department pointed out that all the track elimination was now completed except for the section between Thirtieth and Sixtieth Streets, where the tracks will be depressed. To accomplish this the New York Central Railroad will let a contract for the excavation, involving the removal of about 400,000 cubic yards of material which will be dumped along the Riverside Park waterfront to be used for grading purposes.

On the basis of the bulkhead lines established by the War Department, the Riverside Park fill will extend about fifty feet westward into the Hudson River, and a retaining wall will be built with rock taken from the New York Central excavation between Sixtieth and Thirtieth Streets.

Rock to Save $600,000.

The excavation is expected to yield about 200,000 cubic yards of rock, which will represent a saving of close to $600,000 to the Park Department in the construction of the retaining wall.

"Four thousand relief workers can be put to work immediately on

Continued on Page Five.

REDS RENEW RIOT AT COURT HEARING

300 Protesting Arrests Fight Police When Ejected After Booing Magistrate.

MAN AND WOMAN SEIZED

Blackjacks Rout Agitators in Street Battle—13 Held for Inciting Disorder.

Disorders that were quelled only after the police had blocked all streets leading to the Criminal Courts Building were a sequel yesterday to the riot on Saturday outside the offices of the Department of Welfare at 50 Lafayette Street.

The trouble began with the arraignment of ten men arrested in Saturday's disturbance. As the first of the prisoners faced Magistrate Leonard McGee in Tombs Court, on the first floor of the Criminal Courts Building, about 150 men and women who had crowded into the room began booing his decision to hold the defendants in higher bail than their attorney had requested.

The magistrate ordered the court cleared, and sixty patrolmen who had been sent to the scene in anticipation of disorder began forcing the crowd to leave.

In the corridors of the building the policemen were able to drive the crowd ahead of them. Outside, however, at the White Street entrance, nearly 150 more persons joined the demonstrators. This additional crowd had waited outside, unable to find places in the court.

Couple Arrested in Melee.

Before the neighborhood of the building could be cleared, a half dozen fights between patrolmen and the demonstrators had resulted. A woman and her husband, who was charged with attempting to take her from the custody of a policeman, were arrested and arraigned after the cases of the other prisoners had been acted upon by the court.

By that time the temper of the demonstrators had risen. Groups reformed in the various side streets and attempted to march back to the White Street entrance, the only one used on Sundays.

The police detail on duty, reinforced by the crews of twelve radio patrol cars, formed cordons across White, Franklin, Centre and Lafayette Streets, blocking all approaches to the court building. Thus held back, the crowd finally broke up, marching in detachments through White Street to the East Side and parading for a time in various streets there without police interference.

No injuries were reported, despite the clashes between the police and groups of participants in the mêlée. The patrolmen carried no nightsticks, but used their blackjacks in forcing the throng from the building, rapping sharply on the legs of

Continued on Page Four.

U. S. Envoy Escapes Shots Fired at Home in Havana

Gunmen in Automobile Flee After Attack Timed for Caffery's Usual Departure for Church—Cubans Call With Regrets.

Special Cable to THE NEW YORK TIMES.

HAVANA, May 27.—Gunmen fired several shots at his home today as United States Ambassador Jefferson Caffery was preparing to leave at 10:30 this morning. They sped away in an automobile after seriously wounding a soldier on guard near by.

As the Ambassador was about to leave his residence to enter a waiting automobile, a blue automobile occupied by several men passed along Mendoza Avenue at high speed. The occupants fired at the soldiers.

Mr. Caffery recently leased the beautiful residence in Ninth Street, off Mendoza Avenue, at the highest point in the Miramar residential district. He is accustomed to leave the house at 10:30 Sunday mornings on his way to church. This morning he was a few minutes late.

Early this morning military headquarters was warned that a blue automobile was cruising in the vicinity of the Ambassador's home. Because of recent threats of attacks on the Ambassador a special detail of soldiers was dispatched to the Miramar district.

The attack greatly disturbed government circles. President Mendieta late this afternoon was visibly perturbed when he left the Palace to visit Mr. Caffery.

"This is terrible, terrible!" he exclaimed.

A special Cabinet meeting was called for tonight, allegedly to discuss reform of the recently enacted gold-purchase decree, but it is believed it was called to discuss the attack on the envoy's home.

Colonel Fulgencio Batista, army chief of staff, in commenting on the attack said:

"I greatly regret as a Cuban and as chief of the constitutional army this attack on Mr. Caffery, the Ambassador of the United States to Cuba, both in itself and because of the fatal consequences which it might have meant to us. I wish to express my condemnation of incidents of this nature."

The Ambassador does not believe the attack was the result of a plot to kill him despite the Havana rumors of the past few days. He pointed out that it had occurred at Mendoza Avenue at least 100 yards from his home. He said it was his habit to pass this corner on his way to church but that he was a little late in starting this morning.

Mr. Caffery said he understood that extra soldiers had been sta-

Continued on Page Five.

PARIS AND LONDON PLAN JOINT TALKS ON DEBTS TO U. S.

Barthou and Simon Project Three-Cornered Parley With Davis at Geneva.

FRENCH CONSIDER PAYING

Little Possibility Is Seen, However, of Avoiding Default on June 15.

By The Associated Press.

PARIS, May 27.—France and Great Britain, it was learned today, plan to consider jointly the problem of debts owed to the United States at a meeting of envoys in Geneva.

French Foreign Minister Louis Barthou, it was learned, told the Cabinet yesterday he had sounded out United States Ambassador-at-Large Norman H. Davis, and that he and Mr. Davis, together with Sir John Simon, British Foreign Secretary, plan a three-cornered talk.

M. Barthou expressed little hope of escaping a default in the war debt payment due June 15, but thought it was not impossible that the government at least could announce a disposition to settle speedily, with a bare possibility of recommending to Parliament a token payment.

The French Deputies thus far have been apparently unalterably opposed to payment of any sort on the debt owed to America.

The French Foreign Minister's attitude is that the door is not closed to settlement. This was revealed in his written answer to an interpellation in the Chamber May 23, denying that the United States had taken measures of reprisal against France in the debt matter.

"The United States," he said, "has taken no special reprisal measure against France because of non-payment on the due date of sums owed by France."

He added, however, that the United States had put into effect the Johnson bill, which "in a general manner forbids the floating on the American market of loans by governments which have totally or partially defaulted on debts to the United States."

He did not interpret this as directed specially against France.

European debtor governments, it is understood in France, have been told by the United States that while token payments will be acceptable on June 15, when the next installment is due, such payments will not prevent them from being in default in the terms of the Johnson act.

Sir John Simon has told the British House of Commons that England's course regarding payment of war debts will be determined by circumstances of the moment.

Last week it was indicated in dispatches from London that the British official attitude, heretofore being that the United States must take the initiative in any reopening of the debt question, might be revised to allow an approach to Washington for discussions of the subject.

Continued on Page Five.

NEAR PEACE BASIS IN TOLEDO STRIKE AS RIOTING CEASES

The Mediators, After Parley, Announce the 'Possibility of a Complete Settlement.'

'DIRECT' ADJUSTING IN VIEW

Taft Reports 'Mutual Understanding' of Employers and Union Leaders.

By The Associated Press.

TOLEDO, May 27.—Many hours of negotiation in Toledo's riotous automotive strike were punctuated late today with an official statement from Federal mediators that a "possibility of complete settlement" had appeared.

Issued under the name of Charles P. Taft, chief mediator, the statement said that union leaders and officials of the Electric Auto-Lite Company had been brought together and that a spirit of mutual understanding prevailed.

This was the first definite ray of hope since savage rioting took two lives, and injured nearly 200 within the last six days.

The "possibility of complete settlement" as discussed by Mr. Taft is believed to mean that the mediators have dropped their efforts to achieve merely a basis of arbitration and that they are now trying for a direct and immediate plan to settle differences.

Three plants are involved in the strike, the Electric Auto-Lite Company, the Bingham Stamping and Tool Company, and the Logan Gear Company. Only Auto-Lite officials participated in the three-cornered conference today of Federal mediators, union executives and employers' representatives.

Just after Mr. Taft's statement was issued, the conference adjourned until tomorrow afternoon at 1:30, when officials of the other two companies involved will sit in.

Taft Outlines Negotiations.

Mr. Taft's statement, tracing the course of his negotiations, was as follows:

"Our original efforts were confined to finding a basis for the most prompt settlement of the Toledo strike situation. We therefore made and presented a proposal calling in part for submission to arbitration before the Automobile Labor Board for final decision the many points in controversy. This was rejected.

"We finally concluded to change from our original efforts and to bring about direct negotiations such as we had not previously considered wise. After long conferences during this morning and early afternoon with both the executive committee of the union and officials of the company we brought them together this afternoon, finding an attitude on both sides which made it possible to discuss all problems in an atmosphere of much better feeling and of mutual understanding.

"We feel that we have made very substantial progress in exploring the views of both sides. The pro-

Continued on Page Five.

ROOSEVELT ENDS REGULATION OF THE SERVICE INDUSTRIES, BUT KEEPS CODE LABOR RULE

The President's Statement

Special to THE NEW YORK TIMES.

WASHINGTON, May 27.—Following are the texts of the President's statement announcing changes in the NRA as it affects service industries and of the Executive order promulgating the changes:

Most industries have a national community of economic interests, even though the operation of some of their units is local. There are others which, notwithstanding their having national trade associations, do not actually integrate themselves nationally. Whether an industry can govern and police itself under the fair trade provisions of a national code depends on its degree of actual economic integration on a national scale and on the organization and solidarity within the whole industry.

A trial period of some months has shown that while most industries, after organization for this work and a little experience with it, can secure uniform national results, there are others to whom a greater degree of autonomous local self-government is desirable. Among these are some, but not all, of the so-called service industries—that is, industries engaged in the sale of services rather than of goods.

No industry would give up the gains we have made in the elimination of child labor and in the establishment of minimum wages and maximum hours of labor and, of course, under the law, we cannot give up collective bargaining and the right of the President to cancel or modify codes, orders and agreements.

I am signing an order today which carries these principles into effect as to some of the so-called service industries.

To put it simply: No matter where he is located, no member of any such service industry, as shall have previously been designated by the administrator, may fly the Blue Eagle unless he is living up to the present code provisions governing child labor, maximum hours, minimum wages and collective bargaining.

But trade practices shall be required as a condition of flying the Blue Eagle in these designated service industries only in particular localities in which at least 85 per cent of the members there have proposed as a local code of fair trade practice a schedule of such practices in respect of which they all seek to agree with me to comply with their own proposal.

If the administrator approves

Continued on Page Two.

ROOSEVELT RUSHES 3 VITAL MESSAGES

Forsakes All Recreation on Sabbath to Clear Desk for Departure Wednesday.

COCOANUT OIL A BIG ISSUE

National Program Involved in Water Usage Statement—War Debts to the Fore.

Special to THE NEW YORK TIMES.

WASHINGTON, May 27.—President Roosevelt forsook all recreation today to spend both daylight and evening hours in the White House on the three messages he feels must go to Congress before he leaves Washington on Wednesday for a projected trip lasting several days.

The messages will deal with war debts, the processing tax on coconut oil and a report of a survey by an interdepartmental committee on water usage.

Only one of these messages, that on coconut oils, is expected to recommend legislation, but Mr. Roosevelt is understood to be desirous that Congress have ample time to study the other messages before adjournment date, still set hopefully by Administration leaders as some time early in June.

Mr. Roosevelt also read reports on the agreement reached on the Stock Exchange Control Bill yesterday by House and Senate conferees. The conferees will report to their respective houses of Congress on Tuesday, and it is barely possible that the engrossed copy of the bill will be ready for presentation to President Roosevelt before he leaves Washington Wednesday morning.

The Exchange Control Bill as agreed upon by the conferees differs from the President's previously expressed idea through establishing an independent commission of five members to administer its provisions, instead of placing such administration in the hands of the Federal Trade Commission, but this is believed to be acceptable to Mr. Roosevelt.

Concerned Over Oil Tax.

As for the messages that occupied him today, Mr. Roosevelt was particularly concerned over the one regarding the tax on coconut oil, as he feels that this tax, inserted in the Revenue Act recently enacted, is unfair to the Philippines. The levy of 3 cents per pound on such oil has been described as sufficient to kill off most of the productive sources of income of the islands, while yielding only a negligible return to the Treasury.

The message on war debts is expected to be simply a statement of the status of the debts without legislative recommendations, but the message on water usage probably will cover a broad field overlapping a large portion of the national plan-

Continued on Page Two.

DEFICIT IN BUDGET HALF OF ESTIMATE

Stands at $3,262,484,835 Instead of the Excess of Seven Billions Forecast.

RFC OUTLAY HEAVILY CUT

Public Works Disbursements Are Slightly Over Half the Funds Provided.

Special to THE NEW YORK TIMES.

WASHINGTON, May 27.—Unless there is an unexpected speeding up of emergency expenditures, the Treasury's budget deficit at the end of the current fiscal year, excluding the statutory debt retirement item, will not be much more than half of the $7,309,000,000 estimated by President Roosevelt in his budget message to Congress in January.

As of May 24, the latest detailed figures available, the deficit on this basis stood at $3,262,484,835, and with revenue receipts meeting expectations and expenditures far below estimates some officials are now convinced that it will be well below the $4,000,000,000 level at the year's end.

At the present rate at which outgo is exceeding income the additional deficit for the remaining days of May would bring the total deficit for the first eleven months of the fiscal year to about $3,335,000,000.

On this basis an additional deficit of $665,000,000 would have to be built up in June, the final month of the fiscal year, in order to bring the total to $4,000,000,000. The experts do not believe that money will be poured out at any such accelerated rate, even though public works projects and other emergency measures make increasing demands.

Based on May Estimates.

These deductions are based in part on estimates that the excess of expenditures over receipts, exclusive of debt retirements, for the month of May will be only about $350,000,000. There also is to be taken into consideration that in June a quarterly payment of income taxes falls due, which should, on the most conservative reckoning, supply the government with $150,000,000 more in revenue than will be received in the present month.

On the basis of such calculations experts who recently predicted that the budget deficit would be only slightly in excess of $4,000,000,000, as compared with the President's estimate of $7,309,000,000, are recasting their figures and predicting that the actual deficit may fall considerably short of the four-billion-dollar mark.

The President omitted the statutory debt retirement item of $488,000,000 in making his forecast, the total he named being that by which he estimated the national debt actually would be increased in the

Continued on Page Two.

NRA DRASTICALLY REVISED

But Local Fair Practice Pacts Are Authorized in Executive Order.

85 PER CENT MUST AGREE

Otherwise Blue Eagle Is Permitted if Four Basic Rules of the Law Are Met.

PRICE CONTROL WAS SNAG

Statement by President Cites Handicaps to National Codes for Sale of Services.

Special to THE NEW YORK TIMES.

WASHINGTON, May 27.—President Roosevelt, in an executive order today, authorized the exemption of the service industries from some of the fair trade practices of NRA codes.

The exemption does not apply to minimum wages and maximum working hours, child labor and collective bargaining.

The executive order empowers Recovery Administrator Johnson to cease attempting to enforce open price systems, price fixing and other devices on hundreds of thousands of cleaners, dyers and pressers, barber shops, beauty shops and the like.

In a statement, the President defined service industries as those "engaged in the sale of services rather than goods."

The statement said that "a trial period of some months has shown that while most industries after organization for this work and a little experience with it can secure uniform national results, there are others in which a greater degree of autonomous local self-government is desirable."

Among these are "some but not all" of the service industries, the statement added.

Much Difficulty in Field.

This latest step toward a changed NRA was taken after General Johnson and his aides had found mounting difficulty in the service industries field.

The cleaners and dyers code accounted for more than half the Blue Eagles removed. Under the code a complicated system of minimum prices was set up for various areas in the country.

Widespread violation prompted General Johnson to say that he never should have attempted to write fair trade practice provisions into the pact.

Under the executive order of today, however, fair trade practice provisions for a service industry in a given area may be provided when 85 per cent of the industry in the area agrees to them and they are approved by the NRA.

No member of any service industry may fly the Blue Eagle unless he is living up to the present code provisions governing child labor, maximum hours, minimum wages and collective bargaining. In areas where a local code has been promulgated the members of the industry, to fly the Blue Eagle, must in addition live up to the local code.

Signing Delayed by President.

The decision on whether an industry is eligible for exemption is left to General Johnson and his aides.

While the step was forecast by General Johnson three weeks ago, it is known that the executive order, presumably drafted by the NRA, had been unsigned on the President's desk for almost a week. Some NRA officials had doubted whether he would sign it at all, involving as it does a major change in NRA policy.

Forecasting of the order by General Johnson brought a storm of protest from cleaners and dyers throughout the country.

Since the basic principle of the NRA contemplates meeting the increased production costs of higher wages and shorter working hours with savings by elimination of destructive price cutting and of other practices, much interest in how the new policy would work out was expressed in NRA circles.

NRA officials have for some time recognized a grave problem in handling such codes as come within the scope of today's executive order. They feel there is little that a code can offer in this field in return for

Continued on Page Two.

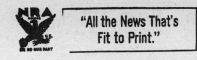

"All the News That's Fit to Print."

The New York Times.

LATE CITY EDITION
WEATHER—Fair and continued warm today; tomorrow cooler.
Temperatures Yesterday—Max., 82; Min., 65

1 Section

VOL. LXXXIII....No. 27,889. | Entered as Second-Class Matter, Postoffice, New York, N. Y. | NEW YORK, SUNDAY, JUNE 3, 1934. | Including Rotogravure Picture, Magazine and Book Sections. | F | TEN CENTS | TWELVE CENTS Beyond 200 Miles. Except in 7th and 8th Postal Zones.

JOHNSON AVERTS A TEXTILE STRIKE; ACCORD IN TOLEDO

PRODUCTION CUT STANDS

25% Textile Slash Goes Into Effect Monday, Johnson Says.

WAGE DEMAND UNDECIDED

But Settlement Orders Fact-Finding and Puts Workers' Adviser on Code Board.

TOLEDO PACT IS RATIFIED

General Strike Collapses as the Auto-Lite and Edison Disputes Are Settled.

Strike Developments.

General Johnson averted the threatened strike of textile workers.

Movement for a general strike in Toledo collapsed as agreements were consummated in the two major labor disputes.

Trolleymen in Northern Indiana went on strike.

Workers in Oklahoma City stockyards quit to get higher wages.

Textile Peril Is Averted.

Special to THE NEW YORK TIMES.

WASHINGTON, June 2.—The strike called by union leaders to tie up the nation's cotton textile industry on Monday as a reprisal against the NRA was averted today under an agreement reached here by General Hugh S. Johnson, NRA Administrator, and Thomas F. McMahon, president of the United Textile Workers.

Under the settlement a 25 per cent machine-hour curtailment order, the ostensible reason for the strike threats, remains unchanged and will go into effect on Monday as scheduled.

General Johnson declared that labor leaders admitted during conferences leading to the agreement that "the strike was not against the order at all but only to secure a 33 1-3 per cent increase in hourly rates of pay and certain other demands."

No decision on this demand was reached in the agreement, but the Research and Planning Division of the NRA is ordered to make a study of the possibilities and report within fourteen days.

The settlement was agreed to by George A. Sloan, chairman of the Cotton Textile Code Authority, a participant in the negotiations. The union and Mr. Sloan both issued statements explaining their positions.

Terms of the Settlement.

Terms of the strike settlement were announced by General Johnson as follows:

"I—Strike order to be countermanded without prejudice to the right of labor to strike.

"II—One representative of employes of the cotton textile industry to be appointed by the Secretary of Labor to Labor Advisory Board.

"III—One representative of employes of the cotton textile industry to be appointed labor adviser to government members on Cotton Textile Code Authority.

"IV—Authority of Cotton Textile National Industrial Relations Board to be defined by administrative order to include all subjects mentioned in VII hereof. Membership to said board to be increased by one representative of employers and one representative of employes from the cotton textile industry.

"V—If these conditions are accepted I will urge the Cotton Textile Code Authority to accept and agree to abide by the foregoing amendment to the Industrial Relations Board provisions.

Investigations to Be Made.

"VI — Investigation and reports upon the following questions to be made by NRA Division of Planning and Research in conjunction with revised Industrial Relations Board:

(a) What productive machine hours are necessary to meet normal demand (within ten days)?

(b) What increase, if any, in wage rates is possible (within fourteen days)?

(c) Have wage differentials above the minimum been maintained (within thirty days)?

(d) What changes have taken place in man-hour productivity?

(e) The Division of Planning and

Continued on Page Twenty-five.

King George 69 Today; To Have Family Gathering

Wireless to THE NEW YORK TIMES.

LONDON, June 2.—King George V will be 69 years old tomorrow. Being Sunday the day will be celebrated quietly with a small family gathering at Buckingham Palace.

The King's birthday will be publicly celebrated Monday. The chief event will be the trooping of the colors on the Horse Guards Parade, and the King will take the salute.

The royal servants will drink the King's health in champagne at noon Monday as the royal salute is fired in Hyde Park. In the evening Sir John Simon will preside at the Foreign Office at the King's birthday banquet, which will be attended by members of the diplomatic corps.

The birthday honors list also will be published Monday.

GOV. ROLPH DEAD AT THE AGE OF 64

Executive Who Upheld Lynching of Kidnappers Succumbs to Lung Congestion.

WAS MAYOR FOR 20 YEARS

Son of Pioneer Family, Made and Lost Fortune in Shipping —Merriam Succeeds Him.

Special to THE NEW YORK TIMES.

SAN JOSE, Calif., June 2.—Governor James Rolph Jr., a prominent figure in the political life of the State and nation, died at 1:30 P. M. today at Riverside Farm, the Santa Clara County ranch where he had been battling against a long illness. He was 64 years old.

The death was due to a mio-carciac malady involving the entire circulatory system. This caused kidney complications and a general disturbance of the nervous system. His illness began in the midst of a stumping tour of the State.

The State Executive had fought his illness with a vigor that was incomprehensible to his physicians. Governor Rolph's restlessness and his will to live made it almost impossible for the doctors to keep him quiet so that he would obtain the maximum rest needed for a completely exhausted mental and physical condition.

Last Tuesday the Governor's condition took a turn for the worse and the physicians summoned his family and his most intimate friend, State Motor Vehicle Director T. J. Roche, to his bedside. This morning all hope for the patient was given up.

Family at the Bedside.

At the bedside when the Governor died were Mrs. Rolph and a son, James 3d, holding his father's hand. In the bedroom also were the Governor's brothers, Will, Ronald and Tom, and the four attending physicians.

By the death of Governor Rolph, Frank F. Merriam, 67, of Long Beach, succeeds to the Governorship of California.

Mr. Merriam was elected Lieutenant Governor Nov. 4, 1930, at the same time Mr. Rolph was elected Governor. Mr. Merriam was nominated by the Republicans in a three-cornered contest with the then Lieutenant Governor, H. L. Carnahan, and State Senator Tallant Tubbs.

As Lieutenant Governor, Mr. Merriam served as presiding officer of the State Senate during the past two sessions of the Legislature.

He was an Assemblyman for ten years. He served as Speaker of the Assembly for two terms. In 1928 he was elected to the State Senate, but he resigned his office to run for Lieutenant Governor. Also in that year he was chairman of the Republican State Central Committee and, as such, he headed the party organization in the successful Hoover Presidential campaign.

New Governor Born in Iowa.

The new Governor, a native of Iowa, came to California in 1910 and engaged in newspaper work at Long Beach for eleven years. He is a widower.

He has long been active in civic, church, club and fraternal circles. He is engaged in the real estate business and also is vice president of the Citizens State Bank of Long Beach.

For many years he was one of California's leading dry advocates,

Continued on Page Thirty-one.

50,000 VISIT FLEET AS BARRED CROWDS BREAK POLICE LINES

Landing Floats Nearly Sink Under Rush of Throngs—22,000 Sailors on Leave.

NAVY PARADES ON 5TH AV.

Army Units Share in Cheers—Sightseers Jam Streets Along the Waterfront.

New York and the navy continued to get along famously yesterday as some 50,000 persons visited the ships of the fleet and 22,000 bluejackets strolled "all around the town."

For the officers and men of the ninety vessels of the fleet anchored in the Hudson or moored to piers in four boroughs New York was still a novel—and therefore an exciting experience—but at the same time some of the city's manifestations of its regard were uncomfortable.

The men-of-war—particularly the battleships—were literally swamped with visitors during the afternoon, and thousands of others who were unable to get aboard the big ships waited for hours in a broiling sun or pushed and struggled in vain attempts to board motor launches.

Police Lines Broken.

At the Seventy-ninth Street dock, where boats from the battleships Maryland, Mississippi, Tennessee, Texas and New York were making their landings, the crowds broke through the police lines in early afternoon, swarmed out on the dock and attempted to board a waiting motor launch. A hundred extra policemen were called, shins were bruised and feelings ruffled before the crowd was finally brought under control.

Earlier in the day the navy had another indication of the interest of the metropolis in the fleet when some 500,000 to 750,000 spectators, according to police estimates, lined Fifth Avenue from Washington Square to Fifty-ninth Street, to applaud 5,000 sailors, marching with rolling stride, in the first large naval parade the city has witnessed since war days.

Following the parade, the flag officers of the fleet were the guests of Joseph E. Widener and Mr. and Mrs. Winthrop Aldrich at two Long Island parties, but for the most part the officers and men of the fleet planned their own parties and were their own guides to New York yesterday.

Last night Broadway and the midtown district was thronged with sailors, many of them ashore for week-end liberty, and Riverside Drive was, as usual, popular. Despite the exuberance of the sailors' good times, the police and shore patrol reported that none of the fleet personnel had been involved in serious difficulties.

In addition to the thousands who inspected the ships of the fleet yesterday and waited in long queues at landing places, hundreds of thousands of persons saw the warships from vantage points ashore. Riverside Drive was packed with vehicular and pedestrian traffic yesterday afternoon and side streets emptied flowing torrents of humanity into the main stream.

Boulevard East, a road atop the Palisades, was also clogged with traffic yesterday as persons came from all over New Jersey to look down upon the ships at anchor in the Hudson, to examine them with binoculars and to take photographs. After dark thousands of others on both banks of the river saw the clashing swords of the searchlights flash about the sky as the fleet staged its nightly searchlight display.

Most of the ships of the fleet—

Continued on Page Three.

Tugwell Fines Father For False Food Label

By The Associated Press.

WASHINGTON, June 2.—Dr. Rexford G. Tugwell, Assistant Secretary of Agriculture, was recently called on to carry enforcement of the Pure Food and Drug Act to an unexpected point.

A prosecution charging violation of the act in misbranding a food shipment was begun in 1932 against his father, Charles H. Tugwell of Wilson, N. Y., a member of the canning firm of Tugwell & Wiseman.

The firm pleaded guilty and on Jan. 6 last the judgment came before the junior Tugwell, acting as Secretary in the absence of Secretary Wallace. He signed it as one of a group of similar actions, thereby levying a fine of $50 on the firm, the customary amount for first violations.

The judgment declared a shipment of canned grapefruit juice and orange juice from Florida to New York bore labels which were "false and misleading," and that part of the shipment labeled as the natural product had been sweetened with sugar.

MAYOR TELLS REDS THEY PREY ON POOR

'You Want People to Starve to Serve Your Ends,' He Says to City Hall Delegation.

HOLDS THEY STIRRED RIOT

225 Police on Guard as 1,500 Mass at Welfare Building in Peaceful Demonstration.

Mayor LaGuardia lost his patience yesterday with leaders of radical demonstrations and bluntly told a group of them who called upon him at City Hall that he considered them "cowardly" and declared that "you really want people to starve to serve your own ends."

The Mayor's plain statement of his beliefs was given to the leaders of a group of about 1,500 men and women who marched to City Hall after holding a demonstration outside the Welfare Department Building at 50 Lafayette Street. The demonstration was peaceful throughout, a strong police detail of mounted men, patrolmen and detectives being on duty to guard against any disorder.

Says Group Prompted Riot.

James Gaynor, chairman of the Greater New York Conference for United Action, was the man who brought down upon himself and his fellow delegates the Mayor's censure. His committee was the sponsor of the demonstration. It was this same group which a week ago was in charge of a similar demonstration outside the Welfare Department Building, which developed into a riot in which a number of policemen were injured. The Mayor said flatly yesterday that it was the radical demonstrators who were responsible for this disorder.

Among those in the party received by the Mayor was A. L. Wirin of the American Civil Liberties Union. Mr. LaGuardia's outburst came after Gaynor had demanded that his group receive representation at the conference on methods of financing relief to be held tomorrow afternoon at City Hall and the Mayor had refused the request.

The Mayor pointed out that such persons as Rabbi Stephen S. Wise, John Haynes Holmes and Arthur Garfield Hays would be among those at the conference and would unquestionably look out for the interests of the jobless.

Accused of Inciting the Poor.

"You want to see these poor people starve so that you can mislead them and incite them to beat the

Continued on Page Twenty-two.

Results in Major Sports Yesterday

Racing—Lady Reigh, 9-2 shot, owned by Mrs. W. Plunket Stewart, scored a surprising five-length triumph in the Coaching Club American Oaks at Belmont Park. The Brookmeade Stable's Cavalcade won the $25,000 added American Derby at Washington Park, Chicago.

Track—John Follows of the New York A. C. provided the feature performance of the 132d Winged Foot games at Travers Island, defeating Joe McCluskey in the two-mile run in 9:17.4. The time was the second fastest for the distance ever made outdoors by an American. Six meet records were broken and one equaled.

Baseball—Manager Bill Terry's hit in the ninth enabled the Giants to beat the Phillies, 5—4. The Yankees downed the Athletics in the tenth, 9—8. The Dodgers lost to the Braves, 16—6. In Eastern Intercollegiate League games Columbia routed Yale, 26—6, and Dartmouth beat Penn in a double-header, 1—0 and 5—4. Fordham overwhelmed N. Y. U., 19—11.

Tennis—Miss Margaret Scriven of England defeated Miss Helen Jacobs of California in the French hard court final, 7—5, 4—6, 6—1. In the men's final Baron Gottfried von Cramm of Germany conquered Jack Crawford of Australia, 6—4, 7—9, 3—6, 7—5, 6—3. The United States took the final two singles matches to score a sweep in its Davis Cup series with Mexico.

Yachting—The old America's Cup yacht Yankee outsailed the new boat, Rainbow, in a brush on Narragansett Bay. At Harwich, England, Velsheda was disabled while leading Endeavour, the English challenger. The race was declared "no contest."

(Complete details of these and other events in Sports Section.)

LEHMAN TO CALL SESSION ON JULY 10 ON COUNTY REFORM

Governor, Formally Acceding to Smith Request, Proposes State-Wide Reorganization.

WHOLESALE CUTS SOUGHT

Special Elections Are Set to Permit Full Legislature to Act on Amendment.

Governor Lehman announced yesterday that he would call a special session of the Legislature on or about July 10 to consider the adoption of a resolution as the first step toward the submission of a constitutional amendment to permit the reorganization, consolidation and abolition of county offices, not only in New York City, but in any county of the State.

The Governor made this announcement in a letter to former Governor Alfred E. Smith, chairman of the New York City Charter Commission, which recently requested him to call such a special session.

Governor Lehman said he would recommend the adoption of a resolution to submit the proposed amendment. If passed at the special session and again at the regular session next year, the proposed amendment can be submitted to the voters of the State in November, 1935. Otherwise under the provision requiring adoption of the resolution by two successive Legislatures, the proposed amendment could not be submitted until 1937.

The Governor, who came here from Atlantic City to attend the wedding of Charles Poletti, his counsel, said he had not decided whether he would broaden the scope of the special session, but indicated that this was probable. The Governor at any time during the course of the special session may broaden its scope by a special message to the Legislature. Reapportionment, taxation and unemployment relief have been mentioned as matters for which consideration may be demanded.

THE GOVERNOR'S LETTER.

Governor Lehman's letter follows:

June 1, 1934.

Honorable Alfred E. Smith,
350 Fifth Avenue,
New York, N. Y.

Dear Governor Smith:

I am in receipt of your letter conveying the request of the New York City Charter Commission that I convene the Legislature in extraordinary session and that I recommend at such extraordinary session the adoption of constitutional amendments which will permit the reorganization, consolidation and abolition of county offices in the five counties within the City of New York.

It is clear that if any constitutional amendments are adopted this year and passed again at the regular session next year they can be approved by the people in the Fall of 1935, and that unless this procedure is followed the amendments cannot be submitted to the people until November of 1937.

I beg to advise you that I will accede to the request of the New York City Charter Commission and will convene the Legislature in extraordinary session on or about July 10, 1934.

As I have previously stated in messages and public utterances, it is my strong conviction that reorganization of county government, through constitutional amendment, should be made readily available throughout the State. We should seek economy and efficency both in the five counties within the City of New York and in the up-State counties as well. I shall, therefore, at this extraordinary session afford the Legislature the opportunity of giving consideration to such constitutional amendments as will permit of the reorganization of government in any county of the State in the interest of economy and efficiency.

Very sincerely yours,
HERBERT H. LEHMAN.

Would Permit Drastic Cuts.

Adoption of the proposed amendment would permit the city administration to do what it has been unable to do under the economy bill and make wholesale cuts and elimination of jobs in the county offices. The recent pay cuts were voluntary on the part of the county officials.

In his letter to Governor Lehman asking for a special session, Mr. Smith said that it was the opinion of a majority of the Charter Commission that no charter revision worthy of the name could be accomplished which left "the five present, independent, wasteful, inefficient and overlapping county governments frozen into the

Continued on Page Thirteen.

RELIEF BILL GIVES PRESIDENT FUNDS NETTING $6,000,000,000; HE ACTS AT ONCE ON DROUGHT

Heat of 90° Is Predicted for City Today As Wave Searing West Spreads to East

The wave of hot weather that has been scorching the Middle West moved over New York yesterday, bringing predictions of a temperature rising to 88 or 90 today. Weather officials said, however, that there was little danger of drought conditions here. Today and tomorrow will be fair, it was forecast.

Meanwhile blistering temperatures throughout the Middle West continued to burn up fields, bringing starvation to cattle and causing inestimable damage to crops.

The mercury soared to 98 in Kansas City and St. Louis and to 102 at Davenport, Iowa, and 100 at Des Moines and Keokuk. The temperature at Bloomington, Ill., was 107, at Taylorville 105 and other down-State Illinois cities reported marks of more than 100. In strange contrast, cities and towns in Montana, Idaho and Washington reported that the first days of June had arrived with snow storms.

Centring in Southern Minnesota, the heat wave spread drought conditions southward to the Gulf and eastward to New York State, where nineteen counties were reported in danger from seared crops and forest fires. From St. Paul, rising temperatures were reported in the Northwest, where the heat wave originated, with a possibility of continued high temperatures in the drought-stricken areas for the next few days.

Showers were expected in some parts of the Middle West, but it was doubtful if they would be sufficient to alleviate conditions that already had resulted in vast damage to crops.

Although the mercury went only a few degrees above normal in New York yesterday, high humidity made the weather oppressive. Rising from a low of 65 at 5 A. M., the temperature reached a high of 82 at 5 P. M. The record temperature for June 2 was 94, in 1895.

BRITAIN WILL PAY DEBT TOKEN JUNE 15

Cabinet Will Then Ask United States for Negotiations on Revision of Terms.

POLICY LONG DETERMINED

Roosevelt's Message on Issue Disappoints Political Leaders in London and Paris.

By CHARLES A. SELDEN.

Wireless to THE NEW YORK TIMES.

LONDON, June 2.—Sir John Simon, Foreign Secretary, who returned today from Geneva, went directly to his home in the country without calling at the Foreign Office. Prime Minister MacDonald is at Chequers, his country home, and other key members of the Cabinet are week-ending in various parts of the country, so there will be no formal consideration by the British Government of President Roosevelt's debt message before Monday.

Perhaps there will be no debt discussion before Tuesday because at the Cabinet meeting on Monday Sir John will report on conditions at Geneva.

The Conservative Morning Post is demanding that Sir John resign from the Cabinet because of the manner in which he handled the British case at the disarmament conference.

Token Payment Is Likely.

Although there is disappointment because President Roosevelt was unable to give special assurance that another token payment in lieu of the full amount due June 15 would absolve the British Government of a default, there is at least no prejudging of the matter. Therefore there is every likelihood that the British will make another small payment on account with the understanding that it is done in anticipation of Anglo-American negotiations for a readjustment of the whole debt question.

It has been the British Cabinet's determination to do that all through the recent discussion on the subject, but a statement of this policy was withheld by Neville Chamberlain, Chancellor of the Exchequer, from Parliament pending the promised Presidential message.

Two things in the message which please the British are President Roosevelt's expressed willingness to negotiate and his agreement with the British argument that international debts have been one of the major factors in the world depression. That was the case which the British Cabinet developed so elaborately in diplomatic notes to the United States just prior to paying the instalment due in December, 1932.

Early Negotiations Doubted.

Those arguments will be reproduced when the two governments get together for consideration of revision. Britain will make no modification of her old arguments because she is now enjoying a budget surplus instead of facing a

Continued on Page Eighteen.

WORK AUTHORIZED AS DROUGHT RELIEF

Roosevelt Approves Program In the Parched Areas to Give Cash to the Destitute.

$500,000,000 TO BE SOUGHT

AAA Heads Will Recommend This to President—Congress Group to Offer Bill.

Special to THE NEW YORK TIMES.

WASHINGTON, June 2.—Following a telephone conversation with President Roosevelt, Harry L. Hopkins, Relief Administrator, made known today that an emergency work program would be started at once in drought-stricken areas to provide cash to destitute families.

Mr. Hopkins added that "during his brief absence from Washington, the President has kept in close touch with the drought situation."

At the same time, the agricultural arm of the government completed a thorough survey of the drought situation tonight and decided that it would cost $500,000,000 to cope effectively with the tremendous relief problem involved.

Recommendations will be carried to President Roosevelt on his return here Monday that this amount be made immediately available.

Agricultural advisers to the President are of the opinion that the money could be obtained from the general relief funds.

The $500,000,000 considered necessary to relieve the drought sufferers in addition to expenditures of up to $150,000,000 by the AAA for the purchase of beef and dairy cattle in drought areas.

For Direct Human Relief.

The new emergency fund would be used chiefly to provide direct human relief through the FERA, feed for live stock and for moving live stock from acute drought areas.

In addition, it is expected by officials that large numbers of families will have to be moved from submarginal areas, and that the drought relief program will in this way be integrated with the broader problem of submarginal retirement.

Recommendations from the agricultural advisers will be in the form of a memorandum to the President, and they expect that this will be made the basis of a message to Congress from Mr. Roosevelt.

Meanwhile, a self-appointed committee of thirty Senators and Representatives conferred on relief programs with Chester Davis, head of the Agricultural Adjustment Administration, and prepared to lay their proposals before Mr. Roosevelt when he returns to Washington Monday.

Senator Shipstead, the chairman, declared that $1,000,000,000 might be needed for drought relief alone, and that it was hoped to put an appropriation bill before Congress Tuesday.

The seriousness of the situation

Continued on Page Twenty-four.

WILL SPEED RELIEF BILL

House to Pass Measure Under Suspension of the Rules Monday

$1,172,000,000 ALLOCATED

But More Than $5,000,000,000 Would Go to Roosevelt From RFC and PWA.

BUDGET DEFICIT LOWER

Even With Increased Outlays in June Figure Would Be Half Estimate.

Special to THE NEW YORK TIMES.

WASHINGTON, June 2.—As a climax to the administration's relief and recovery program, a bill which would put in President Roosevelt's hands a potential emergency fund varying between $2,500,000,000 and $6,000,000,000 was reported for passage today by the House Appropriations Committee.

The measure, to be known as the Deficiency Appropriation Bill of 1934, allocates directly $1,172,000,000 for relief and rehabilitation during the next fiscal year, but it also turns over to the President unobligated savings and balances of the Reconstruction Finance Corporation and Public Works Administration, which, stretched to their fullest in new debentures and collections, run to more than $5,000,000,000.

The bill was reported today so that it might be called up Monday under suspension of the rules. Passage under that procedure would require a two-thirds majority in the House. Leaders were certain that it would be adopted by an overwhelming majority, and they hope it will end, so far as the House is concerned, the legislative program for the Seventy-third Congress.

The bill as reported carries direct appropriations totaling $1,178,269,861.48. Of this, $6,629,861.48 is for items in connection with regular appropriations, leaving $1,172,000,000 for emergency purposes in response to the President's recent message to Congress.

Specific Allocations.

Of this new emergency fund, the President would have absolute control over $899,675,000. The remainder is allocated as follows:

$100,000,000 to emergency construction of public highways.

$6,730,000 for construction of forest roads and trails.

$2,500,000 for roads over public lands.

$2,000,000 for roads on Indian reservations.

$65,000,000 for Federal buildings.

$96,095,000 for various emergency expenditures of the Treasury Department, including additional expenses incurred under the Gold Reserve Act, aid to Federal Land Banks and an increase made necessary in the internal revenue service.

The fund specifically allocated to the President is to enable him to carry out the purposes of the Acts of Congress setting up the Civilian Conservation Corps, the Federal Emergency Relief Administration, the Tennessee Valley Authority and the National Recovery Administration.

In this connection the bill reads: "$899,675,000 to be allocated to the President for further carrying out the purposes of the aforesaid acts and to remain available until June 30, 1935; provided, that any savings or unobligated balances in funds of the Reconstruction Finance Corporation may, in the discretion of the President, be transferred and applied to the purposes of the Federal Emergency Relief Act of 1933 and/or Title II of the National Industrial Recovery Act, and any unobligated balances in appropriations (including allocations of appropriations) of the Federal Emergency Administration of Public Works may, in the discretion of the President, be transferred and applied to the purposes of such Federal Emergency Relief Act of 1933."

Limits Public Works.

The bill contains an additional provision that the amount to be expended for public works under this arrangement shall not exceed $500,000,000, leaving the remainder for more direct relief, which, according to representations to the committee, will be undertaken on a

Continued on Page Twenty-seven.

NRA MEMBER U.S. WE DO OUR PART

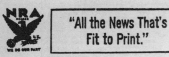

"All the News That's Fit to Print."

The New York Times.

LATE CITY EDITION
WEATHER—Fair, cooler today; fair tomorrow.
Temperatures Yesterday—Max., 84; min., 69.

VOL. LXXXIII....No. 27,893. Entered as Second-Class Matter, Postoffice, New York, N. Y. NEW YORK, THURSDAY, JUNE 7, 1934. P TWO CENTS in New York City. | THREE CENTS Within 200 Miles | FOUR CENTS Elsewhere Except in 7th and 8th Postal Zones

ROOSEVELT DENIES DANGER OF FAMINE IN CROP DISASTER

LARGE REGION DESTITUTE

125,000 Families Need Support for a Year or They Will Starve.

OUR SURPLUS FOOD AMPLE

Drought Is Held Worse Than Burning of City as No Jobs Are Made in Rebuilding.

SHOCK TO BUDGET PLANS

But $525,000,000 Outlay for Relief Cannot Be Avoided, the President Says.

Special to THE NEW YORK TIMES.

WASHINGTON, June 6.—Drought in the West has reached the proportions of a national disaster in that it has cut off the livelihood of a large segment of the population. Thus President Roosevelt appraised the situation today in reviewing the emergency and the government's plans for relief.

The nation's huge carry-over of food stocks from former surpluses removes the danger of famine, the President pointed out, a factor in which he was supported today by an official statement of the Agricultural Department. The department said, however, that market conditions springing from the drought would "materially affect the national food supply."

On the basis of reports made to the President, he estimated that there were 125,000 families in the worst of the drought area who must be provided for until next year's crops are harvested and sold.

Worse Than Destruction of a City.

As many people had been affected by the dry weather in the Northwest, Mr. Roosevelt pointed out, as would have been affected by the burning of a great city, but with worse results, since the destruction of a city would immediately provide a large pool of employment in clearing the wreckage and rebuilding.

No new type of work was created by a drought, and in a large area rains, should they fall now, would be too late, so the government would have to sustain the population until 1935. He pledged the government to do this so far as possible.

The situation was outlined at the President's press conference. It was conceded that the appropriation of $525,000,000 which the administration will seek from Congress will upset the budgetary program, but Mr. Roosevelt saw no choice in the face of the calamity reported by agricultural experts.

It was frankly conceded that the outlay would be in addition to the estimates drawn in January, which contemplated large deficits through this and the next fiscal years, ending June 30, 1935, but a balanced budget thereafter. The question of a possibly unbalanced budget in the fiscal year ending on June 30, 1936, was described as a bridge which would be crossed when the administration came to it.

Prefers Direct Appropriation.

The administration preferred to take the straightforward way of appropriating relief rather than circuitous means possible under existing legislation. The money, it was pointed out, could be taken from the Reconstruction Finance Corporation and not be shown on the government's balance sheets until some future date when the Treasury would have to reimburse the RFC.

A message asking for the funds will go to Congress soon, but Mr. Roosevelt had not decided today whether to request a special measure or to suggest that the Senate provide for the appropriation by an amendment to the pending Deficiency Bill.

The course of the drought's ravages is charted here by the President's advisers on a map showing in red the emergency areas, or those in desperate need, and in blue the areas only partially affected. While the red areas at present represent the homes of about 125,000 families, the colors are constantly changing from blue to red as new reports are received.

The President appeared principally concerned that there would

Continued on Page Six.

Roosevelt's Son Wins Leave for Yale Oarsman

Special to THE NEW YORK TIMES.

WASHINGTON, June 6.—Franklin D. Roosevelt Jr. sent the following telegram from Cambridge today to Marvin H. McIntyre, his father's assistant secretary:

"Just received telegram from friend on Yale varsity who says that David Livingston, rowing No. 4 on junior varsity, cannot go to New London to race against Harvard because of R. O. T. C. engineering camp. Apparently no Senators have been able to excuse him and they wish father to intervene as soon as possible if anything can be done. See you at the races, I hope.

"F. D. ROOSEVELT JR."

The President had the message referred to the War Department which telegraphed permission for Livingston to be excused long enough to row.

BRIBERY IS CHARGED IN PLUMBING TESTS

Witnesses Tell of Paying $400 to Ellis Jungman, Chairman of Board, for License.

M. J. HOGAN ALSO NAMED

Others Accuse an Ex-Member of Death Threat Following Protest on Practices.

Testimony that Ellis Jungman, chairman of the Examining Board of Plumbers, accepted a $400 bribe to grant a master plumber's license to an aspirant who failed to pass an examination was given yesterday by witnesses at the public hearing into the board's activities being conducted by Commissioner of Accounts Paul Blanshard.

A similar charge was brought by two witnesses, one more positive than the other, against Michael J. Hogan of 171 Warren Street, Brooklyn, a Republican politician and a former member of the House of Representatives. The witnesses testified they had paid Hogan $725 on his assurance he could exert influence so that they could get master plumbers' licenses whether they actually passed an examination or not. Hogan flatly denied receiving any money, admitting, however, that he had interceded for the two aspirants.

There was a third sensation at the hearing. It was provided by the testimony of three master plumbers who called at the board offices in the Municipal Building two years ago to protest against improper practices. Two of these witnesses testified that on that occasion John J. Hassett, former member of the board, had, so they considered, threatened them with death unless they stopped their complaints. The third of these witnesses was not sure, he insisted, that Hassett was not joking.

Jungman Won't Comment.

Leonard F. Stampfl, of 5,908 Catawba Avenue, Brooklyn, now a master plumber, and Paul Ambrogio, a tailor and barber, of 157 Wyckoff Avenue, Brooklyn, were the witnesses who charged Jungman with accepting a bribe. Jungman, who will testify today, would not comment on the accusation.

In contrast with most of the previous witnesses in the inquiry, Stampfl and Ambrogio showed no hesitation in telling their story under questioning by Irving Ben Cooper, special counsel to Commissioner Blanshard.

Ambrogio, it developed, had volunteered to aid Stampfl in obtaining a master plumber license and had gone to the examining board offices in the Municipal Building to find out the best way to do it.

He saw Hassett, the witness said, and asked him to teach Stampfl how to get a license. Hassett refused, he said, saying, "I don't know you. Come some other time."

Undaunted, Ambrogio came back to the board offices a week later. This time, he said, he saw and talked with Jungman. Jungman told him to come back after Stampfl had passed the oral part of the plumbing examination. Ambrogio came back to the office again the day Stampfl took his written examination, Dec. 15, 1933. He stood outside in the hall, he said. Finally Jungman came out and after a short conversation told him to come back the next week

Continued on Page Three.

HARRIMAN SWEARS HE KNEW NOTHING OF FALSIFIED SLIPS

Calm and Confident on Stand, He Says He Never Gave Order for Transfer of Stock.

LEFT ALL WORK TO AIDES

Even After Bank Examiners Came, He Testifies, He Had No Inkling of Situation.

Joseph W. Harriman took the witness stand in Federal court yesterday in his own defense. The government has spent more than a year to get him there, over pleas of his counsel that his heart would not stand the ordeal of a trial and that he was no longer mentally responsible. Twice during this waiting period he has attempted suicide, once by jumping in the river and again by stabbing himself slightly in the chest.

Yesterday he denied calmly that he knew anything about the $1,730,080 of false entries or $600,000 misapplication of funds and assets of the defunct Harriman National Bank and Trust Company, for which he was indicted.

Under questioning by his counsel, George S. Leisure, he accepted the contention which the government has spent the last three weeks in presenting—that these transactions were improper—but said that as president of the bank he left all operating details, such as bookkeeping entries and collateral, to his vice presidents.

"I had vice presidents to do that," said Mr. Harriman.

He said he depended principally on Albert M. Austin, his executive vice president. Mr. Austin, who was indicted with him and has sat at the defense table with him since the trial opened, stared at him and seemed to grow older as Mr. Harriman's self-possession returned. Mr. Harriman is 67. Mr. Austin is 40.

Denies Ordering Entries.

He heard Mr. Leisure ask, "Did you give instructions to any one to make false entries in your bank?"

"I did not," said Mr. Harriman.

"Specifically," said Mr. Leisure, "did you give instructions to Mr. Austin to make these fourteen false entries?"

"I did not," said Mr. Harriman.

In this fashion Mr. Harriman disposed of the seventeen counts of the indictment. Although subordinate officers and bookkeepers of the bank who made the fourteen false entries have testified for the government that Mr. Austin told them they represented instructions from Mr. Harriman, he swore that was not so.

Similarly, if the government has succeeded in showing that a loan of $300,000 to Sidney Bernheim was made on such insufficient collateral that the loan constituted a misapplication of funds, Mr. Harriman knew only that he signed an agreement to protect Mr. Bernheim's purchase of bank stock and turned the completion of the transaction over to Mr. Austin.

"I relied on Mr. Austin," said Mr. Harriman.

As to the last two counts of the indictment, that Mr. Harriman had appropriated to his own use a block of 15,000 shares of Standard Oil stock belonging to Dr. Preston Satterwhite and worth more than $300,000, Mr. Harriman said his understanding with Dr. Satterwhite was that he could use the shares, while the doctor's $650,000 art collection was put separately as collateral behind a loan which was completed by Mr. Austin.

Misled Even at the Last.

Mr. Harriman maintained his innocence was so unsuspecting that he was misled as to the agitation of Mr. Austin and the subordinate bank officers in June, 1932, when the false entries were discovered by C. C. Francis, chief national bank examiner, who testified last week for the government.

He thought, he explained yesterday, that they were criticizing a campaign of distribution of Harriman bank stock which he had instituted in 1929 in an attempt to convert depositors into stockholders, in order to hold them against the growing competition of downtown banks which had established branches "on every corner around us."

This campaign, he admitted, had been "necessarily" accompanied by price maintenance operations in the market which involved taking up the Harriman bank stock whenever it offered. Although he started this campaign on his own initiative in 1929 as president and holder of one-third of the stock of the bank, the task of maintaining its market price until the depression was past assumed such proportions that on July 3, 1930, he formed a syndicate of twenty-six of the directors who authorized him individually as syndicate manager to purchase up to

Continued on Page Fifteen.

Sandino's Mother Backs His Foe for Presidency

By Tropical Radio to THE NEW YORK TIMES.

MANAGUA, Nicaragua, June 6.—An interview with the mother of General Agusto C. Sandino, slain revolutionary leader, which the local newspaper Niquino Homo recently printed has caused a stir throughout the country. Señora Sandino told Edgar Torres Leal, a writer, that she would wholeheartedly support General Anastasio Somoza, commander of the Nicaraguan National Guard, if he becomes a candidate for the Presidency.

"I wish I were a man so I could vote for him," she said, "but I have three sons who would cast their ballots for him."

Following the killing of General Sandino and another brother late in February, Gregorio Sandino, their father, accused General Somoza of having instigated the plot. They were ambushed after a conference with government officials.

REPUBLICANS ELECT FLETCHER AS HEAD

Former Ambassador, Choice of Hoover Group as Chairman, Defeats Progressive.

'LIBERAL' PLATFORM WINS

National Committee at Chicago Aligns the Party Against the Roosevelt Program.

The Republican Committee's new declaration of policy, Page 2.

By CHARLES R. MICHAEL.

Special to THE NEW YORK TIMES.

CHICAGO, June 6.—Henry P. Fletcher of Pennsylvania, Rough Rider under Colonel Theodore Roosevelt and an Ambassador under four Presidents, today was elected chairman of the Republican National Committee, succeeding Everett Sanders, who resigned.

Mr. Fletcher's election was heralded as proclaiming a militant Congressional campaign by the party and the charting of a course in opposition to the Roosevelt policies, opposition to which was defined in a declaration of principles of faith adopted by the committee previous to the election of the new chairman. The declaration of principles, drafted by a committee of nine headed by Charles D. Hilles of New York, avoided any specific denunciation of the Roosevelt economic program but in strong and definite language set the Republican party against regimentation of business and abolition of State sovereignty.

The platform was prepared by a committee consisting, in addition to Mr. Hilles, of former Senator Phipps of Colorado, Colonel Ernst Bamberger of Utah, John Richardson of Massachusetts, Mark Requa of California, Miss Dorothy Cunningham of Indiana, Mrs. Worthington Scranton of Pennsylvania, Mrs. Martha McClure of Iowa and R. E. B. Clements of Missouri.

The document represented the composite view of both wings of the committee and closely followed opinions held by Senator Reed and Ogden L. Mills. The latter sat with the committee until the early hours of the morning and virtually phrased the language of the declaration.

While the West, demanding a new deal in party organization and a leader representative of their section, gained much in the declaration of principles, its representatives were disappointed in their

Continued on Page Two.

8c MILK PROMISED BY MAYOR IN FIGHT ON PRICE INCREASE

50,000 Quarts a Day Will Be Sold in Sanitary Cartons Through Health Stations.

STATE ACTION DENOUNCED

LaGuardia Says It Failed to Seek Aid That Would Have Averted the Rise.

Combating the 1-cent-a-quart increase in the price of milk ordered for Monday by the State Department of Markets, Mayor LaGuardia said yesterday that he had arranged with the Borden Company for the distribution of 50,000 quarts of milk at 8 cents a quart here beginning on Monday and daily thereafter.

The Mayor believes the arrangement with the Borden Company is the forerunner of similar arrangements by other milk companies. The Sheffield Farms Company has offered to distribute milk in congested sections of the city from 100-gallon glass-lined tanks at 8 cents a quart. The Borden Company plans to distribute individual quarts in sealed cardboard containers at the same price.

Under authorization by the Sinking Fund Commission yesterday, the milk will be distributed through baby health stations operated by the Health Department in the five boroughs. Health Commissioner John L. Rice has objected to the sale of loose milk because of the sanitary hazards which he says it involves, but he has voiced no objection to the distribution of milk in sanitary individual containers.

Mayor Criticizes State Board.

In announcing his plans, the Mayor took the State Department of Markets to task for not availing itself of Federal aid which other States have received in similar situations. The milk control division of the State Department announced the price increase as an aid to up-State farmers who have suffered from the prolonged drought. The Dairymen's League estimated recently that the drought had increased fodder prices for dairy farmers by about 50 per cent.

"The State authorities could have obtained aid from any one of three sources," the Mayor said. "First, they could have obtained preferential prices on fodder through the Federal authorities. Next, we know that the Federal AAA has been buying dying cattle in other States confronted with the same situation. Thirdly, the farmers could have applied for emergency Federal loans to tide them over the crisis. None of these things has ever been attempted, and I am sure that if appeals had been made to all three sources of aid, at least one or two would have been productive. I find it difficult to understand why the State has made no effort to qualify for this help."

The State Markets Department gave the drought as its reason for ordering the price of Grade B milk delivered increased from 12 to 13 cents a quart.

"We may approach the problem from another angle," the Mayor continued. "The question of loose milk is still under consideration, depending upon the efficacy of the sanitary tanks which the companies are perfecting. Loose milk, however, is a health matter—not a legal one."

Behind the Mayor's plan for the distribution of milk in congested areas at 8 cents a quart is his hope that public health may not suffer through curtailment of the use of milk among the poor. The Mayor said that if the baby health stations

Continued on Page Three.

Banks Will Buy City Bonds Yielding 1½%; Rate on $10,000,000 Is Lowest Since 1931

The successful culmination of negotiations whereby a banking syndicate has agreed to buy $10,000,000 in special revenue bonds due in 120 days and paying an interest rate of only 1½ per cent was announced yesterday by Controller Joseph D. McGoldrick. The issue is in anticipation of the State's contribution to the payment of city teachers' salaries due Oct. 1.

The interest rate, the Controller pointed out, is the lowest granted the city on short-term borrowings since September, 1931, when $44,000,000 in ninety-four-day bonds was sold at an interest yield of only 1¾ per cent.

He explained that it was necessary to obtain the loan to pay teachers' salaries due July 1. For June and July, he said, $17,500,000 was needed, of which $7,500,000 was borrowed from a city sinking fund.

"The improvement in the city's credit, which this administration has been able to bring about, is very graphically reflected in this new rate of 1½ per cent for short-term borrowings," said the Controller. "I am naturally very much gratified, and I am sure the taxpayers of the city will be gratified also. Certainly this low rate tells more emphatically than anything else could how far improved the credit of the city is today."

Records of the Finance Department show that following the low rate borrowing in September, 1931, interest rates on city loans rose rapidly as the city's credit standing was lowered. This rise in interest rates reached its peak in 1933 when the city had to pay as high as 5½ per cent.

The banking syndicate which agreed to buy the short-term bonds includes the Chase National Bank, the National City Bank, the Guaranty Trust Company, the First National Bank, the Chemical Bank and Trust Company and Salomon Brothers & Hutzler.

STEEL EXECUTIVES REJECT JOHNSON PLAN, DEFY UNION; WORKERS ISSUE ULTIMATUM

Text of Statement by the Steel Leaders Reaffirming Their Stand for Open Shop

The statement issued last night by leaders of the steel industry on the impending strike follows:

Representatives of the iron and steel industry conferred here today with General Johnson, National Recovery Administrator, and Donald Richberg, general counsel of the NRA, on the creation of a labor-relations board in connection with the Iron and Steel Code, and on the threatened steel strike.

The steel men stated the demands of the Amalgamated Association do not relate to grievances of the workers, that the sole demand is for a closed shop. As the industry is unalterably opposed to the closed shop, the demand could not be considered.

It was made clear that the industry was definitely committed to the maintenance of employe-representation plans now effective in the industry and to the principle of the open shop.

Meanwhile in Washington no less determined a "rank-and-file" committee of steel workers told Secretary of Labor Perkins yesterday that "all hell will break loose" if the union's demand for a collective bargaining conference with their employers were not met by Sunday.

Union spokesmen in Washington challenged the employers' charge that they were demanding a closed shop. They said that "genuine collective bargaining" was their sole aim, as they had already set forth in a petition of the Amalgamated's president to President Roosevelt.

NRA HEAD PLEADS 2 HOURS

But Industry's Leaders Say They Will Never Discuss Closed Shop.

HOLD TO COMPANY UNIONS

Workers' Grievances Involved in No Way in Demand of the Amalgamated, They Say.

THREAT BY 'RANK AND FILE'

'All Hell Will Break Loose' if Collective Bargaining Is Refused, Miss Perkins Hears.

After listening for two hours and a half to General Hugh S. Johnson plead for a compromise to avert the threatened strike of 100,000 steel workers on June 16, leaders of the steel industry issued a statement here last night reaffirming their unalterable opposition to the labor demands.

General Johnson placed before them his plan for creation of a special labor relations board for steel, similar to that adopted for the automotive industry last March. But apparently it met with no more favor from the steel executives than it had from the union spokesmen, who rejected it on Tuesday.

The sole issue in the present crisis is the demand of the Amalgamated Association of Iron, Steel and Tin Workers, an affiliate of the American Federation of Labor, for a closed shop, the statement issued last night by the employers' group, the American Iron and Steel Institute, declared.

Against the Closed Shop.

The industry "is unalterably opposed to the closed shop," the statement continued, and for that reason the demand of the Amalgamated "could not be considered." The steel men maintained that workers' grievances were in no way concerned in the union's demand.

Emphasizing the intention of the employers to remain firm to the company union system, the statement said that the industry is "definitely committed to the maintenance of the employe representation plans now effective in the industry, and to the principle of the open shop."

This was a direct rebuff to the insistence of the union spokesmen for a meeting "around a table" at which the collective bargaining issue might be threshed out.

The statement reported that General Johnson and Donald Richberg, general counsel of the NRA, had laid before the conferees the plan for a special labor board, but it did not directly report the employers' reaction. The indications were that this concession had met with scant favor. A spokesman of one of the steel companies indicated, however, that the door was not closed to acceptance of the Johnson proposal.

Meet Again Today.

The sixteen leaders of the steel industry who took part in yesterday's all-day conference will meet again this morning for further consideration of the situation. But with grim earnestness as they departed last night they made it plain that they did not intend to yield on what they considered the vital point.

The employers' meeting here yesterday was held in the headquarters of the American Iron and Steel Institute, on the thirty-third floor of the Empire State Building. An air of secrecy surrounded the gathering all day, apparently as the result of General Johnson's determination not to be questioned by reporters.

Although General Johnson had been expected at the conference about 2 P. M., he did not arrive until 4:45, about half an hour after an army airplane had put him down at the Newark airport. He was accompanied by Mr. Richberg and by his secretary, Miss Frances Robinson.

When they finally came in they brushed past the waiting reporters without paying any attention to the questions hurled at them. To avoid being interviewed on their departure they went down a freight elevator to the basement of the skyscraper and out an unwatched exit to the street.

The meeting had been in session

Continued on Page Three.

ARMS COMPROMISE OFFERED BY FRANCE

Plan Given at Geneva Combines Aviation Curb, Security Pacts and Permanent Parley.

ATMOSPHERE IS IMPROVED

Barthou Speech Points to an Effort to Get Germany to Return to Conference.

By FREDERICK T. BIRCHALL.

Wireless to THE NEW YORK TIMES.

GENEVA, June 6.—The bureau (steering committee) of the disarmament conference has held still another session and in a more amiable atmosphere. But it cannot be said that fundamentally the position of the deadlock has changed or that the outcome is any more clear.

Many of the conferees themselves are openly pessimistic. In authoritative British quarters this evening this opinion was expressed:

"We only find the position worse. We cannot get out of it by any form of words, and we see no prospect of a real agreement."

In the American delegation opinion, while not so outspoken, was almost equally pessimistic.

Disarmament Is Goal.

The fact is the divergence between the two camps does not seem susceptible to verbal bridging. The Franco-Russian-Balkan group demands that this become a conference to provide security through promoting regional assistance pacts and "is willing, in fact would rather prefer, to drop disarmament altogether." In this group there is no real desire to see Germany back in the conference. Its actual aim is security through the diplomatic encirclement of Germany.

The Anglo-American group, on the other hand, still clings to disarmament as the conference goal. That can be achieved only by the return of Germany and consent to some measure of German rearmament. The plan this group envisages is the elimination of the more violent and destructive weapons of aggressive warfare and the gradual limitation of the rest. It is willing to consider some guarantees of security alongside and coincident with pursuit of this aim. But it is utterly opposed to maintenance of the status quo by diplomatic means under the guise of security, because it considers such security illusory.

Bureau Meets Tomorrow.

Between the two a great gulf is fixed which endless debate is not serving to narrow. For tonight, all that is certain is that the bureau has not given up in despair yet, but under more tranquil auspices will meet again Friday morning in the hope of presenting something for the general commission to take up in the afternoon.

The bureau, when it met today, had before it a resolution for a long adjournment of the conference, with its program of work meantime that proposed by Arthur Henderson, its president, yesterday and the many amendments to it, which left it a mere wreck of the original. This was immediately supplemented by a

Continued on Page Eleven.

BIDS OF 7 BILLIONS ON TREASURY ISSUES

Flotations of 3% Bonds and 2⅛% Notes Are Subscribed More Than Eight Times.

RESULT PLEASES OFFICIALS

Confidence in Government's Credit and Huge Reserves of Banks Are Main Factors.

Special to THE NEW YORK TIMES.

WASHINGTON, June 6.—Cash subscriptions reaching the surprising total of about $6,900,000,000 (more than eight times the amount sought by the government) were announced today in preliminary reports by the Treasury Department on the government's two offerings of Monday, the $300,000,000 in 3 per cent Treasury bonds and the $500,000,000 in 2⅛ per cent notes. The unusual reception given the two issues by the investment market brought great satisfaction to Treasury officials.

The bonds, although carrying the lowest interest rate quoted since pre-war days on a similar type of security, with the single exception of an $800,000,000-bond issue marketed at 3 per cent in September, 1931, were subscribed eight times. The subscriptions received for the note issue were nine times the amount of the offering.

The sale of 3 per cent bonds at this time came as a test of the market demand for a relatively long-term issue carrying a low interest rate. Some authorities had been skeptical about the reception the issue would receive, and few, if any, officials expected that the demand would be so great.

Large Subscriptions Welcomed.

The Treasury, in offering the bonds, announced that subscriptions up to $10,000 would receive preferred allotment and that the bonds would be parceled out on a percentage basis to those seeking greater amounts.

This was regarded as an invitation to those who desired relatively large blocks of the bonds to increase their subscriptions—bidding, for instance, for five or ten millions of the total in the hope that when the percentage basis was applied to allotments perhaps one-tenth of the amount of the bids would be obtained. Such a practice has been carried on by bidders in connection with other Treasury offerings.

Interest in the reception given the 3 per cent bonds was intensified by the fact that the $800,000,000 issued in September, 1931, was subscribed only after the books had remained open for more than a week and that since then these bonds, although now commanding a slight premium, have more frequently sold under par in the open market.

By some observers it was recalled that only a few months ago predictions were heard that it would be impossible for the government to market its securities, except at prohibitive interest rates, because of the large borrowings expected to obtain funds to carry forward the recovery program.

Confidence in the government's

Continued on Page Five.

WE DO OUR PART

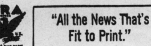

"All the News That's Fit to Print."

The New York Times.

LATE CITY EDITION
WEATHER—Fair and warmer today and tomorrow.
Temperatures yesterday—Max., 67; Min., 57.

VOL. LXXXIII....No. 27,895. Entered as Second-Class Matter, Postoffice, New York, N. Y. NEW YORK, SATURDAY, JUNE 9, 1934. P TWO CENTS In New York City. | THREE CENTS Within 200 Miles | FOUR CENTS Elsewhere Except in 7th and 8th Postal Zones.

ROOSEVELT SETS SECURITY FOR HOMES, JOBS, OLD AGE AS NEW DEAL'S OBJECTIVES

STEEL WORKERS ASSAIL JOHNSON; BOO PEACE PLAN

'Done With You and Institute,' Say Rank and File Men in Reply to Radio Talk.

NEUTRAL BOARD OFFERED

Steel Employers Meet Threat of Strike With Proposal for Settlement of Disputes.

PRESIDENT FAVORS IDEA

Can Create Tribunal, Whether or Not the Amalgamated Union Gives Approval.

By LOUIS STARK.
Special to THE NEW YORK TIMES.

WASHINGTON, June 8.—General Johnson was attacked tonight by the "rank and file" insurgents of the steel workers' union after he had announced a plan agreed upon by the American Iron and Steel Institute by which it was hoped to avert a threatened steel strike June 16.

The labor attack was made after General Johnson had made a radio speech in which he mentioned that steel workers had suggested previously that he should "scorch his Summer pants at an open blast furnace for $24 a week."

Recalling his cavalry service, the general declared that he had worn enough skin off his body sitting in a saddle to "make half a dozen such critics as they."

Thereupon sixteen chiefs of local unions who are in Washington sent an open message to him.

"We, the undersigned steel workers who have just listened to your damnable speech over the radio, denounce you," they said.

"You use your government position and the national radio to call us steel workers who criticize your schemes 'just so much skin off the saddle.' We are done with you and your Steel Institute.

Will "See the President."

"We are going to see the President tomorrow and will go back and report to our lodges."

The institute's proposal called for the creation of an Industrial Relations Board of three neutral members, appointed by the President, which would handle labor disputes in the industry.

While the plan was not formally presented to heads of the Amalgamated Association of Iron, Steel and Tin Workers for approval, General Johnson and Secretary Perkins explained it to a committee of five. They will give their reaction tomorrow.

At a turbulent session in the Department of Labor offices, however, Edward F. McGrady, Assistant Secretary of Labor, was booed by "rank and file" members when he attempted an explanation.

Plan Speeded by Threat.

The Iron and Steel Institute's proposal for a board, worked out jointly by General Johnson and the employers, was stimulated by the threat of a strike.

While the three appointees would be men without any connection with the steel industry, one would represent "the employe interest," one would represent "the employer interest" and the third the "public interest."

As explained by General Johnson tonight, the plan provides machinery to determine the spokesmen of the employes for collective bargaining. It also would permit the employes, if they wished, to scrap any company union and to elect in its place an independent outside organization, such as the Amalgamated Association of Iron, Steel and Tin Workers, the general said.

General Johnson made it clear that the plan for an industrial relations board was agreed to by the industry and that if the President wished to do so he might create the board by executive order.

General Johnson said frankly that acceptance of the plan by the union would have an important bearing on the threatened strike, but he also explained that the proposal had not been put up to the union for its approval or disapproval.

Praised by Roosevelt.

The administrator, it was understood, read the steel industry's proposal to the President over the telephone. Mr. Roosevelt was said to have expressed the belief that the innovation was a distinct advance in industrial relations boards.

The board would have authority to pass upon charges of interference by employers in the choice of representatives for collective bargaining in elections held since Jan. 1.

If such elections are held to have

Continued on Page Four.

Little Entente Joins Soviet In Pacts to Encircle Reich

Russia Officially Recognized, and Rumania and Poland Sign Accords With Her in Which Present Frontiers Are Guaranteed.

By FREDERICK T. BIRCHALL.
Wireless to THE NEW YORK TIMES.

GENEVA, June 8.—While disarmament is making slow and difficult progress the new system of Continental alliances proceeds apace.

It was learned tonight on indisputable authority that the Little Entente had officially recognized Soviet Russia. Thus the way is paved for that Eastern Locarno which is a part of the new policy of keeping Germany peaceful by encircling her with a diplomatic wall of alliances of mutual assistance.

The document putting this into effect was initiated by Foreign Minister Nicolas Titulescu of Rumania as acting chairman of the Little Entente and Foreign Commissar Maxim Litvinoff, representing Russia.

At the same time a triangular understanding has been reached by Poland, Rumania and Soviet Russia mutually guaranteeing the existing frontiers of the three States.

Thus Bessarabia becomes an established entity as part of Rumania, Russia has no longer a grievance against Rumania and a new pan-Slavic alliance arises in the Balkans, with big brother Russia as the apex and the last authority, just as before 1914.

Foreign Ministers Titulescu and Litvinoff leave Geneva tomorrow. Their work is done. An official meeting of the Little Entente will take place in Bucharest between June 18 and 20, at which all these things will be officially ratified.

The new entente, which brings together France and her allies on the one hand and Russia on the other, was precipitated by the only striking success won by the Nazi government in foreign affairs. It made a ten-year non-aggression treaty with Poland, which was hailed in Berlin as a break in France's "iron ring" around Germany.

French concern over this development caused Paris to turn to Russia, taking up vigorously plans for an understanding with Moscow. The Little Entente, after much effort, was induced to enter this combination. Poland also has been drawn back into the understandings.

An important development is the closing of the Bessarabian feud. This territory was given to Rumania at the peace conference at the expense of Russia and the Soviet had steadily refused to recognize Rumania's title. Her desire to secure her frontiers in the west while facing Japan in the east has been a strong factor in causing her to alter her standpoint.

M'KEE TONED DOWN DATA ON MORTGAGE

Induced Bank to Alter Letter Warning Certificate Holders of Foreclosure, Alger Hears.

HELD CITY OFFICE AT TIME

Got $25,000 Fee for Arranging RFC Loan to State Title—Van Schaick Wins Appeal.

Joseph V. McKee, former Acting Mayor of New York City, induced the Bank of the Manhattan Trust Company to delete damaging parts of a letter that would have disclosed to certificate holders of the State Title and Mortgage Company the condition of the mortgage underlying their securities in 1932, according to testimony given yesterday before Moreland Act Commissioner George W. Alger.

Documentary evidence of Mr. McKee's services for the State Title and Mortgage Company was introduced at the hearing at the Bar Association, 42 West Forty-fourth Street, by Kenneth E. Walser, associate counsel to Alfred A. Cook, counsel to Commissioner Alger.

Was President of Aldermen.

Mr. McKee was President of the Board of Aldermen when, according to the testimony, he caused the letter which the trust company sent to the certificate holders to be toned down, and also when he obtained fees totaling $25,000 from the State Title and Mortgage Company for his part in arranging a Reconstruction Finance Corporation loan of $4,700,000. The fees were paid in two equal instalments on Nov. 1 and Dec. 1, 1932, according to vouchers submitted by Mr. Walser.

Mr. Walser also offered in evidence Mr. McKee's bill for $10,225.85 for professional services, including luncheon and dinner conferences on mortgage matters and the dictation of a letter to be sent to certificate holders of the Series C issue. The bill has not been paid, according to Mr. Walser, by George S. Van Schaick, State Superintendent of Insurance, as rehabilitator of the title company.

Intervened in 1932.

Mr. McKee intervened on behalf of the State Title and Mortgage Company in 1932 when the Bank of the Manhattan Trust Company prepared a letter to inform the certificate holders interested in Series C of the status of the $1,500,000 mortgage on the Hotel Victoria, Seventh Avenue and Fifty-first Street, which underlay their securities.

The Victoria Hotel mortgage was substituted in the series for 134 whole mortgages against which the certificates had been sold.

The Bank of the Manhattan Trust Company as depositary held the hotel mortgage and decided to inform the certificate holders by letter of the effect of foreclosure proceedings started by the Chase National Bank.

Mr. McKee's part in the draft of the letter sent to the certificate holders was shown by the copy of a letter he wrote to E. J. Donegan,

Continued on Page Sixteen.

HITLER TO CONFER WITH MUSSOLINI

Will Discuss Arms and Other Issues in Venice, Probably Next Friday or Saturday.

VAST IMPORTANCE IS SEEN

Germany Sought Conference as Relations With Italy Steadily Grew Worse.

Wireless to THE NEW YORK TIMES.

GENEVA, June 8.—It is learned here on excellent authority that a conference between Chancellor Hitler of Germany and Premier Mussolini of Italy has been arranged after long negotiations and will take place in Venice, probably next Friday or Saturday.

It is expected to cover not only the disarmament situation but the project for a Mediterranean pact and other political issues, including the Austrian and Central European problems still unsolved, so its importance can scarcely be overestimated.

It will be the first time the two Western European dictators have met.

Denial Issued in Rome.

By ARNALDO CORTESI.
Wireless to THE NEW YORK TIMES.

ROME, June 8.—A denial was issued here today of the report that a meeting between Premier Mussolini and Chancellor Hitler was being planned and would occur in the near future.

Despite the denial the rumor continues to circulate with the greatest insistence, and there is every reason to believe that even if the meeting has not yet been definitely fixed, intensive pourparlers to that effect have occurred and are continuing between the Italian and German Foreign Offices.

Developments, in any case, are being watched with the closest attention in diplomatic circles here as importance of the very first order would be attached to a meeting of the Italian and German dictators at this time.

Premier Mussolini is now at his estate at Rocca delle Camiante, near Forli. He may come to Rome tomorrow to make the final decision concerning the Italian debt payment to the United States that is due next Friday. If he does, however, he will almost certainly return to his estate immediately afterward. If the meeting with Chancellor Hitler actually does take place, therefore, it is not improbable that it will occur either in Venice or in Milan.

Nations Have Drifted Apart.

After a first moment of rapture following Herr Hitler's accession to power, Italy and Germany have been drifting ever further apart and this slow but constant development has been accompanied by an ever more noticeable Italian rapprochement with France. Indeed, it may be said that never since the World War have Italian relations with France been so good or Italian relations with Germany so bad.

It is regarded as scarcely likely

Continued on Page Six.

ARMS PARLEY VOTES TO CONTINUE WORK; SEEKS REICH ENTRY

General Session Will Adjourn Until Fall and Committees Will Try to Solve Issues.

CORDIALITY NOW PREVAILS

Britain and France Will Carry on Private Negotiations for Return of Germany.

Wireless to THE NEW YORK TIMES.

GENEVA, June 8.—The World Disarmament Conference will carry on. Brought to a realization of the danger of its immediate failure from mere disagreements over procedure, the proponents of the rival theories of continuance succeeded late last night and in further negotiations this morning in reaching a compromise.

The resolution of Arthur Henderson, president of the conference, providing for adjournment pending conference negotiations for Germany's return has been dropped. The French resolution, providing for continuance while the governments separately endeavor to induce Germany to return, has been modified and amended.

This afternoon, in a public session, the bureau (steering committee) of the conference adopted the amended French text after Mr. Henderson himself, with the consent of the proposers of various amendments, had withdrawn his own resolution. The general commission, in a subsequent meeting, endorsed and accepted the bureau's action. Monday it will meet to arrange for the working of the committees provided for in the French resolution during the Summer.

This, however, is a mere detail. The general body of the conference will go into retirement, while its working subsidiaries carry out their separate missions until Autumn.

Germany Is Problem.

What will happen then depends upon developments meanwhile, and especially upon one development not under the conference's control but dependent upon the French and British Governments, which are taking it in hand. If Germany can be induced by these governments to return to the conference its work may proceed and a disarmament convention may come out of it. But unless Germany does return, the achievement of a disarmament convention is all but hopeless. In such a case, the conference may dissolve or it may attempt to continue in some form with the object of providing security in the guise of diplomatic understandings for such participants as are left.

All this was tacitly admitted today in the speeches that wound up the present era of the conference and prepared the way for the new one, with Germany back in it, if she can be induced to return.

It all hangs on Germany. The process is set forth in the amended resolution by Louis Barthou, the French Foreign Minister, as adopted. This resolution provides that:

Taking into consideration the resolutions previously submitted by various groups, and taking into account the clarifications of positions resulting from the French, Italian and British official memoranda, and convinced of the necessity of endeavoring to achieve a general convention for arms reduction and limitation, the general commission decides to continue.

To that end, it invites its bureau to seek, by whatever means it deems appropriate and with a view

Continued on Page Six.

FIXED PRICES STAND IN APPROVED CODES; PROTESTS STIR NRA

Johnson Explains New Policy as Industries Fear Loss of Their Protection.

DEPUTIES ARE HARASSED

Many Were Uninformed of What Was Coming—Authorities Notified to Stop Cuts.

Special to THE NEW YORK TIMES.

WASHINGTON, June 8.—The Recovery Administration's new policy of abandoning price fixing will not be applied to approved codes until after negotiation and agreement by Code Authorities, the NRA announced today.

In a speech telephoned to the International Ladies' Garment Workers Union at Chicago, General Johnson declared that "I cannot use too much emphasis in saying that this policy does not affect codes already approved."

Meanwhile an NRA statement said "while pending codes and codes hereafter submitted for approval will be adjusted to the new policy, codes already approved will be amended to conform only as the result of negotiations with and agreement by the interested Code Authorities."

Relief to Administrators.

These announcements came as a relief to division and deputy administrators, harassed by Code Authorities and members of industries under codes containing price protection, who feared that the NRA had swept away the protection given them in return for the higher labor costs under codes.

Those charged with administration and handling of codes were confused as to how far they were expected to go under the office order, which yesterday bade them to "seek through agreements with Code Authorities of approved codes to amend them to conform with these policies and wherever resistance is encountered, take the subject up with the administrator."

Well over half of the codes now approved have price-fixing or price features, and this number includes such important codes as oil, lumber, coal and retail trade. Oil, however, is administered by a special board under Secretary Ickes.

"Chaos" in Lumber on Coast.

Newspaper reports, it was learned today, sent salesmen out all up and down the west coast cutting prices on lumber under the impression that the price features of the code were dead.

The industry was described as being in a state of chaos over the new policy and from the west coast, where it centres, came reports that buyers were refusing to sign contracts under the impression that the price level would sink immediately.

Wayne P. Ellis, Deputy Administrator, in charge of the Bituminous Coal Code, telegraphed all regional Code Authorities that the policy was not in effect as far as their code was concerned.

A similar bulletin was rushed out from the headquarters of the National Retail Code Authority.

In one industry, already under a code, the situation was so acute that an attempt was made to have a state of emergency declared at once so that present minimum price levels would not suffer. The application was refused, with a declaration that the administration would

Continued on Page Four.

Faber and the Two Millens Found Guilty; To Die for Murder in Bay State Bank Raid

By The Associated Press.

DEDHAM, Mass., June 8—Abraham Faber, youthful college graduate and confessed robber and slayer, and Murton and Irving Millen, brothers, were convicted tonight of murder in the first degree for killing Patrolman Forbes McLeod, one of two policemen slain in a Needham, Mass., bank hold-up last February.

The conviction carries a mandatory sentence of death in the electric chair.

The verdict was returned by a jury before which they had been on trial eight weeks. The jury took the case at 4:51 P. M. and deliberated for four hours and a half.

The fate of the three was placed in the hands of the jury after Judge Nelson P. Brown had delivered a charge that lasted for nearly three hours.

Speaking slowly and deliberately, Judge Brown told the jury it was not to be concerned with public sentiment in arriving at a decision in the case.

The jury was told that sympathy for the bereaved and justice for the accused must not be mixed, and the judge strongly intimated, through citing similar cases, that all three defendants, if guilty, were equally guilty and that their crime, if any, was murder in the first degree.

He dwelt at length on the subject of insanity and said:

"Criminal responsibility does not depend on the mental age of the defendant but whether he knows the difference between right and wrong."

The robbery took place on Feb. 2, shortly after two other similar killings had stirred the entire State.

The Millens were first to be arrested. Resistance was clubbed out of them in the lobby of a large New York hotel, where, with Norma Millen, the clergyman's daughter bride of Murton, the two brothers were staying. At the same time Faber, proprietor of a small Boston radio store, who had never before been in trouble, was being broken down by State detectives at Boston. Eventually, he confessed.

Norma Millen, 19, daughter of the Rev. Norman Brighton, was arrested on a secret indictment after her husband had been brought back from New York. She is awaiting trial on a charge of being an accessory after the murder.

The President's Message

Special to THE NEW YORK TIMES.

WASHINGTON, June 8.—Following is the text of President Roosevelt's message to Congress, outlining a threefold attack on the problems of human security.

To the Congress of the United States:

You are completing a work begun in March, 1933, which will be regarded for a long time as a splendid justification of the vitality of representative government. I greet you and express once more my appreciation of the cooperation which has proved so effective.

Only a small number of the items of our program remain to be enacted and I am confident that you will pass on them before adjournment. Many other pending measures are sound in conception, but must, for lack of time or of adequate information, be deferred to the session of the next Congress. In the meantime, we can well seek to adjust many of these measures into certain larger plans of government policy for the future of the nation.

You and I, as the responsible directors of these policies and actions, may, with good reason, look to the future with confidence, just as we may look to the past fifteen months with reasonable satisfaction.

On the side of relief we have extended material aid to millions of our fellow citizens.

On the side of recovery we have helped to lift agriculture and industry from a condition of utter prostration.

But, in addition to these immediate tasks of relief and recovery we have properly, necessarily and with overwhelming approval determined to safeguard these tasks by rebuilding many of the structures of our economic life and of reorganizing it in order to prevent a recurrence of collapse.

It is childish to speak of recovery first and reconstruction afterward. In the very nature of the processes of recovery we must avoid the destructive influences of the past. We have shown the world that democracy has within it the elements necessary to its own salvation.

Less hopeful countries where

Continued on Page Two.

CONGRESS GETS MESSAGE

Present Legislation Is Tied Up With Program for Next Session.

FOR HOUSING ACTION NOW

Contributory Job Insurance Is Called For—Leaning Toward British Plan Is Seen.

TO END POVERTY FARMING

Incentive to Private Profit Is Held Safe in Ample Scope Left to Initiative.

Special to THE NEW YORK TIMES.

WASHINGTON, June 8.—Disclaiming any intention to oppose "the incentive of reasonable and legitimate private profit," President Roosevelt, in a message today, called upon Congress to coordinate pending measures with prospective social legislation at the next session, which would embark the government upon a sweeping policy designed to provide for "the security of the men, women and children of the nation."

Three factors were presented in the President's analysis of the legislation contemplated. They were:

1. Modernization of existing homes and the building of new homes.

2. Better use of the nation's land and water resources by people who cannot make a living in their present positions, indicating the abandonment of submarginal lands; and definite, annual appropriations to rehabilitate hundreds of thousands of American families on a permanent basis, thus decreasing future costs for relief of destitution.

3. Social insurance, against unemployment and against old age, national in scope, with the States meeting a large share of management costs and the Federal Government investing, maintaining and safeguarding the reserves.

Speaks for the Housing Bill.

No additional legislation at this session was asked for, although by implication Congress was urged to enact the Administration Housing Bill which was reported favorably today by the House Committee on Banking and Currency.

The message, the last but one which the President will send to this Congress, met with generally favorable comment at the Capitol, much of which was enthusiastic. Some Republicans were critical.

Mr. Roosevelt tied up his ideals of social policy in government with a general treatment of the conservation and development of natural resources, particularly water. When the next Congress convenes he hoped "to be able to present to it a carefully considered plan, covering the development and the human use of our national resources of land and water over a long period of years."

In the long range program the President remarked, "ample scope is left for the exercise of private initiative.

Says He Counts on Promises.

"In fact," he continued, "in the process of recovery I am greatly hoping that repeated promises that private investment and private initiative to relieve the government in the immediate future of much of the burden it has assumed will be fulfilled.

"We have not imposed undue restrictions upon business. We have not opposed the incentive of reasonable and legitimate private profit. We have sought rather to enable certain aspects of business to regain the confidence of the public. We have sought to put forward the rule of fair play in finance and industry."

An old-age pension bill has been reported out by both House and Senate committees. No rule has been obtained for its discussion in the House, but it is on the Senate calendar. An employment insurance bill is still in committee in both House and Senate.

The President replied to those critics of the administration program who argue that the cart has been put before the horse. He said "it is childish to speak of recovery first and reconstruction afterward." In the very nature of the processes of recovery "we must

Continued on Page Two.

REPORT ON TUGWELL ORDERED BY SENATE

Committee Instructed to Submit Findings on Nomination by Noon Tuesday.

SMITH IS DEBATE TARGET

Admits He Sanctioned Delay Lasting Since April 24—Byrd Assails Nominee.

Special to THE NEW YORK TIMES.

WASHINGTON, June 8.—On the advice of administration leaders the Senate tonight unanimously instructed its Agriculture Committee to make a report by noon Tuesday on the nomination of Rexford G. Tugwell as Under-Secretary of Agriculture, held in the committee since April 24 through Chairman Smith's opposition.

This action followed a sharp two hours' debate on a motion by Senator Robinson, Democratic leader, to have the Senate discharge the committee from consideration of the nomination, but for which he substituted the motion accepted.

Unexpected fire flamed when Senator Smith resisted the discharge motion as an "insult" to his committee and Senator Byrd declared that Mr. Tugwell did not possess the proper conception of fundamental American ideals.

Tugwell to Be Questioned.

The nominee, about whom controversy has raged for months, will be called by the Agriculture Committee Monday for questioning on his views, the committee sitting if necessary "all Monday and all Monday night," Chairman Smith said.

No doubt exists that the committee will report the nomination favorably Tuesday and that it will be confirmed by the Senate, but only after a debate in which some caustic remarks will be made.

Mr. Smith assured the Senate repeatedly that no motion had ever been made in his committee to bring up the Tugwell nomination, and remarked that he would "have been a fool" to encourage action upon a nominee to whom, he conceded, he was uncompromisingly opposed.

Reproached From Floor.

On all sides Senators charged Senator Smith with bad ethics in refusing to call up the nomination himself, but he reiterated that if no motion was made by committeemen the failure of action was not his fault.

Senator Smith said he had never thought an Under-Secretary necessary, did not, in fact, "like the idea of aping Great Britain."

He said Secretary Wallace sent an appeal to him, but before he could act the legislation creating the office had been sent to the Appropriations Committee, "railroaded through" and "signed by the President."

Thus, he asserted, "the most important function" of the Agriculture Committee was taken away.

He said Dr. Tugwell was an "academic" and not a practical farmer.

Several times, he said, members

Continued on Page Three.

WHEAT ESTIMATE LOWEST SINCE 1893

Federal Report for June 1 Slashes Figure for Crop to 500,000,000 Bushels.

WINTER TOTAL 400,357,000

Spring Yield Only 'Guessed'—Drought Also Cuts Other Prospective Harvests.

Special to THE NEW YORK TIMES.

WASHINGTON, June 8.—The shortest wheat crop for the United States since 1893, amounting to not more than 500,000,000 bushels from both Winter and Spring supplies, was predicted today by the Federal Crops Reporting Board, on the basis of conditions on June 1.

Reflecting the effects on small grains of the worst drought in the country's history, the report put the prospective Winter wheat crop at 400,357,000 bushels. This was a reduction of 61,000,000 bushels from the forecast of a month earlier.

The board declined, in the face of the unusual conditions, to attempt an estimate of the probable yield of Spring wheat, but said it thought it likely to be about 100,000,000 bushels.

Estimates for Other Crops.

Unusually short crops were also predicted for oats, barley, rye and hay. The output of oats was tentatively estimated at less than 700,000,000 bushels, which also would be below that of any years since 1893. Rye production was forecast in 18,800,000 bushels, compared with the short crop of 21,000,000 bushels last year and a preceding five-year average of 40,900,000 bushels.

The board would not hazard an estimate of the probable crop of barley, but said it "appears to have been damaged as much as oats."

The hay crop will depend upon weather conditions during the remainder of the growing season, but the report said that "with pastures bare over a wide area and stock of necessity turned into hay and grain fields, an acute shortage of hay in many States seems unavoidable."

Hay Crop Estimate.

Unless the weather is "exceptionally favorable" in the immediate future, the total crop of tame and wild hay, it was asserted, was not likely to be much beyond 50,000,000 tons. This compares with a short crop of 74,000,000 tons last year and an average from 1927 to 1931 of 84,000,000 tons.

"The records for June in past years show nothing comparable with the situation this year," said the report. "The June 1 condition of oats, for example, is 47.2 per cent this year, whereas the lowest in past years was the 78.3 per cent recorded for 1928. The condition of tame hay is 53.9, and the lowest previously was 76 per cent in 1926. Wild hay prospects are even worse, being 37.7, compared with the previous low of 68.7.

"Reports on the condition of pastures, which have been fairly comparable for perhaps forty years, show 53.2 per cent of normal this year, compared with the previous

Continued on Page Twenty-seven.

NRA WE DO OUR PART

"All the News That's Fit to Print."

The New York Times.

LATE CITY EDITION
WEATHER—Showers today; tomorrow fair, somewhat cooler.
Temperatures Yesterday—Max., 91, Min., 78

Section 1

Copyright, 1934, by The New York Times Company.

VOL. LXXXIII....No. 27,917. Entered as Second-Class Matter. Postoffice, New York, N. Y. NEW YORK, SUNDAY, JULY 1, 1934. Including Rotogravure Picture, Magazine and Book Sections. F TEN CENTS | TWELVE CENTS Beyond 200 Miles. Except in 7th and 8th Postal Zones.

HITLER CRUSHES REVOLT BY NAZI RADICALS; VON SCHLEICHER IS SLAIN, ROEHM A SUICIDE; LOYAL FORCES HOLD BERLIN IN AN IRON GRIP

EXCHANGE, LABOR BOARDS NAMED; FARM BILL SIGNED

KENNEDY IN 'CHANGE POST

The Others Are Mathews, Landis, Healy, Pecora for Varying Terms.

WIRE BOARD IS CHOSEN

Members Are Sykes, Brown, Case, Stuart, Payne, Gary and Walker.

RAIL PENSIONS APPROVED

Clark Howell Heads Air Study—Moffett Made Administrator of the Housing Act.

President Clears His Desk

On the eve of his departure this evening on the cruiser Houston for a month's cruise, President Roosevelt cleared his desk last night.

He named the two commissions to regulate the Stock Exchanges and the operations of telegraph, telephone and radio companies.

He signed the Frazier-Lemke bill setting up new methods for the compromising of agricultural indebtedness.

He signed the railroad employes' pension bill.

He appointed James A. Moffett of New York, prominent oil executive, Administrator of the Housing Act.

He appointed an Aviation Commission, with Clark Howell as chairman.

He created an impartial Labor Relations Board, abolishing the old one and eliminating the NRA from a rôle in settling labor disputes.

Picks Exchange Board

Special to THE NEW YORK TIMES.

WASHINGTON, June 30.—As his last act tonight in cleaning up essential business before sailing from Annapolis for a month's holiday today, President Roosevelt named the personnel of the Securities and Exchange Commission.

He did not designate a chairman, there being some doubt as to his authority to do so, but it was understood in well-informed quarters that responsibility for the commission's work under the sweeping Stock Exchange Control Act would fall upon Joseph P. Kennedy, New York financier, who was designated to serve for five years. Four other commissioners were named for periods varying from one to four years.

The personnel of the commission follows:

JOSEPH P. KENNEDY of New York, five-year term.

GEORGE C. MATHEWS of Wisconsin, four-year term.

JAMES M. LANDIS of Massachusetts, three-year term.

ROBERT E. HEALY of Vermont, two-year term.

FERDINAND PECORA of New York, one-year term.

Messrs. Mathews and Landis are members of the Federal Trade Commission. Mr. Pecora was counsel for the Senate Banking and Currency Committee during the period in which it aired publicly for the first time in twenty years the manifold operations of securities exchanges and investment banking houses. As committee counsel he played a large part in shaping the law under which the commission will operate.

The naming of the Securities and Exchange Commission came after President Roosevelt, in a day of intensive work, had also named the Communications Commission and a commission to plan coordination of aircraft development, and had issued statements announcing the signing of the Frazier-Lemke Farm Mortgage Bill and the Railroad Pensions Bill.

Kennedy Close to Farley.

The membership of the Securities and Exchange Commission had been pretty generally forecast, but even so its composition was full of surprises, particularly the obvious placing in line for the chairmanship of Mr. Kennedy.

This is the first emergence of the New Yorker from what seemed to be political eclipse since the campaign of 1932, when he was distinguished both as a heavy contributor and important raiser of campaign funds, and because of his

Continued on Page Twenty-one.

Major Sports Results

Track—Bill Bonthron of Princeton broke the world's record for the 1,500-meter run in the national A. A. U. championship meet at Milwaukee. Timed in 3:48.8, he beat Glenn Cunningham by two feet. It was the fifth meeting between the stars and the triumph gave Bonthron the edge with three victories.

Tennis—Four Americans advanced at Wimbledon. Frank Shields defeated Christian Boussus of France and George M. Lott Jr. halted Harry Hopman of Australia. Miss Helen Jacobs conquered Mlle. Jacqueline Goldschmidt of France and Miss Sarah Palfrey beat Miss J. Jedrzejowska of Poland.

Baseball—Routing Carl Hubbell, the Dodgers stopped the Giants, 8—4, before 12,000 at the Polo Grounds. At Washington the Yankees were leading the Senators, 4—1, when rain caused the game to be called off in the fifth inning.

(Full details in Sports Section.)

JOHN JACOB ASTOR WEDS ELLEN FRENCH

Notables Fill Newport Church for Ceremony Climaxing Weeks of Social Activity.

ONLOOKERS PACK STREETS

Crowd Delays Both Bride and Bridegroom—Astor's Mother Sits in a Front Pew.

By RUSSELL B. PORTER.

Special to THE NEW YORK TIMES.

NEWPORT, R. I., June 30.—Two of America's oldest families, prominent in both landed wealth and in social position, were united in marriage here today at the wedding of John Jacob Astor 3d and Miss Ellen Tuck French.

The bridegroom is the third of his name in American life. The first John Jacob Astor, fur trader, founded the family in early American days. The second lost his life in the sinking of the Titanic, and the third John Jacob Astor, today's bridegroom, was born a few months later. He is a half-brother of Vincent Astor, and inherited with the latter the great Astor fortune.

The bride is a granddaughter of Amos Tuck French and is related to the Vanderbilt family.

These young members of old families, the bridegroom only 21 years old and the bride 18, were joined together in a setting replete with symbols of early American traditions.

They were married according to the ancient simple ritual of the Protestant Episcopal Church, whose worshipers came to New England with the first settlers, in old Trinity Church, a long, narrow, weather-beaten white clapboard building with a towering white steeple and gilded spire and weather vane. It was all just as it was when the church was built more than two centuries ago, in 1726, eighty-seven years after the founding of Newport in 1639.

Shading the high steeple was a fine, old elm tree, as tall as or taller than the spire itself, with its great spreading branches almost speaking aloud the story of New England. The tree itself was as old or nearly as old as the church.

Church Recalls Colonial Days.

On the other side of the church, so that the wedding procession walked between it and the old tree to enter the building, was the old burying ground with its plain weather-beaten granite headstones bearing the names of men and women who played leading parts in shaping the history of the colonies and of the first days of the Republic.

All around the church, which is right in the centre of this fine old city, old frame buildings of Colonial architecture, with Grecian columns, steeply slanting roofs and gables, crowding close to the building line of the street, bespoke Newport's history.

The time joined with the place in celebrating the event with appropriate ceremony, for not only was it in the midst of the Summer season, when Newport's social colony is always in full swing, but it was coincident with a visit of a large part of the United States fleet. From time immemorial the navy has been associated with Newport, and

Continued on Page Eighteen.

FORD WILL ACCEPT NRA AND ITS CODE, JOHNSON IS TOLD

General Announces He Awaits Signed Certificate From Auto Maker.

SAYS HE ASKED CHANGES

Recovery Head Asserts His Suggestions Have Been Approved in Detroit.

Special to THE NEW YORK TIMES.

WASHINGTON, June 30.—General Johnson believed tonight that he was nearing such a settlement of his ten months feud with Henry Ford as would let the NRA put another feather in its cap and at the same time allow the automobile maker to re-enter the fertile field of government business.

General Johnson today read a copy of an unsigned letter purporting to be from the Ford Motor Company to a local dealer, setting forth the claims that that firm had been complying and would continue to comply with "pertinent" provisions of the Automobile Code.

The Recovery Administrator s. that if the letter, with certain revisions which he suggested, were returned to him signed by Henry Ford or any other authorized executive of the Ford Motor Company, he would consider it a certificate of compliance, would call off his "crack-down" campaign against the company and recommend to President Roosevelt that it be allowed to resume bidding on government contracts.

A large order of motor trucks for the army, which War Department officials prefer should be Ford products, is said to be the immediate stake in negotiations between the NRA and Mr. Ford. Harry H. Woodring Assistant Secretary of War, has made overtures to General Johnson within the last thirty-six hours to learn what the Ford company would have to do to qualify to bid.

Representative Kvale of Minnesota, active in the House Military Affairs Committee investigating War Department purchases, accompanied the Ford dealer when he called to show the unsigned letter to General Johnson this afternoon.

Talks To Ford Adviser.

General Johnson believed the letter to be entirely authentic and to have originated at the Detroit offices of the Ford Company despite the circumstances under which it was shown to him. This belief was intensified by a telephone conversation which he had with William J. Cameron, editorial adviser to Mr. Ford, regarding the suggested revisions.

The letter, according to General Johnson, was addressed to the Northwest Motor Company of Bethesda, Md., the local dealer that has tried so consistently to keep in contractual relations with the governmental departments regardless of Mr. Ford's refusal to sign a compliance certificate for his code.

In its original form the letter said that although the company had complied and would continue to comply with the provisions of the automobile compact, it reserved its "constitutional rights" as guaranteed by the fundamental law.

This was the section to which General Johnson objected. He told R. P. Sabine, president of the Northwest Motor Company, and Representative Kvale that President Roosevelt would not stand for

Continued on Page Twenty-two.

POLICE FILL THE STREETS

Goering's Forces Keep Curious Throngs on Constant Move.

MACHINE GUNS MOUNTED

Public Buildings on Unter den Linden and Wilhelmstrasse Are Heavily Guarded.

NEWS IS AT A PREMIUM

Rumors Are Rampant as Only a One-Sheet Paper Provides Authentic Information.

Copyright, 1934, by The Associated Press.

BERLIN, June 30.—With the peaceful cool of a Summer evening made strangely tense by squads of armed police and the presence of machine guns, this capital city was facing tonight the possibility of a new unnamed, undefined political event.

Crowds of curious spectators, only partly informed as to events through limited press dispatches, surged up and down Wilhelmstrasse, where public buildings were massed with police ever ready to keep them on the move.

In front of the home of Captain Ernest Roehm, suicide deposed leader of the storm troops, were bristling truckloads of Prussian Premier Hermann Goering's special police. They formed an impressive barricade separate from the thousands who dragged their feet in slow response to demands that streets and sidewalks be kept clear.

Show of Force Excites Crowds.

The presence of police everywhere one turned was a direct stimulant to the excitement of the street and thoroughfare. Never in the history of Berlin, it was pointed out, had so many police appeared in the streets at one time with such obvious readiness for action. In addition to the regular police force, augmented by armed reserves, there was the steel-helmeted, green-clad police of Premier Goering.

The sudden appearance of a police machine gun detachment, with ammunition ready, in historic Potsdammer Platz brought a final touch to the grimness of the situation. The sight of another similar detachment riding up and down Unter den Linden left no doubt in the public mind as to the nature of the emergency.

Men and women rushed like hounds on the scent wherever carriers appeared with copies of one newspaper which had printed one page only for free distribution. This carried a brief account of Captain Roehm's discharge by Chancellor Hitler.

Reactions to the news were various and could be read at will on the faces of newspaper readers. Persons obviously of a conservative mind wreathed their faces in smiles as they read what had happened.

Continued on Page Three.

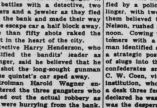

Dillinger Raids Bank in South Bend, Ind., Reported Shot; Officer Slain, Loot $28,000

By The Associated Press.

SOUTH BEND, Ind., June 30.—A bandit quintet with John Dillinger reported to be in command, stormed the Merchants' National Bank today, scooped up $28,439 and fled in a wild barrage of bullets, leaving a slain policeman and four wounded men in their wake.

The ruthless raiders engaged in gun battles with a detective, two officers and a jeweler as they fled from the bank and made their way to the escape car a half block away. More than fifty shots raked the street in the heart of the city.

Detective Harry Henderson, who identified the bandits' leader as Dillinger, said he believed that he had shot the long-sought gunman as the quintet's car sped away.

Patrolman Harold Wagner encountered the three gangsters who carried out the actual robbery as they were hurrying from the bank. He was fatally wounded before he could reach his pistol.

Those wounded were P. G. Stahley, manager of the Birdsell Manufacturing Company; Jake Soloman, Delos N. Coen, a cashier, and Samuel Toth. At Epworth Hospital it was found that a bullet had struck Soloman in the hip and coursed upward. His condition was described as critical. Toth was wounded in the eye as a bullet smashed the windshield of his automobile.

Leaving an outpost, believed to be John Hamilton, on guard at their automobile, and another bandit closer to the bank, the man identified by a police detective as Dillinger, with two henchmen, one of them believed to be "Baby Face" Nelson, rushed into the bank about noon. Cowing the twenty-five customers with a machine gun, the man identified as Dillinger took up a strategic post and sent a score of slugs into the ceiling while his confederates snatched up $28,439. C. W. Coen, vice president of the institution, who took cover under a desk three feet from the gunner, declared he was positive the leader was the desperado Dillinger.

Bundling their loot, the three commandeered Stahley, Coen and several other patrons and used them as human shields as they marched out the door. Wagner ran toward them from across the crowded street. The machine gunner shot him down, three bullets entering the policeman's body.

THREE OF THE LEADERS WHO DIED IN THE REICH MUTINY.

Times Wide World Photo.
Captain Ernst Roehm, ousted Storm Troop head, who committed suicide.

Associated Press Photo.
Karl Ernst, Berlin Storm Troop leader, arrested and later shot.

Times Wide World Photo.
General Kurt von Schleicher, slain by arresting officers.

HITLER COMMANDS NAZI ABSTINENCES

Forbids the Troopers to Spend Money on Banquets and Bans Moral 'Debauches.'

WANTS 'MEN, NOT APES'

Chancellor Asserts All Must Be on Best Behavior or Be Expelled From Ranks.

Wireless to THE NEW YORK TIMES.

BERLIN, June 30.—Chancellor Adolf Hitler issued these eleven commands today to Viktor Lutze, new Chief of Staff of the Storm Troops:

In naming you Chief of Staff of the Storm Troops I expect that you will accept the series of duties that I herewith inform you of.

1—I demand of a Storm Troop leader, just as from a Storm Trooper, blind obedience and unquestioning discipline.

2—I demand that every Storm Troop leader recognize, like every other political leader, that his behavior and reputation must be an example for his organization and for our whole body of followers.

3—I demand that Storm Troop leaders, exactly as in the case of political leaders, be expelled from the Storm Troops without hesitation as soon as their behavior disgraces them in the eyes of the public.

Demands Simplicity.

4—I demand specially from the Storm Troop leader that he be an example of simplicity, not of display. I do not desire Storm Troop leaders to give costly dinners or that they attend such dinners. There was a time when we were not invited to such affairs, and we have nothing to seek there now. Millions of our fellow citizens have not even the necessaries of life. They are not oblivious of those whom fortune has favored, but it is unworthy of a National Socialist to increase the gulf between fortune and misery, which is already great enough.

I probibit the use of Storm Troop or party funds for festivals and the like. It is shameless to stage debauches with the pennies of our poorest citizens. The luxurious headquarters in Berlin, in which it has now been discovered that some 30,000 marks monthly were spent for banquets, is to be done away with immediately.

State Dinners Excepted.

I prohibit for all party groups banquets and dinners paid for with any variety of public funds. I forbid all party and Storm Troop leaders to partake of such banquets. The only exceptions are functions necessary for reasons of State, notably those for which the Reichspresident and the Reich Foreign Minister are responsible. I forbid all party leaders and Storm Troop leaders to give so-called diplomatic dinners. A Storm Troop leader does not need to engage in representation, but simply to do his duty.

5—I do not desire Storm Troop leaders to undertake business trips in expensive limousines or cabriolets, or to employ public funds for such trips. The same

Continued on Page Two.

Hitler Alone Had Power To Order Shooting of 7

Special Cable to THE NEW YORK TIMES.

BERLIN, June 30.—Over its report of the deaths of seven storm troop leaders who yesterday were in power in German, the Völkischer Beobachter, Chancellor Hitler's own newspaper, carried the headline, "Seven Storm Troop Leaders Shot. End of Convicted Traitors."

The German words used for the verb and adjective taken together in this connection carry a wider meaning than the English equivalent, as is the case with so many German words. They imply that the men were proved guilty and executed.

These men were shot on the spot without trial on the mere allegation of their guilt by order of a higher authority. The only authority which could give an order for their execution unchallenged was Adolf Hitler, who, according to the same article in this newspaper, "is the supreme conscience of the German people."

GOERING POLICE NET CATCHES LEADERS

Suicides and Killings Follow Raids on Homes of Notables in Berlin and Vicinity.

By OTTO D. TOLISCHUS.

Wireless to THE NEW YORK TIMES.

BERLIN, June 30.—General Kurt von Schleicher, former Premier, was killed with his wife while "resisting arrest with a weapon in his hand," according to an official communiqué.

The communiqué was one of a long series issued throughout the day as the criminal police of Premier Hermann Goering of Prussia rushed about Berlin and its vicinity, leaving a heavy wake of arrests, suicides and killings among prominent persons.

General von Schleicher met death at his villa in Neubadelsberg, between Berlin and Potsdam. His wife, Frau Elizabeth von Schleicher, it is stated, fell while trying to shield him with her body during an exchange of shots.

From that point tragedy quickly spread. One squad of General Goering's police rushed to the office of Vice Chancellor Franz von Papen in Vos Strasse, next to the Chancellery, and asked the Vice Chancellor to accompany them to his home. There they kept Colonel von Papen under house arrest, and questioned him regarding his relations with General von Schleicher. The amenities were preserved, and later it was stated Colonel von Papen was "at liberty."

Von Papen Visitors Barred.

Visitors to Colonel von Papen's house, however, were not allowed to see him. His secretary and a Reichswehr officer assured every one that Colonel von Papen was in good spirits, had just finished tea and was smoking his afternoon cigar.

His office meanwhile had been occupied by black uniformed special guards, men with field equipment, rifles and hand grenades. To inquirers they insisted they were merely Colonel von Papen's regular guard, placed there to protect him. Visitors noted, however, that all doors of the building stood open, as if a whirlwind had swept through.

In the face of this action, Colonel

Continued on Page Eight.

NAZI CHIEFS TELL OF ENDING REVOLT

Hitler and Lutze Appeal to the Storm Troops to Be Faithful to Their Movement.

RAID DESCRIBED BY PARTY

Leader of War Veterans Urges Them to Be Calm and to Be Loyal to Government.

Wireless to THE NEW YORK TIMES.

BERLIN, June 30.—A series of statements was issued today by German leaders on their success in crushing the radical Nazi revolt.

NAZI PARTY STATEMENT.

A communiqué from the National Socialist party read:

Munich, June 30.

For many months individual elements have been trying to drive a wedge and produce conflicts between the Storm Troops and the party, as well as between the Storm Troops and the State. Suspicions of this became more and more confirmed, but it was also plain that these endeavors were to be charged to a limited clique of certain leanings.

Chief of Staff Roehm, in whom the leader placed an exceptional amount of confidence, not only did not oppose these endeavors but undoubtedly sponsored them. His well-known unfortunate characteristic gradually led to intolerable burdens which drove the leader of the movement and the Highest Leader of the Storm Troops [Hitler] into most serious conflicts of conscience.

Chief of Staff Roehm established contacts with General von Schleicher without the knowledge of Der Fuehrer [the Leader]. His go-betweens were another Storm Troop leader and an obscure person well known in Berlin, to whom Der Fuehrer had always strongly objected.

Since these negotiations also led —of course without the knowledge of Der Fuehrer—finally to contacts with a foreign power, or rather to its representative, it was not possible to avoid intervention both from the standpoint of the party and the State.

Provocative incidents brought about according to the plan caused Der Fuehrer to fly from Bonn to Munich at 2 o'clock this morning, after visiting labor camps in Westphalia, in order to remove and arrest the most seriously compromised group of leaders. Der Fuehrer himself went with only a few companions to Wiessee in order to still any attempts at resistance.

The execution of the arrests revealed such immorality that any trace of pity was impossible. Some of these Storm Troop leaders had taken male prostitutes along with them. One of them was even disturbed in a most ugly situation and was arrested.

Der Fuehrer gave orders for this plague to be done away with ruthlessly. In the future he will not permit millions of decent people to be compromised by a few of such sick men. Der Fuehrer instructed Premier Goering of Prussia to take similar action in Berlin and especially to arrest the reactionary accomplices of this political plot.

At noon today Der Fuehrer

Continued on Page Four.

STORM TROOP CHIEFS DIE

Killed or Take Own Lives as Chancellor and Goering Strike.

REACTIONARIES ALSO HIT

Wife Shot With Schleicher as He Resists Police—Head of Catholic Action Slain.

HITLER FLIES TO MUNICH

Tears Off Rebels' Insignia and Arrests and Ousts Roehm—Papen Held but Freed.

By FREDERICK T. BIRCHALL.

Wireless to THE NEW YORK TIMES.

BERLIN, June 30.—On the eve of a self-proclaimed month of peace Germany has passed today through the throes of a violent purging that must profoundly affect her future. It is neither a revolution nor a coup d'état nor a counter-revolution but authoritative action intended to head off any of the three.

Chancellor Hitler in Munich, backed by General Hermann Wilhelm Goering, Premier of Prussia, in Berlin, has struck simultaneously at the rebel elements in his own Storm Troops and at certain reactionary elements temporarily allied with them or suspected of being so allied for their own ends in an attempt to upset the present régime in Germany.

When the day was over many Storm Troop leaders had been shot to death or had committed suicide.

In addition, General Kurt von Schleicher, Herr Hitler's predecessor as Chancellor, had been slain while resisting police who attempted to seize him as one of the plotters.

[Captain Ernst Roehm, chief of staff of the Storm Troops, committed suicide after having been ousted by Chancellor Hitler, according to The Associated Press, while Heinrich Klausener, chief of the Catholic Action, was shot to death by a Nazi special guard.]

The Official Version.

The official version is that the attempt was a joint effort "to bring pressure" on the government with a threat of violent action behind it. There is mention of a "foreign power" as being involved. The discerning interpret this reference as being to Russia and the ultimate aim of the rebels as a new national bolshevism.

Whatever the cause, Chancellor Hitler has acted swiftly and decisively. Flying to Munich in the early hours of this morning from Bonn, where he had been ostensibly inspecting work camps, he assembled his trusted special guards in that city and proceeded to gather in the suspected leaders, who had already proceeded to preliminary action.

Captain Roehm, the leader of the conspiracy, was arrested in his bedroom in his country house outside Munich by Herr Hitler himself and then and there deposed from all his offices. His fellow-conspirators were gathered in by the dozen in Munich and around it.

The official story told to foreign correspondents by General Goering this afternoon says that some of them, both in Munich and in Berlin, committed suicide and others were shot while resisting.

Goering Acts Swiftly.

Almost simultaneously in Berlin General Goering, by arrangement with Chancellor Hitler, was taking similar action. It came swiftly and unexpectedly just before noon. But here the members of the reactionary group believed to be acting with the rebel Storm Troop leaders were equally the objects of the assault.

Karl Ernst, group leader of the Berlin Storm Troops, was traced to a house near Bremen and surrounded there. He is dead and the official version is that he was shot while resisting arrest. The unofficial version is that he was brought by airplane to Berlin and executed on his arrival.

Police and special guards at the very outset sought to put General von Schleicher under arrest at his villa outside Potsdam. It is said that he attempted to draw a pistol. A volley of shots brought him down and his wife died with him.

Vice Chancellor Franz von Papen, who seems to have been under sus-

Continued on Page Two.

Dr. Albert Einstein, shown here with Mrs. Einstein, was a prime target of Adolf Hitler and his National Socialist Party. While on a vist to the United States, he decided to remain here permanently.

German Chancellor Adolf Hitler and President Paul Von Hindenburg at one of their last public appearances before Hindenburg's death on August 2.

Typical of the rising anti-semitism in Germany, a Nazi forces a Jew to clean the streets.

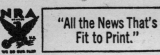

"All the News That's Fit to Print."

The New York Times.

LATE CITY EDITION
WEATHER—Fair, slightly cooler today; fair tomorrow.
Temperatures Yesterday—Max., 84; min., 67.

VOL. LXXXIII....No. 27,933. Entered as Second-Class Matter, Postoffice, New York, N. Y. NEW YORK, TUESDAY, JULY 17, 1934. P TWO CENTS In New York City. | THREE CENTS Within 200 Miles | FOUR CENTS Elsewhere Except in 7th and 8th Postal Zones

DOOLING IS CHOSEN TAMMANY LEADER; BACKS ROOSEVELT

OLD GUARD IS FORCED OUT

Curry Quits Politics—His Successor Pledges 'Good Government.'

NEW CHIEF 'INDEPENDENT'

Warns That Candidates Must Be Qualified and Fit for Public Trust.

WILL SUPPORT LEHMAN

United Fight for Policies of Party Promised—Power of Hines Wanes.

The members of the executive committee of Tammany, many of them veterans in politics, assembled yesterday afternoon at Tammany Hall and unanimously elected James J. Dooling, 41-year-old leader of the Fifth Assembly District, as leader of the organization.

In doing so they ended the factional strife that has torn the organization for many months. They also put Tammany in line with the policies of the State and national administrations and definitely forecast a new era in the city's Democratic machine. In that new era, there may be no place for the political philosophies of some of those who voted for Mr. Dooling yesterday.

The action of the committee came after Stephen A. Ruddy, Mr. Dooling's only opponent, announced his withdrawal from the race, and after the committee had accepted and filed the resignation from its membership of John F. Curry, former leader of Tammany, whom Mr. Dooling succeeds.

The "Old Guard" in the organization had been informally released from its pledges to Mr. Ruddy on Saturday, when Mr. Dooling's election was already assured, and those who favored Mr. Dooling's selection, as well as those who wanted some one with old-line tendencies, all went to Tammany yesterday prepared for what happened.

Mr. Curry's resignation as a district leader was the only surprise, and that was announced before the meeting started. It means his retirement from politics.

Proclaims His Independence.

Mr. Dooling's first act as leader was to make a short speech expressing his thanks to the committee, and then he issued to the press a statement outlining the principles that will govern his actions as leader.

Declaring it to be his belief that a political leader should work for good government in his community, Mr. Dooling said:

"To that end he should do his utmost to see that the men and women selected for public trust are in all respects fit and qualified, and that they remain so."

He went on to say that he was independent, as he had made no pledges to obtain the leadership, but was willing to accept the advice of members of the executive committee and "other loyal voters who are qualified voters in New York County."

The latter remark was interpreted as reassurance that he would not be dominated by Edward J. Flynn, Democratic leader of the Bronx. Opponents of Mr. Dooling's selection had used that as an argument against voting for him.

The Democratic party in Manhattan, he declared, "is in hearty accord with the splendid policies of President Roosevelt and Governor Lehman, and will fight with all its strength to uphold those policies."

Mr. Dooling's Statement.

Mr. Dooling's statement follows:

The Democratic voters of New York County, acting through the executive committee of their county committee, have selected me as the leader of the Democratic party in this county.

I deeply appreciate the honor thus conferred upon me. It is indeed a great privilege to lead the organization which I have served for the past twenty years and which was served for so many more years by my late father, Peter J. Dooling. The post carries with it heavy responsibilities and manifold duties. I shall bend

Continued on Page Six.

Hitler's Talk on Killings Scored by Vatican Paper

By The Associated Press.

VATICAN CITY, July 16.—The Vatican newspaper, the Osservatore Romano, made a bitter attack today on Chancellor Hitler's radio speech on the recent executions in Germany.

Quoting Herr Hitler's phrase that what was done was done for reasons of State and for the decorum of the country, the Osservatore Romano says that reasons of State and the decorum of the country would also have required the most detailed explanation of the events, an explanation that Herr Hitler did not give.

"If the methods of 1934 had been used when Hitler tried his Munich putsch of 1923, the heads of National Socialists would not have been in a position to carry out their proposals for German restoration," the newspaper says.

U.S. BARS ANY DEAL ON GERMAN DEBTS

Firm Memorandum to Berlin Rejects Linking Trade With Reparation Bond Payments.

REICH OPPOSES NEW PACTS

Official Says Treaties Would Not Be Reciprocal While Germany Is Disarmed.

Special to The New York Times.

WASHINGTON, July 16.—In a strongly worded new communication the United States Government has demanded that the German Government give American holders of German bonds the same treatment accorded to bondholders in Great Britain or other countries, and has refused to permit this treatment to be made contingent upon "trade concessions, clearing arrangements or similar measures."

This was revealed by the State Department today when it made public a memorandum that Ambassador Dodd had left at the Foreign Office in Berlin a few hours earlier. Disclosure that Secretary Hull had directed Ambassador Dodd to make these representations was made in a Washington dispatch to The New York Times printed Saturday morning.

The United States Government, the memorandum said, considers that the German Government is under "an inescapable responsibility" to give American bondholders comparable treatment. It was also declared that while this government had always refused to undertake negotiations of private debts, and now thought that the bond settlements should be left to representatives of the bondholders, the government, nevertheless, insisted on equal rights for its nationals.

Apparently touching on reports that the Hitler government desired negotiations regarding the bonds, the memorandum rejected the idea of making equal treatment contingent upon special agreements "as new and additional inducements."

TEXT OF MEMORANDUM.

The memorandum read as follows:

The United States Government considers it essential, in view of the commitments reported recently to have been entered into by the German Government with respect to British holders of German bonds, to insist that measures be taken without delay to assure equally favorable treatment to American holders of such securities.

The German Government is aware, as a result of the repeated representations, written and oral, that have been made to it, both through the American Embassy at Berlin and through its own embassy at Washington, that this government considers as an inescapable responsibility of the German Government the extension to American investors of treatment that is no less favorable than that which is or may be accorded to the investors of other countries.

The American Government does not feel that this expectation can be made contingent upon its entering into special agreements as new and additional inducements to the observance of that obliga-

Continued on Page Eleven.

SMITH OFFERS PLAN ENDING DEADLOCK ON COUNTY REFORM

Suggests Passage of Combined and Separate New York City and Up-State Plans.

LET NEXT SESSION CHOOSE

Proposal at Albany Hearing Wins Acceptance of Dunnigan, Fearon and Lehman.

By W. A. WARN.

Special to The New York Times.

ALBANY, July 16. — Cutting through red tape and non-essentials with characteristic directness, former Governor Alfred E. Smith, at the public hearing here this afternoon on county reform measures affecting New York City and up-State counties, blazed a trail for harmonious action.

He broke the deadlock which had threatened to defeat the proposals for constitutional amendments to eliminate waste and overlapping of functions and introduce efficiency and economy in the county governments.

The man who in the years he was Chief Executive of the State forced through the consolidation of the State's governmental agencies spoke as chairman of the New York City Charter Commission. He suggested that the present extraordinary session pass three measures offered.

One of these is the concurrent resolution introduced by Senator George R. Fearon of Onondaga, minority leader, in which are combined the New York City and up-State proposals for county reforms. The others, sponsored by Senator John J. Dunnigan, president pro tem. of the Senate, and Senator Seabury C. Mastick of Westchester deal with the proposals separately, one providing for the New York City reforms and the other the up-State reforms advocated by Governor Lehman.

Smith's Suggestion.

"Why not pass both the Fearon bill, in which both proposals are bunched together, and the other bills, in which the New York City proposals and the up-State proposal appear separately?" Mr. Smith asked.

"Then we can discuss the matter during the campaign this Fall when we are electing a new set of Senators and Assemblymen and by next year we can reach an agreement on what measure to put through. We should remember that these proposals must be adopted by another Legislature before being submitted to the people for ratification."

"I have no objection to that," said Senator Dunnigan.

"I certainly have none," agreed Senator Fearon.

Governor Lehman, when informed of the suggestion, merely said:

"It is all right with me."

The Governor has received many protests from New York City and up-State against bunching of the reform proposals as is provided in the Fearon resolution.

Speaker Joseph A. McGinnies, when asked after the hearing what stand he would take, said:

"I am in no position to commit myself until there has been a conference on the subject of the Republican members of the Assembly."

Expected to Fall Into Line.

While Mr. McGinnies and some other Republicans in the Assembly are not overfriendly to the plan for up-State county reforms, it is now

Continued on Page Seven.

PEDDLER DETAINED IN CONNOR SEARCH DENIES TAKING BOY

Admits Being Near the Baby's Home, but Says He Knew Nothing of Disappearance.

FOUND ON STATEN ISLAND

Youth Who Wrote Demand for $50 Gets Three-Month Term —Volunteers Hunt Woods.

The eccentric, white-haired peddler of cosmetics who frightened Hartsdale Manor housewives last week by his grandiose and rambling talk was detained yesterday for questioning in the mysterious disappearance of 21-month-old Robert Connor.

The man, who admitted he had been canvassing in this isolated Westchester section a short time before the golden-haired baby disappeared from a sandpile 150 feet from his home, was picked up on Staten Island. After questioning by New York City police he was taken to Greenburg, in which Hartsdale Manor is situated. There he was definitely identified as the peddler who had been sought.

Denies Knowledge of Baby.

The man denied any knowledge of the baby's disappearance. He identified himself as Harry Lee Forestier, 51, of 655 West 187th Street, New York City. He answered questions frankly and admitted that he had been in a mental institution some years ago.

Assistant District Attorney Thomas Scoble Jr. of Westchester County, who described Forestier as a man of "immature mind," said the peddler had declared that he "didn't like children and didn't like policemen."

Although the authorities decided to hold Forestier for further examination today, it was learned they had nothing definite to connect him with the baby's disappearance other than his admitted presence in the neighborhood of the Connor home some time before the child was last seen at 6 o'clock last Thursday.

Forestier's detention, and the sentencing of Bernard Seidenberg, 19 years old, of 855 East 163d Street, to three months in the penitentiary for sending an "annoying letter" to Charles H. Connor, father of the missing baby, were the only tangible developments at the end of the fourth day since the child disappeared.

Woods Are Searched.

Agents of the Department of Justice, State troopers and county and city authorities continued the search for clues yesterday, and "leads" that led to nothing were run down all over Westchester County and as far away as Bridgeport, Conn. During the day 143 men and boys trudged through a square mile of tangled woodland in the vicinity of the Connor home in another vain search for the missing youngster, who dropped out of sight during a ten-minute period when he was left alone near his home.

The search yesterday—the first carefully organized and directed one since the baby's disappearance —will be followed today, it was planned, by an even more extensive beating of the woods in the vicinity. At least 200 volunteer firemen, Boy Scouts, State troopers and relief workers are expected to participate, and a bloodhound will assist the searchers.

Forestier was picked up yesterday as the result of the intensive search

Continued on Page Eight

Fraternity Men at Goettingen Fight Nazis; 10 Held in First Student Revolt Under Hitler

By The Associated Press.

BERLIN, July 16.—An open fight by Göttingen University students against Nazi rule was a fresh contribution today to the general discontent in Germany. In the revolt, the first instance of the kind under the Hitler régime, 1,000 fraternity men battled with brown-shirted Nazi students in defense of their ancient colors.

The fight broke out after the fraternity men had held a meeting at which they protested vigorously against the dissolution of the ancient university society. Fire hose were turned on the combatants and finally order was restored after the arrest of ten leaders, who were charged with "breach of the peace and incitement to revolt."

Two fraternities were suspended until further notice by the university president, acting under pressure of the Nazi-conducted students' federation.

The incident was viewed as significant, since it provided the first instance of open revolt among German students, the vast majority of whom have been ardent supporters of the Nazi movement from its earliest days. It was also taken as an indication of the extent of dissatisfaction that was climaxed by the bloody June 30 "purging" of Nazi ranks.

Wireless to The New York Times.

BERLIN, July 16 (London Times Dispatch).—The national executive body of the Hitler Youth organization has forbidden the public burning of school caps taken from well-to-do youths on the ground that this leads to the destruction of substantial quantities of raw materials, which in Germany's situation cannot be allowed. The collection of the caps and presentation of them to rag dealers is recommended.

It should be explained that local Hitler Youth enthusiasts recently have been making bonfires of these caps as a symbol of that abolition of class distinction which is said to be in progress. The continued wearing of caps after leaving school by youths of the moneyed classes has caused ill-feeling among their fellows in the working classes.

STRIKE PARALYZES SAN FRANCISCO LIFE, BUT UNIONS ALLOW ENTRY OF FOOD AS TROOPS HELP POLICE KEEP ORDER

WASHINGTON SEEKS PEACE

Three Mediators Fly to Coast at the Request of Roosevelt Board.

WAGNER GOES TO PORTLAND

Food Will Be Sent to People in Strike-Ridden Cities if Need Is Shown.

ARMY PLANS NO MOVE NOW

Corps Area Commander Has Power to Protect Federal Property in Emergency.

Special to The New York Times.

WASHINGTON, July 16.— The government rushed additional mediators to the West Coast today to work for settlement of the general strike in San Francisco and to avert another strike threatening the Portland area.

The White House announced that at the request of the special Longshoremen's Board appointed by President Roosevelt, Senator Wagner, who headed the National Labor Board until it was supplanted by the Labor Relations Board, had consented after a telephone conversation with Secretary Perkins to leave at once for Portland.

Chairman Garrison of the Labor Relations Board sent P. A. Donoghue, chief examiner of the board, by plane to San Francisco at the request of the Roosevelt board in that city. The Labor Department ordered Joseph S. Myers, a conciliator, to the strike scene from Dallas.

Mr. Donoghue is expected to arrive in San Francisco at 4:30 A. M. tomorrow, Pacific Coast time. All three mediators will be under the direction of the Longshoremen's Board, which continues the only Federal agency in the strike region.

Meanwhile, President Roosevelt, aboard the Houston in Pacific waters, received detailed accounts by radio of each development. The White House executive offices were open far into the night to keep him fully informed.

Will Guarantee Food.

While maintaining a "hands-off policy" in the strikes on the West Coast, the government is prepared to guarantee food to San Francisco's population. This would be done under the Interstate Commerce Act, which gives the government broad powers in emergencies.

Coast Guard headquarters here made known that cutters at San Francisco had been authorized to transport Federal employes to and from the city while the ferry service is tied up.

The Post Office Department is moving domestic mails in and out of San Francisco on schedule, according to J. M. Donaldson, Deputy Assistant Postmaster General.

The War Department denied that any steps had been taken for the use of Federal troops in the San Francisco area. Acting Secretary Woodring said the Governor of California had made no request for troops.

In a serious emergency the Corps Area commander is authorized under the law to move troops into a troubled area to protect Federal property, guard Federal courts and buildings and maintain the movement of mails. He may act without authorization of the War Department, but it is usual to obtain its sanction.

Navy Has Large Force.

The Navy Department also announced that it was making no plans to intervene at San Francisco. The navy has 4,544 men at San Diego and 933 at San Francisco. The Marine Corps has a contingent of 600 marines at San Diego.

While the use of Federal troops in the strike area is regarded here as a remote possibility, it was pointed out that the Constitution requires the government to protect any State against violence when requested by its Legislature or by its Governor. In 1914 President Wilson sent Federal troops to preserve order in the Colorado coal fields.

Attorney General Cummings canceled plans today to sail from San Francisco for Hawaii July 28. He will probably sail instead from Los Angeles.

American Federation of Labor

Continued on Page Five.

Strike Developments

Major developments in the San Francisco and other strike situations yesterday included:

The general strike which began in San Francisco at 8 A. M. crippled the city's business and transit facilities, inconvenienced its population and increased fears of a food shortage, but only minor instances of vandalism and violence were reported.

Although the tie-up was expected to include the East Bay cities of Oakland and Alameda today, the general strike committee ordered employes of the San Francisco municipal transit lines to return to work, directed highway pickets not to interfere with food trucks, relieved the restrictions on restaurants and "eased up" generally in an effort to win public sympathy and avert bloodshed.

National Guardsmen, 4,500 strong, with tanks, light artillery and machine guns mounted at strategic points, guarded the troubled area from the docks to the produce section. Mayor Rossi charged Communist agitators were fomenting the crisis.

Under the auspices of the Mayor, a committee of 500 was formed to cooperate with the authorities in keeping the district open for the transportation of food.

With General Hugh S. Johnson momentarily expected in the city, the new National Labor Relations Board sent P. A. Donaghue, its chief examiner, there by airplane from Washington to assist in restoring peace.

United States Senator Robert S. Wagner left Newark by airplane for Portland, Ore., to try to avert a general strike there.

Minneapolis truck drivers went on strike at midnight.

Employes of two mills walked out to start state-wide Alabama textile strike scheduled to go into effect at 8 A. M. today.

TRUCKERS GO OUT IN MINNEAPOLIS

Last Minute Efforts to Settle Difficulties Fail—National Guard Ready.

MEDICAL STATION SET UP

Employers' Offer to Arbitrate Called 'Stall'—Union Head Spurs Men to Fight.

Special to The New York Times.

MINNEAPOLIS, July 16.—This Midwest city, which tonight retired to the rumbling of trucks making last-minute deliveries, will awake tomorrow morning with all streets and highways picketed by striking truck drivers.

As last-minute efforts to settle differences with employers failed, the union drivers reaffirmed at a mass meeting their decision of last Wednesday to strike at midnight. Some 4,000 drivers will be affected.

At the same time they voted confidence in the committee which has been conducting negotiations with the employers and in the union officers.

"You have them on the run," William Brown, their president, told the drivers in a speech preceding the final strike action tonight. "The employers either are going to raise workers' wages or we are going to go out and fight like we have never fought before."

In a final conference before the union meeting the last hope of avoiding the strike went glimmering. A proposed peace plan drawn up with the aid of E. H. Dunnigan, Federal Labor Conciliator, and Governor Floyd B. Olson was turned down.

Demands Higher Wages.

The union had demanded that wages be raised before the deadline. This the employers refused to do, at the same time standing firmly against the union representing inside workers, men not directly employed in the business of trucking.

Farrell Dobbs, member of the executive committee, explained to the mass meeting tonight that the employers had offered to arbitrate with the union in so far as the drivers and helpers were concerned, but that he was certain this was "merely another stall." He advised they strike.

A hundred leaders were elected at the mass meeting to supervise the strike, details of which had been completed today. A commissary and medical station already were set up. Wives of the drivers were to be placed in charge of these.

What other trade unions in the city would do was expected to be decided tomorrow. The Central Labor Union last week indorsed the demands of the drivers and announced that its members hold themselves ready to take sympathetic action.

St. Paul Action Deferred.

Across the Mississippi River truck drivers of St. Paul deferred a meeting scheduled to vote on a strike tonight, and in Duluth, Minn., third

Continued on Page Two.

CROWDS SEEK FOOD IN HUNGRY QUEUES

With Only 19 of San Francisco's 3,000 Restaurants Open, Wait Is Long, Irksome.

SUPPLIES QUICKLY GONE

Strikers' Committee Permits Transfer of Food, but This Does Not Meet Demand.

Special to The New York Times.

SAN FRANCISCO, July 16.—Nineteen restaurants!

Last November there were 2,800 restaurants in this city, according to figures by the Bureau of Hotels, Restaurants and Purveyors. Those are the latest figures available officially.

More than twice as many restaurants and beer parlors were opened during the first nine months of 1933 as during the corresponding period the year before because of the repeal of prohibition. Since last November, the number certainly has not decreased. In the first nine months of 1933, 755 new establishments were opened to the public, against 373 in the corresponding period of the previous year. It is believed a reasonable estimate that there are, at the present time, 3,000 eating places in San Francisco.

Nineteen of them were last night "accredited" by the executive strike committee. By 6 A. M. they were all jammed to the doors.

Lines Form Out Into Streets.

By 9 A. M. lines of persons seeking breakfast strung out into the streets, snake fashion, at these nineteen restaurants. The eleven downtown restaurants could not keep up with the demand. Coffee, sugar, ham and eggs were exhausted. The executive strike committee permitted the transfer of more food, but the lines remained. Many could not wait. They were still expected to work. At one alone of the "accredited" restaurants, the line was a block long, and those inside were standing six deep behind the chairs of those who had beat them to it. Normal appetites doubled and trebled as a pure matter of psychology.

The Ferry Building siren blew the noon hour. Thousands poured into the streets. Of the 200,000 estimated on the streets at that time, it is safe to say half of them were in search of food.

The lines formed again.

It was not only the white collar worker who stood in those lines.

Hundreds of those standing there —for an hour, two, three, four— were wearing union buttons. They went on strike at 8 A. M. But it appears that they get hungry, too.

Tempers Give Way; Fights Start.

Tempers frayed, snapped. Disturbances started. There were arguments. Fist fights began. Police cars dashed madly around the city, responding to all sorts of vicious calls. A tabulation of the locations revealed that many were

Continued on Page Two.

CITY'S CAR LINE OPENED

Union Leaders Modify Tie-Up—See Need Now of More Restaurants.

PUBLIC OPINION FEARED

Governor, Mayor Act Promptly and Additional Troops Take Up Strategic Positions.

STERN WARNING ON RIOTS

Citizens Begin Organizing as Federal Circles Forecast a Fight to the Finish.

By RUSSELL B. PORTER.

Special to The New York Times.

SAN FRANCISCO, July 16.—The first day of San Francisco's general strike, which went into effect at 8 o'clock this morning, saw a modification by strike leaders of the transit tie-up, and, to some extent, of the food blockade. There were no mass disorders or looting, and violence were reported they were sporadic and of a minor nature.

Late in the day, after having completely tied up all transportation, except for those private automobiles which could obtain gas; having paralyzed many retail trades and businesses and having seriously inconvenienced the 1,300,000 residents of the metropolitan area in getting to work and in obtaining food and gasoline and such services as the laundry, tailor and barber shops supply, the general strike committees eased up materially in its interference with the normal life and business of the city.

The strike picket lines which had been thrown across the highways leading into the city from adjacent farm areas let food trucks convoyed by policemen pass unmolested. This removed one of the chief fears of violence, as it had been generally understood that serious trouble would follow any attempt to stop food trucks guarded by the public authorities.

The food trucks allowed to pass the picket lines received "permits" from the strike committee, which announced that more permits would be issued tomorrow so that "no one in San Francisco shall go hungry."

Restaurant List Found Inadequate.

At the same time the strike leaders announced that they had no intention of trying to starve out the city. They also indicated that they intended to let all or most of the city's restaurants reopen, inasmuch as the limitation of restaurant services today to nineteen places designated by the union clearly proved inadequate. Long lines waiting on sidewalks outside the favored eating places so attested.

The strike committee also released its grip on the city's transportation by telling the employes of the Municipal Railway to return to work and cautioning against any violence against the city-owned street-car lines. This removed a danger which had been regarded fully as threatening as the possibility of stopping the convoyed food trucks.

Just before the strike committee acted on the Municipal Railway problem the public utilities commissioners had informed the carmen that they must return to work immediately or forfeit their jobs and civil service standing. It was widely believed that if the men did not return to their posts strike-breakers, many of whom are said to be in the city, would be put on the cars, guarded by policemen and special deputies, and that bloodshed certainly would follow.

Service was resumed on the Municipal Railway this evening, with regular employes operating the cars, protected by policemen. It was expected that about 50 per cent of the usual service would be restored before the night was over and that normal operations on this line would be effective tomorrow.

More Troops Enter Strike Zone.

While the strike leaders thus pursued a course obviously designed to keep public opinion from rising against them, State and city officials were taking determined steps to keep the city supplied with food and other necessaries of life, as well as with transportation facilities, before the growing food shortage should become too serious.

Continued on Page Three.

"All the News That's Fit to Print."

The New York Times.

LATE CITY EDITION
WEATHER—Fair today and tomorrow; temperature unchanged.
Temperatures Yesterday—Max., 90; Min., 72

Copyright, 1934, by The New York Times Company.

VOL. LXXXIII....No. 27,937. Entered as Second-Class Matter, Postoffice, New York, N. Y. NEW YORK, SATURDAY, JULY 21, 1934. P TWO CENTS In New York City. | THREE CENTS Within 200 Miles | FOUR CENTS Elsewhere Except in 7th and 8th Postal Zones

50 ARE SHOT IN MINNEAPOLIS AS POLICE FIRE ON STRIKERS; GAS ROUTS SEATTLE PICKETS

PWA READY TO LEND UP TO $100,000,000 FOR CITY PROJECTS

LaGuardia, After Conferring With Ickes, Indicates Full Amount Will Be Borrowed.

$25,000,000 FOR HOUSING

Mayor, Back, Says He Will Seek Only Loans That Can Be Used Constructively.

MOFFETT GETS PLEDGES

Manufacturing, Railroad and Labor Leaders to Cooperate in Vast Housing Program.

Following a conference in Washington yesterday with PWA Administrator Harold L. Ickes, Mayor LaGuardia said New York City could borrow up to $100,000,000 of PWA funds to finance its local improvements.

The Mayor said the city would not borrow any more money than could be constructively employed. The city has submitted projects to the Federal Government calling for an aggregate outlay of $100,000,000, which would indicate that the full amount was to be borrowed.

Shortly after the Mayor's return to the city, it was announced in Washington that manufacturing, railroad and labor leaders from all over the country had pledged Administrator Moffett the "fullest cooperation" with the administration's huge housing program, which would make credit available for repairs and renovation of millions of homes.

Bruere May Get Post.

Those who took part in the conference included W. A. Irvin, president of the United States Steel Corporation; R. V. Fletcher, general counsel of the Association of Railway Executives; Lewis H. Brown, president of Johns-Manville Corporation; Walter P. Chrysler, the automobile manufacturer, and Henry I. Harriman, president of the United States Chamber of Commerce. It became known that Henry Bruere of New York is being considered for appointment as deputy administrator in charge of the financing phases of the program.

Accompanied by Langdon W. Post, Tenement House Commissioner, the Mayor went to Washington by train Thursday night. He and Mr. Post discussed with Mr. Ickes the details of a $25,000,000 Federal loan for the construction of model housing here. After ironing that matter out they talked over PWA and RFC financing generally with Secretary Ickes and Jesse Jones, chairman of the RFC.

Mr. Jones said after the meeting that New York City could expect a substantial amount from the RFC revolving fund of $250,000,000, through which the RFC is authorized to sell on the market bonds held by the PWA. Since the city has already deposited city bonds with the PWA as security for loans already granted, additional financing for local projects could be obtained through sale of these bonds to the RFC. With the money thus obtained the PWA could widen its lending power.

No Limit to Bond Purchases.

"There is no limit to the amount we can buy, and New York City bonds are sound bonds," Mr. Jones said.

While the Washington negotiations have not advanced to the point where details of the bond purchase have been discussed, officials of the Finance Department here believed that the bonds to be bought would be fifty-year 4 per cent bonds.

"I am going to borrow funds only for projects that I can economically and prudently build," the Mayor said after his session with Secretary Ickes. Dwight A. Hoopingarner, associate director of PWA housing, was at the housing conference. Mr. Ickes said Mr. Hoopingarner would accompany Mr. Post back to New York to work out details of the city's housing program. Mr. Post said the difficulties between the local and Federal administrations over the housing loan had been greatly exaggerated.

"I don't see any particular difficulties," he remarked. "The New York City Housing Authority has already taken 54 per cent of the options it needs in the name of the United States Government. There won't be any particular difficulty in working out the details with Mr. Hoopingarner."

The Federal Government has taken the position that it must pass upon the sites where model housing is to be built, as well as upon the prices the city Housing Authority intends to pay for them.

According to Mayor LaGuardia,

Continued on Page Two.

Reich Forced to Cut Mill Output; Hundreds of Thousands Lose Jobs

Raw Material Shortage Causes Reduction to 36-Hour Week in Most of Textile Industry—Others Due to Follow Suit—'Substitute' Workers Hit by Wide Dismissals.

By OTTO D. TOLISCHUS.
Wireless to THE NEW YORK TIMES.

BERLIN, July 20.—The phantom blockade imposed on Germany by her shrinking exports and vanishing gold reserve is beginning to cripple German industry.

Despite Chancellor Hitler's boast that if the world continued to boycott German goods Germany would do without the world, the Reich Ministry of Economics was compelled today to issue a decree placing most of the textile industry on a thirty-six-hour week.

The decree, which becomes effective Monday, frankly states that the reason for this drastic step is the growing shortage of foreign raw materials, imports of which must be curtailed for lack of cash or credit.

In many respects this action constitutes the biggest blow the Hitler régime has suffered thus far. It is an admission of defeat, belying the proud words about the native substitutes that German genius is to stamp out of the domestic earth to replace the products denied to Germany by a hostile world. Moreover, it is fully realized that this is merely a beginning and that similar curtailments of production must come in other industries dependent on foreign raw materials.

Indicative of this trend was another decree issued today which puts the entire rubber trade under government control and forces the tire industry to form a compulsory cartel, principally to prevent any expansion of the existing production capacity.

Government control of industry is rapidly expanding to a point undreamed of under the régime of the republic so vehemently denounced as "Marxist" by the National Socialists.

But to the masses all this means more than a choice between systems of economy. It means decreased working hours, decreased earnings and therewith a decreased standard of living, if not worse. In the textile industry especially the majority of the workers are already living close to the edge of existence and living costs are going up.

Thus far, principally because of the government's labor creation program, official agencies have been able to report that whereas world recovery had stopped, Ger-

Continued on Page Five.

HUGE WAVE FELLS SCORES AT CONEY

One Believed Lost as a Wall of Water Batters Bathers Escaping 90-Degree Heat.

TORRID SPELL TO GO ON

70 Dead in Nation as Drought Peril Increases—Record Temperatures in Midwest.

A miniature tidal wave engulfed hundreds of persons who went to Coney Island yesterday in search of relief from the second day of intense heat and high humidity. As the water receded, it carried several bathers out beyond their depths. One young man was believed to have been drowned and a number of other persons were rescued by policemen, life guards and fellow-bathers. One policeman saved a man and a young woman single-handed.

All of those who went to Coney Island and other beaches escaped high temperatures that reached a maximum of 90 degrees and caused two deaths and several prostrations in the city. Little or no let-up in the torrid weather, which has caused a total of seventy deaths throughout the country since Thursday, according to The Associated Press, was promised for today either in New York or in the drought-stricken parts of the country.

Storm Brings Huge Wave.

About 4 P. M. yesterday a sudden storm broke, kicking up choppy waves. At Coney Island a huge wave, about a quarter of a mile long, smashed in on the five-block stretch of beach between Stillwell Avenue and West Nineteenth Street, coming in with such speed that it took bathers unawares and bowled them over by the hundreds. Some spectators estimated that the onrushing wall of water was eight feet high.

For a few minutes there was pandemonium. Policemen, life guards and hardy swimmers jumped into the water, pulling back to safety a large number of adults and youngsters who were being carried away by the receding waters.

Frank Manghesi, 17 years old, of 344 Water Street, Manhattan, one of those on the beach at the time, was reported missing and the police said he might have been drowned.

Manghesi was reported missing by Joseph Garcia, 18, of 95 Cherry Street, Manhattan, who accompanied him to the beach and who was swimming with him when the sudden storm and miniature tidal wave occurred. Garcia was rescued by Patrolman Joseph Gonzales, 28, of 2,045 Coyle Street, Sheepshead Bay, who was on duty on the beach front, and who swam out to him fully clad.

After the rescue, Garcia looked in vain for his friend and went to the police station with Manghesi's clothing.

After rescuing Garcia, Patrolman Gonzales heard a scream and saw a young woman struggling. The patrolman plunged into the water again, swam about sixty feet, caught her and brought her ashore, unconscious. After being revived by artificial respiration, the girl said she was Betty Cos-

Continued on Page Twelve.

COAL MAN TO TEST NRA PRICE FIXING

Newtown Creek Company Here Attacks Charges for Delivery as Too High.

SEES PROFIT AT $2.50 FEE

Code Sets It at $3 to $3.50—Fuel Authority Will Seek to Enforce It.

The Newtown Creek Coal and Coke Company, 197 West Street, Brooklyn, one of the largest independent retail coal dealers in the city, defying the NRA, announced yesterday that it would stand on its constitutional rights in refusing to abide by the prices fixed by the NRA Retail Solid Fuel Authority.

Dominick Luzino, president and treasurer of the company, declared that the NRA was insisting that retail coal dealers must charge from $3 to $3.50 a ton for making delivery. The Newtown Creek Coal and Coke Company, according to Mr. Luzino, has been able under normal conditions to make delivery at a profit by charging about $2.50 a ton, and will continue to do so with the support of the consuming public.

Fuel Authority to Act.

At the offices of the Retail Solid Fuel Authority, a member of the staff of Nicholas L. Stokes, chairman, declared that the Code Authority would proceed against the Newtown Creek Coal and Coke Company under the NRA and the National Industrial Recovery Act. It will be the first case of its kind, according to the spokesmen for the Code Authority.

The spokesman for the Code Authority would not specify the nature of the proceedings, but he pointed out that the code was designed for the benefit of the trade, and that efforts would be made to compel any recalcitrant member of the industry to observe the provisions of the code.

Mr. Luzino explained that he had served notice of his intention on the Retail Solid Fuel Authority, but that he had not given up his Blue Eagle, nor had he been asked to surrender his insignia.

Mr. Luzino's formal statement follows:

"To our consuming public: We have been selling and serving the general public for the last fourteen years with high-grade anthracite and bituminous coal at reasonable prices. Due to the fact that we are independent from operating companies, have no large affiliated companies or bankers to pay, and that our organization equipment is free from any encumbrances, we have in the past been able to supply hundreds of thousands of customers with good, clean coal, full weight, at fair prices. With the public support we will try our utmost to continue same.

Still Members of NRA.

"We are members of the NRA and paying the schedule of wages to our employes according to the NRA agreement, also according to the union under which we are operating.

"Under the National Recovery Administration it has been our honorable President's intention to

Continued on Page Twelve.

SURPLUS IS SHOWN BY POSTAL SERVICE, FIRST SINCE 1919

Farley Radios Roosevelt That Excess Revenue on June 30 Was $5,000,000.

'DELIGHTED' IS THE REPLY

Accounting Sets Off the Legal Adjustments for Subventions and Free Mailing.

Special to THE NEW YORK TIMES.

WASHINGTON, July 20.—Postmaster General Farley has informed President Roosevelt that a long-elusive goal of the Postoffice Department, a balanced budget, has been achieved.

In a radio message to the President aboard the cruiser Houston Mr. Farley declared that preaudited figures for the fiscal year ended June 30 showed that postal receipts for the first time since 1919 had exceeded expenditures, the surplus being about $5,000,000. This was after making the usual adjustments authorized by law "for certain subventions and free mailing services."

The Postmaster General remarked that this record "was all the more impressive" when the fact was considered that in the last fifty years postal revenues had exceeded operation costs in only seven.

President Sends Congratulations.

President Roosevelt replied to the Postmaster General in a radio message which reached him at San José, Calif., where he has been on a speaking tour. He was "delighted" at the report and congratulated Mr. Farley that such a result had been achieved despite a reduction in postage on local letters and other handicaps.

The President's reply to Mr. Farley read:

"I am delighted to have your report that the Postoffice Department will have a surplus of approximately $5,000,000 for the fiscal year which ended June 30, the first time since 1919 that such a result has been accomplished, and this notwithstanding a reduction in postage on local letters and charges against the postal revenues never before included in the cost of postal service. Congratulations and best wishes."

Message Sent to the President.

Mr. Farley's message to the President read as follows:

"When I assumed the office of Postmaster General you expressed the desire that the postal service be so conducted that the revenues and expenditures would approximately balance each other, and the drain upon the general Treasury and taxpayers in making up the huge deficits experienced in recent years be eliminated. For the fiscal year 1932 the net postal deficit was $152,246,188.50 and for 1933, $50,683,605.46.

"Pursuant to your wishes, every effort was made during the fiscal year just ended to balance the postal budget through systematic, businesslike management and operation of the service and the practice of strict economy wherever practicable.

"As a result of these efforts and the arrest of the decline in postal receipts due to improved business conditions following the adoption of the many reconstructive measures featuring the New Deal, the end desired has been achieved, and I have the honor to inform you that

Continued on Page Twelve.

LONE GUNMAN RAIDS GOVERNORS ISLAND, FREES A PRISONER

Invades Army Headquarters Here and Disarms Sentry of Famed 16th Infantry.

TWO FLEE IN ROWBOAT

Disappear on Brooklyn Shore, Mile and a Half Away—Abandoned Craft Found.

A lone civilian, equipped with a rowboat and a nickel-plated revolver, gave the United States Army one of its most embarrassing moments yesterday by hijacking a military prisoner from Governors Island and rowing him a mile and a half to the freedom of the lower Red Hook section of Brooklyn.

The civilian, a ruddy-faced man of about five feet six, took the prisoner away from Sentry Steven S. Grezegorek, a private doing his first hitch, by the simple but forceful method of shoving the revolver into Grezegorek's ribs and taking from him the shotgun with which he was overseeing the unloading of dirt by three inmates of the disciplinary barracks. The prisoner was Melvin Blanton, 23 years old, who was serving a term for desertion and escapes.

The hijacking took place at the lonely southern end of the island. Grezegorek, a Buffalo (N. Y.) boy, was the only guard in the vicinity. Before help could be summoned the civilian and his liberated companion were well on their way across Buttermilk Channel to the Brooklyn shore. The rowboat was found later, but its occupants were not.

Double Humiliation to Army.

All this was most embarrassing to the army for several reasons. In the first place, Governors Island guards the portal of New York, and as a corporal, on duty at the Fort Jay Ferry yesterday, expressed it, "'Lone bandit steals army prisoner,' the papers say. A devil of a fine thing for the army!"

And there was another phase of the question. Private Grezegorek is a member of Company A, Sixteenth Infantry, First Division. There is no more haughty outfit in the army than the First. It won that designation because it was the first in the World War. Not in all the army was there a prouder insignia than the red "1" worn on the left shoulder by its men back in 1917 and 1918, notwithstanding red arrows and ivy leaves and—though this be treason in New York—the constellation of Orion and the Liberty Statue of New York's own.

Any rear rank private of the Sixteenth Infantry could tell you, in those days, that his regiment was as far above the rest of the division as the division was above the rest of the A. E. F. Battles? Plenty of them. Cantigny, Soissons, St. Mihiel, the Meuse-Argonne, and, in addition, the march to the Rhine.

And there was that other stirring incident in the history of the First. It was men of the Sixteenth Infantry who marched in the grand parade in Paris July 4, 1917, that the French might see the Americans really had come.

Enough of the old-timers are left in the Sixteenth to remember those glories, to keep alive the pride that was. And it was this outfit that was raided by one civilian under the very eyes of New York!

"If only I could of laid on my belly with a Springfield when that boat was about 800 yards out," said

Continued on Page Three.

Shot Kills Daughter of Col. Breckinridge; Girl, 17, Discharges Own Rifle by Accident

Special to THE NEW YORK TIMES.

WASHINGTON, July 20.—Miss Louise Breckinridge, 17-year-old daughter of Colonel Henry Breckinridge of New York City, was killed today by a bullet accidentally discharged from a target rifle which she was carrying.

The tragedy took place at Edgemoor, Md., near Washington. Miss Breckinridge, who lives with her mother, Mrs. Ruth Bradley Breckinridge, at Bethesda, Md., left home about 6 P. M. with two dogs and her .22-calibre target rifle.

She customarily took such a walk of an evening, and sometimes shot at a target. She had walked several blocks, and had reached a wooded area. As she climbed a fence, her rifle apparently became entangled and she fell, discharging the weapon.

The bullet entered her left breast and reached the heart. She is believed to have died instantly.

About 7:45 o'clock, when her daughter had not returned, Mrs. Breckinridge became anxious and began a search. She found her daughter's body, lying about five feet from the fence. The dogs were standing near by.

Mrs. Breckinridge, near collapse, hurriedly called a police emergency squad from Bradley, but the girl was dead. The body was taken to an undertaking establishment in Rockville. Authorities pronounced the death clearly an accident.

Miss Breckinridge was a student at Vassar College, and had completed her sophomore year in June. She was home for the Summer vacation.

Colonel Breckinridge, a lawyer and former Assistant Secretary of War, is attorney for Colonel Charles A. Lindbergh.

Louise Dudley Breckinridge was one of the two children of Colonel Henry Breckinridge, both daughters, by his first wife, Ruth Bradley Woodman of Concord, N. H. Her sister is Miss Elizabeth Foster Breckinridge.

Colonel Breckinridge, who received his military title during his war career from 1917 to 1919, lives at 455 East Fifty-seventh Street. His daughter, Louise Dudley, was named after his mother, who was the former Louise Ludlow Dudley. His father was Major General Joseph Cabell Breckinridge of the regular army.

2,000 QUIT PIERS ON COAST

Mayor Leads 300 Police in Attack After Chief Resigns in a Rift.

ROUT LIKE A WAR SCENE

Fumes Affect All on Both Sides, Including Executive, Overcome at 'Front.'

MANY FELLED BY CLUBS

Stones Hit Police—Trains Start as Docks Are Cleared—Reprisals Expected.

Special to THE NEW YORK TIMES.

SEATTLE, Wash., July 20.—Led by Mayor Charles L. Smith, a former football player, 300 policemen today drove 2,000 dock strike pickets from the Municipal Piers at Smith's Cove.

Virtually all of the combatants, including the Mayor, were affected by the tear gas used by the police. Many pickets were overcome by fumes or struck down by policemen's clubs during the sharp fifteen-minute engagement.

Three newspaper employes were gassed. Scores of men, both strikers and police, suffered cuts and bruises as the police wielded clubs and the pickets hurled stones. While many injured pickets were treated by companions, two of them and three policemen were taken to hospitals.

The pickets, routed, broke ranks and scattered. Many fled up the west side of Queen Anne Hill, a residential district.

Mayor Directing on "Front."

The pickets had been firmly entrenched at the docks since they broke through police lines Wednesday. No effort was made to dislodge them until after Chief of Police George F. Howard resigned last midnight and Mayor Smith took personal command of the department.

The Mayor was gassed slightly at the height of the battle. He held his handkerchief to his face as a wave of tear gas engulfed him while he stood on an overhead bridge to Pier 41, directing the police offensive.

He took refuge in the dock building. Though tears were streaming from his eyes as he reached shelter, he was not affected seriously.

Retreat Likened to War Scene.

The rout of the 2,000 was a spectacular sight for Queen Anne Hill residents as the pickets fled pell-mell before clouds of gas. The shooting of gas guns and exploding of bombs were audible a mile away.

"It sounded like a wartime battle," said one citizen who watched the fight from his porch. "I could hear the shooting plainly. There were clouds of gas. I saw several men falling. Then the whole mob of pickets scattered up the side of the hill and along the streets."

A few minutes after the precipitate retreat, railroad crews started moving freight cars in and out of Piers 40 and 41, where 400 non-union men worked unhindered on nine ships. These tracks had been seized by the strikers in their march through police lines on Wednesday.

After the battle Dr. Don H. Palmer drew a cheer from police when he prescribed beer for those slightly affected by the nauseating gas. He said it would "settle" their stomachs, and a café nearby did a land-office business in selling beer to "cure" the police.

Two arrests were made. J. Munoz, 49 years old, a seaman, was jailed without charge. The police said he was carrying a knife during the battle. George Alexander, 27, a longshoreman, was treated for minor injuries and locked up.

Harold Smith and Frank Potter, photographers, and Richard Sellers, a reporter, all of The Seattle Times, were made ill by gas.

Split With Police Chief.

The police drive today caused a split between Mayor Smith and Chief Howard, which resulted in the latter's resignation. The chief, who retired to his civil service rank of captain, apparently did not favor such drastic police action as the Mayor.

The Mayor then took command of the department, but promised to name either Captain George H. Comstock or Captain Ralph W.

Continued on Page Two.

2,276,000 Days Lost By California Strikers

By The Associated Press.

SAN FRANCISCO, July 20.—Costs of the San Francisco and Alameda County general strikes had mounted to incalculable heights when they were called off.

The millions of dollars' loss, as virtually all business was paralyzed for three days in San Francisco, Oakland, Alameda and Berkeley, cannot be estimated.

But it is possible to figure roughly the time-cost of the strike. The men actually out lost wages for at least 351,000 labor days—141,000 for the 47,000 East Bay workers, on strike three days, and 210,000 for the 60,000 San Francisco strikers, out for three and one-half days.

To this can be added the total of 1,899,920 labor days lost by 27,940 Pacific Coast maritime workers during the sixty-eight days they were on strike prior to the general walkout. They are still striking.

Including also teamsters, street railway employes, butchers, laundry workers and taxi drivers, who struck before the general call, the lost days of labor aggregate around 2,276,000.

Shipping losses to San Francisco alone have been placed at over $1,000,000 a day since the longshore strike started June 9.

TRUCKERS GO BACK AT SAN FRANCISCO

Vote of 1,138 to 283 to Return Unconditionally Is Called Blow at Bridges.

OWNERS FOR ARBITRATION

Johnson Wins Ship Men—Longshoremen Meet Today on Mediation Issue.

By RUSSELL B. PORTER.
Special to THE NEW YORK TIMES.

SAN FRANCISCO, July 20.—Joining the organized labor return to conservative leadership here, the powerful Teamsters Union voted 4 to 1 tonight to go back to work unconditionally. The vote, by secret ballot, was 1,138 to 283 in favor of the following resolution:

"The general strike committee has ordered all men on strike in sympathy with longshoremen to return to work immediately. Are you in favor of returning to work?"

A statement by the teamsters' strike committee said:

"The executive committee of the brotherhood and the strike committee instruct the membership to return to their employment and do all work without reservation."

Michael Casey, head of the Teamsters' Union, added that the men would start hauling all cargo to and from the docks tomorrow morning, regardless of the fact that the longshoremen and marine workers' unions are still out on strike.

Called Blow at Bridges.

J. F. Vizzard, president of the Draymen's Association, said:

"This vote means that the teamsters will return to work 100 per cent, including the transportation of merchandise and freight to and from the docks. More than 70 per cent of the teamsters' work is on the waterfront.

"This vote is a blow at Harry Bridges, chairman of the Maritime Strike Committee. He has been the fly in the ointment and now he is through. The longshoremen, acting sanely, will recognize proper leadership. Bridges is too radical; he doesn't want to settle anything. Why, even now he's going around with eight bodyguards.

"It was agreed between me and Michael Casey, president of the Teamsters Union, that if the men voted to return to work, it would mean all work, including that on the docks.

"I predict that the longshoremen will now choose new leaders and settle their troubles by arbitration."

Johnson Wins Owners.

Coincident with this news came an announcement from General Hugh S. Johnson, NRA Administrator, in Los Angeles, that the ship owners had agreed unconditionally to arbitrate all issues with the eleven marine workers unions who are out on strike with the longshoremen.

The Waterfront Employers Asso-

Continued on Page Two.

TWIN CITY DRIVERS RIOT

Attack Truck Convoyed by Police and Are Met With Bullets.

TROOPS ESTABLISH ORDER

Governor Sends 3,400 More to City and Considers Declaring Martial Law.

GENERAL STRIKE IS URGED

Some Delivery Services Are Shut Off—Police Chief Assailed at Labor Meeting.

Special to THE NEW YORK TIMES.

MINNEAPOLIS, July 20.—About fifty persons were wounded by bullets and twenty others were injured by beatings when police opened fire in a battle with striking truck drivers near the market section here today. The fight started as pickets attempted to halt a wholesale grocery truck moving under guard from the area.

National Guardsmen already in the city hurried into the section and took command after the encounter, and 3,400 others were immediately ordered to Minneapolis by Adjt. Gen. Ellard A. Walsh.

Governor Olson considered declaring martial law as a tense situation prevailed.

First reports that a striker had been killed in the rioting could not be verified late tonight.

Of the wounded, several were reported to be in a critical condition and one was believed to be dying.

In the battle, the police, under orders to shoot into the strikers if necessary, used shotguns and pistols. Most of the wounded, several of whom were merely onlookers, were shot in the arms and legs.

Trucks at First Unmolested.

The two wounded policemen were Sergeant August Brannon, 58, who was slugged, and Patrolman John Green, who was shot in the leg.

During the morning two food trucks had moved out of the district under police guard and had made deliveries to retail stores without molestation from a growing crowd of pickets. By afternoon 150 patrolmen had been sent to the scene to keep the throng in check.

Shortly after 2 P. M. a third food truck moved out from a wholesale house. It was followed by twelve squad cars, each carrying four policemen, all armed with shotguns

The truck turned onto Third Street North; another truck loaded with strike pickets cut in ahead of it. Policemen quickly lined the street, but the strikers plowed through the cordon and drove directly into the front of the truck. Police rushed from the convoy cars and opened fire with shotguns on the pickets' truck. Two pickets fell off, wounded, but the truck continued up the street, being fired on from both sides of the street.

Police Sergeant Beaten.

Sergeant Brannon jumped on the running board, attempting to halt the pickets' truck, but was battered over the head and hurled to the street badly injured.

During this clash more than a dozen were wounded.

Meanwhile, more pickets had poured into the area, breaking through the police lines. Other patrolmen rushed up and forced them back. Then the strikers rallied and began a new charge. The police again opened fire, aiming for the most part in the air and at the sidewalks, but some of the bullets ricocheted and many more in the crowd were wounded. By this time the pickets' truck had run the gauntlet of gunfire and disappeared through the crowds.

At this point four truckloads of National Guardsmen, who had been held in readiness at the armory, arrived at the scene in trucks along with ambulances. Only four wounded strikers were picked up by the City General Hospital ambulances, however. The others had been rushed in private cars to an emergency hospital at strike headquarters, a vacant garage in the Loop district.

With the arrival of the troops the fighting died down.

Thirty minutes later the district had been cleared of pickets and the food truck continued on its way to

Continued on Page Two.

Times Wide World Photo

Clyde Barrow and Bonnie Parker who were killed in Louisiana on May 23 by a party that included former Texas Rangers.

Associated Press Photo

Charles (Pretty Boy) Floyd, one of the most notorious outlaws of the era, was killed on an Ohio farm as he fled from federal agents who were closing in on him on October 22.

Associated Press Photo

The end of George (Baby Face) Nelson's spectacular career of crime came on November 28. His body was found pierced by bullets from the guns of two federal agents whom he fatally wounded in a machine gun battle.

John Dillinger, posing here with the tools of his trade, was considered Public Enemy Number One. He was slain by Hoover's federal agents in Chicago on July 22.

Clyde Barrow poses for a photograph which was later found by police.

J. Edgar Hoover, Director of the F.B.I.

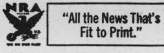

"All the News That's Fit to Print."

The New York Times.

LATE CITY EDITION
POSTSCRIPT
Fair, slightly cooler today; tomorrow fair.
Temperatures Yesterday—Max., 89; min., 73.

VOL. LXXXIII....No. 27,939.
Entered as Second-Class Matter, Postoffice, New York, N. Y.

NEW YORK, MONDAY, JULY 23, 1934.

TWO CENTS In New York City. | THREE CENTS Within 200 Miles | FOUR CENTS Elsewhere Except in 7th and 8th Postal Zones

15 KILLED, 18 HURT AS BUS FALLS 35 FEET AND BURNS ON AN OUTING AT OSSINING

MANY TRAPPED IN FLAMES

Machine Out of Control Plunges Off Ramp Into Lumber Yard.

GASOLINE TANK EXPLODES

Injured Struggle in Vain to Open Jammed Doors of Old-Fashioned Coach.

4, AFIRE, LEAP INTO RIVER

Members of Young Democrats' Club of Brooklyn Bound for Sing Sing Ball Game.

Fifteen persons were killed and eighteen injured, yesterday, when a bus containing about forty men, women and children plunged thirty-five feet from a ramp near the Ossining railroad station and burst into flames.

The bus was one of seven that had been chartered by the Young Men's Democratic League of the Twentieth Assembly District in Brooklyn to take members of the league and their friends to a baseball game in Sing Sing.

Speeding, out of control, down the tortuous Secor Road hill, it mounted the ramp that crosses the New York Central tracks near the Ossining station, crashed through the fragile iron railing on one side of the ramp and landed on its four wheels in a lumber yard.

Gasoline Tank Explodes.

The driver, apparently, failed to turn off the ignition; and as the bus struck the ground the gasoline tank exploded with a deafening roar. Sheets of flame shot out in all directions, and while passengers inside scrambled for the exits, fire enveloped the vehicle and the adjacent lumber piles.

The bus, one of the old-fashioned type with no centre aisle, had eight seats running crosswise and doors on either side of each seat. A few of the doors were opened without difficulty, enabling those inside to escape. But many of the doors, thrown out of alignment by the crash, refused to open.

The occupants of these seats were penned inside, and with the flames mounting around them began screaming for help. Those who had escaped tugged vainly at the closed doors. With the aid of witnesses to the crash they succeeded in opening several doors and releasing some of those inside.

Four Leap Into the Hudson.

Four men, who escaped from the bus with their clothing in flames, rushed to the near-by Hudson River and threw themselves in. Two others raced down along the New York Central Railroad tracks. Those in the river were rescued by Frank McLaughlin, former Fire Chief of Ossining. What became of the two who ran along the tracks could not be definitely ascertained last night, but it is believed that they were taken in charge by near-by residents and rushed to a hospital.

Thomas McGuire Jr. of 828 Halsey Street, Brooklyn, who had escaped from the bus with a broken arm and secondary burns, rushed back to rescue his father, who had been critically burned. Others who had escaped from the bus made every effort to save those still inside. So did witnesses to the accident. George Adcock, an Ossining fireman, got credit for seven rescues. But the old wooden framework of the bus and the sun-dried lumber piled near by burned like tinder and the rescue work had to be abandoned.

All ambulances in Ossining were brought to the scene of the crash and the injured removed to the Ossining, Grasslands and Tarrytown Hospitals. Father John Kelly of Briarcliff, who chanced to be passing in an automobile, had arrived in time to assist in the rescue work. He also administered the last rites of the church to some of the more seriously injured. Afterward, he went to the Ossining Hospital, where he administered the last rites to others.

The regular staff at the Ossining hospital was swamped with work and was reinforced by numerous volunteers. These included Drs. Robert Bloom, James Kearney, John Schofmeister, Edward Huntington of Ossining, Edward Hunt-Miller of Croton.

Many prominent women in the vi-

Continued on Page Three.

Victims of Bus Accident

A partial list of the dead and injured in the bus accident at Ossining, as compiled last night, follows:

THE DEAD.

GALLER, ABRAHAM, 666 Hancock Street, Brooklyn.

HAYES, Mrs. WILLIAM, 27 Cornelia St., Brooklyn.

INCARNATO, FRANK, 28 years old, driver of the bus, 662 Ninety-second St., Brooklyn.

McNICHOLAS, JOHN, Jr., 26, 412 Irving Av., Brooklyn.

An unidentified person.

MISSING (BELIEVED DEAD).

GALLER, Mrs. ABRAHAM, 666 Hancock Street, Brooklyn.

LUFF, ARTHUR, 9 Woodbine St., Brooklyn.

His sister, whose name was not determined.

MEMEY, JOSEPH, 27 Cornelia St., Brooklyn.

McDONALD, Mr. and Mrs. JOSEPH, 109 Gates Av., Brooklyn.

McDONALD, BERNADETTE, 12 years old, their daughter.

MURRAY, Mr. and Mrs. JAMES, 15 Cornelia St., Brooklyn.

THOMPSON, Mrs. ROSE, 9 Woodbine St., Brooklyn.

THE INJURED.

Ossining Hospital.

CONNORS, FRANK, 542 Bainbridge Av., Brooklyn, critical.

CORCORAN, JOSEPH, 666 Putnam Avenue, Brooklyn, not serious.

ELLERY, JAMES, 712 Knickerbocker Av., Brooklyn, left hospital after treatment.

HAYES, WILLIAM, 27 Cornelia St., Brooklyn, not serious.

HAYES, JAMES, 12, his son, critical.

HUPF, FRANK, 831 Monroe St., Brooklyn, not serious.

McCANN, DANIEL, 378 Central Av., Brooklyn, critical.

McGUIRE, THOMAS, 638 Halsey St., Brooklyn, critical.

MERKEL, Mrs. TERESA, 280 Highland Blvd., Brooklyn, left hospital after treatment.

REITMEYER, JOHN, 1,218 Gates Av., Brooklyn, critical.

SCHWARTZ, Mrs. ARCHIBALD, 116 Liberty St., Brooklyn, not serious.

Grasslands Hospital.

KNAUER, FRANK, of 75-07 Sixty-fourth St., Glendale, Queens.

LALOF, MARY, 9 Woodbine Street, Brooklyn; not serious.

McGUIRE, THOMAS, Jr., 828 Halsey Street, Brooklyn; not serious.

SCHNEIDER, EDWIN, 105-11 195th Street, Hollis, Queens; not serious.

SCHWARTZ, ARCHIBALD, 116 Liberty Street, Brooklyn; not serious.

Tarrytown Hospital.

HICKEY, GEORGE, 17 Woodbine Street, Brooklyn; not serious.

MURRAY, WILLIAM, 15 Cornelia Street, Brooklyn; not serious.

BUS BRAKES WEAK, SURVIVORS ASSERT

'We'll Take a Chance,' Driver Said—Stopped Twice for Makeshift Repairs.

MAN SAW WIFE PERISH

Tried to Pull Her From Wreck, but Flames Drove Him Back, He Testifies at Inquest.

Special to THE NEW YORK TIMES.

OSSINING, N. Y., July 22.—Walter Thompson of 9 Woodbine Street, Brooklyn, a survivor of the bus accident that cost fifteen lives here today, testified tonight at the official inquest that the bus driver knew his brakes were bad.

Thompson was the first witness called by Dr. Amos O. Squire, Medical Examiner for Westchester County. His story of the bad brakes and the driver's makeshift repairs was corroborated by other witnesses and in unofficial accounts obtained by newspaper men from other survivors here and in Brooklyn.

"Several times on the way up," Thompson told Dr. Squire, "the driver had trouble with his brakes. I noticed that finally he got up and turned the foot brake around as if he were screwing it on the shaft. After each time the brake held better, and then it seemed to loosen up. At one point the emergency brake held all right, but on the hill in Ossining it was no good.

"In the neighborhood of Tarrytown, where they were fixing the road, the cars ahead stopped for traffic and the driver had to drive off the road because the brakes wouldn't hold.

"We'll Take a Chance."

"I said to him, 'Your brakes are bad.' I told him he'd better be careful and that he ought to stop and fix them.

"The driver said: 'The hell with it. We'll take a chance. I guess we'll get through.' He was completely sober. I thought that he was a good chauffeur—that's what I told the man in the seat with me.

"When we got on the hill on Main Street here and were coming down from the top at a pretty good pace, we got to where he should have taken a turn at Hunter Street [a right-angle turn off Main Street which would have led to the prison] and there were two automobiles parked on the street which partly blocked the turn.

"The driver turned out, swung away over and cleared the automobiles and went on down the hill, swinging from curb to curb almost all the way down the hill. He couldn't get control again.

Yelled to All to Jump.

"Just before the bus crashed through the railing the driver yelled, 'Everybody jump!' We went right through the railing, and the bus fell front first when the hind wheel hit the foundation for the railing, raising up the rear of the bus. The bus struck on the front.

"The motor backed up and drove the steering wheel into the chauf-

Continued on Page Three.

TREASURY OFFERS MORTGAGE BONDS

$100,000,000 in 3% 14-Year Farm Corporation Securities to Go to Highest Bidders.

SALE USHERS NEW POLICY

Marks First Time Treasury Has Acted as Fiscal Agent—Ready Market Expected.

Special to THE NEW YORK TIMES.

WASHINGTON, July 22.—The Treasury Department today announced an offering to the public of $100,000,000 of Federal Farm Mortgage Corporation 3 per cent bonds, thus inaugurating a new policy under which the department acted as the agent of one of the emergency recovery set-ups in floating securities which the corporation is authorized by law to sell to obtain funds.

In the past the Treasury, except in the case of short-term Treasury bills which are sold on a discount basis, has judged the market, determined upon the interest at which a security should be offered and then has sought subscriptions at par or at a small stated premium. Such offerings have been for the purpose of covering the Treasury's own requirements.

In the present offering, however, which the Treasury is making on behalf of the emergency corporations, the department did not have discretion in fixing the interest rate the securities shall carry. It has, therefore, offered the mortgage corporation's bonds to the highest bidders, but in no case at less than par and accrued interest. The bonds will be dated May 15, 1934, mature on May 15, 1949, and may be redeemed on May 15, 1944, or on any subsequent interest payment date which comes semi-annually on May 15 and Nov. 15 of each year.

At present Treasury 3s are selling in the market at slightly over 102, and outstanding bonds of the mortgage corporation are quoted at just over 101. The latter are guaranteed as to principal and interest by law.

Substantial Premium Expected.

In connection with the present offering the Treasury Department expects to market the $100,000,000 issue readily and at a substantial premium. The bonds are exempt both as to principal and interest from Federal, State, municipal and local taxation, except surtaxes, estate, inheritance and gift taxes. They will be issued in denominations of from $100 to $10,000.

The decision to have the Treasury market the bonds and thus further centralize the handling of government-backed security offerings in the public market was reached after conferences between Treasury officials and officials of the Farm Credit Corporation, under the supervision of which the Federal Farm Mortgage Corporation activities are brought.

To a certain extent it is in line with the policy adopted some time ago to suspend the direct sale of debentures by the RFC to banks

Continued on Page Two.

2,320 Planes for Army Asked in Baker Report

Board Declares Congress Should Provide Funds—Separate Unit Plan Rejected —Mail Flying Praised.

Special to THE NEW YORK TIMES.

WASHINGTON, July 22.—Holding that the strengthening of the air forces was essential to adequate national defense, the War Department's special aviation committee recommended today an increase in the aviation strength of the army to 2,320 planes and a corresponding increase in the flying personnel. The present authorized strength of the army air corps is 1,800 planes, which the committee reported to be more than 300 short.

The committee, headed by Newton D. Baker, former Secretary of War, and composed of eleven civilians and generals, declared against consolidation of the army and navy aviation services into a single unit. Its report praised the spirit and manner in which the army carried the mail under difficulties during the period of the cancellation of the air mail contracts. With this was mingled criticism of the actual performance, coupled as it was with fatalities, and whatever there was of failure was attributed to lack of proper equipment and to insufficient training.

While expressing the opinion that the United States was comparatively free from the threat of serious overseas air invasion because of the failure so far to develop an airplane capable of crossing the Atlantic or Pacific with an effective military load, attacking vital areas successfully and returning to its base, the committee held that the army's air corps must be ready at all times for war service.

"The next great war is likely to begin with engagements between opposing aircraft, either sea-based or land-based," the report read, "and early aerial supremacy is quite likely to be an important fac-

Continued on Page Six.

The recommendations of the Baker committee are on page 6.

FALL BUSINESS RISE PREDICTED BY NRA; SUMMER DROP CUT

Upward Trend Held Definite by Leon Henderson, Citing Homely Indicators.

LESS FAMILY DOUBLING-UP

This Despite Increase in Marriages—Small Loans Are Being Rapidly Repaid.

Copyright, 1934, by The Associated Press.

WASHINGTON, July 22.—The NRA has been informed by its experts to "gamble" on a substantial Fall rise in business and a less than usual slump during the remainder of the Summer.

Leon Henderson, chief of the Blue Eagle's research and planning division, held this conclusion today on the basis of a mass of statistical and other data. His advice to NRA is based upon an expectation of an upswing.

Mr. Henderson's searchers have reported to him that the decline thus far this Summer has been less than normal, and that there are now numerous signs of an upward trend in business generally.

There is no expectation, however, of a boom development. Mr. Henderson employs most careful language in his estimate of the future. He himself referred today to his attitude as a "gamble" on the basis of the best facts available.

The research chief is paying especial attention to what he describes as his "homely indicators." For instance, there has been a gain in the sale of living room rugs, one of the first things which housewives like to replace when funds are available.

There also has been a decline in the number of bachelors, he points out. In one city the number of bachelors before the depression was 10,000. This increased to 29,000 at the height of the depression and is now about 22,000, the expert conclusion being that men with funds are less fearful of marriage.

Families Again Spread Out.

For another thing, Mr. Henderson's "doubling up" indicator in reference to housing shows that families which have been crowded now are spreading out and filling vacant apartments and houses.

Small personal loans, his figures show, are being paid up in full at an increasing rate. The index shows the rate of repaying at a record high for the depression, and higher even than in the month when soldiers' cash bonus payments were largest. Similarly, the rate of repayment of building and loan obligations is up and the amount of unrented property held by building and loan associations is down. Repayments to the Home Owners Loan Corporation and Farm Credit Administration are also holding up well.

Mr. Henderson said he was paying increasing attention to this type of statistical indicator because, first, it shows the status of the ordinary person better than the customary type of business statistics, and second, because it tends to get at the beginning of the buying process rather than at the end.

Of particular significance, Mr. Henderson said, are the indicators showing a reduction in personal debt. He holds this to be one of

Continued on Page Two.

FRENCH FACTIONS WARNED BY LEBRUN TO RESTORE TRUCE

President Says Public Will Be Severe With Those Blocking Doumergue's Work.

PREMIER TO SEEK ACCORD

Tardieu Is Said to Be Ready to Make Peace With Herriot to Prevent Cabinet Shifts.

By The Associated Press.

AURILLAC, France, July 22.—President Lebrun took a hand in the bitter Cabinet clash today by warning that there must be no interference with the government of Premier Doumergue.

France will not tolerate anything which blocks M. Doumergue's work of restoration, M. Lebrun said as he unveiled a monument at the birthplace of the assassinated President, Paul Doumer.

M. Lebrun made no direct reference to the Cabinet dissension in which Edouard Herriot and André Tardieu, both Ministers without portfolio and both former Premiers, are the chief figures. But he said pointedly that party fights must be forgotten.

The President expressed pride in M. Doumergue's "wisdom and prudence" and asserted his work must go on.

"Public opinion will not accept a situation that stops his beneficial work," M. Lebrun said. "It will be severe toward those who do not do everything to assure for the future what the wisdom of the efforts of today already is permitting us to hope is being achieved."

Critical Week for France.

Wireless to THE NEW YORK TIMES.

PARIS, July 22.—This coming week seems likely to be as critical for France as was that following the rioting of Feb. 6. There is only this difference in the situation, that this time there is even greater confusion.

It is believed the country as a whole at this vacation time wants a real truce to politics. It has put its trust in Premier Doumergue, and among persons of all classes of opinion one hears expressions of resentment because his Ministers could not keep the truce while his back was turned. Whatever he does will have the approval of most persons, but it also is true that whatever he does is almost certain to arouse resentment in one camp or the other.

In the two camps feeling is running high. André Tardieu's friends on newspapers are reiterating that the Radical Socialists are responsible for breaking the truce and are seeking to thrust them out of the Cabinet because they spoke the truth about Camille Chautemps.

To that the reply of the Radical Socialist press is to describe M. Tardieu as "the man who brought down French bonds."

Newspapers like the Petit Parisien, which more nearly represent average opinion, are being careful to remain outside the quarrel. They are too well aware of its dangers for France, because this quarrel strikes deeper than any political division since the days of the Dreyfus affair. There is no concealment of the fact that below the truce, which is possible only in the person and authority of Premier Doumergue, there is an atmosphere

Continued on Page Four.

DILLINGER SLAIN IN CHICAGO; SHOT DEAD BY FEDERAL MEN IN FRONT OF MOVIE THEATRE

Cummings Says Slaying of Dillinger Is 'Gratifying as Well as Reassuring'

By The Associated Press.

WASHINGTON, July 22.—Smiling in elation, Attorney General Cummings tonight termed the slaying of John Dillinger by Federal agents "gratifying as well as reassuring."

The Attorney General was notified just before he boarded the train for the West, the first leg of a journey to Hawaii. At Union Station he dictated the following statement:

"The search for Dillinger has never been relaxed for a moment.

"He has escaped capture on several occasions by the narrowest of margins.

"The news of tonight is exceedingly gratifying as well as reassuring."

Mr. Cummings said the end of the Indiana bandit reflected great credit on the Chicago office of the division of investigation.

J. Edgar Hoover, chief of the Bureau of Investigation, rushed to his office at word that the desperado had been shot down. He told news men:

"This does not mean the end of the Dillinger case.

"Any one who ever gave any of the Dillinger mob any aid, comfort or assistance will be vigorously prosecuted."

He referred directly to George (Baby Face) Nelson, Homer Van Meter and another gangster. Nelson, named by the department as the killer of Special Agent W. Carter Baum in the Dillinger outbreak in the Wisconsin woods last April, was described by Mr. Hoover as a "rat."

HOT WAVE ABATES; SEVEN DROWN HERE

Highest Temperature Is 89 at 4:30 P. M. After Cool Morning—One Heat Death.

DROUGHT SPREADS IN WEST

Total Dead in Nation From Weather 272—Cattle and Crops Loss Mounts.

After three days of oppressive heat and high humidity, the weather here moderated somewhat yesterday.

The day's maximum temperature was 89 degrees at 4:50 P. M.; but the humidity remained comparatively low throughout the day, and a brisk northerly breeze tempered the heat of the sun.

The combination here of the warm sun and cool breeze made perfect weather for the seashore, and all the near-by beaches again were thronged with large Sunday crowds. For the fourth time this season the crowd at Coney Island was estimated at more than 1,000,000. At the Rockaways, it was estimated, there were more than 450,000; at Long Beach, more than 300,000, and at Jones Beach, more than 150,000.

The crowd at Jones Beach was one of the largest of the year. The causeway there was lined throughout the day with automobiles, and both bathhouses did a near-capacity business.

One heat death and one prostration were reported during the day. An unidentified man about 55 years old was stricken with a heart attack induced by the heat at Sheriff and Delancey Streets and died.

Seven Persons Drowned.

Seven drownings were reported:

JOSEPH CERILLA, 18 years old, of 101 Bergen Street, Brooklyn, drowned while bathing off West Twenty-fifth Street, Coney Island.

JAMES CUNNINGHAM, 24, employed at the Overlook Hospital in Summit, N. J.; drowned off Beach 104th Street, Rockaway Beach.

ALLAN SNYDER, 22, of 533 Wingon Street, West Philadelphia, drowned in Mirror Lake at Browns Mills, N. J.

FRANK SELLTENRICH, 15, of 309 Seventh Street, Jersey City; drowned in New York Bay off Linden Avenue, Jersey City.

CATHERINE LeCONTE, 5, of 948 East Third Street, Brooklyn; drowned in Lake Ronkonkoma, L. I.

WILLIAM MAGUIRE, 72; drowned in Salem Creek at Salem, N. J.

MILTON WEYLANDT, 18, of 282 Watchogue Road, Port Richmond, S. I.; seized with heart attack and drowned in Lake Hopatcong, N. J.

It was said last night at the Weather Bureau that today probably would be fair and slightly cooler.

272 Dead in Nation.

Deaths in the protracted heat wave covering most of the country passed 256 yesterday, The Associated Press reported.

Hundreds of prostrations were recorded.

The Southwest and Midwest were hardest hit. Only slight relief for scattered areas was in immediate prospect.

In the grain belt crops wilted and

Continued on Page Eleven.

THREE DOOMED MEN FLEE TEXAS PRISON

Another Convict Killed Climbing Wall, Two Others Shot in Death House Break.

GUARD ALSO IS WOUNDED

Trio of Killers, One of Them an Aide of Clyde Barrow, Escape in Waiting Car.

By The Associated Press.

HUNTSVILLE, Texas, July 22.—Three of the most desperate killers in the Southwest—Raymond Hamilton, Blackie Thompson and Joe Palmer—escaped from the death house of the State penitentiary here today in a daring break in which one convict was killed, two others wounded and a guard shot.

The three convicts who were shot, all bank bandits and life-termers, were mowed down by the gunfire of guards as Hamilton, Thompson and Palmer scampered over the wall to two waiting automobiles.

Whitey Walker was killed by the shots of guards whom the convicts engaged in battle. Charlie Frazier, the man who engineered the break, was shot from the ladder with which he was scaling the wall and was believed to be fatally wounded. Roy Johnson, the third bank robber, was shot and less seriously hurt.

H. E. George, the guard, was momentarily stunned as a bullet creased his scalp. He was not seriously hurt.

The break occurred while the prison yard was almost deserted. All officials and guards not actually on duty and practically all convicts were attending a ball game between the prison team and a Conroe team at the athletic field beside the walls.

The escape was the first ever made from the death house, which is located in the centre of the prison. In daring and cool execution, the break has no parallel in the annals of the penitentiary.

Guard Forced to Unlock Cells.

At 4:30 P. M. Inside Guard Lee Braswell approached the death house to feed the five inmates. Inside guards are not permitted to carry weapons, as they come closely into contact with the convicts, and it would be possible for the latter on occasions to overpower and disarm them.

As Braswell approached the door, Frazier, crouched against the wall, stepped forward and thrust the muzzle of a .45-calibre revolver against his ribs. In his other hand the convict held another .45.

Frazier marched Braswell into the death house, and compelled him to unlock the cells in which Hamilton, Palmer and Thompson were incarcerated. These convicted murderers came out, and Frazier handed Hamilton his extra gun. Braswell was locked in Hamilton's cell.

The quartet of desperadoes sped from the death house and were joined at the door by Walker and Johnson. A few feet from the death house they encountered W. T. Mc-

Continued on Page Eleven.

REACHED FOR HIS GUN

Outlaw's Move Met by Four Shots, All Finding Their Mark.

HAD LIFTED HIS FACE

Desperado Had Also Treated Finger Tips With Acid to Defeat Prints.

TWO WOMEN WOUNDED

Agents, Tipped Fugitive Was Going to Theatre, Waited While He Saw Show.

Special to THE NEW YORK TIMES.

CHICAGO, July 22.—John Dillinger, America's Public Enemy No. 1 and the most notorious criminal of recent times, was shot and killed at 10:40 o'clock tonight by Federal agents a few seconds after he had left the Biograph Theatre at 2,433 Lincoln Avenue, on Chicago's North Side.

One bullet penetrated the head and another the chest of the desperate outlaw. He died as he was being taken to the Alexian Brothers Hospital. The body was later removed to the county morgue, where the identification of Dillinger was made positive.

According to Melvin H. Purvis, chief of the investigating forces of the Department of Justice in Chicago, and leader of the band of sixteen men who had waited for more than two hours while the desperado viewed his last picture show, Dillinger attempted to put up a fight.

"He saw me give a signal to my men to close in," Chief Purvis said. "He became alarmed and reached into a belt and was drawing the .38-calibre pistol he carried concealed when two of the agents let him have it. Dillinger was lying prone before he was able to get the gun out and I took it from him."

Surgical Disguise Fails.

Dillinger had taken great precautions to prevent his being recognized. His face had been lifted by a surgical process since his last picture was taken and he had dyed his hair a darker shade than its natural light reddish brown.

"It was a good job the surgeons did," Chief Purvis said, "but I knew him the minute I saw him. You couldn't miss if you had studied that face as much as I have."

Two women, passers-by who had no connection with the outlaw, were wounded by stray bullets fired by the Federal agents. They are Mrs. Etta Natalsky, 45 years old, of 2,433 Lincoln Avenue, and Miss Theresa Paulus. Each was struck in the left leg. Their injuries, it was said, were not serious.

Patron of Gangster Film.

Chief Purvis and twelve of his own men, accompanied by Captain Timothy O'Neill and three members of the East Chicago police force, went to the vicinity of the small theatre at about 8:30 P. M.

They had received information during the afternoon that Dillinger would attend the performance of "Manhattan Melodrama," a gang and gun movie featuring Clark Gable and William Powell, in the evening.

The sixteen men were posted strategically, some at all possible exits of the theatre, with groups to the north and south, and one detail on the opposite side of busy Lincoln Avenue. Chief Purvis, seating himself in his automobile a few feet south of the show house, watched.

It was about 8:30 P. M. when Dillinger walked up to the entrance and bought a ticket, or tickets. A Chicago policeman who happened to be at the scene said he was accompanied by two women, one dressed in red, but Chief Purvis said he saw none. Passing into the theatre, Dillinger took a seat.

While he was inside, the agents completed their preparations for his emergence. There were so many of them, and their actions seemed, to the theatre manager and to observers in the neighborhood, to be so suspicious that the police were notified.

Policemen Frank Slattery, Edward Meisterheimer and Michael Garrity, who investigated, were shown Federal badges by the watchers and interfered not at all, al-

Continued on Page Nine.

The dust storms left people homeless, crops destroyed, the land damaged and cattle starved.

"All the News That's Fit to Print."

The New York Times.

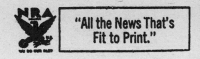

LATE CITY EDITION
WEATHER—Showers, warmer today; tomorrow showers and cooler.
Temperatures Yesterday—Max., 81; Min., 67

Copyright, 1934, by The New York Times Company.

VOL. LXXXIII....No. 27,941. Entered as Second-Class Matter, Postoffice New York, N. Y. NEW YORK, WEDNESDAY, JULY 25, 1934. P TWO CENTS In New York City. | THREE CENTS Within 200 Miles | FOUR CENTS Elsewhere Except in 7th and 8th Postal Zones

VICE-MAYOR VOTED; COMPROMISE WINS ON BOROUGH RULE

SMITH FORCES VICTORS

Local Presidents Lose Executive Powers in Charter Plan.

EARLIER STAND REVERSED

New Official Will Preside Over City Legislature and Act in Mayor's Absence.

SPLIT OVER CITY COUNCIL

Proportional Voting Plan to Be Decided as Separate Issue at Fall Election.

The New York City Charter Revision Commission swung into direct action at its meeting last night in the County Court House.

It voted 15 to 13 for a compromise plan on borough government by which a Borough President would be elected in each borough to preside as chairman over a local or borough council, but he would have no administrative or executive functions. This plan reverses to a great degree the stand which split the commission last week and represents a victory for the forces led by Alfred E. Smith, chairman, and Samuel Seabury.

The commission voted to create the office of Vice-Mayor, elected by direct vote, to preside over the city legislature and to take the place of the Mayor, in the event of the latter's death or disability, for the duration of the disability or for the balance of the Mayor's term.

Split Over Legislature.

It decided that the city legislature "shall have no administrative or executive functions." But the commission split 14 to 14 on whether the legislature should be unicameral or bicameral, and that question was referred back to committee for report Thursday night.

The commission voted to submit to the people, apart from the charter, the question of whether the city legislature shall be elected by proportional representation.

An executive budget and a capital outlay budget, "following as nearly as possible the provisions of the State Constitution," were approved.

A recommendation that all action of the legislative body shall be subject to veto by the Mayor, which may be overruled by vote of two-thirds of all the members of the legislative body, was referred back to the committee on city legislature as being bound up with the question of the form of the legislature.

The city legislature committee was directed to report to the commission Thursday night various forms of unicameral and bicameral councils.

All the recommendations approved last night, except that on proportional representation, had been reached at a joint meeting of three committees in the afternoon, which Mr. Smith had attended.

After a three-hour session, the joint committees reached a tentative agreement for submission to the commission.

The vote on the compromise on borough government, which virtually strips the borough presidents of all their present administrative and executive functions, was accomplished by the swinging over to the Smith-Seabury side of two Queens members of the commission.

Those who changed, according to reliable report, were George J. Ryan, president of the Board of Education and a Democrat, and Robert W. Higbie, a Republican and banker.

Prial Fights Plan.

The vote on the borough government compromise was taken over the protest of Frank J. Prial, champion of the group that last week voted to retain the borough presidents with all their present powers.

"I declared that there were sixty-five organizations in Brooklyn and others in the Bronx which wanted to meet and express their opposition to this contemplated form of borough tyranny, and asked the commission to defer action," said Mr. Prial after the meeting.

Mr. Seabury, in his attacks on the members of the commission voting to retain present borough autonomy, charged that they were controlled

Continued on Page Two.

McGoldrick Not to Ease Brokers' Tax, He Hints

Controller Joseph O. McGoldrick failed yesterday to announce a compromise with brokers' organizations on the city business tax, which is payable on Aug. 1.

Furthermore, it was indicated that he had decided not to make any compromise but to enforce the rules and regulations that he issued on Monday. These rules provide, among other things, that brokers must pay the tax upon transactions consummated in exchanges in this city even though they originated elsewhere.

The brokers contend the city is not empowered to levy the tax on such transactions.

ROOSEVELT REACHES COAST OF HAWAII

President Spends First Day There in Search of Swordfish Near Kailua.

DECLINES TO GO ASHORE

Governor Poindexter Boards the Houston and Welcomes Executive to Islands.

Wireless to THE NEW YORK TIMES.

KAILUA, Hawaii, July 24.—President Roosevelt reached this small town on the Kona coast at 5 o'clock this morning, ending the longest leg of his 12,000-mile cruise of the Atlantic and Pacific Oceans. He came into port in calm, sunny weather, with excellent prospects ahead for his quest for swordfish off the lava flows nine miles to the north.

At his request, no formal welcome was provided except that Governor Joseph Poindexter, who arrived from Honolulu at 6:30 A. M. aboard the Coast Guard cutter Itasca, went aboard the Houston two hours later for a brief conference. With him went a few bouquets of Hawaiian flowers, but, due to the press of time, the Governor was unable to present a lei to the President.

Declining to see members of the press because he wished to get as early a start as possible for his fishing, Mr. Roosevelt announced that he would have something to say tomorrow at Hilo, where he will go ashore to become the first President ever to step on the soil of these islands. He said he wanted no questions to be asked, explaining that he would do all the talking.

His stay at Hilo tomorrow will be brief, as he plans to leave at noon en route to Honolulu, stopping at Lahaina Roadstead and also off the leper settlement at Kalaupapa.

The President and his sons left the Houston at 10 o'clock for some fishing. With them went a Hawaiian expert as guide and half a dozen kapok life preservers from the Itasca, luncheon and the necessary lines, rods and reels. Island fishermen had been barred for two days from the area where Mr. Roosevelt will fish, with expectation that he will have every opportunity for a strike. He expects to spend the remainder of the day at sea, returning in time to board the Houston and sail for Hilo at 8 tonight.

As the Itasca came in this morning and passed the Houston and New Orleans, the crew lined the rails at attention and civilians aboard were asked to stand a few moments. After the cutter came to anchor a boatload of mail was dispatched to the President aboard the cruiser, and an hour afterward he returned to the Itasca to be placed on a naval plane for Honolulu a sack of postal matter addressed to Secretary McIntyre at the White House. This was turned over to the personal care of Charles F. Chillingworth, postmaster at Honolulu, who flew back to the capital city with it.

If Kona had expected to have a holiday today its people were disappointed. Throngs of them were at one small wharf when the cruisers came in this morning, hoping to have a glimpse of Mr. Roosevelt, but he let it be known early that he had no intention of coming ashore. In the welcoming crowd were all of Hawaii's many nationalities. Lei-bedecked and smiling islanders had made ready for the President's angling expedition by taking plenty of live bait and by providing a system of patrol boats, each manned by a veteran of this coast, which cruised offshore look-

Continued on Page Five.

LEHMAN SUBMITS NEW CITY TAX PLEA TO SPECIAL SESSION

Backs Request for Power to Raise Relief Funds—Bill Will Be Offered Today.

PLANS FOR LEVIES ISSUED

Deutsch Lists All Proposals Received, Including One for High Income Taxes.

New York City's problem of financing unemployment relief moved nearer solution yesterday when Governor Lehman sent a special message to the Legislature asking it to grant additional taxing power to the city to raise relief funds.

At the same time the joint committee of the Board of Aldermen and the Board of Estimate, named to consider relief financing, held an executive session in City Hall at which all suggestions made for relief financing were considered. The plans suggested covered a wide range. One of them proposed a graduated scale of city income taxes ranging as high as 75 per cent on incomes of $50,000 or more.

Aldermanic President Bernard S. Deutsch chairman of the committee, made it clear that the committee favored no specific tax, but was merely submitting all the suggestions made at public hearings. In discussing the city income tax proposal he said:

"I can't remember who submitted that one. But if any such tax were enacted it would drive thousands of people out of the city. There need be no fear that the administration will favor it."

The city income tax proposed would apply to all incomes over $5,000. The tax suggested was 12½ per cent on $5,000 to $10,000; 25 per cent on $10,000 to $20,000; 50 per cent on $20,000 to $50,000 and 75 per cent on incomes above $50,000. All other taxes paid to State and Federal Governments would be deductible up to 70 per cent of the tax.

All Suggestions Weighed.

At yesterday's meeting the joint committee went over all the suggestions without deciding to favor any specific ones. Mr. Deutsch said the committee would await the Legislature's grant of additional taxing power before taking a stand on any of the suggestions.

Governor Lehman sent his special message to both houses of the Legislature, laying before them the city's need for additional revenue for relief. He included in the message a letter from Mayor LaGuardia urging the legislation, as well as the report of the joint committee containing all the suggestions for new taxes.

In his letter to Governor Lehman, Mayor LaGuardia said:

"I am compelled to request legislation to permit the City of New York to raise additional revenue to be earmarked and used for the sole purpose of financing unemployment relief.

"As you know, to date we have been financing relief out of the $70,000,000 loan provided for at the time of the bankers' agreement. That fund is now about depleted. We have been contributing on the average of $4,500,000 a month.

"It is my firm belief that current relief from now on should be currently financed. With one exception, this plan has received universal approval and support. I appointed a joint committee of the Board of Estimate and Apportionment and the Board of Aldermen. Several plans of financing have been submitted. Our power to tax is limited and in addition legislation is necessary so that the revenue raised from this source can be set apart and earmarked for relief purposes and not go into the general fund.

"I enclose herewith a report which I received from the joint committee. It is self-explanatory.

"I would greatly appreciate it if you would give this matter your prompt attention. I stand ready to confer, if you deem that necessary, at any time and place at your convenience."

Bill to Be Offered Today.

Assemblyman I. Arnold Ross, New York Republican, will introduce today a bill to give the city the taxing power it wants. The measure is almost identical with a bill he sponsored at the regular session but which was lost in the final shuffle.

Under the Ross bill, the city would have the power to impose any tax which the Legislature had or would have the authority to impose. The taxing power would run from Sept. 1 of this year to Dec. 31, 1937, and it would be possible to earmark the receipts for unemployment relief.

The monthly cost of administering relief here is now about $17,700,000, of which the city contrib-

Continued on Page Four.

$21,160 in Gold Is Stolen From Plane Lying in Nile

Special Cable to THE NEW YORK TIMES.

ALEXANDRIA, Egypt, July 24.—Gold ingots valued at £4,000 [about $21,160 at current exchange] were stolen from the Imperial Airways amphibian Sylvanus while it lay moored in the Nile at Cairo during the early hours of today.

The gold arrived in Heliopolis from South Africa yesterday. It was being sent to England. The shipment was transferred to the amphibian about midnight and must have been stolen before 2 o'clock.

Two native guards are suspected, although there is an alternative theory that the gold never reached the Sylvanus. Those who hold this view believe the ingots might have been stolen during transit from Heliopolis to the mooring station of the Sylvanus.

AUSTRIA NERVOUS, HANGS TERRORIST

Czechoslovak Socialist, 20, Is Executed Three Hours After Hasty Bombing Trial.

COMPANION, 21, IS SPARED

Police Are Making Wholesale Arrests—Search Houses, Guard Dollfuss's Home.

By G. E. R. GEDYE.
Wireless to THE NEW YORK TIMES.

VIENNA, July 24.—The Dollfuss government struck tonight at the intensified terrorism under which Austria has suffered for the last three months. A 20-year-old Czechoslovak Socialist workman, Joseph Gerl, was hanged in the courtyard of the Vienna Assize Court within three hours after a hurried trial.

Gerl and a 21-year-old Austrian worker, Rudolph Anzbaeck, were challenged last Saturday morning by Policeman Ferdinand Forstner while they were waiting to take a train to Czechoslovakia. Forstner began to search Gerl, who suddenly drew a pistol and fired two shots, wounding the policeman seriously, and took to his heels followed by his comrade. After their arrest the two admitted under police pressure that Gerl had tried to blow up a signal mast on a little-used Vienna suburban railroad while Anzbaeck kept guard. The policeman is recovering.

300 More Arrested.

The government's nervousness as to the near future continued today. During the day 300 Socialists were arrested—600 others had been arrested in the previous few days—and were sent to the disused Arnbruster factory because police cells were overcrowded.

The residence of Chancellor Engelbert Dollfuss has been under special guard all day. Tonight "sewer commanders" were sent into the network of Vienna sewers, presumably because of fears that public buildings were going to be blown up. In particular, passages connecting the Chancellor's department on the Ballhausplatz, Parliament and the Rathaus were searched.

Many house searches were made today in various parts of Vienna. The police visited, among other places, the office of the correspondent of the Times Wide World

Continued on Page Seven.

Capital Relief Head Back From Breadlines, Charges Officials Antagonize the Needy

Special to THE NEW YORK TIMES.

WASHINGTON, July 24.—Commissioner George E. Allen, one of the three "Mayors" of the capital city, who returned today from a private inspection of relief operations in several parts of the country, declares that relief is being administered by "snooty" persons who are doing more to antagonize the destitute than to help them.

Mr. Allen spent a week's vacation as a member-in-ranks of the breadlines of Chicago, Milwaukee and other Midwestern cities. He came back to Washington convinced, he said, that 98 per cent of his breadline cronies simply wanted work. He bore personal testimony to the effect that they could not get a job—he tried many times and failed.

"I found beyond question, that, as to 98 per cent of the people you find around relief stations and employment agencies, all they want is a job," Mr. Allen said. "And, furthermore, all of them hope they are going to get one. Tomorrow, perhaps, or the next day. How long this hope will hold out I don't know.

"Furthermore, I found out our employment system is wrong from beginning to end. Around the employment agencies run by the Federal Government you will find the snootiest people. You ask them for a job and they feel they are doing you a favor when they take your application.

"I went from here by train to Milwaukee and traveled by bus to Cleveland, Toledo and Chicago and Detroit. In one I tried to get a job as a bell-hop. In all I tried to get a job at about twenty-five different places, and failed everywhere. But I learned a lot. Even when I went into a pawnshop to pawn my watch, I learned it wasn't worth near as much as I had thought.

"Even the Communists taught me something. I learned the power that the Communists have is gained principally because they will listen to people who are down and out and will work for them and fight for them. That is exactly the attitude the relief people should take, but the relief people won't even listen to you most of the time.

"The crowds that gather around the Communist speakers are made up largely of people who are curious and who have nothing better to do. They stand around listening to a speech about overthrowing the government, and yet if somebody starts a whisper in the crowd that there are jobs to be had somewhere the crowd will melt away and leave the orator talking to himself."

BUS INDICTMENTS FOR MANSLAUGHTER TO BE ASKED TODAY

Grand Jury Will Get Charges Against 'Several Persons' in Ossining Crash.

INSPECTION ORDERED HERE

Mayor Also Directs Check-Up on Owners—Lehman to Ask Special Session to Act.

New York State and city authorities and officials of Westchester County moved swiftly yesterday to fix the responsibility for Sunday's fatal bus crash in Ossining and to "make impossible a repetition of such abuses" as those found by investigators.

Governor Lehman at Albany, aroused by the tragedy and by the subsequent demands for remedial legislation, announced that he would submit to the special session of the Legislature recommendations to safeguard bus travelers.

The New York City Police Department, by order of Mayor LaGuardia, began a rigid inspection of all of the 210 sightseeing buses in the city and started an inquiry into what the Mayor termed the "elusive, irresponsible ownership of these buses." Mayor LaGuardia announced extensive plans for strict municipal control of the speeds and routes of all buses using city streets, and said he was certain a tax could be levied on interstate buses passing through the city.

Indictments to Be Asked.

At Ossining and White Plains, Westchester County authorities aided by experts from the State and city studied the scene of the accident, tested four buses similar to the one that plunged from the railroad ramp and burst into flames, and questioned survivors. Officials announced that evidence would be presented to the Westchester County grand jury at White Plains today, and that manslaughter indictments against "several" persons would be asked.

The death toll rose to eighteen with the recovery from the Hudson River yesterday of the body of William J. Murray Sr., of 13 Cornelia Street, Brooklyn, whose wife also died in the crash. Another man, Daniel Williams, 24 years old, of 45 Cornelia Street, was still tentatively listed as missing, and grappling in the waters of the Hudson near the scene of the tragedy was continued. It is not known definitely that Williams accompanied the Young Men's Democratic League of the Twentieth Assembly District in Brooklyn on the trip to Ossining, but he is missing from his home.

The last of the charred bodies in the morgues in Ossining was finally identified as that of William O'Keefe, 65, of 79 Linden Street, Brooklyn.

None of the thirteen survivors still in Westchester hospitals suffering from severe burns and other injuries is in a critical condition, physicians reported yesterday, although it will be weeks before some recover.

Governor Awaits Report.

Governor Lehman's announcement that he would recommend remedial legislation was made as Charles A. Harnett, Motor Vehicle Commissioner, continued his inves-

Continued on Page Nine.

RECORD HEAT GRIPS WEST; DEATHS TO DATE PUT AT 700; CHICAGO 105°, ST. LOUIS 110.2°

Cattle Die by Thousands in Oklahoma; All Farmers Fighting to Obtain Water

Special to THE NEW YORK TIMES.

GUTHRIE, Okla., July 24.—An increasing number of animals are suffering through the intense heat and lack of water and are dying from thirst in the pastures and on the range in Oklahoma and Kansas. Cattle are being humanely shot where it is impossible to save them.

Farmers and ranchmen in both States are battling day and night against many handicaps to provide water for both man and beast. Never in the history of these two States have cattlemen generally been forced to transport and pump water over such great distances as they are doing today.

Night travelers in South Central Kansas find an atmosphere of oil-boom days, with lighted derricks illuminating the countryside for miles around. Under these derricks engines are churning night and day, sinking wells down to a depth of 200 feet or more to reach water. Crews of engineers and geologists are searching the Southwest for deep underground streams that can be depended upon for a supply of water during drought periods.

Some of these wells will furnish central water supplies for rural communities. Water will be hauled in tanks and barrels five or six miles to livestock on farms.

Both State and Federal Governments are taking a hand in helping farmers to obtain water. Carl Giles, Federal Relief Administrator in Oklahoma, made a request yesterday for an immediate fund of $500,000 to provide for shipping tank cars of water into Southwestern counties and other drought-stricken areas where there is an acute shortage. This money will also be used for drilling wells in counties where water can still be found beneath the surface.

To avoid slaughtering thousands of animals doomed to die from thirst if relief from rain and lower temperatures is not forthcoming, arrangements have been made to use more than fifty tank cars which can be shipped to any point in the State within thirty-six hours. These tanks will transport water only to areas where animals are suffering.

It is estimated that even in many sections outside the seventeen emergency drought-relief districts the existing water supply will last only two more weeks. There is no im-

Continued on Page Three.

63-YEAR MARK SURPASSED

117 Degrees Is Reported in Oklahoma and 106 in Omaha.

DROUGHT RUIN SPREADING

Countless Wells Being Sunk in Frantic Hunt for Water for Humans and Cattle.

1,600,000 LIVING ON RELIEF

Torrid Wave Moves Eastward, but Sea Breezes Promise to Temper It Here.

A vast drought area comprising more than half of the United States suffered yesterday from a continued heat wave that sent the mercury beyond 100 degrees in dozens of places, claimed more than 700 lives to date, seared crops and threatened to reduce great herds of cattle to worthless skeletons.

The Associated Press said heat deaths had occurred yesterday at the rate of ten an hour.

Although the heat wave was moving eastward, the Weather Bureau here said New Yorkers would be spared the extreme temperatures. Officials of the bureau said that the persisting cool weather off the Atlantic seaboard would probably temper the furnace-like blasts from the West.

The temperatures soared as high as 117 degrees at Vinita, Okla., the highest there since 1911. Yesterday marked the thirty-sixth day that that community had suffered temperatures of 100 or more. To add to its troubles prairie fires north of Vinita threatened cattle stocks.

Other high temperatures reported yesterday were: Chicago, 105; Miami, Okla., 112; Tulsa, Okla., 111; Bartlesville, Okla., 113; Omaha, 106; St. Louis, 110.2.

Highest Since 1871.

The marks touched in Chicago and St. Louis were the highest since 1871.

Other communities with high temperatures, as reported by The Associated Press, were: Quincy, Ill., 111; Peru, Ill., 108; Rockford, Ill., 107; Centralia, Ill., 111; Independence, Kan., 112.

In Chicago alone the death toll from the heat reached thirty-seven yesterday, bringing the toll since last Friday up to 126.

With the drought spreading and intensifying, Lawrence Westbrook, in charge of drought relief, announced in Washington that about 400,000 families, comprising 1,600,000 individuals, are being supported by Federal emergency relief projects in the drought area.

Facing a situation unprecedented, the Federal Relief Administration is pushing a far-flung system of water projects as it swings into action to combat the drought.

Frantic Hunt for Water.

In numerous places throughout the drought-stricken States a frantic, almost life-and-death search for water for the parched throats of man and beast is going on.

In Oklahoma, drilling for water took the place of drilling for oil, and hundreds of engines churned incessantly, day and night, sinking wells to a depth of 200 feet or more to reach water.

Crews of engineers and geologists scoured the Southwest countryside in search of deep, subterranean streams that would supply water for human beings, cattle and crops.

State relief administrations in the West hurriedly sunk hundreds of such wells, and in entire neighborhoods owners of land permitted their property to be dug in the universal search for water.

In Wyoming fifty wells have been completed or are under construction, and in South Dakota the total was about 100. Similar programs were being rushed in other range States to save livestock.

Like an Oil Boom.

In South Central Kansas night travelers reported an atmosphere that outwardly resembled oil boom days as the crews of illuminated derricks bored into the earth in search of water.

In many Prairie States turtles, frogs and fish were left high and dry as ponds, lakes and small streams dried up.

Cattle and other livestock ate any green material they could get and even gnawed the very dirt. In many

Continued on Page Three.

EXAMINE REPUTED DILLINGER TIPSTER

Police Find 'Woman in Red' Who Accompanied Him to Theatre.

NAMES OTHER COMPANION

Latter, She Says, Was Outlaw's Sweetheart—Father Takes Body Home.

Special to THE NEW YORK TIMES.

CHICAGO, July 24.—The identity of the "girl in the red dress," who accompanied John Dillinger to the Biograph Theatre Sunday night and saw him shot dead by Federal agents was established tonight as his body was being taken to Indiana for burial.

Examined by the police, she gave her name as Mrs. Anna Miller. She lives at 2,420 North Halsted Street. She said she was formerly known as Anna Gage. The girl whose picture was in Dillinger's watch, Mrs. Miller said, is Mrs. Rita Keele, also known as Polly Hamilton, who was the other woman with the outlaw at the theatre.

Mrs. Keele, divorced from Roy Keele in Gary, Ind., last April, was the latest of Dillinger's sweethearts. The two met in Mrs. Miller's apartment and Captain Thomas Duffy believed Mrs. Miller had sheltered Dillinger for several weeks, knowingly or unknowingly.

Whether Mrs. Miller or Polly Hamilton gave the information about Dillinger was not learned. Captain Duffy said Mrs. Miller was reluctant to talk about the slain man, whom she said she knew as Gene or James Lawrence. She asserted she did not know whether the Hamilton woman had passed the word that meant the end of Dillinger.

Returned to Scene of Death.

Department of Justice agents hastened to the police station and ended further questioning of the woman. By that time, however, Mrs. Miller had said she formerly lived in Gary, Ind., and was well acquainted with Sergeant Martin Zarkovich of the East Chicago, Ind., police department, one of those credited with running Dillinger to earth.

Mrs. Miller admitted that Dillinger had been in her apartment on "three or four evenings," but denied that he had roomed there for several weeks. She said Mrs. Keele was an old acquaintance, whose father is a minister in Fargo, N. D. Mrs. Keele, she said, kept company with Dillinger.

Mrs. Miller said she ran down the alley and to her home less than a block from the theatre immediately after Dillinger was killed. She hurriedly changed her red dress and then joined the crowd in front of the theatre. Mrs. Keele would not go back with her, but hurried to a room she had rented at a hotel and spent Sunday night. Monday she went to the home of her parents in Fargo.

Detective Frank Slattery identi-

Continued on Page Six.

RAYON STRIKE SHUTS MILL PERMANENTLY

Tubize Chatillon to Abandon Hopewell, Va., Yarn Factory, Abolishing 1,500 Jobs.

UNION ATTACKS PROPOSAL

Charges Report of Damage to Idle Machinery Is Ruse to 'Starve Out' Workers.

The Tubize Chatillon Corporation, third largest manufacturer of rayon yarns in the United States, announced yesterday at its offices, 2 Park Avenue, that it would permanently shut down its rayon yarn plant at Hopewell, Va., because of the strike of 1,800 employes, which has closed the yarn and finishing plants since June 29.

In a letter to Miss Anna Weinstock, Commissioner of Conciliation of the United States Department of Labor, made public here, J. E. Bassill, president of the company, explained that the company would shut down the plant because of the damage to equipment caused by its idleness during the strike.

To repair the damage to equipment would entail excessive costs that the company is unwilling to saddle upon its stockholders, since the stockholders already have been burdened with profitless operations continued during the depression, among other reasons, to give employment, it was announced.

1,500 Thrown Out of Work.

The corporation will continue to operate its knitting, dyeing and finishing plant, using yarn produced by its plant at Rome, Ga. About 1,500 of the 1,800 striking employes were on the payrolls of the yarn plant and they will be thrown out of work permanently, it was said. The weekly payroll at Hopewell, Va., was about $43,000.

In announcing the company's plans, Mr. Bassill said most of the employes were loyal and had no grievances against the corporation, as shown by a recent questionnaire.

In his letter to Miss Weinstock, who was in New York recently trying to negotiate a settlement of the strike, Mr. Bassill explained that sudden abandonment of the plant had caused "not only the ruination of thousands of dollars worth of materials in process, but also tremendous amount of damage to the equipment, due to the corrosion of the chemicals and the solidification of the collodion in pipe lines and spinning pumps."

"Our best estimate of the minimum time required to reopen this plant and secure a satisfactory quality of product would be three months," he added. "This would mean heavy losses through the disposal of inferior product produced during such time at sacrifice prices.

"In reviewing the situation which confronts us with respect to the manufacture of nitrocellulose yarn, and taking into consideration the

Continued on Page Two.

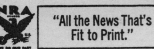

"All the News That's Fit to Print."

The New York Times.

Copyright, 1934, by The New York Times Company.

5:30 A. M. EXTRA

WEATHER—Cloudy, warmer today; local showers tomorrow.
Temperatures Yesterday—Max., 81; Min., 67

VOL. LXXXIII....No. 27,949. Entered as Second-Class Matter, Postoffice, New York, N. Y. NEW YORK, THURSDAY, AUGUST 2, 1934. P TWO CENTS In New York City. | THREE CENTS Within 200 Miles | FOUR CENTS Elsewhere Except in 7th and 8th Postal Zones

TWO REFORM BILLS ARE SIDETRACKED; LEHMAN FIGHTS ON

Quorum Lacking for Report on County Plans as Republicans Walk Out of Committee.

BATTLE ON FLOOR IS DUE

Governor, Assailing 'Despicable' Action, Is Expected to Spur Democrats in Assembly.

SMITH TARGET IN SESSION

Republicans Deny Entering Agreement—Say He Is Trying to 'Bedevil' Situation.

By W. A. WARN.
Special to THE NEW YORK TIMES.

ALBANY, Aug. 1.—The Assembly Judiciary Committee met this afternoon and voted to report eleven minor bills, but failed to take any action on the proposed constitutional amendments, sponsored by Senator Dunnigan and Senator Mastick, to prepare the way for county government reforms.

The Republican majority in the Assembly contrived to block these yesterday after their adoption in the Senate, sending them back to committee.

Governor Lehman pronounced as "despicable" the failure of the committee to act on the measures, the adoption of which he and ex-Governor Smith, as head of the New York City Charter Revision Commission, have so much at heart.

The Governor said he was firmly backing the position taken by Mr. Smith in a telegram transmitted on behalf of the entire Charter Commission to Speaker McGinnies yesterday protesting against the action of the Republican majority in "repudiating" its agreement to pass the County Reform Bills.

Governor Is Silent on Plans.

Governor Lehman has not indicated what further steps he may be contemplating to force favorable action on the two side-tracked measures.

They have both been adopted by the Senate, together with another proposed amendment to the Constitution, in which both the Mastick and Dunnigan proposals are joined and which the Assembly yesterday concurred in by unanimous vote.

While the Judiciary Committee, like the Assembly itself, has a Republican majority, it has become apparent through developments of the last few days that the Democrats in the Legislature are no more eager to pass these constitutional amendments than are a majority of the Republicans.

While engaging on the floor of the Assembly today in an apparent effort to make political capital out of the Republican blockade established yesterday against the Dunnigan and Mastick measures, the Democrats did not bestir themselves to rescue the amendments.

Chance for Steingut to Act.

Assemblyman Steingut, minority leader, has not filed the necessary three days' notice of a motion to take the two resolutions from the Judiciary Committee, possibly on the assumption that the committee had not had an opportunity to act when the Assembly met today.

Now that the committee has met and failed to act the way is open for Mr. Steingut to proceed, but unless action is taken by the Assembly before the end of the week the adoption of the two resolutions would be to no purpose.

Under the Election Law, Monday is the deadline for publication of notice that the amendments are to be submitted to the 1935 Legislature for concurrent action.

Governor Lehman was aroused when he learned of developments at the committee meeting.

"The action in refusing to report or act on the bills is despicable," he said. "I am back of the position taken by Governor Smith 100 per cent.

"Until I learned of the action of the Judiciary Committee in refusing to report the bills, I was convinced that in accordance with the agreement reported by former Governor Smith, the bills would be reported out and passed.

"There is still time to pass these bills, and they should be passed. I am amazed that any condition like this could exist."

Lehman Action Is Expected.

Hence, with the Governor so stirred by the situation, observers at the capital believe he will move to compel more vigorous intervention by the Assembly Democrats to save the measures.

Most of the Democrats, and Republicans also, have already quit their legislative labors for the week and returned to their homes or gone to the Saratoga races or elsewhere. In order to get anything

Continued on Page Four.

Giant Seaplane Tops All Records; Lindbergh Hails Test of Clipper

Sikorsky Machine, Under Transport Conditions With a Full Load, Averages 157.5 Miles an Hour Over a 1,242-Mile Course —Range Would Cover Ocean Trade Routes.

By REGINALD M. CLEVELAND.
Special to THE NEW YORK TIMES.

BRIDGEPORT, Conn., Aug. 1.—All existing world's records for transport seaplane flight (previously held abroad) were toppled like ninepins here today as the giant Sikorsky S-42, the Brazilian Clipper, carrying a full transport load and with Colonel Lindbergh in charge for Pan American Airways, flew 1,242.8 miles at an average speed of 157.5 miles an hour. Eight long-standing and recent world marks were shattered by impressive margins. The two other official ones had already been won by the plane in previous test flights.

As Edwin C. Musick, chief pilot of the airlines, sent the four-engined flying boat four times over a course of 311 miles which included Manhattan's river front, Long Island Sound and the Atlantic Ocean, it was evident that history was being written for American aviation.

Starting at the Stratford Lighthouse, the course ran through five control points, George Washington Bridge, Staten Island Lighthouse, Fire Island Lighthouse, Block Island, Point Judith Lighthouse and back to the place of beginning.

The elapsed time for the flight was 7 hours, 53 minutes, 58 seconds, for a distance equal to that from Newfoundland to the Azores. Yet Pilot Musick used only 69 per cent of the 3,000 horsepower of the four Pratt & Whitney Hornet engines streamlined into the wide silver wing. He had fuel enough for another lap when he landed. The margin of range, with a mail load, for any of the ocean trade routes, Atlantic or Pacific, by way of the islands, had been amply proved.

Cruising speed only was used and less than full horsepower because the flight was an acceptance test for the airline of this craft, which will cut two days' time from the run between Miami and Buenos Aires and put that South American capital within five and one-half days of New York.

Strictly transport conditions prevailed during the flight.

When the plane crossed the starting line against the blue of a morning sky at 9:24:38, Eastern daylight time, she had only six persons aboard. They were Colonel Lindbergh, as official representative of Pan American Airways' technical

Continued on Page Seven.

SMITH ACTS TO QUIT IN CHARTER DISPUTE

Reported Ready to Resign if Board Does Not Agree to Reconsider City Rule Vote.

LETTER ALREADY DRAFTED

Seabury Said to Be Weighing Similar Action—Crucial Meeting Tonight.

Alfred E. Smith will resign from the New York City Charter Revision Commission unless the commission at tonight's meeting changes its decision to retain the city legislature in substantially its present form, according to reports last night in Albany from a source close to the former Governor.

Mr. Smith was said to have long been disgusted with the opposition to thoroughgoing reform of the city charter among members of the commission. According to the report from Albany, Mr. Smith was quoted as saying in private conversation that he was "sick and tired of the bickering and opposition in the commission" and that he "would like a vacation."

The fact that the former Governor has for some time been considering resignation or taking some other drastic action to bring sharply to public attention the failure of the commission to make real progress was confirmed by persons in the city close to Mr. Smith.

Letter Already Drafted.

It was felt that Mr. Smith might be led to resign at tonight's meeting if the commission voted to restore to the Borough Presidents their administrative and patronage powers, as some members of the commission fear will be done. According to a report by The Associated Press, Mr. Smith has already drafted his letter of resignation.

Samuel Seabury, vice chairman of the commission, declined last night to deny or to comment on a report that he also intended to resign. Earlier in the day Mr. Seabury had stated that he would make no comment until after the outcome of tonight's meeting on what he plans to do in case the opposition on the commission succeeds in restoring borough government.

These reports came as fear was expressed by members of the commission and civic organizations favoring drastic charter revision that a successful drive would be made at tonight's meeting to restore to the Borough Presidents their present administrative and patronage powers. Such a result, it was said, would largely nullify all the progress made by the commission. Both Mr. Smith and Mr. Seabury have fought for stripping Borough Presidents of their powers and for a single chamber legislature.

Confusion existed yesterday among members of the commission, as well as among civic organizations, over the effect of the action taken Tuesday night by the commission to retain the Board of Estimate and to revamp the Board of Aldermen into a smaller but much stronger Council.

Many condemned it as merely retaining the present form of city legislature, while others saw in it

Continued on Page Four.

BUSINESS TAX YIELD IS UNDER $3,000,000

$2,092,681 Total, With Mail Returns Still Due, Far Short of $8,000,000 Expected.

BUDGET NOW UNBALANCED

Mayor Denies City Plans to Restore Half of Pay Cut—Chides Levy on Figures.

The city's hope of realizing $8,000,000 from its new business tax received a severe blow last night when Controller Joseph D. McGoldrick announced that the total collected up to 6 P. M. on the final day for payment was only $2,092,681.47.

It was pointed out, however, that a last-minute ruling permitting payment of taxes by mail without penalty, provided the letters containing tax checks or money orders were postmarked before midnight, would probably bring in additional payments today.

Nevertheless it was predicted that the total return, even with the last-minute checks, could not possibly come to much more than $3,000,000—only three-eighths of the sum the city had hoped to garner from the new tax.

McGoldrick Withholds Comment.

Mr. McGoldrick withheld comment on the tax payments pending the final compilation today. It was indicated, however, that he was convinced that the total returns would be materially less than the sum expected when the tax was imposed.

Failure of the revenues from the business tax to come up to expectations will have the effect of unbalancing the city budget, it was said. The budget was balanced after the passage of the City Economy Bill by salary reductions and furloughs and by imposition of new taxes, of which the business tax was one.

A total of $1,094,800.27 was received yesterday in payment of the tax in the City Collector's office in the five boroughs. During the day 16,748 returns were filed.

Several times recently administration spokesmen have expressed the fear that the business tax revenue would be materially below the original estimates. None, however, believed that the revenue would be as small as last night's figures indicated it would be.

In view of the fact that failure to pay the tax on time brings with it a 10 per cent penalty plus payment of 5 per cent interest a month on the whole tax sum due, it was felt in the Finance Department that few concerns would withhold their payments. It was not disclosed how many payments were made under protest and threat of court action to test the constitutionality of the tax measure.

Cut in Reserve Is Hailed.

The revision of the bankers' agreement to provide reduction in the tax delinquency reserve fund in the budgets of 1935, 1936 and 1937 from the original $50,000,000 to $25,000,000 was praised yesterday by Peter Grimm, chairman of the Citizens Budget Commission. Mr. Grimm telegraphed Controller McGoldrick and Governor Lehman, who were mainly responsible for

Continued on Page Nine.

NEW ORLEANS TENSE AS POLICE AWAIT A MOVE BY TROOPS

300 More Patrolmen Sworn In as the Militia Removes Machine Guns From View.

GUARD FORCE IS REDUCED

Gov. Allen Orders Guardsmen to Investigate Alleged Gambling and Vice Graft.

Special to THE NEW YORK TIMES.

NEW ORLEANS, Aug. 1.—New Orleans anxiously watched the growing tension tonight as armed State and city forces faced each other in a political crisis precipitated by the tactics of Senator Huey Long.

George Reyer, Superintendent of Police, completed tonight the swearing in of 500 supernumerary policemen for emergency use. The machine guns manned by National Guardsmen, which have been protruding from the windows of the registration office, were removed.

The 500 emergency policemen, called for service by order of Mayor Walmsley, were armed with automatic shotguns and pistols. They were divided into two platoons, 300 on the day shift and 200 on night duty.

Of the former, 200 will be held at police headquarters, and 100 stationed at the City Hall and the First Precinct station. All of the men on night duty are stationed at police headquarters, with police automobiles and patrol wagons held in readiness to transport them wherever they might be needed.

Policemen now ready for duty number 1,300. All regular members of the department have been instructed to be ready for duty at all times, day or night.

Explains Machine Guns.

The appearance of machine guns in the registration office was explained by Adjt. Gen. Fleming at a conference with Mayor Walmsley this afternoon.

"The members of the artillery unit guarding the registration office," Adjutant General Fleming said, "were relieved Tuesday night by members of the machine gun unit. The machine gun unit always carries its machine guns along wherever it is sent."

He denied the machine guns were intended for intimidation.

Mayor Walmsley and the Finance Commissioner, A. Miles Pratt, in statements issued today, denied there was any intention on the part of the city government to seize any records in the registration office.

The presidents of the chief organizations of business men met today and debated the situation. They adopted a resolution which censured no one and asked the world to understand that "the business of this city is being conducted along the usual, efficient lines with no interruptions whatsoever."

Three members of the new police commission created by the Long-controlled Legislature to take supervision of the police force out of the hands of the Mayor and Council filed their credentials. No attempt was made to call a meeting of the board.

Prosecution of the 500 odd men charged with miscounting ballots in the last election, being regarded as impossible under a law taking effect today, District Attorney Stanley nolle prossed the cases. The charges were brought after a

Continued on Page Fourteen.

Overnight Air Service To West Coast Starts

Starting overnight service between the nation's coasts on the "Lindbergh Line," a fourteen-passenger Douglas plane of the Transcontinental & Western Air Line took off from Newark Airport yesterday afternoon at 5:25 Eastern daylight time. It is due in Los Angeles at 7 this morning.

Elliott Roosevelt, second son of the President; Lieut. Commander Frank M. Hawks, noted speed pilot; two paying passengers, newspapermen and airline officials were aboard as passengers.

The plane also carried two copies of THE NEW YORK TIMES addressed respectively to Frank L. Shaw, Mayor of Los Angeles, and Harry Chandler, publisher of The Los Angeles Times.

20% CUT IN NAVIES URGED BY SWANSON

But Secretary, in Rejoinder to Tokyo Premier, Says 5-5-3 Ratio Should Continue.

OUR PLANE PROGRAM CUT

Navy Now Thinks Equipping of All Ships Will Require 274 Fewer Than 1st Estimate.

Special to THE NEW YORK TIMES.

WASHINGTON, Aug. 1.—A general reduction of 20 per cent in naval armaments by all the powers signatory to the London Naval Treaty was advocated today by Secretary Claude A. Swanson, but he insisted that the 5-5-3 ratio of naval strength fixed by the Washington Treaty of 1922 should stand intact. If agreed to by the powers, the 20 per cent reduction should be a real and not a "blue print" one, he declared.

Meanwhile, Admiral William H. Standley, chief of naval operations, made known that the navy had revised its estimates, but had reached no final decision on the number of planes necessary under the Vinson Naval Building Bill to outfit old and new ships in the next five years. High navy officials now figure that only 910 new planes would be needed, or 274 fewer than previously had been estimated. The navy now has 1,000 planes.

No comprehensive reason was given by naval officials for this reduced estimate, but it was partly explained by the fact that when the earlier estimates were made no decision had been reached to abandon the building of flying-deck cruisers.

Secretary Swanson's statement came as a rejoinder to yesterday's declaration by Premier Keisuke Okada that, while Japan did not expect to attain parity with the United States and Britain at the 1935 naval conference, she could not favor continuation of the present ratio system, which "hurts the self-respect of nations."

Asked to comment on the Japanese Premier's speech, Mr. Swanson said:

"I adhere to the same position I always have. The naval powers met in London and distributed to the naval powers the naval strength they thought was just and right. Naval strength is relative. Both naval and military armaments are relative.

"I represented the navy at the Geneva conference and we offered there the proposition to have any reductions up to 33 1-3 per cent in the different categories of ships,

Continued on Page Three.

Wagner and Prall Hurt in Auto Plunge; Senator Drives Into Brook to Avoid Crash

Special to THE NEW YORK TIMES.

WESTPORT, N. Y., Aug. 1.—Trapped on a curve of a narrow Adirondack highway, Senator Robert F. Wagner drove his automobile over a twenty-foot embankment into a mountain brook rather than have a collision with an oncoming car near here this morning. Senator Wagner and Representative Anning S. Prall, his only companion, were both seriously but not critically injured.

Senator Wagner suffered two fractured ribs on the right side, severe lacerations of the face and knees and numerous body bruises. He may also have concussion of the brain.

Representative Prall suffered a compound fracture of both bones of his lower right leg and lacerations of the hands and forehead.

Witnesses of the crash carried the injured men three miles to the offices of Dr. Harold J. Harris here, where both remained tonight. Dr. Harris said that both were resting comfortably and in no great pain, but that because of the severe shock he did not consider it advisable to move them to a hospital.

Dr. Harris said that he thought it might be best for Senator Wagner to remain in the recovery room in his offices for several days, but that Mr. Prall might be taken to a New York City hospital tomorrow. He said there was "no evidence of skull fractures or concussions, but we never are sure until after twenty-four hours."

The legislators were on their way north on a fishing expedition when the accident occurred. They were bound for the Seigneur Club at Lucerne, Que. Senator Wagner had only recently returned from Portland, Ore., where he attempted to adjust the marine workers' strike and was fired on by mistake.

The highway through the mountains between Wadhams and this village, which is on Lake Champlain, is narrow and winding. Senator Wagner attempted to pass a truck on a curve, only to find another truck approaching from the opposite direction.

Rather than hit either truck he turned his machine off the road. It tumbled down the embankment into the brook but did not overturn. Both occupants were thrown against the windshield and dashboard, but were conscious when they were extricated from the wreckage, and remained so while they were being brought to the office of Dr. Harris here.

VON HINDENBURG DIES AT 86 AFTER A DAY UNCONSCIOUS; HITLER TAKES PRESIDENCY

Times Wide World Photos.

PRESIDENT PAUL von HINDENBURG

END COMES AT 9 A. M.

Reich President Dies at His Home in East Prussia.

MADE A VALIANT FIGHT

Disappearance of House Flag at Neudeck Announces News to World.

THERE HAD BEEN NO HOPE

He Lapsed Into Coma After Hitler Reached Bedside for Last Meeting.

By The Associated Press.

NEUDECK, Germany, Thursday, Aug. 2.—President von Hindenburg died at 9 A. M. today.

The President's death was indicated to correspondents by the disappearance of the house flag from the flagstaff.

Death came to the 86-year-old leader of the German people and former war marshal after a valiant fight against a complication of ailments.

Chancellor Hitler has assumed the Presidency.

Unconscious For Hours.

By GUIDO ENDERIS.
Wireless to THE NEW YORK TIMES.

BERLIN, Thursday, Aug. 2.—A physician's bulletin at 6 o'clock this morning stated that President Paul von Hindenburg remained in the state of unconsciousness into which he lapsed last evening. His death was believed to be a matter only of hours.

The President had consistently lost strength since early morning. All hope that his once rugged constitution would carry him along for a time was definitely dissipated by bedside bulletins that reached Berlin from Neudeck during the day.

At midnight the Propaganda Ministry announced that no further bulletin would be forthcoming during the night. This secretiveness served only to heighten the mystery surrounding Chancellor Hitler's convocation of his Cabinet.

Neither foreign correspondents in Berlin nor those besieging the President's estate at Neudeck had been able to break the news embargo which hedged the Field Marshal's deathbed. Only what seeped through official quarters was placed at the disposal of the German and foreign press.

Hitler Advances Time of Visit.

Chancellor Hitler advanced the time of his flight to Neudeck by more than an hour yesterday morning because of an urgent summons from Professor Ferdinand Sauerbruck, the President's chief physician. It was reported Dr. Sauerbruck notified Herr Hitler that the patient was rapidly sinking.

The last meeting between the President and the man whom he elevated to the Chancellorship after rebuffs which have now become historic, received only brief mention in the day's official bulletins. Herr Hitler found the President momentarily conscious and assured him of the prayerful thoughts of the saddened nation. The President shook the Chancellor's hand and thanked him cordially for his visit; then he dropped into a fresh sleep.

Herr Hitler flew back to Berlin late in the afternoon. Among those who accompanied him to Neudeck was Ernst F. S. Hanfstaengl, chief of his Anglo-American publicity department, but only Herr Hitler was admitted to the sick chamber.

Hope that the President would linger on vanished early last evening when Dr. Sauerbruck, on behalf of the attending physicians, announced that the patient was lapsing into unconsciousness and that his heart action was fast failing. A bulletin issued at 2:30 P. M. stated that the President was then steadily losing ground, despite a restful night. He was conscious most of the forenoon and was able to converse with those around him during part of the afternoon.

Up to two months ago President von Hindenburg's rugged frame and his soldierly bearing gave no evidence of physical decline. The collapse began to set in a month ago when it was discovered the atrophied prostate gland precluded recourse to a major operation be-

Continued on Page B [Preceding Page 4].

SOCIALIST SUPPORT SOUGHT BY AUSTRIA

Neutrality of the Party in Fight With Nazis to Be Rewarded by Release of Leaders.

FOE HANGED IN INNSBRUCK

Minor Rebels to Be Held and Put at Hard Labor—Officials Linked to Putsch.

By G. E. R. GEDYE.
Wireless to THE NEW YORK TIMES.

VIENNA, Aug. 1.—There are signs that the Austrian Government is preparing for radical changes in policy and is contemplating steps calculated to obtain from the Social Democrats assurance of at least neutrality toward the government's fight to the finish with the Nazis.

For eighteen months the Nazis have carried on terroristic activities in Austria, involving a considerable loss of life and enormous property damage. But until yesterday the death penalty had been reserved exclusively for Socialists.

Even the stern ordinance directed against Nazi terrorists, which Chancellor Dollfuss introduced fourteen days before he was slain, proclaiming death as the only admissible penalty for those possessing explosives, had a Socialist for its first victim. He was hanged the night before Dr. Dollfuss was assassinated.

Three Nazis Now Hanged.

Yesterday, however, two Nazis at last were hanged. Today another Nazi was hanged in Innsbruck, Friedrich Wurnig who shot and killed Police Commandant Franz Hickel of Innsbruck on the day of the Dollfuss slaying.

Still more important from the viewpoint of the government, having been committed to a final struggle, is the fact that it has arrested men like Dr. Anton Apold, director of the Alpine Mining Company, and General Karl Bardolf, former adjutant to Archduke Franz Ferdinand, who were always behind the scenes in negotiations between Germany and Austria. Governor Kernmaier of Carinthia, another prominent protector of Nazis, also has been arrested.

The first move to conciliate the Socialists will be the release of prominent leaders who have been imprisoned without trial since February. It is likely they will be free in a day or so. The leaders to be released are Burgomaster Karl Seitz, head of the party, and Herr Danneberg, Herr Helmer, Frau Proft and Frau Postranetzky, members of the central executive committee of the party, and more officers of the Republican Defense Corps, General Koerner, Major Eiffler and Captain Loew.

Whether such release will have

Continued on Page Three.

HITLER CONSULTS CABINET IN SECRET

Ministry Meets Two Hours in Emergency Session—Von Papen in Attendance.

NEW ELECTION POSSIBLE

Friend Says Chancellor Intends to Occupy the Presidency—Army an Unknown Factor.

Wireless to THE NEW YORK TIMES.

BERLIN, Aug. 1.—Chancellor Hitler convoked the German Cabinet for an emergency session at 9:30 o'clock tonight.

The Ministers, among them Vice Chancellor Franz von Papen, had been hastily summoned. They remained with the Chancellor about two hours.

Beyond a more-than-laconic bulletin announcing that the Cabinet had been called, nothing was divulged. There was no indication as to the purpose of the session, and this quickly gave rise to rumors that President von Hindenburg had already died, but that the announcement was being withheld until tomorrow.

The reading public has received only official communiqués concerning the Reich President. The controlled press appears to have been instructed to abstain from any speculative comment on the implications involved in a vacancy in the Presidency.

Hitler Is Seen Taking Power.

Copyright, 1934, by The Associated Press.

BERLIN, Aug. 1.—Adolf Hitler intends to be both President and Chancellor of Germany, one of his close friends told The Associated Press today.

This would give to Herr Hitler a dictatorship as absolute as any in the world.

Despair gripped many Conservatives who had looked upon President von Hindenburg as an anchor against extreme Nazism.

Herr Hitler's plan, The Associated Press informant said, is to call the Cabinet together to read a brief law assigning the dual power to himself.

"The whole thing will take but a few minutes," he said, "for the Cabinet will, of course, endorse the proposal. It will simplify the Führer's [Hitler's] whole work immensely if he need not first ask somebody whether he may do this or that."

An indication of the reliability of this source is that Sunday he revealed the President's turn for the worse and was the first to tip off the fact that Herr Hitler was going to Venice to meet Premier Mussolini.

Under the German Constitution Dr. Erwin Bumke, President of the Supreme Court, would become Act-

Continued on Page Two.

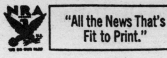

"All the News That's Fit to Print."

The New York Times.

Copyright, 1934, by The New York Times Company.

LATE CITY EDITION
WEATHER—Generally fair today and tomorrow.
Temperatures Yesterday—Max., 77; Min., 66
Detailed weather report, Page 21.

VOL. LXXXIII....No. 27,957. Entered as Second-Class Matter, Postoffice, New York, N. Y. NEW YORK, FRIDAY, AUGUST 10, 1934. P TWO CENTS In New York City. | THREE CENTS Within 200 Miles | FOUR CENTS Elsewhere Except in 7th and 8th Postal Zones

ROOSEVELT NATIONALIZES ALL SILVER AT A PRICE OF 50.01 CENTS AN OUNCE; PROMISES NATION BROADER NEW DEAL

LEHMAN REPORTED READY TO SUPPORT NEW CHARTER BODY

Said to Favor Smaller Group to Be Appointed by Himself and Mayor LaGuardia.

CONFERRED WITH SMITH

Talked Over the Matter Before Ex-Chairman Had Resigned From the Commission.

BROWNELL BILL BLOCKED

Childs Defends Present Board and Holds Views of Smith and Seabury 'Outmoded.'

Special to THE NEW YORK TIMES.

ALBANY, Aug. 9.—While an acrimonious debate over the latest phase of New York City charter revision was in progress in both the Senate and Assembly, reports became current in legislative circles that Governor Lehman in deference to the demand of former Governor Alfred E. Smith and others, was preparing to send in a special message, recommending abolition of the present New York City Charter Commission and the substitution of a new charter revision agency.

The Governor later in the day refused to admit or deny the report. He merely reiterated what he has said before that he was having the matter under very serious consideration. He said in reply to a question that he had discussed the matter with former Governor Smith subsequent to his resignation as chairman and as a member of the present Charter Commission and the resignation of Samuel Seabury as vice chairman and member.

Smaller Board Weighed.

According to the report which made the rounds of the legislative halls, the Governor had in contemplation recommendations for a smaller board with appointment of all the members jointly by himself and Mayor LaGuardia, not as has been proposed in pending legislation, one bloc appointed by the Mayor and another by the Governor. It was said also that the Governor might urge that submission of a new charter be deferred, if not to the 1935 general election, to a special election to be held next year.

In the Assembly the Brownell Bill, providing for a new commission composed of five members to be appointed by the Mayor, came up for advancement to third reading but was blocked by an objection from Assemblyman Carl Pack, Bronx Democrat. Not more than a dozen Assembly members were in their seats when the motion was made to advance the bill.

"This is too important legislation to act upon wantonly with only a dozen members present," Mr. Pack said.

"There is a very general public demand in New York City that we vote on a new charter commission at this session, since there is no hope for real charter revision under the present charter commission," Mr. Brownell said in a plea to the Democratic Assemblyman from the Bronx to withdraw his objection and place the bill in line for final passage. Mr. Pack declined.

Charges Move to Kill Bill.

"There is only one reason for this objection," Mr. Brownell then said. "The Democrats hope to kill this bill."

Then he called upon the Governor to send in a special message recommending charter commission legislation.

"If the Governor fails to take this step," he went on, "he will be repudiating former Governor Smith and slapping Judge Seabury in the face. The time has come when Governor Lehman must assume real leadership in the fight for a new charter for New York City. As Judge Seabury said, he cannot afford to remain neutral."

In the end, Speaker McGinnies, reminding the Assembly that a quorum was not present, ordered action to go over until Monday evening, when the bill will appear on the second reading calendar and no doubt will be advanced to third reading by Republican votes. For passage a two-thirds vote of the Assembly and Senate will be required. Consequently, the bill is doomed unless Governor Lehman should contrive to drum up Democratic support as well for the measure.

In the Senate the charter issue became a topic when the mortgage relief legislation was under heated discussion. Senator Benjamin Feinberg of Clinton, Republican, charged that the eleventh hour exhibition of haste in connection with mortgage legislation was due to the urgent desire of the Democratic majority for a quick adjournment.

Continued on Page Eleven.

New Relief Plan Seeks to Give Aid to 'White Collar' Worker

Similar to CWA Program, It Will Propose 'Real Jobs' for Idle Actors, Playwrights, Artists and Writers—2,000,000 Farm Families May Be Helped.

Special to THE NEW YORK TIMES.

WASHINGTON, Aug. 9.—Details of the broad plan contemplated for care of the masses of unemployed this Winter show that, in addition to its attempting to provide "real jobs instead of alms," it will put "white collar" workers in a separate bracket.

The program, similar in some respects to the CWA, is being studied by the Federal Emergency Relief Administration and will be submitted to President Roosevelt soon after his return to the capital, Aubrey Williams, Acting Relief Administrator, said today.

Among its features for "white collar" workers the plan envisages a little theatre movement in which unemployed actors would give plays written by jobless playwrights; symphony orchestras would be formed by jobless musicians, needy artists would teach art and show their works, and free lance writers would prepare material for study and lectures.

This portion of the program would carry into other fields the artists' relief activities which were carried on by CWA and PWA last Winter. The FERA has already begun to help such professional workers and an additional relief allotment of $10,000,000 for New York State announced today to cover July deficits includes specifically $10,000 for professional projects.

About as many persons were expected on relief rolls this Winter as last, Mr. Williams said in explaining that the new program would differ from the CWA in that it would provide wages for real instead of perfunctory work and from the present relief system in that direct wages would be paid.

About 2,000,000 farm families are expected on the relief rolls as the effects of the devastating drought are fully felt, probably in January and February, according to Mr. Williams, and a gigantic reconstruction program in the drought areas in which irrigation development will be the principal operation is being mapped.

It is felt by the Relief Administration that President Roosevelt's trip through the drought areas has brought out to the fullest extent the need for such aid to the stricken.

Harry L. Hopkins, Relief Administrator, is definitely opposed to further giving of what resembles a dole, Mr. Williams explained, and for that reason the Relief Administration is working rapidly to complete this new program for the President's approval.

Mr. Williams said that in industrial centres the number of families on relief had dropped off by 400,000 since April, so that relief expenditures were now at the lowest point for some time.

The Relief Administration has left some $80,000,000 of the sum allotted it to date for drought relief, Mr. Williams said, and about $200,000,000 of its allotment for normal relief remains, enough to carry on work for about two months more.

KEY MORTGAGE BILL DEFEATED IN SENATE

Creation of Commission to Administer State Relief Fails in 24 to 17 Vote.

RFC HELP IS AUTHORIZED

Second Principal Measure Is Passed—Lehman Had Demanded Immediate Action.

Special to THE NEW YORK TIMES.

ALBANY (Friday), Aug. 10.—After three hours' debate, the Joseph bill providing for the creation of a State mortgage commission of five members to take over from the Insurance Department the administration of relief for holders of guaranteed mortgage certificates, failed of passage by a vote of 24 to 17.

All those who voted for the bill, which had the backing of Governor Lehman, were Democrats. All the Republicans recorded voted against it.

Immediately after the Mortgage Commission Bill had been defeated, the Senate by unanimous vote passed another Joseph bill which would prepare the way for the creation of guaranteed mortgage protective corporations. These would be empowered to loan money to distressed certificate holders and incidentally to negotiate with the Federal Government for RFC funds to aid in that purpose. The two bills were regarded as the key measures in the mortgage relief plan favored by the Governor.

The debate at times was heated and seemed of a strongly political nature as the Republicans denounced the proposed mortgage commission as a political agency.

Feinberg Attacks Plan.

Senator Feinberg of Clinton County made the first attack of this character. He declared that the commission would lead to the creation of "200,000 political jobs, every one of them held by a Democrat." Every manager, janitor and sweeper or other worker on properties that would be under the management of the commission, Senator Feinberg implied, would be a political appointee.

The commission, he said, would be in the "real estate" business and the way would be opened to "unlimited corruption for those willing to use their opportunities to trade and traffic for their own personal profit."

The certificate holders, he said, were not clamoring for this legislation, but another group was making the fight.

"We all know who they are," he added.

Senator Quinn, Democrat of New York City, was the only one on the majority side of the Senate who condemned the Joseph bill which, however, he was compelled on the final vote to support. He charged that the bill would help the property owners and the landlords, but not the certificate holders.

"What we need," he said, "is

Continued on Page Four.

HITLER SETS FREE MINOR OFFENDERS

As New Head of the State, He Decrees an Amnesty, Which Covers 'Overzealous' Nazis.

LINK TO AUG. 19 VOTE SEEN

Swastika Conquest of Church Completed as Mueller Is Voted Dictator.

By OTTO D. TOLISCHUS.

Wireless to THE NEW YORK TIMES.

BERLIN, Aug. 9—Following the precedent usually observed by new heads of States, Chancellor Hitler, who has assumed the German Presidential functions, today decreed an amnesty covering all minor offenses, both criminal and political, committed before Aug. 2, the date of President von Hindenburg's death, and also providing for review of all cases of "protective custody."

The official announcement of the amnesty says it is granted "on the occasion of the union of the office of Reich President with that of Reich Chancellor and the transfer executed therewith of the prerogatives of the Reich President to the Fuehrer and Reich Chancellor, Adolf Hitler." But the fact that in ten days the German people will be asked to confirm this new apotheosis of Herr Hitler by their votes may have something to do with it.

In particular the amnesty includes all such "offenses to which the offender permitted himself to be driven through excessive zeal in the battle for the National Socialist idea." This provision, the Nazi papers stress, includes especially offenses committed by the Hitler and Goering Nazis against the Roehm Nazis, the "reactionaries" and the neutrals on the occasion of Herr Hitler's cleansing of June 30.

Serious Crimes Excluded.

The amnesty excludes "high treason, treason against the country, betrayal of military secrets, all crimes against life, bombings in which persons were killed or injured and all offenses betraying in their execution and motives a base mentality."

This provision excludes from the amnesty Communist leaders like Ernst Thaelmann and Ernst Torgler, who are awaiting trial before the new people's tribunal.

The general amnesty covers offenses committed by first offenders and punished by imprisonment up to six months or fines up to 1,000 marks. Prosecutions of similar offenses still pending are quashed.

The political amnesty covers, in addition to the provision already mentioned, the following:

Slander of the Fuehrer and Reich Chancellor.

Offenses against the welfare or reputation of the Reich committed by word of mouth or writing that have not come from hostile sentiments against the people or the State.

Other slanders or mayhems

Continued on Page Eight

MRS. ANTONIO DIES IN ELECTRIC CHAIR; HOPED TO THE LAST

Woman, Two Men Accomplices Are Put to Death for Murder of Husband for Insurance.

STATEMENT BY GOVERNOR

He Says He Sought Some Fact to Justify Saving Her, but Could Find None.

Mrs. Anna Antonio of Albany and the two men convicted with her of murdering her husband for his $5,000 insurance were put to death last night in the electric chair at Sing Sing.

The 28-year-old mother of three children, who already had received three reprieves, clung, almost to the last, to the hope that Governor Lehman again would grant her another stay. But no word came from the Governor until after the executions.

Then, in a statement issued at his office, he gave his reasons for refusing to intervene. He said that the case had received his "most painstaking consideration" and that the responsibility for carrying out the death penalty on a woman had been "so distressing" that he had sought to find a fact that would justify his interference. But he added that after carefully scrutinizing the records he had been convinced the defendants were guilty.

"Appeals have been made to me to grant Executive clemency to Anna Antonio on account of her sex," the statement said, "but the law makes no distinction of sex in the punishment of crime; nor would my own conscience or the duty imposed upon me by my oath of office permit me to do so.

"Each of the defendants is guilty. The crime and the manner of the execution are abhorrent. I have found no just or sound reason for the exercise of Executive clemency.

"The administration of the criminal law should be fair and just. I am satisfied that it has been in these cases. Likewise, the administration of justice must be definite and certain, so that society may be protected and respect and observance of the law maintained."

Woman Calm to End.

The two men, Vincent Saetta of Albany and Samuel Feraci of Geneva, N. Y., had been placed in pre-execution cells and dressed for the execution early in the afternoon. But Mrs. Antonio, who had been removed from her cell into a corridor of the death house, remained there until shortly before execution time.

Just before she was taken to the execution chamber, Mrs. Antonio told Warden Lawes:

"I don't care what you do to me. I am not afraid to die. I have nothing on my conscience. I never killed any one."

She said, too, that some time before her husband was killed, one of her codefendants had come to her and had told her that he was going to kill her husband.

Her reply, she said, was:

"I don't care what you do. I am only interested in the children."

Father John P. McCaffery, Roman Catholic chaplain of the prison, was with her at the end. Contrary to expectations, she did not break down. When she entered the execution chamber she walked straight to the chair, paying no heed to the wardens and witnesses lined against the wall.

Mrs. Antonio wore a blue gingham dress. She took her place in

Continued on Page Ten.

SPEECH HAILS CONFIDENCE

President at Green Bay Says He Will Forge On to 'End of the Road.'

'LAW OF THE TOOTH' ENDED

People Back Policy and Will Not Let 'Ancient Order' Return, He Asserts.

HE ENDORSES LA FOLLETTE

On Arrival at Chicago He Gets Tumultuous Reception and Leaves for Washington.

The text of the President's speech is printed on page 3.

From a Staff Correspondent.

GREEN BAY, Wis., Aug. 9.—Speaking here on the eve of returning to Washington after an absense of almost six weeks, President Roosevelt declared today that the New Deal had brought a rebirth of confidence and was going to push ahead broadly to its goal.

In his address, delivered at the Wisconsin tercentennial celebration, Mr. Roosevelt asserted that the government intended "no injury to honest business," seeking instead wealth in which all might share.

But he served notice, in breaking a long political silence, that he was prepared if necessary to go to indefinite lengths in extending governmental control over business for the common good.

He contended that the old unregulated, competitive "law of the tooth and the claw" was gone forever and proclaimed his belief that he was following the mandate laid down for him with his election.

"In one year and five months," the President said, "the people of the United States have received at least a partial answer to their demands for action and neither the demand nor the action has reached the end of the road."

He Endorses La Follette.

Mr. Roosevelt surprised even some of those who have been with him constantly during his period in office by holding up the political background of Wisconsin, sometimes termed radical, as a model.

He endorsed Senator La Follette, a candidate for re-election, and praised political acts in Wisconsin which were the work of the Senator's father. The speech was heard directly by a crowd estimated at between 25,000 and 50,000 of the 100,000 who packed this small city to see and hear the President, and in addition was broadcast.

After a long voyage to Hawaii, during which there occurred strikes of major proportions, declines in market values of securities, and an obviously growing demand for a new statement of policy by the administration, he returned to the United States to find his popularity in the great Northwest almost

Continued on Page Three.

Citizens Can Retain Fabricated Silver But All Bulk Metal Must Be Turned In

Special to THE NEW YORK TIMES.

WASHINGTON, Aug. 9.—Mindful of the lengths to which conscientious persons went in turning in gold, officials hastened today to relieve the minds of citizens of any misconception as to silver articles they may not retain under today's order by President Roosevelt. Articles such as the following may be retained:

Silver tableware such as knives, forks, spoons, platters and bon bon dishes, silver rings, silver spectacle rims, silver tooth fillings, silver watches and silver coin of any sort.

What the Treasury wants is bulk silver; "fabricated" silver, including the above items and many others, is decidedly not desired.

There are in the country today 45,000,000 ounces of silver in depositories recognized by the Silver Exchange, Herman Oliphant, chief counsel of the Treasury, said here. He added that unsupported estimates of accumulated stocks run as high as 150,000,000 to 250,000,000 ounces, adding that nobody could do more than guess on the silver stocks.

In the latest available Treasury statement, that of Tuesday, the following stocks of silver were recorded:

Silver bullion under act of May 12, 1933, $1,237,200.
Standard silver dollars, $504,835,460.
Silver bullion, under general fund, $55,128,328.
Subsidiary silver coin, $5,532,985.
Silver certificates outstanding, $495,301,989.

At the end of June there were 30,013,389 silver dollars, $280,400,143 in subsidiary silver and $401,456,099 in silver certificates.

Confidence was expressed by Treasury officials that the seizure of accumulated silver stocks would have a stabilizing effect not only on domestic but international commercial and financial transactions.

They felt that it was a move in the direction of a sound international monetary policy in which the United States, more than any other nation, was in a position to take the lead.

PRESSING PROBLEMS AWAIT ROOSEVELT

Drought Relief, Price Fixing Under Codes and Future of NRA Must Be Met.

HOUSING DRIVE IMPENDS

Also, Unemployment Fund for Cities Is to Be Provided in Time for Winter Needs.

Special to THE NEW YORK TIMES.

WASHINGTON, Aug. 9.—President Roosevelt will return to the White House tomorrow to face new tasks which have accumulated since he left here July 1.

The most pressing will be that growing out of the continued drought in the West. Like many he has faced during his eighteen months in office, the drought problem has emergency and longer range phases, involving not only methods for sending relief to the present victims but plans for averting a food shortage in the coming Winter.

The President is expected to confer with Secretary Wallace and other agricultural authorities early next week in an effort to evolve a better relief program to meet the drought situation. Mr. Wallace is understood to be prepared to assure the President that the country need not fear a food shortage, as there are surpluses in hand sufficient for requirements.

Turning from the drought, the President is expected to make a quick check-up of the new emergency and regulatory agencies set in motion just before his vacation.

Only one of these, the National Labor Relations Board, has got completely under way, although the Housing Administration is about ready to open its drive for modernization and renovation of homes and the Securities and Exchange Commission is to begin next week the registration of stock exchanges as provided by law.

The Labor Relations Board has been hard at work practically ever since the President left. It has devoted itself largely to rendering quasi-judicial decisions relative to the collective bargaining guarantees under the Recovery Act.

Price Fixing Is NRA Problem.

There is some agitation among persons interested in labor for more outright mediation and on this point the President will be called upon to make a decision. The board, so its officials have indicated, will follow its announced policy of interpreting Section 7A of the NRA unless instructed otherwise by Mr. Roosevelt.

The National Recovery Administration will claim much of the President's attention. He will have to decide many pending problems, particularly those growing out of the attempts of organized industries to fix minimum prices. The resistance to this practice by influ-

Continued on Page Three.

BONDS SELL OFF ON SILVER ORDER

Government Securities Drop Sharply, Then Rise in Heaviest Trading Since 1920.

STOCKS, COMMODITIES UP

Sudden Rush Centres on Mining Shares—Silver Futures Trading Is Halted.

The market for United States Government bonds was thrown into confusion on the news at midday of the Silver Nationalization Proclamation, while stocks and the grain markets rose abruptly on heavy buying.

United States Government bonds, in the heaviest trading since Dec. 30, 1920, opened lower, declined in the forenoon, broke badly on the silver announcement, but recovered sharply in the later trading on support attributed to governmental agencies. The bond ticker ran far behind as an avalanche of selling orders came into the market at noon and continued behind as large blocks of bonds were offered to meet the supporting bids.

Total transactions in government bonds on the Stock Exchange reached $21,619,500, with an indicated turnover in government issues in Wall Street yesterday, over-the-counter and in the listed market, of close to $250,000,000. The heavy dealings in government bonds brought the trading total for the listed bond market, including corporation and foreign loans, to $29,910,200, the heaviest since April 12, 1922. Corporation bonds were irregularly lower on the day and foreign loans pointed higher.

Stock Market Rallies.

The stock market, which had been dull and slightly lower during the forenoon, rallied precipitately at noon, with buying centring in the mining shares. The trend was steadily upward during the afternoon and closing prices were 1 to 4¾ points higher on the day.

United States Smelting and Refining, which was selling at 1¾ points below the previous close at noon, closed at 137, up 4¾ points for the day. American Smelting, off 1¼ at midday, finished at 38¾, up 3¼. Anaconda Copper recovered from a loss of half a point at noon and closed at 13, up 1¼, and Cerro de Pasco erased an early loss of ¼ of a point, closing at 40⅞, up 1⅛. Kennecott, Dome Mines, Noranda Mines, Park Utah and Phelps Dodge performed similarly in heavy trading.

Total dealings in stocks, 1,416,000 shares, the heaviest of the month thus far, compared with 692,000 on the Stock Exchange the previous day. The advances carried THE NEW YORK TIMES average of fifty stocks up $1.50 for the day.

The gains were by no means entirely confined to mining stocks.

Continued on Page Twelve.

DUE AT MINTS IN 90 DAYS

Monetary Stock of 1 Part Silver to 3 Parts Gold Is Objective.

MINERS' PRICE STANDS

Imports of the Metal Are Not Affected, but the Government Holds Price Control.

COIN AND ARTS EXCEPTED

Wider Currency Circulation on 100% Metallic Base Held Mild, Harmless Inflation.

Proclamation and orders on nationalizing silver, page 12.

Special to THE NEW YORK TIMES.

WASHINGTON, Aug. 9.—Nationalization of silver was ordered by President Roosevelt in a proclamation and Executive Order made public today by Secretary Morgenthau.

All stocks of silver in continental United States must be turned in at the mints within ninety days, with exceptions which include silver coin, fabricated silver, that which is held under license and that owned by foreign governments and central banks, and other minor holdings.

The government, according to Treasury officials, will seize accumulated stocks at 50.01 cents an ounce. Newly mined silver will be bought as in the past at 64½ cents an ounce. Silver imports are not affected.

Base of Currency Uncheapened.

Today's action was viewed by experts as not inflationary, since it does not cheapen the metallic base of the currency. No change was announced in the policy of issuing currency only on the basis of the purchase price of the silver, but even should the Treasury exercise its authority to issue currency on the basis of the monetary value of the silver, $1.29 an ounce, there still would be a 100 per cent metallic base for silver certificates, it was pointed out.

In other words, it was said, nationalization of silver is simply the final step in the government's policy of concentrating within its physical control all the metallic monetary base, both gold and silver. Inflation of a mild and harmless sort may be effected by today's order, it was admitted, in that it probably will mean a larger amount of currency in circulation, but it was again emphasized that the currency was in no sense cheapened.

The order was hailed by Senators Thomas of Oklahoma and Fletcher of Florida as a long forward step which would prove of value to the country as a whole.

Phones to the President.

Mr. Morgenthau conferred by telephone briefly with Mr. Roosevelt this morning prior to issuing the nationalization order. The action was taken under the President's policy that the United States should increase the amount of silver in monetary stocks with the ultimate objective of having and maintaining one-fourth of their monetary value in silver and three-fourths in gold.

In his proclamation today the President declared that "to effectuate the policy of the Silver Purchase Act of 1934, to assist in increasing and stabilizing domestic prices, to protect our foreign commerce against the adverse effect of depreciated foreign currencies and to promote the objectives of the proclamation of the 21st day of December, 1933, relating to the coinage of silver," nationalization of silver had been ordered.

Under Section 3 of the act of 1934, it was provided that no purchases of silver situated in the Continental United States May 1, 1934, should be made at more than 50 cents an ounce. The Treasury explained that the present acquisition of silver was not a purchase, but a seizure by "eminent domain," and therefore it would not operate under the act. Such was the explanation of the price of 50.01 cents a fine ounce.

To Acquire $2,000,000,000 Worth.

The new program contemplates the acquisition of nearly $2,000,000,000 in silver. Present gold

Continued on Page Twelve.

Canada's Premier Calls Provinces to Confer On Revising Constitution and Creating Dole

Special to THE NEW YORK TIMES.

OTTAWA, Aug. 9.—Premiers of the nine Canadian Provinces are to be called into conference by Prime Minister Bennett to discuss revision of Canada's Constitution and the establishment of unemployment insurance.

Premier Bennett has intimated that he is willing to consider a State-wide unemployment insurance scheme, although he has insisted that it must be one to which employes also contribute.

Provincial autonomy over wages and working conditions, however, stands in the way and Mr. Bennett has made it plain that the Premiers must come prepared to discuss revision of the British North America Act, which is Canada's Constitution.

The Federal Government has found centralization of authority a necessary preliminary to effective action in coping with the depression. Even the new Natural Products Marketing Act, Canada's AAA, requires enabling legislation by the Provinces.

If Canada is to enforce the eight-hour day agreement signed at Geneva, the consent of the Provinces must be obtained.

The Dominion contributes 75 per cent of the cost of old-age pensions, but has no administrative control of them. Aside from the national defense fund, inter-provincial and external trade, there is scarcely a field of action in which there is not conflict between the Federal and provincial authority.

Vested interests which believed they could obtain better terms from provincial governments and racial and religious minorities which feared revision of the British-North America Act since that guaranteed them special rights have hitherto opposed its revision.

By throwing back on the shoulders of the Provinces their constitutional responsibility for relief, which they are scarcely able to finance, Premier Bennett is said to feel that he has a lever to try out consent to the revision of what is now considered to be an outdated Constitution.

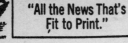

"All the News That's Fit to Print."

The New York Times.

Copyright, 1934, by The New York Times Company.

LATE CITY EDITION
WEATHER—Generally fair today; rain tonight or tomorrow.
Temperatures Yesterday—Max. 78, Min. 61.
Detailed Weather Report Page 46.

VOL. LXXXIII....No. 27,984. Entered as Second-Class Matter, Postoffice, New York, N. Y. NEW YORK, THURSDAY, SEPTEMBER 6, 1934. P TWO CENTS In New York City. | THREE CENTS Within 200 Miles | FOUR CENTS Elsewhere Except in 7th and 8th Postal Zones

ROOSEVELT NAMES BOARD OF THREE TO MEDIATE IN THE TEXTILE STRIKE; TWO DEAD, 24 SHOT IN RIOTS AT MILLS

'BRIBERY' MARKED SUBMARINE SALES IN SOUTH AMERICA

Boat Company Officer Called 'Graft' Basis of All Business There, Senators Learn.

$50,000 TO AN ARGENTINE

Similar Amount Paid to Son of Leguia in Peru—Chile and Brazil Are Mentioned.

SWANSON FOR FULL INQUIRY

British Government Also Backs Investigation—Vickers Head Denies Knowing of Letter.

Special to THE NEW YORK TIMES.

WASHINGTON, Sept. 5.—Evidence of "bribery" in high official quarters in Argentina, Brazil, Chile and Peru in connection with submarine sales was shown in today's hearings before the special Senate committee investigating the munitions industry.

Additional evidence was introduced at the same time to show that a close agreement between the Electric Boat Company of Groton, Conn., and Vickers, Ltd., of England made it possible for those concerns virtually to dominate the world submarine building situation regardless of complications involving other countries.

Seven years ago, when relations between Chile and Peru were far from harmonious and the controversy involving Tacna-Arica was still boiling, the Electric Boat Company, it was shown, was working day and night for contracts to arm Peru for undersea operations.

Representatives of Vickers, ally of the Americans, were just as busy on the other side trying to convince the Chileans that the time was at hand for them to invest in a submarine flotilla or two, testimony revealed.

Briton Was Told of 'Graft.'

It was in connection with the Chilean situation that Lawrence Y. Spear, vice president of the Electric Boat Company, warned Sir Charles Craven, managing director of Vickers, that "graft is the real foundation of all South American business" and that even when the contracts were completed he should bear in mind that "at the last minute something extra is always needed to grease the ways."

The South Americans, according to the testimony, called these payments, which were always included in the price of the submarine or other vessel contracted for, "special commissions."

One official in Buenos Aires, it was disclosed, had received $50,000, while a group of persons high in the Brazilian naval administration had made a demand for $180,000 as their "commission" in the event contracts were signed.

How the American and British submarine makers solved their Peruvian-Chilean problem was disclosed in a letter found in the files of Mr. Spear, written to Sir Charles.

Chilean Deal to Vickers.

For reasons with which Mr. Spear said Sir Charles was "already familiar," he thought it best for the time being to continue talking "nothing but British construction so far as Chile was concerned." The American company, it was made clear, would get its agreed percentage of the profits in the event Vickers was successful in the negotiations in Chile.

The committee started proceedings today with a reference to Peruvian bond transactions in the United States. Senator Clark charged Henry R. Carse, president of the Electric Boat Company, with being in part responsible, although he did not say knowingly, for the sale of $75,000,000 in Peruvian bonds, now in default, to American investors.

In a letter read into the record Mr. Carse had claimed "some credit" for the establishment of Peruvian credit in American banks through the sale of Peruvian obligations to banks to New York, Chicago and other cities in the United States. Mr. Carse declared this had nothing whatever to do with subsequent Peruvian flotations in this country.

Naval Commission Brought In.

Activities of the American naval commission to Peru, which was sent by this government to aid in bringing the Peruvian Navy up to date and also to organize a Peruvian Naval Academy, also came in for much airing. An effort was made to show that the naval officers were working hand in hand with the Electric Boat people to land the submarine contracts for that corporation.

It appeared that considerable diplomacy was resorted to to override Rear Admiral Clark H. Woodward,

Continued on Page Eight

Black Rain Turns Noon To Night in Buenos Aires

Special Cable to THE NEW YORK TIMES.

BUENOS AIRES, Sept. 5.—Black rain fell in Buenos Aires at noon today, giving an unprecedented and weird aspect to the city. The Weather Bureau's analysis showed that the rain water was filled with microscopic particles of burned carbon and unburned petroleum, presumably from the smoke of the recent disaster at Campana, where oil tanks burned for a week following an explosion.

The darkness of night did not lift all afternoon. Buildings were illuminated, electric signs were turned on and street cars ran with lights on.

The heavy rain was accompanied by a cold gale and heavy lightning. Telegraph and telephone wires were torn down and several outlying districts were flooded.

TROLLEYS TO VANISH ON 9 LINES IN CITY

Mayor Reveals Settlement of Suit Over Bus Franchises on New York Railway Route.

RECAPTURE RIGHTS WON

Madison, Fourth, Lexington, 6th and 7th Avenues Are Among Arteries Affected.

The early substitution of motor buses for street cars on Manhattan surface lines operated or controlled by the New York Railways Corporation was envisaged yesterday by Mayor LaGuardia who announced the settlement of pending litigation between the city and the Madison Avenue Coach Company and the New York City Omnibus Corporation.

Both companies, Mayor LaGuardia said, had agreed to modification of their twenty-five-year bus franchises so as to make them recapturable by the city any time after ten years. The franchises were voted during the closing days of former Mayor O'Brien's administration. Their validity was attacked by the LaGuardia administration, but was upheld by Supreme Court Justice Philip J. McCook.

Franchise Terms Modified.

The city dropped its appeal from Justice McCook's decision when the companies agreed to modification of the franchise terms. An appeal is still pending, it is understood, on behalf of a taxpayer in whose suit the city joined. This suit was backed by the Green Bus Lines, Inc., a concern which sought franchise rights on routes awarded to the New York Railways Corporation's subsidiaries.

Mayor LaGuardia intimated that Paul Windels, Corporation Counsel, who negotiated the settlements, was about to close similar deals with the Fifth Avenue Coach Company, the Comprehensive Omnibus Corporation and possibly the East Side Omnibus Corporation, all of which received twenty-five-year grants by the Tammany administration.

The routes affected by the settlements include five longitudinal and four crosstown lines, on which trolley cars are now operated. The longitudinal routes are:

The Madison and Fourth Avenue line.

The Lexington and Lenox Avenue line.

The Broadway and Columbus Avenue line.

The Sixth Avenue line.

The Seventh Avenue line.

The crosstown routes are:

The Eighth Street line.

The Fourteenth Street line.

The Twenty-third Street line.

Continued on Page Fourteen.

M'GOLDRICK WARNS AGAINST 'OLD GANG' AS CAMPAIGN OPENS

Controller at Brooklyn Rally Says Both Opponents Seek Return to Political Rule.

REVIEWS FUSION RECORD

Asks if Balanced Budget and Restored Credit Are to Be Sacrificed at Polls.

Controller McGoldrick's opening campaign speech, Page 11.

Controller Joseph D. McGoldrick opened his campaign last night for both the Republican and Democratic nominations for the Controllership with an appeal to the voters to "look at the record" of the LaGuardia administration and then to refuse to turn over control of the city treasury to "the old gang."

The Controller spoke at a meeting in Erasmus Hall High School, Brooklyn, of which he is a graduate. The Knickerbocker Democrats and the City Fusion party were sponsors of the meeting. A sprinkling of Brooklyn Republican leaders also attended.

Mr. McGoldrick is the organization Republican designee for Controller, being opposed by Lambert Fairchild, and he is contesting the Democratic nomination with Frank J. Taylor, designated by the five Democratic county organizations of the city.

The feature of Mr. McGoldrick's speech was his withering attack on the condition in which the city government had been left by the Tammany administration, and his characterization of both his opponents as "party wheelhorses whose chief claim for office is that they are responsive to party reins."

Asks Who Wants to Turn Back.

Declaring that in the eight months the La Guardia administration has been in office the city has had a government of which it can be proud, Mr. McGoldrick continued:

"Have you forgotten what the old brand was like? Do you wish to substitute uncertainty and default for re-established credit? Do you want to return to the old extravagance? Do you want to return to muddle-head mismanagement, financial bewilderment and the blind staggers?

"The question is not one of voting fusion in or out. The question is: Shall fusion continue to have a power equal to its responsibility?"

Recalling the death of the late Controller, W. Arthur Cunningham, and his selection by Mayor LaGuardia to fill the vacancy, Mr. McGoldrick reminded his audience of the fact that he had been endorsed by the Republican leaders who subscribe to the principles of good government and that he had entered the Democratic primary to obtain the endorsement of the thousands of Democrats of independent leanings.

"After all," he said, "there are hundreds of thousands of Democrats in New York City, followers of Thomas Jefferson, Grover Cleveland, Woodrow Wilson and Franklin D. Roosevelt, who do not regard Tammany Hall and its allies as the fountain of Democratic philosophy or Democratic ethics."

The LaGuardia administration, when it assumed office, found a legacy "of reckless extravagance and gross favoritism," he said. The checking of shortages in accounts, he said, "is a huge task, especially in view of the mass of other dust-covered work which we are trying to fumigate."

Appealing to the city employes, Mr. McGoldrick reminded them that although the administration had found it necessary to impose a

Continued on Page Eleven.

HITLER FORECASTS NO REICH OVERTURN IN NEXT 1,000 YEARS

Proclamation to Nazi Congress Says Movement Won't Yield No Matter What Happens.

REVOLUTION HELD AT END

Chancellor in Speech Scores 'Jewish Intellectualism'—Chides Foreign Press.

Wireless to THE NEW YORK TIMES.

NUREMBERG, Sept. 5.—Chancellor Adolf Hitler today proclaimed the arrival of the Nazi millennium, predicting that the next 1,000 years would not witness another revolution in Germany. He was equally positive that the National Socialist movement had now become absolute master of the Reich and that its leadership rested in the hands of its best men.

The Nazi philosophy and all that it encompasses were served up in huge portions today as the party congress settled down to its first official session. The morning was devoted to the presentation of the Fuehrer's proclamation, a voluminous platform that goes far afield and sets out by announcing that the National Socialist revolution as a revolutionary seizure of power has made way for the process of evolution.

"No revolution can remain a fixture without leading to complete anarchy," says the proclamation. "Revolutions are merely destined to destroy centres of power. Evolution alone can change conditions.

"The National Socialist leadership is unswerving and unshakable. It knows what it wants and wills what it knows."

20,000 Hear Platform Read.

The proclamation was read in Herr Hitler's presence in the Luitpold arena by Adolf Wagner, Bavarian Nazi leader, to an audience of more than 20,000 party faithfuls and distinguished visitors.

Despite its verbosity, the pronouncement made only cursory reference to the economic problems confronting the Third Reich. It was, by and large, a pontifical dissertation on the achievements and political aspects of the Nazi revolution and its cultural aims.

The government's far-flung road-building scheme and homestead projects were again stressed, as was its determination to counter the world boycott with domestic production of raw products. Whatever may happen, the platform warned, national socialism does not intend to capitulate.

Chancellor Hitler made his first formal speech at the congress at the afternoon session, which was wholly devoted to discussion of national socialism's cultural aspirations. It was presided over by Dr. Alfred Rosenberg, director of the party department for culture, who acclaimed Herr Hitler as "not only the greatest political impulse in Germany in the last 150 years, but also its most potent stimulus for art and culture."

Herr Hitler spoke for more than an hour on the party's cultural mission. His speech was in the nature of a highly abstract lecture whose postulations and terminology were cluttered with metaphysical profundities. To be German, he said at one point, meant to be clear.

Hits "Jewish Intellectualism."

"National socialism as a world philosophy is not only the expression of a political system and reform of the State, but also of a reshaping of personal, communal and cultural life," he asserted.

National socialism, he continued, was a reaction to "Jewish intellectualism" and a return to intuition and an organic conception of civilization.

As a cultural movement, he believed, it was faced by two dangers. On the one hand it was menaced by the intrusion of busybodies who hawked about newfangled ideas regardless of their cost. On the other hand, there were unproductive imitators of past forms of expression, which, though respected by National Socialism, were unsuitable for imitation. The Greeks, Herr Hitler said, were akin to the National Socialists.

"The National Socialist State is thinking in long terms of history and could afford to wait for its creative impulses," he declared.

The chaotic period, he added, had come to an end and the new Germany, he believed, was destined to be a breakwater against these tides of the past. He did not propose to look to the ultra-moderns or the imitators for inspiration.

Stresses Blood Ties.

"It is no mere accident that Hellenic art later inspired the Nordic peoples, such as the Germans, Danes, English, Italians and French," he continued. "They worked in a spirit that varied from people to people, but found its roots in the same blood.

"Efforts have been made in State

Continued on Page Thirteen.

Italy Likely to Oust Women From Industry To Employ More Men and Add to Families

By The Associated Press.

ROME, Sept. 5.—Premier Benito Mussolini was reported tonight to be planning to take all women workers out of Italy's industry.

Two reasons, it was reliably learned, influenced him in his decision. He holds, first, that jobs interfere with what he believes to be woman's primary duty, the building up of families and the increase of Italy's population, and, second, that the positions women hold should be filled with men, thus decreasing unemployment and raising the morale of the people.

An editorial in Premier Mussolini's newspaper, Popolo d'Italia of Milan, tended to confirm the report that he would eliminate woman workers.

"The working woman," the newspaper asserted, "creates the problem of population [decrease] as well as that of unemployment. Work, even where it is not a direct impediment interfering with propagation, foments independence and consequent physical and moral habits antagonistic to conception.

"Man, disoriented and above all unemployed, finishes by giving up the idea of family. Oftentimes the working woman saves a family otherwise abandoned, but her work is generally a source of political and moral bitterness. The salvation of a few individuals is paid for by the blood of the multitude. There is no victory without dead.

"The exodus of women from the field of labor doubtless would have economic repercussions in many families, but a legion of men would lift humiliated heads and a hundred times more new families would enter the national life.

"It is necessary to convince ourselves that the same work that causes in woman the loss of her generative attributes brings to man the strongest physical and moral virility."

FIRST CLASH AT TRION, GA.

Violence Follows Trail of Mass Picket Drive Elsewhere in South.

N. CAROLINA CALLS TROOPS

Independent Surveys Show 300,000 Workers Out, or Over 45% of the Employed.

UNION CLAIMS 450,000

Little Disorder in New England, but Movement Is Reported Spreading.

Spreading disorder and scattering violence claimed a toll of two deaths and at least twenty-four persons injured or wounded, most of them in an armed clash at Trion, Ga., as the general strike in the textile industry gained momentum yesterday.

National Guard Ordered Out.

The North Carolina National Guard was ordered out last night after two appeals by labor leaders to pickets, urging them to abandon violent tactics, had been broadcast.

"The power of the State has been definitely challenged," Governor Ehringhaus said. "Local authorities have proven unequal to the test." The Governor acted after calling two times on the strikers to abandon sieges and raids, many of which were made across State lines.

Relative to the inquiry ordered by President Roosevelt, both sides agreed to cooperate. The union has proposed as a basis for settlement a national agreement which covered the issues of the dispute. Encouraged by the success of the picketing manoeuvres, Francis J. Gorman, vice president of the U. T. W. and leader of the walkout, said "the strike will continue until there is a settlement acceptable to the workers."

Independent surveys indicated that more than 45 per cent of the workers normally employed in the industry were idle. It was estimated that the idleness enforced by the spread of mass picketing, crippling of operations, disorder and other factors involved about 325,000 of the 625,000 workmen affected.

The tide of the strike rose to include almost 60 per cent of the textile employes in nine States of the twenty-two in which there are textile mills, accounting for a large part of the rise of 100,000 in the idle in one day. All looms and spindles were idle in New Bedford and Fall River, Mass., centre of the New England textile industry, and in Gaston County, N. C. However, the average idleness of normally employed workmen in thirteen of the States was 17 per cent, with some centres unaffected, according to an Associated Press survey.

Woolen Division Lags.

With the strength of the walk-out movement in the cotton garment division, leaders of the United Textile Workers Union announced in Washington plans for strategic moves in the woolen and worsted divisions, admitted to have many points of resistance.

The union claimed that 450,000 workmen were idle, increasing the total from 400,000 at the close of the day. Spokesmen for the cotton, woolen and silk manufacturers reported the strike to be gaining headway, charging that many willing workers had been intimidated by "flying squadrons," motorcades of hundreds of pickets. Because of incomplete reports, George A. Sloan, president of the Cotton Textile Institute, made no estimate but many mill operators who closed down yesterday announced their intention of reopening today if protection is afforded.

Disorder was widespread throughout the South, the region of the day's violent conflicts. At Trion, Ga., a deputy sheriff and a strike sympathizer were killed and fifteen persons wounded or hurt in a pitched battle between pickets and deputies that lasted more than two hours.

Three men were wounded, one of them critically, when a policeman being trampled by pickets at Augusta, Ga., opened fire from the ground. Ten other persons were hurt, none seriously, when police with nightsticks dispersed the mob. One picket was near death from

Continued on Page Two.

President's Inquiry Order

Special to THE NEW YORK TIMES.

HYDE PARK, N. Y., Sept. 5.—The text of President Roosevelt's executive order creating the board of inquiry for the cotton textile industry follows:

Creation of the Board of Inquiry for Cotton Textile Industry, &c.

By virtue of and pursuant to the authority vested in me under Title I of the National Industrial Recovery Act (CH90, 48 Stat. 195, Tit. 15, U. S. C. Sec. 701) and under joint resolution approved June 19, 1934 (Public Res. 44, Seventy-third Congress), and in order to effectuate the policy of said title and the purposes of the said joint resolution, it is hereby ordered as follows:

Section 1. There is hereby created, in connection with the Department of Labor, a board to be known as the Board of Inquiry for the Cotton Textile Industry (hereinafter referred to as the Board), which shall be composed of Hon. John G. Winant, Governor of New Hampshire, chairman; Mr. Marion Smith of Atlanta, Ga., and Hon. Raymond V. Ingersoll of Brooklyn, N. Y.

Each member of the Board shall receive necessary traveling and subsistence expenses, and (unless he holds another Federal or State office that makes him ineligible for compensation) $25.00 per diem in addition thereto.

Section 2. The Board is hereby authorized and directed to—

(a) Inquire into the general character and extent of the complaints of the workers in the cotton textile, wool, rayon, silk and allied industries; and

(b) Inquire into the problems confronting the employers in said industries; and

(c) Consider ways and means of meeting said problems and complaints; and

(d) Exercise, in connection with said industries, the powers that are authorized to be conferred by the first section of Public Resolution 44, Seventy-third Congress; and

(e) Upon the request of the parties to a labor dispute, act as a Board of Voluntary Arbitration or select a person or agency for voluntary arbitration.

Section 3. The Board shall make, through the Secretary of Labor to the President, a report no later than Oct. 1, 1934, of its activities, findings and recommendations. The Board shall be exempted from making the reports or submitting to the review contemplated by the executive order providing for the creation of the National Labor Relations Board, &c. (Executive Order No. 6,763, June 29, 1934.)

Section 4. The Board is hereby authorized to request existing governmental agencies to render services, furnish information, and otherwise aid the performance of the Board in its duties.

The Board is further authorized, whenever necessary, to appoint additional employes without regard to the civil service laws and the Classification Act of 1923, as amended. The funds necessary for the payment of the salaries and expenses of the Board shall, until other provision is made, be transferred to the Board by the National Labor Relations Board from its own funds.

Section 5. The Board shall cease to exist when, in the opinion of the President, it has completed the duties it is authorized to perform. (Signed) FRANKLIN D. ROOSEVELT.

Poughkeepsie, New York.

Sept. 5, 1934.

TROOPS CALLED OUT IN NORTH CAROLINA

Governor Acts After Motor Squads of Strikers Raid Mills on 110-Mile Front.

By JOSEPH SHAPLEN.
Special to THE NEW YORK TIMES.

CHARLOTTE, N. C., Sept. 5.—With the number of strikers in the cotton textile mills of the South increased to 150,000, nearly 100,000 of them in the Carolinas, and violence spreading in many areas, Governor Ehringhaus of North Carolina tonight ordered Adjt. Gen. J. Van B. Metts to call out what troops he considered necessary to aid local authorities in "policing duties."

Late tonight the adjutant general, after a conference with his staff, took action, under Governor Ehringhaus's authority, and ordered three units of the National Guard to Marion, N. C., after reports a vigilante committee had been formed to repel strikers. The troop units are moving from Asheville, Waynesville and North Wilkesboro. Other troop movements are being planned.

In South Carolina, where martial law was impending, Governor Blackwood today ordered out additional troops to reinforce the five companies now guarding the Greenville area. These developments came after a day in which "flying squadrons" of strike pickets had raided many mill centres in the Carolinas, forcing the closing of several plants. Previously, Governor Ehringhaus had refused to order out the troops despite appeals from many sections of his State.

Meanwhile, some of the larger mills of the Carolinas, facing concerted assaults by masses of pickets, were feverishly preparing to resist. These mills were organizing their own defense by mobilizing special guards equipped with shotguns and tear-gas bombs and by arming workers who remained at the looms.

Governor Ehringhaus, in explaining his call to the troops tonight, said:

"The power of the State has been definitely challenged. Men and women who wish only to be let alone at their peaceful employment are being threatened and terrorized by

Continued on Page Three.

CAPITAL EXPECTS SHORTENED STRIKE

Gorman Voices Faith in President and Promises Aid to His Mediation Board.

By LOUIS STARK.
Special to THE NEW YORK TIMES.

WASHINGTON, Sept. 5.—President Roosevelt's appointment of a mediation board, accepted today by both sides, to study the issues in the textile strike controversy and to make recommendations for a permanent settlement, is expected to result in a shortening of the strike, according to indications in labor and government circles here.

The National Labor Relations Board, unable to shelve all its pending cases in order to plunge into the day and night task of clarifying the issues for the President, will hold itself in readiness to act as a supreme court of appeal in the event that the mediation board is unable to win joint acceptance of its recommendations.

In the meantime, the strike, in which Chairman Francis J. Gorman of the general strike committee now claims 450,000 employes are participating, will continue in effect pending the findings of the mediation board unless President Roosevelt asks the union to call off the walkout.

Will "Go as Far as Possible."

On learning from press reports that the President would name a mediation board, Mr. Gorman said:

"It can be taken as a matter of course that we shall go as far as possible to meet the wishes of the President. We believe he has an understanding of our problems, and that he would not take any step that would jeopardize the welfare of the million men and women who toil in the textile industry.

"Meanwhile, the strike movement is growing stronger every hour and the strike will continue until there is a settlement that is acceptable to the workers."

Later in the day Mr. Gorman said:

"I have been asked throughout the afternoon for further comment on the appointment of a mediation board by the President. I repeat

Continued on Page Four.

ACTS ON GARRISON PLEA

Governor Winant of New Hampshire, a Liberal, Heads Board of Three.

TO MAKE REPORT BY OCT. 1

Marion Smith of Atlanta and Borough President Ingersoll of Brooklyn the Others.

INQUIRY IS FIRST DUTY

But Group Also Will Arbitrate if Request Is Made by Both Sides.

From a Staff Correspondent.

HYDE PARK, N. Y., Sept. 5.—President Roosevelt tonight created a board of three members to investigate the strike in the cotton textile industry and report back to him not later than Oct. 1.

The board, designated in an executive order as the board of inquiry for the cotton textile industry, is composed of the following prominent men:

John G. Winant, chairman, Governor of New Hampshire and a Liberal Republican.

Marion Smith of Atlanta, Ga., an attorney, son of the late Senator Hoke Smith and chairman of the Regional Labor Board for the Southern area.

Raymond V. Ingersoll, President of the Borough of Brooklyn.

To Make General Inquiry.

The board was charged by the President to "inquire into the general character and extent of the complaints of the workers in the cotton textile, wool, rayon, silk and allied industries"; the problems confronting employers; consider means of meeting the complaints and, upon the request of the parties to the dispute, "act as a board of voluntary arbitration or select a person or agency for voluntary arbitration."

In appointing the investigating board, President Roosevelt acted on a recommendation made by Lloyd K. Garrison, chairman of the National Labor Relations Board.

At the same time, the President followed an example set by himself when he appointed a mediation board to deal with the recent strike of longshoremen on the Pacific Coast.

The appointment of the textile board incidentally represented the first act in which President Roosevelt has taken official cognizance of the strike, although he followed closely day-by-day developments that led up to the actual beginning of the strike yesterday morning.

Had to Await Developments.

It was thought in informed quarters that he anticipated that only a minority of the workers in the mills would respond to the strike call and that he had abstained from official participation in the preliminary manoeuvres until events should justify his belief.

Likewise, it was not possible for him to take the definite step accomplished tonight until the strike literally was under way and a situation existed justifying the use of his authority to appoint a special board to examine the causes of the dispute and recommend a method of settlement.

Mr. Garrison based his recommendation that the President appoint a special investigating board on the premise that the National Labor Relations Board is in effect a court of appeals for labor dispute cases and accordingly should not act also as its own investigating body. He set forth this contention in a letter dated Sept. 1, which the President made public here today.

"As a semi-judicial body," Mr. Garrison wrote, "it is desirable that we be as far removed as possible from direct participation in controversies over some aspects of which we may, at a later date, be asked to sit in judgment. The board ought not to be placed in a position which might hamper respect for its judicial activities and hinder its effectiveness as a body for building up public opinion in support of disinterested interpretations of the law."

Request Follows Negotiations.

While recognizing the authority of the board to investigate controversies bearing on interstate commerce, he counseled that this agency

Continued on Page Three.

Men warm themselves at a burning trash can.

Museum of the City of New York

Scavengers were a common sight.

Museum of the City of New York

Despite the Depression, automobile manufacturers brought out new models each year. This is the 1934 DeSoto.

WINNERS IN THE GREAT AIR RACE TO MELBOURNE.

Times Wide World Photo

T. Campbell Black (L) and C.W. Scott, winners of the London-Melbourne Air Derby on October 22, shown beside their plane before the start of the race.

Herds of cattle died searching for food and water in Oklahoma's Dust Bowl.

How Scott and Black Won.

By The Canadian Press.

Here is the record of the flight of C. W. A. Scott and Campbell Black, British fliers, in the London-Melbourne Air Derby. (All times are Greenwich mean time, five hours earlier than Eastern standard time.)

Saturday, 6:33 A. M.--Left Mildenhall Airdrome.

8:15 P. M. Left Kirkuk after short halt to get gasoline.

9 P. M. Arrived Baghdad.

9:33 P. M. Left Baghdad.

Sunday, 9:15 A. M.--Arrived Allahabad.

10:15 A. M. Left Allahabad.

10:23 P. M. Arrived Singapore.

11:42 P. M. Left Singapore.

Monday, 11:08 A. M.--Arrived Darwin.

1:55 P. M. Left Darwin.

10:40 P. M. Arrived Charleville.

Tuesday, 12:59 A. M.—Left Charleville.

5:33 P. M. Arrived Melbourne.

Lamar, Colorado, during the drought and dust storms which ravaged a dozen states and enlarged the New Deal's relief problems.

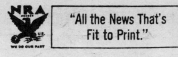

"All the News That's Fit to Print."

The New York Times.

LATE CITY EDITION
WEATHER—Fair today; cloudy, warmer tomorrow.
Temperatures Yesterday—Max., 65; min., 50.
Detailed Weather Report Page 41.

Copyright, 1934, by The New York Times Company.

VOL. LXXXIV....No. 28,031. Entered as Second-Class Matter, Postoffice, New York, N. Y. NEW YORK, TUESDAY, OCTOBER 23, 1934. P TWO CENTS In New York City. | THREE CENTS Within 200 Miles | FOUR CENTS Elsewhere Except in 7th and 8th Postal Zones

PRETTY BOY FLOYD SLAIN AS HE FLEES BY FEDERAL MEN

CORNERED ON OHIO FARM

Melvin Purvis Leads Officers in Shooting Down Outlaw.

BANDIT FALLS IN FLIGHT

Unable to Use Pistols After Ignoring Purvis's Order to Surrender.

LONG SOUGHT AS KILLER

Oklahoma Desperado Blamed for Kansas City 'Massacre' in Which Five Died.

Special to THE NEW YORK TIMES.

EAST LIVERPOOL, Ohio, Oct. 22.—Charles (Pretty Boy) Floyd, one of the most notorious outlaws of the present era, was shot and killed on a farm seven miles from here this afternoon as he fled from Federal agents and East Liverpool police who were closing in on him.

The Chicago Department of Justice head, Melvin H. Purvis, nemesis of the late John Dillinger, was in at the end. Leading four Federal men and four East Liverpool policemen Purvis said he shouted a command to Floyd to halt. The bandit first darted toward a corn crib for cover, then, changing his mind, sprinted toward a wooded ridge. Machine guns and pistols barked and the desperado fell, mortally wounded in the body.

Upon reaching him the agents found he held a .45-calibre automatic in his hand and had a second automatic in a shoulder holster. Neither one had been fired, though the magazines of both were full.

"Who the hell tipped you?" Floyd asked the officers. A moment later he said, "Where is Eddie?" "Eddie," the officers judged, was Adam Richetti, who was captured near Wellsville Saturday, when he and Floyd fought a gun battle with police.

The officers carried the desperado into the farmhouse of Mrs. Ellen Conkle, where he had appeared earlier for food.

Purvis bent close to Floyd, questioning him about the machine gun massacre of five men at the Kansas City Union Station in June, 1933. "I am Floyd," the dying bandit admitted, but to the last he denied complicity in the Kansas City killings. He lived about fifteen minutes after the burst of fire had sent fourteen bullets into his back and one into his side.

Had Meal at Farmhouse.

The body was brought to an undertaking establishment in East Liverpool.

The outlaw's pockets yielded $120 in cash. Little else was found among his personal effects.

The killing climaxed two days of intensive man-hunting in this area by Federal, State and county officers after Floyd escaped in the gun fight with policemen near Wellsville.

This afternoon Floyd appeared at the Conkle farm and asked for something to eat. He received a meal, and after eating it he asked Mrs. Conkle if she could arrange to get him an automobile to take him to Youngstown. She replied that she would have to wait until the men returned from the fields.

Floyd had been sighted on the farm by Arthur Conkle, brother-in-law of Mrs. Conkle, who notified the officers in East Liverpool.

When Purvis arrived with his Department of Justice agents and the four police officers, including Police Chief Hugh J. McDermott of East Liverpool, Floyd was trying to persuade S. L. Dyke, farm hand and brother of Mrs Conkle, to take him to Youngstown.

Leaping out of their cars, the officers closed in on the gunman. Floyd started to run, but the officers' markmanship prevented him from reaching the shelter of the woods.

Richetti Not Told of Death.

Held in jail at Wellsville while Missouri and Ohio authorities quarreled over his custody, Richetti was not immediately told of his chief's death. Richetti had denied that his companion in the Saturday gun fight was Floyd, but the majority of the officers held that the Oklahoma desperado was there.

The first clue of the bandits, both of whom had been sought as

Continued on Page Two.

Nelson Now Takes Place Of 'Public Enemy No. 1'

By The Associated Press.

WASHINGTON, Oct. 22.—The name of George (Baby Face) Nelson tonight was underscored by the Justice Department as the new "No. 1 public enemy."

Only this morning he was "No 2." But he was elevated when Charles (Pretty Boy) Floyd fell this afternoon under a hail of Federal gunfire.

Nelson, a member of the late John Dillinger's gang, is charged with slaying Carter Baum, Federal agent, at a resort near Mercer, Wis., in April.

And John Hamilton, also a member of Dillinger's broken following, is "Public Enemy No. 2," or close enough to tie with any other contestant for that dubious honor.

CITY ACTS TO LIMIT JOBS TO RESIDENTS

Democratic Aldermen Ready to Pass Today Curley Bill Barring Outsiders.

SCHOOL WORKERS EXEMPT

Proposal Is Expected to Meet Strong Fusion Opposition in Board of Estimate.

Democratic Aldermen controlling a majority of the Board of Aldermen prepared yesterday to pass a local law today compelling all city employes except educational employes to reside within the city limits.

The local laws committee of the board reported out the bill yesterday for favorable consideration at today's meeting in City Hall. Alderman Edward W. Curley, Bronx Democrat, originally introduced the measure on June 19 of this year. It was referred to committee and has been there ever since.

On June 15, Borough President James J. Lyons of the Bronx, also a Democrat, introduced companion legislation in the Board of Estimate branch of the Municipal Assembly. The Curley measure, to be acted upon by the Aldermanic branch of the Assembly, provides that the local law shall take effect on Jan. 1, 1935.

Mr. Lyons recently suggested that the effective date of his bill be amended so that it becomes effective on June 30, 1935. It was expected that the two measures would bear the same effective date in their final form. The Lyons bill is now in the local laws committee of the upper branch of the Assembly.

TEXT OF CURLEY BILL.

The text of the Curley bill follows:

Be it enacted by the Municipal Assembly of the City of New York, as follows:

Section 1: No person not a citizen and a bona-fide resident and dweller in good faith in the City of New York shall be eligible to appointment or employment, or to hold any office, in any of the departments, boards, bureaus or branches of the government of the City of New York when such person shall be paid, by reason of such appointment, employment, or holding of office, solely or in part from funds of the City of New York.

Sec. 2. Any person who now is or who shall become after such appointment or employment, a resident and dweller outside of the City of New York, shall thereby forfeit his or her said appointment or employment and shall be removed therefrom.

Sec. 3. Any exception to this local law shall be allowed only by a two-third affirmative vote of the total voting power of each branch of the municipal assembly; nothing herein shall be construed to apply to an official or employe of the City of New York, whose duties regularly require his attendance in places outside the City of New York.

Sec. 4. If any term, part, provision or section of this act shall be held unconstitutional, illegal or ineffective in whole or in part or in its application to any action taken thereunder, or to any effect upon any individual, officer or employe, then to the extent that it is not unconstitutional, illegal or ineffective, such term, part, provision or section shall be in

Continued on Page Sixteen.

BANKING LEADERS BACK COOPERATION WITH WASHINGTON

Determination Is Apparent at Convention as Critics Turn Guns on Administration.

MANY NEW YORKERS THERE

Farm Moratorium Act and the President's Praise of British Bankers Are Attacked.

Special to THE NEW YORK TIMES.

WASHINGTON, Oct. 22.—With an apparent determination of leaders to bring about cooperation with the administration in advancing the recovery program, the four-day sessions of the Americans Bankers Association got under way today.

Speeches sharply critical of some administration policies were heard at divisional meetings, but the general feeling appeared to be that the great majority of bankers favor aiding, not working against, the New Deal's purposes.

Meetings of the general convention will begin tomorrow when Francis Marion Law, president of the association, will make the opening address and Leo T. Crowley, chairman of the Federal Deposit Insurance Corporation, will talk on "Deposit Insurance as an Aid to Banking."

Mr. Law's speech is expected to clarify the atmosphere, which became somewhat beclouded today as a result of the vigorous and critical talks made, particularly at the open meeting of the State Bank Division.

New York Has Large Delegation.

On one point there was general agreement today: Bankers representing the large institutions in the financial centres as well as those from the country banks are awaiting with intense interest President Roosevelt's speech on Wednesday night.

An outstanding feature of the convention is the presence of a large delegation of bankers from New York, leading officials of most of the big institutions of that city having registered. At past conventions, these bankers have not openly taken so direct an interest in the deliberations, and the arrival is giving emphasis to the importance of the issues which are at stake.

This group of bankers did not take prominent part in the preliminary divisional meetings today, restricting their activities chiefly to private gatherings and committee conferences.

The Economic Policy Commission, of which Leonard P. Ayres, vice president of the Cleveland Trust Company, is chairman, has been studying the effect of government policies on the banking structure, and is understood to have completed its findings, but they will not be made public until later.

Branch and chain banking, the operation of the Federal Deposit Insurance Corporation and the extent to which the government has invaded the field of banking are among subjects to be treated.

Committee Procedure Guarded.

The framing of resolutions is still in committee and they will not be made public until Thursday, following an address on Wednesday night by President Roosevelt.

Information as to the trend of

Continued on Page Ten.

Triborough Bridge in Use By Mid-1936, City Is Told

The $50,000,000 Triborough Bridge linking Manhattan with the Bronx and Queens will be completed and in use on or before July 1, 1936, the Sinking Fund Commission was told at City Hall yesterday by Colonel Paul Loeser, engineer for the Triborough Bridge Authority.

The Authority is working out an agreement with occupants of property required for the Manhattan approach, between Ninety-second and 122d Streets on the East River. Robert Moses, chairman of the Authority, recently fixed Jan. 1, 1935, as the date when occupants must vacate their property in that area. Owners of coal pockets in that vicinity, as well as the Washburn Wire Company, asked for an extension. The Washburn company, it was indicated, would be permitted to occupy its present buildings, with access provided by a new overhead roadway.

MOSES ADVOCATES SALES TAX OF 2%

He Comes Out at Binghamton for Levy to Meet Deficit for Present Fiscal Year.

SEES LEHMAN PADLOCKED

Governor, in Address at Utica, Attacks State Milk Board—Sets 9-Point Program.

The text of Mr. Moses's address is printed on Page 15.

From a Staff Correspondent.

BINGHAMTON, Oct. 22.—Robert Moses, Republican nominee for Governor, opened his up-State campaign with a speech at the Central High School here tonight in which he advocated a 2 per cent retail sales tax to meet a State deficit for the present fiscal year which he placed at $100,000,000.

In his opening sentences he declared that Governor Lehman was unwilling to discuss vital issues.

"He wants to claim credit for projects and programs initiated by others, including myself, in which he had little or no part." Mr. Moses said of his Democratic opponent. "He wants to set up straw men labeled 'Old Guard,' 'Power Trust,' 'Big Business,' 'Public Utilities,' 'Reactionaries,' and then knock them down.

"He wants to ignore Farley, Flynn, Basil O'Connor and the Tammany boys. His strategists have put a padlock upon him. They have told him under no circumstances to be drawn into any discussion with me, because he would get the worst of it.

Like "Smokeless Powder."

"It makes a fine picture of the man who called himself 'Silent Dynamite' in the last campaign and who now begins to look more and more like 'Smokeless Powder.'"

About 1,200 gathered in the school auditorium in spite of the rain. The candidate was escorted to the hall through the drizzle by a motor parade and Johnson City's American Legion Band.

Although prominent Republicans in Broome County and throughout the lower tier are understood to have opposed the candidate's advo-

Continued on Page Fifteen.

Rent Strike Voted in Knickerbocker Village; 600 Tenants in Model Apartment Dissatisfied

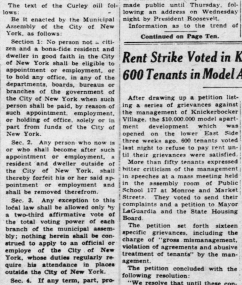

After drawing up a petition listing a series of grievances against the management of Knickerbocker Village, the $10,000,000 model apartment development which was opened on the lower East Side three weeks ago, 600 tenants voted last night to refuse to pay rent until their grievances were satisfied.

More than fifty tenants expressed bitter criticism of the management in speeches at a mass meeting held in the assembly room of Public School 177 at Monroe and Market Streets. They voted to send their complaints and a petition to Mayor LaGuardia and the State Housing Board.

The petition set forth sixteen specific grievances, including the charge of "gross mismanagement, violation of agreements and abusive treatment of tenants" by the management.

The petition concluded with the following resolution:

"We resolve that until these conditions are remedied or complied with to the general satisfaction of the tenants, to withhold payment of rent."

William Hirsch, chairman of the meeting, charged that the management was attempting to make the tenants "feel like objects of charity, although we are paying $12.50 a room rent."

Another speaker, Mrs. Andrew Chaplin, who said she represented the mothers who had rented apartments in the development, declared that none of the play spaces promised for the welfare of mothers and children were available.

In presenting the petition, Joseph P. Seely said the Fred F. French Company, which built Knickerbocker Village, "is violating in almost every respect the agreement under which it obtained an $8,000,000 loan" for building the development.

The "village," which lies just south of the Brooklyn Bridge, was dedicated on Oct. 1 by Jesse H. Jones, chairman of the Reconstruction Finance Corporation. Those present at the ceremonies included former Governor Alfred E. Smith, Mayor LaGuardia and Controller Joseph D. McGoldrick.

The property for the development was acquired by the French Company in the boom days as part of a projected real estate development to supply homes for persons working in the downtown financial area. After the stock market crash, the plan appeared to have been abandoned, but was revived as a "model apartment" project after it became possible to borrow money from the Federal Government.

NRA BOARD DECIDES TO CEASE CURBING INDUSTRY OUTPUT

New Policy Is Looking to Full Production, Lower Prices and Higher Consumer Demand.

EMPLOYMENT SPUR SEEN

White House Sanction Is Indicated for Change—Procedure on Codes Is Pending.

Special to THE NEW YORK TIMES.

WASHINGTON, Oct. 22.—Restriction of industrial output has been definitely discarded as a policy in the recovery program, a high official in the National Recovery Administration indicated today.

The National Industrial Recovery Board, named to administer the NRA after the resignation of General Johnson, has reached a conclusion that the attempt to limit supply, as practiced to a limited extent under him, was a mistake.

Production control, while almost unanimously deprecated by administration advisers, has crept into many of the NRA codes. It has taken these three forms:

1. Machine-hour provisions, whereby manufacturers are bound not to work their equipment more than so many hours a week
2. Restriction of the construction of new plant equipment.
3. Prohibition of sale below cost of production.

The board has not yet decided what to do about the production controls embodied in existing codes, but it was said that no further steps in this direction would be taken.

Roosevelt Approval Expected.

Any broad question of policy of this kind would be subject to review by the Industrial Policy Committee, of which Donald R. Richberg is director, but indications were that the reversal of procedure would meet with approval clear up to the White House.

President Roosevelt was represented as believing that price advances created by increased consumer demand would be of a more healthy nature than those brought into being by artificial restriction of supply. It was admitted that restriction of supply in agriculture had operated to raise price levels, but no permanent results of value from a like procedure were expected in industry.

The NIRB, made up of S. Clay Williams, Arthur D. Whiteside, Sidney Hillman, Leon C. Marshall and Walton H. Hamilton, has been working hard and quietly for nearly a month with very little publicity. It was said that its work so far had been limited largely to studying compliance problems and to assuring a prompt hearing for industrial grievances.

Only within the last few days has the board begun to consider policy procedure, necessarily deferred by the exigencies of routine detail with which the board had to familiarize itself.

The formulation, as yet vague, of the policy against restriction of production is one of the first important conclusions reached.

Stress on Consumer Demand.

From the consideration given to the problem, the board members have apparently reached largely the same conclusions as has the Brookings Institution in two books called "America's Capacity to Produce" and "America's Capacity to Consume." The two works were mentioned and their findings described as "interesting."

Turning from emphasis on overproduction, which was felt to have been much exaggerated, coloring as it did the whole treatment of the industrial problem in the first fifteen months of the NRA, the board was now said to be attacking matters along the line of attracting the consumer by low prices to buy goods.

Prices are to be lowered by permitting mass-production plants to operate at capacity, thus reducing unit costs. Increased demands will cause manufacturers to take on more laborers to produce goods. Increasing consumption will cause prices to stiffen at the same time as employment is increasing and new consumers are being brought into the market.

Textile and Auto Contrasts.

Board members arrived at these conclusions after contemplating the textile industry, whose code contains restrictive provisions and whose nation-wide strike resulted in a decline in employment and a loss of earnings. The automobile industry, which has no limitations, was observed to have enjoyed a comparatively sustained demand for some time for its production.

The new attack will help to relieve unemployment in the heavy goods industries, it is hoped, al-

Continued on Page Eight

SCOTT AND BLACK WIN, FLYING TO MELBOURNE IN 71 HOURS; DUTCH STILL SECOND; 2 KILLED

FINAL LAPS OF RACE AND LEADERS.

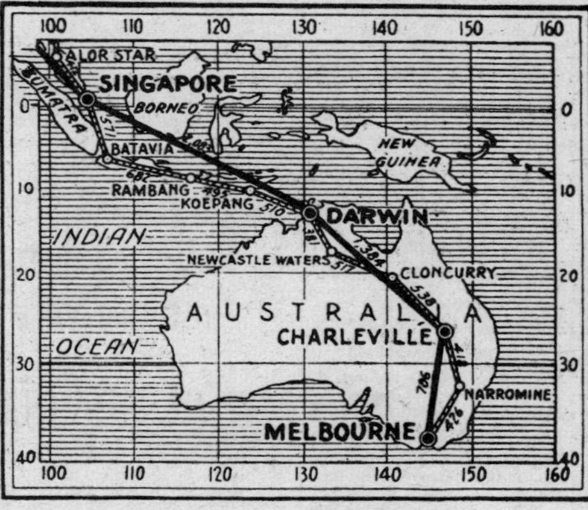

Progress of the Leading Contestants.

1—C. W. A. Scott, T. Campbell Black	British	Landed at Melbourne
2—K. D. Parmentier, J. J. Moll	Dutch	Flying from Darwin
3—Col. Roscoe Turner, Clyde E. Pangborn	American	Landed at Darwin
4—Cathcart Jones, Kenneth W. Waller	British	Approaching Singapore

Captain James A. and Mrs. Amy Johnson Mollison retired from the race and relinquished fourth place at Allahabad, India, because of motor trouble.

ENGLISH AIRPLANE VICTOR

One Motor Failed for a Time, but Fliers Went on After Repairs.

AMERICANS REACH DARWIN

Push On in Wake of Crew From Netherlands, Seeking Second Place.

FATAL CRASH IN ITALY

Britons, Far in Rear Because of Ill Luck, Fall in Mountains and Burn to Death.

Special Cable to THE NEW YORK TIMES.

MELBOURNE, Australia, Tuesday, Oct. 23.—The sleek crimson De Havilland Comet monoplane of C. W. A. Scott and T. Campbell Black of England swooped in here to a landing at 5:33 this morning (Greenwich mean time) to win the $50,000 first prize of the London-Australia air race.

[Greenwich time, officially adopted for the race, is used throughout this dispatch and is five hours later than New York time.]

"We had a lousy trip, and that's praising it," said Scott. "We seem to have been weeks over it and to have lived years." He and Black eagerly drank beer offered to them by Miss Jean Batten, a New Zealand flier, and Mrs. Rose Bonney and Miss Peggy Doyle, Australian airwomen, who were waiting for them as they climbed out of their plane.

The two dauntless airmen had fought against a crack field of twenty starters from all over the world since the start of the race early Saturday morning from Mildenhall Airdrome, just outside London. As they roared across the finish line they were clocked as the time of exactly seventy-one hours.

For the last twenty-four of those seventy-one hours they had been hindered in their progress by trouble with the port motor of the little twin-engined machine. In their long over-water jump from Singapore to Port Darwin, 2,083 miles, it stopped as they passed the halfway mark, and they continued on to Port Darwin, where they landed with one engine dead. After hurried repairs they took off again for Charleville, Queensland, 1,384 miles onward, and the motor was again dead when they hove into sight of the airport a few hours later.

Mechanics Struggle Over Motor.

Mechanics feverishly adjusted the engine, which had been badly burned out during the long strain of overrunning on the 10,539 miles up to that point. The two men were not satisfied with its performance when they took off on the last 786 miles here and were forced to return to Charleville. The mechanics again adjusted the engine to give it sufficient power for the little machine to gain altitude.

It lasted long enough for them to lead their nearest competitor in by a wide margin. Records had been smashed all the way along the line, the pilots had pressed the machine to its utmost, and the MacRobertson Trophy was won for England.

The two airmen swept across the finish line in the centre of the Flemington Race Course here, made a wide circle of the field and then roared off from the Spring afternoon sky. They made their final landing at Laverton Airfield.

Both men almost collapsed as they climbed down from the cockpits. Their lapse was more emotional than physical, however, and was over in a moment. They led their nearest competitor in by more than 800 miles.

Netherlands Entry in Second Place.

K. D. Parmentier and J. J. Moll of the Netherlands, in second place, arrived at Darwin at dawn and hopped off quickly after refueling. Australia was excited over their magnificent performance with a complement of nine persons, including passengers, stopping at every airport. They were last reported over Cloncurry, Queensland, 830 miles out of Darwin, at 2:15 A. M. Greenwich time.

John Wright and John Polando, Americans, left Aleppo for Baghdad at 5:17 A. M.

Colonel Roscoe Turner and Clyde E. Pangborn, the Americans, who are closely pressing the Netherlands

Continued on Page Three.

PRESIDENT URGES AID FOR CHARITIES

He Makes Radio Appeal for Support of '1934 Mobilization for Human Needs' Drive.

NEED FOR GIVING STRESSED

N. D. Baker Opens National Broadcast From Cleveland by Outlining Aims.

Special to THE NEW YORK TIMES.

WASHINGTON, Oct. 22.—Support of private charities by the public was asked tonight in a radio speech by President Roosevelt as a means of lightening as far as possible the relief drain on the Federal, State and local governments.

Mr. Roosevelt spoke on a nation-wide broadcast over the National Broadcasting Company and Columbia Broadcasting System arranged by the "1934 Mobilization for Human Needs," which operates through the Community Chests and other affiliated organizations. He was introduced by Newton D. Baker, who spoke from Cleveland, from where he will lead the campaign. The President said that the government-supported relief program is based on the expectation that the amount of relief done by private organizations "will continue in the future at least at the same pace and in the same amount as in the past."

"I hope that you will well realize," he said, "that it is contrary to a sound public policy to transfer more burdens to the shoulders of government if it can possibly be avoided, and, therefore, that private charity should, as a matter of good citizenship, be maintained at least at current levels."

THE PRESIDENT'S APPEAL.

The text of the President's speech follows:

"For the second successive year I am making a direct and frank appeal to the country to give support to worthy local charities of all kinds.

"You will recognize the necessity of the general rule which prevents the President of the United States from asking for assistance or contributions on behalf of any specific or individual good cause. If I were to begin doing that I would be on the air at least two or three times every evening.

"In this case, however, there is in existence a central organization called the '1934 Mobilization for Human Needs.' The object of this mobilization is to encourage and tie in together the many private organizations which are seeking funds to carry on their very essential and necessary work for the coming year.

"In some communities these organizations seek contributions from the public by means of 'community chests'; in others they are asking for help separately but simultaneously.

"May I very simply explain to

Continued on Page Nine.

WARNS THE LEGION NOT TO 'ROCK BOAT'

Past Commander Johnson Counsels Putting Duty to Nation Before Bonus.

STEIWER URGES PATIENCE

Oregon Senator's Attack on Roosevelt Policies Is Cheered by Miami Convention.

By F. RAYMOND DANIELL.

Special to THE NEW YORK TIMES.

MIAMI, Oct. 22.—In an address which bristled with thinly veiled hostility to the New Deal and which took issue with President Roosevelt's views on the government's responsibility to World War veterans, United States Senator Frederick Steiwer, Republican, of Oregon, urged the American Legion today to make haste slowly in demanding cash payment of the bonus.

The Senator addressed the opening session of the Legion's convention under the waving palms of Bayside Park after Louis Johnson, a past national commander who stemmed the tide of bonus sentiment at Chicago a year ago, had delivered an earnest plea against action this year that would "rock the boat," of national recovery.

Senator Steiwer, coauthor with Senator McCarran of Nevada of the legislation which restored some of the benefits taken from veterans by the National Economy Act, did not refer to President Roosevelt or the New Deal specifically, but his words left his auditors in no doubt as to his meaning.

The delegates and some 4,000 guests, angered by President Roosevelt's speech at Roanoke, Va., last Friday in which he placed the nation's duty to the underprivileged and unemployed above its immediate obligations to World War veterans, cheered the speaker lustily.

Lean to Bonus Payment.

While counseling caution and patience for strategic reasons, both Senator Steiwer and his Democratic colleague from Nevada, who was the chief speaker at the commander's dinner this evening, pledged themselves to support "the first well-ordered proposal" for cash payment of the adjusted compensation certificates when the subject comes before Congress again.

Senator Steiwer departed once from his prepared text in "dealing with the proposition recently advanced," that the government could not pay the bonus now because its first duty was toward the poor and underprivileged. He interpolated these remarks:

"This proposition breeds class conflict. On the one hand you have the underprivileged and on the other you have the veteran who defended his country in time of war. Both deserve better treatment from

Continued on Page Twenty-two.

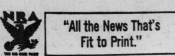

"All the News That's Fit to Print."

The New York Times.

LATE CITY EDITION
POSTSCRIPT
WEATHER—Cloudy and warmer today; tomorrow fair, colder.
Detailed Weather Report, Page 45.

Copyright, 1934, by The New York Times Company.

VOL. LXXXIV....No. 28,046. Entered as Second-Class Matter, Postoffice, New York, N. Y. NEW YORK, WEDNESDAY, NOVEMBER 7, 1934. F+ TWO CENTS In New York City. | THREE CENTS Within 200 Miles | FOUR CENTS Elsewhere Except in 7th and 8th Postal Zones

NEW DEAL SCORES NATION-WIDE VICTORY; LEHMAN WINS, LEGISLATURE DEMOCRATIC; TAYLOR VICTOR, REED AND SINCLAIR LOSE

TIDE SWEEPS NATION

Democrats Clinch Two-Thirds Rule of the Senate

HOUSE LEAD INCREASED

Seaboard States Back the President as Tide Rises in West.

MANDATE FOR PROGRAM

Curley Wins Easily in Massachusetts—Donahey Beats Senator Fess in Ohio.

INDIANA IN PROCESSION

Vandenberg Threatened With Defeat in Michigan—Hyde Park for Roosevelt.

By ARTHUR KROCK.

The President and his New Deal, in its first electoral test yesterday, won the most overwhelming victory in the history of American politics. A record-breaking number of voters for an off-year election gave the President a clear mandate to proceed with his policies in his own way, and, in giving that mandate, they literally destroyed the right wing of the Republican party.

Pennsylvania, the citadel of that Republicanism which has dominated the party since Lincoln's time, rejected for re-election Senator David A. Reed, outstanding critic of the New Deal, and sent to the Senate Joseph F. Guffey, who campaigned as the humble follower of "God's inspired servant"—his characterization of the President.

Apparently the State also chose a Democratic Governor, constituting the most amazing turnover in political history in this country, and the victory was specifically that of the President and his policies.

Increase of Congress Strength.

The nation's voters increased the Democratic strength in the Senate from 60 to 70 or more, assuring two-thirds control, which in itself is a record and something that has never happened before in an off-year. Indications were that the Democrats will increase their preponderant lead of 309 in the House of Representatives.

By their vote yesterday, the people of the United States invested the President with the greatest power that has ever been given to a Chief Executive on the submission of his case. With that power went also the tremendous responsibility that accompanies large and unwieldy majorities.

Upton Sinclair and his plan, under the Democratic aegis, "to end poverty in California" were repudiated because the administration failed to support the party nominee there. But an illustration of the forces Mr. Roosevelt must control came with Mr. Sinclair's statement that yesterday's election was but a "skirmish," that he will move to recall Governor Frank Merriam, and that "EPIC" will be the head and front in 1936 of the Democratic party in the West.

Phalanx of New Deal States.

New York, Massachusetts, Connecticut, New Jersey, Indiana, Ohio, Rhode Island, Illinois, Missouri, Maryland, West Virginia, the Dakotas, Iowa, Nebraska, Nevada, New Mexico, Arizona, Utah, Oregon, Montana, Wyoming, Washington, Colorado and the South were mustered in solid phalanx for the New Deal.

For a time during the night it seemed that a major upset might come in the defeat of Governor Ritchie for a fifth term in Maryland and that Nebraska might reject for the Senatorship Edward R. Burke, militant champion of the President's policies. But later returns revealed that even these satis-

Continued on Page Three.

WINNERS IN NEW YORK

U. S. Senator..	Royal S. Copeland, D.*
NEW YORK STATE	
Governor......	Herbert H. Lehman, D.*
Lt. Governor...	M. William Bray, D.*
Controller......	M. S. Tremaine, D.*
Atty. General..	J. J. Bennett Jr., D.*
NEW YORK CITY	
Controller......	Frank J. Taylor, D.
Richmond County	
Dist. Attorney..	T. J. Walsh, D.-L.P.
COURT OF APPEALS	
Chief Judge....	Fred'k E. Crane, D.-R.
Assoc. Judge...	J. T. Loughran, D.-R.
Assoc. Judge...	Edward R. Finch, D.
SUPREME COURT	
First District...	Kenneth O'Brien, D.
First District...	Lloyd Church, D.
First District...	Francis Martin, D.-R.*
First District...	James O'Malley, D.-R.*
First District...	I. Wasservogel, D.-R.*
Second District.	T. C. Kadien Jr., D.
Second District.	John MacCrate, D.-R.
Second District.	A. G. McLaughlin, D.-R.
Ninth District..	Keyes Winter, R.-L.P.*
Ninth District..	Chas. Garside, R.-L.P.*
COURT OF GENERAL SESSIONS	
N. Y. County..	Otto A. Rosalsky, D-R.*
MUNICIPAL COURT	
Manhattan	
Second District.	Emil N. Hans, D.
Third District..	C. J. Garrison, D.
Bronx	
Second District.	D. V. Sullivan, D.
Brooklyn	
Seventh District.	C. H Haubert, D.*

*Incumbent.

MOORE WINS, DILL ELECTION IN DOUBT

Jersey Executive Ousts Kean From Senate Seat—Race for Governor Close.

HOFFMAN CLAIMS VICTORY

Republicans Lose in Passaic County for First Time—Conflicting Figures.

New Jersey joined the nation-wide swing toward the New Deal, it appeared on the basis of incomplete returns at 4:30 this morning.

Governor A. Harry Moore had ousted Senator Hamilton F. Kean, Old Guard Republican, from the United States Senate. Conflicting compilations made it impossible to determine whether William L. Dill, Democrat, or Harold G. Hoffman, Republican, had won in the Gubernatorial contest fought out on the State issue of reduced taxation.

On the basis of returns from 2,075 districts out of New Jersey's 3,488 election districts, compiled by THE NEW YORK TIMES, Dill had 386,292 votes and Hoffman 359,072, indicating a plurality of 44,824 for Dill.

The Associated Press compilation of tabulations from 2,120 election districts gave Hoffman 419,281 and Dill 369,201, or an indicated plurality for Hoffman of 80,572.

The discrepancy is apparently due to incomplete returns from Hudson County, Democratic stronghold, which has returned a large plurality for Dill and other Democratic candidates. THE TIMES compilation included 504 of the 624 districts of Hudson County. The Associated Press reported at 4:30 A. M. that it had compiled returns from 305 of the Hudson County election districts. The plurality given Dill in the 504 districts compiled by THE TIMES was 63,677.

On the basis of the incomplete returns early this morning, Bernard J. Lamb, campaign manager for Hoffman, claimed the election of the Republican candidate for Governor by 15,000 votes.

Because of the unusally heavy vote and the late hour at which the polls closed—8 P. M.—tabulation of the returns proceeded slowly. They indicated a huge Democratic plurality in the party's normal stronghold in Hudson County and varying leads elsewhere.

"A Deeper Significance."

Governor Moore issued the following statement early this morning:

"Naturally I am delighted at the magnificent vote reported for me at this election and I take occasion publicly to express my heartfelt gratitude to the people for this manifestation of confidence which they have accorded me. I shall ever be grateful to my fellow-citizens for

Continued on Page Eight

PENNSYLVANIA WON

Democrats Elect Guffey Senator in Close Vote

GET ALL STATE OFFICES

Take Governorship and Get 3 New Members of Congress.

REED HOLDS PHILADELPHIA

But His Plurality Is Only 4,086 in the Complete Count of the City.

Special to THE NEW YORK TIMES.

PHILADELPHIA, Wednesday, Nov. 7.—Senator David A. Reed, champion of conservatism and critic of the New Deal, lost his seat in the Senate to Joseph F. Guffey, "original" Roosevelt leader of Pennsylvania, in yesterday's election which threw the Keystone State of Republicanism into the Democratic column.

Voters swarmed to the polling places in almost unprecedented numbers and voted for the man who had put forward President Roosevelt as the only issue in the bitterest campaign in the Commonwealth's recent history.

In electing their first United States Senator in sixty years Pennsylvania Democrats achieved what Republican leaders had termed the impossible, namely, surmounting the obstacle of a Republican registration majority of almost 1,250,000 voters.

Steadily mounting election returns early today indicated that the Democratic triumph would be broad enough to embrace the entire State-wide ticket and increase the present Democratic membership of twelve in the Pennsylvania Congressional delegation of thirty-four.

Earle Wins Governorship.

Attorney General William A. Schnader, the Republican Gubernatorial nominee, who has served under both a Republican and a Progressive Governor, registered totals well ahead of those of his running-mate, Senator Reed. The capitulation of this Republican stronghold to the New Deal, nevertheless, carried to victory his opponent, George

Continued on Page Fourteen.

GOVERNORS ELECTED.

Alabama.....	Bibb Graves, D.
Arizona....	*B. B. Moeur, D.
Arkansas....	*J. M. Futrell, D.
Colorado...	*E. C. Johnson, D.
Connecticut..	*W. L. Cross, D.
Georgia.....	*E. Talmadge, D.
Kansas..	*Alfred M. Landon, R.
Massachusetts.	J. M. Curley, D.
Minnesota..	*F. B. Olson, F. L.
N. Hampshire.	H. S. Bridges, R.
New York..	*H. H. Lehman, D.
North Dakota.	T. H. Moodie, D.
Ohio.....	Martin L. Davey, D.
Oklahoma.	E. W. Marland, D.
Pennsylvania..	G. H. Earle, D.
Rhode Isl..	*Theo. F. Green, D.
S. Carolina..	O. D. Johnston, D.
South Dakota..	*Tom Berry, D.
Tennessee.	*Hill McAlister, D.
Texas....	James V. Allred, D.
Vermont..	Charles M. Smith, R.

*Incumbent.

CALIFORNIA BEATS SINCLAIR AND EPIC

Los Angeles, Primary Stronghold of Former Socialist, Turns to Gov. Merriam.

FRAUD CHARGED BY LOSER

Conceding Defeat, He Says He Will Start Campaign to Recall Republican Victor.

By The Associated Press.

SAN FRANCISCO, Nov. 6.—Upton Sinclair, Socialist who turned Democrat, lost his "end-poverty" bid for the California Governorship today to Acting Governor Frank F. Merriam, Republican.

Mr. Merriam hailed the result as showing that California voters "have rejected radicalism and socialism."

Mr. Sinclair, in a speech addressed to his opponents, said:

"We congratulate you on your brief victory, and we are preparing for the next campaign."

Out of 10,721 precincts in the State, 6,839, complete and incomplete, gave Merriam 594,955; Sinclair, 481,554, and Raymond L. Haight, Progressive and Commonwealth party, 158,674.

Plans Post-Election Fight.

Mr. Sinclair today announced his intention to start a recall campaign against Governor Merriam in the event of the Republican's election.

Even Los Angeles, centre of EPIC in the primary by which Mr. Sinclair won the Democratic nomination, turned against him today.

Mr. Merriam's advantage appeared to be general. In Los Angeles County, which contains approximately 45 per cent of the State's voting strength, Merriam was gain-

Continued on Page Twelve.

Mrs. O'Day Wins Seat in Congress Easily; Race Featured by Aid of Mrs. Roosevelt

Yesterday's election showed that most New York State voters agreed with Mrs. Franklin D. Roosevelt that Mrs. Caroline O'Day, for years a friend of the President's wife, would make a good Representative at Large in the New York delegation in Congress.

Returns from 7,097 election districts of the State's 8,951 gave Mrs. O'Day a plurality of 674,294 over her Republican opponent, Miss Natalie Couch. The vote was 1,726,438 to 1,052,144. Indications were that her lead would be cut slightly, as all the missing districts were up-State, where Miss Couch was running ahead of the Democratic candidate.

Mrs. Roosevelt and Mrs. O'Day met at Democratic headquarters at the Hotel Biltmore last night. They kissed, and with Postmaster General Farley posed for photographers.

"The up-State papers said Mrs. Roosevelt spoke for me because I was too dumb to speak for myself," said Mrs. O'Day. "I resent very much the intimation that Mrs. Roosevelt would speak for a dumbbell. I think many people feel that 'what is good enough for Mrs. Roosevelt is good enough for me.' "

Miss Couch sent a telegram of congratulation to her successful opponent, and Mrs. O'Day replied with a message of thanks.

The participation of Mrs. Roosevelt in the active campaign made the battle between Mrs. O'Day and Miss Couch the outstanding feminine political contest of the national election.

Early in October the President's wife announced that she would take the stump for her old friend, and the announcement reaped an immediate crop of strong criticism. Mrs. Roosevelt met this adverse comment with the unbothered statement that she realized her action was unusual, but Mrs. O'Day was, after all, an old friend, and, moreover, Mrs. Roosevelt was certain that the election of Mrs. O'Day would be in the public interest.

Mrs. O'Day, widow of Daniel O'Day, a Standard Oil Company executive, became assistant State chairman of the Democratic party in 1926. She asked for votes for Representative at Large on a six-point platform: Higher standards for wage earners, adequate relief at lowest cost to the taxpayer, a power program of benefit to the consumer, a sound fiscal policy, friendly foreign relations and wider opportunity for women in government.

In one speech she admitted her admiration for President Roosevelt was so great that she doubtless would be a "yes-woman" in Congress, although if it came to a question of war "I think I would just kiss my children good-bye and start off for Leavenworth."

M'GOLDRICK LOSES

Taylor Victory by 13,855 a Blow To Fusion

BROOKLYN VOTE CLOSE

McGoldrick Carries It and Queens, Runs Well Elsewhere.

CONTROL OF BOARD ISSUE

LaGuardia Strength Will Be Cut to a Bare Majority, Hampering Program.

Carried along by the Lehman landslide in the city, Frank J. Taylor, Tammany candidate, was elected yesterday Controller of the City of New York. His margin was a slender one, Mr. Taylor having a plurality of 13,855 with no election districts missing.

His Republican-Fusion opponent, Joseph D. McGoldrick, the incumbent, made a remarkable run in the face of the landslide, and the only borough he lost by a substantial margin was Manhattan. He carried Queens, carried Brooklyn by a small margin, held the Flynn machine down to a small plurality in the Bronx and did well in Staten Island.

Mr. McGoldrick's defeat reduces the Fusion majority in the Board of Estimate to nine votes against seven, as Borough President George U. Harvey of Queens, elected as a Fusionist, has voted more often with the Tammany bloc.

The Vote by Boroughs.

The figures by boroughs are as follows:

Manhattan—Taylor, 223,062; McGoldrick, 204,886, with no election districts missing. Plurality for Taylor, 18,176.

Brooklyn—Taylor, 287,450; McGoldrick, 289,283, with no election districts missing. Plurality for McGoldrick, 1,833.

Bronx—Taylor, 151,718; McGoldrick, 141,133, with no election districts missing. Plurality for Taylor, 10,585.

Queens—Taylor, 142,117; McGoldrick, 156,566, with no election districts missing. Plurality for McGoldrick, 14,449.

Richmond—Taylor, 25,569; McGoldrick, 24,193, with no election districts missing. Plurality for Taylor, 1,376.

Total Vote—Taylor, 829,916; McGoldrick, 816,061, with no election districts missing.

Mr. McGoldrick's defeat by the slender margin, in the face of the Lehman landslide, wipes out the belief that existed before election that if he were to be defeated it could be construed only as a repudiation of the LaGuardia administration. A normal defeat would have been, but that of the present Controller was not normal.

Fusion Still Holds Voters.

It seemed to indicate that the administration still has a hold on the independent voters in the city and that while its policies may not meet complete approval, a great part of the independents preferred to see it remain in power than to vote for Tammany's candidate. Weakness in the Republican organization which nominated Mr. McGoldrick, and the weakness of the State ticket in the city, appeared to have been the factors that defeated the man appointed to the office last Spring after the death of Controller W. Arthur Cunningham.

Mr. McGoldrick's run in the outlying boroughs, where the home-owner vote counts heavily, appeared to bear out that view. He ran well also in the upper West Side districts in Manhattan, where the apartment house vote is heavy.

In Manhattan Mr. McGoldrick carried the Seventh, Ninth, Tenth, Fifteenth, Eighteenth, Twenty-first and Twenty-third Assembly Districts and ran exceptionally well in the Eleventh, Nineteenth and Twenty-second.

He arrived at his headquarters at

Continued on Page Three.

New York Times Studio Photo.

GOVERNOR HERBERT H. LEHMAN.

FARLEY ACCLAIMS VICTORY FOR PARTY

Democratic Chairman Declares the New Deal Has Been 'Magnificently' Upheld.

EATON LOOKS TO FUTURE

Says Republican Fight Will Go On—Taylor Holds Public Interest Paramount.

Postmaster General Farley, as chairman of the Democratic National Committee, issued the following statement from headquarters in the Biltmore Hotel at 9:30 P. M.:

"The returns have come in sufficiently to show that the Democratic party has won a wonderful victory. The figures are not yet complete enough for us to go into detail of the States we have carried, but we do know that the New Deal has been magnificently sustained.

"Famous Republican figures have been toppled into oblivion. In fact, we must wonder whom they have left that the country has ever heard of.

"The people have shown that they are stronger for President Roosevelt and his administration than they were two years ago. There is no doubt that he would have been given a majority in every State if he had been the Presidential candidate this year.

"We are not going to get into any argument with the campaign methods of our opponents. The people answered that at the polls today.

"Our majority in the United States Senate and our majority in the House of Representatives continues at top figures.

"As all of this was expected and prophesied from our side, any statement that I could make would amount to repetition.

"It will be far more interesting to hear how the Republicans feel."

Points to State Results.

Mr. Farley, as chairman of the Democratic State Committee, issued the following statement at 10:10 P. M.:

"The returns in New York State show the elections of Governor Lehman and Senator Copeland and other State candidates by the greatest plurality ever given to Democratic candidates in the history of the State.

"This election is convincing proof that the people of the State of New York are certain to have a most excellent administration of State affairs for the next two years.

"But far beyond that is the most marvelous endorsement of President Roosevelt's administration in Washington, the greatest ever

Continued on Page Four.

DEMOCRATS WIN STATE ASSEMBLY

Capture Full Control of the Government at Albany in Lehman Landslide.

GAIN STRENGTH IN SENATE

Baldwin Is Victor in Close Race—Dunnigan, Brownell, Moffat Chosen.

By W. A. WARN.

The Democratic tidal wave that swept the State at yesterday's election carried the party into control of both the Senate and Assembly for the first time since 1913, when the Republicans were divided through the Bull Moose revolt.

Complete returns from the legislative elections throughout the State give the Democrats thirty out of fifty-one seats in the Senate, against twenty-six seats in the present body.

In the Assembly, according to the latest figures, they will have a bare working majority of 76 seats out of 150. The Republicans have 84 seats in the present Assembly. The Democrats also defeated one independent who in most votes in the present Assembly made common cause with the Republicans.

Make Inroads Up-State.

Not since the Bull Moose split have the Democrats elected so many members of the Senate and Assembly from up-State districts. Seven of the twenty-nine Democratic members who on the face of the returns have won seats in the upper house will represent up-State districts. Two Democrats from Erie, two from Monroe, one from Rensselaer, one from Albany and one from Westchester County will sit in the 1935 Senate.

Fifteen of the Democratic Assemblymen elected will represent up-State counties; three from Albany, five from Erie, three from Monroe, one from Rensselaer, one from Schoharie, one from Oneida and one from Greene County.

The Republicans lost one Senate seat in New York City, where Jacob J. Schwartzwald, a former Democratic Assemblyman, defeated George Blumberg, Republican incumbent from the Seventh district. To offset this loss, the Republicans succeeded in electing Joseph Clark Baldwin 3d, former Republican leader of the Board of Aldermen, over Albert Wald, the Democratic member of the present Senate.

George R. Fearon of Onondaga, leader of the Republican minority in the present Senate emerged with victory after a stiff fight. All the in the present Senate, emerged with

Continued on Page Six.

STATE TICKET WINS

Lehman Plurality Is Expected to Go to 820,000

HAILED BY THE PRESIDENT

Moses Congratulates Him as Governor Thanks Voters for Approval.

REBUKE TO OLD GUARD

Crushing Defeat for the Faction That Took Over Republican Control.

COPELAND RIDES ON TIDE

Justice Finch Easily Tops His Rival Sears—Vote for Hylan Is Small.

By JAMES A. HAGERTY.

In an overwhelming Democratic victory in New York State, Governor Herbert H. Lehman was re-elected yesterday by an unprecedented plurality in any but a Presidential year.

The Democratic victory in the State was complete. As a result of the sweep, the Democrats increased their majority in the State Senate from one to eight and gained control of the Assembly by electing 76 of the 150 Assemblymen. For the first time in many years the Democrats will have control of both houses of the Legislature as the result of yesterday's election.

In a contest that was marked by the collapse of the Republican party in some up-State counties that usually have been Republican, so far as support of its State-wide candidates was concerned, the voters of President Roosevelt's home State gave overwhelming approval to his New Deal policies and administered a rebuke to the Old Guard faction, which had gained control of the State organization of the Republican party and nominated Mr. Moses for Governor.

The plurality for Governor Lehman, which incomplete returns indicate will be about 820,000, exceeded the 725,000 plurality for Mr. Roosevelt as a candidate for Governor in 1930, and came nearly up to the 847,000 Governor Lehman received in the Democratic landslide in 1932, the last Presidential year.

With the landslide for Governor Lehman, the other candidates on the Democratic State-wide ticket, United States Senator Royal S. Copeland, Lieut. Gov. M. William Bray of Utica, Controller Morris S. Tremaine of Buffalo and Attorney General John J. Bennett Jr. of Brooklyn, were swept back into office.

Mrs. Caroline O'Day and Matthew J. Merritt, candidates for Representatives at large, won by large pluralities over their Republican opponents, Miss Natalie F. Couch and William B. Groat Jr.

The vote for the State ticket now stands as follows:

FOR GOVERNOR.

New York City, complete—Lehman, 1,207,620; Moses, 407,158; city plurality for Lehman, 800,462.

Outside city, 4,635 election districts out of 5,104—Lehman, 942,835; Moses, 908,133; up-State plurality for Lehman, 34,702.

Entire State, 8,482 districts out of 8,951—Lehman, 2,150,455; Moses, 1,315,291; plurality for Lehman in entire State, 835,164 with 469 districts missing.

FOR SENATOR.

New York City, complete—Copeland, 1,122,782; Cluett, 384,252; city plurality for Copeland, 738,530.

Up-State, 3,848 election districts out of 5,104—Copeland, 733,189;

Continued on Page Three.

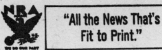

"All the News That's Fit to Print."

The New York Times.

LATE CITY EDITION
WEATHER—Fair today; tomorrow cloudy, warmer, rain at night.
Temperatures Yesterday—Max. 41, min. 24.
Detailed Weather Report, Page 29.

Copyright, 1934, by The New York Times Company.

VOL. LXXXIV....No. 28,084. Entered as Second-Class Matter, Postoffice, New York, N. Y. NEW YORK, SATURDAY, DECEMBER 15, 1934. P TWO CENTS In New York City. | THREE CENTS Within 200 Miles | FOUR CENTS Elsewhere Except in 7th and 8th Postal Zones.

OLD GUARD MOVES FOR LIBERAL PARTY; BARS BORAH VIEWS

First Step to Be Election of a Young Man to Lead the Republican Legislators.

TO FORCE OUT M'GINNIES

Eaton Confers With Moses and Urges Him to Draft Program for Minority at Albany.

LEADERSHIP IS IN DOUBT

Brownell of Manhattan and Ives of Chenango Leading Choices for the Post.

By W. A. WARN.

The making over of the Republican party in this State to have more of a popular appeal will not be delayed. It will be undertaken by the element now in control of the Republican State organization, which, incidentally, hopes to shake off the "Old Guard" tag hung on it by W. Kingsland Macy, former State chairman, and avert State-wide fights in the primary elections next year which would prove disastrous in their effect on the 1936 Presidential campaign.

It is not intended that the more liberal garb in which the party shortly will make its bow to the public shall be a convenient disguise. The leaders whom Mr. Macy denounced as of the Old Guard variety, in league with power and utility interests to the detriment of the people, are determined that the next session of the Legislature shall reflect the new spirit dominating the Republican rank and file and its leadership.

But, it was pointed out yesterday following the addresses delivered at Mecca Temple on the night before by Senators William E. Borah of Idaho and Gerald P. Nye of North Dakota that the liberalization program will not follow the radical Western pattern with which their names are associated in the public mind but will represent a liberal attitude to public problems, adjusted to an Eastern background and environment.

Eaton Makes First Move.

Melvin C. Eaton, State chairman, started the ball rolling at the meeting in Utica of the Republican members who will sit in the 1935 Legislature when he voiced his insistence that a youthful Republican of progressive tendencies should be selected for Republican floor leader of the next House at Albany. This even though he admitted that Speaker Joseph A. McGinnies was the one best fitted by experience and knowledge of the problems confronting the State to serve in that capacity.

Yesterday Mr. Eaton had a breakfast engagement with Robert Moses, late Republican candidate for Governor, whom he invited and urged to prepare a legislative program for the Republican minority in the Senate and Assembly next year. Mr. Moses is taking this proposal under consideration. Mr. Eaton said that Mr. Moses had been accepted pretty generally throughout the State as a liberal and that his profound knowledge of State problems made him better equipped than any other man in the Republican party or in the State for that task.

Liberal leadership in the Assembly, virile enough to compel a following, and a liberal legislative program, Mr. Eaton feels, should place the party on a better footing with the voters and especially with the younger and more progressive element in the party, bringing back to the Republican fold thousands who have deserted and flocked to the Democratic banners in recent State campaigns.

Conference to Be Held.

The whole question, it was learned last night, will come up for discussion at a conference of Mr. Eaton and the Republican legislative leaders within the next week or ten days. Mr. Moses has accepted an invitation to attend this conference. His course will be determined by the outcome, more particularly after the question of leadership has come somewhat nearer a settlement than it was when the Utica conference was adjourned.

While Speaker McGinnies has at present a majority of the votes that will be cast in next year's Republican Assembly caucus, Mr. Eaton left for his home yesterday afternoon, convinced that the veteran leader of the present Assembly would place no obstacles in the way to the selection of a young man for minority leader.

One thing that is giving the advocates of a change in the leadership concern is how to make it possible for Mr. McGinnies to retire

Continued on Page Fourteen.

8 Die, 20 Saved From Sinking Ship In Wild Storm in Mid-Atlantic

Two Rescuers Are Victims With 6 of Crew of Freighter Usworth as Wave Wrecks Lifeboat—Ascania Sprays Oil on Heavy Sea While Belgian Ship Sends Out Craft.

The worst North Atlantic storm of the year brought death to eight seamen yesterday as the British steamer Usworth foundered about 850 miles east of St. Johns, Nfld.

Wallowing helplessly in mountainous seas since last Wednesday night, the Usworth, bound from Montreal to Cobh and United Kingdom ports with a cargo of coal, sent out an urgent call for aid before dawn yesterday after the storm had separated her from the little Belgian freighter Jean Jadot, standing by since Wednesday to give her a tow.

The Cunard White Star liner Ascania, bound from Southampton to New York, via Halifax, answered the SOS and sped to the scene with her men standing by the lifeboats and her engineers preparing to pump oil on the sea.

In the rescue which followed, six men from the Usworth and two volunteer rescuers from the Jean Jadot were lost when a huge wave capsized one of the Belgian lifeboats against the tilting side of the Usworth.

When night fell, the stricken freighter, with her decks awash and her gear torn free by the terrific force of the sea and gale winds, was still wallowing helplessly, abandoned. The two rescue vessels stood off with twenty survivors recovering in ships' hospitals.

A devastating Winter storm was sweeping almost the breadth of the North Atlantic, driving battered vessels into Halifax and other Canadian ports. The Weather Bureau said there were really two storms, creating havoc between them, reaching to the middle of the Atlantic.

One of the storms was centred not far from the Usworth's approximate position, or about 800 miles west of Ireland, and the other swept over the maritime provinces with dangerous force out to sea.

The Jean Jadot, which left New York for Antwerp on Dec. 5, had been standing by the stricken Usworth since Wednesday night, when the latter vessel's steering gear became hopelessly disabled. Although the Usworth had not sent out an S O S at that time, she requested the Jean Jadot to stand by and it was the intention of Captain Sadi Gonthier, master of the Belgian ship, to put a tow line over yesterday morning and tow the Usworth on to the British channel.

But early yesterday, according to meager radio messages sent by the Jean Jadot and the Ascania to The Associated Press and the Mackay

Continued on Page Eight.

SCIENTISTS ADVISE FEDERAL RESEARCH

Program for 6-Year Study to Cost $16,000,000 Is Laid Before President.

WOULD AID IDLE IN FIELD

Group Headed by Compton of M. I. T. Lists Subjects Held Nationally Vital.

Special to THE NEW YORK TIMES.

WASHINGTON, Dec. 14.—Exhaustive study by competent scientists of the principal technical problems facing this country is recommended to President Roosevelt by the Science Advisory Board in a report made public today. The study would continue for six years and cost $16,000,000.

The board, appointed by the President July 31, 1933, tried to get the plan started under the public works program, but Secretary Ickes and his advisers found no legal justification for expending public works funds for such a survey.

The problems recommended for study included long-distance transmission of electric power by new processes, the possibility of creating new industries, natural resources in their economic, social and political relations; study of air masses to further weather prediction, dissipation of fog by artificial means, characteristics and properties of various substances at extreme temperatures and other experimentation that might be of industrial value.

Plan Has Employment Phase.

Besides the material benefits to the nation which might result, the employment relief which the program would afford to scientists and research workers was stressed by the board, which is headed by Dr. Karl T. Compton, president of the Massachusetts Institute of Technology.

The report, in discussion of various subjects recommended for study, said:

"Meteorology—The new technique involves supplementing the meteorological observations taken at the surface of the earth by high altitude measurements of temperature, pressure and humidity obtained by instruments in airplanes or balloons. In this way, the character and motions of the great continental air masses may be studied and their future behavior predicted with much greater certainty than at present.

"Soil mechanics—It is suggested that, under the auspices of several widely distributed engineering schools, the necessary physical constants be obtained for the soils characteristic of various important regions to permit the application of this new theory to the design of future construction projects in these regions.

"Sewage disposal—This is one of America's most important public works problems. The annual investment in sewage treatment works is now comparable with, and probably exceeds, that in water supply and is of the order of $100,000,000 per year.

"Fog dissipation—A method has been invented and tested during the past two years which is successful in dissipating fogs created artifi-

Continued on Page Eight.

600 FLEE FROM FIRE AT BROADWAY SHOW

Film Operator at the Strand Climbs 2 Stories Down Cable With Unconscious Aide.

DENSE SMOKE FILLS HOUSE

Sparks From Roof Shower Into Balconies — Crowd of 10,000 Watches in Times Sq.

A motion-picture machine operator carried his assistant down a cable on the outside of the Strand Theatre Building at 6:45 P. M. yesterday in rescuing him from the projection booth, in which they had been trapped by smoke from a fire in the roof of the building.

While the operators were making the hazardous drop down the cable from the fourth floor to the roof of a second-story extension, fifty feet below, more than 600 in the audience fled from the theatre through the Broadway, the Forty-seventh Street and the Forty-eighth Street exits as a shower of embers fell into the balcony from vents in the ceiling.

Fire apparatus summoned by two alarms fought the blaze, which started in the building's ventilating system in the engine room and was carried up a sheet-iron flue to the roof, where it burned above the auditorium's ceiling, with flames shooting from the roof.

Sparks fell into the theatre, destroying 550 seats in the first five rows of the balcony and damaging the orchestra pit and the wings of the stage. The heat scorched the paint from the ceiling and caused its crystal chandeliers to fall.

Aerial Ladders Used.

Fearing that some of the spectators, confused by the dense, black smoke, might have made their way to the roof, the firemen threw up aerial ladders on the Forty-seventh Street side. No one was found there, but the ladders were used to carry up hose to reach the heart of the blaze.

A crowd, estimated by the police at 10,000, was attracted to the scene from Times Square's pre-theatre throngs and from restaurants in the neighborhood. Two police emergency squads, reserves and mounted police were summoned to hold it in check on the east side of Broadway, the south side of Forty-seventh Street and the north side of Forty-eighth.

Traffic on Broadway was tied up for an hour and a half while firemen fought the blaze, stretching lines of hose into the Broadway entrance of the building as well as on the side-streets. Although vehicles were detoured at Forty-sixth and Forty-ninth Streets, jams resulted, which were not cleared for another twenty minutes.

The flames had made considerable headway in the roof above the theatre's ceiling before smoke began to pour into the balcony. In the projection booth at the top of the balcony, corresponding to the top floor of the four-story building, were Walter Pitchert of Bogota, N. J., the operator of the motion-picture machine, and his assistant, Marcus Rittiner, of 6,811 Narrows Avenue, Brooklyn.

With smoke filling the booth and the heat becoming oppressive, Rittiner collapsed. Pitchert kept the

Continued on Page Fourteen.

POLICE TRY TO LINK BUDD GIRL'S SLAYER TO 3 OTHER CRIMES

Fish Questioned on O'Connor, Collings and Gaffney Cases —He Denies Part in Them.

WESTCHESTER TO TRY HIM

Transfer of Prisoner to That County Now Pending—Child's Skeleton Is Unearthed.

Albert H. Fish, 65-year-old house painter who confessed that he had kidnapped and slain Grace Budd in 1928, will be surrendered to Westchester County for trial on murder charges as soon as the evidence against him is completed, it was announced yesterday.

Tracked down after six years of effort by Detective William King of the Missing Persons Bureau, Fish confessed Thursday night that he had taken the Budd girl to a house in a lonely section near Elmsford, in Westchester County. He killed the child there and left her dismembered body behind a stone wall on the grounds, according to his confession.

Search yesterday along this wall by the police of Greenburg, in whose jurisdiction the crime was committed, resulted in the finding of a virtually complete skeleton of a child of about 10 years, Acting Captain John G. Stein of the Missing Persons Bureau was informed.

Dental Chart Is Clue.

The skull which apparently belongs to this skeleton had been found near the wall by the New York police Thursday night, when they visited the grounds with Fish as their guide, immediately after he had made his confession.

A dental chart, indicating that Grace Budd had undergone treatment at the old New York Hospital, was found by the police at 6 P. M. The dentist who did the work will be asked to inspect two gold fillings in the teeth of the skull today.

It was expected that this would result in a positive identification of the skull as that of the Budd girl, in view of the closeness with which all other facts of Fish's confession have coincided with the physical circumstances of the case.

Meanwhile, it became known, investigation of the prisoner's activities here will continue to determine whether he has been linked with any other cases involving the disappearance of children.

James T. Neary, Assistant District Attorney in charge of the homicide bureau of the District Attorney's office, announced the impending transfer of the prisoner. Although a John Doe indictment was returned here following the Budd kidnapping, the statute of limitations probably has barred prosecution of Fish on the kidnapping count, it was admitted at the Criminal Courts Building.

When Fish will be sent from New York to White Plains, where the trial will take place, cannot be determined at this time, Mr. Neary declared, but will depend on how soon the Westchester authorities are able to complete their case against Fish, including positive

Continued on Page Three.

SENATORS' CHARGES OF 39,231% PROFIT STIR DU PONTS' IRE

Return on $5,000 Invested in Directing Building of Powder Plant Was a Fee, They Say.

STORY OF DELAY DISPUTED

President Presses the Baruch Board to Have Legislation Ready for Congress.

Special to THE NEW YORK TIMES.

WASHINGTON, Dec. 14.—Charges by counsel for the Senate committee investigating the munitions industry that the du Pont Company realized a profit of 39,231 per cent on its cash investment in the Old Hickory Powder plant during the World War provided a tense moment today in the hearing.

His face crimson with feeling, Pierre S. du Pont, who was head of the company during the war, quickly replied with a counter charge that the statement amounted practically to an attempt by the committee to falsify the record, that the statement was ridiculous and of a kind that should have no place in any record of any proceeding.

Nothing in the record of the World War has produced more sleepless nights in the War Department than the long-drawn-out Old Hickory controversy, which started in October, 1917, and has continued to the present day.

Plant Cost $84,000,000.

The plant, which was the keynote of a hurry-up program to guarantee the United States and the Allies the necessary reserve of smokeless powder at a time when the war was nearing a crisis, cost the government about $84,000,000 and in the end was salvaged for less than $4,000,000.

Meanwhile, it became known that quick action is expected by President Roosevelt of the committee which he named on Wednesday to draft legislation to "take the profits out of war."

In response to inquiries as to plans for the committee, Mr. Roosevelt said today that he expected it to meet within two or three weeks and immediately begin discussions with Congressional leaders on legislation to be placed before the new Congress, which will meet three weeks from now.

Bernard M. Baruch, former chairman of the War Industries Board, was named chairman of the committee, which consists principally of Cabinet members.

Negotiations Took Months.

The Old Hickory contracts, three in number, reached the construction stage in the Winter of 1918 after months of negotiations over compensation and the form the contracts should take. Active were Secretary of War Baker, Pierre du Pont, Daniel Willard, then chairman of the War Industries Board; General William Crozier, chief of ordnance of the army, and many other persons in and out of the service.

Finally, under a $1 contract, the government agreed to advance the cost of construction, and at the same time guarantee a compensation which was to be so much per

Continued on Page Six.

Hitler Is Imperiled as His Train Hits Bus; Badly Shaken as 14 in Vehicle Are Killed

By The Associated Press.

BREMEN, Dec. 14.—Chancellor Adolf Hitler's life was imperiled tonight when his special train, en route from Bremen to Berlin, roared into an autobus near here, instantly killing thirteen persons.

A fourteenth died later in the hospital to which the seven other passengers of the bus, all seriously injured, were taken. The bus's occupants were theatrical performers.

Although rudely shaken by the crash, which occurred while his train was returning at high speed from launching ceremonies at Bremen for the new 18,000-ton North German Lloyd liner, Herr Hitler alighted from the train and walked the mile back up the track where the demolished bus and the victims of the collision lay.

After lifting his hand in the Nazi salute over the bodies, the Chancellor helped to pick them up.

Aboard the train were such Nazi notables as General Werner von Blomberg, the Defense Minister; Dr. Hjalmar Schacht, economic dictator of the Reich, and Wilhelm Brueckner, Herr Hitler's adjutant.

A major catastrophe was averted only because the train remained on the track.

Just before the train continued to Berlin Chancellor Hitler stood erect before the bodies, which had been covered, and again gave the Nazi salute. The party was delayed an hour by the accident.

The train had left Bremerhaven at 4:30 P. M. amid wild cheering described by an official communiqué as "the greatest demonstration ever seen in Bremerhaven."

The accident occurred half an hour later when the driver of the bus, unable to see through fog and dusk, drove through lowered crossing gates onto the track near Verden, to be struck by the fast-traveling express.

The bus was filled with an itinerant theatrical troupe en route to its next show. First reports that those killed were members of the Hitler Youth organization proved to be unfounded when the complete death list was announced.

BERLIN, Dec. 14 (AP).—Chancellor Hitler, looking tired and with face drawn, arrived at Lehrter Station here at 11:30 tonight after having narrowly escaped death or injury near Verden.

The locomotive of his special train was so badly damaged by its collision with a bus that another engine was attached to bring the party of Nazi officials back to Berlin.

Herr Hitler, wearing his storm troop uniform, hurried to an automobile while a small group shouted "Heil!" and was driven immediately to the chancellery, guarded by fifteen motor cycle policemen.

JOB INSURANCE BY STATES, WITH A FEDERAL SUBSIDY, ROOSEVELT COUNCIL'S PLAN

NATIONAL STANDARD GOAL

Aid Would Be Cut Off if States Failed to Hold to Lines Laid Out.

BUSINESS MEN BACK IDEA

Those in Council Finally Join Green's Side, Dropping the Wagner-Lewis Measure.

CABINET GROUP ACTS NEXT

Endorsement by President Is Expected if Perkins Committee Approves the Proposal.

By LOUIS STARK.

Special to THE NEW YORK TIMES.

WASHINGTON, Dec. 14.—Federal-State unemployment insurance, administered by the States and providing for a Federal subsidy to States adopting plans which comply with certain national standards, is the form of insurance approved by the President's Advisory Council, it was learned today.

If Secretary Perkins and the Cabinet committee associated with the Committee on Economic Security approve the Advisory Council's action, they will sound the death knell of the Wagner-Lewis bill as the device for encouraging States to adopt unemployment insurance laws.

And if such approval is granted, endorsement by President Roosevelt is expected. Then to bill-drafting experts will be assigned the task of working up the proposal into proper form for presentation to the next Congress.

The advisory council's approval of what is designed to be a nationally supervised system of unemployment insurance came after long debates within its ranks, and after the business members of the group were convinced that this method would be a great improvement over the Wagner-Lewis bill.

Business Group Approves.

In some quarters surprise was expressed that the leading business men on the Advisory Council had finally come out for the national subsidy scheme.

It was learned that the final vote in the council was nine to seven, with all members of the business group joining with William Green, president of the American Federation of Labor; Paul Kellogg, editor of The Survey Graphic; Helen Hall of the Henry Street Settlement, New York, and the chairman, Frank Graham of the University of North Carolina, in approving it.

The others who favored the proposal were Walter Teagle of the Standard Oil Company of New Jersey; Gerard Swope of the General Electric Company; Morris E. Leeds of Leeds & Northrup, Philadelphia; Sam Lewisohn of the Miami Copper Company, New York, and Marion B. Folsom of the Eastman Kodak Company, Rochester.

Besides these nine actually voting there was Mgr. John A. Ryan, who had to leave before the vote was taken but left instructions that he be recorded in the affirmative. Raymond Moley attended the meeting but took no part in the discussion.

According to advocates of the Federal-State subsidy plan, its advantage over the Wagner-Lewis bill is that it would enable the government to formulate standards below which the States might not fall in their job insurance laws, under penalty of forfeiting the Federal subsidies.

Other Plan Embodies Tax.

The Wagner-Lewis bill is a device for a Federal tax on all employers' payrolls. The government would make no payments to the States adopting unemployment insurance laws, but employers in those States enacting such legislation would be credited with their payments into that fund.

For instance, if the Federal payroll tax were 3 per cent and a State insurance scheme called for a 3 per cent contribution by employers, the latter would be freed from the necessity of making any payment whatever on the Federal excise tax.

This plan was evolved to avoid the problem of direct Federal payments out of an excise tax, to which some constitutional lawyers have objected.

Under the Wagner-Lewis device, the government would have no con-

Continued on Page Two.

$590,000 in Securities Vanishes at Bank; Theft Is Discounted in Wall St. Mystery

Fourteen United States Treasury notes worth $590,000 disappeared Thursday from the United States Trust Company of New York, 45 Wall Street, under circumstances which convinced police that they had not been stolen. The police theory was that the loss was an accident.

The notes, which were of the 2⅞ per cent issue due June 15, 1938, were delivered at the securities cage of the trust company at 11:45 A. M. by two messengers. The clerk who received them placed them about two and a half feet from the wicket on the counter within the cage.

There was a misunderstanding about what the messengers were to receive in return, and, while they waited, the clerk made inquiries of officials of the trust company and also talked by telephone with the First Boston Corporation, 100 Broadway, the office from which the notes had come.

He was away from his window no more than ten minutes. When he returned the fourteen notes, which he had left clipped together on the counter, were gone.

Acting Captain Thomas F. Murray, in charge of First District detectives, said that neither the police nor officials of the trust company had the slightest suspicion of any of the six men who were at work in the cage at the time. That disposed of the "inside job" theory.

Captain Murray said also that it would have been impossible for a sneak thief outside the cage in the lobby to have reached the notes unless he "fished" for them through the barred wicket with a spear or a clip attached to a stick more than two feet long.

"There were people around all the time," Captain Murray explained, "and any thief trying to fish for them would have had a hard time. I'm sure it couldn't be done."

That disposed of the "outside

Continued on Page Eight.

MAYOR BACKS TERA ON RELIEF STORES

Denies That City Was Glutted With Food—Minimizes the Potato Spoilage.

CALLS HODSON TO ACCOUNT

Relief Head Told to Explain Why 8,000 Supply Tickets Are Vanishing Monthly.

Following the issuance yesterday of a statement by the State TERA denying that it had glutted New York City with surplus foodstuffs, Mayor La Guardia said an investigation directed by him had shown that the TERA was not at fault in the handling of relief foods.

Carl Anderson, head of the food and clothing distribution division of the Welfare Department, had testified before the Aldermen's committee investigating relief last Thursday that the TERA had sent him 9,000,000 pounds of cabbage when he asked for 300,000. The session disclosed that a quantity of surplus potatoes had frozen and rotted in a Brooklyn warehouse, and the amount was estimated at 1,200,000 pounds. It was also brought out in Mr. Anderson's testimony that the city had not been able to move 11,000,000 pounds of veal from the Bronx Terminal Market because machines for cutting it were lacking.

Sees Facts Misrepresented.

Mayor La Guardia accused the press of misrepresenting the actual state of affairs, although most of the accounts consisted of questions put to Mr. Anderson by members of the Aldermen's committee and his replies.

"A preliminary investigation has been made of the handling of this food," the Mayor said, "and I find that there have been some glaring misstatements of fact—as reported in the press.

"There is no oversupply of cabbage. The last shipment of cabbage was 184 carloads. Sixty carloads went to New Jersey. That left 124. Fifty-one carloads have been distributed and seventy-three remain to be distributed. The seventy-three carloads constitute a ten-day supply.

"Now for the potatoes. There have been no excess shipments of potatoes here, except recently, when cold weather struck Maine and the Federal agencies shipped two shiploads here to prevent them from freezing in Maine. That amounted to 140,000 bags, all of which were properly stored in heated warehouses, except for 20,000 bags, which were sent to a corrugated iron warehouse in Brooklyn. How much of that shipment was frozen and spoiled has not been determined, but the belief is that only the outside bags were spoiled.

"Families on relief are allowed fifty pounds of potatoes a month.

"Concerning the 11,000,000 pounds of veal in the Bronx market, I want to say that the saws for cutting it are all right. I had them examined this morning by the Commissioner of Accounts, Paul Blanshard, and

Continued on Page Fourteen.

1935 COTTON CURB VOTED BY GROWERS

Referendum in South Goes About 9 to 1 for Retention of Bankhead Act.

2 STATES OUTSIDE TREND

Only Oklahoma and California Fail to Give Needed Margin of Two-thirds.

By The Associated Press.

By a majority far more than the necessary two-thirds the South's cotton farmers went on record yesterday for compulsory crop control by voting to continue the Bankhead act in 1935.

Almost from the start of the count the only question was the size of the majority for the legislation which imposes a tax on cotton sold in excess of a quota fixed by the Secretary of Agriculture.

A tabulation early today showed 885,862 votes for continuance and 90,352 against it.

Only Oklahoma and California failed to show the necessary two-thirds majority.

Oklahoma voted 41,741 for continuance of the act and 27,145 against.

In Alabama, home State of Senator Bankhead, whose name the law bears, 132,198 cotton growers voted in favor compared with 6,429 against.

The late tabulation was believed to be nearly final, since it recorded almost one-half of the voters eligible. About 2,600,000 growers were officially registered by the Farm Administration as having the right to vote and Secretary Wallace estimated previously that about half of that number would cast ballots.

Governor Eugene Talmadge of Georgia opposed the measure, but returns in his State showed 108,985 for and 17,543 against.

Tabulation by States.

The latest tabulation showed:

State.	Number Favoring.	Number Against.
Alabama	132,198	6,429
Arkansas	64,389	3,009
Arizona	1,161	459
California	1,051	585
Florida	1,656	60
Georgia	121,329	18,630
Kentucky	92	35
Louisiana	96,173	2,566
Mississippi	164,824	5,143
Missouri	4,413	767
North Carolina	105,022	8,968
Oklahoma	41,741	27,145
South Carolina	29,154	2,109
Tennessee	47,247	4,925
Texas	68,139	9,278
Virginia	7,273	244
Total	885,862	90,352

President Roosevelt endorsed the act and this undoubtedly had much to do with the result.

Georgia Margin Is Large.

ATLANTA, Dec. 14 (AP).—Georgia cotton farmers gave a ratio of more than 6 to 1 for continuance of the Bankhead Cotton Control Act.

The latest returns from the State in today's referendum gave: Yes, 121,329; no, 18,630.

At Athens, Daniel Gilham, a Negro about 60 years old, said he voted for the bill, adding:

"I allows it's better to make a little money on a few bales than to lose money on a heap of bales." He said he owned a fifty-acre farm in the Sandy Creek district.

The interest of Negroes in the

Continued on Page Twenty-seven.

Museum of the City of New York

Cooking in a junk-filled lot.

Museum of the City of New York

The homeless slept in doorways.

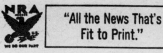

"All the News That's Fit to Print."

The New York Times.

LATE CITY EDITION
WEATHER—Cloudy today; rain and warmer tomorrow.
Temperatures yesterday: Max., 35, min., 28.
Detailed Weather Report, Section 2, Page 8N

Section 1

Copyright, 1935, by The New York Times Company.

VOL. LXXXIV....No. 28,113. Entered as Second-Class Matter, Postoffice, New York, N. Y. NEW YORK, SUNDAY, JANUARY 13, 1935. Including Rotogravure Picture, Magazine and Book Sections. F TEN CENTS | TWELVE CENTS Beyond 200 Miles, Except in 7th and 8th Postal Zones.

MISS EARHART FLIES PACIFIC FROM HAWAII IN 18¼ HOURS; FINDS OAKLAND DESPITE FOG

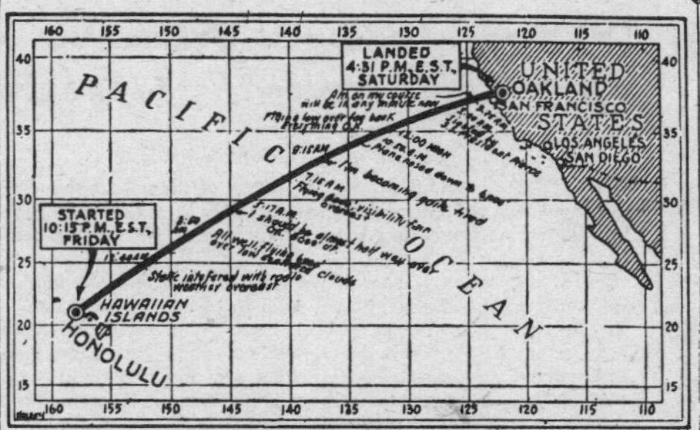

THE HOP FROM HAWAII TO OAKLAND. Amelia Earhart's course over the Pacific and her progress on the 2,400-mile flight as she reported it by radiophone.

WEARY WHEN SHE LANDS

Big Crowd Greets Her at Finish of the Trip From Honolulu.

NEVER LOST, SHE ASSERTS

Perfect Landing Made After Direct Flight of 2,400 Miles Over the Sea.

HOP SETS NEW RECORDS

First Solo Flight Over the Pacific—Doctor Orders Her to Rest After Ordeal.

Special to THE NEW YORK TIMES.

SAN FRANCISCO, Calif., Jan. 12.—Out of the wind and rain-whipped Pacific came Amelia Earhart today, winging low at the end of a transpacific flight which made the whole world wonder, to a tumultuous greeting at Oakland Airport.

In from the Pacific she came in her big, high-winged monoplane after 18 hours 16 minutes of lone flying over the ocean wastes from Honolulu to make a perfect landing before 10,000 cheering onlookers.

It was at 1:31 P. M. [4:31 New York time]—after the huge crowd had been waiting hours for word of her and after rumors and counter-rumors had cast a spell of fear over the crowd—that Miss Earhart, No. 1 woman flier of the United States, slid in to a nonchalant landing from an altitude of scarcely 200 feet.

Surprises the Crowd.

She took the crowd by surprise. They had been scanning the skies for a lone plane searching for its landing field. But in she came, straight as an arrow, spurning a preliminary circle of the field, gliding down to a perfect landing in the centre of the big Oakland Airport.

As the plane swung and taxied toward the hangars there came a roar from 10,000 throats, a cheer louder than any heard before at the field where many distance flights have been concluded. The crowd broke from the police barriers and rushed toward Miss Earhart's plane—a dangerous rush as the propeller was still spinning.

But the police pushed the crowd back—men, women and children—while innumerable automobile horns tooted a clamor of greeting from the road circling the field.

The propeller came to a stop as the engine died, and the isinglass cover of the cockpit opened. Then the first woman—or any person, for that matter—to fly the Pacific alone thrust her tousled head into view.

She smiled wearily at the tremendous greeting. A huge bunch of red roses was thrust into her arms, and she clasped them.

The airport attendants pushed the plane backward into the navy hangar and closed the huge doors on the shouting crowd.

Before she vanished behind the hangar doors, Miss Earhart was heard to remark:

"I had enough gasoline left to fly for several hours."

Hits Objective "On the Nose."

Her speed reduced by headwinds, her course altered time and time again by towering cloud banks and fog, Miss Earhart drove her plane on over the ocean at high altitudes to hit San Francisco "on the nose."

It was a workmanlike job, one that paralleled the historic flight that Colonel Charles A. Lindbergh made across the Atlantic, a flight that climaxed a gallant career with a gallant gesture.

In all of those 18 hours and 16 minutes since Miss Earhart lifted her heavily loaded plane from a soggy runway at Wheeler Field, Honolulu, her ship had been sighted only once.

She had been seen winging toward the coast line, not quite sure of her course, over the Dollar liner President Pierce off the California coast. At that time she asked for directions, requesting that a shore radio station give her a position. The steamer captain estimated that she was south of her course, but apparently she made a hasty correction and drove in for her objective.

All of the communications from the plane through the night hours were by Miss Earhart's voice as she

Continued on Page Twenty-eight.

Amelia Earhart's Own Story Of Her Flight Over Pacific

Her Greatest Hazard Was Adverse Criticism Before the Start—Never Experienced Any Nervousness—Weather Not 'Really Bad.'

By AMELIA EARHART.

Copyright, 1935, by the New York Times Company and NANA, Inc.

OAKLAND, Calif., Jan. 12.—The flight from Honolulu was attempted with no thought of proving anything aeronautical. I can only hope one more passage across that portion of the Pacific succeeds in marking a little more plainly the pathway over which the inevitable air service of the future will fly. To me, also, it seemed good training for other hoped-for long-distance flights.

It came off primarily because the preparation of plane and equipment was admirably handled by Paul Mantz of Burbank, Calif., to whom belongs a large measure of credit. After all, others have flown this stretch, and there are many competent pilots, women as well as men, who will do it again.

As a place to prepare for a flight, Hawaii has one serious drawback. It is so altogether delightful one hates to leave it. But Thursday night I felt that the plane, my Lockheed Vega, was ready and its pilot in condition. Then Lieutenant Stephens, who was very helpful, announced that Friday's weather map would be as favorable as we might reasonably expect.

So yesterday forenoon I rested while the men at the field loaded about 500 gallons of gasoline into the tanks. Then came a final check of weather reports and storing of articles needed on the flight. By 1 o'clock I was ready.

Wanted to Escape Fuss at Start.

This final preparation was accomplished very cautiously. I wanted to escape the fuss and crowds of a preannounced departure. It was easier to have no "Aloha." So I let most of those immediately concerned understand that it was to be simply a test take-off with load, but I was determined that if all went well I'd head for California.

It was at 4:45 P. M., Honolulu time, that I left, and at 5 o'clock I saw Makapuu Point, the last island outpost, fade into the distance. It had been raining, the wind was almost non-existent, and the field was somewhat muddy. When I started out there were clouds all about, and I was among clouds all night. The moon hung brilliantly in the sky until about midnight and millions of stars seemed near enough to touch.

Acting upon the advice of the United States Navy Aerological Bureau, I flew at an average of 8,000 feet, and I ran through many rain squalls during the night. But never, in my many flights, have I ever seen so many stars or clouds. Thus much water was half hidden from my sight by little woolly clouds.

I didn't encounter really bad weather throughout the entire flight, and the greatest hazard I had to overcome was the criticism heaped on my head for even contemplating the flight. For this reason it was infinitely more difficult than my two Atlantic flights. The criticism I had received before taking off from Hawaii was entirely unwarranted and manifested itself in a physical strain more difficult than fatigue. Throughout the night I felt this, yet I never experienced actual nervousness.

Charts for Alternate Courses.

I carried the charts prepared by Clarence Williams, Los Angeles consultant in navigation. These showed alternate courses, one to Oakland, the other to Los Angeles. The choice depended upon weather. Before the takeoff I picked Oakland, shorter by 150 miles, and I was able to stick to this course because of the favorable weather conditions.

The charts required almost hourly changes in compass course, calculated on an average speed of 150 miles per hour, a speed that I did not live up to through the entire trip. On them, too, were plotted the Department of Commerce airway radio beams reaching westerly from Oakland and Los Angeles.

To maintain the flying schedule planned I had three compasses and three clocks. One of the timepieces was set at 12 so that it ticked off from the commencement of the flight the actual minutes elapsed.

Besides being the first solo flight across the Pacific, this was the first long flight in which the radio telephone was used, and I found it almost miraculous in its accuracy. I had remarkable reception throughout the night and had splendid cooperation from Stations KFI and KPO, after 7 A. M., which kept open all night to assist me. I had my responses from them in twelve minutes, and sometimes less.

Wasted Time With Difficult Compass.

I wasted some time in my eighteen hours and fifteen minutes of flying because the type of compass I used proved very difficult to follow at night. Great accuracy is required in using a compass for a successful long flight, and I found it important to keep a true course all the time.

Feeling I was losing time, I throttled down in order to save gasoline. The ship's normal speed is 160 miles per hour, but I averaged throughout the flight a little over 140.

I was constantly over fog banks, but I didn't find these at all disturbing.

For food I carried with me canned tomato juice, hot cocoa, some sandwiches, chocolate and water. I also carried a lunch prepared for me by the wife of an island officer. I sipped a bit of the tomato juice, drank a little water and ate a hard-boiled egg. But I really wasn't very hungry.

For cargo I carried a small bunch of letters and a number of

Continued on Page Twenty-eight.

HAUPTMANN ASKS TO GO ON THE STAND; FIRST FOR DEFENSE

Counsel Reports Him Eager to Deny All Charges and to Tell His Own Story.

WIFE THE SECOND WITNESS

Defense's Experts, Germans Among Them, Begin Close Study of Ransom Notes.

REILLY OUTLINES QUERIES

Concentrates on Handwriting of Fisch but Says He Does Not Seek to Solve Crime.

By RUSSELL B. PORTER.

Special to THE NEW YORK TIMES.

FLEMINGTON, N. J., Jan. 12.—Bruno Richard Hauptmann definitely will take the witness stand in his own defense at his trial here for the murder of Charles A. Lindbergh Jr., it was announced today by Edward J. Reilly, his chief counsel.

Mr. Reilly said he would call Hauptmann as his first witness when the defense begins the presentation of its case, which he expected would be in about two weeks. Mrs. Anna Hauptmann, the prisoner's wife, will be the second defense witness.

C. Lloyd Fisher of defense counsel added that Hauptmann himself demanded of his lawyers this morning that he be allowed to testify from the same chair from which Colonel Lindbergh identified him by the sound of his voice as the man who called to Dr. John F. Condon the night the ransom was paid and from which Dr. Condon identified him as the "John" to whom he paid the ransom and with whom he talked for an hour on a previous night.

From the same chair a taxicab driver identified him as the man who gave him a message to deliver to Dr. Condon during the ransom negotiations, an elderly Hopewell resident identified him as a man he saw near the Lindbergh home in an automobile with a ladder the day of the kidnapping, and a handwriting expert identified his writing as that of the writer of the ransom notes.

Prisoner Eager to Testify.

After visiting the prisoner in his cell in the county jail here this morning, Mr. Fisher said:

"Hauptmann told me that he wanted to get on the witness stand and tell his story, and that was all he asked."

Mr. Reilly said that the first question he would ask Hauptmann on the witness stand would be:

"Did you kidnap the Lindbergh baby?"

After the accused man denies committing the crime, Mr. Reilly said, he would ask the following questions:

"Were you in Hopewell the night of March 1, 1932?"

"Were you in New Jersey that day or night?"

"Did you make the ladder?"

"Did you go up that ladder?"

"Did you write the ransom notes?"

"Did you receive the $50,000 from Dr. Condon?"

On receiving negative replies to all of these questions, according to the lawyer, he will ask:

"Where did you get the money ($14,600 of the ransom money) which was found in your garage?"

The answer will be that the money was left with him by the late Isidor Fisch, the furrier friend of Hauptmann, before Fisch late in 1933 made the trip to Germany where he died.

Reilly Repeats Charge.

Mr. Reilly repeated today his charge that Fisch was the man to whom Dr. Condon paid the ransom in St. Raymond's Cemetery, the Bronx, on the night of April 2, 1932, a month after the kidnapping, and added that handwriting experts consulted by the defense would compare the ransom notes with samples of Fisch's writing in an effort to see whether the furrier wrote the ransom notes.

"Fisch is the man who got the ransom money, and our experts will examine twenty samples of Fisch's writing, which we have in our possession, in comparison with the ransom notes," said Mr. Reilly. "However, our purpose is not to try to solve the crime or to prove who did it, but to prove that Hauptmann is not guilty."

Mr. Reilly said that his handwriting experts had already given him an opinion, based on comparisons of Hauptmann's writing with reproductions of the ransom notes which have appeared in the press,

Continued on Page Thirty.

Capital Debates Gold Issue; Justices Confer for 5 Hours

Speculations on Possibilities of an Adverse Ruling Take Wide Range—Quick Congress Action Is Considered.

By The Associated Press.

WASHINGTON, Jan. 12.—The nine justices of the Supreme Court, who for several days have been hearing arguments on cases attacking the validity of the government's nullification of the gold clause in securities by its monetary legislation, held a long conference today.

The meeting was behind closed doors and lasted until 5 o'clock—an unusually late hour. It was assumed that most of the time was devoted to discussion of the many questions presented by the gold cases.

It is not expected that a decision in these cases will be delivered before Feb. 4, and those closest to the court think it unlikely that a verdict will be handed down until even later.

It is known, however, that the court desires to expedite its opinion in the gold cases as it did in the "hot oil" cases and other New Deal controversies which may reach it for decision.

Meanwhile, quick Congressional action to escape from what administration spokesmen have called possible "chaos" was projected today as a likelihood should the court overturn the Roosevelt monetary program in the "gold clause" cases.

Some persons held that regardless of the coming verdict, the Treasury could make no change in its present method of redeeming maturing government bonds until Congress so ordered.

Although officials would say nothing, and privately expressed confidence that the court would decide in favor of the government, the subject was gone into on Capitol Hill, especially among the inflationist bloc.

A decision against the government would mean, in short, that gold bonds and contracts would be

Continued on Page Two.

JERSEY AIMS TO TAX SALES AND INCOMES

Governor-Elect Hoffman, Here, Works on Program to Be Submitted Next Week.

WOULD AID MUNICIPALITIES

Necessity for Obtaining Relief Funds Vital Factor in the Planning of New Levies.

Governor-elect Harold G. Hoffman of New Jersey will propose a program of new taxes when he takes office at Trenton Tuesday, he indicated yesterday in an interview at the Hotel New Yorker, where he has been for the last few days completing his inaugural address.

Although Mr. Hoffman declined to discuss his contemplated program in detail, it was learned that he has been making a careful study of the financial situation of the municipalities of the State and of the unemployment situation.

It is expected that he will propose both a general sales tax and a State income tax, from both of which New Jersey so far has been free, and also will propose legislation to relieve the real estate taxpayers, whom he believes to be greatly overburdened.

Bars Taxes for Spending.

"I will favor no new taxes unless they are used entirely for relief and not for additional spending," Mr. Hoffman said, maintaining the position he took during his campaign.

In discussing his program with reporters, Mr. Hoffman indicated his belief that new taxes of some sort would be necessary. He declared that eighty-seven municipalities in New Jersey were in default on their borrowings and that the taxes on real estate had become so high in many instances that only a fractional part of them had been collected.

Part of the proposed new taxes, he indicated, would be used for unemployment relief and part to relieve the tax burden of municipalities by having the State assume support of functions the expense of which now is borne by the municipalities.

In New Jersey, he explained, the State does not bear the same proportion of expense of local functions, such as schools, as does New York State. He expressed the opinion that New York State might perhaps have gone too far in aiding local governments and that New Jersey had not gone far enough. He added that he hoped in his program to strike a medium.

Municipal Spending Curb Sought.

Mr. Hoffman, as Governor, will seek to put a curb on the spending of municipalities. He hopes to do this without running counter to home rule sentiment by offering the cities advantages in return for which they will consent to a measure of supervision over their expenditures by a State board.

The Governor-elect expressed approval of the recent action of the acting Governor in abolishing the State codes, established to supplement the codes of the NRA. He added that he believed this action had the approval of the industrialists and the mass of the people of the State.

"The codes were rapidly falling of their own weight," he said. "They were agencies to provide jobs for a few people, tended to price-fixing,

Continued on Page Twenty-seven.

THIEF HURLS WOMAN TO SUBWAY TRACKS

Widow, 53, Saved After Thug Grabs Her Purse and Pushes Her in Path of Train.

CARS HALTED JUST IN TIME

City Employe Risks Life by Leaping to Roadbed to Signal to Motorman.

To facilitate his escape after snatching a woman's handbag containing $8, a sneak thief pushed the owner of the bag, Mrs. Stella Gluckman, 53-year-old widowed mother of four children, on to the northbound tracks of the Independent Subway System at 170th Street and the Grand Concourse, the Bronx, shortly after noon yesterday.

As she toppled headforemost to the tracks, Mrs. Gluckman screamed. She was knocked unconscious when her head hit one of the rails, but a woman on the south-bound platform had heard her. Just then a south-bound train pulled up at the station, and the woman witness excitedly told the train conductor, Ernest Giczi of 370 East 163d Street, of Mrs. Gluckman's plight.

He pulled the emergency lever to open the doors of his train on the side away from the platform station, and jumped down to the track level. As he scrambled over the express tracks toward Mrs. Gluckman's unconscious form, he heard the roar of an approaching northbound train.

Rescuer Halts Train.

Giczi tried to lift Mrs. Gluckman from the tracks, but failed to move her. Still trying to pick her up with one arm, he waved frantically with the other to Motorman Kenneth Kicks of the arriving train and the latter stopped his train only twenty-five feet from the woman.

Meanwhile John J. Quig, a change maker from the north platform, had jumped down to the track level to assist Giczi. Together the two men lifted her to the platform, where she was revived by Dr. Bull, an ambulance surgeon from Morrisania Hospital, who took her to that institution.

Dazed and semi-hysterical, Mrs. Gluckman told Detective William Bechtel of the Bathgate Avenue station that she was on her way from her home at 1,325 Grand Concourse to pay a gas bill. She was waiting for a train near the north end of the station, she said, and the only persons she saw near her were two men, of whom she was able to give only a vague description.

Attacked Without Warning.

Suddenly her bag was torn from her left hand and she was propelled violently over the edge of the platform, toppling to the tracks. She said her bag contained eyeglasses and keys, in addition to the $8.

She did not see her assailant at all, and was not even sure that he was one of the two men she had observed loitering on the station platform, she told the police. From the failure of either man to give the alarm or to go to her aid, however, it was believed probable that they were acting together, one serving as lookout while the other did the actual purse-snatching.

Mrs. Gluckman received severe contusions of the scalp, but X-ray photographs failed to show any fracture of the skull, and last night she was taken to her home.

LA GUARDIA NAMES NEW COMMISSION TO DRAFT CHARTER

Promises It Free Hand and All the Money Needed—Wants Task Done by Fall.

T. D. THACHER IS CHAIRMAN

All Members Are Without Close Political Ties—None of the Smith Board Retained.

A charter revision commission of nine prominent citizens was named yesterday by Mayor La Guardia to undertake the difficult task of drafting a new charter for the city.

The Mayor said the commission, of which Thomas D. Thacher, former Solicitor General of the United States, is chairman, would have an absolutely free hand and all the money needed for its work. It is the Mayor's hope that the commission will have a charter ready for submission to the voters of the city at the election next November.

Appointment of the commission had been awaited ever since last Summer, when the Legislature abolished the commission of which former Governor Alfred E. Smith was chairman and authorized the Mayor to name one of his own. The Smith commission split on the question of abolishing county offices and curtailing the powers of the Borough Presidents. This phase of charter revision constitutes the major problem of the new charter group.

Members of Commission.

The members of the commission are:

Thomas D. Thacher, chairman, of 17 East Seventy-third Street, attorney, former Solicitor General of the United States and a former judge of the Federal District Court. He is a Republican.

Joseph M. Proskauer of 205 West Fifty-seventh Street; former Justice of the Appellate Division of the Supreme Court and a close friend and associate of former Governor Smith. A Democrat.

Thomas I. Parkinson of 270 West End Avenue, attorney and president of the Equitable Life Assurance Society. He is a former dean of the faculty of the Columbia University Law School and is an authority on governmental affairs.

Charles E. Hughes Jr. of Independence Avenue and West 252d Street, the Bronx, an attorney and a former Solicitor General of the United States. He is a son of Chief Justice Charles E. Hughes of the Supreme Court of the United States and is a Republican.

S. John Block of 59 West Twelfth Street, an attorney. He is a prominent Socialist of the Right Wing faction and has several times been a candidate for the Supreme Court, always with the endorsement of the Citizens Union and various bar associations.

Joseph D. McGoldrick of 596 Madison Street, Brooklyn, the former Controller and an authority on municipal government. He is an independent Democrat.

Charles G. Meyer of Bell Avenue, Bayside, Queens, a real estate man connected with the Cord-Meyer concern that built much of Forest Hills. He was chosen to represent the realty interests of the city.

Mrs. William P. Earle Jr. of 120 Willow Street, a former president

Continued on Page Three.

HEAVY SAAR GUARD KEEPS DOWN STRIFE ON PLEBISCITE EVE

Bonfires Across the Frontier Blaze the Nazi Appeal for Return to 'Fatherland.'

FREE CHOICE IS ASSURED

Neutral Officials and Troops to Protect 540,000 Ballots—German Victory Likely.

By FREDERICK T. BIRCHALL.

Wireless to THE NEW YORK TIMES.

SAARBRUECKEN, Jan. 12.—Tomorrow, after fifteen years of peaceful, prosperous existence under the administration of the League of Nations, a half million voters of the Saar Basin territory will cast their ballots to determine the region's future government.

Shall it revert to Germany, shall France take it over or shall it continue under the status quo for a further period, pending some future determination?

France does not want it. Germany does—and ardently. Tonight, as this is written, there are blazing upon hundreds of hills along the German frontier bonfires to express this German longing. They light up all the countryside, bidding the Saarlanders be wakeful and ready to do their duty.

The bonfires repeat the message you see throughout Germany in streamers across highways, high up under the roof of every railway station and again here in shops and in many hotels, but not on public buildings: "Deutsch ist die Saar" (The Saar is German).

And it is. Even after fifteen years of neutral government with French currency and numberless close commercial relations with France, German is the only language you hear here, except from visitors, who are polyglot.

Saar Is Inherently German.

The Saar is German. Its people are German in every trait and every instinct. Tomorrow they will vote by a majority, large or small, for unity with "the homeland." In an issue like this blood tells.

Yet a mere majority may not be decisive. Had this choice been put up to the Saarlanders five years ago, or even three years, there would not have been any doubt as to the result; it would have been overwhelming. But in the meantime Germany has changed. She has fallen under the domination of a militant, intolerant, inelastic political movement, all-possessive of its adherents and bitterly oppressive of its opponents. Germany has become poor and is economically in straits while putting up a brave front so that, in passing through, you would hardly believe it.

The Saar, under neutral rule, has waxed prosperous; it has even been contented.

How many in the territory will now swallow Hitlerism for the sake of reunion with the old land? How many will accept the German slogan, "Better black bread with one's own than white bread with foreigners"? Tomorrow will tell.

There will be a German majority. But there will undoubtedly be a substantial minority for the status quo in the hope that this may be ended if and when Germany changes again and is free. And should that minority be as large as some expect, there will be hesitation at Geneva, where the ultimate decision will be made, over delivering up this minority to Nazism without further guarantees that the

Continued on Page Thirty-one.

2 Policewomen Drag 'Big Shot' to Station After Threatening Him With a 'Mussing-Up'

Two patrolwomen who believe in taking their commissioner literally warned a pickpocket suspect of a "mussing up" if he did not come quietly. They then dragged him half a mile to a station house, it was revealed at the line-up at police headquarters yesterday.

Both the policewomen, Lillian Burck and Martha Mirsberger, are considerably taller and heavier than their prisoner, Frank Madeo, 44 years old, of 1,497 Madison Avenue.

Patrolwoman Burck said that as she was coming to headquarters from her home in Flushing on Friday morning she saw, in the elevator from the Queens line level of the I. R. T. in the Grand Central station, a well-dressed man jostling other persons in the crowded car.

Thinking little about it at the time, she continued to headquarters. Shortly before noon she and her partner received an assignment in Flushing. Getting into the same elevator, Patrolwoman Burck saw the same man, still jostling. She and her companion rode up and down several times, and when the bespectacled man, who was about 5 feet 6 inches tall and weighed about 140 pounds, showed no signs of stopping, they announced that he was under arrest.

"You can't do this to me. I'm a big shot. I'll make trouble for you," they said he retorted.

Warning him that they would stick to the letter of Police Commissioner Valentine's "muss 'em up" order, the patrolwomen closed in. The man's hands were pinned to his side. Unceremoniously he was marched to the street, north nine blocks to Fifty-first Street, then east to the station house. He was booked for disorderly conduct.

The prisoner said he was a contractor. His record showed five arrests since 1911. On Jan. 9 of that year he was sentenced to Elmira for grand larceny and on Jan. 25, 1913, he was sent to Sing Sing for three years on the same charge. His captors casually pointed out to him yesterday that January was a bad month for him.

In Yorkville Court later Magistrate Hulon Capshaw held him without bail for a hearing Tuesday.

NRA WE DO OUR PART

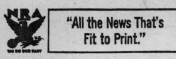

"All the News That's Fit to Print."

The New York Times.

LATE CITY EDITION
WEATHER—Fair today; tomorrow cloudy, rising temperature.
Temperatures Yesterday—Max., 30; min., 20.
Detailed Weather Report Page 20.

VOL. LXXXIV....No. 28,115. Entered as Second-Class Matter, Postoffice, New York, N. Y. NEW YORK, TUESDAY, JANUARY 15, 1935. P TWO CENTS In New York City. | THREE CENTS Within 200 Miles | FOUR CENTS Elsewhere Except in 7th and 8th Postal Zones.

WOMAN SWEARS SHE SAW HAUPTMANN WATCH CONDON BEFORE RANSOM WAS PAID

TESTIMONY A SURPRISE

Model Says Prisoner Spied on 'Jafsie' in Railway Station.

OSBORN FINDINGS BACKED

Second State Expert Asserts That All Ransom Notes Were Written by Defendant.

BOTH CLASH WITH REILLY

Refuse, on Cross-Examination, to Admit Possibility Script Was Imitated.

Digest of yesterday's testimony will be found on Page 14.

By RUSSELL B. PORTER.

Special to THE NEW YORK TIMES.

FLEMINGTON, N. J., Jan. 14.—Another positive identification was added today to the circumstantial evidence which the State of New Jersey is offering against Bruno Richard Hauptmann in his trial for the murder of Charles A. Lindbergh Jr.

Miss Hildegarde Olga Alexander, 26 years old, a saleswoman and clothing model for a gown manufacturer in mid-Manhattan, who lives in the Bronx, swore that she saw Hauptmann watching Dr. John F. Condon, the "Jafsie" of the Lindbergh ransom negotiations, in the Fordham station of the New York Central Railroad on a night in March, 1932.

It was about 6:15 or 6:30 o'clock on a Monday or Tuesday evening between the time Dr. Condon had become publicly known as the "Jafsie" of the ransom negotiations, and the time it was published that he had paid the ransom, Miss Alexander testified. She could not recall the exact date.

Second Link to Condon.

Miss Alexander was the second State witness to corroborate parts of Dr. Condon's testimony that Hauptmann was the "John" with whom he carried on negotiations during March, 1932, and to whom he paid the $50,000 ransom on April 2 of that year. The first was Joseph Perrone, Bronx taxicab driver, who has testified that Hauptmann was the man who gave him $1 during that period to take a message to Dr. Condon's home in the Bronx.

Miss Alexander was a surprise witness. She testified before the Bronx grand jury which indicted Hauptmann for extortion before he was extradited, but the authorities kept her identity a secret because she had asked to be protected from publicity. Bronx authorities brought her to the prosecution headquarters at Trenton last night, accompanied by her mother, and brought her here this morning.

A second handwriting expert testified for the State today that Hauptmann wrote all the ransom notes, and that it was impossible that anybody else could have copied samples of his writing in order to imitate his writing in drafting the ransom notes.

This witness was Elbridge W. Stein of New York, who showed to the jury his own charts illustrating the similarities and peculiarities of Hauptmann's writing and the writing on the ransom notes.

Osborn Ends Testimony.

Albert S. Osborn of New York, the State's chief handwriting expert, completed the testimony he began last week. Repeating his identification of Hauptmann's writing as identical with the writing of the ransom notes, he asserted that the physical evidence was "irresistible, unanswerable and overwhelming."

Prolonged cross-examination by Edward J. Reilly and C. Lloyd Fisher of defense counsel failed to shake either Osborn or Stein in their conviction that Hauptmann and he alone could have written the ransom notes. Defense counsel tried to bring out that Isidor Fisch, Hauptmann's furrier friend, who, according to Hauptmann's story to the police, gave him the ransom money found in the Hauptmann garage, could have written the ransom notes in imitation of Hauptmann's handwriting, but the witness insisted that this could not have happened.

Handwriting experts will occupy the stand for at least one and per-

Continued on Page Fifteen.

Two Handwriting Experts Quit the Defense; Bronx Ladder 'Builder' Not to Be Called

From a Staff Correspondent.

FLEMINGTON, N. J., Jan. 14.—Two of the defense handwriting experts at the Hauptmann trial, Samuel C. Malone and Arthur P. Meyers, quit the case today and returned to their homes in Baltimore.

Edward J. Reilly, chief of the defense, asserted that they had left because "the defense did not have the money to pay them."

In prosecution circles, however, it was pointed out that the announcement of their withdrawal was not made until after Albert S. Osborn, State expert, had said that any one who could not see that the writing of the ransom notes was that of Hauptmann was "either incompetent or dishonest."

The testimony of Miss Hildegarde Alexander that she saw Hauptmann shadowing Dr. Condon was termed "very significant" by Attorney General David T. Wilentz tonight. He interpreted her story as "completely eliminating any defense inference that Ollie Whateley, Isidor Fisch, Henry (Red) Johnson or Miss Betty Gow was implicated in the kidnapping."

C. Lloyd Fisher of the defense attacked Miss Alexander's veracity, however.

"I do not think she was telling the truth," he said. "She testified that in March she knew Dr. Condon was engaged in ransom negotiations for Colonel Lindbergh, when, as a matter of fact, at that time very few people outside of Dr. Condon's family and those close to Colonel Lindbergh knew that he was. That fact alone should discredit her."

After a careful investigation of his story, the prosecution has decided not to call as a witness Abraham Samuelsohn, the Bronx cabinetmaker who claims to have made the kidnap ladder for Hauptmann, it was disclosed by Anthony M. Hauck Jr., Prosecutor of Hunterdon County. Samuelsohn actually did make the box in which the ransom was paid, Mr. Hauck said.

Dr. Condon forgot the cabinetmaker's name and address, however, and it was not until last year that Department of Justice agents located him, Mr. Hauck said. They had him build two replicas of the box, and a miniature reproduction, two feet long, of the ladder, for study by the investigators. Mr. Hauck said he believed Samuelsohn had confused this incident into his tale that Hauptmann had him build a ladder.

POLICEMAN LINKED TO MISSING WOMAN

Admits Signing Her Name to Notes After She Vanished Seven Months Ago.

SUSPENDED BY VALENTINE

Posed as Husband of Queens Divorcee—Says She Left Car on Way to Hospital.

The mysterious disappearance more than seven months ago of Mrs. Florence Neacy Paul of Flushing, divorcee, mother of two children and sister of a Wall Street broker, was revealed yesterday when Patrolman Frank Louis Schultz of the Flushing precinct was suspended from duty.

Police Commissioner Lewis J. Valentine said that the vanishing of Mrs. Paul as she rode to a maternity hospital with Schultz is similar in many ways to the strange disappearance of Agnes Tufverson, middle-aged lawyer, which created a sensation last Summer.

Schultz, tall, with deep-set eyes, sturdy physique and black hair, was stripped of his shield and pistol in the commissioner's presence on Sunday after he had been questioned on the Paul case by the chief and his staff for more than fourteen hours.

No criminal charge was entered against Schultz.

Checking Angles of Case.

"There are several angles in this case that we are trying to check," said Assistant Chief Inspector John J. Sullivan, "but at this time Schultz is only under suspension."

Schultz is 31 years old, a veteran of the World War, is married and has two daughters, Dorothy, 6, and Frances, 3. His family lives in one of a row of houses at 59-30 Fifty-eighth Road, Maspeth. He has been on the force seven years.

Mrs. Paul, a small woman, 32, was divorced from her husband, George Alton Paul, in 1931. She retained custody of her 12-year-old son and her daughter, Lorraine, 8, with whom she lived at that time in Whitestone, Queens.

Schultz Left His Family.

Schultz told his superiors that he became acquainted with Mrs. Paul while he was doing duty at a crossing near the school her children attended in Flushing, in the Spring of 1933. A few months later—in September—he left his family.

He told the commissioner and his staff that he had quarreled with his wife. She had found in his uniform a postcard signed by "Florence"

Continued on Page Three.

WIND LASHES CITY; 10° COLD DUE TODAY

Mercury at 20° as a 55-Mile Blow Topples Signs—Streets Are Coated With Ice.

ROWER MAROONED 5 HOURS

Gale Grounds His Boat on an Island in Jamaica Bay—Middle West Hard Hit.

Ice-glazed streets and a blustery northwest wind caused discomfort and several minor accidents in the metropolitan area yesterday.

In outlying sections tire chains clanked over rutted ice and snow. In the city pedestrians stepped gingerly along sanded sidewalks and shielded their faces from the blasts of a wind that at times reached a velocity of fifty-five miles an hour.

The mercury dropped sharply in the morning, going from 32 degrees at 8 A. M. to 23 at noon. The fall continued last night, the mercury touching 20 at 10 P. M., the last official reading for the night. Before dawn today the city's thermometers were expected to register 10 degrees.

Continued cold, but with diminishing winds, was forecast for today by the Weather Bureau. The day is expected to be fair and temperatures are likely to vary between 10 and 20 degrees, but no snow is expected.

Other Areas Are Hit.

Yesterday's weather was much the same as that in other areas. The northwester whipped the seaboard from the Delaware Breakwater to Boston. Up-State the whistling wind piled snow into drifts that delayed cross-State buses.

The Middle West was much more severely struck, according to The Associated Press. The mercury dropped to 32 below zero at Bemidji, Minn. A man was frozen to death in that State and a 15-year-old unidentified boy was frozen to death in Illinois. Chicago experienced near-zero weather and the cold wave swept into Michigan, Indiana and Ohio.

One accident attributable to ice-covered streets was reported here. Mrs. Faun Wallick, 40, of 410 West Twenty-third Street, suffered a possible fracture of the skull from a fall at Broadway and Twenty-third Street.

The wind, which blew in strong gusts throughout the day, kept police emergency squads active as it loosened signs and other objects exposed to its full force.

Emergency Squad 4 tried to take down a six-foot copper cross atop the Evangelical Church of Holy Trinity, Central Park West and Sixty-fifth Street, but succeeded only

Continued on Page Five.

REVALUED DOLLAR IS URGED IF COURT UPSETS GOLD ACTS

Experts at Capital Consider a Return to Old Weight as Way to Bar Debt Chaos.

WORLD COURT HAS ACTED

Hughes a Member When Brazil Was Ordered to Pay in Gold, but the Cases Differ.

Special to THE NEW YORK TIMES.

WASHINGTON, Jan. 14.—The possibility that a decision adverse to the government in the gold clause cases pending before the Supreme Court might cause Congress to return to the dollar its original gold content and thus effectively prevent further inflation by this route was being discussed today among Federal experts.

Unlike certain Congressional leaders who, through fear of financial chaos, declined even to consider what might happen if the court rules against the government, the departmental experts reached the opinion that such action would have definite advantages.

They believed that President Roosevelt would have ample ground on which to ask Congress to repeal the act whereby it devalued the dollar, and to revalue upward to the level prevailing prior to abrogation of the gold clause and devaluation.

The experts made it plain that they were merely speculating on alternatives should the decision go against the government, and were not engaged in preparing any plan for possible official use.

For Quick Revaluation Act.

The fear among Congressional leaders that financial chaos might follow an adverse decision grows out of the belief that the effect would be to raise gold bonds and gold-clause contracts to 169 per cent of their face value, by requiring payment according to the former value of the gold dollar.

The experts contend that an act of Congress revaluing the dollar upward to meet this contingency not only would be the simplest but probably the most politic thing to do. They hold that dollar devaluation has not measured up to expectations. It has helped domestic prices but little, they contend, and its value in stimulating foreign trade, apparent at first, has largely disappeared.

Speaker Byrns joined the group today which contends that there is too much at stake to fear an adverse decision from the Supreme Court.

"It means too much to the country," he said as he predicted that the court would uphold the government.

Treasury Busy With "Home Work."

Although the Congressional leaders had not considered a course in the event of an adverse decision, Treasury officials were known to have been canvassing the possibilities. Secretary Morgenthau, at a press conference today, said "we are doing considerable home work" on the gold clause cases.

In their search for every possible indication of what the court might do, some Washington observers today ran upon a decision of the Court of International Justice at The Hague, rendered July 12, 1929, holding valid the gold clause in Brazilian bonds.

The case was seized upon as high-

Continued on Page Four.

GOVERNMENT BARS DEAL WITH UTILITY ON LIGHT BILL HERE

Carlisle Rebuffed on Offer to Cut Federal Power Cost by $60,000 a Year.

PLAN FOR PLANT RETAINED

Companies Had Their Chance, Morgenthau Says—Talks With Mayor Awaited.

The Federal Government, through Rear Admiral R. E. Bakenhus, Public Works officer in the New York district, rejected yesterday an offer made by the Consolidated Gas system to cut by $60,000 a year the bills of the government for lighting in Federal buildings and power for other Federal purposes in this district.

In Washington Secretary of the Treasury Morgenthau said in reply to a question that the Federal Government had no intention of abandoning its plans for its own power plant here even if the companies reduced their rates. The companies had had their chance to reduce rates, the Secretary indicated.

Admiral Bakenhus's letter was made public after he had conferred in the afternoon with Mayor La Guardia at City Hall. Although the Mayor offered no comment, it was believed the result would be that the city administration would hold out for substantial concessions from the Consolidated Gas system, both for itself and for consumers, on the strength of its plans for municipal street lighting plants.

The companies are prepared to make concessions that they consider substantial, it also became known. Floyd L. Carlisle, head of the system, is expected to outline those proposals to the Mayor whenever a conference can be arranged. Unless the Mayor balks at attending such a conference it is expected one will be held soon.

Resigned to a Rate Cut.

At the conference the company's representatives are expected to inform the Mayor that they realize a substantial immediate cut in the rates for general consumers must be made to appease public sentiment and to end the anti-utility drive being carried on by the Federal and city governments.

They also are prepared to submit to the Public Service Commission and the city a list of specific items, part or all of which they concede might be wiped from the existing rate base in the formation of a rate base under the Washington plan of rate reduction. Mayor La Guardia called for such a list in his letter to Mr. Carlisle, which was published in yesterday's newspapers.

In addition, it became known, the proposed merger of the seven electric companies in the Consolidated system would include the gas properties of the Consolidated Gas Company itself. The properties and corporate structure would be merged, but separate accounts would be maintained so that the consumers would get their share of the excess profits of the electric system under the Washington plan without having to bear any of the deficits of the gas system.

The gas "deficits" are deficits only in the sense that the company has not been earning the legal rate of return on its investment in the gas business.

The companies in their conference with the Mayor are expected

Continued on Page Two.

Dutch Court Backs U. S. Ban on Gold Clause; Lets Oil Concerns Pay in Devalued Dollars

Wireless to THE NEW YORK TIMES.

THE HAGUE, Netherlands, Jan. 14.—The Netherlands High Court of Justice decided today that the Royal Dutch Shell Company and the Batavia Petroleum Company were no longer obligated to fulfill the gold payment clauses of their dollar bonds floated in Amsterdam and New York.

In February, 1934, a lower court here had ruled that the Royal Dutch Shell Company must meet its payments under the gold clause but that the Batavia Petroleum Company was exempt.

The High Court of Justice held today that the gold clause in the bonds of the Royal Dutch Shell must be regarded as having relation to gold coin and not to gold value.

The court declared that since in the Netherlands the legislators had frequently taken action similar to that of the United States Congress, it could not be said the law abrogating the gold clause was in conflict with the administration of justice in the Netherlands.

The Stockbrokers Association of Amsterdam has already filed notice of an appeal to the Supreme Court of the Netherlands.

Today's judgment caused a great sensation on the Amsterdam Stock Exchange. Royal Dutch Shell 4 per cent bonds fell from 88 to 65, while Batavia Petroleum 4½s declined to 63½, later rallying to 65.

Although the bonds involved in the decision by the Netherlands court were sold both here and in Amsterdam, they contain the promise to pay interest and principal in "United States gold coin." The question involved, it is stated, is virtually the same as that now before the Supreme Court of the United States, on which arguments were held last week.

The contention of the Royal Dutch Shell Company was that the payment of gold coin was impossible because of American legislation in May, 1933, abrogating the gold clause. Holders in the Netherlands, however, maintained that they were not bound by the legislation enacted here, and therefore took the matter to court when the Royal Dutch Company tendered only the equivalent of present currency in payment of interest. It is understood that most of the bonds are held in the Netherlands.

SAAR GOES GERMAN BY 90%; LEAGUE DELIBERATES TODAY; ANTI-NAZIS ALREADY FLEEING

Frick Ready to Take Command of Saar; Little Mercy Seen for Reich Emigres

BERLIN, Jan. 14.—Germany has perfected every detail to enable the reincorporation of the Saar Valley into the Reich within a month, Minister of the Interior Wilhelm Frick said today.

Dr. Frick declared that a month would be more than is needed to accomplish the technical and administrative tasks involved. He is charged with the details of absorbing the Territory in anticipation of the plebiscite victory.

"According to the report of Baron Pompeo Aloisi to the League of Nations Council Dec. 3, 1934," he said, "a minimum term of one month was envisaged. That is quite sufficient for us.

"According to the agreement, the Reich must pay France 900,000,000 francs (about $59,000,000) for the repurchase of the Saar coal mines. The German Reich will have no difficulty in raising foreign exchange to comply with the method of payment prescribed.

"The German Government as early as June 4, 1934, pledged itself concerning all those qualified to vote and even regarding those unqualified who lived in the Saar Valley at least three years, that such persons would neither be persecuted nor even placed at a disadvantage on account of their attitude in the plebiscite campaign. We are willing unequivocally to stick to our promise."

Although Dr. Frick did not refer to the emigrés who flocked to the Saar after Chancellor Hitler's rise to power, there was little doubt such persons may expect little mercy if they agitated against the Third Reich.

Dr. Frick said the Reich will execute a far-flung plan for job creation.

From the administrative point of view the Minister declared:

"The Saar will remain a separate administrative entity within the Reich. Only later, when the Reich has been redistricted, will the Saar be incorporated into one of the districts.

"But its leading political and economic organization, so-called German Front, will not simply be bodily taken over by the Nazi party. On the contrary, every German within the Saar Territory will for himself, freely and without compulsion, be enabled to join the Nazi party or its subsidiary movement."

PRESBYTERY ENTERS CLEAN-FILM DRIVE

Commends Legion of Decency but Votes Down Motion Praising Catholic Church.

PASTORS IN HEATED DEBATE

Moderator Issues Warning of 'Unchristian Attitude' After the Adverse Ballot.

The Presbytery of New York decided unanimously at its mid-Winter meeting yesterday afternoon in the parish house of the Fifth Avenue Presbyterian Church, at Fifty-fifth Street, to enter the crusade against indecent moving pictures.

It voted down, however, a motion "to commend the spirit and purpose of the Roman Catholic Church in the promotion of decency in the motion picture industry."

This motion later was amended, following a half-hour's devotional service, to commend the Legion of Decency, but mention of the Roman Catholic Church was omitted.

The amendment, adopted after many had gone home, was: "That although the program of the presbytery to improve the standard of motion pictures is not in all points the same as that of the Legion of Decency, the presbytery commends the purpose of the legion in the spirit of friendliness."

Urges Bulletins on Films.

The formal report as adopted recommended that lists of approved pictures be put on the church bulletin boards as is being done now in all Roman Catholic churches.

There was some criticism of the Roman Catholic Church during the debate before the first vote was taken. Then came the prayer service, as provided by the docket for the meeting. It was led by the Rev. George M. Duff, pastor of Riverdale Church. At the close of this period, the Rev. Dr. Daniel Russell, the Moderator, said the Presbytery had come "pretty close" to showing an un-Christian attitude "to a great sister communion."

"I wish we could do something about it," he continued. "I regret so many of the men who were here when we took that action have now gone home. But I do not feel satisfied with that action. I wish it had never come before us."

The Rev. Roswell P. Barnes, pastor of the University Heights Church, as chairman of the Social Service Committee of Presbytery, presented the proposed amendment.

The Rev. Dr. A. Edwin Keigwin, pastor of the West End Church,

Continued on Page Twenty-three.

ASKS STATE TO BUY 6,000,000 ACRES

Planning Board Would Acquire Submarginal Land in a 20-Year Program.

PICTURES WIDE BENEFITS

All Citizens Would Gain, Says Report Sent to Legislature by Lehman.

Text of a digest of the report on State planning on Page 2.

Special to THE NEW YORK TIMES.

ALBANY, Jan. 14.—The acquisition by the State, over a twenty-year period, of some 6,000,000 acres of abandoned or submarginal farm land is recommended by the New York State Planning Board in a preliminary progress report presented to Governor Lehman today and transmitted by him, with a special message, to the Legislature.

The report was the first since the unofficial board headed by Dr. A. R. Mann, provost of Cornell University, was appointed by Governor Lehman in March, 1934. A final report of the board, which was one of forty-one such State bodies set up at the instance of the National Resources Board to study State planning, will be made about April 1.

The 6,000,000 acres acquisition recommended in today's report would bring the State's "public domain" to 9,000,000 acres, or more than one-fourth of the total State area.

The acquisition would be of great economic and social benefit, the report holds, and would relieve expense to the State and its citizens. Used for "reforestation, for game and wild life protection, for watershed protection and for public recreation," these lands could become a distinct asset to the State instead of a liability, it is declared.

Would Regulate Billboards.

The board also recommends the regulation of service stations, billboards and other structures along the highways, and says that such control might be vested in the State Division of Highways. It also urges the creation of a permanent State Planning Council, with "planning a continuous process."

In his special message, the Governor commended the report to careful study by the Legislature and the people of the State. While making no plea for immediate legislation based on its recommendations, he declared that they bear out the need of many measures urged in his annual message, such as those for farm-to-market highways, county and town govern-

Continued on Page Two.

VOTE RESULT ANNOUNCED

476,089 for the Nazis, Status Quo 46,613, France 2,083.

TALLY GOES ON ALL NIGHT

Saarbruecken Building Filled With Armed Police—Tellers Not Allowed Outside.

ANTI-NAZIS ARE FEARFUL

Feel Trapped With the French Frontier Closed—Trouble Is Possible Today.

COMMENT OF HITLER

Special Cable to THE NEW YORK TIMES.

BERLIN, Tuesday, Jan. 15.—"A fifteen-year wrong is being corrected," exclaimed Chancellor Hitler when informed that the Saar had voted 90 per cent strong to return to Germany.

"The voice of blood spoke."

He expressed the thanks of the nation to the Saarlanders, whom he welcomed back to the Reich.

"Your vote is a step to peace. After your return, Germany has no territorial demands on France," he added.

By The Associated Press.

SAARBRUECKEN, Saar Basin Territory, Tuesday, Jan. 15.—Germany took 90.8 per cent of the votes cast in Sunday's plebiscite in the Saar Basin Territory.

The official results given out this morning follow:

Total valid votes cast, 524,785.
For Germany, 476,089.
Status quo, 46,613.
France, 2,083.

The status quo percentage was 8.9 and annexation to France .3 per cent.

7 to 1 in Saarbruecken.

The City of Saarbruecken voted seven to one in favor of reunion with Germany, casting its ballots as follows:

For Germany, 73,761.
Status quo, 10,413.
For France, 286.

Voelkingen, seat of Hermann Roechling's steel dynasty, voted ten to one for Germany, casting its ballots as follows:

For Germany, 20,657.
Status quo, 2,206.
For France, 135.

The Communists had boldly asserted they would win the factories of Herr Roechling, a leading Nazi and adviser of Chancellor Hitler of Germany.

The Warndt district, considered one of the greatest French strongholds, went eight to one in favor of Germany, France getting only 137 of the 7,678 votes cast, the status quo 837 and Germany 6,687.

The final decision on the future rule of the Saar rests with the League of Nations.

The strongest of the status quo sections were smothered by the huge vote in the industrial sections, such as Neunkirchen and Sulzbach, which went nine to one in favor of Germany.

Lieut. Col. Franz von Papen's home town of Wallerfangen followed the former Chancellor in voting seven to one for the German rule.

Count Goes On All Night.

By FREDERICK T. BIRCHALL.

Wireless to THE NEW YORK TIMES.

SAARBRUECKEN, Saar Basin Territory, Tuesday, Jan. 15.—Reports from the floor where the count of the Saar plebiscite vote is being made are that there has been an overwhelming sweep by the Nazi Deutsche Front.

At midnight the public counting of the vote in this momentous Saar plebiscite had been in progress for seven hours. The prospect was that another seven hours of steady work would finish the task.

Not only will the result decide the destiny of almost 1,000,000 people in this most crowded section of all Europe, but it will affect the future relations of two great nations—and possibly the peace of all the world.

[The Council of the League of Nations will meet privately this morning to begin its discussion of what disposition to make of the Saar, according to a dispatch from Geneva.]

The big Wartburg Hall, brightly

Continued on Page Eight.

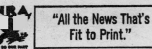

"All the News That's Fit to Print."

The New York Times

LATE CITY EDITION
WEATHER—Generally fair today; snow or rain tomorrow night.
Temperatures Yesterday—Max., 46; Min., 30.
Detailed Weather Report Page 46.

Copyright, 1935, by The New York Times Company.

VOL. LXXXIV....No. 28,118. Entered as Second-Class Matter, Postoffice, New York, N. Y. NEW YORK, FRIDAY, JANUARY 18, 1935. P TWO CENTS In New York City | THREE CENTS Within 200 Miles | FOUR CENTS Elsewhere Except in 7th and 8th Postal Zones.

ROOSEVELT OFFERS HIS SECURITY PLAN FOR JOBLESS, THE AGED AND WIDOWS; PROGRAM SPLITS CONGRESS PARTY LINES

'YOU STOP LYING,' HAUPTMANN RAGES AT FEDERAL AGENT

LEAPS TOWARD THE STAND

Story of Raid on Cache in Garage Provokes Court Outburst.

PRISONER'S TALE DISPUTED

Crock Buried in Floor Cited as Evidence He Did Not Get Ransom From Fisch.

BABY'S INJURY ANALYZED

County Doctor Swears Death Was Due to Skull Fracture—Morgan Employes Testify.

Digest of yesterday's testimony is on Pages 12, 13, 14, 15.

By RUSSELL B. PORTER.

Special to THE NEW YORK TIMES.

FLEMINGTON, N. J., Jan. 17.—Bruno Richard Hauptmann created a scene in the court room late this afternoon when he jumped up and denounced a prosecution witness as a liar.

The witness was Thomas H. Sisk, special agent of the division of investigation, Department of Justice, who was in charge of the Federal agents who arrested Hauptmann in the Bronx last Sept. 19.

He testified after witnesses had told of the finding of the baby's body, and Dr. Charles H. Mitchell, medical examiner of Mercer County, had testified that the child had died almost instantly from a fractured skull. The doctor cited a blood clot in the head as proof that the baby had been alive when the injury was inflicted.

As the twelfth court day of Hauptmann's trial for the murder of Charles A. Lindbergh Jr. drew to a close, Sisk was telling how Hauptmann had made contradictory statements immediately after his arrest in explanation of some of the ransom money found in his possession.

Prisoner's Excitement Increases.

Hauptmann sat shaking his head from side to side in a gesture of disagreement, a frown on his usually impassive countenance, as Sisk described furtive glances which Hauptmann had made from his bedroom window toward his garage while the agents were searching his apartment in the Bronx. They taxed him with having hidden the rest of the money in the garage, according to Sisk, whereupon Hauptmann had denied that he had any more. As the agent said this, Hauptmann shook his head vigorously.

Sisk described the digging up of the garage floor and the discovery of a crock buried one foot under ground, closed with a lid, and covered with dirt. There was no money in it, but at the bottom was water to a depth of two or three inches. Hauptmann denied that he knew anything about it, but the next day, when, after a large amount of ransom money was found, Hauptmann admitted, according to Sisk, that he had kept the ransom money in the crock up to two or three weeks before his arrest.

Leaps From His Chair.

Just as Sisk uttered these words from the witness chair, Hautpmann suddenly rose from his seat between his armed guards inside the rail and directly in front of the bench. With his usually pale face suffused with blood, and with his deep-set eyes blazing with anger, he took a step toward the witness stand too quickly for his guards to stop him. Pointing his finger at Sisk, he shouted:

"Mister, mister, you stop lying."

At this his guards, a New Jersey State trooper at his right and a deputy sheriff in plain clothes at his left, leaned forward, each seizing him by an arm. They pulled him back, but he struggled forward for a moment. He had not finished what he wanted to say.

"You are telling a story," he cried.

A thousand eyes were fixed upon the stolid, muscular figure of the accused man as he stood there in the centre of the court room. There was a noisy stir in the room, then

Continued on Page Twelve.

Hauptmann Friend Says He Saw Bills in His Radio

Special to THE NEW YORK TIMES.

TRENTON, N. J., Jan. 17.—Fred Hahn, baker and former friend of Bruno Richard Hauptmann, who arrived here tonight, is expected to testify that he saw a large roll of banknotes in a radio-phonograph in Hauptmann's home in July, 1932, it became known through prosecution sources. The phonograph is to be offered in evidence.

He came with Detective John McNamara of the New York Bureau of Criminal Identification.

Hahn told New York police that Hauptmann was suffering from a leg injury, producing a limp, for a week after the kidnapping of the baby. He did not say that he himself saw Hauptmann limp, but that on inquiring as to his friend's absence, he learned from Hans Kloeppenburg, their mutual friend, that the man now on trial at Flemington had hurt himself.

CITY PARKS TO GET NEW ARTISTIC TONE

21 Work Relief Artists to Be Put on Job of Creating More Mural Paintings.

ARSENAL IS ON PROGRAM

Historic Scenes to Decorate Walls—Studio Set Up in Natural History Museum.

The Park Department is planning an ambitious art program for 1935, it become known yesterday. Twenty-one work relief artists are being assembled to add a decorative touch to the walls of various park buildings.

The program is in line with Mayor La Guardia's artistic aspirations, but it is understood to have been initiated before the Mayor announced his own plans.

First on the list of Park Department art projects is the adornment of the main hall of the historic Arsenal building in Central Park, headquarters of the department. Preliminary sketches for the murals have been completed, and a studio has been set up in the American Museum of Natural History. Four artists already are at work preparing the big canvas cartoons on which the paintings will be executed.

Other Art Projects.

Other projects in the 1935 program include animal murals for the Central Park Zoo restaurant, animal frescoes for the exterior of the same building, murals depicting the Battle of Long Island for the old Stone House of Gowanus in Brooklyn and additional murals for the Tavern-on-the-Green.

The frescoes will be executed in "scrafito," an Italian process said to have been used little in this country. It consists of the application of a mixture of plaster and cement in layers of different colors, parts of the upper layers being scraped away to show those beneath. They will replace the temporary painted frescoes now on the clerestory walls of the restaurant and the elephant house.

The murals inside the restaurant will depict the inhabitants of the zoo eating and drinking and making merry in human fashion. The waiters will be monkeys. They will be executed from preliminary designs made by Frederick Roth, the sculptor who carved the friezes on the zoo buildings.

The program has been placed under the direction of Allen Saalburg of 223 East Eightieth Street. Mr. Saalburg, who is 35 and has done much mural work between commercial jobs for fifteen years, was "discovered" by the Park Department last Summer when he decorated the popcorn carrettino or pushcart at the zoo. Previously he had been employed by the Public Works of Art project.

For Murals in Big Way

His success with the carrettino brought an assignment to execute murals for the bar in the Tavern-on-the-Green. So pleased were park officials with his rococo lion and unicorn and mid-Victorian horse and barouche that they decided to go in for murals in a big way.

Mr. Saalburg's murals for the Arsenal will cover the four walls of a hall 40 feet long, 25 feet wide and

Continued on Page Twenty-one.

REICH TO GET SAAR MARCH 1, AGREEING TO DEMILITARIZE IT

League Awards the Whole Area 'Under Conditions Resulting From' Versailles Treaty.

LAVAL IN MINORITIES PLEA

Insists Settlement Leave No Bitterness—Bids Germany Enter Security Pacts.

By CLARENCE K. STREIT.

Wireless to THE NEW YORK TIMES.

GENEVA, Jan. 17.—The League of Nations Council at a session tonight awarded the whole Saar to Germany "under the conditions resulting from" the Versailles treaty and fixed March 1 definitely as the date for "the re-establishment of Germany in the government" of this territory.

The Council left all details to be decided by the committee headed by Baron Pompeo Aloisi of Italy with the condition that if any were not thus decided by Feb. 15 the Council itself would rule on them then under the Versailles provisions that enable it to decide such questions by a majority vote. To all this Germany agreed.

This represents a compromise effected only after arduous negotiations all day between Germany and France backed by Great Britain and Italy. One big point at issue was the French desire to get Germany to recognize that the Versailles demilitarization clauses applied to the Sarr Basin Territory and to demilitarize certain military works of small intrinsic value. The compromise on this was deeply hidden.

French Tell of Secret Note.

The French and the British say that recognition of demilitarization is implicit in Germany's agreement to the phrase in the Council resolution that the award to the Reich was made "under the conditions resulting from" the Versailles treaty. The French add that they have a secret note from Germany explicitly recognizing this. The Germans agree that they have consented to demilitarization of the Saar by the League's Governing Commission before March 1.

Another issue involved was Germany's desire that Feb. 15 be fixed for the transfer of the territory without a guarantee that outstanding questions would be settled by that time. The French before agreeing to a definite date wanted an assurance that these questions, particularly those regarding the security of minorities, officials and so forth, and payment for the coal mines, would be settled. The Germans got their definite date, although a later one than they desired, by agreeing to accept the Council's decision by a majority vote on everything outstanding on Feb. 15.

On the proposal of Geoffrey G. Knox, president of the Saar Governing Commission, that as a measure of pacification a general amnesty be proclaimed for all plebiscite offenses in the Saar, the Council authorized the commission to take the necessary measures to this end, This is regarded here as setting an example for Germany to follow.

Laval Appeals for Minorities.

Pierre Laval, the French Foreign Minister, who made the chief speech of the evening, sought in it to protect minorities by stressing that order had been maintained now for fifteen years in the Saar and by citing Chancellor Hitler's plea yesterday to the Saarlanders not to stain their return to Germany by a lack of discipline. This M. Laval interpreted to mean that Herr Hitler desired "to prevent all reprisals against those who used the liberty

Continued on Page Two.

EXTENSION OF NRA TO TEST NEW IDEAS URGED BY WILLIAMS

Head of Recovery Board Tells Retailers More Experience Is Needed for Permanent Plan.

PAYS TRIBUTE TO WEALTHY

They Enrich Treasury at Own Risk, He Says Assailing Radical 'Hangers-On.'

S. Clay Williams, chairman of the National Industrial Recovery Board, told the Retail Dry Goods Association, in convention last night at the Hotel Pennsylvania, that he believed Congress should extend the National Industrial Recovery Act substantially in its present form for another year or two.

Mr. Williams, who is on leave of absence as vice chairman of the board of the R. J. Reynolds Tobacco Company to direct the second phase of the NRA, said the recent hearing looking to the elimination of price-fixing would soon be followed by hearings on code administration and NRA administration, monopolies, small enterprises and production control.

He attacked "camp followers" of the NRA who are preaching the "redistribution of wealth" and defended the wealthy, reminding that they contribute to the government income or inheritance taxes 75 cents of every dollar they make, while risking their funds and supplying the direction of large enterprises that give employment.

Foresees No Radical Change.

Mr. Williams prefaced his speech with the remark that it was reasonable to assume that as far as business was concerned, it would be permitted to follow its course largely along recent lines without radical change. Also, he congratulated the retailers on their enthusiasm and cooperation in the development of NRA measures and praised their recovery program, saying it was one of which any group of business could be proud.

At the conclusion of his address, Dr. Herbert J. Tily, president of the Philadelphia firm of Strawbridge & Clothier and past president of the association, extended to Mr. Williams the thanks of the association "for the sanity of his interpretation" of the NRA and said the organization wanted the NRA to continue.

After asserting that there was general agreement on the good accomplished by NRA codes in abolishing child labor, establishing minimum wages and maximum hours, providing for collective bargaining and setting up fair trade practices, Mr. Williams said:

"But even with respect to most of these provisions there is, in spite of their general acceptability, much doubt as to the best method of establishing them. More experience and study is needed even on these provisions. And when it is realized that these are only a few out of a great number of provisions, many others of which may yet be shown to have great value, the necessity and the wisdom of a further trial period for the act seems apparent.

Hopes Law Will Continue.

"It is, therefore, my thought that the Congress should, and my hope that it will, adopt the policy of extending the National Industrial Recovery Act substantially in its present form for an additional period of one or two years.

"I don't think we are ready to attempt permanent legislation in the field because without more experience and study we could not hope to draft it in form that we could be sure would prove satisfactory. I, therefore, hope we may keep the act as it is for the further trial period necessary for determin-

Continued on Page Four.

Import Duty on Beer Is Reduced One-Half; Roosevelt Sanctions Tariff Board Decision

Special to THE NEW YORK TIMES.

WASHINGTON, Jan. 17.—Presidential approval of an order cutting in half the import duty on beer was announced today by the Tariff Commission, to become effective Feb. 15 by Presidential proclamation.

A report by the commission, after a study of production costs at home and abroad under the provisions of the Tariff Act of 1930, calls for reduction of the present duty of $1 per gallon, or $31 per barrel, to fifty cents per gallon or $15.50 per barrel. This is the maximum reduction permitted under the act.

Since imported beer is not subject to the internal revenue tax of $5 per barrel levied on the domestic product, the protection afforded domestic beer by the present duty is actually only $26 per barrel, or about eighty-four cents a gallon, the commission said.

In its report the commission took into account the rise in alcoholic content permitted to domestic beer under repeal; changes in prices of raw material, and a shift in principal sources of import to Czechoslovakia and Germany for barreled beer, and to England and Ireland for bottled ale and stout.

Little production of bottled ale and stout was found in the United States and a study showed the invoice price of beer from Germany and Czechoslovakia included a cost for transportation that was higher than the cost of Canadian production and exceeded the cost of high-grade domestic beer delivered to New York City, even when the internal tax was added to the cost of the domestic product.

SHARP RIFT OVER DETAILS

All Parties Hail Theory, but Criticism Rises on Methods of Aid.

DIVISION ON OLD-AGE PLAN

Borah and M'Nary Hit $15 Federal Pension as Too Small—Townsend Foes for It.

DEMOCRATS PLEDGE ACTION

Snell Plans Republican Parley—'Program Carefully Worked Out,' Says Robinson.

Special to THE NEW YORK TIMES.

WASHINGTON, Jan. 17.—The reaction to President Roosevelt's social security program, as outlined in his message to Congress, was the shattering of party lines so far as this issue was concerned.

Democrats, Republicans, Progressives and Farmer-Laborites were unanimous in their support of the principle of Federally directed social security. Criticism was confined almost entirely to the methods proposed.

A good deal of immediate comment was averted when Republican leaders in the House decided to call a conference to consider a course of action on the President's proposal.

"I for one do not intend to talk about the program until I have had time to study it and discuss it with the others," remarked Representative Snell of New York, minority leader of the House.

Differences on Old-Age Plan.

A complaint that the program was inadequate in its proposals for old-age pensions came from Senators Borah and McNary, Republicans, while Representative McGroarty, Democrat, of California, who introduced the Townsend Plan Bill in the House, also regretted the old-age provisions.

The message was hailed by Representative Michener, Republican, of Michigan, as a decisive blow to the "Townsend Planners," while many other Republicans, including Senators Couzens, Johnson and Norris and several Representatives, expressed conviction in the soundness of the proposal.

Assurance that legislation for the Roosevelt program would be expedited was given both by Speaker Byrns of the House and Senator Harrison, Democrat, of Mississippi.

Senator Robinson of Arkansas, Democratic leader, struck a keynote for the attitude of many members of his party, when he remarked that the President's message would bring wide improvement in general living conditions.

Comment among members of Congress included:

SENATORS.

ROBINSON, Democrat, of Arkansas—The program of social security contemplated by the President's message has been carefully worked out. Its communication will mark a notable advance in the improvement of living conditions.

HARRISON, Democrat, of Mississippi—The legislation will be expedited as the President has asked. I think that the proposals of the President will prevail.

BORAH, Republican, of Idaho—I would not hastily pass conclusively upon a measure of such complexity, but the first reading leaves the strong impression that as to old-age pensions it is wholly inadequate. I am not satisfied to make an outlay of nearly a billion dollars for armaments and $15 for old age.

McNARY, Republican, of Oregon—I favor social security legislation. I think that a Federal contribution of $15 a month for old-age pensions an inadequate sum.

COUZENS, Republican, of Michigan—The proposal seems sound. My only criticism is that it is too limited in financial scope.

JOHNSON, Republican, of California—The message of the President presents an ambitious program.

NORRIS, Republican, of Nebraska—The plan looks first rate. The idea is a good one.

REPRESENTATIVES.

Speaker BYRNS, Democrat, of Tennessee—He has outlined a pro-

Continued on Page Nineteen.

Old-Age Benefit Plan

Special to THE NEW YORK TIMES.

WASHINGTON, Jan. 17.—While the Wagner social security measure did not give any estimates as to the benefits to be derived by those who will receive old-age annuities under the compulsory contributory old-age insurance plan, the following table of benefits was prepared from expert sources:

MONTHLY ANNUITIES PAYABLE AT AGE 65.

	TRANSITIONAL PLAN.				PERMANENT PLAN.			
	Average Monthly Wage on Which Taxes Were Paid.							
	$75	$100	$125	$150 & Over	$75	$100	$125	$150 & Over
*Age.	Monthly Benefits (a).				Monthly Benefits (b).			
60	$11.25	$15	$18.75	$22.50	$7.50	$10	$12.50	$15.00
55	15.00	20	25.00	30.00	11.25	15	18.75	22.50
50	22.50	30	37.50	45.00	15.00	20	25.00	30.00
45	30.00	40	50.00	60.00	18.75	25	31.25	37.50
40	30.00	40	50.00	60.00	22.50	30	37.50	45.00
35	30.00	40	50.00	60.00	26.25	35	43.75	52.50
30	30.00	40	50.00	60.00	30.00	40	50.00	60.00
25	30.00	40	50.00	60.00	30.00	40	50.00	60.00

*At beginning of tax payments.
(a) Covers those beginning to pay taxes before Jan. 1, 1942.
(b) Covers those beginning to pay taxes on or after Jan. 1, 1942.

These amounts assume that employer and employe have paid the equivalent of at least forty weeks of taxes each year up to the time the employe is 65 years old. The bill provides that the annuity for an individual shall be not less than the actuarial value of the taxes paid on behalf of the individual, together with interest accretions.

Whether this would increase any of the annuities above the figures given here would depend on several factors, such as interest rate, and these factors are not now known.

In order to receive these benefits, the employer and employe jointly would be expected to pay a tax beginning at 1 per cent of monthly wages each year for five years, and gradually increasing until at the end of twenty years they are paying a joint tax into the fund of 5 per cent of the monthly payroll.

Cost of the Security Program

By The Associated Press.

WASHINGTON, Jan. 17.—Here are the appropriations carried by the Wagner Economic Security Bill, introduced today:

Item.	Fiscal Year 1936.	Each Succeeding Year.
Old-age pension	$50,000,000	$125,000,000
Unemployment insurance	4,900,000	49,000,000
Mothers' assistance	25,000,000	25,000,000
Maternal and child health	4,000,000	4,000,000
Crippled children	3,000,000	3,000,000
Child welfare	1,500,000	1,500,000
Public health	10,000,000	10,000,000
Totals	$98,400,000	$217,500,000

SMITH HAILS CHANGE IN TAMMANY SPIRIT

Booed a Year Ago, He Attends Dinner to Praise Dooling and His Altered Policy.

HE WARNS ON 'COCKINESS'

Tells 2,000 Fall Victory Was Endorsement of Roosevelt—Copeland, Farley Speak.

Alfred E. Smith, whose name was booed a year ago at the annual dinner of the Speakers Bureau of Tammany Hall, told virtually the same audience last night that the organization should always conduct itself so that it could go to the people at all times for a vote of confidence, "with a clear heart and a clean conscience."

He told the gathering of nearly 2,000 organization men and women in the Hotel Commodore that the organization here should not be too "cocky," despite the fact that it won in both the city and State in the last election.

"Returns from all over the country show that a large part of that vote was cast as a vote of confidence in the national administration in Washington," the former Governor said.

Mr. Smith's remarks were apparently made with the full knowledge of James J. Dooling, Tammany leader, who sat a few feet away, for Mr. Smith, in paying a compliment to Mr. Dooling's willingness to cooperate with the party's elder statesmen, said: "I am violating no confidence when I say that this is not the first time I have seen him today."

The changed circumstances wrought in the year that had elapsed since the last dinner of the bureau was reflected in the way Mr. Smith was introduced. Last year, he was not at the dinner, the Curry forces were in control, and a telegram of regret that was read was greeted by an organized booing section.

Last night he was introduced by John A. Mullen, toastmaster, as "a man without whom a Speakers Bureau dinner would not be complete—the most distinguished member of the Speakers Bureau, former Governor Alfred E. Smith."

Mr. Smith swung last night into

Continued on Page Ten.

LLOYD GEORGE ASKS BRITISH NEW DEAL

Opening Campaign, He Praises Roosevelt Policies, Urging Like Ones for Britain.

FAVORS BIG PUBLIC WORKS

Suggests 'Prosperity Loan' for Program—Says Accord With Us Would Assure Peace.

By CHARLES A. SELDEN.

Special Cable to THE NEW YORK TIMES.

LONDON, Jan. 17.—In his long-heralded seventy-second birthday speech today proposing a "new deal" program for Britain's economic recovery, David Lloyd George, former Prime Minister, devoted what little he had to say about international affairs almost entirely to Anglo-American relations.

Referring specifically to the situation in the Pacific, he said:

"I would immediately take steps to reach a common agreement with the United States and then act together with that great country in a combined endeavor to secure the pacification of the world."

He also referred chiefly to the United States in his main theme of economic recovery, commenting on President Roosevelt's efforts with warm approval.

"I take my hat off to the American President," he said, "because he is a man of rare courage." The Welsh crowd that heard the speech seemed to share this admiration for the President.

Mr. Lloyd George did not attack the members of the present British Government as individuals, but accused them as a group of nerveless complacency. He cited the appropriation of £2,000,000 for the relief of distressed areas as one illustration of the Cabinet's "incompetence," and called it "piffling with misery."

Attacks Bank of England.

His chief attack was against the Bank of England, to whose advice and guidance of successive governments he attributed most of the country's economic ills. He was careful to say that he did not want the government to assume its ownership, but declared it should be reorganized, and compelled to con-

Continued on Page Two.

PRESIDENT URGES SPEED

Bills Are Introduced at Once to Carry Out His Sweeping Proposals.

AID TO NEEDY AGED NOW

Another Contributory Plan Calls for Equal Payments by Worker and Employer.

A JOB TAX ON PAYROLLS

Program to Cost $100,000,000 at Start—Cooperation of States Essential.

Security Bill and President's message on Pages 16, 17, 18.

Special to THE NEW YORK TIMES.

WASHINGTON, Jan. 17.—In an effort to prevent a recurrence of the social consequences of the business collapse of 1929, President Roosevelt urged upon Congress today a broad Federal-State aid program of permanent unemployment insurance, old-age pensions and benefits to needy and dependent mothers and children. These are designed as safeguards of the average citizen in future periods of depression.

The program was viewed at the capital as the very heart of the social economics of the New Deal. To it was given a place parallel with the business economics of the administration, which has included such measures as control of securities markets, banking reforms and greater supervision of industry.

The third section of the New Deal proposals—a guarantee of comfortable homes for all—is yet to be presented in detail in the President's endeavors to provide for Americans "a more abundant life."

In transmitting his social security program today, the President confessed again that "no one can guarantee this country against the dangers of future depressions," but he reiterated the belief that these dangers would be markedly reduced by such measures as he proposed.

President Asks Swift Action.

Formal submission of the social security plan was through a message from the President to Congress in which he asked for the swiftest possible action on recommendations contained in the report of his Committee on Economic Security, which he attached.

As soon as clerks had finished reading the Presidential message Senator Wagner of New York and Representative Lewis of Maryland introduced identical bills seeking to carry out these recommendations. The bills were referred immediately to the Ways and Means Committee in the House and the Finance Committee in the Senate, where leaders promised the promptest action.

THE PROGRAM IN BRIEF

The President's proposal and the bills as introduced provide:

1. Immediate protection of the needy aged (above 65) through free State pensions, of not to exceed $30 a month, financed on a fifty-fifty basis by the States and the government.

2. A national system of compulsory contributory old age insurance, financed in equal payments by employers and employes without governmental financial participation.

3. A system of voluntary old-age annuities, bought directly from the government, for those in higher income groups.

4. A system of unemployment insurance, financed by a 3 per cent tax on payrolls imposed by the government with credits up to 90 per cent to employers contributing to similar plans in the States.

5. Federal grants to States for assisting widows and children and for the protection of public health. (Not health insurance.)

6. Supervision of the insurance (old age and unemployment) systems by a social insurance board in the Labor Department; supervision of direct benefits to the aged and other dependants by the Federal Relief Administration; supervision of the health benefits by the Public Health Service.

The President estimated that it

Continued on Page Nineteen.

WE DO OUR PART

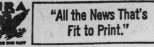

"All the News That's Fit to Print."

The New York Times.

LATE CITY EDITION
WEATHER—Fair and colder today; tomorrow fair and warmer.
Temperatures Yesterday—Max., 28; Min., 14
Detailed Weather Report, Section 2, Page 26.

Section 1

VOL. LXXXIV....No. 28,127. | Entered as Second-Class Matter, Postoffice, New York, N. Y. | NEW YORK, SUNDAY, JANUARY 27, 1935. | Including Rotogravure Picture, Magazine and Book Sections. | F | TEN CENTS | TWELVE CENTS Beyond 200 Miles, Except in 7th and 8th Postal Zones.

TWO INQUIRIES OPENED IN MOHAWK DISASTER; OFFICERS ARE WITNESSES

VEERING OF LINER BLAMED

Master of the Freighter Testifies He Could Not Avoid Crash.

LOWERED NO LIFEBOATS

But Wang Insists He Was Ready to Act if Mohawk Had Asked for Them.

STEERING GEAR GOT TEST

Testimony Indicates Equipment of Mohawk Failed Just Before Collision.

The Federal Government started two investigations here yesterday of the collision of the Ward liner Mohawk and the Norwegian freighter Talisman, in which forty-five were lost Thursday night off the New Jersey coast.

As witnesses were summoned to describe the accident, the search for bodies was continued by a fleet of Coast Guard vessels and army, navy and Coast Guard aircraft and resulted in the finding of the body of a woman passenger. The bodies of a woman passenger and nine of the crew have not yet been found.

The summary of the persons saved and lost in the disaster follows:

	Passengers.	Crew.	Total.
Rescued	39	79	118
Known dead (bodies recovered and identified)	14	21	35
Missing	1	9	10
Total	54	109	163

Thirteen of the officers and crews of the two ships testified at the Custom House, where the United States Steamboat Inspection Service started its investigation during the morning. At the offices of United States Attorney Martin Conboy several members of the Mohawk's crew were questioned. Mr. Conboy refused last night to say whether evidence would be presented to the grand jury.

Witnesses Wear Bandages.

Men in dungarees, sweaters and rude jackets marched into the hearing room of the Steamboat Inspection Service during the four hours it was in session. The hands of some of the witnesses were bandaged for injuries in the accident, and all the men were noticeably affected by the disaster. They described their experiences, but cast no new light on the cause of the collision.

The story of Captain Edmund Wang, master of the Talisman, that his ship was proceeding out to sea at about twelve and one-half knots when the Mohawk came abreast and suddenly veered from her course and into his path, was supported by his log book and by the story of a seaman on the Mohawk. From the testimony it appeared that the steering gear of the Mohawk had failed suddenly.

Captain Wang showed some uncertainty when questioned about the failure of his ship to lower lifeboats. He testified first that the Mohawk had radioed that she did not need lifeboats, but when the record of the communications that passed between the ships was read by Captain Nielsen there was no mention of such a message.

Mr. Weaver pressed this point and brought from Captain Wang an admission that he had not even taken the covers off the four boats which his ship was carrying.

"Then you really used your own judgment in not furnishing lifeboats?" asked Mr. Weaver.

"Well, we had them ready," replied Captain Wang.

Cort M. Pederson, first mate of the Mohawk, replying to a request for a possible explanation of the accident, threw up his arms in a futile gesture.

"I have been thinking, thinking, thinking," he said, "and I cannot figure out yet how it happened."

Say Passengers Were Aided.

The witnesses were questioned about loss of so many passengers. Members of the Mohawk's crew said that quarters had been inspected several times to determine whether all persons had quit the

Continued on Page Three.

Mohawk May Be Raised By Clyde-Mallory Line

Special to THE NEW YORK TIMES.

BRIELLE, N. J., Jan. 26.—Officials of the Clyde-Mallory Line are looking into the feasibility of raising the Mohawk, which they had leased to the Ward Line. The boat now lies in about seventy feet of water in the coastwise steamer lane, and, while it is temporarily marked with a large buoy, it is, nevertheless, considered a menace to navigation. If it is not raised, it may be blown to pieces.

Ten of the thirteen Coast Guard boats that have been searching hundreds of square miles of ocean returned late today to the temporary headquarters here. Commander Simon R. Sands, in command of the Coast Guard of this district, said tonight the search would be abandoned, as he believed it had already been as complete as possible.

35,000 JOIN THREAT OF DRIVERS' STRIKE

If the Teamsters Walk Out Tomorrow, Longshoremen Are Expected to Quit.

CITY-WIDE TIE-UP FEARED

Brotherhood Moves to Keep Situation in Control—Red Activities Are Blamed.

Fear that the one-day strike secretly voted for tomorrow morning by the International Brotherhood of Teamsters, Chauffeurs, Stablemen and Helpers of America without the knowledge of their leaders would spread to the longshoremen and get out of control was voiced yesterday by Michael J. Cashal, vice president, and Edward C. Maguire, counsel for the brotherhood.

Mr. Cashal and Mr. Maguire charged that the Communists were seeking control of the situation and declared the situation was serious. The one-day strike involves between 30,000 and 35,000 teamsters and helpers, and probably will include some 35,000 longshoremen, they said.

Mr. Cashal and Mr. Maguire expressed the fear that a strike of 70,000 might paralyze business to such an extent as to cause general labor unrest and bring on a general strike here like that which paralyzed San Francisco last year.

So secretly was the strike vote taken on Thursday night that Mr. Cashal and other union officials spent most of the next day trying to learn the details and to avert such a course.

Say Longshoremen Must Join.

The men took matters into their own hands, it was said, as a result of the impending order by Supreme Court Justice Humphrey in Brooklyn, enjoining the union from interfering with non-union truckmen hauling freight to and from steamship piers. Union spokesmen point-

Continued on Page Twenty-two.

ICKES CHIEF ISSUE IN BATTLE BREWING ON THE RELIEF BILL

Republicans Declare He and Hopkins Will Rule Despite President's Assurances.

THEY SEEK FULL HEARINGS

Democrats Say Roosevelt Will Take Full Command, but Men Under Fire Will Aid Him.

Special to THE NEW YORK TIMES.

WASHINGTON, Jan. 26.—Despite repeated assurances from the White House that President Roosevelt himself would handle the $4,800,000,000 relief fund he has asked of Congress, Secretary Ickes and the part he might play in the spending continued today to be one of the chief issues in the legislative contest over the new public works program.

Republican Senators, after conferring among themselves on the legislation, said they understood that the fund was to be administered possibly under a new head, but that it eventually would be allocated through the present set-up, including the offices of Mr. Ickes and Harry L. Hopkins, Federal relief administrator.

Some observers thought that the Republicans thus were trying to play upon resentment toward Mr. Ickes which has developed in some quarters and which early this week forced the House leaders to relax the "gag" rule under which they intended to speed the relief appropriation through that body.

The feeling toward the Public Works Administrator has been further intensified in the Senate as a result of a recent attack upon Senator Harrison, Postmaster General Farley and Attorney General Cummings which was given circulation by the Interior Department, which Mr. Ickes heads.

To Get Court Out of Way.

In trying to prevent this resentment from damaging or delaying the relief program, Senate leaders were passing the word around today that Mr. Roosevelt "definitely and personally" would supervise the spending of the new fund.

It is expected that the relief resolution will reach the Senate floor late next week or early in the one following. To that end the Senate helmsmen were trying to clear away other matters, including the protocols for World Court adherence.

The World Court resolutions originally were intended to lie before the Senate for some time, to act as a sort of bone on which the Senators could chew until further items of the President's recovery and relief program were ready for action.

Leaders feel now that the program is well enough under way to warrant disposal of the World Court issue—a feeling which has been heightened considerably by a growing opposition to our entry into the court.

Soon after the relief resolution is acted upon, the Senate expects to have before it the President's social security plan. While this program has not yet been adopted by the House, the body in which it must originate, the Senate Finance Committee has proceeded with hearings in preparation for a quick report should that become advisable.

The most immediate problem before Congress is final action on the relief appropriation. To reach this

Continued on Page Seventeen.

Goering to Be Away on Polish Hunting Trip When Reichstag Divides Prussia Wednesday

Wireless to THE NEW YORK TIMES.

WARSAW, Jan. 26.—General Hermann Wilhelm Goering, Prussian Premier and German Aviation Minister, will arrive here tomorrow morning and on Monday will begin a three-day hunt as the guest of President Moscicki.

Poland is taking elaborate precautions to prevent attempts on General Goering's life. The little town of Bialowitsch, the nearest settlement to the President's hunting lodge, is crowded with police and no strangers are allowed to enter it.

Not since the hated Czar Nicholas visited Bialowitsch when it was Russian territory has so heavy a guard been placed along the roadway to the castle and the entrances to the grounds. The town's 2,000 Jewish inhabitants are being kept under close observation.

The Polish press has not even been allowed to publish the date of General Goering's arrival or the means of transportation he is expected to employ. He will arrive in the early morning in a special car that will halt some distance from the main Warsaw station. From there, without entering the capital, he will proceed by motor car 150 miles northeast to Bialowitsch.

General Goering's hunting trip in Poland, if carried out according to the plan given, will make him miss the session of the Reichstag scheduled for Wednesday. As he is the president of that body and, since the Nazis came into power, has heretofore opened and conducted its sessions, the time chosen for his outing may have large political significance.

The feature of the session will be the adoption of the plan of Chancellor Adolf Hitler to divide Germany into twenty provinces cutting across the old State lines. The State of Prussia, of which General Goering is now Premier, will be split into twelve provinces and will lose its identity.

Power over the provinces passes to Dr. Wilhelm Frick, Reich Minister of the Interior, and so General Goering will be deprived of his chief authority. He fought the plan that would reduce his importance in the country and helped to delay it for almost a year.

Music Union Fines Ship Line $215 For Army Band's Patriotic Airs

Playing of Three Numbers at Induction of the Columbia Into the Merchant Marine Is Barred Until I. M. M. Agrees to Payment of Penalty.

The International Mercantile Marine Company, owners and operators of several United States steamship companies, had to pay $215 yesterday to have three national airs played at the induction of the liner Columbia into the American passenger trade.

The money was paid to the American Federation of Musicians as a penalty for accepting a non-commercial band from Fort Jay as entertainment on the occasion of the raising of the Stars and Stripes at the taffrail of the Columbia, which formerly was the Belgenland of the Red Star Line.

Several hundred guests were aboard the liner at noon when P. A. S. Franklin, Rear Admiral William D. Leahy and others paid tribute to the merchant marine and welcomed into its ranks the reconditioned vessel, which as the Belgenland had made a record as a transatlantic and around-the-world traveler.

Since it was considered an event of importance to the merchant marine and the United States Navy, to which auxiliary units are always welcome, officials of the steamship company asked army officials to provide a band.

After a band from the Sixteenth Infantry had been arranged for, army officials suggested that permission from the national union of musicians would be required before the army band could perform. A request for permission was sent forthwith, and a reply was returned within an hour with the inscription "Request refused."

Subsequent negotiations disclosed that the musicians' union felt that the Columbia was a commercial project and that "the request was not properly made anyhow." A compromise eventually was effected, prescribing that the International Mercantile Marine Company pay the musicians' union $8 for every army musician who appeared on the liner.

It had been planned to use a fifty-four-piece band, but after this union ruling officials of the company asked the army to send only a twenty-five-piece band.

It was understood that Kermit Roosevelt, head of the Roosevelt

Continued on Page Twenty-five.

GRAND JURY CALLED ON PWA 'SWINDLES'

Ickes Asked District of Columbia Inquiry on $4,000,000 Texas Canals.

GLAVIS DATA THE BASIS

Secretary Predicts Ramifications—Aides Seek Graft Evidence All Over.

Special to THE NEW YORK TIMES.

WASHINGTON, Jan. 26.—A special grand jury, the first summoned in the District of Columbia since the Teapot Dome scandals, was called today by Leslie C. Garnett, United States District Attorney, to investigate reports of swindles involving contractors, officials of the Public Works Administration and others in connection with PWA contracts. The jury will sit Feb. 6.

The investigation, Mr. Garnett made clear, is being undertaken at the instigation of Secretary Ickes on information obtained by Louis B. Glavis, chief of the Bureau of Investigation of the Department of the Interior, who has been severely criticized recently in administration and private circles for his widespread activities as head of Mr. Ickes's "Ogpu."

It was remarked that this evidence of activity on Mr. Glavis's part might well be used by Mr. Ickes as ammunition in his assistant's defense.

One case to be investigated by the jury deals with accusations in connection with a $4,000,000 canal project in Texas. Ten or twelve persons are said to be under suspicion in this connection.

Glavis Visited Texas.

The Department of Justice reported today that it had not yet received a detailed report of the charges, and both Secretary Ickes and Mr. Garnett refused to reveal the names of those under suspicion or to make public other information with regard to the action.

"The grand jury investigation will be confined, as far as I know, to the situation in Texas," Mr. Ickes commented. "There may be ramifications to the inquiry, however."

He explained that his force of investigators had been delving into projects "all over the country," in line with his determination to prevent graft in the $3,400,000,000 PWA program.

Asked if PWA officials at headquarters in Washington were involved, Secretary Ickes replied:

"Mr. Garnett said so."

Mr. Glavis has made three trips to Texas in the last six weeks. PWA project lists show two ship channels under construction in Texas, one in Cameron County, financed in part by a PWA loan

Continued on Page Twenty-two.

REMOVAL OF SNOW SPEEDED BY MAYOR

He Says 50,000 Shovelers Will Be at Work by Tomorrow—Orders More Machines Out.

TRAFFIC IS STILL SLOWED

Protests Pouring In From the Rockaways—Cold and Clear Weather Forecast Today.

Mayor La Guardia took personal command of the city's battle against the snow yesterday, ordering that all available snow-fighting forces be mobilized. He drafted deputy commissioners from other city departments to help the fatigued executives of the Sanitation Department.

An army of 40,000—the regular Sanitation Department force, home and work relief contingents and men hired by contractors—was at work all day clearing the city's streets. By tomorrow, the Mayor predicted, the total number of snow fighters will exceed 50,000.

The Mayor devoted nearly all his time to the question of snow removal. After an inspection tour of Manhattan in the morning, he went to the offices of the Sanitation Department, where he conferred for two hours with Commissioner Thomas W. Hammond and his deputies. Later he passed three hours on an inspection tour in Brooklyn and Queens to get a first-hand impression on how the work was going.

As a result of the activities of the snow fighters most of the city's main traffic arteries were at least passable by last night, although there were few, if any, on which vehicular traffic could proceed at a normal rate of speed. Side streets, however, both in Manhattan and in the other boroughs, were largely untouched. The prospects were that little headway would be made in clearing them until tomorrow.

Throughout the State all main roads were reported open, but most of them were ice-coated. Long Island highways were reported in especially bad condition. Motorists wishing to go from New York to Washington were advised by the local Automobile Club that they could probably get through by way of Philadelphia and Harrisburg, provided cars were equipped with chains. To go to Atlantic City, it was said, motorists must travel by way of Trenton.

While the city was confronted with the problem of removing its heavy layer of snow, the lower Mississippi Valley and the Pacific Northwest were still facing serious flood conditions. The Mississippi flood, which affects Mississippi, Tennessee and Arkansas, had taken a toll of twenty-seven lives. The

Continued on Page Twenty-four.

THE NEWS OF THE WEEK IN REVIEW appears in Section 4 of this issue of The New York Times. In the same section are the Editorial, Education and Science pages, Watch Tower and foreign cables, letters to the Editor, and interpretative articles.

HAUPTMANN READY FOR A NEW ORDEAL; REGAINS HIS CALM

Sleeps and Eats Well After Facing Wilentz and Scans Market Deals Again.

HE SCOFFS AT 'CONFESSION'

Defense Declares It Has Found New Witnesses to Back His Alibi Testimony.

By RUSSELL B. PORTER.

Special to THE NEW YORK TIMES.

FLEMINGTON, N. J., Jan. 26.—While Attorney General David T. Wilentz spent the day at his home in Perth Amboy preparing for the resumption of his cross-examination on Monday morning, Bruno Richard Hauptmann had the first of his two days of respite today before he goes back on the stand for another ordeal.

Despite the admissions Mr. Wilentz forced from him in his half hour's cross-examination late yesterday afternoon, Hauptmann was reported to have recovered his composure. Information from the county jail back of Hunterdon County court house was that the prisoner slept well last night, ate well today and did not appear nervous.

Hauptmann will need all the rest and composure he can gain before Monday, which will be the nineteenth court day of his trial for the murder of Charles A. Lindbergh Jr., at Hopewell, on March 1, 1932. Mr. Wilentz is expected to resume the hammer-and-tongs attack which he began yesterday against Hauptmann's denials of kidnapping the Lindbergh baby, building the ladder, writing the ransom notes, and collecting the ransom.

More Books to Be Produced.

The State announced today that it had four more of Hauptmann's account books and diaries found in his Bronx home after his arrest last September, like the little red note-book with the word "boat" spelled "b-o-a-d," which Mr. Wilentz shook in Hauptmann's face yesterday afternoon. This was the same spelling which appeared in the fourteenth and last of the ransom notes.

Although Hauptmann refused to admit that he had written that particular word in the book, he faltered out the admission that it looked like his handwriting, and that the note-book contained his handwriting in other entries. He gave two answers—one that he could not remember having written the word that way in the note-book, and the other that, if he had done so, it must have been eight years ago, before he could write English as well as now.

The prosecution revealed after court that the notebook contained a record of Hauptmann's personal expenditures for 1931, the year before the kidnapping, and that the word "boad," so spelled, appeared in connection with an entry of $2.25 as an expenditure for a boat trip.

Other Samples of Writing.

Other notebooks include a large account book, and in addition the State has samples of Hauptmann's writing when in the German Army and in prison in Germany, with which to attack him either on cross examination or in rebuttal. According to the prosecution, all these documents show that the peculiar misspellings, usages and handwriting characteristics, including the

Continued on Page Sixteen.

Mayor Backs Police on 'Muss 'Em Up' Order; Finds City and Gangs in a 'State of War'

Mayor La Guardia, declaring that the numerous recent killings of policemen by criminals have convinced him that a state of war exists between the city and its underworld, served notice last night that he will give whole-hearted support to Police Commissioner Valentine's edict to "muss up" crooks and gunmen.

"This is no time for sentimentality; this is no time for coddling crooks," the Mayor said, in an address delivered in Madison Square Garden at the annual entertainment and reception of the Patrolmen's Benevolent Association.

Explaining that he was making his remarks at the reception because he wanted to inform the people of the city of his attitude, Mr. La Guardia continued:

"I have been in office but one year, but in that time, together with Police Commissioner Valentine, I have attended funeral after funeral of our great police officers. I say this: The war is on, and you cannot expect that a police officer is going to stand up and be shot down by a cowardly crook without defending his own life. I want you men to know that I understand the situation. I want you men to know that you have complete support from City Hall in the performance of your duty."

He urged that the police deadline be extended to the boundaries of the city, and that criminals be given to understand that "any crook who comes in here must know that he is coming here with notice that we do not want him, and that we are going to drive him out by the use of force."

His remarks were prefaced by a statement that recently there had been much discussion of the treatment of gangsters, racketeers and criminals by the police. He did not repeat Commissioner Valentine's "muss 'em up" phrase, but he expressed his views strongly.

Responding to an introduction by Joseph P. Moran, president of the patrolmen's association, the Mayor praised the policemen for their loyalty. He reiterated his official announcement that promotions to high posts in the department would be made during the rest of his term in office from the ranks.

About 22,000 persons attended the reception, Mr. Moran estimated. Entertainment and dancing, including music furnished by the Police Department Band and the department Glee Club, followed the Mayor's address.

HUEY LONG TROOPS FORCE HIS FOES TO SURRENDER; MARTIAL LAW DECLARED

CIVIL WAR IS AVERTED

Armed Square Dealers Behind Autos Face Deployed Militia.

ONE CITIZEN IS WOUNDED

Senator Long Has Forty of Defiers Seized and Held Incomunicado by Police.

MOB TRAMPLES A 'SPY'

Beaten Back by Soldiers' Tear Gas—Guards of Long Assault a Reporter.

Special to THE NEW YORK TIMES.

BATON ROUGE, La., Jan. 26.—Civil warfare was narrowly averted here this afternoon when 500 National Guardsmen, equipped with machine guns, rifles and gas bombs forced the surrender of 100 citizens who had hastily taken up shotguns, pistols and sporting rifles at the call of the Square Deal Association, sworn to destroy the dictatorship of Senator Huey P. Long.

But fresh fuel was added to the flame of revolt when, after the surrender, the militiamen laid down a gas barrage against a throng of unarmed men, women and children, sympathizers with the Square Dealers.

The bystanders had pressed close to the ranks of the khaki-clad soldiers, when suddenly some one pointed to a short, stout man and shouted:

"There he is! That's the spy!"

Apparently believing that he was the informant who had tipped off Senator Long that the Square Dealers were marshaling their forces, the crowd surged forward angrily.

Their quarry was beaten, knocked down, and trampled despite strenuous efforts to save him by the guardsmen, who eventually were forced to resort to their gas bombs. This soon dispersed the crowd.

Fight Threatened at First.

Earlier, crouching behind a line of thirty automobiles near the woods at one side of the parish airport here, the citizens' army had seemed determined to fight as the first militiamen arrived from this city, which Senator Long's henchman, Governor O. K. Allen, had placed under martial law earlier in the day.

Machine-gun squads of the militiamen crawled forward cautiously on their stomachs across the 500 yards of open space of the airport. The line of the citizens' array held firm and the guardsmen hesitated until further reinforcements arrived. Then their opponents, who were under the command of Ernest Bourgeois, president of the Square Deal Association, realized that resistance was hopeless.

One by one they began to surrender to Colonel E. P. Roy, who was in command of the troops. As the Square Deal line began to break up, a single shot was heard, and George N. Alessi of Independence, La., forty miles from here, was wounded in the arm. Alessi, a Square Dealer, didn't know who shot him, but his wound was caused by buckshot, apparently from the accidental discharge of the weapon of one of his comrades.

No further casualties developed, however, as the Square Dealers reluctantly went forward to the centre of the airport and handed over their arms to the khaki-clad guardsmen. Colonel Roy and his men took their names and addresses and informed them that they were under technical arrest, but then released them.

Arrest of Forty Reported.

About forty leaders of the Square Deal Association and of the mobilization of 300 armed men who held the East Baton Rouge Parish Court House for five hours late yesterday were reported tonight to be under arrest and held incomunicado by police under the control of Senator Long.

Bourgeois, the youthful president of the Square Deal Association, who hurried here this morning simultaneously with Senator Long, refused to discuss the plans of his organization or the purpose of the meeting on the airport this after-

Continued on Page Two.

$30,000 in Gold Falls From Airplane in Gale

Special Cable to THE NEW YORK TIMES.

LONDON, Jan. 26.—Two cases of bar gold worth $30,000 fell out of a Paris-London air liner today during a gale which battered the coasts of England and sent dozens of ships scurrying to harbors for shelter.

The precious boxes are believed to have slid across the floor of the freight compartment while the plane was being tossed in the storm. The passengers and pilot heard nothing, but apparently the heavy boxes tore through the thin sides of the plane and vanished.

When the plane landed at an Essex airdrome a big hole in the fabric was discovered. The gold probably dropped in the Channel, but the police are searching for it along the plane's route over Sussex and Kent. The French police also were notified.

ROB A NEW YORKER OF $250,000 GEMS

Two Bandits Hold Up Mrs. J. E. Bell in Miami Hotel on Return From Races.

HARRY CONTENT A VICTIM

He Rushes From an Adjoining Suite and Is Bound—Party Believed Trailed.

By The Associated Press.

MIAMI, Fla., Jan. 26.—Against a friend's counsel, Mrs. Margaret Bell of New York wore jewels she valued at "probably a quarter of a million" to the Hialeah Park horse races this afternoon, and was robbed of them tonight by two masked men who entered her suite in the Miami Biltmore Hotel with pistols drawn.

Mrs. Bell, wife of J. E. Bell, former New York stock broker, was tied hand and foot, as was Harry Content, a prominent New York broker. Neither was hurt.

Mrs. Bell listed her losses as four pearl necklaces and two rings, a bracelet and a wrist watch, all platinum and set with diamonds. They were insured, she told police, for $350,000.

A member of Mrs. Bell's party described the diamond in one ring as "one of the largest square stones in the world."

Despite Mrs. Bell's scream and telephone alarm to the hotel lobby four floors down, the bandits escaped.

Mrs. Bell, with Mr. Content and Dr. Howard W. Blake, New York dental surgeon, and Mrs. Blake, had returned from Hialeah to the hotel in suburban Coral Gables only twenty minutes earlier.

Victims Tell of Raid.

"I was in my sitting room reading when the two men walked in, handkerchiefs up to their eyes and hold-

Continued on Page Three.

Times Wide World Photo.

MEN AND WOMEN WHO FOUND HAUPTMANN GUILTY OF MURDERING THE LINDBERGH BABY.

The jury which condemned the defendant at Flemington. In the front row, left to right, are Elmer Smith, Mrs. Ethel Stockton, Charles F. Snyder, Mrs. Verna Snyder, Mrs. Rosie Pill and Charles Walton, foreman. In the back row are Robert Cravatt, Philip Hockenbury, George Voorhees, Mrs. May F. Brelsford, Liscom C. Case and Howard V. Biggs.

Bruno Richard Hauptmann

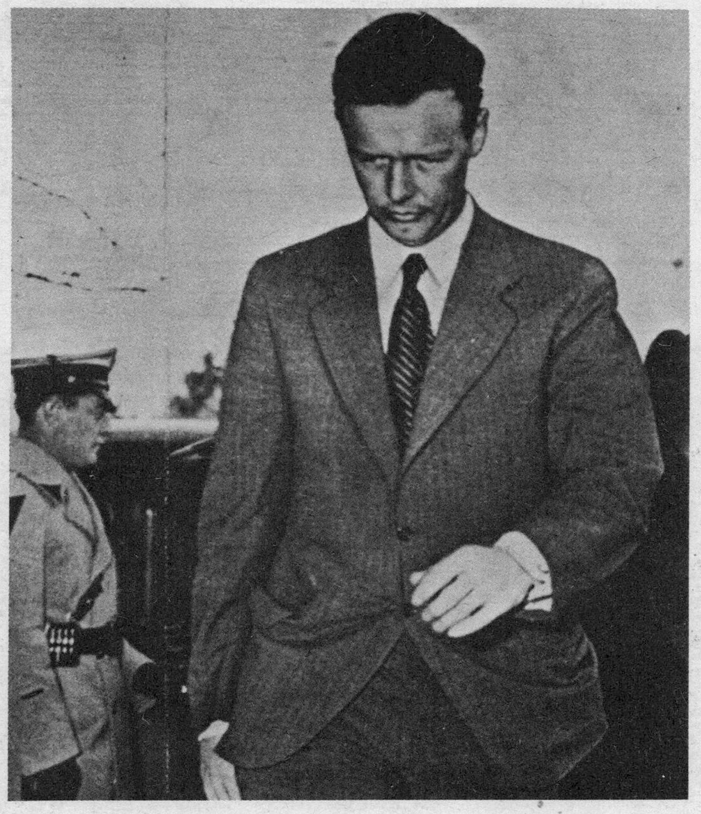

Colonel Lindbergh as he arrived to testify at Hauptmann's trial.

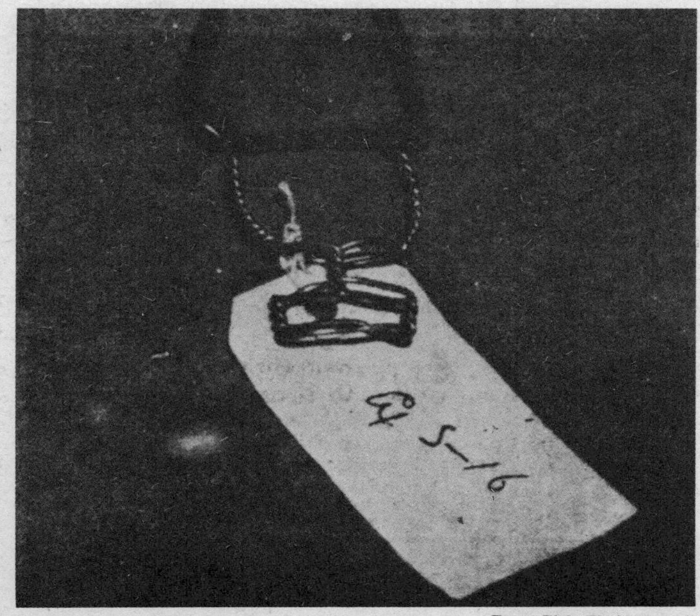

Times Wide World Photo.

The thumbguard worn by the Lindbergh baby and found by Betty Gow the night the child disappeared, which was introduced in evidence.

Chronology of the Main Developments In the Lindbergh Kidnapping Case

A chronology of important developments in the Lindbergh kidnapping follows:

March 1, 1932—Charles A. Lindbergh Jr., 20 months old, was stolen from his crib in the nursery of the Lindbergh home, near Hopewell, Hunterdon County, N. J. A note demanding $50,000 ransom, signed with an identifying symbol, was left on a window sill.

March 9.—Dr. John F. Condon, 70-year-old Bronx educator, received a note with a similar symbol, authorizing him to act as an intermediary, as he had volunteered to do in The Bronx Home News.

March 12.—Dr. Condon met a man who said he was "John," the representative of the kidnapping gang, in Woodlawn Cemetery, the Bronx, and talked with him for more than an hour on a bench in Van Cortlandt Park, across the street.

April 2.—Dr. Condon paid "John" $50,000 in St. Raymond's Cemetery, the Bronx, while Colonel Lindbergh waited in an automobile near by.

May 12.—The baby's body was found in dense underbrush near the Mount Rose Road between Hopewell and Princeton, N. J., about four and a half miles from his parents' home.

Sept. 15, 1934.—Walter Lyle, gasoline station attendant, noted the license number of Bruno Richard Hauptmann's automobile on a $10 gold note with which he had paid for gasoline.

Sept. 19.—Hauptmann arrested in his automobile on Park Avenue between 177th and 178th Streets by detectives who had had him under surveillance since a bank clerk recognized the $10 note as one of the Lindbergh ransom bills.

Sept. 26—Hauptmann was indicted for extortion by the Bronx County grand jury.

Oct. 8.—Hauptmann was indicted for murder by the Hunterdon County grand jury.

Oct. 19.—Hauptmann taken to Flemington, N. J., after the Appellate Division here had upheld his extradition.

Jan. 3, 1935.—Hauptmann's trial started before Supreme Court Justice Thomas W. Trenchard.

Jan. 4—Colonel Lindbergh testified that he recognized Hauptmann's voice as that of the man he heard shout "Hey, dok-tor," to Dr. Condon in St. Raymond's Cemetery.

Jan. 9.—Dr. Condon testified that Hauptmann was the "John" of the ransom negotiations.

Jan. 23—Arthur Koehler, wood technologist for the United States Forestry Service, testified that part of the wood used in the ladder found outside the Lindbergh home came from the flooring in Hauptmann's attic.

Jan. 24—Hauptmann took the stand in his own defense, swearing that he called for his wife at a Bronx bakery on the night of the kidnapping, and that he was home on the night of the ransom payment.

Jan. 30—His wife took the stand and supported his alibis.

Feb. 13—The case went to the jury and after eleven hours Hauptmann was convicted of murder and sentenced to die in the electric chair at Trenton some time during the week beginning March 18.

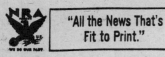

"All the News That's Fit to Print."

The New York Times.

LATE CITY EDITION
WEATHER—Cloudy, rain or snow today; tomorrow rain.
Temperatures Yesterday—Max., 46; Min., 26
Detailed Weather Report Page 42.

Copyright, 1935, by The New York Times Company.

VOL. LXXXIV....No. 28,145. Entered as Second-Class Matter, Postoffice, New York, N. Y. NEW YORK, THURSDAY, FEBRUARY 14, 1935. P TWO CENTS | In New York City. | THREE CENTS Within 200 Miles | FOUR CENTS Elsewhere Except in 7th and 8th Postal Zones.

HAUPTMANN GUILTY, SENTENCED TO DEATH FOR THE MURDER OF THE LINDBERGH BABY

MACON'S MEN LAND, SAVED FROM DEATH IN SKY AND ON SEA

Calm Heroism and Unbroken Navy Discipline Revealed as Survivors Reach Port.

ADMIRAL TELLS OF HORROR

Saw Gasoline Flames Spread Over Water to Airship's Crew as the Cruisers Came Up.

WILEY DESCRIBES PLUNGE

Naval Court Is Ordered for Today as Field Inquiry Into the Cause Is Started.

Special to THE NEW YORK TIMES.

SAN FRANCISCO, Feb. 13.—Eighty-one officers and men of the eighty-three who set out on the dirigible Macon to join the fleet off the California Coast came home today to tell how the giant airship was destroyed yesterday evening and death which snatched at them from sky and sea was beaten back.

They stood huddled on three rescue cruisers in San Francisco Bay, laughing, asking for cigarettes, and between puffs relating this latest epic of man's defeat amid his conquests of space.

But though they could describe the first alarm and the fall, of flying minutes after the Macon struck, and dragging anxiety as the navy swept the misty seas in search of them, they were mute on the cause of the disaster.

Some fabric tore away on her fins and along her backbone; gas cells burst, the great structure shuddered and soared and descended and hit, and suddenly they were tumbled out pell mell into the water, fighting for their lives. Flaming gasoline was ignited about them by calcium flares of mercy.

This was the story in brief, different for every man, yet somehow merging into one clear picture of the whole.

Three Warships Reach Port.

The warships Richmond, Cincinnati and Concord brought in the survivors. Lieut. Commander Herbert V. Wiley, the Macon's skipper, was aboard the Concord. When he described what happened it was in terms of telephone calls, buoyancy and lack of it, jettisoned gasoline and crumbling gas cells and frames. He was in the control car, a city block from the source of trouble.

The story of men is another narrative. The Macon was humming along not far at sea south of Monterey Bay. The weather was dark gray and filled with drizzle, but the world's greatest dirigible had seen many such days. She had met the fleet plowing northward toward San Francisco; she was accompanying it, and soon she would go to her home in Sunnyvale.

The time was a little later than 5 o'clock in the afternoon, and daylight was already failing. There was a slight jar. It jerked at the wheel in the helmsman's hands. Some said they did not feel the jar, but immediately noticed the inclination of the ship, nose upward.

However, there were subsequent "jars." Lieutenant C. S. Rounds described them as a "shudder."

"But it was squally outside," he said. "I doubt if many of us in the first sixty seconds anticipated serious trouble. Even when the 'stand by' orders came, I thought it was a minor crisis of navigation."

Gas Cells Begin to Go.

But those jars were the rupturing of gas units; first No. 1, then No. 2, away aft. Lieutenant Rounds was forward and inside the ship. There was no excitement for the first four or five minutes, excepting among those aft who were whipping telephone calls into the control car. The airship was riding rapidly.

Then No. 9 cell burst. About that time it dawned on all that this was no minor crisis.

They stuck by their posts. They slipped gasoline tanks aft and devalved the forward cells to level her out, but it was no good.

Having soared into the mist in a last living effort, the Macon lost buoyancy and began to fall. It was then that Commander Wiley sent out the message that they were falling and first mentioned abandoning ship.

The man who sent that electric

Continued on Page Two.

Opera Threatened Again As Board Balks at Deficit

Metropolitan Directors Cast Doubt on Next Season Unless Production Costs Are Cut and Popular Subscription Enlarged.

There may be no opera at the Metropolitan next season. The board of directors of the Metropolitan Opera Association has decided that opera cannot be continued on the basis of the enormous losses incurred in the last five seasons.

After a meeting of the executive committee yesterday in the office of Paul D. Cravath, chairman of the board, Mr. Cravath issued the following statement:

"The directors of the Metropolitan Opera Association have decided that it is not feasible to give opera at the Metropolitan Opera House next season on the basis of continuing to incur the large deficits of the last five seasons.

"They have requested the preparation of a plan for reducing the cost of producing opera, and increasing the support of the public through subscriptions for seats, that will render the continuation of opera financially possible."

The members of the committee would not elaborate on this statement last night. One member intimated that the announcement had a twofold purpose; to quiet the rumors that have been at large in the last few weeks and to gauge the public reaction as to its willingness to participate in assuring the Metropolitan's future.

It was emphasized that neither the full board nor the executive committee had abandoned the Metropolitan to whatever fate might befall it, and that, despite the immediate doubts, there was every intention to continue consideration of the opera's future.

Besides Mr. Cravath, the members of the executive committee who attended the meeting were Mrs. August Belmont, Cornelius N. Bliss, Frederic Potts Moore, David Sarnoff and Allen Wardwell. Robert S. Brewster, the new president of the Metropolitan Opera and Real Estate Company, and Myron C. Taylor were the only members absent.

The executive committee has been holding frequent meetings since Fall to determine ways and means of continuing opera at the Metropolitan. The first question before it was the establishment of a policy and financial program. The second, depending on the first, was the naming of a general manager to succeed Giulio Gatti-Casazza, whose resignation takes effect next April.

Many plans for the continuation of Metropolitan Opera were proposed and discussed at these meet-

Continued on Page Twenty-five.

HOPE GAINS IN ROME FOR PEACE IN AFRICA

But Italy Is Reported Ready to Spend $850,000,000 in the Event of War.

REPLY TO DEMANDS ASKED

Plan for Solution Reported in Addis Ababa—Fascist Grand Council to Meet.

By ARNALDO CORTESI.

Wireless to THE NEW YORK TIMES.

ROME, Feb. 13.—The optimistic forecasts made yesterday as to a peaceful solution of the Italo-Abyssinian crisis became more positive today following a meeting between Negradas Yesus, Abyssinian Chargé d'Affaires, and Fulvio Suvich, Italian Foreign Under-Secretary. Although it is stated semi-officially that no actual solution has been reached, the impression is that good progress has been made.

Special emphasis is laid on the fact that Signor Suvich began by assuring the Abyssinian envoy that Italy was animated by the most peaceful intentions, to which the envoy replied that his Emperor also wished to avoid war. Signor Suvich then complained that the demands submitted to Emperor Haile Selassie by the Italian Minister at Addis Ababa remained unanswered.

Then the Italian Under-Secretary went on to discuss possible solutions of the crisis. These include the establishment of a neutral zone on the Abyssinian side of the frontier, but it is positively stated that no indication that this condition will be accepted by the Emperor has yet been received by Italy.

The Abyssinian envoy sent a long report of his conversations with Signor Suvich to Addis Ababa, and it is hoped by Italian officials that a reply will be forthcoming in the next few days.

There has been no let-up in the feverish activities to prepare a strong Italian expeditionary force for dispatch to Africa. In view, however, of today's favorable development hope is beginning to be entertained that it may never be necessary for the force to leave Italy.

Mussolini Studies Note.

By The Associated Press.

ROME, Feb. 13.—Premier Mussolini gave deep study tonight to an Abyssinian note calling Italians the aggressors in recent border conflicts. This note, Italian officials said earlier today, made the situation "very serious."

Nevertheless, there appeared this evening to be less concern in government circles over the prospect of hostilities in Africa, although an authoritative source said Italy was prepared to spend about $850,000,000

Continued on Page Sixteen.

LEHMAN TAX BILLS VOTED BY SENATE

Four-Cent Gasoline Levy and Budget Are Among the 11 Measures Approved.

FEARON ATTACKS FIGURES

He Predicts a $100,000,000 Deficit at Fiscal Year End—Five Proposals Held Up.

By W. A. WARN.

Special to THE NEW YORK TIMES.

ALBANY, Feb. 13.—Eleven of the measures included in Governor Lehman's fiscal program were passed in the Senate today. Action on five was deferred, not because the Democrats did not have the votes to pass them, but because legislative leaders doubted whether passage of them would be within the requirements of the Constitution, until after the main budget bills, already passed in the Senate, had been passed in the Assembly also.

Every Democrat in the Senate voted for the Governor's bills. The Republican vote was split in many instances. Senator Fearon, leader of the Republican minority, voted for the main budget bill, but not until he had first denounced it as a measure which did not comply with the Constitutional provision for a balanced budget and had accused Governor Lehman of financial juggling in drafting his measures.

The Senator cited figures intended to show that Mr. Lehman had constantly blundered in estimating revenues. He declared that these futile processes had been repeated by the Chief Executive in making up his new budget, with the probable result that the Governor would be confronted with a $100,000,000 deficit when the next fiscal year ends instead of the $3,000,000 surplus of the Governor's own estimate, cited in his budget message to the Legislature.

Sees 700 New Jobs.

Senator Fearon accused the Democrats of putting more than 700 new jobs into the budget bill without telling anybody anything about it. He said they had refused the taxpayers a public hearing on the budget bill at a time when the Governor himself was demanding public hearings in towns and counties on local budgets.

Senator Dunnigan, Democratic leader, came to the defense of the Governor and the debate was shot through and through with partisan charges. At times it became quite heated, with Senators Fearon and Dunnigan striding up and down the centre aisle.

Senator Fearon gave Senator Twomey, fiscal leader of the Senate, some moments of embarrass-

Continued on Page Six.

SENATE COMMITTEE ADOPTS WORK BILL; TRUCE OVER WAGES

Drive for Pay Under 'Prevailing' Rates Is Beaten and the 'Dole' Also Is Rejected.

ROOSEVELT RETAINS POWER

But His Scale Must Not Cut Private Wages—Floor Fight Due as Labor Protests.

Special to THE NEW YORK TIMES.

WASHINGTON, Feb. 13.—After hours of struggle today, the administration leadership, supported by Senator Glass, regained control of the Senate Appropriations Committee and finished a redraft of the $4,880,000,000 relief bill deemed acceptable to President Roosevelt.

Mr. Glass expects to report the revised measure formally to the Senate tomorrow or next day. Leaders hope it may be acted upon finally before the diminishing funds in the present relief coffers are depleted entirely.

Today's action in the Appropriations Committee was considered both by the administration and organized labor as a victory for the Roosevelt supporters. Instead of yielding to the demand of the American Federation of Labor for an irrevocable "prevailing wage" provision, the committee adopted an amendment giving the President control over pay rates, but with the added prescription that he must pay the "prevailing" scale if he finds the new works program is depressing, or is likely to depress, private wage structures in any locality.

William Green, president of the A. F. of L., said tonight that the substitute was "unacceptable and unsatisfactory to labor," adding that the federation would make its appeal directly to the Senate membership.

"Dole" Amendment Is Beaten.

The committee also withstood a drive from another group and again voted down, by 12 to 11, the so-called "dole" amendment which would have provided a cut in the appropriation to $2,880,000,000 and thereby, according to its supporters, force the President to rely more on direct relief than upon the more expensive new public works.

Thus, after three weeks of varying degrees of fright, administration leaders apparently had taken hold again. They proposed to move at once to break the log-jam of legislation which has backed up behind the relief program, and expressed confidence in predicting that this measure would be well on its way through the Senate before another week had gone.

Through all of its vicissitudes in the committee, the bill emerged today without any change which leaders regarded as a serious violation of the principles laid down by the President in his annual message. He called then for a lump-sum appropriation and for adequate discretionary authority to spend it in a self-diminishing, largely self-liquidating works program, designed to return 3,500,000 able-bodied persons now on relief to employment at lower than prevailing wages.

All of the trouble on the measure,

Continued on Page Eight.

ELEVATORS TIED UP IN 200 BUILDINGS IN STRIKE FLARE-UP

Union Disclaims Action After New Delay in Decision, but Admits Patience Is Gone.

UPTOWN APARTMENTS HIT

Madison Square Offices Also Are Affected—Spread of the Walkout a Possibility.

A general strike of building service employes in office and apartment house buildings loomed last night after sporadic walkouts affecting more than 200 buildings and 2,500 employes were staged in various parts of the city yesterday.

The strikes were called by a so-called "rank and file committee" of members of the Building Service Employes Union, claiming a membership of 140,000, as the arbitration committee headed by Major Henry H. Curran, appointed last December by Mayor La Guardia to settle the differences between the union and realty interests, was struggling to complete its labors and present an award.

The committee was to have made known its award yesterday. It failed to do so, however, and last night Major Curran announced that the award would not be made public until today. The committee remained in session all evening at Major Curran's office, 280 Madison Avenue.

"Ill Advised," Says Mayor.

Mayor La Guardia on being informed of the walkouts, which occurred in the Harlem, Washington Heights and Madison Square sections, termed the strikes as "ill advised."

At the office of the union, 1,450 Broadway, responsibility for the strikes was disclaimed. The walkouts were characterized as "unauthorized," but the statement was added, "We cannot hold them back any longer—our men have lost patience waiting for the award."

Detectives of the West 123d Street Precinct, cruising in a radio car, arrested sixteen men shortly before 1 o'clock this morning, charging them with disorderly conduct for alleged intimidation of building-service employes in three Harlem apartment houses. According to the officers, the sixteen men, nine of whom were Negroes, had entered the apartment houses and compelled attendants on duty to quit their jobs.

Six of the prisoners were picked up at 50 West 112th Street, three at 56 West 112th Street, and seven at 1,980 Seventh Avenue. They will be arraigned in the Fifth District Court today.

Promised to Work for Peace.

A fortnight ago James J. Bambrick, after a meeting of the union's executive committee and the presidents of its fifteen locals in the city, had promised Major Curran that every effort would be made to prevent any strikes, pending the outcome of the arbitration proceedings.

This was in response to a plea from Major Curran to keep the men from striking lest such action jeopardize the arbitration award.

Continued on Page Eight.

Girl Dies in Leap Off Empire State Tower; Impact Smashes Heavy Marquee in 33d St.

Disconsolate because of a quarrel with her fiancé, a 20-year-old girl jumped from the observation landing of the Empire State Building just before 8:30 o'clock last night, her body crashing into a glass and metal marquee nearly a quarter of a mile below.

The impact of the fall, which shattered frosted glass, light bulbs and the sheet-iron covering of the canopy, was at first mistaken for an explosion by passers-by and shop employes in the vicinity. Witnesses in buildings on the opposite side of Thirty-third Street said the young woman's body had struck a sixth-floor set-back of the building before hurtling onto the marquee.

From the contents of her handbag, which was clutched tightly in her fingers, the girl was identified as Irma P. Eberhardt of the Laura Spelman Hall Branch of the Y. W. C. A., 607 Hudson Street. Except for a Y. W. C. A. membership card the black bag contained only 83 cents in change and a compact of lipstick and rouge.

At the moment Miss Eberhardt jumped from the Empire State terrace, according to the police, Raymond Rebecchi of 5,716 136th Street, Flushing, was at the Charles Street station reporting her disappearance to Detective Frank Campbell. Before he had finished, word of her death was received from the police of the West Thirtieth Street precinct.

Rebecchi is said to have told Detective Campbell that he and Miss Eberhardt had quarreled on Tuesday, but that he had called at the Y. W. C. A. last night in the hope of effecting a reconciliation. He asked her to go to dinner, he said, and while he went to a lavatory to wash his hands the young woman vanished.

Rebecchi is said to have told the police he waited about half an hour in the foyer when he received a telephone call from Miss Eberhardt. "I'm going to kill myself," she said and hung up the receiver. Alarmed, the young man hurried to the police station.

Times Wide World Photo.

BRUNO RICHARD HAUPTMANN

Being taken to his cell after hearing death sentence last night.

HAUPTMANN IN CELL FALLS IN COLLAPSE

After Hearing Verdict Without a Sign, He Breaks Down in Fit of Weeping.

WIFE SOBS AFTER HE GOES

Both Prepared for Worst by Warning of Fisher Against Outburst in Court.

By CRAIG THOMPSON.

Special to THE NEW YORK TIMES.

FLEMINGTON, N. J., Feb. 13.—For the first time since his arrest Bruno Richard Hauptmann was reported tonight to be in a state of collapse.

When he marched out of the court room, manacled to Constable Hovey Low on his left and State Trooper Hugh Stockberger on his right, he was pale but erect and his step seemed firm.

He went through the back rooms to his cell tier, which has been occupied by him alone. The minute the door was slammed shut behind him, according to the reports, he slumped, his face striking the floor.

There was a hush in the court room when Hauptmann came in at 10:30 o'clock tonight. For the first time since the trial started he was in irons, manacled to two of his nine guards. The bell in the belfry had already announced that the jury had reached a verdict, and the shouting of the throng outside was an overtone to the inside hush.

Wife Comes to His Side.

Hauptmann walked across the room from the rear door and took his seat. He sat down stiffly, a little awkwardly, as if the manacles impeded his motions.

At almost the same moment his wife, her normally red face growing pale, edged up the outside aisle and around the seats inside the rail to a place close to her husband. She twisted her lips into a wry smile, but her husband, after one glance, looked away.

In the two minutes that passed before the jurors began to file in there was a vivid little picture. C. Lloyd Fisher, the one member of Hauptmann's counsel who has been closest to him, visiting him in the jail daily and taking his life story before the trial, leaned over and put his arm around the prisoner's shoulder.

He whispered: "This is only the beginning. Don't show a sign, because, if you do, it will count against you."

Then the attorney leaned over and placed his arm around Mrs.

Continued on Page Twelve.

JURY COURAGEOUS, WILENTZ DECLARES

Nation Indebted to Them, He Says—Thanks Aides, Foley and New York Police.

'ENDS OF JUSTICE SERVED'

Peacock Says Verdict Is Reply to 'Mothers' Prayer'—Law Points Raised by Defense.

From a Staff Correspondent.

FLEMINGTON, N. J., Feb. 13.—Attorney General David T. Wilentz, commenting tonight upon the Hauptmann verdict, thanked all those associated with the prosecution, and paid special tribute to the jury.

"The tremendous responsibility imposed upon the Hunterdon County jury was shouldered without flinching," he said. "The nation is indebted to these courageous men and women.

"The proper presentation of the case was due in the main to the work of the New Jersey State police. District Attorney Samuel J. Foley of the Bronx and his assistants labored unceasingly and to them I extend my deep thanks, as well as to Inspectors Henry Bruckman, John J. Lyons, the members of the New York police and the agents of the Federal Government."

Mr. Wilentz added that it had been his unwelcome duty to prosecute the case and said that he hoped society would be served by his efforts and those of his associates.

Former Judge George K. Large of Flemington, special counsel to the State, said, "The verdict was fully justified by the evidence."

"Truth Will Prevail."

Assistant Attorney General Robert Peacock said:

"The verdict proves again that truth will prevail. All during the time I was preparing the case at the request of the Attorney General I felt that the simple truth presented in terms the jury could understand would adequately serve the ends of justice.

"The verdict is the answer to the prayers of the mothers of this nation that those who harm their children shall be punished and that men of the accomplishments of Colonel Lindbergh shall be able to maintain homes in the quiet assurance that their families in the hour of their absence shall be protected by the arm of the law."

Colonel H. Norman Schwarzkopf said:

"I feel that the verdict is in accordance with the evidence and that the ends of justice have been served.

Continued on Page Eleven.

JURY OUT FOR 11 HOURS

One of 2 Women Who Held Out for Mercy Near Tears at End.

DEFENDANT PALE, SILENT

Fails to Glance at Wife as He Is Led Back to Cell—She Is Calm.

DEFENSE PLANS TO APPEAL

Execution Set for the Week of March 18—Court's Charge Attacked as Biased.

Judge's charge to the jury and exceptions granted, Pages 10, 11.

By RUSSELL B. PORTER.

Special to THE NEW YORK TIMES.

FLEMINGTON, N. J., Feb. 13.—Bruno Richard Hauptmann was convicted of murder in the first degree at 10:45 o'clock tonight for the killing of Charles A. Lindbergh Jr. at Hopewell on the night of March 1, 1932.

He was sentenced to die in the electric chair at the State prison in Trenton some time during the week of March 18.

The jury of eight men and four women returned its verdict after having been out for eleven hours and twenty-four minutes since it retired from the court room at 11:21 o'clock this morning to deliberate in the jury room.

Handcuffed to two guards, Hauptmann stood between them silent and motionless, his face ashen white and terror in his deep-set eyes, while he heard the jury state its verdict and the judge pronounce sentence.

A few minutes later he was led away to his cell in the county jail. He did not even cast a glance of recognition toward his wife, who sat a few feet away. She looked at him with red-rimmed eyes, but did not weep.

Colonel Charles A. Lindbergh, who attended every session of the thirty-two court days of the trial from its beginning on Jan. 2, six weeks ago, and who heard Supreme Court Justice Thomas W. Trenchard deliver his charge to the jury this morning, was not in court when the verdict was returned. He had returned to his home in Englewood in the afternoon.

Woman Juror Near Tears.

Mrs. Verna Snyder, juror No. 3, was biting her lips to keep from crying and her eyes were wet with tears as she left the jury box. According to well-founded report, she and Mrs. Rosie Pill, juror No. 2, had held out to the last ballot for a verdict of guilty with a recommendation providing imprisonment at hard labor for life.

All the rest of the jurors were grave but appeared serene, as if they were satisfied that they had done their duty.

At 10:28 Sheriff Curtiss came out of the judge's chambers and gave an order to a deputy sheriff. The latter left the room and mounted the stairs to the cupola on the roof of the white court house. In a moment the 125-year-old bell, older than the court house itself, began to toll. By an old custom, revived a few years ago, the bell is rung to notify the town that a jury has reached a verdict and is about to return to the court room.

"There's the bell!" the whisper spread through the court room.

"Quiet! Quiet!" cried the guards as the reporters murmured among themselves, but both the murmurs and the shouts were drowned out by the noise of the crowd in the street, which at this moment rose to a roar.

Prisoner Is Brought In.

Mr. Fisher of defense counsel came in and indicated that Hauptmann was already on the way from his cell. At 10:31 the prisoner was brought in. The Sheriff and five State troopers led the way.

Hauptmann's gait was unusual as he appeared in the doorway. In a moment the reason was clear. For the first time since the trial began, he was brought into court man-

Continued on Page Twelve.

"All the News That's Fit to Print."

The New York Times.

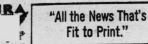

LATE CITY EDITION
WEATHER—Cloudy, followed by rain today; tomorrow fair.
Temperatures Yesterday—Max., 49; Min., 40

Copyright, 1935, by The New York Times Company.

VOL. LXXXIV....No. 28,196. Entered as Second-Class Matter, Postoffice, New York, N. Y. NEW YORK, SATURDAY, APRIL 6, 1935. P TWO CENTS In New York City. | THREE CENTS Within 200 Miles | FOUR CENTS Elsewhere Except in 7th and 8th Postal Zones.

5 BILLION RELIEF BILL VOTED; PRESIDENT READY TO SPEED RECORD PEACE-TIME OUTLAY

TO PUT 3,500,000 TO WORK

House Acts First by 317 to 70, Then the Senate Agrees, 66 to 13.

SCENE STORMY TO THE END

Robinson Insists on Putting Senators on Record and Talk Runs On for Hours.

FREE HAND TO ROOSEVELT

Steps Are Taken to Rush Final Formalities and Speed Act to Florida for Signing.

Text of the work-relief resolution is published on Page 7.

Special to THE NEW YORK TIMES.

WASHINGTON, April 5.—The $4,880,000,000 relief resolution today reached the end of its stormy trip through Congress and tonight was being prepared for delivery to President Roosevelt as the first completed measure in his enlarged program for relief, recovery and reform.

Congressional action was completed late this afternoon when the Senate, after another of the hectic sessions which the measure always evoked in that body, adopted the conference report 66 to 13.

The House had approved it three hours before by the overwhelming majority of 317 to 70.

Democratic leaders hoped that the engrossing of the resolution might be completed tonight so they could rush it by airplane to the President in Florida tomorrow, if necessary. Leaders will not pursue this unusual procedure if they learn that the President will return to Washington in time to sign before relief funds are completely exhausted.

By its action today Congress not only voted the largest single appropriation ever made by the American Congress in peace or war, but it sanctioned overwhelmingly the announced purpose of President Roosevelt to transfer employables from relief rolls to payrolls and return the unemployables as rapidly as possible to the care of local communities.

When the measure was started on its way it was directed primarily to the employment of 3,500,000 men and women—heads of families—who were then on the government's relief list.

Basic Spending Purposes.

So far as committees of Congress were able to determine, no all-embracing plan has yet been evolved for the expenditure of the huge sum. This is to be worked out as the program itself progresses, but a Senate amendment, approved by the President, indicated the general purpose to use the money along these lines:

(a) Highways, roads, streets and grade-crossing elimination, $800,000,000.

(b) Rural rehabilitation and relief in stricken agricultural areas and water conservation, transmountain water diversion and irrigation and reclamation, $500,000,000.

(c) Rural electrification, $100,000,000.

(d) Housing, $450,000,000.

(e) Assistance for educational, professional and clerical persons, $300,000,000.

(f) Civilian Conservation Corps, $600,000,000.

(g) Loans or grants, or both, for projects of States, Territories, possessions, including subdivisions and agencies thereof, municipalities and the District of Columbia, and self-liquidating projects of public bodies thereof, where, in the determination of the President, not less than 25 per cent of the loan or the grant, or the aggregate thereof, is to be expended for work under each particular project, $900,000,000.

(h) Sanitation, prevention of soil erosion, prevention of stream pollution, sea-coast erosion, reforestation, forestation, flood control, rivers and harbors, and miscellaneous projects, $350,000,000.

In order that the President might not be bound irrevocably by these amounts, Congress inserted a further provision that any one of these items might be increased at the expense of any one or more of the others to an extent of 20 per cent

Continued on Page Seven.

Main Points of Work-Relief Bill

Special to THE NEW YORK TIMES.

WASHINGTON, April 5.—Main provisions of the $4,880,000,000 relief resolution, completed by Congress today and sent to the President, are as follows:

Appropriates $4,000,000,000 in a new sum, together with $880,000,000 in existing balances of the Reconstruction Finance Corporation and Public Works Administration, to be used "in the discretion and under the direction of the President," to provide "relief, work relief, and to increase employment by providing for useful projects."

"Ear-marks" the fund in eight general classifications of projects, intended to cover every possible line of public works.

Gives to the President full authority to fix wage scales on these works, with the limitation that he shall pay "prevailing wages," according to the Davis-Bacon Act on strictly Federal building projects, and that other wages shall not lower existing private scales.

Empowers the President to establish any governmental agencies necessary to carry out the purposes of the resolution, but specifies that highway funds must be expended through present channels maintained under the Federal-State Aid Good Roads system.

Provides that of moneys lent or granted to States and political subdivisions thereof for non-Federal works, at least 25 per cent of each separate amount, "in the determination of the President," shall be expended for labor.

Authorizes the President to make loans to farmers, tenants and share-croppers for the purchase of farm lands and farm equipment.

Requires confirmation by the Senate of all central and State administrative officers receiving salaries of $5,000 or more.

Provides penalties for fraud in connection with the use of funds and also for violation of any rules and regulations prescribed by the President in carrying out the purposes of the resolution.

DANZIG HAILS HESS AS HE CALLS ON CITY TO JOIN NAZI FRONT

Hitler's Deputy Holds Up Saar as Example for Germans to Follow at Polls.

ATTACKS RUSSIA BITTERLY

Declares Reich Cannot Enter Pacts With Men Who Plot World Revolution.

DUCE OFFERS STRESA PLAN

Common Front Against Berlin Rearmament Proposed for Discussion by Powers.

The European Arms Situation.

DANZIG—Rudolf Hess, Chancellor Hitler's deputy, in a campaign speech, said the Free City, controlled by the League of Nations, was "an outpost of Germanism" and urged it to coordinate itself with the Reich. He also attacked Russia and Lithuania.

LONDON—Proposals were received from Premier Mussolini of Italy for discussion at the Stresa conference of a common front against German rearmament. Anthony Eden, arriving home, despaired of using the projected Eastern Locarno pact and most of the provisions of the Anglo-French accord as a basis for a European agreement.

PARIS—The War Ministry announced three battalions had been moved to the German frontier in addition to the thousands of men already ordered there. France planned to ask at Stresa for a strong resolution against Reich rearmament.

Hess Cheered Warmly at Danzig.

By OTTO D. TOLISCHUS.
Wireless to THE NEW YORK TIMES.

DANZIG, April 5.—Rudolf Hess, Reichsfuehrer Hitler's personal deputy and a member of the German Cabinet, came to Danzig today to help the local Nazi party machine in its whirlwind close to an election campaign designed to make National Socialism as supreme in this Free City as it is in Germany.

His appearance—which followed that of Air Minister Hermann Wilhelm Goering yesterday and is to be followed by that of Propaganda Minister Paul Joseph Goebbels, Nazism's greatest spellbinder, tomorrow—is a token of the importance attached by the National Socialist régime to the capture and final coordination of Danzig as an eastern equivalent of the Saar.

Like General Goering, Herr Hess was received by a city draped with Nazi flags and resounding to the cheers of thousands of marching men as well as boys and girls, most of them in brown uniforms. The military parade with rifles and steel helmets was absent this time. Instead, Storm Troops bearing torches lined up for miles, making a picturesque streak of light within which Herr Hess rode to Zoppot, a suburb of Danzig and a well-known seaside resort, for the main speech of the day.

Cites Saar as Example.

That speech, delivered in a crowded casino, had nothing whatever to do with any local Danzig issues, but only with issues facing the German people as a whole. Danzig, he said, was "an outpost of Germanism," and the great question facing it was: "Do you want to coordinate yourself with your home, with Germany?" He put before his audience the Saar as an example and the introduction of conscription in Germany as National Socialism's greatest accomplishment.

Beyond that, however, he utilized his presence in this eastern German bulwark to make an important pronouncement on German foreign policy, mainly sharp attacks on Russia and Lithuania, whose policies he contrasted with Germany's "peaceful restraint."

Referring to the Kaunas sentences against Memel Nazis, he declared:

"Nothing testifies to the German love of peace quite as much as the fact that Germany did not use her power for the protection of her sons as England, France or Italy would have done in a like case."

This statement was followed by a new appeal to the powers signatory to the Memel convention to intervene.

His attacks on Russia were connected with a pronouncement on the European pact negotiations and the recent trip of British Ministers to European capitals.

"Can the world object," he asked "that Germany treats with weighty caution all agreements in which Soviet Russia participates? For did not Soviet Russian politicians declare the Soviet State concluded pacts with so-called capitalistic States, with which they must presumably reckon Germany as well,

Continued on Page Four.

Speeding Auto Plunges Into Parade; Kills One, Injures 24 at Elmsford

Car Plows Into Throng of 500 Waiting at Crest of Hill to March Down to Village to Dedicate Veterans' Post—Mayor and Police Chief Among Those Hurt.

Special to THE NEW YORK TIMES.

ELMSFORD, N. Y., April 5.—An automobile traveling at high speed over the crest of a hill on Tarrytown Road at 8:45 o'clock tonight crashed into a group of several hundred persons preparing for a parade of the Veterans of Foreign Wars, killing one man and injuring twenty-four others.

The marchers had congregated just west of the hill crest preparing to march down into the village, where a new veterans' post was to be dedicated, when the automobile driven by Coppola Rocco, 32 years old, a baker of North Tarrytown, plowed into the crowd.

Men and women were sent sprawling in every direction as the driver frantically applied his brakes. The road at this point, between Goodwin Avenue and Evarts Street, is sixty feet wide, but the rain and dim street lights obscured the vision.

The man killed was Herbert R. Halliday, 37, of Pleasantville. He died at 9:45 o'clock at Grasslands Hospital, Eastview, where he had been employed as a clerk in the steward's department.

Among the injured were Mayor Edward Hicks and Police Commissioner Charles Minker. They suffered bruises and cuts when they were thrown to the pavement.

Of the twenty-four injured, eleven were examined at Grasslands Hospital and seven of these were admitted. It was reported that at least two of these were injured seriously.

The hill leads from White Plains into the centre of the village. The paraders had gathered in and about the middle of the road and were about to be placed in the line of march when Rocco's car loomed suddenly out of the dark.

There were about 500 persons as-

Continued on Page Six.

WHITNEY TO QUIT AS EXCHANGE HEAD

Nominating Group Will Retain Him as Member of the Governing Board.

GAY TO GET PRESIDENCY

Change Is Viewed as Victory for Younger Members Who Seek New Policy.

Richard Whitney, who has been president of the New York Stock Exchange since May, 1930, has notified the nominating committee that he will not be a candidate for re-election as president. It is understood, however, that he has received an offer of renomination as a member of the governing committee of the Exchange and has agreed to accept it. Mr. Whitney declined yesterday to comment on the report.

In making this offer to Mr. Whitney, the nominating committee, it was said, was taking a step toward the harmonious settlement of the struggle for the presidency of the Exchange. The committee will make known its slate on Monday, at which time a statement will be made by Mr. Whitney.

The withdrawal of Mr. Whitney from the race will leave Charles R. Gay, senior partner of Whitehouse & Co., unopposed as the candidate for the presidency. There is little doubt that Mr. Gay will be selected by the nominating committee and probably will not have any opposition at the annual election in May.

Mr. Whitney has been a member of the governing committee of the Exchange for many years, and it is felt that his counsel would be invaluable to the Exchange under any circumstances. The continuance of Mr. Whitney as a member of the governing committee and the selection of Mr. Gay as the nominee for the presidency, it is contended, will end what at one time looked like a serious conflict for the presidency of the Exchange.

Victory for Younger Element.

Since Mr. Gay became a serious contender for the presidency of the Exchange a few weeks ago, several efforts have been made to effect a compromise between the faction supporting Mr. Gay and that supporting Mr. Whitney. Mr. Gay has been supported mainly by the younger element in the Exchange, and the withdrawal of Mr. Whitney is considered a victory for the group that has been contending that there should be a change in many policies of the Exchange, particularly with reference to the public and to Washington.

Another contention of the group supporting Mr. Gay is that the Stock Exchange has been dominated by an inner clique that has been slow to accept suggestions and the trend in public psychology. As a result, they have maintained that the Exchange has been subjected to undue criticism from Washington.

Since Mr. Whitney entered office after the collapse of the boom market the Stock Exchange has been the target of much criticism. As a result, his friends have been of the opinion that he should have another year, which probably would be less hectic, after which he could retire voluntarily.

Compromise Proposals Made.

Several compromise proposals have been made, it is reported, in order to avoid an open conflict over the presidency of the Exchange. It has been suggested that Mr. Whitney be re-elected as president and that Mr. Gay be made

Continued on Page Six.

JURY LISTS OPENED TO ALABAMA NEGRO

Gov. Graves Cites Scottsboro Decision in Ordering Courts to Revise Juror Rolls.

CONSTITUTION PUT FIRST

Pending Cases Will Be Continued or Nolle Prossed Till the Jury Boxes Are Refilled.

By The Associated Press.

MONTGOMERY, Ala., April 5.—A revision of Alabama jury lists to include Negroes was called for today by Governor Bibb Graves in view of the United States Supreme Court decision in the Scottsboro case.

The Governor wrote his suggestion to circuit judges and solicitors throughout the State after receiving the official decision and included copies of it.

He also announced that he would ask the Legislature when it reconvenes April 30 for such legislation as may be necessary to cover the dumping and refilling of Alabama jury boxes from which the names of jurors are drawn.

The Supreme Court a few days ago set aside death sentences imposed on two Negro defendants in the Scottsboro attack case, holding that Negroes were "systematically" excluded from jury rolls in Jackson and Morgan Counties with infringement upon the constitutional rights of the accused.

"Supreme Laws of Land."

"Holdings of the United States Supreme Court are the supreme laws of the land," Governor Graves stated. "Whether we like the decisions or not, it is the patriotic duty of every citizen and the sworn duty of every public officer to accept and uphold them in letter and in spirit.

"I have received the Supreme Court's decision in the Scottsboro case, holding in effect that when there is systematic exclusion of Negroes from juries, it is discrimination against the race in violation of the United States Constitution. This decision means that we must put the names of Negroes in jury boxes in every county.

"Alabama is going to observe the supreme law of America."

With reference to pending cases the Governor advised that, if the question of absence of Negroes' names from jury rolls be raised, the case would be continued or nolle prossed until the boxes were refilled to meet constitutional requirements.

Precedent for Rest of South.

ATLANTA, April 5 (AP).—Alabama's action in ordering new jury lists drawn to conform with the United States Supreme Court decision in the Scottsboro case may be followed by other Southern States calling more Negroes for active jury duty, it was indicated today.

No Negroes are barred by law from jury duty in the South but few have actually been called to sit on cases. In most of the States jurors must be qualified voters and this in itself has kept a great many Negroes off the jury list.

The North Carolina Supreme Court has held twice in the past year or so that Negroes were not entitled to new trials when major grounds for appeal were allegations of exclusion of Negroes from the jury.

Jury commissions in South Carolina have discretionary power in selecting jury panels.

Major W. Calvin Wells, president of the Mississippi State Bar Association, said the Scottsboro decision

Continued on Page Six.

RAYMOND HAMILTON CAPTURED IN TEXAS POSING AS A TRAMP

Desperado Who Fled the Death House Seized as He Walks Ties in Disguise.

YIELDS WITHOUT A FIGHT

Had Said He Would Not Be Taken Alive—Man Who Helped Kill Barrow in the Posse.

By [Tel]ephone to THE NEW YORK TIMES.

DALLAS, Texas, April 5.—Raymond Hamilton, fugitive bank robber and slayer, was taken by surprise late today and captured without a struggle by Sheriff Richard Allen (Smoot) Schmid and five aides. The 22-year-old bad man, lieutenant of the slain Clyde Barrow, had boasted he would never be recaptured alive, but was picked up as easily as if he were the tramp he pretended to be.

Clad in overalls, a worn gray coat and a battered felt hat, toting a bedraggled suitcase containing the dapper clothes he had shed in an effort to escape searching parties, he was seized as he was walking the ties in a railroad gorge near Grapevine, north of Fort Worth, thirty miles from here.

He was in the midst of a group of hoboes, but the disguise failed to save him. Hiding at the gorge were Sheriff Schmid, who recognized him on sight, and his five men, four of them from Dallas, Hamilton's home town, where he had received three life sentences.

Silent When Captured.

The posse closed in quickly. Hamilton stopped in his tracks when he realized he was cornered. Crestfallen and sullen, he repressed an ejaculation. Not a word passed his lips as the officers rounded up the hobo party and then manacled him to two men for a swift return to the Dallas County jail.

On the ride to Dallas he ignored the Sheriff's questions as he sat with hunched shoulders and set face. As he was marched into the jail, the Sheriff tried a parting shot.

"How do you feel, kid?" he asked.

"Well," snarled Hamilton, "how do you think I feel?"

Later, however, while the officers were busy fingerprinting the other prisoners and checking their records, he recovered himself and attempted to affect once more the nonchalant air of his desperado character, exchanging quips with his guards.

Sheriff Schmid, in describing the capture, praised his aides, three deputy sheriffs and a city detective. Their weeks of investigation to discover those aiding Hamilton in his evasion of capture, brought the clue today to his whereabouts, he said. They were Chief Deputy Sheriff J. E. Decker and Ed Caster, Bryan Peck and Ted Hinton.

Hinton Helped Kill Barrow.

Hinton was among the officers who killed Hamilton's chief, Clyde Barrow, and his woman companion, Bonnie Parker, in Louisiana. A deputy sheriff from Grapevine completed the posse today.

Sheriff Schmid's story of the capture follows:

"This afternoon three of my deputies were searching in the western part of the city for a stolen automobile when they picked up a stranger in a taxicab, a boy who

Continued on Page Thirty-four.

BIG SECURITY BILL READY FOR HOUSE; 'GAG' RULE SOUGHT

Committee Approves Measure Which Lays New Taxes of $1,800,000,000 by 1949.

FIGHT CERTAIN NEXT WEEK

Republicans Map Hard Attack and Opposition to Too Rigid Procedure Rises.

Special to THE NEW YORK TIMES.

WASHINGTON, April 5.—After nearly three months of hearings and executive sessions on the measure, the Ways and Means Committee formally approved and ordered reported to the House today the administration's social security bill. The form adopted imposes an estimated $800,000,000 of new taxes in 1937 and a minimum of about $1,800,000,000 by 1949.

The present modified version of the omnibus bill originally transmitted by President Roosevelt is expected to be taken up early next week if by that time the wrangle between the Ways and Means group and House leaders over a rule to govern its consideration on the floor has yielded to an agreement.

Seventeen Democratic members of the committee voted solidly in the affirmative to report the measure, while the seven Republican members attending voted "present."

The remaining Republican member, Representative Lamneck of Ohio, was unable to attend the session because of illness.

The 103 Republican members of the House meanwhile were engaged in party caucus to determine their stand when the measure reaches the floor. This, and the possibility that the new taxes involved might cut across party lines and alienate Democratic strength to the opposition forces, stirred the Ways and Means group to press for a decision on a "gag" rule.

Byrns Favors Open Rule.

With a majority of the committee demanding a "gag" that would make out of order any amendments not originating with the committee managers of the bill, Chairman O'Connor of the Rules Committee called a meeting of his group for Monday in the hope that this fundamental question could be disposed of in time to bring the matter before the House on the following day.

Speaker Byrns is known to oppose any such procedure and to favor an open rule under which administration forces would have to rely entirely upon the loyalty of their majority to protect the program from mutilating amendments.

Unless advocates of the restricted procedure can show that this is unlikely of accomplishment, it is probable the Speaker's view will prevail.

With the Republican side certain to concentrate its fire against the taxation provisions of the bill, the opinion was widely held that the rule finally brought in would at least provide that such sections be immune from amendment and lengthy debate.

That the Ways and Means members would not be entirely satisfied in their suggestion for a "gag" rule appeared likely, however, when they concluded a meeting with Messrs. Byrns and O'Connor on this question without arriving at agreement.

There is always a disinclination

Continued on Page Six.

Emperors of Japan and Manchukuo Meet As Public Is Excluded From Tokyo Station

By HUGH BYAS.
Wireless to THE NEW YORK TIMES.

TOKYO, Saturday, April 6.—A storm that blotted out the view of the Inland Sea as the warship Hiei passed through it yesterday ceased at sunset and Emperor Kang Teh's first glimpse of Japan showed him a fairy-like landscape dusted with cherry blossoms under Mount Fuji's snowy cone.

The landing of Manchukuo's ruler at Yokohama this morning proceeded as by clockwork. At 9 o'clock precisely the Hiei, escorted by 150 planes, appeared outside the harbor. As soon as she had tied up at a buoy, launches shot out bearing Prince Chichibu, eldest brother of Emperor Hirohito; Admiral Nobumasa Suetsugu and scores of other notables to the warship.

Introductions were made and champagne was drunk and then Kang Teh landed and was welcomed by the Shinagawa Governor and the Mayor of Yokohama. He heard his fourth twenty-one-gun salute as he boarded a special train for the eighteen-mile journey to Tokyo.

All traffic bound into Tokyo Station was stopped from fifteen minutes before Kang Teh left Yokohama. The great Tokyo Station Plaza was like an empty canvas framed in khaki and steel. A stream of cars filled with dignitaries in gold lace and feathers passed across carrying high ranking Japanese, who alone were permitted to enter the station.

Then all movement ceased, and fifteen minutes later the Emperor of Japan, in an automobile preceded by the imperial standard, passed across the square amid dead silence.

Guns boomed as Kang Teh's train slowly steamed in, but only the privileged high officials witnessed the dramatic meeting of the two young Emperors of East Asia. Kang Teh, in a State coach drawn by four horses, left first. The route chosen took him for a mile between houses, shops, dance halls, cinemas and garages.

Six thousand two hundred policemen guarded the route, which was further protected by 45,000 members of the Young Men's Association. The ordinary public got but a fleeting glimpse of the glittering cavalcade as it flashed past. Kang Teh could not be distinctly recognized. In the beflagged streets the silence could be felt.

CITY BEGINS REPEAL OF ITS INCOME TAX

Board of Estimate Unanimous in Vote—Inheritance Impost to Go Also.

LEHMAN TERMS BEING MET

Taylor Warns of New Levies if the Returns on Sales Fall Below Relief Needs.

By a unanimous vote the Board of Estimate branch of the Municipal Assembly repealed the city income tax yesterday, thus taking the first step to relieve taxpayers of a levy equivalent to 15 per cent of their Federal income taxes. The tax would have become effective on June 1.

The repeal must go through the formality of concurrent action by the Board of Aldermen branch of the Assembly before it is finally effective. By its action yesterday the board carried out part of its agreement with Governor Lehman, under which the city will receive permission to extend other emergency taxes until the middle of next year.

The city inheritance tax, also scheduled for repeal under the agreement, was referred to the committee of the whole for study. Controller Frank J. Taylor suggested this action to pave the way for refunds to those who have already paid the tax.

Levy Was Widely Opposed.

In its brief life on the statute books, the city income tax has aroused a storm of protests and wide demands for its abolition. Controller Taylor's advisory committee on relief taxation urged its repeal, and Governor Lehman wanted it dropped because it, together with the inheritance tax, invaded fields he thought should be reserved for the State. Estimates on the yield of the tax ranged as high as $20,000,000.

Before the repeal was voted, Controller Taylor warned his colleagues that it might be necessary to find additional sources of relief funds. Other members of the board said they were willing to accept this responsibility, although most of them believed the yield from other city levies would suffice to meet relief needs.

When the proposal came before the board, James J. Lyon, Borough President of the Bronx, said:

"This tax was dead from the start—it is now having its funeral service."

Taylor Foresees New Levies.

Controller Taylor's reminder that other forms of revenue might have to be found was based largely on his disappointment at returns from the first quarter of the city sales tax, which have dropped behind badly. The deadline for payment of that tax is today.

"Those who repeal this tax," the Controller said, "must be ready to initiate other legislation if it is found necessary to provide additional revenues."

Mayor La Guardia said last Thursday that the city would be

Continued on Page Two.

LEHMAN WON'T BAR STATE AID INQUIRY

Praising FERA, the Governor Says He Has No Objection to Relief Investigation.

POLITICS MAY BE FACTOR

Leaders Study Possible Effect of Disclosures on Coming National Campaign.

Special to THE NEW YORK TIMES.

ALBANY, April 5.—Governor Lehman said today that he had no objection to a broad legislative investigation of the Temporary Emergency Relief Administration and administration of unemployment relief throughout the State. The prospect for creation of an investigating committee seemed bright tonight.

The Governor made known his views after the introduction of resolutions by Senators Dunnigan and McNaboe providing for establishment of the relief inquiry bodies. At the same time Mr. Lehman expressed full confidence in the TERA officials.

The legislators, stirred by the disclosures in the New York City inquiry about "eurythmic dancing" and "boon-doggling," have hit at city relief administration in harsh terms and have broadened their attack to include the TERA and relief administration through the State generally.

The two resolutions are now in the Senate Finance Committee, and Senator Dunnigan and others declared today that they would press for action early next week. But over the week-end some highly important possibilities of possible political import will be discussed with major leaders before any final decision is reached.

Political Angles Considered.

Under the terms of the Dunnigan and McNaboe resolutions an investigating committee, with wide powers, would be authorized to go anywhere in the State to find out how relief is operating.

An inquiry body of that kind would thus be working in the open in the home State of President Roosevelt just before the 1936 Presidential campaign is beginning to develop, with relief administration through the nation possibly a major topic in the battle.

The Washington administration, it was predicted at the Capitol, will become interested because of possible political repercussions.

In addition, Republicans in the Legislature are now becoming concerned over purely State aspects. An inquiry committee would be controlled by the Democrats, since they have majorities in both Senate and Assembly. The committee would be empowered to go into any hamlet in the State. With the Republicans expected to wage a fight to regain control of the Assembly, invasions of key communities under Republican control might produce an important effect on the Assembly campaign.

The broad social aspect of unemployment relief administration and

Continued on Page Two.

Arrival in the West brought disillusion — little work, meager wages and camping out wherever a bit of unwanted land could be found.

On the road to California.

A family and all their belongings heading west for California and employment.

Two migrant families en route to the fields in California.

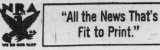

"All the News That's Fit to Print."

The New York Times.

LATE CITY EDITION
WEATHER—Fair today and tomorrow; warmer tomorrow.
Temperatures Yesterday—Max., 63; Min., 50

Copyright, 1935, by The New York Times Company.

VOL. LXXXIV....No. 28,216. Entered as Second-Class Matter, Postoffice, New York, N. Y. NEW YORK, FRIDAY, APRIL 26, 1935. P TWO CENTS In New York City. | THREE CENTS Within 200 Miles | FOUR CENTS Elsewhere Except in 7th and 8th Postal Zones.

M'DONALD ASSAILS REICH AS CHIEF BAR TO EUROPE'S PEACE

Holds Other Nations Justified in Questioning Berlin's Pacific Protestations.

HE ISSUES A CHALLENGE

Signed Article Calls on Hitler to Prove Good Faith by Acting on Stresa Resolutions.

APPEAL TO GERMANS SEEN

Prime Minister Is Viewed as Trying to Go Over Rulers' Heads to Reach People.

By CHARLES A. SELDEN.
Wireless to THE NEW YORK TIMES.

LONDON, April 25.—Prime Minister J. Ramsay MacDonald has written a severe attack on Germany which is to be published Saturday in the fortnightly News Letter, the organ of the Prime Minister's personal following of thirteen members of the House of Commons.

This significant contribution by Mr. MacDonald, however, will reflect the opinion of the much larger Conservative parliamentary group of the dominant pro-French element in the British Foreign Office. It will not have the unanimous approval of the Cabinet.

It reads as if it might have been written under the advice of Sir Robert Vansittart, Permanent Under-Secretary for Foreign Affairs, who has had much more to say than Sir John Simon recently in determining British policy in Continental affairs.

The article says Germany has destroyed the feeling of mutual confidence in Europe and "has broken up the road to peace and beset it with terrors."

"Other nations," says Mr. MacDonald, "will not be satisfied by Germany's assurances and can show ample justification for their refusal."

Appeals to German People.

The Prime Minister in his article repeats the attempt he made in a radio broadcast on April 17 to get an appeal to the German people over the heads of the German Government. There is only a faint trace left of his former attitude that the British peace policy must be based on cooperation with Germany. Instead of his old familiar plea for her to come back to the League of Nations, there is a reference in the last paragraph to the fact that the door is still open and he challenges the German Government to prove its pacific intentions by doing its part in putting the Stresa resolutions into effect.

Members of the British Government who already know what the article contains are curious about what effect it will have in Berlin. It may have an effect similar to that of the British White Paper of March 4, when Reichsfuehrer Adolf Hitler developed a cold that caused the postponement of Sir John Simon's visit to Berlin. This latest utterance by the Prime Minister may give colds to the German naval experts who are expected in London early in May on the invitation of the Foreign Secretary to discuss Herr Hitler's demands for a navy, 35 per cent as big as Britain's.

At any rate, if it is the present mood of Herr Hitler to continue building grievances, he will be able to put Mr. MacDonald's article in the same category as the League Council's recent resolution.

Text of MacDonald's Article.

The full text of Mr. MacDonald's article follows:

Today the lot of the peacemaker is hard. He is suddenly faced by a rapid movement on the part of Germany, which has instilled new fears in the minds of European nations.

Herr Hitler's announcement was accompanied by the usual declaration of peaceful intentions and during his conversations with Sir John Simon and Anthony Eden he committed himself to certain proposals in the nature of peace guarantees of which, although in reality they amount to very little in relation to present requirements, some use can undoubtedly be made when Europe is in a frame of mind to return to a calmer examination of the problems of security.

But peace cannot be pursued over broken roads which the traveler has some grounds for fearing are beset with ambushes and subject to incursions by armed men.

The substance of Germany's general case has a background of reason and human nature. I cannot be accused of ever having approached it "in the mind of Versailles" or in the spirit of one

Continued on Page Eight.

Germany Begins a Drive To End Non-Nazi Press

'Dictator' May Dismiss Editors and Suppress Newspapers—Religious Organs to Go—Owners Must Prove 'Aryan' Descent.

By OTTO D. TOLISCHUS.
Wireless to THE NEW YORK TIMES.

BERLIN, April 25.—A new revolution in the German newspaper publishing field, designed to make the National Socialist press supreme and annihilate even the "coordinated" bourgeois, professional and confessional newspapers still surviving, has been initiated by three orders issued by Max Amann, president of the Reich Press Chamber, who simultaneously has appointed himself Germany's supreme press dictator.

This new revolution, according to an official announcement, has been undertaken to free the German press from the influence of "special and anonymous interests" and make it serve the cultural needs of the entire German community under the publishers' personal responsibility, eliminating those who would "degrade the newspaper to a mere business."

At the same time it is a notorious fact that despite enforced subscriptions and official patronage, the National Socialist press has been losing out in both circulation and advertising compared with the old established bourgeois publications, which still occasionally contain a morsel of news or argument not found in any Nazi newspaper.

Herr Amann, besides being press dictator, is also director of the Eher publishing concern, which publishes the Voelkischer Beobachter and numerous other National Socialist publications, as well as director of the entire National Socialist press.

The first of his orders, entitled "An Ordinance for Safeguarding the Independence of the Newspaper Publishing System," provides among other things that newspapers shall no longer be published by any anonymous stock companies but only by partnerships whose partners can prove their own and their wives' or husbands' "Aryan" descent back to 1800 and who in other respects are entitled to membership in the Reich Press Chamber.

Their publishing directors and editors shall be appointed only with Herr Amann's approval and must be dismissed at his request. They shall also submit to Herr Amann immediately their complete financial status and lists of all the cap-

Continued on Page Nine.

PUBLISHERS COOL TO NEW DEAL BILLS

See Extension of NRA and Other Measures as Wedge Into Private Business.

KEEP RADIO NEWS SERVICE

Press Bureau Broadcasts to Continue Another Year Under Partly Liberalized Policy.

The radio broadcasting of news will continue for another year with a somewhat liberalized policy through the Press-Radio Bureaus established in New York and on the Pacific Coast by cooperation of press associations and broadcasting chains, as a result of action taken yesterday at the annual convention of the American Newspaper Publishers Association.

With 660 publishers registered, a record attendance, the convention adopted a report of its Radio Committee as submitted by E. H. Harris, committee chairman, who is publisher of the Richmond (Ind.) Palladium-Item.

The report recommended, as the result of an agreement by the committee, the press associations and the broadcasting chains, not only that the service be continued but also that newspapers owning or affiliated with radio stations be permitted to broadcast more extensive news reports than the Press-Radio Bureau bulletins. This liberalization will go into effect at once.

Oppose Transportation Change.

A resolution declaring that the association was "unalterably opposed to government ownership of railroads or any other form of transportation" was adopted. It was introduced by E. M. Antrim of The Chicago Tribune as chairman of the Traffic Committee.

The convention adopted a report of its Committee on Federal Laws, of which W. F. Wiley of The Cincinnati Enquirer is chairman, opposing New Deal legislation such as the new NRA extension bill, the AAA, the Wagner labor disputes bill and the Copeland pure food, drugs and cosmetics bill on the ground that all contain provision for governmental "fishing expeditions" into private business affairs in violation of the Fourth Amendment to the Constitution.

It also stated its opposition to the thirty-hour-week bill and suggested changes in the proposed social insurance legislation to make it less burdensome and more efficient.

Views on Radio Vary.

Adoption of the press-radio report followed extensive discussion from the floor, in which Roy Howard, chairman of the board of the Scripps-Howard newspapers, emphasized the seriousness of the problem caused by competition from independent radio stations broadcasting news not authorized by the agreement with the two radio chains the National Broadcasting Company and the Columbia Broadcasting System.

"A rival concern is entering the news distribution field," said Mr Howard. "The newspapers are faced with the developments of a new medium of news dissemination which does not have a century of

Continued on Page Six.

U. S. INQUIRY LIKELY IN PASTRY POISONING

Eggs Laid in Missouri, Packed in Nebraska and Shipped From Chicago Blamed.

VICTIMS NOW TOTAL 683

No More Danger Seen—White Plains Bakery Is Praised by Dr. Nicoll.

With 683 known cases of food poisoning resulting from cream puffs and eclairs sold Tuesday from a White Plains bakery plant, the possibility arose yesterday of Federal prosecution of a national distributer.

Westchester authorities held it possible that the yolks of eggs sent to White Plains by a Chicago house caused the poisoning.

After a conference with Dr. Matthias Nicoll Jr., Health Commissioner of Westchester County and former State Health Commissioner, William R. North, Federal inspector of foods and markets, said:

"This is a Federal matter and will require Federal prosecution if it can be established that impure egg yolks were brought into this State from some other State."

The tabulation yesterday rose from the 479 cases listed Wednesday because of the late arrival in the mails of reports from physicians. The list included sixteen cases in the Bronx, eleven in Greenwich, Conn., and five in Putnam County. Assurances were given by officials that there was no danger of any deaths or of any enlargement of the list other than through delayed reports by doctors. Of the 3,999 cream puffs and eclairs delivered by the company Tuesday, drivers were able yesterday to recover only 119 from customers.

175 Victims in Yonkers.

The list of persons affected, issued last night, was divided as follows:

Yonkers, 175; White Plains, 123; Mount Vernon, 105; New Rochelle, 70; Scarsdale, 36; Mamaroneck, 28; Ossining, 20; Port Chester, 17; Tuckahoe, 17; Bronx, 16; Larchmont, 14; Valhalla, 14; Greenwich, 11; Tarrytown, 8; Pelham Manor, 7; Cold Spring, 5; Bronxville, 5; Hartsdale, 4; Peekskill, 3; Dobbs Ferry, 2; Hastings, 1; Greenburgh, 1.

Specimens of the cream filling are under examination in the State Health Department laboratories at 339 East Twenty-fifth Street. The analysis will not be completed before Saturday.

Meanwhile, Dr. Nicoll discussed the possible cause.

"Circumstantial evidence," he said, "points to a batch of eggs used in the cream mixture Monday night at the White Plains plant of Cushman's, Inc., as the source of the infection. We cannot know definitely until we get the results of the laboratory tests Saturday. The eggs were the only ingredient of the cream which would be a field for bacteria. The eggs were received from a national distributer in Chicago, and were laid in Missouri. They were packed in Nebraska. We could not prosecute the distributer here, but when we have

Continued on Page Three.

SCHULTZ OFFERED TO PAY $100,000 TAX; DEFENSE IS CLOSED

Accountant Testifies He Twice Tried to Settle Federal Income Levy Claims.

TWO LAWYERS WITNESSES

They Say Defendant, in 1926, Sought Advice and Was Told He Was Not Liable.

By MEYER BERGER.
Special to THE NEW YORK TIMES.

SYRACUSE, April 25.—A swift, brief defense against charges that he attempted to evade payment of income taxes totaling $92,000 for 1929-1931 was entered in Federal court here today by Arthur (Dutch Schultz) Flegenheimer. His answer, in effect was:

"I am a rich man, but I tried to pay and the government would not accept; therefore I am not guilty of willful failure to file."

Only three witnesses, an accountant and two lawyers, testified for the defense. The most effective testimony consisted of a sheaf of powers of attorney granted by the defendant to accountants and lawyers who went to Washington in his behalf offering $100,000 to pay the tax and penalties, plus interest, only to be turned down.

Government attorneys, who had spent nine court days showing that Schultz's Bronx beer business had returned a gross of $2,863,000, with a net profit of $1,352,000, and that he had been a fugitive for twenty-two months after his indictment in January, 1933, were surprised by the move.

Government Wins a Point.

John H. McEvers, special assistant to Attorney General Cummings, scored a point after the defense had opened and closed within three court hours, by calling Captain E. A. Baldwin, a Federal agent, and establishing through him that the government had begun its investigation into the Schultz beer income several months before the defendant sent his lawyers to Washington to offer settlement.

James Noonan of the defense staff, tried to block this testimony on the ground that it was improper rebuttal, but he was overruled by Judge Frederick H. Bryant.

When court adjourned until 9 o'clock tomorrow morning for summations and the charge to the jury, all of which should be in by noon, according to attorneys for both sides, Schultz left the chamber with a smile. Earlier in the day he had been extremely nervous, pacing up and down the corridor during recess, with a worried look wrinkling his brow.

"I offered $100,000 when the government was broke and people were talking revolution," he told reporters, "and they turned me down cold. You can see now that at least I was willing to pay."

He amplified this a few minutes later, as he shrugged into his topcoat.

He Says He Is Persecuted.

"Everybody knows I am being persecuted in this case," he said. "I wanted to pay. They were taking it from everybody else, but they wouldn't take it from me. I tried to do my duty as a citizen." Then, as an afterthought: "Maybe I'm not a citizen?" he grinned.

Some one mentioned that it had cost the government more than $300,000 to get him into court.

"Three hundred thousand?" he echoed. "It cost over a million."

The first defense witness today was Edward H. Reynolds of Irvington-on-Hudson, who was Assistant United States Attorney for the

Continued on Page Five.

BONUS ACTION SPED TO BAR LONG FIGHT ON LYNCHING BILL

Harrison Measure Is Reported to Senate as Southerners Threaten Filibuster.

PATMAN PLAN IS BLOCKED

Committee Rejects It as Well as Vinson's—Wagner, Bailey Clash on Lynching Data.

Special to THE NEW YORK TIMES.

WASHINGTON, April 25.—The Harrison compromise bonus bill, liberalized to permit veterans to receive cash or bonds for present value of their adjusted compensation certificates, was rushed to the Senate today as a means of displacing the anti-lynching issue which apparently had involved that body in a hopeless filibuster.

Leaders immediately laid their plans to "adjourn" instead of "recess" for the week-end holiday, beginning tomorrow, or Saturday, in order that the motion of Senator Costigan to take up the Costigan-Wagner anti-lynching bill might be killed without a record vote. The goal of this strategy is to permit Senator Harrison to gain the floor the first thing Monday and move to take up the bonus compromise.

Meanwhile the Finance Committee ordered the bonus compromise reported without record vote after it had rejected the Patman "greenback" bill, already passed by the House, and the Vinson full cash payment plan, sponsored by the American Legion.

As the record of the committee shows it, the committee first voted 13 to 4 to substitute the Vinson plan for the Patman bill, and then voted 12 to 8 to substitute the Harrison compromise for the Vinson plan.

Relief Fund Use Provided.

The principal change which the committee wrote into the Harrison bill was an amendment by Senator Connally, supported by Senator Harrison, permitting veterans to exchange their bonus certificates either for bonds or for cash at the present surrender value, as calculated on the new basis provided in the bill.

The committee also adopted an amendment by Senator Gore permitting the President, in his discretion, to pay the cost of the measure out of the $4,880,000,000 work relief appropriation. Senator Harrison insisted that this amendment was meaningless, as it left the matter entirely to the President. He did not expect that Mr. Roosevelt would ever use the authority.

As the compromise was reported, some Senators raised a question as to whether the President would sign it. Some indicated that the President had intimated to them that he would veto any bonus plan providing payment in any form before 1945 as provided on the face of the adjusted compensation certificates.

Senator Harrison, however, continued in the faith, often expressed, that Mr. Roosevelt would approve his plan.

Southerners Warn of Fight.

A plan of action to put ahead the bonus compromise became imperative late this afternoon when Senator Bailey, following Senator Connally in condemnation of the anti-lynching bill, warned the Senate in behalf of himself and Southern colleagues that "we'll be here all Summer" if necessary to prevent its passage.

"It shall not pass," shouted the North Carolinian. "We'll fight it out on this line, as General Grant once said, if it takes all Summer. As the representative of the sovereign State of North Carolina, I am

Continued on Page Two.

More Than 3 in Front Seat of Car Banned Under Bill Signed by Governor Lehman

Special to THE NEW YORK TIMES.

ALBANY, April 25.—Governor Lehman today signed the Breitbart bill providing that not more than three persons may ride in the front seat of an automobile.

The bill was urged by the State Motor Vehicle Bureau as a safety measure. It is designed chiefly to strike at "joy riders," who frequently pack four and sometimes five in the front seat, thereby interfering with the driver's vision and also with operation of the machine.

Governor Lehman approved the Ross bill, which provides that illuminated signs must be placed at the termination of dead-end streets.

Under the McCall bill, also signed by the Governor, the State Superintendent of Banks receives authority to examine banking corporations once every fifteen months instead of once in each calendar year, as at present.

Four bills were vetoed, including one which would have imposed a license fee of $10 and a registration fee of $15 on manufacturers and wholesalers of narcotics. The Governor said the measure would not aid in the enforcement of the uniform narcotic drug law and that it would unnecessarily increase the cost of government.

Another bill vetoed would have provided for expenditure of $750,000 for construction of a seventeen-mile State highway through forests in Lewis and Herkimer Counties between the villages of Port Layden and McKeever.

Governor Lehman said the highway division had informed him the proposed road would be "a costly venture for the State," and that there was doubt as to its proper location.

A bill which would have compelled the State to pay for documents on file in county clerks' offices was vetoed. The Governor said this would increase the cost of liquidating properties under the jurisdiction of the Banking and the Insurance Departments, and would mean that creditors would get much less for their claims.

JOB INSURANCE BILL SIGNED, TAXING PAYROLLS IN STATE; RELIEF STEPS BY ROOSEVELT

ALLOTMENT BOARD NAMED

Ickes Will Head Group of 22 to Advise President on Money Grants.

WALKER STILL SUPREME

Will Have Greatest Authority Next to Roosevelt—Post for Hopkins Undecided.

RUSH FOR JOBS UNDER WAY

Project Applications Are Also Pouring In, but Await Selection of a Technical Staff.

Text of White House statement is printed on Page 12.

Special to THE NEW YORK TIMES.

WASHINGTON, April 25.—Organization of a works allotment division under the chairmanship of Secretary Ickes, to advise President Roosevelt on final allocation of funds for approved works relief projects from the $4,000,000,000 appropriation, was announced today by the White House.

The announcement of the new allotment division, making public the third of a series of decisions on the program reached in as many successive days, was made coincident with another that President Roosevelt had called his chief relief advisers for a conference at the White House tomorrow night.

The conferees are to be Frank C. Walker, director of the National Emergency Council; Harry L. Hopkins, Relief Administrator; Secretaries Ickes and Morgenthau, Joseph P. Kennedy, chairman of the Securities and Exchange Commission; Rexford Guy Tugwell, Under-Secretary of Agriculture and director of rural resettlement under the relief program, and Charles West, contact man between the White House and Congress.

Group Will Determine Scope.

These men, with the exception of Mr. Tugwell, who has a highly specialized field, were regarded in informed quarters tonight as the ones who will have the final word in determining the scope and activities of the work-relief program. Mr. Kennedy was said at the White House to have been assigned to the special field of studying securities offered for loans for self-liquidating projects.

Establishment of the Works Allotment Division, composed of twenty-two Cabinet members, heads of government agencies and representatives of organizations within the relief set-up, was reported to have marked a shift in original plans under which this group would have been the controlling agency for relief spending, subject only to the will of the President.

Mr. Roosevelt still retained his own authority in the program, but it was made clear that the greatest responsibility other than his own in the organization thus far established rested on Mr. Walker, who is to be chairman of the Division of Applications and Information, established Tuesday.

However, final composition of the relief establishment, which is scheduled for tomorrow, when a final announcement will be made by the White House, still remained a riddle in so far as Mr. Hopkins, author of the work-relief idea, was concerned.

He was still unassigned tonight, and the probability was discussed in informed quarters that he would emerge tomorrow as a highly important figure in the program.

"Third Step" Is Thus Taken.

The White House statement announcing the new agency referred to this as the "third step" in formulating a work-relief program.

It termed the designation of Mr. Walker's group as the first step and grouped in the "second step" action taken yesterday by the President in announcing simultaneously that relief spending would be divided between fifty established government agencies and three new bureaus, and that more than 200 types of projects, divided into eight major groups, offered outlets for application of the program.

The Works Allotment Division, as described at the White House, includes these officials:

Secretaries Ickes, Wallace and Perkins; Mr. Walker; a "director of the Progress Division" yet to be

Continued on Page Twelve.

Roosevelt Will Discuss Relief on Radio Sunday

By The Associated Press.

WASHINGTON, April 25.—President Roosevelt will go on the air Sunday night in a resumption of his fireside radio talks to the nation to discuss the new works relief program. He will speak for half an hour beginning at 10 P. M., Eastern standard time.

It will be the first time Mr. Roosevelt has talked to the people since Sept. 30.

Throughout his recent disputes with Congressional factions over the works relief bill, the President was urged by some advisers to present his problems to the country over the radio but he put these suggestions aside.

With the bill now being put into operation, the President was represented as feeling it was vital that he explain the vast undertaking to the nation.

Mr. Roosevelt suggested today to Senator Lewis, Democratic whip, that the public was looking for Congress to act on important bills and close up business in the early future.

Mr. Lewis reported that he was joshingly chided by the President as a "poor whip-cracker" but he predicted Congress would continue in session until August.

MAYOR HITS BACK ON AIR BASE 'WASTE'

Resents Charge That Cost of East River Relief Work Was $160,000 Over Estimate.

ATTACKS NAVAL ENGINEER

Defends Projects and Holds Witness Who Found Design Foolish Is Ignorant.

Irked by charges that two East River seaplane ramps had been built at almost $160,000 more than their original estimated cost, Mayor La Guardia took a hand yesterday in the aldermanic investigation of relief by denouncing the witnesses who testified to waste and mismanagement on the project.

The Mayor has carefully avoided any direct participation in the inquiry up to yesterday, though he has had transcripts of the testimony every day. When Lloyd Paul Stryker, counsel to the committee, turned his guns on aviation projects, the Mayor was stung into action. The East River bases, at Thirty-first and at Wall Streets, in addition to being used by commercial airlines, form a link in the Mayor's plan to make Floyd Bennett Field in Brooklyn the eastern air mail terminus.

Frank P. Hall, a naval engineer, who testified that the ramps had been improperly built, aroused the Mayor's anger.

"This man is either deliberately and maliciously making false statements, or else he just doesn't know what he is talking about," Mayor La Guardia said. "The ramps have cost about $55,000 each, but that does not cover the shore work that must be provided for seaplane bases."

Mr. Hall had told the Aldermanic committee investigating relief that pontoons under the seaplane decks had been made too large, with the result that it required forty tons of ballast to lower the floats to proper levels.

Mayor Charges Ignorance.

"That shows hopeless ignorance of what the ramps are for," the Mayor said. "These ramps are not to be used just for passengers to stand on. They must be large enough to hold the planes while they are being turned around. They have been planned so that they can handle even large ships of the Clipper type. Transcontinental Western Air, Inc., is planning to use the ramps for an air ferry service between Manhattan and Floyd Bennett Field."

Told that Mr. Hall had designed tugboats, the Mayor said:

"He talks like one. He's qualified, all right—qualified to be a political witness. But I'll bet he couldn't work out a formula or the mathematical calculations for the floats. Of course there have been mistakes made, but did you ever see any new construction that had no 'bugs' in it?

"You must remember that this was an experimental job, and while it was not the first, it was a new type of construction. The ramps

Continued on Page Twelve.

LEHMAN HAILS MEASURE

'Great Step,' He Holds, Wiring Wagner Hope for National Action.

ONLY EMPLOYERS TO PAY

Levies Will Begin March 1, '36—First Benefits Available Two Years Later.

STATE BOARD TO CONTROL

3 Members Will Represent Labor, 3 Employing Concerns and 3 the Public.

Text of Employment Insurance Act is printed on Page 14.

Special to THE NEW YORK TIMES.

ALBANY, April 25.—A permanent State system of unemployment insurance was formally created today when Governor Lehman signed the Byrne-Killgrew bill, establishing the new program.

Victorious in his fight to force the bill through the Senate over objections of rebellious Democrats, the Governor hailed the measure as a great step for the State. At the same time he sent a telegram to Senator Wagner in Washington, expressing hope for early enactment of a national unemployment insurance law.

The measure, as approved by the Governor, takes effect next year, but the first payments toward setting up the reserve funds, out of which benefits will be paid, will not be due until March 1, 1936.

The reserve will be built up by collections from employers only, based on a levy on their payrolls. This levy will be 1 per cent in 1936; 2 per cent in 1937 and 3 per cent in 1938 and thereafter.

With Governor Lehman when he signed the bill were Senator William T. Byrne, Democrat of Albany, and Assemblyman John F. Killgrew, Democrat of New York, who sponsored the legislation. Mr. Killgrew represents the home district of James J. Dooling, Tammany leader.

Recalls Three-Year Fight.

Here is Governor Lehman's memorandum on approving the bill:

"I am most happy to append my signature to this bill which establishes unemployment insurance for the working people of the State of New York. For three years I have repeatedly recommended to the Legislature the passage of such a bill. And so, I am very pleased to be able to place this law permanently upon the statute books of our State.

"In my mind it stands out as the most progressive and enlightened piece of social legislation enacted in this State in many decades.

"The people of the State of New York should feel proud that it is once again leading the nation in legislation which will increase the economic and moral security of its working people, cushion the hardships of economic depressions, and advance the general well-being.

"The bill is approved."

In his telegram to Senator Wagner, Governor Lehman wrote:

"I know you will be deeply interested in learning that I have just signed the Unemployment Insurance Bill which was passed by the Legislature on my recommendation; I am sure you will be happy that our State has once again taken the lead in progressive social legislation. It is my earnest hope that the benefits of unemployment insurance will soon be made available by Congress to the people of the whole nation."

Broader Than Federal Bill.

The new State law is designed to synchronize with administration of a Federal system, although it is broader in one respect. Under the Byrne-Killgrew act, every employer of four or more persons would be required to contribute toward a reserve fund. Under the pending Federal bill, employers of ten or more persons would come under the system.

Elmer F. Andrews, Industrial Commissioner, has already appealed to Washington sponsors of the Federal program to bring it into line with the Byrne-Killgrew act.

Major features of the Byrne-Killgrew act are as follows:

All employers of four or more persons must pay a levy on their

Continued on Page Fifteen.

NRA WE DO OUR PART

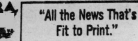

"All the News That's Fit to Print."

The New York Times.

LATE CITY EDITION
WEATHER—Rain, cooler today; tomorrow probably rain, cooler.
Temperatures Yesterday—Max., 77; min., 68.

Copyright, 1935, by The New York Times Company.

VOL. LXXXIV....No. 28,219. Entered as Second-Class Matter, Postoffice, New York, N. Y. NEW YORK, MONDAY, APRIL 29, 1935. P TWO CENTS In New York City. | THREE CENTS Within 200 Miles | FOUR CENTS Elsewhere Except in 7th and 8th, Postal Zones.

PRESIDENT IN TALK TO NATION PROMISES TO EXPEDITE RELIEF; EMPHASIZES SOCIAL SECURITY

NAZIS FIND EXPENSE OF RAW MATERIALS BALKS ARMS PLANS

Costliness of Domestic Goods Bars German Independence of Foreign Products.

CHANGES IN PROGRAM SEEN

Cuts in Purchases of Fibers, Metals, Oils, Timber, Hides and Rubber Are Sought.

TAX RISE TO AID EXPORTS

Officials Plan in Secret to Double the Turnover Levy, Providing $640,000,000 for Subsidy.

By The Associated Press.

BERLIN, April 28.—Germany's dependence upon foreign raw materials was revealed today as the most serious stumbling block in the path of Reichsfuehrer Hitler's comprehensive program to rearm the nation.

The marshaling of war materials, according to authorities in the Nazi administration, is proving more difficult than the mobilization of men. The campaign for self-sufficiency, started two years ago as an emergency measure, is proving more expensive than its initiators had anticipated.

Experts foresee the abandonment or modification of some of the outstanding features of this program. The problem, it was pointed out, lies in reducing further the amounts of imported foreign goods so that Germany, in case of war, can get along indefinitely without importing a single important product.

Imports Show Reduction.

Figures revealed that in 1934 Germany imported 2,600,000,000 marks worth of raw materials from abroad [the mark is currently worth about 40 cents], while in 1933 such commodities costing nearly 6,000,000,000 marks were used in the production of 40,000,000,000 marks worth of industrial goods. In 1928 the raw materials were valued at 17,500,000,000 marks, of which about 40 per cent came from other countries.

Major attention is being paid to reducing the imports of eight commodities: textile fibers, non-ferrous metals, mineral oils, timber, hides, iron ore, wood pulp and rubber.

German textile makers now depend on foreign supplies for 95 per cent of their raw materials. To cut this down a campaign is under way to encourage domestic production of flax and wool.

In 1932 Germany imported 54 per cent of the non-ferrous metals she used, against 71.4 per cent in 1928. Of some metals Germany has no resources and of others the deposits are of poor grade. The government is paying heavy subsidies to develop the home deposits.

More than 30 per cent of Germany's motor fuel needs and 80.7 per cent of her gasoline come from abroad. Of the 250,000 tons of oil produced at home annually, some comes from crude petroleum and the rest is synthetic. The use of alcohol and benzol is being encouraged.

Experts say the trouble is that products manufactured at home are turning out to be two or three times, sometimes six or seven times more expensive than goods imported wholly or in part.

Funds to Aid Exports Planned.

Funds equivalent to about $640,000,000 will be raised during the year to help finance German exports in accordance with a decision of the Hitler Government under which the so-called turnover tax will be doubled.

This tax demands contributions from each individual handling an article in the process of manufacture. Before a shoe could be sold, for instance, the farmer selling the cow formerly paid 2 per cent of the sale price to the government, the butcher selling the hide another 2 per cent, and so on through the tanner, the shoe manufacturer, the wholesaler and the retailer.

The government's decision raises that tax to 4 per cent. Up to now this tax has yielded 1,600,000,000 marks, or about $640,000,000, a year, and doubling it will make the full amount available to compensate exporters for the difference in the sales price in Germany and the lower price necessitated in places like the United States, Britain, Belgium and the Scandinavian countries.

The whole matter is being treated with great secrecy just now so that the enthusiasm of the populace during the May Day activities may not be dampened, for it is anticipated the tax will result inevitably in higher prices for goods, as each processor attempts to pass the added expenditure on to the ultimate consumer.

Soon after the first of May, it was reliably reported, the added tax will go into effect.

Crowds Overflow 35 Churches On Orthodox Easter in Moscow

At Least 75,000 Attend Midnight Services in Soviet Capital—Traditions of the Event Are Followed Even by Some Communists—Anti-Religious Propaganda Sharply Curbed.

By HAROLD DENNY.
Special Cable to THE NEW YORK TIMES.

MOSCOW, April 28.—The thirty-five churches which are all that remain of the thousand that once dotted Moscow were filled to overflowing last night for the celebration of the Russian Easter, the holiest anniversary of the Greek Orthodox calendar.

Every church visited in a midnight tour was crowded to suffocation, and there were great crowds—some numbering as high as 2,000—standing patiently in the churchyards in an intermittent drizzle. These latter persons tried to peer through the windows for a glimpse of the service, and at the climax of the ritual at midnight they lighted candles in unison with those within.

A conservative estimate would be that 75,000 residents of Moscow participated in the Easter celebration. Three-fourths of the worshipers were women, many of whom were elderly and looked as if they had only recently come from villages. There was a liberal sprinkling of young persons, however, and some children.

The services lasted until early hours in the morning. Many persons, however, went home after the midnight services to feasts. Tables were gay with flowers, candles, the traditional Easter cakes—pashki, made of cottage cheese, and kulichi, made of flour, milk and eggs—and Easter eggs, all of which had been sprinkled with holy water. And there were wine and vodka.

This began three days of feasting, in which the devout will go calling among their friends, greeting them with the words, "Jesus Christ is risen"; kissing them thrice on the cheek and exchanging gifts.

Pashki and kulichi are being prepared in the homes of some good Communists also, so strong is the Easter tradition in Russia. But they will not be blessed by priests. They will be served in the feasting that will follow the Red May Day celebration.

In this Easter season, Communist anti-religious activity has been far less than in other years. A few signs urging the people to stay away from church have appeared on the streets, and some anti-Easter handbills have been distributed, but the radio stations, which on preceding Easter eves broadcast anti-religious appeals, ignored the subject last night.

ITALY IS HUMMING WITH WAR ACTIVITY

Mobilization Fills Barracks and Cantonments—Factories Rush Munition Output.

MUSSOLINI WARNS NATION

'Hard Times Approaching,' He Says, With 'Aims' Enlisting All Its Strength.

By ANNE O'HARE McCORMICK.
Wireless to THE NEW YORK TIMES.

MILAN, Italy, April 28.—To enter Italy after a year's absence is to meet at once the "warlike face" described by Premier Benito Mussolini. In this respect the change in the last few months has been spectacular. Signs of military activity are more apparent than in Germany.

While the people's spirit is resigned, more than belligerent, and the general gloom over the war prospect has been somewhat lightened since the Stresa conference—regarded here and in France as a step toward security—the aspect of the country is one of intense preparation for any eventuality.

Factories in this industrial section are engaged in making munitions and army supplies, working day and night. All barracks and many improvised cantonments are full. Not only are last year's conscripts kept mobilized, in addition to the new recruits, but reserve classes have been called up, justifying Il Duce's Stresa declaration that while the international weather remains threatening Italy will have 600,000 soldiers ready to move.

Two Divisions Have Gone.

Two divisions have been shipped to Africa and twice that number, it is estimated, are encamped near the Austrian border warning irredentists on this side of the frontier as well as Nazi agitators on the other. Furthermore, large groups of technicians—engineers, chemists, doctors, former artillery officers, &c.—have been detached from their regular occupations to assist in the concentration of national forces.

Even the international sample fair, which closed yesterday, gave a large space to the display of guns, shells, tanks and other war machines. Second only to the Leipzig fair in size and importance, the Milan exposition this year was the most successful in the sixteen years of its existence. Despite new exchange restrictions, reducing international trade to a minimum, foreign exhibitors were more numerous than ever before, numbering 1,276 out of 5,184. Germany has the largest foreign exhibit and that of the Soviet Union attracted the most interest.

Perhaps the restrictions explain the increased exhibits and the brisk business reported. Quotas were abolished for goods bought and sold at the fair and the results suggest that all countries may have to establish such open seasons to capture any foreign trade.

Gas Masks Form Big Exhibit.

What struck the visitor most forcibly, however, was the display of gas masks and other protective devices against air raids. A well-patronized pavilion was devoted to the exhibit of masks of various styles, models of bombproof cellars, material for camouflaging fac-

Continued on Page Nine.

EXILED DOMINICAN SHOT BY ASSASSIN

Gunman Hunting Dr. Morales Invades Home Here and Fells Insurgent Associate.

STRIFE IN SANTO DOMINGO

Italian Consul Charged With Conspiring Against Life of President Trujillo.

An assassin, seeking Dr. Angel Morales, former Minister of the Dominican Republic at Washington and now in exile from his native land, forced his way last night into the apartment at 87 Hamilton Place that Dr. Morales shares with his friend and ardent supporter, Sergio Bencosme.

Dr. Morales was not at home. Señor Bencosme, who was shaving in the bathroom when the assassin entered, heard the cries of his landlady and rushed into the living room. The invader shot him through the chest.

The attacker, of whom the police have only a scant description, fled down the stairway into the street. Señor Bencosme followed him into the hallway and collapsed.

Other residents summoned an ambulance, which took Señor Bencosme to Knickerbocker Hospital. His condition is critical.

Leader of Opposition.

Detectives of the Wadsworth Avenue Station expressed the opinion that the shooting was the outgrowth of political plotting. Dr. Morales, they pointed out, is a leader of the Opposition party, all the principal members of which have been exiled by President Rafael Leonidas Trujillo.

President Trujillo, a former private in the United States Marine Corps, headed the insurgent forces that, in 1930, overthrew the government of President Horacio Vásquez. Señor Trujillo was elected to the Presidency soon afterward and reelected last year.

According to the police, Dominicans in this country have been secretly fomenting an uprising against President Trujillo with the purpose of making Dr. Morales President. Dr. Morales himself predicted last July that the Trujillo government would be overthrown.

Yesterday afternoon Dr. Morales attended a meeting of Dominican political exiles and did not return home for dinner. Señor Bencosme was making his toilet in preparation for dinner when the assassin knocked at the door of the apartment, which is on the seventh floor The landlady, Mrs. Carmine Higgs, herself a Latin-American but married to an American, went to open it.

She was brushed aside by a man who, pistol in hand, strode in demanding the whereabouts of Dr. Morales. He drove Mrs. Higgs to the kitchen, where, suspecting a hold-up, she hid her diamond rings in a coffee pot and then began screaming for help.

Meeting of Exiles.

Dr. Morales did not return to the apartment until almost midnight. He was greatly shocked when informed of the shooting of his friend. Señor Bencosme, he disclosed, is the son of a general in the Dominican army. The general was killed in political troubles there, his prop-

Continued on Page Three.

ENVOYS OF MEXICO MAKE SILVER PLEA TO MORGENTHAU

Appeal to Ease Buying Policy Believed Presented at Conference in Washington.

MEXICAN BANKS TO REOPEN

Representative Dies Predicts Our Course Will Force World Currency Stabilization.

By The Associated Press.

WASHINGTON, April 28.—Monetary troubles in Mexico, born of world silver prices soaring after United States Treasury offers, today were taken directly to Secretary Morgenthau by representatives of the southern republic.

For an hour President Roosevelt's first financial adviser conferred with Ambassador Castillo Najera and Roberto Lopez, Assistant Secretary of the Mexican Treasury, who was sped to Washington by his government when climbing silver prices forced orders for the surrender of silver coins and closed banks over the week-end.

With Mr. Morgenthau were Herman Oliphant, the Treasury's general counsel, and Herbert Feis, economic adviser to the State Department.

Officials of neither nation would discuss the meeting beyond indicating further conferences. But before the session, Señor Lopez said "it would seem proper that both countries should find a way to cooperate in this matter."

No Change in 77.57 Cent Price.

Mr. Morgenthau's office reiterated there would be no change in the 77.57 cents an ounce price for newly-mined domestic metal before tomorrow at the earliest.

During the day Representative Dies, Democrat of Texas, co-author of the silver purchase act, predicted a continuation of the administration's present silver policy eventually would force international currency stabilization.

Despite the silence in official quarters, the belief was general that the Mexican Government would urge the United States to ease its buying program just as China has asked in the past.

Señor Lopez, in a statement issued late tonight, described the conversations of the Mexican Government officials with Secretary Morgenthau as "mutually satisfactory" to the representatives of the two governments.

He said that despite the fact Mexico's monetary problem had been solved already, the conversations made the outlook even better and promised future collaboration.

Mr. Dies gave his interpretation of the situation in these words:

"The United States, by raising its price for silver to 77.57 cents, is getting or threatening to get the world's floating supply of silver.

Dies Foresees $1.29 an Ounce.

"Many nations have little gold: the United States has half the world's gold. A managed currency without a metallic base is never satisfactory, and the rest of the world knows it.

"So with the United States buying all the silver it can get, some other governments apparently are bidding up the price in order to keep silver within their own borders.

"Eventually the United States

Continued on Page Five.

LEADERS WILL POLL SENATE IN BATTLE TO STOP FILIBUSTER

Robinson Hopes for a Majority Pact Today to Take Up Lynching Bill, Then Shelve It.

ROOSEVELT SEEKING SPEED

But Southerners Say They Will Balk Even This Latest Plan of Getting to the Bonus Bill.

By TURNER CATLEDGE.
Special to THE NEW YORK TIMES.

WASHINGTON, April 28.—Pressed by President Roosevelt for greater speed on his legislative program, administration leaders will try earnestly tomorrow to break the anti-lynching filibuster which has held the Senate at a standstill since early last week.

A poll of the Senate membership will be taken soon after tomorrow's session opens to see if sentiment for the veterans' bonus compromise bill is strong enough to substitute it for the Costigan-Wagner Anti-Lynching Bill, as the pending business before the body.

If that check-up discloses, as it is expected to, that the Senate prefers to consider the bonus, a series of quick moves will be attempted, first to take up the Anti-Lynching Bill and then immediately to lay it aside for the veterans' legislations.

Plans to this effect went forward tonight, despite the warning of certain Southern Senators that they would filibuster indefinitely against even the technical taking up of the Anti-Lynching Bill.

Under the proposed strategy of the leadership, a vote would have to be taken first on Senator Costigan's motion to take up his bill, pending when the Senate recessed yesterday. The Senate has shown in two previous tests that it would adopt the motion if given a chance to vote upon it.

Banking Bill Up in House.

While the Senate is engaged in disposing of this troublesome matter, the House will begin consideration of the Omnibus Banking Bill. The measure will be considered under one of the new "wide-open" rules of that body, with allowances for fifteen hours of general debate and unlimited opportunity for offering amendments.

House leaders hope and expect to complete the Banking Bill in short order and then to place it on the Senate's doorstep alongside of the Economic Security Bill and several other essential measures which they have rushed through with a view, partly, as some members have expressed it, of "shaming the upper body into action."

Senate leaders' plans to break the anti-lynching filibuster were being drawn largely without the cooperation of the group of Southern Senators who announced last Thursday that the Costigan-Wagner measure should not even be considered by the Senate and who spent the remainder of the week carrying out that threat.

Senator Robinson, the majority leader, himself a Southerner, was mapping the strategy to break the deadlock. He was being aided by Senator Harrison of Mississippi, leader of the anti-lynching filibuster in 1922, but who now is more interested in getting early consideration for his compromise bonus plan.

Senators Robinson and Harrison

Continued on Page Four.

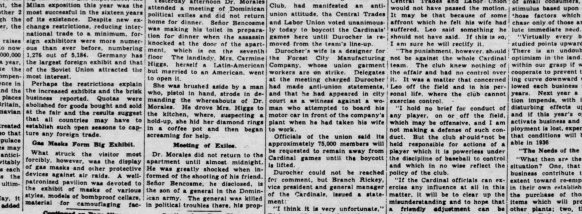

Labor Group Boycotts St. Louis Cardinals; Charges Captain Has Anti-Union Attitude

By The Associated Press.

ST. LOUIS, April 28.—Asserting that Leo Durocher, captain and shortstop of the St. Louis Cardinals National League Baseball Club, had manifested an anti-union attitude, the Central Trades and Labor Union voted unanimously today to boycott the Cardinals' games here until Durocher is removed from the team's line-up.

Durocher's wife is a designer for the Forest City Manufacturing Company, whose union garment workers are on strike. Delegates at the meeting charged Durocher had made anti-union statements, and that he had appeared in city court as a witness against a woman who attempted to board his motor car in front of the company's plant when he had taken his wife to work.

Officials of the union said its approximately 75,000 members will be requested to remain away from Cardinal games until the boycott is lifted.

Durocher could not be reached for comment, but Branch Rickey, vice president and general manager of the Cardinals, issued a statement:

"I think it is very unfortunate," Rickey said, "that the action was taken. I do not think Leo bears animus toward any organization or group and that if the misunderstanding could be cleared up, the Central Trades and Labor Union would not have passed the motion. It may be that because of some affront which he felt his wife had suffered, Leo said something he should not have said. If this is so, I am sure he will rectify it.

"The punishment, however, should not be against the whole Cardinal team. The club knew nothing of the affair and had no control over it. It was a matter that concerned Leo off the field and in his personal life, where the club cannot exercise control.

"I hold no brief for conduct of any player, on or off the field, which may be offensive, and I am not making a defense of such conduct. But the club should not be held responsible for actions of a player which it is powerless under the discipline of baseball to control and which in no wise reflect the policy of the club.

"If the Cardinal officials can exercise any influence at all in this matter, it will be to clear up the misunderstanding and to hope that a friendly adjustment can be made."

Highlights of the Address

Special to THE NEW YORK TIMES.

WASHINGTON, April 28.—Highlights in President Roosevelt's radio speech follow:

My most immediate concern is in carrying out the purposes of the great relief program just enacted by Congress. Its first objective is to put men and women now on the relief rolls to work and, incidentally, to assist materially in our already unmistakable march toward recovery.

While our present and projected expenditures for work relief are wholly within the reasonable limits of our national credit resources, it is obvious that we cannot continue to create governmental deficits for that purpose year after year. We must begin now to make provisions for the future.

The unemployment insurance part of the legislation will not only help to guard the individual in future periods of lay-off against dependence upon relief, but it will, by sustaining purchasing power, cushion the shock of economic distress.

There are chiselers in every walk of life, there are those in every industry who are guilty of unfair practices, every profession has its black sheep, but long experience in government has taught me that the exceptional instances of wrong-doing in government are probably less numerous than in almost every other line of endeavor.

There is pending before the Congress legislation to provide for the elimination of unnecessary holding companies in the public utility field. I consider this legislation a positive recovery measure.

Never since my inauguration in March, 1933, have I felt so unmistakably the atmosphere of recovery. It is more than the recovery of the material basis of our individual lives. It is the recovery of confidence in our democratic processes and institutions. * * * * Fear is vanishing and confidence is growing on every side.

Industry Sees Recovery At Once If Congress Shelves New Laws

Manufacturers Could Spend $20,000,000,000 in Factory Expansion and Rehabilitation, Giving 4,000,000 Jobs, if New Deal Bills Are Sidetracked, They Say.

Special to THE NEW YORK TIMES.

WASHINGTON, April 28.—The United States today is "closer to breaking the back of the depression than at any time since 1932," according to the National Association of Manufacturers, which today made public "a careful analysis" of the business outlook in the nation.

The conclusions of the association are based upon a recently completed study of the economic situation, and the report, it is declared, speaks the views of industrialists throughout the country.

There are billions of dollars, the association statement says, stored up in this country which, if unloosed, would "dwarf" the $4,000,000,000 work-relief program of the administration. If this vast wealth is to go into action, legislation which is not aimed directly at ending the depression or putting millions back to work should be postponed until the next session of Congress, the association asserts.

Included in this legislation which the association says should be shelved temporarily are the Wagner Labor Bill, unemployment insurance, the thirty-hour week and the Utility Holding Company Bill, all of them now pending in Congress.

Statement Cites Surveys.

"Surveys," the statement of the association reads, "indicate that close to $20,000,000,000 in expenditures, which would give employment to 4,000,000 men for two years, is pent up in the field of factory expansion, renovation and rehabilitation alone. The release of this flow of private capital by removing political uncertainties would dwarf the billions appropriated by Congress for relief and make unnecessary the expenditure of much of the taxpayers' money.

"Other billions of purchases, largely within the durable goods field, are dammed up in the hands of small consumers, awaiting the stimulus based upon elimination of those factors which caution purchase only of those articles of absolute immediate need.

"Virtually every business index studied points upward at this time. There is an undoubted spirit of optimism in the land. Recovery is within our grasp if we as a nation cooperate to prevent the disappointing curve downward which has followed each business rise of recent years. Next year a national election impends, with its traditional disturbing effects upon business, and if this year's opportunity to activate business and curtail unemployment is lost, experience dictates that conditions will be less favorable in 1936

"The Needs of the Situation."

"What then are the needs of the situation? One, that industry and business contribute to the fullest extent toward re-employment both in their own establishments and in the purchase of those postponed items which will provide jobs in other plants; two, that Congress and the Federal Government cooperate to the fullest by eliminating uncertainties as to future legislation which forbid long-term commitments by industry.

"This means the laying aside temporarily of any legislation which is not aimed directly and positively at ending the depression, and restoring the millions of idle persons to work within private industry, and the adjournment of Congress as soon as possible.

"Consideration of legislation designed to meet future situations, but which would be a disturbing element during the coming year by compelling a halt while industry makes the necessary adjustments, should be shelved until the next Congress convenes only seven months hence.

"Into this classification would fall the unemployment insurance bill, plainly designed to meet contingencies of the future; the banking bill, the utility holding company bill, changes in the railroad laws which would add millions of dollars to freight charges and increase consumer costs.

"In addition, there is the continuing threat of monetary inflation, the thirty-hour week bill, the Wagner labor disputes bill, extension of the authority of the Secretary of Agriculture, and the Guffey coal bill, which if enacted would compel a waiting period for recovery while business adjusted itself to their provisions.

Huge Purchases "Withheld."

"A survey by the Metal and Allied Products Institute, based upon actual replies from manufacturing plants, shows $18,000,000,000 of machinery purchases withheld over the past five years, which would give employment to 4,000,000 men for two years. This does not take into consideration the current machinery needs of the next two years.

"The Committee for Economic Recovery estimates a delayed demand for durable goods of $49,275,000,000, which would keep this country near the industrial peak for ten years. Colonel Leonard Ayres, noted Cleveland economist, estimates $80,000,000,000 of waiting demand.

"Industry recognizes fully its responsibility to the unemployed, and no group is more sincere in its efforts to bring a speedy end to the depression. We therefore urge at this time that Congress and the administration give every assistance toward eliminating uncertainties which act as obstructions to recovery, and that each individual manufacturer follow with full and complete support of a program which would muster the full force of American initiative against the walls of depression during the next few months.

"Our problems call for a broad understanding in every walk of life, that prosperity is dependent upon the recovery of all groups and that the stirring of antagonisms between

Continued on Page Two.

LISTS CONGRESS PROGRAM

Says He Needs Laws on NRA, Utilities, Transport and Banking.

GIVES BASIS OF WORK PLAN

He Visions Projects Providing Large Sums in Wages and Returns to Treasury.

NOT MOVING HAPHAZARDLY

Each Step Definitely Related to Every Other Step, President Says in 'Fireside Chat.'

Text of the President's radio address appears on Page 2.

Special to THE NEW YORK TIMES.

WASHINGTON, April 28.—Enactment of social security legislation was linked as a "necessity" along side the new $4,000,000,000 emergency work relief program by President Roosevelt tonight, when he went on the air for another 'fireside talk" with the American people

In a speech devoid of dramatic verbal gestures and longer than previous ones of its type, Mr. Roosevelt promised all possible speed in creating jobs for the estimated 3,500,000 employable idle, asked public cooperation in seeing that projects were carried forward efficiently, and defined the basic policies linking the emergency action with the permanent program of his administration.

"The administration and the Congress," he said, "are not proceeding in any haphazard fashion in this task of government. Each of our steps has a definite relationship to every other step."

Mr. Roosevelt also outlined briefly the legislation pending before Congress, in addition to social security, which he wishes enacted at this session of Congress.

The Desired Legislation.

This was as follows:

Extend the life of the National Recovery Act.

Provide for "the elimination of unnecessary holding companies in the public utility field."

Regulate transportation, including that carried by highway, water and air, and strengthen the authority of the Interstate Commerce Commission to "enable it to carry out a rounded conception of the national transportation system."

Amend the banking acts "in the light of past experience and present needs."

This program represented virtually no change in the program reiterated on previous occasions by the President.

Mr. Roosevelt spoke over both the nation-wide broadcasting systems from his study in the White House, reading from manuscript in a quiet, evenly spaced manner. This was his first "fireside talk" since Jan. 4. and in it he broached a feeling of heightened confidence in his program, as when he said:

"Never since my inauguration in March, 1933, have I felt so unmistakably the atmosphere of recovery."

Finds Nation More Cheerful.

Only one critical note was sounded in the speech, when the President said that, while the "overwhelming majority of the people in this country know how to sift the wheat from the chaff," there are "a few who seek to confuse them and to profit by their confusion."

"Americans as a whole are feeling a lot better," he added, "a lot more cheerful than for many, many years."

The President defined his "most immediate concern" as the carrying out of the work relief program, but pointed out that "for the first time in five years the relief rolls have declined instead of increasing during the Winter months."

He then cited the recognition by those in authority of the "possibility and the necessity" of two kinds of remedial measures to be applied to unemployment—a social security program to provide against future unemployment and the work relief program to meet immediate needs.

"Fundamentals" of Work Plan.

President Roosevelt then outlined in numbered paragraphs the "fundamental principles" that will serve

Continued on Page Two.

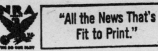

"All the News That's Fit to Print."

The New York Times.

LATE CITY EDITION
WEATHER—Rain and cooler today; tomorrow fair.
Temperatures Yesterday—Max., 60; min., 48.

VOL. LXXXIV....No. 28,241. Entered as Second-Class Matter. Postoffice New York, N. Y. NEW YORK, TUESDAY, MAY 21, 1935. P TWO CENTS in New York City. | THREE CENTS Within 200 Miles | FOUR CENTS Elsewhere Except in 7th and 8th Postal Zones.

ROOSEVELT IS COLD TO BONUS APPEAL BY PATMAN GROUP

The Inflationists Vainly Argue That Treasury's Metal Far Exceeds Greenback Issue.

'DEBT DUE' HELD 'NO DOLE'

President Polishes Message as House Provides for Joint Session Tomorrow.

POST-VETO PLANS SHAPING

Robinson Gives Impetus by Voicing Hope for Working Out Some Kind of Bill.

Special to THE NEW YORK TIMES.

WASHINGTON, May 20.—Presentation to the President today of a 4,000-word brief in behalf of the soldiers' bonus by a committee of twenty-two House members had no effect on his determination forcefully to urge the Congress to uphold the veto message that he will read to a joint session on Wednesday.

The brief was presented by the bonus steering committee of which Representative Patman, author of the bill, is chairman. Mr. Roosevelt received the committee at 10:30 o'clock this morning. Later in the day he spent several hours putting the final touches to his message.

The House, which is expected to override the veto and thus leave to Senate administration adherents the task of upholding the President's action, today adopted a concurrent resolution authorizing a joint session with the Senate on Wednesday and inviting the President to speak at 12:30 P. M.

In the Senate action on the resolution was blocked by the objection of Senator Steiwer, leader of Republican bonus advocates, but it will be taken up under its privileged status tomorrow.

Robinson for New Attempt.

Meanwhile the Senate bonus advocates continued their planning of the course to be followed if and when a veto of the Patman bill is sustained.

The form of further proposals was still in tentative stage, but impetus was added to a post-veto movement by the assertion of Senator Robinson, the Democratic leader, that he hoped that some kind of Bonus Bill would be worked out and passed this session. He did not stipulate what form of legislation he might support.

Senator Robinson was one of the co-planners with Senator Harrison of the Harrison "compromise" which the Senate cast overboard when it adopted the "greenback" bill two weeks ago tomorrow.

The statement by the House committee to the President contained a twofold argument for the Patman bill. It dealt first with the soldiers' adjusted compensation certificates which under the Bonus Bill would be paid immediately instead of when due on Jan. 1, 1945, and then presented arguments designed to show that the issuance of $2,000,000,000 in new currency for this purpose would not constitute a dangerous act of inflation.

Bonus Held a "Debt Owed."

Contending that payment of the bonus would not be a dole but would be "the payment of a debt owed by all classes to one class" and would "prove that Americans still regard heroism as a virtue," the statement said:

"We believe that the country is convinced, after a thorough understanding of the questions among the veterans and non-veterans, that this debt is really past due, although payable in the future, and that it can be paid according to our proposal not only without detriment to the country, but in a way that such payment would be a godsend to the country."

It was signed by Mr. Patman as chairman; Representative Murdock, secretary, and Messrs. Sabath, Scrugham, Greenwood, Colmer, Randolph, Cannon, Connery, Berlin, Hancock, Johnson, Richards, Boileau, May, Hildebrandt, Smith, Dies, Miller, Dondero, Kvale and Ayers.

After reviewing the legislation in which rates of adjusted compensation were fixed for veterans, the committee's statement pointed out that the railroads, other corporations, civilian clerks working for the government and others were "paid in cash" the sums voted by Congress as adjusted compensation for those classes.

Contrasting these payments with the sums allowed veterans, issued on certificates dated in 1925 and made payable twenty years later, the statement added:

"There is no reason why the veterans should not be paid from the time they rendered their services

Continued on Page Six.

High Army Officer Put on Trial Before a Secret Court-Martial

His Name Is Withheld as Session, Excluding Press and Public, Convenes at Capital to Take Up Charge of Accepting Favor From a Lobbyist.

Special to THE NEW YORK TIMES.

WASHINGTON, May 20.—A general court-martial of a high army official, definitely understood to be a general officer, was begun behind closed doors at the Army War College today on charges reported to involve alleged acceptance of a favor from a lobbyist.

Besides excluding the press and the public from the trial the War Department withheld the name of the officer and refused to comment on the case. This practice is followed on the ground that the accused should have the benefit of all doubts pending a verdict. The aim is to prevent a possible injustice to an innocent man.

Although uniforms and side arms are usually worn at courts-martial, the high officers composing the court, which convened on the second floor of the Officers' Club on the reservation, were in civilian clothes so as not to attract attention.

The charges were understood to be an outgrowth of an investigation made by the office of the Inspector General by direction of Secretary Dern, who acted after receiving information from the House Military Affairs Committee.

Information was brought out which in the judgment of officials tended to link the officer with a salesman-lobbyist whose activities have been investigated by the House committee and the Department of Justice.

A grand jury of the District of Columbia considered alleged lobbying conditions at the War Department last year and failed to return any indictments, but a new grand jury is now considering the matter. The accusations in the secret court-martial are rumored to involve a $2,000 loan by the salesman to the officer.

The House committee made a second investigation of the situation last December with the salesman as a witness behind closed doors. There were reports at the time that a black satchel had been brought to the committee from the salesman's hotel room and that it contained important documents.

The committee, in a report to the House, criticized loans or gifts to "at least two War Department officials in high positions."

POLICE OPEN DRIVE ON PUBLIC ENEMIES

Ten With Criminal Records Are Seized in Brooklyn in First Test of Brownell Law.

AN EXODUS IS PREDICTED

Valentine Expects Many to Quit the City—Reticent on Aid by Federal Agents.

The first arrests by the New York police under the recently enacted Brownell amendment to the "public enemy" law were made last night in Brownsville by four detectives under Acting Lieutenant George Colgan. Ten men, all with criminal records and described by the police as petty racketeers, were seized in a group outside a resort at Sutter Avenue and Amboy Street, Brooklyn, about 10 o'clock. The arrests also were believed to mark the beginning of the concerted police and Federal round-up of public enemies in the metropolitan area.

The men will be arraigned this morning in Pennsylvania Avenue magistrate's court on charges of violating Section 722a of the Criminal Code, which forbids known criminals to congregate for illegal purposes or for planning crimes, and which puts the burden of proof of innocent intent on the prisoner. This will be the first test of the new law here.

The men seized were Jerry Pietrasesa, 21 years old, of 89 Alabama Avenue; Rocco Bellarmino, 24, of 138 Powell Street; Irving Schenker, 22, of 142 Amboy Street; Ralph Rabiner, 22, of 426 Chester Street; William Rabinowitz, 21, of 687 Stone Avenue; Irving Moscowitz, 23, of 509 Livonia Avenue; Saul Berman, 28, of 2,114 Atlantic Avenue; Oscar Shapiro, 23, of 201 Barrett Street; Joseph Laurette, 20, of 6,727 Eleventh Avenue, and Barney Gambino, 22, of 2,141 Pacific Street, all of Brooklyn.

Convicted of Various Crimes.

Each of the prisoners has been convicted of crimes such as violation of the Sullivan Law, burglary, assault and robbery, the police said. The detectives would not admit they were conducting any general "round-up" of known criminals under orders from Police Commissioner Valentine, who earlier in the day said he planned to test the Brownell amendment some day this week.

The Commissioner, predicting that "a lot of public enemies are going to leave town,' said that the exodus would not be confined to the notorious characters listed by the police under-cover squad as leaders of the seven worst gangs in the metropolitan area, but that many others would go also.

He declined however, to discuss the report that his men were counting on the cooperation of Federal agents, utilizing the income-tax laws against the gang leaders.

"We always assist other agencies and cooperate with them so far as possible," was all he would say on this phase of the drive.

In Washington, J. Edgar Hoover, director of the Bureau of Investigation of the Department of Justice, told The Associated Press that his special agents here had been instructed to give "full cooperation"

Continued on Page Four.

HUGE BUYING WAVE IS HELD IMMINENT

Threat of Inflation Is Due to Cause Scramble for Goods, Nation's Purchasers Agree.

RAPID PRICE RISE IS SEEN

Federal Spending Attacked—Roper Aide Deplores Refusal to Credit Gains Now Won.

Heavy orders resulting from the belief that commodity prices will rise sharply and business activity itself improve, were forecast yesterday for industry for the rest of this year by executives assembled for the opening of the four-day international convention of the National Association of Purchasing Agents at the Hotel Waldorf-Astoria. Companies represented by the organization's membership spend $8,000,000,000 to $10,000,000,000 annually for durable goods and commodities.

About 1,600 purchasing executives from the United States, Mexico and Canada listened throughout the day to analyses of inflationary and other forces likely to cause durable goods and commodity quotations to advance.

Dr. Edwin Walter Kemmerer, Walker Professor of International Finance at Princeton, warned of the pressing dangers of inflation and predicted that, even on the present basis, prices and the cost of living were bound to double within the next few years.

Dr. Kemmerer's talk came at the close of a three-cornered discussion in which Charles R. Hook, president of the American Rolling Mill Company, and John Dickinson, Assistant Secretary of Commerce, participated, so that the views of finance, industry and the government were represented.

Heavy Spending Assailed.

Pointing out that the government is spending money twice as fast as it receives it, Dr. Kemmerer said these expenditures were being financed by "pumping the banks full of artificial credit" and borrowing from the banks on that credit. At the present rate, this country, through the Roosevelt administration, he said, would have spent by the end of 1936, a sum roughly equal to the $24,500,000,000 spent to cover Federal expenses from the time of Washington down to the close of the Taft administration.

Present ineffectiveness of the forces that ordinarily would check expenditures, he said, was the most serious aspect of the situation. Because the expenditures were being financed by other means than taxation, he pointed out, Congress was not subject to fear of a reaction at the polls.

Attacking the "virus of inflation," Dr. Kemmerer said there was tremendous pressure from inflationists at the present time, and that many "shots in the arm" in the form of depreciated currency, large public expenditures and gold and silver buying policies already had been administered. He said talk of controlled inflation was idle, since history recorded countless instances of inability to check inflationary movements.

Mr. Hook, speaking for industry, devoted the bulk of his address to an attack upon the Wagner bill, which he characterized as the "most vicious piece of legislation ever adopted by Congress in my

Continued on Page Seven.

CUT IN LIGHT RATE IN CITY IS OFFERED; 'YARDSTICK' PUSHED

Public Service Commission Gets Consolidated's Plan, Still in the Informal Stage.

MAY ACT UPON IT TODAY

Mayor to Ask Estimate Board to Approve Municipal Plant at Meeting Friday.

The negotiations between the Public Service Commission and the Consolidated Gas system for a substantial reduction in electric rates for New York City consumers have reached the point where the commission has received informally the outline of the rate cut that the company proposes to make.

The proposal is understood to embody an immediate reduction for residential consumers. Whether the reduction is linked with a profit-sharing arrangement was not ascertained.

The negotiations between the commission and the companies in the Consolidated system have been under way for several weeks. Floyd L. Carlisle, head of the system, and Randall J. LeBoeuf Jr., company counsel, have represented the system at the meetings, and the five members of the Public Service Commission have represented the consumers.

No Formal Offer Yet.

The company offer was made orally. If the commission decides that the plan is sufficiently generous, the company will present a formal written offer on which the commission can act formally. The terms will probably be discussed at the weekly meeting of the commission today, but no formal announcement is to be made after the session.

The negotiations are the result of the rejection by the Public Service Commission, under the leadership of Chairman Milo R. Maltbie, of the Washington plan rate-reduction offer made by the companies earlier this year. The spur behind the company's efforts is the concerted drive by the city, State and Federal authorities against public-utility charges.

Mayor La Guardia, who won a rate reduction for the city's own power needs through the threat of a municipal plant, and who is now keeping alive this threat to force a reduction for the city's residents, made public a letter to the members of the Board of Estimate in which he revealed that he would ask the board at its meeting on Friday to approve his proposed application for a $45,000,000 PWA loan to build a city power system.

The Mayor revealed that the proposed yardstick plant would serve the area between Fourteenth and Seventieth Streets in Manhattan, from river to river. His letter said that the plant would be either on Welfare Island or in the Bellevue Hospital area.

Mayor Tells Plans.

The Mayor's letter, made public by Aldermanic President Bernard S. Deutsch, while the Mayor was in Washington, said in part:

"The power plant will have the latest design of steam electric equipment and a maximum capacity of 140,000 kilowatts providing 40 per cent reserve over the maximum demand.

"The distribution system will be entirely underground and consist of a low voltage alternating current network. A new conduit system will be constructed, except that advantage will be taken of existing ducts in the independent subway

Continued on Page Eight.

PERKINS ASSAILS WIDE POWER GIVEN TO RESERVE BOARD

4 Others of Advisory Council Join National City Head in Attack on Bank Bill.

FEAR MONEY EXPANSION

New Yorker Tells Senators $8,000,000,000 Currency Would Be Made Possible.

Testimony of J. H. Perkins before Glass subcommittee, Page 31

Special to THE NEW YORK TIMES.

WASHINGTON, May 20.—The wide powers proposed for the Federal Reserve Board under Title II of the Omnibus Banking Bill were attacked today by James H. Perkins, chairman of the board of the National City Bank.

He declared that these powers gave opportunity to finance the government "up to many billions of dollars simply on the decision of a small board working in conjunction with the Treasury."

Mr. Perkins was one of five members of the Federal Advisory Council who testified today before a Senate banking subcommittee. The others were Walter W. Smith, president of the First National Bank of St. Louis; Howard A. Loeb, chairman of the Tradesmen's National Bank and Trust Company, Philadelphia; Joseph H. Frost, president of the First National Bank of San Antonio, and Thomas H. Steele, president of the First National Bank and Trust Company of New Haven. Representatives of each of the twelve Reserve Banks make up the council.

The other witnesses joined with Mr. Perkins in urging that the bill be revised to limit the powers projected for the Reserve Board.

Warns of Expansion Scope.

Mr. Perkins declared that under the bill there could be "an expansion of the currency by more than $8,000,000,000, more than double the present amount," without Congressional sanction. He asserted that the authority proposed should be deferred pending an exhaustive study and certainly should not be conferred unless amendments suggested by the council were accepted.

Stating that the powers urged are now virtually all exercised as emergency legislation, he asserted that he could not consider them permanently suitable either in their present form or as contemplated in the bill.

"I know of no present or probable emergency that cannot be met by the law as it now stands, with the re-enactment of a section relating to broadening of rediscount privileges," he declared.

Calling attention to the "powers and responsibilities of a central monetary board," he said:

"The history of control of central banks by governments both abroad and in this country hardly justifies belief in an all-wise exercise of such powers. There is no doubt but that the unsound monetary policies of Germany, which contributed so much to the collapse of the German mark, were facilitated by government control of the Reichsbank."

The testimony of the advisory council members was in contrast to that given recently by Marriner S. Eccles, Governor of the Reserve Board, in favor of the central bank idea, and to that of Secretary Morgenthau, who last week urged government ownership of Reserve Bank stock, with a centralized government credit control agency.

There has been controversy over

Continued on Page Thirty-one.

Hitler Calls Cabinet on Conscription Plan; Talks to Reichstag Today of Arms Tension

By The Associated Press.

BERLIN, May 20.—Reichsfuehrer Adolf Hitler issued a summons tonight for a Cabinet meeting tomorrow afternoon to precede his address to the Reichstag on what the Nazi régime has to offer to alleviate European tension.

Political circles understood that the Fuehrer would obtain final approval for his military conscription law. The Propaganda Ministry, confirming the call for a Cabinet meeting, admitted that conscription would be discussed "in all probability."

Herr Hitler, buoyed up by demonstrations in his honor yesterday at the opening at Frankfurt-am-Main of the first section of a new system of automobile roads, spent most of today writing his speech.

He will again face one of his most critical moments tomorrow night before the largest Reichstag in history, although one of the most impotent. It now has 669 members, including eight newly appointed Deputies from the Saar.

"You take the initiative" has been Great Britain's constant plea to Germany's leader to alleviate the international tension. "We spoke at Stresa and Geneva; now what have you to say?"

Well-informed Wilhelmstrasse circles said London had advised Herr Hitler that he should content himself with an army of about 350,000 men, thereby allaying fears of German aggressiveness, and join the revised Eastern security pact.

Herr Hitler is said to feel, however, that the Reich's entrance into an Eastern pact is impossible since France, Russia and Czechoslovakia have entered a military alliance and Lithuania has been friendly to Soviet Russia.

Herr Hitler is reported to fear if he yields to the demands of the ring of powers about him that it will be interpreted as weakness, with the result that these powers will immediately present additional demands.

ROOSEVELT SETS $19 TO $94 AS MONTHLY RELIEF WAGES; DIVIDES NATION IN 4 GROUPS

Scale of Relief Wages

Special to THE NEW YORK TIMES.

WASHINGTON, May 20.—The schedule of monthly wages by regions and types of work specified in the executive order which President Roosevelt issued this evening was as follows:

COUNTIES IN WHICH THE 1930 POPULATION OF THE LARGEST MUNICIPALITY WAS:

Region.	Over 100,000	50,000 to 100,000	25,000 to 50,000	5,000 to 25,000	Under 5,000
Unskilled Work.					
I	$55	$52	$48	$44	$40
II	45	42	40	35	32
III	35	33	29	24	21
IV	30	27	25	22	19
Intermediate Work.					
I	65	60	55	50	45
II	58	54	50	44	38
III	52	48	43	36	30
IV	49	43	38	32	27
Skilled Work.					
I	85	75	70	63	55
II	72	66	60	52	44
III	68	62	56	48	38
IV	68	58	50	42	35
Professional and Technical Work.					
I	94	[illegible]	77	69	61
II	79	73	66	57	48
III	75	68	62	53	42
IV	75	64	55	46	39

Regions include the following States:

I—Connecticut, Maine, Massachusetts, New Hampshire, New Jersey, New York, Pennsylvania, Rhode Island, Vermont, Illinois, Indiana, Michigan, Minnesota, Ohio, Wisconsin, Arizona, California, Colorado, Idaho, Montana, Nevada, New Mexico, Oregon, Utah, Washington, Wyoming.

II—Iowa, Kansas, Missouri, Nebraska, North Dakota, South Dakota, Delaware, District of Columbia, Maryland, West Virginia.

III—Arkansas, Kentucky, Louisiana, Oklahoma, Texas, Virginia.

IV—Alabama, Florida, Georgia, Mississippi, North Carolina, South Carolina, Tennessee.

WORKERS IN FOUR CLASSES

Rated as Unskilled, Intermediate, Skilled and Professional.

LOWEST IN FAR SOUTH

Highest Is for Technical Services in New York City—All Are Subject to Exemption.

PAYMENT AKIN TO SALARIES

No Deduction Will Be Made for Time Lost From Weather or Other Delays While on Job.

Special to THE NEW YORK TIMES.

WASHINGTON, May 20.—Wage scales for the $4,000,000,000 work-relief program ranging from $19 monthly for unskilled rural workers in the deep South to $94 monthly for professional services in New York City were prescribed today by President Roosevelt in an executive order.

These rates were far below present industrial wages, but no basis of comparison was given, and it was pointed out by officials that several factors involved prevented such comparisons at present.

In setting the wage rates, the country was divided into four regions comprising roughly the deep South, Middle South, Central States and Northern States.

Workers were divided into four classes—unskilled, intermediate, skilled and professional or technical.

Rates of pay also differed according to five population classifications, with pay rates lowest in cities of under 5,000 and rural areas, and highest in cities over 100,000.

The President's order provided that pay on work relief jobs "shall be on a monthly salary basis, the earnings differing according to various regions, degree of urbanization and classes of work prescribed."

Green Predicts Protest Strikes.

Sharp criticisms of the wage scale came from labor leaders. William Green, president of the American Federation of Labor, predicted strikes of the unemployed in protest against the differentials, attacked the zone system set up as too rigid and predicted that the scale would mean a lowering of the wages paid in private industry.

Among the factors that made any comparison with prevailing industrial wages impossible for the moment was the fact that all relief wages are to be paid on a monthly basis with no loss of pay due to temporary interruption of work; that wages for skilled labor are fixed flatly in the President's order, whereas they differ widely for various crafts in the industrial field; and finally that hours of work are not yet definitely fixed, although the order declares that, in general they shall not exceed eight hours a day or forty hours a week.

To assure smooth functioning of the program, Harry L. Hopkins, as director of the Works Progress Division, receives the power to upset the entire scale by exempting projects where necessary in "accordance with local wage conditions" and general authority to set maximum hours of work within the general limit.

Old FERA Rates Form a Basis.

Rates of pay on the work relief program, which was operated on a reduced scale by FERA before the present program was authorized, were used as a basis in determining the new rates.

"The rates paid on this program in the 3,000 odd counties in the United States were typically determined by a local wage committee consisting of one representative of business, one representative of labor and the local relief administrator," said an explanatory statement issued by the Division of Applications and Information, headed by Frank C. Walker.

Wage rates for unskilled labor ran generally far below the $50 a month first suggested for relief wages, from a minimum of $27 to $65 for intermediate workers, from $35 to $85 for skilled labor, and from $39 to $94 for professional and technical services. In general, pay for skilled and professional services was well over $50 a month.

In discussing application of the

Continued on Page Two.

2-YEAR NRA PLAN PROPOSED IN HOUSE

Administration Ignores the Senate Threat of Forcing a Long Filibuster.

RICHBERG URGES APPROVAL

He Tells Committee Failure of Program Would Make 2,000,000 Jobless.

The new NRA two-year extention measure is on Page 8.

Special to THE NEW YORK TIMES.

WASHINGTON, May 20.—Apparently determined to fight to a finish for its seven-point program for NRA reinforcement and extension despite threats of a Senate filibuster beyond the June 16 expiration date, the administration caused to be introduced in the House today a new measure extending the agency's life for two years and placing beyond question many disputed phases of code regulation.

Donald R. Richberg, NRA chief, went before the Ways and Means Committee to lend his support to the substitute resolution it had originated and, while there, denounced the measure recently adopted by the Senate as "administratively impossible," and likely to bring "a reversion to the political and economic chaos that made necessary the constitutional convention of 1787."

Warns of Senate Bill.

Referring later to the Senate measure extending the NRA for ten months, prohibiting price-fixing and placing outside NRA jurisdiction businesses engaged wholly in intrastate commerce, the Recovery Administrator said he knew of no legislation during the last thirty years more likely to defeat its very purpose.

Coming to the aid of the administration's program, General Hugh S. Johnson, former Recovery Administrator, charged in a radio address tonight that the Senate proposed to "kill" rather than to extend the NRA for a limited period. He appealed to all interested parties, and housewives in particular, to make known their insistence upon a two-year extension of the agency in order that business would not be plunged deeper in the "blank uncertainty" that retarded recovery.

The proposed House substitute, drafted by a Ways and Means subcommittee after a series of conferences with Mr. Richberg and Charles R. West, White House liaison with Congress, would provide in the main for the following:

1. Prohibition of price-fixing irrespective of government supervision, except where necessary in the

Continued on Page Eight.

SEE BLOW TO LABOR IN ROOSEVELT SCALE

Green and Other Leaders Are Fearful of Protest Strikes in the Nation.

OPPOSE DIFFERENTIALS

These, Union Men Declare, Will Lower Workers' Pay All Over Country.

Special to THE NEW YORK TIMES.

WASHINGTON, May 20.—Fear of strikes among the unemployed in protest of the wage scales under the $4,000,000,000 work-relief program announced today by President Roosevelt was expressed by William Green, president of the American Federation of Labor, when he was notified of the signing of the executive order. His remarks led the protests of labor leaders.

At the same time, Mr. Green expressed apprehension that employers would use the new wage scale to lower wages in private industry.

"In my opinion the fixing of a wage scale such as has been announced will cause a great deal of dissatisfaction, the labor chief said.

"I understand that zones have been outlined and standard rates set for each zone," he continued. "That means a departure from the fixing of wage scales on the basis of local conditions to a situation where they are established on a zone basis. It means, therefore, going from a system that provides flexibility to one that provides rigidity.

"That will mean injustice. For instance, Washington, in all probability, has a going wage as high or higher than in Canton, Ohio. Yet a security wage will be in force in Washington lower than that in Canton, Ohio. That will cause widespread dissatisfaction in Washington.

"I am fearful of protest strikes among the unemployed, and I am also fearful that private industry will use these rates to reduce the wages they are paying now."

Sees No Additional Work.

Michael J. McDonough, president of the Building Trades Department of the American Federation of Labor, said:

"As far as the organized worker is concerned, the wage rates and conditions in the executive order will do nothing to give him additional employment or relief, as preference is given to those who are on relief rolls," he said.

"A wage of $19 a month in the South for a full month's work is certainly not a living wage. How a man can support a family on that meager income I am sure nobody knows.

"The conditions established under

Continued on Page Two.

On May 27 the Supreme Court ruled that the NRA and its codes were unconstitutional, thus giving the New Deal its first important defeat. The Justices were (left to right, seated) Brandeis, Van Devanter, Hughes, McReynolds, Sutherland, (standing) Roberts, Butler, Stone, Cardozo.

One of the NRA window cards displayed by store owners.

In November, John L. Lewis, leader of the United Mine Workers, defected from the American Federation of Labor to form the Committee for Industrial Organization (CIO) which was dedicated to asserting the workers' power in American industry.

Arthur (Dutch Schultz) Flegenheimer, New York's notorious underworld leader, died on October 24. He was the victim of a gangland killing.

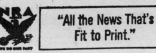

"All the News That's Fit to Print."

The New York Times.

LATE CITY EDITION
WEATHER—Showers tonight, tomorrow; temperature unchanged.
Temperatures Yesterday—Max., 64; min., 55.

Copyright, 1935, by The New York Times Company.

VOL. LXXXIV....No. 28,248. Entered as Second-Class Matter. Postoffice, New York, N. Y. NEW YORK, TUESDAY, MAY 28, 1935. P TWO CENTS In New York City | THREE CENTS Within 200 Miles | FOUR CENTS Elsewhere Except in 7th and 8th Postal Zones.

ALL NRA ENFORCEMENT IS ENDED BY PRESIDENT AS SUPREME COURT RULES ACT AND CODES VOID; WHOLE OF NEW DEAL PROGRAM IN CONFUSION

BALDWIN APPEALS FOR AIR LOCARNO FAVORED BY HITLER

Hopes Treaty to Supplement the 1925 Pact Will Include Limitation of Forces.

URGES ANGLO-U. S. UNITY

It Would Be a Sanction 'No Power Would Dare Face,' Says British Cabinet Leader.

CRITICIZES REICH SECRECY

German Policy Has Increased Europe's Fears, He Asserts—Refers to U-Boat Plans.

By CHARLES A. SELDEN.
Special Cable to THE NEW YORK TIMES.

LONDON, May 27.—Stanley Baldwin, Lord President of the Council, gave the affirmative reply of the British Government tonight to Reichsfuehrer Adolf Hitler's statement of his readiness to supplement the Locarno treaty by an air pact.

"One of the first things to be done," he said, "is to try to pursue—Herr Hitler has expressed his agreement with the principle of this—the idea of embodying a special air pact inside that [the Locarno] treaty, an air pact that may, and I hope will, contain as one of its parts a treaty of limitation."

This pronouncement from the active head of the British Government, who will again be Prime Minister in the very near future, was made in an address at Albert Hall before 10,000 members of the Women's Conservative Association of the United Kingdom.

He chose this occasion as offering him the best platform from which to indicate the Cabinet's considered policy with reference to Herr Hitler's speech in Berlin last Tuesday. It was on the following day that Mr. Baldwin in the House of Commons made a sympathetic response in which he said that the German proposals would receive serious consideration, although at that time he indicated no course of action. Meantime there has been active diplomatic correspondence with both Paris and Berlin, and Sir Eric Phipps, British Ambassador to Berlin, has supplied to the British Foreign Office full details of his discussions of the Hitler speech with Foreign Minister Constantin von Neurath.

Refers to Submarines.

Mr. Baldwin made no definite reference to other points of Herr Hitler's address, but he did refer to the fact that Germany's submarine program had already got beyond the academic stage. This no doubt indicates one point the British will bring up next week in the Anglo-German naval discussions in London.

Mr. Baldwin's revelation of his government's next move toward peace was more pertinent to the current situation but no better received by his great audience than was his confession of his hope that some time there would be an understanding between the United States and the British Empire that no country in the world would dare to disregard.

This reference to a possible future combination of all the English-speaking peoples was out of a clear sky without special connection with what came before or after it in the formal address. It was a spontaneous, almost passionate expression of a hope or dream that many Britons entertain. Mr. Baldwin himself referred to it as a digression "for which I do not apologize."

Regrets Our Absence at Geneva.

"It is in times like these," he said, "when we are talking so much about collective security that I lament so sincerely the absence of the United States from the League.

"For the United States to take part in collective security is, I am aware, not practical politics. But as one who has now been in public life many years and who can't be in high position in this country many years more I may perhaps be allowed one thing that those who follow me may bear in mind.

"I have always believed that the greatest security against war in any part of the world whatever, in Europe, in the East, anywhere, would be the close collaboration of the British Empire with the United States.

"The combined power of the navies, the potential man power, the immediate economic power of refusal to trade or lend money would be a sanction that no power on earth, however strong, would dare to face. It may be a hundred years before that desirable end is attained. It may never come to pass. But sometimes we may have our dreams. I look forward to the fu-

Continued on Page Four.

Graf Zeppelin, Damaged, Forced Down in Morocco

Special Cable to THE NEW YORK TIMES.

MADRID, May 27.—After having wirelessed that she was in difficulties off the Moroccan Coast, the Graf Zeppelin was obliged to land at 9 o'clock tonight at El-Araish (Larache), Spanish Morocco.

SEVILLE, Spain, May 28 (AP).—The Graf Zeppelin was said by Seville Airport officials today to be proceeding to Germany after landing at Larache, Morocco, to leave mail. They said no message had been received here that the giant dirigible had experienced any motor trouble.

Special Cable to THE NEW YORK TIMES.

CASABLANCA, Morocco, May 27.—The wireless station here picked up a message from the Graf Zeppelin stating she had damaged her engine gondola. She asked the airship base at Seville to get everything ready for a landing.

FLANDIN WILL ASK WIDE POWER TODAY

French Premier Is to Request of Parliament Right to Take Steps to Revive Industry.

GOLD LOSS SETS RECORD

Newspaper Says $79,949,000 Was Withdrawn From the Bank of France Yesterday.

By P. J. PHILIP.
Wireless to THE NEW YORK TIMES.

PARIS, May 27.—Powers not much less extensive than those Congress accorded to the President of the United States will be asked for tomorrow in the French Parliament by Premier Pierre-Etienne Flandin to enable him to protect the franc.

He is not going to content himself with the right to proceed with certain economies by decree. He wants, without having to wait for passage of certain bills by Parliament, to have the right himself to take whatever measures he believes will revive economic activity in the country.

For the Premier's view of the situation is that merely to cut expenditure would be the least effective of all remedies. To increase taxation is impossible just now. What must be done is to obtain a fuller return of revenue into the State coffers by getting the wheels of industry and commerce moving again. For if business were normal there would be no treasury shortage, such as there is, and no danger whatever to the franc, which has more than sufficient gold cover to meet all emergencies.

Huge Sums Withdrawn.

According to the Petit Parisien, the Bank of France lost the unprecedented sum of 1,123,000,000 francs ($73,949,000) in gold today in the form of withdrawals for hoarding, export and speculation. If this figure is true, it shows a striking acceleration in the already huge withdrawals and it will give the government a powerful weapon in its efforts to impress Parliament with the necessity of acting quickly and firmly.

The Petit Journal will make tomorrow morning the most striking reply of all as to what should be done about the franc. Its first four pages are entirely given over to a plea for devaluation. Not only does Raymond Patenotre, the publisher, write an urgent appeal, but a number of Deputies and Senators, taken from the Right and the Left, give their opinion that the franc must be reduced to save French economy.

Two whole pages are devoted to Belgium's experiment, in which it is asserted that devaluation there had been a great success.

How far the Premier intends to go in trying to restore business by one-man government is still a Cabinet secret. All that was divulged today, after a Ministerial council, was that the terms of the bill had been drawn up and unanimously approved and that it conferred on the government "extensive powers in economic and financial matters."

Bill Before Cabinet Today.

This bill will be submitted to another Cabinet meeting tomorrow morning and to the Chamber of Deputies in the afternoon by Finance Minister Louis Germain-Martin.

Premier Flandin's broken arm is said to be now mending satisfactorily and the Premier is suffering less pain and is able to sleep well. But it will not be until probably Monday or Tuesday that he will be able to go before Parliament.

Meanwhile, the bill will be examined in commission. If it gets quick approval there it is not impossible that it will be debated Friday, in which case the Premier will almost

Continued on Page Forty-five.

WEYERHAEUSERS IN SECRET PARLEY ON KIDNAP CLUES

Parents Meet With Officials After Plea to Federal Men to End 'Interference.'

FAIL TO RAISE $200,000

Banker Says That Family Has Toiled '24 Hours a Day' in Vain to Get Money.

RANSOM NOTE PUBLISHED

Car Containing Boy Who Looked 'Exactly Like' Picture of Victim Is Hunted.

By The Associated Press.

TACOMA, Wash., May 27.—Racing against the deadline set for payment of $200,000 ransom, the parents of 9-year-old George Weyerhaeuser met secretly today with officials while Department of Justice agents began a search for "at least three men" as the suspected kidnappers.

A report from Port Angeles said that Sheriff's deputies had begun an intensive check of highways west of that town tonight upon receiving reports that a boy resembling the kidnapped George Weyerhaeuser had been seen there in a dark blue sedan with California license plates.

A man, whose name was not learned by the officers, reported that the car, carrying three men, a woman and a child, had stopped him on the street at about 6 P. M. and the driver had asked directions.

Officers quoted the informant as saying he had thought nothing of the incident until he saw an enlarged photograph of the kidnap victim in a newspaper. He declared that the boy in the car looked "exactly like the picture."

Officers Block Road.

The occupants of the machine were said by officers to have inquired how to get out to a resort at Lake Crescent, a few miles west of here on the Olympic Highway.

The highway was blocked at Forks by Sheriff's deputies and a thorough check of all resorts between here and the ocean was begun.

The heir to a lumber fortune was kidnapped Friday noon and the abductor's note, signed "Egoist," gave his parents five days to comply with demands for the ransom.

It was believed that the meeting of officials and members of the child's family in the offices of the Weyerhaeuser Company was to determine the next step for the boy's recovery.

A banker close to the family, who asked that his name be withheld, said that the family had been "working twenty-four hours a day since last Friday, but that they had not succeeded in raising the money."

Hear of Men Near Scene.

Movements of the government's agents were shrouded in secrecy, but it was learned they were making complete checkups of stories that from one to three men were seen lurking near the spot where the child was kidnapped.

A fourth resident of the district today informed police that he saw three men and a boy leaving the vicinity Friday. Three other persons had reported seeing three men in a tan sedan bearing California license plates.

It was reported that the fourth informant was able to give a de-

Continued on Page Three.

This Year's Court Rulings On New Deal Program

By The Associated Press.

WASHINGTON, May 27.—Here is the way the New Deal has fared this year in the Supreme Court:

Won (By 5-4 Vote)—The gold-clause cases. In one case the court held that, although the government had no right to abrogate the clause on its own bonds, the holders had failed to show damages.

Lost (By 8-1 Vote)—The decision holding that NRA's Section 9c, giving to the President authority to prevent shipments of illegally produced oil, was an improper delegation of legislative authority.

Lost (By 5-4 Vote)—The Rail Pension case. (This was not an administration measure, but it embodied New Deal principles.)

Lost (Unanimous) — Schechter case, involving the NRA, Frazier-Lemke mortgage moratorium case and Humphrey removal case.

PRESIDENT CURBED IN REMOVAL POWER

Supreme Court Overrules Dismissal of W. E. Humphrey as Trade Commissioner.

CERTAIN OFFICERS EXEMPT

Those of Legislative or Judicial Agency Are Not Subject to Ouster 'at Mere Will.'

Special to THE NEW YORK TIMES.

WASHINGTON, May 27.—President Roosevelt's action in demanding removal of the late William E. Humphrey from the Federal Trade Commission was held illegal by the Supreme Court today.

In an opinion by Justice Sutherland, the court unanimously declared that the President exceeded his powers in dismissing Mr. Humphrey, not for the statutory "inefficiency, neglect of duty or malfeasance in office," but upon other grounds, which actually were, Mr. Roosevelt then stated, that he did not think that his mind and Mr. Humphrey's were linked either on the policies or administering of the commission.

The court decided that the term of Trade Commissioners was fixed by law, that they must not be removed except upon statutory reasons, and that to hold that the commissioners must continue in office "at the mere will of the President, might be to thwart in large measure the very ends which Congress sought to realize by definitely fixing a term of office."

Wilson Case Held Not to Apply.

This case, which has attracted intense interest because Mr. Humphrey was a Republican of the old high protective tariff school, was argued some weeks ago. William J. Donovan, former assistant to the Attorney General, appeared for Samuel F. Rathbun, executor of the Humphrey estate.

The government, in this argu-

Continued on Page Nineteen.

School Children Suffer From Tear Gas, 20 Others Hurt in Ohio Strike Rioting

By The Associated Press.

CANTON, Ohio, May 27.—Twenty persons were injured today, one seriously, in a burst of gunfire and rioting at the plant of the Berger Manufacturing Company, where a strike began this morning.

Herbert Blazer, aged 26, a passer-by, was shot in the back and was in serious condition. He was on his way home from work. Four others were shot, three in the legs and one in the hand. Another man was clubbed on the head and suffered scalp injuries.

Fifteen school children, herded into a restaurant, suffered from tear gas but were not sent to hospitals. Most of the persons injured were bystanders.

The violence started as several automobile loads of workers were being escorted out of the company yard by guards. Witnesses said the strike sympathizers hurled stones at the workers. An armored car, containing about ten men, followed the escort out of the yard and stopped about 500 yards from the plant. Then its occupants opened fire into the crowd, witnesses said.

A large group of men rushed toward the armored car and seized the ten armed men and a general mêlée ensued. No official estimate of the number of persons clubbed could be ascertained. In addition to the twenty admitted to a hospital, others were treated for minor lacerations and bruises by women who went to the scene with bandages and other medical supplies. No arrests were made.

Executives of Loyalty Local, No. 18903, of the Amalgamated Association of Iron, Steel and Tinplate Workers declared the strike. The outbreak followed earlier violence which occurred on the picket lines when union strikers sought to prevent non-union men from entering.

The union is asking for recognition as a collective bargaining unit for all the workers. Company officials said not more than 36 per cent of the plant's 450 workers are members of the union.

RICHBERG ISSUES PLEA

He Calls on Employers to Maintain Labor, Fair Practice Standards.

NRA, AAA, FACA END FEARED

Both Branches of Congress in Turmoil, Halt Work on New Legislation.

HOUSE DELAYS NIRA BILL

Administration Aides Seek Way Out of Dilemma as Opposition Cheers the Ruling.

Special to THE NEW YORK TIMES.

WASHINGTON, May 27.—Immediate suspension of all NRA code enforcement was announced tonight by Donald R. Richberg, chairman of the National Industrial Recovery Board, who appended to the announcement an appeal to employers to maintain the standards of labor and fair practice achieved under the code system.

The announcement followed a White House conference between President Roosevelt, Mr. Richberg, Attorney General Cummings and Solicitor General Reed, and after a day of unutterable legislative and administrative confusion in which officials attempted to assay the havoc wrought in nearly every department of the government by the overthrow of the National Industrial Recovery Act by the Supreme Court.

THE RICHBERG STATEMENT.

Mr. Richberg's statement read as follows:

"On June 16, 1933, when the National Industrial Recovery Act was approved, the President stated the simple truth that the act was a challenge to industry, to labor and to our whole people—a challenge to 'sink selfish interest and present a solid front against a common peril.'

"He stated that the law put to our whole people the simple but vital test: 'Must we go on in many groping, disorganized separate units to defeat or shall we move as one great team to victory?'

"In the two years which have followed we have engaged in a great cooperative movement for the rehabilitation of trade and industry, for the improvement of the condition of the workers and their standard of living, and for the elimination of sweatshop wages, child labor and unfair competitive practices.

"According to the opinion of the Supreme Court, the Congress did not sufficiently define in the law the policy and standards of the wise and beneficent measures which we have undertaken, but delegated to the President 'unfettered discretion' to approve all provisions in codes of fair competition which he deemed 'beneficial in dealing with the vast array of commercial and industrial activities throughout the country.' The court held that: 'The code-making authority thus conferred is an unconstitutional delegation of legislative power.'

Code Regulations Suspended.

"This decision of the court makes codes of fair competition unenforceable as a matter of law; and in deference to that ruling all methods of compulsory enforcement of the codes will be immediately suspended. This will not affect the enforcement of any contractual obligation which may have arisen by agreement of the parties requiring no sanction of Federal authority.

"We face now the question of maintaining the gains which have been made in the last two years and retaining the values which have been created under the National Recovery Administration. It seems clear that that question must be decided by the administration and the Congress and the people of the United States within a very short time.

"Pending the determination of this question, it would be most harmful to the general welfare if unfair competitive practices, universally recognized as such, were to be revived, and if the fair standards affecting labor were to be disregarded.

"Therefore, pending the determination of this question, I hope that all employers heretofore operating

Continued on Page Twenty.

The Three Court Rulings

Special to THE NEW YORK TIMES.

WASHINGTON, May 27.—Here is the gist of the three Supreme Court decisions in which the Roosevelt administration was reversed today:

National Industrial Recovery Act.

The entire code structure of NRA was invalidated, the court holding that the code-making provisions of the act constituted an invalid delegation of power by Congress of its authority to legislate to persons wholly disconnected with the legislative functions of the government.

Exercise of Congressional powers over commerce was definitely restricted to interstate commerce, or to such activities as had a provable direct connection with interstate commerce. The court held that no economic emergency could justify the breaking down of the limitations on Federal authority as prescribed by the Constitution or of those powers reserved to the States through the failure of the Constitution to place them elsewhere.

Frazier-Lemke Farm Mortgage Moratorium.

The legislation authorizing a five-year moratorium on mortgages when efforts to scale a farmer's debts down collapse, was declared unconstitutional. The court held that under the Fifth Amendment to the Constitution private property could not be taken without just compensation. There has been no previous instance, the court said, where a mortgagee was forced to relinquish property to a mortgagor free of lien unless the debt was paid in full.

Removal of Federal Trade Commissioner.

President Roosevelt's dismissal of the late William E. Humphrey from the Federal Trade Commission was held illegal because the President did not remove Mr. Humphrey for the statutory grounds of inefficiency, neglect of duty or malfeasance in office, but, as the President stated, because their minds did not meet upon the policies or administration of the commission. The court held that trade commissioners' terms are fixed by law and that their removal must be for the grounds stated in the act.

WALL STREET HAILS NEW DEAL DEFEATS

Some Bankers and Industrialists Call NRA Decision 'Best Thing in Years.'

SEE UNCERTAINTY ENDED

Check on Social and Economic Legislation Predicted—Steel Men Fear Deflation.

Wall Street's first reaction to the news of yesterday's three decisions of the Supreme Court invalidating the NIRA and the Frazier-Lemke Act and overruling President Roosevelt's removal of a Federal Trade Commissioner was in general one of rejoicing. In some quarters the fear was expressed that, unless Congress should enact a substitute measure providing for the continuance of price-fixing and wage agreements in certain industries, deflationary consequences might ensue, but for the most part this point was overlooked in the general approval of the "conservative" stand displayed by the Supreme Court.

The stock market had only about twenty minutes in which to register a response and its action in that period was not conclusive, but prices displayed a firmer trend for the most part after the decision was out, in contrast to highly irregular movements earlier in the day.

Leading bankers and a number of industrialists characterized the decision on the NRA as "the best thing in years," although they declined to comment formally, on the plea of not having read the entire decision.

The approval shown was not entirely based on the financial community's dislike of certain types of New Deal legislation. It was felt that the decision had the practical merit of removing a source of uncertainty which has hampered business. This uncertainty arose from the fact that large corporations have had to conform to the NRA without being able to count upon its permanence because their own counsel assured them it was unconstitutional.

Speculation on Effect on SEC.

The belief prevailed among Wall Street men that the Supreme Court's decision with respect to the NRA might reflect upon the constitutionality of other New Deal legislation, including the Securities and Exchange Act, and might have an important bearing upon the character of future legislation. It was felt that, with three such decisions in the record, Congress would be much less disposed to enact without question future proposals for legislation of a far-reaching social and economic character.

Executives of the oil and copper industries agreed that the invalidation of their respective codes would not adversely affect the industries.

Continued on Page Twenty-one.

FULL BENCH ANNULS FARM MORATORIUM

Frazier-Lemke Act Takes Property Without Compensation, Brandeis Holds in Opinion.

5TH AMENDMENT VIOLATED

Despite Rent and Title, Mortgagee Is Declared to Lose 'Rights' in 5-Year Period.

Special to THE NEW YORK TIMES.

WASHINGTON, May 27.—The Frazier-Lemke Farm Mortgage Moratorium Law was unanimously declared unconstitutional by the Supreme Court today on the ground that private property cannot be taken for public use without just compensation.

This law, driven to completion last June under the spur of Senator Long, provided a five-year moratorium in case of the collapse of efforts to scale a farmer's debts down to a figure that would have enabled him to pay off the mortgage. Insurance companies and other mortgagees complained that they would suffer severely if farmers used the law to evade debts they actually could pay.

President Roosevelt, signing this bill ten days after Congress adjourned in 1934, said it was in some respects "loosely drawn," but, although it was not an administration measure, he defended it, and said he did not share the fears of insurance companies and other mortgagees, as:

"I have sufficient faith in the honesty of the overwhelming majority of farmers to believe that they will not evade the payment of just debts."

Bank's Right to 6 Per Cent.

The court's undivided opinion was written by Associate Justice Brandeis, and it was the first that he has rendered on main recovery legislation.

The issue was an appeal brought by the Louisville Joint Stock Land Bank against William R. Radford Sr., a Kentucky farmer, who had mortgaged his lands for $9,000, but who, under the Bankruptcy Law, of which the Frazier-Lemke act is a part, could have redeemed this property for $4,445.

Justice Brandeis said that the mortgage law, passed just two days before Radford's property was foreclosed upon, "took away" the rights of the land bank, while it gave Radford the right to buy the farm back on deferred payments at a 1 per cent year interest.

"Obviously 1 per cent is not the value of money," Justice Brandeis stated for the court. "The legal rate of interest in Kentucky is 6 per cent."

The court's opinion focussed on the Fifth Amendment to the Constitution, which states, among other things, "Nor shall private property be taken for public use without just compensation." With

Continued on Page Fourteen.

COURT IS UNANIMOUS

President Cannot Have 'Roving Commission' to Make Laws by Code.

NO INTRASTATE WAGE PACT

Indirect Effect of an Activity on Interstate Commerce Is Held to Be Insufficient.

PARLEY AT WHITE HOUSE

AAA Officials Also Plunge Into Study of Effect of Opinion on Farm Legislation.

Decision of the Supreme Court on the NIRA, Pages 16 and 17.

By ARTHUR KROCK.
Special to THE NEW YORK TIMES.

WASHINGTON, May 27.—By a unanimous decision in the Schechter poultry case the Supreme Court today held unconstitutional the National Industrial Recovery Act, due to expire by limitation on June 16, and, by voiding the 750 codes which are the heart of the National Recovery Administration and denying the right of Congress or its agents to fix wages and hours in intrastate trade activities, demolished the chief administrative recovery weapon of the New Deal.

Immediate cessation of NRA code enforcement was announced by Chairman Richberg of the National Industrial Recovery Board following a conference at the White House in which President Roosevelt, Attorney General Cummings, Solicitor General Reed and Mr. Richberg participated. Mr. Richberg coupled with his announcement a plea to employers not to scrap the achievements in the field of fair practice and labor relations which had flowed from the Recovery Act.

The court, speaking through the Chief Justice, who read the passages vehemently, once more declared that Congress cannot give to the President or to private persons what Justice Cardozo, in a separate assenting opinion, called "a roving commission" to make laws in the form of codes or otherwise. Congress must specify standards and list objectives and provide a definite range of action.

But even when Congress has done that, said the court, its delegation of authority cannot apply to those engaged in intrastate industry, which was defined as any not "directly" affecting the current or flow of interstate commerce. The court specifically included mining, agriculture and manufacture.

Hour and Wage Rules Collapse.

Justice Cardozo pointed out that the attempted regulation of wages and hours was "the bone and sinew of the codes," and that therefore by the decision of the court they "collapse utterly." Since industry directly affecting interstate commerce is too small a group on which to base the NRA recovery plan, the theory and practice of NRA were killed by the decision, even though Congress should rewrite the law.

Realizing this, Congressional leaders at once took steps to substitute for the fallen code system such interstate trade regulations as those contained in the Black Thirty-Hour Bill and the Guffey coal legislation, and such labor wage-bargaining as is provided in the Wagner bill.

Government attorneys had been optimistic about the Schechter case and to them the decision was a bombshell. Donald R. Richberg and Solicitor General Reed, who had defended NIRA, left the court room with downcast faces. The Attorney General in his office stopped chewing a ham sandwich. The argument between the House and Senate over the time extension of NIRA and the terms thereof was temporarily laid aside. At the headquarters of Triple-A, which is administering some of the codes, the opinions were studied to determine whether they foreshadow the doom of that recovery experiment also.

Conferences were held at the Department of Justice, and then the Attorney General, the Solicitor General and Mr. Richberg were summoned to a late afternoon conference at the White House—the first of many—to ascertain what could

Continued on Page Twenty-one.

NRA U.S. WE DO OUR PART

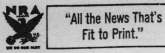

"All the News That's Fit to Print."

The New York Times.

LATE CITY EDITION

WEATHER—Possibly showers today, cooler tonight; tomorrow fair. Temperatures Yesterday—Max., 75; min., 66.

VOL. LXXXIV....No. 28,255. Entered as Second-Class Matter. Postoffice, New York, N. Y. NEW YORK, TUESDAY, JUNE 4, 1935. PP TWO CENTS In New York City. | THREE CENTS Within 200 Miles | FOUR CENTS Elsewhere Except in 7th and 8th Postal Zones.

NORMANDIE HAILED BY THRONGS HERE; SETS NEW RECORDS

4-DAY 11-HOUR CROSSING

World's Largest Ship Averages 29.6 Knots, Cuts Time 2 Hours.

HARBOR SHRIEKS WELCOME

Crowds Line Shore to Watch as Planes and River Boats Escort Liner to Pier.

DOCKED WITHIN AN HOUR

Mme. Lebrun, Feted by City at Reception, Brings a Greeting From France.

By F. RAYMOND DANIELL.

The great new French liner Normandie completed her maiden voyage safely yesterday afternoon and brought the continent of Europe a few hours nearer to the United States. The world's largest ship had proved she was faster than all her older rivals.

Proudly her Gascon skipper, Captain René Pugnet, ordered the blue pennant of speed supremacy run up on her main truck at 11:02 A. M. when she glided past Ambrose Lightship four days, eleven hours and forty-two minutes after putting Southampton Nab behind her.

So, like the queen that she is, the great ship sailed into the harbor and up the Hudson to her unfinished berth at West Forty-eighth Street with most of her 1,013 passengers standing at her rails and gazing at one of the most tumultuous harbor receptions any ship ever received.

Takes Hour to Dock.

After nearly an hour of puffing and snorting and straining, a dozen tugs succeeded in easing the 79,280-ton vessel alongside her pier, but not until she had snapped two hawsers, smashed a small cushion raft, imperiling a workman's life, and lunged menacingly at the pier next above her own. There she will remain until Friday, when she will begin her first voyage homeward.

In spite of fog, which cut down her speed by one-third for five hours after she left England, the Normandie maintained an average speed of 29.64 knots for the 3,192 miles between Southampton and Ambrose lights. Thus she beat the record set in August, 1933, by the Italian liner Rex, which averaged 28.92 knots for the 3,181 miles between Gibraltar and Ambrose, crossing the Atlantic in four days, thirteen hours and fifty-eight minutes.

Not only did the vessel set the record for the fastest westward crossing of the Atlantic and the best average speed—she wrested from the Rex the banner for the best day's run as well, topping by twelve miles the 736 miles the Italian liner covered in a single day.

Although officials of the French Line had insisted during her entire voyage that the liner was not trying for any speed record, her passengers were all wearing composition medals backed with blue ribbons to commemorate the record crossing when the ship reached Quarantine. They were distributed soon after the blue pennant was hoisted, and they were "Made in France."

Celebrities Are Aboard.

There were many distinguished passengers aboard the vessel, including Mme. Albert Lebrun, wife of the President of France and sponsor of the Normandie; the Maharajah of Kapurthala and Colette, the novelist.

Mrs. F. H. La Guardia, the Mayor's wife, and scores of silk-hatted dignitaries met the ship at Quarantine to welcome Mme. Lebrun with flowers and fine phrases on behalf of the city and the nation, but it was the great floating mass of powered steel to which the crowds paid homage.

The streamlined, dark hull of the Normandie, 1,029 feet long, loomed out of the slight mist that hung over the outer harbor a little before noon. Coast Guard cutters bearing the French Ambassador and the French Consul General, the Riverside, with the Mayor's reception committee, headed by State Senator Joseph Clark Baldwin, and a score of other craft hastened out to greet her.

In their wake was a flotilla of

Continued on Page Two.

Public May Visit Ship 10 A. M. to 5 P. M. Today

The French Line announced last night that the Normandie would be open for public inspection today between 10 A. M. and 5 P. M. and tomorrow from 1 to 5 P. M. An admission charge of 50 cents a person will be made. The income will be donated by the French Line to relief funds for American and French sailors.

Officials of the line explained that they had decided to charge for admission because of the flood of requests to view the ship. Thousands of persons made application and it was considered impossible to accommodate all applicants. The new city pier at which the ship is docked will also be open for inspection for the first time.

BRITAIN TO OPPOSE GERMAN NAVAL BID

Will Declare Desire for 35% of Her Strength Unreasonable Because of Limited Coast.

HITLER DIPLOMACY SCORES

Raising of Ribbentrop's Rank Forces London Ministers to Receive Him Before Talks.

By CHARLES A. SELDEN.

Wireless to THE NEW YORK TIMES.

LONDON, June 3.—Joachim von Ribbentrop, head of the German delegation that is to begin naval talks with the British tomorrow, was received today by Prime Minister Ramsay MacDonald and Sir John Simon, Foreign Secretary, in their private rooms at the House of Commons and afterward by Sir Bolton Eyres-Monsell, First Lord of the Admiralty, in his Admiralty Office.

Simultaneously it became known that the Germans would be informed that their desire for a fleet 35 per cent as strong as Britain's was unreasonable inasmuch as Germany had a limited sea coast to protect, while the British Navy had to cover possessions scattered all over the world.

Talks of Experts Planned.

When the plans for these naval conversations were announced a week ago in London it was said that they would be entirely between experts of the two countries and that no British Cabinet Ministers would participate either socially or technically. But on the eve of Herr von Ribbentrop's departure from Berlin, Reichsfuehrer Hitler suddenly raised him to the rank of Ambassador Extraordinary and Plenipotentiary on special mission. This bit of diplomacy was interpreted in London as indicating that Herr Hitler was determined to give more importance to these naval talks than the British seem inclined to accord them.

At any rate, Herr von Ribbentrop's new rank undoubtedly was responsible for the receptions he had today from Ministers.

Not Taken Seriously Before.

When Herr von Ribbentrop was here before he was not taken very seriously, and when Dr. Alfred Rosenberg came from Berlin in 1933 as a representative of the Nazi political department to ascertain British official opinion of Germany, both Stanley Baldwin, Lord President of the Council, and Mr. MacDonald refused to see him. Dr. Rosenberg had no diplomatic title whatever.

Now it is expected that Sir John Simon himself will open the discussions tomorrow, but will retire after the formalities, leaving the British case in the hands of Robert L. Craigie of the Foreign Office, Vice Admiral C. J. C. Little, expert on submarines, and Captain V. H. Danckwert, assistant director of naval plans of the British Admiralty. Admiral Little's assignment is attributable largely to Britain's interest in the fact that Germany has admitted she already has twelve small submarines, contrary to the Versailles treaty restrictions.

Legality Not to Be Discussed.

But the legality of Germany's naval program with reference to the terms of the Versailles treaty is not to be discussed at all in these London talks, which are expected to last two or three days. Britain takes the violation of that treaty in naval as well as in army and air

Continued on Page Nineteen.

ETHIOPIANS ATTACK 2 ITALIAN OUTPOSTS; 30 NATIVES SLAIN

Drive Off Several Thousand Head of Cattle in Raid at Somaliland Border.

SECOND CLASH IN ERITREA

Incidents Mar First Conciliation Meeting Today—Italian Press Bitter at British.

By ARNALDO CORTESI.

Wireless to THE NEW YORK TIMES.

ROME, June 3.—At least thirty African subjects of Italy and an undetermined number of Ethiopians are reported to have been killed in one of two clashes on the Eritrea and Italian Somaliland frontiers. Both conflicts are said to have been caused by Ethiopian incursions into Italian territory.

A strong Ethiopian force, it is stated, attacked a small Italian post at the southern extremity of Eritrea in the Danakil area. The attackers, it is added, made off with several thousand head of cattle.

Near Gublei in Somaliland, according to a second dispatch, a band of twenty armed Ethiopians opened fire when challenged by Italian native troopers while trying to cross the frontier. The Ethiopians are said to have retreated, suffering an undetermined number of casualties.

Incidents Menace Conciliation.

These incidents will be made the subject of an official representation by the Italian Government to Ethiopia. Their gravity is the greater, it is held here, by reason of their occurrence just before the first meeting of the Italo-Ethiopian conciliation commission at Milan.

The Italian press has launched a powerful anti-British campaign. Great Britain is accused of unwarranted interference in Ethiopian affairs and of stiffening Ethiopia's resistance by giving the impression that the whole might of the British Empire would be ranged against Italy in event of a conflict in East Africa.

The blame is not attributed directly to the London Government. Indeed, the semi-official Giornale d'Italia lays the guilt at the door of British colonial officials in Africa, adding that their action "is certain to be deplored in London."

It is argued however, that, as long as Ethiopia believes, rightly or wrongly, that she can count on British support, there is little hope that the conciliation commission can arrange a peaceful settlement.

It is further charged that large quantities of war materials for Ethiopia are passing through British colonies. One hundred motor trucks are said to have been unloaded at Berbera, British Somaliland, in transit to Ethiopia.

After the Ualual incident, it is asserted, the Ethiopians, on the advice of British agents, dug deep holes along the frontier to prevent the advance of Italian tanks.

A report that Ethiopia, in case of a conflict with Italy, would place herself under a British protectorate, is said to have been traced to Lieut. Colonel Clifford, head of the British delegation on the Anglo-Ethiopian commission for the de-

Continued on Page Nineteen.

Nazis Aided Marriages With 400,736 Loans

Wireless to THE NEW YORK TIMES.

BERLIN, June 3. — Between August, 1933, and March, 1935, the German Government granted to newly married couples 400,736 marriage aid loans averaging 500 marks each.

During the same period it granted subsidies for 185,475 children born of these marriages consisting of cancellation of 25 per cent of the loan for each child. During the first quarter of 1935 the subsidies for newly born children exceeded the number of new marriage loans.

According to the official figures for 1933, divorces showed a slight increase under the National Socialist régime compared with 1932. The German divorce rate, although only half that of the United States, is among the highest in the world. The greatest percentage of divorces came after four years of married life.

CITY REVIVES HOPE ON CIVIL WAR CLAIM

Heartened by Senate's Move to Repay Money Used to Equip Soldiers in 1861.

TOTAL DUE IS $764,143

Wood Made First Effort to Collect in '64—Even Cockran and Platt Failed.

City officials were encouraged slightly—ever so slightly—yesterday at news from Washington that the Federal Government at last was moving toward payment of the city's claim for $764,143, incurred seventy-three years ago for arming and equipping 15,000 Civil War troops.

Their lack of enthusiasm was based upon past experiences with the claim, which has been presented on numerous occasions without success. The Senate Judiciary Committee, according to The Associated Press, approved a bill yesterday which would satisfy the claim. Finance Department officials recalled that similar bills had even been passed by previous Senates, only to die before payment was actually made.

Going back through city records, members of the Controller's staff uncovered a little-known chapter in New York's history. On April 22, 1861, the city's Board of Councilmen responded to President Lincoln's appeal for troops by authorizing a million-dollar bond issue to train and equip the men. To all intents, the city itself went to war, since it not only armed, equipped and transported the troops to Washington, but also made provision for their families here.

Defense Committee Formed.

The city established wholly or in part at least fifty military units of the New York State Militia and the New York Volunteers. The "Union Defense Committee" was organized at a great public mass meeting in April, 1861, to "aid in suppressing the Rebellion." In addition to the heads of the city government the committee consisted of such citizens as John Jacob Astor, Alexander T. Stewart, Hamilton Fish and William F. Havemeyer. The commit-

Continued on Page Eleven.

Austrian Legion Reassembled in Germany; Trucks With Newly Equipped Men Go South

Wireless to THE NEW YORK TIMES.

MUNICH, June 3.—There are increasing indications that the Austrian Legion, supposedly dissolved last Summer, is being concentrated again and equipped with new uniforms.

Half a dozen trucks passed through Munich today loaded with legionaires in brand-new equipment, including complete marching kits. They were remarkable for their smart appearance, which contrasted sharply with their dilapidated state last Summer.

According to reports from Bad Aibling, Upper Bavaria, the Austrian Legion camp there is being occupied by a larger number of men than six months ago.

German citizenship has been granted to some of the legionaires, but even those incorporated in the German Nazi Storm Troops continue to wear the strawberry-colored insignia that is the Austrian Legion's mark.

By The Associated Press.

MUNICH, June 3.—Lorries filled with cheering Austrian legionaires rolled southward from Munich in the direction of Innsbruck, Austria, sixty-two miles distant, today, but all the occupants were silent as to their objective.

Reports were current in Berlin that Alfred Frauenfeld, Austrian Nazi leader, had received a high position in the Reich Culture Chamber, which is headed by Dr. Paul Joseph Goebbels, Minister of Propaganda.

Wireless to THE NEW YORK TIMES.

VIENNA, June 3.—Many more arrests were made today in connection with the Illkor, illegal Nazi news sheet. The wives of Dr. Hermann Senkowsky, a high employe of the Ministry of Finance, and Dr. Erich Stiassny, former Nazi newspaper man, who were seized last week, were among those arrested.

Many university men were jailed on suspicion of being connected with the news sheet. Altogether thirty persons are now under arrest in this connection.

The police suspect that the little newspaper was actually prepared in Budapest and sent here for distribution. It is also alleged in the press that the arrested men were in close contact with Nazis in Munich. All those arrested strenuously deny any connection with the news sheet.

Despite the cornering of the Illkor's alleged staff, the news sheet appeared again today as usual.

The police tonight arrested one of the leading foreign correspondents in Vienna, Dr. Hans Hartmeyer, president of the Association of German Correspondents in Austria and a member of the committee of the Union of Foreign Correspondents.

RANSOM CAR FOUND; TURNS KIDNAP HUNT TO GANG ON COAST

Tan Sedan, Seized in Seattle, Is Searched for Clues to the Weyerhaeuser Abductors.

OWNED BY BOY'S UNCLE

He Admits Using It in Payoff, but Is Silent on Loss—Suspicion of Karpis Wanes.

By The Associated Press.

TACOMA, Wash., June 3.—A motor car found abandoned in Seattle was disclosed tonight to be a vital clue in the government's determined drive to trap George Weyerhaeuser's kidnappers, now indicated as being members of a Northwest criminal gang.

The car, a tan sedan owned by F. Rodman Titcomb, uncle of the ransomed 9-year-old timber fortune heir, presumably was used to convey $200,000 to the abductors a few hours before they released their victim.

"Yes, that is my car," Mr. Titcomb said, breaking a silence he has maintained since George was returned home last Saturday.

At the same time it appeared that suspicion toward the notorious gang of Alvin Karpis, co-engineer of the $200,000 Edward G. Bremer kidnapping, was on the wane and that a band of Northwestern outlaws was being sought.

As for Volney Davis, the Karpis lieutenant who pleaded guilty today in St. Paul in the Bremer kidnapping, Federal agents said they had learned that he was not in Tacoma during the week of the Weyerhaeuser abduction.

At the same time the Federal men distributed lists containing the numbers of the bank notes given to the Weyerhaeuser kidnappers. Strategic points were asked to watch for appearance of the bills.

Minute Scrutiny of Car.

The boy himself named Mr. Titcomb as the pay-off man and there were reports that the abductors seized the car and forced the uncle to walk for several miles after making the payment. The sedan was found in Seattle a few hours after George turned up safely.

Department of Justice agents seized the car and closely guarded it while presumably searching for finger prints and other evidence.

If government criminologists can do with the automobile what Walter J. Koehler, government wood expert, did with the Lindbergh kidnap ladder, it may tell them a long story about the kidnappers.

Any fingerprints obtained will open the way toward determining whether the car was used by any one of the thousands of criminals recorded by the Bureau of Identification.

Under the microscope the tires of the car may yield clues as to its movements immediately before it was abandoned. Minute particles of soil in the tread may reveal the road it followed.

If the kidnappers dropped any small article in the car or left even the finest threads from their clothing or from other personal effects, these things may tell much to the eye of a laboratory detective.

Only One Ransom Note.

New information concerning how contact was arranged with Mr. and Mrs. J. P. Weyerhaeuser, parents of the boy, came from close family sources which said that but one ransom note was received.

Telephone conversations to which justice agents in the house could have listened were understood to have been the other means of communication.

No definite information could yet be obtained as to when and where the ransom was paid, and neither Mr. Titcomb nor justice agents would comment on reports that the meeting place was near Elma, about sixty miles southwest of here.

Mr. Titcomb, a high official in the Weyerhaeuser lumber organization, would not affirm or deny that the car had been taken from him by the abductors.

The fact that the machine was found abandoned in Seattle gave definite indications that at least some members of the gang had fled in that direction.

No "Hot Money" Turns Up.

Soon after copies of the ransom note serial numbers were distributed to banks and various other places here, Justice Department headquarters heard from people who thought they had obtained some of the ransom money.

Agents were kept busy checking through the long list of the bills, but found none of the "hot" money.

Belief that the kidnap gang still was in the Pacific Northwest, or at least on the Coast, was strengthened when it was said there would be more safety in passing the ransom money here than in the East.

The $200,000 fund, all except nine

Continued on Page Ten.

ROOSEVELT MOVES TODAY TO REMEDY NIRA IMPASSE; CALLS THREE CONFERENCES

Steel Institute Leads Wide Move To Retain NRA Rules Voluntarily

Big Metal Producers' Pledge Against Wage Cuts and Unfair Rivalry Is Echoed by the Textile and Dry Goods Industries, Garment Trades and Other Powerful Groups.

Industry and business pressed their efforts yesterday to maintain observance of NRA wage and labor standards and code rules of fair trade practices on a voluntary basis.

Leading the movement was the American Iron and Steel Institute, supported by the textile industry, the Wholesale Dry Goods Institute and the National Retail Dry Goods Association. Employer associations in the garment trades likewise gave the movement their support.

From other directions, including the Radio Corporation of America, came indications that although the NRA no longer existed, business men and industrialists were eager to preserve its positive features as far as voluntary effort made this possible.

Resoutions calling upon individual members of the American Iron and Steel Institute to maintain voluntarily present rates of pay, maximum hours of work and standards of fair competition, as set forth in the Steel Code, were adopted by the directors of the institute at a special meeting here. All the important steel corporations are members of the institute.

The board also urged its members to continue to protect the employes' rights of collective bargaining, which also were outlined in the Steel Code.

The action of the board was preceded last week by statements of heads of most of the leading producers announcing their intention to maintain the principles of the code.

Since the directors of the institute are the former members of the Steel Code Authority, and since they are the heads of the principal companies in the industry, the statement gave assurance that there would be no cutting of wages or abandonment of the fair-trade practices of the Steel Code.

By pledging themselves to maintain the basic principles of their code the steel executives are making it impossible for them to reduce prices of steel products without incurring losses. With steel operations at a little less than 40 per cent of capacity, the industry as a whole is probably hardly breaking even under the present prices, steel executives declare.

For this reason it is believed an

Continued on Page Six.

NRA FORCE KEPT INTACT

Richberg Is Told Not to Serve Notice Ending 5,400 Jobs June 16.

CABINET MEETS AT 11 A. M.

Congress Chiefs and Recovery Aides Summoned to White House in Afternoon.

PRESS IS INVITED IN LAST

Capital Expects Legislative Steps, Leaving Constitution Issue to the Future.

Special to THE NEW YORK TIMES.

WASHINGTON, June 3.—Promulgation tomorrow by President Roosevelt of a new program to supersede the unconstitutional National Industrial Recovery Act was clearly indicated at the White House tonight.

After instructing Donald R. Richberg, chairman of the National Industrial Recovery Board, to maintain the NRA force of 5,400 employes intact, and not to serve notice that their jobs would terminate on June 16, Mr. Roosevelt called the Cabinet to meet at 11 A. M. tomorrow, invited Congressional and administration leaders concerned with recovery legislation to meet at the White House at 3:30 P. M., and set 5 P. M. as the hour for a special press conference.

No hint was given as to the program the President had in mind, but this activity was taken as evidence that he did not consider tonight that the administration's recovery program was in as dangerous a position as he pictured it on Friday at his last press conference, when he explained his views on the effects of the Supreme Court's decision in the Schechter case, invalidating the NIRA.

It was expected that the program forecast for tomorrow would be purely legislative in character, leaving for future consideration suggestions of amending the Constitution. Mr. Roosevelt himself has termed the amendment route too long for immediate practical purposes.

Those Invited to the Conference.

Those invited to the White House conference, which will follow the Cabinet meeting tomorrow, were Attorney General Cummings, Secretaries Perkins and Morgenthau, Senators Robinson, Harrison and Wagner; Speaker Byrns, Mr. Richberg, Representatives Doughton and O'Connor, Solicitor General Reed, Acting Secretary Dickinson of the Commerce Department and Charles West. Others are yet to be designated.

The rapid fire of events foreshadowing an early, although probably temporary solution came after a long day devoted by the President and his advisers principally to study of the problem.

Members of the NIRB labored over a dozen plans providing possible answers to the question of what to do next. Scores of other suggestions were studied at the Department of Justice by Attorney General Cummings and Solicitor General Reed, already designated by the President as official reviewers for proposed plans.

Mr. Roosevelt personally was in touch with these offices frequently by telephone. He began the day with a conference in the White House residential quarters with Speaker Byrns and ended it with his conversation with Mr. Richberg. He spent half an hour talking to Senator O'Mahoney, who proposed a Federal incorporation statute for companies doing interstate business.

Congress Leaders Hopeful.

While this work was going forward in the executive agencies, Congress went ahead with its work, awaiting word from the President but confident, according to its leaders, that a substitute would be found for the NRA.

Despite constitutional questions raised by the court decision as cited by the President on Friday, the Senate proceeded today to consider the Wheeler-Rayburn bill to regulate utility holding companies, and in the House the way was paved for consideration of the Wagner Labor Disputes Bill.

The bill amending the Agriculture

Continued on Page Eight.

JERSEY SALES TAX PASSES ASSEMBLY

Hoffman's Proposal for a 2% Levy for Relief Wins by Vote of 31 to 27.

INCOME IMPOST IS LOST

House Also Defeats Clee Bill to Divert $10,000,000 State Funds to Relief.

Special to THE NEW YORK TIMES.

TRENTON, N. J., Tuesday, June 4.—Governor Harold G. Hoffman forced the passage of his bill for a 2 per cent sales tax to finance emergency relief in the New Jersey Assembly early today. The measure was approved by a vote of 31 to 27. The concurrence of the Senate is believed certain.

A companion administration bill for income levies to ease the tax load on real estate was decisively defeated.

The Assembly previously rejected the bill sponsored by its Speaker, the Rev. Lester H. Clee of Newark, for a special appropriation of $10,784,266 to aid the needy. The measure would have authorized diversion of nearly $7,500,000 from highway funds and utilized anticipated surplus revenue in the general treasury as well as municipal contributions.

Voting on the bills, followed the appearance of State officials summoned to report on the State's actual financial condition. They read off figures for an hour and then the minority floor leader, Assemblyman John J. Rafferty of Middlesex, announced he was ready to support the sales tax. He said he was not convinced the Clee proposal was sound.

Vote on Two Bills.

The Clee bill was defeated by a vote of 28 to 28, the number required for adoption being 31. The Income Tax Bill was beaten by a vote of 16 to 42.

The Sales Tax Bill was opened to amendment before being considered on third reading. An amendment to provide $700,000 for establishing offices and for administration purposes the first year was defeated, 24 to 34, after Dr. Clee, leading opponent of the sales tax idea, charged "this $700,000 is really the reason for the sales tax."

The bill was amended to provide the tax be levied as follows: 12 cents or less, no tax; 13 to 60 cents, 1 cent; 61 cents to $1.13, 2 cents, with 2 cents on each additional dollar purchase plus the fraction.

An amendment to exempt milk and cream sales was defeated. Adopted were two amendments setting July 1 as the effective date and specifying that $1 license fee shall be effective after July 1.

In a dramatic plea against new taxes, Speaker Lester H. Clee, leader

Continued on Page Ten.

WORKS WAGES GET BIGGER FUND SHARE

Projects for Which the Cost of Materials Is Low Will Receive Preference.

PRESIDENT FORCES RULE

Cites Total of Idle at Meeting With ACA—New York City Plans Affected.

Special to THE NEW YORK TIMES.

WASHINGTON, June 3.—A decision that work relief projects for which the cost of materials is low will receive preference in apportioning the rest of the $4,000,000,000 fund, a course adverse to some large projects proposed for New York City, was made today by the Advisory Committee on Allotments, which met with President Roosevelt at the White House.

A program somewhat similar to that developed by CWA, but with better conceived and more useful projects, will be pushed through as a result of this decision. Housing, public works and other projects on which material costs are relatively high will take a secondary place.

The President, who presided at the meeting, insisted upon this procedure. He informed the committee that on more than $1,000,000,000 of projects approved to date the cost of employing each person ran to about $2,000. If 3,500,000 persons are to be employed under the program, the average cost per person cannot be much over $1,140, he pointed out.

City to Get Large Aid.

While the decision is expected to make impossible the undertaking of some of the larger work projects suggested for New York City by Mayor La Guardia, it will not hamper a useful work-relief program there, officials here stressed.

Paving materials for large cities, for instance, will naturally cost more than for country roads, but it was promised that New York would receive whatever funds were necessary for this kind of work.

"White collar" projects are especially harmonious with the new rule since overhead costs in the taking of various types of censuses and other clerical jobs are exceedingly low, officials added. New York City has a particularly high ratio of "white collar" unemployed.

River and harbor projects, the construction of roads and rural airports and CCC projects also involve low material costs, it was pointed out.

"Figures were submitted to the committee showing that many projects already tentatively approved, because of their high material cost, entail a work-relief cost in excess of the average amount needed to give sufficient work," said a statement given out after the White House meeting.

"It was decided, therefore, to

Continued on Page Nine.

"All the News That's Fit to Print."

The New York Times.

LATE CITY EDITION
WEATHER—Rain today, continued warm; tomorrow showers.
Temperatures Yesterday—Max., 79; min., 66.

Copyright, 1935, by The New York Times Company.

VOL. LXXXIV....No. 28,268. Entered as Second-Class Matter. Postoffice, New York, N. Y. NEW YORK, MONDAY, JUNE 17, 1935. PP TWO CENTS in New York City. | THREE CENTS Within 200 Miles | FOUR CENTS Elsewhere Except in 7th and 8th Postal Zones.

PRESIDENT SETS UP NEW NRA AND PICKS STAFF TO RUN IT; $300,000,000 WHITE COLLAR AID

U.S. RESCUED FRANC IN RECENT CRISIS, TANNERY REVEALS

Chief of Bank of France Says Treasury Supplied Market With Badly Needed Dollars.

HE PRAISES MORGENTHAU

'Broad Understanding of the Situation' Averted Trouble, He Declares at Basle.

BANKERS ARE IMPRESSED

Discern a Major Development of American Policy and Aid to de Facto Stabilization.

By CLARENCE K. STREIT.
Wireless to THE NEW YORK TIMES.

BASLE, Switzerland, June 16.—The United States Treasury played the decisive rôle in saving the franc in the recent crisis, Jean Tannery, Governor of the Bank of France, disclosed here today at the monthly meeting at the World Bank of the governors of Europe's central banks.

M. Tannery paid a special personal tribute to Secretary Morgenthau's "broad understanding of the situation," which had enabled the French to keep the exchange rate from getting out of hand, as it seemed likely to do on May 31 because of the Bank of France's difficulty, despite its gold, in getting enough dollars to meet the demand.

M. Tannery declared that at this juncture in the crisis, in which, he said, France lost nearly 10,000,000,000 francs' worth of gold—half to the United States—the United States Treasury had stepped in with its tremendous resources and "constantly supplied the market with dollars."

Bankers Favorably Impressed.

The fact that the United States Treasury thus intervened to allow the smooth working of the gold standard and to prevent devaluation of the franc—which is to say of the gold bloc currencies—made, there is good reason to believe, a tremendous and favorable impression on the bank governors who were aware of the incalculable consequences of such a monetary upset.

There had been rumors that Washington had cooperated with France in this crisis, but even the bank governors, it is understood, showed surprise at learning the degree of support Washington had given, the like of which they had not seen since 1931. They were obviously happy when they left the bank; in fact, such cheerful faces have not been seen here in years. The American move is regarded as a major development in American policy and one greatly encouraging to the gold bloc and accepted by others as making for de facto stabilization.

The American rôle in the crisis of the franc became public when the Bank of France issued a communiqué this evening after the meeting saying that M. Tannery had explained the crisis to the governors and given a summary of his statement containing prominently this passage:

"M. Tannery brought out the importance of the aid that had been given by the United States Treasury which, thanks to Secretary Morgenthau's broad understanding of the situation, constantly supplied the market with dollars to prevent the dangerous consequences of any cessation of gold purchases."

Saving of Franc Described.

Inquiry into what lay behind this passage brought out bit by bit what seemed the main elements of the part the United States had played. The inside story M. Tannery told to the governors of how the franc had been saved was not lacking in excitement. The situation he described may be thus summarized:

The flight of francs to dollars, pounds and gold had jumped from 60,000,000 francs a day at the beginning of May to nearly 1,000,000,000 a day when the month-end neared and a fantastic but very real difficulty threatened then to upset the franc. The fantastic thing was that the Bank of France with $5,000,000,000 worth of gold in its cellar and anxious to buy dollars with it to meet the market demand and thus keep the exchange rate in hand could no longer be certain of getting even 100,000,000 paper dollars with its gold.

Here are the reasons: The run had then reached such dimensions that, it is understood, Paris banks were handling as much as $30,000,000 a day in dollar sales, and by the last week in May only one bank was still buying francs with dollars.

Others knew that all ships, from the giant Normandie to the smaller cabin boats of the American merchant lines, which rarely get gold shipments, were loaded then to

Continued on Page Seven.

Long-Sought Gunman Slain By Police in Country Club

Fugitive, Listed as Public Enemy Here, Trapped in Fashionable West Orange Resort, Is Beaten to Draw by Officer.

Special to THE NEW YORK TIMES.

WEST ORANGE, N. J., June 16—Vincent Diauon, 27-year-old gunman, listed as one of the most-sought public enemies on the rolls of New York's recently organized State "Scotland Yard" and wanted here for a series of burglaries and assaults upon women, was shot and killed by police tonight in the crowded bar of the fashionable Mayfair Country Club atop Eagle Rock.

Entering the barroom after he had left a blond woman companion at a table, he recognized two of the five policemen who were waiting in the hope of capturing him without gunplay. Diauon reached for a revolver.

As the weapon was half out of the man's hip pocket, Captain William Wylie of the West Orange police drew his own revolver and fired once. The bullet struck Diauon in the head. Turning, the gunman started to run from the barroom, just as the police captain fired again. The second bullet struck Diauon in the back. Despite this, however, the wounded man succeeded in getting out of the barroom and crossed the entrance lobby to a small dining room, where he collapsed and died.

The weapon he sought vainly to use was found on examination to bear marks linking it with the Rochester (N. Y.) Police Department, and police upon investigation declared that he had held up two plainclothes detectives in that city, robbing them of their weapons before he returned recently to the Oranges.

More than 100 persons, about half of them women, were in the club when the shooting occurred. Screaming as the two shots echoed through the dining room, adjoining the barroom, women leaped from their tables and sought to run from the place. About twenty couples halted on the dance floor as the orchestra, playing "She's My Cookie," brought the music to an abrupt halt.

In the barroom, where about twen-

Continued on Page Three.

CATHOLICS DEMAND LIBERTY IN MEXICO

15,000 Demonstrate Before Rotarians—Youth Seized for Threat to President.

ECLIPSE OF CALLES SEEN

Ex-President Announces He Is Quitting Public Life—Retires to Ranch.

Special Cable to THE NEW YORK TIMES.

MEXICO, D. F., June 16.—Fifteen thousand Catholics paraded in this city this morning in a demonstration to impress 4,000 Rotarians, now here for their international convention, with their struggle for religious liberty.

The marchers carried banners inscribed "We protest against religious persecution" and "We are friends of the American people but not of Ambassador Daniels."

The procession, in passing the National Palace, sang the national anthem. Soldiers on guard at the palace stood at attention with fixed bayonets. Police were conspicuously absent.

On their arrival at the Palace of Fine Arts, the Rotarian headquarters, the paraders stopped. Speakers addressed the visitors in English.

"We can thank you for this liberty," declared one orator. "We are parading for religious liberty, the same as you have in your countries." Rotarians applauded as the paraders dispersed after a peaceful march past the Palace of Fine Arts.

Washouts Delay 2,000.

The 4,000 visiting Rotarians will open their convention officially tomorrow morning at the Palace of Fine Arts. Executive committee sessions have been held during the past five days at the resort of Cuernavaca.

Two thousand more Rotarians expected here today were held up by bridge washouts between the United States border and Monterrey. Twelve special trains were delayed. They are now expected to arrive here by daybreak.

United States Ambassador Josephus Daniels, returning here after a vacation, was delayed with the Rotarians, but he transferred to plane and arrived at the Central Airport early this afternoon.

He will attend the Rotary sessions, making one of the principal speeches.

Two thousand of the Rotarians are housed in Mexico's new Pullman city. Hotel and private accommodations in this capital are crowded. During the next five days an unprecedented series of festivities will be held for the largest group of visitors ever to come to Mexico.

Calles Retires to His Ranch.

By The Associated Press.

MEXICO, D. F., June 17.—The political conflict between President Lazaro Cardenas and former President Plutarco Elias Calles ended today with a statement by Señor Calles that he was leaving for his Sinaloa ranch and stepping out of public affairs.

Señor Calles asserted he was departing so that his declarations concerning political and economic conditions "might not be misinterpreted as meaning I desire to intervene in public affairs."

Fifteen thousand Catholics paraded unmolested past the National Palace today while their speakers

Continued on Page Seven.

FINGERPRINTS' TALE NOW LEFT ON CLOTH

New Methods Used by Police Reveal Marks of Hands on Almost Any Substance.

BODY CHEMISTRY IS KEY

With Help of Hauptmann Case Expert, Detectives Even Hope to Trace Gloved Criminal.

The crook, so familiar in motion pictures, who carefully wipes his fingerprints from a polished surface with his handkerchief, no longer saves himself from detection if he inadvertently leaves the handkerchief as he makes off with the jewels.

He is no longer safe if his bare hands have touched sheets, pillow slips, the embroidered doily on the mahogany table, or even the black alpaca lining of his victim's coat as he extracts valuable papers.

These are some of the advancements of fingerprint detection now in use by the New York Police Department, as announced yesterday by Commissioner Lewis J. Valentine.

Although Mr. Valentine did not touch upon it in his announcement, the workers in the department's technical research laboratory will be disappointed if, in a short time, he is not able also to announce that the use of gloves will no longer mask the whorls, loops and ridges by which human fingers are identified wherever they have left discernible marks.

The processes of making these marks discernible are fields in which the department is advancing by means of new techniques. With them a piece of clean cloth can be converted into a portrait of the hand that has touched it, regardless of whether the cloth is black or white. Mathematical probabilities, according to experts, proclaim that only once in 640 billion times will two different fingers leave identical portraits.

The research on fingerprinting has been done in the department laboratory under plans made by Assistant Chief Inspector John J. Sullivan and Deputy Chief Inspector John J. O'Connell. The work has been carried out by Lieutenant William J. McMahon and Detectives Maurice Harnett and Francis D. Murphy, with the expert assistance of Dr. Erastus Mead Hudson, a specialist in body chemistry of 30 East Seventy-sixth Street.

Dr. Hudson, whose position as an expert on fingerprinting came through his pursuit of a hobby, figured in the trial of Bruno Richard Hauptmann for the Lindbergh kidnapping when he testified that he had raised 500 prints on the kidnapper's ladder after the police had failed to reveal any.

The method he used on wood in the ladder is essentially the same as that used by the New York police on white and light-colored cloth. The principal agent is silver nitrate.

Every time a human being puts his hands down on any surface he leaves an impression. On most surfaces the marks are invisible, but they consist of a deposit of a substance called body wax, in which there is a quantity of sodium chloride, the technical term for common salt.

If the cloth on which this deposit

Continued on Page Three.

BOYS STEAL PISTOL IN POLICE STATION, ROB AND KILL MAN

Three, Aged 11 to 13, Use Ruse to Take Weapon From Coat of Jamaica Patrolman.

TRY TO HOLD UP A WOMAN

Run When She Slaps Leader—Wake Drunken Man, Demand Money, Then Shoot Him.

Three boys, two of them 13 years old and one only 11, stole a revolver from a policeman's coat in a Jamaica police station Saturday afternoon and embarked on a career of crime.

They tried to hold up a woman in the street, but she slapped one of them and sent them all on their way. Their next victim was a man lying, in drunken sleep, in a nearby lot.

They woke him and, when he refused to turn over his money, one of the youngsters shot and killed him. The boys are to be arraigned on homicide charges this morning in Jamaica Court.

District Attorney Charles P. Sullivan of Queens County said last night that he would ask that the boys be held without bail for the grand jury on the homicide charge and that he would let that body decide whether the case should be disposed of in the Children's Court, where juvenile delinquency would be the charge, or in County Court, where homicide would be the final charge against them.

Those under arrest are Frank Damato, 13, of 144-04 South Street, Jamaica, Queens, his 11-year-old brother, Julius, and Libson Lawrence, 13, a Negro, of 105-04 Liverpool Street, Jamaica. The two Damato boys are the sons of John Damato, a bricklayer, who has been out of work for three years. Their mother died two years ago, and they are members of a family of five children. The Lawrence boy is the son of the Rev. Edward Lawrence, Negro pastor of the Mount Calvary Baptist Church, 105th Avenue and Elaine Street. Libson is one of thirteen children.

Boys Confess the Killing.

Their victim, whose murder they have confessed, was William Walsh, 36 years old, who lived with his sister at 205-28 110th Avenue, Belleaire. Walsh, who had a police record dating back to 1915, had been sentenced to thirty days for vagrancy on Feb. 4, of this year.

Walsh had a wife, Tillie, and two children, Virginia, 13, and Adolph, 8. Mrs. Walsh and the children, separated from Walsh for a number of years, live at 105-17 Rockaway Road, Jamaica.

According to the boys' story to the police, the three, with Frank Damato as leader, had decided to organize the boot-blacking business along Jamaica Avenue. Frank was quoted as saying that he was going to prevent competition from "muscling in."

Crime was not a novelty to Frank and Julius. On June 2 they broke into a tavern in Jamaica and came out ten minutes later with $140.

They were arrested the next day, and two days later paroled in the

Continued on Page Eighteen.

Quezon Gets Nomination For Filipino Presidency

By The Associated Press.

MANILA, June 16.—Manuel Quezon was nominated tonight for the Presidency of the projected Philippine Commonwealth by two principal political parties, holding separate conventions.

This coalition ticket, which included the nomination of Senator Sergio Osmena for Vice President, was put forth in opposition to General Emilio Aguinaldo and Gregorio Agilpay, head of the Independent Catholic Church of the Philippines and former Roman Catholic priest.

At the election, to be held next Sept. 17, members of the first National Assembly also will be chosen.

The identical platforms of the two parties said "the question of independence has been settled" by the Tydings-McDuffie Act, which provides establishment of complete independence after a transition period of ten years.

TWO DIE, 5 ESCAPE AS BOAT CAPSIZES

Pair on Jamaica Bay Outing Drown, Third Man Saved and Four Swim Ashore.

HAD TIN CAN FOR BAILING

They Were Rowing in Rented Craft to Inspect a Vessel of the Byrd Expedition.

Two men were drowned yesterday when a rowboat capsized in Jamaica Bay, near the Floyd Bennett Airport. A third man was rescued by three policemen. Four other occupants of the boat swam ashore.

The seven men had started from the Barren Island Beach, several hundred feet away, for the pier at which Admiral Byrd's Antarctic vessel, the Jacob Ruppert, had tied up at 6 o'clock in the morning.

The dead men were Albert Delissio, 34 years old, of 584 Sackett Street, Brooklyn, married and the father of one child, and Henry Cataldo, 26, of 572 Sackett Street, married and the father of two children.

The others in the party, all of Brooklyn, were Delissio's brother, Michael, 38; Richard Sarentino, 30, and his brother, Alfred, 19, both of 117 Navy Street, and Dominick Desimione, 26, and his brother, Joseph, 25, of 555 Union Street.

Boat Rented for Outing.

All were members of the Union Boys Social Club of Brooklyn. They went to the beach with musical instruments for an outing. About 2 P. M. they rented a rowboat at 25 cents each.

The owner of the boat, Tony Caruso, of 306 Degraw Street, Brooklyn, later was questioned in the Vanderveer Park police station about the condition of the boat. Caruso, the police said, had provided a tin can for bailing.

After having questioned Caruso and others, Assistant District Attorney Anthony D. Giovanni said there was no evidence of neglect and no reason to hold him.

It was about thirty feet from the Jacob Ruppert's pier and about 100

Continued on Page Ten.

Fokine Home on Riverside Dr. Ransacked; $25,000 Loot Taken in Absence of Dancer

Burglars entered the home of Michel Fokine, ballet master, at 4 Riverside Drive and escaped yesterday with loot tentatively valued at $25,000, police revealed early today.

Entry to the four-story white granite structure, which is between Seventy-second and Seventy-third Street, was effected sometime between 4 and 10 P. M. while the Fokines were away and the servants were off. Apparently the thieves forced an iron grill door under the stoop and leading to the basement.

The burglars ransacked the house, strewing clothing and silverware and turning furnishings upside down. Articles listed as taken included several diamond-studded pendants, a lavallier, ear rings, a brooch valued at $10,000; two mink coats and a mink cape, valued at $6,000, and several hundred dollars in cash. The jewelry was taken from a wall vault in Mrs. Fokine's bedroom on the second floor.

The intruders seemingly were scared off in the middle of their work, for a considerable part of the silver service was found in the dining room as if prepared to be carted away.

How they managed to make off with the loot was puzzling to the police. They could not have taken it out through the front to a parked car, it was believed, because parking is restricted. Moreover, two policemen were on duty a few feet away directing traffic.

In addition, Riverside Drive had been bustling with traffic during the time when the burglars were at work. The police pointed out that the stream of cars on the Drive was larger yesterday than average for a Sunday owing to the return of thousands of motorists who had taken advantage of the fine weather to spend the day in the country.

The robbery was discovered shortly after 10 o'clock by Vitale Fokine, 20 years old, son of the ballet master. He, like his parents, had been out for the evening and upon his return noticed that the glass panel in the main entrance door had been broken. He unlocked the door and entered. His first glance into the hallway disclosed that the home had been ransacked by burglars. He notified the police.

The ground floor of the building contains the servants' quarters; the first and second, living quarters of the Fokines, and the third, dancing studios. The fourth contains guest rooms. The house is furnished with many costly paintings, but none of these was touched, according to the police.

Mr. and Mrs. Fokine returned while policemen were checking up on the stolen articles. They told the police they had left the house at 4 P. M., soon after their son had left. All the servants were away, they said, and the house was unguarded.

FERA REVEALS BIG PLAN

New Projects Designed Primarily to Help the Clerical Class.

SOME CRITICISM EXPECTED

But Hopkins' Aides Say They Have Not Dodged Work Which They Believe Useful.

PAROLES OFFER NEW FIELD

Carefully Selected Persons Urged as Court Officers—Art Program Included.

Special to THE NEW YORK TIMES.

WASHINGTON, June 16.—A $300,000,000 "white collar" program, more carefully conceived than either of those carried out by the CWA or the "direct" relief administration, has been virtually completed by Harry L. Hopkins's Work Progress Administration.

Although not complete in all details, the program to provide "assistance for educational, professional and clerical persons," who in New York City comprise 25 per cent of all those on relief rolls, represents the culmination of two years' experience in administering aid to professional and "desk" workers.

"We have not dodged projects which may be criticized by some in drafting our 'white collar' plans," one high FERA official said today, "but we have chosen projects which experience shows us will give useful occupations to specialized groups.

"While we have planned for amplified aid in their own fields for theatrical, artistic and other specialized groups, we have concentrated on projects to assist clerical workers who comprise the large bulk of the needy 'white collar' workers."

Project Suggested by Bates.

Among the most interesting of the clerical projects being developed is one under which carefully selected persons would act as parole officers for courts and prison bodies on a nation-wide scale.

This project, suggested by Sanford Bates, Federal Director of Prisons, would have an influence in restricting the improper use of the parole system, which President Roosevelt recently criticized, and would offer a means by which those truly worthy of parole could secure aid in rehabilitating themselves, officials said.

Officials seeking to investigate causes of distress in certain major industries and means of eliminating them have encountered a lack of proper information, it was said, and therefore it is planned to conduct studies of all major industries and agricultural pursuits for which more adequate information is required.

"We plan also to get more definite information about people, how much they earn, how they earn it, and other vital information," the FERA spokesman remarked.

"A great deal of useful and practical work will also be carried out with the cooperation of major universities," he continued. "We are not ready to disclose our plans in this regard as yet.

Aim to Equalize Wages.

"We no longer fear criticism of boon-doggling and other such activities. We have found out what projects of this kind really serve a useful purpose, and we are going ahead with them.

"Art, theatrical, and other such projects may not be appreciated by all, but they offer valuable contributions to American life. They represent only a minor part of this program, of course.

"Moreover, persons will have a sense of security they have not had under previous 'white collar' programs. They will work on one project for the time they are employed, rather than being shifted from one program to another after two or three weeks."

Newly appointed State Works Progress Administrators from all over the nation were arriving here tonight for their two-day conference with Mr. Hopkins. During the meeting, they will be informed of their duties under the new program, and the general policies for the $4,000,000,000 works program, developed during the two past months of preliminary work, will be explained to them in detail.

All Soft-Coal Operators Agree to Strike Truce

By The Associated Press.

WASHINGTON, June 16.—The United Mine Workers reported today that all soft-coal operators had agreed to President Roosevelt's strike truce.

This agreement to continue present wages, hours and working conditions through June 30 removed the last possibility of any walkout tomorrow.

Several producing districts did not send representatives to the joint wage conference yesterday which ratified the contract extension Mr. Roosevelt proposed to avert the nation-wide strike originally set for midnight tonight.

Absence of these representatives gave rise to reports that scattered strikes might result.

The union canvassed operators in these districts, however, and reported them willing to abide by the President's proposal.

GUFFEY COAL BILL IS MADE 'NO. 1 MUST'

Administration Chiefs Plan Drive for Early Passage to Avert Mine Strike.

DEMANDED BY ROOSEVELT

Congress Nears Its 24th Week With Heavier Task Ahead Than It Faced Jan. 3.

By TURNER CATLEDGE.
Special to THE NEW YORK TIMES.

WASHINGTON, June 16.—Answering an urgent request from President Roosevelt, Congressional leaders will attempt this week to drive the Guffey Coal Bill toward final passage as a preventive against the threatened strike of 450,000 miners in the bituminous fields.

Senate chieftains hope to call up the measure early in the week, following passage of the Social Security Bill, first of President Roosevelt's major reform measures. There was some question tonight as to whether the Guffey bill should not originate in the House, but plans called for quick action in the Senate, regardless of what adjustments on procedure might be necessary to bring its passage within strict conformity to the Constitution.

Mr. Roosevelt has practically demanded final enactment of the bill before June 30, the date on which the miners threaten to walk out unless wage and hour provisions they enjoyed under the NRA are now renewed by contract.

Guffey Bill an "Added Starter."

The Guffey bill, an "added starter" on the Administration program, now finds itself as No. 1 on the President's "must" list, taking the preferred place of the NRA extension which was finally enacted Friday, just two days ahead of tonight's deadline.

The first session of the Seventy-fourth Congress will enter its twenty-fourth week Wednesday, when it will face a list of legislative tasks even greater than when it convened on Jan. 3. From that January day until now, only one of the really important New Deal measures has been finally approved—the $4,880,000,000 work relief resolution—and only one other, the Social Security Bill, is in position for early enactment.

The additional work piled up on Congress was necessitated largely by the Supreme Court's practical destruction of the NRA through the Schechter decision. The first obstacle thrown up by this decision, that of extending the recovery agency in a skeleton form, was finally hurdled last week with a maximum of effort, but this left at least six additional measures which must be soon dealt with to repair the actual and potential damage to other New Deal policies.

Model Code Is Sought.

First of these is the Guffey Coal Bill. Urged now as an emergency measure to meet the threat of a miners' strike, Mr. Roosevelt nevertheless hopes to develop from its operation a model code for natural resource industries. It provides for a national coal commission to superintend and administer trade agreements and wage and hour provisions through which its sponsors hope to stabilize the soft coal indus-

Continued on Page Two.

O'NEILL IS ACTING CHIEF

Marshall, Coonley, Berry and Others From Old Set-Up Get Posts.

PERMANENT PLAN HINTED

President, in Executive Orders, Suggests 'Possibility of Further Legislation.'

GENERAL STRUCTURE KEPT

But Present Functions Are Narrow and Staff Is to Be Cut Steadily.

Special to THE NEW YORK TIMES.

WASHINGTON, June 16.—President Roosevelt, in executive orders tonight, set up an organization to carry out the skeletonized National Recovery Administration until April 1, 1936, as provided in Congressional passage of the resolution extending the recovery agency's life under restrictions limited by the Supreme Court decision in the Schechter case.

The functions of the deflated NRA will be to assemble statistics concerning the effect of the defunct codes on industry and labor and to aid in the maintenance of voluntary codes of fair competition.

The resolution restored the Anti-Trust Laws suspended under the NRA, and the Federal Trade Commission will now be called upon to see that fair trade practices are maintained and monopolies controlled under those statutes.

The executive orders terminated the life of the National Industrial Recovery Board created Sept. 27, 1934, and named officers to carry out the restricted program of the extended act.

OFFICERS APPOINTED.

Officers appointed under the orders are:

James L. O'Neill, New York, acting administrator.

Leon C. Marshall, director of the Division of Review.

Prentiss L. Coonley, director of the Division of Business Cooperation.

George L. Berry, assistant to the administrator, to represent labor.

An advisory council, consisting chiefly of present members of the National Recovery organization, was established with the following members:

Charles Edison, Howell Cheney, Philip Murray, William Green, Emily Newell Blair and Walton H. Hamilton.

President Roosevelt, in connection with the signing of the executive orders, stated:

"The administration of the amended act will proceed as rapidly as possible to adjust activities and personnel to conform to present limited objectives.

"So long, however, as there is a possibility of further legislation it will be desirable to maintain the general structure of the recovery administration in Washington and in field offices, and to retain those essential members of a trained personnel who can be usefully employed. There will be lasting values in a careful appraisal of the two-year accomplishments of the NRA and in preserving for permanent use the records of that experience. This can be done most efficiently and economically by those heretofore engaged in the work of codification.

To Cut Force Gradually.

"Steady but gradual reduction of personnel is, therefore, a sound public policy which will also avoid imposing undue hardships on faithful public employes who can continue to render a service of exceptional value to the government. It will be necessary, of course, to retain a sufficient field force to report on the effects of code abolition. This will include information covering changes in labor and fair-practice standards."

The NRA will continue without its most important functions. The enforcement of business codes is eliminated. It will have no authority to enforce hours of labor or minimum wage scales, but will endeavor to aid corporations which wish to work under voluntary agreements.

It will gather statistics to show how far corporations are operating under voluntary agreements and to determine whether business will operate under voluntary fair prac-

Continued on Page Two.

"All the News That's Fit to Print."

The New York Times.

LATE CITY EDITION
WEATHER—Fair, continued warm today; tomorrow rain, cooler.
Temperatures Yesterday—Max., 87; Min., 69

VOL. LXXXIV....No. 28,287. Entered as Second-Class Matter, Postoffice, New York, N. Y. NEW YORK, SATURDAY, JULY 6, 1935. P TWO CENTS In New York City. | THREE CENTS Within 200 Miles | FOUR CENTS Elsewhere Except in 7th and 8th Postal Zones.

PRESIDENT REJECTS ETHIOPIA'S APPEAL FOR PEACE EFFORT

Declines to Invoke Pact, as Dispute Is Being Considered by League of Nations.

HE VOICES HOPE OF ACCORD

Says U. S. Is 'Loath to Believe' Either Party Will Use 'Other Than Pacific Means.'

FRENCH REBUFF BRITAIN

Refuse to Pledge Themselves to Joint Action on Africa or Naval Parley Plans.

Special to THE NEW YORK TIMES.

WASHINGTON, July 5.—The Independence Day appeal of Emperor Haile Selassie of Ethiopia for the United States to invoke the Briand-Kellogg Pact against Italy in her threatened African war was promptly rejected by President Roosevelt today. His reply recalled that the issue already was in process of arbitration by the League of Nations.

The President said a good word for the peace treaty, known officially as the Pact of Paris, but did not send Italy a reminder of her obligations under it.

Mr. Roosevelt emphasized as "of great importance" the view that the United States Government "would be loath to believe" that either Ethiopia or Italy "would resort to other than pacific means as a method of dealing with this controversy or would permit any situation to arise which would be inconsistent with the commitments of the pact."

The President announced that the reply would be sent after a Cabinet meeting and after he had conferred with Secretary of State Cordell Hull, who had indicated earlier that no action would be taken today.

Sees No Gain in Delay.

It appeared obvious that Mr. Roosevelt felt that, inasmuch as he had no question concerning our position, there would be nothing gained by delaying the reply, and even some good might be gained by not permitting time for further conjectures as to our attitude.

The reply, Mr. Roosevelt said, was simple and clear. It took the form of instructions to William Perry George, United States Chargé d'Affaires in Addis Ababa, which were announced by the State Department tonight as follows:

The Emperor of Ethiopia on the evening of July 3 summoned the American Chargé d'Affaires ad interim at Addis Ababa to the palace and handed the Chargé a communication in which the Emperor stated that he felt it to be his duty to ask the American Government to examine means of securing observance of the Pact of Paris.

The Chargé has been instructed to reply to the Emperor as follows:

"I have the honor to acknowledge the receipt of Your Imperial Majesty's note of July 3, 1935, and to inform Your Imperial Majesty that I immediately communicated its contents to my government. I have been instructed by my government to reply to your note as follows:

"'My government, interested as it is in the maintenance of peace in all parts of the world, is gratified that the League of Nations, with a view to a peaceful settlement, has given its attention to the controversy which has unhappily arisen between your government and the Italian Government and that the controversy is now in process of arbitration.

Hopes for Peaceful Solution.

"'My government hopes that, whatever the facts or merits of the controversy may be, the arbitral agency dealing with this controversy may be able to arrive at a decision satisfactory to both of the governments immediately concerned.

"'Furthermore, and of great importance, in view of the provisions of the Pact of Paris, to which both Italy and Abyssinia are parties, in common with sixty-one other countries, my government would be loath to believe that either of them would resort to other than pacific means as a method of dealing with this controversy or would permit any situation to arise which would be inconsistent with the commitments of the pact.'"

The reply was sent without awaiting the text of the written memorandum Emperor Haile Selassie gave to Mr. George. Mr. George reported to the State Department that the Emperor had orally informed him of his understanding of the situation and had then asked the United States to consider means to induce Italy to live up to the

Continued on Page Five.

Chinese Province Gets Japanese Army Adviser

Special Cable to THE NEW YORK TIMES.

SHANGHAI, July 5.—A spokesman for the Japanese Embassy here revealed today that Lieut. Col. Gennosuke Matsui, resident Japanese observer at Kalgan, Inner Mongolia, had been appointed military adviser to the Chinese province of Chahar.

This was an aftermath of China's acceptance of Japanese demands for demilitarization of Southeastern Chahar and removal of Sung Cheh-yuan as Governor because of various incidents.

In reply to a question the spokesman said he was uninformed as to whether the Chinese authorities had invited Japanese military, political and economic advisers for Hopei, Suiyuan and Shantung Provinces.

'THIRD PARTY' MEN HUNT FOR LEADERS

250 'Native Radicals' Meet at Chicago to Form Lines for Possible '36 Fight.

THEY BAR COMMUNISTS

Seek Change Only 'Through Ballots'—'Production for Use' May Be the Main Plank.

Special to THE NEW YORK TIMES.

CHICAGO, July 5.—Creation of a leadership for a national "third party," if the advisability of one should develop prior to the 1936 political campaign, was the goal of about 250 "native American radicals" who held today the first session of a two-day conference here.

Representatives of radical organizations, exclusive of Communists, from twenty-seven States presented their credentials. They had responded to a call from five members of Congress, acting with the Farmer-Labor Political Federation, the League of Independent Action and the People's Political Alliance of Chicago.

Signers of the call were Representatives Thomas R. Amlie and George Schneider, Wisconsin Progressives; Vito Marcantonio, New York Republican; Ernest Lundeen, Minnesota Farmer-Laborite, and Byron Scott, California Democrat. Only two Representatives, Mr. Amlie and Mr. Marcantonio, were present today.

Paul Douglas Chairman.

Paul H. Douglas, Professor of Political Economy at the University of Chicago, was elected permanent chairman of the conference. Alfred M. Bingham of New York, acting secretary of the Farmer-Labor Political Federation, was named secretary. He is a son of former Senator Hiram Bingham, Republican of Connecticut. Committees on platform, organization and press also were named.

"We are organizing," said Mr. Amilie, "so that if a third party is inevitable in 1936 we will have the leadership ready. Our aim is to unite all the groups who want a change to come through the ballot box, which excludes Communists."

Mr. Marcantonio also declared that the purpose of the conference was to develop a leadership for a possible third party rather than to begin a third party at present.

"We are opposed to a third party at this time," he said, "but we are for the organization of a political federation to be held ready for action in 1936, if necessary."

Mr. Bingham characterized the delegates as "a cross section of the native American radical movement without the benefit of the European idea."

"These people are the direct de-

Continued on Page Two.

JOHNSON TO SPEND $19,500,000 IN JULY; KNAUTH QUITS POST

$17,500,000 of Federal Funds Allotted — State TERA to Advance the Remainder.

LAY-OFFS ARE PREVENTED

Details of City Projects to Be Announced Today—Knauth's 2 Chief Aides Also Resign.

General Hugh S. Johnson, Works Progress Administrator for New York City, was advised yesterday by Harry L. Hopkins, Federal Works Progress Administrator, that $17,500,000 of Federal funds would be available for New York City for July.

In his telegram, Mr. Hopkins further said that he had been informed by Frederick I. Daniels of the State TERA that this fund would permit a total of $19,500,000 to be used by New York City in July and that it meant no workers would be laid off in the period in which the Works Progress Administrator takes over the Works Division from the Emergency Relief Bureau.

Declaring that the reorganization of the Emergency Relief Bureau is well under way and that his work had been substantially completed, Oswald W. Knauth, director of the bureau, announced yesterday his resignation, effective on or before Aug. 1. His letter was dated June 27. At the same time he announced the resignation of Francis Boardman, director of the Works Division; of Major Irving V. A. Huie, deputy director, and of the six business men he had drafted as his special assistants.

General Johnson pointed out that while $78,657,310 had been allotted to New York City from the work projects fund his division as yet had received none of it. He presumed that the allotment would be used to complete old projects already under way and to launch new projects providing employment for about 60,000 men. General Johnson and Major Joseph C. Mehaffey, his aide in charge of projects and works, will give details at a press conference today of the projects to be financed by the New York City allotment.

More Active Next Week.

Early next week General Johnson announced, he expects to have a good knowledge of the system employed by the local relief organization and to be in a position to take more active control of the situation. He said he would have daily reports on the number and type of projects and the number of relief workers employed on those projects.

Ten of his former aides whom he brought here from Washington are making a thorough study of the local work-relief system, reporting to him daily their findings in different departments and making recommendations for improvements.

In his press interview at noon yesterday General Johnson referred to the slowness with which the works program in New York City had been carried on. After the installation of new elevators in the Municipal Building had been cited as a case in which the contract was not let until ten months after the application for funds had been filed, General Johnson said:

"My purpose is to see that there is no delay in these projects in the future. I don't know what those in charge have done in the past, but it is part of my job to eliminate any such needless delays."

General Johnson is preparing a detailed study not only of the per-

Continued on Page Three.

Objector to New Reich Army Service Jailed; Deacon Would Not Wear Swastika Insignia

Wireless to THE NEW YORK TIMES.

BERLIN, July 5.—Gerhard Handrock, a Protestant deacon and candidate for the ministry, was sentenced to four months' imprisonment today as the first young German who has conscientious objections to serving in the new universal service army.

He was charged with and convicted of insulting the Reich colors and attacking the army on the basis of a letter he wrote to the military authorities referring to the swastika as a pagan symbol and asserting "Jesus does not desire His children to carry the sword."

The letter said that its author regarded it as his duty to pray for the German people threatened with a revival of paganism rather than to serve in the army. Mr. Handrock also asserted that he could not be expected as a candidate for the Christian ministry to put on a uniform on which the "heathen swastika" was so prominently displayed.

The judge, commenting on the case, declared:

"There can be no question in the new Germany that fulfilling a citizen's duty takes precedence over all other duties. If some one interests himself in religious things, that is a private affair."

Under amendments to the criminal law issued today no male German may leave the country, even on a visit, until he has done military service, unless he has special police permission.

Any German who emigrates or attempts to emigrate until he is released from the reserve at the age of 45 is threatened with six months to a year's imprisonment if the German police succeed in laying hands on him.

This law restores the pre-war situation, when many American citizens were not recognized as such by the German Government and were subject to arrest as soon as they set foot on German soil. The constant ill feeling engendered by such incidents helped to embitter German-American relations.

Japan and Soviet Agree on Board To Settle Grave Boundary Issues

Accord, Ending Long Dispute, Is Seen as a Form of Russian Recognition of Manchukuo—Japan Plans Vast Economic Enterprises in North China That Will Also Aid Defense.

By HUGH BYAS.
Wireless to THE NEW YORK TIMES.

TOKYO, Saturday, July 6.—Ambassador Constantin Yureneff informed Foreign Minister Koki Hirota that the Soviet accepted the proposed tripartite frontier commission to regulate disputes arising over the Siberian-Manchurian boundaries.

The suggestion that Russia submit a draft organization was accepted on condition that Japan and Manchukuo also prepare drafts.

The newspaper Asahi sketches the form of a commission that would be acceptable to Japan. It would be composed of representatives of the Soviet, Manchukuo and Japan and would sit permanently at Harbin, with subcommissions at Manchuli, Manchuria, and Blagoveshchensk and Pogranichnaya, Siberia.

All disputes along the frontier would be submitted to the commission, which would investigate and propose solutions but would refer to the three governments any cases it failed to settle.

The long delay in realizing this seemingly common-sense device, which Russia had already adopted on eight of her frontiers, was due to its implications. Other commissions deal with agreed frontiers, but parts of the Siberian-Manchurian boundary are not defined. The commission consequently cannot avoid becoming in some degree a body for fixing the boundaries of Manchukuo, thereby giving the new State a tangible form of recognition.

The Japanese realize that the Soviet's action is one more proof of its peaceful intentions.

Military comment, as reported in the press, is somewhat sour. The army is said to think that by bringing up eight complaints over border incidents last week, the Soviet wanted to gain some advantage from the commission. As it is a diplomatic matter the army will not oppose, but will watch developments and observe if the Soviet displays "sincerity." That hard-worked

Continued on Page Four.

MERCURY AT 87.2°, HOTTEST OF YEAR

Three Prostrations Reported in the City as Torrid Wave Sweeps the Country.

CROWDS AT THE BEACHES

Holiday Aspect at Coney Island —3 Drowned in Minnesota as Winds Upset Boats.

Those who stayed behind this week-end and did not join the exodus to the great open spaces experienced New York's hottest day of the year yesterday. The temperature rose to 87.2 degrees at 1:05 P. M. The previous high for the year was 86.7, June 13.

Weather Bureau officials forecast generally fair weather today and predicted that the thermometers would reach 86. Tomorrow showers and somewhat cooler weather are indicated.

Throughout yesterday the winds were southwest to west.

Temperatures for the day, as recorded by the Weather Bureau here, were as follows:

12 Midnight	73	4 P. M.	84
3 A. M.	71	5 P. M.	84
6 A. M.	69	6 P. M.	82
8 A. M.	72	7 P. M.	82
9 A. M.	73	8 P. M.	81
10 A. M.	77	9 P. M.	80
11 A. M.	79	10 P. M.	79
12 Noon	81	11 P. M.	78
1 P. M.	87	12 Midnight	*78
2 P. M.	86	1 A. M.	*80
3 P. M.	84	2 A. M.	*76

*Unofficial at Times Square.

The Associated Press reported high temperatures throughout the country, with one of the highest marks recorded at Dresden, Kan., where the mercury rose to 104 degrees. The same source also reported three persons drowned in Minnesota lakes when winds upset boats, and the derailing of a passenger train near Bainville, Mont., as a result of storm damage. Boston suburbs had temperatures ranging from 90 to 95 degrees.

Overcome by Heat.

In New York, Harry Jarvin, 35 years old, of 2,327 Walton Avenue, the Bronx, was overcome by heat in the afternoon while standing at Jerome and Burnside Avenues. He was treated at Morrisania Hospital and sent home.

Gertrude Slater, 19, of 60 West 142d Street, was overcome by the heat at Westchester Square, the Bronx, and taken to Fordham Hospital.

While on the stairs of the southbound platform of the Simpson Street Station of the I. R. T. at 9 P. M. Isadore Gold, 38, of 736 Fox Street, the Bronx, collapsed from the heat and was taken to Lincoln Hospital.

Thousands who remained in the metropolitan area rather than take advantage of the holiday week-end in the country swarmed to the beaches and indicated that many of them would stay there for the night. As evening came on, parking spaces which generally lose many of their patrons at that time were maintaining an afternoon average. The water was exceptionally warm, attracting many who ordinarily get into bathing suits but do not go near the water.

At Coney Island Police Captain Henry E. Bauer estimated the crowd at more than 300,000. The beach and boardwalk had a holiday aspect. There were the usual reports of lost children, all eventually being returned to their parents, and police arrested a score of peddlers who probably thought they were immune on week days.

Similar situations were in evi-

Continued on Page Three.

WALL ST. BANKERS SPLIT ON GLASS BILL

Association Members Differ Sharply on Modifying Ban on Underwriting.

CLASH IN CAPITAL SURE

Investment Houses Also Are Hostile, but Hesitate to Make Direct Attack.

A wide split between members of the Wall Street banking community has been caused by the amendment to the Banking Act of 1935 restoring to banks of deposit a part of the security business which was taken away from them by the Banking Reform Act of 1933.

Opponents of the change, recovering from the surprise with which they received the news of the amendment last week, are beginning to prepare to combat it. On Wednesday the American Bankers Association's special committee on the Banking Act of 1935 will meet in Washington to consider the act as revised by the Senate Banking Subcommittee under the chairmanship of Senator Carter Glass.

The committee will be urged to oppose vigorously the attempt to put banks of deposit part-way back into the securities business, as well as other features of the bill, including one which specifically authorizes interlocking bank directorates. Failing a strong opposition stand by the committee itself, individual members are expected to make known their own objections to the measure.

While strong forces within the American Bankers Association are thus preparing to move against the Glass committee's version of the bill, leading investment bankers and dealers are endeavoring to have the Investment Bankers Association record itself in opposition to the plan to restore the privilege of underwriting securities to the commercial and private banks.

The investment bankers and dealers are moving cautiously, for the larger ones fear that they may be accused of a too obvious self-interest and the smaller ones have no desire at this time to gain the enmity of powerful banks and bankers who may, if the proposed bill goes through, shortly be once more in a dominant position in the security business.

The dealers, furthermore, are not unanimous. While many feel that the opportunity for larger operations which had appeared to be opening before them in the past year will be snatched away under the new bill, causing a reversion to former conditions where a few large institutions dominated the capital market, others hold that the re-entry of banks into the business of underwriting will mean a rise in new financing which will in turn entail more business and profits for all.

The special committee of the American Bankers Association which will consider the new bill at its meeting in Washington next Wednesday, includes Rudolf S. Hecht, president of the A. B. A.; Robert V. Fleming, vice president of the association and president of the Riggs National Bank, Washington, D. C.; Tom K. Smith, president of the Boatmans National Bank, St. Louis; Winthrop W. Aldrich, chairman of the Chase National Bank, and Ronald Ransom,

Continued on Page Two.

ROOSEVELT SIGNS THE WAGNER BILL AS 'JUST TO LABOR'

It Is Important Step Toward Industrial Peace but Will Not Stop All Disputes, He Says.

MEDIATION NOT AFFECTED

President Explains New Board Will Act Only on Violations of the Right to Organize.

Special to THE NEW YORK TIMES.

WASHINGTON, July 5.—The Wagner Labor Disputes Bill, enacting into permanent law a Federal authorization for labor to organize for the purpose of collective bargaining, a definition of unfair practices, the creation of an organization to review disputes between employers and labor, was signed by President Roosevelt today.

The signing had been postponed several days in an effort to arrange a ceremony, but after it had been found impossible to get together all the leaders who sponsored the legislation, Mr. Roosevelt approved the bill at the White House this morning before going to the executive offices.

Later he hailed the measure as "an important step toward the achievement of just and peaceful labor relations in industry," but at the same time warned the public that "it will not stop all labor disputes."

He used two pens in signing the bill, directing afterward that one be presented to Senator Wagner, co-author of the bill with Representative Connery, and that the other go to William Green, president of the American Federation of Labor, who has called the bill the "magna charta of labor."

The bill provides Federal machinery for the adjudication of disputes over the right of labor to organize when "violation of the legal right of independent self-organization would burden or obstruct interstate commerce," the President announced.

Adjudication would be placed in the hands of a permanent National Labor Relations Board, to supersede the board carrying the same title which was organized under the National Recovery Act.

None of the personnel of the new board had been designated or even considered finally by Mr. Roosevelt, he said today.

The temporary board, the tenure of which was recently extended to Aug. 1, is expected to lapse immediately. Francis Biddle, chairman of the NLRB, who had announced he would leave office upon signing of the Wagner bill, called at the White House today to bid good-bye to the President.

THE PRESIDENT'S STATEMENT

Mr. Roosevelt's statement of the bill's purposes read as follows:

"This act defines, as a part of our substantive law, the right of self-organization of employes in industry for the purpose of collective bargaining, and provides methods by which the government can safeguard that legal right.

"It establishes a National Labor Relations Board to hear and determine cases in which it is charged that this legal right is abridged or denied, and to hold fair elections to ascertain who are the chosen representatives of employes.

"A better relationship between labor and management is the high purpose of this act. By assuring the employes the right of collective bargaining it fosters the development of the employment contract on a sound and equitable basis. By providing an orderly procedure for determining who is entitled to rep-

Continued on Page Two.

Canadian Yacht Asks Aid, Adrift 7 Days Off Cuba

By The Associated Press.

PALM BEACH, Fla., July 5.—Radiomarine station WOE of Palm Beach tonight notified the Cuban Government of S O S signals received from the Casarco, a small ketch becalmed and leaking badly 100 miles south of the western tip of Cuba.

Messages received here said that the Casarco, owned by M. C. Rice of Toronto, Canada, had been adrift for seven days. Aboard the ketch were Mr. and Mrs. Rice and three unnamed men. Mrs. Rice was said to be seriously ill.

The Casarco left Cuba a week ago en route for the Isle of Pines.

HAVANA, July 5 (AP).—Naval headquarters tonight ordered the gunboat Santa Clara to sail from Batabano immediately to search for the Canadian yacht Casarco.

EX-CONVICT SLAIN IN STREET; 2 SEIZED

Policeman Subdues Pair as They Start to Drive Away After Brooklyn Killing.

THREE BYSTANDERS SHOT

Murder of Racketeer Laid to War Between Rival Rings of Loan Sharks.

An ex-convict was shot dead and three other persons were struck by gunmen's bullets last night on New Utrecht Avenue near Seventy-eighth Street, Brooklyn. A few minutes after the body of the ex-convict, Girardo (Big Jerry) Mugavero, a racketeer recently released from Sing Sing Prison, slumped to the pavement, a policeman cornered two men who are believed to have been his assailants.

After their arrest one of the men struck the officer, Patrolman Harry Leftwich of the Bath Beach station, behind the ear and almost escaped, but before the battle was over the two prisoners were well in hand and one of them was suffering from a fractured skull.

Those struck by bullets during the affray are Julian Dargeno, 12 years old, of 1,568 Seventy-eighth Street; Dominic Di Martini, 24, of 1,618 Seventy-sixth Street, and Patsy Orlando, 26, of 1,847 Seventy-fourth Street. All suffered flesh wounds.

The prisoners are Benny Minoe, address unknown, and Alfred Di Stefano, 21, of 190 Madison Street, Manhattan. Minoe was taken to the prison ward at Kings County Hospital after his attempt to escape. Di Stefano said he had a paper bag business at Seventy-fourth Street and Thirteenth Avenue, Brooklyn, and had been forced at the point of a pistol to accompany the other man.

Crowd Flees Shots.

Shortly after 10 P. M. Patrolman Leftwich, who was detailed to the Hollywood Theatre cashier's booth on the northeast corner of Seventy-eighth Street and New Utrecht Avenue, heard a series of shots in the street. He hesitated a moment, believing they were firecrackers, and then saw scores of persons running toward Seventy-seventh Street.

As he reached the pavement some one shouted: "There's a dead man up the street." Leftwich noticed that all traffic with the exception of one automobile was immobile. That one car was just about to leave the corner opposite the theatre.

With his revolver drawn he ran to the car and ordered the driver to stop. One of the men, according to the policeman, reached down as if for a weapon.

"I'll blow your heads off at the

Continued on Page Twenty-eight.

Vatican Bans the Latest Book by d'Annunzio; Declares It Is Immoral and Blasphemous

Wireless to THE NEW YORK TIMES.

VATICAN CITY, July 5.—The Vatican placed on its index of forbidden books today Gabriele d'Annunzio's recently published work "A Hundred and a Hundred and a Hundred and a Hundred Pages From the Secret Book of Gabriele d'Annunzio, Tempted to Die."

The Vatican states that in this book "the effrontery of immorality rivals with the affirmation of errors that are often impious and blasphemous."

The banned d'Annunzio volume is made up chiefly of souvenirs, personal experiences, spiritual adventures, meditations, observations, episodes of all kinds, aphorisms and obiter dicta. It is full, of course, of fine images, poetical beauties, exquisite expressions; of bizarre thoughts, luminous fantasies, and of that superb egotism, that sensual paganism and frantic passion for action and glory that are typically d'Annunzian.

The book is divided into two parts: Part One, under the title of "Via Crucis, Via Necis, Via Nubis," tells strange stories of his youth, of his tormenting visions, and his wild longings. Part Two is the proper "secret book," and bears the following subtitle, "Regimen hinc animi." At one point the poet says, "Whoever today and in the centuries to come will be able to gaze on what I deliberately concealed of myself?" The question, giving an explanation of the title, will probably remain unanswered.

Further on one finds this aphorism: "If Italy is an enigma to me, am I not an enigma to Italy?"

Part Two recalls many episodes of the war and the martial ardor of the poet-warrior. Here and there his imperial dream explodes. "Is there a God of Italy who shall raise tomorrow our stature by one thousand cubits? Who shall give us the will of power, of the divine right and of the hereditary empire?"

LEHMAN APPEALS TO 'RACKET RIDDEN' FOR AID IN INQUIRY

Urges the Exploited and Those With Knowledge of Crooks to Help Stamp Out Crime.

HE CONFERS WITH DEWEY

Governor Says That He Sees 'Eye to Eye' With Young Special Prosecutor.

POLICE HEADS LECTURED

Seery Summons Officers and Demands All Data Bearing on Schultz's Activities.

Governor Herbert H. Lehman called upon "the racket-ridden and the exploited" yesterday to support Thomas E. Dewey's investigation of racketeering and vice as the Police Department took steps to carry out Commissioner Lewis J. Valentine's promise to cooperate fully with the young special prosecutor.

The Governor's appeal to the public was contained in a formal statement issued at Albany following a conference with Mr. Dewey, who was appointed a Special Deputy Assistant by District Attorney William C. Dodge at Governor Lehman's direction. Mr. Lehman said that he and Mr. Dewey saw "eye to eye" on the various problems connected with the inquiry.

While the 33-year-old special prosecutor conferred with the Governor at Albany the Police Department here made preparations for the inquiry that will open on July 29, when Supreme Court Justice Philip J. McCook, chosen by Mr. Lehman to preside over an extraordinary term of court, will swear in the special grand jury to hear the evidence gathered by Mr. Dewey.

Police Officers Hear Lecture.

All the commanding officers of Manhattan and the Bronx were summoned to police headquarters during the day to listen to a lecture by Chief Inspector John J. Seery. He told them he wanted them to assemble and turn in all the data in their possession on the activities of Arthur Flegenheimer, who is better known as Dutch Schultz, beer runner and racketeer.

Ostensibly the information is for the use of former United States Attorney Martin Conboy, who is to prosecute Schultz at his second trial for income tax evasion at Malone, N. Y. Actually, the material is as much for the use of Mr. Dewey as for the Federal officials, for Schultz and the political leaders who have befriended him in the past are among the chief targets of the special prosecutor's inquiry.

The officers summoned to Police Headquarters for a conference with Inspector Seery and Assistant Chief Inspector John J. Sullivan, included commanders of the uniformed and detective forces. Among them were Deputy Chief Inspector David J. McAuliffe, commanding the uniformed police of Manhattan; Acting Deputy Chief Inspector Francis J. Kear, in charge of Manhattan detectives; Inspector Joseph P. Loonam, chief of the uniformed men of the Bronx, and Acting Deputy Chief Inspector Henry Bruckman, head of the Bronx detective bureau. Division, precinct and detective squad commanders attended also.

After their talk in Albany, Governor Lehman issued a statement, which Mr. Dewey said expressed his views adequately, asserting that the impending investigation was designed not merely to stop gambling and exterminate organized vice, but to "stamp out, so far as possible, organized crime and racketeering of all kinds."

THE GOVERNOR'S STATEMENT

The full text of the Governor's statement follows:

Mr. Thomas E. Dewey and I have had a long talk this afternoon and have carefully gone over plans. I have outlined to him my views and expectations with regard to the concerted drive against racketeering and organized crime. The drive will be of the broadest possible character and I have expressed the desire that it will proceed without any avoidable delay. I am satisfied that I have entrusted this very important public work to a man who is well equipped to carry it on.

Thus far I have provided the following powerful weapons:

(1)—I have convened an extraordinary special and trial term of the Supreme Court under the direction of Mr. Justice Philip J. McCook;

(2)—I have directed Judge McCook to empanel a special grand jury which will have the broadest powers to investigate every kind

Continued on Page Twenty-eight.

THE FACES OF POVERTY

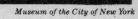

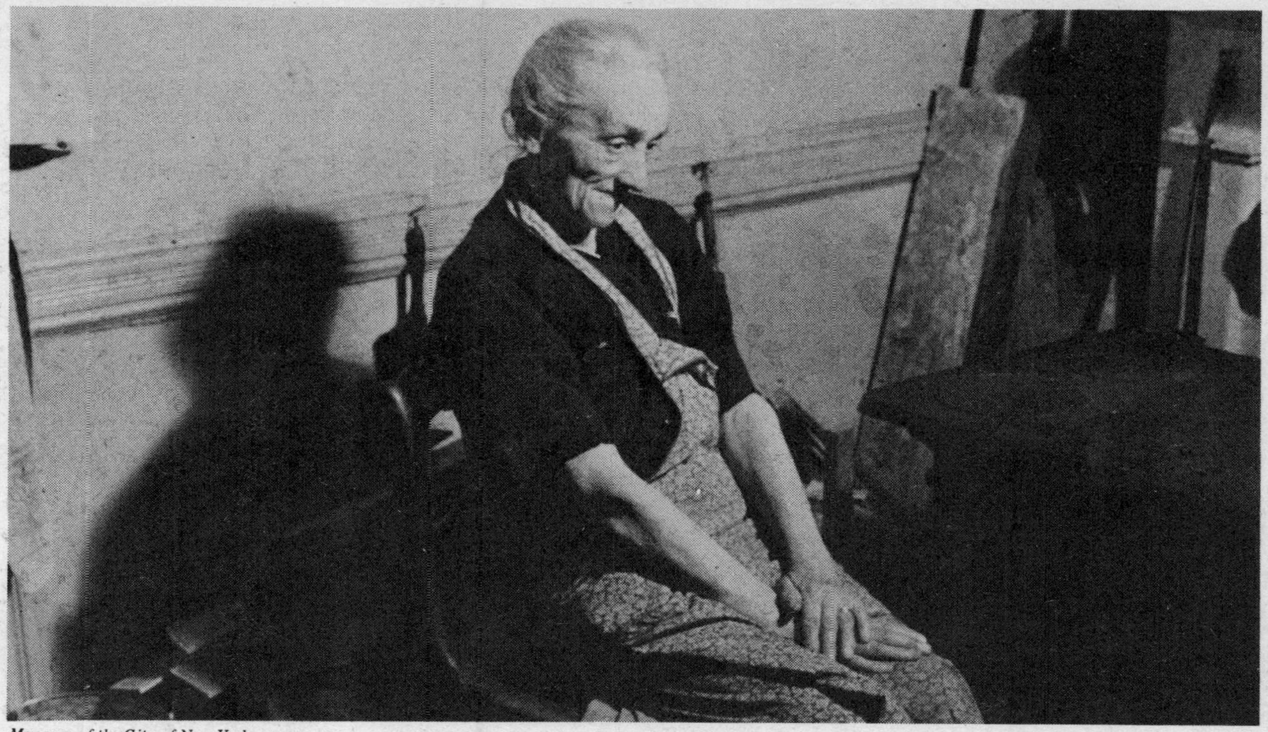

Museum of the City of New York

Museum of the City of New York

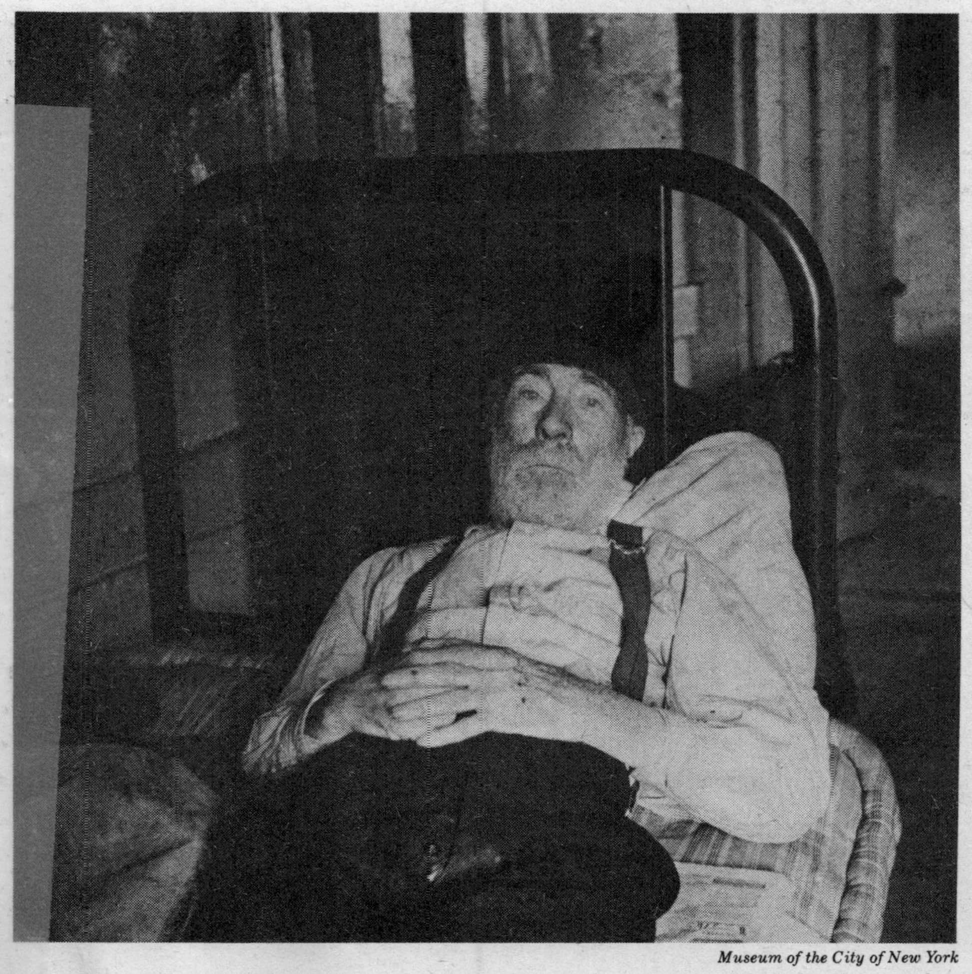

Museum of the City of New York

Museum of the City of New York

"All the News That's Fit to Print."

The New York Times.

LATE CITY EDITION
WEATHER—Fair today and tomorrow; temperature unchanged.
Temperatures Yesterday—Max., 80; Min., 71

Copyright, 1935, by The New York Times Company.

VOL. LXXXIV....No. 28,307. Entered as Second-Class Matter, Postoffice, New York, N. Y. NEW YORK, FRIDAY, JULY 26, 1935. P TWO CENTS In New York City. | THREE CENTS Within 200 Miles | FOUR CENTS Elsewhere Except in 7th and 8th Postal Zones.

MUSSOLINI OFFERS CONCILIATION PLAN IN ETHIOPIAN ROW

SENDS PLEA TO LEAGUE

Consents to Inquiry on Clashes if Frontier Issues Are Barred.

LEAGUE TO MEET JULY 31

Officials Expect Council Will Pass On Dispute Despite Manoeuvre of Italy.

ARMS HALTED BY BRITAIN

Will Stop Exports to Ethiopia Until League Has Acted—Program Not Made.

The Italo-Ethiopian Clash.

ROME—Mussolini sent an offer to the League of Nations to continue conciliation efforts with Ethiopia if questions of frontiers were barred. A great demonstration of Fascists, however, was held in favor of war.

GENEVA—The Italian offer was received, but League officials still believed a meeting of the Council would be held next week to take up the dispute.

PARIS—The Foreign Office announced the League Council meeting would be held July 31.

LONDON—Britain decided not to permit export of war materials to Ethiopia or Italy until after the League meeting, but to let British facilities be used for this traffic under treaty. Britain and France were still divided as to procedure in the League.

Mussolini Sends New Offer.

By ARNALDO CORTESI.
Wireless to THE NEW YORK TIMES.

ROME, July 25.—Premier Benito Mussolini in his capacity as Foreign Minister sent a telegram today to Joseph A. C. Avenol, Secretary General of the League of Nations, declaring he was ready to resume the efforts that failed a fortnight ago in Scheveningen, Holland, to find a solution for the Ualual and other Italo-Ethiopian incidents.

[The League of Nations Council will meet next Wednesday, July 31, to take up the Italo-Ethiopian dispute, the French Foreign Office announced last night, according to The Associated Press.]

Only a few hours later Deputy Orazi, in his capacity as delegate of the Fascist party, was whipping a vast crowd in the centre of Rome into a state of patriotic frenzy by promising them victory in a war against Ethiopia.

Would Bar Council Meeting.

Mr. Mussolini's telegram to Mr. Avenol—a copy of which was sent to the Ethiopian Government—was a last-minute effort to stave off the impending meeting of the League Council. Mr. Mussolini said he was willing to submit Italy's case again to the Italo-Ethiopian conciliation commission provided Ethiopia undertook to keep the discussion within limits set by the League itself in its deliberation of May 25—or, in other words, provided Ethiopia does not attempt to drag into the discussion questions pertaining to the delimitation of frontiers and the interpretation of border treaties.

Before the commission begins sittings, however, Mr. Mussolini wants Ethiopia to give him a yes-or-no reply on this point.

The future course of events in Geneva depends very largely on the answer to this step by Mr. Mussolini. If Ethiopia agrees to his request the Italo-Ethiopian conciliation commission will resume its sittings and Italy will be able to plead that the procedure set forth by the League Council on May 25 be scrupulously followed.

Italy holds that it would follow naturally from this that there would be no need at present for interference by the League since it was agreed that the Council would meet only if the Italo-Ethiopian Commission failed to reach an agreement by July 25.

If Ethiopia rejects this plan, Italy believes she will have strengthened her position very greatly when the matter comes up for discussion in Geneva.

It is authoritatively denied that Italy has any present intention of abandoning Geneva, although it is evident such a possibility is always at the back of Italy's mind and that she is using this threat as a

Continued on Page Eleven.

Davis Predicts League Will End African Threat

By The Associated Press.

WASHINGTON, July 25.—A prediction was made tonight by Norman Davis, United States Ambassador at Large, that the League of Nations would bring Italy and Ethiopia to a peaceful settlement of their threatened war.

The statement was made to newspaper men by Mr. Davis as he came from a meeting of members of the Senate Foreign Relations Committee and State Department officials at which neutrality legislation had been discussed.

"It appears to me," Mr. Davis said, "that France is not going to break with the League and with England at the same time just to support Italy in its present position. The League was not called into session just for a pleasant gathering."

AID TO FOREIGNERS BY PWA IS CHARGED

Grace Tells of Recent Order Requiring Purchases Abroad if 15% Can Be Saved.

STEEL MEN FILE PROTEST

Lower Wages Enable European Producers to Underbid U. S. Mills, They Declare.

The American steel industry's potential share in the $4,000,000,000 public works funds has been impaired, to the advantage of foreign producers, as a result of an order signed by a deputy administrator of the PWA dated May 25, Eugene G. Grace, president of the Bethlehem Steel Corporation, said after a meeting of the company's directors yesterday.

Workmen in the United States may suffer as a result, he said, and increased unemployment among steel workers might well be a consequence of the order's rigid application.

The order specifies that "a borrower of money must buy foreign material where the value of the order is $10,000 or more and the price is 15 per cent less," Mr. Grace said. This applied not only to steel but to all other materials entering into construction, he said, but it was the potential effect on the steel industry that was actively engaging his attention.

Protest Made in Washington.

A protest already has been entered "through channels" in Washington against this administrative order, Mr. Grace said, the American Iron and Steel Institute having been entrusted with the presentation of objections to the ruling.

The ruling came to Mr. Grace's attention only this week, he said, although dated May 25. He was unable to explain this fact, and was unwilling to interpret the objective sought by the person or persons who drew up the clause objected to.

In any event, Mr. Grace asserted that foreigners could ship steel and sell it in the United States at 15 per cent and more below the domestic price and still make a profit. Imports of foreign steel are mounting at an alarming pace, he said, drawing attention to a statement issued by the institute ten days ago, in which steel imports for the first five months of 1935 were shown to be 65 per cent above the 1934 period, while domestic production was less than 3.5 per cent higher for the same periods.

Wages Up, Prices Down.

The American steel industry has increased wages since 1929 and at the same time has reduced prices, Mr. Grace said. The July, 1926, selling price for American steel was $37.68 a ton. In July, 1929, it was $36.71; in July, 1934, it was $32.32, and in the first three weeks of the current month it was $32.40.

As to wages, he said, the average United States hourly rate in May this year was 65½ cents, an increase of 7 per cent from the average in effect in 1929. Abroad, he said, the average hourly rates were 25 cents for England, 17 cents for Belgium and 29 cents for Germany. He regarded Germany as the greatest competitor of the American steel industry.

Regardless of the May 25 ruling, the American steel industry is not

Continued on Page Six.

WORLD REDS CAST LOT WITH LIBERALS TO FIGHT FASCISM

Congress of International in Moscow Decides to Lend Aid to Moderate Parties.

REVOLUTION IS PUT ASIDE

Action Is Declared Emergency Move to Combat Political Trend and War Peril.

By HAROLD DENNY.
Special Cable to THE NEW YORK TIMES.

MOSCOW, July 25.—The Communist International in a remarkable change of front has decided to cast its lot with the more moderate elements in capitalistic countries in order to combat the growing menace of fascism.

At a congress here, which began behind closed doors today, the International will launch a world labor party with the object of enlisting workers of all countries and of varying shades of political belief, including even liberals, among whom Communists would necessarily be greatly outnumbered and whom they could hardly hope to control.

The emergency created by fascism is considered to be so great—especially in Germany, where it is held to constitute a direct threat of war against the Soviet Union—that the Communist International is even willing to struggle to save the remnants of bourgeois democracy (at which it sneers) in countries where fascism threatens it.

World Revolt in Background.

Thus the theme of world revolution, for which the Communist International was established, is pushed into the background for the time being. And thus the International cleverly escapes the dilemma of how to hold a congress without affronting or alarming the capitalist States with which Soviet Russia is diplomatically engaged in the hope of having allies in case of war. These States do not include Fascist countries.

The reasoning behind the new policy is outlined today in a long and carefully framed editorial in Pravda, the chief spokesman of the Russian Communist party.

"The most important task of the international workers' movement at the present juncture is to effect a united front for the struggle of the working class," says Pravda. "Can Communists wait until a majority of the working class unites on a general program to overthrow capitalism and bring about a victory of proletarian revolution? Can they wait until a majority of workers accepts the program of the Comintern? No, they cannot.

"It is essential that the struggle against the onslaught of Fascism be organized immediately, for Fascism is our bitterest enemy, both nationally and internationally. The masses must be shown that what must be done today is to rebuff capital and defend themselves against Fascist barbarism and the horrors of war.

"Communists do not conceal the fact that they are fighting to replace capitalism with socialism—to replace the bankrupt bourgeois democracy with a proletarian democracy through a dictatorship of the proletariat. Therefore, the most important slogan of Communists throughout the world was,

Continued on Page Nine.

Germany Prescribes Axe For Treasurer of Reds

Wireless to THE NEW YORK TIMES.

BERLIN, July 25.—Rudolf Claus, 41 years old, of Brunswick, a lieutenant of Max Hoelz in the Communist uprising in Saxony in 1920, was sentenced today by the People's Tribunal to be beheaded for acting as treasurer of Red Help, a Communist secret organization. No other serious charge was brought against Claus, but the court announced that it had taken into consideration the defendant's intentions as revealed by his previous record.

Claus was sentenced to life imprisonment by a republican court in 1921 for fomenting insurrection. Released under an amnesty in 1923, he was later sentenced to eight years' penal servitude for robbery and again received amnesty.

Three other Communists, one a woman, received sentences of four to thirteen years for acting as couriers for the Red headquarters in the Saar.

JUDGE IMPRISONS 4 SCHULTZ AIDES

Court Acts When One Proves an Unwilling Witness at the Trial in Malone.

MISTRIAL PLEA IS DENIED

Defense Counsel Fights Vainly to Block Evidence Sought by Federal Prosecutor.

By MEYER BERGER.
Special to THE NEW YORK TIMES.

MALONE, N. Y., July 25.—Federal Judge Frederick H. Bryant committed four aides of Arthur (Dutch Schultz) Flegenheimer to the county jail today "to be sure they will be available as witnesses" at Schultz's second trial for income tax evasion, which opened here Tuesday. The defendant himself was committed when the trial started.

Sol Rosnoff, alias Charlie Miller, who answered the telephones at Schultz's beer headquarters at 215 East 149th Street in the Bronx when Schultz was piling up a $3,000,000 net income during 1929-31, was more or less responsible for the judge's order this morning.

Brought here on a government subpoena, as were Abe (Bo) Weinberg, Rocco Di Larmi and Moe Margolese, the other Schultz associates, he wriggled in the witness chair for more than three hours, evading answers as John W. Burke Jr., special assistant to the Attorney General, pinned him with sharp questions.

Judge Bryant's kindly features grew more grim with each new contortion of the witness. Rosnoff tried to parry questions with "I don't remember," "I don't know," "It was so long ago." Finally the court stopped him in the middle of a mumbled sentence that no one quite heard.

"You'd better tell the truth," the judge said sharply.

James M. Noonan, chief defense lawyer, leaped to his feet.

"I object to Your Honor's remark," he said, "and move at this time for a mistrial. I ask that a juror be withdrawn and that a mistrial be declared."

The motion was denied.

Rosnoff had been preceded on

Continued on Page Two.

Rain Ends Grip of 21-Day Heat Wave Here; Sustained Humidity Established Record

The twenty-one-day heat wave that has caused discomfort and distress to the city's millions was broken yesterday by a series of gentle showers.

The high humidity that accompanied the heat wave continued, however. The unusual combination of high temperatures and high humidity over a period of twenty-one days established a new record.

A study of humidity records at the Weather Bureau revealed that the ancient wheeze, "It's not the heat, it's the humidity," is meteorologically incorrect. Neither the heat nor the humidity alone is the cause of the extreme discomforts of a heat wave, but a combination of both, designated by Weather Bureau officials as the "effective temperature."

The average temperature yesterday was only one degree above normal. After rising to a high of 80 at 2:10 o'clock in the afternoon, showers cooled the atmosphere and sent the mercury to a low of 71 at 7 P. M., setting an average temperature of 76. The hottest July 25 was in 1892, when the mercury rose to 94, and the coolest was in 1920, with a temperature of 58.

Fair weather today and tomorrow with not much change in temperature is forecast.

In this city Bernard Newmark, 60, proprietor of a clothing store at 529 Broadway, died there from the effects of the heat. His home was at 881 East Seventh Street, Brooklyn, where he leaves a widow and two sons.

Patrolman Frank Warren, 33, of 374 Eastern Parkway, Brooklyn, and attached to the Miller Avenue station in Brooklyn, was drowned in Great South Bay near West Islip, L. I., while hunting for clams with two friends. The body was recovered.

In an analysis of high temperatures and high humidity of the heat wave this month Dr. David R. Morris, junior meteorologist in charge of the observatory in Central Park, explained that "effective temperature" was a term to designate the combination of temperature, humidity and wind movement.

"The average humidity during the last twenty-one days," he said, "has been much above normal and the wave has been unusually long."

Figures show that the July average so far for humidity has been 81 per cent of saturation at 8 A. M., and 74 per cent at 8 P. M. This has been exceeded only twice in previous years, in July 1896 and in July, 1916. The normal figures for July are 75 and 69.

GLASS HITS ECCLES IN BANKING DEBATE AS AN INFLATIONIST

Senator Also Attacks a 'Certain Great Banker' as Foe of Private Institutions.

TITLE I APPROVED INTACT

Nye Central Bank Amendment Submitted, With Senate Ready to Reject the Idea Today.

Special to THE NEW YORK TIMES.

WASHINGTON, July 25.—Plans by which it was hoped to drive the Banking Bill to a final vote tomorrow were made in the Senate today after a five-hour session during which Title I, affecting Federal deposit insurance, was approved without change, Senator Glass completed an exposition of the bill, and Senator Nye urged his central bank proposal.

Senator Glass criticized Marriner S. Eccles, Governor of the Federal Reserve Board, as the greatest inflationist in the United States, denounced the Federal Reserve Board for failure to defy "one of the most notorious speculators in the New York stock market," and charged that a "great banker's enmity and jealousy of one or two private bankers in his city" was chiefly responsible for criticism of the banking committee plan to let a banker serve simultaneously on two bank boards.

By a viva voce vote the Senate defeated Senator Murphy's effort to scrap a section of Title I which requires State banks with deposits of $1,000,000 and more to join the Federal Reserve System by July 1, 1937, or lose their deposit insurance and that State banks organized in future must join the system to obtain insurance.

Vote Today on Nye Proposal.

Leaders in charge of the bill were ready to reject Senator Nye's amendment for a central bank as soon as he finished speaking, but before he sat down he said he hoped a quorum would be present to act. It was then too late to summon the quorum and the vote went over until tomorrow, with predictions that the North Dakota Senator would muster no more than ten to eighteen votes for his amendment, which carries out ideas of the Rev. Charles E. Coughlin.

Senator La Follette will bring pressure tomorrow for his amendment to eliminate the underwriting section and to bar any interlocking directorates whatsoever; possibly also he will bring up his scheme to constitute the Reserve Board as the open-market committee, with Reserve Bank representatives acting solely as advisers.

Senator Thomas of Oklahoma has an amendment said to be a proposal to have the government buy the stock of the Reserve Banks. Senator Borah may offer the Goldsborough "rubber dollar" amendment.

Leaders said that with the possible exception of the underwriting section, all the amendments will be beaten and the bill will go to conference with the House virtually as it stood when unanimously approved by the Banking Committee.

Senator Fletcher, who has put forward suggestions akin to those of Senator La Follette, says he will not press them if such a course would put the bill in jeopardy.

Glass Attacks Eccles.

Senator Glass's sarcastic allusions to Mr. Eccles came almost at the outset of his speech. First he stoutly denied that the Banking Bill was in any way an administration measure. Then he suddenly brought in the Reserve Governor's name with this statement:

"I speak of it simply as the Eccles bill because nobody, with a single exception, who has appeared before either of the banking committees has advocated this bill.

"It is suggested," he continued, "that the chief advocate of Title II is in a nervous state, and has a large measure of anxiety lest we should have inflation in the country; that he wants to prevent inflation and deflation where we already have more deflation than may be remedied in the next ten or twenty years to come.

"As a consequence I am amused at the pretense that the sponsor of Title II of the bill is anxious to prevent inflation, because of all the inflationists in the country he has exceeded the group in his advocacy of inflation."

"The 1933 Banking Act," the Virginian added, "averts all danger of a return to the frightful conditions of 1929 which brought on the collapse due to the excessive speculation on the stock market."

Then, alluding to the former fifteen-day loans on government securities, he continued:

"It was under this fifteen-day and ninety-day provisions of the old act that the facilities of the Federal

Continued on Page Six.

DEMOCRATS DRAFT TAX BILL TO TAKE $150,000,000 MORE FROM RICH AND BIG BUSINESS

Tentative Provisions of New Taxes Being Considered by House Committee

Special to THE NEW YORK TIMES.

WASHINGTON, July 25.—Tentative provisions of the tax program being considered by the Ways and Means Committee, which approached a final draft today, include:

1. A surtax on personal incomes greater than $150,000, with rates graduated up to 75 per cent of that portion in excess of $10,000,000. Estimated to yield $20,400,000 a year.
   Tentative schedules made public yesterday and superseded by those agreed upon today, called for individual income surtaxes ranging from 60 per cent on incomes of $1,000,000 to $1,500,000 to 75 per cent on incomes ranging from $5,000,000 to $10,000,000 and 80 per cent on all over $10,000,000.
   The present law taxes individual incomes starting at 4 per cent and ranging upward to 58 per cent on income between $700,000 and $1,000,000, with no provision for increased taxation on incomes over $1,000,000.
2. A graduated corporation income tax, ranging from 13¼ to 14 per cent, instead of the present flat rate of 13¾ per cent, or the schedule tentatively agreed upon yesterday ranging from 10 to 17½ per cent. Estimated to yield about as much revenue as the existing rate.
3. An excess profits tax on corporations, on the following graduated scale: "Excess" profits of from over 8 to 12 per cent, 5 per cent tax; from 12 to 16 per cent, 10 per cent tax; from 16 to 25, 15 per cent; over 25, 20 per cent tax. No estimate of yield was made.
4. An inheritance tax, in addition to existing estate taxes, to be levied at graduated rates running as high as 75 per cent on that portion of an inheritance in excess of $10,000,000. Estimated to yield about $95,000,000 a year. These taxes probably would start at 4 per cent on $300,000 and range up to 70 per cent on inheritance from $7,000,000 to $10,000,000, with 75 per cent on all over that high total.
5. A gift tax, to prevent evasion of the inheritance tax, at rates about three-fourths of the inheritance rates in corresponding brackets. Estimated to yield about $26,000,000.

FIVE MAIN LEVIES IMPOSED

Corporation Tax Set at 13¼ to 14¼% With Impost on Excess Profits.

INCOME SURTAXES RAISED

Starting Above $150,000, It Advances Rates to 75% on Earnings Over $10,000,000.

INHERITANCE EXEMPTIONS

Blood Relatives Are Favored Over Non-Kin Heirs—Republicans Hit at Bill.

Special to THE NEW YORK TIMES.

WASHINGTON, July 25.—A tax program estimated to bring to the government an added revenue of about $150,000,000 a year was tentatively decided upon today by Democratic members of the Ways and Means Committee.

A bill embodying the rates and schedules agreed upon will be printed in time for consideration by the full committee Monday.

Republican members of the committee, who have not been consulted thus far, made little comment upon the Democratic draft.

Representative Crowther of New York said that the measure, as he understood it, was neither an instrument of social reform nor an aid to the government's financial standing.

Another member, who preferred not to be quoted, called it a "hell raiser, not a revenue raiser," but admitted that he would probably vote for it.

Five Principal Taxes.

The bill as outlined by Chairman Doughton at the end of the day's meeting of the Democrats on the committee was tentatively approved by a close vote and will consist of these five principal taxes:

A surtax on personal incomes greater than $150,000, probably less than 1,000 in the country, with rates graduated up to 75 per cent of that portion in excess of $10,000,000. Estimated to yield $20,400,000.

A graduated corporation income tax varying from 13¼ to 14¼ per cent on brackets not made public. Estimated to produce about the same revenue as the existing flat tax of 13¾ per cent.

An excess profits tax on corporations, ranging from 5 per cent on profits in excess of 8 to 12 per cent to 20 per cent profits over 25 per cent. Yield not estimated.

An inheritance tax, in addition to the existing estate tax, to be levied at graduated rates, going as high as 75 per cent on that portion of inheritance over $10,000,000. Estimated to yield about $95,000,000.

A gift tax, to prevent evasion of the inheritance tax, at rates of about three-fourths of the inheritance tax rates on corresponding brackets. Estimated to yield about $26,000,000.

Under the schedules the recipient of an income of $200,000 a year would be taxed $89,000; an income of $10,000,000 would pay a tax of $7,493,000. The surtax rates would start at 54 per cent on the portion in excess of $150,000, and would be superimposed on the normal rate of 4 per cent.

Question of Income Levy Yield.

President Roosevelt, in his tax message, pointed out to Congress that existing income rates taxed all incomes of more than $1,000,000 at 59 per cent, the same rate applying to an income of $5,000,000 a year as to one of $1,000,000.

This was taken to mean at first that the President wanted only an increase in rates on incomes over $1,000,000 a year, but experts soon pointed out to the committee that in 1933 only forty-six persons in the country had incomes that great and that only one of them received in excess of $5,000,000.

Obviously little revenue could be obtained from that level of wealth, inasmuch as it was estimated that confiscation of all income in excess of $5,000,000 would bring in considerably less than $35,000,000 a year.

The committee, accordingly, decided to dig down a little deeper in the financial scale, but the schedules adopted today affect a negligible number of citizens. In 1933 only 693 reported incomes of be-

Continued on Page Three.

MAYOR REBUFFED ON GERMAN CURB

State Department Denies It Got Complaint That Reich Violated Trade Pact.

WINDELS REPEATS STAND

Overruled Again by La Guardia—Germany Fears License Ban May Set Precedent.

Paul Windels, Corporation Counsel, was advised yesterday by the State Department that the German-American commercial treaty of 1925 was still in effect and that no complaints had been received that Americans have been discriminated against in Germany in violation of the provisions of the treaty.

Thereupon Mr. Windels submitted a second opinion to Mayor La Guardia, reaffirming his previous statement that the refusal of a city license as a massage operator to a German citizen was illegal because it contravened the terms of the treaty.

The Mayor, who on Tuesday had rejected Mr. Windels's first opinion and had directed him to study the matter further, declared that his ruling would stand unchanged. He said that Mr. Windels's opinion was "an interesting, learned, academic discussion of the general subject," but that it had not changed his determination.

"I am concerned with the policy in the enforcement of a city ordinance," the Mayor said. "My order to the Commissioner of Licenses stands."

Challenges Report.

Mayor La Guardia said that he had not been in communication with official Washington himself, and that he did not know that Mr. Windels had been in touch with the State Department. He said that he doubted the accuracy of newspaper reports that the State Department had no complaints of discrimination on file.

"That's contrary to information I received as a member of Congress during the latter part of my last term," he said.

Mr. Windels declined to make public the text of his second opinion, on the ground that it should come from the Mayor, but when he was asked if it differed in content from his first opinion, in which he maintained that the treaty until abrogated was binding on all legislative bodies, courts and public officials, he said emphatically that it did not. He said that the law on the subject was "elementary."

Mr. Windels telephoned the State Department yesterday, asking several specific questions about the treaty and the treatment of Americans in Germany. In refusing his first opinion Mayor La Guardia had told him that the department had complaints on file of discrimination against Americans.

The State Department denied

Continued on Page Eight.

BERLIN RIOTS MAR OLYMPIC PLANNING

Assaults on Jews in Midst of City's Rebuilding to Impress World Cause Consternation.

RE-PLEDGE MAY BE ASKED

A. A. U. Head Will Oppose Our Taking Part if Athletes Are Discriminated Against.

By FREDERICK T. BIRCHALL.
Wireless to THE NEW YORK TIMES.

BERLIN, July 25.—About this time a year hence Berlin, as the scene of the eleventh world Olympics, expects to be "host to all the world." Not only Berlin but all Germany is looking forward to this and is preparing for it with a thoroughness and concentration such as few countries, if any, could manifest. It is to be the occasion for "showing the world what Germany really is."

In consequence, never within living memory has the German capital presented to visitors and residents alike so organized a mass of new construction and rebuilding as at the present time. All over the city old buildings are coming down and new ones are replacing them. Other buildings are being refaced and refurbished. Streets are being made over. Activity is most marked along the principal thoroughfares.

Unter den Linden and the borders of the Tiergarten near by are a welter of excavations and sandpiles surrounded by high board fences painted green to modify their ugliness. Within steam shovels are noisily at work and giant piledrivers bang twenty-four steel uprights into the sand on which Berlin is built. Most of the trees along Unter den Linden have come down and gaping holes or huge sandpiles replace them.

The reason is that a new cross-town subway linking all the existing ones is being constructed.

At the far western end of the city on the edge of the Gruenewald 1,000 workers are preparing the site for the games—a stadium, a swimming pool and an athletic plant, the largest and most elaborate the world has ever seen. The stadium will seat 100,000 persons. The swimming pool is in proportion. Alongside it is a Greek theatre for dramatic performances. Next door is the great House of German Sport.

For the competing teams the army is building a model village of 150 houses and a restaurant of twenty dining rooms, each seating fifty persons. There are to be open and enclosed exercising spaces close at hand.

All these buildings are specially designed and are to be as beautiful as they are to be convenient. Reichsfuehrer Adolf Hitler is giving his personal attention to supervision of the plans. He often visits

Continued on Page Nine.

"All the News That's Fit to Print."

The New York Times.

LATE CITY EDITION

WEATHER—Showers today, continued warm; tomorrow fair.
Temperatures Yesterday—Max., 89; Min., 72.

VOL. LXXXIV....No. 28,327. Entered as Second-Class Matter, Postoffice, New York, N. Y. NEW YORK THURSDAY, AUGUST 15, 1935. PP TWO CENTS In New York City. | THREE CENTS Within 200 Miles | FOUR CENTS Elsewhere Except in 7th and 8th Postal Zones.

FIGHT TO DELAY TAX BILL DEFEATED IN SENATE, 55-19; TEST SPEEDS FINAL VOTE

AMENDING STAGE TODAY

Eight Democrats Join Eleven Republicans for Postponement.

NEXT SESSION HELD TIME

Vandenberg Leads Attack as Committee Minority Report Denounces Measure.

MAJORITY DEFINES LEVIES

Leaders See Shift to Retain Estate Instead of the Inheritance Tax Feature.

Senate committee majority and minority tax reports, Pages 8, 9.

Special to THE NEW YORK TIMES.

WASHINGTON, Aug. 14.—An effort to block action on the Tax Bill at this session, begun with a sharp attack from the Republican side, was overwhelmingly defeated today by the Senate. By a vote of 55 to 19, a motion by Senator Vandenberg of Michigan to recommit the measure to the Finance Committee for further study was rejected.

Although eight Democrats joined with eleven Republicans in voting for the Vandenberg motion, Senator Copeland was the only Democrat who spoke in its behalf. He denounced the wealth-tax provisions as unjust and unfair.

Encouraged by their show of strength, administration leaders purposed to head the measure straight into the amending stage tomorrow, confident that they could beat off all other opposition and send it to conference by Saturday night in a form still more in keeping with the desires of President Roosevelt.

At the same time, a possibility developed that the inheritance levy, chief feature of the President's wealth-sharing tax plan, might be dropped for this session because of the increasing difficulties in working out proper administrative provisions for enforcement. A consequence might be final approval by both the Senate and House of increased estate tax rates, as substituted for the inheritance levy by the Senate Finance Committee.

Consent Is Held Probable.

If the inheritance tax proposal should be dropped, it will be with administration consent. An indication that the administration is amenable to deferring this levy for further study of administrative features and to accepting the Senate estate tax provisions was seen in the attitude of Senate leaders who originally announced their firm determination to reinsert the inheritance tax on the floor.

None of them would say definitely today that he would attempt to reincorporate this provision. Meanwhile, the Senate's tax experts were laboring fruitlessly to work out satisfactory administrative details.

These same leaders have also insisted lately that if the inheritance tax goes back into the bill special exemptions must be allowed for inheritances passing in the form of going industrial enterprises and for proceeds from insurance policies.

The immediate task before the leadership was to get the bill to conference, however, and they believed that they weathered the first of two main tests when they defeated the effort to block action this session.

The second test will be faced early tomorrow when the offering of amendments starts. At least three proposals are pending. Senator La Follette favors higher personal surtax rates all along the line and the lowering of the personal income tax exemptions. Senator Clark would tax immediately the income from tax-exempt securities instead of waiting for a constitutional amendment as suggested by the President. Senator McCarran seeks the repeal of certain permissive features of the Silver Purchase Act of 1934. Senator Long is expected, also, to offer an amendment carrying out his share-the-wealth plan.

Vandenberg Assails Measure.

The Republican broadside against the measure was thought to have been spent in the debate that pre-

Continued on Page Eight.

Return to Gothic Letters Widened by Reich Army

Special to THE NEW YORK TIMES.

BERLIN, Aug. 14.—Official Germany appears to be determined to return to the Gothic letter form that makes so many editions of the German classics practically unintelligible to foreigners who know German but are unfamiliar with this type.

This medieval letter form, which was replaced after the war by the simpler and clearer Latin letters, is asserted to be more German and, therefore, more patriotic and more National Socialist.

Accordingly, General Werner von Blomberg, War Minister, has now issued orders that all notices on military property shall be printed in the old Gothic letters. The idea is that through reading them the soldiers will become more thoroughly German.

In Offenbach-on-the-Main a special school has been opened for young missionaries of the Gothic letter form, who will be sent throughout the country to point out the "unpatriotic" character of the "foreign" letter form now in general use.

CITY TO BAR RELIEF TO WPA STRIKERS

Mayor Says Bricklayer With Ill Wife Who Got Cash for Food Is Isolated Case.

TO BACK FEDERAL POLICY

Has Talk With Johnson, Who Repeats Warning—Walkout Spreading, Labor Insists.

Striking Works Progress Administration workers will not receive relief from the city administration, Mayor La Guardia indicated yesterday. It was the first official intimation of the course the city will pursue.

This decision by the Mayor came at about the same time that Thomas Martin, a striking bricklayer of 773 East 155th Street, the Bronx, received $5 for food and a supplementary relief voucher for $23.50 from Miss Rosetta Fisher, case supervisor at the Home Relief district office, 797 Prospect Avenue, the Bronx. The Martin case, the Mayor suggested, was an isolated one and established no precedent.

In other respects the strike was dormant yesterday. Union leaders continued to maintain that they were making progress, and said more than 1,000 were on strike. Figures on the number of workers out were not forthcoming from Administrator Hugh S. Johnson's office, except that it was declared there were fewer men out than on any day since last Thursday. This meant less than 400.

Martin, whose wife, Lena Martin, is ill and who has six children

Continued on Page Six.

CONGRESS MAY QUIT AS TAX BILL PASSES, POSSIBLY TUESDAY

Hasty Adjournment Would Hit Roosevelt Program, Mean Death of Many Measures.

COAL BILL IS AMONG THEM

Meanwhile, Senate Adopts Oil Control Plan—House Bars Liquor Bill Changes.

Special to THE NEW YORK TIMES.

WASHINGTON, Aug. 14.—An impression was current at the Capitol today that Congress might adjourn as soon as the Tax Bill was disposed of, and some estimates from trustworthy sources set the date as early as next Tuesday night.

Such a sudden quitting would involve jettisoning many elements of the session's legislative program, but it was represented that the temper of the legislators, and of the Senators in particular, was such that leaders could not hold members in Washington any longer.

Unless the strongest kind of pressure from the White House brings a change of heart to Capitol Hill, victims of the heat and the legislative confusion would include the Guffey-Snyder bill for the regulation of the bituminous coal industry, the Banking Bill, the Utility Holding Company Control Bill and the amendments to strengthen and enlarge the Tennessee Valley Authority.

Reminders that the United Mine Workers have postponed their thrice-threatened national coal strike until Sept. 16 only on direct promise from President Roosevelt that Congress will at least act upon the Guffey-Snyder bill have apparently had no effect on the Senators longing for cooler places than Washington.

Death of Bill Predicted.

It was privately asserted by some Senators in close touch with the general situation that the coal measure would not be considered in the upper branch. If this estimate is believed in the House, it is likely that administration leaders there will abandon the fight for the bill and neglect to bring the measure to the floor.

Chairman Doughton of the Ways and Means Committee said today, however, that he understood the agreement with Senate leaders to consider the bill still held good. He planned to report the bill to the House tomorrow and bring it up on the floor in an effort to pass it before week-end adjournment on Saturday.

Yet in the face of such considerable opposition that even the stanchest administration supporters are doubtful of enough votes to push the measure through the House, it was regarded as unlikely that Mr. Doughton and colleagues would risk their prestige to jam it through, only to have the Senate force adjournment without having acted upon it.

Six of the seven Republican members of the Ways and Means Committee made public today their minority report on the measure, opposing its passage. They were Representatives Treadway of Massachusetts, Bacharach of New Jersey, Crowther of New York, Knutson of Minnesota, Reed of New York and Woodruff of Michigan.

"In his advocacy of this legislation," the minority report said, "the President continues to show

Continued on Page Ten.

Democrats Are Sounding Out Sentiment On Changing the National Constitution

By The Associated Press.

WASHINGTON, Aug. 14.—Soundings to ascertain national sentiment on a constitutional amendment to broaden the powers of the Federal Government have been undertaken by Democratic strategists.

Informed persons said the survey was being made by neither the Democratic National Committee nor the White House, but that the results probably would be passed along to President Roosevelt before he leaves on his Western trip in September.

They added that the results of the survey probably would have much to do with guiding the President's decision on whether to nail the constitutional issue to his standard for the next campaign.

There was some speculation in Washington over whether former President Hoover had heard of these plans before issuing his Chicago statement. In that statement he called upon the President for a declaration of what he intended to do about the Constitution.

Many party men in widely scattered areas are said to be involved in the survey so as to present the rounded picture of the situation which the President has desired ever since the Supreme Court overthrew the NRA.

At that time, in his "horse and buggy" press conference statement, Mr. Roosevelt indicated that he might take the question to the country by proposing a constitutional amendment which would give the Federal Government much wider powers upon which to base social and economic legislation.

There has been little talk on that subject around the White House for some time now. Some published reports have said that the response to the President's original statement was lukewarm. Other reports have said the matter depended on what New Deal laws were discarded by the Supreme Court.

Advocates of such an amendment were watching closely for the reaction in Southern States. States' rights have been a Democratic talking point there for years.

Republicans have predicted that several Southern States would desert the Democratic Party in 1936 if it espoused greater Federal powers.

Social Security Bill Is Signed; Gives Pensions to Aged, Jobless

Roosevelt Approves Measure Intended to Benefit 30,000,000 Persons When States Adopt Cooperating Laws—He Calls the Measure 'Cornerstone' of His Economic Program.

Special to THE NEW YORK TIMES.

WASHINGTON, Aug. 14.—The Social Security Bill, providing a broad program of unemployment insurance and old-age pensions, and counted upon to benefit some 30,000,000 persons, became law today when it was signed by President Roosevelt in the presence of those chiefly responsible for putting it through Congress.

Mr. Roosevelt called the measure "the cornerstone in a structure which is being built but is by no means complete." He was referring to his program for economic rehabilitation.

He added that the present session of Congress would have become historic had it done nothing beyond completion of this law. The text of the measure as originally introduced was published in THE NEW YORK TIMES Jan. 18.

The President said he hoped that three members of a board provided by the law to supervise the social projects could be named before the Congress session ended.

He gave no indication of the persons he had in mind for these posts, but it was reported that among possible appointees are Arthur J. Altmyer, Assistant Secretary of Labor, and Murray Latimer, chairman of the Railroad Pensions Board, an organization now in abeyance because the Supreme Court declared unconstitutional the law establishing the board. The third member will be a political appointee.

The signing took place in the Cabinet Room of the White House offices, where motion picture and still photographers had been invited to record the event as a result of the President's desire to obtain the widest possible publicity for the measure, which he said had not received due publicity because of the press of other news.

Among about thirty persons who stood grouped around the President as he read a statement and then signed the act were Secretary Perkins, Senator Wagner, who was one of the first advocates in Congress of legislation of this character; Representative Lewis of Maryland, co-author with Senator Wagner of the bill; members of the Senate Finance Committee, headed

Continued on Page Four.

BRITISH WILL CITE 1906 PACT TO ITALY

Feel Ban on Interference in Ethiopia Without Consent of Signatories Is Pertinent.

EDEN CONFERS WITH LAVAL

Italians to Give Views Today —Plan for Special Rights in Addis Ababa Gaining.

By FREDERICK T. BIRCHALL.
Wireless to THE NEW YORK TIMES.

PARIS, Aug. 14.—The clearing of ground for the formal three-power conference to save Ethiopia from the disasters of a war with Italy and the League of Nations from a dilemma that is likely to wreck it as a vital institution, whichever horn it may choose, began here today when Premier Pierre Laval received the British delegates at the Quai d'Orsay.

Conversations were held between Anthony Eden, British Minister for League of Nations Affairs, and Mr. Laval. British and French experts on African questions got together later to put into form various technical questions regarding past treaties, which later may play an important part in the negotiations.

The French part, it became clearer than ever today, is to be that of mediator—an honest broker who wants nothing much for himself except good-will and such a quid pro quo as may voluntarily be vouchsafed him in return for reconciling the two opposing parties.

Today Mr. Laval heard the British argument. Tomorrow he will listen to the Italian views when Baron Pompeo Aloisi arrives. The Ethiopian aspect of the matter Mr. Laval has learned already from Bedjirond Tecle Hawariate, the Emperor's Minister to Paris. That, however, as is quite clearly established, will count for very little. Ethiopia is expected to do what the greater powers decide is best for her. Also she probably will, the only alternative being her utter extinction.

Italy's Stand Awaited.

It was said tonight in British quarters that "some progress, in fact all that could be expected from a mere preliminary meeting," had been made today. This probably covers the facts that little had been expected and little was accomplished because both the British and the French are merely waiting to hear what the Italians say tomorrow before any definite proposals are advanced.

Mr. Eden pointed out to Mr. Laval that both Britain and France were deeply concerned in the Ethiopian matter because it involved not only peace in Africa, where both have extensive colonies, but probably European peace as well and certainly the League's future influence.

Beyond this, however, it is understood, the conversations proceeded along the most general lines as to the prospect of effecting a settlement and the part that may be played in such a settlement by the old tri-partite treaty of 1906, the Italo-Ethiopian Arbitration Treaty of 1928 and the exchange of notes between Italy and Britain in 1925. Concrete proposals were not

Continued on Page Two.

10 MORE CATHOLICS ON TRIAL IN BERLIN

7 Sisters of Good Shepherd Punished for Violation of Foreign Exchange Rules.

JEW IS ARRESTED IN SAAR

Anti-Semitic Drive Spreads to Protected Territory—More Prosecutions Threatened.

By OTTO D. TOLISCHUS.
Wireless to THE NEW YORK TIMES.

BERLIN, Aug. 14.—Three of the highest officials in Germany of the Catholic Brothers of Mercy order and seven nuns of the Sisters of the Good Shepherd went on trial in Berlin today on charges of violating German foreign exchange regulations.

[One of the nuns was sentenced to four months' imprisonment and fined 900 marks and the six others were fined 1,200 to 4,500 marks, according to The Associated Press.]

These trials are part of a series of about fifty separate prosecutions started by National Socialist authorities against institutions, leading invariably to long terms of imprisonment for individuals and almost confiscatory fines for their institutions

The convictions give the National Socialists their heaviest ammunition against the Catholics and may be expected, together with the charges of "race ravishing" against Jews, to play a big part in the speech with which Julius Streicher will whip up National Socialist fervor at his first mass meeting in Berlin tomorrow night.

Also Accused of "Treason."

The three Brothers of Mercy, who are also charged with "treason against German economy," are Ottmar Vey, 57 years old, superior general; Josef Bruemmer, 56, general administrator, and Stephan Kok, 56, assistant general administrator. They are accused of having smuggled 100,000 marks from Germany and having failed to report assets held abroad, including a claim of $3,700 against the order's branch in Buffalo, N. Y.

The seven Sisters of the Good Shepherd are accused of similar offenses involving 62,000 marks.

The Catholic Youth camp at Hungenberg near Baireuth, containing thirty-four youths under the guidance of Father Luhn, has been dissolved on the ground that it had indulged in sports and military exercises which are reserved for the Hitler Youth alone.

Provost Adam Schrull of Teltge, Westphalia, a pilgrimage place, was sentenced to three months' imprisonment for tearing down National Socialist posters against political Catholicism.

Viktoria Kern of Freudenberg, a member of a Catholic young women's organization, was jailed for two months for the same offense.

Father Peter Hunstiger of the Catholic congregation at Nordhausen, who had refused a church burial for a Storm Trooper, was in "protective custody" together with his assistant.

Symptoms of the anti-Jewish campaign began to appear in the Saar today when Erich Oppenheimer, owner of a store at Saarbruecken, was arrested on charges of "race

Continued on Page Three.

700 SEIZED IN PARKS AS 200 POLICE OPEN DRIVE TO END CRIME

Squads Round Up Derelicts in Campaign Spurred by a New Assault in Central Park.

MOSES PROMISES HIS AID

Valentine Adds Guards After Parley Attended by Mayor, Who Chides Magistrates.

Aroused by an assault and robbery of an elderly man, the latest in a series of crimes committed in the public parks, the city marshaled its forces yesterday for a campaign to make all park areas safe by night as well as day.

After a morning conference at police headquarters, attended by Mayor La Guardia, Chief Magistrate Jacob Gould Schurman Jr. and high police officials, Police Commissioner Lewis J. Valentine organized a special force of 100 detectives and 100 patrolmen. This squad was sent into action last night.

The special force and the regular precinct police acted with results that gratified their superiors. As the campaign gained momentum the number of arrests soared to more than 700 with the police sallying beyond the bounds of the parks. They raided many of the more evil nooks of the city, ferreting out mendicants, the polite police characterization for drunkards, panhandlers and beggars. It was believed the number might have been even greater if the rain had not driven them to cover.

Derelict Centres Combed.

The police roved the waterfronts, the "Bums Clothing Exchange" in the Bowery, the produce market at Pier 17, North River; the site of the former "Hoover City" of derelicts at the foot of East Tenth Street, Chinatown, Avenue B's "gas house" district between Eleventh and Twelfth Streets, and the tenement streets in the heart of the East Side.

By 1:30 o'clock this morning 344 of the prisoners had had hearings in Night Court on charges of disorderly conduct. They were sentenced to two days in jail, none being able to take the alternative of paying a $2 fine. In imposing the sentences, Magistrate Smith said he would have given the prisoners longer jail sentences if the city had the facilities to handle them.

The police round-ups on the various parks caused the Night Court last night to have the heaviest calendar in ten years and one of the heaviest in its history. Altogether, 449 persons appeared in the court, including the park loiterers, theatre pickets and others.

Most of the men arrested were pitiful, unkempt derelicts who had been using doorways and parks for homes, paper for sheets and their arms for pillows, eking out near-starvation existences by panhandling. They were men so lacking in morale and so long unused to personal discipline that they shunned the municipal lodging houses because of the simple routine that would require them to appear thrice daily for meals and at stated times for bath and bed.

Before the police and the courts have finished with them they will be fingerprinted, and it was pre-

Continued on Page Thirteen.

SENATE-HOUSE RIFT GROWS AS O'CONNOR HOLDS HOPSON, IGNORING CONTEMPT ORDER

Mayor Sets Up Recorder Of Noise in His Office

Mayor La Guardia extended his anti-noise campaign to his own office at City Hall yesterday, installing a noise measuring device there, without the knowledge of his staff, to test the number of decibels which hover around his sanctum.

At 6 o'clock, just before he left for the day, the Mayor hauled out the hidden device and found it had registered a maximum of thirty-eight decibels of sound. The Mayor made no comment on this reading and no one else at City Hall could explain it. It was pointed out, however, that noise readings at fairly busy street intersections show about seventy-seven decibels. Incidentally, it was noted that the windows in the Mayor's office were open all day.

The anti-noise campaign was given the support yesterday of the Motorcycle Chamber of Commerce, representing 15,000 motorcycle owners.

ICE CREAM LOBBYING PUT UP TO THE FTC

Counter Freezer Makers Open Fight to Have Charges of Such Activity Restored.

ONCE STRICKEN FROM BRIEF

Commission Then Held It Had No Jurisdiction in State Law Drives—6 Dairies Targets.

Special to THE NEW YORK TIMES.

WASHINGTON, Aug. 14.—A fight to restore charges of undue legislative activity to the complaint in which the Federal Trade Commission alleges unfair competition in the suppression of counter ice cream freezers was started today. The complaint is drawn against the International Association of Ice Cream Manufacturers and six of the country's largest dairy companies.

Three paragraphs of the complaint, alleging that the respondents sponsored and urged State laws which would outlaw counter freezers; that they drew these laws to the attention of prospective purchasers of counter ice cream freezers and worked with local sanitary and other officials to prevent their use, were stricken from the complaint last week on motion of counsel for the association.

Today the National Association of Counter Freezer Manufacturers filed a petition to intervene in the case and to vacate the granting of the motion.

Granting of the motion to strike out the original paragraphs which was based on a contention that the Federal Trade Commission had no jurisdiction over activities and relations between citizens and State Legislatures, caused considerable comment at the time.

The original complaint, which was

Continued on Page Four.

DEFIES BLACK COMMITTEE

Utility Man Vanishes Refusing to Appear Despite Subpoena.

SENATE THEN CITES HIM

O'Connor Says He Has A. G. E. Head in Custody and Won't Surrender Him.

SENATE ALSO CALLS HILL

Cox of Georgia Threatens to 'Kick' Hopson Out of House Committee Hearing.

Special to THE NEW YORK TIMES.

WASHINGTON, Aug. 14.—A fight between the Senate and the House for the possession of Howard C. Hopson as a witness in their respective investigations of lobbying against the Utility Holding Company Bill was on tonight after the Senate had cited the "master mind" of the Associated Gas and Electric System to appear before it tomorrow and show cause why he should not be adjudged in contempt.

While Chesley W. Jurney, sergeant-at-arms of the Senate, pursued a vain hunt for the utility man, seeking to serve the Senate citation on him, Chairman O'Connor of the House Rules Committee, before which Mr. Hopson had testified during the day, declared that the witness was in his custody and would not be surrendered to the agents of the Senate.

Late this evening Mr. O'Connor notified the Senate officer that he had Mr. Hopson in custody and added, according to Mr. Jurney: "We'll hold him until we get through with him."

Plans to Apply for Warrant.

The sergeant-at-arms announced that he would apply tomorrow to the Senate for a warrant calling for the arrest of Mr. Hopson. Chairman O'Connor countered by saying that a resolution calling for the delivery of Mr. Hopson to the House sergeant-at-arms would be presented in the House tomorrow.

The Senate also cited William A. Hill of Boston, counsel for Mr. Hopson, to appear and show cause why he too should not be adjudged in contempt.

Mr. Hopson was cited because of his failure to respond to a "subpoena instanter" of the Senate committee served on him just before noon. Mr. Hill was cited on the ground that he "physically interfered" yesterday with a Senate committee agent who vainly sought to serve Mr. Hopson with a subpoena.

Mr. Hopson's defiance of the Senate committee is understood to have been based on the advice of a "responsible personage," who, it was said, had advised him that he was in the custody of the House Rules Committee and therefore could not be compelled at this time to recognize a subpoena of the Senate committee.

After succeeding in serving the subpoena today, the Senate committee waited four hours and fifteen minutes for Mr. Hopson to appear. The time limit was 4 P. M. Promptly on that hour Senator Black recessed the committee and ten minutes later the citation resolution was pending before the Senate.

Jurney Seeks Legal Advice.

The Senate sergeant-at-arms was not certain how he would use a Senate warrant, but planned to consult legal advisers on the technicality of whether the Senate could arrest a man already in the custody of the House.

"I know, of course, that I can't arrest him while he's testifying before the House committee, but maybe I can nab him as soon as the committee recesses," Mr. Jurney said.

Mr. Jurney was apprised of Representative O'Connor's coup in taking Mr. Hopson into friendly custody when he saw the Representative at his office late in the evening. Mr. Hopson was not present at that meeting.

About midnight Mr. Jurney went to the Shoreham Hotel, Mr. O'Connor's Washington residence, to await him for another conference. While there he met Mr. Hill, who already had accepted service of the

Continued on Page Ten.

Canadian Parliament Is Dissolved; General Election Is Set for Oct. 14

By The Canadian Press.

OTTAWA, Aug. 14.—After effecting a partial reconstruction of his Cabinet, involving the swearing in of four Ministers, Prime Minister R. B. Bennett today obtained dissolution of Parliament. He announced that a general election would be held Oct. 14. Writs will be dated tomorrow and be returnable on Nov. 9.

The Earl of Bessborough, Governor General, made a special trip to the capital from Quebec, where he is in Summer residence, and signed the dissolution.

Chosen to fill gaps in the Cabinet ranks created by appointments and retirements, the new Ministers are Lieut. Col. G. R. Geary of Ontario, Minister of Justice; J. Earl Lawson of Ontario, Minister of National Revenue; William G. Ernst, a Nova Scotia member, Minister of Fisheries, and Samuel Gobeil of Quebec, Minister without portfolio.

Further Ministerial changes awaiting completion involve the portfolios of Marine, Postoffice and Finance. Maurice Dupré, Solicitor General, is expected to become Postmaster General. The portfolio of Finance may not be filled before the election. E. N. Rhodes, who has been Minister of Finance since 1932 and who was recently appointed to the Senate, will remain in office for some time to complete important refunding operations he has in hand, Mr. Bennett said.

It was necessary for the government to pass an order-in-council rescinding that passed some months ago which fixed Oct. 14 as Thanksgiving Day and changing the national holiday to Oct. 24. Originally it had been planned to hold the elections on Sept. 30, Mr. Bennett said, but in order to complete the necessary preliminaries, it was then decided to delay polling until Oct. 7.

When it was brought to the attention of the government that Oct. 7 was the Jewish Day of Atonement, Mr. Bennett said that to have polling on that date would disfranchise a large number of electors.

Since the statute requires that general elections must be held on Monday, it was then necessary to select Oct. 14.

With the decks practically cleared for campaigning, it is understood the government forces will take the field next week. First activities of the Prime Minister are to be a series of radio broadcasts.

Senator Huey Long of Louisiana after one of his famous filibusters. He died on September 10 of the wounds inflicted by his assassin.

Times Wide World Photo

Amelia Earhart tuning up her plane at Wheeler Field in Honolulu. She flew from Honolulu to Oakland, California, in 18¼ hours on January 12.

Dr. Carl A. Weiss, the man who put an end to Huey Long's dictatorship before it could spread outside Louisiana.

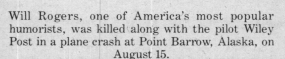

Will Rogers, one of America's most popular humorists, was killed along with the pilot Wiley Post in a plane crash at Point Barrow, Alaska, on August 15.

Record of Miss Earhart's Flight Over Pacific; Flier Enjoyed 'Scenery' on 2,408-Mile Hop

By The Associated Press.

(All Times are Eastern Standard.)

FRIDAY, JAN. 11.

10:15 P. M.—Amelia Earhart left Wheeler Field, Honolulu, to attempt first solo flight from Hawaii to California, 2,408 miles.

10:21 P. M.—2,000 feet up, headed for Diamond Head and the open Pacific.

11:15 P. M.—Radioed, "Everything OK."

SATURDAY, JAN. 12.

12:40 A. M.—Tremendous static interfered with radio communication but land stations heard: "Flying 8,000. Weather overcast outside. Temperature 45 degrees."

2:50 A. M.—Flying at 3,000 feet through fog.

3:15 A. M.—"Everything OK" at 8,000 feet.

3:50 A. M.—All well, flying at 6,000 feet over low scattered clouds.

4:19 A. M.—"All OK." Thanked husband for broadcast greeting.

4:48 A. M.—"All OK."

5:17 A. M.—"I should be almost half way. OK." 8,000 feet up.

5:57 A. M.—"All OK."

6:17 A. M.—Flying in scattered clouds, visibility good. "OK."

6:50 A. M.—"All OK."

7:15 A. M.—Flying at 8,000 feet; overcast; visibility fair.

7:20 A. M.—Ran into high fog at 7,000 to 8,000 feet.

7:49 A. M.—"Am still OK."

8:12 A. M.—Out of the fog at 6,000 feet.

8:22 A. M.—"OK."

8:48 A. M.—"OK."

9:15 A. M.—"I'm becoming quite tired."

10 A. M.—"All is well. Enjoying the scenery."

10:40 A. M.—"All is well."

10:50 A. M.—Plane nosed down to 700 feet from altitude of 6,000 feet.

11:18 A. M.—"All OK."

11:48 A. M.—"Everything OK."

12 NOON—"Flying low over fog bank. Everything OK."

2 P. M.—Sighted by steamer President Pierce, 250 miles off San Francisco.

2:35 P. M.—Radio stations reported plane flying through fog and off course.

3:25 P. M.—"Am on my course; will be in any moment now."

4:15 P. M.—Sighted off Lobitos, twenty miles south of San Francisco.

4:31 P. M.—Landed at Oakland Airport, completing first solo flight ever made between Hawaii and California.

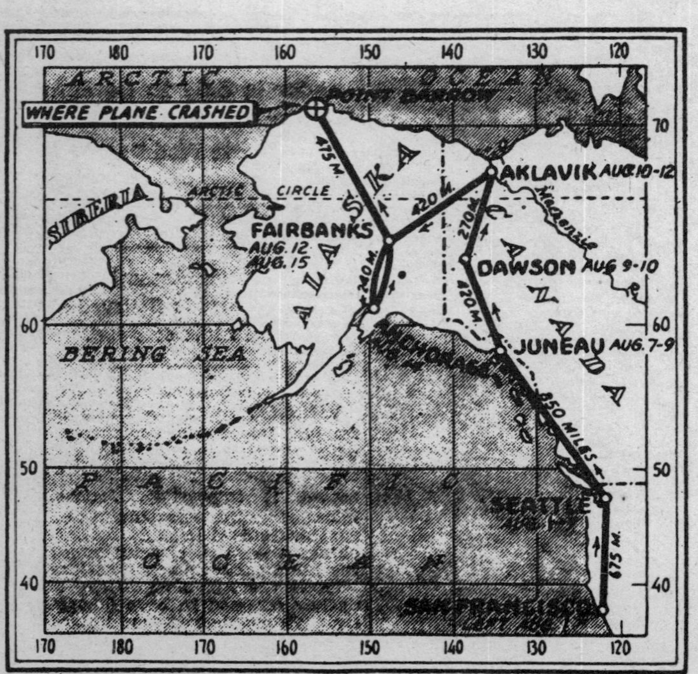

Map showing the route of the Rogers-Post flight. The black line shows the areas covered, from San Francisco to Point Barrow, on the fatal trip.

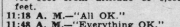

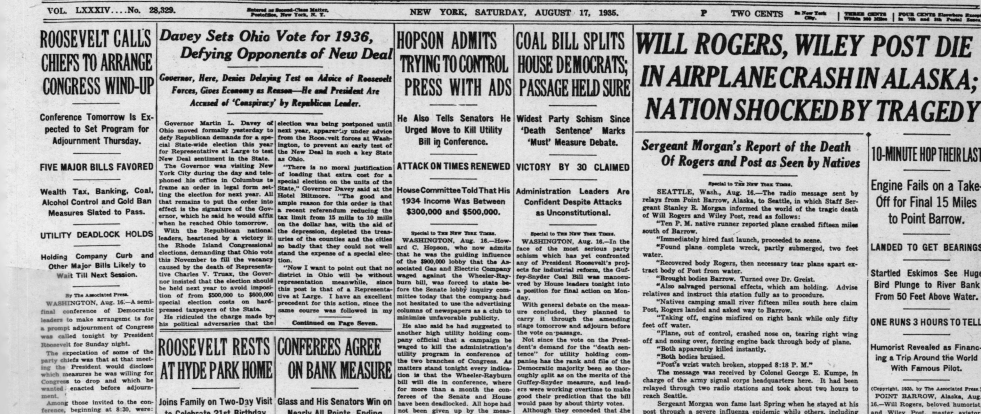

"All the News That's Fit to Print."

The New York Times.

LATE CITY EDITION
WEATHER—Fair, continued warm today; tomorrow cloudy, showers.
Temperatures Yesterday—Max., 85; Min., 72

Copyright, 1935, by The New York Times Company.

VOL. LXXXIV....No. 28,329. Entered as Second-Class Matter, Postoffice, New York, N. Y. NEW YORK, SATURDAY, AUGUST 17, 1935. P TWO CENTS In New York City. | THREE CENTS Within 200 Miles | FOUR CENTS Elsewhere Except in 7th and 8th Postal Zones.

ROOSEVELT CALLS CHIEFS TO ARRANGE CONGRESS WIND-UP

Conference Tomorrow Is Expected to Set Program for Adjournment Thursday.

FIVE MAJOR BILLS FAVORED

Wealth Tax, Banking, Coal, Alcohol Control and Gold Ban Measures Slated to Pass.

UTILITY DEADLOCK HOLDS

Holding Company Curb and Other Major Bills Likely to Wait Till Next Session.

By The Associated Press.

WASHINGTON, Aug. 16.—A semi-final conference of Democratic leaders to make arrangements for a prompt adjournment of Congress was called tonight by President Roosevelt for Sunday night.

The expectation of some of the party chiefs was that at that meeting the President would disclose which measures he was willing for Congress to drop and which he wanted enacted before adjournment.

Among those invited to the conference, beginning at 8:30, were: Vice President Garner, Speaker Byrns, Senator Robinson of Arkansas, the Democratic leader; Chairman O'Connor of the House Rules Committee, Chairman Harrison of the Senate Finance Committee and Chairman Doughton of the House Ways and Means Committee.

It was indicated by one of the conferees that any agreement reached Sunday night, however, would be subject to possible modification if particular pressure developed for the enactment of any measure.

Conjecture on Program.

From what they already had heard directly and indirectly from the President, some of the conferees, talking privately, said the meeting made more clear the possibilities of an end to the present session by the end of next week at the latest.

Some were talking about an adjournment Tuesday, or Thursday. Most agreed that it probably would be the latter part of next week before everything could be wound up to their satisfaction or to that of the President.

The expectation of some of the conferees was that the President would renew his insistence upon enactment of:

1. The Guffey Coal Stabilization Bill, which proponents and some opponents say will pass the House Monday and be approved by the Senate early next week:
2. The Federal alcohol control plan.
3. The $250,000,000 Tax Bill.
4. The Omnibus Banking Bill, on which conferees reached an agreement late today.
5. The measure forbidding suits for gold payments on government contracts.

Six Bills May Be Shelved.

Their belief was that unless action was hastened the following would be left behind when this session ended, with their present status remaining the same until the next session:

1. The Utilities Bill;
2. The rivers and harbors legislation;
3. The measure expanding Federal control over food and drugs;
4. Railroad reorganization;
5. General oil regulation;
6. The Ship Subsidy Bill.

Leaders said the Utilities Bill probably would be left behind, not because the President did not want the legislation, but because the conference deadlock could not be broken.

A possibility was seen by some that the Rivers and Harbors Bill might be insisted upon because it would legalize the millions already spent by the Federal Government on a number of projects, such as the Parker Dam. And they added that they had but scant doubt that before Congress had adjourned it would ratify the oil compacts entered into in Dallas last February.

House Tax Conferees Named.

Special to THE NEW YORK TIMES.

WASHINGTON, Aug. 16.—A determined drive to adjourn Congress by Tuesday night, with Thursday as the latest alternate date, was started today following formal commitment of the Wealth-Tax Bill to conference and a conference agreement on the Eccles Banking Bill.

The promise of Tuesday adjournment was held out by Senator Robinson as the Senate voted to take a recess until Monday. Early in the day he had informed the Senate of his desire to quit at that time and in so doing issued a warning

Continued on Page Fourteen.

Davey Sets Ohio Vote for 1936, Defying Opponents of New Deal

Governor, Here, Denies Delaying Test on Advice of Roosevelt Forces, Gives Economy as Reason—He and President Are Accused of 'Conspiracy' by Republican Leader.

Governor Martin L. Davey of Ohio moved formally yesterday to defy Republican demands for a special State-wide election this year for Representative at Large to test New Deal sentiment in the State.

The Governor was visiting New York City during the day and telephoned his office in Columbus to frame an order in legal form setting the election for next year. All that remains to put the order into effect is the signature of the Governor, which he said he would affix when he reached Ohio tomorrow.

With the Republican national leaders, heartened by a victory in the Rhode Island Congressional elections, demanding that Ohio vote this November to fill the vacancy caused by the death of Representative Charles V. Truax, the Governor insisted that the election should be held next year to avoid imposition of from $500,000 to $600,000 special election costs on hard-pressed taxpayers of the State.

He ridiculed the charge made by his political adversaries that the election was being postponed until next year, apparently under advice from the Roosevelt forces at Washington, to prevent an early test of the New Deal in such a key State as Ohio.

"There is no moral justification of loading that extra cost for a special election on the units of the State," Governor Davey said at the Hotel Biltmore. "The good and ample reason for this order is that a recent referendum reducing the tax limit from 15 mills to 10 mills on the dollar has, with the aid of the depression, depleted the treasuries of the counties and the cities so badly that they could not well stand the expense of a special election.

"Now I want to point out that no district in Ohio will be without representation meanwhile, since this post is that of a Representative at Large. I have an excellent precedent for this action, since the same course was followed in my

Continued on Page Seven.

ROOSEVELT RESTS AT HYDE PARK HOME

Joins Family on Two-Day Visit to Celebrate 21st Birthday of Franklin Jr.

AVOIDS ISSUE ON HOOVER

President Intercedes for Man Caught at Baltimore While Stealing Ride on His Train.

From a Staff Correspondent.

HYDE PARK, N. Y., Aug. 16.—President Roosevelt returned to Hyde Park House today for a brief period of quiet contemplation before undertaking the direction of strategy designed to bring the current session of Congress to a satisfactory conclusion from the administration standpoint.

He came here overnight aboard a special train which arrived at 8:30 o'clock this morning for the announced purpose of attending a family party tomorrow in celebration of the twenty-first birthday anniversary of Franklin D. Roosevelt Jr., his third son.

However, an impromptu "press conference" held by Mr. Roosevelt while he sat in an automobile for the ride from the train to his mother's estate overlooking the Hudson River gave ample indication of the many problems awaiting a directing hand, if not a definite solution, by the President.

These problems he plans to tackle actively on Sunday, when he will return to the White House for a long series of conferences with the individuals and groups representing the administration leadership on Capitol Hill.

A cheery confidence was radiated by Mr. Roosevelt today as he was subjected to a barrage of questions by reporters who clustered around his automobile in the bright morning sunlight.

Questioned on Utility Bill.

The questions dealt principally with the Utility Holding Company Bill, which has been deadlocked in conference between the House and Senate for some time, and the Tax Bill which was sent to conference yesterday after the Senate had approved a measure considerably different than the House bill.

Asked if he expected enactment of the Utility Bill this session, Mr. Roosevelt replied smilingly that he hoped so, with an inflection in his voice which some reporters interpreted as indicating that he intended to have this done.

Would he be willing, he then was asked, to accept the House bill, which differs from the Senate bill and administration recommendations in its omission of the celebrated "death sentence" section? At this question, Mr. Roosevelt smiled and closed the topic with the assertion that he could not comment on details.

A request for comment on the action of the Senate in passing the Tax Bill in changed form brought the rejoinder from the President that the Tax Bill had not been finally passed by Congress yet; that it was still an open question.

Renewed efforts by correspondents to get specific comment from the President on the recent statement by former President Hoover requesting Mr. Roosevelt to set forth definitely his plans regarding possible changes in the Constitution, elicited from the President only the reply that he had read Mr. Hoover's statement very hurriedly and therefore was in no position to comment.

Aside from the conferences Mr.

Continued on Page Fourteen.

CONFEREES AGREE ON BANK MEASURE

Glass and His Senators Win on Nearly All Points, Ending Long Battle on Bill.

ONE VICTORY FOR HOUSE

Effort to Force State Banks Into Reserve Is Put Off—Swift Finish Planned.

Special to THE NEW YORK TIMES.

WASHINGTON, Aug. 16.—Unanimous agreement on every feature of the hotly contested bill to change the nation's banking laws was reached by Senate and House conferees late today and arrangements were made to hurry this highly important measure through both branches of Congress early next week.

Senator Glass and his conservative colleagues of the Senate conferees won a smashing victory over Representatives Steagall and Goldsborough of the House conferees in almost every particular, but the two House liberals succeeded in postponing efforts to force State banks into the Federal Reserve System.

Senator Glass was delighted by the outcome. He and the other members of the conference asserted that the bill would go through both branches with ease.

Action will be taken on the conference report in the House Monday. The conferees arranged to file formal reports to both branches tomorrow.

The end of the conference marks a long and bitter fight over the policies of Marriner S. Eccles, governor of the Federal Reserve Board, as expressed in the bill passed by the House, and the views of the Glass group as set forth in the Senate bill.

Opinion tonight was that Mr. Glass, veteran banking legislator, had once more come out the victor.

Reserve Board Is Increased.

He and the other Senate conferees succeeded in carrying out their views on the open market committee, particularly in the aspect that government securities must be purchased on the open market and not direct from the Treasury.

Likewise, Senate conferees prevailed in their insistence that the Federal Reserve Board must be increased from the present six to seven members, with the Secretary of the Treasury and the Controller of the Currency eliminated as members ex officio.

The suggested permission of the Senate bill for banks of deposit to underwrite securities was stricken out at the request of President Roosevelt, Senator Glass stated.

The provision of the Senate bill that bankers may serve on not more than two bank boards simultaneously was retained but made subject to the discretion of the Reserve Board, however.

A big feature of the bill is the arrangement for the open market committee, which would be composed of seven Reserve Board members and five representatives of the twelve regional Reserve Banks. This committee would have power to influence the flow of credit by purchase and sale of government bonds by the Reserve Banks.

Policy Is Mandatory.

The policy laid down by the committee would be mandatory upon the Reserve Banks.

Following the view of Mr. Eccles, the House gave complete voting control of open market operations entirely to the Reserve Board, with

Continued on Page Fourteen.

HOPSON ADMITS TRYING TO CONTROL PRESS WITH ADS

He Also Tells Senators He Urged Move to Kill Utility Bill in Conference.

ATTACK ON TIMES RENEWED

House Committee Told That His 1934 Income Was Between $300,000 and $500,000.

Special to THE NEW YORK TIMES.

WASHINGTON, Aug. 16.—Howard C. Hopson, who now admits that he was the guiding influence of the $900,000 lobby that the Associated Gas and Electric Company waged against the Wheeler-Rayburn bill, was forced to state before the Senate lobby inquiry committee today that the company had not hesitated to use the advertising columns of newspapers as a club to minimize unfavorable publicity.

He also said he had suggested to another high utility holding company official that a campaign be waged to kill the administration's utility program in conference of the two branches of Congress. As matters stand tonight every indication is that the Wheeler-Rayburn bill will die in conference, where for more than a month the conferees of the Senate and House have been deadlocked. All hope had not been given up by the measure's advocates, however.

Earlier in the day, before the House investigating committee, Mr. Hopson for the first time gave figures on his income last year. He said he had received "some three or four or five hundred thousand dollars" from his private companies.

Admits Borrowing Millions.

He also said that the A. G. E. had borrowed several million dollars since the first of the year, and that had it not been for the Wheeler-Rayburn bill the borrowings might have been a million dollars less.

He was directed to supply the names of the banks from which the money was borrowed, and said he would do so.

Before the Senate committee Mr. Hopson again made charges involving THE NEW YORK TIMES. He asserted that the newspaper was under "the strong influence" of the Morgan and Carlisle interests, and that because of this alleged influence the A. G. E. should expect at "more or less frequent intervals" more "unpleasant attacks from that quarter."

The charges were made in a telegram to the H. C. Hopson Company, New York, which was signed by Duncan Robertson, Mr. Hopson's private secretary.

The telegram was in fact his own, said Mr. Hopson, explaining that it was his custom to have Mr. Robertson sign practically all of his messages to his New York office.

Messages to Hearst Admitted.

William Randolph Hearst was pictured before the committee as the writer of an editorial printed in the Hearst newspapers Sunday, June 2, which Senator Black asserted was strikingly along lines suggested by Mr. Hopson in a telegram to Mr. Hearst dated May 31.

Mr. Hopson admitted sending frequent messages to Mr. Hearst, who was dubbed by Senator Minton "the sage of San Simeon," but insisted that he had no reason to believe his messages inspired editorials or news articles in the Hearst papers.

Arthur Brisbane, Hearst writer, was pilloried, however, and documents placed in evidence showed

Continued on Page Twenty-six.

Lawyer Charges Judge Downs Beat Him; Sues for $50,000 in Contempt Case Row

County Judge Thomas Downs of Queens was sued in the New York Supreme Court yesterday by Lorenzo C. Carlino, a lawyer, for $50,000 damages. The lawyer charged that Judge Downs, after finding him guilty of contempt of court in a trial, and fining him $250, had knocked him down and kicked him at the St. Albans Golf Club in Queens.

Mr. Carlino alleges that his appeal from the contempt order was based on the ground that it was a violation of the section of the Judiciary Act which requires that a contempt order cite the specific facts upon which it is based. The lawyer further asserts that he got an order from the Appellate Division restraining Judge Downs from making any change in the order pending the appeal.

Mr. Carlino served the order on Judge Downs at the golf club on May 7 last, he alleges, when the jurist was about to step into his car. He says that as soon as he showed a signature of Presiding Justice Lazansky on an injunction order, "the defendant, Thomas Downs, struck the plaintiff, knocked him down, then kicked him while on the ground and trampled upon the order which was served upon him. Defendant called plaintiff vile, filthy names and otherwise used vile and filthy language."

In addition to the suit against Judge Downs the lawyer asks $25,000 damages from Sheriff Peter J. McGarry of Queens for brutal treatment when he was arrested on the contempt order, which was later set aside by the Appellate Division.

Judge Downs denied last night he had assaulted Mr. Carlino.

"I was getting into my automobile parked in front of the clubhouse about 10 o'clock one night more than three months ago," the judge explained, "when a man I did not recognize in the darkness rushed out at me from some shrubbery. I was all alone and had received only a few days before an anonymous threat against my life. I hit the man at once. He fell down and a paper dropped to the ground. The man picked up the paper and ran away."

COAL BILL SPLITS HOUSE DEMOCRATS; PASSAGE HELD SURE

Widest Party Schism Since 'Death Sentence' Marks 'Must' Measure Debate.

VICTORY BY 30 CLAIMED

Administration Leaders Are Confident Despite Attacks as Unconstitutional.

Special to THE NEW YORK TIMES.

WASHINGTON, Aug. 16.—In the face of the most serious party schism which has yet confronted any of President Roosevelt's projects for industrial reform, the Guffey-Snyder Coal Bill was manoeuvred by House leaders tonight into a position for final action on Monday.

With general debate on the measure concluded, they planned to carry it through the amending stage tomorrow and adjourn before the vote on passage.

Not since the vote on the President's demand for the "death sentence" for utility holding companies has the rank and file of the Democratic majority been so thoroughly split as on the merits of the Guffey-Snyder measure, and leaders were working overtime to make good their prediction that the bill would pass by about thirty votes.

Although they conceded that the final count would be close, all said enough votes had been obtained to assure passage of the administration "must" measure. Their estimate of thirty votes was verified by Republican leaders.

"Stalwarts" Oppose Measure.

Shouts of "unconstitutional," "communism," and "regimentation" from some of those who have been among the stanchest supporters of the administration on some other reform programs marked consideration of the bill on the floor today.

The opposition among Democrats was so strong that Republicans either sat back to watch them denounce the measure or left the floor entirely.

Emphasizing the broad difference of opinion on the constitutionality of the measure was the performance of such Ways and Means Committee "stalwarts" as Representatives McCormack of Massachusetts, Cooper of Tennessee and Fuller of Arkansas, all of whom took the floor to oppose it, and sometimes on Republican time. The bill had been reported favorably by the committee by a vote of 12 to 11.

The special rule for consideration of the bill was adopted 241 to 94, after a perfunctory debate. Representative McCormack, one of the two Democrats on the Ways and Means Committee who abstained from voting on reporting out the measure, said that he would vote for the rule but against the bill.

He told other members that there would be no inconsistency in such a position, and that he thought the bill should have a chance for consideration on the floor.

Representative Fuller of Arkansas called Speaker Byrns's attention to the distribution by pages in the hall of copies of the bill bearing typewritten slips which said:

"Bituminous Coal Bill as amended and reprinted. Controversial propaganda largely eliminated. Two-thirds of tonnage output operators favored bill and more than 95 per cent of labor."

Representative Snyder of Pennsylvania, co-author of the bill, said that he had pasted the slips on the measure and had instructed the

Continued on Page Seven.

WILL ROGERS, WILEY POST DIE IN AIRPLANE CRASH IN ALASKA; NATION SHOCKED BY TRAGEDY

Sergeant Morgan's Report of the Death Of Rogers and Post as Seen by Natives

Special to THE NEW YORK TIMES.

SEATTLE, Wash., Aug. 16.—The radio message sent by relays from Point Barrow, Alaska, to Seattle, in which Staff Sergeant Stanley R. Morgan informed the world of the tragic death of Will Rogers and Wiley Post, read as follows:

"Ten P. M. native runner reported plane crashed fifteen miles south of Barrow.

"Immediately hired fast launch, proceeded to scene.

"Found plane complete wreck, partly submerged, two feet water.

"Recovered body Rogers, then necessary tear plane apart extract body of Post from water.

"Brought bodies Barrow. Turned over Dr. Greist.

"Also salvaged personal effects, which am holding. Advise relatives and instruct this station fully as to procedure.

"Natives camping small river fifteen miles south here claim Post, Rogers landed and asked way to Barrow.

"Taking off, engine misfired on right bank while only fifty feet off water.

"Plane, out of control, crashed nose on, tearing right wing off and nosing over, forcing engine back through body of plane.

"Both apparently killed instantly.

"Both bodies bruised.

"Post's wrist watch broken, stopped 8:18 P. M."

The message was received by Colonel George E. Kumpe, in charge of the army signal corps headquarters here. It had been relayed through two radio stations and took about two hours to reach Seattle.

Sergeant Morgan won fame last Spring when he stayed at his post through a severe influenza epidemic while others, including his wife and 2-year-old son, Barrow, lay seriously ill. Sergeant Morgan and Dr. Henry W. Greist, the Presbyterian medical missionary, waged a bitter fight against the epidemic. While Dr. Greist ministered to the sick, Sergeant Morgan radioed for the aid which finally defeated the epidemic.

10-MINUTE HOP THEIR LAST

Engine Fails on a Take-Off for Final 15 Miles to Point Barrow.

LANDED TO GET BEARINGS

Startled Eskimos See Huge Bird Plunge to River Bank From 50 Feet Above Water.

ONE RUNS 3 HOURS TO TELL

Humorist Revealed as Financing a Trip Around the World With Famous Pilot.

(Copyright, 1935, by The Associated Press.)

POINT BARROW, Alaska, Aug. 16.—Will Rogers, beloved humorist, and Wiley Post, master aviator, were crushed to death last night when a shiny, new airplane motor faltered and became an engine of tragedy near this outpost of civilization.

Both were killed when their red Arctic sky cruiser slipped and fell fifty feet head-on into a river bank. The 550-horse-power motor, driven back into the fuselage, snuffed out the lives of the two men instantly.

A native runner raced to Point Barrow with word of a plane crash. Sergeant Stanley R. Morgan of the Army Signal Corps dashed to the scene to learn the full significance of the tragedy.

First he took the body of Rogers from the cabin. Then he was forced to tear the plane apart to recover that of the flier who twice had flown around the globe—once alone.

Bodies Are Taken to Barrow.

The bodies were brought here and given to the care of Dr. Henry W. Greist, a Presbyterian medical missionary.

It was a trifling ten-minute flight that ended the careers of two famous figures long accustomed to flying. Although Rogers—gentle master of the "wise crack"—never became a pilot, he was perhaps the world's foremost airplane passenger.

Resuming a happy-go-lucky aerial tour of Alaska, a prelude to a flight to Siberia and on to Moscow, the noted travelers left Fairbanks late yesterday for a 500-mile hop to Point Barrow, northernmost white settlement in America.

Fifty miles out they encountered fog. Post "sat down" on Harding Lake for a while, but resumed the journey soon.

Apparently uncertain of his bearings, he again brought his pontooned plane to the surface of a shallow river fifteen miles southwest of here to ask natives the way to Point Barrow.

Rogers chatted with the Eskimos. Post tinkered with the plane during the brief stop. Soon after 5 P. M. (11 P. M. Eastern daylight time) they took off for the last little hop.

Motor Misfires on Take-Off.

The natives told the story to Sergeant Morgan. They said the motor of Post's new specially built plane misfired soon after it rose. The pilot quickly banked to the right; then the ship plummeted nose first, out of control. It dived into the edge of the stream, where the water was only two feet deep.

When Sergeant Morgan arrived at the scene by launch, he said today, he found the monoplane a complete wreck, partly submerged. The right wing was broken off.

The soldier said Post's watch had stopped at 8:18 P. M., apparently the time of the accident. [The difference in time indicated by the aviator's watch and that reported by the natives probably is accounted for by the time zones through which he had flown.]

The runner arrived here at 10 P. M. with word of the tragedy. Recovering the flier's personal effects, Sergeant Morgan turned them over to Dr. Greist, awaiting instructions from Mrs. Rogers and Mrs. Post and from Morgan's superior, Colonel George E. Kumpe at Seattle.

The unrelenting Arctic, grave of other such noted fliers as Carl Ben Eielson and Frank Dorbandt, played a leading part in this new tragedy.

Rogers and Post had left Fairbanks in the face of poor flying conditions. The stop at Harding Lake enabled them to await the

Continued on Page Four.

ETHIOPIANS OFFER ITALY GUARANTEES

Bar Military Occupation, but Propose Mine, Rail, Trade and Settlement Rights.

ASK ROME TO STATE CASE

Britain and France Hold That Frank Presentation of Demands Is Essential.

By FREDERICK T. BIRCHALL.

Wireless to THE NEW YORK TIMES.

PARIS, Aug. 16.—Throughout the day and until late this evening, with only an interval for luncheon, Premier Pierre Laval, Anthony Eden of Great Britain and Baron Pompeo Aloisi of Italy have been in conference at the Quai d'Orsay over the Italo-Ethiopian problem in an effort to avert a war, with its resultant repercussions in Europe.

The first day's deliberations closed tonight with one definite, positive step taken toward results. The British and French have made a joint formal request to the Italians to state fully and frankly their complaints against Ethiopia and their consequent claims upon her.

From a British source it is learned that the Ethiopian Government, which is not represented at this conference, has shown a disposition to concede several points that may go far toward satisfying the Italian claims when these are made.

Offers Security Guarantees.

The Addis Ababa government, for instance, has expressed willingness to provide the most complete guarantees of security from Ethiopian aggression for the present Italian colonies and such economic concessions as may be agreed upon, provided the guarantees expected fall short of military occupation.

Emperor Haile Selassie is willing to grant reasonable rights for developing mineral and commercial possibilities within the Ethiopian territory, specific concessions to Italy being made in both fields.

He is further willing to consider granting some rights to Europeans to settle in Ethiopian territory and develop it while maintaining their original nationality. This last point would go a long way toward compliance with the Italian wishes.

Finally, he is willing to renew and even extend by making further concessions the old understanding with Italy, giving her permission to undertake a certain amount of commercial road and railroad construction in this country. This again anticipates an obvious Italian demand.

No answer to the Franco-British query was forthcoming from Rome tonight. Indeed, an immediate response was not expected. Baron Aloisi agreed to submit the request to Rome and to report the result as soon as possible. He received assurance from the others that if Italy would comply with this re-

Continued on Page Three.

CAPITAL SADDENED BY ROGERS DEATH

Both House and Senate Halt Business for Tribute to the Humorist and to Post.

GARNER DEEPLY AFFECTED

Robinson Hails 'Best Loved Citizen'—Deaths 'Real Loss,' Speaker Byrns Says.

Special to THE NEW YORK TIMES.

WASHINGTON, Aug. 16.—The death of Will Rogers and Wiley Post shocked and saddened the capital, which knew Rogers as a frequent visitor and liked him as an amiable "josher" of politicians.

Legislative machinery stopped briefly in tribute. The Senate dropped other business to honor the humorist, a friend of Presidents, diplomats and political leaders. The House also listened to a speech of eulogy, while from all quarters came expressions of sorrow over his death.

As soon as the Senate convened, Senator Robinson, the Democratic leader, took the floor and said:

"Probably the most widely known private citizen in the United States and certainly the best beloved met his death some hours ago in a lonely, far-away place.

"We pause for a moment in the midst of our duties to pay brief tribute to his memory and to that of his gallant companion, Wiley Post.

"I do not think of Will Rogers as dead. I shall remember him always as a sensible, courageous, loyal friend, possessed of unusual and notable talents.

"He made fun for all mankind. In nothing that he ever said was there an intentional sting. He was kind, generous, patriotic.

"His companion was a courageous representative of a gallant group who, on wings of adventure, sought remote places and conquered long distances."

News Saddens McNary.

Senator McNary, the Republican leader, said:

"Mr. Rogers has brought happiness, joy and good feeling to the hearts of millions of Americans. In common with all his fellow-citizens, I regret his tragic end and that of his doughty and valiant companion."

Vice President Garner, a friend of long standing, who shared the humorist's dislike of ceremonial attire, could only say, when informed of his death:

"Awful bad! Awful bad!"

Mr. Rogers had boomed Mr. Garner for the Presidency three years ago, and the two had a gay time together Jan. 17 when the Vice President entertained for President Roosevelt.

Speaker Byrns, addressing the House, mentioned Mr. Rogers's in-

Continued on Page Four.

"All the News That's Fit to Print."

The New York Times.

7 A. M. EDITION

WEATHER—Fair today, temperature unchanged; tomorrow fair. Temperatures Yesterday—Max., 71; Min., 56.

VOL. LXXXIV....No. 28,353. Entered as Second-Class Matter, Postoffice, New York, N. Y. NEW YORK, TUESDAY, SEPTEMBER 10, 1935. TWO CENTS In New York City. | THREE CENTS Within 200 Miles | FOUR CENTS Elsewhere Except in 7th and 8th Postal Zones.

ITALIANS REFUSE PLEDGE TO AVOID WARLIKE MOVES

Ethiopia Agrees to Prevent Hostile Acts as League Group Deliberates.

ROME TO IGNORE EFFORTS

League Leaders Fear Order to Advance Will Be Given by Mussolini Saturday.

ASSEMBLY AVOIDS ISSUE

Haile Selassie Is Willing to Accept Advisers—Reich May Demand Colonies.

By FREDERICK T. BIRCHALL.
Wireless to THE NEW YORK TIMES.

GENEVA, Sept. 9.—Hope that out of the new conciliation committee of five powers established by the League of Nations Council last Friday there may come some solution of the Italo-Ethiopian problem received a decided setback this evening.

The theory in more optimistic League circles has been that Italy by refraining from voting in the Council and thus permitting the committee's appointment tacitly left the door open for further negotiations and that she would refrain from hostile action until such negotiations proved actually fruitless.

The first thing the committee did Saturday after its appointment was to authorize Salvador de Madariaga, its president, to write to the Italian and Ethiopian delegations expressing the hope that neither would complicate its task by any overt act. Ethiopia immediately gave a pledge to that effect.

Italy Balks at Pledge.

But tonight Mr. de Madariaga, calling upon Baron Pompeo Aloisi of Italy with the idea of keeping in touch on the ground and acquainting him with the fact that today the committee had appointed a subcommittee to study the Italian memorandum indicting Ethiopia and such reply to it that Ethiopia might make, found this entire theory baseless.

Baron Aloisi informed him that Italy was unable to comply with the wish expressed in the committee's letter Saturday. She could not promise to refrain from hostilities until the committee finished its exploration of the possibilities of settlement but must retain her entire freedom of action, he said.

By refraining from voting in the Council, Baron Aloisi explained, Italy had no intention of signifying her consent to the appointment of the new committee. Her position was rather that she was ignoring the committee's existence and thus leaving it free to take any steps it thought desirable toward bringing Ethiopia into conformance with the Italian wishes. And the last thing Italy intended to do was to tie her own hands because fresh negotiations were in progress.

This was cold water dashed upon the Council's entire scheme. It confirmed the worst prognostications as to the imminence of an Italian invasion of Ethiopian territory. How the committee can continue under that menace is not at all clear, and Premier Pierre Laval's return from Paris tomorrow is anxiously awaited in the hope that he may be able to suggest to Italy some modification of this attitude.

Impasse Again Reached.

As for the rest of the conversation it is understood that Baron Aloisi listened to all that Mr. de Madariaga had to communicate, but did not make commitments. The negotiations, therefore, have again reached an impasse and the outlook for peace is as dark as it ever was.

Premier Laval left Paris for Geneva tonight. Sir Samuel Hoare, British Foreign Secretary, attended the Assembly session and took no part in Ethiopian matters.

The new committee of five held a short session, Alexis Leger taking the place of Premier Laval. The committee's only action was to appoint a subcommittee of experts, one from each nation, to consider the Italian memorandum detailing with Ethiopian sins and the Ethiopian reply when that is received.

This was a concession to Italian sensitiveness. Some grievance, it is understood, has been felt by the Italian delegation over the reception to this memorandum, prepared with so much labor. Nobody has paid any serious attention to it, the chief comment it has evoked having been principally concerned with the bad taste of the distribution so widely of exhibits usually confined

Continued on Page Twelve.

23 Ships Ordered by Navy In Drive for Treaty Fleet

Private Yards Get Contracts for 12, Including Carrier, and Government Yards Will Build 11, Including Cruiser Here.

Special to THE NEW YORK TIMES.

WASHINGTON, Sept. 9.—Another long step in the administration's program to build to full London treaty strength was taken today, when the Navy Department authorized construction of twenty-three fighting ships, including an aircraft carrier and a 10,000-ton cruiser.

All bids for construction of the twenty-fourth vessel of the 1935 program, a 10,000-ton light cruiser, were rejected as "unsatisfactory" because they were from $1,000,000 to nearly $2,000,000 in excess of the bids submitted for the same type of ship last year.

Twelve ships, to cost $59,225,500, will be built by private companies and eleven by navy yards. Ships to be built in navy yards include the 10,000-ton light cruiser to be constructed at the New York Navy Yard. Three 1,500-ton destroyers will be built at Kearny, N. J., by the Federal Shipbuilding and Drydock Company.

The awards disclosed that a second private yard has entered the aircraft-carrier construction field, which in recent years has been solely occupied by the Newport News Drydock and Shipbuilding Company.

The contract for the aircraft carrier in this year's program was awarded to the Bethlehem Shipbuilding Corporation of Quincy, Mass. The construction of this ship, which will displace 14,000 tons and will cost $20,737,000, will bring the aircraft carrier force of the navy to virtual treaty strength. It will give the navy four of the greatest and newest aircraft carriers in the world.

One of the four—the Ranger—is now in commission and two others are under construction by the Newport News company. The building of this squadron was the dream of the late Admiral William A. Moffett, who for years urged these ships as absolutely essential to the national defense. The admiral, who lost his life in the Akron disaster, lived to see the keel of the Ranger laid.

The other awards to private yards, all subject to adjustments within limits for changes in the

Continued on Page Nine.

NOISE DRIVE OPENS, CITY TAKING LEAD

As Hammers Pound Outside, Mayor Pledges Scrapping of Clanking Refuse Trucks.

BAN ON HORNS AT NIGHT

11 P. M. to 7 A. M. Quiet Period to Go Into Effect Oct. 1, Civic Leaders Are Informed.

New York's noise abatement campaign got under way at City Hall yesterday with a general agreement among speakers at the first conference that unnecessary noise could be largely eliminated if the populace remembered its good manners.

Mayor La Guardia, heading the speakers, said the city would set an example by replacing its outworn and noisy Sanitation Department trucks. He said the noise now made by these vehicles was traceable to improper design, which would be corrected in the new equipment.

Deputy Police Commissioner Harold Fowler announced that beginning Oct. 1, tooting of motor horns would be forbidden between 11 P. M. and 7 A. M. Later, he said, the restriction would be extended to the entire twenty-four hours.

Others who addressed the gathering of more than 100 civic and business representatives were Police Commissioner Valentine, Major Henry Curran, the Mayor's noise-abatement commissioner; Chief City Magistrate Jacob Gould Schurman and Acting Health Commissioner William Best.

Curran Lists Nuisances.

Major Curran listed the ten most annoying noises in a way that amused his listeners, though his own anguish over them was quite evident. First, he said, was the unnecessary use of automobile horns, with truck noises a close second.

"Third," he went on, "is the newspaper vendors—those loud-lunged adults who bawl and bellow at the top of their lungs to sell an extra that is not an extra and that has no news in it. Then come noises from drills, and fifth we have street cars, though the Mayor is happily giving street cars the bum's rush in favor of buses. Sixth comes the elevated trains—I believe they were built by Noah and I'm certain they will outlive me."

"No, they won't," interjected Mayor La Guardia.

"In seventh place is the noise from radios," Major Curran went on, "which is a cruel and unusual form of punishment. Riveting noises take eighth place, and ninth goes to the airplanes that fly low over the city in the middle of the night. The tenth class consists of noise from whistles and fog horns on the rivers."

After describing how noise had been quelled in numerous European cities, Major Curran said the same thing could be done here if the people get behind the Mayor.

"Good manners and common courtesy on the road would do much to end traffic noise," Major Curran said.

Commissioner Valentine thanked those who attended the meeting for allying themselves with the police in the anti-noise drive.

"We know from experience that cars can be driven in this city without use of a horn," he said. "All

Continued on Page Eight.

CITY WORKERS FACE PAYLESS FURLOUGHS

M'Gahen Aide Holds Move May Be Necessary to Find Way Out of Financial Straits.

COLLEGES ASK FOR MORE

Three Institutions Seek Rise of $1,186,650—Taylor Items Will Be Lower.

A strong possibility that the city will have to resort to another payless furlough for municipal employes in its effort to find a road out of its budgetary problems for 1936 was indicated yesterday by Leo J. McDermott, Assistant Budget Director, at a hearing on the Board of Higher Education estimate for next year.

The board had asked an increase of $1,186,650 over the $6,644,652 it was allowed this year to meet the operating expenses of the three city colleges. Of the increase $856,633 was to go for personal service, most of it representing mandatory rises under the State law.

Rufus E. McGahen, Director of the Budget, raised the question of "how far the city can go in meeting the provisions of the law relative to mandatory increases."

Robinson Defends Demands.

He was answered by Dr. Frederick B. Robinson, president of the City College, who was defending the requests of his institution. Dr. Robinson said:

"The fiscal authority of the city has no legal right to revise the figures of the Board of Higher Education. In permitting you to impose reductions in the past, the board has simply been helping the city through a trying time. We could have mandamused you through the courts and we would have won, as we did in the Hylan administration.

"I want to point out that the city colleges operate at the lowest per capita cost and the lowest unit student-hour cost in the nation."

The hearing proceeded in routine fashion for a few minutes, with Dr. Robinson repeatedly calling attention to statutory considerations. Then Mr. McDermott put in:

"I think it only fair to point out that you will just get another furlough if every one insists on what he believes to be his rights. It is not a question of what your rights are, but what the city's pocketbook can stand."

And a few minutes later, after Dr. Robinson had declared his willingness to waive further discussion of legal claims, Mr. McDermott added:

"Even when you waive all those things I very much fear that there will be another furlough."

"I don't care," the college head said, shrugging affably.

Sorry for Low-Salaried.

Mr. McDermott looked up.

"Well, I care," he retorted. "I care on behalf of those 80,000 to 90,000 persons who are getting very low salaries. Bringing in all these people in higher-salary brackets doesn't add a nickel to their purchasing power."

"You didn't understand what I

Continued on Page Eighteen.

PWA SPEEDS PLANS TO PUT $420,000,000 A MONTH INTO JOBS

Applications on File When the Books Closed Represent 8,000 Projects.

125 REJECTED IN STATE

$18,500,000 Court House and Queens Centre on List—$88,000,000 Pleas Denied.

TALES OF DISCORD DENIED

Washington Had Heard That Ickes and Hopkins Again Had Differed on Policy.

Special to THE NEW YORK TIMES.

WASHINGTON, Sept. 9.—The government moved rapidly today to clear the decks for the expenditure of $5,000,000,000 of State and Federal funds for work relief, at the rate of $420,000,000 monthly, as PWA announced the closing of its books on new applications four days before the deadline set by President Roosevelt for that act.

Works Progress Administration officials said that they would have sufficient applications on hand by the deadline on Thursday to carry the WPA program to conclusion, but decided to admit new applications until that time.

Meanwhile, revelations that Harry L. Hopkins, Works Progress Administrator, had recommended to the Advisory Committee on Applications the rejection of 1,908 projects which had been approved by the PWA caused much comment here.

Reports that there was serious discord between Mr. Hopkins and Secretary Ickes, PWA Administrator, were emphatically denied, however, by both PWA and WPA officials. Revelation of the number of projects refused came after the Advisory Committee on Allotments, at the instance of Mayor La Guardia of New York, had ruled that sponsors of all projects sent to various government agencies should be notified if their applications were rejected.

Not Enough Work Provided.

Most of the applications were turned down by Mr. Hopkins on the ground that they did not provide enough employment, it was learned.

PWA applications, which doubled in number over the week-end, totaled about 8,000 today, and called for the expenditure of some $1,000,000,000, of which $550,000,000 would represent local contributions and $450,000,000 outright Federal grants. New York State projects on hand numbered 440, totaling $290,000,000.

Works Progress applications on hand were understood to total over $2,000,000,000, and Harry L. Hopkins, Works Progress Administrator, indicated that local contributions would add 25 or 30 per cent to this sum. With the closing of PWA books on applications it was possible to calculate that local contributions would add at least another $1,000,000,000 to the $4,000,000,000 set aside by the Federal Government for work relief.

The army of officials administering the program, the development of which will be speeded as soon as the Advisory Committee on Allotments approves the new applications at its meeting Sept. 17, has

Continued on Page Six.

Moses Charges WPA Sent Him 1,000 'Bums'; Will Reject Them as Useless in Park Jobs

Park Commissioner Robert Moses charged yesterday that the Works Progress Administration had been sending him "Bowery bums" for his relief projects. He declared that he could not and would not use "bums" for his park work and announced his intention of "sending them back within twenty-four hours."

Of 9,000 men furnished the Park Department to date in the work relief expansion program, Mr. Moses estimated that at least 1,000 were "riff-raff picked up by the police as vagrants." He said he had received 250 of them within the last twenty-four hours for assignment to the rehabilitation of the old reservoir site in Central Park.

"They are not suitable for park work; they can't work, anyway, and I won't use them," Mr. Moses declared. "We have enough trouble in Central Park as it is."

Mr. Moses refused to name any one in the relief administration whom he considered responsible. In describing the situation he referred to the relief authorities indefinitely as "they."

He said that the men had been picked up by the police as vagrants and brought into magistrates' court. They were then turned over to the welfare authorities and in some way eventually certified to the WPA for jobs and "sent to us as competent workers."

Mr. Moses's objection to the men was based in part on the fact that they were not in his opinion capable of working and in part on the belief that they were not the right kind to assign to jobs involving contact with the public, and particularly with children. His contention is that the work-relief program involves the completion of certain definite and relatively ambitious projects and that to do this he must have qualified workers.

In this connection he disclosed that of the 9,000 men assigned so far only 10 per cent were skilled workmen. Most of the jobs call for a much higher percentage than this. Furthermore, he said he had received only six foremen and twelve supervisors for the entire number.

General Hugh S. Johnson, head of the WPA here, would not comment on Mr. Moses's statement last night. One official, however, said:

"Does Mr. Moses intend to make dress the qualification for a job in the parks? Until we hear something more specific from Mr. Moses as to his reported objections we do not care to discuss this question."

SENATOR HUEY LONG DIES OF WOUNDS AFTER 30-HOUR FUTILE FIGHT FOR LIFE; TROOPERS GUARD LOUISIANA CAPITOL

PRESIDENT IS GRIEVED

He Deplores Resort to Violence, Calls Spirit Un-American.

FOR CALM, NOT PASSION

Sent Message of Sympathy to Mrs. Long Early in Day on News of Shooting.

SENATOR'S FOES SORROW

His Washington Office Centre of Expressions Denouncing Baton Rouge Attack.

Special to THE NEW YORK TIMES.

HYDE PARK, N. Y., Sept. 9.—The resort to violence was denounced as un-American by President Roosevelt today in a statement expressing deep regret over the attack last night on Senator Long.

The attack on the Senator occurred after President Roosevelt had retired last night, and accordingly word did not reach him until he read the news in this morning's newspapers. His statement was his first act of the day.

"I reeply regret the attempt made upon the life of Senator Long of Louisiana," the President said. "The spirit of violence is un-American and has no place in a consideration of public affairs, least of all at a time when calm and dispassionate approach to the difficult problems of the day is so essential."

Coincident with the issuance of this statement from the Hyde Park house, the President joined with Mrs. Roosevelt in sending a private message of sympathy to Mrs. Long.

No one has opposed President Roosevelt's policies in more emphatic terms than the Louisiana Senator, but Mr. Roosevelt has been careful never to say or do anything that would bring the political disputes between them down to a personal level. His attitude, rather, has been one of patient waiting in the belief that time would demonstrate the wisdom of administration projects for which Senator Long wished to substitute his "share-the-wealth" program.

Special to THE NEW YORK TIMES.

NEW ORLEANS, La., Sept. 9.—The message received by Mrs. Long was signed by Marvin H. McIntyre, assistant secretary to the President. It read:

"The President and Mrs. Roosevelt ask me to extend to you and to the Senator their sympathy and good wishes for his recovery."

Capital Deplores Shooting.

By The Associated Press.

WASHINGTON, Sept. 9.—Senate colleagues and friends kept the telephone in Senator Long's Capitol office ringing almost unceasingly today with anxious inquiries. Politi-

Continued on Page Two.

House Inquiry Is Urged to Find Those 'Instigating' Long Shooting

Representative Finerty Asks That Elections Committee Act and Defends Filibuster Which Stopped Funds—Washington Observers Discuss the Political Phase.

Special to THE NEW YORK TIMES.

WASHINGTON, Sept. 9.—An investigation of the attempted assassination of Senator Long, and the men responsible for it, was proposed today by Representative Clare G. Fenerty of Pennsylvania, a member of the special committee appointed recently by Congress to inquire into the political activities of the Louisiana Senator.

"The murderous attempt on the life of Senator Long is to be deplored by all Americans who believe in our system of government," he said. "A Congressional committee which is about to investigate the political activities of Senator Long in Louisiana should investigate the men who were responsible for instigating the attempted assassination.

"I regard the attempt to wipe out Senator Long's life as much worse than the things that have been taking place in Louisiana. It is only fair at this juncture to say that Senator Long should not be severely criticized for stopping, by his filibuster, the funds for carrying out the provisions of the Social Security Act. As a matter of fact, every one knows that the President has ample funds to inaugurate the social security machinery.

"The attempted assassination may prevent the rise heretofore expected of an ultra-radical third party, headed by Senator Long, probably the most outstanding enemy of the administration in the Democratic ranks. Senator Long, according to his friends here, as the head of a new party, had fully determined to oppose the re-election of President Roosevelt. With him, according to political information here, were aligned Governor Talmadge and several other Democrats who have strayed away from the party as a result of New Deal policies, and particularly fears of a move to amend the Constitution vitally."

Even should Senator Long recover from his wound, the present indications are that he might not be able to make an aggressive campaign next year, such as he had planned, against the administration. However, politicians say that if he should regain his health quickly,

Continued on Page Three.

LONG BILLS PASSED BY GUARDED HOUSE

Gerrymandering Measure for Ousting Dr. Weiss's Father-in-Law Is Approved.

ONE FORCES GUN LISTING

Others Hit at Roosevelt, Fixing Jail Term for Federal Men 'Who Violate Constitution.'

By The Associated Press.

BATON ROUGE, La., Sept. 9.—In a subdued session, the House of Representatives today pushed through passage a new batch of bills which were sponsored by Senator Long and aimed at the Federal administration.

Even in the absence of their leader, the legislative followers of the Senator held firm against sporadic opposition, pushing ahead the program which had been described by the Senator as preserving "State's rights" against any encroachment by the Federal Government.

The Senate held a brief night meeting, remaining only long enough to refer all of the House-approved bills to the Finance Committee.

The Senators opened their session with a prayer by the Rev. C. E. Bordelon, pastor of the Church of the Nazarene, for the "life and health of a fellow citizen, our beloved senior Senator of Louisiana."

Armed guards stood at every door in the Capitol today, while all who entered were searched for weapons. Otherwise, legislative business proceeded much as if Senator Long were giving it his energetic personal attention.

Before tackling the anti-Roosevelt measures, the House passed a bill aimed at Judge B. H. Pavy of Opelousas, father-in-law of Long's slain assassin. Judge Pavy has been one of the Senator's principal opponents in St. Landry Parish for some time.

The bill, designed to open the way for Long's followers to oust Judge Pavy in the next election, would change the boundaries of his judicial district.

Anti-Roosevelt Bills Fought.

Few bills except those slapping at Roosevelt drew debate. Those were described by opponents as "political propaganda" to be "used on the stump."

One of the measures fixes a jail term for Federal agents exercising "unconstitutional" powers in the State.

It was aimed at Senator Long's opponents who have been placed in charge of New Deal activities in Louisiana.

Representative Isom Guillory, administration floor leader from St. Landry Parish, said the bill "provides that no Federal agent can come into the State and exercise a

Continued on Page Three.

STORY OF SHOOTING HEARD AT INQUEST

Reporter Tells Coroner He Saw Dr. Weiss Struggle With Long Bodyguard.

SIX THEN OPENED FIRE

Poured Bullets Into Prostrate Body as Senator Walked Away Holding Side.

By The Associated Press.

BATON ROUGE, La., Sept. 9.—The dramatic story of the attempt to assassinate Senator Huey P. Long in the $5,000,000 State House and the killing of his assailant, Dr. Carl A. Weiss, was related today by eye-witnesses at a coroner's inquest.

The coroner said an examination of Dr. Weiss's body showed it had thirty bullet holes in the front, twenty-nine in the back and two in the head.

C. E. Frampton, statistician for the State Attorney General's office and a reporter for The New Orleans Item-Tribune, told how he emerged from an office after hearing a shot and saw the Senator walking down the corridor, clasping his side.

He said he saw Murphy Roden, one of Long's bodyguards, and Dr. Weiss struggling. Then he told how Weiss was killed.

District Attorney John Fred Odom adjourned the inquest until 4 P. M. after the coroner's jury had heard Frampton and John d'Armond, who was near the scene of the shooting.

Heard Thirty or Forty Shots.

D'Armond said he was in the office of Governor Allen's secretary when he heard thirty or forty shots fired.

Frampton said only three or four second elapsed between the shots Weiss fired at Long and the volley from bodyguards, which killed the young physician.

Frampton, under questioning by the District Attorney, said:

"Immediately preceding the shooting I talked with Senator Long and then went to the Governor's office and telephoned my office in New Orleans. In response to questions propounded by my office, I again called Senator Long at the sergeant-at-arms office in the House and talked with him.

"Then I left and was about to open the double doors leading into the corridor where the shooting occurred when I heard a shot. As I opened the door, I saw Senator Long walking down the corridor clasping his side. As I stepped through the door I saw two men struggling, Murphy Roden and a man later identified as Dr. Carl A. Weiss. Then half a dozen men began firing at Dr. Weiss."

District Attorney Odom then drew

Continued on Page Two.

END COMES AT 6:10 A. M.

State Ruler Succumbs to Assassin's Bullet, in Coma at End.

THREE TRANSFUSIONS FAIL

Farewells Spoken by Family and Officials at Bedside When Hope Is Abandoned.

CHURCH RITES FOR SLAYER

Troops Ready for Baton Rouge, Quiet but Tense as Details of Tragic Drama Unfold.

Special to THE NEW YORK TIMES.

BATON ROUGE, La., Tuesday, Sept. 10.—United States Senator Huey P. Long died at 4:10 o'clock this morning (6:10 A. M., New York Time).

The last vestige of hope for recovery of the Senator, who was shot about 9:30 o'clock Sunday night by Dr. Carl Austin Weiss Jr., was abandoned just before midnight.

Frankly expressing the opinion that nothing could be done, physicians nevertheless had attempted a third blood transfusion at 11 P. M. in a last desperate effort to prolong his life.

Fighting for his life in Our Lady of the Lake Hospital here, where he was removed after a bullet had made two punctures in the colon and pierced a kidney, Senator Long had withstood an emergency operation and responded to a blood transfusion in such manner as to give his friends and family hope that with no complications he might survive.

Transfusions Fail to Help.

Just after noon yesterday, however, word spread in the capital that the former dictator of Louisiana had taken a turn for the worse. A second transfusion was hastily administered, and when this failed to result in immediate improvement in the Senator's condition, physicians began to despair of his recovery.

A third blood transfusion was administered just before midnight last night, a half hour after Senator Long had been placed under an oxygen tent.

After a hasty test of several volunteers, Dr. Willard Ellender, a member of the staff of the New Orleans Charity Hospital, and a brother of Allen Ellender, Speaker of the Louisiana House of Representatives, was selected.

The vitality of the powerful political figure continued to weaken despite all emergency measures.

Members of the Senator's immediate family and Governor O. K. Allen had left the hospital about 10:20 o'clock (12:20 A. M., E. S. D. T.) after having bade farewell to the Senator. He was then in a comatose state.

At times he slipped into delirium, although at less frequent intervals he would recognize those gathered at his bedside and talk rationally.

During the delirious periods, according to Earl Long, a brother, the Senator referred frequently to his new book, "My First Year in the White House," which was scheduled for publication in the near future.

Capital City Closely Guarded.

Legislators were inclined to regard the shooting as an individual affair with no indications of a general uprising in the State which might conceivably modify their program.

Nevertheless Baton Rouge swarmed all day with State troopers, holding off thousands of citizens who sought to approach the five-million-dollar skyscraper Capitol, where the shooting occurred, and the Our Lady of the Lake Hospital, where the Senator lay waging a desperate fight for his life.

While State police, armed with submachine guns and sawed-off shotguns, patrolled the city, Colonel E. P. Roy, their commander, issued orders to shoot down any photographer who attempted to make pictures near the Capitol or the hospital.

All persons approaching either building were compelled to undergo

Continued on Page Two.

Museum of the City of New York

The famous Lyric Theatre, on Third Avenue between 12th and 13th Streets in New York City.

Museum of the City of New York

The window of an A & P food store.

"All the News That's Fit to Print."

The New York Times.

LATE CITY EDITION
Partly cloudy today, temperature unchanged. Tomorrow cloudy, probably snow.
Temperatures Yesterday—Max., 21; min., 14.

VOL. LXXXV.....No. 28,466. Entered as Second-Class Matter, Postoffice, New York, N. Y. NEW YORK, WEDNESDAY, JANUARY 1, 1936. P TWO CENTS In New York City. | THREE CENTS Within 200 Miles | FOUR CENTS Elsewhere Except in 7th and 8th Postal Zones.

SWEDES ARE SLAIN AS ITALIANS BOMB A RED CROSS UNIT

9 REPORTED AMONG DEAD

23 Ethiopians Said to Be Victims in Wreck of Ambulance Corps.

STOCKHOLM IS INDIGNANT

Rome's Legation There Is Put Under Guard and Italians in City Are Menaced.

GREEK SYNOD PROTESTS

Orthodox Group in Athens Takes Italian Army to Task for Burning of Churches.

Special Cable to THE NEW YORK TIMES.

ADDIS ABABA, Dec. 31.—A radiogram received here this morning from the headquarters of Ras Desta Demtu at Nogheilli in southernmost Sidamo Province reported that a Swedish Red Cross unit near Dolo, on the Ethiopian-Italian Somaliland frontier, had been destroyed by Italian bombing planes yesterday morning. The unit was said to have been twenty miles from Dolo on the banks of the Ganale Doria River.

[Nine Swedes and twenty-three Ethiopians composing the unit were reported killed, according to The Associated Press, but a Reuters dispatch from London reported that the leader of the unit, Dr. Fride Hylander, and three other Swedes had been wounded instead of slain.]

The first news came from a wireless operator, who briefly announced to the government the total destruction of the unit. Ras Desta Demtu followed with a message to Doctor Hanner, the Swedish Consul here and head of the Swedish hospital, stating that the staff and equipment of the ambulance unit had been "destroyed" and asking for Red Cross airplanes to carry the leader of the unit, Doctor Fride Hylander, who was severely wounded, back to Addis Ababa. An airplane left Dessye this morning but was recalled. It is expected here tomorrow morning, as Italian mastery of the air makes flights in the Dessye area unsafe during the day.

The government meanwhile has asked Ras Desta Demtu for fuller details. Representatives of the Ethiopian Red Cross will fly to the Dolo area tomorrow to make a thorough inquiry.

Grave fears are entertained here for the lives of the rest of the unit. The Swedish flag on the Consulate and the Red Cross flag on the Red Cross office were lowered today.

Personnel Reported Killed.

By The Associated Press.

ADDIS ABABA, Dec. 31.—A report that a Red Cross ambulance unit of thirty-two persons was obliterated by a bombardment from Italian airplanes was received here today. Ras Desta Demtu, son-in-law of Emperor Haile Selassie and Ethiopian commander in the South, said in a wireless message that nine Swedes and twenty-three Ethiopians were killed in the rain of bombs. Red Cross officials here were without details.

Before this report was received the government issued a communiqué saying:

"Yesterday morning a Swedish Red Cross ambulance was bombarded by Italian planes 30 kilometers (about 19 miles) from Dolo, on the Ganale Doria River. The ambulance chief was injured.

[Dolo is on the frontier, between Ethiopia and Italian Somaliland.]

Casualty Reports Conflict.

LONDON Wednesday, Jan. 1 (Reuters). — Conflicting reports reached London today regarding the number of casualties in the bombing of a Swedish Red Cross unit in Southern Ethiopia by Italian planes.

Although Ras Desta Demtu, commander of the army to which the unit was attached, wirelessed Addis Ababa that all its members had been wiped out, another report reaching here from Paris said that all of the nine Swedes on the staff were believed killed except the commander, Dr. Fride Hylander; Dr. Eric Smith, Dr. Ake Holm and one unnamed assistant, all of whom were wounded. The Swedish Red Cross at Stockholm was informed

Continued on Page Twenty-four.

Carter Glass, Near 78, Snowballs a Reporter

By The Associated Press.

WASHINGTON, Dec. 31.—Senator Carter Glass came away from a White House luncheon today throwing snowballs—not at President Roosevelt but at a reporter.

"I landed a good one and then escaped in the automobile," the Senator announced as he arrived at his office, still chuckling.

"That boy acted as if he were going to throw one at me, so I picked up a large piece—it was hard, too—from the running board of the car and landed a good one."

The senior Virginia Senator will be 78 on Saturday.

NEUTRALITY POLICY PLIANT IN NEW BILL

Roosevelt, Hull and Congress Leaders Shape Measure for Discretionary Power.

MAY BE FIRST IN HOPPER

Speed Planned Both Because of African Situation and to Get the Jump on Nye.

Special to THE NEW YORK TIMES.

WASHINGTON, Dec. 31.—A comprehensive neutrality bill embracing both mandatory and discretionary features was agreed upon for submission to Congress at a White House conference this afternoon.

It will be one of the earliest legislative proposals made to the session, signifying the importance the administration attaches to it. The bill may be introduced the first day of the session; or, at least, that is the hope of Chairman Sam D. McReynolds of the House Committee on Foreign Affairs.

President Roosevelt summoned for the conference Secretary of State Cordell Hull; R. Walton Moore, Assistant Secretary of State; Senator Key Pittman, chairman of the Senate Foreign Relations Committee, and Mr. McReynolds. Late in the discussions, which lasted for an hour and a half, Representative John J. O'Connor of New York, chairman of the Committee on Rules, was called in. Significance was attached to the summarizing of the rules chieftain, in view of the desire for immediate action.

One reason for the prompt move contemplated is not only the uncertain East African situation, with its European aspects, but the fact that the present neutrality resolution expires on Feb. 29 and Congress probably will debate the proposals at length.

Seek to Get Jump on Nye.

Immediate submission of a neutrality bill also would give the administration the advantage of "getting the jump" on Senators Gerald P. Nye and Bennett C. Clark of the Senate Munitions Committee. These Senators are drafting a measure of an extreme mandatory character in contrast to the combined discretionary and mandatory provisions of the administration proposals.

Being first in with its bill, it was believed, would give the administration a tactical advantage in the battle that looms.

No final draft of the measure was completed today, but further conferences will be held by administration officials for this purpose.

In the absence of any authoritative word as to the details of the bill, it appeared that it would contain mandatory features with respect to the imposition of embargoes against belligerents on arms, ammunition and implements of war. This is expected to be a policy to be applied against both belligerents in any conflict.

In the field of conditional contraband, however, lies the possibility of discretionary authority for the President to impose embargoes in his judgment against belligerents with respect to shipments from this country of such prime war materials as oil, cotton, copper, steel and iron scraps.

Handicapped by Present Act.

No such authority resides in the present neutrality resolution, a circumstance which required President Roosevelt, in order to discourage the East African war, to appeal to American business men not to ship these goods in more than

Continued on Page Twenty-four.

EXUBERANT CITY GREETS LEAP YEAR WITH FESTIVE DIN

Noisy Thousands Jam Times Sq. —Record Spending Reported by Night Clubs and Hotels.

BARS ARE OPEN ALL NIGHT

Throngs Overflow Sidewalks —Theatres, Movies Crowded —Services at Cathedrals.

New Yorkers let themselves go last night in one of the most delirious welcomes to a New Year that even the most hard-bitten Broadway veterans could recall. Happier faces, more spontaneous shouting and clamoring with noise devices, heavier spending in night clubs, hotels and barrooms seemed to reflect, beyond all doubt, a definite return of mass confidence.

Police officials, white light habitues and veteran bartenders were unanimous in the opinion that many decades have passed since Broadway had witnessed any such demonstration as that which rocked the midtown district at midnight when the globe of white electric lights slid down the pole atop The Times Building and "1936" flashed into view.

Night clubs, hotels, dance halls, theatres, motion picture houses, etc., were jammed to the doors, and at the bars drinkers stood three deep, in most places, shouting their orders. In the better night clubs and in the leading hotels champagne actually flowed like water, though it was selling at from $6 to $15 a bottle. Most of the places patronized by the wealthy served nothing else.

Crowd Gathers Slowly.

It was a slow-gathering crowd at first, and observers mounted on hotel galleries pointed out great bare patches at various spots along Broadway and Seventh Avenue, but after 11:15 P. M., as if answering some mysterious summons, tremendous crowds began to pour in from the sidestreets, sweeping everything before them.

Chief Inspector John Seery, who is not easily awed by great assemblages, surveyed the spectacle from the police booth at Forty-sixth Street and Broadway and pronounced it "the greatest crowd in the history of Broadway."

"I've been at these things the past thirty years," he exclaimed, "but I've never seen anything like this." He estimated the crowd, at its height at midnight, numbered well above 1,000,000 persons.

At 10:30 P. M. single-lane traffic moved with difficulty through the horn-blowing, bell-jangling human tides, and the Chief Inspector sent his couriers out to order that pedestrian traffic be made one-way on the main arteries, to prevent serious jams. As best they could, the 1,200 policemen on duty kept the northbound crowds on Seventh Avenue, the southbound on Broadway.

Crowds Bulge Into Roadways.

By 11 P. M., despite the most earnest efforts of the patrolmen and the mounted men, the crowds bulged out over the curbs and began to cover the motor roadways. Mounted men had to be detached from curb duty to ride on the flanks of northbound and southbound trolley cars to clear the way for them. The laughing, riotous crowds made way,

Continued on Page Twenty-one.

New Taxes, Other Laws In Effect as 1936 Opens

By The Associated Press.

WASHINGTON, Dec. 31.—Here are some of the Federal enactments just becoming effective at midnight:

Social Security—Taxable year for unemployment pension levies begins, but operations of law involves future enactment of complementary legislation by States.

Gold Clause—Suits against the government for damages claimed from abrogation of the gold-payment clause in its contracts are barred henceforth.

Foreign Trade—Reciprocal trade pacts with Canada and Brazil and a convention with France ending "double taxation" of American firms there become operative.

Wealth Tax—Levies on gifts and new graduated taxes on corporate incomes.

Other legislation of less general effect, including safety-at-sea rules governing ship personnel discipline, watches and navigation, also went into effect.

NEW 'SHAKER' AIDS FIGHT ON QUAKES

Ruge Machine Reproduces Any Tremor, for a Study of Effects on Buildings.

VISION 100-MILE ROCKET

Scientists at St. Louis Meeting Hail the Goddard Ship's Future in Research.

By WILLIAM L. LAURENCE.

Special to THE NEW YORK TIMES.

ST. LOUIS, Dec. 31.—A new "earthquake machine," which makes it possible to reproduce in the laboratory for the first time all the intricate motions of destructive earthquakes hundreds of miles below the surface of the earth was described here today before the American Association for the Advancement of Science.

The new mechanical "earth shaker" was designed by Arthur C. Ruge of the Massachusetts Institute of Technology, and will be used to study the effects of earthquakes on buildings and other structures by means of scale models.

The report was presented for Mr. Ruge by Captain N. H. Heck of the Coast and Geodetic Survey.

The apparatus is a veritable "thinking machine," with a "memory" which can reproduce at will any earthquake ever recorded by a seismograph from any part of the world.

In studying the patterns of the forces which shake the earth in various localities, engineers will now be able to design buildings that could counteract these forces.

"Personalities" in Quakes.

Earthquakes have their individual "personalities," the lines of force in the bowels of the earth traveling different routes and creating their own patterns. To reproduce these patterns gives engineers a new weapon for controlling these forces of destruction.

Though complex in details, the general principles of the earthquake machine are relatively simple, and its control is scarcely more difficult than the operation of a radio receiving set.

A "shadowgraph," which is really an optical cam, is made from an

Continued on Page Eighteen.

British Air Liner Crashes in Mediterranean; Warship Finds Wreckage and Picks Up Pilot

By The Associated Press.

LONDON, Wednesday, Jan. 1.—The British destroyer Brilliant reported early today it had discovered the wreckage of the Imperial Airways liner City of Khartoum in the Mediterranean Sea, but had found only one member of the crew and none of the passengers. The plane was forced down between Mirabelle, Crete, and Alexandria, Egypt, yesterday.

The number of passengers was unknown, but the air liner carried a crew of four. The Brilliant wirelessed that it had picked up Pilot Vernon Gorry Wilson, who apparently had been swimming in the water from the time the plane came down, but that there was no trace of any other occupants.

Besides Wilson, the crew included Flight Engineer Amor, Wireless Operator Baker and Steward Richardson.

Two flying boats left Crete bound for Alexandria yesterday, but the passenger lists in London did not indicate which passengers were on the City of Khartoum.

After leaving Mirabelle at noon yesterday, the plane sent word at 5:30 P. M. to the Alexandria airport that it was "winding in" its wireless aerial preparatory to landing.

A party that set out in search of the City of Khartoum reported that it was still flying over the sea at 5:55. From that time it was not sighted and there was no word of it until the Brilliant radioed that it had found the wreckage of the flying boat.

A British destroyer from Alexandria and the air liner Hannibal were ordered to join the search.

Imperial Airways has several planes operating on the route between Europe and Africa, each of which is designed to carry sixteen passengers in addition to the crew.

The most recent serious airplane accident abroad resulted in eleven deaths when a Belgian air liner, en route to the airport at Croydon, England, crashed in the Tatsfield district of Surrey on Dec. 10. Seven passengers, including Sir John Carden, designer of airplane engines and army tanks, and the four members of the crew were killed.

The formation of ice on the wings was blamed for that accident. The French air service from Paris to Croydon had been cancelled earlier in the day because of the weather.

ERIE REPUBLICANS WILL CARRY FIGHT TO THE ASSEMBLY

Shun Caucus After Jaeckle Accuses Eaton of $100,000 Delegate Deal.

LATTER ADMITS AN OFFER

But Says He Rejected It—Ives Is Nominated for Speaker.

By W. A. WARN.

Special to THE NEW YORK TIMES.

ALBANY, Dec. 31.—With the six Republican Assemblymen from Erie County ready to take their fight over organization of the Assembly to the House floor at the opening of the Legislature tomorrow, the Republican Assembly caucus took a recess at 11:30 this evening until 10:30 A. M. tomorrow.

Before adjourning the Assemblymen nominated Irving M. Ives of Chenango, home county of Melvin C. Eaton, the State chairman, for Speaker of the Assembly. He served as floor leader last year.

The nomination was by a unanimous vote. The caucus also made nominations for other elective Assembly posts with the exception of that of clerk.

In addition to the Erie group, John G. Downs and Hamilton F. Potter, representatives of Suffolk County, where the former State chairman, W. Kingsland Macy, is the leader, remained away from the caucus. Mr. Macy, however, said he thought they would attend the caucus tomorrow.

Mr. Ives said he was still optimistic that the differences would be adjusted in time to effect organization of the lower house at the opening session.

Only Seventy-two Votes for Ives.

As things stood when the caucus ended for the night Mr. Ives was assured of only seventy-two votes including his own. Should the six Assemblymen from Erie and the two from Suffolk decide to take their fight to the floor, he would fail of election unless a number of Democratic Assemblymen should absent themselves. With all of the 149 members in attendance, seventy-five votes would be required for election.

It has been rumored that advances have been made to the Democrats to help Mr. Ives in the event of insurgency on the floor. But it was learned tonight that there was only a slim chance that any Democrat will be absent from his seat tomorrow when Governor Lehman is scheduled to address a joint session of both houses.

Assembly Democrats held a short and peaceful caucus and put forward Irwin Steingut as their choice for Speaker and Homer W. Story as their selection for Clerk. The action was merely a formality but it did insure the position of minority leader for Mr. Steingut, who served as Speaker in the last session, when the Democrats were in the majority.

Caucus After Hectic Day.

The meeting on Capitol Hill was opened after a hectic day replete with developments, of which the chief one was the charge made by Edwin F. Jaeckle, leader of Erie County, that Melvin C. Eaton, chairman of the State committee, had revealed to him that he had been negotiating for a $100,000 contribution to the State party fund in return for assurances that he would promote the election of one of two "metropolitan Republicans" as a delgate to the national convention.

When a recess of the caucus was first called Mr. Ives went into conference with the party Assemblymen from Erie in an effort to iron out differences which threaten to result in open warfare on the floor of the Assembly at the opening session of the Legislature tomorrow.

This was the second attempt by Mr. Ives to bring about harmony in his flock. Prior to the meeting of the Assemblymen, the six members from Erie, responding to a summons from him, appeared in his office at the Capitol, but they refused to be placated.

At the first conference Mr. Ives told the Erie men that the clerkship of the Assembly was at their disposal and that if they had no candidate he would suggest Walter J. Mahoney of Erie, president of the Association of Young Republican Clubs of the State of New York.

He was told by the Erie group that Mr. Mahoney was not acceptable. In his place they proposed former Assemblyman Ansley B. Borkowski of Buffalo.

"It would be to no purpose to discuss Mr. Berkowski because there can be no agreement on the first condition involving New York and Nassau Counties. Mr. Ives said.

At this the Erie Assemblymen marched down the hill to their hotel just as the caucus was about to start.

Meanwhile a tentative agreement

Continued on Page Twelve.

CONGRESS TO HEAR PRESIDENT IN A NIGHT SESSION FRIDAY; HE SEEKS A 'FIRESIDE' CHAT

Gold Clause Suits Are Rushed As Bondholders Beat 'Deadline'

New Actions Against Government Are Begun in Capital—Swiss Group Attacks Law as Unconstitutional—Another Case Involves Effect on Foreign Securities.

Special to THE NEW YORK TIMES.

WASHINGTON, Dec. 31.—The deadline was reached today for filing suits to compel payment of government obligations in gold or $1.69 for each dollar and litigants rushed to the courts with cases whose outcome may affect more than $8,000,000,000 in government securities.

Through a joint resolution adopted at the last session of Congress, the government gave holders of gold-clause securities until Jan. 1, 1936, to sue for the full gold value, outlawing suits attempted after that limit.

Among actions brought today were thirteen filed with the Court of Claims by Swiss holders of American obligations who protested the constitutionality of the Gold Reserve Act of 1934 and President Roosevelt's subsequent proclamation reducing the gold content of the dollar.

Typical of these cases, all filed by Waldron Kintzing Post of New York, was that of Fritz Muller, who demanded for his Liberty Bond $500 in former gold coin, or $846 in present equivalent.

It was said that these suits were the first attack on the government's gold laws made by foreign interests. The thirteen obligations involved totaled $110,000 and were all Liberty Bonds, except one Treasury note.

One Case in Supreme Court.

Otis Beall Kemp, a Washington lawyer, presented $100,000 in government gold bonds to the Treasury and demanded payment in gold or present equivalent. His request was refused, and he filed a suit before the Court of Claims closed its doors.

Notifying the District of Columbia Supreme Court that the Treasury had declined to pay more than the face value of six $1,000 Fourth Lib-

Continued on Page Six.

ERB TO CUT STAFF 1,662 MORE BY FEB. 1

Reduction of 4,762 Since Nov. 1 Will Reduce Expense to City by $509,000 a Month.

DUE TO TRANSFER TO WPA

23.8% Administrative Costs Held Too High and Move to Retrench Is Started.

Plans for dismissal of 1,662 more staff employes by Feb. 1 were announced yesterday by the Emergency Relief Bureau, bringing the total of staff curtailments to 4,762. The number of ERB staff employes by February will be 13,313 as compared with 18,075 on Nov. 1. The city will save $509,000 a month as compared with home relief expenditures in October.

A statement from the ERB headquarters at 902 Broadway yesterday declared that the retrenchment was necessary to reduce the administrative expense and place it in harmony with the reduction in the ERB clientele.

Since Aug. 1, when the Federal Government through the WPA took over the financing and administration of work relief, heretofore administered by the ERB, 170,000 heads of families and individuals have been taken off the home relief rolls and transferred to WPA jobs.

23 Per Cent for Administration.

An accounting made public yesterday by the ERB revealed that in November the ERB spent $7,933,000. Of this sum $1,890,000 was spent on salaries, supplies, electricity and telephone service, so that due to "exceptional and temporary conditions" approximately 23.8 cents of every dollar spent by the ERB that month went for administration.

Of the total of $8,584,000 spent in December, $1,844,000 was spent for salaries, supplies, rentals and telephone service.

"This means," the ERB statement explained, "that 21.4 cents of every dollar spent by the relief bureau went for administration. More than 90 per cent of these administrative expenses went for salary disbursements.

"This administrative ratio is too high and the share of the relief dollar going to the unemployed is too low. Our administrative overhead must be cut. We recognize that this was a temporary condition caused by the transfer of a large number if our clients to the WPA payroll. The high administrative ratio resulted from a drop in relief expenditures caused by WPA transfers and not by any increase of payroll. The Emergency Relief Bureau has pursued since August the policy of not hiring new personnel and not filling vacancies as these occurred. Until the WPA program was completed it was obviously impossible to curtail our administrative expenses because of the added burden placed upon the bureau by the task of transferring 170,000 clients to WPA jobs.

"Now that these transfers have

Continued on Page Eleven.

ICKES IN NEW ROW OVER BUILDING SITE

Plot Held by Pan American Union Is Wanted for the New Interior Building.

UNION'S PLANS ARE READY

Tunnel Is Already Built on Property to Connect Old and Projected Edifice.

Special to THE NEW YORK TIMES.

WASHINGTON, Dec. 31.—Secretary Ickes has become involved in another struggle here by seeking to acquire the site at Constitution and Virginia Avenues, already voted by Congress to the Pan American Union for construction of a new Pan American Building.

That the Secretary is trying to obtain a transfer of this land to the Department of the Interior for use in connection with the new $10,000,000 Interior Building was disclosed today by an official of the Pan American Union, who refused to be quoted.

This official revealed, however, that Secretary Ickes regarded possession of the land adjacent to the new Interior Building, which already is well advanced in construction, as essential to the plans of his department.

Rumors that President Roosevelt was supporting Mr. Ickes in his stand and that the transfer might be made without consent of Congress could not be confirmed.

Tunnel Is Already Built.

Pan American officials were determined not to cede the property, since plans for the construction of their own additional edifice already have been completed and a tunnel to connect it with the present Pan American Building has been finished.

According to one unconfirmed report, the President has placed a plan for transferring this valuable property to the Interior Department in the hands of the Fine Arts Commission, which passes upon building undertaking in the capital, with his recommendation for its adoption.

Officials of the Fine Arts Commission refused to comment upon this report, but indicated that the matter of transferring the property was under consideration in official circles.

Some sources were of the opinion that, since the land was put at the disposition of the Pan American Union by Congress, legal permission of Congress to transfer it would be required. Others said that it was possible that Mr. Roosevelt would commend to Congress that it approve an amendment granting Mr. Ickes's wish.

Reference to Congress Asked.

Senator King, chairman of the District of Columbia committee, said today that it appeared to him that Congress should have the right to act upon the question of any such transfer.

"While it might be desirable to transfer this property to the Interior Department, and I know nothing of the details of the situation,

Continued on Page Two.

SURPRISE TO THE CAPITOL

Sudden Shift in Plans Sets a Precedent for Opening a Session.

NATION WILL BE AUDIENCE

House Rule a Stumbling Block, but Leaders Agree on Ways to Preserve Formalities.

SNELL JOINS IN THE PACT

Washington Promptly Begins Asking if the Message Will Be Campaign Keynote.

By TURNER CATLEDGE.

Special to THE NEW YORK TIMES.

WASHINGTON, Dec. 31.—In a sudden change of plans for the opening of Congress President Roosevelt and Congressional leaders of both major parties agreed tonight to arrange a joint meeting of the Senate and House on Friday night to hear a personal delivery by the President of his annual message on "the state of the Union."

The Congressional leaders agreed to lay the proposal before both houses when they convene formally Friday noon. They understood that the President wanted to make his message a combination of sailing orders to Congress and fireside radio chat with the people on the accomplishments of his administration.

It will be the first time a President ever has delivered his opening message to Congress at a night session and the second time in history that a Congress has assembled at night to hear a Presidential communication delivered in person by the Chief Exectuive. President Wilson was the first, when he read his historic war message in April, 1917.

The suggestion of this unusual procedure was said to have come from the President himself. The first intimation that Speaker Byrns and other Congressional authorities had that any such plan was afoot was when radio brodcasters sought permission to install broadcasting equipment in the House chamber, where all joint sessions are held.

The House leaders were at first a bit upset over the idea that they had not been consulted, particularly since the rules furnished an obstacle which would have to be overcome if it was to be carried out. They were quickly appeased, however, and some time later, when Speaker Byrns and Representative Snell, the Republican floor leader, came from a conference with Vice President Garner and Senator McNary, the Republican Senate leader, they appeared in excellent spirits and pledged their best efforts to remove this obstacle.

House Rule Is a Problem.

The House has a rule that it may not be reconvened on the same day it is adjourned except by unanimous consent. Under the plan as agreed upon, both houses would be convened in regular session Friday noon, as provided by the Constitution, and would be adjourned or recessed until 9 P. M.

Should one member of the House object, unanimous consent to reconvene the House for the joint session would be denied. The Rules Committee could immediately submit a resolution, however, providing for suspension of the rule, which could be amended on two-thirds vote of the House.

Representative Snell, as the Republican leader, was understood to have included in his part of the agreement a pledge of his offices, first, to see to it that no Republican sharp-shooter objects to reconvening, and, second, to help pass the resolution suspending the unanimous consent rule should objection be made.

A concurrent resolution authorizing the joint session must be adopted by both the Senate and House, but leaders of each believed its adoption would be perfunctory.

The sudden shifting of plans for the opening day focused attention sharply upon the President's annual message. For the last few days it had been discussed but little in Congressional and political quarters, the chief attention being centered on the budget measure, in which the President is expected to disclose his policies with regard to

Continued on Page Two.

"All the News That's Fit to Print."

The New York Times.

LATE CITY EDITION
Cloudy, preceded by light rains this morning; temperature unchanged. Tomorrow fair, colder.
Temperatures Yesterday—Max., 56; min., 36.

Copyright, 1936, by The New York Times Company.

VOL. LXXXV....No. 28,472. Entered as Second-Class Matter, Postoffice, New York, N. Y. NEW YORK, TUESDAY, JANUARY 7, 1936. P TWO CENTS in New York City. | THREE CENTS Within 200 Miles | FOUR CENTS Elsewhere Except in 7th and 8th Postal Zones.

SUPREME COURT FINDS AAA UNCONSTITUTIONAL; 6 TO 3 VERDICT DOOMS OTHER NEW DEAL LAWS; ROOSEVELT STUDIES UPSET; MORE TAXES NEEDED

MAYOR REVIEWS 2-YEAR PROGRESS OF FUSION RULE

Defends City's Relief Program and Urges Cooperation to Uphold Sales Tax.

HAILS GAINS IN FINANCES

Expresses Hope That Bankers' Agreement Soon Will End—Housing Advance Praised.

REORGANIZATION IS PUSHED

Early Action by Aldermen Asked to Abolish Unnecessary County Offices.

Text of the Mayor's statement is printed on Page 16.

Mayor La Guardia marked the half-way point in his four-year term yesterday by reviewing sixteen of the city's major problems before the new Board of Aldermen, which met for the first time at City Hall.

At the same meeting Timothy J. Sullivan was re-elected vice chairman and became Acting Aldermanic President. He named thirteen Democrats to succeed Fusion appointees on the Aldermanic President's office staff, leaving two vacancies to be filled. Alderman Murray W. Stand, Manhattan Democrat, was elected floor-leader, and Alderman Frank A. Cunningham, Brooklyn Democrat, succeeded himself as chairman of the finance committee.

Relief problems occupied most of the Mayor's lengthy address to the Aldermen. In this, as well as in other city problems, he bespoke their cooperation, praising their previous contribution toward putting relief upon a pay-as-you-go basis. The Mayor said relief seemed to be a popular subject of attack inviting the fire of both the ultra-conservatives, who wanted no relief, and that of the ultra-radicals. Despite these circumstances, he said, the city had 170,000 cases on home relief and about 240,000 cases on work relief.

Changed Twice in Two Years.

In the last two years, he declared, the relief system has changed twice: once when the Federal Government took over CWA and then gave it back, and secondly when the Federal Government took over WPA. Praising the Federal Government's contribution toward the relief burden the Mayor said that for every dollar spent by the city for relief three additional dollars had come into the city from Federal and State sources.

He traced his efforts to cut the administrative cost of relief, mentioning his recent rejection of the January relief budget because this cost was too high. He challenged the spread of misinformation about relief, criticizing the stories of exaggerated salaries. Specifically, he said only five of the 15,466 relief employes on the payroll last month received more than $100 a week. By contrast with the Police, Fire, Hospitals and Sanitation Departments he said these salaries were small.

The Emergency Relief Bureau, the Mayor added, was strictly a non-political board, as its members had been recommended by private philanthropists. He said they received no salary, but a great deal of abuse despite the fact that no investigation had shown political dominance over them. The Mayor combated agitation about "carpetbaggers" on relief rolls. He showed that in 1934 the city had spent $49,000,000 for relief, the State $26,000,000 and the Federal Government $140,000,000 here. In 1935, he said, the city had spent $52,000,000, while $29,000,000 came from the State and $210,000,000 from the Federal Government.

With relief problems increasing through additional demands for hospitalization and other collateral relief services the Mayor insisted upon the need for extending the city's emergency relief taxes through 1936. He asked the Aldermen to cooperate in continuing the 2 per cent sales tax, and 3 per cent utility tax and the city's tax on gross business, all of which go directly for relief.

Great Strides in Housing.

Housing, with Federal aid, has made great strides in the last two years, Mayor La Guardia said. He pointed to the recently completed "First Houses" at Third Street and Avenue A as an example of modern progress. Model housing is going forward in the Williamsburg section of Brooklyn and in West Harlem, he added.

Turning to the referendum authorizing reorganization of county offices, he reminded the Aldermen

Continued on Page Sixteen.

Britain Fortifying Coast Of East African Colony

Wireless to THE NEW YORK TIMES.

NAIROBI, Kenya, Jan. 6.—The British Government has decided to fortify the port of Mombasa and two guns and a number of searchlights will arrive shortly. The East African Government will share the cost.

The Kenya Government contemplates the formation of a volunteer European unit of engineers and artillery. Mine-sweeping gear also is being introduced, for which Arab and African boatmen are being recruited by the local unit of the Royal Naval Volunteer Reserve.

The decision is not connected with the war in Ethiopia, because it has been planned for a considerable time.

GEM SHOP LOOTED AMID 5TH AV. CROWD

Thugs Also Brave Throngs in Rockefeller Center Plaza to Escape With $100,000.

PICK JEWELS CAREFULLY

Take Less Than 5 Minutes to Cow 3 in Store and Choose Most Valuable Pieces.

While thousands of out-of-town visitors wandered about the Sunken Plaza in Rockefeller Center at 11:10 A. M. yesterday, four armed robbers held up a jewelry store on the north side of the promenade in Rockefeller Plaza, Fifth Avenue, between Forty-ninth and Fiftieth Streets, and escaped with jewelry valued at from $100,000 to $150,000.

The store, owned by the Greenleaf & Crosby Company, Inc., is in the British Empire Building, 620 Fifth Avenue, and has two entrances. One is from the promenade, about twenty feet in from Fifth Avenue, and the other from the corridor of the building. Frosted glass windows on one side and heavy velvet drapes on the other effectively shield the interior from passers-by.

It took the four neatly dressed robbers less than five minutes to complete the hold-up. In that time they cowed the three men in the place, partly handcuffed one to a desk and put a piece of adhesive tape across his mouth, and selected thirty choice pieces of jewelry from the five show cases in the small store. The most valuable piece, the police said, was worth about $30,000. Then they stuffed the loot in a black leather zipper portfolio and walked out the promenade side and were lost in the crowd.

Workmen Busy Near By.

Directly outside of the store workmen on ladders were removing Christmas decorations from arches over the open court that divides the British Empire Building from the La Maison Française. On Fifth Avenue many worshipers were hastening toward St. Patrick's Cathedral, diagonally across the street, to attend services marking the Feast of the Epiphany.

Less than 200 feet from the scene of the hold-up a large number of persons were looking at the gondola used in the National Geographic Society's stratosphere flight.

Their first knowledge of the robbery was about two minutes after it had been completed, when the first of nine radio cars, that participated in the fruitless search for the bandits, arrived in response to an alarm sent through a protective agency.

As the other radio patrol cars came racing up Fifth Avenue with their sirens screaming, several thousand curious persons gathered near the store and it required several patrolmen to keep them in check.

Three of the robbers with pistols drawn came into the store from the building side as their companion entered from the other.

Seated at his desk in a corner of the store was the manager, Robert Mercadal of 33-12 Eighty-fifth Street, Jackson Heights, Queens. Standing near a showcase next to the desk were Walter Gibson, a salesman, of 30-26 Eighty-eighth Street, Jackson Heights, Queens, and Harry Oppenheimer of 1,185 Park Avenue, a jeweler associated with L. Heller & Son, Inc., of 608 Fifth Avenue, who was in the store on business.

The robbers went briskly to work. In a low-pitched voice the leader announced "This is a stick up." Then he motioned to Gibson and Oppenheimer to stand grouped around the seated manager as if they were in conference. "Stay there and keep your hands on the desk," he warned.

Loot Carefully Selected.

While two of the robbers kept the victims under guard the others carefully selected from the five showcases the jewelry they thought most valuable, pointedly ignoring

Continued on Page Six.

ROOSEVELT BUDGET ASKS $6,752,000,000; RELIEF AID NOT SET

$893,000,000 Cut in 'Regular' Estimates Is Upset by Court's Ban on AAA Taxes.

MESSAGE ON RELIEF LATER

Marked Reduction Planned in New Outlay—Deficit Is Put at $1,098,000,000 So Far.

The budget message and tables are printed on Pages 14 and 15.

By TURNER CATLEDGE.
Special to THE NEW YORK TIMES.

WASHINGTON, Jan. 6.—Hailing a turning point in the fiscal affairs of the government, with expenditures definitely declining and revenues at a peace-time high, President Roosevelt today submitted his budget to Congress with recommendations for a total of at least $6,752,000,000 to finance the multitudinous Federal activities for the fiscal year beginning July 1, 1936, and ending June 30, 1937.

This figure was $893,000,000 below the revised estimates for the current fiscal year, ending next June, but did not include any new recommendation for recovery and relief, which the President said he would submit later but in ample time for Congress to act at this session.

Rosy as was the President's budget picture when it left the White House, with its promise of a reduced deficit and no new taxes, it was dimmed while being delivered to the Senate and House by the decision of the Supreme Court invalidating the Agricultural Adjustment Act. The President contemplated tax collections of $5,654,000,000, more than $547,000,000 of which was to be from the processing levies outlawed by the court.

Counts Unexpended Relief Funds.

The budget figure was not final because of the undetermined amount to be asked for work relief. It contained only the unexpended balances carried over from former appropriations for this purpose, amounting to $1,103,000,000.

In its inconclusive form, the budget indicated a gross deficit for the fiscal year 1936-37 of $1,098,000,000, inclusive of a statutory payment of $580,000,000 on the public debt, or $2,136,000,000 less than the $3,234,000,000 estimated for the present fiscal year.

After the deduction for debt retirement, and a smaller item for retirement of national bank notes, the message forecast a net increase in the public debt of upward of $418,000,000, sending it to a total of $31,351,000,000.

The President indicated that he would be ready within two months to make a final estimate for work relief. The only assurance he ventured at this time was that the amount would not be nearly so large as the $4,880,000,000 of last year.

With continuing improvement in private business, and consequent lessening of unemployment rolls, the President hoped the item would not go appreciably higher than the unexpended balances, carried over from the $4,880,000,000 and other recovery and relief funds of the two previous years. He indicated with complete confidence that the amount would not be so high as to wipe out the estimated reduction in the deficit.

As to the Regular Budget.

Except for the missing relief estimate, the President asserted that the regular budget not only would be balanced during the fiscal year, but an actual surplus of $5,000,000 would be shown by June 30, 1937. He made his prediction despite a sharp increase in permanent expenditures, amounting to $843,000,000 over the like outlay for the present fiscal year.

The regular budget was placed at $5,069,000,000, which, with the preliminary relief estimate of $1,103,000,000 and the statutory debt retirement of $580,000,000, made up the gross recommendation of $6,752,000,000. The over-all total of new appropriations recommended, which are not necessarily identical to expenditures, totaled $6,400,000,000, including probable supplemental items, estimated at $600,000,000, for administering the Social Security, Railway Pensions, Guffey Coal and other acts passed at the last session.

Having no apparent inkling as to what the court might do with the processing taxes, the President reiterated the assurance that there would be no new taxes asked at this session; that is, if Congress made no demands upon the Treasury outside of present laws.

The court ruling made it almost certain, however, in the minds of Congressional leaders that new taxes would have to be found and a new plan evolved to continue the distribution of benefit payments to

Continued on Page Fifteen.

AAA Doubts Payers of Tax Can Regain $979,000,000

Special to THE NEW YORK TIMES.

WASHINGTON, Jan. 6.—AAA officials estimated, following the Supreme Court's decision today, that about $979,000,000 of processing taxes had been collected by the end of October, when the multitude of suits to prevent further imposition of the taxes first became apparent.

The officials were of the opinion that, since these collections already had been disbursed in benefit payments, they could not be recovered. The right of recovery, officials said, would hinge upon the consent of the Federal Government to be sued for payment of such disbursed amounts and the ability of processors to show that they had sustained financial loss as a result of the tax collections.

While there was no formal announcement of the government's position on the matter, the opinion of AAA heads was that the government would not consent to be sued in the first instance, and that, in the second, processors would be unable to show a financial loss by payment of the taxes because they had passed them on to the consumers in the form of higher prices.

FOOD SHARES RISE; STORE PRICES FALL

Food, Textile and Tobacco Stocks React Quickly in Market to AAA Decision.

INDUSTRIALS ARE LOWER

Drop Is Based on Fear That the Farmers' Buying Power Will Be Cut Down.

Prices of food, textile and tobacco stocks advanced sharply yesterday in response to the decision of the Supreme Court scrapping the AAA. Other groups of stocks advanced for a short time, and then sagged abruptly, as it became apparent that the court's ruling not only invalidated the processing taxes levied by the AAA, but also outlawed benefit payments to farmers, through which the purchasing power of rural areas has been sustained.

Gains of the food, textile, tobacco and other companies which have been paying processing taxes to the government ranged from 1 to 4½ points on the Stock Exchange. These advances were offset by losses ranging from 1 to 3¼ points in automobile, farm equipment and mail order stocks when the sweeping nature of the court's decision became known.

Confusion and uncertainty ruled the financial markets. At first, Wall Street was disposed to place emphasis on the scrapping of the processing taxes, and a heavy buying movement occurred in the food stocks. Gradually, however, traders began to look at the other side of the picture, the cessation of benefit payments to farmers, which have stimulated buying of automobiles, farm equipment and other manufactured goods in all agricul-

Continued on Page Twelve.

EMERGENCY PLAN FRAMED

Congress Would Vote $250,000,000 to Pay Sum Due Farmers.

TREASURY STOPS CHECKS

Benefit Payments and Even AAA Administrative Expenses Are Cut Off.

WON'T ABANDON CONTROL

Officials Determined to Find Some Way of Replacing Invalidated Processing Taxes.

Special to THE NEW YORK TIMES.

WASHINGTON, Jan. 6.—Visibly stunned by the sweeping nature of the Supreme Court's AAA decision, commodity and legal chiefs of the Agricultural Adjustment Administration met throughout the day and up to late tonight, seeking some way of keeping farm crops of the future within the limits of actual demand.

Plans were completed at a White House conference among President Roosevelt, AAA heads and the chairmen of the Senate and House Agricultural Committees for the immediate introduction of a bill appropriating $250,000,000 with which to meet the government's obligations to farmers for their actual fulfillment of 1935 production-control contracts.

The mailing of all benefit checks was halted under a ruling of the AAA controller as soon as the the court's decision had been read. It was announced on behalf of Secretary Morgenthau that "no further steps would be taken for the collection of processing taxes, new or old," and that "for the present no checks will be issued for rental or benefit payments or refunds or for administrative expenses."

Official Silence Ordered.

Early in the day all agencies affected by the court's decree clamped a tight lid on all official conjecture as to what course might be pursued by the administration. This enforced reticence was attributed to instructions received from the White House secretariat.

One thing was apparent from the feverish activity and conferences of officials at the White House and elsewhere. That was that the administration did not intend to take the Supreme Court opinion as meaning an end to production control programs. Chester C. Davis, AAA Administrator, said after his talk with the President that a number of plans were under discussion.

Prominent among these, he said, was a suggestion that processing taxes might still be levied in the form of special excise taxes on the commodities now called basic under the Adjustment Act. These funds, it was thought, might be used to finance intrastate crop adjustments under a plan for making Federal grants to States similar to those for road building.

The belief that "something might be worked out along these lines"

Continued on Page Eleven.

Payments Under AAA Were $1,200,000,000; Rental and Benefit Aid Over $927,459,777

Special to THE NEW YORK TIMES.

WASHINGTON, Jan. 6.—The Agricultural Adjustment Administration has paid out about $1,200,000,000 in various benefits and administrative costs under its program for restoring prosperity to farmers, according to official estimates.

For administrative expenses alone about $50,000,000 was disbursed from the proceeds of processing taxes and from an original appropriation of $100,000,000 carried in the law for financing incidental undertakings not properly deductible from the commodity levies.

For rental and benefit payments alone the AAA had paid out $927,459,777 through Sept. 30, 1935. This amount was exclusive of nearly $100,000,000 realized by cotton farmers from the sale of options taken on Farm Board supplies, profits on surplus stocks pooled with the Federal Government and later sold at higher prices, and other amounts obtained from disposition of exemption certificates under the Bankhead Act which were not needed in localities having short crops.

The total of all payments had increased by Dec. 19, 1935, to $1,126,190,080, on the basis of a capitulation of benefit checks signed in the AAA audit division.

By The Associated Press.

WASHINGTON, Jan. 6.—The AAA issued a statement tonight saying that $283,250,349 was due to farmers on 1935 adjustment programs. Total paid under the 1935 programs was $324,229,789.

The figures for cotton were $110,318,820 paid and $12,681,180 due; for wheat, $60,210,198 and $55,389,802; corn-hogs, $79,114,945 and $106,885,055; tobacco, $7,757,835 and $5,620,665; sugar, $55,000,000 and $35,000,000; peanuts, $2,429,249 and $1,153,534, and rice, $9,398,042 and $520,112.

For Winter wheat 1936 compliance program $66,000,000 was due.

AAA officials said that they have paid out $200,000,000 more than has been received in processing taxes.

Roosevelt Receives Decision With a Smile; Starts Conferences on Steps to Be Taken

Special to THE NEW YORK TIMES.

WASHINGTON, Jan. 6.—In an atmosphere of tranquillity President Roosevelt received word of the Supreme Court's decision against the AAA and the administration's farm program.

The President had just ended a conference with Secretary Wallace and other officials regarding new legislation designed to permit farm tenants to obtain loans, and was seated at his desk chatting with Secretary Dern and Marvin McIntyre, one of his secretaries, when the news bulletin of the decision was laid before him.

According to Secretary Dern, Mr. Roosevelt held the sheet of newsprint before him and "smiled."

"He seemed to take it all right," the Secretary said.

Within five minutes, Stephen T. Early of the White House secretariat announced that there would be "no comment today" by the President on the decision.

Possibly anticipating an adverse decision, Mr. Roosevelt had made no appointments for the afternoon. He immediately summoned a group of his advisers to the White House at 2:30 P. M. to discuss the court's majority and dissenting opinions.

Those in attendance were Secretary Wallace, Attorney General Cummings, Chester Davis, AAA Administrator; Senator Bankhead and Chairman Marvin Jones of the House Agriculture Committee.

Apparently the only definite decision made was to seek an appropriation from Congress to pay "up to today" payments on AAA contracts "entered into in good faith." Several drafts of bills were discussed at the meeting, according to Mr. Davis, but he indicated that no decision was made regarding them.

DECISION ASTOUNDS CONGRESS MEMBERS

Political Issue Involved Keeps All but a Few From Voicing Their Approval.

COMMENT ON PARTY LINES

Administration Men and Progressives Dispute Court's Right to Act.

Special to THE NEW YORK TIMES.

WASHINGTON, Jan. 6.—The far-reaching scope of the Supreme Court's decision invalidating the Agricultural Adjustment Act astounded members of Congress. There were few outspoken expressions of approval, however much certain members may have been pleased at the court's action, for farm relief, like the veterans' bonus, is a delicate question which cuts across party lines.

Senator Robinson, the majority leader in the Senate, said that it "is not practicable now to anticipate what action will be taken by the Congress."

Speaker Byrns expressed the opinion that "we will try to pass some sort of substitute legislation." The Democratic House floor leader, Representative Bankhead of Alabama, called the decision "distressing and disappointing."

If, as is generally believed, the administration has perfected plans to meet the situation created today, its legislative leaders have not been informed of them, to judge by their hesitant comment on the decision.

News Reaches the Senate.

The news reached the Senate while the clerk was reading President Roosevelt's budget message. A buzz of conversation between members broke out immediately and practically drowned out the clerk's voice

In the House, Democratic members seemed stunned by the news and it was obvious that the administration stalwarts and the farm group were overwhelmed by the extent of the court's dictum.

The Republicans were overjoyed, but few of them wanted to comment owing to the ticklish political situation. Those who did said that they had expected the decision and that it would be an aid to recovery.

Representative Warren of North Carolina took the floor to declare the House would continue some aid to farmers. Describing the decision as "a sickening and deadly blow" to farmers, he exclaimed:

"There are enough gentlemen in this Congress interested in the plight of the farmers to keep this Congress in session until Christmas if necessary in order to pass appropriate legislation."

Comment at the Capitol.

Some typical comments at the Capitol were:

SENATORS.

Republicans.

McNARY—I intend to introduce within a few days my own farm bill, providing for export debentures, domestic allotments and the equalization fee. The AAA is

Continued on Page Thirteen.

FARMERS ARE SPLIT ON END OF THE AAA

E. A. O'Neal, Federation Head, Urges Immediate Steps to Amend Constitution.

'FIGHT IS ON,' HE DECLARES

Independence Council Hails Blow to 'Bureaucrats Masquerading as Benefactors.'

Special to THE NEW YORK TIMES.

CHICAGO, Jan. 6.—Comment of farm leaders on the Supreme Court decision invalidating the Agricultural Adjustment Act varied widely tonight.

Edward A. O'Neal, head of the American Farm Bureau Federation, termed the ruling "a stunning blow to national economic recovery," while Stanley F. Morse, vice president of the Farmers Independence Council, welcomed it as a blow to "bureaucrats masquerading as benefactors."

Various shades of opinion were represented in between.

"The fight is on," said Mr. O'Neal. "And this time all gloves are off.

"Those who believe the American farmer is going to stand idly by and watch his program for economic equality and parity, for which he has fought more than a decade, swept in to the discard, will be badly mistaken.

"I consider this decision a stunning blow to national economic recovery.

"The program launched by organized agriculture must go forward. The American farmer will continue to fight for economic parity. Under the operations of the Agricultural Adjustment Act, the agricultural march toward parity, by giving farmers a purchasing power, has stimulated business revival throughout the country.

"We are going to look to Congress to take specific steps which will provide by legislation the mechanism by which agricultural parity is to be continued.

Change in Constitution Urged.

"It is up to Congress to provide that legislation within the provisions of the Constitution.

"If the Constitution in its present form makes it impossible for all groups to enjoy economic equality, steps will be taken immediately to amend the Constitution so that the rights of all groups and of all citizens will no longer be jeopardized.

"The laws of this country must protect equally all groups and classes. The day of special privilege for certain groups is over. The program which has just been overthrown by the court's finding is the farmers' own program. It was written by the farmers, and by no one else.

"Those who attacked this program, in preliminary hearings before Congressional committees, and in suits against the United States Department of Agriculture and the Agricultural Adjustment Administration, are enemies of the Republic.

"By their selfish attitude and

Continued on Page Twelve.

FARM ACT IS SWEPT AWAY

States' Rights 'Invaded' and Compliance Bought, Roberts Declares.

STONE LEADS HOT DISSENT

With Brandeis and Cardozo He Ridicules a 'Tortured' View of Constitution.

CONFUSION IS WIDESPREAD

Effect on Payments in Doubt—Republicans Are Jubilant, Seeing Campaign Aid.

Text of majority decision is on Page 10; minority, Page 11.

By ARTHUR KROCK.
Special to THE NEW YORK TIMES.

WASHINGTON, Jan. 6.—The Supreme Court by a two-thirds majority vote today demolished the Agricultural Adjustment Act (the AAA) as completely as last year it destroyed the NRA. These two were the major legislative devices of the New Deal for orderly recovery in industry and agriculture, and for economic parity between them.

The AAA, like the NRA before it, was held by the court majority to be an invasion of the rights of the States to regulate their local activities. It specifically banned the use of processing taxes to regulate crop production. The minority of three, in a bitter attack on the reasoning of their brethren, termed the decision a "tortured construction of the Constitution."

The decision definitely forecast the later invalidation of the cotton, potato, tobacco and other crop control laws, appeared definitely to doom the TVA, railroad pensions and Guffey coal-mining regulation acts, and seemed to offer to the New Deal only the device of a constitutional amendment to legalize all its recovery methods unless a State-aid plan can be used in the case of AAA.

Longer Congress Session Likely.

It foreshadowed a longer session of Congress, if the President and his aides decide to try to find a way around the stone-wall decision; cut down expected government revenues by at least half a billion; jeopardized the legality of $1,126,000,000 already distributed, and $979,000,000 already collected, in the processing taxes under AAA; and threw back the whole farm-relief issue into the lap of partisan politics, with a Presidential campaign at hand. Its finality struck the Department of Agriculture with bewilderment, brought silence to the White House and a general order that all the government agencies should be silent also.

But, while the NRA decision in the Schechter case was unanimous, today's evoked from Justice Stone, speaking also for Justices Brandeis and Cardozo, words burning enough to light fires of dissatisfaction in the vast areas where AAA enjoys great popularity. The objects of his legal attack, and sometimes scorn, were the Chief Justice of the United States, Justices Van Devanter, Sutherland, Butler, McReynolds and Roberts, who read the opinion of the majority.

Justice Stone, in brief, denied the view of his six colleagues that Congress, which they admitted had the right to levy processing taxes, had not the right to use them as they have been used.

The fate of the AAA came before the court with more dignity than did the NRA, which perished in a chicken-coop in Brooklyn. Receivers of the Hoosac Mills in 1933 declined to permit the company to pay the government's claim for processing taxes. A district court in Massachusetts ordered the moneys paid. The Circuit Court of Appeals reversed this ruling, and today the Supreme Court majority upheld the secondary Federal tribunal.

Budget Estimates Involved.

Since the lower court spoke, the AAA had been amended in an effort to cure defects arising out of loosely delegated power by Congress to the Secretary of Agriculture. But in a curt last sentence Justice Roberts swept away this Congressional effort, saying that,

Continued on Page Eleven.

"All the News That's Fit to Print."

The New York Times.

LATE CITY EDITION
Cloudy, slowly rising temperature today. Tomorrow cloudy, probably followed by rain or snow.
Temperatures Yesterday—Max., 31; min., 13.

VOL. LXXXV.....No. 28,486. Entered as Second-Class Matter, Postoffice, New York, N. Y. NEW YORK, TUESDAY, JANUARY 21, 1936. P TWO CENTS In New York City. | THREE CENTS Within 200 Miles | FOUR CENTS Elsewhere Except in 7th and 8th Postal Zones.

KING GEORGE V DIES PEACEFULLY IN SLEEP; PRINCE OF WALES BECOMES EDWARD VIII

BONUS BILL PASSES IN SENATE, 74 TO 16; HOUSE TO CONCUR

BOND PLAN IS TRIUMPHANT

All but 2 Minor Changes Are Beaten in 3-Hour Final Session.

INFLATIONISTS FIGHT HARD

But Neely Move to Pay With Currency and 'Protect' the Taxpayer Loses, 65-23.

14 'ANTIS' SWING OVER

Cost Put at $2,491,000,000 to $2,664,000,000 or More—House Acts Tomorrow.

Special to THE NEW YORK TIMES.

WASHINGTON, Jan. 20.—By a vote of 74 to 16 the Senate today passed after about three hours' further consideration the "baby bond" Soldiers' Bonus Bill, whose total cost in outlays soon and eventually is estimated at from $2,491,000,000 to $2,664,000,000.

The measure now goes to the House, where concurrence, in a vote set for Wednesday, is regarded as certain. The vote there is being deferred, Speaker Byrns said, to allow absent members to return in time to go on record on final passage.

The overwhelming Senate support of nearly 5 to 1 for prepayment of the adjusted compensation certificates, due in 1945, was furnished by fifty-six Democrats, fifteen Republicans, two Farmer-Laborites and one Progressive.

Only nine Democrats and seven Republicans were recorded against. Thirteen names had been called without a dissenting vote before Senator Brown answered "no."

Senator Bulkley voted against, as did Senators Burke and Byrd. Ten more names were called before the next opposing vote, that of Senator Couzens, the first Republican to vote "no."

The following, who voted for the baby bond bill today, had stood against the Patman currency bonus bill May 7:

Ashurst, Bailey, Barkley, Dieterich, Guffey, Harrison, Lonergan, Radcliffe, Robinson and Walsh, Democrats; Austin, Barbour, McNary and White, Republicans.

The following Senators who did not vote on passage of the Patman bill last May voted affirmatively today: Gore, O'Mahoney and Reynolds, Democrats, and Norbeck and Nye, Republicans.

Many Veterans in Gallery.

Veterans packed the galleries today and even the diplomatic section was well filled. Some of the veterans wore overcoats issued to them years ago or bought at salvage stores since. Some had apparently not shaved for several days. They had but one concern: this vote. They listened intently to the debate, to the voting—and departed jubilant.

High up in one of the public galleries Ray Murphy, National Commander of the American Legion, and James E. Van Zandt, National Commander of the Veterans of Foreign Wars, took their seats soon after the session began.

On the final roll-call they kept pace with the vote on their own tally sheets.

"I am pleased, that is all, and I have nothing more to say," Mr. Murphy said afterward as he was being congratulated on all sides.

The Senate had met at noon and at 3:14 P. M. the vote was over and adjournment was quickly taken. Most observers agreed that practically every member who voted for the bill today would vote to override a veto, should President Roosevelt return the bill after the expected concurrence of the House. That would more than suffice to override.

Instead of paying the cost of the certificates in cash, as provided in

Continued on Page Fourteen.

House Votes Bill to Bar Foreign Mail Divorces

Special to THE NEW YORK TIMES.

WASHINGTON, Jan. 20.—A bill designed to restrict "mail order" divorces from Mexico, by closing the mails to all correspondence about them, passed the House and went to the Senate today.

Introduced by Representative Healey of Massachusetts, the bill provides that every sort of communication designed to give information or to solicit divorce business in a foreign country is not mailable. The bill provides a fine of $5,000 and a maximum prison sentence of five years or both.

There has been much agitation for such a bill owing to the issuance of many fraudulent Mexican divorces.

DR. ROBINSON UNFIT, ALUMNI UNIT FINDS

City College Committee Holds President Lacks Qualities Vital to Leadership.

MINORITY DEFENDS RULE

12-to-4 Report on Long Study of Campus Disorders Is Sent to Graduates.

Dr. Frederick B. Robinson, president of City College, lacks "the human qualities necessary to achieve the widespread confidence of his faculty and his student body and to provide genuinely inspired, resourceful and socially imaginative leadership," in the opinion of a special committee of the Associate Alumni of the college. The committee for more than a year has been studying the factors responsible for the frequency of undergraduate demonstrations at the institution.

Twelve members of the committee signed the report, which was mailed last night to 1,500 members of the association. Four others signed a minority draft, warmly defending the record of the Robinson administration. One committeeman did not vote because of his inability to attend meetings.

The committee was appointed on Dec. 17, 1934, by Dr. Stephen P. Duggan, director of the Institute of International Education and then president of the alumni organization. His action followed adoption at the association's annual meeting of a resolution directing him to appoint a committee to "seek all significant facts concerning present conditions in the City College and the nature of the present relations between the administration and the student body and the staff."

The group was to have reported its findings at a special meeting of the alumni a month later, but the mass of testimony gathered by it in "tapping every disclosed source of authentic information" soon made it apparent that the committee's deliberations must be extended.

Alumni Meeting Called.

A special meeting of the Associate Alumni has been called for next Monday night at the college's Twenty-third Street building by Federal Judge Clarence G. Galston, president of the association. Both the majority and the minority reports will be discussed.

Signers of the majority draft were Dr. Henry Moskowitz, '99, chairman of the committee and executive adviser of the League of New York Theatres; Dr. Paul Abelson, impartial chairman in the arbitration of labor disputes; Dr. Louis I. Dublin, '01, third vice president of the Metropolitan Life Insurance Company; Waldemar Kaempffert, '97, science editor of THE NEW YORK TIMES; Professor Charles V. Morrill, '03, of the medical faculty of Cornell University; Dr. Henry Neumann, '00, leader of the Brooklyn Society for Ethical Culture; Louis Salant, '98, attorney; Jonas J. Shapiro, '18, attorney; Professor Herbert Wechsler, '28, of Columbia

Continued on Page Two.

QUICK AAA REFUND SHARPLY ORDERED BY SUPREME COURT

Mandate Is Swiftly Issued as Government Fights for 200 Millions Held in Escrow.

CONTRARY RULING CITED

President Calls Conference of Congress Leaders and Aides to Seek Way Out.

Special to THE NEW YORK TIMES.

WASHINGTON, Jan. 20.—With sudden swiftness breaking a precedent of years, the Supreme Court today issued mandates making immediately effective its recent decisions declaring the Agricultural Adjustment Act unconstitutional and ordering $200,000,000 of impounded AAA taxes returned to processors.

The impact of the action was immediately felt in administration circles. President Roosevelt summoned a group of Congressional and farm leaders to meet at the White House tomorrow to discuss the situation created by the release of the $200,000,000, and the farm situation in general.

Announcement of the court's mandates came two and a half hours after the justices had left the bench and entered upon a two-week recess to catch up with their work. Court attachés said they could not remember when the justices had acted so quickly except in urgent matters such as murder cases. Usually all orders are handed down from the bench while the court is in session, and it was assumed that this would be the procedure today.

One of the orders tersely refused a government request made earlier in the day for reopening of the Louisiana rice millers' case through which the $200,000,000 was ordered turned back to the processors. It also granted the mandate sought by the rice millers and directed that their own impounded $200,000 taxes be released. The other order directed immediate issuance of a mandate releasing $80,000 in the receivership proceedings of the Hoosac Mills, victors in the AAA case decided on Jan. 6.

President Is Urged to Act.

Court action came even while government officials were studying plans to prevent the sequestered $200,000,000 from being recovered by processors without stern legal fights. In the face of the justices' swift moves, the President's advisers urged him to call tomorrow's conference as the present tentative strategy might have to be materially altered.

At the White House, it is understood, will be Senators Bankhead and Smith, and Representative Jones of Texas, Congressional farm leaders and possibly Senator Robinson, Democratic floor leader and and Speaker Byrns. Secretary Wallace and Chester C. Davis of the AAA, M. G. White, solicitor for the Agricultural Department and representatives of the Treasury and Department of Justice are also expected to participate.

Government legal officers said it would be necessary for all processors with taxes impounded as part of the $200,000,000 to make applications in the Federal courts before their money could be released. The money, it was stated, would not be automatically given back without

Continued on Page Fifteen.

NEW KING 41 YEARS OLD

Adopts Name Edward in Signing Notice to London's Mayor.

FACES AN ARDUOUS LIFE

An Ardent Rider and Flier, He Must Settle Down to More Prosaic Tasks.

CORONATION A YEAR AWAY

Period of Court Mourning Will Precede It—Heir to Throne Flew to Sandringham.

By FREDERICK T. BIRCHALL.

Special Cable to THE NEW YORK TIMES.

LONDON, Tuesday, Jan. 21.—Edward VIII, who at the age of 41 became King at the moment of his father's death just before midnight, will be publicly proclaimed as sovereign today.

According to ancient custom, a crier will call out from the steps of the Royal Exchange, "The King is dead, long live the King!" Ceremonial announcements of the same description will be made in every city, town and village in the country.

The new King himself, who is still at Sandringham, may be expected to remain there in such seclusion as can be permitted to him. His great loss came to him last night after a day more strenuous than most of those he has experienced in a life already inured to ceremonial hardships and quick movement.

Visited London Sunday.

King Edward, then the Prince of Wales, was in London Sunday night, having come here in the afternoon to see Prime Minister Stanley Baldwin and to arrange for a special meeting of the Privy Council at Sandringham which, in King George's presence, would appoint a Council of State, now useless and obsolete, to act should the late monarch's illness have continued over a long period.

Edward, with his brother, the Duke of York, flew back to Sandringham yesterday morning and was present when the Privy Council appointed this intended Council of Regency. Thereafter he was close by his father's death chamber until the end came.

His first task was to console his weeping mother, to whom he is deeply attached and whose favorite son he is. But his duties as King brooked no delay. Already they pressed upon him, and within less than an hour of his father's death and his own accession to the throne he had undertaken his first official act as King by sending the following telegram:

Sandringham, 12:28 A. M.
Lord Mayor, London.
I am deeply grieved to inform you that my beloved father, the King, passed away peacefully at 11:55 P. M. tonight.
EDWARD.

In the next few days, until the funeral is over, he will have a foretaste of the strenuous life of duty awaiting him. He will be consulted upon a thousand matters of procedure. He must preside over

Continued on Page Nine.

THE DEAD KING.

THE NEW KING.

MONARCH'S DEATH STIRS WASHINGTON

Roosevelt Cables Condolences—He Is Expected to Appoint Special Envoy for Funeral.

GRIEF IN WORLD CAPITALS

Bitterness Abates in Rome—New Ruler Wins Praise in Berlin—Paris Is Moved.

Special to THE NEW YORK TIMES.

WASHINGTON, Jan. 20.—The death of King George caused deep sorrow and brought many expressions of grief here tonight. Official messages of condolence were sent to London by President Roosevelt and Secretary of State Cordell Hull.

Sir Ronald Lindsay, the British Ambassador, and the Ministers of Legations maintained here by British Dominions were deeply grieved. They refrained, however, from making any statements until they had been officially notified of the death by their governments.

Official periods of mourning will be declared by these missions by authority of royal decree. In addition to the British Embassy, there are maintained here legations of Canada, the Irish Free State and the Union of South Africa.

It is likely that President Roosevelt will designate a Special Ambassador to represent him at the funeral. A decision on this question, however, is being delayed until official information on the funeral arrangements has been received from the United States Embassy in London.

Messages by the President.

The following message was sent by the President to the new King:

It is with deep sorrow that I learn of the death of His Majesty your father. I send to you my profound sympathy and that of the people of the United States, in whose respect and affection he occupied a high and unique place. I had the privilege of knowing His Majesty during the war days and his passing brings to me personally a special sorrow.

To Dowager Queen Mary the President sent this message:

Mrs. Roosevelt and I extend to Your Majesty and to the members of your family our heartfelt sympathy and join you in mourning the loss of one whose high qualities of kindness and wisdom have been so powerful an influence for universal peace and justice.

Mr. Roosevelt also sent condolences to the governmental heads of the British Dominions—Australia, Canada, the Irish Free State, New Zealand and the Union of South Africa. The message to Lord Tweedsmuir, Governor General of Canada, was typical. It follows:

Upon the sad occasion of the death of His Majesty King George, I offer to Your Excel-

Continued on Page Five.

Death Bulletin Posted At Sandringham House

By The Associated Press.

SANDRINGHAM, England, Tuesday, Jan. 21.—The last bulletin posted at "Jubilee Gate" of Sandringham House was done with rural simplicity.

Down the darkened drive a bareheaded youth rode a bicycle with a dim oil lamp flickering in front of him.

In an old brown leather case, which he carried in one hand while the other gripped a handlebar, he brought the announcement of the death of the Sovereign of the world's largest empire.

The chimes of the Sandringham church clock, striking half an hour after midnight, had just died away. Only the moaning of the wind through the elms bordering the drive broke the silence.

The youth, without dismounting, delivered the case at the lodge gate to one of the King's servants. The bulletin was taken out of the case and slowly, in the light of two great lanterns of the lodge, the gatekeeper walked across the drive and posted it.

DEATH IS MOURNED BY WHOLE EMPIRE

Aga Khan Honors the King's Memory in Bombay—Salute Is Fired in Singapore.

Special Cable to THE NEW YORK TIMES.

LONDON, Tuesday, Jan. 21.—Within a few minutes of the King's death almost every corner of the earth had heard the news.

In Bombay, India, the Aga Khan declared that the "King Emperor was not only a great ruler but also a great man." He added:

"I am sure that the new King Emperor will, with his knowledge of the world and the whole empire, be a worthy successor."

Mahatma Gandhi announced from his Bombay sick bed that he had sent "respectful condolences" to the royal family through the Viceroy, the Earl of Willingdon.

In Cape Town most persons were asleep when the news of the King's death was received, but at the Government House high officials waited near telephones.

In Singapore a Royal Air Force airplane flying a long black streamer gave the first general indication that the King was dead. Later a battery fired a salute of seventy guns. Mohammedans, Hindus, Buddhists, Chinese and Jews, as well as Christians of all denominations, plan memorial services. The news of the death caused a suspension of Chinese New Year festivities and all markets were closed.

When Melbourne, Australia, received the news in the middle of the morning public offices were closed. All sports were canceled. Sir Isaacs, performing his last duty as Governor General of the Commonwealth, sent a message of sympathy to the royal family.

Hushed crowds in Wellington,

Continued on Page Five.

LONDON SADDENED BY NEWS OF DEATH

Hushed Crowd at Buckingham Palace Receives Word From Mourning Servant.

END SEEMED ANTICIPATED

Quietness in Piccadilly Circus Long Before Midnight Showed Stress of Nation.

By FERDINAND KUHN Jr.

Special Cable to THE NEW YORK TIMES

LONDON, Tuesday, Jan. 21.—The hand of death lay upon London last night. It was a stunned and silent crowd of several hundreds that stood outside Buckingham Palace just after midnight when the notice announcing that the King had died was posted on the railing.

Few in the crowd could read what it said, but all knew what it meant. Heads were bared as if by a common signal, and all conversation was hushed to whispers.

One light glowed in a window high up in a corner of the palace, but nothing else broke the gloom except the incessant popping of photographers' flashlights and the glare of headlights from automobiles that drew slowly up to the palace gates and then passed on.

Sentry Continues March.

The front of the palace loomed up dimly in the darkness across the great courtyard. A sentry in gray tramped back and forth along the sidewalk as though nothing had happened.

The crowd stayed long after midnight, apparently unwilling to believe or unable to realize the King had died. Some attraction had drawn those hundreds to the palace, although the King was lying at Sandringham far away. After all, it was his home in his capital and it was to this building that thousands had come to acclaim him on Armistice Day and hundreds of thousands on the sunlit morning of his Jubilee.

Slowly the crowd melted away. By this time newsboys were shouting through the empty streets near by and their black-bordered placards announced that a great reign had ended.

But the palace sentry still marched up and down as he had done all evening. One King had died but another was on the throne and Great Britain had not changed at all.

Even before the sad news came the King's capital seemed to anticipate it. The electric signs of Piccadilly Circus flashed their messages as brightly as ever, but all the gayety had gone out of the life of the great city.

The theatres were half empty and the streets were strangely deserted as millions sat at their radios listening for news from Sandringham.

Early in the evening a vaudeville program from a broadcasting studio

Continued on Page Ten.

FAMILY WITH KING AT END

Queen Breaks Down as Long Vigil Closes at Sandringham.

HOPE HAD RISEN A LITTLE

Ruler, 70, Had Signed Paper Naming Council of State to Act in Illness.

PARLIAMENT MEETS TODAY

Theatres and Stock Exchange to Be Closed and Ships at Sea Will Lower Flags.

Outline of the life and reign of King George V, Pages 5 to 10.

By CHARLES A. SELDEN.

Special Cable to THE NEW YORK TIMES.

LONDON, Tuesday, Jan. 21.—George V, King and Emperor, passed peacefully last night in the twenty-sixth year of his reign and the seventy-first year of his life out of a world in which he had faced manfully much tribulation. His eldest son, as Edward VIII, now reigns in his stead over Great Britain, Ireland and the great British Empire overseas.

The King died five minutes before midnight in his own house of Sandringham in Norfolkshire, where he had spent the happiest hours of his life. His Queen and his children, all except one—Henry, Duke of Gloucester, who is himself ill in London—were at the bedside as the King's life ebbed away.

He suffered no pain, the doctors say. Throughout the last twelve hours his strength slowly failed until he fell asleep.

Canterbury Blesses Him.

Just before the end came the Archbishop of Canterbury, the King's lifelong friend, who had shared this last vigil with the royal family, bent over the dying monarch and gave him a last blessing.

A few moments later life was extinct and the news was being telephoned to Prime Minister Stanley Baldwin by Sir John Simon, Secretary of State for Home Affairs, who in virtue of his office had also remained at Sandringham near the King's chamber, and the news was being flashed also to the whole world.

The official bulletin of the death was as follows:

Death came peacefully to the King at 11:55 o'clock tonight in the presence of Her Majesty the Queen, the Prince of Wales, the Duke of York, the Princess Royal and the Duke and Duchess of Kent.

FREDERIC WILLANS,
STANLEY HEWETT,
DAWSON OF PENN.

From the death chamber there are already coming affecting stories of the last solemn scene. The Queen, who had maintained a constant watch both day and night in the room adjoining the King's bedroom, had at last been persuaded to take some food. Then she joined the others at the bedside. When the end came the iron self-control she had kept through the long, anxious days broke down at last. She turned to her son, the new King, and they exchanged an affectionate embrace. Each looked lovingly at the dead monarch, then with slow steps they turned away and went to another room, where they did their best to console each other.

Ships to Lower Flags.

Immediately on hearing the news from Sandringham the Admiralty Office in London flashed it to all British warships on the seven seas. Today all their flags will fly at halfmast.

Parliament will convene today as by law it must without summons whenever a sovereign dies. Mr. Baldwin has fixed the hour for the session at 6 o'clock in the evening.

In the House of Commons the Speaker will take the chair wearing white bands on the sleeves of his black gown and black shoe-

Continued on Page Five.

Lieut. Giovannoli Named for Cheney Award; Faced Death in Rescues From Burning Plane

Special to THE NEW YORK TIMES

WASHINGTON, Jan. 20.—Lieutenant Robert K. Giovannoli of Lexington, Ky., on duty with the Army Air Corps at Dayton, was selected today to receive the Cheney Award for 1935, in recognition of his "extreme bravery" in the rescue of two men from a burning plane at Dayton on Oct. 30.

Lieutenant Giovannoli was born in 1904 in the District of Columbia, is a graduate of the University of Kentucky, and was commissioned in 1930.

"Probably not in the entire history of the Air Corps has a more heroic action been recorded," the War Department said of Lieutenant Giovannoli's act. An experimental bombing airplane crashed at Wright Field, the citation said in part, the wreckage catching fire. Three of the crew were rescued, but Major Ployer P. Hill, pilot, and Leslie Tower, civilian test pilot, were trapped in the all-metal cockpit.

Lieutenant Giovannoli extricated Tower through a window of the cabin. He returned, entered the compartment through the window, and began the task of releasing Major Hill. He worked with "seemingly superhuman energy" four or five minutes and cut loose with a pocket knife the pilot's shoe which had become wedged in the wreckage. He then raised the pilot and passed him through the window to waiting hands.

"His own escape from a perilous position in which he suffered serious and painful burns was considered miraculous," the citation said.

Major Hill died several hours later and Mr. Tower several days later.

"All the News That's Fit to Print."

The New York Times.

LATE CITY EDITION

Fair, slowly rising temperature today. Tomorrow cloudy, rising temperature, probably snow at night.

Temperatures Yesterday—Max., 25; min., 7.

VOL. LXXXV.....No. 28,493. Entered as Second-Class Matter, Postoffice, New York, N. Y. NEW YORK, TUESDAY, JANUARY 28, 1936. P TWO CENTS in New York City. | THREE CENTS Within 200 Miles | FOUR CENTS Elsewhere Except in 7th and 8th Postal Zones.

GRAZIANI'S DRIVE IN SOUTH MENACES ETHIOPIAN CAPITAL

Italians Close to Allata, Key to Mountain Range Guarding Addis Ababa.

DEFENDERS LOSE 15,000

5,000 Slain in 3-Day Fight in North and 10,000 in Two Southern Battles.

ETHIOPIA ADMITS CONCERN

Ras Desta Demtu's Armies Are Believed Shattered—Red Cross Unit Is Bombed.

By ARNALDO CORTESI.

Wireless to THE NEW YORK TIMES.

ROME, Jan. 27.—Today's official war bulletin again shifts interest to the Somaliland front, where General Rodolfo Graziani's smashing victory last week is assuming ever greater proportions. One index of the damage inflicted by the Italians is given by the Ethiopian casualties, which are now stated to total 10,000 killed.

At the same time it is announced that Italian columns commanded by the Fascist Militia General Agostini occupied Malca Murri on the Kenya frontier and that some Italian columns have advanced as far as Wadara, forty-three miles beyond Noghelli on the road to Allata.

With this latest move the Italians are now 280 miles beyond Dolo, the point from which their offensive started. Operations around Wadara bring Allata definitely within the range of General Graziani's threat.

Allata Key to the Capital.

Allata is a point of great strategic importance, because it not only controls all the principal Ethiopian lines of communication between Addis Ababa and the south, but also dominates a broad valley of great lakes, which are flanked on either side by tall mountain ranges, forming an accessible avenue of approach to Addis Ababa itself.

If General Graziani occupies Allata, it may be said that he is definitely within striking distance of the Ethiopian capital.

A glance at a map reveals the reasons why Allata is a point whose occupation may have far-reaching consequences on the progress of the campaign. It is the key to Addis Ababa from the south. It is on high ground, about 7,000 feet above the sea level, and easily defendable.

It is protected on the east by a region of rugged mountains, through which an army could advance only with the greatest difficulty, and to the west by the great lakes. It commands a corridor across comparatively flat low-lying ground, which leads to the foot of the mountain on which Addis Ababa rises.

Whether General Graziani has the strength to make a direct advance on Addis Ababa from the south is a matter on which opinions of military experts are divided. The difficulties are certainly enormous, owing chiefly to the great distances that have to be covered by Italian lines of communication. Allata is almost 600 miles from the Italian base at Mogadiscio, and Addis Ababa is another 170 miles further on.

Supply Problem Serious.

The problem of keeping an army supplied in enemy territory at great distances from its base over roads that would not be recognized as roads in any civilized country is one that seems absolutely insoluble to many critics. Mere possession of Allata, however, would place General Graziani in a very favorable position, since it would probably oblige the Ethiopians to split their forces. They would have no way of knowing whether the Italians intended to continue their advance on Addis Ababa from the south or to resume operations against Harar. They would have to guard both these danger spots and at the same time maintain their greatest army in the north to keep an eye on Marshal Pietro Badoglio, who may decide to resume operations at any moment.

General Graziani is thus able to select the weakest point in the Ethiopian defenses and to concentrate on it.

Today's war bulletin, after giving details of the booty captured by the Italians in their advance upon Noghelli, says that heavy iron chains and stocks were found, which had apparently been used by the Ethiopians for their slaves. Newspapers supplement this information with statements that in some places the Ethiopians, unable to remove their

Continued on Page Ten.

Edward Is Host to Five Kings On Eve of His Father's Funeral

Only Royalty and French President at State Dinner in London Palace—New Ruler Shows Great Interest in German Envoys at Later Reception to World Delegations.

By FERDINAND KUHN Jr.

Special Cable to THE NEW YORK TIMES.

LONDON, Jan. 27.—King Edward followed his father's precedent tonight by giving a dinner at Buckingham Palace for five Kings, Haakon of Norway, Christian of Denmark, Leopold of the Belgians, Boris of Bulgaria and Carol of Rumania, who have come to London for tomorrow's funeral of King George V.

President Albert Lebrun of France also was a guest of honor, for he is the head of a State and ranks as a reigning sovereign.

The dinner was served in the white and gold dining room on the famous gold plate which is used only on occasions of the greatest splendor. It was a smaller gathering than King George's dinner on the eve of King Edward VII's funeral in 1910, for the new King decided to invite only visiting Kings and royal personages, great and small.

It was said the King did not want Grand Duke Dimitri of Russia, one of his Romanoff cousins, to be asked to sit at the same table with Maxim Litvinoff, envoy of the Soviet republic which killed the Czar and drove the surviving Romanoffs into exile.

The result was that Norman H. Davis, the representative of the United States, Mr. Litvinoff and the representatives of other countries without crowns did not attend the dinner. They came afterward to a reception at which King Edward greeted all foreign dignitaries who had come for tomorrow's ceremonies.

A long line filed past the new King, each delegate receiving just a cordial handshake and a few words of greeting until the German Ambassador, Dr. Leopold von Hoesch, and Baron Constantin von Neurath, the German Foreign Minister, reached the King. Then the line had to wait while the King held a long, animated conversation with the Germans.

Every one in the room noticed the incident, which seemed to bear out stories of the new King's personal liking for Germans. It recalled

Continued on Page Nine.

GUN-RUNNING LAID TO AIRCRAFT HEADS

Four Men and Three Companies Are Indicted for Conspiracy During Gran Chaco War.

EXPORT LIST HELD FALSE

First Case Under Neutrality Law Is Based on Packing of Arms in Plane Crates.

Three corporations and four individuals were indicted here yesterday by a Federal grand jury for running machine guns to Bolivia during the war between that country and Paraguay growing out of the Gran Chaco boundary dispute.

The indictment, the first of its kind based on charges of violation of Congress's neutrality resolution, names the Curtiss-Wright Export Corporation, the Curtiss Aeroplane Motor Company and the Barr Shipping Company.

The individual defendants are John S. Allard, president of the Curtiss-Wright Export Corporation; Robert R. Barr, vice president of the Barr Shipping Company; Samuel J. Abelow, a shipping clerk employed by the Curtiss-Wright Export Corporation, and Clarence W. Webster, president of the Aircraft Export Corporation, which is not a defendant.

Two Counts Are Listed.

The indictment contains two counts, each of which is punishable by a maximum prison sentence of two years and a fine of $10,000. The first count charges that from May 29 to Sept. 28, 1934, the defendants "conspired to sell fifteen machine guns to Bolivia in violation of the joint resolution of Congress which prohibited the sale of arms, and to violate the proclamation of the President of the United States dated May 28, 1934."

The second count alleges that the defendants "conspired to defraud the United States of and concerning its governmental function and of the right to administer the Bureau of Customs of the Treasury Department in the clearance of vessels from ports of the United States to foreign ports."

It was a part of this conspiracy, according to the indictment, "that fifteen machine guns were packed and inserted for shipment in thirteen cases which contained three Curtiss Hawk planes and two Curtiss Falcons."

To conceal the true nature of the contents of the cases, the indictment charges, the defendants made out a shipper's export declaration "falsely describing the merchandise as airplanes and omitting to state that fifteen machine guns were included therein."

Inquiry Not Yet Completed.

The indictment was obtained by Martin Conboy, Special Assistant Attorney General, and his aides, Robert E. Pratt and John Goldstone. They have not completed their investigation, which was begun last year.

The guns mentioned in the indictment were said to have been packed in two of the fifteen cases which contained the five airplanes. The Secretary of State had permitted these and two guns mounted on parts of each of them to be shipped to South America, as they had been bought and paid for prior to the embargo.

The fifteen additional guns and

Continued on Page Ten.

GENERAL MOTORS EARNS $167,226,000

Net for 1935 Is Largest in 6 Years, Equaling $3.69 a Share on Common.

4TH QUARTER SETS RECORD

Income of $52,743,074 Is the Largest for Such a Period in Company's History.

The General Motors Corporation announced yesterday that its preliminary statement for 1935 showed a net profit of $167,226,000, equivalent to $3.69 a share on the average number of common shares outstanding during the year.

This represents the largest profit for any year since 1929. In 1934, the net profit was $94,769,131, equivalent to $1.99 a share on the common stock.

For the fourth quarter of last year, the indicated net profit was $52,743,074, equivalent to $1.23 a share, the largest fourth quarter profit in the twenty-eight years of the corporation's existence. In the fourth quarter of 1934, the net profit was $2,323,790.

The sharp gain in earnings in the final quarter of 1935 was caused partly by the presentation of the new 1936 auto models, which stimulated sales by giving the corporation its second introductory season of the year. In 1934, new models were not introduced until January.

Third Consecutive Increase.

Last year's gain in earnings represented the third consecutive increase in earnings. In 1932, the corporation's net profit was only $164,979; in 1933, it was $83,213,676, and in 1934, $94,769,131. The total for 1935 was exceeded only four times in the history of the company—in 1926, 1927, 1928 and 1929. The record, $276,468,108, was established in 1928, while the total for the following year, $248,282,268, represented the second largest earnings.

Including the profit for 1935, General Motors total net profit for its twenty-eight years amounts to $2,031,000,000.

Alfred P. Sloan, president of General Motors, said the report for last year was subject possibly to final adjustments.

"Preliminary net earnings available for dividends," he said, "including equities in the undivided profits or losses of subsidiary and affiliated companies not consolidated, for the year ended Dec. 31, 1935, amounted to $167,226,000. This compares with net earnings of $94,769,131 for the year 1934. After deducting dividends of $9,178,000 on the preferred stock, there remains $158,048,000, being the amount earned on the common shares outstanding, which compares with earnings on the common stock of $85,590,911 for the year 1934. These earnings for the year 1935 are after providing for depreciation of real estate, plant and equipment, amounting to approximately $35,000,000, which compares with a provision of $32,616,832 in the year 1934.

Liquid Assets Increase.

"The preliminary figure for cash, United States Government and other marketable securities at Dec. 31, 1935, amounted to $200,100,000, compared with $186,966,609 at Dec. 31, 1934. Preliminary net working capital at Dec. 31, 1935, amounted

Continued on Page Twelve.

RELIEF DUE TODAY AFTER FRIGID WAVE AGAIN GRIPS CITY

Slowly Rising Temperatures Also Expected Tomorrow—Snow Possible at Night.

31,603 WORK ON STREETS

Municipal Lodging House Cares for 7,000 Nightly—Nation's Toll 250.

Following a new cold wave that struck the city yesterday and was expected to drive the mercury to zero or lower early this morning, the weather will moderate somewhat later in the day, according to the official forecast last night. Continued rising temperatures were predicted for tomorrow, with light snow probable tomorrow night.

The renewed wave of cold swept into New York late yesterday while most of the nation continued to shiver in a vast ice-locked area from Maine to Montana and as far south as the Gulf States.

Weather observers in Chicago and other parts of the Midwest described the cold as the most severe and prolonged of the century. Fifteen additional deaths attributed to the weather during the day by The Associated Press brought the nation-wide total to 250.

In New York an army of snow-removal forces continued its battle to clear the ice-coated streets, its work slowed by temperatures that steadily fell to a low of 7 above at 5 P. M. and by the strong north to northwest winds that lashed the city.

Record Cold Likely Today.

The record low for the date, 1 below zero, was established in 1927. The same mark is the record for Jan. 28, set in 1925, and weather officials said last night that this mark might be equaled or shattered early this morning. Today the temperature is not expected to rise higher than 15 above zero at any time.

Yesterday's hourly temperatures were:

Midnight	25	2 P. M.	13
1 A. M.	22	3 P. M.	10
2 A. M.	22	4 P. M.	10
3 A. M.	20	5 P. M.	7
4 A. M.	19	6 P. M.	8
5 A. M.	20	7 P. M.	9
6 A. M.	18	8 P. M.	8
7 A. M.	19	9 P. M.	9
8 A. M.	20	10 P. M.	9
9 A. M.	18	11 P. M.	9
10 A. M.	15	Midnight	*12
11 A. M.	14	1 A. M.	*12
Noon	12	3 A. M.	*12
1 P. M.	10		

*Unofficial, at Times Square. The last official registration was at 11 P. M., at which time the unofficial reading was 3 degrees higher.

Traffic Accidents Continue.

Traffic accidents, fires, minor mishaps of pedestrians on treacherous thoroughfares and victims of frostbite and exposure continued to be reported.

Thomas W. Hammond, Commissioner of Sanitation, said yesterday afternoon that 31,603 men were working at snow removal. Of these 9,500 were regular Sanitation Department employes, 1,200 extra drivers, 1,397 Borough Presidents' employes; 5,352 contractors' employes, 9,618 Emergency Relief Bureau men and 4,536 WPA workers.

Those in the Sanitation Department used 637 pieces of its automotive equipment, including cross-walk plows, truck plows for piling ice and snow, loading machines and

Continued on Page Thirteen.

HOUSE DEMOCRATS APPLAUD ATTACK ON SMITH SPEECH

Rise in Ovation as Woodrum Calls Him the 'Party's Best Walker-Outer.'

FISH, REPLYING, IS BOOED

Republicans at Albany Lay Plans to Make Campaign Use of New Aid.

Special to THE NEW YORK TIMES.

WASHINGTON, Jan. 27.—Alfred E. Smith's speech before the American Liberty League stirred up a caustic debate in the House today, and an attack on the New Yorker by Representative Woodrum of Virginia for his threat to "take a walk" from the Philadelphia convention brought the Democratic members to their feet in a noisy ovation. The chamber was unusually well filled for a Monday.

Mr. Woodrum declared that the former Democratic nominee for the Presidency had already taken his walk and "moved up town," where he could enjoy daily the plaudits of such people as sponsored his address here Saturday night.

The Virginian drew a quick reply from Representative Fish of New York, who, after being jeered and booed, asserted that "where the feathers fly is where the shot hit."

Senate Democrats held their fire today, committed to a gentleman's agreement to keep quiet until Senator Robinson, their leader, delivers the official party answer to Mr. Smith tomorrow night. Mr. Robinson today gave his intended radio speech the title: "The Hands of Esau."

Assails League's Membership.

Opening with the assertion that Mr. Smith had "moved up town," Mr. Woodrum assailed his speech, saying it reminded him of county fairs where two locomotives were run together head on because an American "will go anyhere to see somebody bust hell out of something."

The Liberty League, said Mr. Woodrum, was made up of three groups: first, the Republicans; second, "a small group of disgruntled, disillusioned, disappointed political has-beens," and third, "political nondescripts who hope to manipulate parties to their own interest and advantage."

The last, he said, would be for any party they could control, although they might contribute to the war chest of two parties.

Mr. Woodrum charged Mr. Smith with running out on the Democrats' original prohibition plank at Houston in 1928, thus causing his own State of Virginia to go into the Republican line that year.

"He took a walk some time ago, for I submit you can't walk out of a place you have never been in," he said. "In fact he is the party's best walker-outer. How well do we remember the little walk he took in Chicago, he and little Johnny Raskob, and little Jouett Shouse, and those other spoiled little boys who can't take it. No, he took the walk in Chicago and is still walking and he just happened to stop in Washington the other night on his hike."

Fish "Endorses" Smith Ideas.

When Mr. Woodrum closed, the Democrats arose as a unit and cheered.

Representative Fish, in joining

Continued on Page Four.

Mexican Catholics Denounce Curbs Anew; Prelates Dispute Cardenas in Open Letter

By The Associated Press.

MEXICO, D. F., Jan. 27.—Declaring that "a state of religious persecution exists in Mexico," the Catholic Episcopate of Mexico, in an open letter to President Lazaro Cardenas made public today, asked for the restoration of certain church liberties.

The statement, dated Nov. 23, 1935, and signed by all Mexican Archbishops and Bishops, replied to a government announcement of Nov. 1 that turned down a petition for modification of laws regulating the church's activities and its rights to own property.

The Archbishops and Bishops said they could not accept the official viewpoint that the church enjoyed religious liberty, and they took special exception to the statement that socialistic education, by preventing instruction in any specific religion, "respects all religions."

"The real reason why religious instruction is not allowed has been repeatedly given," the church statement said. "It has been said to the point of satiation that religious education is prohibited because it is harmful to the souls of children, since through it are communicated errors, superstitions and all kinds of blunders."

The statement contained a petition in which the church asked the government:

That it restore to Catholics all churches seized or closed since 1914, as those now open are insufficient for the 16,000,000 Catholics in Mexico.

That it approve future petitions for the opening of new churches.

That State Legislatures be forced to abrogate laws "illegally" limiting the number of priests allowed to officiate in each State.

That Catholic seminaries "illegally" closed be permitted to reopen.

That church annexes be restored in order to permit installation of offices and homes for priests.

That the Secretariat of Education be ordered to prohibit teachers from giving anti-religious instruction and that anti-religious posters and propaganda be removed from the schools.

BONUS BILL BECOMES LAW; REPASSED IN SENATE, 76-19; PAYMENT WILL BE SPEEDED

Procedure to Get Bonus

By The Associated Press.

WASHINGTON, Jan. 27.—Here are the steps necessary for a World War veteran to exchange his bonus certificate for cashable bonds, based on the advice of the White House and veterans' organizations:

Blanks to be used in applying for bonds will be mailed by the Veterans Administration to all its field officers and local offices of the veterans' organizations.

If a veteran has not borrowed on his certificate and has it in his possession, he should send it with his application to the nearest regional office of the Veterans Administration or to the central office in Washington.

If a loan is outstanding against the certificate, the application should be sent to the Veterans Administration office where the loan was obtained.

If the veteran has made a certificate loan at a bank, he should send his application direct to the Veterans Administration in Washington.

After filing his application, the veteran need take no further action, as his account will be checked by the Veterans Administration, forwarded to the Treasury, and the amount due him will be sent him in bonds dated June 15, 1936, of $50 each. Odd amounts will be paid by a government check.

JAIL THREAT AIMED AT TOWNSENDITES

Congressmen Consider Invoking Act Requiring Reports on Campaign Funds.

NONE OFFERED BY GROUP

Chicagoans Receive Senate Query on Money Given to Anti-New Deal Bodies.

Special to THE NEW YORK TIMES.

WASHINGTON, Jan. 27.—Invocation of the Corrupt Practices Act, with its heavy fines and jail sentences, against the leaders of the Townsend old-age pension movement, is being considered in Congress.

The charges would be based on the failure of the movement to file with the clerk of the House an accounting of receipts and expenditures for the past year, as required of all organizations attempting to influence Federal elections in two or more States under the terms of that act.

It was made clear, however, that there is no present intention to press for criminal action, although it is contended that the Townsend leaders, who have claimed the credit for the success of candidates in numerous Federal elections, are at the present time subject to the penalties of the act.

Warning to Be Given.

Instead, the plan is to take the floor of the House and call the attention of the heads of the Townsend movement to their alleged derelictions. In this way, it is hoped, the Townsendites will be induced to file their accounting and the inner activities of the group will thus in some measure be revealed.

The attack on the floor will be made with the implied threat of a complaint to the Department of Justice should the Townsendites fail to comply.

Behind the immediate strategy lies the fact that at least one resolution for an investigation of the entire Townsend movement has already been introduced by Representative Zioncheck of Washington. Should the present movement succeed in forcing filing under oath, the leaders of the group feel that these statements would make useful material for any investigation.

Charges that the plan itself constitutes a "racket" were made by Representative Zioncheck in introducing the resolution.

Records Not Filed by Group.

No record of expenditures has been filed by the Townsend group for March, June or September or on Jan. 1 of this year, when reports were required under the law.

Representative Engle of Michigan today presented a detailed analysis of the cost of the Townsend plan, which would pay a pension of $200 per month to every person over the age of 60 upon his promise to spend it every month and to engage in no gainful labor. The pensions would be financed by a transaction tax of 2 per cent.

Assuming that the plan would cost $24,000,000,000 per year, Mr. Engle found that the per capita cost of paying it would be $195 per man, woman and child in America.

Special to THE NEW YORK TIMES.

CHICAGO, Jan. 27.—Questionnaires issued by the Senate Lobby

Continued on Page Three.

FARM PLAN TO RELY ON STATES' RIGHTS

Permanent Program Starting in 1938 Will Be 'Wholly Constitutional,' It Is Said.

DOUBT ON STOP-GAP LAW

But C. C. Davis Says Neither He Nor Wallace Is Uneasy Over Conservation Scheme.

Special to THE NEW YORK TIMES.

WASHINGTON, Jan. 27.—Through Chester C. Davis, Farm Administrator, the Roosevelt administration today gave word of its intention to rely entirely on the principle of States' rights in carrying out its permanent program of agricultural recovery. The program calls for operation within limits prescribed by the Supreme Court in its AAA decision.

With this explanation passed all prospect of an administration drive within the next few years for a constitutional amendment to make valid the production control contracts outlawed by the court's decision in the Hoosac Mills case.

Although the probability of such a move had been diminishing from day to day, Mr. Davis sounded the death knell to any such procedure when, after several appearances before Senate and House Committees on Agriculture in executive sessions, he agreed this afternoon to outline the administration's objectives.

Mr. Davis agreed that there remained some doubt in the minds of members of both Congressional committees as to the constitutionality of the so-called stop-gap program provided in the pending Bankhead bill permitting federally subsidized soil conservation practices but said that neither he nor Secretary Wallace had any such doubts.

As to the more permanent program, proposed to be started in 1938, Mr. Davis said:

"I think there isn't any question at all that when the program gets on a States' relation basis, the program will be wholly constitutional in every respect."

Mr. Davis replied to inquiries as to the fundamental constitutionality of the proposed interim program with a citation from the Supreme Court's decision in McCullough v. Maryland, wherein it was held:

"Let the end be legitimate, let it be within the scope of the Constitution, and all means which are appropriate, which are plainly adapted to that end, which are not prohibited but consistent with the letter and spirit of the Constitution are constitutional."

The objectives sought to be attained by the administration in its substitute farm program were listed by Mr. Davis as the protection and upbuilding of the soil, the assurance of an adequate supply of farm products to consumers, and the reestablishment and maintenance of the purchasing power of the farmers.

He differed with the Supreme Court as to the primary purposes sought to be attained through the Agricultural Adjustment Act, explaining that the end was to reestablish the purchasing power of

Continued on Page Five.

PRESIDENT ACTS QUICKLY

Sets Machinery Going but Asks Veterans to Be Patient.

HUGE TASK BY JUNE 15

Seven Million Interest Calculations Required With 3,000 More Clerks to Be Hired.

PLEA MADE TO HOLD BONDS

Ex-Service Men's Leaders Urge Against Cashing In at Once Unless Need Is Pressing.

Special to THE NEW YORK TIMES.

WASHINGTON, Jan. 27.—The $2,491,000,000 "baby bond" Bonus Bill became law at 1:30 o'clock this afternoon when the Senate voted 76 to 19 to override President Roosevelt's veto. Every member voted.

Acting quickly after the vote was announced, President Roosevelt ordered the Veterans Administration and coordinated agencies to make preparations for carrying out the new law "as expeditiously as accuracy will permit." He called attention at the same time to the fact that it would be a tremendous job to issue and distribute the bonds and cash by June 15.

Secretary Morgenthau, who will supervise the printing of the bonds and probably their distribution to the veterans, likewise stated that it was a tremendous job. He said, however, that everything humanly possible would be done to complete the task on time.

Confer With the President.

From the Capitol, where they listened to the debate and vote on overriding the President's veto, the national commanders of three veterans organizations went to the White House to assure Mr. Roosevelt that they would do everything within their power to dissuade veterans from cashing the bonds until the maturity date in 1945.

A statement issued later said that "the President, as well as the commanders of the ex-service organizations, feel that the veterans should consider first of all the protection of their families."

The veterans' leaders who conferred with the President included Commanders Ray Murphy of the American Legion, James E. Van Zandt of the Veterans of Foreign Wars and M. A. Harlan, Disabled American Veterans.

Despite the order from President Roosevelt, it was reported tonight that it would be almost impossible to complete the preliminary work in time to distribute the baby bonds to applicants by June 15, the date provided that veterans may cash them at postoffices or other places designated by the Secretary of the Treasury.

Veterans in Galleries Cheer.

Cheers from veterans gathered in the Senate galleries, and scattered applause from the floor, greeted the announcement of the vote by Vice President Garner. He made no effort to still the cheering, and veterans piled quickly from the galleries.

Commanders Murphy, Van Zandt and Harlan sat silent when the vote was announced, but John Thomas Taylor, head lobbyist for the American Legion, stood and waved his hand as he beamed upon near-by persons who were cheering.

So great was the throng seeking admission to the galleries that wives of Senators and other "privileged" guests were unable to get inside.

Fifty-seven Democrats and sixteen Republicans, with the lone Progressive and two Farmer-Labor Senators, voted to override the veto, while twelve Democrats and seven Republicans voted to sustain the President.

On passage of the bill last Monday in the Senate the vote was 74 to 16. Today Senators Connally and Fletcher, then paired against the bill, and Senator Tydings, who was absent, voted to sustain the President.

TEXT OF FIRST STATEMENT.

The first White House statement, that on the President's order for preparations to pay the bonus, read:

"In view of the fact that Congress has enacted the law authorizing the

Continued on Page Two.

"All the News That's Fit to Print."

The New York Times.

LATE CITY EDITION
Rain or snow today, colder tonight. Tomorrow fair and somewhat colder.
Temperatures Yesterday—Max., 45; min., 32.

VOL. LXXXV.....No. 28,514 | Entered as Second-Class Matter, Postoffice, New York, N. Y. | NEW YORK, TUESDAY, FEBRUARY 18, 1936. | PP | TWO CENTS in New York City. | THREE CENTS Within 200 Miles | FOUR CENTS Elsewhere Except in 7th and 8th Postal Zones.

LEHMAN MESSAGE DEMANDS PASSAGE OF HIS CRIME BILLS

HE WARNS OF REAL FIGHT

Executive Repeats State Must Have Modern 'Defense Weapons.'

ASKS LEGISLATURE'S AIMS

Assembly Asks Him to Name Groups He Accused — He Promises Reply on Radio.

CITY INQUIRY IS SOUGHT

Assemblyman E. S. Moran Demands Investigation of La Guardia.

The text of Governor Lehman's message is printed on Page 4.

By W. A. WARN.
Special to THE NEW YORK TIMES.

ALBANY, Feb. 17.—Governor Lehman sent to the Legislature a message today renewing his declaration of war on organized crime, asserting that he intended to discharge his "full duty and responsibility" and asking the lawmakers to discharge theirs.

In reply the Assembly late tonight adopted a resolution calling upon the Governor to name the members of that body whom he had reason to believe might have been improperly influenced in their actions in opposition to some of his anti-crime bills.

In a statement last week the Governor said that he was "disturbed" at the attitude of "certain" members of the Legislature toward his anti-crime bills and added that "strong groups" were intent upon killing as much of his law enforcement program as they dared.

The resolution sponsored by Assemblyman W. Allan Newell of St. Lawrence and drafted by Republican leaders was adopted by a party vote, all but three of the Democrats voting against it.

The vote was 83 to 61, three Tammany Democrats, Assemblymen Byrnes, Keenan and Sheldrick, voting with the Republicans for it.

Lehman Gives Notice of Reply.

Immediately after the resolution was adopted, the Governor sent the Assembly the following message:

"I have been advised that the Assembly has just adopted a resolution concerning the anti-crime program.

"I beg to advise you without loss of time that I shall answer the resolution publicly in a radio address to the people of the State within the next few days.

"The people of the State are very deeply concerned and interested in what the Assembly may do to the anti-crime program.

"A copy of my radio address will be transmitted to the Assembly."

Several Republicans protested against the informality of this message, charging that it was disrespectful to the Assembly.

Action on the resolution was preceded by a drawn-out debate with heated exchanges.

Ostensibly the resolution was designed to make it possible for the Assembly to deal under the law with members who might have been yielding to outside influence in opposing the anti-crime legislation.

The Democrats, however, view the resolution as an attempt to embarrass the Governor and prepare the way for further opposition to his anti-crime measures.

Message Impresses Throng.

The Governor's message was read soon after the opening gavel had fallen in the Senate and in the Assembly.

The impressive language used by the Governor was not lost on the record crowd which filled the galleries and all available spaces in the Assembly chamber set aside for visitors.

Telling the legislators he felt that they "fully realize that racketeering and organized crime have been steadily increasing," the Governor declared that crime in this State was no longer "a haphazard or sporadic manifestation."

He explained that his measures had been drafted by experts for the purpose of giving to law-enforcement agencies modernized "defense weapons" with which to combat criminals who now had weapons and means of evading punishment

Continued on Page Four.

Roosevelt Puts His Veto On 5 Private Claim Bills

Special to THE NEW YORK TIMES.

WASHINGTON, Feb. 17.—Five veto messages affecting private-claim bills went to Congress from the White House today in one batch as President Roosevelt continued his campaign against legislation of this type, which reverses carefully considered judgments already made by official departments.

He vetoed three bills that would have removed from the records of former enlisted men in the army the stigma of dishonorable discharges, and disapproved another bill that would have conferred not only an honorable discharge but the retirement pay of a captain on an officer similarly dismissed.

The remaining veto turned down a bill that would have provided for a small tax refund to an estate.

PLANES SPEED ROUT OF ETHIOPIAN FORCE

Italians Bomb Remnants of Mulugheta's Army, Fleeing After Enderta Defeat.

COUNTER-ATTACK 'FOILED'

Attempt Said to Have Failed to Cut New Lines—6 Fliers Die as Craft Burns.

By HERBERT L. MATTHEWS.
Wireless to THE NEW YORK TIMES.

ENDA JESUS, Ethiopia, Feb. 16 (Delayed. By Military Plane to Asmara).—The Ethiopian force was in full flight southward today after a smashing defeat in the six-day Enderta battle. Italian aviators, who made more than 100 reconnaissance flights, sighted retreating columns almost as far south as Alaji and bombed some of them. From the fact they made no effort to hide or shoot back it is deduced that the Ethiopians are completely demoralized.

Mopping-up operations are being carried out along the top and sides of Amba Aradam, a mountain five miles wide and two miles deep, pitted with caverns and trenches. However, virtually all the soldiers of War Minister Ras Mulugheta's force appear either to have been killed or to have fled. Only a few prisoners were taken.

Decorations said to belong to Ras Mulugheta, found in one cavern, included the British Royal Victorian Order. A great many chains such as are used on slaves and prisoners were also exhibited as part of the loot. It was explained that the wearers of these evidently has been freed so they might escape.

It was learned today that Emperor Haile Selassie had ordered Ras Kassa Sebat to attack an Italian force early in the battle to create a diversion against the flank, but apparently Ras Kassa Sebat was unable to do so, presumably because his force had been too badly smashed in the Tembien battle last month to wage another combat.

6 Reported Dead in Air Crash.

ADDIS ABABA, Feb. 17 (AP).—An Italian tri-motored plane fell in flames and its six occupants were burned to death during a bombardment last week of the northern Lake Haik monastery, Ethiopian officials reported today.

An Ethiopian communiqué said today that 4,000 Italian native troops had deserted on the southern front and reached the British Kenya Colony safely, despite a pursuit by Italian land and air forces.

It was understood the alleged deserters were disarmed and interned by the British for the duration of the war.

The communiqué said:

"Since the beginning of the war the total of Eritrean deserters has been 10,000."

Rome Awaits Details of Battle.

Wireless to THE NEW YORK TIMES.

ROME, Feb. 17.—Two official war bulletins issued today described various phases of the Enderta battle and gave additional details of the present situation in Northern Ethiopia. Both tended to increase the proportions of the Italian victory.

Broken remnants of Ras Mulugheta's army were stated to be in full flight, part of them southwest toward Fenaroa and part of them

Continued on Page Six.

RIOTS SWEEP SPAIN ON LEFT'S VICTORY; JAILS ARE STORMED

'State of Alarm' Is Decreed in Post-Election Disorders—President's Family Moves.

STRICT CENSORSHIP IS SET

Lepers Freed by Extremists in Alicante—Convicts Mutiny, Set Fire to Their Beds.

By WILLIAM P. CARNEY.
Wireless to THE NEW YORK TIMES.

MADRID, Tuesday, Feb. 18.—Jubilant Socialists and their extreme Leftist allies yesterday tried to celebrate their victory in Sunday's general election with a wholesale delivery of "model prison" inmates here. A principal plank in the Left coalition's campaign platform was amnesty for "political prisoners."

A crowd of 3,000 demonstrators marched on the big municipal jail with the object of releasing every one confined there. They were met at its gates by Civil Guards, who fired at them. The demonstrators dispersed, leaving one youth dead and many wounded.

The result was a proclamation of a "state of alarm," modified martial law, throughout Spain, with a reimposition of press censorship.

Premier Manuel Portela, whose government was appointed solely to conduct the election, appealed to the Socialist leaders to discourage their followers from acts of rowdyism and violence.

Amnesty Cry Is Raised.

The demonstrations in Madrid threatened to become serious when hundreds of Socialist marchers arrived in the Puerta del Sol. They were joined by a number of shock policemen guarding the Interior Ministry, who raised clenched fists and shouted with the others: "Amnesty! Amnesty!"

The Socialist executive committee finally issued orders to all its followers to "be prudent and refrain from all hasty and unlawful acts before the legal power to right all wrongs is put into our hands."

Elsewhere in the country rioters apparently interpreted the Left election victory as a mandate to liberate all prisoners.

In Cartagena Prison, where Luis Companys, former President of the rebellious Catalan Generalidad, and six members of his Cabinet are confined, convicts mutined and set fire to their beds. They were subdued with difficulty. Mr. Companys and his companions have all been elected as Deputies to the Madrid Cortes, but they cannot take their seats until an amnesty decree frees them.

Valencia Convicts Rebel.

In Valencia Penitentiary prisoners revolted, killing one jailer and wounding two. Several convicts who had obtained firearms were finally disarmed after troops had rushed to the prison.

In Saragossa Prison convicts also rioted and burned their beds. They were eventually subdued.

Extremists for some inexplicable reason broke into a leper colony near Alicante and informed all the inmates they were free. Many refused to leave.

The Left gains in the election were attributed chiefly to the heavy Anarcho-Syndicalist vote in Madrid, Catalonia and Andalusia. The fact that there are 30,000 political prisoners in Spanish jails is believed to have influenced many women to vote for the Leftist ticket. The Syndicalists, who heretofore abstained from voting because they believed in direct action, are said to have been no less sentimental than the women.

Rightists' Vote Divided.

The Rightists are known to have lost many seats in Parliament, moreover, because, unlike the Left, they were unable to count on the solid backing of their followers. While the Socialists, with their perfectly disciplined machine, were able to deliver the organization vote in Madrid to the Left Republicans led by former Premiers Manuel Azana and Diego Martinez-Barrios, the Right was divided. Monarchists were unwilling to vote for Conservative Republicans on the Right ticket and Conservative Republicans scratched out the names of Monarchist candidates.

In Barcelona, where syndicalism originated and still is strongest, the Left won by 750,000 votes.

Premier Portela yesterday appointed Juan Moles, former High Commissioner of Spanish Morocco, to be Acting Governor General of Catalonia, replacing José Escala, a Center party man, who resigned Sunday night after the sweeping Left victory. The Premier had promised to have a new Governor

Continued on Page Nine.

Sleighs Carry Supplies To Snowbound Village

By The Associated Press.

HATFIELD, Mo., Feb. 17.—A month's imprisonment by snow of 200 villagers ended tonight amid joyous shouts as five horse-drawn sleds arrived with sorely needed food and fuel, after struggling six miles through deep drifts.

Eagerly the villagers unloaded cans of kerosene to burn in stoves ordinarily used only for Summer cooking. Coal gave out three weeks ago.

Others snatched up sacks of flour, sugar, rice and beans to replenish larders that held only enough food for two or three days at the most. Medical supplies also were brought in.

In desperation, a plane had been chartered at St. Joseph and plans made to rush supplies here tomorrow by air had the sleds failed to get through.

NEUTRALITY PLAN PASSED BY HOUSE

Compromise, Extending Present Law, Wins, 353 to 27, Under a 'Gag' Rule.

SENATE ACTION DELAYED

Consideration Goes Over Until Today to Let Nye and Clark Attend Debate.

Special to THE NEW YORK TIMES.

WASHINGTON, Feb. 17.—Under procedure permitting only twenty minutes of debate on each side of the question and prohibiting the offering of amendments, the House today passed the compromise resolution to extend the existing Neutrality Act until May 1, 1937, with the addition of a prohibition on loans and credits to belligerents and an exemption in favor of American republics in any conflict with non-American powers. The vote was 353 to 27.

In the Senate, Chairman Pittman of the Foreign Relations Committee attempted to obtain consideration of the resolution today, but finally agreed to put it off until 11 o'clock tomorrow morning. Senators McNary and Vandenberg asked the postponement on the ground that Senators Nye and Clark, who are opposed to the compromise plan, were absent from Washington today.

In both houses, leaders explained that haste was necessary because the arms embargo provisions of the existing law expire on Feb. 29. If the embargo now in effect should become legally inoperative, it was held, Italy and Ethiopia might consider its reimposition at a later date an unneutral act.

Provisions of the Measure.

As the measure passed the House it would direct the President to forbid the export of arms, ammunition and implements of war or their transport by American ships to all belligerents; would make illegal any loans and credits to belligerent governments; would exempt American countries at war with non-American powers; would warn American citizens that they could travel on belligerent vessels only at their own risk, and would empower the President to restrict the use of American ports as bases of supply for belligerent war vessels or submarines.

Chairman McReynolds of the House Foreign Affairs Committee justified the action of the leader-

Continued on Page Five.

ARMY REBELS SEIZE PARAGUAY CAPITAL IN HARD FIGHTING

Troops, Angered Over Results of Chaco War, Rise Against the Ayala Government.

PRESIDENT IS HOLDING OUT

Asuncion Is Isolated All Day —Rebels Look to Franco, War Hero, as Leader.

By JOHN W. WHITE.
Special Cable to THE NEW YORK TIMES.

BUENOS AIRES, Argentina, Tuesday, Feb. 18.—A revolutionary movement in Paraguay, backed by soldiers who defeated Bolivia in the Chaco war, has apparently succeeded.

The revolutionists are victorious in Asuncion and fighting that had been going on all day ceased at 10 o'clock last night, according to a censored radio message that was received at 1 o'clock this morning by the newspaper the Nacion from its office in Asuncion.

The government of President Eusebio Ayala apparently had not surrendered, but the message said the revolting army had dominated the situation, which was rapidly returning to normal.

The movement was led by Lieut. Cols. Smith and Recaldo, commanders of two regiments that had made themselves famous during the Chaco war. Colonels Smith and Recaldo proclaimed Colonel Rafael Franco, Chaco war hero, supreme leader of the revolutionary movement, the message said, and he is expected to go to Asuncion shortly.

Artillery Used in Fighting.

The fighting began at 7 o'clock yesterday morning and continued intermittently all day, including considerable artillery firing, in which river gunboats participated.

The movement seems to have taken the government completely by surprise. The rebels quickly seized strategic buildings, including the Asuncion railroad station, and then entrenched themselves in the Plaza Uruguay, 500 yards from police headquarters. The aviation forces were with the rebels from the beginning.

There are no reports of fighting outside Asuncion, but the rebels appear to have cut all lines of communication and effectively prevented the government from calling in troops from the interior.

Since the revolt was led by the most prominent army leaders, it is expected they will meet little resistance in their efforts to consolidate their position.

The government of President Ayala was said to have taken refuge in a naval arsenal, where, according to the reports, it was defended by sailors and police against an onslaught by four infantry regiments that had fought in the Chaco. The sailors defending the officials belonged to Paraguay's small navy of river gunboats that patrol the Upper Paraguay River, which forms the frontier between Brazil and the Chaco.

The military commander at Villa Encarnación, Paraguayan city on the Argentine frontier 230 miles southeast of Asuncion, is said to have received orders in the morning to recruit the largest possible force and rush it to Asuncion to defend the government. The orders were canceled later in the day, it is declared, with the explanation that the rebels had cut the railroad line

Continued on Page Nine.

Britain and Free State Ease Trade War; Further Mutual Concessions Pledged Soon

Wireless to THE NEW YORK TIMES.

LONDON, Feb. 17.—There is every indication that the disastrous four-year trade war between Great Britain and the Irish Free State is being gradually abandoned without any great political palaver.

The situation was further eased today when an agreement on a fifty-fifty basis was announced which, by reducing duties on Irish cattle and allowing freer importation of certain classes of British goods, will permit between the two countries a greater flow of trade than has existed since 1932.

At that time it looked as if all commercial intercourse would end, as a result of a disagreement over payment of Free State annuities to Britain. Last year the Free State exchanged cattle for coal on a pound-for-pound basis. Recently the Free State removed the duty of 5 shillings a ton on British coal.

Today Captain Douglas Hacking, British Under-Secretary for Dominion Affairs, announced that Britain would reduce by 10 per cent the existing duties on live animals and meat, and would make additional reductions in duties on horses, sheep, live lambs, mutton and lamb, and minor adjustments in reduced cattle duties. Arrangements for the regulation of Irish bacon and ham exports to Britain in 1936, Captain Hacking said, would provide for an increase of 10 per cent in supplies from the Free State, as compared with 1935.

The Free State will reserve for Britain one-third of its imports of cement and reduce by 10 per cent the existing duties on electrical goods, machinery, various iron and steel products, cycles, cement and sugar.

Malcolm MacDonald, Minister for Dominions, following his victory in the Ross and Cromarty by-election as a National Laborite, took his seat in the House of Commons this afternoon to the accompaniment of cheers, counter-cheers and shouts such as "Another good Tory" and "Where's your kilt, Malcolm?"

A Laborite asked whether the change in Irish relations was due to a change of Ministers, but Mr. Hacking retorted that today's reduction of duties was "a continuation of what was done" when J. H. Thomas held the office.

SUPREME COURT, 8 TO 1, BACKS TVA ON THE SALE OF POWER PRODUCED FROM WILSON DAM

New Federal Power Plans

Special to THE NEW YORK TIMES.

WASHINGTON, Feb. 17.—Plans are being prepared by administration officials for setting up additional power authorities similar to the TVA to make possible the marketing of electricity produced from Federal dams to three sections of the country. Enabling legislation had been held up pending the Supreme Court's decision on the TVA.

The plans call for the creation of a Mississippi Valley Authority to supply power in the neighborhood of the junction of the Mississippi and Ohio Rivers, including parts of Ohio, Indiana, Kentucky, Illinois, and perhaps extending as far South as the State of Mississippi. A Red River Authority would also be created to "electrify" parts of Texas and Louisiana.

The giant Bonneville and Grand Coulee Dams would be linked with the Skagit development, near Seattle, to supply cheap power to Washington, Oregon and Northern California. This plan, upon which J. D. Ross, attorney for the Security Commission, has been working, would not require Congressional action but would be carried out in cooperation with the three States.

It had been thought that the $37,000,000 Passamaquoddy tidal-power project in Maine would also be carried out along State-development lines, but the administration is now inclined to make no effort toward having the Senate reintroduce an appropriation for continuing work, which the House last week denied.

Complications were said to have made it desirable to shelve this enterprise, for the time being at least. One reason is understood to be that the Boston Edison, General Electric and Westinghouse companies still contend that they have claims against the Dexter Cooper Company, which originally planned the Quoddy project.

O'CONNOR'S THREAT STIRS HOUSE UPROAR

Members Cheer His Telegram —Supporter Says Coughlin 'Accepts' Challenge.

NEW ATTACK ON PRIEST

Congressman Says Clergyman Seeks to Run Government —He Is Silent.

Special to THE NEW YORK TIMES.

WASHINGTON, Feb. 17.—The threat of Chairman O'Connor of the House Rules Committee to kick the Rev. Charles E. Coughlin "from the Capitol to the White House" in retaliation for derogatory remarks made yesterday by the Detroit radio priest in a broadcast brought cheers and shouts from both sides of the House today when the telegram sent by Mr. O'Connor to Father Coughlin was read on the floor by Representative Sweeney of Ohio.

Mr. Sweeney, a supporter of Father Coughlin, received one minute by unanimous consent. It required that time to read the duplicate of the O'Connor telegram, but as he sat down Mr. Sweeney yelled:

"He accepts your challenge and will be here at 10 o'clock tomorrow morning."

It was learned later at the Capitol that the radio priest, whom Mr. O'Connor accuses of having "libeled" him yesterday, will not come to Washington until Feb. 26.

Mr. O'Connor, from his office late today, repeated his intention to chastise Father Coughlin.

"I will kick him," Mr. O'Connor said. "What I said goes.

"Every decent Catholic in America has been ashamed of him since he came to this country. There isn't a clergyman of the Catholic Church except one (Bishop Gallagher of the Diocese of Michigan), that I know of, who has approved of his desecration of the cloth by his intrusion into politics.

Bishop Cannon Issue Recalled.

"I personally never heard a Catholic priest talk politics from the pulpit. In the old days of prohibition and the Ku Klux Klan the cry of many of us to Bishop Cannon was 'Back to the pulpit; stay where you belong.'

"Just because Father Coughlin is obviously an egomaniac he thinks he can run the government. He stepped into the bonus and the World Court issues, but had as much to do with Congressional action on them as any elevator operator in the Capitol.

"When he saw the Frazier-Lemke bill needed only four signatures he stepped into that.

"He is ineligible to run for President, but most people would welcome his attempt to run for any other office.

"While purporting to be for the bonus, he told American Legion commanders that he was for the Economy Bill; that the soldiers had too much already.

"In a conference with fifteen Senators last year, after the House had passed the Patman (bonus) bill,

Continued on Page Two.

MARKET BOUNDS UP, BUT DROPS SHARPLY

Speculators' Attempt to Guess Purport of TVA Decision Spurs Utility Issues.

REACTION IS SPECTACULAR

It Extends to Other Shares, Pulling Down Nearly All in Excited Selling.

Vain attempts of speculators to guess the purport of the TVA decision of the United States Supreme Court yesterday resulted in a wild upward rush of public utility stocks soon after noon, and an even more spectacular liquidation extended to the entire market thirty minutes later, when it became apparent that the first guess of the traders was wrong.

Although the trading volume for the greater part of the day was the highest since the collapse of commodity prices determined stock market liquidation in July, 1933, there were only a few scattered interruptions in normal trading.

Public utility shares started their brief boom as soon as the news tickers announced that Chief Justice Hughes had begun reading the TVA decision. It was then 12:13 P. M. here. In fifteen minutes most utility stocks had soared 1 to 4 points to new highs for the year, several reaching the best levels since 1933 and in rare instances the highest marks since 1931.

Excerpts of the opinion appeared on the tickers every few minutes, and as time went on with no "flash" indicating a defeat of TVA, trading grew cautious, but prices held. At 12:40 the Chief Justice was quoted as saying that "the claims of assumed potential action by TVA are not sufficient for court intervention" and prices began to sag.

Rest of Market Pulled Down.

It was not until 1:08 that the traders were convinced that TVA apparently had won out, and the pace of selling grew as utility stocks declined as rapidly as they had risen, pulling down most of the market in their wake.

Throngs of brokers surrounded the specialists in most leading stocks. On the Stock Exchange trading had to be delayed for ten to fifteen minutes in United States Steel, Chrysler, Commonwealth & Southern, Columbia Gas and Electric, National Power and Light and nearly a score of other principal stocks to give the specialists time to record buying and selling orders. Members of the Committee on Arrangements stood by to observe these operations, which were conducted methodically.

On the New York Curb Exchange trading in Electric Bond and Share Company was delayed for thirteen minutes for similar reasons. On both markets quieter conditions prevailed after 2 P. M., and many stocks showed an improved tone by the close of trading. The Stock Exchange ticker was seven minutes late at one time, but kept

Continued on Page Thirteen.

BUYING OF LINES UPHELD

But Decision Is Limited Strictly to Case Before the Court.

HUGHES READS THE OPINION

Status of TVA as Operator of Consumer Systems or of Its Social Aims Passed By.

DISSENT BY M'REYNOLDS

Brandeis, Stone, Roberts, Cardozo Join the Majority but Wanted Suit Dismissed.

Texts of majority and minority opinions are on Pages 10-11-12.

By ARTHUR KROCK.
Special to THE NEW YORK TIMES.

WASHINGTON, Feb. 17.—The Supreme Court ruled today, 8 to 1, that the Wilson Dam at Muscle Shoals was constitutionally constructed, and it validated also the Tennessee Valley Authority's purchasing contract with the Alabama Power Company of transmission lines to carry surplus power to a market. It held the TVA test rigidly to this narrow field.

Speaking through the Chief Justice, the court declined to go further in weighing the constitutionality of the TVA as operator of electrical distribution systems to consumers or in deciding the actual legality of other projects and social objectives the Authority has enunciated.

The administration was left with this finding:

Congress may construct dams to control navigation and floods and for national defense. It may contract for privately owned transmission facilities to carry its surplus to market. To this basis TVA counsel narrowed the whole case, and the court abided within these limits. Specifically, the TVA's contract of Jan. 4, 1934, with the Alabama Power Company is legal, and the preferred stockholders who sued have no case.

Four Were for Dismissing Case.

Four justices—Messrs. Brandeis, Stone, Roberts and Cardozo—agreed with these conclusions, but held that the plaintiffs, having no case, had no proper standing in court and their action should have been dismissed on that ground, especially since the court always seeks to avoid ruling on a constitutional question when it can invalidate a suit on other findings.

Joining the Chief Justice and Messrs. Sutherland, Van Devanter and Butler in their view that the plaintiffs were entitled to adjudication, Justice McReynolds, however, dissented from the constitutional conclusions of his eight brethren. His main point was that the purpose of the TVA must be judged on all available facts, and not narrowed down to the Wilson Dam power contract. On that contention, Justice McReynolds found the whole scheme unconstitutional.

Thus the court divided 8 to 1 on constitutionality and 5 to 4 on the legal point of the right of the preferred stockholders of the Alabama Power Company (the plaintiffs) to sue.

O'Brian Formulated Strategy.

The government was highly successful in its strategy, formulated by John Lord O'Brian of Buffalo, who was specially hired by the TVA for this action, to limit the constitutional question to the Wilson Dam contracts and to exclude many published evidences—official and otherwise—that the conception and practice of TVA far exceed a mere agency to dispose of a power surplus produced during the process of regulating navigation and preparing for war.

Mr. O'Brian used to be Assistant Attorney General in Republican administrations. The court majority permitted him to concentrate the issue on the power company contract, and thus availed itself of its first recent opportunity to uphold a government contention growing out of an act of Congress. To do this it sternly—Justice McReynolds alone protesting—turned its back on James M. Beck and Forney Johnston, the plaintiffs' lawyers, and

Continued on Page Twelve.

"All the News That's Fit to Print."

The New York Times.

LATE CITY EDITION
Fair and somewhat warmer today. Tomorrow rain and warmer.
Temperatures Yesterday—Max., 36; min., 17.

Section 1

VOL. LXXXV....No. 28,533. Entered as Second-Class Matter, Postoffice, New York, N. Y. NEW YORK, SUNDAY, MARCH 8, 1936. P Including Rotogravure Picture, Magazine and Book Review. TEN CENTS | TWELVE CENTS Beyond 200 Miles Except in 7th and 8th Postal Zones.

STRIKE PEACE HOPE REVIVED AS MAYOR OFFERS A NEW PLAN

OWNERS ARE RECEPTIVE

Realty Board Acts Today on Move to Submit to Arbitration.

UNION ASSENT IS HINTED

Resumption of Negotiations Is Held Likely After La Guardia and Strikers Confer.

300 AT TUDOR CITY QUIT

More Park Av. Buildings Also Affected—Closed-Shop Issue No Longer a Factor.

Hope for settlement of the strike of elevator operators and other building service employes was revived last night after another appeal to both sides by Mayor La Guardia to submit the dispute to arbitration.

The Mayor made his proposal in identical telegrams addressed to the Building Service Employes Union, the strike organization, and the Realty Advisory Board, which has played the rôle of spokesman for large realty interests in the strike. Accompanying the Mayor's proposal was a detailed plan of settlement minus the closed shop.

The fact that the Mayor dispatched his peace plan after he had conferred at City Hall with strike leaders was taken as a clear indication that it was acceptable to the union, which had previously indicated its readiness to abandon the closed-shop demand.

William D. Rawlins, executive secretary of the Realty Advisory Board, declared after receipt of the Mayor's telegram that the peace plan might be looked upon with favor in the form in which it was submitted.

He announced that the directors of the Realty Advisory Board would consider the Mayor's proposal at a meeting this afternoon at the board's offices, 12 East Forty-first Street. The proposal will be analyzed by Walter Gordon Merritt, counsel for the board, after which a reply to the Mayor will be drafted.

New Negotiations Hoped For.

It was hoped last night that today's meeting of the Realty Advisory Board's directors would lead to a resumption of negotiations at City Hall tomorrow morning and to a settlement of the strike.

The Mayor's appeal for peace came after another day in which there were no important strike developments.

Although the union called out some 300 employes in Tudor City, preliminary to extending the walkout in the Grand Central area tomorrow, and appeared to be holding its lines in other parts of the city, there was no marked extension of the strike during the day.

Upon the intervention of the Mayor the union called off the strike in some 170 buildings controlled by the New York State Mortgage Commission after the commission had agreed to abide by any settlement ultimately reached with the realty interests of the city. The commission controls about 140 buildings in Manhattan and thirty in the Bronx.

In making known the dispatch of telegrams to the contending groups, pleading with them to bring the strike to a termination, Mayor La Guardia said:

"I am convinced that the strike can be settled if both sides are willing to do so. Resistance on one side and provocation on the other will get nowhere. Misrepresentations from either side are not helpful. The real issue now is wages and working conditions, and surely arbitration should be accepted by both sides.

"The Mayor will maintain law and order, protect life and property, and that goes for both sides. He will continue his efforts to end this controversy regardless of abuse from either side."

Closed-Shop Demand Eased.

The Mayor's plea was made public after he had conferred again with James J. Bambrick, strike leader, and other union spokesmen. His statement that "the real issue now is wages and working conditions" was taken as another indication that the union was will-

Continued on Page Thirty-seven.

Butler and Shaw Swap Retorts Not 'Courteous'

By The Associated Press.

SAN PEDRO, Calif., March 7.—Nicholas Murray Butler and George Bernard Shaw let go with both barrels of caustic sarcasm today at each other through the medium of interviews.

Said Dr. Butler, president of Columbia University, with regard to the gibes of G. B. S. at the American Constitution and the President:

"Anything George Bernard Shaw may say about politics is too ludicrous to comment upon. This won't surprise Mr. Shaw because it represents an opinion I have had about him for a long time. And he knows it."

Said G. B. S.:

"I suppose if Dr. Butler had an automobile that had been running for thirty years and was still running he would insist that it shouldn't be exchanged for a new motor car. That is the way with your Constitution. Dr. Butler's antiquated automobile wouldn't bring much of a 'trade-in.'

"Anyway I'm 'G. B. S.' and Dr. Butler isn't 'N. M. B.'"

LEHMAN CRIME PLEA POLITICS, SAYS IVES

Speaker Ascribes Attack on Assembly Members to Quest for Re-election Issue.

DEFENDS ALL COLLEAGUES

He Calls on the Governor for 'Appropriate Action' on Dodge and Geoghan.

The text of Mr. Ives's address is printed on Page 38.

Special to THE NEW YORK TIMES.

ALBANY, March 7.—Governor Lehman is making a "political football" of his crime program and picking a fight with the Legislature merely to develop an issue on which to run for re-election, Speaker Irving M. Ives of the Assembly asserted tonight in a State-wide radio broadcast.

The Speaker went on the air over WOKO and a chain of stations to reply to the radio attack of two weeks ago in which the Governor charged that "powerful groups of lawyer legislators" were banding together to hamstring his program in the Assembly.

Mr. Ives offered a detailed statement of his position on the crime bills, saying that his attitude was that of many Democrats and Republicans, and demanded that Governor Lehman "take appropriate action" in the cases of District Attorney William C. Dodge of New York and District Attorney William F. X. Geoghan of Kings. He said:

"Two glaring examples of the failure of law enforcement are to be found in New York City. The first is the case of District Attorney William F. X. Geoghan of Brooklyn, who, unable to secure convictions in the notorious Drukman case, was superseded by Special Prosecutor Hiram C. Todd, who obtained these convictions with admirable promptness.

Demands Governor Act.

"The second example is that pertaining to District Attorney William C. Dodge of New York County, who, after having shown himself unable to break up racketeering gangs which for years have been preying upon the public of New York, was finally superseded in this assignment by Attorney Thomas Dewey as special prosecutor. Where Mr. Dodge failed, Mr. Dewey has not failed and instead has obtained a number of convictions.

"Obviously, there must be some laxity of law enforcement somewhere in these cases, and I recommend that the Governor, in view of the facts, take appropriate action."

The Speaker enumerated "certain basic truths that have emerged from the confusion and misunderstanding which this anti-crime controversy has provoked."

He declared that "the intemperate charges directed at the Assembly by the Governor are utterly false and ridiculous."

He asserted that "the Governor has sought to claim credit for inaugurating all anti-crime programs offered in this State since the 1935 session of the Legislature, to the

Continued on Page Thirty-eight.

HOOVER DECLARES FREEDOM IN PERIL, LIFE 'MORTGAGED'

He Tells Colorado Republicans We Face Enslaving Taxes, Repudiation or Inflation.

'COMMON MAN' MUST PAY

Future 'Fireside Talks' Will Be With Collector, He Says—Hits 'Planned Economy.'

The text of Mr. Hoover's speech is printed on Page 36.

Special to THE NEW YORK TIMES.

COLORADO SPRINGS, March 7.—Crushing taxes, repudiation of debts or inflation are certain sequels to the New Deal, Herbert Hoover declared tonight before the Young Republican League of Colorado in a speech which was broadcast nationally.

The administration's spending and what he regarded as its steps toward dictatorship have failed to solve the problems of the depression or end unemployment, he said.

The former President asserted that the youth of the nation faced a choice between the old American system, with its political liberty and equality of economic opportunity, and a "planned economy" involving regimentation and bureaucracy.

The freedom and opportunities of youth "are being mortgaged," Mr. Hooover asserted, adding that "taxation enslaves as well as dictatorship."

More Taxes "Inevitable."

He warned that the nation's "future fireside talks" would be with the tax collector, and some believed that present taxes on wealth, designed to complete the cycle of "shirtsleeves to shirtsleeves in three generations," take the shirt also.

"Do not mistake," he went on. "The new taxes of today are but part of them. More of them are as inevitable as the first of the month. The only alternatives are repudiation or inflation. No matter what nonsense you are told about corporations and the rich paying the bill, there will be two-thirds of it for the common man to pay after the corporations and the rich are sucked dry."

He said, further:

"And where do we get to after all this attempt to supplant the American system? At the time of the election in 1932 the American Federation of Labor reported 11,600,000 unemployed. Today, after three years of the New Deal, they report 11,600,000 unemployed.

"To get these people back to their jobs was the outstanding job of our government. It was the excuse given for all these doings. But the grim fact remains that it has failed in its primary purpose. And $15,000,000,000 will be added to the national debt before the New Deal is over."

The Record on Platform Pledges.

Mr. Hoover contrasted the administration's actions and party platform promises of 1932, and said that when he was President all but two of the thirty-seven Republican platform promises were carried out, despite depression difficulties. Two secondary promises, he said, "broke against the obstinacy of a Democratic Congress."

The trend of events in this country since 1932, he said, followed the pattern of European nations that succumbed to dictatorship, and he added that the New Deal had "imitated the intellectual and vocal technique of typical European revolution."

The great contributions to civili-

Continued on Page Thirty-six.

HITLER SENDS GERMAN TROOPS INTO RHINELAND; OFFERS PARIS 25-YEAR NON-AGGRESSION PACT; FRANCE MANS HER FORTS, BRITAIN STUDIES MOVE

Rumania's War Council Called to Special Session

By The Associated Press.

BUCHAREST, March 7.—The Rumanian Defense Council tonight was called to a special session Monday, to devise means for improving and rapidly increasing the nation's armaments. The council consists of King Carol, former Premiers and the general staff of the army.

The semi-official newspaper, Dimineata, predicted that the League of Nations would apply economic sanctions against Germany as a result of remilitarizing the Rhineland.

Commenting on Chancellor Adolf Hitler's speech before the Reichstag, the newspaper said, "Germany is laughing today, but France and England will be laughing tomorrow."

MUSSOLINI ACCEPTS PEACE PARLEY BID

League Invitation Satisfactory in Principle as Basis for Talks, He Tells Cabinet.

ITALY WILL NOT AID PARIS

Imposition of Sanctions Said to Have Freed Nation of Locarno Obligations.

By ARNALDO CORTESI.
Wireless to THE NEW YORK TIMES.

ROME, March 7.—At almost the minute when Chancellor Adolf Hitler, in Berlin, was announcing the reoccupation of the Rhineland, Premier Benito Mussolini, in Rome, was informing the Italian Cabinet Council that he had decided to accept "in principle" the invitation of the League of Nations to negotiate peace with Ethiopia.

These two facts, though seemingly unrelated, are likely to have some important repercussions on each other. The turmoil created in Europe by Hitler's move, which has directed attention from East Africa and pushed sanctions into the background, is expected to help Mussolini to drive a hard bargain with the Negus and to settle the Italo-Ethiopian conflict with all possible speed.

Italy, as soon as her best energies are no longer fettered in Africa, will be able to make her weight felt in the European balance of power and participate in the process of readjustment in the next few years.

The text of Mussolini's reply to the League's peace appeal is not yet known and will not be made public until it has arrived at Geneva. Therefore, it is still uncertain whether he has agreed unreservedly to negotiate or whether he has pledged his acceptance with important reservations.

Newspapers, usually regarded as the government's mouthpieces, are at variance on this point. The Giornale d'Italia thinks, as the invitation of the League contained no limitations, there are no conditions in Mussolini's reply. The Tribuna on the contrary says that Mussolini's acceptance does not tie him down to anything and implies the widest reservations. It also

Continued on Page Thirty-nine.

Brief Attack of Cold Is Repelled by Sun; Rising Temperatures Forecast for Today

Winter tried to take possession of the city again yesterday, just two weeks before the official arrival of Spring. But a bright sun in a clear sky turned Winter back with a jump of 7 degrees in temperature within little more than an hour in the afternoon.

A forecast for continuing rising temperatures and fair skies is expected to bring a moderate day of above-freezing weather today and warmer weather and rain tomorrow.

From midnight Friday until 3 o'clock yesterday afternoon the mercury remained below freezing and brought a renewed touch of Winter to the city. At 8 A. M. the temperature dropped to a low of 17—the coldest since the days of snow and ice on Fifth Avenue and Broadway.

Within the next hour the mercury rose ten degrees and then dropped back for several hours before renewing an upward course at noon. At 3 P. M., when the mercury stood at 32, a shift in light winds from the north to the southwest sent it up quickly to a high of 39 at 4:15, after which it fell slightly.

The average temperature for the day was 28, which is seven degrees below the normal. The coldest March 7 in the records of the Weather Bureau was in 1890, when the mercury dropped to 6, and the warmest was in 1921, when it rose to 69.

Since Jan. 1, when the day was 9 hours and 17 minutes long, the length of the day has increased gradually and will be 11 hours and 32 minutes long today. On March 18 the vernal equinox will begin with the day and night each 12 hours long. Two days later, on March 20, at 1:58 P. M., Spring will begin.

PARIS APPEALS TO LEAGUE

Rejects Reich Proposal of a Substitute for Locarno Treaty.

ALLIES SUPPORT PROGRAM

Russia and Czechoslovakia to Aid to 'Limit' in Effort to Clear Rhineland.

BELGIUM ACTS AT BORDER

French Officials Say Military Moves to Drive Back Germans Await Geneva Decisions.

By P. J. PHILIP.
Wireless to THE NEW YORK TIMES.

PARIS, March 7.—France has laid Germany's latest treaty violation before the Council of the League of Nations. That is the procedure called for in the situation.

At the same time the French Government today made it quite clear that there could be no negotiation with Germany of any substitute for the Treaty of Locarno or anything else as long as a single German soldier remained in the Rhineland in contravention of Germany's signed undertakings.

While no public mention of French troop movements is being made here, it is obvious that the necessary precautions will be taken, probably on the same scale as last March, when the Reich government denounced the military clauses of the Treaty of Versailles and reorganized her army.

[France ordered all northeastern border fortifications garrisoned at full strength, The Associated Press reports, and Belgium canceled leaves for troops garrisoning her eastern frontier.]

Withdrawal Held Essential.

What is essential, in the French view, is that the German Government must be compelled, by diplomatic pressure first and by stronger pressure if need be, to withdraw from the Rhineland. For what is found most intolerable in all today's happenings is this renewed appearance of the mailed fist in diplomacy—not, in French opinion, in the service of common peace and order, but as a menace and provocation.

Everything that can be done to avoid war will be done. But there should be no mistaking this fact in Germany or elsewhere: that rather than submit to this last crashing piece of Teutonism, France will fight.

Meanwhile, as always, the French have presented their case. The Cabinet met twice today, once in reduced numbers at the Elysée Palace with President Albert Lebrun and later at the Quai d'Orsay. Between the two meetings Foreign Minister Pierre-Etienne Flandin called in the Ambassadors of all signatory powers of the Locarno agreements for consultation and to acquaint them with his government's views.

General Marie Gustave Gamelin, chief of the General Staff, took part in the Elysée Palace meeting.

The Cabinet has been summoned for tomorrow morning to be kept fully apprised of the situation and to learn the attitude of other governments whose opinions have been sought by French diplomatic representatives.

After the second Cabinet meeting, Mr. Flandin, in the famous clock room at the Quai d'Orsay, read to the biggest assembly of newspaper men there had been there since the days of the Versailles treaty a long declaration setting forth his government's views and decisions. It was a direct indictment of German veracity and an exposure of all treaty infractions involved in today's actions.

Invokes Mediation Clause.

One of his most damning declarations was the invocation of that section of the Locarno Pact by which France and Germany agreed that if any difference should arise between them which could not be dealt with by ordinary diplomatic means, they would submit it to conciliation and arbitration.

That procedure, it is argued here,

Continued on Page Thirty.

GERMAN ARMY AGAIN ON THE RHINE.

The shaded portion of the map shows the district demilitarized under the Treaty of Versailles. It included all German territory on the west of the Rhine and a zone fifty kilometers wide along the east bank. The stars show where the principal garrisons were established.

GERMANY'S ACTION ASSAILED BY EDEN

He Uses Severe Tone Toward Reich Envoy, but Attitude of Cabinet Is Deemed Milder.

By AUGUR.
Special Cable to THE NEW YORK TIMES.

LONDON, March 7.—Foreign Secretary Anthony Eden used strong words to condemn the German Government's action when Ambassador Leopold von Hoesch of Germany presented to him this morning Chancellor Adolf Hitler's memorandum concerning the Rhineland.

Mr. Eden said the British Government must consider the entry of German regular troops into the forbidden zone to be in defiance of treaty obligations and a flagrant breach of a territorial frontier. The terms of the Treaty of Locarno impose definite duties on the British Government. The implications of the situation now created will therefore be carefully gone into.

But to Charles Corbin, the French Ambassador, Mr. Eden said that the government, while determined to comply with treaty obligations, was equally desirous of avoiding hasty action and it advised the French Government to study the points of the German offer, for they appear to be not without value.

Action Had Been Expected.

The fact is that at the bottom of their hearts Cabinet Ministers here are not so displeased with Hitler's proposals as it officially must be said they are. For sometime past the demilitarized zone has been written off as lost. A chance to obtain a solid counter-value for a hopeless item on the balance sheet appears attractive for practical politicians in London.

The real question awaiting reply is whether Hitler offers advantages that upon closer inspection may be found ephemeral once the fact of the illegal military occupation of the Rhineland is accepted without demur.

Officials in Berlin, it is known here, were alarmed when Foreign Minister Pierre-Etienne Flandin of France put a direct question to Mr. Eden concerning British aid in case of an infraction by Ger-

Continued on Page Thirty-three.

ARMY MARCHES IN AS HITLER SPEAKS

In Full War Equipment It Goes to Rhineland, Ending Its Advance Near Frontier.

By OTTO D. TOLISCHUS.
Wireless to THE NEW YORK TIMES.

BERLIN, March 7.—Germany today resumed her "watch on the Rhine" when, with an astonishing bravado that dared challenge Europe to war or to peace and left the world breathless for the moment, the new German Army crossed the military frontier, which hitherto has separated it from France, and occupied the demilitarized Rhineland zone created by the Versailles treaty and reaffirmed at Locarno.

The move was carried through with that German efficiency which drew from foreign military experts tribute to the German Army command and amid manifestations of both popular enthusiasm and grave apprehension. It brought back echoes of the last German westward march nearly twenty-two years ago, but also it was made to look like a dress rehearsal for more serious business.

Even while Chancellor Adolf Hitler was serving notice of the contemplated move to diplomats of the Locarno powers assembled in the chancellery at 11 A. M. field-gray masses of the troops of occupation were already on the march.

Planes Circle Cologne.

A few minutes before Hitler began to announce this move to the world in his speech before the Reichstag the first military flying squadrons already were circling Cologne's cathedral spires. As he began to talk infantry, artillery, motorized cavalry, tanks, machine-gun units, anti-aircraft artillery and all other paraphernalia of modern warfare already were closing the Rhine bridges, and two hours after he had finished, his advance guards already had reached Saarbruecken, their westernmost point for the present, only three kilometers from the French frontier.

According to an official announcement, troop movements will continue all day tomorrow. Occupation of the zone, which comprises

Continued on Page Thirty-one.

VERSAILLES CURB BROKEN

Hitler Smashes Locarno Citing Franco-Soviet Treaty as Reason.

READY TO REJOIN LEAGUE

Battle for Equality Ended, He Tells Joyous Reichstag—Sets Vote for March 29.

URGES AIR PACT IN WEST

Bilateral Neutralization of Rhine Proposed—Hand Is Extended to Lithuania.

Hitler's Reichstag speech and other texts on Pages 31, 32, 33.

By GUIDO ENDERIS.
Wireless to THE NEW YORK TIMES.

BERLIN, March 7.—Germany today cast off the last shackles fastened upon her by the Treaty of Versailles when Adolf Hitler, as commander-in-chief of the Reich defense forces, sent his new battalions into the Rhineland demilitarized zone.

The Chancellor's marching orders were timed to synchronize with Germany's notification to the powers concerned and to a listening Reich that she no longer considered herself bound by the Locarno terms because the fundamental basis and inherent purpose of that pact had been destroyed through the conclusion of the mutual assistance treaty between France and the Soviet Union.

Hitler related to the Reichstag all he had done. After he had proposed a daring peace program he was greeted with a burst of enthusiasm when he announced that with complete sovereignty over all German territory restored, the Reich was prepared not only to return to the League of Nations, but also to cooperate in any system of collective security that gave promise of success.

Sees Struggle Closed.

"After three years of ceaseless battle," Hitler concluded, "I look upon this day as marking the close of the struggle for German equality status and with that re-won equality the path is now also clear for Germany's return to European collective cooperation."

To give the German people an opportunity to pass judgment on his leadership, Hitler said, he decided to dissolve the Reichstag and order a plebiscite on Sunday, March 29, in which German voters will be able to record their confidence or lack of it in the government's home and foreign policies.

The announcement of Germany's denunciation of the Locarno pact, which she voluntarily negotiated with France and Belgium in 1925 and for which Great Britain and Italy stood sponsors, provoked less jubilation in the Reichstag than did the news that German troops at that very hour were again marching to their peace garrisons in the Rhineland. That news unloosed a cyclone of rejoicing as the 660 Deputies rose to greet it.

But the Chancellor's speech as a whole must be counted an outstanding political pronouncement and oratorical achievement with respect to both its contents and forceful delivery and also the intense sincerity that marked the recital of the reasons that had determined him to abrogate Locarno.

Offers Non-Aggression Pacts.

The speech was easily Hitler's boldest utterance on German foreign policy. While it was not free from recriminations and indictment of France's refusal to grasp Germany's outstretched hand, that hand was once more revealed as offering France and Belgium a twenty-five-year non-aggression pact at the very moment when the roll of German regimental drums was being heard along the Rhine for the first time since 1919.

The proposed non-aggression pact, which Hitler said was open also to the Netherlands, constituted the only part of his seven-point peace scheme that he offered as a substitute for the discarded Locarno accord.

Germany is also prepared, he continued, to negotiate immediately for the creation of a demilitarized

Continued on Page Thirty.

"All the News That's Fit to Print."

The New York Times.

LATE CITY EDITION
Rain and colder today Tomorrow generally fair, with little change in temperature.
Temperatures Yesterday—Max., 56; Min., 36

VOL. LXXXV.....No. 28,546. | Entered as Second-Class Matter, Postoffice, New York, N. Y. | NEW YORK, SATURDAY, MARCH 21, 1936. | P | TWO CENTS In New York City. | THREE CENTS Within 200 Miles | FOUR CENTS Elsewhere Except in 7th and 8th Postal Zones.

4 POWERS TO FORM ALLIANCE IF GERMANY REJECTS TERMS; HITLER 'WON'T RETIRE AN INCH'

BORDER FORCE PROPOSED

12½-Mile Strip Along Reich Frontier Would Be Re-Occupied.

NO ULTIMATUM INVOLVED

British Prepare to Plead for Concessions by Paris if Germany Rejects Move.

FRENCH HAIL PLEDGED AID

But Other Features of Speech by Flandin Win but Scant Applause From Deputies.

Texts of British White Paper and Eden's speech on Page 4.

By CHARLES A. SELDEN
Wireless to THE NEW YORK TIMES.

LONDON, March 20.—The British and French Governments made public today their proposals, framed in collaboration with Belgium and Italy, for rectifying the menacing European situation caused by Germany's violation of the Locarno treaty two weeks ago when she sent her troops into the demilitarized zone.

The next vital move belongs to Chancellor Hitler, to whom the text of the proposals has been sent by Joachim von Ribbentrop, Ambassador at Large, now in London in charge of Germany's case. No instructions have yet been received from Berlin, but it is assumed in advance not only by Mr. von Ribbentrop and his associates but by the British Foreign Office that Chancellor Hitler will reject the plan because it demands another surrender of sovereignty over a part of German territory.

Anthony Eden, British Foreign Secretary, told Mr. von Ribbentrop that he could see him any time during the week-end. Pierre-Etienne Flandin, French Foreign Minister, is expected back here Monday.

4-Power Alliance Set Up

The plan imposes "obligations of mutual assistance between Belgium, France, Britain and Italy or any of them, with suitable provisions to insure prompt action by the signatories in case of need as well as technical arrangements for the preparation of such measures as would insure effective execution of these obligations."

In other words, there has been set up to meet the present emergency a new four-power military alliance to continue so long as Germany's behavior makes it necessary. The apparent incongruity in the fact that two of these powers—Britain and Italy—have been at sword's points for months because of the Italo-Ethiopian war is met by the British Government with the assurance that the troubles in Africa and Europe are in watertight compartments with no bearing on each other.

The text of the plan was submitted this afternoon to the League Council, which will convene Monday to consider what action to take to further the new adventure of the four nations chiefly concerned. The program devised by the Locarno powers ranges widely from immediate demands upon Germany that she submit to demilitarization of another part of the Rhineland and to harboring of foreign troops to a promise of a world conference some time in the future for limitation of armaments, establishment of security and improvement of international commercial delegations.

Between the first and last steps of the program there is a multitude of provisions for negotiations and special military arrangements, one of which is that Britain and Italy prepare immediately for giving France and Belgium military assistance in the event of Germany's refusal to accept the terms that the other four Locarno powers have now laid down for her.

World Court Decision Sought

The plan also provides by a special set of resolutions for bringing in the League Council to take action for better future protection of the sanctity of treaties. And there is a demand that Germany submit to a decision by The Hague Court on the validity of her assertion that France first violated the Locarno treaty by making a military alliance with Russia, thereby absolving Germany from her agreement

Continued on Page Four

Aims of 4-Power Plan

By The Associated Press.

LONDON, March 20.—Highlights of the four-power plan published today in a British White Paper are:

The German Government is invited to present its argument against the Franco-Soviet mutual assistance pact to the Permanent Court of International Justice at The Hague.

All movement of German troops or war material into the Rhineland would be suspended and a limit placed on troops already there.

An international force composed of troops of the Locarno guarantor powers would be stationed in a buffer zone in Germany along the borders of France and Belgium until a new security treaty was drawn up. The zone would be 20 kilometers (12½ miles) wide, paralleling the frontier. German troops would be withdrawn from the zone.

An international commission would be formed to supervise the new zone.

Support would be given to a motion before the League of Nations to call an international conference to consider peace and revision of the League covenant, armament limitation, economic relations and Adolf Hitler's peace suggestions.

In letters attached to the accord, Great Britain and Italy agree, if Germany refuses the suggestions, to consult with Belgium and France on "all practical measures for the purpose of insuring security against unprovoked aggression."

Contacts among the general staffs of the four powers are to be established or continued.

FLANDIN WORKING TO END AFRICA WAR

Seeks 'Early Simultaneous Cessation of Hostilities and of Sanctions.'

PARIS-ROME 'DEAL' DENIED

But Reports Persist in London of Pressure on Ethiopia for Terms Italy Can Accept.

By P. J. PHILIP
Wireless to THE NEW YORK TIMES.

PARIS, March 20.—Foreign Minister Pierre-Etienne Flandin told the Chamber of Deputies today that he was seeking "rapidly to bring about simultaneous suspension of hostilities in Ethiopia and of sanctions against Italy."

The Foreign Minister was presenting to the Chamber his account of the London negotiations over the situation created by Germany's reoccupation of the Rhineland.

"Mr. Grandi (the Italian Ambassador to London), whose attitude in what was a most difficult situation for him has never ceased to be distinguished by the frankest friendship, gave his adhesion to the proposal," said Mr. Flandin.

"Shall I also stress," asked Mr. Flandin, "how much I endeavored—and how much I rejoiced in so doing—to prepare for reconstruction of the pacific front of Stresa, which now should be realized, thanks to the opening of peace negotiations which I succeeded in obtaining at Geneva recently and which are intended rapidly to bring about a simultaneous suspension of hostilities and of sanctions?"

Questioned this evening about that passage of his declaration relating to the removal of sanctions against Italy, Mr. Flandin replied that he did not refer to any special negotiation that had been carried on with Rome. His statement had been made, he said, with the intention of creating as speedily as possible a more favorable atmosphere among the Stresa powers.

London Peace Hopes Revived
Wireless to THE NEW YORK TIMES.

LONDON, March 20.—The announcement that the League of Nations Conciliation Committee of Thirteen would meet again Monday after many postponements suddenly revived hopes today that hostilities in Ethiopia would be ended soon and that sanctions against Italy would be dropped without long delay.

London buzzed with rumors of a "deal" when an incorrect version of Foreign Minister Pierre-Etienne Flandin's speech in the French Chamber of Deputies was displayed prominently on the front pages of afternoon newspapers. It turned out, however, that instead of announcing the end of sanctions, Mr. Flandin had merely expressed the hope that they could be lifted soon.

Fulfillment of this hope must depend more upon the temper of Emperor Haile Selassie than upon any real or rumored "deal" between the British, French and Italians. It takes two belligerents even to declare an armistice, and there was an impression in London tonight that the Ethiopian Emperor would need at least one more serious defeat in the field before he would be

Continued on Page Six

HITLER STIRS 40,000 IN FIGHTING SPEECH

Hamburg Crowd in Uproar as He Says Reich Won't Submit to Further Defamation.

REPLY TO POWERS HELD UP

Berlin Calls Plan for Foreign Force on Rhine Reversion to 'Versailles Mentality.'

Wireless to THE NEW YORK TIMES.

HAMBURG, March 20.—Chancellor Adolf Hitler delivered a stormy oration here tonight on the old thesis of German equality which outdid in fury any of his preceding campaign speeches and aroused an audience of 40,000 in the huge hall erected for the Max Schmeling-Steve Hamas fight to new heights of patriotic hysteria.

He warned the statesmen of Europe that the German people would not submit to further defamation and that Germany, whatever confronted her, would under no circumstances "retreat one inch" from her equal rights.

Unless his offer of cooperation in the task of achieving a European settlement were accepted on terms of strict equality, he reiterated, Germany would prefer retirement into "honorable isolation."

Reply to Locarno Powers

The Fuehrer's challenge was received as an answer to the memorandum of four Locarno powers which was handed to Joachim von Ribbentrop, Hitler's special Ambassador at Large, in London last night.

The speech went slowly, for the crowd was on its feet in a delirium of shouts and applause for almost as much of the evening as Hitler himself devoted to expressing his opinions.

"I need the German people in the struggle that I carry on for its own sake, in the struggle for German equality, in the struggle against the insolence of others who still regard Germany as an inferior or as enjoying inferior rights or who try to act as if such were the case," he declared.

"I need the German people to demonstrate therewith to the whole world that whatever happens we will not retreat one inch from our equal rights—not because we want to disturb European order but because we are convinced, contrary to the opinion of temporary and mortal politicians, that permanent order in Europe is possible only on a foundation of peoples enjoying equal rights.

"The opinion that European order can be founded permanently on the defamation of a people numbering 67,000,000 is lunatic and madness. They do not need to think that the German nation has rebelled simply because a certain man, Adolf Hitler, stands at its head. No, if I were not there, another would have come sooner or later. Germany will live longer than such an opinion will live.

"The German nation in its history has often suffered a bitter fate, as other nations have. It is alone in that it has never been destroyed by such events, as our enemies once believed. When they struck at Ger-

Continued on Page Six.

AAA Details New Program At Cost of $470,000,000

Shift of 30,000,000 Acres to Soil-Saving Plants Is Planned—Proposal Is Rushed as Renewed Surplus Is Threatened.

Special to THE NEW YORK TIMES.

WASHINGTON, March 20.—A soil conservation program designed to shift at least 30,000,000 acres of commercial crop land to grasses and legumes at an estimated cost of $470,000,000 this year was announced today by the Agricultural Adjustment Administration amid official misgivings as to its popularity in other than single crop sections.

Even experts admitted the plan is so far-reaching and complicated that they are confused as to the exact meaning of some provisions.

Gravely concerned at the prospect of renewed surplus production, particularly of grains and of resulting falling prices, AAA officials worked late into the night to get the outline of the program out to the "Grass Roots" in time to affect 1936 planting.

Embracing thirteen field crop classifications, the new program would make benefit payments to farmers at an average rate of $10 an acre in return for shifting 15 per cent of their intensively cultivated land to approved "soil conserving" crops. Farmers who engaged in recognized soil improving practices, such as terracing to prevent erosion, also would qualify for this payment.

This soil conserving payment would be based upon the past and present productivity of the land and for this reason might rise as high as $40 an acre or fall as low as $4 or $5. A farmer's production rec-

Continued on Page Two

YOUTH GROUPS URGE $3,500,000,000 AID AT SENATE HEARING

Delegates From All Sections Mass in Appeal for Bill to Give 5,000,000 Jobs.

EARLY ACTION UNLIKELY

Committee Opposition Believed Strong — Foes of Plan Predict $14,000,000,000 Cost.

Special to THE NEW YORK TIMES.

WASHINGTON, March 20.—Mass power of more than 2,250,000 young men and women was thrown behind the "American Youth Act" as the Senate Committee on Education and Labor today held hearings on this bill which proposes to pay wages and living expenses to 5,000,000 unemployed young persons and needy students at a cost of $3,500,000,000 to the United States Government.

Delegates from youth societies in many parts of the country crowded the committee room and applauded the witnesses testifying for the bill recently introduced by two liberals, Senator Benson of Minnesota and Representative Amlie of Wisconsin. A vivid cross-section of American youth was present, representing varying creeds and colors.

William Wattenberg of New York, one of the witnesses for the bill, set the cost at $3,515,410,000, but Kenneth Holland of the American Youth Commission, who criticized the measure, said the total could amount to from $14,000,000,000 to $20,000,000,000 if the age limits were extended.

Present Efforts Scored

Strong dissatisfaction with the National Youth Administration, the government's effort to cope with the youth problem, was expressed by some witnesses.

Francis J. Gorman of the United Textile Workers and Professor Charles A. Beard, the historian, were among the twoscore witnesses backing the bill. Mr. Gorman asserted that the young men and women were being used "as a bludgeon" to defeat conditions for which trade unions had fought. Dr. Beard said the "tragic figures of 5,000,000 to 8,000,000 young people between 16 and 25 wholly unoccupied are a frightful challenge."

Gilbert Green of New York, secretary of the Young Communists, declared there was a "surging wave of anger and resentment" among modern youth who demanded a new social order like that of Soviet Russia to govern this country.

No great sympathy was shown by the committeemen toward the $3,500,000,000 scheme, and there is general belief that it will repose in the committee for a considerable period, even if eventually reported out at this session of Congress.

Minimum Weekly Wage

Under the measure the Secretary of Labor and Commissioner of Education are told to establish immediately a system of vocational training and employment "on public enterprises," to pay prevailing wages, but not less than $15 weekly plus $3 for each dependent, to youths between the ages of 16 and 25. Further, full payments of fees, plus weekly living expenses, must be paid to needy high school and vocational training students, and the compensation exclusive of fees must not be below $15 monthly.

The act provides for the necessary Treasury appropriation, but it adds:

"Further taxation necessary to provide funds for the purposes of this act shall be levied on inheri-

Continued on Page Three

WOMEN HOSTAGES SEIZED AS ROBBERS LOOT NANUET BANK

Two Sisters Kidnapped and Used to Shield Flight to Newark With $12,000 Booty.

AUTOIST SHOT TO GET CAR

Federal Agents Find Escape Machine Abandoned and Bandits' Fingerprints.

Special to THE NEW YORK TIMES.

NANUET, N. Y., Saturday, March 21.—Federal agents, New Jersey and New York police joined forces early this morning in a hunt for four armed bandits who held up the Nanuet National Bank yesterday afternoon and escaped by kidnapping two sisters in stolen cars.

The four thieves escaped in two cars—one of which was found later in Newark—after smashing one stolen car when their own vehicle stalled here a few minutes after the hold-up, which netted them nearly $12,000.

A motorist was shot in both legs a short distance from the hold-up scene when he objected to the seizure of his car.

The search for the bandits centered after midnight in New York City, Newark and near-by New Jersey cities.

Two Hold Up Bank

The four men appeared in a black sedan on Main Street here shortly after 2:30 P. M. yesterday. Near the bank they stopped the car and two of the men got out and entered the bank. As they walked toward the building, the other two men drove the car around the block.

In the bank were Edward Straub, cashier; his assistant, John Stefan, and Paul Bernreiter, a clerk. One of the two thieves drew a pistol and warned the employes to make no outcry. Then while the bank employes held their hands over their heads, the robbers scooped up all available cash, nearly $12,000.

Again warning the three employes

Continued on Page Three

Permanent State Relief Plan Approved By Gov. Lehman and Legislature's Chiefs

Special to THE NEW YORK TIMES.

ALBANY, March 20.—After conferences between Governor Lehman, leaders of the Legislature and relief experts, which have been in progress at different times for more than a month, an agreement was reached in the early morning hours today on a plan for putting the administration of unemployment relief on a basis of permanency as a division of the State Department of Social Welfare. Such relief is now administered by the Temporary Emergency Relief Administration.

It became known today that a bill to carry the plan into effect was being prepared for introduction next week as soon as some details, still awaiting a decision, had been worked out.

The agreement ends a controversy which has been in progress since the plan for making unemployment relief a regular State activity was first broached.

The differences, it has been apparent, have been not on partisan grounds or between the legislative leaders but among various groups of relief experts, who now, it was said, had been brought together in support of a compromise plan for which the bill will provide.

Governor Lehman said today that he was well pleased that the controversy had come to an end and held that the transfer from the TERA can go into effect at the beginning of the next fiscal year, July 1.

It is not intended to abolish the TERA as soon as the transfer has been effected. As part of the new plan another measure extending its life, possibly until Jan. 1, 1937, is to be put through in the Legislature, making it possible for the TERA to wind up its work without haste and also giving the new division time to become properly organized.

The conference at which the agreement was reached was the fourth on the subject held at the Executive Mansion. The TERA, the Department of Social Welfare and the Wardwell Commission, which, after a protracted investigation of social welfare and relief activities in the State, reported to the Governor and the Legislature early this session, all were represented at the conferences.

The Democratic and Republican leaders of the Legislature, of course, and at the final conference, last

Continued on Page Three

FLOOD PARALYZES HARTFORD; WIDE RUIN IN NEW ENGLAND; WATERS ELSEWHERE RECEDE

The Flood Situation

By The Associated Press.

As rivers in New England raced toward record crests and laid waste new areas in that region, the industrial Northeast from the Ohio Valley to Maine, overwhelmed by the worst flood disasters since the turn of the century, counted 152 dead. Meanwhile, the flood-ravaged regions from which the waters had begun to recede found themselves confronted with disease, thirst and discouraging heaps of wreckage. The Red Cross was caring for 270,000 in thirteen States, and property damage was estimated at $300,000,000.

In brief, by regions:

NEW ENGLAND—Scores of communities, including Hartford, Conn., were struck by new floods. Dead, 22; homeless, 100,000; damage, $100,000,000. In Hartford water spread over a large part of the city and threatened to disrupt all business activity. Three persons were missing; damage was estimated at $5,000,000.

OHIO VALLEY—Hundreds fled their homes between Marietta and Portsmouth as the Ohio River flood rolled southward, subsiding gradually. Seventeen were dead in West Virginia; property damage was $20,000,000. The damage in Ohio was $7,000,000.

PENNSYLVANIA—Flood-ravaged sections combated disease, food and water famines. Dead, 99; damage $150,000,000. Pittsburgh had only partial light, heat and power service, and faced threats of epidemic and water famine. Throughout Western Pennsylvania solemn crowds filed through temporary morgues identifying the remainder of the 69 dead in that region. Metropolitan Pittsburgh accounted for 45 of the victims.

WASHINGTON—President Roosevelt deferred his vacation to organize relief work; Congress considered spending $400,000,000; donations to the Red Cross relief fund poured in.

NEW YORK—Floods receded in most sections; sleet storms isolated mid-State towns.

BIG HARTFORD AREA IS HIT

Thousands Flee From Homes as River Passes the 37-Foot Level.

LIGHT AND POWER CUT OFF

Waters Inundate Business District and 650 Troops Are on Guard Against Vandals.

WPA MEN RUSH SANDBAGS

Lobbies of Hotels Are Flooded —Debris Floats Into City, Causing Disease Warning.

By LEO KIERAN
Special to THE NEW YORK TIMES.

HARTFORD, Conn., March 20.—With confusion and excitement reigning in Hartford's streets while more than a fifth of its area was covered by the waters of the raging Connecticut River, this capital city of the State today bore the brunt of the great flood in the Connecticut Valley.

Throughout the length of the Connecticut River dams and bridges still standing were in imminent danger of being swept downstream to increase the disastrous effects of the flood in the lower reaches of the valley.

Damage has already reached an estimate of $5,000,000 in this city itself. North from here along the river the countryside was completely isolated. It was estimated here today that more than 30,000 persons in the Connecticut Valley have been rendered homeless and destitute.

Power, light and communication systems in Hartford were almost paralyzed during the day and tonight. Water poured into the lobbies and flooded the cellars and basements of hotels. There was fear of a general food shortage as housewives from the non-flooded areas rushed the stores at an alarming rate.

Force of Troops Increased

Meanwhile the city itself was practically under martial law. National Guard forces were increased today at the request of Mayor Thomas J. Spellacy, and tonight special emergency orders were issued by Governor Cross to mobilize units in other cities for possible duty here. Police restricted the activities of rowboats and other water craft to persons duly authorized and accredited from the Mayor's office.

Crowds of pedestrians were on the streets tonight despite the darkness. Many individuals suffered head-on collisions with others, the occasional beams of hand torches and moving automobile headlights only making the shifting shadows more confusing.

Fire apparatus from headquarters was garaged on the street corners high above the former fire building, where half the garage space was submerged. Workmen were toiling on a temporary structure of wood to serve as fire headquarters until the flood recedes.

According to the city officials tonight, the high mark of the flood has been reached. From a reading of 37.75 feet at 4 P. M., the official gauge dropped by 7 o'clock to 37.2 feet, but the waters were still eight feet higher than in the record 1927 flood.

40,000 Phones Out of Order

Meanwhile, the emergency forces of the city doubled their efforts to prevent looting in the flooded areas.

Telephone service collapsed save for a few official lines operating on battery power, and more than 40,000 telephone lines were reported out of commission.

All highways were closed to the north and east. Telegraphers worked by candle light with swamped wires. The closing of the roads to the south was being considered momentarily as the flood tide continued on toward Long Island Sound.

To relieve the congestion in the non-flooded parts of the city, the police tonight barred all except relief and reconstruction vehicles from the clear streets of the city.

The Connecticut tobacco crop has been virtually destroyed by the floods, the shade and stalk plants on which the cigar industry depends having been ravaged over a wide

Continued on Page Ten

PITTSBURGH FIGHTS MENACE OF DISEASE

Fire Danger Is Also Feared as Water Runs So Low That Famine Is Threatened.

By F. RAYMOND DANIELL
Special to THE NEW YORK TIMES.

PITTSBURGH, March 20.—With the rivers which flooded Pittsburgh once more within their banks, two facts stood out clearly today. The first was that the damage was much greater than even the most extravagant of the earlier estimates. The second was that the nation's industrial center, because of crippled power service, faces a long and indefinite period of enforced idleness in its great mills and factories.

At present, the city and the metropolitan area, with a population of nearly 1,500,000 in all, is threatened by the two-edged sword of fire and disease, with water supplies falling constantly lower despite desperate efforts to conserve them. The fire hazard is a real one.

The threat of disease in the wake of the flood, which caused deaths estimated at between thirty and forty-five in Allegheny County, appeared less imminent. Residents of Pittsburgh have been warned to boil their drinking water, and Dr. Ray P. Moyer, Director of Public Health, has condemned more than 500 carloads of foodstuffs which it was feared might have been contaminated by flood waters.

Troops continued today to patrol

Continued on Page Eight

FLOOD IS SWEEPING DOWN OHIO VALLEY

High Waters Rush On and Inundate Towns in Ohio and West Virginia.

Copyright, 1936, by The Associated Press

PORTSMOUTH, Ohio, March 20.—Ohio River Valley flood waters pushed on relentlessly tonight, with ever-increasing refugee lists and devastation.

From out of the upper valley tri-State region of Ohio, Pennsylvania and West Virginia the crest of the flood moved past Marietta, Ohio, into Pomeroy, Ohio, and menaced Kentucky river towns.

In the lower valley thousands evacuated their homes. Nineteen hundred were moving out in Kentucky cities in the Cincinnati area. Unofficial estimates of homeless ranged between 25,000 and 30,000.

Rehabilitation and relief for flood sufferers progressed slowly between Pittsburgh and Marietta. Waters receded steadily, however, from the worst flood in the upper valley's history.

Damage was heaviest to the steel, pottery and mine district in that area. Newspaper men who surveyed it agreed that it would vary between $10,000,000 and $15,000,000.

Cities and villages southward from Marietta were adequately prepared for the destructive, débris-filled waters. Some took the flood as an "annual event." The crest moved ten to twelve feet under record marks set by the disastrous flood of 1913.

While the river dropped steadily in the rich upper valley Tri-State region of Ohio, Pennsylvania and West Virginia, the crest moved past Marietta, Ohio, toward Pomeroy, Gallipolis and Portsmouth, menacing towns both in Ohio and Kentucky.

The water stood at 52.8 feet at Gallipolis, with a 59-foot crest expected by morning.

Portsmouth had slightly more than fifty-three feet lapping against a 60-foot flood wall.

Baggage Station Carried Away

Swift waters advancing ahead of the crest swept a railroad baggage station from the riverfront business district of Pomeroy, which has a population of 3,500. Six feet of water ran through its streets and was rising slowly. The fronts of all business places were boarded up. Five hundred were homeless.

The little boat-building town of Point Pleasant, W. Va., at the mouth of the Kanawha River, was isolated. Water poured through its streets, but a large number of its residents had taken refuge in a National Guard camp five miles back in a hilltop region.

Relief agencies cared for 400 homeless in the Gallipolis lowland areas. A fifty-nine-foot crest, eleven feet under 1913, was expected there tomorrow morning. The main business and residential sections were safe on high ground.

The Federal Government's $5,000,000 partly completed dam, seven

Continued on Page Nine

Eviction scene, New York City.

Museum of the City of New York

Day after day, crowds waited outside employment agencies in New York.

Museum of the City of New York

"All the News That's Fit to Print."

The New York Times.

LATE CITY EDITION
Local showers, little change in temperature today. Tomorrow fair, cooler, preceded by showers.
Temperatures Yesterday—Max., 86; min., 58.

Copyright, 1936, by The New York Times Company.

VOL. LXXXV....No. 28,619. Entered as Second-Class Matter, Postoffice, New York, N. Y. NEW YORK, TUESDAY, JUNE 2, 1936. P TWO CENTS In New York City. | THREE CENTS Elsewhere Except Within 200 Miles | FOUR CENTS Elsewhere Except in 7th and 8th Postal Zones.

NEW YORK GREETS THE QUEEN MARY WITH MIGHTY DIN

HER SPEED CUT BY FOG

British Liner Misses the Normandie's Record by 42 Minutes.

SALUTED BY HARBOR CRAFT

Boats Swarm About as Planes Dip Wings and Throngs Cheer From Shore.

GIANT DOCKED SMOOTHLY

Passengers Praise Steadiness of Vessel—Line's Head Calls Her 'Ship of Peace.'

By F. RAYMOND DANIELL

Cheered by thousands ashore and afloat, Great Britain's new 80,000-ton challenger for supremacy among the merchant vessels of the world, the 1,018-foot Queen Mary, completed her maiden voyage to the United States yesterday afternoon, sliding into her berth at West Fiftieth Street as smoothly and easily as a yacht.

She had failed by the narrowest of margins to win back for Britain the coveted blue pennant that the Normandie, on her record-breaking maiden voyage a year ago, captured for France. Her officers, with British tenacity and sportsmanship, promised to try again and made no excuses, although fog cut down the new ship's speed materially.

Even though the Queen Mary had failed to prove herself the fastest ship afloat, and while her great bulk was equaled, if not exceeded, by the Normandie, on her record-breaking maiden voyage a year ago, and the harbor craft and the people of the city joined in giving her the royal welcome that was due the first Cunarder to be christened by a Queen with her own name. She accepted the homage of lesser craft with gracious dignity, responding to the shrill salutes with her deep-throated voice two octaves below middle A.

Small Craft Surround Her

From the moment she dropped her sixteen-ton bow anchor at Quarantine, this 10 A. M., until 4:10 P. M., when she began discharging her 1,849 passengers after an up-river wind had snapped an eight-inch hawser, the great, proud ship was surrounded by a flotilla of tugs, yachts, excursion boats and other small craft, while airplanes aloft dipped their wings in salute. Thousands of persons lined the shore and admired her trim lines from afar.

Although this newest ship, which must compete not only with the French liner Normandie but with the German dirigible Hindenburg as well for speed-conscious passengers in the North Atlantic trade, did not establish any new record for the ocean crossing, she failed by only forty-two minutes to match her rival's time. The competition between the two liners for the speed record probably will be as keen in the future as the old rivalry of Mississippi River steamboats, for few maritime experts believe that either ship has been unthrottled to the limit.

The Queen Mary averaged 29.13 knots on a measured course of 3,158 nautical miles between Cherbourg Breakwater and Ambrose Light, completing the journey between those two points in 4 days 12 hours 24 minutes at 9:03 A. M. The Normandie, sailing a slightly different course of 3,192 nautical miles from Southampton Nab to Ambrose a year ago, averaged 29.64 and completed the ocean crossing in 4 days 11 hours 42 minutes, which is about two days longer than the airship Hindenburg's best time between Germany and Lakehurst.

Passengers Praise Liner

The passengers aboard the new liner, one of the lifeboats of which will carry more passengers than the total complement of the Britannia, the first Cunarder, praised her highly for her steadiness and absence of vibration, even when running at her top speed of more than 30 knots. Among them were Robert W. Bingham, Ambassador to the Court of St. James; the Marquis and Marchioness of Milford-Haven, Sir Joseph and Lady Robinson and the Marquis of Donegal.

Mayor La Guardia's official reception committee, headed by Samuel Seabury, first saw the faint outline of the ship through the spindrift from the bow of the Riverside

Continued on Page Two

Normandie Reaches Port With Blue Ribbon Flying

Wireless to THE NEW YORK TIMES.

PARIS, June 1.—The French liner Normandie returned to Havre this afternoon with the blue ribbon flying and general content aboard and ashore that the Queen Mary had not on her first trip deprived her of that honor.

On Friday, May 29, the Normandie averaged 29.43 knots. Even at 30 knots, it is maintained, the vessel is steady. With her new propellers the vibration that marked last year's trips has been overcome.

On her homeward trip her speed was not pressed at any time and there is plenty of confidence here that the Normandie has an extra turn of speed in her boilers which will be forthcoming if and when the blue ribbon is endangered.

HOFFMAN TO OUST COL. SCHWARZKOPF

Kimberling Named by Governor to Head New Jersey Police—Approval Up to Senate.

PLEAS OF PUBLIC IGNORED

Executive Also Flouts Wish of Party Leaders After Feud in Lindbergh Case.

Special to THE NEW YORK TIMES.

TRENTON, N. J., June 1.—Governor Harold G. Hoffman sent to the Senate for confirmation tonight the appointment of Colonel Mark O. Kimberling, warden of the State penitentiary, as superintendent of the New Jersey State Police to succeed Colonel H. Norman Schwarzkopf.

The appointment of his personal friend was made without comment by the Governor and against the wishes of leaders in his own political organization. It completely ignored many prominent individuals and organizations that had petitioned for the reappointment of Colonel Schwarzkopf.

The selection was announced on slips of paper given to newspaper men shortly after 9 P. M. on which the Governor also announced the reappointment of Thomas A. Mathis as Secretary of State and the appointment of Senator President John C. Barbour of Passaic County as judge of the Circuit Court to succeed the late Worrall F. Mountain.

Word of the Governor's choice for the head of the State Police was given to Colonel Schwarzkopf by newspaper men. He refused to make any comment. The Governor also refused to speak about the appointment.

Hundreds Back Schwarzkopf

The appointment of Colonel Kimberling had been expected for some time and recently hundreds of letters and petitions were received by the Governor asking him to keep Colonel Schwarzkopf in office.

The Senate adjourned at 10:30 P. M. until noon tomorrow without confirming Colonel Kimberling's appointment.

To vote on the appointment tomorrow it will be necessary to suspend the Senate rules, which require that a nomination cannot be considered on the same day on which it may be reported from committee. Should the Senate fail to confirm the appointment, it could not take action until after the ten-day adjournment that is expected.

Considerable opposition to the appointment of Colonel Kimberling was expressed tonight by political leaders who have opposed the Governor recently. Senator Lester H. Clee, leader of the Republican Clean Government forces of Essex County, who has been a leader in opposing the Governor's policies, said he would support Colonel Schwarzkopf for reappointment against the wishes of Governor Hoffman, the nominal leader of the State party organization.

Governor Hoffman and Colonel Schwarzkopf have been at odds for some years. During the recent investigation carried on by the Governor in the case of Bruno Richard Hauptmann, convicted slayer of the Lindbergh baby, the Governor referred to the State Police handling of the whole kidnapping case as the "worst bungled police job in history."

The feud of the Governor and the head of the State Police, however, goes back to a time during the Governorship of A. Harry Moore.

Continued on Page Fifteen

SOVIET TO PROTECT RIGHTS OF CITIZEN UNDER NEW CODE

Revised Constitution Shifts Stress From Guarding State to Guarding Individual.

JUDGES WILL BE ELECTED

Prosecutor Reveals Accused Person Will Present His Own Story Before Indictment.

By HAROLD DENNY

Special Cable to THE NEW YORK TIMES.

MOSCOW, June 1.—Reorganization of the Soviet judicial system so as to protect the civil rights and personal dignity of citizens will be provided for in the new Constitution of the Union of Soviet Socialist Republics. This was announced today by Andrei Vyshinsky, the Soviet's chief prosecutor, who is a member of the commission headed by Joseph Stalin that has framed the Constitution.

Mr. Vyshinsky's statement contains the highly significant information that the emphasis of the "revolutionary law" will be shifted from its present almost complete preoccupation with protection of the State to protection as well of the individual, even against wrongful prosecution by the State.

The statement is the first disclosure of any details of the new Constitution. That document is closely held among the highest members of the government preparatory to being made public, possibly this month. It will be adopted at the next All-Union Congress of Soviets.

Aim of Present System

The first principle of the present judicial system, as Mr. Vyshinsky described it today, is "to defend the interests of the proletarian State and the Socialist property which forms the economic basis of the Soviet régime from any inroads of class enemies and other criminal elements antagonistic to the cause of socialism by suppressing any resistance of those enemies and by developing a large-scale system of forced reformatory measures."

Mr. Vyshinsky officially confirmed earlier reports that judges under the new Constitution would be elected by direct secret ballot instead of being appointed by executive committees of soviets.

"This will connect the judge more closely to the broad masses of the working people," he continued, "and in the eyes of the population will increase the significance of the people's judge as guardian of the interests of the proletarian State and of all the workers.

"The basic defect of the criminal code is its unwieldiness, its lack of clarity and its insufficiency of attention to defense of the rights and interests of individual working people."

Criminal Code Redrawn

Therefore, said the prosecutor, the criminal code will be revised from the ground up, with the special object of providing maximum precautions against unwarranted indictments and unjust convictions. One reform will consist of allowing the accused to tell the judge his own story before indictment. The defendant may, bring his own lawyer or the lawyer may confer alone with the judge on his behalf.

The legal profession also will regain some of its ancient prerogatives, which will give defense lawyers more scope in protecting their

Continued on Page Eight

British African Colonies Discuss Defense Today

By The Associated Press.

NAIROBI, Kenya, East Africa, June 1.—The Governors of five British colonies of East Africa will gather tomorrow at Dar es Salaam, Tanganyika, to discuss the defense of East Africa.

The Governors of Kenya, Uganda, Tanganyika, Nyasaland and Zanzibar will be present.

It is understood they will also consider plans for the unification of civil aviation in East Africa.

Italy's possession of Ethiopia brings her to the northern border of Kenya and close to the northern border of Uganda. The other colonies lie to the southward.

Native unrest has been caused in their territories by the Italian conquest.

CONVICTS MURDER LIFER AT SING SING

Jewel Thief and Member of Prison Band Is Clubbed to Death in Recreation Room.

7 SUSPECTS ARE ISOLATED

Cut in Pay to Musicians Is Believed to Have Been Cause of Fatal Row.

Special to THE NEW YORK TIMES.

OSSINING, N. Y., June 1.—A lifeterm convict was struck on the head and fatally injured in Sing Sing late today by other prisoners. The dead man was a musician in the prisoners' band and officials expressed the belief that other members of the band might have considered him responsible for a recent cut in their small salary.

The victim was Frank Lopez, 44 years old, who formerly lived at 1,500 Boston Road, the Bronx. He had served nearly all of the past twenty-eight years in prison and had received a life sentence in 1930 under the Baumes Law.

Lopez had blamed a skull fracture received many years ago for his criminal tendencies.

The murder was disclosed by Warden Lewis E. Lawes shortly after Lopez died in the prison hospital at 9:20 P. M. According to the warden, the prisoner had been allowed to go to the recreation building for his free hours this afternoon.

Shortly after 5:30 P. M. Keeper Henry Lashway, patrolling the recreation building, saw a group of seven prisoners huddled together on the third floor. On the floor are a number of chairs and tables. The band instruments are kept in one corner.

As the keeper appeared, the prisoners separated hurriedly and attempted to leave the floor. Discovering a man on the floor, Lashway called to Keeper Edward Farrell. They kept the seven men together. They identified the victim as Lopez and found that he was unconscious from a severe blow on the head.

The injured man was rushed to the prison hospital where physicians under Dr. Charles C. Sweet attempted to save his life. Warden Lawes said that Lopez never regained consciousness.

The seven prisoners were put into separate cells and Warden Lawes started an investigation. He said that several of the men declared that Lopez had suddenly become dizzy and fallen. One of the prisoners, the warden said, declared that Lopez had complained of feel-

Continued on Page Three

Suspect Seized in Queens '3X' Murders; Reported to Have Confessed Shooting Two

A possible solution to the "3X" murders that terrorized nocturnal couples in sparsely settled sections of Queens in 1930 was provided yesterday by the arrest of a man in Elizabethtown, N. Y., who, the police declared, confessed to the crimes.

The prisoner, a powerfully built man just under six feet tall, identified himself as Frank Engel, 29 years old, of 9-11 125th Street, College Point. State Troopers Elmer Salisbury and Walter Rockburn said they arrested Engel because of his "queer actions" in an Elizabethtown garage and that his confession of the Queens slayings followed their questioning.

Notified of the arrest, District Attorney Charles P. Sullivan of Queens left by automobile for Elizabethtown last evening, accompanied by, James J. Conroy, his chief assistant; Captain Edward Burke and Lieutenant Hugh McGovern of the Queens homicide squad.

Engel and a friend, Felix Nowicki of 125-11 Tenth Avenue, College Point, left last week in Engel's car to seek employment at various Summer resorts in the Adirondacks. An expert swimmer, Engel had worked at up-State resorts for several seasons as a lifeguard and swimming instructor. At other times, according to his parents, he drove a taxicab in Queens.

Engel is a son of Mr. and Mrs. Joseph Engel and is the second oldest of five boys and four girls in the family. He was born and educated in Queens, having been graduated from the St. Fidelis Parochial School. He was a member of the College Point Volunteer Life-saving Corps and in 1928 he rowed in a crew that won a race around Manhattan Island. The latter event was sponsored by the United States Coast Guard.

The slayer who killed two victims with a pistol as they sat in parked cars accompanied by women did not leave papers on the bodies of his victims describing himself as "3X" but wrote to newspapers boasting of his exploits and predicting "fourteen others" to follow.

When the search for the killer was at its height 2,000 patrolmen and detectives combed the lover's lanes of Queens and hundreds were assigned to lonely sections for weeks at a time. The killer suddenly ceased his activity, however, and no trace of him was ever found.

The two victims of the "3X" murders were Joseph Moyzynsky, a grocer, and Noel Sowley, 26-year-old radio salesman.

2 TAX BILL REPORTS FILED WITH SENATE DRAW BATTLE LINE

Black and La Follette Demand Higher Levy on Profits and Oppose Committee Bill.

DEBATE WILL START TODAY

Couzens Threatens Filibuster to Bar Acceptance of House Terms in Final Drive.

Text of minority report and summary of Tax Bill, Pp. 21, 22.

By TURNER CATLEDGE

Special to THE NEW YORK TIMES.

WASHINGTON, June 1.—Warnings of a bitter fight ahead over the Tax Bill, supported by the filing in the Senate of a minority report against the Finance Committee compromise, failed to deter administration leaders today in their drive to end the present session of Congress by Saturday or Monday.

The tax measure was in position tonight to be taken up in the Senate tomorrow. With passage of the $1,425,000,000 relief appropriation today, the revenue bill became the last major hurdle for the leadership to clear on its way to the adjournment goal.

A "dummy" majority report on the Tax Bill was filed soon after the Senate convened this morning. This was to make sure that it would be in order for consideration tomorrow. The Finance Committee's formal argument, which actually comprises the report, will hardly be ready before the bill is called up by Acting Chairman King, who will pilot it in the absence of Chairman Harrison. The latter is ill at his home.

Black and La Follette Act

Soon after the text of the revised bill was made available this afternoon, Senator Black, acting for himself and Senator La Follette, submitted a minority report as the basis for their threatened fight to restore to the bill by floor amendments levies nearer in accord with the theory of an undistributed corporate profits tax requested by President Roosevelt in his message of March 3.

Simultaneously, Senator Couzens, the only Finance Committee member who voted against any form of undistributed profits levy, gave emphatic notice that a coalition of Republicans and conservative Democrats would resist to the last ditch any impost of this kind other than that provided in the committee compromise.

He intimated that if the leaders rushed the bill through the Senate and to conference, and there evolved a measure approximating the House's version of the President's plan, an interminable filibuster would result, notwithstanding adjournment plans in the contrary.

Follows Compromise Lines

As reported today, the compromise bill followed exactly the lines agreed upon in committee last week. It included a combination of corporate income tax, with rates ranging from 15½ to 18 per cent, to be substituted for the present schedule of 12½ to 15 per cent, and a 7 per cent flat surtax on undistributed corporate profits; a step-up of 1 per cent in each individual surtax bracket on incomes between $6,000 and $50,000; full application of the normal income tax rate of 4 per cent to dividends in the hands of individual shareholders, and a "windfall" tax of 80 per cent on unjust enrichment resulting from the return or abatement of formerly impounded or uncollected agricultural processing taxes.

The bill also reasserted the House provisions liberalizing taxes on corporate liquidations, designed to induce the distribution of assets of many personal holding companies so that such proceeds might be levied upon as income in the hands of their eventual recipients.

In the form presented today, the Treasury calculated that the bill would produce $702,000,000 in additional revenue for the first year and $620,000,000 annually thereafter.

The President had asked for a measure that would bring in at least $793,000,000 in new funds annually for the first three years and $620,000,000 permanently thereafter. It was only by this additional yield, he said, that provision could be made through taxes for financing the new farm program and prepayment of the veterans' bonus, and for making up over a short term of years the current budget deficiency caused by the Supreme Court's invalidation of the Agricultural Adjustment Act.

Senators Black and La Follette argued in their minority report that the compromise failed to meet the revenue requirements. But more than that, they said, it sought to raise the additional funds through additional taxes

Continued on Page Twenty

SUPREME COURT, 5-4, VOIDS STATE MINIMUM WAGE LAW; ANOTHER BLOW, SAYS A. F. of L.

Wage Ruling Stirs Indignation In Congress and in Labor Ranks

Many in Capital Voice Astonishment and Call Court Inconsistent —Lehman Deplores Lost Protection for Millions— Officials of Woman's Party Pleased.

Special to THE NEW YORK TIMES.

WASHINGTON, June 1.—Astonishment, indignation and disappointment greeted the Supreme Court's decision in the New York minimum wage case from the ranks of labor, Congress and women advocates of such laws. The National Woman's Party, ardent supporter of equal rights for women, hailed the decision with delight on the ground that laws seeming to "protect" women really exploited them.

William Green, president of the American Federation of Labor, said:

"The decision of the Supreme Court holding the New York State Minimum Wage Law invalid can only be regarded as another blow to labor and its friends throughout the entire country.

"The one ray of hope to labor arising from the decision is to be found in the five-to-four opinion of the court. We hope that a study of the decision will show that a way can still be found to enact a minimum wage law which can and will be held constitutional.

"Labor will fight on. It cannot and will not assume a defeatist attitude in its fight for the enactment of social justice legislation."

Mary Anderson, chief of the Women's Bureau, Department of Labor, a leader in the legislative battle for minimum wages, said that while she could not officially comment on the decision, those who favored such laws would be deeply disappointed at the outcome, which would affect more than 3,000,000 working women in sixteen States.

The decision probably caused more astonishment among members of Congress than any of the previous rulings during the past year. Disbelief at first greeted the news conveyed by newspaper men to individual members, but soon gave way to perplexity.

"I am just wondering if there are any States' rights," said Representative Bankhead of Alabama, House majority leader, summing up the situation as expressed by others. Then he added:

"What power have the Federal authorities to pass upon State legislation?"

Senator Wagner, who had much

Continued on Page Nineteen

TREASURY LOAN OVERSOLD IN DAY

Heavy Oversubscriptions Are Indicated for Tax-Exempt, Low-Interest Issues.

MORGENTHAU IS PLEASED

Allotments Will Be Announced on Thursday — Conversion Offering Ends Tomorrow.

Special to THE NEW YORK TIMES.

WASHINGTON, June 1.—Indicating a heavy oversubscription of the Treasury's offering of $600,000,000 of 2¾ per cent bonds and $400,000,000 of 1⅜ per cent notes, Secretary Morgenthau announced that the subscription books would be closed this midnight.

No indication as to the amount of the oversubscription was given by Mr. Morgenthau, although he declared that he was well pleased with the response. There were large oversubscriptions to the Treasury issues of 2¾ per cent bonds and 1⅜ per cent notes on Dec. 15 and March 15.

On both of the previous major offerings of Treasury bonds and notes the subscriptions were closed in one day, as was the case of the current securities.

Subscriptions for the cash offerings on bonds and notes, terminated at the close of business today, were to be considered if placed in the mails before midnight.

Indication of Popularity

A further indication of the popularity of the two issues was seen in the fact that the books will be closed Wednesday, June 3, for the receipt of subscriptions in payment of which Treasury notes maturing June 15 and Aug. 1 are offered in payment. On June 15 there is a maturity of $686,616,400 in notes and on Aug. 1 of $364,138,000 in the same type of security. The closing of the books for an exchange offering was made in record time, although on cash offerings it has been customary to close the books in one day.

Official announcement of the allocations by Federal Reserve districts was expected to be made Thursday.

Mr. Morgenthau described the offering as a big success, with the implication that it was as well oversubscribed as those of last December and last March.

Statement by Morgenthau

His official announcement follows:

"Secretary of the Treasury Morgenthau announced last night that the subscription books for the current offering of 2¾ per cent Treasury bonds of 1951-54 and of 1⅜ per cent Treasury notes of Series B, 1941 closed at the close of business Monday, June 1, for the receipt of cash subscriptions.

"Cash subscriptions for either is-

Continued on Page Nineteen

RELIEF BILL PASSED BY SENATE, 62 TO 14

Borah Attacks Vandenberg's Substitute, Which Is Defeated by 57 to 14.

PWA GRANT LIMIT LIFTED

Chamber Strikes Out Clause Which Restricted Aid to 30% of Projects' Cost.

Special to THE NEW YORK TIMES.

WASHINGTON, June 1.—The Senate passed late today, by a vote of 62 to 14, the Deficiency Appropriation Bill containing $1,425,000,000 for work relief and $300,000,000 for public works to be expended during the coming fiscal year. The upper chamber sat late to complete action on the measure as part of administration leaders' plans to effect an adjournment of Congress by the end of this week.

Before the final vote, the Senate rejected the substitute work relief plan offered by Senator Vandenberg, which would have turned over the administration of relief funds to the States, by 57 to 14. Senator Borah spoke against the Vandenberg proposal and voted against it on the ground that it would be less efficient than the present arrangement.

On the final passage of the bill, three Democrats joined eleven Republicans in voting "no." They were Senators Tydings of Maryland, Byrd of Virginia, and Bulkley of Ohio. Mr. Bulkley announced that his colleague, Senator Donahey, would have voted against the bill had he been present.

Bill Gets Republican Support

A number of Republicans joined administration supporters in voting for the bill. Their number included Senators Borah, Capper, Carey, Davis, Frazier, Johnson, La Follette, and McNary, the minority floor leader.

Mr. Vandenberg called up his substitute amendment toward the end of the session, and there was relatively little debate. In offering it, he announced that he had no illusion as to what the result would be.

"I want to get this on the record," he told the Senate, "because the record may be useful."

He declared that the government would never eliminate waste and political exploitation from the administration of relief funds until that supervision was turned over to the States and controlled by the people who best knew local conditions.

It was on that point that Mr. Borah differed with him. The Idaho Senator held that efficiency and economy would be impossible under a scheme where one sovereignty administered the expenditure of funds granted by another sovereignty. He said that he had made a close study of the problem

Continued on Page Seventeen

RULING BARS ALL CURBS

Majority Decision Blocks Both State and Federal Limitations.

HITS 17 COMMONWEALTHS

Hughes in Dissenting Opinion Holds N. Y. Act Safeguarded Employer and Employe.

STONE ATTACKS FINDING

He Refers to Majority Attitude as Expression of 'Personal Economic Predilection.'

Texts of the three opinions rendered are on Pages 18 and 19.

Special to THE NEW YORK TIMES.

WASHINGTON, June 1.—One more item of industrial reform legislation was nullified by the Supreme Court today when the justices, in a 5-to-4 decision, declared the New York State Minimum Wage Law for Women and Children unconstitutional as violating the due process clause of the Fourteenth Amendment.

The majority opinion, written by Justice Butler, asserted that neither New York State nor the Federal Government had authority to fix wages for women workers. This opinion appeared to bar all efforts either by the States or the government toward regulation of wages and hours.

Sharing the majority opinion were Justices Van Deventer, McReynolds and Sutherland of the "fundamentalist" bloc, and also Justice Roberts who once more voted with the conservatives.

The dissent, vigorous in character, was written by Chief Justice Hughes, who sided with the three liberals, Justices Brandeis, Cardozo and Stone. They in turn presented through Justice Stone an independent argument attacking the majority attitude as an expression of "personal economic predilection."

Say Miners Escape Ruling

While the case at hand mentioned the wages of women only, and not those of children, there was a strong feeling here that the court's action invalidated the entire New York law, and thus the wages of minors. However, there was a hope among some lawyers that minors might not be affected, as they are legally prevented from making contracts.

Seventeen States have minimum wage legislation. Seven of these with laws similar to the New York State statute had asked the Supreme Court to sustain that law.

Justice Butler in the majority opinion unqualifiedly asserted that the New York law, despite its qualifying clauses, presented no issue different from the District of Columbia Minimum Wage Law rejected in the Supreme Court by a 5-to-3 opinion thirteen years ago, and upon which the New York Court of Appeals depended when it held the State law unconstitutional.

The New York case arose when efforts were made to prosecute Joseph Tipaldo, manager of the Spotlight Laundry in Brooklyn, charged with falsifying records to show he had paid the minimum wage to women working in his laundry.

Eventually he sued for a writ of habeas corpus on the ground that the law violated the due process clauses of the State and Federal Constitutions. The court finding today releases him from the custody of Frederick L. Moorehead, warden of the city prison of the borough of Brooklyn.

Contrast With Guffey Ruling

Although the celebrated case does not directly involve a New Deal issue, government officials had been tensely awaiting the court's decision, especially inasmuch as in the Guffey case the majority found that wage regulation to be a purely local matter, and in the Nebbia case, to which Justice Stone today called attention, the court said that despite due process a State could adopt whatever economic policy it may reasonably be deemed necessary to promote public welfare.

Members of Congress, already surprised by the hard-and-fast attitude of the court during this term, were astonished and perplexed.

Continued on Page Eighteen

"All the News That's Fit to Print."

The New York Times.

LATE CITY EDITION
Mostly cloudy, probably occasional showers today and tomorrow with little change in temperature.
Temperatures Yesterday—Max., 74; Min., 62

VOL. LXXXV.....No. 28,628. Entered as Second-Class Matter, Postoffice, New York, N. Y. NEW YORK, THURSDAY, JUNE 11, 1936. PP TWO CENTS In New York City. | THREE CENTS Within 200 Miles. | FOUR CENTS Elsewhere Except in 7th and 8th Postal Zones.

HOOVER EXCORIATES NEW DEAL AS FASCISM, DEMANDING A 'HOLY CRUSADE FOR FREEDOM'; CURRENCY PLANK PLEDGES STABILIZATION

ROOSEVELT CALLS FOR BROADER VIEW OF CONSTITUTION

SEES NO CHANGE NEEDED

Its Breadth Includes Nation's Welfare, He Says in Arkansas.

JEFFERSON'S ACT CITED

No One Took Louisiana Purchase to Supreme Court, He Recalls in Historical Speech.

CROWDS HAIL PRESIDENT

Thousands Pack Little Rock Stadium After Throngs Greeted Him in Tour of State.

Text of the President's speech appears on Page 9.

By CHARLES W. HURD

Special to THE NEW YORK TIMES.

CENTENNIAL STADIUM, LITTLE ROCK, Ark., June 10.—In a speech which constituted a virtual challenge to the Republican National Convention, President Roosevelt tonight opened a totally unexpected campaign for broadening interpretation of the Constitution to embrace all legislation necessary to safeguard human welfare under modern conditions.

He took the position that amendment of that document is not necessary to safeguard self-government, but argued that the Central Federal Government has authority to control all conditions too widespread to be handled by the individual States.

While Mr. Roosevelt did not criticize directly the numerous adverse decisions on New Deal legislation and New York's Minimum Wage Law, handed down in the past year by the Supreme Court, he pointed out that the Louisiana Purchase, which brought Arkansas and other States, including Kansas, home of Governor Landon, into the Union was consummated by President Jefferson "without the full and unanimous approval of every member of the legal profession."

He remarked pointedly of that action that "nobody carried the case to the Supreme Court."

Address Held Platform Basis

Although the President's speech, delivered at Centennial Stadium here in commemoration of a century of Statehood for Arkansas, had been described repeatedly in advance by the White House as "historical," it contained general statements woven into a background of historical allusion which observers believed would be restated as the basic policies in the Democratic platform.

While the speech contained no specific recommendations, it was one of the broadest discussions made by Mr. Roosevelt as President, covering the fields of self-government, States' rights, control of predatory groups and related topics in the realm of political discussion.

Mr. Roosevelt stated as firmly as possible his belief in the doctrine of States' rights and the right of self-government by all subdivisions of population, arguing exceptions to this rule only on the basis that there are social and economic problems in modern life which cannot be handled individually by State units.

"The Federal Union itself was organized under a Constitution," he said, "because in the days following the Revolution it was discovered that a mere federation of States was such a loose organization, with constant conflicts between the thirteen States themselves, that a Constitution and a national organization to take care of government beyond State lines was necessary.

Speech Is a Surprise

"The Constitution provided the best instrument ever devised for the continuation of these fundamental principles," he continued. "Under its broad purposes we can and intend to march forward, believing as the overwhelming majority of Americans believe, that it is intended to meet and fit the amazing physical, economic and social requirements that confront us in this generation."

He stated that "self-government we shall and will maintain," saying that "it will never be possible for any length of time for any

Continued on Page Nine

China Led in Purchases Of Arms From Us in May

Special to THE NEW YORK TIMES.

WASHINGTON, June 10.—Arms, ammunition and implements of war having a total value of $1,390,102 were exported from the United States to China during May, according to a report by the State Department today.

China was the heaviest purchaser of any country, although commercial aircraft accounted for $966,835 of the total. Military aircraft and parts accounted for purchases in the amount of $421,140.

Second on the list was Greece, which bought guns, howitzers and mortars valued at $150,000 and ammunition worth $950,000, a total of $1,100,000.

The total purchases of arms, ammunition and implements of war by all countries during May was $5,108,626.73.

CHAMBERLAIN ASKS REGIONAL TREATIES

Chancellor of the Exchequer Calls for Guarantees to Localize Danger Zones.

WOULD REVOKE SANCTIONS

Favors Limiting the Functions of League to Accord With Its 'Real Powers.'

Special Cable to THE NEW YORK TIMES.

LONDON, June 10.—Neville Chamberlain, Chancellor of the Exchequer, gave a further indication tonight of the line the British Government may take in reform of the League of Nations. He suggested to the members of the 1900 Club that regional arrangements or guarantees might be concluded to localize world danger spots.

The policy of collective security based on sanctions, he declared, had been tried out in the case of the Italian invasion of Ethiopia and had failed.

"It failed to prevent the war, it failed to end the war and it failed to save the victim of aggression," he said. "I am not blaming any one for its failure. I merely record it now because I think it is time we reviewed the history of those events and seek to draw what lessons and conclusions we should from those events."

Mr. Chamberlain described the appeal of Viscount Cecil of Chelwood, president of the British League of Nations Union, Sunday urging that increased sanctions might save Ethiopian independence as "the very midsummer of madness."

Holds Task Beyond League

"We must admit that we tried to impose upon the League a task which was beyond its powers," he continued. "It is time to limit the functions of the League so that they may accord with its real powers."

If the League were limited in that way it could no longer be relied upon to secure the peace of the world by itself, Mr. Chamberlain admitted, and he then suggested a system of regional arrangements.

"I put these to you merely as provisional conclusions," he explained. "Before we can translate them into action it is clear that we would have to take counsel with others and in particular that we would have to consult those dominions whose partnership with us means so much for the influence of the British Empire in the world. And who, if they act with us, can influence so great an effect upon the nations of the world itself?

"But whatever may be the policy whereby we seek to secure peace for ourselves and others, it is quite impossible for us either to protect our own interests or to play an effective part in making an adequate contribution to the system of collective security unless we are adequately armed."

Delbos Sees Italian Envoy

Wireless to THE NEW YORK TIMES.

PARIS, June 10.—Yvon Delbos, French Foreign Minister, today received Vittorio Cerruti, the Italian Ambassador, and discussed impending League of Nations negotiations with him.

The visit was said to be a formal one and Mr. Cerruti did not deliver any official message. It is known, however, that he took the opportunity of declaring that the removal of sanctions in his estimation was all that stood in the way of Italian collaboration in Central Europe.

ACCUSER PLOTTED DRUKMAN BRIBERY, SINGER TELLS JURY

Defendant, Taking Over Case, Charges Ex-Representative Hogan Is Solely Responsible.

WITNESS NAMES SOLOVEI

Says Brooklyn Lawyer Asked Him to Intercede With Juror in Luckmans' Behalf.

Henry G. Singer, former Chief Assistant United States Attorney and hitherto one of the most silent of the five defendants in the Drukman conspiracy trial, rose unexpectedly in court yesterday to defend his name against the accusations of a man he convicted of bail-bond frauds four years ago.

The youthful defendant took over from his attorney, I. Gainsburg, the cross-examination of Charles Nittoly, former Assistant United States Marshal, and Michael J. Hogan, a former United States Representative, who gave testimony linking, directly or indirectly, the former prosecutor to the alleged bribery plot.

When Singer finished with them he had drawn admissions as to unsavory details in their past and had got on the record for the first time the defense version of the Drukman conspiracy.

He flatly accused the former Representative, who was convicted in 1935 of naturalization fraud charges, of having thought up and executed, alone, the scheme to "contact" Theodore Cohn, member of the April (1935) grand jury that exonerated Meyer and Harry Luckman and Fred J. Hull, the murderers of Samuel Drukman.

He gained from Nittoly admissions that he had perjured himself in other courts and had pleaded guilty to bail bond charges involving an extensive graft.

A Relentless Questioner

Not only did the former prosecutor gain a number of admissions tending to impugn the credibility of the testimony of his accusers, but he conducted his cross-examination with an aggressiveness and relentlessness, hitherto absent in the trial, which is in its second week before Supreme Court Justice Erskine C. Rogers in Brooklyn.

Weaving back and forth across the courtroom, thrashing his arms and hurling rapid-fire questions at both witnesses, Singer held the jury in rapt attention.

Hogan and Nittoly were only two of a parade of witnesses in the trial yesterday. Cohn, the grand juror who turned down a $100 bribe offer to vote against an indictment of the Drukman murderers, gave corroboratory testimony as to that phase of the alleged plot. He engaged in a give-and-take tilt with Mr. Gainsburg on cross-examination that provided a bit of humor for the spectators, but he yielded no points to the defense.

There was, also, Mrs. Fay Braff, daughter of Max Silverman, a fugitive named in the conspiracy indictment, who bristled with hostility for the State. Both sides questioned her concerning her father's relations with Assistant District Attorney William W. Kleinman.

Wife of Juror Testifies

Mrs. Cohn, the wife of the grand juror, testified concerning her knowledge of the attempt to "reach" her husband, and a Negro servant in the Silverman household gave testimony to substantiate the State's contention that Silverman and Kleinman were sufficiently acquainted to dine together.

The State, however, by the end of yesterday's session had got well started on its theory of why the April grand jury did not indict the three men who were found in the locked and darkened Luckman ga-

Continued on Page Two

With Bridges on Ticket Landon Men Fear Slogan

Special to THE NEW YORK TIMES.

CLEVELAND, June 10.—The Landon forces held a conference last night on a candidate for Vice President, interrupted by telephone calls to Governor Landon at Topeka and reports from the resolutions committee drafting the platform.

"What about Governor Bridges of New Hampshire; he is a progressive and an able speaker?" one of the Landon managers asked.

"That's true, but we have to be careful that we do not give the opposition a slogan," remarked Roy C. Roberts, managing editor of The Kansas City Star and a keen observer of the political scene.

"How would 'Landon Bridges falling down' sound?"

85 NEW YORK VOTES POLLED FOR LANDON

Stand for First Ballot Bared at Open Meeting to Check Reports of Friction.

MOVE FOR DELAY BEATEN

Mills Halts Plan to Wait Till Hoover Speaks—Gannett Backed by Two.

By WARREN MOSCOW

Special to THE NEW YORK TIMES.

CLEVELAND, June 10.—New York State will cast a minimum of eighty-five votes for Governor Landon on the first ballot, it was disclosed today at an open poll of the delegation. With eighty-nine of the ninety delegates present or represented by alternates, there was one vote for Hoover, two for Frank E. Gannett and one for Alfred P. Sloan Jr. All the rest were for the Kansas Executive.

When Charles D. Hilles, national committee member, the first called upon to declare his stand, cast his vote for Landon, near unanimity was assured. Mr. Hilles recalled that the party leaders, feeling that States west of the Mississippi must be carried by the party in November, had decided to let Western sentiment crystallize on a candidate. That sentiment has crystallized substantially on a candidate, he told the gathering, and then he announced his vote for Landon.

He recalled that New York had decided to have an unpledged delegation to the convention, and added:

"You now ask me to cast a ballot. We felt, all of us who had been studying the matter carefully, that it would be necessary for us to carry States west of the Mississippi, casting at least fifty-two electoral votes. There was feeling that the candidate should be from the West, and there has been resistance in the East to letting the Middle West and the farm West develop the candidate.

"While there has been no absolute crystallization of sentiment, there has been substantial crystallization. It can be fairly said that the West has indicated a candidate, and I cast my vote for Landon."

The recording by New York of its vote today was unusual from start

Continued on Page Sixteen

Convention Profit Assured to Cleveland; Delegates' Spending May Reach Million

Special to THE NEW YORK TIMES.

CLEVELAND, June 10.—The enterprising business men of Cleveland who paid $150,000 to play host to the Republican National Convention will not lose on their investment but may even get a dividend, James L. Jappe of the convention committee disclosed today.

Mr. Jappe said that advertising in the souvenir booklet of the convention would bring the committee a net profit of about $50,000. Another $45,000 he thought might be realized from the sale of the book at $2.50 a copy.

The committee had 25,000 copies of the book published. Of these some 7,000 were given away free to national committeemen, the press and subscribers to the convention fund. Most of the balance have been sold already.

Mr. Jappe said that in spite of more liberal entertaining than was originally intended it may cost less than was estimated to play host to the Republicans, who, he added, have turned out to be better spenders than any one had hoped.

He estimated that before the delegates finish up their work here they will have spent between $800,000 and $1,000,000 on food, lodging, taxicab fares, knickknacks and souvenirs. Most of the money will land in the bank accounts of the hotels, but that is considered fair enough because they subscribed the largest part of the convention fund.

The convention, Mr. Jappe said, had brought about 25,000 visitors to Cleveland, adding that reports indicated that the convention guests were models of good behavior.

PLATFORM DRAFT IS READY

Readjusting Currency Would Be Timed to Nation's Good.

COMPROMISE WITH BORAH

'Still Not Altogether Satisfactory,' He Says, but It Is Better Than First Draft.

LANDON APPROVAL SOUGHT

2,400-Word Document Is Wired to Topeka and Work Awaits Governor's Judgment.

By CHARLES R. MICHAEL

Special to THE NEW YORK TIMES.

CLEVELAND, Thursday, June 11.—Platform declarations which would commit the Republican party to a "sound and stable currency" to be attained by a balanced budget, repeal of the Presidential power to fix the value of the dollar and avoidance of foreign alliances through the League of Nations or the World Court were among planks laid before the full resolutions committee late last night for final ratification.

It was also set forth that relief and minimum wages and hours of employment could be best administered by the States and that no constitutional amendment giving additional powers to the States was necessary.

These and other planks were submitted by a subcommittee for approval after its fifteen members had labored forty-eight hours with only brief intermissions for sleep.

Consulting of Landon

In a sudden reversal of plans, the subcommittee announced a decision not to make public the platform until it had been approved by Governor Landon.

The text of the accepted planks were telegraphed to the Governor at Topeka and his attitude regarding each was to be laid before the reassembled group in the morning.

William Allen White said that the Governor wanted to look over the platform himself.

Herman Langworthy, chairman of the committee, said he did not believe that Governor Landon would offer any serious objections. But some of the Governor's friends on the committee thought that he should be advised of certain changes in the social security and utility planks and they insisted that the platform conform with his ideas because of the likelihood that he must run upon it.

Emerging from the full committee meeting at its adjournment a few minutes after midnight, former Senator Reed of Pennsylvania said the completed platform comprised about 2,400 words, requiring thirteen pages of double-spaced typewritten copy. This compares with the 8,000-word platform of 1932.

Although ratification by the full committee and adoption by the convention are required to put the party on record, there is little doubt that the needed sanction will be obtained.

The platform remained a Landon-sponsored declaration of principles. In virtually every instance, however, the planks were modified in the direction of conservatism, as compared with the tentative form originally submitted by the Landon managers.

Neutral on Monetary Policy

Outstanding among the platform items was that dealing with monetary policy. Entirely neutral in character and designed particularly to appease Senator Borah and to prevent his threatened bolt of the party, it made no mention of the gold standard but declared for a fixed "metallic standard" instead.

Throughout, the plank represented a compromise with forces led by Senator Borah. While it avoided the somewhat inflationary course he had espoused, it contained no promise of a return to the monetary gold standard at any time.

The text of the currency plank is as follows:

"We advocate a sound currency, to be preserved at all hazards.

"The first requisite to a sound and stable currency is a balanced budget.

"We will restore to Congress the authority lodged by the Constitution to coin money and to regulate

Continued on Page Sixteen

Mr. Hoover's Speech

By The Associated Press.

CLEVELAND, June 10.—Former President Hoover's address to the Republican convention tonight was as follows:

In this room rests the greatest responsibility that has come to a body of Americans in three generations. In the lesser sense this is a convention of a great political party. But in the larger sense it is a convention of Americans to determine the fate of those ideals for which this nation was founded. That far transcends all partisanship.

There are elemental currents which make or break the fate of nations. There is a moral purpose in the universe. Those forces which affect the vitality and the soul of a people will control their destinies. The sum of years of public service in these currents is the overwhelming conviction of their transcendent importance over the more transitory, even though difficult, issues of national life.

I have given about four years to research into the New Deal, trying to determine what its ultimate objectives were, what sort of a system it is imposing on this country.

To some people it appears to be a strange interlude in American history in that it has no philosophy, that it is sheer opportunism, that it is a muddle of a spoils system, of emotional economics, of reckless adventure, of unctuous claims to a monopoly of human sympathy, of greed for power, of a desire for popular acclaim and an aspiration to make the front pages of the newspapers. That is the most charitable view.

To other people it appears to be a cold-blooded attempt by starry-eyed boys to infect the American people by a mixture of European ideas, flavored with our native predilection to get something for nothing.

You can choose either one you like best. But the first is the road of chaos which leads to the second. Both of these roads lead over the same grim precipice that is the crippling and possibly the destruction of the freedom of men.

Which of these interpretations is accurate is even disputed by alumni of the New Deal who have graduated for conscience's sake or have graduated by request.

In Central Europe the march of Socialist or Fascist dictatorships and their destruction of liberty did not set out with guns and armies. Dictators began their ascent to the seats of power through the elections provided by liberal institutions. Their weapons were promise and hate. They offered the mirage of Utopia to those in distress. They flung the poison of class hatred. They may not have maimed the

Continued on Page Fourteen

SNELL WINS CHEERS IN ATTACK ON FOES

He Invites Aid of Democrats, Charging Broken Promises to Roosevelt.

10,000 HEAR CHAIRMAN TALK

Pattangall, Ex-Democrat, Is Applauded as He Appears on Convention Platform.

Text of Representative Snell's speech appears on Page 17.

Special to THE NEW YORK TIMES.

PUBLIC AUDITORIUM, CLEVELAND, June 10.—An invitation to "constitutional Democrats" to join the Republicans in the campaign against the "unconstitutional dictatorship" and "arrogant individualism" of President Roosevelt was issued today by Representative Bertrand H. Snell in his speech on assuming the permanent chairmanship of the Republican National Convention.

Mr. Snell, who as minority leader of the House has taken the lead in the fight against New Deal legislation, attacked the President for broken promises and repudiated pledges. He assailed the Roosevelt administration for planned extravagance, waste, debasement of the dollar, increase of taxes, imposition of a burden on the backs of youth, use of public money to create a gigantic political machine and failure, with reckless squandering of money and political boondoggling, to find jobs for 11,000,000 unemployed.

Mr. Snell stressed the danger of "cataclysmic inflation" and a "government - dictated collectivist order," if President Roosevelt should be re-elected, and charged that the President had sought continually to usurp the powers of the Supreme Court.

Snell Applauded by 10,000

Nearly 10,000 delegates and spectators in the Public Auditorium applauded Mr. Snell's attacks on the President and the Roosevelt policies. Several times those in the hall rose to cheer his points, and the convention, which so far has shown only few signs of real enthusiasm, arose en masse with a cheer when Mr. Snell closed his speech by declaring that the Republican party in the coming election would appeal to the hearts and consciences of the American people and would win.

It was a minute after noon when Senator Frederick Steiwer of Oregon, temporary chairman, called the convention to order.

After prayer by the Right Rev. Ernest Lynn Waldorf, Bishop of Chicago, and singing by a trio of crooners, Walter S. Hallanan of West Virginia, chairman of the

Continued on Page Seventeen

HOOVER ACCLAIMED IN DAY OF OVATIONS

Great Demonstration at Convention Follows Welcome at Railroad Station.

DISCUSSED AS NOMINEE

California Delegation, Stirred by Speech, Studies Advisability of Offering His Name.

By TURNER CATLEDGE

Special to THE NEW YORK TIMES.

CLEVELAND, June 10.—Former President Hoover arrived here today to become the center of a series of rousing demonstrations leading up to his speech tonight before the Republican convention. As a result his political stock again was put on a rising market.

Following his attack on the New Deal and, for him, the virtually unprecedented demonstration which came after he called his party members to a "Holy crusade for freedom," the California delegation went into session to discuss, among other things, the possibility of placing Mr. Hoover's name before the convention for the Presidential nomination.

Whether his home-State representatives or any other delegation nominate him or not, the opinion here was that his speech tonight, and the day of adulation preceding it, had put the former President in the position of an elder statesman whose advice and assistance will be sought and used during the coming campaign.

From the time he arrived here this morning from Chicago until he departed tonight for New York, Mr. Hoover was the center of attention.

Landon Supporters on the Alert

His presence was watched closely by those interested in the candidacy of Governor Landon of Kansas to see whether Mr. Hoover would give any encouragement to the groups which previously had been unable to get together to prevent the Kansan's nomination.

Mr. Hoover avoided private conversations during the day with any of the leading candidates. He and his spokesmen sought in every way to dispel the idea that he had come to Cleveland to rally the anti-Landon forces, as many had thought he would. He insisted on confining to his speech what he had to say, leaving interpretations to the delegates.

Tonight, after the speech and the tumultuous reception given him, many party leaders closely watched for the results of the session of the California delegates. The delegation adjourned late tonight, however, without taking any action relative to Mr. Hoover, but planned to meet again tomorrow.

An ovation that continued for fif-

Continued on Page Fourteen

PATH CLEARED FOR LANDON

Borah Remains a Man of Mystery, but Kansan Has Votes Needed.

HOOVER'S SPEECH AIDS HIM

Fear Ex-President Would Picture Another Man Fades on His Arrival in Cleveland.

HINTS ON SECOND PLACE

Knox Gets a Bit of a 'Run' From Governor's Men but They Do Not Exclude Others.

By ARTHUR KROCK

Special to THE NEW YORK TIMES.

PUBLIC AUDITORIUM, CLEVELAND, June 10.—The Republicans of the East capitulated to the Republicans of the Mississippi River basin today, having received certain assurances on the platform, and, unless William E. Borah can prevent the nomination of the Governor of Kansas—a slight possibility indeed—he will be chosen on the first or second ballot.

An ecstatic uproar of approval which followed the address of Herbert Hoover tonight and prevented the transaction of further business put hope in the hearts of the Californians that perhaps, after all, the former President could be renominated. They caucused instantly. But no experienced leader or observer on the scene believes that the tribute represented any real wish among the delegates to change the prospect of Mr. Landon's nomination.

This conclusion of the pre-convention campaign, increasingly indicated by recent political events, entered the realm of inevitability today when the New York and Pennsylvania delegations were polled and disclosed eighty-five New Yorkers and fifty Pennsylvanians for Mr. Landon on the first ballot. John D. M. Hamilton, manager of the Kansas candidate, did not await the overwhelming news from New York, but, as soon as he heard from Pennsylvania, claimed a first-ballot nomination.

The polls were taken in a flurry of rumors about the convention speech tonight of Mr. Hoover and before any one knew whether or not his remarks would weaken the prospective nominee of the conventon. They were taken while the Landon spokesmen on the platform were still negotiating with Senator Borah in the hope of obtaining his campaign support, and with indifference to the outcome of those negotiations.

New Deal Sole Hoover Target

Mr. Hoover's speech disposed of the reports that he would attempt to draw the lineaments of a Republican candidate which could not possibly be recognized as Mr. Landon. His words constituted the bitterest arraignment of the New Deal and of the President which he or any other Republican orator of the first rank has yet made, and repeatedly brought the delegates to their feet, thrilled, cheering tumultuously, persuaded that their cause was so just and so vital that victory must be possible.

It was a trumpet call to battle from the defeated but still belligerent former general of the forces. It vetoed no standard bearer the party might choose to renew the fight. Had conditions been otherwise it might have brought about the renomination of Mr. Hoover himself, but, that being impossible, the Landon forces led in the ecstatic cheering, the first spontaneous cheering of the convention. After he appeared on the platform, it required fifteen minutes to quiet the shouting audience.

Among the most important events of the crowded day and night was an agreement by the subcommittee of the resolutions group on a platform which late tonight was being considered by the full committee. The currency plank omits mention of gold, resting the party position on a balanced budget as the essential precursor of international monetary stabilization, presumably on gold.

In addition to this concession to Senator Borah, the subcommittee is said to have acceded to his text on the monopoly and foreign affairs party positions. Should he retain these triumphs before the convention the expectation of the Landon

Continued on Page Fifteen

Alfred M. Landon, the hope of the Republican Party, on a whistle-stop campaign tour.

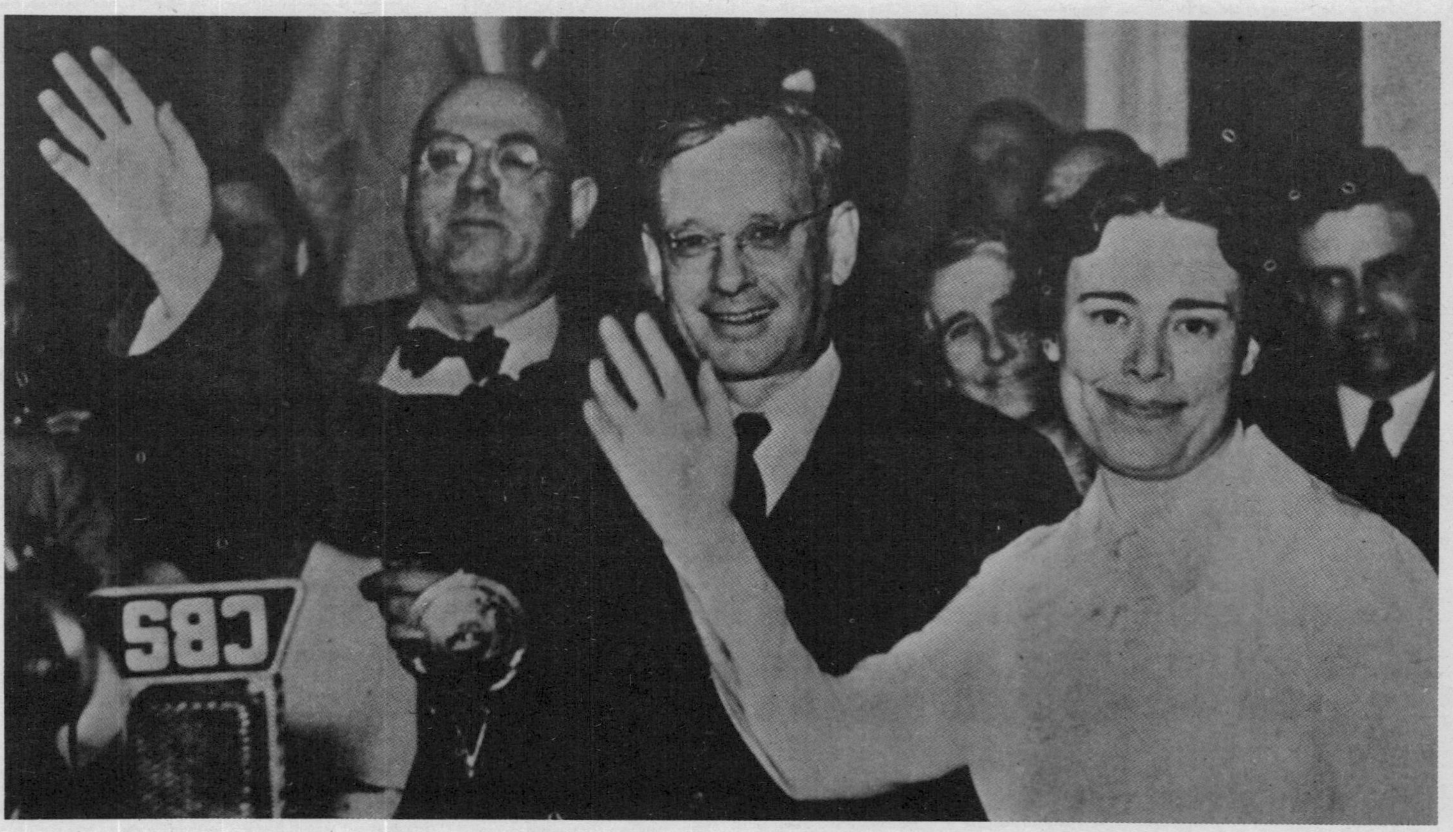

Mr. and Mrs. Landon wave to supporters after the Republican convention chose Landon as its candidate for President.

President Roosevelt makes a campaign speech in Massachusetts. His wife, Eleanor, is at left.

"All the News That's Fit to Print."

The New York Times.

LATE CITY EDITION
Generally fair and slightly cooler today. Tomorrow fair and warmer.
Temperatures Yesterday—Max., 77; Min., 62

Copyright, 1936, by The New York Times Company.

VOL. LXXXV....No. 28,629. Entered as Second-Class Matter, Postoffice, New York, N. Y. NEW YORK, FRIDAY, JUNE 12, 1936. PP TWO CENTS In New York City. | THREE CENTS Within 200 Miles. | FOUR CENTS Elsewhere Except in 7th and 8th Postal Zones.

REPUBLICANS NAME LANDON UNANIMOUSLY; HE ACCEPTS PLATFORM, ADDING OWN IDEAS

SOVIET TO SET UP NEW PARLIAMENT WITH TWO HOUSES

One Chamber to Be Composed of Deputies Elected by Secret Vote of the People.

'SENATE' WILL BE PICKED

It Will Contain Delegates of the Republics—Freedom of Speech Due for All.

PRESS ALSO IS AFFECTED

Liberty of Worship and Equal Rights for Women Among Features of Charter.

By WALTER DURANTY
Wireless to THE NEW YORK TIMES.

MOSCOW, June 11.—The proposed new Soviet Constitution, which will be published tomorrow, is strikingly different from the earlier Constitution, which became law July 6, 1923.

The first difference is that in the initial section there is no reference as before to the severance of the world into the camps of socialism and capitalism—no mention of imperialist hostility or of a union of international workers or that "the bourgeoisie of the world have been unable to organize the collaboration of peoples."

Allows Private Farming

Instead, the new first section stresses the success of socialism in the Union of Soviet Socialist Republics, declares the means of production, commerce, finance, the railroads, &c., now belong to the State and outlines the position of collective farms, with the note that their property belongs to them "eternally," but the Constitution allows private farming and private sale of produce on the condition that it be direct and not involve any profit from or exploitation of a third party.

That, in short, is the basic principle of the Soviet State today as expressed by the new Constitution—that no individual or group can profit by the labor of others and that everything that matters is the property of the community, worked for the community's benefit.

The first section concludes with these significant sentences: "The economic life of the U. S. S. R. is directed by the State's economic plan toward increasing the general wealth.

"In the U. S. S. R. there is established the principle of socialism. 'From each according to his capacity, to each according to his work.'"

Here you get the basic principle of Stalinism, or Soviet socialism, at its present stage as compared with the ultimate goal of Marxian communism, the motto of which is, "From each according to his capacity, to each according to his needs." In other words, the Socialist principle of greater rewards for greater service still prevails over the ultimate ideal of Communist equality.

The second change is that instead of seven federated republics in the U. S. S. R. there will henceforth be eleven, the Caucasian Federation being split into three—Georgia, Azerbaijan and Armenia—and Kirghizia and Kazakstan are added. This is only a formal difference for administrative purposes, and the federated republics, as before, retain the right to secede from the union at will.

New Parliament Provided

The third change, however, is more important, affecting the whole electoral system. Instead of provincial Soviets being elected by lists on open ballot and then their choosing delegates to the All-Union Soviet Congress, there are now to be secret ballots for individual Deputies on the basis of one Deputy to each 300,000 members of the population.

These Deputies will be elected to what will be equivalent to the House of Representatives in the United States. And instead of these Deputies sitting jointly with the Congress of Nationalities, there will henceforth be two houses with equal powers of action and initiative, in which the House of Nationalities will be chosen by provincial councils in the ratio of ten Deputies from each federated republic, five from each autonomous

Continued on Page Five

Hoover Calls Platform 'Fighting, Progressive'

Former President Herbert Hoover last night called the Republican platform and Governor Landon's specific statements upon it, as read at the Cleveland convention, "fighting and progressive."

Through his secretary Mr. Hoover made public this statement:

"The platform admirably covers the principles and methods I have so repeatedly advocated. The platform is the fighting, definite and progressive statement the country needs.

"When put into force by the American people, these principles will regenerate the country. Governor Landon's statement amply covers any other points that may be in question."

BORAH IS 'STUNNED' BY LANDON'S PLEA

Nominee Should Have Acted 'Sooner,' He Says When Told of Gold, Wage Demands.

SILENT AS TO HIS SUPPORT

Senator Leaves for Washington After Winning Victory on His Platform Goals.

By The Associated Press.

CLEVELAND, June 11.—The Plain-Dealer says Senator Borah appeared "stunned" when informed at Akron tonight that Governor Landon had declared for a gold-backed currency and a constitutional amendment, if necessary, to permit State regulation of wages and hours.

Informed of the nominee's telegram to the Republican convention, Mr. Borah said:

"Well, that's his business. Why didn't he send it sooner?"

The Plain-Dealer says Mr. Borah ran his hands over his face four or five times. Asked if he had any more comment, he said:

"I shall wait until morning and see what they do."

Mr. Borah was on a train en route to Washington, having left Cleveland just a few minutes before the delegates adopted the platform. He had fought to have any mention of the gold standard eliminated from the platform.

Platform Pleases Him

Special to THE NEW YORK TIMES.

CLEVELAND, June 11.—Senator Borah expressed himself this afternoon as well pleased with the platform sent to the national convention by the committee on resolutions.

But the question whether he would support the man whom the convention was to select as party standard bearer remained unanswered when the Idaho Republican left for Washington.

After the final draft of the platform had been completed and become available for examination, it was reported that Senator Borah had examined it and was satisfield with the language of the planks in

Continued on Page Fourteen

'VICTORY' LANDON PLEDGE

He Promises to Wage One of Party's Most Forceful Campaigns.

THANKS HIS TOWNSMEN

With Wife at His Side on the Front Porch He Hails Their Loyalty.

TOPEKA HAILS THE CHOICE

Citizens Decorate City and Parade to Governor's Home When Nomination Is Flashed.

By WARREN MOSCOW
Special to THE NEW YORK TIMES.

TOPEKA, Kan., June 11.—With thousands of his neighbors and other citizens of Topeka gathered around the yellow brick Executive Mansion at Eighth and Buchanan Streets, Governor Alfred M. Landon delivered to them tonight a simple message of his appreciation of their loyalty and affection as they gathered to celebrate his nomination as the Republican candidate for President.

Earlier, in a statement issued to the press, he had pledged himself to lead a harmonious party to victory next November.

It was exactly 11:14 o'clock, Central standard time, when the Governor and Mrs. Landon stepped out to meet a deafening roar of applause from the crowd.

The air rang with cheers, torches and flares blazed and band after band blared "Oh, Susanna" as the Governor and Mrs. Landon left the study in which they had spent most of the evening to appear on the front porch.

Thanks His Townsmen

The Landons' neighbors and all Topeka had been preparing to celebrate his actual nomination and had been awaiting only a radio flash from the convention hall in Cleveland apprising them of the fact. The city was decorated with flags and bunting, and paraders formed in line, with all the city's bands and bugle and fife and drum corps ready to blow their heartiest. Finally word of the nomination came and the paraders marched to the Executive Mansion.

Governor Landon, when he stepped forward into the glare of the floodlights arranged around the house, was at ease, though toward the end of his talk he was plainly affected. He wore a gray business suit, with a white shirt and attached soft collar.

Mrs. Samuel E. Cobb, Mrs. Landon's mother, and Joe Cross, a cousin of Mrs. Landon, were with the Governor and his wife. They took seats on the porch swing, while the Governor and Mrs. Landon faced the cheers of the more than 15,000 paraders.

Governor Landon in his greeting said:

Mrs. Landon and I are deeply touched by this expression of your good will and good wishes. We are proud, too, that so many of our friends from surrounding towns

Continued on Page Thirteen

Roll-Call of the States On Landon's Nomination

Special to THE NEW YORK TIMES.

CLEVELAND, June 11.—Following is the vote by States for Governor Landon when roll was called on the nomination for President:

State or Territory.	No. of Deleg.	State or Territory	No. of Deleg.
Alabama	13	New Jersey	32
Arizona	9	New Mexico	6
Arkansas	11	New York	90
California	44	North Carolina	23
Colorado	12	North Dakota	8
Connecticut	19	Ohio	52
Delaware	9	Oklahoma	21
Florida	12	Oregon	10
Georgia	14	Pennsylvania	75
Idaho	8	Rhode Island	8
Illinois	57	South Carolina	10
Indiana	28	South Dakota	8
Iowa	22	Tennessee	17
Kansas	18	Texas	25
Kentucky	22	Utah	8
Louisiana	12	Vermont	9
Maine	13	Virginia	17
Maryland	16	Washington	16
Massachusetts	33	West Virginia	15
Michigan	38	Wisconsin	6
Minnesota	22	Wyoming	6
Mississippi	11	Alaska	3
Missouri	30	Dist. of Columbia	3
Montana	8	Hawaii	3
Nebraska	14	Philippine Islands	3
Nevada	6	Puerto Rico	2
New Hampshire	11	Total	984

West Virginia gave one vote for Borah. Wisconsin gave 18 votes to Borah.

VANDENBERG LOOMS AS RUNNING MATE

Senator Agrees to Reconsider Refusal and Landon Men Believe He Will Aeccept.

STEIWER SECOND CHOICE

Kansans May Pick Him if Other Plan Fails—Borah Backs Gannett—Knox Boomed.

By CHARLES R. MICHAEL
Special to THE NEW YORK TIMES.

CLEVELAND, June 11.—The Landon forces have not yet abandoned the hope of persuading Senator Vandenberg to accept the nomination for Vice President, despite reiteration of his announcement of last week that his decision to remain in the Senate was "final."

Although he continued his refusal earlier in the day, the Michigan Senator agreed this evening to confer again with the Landon forces after adjournment tonight. At this time he was expected to determine whether he would bow to the request of Governor Landon.

Confidence was expressed at the Kansan's headquarters that Mr. Vandenberg would be nominated tomorrow.

There is a strong movement in favor of Colonel Knox. His selection, however, is opposed by Colonel Robert R. McCormick, publisher of The Chicago Tribune.

Frank E. Gannett of Rochester, N. Y., a Borah supporter, came into the situation as a compromise candidate. Members of the New York delegation were told that Senator Borah desired his nomination and "would vigorously support

Continued on Page Twelve

THE PLATFORM IS VOTED

Containing 14 Planks, It Is Declared Largely a Liberal Victory.

WORLD COURT IS BARRED

States' Rights Are Stressed—Social Security Would Be on Pay-as-You-Go Basis.

BANS 'SCARCITY' POLICY

Farm Statement Sets Broad Aims on Crops and Credit Help—Trading Act Repeal Urged.

By FELIX BELAIR Jr.
Special to THE NEW YORK TIMES.

CLEVELAND, June 11.—After laboring for three days and nights to draft a declaration of political principles that would come near to satisfying the expected Presidential candidate and placate potential party bolters, the resolutions committee of the Republican National Convention brought forth tonight a platform on which it hopes the party can carry the national elections in November.

It was a composite of compromises in which the demands of Governor Landon, the assured nominee, were subordinated in several important instances to those of the more conservative Eastern delegations on matters of social and economic progress.

Throughout its preamble and fourteen planks the document condemned abuses it connected with the present administration.

While it urged continuance of several reforms inaugurated by the Roosevelt administration, such as regulation of security markets for the protection of investors, social security and unemployment relief—with the latter two administered by the States—these were far outnumbered by the departures from present national policy that it proposed.

Main Points of Platform

The outstanding declarations of the platform were:

1. Constitutional and local self-government must be preserved as well as the authority of the Supreme Court as final protector of citizens' rights, and maintenance of our system of free enterprise, private competition and equality of opportunity.
2. Absorption of the unemployment by private industry and agriculture holds the only answer to that problem, and to that end restriction of production should be abolished, and all policies that raise production costs and cost of living discontinued. Legitimate business should be encouraged and the government withdrawn from competition with industry.
3. Responsibility for relief of the needy must be returned to the States, which should receive Federal grants in proportion as the States contribute. This should be combined with a system of public works, such projects to be undertaken only on their merits.
4. The States should enact Old-Age Pension Laws for persons over 65 and the government make contributions to support such systems according as States contribute, but all such programs should be financed on a pay-as-you-go policy, by widely distributed taxation.
5. Labor's right to organize and bargain collectively through representatives of its own choosing without interference must be protected. State laws and interstate compacts should be undertaken to abolish sweatshops and child labor.
6. Scarcity economics should be abolished in agriculture; a national land use program should be pursued for the protection and restoration of land resources; experimental aid to farmers should be developed for production of new crops and promotions of new industrial uses of non-food crops; farmers protected from foreign importations. Farm credits at rates comparable with those in industry should be fostered together with decentralized nonpartisan control of the farm credit administration. A form of subsidy should be instituted to take care of exportable surpluses with benefits based on the domes-

Continued on Page Fourteen

© New York Times Studio Photo.

NOMINATED FOR PRESIDENT
Alfred Mossman Landon

The Text of the Platform

Special to THE NEW YORK TIMES.

CLEVELAND, June 11.—Following is the text of the party platform as adopted by the Republican National Convention tonight:

America is in peril. The welfare of American men and women and the future of our youth are at stake. We dedicate ourselves to the preservation of their political liberty, their individual opportunity and their character as free citizens, which today for the first time are threatened by government itself.

For three long years the New Deal administration has dishonored American traditions and flagrantly betrayed the pledges upon which the Democratic party sought and received public support.

The powers of Congress have been usurped by the President.

The integrity and authority of the Supreme Court have been flaunted.

The rights and liberties of American citizens have been violated.

Regulated monopoly has displaced free enterprise.

The New Deal administration constantly seeks to usurp the rights reserved to the State and to the people.

It has insisted on passage of laws contrary to the Constitution.

It has intimidated witnesses and interfered with the right of petition.

It has dishonored our country by repudiating its most sacred obligations.

It has been guilty of frightful waste and extravagance, using public funds for partisan political purposes.

It has promoted investigations to harass and intimidate American citizens, at the same time denying investigations into its own improper expenditures.

It has created a vast multitude of new offices, filled them with its favorites, set up a centralized bureaucracy and sent out swarms of inspectors to harass our people.

It has bred fear and hesitation in commerce and industry, thus discouraging new enterprises, preventing employment and prolonging the depression.

It secretly has made tariff agreements with our foreign competitors, flooding our markets with foreign commodities.

It has coerced and intimidated voters by withholding relief to those opposing its tyrannical policies.

It has destroyed the morale of many of our people and made them dependent upon government.

Appeals to passion and class prejudice have replaced reason and tolerance.

To a free people, these actions are insufferable. This campaign cannot be waged on the traditional differences between the Republican and Democratic parties.

The responsibility of this election transcends all previous political divisions. We invite all Americans, irrespective of party, to join us in defense of American institutions.

CONSTITUTIONAL GOVERNMENT AND FREE ENTERPRISE

We pledge ourselves:

1. To maintain the American system of constitutional and local self-government, and to resist all attempts to impair the authority of the Supreme Court of the United States, the final protector of rights of our citizens against the arbitrary encroachments of the legislative and executive branches of government. There can be no individual liberty without an independent judiciary.

2. To preserve the American system of free enterprise, pri-

Continued on Page Fourteen

LANDON SENDS TELEGRAM

To Back Constitutional Amendment if States' Wage Laws Fail.

FOR GOLD AT PROPER TIME

In His Message to Convention He Specifies Exceptions in Accepting the Platform.

BORAH WINS HIS PLANKS

Vandenberg Is Expected to Be Vice Presidential Choice at Final Session Today.

By ARTHUR KROCK
Special to THE NEW YORK TIMES.

CLEVELAND, Ohio, June 11.—An unbossed Republican National Convention, yet working like a machine, at 11:41 o'clock tonight unanimously nominated Alfred M. Landon of Kansas for President, adopted unanimously a platform embracing certain social welfare ideas of the New Deal (which otherwise is excoriated) and seated party control in a group of young Kansas politicians and editors who entered the national political field less than two years ago.

At a final session tomorrow Arthur H. Vandenberg of Michigan is expected to accept the Vice Presidential nomination.

Eighteen Borah delegates from Wisconsin and the Senator's campaign manager (Delegate Carl G. Bachmann of West Virginia) voted for Mr. Borah on the first ballot, which prevented a nomination by acclamation under the rules. But Wisconsin then moved to make the nomination unanimous, and it was done.

Hamilton Reads Message

Two dramatic events colored the night session. Before John D. M. Hamilton, the chief of staff of the nominee, presented his name to the convention, he read at Mr. Landon's request a telegram from the Governor "interpreting" three planks of the platform and stating reservations. These planks, relating to currency, civil service and State control of wages and hours, had been revised by the resolutions committee from the text submitted by the Governor as a part of the week-long effort to placate Senator Borah and win his support in the campaign.

Governor Landon "interpreted" a "sound currency" to mean a currency eventually convertible into gold, insisted that the civil service should extend as far as the government's under-secretariat and pledged himself to support a constitutional amendment to permit the States to regulate wages and hours if the statutory method were not effective. He said "in good conscience" he must make these intentions known in advance.

The other element of drama was when all the other Presidential candidates but Senator Borah, who had already left for Washington, took the platform and seconded the nomination of Mr. Landon. Mr. Borah is only fairly well-pleased with the platform, and he expects to survey Mr. Landon's speeches and the personnel of his campaign cabinet for a couple of months before deciding whether to support the candidacy. Herbert Hoover, the other eminent Republican whose opposition was feared by the Landon group, phoned here today that he was satisfied with the platform.

Senator Vandenberg was among those seconding the nomination. Colonel Knox, L. J. Dickinson, Robert A. Taft and Harry Nice, the other aspirants, followed.

Harmony the Landon Goal

Harmony among all Republicans and the support of anti-New Deal Democrats have all along been stated as the twin goals of the Landon managers, and, except for Mr. Borah, the harmony seems to have been effected.

The end of the session, amid a series of ecstatic demonstrations for Mr. Landon and Mr. Vandenberg, came after a day of anxious concern to the Kansas syndicate which, at midnight last night believed that all its worries were over. Mr. Landon's differences with the resolutions subcommittee, and with Mr. Borah, and the latter's objections to revision of planks he had been asked to submit, caused the snarl.

But by 7 o'clock tonight, except

Continued on Page Twelve

Gov. Landon's Statement on Platform

Special to THE NEW YORK TIMES.

CLEVELAND, June 11.—Governor Landon, while approving most sections of the platform, sent the following message which was read to the convention before he was placed in nomination by John M. Hamilton:

To the delegates of the Republican National Convention:

My name is to be presented for your consideration as a candidate for the nomination for President of the United States. The platform recommended by your committee on resolutions and adopted by the convention has been communicated to me.

I note that according to the terms of the platform, the nomination tendered by this convention carries with it, as a matter of private honor and public good faith, an undertaking by each candidate to be true to the principles and program herein set forth.

If nominated, I unqualifiedly accept the word and spirit of that undertaking.

However, with that candor which you and the country are entitled to expect of me, I feel compelled before you proceed with the consideration of my name to submit my interpretation of certain planks in the platform so that you may be advised as to my views. I could not in conscience do otherwise.

Under the title of Labor the platform commits the Republican party as follows:

"Support the adoption of State laws and interstate compacts to abolish sweatshops and child labor, and to protect women and children with respect to maximum hours, minimum wages, and working conditions. We believe that this can be done within the Constitution as it now stands."

I hope the opinion of the convention is correct that the aims which you have in mind may be attained within the Constitution as it now stands. But, if that opinion should prove to be erroneous, I want you to know that, if nominated and elected, I shall favor a constitutional amendment permitting States to adopt such legislation as may be necessary adequately to protect women and children in the matter of maximum hours, minimum wages and working conditions. This obligation we cannot escape.

The convention advocates "a sound currency to be preserved at all hazards." I agree that "the first requisite to a sound and stable currency is a balanced budget."

The second requisite, as I view it, is a currency expressed in terms of gold and convertible into gold. I recognize, however, that the second requisite must not be made until and unless it can be done without penalizing our democratic economy and without injury to our producers of agricultural products and other raw materials.

The convention pledges the party to the merit system and to its restoration, improvement and extension.

In carrying out this pledge I believe that there should be included within the merit system every position in the administrative service below the rank of assistant secretaries of major departments and agencies, and that this inclusion should cover the entire Postoffice Department.

ALF M. LANDON.

"All the News That's Fit to Print."

The New York Times.

LATE CITY EDITION
Cloudy, possibly showers today, somewhat cooler. Tomorrow cloudy, possibly showers and cooler.
Temperatures Yesterday—Max., 86; Min., 63

VOL. LXXXV....No. 28,644. Entered as Second-Class Matter, Postoffice, New York, N. Y. NEW YORK, SATURDAY, JUNE 27, 1936. PP TWO CENTS In New York City. | THREE CENTS Within 200 Miles. | FOUR CENTS Elsewhere Except in 7th and 8th Postal Zones.

ROOSEVELT NOMINATED BY ACCLAMATION; DEMONSTRATIONS FOR HIM AND LEHMAN

RAIL PENSION LAW VOIDED BY COURT; WRIT HALTS TAXES

District of Columbia Court Rules 1935 Act and Its Tax Legislation Unconstitutional.

CITES FINDING ON 1934 LAW

Bailey Holds Supreme Court Decision on This Also Invalidates Substitute Measures.

CARRIERS WIN INJUNCTIONS

Federal Board Plans a Quick Appeal as 1,000,000 Workers Face Loss of the Benefits.

Text of Justice Bailey's decision on rail pensions is on Page 28.

By LOUIS STARK
Special to THE NEW YORK TIMES.

WASHINGTON, June 26.—On grounds similar in part to those expounded by the United States Supreme Court majority on May 6, 1935, in invalidating the 1934 Railroad Retirement Act, Justice Jennings Bailey in the District of Columbia Supreme Court today declared unconstitutional the 1935 Railroad Pension Law and its companion tax measure, providing the levying and collection of taxes to finance railway men's pensions.

The Tax Act and the Pension Act itself were "inseparable," the two dovetailing "into one another so as to create a complete system," the court declared in the ruling.

The decision was the second blow delivered to the pension aspirations of a million railway workers in the last fourteen months, the Supreme Court having previously held the first Pension Law invalid as a violation of the due process clause of the Constitution.

The first decision was announced while the Social Security Act was pending, and gave rise to the question whether the taxation feature of the Social Security Act would stand up when attacked in the Supreme Court. Today's decision revived the doubts as to the constitutionality of the Social Security Act.

In today's decision, Justice Bailey stated that on Aug. 29, 1935, Congress had approved two acts, one creating a pension system for railway employes and the other levying an excise tax of 3½ per cent of the payrolls, to be paid by the carriers, and a similar tax to be deducted from the employes earning up to $300 a month.

Laws Held Interdependent

"The provisions of the two acts in question are so interrelated and interdependent that each is a necessary part of one entire scheme," the opinion stated. "This is not only apparent from the terms of the acts themselves but is shown by their legislative history. It was clearly the intention of Congress that the pension system created by the Retirement Act should be supported by the taxes levied upon the carriers and their employes."

Holding that the Taxing Act was unconstitutional, Justice Bailey said that it sought to collect revenue, not to provide for the expenses of government, "but solely for a purpose which the United States Supreme Court has held not to be within the domain of the Fedetral Government."

Whether the twenty-one standard railway unions would attempt to open direct negotiations with the Class I roads, which won a victory by the decision today, in an effort for an agreement on a voluntary pension arrangement, could not be ascertained in advance of early conferences among the unions.

Counsel Will Meet Judge

It was assumed that the decision would be appealed to the Supreme Court, but in the absence of Attorney General Cummings no statement was forthcoming from the Department of Justice.

Counsel for the Railroad Retirement Board and the Federal law officers will meet in Justice Bailey's chambers on Tuesday to draw up the formal court order.

The decision enjoined the Railroad Retirement Board from compelling the railroads to "assemble, compile or furnish any of the information and records required, or which may be required to be furnished under said Retirement Act."

It also enjoins Commissioner of Internal Revenue Guy T. Helvering

Continued on Page Twenty-eight

Warships of Five Nations To Meet in Chilean Fete

Special Cable to THE NEW YORK TIMES.

SANTIAGO, Chile, June 26.—Warships of five Latin American nations—Argentina, Brazil, Peru, Ecuador and Chile—will meet in Valparaiso Bay early in September, it was announced today.

They will be present to participate in celebrations marking the 400th anniversary of the founding of the city of Valparaiso.

The meeting is considered an excellent occasion to reawaken cordiality among Latin Americans.

A great display of Chile's air forces is contemplated.

DRUKMAN JURORS DEBATE FOR HOURS

Get Case Accusing Five of Plot in Brooklyn Murder at 2 P. M. and Sit Into the Morning.

POLICE GUARD JURY ROOM

Judge Holds Charges 'of Great Importance' and Menace to the Jury System.

The Brooklyn blue ribbon jury which listened for four weeks to testimony in the Drukman conspiracy trial had not yet agreed, at 3:30 A. M. today, on verdicts for the five defendants charged with plotting to obstruct justice in the Samuel Drukman murder case.

Shortly before midnight the police cleared hundreds of persons out of the building and an army of scrubwomen took possession of the marble floors and corridors. The ousted crowds milled about in the street where ordinarily the sidewalks are deserted at that hour of the night. Scores of persons coming from the theatres drew up in taxicabs to get news.

At that time there had been no word from the jury room since the jurors returned from dinner. No persons were allowed above the ground floor of the building, except the uniformed court officers guarding the vicinity of the jury room. Justice Rogers had given no indication whether he would lock up the jury for the night.

Get Case at 2 P. M.

The jury had been deliberating, with time out for dinner, since 2 P. M. yesterday. Supreme Court Justice Erskine C. Rogers, presiding at the extraordinary term of the court, charged the jury for an hour and forty-five minutes in the morning. Then the jurors went out to lunch, and at 2 o'clock began their deliberations.

Shortly before 5 o'clock they sent two communications to the judge, one asking for testimony dealing with certain tapped-wire conversations and for the testimony of witnesses whose stories, partly contradicting each other, dealt with the State's charge that the defendant, William W. Kleinman, had been seen in an automo-

Continued on Page Four

LEHMAN FOR SOCIAL ISSUE

He Denounces 'Callous' Republican Fight on Security Plan.

'GHASTLY' PHILOSOPHY HIT

President's Program Is Held 'Most Humane Measure of Our Lifetime.'

'MIRACLE' UPTURN HAILED

Governor Also Predicts Fresh Business Expansion—He Will Confer With Roosevelt.

Text of Governor Lehman's seconding speech is on Page 7.

By W. A. WARN
Special to THE NEW YORK TIMES.

THE MUNICIPAL AUDITORIUM, PHILADELPHIA, June 26.—In one of the most impressive addresses of his public career, Governor Lehman of New York appeared before the Democratic National Convention tonight amid a great ovation to second the nomination of President Roosevelt on behalf of the President's and his own home State. He painted a picture of the reaction which would follow in the event of a Republican election victory this Autumn.

Governor Lehman said that in New York the Republicans in the Legislature had bitterly fought progressive measures, especially the social welfare legislation that had been recommended by himself and his immediate predecessor in the Governorship, now the President.

At no time did Governor Lehman mention former Governor Smith, with whom he has been on terms of warm friendship since he entered public life.

"Callous" Policies Scored

In his arraignment of Republican leaders in New York Governor Lehman described their policies as "cruel," "callous" and "reactionary," and declared that the social philosophy which inspired their action was undoubtedly the guiding star of Republican leaders in the nation.

Mr. Lehman declared that President Roosevelt had supplied leadership which was needed as never before when he took office and had lifted the country out of an abyss of despair and panic as by "a miracle." The Governor predicted that upon the foundation laid by the President there would be witnessed an expanding improvement in business during the present year.

"For the real progress that has been made, for the great economic reconstruction of this country, for the hope and confidence that again lie in the breasts of millions of our people—one man above all others deserves our gratitude—Franklin D. Roosevelt," Governor Lehman said.

Governor Lehman met a charge

Continued on Page Seven

President Thanks Lehman, Hails Tribute to Him

Special to THE NEW YORK TIMES.

MUNICIPAL AUDITORIUM, PHILADELPHIA, June 26.—President Roosevelt tonight sent the following telegram to Governor Lehman:

"I thank you, my old friend, from the bottom of my heart for all you said tonight.

"That wonderful tribute to you came from the hearts of every State, and you rightly deserved it. My love to you both.

"FRANKLIN D. ROOSEVELT."

The both includes Mrs. Lehman.

ROOSEVELT HINTS OF FARLEY DECISION

His Deferring of Reply Till End of Convention Is Construed as Forecasting Cabinet Change.

CLOSER TO PHILADELPHIA

President Keeps Telephone Busy—Acceptance Speech Will Dwell on Platform.

By CHARLES W. HURD
Special to THE NEW YORK TIMES.

WASHINGTON, June 26.—President Roosevelt hinted today of early settlement of the question as to how long Postmaster General Farley would remain in the dual position of Cabinet member and chairman of the Democratic National Committee.

In response to a question at a White House press conference whether he was prepared to discuss Mr. Farley's expected resignation, President Roosevelt replied that he could not say anything until after the convention. His remark was construed as at least partial confirmation of reports that Mr. Farley would resign from the Cabinet in the near future.

Mr. Farley has remained in the Cabinet for more than two years since the President issued a dictum that party officials could not also hold government office, a rule which he enforced with severity except in the case of the party chairman.

Keen Over Convention

The press conference, the President's last before he will go to Philadelphia tomorrow night to accept renomination, came in the midst of a day divided about equally between routine work on bills left by Congress and political work, including the polishing of his speech of acceptance.

The President was cheerful over the smooth running of the Philadelphia convention, but marks of fatigue on his face reflected the late and irregular hours he has kept during the week.

For the first time he admitted an active interest in the convention, saying that he had used the telephone at 1:30 this morning. Denying reports that memoranda on the final draft of the platform had been sent to him by airplane for approval, he laughingly asked newspaper correspondents if they did not agree that the telephone was a simpler means of communication.

His early morning call to Philadelphia was made to congratulate Senator Wagner, chairman of the resolutions committee, on his delivery of the platform before the convention. The radio brought it to the White House.

Mr. Roosevelt said that he also tried to reach Marvin H. McIntyre, one of his secretaries sent to Philadelphia as an observer, but was unable to do so at that hour.

Rough Draft Still "Too Rough"

As for the platform, much of which obviously was substantially written in advance of the convention with the close cooperation of, if not by, Mr. Roosevelt, he said that he had only read part of the final text.

What the President wishes to say publicly about the platform will constitute the main portion of his speech tomorrow night.

This speech, a comparatively brief document of about 2,000 words, was almost completed, having been dictated last night by the President, but he said that he probably would make several changes in it because the rough draft, in second reading this morning, appeared to be literally "too rough" in spots.

In further conversation the President said that he intended to stay within the borders of the United States until after election and that there would be no cruises to Hawaii

Continued on Page Nine

DRAMA IN NIGHT SESSION

One Big Moment Is Held Back When Lehman Speech Is Delayed.

HE GETS TWO OVATIONS

Acclaim in Drafting Movement Rivals That for President as Name Is Ratified.

DOOLING LEADS PARADE

'It Was Swell,' Says Governor, but Gives No Intimation of What Answer Will Be.

By TURNER CATLEDGE
Special to THE NEW YORK TIMES.

THE MUNICIPAL AUDITORIUM, PHILADELPHIA, Saturday, June 27.—With two prolonged demonstrations for Governor Herbert H. Lehman and another for President Roosevelt, the Democratic National Convention, at its session which ended nearly an hour after midnight this morning, attempted by a frank show of its enthusiasm to tie together the personalities of these two leaders for the campaign.

When the convention adjourned at 12:55 this morning until 10 A. M. today, it was in the midst of an ovation to President Roosevelt. It was the second given him during the day's two sessions, the other, lasting an hour and four minutes, being when he was placed in nomination in the afternoon.

The first outburst for Governor Lehman rivaled anything seen at this convention. It came when Chairman Robinson announced at about 10 P. M. that the New York Governor would take the rostrum to second the nomination of President Roosevelt.

Culmination of "Draft" Move

It was the culmination of the "draft Lehman" movement which started even before the convention began and which last night saw every State, Territory and district represented here join in a concerted movement to add what they all considered a "dynamo of strength" to the Democratic ticket next Fall.

The demonstration was started by the New York delegation, led by James J. Dooling, leader of Tammany; Frank V. Kelly, Brooklyn leader; Senator Robert F. Wagner, and Borough President James J. Lyons of the Bronx. Just behind came George Gordon Battle. The New Yorkers were smiling and shouting as they were joined by delegates from other States.

The instant Governor Lehman's name was mentioned by Senator Robinson, permanent chairman of the convention, the delegates, alternates and spectators literally exploded with enthusiasm. They had been waiting impatiently for nearly an hour while representatives of other States paid their respects to the candidacy of Mr. Roosevelt.

The demonstration bade fair to go on and on, but Senator Robinson pleaded for quiet so that Governor Lehman could begin his speech. When he began the aisles were jammed with marching delegates and alternates, each delegation headed by a banner advocating the drafting of the Governor for renomination.

Lehman Stops the Outburst

As Mr. Lehman raised his voice, however, the demonstration quickly subsided. The demonstration lasted eleven minutes and might have gone on for an hour had it not been halted.

The New York delegation started a new demonstration for Governor Lehman after he had completed his speech. The Buffalo women's drum and bugle corps started playing again and the "Lehman Must Run" banners began moving in all sections of the hall.

Chairman Robinson rapped for order and tried to stop it. He wanted to proceed with the seconding speeches and was ready to present Mrs. Emma Guffey Miller to speak for Pennsylvania, but the New Yorkers kept parading, Alabama joined in, then followed Pennsylvania, Minnesota, Texas, Kansas—headed by a banner making light of Governor Landon's claims of balancing his budget—a delegate bearing the standard of the National Colored Democratic Association, North Dakota, Michigan, the Virgin Islands and others.

Other delegations waved their standards.

The second Lehman demonstration continued for ten minutes be-

Continued on Page Nine

© Photo by New York Times Studio.

RENOMINATED FOR PRESIDENT
Franklin Delano Roosevelt,
from a photograph for which he posed at the White House last Saturday

ENTHUSIASM RUNS HIGH

Eight Hours of Oratory Precede Acclamation in Early Morning.

CHEER PRESIDENT AN HOUR

Delegates in Ecstatic Climax When Name Is Presented to Convention by Mack.

LEHMAN TOPS SECONDERS

Received So Enthusiastically as to Leave No Doubt of Desire That He Run Again.

Text of former Justice Mack's nominating speech is on Page 6.

By ARTHUR KROCK
Special to THE NEW YORK TIMES.

THE MUNICIPAL AUDITORIUM, PHILADELPHIA, Saturday, June 27.—After more than eight hours of eulogistic oratory and demonstrations, which kept the Democratic National Convention in session from 1 P. M. yesterday until 12:55 o'clock this morning, Franklin Delano Roosevelt was nominated for re-election by acclamation. Vice President Garner will be similarly honored this afternoon.

Fifty-seven speeches were made by the orators in the seconding talkathon, representing every State, territory, possession and the District of Columbia. They included twelve Governors, eight Senators, one Senator-elect, eight women, a Cabinet officer and the Governor General of the Philippine Islands. Senator McAdoo, when called to the chair, also spoke in favor of the nomination but his was not strictly a seconding speech.

On motion of Governor Berry of South Dakota the rules were suspended and the roll-call was dispensed with, the nomination coming at 12:42 A. M.

Final, Noisy Celebration

Senator Robinson's announcement from the platform that the President had been chosen by acclamation—thus "beating Cleveland"—loosed another and the final demonstration of the all-day, all-night session. It was just like the rest and was still in progress when the chairman heard, put and declared passed a motion to recess until 10 o'clock this morning—an action unknown to nearly all the shouting, parading, horn-tooting demonstrators.

Rarely has the flow of harmonious oratory been equaled in a national political gathering as a few conservatives joined a long parade of New Dealers in extolling the President. Going a step beyond the Repubican convention at Cleveland two weeks ago, the Philadelphia delegates cast not a single vote against Mr. Roosevelt. A score of votes from Wisconsin and West Virginia kept Governor Alf M. Landon from enjoying the same distinction.

Much more exciting than the actual nomination was a series of tumultuous uprisings to honor Governor Herbert H. Lehman of New York, who made the chief seconding speech at 10 o'clock last night. The effort was in part prearranged to convince Mr. Lehman that he must stand for re-election. At the same time a great deal of it was spontaneous and sincere. When Mr. Lehman was finally permitted to leave the platform he received a telegram of thanks from the President at Washington. Though beset with importunities, he declined to admit any change in his intention to retire.

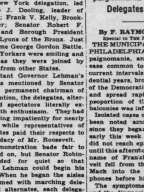

Stresses President's Record

The Governor stressed the President's bent and record in behalf of social welfare, and, by his scathing attack upon the Republican leadership at Albany, intimated what the chief campaign issue in that State will be if the Democrats can make it so.

When the President's name was formally proposed by John E. Mack of Poughkeepsie, who rendered the same service in 1932, a demonstration of more than an hour's duration interrupted the proceedings. Whatever the feelings of many Democrats who will go along this year for a number of reasons, and some of whom excused themselves from prominent participation in the oratory of the day, there is no doubt that the tumult expressed the feeling of the overwhelming majority of the delegates.

Although a fair percentage of the

Continued on Page Eight

OUTBURSTS ALARM PROF. CEREBELLUM

Psychiatrist Diagnoses Campaignomania Which Affects Delegates at Times.

By F. RAYMOND DANIELL
Special to THE NEW YORK TIMES.

THE MUNICIPAL AUDITORIUM, PHILADELPHIA, June 26.—Campaignomania, an occupational disease common to politicians at recurrent intervals, notably in Presidential years, broke out on the floor of the Democratic convention today and spread rapidly until a large proportion of the visitors in the balconies was infected.

Isolated cases of the malady have been noted among the delegates since they began assembling here early this week but the outbreak did not reach epidemic proportions until this afternoon, when the magic name of Franklin Delano Roosevelt fell from the lips of John E. Mack into the cluster of microphones before him.

The symptoms were recognized and the diagnosis provided by Professor Cerebrus Cerebellum, a noted psychiatrist from Brownsville, Brown County, Ind., close friend of those other Brown countians, Godfrey Gloom and Abe Martin, who once remarked that a "lot of people believe in Providence who never heard of Rhode Island."

As the professor explained it, campaignomania is a disease characterized by more or less violent manifestations of short duration. There is no immunization against it, he said, and the more dignified statesmen are especially susceptible to its ravages at convention time.

Case History Is Revealing

In the interest of science, the professor suggested that a detailed and objective study of the apparent aberrations of reflexes of the patients be made and published for the benefit of students of psychiatry and politics. Therefore the following:

At 1:23 P. M. when Mr. Mack mentioned the name of Mr. Roosevelt, the delegates and guests were slumped in their seats, listening politely and to all outward appearances behaving like perfectly normal average citizens.

A second later the entire scene had changed from a relatively dignified assemblage of patriots to one resembling what might take place in the psychopathic ward of a great

Continued on Page Eight

GARNER ON SCENE, MET WITH ACCLAIM

Vice President Passes Through Cheering Crowds From Station to His Hotel.

By CHARLES R. MICHAEL
Special to THE NEW YORK TIMES.

PHILADELPHIA, June 26.—Jovial Jack Garner, Vice President, arrived here at 7 o'clock tonight to participate with President Roosevelt in the notification ceremonies tomorrow night. Escorted by 175 mounted policemen from the Thirtieth Street station, he was cheered by the crowds, whose attention was attracted by shrieking sirens as he and the reception committee proceeded to his hotel. He acknowledged the acclaim from the sidewalks by standing up in his car.

At the hotel the Texas delegates, massed in the street under their Lone Star banner, gave him a rousing welcome.

Mr. Garner was met at the station by a committee composed of Attorney General Cummings, Postmaster General Farley, Senators Robinson and Connally and Governor and Mrs. Earle. As he left his car he turned to the captain commanding the police escort and said:

"I have never seen a better lot of officers than you have here. You remind me of the Texas Rangers and your presence makes it homelike."

Is Guest at Reception

The Vice President attended a reception given in his honor by the Texas delegation and later participated briefly in the dinner of the Young Democrats. He did not make a speech and tarried only long enough to greet them. He told them as he left that the future of the country and the Democratic party depended upon their efforts.

Mr. Garner spent the evening in his hotel chatting with old friends. Many came to visit him. He will not make any public appearance until tomorrow night, when he is scheduled to accept renomination for the Vice Presidency before President Roosevelt makes his acceptance speech.

Since becoming Vice President, Mr. Garner has refrained from discussing public questions. He remained true to that policy tonight and declined to comment upon the platform.

He, however, did discuss the political outlook with Chairman Farley and other Democratic chieftains

Continued on Page Nine

3 Guilty of Fraud, Fourth's Fate in Doubt In Failure of $81,000,000 Title Company

J. Crawford Stevens, president, and Reginald P. Ray, vice president, of the defunct Westchester Title and Trust Company, were found guilty at 12:20 A. M. today on all counts of a twenty-count mail fraud indictment by a Federal court jury which had deliberated for more than eight hours.

Philip H. Kuss, also a vice president, was found guilty on twelve of the twenty counts, and the jury failed to reach an agreement on the guilt or innocence of Frederick P. Condit, chairman of the executive committee, who is also a vice president and trustee of the Title Guarantee and Trust Company.

Judge Robert P. Patterson ordered the jury locked up for the night. It will continue its deliberation this morning on Condit.

Stevens and Ray face prison terms up to ninety-seven years and fines totaling $29,000 each, while Kuss is subject to imprisonment for up to fifty-seven years and fines totaling $22,000.

Shortly before midnight Judge Patterson called the jury into the court room and asked whether they had been able to approach a verdict. Fletcher Swain, foreman, said that agreement had been reached regarding three of the defendants but that the jury was deadlocked as to the fourth. Judge Patterson then said that he would accept a partial verdict and the jury retired, to return about twenty minutes later.

Former Mayor John J. Fogarty, of Yonkers, representing Stevens and Kuss, and Monroe Cahn, attorney for Ray, objected strenuously to the court's procedure in accepting an incomplete verdict.

The Westchester Title and Trust Company failed in August, 1933, with $81,000,000 of its securities in the hands of the public. The trial has been in progress for more than seven weeks.

Of the twenty counts in the indictments, nineteen concerned the mailing of sales-promotion literature containing statements which the government charges were misleading. The twentieth charged conspiracy. Some of the challenged statements were that mortgage certificates issued by the company were absolutely safe, depression proof and secured by Westchester County homes or improved property.

Judge Patterson pointed out that Mr. Condit was not a salaried officer of the company and was not active in its affairs. The jury's duty, he explained, was to determine only whether he participated in arranging for year-end loans in 19[illegible] and 1932 and whether, if he did so, he knew this was done to produce financial statements which might mislead the public.

Wide World Photo

FDR campaigning for re-election.

The Republican campaign button featured Alf Landon's smile surrounded by the petals of a yellow sunflower.

Sheep in search of grass and water in South Dakota, one of the states hard hit by drought in July.

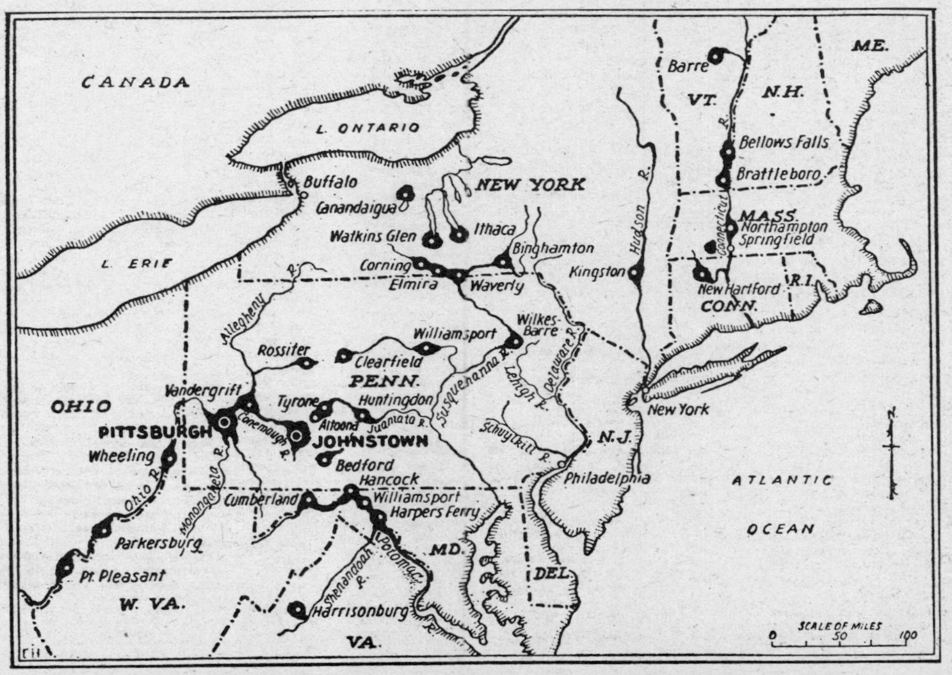

Map showing the wide area hit by floods in March causing heavy losses. The shaded towns and cities are those where overflowing rivers caused the worst damage.

Automobiles and trucks clog a main thoroughfare in Hartford as the water from the Connecticut River swirled through the city in March.

"All the News That's Fit to Print."

The New York Times.

LATE CITY EDITION
Fair and warmer today. Tomorrow generally fair and continued warm.
Temperatures Yesterday—Max., 95; Min., 66

Copyright, 1936, by The New York Times Company.

VOL. LXXXV.....No. 28,655. Entered as Second-Class Matter, Postoffice, New York, N. Y. NEW YORK, WEDNESDAY, JULY 8, 1936. P TWO CENTS In New York City. | THREE CENTS Within 200 Miles. | FOUR CENTS Elsewhere Except in 7th and 8th Postal Zones.

RELIEF TO 134,000 FAMILIES PLANNED FOR DROUGHT AREA; ROOSEVELT TO VISIT REGION

Mercury Hits 120, No Rain in Sight, As Crops Burn in the Drought Area

Twenty-five Die From Heat and 26 Are Drowned—Grain Prices Soar—Federal Grants of $17.50 Per Family for July Arranged—Forest Fires Spread.

Special to THE NEW YORK TIMES.

CHICAGO, July 7.—The heat wave again set records over the 100 degree mark in its fifth day of dominance in the drought stricken regions of the Central and Northwest States.

The mercury was on its way to the 100 degree mark in Chicago today when a light lake breeze set in, after a maximum of 95 degrees had been reached. But in the western and southwestern suburbs there was no relief. Unofficial marks as high as 120 at Mishek, N. D., and 118 at Des Plaines, Ill., were recorded.

Temperatures above 100 degrees outside of Chicago were recorded: Phoenix, Ariz., 110; Rockford, 105; Rockford Airport, 118; Aurora, 106; Ottawa, 106; Mishawaka, Ind., 116; Evansville, 106; Champaign, Ill., 101; Bismarck, N. D., 103; Devils Lake, N. D., 106; Waterloo, Iowa, 101; Fairbault, Minn., 103; La Crosse, Wis., 102; Green Bay, Wis., 104; Glendive, Mont., 112; Glasgow, Mont., 106; Bemidji, Minn., 100; Mason City, Iowa, 102, and Duluth, Minn., 100.1.

As the forecaster examined meteorological conditions and predicted more torrid weather and no rain for the parched grain and stock belt, members of the Board of Trade saw wheat reach a new seasonal high of $1.10 a bushel and then recede a few cents later in the day on reports of showers in Western Canada. Corn, however, advanced to a new high of 78 cents a bushel. Oats and rye also reached new highs but were a few points lower than these at the close of the market.

Central Illinois farmers anxiously scanned the cloudless skies for rain, which can save a good portion of their crops if it comes soon. In many sections of the State the wheat crop has not been seriously damaged, although corn is badly hit. Near Champaign, oats are practically worthless, it was report-

Continued on Page Three

BROAD PROGRAM BEGUN

Hundreds of Men to Be Hired Daily for 'Useful' Work to Yield Cash.

FOOD SUPPLY HELD AMPLE

President Makes Plain That Wheat and Corn Plantings Exceeded Average.

AAA CHANGES CONTRACTS

Farmers May Now Grow Feed and Not Lose Their Benefits—'Emergency' in 97 Counties.

Special to THE NEW YORK TIMES.

WASHINGTON, July 7.—A comprehensive program to give work relief or subsistence to 100,000 families impoverished by the drought and provide soon for another 34,000, in addition to 70,000 families already on subsistence relief in the drought areas, was set in motion today by President Roosevelt.

He approved this program and assumed personal direction of it during a two-hour conference with his emergency drought committee, and immediately afterward announced his plans in detail at a press conference.

The President also said that he would take a trip to the Dakotas and Minnesota in August to see at first-hand the progress made in the program he has set in motion. In reply to a direct question whether his proposed trip would have political significance he replied with asperity that it would not.

When asked what the cost of this new relief undertaking would be, and where the funds would be obtained, he said that he was concerned at the moment with matters more important than cost estimates; that the money would come from a number of sources.

Expects No Food Shortage

In discussing the drought the President emphasized two other points:

First, that there would be no national food shortage.

Second, that any possible curtailment of normal supplies of foodstuffs would be due to the drought alone and not to crop-restriction activities, since more wheat and corn were planted this year than in 1933 or in the average year from 1928 to 1932.

As for the wheat outlook, he said he expected that a report due later this week would show an estimated crop of 600,000,000 bushels, which, combined with a carry-over of 150,000,000 bushels, would give the United States an excess of 125,000,000 bushels above the average normal annual consumption of 625,000,000 bushels. The drought has destroyed all but 15 per cent of the Spring wheat crop, he added.

While the President was outlining relief plans the Weather Bureau announced that no rain appeared to be in prospect for the drought areas in the next thirty-six hours.

The Department of Agriculture designated ninety-seven counties in the Northwest, where the drought is more severe, as "emergency drought counties," thereby permitting railroads automatically to reduce freight rates in those regions.

Traces Drought's Spread on Maps

The President opened his discussion of the drought as soon as reporters had filed into his office.

Before him he had numerous charts and maps, and seated behind him were members of the drought committee, including Rexford G. Tugwell, Resettlement Administrator; Aubrey Williams, Assistant Works Progress Administrator, and J. B. Hudson of the Agricultural Adjustment Administration.

With the remark that he thought he would talk about agriculture first, Mr. Roosevelt began a half-hour discussion in which he showed three maps bearing witness to the spread of the drought area as well as the steadily declining water tables in the affected regions.

These maps showed that fairly severe conditions existed in Southern Kentucky, Northern Tennessee, Georgia and North and South Carolina, and in a small area to the westward embracing parts of Western Arkansas and Eastern Oklahoma.

The really severe drought region was shown as in North and South Dakota, Eastern Montana, Western Wyoming and parts of Minnesota.

The 204,000 families in need of relief, the President went on, are

Continued on Page Three

GREEN DECLARES LEWIS IS BLOCKING STEEL UNION PLAN

Labor Chief Asserts on Eve of Council Meeting Move of C. I. O. Can't Succeed.

LEWIS ASKS COOPERATION

Retorts That No Effort Was Made by the Federation to Organize Steel Forces.

UNIONIZATION IS PRESSED

Murray Puts More Organizers in Field and Defies Any Action by the A. F. of L.

Steel Unionization Moves

President Green of the A. F. of L. asserted that the federation was preparing to unionize steel and that the industrial union movement headed by John L. Lewis cannot succeed without the backing of the federation.

Phillip Murray, director of the steel unionization drive of the Amalgamated Union, declared that it would go on regardless of what action the American Federation of Labor takes.

European labor leaders, gathered for the congress of the International Federation of Trades Unions in London, feared the growing split in the A. F. of L. might lead to weakening of united labor resistance against fascism.

Green Issues Statement

By LOUIS STARK

Special to THE NEW YORK TIMES.

WASHINGTON, July 7.—On the eve of a momentous meeting of the American Federation of Labor's executive council tomorrow, President William Green today charged the committee for industrial organization, led by John L. Lewis, with thwarting the federation's plan to organize the steel industry by the united action of the labor movement.

Mr. Green emphasized the division of sentiment in labor's ranks by asserting that the C. I. O. since its organization last November had achieved "nothing whatever except division, discord and confusion within the ranks of organized labor."

The statement evoked an immediate reply from Mr. Lewis, who asserted that the executive council had no plan to organize the steel industry, that the instructions of the last two conventions to begin such action had not been executed and that it was not too late to join the C. I. O. in its present campaign.

If the council, he said, elected "to join with the corporations composing the American Iron and Steel Institute in fighting the C. I. O., now engaged in this major effort, the shame of such a dishonorable action will lie on the heads of Mr. Green and his irreconcilable associates."

The "fighting words" of the two labor leaders further widened the rift between the advocates of industrial unions in the mass production industries and the craft union leadership. In view of the widening chasm between the two groups the question as to whether the council would suspend the twelve C. I. O. unions, comprising one-third of the federation's membership, was uppermost in labor circles here today. In some quarters the Green statement was regarded as presaging such action.

Seek to Avoid Labor Split

However, some "middle of the road" leaders were still seeking for a formula that would avoid splitting the labor movement into two warring camps, one of which would be suspended from its membership with the added threat that it would be ousted from the federation at the next convention if it refused to dissolve the C. I. O.

One of the questions to be considered by the executive council is whether to furnish a "bill of particulars" to the C. I. O. unions stating specifically and in detail why they are considered as a "dual" or rival organization to the federation.

Demand for such a "bill of particulars" before formal charges are heard has been made to Mr. Green by John Brophy, director of the C. I. O., who said that such action was in accordance with usual trade union procedure.

Associates of Mr. Lewis said today that the office of the United Mine Workers had been deluged with telegrams and telephone messages commenting on the radio address of the miners' chief last night on the steel organization drive.

The radio will again be used in the campaign, it was said.

Mr. Green's statement against the Committee for Industrial Organization follows:

"As the plans of the organizing campaign launched by the Commit-

Continued on Page Two

Hoffman Bars Parker Extradition; Calls Wendel Unworthy of Belief

Governor Contrasts Complainant's Record and Detective's Long Service—Questions Motive in Prosecution—To Sue Radio Commentator Over Hauptmann Case Broadcasts.

Special to THE NEW YORK TIMES.

TRENTON, July 7.—Governor Hoffman refused today to grant the extradition of Ellis H. Parker Sr. chief of Burlington County detectives, to Brooklyn, where he is under indictment for the kidnapping of Paul H. Wendel.

The Governor's action was not unexpected. He said some weeks ago that if the facts proved to be as he then understood them he would not "sacrifice" either the detective or the latter's son, who is a fugitive on a similar indictment.

Governor Hoffman issued a statement in defense of his refusal to honor New York State's requisition. He cited instances in which United States Senator A. Harry Moore, a Democrat, when Governor of New Jersey, declined to order the return to Georgia of a chain gang fugitive and President Roosevelt, when Governor of New York, denied New Jersey requisitions for the return of five fugitives wanted in Monmouth County.

Another aftermath of the Lindbergh kidnapping investigation developed tonight when Governor Hoffman announced that he had authorized the filing of a $100,000 suit against Boake Carter, radio news commentator, and others.

Charges in the action are to be based on broadcasts by Mr. Carter before and on the day of the Hauptmann execution at Trenton, according to William Conklin, the Governor's secretary, after a conversation on the subject with Mr. Hoffman. The Governor authorized the suit, Mr. Conklin said, after a conference at Trenton yesterday with Harry Greene, his attorney, who has offices at Newark.

In the Parker case, the Governor declared, neither Wendel nor Murray Bleefeld, whose affidavits accompanied the request for extradition, was "worthy of belief."

"Placing the forty-two years of devoted and zealous service of Ellis Parker Sr. to the State of New Jersey against the mendacity and criminality of Wendel, I could not

Continued on Page Five

LEHMAN TO SET UP TWO GRAND JURIES IN DEWEY INQUIRY

Prosecutor, in Albany, Wins Plea to Have Machinery for Racket Drive Doubled.

GOVERNOR PRAISES WORK

Garment District Concern Is Raided in War on Gangs Preying on Industry.

Special to THE NEW YORK TIMES.

ALBANY, July 7.—Governor Lehman announced tonight after a three-hour conference with Special Prosecutor Thomas E. Dewey and Supreme Court Justice Philip J. McCook, who have been investigating rackets in New York City, that he would impanel immediately two more special grand juries and call Special Terms of the Supreme Court to continue the work started by Mr. Dewey.

One of these Special Terms will be presided over by Justice McCook and the other by a justice whom the Governor said he would name as soon as he could find one available. Then the present city grand jury will be dismissed, the Governor said, explaining that it had been working six hours a day for about six months and wished to be relieved of its duties.

Mr. Dewey and Justice McCook arrived at the Governor's office at 3 o'clock this afternoon and were closeted with him until about 6:30. Mr. Dewey had nothing to say about the conference and Justice McCook was equally silent, referring all questions to Governor Lehman.

Asked for Report

Governor Lehman in his talk with the newspaper men said:

"I have had a long talk with Mr. Dewey and Justice McCook, who on my invitation came to see me to tell me what has happened in the prosecution of rackets and what they propose to do in the immediate present.

"I had a long talk with both of them and the situation was very carefully gone over. I am very well satisfied and pleased with the progress that has been made in both the investigation and the prosecution that has been carried on by Special Prosecutor Dewey and Justice McCook.

"We went over the future situation and discussed the presentment of the city grand jury, which in a report to me outlined that the work was too great to be carried on by only one grand jury and recommended that they be relieved, and in place of one I now convene two Special Terms and two grand juries.

"In view of the fact that this grand jury has been sitting for six months and devoting six hours a day and that in spite of this the work has backed up to a certain extent, I decided to impanel two grand juries and two Special Terms.

To Issue Order Soon

"One, of course, will take the place of the present grand jury, which will continue until the other can become effective. The other additional one will supplement the work that has been carried on. The orders for these grand juries and Special Terms will be issued as soon as possible. I shall redesignate Justice McCook to preside over one and will select the other as soon as I am able."

Governor Lehman, in answer to a question, said Mr. Dewey did not say how much longer his investigation would continue. Closing the interview, Governor Lehman said:

"The recommendation of the grand jury, I felt, was sound. Mr. Dewey will continue the work and I am confident from his past ex-

Continued on Page Four

LANDON ASKS STATE FOR 2 AMENDMENTS ON SOCIAL SECURITY

Special Legislative Session Urged to Pave Way for Unrestricted Program.

RESOLUTIONS ARE SPEEDED

Republican Nominee Confers With National Party Leaders —Gets Optimistic Reports.

By WARREN MOSCOW

Special to THE NEW YORK TIMES.

TOPEKA, July 7.—Governor Landon, in a message to the special session of the Kansas Legislature, and a later statement to the press, took a broad stand today in favor of social security legislation, likening it to a dike built after some great disaster to prevent its repetition in the future.

Mounting the rostrum of the House Chamber in the State Capitol, and facing the joint membership of Senate and House, he asked them to adopt broad amendments to the Kansas Constitution to enable the State to conform with a Federal social security program, be it the one now in force, or be it along the lines outlined in the Republican national platform.

He did not deem it a fitting time to enter into a discussion of the relative merits of the present act and the proposals set out in the Republican platform, he told the assembled lawmakers.

Later, in his statement to the press, he said:

"Social security in the end can only be built upon character, and religion, and industry, but in the meantime our natural humanity and the employment problem of a great industrial civilization require the community through its government to protect those who by reason of age or other misfortune may have claims upon us.

Hopes For Amendment

"Flood and disaster lead us to build dikes and to take other means to protect us from a recurrence of the calamities we have known. We have passed through such a period. We know its effects on individuals and the country as a whole. The thought behind social security is to create such a dike and other means as will protect us from a repetition of the troubles of the past years, or minimize their effects.

"The Constitution of Kansas prevents our State from properly joining in this worthy effort. I hope the present special session of our Legislature will submit such amendments to that Constitution as will enable this State to join in securing all proper assistance to our people."

In his message to the Legislature, the Governor said:

"Such amendment should not, in my judgment, contain the details of a plan which may finally be adopted in this State. It should merely be a grant of power. The methods of administration have no part in the Constitution of the State, but should be left to the wisdom and sound judgment of the Legislature. This is the procedure followed in the original drafting of our Constitution, and the subsequent amendments.

"My confidence in the legislators of this State assures me that if this power is entrusted to them it will be exercised in a wise, sound and just manner to the end that the obligation of the State to its less fortunate may be fulfilled and the rights of all our people justly protected."

Meanwhile, the legislative leaders, working through the Judiciary Committee and of both houses, came to an agreement on the wording of the two amendments which

Continued on Page Eight

CITY REPUBLICANS TO IGNORE MAYOR

Leaders, Angered by Lack of Patronage, Plan to Name Straight Party Ticket.

WILL CONFER TOMORROW

Expected to Let Queens Pick Candidate to Head the Board of Aldermen.

As the five Republican leaders of New York City prepared to pick a designee for the Presidency of the Board of Aldermen it was learned last night that they will make their selection without consulting Mayor La Guardia, who though nominally a Republican was elected on a Fusion ticket.

"Why should we consult Mayor La Guardia?" one county leader asked last night. "He has never consulted with us."

Several of the leaders have made no secret of their antagonism to the Fusion Mayor because of his refusal to consider their patronage needs. As a result it is expected that the Republicans will select a straight party ticket for the city-wide offices at the municipal election next year.

The Republican leaders will meet tomorrow in the National Republican Club to pick a candidate to oppose Sheriff William F. Brunner of Queens, who was chosen by the Democratic leaders as their choice for the remaining year of the late Bernard S. Deutsch's four-year term. Mr. Deutsch was a running mate of Mayor La Guardia on the Republican-Fusion ticket of 1933.

Choice Likely to Go to Queens

The consensus is that the opportunity of naming the designee will go to Queens because Mr. Brunner is a resident of that borough. It was intimated that the final choice would not be agreed upon by the Queens organization for several days.

The leaders who will gather around the table are Kenneth F. Simpson, Manhattan leader; John R. Crews, Brooklyn; Warren B. Ashmead, Queens; John J. Knewitz, Bronx, and Sheriff John Timlin, Staten Island.

Mr. Ashmead, Jamaica banker, indicated last night that the other leaders would agree to a Queens Republican. He said the move had been inspired by the action of the five Democratic leaders in picking Sheriff Brunner.

"To date no personalities have been discussed," Mr. Ashmead said. "But I think the candidate will be designated within two or three days after our conference Thursday, when we shall decide on which county organization is to name the candidate."

Fusion Support in Doubt

Whether the Republican designated will have Fusion support from the organization that backed Mr. La Guardia, the late Controller W. Arthur Cunningham and the late Mr. Deutsch could not be ascertained last night. Sheriff Brunner ran for his present office in Queens last year with the Fusion endorsement.

The Queens Democratic Executive Committee met yesterday afternoon at its Woodside headquarters and unanimously approved of the action of the five county leaders and its own membership in the State committee for selecting Sheriff Brunner to run for the aldermanic presidency.

James C. Sheridan, Queens leader,

Continued on Page Seven

LEAVE OF ABSENCE IS GIVEN TO FARLEY

President Represented as Rejecting Postmaster General's Suggestion of Resigning.

HOWES ACTING SUCCESSOR

National Chairman Expected to Return to the Cabinet if Roosevelt Is Re-elected.

Special to THE NEW YORK TIMES.

WASHINGTON, July 7.—President Roosevelt granted to Postmaster General James A. Farley today a leave of absence from that office, effective from Aug. 1 until after the November elections.

W. W. Howes, First Assistant Postmaster General, was designated as Acting Postmaster General during Mr. Farley's absence.

It was understood that the President declined to grant Mr. Farley's request that he be permitted to resign in order to devote all his time to his duties as chairman of the Democratic National Committee and chairman of the New York State Democratic Committee. Instead, Mr. Roosevelt decided that Mr. Farley should take a leave of absence without pay from his Cabinet post. It is expected that he will resume his position as Postmaster General if President Roosevelt is re-elected.

Mr. Farley is said to have informed the President that he was ready to resign to silence the administration's critics, especially Senator Norris and some Democratic Senators. The President is understood to have declined to accede to this informal proffer and to have held that the same purpose would be effected if Mr. Farley left the Cabinet temporarily and was on leave without pay during the campaign months.

Pleased by Farley's Record

Mr. Roosevelt was represented as believing that Mr. Farley had made a good record as Postmaster General and was entitled to another term if the administration continues in power.

The President's decision that he should not leave the Cabinet permanently was understood to be especially pleasing to Mr. Farley. Some influential administration advisers had counseled the President to accept Mr. Farley's resignation. The action of the President in ignoring such advice was accepted by Mr. Farley as a tribute not only to his work as a Cabinet member but as head of the national committee.

Under the law, Mr. Farley as a Cabinet member on leave cannot solicit contributions from other Federal office holders. The President was asked about this prohibition today. He said that he had not studied the law enough to say whether this would operate. An official of the Democratic National Committee, however, explained that the law forbade a Federal office holder from soliciting funds from other officials, and that Mr. Farley as chairman would not make requests for funds from this class.

"The law does not prohibit him receiving such funds," it was explained at the Democratic committee offices.

Farley Comes to New York Aug. 3

During the next few weeks Mr. Farley will be busy making up his official reports. He will assume active direction of the campaign Aug. 3, when he will take up his headquarters in New York City.

President Roosevelt is expected

Continued on Page Seven

STATE DEFICIT CUT $41,171,323 IN YEAR

$97,048,752 of 1935 Nearly Halved, Best Showing in New York's History.

EMERGENCY TAXES FACTOR

Lehman Cites These and 1933 Economies—Assembly Called New Budget Menace.

Special to THE NEW YORK TIMES.

ALBANY, July 7.—In the fiscal year just ended, the State nearly halved its deficit, cutting it from $97,048,752.52 to $55,877,428.89 with the aid of emergency taxes, figures prepared by Controller Tremaine and released today by Governor Lehman showed.

The State's receipts for the year amounted to $330,543,774.53 and expenditures to $289,372,450.90, leaving a balance of $41,171,323.63 to go automatically into the accumulated deficit fund for the reduction. Incidentally, the deficit as it now stands is $1,597,632.80 less than the Governor had estimated in January.

Of the emergency taxes, the 4-cent motor fuel levy, carrying a 2-cent emergency tax, produced $52,699,614.23 revenue, while the personal income tax, 1 per cent of which is in the emergency category, yielded $74,328,921.94. The 1½ per cent corporation franchise tax produced $27,016,927.19 and the tax on unincorporated business $3,626,347.05.

Governor Lehman was elated, saying the State would begin its new fiscal year in a stronger financial position than at any time for many years.

State's Best Year

"Measured by the size of the surplus from the year's general fund operations," he said, "the fiscal year 1936, with its operating surplus of over $41,000,000, stands out as the most successful single year in the State's financial history.

"Never before has the State in a single year received so much more than it spent."

Another cause for elation on the part of the Governor was that the revenue estimates made six months ago were accurate within one-seventh of 1 per cent. The executive budget estimated State expenditures at $290,510,941.53; the amount actually spent was $289,373,450.90, or $1,138,490.63 less than the estimates.

It was also estimated in the official budget that the State would be $39,573,690.83 ahead as the result of the year's operations; actually it is $41,171,323.63 ahead. It was estimated that the accumulated deficit would be reduced from $97,098,752.52 to $57,475,061.69; actually the reduction was $55,877,428.89.

"Such a close correspondence between prediction and realization," Mr. Lehman said, "is extremely gratifying, particularly in view of the great difficulties in forecasting the various items of the State's revenue system."

He emphasized that during the

Continued on Page Nine

CANADA SEES DOOM OF WHEAT SURPLUS

Drought Damage to Crop May End One Problem, but Raise Another in Relief Needs.

70% HARVEST FORECAST

Meanwhile Scattered Showers and Cool Breezes Halt Rise Toward $1 Market Price.

Special to THE NEW YORK TIMES.

MONTREAL, July 7.—The wheat surplus which has haunted the imagination and embarrassed the exchequer of two Canadian governments practically ceased to be a factor today when an official crop report confirmed Western reports of damage from sweltering heat and drought.

While the report does not estimate the total damage in detail it confirms a Winnipeg estimate today of a 70 per cent crop of 250,000,000 bushels, instead of the expected 375,000,000. This would be a drop of 125,000,000 bushels, which probably will mean that the carry-over at the end of the present crop year will be the normal 50,000,000 bushels or even less.

The new Canadian Wheat Board appointed by the present government took over 298,356,000 bushels of cash and future wheat on Dec. 7, and by the end of January had sold 76,000,000 bushels and acquired 15,000,000 more from producers. It has been selling actively since then, although the price level which ruled meant that the government was bound to incur a loss on its total holdings and pegging transactions since 1931.

Winnipeg Market Lower

If dollar wheat comes, and it is said, moreover, that it might have already been reached had the 5-cent trading limit not existed, the government will begin to recoup some of this loss. At the close of operations in the Winnipeg Grain Exchange today, as a result of scattered showers and cooling breezes in the West, prices were a little lower than yesterday, July at 91¼ and October at 90¼.

What the government gains in one way, however, it will lose in another. The calamitous weather conditions which have belatedly justified former Prime Minister R. B. Bennett's policy of holding Canada's accumulating surpluses off the market have put grain crops in many parts of Manitoba, Saskatchewan and Alberta beyond repair.

"Severe drought conditions," says today's crop report, "extend westward over a wide area from Southeastern Manitoba to the southern foothills of Alberta, having its greatest width in Western Saskatchewan. Practically all of Manitoba is included in this drought area except parts of the Red River Valley and extreme Northern districts.

"The Northeastern and East Central areas of Saskatchewan have fair prospects as yet, but the re-

Continued on Page Three

£27,000,000 More Asked for British Arms, Showing Uneasiness Over Foreign Outlook

Wireless to THE NEW YORK TIMES.

LONDON, July 7.—Tangible evidence of the government's uneasiness over the foreign outlook is found in the increasing pressure to accelerate rearmament.

Additional estimates for the navy, army and air expenditures are to be presented Thursday. Parliamentary approval will be asked by the government next week, before the House of Commons adjourns for the Summer.

It was only last April when the navy asked for an extra £10,300,000 to be added to the £70,000,000 originally appropriated for this year. The announcement of another addition so soon has surprised even those members of Parliament who have been urging speed on the new arms policy, despite the recent warning of Neville Chamberlain, Chancellor of the Exchequer, that the cost of rearming was bound to create a deficit in the 1936 budget.

The additional sum the Air Ministry will demand is about £10,000,000 and the army wants another £7,000,000.

By The Associated Press.

LONDON, July 7.—With the empire already facing an overdraft as the result of the rearmament program, the army, navy and air force are seeking additional money to build ships and airplanes and to whip the mechanization of land forces into first-class shape.

The navy, which has had ample opportunity to test its theoretical strength or weakness during the Mediterranean crisis, may ask as much as £10,000,000 extra, Members of Parliament believed.

The air force is carrying out plans to triple its strength.

The navy has already received grants of £80,230,000, representing £69,930,000 provided in the budget, plus £10,300,000 voted in the Commons since that time.

The War Office announced seventeen units of territorials (the home guard) were being converted into anti-aircraft brigades to defend the industrialized midlands in Northern England.

Jeannette MacDonald and Nelson Eddy in one of the films they appeared in together, *Rose Marie*.

W.C. Fields in a classic pose.

Science fiction first came to the screen in the 30s. Buster Crabbe starred as Flash Gordon.

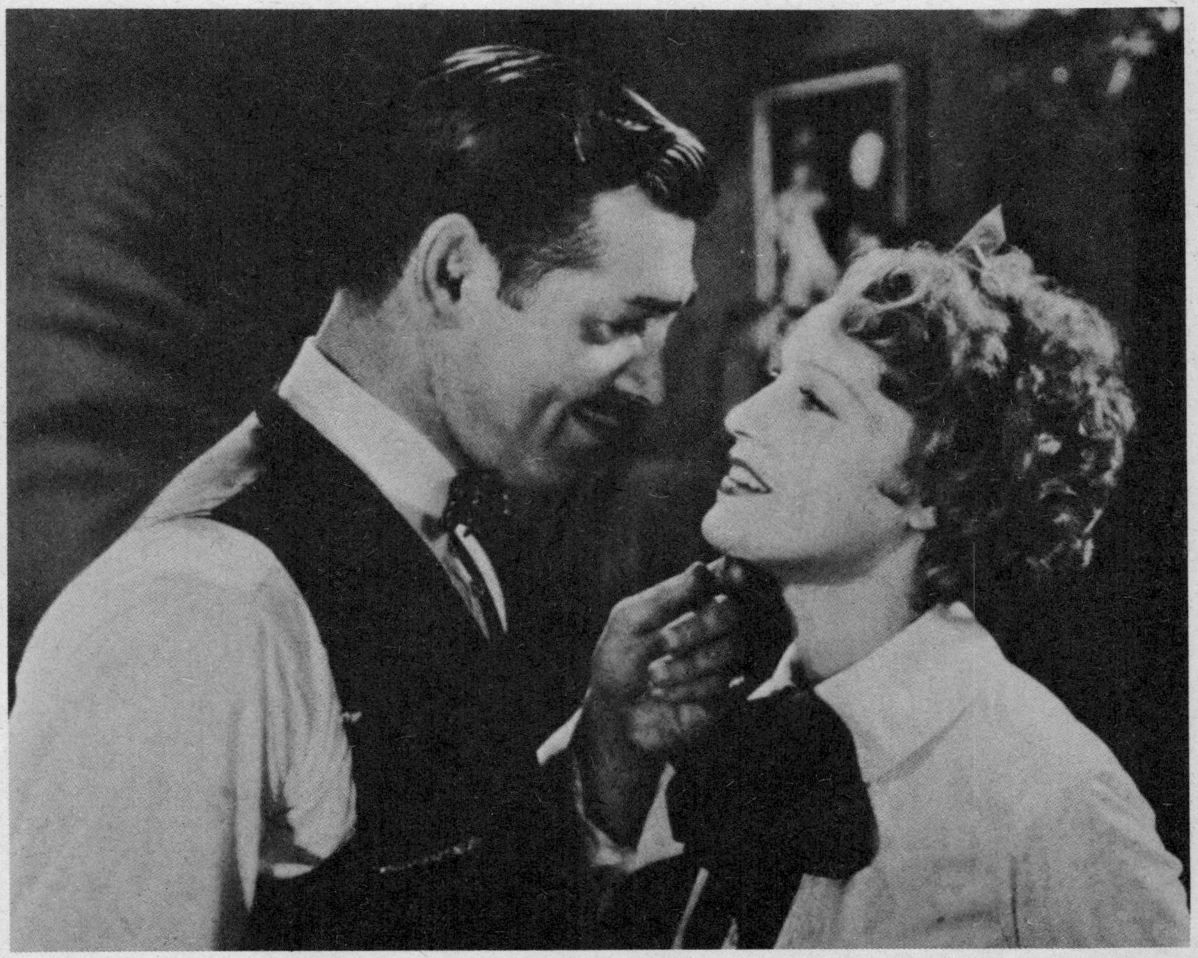

Clark Gable and Jeannette MacDonald starred as Blackie Norton and Mary in *San Francisco*, a story about the 1906 earthquake that destroyed the city.

The dedication of the Tennessee Valley Authority facilities brought FDR to Chickamauga Dam.

President Roosevelt, whose New Deal fathered the Triborough Bridge, with New York Governor Herbert Lehman (L) and New York City Mayor Fiorello La Guardia (R).

THE NEW $60,300,000 TRIBOROUGH BRIDGE

The first cars go over the bridge as the President's party arrives at the Manhattan approach.

Times Wide World Photo

"All the News That's Fit to Print."

The New York Times.

LATE CITY EDITION
Fair, except thunder showers this afternoon; continued warm. Tomorrow afternoon thunder showers.
Temperatures Yesterday—Max., 96; min., 76.

Section 1

Copyright, 1936, by The New York Times Company.

VOL. LXXXV....No. 28,659. Entered as Second-Class Matter, Postoffice, New York, N. Y. NEW YORK, SUNDAY, JULY 12, 1936. Including Rotogravure Picture, Magazine and Book Review. PP TEN CENTS | TWELVE CENTS Beyond 200 Miles Except in 7th and 8th Postal Zones.

RAIN FAILS TO END HEAT HERE AFTER 72 DIE IN FOUR DAYS; RELIEF FORECAST IN WEST

RESPITE IN CITY IS BRIEF

Mercury Touches 96.2°—Today Also Is Due to Be Torrid.

35 DEATHS IN THIS AREA

Humidity Adds to Suffering on Hottest July 11—Crowds Sleep at the Beaches.

700 DEAD IN THE NATION

Toll in the East Is Nearly 200—Hot Spell May Not End Until Wednesday.

The heat wave that swept across the country from the drought-baked Middle West last week continued to scorch New York and virtually the entire East yesterday on its fourth successive day.

Blazing down relentlessly except for a few brief periods of respite from local showers, intermittent clouds and breezes, the torrid rays of the sun prostrated persons in many sections of the country.

Thirty-five more deaths were reported as due to the heat in New York City and the metropolitan area, bringing the death toll attributed wholly or partly to the heat wave in this vicinity to seventy-two. There were two drownings up-State and two in the metropolitan area.

Hourly Temperatures

The official Weather Bureau temperatures hour by hour yesterday were as follows:

12:00 P. M.	85	2:00 P. M.	92
1:00 A. M.	83	3:00 P. M.	96
2:00 A. M.	81	3:10 P. M.	96.2
3:00 A. M.	80	4:00 P. M.	91
4:00 A. M.	78	5:00 P. M.	89
5:00 A. M.	77	6:00 P. M.	86
6:00 A. M.	76	7:00 P. M.	82
7:00 A. M.	79	8:00 P. M.	80
8:00 A. M.	82	9:00 P. M.	80
9:00 A. M.	84	10:00 P. M.	79
10:00 A. M.	88	11:00 P. M.	80
11:00 A. M.	88	Midnight	*76
Noon	92	1:00 A. M.	*76
12:30 P. M.	96	2:00 A. M.	*75
1:00 P. M.	93	3:00 A. M.	*74

*On twelfth floor of Times Annex.

Throughout the country there were more than 250 deaths not previously reported, making the nation-wide total upward of 700, according to a compilation made by The Associated Press. These deaths were attributed to the heat, the drought, drownings and other effects directly or indirectly caused by the weather.

Deaths in the East reached a total of nearly 200, with 39 in New York State outside of this city, 28 in New Jersey, 31 in Pennsylvania, 5 in Delaware, and 31 in New England.

The showers yesterday afternoon began about 5:10 o'clock and did not last long. They were scattered and little rain fell. Although the air was cooled, the rain failed to decrease the humidity.

A more general storm, affecting a large part of the city, began at 6:50 o'clock last night, with thunder and lightning. It was raining quite hard in some sections about 7:10. The showers were followed by cool breezes and lower temperatures, which alleviated the suffering from the day's heat. By daybreak, however, it was said the effect probably would have worn off and the heat would continue.

Hottest July 11 on Record

Although the temperature did not reach the high marks of 102.3 degrees of Thursday and 100 degrees of Friday, it broke all records for July 11 when it climbed to 96.2 degrees at 3:10 P. M. yesterday. After having gone to 96 at 12:30 P. M., it receded several degrees as the prevailing light westerly wind shifted to the south, but at 3 P. M. it jumped back to 96 and then went to 96.2 before dropping to 91 at 4 P. M.

Later in the afternoon showers fell over New York and the blinding sun retreated behind the clouds, cooling the air and the streets by 7 o'clock, after which it continued to decline slowly. The United States Weather Bureau predicted, however, that this interlude of comfort would be only temporary. The lowest temperature during the night was expected to be 75, and another hot day was predicted for today.

The highest previous temperature for a July 11 on record at the Weather Bureau was 95, which occurred in 1911. The average normal temperature for July 11 is 74 de-

Continued on Page Three

Cool Air Sweeping From Rockies Holds Hope for Sizzling Midwest

Residents of Montana and North Dakota Stand in Rain as the Temperature Falls to 60 and Showers Move On Eastward—Grain Prices Tumble.

By The Associated Press.

CHICAGO, July 11.—In a mass of cooling air ballooning over the Rocky Mountains, weather forecasters sighted tonight the end of the worst heat wave of recent years in the northern section of the nation.

With showers already fallen in parts of the mountain and Western Plains States, Forecaster J. R. Lloyd here said that the natural course of the refreshing current would be eastward.

Just how deeply rains predicted by Mr. Lloyd would cut into the drought's wide Western domain remained to be seen, but the mere possibility of their coming cheered millions.

Rejoicing residents of almost a dozen counties in Southwestern North Dakota and Eastern Montana, weary from their battle with the heat and drought, ran from their homes to stand in showers that dropped the mercury to 60 degrees tonight. The rains were too late to revive crops and even pasturage in some regions.

The millions cheered by the rains included the farmers who have suffered the bulk of the estimated $300,000,000 loss from the drought and the city residents who have wilted under one of the longest successions of days of higher than a 100-degree heat in recent years. Today's was the ninth, with the ravages from the heat and the drought continuing over most of the West, the North and Southern sections.

Fatalities from the heat kept mounting as the mercury took its daily flight, reaching a high of 111 degrees at Danville, Ill. At Rockford, Ill., a new all-time high mark of 108 was established. A high record also was recorded at Grand Forks, N. D., with a 108 maximum, in the State which has suffered one of the heaviest drought losses. For

Continued on Page Two

DROUGHT SERIOUS IN 3 MORE STATES

Government Officials Add Oklahoma, Georgia and Kentucky to Emergency List.

RELIEF STEPS ARE PUSHED

Federal Reclamation Projects Oases in Arid Areas—Ducks Flee Great Plains.

Special to THE NEW YORK TIMES.

WASHINGTON, July 11.—Government agencies continued today their efforts to relieve suffering, both human and animal, in the blistered regions, as Oklahoma, Georgia and Kentucky were added to the official list of States which are at least partly suffering from severe drought.

The rains which ended the eighty-five day drought in Tennessee a week ago did not help the neighboring States, and the Department of Agriculture today placed fifty-nine counties in Kentucky and Georgia on the emergency list.

In the whole country 336 counties are now thus listed. In those sections the crops are considered by now to be a total loss and relief efforts are being devoted to saving the livestock. The Department of Agriculture is buying some of it, the railroads are offering reduced freight rates to ship the animals to fresh pasture, to be returned later when conditions have improved.

The Works Progress Administration is providing relief projects of deep-well drilling and the construction of dams to make storage reservoirs for the rain that will come some day, and the Resettlement Administration is lending money to farmers to keep them going until new crops can be planted and harvested.

Water Conservation Planned

The water conservation projects of the WPA will be pushed to rapid conclusion in Oklahoma, North Dakota, South Dakota, Minnesota, Montana and Wyoming, it was announced.

Indications of crop damage sent the price of wheat up 10 to 12 cents a bushel, corn up 20 cents a bushel, oats up 6 to 7 cents a bushel, barley up 12 to 15 cents a bushel and cotton up 105 points in the week ending yesterday, the Bureau of Agricultural Economics reported today.

Farmers living on 3,000,000 acres of land irrigated by Federal Reclamation Works, in the midst of the drought area, will have almost normal crops and will profit by the high prices, John C. Page, Acting Commissioner of Reclamation, reported to Secretary of the Interior Ickes today. He said that, in fourteen States affected by the drought, there are 19,000,000 acre-feet of water stored in reservoirs—enough water to cover the State of South Dakota to a depth of five inches.

"The healthy condition of our reclamation projects, where there has been hardly any need for Federal relief even during the height of the depression, indicates that

Continued on Page Two

MAP HUNGER MARCH ON HARRISBURG, PA.

Philadelphia Idle, Incensed by Stoppage of Relief, May Approach Legislature.

SENATORS ARE PICKETED

Earle Asks Pew, Grundy Mellon and Weir to 'Release' Republican Legislators.

Special to THE NEW YORK TIMES.

PHILADELPHIA, July 11.—Plans for a hunger march on Harrisburg, timed to coincide with the start of the eleventh week of the special session of the Legislature next Monday, were discussed here today as most of the 58,000 families on relief in the city continued to shift for themselves.

With the State's relief funds exhausted since last Monday and Governor Earle and the Republican-controlled Senate at a stalemate on the estimated needs, Philadelphia police distributed emergency rations here upon orders from Mayor S. Davis Wilson. Heavy demands were being made on social agencies and charities, but the bulk of the relief recipients apparently were maintaining themselves through credit with grocers or the bounty of friends.

The threat of a hunger march apparently originated with the Philadelphia Citizens' Committee on Unemployed Needs. Herbert Grossman, the chairman, has distributed 2,500 postcards to be sent to State Senators by unemployed persons.

"I demand that you vote for the $54,000,000 relief appropriation, in itself inadequate, but immediately necessary to stave off hunger and disease," the cards read. "Your present obstinate stand indicates a conscienceless political game which I utterly condemn."

Senators' Homes Picketed

The amount named on the cards is the sum Governor Earle and Karl de Schweinitz, the State relief director, declare is needed to care for relief needs until Jan. 31. Republican Senators this week have been figuring on an estimate of $35,000,000, which is only half the total sought by the Governor at the outset of the legislative session.

Picketing of the homes of the five Republican members of the Senate from this city was begun by unemployed groups early this afternoon. Carrying placards reading "Help Us Fight for the Right to Live" and "We Want $55,000,000 for Relief of Starving People," about 100 men and women joined a picket line at the residence of Senator Max Aron.

While the crowd booed and two policemen watched, Senator Aron was interviewed by a committee of the pickets. Mr. Aron, declaring the $55,000,000 relief estimate of the Governor too high, alleged that the picketing was "a political trick, instigated by Democratic committeemen."

"They are using questions of relief for political fodder," he declared. "Relief is not a political matter."

The other Senators included in

Continued on Page Sixteen

Major Sports Yesterday

OLYMPIC TRACK AND FIELD TRIALS

Jesse Owens of Ohio State captured the 100-meter dash and broad jump to qualify for two places on the American team as the final Olympic tryouts opened at the new Randalls Island Stadium. Ralph Metcalfe and Frank Wykoff also gained places in the sprint. The first three hammer throwers were Henry Dreyer, Bill Rowe and Don Favor. A crowd of 15,000 saw Owens and Forrest Towns better Olympic records. In Berlin Miss Gisela Mauermeyer beat the women's world discus mark at the German championships with a toss of 158 feet 6 inches.

BASEBALL

Dizzy Dean suffered a bad concussion when hit on the head by a line drive from Burgess Whitehead's bat in the sixth inning of a game at St. Louis which the Cardinals won from the Giants, 9 to 3. An X-ray examination revealed that there was no fracture of the skull. With the Dodgers stopping the Cubs at Chicago, 5 to 3, the Cards increased their league lead by a full game. At the Stadium, the Yankees were crushed by the Indians, 10 to 2.

RACING

Alfred Gwynne Vanderbilt's Good Gamble ran a mile and three-sixteenths in 1:58 1/5, breaking the track record by two seconds, to win the Butler Memorial Handicap at Empire City. Esposa, the favorite, was second, and Split Second third. The Wakefield Handicap, secondary feature, went to Billionaire. Before 25,000 at Arlington Park, Nation's Taste captured the Hyde Park Stakes, defeating Apogee by a head.

OLYMPIC SWIMMING TRIALS

Miss Katherine Rawls won both the 100-meter free-style and three-meter springboard diving in the women's final Olympic swimming tryouts at the new Astoria pool. Adolph Kiefer took the 100-meter back-stroke final, bettering the accepted world record, and Ralph Flanagan annexed the 400-meter free-style final in the men's meet at Warwick, R. I.

(Complete details of these and other sports events in Section 5.)

ROOSEVELT AVOIDS ANY INTERVENTION IN LABOR UNION ROW

Administration Leaders Are Confident Both Sides Will Support President.

LA GUARDIA TAKES HAND

Mayor Asks Clash Data From Wagner—A. F. of L. Members See Steel Drive Imperiled.

By LOUIS STARK

Special to THE NEW YORK TIMES.

WASHINGTON, July 11.—Whatever the outcome of the industrial-craft union fight in the American Federation of Labor the Roosevelt administration—unless its services are requested—will meticuously avoid taking sides or intervening in any way before election, it was reported here today. Edward F. McGrady, Assistant Secretary of Labor, gave the President a last-minute report last night at the station just before his train left for New York, but this was only a continuation of the President's policy of keeping informed.

Democratic leaders, convinced that organized labor to a major extent is solidly behind President Roosevelt, profess to feel that the internal labor conflict will have no effect on the election.

As evidence of their confidence in the support of labor, these leaders say that, even though support is divided into two parts, they are both animated by the same object—the election of the President.

Labor's Non-Partisan League was formed by John L. Lewis, president of the United Mine Workers; Sidney Hillman, president of the Amalgamated Clothing Workers, and George L. Berry of the International Printing Pressmen's Union. Messrs. Lewis and Hillman are members of the committee for industrial organization, which is at odds with the executive council of the federation on the craft-industrial union issue.

Would Avoid Pre-Election Split

At the same time Daniel J. Tobin, president of the International Brotherhood of Teamsters, is expected to lead the labor committee of the Democratic National Committee in rounding up votes for Mr. Roosevelt. While there are many differences between Mr. Lewis and Mr. Tobin on the issues now disturbing the labor movement, both are ardent supporters of the President.

While the administration does not wish to take any part in the quarrel which threatens to split the federation, it is known that Democratic leaders are following the situation carefully and are desirous of seeing a united labor movement.

Since the administration counts greatly on support from labor, its spokesmen would like labor unity to continue after election, assuming that the President is re-elected, in order that there may be solid backing for his projects in the way of social welfare measures. Two groups, split on important measures such as the President has in mind for his next term, would weaken the possibility of Congressional action on such measures.

Mayor La Guardia of New York, it became known today, has asked for information on the labor dis-

Continued on Page Seven

GERMANY CONCEDES AUSTRIAN FREEDOM AS PACT ENDS FEUD

Gives Pledge That She Will Not Intervene in Neighbor's Internal Affairs.

AUSTRIA 'GERMAN STATE'

Will Make Policies Conform With That Fact—Vienna Public Taken by Surprise.

By FREDERICK T. BIRCHALL

Wireless to THE NEW YORK TIMES.

BERLIN, July 11.—An agreement between Germany and Austria adjusting in principle the differences between them on lines forecast in recent dispatches from London, Berlin and Vienna to THE NEW YORK TIMES was announced simultaneously in Berlin and Vienna tonight.

Germany has agreed to recognize Austrian sovereignty on the lines laid down in Chancellor Adolf Hitler's speech on May 27 of last year. In that speech he said:

"Germany has neither the wish nor the intention to mix in internal Austrian affairs or annex or unite with Austria.

"The German people and government have, however, from a simple feeling of solidarity and common ancestry the wish that not only foreign people but also German people shall be granted the right of self-determination. I do not believe that any régime not anchored in and by the people can be enduring."

Non-Interference Pledged

Both parties to this agreement have pledged themselves not to interfere in each other's internal affairs. Austria never having attempted to interfere in German affairs, this provision is of importance only as binding Germany.

Austria, however, agrees to bring her policies in so far as they affect Germany into conformity with the fact that Austria professes herself to be a German State. But those Rome protocols of 1934 and their supplements of 1936 and Austria's relations with Italy and Hungary as partners in those protocols are not to be affected.

The necessary measures for lessening the tension between Austria and Germany are to be taken by each in the form of decrees. This means that Germany will remove the 1,000-mark tax she has imposed for each visa permitting a German to visit Austria and certain other restrictions she has placed on trade with Austria.

The Austrians will abolish certain mild counter-restrictions they had imposed upon the Germans. The 1,000-mark charge for a German visa was originally imposed as a reprisal for the expulsion of German Nazi agitators from Austria.

Announcement of the agreement was made in the form of a communiqué jointly issued by the two governments. In Berlin it was read over the radio by Dr. Joseph Goeb-

Continued on Page Twenty

PRESIDENT, BACKING U. S. AID, OPENS THE TRIBOROUGH SPAN; MOSES AND ICKES END FEUD

200,000 Rush to Use New Bridge By Auto, Bus, Cycle and on Foot

Presidential Party First to Drive Over 17½ Miles of Span—Rush at All Approaches When Barriers Are Lifted on Word Flashed by Police Radio—Boy Bicyclist First at Toll Booth.

More than 200,000 New Yorkers journeyed by car, by bus and on foot yesterday to the confluence of the Harlem and East Rivers to dedicate by use the new $60,300,000 Triborough Bridge.

The huge bridge, whose water crossings, viaducts and highways sweep out for seventeen and one-half miles into Manhattan, Queens and the Bronx from a junction on Randalls Island, was opened to traffic at 1:30 o'clock, following formal dedication of the structure at ceremonies on the island and a tour of inspection by President Roosevelt.

The word to open the bridge to toll traffic was flashed from a special short-wave field station to police radio cars and motorcycles at the bridgeheads. It was the first time the Police Department has used radio transmission in the field, and was said to represent the beginning of two-way communication here.

"The Triborough Bridge is now officially open to the public," came the voice over the air of Gerald S. Morris, Superintendent of Telegraph, and a moment later the barriers at the Queens and Bronx bridgeheads were lowered and the huge lift span across the Harlem River began to descend slowly.

Private automobiles, taxicabs, motorcycles and even a tandem bicycle raced forward, eager to gain the honor of being the first paying vehicle across the bridge. For a few minutes cars jammed the six toll booths on the Manhattan arm, but as soon as the race of "first-over" enthusiasts had subsided, the traffic moved with a minimum of delay.

Some motorists were there just to look over the new bridge, which for so many years had been discussed as a fantastic dream. Others were putting it to the test for which it was built, using it to save time in going out to Long Island for the

Continued on Page Twenty-four

GREAT LINK IS ACCLAIMED

People Demanding Such Up-to-Date Projects, Roosevelt Says.

TALK SEEN AS CHALLENGE

Ickes and Moses Praise Each Other as They Meet for the First Time.

LEHMAN GRATEFUL TO U. S.

Mayor Also Hails Government—Olympic Stadium on Island Dedicated.

The speeches at the opening of the Triborough span, Page 23.

The new Triborough Bridge, a colossus of steel and concrete straddling Wards and Randalls Islands and flinging itself across the East and Harlem Rivers, Little Hell Gate and the Bronx Kills to link Queens, Manhattan and the Bronx in a Y-shaped sky highway, was opened officially to the public yesterday with elaborate ceremonies in a country-picnic setting.

The principal dedicatory exercises took place on a ramp leading to Randalls Island and the new Municipal Stadium. The Stadium was opened formally with oratory as the final Olympic track and field trials were held before a crowd of more than 15,000 in the blistering sun. The Stadium is a part of an integrated park and recreational system made possibl by the bridge.

President Roosevelt himself stopped off on his way from Washington to Hdye Park to take part in the celebration marking the opening of the bridge and to inspect it with Governor Lehman, Mayor La Guardia and Park Commissioner Robert Moses. Heavily guarded by police and Secret Service men, President Roosevelt was cheered by crowds which lined the streets through which he passed on his brief visit to the city.

While the President's speech was non-political and was delivered before a mixed audience of 4,000 invited guests, many of those who heard it regarded it as a reply to critics of the government's policy of financing public works and a challenge to those who oppose Federal spending on local projects.

Interstate Value Noted

Pointing out that the bridge, providing easy access to Long Island and Connecticut, had an interstate as well as an intracity value, Mr. Roosevelt said:

"People require and people are demanding up-to-date government, just as they are requiring and demanding tri-borough bridges in the place of ancient ferries."

The President was introduced by Mayor La Guardia, who said that in dedicating the bridge "we dedicate ourselves to the building of a greater bridge which will permanently join the land of liberty and equality to a system of economic security." Presenting Mr. Roosevelt to the crowd, Mr. La Guardia called him the chief engineer, the master builder, the leader of this great march of the American people."

Not only did the opening of the bridge provide a motor highway between three of the city's five boroughs but it served to bring together also the participants in a political feud of long standing, Public Works Administrator Harold L. Ickes and Commissioner Moses, secretary and chief executive officer of the Triborough Bridge Authority.

Mr. Ickes and Mrs. Moses, despite their exchange of correspondence during the controversy over the Park Commissioner's dual office-holding, had never met until they came face to face upon the speakers' platform. There they were introduced by Paul Moss, License Commissioner, just before Mr. Moses took over his duties as chairman.

Under the smiling eye of Postmaster General James A. Farley, who while present at the ceremonies was unheard, Mr. Moses introduced Mr. Ickes, who vainly sought his removal from the Bridge Authority, in an address which brought appreciative laughs and chuckles from the audience seated on folding chairs in the tractor-marked dust eighteen feet below the rostrum on the ramp.

"There have been times," said

Continued on Page Twenty-two

U. S. RAISES DUTIES ON GERMAN GOODS

Retaliatory Levies Imposed in Reply to Reich Subsidies for Certain Exported Articles.

PLEAS FOR STAY FUTILE

But Berlin Experts Continue Talks in Washington—Move Held Compulsory Under Law.

Special to THE NEW YORK TIMES.

WASHINGTON, July 11.—The Treasury Department announced today it would put into effect at midnight the countervailing duties that it ordered a month ago under the authority of the Tariff Act of 1930. The action was taken despite pleas for a stay by American importers and despite the official representations of a German governmental delegation now discussing the whole situation with Treasury experts.

The extra duties, ranging from 22½ per cent to 56 per cent on a number of German exports to this country, were imposed to compensate for bounties granted by the German Government to exporters of those articles. The step is not to be confused with the earlier action of the State Department in denying to Germany the benefit of generalization of tariff concessions granted in the course of negotiating reciprocal trade agreements. The State Department's action was a purely retaliatory measure, resulting from German discriminations against certain American imports. Such retaliatory measures were authorized by the Trade Agreements Act of 1934.

The countervailing duties were put into the 1930 enactment as part of the high protectionist philosophy reflected in that law. They were based largely on the same school of economic thought that actuated the inclusion in most of the NRA codes of prohibitions against selling below cost of production.

Action Taken Reluctantly

The Treasury's action of a month ago was taken reluctantly by the officials concerned. It was only after Attorney General Homer S. Cummings had given an opinion, confirming the opinion of the Treasury's own legal department, that the provisions of the 1930 act were mandatory and must be enforced, that the announcement was made. That part of the law reads as follows:

Whenever any country, dependency, colony, province, or other political subdivision of government, person, partnership, association, cartel, or corporation shall pay or bestow, directly or indirectly, any bounty or grant upon the manufacture or production or export of any article or merchandise manufactured or produced in such country, dependency, colony, province, or other political subdivision of government, and such article or merchandise is dutiable under the provisions of this act, then upon the importation of any such article or merchandise into the United States, whether the same

Continued on Page Twenty-four

MRS. OWEN IS WED TO CAPTAIN ROHDE

Nation's First Woman Diplomat Becomes Bride of Danish Officer at Hyde Park.

ROOSEVELTS AT CEREMONY

Distinguished Guests Gather at St. James Church—Storm Ends Supper Party.

From a Staff Correspondent

HYDE PARK, N. Y., July 11.—A romance involving America's first woman diplomat culminated here today when Mrs. Ruth Bryan Owen, standing in an ivy-covered church where President and Mrs. Roosevelt sat in the pew they have held for thirty years, was married to Captain Boerge Rohde, Captain of the Royal Life Guards of King Christian X of Denmark, to whose court Mrs. Owen is Minister.

Mrs. Owen went to the church from Hyde Park House, where she was a guest today while awaiting the time for the ceremony at 5 o'clock. She went immediately afterward with her husband to the President's cottage at Val Kil where Mrs. Roosevelt was hostess at a wedding supper.

Wedding Service Simple

The wedding service was a simple one, following the ordinances of the Episcopal Church. It took place in St. James's Church, which was built here in 1811. However, instead of being conducted by the Rev. Frank R. Wilson, pastor of the President's church, the service was read by the Rev. Samuel M. Shoemaker, rector of Calvary Protestant Episcopal Church, of New York City.

The bride, who is a daughter of William Jennings Bryan, wore a blue chiffon afternoon gown and a big blue hat and carried a bouquet of small roses and garden flowers.

The bridegroom's uniform consisted of a dark blue tunic with high collar, around which were rows of silver bands. The tunic was fastened with double rows of gilt buttons. His trousers were of pale blue, and his sword was suspended from a gilt belt. In his hand he carried a peaked dress hat, similar to that worn by American naval officers, except that it was decorated with silver and gilt bands and a crest of blue and cock's feathers.

Miss Fannie Hurst, the novelist, who was matron of honor, wore a gown of black and white and a crystal hat. The best man was Robert Lehman, son-in-law of Mrs. Owen. Mrs. Lehman was unable to be present because of illness, but Bryan Owen, son of the bride, was among the guests.

Bride Appears Youthful

Mrs. Rohde looked particularly youthful in her costume, and smiled radiantly after the ceremony.

The bride did not walk down the aisle of the church, but entered with Captain Rohde from a side door, after they had posed out of doors for pictures together. The wedding ceremony lasted just thirteen minutes, and guests were in-

Continued on Page Twenty-four

Mussolini (L) is Hitler's guest. Italian troops were fighting in Ethiopia and Spain.

Generalissimo Francisco Franco, rebel leader of the Spanish Civil War.

German troops in the streets of Cologne. Hitler sent his troops into the Rhineland in March, thus ending the Treaty of Versailles.

Franco (pointing) speaks to the people shortly after he established the Nationalist (Insurgent) Government in October.

"All the News That's Fit to Print."

The New York Times.

LATE CITY EDITION
Generally fair today, little change in temperature. Tomorrow fair, not much change in temperature.
Temperatures Yesterday—Max., 88; min., 64.

Copyright, 1936, by The New York Times Company.

VOL. LXXXV.....No. 28,667. Entered as Second-Class Matter, Postoffice, New York, N. Y. NEW YORK, MONDAY, JULY 20, 1936. PPP TWO CENTS In New York City. | THREE CENTS Within 200 Miles. | FOUR CENTS Elsewhere Except in 7th and 8th Postal Zones.

LEMKE PLEDGES AID TO TOWNSEND PLAN; CONVENTION CLOSES

Candidate Also Promises to Make Good Some of Huey Long's Dreams.

WINS BACKING IN HIS RACE

Townsend Avoids Committal, but Rev. Mr. Smith Hails 'Only Real Democrat.'

ONLY 5,000 AT THE FINALE

But They Are Aroused to a High Pitch by Attack on Roosevelt—To Seek Youths' Help.

Text of Representative Lemke's speech at convention, Page 6.

By F. RAYMOND DANIELL
Special to THE NEW YORK TIMES.

CLEVELAND, July 19.—The second annual convention of Townsend Clubs came to a prayerful end tonight in a great outdoor stadium where Representative Lemke, third party candidate, promised to save the country, and won the approval of the Rev. Gerald L. K. Smith, one time exponent of the Share-the-Wealth Plan and now an ardent Townsendite.

Only about 5,000 persons came into the field, which has a capacity of 80,000 to 90,000, although admission to the closing session was free.

Dr. Francis E. Townsend, founder of the organization which aims at retiring the aged on taxes paid by the rest of the population, avoided any specific promises tonight as to support of a Presidential candidate.

He urged his following, which he estimated at 20,000,000 souls, to go home and devote their energies to electing members of Congress sympathetic to their cause while he went "after bigger game."

He and the Rev. Mr. Smith are soon to go on a barnstorming tour with the Rev. Charles E. Coughlin, head of the National Union for Social Justice and the North Dakota Representative's chief political supporter.

Many Threats of Resignations

Just what will be the effect of this week's pow-wow on the Townsend organization itself remains to be seen. Half of the directors are threatening to kick out the other half and the latter are making threats of resignations galore.

With the faithful on their way home the directors are to meet tomorrow and fight it out among themselves. Dr. Townsend appears to have everything "under control" as far as the rank and file are concerned, however.

Gomer Smith, the Oklahoma office-seeker who evoked the displeasure of Dr. Townsend by speaking out in meeting in defense of President Roosevelt and in criticism of Father Coughlin and the Rev. Mr. Smith, was missing from tonight's program.

Sheridan Downey of California, however, another Roosevelt man, got a chance to announce in public that he was for tolerance and forbearance even in this heated campaign.

Gomer Smith bought himself some radio time in the afternoon and told his followers in the Southwest that Dr. Townsend was being taken into camp by two designing clerics. The Rev. Mr. Smith, he said, was "indecent" in his vilification of the President and had worked up his audience "to a pitch equalled only by good old-fashioned Negro revivals in the deep South."

Father Coughlin, who he said had ripped off his "coat and his shirt" and stood there showing his manly chest, had made the "most radical and un-American speech" he had ever heard, the Oklahoman charged.

Calls Lemke "Real Democrat"

It was so vituperative and disgraceful, he said, that even Republicans in the North were disgusted at the priest's attack on the President.

Mr. Lemke, a freckle-faced man with thinning hair, opened the meeting with an endorsement of the Townsend Plan and a pledge to make good Huey Long's promise to make every man a king and every woman a queen, by means of inflation and old-age pensions.

The Rev. Mr. Smith closed the ceremony with the statement that he as a good old Southern Democrat would have to vote for Mr. Lemke because the North Dakotan was the only real Democrat in this year's Presidential race.

Mr. Lemke, he said, believed in Share Our Wealth and old-age pensions and if he showed any signs of wabbling "a Louisiana preacher and a country doctor will chop his dad-gummed head off."

Mr. Smith hinted at the immediate organizing of an army of storm troopers to guard the polls and insure an honest count for his candidate; he promised the people

Continued on Page Six

Russian Astronomer Is Accused Of 'Servility' to Foreign Science

Prof. Boris Gerasimovitch, Internationally Famous, Denounced for Publishing Works of Observatory Staff Abroad First—Campaign Aims to Foster the National Spirit.

By HAROLD DENNY
Special Cable to THE NEW YORK TIMES.

MOSCOW, July 19.—Professor Boris Gerasimovitch, head of the Pulkovo Observatory in Leningrad, was accused today of "servility" toward foreign science by the newspaper Leningrad Pravda, chief organ of the Communist party in that city. The attack has created a stir in scientific circles here.

Professor Gerasimovitch is the foremost astronomer of the Soviet Union, and he possesses an international reputation as one of the world's greatest astro-physicists. He is especially well known in the United States, where he spent the year 1928 in research at Harvard and visited several American observatories.

At the Lick Observatory he cooperated with Dr. Donald Menzel in studies on the source of stellar energy, which won a prize of the New York Academy of Sciences.

Professor Gerasimovitch took a leading part in bringing scores of foreign scientists to Russia to study the recent solar eclipse, and he headed the Pulkovo Observatory's expedition to Ak-Bulak, alongside the Harvard-Massachusetts Institute of Technology group. He is widely known for the praise of scientists of many nationalities for his unstinting cooperation with them.

The attack on him, which betrays some personal heat, is evidently part of a campaign now being waged against alleged servility among Soviet scientists to foreign science. This campaign is a new manifestation of the national spirit that the Soviet Union has been sedulously cultivating for the past two years.

The Leningrad Pravda writer charges Professor Gerasimovitch engaged a young and unqualified astronomer, named Voronoff, merely because Voronoff had had work published abroad, and asserts all

Continued on Page Two

THREE CONTRADICT ALIBI OF VIOLINIST IN CO-ED'S MURDER

Two Women and Waiter Assert They Saw Him Out When He Says He Was at Home.

REDDISH STAINS ANALYZED

Found on Prisoner's Clothing—Landlady's Daughter, Who Backed His Story, Held.

Special to THE NEW YORK TIMES.

ASHEVILLE, N. C., July 19.—Officers today exposed seeming discrepancies in the story told by Mark Wollner, concert violinist, of his movements subsequent to the time when Miss Helen Clevenger of Staten Island, New York University co-ed, was shot to death in her room at the Battery Park Hotel here early Thursday morning.

Three witnesses have made sworn statements that Wollner was not in bed at his home at times when he told officers he was.

Although Wollner protests his innocence, he is being held in the county jail "for questioning" and will probably be confronted tomorrow with witnesses who contradict details of his statement.

Early tonight Miss Mildred Ward, 19, daughter of Mrs. Essie Ward, at whose home Wollner roomed, was taken into custody. She made a statement last night corroborating Wollner's contention that he was at her mother's home from 9:30 P. M. Wednesday until 8 A. M. Thursday.

"Their stories tally too closely to suit me," Sheriff Laurence E. Brown said tonight in ordering the detention of Miss Ward. "I'll give her another chance to tell the truth about this case. She may not have had a hand in it, but her story doesn't suit me."

Miss Clevenger was slain at about 1 A. M., Thursday, according to medical opinion, and the crime was discovered at about 8:30 A. M., Thursday.

Held on "Investigation Charge"

Miss Ward was hustled into the jail elevator as she tried to hide from photographers. She did not seem to be excited about her arrest. Sheriff Brown said she was being held on an "investigation charge."

Wollner has not been questioned since he made his first statement last night.

Also in the jail is Daniel H. Gaddy, night watchman at the hotel, who was on duty the night Miss Clevenger was slain. He also is being detained on an "investigation charge."

Joe Urey, Negro bellboy at the hotel, was released today when officers decided he knew nothing about the case. He was arrested Friday night.

Miss Lavada Whitaker, 30, and Mrs. Roy Bailey, who live next door to the Wollner boarding house, made sworn statements today that Wollner returned to his boarding house about 6:30 Thursday morning and walked up a flight of steps as if "his feet hurt him."

An examination by the county health officer last night revealed that one of Wollner's toes was split. He did not explain how he received this injury.

Charles English, 19, waiter at a small café near the Battery Park Hotel, told officers that Wollner came into the café about 6:15 Thursday morning and ordered a cup of coffee. He remarked that he had been up all night and had "had a bad night," the waiter said.

English was certain it was Thurs-

Continued on Page Four

CANTON CIVIL WAR SEEN AS KWANGSI MOVES TO GET CITY

Japanese Sailors Are on Guard to Aid Police in Protecting Lives and Property.

REBEL CHIEF IN HONGKONG

Gen. Chen's Collapse Is Said to Have Resulted When He Hired Fliers From Japan.

Wireless to THE NEW YORK TIMES.

SHANGHAI, Monday, July 20.—Although Canton is reported to be outwardly quiet, with posters welcoming the troops of Generalissimo Chiang Kai-shek and General Yu Han-mou, Japanese sailors landed late Saturday night from the gunboat Sagi to protect Japanese lives and property with the aid of the Japanese consular police.

The most serious phase of the situation is the possibility of a clash between the Kwangtung and Kwangsi forces. The Kwangsi army was frustrated in its attempt to enter Canton by a forward movement of the Kwangtung units garrisoning the city and the timely arrival of heavy reinforcements from Fukien.

[Nanking government troops have entered Canton, according to the Japanese Domei news agency, as reported by The Associated Press. The soldiers were the advance guard of an army under General Yu Han-mou, who was expected to reach Canton tonight.]

There have been large troop movements near Canton. Some are attributed to advances against the Kwangsi forces. Others are said to be divisions which refuse to acknowledge Nanking's authority and intend to offer their services to Kwangsi against General Yu Han-mou.

Loyal Fliers Invite Chiang

Carrying 130 Kwangtung pilots and mechanics, forty of the more than sixty military airplanes which deserted Canton on Saturday landed today at Nanchang, the capital of Kiangsi Province. At Nanchang the Kwangtung airmen telegraphed to Generalissimo Chiang Kai-shek, asking him to come to Nanchang to inspect the planes and aviators.

The telegram explained that the Kwangtung fliers had deserted Canton because they were opposed to civil war and also to prevent use of their machines by thirty Japanese aviators who were said to have been engaged by the Southern militarists to organize a pursuit squadron for use against Nanking.

What is considered the culminating blow to the dangerously aggravated Chinese-Japanese relations in Shantung Province was the shooting and killing yesterday morning of a Japanese resident of Fangtse, a small station on the Tsinan-Tsingtao railway, by an unidentified gunman.

The seriousness of this incident was emphasized because this was the second killing of a Japanese resident in Shantung in a month. A Japanese woman was wounded and two Japanese vessels were fired at by customs guards during the same period.

The Japanese navy recently threatened "to take appropriate measures" and the Japanese army issued a formal statement on the seriousness of Shantung attacks.

Chen Guarded in Hongkong
Wireless to THE NEW YORK TIMES.

HONGKONG, Monday, July 20.—The future movements of General

Continued on Page Two

REBELS GAIN IN SOUTH SPAIN; CIVIL WAR RAGES IN CITIES; TWO MADRID CABINETS FALL

Developments in Spain

While the government in Madrid was so confused that it had three Premiers in twenty-four hours the Spanish military revolt gained headway.

The rebels who had seized control of Spanish Morocco on Saturday sent a force to Cadiz which formed a junction with the revolutionaries of Seville, where the commandant had raised their standard. Garrisons in Andalusia were reported to be joining the cause.

Paris heard that the rebels held a large part of southern Spain and had the upper hand in some other sections of the mainland.

Travelers reaching France told of heavy fighting in Valencia, Cadiz, Bilbao and Seville. The government asserted it had put down "movements of particular intensity" in Barcelona, Seville and Malaga and completely dominated the situation. Madrid was quiet.

Three government warships sent to Morocco were reported to have joined the rebels. Loyal aviators bombed the High Commissioner's residence at Tetuan. Other aviators are said to have refused to aid the revolt.

The Leftist Cabinet, headed by Premier Santiago Casares Quiroga, which resigned early yesterday, was succeeded by another under Diego Martinez Barrio. This, after a few hours, gave way to one headed by José Giral, former Minister of Marine.

Soldiers were reported quitting the rebels under a governmental decree releasing them from their commanders' orders.

A column of miners was reported marching from Asturias to help the government, which was arming the workers.

A small rebel force was said to be holding out at Las Palmas, Canary Islands.

REVOLT'S CHIEF AT CADIZ

Moroccan Force Franco Brings Joins With Seville Troops.

ALL ANDALUSIA CLAIMED

But Leftist Regime Insists It Completely Controls Country After Fighting.

GIVES THE WORKERS ARMS

Asturian Miners Are on Way to Defend the Capital—Giral Takes Over Premiership.

Wireless to THE NEW YORK TIMES.

LISBON, Portugal, July 19.—General Francisco Franco, leader of the Spanish Rightist rebellion, landed at Cadiz today with troops of the Foreign Legion from Morocco.

General Queipo de Llano, commanding the garrison in Seville, who has joined the revolutionary movement, broadcast an enthusiastic message sent to him by General Franco.

The message said that all the garrisons in Andalusia were gradually joining the movement, as was the Spanish Navy. It ended with the words, "No earthly power can check our triumphant movement. Spain is saved!"

General Franco urged that the government should resign collectively and intimated that the rebels intended to march on Madrid.

[Although the Leftist Government in the capital, headed by its third Premier in twenty-four hours, insisted it had gained complete control over the rising in various cities of the peninsula, reports reaching Paris said the rebels held a large part of Southern Spain and had the upper hand in some other sections of the mainland, according to The Associated Press.]

Frontier towns reported a heavy influx of Spaniards into peaceful Portugal to escape the tumult in Spain.

Rebels Marching on Seville
Wireless to THE NEW YORK TIMES.

GIBRALTAR, July 19.—It is reported that infantry troops who landed at Cadiz from Spanish Morocco this morning are now en route to Seville to join the rebel forces there and then march together to take over the government.

[A Havas News Agency dispatch received in Paris last night from Gibraltar said that the rebels advancing from Cadiz had effected a junction with the Seville revolters. Another Havas dispatch declared that the entire Spanish region north of Gibraltar had surrendered to the rebels, according to The Associated Press.]

A troopship packed with troops from Morocco arrived at Algeciras this morning. More troops landed this afternoon and marched out toward La Linea.

A Spanish torpedo boat arrived off La Linea and fired a number of shots, some hitting the infantry barracks, to warn the troops and carabineers there to surrender. When the sixth shot was fired, white flags were immediately displayed all over La Linea, all the troops declaring for the rebels.

[The warship that bombarded La Linea was a rebel destroyer, according to an Associated Press dispatch from Gibraltar. The troops in La Linea were declared to have revolted in support of the Fascist rebellion supporting the Republic before the warship caused their surrender.]

Gibraltar Hears Rifle Fire

Much rifle fire is heard here from the direction of the village of Campamento, but it is impossible to obtain trustworthy news, as British forces are patrolling the bayside barrier and half a mile of the actual frontier.

According to one account, about 1,700 of the insurgent Moroccan native troops arrived at La Linea to take over the military command of the district. It appears that a few were left to guard Campamento, where civilians disarmed them and went toward La Linea in an endeavor to rouse the civilian population against the insurgents.

Still another version, which ap-

Continued on Page Three

LANDON LEADS POLL OF FARM JOURNAL

First Returns Give Kansan 25,307, Roosevelt 20,869, Thomas 461, Lemke 291.

32 STATES REPRESENTED

Republicans Ahead in 21 of Them—'Reliable Sample of Farmers' Views,' Says Editor.

Special to THE NEW YORK TIMES.

PHILADELPHIA, July 19.—Governor Landon has a lead over President Roosevelt in the first returns made public today by The Farm Journal in its Presidential straw vote conducted among the nation's farmers.

The tabulation gives the Republican nominee 25,307 votes, and the President 20,869, with relatively light totals for the other candidates. Although the poll so far has touched only thirty-two States, so many counties have been covered that the result is a "reliable sample" of the farmers' views up to July 10, The Farm Journal asserts.

"The individual States, however, show striking differences in trend, as, for example, between Missouri, with a pronounced Republican preference, and Iowa, which so far is standing by Mr. Roosevelt," says The Farm Journal.

"This is one of the oldest of straw votes. The Farm Journal having taken this poll in every Presidential campaign since 1912. Beginning with 1916, this has correctly forecast the result of all elections, including the very close Wilson-Hughes campaign. It even showed in 1928 the capture of Virginia, Florida and Texas by the Republicans.

Personal Calls on Farmers

"All ballots in this first tabulation have been obtained by personal calls on farmers in their homes. In most of the thirty-two States for which figures are given many counties have been covered, so that the result is a reliable and representative sample of farm opinion up to the 10th of July.

"It may be added that the latest figures show a slight Republican trend, the Republican share of the total vote having risen from 49.8 per cent to 54.7 per cent since the nomination of Governor Landon. As pointed out above, however, the situations in different States vary sharply."

In a single column the paper includes the total vote recorded for all candidates other than Landon, Roosevelt, Thomas and Lemke. It was explained tonight by Arthur H. Jenkins, the editor, that by far the greatest number of ballots in this column was cast for Dr. Francis Townsend, although Senator Borah received "a few" and there was a scattering of Prohibition votes.

In the territory covered so far, Washington, with 317, was represented with the most votes in this column, while Massachusetts, Missouri and Ohio also contributed more than the general average.

Interest in New York Vote

Of unusual interest was the vote in New York, which has been claimed vigorously by both National Democratic Chairman Farley and National Republican Chairman Hamilton in recent weeks on behalf of their candidates. Among the farmers polled so far Governor Landon has a four-to-one lead over the President in New York. In Pennsylvania, which is likewise claimed by both major-party chair-

Continued on Page Five

SEE DROUGHT BOON TO MOST FARMERS

Rail Experts Say Price Rise May Bring More Return Than Would Bumper Crops.

MANY SECTIONS GET RAIN

High Wind Damages Buildings and Electric Lines at Omaha and Other Places.

Copyright, 1936, by The Associated Press.

CHICAGO, July 19.—Predictions that the drought may yet be a boon to the farmers generally rose tonight from the Grain Belt as week-end showers poured new life into the corn crop. The rains were attended by high winds in some sections and there was some damage to buildings and electric lines.

If the rains, which have been scattered over Minnesota, Wisconsin, Iowa, Missouri, Illinois, Indiana, Nebraska, the Dakotas and other States, continue and spread, farm experts of Western railroads declared that, although thousands engaged in agriculture were ruined, most farmers would be better off than with a bumper crop.

The drought had done staggering damage in some States, they said, but it was not nearly as devastating or widespread as the 1934 disaster.

Weather Bureau crop forecasters agreed with the railroad men that a good corn crop was still possible and that fair yields would be made in other crops in some sections.

The result, they said—always counting on moderate to heavy rains—would be that crops would be cut enough to give the farmers as a whole a good price at a good quantity. His income, they went on, would be better than on a market flooded by products.

Dakotas May Save Something

Even in the heart of the drought furnace, with thousands of farmers dependent on WPA for a livelihood in the Dakotas, Montana, Wyoming and Minnesota, observers saw hope of saving something from the ruin.

Spring wheat in the fertile Red River Valley in North Dakota and Minnesota—the "nation's bread basket"—was the last to feel the drought's scorching breath. The railroad men reported "prospects excellent" in irrigated sections of Northern Colorado, Wyoming and Western Nebraska. The Winter wheat crop, harvested now, was "better than expected" almost everywhere. In 1934 it was a failure. The rest of the 1936 Spring wheat, however, was gone.

As far as cattle were concerned, C. B. Denman of Farmington, Mo., president of the National Livestock Marketing Association, which has 300,000 members, said that "the drought has not been on long enough to force heavy receipts." The cattle which were sold because of drying pastures, he said, were "good fat beef."

The grain markets are expected to continue jumpy tomorrow because of the week-end rains, which began Friday night. Corn dropped the 4-cent limit yesterday, its worst loss since the drought started it on an almost vertical rise of 32 to 34 cents from June levels.

Minnesota Tension Is Eased

The showers brought greatest cheer to the growers of corn.

In Iowa, where six weeks ago farmers were worrying about low prices because of an anticipated bumper yield, the rain brought "considerable recovery" from the hot weather's damage. Other crops were definitely improved, although

Continued on Page Eight

Electrified Dairy Affords Cows Luxury; Virginia Farm Is World Power Exhibit

Special to THE NEW YORK TIMES.

WASHINGTON, July 19.—Farm boys who remember getting up at dawn to drive in the cows from the pasture for the morning milking are not going to believe what they hear about the Rosedale Dairy Farm, which is to be formally opened Wednesday over in near-by Virginia as an exhibit of the forthcoming third World Power Conference.

Rosedale Farm is an electrical engineer's idea of what a dairy farm should be like. The builders hope the cows will like it.

All the milking, of course, will be done by electricity. Most modern cows are used to that. At Rosedale, however, there will be ventilating fans and hot and cold running water for each "bossy," and each cow will have her private drinking fountain.

Whether there will be a radio in every stall is not disclosed, and what use will be made of electric vibrators, hair dryers and sun ray lamps has not been explained, but Rosedale Farm will not be dark. Likewise the wood will be chopped, the churns will be run and even the old dinner bell that calls in the hands from the fields will be operated by electricity.

If the cows want to stay up late at night they may enjoy themselves in the glow of electric floodlights which will illuminate the farm when there is night work to be done.

The flies better stay away from the dairy house, however, for the screens are electrically charged and they will fly no more if they touch them.

When Rosedale is formally opened on Wednesday, Harold L. Ickes, Secretary of the Interior; Governor George Peery, Senator Harry F. Byrd and Representative Howard Smith, all of Virginia; Morris L. Cooke, Rural Electrification Commissioner, and a number of specially invited government officials, industrialists and farm leaders will participate in the ceremonies. They will pay tribute to the power of electricity to take some of the drudgery out of farming and will point out what rural electrification holds in store for the farmer of the future.

When the third World Power Conference meets Sept. 7-12, thousands of engineers from all parts of the world are expected to visit Rosedale.

VENEZUELANS SEEK TO OUST OIL FIRMS

Workers Urge Cancellation of Concessions and Local Control of Production.

SOLDIERS SENT TO AREAS

Labor Agitators Warned the Government Won't Tolerate Molestation of Foreigners.

Special Cable to THE NEW YORK TIMES.

PANAMA, Republic of Panama, July 19.—The government of Venezuela is sending additional troops to the oil fields, where a dozen police sufficed to keep order during the régime of the late dictator, Juan Vicente Gomez.

Five hundred soldiers were sent to Lagunillas and 150 are quartered inside the oil companies' compounds, where a permanent barracks is being built. The government has warned labor agitators it will not tolerate molestation of foreigners and it ordered soldiers to shoot to kill when necessary to protect them.

Oil employes complain about the prohibition on carrying arms for self-protection. A cashier was fined 2,500 bolivars (about $600) recently when he was found guilty of possession of a .25 caliber automatic.

Workers in the syndicates are demanding a cancellation of oil concessions and propose working the fields only by and for Venezuelans. They hold meetings in defiance of the authorities by keeping women and children, wrapped in Venezuelan flags, between them and the troops, knowing the soldiers will not fire on the flag or women.

The strikers disrupted oil field operations recently by stealing vital parts of the pumps and other machinery and by removing magnetos from 250 trucks and automobiles. Apparently fearing more trouble, the companies are exporting stored oil. The amount in storage tanks has dropped 80 per cent in the last three months.

It is explained by stating that the tanks are being emptied to reduce the fire risk, but well-informed observers contend the object is to avoid sabotage and possible confiscation.

Labor leaders are inciting workers against all foreigners, many of whom are sending their families away. The oil companies have informed their foreign employes, largely British and American, not to bring their wives and families to Venezuela. President Eleazar Lopez Contreras is making every effort to keep the situation under control.

Standard Active in Country

The principal oil companies operating in Venezuela are the Standard Oil Company of New Jersey and the Royal Dutch Company, which in 1935 produced in that country 66,100,000 barrels and 8,469,447 metric tons of oil, respectively. Although Royal Dutch has a plant at San Lorenzo, little refining is done in Venezuela, most of its crude oil being transported by tanker to the company's refineries

Continued on Page Two

REBELS IN MOROCCO BOMBED BY PLANES

But Insurgents Are Reported Still in Full Control of Zone—Death Toll Is Put at 60.

3 WARSHIPS JOIN RISING

Fierce Fighting at Larache—Loyal Troops Reach Ceuta—Revolt Laid to Gil Robles.

By The Associated Press.

TANGIER, International Zone, Morocco, July 19.—Loyal Spanish aviators were reported tonight to have bombed the High Commissioner's palace in Tetuan, capital of Spanish Morocco, killing twenty persons, while a rebellious army claimed firm control of the zone and announced sweeping gains on the mainland itself.

The Tetuan reports augmented a death toll already estimated at more than forty, with many wounded, since General Francisco Franco and his revolutionary soldiers smashed the authority of Leftist Spain in Morocco at the start of the week-end.

With three government warships reported to have deserted to the rebels they had been sent to fight, General Franco was understood to have arrested and imprisoned the High Commissioner in Tetuan.

Revolt Laid to Gil Robles

At Elksar the Police Commissioner and fifty Leftist leaders were jailed by soldiers of the revolt, while one aviator who had fled from the rebel command said had been instigated by José Maria Gil Robles, powerful Spanish Catholic leader.

Three children, reports from Tetuan said, were killed in the palace bombing, while loyal members of the aviation forces smashed their planes rather than let them fall into rebel hands. The high priest of the Tetuan mosque died of excitement during the bombing. A delegation of native officials protested to the Sultan over the bombing.

Estimates of the number of rebels in Morocco ranged from 18,500 to 40,000, the larger number being virtually all the Spanish troops garrisoned in the Spanish zone. Advices filtering through to French Morocco said the rebels in the Spanish zone were restoring order.

Stories of fierce fighting at Larache, where two officers and two of the loyal forces were slain in defending the telephone offices, reached Rabat. There one of three aviators, who had fled to French Morocco rather than fight government planes under rebel orders, said a government plane had bombed Larache. However, the bombing tactics were reported to have ceased.

Rebels Search Passenger Ships

A traveler who crossed the border into the French zone declared rebel warships were searching all passenger vessels entering Moroccan ports.

Rebels tried to seize the Spanish postoffice here, but were disarmed and imprisoned. Hostilities

Continued on Page Three

"All the News That's Fit to Print."

The New York Times.

LATE CITY EDITION
Showers with moderate temperatures today. Tomorrow possibly showers, temperature unchanged.
Temperatures Yesterday—Max., 81; Min., 71

Copyright, 1936, by The New York Times Company.

VOL. LXXXV....No. 28,684. Entered as Second-Class Matter, Postoffice, New York, N. Y. NEW YORK, THURSDAY, AUGUST 6, 1936. PP TWO CENTS In New York City. | THREE CENTS Within 200 Miles. | FOUR CENTS Elsewhere Except in 7th and 8th Postal Zones.

A. F. OF L. SUSPENDS 10 UNIONS WITH MEMBERSHIP OF 1,000,000 UNLESS THEY QUIT THE C. I. O.

PARIS PUSHES CURB ON ARMS FOR SPAIN AS FRENCH ENLIST

Soviet, Britain and Belgium in Neutrality Move—Reply of Italy Expected Today.

PORTUGAL LIKELY TO JOIN

France Contends Volunteers Who Leave to Aid Madrid Are Not Violating Its Program.

REBELS DRIVE FOR COAST

Hold Pass 35 Miles From Capital—Land 2,000 From Morocco After Battle Off Gibraltar.

Developments in Spain

French volunteers streamed across the border into Spain to fight against the rebels as France pressed yesterday for a seven-power neutrality pact. With Britain, France and Belgium already lined up, Russia agreed to the accord, expressing a desire for the inclusion of Portugal, which is expected to accept. Italy's reply probably will be a conditional acceptance and Germany's is still in doubt.

Spanish insurgents, battling for a northern sea outlet, intensively bombarded Tolosa and opened an offensive near Gijon. In the Guadarrama Mountains they declared they were thirty-five miles from Madrid.

Two troopships from Ceuta, Morocco, landed 2,000 rebels in Spain after a destroyer, planes and land guns had fought off a loyalist destroyer in the Straits of Gibraltar.

Government forces reported the defeat of insurgents at Sastago near Saragossa.

Volunteers Flock to Spain

By The Associated Press.

PARIS, Aug. 5.—France sought tonight to clamp an arms embargo on Spain as the first step toward preventing the civil war from becoming an international conflict.

Frenchmen meantime streamed across the border at Perpignan to volunteer in the fight on the side of the Spanish Government. That was regarded as within the meaning of neutrality as long as the men had their passports in order.

At the Toulouse airport fourteen pursuit planes were reported lined up and ready to take off for Spain for delivery to a Spanish buyer. They were held while France pressed the non-aggression agreement.

French newspapers hostile to the Madrid government said the planes were sold to Spanish rebels when the Lithuanian Government canceled its order for them.

Embargo Is Urged in Rome

Particular emphasis, officials said, was placed upon success of the arms embargo in negotiations at Rome for a proposed seven-power agreement on neutrality because Italian planes already have been flown to Spanish Morocco, where the rebels hold sway.

Britain, France and Belgium already are in accord and Russia expressed willingness tonight to join. Germany was said to be awaiting what the others will do. Portugal was expected to agree readily.

Italy's reply, which is likely to accept the principle of non-intervention, French sources said, might declare airplane and arms traffic difficult to control. It also was expected to raise the question of Soviet propaganda and Communist contributions of money to anti-Fascist forces in Spain.

The French People's Rallying Committee, which is the executive organization of Leftist government parties, appealed for 1,000,000 francs by Aug. 15 to provide medical care for Leftist fighters in Spain and food for their families.

"Spanish fascism, the sower of ruin and death, is finding support in international fascism," said the appeal. "Torturers of the German and Italian peoples are furnishing Spanish torturers with the means to establish on our Pyrenees frontier a military dictatorship which would complete the encirclement of France."

Deputy Urges Intervention

While Premier Leon Blum's own government was trying to get most of Europe to enter a non-intervention agreement, some of its own Leftist supporters still advocated aid for the Spanish loyalist government.

One Deputy of Mr. Blum's Socialist party supported Communist Deputies in favoring intervention in a discussion of the situation by the Foreign Affairs Committee of the Chamber of Deputies.

On the other hand, Georges Bonnet, a prominent member of the Radical Socialist party, which is al-

Continued on Page Two

Owens Completes Triple As 5 Olympic Marks Fall

U. S. Ace Sprints 200 Meters in 0:20.7, a Record Feat—Meadows Takes Vault After Dramatic Struggle—Carpenter Wins.

By ARTHUR J. DALEY

Wireless to THE NEW YORK TIMES.

BERLIN, Aug. 5.—The imprint of American domination, so indelibly stamped on the men's track and field program to date, stood forth in bold relief again today as the eleventh Olympic Games moved through their fourth day. The United States won three of the four finals to make its championship harvest nine out of fifteen.

Jesse Owens, phenomenon from Ohio State, rocketed to his third crown, taking the 200 meters in world and Olympic record time. Earle Meadows of Southern California carried on the American tradition of pole-vault victories by winning that test at an Olympic record height, and Ken Carpenter of Compton, Calif., set an Olympic mark in annexing the discus throw.

Only the 50,000-meter walk championship was beyond the reach of the Star-Spangled contingent, that going to Harold Whitlock of Great Britain, also in Olympic record figures.

One of the greatest shows of the huge athletic carnival was unfolded at the Reich Sports Field Stadium before the eyes of 90,000 persons in the morning and the fifth successive gathering of 100,000 in the afternoon. The spectators were somewhat glum and disconsolate

Point Score

U. S.	140	Sweden	6 1/11
Germany	79 3/4	Norway	5
Finland	30 1/4	Latvia	4
Japan	25 15/22	Philippines	4
Poland	17 1/11	Austria	3 2/11
Great Brit.	12 1/11	Czechoslo'kia	3 1/11
Italy	11 13/22	Brazil	2
Canada	11 1/11	Greece	2
Netherlands	9	Argentina	1
Switz'land	8	Hungary	2/11

Table includes only men's and women's track and field.

Points are unofficial, based on 10 for first place and 5, 4, 3, 2, 1 for the next five places respectively.

because Germany, having shot her bolt early in the proceedings, left them little for which to cheer, yet they certainly witnessed a grand meet.

Here were the high spots:

Records—Owens, doing 20.7 seconds around a turn, shattered Eddie Tolan's world mark of 0:21.2, while just missing by the picayune margin of one-tenth of a second the straightway standard, 0:20.6; Meadows, vaulting 4.35 meters (14 feet 2 15-16 inches), broke Bill Miller's standard of 4.31 meters ten hours after he started to compete; Carpenter,

Continued on Page Twenty-five.

PUP GETS 2 YEARS IN BOY'S DROWNING

Idaho Escapes Death, but Is to Be Shot if Owner Fails to Keep Him at Home.

CROWD CHEERS OUTCOME

But Brockport Victim's Mother Threatens to Kill the Dog—Prosecutor Goes 'Soft.'

By MILTON BRACKER

Special to THE NEW YORK TIMES.

BROCKPORT, N. Y., Aug. 5.—A lustrous-eyed mongrel pup, accused of drowning a boy, slept through most of his trial for life here today while 500 men, women and children muttered, gaped and fidgeted in the weathered Village Hall during an unparalleled "legal" proceeding.

Idaho, the 7-month-old dog, escaped a death sentence, and a weary throng cheered. But under the decision read by the presiding justice of the peace, Homer B. Benedict, the pet faces two years of far more restricted life than in his carefree past.

Until Oct. 1, 1938, it was ruled, he must be confined to his master's home, on penalty of death. His owner lives in a dun-colored, six-room house, whose modest yard is not exactly paradise as a dog's romping ground.

The sentence was not popular in one quarter. The drowned boy's mother said, on hearing of it, that if she had a gun she would shoot the dog herself.

The Transcript Is Long

Before sentence was pronounced there had been written into the records of Sweden Township an amazing profusion of testimony, cross-examination and re-direct examination, oratory and irrelevance.

Technically, the hearing concerned a civil suit demanding that the animal's owner be required to show cause why the dog should not be destroyed. Though the framework of a modern murder trial was there, with its conscious theatrics, in the hard, hot glare of Kleig lights the fundamental facts remained peculiarly simple and dramatic.

The facts were:

Russell Maxwell Breeze, 14-year-old son of a WPA worker, was drowned in the sleepy old Barge Canal late in the afternoon of July 4. A dog was said to have attacked him and forced him under. Idaho was picked up, but his owner, Victor Fortune, 25, a former CCC worker, insisted that his pet was innocent.

Two weeks ago Justice Benedict interrupted preliminary hearings by turning the shaggy brown and black "defendant" over to a group of experts. Idaho, until today, was under the care of Mary Foubister, executive secretary of the Rochester Dog Protective Association. The animal lay at the foot of her bed every night.

As the trial date neared the justice of the peace noted his swelling mail each morning and transferred the proceeding from his small office to the fifty-two-year-old

Continued on Page Eight

WEST POINT FIGHTS FOR POSTMISTRESS

Storm Rages as Daughter of Man Who Died With Custer Faces Loss of Her Job.

'SPOILS SYSTEM' BLAMED

Farley Is Accused of Plot to Squeeze Her Out in Favor of a Local Democrat.

Special to THE NEW YORK TIMES.

WEST POINT, N. Y., Aug. 5.—Miss Grace A. Harrington, 62-year-old postmistress at West Point, is making a last stand like her father who died with Custer at the massacre of the Little Big Horn in 1876.

Miss Harrington, postmistress to the 5,000 officers, cadets and soldiers attached to the Military Academy here, and friend and confidante of many of them, is quietly fighting to hold the $2,700-a-year position which she has filled for eight years, and which is now threatened, army personnel believe, by partisan politics.

Not only the army personnel here at West Point (who are fighting behind the scenes for Miss Harrington, but decline to comment for publication), but a large part of the service generally, and The Army and Navy Journal, service paper, are considerably exercised over the threatened replacement of Miss Harrington.

Miss Harrington, who by virtue of her parentage is a member of that select circle of "army juniors," is the third "army orphan" who has held the position of postmistress at the Point since 1847. The post traditionally has been removed from politics, and has usually gone to one of the army's own as a permanent nonpartisan assignment, not subject to political change.

Named to Post in 1927

This soldier's daughter, who knows her boys (the cadets) by their handwriting, and to whom West Point history and West Point tradition are almost as sacred as to the corps itself, was appointed postmistress by President Coolidge in 1927. Her term expired last January, but reappointment was taken for granted until last December, when rumors of a political patronage deal began to be heard about Highland Falls and West Point.

Jacob Hicks, recently appointed Democratic leader in Highland Falls, backed a deserving Democratic woman of Highland Falls, not an "army junior," for the job, and apparently had won Postmaster General Farley's approval. However, the publicity which resulted when the proposed ousting of Miss Harrington became known ended, it was thought for all time, the intrusion of partisan politics into the ivy-clad gray stone walls and turreted battlements of West Point.

Miss Harrington stayed on her old job, distributing the 1,000 letters her postoffice receives in an average morning's mail, and expecting as a matter of course a reappointment. But apparently her opponents are as unrelenting as the Sioux Indians who in that battle of the Little Big Horn massacred

Continued on Page Twelve

METAXAS CRUSHES STRIKE IN GREECE; DICTATORSHIP SEEN

Troops Occupy Athens Under Martial Law After Premier Charges Red Plot.

GOVERNMENT DENIES COUP

Serious Clashes Are Said to Have Taken Place in the Capital and Salonika.

Wireless to THE NEW YORK TIMES.

ATHENS, Greece, Aug. 5.—Following the publication of a royal decree enforcing martial law and dissolving the Chamber of Deputies and the occupation of Athens by troops, the twenty-four hour general strike called by Leftist trade unions was crushed early today and the capital resumed its normal aspect save for frequent patrols.

The strike had been called for last midnight in protest against a recent law fixing minimum-wage scales and subjecting workers' claims to obligatory arbitration.

Late last night Premier John Metaxas announced that his government had found it necessary to adopt exceptional measures in order to combat "a Communist plot tending to cause serious trouble in Athens and other cities."

After telling the Cabinet council of the alleged Communist plans to turn the general strike into a revolt, Premier Metaxas, with King George's consent, published the royal decree.

An official proclamation declares that the government's action tends to save the Greek people from the clutches of Communists, who threaten to disturb social peace and order. Governmental circles insist the Premier's action was entirely nonpartisan, which would explain why political leaders have not been molested.

Metaxas Takes Cabinet Posts

By The Associated Press.

ATHENS, Greece, Aug. 5.—In a Cabinet shake-up tonight Premier John Metaxas took for himself the portfolios of the Army, Navy, Air and Foreign Affairs and retained his friend George Skylakakis as Minister of the Interior.

He named Constantine Zavitziana, veteran politician, as Vice President of the Council and changed the Under Secretaries of the Ministries of Finance, Labor, Public Assistance, Hygiene and Air.

In a proclamation General Metaxas promised enforcement of an eight-hour day and a minimum wage and the institution of a social insurance system.

New elections for the Chamber of Deputies will be held when the situation permits, it was stated. The old Chamber's dissolution wiped out the power of fourteen Communists who have held the balance between the Venizelist and anti-Venizelist factions.

Dispatches to Vienna Scanty

Wireless to THE NEW YORK TIMES.

VIENNA, Aug. 5.—The only dispatches allowed to pass the rigid Greek censorship tonight were scanty.

The unusually long period during which all communications have been interrupted with other countries seems to indicate that Greece's present rulers do not consider the situation entirely stable and are awaiting developments.

The events of the last twenty-four hours cannot yet be chronicled, as telephonic communications are still interrupted. But from reliable reports that have filtered through

Continued on Page Four

Pigs Feast Daily on Eight Varieties of Pies, Ordered on Contract for Quoddy Workers

Special to THE NEW YORK TIMES.

PERRY, Me., Aug. 5.—The world is full of pigs in clover, but Perry pigs are feasting on pie—many kinds of pie, served daily.

It all came about from the collapse of Quoddy, the tide power dam across the bay, and it proves again that it's an ill wind that blows no good.

When Quoddy was started and thousands of men were at work there contracts were made with the bakers in Bangor and elsewhere to supply the commissary with 500 pies and 800 loaves of bread daily to supplement the produce of the Quoddy kitchens. The pies and loaves came on schedule and were eaten to the last bite, the supply barely keeping pace with demand.

Then a few weeks ago, when President Roosevelt announced that there could be no more money for Quoddy until Congress had given the dam its blessing, workers were discharged in thousands, until only a corporal's guard remained to eat the 500 pies and the 800 loaves.

Still the pies and the loaves continued to arrive by the truckload every morning, because the government had bought them on time contracts, and the contracts had many days to run.

With 500 pies and 800 loaves pouring in daily, and only six pies and eight loaves required, a serious problem was presented. There being nothing in the New Deal regulations providing for the distribution of surplus pies and loaves to the poor, but one course remained. The surplus must go to the garbage dump. And there it has been going for a week or two.

Farmer Ed Pottle of Perry, who keeps a lot of pigs, has the contract to remove Quoddy garbage, and that is how he has been able of late to feed his pigs on pie—eight kinds. Of course this can't last forever. The pie contracts may be terminated any day.

Pottle rather expects that next Winter he may be able to furnish pork loins and hams flavored with raspberry, lemon, prune and pineapple.

PRIAL ENTERS RACE TO HEAD ALDERMEN; BERLE NOT TO RUN

Former Deputy Controller Will Oppose Brunner—Calls Him Product of 'Boss Rule.'

CHAMBERLAIN FOR MORRIS

Praises Republican as Logical Man but La Guardia Still Seeks Own Candidate.

Former Deputy Controller Frank J. Prial announced yesterday that he would be a candidate for the Democratic nomination for President of the Board of Aldermen, while City Chamberlain A. A. Berle Jr. announced that he would not be a candidate for any nomination for that post.

Mr. Prial coupled with his announcement an attack on "boss rule," striking at the selection by the five Democratic county leaders of Sheriff William F. Brunner of Queens as the organization candidate for the nomination for Aldermanic President.

Mr. Berle, who was put forward by Mayor La Guardia as his choice for a Fusion nomination for the place, included in his announcement high praise of Newbold Morris, Republican designee.

Move Interests Leader

The two developments caused unusual interest among political leaders and gave rise to numerous surmises as to their effect on the State, national and local election as far as New York City was concerned.

Mayor La Guardia, with whom Mr. Berle consulted before making public his announcement, declared he was still ready to discuss with Republican leaders the selection of any Fusion candidate who would meet his requirements, adding that he felt Mr. Morris did not.

At the same time it was indicated that Mayor La Guardia might throw in his fortunes with the newly formed Labor party if it nominated a candidate for Aldermanic President, to pave the way for formal alliance with that body for re-election as Mayor next year as a Labor party candidate.

Morris and Simpson Pleased

Mr. Morris and Kenneth F. Simpson, Republican County Chairman, expressed pleasure at Mr. Berle's statement, and Mr. Morris indicated that he expected Mr. Berle's support in the campaign. Mr. Simpson and other Republican leaders were further pleased when they learned that Mr. Prial intended to enter the Democratic primary against Sheriff Brunner. These leaders felt that a rift among the Democrats would not only aid Mr. Morris but the Landon-Knox campaign in the city as well.

Mr. Prial declined to augment his formal statement, in which he said:

"A large number of organizations, both civic and political, and many individuals have urged me to enter the Democratic primaries as a candidate for the office of President of the Board of Aldermen.

"Representatives of these groups particularly stressed the fact that the direct primary was created for the purpose of giving the enrolled voters in a party the opportunity to select their candidates for public office.

"They complained that unless a candidate is designated to run in the primaries the nomination would go by default to William F. Brunner, who was hand-picked for this office, not because of any qualification or experience but solely to meet a political situation.

"I agree with these contentions

Continued on Page Fourteen

Labor Leaders' Statements

Special to THE NEW YORK TIMES.

WASHINGTON, Aug. 5.—Here are the statements of the four principal figures in the controversy between the A. F. of L. and the C. I. O., issued after the vote of the executive council suspending the ten groups supporting the industrial union movement:

William Green

President American Federation of Labor

The Executive Council of the American Federation of Labor decided that the Committee for Industrial Organization is a dual organization and that its originator and leader is John L. Lewis, president of the United Mine Workers of America.

This decision was reached after the Executive Council had made a careful study of the charges filed by President Frey of the Metal Trades Department against the Committee for Industrial Organization and of the evidence offered in support thereof.

This is the first attempt ever made during the existence of the American Federation of Labor, covering a period of more than fifty years, to set up a dual movement within it. It was the opinion of the Executive Council that it could not condone the setting up of a rival organization within the officially recognized family of labor, or tolerate and countenance it without sacrificing its self-respect, or making an unconditional surrender to a minority group composed of members who are in open rebellion to democratic procedure and majority rule, as exemplified at the latest convention of the American Federation of Labor.

The decision of the executive council to suspend those organizations from affiliation with the American Federation of Labor which hold membership in the dual organization (the Committee for Industrial Organization) within thirty days unless they withdraw therefrom means that said organizations are required to do nothing more than to discontinue holding membership in, and to cease fostering, financing and maintaining

Continued on Page Fifteen

PHILCO SUIT SAYS RCA HIRED SPIES

Charges Girl Employes, Feted at Night Clubs, Divulged Radio Trade Secrets.

RETURN OF DATA IS ASKED

Detective Agency Is Accused—Counsel for Defendants Makes Vigorous Denial.

The Philco Radio and Television Corporation accused the Radio Corporation of America and its subsidiary, the RCA Manufacturing Company, in Supreme Court here yesterday of using agents of a detective bureau to furnish liquor and entertainment to women employes of the Philco Company to obtain confidential information about the manufacture of radio sets.

The agents of the detective bureau were alleged to have taken Philco women employes to hotels, night clubs and restaurants in Philadelphia and vicinity "and involving them in compromising situations." The accusations were made in a suit for an injunction to restrain the defendants from alleged unfair and illegal business practices.

The plaintiff also asked for an order forcing the return of any information obtained by such practices and for whatever damages the court may find the Philco Corporation has suffered as a result of the defendants' alleged acts.

Defendants named in the action include John S. Harley, Inc., described as a detective agency; Charles A. Hahne, said to be vice president of that agency, and Lawrence Kestler Jr., an alleged agent for the detective bureau.

Makes a Vigorous Denial

The following comment on the suit was made by Manton Davis, vice president and general counsel of the Radio Corporation of America:

"We intend to answer this complaint and vigorously deny its allegations. There is no foundation whatsoever to the charge that RCA has by espionage or by any improper means attempted to obtain information as to the laboratory research, designs, distribution policies or any other trade secrets of Philco."

At the office of the Harley firm it was said that no statement would be made concerning the alleged activities of the company. It was denied that any one named Hahne is connected with the agency.

The Philco company says it has obtained a leading position in the sale of radio receiving apparatus in the United States and that 98 per cent of its stock is owned by its officers and employes. The Radio Corporation of America is described as having assets of more than $100,000,000 and owning or controlling the great majority of patents covering radio appliances and apparatus.

"By the exercise of its financial power and patent monopoly it dominates and controls the radio industry of the United States and by the acts alleged herein is seeking further to extend and strengthen its

Continued on Page Ten

LANDON WINS CUT IN FARM RAIL RATES

Roads Accede to Demand and Sharply Reduce Feed Tariffs to Drought States.

EASTERN DATES ARE SET

Governor Will Speak at West Middlesex Aug. 22—Dickinson Hopeful for Iowa.

By JAMES A. HAGERTY

Special to THE NEW YORK TIMES.

TOPEKA, Aug. 5.—Efforts of Governor Landon to obtain reduced freight rates on shipments of water and feed to farmers in the drought areas of Kansas brought results today. The Western trunk-line committee at Chicago submitted to him a satisfactory plan for emergency rates on feed shipments and the Santa Fe Railroad reduced its rates on water shipments 50 per cent.

An arrangement for emergency rates for shipments of cattle to better pasturage is expected soon, the Governor said.

Late in the afternoon the Governor made public the dates for his first Eastern campaign trip. He will speak at West Middlesex, Pa., his birthplace, on Saturday, Aug. 22, at 3 P. M.; at Chautauqua Monday evening, Aug. 24, and at Buffalo Wednesday evening, Aug. 26.

Mr. Landon was told today by Senator L. J. Dickinson and others that he would carry Iowa and was informed by Governor Frank D. Fitzgerald that the swing toward him in Michigan would result in his carrying that State.

Pleased at Capper's Victory

Governor Landon had no comment on the results of the Kansas primary election yesterday except to express gratification at the renomination of Senator Capper.

Although the Democratic primary vote was the largest ever cast, the Governor's supporters felt no uneasiness that it held a menace to his chance of carrying his home State, but were willing to admit that the contest might be a lively one.

By the nomination of Walter A. Huxman for Governor over former Governor Jonathan M. Davis and the nomination of Omar Ketchum for Senator over Dempster O. Potts, the Roosevelt wing of the Democratic party, under the leadership of Harry H. Woodring, Assistant Secretary of War, and Guy T. Helvering came into complete control of the party organization.

Mr. Davis and Mr. Potts ran with the endorsement of the Townsend clubs, the members of which may hold the balance of political power in the State, although the Townsendite candidates made a poor showing in the Republican primary.

Trembley Defeat Called a Blow

The results of the Republican primary were generally satisfactory to Governor Landon and his immediate friends, although The Topeka State Journal, of which former Senator Allen is an owner, said today of the contest for the Republican nomination for State Treasurer:

"The State Republican organization built up under Governor Lan-

Continued on Page Thirteen

TIME IS SET FOR SEPT. 5

Executive Council Votes 13 to 1 as Dubinsky Urges Delay.

LEWIS REFUSES TO YIELD

He Says His Organization Will Not Disband, but Will Press Activities.

CALLS OUTCOME 'STUPIDITY'

Green Declares Action Was Forced in Defense of Federation's 'Self Respect.'

By LOUIS STARK

Special to THE NEW YORK TIMES.

WASHINGTON, Aug. 5.—The executive council of the American Federation of Labor today suspended ten affiliated unions with more than 1,000,000 members, effective on Sept. 5, unless they withdraw from the Committee for Industrial Organization, which was held to be an attempt to set up a dual or rival labor movement.

John L. Lewis, chairman of the C. I. O., immediately announced that the committee would not disband.

The council's action, decided upon yesterday, was not stayed by the last-minute appeal of David Dubinsky, president of the International Ladies Garment Workers Union and a member of the council, who urged postponement for a few days with the assurance that the situation could be saved without a split in the labor movement under a compromise plan he presented. He was the only member of the council to vote against suspension.

Mr. Dubinsky's appeal, following his arrival here from New York today on his return from Europe, delayed the action a few hours, during which he was heckled by council members, several of whom questioned his right to be present as he was a member of one of the ten unions found guilty. Mr. Dubinsky retorted that President William Green of the A. F. of L., a member of the United Mine Workers, was in the same position.

Legality Is Questioned

In the end the council adopted the policy it had been ready to put into effect three weeks ago at its last meeting here but which was postponed because of certain legal steps, deemed necessary to bolster its case if the suspended unions appealed to the courts.

Mr. Dubinsky, in a statement, attacked the council for its "so-called enabling rule to put a color of legality on this illegal procedure" and said that "aside from the undemocratic and high-handed technical side of this act of the executive council" it was "calculated obviously to disfranchise in advance a large minority of unions from taking part in the next convention of the A. F. of L. and be heard in their defense before the only proper tribunal in organized labor qualified to pass on their guilt or innocence."

Pleading for more than an hour that the council postpone action until the next convention in November, Mr. Dubinsky said that his union would be willing to forego a two-thirds vote and abide by whatever decision a majority might take at the convention.

Lewis Calls Act "Stupidity"

Mr. Lewis, who is president of the United Mine Workers of America, as well as chairman of the C. I. O., lost no time in characterizing the council's action as "an act of incredible and crass stupidity," saying that "the executive council would not trust the judgment of a convention of the federation which meets in November" and "hastened to prejudice the action of the convention by stripping the defendant unions of their voting privilege."

Declaring that he and his associates would not disband the C. I. O., Mr. Lewis said that the decision would not have any effect upon its organizing activities.

Daniel J. Tobin, president of the International Brotherhood of Teamsters and chairman of the Labor Division of the Democratic National Campaign Committee, said that while suspension of the ten unions was a "serious division" in the ranks of labor, it would not destroy its efficiency.

From the political standpoint, Mr.

Continued on Page Fifteen

New York welcomes Jesse Owens, winner of 4 medals at the Berlin Olympics, with a ticker-tape parade.

Governor Lehman appointed Thomas E. Dewey special prosecutor to investigate crime in New York. He and his staff, seen here at a press conference, were responsible for putting Charles (Lucky Luciano) Lucania behind bars.

"All the News That's Fit to Print."

The New York Times.

LATE CITY EDITION
Occasional showers today, with moderate temperatures. Tomorrow showers, temperatures unchanged.
Temperatures Yesterday—Max., 86; Min., 76

VOL. LXXXV.....No. 28,704. Entered as Second-Class Matter, Postoffice, New York, N. Y. NEW YORK, WEDNESDAY, AUGUST 26, 1936. P TWO CENTS In New York City. | THREE CENTS Within 200 Miles. | FOUR CENTS Elsewhere Except in 7th and 8th Postal Zones

ROOSEVELT, IF RE-ELECTED, MAY CALL KINGS, DICTATORS AND PRESIDENTS TO GREAT POWER PEACE CONFERENCE

RULERS WHO MAY BE INVITED TO CONFER

Edward VIII Mussolini Hitler Stalin Lebrun

Times Wide World Photos.

PLANS NO COMMITMENTS

President Would Have Heads of States Unite Voices for Peace.

TO CONSIDER WAR CAUSES

And Discuss Disarmament—Vigorous Public Support Is Expected to Develop.

SITUATION UNLIKE 1918

No Victors and Vanquished Are Now Concerned—Opposition Here Expected.

By ARTHUR KROCK

The President is seriously considering a plan—his own—in the event of his re-election to propose a joint conference soon thereafter with the heads of the most important nations in an effort to assure the peace of the world. He has mentioned his idea to a few intimate friends, stressing the fact that, while he has not definitely decided upon the plan and has thought out but a few details, he is earnestly weighing the possibilities.

The conference, to meet in the place considered fittest by those participating, would include the President, King Edward VIII, Joseph Stalin, Benito Mussolini, Adolf Hitler, President Lebrun of France, effective representatives of Japan and China and a few others. It would be small in numbers, which the President considers important for its impressive functioning. He believes that, in view of the power and prestige of the conferees, and because of the fact that detailed programs and commitments would not be asked, retinues of economic experts and diplomats—the usual accompaniment of international conferences—could be dispensed with.

President's Idea Outlined

As the President has outlined his idea thus far, the eminent members of the conference would generally discuss the prospects and hopes of disarmament and peace, consider the seeds of war, and unite in a proclamation of personal purpose to use all their influence to prevent war in any part of the world. Public opinion would be expected to take more vigorous and definite form behind the conferees than it has attained on the present separate nationalistic basis. While carefully refraining from assuming for the United States any obligation or responsibility for militant action for peace in the Eastern Hemisphere, and making no request of any foreign States to assume these, the President would point to conditions in the Western Hemisphere and urge the Pan-American agreements as a model.

In such a conference the administration policy, pursued by Secretary of State Hull, for international trade agreements, the leveling of tariff barriers and the elimination of quotas would naturally be discussed with a view to extending the policy, and the importance of economic causes of war would be stressed.

The President has said to his friends that, if he is re-elected over the intense opposition he is facing, he believes he will be in the best position any American President has ever been to promote the cause of world peace, and he has given several reasons. One is that his prestige will have been greatly increased, which will lend additional weight to his initiative in the matter of a conference. He will have entered upon a new term of office, of fixed duration, in the course of which he can greatly assist in any peace efforts on which the conference may agree.

Unlike Wilson's Position

The President, recalling the paramount position of Woodrow Wilson in the world in 1918, feels he is fortunate in possessing several accidental advantages over that President at the Versailles Peace Conference. As he sees them, they are:

The 1937 meeting would not be meeting after a long, bloody and bitter war, but in time of peace. There would be no victors, no van-

Continued on Page Seven

LANDON WILL AVOID BACKING CANDIDATE FOR GOVERNORSHIP

Feels Presidential Nominee Should Not Interfere in a State's Affairs.

BUT HAMILTON MAY HELP

Race Is Seen Narrowing Down to Fearon and Bleakley, Who Is Aided by Jaeckle.

KANSAN MEETS LEADERS

He Will Carry New York, Assisted by Heavy Vote Up-State, Colonel Roosevelt Asserts.

By JAMES A. HAGERTY
Special to THE NEW YORK TIMES.

BUFFALO, Aug. 25.—A "hands off" policy, as far as taking personal part in the selection of a Republican candidate for Governor of New York is concerned, was announced by Governor Landon in talks with party leaders.

Those who discussed the New York political situation with him said that Mr. Landon regarded it as no part of the function of a Presidential candidate to interfere in party affairs in a State or to favor one candidate for any office at the expense of another.

Members of Mr. Landon's personal party told the leaders that, if there was to be any advice from the national party organization on a Gubernatorial candidate, it would come from John D. M. Hamilton, national chairman, instead of Mr. Landon.

Mr. Hamilton will arrive tomorrow from Chicago and accompany Governor Landon on his return trip as far as that city.

In the opinion of many leading Republicans here, the race for the Republican nomination for Governor has narrowed just at present to a contest between George R. Fearon of Syracuse, minority leader of the Senate, and William F. Bleakley of Yonkers, Supreme Court justice.

Candidates to See Landon

Mayor Marvin of Syracuse remains in the race, however, as does George U. Harvey, Borough President of Queens, and there will be several candidates of the "favorite son" variety, such as Eppis J. Staley of Albany, former Supreme Court Justice, and O. Byron Brewster of Essex County, Supreme Court justice, to hold the votes of their respective counties in the early ballots at the State convention.

Friends of Frank E. Gannett, Rochester newspaper publisher, have suggested that he might be a good compromise candidate.

Senator Fearon and Justice Bleakley are here, and Mayor Marvin is expected. Justice Bleakley, accompanied by Charles H. Griffith, Westchester County leader, had a talk with Governor Landon. Senator Fearon and Mayor Marvin will see him tomorrow.

The question of a Republican Gubernatorial candidate will probably be discussed further at a meeting of the executive committee of the State committee. It was believed at first that the meeting had been called because of Mr. Hamilton's expected presence, but Clarence R. King, executive committee chairman, said it was decided at Syracuse a week ago to get members together again here. Charles D. Hilles, national committeeman, is expected here in time for the meeting.

Supporters of Senator Fearon declared that he was already assured of slightly more than 600 delegates out of the 1,228 in the State convention, and that at least forty county leaders were for him. These leaders do not include the leaders of any of the five counties of New York City, Erie or Monroe.

Mayor Marvin has no such support throughout the State, but is strong in his territory. Mr. King, the Onondaga County leader, who is here, has not declared thus far for either Syracuse candidate.

Jaeckle Said to Aid Bleakley

A strong movement has developed for the nomination of Justice Bleakley. It is apparently being fostered by Edwin F. Jaeckle, Erie County chairman, who has made no definite commitment but is believed to favor the Yonkers jurist over Senator Fearon. Justice Bleakley has the support of the Ninth Judicial District, of which Westchester County is a part, and considerable support in New York City.

Although the convention delegates will not be elected until Sept. 15, when the primary election will be held, there are comparatively few contests and the results of these are not likely to have any particular effect on the contest for the Gubernatorial nomination.

Arrangements for Governor Lan-

Continued on Page Twelve

State Labor Backs Roosevelt And Lehman for Re-election

Syracuse Convention Becomes Virtually a Rally for Them—Governor After Great Ovation Declares for Amendment 'if Necessary' to Win Labor Reforms—Green Denounces C.I.O.

By JOSEPH SHAPLEN
Special to THE NEW YORK TIMES.

SYRACUSE, N. Y., Aug. 25.—Unanimous endorsement of President Roosevelt and Governor Lehman for re-election was voted by the convention of the State Federation of Labor at its opening session here today.

Governor Lehman, who in an address assailed "the reactionary and short-sighted opposition" in the Legislature which defeated his eight-point Social Security Bill and other social and labor legislation, received a tumultuous ovation.

He pledged himself anew to support of advanced legislation for the benefit of wage earners and expressed himself as favoring a constitutional amendment, "if necessary," to meet objections of the courts to social and labor laws.

The Governor's address was, in substance, an accounting of his stewardship in this field and an appeal for continued effort in the direction of social betterment, notably passage of his Social Security Bill. He was repeatedly cheered.

William Green, president of the American Federation of Labor, who followed the Governor on the platform, added his praise of the New York Executive to that of the convention and appealed to the 1,100,000 workers represented in the State federation "to rally behind the Governor and march to the polls in November as one man to insure his re-election."

"The Governor of this great State, who has made so many sacrifices for the working people, ought to be re-elected by the greatest majority ever given to any Executive," Mr. Green declared to the applause of the delegates.

Similar sentiments were expressed by George Meany, president of the State federation, in opening the session. Mr. Meany also issued a statement declaring that the re-election of President Roosevelt was a matter of vital necessity to the workers of the nation.

The Governor's address, the ovation given him, the endorsement voted by the convention of his and President Roosevelt's candidacies, the appeals by Mr. Green and Mr. Meany, and the enthusiasm displayed by the delegates turned the

Continued on Page Ten

FRENCH SEEK WAY TO PARALLEL REICH IN MILITARY RACE

Urgent Meeting of Chamber's Army Group Asked to Take Up Berlin's Move.

REDS FOR NATIONAL UNITY

Thorez Echoes Lebrun in Call for Firm Stand in Face of 'Hitler War Danger.'

By The Associated Press.

PARIS, Aug. 25.—French parliamentarians tonight cast about for ways and means to meet the challenge of the expanded war machine of Nazi Germany.

Convinced, they indicated, that Chancellor Adolf Hitler was preparing to go to war over the wheat fields of the Russian Ukraine, government Socialists heaved overboard their previous efforts to reduce France's military service period. Hitler, they said, was going to make war on them "under [guise of] a crusade against the Red peril."

The Nazi Chancellor, in extending the German compulsory military training period from one to two years, thus swelling the ranks of those under arms or in training to some 1,000,000 men, cited "Bolshevist perils" as motivating the German action.

Fears Germany's Strength

Tonight France's leaders apprehensively faced the problem of matching the new man-power of the German Army, expressing fears that Germany would crush France's fighting forces if it came to a showdown under the existing comparative sizes of the armies of the two nations.

French officials listed their nation's fighting forces at 605,000, as against the Reich's reported goal of 1,000,000 men by October.

Further weighting the war scales in Germany's favor, French officials declared, was the fact that France would have to delegate some 200,000 of her troops to duty in her colonies in the event of war, while Germany, they estimated, with 500,000 additional potential fighting men in semi-military organizations, would be able to put 1,200,000 men in the battle lines in a short time.

Fernand Laurent, member of the Chamber of Deputies' army committee, asked the chairman, Guy La Chambre, to call an emergency meeting to discuss what could be done to strengthen the French forces. Hardly had his urgent request been made when Léon Archimbaud, one of the government's army authorities in the Chamber, said "there can be no question of lengthening, our military service," which is now two years.

Some way to raise the size of the French standing army was considered imperative in parliamentary circles. Mr. La Chambre said France's only alternative would be a revival of the arms limitations conference, which has been one of Premier Blum's policies but which the Premier's critics have termed hopeless.

See More Danger of Two Camps

French authorities said that Hitler, by raising his army from "equality to superiority," had heightened the danger of Europe's being divided into two armed camps with the Chancellor in the rôle of protector, attracting the smaller nations to his banner.

General Auguste Hirschauer, former Military Governor of Stras-

Continued on Page Three

HARRISON IS VICTOR IN PRIMARY BY 2 TO 1

Mississippi Senator Swamps Conner, Who Ran With the Support of Bilbo.

BYRNES GAINS HUGE LEAD

Distances 2 New Deal Critics in Carolina Vote—Townsend in California Test.

By FELIX BELAIR JR.
Special to THE NEW YORK TIMES.

JACKSON, Miss., Aug. 25.—By a margin of more than two to one, Senator Pat Harrison swept aside all opposition in the primary today to win the Democratic nomination to succeed himself and begin his fourth term in the United States Senate.

He rode rough-shod over what had been termed "an unbeatable combination" of Senator Theodore Bilbo and former Governor Mike Sennett Conner, the opposing candidate.

Returns from 1,502 out of 1,659 precincts gave Harrison 123,364, Connor 61,673 and State Senator Frank Harper 2,275.

So decisive was Senator Harrison's victory that it raised serious doubts in the minds of some observers concerning the political future of Senator Bilbo, who set a precedent in Mississippi politics by seeking the defeat of his senior colleague. In Pearl River County, home county of Senator Bilbo, Mr. Harrison received 1,527 votes to 1,020 for Conner in returns from 23 of 24 precincts.

Nearly complete returns from the seven Congressional districts indicated victory for the six incumbents, including Representatives Rankin, Whittington, Doxey, Colmer and McGehee. Former Representative Ross Collins was running far ahead of Adam Byrd in the Fifth district and Representative Wall Doxey was unopposed in the Second district.

At his home in Gulfport, Senator Harrison issued the following statement tonight:

"The result of the election is even better than I anticipated. It is a glorious victory and my heart goes out to every man and woman in Mississippi who assisted in making this victory so complete."

Long before fragmentary returns began to show a trend toward Senator Harrison, spokesmen at his headquarters here were prepared to hail his victory as one for President Roosevelt and the New Deal. Although the administration and its policies were not an issue in the fight, Harrison supporters pointed to the Senator's support of the President.

Byrnes Piles Up Lead
By The Associated Press.

COLUMBIA, S. C., Aug. 25.—Senator James F. Byrnes, stanch supporter of the New Deal, buried two anti-administration opponents under an avalanche of votes in today's Democratic primary on the basis of incomplete returns.

From every part of the State came reports of huge majorities for the junior South Carolina Senator over Thomas P. Stoney, former Mayor of Charleston, and Colonel William C. Harllee, retired marine, of Dillon, both of whom made criticism of the Roosevelt administration the dominant note in their campaigns.

Returns from 944 of 1,474 pre-

Continued on Page Eleven

TODD TO CALL BYK IN GEOGHAN INQUIRY

Slot-Machine Man Will Be a Witness Against Friend at Hearing Opening Today.

PROSECUTOR IN ALBANY

Confident Governor Will Acquit Him—Takes His Chief Aides With Him.

From a Staff Correspondent.

ALBANY, Aug. 25.—Governor Lehman's hearings of the grand jury's charges demanding the removal of District Attorney William F. X. Geoghan of Brooklyn will open here at 2 o'clock tomorrow afternoon. The Governor has called a conference at 11 o'clock in the morning between counsel for Mr. Geoghan and Special Prosecutor Hiram C. Todd.

Mr. Geoghan arrived late tonight from New York, following his attorney, Lloyd Paul Stryker, by a few hours.

"I feel in splendid condition," he said. "I have never felt better in my life. I am confident that the Governor, after hearing me, will dismiss the charges. I was detained in New York this afternoon on a routine office matter before the August grand jury. As soon as I was finished with that I took the train for Albany. Mrs. Geoghan will join me tomorrow."

Mr. Geoghan's party also included Frederick L. Kopff, his chief assistant; Edward H. Levine, a law expert on his staff, and William F. McGuinness, an Assistant District Attorney, who has been subpoenaed by the prosecution. Mr. McGuinness was the first member of Mr. Geoghan's staff to question witnesses on the night of the Samuel Druckman murder.

Mr. Todd and members of his staff arrived during the afternoon and retired behind closed doors to

Continued on Page Fourteen

President Departs for Drought Area Tour; Puts Landon on Footing of All Governors

Special to THE NEW YORK TIMES.

WASHINGTON, Aug. 25.—President Roosevelt left Washington late this evening for a tour of the drought regions, including visits to eight States and conferences with sixteen Governors.

With him went a group of officials concerned with administering the relief program in the "dust bowl," including Secretary Wallace; Harry L. Hopkins, Works Progress Administrator; William I. Myers, governor of the Farm Credit Administration, and Robert Fechner, director of the Civilian Conservation Corps and half a dozen technical experts and advisers, in addition to a large White House secretarial staff.

On the eve of departure, the White House reiterated the President's statement that the purpose of the tour is to give him a first-hand picture of the drought regions and that it is not political.

However, principal public attention already was focussed on his scheduled call at Des Moines, Iowa, next Tuesday, when he will meet Governor Landon, the Republican candidate for the Presidency. Every effort is being made by the White House to keep this from appearing an extraordinary occasion, and the schedule for that day has been arranged so that while the President and Mr. Landon will have both luncheon and dinner together, they will meet only in company with four other Governors.

The President's itinerary calls for the first stop Thursday at Bismarck, N. D. There Mr. Roosevelt not only will meet the Governors of the Northwestern States but the members of the Great Plains Drought Committee.

From Bismarck, President Roosevelt will go to Pierre, S. D., and then double back through Minnesota and Wisconsin before going to Des Moines. From there he will travel eastward through Illinois, stopping at Springfield, and through Indiana, where he will make a final stop at Indianapolis before returning to Washington.

Only one speech is scheduled, a brief one, to be delivered at dedication ceremonies for a bridge at Hannibal, Mo., but it is considered quite probable that Mr. Roosevelt will give a radio address either at Des Moines or Indianapolis on his impressions of the drought problem.

BULLITT SUCCEEDS STRAUS IN FRANCE

Transferred From Moscow as Paris Envoy Resigns Because of Ill Health.

BOTH ARE IN THIS COUNTRY

President, Acquiescing 'With Regret,' Praises Service of Retiring Ambassador.

Special to THE NEW YORK TIMES.

WASHINGTON, Aug. 25.—President Roosevelt today named William C. Bullitt, Ambassador to Russia, to be Ambassador to France to succeed Jesse Isidor Straus, and announced acceptance with "deep regret" of the resignation of Mr. Straus, who pleaded that acute illness would require an extended period of rest.

The major shift in America's diplomatic representation puts one of the youngest Ambassadors in a new key post at a crucial time in European affairs.

The President announced the resignation of Mr. Straus at a White House press conference, making public the letters of resignation and of acceptance. Within an hour the White House offices issued an announcement of the appointment of Mr. Bullitt.

Both Mr. Straus and Mr. Bullitt are in the United States, the former having taken a leave of absence because of his health and the other having returned in June, openly stating his desire to resign from the Russian post.

Resented Repudiation

Mr. Bullitt was named by President Roosevelt as the first Ambassador to the Soviet Union after American recognition and completion of a debt agreement, which the Soviet has since repudiated.

This repudiation appeared to observers to have changed Mr. Bullitt from an ardent defender of Soviet recognition. He left the Embassy in charge of Loy W. Henderson, Second Secretary, and returned to request that he be relieved.

After several talks with Mr. Roosevelt, he consented to remain an Ambassador in rank and take an assignment to conduct special studies at the State Department. When Mr. Straus became acutely ill the President decided on Mr. Bullitt as his successor.

Mr. Straus, who was president of R. H. Macy & Co., New York department store concern, was named Ambassador to France immediately after President Roosevelt took office in 1933. He and the President are close friends.

Straus Letter of Resignation

Mr. Straus's letter of resignation was as follows:

"Aug. 18, 1936.

"My dear Mr. President:

"When I left Paris at the beginning of the month, I had hoped to return about the first of October. Upon arriving at home, however, my physicians informed me that I was in a very run-down condition and that I must have a complete rest for six months.

"In view of the fact that there is much work to be done in Paris at the moment, I feel that it is imperative to keep the embassy staff at its full complement. I,

Continued on Page Three

Spain Orders No Mercy For Moorish Invaders

By The Associated Press.

MADRID, Aug. 25.—The government called on citizens tonight to rise against the "Moorish invasion," following reports that Moorish troops brought to Spain by the Rebels had increased their activity.

Officials declared "no mercy will be shown these uncivilized barbarians."

It was asserted that 500 Moors had charged government troops in the Navalperal sector armed with hand grenades, but had been driven off, losing eighty killed and many wounded. The bodies of the Moors were cremated on the field after being covered with gasoline-drenched brush.

2 JAPANESE SLAIN BY A CHINESE MOB

Attacked by Crowd Protesting Against Plan to Station a Consul in Chengtu.

Wireless to THE NEW YORK TIMES.

SHANGHAI, Aug. 25.—Two Japanese were killed and another was injured in Chengtu, the capital of Szechwan Province, yesterday afternoon when a Chinese mob attacked a group of four Japanese visitors at their hotel. The fourth member of the party is missing.

News of the attack was reported here by the Domei [Japanese] News Agency.

The assault was said to have followed a mass meeting opposing the planned reopening of the Japanese Consulate in Chengtu. Incited by anti-Japanese oratory, the crowd was said to have left Hsiao Cheng Park and to have gathered at the inn where the Japanese were staying and there assaulted the group despite police efforts to beat off the rioters.

The members of the party were Kozaburo Watanabe, correspondent of the Osaka Mainichi and the Tokyo Nichi Nichi; Takeo Tanaka, an employe of the Shanghai office of the South Manchuria Railway; Keiji Fukagawa, a reporter for the Shanghai Mainichi, and Shoichi Seto, Hankow merchant. The group arrived in Chengtu Aug. 17 from Shanghai. Which members of it were killed is not known. The injured man was taken to the Provincial Government offices.

Vigorous Protest Lodged

Yakichiro Suma, Japanese Consul General in Nanking, was reported to be lodging vigorous representations today with Foreign Minister Chang Chun, who was hurrying to Nanking from Kuling, the "Summer capital," to deal with the situation.

The Chengtu rioting is believed to have been the outgrowth of widespread popular opposition to the Japanese plans to reopen the consulate, which has been closed since 1932. The Chinese declare that Chengtu is not a treaty port and foreign powers do not possess the right to station consuls there.

Foreign consuls have been residing there for many years because the Chinese previously have not made an issue of the question, but last week the British and French agreed to withdraw their consuls.

Continued on Page Five

REBEL ARMY GAINS NORTH OF MADRID

One Force of Insurgents 24 Miles From Capital—They Claim Navalperal Victory.

CITIES OF RIGHTISTS RAIDED

Government Bombers Attack at Cadiz and 3 Other Centers—Anti-Cruelty Pact Sought.

Special Cable to THE NEW YORK TIMES.

LISBON, Portugal, Aug. 25.—The Spanish insurgents claimed a long series of successes today.

In Aragon, they announced, their forces, despite repeated attacks by government supporters, gained a footing on the right bank of the Ebro River, between Quinto and Fuentes de Ebro. Near Medinaceli, in Old Castile, an insurgent column, after a long night march, occupied the village of Guijoza and cut railway and telephone lines and the high-tension cables of Siguenza.

In Asturias, the Rebels assert, their forces have occupied Cangas de Narcea, dislodging government forces from Puerto de Infierno and driving them back eight miles.

Insurgent forces also are reported to have occupied Navafria on the Guadarrama front, where an artillery duel has raged for twenty-four hours.

The government, for its part, asserts its troops have dispersed a column from Saragossa. The advance toward Teruel, about 100 miles southeast of Saragossa, continues, and Loyalists have occupied parts of Escatron in that area.

[Loyalist troops were seven miles from Teruel yesterday, according to an announcement in Madrid, but the Rebel command at Seville asserted that Civil Guards had defeated a government force in the town, "killing many and not taking a single prisoner."]

Report Two Planes Shot Down

The Loyalists also announce that they are now well established on the island of Majorca and have shot down two of three anti-government seaplanes that set out to bomb their positions.

[The Rebel headquarters at Seville reported that a Loyalist aerial squadron had bombed Cadiz, killing ten civilians. Madrid authorities announced that government planes had attacked Seville, Granada and Huesca.]

Insurgent aircraft are active in the Teruel area and have dropped supplies of food on the Alcazar at Toledo, in which several hundred Rebels, besieged since the beginning of the war, are still holding out.

[Persistent but unconfirmed rumors in Madrid said that the Alcazar had fallen to Loyalist troops, according to The Associated Press.]

Government forces are pressing strongly on Cordoba, where the defenders are under fire of artillery.

In the northern area Asturian miners are reported to have entered the suburbs of Oviedo at several places, dynamiting houses as they did at Gijon.

There were further executions of

Continued on Page Two

"All the News That's Fit to Print."

The New York Times.

LATE CITY EDITION
Cloudy, mild, with occasional rain today; clearing, colder tonight. Tomorrow colder.
Temperatures Yesterday—Max., 53; Min., 38.

Copyright, 1936, by The New York Times Company.

VOL. LXXXVI....No. 28,811. Entered as Second-Class Matter, Postoffice, New York, N. Y. NEW YORK, FRIDAY, DECEMBER 11, 1936. P TWO CENTS In New York City | THREE CENTS Within 200 Miles | FOUR CENTS Elsewhere Except in 7th and 8th Postal Zones.

EDWARD VIII RENOUNCES BRITISH CROWN; YORK WILL SUCCEED HIM AS GEORGE VI; PARLIAMENT IS SPEEDING ABDICATION ACT

CODE FOR INDUSTRY VOTED HERE TO BACK AIMS OF NEW DEAL

Association of Manufacturers Pledges Cooperation for 'Era of Good Feeling.'

ASKS FOR CENSUS OF IDLE

Moley Urges Business Join in Federal Planning—McCarl for Industrial Board.

LABOR GIVES 30-HOUR PLAN

Industrial Progress Council in Washington Hears Program for a Shorter Week.

Industry and New Deal

The National Manufacturers Association meeting here adopted a code for industry pledging "era of good feeling" and cooperation with social aims of New Deal. The text of the code is on Page 30.

The Council for Industrial Progress in Washington heard labor's plan to promote employment by a thirty-hour week and Federal regulation of working conditions. Employers did not oppose new labor laws, but spokesmen insisted that they should conform to the Constitution. Page 33.

Code Is Adopted Here

A declaration of principles for American industry, calling for an era of good feeling both at home and abroad, pledging cooperation with the government in the national interest and embracing, at least in principle, some of the most important social reforms of the New Deal, was adopted yesterday afternoon at the final session of the forty-first annual convention of the National Association of Manufacturers, held in the Waldorf-Astoria Hotel.

The declaration was in harmony with the keynote speech delivered at Wednesday's session by Colby M. Chester, chairman of the General Foods Corporation and president of the association, and in striking contrast to the bitter criticisms of the New Deal uttered by industrialists at previous meetings.

In closing the convention Mr. Chester asserted his belief that it had "written a new, sound and progressive note in the industrial life of this nation in its declaration of principles," and predicted that it would have the support of "a united industry" within the year.

Census of Idle Is Urged

Resolutions were adopted urging a government census of unemployed and opposing governmental ownership of the railroads or any transportation system.

Addresses were made by Raymond Moley, editor of the magazine Today; John R. McCarl, former Controller General; George H. Mead, president of the Mead Corporation and chairman of the business advisory council to the Department of Commerce, and James A. Emery, general counsel of the association.

Mr. Moley urged joint economic planning by the government and business. He warned industry that it must recognize the meaning of the election returns—that the people voted for security of wages and living standards—and offer them a rational plan to attain these ends if it does not wish to be compelled to submit to impractical and drastic legislation.

A balanced budget through the reduction of relief expenditures and other government spending was advocated by Mr. McCarl. He urged industry to accept the responsibility for reducing the need for relief by giving more jobs. He also suggested the business organize a National Industrial Board to cooperate with the government in the "collective" solution of social and economic problems.

According to Mr. Mead, business wants "constructive regulation," contrary to a general public impression, although it is opposed to "government ownership or control." Business also believes in economic security, he said, adding that a "practical" economic security and

Continued on Page Thirty-one

4,336,000,000 Francs Set As French Budget Deficit

Wireless to THE NEW YORK TIMES.

PARIS, Dec. 10.—There will be a deficit of 4,336,000,000 francs in the French budget during the coming year, according to figures put before the Chamber of Deputies this morning by the finance commission.

The ordinary expenditure under the budget is estimated at slightly more than 48,000,000,000 francs and the income at 43,685,000,000 francs. With these figures before them, the Deputies began to vote in rapid succession for most of the 140 articles in the law having to do with the collection of revenue despite the protest of one Right Deputy who argued that to vote revenues before expenditures was contrary to all good sense and logic.

JAPAN WITHDRAWS DEMANDS ON CHINA

Indicates Dropping of Moves for Anti-Red Cooperation and Autonomy of North China.

ARMY IS UNDER CRITICISM

Foreign Office Wants Public to Know the Military Interfere With Major Policies.

By HUGH BYAS

Wireless to THE NEW YORK TIMES.

TOKYO, Dec. 10.—Withdrawal of all the Japanese demands regarding North China autonomy and of that for cooperation against communism was implied in a statement issued to the press today by Eiji Amau, Foreign Office spokesman.

Japan asks Nanking to fulfill the agreements already reached on lesser points, but the request is not accompanied by a threat or warning except that if Japanese lives or property are endangered or Japanese rights violated the government will take "adequate measures."

Ambassador Shigeru Kawagoe's failure to obtain satisfaction from China, even in minor matters, is explained as due to Chinese indignation over the invasion of Suiyuan Province by Mongols and Manchukuoans.

Mr. Amau said nothing to connect the Japanese Kwantung Army with these events, but the public was already aware that Manchukuo's Premier had proclaimed sympathy with the Mongolian rising and knew he would not have taken such a step without being prompted.

Mr. Amau's statement, read in conjunction with Foreign Minister Hachiro Arita's answer to the Privy Council yesterday, suggested that the Foreign Office wants the public to know how the Kwantung army interferes with major policies on which all branches of the Tokyo government have agreed.

The statement claims that a definite agreement was reached with China regarding suppression of anti-Japanese movements—including revision of the control of the press and of Kuomintang (Nationalist party) branches—engagement of Japanese advisers, control of Korean exiles and reduction of tariffs.

Consulate Involved

China further agreed to reopening of the Chengtu Japanese Consulate and accepted most of Japan's demands for settlement of recent incidents.

A hitch occurred over air services. No agreement was reached regarding joint defense against communism though both sides concurred on several items.

Economic cooperation in North China was agreed on in principle. This stage having been reached, the Chinese, "taking advantage of the Suiyuan affair," broke off negotiations, threatened to repudiate all the concessions already made and evaded Ambassador Kawagoe's repeated requests for a further interview with Foreign Minister Chang Chun. Mr. Kawagoe was said to have handed Mr. Chang a note embodying the agreed points, requesting that they be put into effect.

"Japan is now watchfully waiting for China's response and is prepared to take adequate measures if China fails to control anti-Japanese movements or if Japanese life and property interests are jeopardized," the statement said.

It is pertinent to recall that Mr.

Continued on Page Twelve

CROWDS IN LONDON CALM

News Is Received With British Reserve as Thousands Gather.

QUEEN MARY IS CHEERED

Many Break Through Police Lines When She Calls at Home of Duke of York.

TENSION OF WEEK ENDED

People Sad at Losing Edward but Relieved the Suspense at Last Is Over.

Wireless to THE NEW YORK TIMES.

LONDON, Dec. 10.—As the news of King Edward's abdication sped to the far corners of the empire this afternoon Britain received confirmation of her worst fear with mixed emotions, sadness at losing so popular and beloved a sovereign and relief that the gnawing suspense of the last week at last had drawn to an end.

Massed thousands stood silently outside the towering iron gates of Parliament while the terse, restrained statement of the first monarch in England's history ever to renounce the throne voluntarily was read to the House of Commons. Presently, as the twilight shadows of Westminster Abbey lengthened over Parliament Square, word sped from mouth to mouth that the reign of Edward was coming to an end.

Although the atmosphere a few minutes before had been highly charged with tension and anxiety the news was received calmly and with typical British reserve. There was no demonstration and no show of feeling save for the serious, strained faces in the crowd and the flutter of women's handkerchiefs here and there.

Crowds Gather Throughout Day

Throughout the day, from dawn until after midnight, crowds of varying proportions gathered outside all the buildings associated with the historic happenings of the day. People clustered about No. 10 Downing Street, the Houses of Parliament and all the royal residences, standing stolidly and silently when allowed or moving along without protest if required. If any emotion was perceptible that could be described as a corporate reaction, it was one of bewilderment and incredulity that such a thing ever could actually happen.

A throng composed mostly of women, which at times reached 10,000 or more, stood on the pavement before Buckingham Palace forming

Continued on Page Twenty

Edward Plans Radio Talk To British Empire Tonight

Special Cable to THE NEW YORK TIMES.

LONDON, Dec. 10.—King Edward will broadcast to the empire tomorrow night at 10 o'clock, immediately after he has signed the Abdication Act and ceased to be King, in the character of a private person. It is expected Parliament will have disposed of its business by then.

[American networks will broadcast the message at 5 P. M., Eastern Standard Time.]

The British Broadcasting Corporation has arranged for a worldwide hook-up.

Many persons feel the King's decision to broadcast is not wise. He has already sent a message to Parliament with a penciled note to the Prime Minister, commending the Duke of York to the support of the whole empire. These will be broadcast four times tonight and printed in every British newspaper.

MRS. SIMPSON CRIES LISTENING AT RADIO

Shaken and Exhausted by the Climax in Career of King Who Forsook Throne for Her.

WILL REMAIN AT CANNES

Edward Will Not Visit Her Now—Britons in France Question Her Course.

Wireless to THE NEW YORK TIMES.

CANNES, France, Dec. 10.—With tears streaming down her face, Mrs. Wallis Warfield Simpson, for whose sake Edward VIII has abdicated as King and Emperor of the greatest empire the world has ever known, listened today as did all the rest of the world to the news over the radio from the scene in the British Parliament.

She heard the words announcing that the King Emperor of whom so much had been expected had laid down his scepter and crown so as to be free to marry her some months hence and live the life of an ordinary mortal.

Says King Won't Go to Riviera

At 1 o'clock this afternoon the following statement was made by Herman L. Rogers, at whose villa Mrs. Simpson is staying:

"There is definitely no change so far as Mrs. Simpson's plans are concerned. She will stay here until after Christmas. She is now at the villa and in the best of health. There has been no change in the household.

"It cannot be stated if she has

Continued on Page Twenty

Soviet Orders Militia Punished for Arrests Without Warrants in Spite of New Charter

Special Cable to THE NEW YORK TIMES.

MOSCOW, Dec. 10.—The first charges of violating the new Constitution were brought at Kazan today in connection with the arrests of eleven persons there by the militia on its own initiative.

According to the new Constitution, "no one may be subjected to arrest except upon the decision of a court or with the sanction of the prosecutor." Apparently no such authorization was obtained, and Moscow authorities have called the Kazan militia's action an "outrageous violation" of the Constitution and ordered that the guilty be suitably punished.

According to an investigation in Kazan, a doorman at a restaurant was arrested this week purely on suspicion. When he failed to arrive home his father made inquiries, and on finding his son in jail complained to the public prosecutor. The latter showed little interest. A correspondent of the Moscow newspaper Izvestia then took up the matter and spurred the prosecutor to visit the jail, where he found eleven persons arrested without warrants.

Today also the first Soviet death sentence for the infringement of private ownership and personal property and the murder of a private individual was imposed in a Moscow court.

Two employes of a State antique shop had been selling valuable old books to two highly paid ballet dancers. Thus the employes had learned their clients had money and valuables. They invaded the young dancers' home in their absence, killed their mother and cook with a brass pestle and looted the apartment. The criminals were traced, arrested, convicted and tonight they will be shot.

Hitherto the death penalty has been imposed in murder cases only where the safety or welfare of the State was involved, the normal penalty for an ordinary murder being not more than ten years.

Nikolai V. Krylenko has assumed his duties as head of the All-Union Commissariat for Justice, newly created under the Constitution. Today he began reorganizing the whole legal profession of the country into voluntary associations, which will give legal aid to any accused persons demanding their services. Any accused person is entitled to free legal counsel if he desires. Legal aid offices are also being established by trade unions.

Because of the new legal guarantees many more lawyers than hitherto will be needed. Accordingly steps are being taken to enroll thousands more students in the law schools already established, and plans are being formed for the creation of many more schools in the various republics.

BALDWIN TELLS OF EVENTS

Relates to the Commons How He Warned King Against Marriage.

DENIES ANY BITTERNESS

Says Ruler, Far From Feeling Resentment, Had Become a Firmer Friend to Him.

LEGAL ISSUE IS REFUTED

Churchill Declares It Is Now Clear That There Was Never a Constitutional Crisis.

By CHARLES A. SELDEN

Special Cable to THE NEW YORK TIMES.

LONDON, Dec. 10.—The momentous session of Parliament that received today King Edward's message of abdication was best described by Prime Minister Stanley Baldwin himself when he said near the close of his narrative of the crisis:

"This House of Commons today is a theatre which is being watched by the whole world."

Never since the first British Parliament was called by Simon de Montfort 672 years ago had it been the theatre for such an impressive tragedy as that enacted today.

There have been greater political issues, perhaps, and more fateful struggles between Crown and Commons. There have been long Parliaments, short Parliaments and rump Parliaments. But there has been no precedent for today's enactment of the tragedy in which a monarch signed away his sovereignty over an empire of 500,000,000 people for his love of a woman.

And while the play was on, the wars of one hemisphere and the efforts in the other hemisphere to end wars were merely side shows.

Extra Police on Hand

Standing room only was the situation in the legislative chamber itself, while there was not even standing room left in the acres of lobbies and for many blocks outside on the streets that lead to the Houses of Parliament.

So many extra companies of police were assigned to duty around the buildings that it was feared serious disorder was anticipated by the authorities, but nothing could have been further from the fact. There was as much decorum in witnessing this self-effacement of Edward VIII as there was last January when the multitudes gathered to mourn for his father and to proclaim him.

Needless to say, the House itself was filled as it had not been since the session at which war was declared in 1914. In the diplomatic gallery, every seat was taken by Ambassadors and Ministers from nearly all nations.

What little daylight sometimes seeps into the Commons chamber on a Winter afternoon was completely shut out by a dense fog, so there was nothing but mellow illumination from the lights above the stained glass ceiling.

House Is Ill at Ease

The House was ill at ease during the hour's interval prior to the great moment when Prime Minister Baldwin entered with the King's message of abdication. The familiar cry, "Prayers are over," after the customary, brief devotional exercise with which every session opens, was followed by many involuntary, at least unusual, "Amens," suggestive of a devout wish that for this once they might be answered quickly.

There were no "King's men" in this House. But it was equally true there were no anti-King men.

The King's own message was received with sorrow and sympathy. When Mr. Baldwin made his long statement of the events that preceded the decision to abandon the throne, there vanished the last trace of the bitterness that had developed in the last week from fear that the Crown might try to override the Commons.

"We are not judges," said Mr. Baldwin, and it was one of his utterances to which members gave their warmest assent.

"While there is not a soul among us who will not regret this from the bottom of his heart," said the

Continued on Page Sixteen

Associated Press Photo.

SUCCESSOR TO THE BRITISH THRONE
The Duke of York

YORK GETS OVATION AT HOME IN LONDON

Cheering and Singing Theatre Crowds Surge About His Car While Auto Horns Salute.

HE DOFFS HAT TO THRONG

New Monarch Expected to Use Name 'George' as Symbol of Strength and Steadiness.

Special Cable to THE NEW YORK TIMES.

LONDON, Dec. 10.—Thousands of Londoners shouted a welcome tonight to a shy and awkward young man who was ready to step into the dazzling light of the greatest throne on earth.

With the abdication of King Edward VIII, the 41-year-old Duke of York was about to take his place on the world wide stage as the latest in the long line of English sovereigns. And tonight, in front of his town house at 145 Piccadilly, the crowds had their first chance to show him that they were glad.

A surging throng of theatre-goers on the way home surrounded his car as he returned after having dinner with Edward at Fort Belvedere. Cheering and waving hats, they filled the wide roadway in front of the house and blocked traffic so completely police were powerless to keep it moving.

Before the Duke entered the house he turned to the crowd and raised his hat several times. That was the signal for a great demonstration. Hundreds of motorists set up a deafening salute with their horns, while the crowd began singing the national anthem and "For He's a Jolly Good Fellow."

Popular Reign Indicated

It was a demonstration of some importance in the story of the British throne, for it showed that the Duke may be a popular King even without any of the brilliant qualities of his elder brother.

Tomorrow night he will become King, and Saturday morning his accession will be proclaimed with the stately pageantry that has come down unchanged from medieval times. For individual kings may come and go, but the British monarchy that has survived many shocks before this will keep its place as the keystone of the vast and loosely jointed empire.

Heralds in uniforms of gold will

Continued on Page Eighteen

EDWARD CHEERFUL AFTER TAKING STEP

Reported Like Man Who Has Had Crushing Load of Worry Lifted From Shoulders.

PACKS FOR HIS DEPARTURE

Knowledge That He Will Not Be Barred From Returning to England Relieves Him.

By FERDINAND KUHN Jr.

Wireless to THE NEW YORK TIMES.

LONDON, Dec. 10.—The blue and white flag of the Duchy of Cornwall fluttered slowly to the foot of its mast at 10 o'clock this morning on the high turret over Fort Belvedere.

It was a signal that made history, for at that moment King Edward was renouncing the greatest throne on earth so that he could marry the woman he loved. With his three brothers as his only witnesses, he signed the instrument of abdication as his "final and irrevocable decision" to retire into private life.

He will remain King until tomorrow afternoon, when the Abdication Bill is expected to reach him from Parliament. As soon as he signs it, however, his unhappy days as King will come to an end after the shortest reign in 453 years. The Duke of York will come to the throne as George VI and Edward will leave England as the first man in all the 1,000 years of the British monarchy to have left the throne of his own accord.

Edward Again Cheerful

Although he has not shown himself to the public for almost a week, it was reported on good authority tonight that he was like a man who had had a crushing load of worry lifted from his shoulders.

The depression and jumpiness of the last few days had vanished and the King was said to be cheerful and purposeful, superintending the packing of his belongings, dealing with State papers, which arrived incessantly from London, and looking forward to more happiness than he has known in a long time.

Workmen and tractors were busy all day on Edward's private flying field at Smith's Lawn in Windsor Great Park, apparently preparing it for the take-off of an important airplane. Four police cars were on duty and a cordon of police and

Continued on Page Sixteen

KING MAKES HIS DECISION

Chooses Woman Over Throne After 'Long and Anxious' Thought.

FINALE LIKELY TOMORROW

New Reign, Expected to Bring Back Calm of George V's, Is to Be Proclaimed Then.

CROWNING PLAN MAY HOLD

Edward Can Use Either of Two Titles, Earl of Rothesay or Baron of Renfrew.

Edward's letter, the Abdication Bill, Baldwin's speech, Page 17.

By FREDERICK T. BIRCHALL

Special Cable to THE NEW YORK TIMES.

LONDON, Dec. 10.—Some time Saturday morning, perhaps even as soon as tomorrow night, Edward VIII will cease to be a King and Emperor. He has made his choice between a woman and a throne and the woman has won.

Today at Fort Belvedere, his country home near Windsor Castle, and in the presence of his three brothers, the Dukes of York, Gloucester and Kent, the King signed a message to his Ministers announcing his determination "after long and anxious consideration" to renounce the throne to which he had succeeded on the death of his father. This, said the message, is "my final and irrevocable decision."

The message was carried by Prime Minister Stanley Baldwin this afternoon to a crowded session of the House of Commons and there read, not without emotion, by the Speaker.

Bill Introduced in House

There is no question of whether the House should accept it. Under the British Constitution there can be none, for it was an expression of the King's will and the King rules, though he does not govern, Britain and the empire. But immediately afterward, as soon as the Prime Minister in a speech that will be memorable for the restrained feeling it expressed and the leaders of the Opposition each after his fashion had voiced their regret, a bill was introduced that will implement the monarch's decision.

Tomorrow this formal bill of abdication will be rushed through all its stages in both houses, Commons and Lords. It will then be carried to the King for his royal assent. The moment he signs it he ceases to be King and his brother, the Duke of York, who is nearest to him, will reign in his stead.

The new King will take the throne, according to the best information available tonight, as George VI and for that choice there is a reason. It is desired, now that this storm is over and the skies are clearing, to get back to the ordered peace and quiet stability of the monarchy under the last King George, to leave behind this brief era of conflict between will and duty and to concentrate anew on the empire and its common destiny.

Proclamation Likely Tomorrow

Another era will begin probably at noon on Saturday when the accession of the new King is proclaimed from the balcony of St. James's Palace, again at old gray Charing Cross and finally from the steps of the Royal Exchange in the City of London, each time with all the pomp and ceremony that the monarchy has upheld here throughout a thousand years. Kings may change but the old order remaineth; that is to be Britain's watchword still.

And thus, in circumstances that will arouse wonder and pity as long as history continues to be written, ends the brief reign of King Edward VIII. It has lasted ten months and twenty-two days before this strange storm that love of woman created has brought it to a close, and the empire still endures. Even a newcomer can

Continued on Page Sixteen

"All the News That's Fit to Print."

The New York Times.

THE WEATHER
Fair today and tomorrow; warmer tomorrow; moderate winds.
Temperature yesterday—Max. 70, min. 60.
For weather report see Page 34.

VOL. LXXXVI....No. 28,813. | Entered as Second-Class Matter, Postoffice, New York, N. Y. | NEW YORK, SUNDAY, DECEMBER 13, 1936. | Including Rotogravure Picture, Magazine and Book Review. | PP | TEN CENTS | TWELVE CENTS Beyond 200 Miles Except in 7th and 8th Postal Zones.

GEORGE VI PROCLAIMED KING; EDWARD ON TRAIN FOR VIENNA; HE WILL BE DUKE OF WINDSOR

ANCIENT RITUAL ENACTED

Hundreds of Thousands Mass as New Reign Is Opened by Pageantry.

QUEEN MARY A SPECTATOR

She Looks On as News of Her Son's Sovereignty Is Read to Throngs in Drizzle.

RULER RECEIVES FEALTY

Accession Is Heralded in All the Land—Coronation Date Remains May 12, 1937.

By FREDERICK T. BIRCHALL
Special Cable to THE NEW YORK TIMES.

LONDON, Dec. 12.—Under a gray sky and amid a mild drizzle characteristic of London in mid-December, a new régime, which is in a measure nothing more than a return to the old order of things, began in Great Britain today with the proclamation of George VI as King and Emperor.

It was initiated under the old forms observed in the case of the preceding monarch less than a year ago, but it was ushered in in a different spirit. The reign of Edward VIII was ushered in last January with a popular ebullience that was lacking today.

This was a more sober inauguration of the King-Emperor, despite the absence of mourning attire that characterized the previous one. It was obvious that the countless thousands who gathered about the scenes of the proclamation were thinking hard—thinking and hoping after a great disappointment.

Council Takes New Oath

But otherwise little was changed. The Accession Council, comprising the 300 members of the King's Privy Council, reinforced by the Lord Mayor, Aldermen and Sheriffs of the City of London, assembled this morning in the Throne Room in St. James Palace, all in full panoply of office, and the new King, in naval uniform, appeared before them. He walked to his place by the great crimson and gold throne and those present took their oaths of allegiance to him in his presence.

In his turn the King made his initial declaration. Then he subscribed, as is customary, to the oath for the security of the Church of Scotland.

Finally the council adopted the accession proclamation and the King signified his assent to its promulgation [The texts of the proclamation and the King's response appear in the adjoining columns.]

The signatures of those present, beginning with the Duke of Gloucester and the other royal Princes, were appended.

Hundreds of Thousands Gather

Hundreds of thousands of persons meantime were massing around St. James's Palace, along the Mall, at Charing Cross and down the Strand, Fleet Street and Cheapside as far as the Royal Exchange to hear the Accession Proclamation and see the heralds who came in procession to make it.

Along the route were lined 30,000 troops, comprising battalions of Foot Guards, some of Highlanders and a selection of regiments of the line to help the police to keep the roadway clear. In Pall Mall at one stage the crowd broke through the police lines and guards had to assist in restoring the cordon.

Another great crowd had waited outside the new King's home in Piccadilly to cheer him when he emerged to attend the Privy Council. It patiently stood there afterward until his return.

At 3 o'clock Sir Gerald Wollaston, the Garter Principal King of Arms, walked out on the floodlighted balcony of old St. James's Palace overlooking Friary Court, followed by pursuivants and heralds of the realm and their trumpeters. The trumpets sounded a fanfare and the Garter Principal King of Arms read the proclamation, ending with a resonant: "God save the King!" The troops below came to present arms, the massed bands played the national anthem and the crowd joined in singing it with a will.

Behind the closed windows of

Continued on Page Forty-eight

Accession Proclamation

Wireless to THE NEW YORK TIMES.

LONDON, Dec. 12.—The texts of the Accession Council's proclamation today declaring George VI King and of his initial declaration follow:

Whereas, by an Instrument of Abdication dated the Tenth day of December, instant, His former Majesty, King Edward the Eighth, did declare it his irrevocable determination to renounce the throne for himself and his descendants, and the said Instrument of Abdication has now taken effect, whereby the Imperial Crown of Great Britain, Ireland and all other of His former Majesty's Dominions is now solely and rightfully come to the High and Mighty Prince Albert Frederick Arthur George:

We, therefore, the Lords Spiritual and Temporal of this realm, being here assisted with these of His former Majesty's Privy Council, with numbers of other Principal Gentlemen of Quality, with the Lord Mayor, Alderman and citizens of London, do now hereby with one voice and consent of tongue and heart publish and proclaim that the High and Mighty Prince Albert Frederick Arthur George is now become our only lawful and rightful Liege Lord, George the Sixth, by the Grace of God, of Great Britain, Ireland and the British Dominions Beyond the Seas King, Defender of the Faith, Emperor of India:

To whom we do acknowledge all faith and constant obedience with all hearty and humble affection: Beseeching God, by whom Kings and Queens do reign, to bless Royal Prince George the Sixth with long and happy years to reign over us.

Given at St. James's Palace this twelfth day of December in the Year of Our Lord One Thousand Nine Hundred and Thirty-six.

King George's Declaration

I meet you today in circumstances which are without parallel in the history of our country. Now that the duties of sovereignty have fallen on me, I declare to you my adherence to the strict principles of constitutional government and my resolve to work before all else for the welfare of the British Commonwealth of Nations.

With my wife as helpmeet by my side, I take up the heavy task which lies before me. In it I look for the support of all my peoples.

Furthermore, my first act on succeeding my brother will be to confer on him a dukedom, and he will henceforth be known as His Royal Highness, the Duke of Windsor.

EDWARD REACHES FRANCE ON WARSHIP

Transfers to Train Under Heavy Guard at Boulogne—Bars All Visitors.

HE MAY GO TO INNSBRUCK

Vienna Expects Him Today and Believes He May Visit Tyrol for Winter Sports.

By P. J. PHILIP
Wireless to THE NEW YORK TIMES.

PARIS, Dec. 12.—While his brother was being proclaimed King-Emperor in London with all the time-honored ceremony with which he himself succeeded to the throne less than a year ago, the Duke of Windsor, formerly Edward VIII, landed in France this afternoon to begin his self-imposed exile.

On the destroyer Fury, on which he embarked at Portsmouth last night, he reached Boulogne this afternoon at 4 o'clock and from there this evening took a train for Basle and some unannounced destination in Switzerland, Italy or Austria.

Previously it had been supposed the Duke was aboard the Admiralty cruiser Enchantress.

[Edward's immediate destination was Vienna, train officials told The Associated Press. It was reported in the Austrian capital he was going to Innsbruck.]

Boards Train After Dark

It was dark when the party left the destroyer to board a special railway coach which waited at the dockside.

The Duke of Windsor, wearing a gray suit and a dark overcoat and derby, was accompanied by his equerry, Lieut. Col. Piers Leigh, and by a valet leading the Duke's small terrier.

Five French Sûreté agents went aboard the special coach, occupying four of the eight compartments.

Several French officials, including the Mayor of Boulogne and the Subprefect, saluted the former King as he boarded the train.

Just as the train pulled out, several news men succeeded in breaking through the police lines and boarding other cars. They were unable to gain access to the Duke's coach.

When the train stopped at Amiens at 9:25, a large force of police was drawn up at the station and surrounded the Duke's coach on both

Continued on Page Forty-eight.

FREE STATE ACCORD WITH BRITAIN SEEN

London Is Pleased by Dublin's Intention to Stay Within the Commonwealth.

NEW LEGISLATION HAILED

No Resentment Expressed at Abolition of Last Pretense of King's Prerogatives.

Wireless to THE NEW YORK TIMES.

LONDON, Dec. 12.—The British people noticed for the first time today that something important and immensely encouraging had happened across the Irish Sea while they were immersed in their crisis over the monarchy.

Officials here rubbed their eyes, then smiled as they read the news of the constitutional changes in the Irish Free State which passed the Dail Eireann this afternoon. For although the Irish have abolished the last pretense of the King's prerogatives they have chosen of their own free will to stay within the British Commonwealth and accept George VI as their King.

This, at least, is London's interpretation of what President Eamon de Valera has just done during the constitutional crisis in the empire. It may turn out to be one of the

Continued on Page Forty-eight

Pact for American Peace Ratified by Parley Chiefs

Final Approval Sure After Unanimous Vote by the Committee on Two Measures—Hull Hails First Major Step.

By HAROLD B. HINTON
Special Cable to THE NEW YORK TIMES.

BUENOS AIRES, Dec. 12.—In an emotional, excited atmosphere reminiscent of a really inspired religious revival meeting, the Inter-American Conference for the Maintenance of Peace took today its first important step toward trying to assure the Western Hemisphere against any threats of war from within or without.

A hastily summoned session of the standing Committee on Organization of Peace, at which most countries were represented by their Foreign Ministers, unanimously adopted favorable reports on conventions for maintenance, preservation and re-establishment of peace and on non-intervention.

Since both measures had been introduced in the name of all the twenty-one nations represented here, the committee's action was a foregone conclusion, as is adoption by the plenary conference, which will probably act Tuesday.

Secretary of State Cordell Hull, in a radio speech tonight, described the day's events as "most enheartening progress in formulating concrete proposals for enduring inter-American peace."

[The text of the radio speech by Secretary Hull is on Page 43.]

In addition to the two instruments approved by the committee today, another convention coordinating existing treaties between American States and extending them in some respects was introduced with the same unanimous backing and will go through the standing Committee on Neutrality with equal ease, probably Monday.

The more important of the two conventions whose adoption was assured today may be described as a collective security pact. While obligations would be limited to consultation and peaceful cooperation in the event that the "peace of American republics should be threatened," the intent of the instrument is understood, by Latin-American delegates at least, as a demonstration of American solidarity in a world where war threats are only too abundant.

The instrument would provide for mutual consultation in case of war between American States, and equally in the case of international war outside that might menace the peace of American republics.

While this draft convention carries out ideas of the original United States neutrality proposal which was junked in favor of the concerted proposal approved today, the

Continued on Page Forty-two

BILL FOR NEW NRA PLANNED BY BERRY FOR QUICK ACTION

Measures Urged by Industrial Progress Council Will Be Drafted This Week.

CONSTITUTIONAL LAW AIM

Committee Will Try to Fit It to Supreme Court View—Census of Idle Sought.

Special to THE NEW YORK TIMES.

WASHINGTON, Dec. 12.—A draft of proposed legislation which would embody the three-point program for industry as adopted yesterday by the Council for Industrial Progress will be started within the next week, according to George L. Berry, the President's Coordinator for Industrial Cooperation.

Included in the council's recommendations are a revised NRA, favorable to the "little man," amendments to the anti-trust laws to make them more workable and a system of Federally guaranteed loans to small businesses along the lines prescribed in the Federal Housing Act for assistance to home owners.

Mr. Berry hopes to have bills for carrying out these objectives ready for presentation to President Roosevelt soon after he returns from South America. Whether he will turn them over to the President as suggestions in formulating his own program for business legislation or he and the council will seek to push them as independent measures at the forthcoming session of Congress is a question which Mr. Berry was not prepared to answer today.

In addition to the specific legislative recommendations Mr. Berry will transmit to the President a

Continued on Page Thirty

LEFTIST SUBMARINE SUNK OFF MALAGA; 47 OF CREW LOST

C-3 Is Torpedoed by Another Undersea Craft, 'Evidently Foreign,' Valencia Reports.

MEDIATION NOW OPPOSED

Madrid's Defenders Insist Upon Peace With Victory—League Sidetracks Spanish Issue.

By The Associated Press.

VALENCIA, Spain, Dec. 12.—The Ministry of Marine of the Leftist government issued a communiqué tonight saying that its submarine C-3 had been torpedoed and sunk. The C-3, the Ministry asserted, was torpedoed by another submarine, "evidently foreign."

The Spanish craft was said to have gone down with forty-seven of her crew aboard, off Malaga, seaport on the southern coast of Spain, near the Straits of Gibraltar.

As far as was known, officials said, only the submarine's captain, Agustin Garcia, and two seamen were saved. They were reported picked up later by the vessel Artabro.

Vessel Was Built in 1928

The C-3 was built at Cartagena, chief naval arsenal of Spain, in 1928. Her displacement was 915 tons on the surface and 1,290 tons submerged. She was 247 feet long.

With two sets of eight-cylinder Diesel engines delivering 2,000 horsepower, the vessel had a speed of sixteen knots on the surface and eight and one-half knots when submerged.

Her armament consisted of one 3-inch anti-aircraft gun and six 21-inch torpedo tubes, four in the bow and two in the stern.

Madrid Cool to Mediation

By HERBERT L. MATTHEWS
Wireless to THE NEW YORK TIMES.

MADRID, Dec. 12.—The present session of the Council of the League of Nations at Geneva and the Anglo-French effort to mediate the Spanish conflict have stirred very definite reactions here, but they are all unfavorable. There is certainly a great desire for peace, but only for peace with victory.

A month ago it might have been different, but the government and particularly those who are conducting the military side of the war feel that they have turned the tables on the Insurgents and will win sooner or later. Such being the case, they see no reason to accept any solution except complete capitulation by the Rebels.

The government has indicated clearly that it would favor any effort to prevent interference by foreign countries in the civil war, but in view of past performances little hope is held that anything constructive will be accomplished.

The newspaper Liberal declares ominously:

"Even if Franco [Generalissimo

Continued on Page Forty.

Roosevelt Catches 34 Fish in Three Hours; Presidential Flotilla Then Heads for U. S.

By The Associated Press.

WITH PRESIDENT ROOSEVELT AT SEA, Dec. 12.—President Roosevelt found a rich fishing spot today, close to tiny Bird Island in the Caribbean, about 350 miles north of Trinidad.

He caught thirty-four fish in three hours, including pompano, barracuda and other varieties.

Mr. Roosevelt had splendid weather and the smoothest water of the entire trip when he put over the side of the cruiser Indianapolis in a whaler to try his luck.

The fishing expedition, four boats in all, carrying other members of the Presidential party, left the Indianapolis and the Chester, its convoy cruiser, at 7:15 A. M., after the earliest breakfast on the whole South American voyage.

The fishermen were able to see "those that got away" swimming on the ocean floor under 25 feet of clear blue water.

The President wore his oldest fishing togs and appeared to enjoy one of the most restful days of his post-election vacation and peace mission.

The Presidential flotilla steamed northward again tonight. Its course was to be by way of the Bahamas to Charleston, S. C., where it was due Tuesday morning.

A long-rehearsed musical comedy was given tonight on the Indianapolis, with the President and his party in the audience.

During the day Mr. Roosevelt worked on two pouches of mail taken aboard yesterday at Trinidad. The destroyer Phelps met the party at Bird Island this morning and took off signed mail to be air-mailed to Washington from San Juan, P. R.

CHIANG KAI-SHEK IS PRISONER OF MUTINOUS SHENSI TROOPS, DEMANDING WAR ON JAPAN

Tokyo Sees Danger in Chinese Rebellion; Officials Anxiously Await Next Move by Foe

By The Associated Press.

TOKYO, Sunday, Dec. 13.—The seizing of Generalissimo Chiang Kai-shek by anti-Japanese rebels in China is considered here to have thrown the whole Far Eastern situation into confusion, the outcome of which it is impossible to foresee. Official quarters said the Japanese Government was most gravely concerned about immediate developments and possible future consequences of General Chang Hsueh-liang's rebellion. Official comment, however, was withheld until the situation becomes clearer.

Coming so soon after the recent conflict on the borders of Suiyuan and Chahar Provinces, in which Chinese troops loyal to General Chiang repulsed Mongol and Manchukuoan irregulars aided by Japanese military, the virtual kidnapping of the Chinese generalissimo by his subordinate shocked Tokyo.

Recently General Chiang has been trying—hitherto successfully—to re-establish Nanking's authority in the Northwest. An important point in this campaign was the elimination of General Chang, whose loyalty to General Chiang and the Nanking government had been gravely questioned, especially since his troops were reported fraternizing with the Chinese Communists they were supposd to fight.

The generalissimo had intended, it was believed, to surround General Chang's forces with troops loyal to himself. The necessity of reinforcing the loyal Suiyuan provincial levies fighting the Mongol-Manchukuoan invaders caused postponement of this plan. The growing insubordination of General Chang and his followers was known to the generalissimo, who arrived at Sian earlier this week by air to take drastic action to suppress the incipient rebellion.

The uprising followed yesterday. Along with the generalissimo the rebels captured several of his highest aides, including General Cheng Chen, his chief of staff and right-hand man; General Yu Hsueh-chung, the Governor of Kansu Province; General Chiang Tso-pin, former Ambassador to Japan and high in the Nanking government, and others.

MANCHURIAN IN REVOLT

Chang Hsueh-liang for Return of Communists to Nanking Regime.

LOST TERRITORY SOUGHT

Generalissimo Seized in Midst of Preparations to Discipline Those Friendly With Reds.

NANKING MOVES SWIFTLY

Names Leader for Armies in Field—New Risings Feared—Students Plead for War.

By HALLETT ABEND
Wireless to THE NEW YORK TIMES.

SHANGHAI, Sunday, Dec. 13.—Generalissimo Chiang Kai-shek has been seized by General Chang Hsueh-liang in Shensi Province in an effort to force the Nanking Government to declare war against Japan.

General Chang, former Manchurian commander, guaranteed the life of the generalissimo in a telegram to military leaders throughout China. The telegram also carried these demands:

1. An immediate declaration of war against Japan.
2. A pledge by the Nanking government to recover all lost territories, including Manchuria.
3. Reorganization of the Kuomintang [Nationalist party] to readmit Communists to membership on the basis existing before the anti-Communist purge began in 1927.

Seizure Follows Mutiny

The arrest of Generalissimo Chiang followed a mutiny yesterday at Sian, the capital of Shensi Province. Part of the former Manchurian forces commanded by General Chang Hsueh-liang and part of the Shensi provincial troops commanded by General Yang Fu-cheng mutinied and presented demands for immediate cooperation with the Chinese Communists and military action to stop Japan's encroachments on China's territorial and administrative integrity.

Following the mutiny General Chang, his executive officers and General Yang sent an urgent telegram to the Executive Yuan at Nanking advocating cooperation with the Communists and formal approval of a policy of armed resistance to Japan.

When the mutiny started the generalissimo was resting at the hot springs twenty miles from Sian. When informed of the turmoil in the provincial capital he disregarded personal danger and hastened there, hoping to regain control.

Nanking Acts Swiftly

The central government moved swiftly to cope with what was admitted to be a large-scale revolt. A joint all-night meeting of the standing committee of the Central Executive Committee and the Political Council in Nanking decided on four important measures:

First—The Executive Yuan, with Finance Minister H. H. Kung as vice chairman, received full responsibility during the detention of the chairman, Generalissimo Chiang.

Second—The standing committee of the National Military Council was increased to include General Ho Ying-ching, the War Minister; General Chen Chien, the chief of staff, and Generals Li Lih-chun, Chu Pei-teh and Tang Sheng-chih and Admiral Chen Shao-kwan, the Navy Minister.

Third—Responsibility for the conduct of affairs of the National Military Council, of which Generalissimo Chiang is chairman, was given to General Feng Yu-hsiang, the vice chairman, and the other members.

Fourth—Movement of the armies in the field was entrusted to the command of General Ho Ying-ching.

General Chang Hsueh-liang was dismissed from all government and military posts. Punishment by the National Military Council was recommended. The council was instructed to assume command over

Continued on Page Thirty-eight

LA FOLLETTE MOVES TO OUST DR. FRANK

Wisconsin Governor Calls Regents of University to Act on President's Removal.

HE WITHHOLDS DECISION

Political Differences and Alleged Radicalism Are Factors in the Strife.

Special to THE NEW YORK TIMES.

MADISON, Wis., Dec. 12.—An effort to force the dismissal of Dr. Glenn Frank from the presidency of the University of Wisconsin has been renewed by the Wisconsin Progressive party, headed by Governor Philip F. La Follette.

The board of regents, dominated by a majority composed of La Follette appointees, has been summoned to attend a special session on Wednesday to approve a statement of legislative budget requests and to act on proposals for the dismissal of President Frank.

Governor La Follette called to his office on Monday Harold M. Wilkie of Madison, president of the regents, and Clough Gates of Superior, also on the board, and, according to some reports, told them to speed up the dismissal action.

The regents met the following day and Wilkie and Gates conferred for nearly two hours behind locked doors with Dr. Frank.

Told to Retire Quietly

Reports published here stated that at the conference Dr. Frank was told to retire quietly or face outright dismissal. He was reported to have agreed to forego a controversy, but when he was asked whether he had agreed to resign, he replied:

"That is news to me."

He has refused to make any other comment.

On the day of the conference, the regents met in open session and instructed Wilkie to prepare a statement of budget needs to be presented to the Governor Thursday and later to the Legislature.

This action was at variance with the practice of recent years. In the past the president of the university has conferred with the deans and department heads, has prepared a budget, submitted it to the regents for approval and has then taken it to the Governor and the Legislature.

By their action last week, the regents gave notice to Dr. Frank that he may make whatever budget statement he chooses to the Governor, but that they will make their own statement, independent of his.

When Gates was asked if that meant that Dr. Frank's statement would be a personal one, not representing the university, his reply was "yes."

Verified reports point clearly to

Continued on Page Three

SEIZED AS FUGITIVE FROM GUILLOTINE

Pier Worker Held as Suspect Who Killed Two and Fled France After Sentence.

ARRESTED IN PARKED CAR

Denies He Ever Was in France, but Description Tallies With the Man Wanted.

Charged with being a fugitive from justice from France, whence he escaped in 1924 after being sentenced to be guillotined for the murder of two men, a 42-year-old longshoreman was arrested yesterday afternoon as he sat in his parked automobile in front of the Supreme Court Building in Foley Square.

The arrest, which ended a month's search for the prisoner, was made after the police had received an application for an extradition warrant from the State Department in Washington. The application was issued on the request of André de Laboulaye, French Ambassador.

The application was accompanied by a letter from the French authorities in Washington which said that a man known as Gennero Caputo, who used the alias of John Caputo, a native of France, and who had been sentenced to death for murder by the Court of Assizes of Bouche-du-Rhone on Jan. 31, 1924, was believed to be in the city. The letter gave a description of the fugitive.

When the communication was received by Assistant Chief Inspector John A. Lyons, he assigned Detectives Edward Fitzgerald, George McNulty and Charles Dinegar to the case. McNulty remembered that a man whose last name was Caputo and resembling the descriptions had been taken into custody for questioning by the customs authorities on Nov. 18 in connection with illegal narcotic activities, but had been freed the same day.

Haunt the Waterfront

For more than a month the three haunted the waterfront gathering places for their suspect, but until yesterday they were unsuccessful. Shortly before noon yesterday they saw their quarry—the man who had been questioned by the Customs authorities, who then said he was John Caputo, 42 years old, of 9 Second Street, Brooklyn.

Caputo was sitting in his automobile at James Slip on the East Side waterfront. The detectives followed him while he drove his car to Foley Square, where he again parked for about an hour and a half. After watching him for that time the detectives approached and made the arrest.

According to the police, Caputo said he was born in California. He

Continued on Page Twenty-six

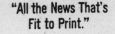

"All the News That's Fit to Print."

The New York Times.

LATE CITY EDITION
Occasional rain and warmer today. Tomorrow partly cloudy, mild temperatures, possible rain.
Temperatures Yesterday—Max., 44; Min., 35

Copyright, 1936, by The New York Times Company.

VOL. LXXXVI....No. 28,830. Entered as Second-Class Matter, Postoffice, New York, N. Y. NEW YORK, WEDNESDAY, DECEMBER 30, 1936. P TWO CENTS In New York City. | THREE CENTS Within 200 Miles. | FOUR CENTS Elsewhere Except in 7th and 8th Postal Zones.

NEUTRALITY LAW REVISION IS SPEEDED BY PRESIDENT TO HALT ARMS FOR SPAIN

LICENSEE IS SCORED

Sending Planes Is Legal but Unpatriotic Step, Says Roosevelt.

PITTMAN STUDYING BILL

Committee to Draft Measure Making Act Cover Civil Wars —Leaders Approve Idea.

REBELS OPEN NEW DRIVE

Use Most of Their Germans in Attack in Cordoba Sector— Madrid Front Still Quiet.

The Spanish Situation

WASHINGTON—President Roosevelt favored extension of the neutrality law to prevent shipments of arms to belligerents in civil wars. He denounced the sale of American airplanes and engines to the Spanish Government.

BERLIN — A German cruiser forced the release of the freighter Palos by the Loyalists at Bilbao, but demanded also that a "guest" Spaniard and arms taken from the vessel should be given up. Page 1.

PARIS—Resentment against their German allies on the part of the Rebels was reported as authorities heard Berlin was trying to align Italy and Portugal against Britain and France. Page 13.

LONDON—Officials were relieved on learning the United States would probably forbid the shipment of arms to Spain. Page 12.

MADRID—A Rebel drive, aided by Germans, has begun in Southern Spain with the apparent object of cutting off Madrid from the sea. Page 13.

Neutrality Law to Be Changed

Special to THE NEW YORK TIMES.

WASHINGTON, Dec. 29.—President Roosevelt gave his approval today to plans of legislative leaders to have enacted immediately after Congress convenes next week an amendment to the Neutrality Act extending it to Spain and, with certain discretionary features, to all other countries where internal strife occurs.

In making this clear at his press conference today Mr. Roosevelt denounced the action of Robert Cuse of Jersey City in insisting upon obtaining a license from the State Department to export to the Loyalist government in Spain $2,777,000 worth of airplanes, engines and parts.

It was a thoroughly legal but unpatriotic act, the President said, and one concerning which he felt very strongly. He declared it represented the attitude of 10 per cent or less of the business community in this country that did not hesitate to act unethically, whereas the other 90 per cent or more wanted to act ethically and patriotically.

The assertion of Mr. Cuse today that the order would provide employment for Americans, Mr. Roosevelt declared, is similar to arguments made in behalf of the munitions business during the World War, and does not make the move by Mr. Cuse the right thing to do.

Pittman Calls Committee

Earlier, Senator Key Pittman, chairman of the Foreign Relations Committee, called a meeting of this committee for Jan. 6 to consider an amendment, which he will draft in cooperation with the State Department, to extend the Neutrality Act to countries in which civil war prevails, with special reference to the Spanish situation. His plan met with general approval among Congressional leaders.

The situation aroused intense interest today among members of Congress assembling for the opening next week. Senator William E. Borah and others who have advocated strong neutrality laws asked swift action to close the loophole in the present law. Even conservative members were not hesitant in denouncing the sale of airplanes to the Spanish Loyalists by an American as an unpatriotic act and one that naturally would encourage other countries to continue their

Continued on Page Thirteen

Blind Musician, Groping in Subway, Miscounts Steps, Is Killed by Train

'Nobody Offered to Help Us; as a Rule Somebody Does,' Says Companion, Saved From Death by Friend's Cry—34-Year-Old Accordion Player Was on Way Home to Wife and 3 Children.

By MEYER BERGER

The sixth sense that had preserved Oscar England from harm through the thirty-four dark years of his life betrayed him yesterday. One step too many in the B. M. T. Union Square station and he was wedged, lifeless, between a northbound express and the concrete platform.

His cry, as he was torn from the grip of James Sumners, fellow musician in a blind men's orchestra, prevented a second death. Pale and frightened, Sumners backed away, until some one led him to the center of the platform.

Last night, in that part of the Bushwick district of Brooklyn where Broadway's blind musicians have a little colony of their own, the sightless players tapped their way from door to door to discuss in low tones the tragedy of one of their band.

Sumners, a clean-cut man about England's age, still showed signs of nervous shock as he sat in a deep armchair in the spotless parlor of his home at 257 Cooper Street. His fingers laced and interlaced and his facial muscles worked.

"Nobody offered to help us," he said, brokenly. "As a rule, somebody does. We've been through that subway—all the subways—over and over again."

He could not quite understand how the accident happened. He seemed bewildered.

"Fewer blind people are killed in that way than normal people," he said, in answer to a question, "even in proportion to their number. Please don't ask me any more. When your best friend goes and you've known him thirty years"—

England, blind since babyhood after an attack of smallpox; Sumners and Ray Dinsmore, who lives at 282 Cooper Street, usually rode in the subways together because they lived in the same district and were all members of the Capitol Dance Orchestra.

England with his accordion, Sumners with his banjo and Dinsmore with his saxophone, were familiar figures on Broadway until they got on the radio through a WPA music project. England earned $23.75 a week as his share. None of his friends could say last night what will happen now to Lelah, his wife, and their three children.

The orchestra has broadcast sev-

Continued on Page Four

GERMAN FREIGHTER IS FREED BY SPAIN

But Loyalists Refuse to Meet Cruiser's Demand for All of Cargo and a Passenger.

NAZI CHIEFS MEET TODAY

Hitler Aides to Discuss Reply to Franco-British Plea for Ban on Aid to Civil War.

By FREDERICK T. BIRCHALL

Wireless to THE NEW YORK TIMES.

BERLIN, Dec. 29.—The German Government announced through its official news agency today a partial victory in Spain in these terms:

"The German steamer Palos has been released on the demand of the cruiser Koenigsberg and has continued her voyage. However, the Spanish citizen aboard the ship, and therefore on German sovereign territory, as well as part of the ship's cargo, has been retained. A complete settlement of the matter therefore is still to be made."

It is worth noting that this announcement was printed in newspapers here almost inconspicuously and no comment on it has been permitted.

In amplification of the official news it is learned that the Koenigsberg—a modern 6,000-ton cruiser with a main battery of nine 6-inch guns—appeared before the port of Bilbao with an accompanying destroyer, and her commander sent a formal demand to the port authorities for the release of the Palos.

Threat Behind the Request

The demand was not couched in the form of an ultimatum nor was any threat made as to the consequences which non-compliance might entail. Just the same, there was behind it, without any need for repetition, the notice recently sent to the Spanish naval authorities by Vice Admiral Rolf Carls, then commander of the German forces in Spanish waters:

"I have ordered my ships to meet with force every unjustified act of force on the part of yours."

Since sending that notice Vice Admiral Carls was made commander-in-chief of the German fleet, succeeding Admiral Richard Foerster. There could be no doubt, therefore, as to the significance of the message to Bilbao.

The German Government is now demanding the release of the Spaniard seized on the Palos and the return of that part of the cargo retained ashore. The seized cargo consists admittedly of war material. However, the German Government is understood to be willing to transport this back to Hamburg instead of delivering it to the Rebels, for whom it was intended.

Until the German demands are met, however, the Koenigsberg and the accompanying destroyer will

Continued on Page Thirteen

KILLS BOY IN COURT TO AVENGE HER SON

Kentucky Woman Opens Fire Just as Breathitt County Judge Starts Trial.

2 ONLOOKERS WOUNDED

Assailant Is Seized and, With Her Husband and 2 Others Near By, Is Hurried to Jail.

By The Associated Press.

JACKSON, Ky., Dec. 29.—A mountain woman, seeking to avenge the slaying of her son, loosed a burst of gunfire in Breathitt County court room today, killing the accused youth and wounding two spectators.

The pistol shots were fired at the opening of court in which in the past many men have been tried for feud killings. They fatally wounded Johnny Shepherd, 18, charged with shooting to death 17-year-old Harvey Gabbard on Christmas Eve, and sent some 150 spectators scurrying for safety.

Mrs. Viola Wickline, 35, the mother, had leaped to her feet and fired four times, according to County Attorney Alfred M. Russell, with no warning other than "shouting a vile name at Shepherd."

Shepherd, a cripple, crumpled before the trail, two bullets through his leg. George Shouse, 27, fell with a punctured lung. Moss Noble, 25, a lawyer, who at one time was on the secretarial staff of former Senator Frederic M. Sackett Jr. and was present like Shouse as a spectator, received a bullet in his leg.

One of the bullets knocked a hat from the knee of Howard Moore, another spectator, and bruised his kneecap.

Shepherd died several hours later. Shouse was expected to recover. Noble was taken home after a bullet had been removed from the muscles in his leg.

Mother Takes Full Blame

Mrs. Wickline's husband and two other persons were arrested with her after the shooting. An opinion that two women fired guns in the court room was expressed by Henry L. Spencer, attorney for Shepherd, but he identified only Mrs. Wickline.

According to Deputy Sheriff John F. Rice, Mrs. Wickline took sole blame tonight, saying "no one" aided her in the shooting. He said she "calmly voiced regret that wild shots" had wounded Noble and Shouse.

About 150 persons were in the court room when County Judge George W. Little rapped for order for the examining trial of Shepherd. Mrs. Wickline sat with her

Continued on Page Two

POPE FAILS TO GAIN; ITALIAN CHURCHES TO RECITE PRAYERS

Gloom at Vatican as Pontiff Suffers Intense Pain— X-Rays Used on Leg.

SEDATIVES HELP HIM REST

Physician Stays Near, Making Frequent Checks on the Condition of Patient.

By ARNALDO CORTESI

Wireless to THE NEW YORK TIMES.

VATICAN CITY, Dec. 29.—The papal physician, Dr. Amanti Milani, administered a sedative to his patient last midnight, and Pope Pius slept for a few hours quietly under its influence, awaking in the morning considerably refreshed. The improvement, however, was brief, for intense pain in his left leg began again shortly afterward, quickly neutralizing the benefit derived from his rest.

By the time Cardinal Pacelli, Secretary of State, went to see him—at about 10 o'clock—the Pontiff was back in about the same state as the day before. Semi-official advices from the Vatican described the Pope's condition as stationary.

But anxious observers could find little comfort in this fact, for he was so weak that every day that passed without energetic reaction against his maladies was regarded as marking a step backward. Yet reports spreading through Rome for two days that the Pontiff was rapidly sinking were categorically denied. The general impression was that he was not in immediate danger, for his constitution, though weakened, was still strong.

Electric Massage Futile

The bursting of one or more veins between the Pope's left ankle and heel was confirmed in various sources, as also was the fact that the excruciating pain he was suffering was due to an affection of a group of nerves in the leg. An attempt was made to allay the pain by electric massage, but the whole limb was so sensitive the Pope could not bear it.

It was established, moreover, that the nerve affection produced advanced muscular atrophy. X-ray treatment was applied today for the first time.

The catarrh from which the Pope also suffers, as revealed when he made the radio broadcast Christmas Eve, obliged his doctor to raise the room temperature considerably for fear that pneumonia might set in. The heat of the room produced a feeling of heaviness in the Pope and caused him to perspire freely.

Nevertheless, those around his sickbed said he bore all his afflictions with admirable fortitude, never complaining. When the leg pain became unbearable, he occasionally uttered a few groans, but never a word of complaint, they said.

The absolute immobility that the Pope has maintained for the last three weeks has not been beneficial to his blood circulation, but his heart, which in the early stages of his illness gave the doctor considerable apprehension, has behaved unexpectedly well—so well, indeed, that it has not been necessary to administer any stimulants. The Pontiff's asthma also was greatly

Continued on Page Twelve

RANSOM PAYMENT FOR MATTSON BOY IS DECLARED NEAR

Negotiations With Kidnapper Are 'Definitely Under Way,' Friend of Family Says.

RELEASE IN 12 HOURS SEEN

Note Demanding $28,000 Hints Educated Person Was Accomplice in Crime.

By The Associated Press.

TACOMA, Wash., Dec. 29.—A friend of the family declared tonight that negotiations for the return of kidnapped Charles Mattson, 10, son of Dr. W. W. Mattson, were "definitely under way" and that the $28,000 ransom would probably be paid within twelve hours.

The spokesman refused to allow his name to be used.

He said a "truce" called by Department of Justice agents searching for the boy stolen from his home here Sunday night had opened the way for negotiations between the family and the abductor.

Dr. Mattson was reported ready to pay the $28,000 ransom demand "in his own way," after refusing dozens of offers of financial aid. He lacked any such amount in cash when Charles was stolen, but had obtained it since, it was said.

Officers had stayed their activities to give the kidnapper full opportunity to return the boy safe.

Dr. Mattson and officials of The Seattle Times said they knew of no connection between the kidnapping and a classified advertisement in the newspaper which drew speculation whether it was an attempt to contact the kidnapper.

Grandparents Make Offer

The advertisement read:

"Mabel: Please give us your address. Ann."

Authorities denied all knowledge of the advertisement.

Arrival of a special delivery letter this morning at the Mattson home stirred surmise that it contained word from the kidnapper.

The boy's grandparents offered to surrender their small home and all that remains of a once sizable fortune for his safe return. His grandmother, Mrs. Charles Fletcher, appealed to the kidnapper to contact her if he feared to communicate with the boy's parents.

"No one comes here very much," she said. "It would be easy for him to come and go and no one would notice us."

She fondled a photograph of her own son and said:

"He went to France—and never came back. But this—this is so much worse.

"I'm afraid Charles is cold. He wasn't very well, you know, and he wasn't warmly dressed."

A bitter wind and freezing temperatures came to this area today.

Aid in Crime Evidenced

Special to THE NEW YORK TIMES.

TACOMA, Wash., Dec. 29.—Search for an accomplice of the man who kidnapped ten-year-old Charles Mattson and indication that the abductor had attempted to kidnap the son of another family in the fashionable Tacoma neighborhood were developments today in the na-

Continued on Page Four

Dr. Iyenaga Drowns in Fall Through Ice; Was Famous as a Diplomat and Lecturer

Special to THE NEW YORK TIMES.

ONEIDA, N. Y., Dec. 29.—Dr. Toyokichi Iyenaga, 74 years old, retired publicist, lecturer and Japanese diplomat, living at Fish Creek, near Oneida Lake, was drowned today while fishing through the ice.

With his son and a Japanese neighbor he started on an ice fishing expedition ten miles from his home. The younger men fished some distance out on the lake while Dr. Iyenaga remained close to shore.

Dragging a sled along, Dr. Iyenaga walked cautiously over the ice until he suddenly fell through a crack and disappeared. No one saw him go. Some hours later the younger men walked toward shore and discovered the ice crack.

They drove to Sylvan Beach and summoned State Troopers and conservation workers. The men used a fish line with heavy hooks on the end to locate the body in seventeen feet of water. They fastened three pike poles together and with a hook on the end succeeded in hooking on the clothing and recovering the body.

Dr. Iyenaga leaves a widow, one son and two grandchildren.

Dr. Iyenaga served his country for many years in the United States as an unofficial or semi-official spokesman. He frequently addressed American gatherings, upholding Japan's course in various matters, and wrote articles for American publications.

From 1914 to 1922 Dr. Iyenaga, who previously had lectured at American colleges, was director of the East and West News Bureau, with headquarters here. He formerly acted as an adviser to the Japanese consulate general here.

Born in Yanagawa, Japan, Dr. Iyenaga received his Ph. B. degree at Oberlin College in 1887 and his Ph. D. at Johns Hopkins University in 1890.

From 1890 to 1895 he was Professor of Political Science at Waseda University and also the Higher Commercial College, Tokyo. In 1895 he became a secretary with the Japanese Department of Foreign Affairs, leaving that post to become, in 1898, a Commissioner of the Formosan Government to India, Persia, Turkey and China. He held that position until 1899.

In 1901 he returned to the United States to become a professional lecturer on political science at the University of Chicago, remaining in that post until 1920. In 1913 he lectured at Columbia University.

In late years he had been in semi-retirement, living on a farm with his son at Sylvan Beach and going fishing almost daily.

He was the author, with Kenoske Sato, of "Japan and the California Problem."

ROOSEVELT FAVORS ACTION TO END STARVATION WAGES, LONG HOURS, CHILD LABOR

The President's Budget Message To Embody Relief Fund Request

He Refuses to Disclose the Amount Needed as He Reveals Plan to Give Congress Complete Picture Jan. 8—Also Silent on Whether Balance Will Be Shown for 1938.

Special to THE NEW YORK TIMES.

WASHINGTON, Dec. 29.—President Roosevelt said today he would include in his annual budget message to Congress his request for additional relief funds for the fiscal year 1937, which ends next June 30, and that the budget message would probably be sent to Congress on Friday, Jan. 8, two days after his message on the state of the Union.

He disclosed nothing as to the total that would be asked for relief, explaining that the question was still in the discussion stage. But by inclusion of the request in the budget message, he pointed out, the complete picture for 1937 would be presented.

The President refused to indicate whether the message would show a balanced budget for the fiscal year 1938. He said it would contain figures on estimated receipts and expenditures and on a surplus or a deficit. It would be complete with respect to 1938, he added, except for relief figures, which would be sent to Congress in March for that fiscal year.

Mr. Roosevelt made the announcement at his press conference, after he had discussed the deficiency appropriation extensively with administration aides and Cabinet members. He took up the question first during the morning when Secretaries Morgenthau, Wallace and Ickes, Rexford G. Tugwell, resigned Under-Secretary of Agriculture, and Harry L. Hopkins, WPA Administrator, called on various other subjects in their fields of administration.

Taking advantage of their joint presence, they had discussed the relief matter at some length but not to a final conclusion, the President said later.

The other officials threw little light on the conference. Mr. Hopkins said he had presented a tentative estimate of the sum needed for relief, but indicated that reports of a deficiency request for $750,000,000 for relief activities were inaccurate. Mr. Roosevelt has previously indicated that he might ask for around $500,000,000.

"I'm not prepared to do any talking yet," Mr. Hopkins said after leaving the White House.

WAY BEING STUDIED

But President Is Silent on Question of Change in the Constitution.

STANDARDS GOING DOWN

Of That There Is No Doubt, He Says After Talk With Hillman, Formerly of the NRA.

MANY PLEAS REACH HIM

From People Who Think He Still Has the Power, Shorn by Court, to Control Industry.

Special to THE NEW YORK TIMES.

WASHINGTON, Dec. 29.—President Roosevelt made clear today that he believed something should be done by the government for the elimination of child labor, long working hours and starvation wages, but he left open to question whether he would make specific recommendations to Congress in the coming session.

In denouncing at a press conference the gradual breaking down of standards governing child labor, minimum wages and maximum working hours which were contained in the defunct NRA, he did not go so far as to declare for restoration of the National Recovery Administration, but his remarks left no doubt that he felt a revival of some of its principles was essential.

Moreover, he made it plain that he felt State action would not suffice; there should be some assistance by the government.

Lacks Power Over Hours Now

Something must be done, and it was obvious, he added, that something should cover child labor, long hours and starvation wages. But beyond that he would not go. He refused to say whether he felt a constitutional amendment, he refused to express an opinion.

As things now stand, in the light of the Supreme Court's NRA decision, the President does not have the power to check the abandonment of the hours, wages and working conditions that were in existence two years ago.

Yet many in the country apparently think he has, judging from the number of appeals he has been receiving to stop the movement.

The whole question, he continued, is under consideration by the Department of Justice, which is studying various proposals made in Congress and by individuals.

These include Senator O'Mahoney's bill for Federal licensing of corporations, and many other plans.

Of the breaking down of maximum hour and minimum wage limitations since the death of the NRA there is no question, Mr. Roosevelt declared.

He went on to say that he had discussed this question only today with Sidney Hillman, president of the Amalgamated Clothing Workers of America, but with what results he did not divulge.

Recalls Campaign Incident

The departure from the standards of two years ago has been constant and increasing, the President emphasized.

He recalled an incident during the campaign, when he was in New Bedford.

He had noticed the police pressing back a girl who was trying desperately to reach him with an envelope, and he directed the late "Gus" Gennerich, his bodyguard, to "get that note from that girl." This was promptly done and the President found that the note read as follows:

"I wish you would do something to help us girls. You are the only recourse we have left. We are working in a garment factory and a few months ago our minimum wages were $11. Today they have been cut down to $4 and $5 and $6. Please send some one from Washington to restore our minimum wage so that we can live."

The President said he had referred the note to Massachusetts officials. He declared that the incident was a good example of many similar campaign occurrences; many people thought that he had the direct power to alter the wage scale.

In connection with the breaking down of wages and hours stand-

Continued on Page Four

NEW DEVICE SCRUBS SMOKY AIR OF CITIES

Poisonous Fumes Removed at Smokestacks by Technique Described to Chemists.

SULPHUR A BY-PRODUCT

Dr. Kimball Hails Discovery, Saying Practical System Would Be Boon to Nation.

The development of a new engineering technique for purifying the smoke-laden air over big cities was announced here yesterday.

The discovery, which promises to promote the health of millions and safeguard property, besides tapping a vast new reservoir of mineral wealth, was described at the closing session of the two-day symposium on "Absorption and Extraction," sponsored by the American Chemical Society, at Columbia University. It is the work of Dr. H. F. Johnstone, Associate Professor of Chemical Engineering, and A. D. Singh, research chemical engineer, both of the faculty of the University of Illinois.

The new technique, which was described as "air conditioning a city's atmosphere," passes air through a "scrubbing" process which eliminates sulphur chloride, nitrous and hydrochloric acid fumes, the three gases chiefly responsible for poisoning the air we breathe. These gases in the atmosphere of big cities are believed to be extremely harmful. In heavy concentrations they cause death, while continued exposure to air containing even very small quantities of the fumes leads to generally lowered health and may be responsible for lung and stomach ailments.

Danger to Health Here

The atmosphere of New York, Pittsburgh, Chicago and other highly industrialized cities contains a quantity of these fumes which may measure from two to six parts per million cubic feet of air, Professor Johnstone and Mr. Singh estimated. They explained that about three parts of the gases per million cubic feet of air can affect the vegetation and injure the health.

The new technique not only purifies the air by ridding the city atmosphere of this pollution, but yields, at the same time, new stores of sulphur, thus opening up the prospect of the day when, the nation's natural sulphur deposits exhausted, chemists may mine the air for the mineral.

Dr. James H. Kimball, meteorologist in charge of the United States Weather Bureau, commented last night that any process for purifying the air of "our smoky big cities" would mean "a great boon" for the country. He explained that experimenters in the past had been unable to overcome what appeared to be the prohibitive cost of install-

Continued on Page Ten

EXPERTS WILL PLAN SAFER AIR TRAVEL

Commerce Department to Hold Conference Soon of All Aviation Interests.

SPURRED BY RICKENBACKER

Johnson Confident Most of Accidents Like Recent Series Can Be Averted.

Special to THE NEW YORK TIMES.

WASHINGTON, Dec. 29.—On the heels of three airplane accidents this month, whose fatalities brought the year's total on transport lines to sixty, J. Monroe Johnson, Assistant Secretary of Commerce, announced today that a conference would be called soon to take steps to make air travel safer.

Air line operators and officials from all government departments who have anything to do with operation of aircraft will be called to the meeting, which, Mr. Johnson indicated, will not be held until after all phases of the three crashes this month, in the last of which twelve died, have been investigated by Federal officials.

Rickenbacker Suggests Steps

Decision to hold the conference was the direct outcome of a letter sent to Mr. Johnson by Eddie Rickenbacker, general manager of Eastern Airlines, wherein improvements in Federal aid to aviation were suggested.

As an example of this need the recent forced landing of a transport plane at Port Jervis, N. Y., in which Pilot Dick Merrill saved his passengers by his skill, was cited.

Four improvements were suggested, as follows:

That the Department of Commerce make every effort to modernize and raise to the highest standard of efficiency all of its present air aids as soon as Congress appropriates the necessary money.

That all modern air transports be equipped with radio compasses qualified to operate both day and night, with antennae shielded against rain, sleet and snow static.

That the Department of Commerce equip all of its ground stations with T-L antennae, offering the transport ships in the air a twenty-four-hour a day service, with special identification for each city or airport where the facilities of the department are located, thus eliminating the necessity, as at present, of using commercial stations on any other frequency in announcing their designations on the air twenty-four hours a day.

That all Department of Commerce radio stations be equipped with radio direction finders on special frequencies, with personnel qualified to man them twenty-four hours a day, that any pilot unable to ascertain his position at any time may obtain a bearing from them from any operator's ship which may be temporarily lost

Continued on Page Twenty-two

Auto workers on a sit-down strike in Flint, Michigan.

John L. Lewis, chairman of the CIO. By 1937, the CIO had over three million members and was making most of the nation's labor news.

UAW members staged a sit-down strike at the Ford plant in Kansas City.

Walter P. Chrysler signing the agreement with the UAW. John L. Lewis (left) and Michigan Governor Frank Murphy (center) look on.

"All the News That's Fit to Print."

The New York Times.

THE WEATHER
Fair today and tomorrow, not much change in temperature.
Temperature yesterday—Max., 68; min., 53.
For weather report see Page 54.

VOL. LXXXVI.....No. 28,843. Entered as Second-Class Matter, Postoffice, New York, N. Y. NEW YORK, TUESDAY, JANUARY 12, 1937. P TWO CENTS In New York City. | THREE CENTS Within 200 Miles. | FOUR CENTS Elsewhere Except in 7th and 8th Postal Zones.

MATTSON BOY FOUND SLAIN; BODY LEFT IN LONELY BRUSH; KILLER'S FOOTPRINTS IN SNOW

BEATEN TO DEATH

Hunter Stumbles Over Frozen Child Hidden Near Everett, Wash.

CARRIED THERE IN AUTO

Tracks Lead From Car—Dogs' Baying Sets Time at Sunday Night.

DEATH PUT ON THURSDAY

River Silt on Face Indicates Previous Hiding Place—'G-Men' Go Into Action.

Special to THE NEW YORK TIMES.

TACOMA, Wash., Jan. 11.—The savagely battered body of 10-year-old Charles Mattson was found today lying nude and frozen stiff in snow-covered brushland near Everett.

A youth hunting a rabbit discovered the murdered child, who was kidnapped two weeks ago last night from the home here of Dr. W. W. Mattson, his father. Everett is about fifty miles from Tacoma.

Coroner Otto Mittelstadt of King County, Seattle, said death apparently had occurred Thursday. The boy's skull was crushed, as if with a blunt instrument; several front teeth were knocked out, and the bruised face and body gave further evidence of a terrific beating. The body was brought to Tacoma tonight.

Federal Men Go to Work

"G-men" unloosed their full forces in an intensive hunt for the kidnapper.

Positive identification of the body was made by James Gowdy of Everett, a relative of the Mattson family, and Paul Sceva of Tacoma, old friend of the family who had been mentioned frequently as the possible intermediary in ransom negotiations.

The kidnapper had asked $28,000 for the boy's release, but the money was not paid, although repeated efforts were made to arrange this.

Fine silt on the boy's face and hands indicated that the body previously had been hidden along a river's edge or by a mudflat.

The lonely region where the child was found, shortly before noon, is thickly covered with brush and is chiefly populated by chicken ranchers.

Body Half-Mile From Road

The body lay a half-mile west of the Pacific Highway and six miles south of Everett.

Tire marks and the footprints of one man in the snow told the story of the slayer's visit to the scene to dispose of his burden. The time is set at 9 o'clock last night by the frantic baying of ranchers' dogs in the vicinity, recalled today.

Gordon Morrow, 19 years old, who lives near by, found the body.

A graveled road running from Edmunds to Beverly Park passes within 150 feet of where the Morrow boy made his discovery. Tire tracks showed where a car had swung off at the side of the road. Deputy sheriffs of Snohomish County, under the direction of Sheriff Walter F. Faulkner, immediately threw a guard around the area to preserve the evidence.

Agents of the Federal Bureau of Investigation rushed from Tacoma to the scene and the State patrol under Chief William Cole threw a widespread dragnet for the kidnapper. It is considered possible that he is demented.

Dr. Mattson was in his office here when the news was broken to him.

"I feared it," he said. "When that man pulled Charles out into the night that way I feared something like this would happen." Dr. Mattson added that he had made every possible effort to pay the ransom. Later, at his home, he was reported to have broken down for the first time since the kidnapping. Mrs. Mattson was put under the care of a nurse.

Youth Stumbles on Body

Pat Ryan, chief criminal deputy sheriff of Snohomish County, and an Everett reporter and photographer were the first at the scene after discovery of the body.

Young Morrow told Deputy Ryan that he was seated in his house when he saw a rabbit dash into the woods. He grabbed up a rifle and ran after it. Suddenly he stumbled

Continued on Page Sixteen

Young Bride Slain in Queens Home; Husband Finds Body in Bathtub

Woman Clubbed and Strangled in Jackson Heights Kitchen, Then Dragged to Bathroom—Hammer and Looted Purse Found in Incinerator Near Apartment Door.

Felled by heavy hammer blows in the head while working in her kitchen, Mrs. Mary H. Case, 25 years old, a bride of one year, was found slain at 6:35 o'clock last night in the overflowing bathtub of her three-room apartment on the fourth floor of 37-06 Eightieth Street, Jackson Heights, Queens.

Her husband, Frank, discovered the body in the bathtub, almost submerged in water underneath a bedsheet which had been thrown across the tub. He had pulled her out and dragged her across the threshold of the bathroom when the apartment bell was rung by John Caldy, the superintendent, who had gone up to investigate water seeping through the floor to the apartment below.

"Where is the leak?" Caldy asked.

Bitterly, Case replied, "Look in the bathroom."

The young husband left the superintendent by the body of his wife to call Dr. Lee Anderson of 35-63 Eighty-third Street, a neighboring physician. Dr. Anderson, after pronouncing the woman dead, procured a thermometer and tested the temperature of the water in the cascading tub in an effort to fix the time of the murder. The instrument registered 75 degrees.

Caldy meanwhile called the owners of the building, the Queensboro Corporation, who notified the police. High officials hastened to the scene and said the crime closely paralleled the Titterton case of April 10, 1936, in which Mrs. Nancy Evans Titterton, 34-year-old writer, was slain in her apartment at 22 Beekman Place. Mrs. Titterton's slayer, John Fiorenza, 24-year-old upholsterer's helper, is awaiting execution in Sing Sing prison.

As in the Titterton case the victim was also strangled, fingernail marks having been found in the neck. Because the parallel was so close, the detectives placed their greatest reliance for the solution of the case on the Police Crime Laboratory, which photographed every object in the apartment and removed for analysis hair from a comb, a part of the stained rug and other articles.

Mrs. Case was last seen alive at 8 o'clock in the morning when her husband, an accountant and a

Continued on Page Three

REALTY MAN PAYS $2,000,000 U.S. TAX

Record Settlement Is Made by M. L. Parshelsky in Brooklyn for Income Levy Fraud.

SENTENCE IS SUSPENDED

Collectible Total Reduced by Statute of Limitations—4 Concerns Involved.

Moses L. Parshelsky, Brooklyn realty man, yesterday paid the Federal Government $2,000,000 in back income taxes, pleaded guilty to an indictment charging income tax evasion and then received a suspended sentence from Federal Judge Robert A. Inch in Brooklyn, carrying five years' probation. Unite States Attorney Leo J. Hickey said he believed the acceptance of the $2,000,000 was "the largest money settlement in income tax fraud in the history of the country."

The government had charged that Parshelsky, with his deceased brother, Isaac, and four concerns in which the brothers were interested, owed a total of $4,000,000 in taxes, penalties and interest. The total tax, the government charged, was $2,367,323. Some of the evasions, according to the government, went back to 1919. The investigation began in November, 1932.

The indictment to which Parshelsky entered a plea of guilty also charged that the firm of Parshelsky Brothers, Inc., of 131 Morgan Avenue, Brooklyn, also evaded tax payments. Judge Inch fined the company $500.

Promise by Defendant

In a memorandum made public by Mr. Hickey's office, it was disclosed that the offer of the $2,000,000 settlement made by Parshelsky also carried the promise that the defendant would enter unconditional pleas of guilty to the third count in the indictment and would "abide the sentence of the court thereon without any recommendation on the part of the United States as to sentence but with full disclosure by the United States to the court of the facts concerning the conduct of the defendant through his counsel during the investigation of the offenses charged, as well as the facts concerning the settlement of the civil liability of Moses L. Parshelsky and the other taxpayers on behalf of whom this offer is submitted."

The memorandum also pointed out that Attorney General Homer S. Cummings was a party to the compromise. The Attorney General, it was explained, requested that all payments be made in advance of the guilty pleas and that the court be advised of all of the facts.

Assistant United States Attorney James D. Saver, who informed the

Continued on Page Three

JERSEY DEMOCRATS DROP 'STRIKE' PLAN

Senators Decide at Meeting Here to Make Political Capital of the Seating of Hunt.

'ADVISE' FOES TO WAIT

Republicans May Balk Them by Accepting Proposal to Delay Until Court Rules.

Democratic members of the New Jersey Senate abandoned last night the projected "stay-away" strike to prevent organization by the Republicans of the upper house when it convenes at Trenton today.

At a conference here at the Hotel Waldorf-Astoria they decided, it was understood, to make as much political capital as possible out of the contested seat of Senator William C. Hunt, Republican, of Cape May County, for use in the Gubernatorial campaign next Fall.

The strike had been planned to prevent the Republicans from having a quorum and seating Senator Hunt, whose election would give them eleven of the twenty-one seats, or a majority of one. In order to be seated Senator Hunt must get the vote of Senator Lester H. Clee, Clean Government Republican from Essex County.

"Sacrifice Play" Planned

Senator Clee is regarded as the probable Republican Gubernatorial nominee for next Fall, to run against Senator A. Harry Moore. The plan of the Hague machine,

Continued on Page Two

Hitler Trades Assurances On Spain With French Envoy

Formal Pledges on Status Quo Are Given at Berlin Fete—Paris, Relieved, Calls the Moroccan Incident Closed.

BERLIN—*Chancellor Hitler and the French Ambassador exchanged pledges at a New Year reception to respect the status quo of Spain, including Spanish Morocco. Page 1.*

TANGIER—*German penetration in Spanish Morocco is found to be going forward rapidly in economic, administrative and military spheres. Melilla, which is being fortified, is regarded as practically a German naval base. Page 4.*

THE FRONT—*Loyalists claim to have halted General Franco's latest drive. The Spanish envoy here reported recovery of all ground lost to the Rebels in the past two days. Page 5.*

By FREDERICK T. BIRCHALL

Wireless to THE NEW YORK TIMES.

BERLIN, Jan. 11.—The Franco-German quarrel over Spanish Morocco, which last night assumed a distinctly formidable aspect, seems tonight on its way to settlement as a result of formal pledges exchanged by the French Ambassador and Chancellor Adolf Hitler himself at the Fuehrer's New Year reception for the diplomatic corps at noon. In this exchange Germany and France have given each other formal assurances that neither has any intention of changing the status quo in Spain or any of her possessions, including Morocco.

The New Year reception, the scene of this dénouement, was held as usual in the Presidential palace in Wilhelmstrasse, which President Paul von Hindenburg last occupied and which is now reserved solely for state functions. The entire diplomatic corps attended to pay its respects to the Chancellor and a congratulatory address was read to him, after which he suitably replied.

By one of those odd coincidences that sometimes occur in international relations the Papal Nuncio, ex officio dean of the corps, who should have read the address, is ill. In his absence that duty fell on Andre Francois-Poncet, the French Ambassador, who is the

Continued on Page Four

SOVIET WAR BUDGET INCREASED A THIRD; FASCISM IS CITED

20,102,000,000-Ruble Total for 1937 Is a Fifth of the State's Expenses.

EDUCATION ALSO HELPED

Health Outlay Augmented Under Plan Presented to the Executive Body.

By HAROLD DENNY

Special Cable to THE NEW YORK TIMES.

MOSCOW, Jan. 11.—Another big increase, bringing the Soviet military budget to 20,102,000,000 rubles for 1937, was announced by Gregory T. Grinko, Finance Commissar, at the opening session tonight of a full meeting of the Soviet Central Executive Committee in the Kremlin Palace. The 757 members and 400 visitors from factories and farms, who attended as specially honored guests, cheered the announcement.

This year's military budget is a 35.7 per cent increase over last year's expenditures of 14,815,000,000 rubles and is more than a fifth of the nation's entire budget—which here, of course, in this socialized State, includes virtually all industry and commerce as well as ordinary governmental expenditures.

And because the Soviet budget includes so much that under capitalism is left to private enterprise the proportion of military expenditures to others is all the more impressive. The military expenditures alone this year will cost the average family 587 rubles.

Diplomats Attend in Force

No hint was given by any speaker tonight that the increased budget presaged an increase in the size of the army from its total of 1,300,000, to which it was raised a year ago. However, some high-ranking Red

Continued on Page Six

LABOR BARGAINING BY LAW HELD VOID IN COURT DECISION

Wagner Act Unconstitutional in Forcing Contract Upon Employer, Ruling Says.

BOARD LOSES MACKAY SUIT

'Due Process' Basis of 2-to-1 Edict of Coast Circuit Bench —Dissent Cites 'Welfare.'

Special to THE NEW YORK TIMES.

SAN FRANCISCO, Jan. 11.—The National Labor Relations Board lost by a two-to-one decision of the Ninth United States Circuit Court of Appeals today in an action seeking enforcement of a ruling by the board against the Mackay Radio and Telegraph Company.

The board had ordered that five discharged Mackay employes, members of the American Radio Telegraphists Association, be rehired and paid for the time they were off the job because of a strike by their union in 1935. The board also asked the Circuit Court to enforce its demands that the Mackay company "cease and desist" from interfering with the union or threatening employes who sought to join the union.

The Wagner act was declared unconstitutional, in so far as it would "require collective bargaining," in the majority decision written by Presiding Justice Curtis D. Wilbur, Secretary of the Navy under President Coolidge.

Justice Wilbur based his opinion on the "due process" clause of the Constitution.

Separate Concurring Opinion

Justice Clifton Mathews, concurring in Justice Wilbur's verdict, held that, assuming the Wagner act as constitutional, the board had not acted legally.

Justice Francis A. Garrecht, dissenting, upheld the power of Congress to act, through the National Labor Relations Board, for the "general welfare" in industrial strife.

Justice Wilbur voiced disagreement with a recent decision of the Second Circuit Court of Appeals in the National Labor Relations Board's suit against The Associated Press in the Watson case, in which the court found in favor of the board.

Quoting the United States Supreme Court decision on the Guffey Coal Act, Justice Wilbur said he considered that had an important bearing on the National Labor Relations Act, adding he regarded Congress within its rights in regulation of interstate commerce, admittedly performed by the Mackay company.

But, he declared, the right of the company, under both the declaration of liberty and the constitution, "freely to contract with its employes, is taken away without due process of law."

Act Called Coercive

"The act," Justice Wilbur continued, "by prohibiting the employer from negotiating with any individual or group of employes other than the selected representatives of a group or unit designated by the board, in effect destroys the right

Continued on Page Thirteen

Senate Votes Pension for Mrs. Coolidge; Carter Glass Surprised at Delay in Acting

Special to THE NEW YORK TIMES.

WASHINGTON, Jan. 11.—The Senate today approved a pension of $5,000 a year to Mrs. Grace G. Coolidge, widow of President Coolidge, the action being taken more than four years after the death of Mr. Coolidge.

On motion of Senator Glass the Senate suspended its rules and passed without a dissenting vote his resolution directing payment of the pension.

"I was astounded," said Senator Glass, "when it was brought to my attention that such action had not been taken in behalf of Mrs. Coolidge four years ago, and that nothing had been done to provide this pension for her. The action taken is in conformity with Congressional policy in such matters."

The Administration of Veterans' Affairs is directed to pay the pension.

The widows of Theodore Roosevelt and Woodrow Wilson are now receiving annual pensions of $5,000 each. Mrs. William Howard Taft, Mrs. Benjamin Harrison and Mrs. Frances Folsom Cleveland Preston are not on the pension roll because of "special reasons," Senator Glass said.

The "special reasons" were not stated. It is understood that Mrs. Taft draws an annuity from the Carnegie Foundation, while the widow of President Cleveland is now the wife of Professor Thomas J. Preston of Princeton University.

Mrs. Harrison, widow of President Benjamin Harrison, is said to have declined the pension on the ground that she was amply provided for.

By The Associated Press.

NORTHAMPTON, Mass., Jan. 11.—Mrs. F. B. Adams, with whom Mrs. Grace Coolidge makes her home, today said Mrs. Coolidge would not comment on the Senate's action to grant her a pension.

24 HURT IN FLINT STRIKE RIOT; POLICE BATTLE STREET MOBS; GOVERNOR RUSHES TO SCENE

MILITIA MOBILIZED

Troops Ready as Auto Strikers in Plant Repel Gas Attack.

BOTH SIDES HAVE DUG IN

Workers Tear Up Paving for Missiles and Drive Police Back With Fire Hose.

PLANT GUARDS OVERCOME

'Sit-Downers' Who Had Held Floor for 2 Weeks Suddenly Take Whole Building.

Special to THE NEW YORK TIMES.

FLINT, Mich., Tuesday, Jan. 12.—After more than five hours of hand-to-hand fighting with the police, in which at least twenty-four persons were injured by bullets, stones, clubs, knives and tear-gas bombs, a siege was on this morning at the Fisher Body plant No. 2, where "sit-down" strikers are defying the courts and the State authorities.

Governor Murphy, who rushed to Flint by automobile, was in conference at the Hotel Durant on steps to be taken to end the fighting. Under his orders a company of the 125th Regiment of the Michigan National Guard was mobilizing for riot duty at the Flint armory, prepared to prevent further bloodshed and rioting.

In addition it was reported that forty State policemen, in response to appeals by Flint officials for aid, would soon arrive to enter the fray.

The police meanwhile could do little more than hold their lines against some 800 strikers, pickets and sympathizers who were being directed by the broadcasting apparatus of a sound truck parked near the plant gate. The truck was surrounded by the automobiles of strikers as a barricade to prevent the police from approaching.

Some Strikers Believed Armed

Virtually every window in the two-story factory building appeared to have been broken. The street before the plant, which is opposite the Chevrolet factory in Chevrolet Avenue, was littered with débris.

Rioters had torn up stretches of the asphalt pavement to obtain missiles to hurl at the police. At another point along the avenue the curb stones had been pried up and had been broken into pieces by the strikers.

That some of the strikers were armed was held certain, because at one point a message was shouted from the sound truck:

"Go home and get your guns and come back again."

The wounded, however, were believed to have been injured mostly by fragments of exploding tear gas shells fired by the police, and by missiles, rather than by gunfire.

Of those hurt twenty persons were taken to hospitals, among them five policemen.

Driver Is Badly Injured

One of the strikers, Earl de Long of Flint, described as a driver, was said at the hospital to be in a serious condition, with a wound in the abdomen.

Most of the others were reported wounded about the legs, as if by fragments of tear-gas grenades that had exploded near them.

Three of the injured refused hospital aid. The twenty-fourth of the known casualties was a Detroit newspaper photographer, who was slashed on the hand when he attempted to obtain pictures of the rioters in action.

Two other photographers, employed by The Flint Journal, were beaten by rioters, but not seriously hurt, and it was believed that others who approached too close to the front line of battle had also been roughly handled.

Governor Murphy arrived shortly after 1 A. M. with Adjutant General John Bersey, commanding the National Guard; Oscar Olander, commandant of the State police; Caesar J. Scarvada, captain of the State police, and Edward Kemp, Assistant Attorney General, who acted as legal adviser to the Governor.

The party, which had traveled by automobile from Lansing, met immediately with City Manager John M. Barrinber and Chief of Police James B. Wills.

At that time the number of policemen who had been dispatched to the Fisher Body factory numbered

Continued on Page Twelve

5 More Plants Shut or Curtailed; Idle Auto Workers Rise to 112,800

19,500 Are Losing Jobs With New Closings, With All Chevrolet and Cadillac-La Salle Production Now Cut Off—5,000 Lansing Employes Ask Presidential Aid.

By RUSSELL B. PORTER

Special to THE NEW YORK TIMES.

DETROIT, Jan. 11.—The General Motors Corporation announced today the complete or partial closing of five additional factories, throwing 19,500 more employes out of work, because of the shortage of glass and other consequences of the widespread strikes in the automotive and allied industries. The new shutdowns will begin tonight and be spaced over tomorrow and Wednesday.

By Wednesday thirty-four of the sixty-nine General Motors factories throughout the country will have closed, with 112,800 of the company's 175,000 hourly wage-workers in automotive trades forced into unemployment.

Further shutdowns during the week are expected.

As most of the General Motors factories still running are engaged in the production of other goods and are not essentially automobile factories, today's developments mean that the mammoth General Motors automobile production machine, the largest in the country, has been brought near to a standstill, which may be fully realized in the next few days.

All Chevrolet and Cadillac-La Salle production has been stopped, and Pontiac and Oldsmobile production has been seriously curtailed by the newest shutdowns.

It is learned that the company has no intention of attempting to open any of its plants with strikebreakers. It feels that this would not be necessary, even if it wished to do so, as it has plenty of loyal workers who would like to work if they could.

Moreover, it is held in company circles that G. M. has not made a practice of using strikebreakers in the past and it does not desire to do so now.

The most important units still running at full force are five Chevrolet assembly plants, in various parts of the country, and their adjacent Fisher Body plants. It is only a matter of time before the shortage of engines, glass and parts

Continued on Page Twelve

TAMMANY TO ACT ON LEADER TODAY

Collapse of Fight on Dooling Forecast After Hurried Call for 'Showdown' Meeting.

END OF TRIUMVIRATE SEEN

Developments of Last Week Said to Have Strengthened Position of the Chief.

The Tammany Hall executive committee will convene at 4 P. M. today for a meeting designed to end the controversy over the leadership of the organization. The session was decided upon yesterday by James J. Dooling, Tammany leader, and was called at his request, Mr. Dooling's friends said.

Telegrams were sent to the individual leaders in the name of William P. Kenneally, chairman of the executive committee. The purpose of the meeting, it was made clear, was to force a "showdown" to end the reports that Mr. Dooling soon was to be superseded by a new leader.

The fact that the meeting is being held was taken in informed quarters as a fairly clear indication that no new leader was to be chosen today. The meeting comes at a time when the friends of Mr. Dooling are in a better strategic position than they have been for some time, and with the opposition to him in the executive committee more divided than ever, it is believed.

Result of Sullivan Boom

This is a result of the recent boom for Representative Christopher D. Sullivan for leader, and then its decline. The three principal contenders for the leadership now are said to be Mr. Sullivan from the Second Assembly District, Charles Culkin of the Third, and Stephen A. Ruddy of the Sixteenth. Mr. Sullivan faced a coalition of members of the two other groups, opposed to his election, and this appears to have worked toward the retention of Mr. Dooling as leader. Then Mr. Sullivan suffered a further loss of strength as a result of a mix-up in a recent patronage matter—the appointment of a Supreme Court Justice to succeed John L. Walsh.

Another favorable turn for Mr. Dooling was that Jeremiah T. Mahoney, least popular with his fellow-members of all of the district leaders, demanded that a meeting be held to elect a new leader. The result was that leaders who had been clamoring for a showdown pledged anew their loyalty to Mr. Dooling.

Former Sheriff Culkin is believed to have the support of the Hines bloc for the leadership if a change is made, but there are some Culkin and Ruddy supporters who are represented, by friends of Mr. Dooling,

Continued on Page Two

790 MILLION ASKED FOR IDLE TO JULY 1

President's Relief Message to Congress Calls On Business Again to Increase Jobs.

HOUSE LEADERS GET BUSY

Line Up Forces in an Effort to Checkmate Group Mapping a Fight for Larger Fund.

The text of the President's letter on relief is on Page 14.

By TURNER CATLEDGE

Special to THE NEW YORK TIMES.

WASHINGTON, Jan. 11.—President Roosevelt submitted to Congress today a request for an immediate appropriation of $790,000,000 to continue relief and work relief for the next five months, coupled with another warning to private business that costs for these activities could be reduced only by re-employment of the idle in industry.

The President gave notice in his budget message, delivered Friday, that the supplemental appropriation would be asked. If was made necessary, he said, by the extra Federal relief load occasioned by the drought of last Summer. Without the new appropriation, relief funds will be exhausted by Feb. 1.

The additional funds would continue the relief program until the end of the fiscal year on June 30, and enable limited commitments for the first few weeks of the fiscal year 1938.

Message a Letter to Speaker

The message today was addressed in the form of a letter to the Speaker of the House. Speaker Bankhead and Representative Rayburn, the majority leader, began preparations for early consideration, but one of their main tasks, as they saw it, was to align their forces so that Congress might not increase the appropriation asked for by the President. This was the result of the formation of a bloc of Western Senators and Representatives, led by Senator Bone of Washington, for the purpose of increasing relief appropriations to an amount they regard as more nearly adequate.

In submitting his estimate, the President said that even though industry might not be doing its full share in re-employment, the need for government assistance to the unemployed is being reduced. He estimated a reduction in relief rolls of more than 800,000 since last March, and said that at the beginning of the present Winter at least 6,000,000 more workers were employed in non-agricultural jobs than in March, 1933. More than 1,000,000 of this number had returned to private employment during the past year, he said.

The President complimented in-

Continued on Page Fourteen

"All the News That's Fit to Print."

The New York Times.

LATE CITY EDITION
Rain and warmer today. Tomorrow rain and colder.
Temperatures Yesterday—Max., 35; Min., 30

Copyright, 1937, by The New York Times Company.

VOL. LXXXVI.....No. 28,852. Entered as Second-Class Matter, Postoffice, New York, N. Y. NEW YORK, THURSDAY, JANUARY 21, 1937. P TWO CENTS In New York City. | THREE CENTS Within 200 Miles. | FOUR CENTS Elsewhere Except in 7th and 8th Postal Zones.

ROOSEVELT PLEDGES WARFARE AGAINST POVERTY, BROADER AID FOR 'THOSE WHO HAVE TOO LITTLE'; THRONGS SEE INAUGURATION IN PELTING RAIN

NEW AUTO PARLEY IN CAPITAL FAILS; MURPHY GLOOMY

Sloan, Knudsen and Aides Meet All Afternoon With Governor and Miss Perkins

CONFEREES ARE ANXIOUS

But Secretary Is Hopeful—Further Talks in the East May Be Arranged

ENTIRE BUICK PLANT SHUT

Closedown Makes Total of Flint Idle 38,000 and Accentuates Relief Problem

Day's Strike Developments

WASHINGTON—A parley in which Secretary Perkins, Governor Murphy and General Motors officials participated failed to find a solution of difficulties.

FLINT—The Buick plant shut down completely last night, adding 10,000 to the ranks of the idle, which previously numbered 28,000. Danger that the relief problem will soon become acute is seen.

DETROIT—As a matter of strategy, affiliates of the C.I.O. moved to settle the local Bohn Aluminum plant strike and the glass strike in Pittsburgh.

PITTSBURGH—Union and Pittsburgh Plate Glass officials reached an agreement on wages in five company plants which will send 7,000 back to work at once. The workers will get 8 cents an hour more.

Capital Negotiations Futile

Special to THE NEW YORK TIMES.

WASHINGTON, Jan. 20.—Governor Murphy of Michigan, at the end of another long conference here today on the General Motors strike situation indicated that it seemed difficult, if not impossible, to break the deadlock through State action.

Possibility of Presidential intervention within a week loomed as the eventual action to end the strike.

This was the conclusion forced on observers, after Governor Murphy had participated in an all-afternoon conference with Secretary Perkins, Alfred P. Sloan, president of General Motors: William S. Knudsen, executive vice president; Donaldson Brown, chairman of the corporation's finance committee, and John Thomas Smith, general counsel.

There was a possibility that Mr. Murphy might go to New York to continue his efforts to arrange resumption of the truce which he had brought about last Friday at Lansing where, for the first time, he had General Motors officers and the union officials in one room at the same time.

Following today's meeting neither the Governor nor any participant concealed his anxiety over the fact that the situation was reaching a critical stage.

For the present it appeared that President Roosevelt would not be called upon to mediate the strike issues, for Secretary Perkins was determined to avoid this if possible. However another week, it was said, will probably tell another story.

Negotiations Kept Secret

The utmost secrecy surrounded the afternoon deliberations. All sorts of reports were current, including one that the parley would be resumed tomorrow and that John L. Lewis, chairman of the Committee for Industrial Organization, might then be called into a conference with Mr. Sloan.

Governor Murphy said that he would exhaust all efforts "in the East" to arrange for resumption of joint negotiations, but did not explain what he meant. He was holding further talks tonight.

Mr. Lewis has repeatedly charged that a "united front" of financial groups interested in the steel, automobile, rubber and glass and coal industries is intent on ending what they consider the "menace" of the C. I. O., which has for its objective the organization of these mass production industries.

Mr. Murphy would not say whether he would confer tomorrow with officers of the United Automobile Workers of America, who left Detroit tonight for Washington, nor would he indicate whether he would again see Mr. Lewis.

Secretary Perkins declined to discuss the situation with reporters, but a statement was issued in her behalf to the effect that she and the Governor were still striving to reopen negotiations on a "fair and honorable" basis.

Statement by Miss Perkins

Her statement was as follows:

"We discussed all aspects of the problem and particularly the break-

Continued on Page Four

Berlin-Tokyo Body Named To Carry Out Agreement

By The Associated Press.

BERLIN, Jan. 20.—A mixed German-Japanese commission has been named to carry out provisions of the anti-Comintern agreement of last November, it was learned from a semi-official source tonight.

Names of the members have not been disclosed.

The agreement binds the two nations "to execute in close cooperation with each other" such measures as are deemed necessary to counteract "the disruptive activities of the Communist International."

EX-CONVICT SLAYS SHACKLED TROOPER

Prisoner Attacks Michigan Officer in Patrol Car and Handcuffs Him to a Mail Box

CAUGHT IN 3-STATE HUNT

Gunman Cornered on Highway in a Commandeered Car—Confesses to Murder

By The Associated Press.

MONROE, Mich., Jan. 20.—State Trooper Richards G. Hammond was killed early today after he had been overpowered by a prisoner in a patrol car and had been shackled to a rural mail box with his own handcuffs. The prisoner, a paroled convict, shot the trooper through the head.

Tonight, after the most intensive man-hunt in Michigan's history had spread to the States of Ohio and Indiana, the fugitive felon, Alcide (Frenchy) Benoit, 24 years old, was captured by State Police and, according to Sheriff Joseph J. Bairley of Monroe County, later confessed that he had slain the policeman.

Sheriff Bairley said that Benoit admitted after questioning that he slugged Hammond following his arrest at midnight last night at almost the exact spot where he was captured tonight, and that he had dragged the dazed trooper from his automobile, handcuffed him to the mail box post and then shot him.

Prosecutor Francis C. Ready and State Police Captain Lawrence A. Lyon declared that Benoit admitted in an oral statement that he fired the fatal shot, but insisted that it was fired during a fight he had with the trooper, and not while the officer was in a dazed condition.

Escaped With Posse Near By

After handcuffing Trooper Hammond to the mailbox post, the officials quoted Benoit as saying, and firing the fatal shot, he fled, hiding in a field while a posse flashed lights within a few feet of him. After the posse had gone, he said, he spent the remainder of the night and all of today in a barn near Monroe.

He admitted, the officials said, that he had committed robberies in Detroit, Flint, Grand Rapids, Lansing and Pontiac, Mich.; Toledo, Cleveland and Chicago.

The capture of Benoit came after Captain Lyon had expressed fear early in the evening that Benoit had eluded the net set for him.

At 7 P. M., a man later identified as Benoit, knocked on the door of a farmhouse near Fetterman, occupied by Paul Balog, 56: his wife and two children. The man asked Balog and his son, Steve, 16, to help him dig his car out of the mud. Balog said later that the man threatened to shoot them if they did not help.

They went to the barnyard, Balog said, where the man declared he was the man who had shot the trooper, and with two guns—one his own and other taken from Trooper Hammond—forced the Balogs to start their pick-up truck and drive him toward Monroe.

At the edge of the city they were met by State police, but Benoit, who was driving, swerved his car, narrowly missing a trooper who sought to question him, and eluded capture.

Balog said that they drove around in the vicinity of Monroe for an hour, dodging police cars by driving in private lanes and leaving lights off, but finally again approached the intersection of Michigan State Route No. 50 and Telegraph Road, where Benoit and John Smith, 29, alias Delberto, also a former convict, had been arrested by Troopers Hammond and Sam Sineni last night as suspects in the kidnapping of Fred Williams, a Detroit used-car salesman.

Surrenders to Four Troopers

As Benoit dodged into a driveway tonight, a State police car followed and fired one rifle shot into the back of the truck, Balog told newspaper men. The bullet penetrated the end gate and the seat on which the three sat, but failed to strike any of them.

Balog said that Benoit resisted when four troopers sought to handcuff him, but that when he saw the

Continued on Page Two

OPEN DOOR URGED IN WORLD COLONIES BY TOKYO MINISTER

Arita Says This Is Way to End Much Unrest Among Lands Lacking Raw Materials

DEFENDS PACT WITH REICH

Attributes World's Troubles to Communism—Sees Gain in Relations With U. S.

By HUGH BYAS

Wireless to THE NEW YORK TIMES.

TOKYO, Thursday, Jan. 21.—An appeal that the world adopt an "open door" policy of free trade in all colonies to give poor nations access to essential raw materials was made at the opening of the Diet (Parliament) today by Foreign Minister Hachiro Arita.

Mr. Arita declared that if the colony-owning nations would agree to pursue this policy, it would go far toward eliminating world unrest and dissatisfaction.

He defended the Japanese "anti-Communist" pact with Germany by describing how he felt communism was menacing the world, but added that the accord had no ulterior implications and was not a threat to any country. He went further, in fact, and urged that other lands join in it.

Both Mr. Arita and Premier Koki Hirota, who opened the Diet session, laid great emphasis on Japan's efforts to promote friendship with the United States and Britain.

Defense Needs Stressed

Mr. Hirota also emphasized the necessity for rapidly expanding Japan's armaments.

"Of all the questions before the House, promotion of defense is the most important," he said. "We require this in order to insure the safety of the country, to carry out its policies and to maintain our position as the stabilizing power of East Asia. No weakness in defense can be permitted at this time.

"The reason is apparent when we survey the international situation. The army is compelled to expand its defenses without delay in order to attain security."

His references to the navy were expressed in milder terms. The navy, also, he said, is obliged to adjust its defenses to meet the new non-treaty situation, but it goes without saying that Japan will not be the first to start a naval race.

"Our naval program will continue to be governed by the principle of non-menace and non-aggression," he declared.

Mr. Hirota also defended the German pact, asserting that the Comintern's activities had been increasing in recent years.

Japan, he said, will continue to seek a settlement of outstanding problems with the Soviet.

Treaty Plan Suggested

Special to THE NEW YORK TIMES.

WASHINGTON, Jan. 20.—Foreign Minister Arita suggested to the Tokyo Diet that the problem of colonial trade be settled universally in the spirit of the Congo Basin treaty, according to the text of his address as given out here by the Japanese Embassy.

It was assumed that Mr. Arita referred to the rules and regulations established in 1884 in the Congo Basin for States that had obtained grants of territory there under the supervision of the International Association of the Congo.

By declaration of the association, foreign citizens who established themselves in the Congo received

Continued on Page Ten

ADDRESS IS PRAISED

Many Republicans Join Democrats in Hailing Tone of the Speech

CALLED A 'FINE SERMON'

Senator McNary's Remark Gets No Disagreement Even From the Partisan Critics

NO DETAILS OF PROGRAM

Those Who Expected Outline of the Next Four Years Alone Voice Disappointment

By TURNER CATLEDGE

Special to THE NEW YORK TIMES.

WASHINGTON, Jan. 20.—The elevated tone of President Roosevelt's inaugural address, especially his redeclaration of the principle that government should be the instrument of our "united purpose to solve for the individual the ever-rising problems of a complex civilization," was the memory which thousands of visitors took home with them tonight.

Democrats, of whom there were hundreds of thousands in Washington, hailed the address, in the words of Senator Harrison, as the "Roosevelt gospel of real democracy," and Republicans could do nothing but agree that it was "a fine sermon," as Senator McNary of Oregon, Republican leader of the Senate, commented.

Those who had looked for a detailed outline of the President's purposes for the next four years, especially for an elaboration of his program for the new Congress, were in part disappointed. Those who had expected that he would expand upon his view of international relations, particularly his plans for keeping the United States out of war, were also short of specifications. But within the 2,000 words of his address could be read the credo of his whole political philosophy, which, as he asserted, was ratified by the American people in the most recent expression of the popular will.

Many in Crowd Fail to Hear

The address brought no wild burst of applause from the rain-drenched audience. In fact, it was hardly heard by many of the thousands who gathered in the Capitol plaza. Those who were more interested in what he had to say than in the spectacle stayed by their radios to hear the words which the falling sleet and rain prevented the crowd from hearing.

There was a rush for copies of the address tonight, however, and newspapers carrying it in full were much in demand. It was a speech which provoked reference to no particular part. It was interesting from the standpoint of the whole, for it was the overtone that was significant: "Forward! Forward! Forward!"

Contrary to expectations, even to

Continued on Page Fifteen

Times Wide World Photo.

FRANKLIN D. ROOSEVELT BEGINS HIS SECOND TERM
Chief Justice Charles Evans Hughes administering the oath of office to the President

PRESIDENT SPEAKS

Calls for Leadership of the People Along Road They Have Chosen

SCORNS 'BLINDLY SELFISH'

But He Repeats His Reliance on 'General Welfare' Clause of the Constitution

HEAD BARED TO DOWNPOUR

'If Crowd Can Take It, I Can,' He Says—Mrs. Roosevelt Joins Him in Open Car

By ARTHUR KROCK

Special to THE NEW YORK TIMES.

WASHINGTON, Jan. 20.—On the main portico of the Capitol, his head bared to a chill, driving rain, Franklin Delano Roosevelt soon after noon today took for the second time the oath as President of the United States; and to a streaming crowd in front of, beside and behind him reconsecrated the government to leadership of "the American people forward along the road over which they have chosen to advance."

Under the terms of the Norris Amendment to the Constitution, adopted Feb. 6, 1933, this was the first inaugural to be solemnized on a date other than March 4. But the elements made it one to be remembered for another reason by visiting the capital city with a frigid downpour which was responsible for many empty places, a bedraggled parade and a rush of auditors from the space in front of the Capitol as soon as the President completed his address.

His reconsecration was in general terms, omitting specifications of program which members of his Cabinet had expected. The President briefly reviewed the dispersal of "stagnation and despair" after he took office in 1933 and pledged government to "solve for the individual the ever-rising problems of a complex civilization." He spoke scornfully of "blind economic forces" and castigated "blindly selfish men"; and once more he admonished any who may doubt it (courts, people or Congress) that the powers implied in the Constitution of 1787 were "sufficient then and now to solve problems utterly beyond individual or local action."

As to the Law and Welfare

The President, stressing once more the preamble of the national charter, emphasized that by it government is ungrudgingly entrusted with the "general welfare," and indicated that he expects from all concerned a liberal construction of laws which have general welfare for their purpose.

Of his own four-year record, this was his epitome:

"By using the new materials of social justice we have undertaken to erect on the old foundation a more enduring structure for the better use of future generations."

Again, as on March 4, 1933, the President won a shower of golden opinions by his inaugural address. Among his divergent groups of political supporters none saw in its general terms any policy in conflict with their own. Praise came from all types of political partisans in the capital (Republicans referred to the speech as a "sermon" and Democrats as a "gospel"): and there was a bull market in Wall Street.

"A Change in Moral Climate"

The President selected as the greatest alteration in the nation since he first took office "a change in moral climate" and expressed confidence that there were enough men and women of "good-will" in the country to make permanent that change. He did not find that the "happy valley" had been reached in his four years, pointing to the "indecent" living conditions of millions, with education, recreation and advancement denied them, a third of the nation ill-housed, ill-clad and ill-nourished, their poverty a brake on prosperity's wheel. Because of that prevailing condition, he said, the government will "carry on" until the happy valley is reached, paying no heed to the counsels of comfort, opportunism or timidity.

Despite the cold, pitiless beat of the rain, the President's speech was continuously interrupted with applause. And though the crowd

Continued on Page Fourteen

CROWD UNDAUNTED BY STREET FLOODS

Mud, Rain and Sleet Forgotten as Thousands Cheer the President's 'Challenge'

STAY THROUGH PARADE

Army and Naval Units March Over an Hour in Storm—Governors Ride in Autos

By F. RAYMOND DANIELL

Special to THE NEW YORK TIMES.

WASHINGTON, Jan. 20.—Ankle deep in mud, huddled under umbrellas, with rain that was half sleet pelting them in the face, thousands stood shivering in a raw wind today while Franklin D. Roosevelt swore for the second time, upon the Bible of his ancestors, to "preserve, protect and defend" the Constitution of the United States.

These and other thousands scrambled over pavements running with water like trout streams to places along Pennsylvania Avenue to see the procession of military strength, actual and potential, which the President, scorning the protection of bullet-proof glass, reviewed as he stood for more than an hour and a half on the portico of a replica of Andrew Jackson's Hermitage after his inauguration.

When the President in his inaugural address, delivered immediately after he took the oath, promised to carry on the reforms as well as the reconstruction that he had begun in the name of the New Deal, he made this "challenge:"

"The test of our progress is not whether we add more to the abundance of those who have much; it is whether we provide enough for those who have too little."

At these words, the crowd forgot its umbrellas, forgot its wet feet, forgot its discomfort and cheered and applauded. These were the sort of words that the New Dealers, engaged in a devotional demonstration of patriotism, with their acres of umbrellas swinging like black mushrooms in a mucky field, had come to hear.

Taking of the Oath Is Dramatic

The unexpected, the unscheduled, the more dramatic incident took place before the President began his inaugural address. It was indefinable, intangible and yet it impinged upon the consciousness of almost every one there as Lincoln's eloquence at Gettysburg must have impressed those fortunates who heard it. It came as he repeated after Chief Justice Charles Evans Hughes the traditional oath of office taken by the thirty-one Presidents who have preceded him.

John N. Garner, who was sworn in by Senator Joseph T. Robinson, majority leader of the Senate, responded with the simple words. "I do," after the senior Senator from Arkansas had administered the oath. Not so the President when he took the oath from Chief Justice Hughes, who has been lined up with the anti-New Deal majority of the Supreme Court on most admin-

Continued on Page Fifteen

The Inaugural Address

By The Associated Press.

WASHINGTON, Jan. 20.—The text of President Roosevelt's inaugural address, delivered immediately after he took the oath, was as follows:

My Fellow-Countrymen:

When four years ago we met to inaugurate a President, the Republic, single-minded in anxiety, stood in spirit here. We dedicated ourselves to the fulfillment of a vision—to speed the time when there would be for all the people that security and peace essential to the pursuit of happiness. We of the Republic pledged ourselves to drive from the temple of our ancient faith those who had profaned it; to end by action, tireless and unafraid, the stagnation and despair of that day.

We did those first things first.

Our covenant with ourselves did not stop there. Instinctively we recognized a deeper need—the need to find through government the instrument of our united purpose to solve for the individual the ever-rising problems of a complex civilization.

Repeated attempts at their solution without the aid of government had left us baffled and bewildered. For, without that aid, we had been unable to create those moral controls over the services of science which are necessary to make science a useful servant instead of a ruthless master of mankind. To do this we knew that we must find practical controls over blind economic forces and blindly selfish men.

We of the Republic sensed the truth that democratic government has innate capacity to protect its people against disasters once considered inevitable—to solve problems once considered unsolvable. We would not admit that we could not find a way to master economic epidemics just as, after centuries of fatalistic suffering, we had found a way to master epidemics of disease. We refused to leave the problems of our common welfare to be solved by the winds of chance and the hurricanes of disaster.

In this we Americans were discovering no wholly new truth; we were writing a new chapter in our book of self-government.

Forefathers Found Way Out of Chaos

This year marks the one hundred and fiftieth anniversary of the constitutional convention which made us a nation. At that convention our forefathers found the way out of the chaos which followed the Revolutionary War; they created a strong government with powers of united action sufficient then and now to solve problems utterly beyond individual or local solution. A century and a half ago they established the Federal Government in order to promote the general welfare and secure the blessings of liberty to the American people.

Today we invoke those same powers of government to achieve the same objectives.

Four years of new experience have not belied our historic instinct. They hold out the clear hope that government within communities, government within the separate Sates, and government of the United States can do the things the times require, without yielding its democracy. Our tasks in the last four years did not force democracy to take a holiday.

Nearly all of us recognize that as intricacies of human relationships increase, so power to govern them also must increase—power to stop evil; power to do good. The essential democracy of our nation and the safety of our people depend not upon the absence of power but upon lodging it with those whom the people can change or continue at stated intervals through an honest and free system of elections. The Constitution of 1787 did not make our democracy impotent.

In fact, in these last four years, we have made the exercise of all power more democratic; for we have begun to bring private autocratic powers into their proper subordination to the public's government. The legend that they were invincible—above and beyond the processes of a democracy—has been shattered. They have been challenged and beaten.

Our progress out of the depression is obvious.

Seeks More Enduring Social Structure

But that is not all that you and I mean by the new order of things. Our pledge was not merely to do a patchwork job with second-hand materials. By using the new materials of social justice we have undertaken to erect on the old foundations a more enduring structure for the better use of future generations.

In that purpose we have been helped by achievements of mind and spirit. Old truths have been relearned, untruths have been unlearned. We have always known that heedless self-interest was bad morals; we know now that it is bad economics. Out of the collapse of a prosperity whose builders boasted their practicality has come the conviction that in the long run economic morality pays.

We are beginning to wipe out the line that divides the practical from the ideal, and in so doing we are fashioning an instrument of unimagined power for the establishment of a morally better world.

This new understanding undermines the old admiration of

Continued on Page Fourteen

Rail Brotherhoods to Ask 20% Wage Jump; $116,500,000 Annual Rise in Joint Demand

Special to THE NEW YORK TIMES.

CHICAGO, Jan. 20.—Leaders of the five big railroad brotherhoods voted here tonight to demand a 20 per cent pay increase for about 300,000 members of the unions.

The vote came after nine days of negotiations among the brotherhood chiefs in conference here. The brotherhoods embrace all employes in the train service classifications.

Based on the October, 1936, payroll statistics issued by the Interstate Commerce Commission, the 20 per cent rise would require an increase of $116,500,000 in the annual payrolls of the country's railroads.

Formal notice of the demand for increased pay will be served on the country's carriers as soon as the necessary steps can be taken, David B. Robertson of Cleveland, president of the Brotherhood of Locomotive Firemen and Enginemen, asserted.

The brotherhood leaders did not act on a six-hour day, thirty-hour week proposal, presented at the start of their meeting.

Besides the firemen's brotherhood, the unions involved in the joint demand are the Brotherhood of Railway Trainmen, Brotherhood of Locomotive Engineers, Order of Railway Conductors and the Switchmen's Union of North America.

Mr. Robertson's group has 65,000 members. The largest brotherhood is that of the railroad trainmen, headed by A. F. Whitney of Cleveland, which has 145,000 members. The conductors have 20,000 members; engineers, 65,000, and the switchmen, 7,000.

James A. Phillips of Cedar Rapids, Iowa, is president of the conductors; Alvaney Johnson of Cleveland is president of the engineers, and Thomas C. Cashen of Buffalo is chief of the switchmen. The latter union is the only one of the five affiliated with the American Federation of Labor.

Under the Railway Labor Act the railroads of the country within thirty days after the filing of notice of demands by the unions must set a time and place for meeting with brotherhood leaders for the opening of wage negotiations. If no agreement can be reached the whole matter is then referred to Railway Labor Board for adjudication.

"All the News That's Fit to Print."

The New York Times.

LATE CITY EDITION
Fair today, little change in temperature. Tomorrow cloudy and warmer, followed by rain.
Temperatures Yesterday—Max., 37; Min., 27

VOL. LXXXVI.....No. 28,868. Entered as Second-Class Matter, Postoffice New York, N. Y. NEW YORK, SATURDAY, FEBRUARY 6, 1937. P TWO CENTS In New York City. | THREE CENTS Within 200 Miles. | FOUR CENTS Elsewhere Except in 7th and 8th Postal Zones.

ROOSEVELT ASKS POWER TO REFORM COURTS, INCREASING THE SUPREME BENCH TO 15 JUSTICES; CONGRESS STARTLED, BUT EXPECTED TO APPROVE

PROGRESS IS MADE IN MOTORS PARLEY; EVICTION DEFERRED

WORKING ON TERMS

Subcommittee Begins Study of Specific Issues in Strike

WILL REPORT THIS MORNING

Pressure From Roosevelt Is Credited With Averting Complete Collapse

MURPHY BLOCKS OUSTERS

Halts Arrest of Union Men After Court Issues Eviction Writs at Flint

Developments in Auto Strike

DETROIT—President Roosevelt's pleas avert a new deadlock in the auto strike conferences. After all-day sessions a subcommittee is named and begins a study of specific issues pending a new joint meeting today.—Page 1.

FLINT—Judge Gadola signs writs for arrest of union leaders and sit-down strikers, but Sheriff, after asking aid of troops, delays action.—Page 2.

NEW YORK—Federal Council of Churches of Christ in America condemns sit-down strikers as a "dangerous weapon." It also assails General Motors for its speed-up program.—Page. 2.

Negotiations Go On

By LOUIS STARK

Special to THE NEW YORK TIMES.

DETROIT, Feb. 5.—John L. Lewis, chairman of the Committee for Industrial Organization, and William S. Knudsen, vice president of General Motors Corporation, comprising a subcommittee designated at today's joint conference of spokesmen for both sides in the automobile strike dispute, sat down tonight with Governor Frank Murphy to formulate a report to go before the full committee tomorrow.

The subcommittee was named today after President Roosevelt's repeated telephonic intervention had saved the deadlocked automobile conference from collapsing. When the second session of the conference closed at 8 o'clock this evening Governor Murphy announced that progress had been made.

While the Governor divulged no details of the conference session today, it was learned that Mr. Lewis had made an important concession toward meeting General Motors spokesmen part way. He agreed to drop his demand that the union be the sole bargaining agency in all the sixty-nine plants of the corporation and to limit this demand to twenty plants where union men are on strike.

Company Reported Wavering

The corporation committee, it was reported, appeared tentatively to be willing to grant sole bargaining rights to the union in six plants on certain conditions, but made no definite commitment that could be regarded by the union as unqualified acceptance of its position in these six plants. Actual and positive agreement on this point awaited further clarification at the hands of the subcommittee tonight.

In announcing progress tonight Governor Murphy, flushed and beaming, warned against over optimism. He indicated that as yet there was no absolute assurance that whatever progress had been made would broaden out until a complete settlement had been written.

Nevertheless, Mr. Murphy's announcement that a sub-committee had been appointed to meet tonight to explore the various subjects in dispute, presumably collective bargaining, wages, hours and creation of machinery for the settlement of disputes, gave rise to hope in many quarters that a settlement might be in sight.

The full joint conference of three on each side will convene again at 10 o'clock tomorrow morning to hear the reports being prepared tonight by the sub-committees.

Presses Roosevelt Plea

Governor Murphy pressed home to both sides today the admonition of President Roosevelt that the nation looked to them to settle their dispute in a manner betokening public-spirited citizens in a civilized community, and without the indus-

Continued on Page Two

Great-Grandmother, 72, Joins Picket Line in Flint

By The Associated Press.

FLINT, Mich., Feb. 5.—A 72-year-old great-grandmother joined union pickets today in front of Fisher Body Plant No. 1, held by sit-down strikers.

She was Mrs. Rebecca Goddard of Clio, Mich., who said she had nine or ten relatives, including a son, inside the plant.

"I just came down from Clio to show some of my neighbors," she said. "There are a lot of sit-down grouches up there. You don't know what sit-down grouches are? Why, they're people who don't believe in the union."

She was asked if it was true she was a great-grandmother.

"Certainly," she replied. "I have six children, twenty grandchildren and about ten great-grandchildren. My youngest son, Robert, is in that plant right now."

She said she also had some grandchildren and nephews in the plant.

FRIARS FACE TRIAL AS SPANISH REBELS

'People's Court' Will Assemble Monday for Case Against 60 Escorial Guardians

1,500 OTHERS ARE INDICTED

Speedy Hearings Are Planned for Prisoners Who Fill the Jails in Madrid

By The Associated Press.

MADRID, Feb. 5.—A special "people's court" will sit in judgment on the Augustinian friars who dwelt in the Escorial monastery built by King Philip II nearly 400 years ago, the government announced today.

The monks are charged with holding "anti-government tendencies" in the civil war. So far the government has kept possession of Escorial, northwest of Madrid, despite encirclement and siege by insurgent armies.

There are perhaps 60 of the friars and there are nearly 1,500 more persons who are similarly indicted by the Leftist régime in Spain.

Trials Begin Monday

The friars will be tried by a court made up of a judge and two "representatives of the people." The court's session will begin Monday, and it has been instructed to conclude the trial within twenty days.

Simultaneously, Wenceslao Carrillo, Director General of Public Safety, announced he would immediately begin to examine the cases of all prisoners in Madrid's teeming jails with a view to liberating those against whom there is insufficient evidence of Rebel activity. The others will be rushed to trial.

The Augustinian friars were custodians of the edifice which housed the tombs of Spanish Kings since Philip II had it built to commemorate a victory over the French in 1557. He intended it as a retreat from Madrid's court gayety.

When the military uprising plunged Spain into civil war the large Escorial monastery was converted into a temporary prison for 500 Summer residents of the town. On their release a wing of the vast, rectangular structure was converted into barracks. The treasures the monks had guarded were stored in other parts of the building.

Constant improvements on the building, even in modern times, gave Spaniards a figure of speech. They have come to say "This is work on Escorial" when they wish to describe some task never finished.

State Monument Planned

Since the advent of the Spanish Republic it had been planned to remove the friars to allow conversion of the monastery into a national monument along with royal palaces and other properties. But the war gave a different aspect to their evacuation.

The mausoleum has but one vacant sepulcher, that reserved for former King Alfonso XIII, now an exile with slight chance of lying with his predecessors.

One of the friars' most-prized possessions was a rich library of Arabic, Hebrew and Spanish manuscripts. They had a school of higher education bearing the name of Alfonso's father, Alfonso XII, and a university, similarly named, devoted to the education of the sons of the Spanish nobility.

$100,000 CAFE SHUT BY RACKET BOMBS, OWNER TESTIFIES

Stench Missiles Used for Ten Months After He Refused to Pay $3,000, He Says

FOUR OTHERS TELL ILLS

Restaurant Manager Describes Threats to His Children and $2,000 Demand

A $100,000 example was given to the Supreme Court jury hearing evidence in the restaurant racket trial yesterday by Hyman Gross, who had been one of the owners of the Gerard Cafeteria, on Broadway at Times Square, which was closed by a stench bombardment ten months after it opened.

The experience of Mr. Gross, who had refused to pay Louis Beitcher, the racket's collector, $3,000, was one of five cases, three of attempted extortion and two of extortion placed in the record before Justice Philip J. McCook during the day.

In another, John A. Miller, manager of the Anne Miller restaurant, then at 43 West Eighth Street and a place patronized by Juror No. 5, Franklin H. Middleton, told of kidnap threats against his children and a demand for $2,000. Harry A. Vogelstein, one of the defendants, Miller said, told that "only saps" picketed.

Tells of $1,750 Payment

Isidoris Coviris, one of three owners of the Broadway Cafeteria at 2,230 Broadway, testified that he paid Beitcher $1,750 to purchase protection from the "rights of the union," and Richard M. Decker, owner of a night club called the Congress Restaurant at 1,657 Broadway, told of a sudden strike called by Local 16 of the Waiters Union to force him to join the Metropolitan Restaurant and Cafeteria Association, an employers' association, which he did at a cost of $285.

Two of Mr. Decker's waiters had worked for Jules Martin, the man who organized the racket for Arthur (Dutch Schultz) Flegenheimer, when he operated a restaurant in West Forty-eighth Street.

The flow of witnesses was speeded up by the fact that attorneys for the eight defendants, including three officials of Local 16 of the Waiters Union, two of Local 302 of the Cafeteria Workers Union, and three others, two of them lawyers, connected with the Metropolitan Association, shortened their cross-examination.

Run Short of Witnesses

Toward the end of the day the prosecution, conducted by William B. Herlands and Milton C. Schilback, two of Special Prosecutor Thomas E. Dewey's chief assistants, ran short of witnesses and a half-hour wait followed while more were produced after telephone calls.

Mr. Gross was examined by Mr. Schilback. He said his regular business was real estate, but in July, 1933, after he and associates "had spent $100,000 to build the place," the Gerard was opened at 1,508 Broadway. He had personally put up $40,000, he said.

Before they opened, Max Pincus, then in Local 302 but now dead,

Continued on Page Thirty-six

Supreme Court Keeps Up With Its Work, Say Aides

By The Associated Press.

WASHINGTON, Feb. 5.—Supreme Court attachés said today that the tribunal was up to date in handling its business.

They explained it had been so since soon after William Howard Taft became Chief Justice in 1921.

When he went on the bench, fulfilling a lifelong ambition, the tribunal was from two to three years behind in its work. He speeded up disposition of the litigation so that soon afterward it was abreast of the docket.

SIX ON HIGH BENCH ELIGIBLE TO RETIRE

They and Six Justices of the Circuit Courts Could Come Under Roosevelt Plan

13 OTHER JURISTS LISTED

These Members of the Lower Courts Also Have Reached 70, With 10 Years of Service

Special to THE NEW YORK TIMES.

WASHINGTON, Feb. 5.—Not only six of the nine justices of the Supreme Court but half a dozen of the judges of the Federal Circuit Courts and an undisclosed number of the judges of the District Courts would be eligible for retirement as having reached the age of 70 after ten years of service on the bench, as urged by President Roosevelt.

There are forty-three judgeships in the Circuit Courts and 163 in the District tribunals, but in some instances there are still vacancies in appointments.

Preferring not to single out individuals, the Department of Justice refused to reveal the details today, but it was established from other sources that about six of the Circuit justices could retire on these qualifications.

As President Roosevelt stated that twenty-five out of a total judiciary of 237 could thus leave the bench, and as it is known that six Supreme Court and six Circuit justices were so classed, the thirteen others must be members of the district benches and special Federal courts.

Chief Justice Hughes is, of course, among those who will be in the 70-year-old, ten-year service class this year. In fact, he will be 75 years old April 11, and Justice Van Devanter will be 78 just six days later.

Justice McReynolds's seventy-fifth birthday fell on last Wednesday. Justice Brandeis, oldest member of the court, reached the age of 80 Nov. 13 last. Justice Sutherland will be 75 on March 25 and Justice Butler 71 on March 17.

Justice Stone will be 65 Oct. 11,

Continued on Page Ten

West Virginian Saved After 8 Days in Mine; Had No Food, Forced to Drink Sulphur Water

By The Associated Press.

FLEMINGTON, W. Va., Feb. 5.—Eight foodless days of utter darkness while lost in the débris-choked passageways of an abandoned mine ended today for Robert Johnson, 36-year-old rural mail carrier.

"I sure thought I was a goner," he said.

Johnson told from his cot in a hospital of praying through the long hours in the damp mine, of giving up all hope, then of seeing a dim glow of lamps carried by rescue workers.

"Thank God, my prayers were answered," he sobbed fervently before a sleeping potion administered by physicians put him to sleep.

Doctors had broken his long fast—he had only sulphur water to drink in the mine—with plenty of black coffee, then with bowls of strained soup.

Rescue crews found Johnson nearly two miles from the mine entrance early today. He was huddled behind a heap of jagged chunks of slate in the mine which he operated to dig coal in his spare time for sale to neighbors.

The crews had expected difficulty in removing the slate, but had little actual trouble in reaching the imprisoned man.

Three of the scores of volunteers who had searched the mine day and night since Johnson disappeared on Jan. 27 heard his feeble cries for help while exploring a narrow tunnel.

His first words were to assure himself he hadn't merely imagined a light had cut through the dark.

C. P. Pride, assistant safety director for the State Department of Mines quoted him:

"I told myself, 'Bob, please don't lose that light.'" He didn't.

As the rescue party came closer he called to Mike Stanko Jr., Edward Whitehair and William Westfall, all his friends and neighbors:

"Take your time, I'll guide you by your light."

They cautiously approached the heap of slate, reached through a hole and gripped Johnson's hand—assurance he was safe.

Then word went to the surface, sped through this little community of about 400 population in Northeastern West Virginia. Pride and eight others gathered stretchers and blankets. They hurried into the mine, waded and swam through a deep pool of water covering nearly an acre where originally, many believed, Johnson had drowned while trying to open clogged drains.

After Johnson was taken out on the mountainside, he was carried a quarter of a mile down a snow-covered path to a waiting ambulance. There he was joined by his wife—among his first questions was "How's my wife?"—and hurried to a hospital fifteen miles away in Clarksburg, the nearest large city.

BILL IS INTRODUCED

Robinson and Bankhead Act for Passage by Senate and House

MAJORITY FOR PROPOSAL

But Most Conservative Democrats Are Silent and Republicans Are Hostile

SPECULATION ON JUSTICES

Those Mentioned for New Places Include J. M. Landis, Richberg and Frankfurter

By TURNER CATLEDGE

Special to THE NEW YORK TIMES.

WASHINGTON, Feb. 5.—President Roosevelt's proposals for a comprehensive reform of the Federal judiciary fell today like a bombshell upon a Congress which thought it already had experienced the ultimate in surprises when it heard his recent messages on reorganization of the executive branch.

Not even the closest of the President's Congressional advisers knew of the plan until they were called to the White House this morning and told to prepare for the shock at noon.

Regardless of the far-reaching nature of the proposals, the balance of Congressional reaction was decidedly in their favor. Judging from the content of the comment, this was due to three main factors—the resentment in Congress at recent decisions of the Supreme Court holding its acts invalid, the continuing faith of the so-called "liberal" element in Mr. Roosevelt and his works, and the unquestioning loyalty of the leadership in both houses to him and his program.

Republican Protest Vehement

On the other side of the scales were the spontaneous objections of the Republicans, characterized by a vehemence akin to that of the last Presidential campaign, and the disapproving attitude of a number of conservative Democrats.

Most of the conservative Democrats declined to comment.

Although the President's plan for a non-amendment approach to the issues raised by the court's interpretations ran counter to the plans of several outstanding legislators, notably Senator Robinson and Senator Ashurst, the leadership started laying general plans for its enactment. Senator Robinson predicted that the recommendations would receive "favorable consideration" in the Senate, and Speaker Bankhead promised quick action in the House on what he considered a "sound principle" of judicial reform.

The details of the plan, particularly the effective proposal for appointment of six new justices to the Supreme Court, brought forth limitless speculation as to the possible appointees. High on practically every list of possibilities were Senator Robinson, James M. Landis, who will shortly resign as chairman of the Securities and Exchange Commission to become dean of the Harvard Law School; Felix Frankfurter, Professor of Law at Harvard; Donald R. Richberg, former general counsel of the National Recovery Administration; Senators Wagner and Ashurst and Chairman Summers of the House Judiciary Committee.

The reform proposals were submitted in accordance with the best approved New Deal practices. They were worked out in every essential detail by the President with his administrative advisers, then the Congressional leaders were called in and informed of the schema. Later a message, with supporting data and the draft of a bill, was sent to Congress.

The only difference today from the practice followed with most of the other measures of major importance was that the three documents—message, supporting data and bill draft—were appended together in a single sheaf of papers, and representatives of the press were called in to be informed in advance of their specifications. The latter was not exactly an innovation, as the President follows this practice regularly on involved budget matters and recently used it in presenting and explaining his plan on executive reorganization.

The President's attitude in explaining the proposal today was in

Continued on Page Nine

President's Message

Special to THE NEW YORK TIMES.

WASHINGTON, Feb. 5.—Following are the text of the President's message to Congress on the judiciary, the draft of his proposed bill and the text of the letter of Attorney General Cummings to the President:

I have recently called the attention of the Congress to the clear need for a comprehensive program to reorganize the administrative machinery of the executive branch of our government. I now make a similar recommendation to the Congress in regard to the judicial branch of the government, in order that it also may function in accord with modern necessities.

The Constitution provides that the President "shall from time to time give to the Congress information of the state of the Union, and recommend to their consideration such measures as he shall judge necessary and expedient." No one else is given a similar mandate. It is therefore the duty of the President to advise the Congress in regard to the judiciary whenever he deems such information or recommendation necessary.

I address you for the further reason that the Constitution vests in the Congress direct responsibility in the creation of courts and judicial offices and in the formulation of rules of practice and procedure. It is, therefore, one of the definite duties of the Congress constantly to maintain the effective functioning of the Federal judiciary.

The judiciary has often found itself handicapped by insufficient personnel with which to meet a growing and more complex business. It is true that the physical facilities of conducting the business of the courts have been greatly improved, in recent years, through the erection of suitable quarters, the provision of adequate libraries and the addition of subordinate court officers. But in many ways these are merely the trappings of judicial office. They play a minor part in the processes of justice.

Since the earliest days of the republic, the problem of the personnel of the courts has needed the attention of the Congress. For example, from the beginning, over repeated protests to President Washington, the justices of the Supreme Court were required to "ride circuit" and, as circuit justices, to hold trials throughout the length and breadth of the land—a practice which endured over a century.

In almost every decade since 1789, changes have been made by the Congress whereby the numbers of judges and the duties of judges in Federal Courts have been altered in one way or an-

Continued on Page Eight

STOCKS DROP FAST ON COURT MESSAGE

Sweeping Declines Stop a Rise, Making Market the Year's Second Largest

BRIEF RALLIES ARE FUTILE

List Closes Only Slightly Above Day's Lows—Some Bankers Say Effect Will Be Mitigated

President Roosevelt's proposals for changes in the Federal judiciary came as a stunning surprise to the financial community yesterday. They evoked uncertainty and alarm among bankers and business men which found expression in a sweeping decline of stock prices.

Prices of representative issues on the New York Stock Exchange, which had been advancing during the morning, broke swiftly as the President's message was being read. The volume of dealings increased, the stock ticker fell five minutes behind the pace of trading and earlier gains were quickly turned to losses of one to three or four points.

Brief rallies in the afternoon gave way repeatedly to renewed selling and closing prices were only slightly above the lowest levels of the day.

From the standpoint of number of shares dealt in, the market was the second largest of the year, the total of transactions being 3,321,000. On the basis of number of issues to appear on the tape, 975, it was the broadest market since Nov. 12.

Course Unexpected by Bankers

A sample of the net declines among important issues showed: United States Steel down 2⅜ points at 96⅝; Bethlehem Steel, off 2⅜ at 81¼; Allied Chemical, 5 points lower at 235; Allis Chalmers, off 2½ at 75½; Anaconda Copper, down 1¼ at 54⅜; Chrysler, off 2 at 126¼, and Standard Oil of New Jersey, off 1⅝ at 70⅝.

Domestic corporation bonds were irregularly weaker, while the market for government securities showed declines fairly evenly matched by advances.

The response of financiers to the news was based upon concern and uncertainty over its implications rather than upon disagreement with the President's objectives. In spite of rumors which have been heard from time to time that Mr. Roosevelt might seek to enlarge the Supreme Court, it had been felt by most bankers that such a course was unlikely.

Consequently, as the chief executive of one big bank expressed it, the financial community was "flabbergasted" at the suddenness of the announcement, the drastic character of the changes proposed and the implications of criticism of

Continued on Page Ten

AIM TO PACK COURT, DECLARES HOOVER

Roosevelt Move Transcends Any Partisanship Question, Ex-President Holds

WIDELY CRITICIZED HERE

'Shameful Day' in Our History, Colby Asserts—Justice Black Hails 'Greatest Advance'

President Roosevelt's message to Congress asking for authority to appoint Federal judges in addition to those more than 70 years old was characterized last night by Herbert Hoover, his predecessor in the White House, as a proposal for "packing" the Supreme Court to get through New Deal measures.

Mr. Hoover declared that the President's proposal went far beyond any question of partisanship, and advised that Congress delay action on it until the people had time to formulate their views. His comment, made public at his suite in the Waldorf-Astoria, was as follows:

"Stripped of subsidiary matters, some of which are admirable, the President's action amounts to this:

"The Supreme Court has proved many of the New Deal proposals as unconstitutional. Instead of the ample alternatives of the Constitution by which these proposals could be submitted to the people through constitutional amendment, it is now proposed to make changes by 'packing' the Supreme Court. It has the implication of subordination of the court to the personal power of the Executive. Because all this reaches to the very depth of our form of government, it far transcends any question of partisanship.

"The Congress should delay action until the people have had ample time to formulate their views on it. In the long sweep of the Republic a few months are not too much to consider a vital change in the repeated judgment of the American people over 150 years. That judgment has always been that their liberties have depended greatly on the independence of the court and that they themselves should determine changes in the Constitution."

Reaction to the President's proposal among New York City lawyers was generally strongly unfavorable. Former Justice Clarence J. Shearn, president of the Bar Association of the City of New York, asserted that it was plainly an attempt to pack the Supreme Court for cases in which the Federal administration would have a political interest and called on all opposed to "mobocracy" or dictatorship to fight it.

Bainbridge Colby, Secretary of State during the Wilson administration, declared it was an attempt to

Continued on Page Nine

SURPRISE MESSAGE

Asks Authority to Name New Justices if Old Do Not Quit at 70

SEES NEED OF 'NEW BLOOD'

Constitutional Amendment and Statutory Judiciary Curb Would Be Side-Stepped

LOWER COURTS AFFECTED

Bench Would Be Expanded, Appeals Speeded and Defense Assured in Injunctions

By ARTHUR KROCK

Special to THE NEW YORK TIMES.

WASHINGTON, Feb. 5.—The President suddenly, at noon today, cut through the tangle of proposals made by his Congressional leaders to "bring legislative and judicial action into closer harmony" with a broadaxe message to Congress recommending the passage of statutes to effect drastic Federal court reforms.

The message—prepared in a small group and with deepest secrecy—was accompanied by a letter from the Attorney General and by a bill, drawn at the Department of Justice, which would permit an increase in the membership of the Supreme Court from nine to a maximum of fifteen if judges reaching the age of 70 declined to retire; add a total of not more than fifty judges to all classes of the Federal courts; send appeals from lower-court decisions on constitutional questions direct to the Supreme Court, and require that government attorneys be heard before any lower-court injunction issue against the enforcement of any act of Congress.

Avoiding both the devices of constitutional amendment and statutory limitation of Supreme Court powers, which were favored by his usual spokesmen in Congress, the President endorsed an ingenious plan which will on passage give him the power to name six new justices of the Supreme Court.

Power Left to the President

Under the provisions of the bill drawn by the Department of Justice for Congress, if the six now sitting justices who are more than 70 years of age do not resign, the President is empowered to name a new member for each justice in that category. These are the Chief Justice and Justices Brandeis, Van Devanter, Butler, McReynolds and Sutherland. Thus, after the passage of the bill, which is generally expected, the court will number anywhere from nine to fifteen justices.

Although the message—an unusually long one for the President—was a general criticism of the effects upon government and private litigants of overburdened courts and superannuated judges, and stressed a general plea to Congress to make provision for "a constant and systematic addition of younger blood" to "vitalize the courts," Congress instantly recognized its outstanding feature and purpose.

Although the message outlined basic defects in the administration of justice in the United States, and contained many reforms to which no exception will be taken, Congress quickly sensed that the President had hurdled the present majority of the Supreme Court on his way to the goal he outlined in his opening message of the session. This, as he stated it, is to find "means to adapt our legal forms and our judicial interpretation to the actual present needs of the largest progressive democracy in the modern world."

Variety of Emotions Aroused

That passage was the one which had brought the most cheers from the floors of Congress when the President uttered it. To achieve its aim was the object of all the proposed amendments and statutes which have heaped high in the Congressional hoppers since the opening of the session. When members of the Senate and the House became aware of the ingenious but effective manner in which the President planned to attain his objective without touching the Constitution or the powers of the court, they were torn by a variety of emotions.

Senator Robinson, the majority leader in his branch, said the mes-

Continued on Page Eight

"All the News That's Fit to Print."

The New York Times.

LATE CITY EDITION
Fair today, temperature unchanged. Tomorrow cloudy, warmer; rain or snow in afternoon or at night.
Temperatures Yesterday—Max., 45; Min., 30

VOL. LXXXVI.....No. 28,873. Entered as Second-Class Matter, Postoffice, New York, N. Y. NEW YORK, THURSDAY, FEBRUARY 11, 1937. PP TWO CENTS In New York City. | THREE CENTS Within 200 Miles. | FOUR CENTS Elsewhere Except in 7th and 8th Postal Zones.

ROOSEVELT BARS SPLITTING OF COURT REFORM PROGRAM; HOUSE PASSES PENSION BILL

ROOSEVELT IS FIRM

Halts Sumners Move to Handle Controversial Issues Separately

CALLS IN SENATE LEADERS

Of 5 Committeemen at Hour's Parley Only One Voices Wholehearted Support

CONGRESS DEBATES SHARP

President's Drought Message Is Read to Cool Off the House—Democrats Lead Attack

Court Reform Contest

President Roosevelt won the first legislative tilt over his program for reforming of the judiciary, insisting that the less controversial parts not be split off for separate action in Congress. The House passed the Sumners bill to permit Supreme Court justices to retire at 70 at full pay. Page 1.

Sharp debate developed in both the Senate and the House on court proposals. Page 14.

An informal poll and other statements showed that twenty-two Senators opposed the President's plan to change the personnel of the Supreme Court, nineteen favored it and thirty-six were not yet committed. Page 15.

The Kansas House condemned the President's proposal, the Delaware House upheld it, while the Pennsylvania Senate, the Indiana House and Ohio Senate blocked moves opposing it. Other States prepared to act. Page 14.

Republican members of the Albany Legislature were ready to open a fight for a memorial to Congress against the change. Page 1.

President Calls In Leaders

By TURNER CATLEDGE

Special to THE NEW YORK TIMES.

WASHINGTON, Feb. 10.—President Roosevelt won the first legislative move today on his judiciary reform proposals when, by personal intervention, he stopped the splitting of the program in the House and prevented immediate consideration of the less controversial sections, as independent from his plan to remake the Supreme Court.

The House passed by a vote of 315 to 75 the bill previously reported by its Judiciary Committee providing for voluntary retirement of Supreme Court justices at 70 at full pay, by which its leaders hope eventually to reach a compromise on the disputed part of the President's proposed reforms.

As soon as this was done, however, the leaders suddenly abandoned a plan to push through another measure embodying the President's recommendation for speeding appeals on constitutional matters from the lower courts to the Supreme Court and permitting the Attorney General to intervene in any case, whether the government is a party or not, involving a constitutional issue.

Representative Sumners, chairman of the Judiciary Committee, who visited the White House this morning, stated frankly that plans for consideration of the bill were changed because the President wanted "to discuss the matter further."

Foes' Strategy Is Upset

Favorable action today on that bill would have divided the President's program and left strictly on its merits the proposal to appoint six new members to the Supreme Court to replace or supplement justices who have passed the age of 70. This would have been a successful use of the strategy which opponents of the President's program intend to follow in the Senate, and House adversaries had counted on voting for the bill in the hope that it would complicate action on the other proposal.

Debate over reform of the Supreme Court broke today in the House over the retirement bill and in the Senate over a proposal of Senator McKellar to prevent lower courts from holding acts of Congress unconstitutional or restraining their enforcement.

Further indicating that he had assumed personal leadership in the face of mounting opposition to his

Continued on Page Fifteen

Fight Over Court Reform Looms As Albany Republicans Lay Plans

Legislators Draft Protest to Congress Against Roosevelt Proposals—Issue Comes Up in Many States, With Four at Least Giving Tacit Approval

Special to THE NEW YORK TIMES.

ALBANY, Feb. 10.—President Roosevelt's judiciary reform program was put to the fore today in the Legislature and it was predicted that within a short time the issue would become one of sharp dispute on partisan lines in the Senate and Assembly.

Senator Thomas C. Desmond, Republican, announced that tomorrow he would offer a resolution to memorialize Congress to reject the proposal. Assemblymen Wadsworth and Peterson, both Republicans, stated that they would offer similar resolutions in the lower house Monday night.

Meanwhile, George H. Bond of Syracuse, president of the State Bar Association, made known plans for a meeting of the executive committee of that body here on Feb. 20 "to take such action as may be proper." In view of recent statements by leading attorneys in the State, "the proper action" in all probability will be condemnation of the judiciary proposals of the President.

Assemblyman Wadsworth and Senator Desmond, it is understood, are not acting officially for the Republican party in drafting a memorial, but it is forecast that once they present the issue to the Legislature it will gain solid Republican support. Likewise, it is believed here, the Democrats will be against it just as solidly.

"President Roosevelt is attempting to pack the Supreme Court," said Mr. Wadsworth, "so that his New Deal proposals will be declared constitutional. It is time that the Republican Assembly went on record against such a brazen proposal.

"It is to be hoped that Congress administers a stern rebuke to Mr. Roosevelt by defeating his plan."

The Republicans control the Assembly with 76 votes to 74 votes for the Democrats. If, as expected, the issue is decided strictly on party lines, absence of a few members on either side may decide the fate of the measure.

The Senate is dominated by the Democrats by a good margin, and there, it is believed, the measure will stand very little chance of

Continued on Page Fourteen

LEHMAN BILL WINS ON SOCIAL SECURITY

Assembly Finally Passes the Measure, 115 to 20, and the Senate Completes Action

WADSWORTH FIGHT FAILS

Heck, Ives, Moffat Are Among Those Voting for Bill—Governor to Sign This Week

By W. A. WARN

Special to THE NEW YORK TIMES.

ALBANY, Feb. 10.—Governor Lehman's long fight for adoption of his social security program ended in victory today when the Assembly, with its Republican majority, passed by a vote of 115 to 20 the Dunnigan Social Security Bill, which had been sent to the Assembly for concurrence following passage by the Democratic-controlled Senate.

The Senate passed the Governor's bill on Jan. 13, just one week after the legislative session began. But after the bill reached the Assembly it was amended in some minor details following conferences between the Governor and leaders of the Assembly. Consequently it had to be sent back to the Senate to enable that branch to concur with the Assembly in the amendments.

The Senate, after marking time to allow the Assembly to act, received the bill and passed it for a second time without debate and without dissent.

Governor Lehman said tonight that he would sign the Dunnigan bill before the end of the week. The measure is adjusted to fit into the Federal social security plan, and will place the State in line to have its own disbursements for aid to the under-privileged matched by contributions to the State from the Federal Treasury. The counties will be charged 50 per cent of the cost of the social security service, the remaining half being defrayed by the State and the Federal Government.

In the bill which was defeated in the Republican Assembly last year, the Governor had put forward a social security program providing for continuation, with some changes, of the State old-age pension system, aid for the blind, for maternal and child health work, for dependent children, for service to crippled childen and for public health work in the counties. This year's version provides for all these except the old-age pension system, since the Republicans last year put through in the Legislature an Old-Age Pension Bill which the Governor finally approved.

"I greatly rejoice in the passage of the Social Security Bill," Governor Lehman said tonight. "It is a liberal piece of legislation and a great step forward for the benefit of the handicapped and under-

Continued on Page Six

$50,000 SHAKEDOWN OF S. KLEIN FAILED

Merchant Was 'Not Interested' in Offer to Remove Pickets From Store Restaurant

CAFE MAN INTERMEDIARY

Beitcher's Liaison Man Tells of Reporting on Grand Jury to Association Lawyer

S. Klein, Union Square clothing merchant, was asked to pay $50,000 for the removal of a picket line in front of an eating place in one of his store buildings, the Supreme Court jury hearing the restaurant racket trial was told yesterday.

The demand was taken to a Klein executive by Samuel Gershowitz, a constant contributor to the gangsters dominating the racket and more than once the liaison man between Louis Beitcher, collector for Jules Martin, and intended victims with whom Beitcher avoided direct dealing.

When Mr. Gershowitz took the stand William B. Herlands, assistant prosecutor, told Justice Philip J. McCook that the testimony to be adduced was offered as bearing on all forty-eight counts of the indictment rather than on any specific one. The indictment contained no specific count on any of three payments that the witness said he had made, one to Martin and two to Beitcher.

After Martin's Murder

The attempted "shakedown" of Klein, according to Mr. Gershowitz, took place in the Spring of 1935, which was at about the time that Martin was murdered in Troy, N. Y., and his place at the head of the restaurant racket was taken over by Samuel Krantz, now a fugitive.

Mr. Gershowitz had recently opened a place called the Ritz Diner at 27 Union Square, on property owned by Mr. Klein. On two other restaurants he had previously paid $3,700, and on the Ritz, a small enterprise, he was merely required to join the Metropolitan Restaurant and Cafeteria Association, of which he is still a director.

At this time a picket line was in front of the restaurant in the Klein store. Beitcher asked Mr. Gershowitz to go to a man identified only as "Mr. Simon," who had charge of the Klein properties, and offer, on the gangster's behalf, to get the picket line removed for $50,000. "Mr. Simon" replied that "they weren't interested." This information was conveyed to Beitcher.

The Klein eating place was subsequently closed and was never unionized.

This was only one incident in a long series of meetings and deals with Martin and Beitcher, and also the Metropolitan association, which

Continued on Page Twenty-four

ROAD TO VALENCIA IS STILL PASSABLE, WRITER DISCOVERS

He Taxis Along Highway and Bridge Under Rebel Artillery and Machine-Gun Fire

MORE CATALANS MOBILIZE

Cabinet Acts After Barcelona Is Shelled by an Insurgent Ship for an Hour at Night

By HERBERT L. MATTHEWS

Wireless to THE NEW YORK TIMES.

MADRID, Feb. 10.—The Valencia road is not cut and has not been cut despite the claims by the Insurgents that they had cut it.

The writer can make this statement tonight positively, having just driven with a colleague, Irving Pflaum of The United Press, along the road and across the Arganda bridge under machine-gun and artillery fire to Arganda, sixteen miles southeast of Madrid, from where there is a clear, untouched road to the coast.

To the right of the road going toward Valencia, in fact, government troops as we drove along were successfully pushing the Insurgents back from Vaciamadrid.

At staff headquarters when we set out we were told that the officers directing operations were well down the road, where the writer had seen them yesterday on a similar but fruitless trip. At that point we talked to couriers who had just driven up from Arganda on motorcycles, and they drew a clear picture of what to expect.

Warned to Drive Fast

"Yes," they said, "the road is open and you can be blankety-blank sure that it is going to stay open! But it is under fire. From Kilometer Eighteen to Nineteen you will come under machine-gun fire, but go as fast as you can and the chances of being hit will be slight.

"Then you will reach the Arganda bridge, which has been the Insurgents' unsuccessful objective for five days. They are attacking now, but we are holding them. The bridge will probably be fired upon by artillery, but bowl across at top speed and pull up in front of a solid red brick house, where you will find a large group of soldiers."

That seemed fair enough to us, but Ramon, our chauffeur, refused flatly to go, pointing with some justice to the ramshackle old taxicab that constituted our only form of locomotion. The militiamen around us laughed at him.

"You're a fine chauffeur," they said, "but you're afraid."

That is one thing that Spanish pride cannot stand. Ramon got purple in the face, exploded into a torrent of expletives and said that if we insisted on going he would take us. So back we got into the car and started off.

Window Is Lowered

We lowered one window on the side from which the firing would come, for glass does not stop a bullet and on the contrary adds its own danger. The back window next to the seat would not come down, so I shielded my face with my right arm.

We conversed until we passed Kilometer Eighteen, and then the conversation stopped. The cab, which was following two couriers on a single motor cycle, rattled and bumped at its top speed of about forty miles an hour.

Suddenly the ugly sound of machine-gun bullets crackling against

Continued on Page Twelve

HULL CALLS PACTS FOR FOREIGN TRADE PEACE INSURANCE

Letter to Senate Committee Warns of Peril if Reciprocal Policy Is Scrapped

SAYRE GRILLED ON STAND

Democrats Lead Republicans in Critical Examination of Administration Program

Secretary Hull's letter to the committee appears on Page 2.

Special to THE NEW YORK TIMES.

WASHINGTON, Feb. 10.—Even if the United States should be able to escape actual military participation in any large-scale international war it would be certain to suffer heavily from the economic upheaval the war would cause, Secretary Hull told the Senate Finance Committee in a letter to its chairman, Senator Harrison, made public today.

The nation's best chance to avoid such suffering, Mr. Hull wrote, was to promote peace through prosecution of the administration's reciprocal agreement program for the revival of international trade and the promotion of universal prosperity.

The Secretary of State wrote his letter to be read in lieu of his appearance before the committee as it began its hearings on a resolution to extend for another three years the tariff bargaining powers granted to President Roosevelt in 1934. The House adopted the resolution yesterday.

Between the lines of the letter was apparent Mr. Hull's concern at the existing international situation and his feeling that this country's economic contribution to peace, the only one it could make, must be hastened lest it come too late. He declared that economic distress was the most dangerous cause of war and had already forced many nations in the direction of military conflict.

Policy Is Declared Vital

Though Mr. Hull told the committee that international economic warfare showed signs of abating, he added that abandonment by this country of its trade agreements program would start it up again.

"A recrudescence of international economic warfare will spell unimaginable disaster to the whole recovery process," he declared.

In Mr. Hull's absence the administration put forth its star witness in the person of Francis B. Sayre, Assistant Secretary of State.

Mr. Sayre was clearly appearing before a body of men generally less sympathetic with the administration's program than was the House Ways and Means Committee, before which he had previously testified.

During the entire day hardly a single question was asked of him or a single observation made which indicated a friendly interest on the part of any questioner. Such conservative Democratic Senators as Connally of Texas, Bailey of North Carolina and Gerry of Rhode Island asked more skeptical and critical questions than did the Republican members of the committee.

Vandenberg Leads Attack

Senator Vandenberg led the Republican attack on the witness, aided to some degree by Senator Capper and Senator Davis.

Although Mr. Vandenberg's examination of the witness today was

Continued on Page Two

Name 'Tim' and a Tip Trap Mattson Suspect; Woman Companion of Ex-Convict Also Sought

By The Associated Press.

SEATTLE, Feb. 10.—State police said tonight that a man held here in connection with the kidnapping of Charles Mattson was arrested at a hotel, where he registered as "Tim Donovan," the same first name used in the crudely printed $28,000 ransom note left at the Mattson home by the kidnapper on Dec. 27.

The prisoner, booked as H. A. Post, a 32-year-old seaman, was arrested yesterday. Also known as James G. McDonald, he had been sought since Feb. 5 on "general pick-up orders." Detective A. E. Kuehl said the man was picked up on an "underworld tip."

The prisoner, a former convict of San Quentin prison, California, has denied knowledge of the kidnapping and death of the 10-year-old boy, whose nude body was found battered near Everett, Wash., on Jan. 11.

Chief William Cole of the State patrol, who ordered the arrest last night, said Post answered the kidnapper's description. Many other persons, however, have been arrested for their resemblance to the dark, unshaven man who broke through a French door into the living room of the Dr. W. W. Mattson home at Tacoma and took his son away. All others have been released.

Federal agents suddenly started an exhaustive perusal of police bulletins after three of them questioned Post. They declined to comment.

State and Tacoma police at American Lake, near Tacoma, sought for questioning a red-headed woman, described by State Patrol Chief William Cole as the prisoner's recent companion.

A police official said Virginia Chatfield, 15, and the Mattson boy's brother and sister, William, 16, and Muriel, 14, who saw the kidnapper, would confront the prisoner in a police line-up. The families of the children said, however, that they knew of no such plans.

Chief Cole said the prisoner was in Tacoma on the day of the kidnapping and had been at Bothell, between Seattle and Everett, several days later.

AUTO SIT-DOWN STRIKE ENDS; AGREEMENT WILL BE SIGNED AT 11 A. M. TO QUIT PLANTS

Great Plains War on Droughts Mapped for Action by Congress

Vast Plan to Make Over, Under a New Federal Agency, Lands and Life of People in Ten States Is Urged by the President in a Special Message

Special to THE NEW YORK TIMES.

WASHINGTON, Feb. 10.—A gigantic program designed to make over lands in ten States and help 4,000,000 persons to escape the scourge of duststorms, with their consequent ruin of the nation's granary lands, was urged on Congress today by President Roosevelt.

With a report of his Great Plains Committee mapping the strategy of a war for a "new economy" for the arid areas of the Great Plains States, the President sent a message declaring that the drought and dust storm problems could be solved, but that "the solution would take time." He said the program should be adopted and put into effect without undue delay.

The committee, headed by Morris L. Cooke, retiring administrator of the Rural Electrification Administration, recommended a new Federal agency to work with State, local and private organizations in directing a "program of constructive action" in the region between the Canadian and Mexican borders and the Mississippi River and the Rockies.

The work would be along the lines of land, economic and social readjustments and would be designed to coordinate all activities involved in the solution of the Great Plains problem.

The Great Plains committee's report covered in detail every angle of the drought problem in Texas, Colorado, Kansas, Nebraska, Oklahoma, Montana, New Mexico, North Dakota, South Dakota and Wyoming.

The work of the Federal Agency would dovetail with the proposals of the National Resources Committee "in the larger aspects of public planning," the President said. The National Resources Committee's report, sent to Congress a week ago, projected a six-year program of land and water control, involving $5,000,000,000.

"Depression and drought have only accentuated a situation which has long been developing," the President said. "The problem is one of arresting the decline of an

Continued on Page Twenty-one

REICH TO OPERATE BERNSTEIN LINES

Trustee to Run Ship Concerns Pending Outcome of Charges Against Three Officials

EXCHANGE VIOLATION CITED

Bernstein and 2 Subordinates Can Be Executed Under the Law if Found Guilty

Wireless to THE NEW YORK TIMES.

HAMBURG, Germany, Feb. 10.—The prosecuting attorney announced here today that the Arnold Bernstein and Red Star Lines, both controlled by the Jewish shipping man, Arnold Bernstein, were formally charged with breaches of the exchange laws and that a State trustee had been appointed to operate them pending the outcome of the trial.

The lines were the only shipping companies here under Jewish control. The trustee appointed by the "Fuehrer of German Shipping" is Marius Boeger, formerly associated with Hapag [Hamburg-American Line]. Before appointing a trustee the State secured the consent of creditors representing chiefly American interests.

However, the prosecutor explained that such consent was not essential, as the appointment of a trustee is not provided as an element in criminal or civil procedure, but is apparently done simply on the government's dictatorial authority.

Bernstein Still Imprisoned

As is the custom in Germany no details of the indictment are allowed to be published before the trial, and the official communiqué stated merely that the lines are charged "with violations of the exchange law."

Mr. Bernstein and two associated with him, are still imprisoned here. Whether charges will be brought against them privately could not be ascertained. Charges of exchange irregularities brought against individuals can involve the death penalty under the economic treason act.

Under further exchange laws issued in February, 1936, authorities now are empowered to administer the two shipping firms' properties so long as there is a "suspicion that they might intend to smuggle any part of their holdings abroad."

The prosecutor asserted that the State trustee was appointed to calm the creditors by guaranteeing the continued operation of the companies' ships and a trustworthy administration of their funds. On the other hand the opinion was expressed in Hamburg shipping circles that the trustee was appointed to keep the lines under the German flag and not to let them fall into the hands of foreign creditors. It is assumed in any case that Mr. Bern-

Continued on Page Seven

CHURCH BAN LIFTED BY MEXICAN STATE

Action by Vera Cruz Seen as Beginning of New Era With Services on Freer Scale

MOVES ELSEWHERE LIKELY

Catholics of Orizaba Praise President—Many Hasten to Mass, Weeping for Joy

By FRANK L. KLUCKHOHN

Wireless to THE NEW YORK TIMES.

MEXICO, D. F., Feb. 10.—Church bells rang today in the State of Vera Cruz and eager people filled the churches after the State Legislature late last night repealed the law preventing religious ceremonies in the State.

The Legislature's action was taken after President Lazaro Cardenas yesterday instructed the Secretary of the Interior personally to investigate the killing of a girl and the arrest of more than seventy Catholics, including a priest, when the police broke up a clandestine mass in a private home in the town of Orizaba Sunday.

Vera Cruz has been one of the States where religious persecution has been the most unrelenting and the Mexican press interprets the action of the Legislature as having been caused by President Cardenas's determination to permit the freer holding of masses in all Mexico. It is thought in some informed circles that President Cardenas will and perhaps already has brought pressure for similar action on the Legislatures of such States as Tabasco, where a priest can legally officiate only if married; Chihuahua, where only one priest is permitted to officiate in the whole State, and Chiapas in the South.

Repeal Held Retroactive

Just how the Legislature of Vera Cruz succeeded in acting in such quick fashion upon President Cardenas's insistence is unknown, since no press dispatches from the State capital indicate that the body met. It is presumed, however, that the repeal law will be held retroactive and that Sunday's tragic mass will be declared legal so the offenders will not be prosecuted.

The girl killed Sunday. Leonor Sanchez, already is regarded as a martyr in Catholic circles here since it is widely felt that her death will open a new era with regard to holding church services in Mexico, already permitted on a much freer scale than heretofore under the Cardenas administration.

More than a hundred Catholics of Orizaba sent the following telegram to President Cardenas congratulating him on the Legislature's action:

"The Catholic people of Vera Cruz and especially of the town of Orizaba are proud of having an Execu-

Continued on Page Seven

HALT COURT ACTION

'Reason Has Prevailed,' Says Murphy of Both Sides in Dispute

GOVERNOR WORKS TO LAST

Full Terms to Be Announced Today, He Declares When Parley Winds Up at 2:45 A. M.

TO CLEAR PLANTS TODAY

Troops Ordered to Take Preliminary Steps for Their Evacuation of Flint

By LOUIS STARK

Special to THE NEW YORK TIMES.

DETROIT (Thursday), Feb. 11.—Governor Murphy announced at 2:45 o'clock this morning that an agreement had been reached to end the automobile strike which has crippled production in General Motors Corporation since late December.

The announcement was made by the Governor dramatically in the Hotel Statler after all-night sessions with spokesmen for General Motors Corporation and the United Automobile Workers of America.

Under the terms of settlement, the Fisher Body and Chevrolet plants at Flint will be evacuated of sit-down strikers by the union and on its side General Motors will drop the mandatory court injunction which it obtained a fortnight ago.

The agreement will have to be ratified by the men in the plants, but this is considered a formality.

Governor Murphy credited James F. Dewey, veteran Labor Department conciliator, with a large share of the final settlement.

Statement by Murphy

Surrounded by several score newspaper men, Governor Murphy said:

"An agreement has been reached, under the terms of which the union agrees to end the strike. The signing of the agreement will take place at 11 A. M. today. The terms will then be announced.

"All parties will be present. Mr. Lewis and his associates and the representatives of General Motors have contributed all they could with earnestness and in fairness to bring to a conclusion this great industrial conflict. I gratefully thank them.

"It is also a great duty of mine to acknowledge the wise counsel and assistance of James F. Dewey, Federal conciliator.

"It has been a difficult job, but reason has prevailed. I hope it will be a contribution toward ending forever in the United States——"

At this point the Governor was interrupted by news photographers, who flashed their lights to take pictures and halted his statement for the time being.

He finished the sentence—"anything but peaceful, reasonable and conciliatory methods."

It is hoped that the Flint plant will be evacuated simultaneously with the signing of the agreement in the office of Judge George Murphy, brother of Governor Murphy.

Governor Murphy immediately called the National Guard officers at Flint, complimented the men under their command "as peacemakers" and requested them to take the necessary preliminary steps to arrange for their evacuation of Flint, where they have been stationed for five weeks.

The Governor and his associates are particularly pleased that this important industrial dispute was not marked by a single fatality, despite the tense situation that has existed in Flint for weeks.

Murphy Wearied by Efforts

Definite progress had been reported early in the evening by Governor Murphy after a hectic day of conferences and negotiations which began in the office of his brother, Judge George Murphy, at the Recorder's Court, and then switched to Mr. Lewis's hotel room.

While Governor Murphy indicated then that the situation had never looked better, he warned against excessive optimism.

The Governor, fatigued from lack of sleep, stuck to his task of keeping the conference going just as long as possible and was confident that it would end peacefully instead of breaking off without result.

"I intend to keep the parties in

Continued on Page Twenty-four

"All the News That's Fit to Print."

The New York Times.

LATE CITY EDITION

Partly cloudy, warmer today. Tomorrow cloudy, moderate temperatures, followed by rain at night.
Temperatures Yesterday—Max., 34; Min., 19

Copyright, 1937, by The New York Times Company.

VOL. LXXXVI.....No. 28,874. Entered as Second-Class Matter, Postoffice, New York, N. Y. NEW YORK, FRIDAY, FEBRUARY 12, 1937. P TWO CENTS In New York City. | THREE CENTS Within 200 Miles. | FOUR CENTS Elsewhere Except in 7th and 8th Postal Zones.

PROGRAM OFFERED TO SOLVE TENANCY ON 3,000,000 FARMS

MISERY PICTURED

President's Committee Urges Land Purchase by Federal Aid

40-YEAR PAYMENT PERIOD

Interest at 2½ Per Cent Plus Reserve Fund Proposed for Amortization Plan

SPECULATION CURB ASKED

Turnover Tax on Any Farm Held Less Than Three Years Suggested in the Report

By FELIX BELAIR Jr.
Special to THE NEW YORK TIMES.

WASHINGTON, Feb. 11.—The special committee appointed by President Roosevelt to study farm tenancy completed its labors today after adopting a report calling his attention to the fact that fewer than half of the farmers of the nation own the land they operate and that "rural civilization is threatened with decadence."

Finding that nearly 3,000,000 farmers were living under conditions directly attributable to tenancy which "make them equally easy prey to economic and even political parasites," the President's committee, headed by Secretary Wallace, proposed legislation establishing a farm security administration built around the present Resettlement Administration and supplemented by a farm security corporation.

The committee proposed that the new agency be empowered to acquire farm lands and buildings, financed at the outset by regular appropriations by Congress, and to contract with present tenants for the purchase of such farmsteads over a forty-year period so that they would be secure in their tenure and immune to land speculation.

Aid to Farm Owners Urged

The report made no mention of the amount of money the program might require, but some members were of the opinion that at least $10,000,000 a year should be provided.

The tenant-ownership program would be augumented, under the committee's proposals, by legislation to help farm owners avoid the loss of such farms, to provide ordinary housing and sanitary facilities for the army of migratory farm laborers, to safeguard civil liberties of tenants and to place definite curbs on land speculation.

To the latter end, it was proposed that Congress enact a form of windfall tax on the proceeds of land sales undertaken within three years of the time the land was first acquired by the seller.

The report mentioned that the Federal Reserve Board and the Farm Credit Administration were "well aware of the dangers" in overcapitalization of land resulting from widespread speculation, and were "in a strong position to insist that appraisals and loan policies be kept well below advances in price and current farm incomes until the degree of permanence in such advances can be determined."

Large Land Sale Tax Favored

But the committee was of the opinion that further restraint on land speculation was needed and in connection with the proposed tax of such sales said that 'such a tax, taking a large percentage of the increment, would materially discourage buying land merely for the purpose of early resale, and would tend to keep land values on a level where farmers could better afford ownership."

"Special safeguards should prevent evasion through fictitious forms of ownership, and also prevent the tax working severe hardship in cases of unavoidable resale," the report said.

The report, adopted after several minor amendments, including one providing for the amortization of tenant sales contracts within twenty years at the option of purchasing tenants, is expected to be "boiled down" prior to its submission to the President, probably before the end of the week. It is also likely to be accompanied by at least two minority expressions representing views of members who

Continued on Page Five

'Mosquito Fleet' Saved 13,500 Marooned by Flood

By The Associated Press.

MEMPHIS, Feb. 11.—Dr. Louis Leroy returned to his practice last night after directing the rescue of 13,500 flood-marooned farmers with his "mosquito fleet."

"We have detailed records of 10,986 persons brought out by our boats since evacuation began with the flooding of the Mississippi," he reported to Red Cross officials, "and at least another 2,500 persons were saved by volunteer help working under our direction."

Dr. Leroy said his flotilla was dubbed "the mosquito fleet" because many of the smaller boats were powered by outboard motors which made a buzzing noise.

Dr. Leroy's rescue work was exclusive of that performed by Coast Guardsmen, army engineers and other groups.

GREEN IS CONVICTED IN THE FIRST DEGREE

Negro Must Die for Murder of Mrs. Case—Jury Confers Less Than Two Hours

DEFENSE TESTIMONY BRIEF

Only Three Witnesses Called—Porter Cries Out a Denial During Lawyer's Summary

Major Green was convicted of first-degree murder in Queens County Court at 8:34 o'clock last night, barely more than an exact month since the body of Mrs. Mary Harriet Case was found in her apartment at 37-06 Eightieth Street, Jackson Heights.

The blue-ribbon jury required three hours and two minutes, of which an hour and ten minutes was spent at dinner, to find the 33-year-old Negro porter guilty.

Judge Charles S. Colden, who will sentence Green to the electric chair a week from today, told the jurors before dismissing them:

"With reference to your verdict, in the opinion of the court it is entirely correct. It is difficult to see how you could have rendered any other verdict."

Defendant Is Tense

The persistent half-smile which was the prisoner's most characteristic expression during the trial was gone when he stood to face the twelve married men who condemned him. He braced himself with his hands, pressing them palms down on the table at which he had sat.

Chief Clerk B. F. Funke delivered the traditional question: "Gentlemen of the jury, have you agreed upon a verdict?"

"We have," said the foreman, Thomas A. Dillon, from the first seat in the rear row.

"What is your verdict?"

"Guilty of murder in the first degree."

The jury was polled. Each member answered affirmatively, a few precipitately, as if they could not wait to be called.

Green was led before the bench. His slight frame seemed even more slumped than usual and his voice was a whisper as he gave his name and other facts.

"Born?"

"Barco, Fla."

"Go to school?"

"Two and a half years."

"Go to church?"

"Regular."

"Drink?"

His head bobbed. "Moderately," said the clerk, who had to repeat all the answers so the stenographer could hear them.

Chief Assistant District Attorney James J. Conroy had asked the jury to disregard the commission of a felony murder and base their decision on whether Green had "deliberately and with premeditation" hammered and choked Mrs. Case to death. The promptness of the verdict left no doubt as to how they felt.

Interruption by Green

The careful phrasing of Mr. Conroy's final appeal for the death penalty was dramatically interrupted during the afternoon by the defendant's only audible comment of the trial.

Mr. Conroy was telling the jury of the difficulty that surrounded the search for the wedding ring.

"And it was not until that defendant told Roberts—" he was saying, pointing to Green, when the narrow-shouldered porter straight-

Continued on Page Three

ROOSEVELT DRIVES FOR COURT REFORM AS CONGRESS WAITS

He Tells Five More Senators, Including Norris and Wagner, Views of Need for Bill

NEBRASKAN HOLDS IT 'BAD'

But Is Noncommittal on Vote—President Against Wait of 'Years' for Amendment

By TURNER CATLEDGE
Special to THE NEW YORK TIMES.

WASHINGTON, Feb. 11.—President Roosevelt moved with greater vigor today to head off an incipient Congressional revolt against his judiciary reform proposals, particularly the one permitting him to remake the Supreme Court with more "liberal" personnel.

While official circles represented the President as unalterably opposed to any change in his program, he called to the White House another group of Senators for the double purpose of dissipating any feeling they might have at not having been consulted previous to its announcement, and to make his own arguments in its behalf.

Among the Senators consulted today were Norris of Nebraska, Pittman of Nevada, Dieterich of Illinois, Wagner of New York and McAdoo of California. Some of these had expressed favor for all of the plan and others had demurred to the part affecting the Supreme Court. He discussed the subject with six others yesterday.

Senators Silent About Parley

Upon leaving the White House Senator Norris reasserted his advocacy of a more "fundamental" approach to the problem of Supreme Court adjustment than proposed by President Roosevelt. He suggested submission of two constitutional amendments, one limiting the tenure of office of justices and judges and another giving Congress authority to override Supreme Court decisions, perhaps by a two-thirds majority, as it now has to override Presidential vetoes. Although he complained that the President's program did not go to the heart of the issue, Senator Norris declined to indicate whether he would vote for or against it if and when it reaches the Senate floor.

The Senators were all silent as to their discussions with the President. Some seemed to be in better spirits, however, than when they entered the President's office. In fact, the general tension caused by the President's message to Congress Friday appeared to ease perceptibly today. Members of both houses seemed to be waiting and watching—watching principally for the reaction from the country.

Opposition Checks Strength

The outright opponents of the proposals were busy, however, making informal checks of their probable strength and prophesied they would start out with a "bloc" of thirty-six to forty Senators when the measure reaches the floor.

Regardless of the apparent White House opposition to a compromise on the more controversial section of the plan, that allowing the President immediately to appoint six new members to the Supreme Court to replace or supplement justices who have passed 70 years of age, some of the Congressional leaders hoped that an "arrangement" might be worked out that would soften its impact.

They were hoping that the Supreme Court Justices Full-Pay Retirement Bill passed yesterday in the House might open the way. They planned to rush this measure to the Senate for action as soon as possible, in the somewhat desperate hope that two or more of the present Supreme Court justices might retire under its terms, thus permitting the President to "re-

Continued on Page Two

Big Fetes in Japan Mark 2,597th Year of Empire

By The Associated Press.

TOKYO, Feb. 11.—Emperor Hirohito discarded his customary modern dress today for a dazzling medieval court costume to receive the congratulations of his people on the 2,597th anniversary of the founding of his royal dynasty and the Japanese Empire.

A gala parade of 200,000 persons converged on the palace and shouted their "banzais" while the Emperor and Empress and the princes of the blood worshiped the spirits of their ancestors.

Afterward, at a glittering banquet, the head of the world's oldest empire acknowledged the congratulations of envoys of other countries, including Ambassador Joseph C. Grew of the United States.

20,000 IN MEXICO OCCUPY CHURCHES

Orizaba Crowd Acts After the Veracruz Governor Makes Effort to Close Edifices

LEFTISTS BRING PRESSURE

Catholics Post Citizen Guards to Prevent Shutting of Doors—Cardenas Urged to Act

By FRANK L. KLUCKHOHN
Special Cable to THE NEW YORK TIMES.

MEXICO, D. F., Feb. 11.—More than 20,000 Catholics today took possession of eleven churches in the town of Orizaba in the State of Veracruz after Governor Miguel Aleman had ordered them closed at 8 A. M. under pressure from Leftists.

Yesterday Interior Department officials in Mexico, D. F., announced that the strict Veracruz religious law, permitting only one priest to each 100,000 persons, had been repealed by the Legislature under a special form sometimes used in Mexico when State bodies are in recess. Apparently the understanding between President Lazaro Cardenas and the Governor on this point has broken down, at least temporarily, for Orizaba churches, opened yesterday, were closed upon the Governor's arrival at Orizaba this morning.

Crowds immediately appeared on the streets and demonstrated. At 11 A. M. they rushed the churches guarded by Federal troops and were permitted to enter unhindered. They posted their own citizen guards. A similar incident occurred at the near-by town of Rio Blanco.

Demonstration Is Peaceful

For a time it was feared that violence would occur as business concerns quickly closed their stores and shuttered their windows. However, although one soldier did shoot over the heads of the crowd, Catholic leaders persuaded their followers to carry on a peaceful demonstration.

The early morning crowd surrounded the building where the Governor had his headquarters to demand the formal reopening of the churches. Governor Aleman appeared on the balcony and told them that the law still required the closing of churches. Immediately the crowd, now swelled by many from near-by villages, took possession of the churches.

Later in the afternoon there was another demonstration but it was learned that the Governor had left to return to the State capital at Jalapa. He told Catholic leaders before leaving Orizaba that they should petition the Finance Ministry handling church affairs for the right to have the churches turned over to groups of local Catholics. Learning that the Governor had left, the crowd took possession of

Continued on Page Fourteen

Plane Crashes in Berlin Square, Killing Six; Hits Trolley and Burns Near Cage of Lions

By The Associated Press.

BERLIN, Feb. 11.—Six persons died today when a tri-motored army plane, cut off from a near-by landing field by a curtain of driving snow, crashed into a crowded Berlin market place, caromed off a trolley car and burst into flames near a cage of circus lions.

Five of the dead were occupants of the plane. The sixth was the conductor of the trolley car, burned fatally by a charged wire that the plane had ripped away. Another trolley worker was injured and several other persons were burned. An automobile in the square caught fire and burned.

Panic swept the square for an hour, and the roar of the fifteen lions, part of a traveling circus, rose above the cries of terrified trolley passengers and pedestrians.

The plane fell about a half mile from the new barracks of the regiment named after Air Minister Hermann Goering and a short distance from a wide meadow in Schillerpark which offered safe landing had the pilots been able to find it.

The plane, en route from Stargard to Jueterbog, was several miles off its course. Residents of the Tiergarten section reported having seen it skirt housetops, apparently seeking a landing place, a few minutes before the crash into one of the city's busiest intersections, the corner of Muellerstrasse and Seestrasse.

Lieutenants Schultz and Hajok were the pilots, the Air Ministry announced. The other occupants were an engineer and two corporals.

The military cleared away the wreckage and traffic was restored to normal one hour after the crash.

BRITAIN WILL RAISE A £400,000,000 FUND FOR REARMAMENT

30-Year Loans Spread Over Five Years Will Supplement Surpluses for Purpose

PLAN IS WARNING TO REICH

Chamberlain Outlines Proposal Just Before Ribbentrop Tells London of German Desires

By FREDERICK T. BIRCHALL
Special Cable to THE NEW YORK TIMES.

LONDON, Feb. 11.—Germany, engrossed in her own great rearmament, received today from Great Britain a significant warning, of what an aggression, should it affect British rights and possessions, would have to meet. It was a warning all the more impressive in that it did not take the shape of a threat, but came in the order of ordinary legislative procedure. Moreover, it conforms to the Nazi preference for deeds rather than words.

In the House of Commons Neville Chamberlain, Chancellor of the Exchequer, gave notice that the government would shortly introduce a bill giving it authority to raise capital for defense expenditures up to an amount not exceeding £400,000,000 spread over a period not exceeding five years. The government proposed to obtain the capital by use of budget surpluses when available and by a series of loans issued in convenient form as needed.

This will be for capital expenditures, such as for new battleships; naval, military and air bases; arms factories and similar major permanent investments. It will be additional to the £1,000,000,000 already envisaged and now being spent at the rate of £200,000,000 annually during the same five years for maintenance and replacements of the huge military, naval and aerial defense machine that Britain is building up.

Some £188,000,000 of this sum has already been expended this year, and warning has been given that as the machine grows so will its cost increase.

What Plan Would Mean Here

Thus a country with one-third the population of the United States is preparing to spend in the next five years £1,400,000,000 purely on defensive measures. Translated into American terms, it would mean, if applied to the United States on the basis of our larger population, a total of almost $21,000,000,000 solely for armaments, engines of war and destruction, and protection of the population against bombs, poison gas and all that the air menace implies.

It entails inevitably an increase of taxation, already at a crushing level for purposes of meeting the cost of a military establishment swollen beyond anything ever known in peacetime.

The ordinary British income tax, without the surtaxes laid upon larger incomes, now stands at a standard rate of 23.75 per cent. Its rise to a level of 25 per cent, if not higher, under the next budget, to be framed in April, has been forecast for some time on the basis of the huge expenditures already being incurred. To these will now be added, while such expenditures are increasing with the growth of the military machine, interest on the loans for which Mr. Chamberlain is now preparing.

"It is necessary," said Adolf Hitler in defending German rearmament in his Reichstag speech on Jan. 30, "that the amount of a country's defensive armaments be determined by the degree of the dangers that threaten that country. Each nation is competent and alone competent to judge that point. The estimate of our own need is being decided exclusively in Berlin."

Chamberlain Gives Answer

Mr. Chamberlain's statement today is apparently Britain's answer. She also is "determining her armaments by the degree of the danger" that threatens her.

It is perhaps significant that the Chancellor of the Exchequer's announcement was made in the House of Commons just about an hour before the German Ambassador, Joachim von Ribbentrop, went to the Foreign Office by appointment to make his first official call since Chancellor Hitler's speech and his own return from Berlin. As he drove toward Downing Street news vendors along the curb were already displaying placards of the evening papers just issued:

"Four Hundred Millions for Defense—Official Announcement."

It may have been a mere coincidence and again it may have been considered wise that the Ambassador, making his first call with new instructions supposedly covering German desires, should have this

Continued on Page Thirteen

STRIKERS QUIT AUTO PLANTS; OPERATIONS RESUME MONDAY; $25,000,000 RISE IN WAGES

Strike Settlement in Brief

Terms of the Agreement

General Motors Corporation agrees:

To recognize the United Automobile Workers as bargaining agent for its members.

Not to bargain on "matters of general corporate policy" with any other group from twenty struck plants without Governor Murphy's sanction.

Not to discriminate against members of the union or the union in favor of any other group.

To drop court proceedings in the sit-down strikes.

To return all employes to their usual work without prejudice.

To resume full operations as soon as possible.

The union agrees:

To call off the strike and evacuate occupied plants forthwith.

To refrain from intimidation and coercion of employes, on or off the premises, in efforts to gain members.

To refrain from recruiting on company property.

To exhaust every possibility of negotiating grievances before calling any other strike.

To refrain from calling strikes or interfering with production pending negotiations.

The corporation and the union agree:

To begin collective bargaining negotiations Tuesday on wages, hours, production "speed-up" and other working conditions.

Results of the Agreement

Settlement ends forty-four days of striking, and eight days of mediation conferences.

Will put 105,000 of the corporation's employes, now idle, back to work and 120,000 now on part time back on full time.

Ends loss of $1,000,000 daily to the workers, and untold company losses.

Operations to start at once, with complete resumption in twelve days and capacity, 225,000 cars a month, by March.

Corporation announces a previous decision, raising average wage rate five cents an hour at a normal annual cost of $25,000,000,

PEACE PACT SIGNED

Action Officially Ends 44-Day Strike That Tied Up Plants

WITNESSES TO ACT CHEER

Officials on Both Sides, as Well as Gov. Murphy, Laud Outcome of Conferences

MEET ON DETAILS TUESDAY

Committees Will Settle Wage, Hour and Other Demands at New Sessions

By LOUIS STARK
Special to THE NEW YORK TIMES.

DETROIT, Feb. 11.—The nation's first major labor dispute in the automobile industry ended at noon today when representatives of General Motors Corporation and the International Union, United Automobile Workers of America, signed an agreement terminating the forty-four-day strike which had crippled the production of automobiles by the corporation.

While the signatures were being affixed to the document in Judge George Murphy's court, with Governor Frank Murphy, his brother, the focus of Kleig lights and newsreel cameras, Alfred P. Sloan Jr., president of General Motors, in New York, announced a $25,000,000 wage increase to General Motors employes.

A mile from the court room where an excited crowd applauded the speeches of the principals on both sides, John L. Lewis, strike generalissimo and chairman of the Committee for Industrial Organization, smiled happily as the radio carried the news to him in the hotel room where he has been confined with influenza for two days.

Sit-Downers Quit Plants

Late today three General Motors plants in Flint were evacuated by sit-down strikers, who embraced each other with joy as they were told by their leaders that their union had been recognized by the company.

To members of the C. I. O. in the steel and rubber industries, as well as those in the automobile industry, the agreement, they felt, was the first major offensive won by them in their program of unionizing the nation's basic industries.

A crowd formed an eager circle around the signers of the agreement in the high vaulted court room. In seats arranged for them and flanked by two court officers, were James F. Dewey, Federal conciliator; W. S. Knudsen, vice president of General Motors; Governor Murphy and Wyndham Mortimer, vice president of the union. Behind them stood John Thomas Smith and Donaldson Brown, vice presidents of the company, and Lee Pressman, general counsel of the C. I. O. On the judge's dais behind these participants were other union officers and reporters.

The court was crowded with municipal employes, attendants, and a large crowd of men and women attracted to the event. Many stood on chairs in the jury box.

As the Governor entered, weary from his long labors but still smiling, court attendants made way for him and for the union and corporation chiefs.

Murphy First to Sign

The spectators burst into applause as the principals took their places. The Governor sat down with Mr. Knudsen at his left and next to him Mr. Dewey. On the Governor's other side was Mr. Mortimer. Behind them were Messrs. Smith, Brown and Pressman.

Governor Murphy and Mr. Dewey signed the agreement first. The crowd was tense and hushed at first. Then Mr. Knudsen signed, followed by Messrs. Mortimer, Pressman, Brown and Smith.

The cameras clicked, the newsreel recorded the scene for posterity, and a radio announcer tried to talk above the buzz in the court which grew louder as the event was recorded.

When Governor Murphy announced that the peace pact had been signed, "thanks to these gentlemen here," the crowd again applauded.

"Let us have peace and make automobiles," said Mr. Knudsen

Continued on Page Nineteen

POLAND PLANNING ONE-PARTY STATE

Government Program Going to Sejm Today Would Make Smigly-Rydz Leader

CALLS FOR GRAND COUNCIL

New Organization Is to Unite Country—End of Political Stagnation Is Sought

By OTTO D. TOLISCHUS
Wireless to THE NEW YORK TIMES.

WARSAW, Poland, Feb. 11.—The government program for Poland's political reorganization, long-heralded and long-delayed, is now to be outlined before a committee of the Sejm tomorrow.

Unless all signs deceive, it will launch Poland on the road to an authoritarian one-party State under the leadership of Marshal Edward Smigly-Rydz, direct successor of the late Marshal Josef Pilsudski.

On this program Colonel Adam Koc, former Governor of the Bank of Poland and commander of the Pilsudski Legionnaires, has been working for months under Marshal Smigly-Rydz's instructions. According to present information, it calls not only for the proclamation of a leader equivalent to the Fuehrer or Duce, but also for the appointment of a grand council equivalent to the Fascist Grand Council.

In addition, it provides for the creation of one totalitarian, authoritarian and apparently self-perpetuating political organization that will ultimately supplant the political parties of the moribund Polish democracy. In it are to be merged all the classes and interests in the country under the banner of nationalism, military preparedness, and social and economic reform.

Poles to Be "Ruling Nation"

Particularly the new scheme of things is apparently supposed to complete "Polonization" by proclaiming the Poles, numbering about 22,000,000 of the 34,000,000 inhabitants of Poland, as the "ruling nation." This presumably means that the Poles will reserve the government and key positions for themselves while the minorities will probably continue enjoying the "rights of citizens," but not those of the "rulers."

This program, which has hitherto been as much of a mystery in Polish politics as the proverbial sea serpent in zoology, is offered as a solution for the disconcerting era of political stagnation which began with Marshal Pilsudski's death and which has already led to a slow but perceptible decline in governmental authority and a revival of opposition, which in turn is one explanation of the outbreak of anti-Semitic violence.

The program is especially designed to appeal to rising youth, which has learned to look to an authoritarian rather than a demo-

Continued on Page Nine

STRIKERS AT FLINT MARCH AS VICTORS

Leave Plants, 'Heads High,' Singing 'Solidarity' and Greeting Families

PEACE HAILED BY CITY

Payroll Prospect Is Cheering After Long Trade Tie-Up—Troops Still on Hand

By RUSSELL B. PORTER
Special to THE NEW YORK TIMES.

FLINT, Mich., Feb. 11.—The sit-down strikers who stalled the General Motors production machine and paralyzed the economic life of this city of 165,000 persons evacuated the three occupied plants late this afternoon and tonight.

About 400 men left Fisher Body Plant No. 1, 125 quit Fisher 2, and 200 to 300 walked out of Chevrolet 4 engine plant. The sit-downers had held possession of the two Fisher plants for forty-four days and the Chevrolet plant for ten days.

During the last ten days the occupants of Fisher 2 and Chevrolet 4 have been held virtually incomunicado as voluntary prisoners in those plants, which were surrounded by National Guard troops after the rioting a week ago Monday.

The 3,500 troops are still on duty here. They continue to hold an eighty-acre military zone around the Fisher 2-Chevrolet plants, although they withdrew their sentries and patrols from Chevrolet Avenue tonight while the sit-downers evacuated the plants.

Military headquarters said no orders for demobilization had been received.

Town Hails Pay Prospect

More than 35,000 General Motors workmen who have been forced off the payroll by the strike will return to work during the next week or ten days.

The city was overjoyed at the prospect of $250,000 to $300,000 daily in wages being paid out again and of the end of potential civil warfare. While the strikers celebrated their "victory" in mass demonstrations in front of the evacuated plants and in an automobile parade through the center of the city, the rest of the town celebrated the coming return to work.

Before the evacuation the sit-downers in the plants voted to accept the peace settlement and leave the plants. They questioned the first clause, in which the union was recognized as the bargaining agency for its own members only, and not as the exclusive bargaining agency for all G. M. employes.

Some of them accepted this with reluctance after a union official read the letter from William S. Knudsen to Governor Murphy, in which the company agreed not to bargain with or enter into agreements with any other representatives of the plants on strike during

Continued on Page Fifteen

Museum of the City of New York

A WPA project for the New York City Housing Authority, Demolition Division.

Museum of the City of New York

A New York City street scene. On a billboard, Childs restaurant offers a complete dinner for 60¢.

"All the News That's Fit to Print."

The New York Times.

LATE CITY EDITION
Generally fair slightly colder today. Tomorrow fair with rising temperatures.
Temperature Yesterday—Max., 40; Min., 26

VOL. LXXXVI.....No. 28,900. Entered as Second-Class Matter, Postoffice, New York, N. Y. NEW YORK, WEDNESDAY, MARCH 10, 1937. P TWO CENTS In New York City. | THREE CENTS Within 200 Miles. | FOUR CENTS Elsewhere Except in 7th and 8th Postal Zones.

CHILD LABOR BILL DIES IN ASSEMBLY; VOTE IS 102 TO 42

MARGIN A SURPRISE

Defeat Made Emphatic by 102-35 Ban on Reconsideration

PARTIES SHARPLY DIVIDED

41 Democrats, 61 Republicans Are Recorded Against the Ratification Measure

THRONGS HEAR THE DEBATE

Lehman Is Disappointed, but Declines to Say Whether He Plans New Drive

By W. A. WARN
Special to THE NEW YORK TIMES.

ALBANY, March 9.—After a debate of more than three hours the Assembly late this afternoon overwhelmingly defeated the Kleinfeld resolution for ratification of the child labor amendment to the Federal Constitution. The vote was 102 to 42.

To make doubly sure that the resolution would remain dead, the Assembly then defeated by 102 to 35 a motion to reconsider the adverse vote.

This prompt rejection of the motion to reconsider was a departure from Assembly practice and from the practice of either branch of the Legislature for the last generation or so. The motion to reconsider was made by Assemblyman Bernard J. Moran, Kings Democrat, for the purpose of definitely killing the resolution. The Assembly with a whoop advanced to slaughter the motion.

The Senate, with its Democratic majority, rushed through the resolution without much debate in a surprise move Feb. 2. But in the Assembly today 41 Democrats voted against it and only 33 for it. Sixty-one Republicans voted against it and 9 for it.

Speaker Heck was not recorded on the roll-call, but former Speaker Irving M. Ives, now Republican floor leader voted in the negative.

Adverse Strength Unexpected.

President Roosevelt and Governor Lehman have made repeated appeals for ratification, and Governor Lehman, in a radio address Friday night, made a special plea to the Republicans in the Assembly to supply enough votes for the Kleinfeld resolution to match those cast by Democrats. This, he predicted, would make this State the twenty-ninth State of the thirty-six needed to make the amendment part of the Constitution.

The showing in the Assembly today proved that the Governor, as in the case of most other observers, had underestimated the defection within his own party. Even had the Republicans met his plea, ratification would have been defeated.

The Governor expressed great regret at today's Assembly action. He did not disclose his plans, but it is not believed he is ready to give up the fight. Any early move, however, is doubted.

"I am deeply disappointed at the defeat of the resolution to ratify the child labor amendment," he told reporters who went to the Executive Chamber after the vote.

"The child labor amendment was adopted by an overwhelming vote in Congress as a nonpartisan measure to protect the children of America against exploitation.

Looks to Public Judgment

"While the then President was a Republican, Democratic as well as Republican members of the Congress voted for it. Since then it has had the strong support of both Republican and Democratic Presidents and other public officials.

"I regret that the resolution to ratify the child labor amendment did not receive in the Assembly the support of the members of the two parties which it received in the State Senate. Had it done so, it would, of course, have been easily ratified. The record speaks for itself. The people of this State will form their own judgment on that record."

Asked whether he had any plans in connection with the situation, he said:

"I have nothing to add to my statement."

A crowded gallery heard the debate. Mrs. Lehman was present throughout the proceedings.

Before the Assembly took up the

Continued on Page Twenty

Asks Quebec to Padlock Red Propaganda Sources

Special to THE NEW YORK TIMES.

QUEBEC, March 9.—Property in Quebec Province used for the purposes of Communist propaganda would be padlocked, as are places used for illegal purposes, under a law which Premier Duplessis is laying before the Legislative Assembly.

All that lies within provincial jurisdiction will be exercised to prevent the spread of Communistic doctrine in Quebec, it was revealed and the necessary provisions to that effect are contained in the bill.

There is to be no attempt in provincial anti-Communist legislation to infringe upon the criminal code of the Federal Parliament, but it is pointed out that the Province, while not having authority to enact punishment for Communists, would have power if the padlock measure is made law to deal with propaganda, notably in the holding of public meetings.

BRESLIN HUNTING SCHULTZ GUNMAN

Dealer Says Redwood Murder Pistol Was Among 300 He Sold to Gang in 1933

BAIL DENIED TO WITNESS

Moe Saraga, on Return From Europe, Bares His Trade in Underworld Arms

Orders were issued last night for the arrest of a former henchman of Arthur (Dutch Schultz) Flegenheimer in connection with the murder of Norman Redwood, sandhog union leader, at Teaneck, N. J., on Feb. 19.

This action followed an admission by the self-confessed Zaharoff of the murdered beer baron's gang, that one of the pistols used in Redwood's murder was part of a consignment of 300 weapons he sold to the racketeer in 1933.

The informant was Moe Saraga, former New York dealer in firearms, who returned from Europe early yesterday aboard the Queen Mary. Detectives, with the assistance of immigration officials, whisked him from the ship to Hackensack, N. J., where John J. Breslin Jr., prosecutor of Bergen County, caused him to be held without bail as a material witness in the murder.

Fears for Family's Safety

The statements made by Saraga, a heavy-jowled six-footer, lent weight to the theory advanced by Mr. Breslin that Redwood's murder was committed by paid gunmen acting for higher-ups who wanted the union official out of the way. Saraga, seemingly unconcerned about his predicament, told his story without reluctance, officials said. Later he expressed concern for the safety of his wife and three children, who live at 1,223 White Plains Road, the Bronx.

Known to the underworld as "Luger Mike," Saraga had been in trouble before over pistols sold by him and subsequently found near the bodies of victims of gangster feuds. He had succeeded in avoiding serious trouble before, however, by asserting that the weapons were part of a consignment he had sold to the Cuban Government.

The pistol found near the scene of Redwood's body and identified by ballistics tests as one of the weapons used in the murder was traced to Saraga, who was found to be in Europe. Before consulting him about it, detectives under Inspector Richard F. Oliver ascertained that the pistol never had been shipped to Cuba. Then they went about the task of getting him back from Europe.

Induced to Return

It was found that he was out in $1,000 bail awaiting sentence for concealment of assets in a bankruptcy case and that he had received permission by Federal authorities to go to Europe in the interim between conviction and sentence as agent for an importer for whom he was working.

With the aid of his lawyer, Frederick Weisler, and John Burke, Assistant United States Attorney, Inspector Oliver induced Saraga to return at once for questioning. Facing a sentence of as much as twelve years on the concealment of

Continued on Page Forty-eight

CHRYSLER IS FIRM ON 'CLOSED SHOP'; PLANTS STILL HELD

Company Talk With Union Fails to Solve the Issue of Sole Bargaining Right

BAR OFFICIALS AT PLANTS

But Sit-Downers Are Finally Ordered to Admit Them—Hudson Strike Unbroken

Auto Strike Situation

Strikers held full control of Chrysler plants in Detroit, even barring company executives for a time. Conferences on the issue of sole bargaining power continued, with no progress made. The company puts its idle at 69,000. Page 1.

Hudson Motor Company plants also remained shut down, with a conference set for today. Page 1.

In Flint General Motors plants resumed production. Page 2.

Governor Murphy cut short a Florida vacation to return to Detroit to renew peace efforts in the industry. Page 2.

Stoppage in Detroit

By RUSSELL B. PORTER
Special to THE NEW YORK TIMES.

DETROIT, March 9.—Stay-in strikers held complete control of the nine Chrysler Corporation's automobile plants in the Detroit area tonight after the largest and most effectively organized sit-down strike on record, but failed in their principal demand: recognition of the United Automobile Workers of America as sole bargaining agency for all company employes.

The company stuck to its contention that to grant this would inevitably mean the closed shop, whereas the union officially insisted that this was not the fact.

Individual union men interviewed in the occupied plants by this reporter admitted, however, that they hoped sole bargaining would bring the closed shop "later on."

After a two and a half hour conference between company and union representatives at the company's general executive offices in Highland Park this afternoon, B. E. Hutchinson, vice president of the company, said that the situation was unchanged as far as collective bargaining was concerned.

He said that the company's reply was still "no" to the union's ultimatum demanding a "yes or no" answer on the sole bargaining question.

"It should be understood," he added, "that we have dealt with the United Automobile Workers of America in the past, are dealing with them now, and will continue to deal with them in the future. The men are out of their own choosing."

Union Explains Demands

George Addes, secretary-treasurer of the United Automobile Workers of America, declared tonight, in a statement setting forth the basis of the union's demands, that 95 per cent of the workers in the Chrysler plants belonged to the union, and that the majority was entitled to exclusive bargaining rights under the Wagner Labor Act.

This was regarded as a reply to the assertion last night by Mr. Hutchinson that sole bargaining would inevitably lead to a closed shop.

Mr. Hutchinson said that he had not heard from Governor Murphy, who was on the way back to Detroit from Florida because of the strike.

Last month Mr. Murphy settled the forty-four-day General Motors strike by getting an agreement whereby the company recognized the union as the bargaining agency for its own members only, whereas the union originally demanded sole bargaining rights for all G. M. employes.

The sit-down strike which tied up the three Hudson Motor Car Company plants here yesterday morning continued today with about 1,000 men staying in.

According to representatives of the United Automobile Workers, this strike was called because the men believed that the management was "stalling" in negotiations which had been going on for two weeks.

The Hudson Company employs more than 10,000 men, of whom the union claims over 90 per cent. The union is demanding sole bargaining rights, 75 cents an hour minimum for women and 85 cents for men, and other wage adjustments. A meeting with the management has been scheduled for 4 P. M. tomorrow.

Conferences Are Interrupted

Although no court action is contemplated as yet against the Chrysler sit-downers for taking and holding company property, Mr. Hutchinson said, counsel for the company are studying the situation.

He emphasized the fact that union

Continued on Page Two

'Stuck in Mud' Striker Insists Town Fix Road

By The Associated Press.

JOLIET, Ill., March 9.—Cheek-nipping cold harassed Frank Peterlin today but he was too hot under the collar to quit the nation's only "stuck in the mud" strike.

For the second day he sat steadfastly in his car—stalled in mire up to the hub caps in unpaved May Street. Persons who watched the temperature fall to 15 above zero expected to find him gone with the Wintry wind. But he remained in his machine, reiterating his intention to sit there until city officials agreed to coat the thoroughfare with cinders.

Mayor George Jones pondered the problem, decided Peterlin was not obstructing traffic and announced he could "just go ahead and sit there."

"I'll stick until they do something about this muck," Peterlin said.

C. I. O. TO CHARTER OWN LABOR BODIES

Lewis Group Carries War to A. F. of L.—Will 'Certify' State, City Affiliates

MAPS TEXTILE, OIL DRIVES

Committees Under Hillman and Howard Formed—Green Says Rivals' Expulsion Is Likely

By LOUIS STARK
Special to THE NEW YORK TIMES.

WASHINGTON, March 9.—Organization drives which will seek to enroll a large segment of the 2,250,000 workers in the textile and oil and refining industries will be started soon under the auspices of the Committee for Industrial Organization, it was announced today by John L. Lewis, chairman, at the close of a meeting where spokesmen for the fifteen affiliated unions reported the progress of campaigns in the steel, automobile and rubber industries.

At the same time the C. I. O. took its first overt step to begin the creation of State labor federations and city central labor bodies as rivals to similar bodies now existing in the American Federation of Labor.

The executive officers were authorized "to issue certificates of affiliation to national, international, State, regional, city central bodies and local groups whenever it is deemed such action is advisable."

Rivalry Clear, Says Green

William Green, president of the American Federation of Labor, immediately declared that the C. I. O. had acted as he had predicted a year ago when he and the executive council of the A. F. of L. asserted that the new Lewis organization aimed to set itself up as a rival to the federation.

The next step, said Mr. Green, would be for the C. I. O. to set itself up as a national labor organization, with a name of its own clearly indicating that it was the federation's rival.

"It was clearly evident from the beginning that this objective would be reached," Mr. Green stated. "By that I mean that the C. I. O. would reach the point where they desired to function as a rival to the American Federation of Labor. You recall that the executive council classified the C. I. O. as a rival organization a year ago. That was vehemently denied at the time. There will be no question about it, I guess."

Before the A. F. of L. takes any action in reprisal, Mr. Green said, members of the council would be

Continued on Page Three

ARMS SHIP TRACED BY BETRAYAL HERE; SINKING IS DENIED

Mar Cantabrico's Route, Code and Plan for Disguise Given to Spanish Rebels Jan. 6

VESSEL REPORTED AFLOAT

Franco Uses Two Divisions of Italians in New Drive on Guadalajara Front

The Spanish Situation

LONDON—Diplomatic circles revealed that the Spanish Rebels had had full information on the movements of the arms ship Mar Cantabrico before she was overtaken in the Bay of Biscay. Details of her plans were obtained in New York. Page 1.

ARCACHON—Officers of British destroyers said the Mar Cantabrico was still afloat yesterday morning, being convoyed to a Rebel port. [Follows above story.]

THE FRONT—Rebels advanced northeast of Madrid and the Loyalists charged two divisions of Italians, 14,000 to 16,000 men, were in the drive. Page 12.

Arms Ship Secrets Revealed

By FREDERICK T. BIRCHALL
Wireless to THE NEW YORK TIMES.

LONDON, March 9.—The real story behind the seizure of the Spanish motorship Mar Cantabrico came out here today from diplomatic sources that long had been expecting some such development as occurred yesterday in the Bay of Biscay. From the very day the freighter left New York the Spanish Insurgents were aware of her every movement and her fate was sealed.

[Contrary to first reports that the Mar Cantabrico had been sunk, officers of two British destroyers in the Bay of Biscay reported last night, according to The Associated Press, that the ship had still been afloat yesterday morning and, as a prize of the Rebels, had been moving under her own power toward an Insurgent port.]

On the evening of Jan. 6, the day on which the Mar Cantabrico escaped from the clutches of United States Coast Guards and customs watchers and steamed out past Ambrose Lightship a few hours before Congress adopted neutrality regulations that could have held her, a mysterious person visited the apartment of an agent of the Rebel generalissimo, Francisco Franco, in New York. Without saying a word he left a package there and departed.

Package Contains Documents

The package, when opened, was found to contain what purported to be copies of correspondence between the Spanish Ambassador in Washington and his agents in New York. One document referred to the sailing of the Mar Cantabrico from New York to Mexico and thence to Europe. Another contained a plan for transformation of the ship at sea into an imitation of an Elder Dempster liner that somewhat resembled her in general outline. Still other documents gave the wireless code to be used at sea for communication with the Spanish Government.

The person with whom the mysterious stranger had left the documents was not at first greatly impressed with their importance. He duly communicated them to col-

Continued on Page Twelve

Paris Chamber Halted by Women's Dispute; Mrs. Blum Rebukes Critic of Her Husband

Wireless to THE NEW YORK TIMES.

PARIS, March 9.—During today's debate in the Chamber of Deputies, Mrs. Léon Blum, wife of the Premier, who always attends important debates, was involved in an incident that caused several minutes' disturbance in the visitors' gallery.

While Premier Blum was speaking and afterward another woman in the gallery made audible sneering remarks. At last Mrs. Blum's patience gave out. Turning around, she retorted that the visitors' gallery was not the place for such comment and that it was extremely ill-mannered.

Rival factions immediately formed in the gallery, and the argument became so heated that it drew the attention of the President of the Chamber and the Deputies present. Ushers were ordered to clear the gallery, and the sitting was suspended.

Mr. Blum had just finished speaking when the incident occurred. Louis Marin, a Rightist leader, was at the tribune. For a few moments the argument in the gallery was carried on in semi-whispers, but suddenly a feminine voice rang out, clear and shrill.

Every head in the Chamber turned and every eye was directed on the part of the gallery reserved for guests of the President of the Chamber, in the front row of which Mrs. Blum sat. After her first remonstrance, she had taken no part in the argument, but her face flushed slightly under the scrutiny of the whole Chamber, while cries of protest were raised by the Right benches.

As soon as the sitting was suspended Mr. Blum went around to the visitors' gallery to talk with his wife and find out for himself what had happened. It is, however, his usual custom to pay her a visit when she attends a sitting of the Chamber.

The woman who was the original cause of the incident was mildly rebuked by the Chamber authorities for having broken the rule that visitors must not comment on debates.

ROOSEVELT ASKS THAT NATION TRUST HIM IN COURT MOVE; RESENTS 'PACKING' CHARGES

The President's Address

Special to THE NEW YORK TIMES.

WASHINGTON, March 9.—Following is the prepared text of President Roosevelt's radio address tonight on his proposals for reorganization of the Federal judiciary:

Last Thursday I described in detail certain economic problems which every one admits now face the nation. For the many messages which have come to me after that speech, and which it is physically impossible to answer individually, I take this means of saying "Thank you."

Tonight, sitting at my desk in the White House, I make my first radio report to the people in my second term of office.

I am reminded of that evening in March, four years ago, when I made my first radio report to you. We were then in the midst of the great banking crisis.

Soon after, with the authority of the Congress, we asked the nation to turn over all of its privately held gold, dollar for dollar, to the Government of the United States.

Today's recovery proves how right that policy was.

But, when almost two years later, it came before the Supreme Court its constitutionality was upheld only by a five-to-four vote. The change of one vote would have thrown all the affairs of this great nation back into hopeless chaos. In effect, four justices ruled that the right under a private contract to exact a pound of flesh was more sacred than the main objectives of the Constitution to establish an enduring nation.

In 1933 you and I knew that we must never let our economic system get completely out of joint again—that we could not afford to take the risk of another great depression.

We also became convinced that the only way to avoid a repetition of those dark days was to have a government with power to prevent and to cure the abuses and the inequalities which had thrown that system out of joint.

We then began a program of remedying those abuses and inequalities—to give balance and stability to our economic system—to make it bomb-proof against the causes of 1929.

Today we are only part way through that program—and recovery is speeding up to a point

Continued on Page Fifteen

TIME IS HELD VITAL

He Declares Bench Has Set Itself Up Today as 'Super-Legislature'

CALLS FOR MODERN MINDS

Constitution to Be Saved From Justices, He Says—Will Not Pick 'Spineless Puppets'

SENATE STILL HAS ITS SAY

Real Purpose Is to Stop Usurpation of Power, He Asserts in His 'Fireside Chat'

By TURNER CATLEDGE
Special to THE NEW YORK TIMES.

WASHINGTON, March 9.—In a second appeal within six days for popular support for his plan to reorganize the Federal judiciary, President Roosevelt tonight sought to assure millions of Americans gathered around their radios that in this new project he was seeking only to protect them from the usurpations of a Supreme Court which had left its place at the scales of justice to set itself up as a "super-legislature."

Seated in the diplomatic reception room at the White House and speaking into the microphones of the three national broadcasting chains, the President asked most of all that the country trust him to do the right thing by American democracy.

He had no intention, he said, of packing the bench with "spineless puppets." He simply proposed to return the court to its "rightful and historic place," and save the Constitution from "hardening of the judicial arteries."

Again he shoved aside as impractical or too slow proposals for amending the Constitution to bring about the results he desired. He put forward the proposed legislation as the best method, first, because he believed it could be passed at this session of Congress, and second, "because it would provide a reinvigorated, liberal-minded judiciary necessary to furnish quicker and cheaper justice from bottom to top."

Speaks on Eve of Hearings

The President's broadcast came on the eve of public hearings on his Supreme Court enlargement bill, which will open before the Senate Judiciary Committee tomorrow with Attorney General Cummings as the first witness.

Senate opponents of his plan were preparing tonight to put the Attorney General through a cross-examination and one of their number, Senator Wheeler of Montana, was on his way to Chicago to deliver their official answer to the President's Victory Dinner speech last Thursday and tonight's "fireside chat." Senator Wheeler will appear in a joint discussion of the subject with James M. Landis, chairman of the Securities and Exchange Commission, before a congress of Midwest women.

In another development considered as linked in part with the administration's strategy, President Roosevelt today announced the appointment of District Judge J. Earl Major of Illinois to be United States judge for the Seventh Circuit. Judge Major was backed for his new appointment by Senator Dieterich, a member of the Senate Judiciary Committee, who recently has been listed as favorable to the President's program.

The President also sent to the Senate for confirmation the nomination of John Caskie Collet of Missouri to fill a new judgeship created at the last session of Congress. Mr. Collet's appointment was a compromise between Senator Clark, an opponent of the proposed judicial reorganization, and Senator Truman, who only recently declared in its favor.

Appeals to "You Who Know Me"

Definitely assuming command of the campaign to arouse sentiment in the country for the program, President Roosevelt asked the nation to trust him personally.

"You who know me," he said, "will accept my solemn assurance that in a world in which democracy is under attack, I seek to make American democracy succeed."

He referred to his own record as Governor and President to prove his devotion to the essential liber-

Continued on Page Fifteen

KEECH ENDS LIFE BY LEAP IN SUBWAY

71-Year-Old Broker, Indicted in Burning of Tuxedo Park Mansion, Dies Under Train

HAD BEEN IN POOR HEALTH

Once Big Operator in Market, Hard Hit by Crash—Colonel, Veteran of Two Wars

A northbound subway train roaring into the Fifty-first Street station of the Lexington Avenue line at 3:32 P. M. yesterday ended the life of Colonel Frank Browne Keech, former large-scale operator in the stock market, who twelve days ago was indicted for the burning of his mansion at Tuxedo Park on Feb. 26, 1932.

Detective Charles McGowan of the East Fifty-first Street police station said the veteran financier and soldier, who was 71 years old, was a suicide. Lee McCanliss of 31 Nassau Street, an attorney for the victim, pointed out that his health had been poor and that he suffered from a heart condition that made him susceptible to falls.

On Feb. 27, before Supreme Court Justice Graham Witschief in Newburgh, Mr. Keech was arraigned on charges of second and third degree arson and willful destruction of insured property. He was freed in $50,000 bail, the justice forbidding Under-Sheriff Bert Truesdell to fingerprint the defendant, saying: "He is sufficiently prominent and sufficiently well known."

Alleged Tool Likely to Go Free

Charles F. Smith, once chauffeur for the broker, was lodged in Newburgh jail, named in similar indictments. District Attorney Henry Hirschberg of Orange County, who had expected to prove that the colonel had paid Smith to destroy the home, said yesterday, when identification of the dead man was still only tentative: "The chances are I wouldn't prosecute the tool if the principal was dead."

Following his arraignment Colonel Keech left the court room leaning heavily on the arm of his counsel. He returned to his New York residence, at the Hotel Gotham, Fifth Avenue and Fifty-fifth Street, where he lived with a valet.

He had lunch at the hotel yesterday, and after some indecision said he was going for a walk.

According to witnesses, Colonel Keech leaped in front of a Pelham Bay local, only a few feet from the south end of the platform, where the entering train's speed was at a maximum. Motorman Sidney Baldwin of 480 Concord Avenue, the Bronx, was unable to stop until all four cars had passed over the body.

Power on the line was shut off for fifteen minutes as Emergency Squad No. 3 removed the body.

At the station house, tentative identification was established by checks, a bill fold containing about $35 and a watch in pockets of the dead man's brown suit. A $5 check on a Washington bank was signed

Continued on Page Seven

REVERSAL UPHOLDS STATE'S PRICE LAW

Appeals Bench in a 5-to-1 Decision on Bourjois Case Bars Drug Store Cuts

BOWS TO SUPREME COURT

Washington Ruling in Illinois Suit Guides the Change—Wide Effect Seen Here

Special to THE NEW YORK TIMES.

ALBANY, March 9.—Reversing its previous position in view of recent Supreme Court rulings, the Court of Appeals today upheld the State Fair Trade Law, which it had declared unconstitutional on Jan. 7, 1936. The court divided 5 to 1.

The Supreme Court has sustained similar legislation in California and Illinois.

The Court of Appeals, in its decision a year ago, declared, in the case of Doubleday, Doran & Co., Inc., vs. Macy & Co., that the Fair Trade Law was unconstitutional as "an unauthorized restriction upon the disposition of one's own property and unconstitutional within former decisions of the United States Supreme Court."

The suit decided today was brought by the Bourjois Sales Corporation of Brooklyn, which sought and is now to receive an injunction prohibiting Abraham Dorfman, a Brooklyn druggist, from selling Bourjois products at a price below that stipulated in contracts.

Chief Judge Crane, writing the majority opinion, said:

"The complaint in this appeal now before us is in no way different from that before the Supreme Court under the Illinois act so that we feel it to be our duty to submit our own judgment to the rulings of the Supreme Court on the Constitution of the United States and the interpretation of its own decisions."

Seagram Case Is Cited

Referring further to this Illinois case, which was Old Dearborn Distributing Company vs. Seagram-Distillers Corporation, the 600-word opinion said:

"Had the Seagram case been decided before the argument in the Doubleday case, we certainly would have followed the Supreme Court's ruling on the Federal Constitution. We do now by sustaining the complaint in this case and reversing the order of the special term."

Judges Lehman, Hubbs, Loughran and Rippey concurred with the chief judge and Judge O'Brien dissented, but wrote no opinion. Judge Finch took no part in the case.

Between the Doubleday Doran and Seagram cases said Judge Crane, "distinctions may be drawn, but these are matters of emphasis, not of principle."

He also remarked that "the Seeck & Kade, Inc., case, decided at the same time on the authority of the Doubleday case, was similar to the Seagram case in that the facts establishing good-will were set forth in full."

The Doubleday Doran suit arose

Continued on Page Eighteen

"All the News That's Fit to Print."

The New York Times.

LATE CITY EDITION

Fair today, temperature unchanged. Tomorrow probably rain or snow, little change in temperature.

Temperatures Yesterday—Max., 44; min., 29.

VOL. LXXXVI.....No. 28,920. Entered as Second-Class Matter, Postoffice, New York, N. Y. NEW YORK, TUESDAY, MARCH 30, 1937. P TWO CENTS In New York City. | THREE CENTS Within 200 Miles. | FOUR CENTS Elsewhere Except in 7th and 8th Postal Zones.

MINIMUM WAGE LAW CONSTITUTIONAL; SUPREME COURT SWITCH DUE TO ROBERTS; GLASS EXCORIATES ROOSEVELT'S PLAN

COMPROMISE PACT NOW HELD LIKELY IN CHRYSLER STRIKE

Murphy Presses Points as the Conferees Agree to Meet Again Today

HE HAS TALK WITH LEWIS

Auto Manufacturer Cancels Plans to Leave Lansing as Peace Efforts Proceed

RANK AND FILE IS FEARED

Their Envoys Arrive in Lansing and Oppose Any Concession on Sole Bargaining

Day's Strike Developments

A compromise agreement was held likely as Governor Murphy pressed for a settlement of the Chrysler strike. Walter P. Chrysler remained in Lansing for another peace conference today. Page 1.

Chairman Madden of the Labor Board intimated at Washington that delay of court ruling on the Wagner act was a factor in industrial unrest. Representative Dies asserted that Lewis had "outlawed" sit-down strikes. Page 12.

Lewis denounced Green's attitude on sit-downs as "characteristically cowardly and contemptible." Page 13.

Fight for Peace Pressed

By RUSSELL B. PORTER

Special to THE NEW YORK TIMES.

LANSING, Mich., March 29.—Walter P. Chrysler, chairman of the Chrysler Corporation, remained here today and participated in six hours of negotiations with auto union leaders on the sixth day of Governor Murphy's peace conference on the Chrysler strike, while John L. Lewis, chairman of the C. I. O., who left yesterday, was trying to settle the soft coal labor dispute in New York.

Mr. Chrysler was to have left here this afternoon, but canceled his plans and attended both the morning and afternoon sessions. Tonight he announced that he would be present when the conference resumed at 11 o'clock tomorrow morning in Governor Murphy's offices.

The C. I. O. chief is expected back here by Thursday morning to resume his leadership of the union negotiating committee, which is now headed by Lee Pressman of New York, counsel for the C. I. O., with Homer Martin, president, and Richard T. Frankensteen, Detroit organizational director, of the United Automobile Workers of America, as his associates.

Recess Tomorrow Likely

If Mr. Lewis is unable to get back on Wednesday, it was understood tonight, there may be a recess on that day until he returns.

Both Governor Murphy and union leaders talked with Mr. Lewis by telephone today in what was believed to be an attempt by the Governor to get his agreement to a formula which apparently was satisfactory to the automobile manufacturer on the degree of representation the U. A. W. A. should have in collective bargaining for Chrysler employes.

Since Mr. Lewis last week made the agreement which resulted in the evacuation of the eight Chrysler plants in Detroit by 6,000 sit-down strikers, he is also understood to have agreed to leave the word "sole" or "exclusive" out of any contract the workers may sign with the Chrysler Corporation describing the form of collective bargaining to be granted by the company.

Mr. Chrysler is represented as having rejected various formulas which in his opinion would have granted "sole" or "exclusive" bargaining to the union, even though those particular adjectives were omitted from the proposal, but to have been willing to reach an accord on one which would preserve his rights to bargain with company unions and American Federation of Labor craft unions as well as the U. A. W. A.

Believe Compromises Point Way

It is believed that both sides have now made sufficient compromises to make an agreement possible on a basis which, in the opinion of each side, will enable it, from the union standpoint, to consolidate its gains and increase its already majority representation among Chrysler employes, and from the company standpoint, to wean its workers away from the union sufficiently to protect it from what it regards as the paramount danger, a closed shop.

Although Governor Murphy is pressing the points he has already scored in an effort to bring about an agreement by tomorrow, it is

Continued on Page Thirteen

Clipper Reaches New Zealand Goal, Finishing 7,000-Mile Survey Flight

Huge Flying Boat Alights at Auckland as Trade-Route Pioneer After Hop From Pago Pago—Few Anchorages Noted on Final Leg, Covered in Varied Weather Conditions

By The Associated Press.

AUCKLAND, New Zealand, Tuesday, March 30 (Via Pan American Airways Radio).—The Pan American Clipper, pioneering a commercial air route of 7,000 miles between California and Australasia, landed in the harbor here today, completing the final leg in the journey, an 1,800-mile flight from Pago Pago, American Samoa.

The four-motored flying boat, which had left Alameda, Calif., on March 17, arrived here at 5:54 P. M. [1:24 A. M., New York time].

By EDWIN C. MUSICK
Captain, Pan American Clipper

Copyright, 1937, by The North American Newspaper Alliance, Inc.

ON BOARD THE PAN AMERICAN CLIPPER, Tuesday, March 30.—On the way to completion of the final stage of our 7,000-mile flight to survey a new aerial trade route between the United States and Australasia, the Pan American Clipper has just passed over the Kermadec Islands, referred to by mariners as the outlying islands of New Zealand. We had covered some 1,300 miles of the distance scheduled.

These islands are about 500 miles from the main coast of New Zealand and the City of Auckland, the final goal of our flight. In order to inspect the four tiny, widely separated islets that compose this group we swung several hundred miles off our course and delayed a direct crossing of the international dateline. With the crossing of this imaginary line we have flown in all four hemispheres of the world since beginning this aerial assignment.

As on the three previous stages of this undertaking, we encountered every type of weather after leaving Pago Pago, American Samoa.

This last portion of the flight was in many respects the most interesting from the viewpoint of the aerial observer, as it has taken us over a long series of tropical islands never observed before by man from the air. It was for this reason that we tried to make this 1,800-mile flight completely in daylight.

It was with the greatest reluctance that we said farewell to the many friends we were fortunate enough to make in Samoa during our brief stay, particularly the naval personnel headed by Captain

Continued on Page Seven

SOCIALISTS VOTE TO ENDORSE C. I. O.

Resolution Accusing A. F. of L. of 'Disruptive Role' Adopted by National Convention

NEW CHARTER IS DRAFTED

Committee Is Named to Spur Party Action—Farmer-Labor Cohesion Is Authorized

Special to THE NEW YORK TIMES.

CHICAGO, March 29.—Endorsement of John L. Lewis's Committee for Industrial Organization was voted by the convention of the Socialist party of America today in a resolution urging party members to support the new labor group.

The resolution charged the American Federation of Labor with taking "organizational steps in order to destroy" the C. I. O., which was termed "one of the most significant developments in the American labor movement."

The A. F. of L. executive council's suspension of unions affiliated with the C. I. O., the resolution said, "created the danger of a split in the American labor movement." This danger was increased, it added, by the suspension of C. I. O. locals recommended in a letter of William Green, A. F. of L. president, to central labor unions.

"Shortcomings" of the C. I. O.

The resolution also charged that the A. F. of L. "played a disruptive rôle" in the automobile and steel strikes "by fighting recognition of unions as the sole bargaining agencies for the workers."

At the same time, the resolution mentioned "shortcomings" of the C. I. O., especially objecting to dependence of its leadership upon a "political alliance with the Democratic party."

Unions were advised against hasty abandonment of affiliation with the A. F. of L., which, it was set forth, would continue to hold a substantial section of organized workers.

This action on the C. I. O. issue came at the end of a closed session at which the delegates voted to instruct the party's national executive committee to "collaborate in building a national Farmer-Labor party whenever circumstances are favorable."

The national executive committee was directed to "advise and confer with local and State subdivisions of the Socialist party concerning local Socialist participation in local and State Farmer-Labor parties."

Anti-Semitism Condemned

Other resolutions endorsed the program of the Southern Tenant Farmers Union and condemned anti-Semitism as reflecting the "tactics of fascism."

Earlier action by the delegates included the passage of a resolution calling upon Great Britain to release immediately political leaders "now under arrest" and to lift the ban on "political meetings" in India.

A new Socialist party constitution was drawn at the meeting and a new National Action Committee was appointed to speed up party activities. Its membership was drawn from party officers and whatever business they transact will be subject to the approval of the executive committee at its quarterly meetings.

Norman Thomas, three times So-

Continued on Page Twelve

BRITISH HEAR PLOTS BESET INSURGENTS

30 Officers and Men Declared Shot in Spanish Morocco—Italians Reported Executed

MALAGA IS TERMED CENTER

New Fighting Is On in Cordoba Zone—Loyalists Make Gain in Guadalajara Region

By FREDERICK T. BIRCHALL

Wireless to THE NEW YORK TIMES.

LONDON, March 29.—Reports of dissension in the Insurgent ranks, both behind the lines and on the fighting fronts in Spain, are coming from many sources so persistently that neutral observers are beginning to believe them well founded. A German broadcast today even spoke of a "revolt" against Generalissimo Francisco Franco at Malaga and at other critical spots.

A military conspiracy is reported from Spanish Morocco, where, it is declared, thirty officers and soldiers of the Tetuan aircraft station have been shot as a result. Another report says that Captain Jiminez, the commandant at La Linea, the Spanish town nearest Gibraltar, has been relieved of his post without notice and that Captain Herrera of the garrison at San Roque has succeeded him.

A Reuters report from Malaga says twenty Italian carabineers and a number of non-commissioned officers and recruits of the Pavia Regiment, now at Algeciras, have been shot during the week-end on suspicion of attempted conspiracy against the Insurgents there.

Center Put at Malaga

A usually well-informed diplomatic correspondent here asserts that the reports of a conspiracy against the Spanish Rebel junta are true. He declares it had spread to several towns and seems to have been most formidable at Malaga. The purpose was to release the prisoners in Rebel hands and to start an armed uprising behind the lines.

According to this authority, the reported conspiracy was discovered by the German espionage service. It involved, he declares, a number of officers whose nationality was not disclosed. The discovery is declared to have resulted in the execution of eighteen persons.

There is a British tendency to attribute this development, always supposing that it is true, to two causes—disillusionment among the Italians serving in Spain, many of whom believed they were going out to service in Ethiopia, and growing uneasiness among the Spaniards over the spread of Italian military, political and commercial influence in their country.

Defeat of Italians a Factor

The recent setback suffered by the Italians and the apparent revelation that they were not such wonderful fighting men as had been believed intensified this discontent and brought matters to a crisis.

One suggestion heard here tonight is that the opposition of Count Dino Grandi of Italy in the European Non-Intervention Committee a few days ago to the effort to withdraw all alien volunteers from Spain was probably due to

Continued on Page Four

HAIR IS SOLE CLUE IN TRIPLE MURDER; POLICE BAFFLED

Several Short Gray Strands Under Model's Nails Indicate She Fought With Killer

50 DETECTIVES ON CASE

'Groping in Dark,' Inspector Says—Man Who Roomed With the Gedeons Is Questioned

Several strands of short gray hair found under the fingernails of Veronica Gedeon, 20-year-old commercial model, offered virtually the sole remaining clue last night to the man who murdered the girl, her mother, Mrs. Mary Gedeon, and a roomer, Frank Byrnes, in their apartment at 316 East Fiftieth Street early Sunday morning.

After a day that saw the collapse of several promising leads furnished by the intensive work of fifty picked detectives, John A. Lyons, assistant chief inspector, in command of detectives, said the investigators were "up against a stone wall." They had developed nothing that pointed to either the identity of the slayer or the motive for the brutal series of crimes, he said.

"We are simply groping in the dark, hoping that something will turn up," he declared.

Reminded that the police had made similar statements in the investigation of the murder of Mrs. Nancy Titterton last year, only about a block from the Gedeon home, and again in the investigation of the death of Mrs. Mary Case in Queens, Inspector Lyons laughed and said "this time it goes."

Former Roomer Questioned

He declared that George (Frenchy) Guret, who had been questioned at length at the East Fifty-first Street police station from 11:30 A. M. on, had been definitely eliminated from suspicion after a check of his movements Saturday night and that he would be released. Despite that, Guret was still being questioned early this morning.

Guret, who had roomed with the Gedeons when they lived at 240 East Fifty-third Street, was brought in for routine questioning because he had been seen in the vicinity of the murder Saturday night. When the police found two blood-stained handkerchiefs in his furnished room at 201 East Fiftieth Street they thought they were on the right track. Guret, however, explained that he was subject to nosebleeds and gave an alibi confirmed by his landlady, Mrs. Ella Peterson.

The gray hairs and tiny particles of skin from under Miss Gedeon's nails were found by Dr. Thomas A. Gonzales, acting Chief Medical Examiner, when he performed autopsies on the three bodies at Bellevue. He said that because rigor mortis had set in it was impossible to fix the time or order of their deaths.

Miss Gedeon had been drinking heavily before her death, an analysis of her organs showing an alcoholic intensity of three-plus, one short of the maximum. Dr. Gonzales said the external indications were that both mother and daughter had been criminally assaulted, but that he would not be able to determine this definitely until a chemical analysis had been completed today.

Both Women Strangled

The autopsy showed that both women died of strangulation after each had received a brutal beating. Mrs. Gedeon's knuckles were badly bruised, indicating that she also had tried to defend herself, the medical examiner said. The daughter had received a blow on the chin that probably dazed her so that her resistance was feeble.

Byrnes was killed while he was

Continued on Page Two

VIRGINIAN IS BITTER

'Frightful' Scheme by White House Aims at Autocracy, He Says

HELD 'EVIL' PACKING PLAN

Senator, Over Radio, Declares Court Proposal Is 'Destitute of Moral Sensibility'

SENATE DEBATE STORMY

Holt of West Virginia Charges He Received Suggestion of a 'Trade' for His Vote

The text of Senator Glass's speech is printed on Page 16.

Special to THE NEW YORK TIMES.

WASHINGTON, March 29.—Carter Glass, oldest member of the Senate, assailed tonight President Roosevelt's plan for reorganization of the Supreme Court. He was speaking, he admitted, "from the depths of a soul filled with bitterness" against a proposition "utterly destitute of moral sensibility."

The Virginian, who is in his eightieth year, referred to the plan as "the frightful suggestion" from the White House and as a "repugnant scheme." He declared it an effort to substitute for the deliberate judgment of an independent court "the previously pledged opinions of judicial subalterns," a proposal to make "an Executive's puppet" of the court and an "attempt to replace representative government with an autocracy."

"No threat to representative democracy," he asserted, "has exceeded in its evil portents this attempt to pack the Supreme Court of the United States and thus destroy the purity and independence of this tribunal of last resort."

His address, over a Columbia Broadcasting Company network, followed a Senate debate of the issue today in which a dozen Senators, all Democrats and most of them supporters of the reorganization plan, participated.

McKellar Sets Off Debate

The debate was set off by a speech by Senator McKellar of Tennessee, a supporter of the President's plan, who charged the Supreme Court "shrouds its procedure in un-American secrecy" and has a habit of ignoring the rights of litigants in refusing to hear cases appealed from the lower courts.

Senator Wheeler of Montana sprang to the defense of the court, as did Senator Burke of Nebraska and Senator Connally of Texas. All the others who took part in the debate, including Senators Robinson of Arkansas, Ashurst of Arizona, Minton of Indiana, Schwellenbach of Washington and Barkley of Kentucky, championed the President's plan. They denied that patronage, propaganda or other pressure has been or is being exerted to force into line Senators still undecided on the issue.

Near the close of the debate there were a few heated moments when Senator Holt, rebellious Democrat from West Virginia, asserted that Assistant Attorney General Joseph

Continued on Page Sixteen

Dr. Townsend Asks for a $5,000,000 Loan For Campaign to Put Over His Pension Plan

Special to THE NEW YORK TIMES.

CHICAGO, March 29.—An "extraordinary proposal" for a loan of $5,000,000 to be used in a campaign to "put the Townsend plan over now" by promoting the General Welfare Act of 1937, now before Congress, was made by Dr. Francis E. Townsend today to his alleged 4,500,000 followers.

Dr. Townsend, founder of the Old Age Revolving Pension Plan, appealed for individual loans ranging from $10 up, and offered as "collateral" only his total assets of $500 and his unsecured promissory note. The loans would be payable in twenty-four months and pay 4 per cent interest under his proposal.

Dr. Townsend makes his appeal in The Townsend National Weekly, stating assurance that the money is to be used in a revolving fund under his personal control and that it will be repaid.

"I am going to put the Townsend plan over now," said the announcement. "I am going to do this in a constitutional way by arousing the people of America to the need of the Townsend plan; by arousing voters in every Congressional district to the importance of seeing to it that their Congressmen truly represent their wishes in the national Congress."

Plans for "promoting the General Welfare Act," which Dr. Townsend said "would put the Townsend plan in operation," include educational campaigns in Congressional districts, mass meetings, State conventions, radio broadcasts and a national convention of Townsendites and their supporters in Washington.

New Farm Mortgage Law Upheld; Revision Saves Frazier-Lemke Act

Measure Provides Three-Year Moratorium, Applying Principle of Bankruptcy Statute—Supreme Court Is Unanimous for Opinion by Brandeis, Who Wrote Adverse Ruling on Original Draft

Special to THE NEW YORK TIMES.

WASHINGTON, March 29.—The Supreme Court today unanimously upheld the constitutionality of the revised Frazier-Lemke Farm Mortgage Moratorium Law, which was designed to extend to bankrupt agricultural proprietors the same aid provided for facilitating corporate reorganizations. The opinion was given by Justice Brandeis, who was also the author of the decision which ruled out the original moratorium measure.

Under the present law, any farmer, unable to pay his debts and unable to obtain a composition or extension, may ask to be adjudged a bankrupt, that his property be appraised, and that he be permitted to retain possession, under supervision and control of the court, of all or part of the property, according to conditions prescribed in the law.

The law authorizes the court to stay all proceedings against a bankrupt farmer for three years, during which time the debtor is permitted to retain possession of his farm provided he pays a reasonable rental for whatever part he retains. Such payments would be paid to the court and used for taxes, upkeep and payments on claims of secured and unsecured creditors.

At the end of three years, or prior thereto, the property having been appraised, the debtor could regain, unencumbered, possession of it by paying into court "the amount of the appraisal of the property of which he retains possession, including the amount of encumbrances on his exemptions, up to the amount of the appraisal less the amount paid on principal."

The court held that Congress, in revising the outlawed act, had succeeded in spirit, at least, in removing the objectionable features which proved fatal in the first case. Although still loosely drawn, the new measure, according to the decision, was a proper exercise of Congressional power to establish uniform bankruptcy laws and promote amicable composition of debtors' liabilities.

Generally speaking, the court held

Continued on Page Seventeen

STATE TO RE-ENACT MINIMUM WAGES

Lehman Holds Way Cleared for Prompt Action to Replace Wald Act of 1933

DECISION IS WIDELY HAILED

Andrews Sees Salvation for 'Thousands' of Women Earning Under 20c an Hour

Special to THE NEW YORK TIMES.

ALBANY, March 29.—New York State will have a new minimum wage law within a few weeks, according to forecasts made tonight as a result of the decision of the United States Supreme Court on the Washington State law.

Governor Lehman and Attorney General Bennett hailed the Supreme Court ruling, and meanwhile it was indicated that the Republicans would probably withdraw their objections to the Fischel bill in the form desired by the Governor.

Since the Legislature is due to reconvene next week and seek final adjournment within a week or so after that, the enactment of a new measure to replace the Wald Minimum Wage Act, previously ruled unconstitutional by the Supreme Court, will necessarily take place within a short time.

"This decision," said Governor Lehman, "clears the way for prompt enactment of a minimum wage law to protect women and minors in this State.

"I am very glad to hear of the decision in the Washington case. It would appear definitely to dispose of all the objections made heretofore against our own Minimum Wage Act of 1933, which was one of the great forward-looking steps in social legislation."

Bennett Is "Gratified"

Attorney General Bennett said:

"We are very much gratified by the decision. We will have more comment when we have seen the entire text of the opinion."

The Fischel bill, advocated by the Governor, would establish a minimum wage law for women and minors. The Senate already has passed it. But in the Assembly it has been held up because amendments backed by Assemblyman Abbot Low Moffat have been put in the measure.

These amendments would include men in the minimum wage provisions, and the Republicans had indicated up to today that they were ready to make a fight to pass the bill in that form. With the announcement of the decision, however, those available at the Capitol expressed the belief that the battle would be abandoned.

However, final plans for putting a new law on the statute books will not be mapped until a thorough study of the decision has been made.

The Wald law, which was thrown

Continued on Page Fifteen

RAILWAY LABOR ACT WINS IN HIGH COURT

Unanimous Opinion Written by Stone Upholds the Law Under Commerce Clause

MUST BARGAIN WITH MEN

Virginian Road Is Told Even Repair Shop Workers Are in Interstate Activity

Special to THE NEW YORK TIMES.

WASHINGTON, March 29.—Sections of the Railway Labor Act requiring railroads to engage in collective bargaining with their employes were unanimously upheld by the Supreme Court today in an opinion by Justice Stone.

The decision was eagerly studied by government leaders, who sought to ascertain how the court might decide the Wagner Labor Act cases also involving the principle of collective bargaining, but in which railroad workers are not concerned.

The decision was handed down in a suit by the Virginian Railway against System Federation No. 40, Railway Employes Department, American Federation of Labor. The railroad had been defeated in the Fourth Circuit Court of Appeals.

The Stone opinion, twenty printed pages, held that the Railway Labor Act, built under the commerce clause of the Constitution, was a proper measure to protect interstate commerce from interruptions due to labor disputes. The court stated emphatically that Congress possessed power to maintain interstate transportation in the face of industrial troubles.

A high point was the conclusion that "back shop" employes are a part of interstate activity, although the railroad contended that their work of repair of equipment kept them within the State and thus not within the province of the commerce clause.

To Deal With "True" Agent Only

The decision dealt principally with a section compelling the railroad to "treat" with the recognized representatives of the majority of the workers. In an exhaustive review Justice Stone expressed the court's views on the entire Section 2 of the act, the labor bargaining section which had been challenged by the railroad under the Fifth Amendment, which prevents the government from taking life, liberty and property without due process of law.

Discussing collective bargaining, Justice Stone said that the railroad had "misconstrued" a decree of a lower court forbidding it to enter into employment contracts with individual workers.

"Both the statute and the decree," he said with great earnestness, "are aimed at securing settlement of labor disputes by inducing collective bargaining with the true representative of the employes and by

Continued on Page Seventeen

A 5-TO-4 DECISION

Washington Law Akin to Voided New York Act Is Sustained

ADKINS RULING REVERSED

Hughes Reads Opinion—Sutherland, Van Devanter, Butler and McReynolds Dissent

PUBLIC INTEREST DECISIVE

But Minority Says Changes in Economic Conditions Do Not Abrogate Due Process

The majority opinion, Page 14; minority opinion, Page 15.

By TURNER CATLEDGE

Special to THE NEW YORK TIMES.

WASHINGTON, March 29.—By a 5-to-4 decision, the numerical division by which it struck down the New York Minimum Wage Law for Women and Children last June, the Supreme Court today held constitutional a similar statute of another State, the Minimum Wages for Women Act of the State of Washington.

But while the numerical division was the same, the line-up was changed. Justice Owen J. Roberts switched from the "conservative" to the "liberal" side and turned what for fourteen years had been a minority view, into the controlling opinion of the court.

Justice Roberts found sufficient reason today to join with Chief Justice Hughes and Justices Brandeis, Stone and Cardozo in validating the Washington act, leaving Justices Sutherland, Van Devanter, McReynolds and Butler, with whom he had acted in overthrowing the New York law, powerless to do anything but issue a vehement dissent.

Reports of the court's decision, rushed to the Senate floor by a messenger, found that body engaged in a heated debate over President Roosevelt's judiciary reorganization program. Breaking into the discussion to tell the Senate what had happened, Senator Robinson shouted that the Supreme Court had "reversed" itself.

Other States' Wage Laws Spared

Not only did the decision settle the constitutionality of the 24-year-old Washington statute, but it expressly reversed the basis upon which the New York law had been invalidated and the minimum wage laws of fifteen other States jeopardized.

That basis was the decision in the Adkins case, long considered a barrier against the fixing by Congress of minimum wages for women in Federal jurisdiction, and cited as the controlling factor in the adverse opinion in the New York case, even though the latter involved a State law. Senator Robinson told the Senate that the reversal on the Adkins case probably validated the New York law, which was ruled unconstitutional ten months ago.

In the Adkins case the Supreme Court invalidated a minimum wage law for women enacted by Congress for the District of Columbia, a strictly Federal territory. In view of this new ruling of the court, Elwood Seal, Corporation Counsel for the District of Columbia, held tonight that the old law, which was in effect from 1919 to 1923, "is fully effective" and began preparations to re-establish the Minimum Wage Board which administered it.

The court's opinion today, read to a packed court room by Chief Justice Hughes, said specifically:

"Our conclusion is that the case of Adkins vs. Children's Hospital should be and is overruled."

The opinion pointed out that in the New York case the court had not been asked to overthrow the Adkins decision, and therefore could not, while in the Washington case it had been made a vital point by the refusal of the State Supreme Court, in its decision upholding the validity of the statute, to consider the Adkins case as controlling.

Doubt Effect on Congress Fight

With the disclosure of this new attitude of the court on State powers in dealing with industrial reform legislation, speculation sprang high as to its probable influence on President Roosevelt's plan to re-

Continued on Page Fourteen

"All the News That's Fit to Print."

The New York Times.

LATE CITY EDITION
Generally fair and somewhat colder today. Tomorrow cloudy, with rising temperatures.
Temperatures Yesterday—Max., 70; Min., 47

VOL. LXXXVI....No. 28,928. Entered as Second-Class Matter, Postoffice, New York, N. Y. NEW YORK, WEDNESDAY, APRIL 7, 1937. P TWO CENTS In New York City. | THREE CENTS Within 200 Miles. | FOUR CENTS Elsewhere Except in 7th and 8th Postal Zones.

CHRYSLER STRIKE IS SETTLED; 65,000 WILL RETURN TO WORK; NEW PARLEYS OVER DETAILS

MARTIAL DISPLAYS, PEACE PLEAS MARK WAR ANNIVERSARY

President Reviews Parade Held in Coincident Celebration of Army Day

STRIFE FOUGHT IN HOUSE

Varied Proposals for Lasting Tranquillity Urged—Sayre, Here, Asks Freer Trade

BRITISH DISREGARD DATE

With Qualms About Our Policy Allayed, They Find No Need to Rekindle 1917 Spirit

War Anniversary Marked

WASHINGTON—President Roosevelt led nation in observance of the twentieth anniversary of its entrance into the World War. He reviewed a parade marking the coincident celebration of Army Day. Moves to foster peace featured the House session. —Page 1.

NEW YORK—Freer world trade as one way to prevent war was urged by Francis B. Sayre, Assistant Secretary of State, in address here.—Page 20.

LONDON—The anniversary passed unnoticed in Britain. Statesmen, reassured as to American policy in the event of war, saw no need to rekindle the emotions of 1917. —Page 20.

Parade in Nation's Capital

Special to THE NEW YORK TIMES.

WASHINGTON, April 6.—President Roosevelt led the nation today in commemoration of the twentieth anniversary of America's entrance into the World War and in celebration of Army Day, which he designated by proclamation.

Flanked by Secretary Woodring, General Malin Craig, chief of staff of the army, and his military and naval aides, Mr. Roosevelt stood in front of the reviewing stand for more than an hour as army, navy and marine corps units, cadets and members of patriotic organizations passed in one of the most colorful parades Washington has seen of late. Behind the President sat Congressional leaders, diplomats and high ranking officers of the military and naval services.

The President was grave as he responded to the honors of the marching units. Almost a hundred times he doffed his high hat and stood rigid in acknowledgment of salutes. A warm sun beat upon his bronzed face. The temperature was around 70.

In the parade were veterans of the nation's wars back to the Indian wars, high school cadets and Sons of the Legion hardly big enough to shoulder their rifles.

Peace Efforts Get Stress

But it was not a day given over completely to martial display. The occasion gave opportunity to stress movements for lasting peace.

In the House, Representative Ludlow of Indiana introduced a petition seeking 218 signatures for discharge of a committee from further consideration of his bill that would require a national referendum before the United States could enter a future war. He was supported by Representative Case of South Dakota, sponsor of a similar measure.

Representative Knutson of Minnesota, only present member of the House who voted against war with Germany on the morning of April 6, 1917, took the floor to plead for permanent peace.

He told the House that of the fifty-six Senators and Representatives who voted against our entrance into the World War, only twenty-six are alive today. He gave details of the plans for the reunion tonight at which eleven of these assembled. He warned that another war impends, with "great powers arming themselves for the conflict."

His assertion that the United States was driven into the last war against the wishes of the majority of Congress and the American people was disputed by Representative Fish of New York. Mr. Fish asserted that President Wilson was right when he asked for a declaration of war.

"Knew What It Was Doing"

"We were forced into the war because Germany torpedoed our ships without warning," Mr. Fish declared. "We had warned Germany frequently that this would lead to war. Congress knew what it was doing. The time to fight war is in peace, before it is too late."

He proposed that Congress call an International Disarmament Conference "if the President does not do so." Signatories to the last

Continued on Page Twenty

Four Navy Fliers Are Killed In Crash of Bombers in Air

Planes Sink in Pacific 40 Miles Off San Pedro—Wreckage of Transport, Lost With 8 on Board, Is Sighted in Arizona

By The Associated Press.

SAN DIEGO, Calif., April 6.—Four naval fliers plunged to death in the sea today after two fast scout bombing planes crashed head-on during manoeuvres over the fleet drill grounds, forty miles off shore, naval authorities reported.

The dead:

Ludwell R. Pickett, lieutenant, junior grade, Coronado, Calif.

Joseph L. Loughlin, lieutenant, junior grade, Long Beach, Calif.

Harry M. Bradley, chief machinist's mate, San Diego, Calif.

John Joseph Carney, aviation machinist's mate, first class, National City, Calif.

Official naval release of information on the tragedy said it occurred about 2:40 P. M. as the two land planes were being put into position to form a flight squadron from the aircraft carrier Lexington.

It was stated unofficially they had taken off from the landing deck of the Lexington a few minutes before the collision.

Boat crews were put over from the Lexington immediately, but naval officials said the planes sank as soon as they hit the water, and only the body of Lieutenant Loughlin was recovered.

The Lexington was ordered back to port and arrived shortly after sundown, transferring the body to a shore boat.

Bradley had served more than nineteen years in the navy and would have retired in a few weeks. All the men except Lieutenant Loughlin are survived by wives. His mother lives at Long Beach.

Special to THE NEW YORK TIMES.

ALBUQUERQUE, N. M., April 6.—The tangled wreckage of a new Douglas skyliner, missing since Saturday, as it was being "ferried" to New York for shipment to Holland, was sighted this morning twenty-five miles northwest of the rugged slope of Mount Baldy on the eastern central border of Arizona, at an altitude of 8,500 feet.

A ground searching party of thirty-five men immediately began plodding through heavy snow up the trailless slopes, but it was doubted that they could reach the scene of the crash for several days. There was no hope that any of the eight persons on board the plane were alive.

"It would be impossible for any one to be alive in that wreck," Captain A. D. Smith, Transcontinental and Western Air district superintendent here declared upon returning from a flight in which he

Continued on Page Three

'NO FOREIGN WAR,' CRY NEW CRUSADERS

Nation-Wide Emergency Peace Campaign Opened From White House

BROADCAST TO THE NATION

Rear Admiral Byrd and Mrs. Roosevelt Speak There, Dr. Fosdick Here

Addresses by Mrs. Roosevelt, Admiral Byrd, Dr. Fosdick, P. 21.

Special to THE NEW YORK TIMES.

WASHINGTON, April 6.—Rear Admiral Richard E. Byrd, retired; Mrs. Franklin D. Roosevelt and the Rev. Dr. Harry Emerson Fosdick stressed the need for effective international action to prevent war in radio addresses tonight, marking the opening of a nation-wide "No-Foreign-War Crusade" sponsored by the Emergency Peace Campaign.

Rear Admiral Byrd and Mrs. Roosevelt spoke from the White House, where the aviator-explorer had been a dinner guest of President and Mrs. Roosevelt. Rear Admiral Byrd, honorary chairman of the crusade, held up President Roosevelt's good-neighbor policy as an ideal which, if followed by all nations, would make peace "a fact."

The Rev. Dr. Fosdick, chairman of the crusade, who spoke from New York, pointed out that "in the last war we were unmercifully gypped" and pleaded that the peace movement in the United States be an inclusive, non-sectarian one.

Timed to coincide with the twentieth anniversary of the entrance of the United States into the World War, the three speeches were broadcast over the National Broadcasting Company's WJZ network from 10:30 to 11 P. M. The Emergency Peace Campaign, with headquarters in Philadelphia, was launched in the Spring of last year by the American Friends Service Committee. It is a member of the National Peace Conference, comprising thirty-four national peace organizations. Its "No-Foreign-War Crusade" will continue until some time next month, moving into more than 2,000 communities from coast to coast.

Affirms Right to Protest

Admiral Byrd declared that the most important piece of unfinished business since this country's entrance into the World War was the "establishment of an efficient international organization and the job of ending war."

He argued that "if the nations of the world put one-fourth as much money and effort into stopping war as they do into preparing for it with the ever-increasing armaments, war would most certainly be licked." It was this country's solemn duty "to prevent other nations from warring" because we would be "vitally affected by a major conflict anywhere on the face of the earth."

"Any nation," he continued, "should have the right to protest against any war, anywhere in the world. The Kellogg Pact, forgotten by some nations in so short a

Continued on Page Twenty

SWIFT NEW PLANES HELP STEM REBELS IN DRIVE ON BILBAO

Two Attacks Repelled With Aid of Russian 'Chatos' Craft, Loyalist Officials Report

BUT FOE CLAIMS ADVANCE

Insurgents Tell of Taking 12 Square Miles—Leftists Push Gains in Cordoba Region

Wireless to THE NEW YORK TIMES.

BILBAO, Spain, April 6.—For the first time, today the Spanish Government brought its new "chatos" pursuit aircraft [swift, snub-nosed Russian planes] into action on the Basque front. Officials reported later that the planes, of the type that have given the Loyalists superiority in the air on other fighting fronts, had stemmed the Rebel bombing force, which had dropped 4,000 bombs on Sunday.

General Emilio Mola's Insurgents again attacked heavily between Mount Gorbea and Puerto de Dima. After artillery preparation, their infantry advanced, but later was forced to retire.

Two more attacks, led by bombing planes, were launched later in the day, but the new Loyalist craft went into action and two Insurgent planes fell in flames. The Loyalists' lines held and, it is asserted, they even recovered some ground at Puerto de Dima.

The Loyalist line extends from Gorbea through the Puerto de Dima pass above Ochandiano and Puerto de Urquiola, opposite Mount Amboto, to Aramayona. This is characterized in the Basque press as the second line of defense.

Rebels Report New Gains

VITORIA, Spain, April 6 (AP).—Leaders of the Insurgent northern army driving toward Bilbao asserted tonight they had "thrust a foot in the half-open door" of the Basque region and that the road to the sea could now be considered open to them.

In today's drive alone, they said, twelve square miles of mountainous territory was captured as General Emilio Mola's soldiers battled through rainstorms toward Durango, key to Bilbao, the Basque capital, sixteen miles farther on.

Insurgents declared the Basque forces disputing the mountain fastnesses with them had lost 10,000 of their best men in killed, wounded and captured in the six days of the offensive. The Basque dead alone were estimated at 2,000. Officers of the attacking forces said the toll had seriously weakened the Basque Separatists, Anarchists and Communists allied in the defense of the Basque country.

Insurgents Beyond Ochandiano

Special Cable to THE NEW YORK TIMES.

VITORIA, Spain, April 6.—The Insurgent troops driving toward Bilbao were reported by their officers tonight to have advanced three and a half miles beyond Ochandiano on their way to Durango, the gateway to Bilbao.

Villages and positions taken in the fighting yesterday and today were said to include Olaeta, Gardovilla, Santa Cruz, Hermitage, Mt. Arancho and Mondrote. The Leftists were reported to have left more than 800 dead on the battlefield, and 800 others were claimed as prisoners. The desertion of fifty Basques to the Insurgent side was reported.

Much war material—including

Continued on Page Fourteen

ALL LEADS FUTILE IN HUNT FOR SLAYER

Police Vainly Follow Tips That Sculptor Has Been Seen in Dozens of Places

HIS FRENZIES REVEALED

Psychiatrist Who Studied Him Asserts That Artist Tried to Strangle Several Persons

Despite dozens of reports that Robert Irwin had been seen at various places in the Northeast, the police asserted last night they were without a definite lead in their search for the man they have accused of the murders of Mrs. Mary Gedeon, her daughter Veronica, and their roomer, Frank Byrnes, on the night before Easter.

One by one promising tip after another exploded almost as fast as they were received, high officials of the department turned to scientific counsel to amplify their information about the 29-year-old sculptor, former divinity student and voluntary inmate of an insane asylum.

Irwin was described as a victim of dementia praecox, with homicidal tendencies that had found partial expression in attempts to throttle several persons who had aroused his rage, by an eminent psychiatrist who had studied the young man's case when he was a patient at Bellevue Hospital in the first three months of 1933.

John A. Lyons, assistant chief inspector in command of detectives, consulted this psychiatrist yesterday to obtain a more complete picture of the mental characteristics of the man who is so eagerly sought. Mr. Lyons withheld his name, but said he was one of the leading psychiatrists in the city.

Accused of Attack in 1933

The detective chief added that from other sources he had obtained information that Irwin once attempted the criminal assault of a woman employe of Burke's Foundation at White Plains, N. Y., where Irwin held a $40 a month job early in 1933. Irwin was said to have boasted later that he escaped prosecution because of the woman's fear of him.

Several detectives were assigned yesterday to keep guard over Mrs. Ethel Kudner, daughter of Mrs. Gedeon, and others were detailed to watch her home at 3,083 Twenty-ninth Street, Astoria, although on the advice of police officials she had temporarily taken up residence elsewhere.

The police believe that Irwin was infatuated with Mrs. Kudner when he roomed with the Gedeons about five years ago and that he killed Mrs. Gedeon and Veronica because he blamed them for having broken up his romance. They thought it possible that Irwin might try to harm Mrs. Kudner because she rebuffed him.

Inspector Lyons and other high police officials working on the case refused to discuss in any way the nature of the physical evidence by which they claim to have placed Irwin in the Gedeon apartment at

Continued on Page Nine

GROUP IN CONGRESS SEEKS RELIEF CUT TO HALT NEW TAXES

Forms as House Bloc Demands $2,400,000,000 in Added Levies for Public Works

ASKS 20% WPA PAY RISE

Lasser Sees Hopkins—Billion a Year Move for the Jobless Is Rumored in Capital

Special to THE NEW YORK TIMES.

WASHINGTON, April 6.—The threat of new taxes inherent in the failure of government revenues to meet Treasury estimates brought about today the formation of a Congressional bloc which will insist that President Roosevelt revise his indicated recommendation for a $1,200,000,000 work relief fund to a lesser amount in order to avoid additional levies.

A rumor also was heard at the Capitol that another bloc, consisting principally of House members, was being formed to demand a permanent Works Progress Administration with an annual appropriation running well above a billion dollars.

Into this clash of purposes came a third bloc, claiming 100 House members, headed by Representative Maverick of Texas, which met today and demanded a $2,400,000,000 Public Works program next year, financed out of new taxation, to care for 3,000,000 jobless, despite the assertion of Secretary Ickes at his first press conference in the new Interior Building that the PWA's job is done. He suggested that its program be carried on with only a skeleton organization.

Demand Higher Relief Wages

Still another development in the relief situation was a conference between officials of the Workers' Alliance of America and the WPA Administrator, Harry L. Hopkins, at which he was told there was a need for an immediate 20 per cent increase in the monthly wages of relief workers, to enable them to meet the rising cost of living and that Alliance-sponsored strikes for higher wages would be continued.

David Lasser, leader of the Alliance, said the group on the West Coast was considering extending to Los Angeles a strike of 16,000 relief workers at San Francisco. Mr. Lasser said he asked Mr. Hopkins to support the Boileau bill calling for $3,000,000,000 for the WPA during the coming year and for a $1,000,000,000 Federal contribution to State relief. The conference between the Alliance officials and Mr. Hopkins will continue tomorrow.

These new demands apparently have alarmed influential members in both houses who are opposed to any new taxes, and favor strongly a balancing of the budget through decreased expenditures, particularly of relief funds. This group is described as determined to block any attempt to levy new taxes. They believe that the President can avoid new imposts by the simple expedient of asking for less than the $1,200,000,000 relief fund he is reported to have been considering.

The Senate bloc members, some of whom come from agricultural States, believe the economic trend has brightened to such an extent that the previous huge expenditures for relief are not now needed. They believe also that a curtailing of

Continued on Page Seven

Vermont Legislature Outlaws Sit-Downs; Two Years or $1,000 Fine for 'Conspiracy'

By The Associated Press.

MONTPELIER, April 6.—Vermont's Legislature tonight became the first in the nation to vote to outlaw sit-down strikes.

The Senate sent to Governor Aiken a bill providing a maximum sentence of two years' imprisonment or not more than $1,000 fine for violation.

The act provides the penalties, on conviction, for each person when "three or more conspire together or act in concert for the purpose and with the intent of forcibly and unlawfully occupying, holding or possessing any store, factory, mill, plant, dwelling house or any part thereof against the will and without the consent of the owner, lessee or management thereof."

The bill went through its final stage, approval of a minor House amendment, without record vote. Two months ago the Senate had passed the measure by 27 to 2.

It was then held in the House Judiciary Committee until two weeks ago, when it was called up for action on motion of Representative Carpenter of Waterbury.

An adverse report by the committee was overturned 152 to 63, but the bill was changed slightly, forcing it back for final action in the Senate.

The Senate defeated two attempts at the last minute to reduce the penalty. The amendments were offered by one of the body's seven Democrats, Senator Comings of Richford.

His proposal that maximum penalties be cut from two years to six months and the maximum fine from $1,000 to $200 was defeated by 22 to 7.

The House amendment approved by the Senate made the penalties "imprisonment or fine," instead of "imprisonment and fine."

AUSTIN, Texas, April 6 (AP).—Sit-down strikers in Texas will face severe penalties if a bill, passed today by the Senate, is enacted into law.

The bill, introduced by Senator R. A. Weinert, provides punishment of thirty days in jail to five years in the penitentiary for violation of its prohibition against two or more persons entering premises or "remaining therein" with the intent to force the owner, representative or manager to do "or refrain from doing any act or thing whatsoever."

The Senate action followed a statement three days ago by Governor Allred that he would use every means at his command to prevent sit-down strikes in Texas.

Sit-Downs Close 3 G. M. Plants; One 'All a Joke,' Martin Declares

Olds Factory at Lansing Halts, and Forces Shutdown of the Fisher Body Unit—Gear and Axle Workers at Saginaw Also Seize Shops

By The Associated Press.

LANSING, Mich., April 6.—Two new sit-downs today closed three General Motors plants, two of them here and one in Saginaw.

A sit-down in the Olds Motor Works tonight caused the closing of that factory and the Fisher Body plant here, which assembles bodies for Olds. The strike was the first of the present unrest in the automotive industry in the Olds plant. Both it and the Fisher plant were shut during the January-February strike.

The Olds factory employs between 7,000 and 8,000; Fisher, 4,000.

A company official said that the committee of the United Automobile Workers of America which has been discussing wages with the management tried to prevent the strike. He said about "a score" of workers started the sit-down.

The strikers took charge of the Olds plant gates. Non-union workers left.

Later Bernard Wilcie, president of the U. A. W. A. local at the Olds plant, said after a conference with company officials that the strike "was all a mistake."

He said he would ask the men to leave the factory and return to work at 7 A. M. (E. S. T.) tomorrow.

Homer Martin, U. A. W. A. president, said the strike resulted "from a joke." He said the strike began at 4:20 P. M., when the day shift completed its production ten minutes before quitting time and jokingly sat down. Other workers, he said, took the demonstration seriously and the sit-down spread until the Olds factory was closed at 6:30.

The Fisher Body plant, which supplies Oldsmobile bodies, also was closed then.

SAGINAW, Mich., April 6 (AP).—More than 500 employes in the General Motors steering gear plant here started a sit-down strike soon after noon today demanding recognition of a shop steward system. Company officials said the strike was called by local leaders of the United Automobile Workers Union.

Some non-union employes left the plant in small groups, but between

Continued on Page Seven

URGES STATE TAX ALL ITS OFFICIALS

Lehman Asks the Legislature for Measure Now to End Income Exemptions

NO COURT RULING BARS IT

Levy Would Hit Governor and Legislators—Assembly Chief for Constitutional Study

Special to THE NEW YORK TIMES.

ALBANY, April 6.—Governor Lehman called upon the Legislature today to enact a measure fixing it as State policy that all State officials be required to pay State income taxes.

The Governor sent a special message to the Legislature, remarking that certain officials, including himself and the other three State-wide elected officers, the Lieutenant Governor, Attorney General and Controller; also the members of the Legislature, of the Court of Appeals, the Supreme Court and others were considered exempt from State income taxes.

He recounted his surprise at finding that this was not the result of court decisions, but of opinions of Attorney General Newton in 1920 and Attorney General Ottinger in 1925.

He cited the fact that the Court of Appeals had not yet ruled upon the question.

He requested action at the present session of the Legislature, which, he said, would have great weight in adjudication by the courts of any constitutional question involved.

The Governor's Message

In his message, the Governor said: "I wish to submit for your consideration legislation to bring within the State Income Tax Law the salaries of all officers named in the State Constitution who are now exempt from the payment of State income taxes.

"It is well settled that neither the Federal Government nor the States may constitutionally tax the property of the other or the means or instrumentalities employed by each in the exercise of governmental powers.

"Because of this, the State of New York cannot impose an income tax upon the salaries of Federal officers and employes engaged in the performance of governmental duties. By the same token the Federal Government cannot tax the salaries of New York State officers or employes engaged in the performance of governmental functions. This relationship clearly cannot be changed by any action that the Legislature of this State could take.

"At the present time, however, certain State officers who are named in the Constitution are also exempt from the payment of State income taxes. These include the four elective State officials, members of the Legislature, judges of

Continued on Page Two

WAGE ACT VALIDITY STIRS COURT ISSUE

Cummings Opinion, Holding Old District Law in Force, Is Sent to Congress

REVERSAL ON NRA POSED

Possibility Raised of Power, if President Picks Judges, to Revive 'Dead' Measures

Special to THE NEW YORK TIMES.

WASHINGTON, April 6.—Attorney General Cummings today gave an opinion that the District of Columbia Minimum Wage Law became once more effective, without further legislative action, when the Supreme Court last week reversed its decision in the Adkins case, in which the law was found unconstitutional in 1923.

The opinion, which was given to the President and transmitted by him to Congress, was considered interesting in view of the President's plans for reorganization of the Supreme Court.

Some observers suggested that, should the court, if it were reorganized, decide to reverse decisions which invalidated such New Deal laws as the NIRA and the AAA, and should Mr. Cummings's opinion be generally accepted, the invalidated laws might again come into effect without further action on the part of Congress.

However, it was recalled that, even if the President should receive power to appoint six new justices and should all of these hold NIRA constitutional, at least two of the present bench would have to shift their positions to validate the law that established it. The decision against the NIRA was unanimous.

In identical letters to Vice President Garner and Speaker Bankhead, the President suggested, in transmitting the opinion on the District's Minimum Wage Law, that Congress might want to amend it in view of the long period of invalidity. He said he had suggested to the District Commissioners that they delay until May 1 appointment of the Minimum Wage Board to administer it.

THE PRESIDENT'S LETTER

The President's letter read:

"Sir:

"Fourteen years have elapsed since the Supreme Court, by its decision in the case of Adkins v. Children's Hospital, 261 U. S. 525, rendered the District of Columbia Minimum Wage Law inoperative. I submit herewith the opinion of the Attorney General, which makes clear that the recent decision of the Supreme Court, in the case of West Coast Hotel Company v. Parrish, overruling the previous decision, has rendered the statute once more effective.

"In view of the long interval, during which it was impossible to administer the statute, many developments have taken place and

Continued on Page Six

SIT-DOWNS BARRED

Lewis Gives His Pledge to Prevent Further Work Stoppages

BARGAINING RIGHT LIMITED

C. I. O. Is to Act for Its Members Only, but Company Agrees to Avoid Aid to the Others

'RED' OPPOSITION FEARED

Labor Officials Admit Probable Difficulty in Winning Rank and File Approval

Day's Labor Developments

Chrysler automobile strike settlement was reached between Walter P. Chrysler and John L. Lewis. The 65,000 workers are to go back to work quickly.—Page 1.

Three General Motors plants, the Olds and Fisher units in Lansing and the gear and axle shops in Saginaw, were closed by new sit-down strikes.—Page 1.

Administration leaders in Senate drafted a compromise resolution condemning sit-down strikes, but denouncing as well industrial espionage and refusal by employers of collective bargaining. —Page 8.

Chrysler Contract Drawn

By RUSSELL B. PORTER

Special to THE NEW YORK TIMES.

LANSING, Mich., April 6.—The Chrysler automobile strike, now in its thirtieth day, was settled at 9:05 o'clock tonight by an agreement between Walter P. Chrysler and John L. Lewis on collective bargaining and related issues. The agreement was signed at 11:15 P. M. Governor Murphy said that the 65,000 workers on strike would be back at work in the Chrysler plants in Detroit as quickly as possible.

The Governor said that demands of the United Automobile Workers of America on wages, hours and working conditions would be taken up at a new series of negotiations to begin Thursday in Detroit.

Both Leaders "Satisfied"

Both Mr. Chrysler and Mr. Lewis expressed satisfaction with the terms of the contract, which is to run until March 31, 1938. Mr. Chrysler told the Governor that he would resume production as soon as possible, although it probably would be two weeks before full production is reached.

The agreement, coming on the eleventh day of Governor Murphy's peace conference, includes guarantees by the union that it will prevent unauthorized sit-down strikes in the Chrysler plants for the life of the agreement, such as have occurred in General Motors plants since that company signed a contract with the union after its long strike in January and February.

Bargaining Right Limited

The Chrysler contract is worded so carefully as to leave, in the opinion of the Governor and the conferees, no room for misunderstanding over the adjustment of grievances by the shop steward system, such as have been used by "outside elements" to stir up trouble and provoke sit-down strikes in the General Motors plants.

It gives to the union recognition as agent for its own members only in collective bargaining, but provides guarantees which protect it from "competition" from company or other unions, from American Federation of Labor craft unions or from other labor organizations which it fears might be fostered by the company.

The union's original demand for "sole" or "exclusive" bargaining rights was abandoned, but the union believes the contract gives what amounts to "preferential" bargaining.

Will Not Undermine Union

The corporation also agreed not to "aid, promote or finance" any other labor organization or any agreement with an organization "for the purpose of undermining the union," and not to interfere with or discriminate against workers because of union membership.

In return the union agreed not to intimidate or coerce non-union

Continued on Page Four

"All the News That's Fit to Print."

The New York Times.

LATE CITY EDITION
Cloudy today, probably rain tonight; temperature unchanged. Tomorrow cloudy, probably rain.
Temperatures Yesterday—Max., 55; min., 46.

VOL. LXXXVI....No. 28,929. Entered as Second-Class Matter, Postoffice, New York, N. Y. NEW YORK, THURSDAY, APRIL 8, 1937. P TWO CENTS In New York City. | THREE CENTS Within 200 Miles. | FOUR CENTS Elsewhere Except in 7th and 8th Postal Zones.

FARMERS OUST 500 SIT-INS IN BATTLE AT HERSHEY PLANT; HENRY FORD BARS ALL UNIONS

CAFE RACKETEERS GET 5 TO 20 YEARS; SCORED BY JUDGE

Justice McCook Denounces 7 as Sordid Extortionists and Betrayers of Labor

LENIENCY PLEAS UNHEEDED

'Unrepentant' Gangsters Have Made No Move to Aid Dewey Since Trial, Court Says

COULCHER CACHE REVEALED

$3,500 He Left With Restaurant Man Produced—Action on Beitcher Is Delayed

Characterizing them as "hypocritical scoundrels" who posed as "respectable professional and business men and honest union leaders," Supreme Court Justice Philip J. McCook imposed prison sentences yesterday afternoon on the seven men convicted of conspiracy and extortion in the restaurant racket trial.

In sentencing the four union leaders among the defendants, Justice McCook upbraided them for wrapping themselves "in the mantle of labor" and trying to create the impression that Special Prosecutor Thomas E. Dewey sought to "disrupt the unions and to discredit and injure the cause of unionism."

"Even after the trial began some of your lawyers were still echoing this fake charge until the pressure of the people's evidence was great enough to force you to abandon that contention and invent the shallow defense in which most of you indulged," the court said.

List of Defendants

The defendants and their sentences follow:

Paul N. Coulcher, secretary of Local 16, Waiters Union, convicted of conspiracy, five counts of attempted extortion and twenty-three counts of extortion, 15 to 20 years.

Abraham Cohen, counsel for the Metropolitan Restaurant and Cafeteria Association, convicted of one count of conspiracy, four of attempted extortion and twelve of extortion; 10 to 15 years.

Irving Epstein, business agent of Local 302, Cafeteria Workers Union, convicted on same counts as Coulcher; 10 to 15 years.

Philip Grossel, secretary of the Metropolitan, convicted of one count of conspiracy, four of attempted extortion and fifteen of extortion; 10 to 15 years.

Aladar Retek, organizer for Local 16, convicted on same counts as Coulcher; 7½ to 15 years.

John J. Williams, business agent of Local 302, convicted on same counts as Coulcher; 7½ to 15 years.

Harry Vogelstein, lawyer, one of the organizers of the Metropolitan, convicted on same counts as Coulcher; 5 to 10 years.

By 10 A. M., the time set for sentencing, the corridors of the Supreme Court building were crowded with relatives and friends of the defendants and scores of uniformed and plainclothes policemen stood on duty in the small courtroom and throughout the building. At the last minute, however, the time was changed to shortly after noon to allow the completion of some probationary reports.

At 12:10 Justice McCook ordered the defendants brought before him. As they filed into the courtroom and took their stand before the bench, all, with the exception of Coulcher, showed nervousness.

Court on Racket Menace

Justice McCook told them that he intended to sentence them separately, but first wanted to address them as a group.

"In relatively recent years, and especially within the past decade," he said, "the industrial racket has emerged as a grave menace to the larger communities throughout this country.

"Two lawyers, one business man and four union officials, you stand convicted of systematically, over a period of years, engaging in a criminal conspiracy, with the aid of gangsters, to carry on one of these rackets in the form of wholesale extortions from owners of restaurants, cafeterias and other similar establishments in New York County.

"As a part of this enterprise, hundreds of business men have been subjected to a veritable reign of terror. If anything can be worse than deliberately and sordidly preying on substantial employers through the underworld, it is by the same means betraying the members of two great unions who serve those employers.

"One of the most shocking pieces of testimony in this case related to the dissipation and diversion by the four union leaders of the funds of these two unions, built out of the small contributions made by their honest, decent and hardworking fellow members.

"The State of New York stands

Continued on Page Ten

Chill Winds Blow Snow, Rain and Dust Over West

By The Associated Press.

DENVER, April 7.—Dust, snow, rain and chill winds blew over Western States today.

A Spring blizzard swept across the Rocky Mountains, interrupting plane and highway traffic. Airplane schedules out of Denver were canceled as the snowfall reached three inches. Five inches of snow, whipped by a north wind, blanketed the country around Cheyenne, Wyo.

Over Eastern New Mexico and West Texas billowed thick, brown clouds of dust, described as the worst this year, which closed schools and halted bus travel. Visibility was zero in some places.

A sandstorm at Tucumcari, N. M., reduced visibility to 100 yards, and at El Paso, Texas, the brown haze cut visibility to one mile. A chill wind swept most of Texas.

Precipitation was spreading over the western half of Kansas.

WENDEL ABDUCTORS GET 20-YEAR TERMS

Schlossman and Weiss Hear Sentences for Their Part in Lindbergh Case Plot

INNOCENT, THEY INSIST

But Court Recalls Admission of Guilt to Grand Jury—Prison Trip Is Put Off

Martin Schlossman and Harry Weiss, each 27 years old, received mandatory sentences of twenty years to life imprisonment yesterday for kidnapping Paul H. Wendel in a plot to compel him to "confess" the kidnapping of Charles A. Lindbergh Jr.

The sentences were imposed by County Judge John J. Fitzgerald in Brooklyn, before whom the two men were convicted on March 11 by a blue-ribbon jury which deliberated only fifty-three minutes. Asked if they had anything to say before being sentenced, Weiss and Schlossman, white-lipped and nervous, replied:

"We are innocent."

"You admitted your guilt before the grand jury," Judge Fitzgerald commented, "and at your trial you did not contradict that testimony."

Trip to Prison Delayed

Schlossman asked whether he could remain in Brooklyn until his attorney, who was not in court, could apply for a certificate of reasonable doubt preparatory to appealing to the higher courts. Judge Fitzgerald said he would permit both men to stay in Brooklyn until they could confer with their lawyers. The sentences are to be served at Sing Sing prison.

Schlossman and Weiss were convicted after a second trial for the kidnapping of Wendel. On Feb. 13 another Kings County jury disagreed on their guilt, after deliberating for more than twenty hours.

A third defendant, Murray Bleefeld, pleaded guilty before the end of the first trial. He is at liberty on $7,500 bail, awaiting sentence for which no date has been set. He is to be the government's star witness in Newark on April 19, when Ellis H. Parker Sr., the New Jersey county detective, and his son, Ellis Jr., are scheduled to go to trial for violating the Federal kidnapping law.

Wendel testified at both trials that he was forced into an automobile by the three defendants in front of a Manhattan hotel on Feb. 14, 1936, and taken to Bleefeld's home at 3,041 Voorhies Avenue, Brooklyn. He was held a prisoner until Feb. 24, during which time he was tortured until he made a "confession" that it was he who had kidnapped the Lindbergh baby.

Thought Work Was "Legal"

When the three defendants were arrested they admitted they had participated in the kidnapping, but did it at the request of the two Parkers, believing that they were performing "legal" police work.

The kidnapping indictment also named the two Parkers, but Governor Harold G. Hoffman of New Jersey, a lifelong friend of the elder Parker, refused to grant the request of District Attorney Geoghan of Brooklyn that they be extradited.

Schlossman, in court, gave his address as 801 Avenue M, Brooklyn. He said he was a salesman, a graduate of public school, high school and had attended the Columbia School of Architecture. He is the father of one child.

Weiss gave his address as 2,858 West Twenty-fourth Street, Brooklyn. He said that he was a taxicab chauffeur and a graduate of public school. He is the father of two children.

None of the prisoners' families or relatives was in court at the proceeding.

ROME SAYS FRANCE DIRECTS LOYALISTS AND TRAINS FLIERS

General and 25 French Staff Officers in Spain Prepare Offensive, Gayda Charges

SENDING OF ARMS ALLEGED

Paris Suspects Attack May Be Move to Pave the Way for New Italian Aid to Rebels

By ARNALDO CORTESI
Wireless to The New York Times.

ROME, April 7.—While rumors are circulating with increasing insistence that Colonel General Hermann Goering, the German Air Minister, will return to Rome toward the end of the month to discuss recent developments in the Spanish situation with Premier Benito Mussolini, the Italian press has thrown itself with redoubled vigor into a campaign intended to prove that the powers supporting the Valencia government are guilty of gross infractions of the non-intervention agreement.

The newspapers give a prominent place to every scrap of information bearing on the traffic in volunteers and war material for Spain.

Virginio Gayda enters the lists today with an article in the Giornale d'Italia accusing France of flagrantly intervening in Spain in favor of the Valencia régime, even to the extent of sending officers of her general staff.

He cites such a wealth of instances and goes into such minute detail that it is evident his article is based on official information.

Importance of Goering Visit

If the report of General Goering's projected visit to Italy is confirmed, it will assume much greater importance than his last one, since the moment is much more critical. Help can no longer be sent to General Francisco Franco, the Insurgent commander, on a large scale without first denouncing the non-intervention agreement, which would certainly cause a most undesirable reaction in France and Russia.

On the other hand, Italy and Germany are committed to secure General Franco's triumph and cannot easily at present consider an offer of British mediation since a compromise solution of the Spanish affair as things now stand would resolve itself into at least a moral defeat for General Franco.

It is evident, therefore, the offensive decided on in the last Mussolini-Goering meeting having ended in failure, that new measures must be devised and put into practice immediately.

Well-informed Italian circles continue to state that there is at present no intention on Italy's part to denounce the non-intervention agreement. Mr. Gayda says the same thing in his article today.

"Italy," he declares, "remains firm in the non-intervention policy and merely asks that this policy become operative beyond mere words.

"She is determined to give it her cooperation, but she again demands vigorously that this policy be something serious and not reduced to

Continued on Page Six

Move for Canadian Bonus Finds Government Cool

Special to The New York Times.

OTTAWA, April 7.—A movement to pay bonuses to Canadian veterans of the World War of a kind similar to those granted in the United States has begun in Canada, but according to a statement made in the House of Commons today by C. G. Power, Minister of Pensions, it will not be heeded by the government.

Mr. Power, who went to France with the first Canadian contingent as a private and was demobilized as a major, told the House that Canada had paid $1,000,000,000 to disabled soldiers since the war.

"An agitation has arisen, probably strengthened by what happened in the United States, that every man who served in the war should receive a bonus," he said. "I don't think the Canadian people or this House wish to reopen the bonus question."

21ST ST. IS SHAKEN BY SUICIDE'S BLAST

Gas Explosion Demolishes Two Apartments and Shatters Hundreds of Windows

SAMUEL WITTLIN IS VICTIM

Former City Official, Out of Work, Found in Debris—Jets of Range Open

The body of Samuel Wittlin, 38 years old, a former Assistant Corporation Counsel and later connected with the Department of Labor in Washington, was found in the débris of his tenth-floor apartment at 245 East Twenty-first Street shortly after 2 P. M. yesterday, following an explosion. The blast demolished his and an adjoining apartment, shook other buildings within a two-block radius and shattered several hundred windows in the neighborhood.

Mr. Wittlin, whose suicide by gas is reported to have caused the blast, was dead when the police and ambulance surgeons arrived. Acting Chief Medical Examiner Thomas A. Gonzales, who examined the body, expressed the belief that his death was a suicide, and that the accumulated gas from the four open jets of the range had been ignited by a spark from the electric refrigerator.

Explosion Attracts Throng

Several thousand persons thronged the near-by streets. Fire Commissioner John J. McElligott ordered firemen and the police to rope off the entire block, as he noted a bulge on the face of the sixteen-story building and feared the structure might buckle. Chief Inspector Frederick C. Kuehnle of the Building Department later reported that the building was safe, however.

Mayor La Guardia and Police Commissioner Lewis J. Valentine arrived a few moments after the blast and went to the tenth floor. Upon their return to the street they were surrounded by reporters, but the Mayor shook his head and said

Continued on Page Fifteen

ASSEMBLY BEATS LEHMAN TAX PLAN; MESSAGE IS FUTILE

79-70 Vote Kills Extra Gasoline Levy After Governor Warns the House 'of Its Duty'

SIX DEMOCRATS IN BOLT

Republicans, Criticized by the Executive, Deny Blame for $20,000,000 'Unbalancing'

Governor Lehman's message to the Assembly is on Page 8.

By W. A. WARN
Special to The New York Times.

ALBANY, April 7.—After hearing the reading of a special message sent in by Governor Lehman, in which he put responsibility for balancing his $370,000,000 executive budget upon the Republican majority in the lower house, the Assembly Republicans today permitted the budget to be thrown out of balance by withholding votes which it was within their power to furnish. The vote was on the Governor's bill to restore the fourth cent of the tax on gasoline by the gallon.

This bill was defeated, 70 to 79.

The Governor's message asserted that the Budget Bill already passed by the Assembly failed to provide for $20,000,000 of the total of the budget, the amount he estimated that an extra penny on the gasoline tax rate would provide.

On the final roll-call the Republicans lived up to their agreement to supply the Democrats with two Republican votes which, in addition to the 74 Democratic votes, would have rounded out the constitutional majority of 76 votes required to pass the Governor's tax bill—provided all the Democrats had remained in line for the measure. But six Democratic members of the Assembly refused to vote for Mr. Lehman's plan to increase the tax on gasoline.

Two Republicans Give Votes

The two Republicans who joined a majority of the Democrats in supporting the bill were Assemblymen Abbot Low Moffat, chairman of the Ways and Means Committee and fiscal leader of the Lower House, and William E. Morris of Saratoga.

The Democrats who bolted their party in the final vote were Assemblymen Anthony J. Canney, Fred Hammer and Edwin L. Kantowski of Erie, Paul B. Mercier of Oneida, Bernard J. Moran of Kings and Emmett J. Roach of Clinton County.

The vote came after a long debate in which Democratic speakers assailed Republican statements that the Governor had proved "unbending" and had turned a deaf ear on Republican pleas for a fiscal plan which would produce a "really balanced" budget covering all expenditures falling due during the next fiscal year, would lower taxes and would provide a long-term arrangement for capital outlays.

Assemblyman Steingut, leader of the Democratic minority, declared that at their conference with the Governor last week the Republican legislative leaders had presented no plan which had the backing of their party and that the only proposal submitted was one sponsored personally by Mr. Moffat.

Irving M. Ives, the Republican floor leader, replied that the Governor himself was to blame if his budget got out of balance and that the Governor's program had been short by $40,000,000 in its provisions for the needs of the State during the fiscal year beginning on July 1.

Ives Accuses the Governor

"I charge the Governor of the State with having been derelict in his constitutional duty to a greater extent than the Assembly be," Mr. Ives said. "During the years since he has been Governor we have never had a balanced budget.

"His latest budget, on the face of it, was $40,000,000 out of balance when he submitted it to the Legislature. His 'emergency' taxes are partisan taxes. We have had nothing to do with his revenue program. You and your Governor alone are responsible.

"We are charged with providing the necessary revenues—yes—and we propose to supply the necessary votes to provide for a technically balanced budget if you Democrats will supply the financial program of your Democratic Governor."

The debate on the Governor's bill got under way after the reading of his message.

However, it was read only after it had reposed for hours on the Speaker's desk, although the reading of a message from the Governor is in order at any stage of Assembly procedure. Mr. Steingut called attention to the fact that the Governor had sent a message to the Assembly and insisted that the Assembly ought to show courtesy to

Continued on Page Eight

Three Priests Among Seven on Trial in Reich Charged With Plotting Catholic-Red Front

Wireless to The New York Times.

BERLIN, April 7.—Three Catholic priests and four laymen stood before the People's Court here today charged with high treason. The indictment, covering 154 typewritten pages, charges a vast conspiracy between the Catholic priests and Communists to undermine the National Socialist government.

The seven also are accused of seeking to further a "Catholic-Communist united front," which, authorities allege, was one of the aims of the old Communist party in Germany.

This is the first time that members of the Catholic clergy have been brought before the People's Court, and the trial, which is expected to last several weeks, is fully reported in the official press. This is quite unusual, the general procedure being to ignore trials—even for treason—until sentence is passed.

The priests are Joseph Rossaint of Duesseldorf, described as chaplain of a "storm detachment" of the German Catholic Young Men's Association; Karl Cremer of Remscheid and Jakob Clemens of Duesseldorf, the latter secretary general of the German Catholic Youth Association. Father Rossaint is described as the ringleader and the movement's "soul."

Three laymen were named and the fourth was referred to only by the initial "J"; he is described as a Jew converted to Catholicism in 1933. The prosecution alleges he went to Father Rossaint for advice about marrying a Catholic, but their conversation was largely devoted to politics such as the economic situation, Germany's position among the powers, and the National Socialist question.

The accused are Franz Steder of Matzendorf, Peter Himmes and Herman Julich, both of Duesseldorf. Steder is accused of being Father Rossaint's chief aid as "Reich Fuehrer" of the so-called storm detachments and plotting in a "treasonable manner." Himmes and Julich are charged with distributing communistic propaganda and with the possession of treasonable leaflets.

Father Clemens, who was the only priest wearing a cassock in court, objected to being called chaplain. He said he was a member of the clergy but his chief function was his post as secretary-general of the Youth Association. He is in precarious health and was allowed bail.

He denied ever engaging in political activities until 1933 when he attended a meeting of Catholic youth at Lyon, France, and in 1934 a similar meeting in the Saar, where he spoke supporting national socialism.

Father Rossaint also is accused of having helped a Communist named Schwyppert who escaped to the Netherlands in 1934. He is charged with having sent Schwyppert money, given him political information and sent warnings.

Father Cremer was closely questioned regarding allegedly defeatist activities. Twenty-seven witnesses will appear for the prosecution.

'Will Never Recognize Any Union,' Ford Asserts as New Strike Ends

He Reveals Short-Lived Sit-Down in St. Louis Plant and Declares Strikers Were 'Escorted Out'—Union Leader Calls 'Brief Cessation' a Misunderstanding Over Discharges

By The Associated Press.

WAYS, Ga., April 7.—Henry Ford today announced a short-lived "sit-down" strike in his St. Louis assembly plant and said his company had no intention of recognizing the United Automobile Workers union as a bargaining agency.

"We'll never recognize the United Automobile Workers union or any other union," the 73-year-old manufacturer said at his Winter home here.

Mr. Ford revealed the St. Louis strike after talking by telephone with his son, Edsel Ford, president of the company, in Dearborn, Mich. The elder Ford said he learned a few men struck in the St. Louis plant and were "escorted out peacefully today. Any of our workers who strike will be led out of the plant involved."

"But we don't hold any grudge against them and would rehire them," he added. "We would regret taking such action because we know the men are simply being duped by the leaders and coerced."

The manufacturer, who advised workers last month "to stay out of labor unions" for their own good, said he felt public officials should protect industry from sit-down strikers.

"Those who seize property not their own are in the same category as housebreakers," he added. "The politicians who were elected as our public servants are policemen in a sense and should protect our rights."

He felt workers participating in recent strikes "have lost."

"They're being organized and held in a body and they're paying for their freedom taken away," he declared. "They'll pay money to the unions and get nothing in return.

"History shows that all improvements in labor have come out of industry and never out of coercion or politics. This is quite logical. If we don't do our part to create a market by paying good wages, we can't sell our goods."

Mr. Ford is just back from Dearborn, where he conferred with company officials during the settlement of the strike in the plant at Kansas City.

"We made no concessions," he asserted. "Our men know what we

Continued on Page Eighteen

SENATE DENOUNCES SIT-INS AND SPIES

Company Unions Are Included in Resolution Amended to Aim at Both Sides in Strikes

ONLY THREE NOES, 75 AYES

Measure Does Not Require Signature of President—It Goes to the House for Action

By TURNER CATLEDGE
Special to The New York Times.

WASHINGTON, April 7.—By the overwhelming vote of 75 to 3, the Senate passed today and sent to the House a concurrent resolution intended as a rebuke by Congress to both sides in labor controversies. The three negative votes were cast by Senators Borah, Frazier and Lundeen.

The text of the resolution was as follows:

"Resolved by the Senate (the House of Representatives concurring), that it is the sense of the Congress that the so-called sit-down strike is illegal and contrary to sound public policy;

"That the so-called industrial spy system breeds fear, suspicion and animosity, tends to cause strikes and industrial warfare and is contrary to sound public policy; and

"That it is likewise contrary to sound public policy for any employer to deny the right of collective bargaining, to foster the company union or to engage in any other unfair labor practice as defined in the National Labor Relations Act."

Passage by House Expected

The resolution will be reported tomorrow to the House, which is scheduled to take up the Dies proposal for a special investigation into sit-down strikes. House leaders had made no plans tonight for consideration of the Senate measure, but assumed that it would be brought up and passed in the next few days, as they saw little controversy in it. One of them remarked facetiously that any measure which the Senate adopted by such a majority could not contain much "fire" anyway.

The vehicle for the Senate's action was the resolution introduced by Senator Pittman immediately after the Byrnes anti-sit-down strike amendment to the Guffey-Vinson Coal Bill had been defeated Monday.

In its original form, the Pittman resolution was a simple Congressional denunciation of sit-down strikes in those inter-State industries over which Congress has jurisdiction under the Constitution. It was broadened later by its author to include condemnation of the industrial espionage system.

The resolution was amended further today by a proposal offered by Senator Robinson, the Democratic floor leader, to include also a rebuke to companies fostering com-

Continued on Page Seventeen

25,000 CHEER LEWIS AT CHRYSLER RALLY

Strikers in Fair Grounds Hear Union Chiefs Say Contract Gives Sole Rights

THREAT TO FORD IS MADE

Meanwhile, Governor Murphy Brings About a Settlement of the Reo Sit-Down

By RUSSELL B. PORTER
Special to The New York Times.

DETROIT, April 7.—A crowd estimated at 25,000 automobile workers, friends and sympathizers crowded the Coliseum at the State Fair Grounds to capacity tonight, cheering John L. Lewis, chairman of the Committee for Industrial Organization; Homer Martin, president of the United Automobile Workers of America, and other union leaders as they hailed last night's Chrysler strike settlement as a great union victory.

Mr. Lewis urged the 65,000 Chrysler strikers to return to work and stay on the job without going out on unauthorized sit-down strikes such as have occurred in General Motors plants since the union's agreement with that company.

He Warns Against Reds

Advising the unionists that contracts were made to be kept, not to be broken, Mr. Lewis warned them that if the wave of unauthorized sit-downs continued it might ruin the future of the union and of collective bargaining in the automobile industry.

He also warned union members to beware of following wrong advice from persons who have "wormed their way into positions of responsibility" and who may take advantage of their positions to bring about trouble and confusion for the union.

This was interpreted as referring to Communist and other radical agitators who are now being "purged" by the union leadership because of their suspected instigation of some of the unauthorized General Motors sit-downs.

Mr. Lewis received a series of prolonged demonstrations, and the audience gave three cheers, with no expression of disapproval, when asked to show whether it approved his statement on upholding the contract.

The C. I. O. chief also aroused much enthusiasm when he declared that Henry Ford, the only one of the "big three" auto manufacturers not yet organized, would have to recognize the union sooner or later. But he urged Ford workers not to try to take any action until they were well organized.

Several thousand persons were unable to get inside the crowded auditorium and heard the speeches through amplifiers in the street. The crowd was enthusiastic. Every mention of Henry Ford's name was

Continued on Page Eighteen

SCORE HURT IN RIOT

C. I. O. Strikers, Cut and Bones Broken, March Out in Surrender

PELTED WITH STONES, COAL

Women Join Angry Attack in Chocolate Town, Prompted by Loss of Milk Sale

MENNONITES LOOK ON

Flag Is Raised After Factory Is Restored to the Management —Earle Orders 'Prosecution'

Day's Strike Developments

Three thousand farmers ousted Hershey factory strikers from the plant in sharp fight. Page 1.

Upward of 25,000 Chrysler workers in Detroit heard union leaders explain the strike contract, and yelled their approval. Company officials sped plans to resume operation of the plants. Page 1.

Unofficial estimates put the Chrysler strike cost at $87,000,000, with nearly $9,000,000 lost in wages by Chrysler employes. Page 17.

Henry Ford declared he "would never recognize any union" as a short-lived strike ended in his St. Louis assembly plant. Page 1.

The Michigan Senate passed two bills making sit-down strikes and negotiations felonies and providing for fine and imprisonment. Page 18.

The Senate at Washington denounced sit-down strikes in a two-edged resolution rebuking labor espionage and company unions as well. Page 1.

Fight for Hershey Plant

By ROBERT S. BIRD
Special to The New York Times.

HERSHEY, Pa., April 7.—A crowd of 3,000 or 4,000 angry Central Pennsylvania farmers, bred in the tradition of a seven-day week and a dawn-to-sundown day, descended today on this model industrial town armed with clubs and improvised weapons, and put a pretty severe crimp in a C. I. O. sit-down strike in the mammoth Hershey chocolate plant.

The farmers were chiefly angry at the strikers' action in blocking their market for some 800,000 pounds of milk each day, which meant a daily loss of $10,000 to them.

But they were equally aroused over the whole idea—foreign in their opinion—of a sit-down strike in this intensely patriotic community.

They reached the boiling point today, and all morning long, in automobiles and buggies, they poured into town, filling the huge Hershey arena with indignant oratory.

When the strikers failed to budge, after a warning to leave the plant, the farmers marched into the factory and simply threw them out.

They were supported by more than 1,000 of the non-strikers, who were prevented from working by some 500 or 600 of the strikers, and received at least the passive approval of some 2,000 townspeople who were merely onlookers at the battle.

Farmers Hurry Home to Chores

The strikers, upon emerging from the plant with their hands high above their heads in surrender, were run through a long gantlet and forced to suffer the indignity, not to say the physical pain, of a good old-fashioned walloping.

The women and young girls alone were spared.

There were many bloody faces, and first reports in the hundreds, but a check-up tonight at the Hershey Hospital disclosed that not more than twenty or so were really hurt, and none seriously. These included both strikers and farmers.

The plant was quickly evacuated and as soon as the company officials were able to enter it, the farmers threw down their weapons and went to work picking up the injured and the merely frightened. They worked quickly because they had to get back to tend their live-

Continued on Page Sixteen

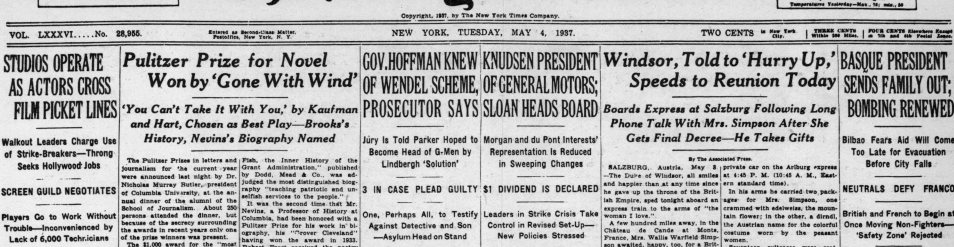

"All the News That's Fit to Print."

The New York Times.

LATE CITY EDITION
Fair, little change in temperature today. Tomorrow probably fair, temperature unchanged.
Temperatures Yesterday—Max., 78; min., 60

Copyright, 1937, by The New York Times Company.

VOL. LXXXVI.....No. 28,955. Entered as Second-Class Matter, Postoffice, New York, N. Y. NEW YORK, TUESDAY, MAY 4, 1937. TWO CENTS in New York City. | THREE CENTS Within 200 Miles. | FOUR CENTS Elsewhere Except in 7th and 8th Postal Zones.

STUDIOS OPERATE AS ACTORS CROSS FILM PICKET LINES

Walkout Leaders Charge Use of Strike-Breakers—Throng Seeks Hollywood Jobs

SCREEN GUILD NEGOTIATES

Players Go to Work Without Trouble—Inconvenienced by Lack of 6,000 Technicians

STEEL STRIKE THREATENED

C. I. O. Unit Demands Republic Corporation Act at Once on Labor Contract

Day's Strike Developments

With actors passing through picket lines unmolested, Hollywood studios continued operation despite a strike of 6,000 film technicians, whose leaders charged the use of strike-breakers. Page 1.

C. I. O. union demanded an immediate date for a contract conference with the Republic Steel Corporation, on threat of a strike. Page 15.

Executives of the sixteen hotels affected by the San Francisco strike met and named a policy committee, but made no move for a conference with the strike leaders. Page 15.

The Montreal garment strike and its handling by the Provincial Government stirred warm debate in the Legislative Assembly. Premier Duplessis defended his course, and criticized the Ottawa government for failure to "combat communism." Page 16.

Pickets Encircle Film Studios

Special to THE NEW YORK TIMES.

HOLLYWOOD, May 3.—Nine major motion picture studios were picketed by strikers today, but production went on, actors passing undisturbed through the picket lines, and there was no disorder.

Leaders of the 6,000 strikers, however, assert that the studios were using strike-breakers.

Bridgeon Smith, chairman of the Central Strike Committee for the Federated Motion Picture Crafts, which called the walkout, charged that strike-breaking make-up artists and painters were passed through thin picket lines during the night.

William McDowell, in charge at Paramount's main gate, reported that many women said they were telephone operators when they applied for permission to enter the enclosure. Others identified themselves as make-up artists.

Those who got through rushed out to the personnel manager and applied for jobs. Asked what kind of work they wanted, they generally replied: "Any kind of job."

Other Unions Being Polled

The eleven unions of technicians on strike comprise the scenic artists, painters and make-up artists, which polled their members last week; and the stationary engineers, plumbers, molders, utility workers, machinists, boilermakers and welders, costumers and cooks.

Other crafts in the Motion Picture Federation are being polled on joining the strike for recognition of the federation as the sole bargaining agency for its seventeen unions, claiming a total of 16,000 members and all affiliated with the American Federation of Labor.

The powerful Screen Actors Guild, which includes most of the stars and virtually all of the lesser actors, has deferred action for a week on the question of joining the walkout.

The guild, which is not a member of the federation, has opened its own negotiations with the producers, seeking recognition of itself as sole bargaining agency for the film players.

Procedure of the Actors

At a meeting last night attended by 2,000 of its 5,600 members, the guild instructed its directors to begin conferences with producers on Wednesday and report results to a general meeting Sunday. The producers, who regard the guild's stand as a major factor in the outcome of the strike, readily agreed to negotiate.

Aubrey Blair, secretary of the guild, said that its demands were principally in behalf of free-lance, small-part and "bit" players and "extras."

"The only things asked for people in the higher wage brackets are working conditions and hours that would aid small players to get more employment," he said.

The guild also decided at its meeting that its members would continue to pass through the picket lines until final action is taken on its stand.

Pickets made no efforts to halt the actors or delegates to the an-

Continued on Page Fifteen

Pulitzer Prize for Novel Won by 'Gone With Wind'

'You Can't Take It With You,' by Kaufman and Hart, Chosen as Best Play—Brooks's History, Nevins's Biography Named

The Pulitzer Prizes in letters and journalism for the current year were announced last night by Dr. Nicholas Murray Butler, president of Columbia University, at the annual dinner of the alumni of the School of Journalism. About 250 persons attended the dinner, but because of the secrecy surrounding the awards in recent years only one of the prize winners was present.

The $1,000 award for the "most distinguished" novel of the last year went to Margaret Mitchell, author of "Gone With the Wind," a best seller published by the Macmillan Company. The prize for the most distinguished play was awarded to George S. Kaufman and Moss Hart, co-authors of "You Can't Take It With You," now playing at the Booth Theatre. Mr. Kaufman won the prize once before, for "Of Thee I Sing," a political satire with music.

For the most distinguished book on the history of the United States, the committee selected the "Flowering of New England," written by Van Wyck Brooks and published by E. P. Dutton & Co., for the $1,000 prize. Allan Nevins's "Hamilton Fish, the Inner History of the Grant Administration," published by Dodd, Mead & Co., was adjudged the most distinguished biography "teaching patriotic and unselfish services to the people."

It was the second time that Mr. Nevins, a Professor of History at Columbia, had been honored with a Pulitzer Prize for his work in biography, his "Grover Cleveland" having won the award in 1933. Robert Frost received the poetry award for the third time in his career, with "A Further Range," published by Henry Holt & Co.

Anne O'Hare McCormick, a member of the editorial staff of THE NEW YORK TIMES, received the $500 prize for the most distinguished foreign correspondence for her "dispatches and feature articles from Europe in 1936." The terms covering this award read:

"For distinguished services as a foreign or Washington correspondent during the year, the test being clearness and terseness of style, preference being given to fair, judicious, well-balanced and well-informed interpretive writing, which

Continued on Page Twenty

HALF BILLION CUT IN RELIEF SPURRED

Woodrum in House Moves to Put Plan Up to Committee and Thinks It Will Carry

BYRNES APPEALS ON RADIO

Roosevelt in Letter Asks for Ban on Flood Control—Army Housing Is Slashed

By TURNER CATLEDGE

Special to THE NEW YORK TIMES.

WASHINGTON, May 3.—Government economies and budget-balancing were the chief topics of discussion in the halls of Congress today, and the movement for reducing the relief outlay for 1938 to $1,000,000,000, instead of the $1,500,000,000 asked by President Roosevelt, appeared to be gaining ground.

Senator Byrnes of South Carolina broadcast an appeal tonight for public support of the proposal to pare the relief appropriation and other economies in an address over a National Broadcasting Company network.

Representative Woodrum of Virginia, second ranking member of the House Appropriations Committee, announced that he intended to propose the reduction in the relief appropriation when the committee begins consideration of the President's new recommendations later this week. Mr. Woodrum expressed the belief that the House would approve the suggested cut of one-third in the 1938 request for relief.

President Writes a Letter

That the President and Congressional committees intend to use every means to hold new appropriations down at least to the estimates presented by the Budget Bureau was clearly indicated.

Representative Whittington of Mississippi, chairman of the House Flood Control Committee, revealed that Mr. Roosevelt had written him a letter urging postponement until next session of action on an extensive power and flood control program for the Ohio and lower Mississippi Rivers.

Meanwhile, extension of the active life of the Public Works Administration as a recovery agency for two years was recommended to a House subcommittee by Secretary Ickes and Horatio B. Hackett, Assistant PWA Administrator. They proposed that the revolving fund of the PWA, now amounting to about $150,000,000, be used to continue the agency, the activity of which will expire June 30, 1938, if it is not extended by Congress.

Their recommendations entailed no new appropriations and hence did not conflict directly either with the President's or Congress's economy movement. Mr. Woodrum, head of the subcommittee that heard the plea of Mr. Ickes and Colonel Hackett, said there was little disposition within the committee to oppose continuing the PWA under such conditions.

Army Housing Plan Rejected

Reports were confirmed that the Budget Bureau had disapproved a projected $162,000,000 long-range housing program for the army as recommended by the War Department, as it would interfere with the President's economy program.

On the other hand, backers of legislation calling for new expendi-

Continued on Page Thirteen

COURT COMPROMISE IS HINTED BY LOGAN

First Intimation Given by Aide of Administration That One Might Be Accepted

BURKE ALSO CONCILIATORY

Friendly to Hatch Amendment —Pettengill Tells House Bill Is Unconstitutional

Special to THE NEW YORK TIMES.

WASHINGTON, May 3.—The first intimation by an administration supporter that a compromise on the bill to reorganize the Supreme Court might be acceptable came today from Senator Logan.

At the same time, Senator Burke, a leader of the opposition, said that if the administration was willing to put aside its bill, a compromise as suggested by Senator Hatch "would have a real chance for favorable consideration." The Hatch amendment would provide for a flexible number of justices, but permit the President to appoint only one additional justice in a year, instead of six as he might under the administration bill.

The constitutionality of the court bill was challenged in a House speech today by Representative Pettengill of Indiana, who asserted that it would be a delegation of legislative power to the court itself, since the number of justices on the bench would depend on the decision or reluctance of any over 70 to retire.

He turned the words of both President Roosevelt and Attorney General Cummings to his use in making an argument which Senator Borah later called "unanswerable."

Proposes Change of Procedure

Senator Logan suggested that the Judiciary Committee vote first on the bill as it came from the White House, and after the vote was taken proceed to consider amendments and substitutes now pending before or to be submitted to the committee.

This would be a reversal of the regular committee rule, which is to dispose of all amendments before voting on a bill.

Some Senators saw in the Logan proposal a move to avert an adverse report to the Senate.

The committee would be in a position, if a majority voted against the bill, to continue consideration in an effort to work out some compromise that a majority would support, thereby making possible a favorable report on an amended bill. This would give the advocates of the bill an opportunity to offer the original bill as a substitute, from the floor of the Senate.

Senator Logan's proposal was discussed at some length in committee today, but no decision was reached. The matter will probably come up again tomorrow.

Pettengill's Argument in House

Mr. Pettengill said in his speech in the House that changes in the number of the court members made prior to 1869 were not challenged as unconstitutional, and because of this, the validity of the present bill had not heretofore been questioned. But these prior changes, he said, afford no precedent in the present case because the age of justices was not mentioned, nor was the size of

Continued on Page Fourteen

GOV. HOFFMAN KNEW OF WENDEL SCHEME, PROSECUTOR SAYS

Jury Is Told Parker Hoped to Become Head of G-Men by Lindbergh 'Solution'

3 IN CASE PLEAD GUILTY

One, Perhaps All, to Testify Against Detective and Son —Asylum Head on Stand

From a Staff Correspondent

NEWARK, N. J., May 3.—The Federal Government opened its case in the Parker conspiracy trial here today by charging that Governor Hoffman of New Jersey knew about the alleged scheme whereby Paul H. Wendel was produced as the "real" kidnapper of the Lindbergh baby, a few days before Bruno Richard Hauptmann was to be put to death for the crime.

United States Attorney John J. Quinn, outlining his case before the jury of eight housewives and four men, depicted the Governor as a background figure in what was described as a ruthless and barefaced plot by Ellis H. Parker Sr. to gain fame and political fortune for both.

"There will be evidence here," Mr. Quinn said, "that Governor Hoffman knew about this proceeding. Whether or not the bill of goods was sold by the Parkers to Governor Hoffman, I do not know. That is for the jury to determine."

"Or Whether the Governor—"

Mr. Quinn, in a press conference after the court, insisted that he also made to the jury the alternative remark, "or whether or not the Governor sold a bill of goods to the Parkers," but these words were not recorded by the court stenographer.

The prosecutor pictured the 67-year-old county detective as an "egocentric" person who had hoped to gain credit for "solving" the Lindbergh crime and thereby win for himself a position as head of the Federal Bureau of Investigation, and for his lifelong friend, the Governor, the Vice Presidency of the United States.

Wendel, a former Trenton attorney who had got into trouble on one or two occasions, was regarded by his former friend, Parker, as having a peculiar "mental twist," according to the prosecutor.

Parker, who was depicted by Mr. Quinn as having almost hypnotic powers over people, planned to make Wendel confess the Lindbergh kidnapping and thereby take advantage of the confusion in the public mind concerning Hauptmann, who was about to die for the crime.

"Will Make Me a Big Man"

Mr. Quinn said that Parker told Wendel, as he was about to be surrendered after his abduction and torture: "You can go to State's prison for a short length of time. You know what I can do. You know the power I have got. This condition will make me a big man; I may even take Hoover's place." This last apparently referred to J. Edgar Hoover, head of the Federal Bureau of Investigation.

Parker also told Wendel, according to the prosecutor, that the condition of public opinion resulting from the "solution" of the crime would make "Governor Hoffman Vice President of the United States, and as such would make him a big man, naturally."

As the actual trial got under way today, the issues were narrowed down to those involving the two Parkers, the detective and his son,

Continued on Page Two

KNUDSEN PRESIDENT OF GENERAL MOTORS; SLOAN HEADS BOARD

Morgan and du Pont Interests' Representation Is Reduced in Sweeping Changes

$1 DIVIDEND IS DECLARED

Leaders in Strike Crisis Take Control in Revised Set-Up—New Policies Stressed

Declaring a common dividend of $1 a share for the first quarter, the directors of the General Motors Corporation, at a meeting that lasted two hours and a quarter yesterday afternoon, reorganized the high executive personnel of the company. The directors met in the General Motors Building here.

In the sweeping changes, the finance committee and executive committee were abolished and a policy committee and an administration committee with well-defined duties were created, with Alfred P. Sloan Jr. as chairman of both.

Mr. Sloan, who submitted the proposed changes to the board, remains chief executive officer of the corporation, but as chairman of the board. William S. Knudsen was elected president in his place.

Mr. Sloan succeeds Lammot du Pont, who declined re-election as chairman because of his other business responsibilities. Donaldson Brown, formerly vice president and chairman of the finance committee, was elected vice chairman of the board.

Knudsen's Duties Widened

As president, Mr. Knudsen will assume complete responsibility as to administration of all the corporation's operating divisions and subsidiaries other than those of a strictly financial nature.

Elimination of the finance and executive committees carried with it a reduction in the representation of the Morgan and du Pont interests in executive capacities in General Motors affairs. At the same time several of the less active officers were dropped and replaced by other men on the two new committees.

In addition to the other changes, Marvin E. Coyle, general manager of the Chevrolet Motor Division, and Floyd O. Tanner, who will deal with labor relationships as a member of the general staff, were elected vice presidents of General Motors Corporation.

To the policy committee were elected Mr. Brown, Albert Bradley, Walter S. Carpenter Jr., Lammot du Pont, Mr. Knudsen, John Thomas Smith, George Whitney and C. E. Wilson, with Mr. Sloan as chairman. All are officers of the company except Mr. Carpenter and Mr. du Pont, who represent du Pont interests, and Mr. Whitney of J. P. Morgan & Co.

Members of the former finance committee dropped in the reorganization are George F. Baker, Henry F. du Pont, Irenee du Pont, Pierre S. du Pont, Junius S. Morgan, Charles S. Mott, Seward Prosser and John J. Raskob. Mr. Mott, although a vice president and a large stockholder, has been semi-active in recent months.

New Administrative Group

The new administrative committee consists of Mr. Bradley, Lawrence P. Fisher, R. H. Grant, O. E. Hunt, Mr. Knudsen, James D. Mooney, Mr. Wilson, R. K. Evans, Mr. Tanner and Mr. Sloan as chairman. All are officers of General Motors Corporation.

Members of the former executive committee who do not appear on

Continued on Page Three

Strike Ties Up a Weehawken Ferry Line; Hundreds of Waiting Autos in Jam Here

With horns blaring impatiently in an incessant din, hundreds of Jersey-bound trucks and automobiles stood still four abreast for more than an hour yesterday in a line from Fourteenth to Twenty-eighth Street along the West Side waterfront as fifty-seven employes of a ferry company went on strike.

At 4:20 P. M., as a boat of Electric Ferries, Inc., inbound from Weehawken, nestled into its slip, the captain and mate and all hands on the ship and on the dock walked away from their posts and announced quietly that a strike had been called. At the same time two other boats of the company were abandoned at the Weehawken terminal at the foot of Baldwin Avenue.

Truck drivers and motorists out for a drive on a fine day were not warned of the strike and grew steadily more confused and angry as they were wedged into a traffic jam that met itself in opposition at Twenty-third Street. Finally radio car policemen forced back the ends of the line as it formed to the north and south, while twenty other policemen turned the center to the slips of four other near-by ferry lines.

Last night the three ferry boats still lay idle at their slips, while company officials met at the Weehawken pier to plan a restoration of service.

The strike was called by the Harbor Towboatmen's Union, Local 933-3 of the International Longshoremen's Association, at the expiration of a contract between the company and the Masters, Mates and Pilots Union. William Bradley, business manager of the towboatmen's union, said that the strike had been called because Clarence H. Walker, vice president and director of operations of the ferry company, had refused to recognize the towboatmen's union.

Mr. Walker said that the company was in a quandary over the recognition of three unions of ferry boatmen. Most of them, he said, had signed petitions for representation by both the Masters, Mates and Pilots Union and the Towboatmen's Union. There is also a Marine Engineers Union. All three have been fighting for recognition.

Windsor, Told to 'Hurry Up,' Speeds to Reunion Today

Boards Express at Salzburg Following Long Phone Talk With Mrs. Simpson After She Gets Final Decree—He Takes Gifts

By The Associated Press.

SALZBURG, Austria, May 3.—The Duke of Windsor, all smiles and happier than at any time since he gave up the throne of the British Empire, sped tonight aboard an express train to the arms of "the woman I love."

A few hundred miles away, in the Château de Cande at Monts, France, Mrs. Wallis Warfield Simpson awaited, happy, too, for a British divorce court had removed the last legal barrier to their marriage.

Each hour brought him closer to the dark-eyed, American-born woman. Tomorrow another chapter will be written in the world-stirring romance, for the Duke will see her for the first time since he stepped down from the throne on Dec. 10.

The Duke ended twenty-two long weeks of exile in Austria, restless and impatient to go to her side.

They talked by telephone within a few minutes after the British tribunal said she was free.

She told him to "Hurry up!" He did.

Loaded down with edelweiss, suitcases and smiles, he boarded his private car on the Arlburg express at 4:45 P. M. (10:45 A. M., Eastern standard time).

In his arms he carried two packages for Mrs. Simpson, one crammed with edelweiss, the mountain flower; in the other, a dirndl, the Austrian name for the colorful costume worn by the peasant women.

Seventeen suitcases were scattered about the Duke's car.

Twenty-two weeks ago he came here in voluntary exile, haggard and worried. The change in his mien, once he reached Salzburg today, was apparent immediately.

Leaving an automobile, he fairly sprinted along the sunny station platform, radiating happiness. He wore no hat and he had, perhaps, the best coat of tan that Austria has produced this season.

Before leaving Appesbach he posed cheerfully for photographers, smiling broadly and joking with newspaper men.

As evidence of his enthusiasm and eagerness to leave, he told

Continued on Page Twenty-seven

WORLD BANK URGES LOWER GOLD PRICE

Report Holds Move Would Aid in Coping With Problems of Over-Abundant Production

NIEMEYER IN NEW POST

Briton Heads Board—Beyen of Netherlands Succeeds Trip as President

By CLARENCE K. STREIT

Wireless to THE NEW YORK TIMES.

BASLE, Switzerland, May 3.—The gold and arms situations appear as the darkest shadows in the picture of the world-wide upswing that the Bank for International Settlements draws in its annual report surveying the monetary and economic world. President L. J. A. Trip submitted the report to the bank's general assembly here today, which approved it.

The general assembly approved change in the statutes proposed by the bank board, dividing the present functions of the bank's presidency between two officers, one to be chairman of the board and the other president of the bank, both to be elected for three-year terms.

As President Trip's resignation took effect today the board, as expected, elected as its chairman Sir Otto Niemeyer of Great Britain and as the bank's president J. W. Beyen of the Netherlands, who has been Dr. Trip's alternate for the past two years.

Central Bank Heads Present

The assembly was attended by delegates from twenty-five member banks, including Montagu Norman of Great Britain, Emile Labeyrie of France, Dr. Hjalmar Schacht of Germany and almost all European central banks' governors. Samuel Welldon, vice president of New York's First National Bank, represented American stockholders.

The report, which was the meeting's main event, was chiefly the work of the bank's Swedish economic advisor, Per Jacobsson, although signed by Dr. Trip and issued under the bank's responsibility.

The report finds that the lowering of the price of gold would help cope with the serious problems resulting from over-abundant production. But it points out the difficulties and dangers and makes no recommendation.

The report, which was written before the recent price break, agrees with President Roosevelt that "concern should be felt about the strength of recent price developments," and also approves the policy of restricting credits and decreasing government expenditures. It repeatedly stresses the need for lowering trade barriers if recovery is to endure.

The world's gold production increased in 1936 by thirteen and a half per cent, the report says, pointing out that this was the highest rate of increase the world has ever known except during the three big gold strikes in the Transvaal, California and Australia.

Even these records were beaten in two respects by 1936, the report says, for the year's total of 35,254,000 fine ounces not only was the greatest in history but represented an increase over 1935 of more than 4,300,000 ounces which is the larg-

Continued on Page Forty-three

NEURATH IN ROME; AMITY EMPHASIZED

Reich Foreign Minister Has a Talk With Mussolini After Warm Welcome at Station

ALLIANCE PLAN IS DENIED

Italy Not Willing to Fight War for Germany—Arming by Britain to Be Studied

By ARNALDO CORTESI

Wireless to THE NEW YORK TIMES.

ROME, May 3.—Foreign Minister Constantin von Neurath of Germany arrived in Rome at the head of a large German delegation at 11:35 o'clock this morning and got a reception in which every possible emphasis was laid on Italo-German friendship. Count Galeazzo Ciano, Italian Foreign Minister, welcomed him cordially at the station amid much waving of Italian and German flags, playing of the Italian and the German national anthems, inspecting of guards of honor and shouting and cheering.

Europe's present political line-up was stressed by the fact that besides officials of the two countries actually concerned, only the Ministers of Austria and Hungary were at the station.

Only a preliminary conversation lasting one and a half hours between Baron von Neurath on one side and Premier Benito Mussolini and Count Ciano on the other was held today. In the afternoon Baron von Neurath performed such usual duties as laying wreaths on the tombs of the Italian Kings in the Pantheon and on the tomb of the Unknown Soldier. Earlier in the day he had called at the Palazzo Chigi to pay his respects to Count Ciano and then received Count Ciano for a return visit at his hotel. These purely formal meetings lasted only a few minutes.

Talk at Palazzo Venezia

The sole political conversation of the day was held at the Palazzo Venezia from 5 P. M. to 6:30. In the evening Baron von Neurath was honored at an official dinner given at Villa Madama, the beautiful residence for distinguished guests inaugurated by the German Air Minister, Col. Gen. Hermann Goering, last January.

Premier Mussolini, Baron von Neurath and Count Ciano will get down to real business in the Palazzo Venezia tomorrow and will probably continue their discussions Wednesday morning.

No direct contacts between the responsible heads of Italian and German foreign policy have taken place since Count Ciano's visit to Germany last October and events have progressed so rapidly since then that the need is felt on both sides to take stock of developments.

The most notable changes that have occurred in Europe, which will certainly be carefully studied by the Italian and the German statesmen, are British rearmament, the stalemate in the Spanish civil war and the new Italian attitude toward Austria, revealed in the recent Venice meeting between Mussolini and Chancellor Kurt Schuschnigg of Austria.

British rearmament has heightened the prestige of the democracies and correspondingly lowered that of the dictatorships as shown by the fact that some smaller countries that at one time showed symp-

Continued on Page Ten

BASQUE PRESIDENT SENDS FAMILY OUT; BOMBING RENEWED

Bilbao Fears Aid Will Come Too Late for Evacuation Before City Falls

NEUTRALS DEFY FRANCO

British and French to Begin at Once Moving Non-Fighters—'Safety Zone' Rejected

REBELS IN BERMEO TRAP

Loyalists Say Foe Has Lost Many in Siege of Biscayan Town—Madrid Battle Resumed

The Spanish Situation

SAINT-JEAN-DE-LUZ—The wife and two children of President Aguirre, of the Basque Republic, fled from Bilbao to France. Their action was taken to indicate the seriousness of the city's plight. Page 1.

LONDON—The British Government announced it would go ahead with the rescue of Bilbaoan women and children despite General Franco's objections. (Follows above dispatch.) Page 8.

THE FRONTS—Basque forces held the Rebels in the day's fighting near Bermeo and Durango. Loyalists said Rebels were still trapped at Bermeo and had suffered severe losses. Fighting was renewed outside University City at Madrid. Page 9.

BERLIN—The press joined in a strong campaign against British "lies." Accounts stating Guernica was destroyed by German aerial bombers were particularly denounced. Page 9.

Flight of President's Kin

By The Associated Press.

SAINT-JEAN-DE-LUZ, France, May 3.—The wife and children of the Basque President, Juan Antonio Aguirre, arrived today at Biarritz, France, after a flight from Bilbao, the besieged capital of their country, from which French and British warships began evacuation of their own nationals.

The flight of the President's family was regarded as indicating the grave view taken by Basque leaders of the situation of their chief city. Mrs. Aguirre and her children joined families of other Basque leaders who had preceded them into France.

To Saint-Jean-de-Luz the British destroyer Faulknor brought the first refugee contingent, arriving from Bilbao with twelve passengers, including the British consul and vice consul. A little later came the French dispatch ship Somme, carrying seventy-two French and Belgian refugees.

The British battleship Royal Oak, four British destroyers and a French sloop are at Saint-Jean-de-Luz, ready to guard refugee vessels once they have passed outside the Spanish three-mile limit.

Evacuation Not Yet Begun

Except for the departure of the President's family, evacuation of Spaniards from Bilbao, on which the Insurgent armies are pressing, had not begun today, as far as could be determined here.

In view of the increasing military pressure on the Basque capital, diplomats here expressed doubt that any large-scale evacuation of Bilbao noncombatants could be carried out.

The war zone around Bilbao is becoming increasingly dangerous, they pointed out. General Francisco Franco's Insurgent planes daily are bombarding Bilbao's ports along the Nervion River. In spite of official statements in London and Paris that evacuation plans will be carried out as announced, regardless of General Franco's refusal to accept them, it was believed any mass rescue of Bilbao's women, children and aged men had become impossible.

A few thousand women and children, however, will be brought to France. Three requisitioned French steamers are leaving Bordeaux for Bilbao Tuesday night, but they can carry only 2,000 persons.

The part to be played by the British freighters that ran the Insurgent blockade with food cargoes for Bilbao and are still there remained uncertain. It was planned they should carry iron ore cargoes when they left, but that plan has been abandoned in the fear that the ore cannot be loaded before the city falls.

The Faulknor's trip to Bilbao today was her second in three days. Insurgent airplanes dropped bombs near her when she slipped into port there Saturday to discuss evacuation with the British consul.

Britain Defies Franco

Wireless to THE NEW YORK TIMES.

LONDON, May 3.—The British Government announced today that

Continued on Page Eight

THE HINDENBURG AS SHE SAILED OVER MANHATTAN

The giant dirigible as it flew over New York's financial district enroute to Lakehurst, New Jersey.

The *Hindenburg* bursting into flames as it nosed toward the mooring post.

Associated Press Photo.

The huge skeleton of the *Hindenburg* settled to the ground as smoke continued to pour from it.

Times Wide World Photo

"All the News That's Fit to Print."

The New York Times.

LATE CITY EDITION
Fair today, temperature unchanged. Tomorrow fair, little change in temperature.
Temperature Yesterday—Max., 71; Min., 56

VOL. LXXXVI....No. 28,958. Entered as Second-Class Matter, Postoffice, New York, N. Y. NEW YORK, FRIDAY, MAY 7, 1937. P TWO CENTS In New York City. | THREE CENTS Within 200 Miles. | FOUR CENTS Elsewhere Except in 7th and 8th Postal Zones.

HINDENBURG BURNS IN LAKEHURST CRASH; 21 KNOWN DEAD, 12 MISSING; 64 ESCAPE

ANARCHISTS RENEW BARCELONA STRIFE; 5,000 LEAVE BILBAO

Revolters, Regaining Part of Catalan Capital, Demand Shock Troop Dissolution

SOCIALIST MINISTER SLAIN

Insurgents Reported Gaining Unresisted in Aragon as Foes Withdraw 12,000

EVACUATION IN NORTH SPED

British Warships Protect Craft Taking Women and Children From Bilbao to France

The Spanish Situation

PERPIGNAN—Anarchists were reported to have regained positions in Barcelona and to have demanded the dissolution of the government's shock troops. Withdrawal of 12,000 men from the Aragon front, to deal with the situation, was also reported, leading to an advance by the Rebel armies. Page 1.

ROME—A heavy concentration of Rebels, including Italians, to rescue the Italians cut off at Bermeo, was under way on the Bilbao front. Page 10.

BILBAO—Five thousand women and children were taken from the city, and vessels carrying them to France were guarded by British warships. More refugees were preparing to leave. (Follows the above.) Page 10.

LONDON—Foreign Secretary Eden revealed that the British Government had evidence that Guernica was destroyed by airplanes. He favored a neutral inquiry. Page 10.

Anarchists Give Ultimatum

Special Cable to THE NEW YORK TIMES.

PERPIGNAN, France, May 6.—The Anarchists are reported to have regained control in parts of Barcelona this afternoon after the Catalan Generalidad believed it had dominated the situation.

The Anarchists issued an ultimatum to the government demanding the dissolution of the shock troops patroling the city, the government's chief support, within twenty-four hours and declaring that otherwise they would take matters into their own hands and use every means in their power to suppress the shock troops.

The Anarchists also have obtained the upper hand at Junquera in addition to Figueras, according to news received here, and threaten, it is alleged, to use asphyxiating gas unless their ultimatum is obeyed.

Anarchist broadcasts have been picked up here stating that the casualties in the disorders in Barcelona since the Anarchist rebellion Tuesday amounted to 400 dead and 2,000 wounded. Declaring that "enough blood has flowed," the broadcasts continue to appeal for calm every ten minutes, and it is therefore believed that trouble still persists in Barcelona.

French Consulate Menaced

The French Consulate was threatened by Anarchists, who asserted that Rightist sympathizers had taken refuge there. The consul appealed to French warships in the harbor and 200 armed sailors reinforced the consulate guard.

Telephonic communication with Barcelona is still cut off tonight, and telegraphic and telephonic communication with the interior of Catalonia, which was re-established yesterday, was again interrupted this morning.

The Spanish Consul at Perpignan has recommended that Frenchmen and others should not go further than Figueras, and trains do not proceed beyond Gerona.

Francisco Ascasso, leader of the Anarchists in the Aragon Government, is reported to have been murdered.

Rebels Gain on Aragon Front

By The Associated Press.

PERPIGNAN, France, May 6.—Reports of an unresisted Insurgent advance along the whole Aragon front of Northeastern Spain and of the withdrawal of 12,000 government troops from it to keep the peace in troubled Barcelona, put a new and serious face on the Catalan Anarchist insurrection tonight. The reports emanated from Insurgent

Continued on Page Ten

Judge Sentences Himself By Signing Papers Unread

Wireless to THE NEW YORK TIMES.

MOSCOW, May 6.—A judge on one of the most important benches of the Moscow District Court who has the bad habit of signing unread any document placed before him has just sentenced himself to jail.

The court clerks, deciding he needed a lesson in "Bolshevik vigilance," presented to him a sheaf of papers including one reading "To the chief of Butyrky prison: Under Magistrate Abramson is sent to you for further detention." Judge Abramson signed all the papers and picked up his newspaper again.

The clerks, of course, extracted the sentence and were passing it around laughingly when the judge found out about it. He destroyed it in a rage, declaring such jokes tended to undermine Soviet justice.

The government learned about it, however, and today Izvestia delivered to Judge Abramson a stinging rebuke for perfunctoriness, reminding him that he dealt not in inanimate goods but in human fate.

HUGHES SEES CHOICE IN LAW OR TYRANNY

Courts Must Be Maintained, He Tells Law Institute, or We Replace Reason by Force

TEST OF BAR TO ROOSEVELT

Stewardship Is Questioned by Laymen, He Writes in Warning of 'Critical Audience'

Text of Chief Justice Hughes's address is on Page 17.

Special to THE NEW YORK TIMES.

WASHINGTON, May 6.—Chief Justice Hughes made what his hearers construed as a reference to the Supreme Court when he told the American Law Institute today that if society is to choose the processes of reason as opposed to the tyranny of force, "it must maintain the institutions which embody those processes." It was the second time that the Chief Justice of the United States has broken his silence since the controversy over reorganization of the Supreme Court started three months ago.

Vigorous applause, lasting more than a minute, followed the Chief Justice's words, with which he concluded a speech in which he avoided any direct reference to the court issue.

President Roosevelt in a message to the institute likewise refrained from any positive statement about the Supreme Court, but remarked that "law interpreters," among other legal experts, are facing a sometimes critical audience.

President on Lawyers' Position

"I am happy to greet you members of the bench, the bar and the law school faculties who have assembled for the fifteenth annual meeting of the American Law Institute," the President stated.

"I have followed with interest your accomplishments within recent years in the restatement of the law and your proposals for improvement in the administration of criminal justice.

"Today our stewardship as lawyers is being questioned. The laymen of America are not, perhaps, quite so disposed to make a complete delegation of law matters to law men. At least the layman asserts his right to evaluate us.

"Law scholars, law practitioners, lawmakers, law administrators and law interpreters have the stage today. But more significant, they must play their rôles before an intense and sometimes critical audience.

"But this is well. The virtue of the common law was its adaptability to growth and improvement. In generations present and future the lawyer likewise will be measured by the same test.

"It is encouraging today that so many outstanding leaders of the profession assemble to give service in the important and worth-while task to which the American Law Institute is dedicated. I extend again my warm and cordial greetings to your membership and my best wishes for continued success."

Only at one other time since President Roosevelt made his recommendations to Congress on Feb. 5 has the Chief Justice made any

Continued on Page Seventeen

NOTABLES ABOARD

Merchants, Students and Professional Men on the Dirigible

LEHMANN IS A SURVIVOR

Veteran Zeppelin Commander, Acting as Adviser on Trip, Is Seriously Burned

CAPT. PRUSS IS ALSO SAFE

C. L. Osbun, Sales Manager, Who Survived a Plane Crash, Escapes Second Time

Notables from many walks of life were among the passengers on the ill-fated Hindenburg. They included merchants, students and business and professional men and women.

Many of the survivors owed their lives to the fact that they were apparently near windows in the dirigible when the accident happened and were able to leap through them to the ground in safety.

Among the survivors listed were Captain Ernst Lehmann, veteran Zeppelin commander; Captain Max Pruss, the new Hindenburg commander; Herbert O'Laughlin of Chicago, employed by the Consumers Company of Elgin, Ill.; Clifford L. Osbun, export sales manager of the Oliver Farm Equipment Company of Chicago, and Ferdinand Lammot Belin Jr. of Washington, D. C.

Lehmann's Condition Grave

Early this morning Dr. E. G. Herbener, staff surgeon at the Paul Kimball Hospital in Lakewood, said that Captain Lehmann was on the doubtful list. Captain Lehmann is suffering from shock and second and third degree burns of the face and body. Captain Pruss is suffering from second and third degree burns of the face, forehead and arms and will probably recover, Dr. Herbener said.

Among the passengers who were still unaccounted for were John Pannes, passenger traffic manager of the Hamburg-American Line and North German Lloyd at New York, and his wife; Ernst Rudolf Anders, partner of the firm of Seelig & Hille, tea merchants of Dresden, Germany, and his son, R. Herbert Anders, and Hermann Doehner of Mexico, D. F.

Captain Lehmann and Captain Pruss were in the control gondola when the crash occurred. Both officers, together with several other members of the crew, leaped through the gondola windows to safety

Lehmann an Adviser

Captain Lehmann, who was serving as adviser aboard the Hindenburg, had been commander of the ship until this year. He has had long experience with the lighter-than-air craft, and has been associated with Hugo Eckener, world-famous authority on Zeppelins, since 1931.

He was born March 12, 1886, at Ludwigshafen, on the Rhine, the son of a chemist. He became a naval cadet in 1905 and later entered the Polytechnic Institute at Charlottenburg, a borough of Berlin.

During the World War Captain Lehmann received the German Iron Cross award. After the war, as second in command to Eckener, he brought the dirigible Los Angeles to Lakehurst in 1924. When the Hindenburg was completed in 1936 Captain Lehmann was placed in command, a position he held until recently, when Captain Pruss was elevated as commander of the ship.

Mr. Osbun's escape from the disaster marked the second time that he had narrowly missed death as the result of a flying accident. Last year he was aboard a transport plane when it was forced down en route from Puerto Rico to Buenos Aires. Soon after he was transferred to a motorboat with other passengers and the motorboat blew up. Mr. Osbun escaped injury, but two other passengers were seriously burned.

Mr. Osbun declared that he was talking to fellow passengers in the dining salon, looking down through the observation window watching the ship being moored, when the disaster occurred. He was apparently blown through the window and thrown to the ground, suffering injuries. He was taken to the Paul Kimball Hospital in Lakewood, where his condition was said to be not serious.

Mr. Osbun is 37 years old, the fa-

Continued on Page Nineteen

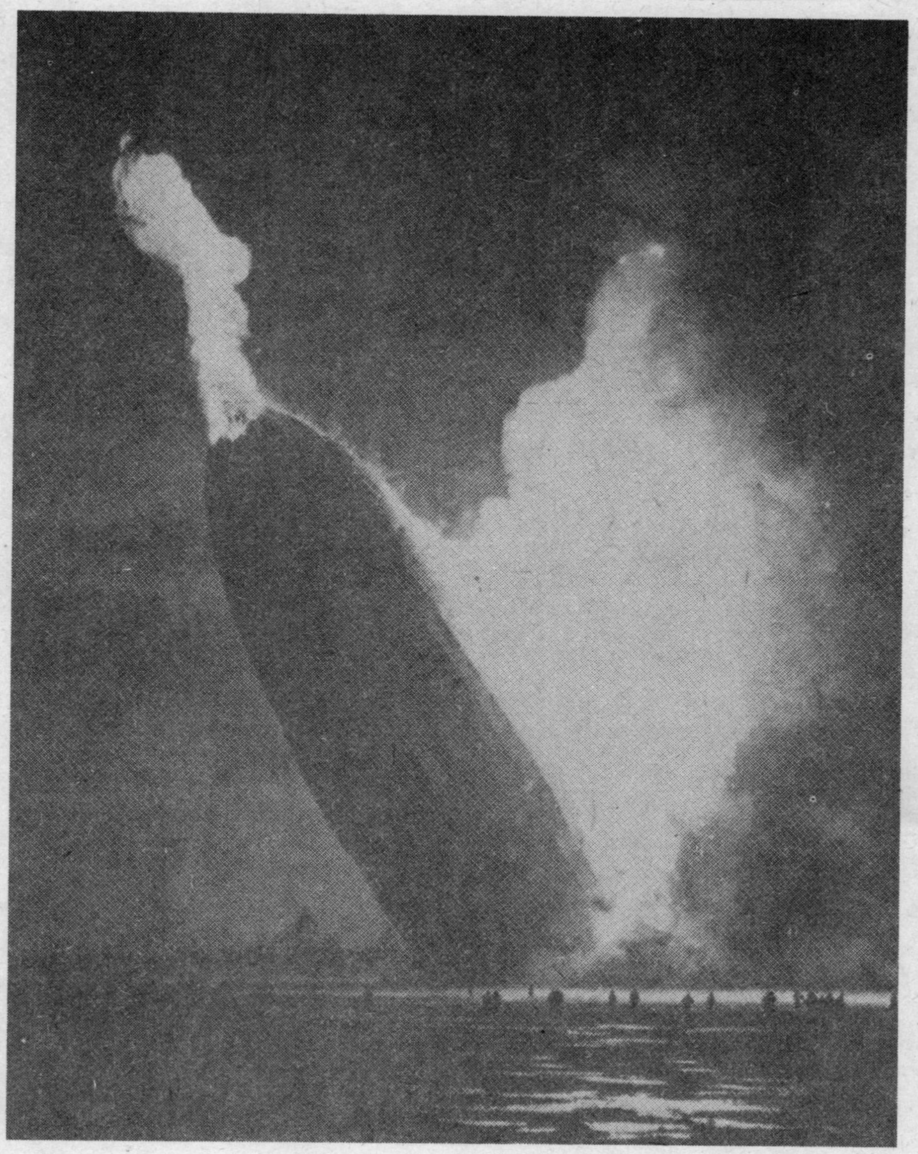

Associated Press Photo.

THE HINDENBURG IN FLAMES ON THE FIELD AT LAKEHURST

The giant airliner as she settled to the ground near her mooring mast at 7:23 o'clock last night

SHIP FALLS ABLAZE

Great Dirigible Bursts Into Flames as It Is About to Land

VICTIMS BURN TO DEATH

Some Passengers Are Thrown From the Blazing Wreckage, Others Crawl to Safety

GROUND CREW AIDS RESCUE

Sparks From Engines or Static Believed to Have Ignited Hydrogen Gas

A page of photographs of the disaster and survivors Page 20.

By RUSSELL B. PORTER

Special to THE NEW YORK TIMES.

NAVAL AIR STATION, LAKEHURST, N. J., May 6.—The zeppelin Hindenburg was destroyed by fire and explosions here at 7:23 o'clock tonight with a loss of thirty-three known dead and unaccounted for out of its ninety-seven passengers and crew.

Three hours after the disaster twenty-one bodies had been recovered, and twelve were still missing. The sixty-four known to be alive included twenty passengers and forty-four of the crew. Many of the survivors were burned or injured or both, and were taken to hospitals here and in near-by towns.

The accident happened just as the great German dirigible was about to tie up to its mooring mast four hours after flying over New York City on the last leg of its first transatlantic voyage of the year. Until today the Hindenburg had never lost a passenger throughout the ten round trips it made across the Atlantic with 1,002 passengers in 1936.

Two Theories of Cause

F. W. von Meister, vice president of the American Zeppelin Company, gave two possible theories to explain the crash. One was that a fire was caused by an electrical circuit "induced by static conditions" as the ship valved hydrogen gas preparatory to landing. Another was that sparks set off when the engines were throttled down while the gas was being valved caused a fire or explosion.

Captain Ernst Lehmann, who commanded the Hindenburg on most of its flights last year and was one of tonight's survivors, gasped, "I couldn't understand it," as he staggered out of the burning control car. Captain Max Pruss, commanding officer of the airship, and Captain Albert Stampf were also among the survivors.

Captain Lehmann was critically burned and injured; the other officers were also burned, but less seriously.

Experts in lighter-than-air operations who saw the accident said tonight that when the two landing lines were dropped by the dirigible at 7:20, they were immediately made fast to the mooring cars on the circular track about the mooring mast. The crew began to make the lines taut, but the ship had gathered too much momentum, according to these observers, and drifted several hundred yards past the mast. The starboard line pulled hard as the nose of the ship passed over the mooring mast at the top.

Order Not Heard

Captain Pruss, making his first trip in command of the dirigible, signaled and shouted, "Pay out!"

This order was heard by the operator on one mooring car, but not by the other, as the shout went against the wind and could not be heard. Consequently, one mooring car paid out and the other did not. The result was that the ship was thrown off its balance and lost the perfect equilibrium it had previously had.

Its nose dipped, forward ballast was dropped and the elevators were set to raise the ship. Instead the ship was held tight by one yaw line. The nose was pulled over and the elevators had an effect opposite to that which they were intended to have, according to this version. The tail dropped sharply and the bottom rudder hit the

Continued on Page Nineteen

DISASTER ASCRIBED TO GAS BY EXPERTS

Washington Sees Dangerous Combination of Hydrogen and Blue Gas as Cause

Special to THE NEW YORK TIMES.

WASHINGTON, May 6.—Washington airship experts and Congressional leaders received the news of the Hindenburg disaster with amazement and expressions of sorrow. But in every instance those who commented pointed out that the three disasters of the United States Navy were structural, while that of the German craft was due to the use of a combination of hydrogen and blue gas, the most dangerous of all gases for inflation of airships.

Dr. Hans Luther, the German Ambassador, said the disaster must not cause the world to lose faith in dirigibles and that it could not have been caused by technical defects.

"It is terrible," the Ambassador said. "I was horrified by the news, but it could not have been a technical matter. It must not cause us to lose faith in dirigibles because the Graf Zeppelin has operated safely and efficiently for eight years on the run from Europe to South America and elsewhere."

Secretary Hull sent the following message tonight to Konstantin von Neurath, the German Minister of Foreign Affairs:

"I extend to you and to the people of Germany my profound sympathy at the tragic accident to the dirigible Hindenburg and the resultant loss of life to passengers and crew."

"It is too terrible to believe," Admiral A. B. Cook, Chief of Naval Aeronautics, said. "From what I

Continued on Page Twenty-one

Airship Like a Giant Torch On Darkening Jersey Field

Routine Landing Converted Into Hysterical Scene in Moment's Time—Witnesses Tell of 'Blinding Flash' From Zeppelin

By CRAIG THOMPSON

Special to THE NEW YORK TIMES.

LAKEHURST, N. J., May 6.—The Hindenburg, giant silver liner of the air, suddenly became a torch above the naval air station here tonight. What began as a routine landing of the transatlantic airship ended in a holocaust.

The ground crew, officials of the naval air base, spectators, reporters and press photographers were going about their customary business of aiding or watching the ship nose into the mooring mast.

Two ground lines had been dropped from the nose. These, attached to the cars running on a circular track around the mast, were holding the ship nose down at a thirty-degree angle, and helping it jockey into a position favorable with the wind for a mooring.

A thunderstorm had passed over the field a short time before and a drizzly rain was still falling. Twilight was beginning, although the visibility was still good.

So suddenly that it left spectators on the verge of hysteria for some time afterward, the ship burst into flame. Some one in the ground crew yelled "Run for your lives!" and the crew did. The stern of the ship settled and the photographers, squinting through the view finders of their cameras, ran toward the ship.

The occurrence sounded, witnesses said, like two explosions, one following the other about thirty seconds apart. Some said they saw one burst of flame, others two, but the noises they described as explosions gave way to the sounds of human screams.

In the "heavier-than-air" hangar, the pilot of an American Air Lines plane, waiting to ferry passengers from the airship into Newark, watched from a window.

"It seemed to happen so fast that I didn't think anybody could escape," he said afterward.

He was wrong, for about at that moment a man ran into the hangar.

"His face was black, but he seemed to be all right otherwise. He wanted to telephone his mother in Chicago."

The passenger was Herbert James O'Laughlin of Chicago.

On the field was an army detachment from Philadelphia, detailed there for just such an emergency. This detail promptly went to work, trucks scurrying over the field seeking the injured, while in the hangar telephone calls were being put through to all points in New Jersey and New York City calling for ambulances, doctors, nurses, medicine.

All this occurred while the flames spread toward the uptilted nose of the ship, while the stern sank to the ground to be followed shortly by the entire length, girder and strut, the bared ribs of the ship from which the skin had disappeared.

Robert Seelig, Murray Becker and Larry Kennedy, all newspaper camera men, related what they had seen.

"There was a noise that sounded like bullets coming out of the gondolas," Seelig said. "I saw nobody

Continued on Page Twenty-one

GERMANY SHOCKED BY THE TRAGEDY

At First Disbelieving, Line's Officials Tell of Receiving Message of Landing

Special Cable to THE NEW YORK TIMES.

BERLIN, Friday, May 7.—It was a few minutes after 1 o'clock this morning when the first news of the disaster to the Hindenburg reached Berlin by telephone from The New York Times Bureau in London. The bureau forwarded the brief bulletin to the effect that the airship had been destroyed while making its landing. No details were given.

At that hour the German newspapers were without news. Several first editions, in fact, had reported the Hindenburg's supposedly safe arrival on the strength of an erroneous telegram received by the company in Frankfort on the Main. It was almost two hours later before the news of the disaster with some few details reached the newspapers through the medium of the German official news agency.

Facts Difficult to Get

In the meantime such facts about the airship and its passengers proved difficult to obtain. The Frankfort and Berlin offices of the Zeppelin company were closed and no complete list of the passengers or crew was available. A list of twenty-one names comprising foreign passengers out of a total list of thirty-nine was obtained by telephone from Frankfort, where this correspondent had retained it since the sailing day.

Dr. Hugo Eckener, veteran chief of the Zeppelin service, was in Austria, where he had lectured last night in Vienna. The Vienna bureau of THE NEW YORK TIMES traced him to Graz and obtained his ad-

Continued on Page Nineteen

Times Wide World Photo

King George VI and Queen Elizabeth who were crowned on May 12.

Margaret Mitchell and her editor, Harold Latham, read the announcement that her best-selling novel, *Gone With the Wind*, won the Pulitzer Prize on May 3.

Amelia Earhart who was lost at sea on an attempt to be the first woman to circle the globe.

New York Times Studio Photo

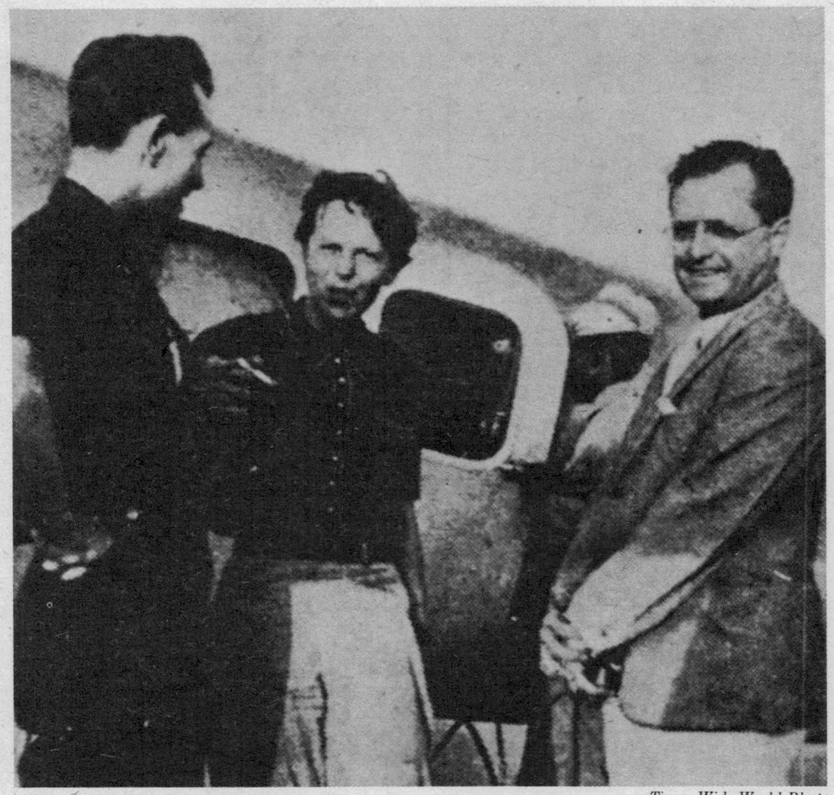

Times Wide World Photo

Miss Earhart as she landed at the Karachi airport in India on June 15. This is one of the last photographs of her to reach the United States. At the left is Fred J. Noonan, her navigator, and at the right is Viscount Sibour of the Standard Oil Company.

Miss Earhart's plane, *The Flying Laboratory.*

Times Wide World Photo

"All the News That's Fit to Print."

The New York Times.

LATE CITY EDITION
Showers and cooler today. Tomorrow generally fair and continued cool.
Temperatures Yesterday—Max., 73; Min., 56

VOL. LXXXVI.....No. 28,964. Entered as Second-Class Matter, Postoffice, New York, N. Y. NEW YORK, THURSDAY, MAY 13, 1937. PP TWO CENTS in New York City. | THREE CENTS Within 200 Miles. | FOUR CENTS Elsewhere Except in 7th and 8th Postal Zones.

GEORGE VI AND ELIZABETH CROWNED IN ABBEY; MILLIONS OF THEIR SUBJECTS ACCLAIM THEM; KING, ON AIR, PLEDGES SERVICE TO THE EMPIRE

Times Wide World Radiophoto.

THE ROYAL FAMILY ACKNOWLEDGES GREETINGS OF CORONATION CROWDS

King George VI, Queen Elizabeth and the Princesses Elizabeth and Margaret Rose on the balcony of Buckingham Palace after the ceremony at Westminster Abbey. Behind the Queen, on the left, is Lady Ursula Manners, daughter of the Duke of Rutland, and on the right Lady Diana Legge, daughter of the Earl of Dartmouth, both train bearers for the Queen. Behind King George are two members of the Palace staff.

C. I. O. STEEL STRIKE SHUTS TWO PLANTS OF JONES-LAUGHLIN

27,000 MEN ARE IDLE

Corporation Puts Blame on Murray, Says It Will Sign Pact

DRIVE AT INDEPENDENTS

Picketing Begins at Pittsburgh and Aliquippa Mills, Backing Recognition for Union

REPUBLIC BARS CONTRACT

Cleveland Letter Tells 55,000 Workers Company Will Not Agree to a Closed Shop

By The Associated Press.

PITTSBURGH, May 12.—Thousands of union steel workers picketed the giant plants of the Jones & Laughlin Steel Corporation tonight in the first major steel strike since John L. Lewis began his drive to organize the nation's millmen into one big union.

The strike began at 11 P. M. as the first move in the campaign of the Steel Workers Organizing Committee to obtain written collective bargaining contracts with the independent steel producers of the country, employing about 202,000 men.

Cheers from the picket lines greeted union members on the early night shifts who walked from the mills in Pittsburgh and Aliquippa, in answer to the strike order of Philip Murray, chairman of the S. W. O. C.

Walkout on Murray's Order

Mr. Murray ordered the walkout after a two-hour conference with H. E. Lewis, chairman of the board of Jones & Laughlin had failed to effect an agreement on the union's demand.

The corporation, in a formal announcement, stated that it had offered to sign a contract provided an identical contract could be granted to non-union workers among its 27,000 employes.

The company also announced that it had offered to grant a sole collective bargaining contract to the group obtaining a majority vote at an employes' election, supervised by the National Labor Relations Board.

A company representative said no attempt would be made to operate the plants "for the time being."

Mr. Murray declined to state what effect the Jones & Laughlin strike would have on union activities at other independent companies, and he would not comment on the company's statement.

The Steel Workers Organizing Committee, as an affiliate of the Committee for Industrial Organization, received a rebuff from Republic Steel Corporation at Cleveland during the day.

The Republic corporation, with 55,000 employes, made public a letter to its workers, refusing to sign a C. I. O. contract. It said, "Republic does not believe in the closed-shop principle."

Biggest Steel Strike Since 1919

The Jones & Laughlin walkout is the biggest strike blow aimed at the steel industry since 1919. The 1919 strike cut production 40 per cent.

Mr. Murray said the Jones & Laughlin mills would be shut "tight," except for maintenance crews, which were ordered to keep up the blast furnaces.

A further conference would be held with the company tomorrow, Mr. Murray said.

Flames from the blast furnaces shot high into the air, intermittently lighting up the faces of the crowds of men, women and children who packed the streets in front of mill gates more than an hour before the strike call went into effect.

Two score municipal police mingled with the crowd, but made no attempt to break the picket lines.

Without disorder, the union men prevented non-union workers from entering the mill gates.

They held two American flags across the main entrance at the Aliquippa works.

Night Shift Men Parade

The throng was increased by the night shift members who fell into line, clasped arms with one another, and paraded in front of the gates.

A light rain before midnight sent many of the women and children of the strikers' families to their

Continued on Page Four

Home Relief Families Get $1,200,000 WPA Clothes

Distribution to home relief families of 2,056,989 articles of clothing made by seamstresses on WPA sewing projects was reported yesterday by Miss Charlotte E. Carr, executive director of the Emergency Relief Bureau. The clothing, which had an estimated retail value of $1,200,000, was distributed between April 13, 1936, and April 23, 1937.

In addition to these WPA products, home relief families received $2,562,410 in cash for the purchase of apparel.

The cash sum to be distributed by the ERB as a clothing allowance for the quarter ending June 30 has been raised to $1,500,000, Miss Carr announced. Of this amount $750,000 was disbursed last month.

REBELS BEAT BACK ATTACK ON TOLEDO

Report Loyalists Have Lost 3,000 There—Government Claims 7-Mile Gain

BILBAO SUBURBS BOMBED

More Than 100 Missiles Were Dropped—Madrid Shelled, Toll Rising to 217

By The Associated Press.

TOLEDO, Spain, May 12.—Heavy government attacks against Insurgent-held Toledo developed today into a mass offensive in which, Insurgents said, the attackers suffered "unprecedented slaughter."

Government prisoners estimated their dead in the campaign at more than 3,000, with total casualties not calculated, Insurgent reports said.

Waves of government infantry charged Insurgent positions south of the Tagus River as a climax to four days of fighting.

Insurgents braced their lines tonight along a six-mile front south of the Tagus. Estimates of government troops in the offensive ranged from 18,000 to 22,000 men.

No-man's land was covered with dead and wounded after a terrific battle yesterday. Squads from both armies roamed the area in the night looking for wounded.

The brilliant defense of Insurgent militiamen in one sector, it is stated, won for them the collective award of the Laureada, the highest honor for bravery in the Spanish Army.

Prisoners taken by the Insurgents were quoted as saying the government army in the Toledo sector included two brigades of the Lister Division and two other international outfits, the Campesina Brigade and the Dimitroff Battalion, in addition to the units already on the front. Apparently they were sent to reinforce government troops trying to recapture the city won by Insurgents last October, when they freed comrades besieged in the Alcazar.

[The government asserted its troops had advanced about seven miles on the Toledo front.]

100 Bombs Dropped Near Bilbao

BILBAO, Spain, May 12 (AP).—Insurgent airplanes dumped more than 100 bombs into the suburbs of Bilbao today but did not fulfill General Emilio Mola's threat to blast the Basque capital to bits.

Terror-stricken inhabitants, mindful of the Insurgent Northern commander's warning he would bombard the city "without mercy" if it did not surrender by today, ducked for cover three times as nine bombing planes and seven pursuit planes roared over Bilbao. Several gasoline tanks were set afire and nearby buildings were destroyed. Clouds of dark smoke billowed over the city.

Basque officials asserted they were informed General Mola had chosen today for the expiration of his ultimatum because the eyes of the world would be turned away from the Spanish civil war toward the London coronation. The indignation that would follow a violent attack on the civilians in the city thus would be lessened, they said.

One person was killed and several wounded in the air bombing of the town of Sorroza. Planes also bombed Larrauri and Manguia, north of Bilbao.

Bilbao's food situation was grave again. Bread supplies were almost exhausted. Only enough re-

Continued on Page Thirteen

142 PLAYGROUNDS, CLOSED BY MOSES, SEIZED BY POLICE

Patrolmen Force Locks to Reopen Them as Park Head Defies Mayor on Control

STAFF FURNISHED BY WPA

Somervell, in Control Again, Provides Labor That Moses Lost in Personnel Cuts

One hundred and forty-two playgrounds in the city became the battlefield yesterday for confused conflict between Mayor La Guardia, Lieut. Col. Brehon B. Somervell, WPA Administrator, and Police Commissioner Lewis J. Valentine on the one side, and Park Commissioner Robert Moses on the other. By nightfall, however, "New York's finest" were in full control.

With the Mayor heading by train for California but keeping in touch with the situation by long-distance telephone, the police late in the afternoon picked or broke the padlocks on the playgrounds which had been closed by Mr. Moses because WPA play directors had been withdrawn, and replaced them with police padlocks.

Facilities Normal Today

Today the playgrounds will be reopened to the children, with WPA directors working for the Police Department under direct WPA jurisdiction, aided by 135 men and women from the police juvenile aid bureau. The children can play in safety, the police promised.

The police advanced on the locked gates of the playgrounds only after Mr. Moses had announced to the press there would be "no armed conflict between his park guardsmen and the police" and after he had refused the request of Commissioner Valentine for keys to the padlocks.

The Park Commissioner, asserting that no one was more interested in keeping the playgrounds open for the children than he, stood off the Police Commissioner on legal grounds. The Mayor's order to have the police take over any closed playgrounds, in effect transferring jurisdiction to the police, was a "clear violation of the charter and absolutely illegal," he declared.

Keep Up Other Play Areas

Playgrounds that had been locked "because of the outrageous way in which the WPA has done this" will stay locked, Mr. Moses said, but he added that "if the police want to take the locks off, it will be all right." The 215 playgrounds which were manned by Park Department employes will continue to be run by the department, he said.

The Mayor, anticipating a playground crisis because of the long feud between Mr. Moses and the WPA administrator, had issued his order to the police Tuesday night when he left for California. The order was made public at City Hall by his secretary, Lester Stone, after Mr. Moses had announced the closing of the playgrounds.

With the playgrounds still locked at 3 o'clock, Mr. Stone put in a telephone call for the Mayor at Toledo, and when the Mayor's train arrived informed him of the general situation. He then announced that the Mayor issued the following statement:

"I confirm my order to keep all the playgrounds open. The children of the city, for whom the playgrounds were built, cannot be made to suffer, and I expect the Police Department to reopen the play-

Continued on Page Two

YOUNGER PRINCESS IS BORED BY AFFAIR

Margaret Rose, 6, Even Goes to the Extent of Yawning at Archbishop of Canterbury

OLDER SISTER NUDGES HER

Elizabeth, for the First Time, Takes Precedence Over Other Ladies of Royal Family

By The Associated Press.

LONDON, May 12.—Two little Princesses saw their father crowned King today, but their reactions were very different.

Eleven-year-old Princess Elizabeth sat primly in her seat in the royal box, her attention fastened on the dramatic spectacle before her. One day she may play the leading rôle in such a ceremony, for she is heir presumptive to the throne.

Beside her, Princess Margaret Rose, 6½, tried her best to act as a princess should at a coronation. But she couldn't keep from squirming and lounging in her seat as the proceedings went on, and once she yawned right at the venerable Archbishop of Canterbury, head of the Anglican Church.

The little girls had risen at 7:30 for the great day. They peeped out of the nursery windows of Buckingham Palace to see thousands

Continued on Page Sixteen

Vast Throngs Cheer Royalty In Procession and at Palace

Rain Fails to Lessen Enthusiasm of More Than 1,000,000 on London Route—Queen, Queen Mother, Baldwin Get Ovations

By CHARLES W. HURD
Wireless to THE NEW YORK TIMES.

LONDON, May 12.—The most representative military spectacle the British Empire could muster escorted King George today through six miles of London streets to signalize his coronation, while more than 1,000,000 Londoners and visitors from all countries looked on and cheered even in the last hour, when a cloudburst fell from the skies.

The procession was at once a display of most impressive pageantry and a graphic demonstration of British feeling that the monarchy is an integral part of the empire's soul.

There were plenty of cheers for the troops and the famous personages in line, but most were reserved for four persons—the King and Queen, who got the greatest ovation; Queen Mary, whose popularity is undimmed, and Prime Minister Stanley Baldwin, who steered the throne through its greatest modern crisis last December.

Following their triumphal ride the royal family had another great ovation from the crowds at Buckingham Palace when, in response to cheers, the King appeared on the balcony wearing his robe and crown. The crowd roared, "God save the King!" and then sang "For He's a Jolly Good Fellow."

More prolonged cheers were given Princess Elizabeth and Princess Margaret Rose when they joined their parents. There was an ovation for Queen Mary when she appeared to stand between the King and Queen.

The King and Queen, although tired by the day's responsibilities, made four more appearances later in the evening. Responding to the cheers of the crowds, they walked out on the balcony at 9 o'clock. Immediately after the loud-speakers were employed to announce that they would appear no more tonight. However, they made bows from the balcony three more times, the last at 11:50.

Heavy Rain in Afternoon

By seven o'clock this morning most of the stands along the parade route were filled by ticketholders who had tucked their lunches and mackintoshes under their chairs and hoped they would not have to use the coats despite the lowering skies. Hope for good weather became large when, almost coincident with the King's departure from Buckingham Palace, the sun peeked momentarily through the clouds, but it was its first and last appearance. Thenceforward the clouds yielded intermittent showers, followed by a heavy downpour starting at 3 o'clock.

With the coming of the heavy rain those who had yet to see the procession pulled on their coats, raised their umbrellas and waited. The newspapers they brought to read while waiting were used to wrap legs and feet and to cover women's hats.

Those who left their umbrellas up after the parade appeared were pelted with balls of wet paper until they gave up the struggle to keep dry either in the open seats or among the standing crowds. It was notable that few yielded their places until they had seen the King and Queen at the close of the procession.

Britons saw their King in his full story-book rôle attired in royal raiment—the symbol of all honor and protection—riding with the Queen in a golden coach surrounded by the panoply of greatness which every Briton loves as the symbol of spiritual possessions that all share alike.

Affection for King Displayed

George, looking through the glass windows of his coach, obviously sincere but modest to the point of shyness, saw manifestations of affection and regard which promise at some future day to raise him to a status approximating that of his father, George V, as the average Briton's ideal of a modest gentleman.

Some enthusiastic reports placed the size of the crowd greeting the King at 3,000,000 to 5,000,000, but a conservative estimate would reduce this—possibly to less than the number that turned out for George V's funeral early last year, but an extraordinary number considering the threatening weather and the bus strike which paralyzed this highly important transportation system.

Moreover, with the exception of the estimated 250,000 persons who bought reserved seats, most of the spectators had stood eight to fifteen hours by the time they saw the procession. They paid a heavy price, fainting by thousands, requiring attention by a large corps of doctors, nurses and ambulances. During the wait for the Westminster Abbey ceremonies the writer saw hundreds of them in one limited area drop down to rest or sleep on the soaked ground.

Show Love of Triumphs

This picture of the sleepers on the wet ground encompassed the whole story, the love of government, King and pageantry by average Britons and their dogged determination to participate in the nation's triumphs even though many

Continued on Page Eighteen

GEORGE VI THANKS PEOPLE OF EMPIRE

His Broadcast Is Received as Promise of a Reign Like That of His Father

HE GREETS THE DOMINIONS

Recalls That Kingship Arises From 'Will of Free Peoples' Associated in Amity

By FERDINAND KUHN Jr.
Wireless to THE NEW YORK TIMES.

LONDON, May 12.—With the cheers of London crowds still ringing in his ears, King George gave his personal thanks tonight to his peoples throughout the empire and promised to serve them faithfully in the years ahead.

He chose the evening of his coronation day to speak into the microphone from his study in Buckingham Palace as his father had after his silver jubilee two years ago. He talked not only as a king who had just had a crown placed on his head but as a simple young man without great brilliance who had been called to great responsibilities and was determined to live up to them.

Voices Thanks for Loyalty

It was an unassuming little speech, and there was more than a hint of George V in the new King's voice when he said:

"I cannot find words with which to thank you for your love and loyalty to the Queen and myself. Your good will in the streets today and your countless messages from overseas and from every quarter of these islands have filled our hearts to overflowing. I will only say this: that if in the coming years I can show my gratitude in service to you that is the way above all others that I should choose."

All this, so sincerely meant and so modestly spoken, might have come from the lips of George V if there had been a broadcast on the day of his coronation. It was evident in every sentence that in his coronation George V had set the pattern for this reign of the son who resembles him so closely in his temperament and in his attitude toward his royal job.

Later in his speech King George recalled that he had assumed his crown not only by the grace of God, but "by the will of the free peoples of the British Commonwealth," a reminder that he, like his father, realizes the source whence his kingship comes.

He talked, too, of today's ceremonial as a solemn "dedication" of himself and his Queen, and in one moving passage he reminded unnumbered millions of listeners that "the highest of distinctions is service to others."

Finally there was a reference to

Continued on Page Seventeen

RITE IS MEDIEVAL

WestminsterRelivesPast Age as Ruler Comes Into His Kingdom

KING A FRAIL, GRAVE FIGURE

Anointed and Robed in Regal Garb, He Receives Crown and Is Cheered by Peers

GIVES VOW WITH EMOTION

Queen, Serious and Nervous, Takes Place on Throne—Historic Service Drags

By FREDERICK T. BIRCHALL
Wireless to THE NEW YORK TIMES.

LONDON, May 12.—In a setting of medieval splendor such as seemed scarcely to belong to this day and age George VI was crowned King and Emperor in Westminster Abbey today.

He rode there with his Queen in their golden coach drawn by eight gray horses through streets lined with troops brought from all parts of the empire, and millions of his subjects acclaimed him as he passed.

In the Abbey he went through the ceremony of being accepted by his people. He took a vow to care for their welfare, to maintain and obey the laws passed by their Parliament, to be just and to temper justice with mercy.

Anointed With Holy Oil

He was disrobed of the outer garments he had worn on entering and anointed on his hands, breast and forehead with holy oil and thus dedicated to the kingship. Then he was freshly robed in cloth of gold and royal purple. The Sword of State was girt to his side and his heels were touched with the Spurs of Power.

They put the Ring on his finger. Two scepters—emblems of power and justice, equity and mercy—were placed in his hands. Then St. Edward's ancient crown of pure gold and costly jewels was pressed upon his bowed head with a prayer to God to crown him with all princely virtues.

Trumpets sounded, drums rolled and the Abbey sprang into full illumination at his crowning, while outside the church bells rang for joy and guns thundered a royal salute. The peers of his realm surrounding him put on their own coronets and the great edifice rang with the shout, "God save the King!" Archbishops, Bishops, the King's royal brothers and the nobles of his realm knelt in turn before him and swore fealty.

Then Queen Is Crowned

Then the Queen was anointed and crowned in like manner and took her place on her lower throne beside him. They went together to the high altar, knelt in prayer and partook of the communion. Finally, in a new splendid procession, they passed down the great nave and out among the plain people, who are the mainstay of their kingdom, yet had had little share in all this ceremony. And throughout the long drive they were again acclaimed in a thunder of cheers echoing through all London—"God save the King!"

The pageant within the Abbey followed the lines that already have been so fully described in advance. The King and Queen entered the Abbey at 11:20 A. M. from the temporary annex, to which the street procession had carried them. They left it at 2:40 P. M. The historic service had dragged a little.

Most of those within the edifice had arrived before 7 o'clock. Few were able to depart before 3:30. The last did not get away before 8. That was due to bad management and it made a long day for many persons no longer young.

So the sixth George and the second Elizabeth, his consort, came at last into their kingdom. Into more than a kingdom; into an empire of kindred and equal great States that overspreads the world. To keep these firmly linked and insure justice to their countless millions is no easy task in these troublous times. But that is of tomorrow.

Scene One of Splendor

The splendor of the scene in which this pageant was enacted is not easy to convey.

Picture the great gray Abbey, shrine and temple of the English race throughout a thousand years,

Continued on Page Sixteen

Housewives Entitled to Fixed Salaries, Like Any Worker, Mrs. Roosevelt Holds

The suggestion that wives who stay at home to look after the household should receive a definite salary for their work was advanced last night by Mrs. Franklin D. Roosevelt, wife of the President.

Remarking that a housewife earns the right to a salary, "without any question," Mrs. Roosevelt added that "any girl who is needed at home has a job just as surely as the girl who operates a machine in a factory; if she is not needed at home, she loses out by not working."

Mrs. Roosevelt expressed her views in a discussion of "The Home vs. Work for Women," with Miss Rose Schneiderman, president of the Women's Trade Union League and secretary of the New York State Department of Labor. The discussion was broadcast over a radio network.

Asked for her opinion of the most vital question facing working women, Miss Schneiderman said it was "getting over their economic inferiority complex." Women often carry a feeling of inferiority into business and industry and are willing to work for much less pay, she said.

Mrs. Roosevelt remarked that there was no question that "a woman who works to give her children the necessities and some of the advantages of life should have her work day limited to eight hours."

Miss Schneiderman said that when the working conditions of women were bettered "those of men automatically rise too."

"When women work long hours and for next to nothing," she continued, "they are not only competing against each other, but are pulling down the wages of their men folks."

Asked by Mrs. Roosevelt if she thought men resented women in industry, Miss Schneiderman replied that emotionally they did, "sometimes."

"But can you imagine," she continued, "what would happen if the 11,000,000 working women in the United States suddenly quit their jobs and just waited for the men to support them?"

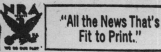

"All the News That's Fit to Print."

The New York Times.

LATE CITY EDITION

WEATHER—Generally fair today; showers, cooler tomorrow.

Temperatures Yesterday—Max., [illegible]; Min., [illegible]

Copyright, 1934, by The New York Times Company.

VOL. LXXXVI.....No. 28,976. Entered as Second-Class Matter, Postoffice, New York, N. Y. NEW YORK, TUESDAY, MAY 25, 1937. P TWO CENTS in New York City. | THREE CENTS Within 200 Miles. | FOUR CENTS Elsewhere Except in 7th and 8th Postal Zones.

SUPREME COURT BACKS SECURITY ACT ON JOB INSURANCE, 5-4, PENSIONS, 7-2; ROOSEVELT ASKS A WAGE-HOUR LAW

BILL IS INTRODUCED

Embodies Policies of Message Calling on Congress to Act

CHILD LABOR ALSO BANNED

Sponsors Leave 40-Hour Maximum Formula Blank—May Seek Range of 30 to 40

40-CENT MINIMUM THE AIM

President Assails Past 'Subterfuges' of Supreme Court on Commerce Clause

Text of the Federal Minimum Wages Bill is on Pages 20-21

Special to THE NEW YORK TIMES.

WASHINGTON, May 24.—President Roosevelt called upon Congress today to "extend the frontiers of social progress" by enacting a maximum hour-minimum wage law which also would abolish child labor. A bill embodying those aims was introduced in both houses immediately after the reading of the Presidential message.

Sponsored by Senator Black and Representative Connery, chairmen of the committees on labor, the bill contained no specific formula on maximum hours and minimum wages, but both sponsors indicated that they would press for a "ceiling" of forty hours for a maximum work week, with discretion left to a five-man labor standards board to fix the week as low as thirty hours.

Mr. Roosevelt based his recommendations upon the power of Congress to regulate interstate commerce, and the bills, identical except as to one provision, carry out the aims advanced by the President, as follows:

1. A general maximum work week, with time and a half to be paid for time worked in excess of the maximum.

2. A minimum wage, yet to be fixed.,

3. Abolition of all labor by children under 16 years of age, and 18 years in the case of hazardous employment.

4. Denial of movement in interstate commerce of all goods produced under "oppressive hour or wage conditions," and by children under 16.

Issue Put Up to Congress

After last minute conferences with the White House, Senator Black and Mr. Connery deleted from the draft of the bill figures providing a maximum forty-hour week and a minimum wage of 40 cents an hour, and announced they would ask Congress to give to the proposed labor standards board the power to fix by industries not less than thirty nor more than forty hours as the basic week. Both for

Continued on Page Twenty-one

The Roosevelt Proposal

Special to THE NEW YORK TIMES.

WASHINGTON, May 24.—The text of President Roosevelt's labor message to Congress follows:

To the Congress of the United States:

The time has arrived for us to take further action to extend the frontiers of social progress. Such further action initiated by the legislative branch of the government, administered by the Executive and sustained by the judicial is within the common sense framework and purpose of our Constitution and receives beyond doubt the approval of our electorate.

The overwhelming majority of our population earns its daily bread either in agriculture or in industry. One-third of our population, the overwhelming majority of which is in agriculture or industry, is ill-nourished, ill-clad and ill-housed.

The overwhelming majority of this nation has little patience with that small minority which vociferates today that prosperity has returned, that wages are good, that crop prices are high and that government should take a holiday.

The truth of the matter, of course, is that the exponents of the theory of private initiative as the cure for deep-seated national ills want, in most cases, to improve the lot of mankind. But, well-intentioned as they may be, they fail for four evident reasons—first, they see the problem from the point of view of their own business; second, they see the problem from the point of view of their own locality or region; third, they cannot act unanimously because they have no machinery for agreeing among themselves, and, finally, they have no power to bind the inevitable minority of chiselers within their own ranks.

Though we may go far in admitting that innate decency of this small minority, the whole story of our nation proves that social progress has too often been fought by them. In actual practice it has been effectively advanced only by the passage of laws by State Legislatures or the national Congress.

Today, you and I are pledged to take further steps to reduce the lag in the purchasing power of industrial workers and to strengthen and stabilize the markets for the farmers' products. The two go hand in hand. Each depends for its effectiveness upon the other. Both working simultaneously will

Continued on Page Nineteen

NEW DEAL VICTORY

Welfare Clause Is Not 'Static,' Says Cardozo for the Majority

OUR NEEDS 'INTERWOVEN'

Age Law Seeks to Save Folk From 'Haunting Fear' as to 'Journey's End'

MINORITY SEES 'COERCION'

McReynolds Holds 'No Appeal to Humanity' Can Expand Powers of Congress

Majority opinion on Insurance, Page 22; Minority, Page 23; Majority on Pensions, Page 24.

Special to THE NEW YORK TIMES.

WASHINGTON, May 24.—The Supreme Court upheld today in three historic opinions the constitutionality of the Social Security Act affecting 26,000,000 workers and 2,700,000 employers. It was a decisive victory for the administration.

The decisions sustaining the broad program, although achieved in two instances by five-to-four divisions only, showed that the majority of the court now tends to favor the liberal aims of the administration; the record of affirmative opinions for the New Deal and other progressive legislation at the present term of the court remains unbroken.

The unemployment insurance and old-age pensions sections of the Federal law were approved, respectively, by five-to-four and seven-to-two, while auxiliary State laws were backed by a five-to-four vote.

Justice Cardozo, celebrating his sixty-seventh birthday, wrote both decisions on the Federal act; Justice Stone, another liberal, was author of the opinion on the State-law test.

Government forces construed the rulings to mean that the administration could now go ahead with its social plans in full possession of constitutional authority to lay down taxes for the general welfare. Not long ago the Wagner labor act decisions widely extended the Congressional power to regulate commerce among the States.

Broad View on Welfare Clause

Behind the Cardozo opinions lay the philosophy that the Social Security Act was not only entirely legal but was also unquestionably justified by the economic conditions of the day. The concept of the general welfare clause cannot be "static," he held, saying:

"Needs that were narrow or parochial a century ago may be interwoven in our day with the well-being of the nation. What is critical or urgent changes with the times.

"The hope behind this statute is to save men and women from the rigors of the poorhouse as well as from the haunting fear that such a lot awaits them when journey's end is near."

The justices divided as follows on the three tests:

Unemployment insurance: For, Cardozo, Stone, Brandeis, Roberts, Chief Justice Hughes; against, McReynolds, Sutherland, Van Devanter, Butler.

Old age pensions: For, Cardozo, Stone, Brandeis, Roberts, Van Devanter, Sutherland, Chief Justice Hughes; against, Butler, McReynolds.

State law: For, Stone, Cardozo, Brandeis, Roberts, Chief Justice Hughes; against, Sutherland, Van Devanter, Butler, McReynolds.

How the Dissenters Stood

Three separate dissents were entered on the unemployment feature. Justice McReynolds, who went further in his objections than the other three conservatives, departed from a written dissent to deliver a pungent lecture from the bench. Justice Sutherland wrote an objection concurred in by Justice Van Devanter, and Justice Butler presented a third document.

In the old age case Justice Cardozo announced that Justices McReynolds and Butler were opposed but they offered no written opinion.

In the State-law case Justice Stone said that Justice McReynolds could not agree with the majority, while Justice Sutherland read a dis-

Continued on Page Twenty-four

BRITISH TO PROPOSE TRUCE TO RID SPAIN OF FOREIGN TROOPS

Are Said to Envisage a Nonpartisan Regime Under a Leader Like Madariaga

ITALY OFFERS AN OBSTACLE

Claims Full Support of Reich in Barring Halt in Fighting During Bilbao Drive

VALENCIA'S 'NO' EMPHATIC

Loyalists Would Oust Outsiders but Reject Armistice While They Feel They Are Winning

By CLARENCE K. STREIT

Wireless to THE NEW YORK TIMES.

GENEVA, May 24.—The League of Nations Council began its ninety-seventh session today with a meeting headed toward becoming a drive for withdrawal of all foreign troops from Spain.

Foreign Secretary Anthony Eden of Great Britain, sure of the support of Foreign Minister Yvon Delbos of France and most of the Council, wants to limit the Council's resolution on the Spanish war to blessing London's troop-withdrawal proposal and engaging the Council members to execute it as regards their nationals if Germany, Italy and the Valencia and Burgos groups in Spain will agree. The real aim of this manoeuvre is to bring Italy around by isolating her.

Julio Alvarez del Vayo, delegate of the Spanish Republic, strongly gives the impression that Valencia is ready to send away all foreigners fighting on its side if General Francisco Franco will do the same. Valencia apparently figures the republic could then suppress the rebellion in one month.

Guarantees Offered

It is also understood that Valencia is prepared to go further to the right to stress the democratic character of its government and to give guarantees against communism in Spain, but it will not consider giving way to any compromise "nonpartisan" government.

There is reason to believe Mr. Alvarez del Vayo will not object to leaving the details of troop withdrawal, including truce terms, to the London non-intervention committee instead of to the League to work out and submit to both sides. Since Valencia is not represented in the non-intervention committee, as it is in the League Council, this method saves its having to make proposals itself and leaves it in a stronger bargaining position where everything comes up to it.

The White Book Mr. Alvarez del Vayo plans to submit to the Council on German-Italian intervention fits into this picture as a part of his means for bringing pressure on Berlin and Rome to accept general withdrawal of foreign combatants. It is understood Mr. Alvarez del Vayo wants Italy and Germany mentioned by name in a Council resolution urging troop withdrawal, but Mr. Eden shies at naming any country.

Britons Are Optimistic

A British spokesman said his delegation was rather optimistic because of the reception accorded to its moves in Berlin and Valencia, despite the attitudes of Premier Benito Mussolini of Italy and General Franco.

One gets the impression that the maximum goal of the British is to work into an armistice in due time the idea of a provisional "nonpartisan" government headed, say, by Salvador de Madariaga, all in the hope of keeping the fighting ended once the guns cease firing. The main British objective, however, would seem to be their minimum goal—getting all foreign soldiers out of Spain. They stress that this alone is sufficiently difficult, important and distant.

The Council met today only in a private session to adopt its agenda and accept the addition thereto of the Spanish appeal, which is not likely to be heard before Friday.

Truce Plan Sidetracked

Special Cable to THE NEW YORK TIMES.

LONDON, May 24.—In a three-hour session at the Foreign Office here this evening, the Spain Non-Intervention Committee's Steering Committee decided that an appeal should be made to both sides in the Spanish civil war to conduct their operations with regard for humanitarian considerations.

The committee also had before it a seventy-page report of its technical subcommittee, outlining in great detail how foreign volunteers could be gradually withdrawn from Spain. The basis of the plan is a temporary truce in the hostilities.

The committee postponed action on this report, realizing that the present prospects of putting any

Continued on Page Nine

Recruits for Spain Drilled in U. S., Deserter From Group Says in Paris

Young Communist Asserts He Enlisted as a Worker, but Was Forced to Undergo Military Training in Camp Near New York—Conditions Made Him Quit Contingent of 30

By GEORGE AXELSSON

Wireless to THE NEW YORK TIMES.

PARIS, May 24.—Despite the State Department's ban on United States volunteers for Spain, recruiting continues in the United States. Proof of this was obtained by the writer today when he interviewed Paul Burke, 26-year-old Minneapolis bricklayer who arrived at Havre last night aboard the steamer Georgic with twenty-nine fellow-volunteers, who had all enlisted at various points in the United States and had undergone hasty military training prior to leaving.

Burke showed documents, including his passport, as proof of his contentions. He said he had run away from the party as soon as he had arrived in Paris because his experiences since having enlisted had made him change his mind about wanting to fight for Spanish democracy. His story follows:

"I was born at Coleridge, Neb., where I joined the Communist party. At one time I suffered detention in a Federal institution for my activity in propagandizing among Nebraska farmers. When I was released I went to Minneapolis to work at bricklaying. Last month I saw an ad in a Minneapolis morning newspaper for skilled workers for Spain to take the places of men who had gone to the front. The ad was signed by the Society for Technical Aid to Spanish Democracy.

"I applied and soon received a ticket to New York. Only when I reached New York did I begin to suspect that the tools of my 'trade' were to be a rifle and bayonet. In New York City I met eleven other young men who had come from different parts of the country in response to the same kind of ads. We were herded together and bundled off in automobiles to a camping place near New York. We left New York after midnight and arrived at our destination around 3 A. M.

"At the camp we were told we were to be put through two weeks' military training. A drill sergeant who said he had been in the regular army for eighteen years told us he would teach us in two weeks what normally required sixty to ninety days. Some fellows already were ahead of us in the camp, so we now were a group of thirty.

"A difficult period began, which was made still more difficult by

Continued on Page Nine

VALENTINE ASSAILS REDWOOD INQUIRY

'Killers Came From Atlantic City, Went Back There and Are Known,' He Asserts

CHALLENGED BY BRESLIN

Bergen Prosecutor Offers to Call Grand Jury to Hear Commissioner's Evidence

The unsolved murder of Norman Redwood, leader of a New York sandhog's union, at Teaneck, N. J., three months ago was the subject of an angry exchange of statements yesterday by Police Commissioner Lewis J. Valentine and John J. Breslin, Prosecutor of Bergen County, N. J.

Mr. Valentine chided Mr. Breslin for taking a holiday in Florida in the midst of the investigation in which New York detectives have been cooperating with the New Jersey authorities. The manner in which Samuel Rosoff, the subway builder against whom Redwood was directing a strike, was permitted successfully to defy the efforts of New Jersey to compel him to go there and testify, the Police Commissioner said, was "disgusting."

At the start of the commissioner's criticism of Mr. Breslin, First Deputy Police Commissioner Harold Fowler, who was with him at the time, seized his arm and tried to dissuade him from saying more. Mr. Valentine, however, shook off the deputy's restraining hand and, asserting that he was "sick of it," declared it was "time the truth came out." He added:

"If I were the prosecutor I wouldn't be kidded and I wouldn't go to Florida. We know that the killers came from Atlantic City. The gun has been traced there. All of that information has been turned over to Mr. Breslin. Why doesn't he indict them? The information shows that the killers came from Atlantic City and went back there and they are known."

"Crime Not Planned in New York"

Later Mr. Valentine said:

"I'm convinced that the crime was not planned in New York by any New York gunmen or assassins. It's possible it may have been ordered from here. Of course the man who was killed was a labor leader over here."

Mr. Valentine declared that the evidence turned over to Mr. Breslin by Deputy Inspector Richard J. Oliver and other New York detectives assigned to the case should have been presented to the grand jury of Bergen County. He added:

"If it were a New York case arrests would have been made for homicide and the facts presented to a grand jury."

Mr. Valentine said he planned to ask Mr. Breslin to confer with him soon and tell what he planned to do about prosecuting those responsible for Redwood's murder. Mr. Breslin, however, lost no time in calling upon the commissioner to produce the evidence. He sent the following telegram to Mr. Valentine:

"According to press reports printed today you are quoted as follows with reference to the Redwood case: 'We are convinced that the killers came from Atlantic City and that they are there now. The evidence we have clearly shows that the killers were traced to that city. Their guns were traced there. Why

Continued on Page Two

PROFITS TAX BILL PRESSED IN BRITAIN TO GET ARMS FUND

Chamberlain Measure Is Little Modified on Introduction in House of Commons

SCALE OF LEVY IS REVISED

Yardstick to Measure Growth of Firm's Gains Is Altered, but Main Idea Remains

By FERDINAND KUHN Jr.

Wireless to THE NEW YORK TIMES.

LONDON, May 24. — Within a week of becoming Prime Minister, Neville Chamberlain, the Chancellor of the Exchequer, showed the nation today that he could stand firm against the bitterest attack he has ever had to face from the financial and business community.

The text of his eagerly awaited finance bill, submitted to the House of Commons this afternoon, contained only minor modifications of his proposed new tax on the growth of profits, a tax so severe that the first announcement of it precipitated a collapse on the Stock Exchange a month ago.

The clamor against the tax has grown more intense since then and pressure has been brought on Mr. Chamberlain to weaken it drastically or to withdraw it altogether. Business leaders have complained loudly of "the injustice in the tax proposals"; financiers have denounced the scheme as emphatically as if they had been in Wall Street in the early days of the New Deal.

Moves to Reassure Workers

But Mr. Chamberlain has given little comfort to his critics, although he has listened patiently during the past fortnight to their complaints. He is determined that a stiff tax on profits must be placed on the statute books this year, not only to tap a new source of future revenue, but also to convince the working people that no inordinate profiteering will be permitted in the British rearmament program.

In his original proposals the yardstick to measure the growth of profits would have been the average of 1933, 1934 and 1935. Now Mr. Chamberlain has relented somewhat by allowing the taxpayers to choose. They can take the average of three or four years from 1933 to 1936 inclusive or any two of the three years 1933 to 1935.

This will remove some of the inequalities of his original scheme but it will not satisfy the rubber industry, which wanted 1930 to be used as the yardstick, or most other companies which hoped the unusually profitable 1936 would be used as the measuring rod.

Mr. Chamberlain has also made a slight concession in the sliding scale of the tax. Originally he proposed to tax the growth of profits at 20 per cent wherever the increase amounted to 6 to 10 per cent of the company's capital and 25 per cent wherever the growth of profits was 10 to 15 per cent. Now he has decided to take 20 per cent in the zone between 6 and 12 per cent of capital and 25 per cent in the zone between 12 and 16 per cent of capital.

He has also clarified the definition of "capital" by ruling that the basis will be the actual cost of a company's assets less deduction for depreciation. He rejected demands from business leaders that investments or borrowed money or deben-

Continued on Page Four

THIRD SON IS BORN TO THE LINDBERGHS

News, Phoned by Flier to U. S. Embassy in London, Kept Secret Since Birth May 12

HOME IN KENT IS GUARDED

Mother and Child Are 'Doing Nicely,' Says Aunt of Mrs. Lindbergh in Cleveland

By The Associated Press.

WEALD, Kent, England, May 24.—The birth of a third son to Colonel and Mrs. Charles A. Lindbergh was disclosed today by the famous aviator in the family's English retreat.

He withheld details, but an aunt of Mrs. Lindbergh in Cleveland, Ohio, announced that the baby had been born on the night of King George VI's coronation—May 12. Colonel Lindbergh had declined an invitation to attend the coronation.

The aviator broke his closely guarded secret in a telephone conversation with United States Embassy officials in London. He told them the child had been born more than a week ago.

He pledged all his friends to secrecy, then went for a lonely walk in the hills near Long Barn, at Sevenoaks, Kent, where the flier and his wife have lived with their son, Jon, since soon after they fled to Europe following the kidnapping and murder of their firstborn.

Not Registered at Weald

Weald officials said the birth had not been registered, but British law allows this formality to be carried out within six weeks. Registration at the United States Consulate is not required, but is the customary procedure for Americans residing abroad.

There were reports that the baby had not been born in the Lindberghs' straggling, half-timbered country home. The vicar of Weald said he "understood" there had been a birth, "but not here."

The little village of Weald was not excited over the event. Villagers know little about the Americans, who live a cloistered existence in their rambling old house at the bottom of a long hill just where it forks off toward the Weald, or valley of Kent.

The house is isolated from the rest of the village and shut off from the road by high brick walls. About the only thing visible through the gate is a large earthenware urn about three feet high.

News of the birth of a brother to Jon—who was born Aug. 16, 1932—had not even reached the village postoffice, which, like the general store of an American village, is the center of gossip. But the villagers have been absorbed with the coronation, and as the Lindberghs wanted to be let alone, they have paid little attention to them.

Only two lights could be seen burning tonight in Long Barn, and a person resembling Colonel Lindbergh leaned from a window overlooking an expanse of rolling downs lighted by an almost full moon. Soon the figure disappeared and the curtain was drawn.

Two policemen in a touring car were stationed outside the house. They said they had orders to pre-

Continued on Page Four

WPA Writers Strike for Larger Relief Fund; Expect City to Provide for Their Support

WPA writers, beginning a combination sitdown strike and walkout yesterday against prospective cuts in the Congressional appropriation for work relief, instructed their families to apply at once for home relief to carry them through the period of the strike.

Insisting that the city, through its Emergency Relief Bureau, foot the bill for the writers' demonstration, officials of the Workers Alliance announced that the strike would continue until the House of Representatives substituted a larger sum for the $1,500,000,000 relief allowance it has voted for the fiscal year 1938. The alliance believes the sum should be increased to $3,000,000,000.

That a demand for temporary home relief will be part of the organization's strategy in its frequent strikes against Federal relief policy here was indicated last night by Michael Davidow, general organizer.

If a referendum now being taken among 100,000 WPA workers on the question of a general strike leads to a walkout on all projects, the city relief authorities will be asked to provide for all strikers whose families are in need, he said.

What stand the ERB will take on such a demand could not be ascertained yesterday. It was believed that no definite formulation of policy would be made until actual cases were presented for consideration.

Work in the offices of the WPA Federal Writers Project on the second floor of 235 East Forty-second Street, between Second and Third Avenues, was halted by the strike, which began at 10:15 A. M. after the writers had been told at a staff meeting that the $1,500,000,000 appropriation probably would necessitate a 25 per cent cut in personnel.

Leaders of the demonstration, called by the City Projects Council, an affiliate of the Workers Alliance, in conjunction with five other organizations, declared that virtually all of the project's 525 employes were on strike. At the request of the strike strategy committee, 160 men and women sat down and the others walked out to picket and to muster support for the sitters.

Cooperating with the City Projects Council in sponsorship of the strike were the WPA unit of the New York Newspaper Guild, the Bookkeepers, Stenographers and Accountants Union; the American Writers Union, the Negro Writers Guild and the Jewish Writers Union.

'RED' C. I. O. ASSAILED IN A. F. OF L. PARLEY

Leaders Heckle Howard, Defy Him to Disprove That Lewis Group Is 'Communistic'

'SEEING RED,' HE RETORTS

Federation Council in Call for War Charges Lust for Power and Violence to C. I. O.

Report of the A. F. of L. executive council is on Page 18.

By LOUIS STARK

Special to THE NEW YORK TIMES.

CINCINNATI, May 24.—An overwhelming demand for war against the Committee for Industrial Organization dominated the special conference of the American Federation of Labor today after the 300 delegates heard the executive council's recommendations calling for creation of a war chest and for a purge of C. I. O. unions from State federations and city central labor bodies.

The discussion today evoked few evidences of peace sentiment among the delegates although the recommendation itself, in a brief paragraph, expressed willingness of the federation "to entertain any honorable basis of terminating the controversy."

That a war already existed between the federation and the C. I. O. was attested by speakers like Thomas L. Hughes of the teamsters union who pleaded for an increase in the assessments of 1 cent a month per member by the national unions of the federation.

Plenty of "Ammunition" Urged

If "an army" is to be equipped with the latest weapons it also should be furnished with plenty of "ammunition," Mr. Hughes said.

After John P. Frey, president of the Metal Trades Department, had charged that the C. I. O. was "infiltrated" with Communist organizers, he challenged Charles P. Howard, president of the International Typographical Union and secretary of the C. I. O., to deny the charges. Mr. Howard's answer did not satisfy Mr. Frey, and the typographical chief was heckled from the chair by President William Green, and later from the floor by Thomas Duffy of the potters' union.

Mr. Howard, who is a member of the C. I. O. in his individual capacity and therefore not a member of the ten union groups suspended by the A. F. of L., asserted that the "state of war" now existing between the C. I. O. and the A. F. of L. was caused by the executive council's "usurpation" of powers never delegated to it by the federation's constitution.

Called upon to explain why he had said early in the C. I. O.'s career that it was not the intention of that organization to "raid" ex-

Continued on Page Eighteen

WAGNER NOW ASKS BROADER SECURITY

Calls for Covering Groups Not in Act, Wage-Hour Law, Cabinet Welfare Post

HOLDS COURT LAID BASIS

Senator Tells Social Work Session at Indianapolis That Housing Will Absorb the Idle

From a Staff Correspondent

INDIANAPOLIS, Ind., May 24.—The Supreme Court's decision today upholding the Social Security Act and its previous decision on the National Labor Relations Act "makes it certain now" that Congress may enact laws to fix maximum hours, minimum wages and abolish child labor, Senator Robert F. Wagner declared here tonight.

Addressing the National Conference of Social Work, amid repeated applause, the Senator said:

"It is my view that the Supreme Court decision in interpreting the Labor Relations Act as to interstate commerce, because it has widened in its decision the area in which Congress may act, and the decision today which held that Congress may levy a tax to serve the general welfare, under the welfare clause, makes it certain now that we may enact laws in Congress to fix maximum hours, minimum wages and abolish child labor.

"I believe that public welfare is a major responsibility of government, and therefore, I have enlisted my aid in the plan to establish a Federal Department of Public Welfare with the director a Cabinet officer."

He referred to the plan proposed recently by the President's Committee on Administrative Management, of which Louis Brownlow is chairman.

"Magna Charta" for Worker

The Senator declared the Labor Relations Act the "magna charta" for the worker, raising him from "economic slavery in many large industries" to the status of a "free man" with the right to organize and bargain collectively.

"And we have had some recent elections which show how peacefully those relations can be carried on," he added.

Denying a charge that the law is "one-sided," he argued that the employers had the right to organize, to bargain with their own stockholders or with their competitors.

"The very right we have given to the workers has long been enjoyed by the employers in this country, and rightly so, and this law simply treats them both on an equality," he said.

With the court's decisions laying the basis for legislation on all social and economic subjects "deemed by Congress to be national in scope," the Senator said the time had come to extend the Social Security Act to "those groups as yet

Continued on Page Sixteen

"All the News That's Fit to Print."

The New York Times.

LATE CITY EDITION
Showers and cooler today. Tomorrow cloudy, probably showers with moderate temperatures.
Temperatures Yesterday—Max., 78; Min., 61

Copyright, 1937, by The New York Times Company.

VOL. LXXXVI.....No. 28,978. Entered as Second-Class Matter, Postoffice, New York, N. Y. NEW YORK, THURSDAY, MAY 27, 1937. P TWO CENTS in New York City. | THREE CENTS Within 200 Miles. | FOUR CENTS Elsewhere Except in 7th and 8th Postal Zones.

REBEL PLANES SHOOT DOWN A FRENCH TRANSPORT LINER IN AN ATTACK NEAR BILBAO

WOMAN IS INJURED

Three Other Passengers Unhurt in Crash, but Pilot Is Cut by Glass

ATTACKED FROM BEHIND

Craft, Disabled by Bullets, Lands in Field—Insurgents Warned 'Blockade Runner'

ANARCHISTS SET UP 'STATE'

A Free Republic in Huesca Is Reported—Mola Pushes to Town 8 Miles From Bilbao

The Spanish Situation

BILBAO—Insurgent planes shot down a French transport ship flying from Biarritz to Bilbao. The pilot and a woman, one of four passengers, were hurt and the plane was damaged in landing in a field twelve miles from the Basque capital. The Rebels had termed the craft an "aerial blockade runner."—Page 1.

THE FRONT—Despite denials by Loyalist sources, travelers confirmed the anarchist rising in Huesca Province, saying a free republic has been set up. The Insurgents on the Basque front pushed to Lemona, eight miles from Bilbao.—Page 12.

MADRID—The United States Embassy received 880 pounds of food from Valencia. The food situation in the city is easing slowly but steadily.—Page 12.

LONDON—The Non-Intervention Committee adopted a plan for the withdrawal of foreign volunteers from Spain and referred it to the member governments for approval. An appeal to end airplane bombings was delayed.—Page 12.

French Aircraft Attacked

Wireless to The New York Times.

BILBAO, Spain, May 26.—A French commercial plane that has been engaged in regular passenger service between Biarritz, France, and Bilbao for the past six weeks was shot down by Insurgent fighting planes this morning at Sopelana, twelve miles northwest of Bilbao.

Cut in the face by flying glass, Leopold Galli, the French pilot, managed to bring down the twin-engined Airspeed Envoy (British manufactured) plane in a plowed field, avoiding near-by houses. The plane was, however, badly damaged, since Galli had had no time to lower the retractable undercarriage. A woman, one of four passengers, was injured.

"Tell my family I am quite all right," was Galli's first request after he had been brought to a hospital here.

Between sips of strong coffee Galli gave a detailed account of the attack, which was followed by a decision of the operators of the Air Pyrenees Line to suspend the hazardous service.

Was Flying at Low Altitude

"I had just flown up from the sea very low—at 600 feet at most—over the coastland between Cape Villano and the mouth of the Nervion River," Galli said, "when I was attacked by a flight of planes that had dropped unseen from the clouds 400 feet above me.

"I was definitely in Basque government territory. Bullets from the first machine-gun attack stopped my port engine and also perforated the wings. The plane listed over and I immediately looked for a landing place.

"The planes made machine-gun attacks, diving on me from behind. I counted five, but there may have been more.

"I had no time to let down the undercarriage and I scarcely know how I landed. I remember a violent blow on the head. I think, although I am not absolutely certain, that the Insurgent planes continued machine-gunning us after we had crashed."

Little information came from the passengers. One explained that "I did not see much as I ducked low," but residents of Sopelana said they had seen the Insurgent planes dive and machine-gun the passenger plane after the crash.

Both Galli and ground witnesses said the attacking planes had been

Continued on Page Twelve

Leader of the Rebellion In Albania Is Killed

Wireless to The New York Times.

TIRANA, Albania, May 26.—Ethem Toto, former Minister of the Interior, who led the revolt that broke out May 15 at Argyrokastron against the government of King Zog, has been tracked down and shot.

A gendarme patrol caught Toto and four of his followers near the village of Golemas in Southern Albania. The group resolutely defended itself, but after a sharp exchange of shots Toto and one follower were killed and the others were captured.

NORTH POLE HAILS SUPPLY AIRPLANE

Molokoff's Machine Is on Ice Floe at the Side of the First Craft to Reach Soviet Base

MISSING PLANE IS FOUND

One of the Three Pilots Failed to Report After Getting 35 Miles From His Goal

By MARK TROYANOVSKY

Copyright, 1937, by The New York Times Company and North American Newspaper Alliance, Inc.

Wireless to The New York Times.

NORTH POLE, May 26.—Today we are immensely happy, for into the ice camp at the North Pole came the airplane of Vassily Molokoff. His machine stands on an ice floe alongside Mikhail Vodopyanoff's plane.

The enormous ice fields serve as an airdrome. The flying field sparkles with myriad diamond flashes in the glaring light of the sun. Tents of the expedition are walled about with snow fences and look like the forts from which Moscow youngsters bombard each other with snowballs.

With the arrival of the expedition's second ship the population at the camp almost doubled. There are now twenty-two men in the camp.

The plane piloted by A. D. Alexieff landed twenty to thirty miles from our camp. Everything was in order there.

As I am writing this dispatch, the weather in the North Pole region has begun to grow worse. Clouds have appeared and the temperature has started to rise. Until almost 7 P. M. there was no connection between Rudolf Island and other stations. That apparently is due to atmospheric conditions.

Weather Growing Worse

The weather is growing worse and less fit for flying every minute. Dickson Island has reported that the radio station of the wintering camp at Udinenie Island has heard signals of I. P. Mazuruk's plane at 3:30 and 3:45 A. M.

Now a snowstorm is raging. Flights are impossible. The polar radio center at Dickson Island and other polar stations are sending signals into the ether every half hour so that the navigator of Mazuruk's plane, who also operates its radio, can determine the direc-

Continued on Page Thirteen

CITY REPUBLICANS WEIGH DEMOCRAT TO OPPOSE MAYOR

Simpson Intimates if Rivals Run Man Unlinked to Tammany He Will Be Supported

CLUB IN STORMY DEBATE

Group of 27 Headed by Warburg and Hughes Backs La Guardia, but Is Opposed

The clear inference that the Republican party will not renominate Mayor La Guardia unless it has to, and that it might support a Democratic candidate provided that he is not of the Tammany Hall type, was contained last night in a statement issued by Kenneth F. Simpson, Republican county leader. Mr. Simpson generally is believed to be the man who eventually will determine whether the Mayor will get the support of the Republican machine in the coming election.

Mr. Simpson, from his sick bed in his home at 109 East Ninety-first Street, issued the statement which praised the Mayor's administration but viewed him also as a national menace, just a few hours before the club members of his home district, the silk-stocking Fifteenth, stormed their clubhouse at 122 East Eighty-Third Street, to vote, if club rules permitted, and express their distinctly unfavorable view of the Mayor.

Meeting Is Stormy

The meeting, one of the stormiest and rowdiest in the history of the party in the city, broke up at 11:20 last night, with a vote on an anti-La Guardia resolution blocked by the ruling of the chairman that the by-laws prohibited passage of a resolution except on due notice to the members.

Anti-La Guardia leaders charged that the adjournment resolution had been steam-rollered; neutral observers noted that while the sentiment of the gathering was decidedly anti La Guardia, the heat and the lateness of the hour had led to a favorable vote on the adjournment motion.

The club members were faced, at the meeting last night, with an appeal from twenty-seven of their fellow members headed by Charles Evans Hughes Jr. and Felix M. Warburg, asking them to go on record as favoring the renomination of the Mayor, in the interests of good government.

Mayor or "Tin-Box" Era Seen

"As Republicans and citizens we face only two alternatives: to permit our city to sink back into the reproach of the old tin-box government or to re-elect the present administration of Mayor Fiorello H. La Guardia," the Hughes-Warburg communication stated.

Mr. Simpson in his statement was franker than is the custom of political leaders. He declared that while the Republicans probably could not elect a Mayoralty candidate of their own they held the balance of power and, after discussing the Mayor's own record, he challenged somewhat indirectly the Democrats to produce a candidate not definitely tied up with either Tammany Hall or too closely allied with the New Deal who could command Republican support. The chances of the Republicans putting a third candidate in the field dwindled somewhat as a result of his statement.

He criticized the Mayor as a clear and avowed radical, who favored collectivism versus constitutionalism as to issues in 1940, with the Mayor definitely on the collectivist

Continued on Page Ten

Aide to Slain Dr. Speer Held on Assault Charge

Thomas E. Elder, Retired Mt. Hermon School Dean and Important Figure in Unsolved Murder, Is Accused by Former Colleague

Special to The New York Times.

GREENFIELD, Mass., May 26.—Thomas E. Elder, 65, retired dean of the Mount Hermon School for Boys at Northfield, scene of the unsolved shotgun slaying of Dr. Elliot Speer, headmaster, in 1934, was brought here tonight from the Holden Barracks of the State police, under arrest on the charge of assault with intent to murder S. Allen Norton of this town, former treasurer of the school. He will be arraigned in the District Court here tomorrow.

Found by police today at his home in Alton Bay, N. H., after Mr. Norton had declared that he was the man who menaced him with a shotgun here late Tuesday night, the prisoner calmly protested his innocence, waived extradition and returned to Massachusetts to face charges, which include illegal possession of firearms.

He said he could prove that he spent Tuesday night at a Keene (N. H.) hotel.

Accused and accuser were colleagues on the staff of the Mount Hermon School for twenty-two years and both were witnesses at the inquest into the death of Dr. Speer, who was killed by a blast fired through the window of his study. They gave contradictory testimony.

"I know Tom Elder as well as I do a member of my own family," Mr. Norton told police in reporting the attack on him at his home, 71 Hayward Street.

Elder appeared at Alton Bay at 10:30 A. M. today, nearly twelve hours after the Greenfield incident and after police of Massachusetts, New Hampshire and Vermont had been warned to watch for him. He was questioned by the Alton police and remained at the police station in the New Hampshire town until the arrival of Massachusetts State detectives.

His counsel, Charles Fairhurst, a former District Attorney of Franklin County, who represented him at the Speer inquest, issued this statement tonight:

"I have talked with Mr. Elder and I told him I would take care of him again. I asked him if he wished to waive his constitutional rights to extradition and he said that he did, that he did not want to make any

Continued on Page Sixteen

REICH POLICE JAIL PROTESTANT BOARD

Arrest All Five Members of the Executive Committee of the Confessional Government

DETENTION SITE UNKNOWN

Goebbels Expected to Answer Cardinal Mundelein on the Radio Tomorrow Night

By The Associated Press.

BERLIN, May 26.—The fight of Protestant Confessional churchmen against Nazi domination entered a new acute phase today following the imprisonment by the secret State police of all five members of the executive committee of the Confessional Synod's provisional church government.

The five pastors, it was disclosed, were taken into custody last night, but neither their names nor their whereabouts—whether they were in concentration camps or in preliminary custody—were revealed.

The present membership of the committee could not be determined officially because the personnel changes frequently and church sources could be arrested if they gave the names of the imprisoned pastors.

The arrests were understood to have been based on alleged violation of a recent government decree prohibiting provisional church governing committees from exercising jurisdiction until after the general synodical elections ordered last Feb. 15 by Chancellor Adolf Hitler.

Goebbels to Answer Cardinal

Now embroiled with both Catholics and Protestants in disputes that appear to be heading toward a climax, the Nazi Government will carry its argument to the people Friday night when Dr. Joseph Goebbels, the Propaganda Minister, will deliver a speech in which, it was announced, he will aim his oratorical guns primarily at Cardinal Mundelein, Archbishop of Chicago.

Dr. Goebbels will deliver his speech in Deutschland Hall, which accommodates 20,000 persons, while a radio hook-up will carry to millions of German homes what is expected to be a challenge to the Vatican over the recent anti-Nazi speech by Cardinal Mundelein.

The imprisonment of the five members of the Confessional Synod's church-governing executive committee marked the latest step in the long struggle of independent Protestant churchmen for freedom from State domination.

The Reich Church Commission, set up by Nazi authorities to coordinate the Protestant church, resigned Feb. 13 and two days later Hitler issued a decree ordering elections in which the church members themselves were to decide what kind of a church government they were to have by electing a new synod.

A controversy quickly arose over who should be allowed to vote, however, and the election date was put off. Hanns Kerrl, Reich Minister for Church Affairs, meanwhile reconstituted the Evangelical church government to continue the status quo until the church elections.

The fixing of the election date has been delayed repeatedly, either because of the controversy over the eligibility of church voters or for some other reason.

NETHERLANDS VOTE IS BLOW TO NAZIS

Moderates Supporting Colijn Win Approval of Greater Part of Electorate

DEMOCRATS MAKE BIG GAIN

Communists Lose One Seat as the Premier Strengthens His Position in Country

Wireless to The New York Times.

THE HAGUE, The Netherlands, May 26.—Premier Hendryk Colijn's "policy of adaptation" to the economic crisis won the approval of a greater part of the Netherland electorate judging by the results of today's election for both houses of the States General.

All the returns have not yet come in, but enough ballots have been counted to show which way the election is going. Furthermore, the ballots show a setback for the National Socialist movement, which presented candidates for the first time in any national elections.

Premier Colijn's Calvinist party increases its representations from fourteen to sixteen. The Roman Catholics and the Socialists—the two strongest parties in the last Parliament—remain stationary.

The surprising feature is the rise of the Liberal Democratic party from six to eleven representatives. This party stands to the right of the Socialists and its most prominent leader is P. J. Oud, Finance Minister in Premier Colijn's Cabinet. The Liberals, or the League of Liberty, on the other hand, fell from seven members to four. The Communists dropped from four representatives to three. Most of the other small parties seem to have disappeared.

Premier's Position Strengthened

The main outcome of the polling is the great strengthening of the Premier's position. It represents a national vote of confidence in Premier Colijn, since those electors who desired to support him without being themselves dogmatic Calvinists voted for his Finance Minister's ticket.

During the electoral campaign it was noteworthy that the Premier's speeches were not demagogic and that they did not contain promises for any panaceas. Nor did he assail the other parties; he simply took his stand on his record of having steered the country on a safe course despite the relative unpopularity of his vigorous "adaptation policy."

Nevertheless the Nazi movement remained an unknown quantity till the result was known this evening. Many thought it would win at least ten seats. It had also been thought that the Communists might win a few seats at the expense of the Socialists. But the results prove that the Netherlands does not care for extremists.

Nazis Get Four Seats

AMSTERDAM, Thursday, May 27 (AP).—The government coalition headed by Premier Hendryk Colijn was shown early today by final returns in yesterday's Parliamentary election to have administered a sharp setback to a Nazi challenge for power.

National Socialists under the leadership of Anton Adrian Mussert had expected to capture 10 of the 100 Parliament seats at stake in the election. Final tabulations gave them four seats.

ATTEMPT TO QUELL 'PORK BARREL' BOLT OVER RELIEF BILL

Leaders in House Map Counter Attack to Beat Amendments Earmarking $505,000,000

WARNING FROM HOPKINS

Half-Million Must Be Dropped From Rolls Plus 400,000 Cut Contemplated, He Says

Special to The New York Times.

WASHINGTON, May 26.—House leaders mapped plans today to quell the revolt which resulted yesterday in the earmarking of $505,000,000 of the $1,500,000,000 Relief Bill for so-called pork barrel projects in defiance of administration wishes.

Representative Rayburn of Texas, the majority leader, and other administration stalwarts were in conference all afternoon with Harry L. Hopkins, Works Progress Administrator. Afterward they asserted that unless the earmarking amendments are defeated when the bill is considered again tomorrow it was possible that 500,000 to 600,000 persons would have to be dropped from the relief rolls, in addition to the 400,000 who will be dropped anyway, through curtailment of the program.

Mr. Rayburn announced that he would demand separate roll-calls on the amendments, a method which New Deal leaders seldom have employed to hold their forces in line. Practically all Republican members present yesterday supported the revolting group because of opposition to the size of the relief fund, and the Democratic side can hope for no changes in votes there.

Democrats to Be Rounded Up

The House majority whip, Representative Boland of Pennsylvania, was instructed to see that all Democratic members are in their seats when the House reconvenes tomorrow. Then Mr. Rayburn expects to corral enough votes to eliminate the amendments. The revolt caused the earmarking of $55,000,000 for flood control projects $300,000,000 for Public Works Administration projects and $150,000,000 for Federal system roads.

"These amendments," said Mr. Rayburn, "if allowed to remain in the bill, will be destructive to the relief program. If $505,000,000 of the $1,500,000,000 is earmarked for other purposes, Mr. Hopkins says that between 500,000 and 600,000 persons will have to be dropped from relief rolls, in addition to the approximately 400,000 who will go off, due to some curtailment in the relief program from last year.

"It was decided to demand separate roll-calls on these three amendments."

Asked whether he knew that the leaders of the revolting group, Representatives Beiter of New York, Stearns of Alabama and Cartwright of Oklahoma, had been writing letters to the 170 or more members who supported the amendment, Mr. Rayburn said:

"Yes, I understand they are busy trying to hold their forces in line. But I will say this—tomorrow we expect to be in better shape than we were yesterday."

Representative Woodrum of Virginia, chairman of the appropriations subcommittee in charge of the bill, denounced members who fought his efforts earlier in the week to cut the relief appropriation to $1,000,000,000 and then joined in a "pork barrel feast."

He recalled that some of these members "spoke in touching terms of the poor, unfortunate people who would be dropped from the re-

Continued on Page Six

FORD MEN BEAT AND ROUT LEWIS UNION ORGANIZERS; 80,000 OUT IN STEEL STRIKE

Baldwin Will Announce Commons Pay Rise Today

By The Associated Press.

LONDON, May 26.—Prime Minister Stanley Baldwin in one of his final acts as head of the government will announce in the House of Commons tomorrow a rise in pay for its members. This was decided by the Cabinet today, it was learned.

The members, who now receive £400 [approximately $2,000 at current exchange] a year in contrast to the $10,000 salary of United States Representatives, will receive an increase of £100 or £200.

Today's decision follows the recent voting of salary increases for Cabinet Ministers.

27 BIG STEEL MILLS DARKENED BY STRIKE

Walkout at Republic, Inland and Youngstown Plants Starts Peacefully

FIVE STATES ARE INVOLVED

Picket Lines Form in Night—Companies Refuse to Sign Contracts With C. I. O.

By LOUIS STARK

Special to The New York Times.

YOUNGSTOWN, Ohio, May 26.—Strikes affecting between 75,000 and 80,000 employes in the plants of the Republic Steel Corporation, Youngstown Sheet and Tube Company and Inland Steel Company became effective at 11 o'clock tonight. The strike order was issued late this afternoon by Philip Murray, chairman of the Steel Workers Organizing Committee, after he and his associates held a "war council" here.

The strikes affect employes in twenty-seven plants in five States—Ohio, Illinois, Indiana, Pennsylvania and New York. In this area the walkout was peaceful. Crowds of pickets and strike sympathizers gathered at mill gates, waited for the men to go off the shift at 11 o'clock and cheered them as they left with their lunch buckets.

The chief strike zones are the Youngstown district, with 35,000 employes divided between the Republic and Youngstown Sheet and Tube, and the Chicago area, with about 23,000 employed by these two and the Inland company.

Following a three-hour session with sixty officers and regional staff members, Philip Murray, chairman of the Steel Workers Organizing Committee, announced that all the "mechanics" of strike preparation were ready and that local meetings would be held at once.

Mr. Murray said it was the union's intention to conduct the strike peaceably, but that he had been advised the Republic corporation had large stores of munitions at each plant, "including machine guns."

The corporation denied this charge and, in a statement furnished to its employes, denounced the "coercion" of a closed shop, saying that was what the union would ultimately demand. Signing of an agreement now, it was said, would

Continued on Page Two

16 HURT IN BATTLE

C.I.O. Leader, 7 Women Are Among Injured at Dearborn Plant

FORD PROPERTY CLEARED

Fight Blocks Distribution of Leaflets—Union and Company Blame Each Other

NLRB INVESTIGATION BEGUN

County Prosecutor Also Takes Action — U. A. W. A. Asks National Demonstrations

Day's Strike Developments

Ford workers beat union organizers and chased them from the Ford Company property in the first battle of the C. I. O. drive at the Rouge plant. Sixteen were reported injured, including seven women. National Labor Board and Wayne County prosecutor began investigations as the company charged a "frame-up" by the union.—Page 1.

Strikes in twenty-seven plants of Republic Steel, Youngstown Sheet and Tube and Inland Steel, employing nearly 80,000 men, and called by S. W. O. C., began at 11 o'clock last night.—Page 1.

The A. F. of L. decided to organize a new maritime department to combat the C. I. O. in shipping centers and offered an industrial union charter to a Chevrolet group in Indianapolis.—Page 2.

The Ford plant at Richmond, Calif., was closed by a strike called by the U. A. W. A. Pickets barred company officials and office workers from the factory and 1,800 workers were made idle.—Page 3.

Battle at Ford Plant

Special to The New York Times.

DETROIT, May 26.—An outburst of violence, in which union representatives were beaten, kicked and driven away, marked today the first attempt of the United Automobile Workers of America to organize the employes of the Ford Motor Company.

Richard T. Frankensteen, directing the membership drive in behalf of the auto affiliate of the Committee for Industrial Organization, and Walter Reuther, president of the West Side local of the automobile workers' union, were set upon by a group of employes at No. 4 gate of the Ford Rouge plant in Dearborn. With two other men who had accompanied them to oversee the distribution of union handbills, they were knocked down repeatedly, kicked, and finally forced away from the gate, despite efforts of Frankensteen to fight off his assailants.

Subsequent fighting, in which employes routed union representatives who had come to distribute leaflets, resulted in the injury of twelve more persons, seven of them women, the union stated.

"It was the worst licking I've ever taken," Frankensteen declared. "They bounced us down the concrete steps of an overpass we had climbed. Then they would knock us down, stand us up, and knock us down again."

Both Frankensteen and Reuther, together with several of the other victims, were treated by physicians.

Accuses Ford Service Men

Members of the Ford service department participated in the attack in an effort to block any union contact with the workers, the union charged in a statement issued later. Spokesmen for the Ford Company denied this, however, and said that the attack had been provoked when the union representatives shouted "scabs" at Ford workmen, in an effort, the company said, to provoke a clash that could be brought to the attention of the Senate's La Follette civil liberties investigation.

Two investigations of the outbreak were under way tonight, one by representatives of the National Labor Relations Board; the other by Duncan C. McCrea, Wayne County prosecutor.

In addition, the union, at headquarters guarded by a watchman with a shotgun, was endeavoring to get an inquiry on charges that the

Continued on Page Three

Doriot, French Rightist Leader, Is Ousted As Mayor of 'Red' Town for 'Irregularities'

Wireless to The New York Times.

PARIS, May 26.—Jacques Doriot, leader of the Rightist French Popular party and a former Communist leader, was removed tonight from his office as Mayor of Saint Denis, a "Red" suburb of Paris, under a decree of the Ministry of the Interior charging him with irregularities in office.

The expulsion order, signed by President Albert Lebrun, charged that coal and electricity contracts had been awarded under irregular conditions and that merchandise delivered to the City Hall had not been of the quality specified in the bids. It was also charged that the quantities of materials received had not corresponded to the amounts paid for.

The expulsion came after an investigation by a local inspector and Ministry of Finance agents had brought a reply deemed unsatisfactory by Marx Dormoy, the Minister of the Interior.

Legally Mr. Doriot cannot protest against the Ministry's decision, nor can he run for re-election within a year.

Marcel Marshal, the Vice Mayor, who now takes over the Mayor's office temporarily, asserted in a statement to the press that no "specific act" had been cited against Mr. Doriot and that the Ministry's action had been "arbitrary and inadmissible."

The press bureau of the Popular party issued a statement asserting that Premier Léon Blum's Popular Front government was "fighting against insoluble financial problems" and hence sought "to divert attention by pointing to side issues."

The statement added that the expulsion had been a result of Communist instigation and that it had been carried out despite Mr. Doriot's "refutation" of the investigators' report on his administration. In conclusion, the statement said:

"It is only because of the boom in the French Popular party and also Mr. Doriot's taking over of the editorship of the newspaper Liberté and his success in launching a 'Liberty Front' that Dormoy has given in to Communist threats."

Smith Is Greeted by Pope as an Old Friend; Amazed, at First Audience, by Pontiff's Vigor

Wireless to The New York Times.

ROME, May 26.—Alfred E. Smith held a long conversation with Pope Pius XI, who received the former Governor of New York and his party this morning in the Papal Summer residence, Castel Gandolfo. On leaving the Pope's presence Mr. Smith declared he had been pleasantly surprised to find the Pontiff in a much better mental and physical condition than he had expected.

"I know many men who are not as old as he is," he said, "and have not half the keenness of mind and bodily vigor that he has."

The Pope greeted Mr. Smith as an old friend, saying that he felt that he had known Mr. Smith all his life as he always had been an admirer of the New York leader and was acquainted with every detail of his career. Mr. Smith replied that for many years he had looked forward to this opportunity to pay his respects to the Pope and to obtain his blessing. From this point the conversation branched out to other subjects that were not disclosed.

Mr. Smith and his party were accompanied to Castel Gandolfo by Mgr. Ralph L. Hayes, rector of the North American College at Rome, and Mgr. Fulton J. Sheen of the Catholic University in Washington. They were greeted at the entrance to the Papal palace by eighteen students of the North American College from New York, who were introduced by Mgr. Hayes. In one place in the courtyard Mr. Smith was recognized by a group of newly ordained Irish priests, who greeted him with cheers.

At the end of the audience the Pope gave to Mr. Smith a miniature of himself with an autograph dedication, and to Mrs. Smith a medal and rosary. Mr. Smith gave a small reproduction in gold of the Empire State Building to the Pope.

In the evening Mr. Smith held a long conversation with Cardinal Pacelli in the Vatican.

"All the News That's Fit to Print."

The New York Times.

LATE CITY EDITION
Fair, slightly warmer today. Tomorrow cloudy, continued warm, local thunder showers, cooler.
Temperatures Yesterday—Max., 81; min., 66.

Copyright, 1937, by The New York Times Company.

VOL. LXXXVI.....No. 28,982. Entered as Second-Class Matter, Postoffice, New York, N. Y. NEW YORK, MONDAY, MAY 31, 1937. P TWO CENTS In New York City. | THREE CENTS Within 200 Miles. | FOUR CENTS Elsewhere Except in 7th and 8th Postal Zones.

4 KILLED, 84 HURT AS STRIKERS FIGHT POLICE IN CHICAGO

STEEL MOB HALTED

1,000 Marchers Fail in Effort to Close Republic Plant

MANY FELLED BY SHOTS

Crowd Uses Guns and Rocks, Police Employ Clubs, Tear Gas and Bullets

HORNER REACHES THE CITY

Immediately Arranges Parley With Both Sides—Loyal Workers Hold Mill

Day's Strike Developments

Four were killed and eighty-four injured when about 1,000 C. I. O. strikers, marching on the Republic Steel plant in South Chicago, were repulsed by police. The strikers hurled rocks and bolts and fired some shots. The police used their clubs, tear gas and guns. Page 1.

A battle line was drawn at Youngstown between steel strikers and civic authorities over the supplying of food to maintenance men within the plants. Union planes failed to prevent company aircraft from dropping supplies for the besieged. Page 5.

Rival steel worker rallies were held near the Weirton company's mills in West Virginia, with some members of the Security League booing a C. I. O. parade and snatching flags off cars. Page 5.

The City Industrial Relations Board promised the C. I. O. taxi drivers' union to consider its request for a referendum of the employes of the Parmelee System.

Battle in Chicago

Special to THE NEW YORK TIMES.

CHICAGO, May 30.—Four men were killed and eighty-four persons went to hospitals with gunshot wounds, cracked heads, broken limbs or other injuries received in a battle late this afternoon between police and steel strikers at the gates of the Republic Steel Corporation plant in South Chicago.

One of the dead was identified as Earl Hanley, 37, of Indiana Harbor, Ind. He died tonight in the Burnside Hospital of a fractured skull.

Twenty-nine of the injured were victims of gunfire. Twenty-three were policemen, all hit by missiles.

The clash occurred when about 1,000 strikers tried to approach the Republic company's plant, the only mill of the three large independent steel manufacturers in this area attempting to continue production. About 22,000 steel workers are on strike in the Chicago district.

The union demonstrators were armed with clubs, slingshots, cranks and gear-shift levers from cars, bricks, steel bolts and other missiles. Police charged that some of the men also carried firearms.

After their repulse in the march, which began at 4 P. M., the strikers tried to reassemble for another attack on the plant, but gave it up with the arrival of police reinforcements.

Police Discharge Tear Gas

The police said they stood their ground but made no effort to harm the invaders until showered with bricks and bolts. The police then used tear gas. When the rioters resorted to firearms, the police said, they were forced to draw their revolvers to protect themselves. Even then, the police declared, they first fired into the air as a final warning.

At a late hour three of the dead were still unidentified. Police interpreted this as a confirmation of reports that outside agitators had played a leading part in the raid on the plant.

Governor Horner arrived from Springfield shortly after the battle, accompanied by Adj. Gen. Carlos E. Black. He left the Congress Hotel with General Black and said he was going into conference with both sides.

"Are you going to call out the military?" the Governor was asked.

"I can't determine what I shall do until I know what the situation is," he replied.

It was understood that he was hoping to arrange a conference with James P. Allman, Police Commissioner, and Van A. Bittner,

Continued on Page Five

C. I. O. Wins Test Votes In 2 Maine Shoe Plants

By The Associated Press.

LEWISTON, Me., May 30.—The first voting test of the relative strength here of the Committee for Industrial Organization and a local shoe workers' union has given the Lewis faction a decisive victory.

The United Shoe Workers of America defeated the Lewiston-Auburn Shoe Workers' Protective Association in Wagner Act "consent" elections in two of nineteen Lewiston-Auburn factories, normally employing 6,400, which are involved in a general strike now in its third month.

In balloting yesterday employes of the Clark Shoe Company cast 343 votes for the C. I. O. affiliate and 289 for the protective association. In the Augusta Shoe Company plant the vote was 293-141 in favor of the Lewis union.

Previous elections, in which the local union had no place in the ballot, had given bargaining rights to the C. I. O. in three factories. Three others had given recognition, without elections, to the protective association, and another had recognized an independent union.

SOCIALISTS FIX WAY TO AID LA GUARDIA

Federation Constitution Allows Help if Labor Party Independently Backs Race

TIE-UP WITH REDS BARRED

Group Appeals for End of C. I. O.-A. F. L. Feud as Vital for Third Party Start

By JOSEPH SHAPLEN
Special to THE NEW YORK TIMES.

PITTSBURGH, May 30.—The convention of the Social Democratic Federation, which will seek to become the nucleus of a third party in the United States by uniting all labor and progressive elements, today completed the federation's organization and elected Mayor Jasper McLevy of Bridgeport its national chairman.

As a step deemed essential to uniting the forces of labor on the political field, in expectation of a basic realignment for the campaign of 1940, the convention appealed for unity between the American Federation of Labor and the Committee for Industrial Organization.

Another step taken designed to facilitate the cooperation of labor and progressive forces in the task of building a third party was the adoption of a constitution for the Social Democratic Federation under which Socialists affiliated with the organization in the respective States will be enabled to support candidates of State Labor parties functioning as independent organs of political action.

Political Cooperation Sought

This will enable Socialists in New York to support Mayor La Guardia for re-election in the event he obtains the endorsement or nomination of the American Labor party, the New York State affiliate of Labor's Non-Partisan League, provided the campaign of the American Labor party is conducted separately from any other party supporting Mr. La Guardia. Similar cooperation between Socialists affiliated with the Social Democratic Federation and political organizations of labor in other States will be promoted by the newly formed federation.

Leaders of the convention hoped that a national conference of forces interested in the promotion of a third party would be called within a year. It was stipulated, however, that no cooperation was to be sought with Communists or organizations promoted by Communists.

Holds Feud Imperils Labor

With respect of the conflict between the American Federation of Labor and the Committee for Industrial Organization, the convention took the position that continuance of the feud would not only injure seriously the cause of the labor movement on the industrial field but would divide labor politically and thereby weaken if not destroy its influence upon government.

In appealing for unity between the A. F. of L. and C. I. O., the convention declared:

"We, the Social Democratic Fed-

Continued on Page Seven

GEORGE F. BAKER, 59, DIES OF PERITONITIS ON YACHT IN HAWAII

Banker, Who Was Operated On at Sea, Succumbs After 300-Mile Race to Honolulu

PLANES TAKE WIFE TO SIDE

Chairman of First National of New York Is Said to Leave Holdings of $50,000,000

By The Associated Press.

HONOLULU, May 30.—George F. Baker, 59 years old, New York banker, died today aboard his yacht Viking in Honolulu Harbor, a victim of peritonitis, despite efforts by air and sea to save his life.

Mr. Baker, chairman of the First National Bank of New York, succumbed at 6:15 A. M. [12:45 P. M. Eastern daylight-saving time] after physicians and nurses had worked fruitlessly throughout the night and had seen his condition become progressively worse.

At least one blood transfusion was given and oxygen was reported used.

The battle was lost despite the combined efforts of three government agencies, an ocean liner and a 300-mile race into port with the stricken financier. In addition Mrs. Baker made a 5,500-mile air dash from New York to Honolulu.

Father Died in 1931

Mr. Baker's death was the second in recent years to affect the family and the bank. His father, George F. Baker Sr., died in May, 1931, at the age of 91.

The father was regarded as a Colossus of the financial world and was noted for his dislike of the spotlight. His son, in taking up the position and responsibilities left by the father, likewise acquired a reputation for reticence and a dislike of publicity. Associates said that despite his condition he had exhibited annoyance on learning yesterday of the notice given to his illness and the strenuous effort in his behalf.

Mr. Baker became ill last Tuesday as the yacht, with a party of friends, was heading toward Honolulu from the Fiji Islands.

Seeking medical assistance, the yachting party hailed the Canadian Pacific liner Niagara as she passed. Dr. John A. Newell, 70-year-old Australian specialist, a Niagara passenger, volunteered to assist and with an English nurse boarded the Viking in mid-ocean.

Operated On at Sea

Immediately Dr. Alfred S. Ambler, Mr. Baker's personal physician and a member of the yachting party, performed the operation, assisted by Dr. Newell and the nurse.

The Niagara resumed her course and the Viking put on full steam for Honolulu. A few hours later the yacht sent a call for medical assistance.

Coast Guards converted their cutter Taney into a hospital ship, picked up Dr. D. J. Zaugg of the Public Health Service and three nurses and sped out of Honolulu to the rescue. An hour later a naval plane collected serums that Dr. Zaugg had not had time to gather, overtook the cutter and dropped them. The Taney picked them up and sped on. Dr. Zaugg and the nurses boarded the Viking.

Mrs. Baker, meanwhile, left New York by airplane for Honolulu. The yacht reached port Friday morning and Mrs. Baker arrived the next day aboard the Philippine Clipper.

Physicians reported Mr. Baker

Continued on Page Fifteen

Major Sports Results

Tennis—The United States Davis Cup team advanced to the interzone final by scoring its third straight victory over Australia at Forest Hills yesterday. Donald Budge and Gene Mako beat Jack Crawford and Vivian McGrath in the doubles, 7—5, 6—1, 8—6, to clinch the series.

Baseball—The Yankees routed the Athletics, 13—1, the eight-game winning streak of the Giants was snapped by the Phillies, 6—3, and the Bees downed the Dodgers, 11—4. The Pirates strengthened their hold on the National League lead by defeating the Cards, 7—4, dropping the losers to fourth place.

Golf—Denny Shute retained the P. G. A. title by overcoming Harold (Jug) McSpaden in a thirty-seven-hole match at the Pittsburgh Field Club. McSpaden had a two-hole lead with three to go, but Shute drew even and won on the first extra hole.

(Full details on sports pages.)

WAR DEAD HONORED; ARMS RACE SCORED

Services Held by Religious and Patriotic Organizations Throughout the City

THOUSANDS MARCH TODAY

Three Memorial Parades to Be Held Here—Holiday Travel Is Unusually Heavy

The observance of Memorial Day, which will be celebrated officially today, began yesterday with religious and veterans' organizations throughout the city holding services in tribute to the nation's military dead.

From the pulpits of some of the city's churches, preachers raised their voices in protest against the world-wide armament race between the nations, pointing out that many of the soldier dead who were being honored had gone to France to fight in a "war to end wars." They contended that Christianity, with its message of universal brotherhood and love, demands that the peoples of the world take a firm stand against war.

At Governors Island and other military and patriotic sites, the bugle notes of taps were sounded at memorial services held under the auspices of various veterans' organizations who paid homage to their departed comrades-in-arms.

Thousands Make Holiday

Elsewhere in the city and throughout the metropolitan area, thousands, taking advantage of the clear day and Summer warmth which reached a high of 81 degrees at 2:15 P. M., crowded the beaches and resorts to bask in the sunshine and even to bathe in the waters which were still somewhat chilly.

Automobile traffic on the ferries, bridges and through the Holland Tunnel, leading in and out of the city, was extremely heavy, as was traffic on the main highways surrounding the metropolitan area. Automobile accidents took their toll of dead and injured.

While thousands of city residents already had left the city on Friday and Saturday to spend the three-day holiday in the country, an almost equal number of out-of-towners crowded into the city by every available means of transportation. Hotels in the midtown area reported they were filled to capacity, while railroads, bus and air lines declared that they were pressing

Continued on Page Two

Roosevelt, at Hyde Park, Rests and Swims; Visits With Mother and Meets Vestrymen

From a Staff Correspondent.

POUGHKEEPSIE, May 30.—With his message suggesting to Congress concerted action against evaders and avoiders of income taxes in the higher brackets virtually ready for transmission Tuesday, President Roosevelt tonight settled down for a quiet week-end with his mother at her house at Hyde Park, six miles up the Hudson from here.

Mr. Roosevelt arrived at Hyde Park early this morning aboard his special train and drove directly to his mother's house.

Only a small group of old friends and neighbors was waiting at the Hyde Park station when the President arrived, the members of the Roosevelt Home Club, which usually sponsors homecoming celebrations, being absent sightseeing in Washington.

This was the first visit to Hyde Park, where he lives and votes, which the President has made since soon after his re-election last Fall. Beyond the very minimum of staff necessary to set up temporary White House offices here, the President was completely alone.

The President showed no ill effects from the cold which has been bothering him during the past week. He spent most of the day with his mother. In the afternoon he drove about the family place and swam in the pool at the nearby Val-Kil Cottage, which he owns himself.

His mother, Mrs. James Roosevelt, who is 82, broke her ankle recently and was reported as recovering satisfactorily.

Also during the afternoon Mr. Roosevelt presided at a meeting in the Roosevelt home of the vestry of St. James's Protestant Episcopal Church of Hyde Park, of which he is senior warden. The other members of the vestry present were the Rev. Frank R. Wilson, the pastor; A. S. Halpin, Henry Hackett, Allan D. Macy, D. M. Crapser, Arthur S. Degroff and Gerald Morgan.

Herbert C. Pell, newly appointed Minister to Portugal, and Mrs. Pell called on Mr. Roosevelt late in the day. Mr. Pell said his visit was "purely social."

Another visitor was Edward E. Perkins, a leader of Democrats of Poughkeepsie.

The President does not expect to leave Hyde Park until Tuesday night, arriving in Washington early Wednesday morning.

PROTESTANTS DEFY MOVE BY THE NAZIS TO SILENCE CLERGY

National Synod Urges Pastors to Combat Restrictions on Services and Publications

STATE'S ATTACKS LISTED

Propaganda Is Said to Deride Bible, Clergy, Church and Christianity Generally

Wireless to THE NEW YORK TIMES.

BERLIN, May 30.—The anti-church campaign here has reached such a pitch that the National Confessional Synod has issued special instructions to Protestant pastors for combating propaganda and National Socialist party official interference with church life. A commission has been organized to the same end.

Consisting largely of a series of warnings the instructions to the pastors can be regarded as evidence of the unusual difficulties facing the church throughout the Reich. The Synod leaders say:

"We must report—painful as it is—that everywhere in the training courses [National Socialist], in public assemblies, newspapers and magazines, the Bible is attacked and the Gospel and the church are spoken of with contempt. We warn all Christians not to be silent, but to protest against such attacks. Against anti-Christian declarations made during service [in the Storm Troops or in the party] protest should be made as soon as the period of service is completed.

"Parishioners are subject to a very special danger to their faith through the many assemblies of party organizations which are so scheduled as to prevent attendance at divine service. We warn Protestant Christians to allow nothing to interfere with their attendance at church services.

Nazis Enter All Fields

"The National Socialist ideology mobilizes all aspects of life within its sphere of activity and claims exclusive control in all fields of activity. The National Socialist People's Welfare Organization has taken over charity activities. Recreation has been absorbed by the Strength Through Joy organization. Education is absorbed by the Hitler Youth high command and the National Socialist Teachers League.

"The basis for all this is the conviction that National Socialism itself is the church. Accordingly all State activities assume a religious character. Politics is a divine mission. Service to the nation is divine service. National Socialism, therefore, has a definite mission, for the fulfillment of which it claims the whole nation. By its very principles it cannot allow other bodies to engage in the same activities in which it is engaged.

"Thus members of the German nation are made incapable of understanding their Christian mission or fulfilling their Christian duties. The one-sided deification of racial and biological values and concrete accomplishment has created a hard-heartedness regarding the 'inferior and useless' which is a contradiction of neighborly love.

"The church's work has been hindered in the following specific instances:

"The Minister for Church Affairs suppressed by a decree on Dec. 2, 1935, a great part of the activity of the Confessional Church which has since been subjected to prohibitions, house searches and confiscations of all sorts. Sunday is regularly employed for exercises, training courses and propaganda.

Pastors Isolated from Public

"Public church assemblies are no longer allowed outside church buildings. Church collections have been strictly limited. Pastors and young theologians, wherever possible, are isolated from public life. They are not allowed to belong to the Storm Troops, Hitler Guards or Hitler Youth.

"They are set apart from others in labor service. Pastoral work in the labor service camps is prevented. The courts have been excluded from jurisdiction in church cases by the creation of the Church Affairs Judicial Bureau under the Reich Church Minister. Civil servants are forced to remove their children from church youth organizations."

The document continues with twenty further examples of similar practices.

A separate section is devoted to the church's rôle in the press. It says:

"The columns of the daily press have been closed to the churches. The Propaganda Minister decides on the character of the reports regarding the church appearing in the press and thereby determines the picture the public receives of the condition of the church. The ideological press has almost unlimited power to attack the church. The German Christians Society's

Continued on Page Four

SPANISH ATTACK STIRS REICH; ALL NAVY LEAVES CANCELED; BOMBS KILL 23 ON WARSHIP

Reich and Italy to Act in Concert; May Take Law in Their Own Hands

Two Nations Expected to Proceed Directly Against Valencia Government for Attacks on Their Ships—Valencia Seen in Effort to Draw Berlin and Rome Into Conflict

By ARNALDO CORTESI
Wireless to THE NEW YORK TIMES.

ROME, Monday, May 31.—News of the bombing of the German warship Deutschland Saturday by airplanes of the Valencia Government spread in Rome last night and caused a profound sensation.

The general impression is that decisive measures are about to be taken and that Italy and Germany will act in concert to exact reparations for actions against their ships. It is thought the two governments will take the law in their own hands and proceed directly against the Valencia Government, merely informing the non-intervention committee in London, as an act of courtesy, of what they propose to do.

It is the view here that recent bombings of Italian and German warships can no longer be attributed to error. It is now definitely assumed that they take on the character of willful provocation and public opinion in Rome is in no mood at present to permit the challenge to pass unheeded.

The Spanish civil war is considered to have developed long ago into a struggle between communism and fascism and it is asserted that this aspect can no longer be denied now as the Valencia government is accused of going out of its way to draw the Italian and German governments into the fight.

Up to a few days ago the Italian Government seemed ready to accede to a compromise solution of the civil war under certain conditions, but the events of the week-end seem to have ruled out such a possibility since both Italy and Germany seem compelled to assume a strong line of action.

There can be no doubt that Italy and Germany will find themselves side by side in whatever measure is taken. The policies of the two governments for many months have been running on parallel lines and the two countries now have suffered an affront by Valencia in almost identical conditions. Their reactions, therefore, certainly will be similar and their actions parallel.

Premier Benito Mussolini, who is still at his country estate near Forli, is expected to hasten his return to Rome to take charge of the situation. The decision of the Italian Government probably will be announced today simultaneously with the German action.

Special Cable to THE NEW YORK TIMES.

LONDON, May 30.—A special meeting of the steering committee

Continued on Page Three

WPA JOB-DODGERS TO BE WEEDED OUT

Somervell Moves to Replace Those Failing to Seek Work With Home Relief Clients

BANS PUBLIC-AID 'CAREERS'

Persons on the Rolls Longest Face Test as to Need for Continued Federal Wage

Disturbed by the apparent willingness of thousands of WPA workers to make careers of their relief jobs, Lieut. Col. Brehon B. Somervell, Works Progress Administrator here, disclosed yesterday that he had drawn preliminary plans for returning such workers to the home relief rolls and replacing them with jobless men and women more eager to equip themselves for an early return to private employment.

To determine the extent to which WPA workers are "frozen" into their present posts, Colonel Somervell has directed his statistical division to prepare an analysis of "the life on work relief" of each of the 170,000 persons now receiving Federal aid here.

The records of those who have been on work relief longest then will be examined to establish whether any socially useful purpose would be served by continuing their WPA employment.

"Some people who have not stirred since they got their first work relief job under the Civil Works Administration of 1933 may find it less comfortable on home relief, with half their present monthly allowance," Colonel Somervell said.

ERB Clients Get More Jobs

With home relief recipients finding private jobs at twice the rate of WPA workers, officials of the Federal agency have long felt that a way must be found to disabuse relief employes of the notion that WPA will provide a permanent haven for those on its rolls, regardless of improvements in the outside employment situation.

Most WPA workers are eager to free themselves of the necessity for government aid, Colonel Somervell and his associates believe, but among the 170,000 there are also many who are ready to accept without question the view that there are no jobs and that it is pointless to look.

Mindful that WPA's goal has been rehabilitation as much as relief, officials here feel it is their duty to dislodge those whose records show them incapable of reabsorption in industry. In the opinion of these officials, many persons classed as employables when they were assigned to work relief are no longer equipped to fill any kind of private job.

A special problem is presented by

Continued on Page Six

CUBAN HOUSE BACKS SWEEPING AMNESTY

Passes Island's Most Inclusive Pardon Bill in Stormy Sitting—Senate Likely to Concur

WOULD FREE THOUSANDS

Machado and Officials of His Regime Included in Measure—Emptying of Jails Seen

By J. D. PHILLIPS
Wireless to THE NEW YORK TIMES.

HAVANA, May 30.—The most sweeping Amnesty Bill in the history of the republic was approved by the House of Representatives early today after more than twelve hours of stormy debate. Twice during the night reporters and spectators were ejected and secret sessions were held.

The bill would pardon crimes committed up to May 20, 1937. If it is accepted by the Senate, which is not unlikely, it will virtually empty the prisons of the island both of common convicts and political offenders, and will clear the jammed court dockets. It is estimated that about 6,000 criminals are in the jails, in addition to hundreds still awaiting trial.

Former President Gerardo Machado, who fled Cuba during the 1933 revolution, would be pardoned on all the counts against him, along with officials of his administration and members of his police force and his hated "Porra," or strong-arm squad.

About forty members of the Machado régime are now in Cabanas Fortress, many under death sentence. Among them is Antonio Zubizarreta, former Secretary of the Interior, who would be freed. Thousands, including Machado Cabinet officials now living in exile, would be able to return to Cuba with the slate wiped clean.

Would Commute Death Sentences

The amnesty also would be applied to political prisoners serving sentences for offenses during the 1935 revolutionary strike, thus including students and public employes. The crimes of terrorism and gangsterism would not be included, although death sentences imposed for such offenses would be commuted to life imprisonment along with death sentences for common crimes.

Most of the youths serving sentences under charges of terrorism and gangsterism were members of the outlawed revolutionary organization Joven Cuba and are bitter enemies of the present military clique headed by Colonel Fulgencio Batista, Army Chief of Staff.

Death sentences imposed since 1933 have been held in abeyance except in the cases of several civilians

Continued on Page Four

CABINET IN SESSION

All German Navy Craft Wait With Steam Up for Instructions

LONDON MEETING CALLED

Non-Intervention Group to Consider Safety Measures for Warships Off Spain

SPANISH LINER IS SUNK

Vessel With Heavy Passenger List Is Torpedoed by Rebel Submarine Off Barcelona

By GUIDO ENDERIS
Wireless to THE NEW YORK TIMES.

BERLIN, Monday, May 31.—A session of the German Cabinet was held here last night to deal with the bombing of the German pocket battleship Deutschland by Spanish Government airplanes Saturday. [The Admiral Scheer was erroneously reported yesterday as the ship bombed.]

Afterward an official communiqué was issued in which it was said that "the German Government is forced to take measures which will be communicated immediately to the non-intervention committee in London."

It also disclosed that the Deutschland had reached Gibraltar and had reported that the bombing had caused twenty-three deaths and that nineteen members of the crew had been seriously injured and sixty-four slightly wounded.

"Measures" Not Divulged

The nature of the measures to be taken was not disclosed. Propaganda Minister Joseph Goebbels summoned the representatives of the German press to his office, but apparently confided nothing that would expand the official statement. The Foreign Office was in communication with Ambassador Joachim von Ribbentrop in London but was inaccessible throughout the day.

[All shore leaves in the German Navy were canceled, according to an Associated Press despatch from Berlin, and every warship was waiting with steam up for further instructions. Orders to this effect were said to have been relayed from ship to ship around the world.]

Chancellor Adolf Hitler was in Munich, attending the opening of the Reich's food show, when apprised of the bombing. Accompanied by Foreign Minister Baron Constantin von Neurath and Admiral-General Erich Raeder, he immediately returned to Berlin by special airplane. Colonel-General Hermann Goering flew up from Weimar, where he had made an address on the Four-Year Plan.

Field Marshal Werner von Blomberg and other members of the Cabinet were summoned to a meeting. The session continued to a late hour.

TEXT OF COMMUNIQUE

At its conclusion the following communiqué was issued:

Following attacks by Red airplanes on British, German and Italian warships in the harbor of Majorca in which six officers were killed on an Italian ship, it became impossible for German ships to remain in that harbor. On Saturday, May 29, 1937, the battleship Deutschland was in the harbor of Iviza. This vessel belongs to the forces of international maritime control. Despite this, the battleship was attacked suddenly between 6 and 7 P. M. and bombed by two airplanes of the Red Valencia government.

As the ship rode at anchor, the crew was gathered forward in unprotected crew's quarters.

One of the Red bombs struck in the midst of the crew's mess—as recently an Italian ship's officers' mess was hit.

Twenty-three dead, nineteen seriously and sixty-four slightly wounded are the consequences of this criminal attack.

A second bomb struck the side deck but caused only small damage. The ship, which was entirely fit for action and navigation, proceeded to Gibraltar to land the wounded there. The ship had not fired against the airplanes.

Since the Valencia government had been twice warned by the Non-Intervention Committee and

Continued on Page Three

"All the News That's Fit to Print."

The New York Times.

LATE CITY EDITION
Partly cloudy, local showers today, slightly cooler. Tomorrow fair, little change in temperature.
Temperatures Yesterday—Max., 75; Min., 65

VOL. LXXXVI.....No. 28,991. Entered as Second-Class Matter, Postoffice, New York, N. Y. NEW YORK, WEDNESDAY, JUNE 9, 1937. P TWO CENTS In New York City. | THREE CENTS Within 200 Miles. | FOUR CENTS Elsewhere Except in 7th and 8th Postal Zones.

MONROE, MICH., CALLS CITIZENS TO ARMS TO GUARD MEN RETURNING TO STEEL JOBS; FIGHTS IN OHIO AS PICKETS ARE DISARMED

SUN'S ECLIPSE SEEN BY EXPERTS AT SEA, ON LAND AND IN AIR

Princeton Scientists on Ship in Mid-Pacific Lengthen View by Speeding With Shadow

PHOTO PLANE UP 5 MILES

Major Stevens and Aides Take Movies and Stills in 4-Hour Flight Above Peru

A NEW STAR REPORTED

Phenomenon Frightens Indians—Astronomers on Canton Island Get Rare Pictures

Dr. JOHN Q. STEWART,
Member of the Staff of Princeton University
By The Associated Press.

ABOARD S. S. STEELMAKER IN MID-PACIFIC, June 8.—The eclipse was viewed successfully from this ship today for the entire duration of seven minutes, six seconds. An unidentified faint star was sighted near the sun by a member of the crew.

The star was reported by Mate Greene about three degrees west of the sun, while astronomers and members of the crew were viewing the eclipse.

Numerous photographs of the spectacle were made by Dr. James Stokley of the Franklin Institute and will be developed when the expedition returns to New York.

At the height of the eclipse, the inner corona was very narrow, and at least seven distinct streamers started out, it seemed, from the very edge of the moon. The longest, to the northwest, seemed about two diameters of the sun in extent, and there was another long streamer to the southwest.

All thirty-six persons aboard the Steelmaker saw the longest modern eclipse at practically its maximum point, 1,000 miles southwest of Honolulu.

Weather Conditions Fine

Weather conditions were fine but not perfect. Cumulus clouds ringed the horizon and much of the sky was slightly hazed by a thin, high alto cirrus cloud formation. Consequently illumination was brighter than we had hoped.

We needed no flashlights and could read newspapers easily. Only stars and planets of the first magnitude, including Venus, Mercury and Rigel, could be seen.

The sky near the corona was dark blue, the same color as the sea. The motion of the moon's shadow in the east was conspicuous in the twilight zone beyond it. As totality ended, the dark blue shadow could be seen receding down the eastern sky.

Dr. Stokley, who measured the brightness of the corona by the Macbeth illumination meter, made a preliminary estimate that the total brightness was, perhaps, twice that of a full moon.

The theoretical time of the total eclipse was 7 minutes 2 seconds, but an additional four-second observation was obtained by the eight-knot eastern speed of the Steelmaker, which kept the ship in the shadow cast by the moon more than a half hour.

The time of totality was 11:27 to 11:34 A. M. ship time, or 4:27 to 4:34 P. M. Eastern daylight time. The longitude was 133.40 West and the latitude 9.49 North.

Plane 5 Miles Up Gets Photos

By CAPTAIN C. R. DISHER

Copyright, 1937, by The New York Times Company and the North American Newspaper Alliance, Inc.

LIMA, Peru, June 8.—In a flight career of more than a decade I have had many a wonderful experience—seen many a sight far beyond my powers of description. But the magnificent adventure those of us in the Pan American-Grace flying observatory had this afternoon while making a photographic record of the solar eclipse from a point five miles above the coastal plain of Peru undoubtedly tops them all.

Aboard our Douglas airliner Santa Silvia, as we lifted off Limatambo Airport at 3:30 P. M., Eastern daylight time, were myself, E. W. Gray, Pan American-Grace copilot and radio operator; Major Albert W. Stevens, assigned to our observatory by the American Museum of Natural History, and J. W. Runcie of Lima, known as one of the best photographers on the West Coast of South America.

Climb to 14,000 Feet

Climbing steadily toward the northward, we reached 14,000 feet over Huarmey at 4:45. Passing back into the rear compartment while Gray took the controls, I found Major Stevens and Runcie puttering about their cameras, taping up every possible crack that might permit light leaks. Stevens, like a mother with a delicate child,

Continued on Page Fourteen

Birth Control Is Accepted By American Medical Body

Association Backs Doctors in Use of 'Legal Rights' on Contraceptive Advice—Hearing Today on Public Health Issue

By WILLIAM L. LAURENCE
Special to THE NEW YORK TIMES.

ATLANTIC CITY, June 8.—After a struggle of many years birth control received its first official recognition here today from the American Medical Association, which represents organized medicine in the United States.

The association's house of delegates, supreme court of American medicine, meeting during the association's eighty-eighth annual assembly here this week, adopted today the report of its committee to study contraceptive practices, appointed two years ago, which recommends that the American Medical Association officially approve birth control as having a definite place in medical practice.

The house of delegates adopted two far-reaching recommendations of the committee—first, that the American Medical Association investigate the various forms of contraception with a view to disseminating authoritative information on the subject to the medical profession, and second, that the association promote the teaching of proper methods of birth control in the medical schools.

The action marks another landmark in the 'annals of American medicine. For many years all efforts to gain official status for birth control, as a legitimate part of medical practice, have been bitterly fought and successfully blocked by powerful groups, religious and otherwise, within the ranks of American medicine.

With the settlement of this issue the house of delegates settled down to give further consideration to the most important problem facing American medicine today, whether to give official recognition to the principle, introduced in a resolution yesterday by the Medical Society of the State of New York, that "the health of the people is the direct concern of government and that a national health policy directed toward all groups of the population be formulated."

This resolution, the adoption of which would mark a distinct turning point in American medical practice, was referred back to committee at the meeting of the house of delegates this afternoon. It will be acted upon at the scheduled meeting Thursday morning.

Meantime, there was evidence of much heated discussion behind the scenes. Tomorrow an all-day "public" hearing will be held by the committee, at which every member

Continued on Page Twenty-six

REBELS OPEN DRIVE IN CORDOBA REGION

Casualties Heavy in Vigorous Attack Near Penarroya That Aims at Mercury Mines

LOYALISTS GAIN IN NORTH

Advance 3 Miles on Asturian Front—Bilbao Zone Quiet—Madrid Bares 'Spy Ring'

By HERBERT L. MATTHEWS
Wireless to THE NEW YORK TIMES.

MADRID, June 8.—The Insurgents launched what appears to be one of the major offensives of the war on the Cordoba front today while Madrid cleaned up after the most severe night bombardment it has yet experienced.

Few details about the Rebel offensive are available, except that it has been launched against government positions on the heights above Penarroya and that it is accompanied by an extremely heavy concentration of men and materials. Thirty-five Insurgent planes bombed the government positions as a prelude to an attack that, it is understood, culminated in fierce hand-to-hand fighting—a relatively rare thing in this war.

Reports from Andujar admit heavy casualties, but they assert that the Rebels suffered more than the Loyalists.

New Struggle for Mines

The struggle for Pozoblanco and the Almaden mercury mines therefore enters a new phase. It will be recalled that all Winter the Insurgents drove hard, at first with some success, against Pozoblanco, getting almost to the edge of the town. Then in March the government launched a counter-offensive, which for a while gave evidence of being the most successful drive on the Loyalist side since the war started.

The government's extreme right wing took Blasquez, while the center drove almost to Fuenteovejuna and Penarroya and the left wing all but succeeded in capturing Villaharte and Ovejo. In fact, there was steady progress until the end of April, when the drive petered out for a reason that has been all too common in this "poor man's war"—a lack of materials.

Loyalists Kept Positions

However, the government held its advance positions and it was the understanding here that preparations were being made for a resumption of the offensive soon on an even heavier scale. The Rebel attack, therefore, seems to be an effort to forestall the Loyalists with a counter-offensive or else just an attempt to prevent the government drive. From the amount of material the Insurgents are using it appears tonight to be an important offensive, but it will take a few days for one to be sure.

Last night's bombardment here was unusually terrifying, for it was directed not only against the usual central areas but also against the neutral and diplomatic zones, including the United States Embassy street, which received four shells. It is officially estimated that about 1,000 shells poured into the city be-

Continued on Page Eighteen

HITLER DEFENDER NOW ATTACKS HIM

Macfarland Charges Leader Broke 1933 Promises to Him to Respect Religion

CHURCH BODY ALSO ACTS

Council Holds the Nazis Show 'Hostility' to Christians by Barring World Parley

Text of Dr. Macfarland's letter will be found on Page 16.

The Rev. Charles S. Macfarland, venerable American churchman, who wrote a book in 1934 disapproving the boycott of Nazi goods and urging Americans to give Chancellor Hitler the benefit of the doubt in his attitude toward the German churches, made public yesterday a scathing indictment of the German Fuehrer, comparing him with Herod in his persecution and despoliation of the Jews, and denouncing him for undermining the basic ideal of Christianity.

The Federal Council of the Churches of Christ in America, of which Dr. Macfarland is general secretary emeritus, simultaneously issued a resolution adopted by its executive committee last week declaring that the Nazi government's ban against German delegates attending the World Conference of the Churches on Church, State and Society in Oxford next month was proof of its hostility to the Christian church.

Both statements emphasized the "broken" promises on the religious question given by Chancellor Hitler early in his régime, which the resolution held were responsible for many Germans accepting the Nazi régime. Dr. Macfarland, who conferred and corresponded with Chancellor Hitler, declared that the Nazi leader had violated every assurance made to him on the church problem.

Dr. Macfarland's attack on the Nazi government was made in the form of an "open letter" to Chancellor Hitler, which he explained was written in his personal capacity and not as a representative of the Federal Council. The letter was mailed on the Europa a week ago, to be sent by airmail to Berlin. Publication was deferred to allow time for it to reach the Chancellor.

Taxes Hitler With Seizing Church

He accused the German Chancellor of seizing control of the church, arresting multitudes of pastors, imprisoning many and allowing unrebuked attacks on some.

The writer emphasized his background of more than thirty-five years of friendship for Germany and his study of the religious situation there at Hitler's invitation late in 1933, which resulted in the book published the next year under the title, "The New Church and the New Germany: A Study of Church and State." As a young man Dr. Macfarland studied in Germany. Since then he has made frequent trips there and has lectured at the University of Berlin on many occasions.

The resolution of the Federal Council represents twenty-three denominations. The Federal Council is the American section of the

Continued on Page Sixteen

WAGNER WON'T RUN AGAINST THE MAYOR, FRIENDS HERE SAY

Desire to Stay in Senate and Friendship With La Guardia Given as Reasons

MOVE TO DRAFT HIM GAINS

He Will Be Subject to Severest Pressure as the One Man Held Certain of Winning

Senator Robert F. Wagner, virtually the unanimous first choice of the party leaders for the Democratic nomination for Mayor, will not run against Mayor La Guardia in any circumstances, according to close friends here.

Two reasons are given for Senator Wagner's unwillingness to enter the Mayoralty race: First, because he wants to continue as Senator, a post he regards as the highest in his reach because of his German birth; and, second, because of his personal friendship with the Mayor, with many of whose views he is in accord.

Of course, Senator Wagner's reported unwillingness to run for Mayor will not end the movement to draft him, which has spread rapidly during the last few days. He is the one candidate upon whom James J. Dooling, leader of Tammany; Frank V. Kelly, Brooklyn leader, and Secretary of State Edward J. Flynn of the Bronx and the other county leaders can unite, and the one candidate regarded as certain to defeat Mayor La Guardia.

Pressure to Be Brought

That Senator Wagner will be subject to the severest kind of pressure to run during the next two weeks is certain. He will be told that his candidacy is almost a life and death proposition for Tammany and will be urged to sacrifice his personal inclinations for the good of the organization.

Word of Senator Wagner's unwillingness to leave his Senate seat for the chance of occupying the Mayor's chair at City Hall was received here as the boom for him was gaining headway, as shown by the remarks of Tammany district leaders who gathered at Tammany Hall for the regular appearance of Mr. Dooling. It received further impetus when Samuel Untermyer, who called upon Mr. Dooling to discuss the Mayoralty situation, spoke approvingly of Senator Wagner as a possible candidate, but expressed doubt that the Senator would accept the nomination.

Neither Mr. Dooling nor Mr. Untermyer would discuss their conversation, Mr. Dooling saying that he was "on the receiving end." Talk of the possibility of nominating Borough President Samuel Levy, Tammany's only Jewish candidate, revived after Mr. Untermyer's visit.

Sees Hard Fight for Party

After his call on the Tammany chieftain, Mr. Untermyer expressed the opinion that the Democratic party had a hard fight ahead and that Mayor La Guardia might be a hard man to beat.

"Of course, Senator Wagner could beat him," Mr. Untermyer added. Mr. Untermyer added that he might go to Washington soon and would see Senator Wagner.

Mr. Dooling said that he knew that the movement to nominate Senator Wagner was growing. He added that he expected to see Sen-

Continued on Page Twenty-six

Puerto Ricans Fire Shots at Judge Cooper Soon After 8 Nationalists Go to U. S. Prison

Special Cable to THE NEW YORK TIMES.

SAN JUAN, Puerto Rico, June 8.—Three or four unidentified men fired more than a dozen shots at United States District Judge Robert A. Cooper late this afternoon less than eighteen hours after Pedro Albizu Campos and his seven Nationalist party associates entered Atlanta prison to serve sentence of six to ten years for conspiracy to overthrow the United States Government in Puerto Rico.

Judge Cooper, a former Governor of South Carolina and former Governor of the Federal Farm Loan Board, tried and sentenced the Nationalists.

The shots went wild and Judge Cooper was not injured. One bullet pierced the windshield of his car, barely missing Detective Francisco Davila who since the Nationalists' trial has been Judge Cooper's bodyguard.

The shooting occurred at the entrance to the Condado residential district just after Judge Cooper's car passed over the Dos Hermanos bridge. Beside the unoccupied home of Colonel Sosthenes Behn the judge said he saw a public car with three or four men about it, seemingly trying to start it.

As the Cooper car passed, the motor of the public car started and pistol firing commenced almost simultaneously. The judge said he believed two and possibly three pistols were fired at the same time and that there were twelve to fifteen shots.

Detective Davila, who was riding in the front seat while Judge Cooper was in the rear, said his only thought was to save the judge and instead of returning the fire he covered the judge as he leaned forward in his seat.

Acting Governor Rafael Menendez Ramos, Police Chief Enrique de Orbetta and Robert Thompson, a Federal agent who was recently stationed here, quickly joined Judge Cooper at his home.

The Acting Governor and others connect the attack on Judge Cooper with the departure of the Nationalists for prison and with the recent investigation by Arthur Garfield Hays of the Civil Liberties Union into the Palm Sunday killings at Ponce. The Acting Governor said he had complained to Dr. Ernest Gruening, Director of the Interior Department Division of Territories and Island Possessions, that Dr. Gruening and Secretary of the Interior Harold L. Ickes had been listed by the Civil Liberties Union as members of the organization to give a false appearance of government sanction for disturbing influences.

STRIPPED OF CLUBS

Moves by the Mahoning Valley Sheriffs Start Minor Violence

MILL GATES ARE CRASHED

Two Republic Watchmen Are Beaten at the Company's Plant in Youngstown

NEW DEPUTIES ATTACKED

Steel Strikers Threaten March on Jail to Free Three Men Held There

By F. RAYMOND DANIELL
Special to THE NEW YORK TIMES.

YOUNGSTOWN, Ohio, June 8.—Bitterness, smoldering for nearly two weeks like the banked furnaces of the steel mills made idle by a strike of C. I. O. workers against independent steel companies, flared today in minor outbreaks of violence as the Sheriffs of two Mahoning Valley counties acted simultaneously to disarm the pickets around the plants.

At Massillon, Ohio, according to an announcement of the Republic Steel Corporation, a mob of fifty pickets broke through a company gate and beat up two watchmen, injuring one seriously, before it was driven off. Here in Youngstown three men were arrested for participating in an attack on twelve deputies as they were buying uniforms in a downtown store.

The deputies were attacked by a mob of more than 250 as they came out of the store to which they had been sent by Sheriff Ralph Elser, who was busy all day swearing in husky young men to help him enforce his order to the pickets to comply with the law against carrying weapons. A carload of city police and two truckloads of deputies were rushed to the scene of the mêlée.

Attack on Jail Proposed

They succeeded in dispersing the mob and arresting three men accused of taking part in the attack, but not until four of the deputies who were the objects of the attack had been beaten up, though not severely. The Sheriff declined to let newspaper men see the victims or release their names. He gave the names of his three prisoners as Frank Komack, Pat Prechok and Fred Fortunato.

A report was received at the Sheriff's office from a member of the rescue party that as the crowd dispersed a man shouted to the mob urging every man to go home and get his gun and march upon the jail to deliver the prisoners.

Immediately the jail was surrounded by more than fifty uni-

Continued on Page Four

Republic Steel Tells Farley to Get Mail to Strike Mills or Face Suit

Formally Protests Refusal of Postmasters to Accept Any Food Packages in 'Irregular' Course—Department Refuses to Act—President Declines to Comment

By TURNER CATLEDGE
Special to THE NEW YORK TIMES.

WASHINGTON, June 8.—A formal protest against the refusal of postoffice officials to accept food and other shipments for delivery in strike-bound steel plants of the Middle West was addressed to Postmaster General Farley today by the Republic Steel Corporation. It failed, however, to alter the administration in its course of non-intervention in the labor disputes, this policy going to the extent of denying as "irregular" mail deliveries which under ordinary circumstances might be termed "regular."

The corporation's complaint was made in a letter to Mr. Farley, signed by John S. Brookes Jr., member of the executive committee and the board of directors and counsel. Unless the Postmaster General ordered the postmasters at Niles and Warren, Ohio, to accept parcels for delivery to the Republic plants, the letter asserted, "we shall feel compelled to take such legal steps as may be available to us in the premises."

The letter said, in effect, that if the Postoffice Department was afraid to send its mailmen into the plants for fear of violence, the corporation was ready to be deputized by the department to make the deliveries and would place both means of transportation and personnel at its service.

The department maintained the position that it would not make "irregular" deliveries to the plants, whether they were on regular routes or not. Officials said that certain articles, such as foodstuffs and clothing addressed to the men in the strike-bound plants, which would be accepted for delivery and would be within the definition "regular" under normal conditions might in emergencies such as the steel strike become "irregular."

Similar articles have been refused in the past, officials said. They mentioned cases during the recent floods and also in other labor disturbances. Primary discretion as to what will or will not be accepted for delivery is left to the postmaster at the scene.

Replying specifically to the steel company's proffer of facilities for handling the mails if it should be deputized, officials said there was

Continued on Page Two

CITY SUBWAY UNION SEEKS CLOSED SHOP

Taking Mayor at His Word, Independent Employes Will Prepare Demands Tonight

EXECUTIVES GET PAY RISE

Board Lists Salary Increases—B. M. T. Head Is Ready to Discuss Workers' Vote

Mayor La Guardia's declaration on Sunday in favor of the closed shop rebounded yesterday when the Transport Workers Union, C. I. O. affiliate, announced that it would meet tonight to formulate demands for a closed shop on the city's own Independent Subway System.

The union, which claims 3,500 of the 4,000 employes of the city system, has already achieved a closed shop agreement with the Interborough as a result of the changed labor policy of that company. Its recent demands for an election on the city system in which the employes could designate a union to represent them in collective bargaining have been ignored. An election of individual representatives was held in January.

The union made no mention of the Mayor's recent pronouncement, simply announcing that the meeting would be held tonight at the union headquarters at 153 West Sixty-fourth Street "in preparation for a campaign of action to obtain a closed-shop agreement on the Independent System."

Concession from B. M. T.

Meanwhile, the union won what appeared to be a substantial concession from the B. M. T. management when William S. Menden, head of that system, made public a letter to the Transport Workers Union setting forth the company's willingness to discuss an employe vote on a bargaining agency at any convenient time.

Mr. Menden's letter to Douglas L. MacMahon, business agent of the union, said:

"Under the Doyle-Neustein act recently passed by the Legislature and signed by the Governor, and effective July 1, 1937, provision is made for the secret election of representatives of the employes in an election supervised by the Labor Relations Board of the State of New York. The act further provides that the board shall determine the appropriate unit for the purpose of collective bargaining, which unit shall be either the employer unit, craft unit, plant unit or any other unit determined by the board to insure to the employes the full benefit of their right to collective bargaining.

"If the employes of the various companies wish to change the representatives elected in December, 1936, by an election pursuant to this

Continued on Page Two

STRIKE THREATENS CANNED FOOD TIE-UP

75 General Warehouses Forced to Close Doors as Result of Teamsters' Walkout

COMPROMISE IS REJECTED

Strike May Spread to Ranks of Longshoremen—Crisis in Situation Due Today

New York City's supply of canned and cold storage food is in danger of being shut off by a teamster strike which began on Monday and threatened yesterday to spread to the longshoremen.

Demanding higher wages and shorter hours, the International Brotherhood of Teamsters, Local 818, called the strike against the Warehousemen's Association of the Port of New York. The union asked for recognition, a 40-hour week and wages of $36 a week for laborers and $37 for checkers.

Union spokesmen declared that warehouses were paying $16, $17, $20 and $28 a week, and that after the union submitted a contract, the employers proposed a substitute contract that was unacceptable.

Concedes 1,000 Walked Out

The union contends that between 1,800 and 2,000 men involving 150 general warehouses refused to work, and that no food products were moving to and from those warehouses. The warehousemen conceded that about 1,000 men walked out and caused seventy-five general warehouses to close their doors.

The Warehousemen's Association, through its president, E. W. Forbes of Baker & Williams Bonded & Free Warehouses, Inc., and other spokesmen, pointed out that the warehouses already were paying an average of $25 a week to the teamsters as against an average of $21 paid by Philadelphia warehouses.

They maintained that if they paid the wages demanded by the union they could no longer hope to compete with Philadelphia, Boston and other rival ports. The Warehousemen's Association offered $30 a week and a 44-hour week to the employes of the general warehouses.

Countering the demands of the union for a 40-hour week and $40 a week for the cold-storage warehouse employes, the Warehousemen's Association offered a contract providing for a 44-hour week and $34 a week. The warehousemen insist that it would be out of the question to meet the union's demand for $40 a week for cold storage employes.

Crisis Is Expected Today

The Warehousemen's Association estimates that about 1,000 men are involved in the dispute with the cold-storage warehouses which may reach a crisis today. According to

Continued on Page Two

MURPHY BARS AID

Mayor Seeks to Enlist Men With Military Experience

PLANT TO OPEN TOMORROW

City Officials Are Warned of Invasion by 5,000 C. I. O. Men to 'Seal' Mill

WORKERS VOTE TO RETURN

Straw Ballot Shows 1,331 Republic Men Want to Work, and Only 20 Do Not

Day's Strike Developments

Monroe (Mich.) Mayor called for volunteers to help reopen the Republic Steel plant there. Page 1.

Mahoning Valley Sheriffs and Youngstown Mayor ordered steel pickets to disarm. Three were held for attack on deputies. Page 1.

The eighth victim of the Memorial Day steel riot died in Chicago, as C. I. O. invoked the Wagner Act. Page 2.

Republic Steel Corporation called upon the Postoffice Department to accept food and other mail parcels for its strikebound plants. Page 1.

In Detroit strikes called by the U. A. W. A. closed the Budd Wheel Company and Ternstedt Manufacturing Company plants. Page 3.

At Waukegan thirty-nine C. I. O. sit-downers in the Fansteel factory were fined and jailed. A La Follette agent was declared in contempt. Page 3.

Lansing was tied up a second day when A. F. of L. building workers followed the C. I. O. automobile employes and declared a work holiday. Page 3.

Teamsters' strike here may spread to longshoremen and tie up canned goods and cold storage supplies. Page 1.

The Transport Workers Union here will plan tonight for demanding a closed shop on the Independent subway system. Page 1.

Monroe Organizes Defense

Special to THE NEW YORK TIMES.

MONROE, Mich., June 8.—In preparation for the first showdown in the struggle between the Republic Steel Corporation and the C. I. O., Mayor Daniel A. Knaggs issued a call tonight for civilians with military experience to enlist as special policemen to permit the Newton Steel Company, a Republic subsidiary, to reopen its strike-closed plant Thursday morning.

Mayor Knaggs issued the call by telephone from Lansing, where Governor Frank Murphy informed him that the State would not intervene "unless local resources are exhausted."

Hurrying home to what he described as "this town of twenty-thousand American citizens," Mayor Knaggs said he expected that several hundred volunteers would be sworn in as special policemen tomorrow. They will reinforce the twenty regular policemen and twenty-two Sheriff's deputies here.

The Mayor's call was made in the face of what he termed "threats" that from 5,000 to 10,000 C. I. O. automobile workers and sympathizers were going to flock here from Detroit and Toledo.

A few hours after his call was issued, the Mayor said, offers poured in from all parts of the community.

"There seems to be no age limit to the volunteers," he said. "Offers have been made by youths and by men 70 or 75 years old."

Hints at Use of Deer Guns

Asked if the special policemen would be armed, the Mayor answered that they would be, but he and his police chief, Jesse Fisher, had not decided what kind of arms with which the extra men would be equipped.

He added significantly that "this is a great deer hunting country," and a large number of citizens have firearms for hunting.

The Mayor explained that a straw vote had been taken among the 1,351 workers at the Newton plant, and it showed that 1,331 wished to

Continued on Page Four

"All the News That's Fit to Print."

The New York Times.

LATE CITY EDITION
Showers early, generally fair and warmer today. Tomorrow generally fair, possibly thunder showers.
Temperatures Yesterday—Max., 76; Min., 64

Copyright, 1937, by The New York Times Company.

VOL. LXXXVI.....No. 29,015. Entered as Second-Class Matter, Postoffice, New York, N. Y. NEW YORK, SATURDAY, JULY 3, 1937. PP TWO CENTS In New York City. | THREE CENTS Within 200 Miles. | FOUR CENTS Elsewhere Except in 7th and 8th Postal Zones.

PHILADELPHIA DRIVERS STRIKE IN A.F.L. HOLIDAY AGAINST C.I.O.; BITTER LABOR ROW IN HOUSE

ALL TRUCKS HALT

Newspapers Suspend as the Strike Brings City Near Paralysis

MILK SHORTAGE IS FEARED

Mayor Ready to Add 10,000 Police—Other A. F. L. Groups Uphold Contracts

TAXI MEN REFUSE TO QUIT

C. I. O. Pacts Signed by Two Bakeries Cause Issue—NLRB Elections Demanded

Day's Strike Developments

Teamsters' council called a "holiday" for 25,000 drivers, halting the movement of food, freight, merchandise and newspapers in Philadelphia. Page 1.

Republic Steel mills at Massillon, Ohio, were reopened under protection of National Guardsmen. Page 6.

Johnstown remained quiet on eve of tomorrow's strike rally while Mayor and State police prepare for gathering of 40,000. Page 6.

A bitter attack by Representative Cox on Representative Maverick as defender of C. I. O. was vigorously applauded in the House. Page 1.

Members of Senate Civil Liberties Committee saw pictures of Chicago Memorial Day strike riot. Page 5.

Third Avenue system signed C. I. O. contract covering bus and trolley operators. Pay rises and preferential shop granted. Page 11.

Labor War in Philadelphia

Special to The New York Times.

PHILADELPHIA, July 2.—A "general holiday" of 25,000 American Federation of Labor truckmen, called in a test of strength with the C. I. O., brought business activity in Philadelphia and its surrounding area to the edge of paralysis tonight.

The immediate occasion of the "holiday" was what the A. F. of L. leaders called an "invasion" of the truck union field by the C. I. O. through the signing of contracts with the Ward and Freihofer Baking Companies after the expiration of A. F. of L. contracts Wednesday night.

Eight hours after the "holiday" began at 2 P. M. today, virtually all deliveries were suspended. In the commission market district of the city between $1,500,000 and $2,000,000 worth of foodstuffs lay in warehouses, with little probability that they would be distributed before much of them spoil.

This evening at least a temporary milk shortage threatened. A statement by the Joint Teamsters Council, A. F. of L. organization which controls almost all the Philadelphia truckmen, promised that emergency milk and bread deliveries would be made tomorrow.

But parents who feared their children might go without food had bought up a large part of the milk supply immediately available.

Newspapers Suspend

At 10:30 this evening, after a conference of the publishers of all Philadelphia newspapers, it was agreed to suspend publication in line with the suggestion of Mayor Wilson "in order not to endanger the lives of citizens or policemen."

Conferences of the publishers were held in the office of Robert McLean, publisher of The Evening Bulletin, and the announcement was made after first editions of morning newspapers had been printed, though not generally distributed, because of the lack of trucks.

The suspension of publication, it was announced, will be indefinite. The Philadelphia newspapers affected are The Bulletin, The Daily News and The Evening Ledger, evening publications, and The Inquirer and The Record, morning newspapers. Their total circulation is about 1,500,000 copies. In Camden, N. J., The Camden Post and The Camden Evening Courier also suspended.

A statement released by the publishers and broadcast through radio stations and news services not affected by the "holiday" said that

Continued on Page Five

Cox Assails Maverick on the C.I.O. Amid Cheers of Representatives

Georgian Calls Texan More of a Buffoon Than a Public Servant and Asks if He Favors 'Terrorism'—Latter Angrily Defends Lewis and Warns 'Hysteria' Brought on Civil War

Special to The New York Times.

WASHINGTON, July 2.—Supporters and opponents of the C. I. O. labor movement staged the bitterest debate of the session in the House today and suggestions were made that fist fights would result unless "these insulting remarks" were discontinued.

Representatives Maverick of Texas and Cox of Georgia were principals in the tussle, aided by Representatives Hill of Washington and Hoffman of Michigan.

After Mr. Maverick had answered Mr. Cox's speech of Wednesday attacking the C. I. O. movement as one which, if not halted, might plunge the country into civil war, the Georgia Representative took the floor for a speech in which language he used was bitterly objected to by Mr. Maverick.

The House, however, on a demand for a determination of the matter by Mr. Maverick, overwhelmingly voted to leave intact in the record Mr. Cox's words describing the Texan as "more interested in provoking amusement by his extravagance and buffoonery than in molding sound public sentiment."

In a parliamentary move rarely resorted to, Mr. Maverick had demanded that "the gentleman's words be taken down," after which it becomes the privilege of the House to determine whether the member's words reflect upon the integrity, character or standing of the offended colleague.

After the House, by a voice vote, had backed Mr. Cox, Mr. Maverick shouted that "a quorum is not present—they can put this on record if they want to." But Mr. Maverick withdrew his point of no quorum after Speaker Bankhead, striving to maintain order and enforce the rules, had observed that there obviously was no quorum present.

Mr. Maverick had defended the C. I. O. movement and had asserted Mr. Cox was "one of those" who sought to oppose the President in some points of his program.

"I want to think better than well of the gentleman (Mr. Maverick)," Mr. Cox said in reply. "However, it would be difficult for me to esteem him as highly as he might wish. I do want to believe, Mr. Speaker, that the gentleman loves his government and would not willingly lend himself as an instrument to its overthrow."

Quoting Andrew Jackson's words, "Our Federal Union, it must be preserved," Mr. Cox continued:

"Then I want him (Mr. Maverick) to join with me in asking the ques-

Continued on Page Six

NEW COURT BILL OFFERED IN SENATE TO END CONFLICT

Leaders Abandon President's Program in Effort to Save Him From Defeat

RETIRING AGE SET AT 75

Measure Limits Appointments to One a Year—Opponents Reject Compromise

The text of the new Court Bill will be found on Page 4.

By TURNER CATLEDGE

Special to The New York Times.

WASHINGTON, July 2.—A substitute court bill, providing an addition of one justice a year to the Supreme Court to supplement those passing 75 years of age and refusing to retire, was introduced in the Senate today by Senate leaders, formally abandoning the President's original program.

It was presented by Senator Logan in the name of himself and Senators Ashurst and Hatch, but it represented the results of three weeks or more of negotiations by Senator Robinson, which he started when President Roosevelt gave him full authority to salvage what he could out of his judiciary reorganization plan and end the five-month controversy over the issue.

At the same time it started a drive to win such a compromise as might save Mr. Roosevelt from utter defeat on this most bitterly contested of all his measures to date.

Friends and foes of the proposal to enlarge the Supreme Court by the immediate addition of six new justices to replace or supplement those over 70½ years of age agreed that the new bill would be passed by a comfortable majority if it should ever reach a vote in the Senate.

This left a large "if," however, for opponents of the original six-justice bill vowed anew their determination to fight any increase in the membership of the high tribunal and boasted that they would filibuster for weeks to prevent the compromise plan from coming to a vote in the Senate.

Fighting "On Principle"

They said they were fighting the bill on a matter of principle, and that the principle was the same whether it increased the court by one or a dozen, if to increase it was to attempt to interfere with its line of decisions.

Whether the court-enlargement foes would attempt to make good on their threat, or whether, if they did, the administration leaders would try to ride out a filibuster were other unknown quantities in the equation. Any definite forecast of what might happen was, therefore, impossible.

The substitute bill will be brought up early next week, according to present plans. It may be debated for several days, possibly two or three weeks, without any suggestion of obstructionist tactics.

Should a filibuster then develop, however, it would be for the Senate leaders to determine whether they would attempt to ride it out, which most observers agreed they could do if they were willing to stay in session indefinitely, or whether, in the interest of early adjournment and greater harmony in the Democratic party, it would be better to postpone the matter indefinitely and recommit the bill to the Judiciary Committee for further study.

In view of all the circumstances

Continued on Page Four

SOVIET WITHDRAWS FORCE FROM AMUR AT SCENE OF FIGHT

Japanese-Manchukuoan Guard Also Gone, So Danger of New Clash Is Removed

PARLEYS WILL FIX BORDER

Tokyo Hails the Settlement as Evidence That Recent Purge Weakened Moscow

By HAROLD DENNY

Wireless to The New York Times.

MOSCOW, Saturday, July 3.—The Commissariat of Defense issued an order early today for the withdrawal of Soviet armed patrols and naval cutters from Amur River islands, the ownership of which is in dispute between the Soviet Union and Japanese-controlled Manchukuo.

The islands were the scene of recent fighting with losses to both Soviet and Japanese forces. The ownership of the contested land will be determined by future negotiations.

Thus another threatening Far Eastern crisis appears to have blown over. The Soviet's order for withdrawal of its forces followed a half-hour conference at the Foreign Office late last night between Foreign Commissar Maxim Litvinoff and Mamoru Shigemitsu, the Japanese Ambassador, at which the envoy informed the Commissar that he had received telegraphic information from Tokyo that Japanese-Manchukuoan cutters had been withdrawn from the islands. He added that he expected the Soviet naval land and air forces would be promptly withdrawn also.

Both Statements Agree

According to the Soviet Foreign Office communiqué, the content of which was in harmony with the Japanese Ambassador's account of the conversation, Mr. Litvinoff agreed that the Japanese-Manchukuoan withdrawal met the suggestion he had previously made, that both sides withdraw and take up the sovereignty issue later. He promised immediately to inform military authorities so they could give the necessary orders.

The communiqué then continued:

"To the Ambassador's question as to whether the withdrawal would establish the status quo ante Mr. Litvinoff answered affirmatively. Explaining it would restore the status quo of both parties laying claim to the islands, he said that after the restoration of order it would be possible to start to review those claims.

"The Ambassador agreed that in the future it would be possible to begin demarcation of the border line on the Amur. Mr. Litvinoff made clear that such demarcation would determine the possession of the islands by one or the other party."

Border Issue Is Difficult

The solution, though it seems to dispose of the immediate danger, leaves the basic question of the Amur boundary unsettled. There are indications that will be a knotty problem. In the past two years the Soviet Union and Japan made proposals and counter-proposals for demarcation commissions without approaching agreement. The Japanese insisted the commission should be composed of three members, a Soviet citizen, a Manchukuoan and a Japanese. To this the Soviet objected that it would be tantamount to giving Japan two representatives to the Soviet's one.

Japanese Embassy officials asserted before Mr. Shigemitsu's confer-

Continued on Page Two

PRIAL AND TAYLOR IN CONTROLLER RACE

Democrats Face Hard Fight in Primaries as Both Announce Candidacies in Day

LABOR COOL TO WAGNER

Party Reported to Be Loyal to La Guardia—Republicans Considering Smith

A primary fight for the Democratic nomination for Controller was indicated yesterday when former Deputy Controller Frank J. Prial announced his candidacy for that office and Controller Frank J. Taylor declared that he would be a candidate for re-election on his record.

Mr. Prial's announcement came just before the five Democratic county leaders, James J. Dooling, leader of Tammany; Frank V. Kelly of Brooklyn, Secretary of State Edward J. Flynn of the Bronx, James C. Sheridan of Queens and William T. Fetherston of Richmond, met in secret conference to prepare a slate for the Democratic city ticket. These five leaders were reported to be united on Senator Robert F. Wagner as the candidate for Mayor if he would consent to run.

There was no such unanimity on the candidate for Controller. Mr. Dooling was reported to favor the designation of Mr. Prial as the organization candidate in the interest of party harmony. Mr. Kelly was said to have insisted upon the designation of Controller Taylor. With agreement seemingly impossible, a bitter primary fight was in prospect with every indication that Mr. Prial would receive strong Tammany support.

The leaders made no definite decision. Mr. Sheridan insisted that the organization designate William F. Brunner, President of the Board of Aldermen, as its candidate for President of the new City Council.

Owen J. Brady, secretary of the Amalgamated Irish Societies, announced that this organization had sent a message to Mr. Dooling protesting against the nomination of Senator Wagner. The message read:

"Amalgamated Irish Societies of Greater New York strongly oppose nomination of Robert Wagner, consistent enemy of Irish race and leading advocate of American membership in League of Nations and World Court."

"I have decided to run for Controller," was Mr. Prial's laconic announcement, which he declined to amplify.

"Have you anything to add to this?" he was asked.

"No," he replied.

Mr. Taylor's declaration of his

Continued on Page Six

TREASURY DEFICIT IS $2,707,000,000 NET

Roosevelt Estimate In April Exceeded by $150,000,000 in Year-End Figures

DEBT ROSE $2,646,000,000

Receipts Up $1,178,000,000 —Outlay Exceeded Estimate by $220,000,000

Special to The New York Times.

WASHINGTON, July 2.—The government ended the fiscal year on June 30 with a net deficit of $2,707,000,000 and a gross public debt of $36,425,000,000, according to final figures made public today by Secretary Morgenthau. The deficit was about $150,000,000 more than estimated by President Roosevelt on April 20. The debt was an increase of $2,646,000,000 for the fiscal year.

General receipts will be $5,294,000,000, exceeding those for 1936 by $1,178,000,000, and about $70,000,000 more than estimated in April. Total expenditures exclusive of $104,000,000 for statutory debt retirement were $8,001,000,000, or about $220,000,000 over the April estimate.

In addition to the gross public debt, Secretary Morgenthau said, the government has certain contingent liabilities in guarantees as to principal and interest on outstanding obligations of the Reconstruction Finance Corporation, Federal Housing Administration and the Home Owners Loan Corporation amounting as of June 30 to about $4,725,000,000, as compared with a total of $4,750,000,000 on June 30, 1936.

$3,889,000,000 of Assets Held

On May 31 the government held net assets in loans and other investments of governmental corporations and credit agencies of about $3,889,000,000, a decrease of $406,000,000 from May 31, 1936, the reduction representing mainly net recoveries by the government.

Daniel W. Bell, Director of the Budget, said he felt the government would come very close to the forecasts of a balanced budget in the year 1938 if revenues held up to estimates and Congress did not place any further burdens on the Treasury. The earlier forecasts had been for a deficit in 1938 of about $400,000,000, which it was hoped could be wiped out by economies.

Should that objective substantially be attained, it was estimated, with receipts of around $1,000,000,000 from social security legislation about $600,000,000 of outstanding government securities could be retired in the year. There would be issued, however, a like amount of special government securities which would be a charge against the public debt. Actual reduction of the

Continued on Page Twenty-six

A. A. U. Declines Invitation to Germany; Religious Persecution Is Cited by Mahoney

Special to The New York Times.

MILWAUKEE, Wis., July 2.—In the first rebuff given to a foreign nation in the half century of its existence, the Amateur Athletic Union of the United States tonight declined to permit a track and field team to compete in Germany this Summer.

The decision was made by the combined executive and foreign relations committee and the vote was unanimous. That part of the tour by a ten-man team that took it to Sweden, the Netherlands and Hungary was approved, but the athletic invasion of the Reich was banned.

In announcing the move, President Jeremiah T. Mahoney said.

"This is consistent with the stand that I have always taken. I do not believe that our American athletes should go to a country where freedom of speech, religion and action have been abolished. Since I first started the fight to keep our fine young boys out of a land that persecuted the Jews, the Nazis have begun to attack and stifle Catholicism and Protestantism as well. Nazi ideology cannot conform with American democracy."

The same leaders who made the unsuccessful fight to keep the United States out of the Olympic Games last Summer were behind tonight's move with reinforcements from other quarters.

Judge Mahoney was the ex-officio chairman of the double committee meeting. Others there were Jack Rafferty of Houston, Texas; Charles L. Ornstein of New York, Louis Di Benedetto of New Orleans, George W. Graves of Detroit, John J. Magee of Bowdoin College, Daniel J. Ferris of New York, Raymond N. Sellon of Milwaukee, Ward Haylett of Kansas State College and Charles F. Hunter of San Francisco.

The Houston convention last December saw this group come back into power in A. A. U. affairs after the Avery Brundage forces had held control in the Olympic year.

Mr. Ferris, as secretary-treasurer of the world's largest sport governing body, cabled to other inviting countries that their bids had been approved and to Germany that her offer had been declined.

MISS EARHART FORCED DOWN AT SEA, HOWLAND ISLE FEARS; COAST GUARD BEGINS SEARCH

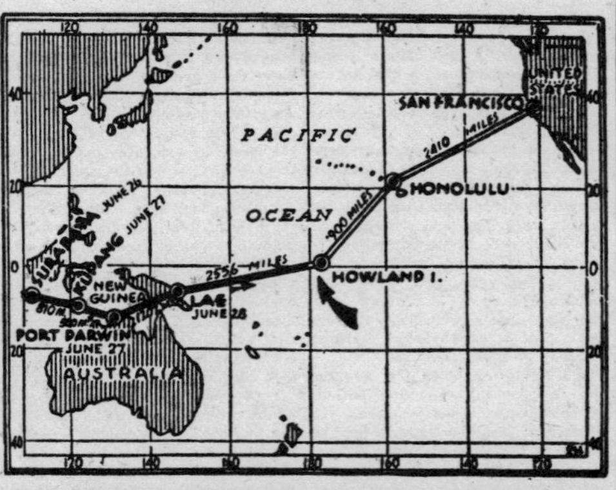

ROUTE OF EARHART PLANE IN PACIFIC

The flier took off from Lae, New Guinea, at 8 P. M., New York time, Thursday, and was in the vicinity of Howland Island at 4:43 P. M. Friday, when she was in communication with the Coast Guard cutter Itasca. She had intended to fly from this island to Honolulu and thence to the mainland for the completion of her world tour.

FUEL HAD RUN LOW

Fliers Were Near Goal When Last Reported but Saw No Land

PLANE EQUIPPED TO FLOAT

Has Sealed Gasoline Tanks and a Rubber Lifeboat for Emergency at Sea

RADIO BELIEVED HEARD

Los Angeles Amateurs Pick Up Weak Signals on Frequency Assigned to the Plane

By The Associated Press.

WASHINGTON, July 2.—Coast Guard headquarters was advised tonight that Amelia Earhart was believed to have alighted on the Pacific Ocean near Howland Island shortly after 5 P. M. Eastern daylight time today.

A message from the cutter Itasca, stationed in the vicinity of the island in the mid-Pacific, said:

"Earhart unreported at Howland at 7 P. M. [E. D. T.]. Believe down shortly after 5 P. M. Am searching probable area and will continue."

Admiral William D. Leahy, chief of naval operations, instructed the commandant of the naval station at Honolulu tonight to render whatever aid he may deem practicable in the search for Miss Earhart.

Plane Joins in Search

[A navy flying boat hopped off from Honolulu late last night for Howland Island, 1,900 miles distant, to join the cutter Itasca in hunting for Miss Earhart, The Associated Press reported. Two Los Angeles radio amateurs were said to have picked up weak signals on the frequency assigned to the Earhart radio.]

Coast Guard headquarters here received information that Miss Earhart probably overshot tiny Howland Island because she was blinded by the glare of an ascending sun. The message from the Coast Guard cutter Itasca said it was believed Miss Earhart passed northwest of Howland Island about 3:20 P. M. [E. D. T.], or about 8 A. M., Howland Island time. The Itasca reported that heavy smoke was bellowing from its funnels at the time, to serve as a signal for the flyer. The cutter's skipper expressed belief the Earhart plane had descended into the sea within 100 miles of Howland.

Husband Asks Assistance

In a message to Washington, the flier's husband, George Palmer Putnam, who is awaiting her return to this country at the Oakland, Calif., airport, said:

"Technicians familiar with Miss Earhart's plane believe, with its large tanks, it can float almost indefinitely. With retractable landing gear and smooth seas, safe landing (on the sea) should have been practicable.

"Request such assistance as is practicable from naval aircraft and surface craft stationed at Honolulu. Apparently plane's position not far from Howland.

"The plane's large wing and empty gasoline tanks should provide sufficient buoyancy if it came to rest on the sea without being damaged.

"There was a two-man rubber lifeboat aboard the plane, together with lifebelts, flares, a Very pistol and a large yellow signal kite which could be flown above the plane or the liferaft."

Mr. Putnam said his wife had planned to take emergency food rations and plenty of water on the hazardous flight, the most dangerous on her trip around the world.

Earlier the Coast Guard had ordered the cutter Roger B. Taney to proceed from Honolulu to Howland Island to aid the cutter Itasca in the search for Miss Earhart. A message from Honolulu, however, said the Taney was undergoing repairs and could not participate.

Amateurs Pick Up Signals

LOS ANGELES, July 2 (AP).—Two amateur radio operators claimed to have picked up signals tonight on frequencies officially assigned to the plane of Amelia Earhart.

Walter McMenamy said he picked up weak signals on 6210 kilocycles

Continued on Page Three

SOVIET 'LIQUIDATES' 120 MORE AS SPIES

Disclosure Indicates Others May Have Been Shot as the Agents of Estonia and Poland

AVIATOR IS AMONG THEM

Government Is Now Trying to Check Persecution of the Innocent in Campaign

Wireless to The New York Times.

MOSCOW, July 2.—The detection and "liquidation" of two large groups of alleged spies—one of seventy members, said to be in the service of Estonia, and the other of fifty to seventy members, said to be in the service of Poland—were disclosed today by Leonid Zakovsky, chief of the Leningrad district of the Commissariat of Internal Affairs [the secret police department].

Mr. Zakovsky received the Order of Lenin on June 26 for "self-sacrificing fulfilment of most important orders of the government." The nature of the orders was not disclosed.

The detection of these groups apparently occurred in the past year, although many members were accused of having carried on activities for many years. Mr. Zakovsky did not say in so many words that all these 120 or more had been shot, but the plain inference is that they were.

Gives Details on Seizures

Mr. Zakovsky's disclosures, giving far more details than usual in such cases, are contained in an article he wrote for Komsomolskaya Pravda, Young Communist newspaper, instructing youth on the necessity of being on guard against foreign spies who invidiously worm their way into confidences.

He said the alleged Estonian group was led by the son of a Kulak [individualist farmer] in the Leningrad region and that that leader after training by the Estonian General Staff, returned to Russia and installed a secret radio station in a forest in the Leningrad region. By that means, it is said, he received and sent code messages.

Gradually, he recruited bands of saboteurs and spies in villages, factories and even in the Red army, but at length he was caught with the radio in the forest, resisted and was shot by secret police officers.

Mr. Zakovsky declared the Polish Intelligence Service organized bands in White Russia who, on the outbreak of war, were to become "Polish partisan rioters" commanded by Polish officers who would arrive on Soviet soil a few days before the outbreak of war.

Among other instances of alleged spying there was the case of a Soviet military aviator, who, Mr. Zakovsky said, became involved with a woman whose husband was a foreign spy. The husband and wife, after gaining important military information from him, blackmailed him into becoming a full-fledged spy and finally into organizing within his squadron a sabotage group that put planes out of repair, causing a number of accidents. The aviator was discovered and shot.

Indications that authorities are trying to check the distortion of the hunt for "spies" and wreckers

Continued on Page Three

VALERA FAR AHEAD IN IRISH ELECTION

His Return to Power in Dail Seems Assured by Early Count in Free State

VOTE ON CHARTER CLOSE

Heavy Adverse Sentiment Is Indicated—Larkin, Labor Leader, Wins Seat

Special Cable to The New York Times.

DUBLIN, Irish Free State, July 3.—The first returns in the Free State general election received tonight indicate that the De Valera party, the Fianna Fail, is running ahead in many constituencies and the Cosgrave party faring badly.

Lord Mayor Alfred Byrne was the first candidate to gain election when he headed the poll in Northeast Dublin, far ahead of all other candidates. He received 12,068 votes. Next to him came Oscar Traynor, President Eamon de Valera's Minister for Posts and Telegraphs, with 9,693. The quota to insure election was 9,051.

Larkin Wins Seat

This constituency provided an election sensation when James Larkin, a labor leader, and once an inmate of Sing Sing prison in New York, won the third seat here by defeating General Richard Mulcahy, one of ex-President William Cosgrave's most effective front benchers. General Mulcahy was chief of staff of the Republican army during the fight against the British, and later was Minister for Defense in the Cosgrave administration. Subsequently he was a Minister in the local government. His defeat by Larkin is a big blow to the Cosgrave party.

Mr. de Valera easily headed the poll in Clare, where he was elected with 14,012 votes on the first count of a total of 63,000. This figure actually shows a decrease in de Valera's poll, compared to the 1933 election, when he received 18,000 votes of a total of 55,000. The decline is attributed to local dissensions over the selection of Fianna Fail candidates for this constituency.

In Cork City Mr. Cosgrave fared much worse than Mr. de Valera. Of a total of 53,019 votes the former President polled only 9,000-odd votes against the 14,863 he received in the 1933 election of a total of 68,000. Mr. Cosgrave headed the poll and was elected on the first count, but generally his party fared badly.

Results in Cork

His party's second candidate, Alderman William Desmond, polled only 2,008 and defeated the Labor candidate. On the other hand, the Fianna Fail held both its seats in Cork City with the return of Hugo Flinn, Parliamentary Secretary, and Thomas Dowdall. Already, before one-fourth of the results have been announced, the Cosgraveites have suffered two heavy defeats in Dublin and Cork.

In two other Dublin constituencies where results were available tonight the de Valera candidates headed the polls. Sean MacEntee, the Minister of Finance, was elected in Dublin Township on the first count with 10,124 votes.

Next to MacEntee came Cosgrave's former Attorney General, John Costello, with 8,418, who also was returned. In Dublin County

Continued on Page Two

"All the News That's Fit to Print."

The New York Times.

LATE CITY EDITION
Generally fair, continued warm today and tomorrow. Showers and cooler tomorrow night.
Temperatures Yesterday—Max., [illegible]; Min., [illegible]

Copyright, 1937, by The New York Times Company.

VOL. LXXXVI.....No. 29,035. Entered as Second-Class Matter, Postoffice, New York, N. Y. NEW YORK, FRIDAY, JULY 23, 1937. P TWO CENTS in New York City. | THREE CENTS Within 200 Miles. | FOUR CENTS Elsewhere Except in 7th and 8th Postal Zones.

TAMMANY NAMES COPELAND, SUPPORTING DOOLING 2 TO 1; PRIAL AND LEVY DESIGNATED

ALLIANCE WINS DAY

Former Foes of Leader Desert Whalen to Join in Fight on New Deal

SOME CHIEFS DEFIANT

Hines and Kenneally Break With Organization to Side With 4 County Heads

PRIMARY FIGHTS SURE

County and District Contests Foreseen—Court Bill Defeat a Factor in Outcome

By JAMES A. HAGERTY

The Tammany executive committee threw down the gauntlet last night to the Democratic leaders of the four other counties of the city and the Roosevelt administration and adopted a resolution designating United States Senator Royal S. Copeland as the Tammany candidate for the party nomination for Mayor by a vote of 15 11-12 to 8 5-12.

Included in the resolution were designations of former Deputy Controller Frank J. Prial as the Tammany candidate for Controller and Borough President Samuel Levy as the Tammany candidate for President of the Council.

The vote was on the adoption of the resolution and the negative votes were by those in favor of the designation of Grover A. Whalen for Mayor, Controller Frank J. Taylor for renomination and Max J. Schneider for President of the Council.

Victory for Dooling

The vote was a victory for James J. Dooling, ailing leader of Tammany, who failed to attend the meeting, his friends explaining that the condition of his health made it inadvisable.

The result of the meeting insured a lively Democratic primary fight, with indications that it might spread from a contest for nominations on the city ticket to become an issue in leadership fights in Assembly districts throughout the city.

James J. Hines, leader of the Eleventh Assembly District, who headed the group favoring the designation of Mr. Whalen and his running mates, said he intended to support Mr. Whalen and his running mates against the Tammany executive committee slate. William P. Kenneally, chairman of the executive committee, also said he would support Mr. Whalen in the primary election.

The opinion was expressed by supporters of Mr. Whalen that virtually all the members of the executive committee who voted against the designation of Senator Copeland would support Mr. Whalen in the primary.

Copeland Is Silent

When informed of the outcome by telephone at his Summer home at Suffern, N. Y., Senator Copeland declined to make any statement. He indicated, however, that he would have something to say this morning.

On being informed of the action of the Tammany executive committee, Mr. Whalen, as expected, declared that it meant a primary fight. He said:

"The regular Democratic ticket of Whalen, Taylor and Schneider was unanimously endorsed Tuesday by the executive committee of the Bronx, was unanimously endorsed today by the executive committee of Kings County and will be endorsed by the committees of Queens and Richmond as soon as, under their rules, they may convene.

"The fact that two opposition groups, hostile to each other in the New York County executive committee, had to combine in order to defeat a resolution endorsing Whalen, Taylor and Schneider and then by such a slim margin that four votes would have changed the result, is indicative of an overwhelming victory, particularly as the leaders in favor of the regular ticket represent more than 50 per cent of the enrolled Democrats in New York County.

"We will conduct an aggressive and clean campaign and confidently expect that after the primaries all Democrats will rally to the support of the Democratic nominees."

Informed of the action taken at Tammany Hall, Mr. Prial said:

"My candidacy for Controller in

Continued on Page Seven

Fusionists Name Steering Group To Aid La Guardia's Re-election

Seabury and Burlingham Head Committee to Seek Agreement on Other Candidates—Seven Are Selected for Executive Body—Resolutions Praise Mayor's Administration

The creation of a fusion steering committee, known as the Citizens Non-Partisan Committee, headed by Samuel Seabury and Charles C. Burlingham, to back the candidacy of Mayor La Guardia, was announced yesterday following a conference of Fusion leaders at the City Club, 55 West Forty-fourth Street.

The conference was attended by many who were present at similar conferences in 1933, when Fusion sought for the first time to elect Mayor La Guardia. Mr. Seabury almost automatically was chosen chairman and Mr. Burlingham was his first choice for membership on the executive committee he was authorized to name.

The purpose of the group will be to seek agreement on candidates for Controller and President of the City Council, and then, dividing into borough groups, seek satisfactory nominees for the various local offices.

The executive committee named by Mr. Seabury consisted of himself, ex officio; Mr. Burlington, William M. Calder, former United States Senator; Charles Evans Hughes Jr., former Solicitor General; George Z. Medalie, former Federal Attorney; Thomas D. Thacher, chairman of the Charter Revision Commission; Mrs. H. Edward Dreier and Charles H. Tuttle, former Federal Attorney. These were named from those who attended the conference. Mr. Seabury pointed out that he had power to name nine or more members on the executive committee, and that he intended to see to it that other groups were represented.

Others who attended the meeting were Richard S. Childs of the City Club, George Brokaw Compton, Maurice P. Davidson of the Progressive City Committee, Mrs. Louis I. Dublin, Mrs. William P. Earle Jr., Ben Howe, head of the city Fusion party; Bernard Katzen, Richard W. Lawrence, Oscar A. Lewis, Arthur

Continued on Page Seven

SHIPYARD PICKETS STONE POLICE AGAIN

Crowd Jeering Robins Workers Is Routed After Sergeant Is Cut in the Face

HEARING ON EARLIER CLASH

Mayor Orders Inquiry After the Strikers Tell of Beatings by Brooklyn Patrolmen

Violence flared out again yesterday in the shipyard strike in Brooklyn as Mayor La Guardia, on demand of the Industrial Union of Marine and Shipbuilding Workers, ordered an investigation of charges of police brutality against pickets at the Robins Drydock and Repair Company.

While the investigation was in progress at Brooklyn police headquarters during the afternoon, with Paul Blanshard, Commissioner of Accounts, representing the Mayor, more than 1,000 strikers and sympathizers staged their biggest mass picketing demonstration in front of the Robins plant at the foot of Dwight Street. As during the clash last Friday, they hurled stones at the police assembled at the plant in large numbers and bombarded with bricks and other missiles automobiles bearing workers to their homes under police escort.

Two Men Arrested

During the demonstration Sergeant Leo Russ of Mounted Squad 2 was severely cut in the face by a stone and an unidentified man and woman also were hurt. Two men were arrested for disorderly conduct. Earlier in the day three Robins employes on their way to work reported to the police that they had been attacked with stones by strikers in the vicinity of the plant.

The demonstration was intended to show the strikers' strength, with the company equally determined to continue operation. More than 800 of the plant's 1,400 employes reported for work yesterday. The picketing continued all day, reaching its climax at 4 P. M. as the workers inside the plant prepared to leave. Their emergence from the plant in automobiles escorted by motorcycle police was greeted by the pickets with cries of "scab," jeers and catcalls.

Police Break Up Crowd

Nearly 300 policemen, dozens of them stationed on near-by roofs, were alert against disorder. They did not interfere, however, until a stone hurled from the midst of the pickets struck Sergeant Russ. He jumped from his horse and dashed into the crowd, followed by twenty-five other policemen. At first the crowd did not give way, but soon fled in all directions. Sergeant Russ was treated at the Long Island College Hospital and then sent home.

Acting Police Commissioner Harold Fowler and Deputy Inspector George Bishop, in charge of Brooklyn police, were on the scene

Continued on Page Three

LUCANIA IS CLIMBED BY HARVARD PARTY

Highest Mountain Hitherto Unscaled in North America Is Conquered by 2 Men

PEAK TOWERS 17,150 FEET

Bradford Washburn Jr. of Cambridge and R. H. Bates of Philadelphia Reach Top

By The Associated Press.

VALDEZ, Alaska, July 22.—Conquest of Mount Lucania, highest mountain hitherto unclimbed in North America, was announced today by Bradford Washburn Jr. of Cambridge, Mass., and Robert H. Bates of Philadelphia, on their arrival here by plane from Burwash Landing in the Canadian Yukon.

The two youthful climbers said they attained the 17,150-foot high summit of Mount Lucania on July 9, planting there a special flag of the National Geographic Society.

Two days later they scaled near-by Mount Steele, 16,600 feet high, the second ascent of this peak, Mr. Washburn said.

Magnificent weather during both ascents enabled them to bring back a complete photographic record of the climbs. The expedition was sponsored by the Harvard Institute of Geographical Exploration and the New England Museum of Natural History.

The explorers said theirs was the first crossing on foot from Alaska to Canada over the Great Northern peaks of the St. Elias Range.

The exploration started June 18 when Pilot Robert Reeve of Valdez landed Mr. Bates and Mr. Washburn in a plane equipped with skis at a base camp on the surface of Walsh Glacier.

Glacier Surface Cracked

The surface of the glacier proved so badly cracked that Reeve was able to return only after three take-off attempts, and plans to fly in Russell Dow of Woodsville, N. H., and Norman Bright of Sunnyvale, N. H., to join the climbing party had to be abandoned.

Mr. Washburn said that the pair at once began the laborious task of transporting supplies over a shoulder of Mount Steele.

On June 26 they dragged a 300-pound sledge load of supplies to a cache five miles farther up the valley. Fresh snow continually blotted out the trail, making it necessary to keep camps close together and move forward by short relays, marking the trail by willow twigs in the snow.

An advance camp stocked with thirty days' food supply was set up July 1 at a height of 10,000 feet, at the base of the great buttress which rises from the head of Walsh Glazier to the lofty pass between Mount Lucania and Mount Steele.

Climbing conditions became so bad that on July 3, after an extra heavy snowfall, Mr. Washburn and Mr. Bates were forced to abandon one sleeping bed and air mattress

Continued on Page Six

PEACEFUL SOLUTION OF CRISIS IN CHINA NOW IN PROSPECT

Nanking Is Reported to Have Agreed to Local Deal to Settle the Issues

TROOPS BEING DRAWN BACK

Chiang Said to Have Prevailed Over Chinese, While Civilians Gain Strength in Tokyo

By HUGH BYAS

Wireless to The New York Times.

TOKYO, Friday, July 23.—Hopes that the crisis in North China will end peacefully and speedily are now strong here. The withdrawal of the Chinese Thirty-seventh Division from its points of contact with Japanese troops is proceeding on a large scale, thus removing the main source of immediate danger in North China.

Even more important than the local improvement is the circumstance that this withdrawal, according to the Tokyo newspaper Asahi's correspondent in Nanking, has been sanctioned by the Central government. Nanking announces that the Chinese withdrawals are being effected simultaneously with Japanese withdrawal.

That is a somewhat optimistic version, as the Japanese have not announced any change in their policy of watching the Chinese carry out their agreement, but it only anticipates events. When those Chinese troops have withdrawn the Japanese will return to their barracks.

Face-Saving Gesture Seen

Their retirement is a gesture that will save Nanking's face and so remove one of the greatest practical difficulties in restoring peace conditions.

The change in the Central government's attitude follows its study of the local settlement arranged last Monday between the Japanese military and North China authorities. Evidently its terms have been found to correspond with Japan's declaration that they did not contain political conditions or clauses affecting China's territorial and administrative integrity.

It is announced here that the Japanese Government intends to publish those terms in full to dispel misunderstandings abroad. As this correspondent has already reported, they have been kept secret at the Northern Chinese administration's request in order to get the Thirty-seventh Division out of the danger zone before disclosing publicly its transfer from the vicinity of Peiping.

This division, said to be officered by diehards of the old Manchurian army, has been a source of continuous trouble with Japanese troops, and its removal was held necessary in the interests of calm. It is being transferred to Paoting, about eighty miles south of Peiping, where it will be at an entirely safe distance from Japanese troops.

Three Points Regarding Japan

The following statements, which are believed to be absolutely correct, are important in any estimate of the situation as far as it depends on Japan:

1. The only troops that have left Japan are the contingents announced on July 15. They can be described as varied and supplementary in character and numerically small.

2. Only preparatory mobilization measures on a restricted scale are in progress here. "Full mobiliza-

Continued on Page Eight

POLICE DENOUNCED IN SENATE REPORT ON RIOT IN CHICAGO

Action in Memorial Day Strike Clash Was 'Unwarranted,' Says La Follette Body

FILM EVIDENCE STRESSED

Chicago Officials Hit Findings as 'Biased,' Assert Their Witnesses Were Not Heard

Official summary of La Follette subcommittee report, Page 4.

Special to The New York Times.

WASHINGTON, July 22.—Severe censure of the Chicago Police Department for the conduct of its members during the Memorial Day clash with strikers and strike sympathizers at the Republic Steel Company's plant on the outskirts of the city was contained in a report submitted to the Senate today by the La Follette subcommittee investigating violations of free speech and rights of labor.

A Cook County coroner's jury in Chicago on Tuesday exonerated the policemen concerned in the affair, in a verdict which described the killings of ten of the paraders as "justifiable homicides."

The subcommittee's report was signed by the two members, Senators La Follette and Thomas of Utah.

It summarized the facts that ten strike marchers were fatally injured in the Memorial Day conflict, ninety were wounded, including thirty by gunfire, and thirty-five police were injured.

All of this loss of life and injury could have been avoided, the report held. It charged that the Chicago police used force "far in excess of what the occasion required."

Future Incidents Warned Of

"Its use must be ascribed either to gross inefficiency in the performance of police duty or a deliberate effort to intimidate the strikers," the two Senators asserted.

"We conclude that the consequences of the Memorial Day encounter were clearly avoidable by the police," they continued.

"The action of the responsible authorities in setting the seal of their approval upon the conduct of the police not only fails to place responsibility where responsibility properly belongs but will invite the repetition of similar incidents in the future."

The report strongly criticized Police Commissioner Allman and other Chicago officials for alleged failure to lay down a clear policy for the police to follow on strike duty or to give clear orders to the policemen sent to the Republic plant in East Chicago May 30.

It further assailed these officials, including Assistant Corporation Counsel Daly, for allegedly hampering the Senate investigation.

Besides their regulation weapons, the report said, the police at the scene armed themselves with hatchet handles, apparently from the Republic plant.

Treatment by the police of the injured after the clash, it stated, "was characterized by the most callous indifference to human life and suffering. Not only did the police neglect the wounded; they prevented the union from giving aid."

Senator La Follette, in offering the report, asked the Senate for an additional appropriation of $50,000 to continue the subcommittee's inquiries. He said the $55,000 pre-

Continued on Page Four

Nye Criticizes the NLRB as 'a Partisan Body'; Says Average Man Thinks It a C.I.O. Adjunct

Special to The New York Times.

WASHINGTON, July 22.—Senator Nye, Republican of North Dakota, asserted in a statement issued today, that the National Labor Relations Board "seems to have gone out of its way to demonstrate to the public that it is a partisan body rather than a judicial institution."

"It has disqualified itself as a referee between management and workers," he said. "No governmental body enjoying the powers and privileges of this group can afford to take sides.

"We cannot try any industrial dispute before a kangaroo court and expect either satisfactory results or public approval. The NLRB has such a pronounced pro-C. I. O. bias that the average man regards it as an adjunct. It would be equally bad or worse if it had a pro-capital bias.

"We would be less than truthful if we acted on the presumption that the NLRB has been non-partisan and dispassionate in its activities."

After declaring that he did not wish "to see the governmental umpire battling for either side," Mr. Nye said that the "friends of labor who hail the obvious partisanship of the NLRB should bear in mind that it is quite possible that we will see a day when another governmental body of the same type will use its tremendous power to oppress labor.

"Governmental partisanship," he continued, "can do nothing but increase bitterness, promote discord, awaken cries of unfairness and destroy the great hope of economic advancement at a time when such destruction would certainly bring disaster.

"If management is unfair, oppressive or tyrannical, let us punish management.

"If labor organizations are unfair, ruthless or violent, let us punish labor organizations.

"But the government is not dedicated to the penalization of any group or class; on the contrary, we are striving for a harmonious meeting of minds which will enable us to go forward."

COURT BILL IS KILLED, 70 TO 20, AS SENATE GALLERIES CHEER; LOWER COURT CHANGE LIKELY

Court Recommittal Vote

Special to The New York Times.

WASHINGTON, July 22.—The vote by which the Senate sent the Roosevelt court bill back to committee today was as follows:

FOR RECOMMITTAL—70

Democrats—53

Adams (Colo.)	Gerry (R. I.)	Murray (Mont.)
Andrews (Fla.)	Gillette (Iowa)	O'Mahoney (Wyo.)
Ashurst (Ariz.)	Glass (Va.)	Overton (La.)
Bailey (N. C.)	Harrison (Miss.)	Pepper (Fla.)
Barkley (Ky.)	Herring (Iowa)	Pope (Idaho)
Brown (Mich.)	Holt (W. Va.)	Radcliffe (Md.)
Brown (N. H.)	Johnson (Colo.)	Reynolds (N. C.)
Bulow (S. D.)	King (Utah)	Russell (Ga.)
Burke (Neb.)	Lee (Okla.)	Sheppard (Texas)
Byrd (Va.)	Lewis (Ill.)	Smith (S. C.)
Byrnes (S. C.)	Logan (Ky.)	Thomas (Okla.)
Clark (Mo.)	Lonergan (Conn.)	Thomas (Utah)
Connally (Texas)	Maloney (Conn.)	Tydings (Md.)
Copeland (N. Y.)	McAdoo (Calif.)	Van Nuys (Ind.)
Deitrich (La.)	McCarran (Nev.)	Wagner (N. Y.)
Donahey (Ohio)	McGill (Kan.)	Walsh (Mass.)
Duffy (Wis.)	Minton (Ind.)	Wheeler (Mont.)
George (Ga.)	Moore (N. J.)	

Republicans—16

Austin (Vt.)	Gibson (Vt.)	Steiwer (Ore.)
Borah (Idaho)	Hale (Me.)	Townsend (Del.)
Bridges (N. H.)	Johnson (Calif.)	Vandenberg (Mich.)
Capper (Kan.)	Lodge (Mass.)	White (Me.)
Davis (Pa.)	McNary (Ore.)	
Frazier (N. D.)	Nye (N. D.)	

Farmer Laborite—1

Shipstead (Minn.)

AGAINST RECOMMITTAL—20

Democrats—18

Bilbo (Miss.)	Ellender (La.)	McKellar (Tenn.)
Black (Ala.)	Green (R. I.)	Neeley (W. Va.)
Bone (Wash.)	Guffey (Pa.)	Schwartz (Wyo.)
Bulkley (Ohio)	Hatch (N. M.)	Schwel'nback (Wash.)
Caraway (Ark.)	Hitchcock (S. D.)	Smathers (N. J.)
Chavez (N. M.)	Hughes (Del.)	Truman (Mo.)

Progressive—1

La Follette (Wis.)

Farmer-Laborite—1

Lundeen (Minn.)

PAIRED—2

Bankhead (Ala.), for, and Norris (Neb.), against

A FULL SURRENDER

Barkley Declines, and Logan Makes Motion to Bury Measure

OPPONENTS IN FULL SWAY

Agree to Procedural Reforms in Lower Bench to Expedite Constitutional Cases

PRESIDENT MAY FIGHT ON

Garner, Active in Solution, Is Revealed as Having Praised Wheeler for Opposition

By TURNER CATLEDGE

Special to The New York Times.

WASHINGTON, July 22.—The surrender by the Senate leadership of President Roosevelt's plan for changing the Supreme Court at this session of Congress was made formal and complete at 2:55 o'clock this afternoon.

At that hour the Senate, in a session as dramatic as any witnessed in the historic chamber in many years, voted, by agreement of the administration leaders, 70 to 20, to send the controversial measure back to the hostile Judiciary Committee. By the same ballot the committee was instructed to report within the next ten days another bill dealing with "procedural" reforms in the lower courts.

But the Supreme Court section was dead. By the Senate's action it was returned to the archives of the Judiciary Committee to be interred under assurances from the administration leaders that there would be no attempt to revive it this session.

Although the vote was not of itself a measure of the strength of the opposition, the outcome was appraised by many Senators as the worst defeat suffered by a President since the Senate rejected President Wilson's League of Nations covenant in 1920. The same Senators gave credit for settling the controversy to Vice President Garner, who, returning to Washington Monday night, proceeded to bring a solution about.

Motion Is Made by Logan

The motion to recommit was made by Senator Logan, co-author of the one-justice-a-year compromise bill. He was designated after Senator Barkley, newly elected majority leader, attending a peace council of the Judiciary Committee this morning at which the Vice President and Senator Wheeler, field marshal of the opposition, were present, declined to make the motion.

Senator Logan took the floor just after the Senate had delivered another blow to the President, overriding by a vote of 71 to 19 his veto of the farm mortgage interest reduction bill. As the Kentuckian made the motion, Senator Johnson of California sought definite assurances that the Supreme Court sections of the bill would be dropped in any redraft.

"The Supreme Court is out?" asked Senator Johnson.

"The Supreme Court is out," replied Senator Logan in a firm, clear voice.

"Glory be to God!" shouted the Californian as he dropped into his seat. The galleries burst into applause.

In the recommital vote, many administration stalwarts, including Majority Leader Barkley, joined with the unbroken phalanx of the opposition to send the measure back and end the controversy. The division of 70 to 20 was not, therefore, an adequate test on the court issue.

Among the twenty negative votes were those few Senators who enthusiastically favor Supreme Court reorganization, and those who wanted to keep their records of administration support unblemished by any compromise that would appear a setback for President Roosevelt.

Adjournment Zeal Kindled

After the vote the Senate appeared exhausted, as if a five and one-half months fever suddenly had left it. In this state an adjournment drive became infectious, and certain leaders predicted that the session would be wound up within the next three weeks, possibly by the night of Aug. 7, even if certain important measures on the President's "preferred" list

Continued on Page Two

CONGRESS REPEALS FEDERAL JOB LAW

Economy Act Clause Barring Man and Wife From Government Posts Rescinded

WOMEN HAD PROTESTED

Business Federation Sent Plea For Action to McKellar—Miss White Nominated

Special to The New York Times.

WASHINGTON, July 22.—The Senate late today voted unanimously for repeal of the so-called married persons clause of the Economy Act. The House already has passed the repeal bill and it now goes to President Roosevelt for his signature.

The Senate action was taken after Senator McKellar had filed a favorable report of the Civil Service Committee on the bill. Senator McKellar explained that the purpose of the bill was to remove any discrimination against government employes merely because of their marital status.

Section 213 of the Economy Act, which is now repealed unless President Roosevelt should veto the bill passed today, provided that whenever reductions in force become necessary in any government bureau, an employe whose husband or wife also was employed by the government would have to be let out first.

Women Urged Repeal

By KATHLEEN McLAUGHLIN

Special to The New York Times.

ATLANTIC CITY, July 22.—Delegates to the convention of the National Federation of Business and Professional Women here voted by acclamation this morning to appeal to Senator McKellar to do his utmost to expedite repeal of the law prohibiting man and wife from holding government positions. Then they sat back and heard their former national head, Miss Lena Madesin Phillips, charge that this measure, discriminating against married women, would have been halted at its source if they had acted in unison at the proper moment.

Miss Phillips, who is president of the International Federation, said she was "highly gratified," on being informed tonight of the Senate's repeal of Section 213 of the Economy Act. She expressed the hope that the action would "encourage the average woman to take an even more active part in righting wrongs against their sex, about which they so often complain."

Miss Charl Ormond Williams, na-

Continued on Page Five

SENATE OVERRIDES FARM LOAN VETO

Enacts Low Interest Law by Vote of 71 to 19 After President's Protest Is Assailed

LEVITY MARKS ROLL-CALL

19 Democrats Back Roosevelt and Vandenberg Solemnly Utters Sole Republican 'No'

Special to The New York Times.

WASHINGTON, July 22. — The Senate overrode President Roosevelt's veto of the bill to continue in effect existing reductions in interest on mortgage loans made by the Federal Land Banks. The vote was 71 to 19, eleven more than the required two-thirds majority.

The House already had passed the measure over the veto, so that it now becomes law, "the objections of the President of the United States to the contrary notwithstanding," as the result was announced by Senator Connally, acting presiding officer of the Senate.

As the roll-call proceeded, Senators cast their votes in the manner of schoolboys during recess. Joking comments and laughter went through the chamber.

Usually stanch advocates of economy such as Senators Glass, Townsend and White voted to enact the measure which the President had vetoed because it would add an unexpected $30,000,000 to the Federal budget for the current fiscal year and would upset his program for bringing equilibrium to the Federal finances before June 30, 1938.

All of the Republicans who were present voted to override the veto except Senator Vandenberg. With a serious mien he cast his negative vote, despite the capers of some colleagues on his side of the aisle.

Barkley Sounds Warning

Acting for the first time in his rôle of majority leader, Senator Barkley asked the Senate to sustain the President. Although he originally reported the bill favorably for the Banking Committee, he said that the reasons advanced by the President were sufficient to justify letting it lapse.

"No one can predict whether another attempt will be made to get another extension after the one we now propose has expired," he said. "If this is to continue as a policy of the government regarding farm loans, it will be difficult to resist the same requests which will come from borrowers from other Federal agencies."

In reply, Senator Smith, chairman

Continued on Page Two

"All the News That's Fit to Print."

THE NEWS INDEX IS ON PAGE 33, THIS SECTION

The New York Times.

LATE CITY EDITION
Fair, little change in temperature today. Tomorrow fair, temperature unchanged.
Temperatures Yesterday—Max., 85; min., 64

Section 1

VOL. LXXXVI....No. 29,044. Entered as Second-Class Matter, Postoffice, New York, N. Y. NEW YORK, SUNDAY, AUGUST 1, 1937. Including Rotogravure Picture, Magazine and Book Review. PP TEN CENTS | TWELVE CENTS Beyond 200 Miles Except in 7th and 8th Postal Zones.

JAPANESE BATTER TIENTSIN AS CHINESE STILL HOLD OUT; 'PUPPET STATE' IS IN REVOLT

RAIN HOLDS PLANES

Japanese Craft Unable to Assist Troops in Tientsin Fight

FOREIGNERS ASKED TO AID

Invaders Think They Should Help in Removing the Dead to Prevent Epidemic

REBELS MENACE RAILWAY

East Hopeh Forces, Armed and Trained by Japanese, Have Upset Friendly Regime

By HALLETT ABEND

Wireless to THE NEW YORK TIMES.

TIENTSIN, China, Sunday, Aug. 1.—The Japanese Army in North China at dawn today resumed its attempt to clean out "the nests of Chinese snipers" in this area.

The planned aerial review by Japanese Army planes which was intended to awe and intimidate the Chinese populace was postponed because of a low ceiling and bad flying conditions. Soon after noon yesterday, when a drizzling rain alternated with almost tropical downpours to immobilize Japanese bombers by turning the airfield into a mucky clay, trench mortars again began belching fire on many places along the north bank of the Pei River opposite the British and French Concessions and farther westward.

Despite this chaos on the north bank of that river, where the railway tracks leading to Tangku run, many trains shuttled back and forth all afternoon, with Japanese reinforcements, which were reported arriving in large numbers.

Communications Are Down

Tientsin continues to be cut off from news of the Peiping district, and the promised resumption of communication has again been deferred indefinitely.

The Japanese Army spokesman hinted at some resentment against foreigners at army headquarters, saying that only the Italians "were very kind about allowing travel through their concession." He expressed the opinion that the powers proclaiming the Boxer protocol should coordinate in efforts to sweep away the rioting Chinese troops.

"In my opinion," he said, "the other powers are offering every convenience to the Chinese side." He also expressed the belief that troops of other nations here should help the Japanese clean up the areas where fighting has ceased. He declared the delay in disposing of the hundreds of bodies now littering the streets might cause an epidemic or plague.

"In Tientsin today," the spokesman said, "we are firing on every place where we find Chinese troops or police."

The revolt against the Japanese Army by General Yin Ju-keng's Tungchow Peace Preservation Corps in the East Hopeh "puppet State" appears to have developed into a serious affair. The Japanese spokesman admitted that the army had to use bombing planes against the Tungchow rebels both on Thursday and Friday and that the rebels were driven out only after reinforcements had arrived. Casualties in the Japanese Army were two officers and eighteen men killed and twelve wounded. Chinese losses were described as unknown but enormous.

General Revolt Seen Spreading

This revolt of Yin Ju-keng's men possibly has spread along the Tientsin-Shanhaikwan Railway, for General Yin had about 17,000 men scattered over about twenty-two hsien (counties) in East Hopeh. Ironically, these men were all armed, drilled and equipped by the Japanese; their very ammunition is from Japanese factories, and this revolt seems to indicate that a southward extension of Manchukuo's "new paradise" did not entirely satisfy East Hopeh's 6,000,000 people.

The Japanese spokesman now admits that General Yin Ju-keng was arrested by men from his own Peace Preservation Corps. The spokesman said he was safe and that his life was not in danger, but meanwhile Lieut. Gen. Kiyoshi Katsuki, Japanese Commander in Chief, appointed a successor to take over Yin's responsibilities.

Two independent regiments and

Continued on Page Thirty-one

Chinese Preparing for War in Air; Tokyo Pushes Troop Movements

Sugiyama Tells Peers Japan Is Preparing to Meet Concentration of 170,000 Men in Hopeh—Says Peiping City Will Not Be Bombed Unless Chinese Provoke Action

By HUGH BYAS

Wireless to THE NEW YORK TIMES.

TOKYO, Sunday, Aug. 1.—General Gen Sugiyama, War Minister, repeated before the House of Peers yesterday that future developments in China depended entirely upon the attitude of the Chinese. The implication of this statement, taken in conjunction with other official declarations, is that the Chinese will not carry the hostilities beyond the Yungting River, but General Sugiyama did not say so directly.

The War Minister said that while no Central Government planes had participated in the fighting as yet, the Nanking régime was making extensive preparations.

Chinese air forces, it is said, are being concentrated along the Lunghai Railway and emergency airdromes are being built at strategic points along railways. Fuel and bombs are being rushed to all air positions in the north, according to Japanese reports.

General Sugiyama told the Peers that the War Department would leave nothing undone in preparation to meet the situation created by the concentration of 170,000 Chinese troops in or near Hopeh. There were now, he said, 70,000 Nanking troops in Hopeh, making the total number concentrated near Tingchow 120,000 with 50,000 more at Haichow and others assembling near Tsinan.

Recounting the development of the affair from Japanese official information, General Sugiyama said that Chinese attacks at Langfang and Peiping had shown that they did not intend to fulfill their agreement, and the Japanese commander, "who had borne what is unbearable," resolved on punitive actions.

In doing so, said General Sugiyama, the Japanese Army was operating against a Chinese army that had challenged it, not against the Chinese people. Further, he said, with implied reference to American and British representations, the Japanese would not use force in Peiping unless the Chinese attacked first.

The rest of the speech was a fac-

Continued on Page Thirty-one

JAPANESE RAIDERS BOMB TROOP TRAINS

20 Rolling Toward Peiping Are Attacked From Air, Reports to Shanghai Declare

DAMAGE DONE AT PAOTING

War Planes Set Fire to Rail Station—Nanking Determined to Fight, Official Insists

Wireless to THE NEW YORK TIMES.

SHANGHAI, Sunday, Aug. 1.—Japanese air raiders bombed twenty trains filled with Chinese Government troops rolling northward yesterday from Paoting, the capital of Hopeh Province, toward the Japanese lines just south of Changsintien, near Peiping, according to Japanese press reports from Nanking today.

The extent of the casualties in this attack was not indicated, but in other raids, it was reported, the Paoting railway station was set afire and much damage was done.

Twenty-five trains loaded with Government soldiers were reported seen near Tsangchow, on the Tientsin-Pukow Railway. It was declared also that feverish military activity was in progress, particularly in airfield construction, in Shantung Province and along the Lunghai Railway.

Attack Order Reported

The Japanese reports declare that the northward advance of the Chinese was a result of a general attack order given at Paoting by General Chen Cheng, field commander of the anti-Japanese drive.

Despite a widespread public demand for a specific announcement and evidence of an intention to challenge Japan with immediate and determined wide-scale military resistance, the Chinese Government continued to blanket its activities in silence. Only Japanese sources carry the reports of army movements northward.

Says Nanking Is Determined

The Chinese Government is united in a determination to carry through a fight to the finish with Japan, Sun Fo, president of the Legislative Yuan, who is on a week-end visit here, said in an interview this morning. He thus answered Japanese reports of dissension in the government ranks and of hesitancy and uncertainty in the prosecution of military resistance of the Japanese invasion of North China.

"Ridiculous! Ridiculous!" he exclaimed scornfully when his attention was directed to Japanese press reports of differences between Generalissimo Chiang Kai-shek and leading subordinates.

"The Japanese are just trying to stir up trouble," Mr. Sun asserted.

Chiang Kai-shek's four minimum conditions, enunciated two weeks ago, for the settlement of the Hopeh trouble remain the basis for peace

Continued on Page Thirty-one

REBEL DRIVE GAINS IN EASTERN SPAIN

Loyalists Admit Evacuating Towns Before Push to Cut Madrid-Valencia Road

GRANADA TROUBLE DENIED

But Government Hears Spanish Troops Rebelled at Alleged Favoritism to Italians

By The Associated Press.

HENDAYE, France, July 31.—Both the Insurgent and the Government high commands today reported an Insurgent victory in Eastern Spain, where General Francisco Franco is trying to drive a wedge between Madrid and Valencia.

Frequently in recent weeks official Government announcements have confirmed Insurgent reports of reverses suffered by the Madrid-Valencia forces.

The Government announcement said violent Insurgent pressure on the boundary of Cuenca Province, about 100 miles east of Madrid, supported by intensive shelling, had forced the Madrid-Valencia troops to retreat from positions at Terriente and Saldon. Those villages are about sixty miles north of the Madrid-Valencia road, toward which General Franco's new Teruel offensive is aimed. Cutting off the road, the only direct line of communication between inland Madrid and Valencia, temporary seat of government, might be the deciding blow of the year-old civil war.

Dominates Road Link

Terriente is of strategic importance because of its location on a road running south from Albarracin which connects that Insurgent field base with a highway running between Teruel and Canete. The latter city lies deep within Cuenca Province, into which General Franco's army was driving. From Canete an improved road runs circuitously through mountainous country to Cuenca, the provincial capital, only about thirty miles to the west.

The Insurgent drive had split into two columns. One, skirting the Universales Mountains, was reported already to have crossed the Teruel-Cuenca provincial border. The other apparently was driving southeastward toward a small territory known as Rincon de Ademuz, about seventy miles northwest of Valencia. Possibly this latter movement foreshadowed a drive on the Mediterranean stronghold of the Government from a new angle. Months ago the Insurgents' Teruel offensive was aimed at the coast north of Valencia in a futile attempt to cut the city off from autonomous Catalonia.

Without giving a specific location, the Insurgent communiqué said the Government attempted an attack on the Granada front, in Southern Spain, which General Franco's men

Continued on Page Twenty-nine

Ranger Beats Endeavour II As Yachts Start Cup Races

Harold S. Vanderbilt's Ranger, defending the America's Cup, triumphed easily over T. O. M. Sopwith's Endeavour II in the first race of the series off Newport yesterday. The British yacht finished 17 minutes 5 seconds behind, the margin being the biggest in a cup match for fifty years.

Endeavour II fell behind in the first few minutes of the contest and after that the American craft drew steadily away. Ranger led by a mile at the half-way mark over the thirty-mile windward and leeward course.

A huge fleet put to sea to follow the racers, which sailed in a light breeze. The series will continue until one yacht wins four times, with the next contest scheduled tomorrow.

Results in Other Sports

HORSE RACING

Esposa captured the Saratoga Handicap by half a length from Maeriel, with Blackbirder third. Chaps, a 15-1 shot, took the United States Hotel Stakes. At Chicago, Tiger and Teddy's Comet raced a dead heat in the $45,000 Arlington Futurity and Dellor annexed the $20,000 added Arlington Handicap.

BASEBALL

The Cubs crushed the Giants, 7 to 1, at Chicago, increasing their National League lead to five games. Tex Carleton allowed only three hits. Despite Joe DiMaggio's twenty-ninth and thirtieth home runs, the Yankees lost to the Browns in the tenth, 9 to 6, at the Stadium. The Cardinals beat the Dodgers, 4 to 3, at St. Louis.

GOLF

Clipping seven strokes from par with a 65 that equaled the Shackamaxon course record at Westfield, Craig Wood tied Victor Ghezzi for the New Jersey State open championship with a seventy-two-hole total of 278. They will stage an eighteen-hole play-off for the title today.

(Complete Details of These and Other Sports Events in Section 5)

FUSION CAMPAIGN IS IMPEDED BY RIFT ON SEABURY SLATE

Harvey Definitely Rejected by Labor Group and Queens Council of City Party

MAYOR MAY SHUN CONTEST

Republican Backers Worried—Tammany Executive Body to Meet Tomorrow

Republican supporters of Mayor La Guardia were somewhat worried yesterday as to whether he would be willing to enter a contest in the party primary, as it became evident that the Mayor would not be endorsed by the Bronx and Queens organizations.

The Mayor has said he would accept the Republican nomination, which can only be given him by vote of enrolled party members at the primary election. He has not said that he would go into a primary contest to get it. Neither Kenneth F. Simpson nor any of his associates have any further information from the Mayor than that contained in his statement accepting as running mates, Joseph P. McGoldrick and Alderman Newbold Morris, the candidates put forward for Controller and President of the Council.

One of the candidates proposed by the Nonpartisan Citizens Committee, of which Samuel Seabury is chairman, has been definitely rejected by all the groups in the proposed Fusion combination, except the Republican party. He is George U. Harvey, Borough President of Queens, who is scheduled for renomination by the Republicans.

Labor Party Rejects Harvey

Officers of the American Labor party asserted with authority that they would not accept Mr. Harvey. The Queens division of the City Fusion party upheld the action of the City Council of the party and rejected Mr. Harvey, as did Maurice P. Davidson, chairman of the Progressive City Committee, a member of Mr. Seabury's committee.

"A group of Manhattan citizens, who are not well informed about the political situation in Queens, have asked the City Fusion party to take George U. Harvey as its candidate for Borough President," said E. C. Ahrens, chairman of its Queens County Committee. "This group did not consult with the Queens City Fusion party and, as we had no voice in the selection, we consider this an encroachment upon the rights of our organization.

"We believe that the voters of Queens and particularly the civic-minded group that comprise the City Fusion party in this borough are in a better position to say who shall be the candidate, at least of their own party. My county committee has authorized me to say that so far as the Queens City Fusion party is concerned we will not recognize any action the Citizens Nonpartisan Committee may take for borough candidates and we will not be bound by their announcements.

"Judge Seabury and his committee might better study local conditions carefully before submitting any candidates for borough office. Their slant on Queens is merely through the windows of a Manhat-

Continued on Page Three

CHAMBERLAIN SENDS NOTE TO MUSSOLINI AS PEACE GESTURE

Prime Minister Brushes Aside Diplomatic Custom in Effort to Bring Nations Together

MAY RECOGNIZE CONQUEST

Guarantees Asked, However, on Italy's Policies in Near East and Mediterranean

Wireless to THE NEW YORK TIMES.

LONDON, July 31.—Just after Prime Minister Neville Chamberlain, wearing a light sporting jacket and jaunty soft felt hat, had shut the door of No. 11 Downing Street behind him today and started his vacation it became known that he had brushed aside diplomatic custom and had written a "personal letter of friendship" to Premier Benito Mussolini.

On Tuesday Mr. Chamberlain took an unusual step for a British Prime Minister and sent for Count Dino Grandi, the Italian envoy, with whom he had a ninety-minute talk. Now it is said that Mr. Chamberlain's letter was a reply to the cordial message from Rome which Count Grandi delivered on that occasion.

There are few facts but much speculation regarding the interview which now has assumed considerable importance in London and Rome. The text of the letter to Mussolini has not been disclosed here. However, in quarters usually well informed, it is stated that the purpose of the interview was to remove the underlying suspicions between the two countries, particularly with regard to the Mediterranean, resulting from the sanctions crisis.

That, it is assumed, means British recognition of Italy's Ethiopian empire—a subject, as The Sunday Observer points out, left in abeyance when the "gentlemen's agreement" with Italy was signed in January.

"It is assumed in some quarters," proceeded The Observer, "that as the League Assembly meets in September there is a strong desire on the part of Italy that this stumbling-block to cooperation should no longer stand in the way of the more friendly cooperation now begun. In such a comprehensive survey of the political landscape, intervention in Spain and, in general, the European situation could hardly have been avoided but the main purpose of Chamberlain, it is understood, was to assure Italy of the good-will of the British Government to overcome all possible points of friction in a situation admittedly difficult."

The Sunday Observer adds that the favorable impression made in Rome "owes something to Chamberlain's name because both his father and the late Sir Austen were known as friends of Italy."

Recognition Held Possibility

Wireless to THE NEW YORK TIMES.

ROME, July 31.—Premier Benito Mussolini today received a letter from Prime Minister Neville Chamberlain and another from King Leopold of the Belgians which accompanied Premier Paul van Zeeland's plan for the establishment of an international economic body.

Mr. Chamberlain's letter, accord-

Continued on Page Thirty

SENATE, 56 TO 28, VOTES BILL FIXING WAGES AND HOURS; CURBS CHILD LABOR GOODS

Drive to End Session Is Renewed; Success Hangs on House Action

Chief Factor Is Speed With Which Lower Body Handles Labor Bill—Republicans Insist Adjournment Should Come Saturday, but Some Democrats Demand All of President's Program

By TURNER CATLEDGE

Special to THE NEW YORK TIMES.

WASHINGTON, July 31.—The drive to end the Congress session quickly, quiescent during the last two days of debate in the Senate, began anew tonight following the passage of the Administration's Wages and Hours Bill.

As soon as Vice President Garner had announced the passage of the labor measure Senator Wagner put his housing bill before the Senate for consideration the first thing Monday. It was second on the five-point legislative program outlined at the White House early this week by President Roosevelt and his Congressional leaders.

The tentative adjournment date again was set unofficially for Aug. 14.

Senator McNary, the Republican leader, insisted that the session could and should be ended next Saturday night, while others maintained that Congress should remain in Washington not only until the remainder of the five-point program is enacted, but until general farm legislation, tentatively sidetracked, is considered.

The program demanded by the President includes final action on the wage-hours bill, the Wagner housing plan and amendments to the tax laws plugging up the loopholes through which revenues have been escaping the Treasury. Sugar quota legislation is also on the preferred list and constitutes the fifth of the five-point program, but the President is understood to feel that if a suitable bill cannot be agreed upon, this question might be put off until the next session.

The adjournment situation depended tonight on two considerations, the speed with which the House acts upon the wage-hours bill and frames legislation plugging income tax loopholes.

The major consideration is action by the House on the labor measure. Some hostility to the measure has developed in the lower body, but with the reassertion of the Administration's control over the Senate in passing the bill today the President is expected to hold Congress

Continued on Page Three

SOME CHANGES WIN

But Main Aims Emerge Unscathed in Hard Amendment Drive

CHILD LABOR PART REVISED

Wheeler-Johnson Plan Is Used, Shearing Board Powers, but With 3-Fold Prohibition

15 DEMOCRATS IN NAY LIST

Mostly From South, They Are Joined by 13 Republicans—Lynching Rider Beaten

Special to THE NEW YORK TIMES.

WASHINGTON, July 31.—The Senate passed the Wages and Hours Bill late today by a vote of 56 to 28, after crushing most of the important amendment proposals put forward at the close of sharp and sometimes bitter debate.

The measure now goes to the House, where a hard fight appears to await it.

Before adopting the proposal, the Senate threw out of the administration bill all its child-labor provisions and substituted the Wheeler-Johnson bill, a move which converted many votes and helped to account for the large margin in its favors at final passage.

The measure's other two objectives, establishment of minimum wages not to exceed 40 cents an hour and a maximum work week to be placed not lower than forty hours, emerged substantially untouched.

In the House, however, a determined effort will be made to raise the possible minimum wage to 70 cents an hour, and to lower the possible work-week to thirty-five hours.

As passed by the Senate the measure would set up a Labor Standards Board of five members which would be authorized to establish minimum wages and maximum working hours, within the limits set, for industries throughout the country.

Only Two Republicans for It

Fifteen Democratic Senators, mostly from the South, joined with thirteen Republicans to vote against the bill on final passage.

Senator Davis of Pennsylvania, former Secretary of Labor under Presidents Harding, Coolidge and Hoover, and Senator Lodge of Massachusetts were the only Republicans who supported it. Senator LaFollette, Progressive, and Senators Shipstead and Lundeen, the Farmer-Laborites, voted for the bill.

The administrative board would have no authority over child labor under the accepted amendment, for the problem of child labor would be attacked along the lines of the Sumners-Ashurst act dealing with prison-made goods.

There would be absolute prohibition of transportation or sale in interstate commerce of the produce of child labor, and all goods produced by child labor would be so labelled, to warn prospective buyers.

Child labor goods, when shipped in interstate commerce, would be liable to State prohibitory laws where they existed.

After Jan. 1, 1938, it would be unlawful for any producer of goods made by child labor, or for any commission merchant or agent, to transport in interstate commerce or sell in interstate commerce such goods.

Seek to Avoid Invalidation

Senator Wheeler, co-author of the bill, explained to the Senate that these three approaches to the problem were included as a safeguard against court invalidation of any one of them.

The Interstate Commerce Committee felt, he said, that any one of the methods of prohibition would prove a deterrent to child labor, and that the three of them taken together would outlaw it altogether.

Child labor was defined as the labor of persons below 16 years of age, or below the age of 18 in hazardous occupations.

The same age limits were, in a general way, prescribed in the child labor provisions of the Black-Connery bill which today's amendment replaced.

The major difference between the two methods of dealing with the problem was the degree of adminis-

Continued on Page Two

PARTY BOOKS COST MRS. BIDDLE $20,000

Wife of Ambassador Paid the Largest Sum for Democratic Souvenirs, Report Shows

BETHLEHEM STEEL ON LIST

Corporation's $7,500 Was the Second Highest Purchase in Pennsylvania, Ditter Asserts

Special to THE NEW YORK TIMES.

WASHINGTON, July 31.—Mrs. Margaret Biddle of Pennsylvania, wife of A. J. Drexel Biddle Jr., Ambassador to Poland, paid $20,000 for Democratic souvenir convention books, autographed by the President, according to a summary for Pennsylvania made public today. This is the largest amount received by the Democratic National Committee for this publication, which is being sold to wipe out the deficit of the last convention.

The Bethlehem Steel Corporation was the next highest purchaser in the Pennsylvania list, made public by Representative Ditter through the Republican Congressional Committee, which compiled the receipts from the records filed with the clerk of the House. Bethlehem Steel contributed $7,500, but the Pennsylvania Railroad, chief corporation in Pennsylvania bought only one book, paying $100.

The committee reaped about $100,000 from the sale of these books to individuals and corporations in Pennsylvania. Representative Snell of New York, minority House leader, is insisting that the House investigate the sale of the books, charging that it is a violation of the law for corporations to make campaign contributions.

List of the Purchasers

Among the purchasers in Pennsylvania were:

Everett Zurn, Erie	$250
Melvin Zurn, Erie	250
J. M. Magenau and Eugene W. King, Erie	250
Planters Nut and Chocolate Co., Wilkes-Barre	250
Samuel P. Wetherill, Philadelphia	250
Kehoe-Barge Coal Co., Pittston	250
Vincent Ventresoa, Philadelphia	250
John Durkan, Scranton	250
F. G. Vogt & Sons, Inc., Philadelphia	250
Stegmaier Brewing Co., Wilkes-Barre	375
National Portland Cement Co., Philadelphia	375
Ritter Brothers, Harrisburg	375
Robert H. Graupner Brewing Co., Harrisburg	500
The Rust Engineering Co., Pittsburgh	500
Tom Walker & Co., Inc., Pittsburgh	500
F. A. Merrick, Pittsburgh	500
Frank M Speakman, Philadelphia	500
Charles A. Devlin, Philadelphia	650
E. F. Houghton & Co., Philadelphia	800
Tom Walker, Inc., Pittsburgh	800
Air Defense League, Philadelphia	800
Shoup Voting Machine Corporation, Philadelphia	1,000
American Federation of Hosiery Workers of Philadelphia and vicinity	1,000
Brotherhood of Transportation Workers, Highway Drivers and Helpers Local No. 107	1,000
W. V. Pangborne & Co., Philadelphia	1,500
Hookless Fastener Co., Meadville	2,000
Hammermill Paper Co., Erie	2,500

Representative Ditter, vice chairman of the Republican Congres-

Continued on Page Three

C. I. O. PUTS $100,000 INTO SHIPYARD ROW

Thousands of Pickets to Help Strikers Here Also Pledged at Leaders' Parley

$5,000 CHECK FROM LEWIS

Union Head in Demand to End Dispute Urges Employers to Consent to Meeting

A $100,000 fund and thousands of pickets to aid the strike of shipyard workers here were pledged yesterday by leaders of a score of international C. I. O. unions at a closed meeting at C. I. O. headquarters, 1,133 Broadway.

Later members of the conference disclosed that they had already turned over checks for $10,000, including one of $5,000 from John L. Lewis, to a board of strike strategy organized to aid in conducting the strike.

John Green, president of the Industrial Union of Marine and Shipbuilding Workers of America, declared that "the magnificent support" pledged by the twenty C. I. O. unions "should sound the death knell for the miniature Tom Girdlers of the shipbuilding industry." Earlier in the day Mr Green sent to the major shipyards of Brooklyn and Staten Island the following telegram:

"Decent consideration for public interests requires an end to paralysis of shipping and widespread hardships caused by strike. I now suggest you agree to settle this in a civilized manner, by negotiations and round-table. We are prepared to discuss a fair basis of strike settlement at any convenient time and place. Please wire reply."

Protest Meeting Wednesday

Protest against hardships which he said the strike was causing to the public was voiced meanwhile by E. S. Rothstein, chairman of the American Labor party of the Seventh Assembly District, Brooklyn. Mr. Rothstein announced that citizens would hold a mass meeting on Wednesday at Holy Trinity Church, 157 Montague Street, Brooklyn, to protest against the strike which he said had cost local merchants more than $1,250,000.

The notice of the meeting charged shipyard owners with prolonging the strike by refusing to bargain collectively. Manuel Maxwell of the City Progressive Committee will address the rally which plans to organize a citizens' committee to work for the end of the strike.

About 700 employes of the Robins Dry Dock and Repair Company, Erie Basin, Brooklyn, reported for work yesterday for a half day. They arrived and departed under protection of a guard of several hundred police without interference from 150 pickets gathered in front of the gate of the plant.

At the C. I. O. strike fund meeting, Samuel Wolchok, president of

Continued on Page Four

"All the News That's Fit to Print"

The New York Times.

LATE CITY EDITION
U. S. Weather Bureau Report (Page 44) forecasts: Mostly fair, hot, humid, chance of showers late today, part of tomorrow.
Temp. range: 94—75; yesterday: 93—72.
Temp.-Hum. Index: low 80's; yesterday: 82.

VOL. LXXXVI.....No. 29,056. Entered as Second-Class Matter, Postoffice, New York, N. Y. NEW YORK, FRIDAY, AUGUST 13, 1937. P TWO CENTS In New York City. | THREE CENTS Within 200 Miles. | FOUR CENTS Elsewhere Except in 7th and 8th Postal Zones.

FIRST CLASH IN SHANGHAI; CHINESE RUSH AID TO CITY; FOREIGNERS FEAR ATTACKS

BATTLE IS AWAITED

5,000 Japanese Naval Men Raise Defenses as Foes Increase

TOKYO SHIPS ALSO READY

Foreigners Think Settlement Will Not Be Immune as in 1932 Fighting

U. S. MARINES ON PATROL

Katsuki Says China Invites War in North by Sending Troops Against Him

The Chinese Situation

SHANGHAI—Fighting began in Shanghai between the Japanese naval patrol and Chinese. Foreign troops prepared to defend the International Settlement in an expected extensive battle, because Chinese troops are converging on the city. Page 1.

TOKYO—The Cabinet in an emergency session decided to negotiate with the Chinese on the alarming Shanghai situation. Page 1.

TIENTSIN—Lieut. Gen. Kiyoshi Katsuki, Japanese Army chief in North China, said Nanking was inviting war by sending more troops to Southern Hopeh Province. He said he would take the offensive as soon as the Chinese troops increased to numbers that would imperil his forces. Page 8.

WASHINGTON—Officials believed the 1,100 marines stationed in Shanghai constituted a force sufficient to protect the Americans there and did not plan to send reinforcements. Page 7.

Snipers Open Fire

Wireless to THE NEW YORK TIMES.

SHANGHAI, Friday, Aug. 13.—Alleged Chinese snipers started firing at Japanese patrols along the Chapei border this morning.

Your correspondent visited the district and found intense activity among the Japanese naval landing parties seeking to locate the sources of sporadic shooting. They said the firing was coming from a building across the Woosung railway in Chapei.

I drove down the North Szechuen Road and on returning found the road barred to traffic. "Snipers," the police explained, indicating the rapid spread of the firing into an area completely controlled by Japanese naval contingents.

Refugees Return to Hongkew

Hongkew was teeming with frightened Chinese who evacuated yesterday and today were returning to salvage their belongings. Japanese naval reservists were herding people about, detouring them around Japanese concentrations.

Chinese early this morning sank a string of junks across the Wangpoo River between the Nantao and Pootung sides, apparently with the object of blocking the stream to protect the naval arsenal and dockyard upstream.

The Japanese Consul General, Mr. Okamoto, is demanding that the Chinese reveal the whereabouts of and return three Japanese civilians, one a news photographer who disappeared in Chapei yesterday and allegedly are being held by Chinese.

Giving the Chinese version of the sporadic clashes in Chapei, Mayor Yui issued a statement saying that a Japanese force made a foray into Chinese territory at 9:15 o'clock this morning, violating the existing truce. He said they clashed with Chinese at three points along the Chapei border.

"The Chinese," he added, "are putting up determined resistance."

Peace Efforts Fail

Diplomatic efforts failed yesterday to alleviate the threat of large-scale Sino-Japanese hostilities in the Shanghai area.

While Japanese marines and Chinese regular army units faced each other menacingly along the northern boundary of the International Settlement Mayor O. K. Yui rejected the Japanese demand for the withdrawal of the Chinese troops at a meeting of the International Commission, set up in 1932 to supervise the carrying out of the demilitarization agreement terminating

Continued on Page Eight

Japanese Decide to Negotiate; Alarmed by Shanghai Situation

Cabinet in Three-Hour Emergency Session Agrees to Seek Settlement There, Although Premier Asserts 'Right of Self-Defense' May Be Invoked

By HUGH BYAS

Wireless to THE NEW YORK TIMES.

TOKYO, Friday, Aug. 13.—The Japanese Cabinet has decided to negotiate with the Chinese authorities for the cessation of hostile or provocative movements in Shanghai.

This decision was announced at 12:30 P. M. today, after the Cabinet had discussed the situation in a special session for three hours, by Akira Kazami, the Cabinet's chief secretary.

He said that a very critical position had arisen in Shanghai because the Chinese were moving a force into a demilitarized zone and that the Cabinet, after considering the matter, had decided to negotiate with China on the lines described and had also considered measures to protect Japanese residents.

"If the worst should happen," said Mr. Kazami, "the responsibility will rest solely on the Chinese."

Up till noon today the War Office had not received or given any fresh orders regarding Shanghai. All messages received from Shanghai in the last twenty-four hours, however, have revealed acute and rapidly mounting alarm. The Japanese are virtually besieged in their concession.

Members of the Chinese Preservation Corps, highly armed, intoxicated with hatred of the Japanese and imperfectly disciplined, have advanced to the line between the Japanese city and the International Settlement, where they are erecting barricades and machine-gun emplacements. With them are part of the Eighty-eighth Central Division, one of Generalissimo Chiang Kai-shek's so-called crack divisions.

The preservation of peace in Shanghai, it is felt, does not depend on the will of the Japanese and Chinese Governments, but on any unit or individual of these half-disciplined Chinese soldiers.

Japanese marines, strengthened by 1,000 reinforcements landed from Japan, are on guard around the Japanese concession.

Japanese residents in the outlying suburbs who had saved only the clothes they were wearing were

Continued on Page Nine

DICTATOR OF IRAQ SLAIN BY SOLDIER

Assassin Said to Be Relative of Minister Killed in General Sidky's March to Power

AIDE DIES IN HEROIC ROLE

Major Jawdat Also Falls Victim When He Tries to Wrest Gun From the Assailant

Wireless to THE NEW YORK TIMES.

BAGHDAD, Iraq, Aug. 12.—An Iraqi soldier, reliably stated to be a distant relative of General Jafar Pasha al-Askari, Iraqi Minister of Defense, whose murder prepared the way for General Bakr Sidky Pasha's coup d'état last October, assassinated the dictator last night at the airport at Mosul.

Major Mohamed Ali Jawdat, Commander of the Iraqi Air Force, his lieutenant in his rise to power, died trying to save his chief's life.

The bodies of the two leaders were brought to Baghdad by airplane early today and the funeral was held immediately afterward. The presence of two armed policemen at the end of every street was the only indication of any unusual occurrence.

The road from the Ministry of Defense Building, from which General Sidky ruled the country as permanent chief of the Iraqi General Staff, was lined with troops of cavalry. Although King Ghazi did not attend he sent a representative and Prime Minister Hikmet Beg Suleiman, members of the Cabinet, the Diplomatic Corps and the British Military Mission attended. A salute of nineteen guns was fired as the coffins were lowered into the grave.

Dictator's Slayer Arrested.

The first news of the assassination was given out at 10 A. M. today in a Government communiqué, which said that the dictator's slayer had been arrested. General Sidky was en route to Turkey to attend the Turkish Army manoeuvres at the invitation of the Government and Major Jawdat had flown from Baghdad to say good-bye to his chief before he crossed the frontier.

The two friends were sitting and watching the sunset opposite the officers' mess at the airport when a passing soldier without warning fired several shots at General Sidky, whose death was instantaneous. Major Jawdat leaped at the assailant only to fall victim to the assassin's bullets.

General Sidky's journey to Turkey reflected his sympathy with the Government in whose army he served until after the World War.

After the murder of General Jafar, last October, General Sidky marched on Baghdad at the head of his army while his lieutenant, Major Jawdat, and his aviators dropped pamphlets calling on the people to surrender.

The Prime Minister and the Cabinet fled and General Sidky took

Continued on Page Seven

BODIES OF 19 FOUND IN BUILDING'S RUINS

Two Still Missing, Five Hurt After Collapse of Tenement in Staten Island Storm

INQUIRY TO OPEN MONDAY

Grand Jury Will Look Into Possible Negligence—Site Lies Between Hills

Nineteen bodies were recovered yesterday from the mud-packed debris at 1, 3 and 5 New Street in New Brighton, S. I., where rainstorm floodwater swept away the foundations at 10 o'clock Wednesday night and sucked poverty-stricken tenants, brick walls, beams and furniture anywhere from 50 to 100 feet northward, toward Kill Van Kull.

Two persons are still missing and five are in hospitals. Firemen, policemen, Department of Sanitation workers and WPA workers toiled all day through the intense heat, carefully going over each fresh mound for the missing.

The search was continued until after midnight, when it was halted by a downpour, with the crews working under acetylene lamps, search-lights and motor-car beams, just as they had through the storm on Wednesday and early yesterday morning. It will be renewed at 8 A. M. today.

Held "Act of Providence"

Borough President Joseph A. Palma, who remained at the spot through the morning and late into the afternoon, seemed convinced from what he saw and from official reports that the tragedy "was an act of Providence," in no way due to criminal neglect on the part of the owners of the dwellings. Richmond's Building Superintendent, Henry J. Langworthy, apparently concurred.

District Attorney Frank Innes announced last night that he would gather all the facts in the case and present them on Monday to the Richmond County grand jury. Inquiries are also being made by the Police, Fire and Building Departments. Mr. Palma pleaded for contributions to a fund to feed and clothe the survivors and to bury the dead.

All the tenants in the old flats were virtually penniless. Employes in the Borough President's office contributed $500 to the fund yesterday, a Mrs. Dreyfus $100 and Mrs. Martha Sullivan Quinn $25.

Mayor La Guardia, who had gone down into the pit early in the morning, praised the courage of Patrolman Joseph J. McBreen of Emergency Squad 10, who lost his life in an attempt to save Patricia Hurley, 2 years old. McBreen's body, his arms holding the dead child, was found in the ruins later. The ladder by which he had reached her lay under them, snapped in more than

Continued on Page Three

Eclipse Photos Give the Sun A Halo Million Miles Deep

Pictures Made From a Plane 25,000 Feet Up Cause Scientists to Revise Their Conception of Its Corona

Study of photographic records of the recent solar eclipse indicates that science must revise its conception of the corona and may lead to a new understanding of the sun's structure, particularly those mysterious sunspots that have an appreciable effect on human destinies, it was announced yesterday jointly by Harvard University and the American Museum of Natural History.

Extraordinarily clear still and motion pictures of the total eclipse of June 8, taken for the first time from the stratosphere and carefully examined since then by astronomers and optical experts, have conclusively proved the existence of a gigantic globular envelope, more than a million miles deep, about the earth's source of light and heat. This outer shell, or atmosphere, of the sun, astronomers explained, may be as much as one hundred times the sun in volume.

This major discovery regarding the structure of the sun was revealed on photographs made from an airplane flying between 25,000 and 30,000 feet up near the jagged, snow-capped peaks of the Andes. The pictures were taken by Major A. W. Stevens, one of the army's crack stratosphere fliers and a member of the Hayden Planetarium-Grace Eclipse Expedition to Peru.

The pictures were flown back from Peru to laboratories here. Experts at the Harvard College Observatory were "amazed" when they began to study the pictures taken from an atmosphere where there is no dust and almost no sky or atmospheric haze. The familiar coronal streamers which appear on eclipse photographs taken from the ground as tongues of flame spurting from the sun's surface, so much so that some astronomers have nicknamed the sun "a five-point star," were almost indistinguishable.

Instead, the stratosphere pictures were completely dominated by a giant halo pervading the solar atmosphere on all sides. The coronal streamers appeared as "relatively insignificant" bright tracery in this immense globular envelope.

The astronomers hesitated to make a public announcement of the discovery, which in many ways upset traditional views of the sun's struc-

Continued on Page Nineteen

LEVANEVSKY IS OFF FOR U. S. VIA POLE WITH 5 IN BIG PLANE

Flier Leaves Moscow Planning Trip to New York, but Seattle Attache Reports New Goal

SOARS OVER BARENTS SEA

Four-Motored Craft to Refuel at Fairbanks—Will Travel in the Substratosphere

By HAROLD DENNY

Wireless to THE NEW YORK TIMES.

MOSCOW, Friday, Aug. 13.—Blond Sigismund Levanevsky, whose appearance and accomplishments have won for him the sobriquet "the Soviet Lindbergh," took off last evening at 6:13 o'clock [10:13 A.M., Thursday, Eastern daylight time] in a gigantic four-motored airplane for the United States via the North Pole.

His first stop will be Fairbanks, Alaska, where he will refuel. Thence he was to steer a course toward New York, his eventual destination, with a refueling at Edmonton, Alberta, and possibly another at Chicago.

[A. Vartanian, Soviet representative in Seattle, Wash., was quoted by The Associated Press as saying an official change in plans made the plane's destination the Oakland, Calif., airport instead of New York. He said the plane would pass over the North Pole about 11 P. M. Thursday (3 A. M. Friday, Eastern daylight-saving time).

[Mr. Vartanian reported the fliers had radioed at 9 P. M. (midnight, Eastern daylight time) that they had passed over Alexandra Land on the European side of the North Pole, about 600 miles from the Pole.]

Allows 30 Hours to Alaska

Levanevsky hopes to land in Alaska in a little more than thirty hours. He could not estimate his time after that, for it will depend on refueling arrangements.

Although two Soviet flights across the pole to America have been carried out this Summer with such regularity and precision as to make them almost routine events, this flight has several unique features. It is being made under conditions closely approximating those that Soviet aviation authorities envisage in the event that their dream of a regular airline between the Soviet Union and America via the Arctic becomes an everyday reality.

The plane, a new one and to judge by its appearance one of the finest Soviet engineers have ever constructed, was specially designed by Bolkhovitinoff for safely carrying passengers and freight to America. On its present flight it is carrying a crew of six men, all of whom have flying duties. This is twice the size of the crews that manned the preceding transpolar ships.

In addition to Mr. Levanevsky, the members of the crew are:

Co-pilot Nikolai Kastanaeff, 33 years old, one of the well-known Soviet test pilots.

Navigator Victor Levchenko, 31,

Continued on Page Eleven

BOND TO WITHDRAW TO HELP COPELAND; DEWEY BOOM GAINS

Action of Ex-Representative Lets Party Foes of Mayor Center on One Man

HE WILL RUN KINGS DRIVE

Senator's Petitions Checked —Friends Hopeful Racket Prosecutor Will Run

Former Representative Charles G. Bond announced last night that he would decline the designation for the Republican nomination for Mayor in favor of Senator Royal S. Copeland, Tammany's candidate for Mayor in the Republican primary, and would act as the Senator's Brooklyn campaign manager.

Mr. Bond's decision to withdraw will enable Republicans opposed to the renomination of the Mayor to concentrate on one candidate. Jacob A. Livingston, leader of the anti-La Guardia Republican forces in Brooklyn, expressed approval of Mr. Bond's withdrawal and declared that there was now a clear New Deal issue in the Republican primary between Senator Copeland, opponent of the Roosevelt policies, and Mayor La Guardia, a supporter of the President. Mr. Livingston added that he had no doubt that Senator Copeland would defeat Mayor La Guardia in the Republican primary.

Backers Count on Mayor

Despite the fact that Mr. Bond's withdrawal will make it more difficult for Mayor La Guardia, Republican leaders supporting the Mayor were confident last night that he would continue in the Republican race. They admitted, however, that this was not absolutely certain.

There also was increasing pressure upon Thomas E. Dewey, whose success as a prosecutor of racketeers has won him nation-wide reputation, to take the Republican

Continued on Page Two

Cardinal Hayes Resting in Hospital Here After 100-Mile Ambulance Ride in Storm

Cardinal Hayes was reported last night to be resting comfortably at St. Vincent's Hospital, where he was brought early yesterday after an ambulance trip at night through a driving rain from his Summer residence near Monticello, N. Y.

Mgr. John J. Casey, his secretary, said that the Cardinal had suffered an attack of indigestion and that it had been decided to make a 100-mile journey by ambulance so that he could have the best attention at the hospital here. Mgr. Casey said that after resting at the hospital for a few more days the Cardinal expected to return to Monticello.

Cardinal Hayes was at St. Joseph's Camp in Sullivan County, where he generally spends several months each Summer, when he became ill on Tuesday. The attack did not appear serious, but it was decided to notify Dr. Raymond P. Sullivan and Dr. Oswald La Rotonda, staff physicians at St. Vincent's.

After a consultation the two physicians decided late Wednesday that it would be best to bring the Cardinal to New York for treatment. They went to the Summer residence in a private ambulance Wednesday night and immediately began the return trip with the Cardinal at about midnight.

The ambulance arrived at the hospital after a trip of about four hours through a thunderstorm.

The Cardinal was reported to have stood the trip easily and to have shown improvement soon after arriving at the hospital. Mgr. Casey remained at his bedside but said there was no cause for alarm.

Cardinal Hayes, who is 69 years old, had gone to St. Joseph's on July 1.

The prelate has been in generally good health in recent years. In 1932, while he was attending the Eucharistic Congress in Dublin, illness caused him to postpone his return to this country for several days. In 1931 he had influenza, but recovered after a tour of the South.

SENATOR BLACK NOMINATED AS SUPREME COURT JUSTICE; QUICK CONFIRMATION BALKED

Selection of Black Splits Congress; Both Green and Lewis Praise Him

Division Viewed in Capitol as Presaging Another Controversy to Complicate Remaining Days of the Session—Many Decline to Express Their Views

Special to THE NEW YORK TIMES.

WASHINGTON, Aug. 12.—The first reaction following President Roosevelt's nomination of Senator Black to the Supreme Court today indicated that another bitter fight might further complicate the last days of this session of Congress.

Certain Senators, including Glass, King, Burke, Austin, Vandenberg and Bridges, made it known publicly that they would oppose his confirmation and others, not so vocal, intimated that they expected a fight.

Involved in the issue were not only Senator Black's distinct leanings toward the more radical of the New Deal policies but also a number of hurts that he had inflicted in his famous Senate investigations of air and ocean mail contracts and lobbying in Congress.

Also involved was a resentment in certain Senatorial quarters against the surprise tactics of the President in making the nomination.

On the other hand, the Administration leadership from the White House down and the young liberal Senators, of whom Senator Black was a champion, were preparing to make a determined fight in his behalf. They freely predicted that they would send his confirmation to the President by the middle of next week.

Opponents of Senator Black's appointment were as yet a leaderless group.

Meanwhile, comment both favorable and unfavorable to his selection was forthcoming from both Houses, divided chiefly along New Deal and anti-New Deal lines. Organized labor through William Green, president of the American Federation of Labor, and John L. Lewis, head of the Committee for Industrial Organization, were among the first to announce in favor of Mr. Black and an intention to press for his confirmation.

Following are some of the comments:

POSTMASTER GENERAL FARLEY—I am confident that Senator Black's appointment will be highly pleasing to millions who desire that our Government shall be conducted along liberal and progressive lines. He has never faltered in his support of liberal legislation and he has never failed to oppose legislation which in his opinion would give undue privileges to special interests.

SECRETARY PERKINS—I am

Continued on Page Four

BARS BOOK INQUIRY AFTER SNELL PLEA

House Committee, 9 to 3 on Party Lines, Tables Study of Democratic Sales

NEW YORKER GIVES DATA

Dictaphone Transcript Recites Alleged Pressure by Lasker on J. E. Jones, Broker

Special to THE NEW YORK TIMES.

WASHINGTON, Aug. 12.—By a strict party vote, 9 to 3, the House Rules Committee today tabled Representative Snell's resolution for an investigation by the House into the sale by the Democratic National Committee of its 1936 convention books autographed by President Roosevelt.

In arguing for the investigation Mr. Snell laid before the committee twenty-one exhibits to uphold his charge that the committee had collected more than $1,000,000 from the sale of the books to "more than 900 corporations." This he contended was in violation of the Corrupt Practices Act, which prohibits corporations making political contributions.

In the course of his testimony, the House Republican leader read to the committee what he said were excerpts from a transcript of a dictaphone record of an interview J. Edward Jones, New York broker, had with Myles Lasker, who was at one time an agent of Mrs.

Continued on Page Five

NEW TURN SPEEDS ADJOURNMENT AIM

Settlement of Senate's Anti-Lynching Filibuster Gives Hope of End in 10 Days

MOST BILLS WILL GO OVER

Housing as Well as Wages and Hours Measures Imperiled in the House

Special to THE NEW YORK TIMES.

WASHINGTON, Aug. 12.—A pacific settlement of the anti-lynching bill filibuster in the Senate and the perceptibly growing lassitude of the House of Representatives made it appear today that the end of this session of Congress is distant not more than ten days or a fortnight. The general sentiment was that most pending major legislation would be left to be disposed of at the next session.

Two of these major measures, the Wages and Hours Bill and the Housing Bill, are stymied in committees on the House side of the Capitol. The deadlock in the Rules Committee over the wages and hours measure continued today, and House leaders announced that they had formed no plans for forcing the bill to the floor in the event it could not be put through the Rules Committee.

"I am not in close touch with the Rules Committee situation on the Wages and Hours Bill," Speaker Bankhead said, adding that "of course, the leadership would like to have such a bill passed this session."

Representative Rayburn of Texas, majority leader, declined to make any predictions about the fate of specific legislative items, but repeated his opinion that Congress would adjourn by Aug. 25 at the latest.

Housing Draft Is Delayed

The housing bill once again failed to emerge from the House Banking and Currency Committee, which has had it under consideration for several days. House leaders had expected to bring it up for debate on the floor early this week, but the banking committee apparently cannot complete a draft satisfactory to a majority of its members.

A straw showing which way the wind is blowing was found in the announcement today that the Rules Committee would meet tomorrow morning to consider a recess resolution, which is a routine formality normally adopted a few days before the final adjournment of a session of Congress. The resolution authorizes the House to recess, instead of adjourning, at any time, from hour to hour or from day to day.

The procedure can be used, if the House leadership desires, to keep a

Continued on Page Five

SENATE IS STARTLED

Message by Roosevelt Is Kept Secret Till Divulged on Floor

ASHURST INVOKES CUSTOM

But Johnson and Burke Abrogate 'Courtesy' Rule by Call for Committee Study

COURT BATTLE FLARES UP

Choice of Wage Champion Rankles Some of South, but He Is Expected to Win

By TURNER CATLEDGE

Special to THE NEW YORK TIMES.

WASHINGTON, Aug. 12.—President Roosevelt today nominated Senator Hugo Black of Alabama, an ardent supporter of the New Deal and co-author of the Black-Connery Wage-Hour Bill, to be Associate Justice of the Supreme Court, filling the vacancy caused by the retirement of Justice Van Devanter.

The nomination of the 51-year-old Alabaman was sent in a sealed envelope to the Senate at noon, attended by all the secrecy that had surrounded the President's earlier and ill-fated proposal to add six new justices to the court.

It dropped like salt into the political wounds already rubbed raw by the court issue, the wage-hour bill and the many other controversies worked up between the Administration and Congress in the drive to adjourn.

The first manifestation of this was the blocking by Senators Johnson of California and Burke of Nebraska of an attempt by Senator Ashurst to rush confirmation of Mr. Black's nomination without sending it to the Judiciary Committee.

Disregard for Courtesy Rule

The Senate's rule of courtesy by which executive appointees from its membership are confirmed promptly and unanimously was thus abrogated for the first time since L. Q. C. Lamar of Mississippi was nominated to the court in 1888.

Neither Senator Johnson nor Senator Burke voiced outright opposition to Senator Black's surprise nomination, but they insisted that it should be carefully studied by the Judiciary Committee in light of the controversies which so recently had been raging about the court.

The nomination, therefore, was referred to the Judiciary Committee and by it to a subcommittee composed of Senators Neely, Logan, Dieterich, McGill, Austin and Borah for study and report. A public hearing by the subcommittee was set for tomorrow morning at 10:30 o'clock.

Senator Black's friends and Administration leaders had little doubt tonight that he would be confirmed by a decisive vote regardless of the undercover rumblings of opposition.

Southern Resentment Felt

Only a few Senators had expressed themselves as opposed to the confirmation—among them Senators Glass, King, Vanderberg, Austin and Bridges—but others were obviously unhappy over the choice, particularly among the conservative Southern contingent who regarded Mr. Black's selection as another White House slap at them.

Whether the antagonism of the nominee's Southern colleagues would flare into the open was a question. They disliked the choice for several reasons, among them Senator Black's own activities in behalf of such measures as the wages and hours and the thirty-hour week bills.

But they disliked most of all what they construed as a deliberate effort of Mr. Roosevelt further to slice up the Democratic party in the South.

Drama at White House

Regardless of the repetition of White House surprises, Senator Black's nomination came with startling effect upon the Senate membership.

A scant two hours before it was sent to the Capitol a White House spokesman, Stephen T. Early, assistant secretary to the President, had indicated that the appointment might not be made at this session. He said that the President was still studying a list of sixty or seventy names of possible appointees.

Soon after making this announcement Mr. Early called regular

Continued on Page Four

Japanese forces entering Tientsin, China, in July.

The Supreme Court after FDR's appointment of Hugo L. Black (Standing, at extreme right). (Seated, left to right) George Sutherland, James Clark McReynolds, Chief Justice Charles Evans Hughes, Louis D. Brandeis, Pierce Butler. (Standing) Benjamin N. Cardozo, Harlan Fiske Stone, Owen J. Roberts.

"All the News That's Fit to Print."

The New York Times.

LATE CITY EDITION
Generally fair, slightly colder, probably preceded by snow early today. Tomorrow fair, warmer.
Temperatures Yesterday—Max.,36; Min.30

Copyright, 1938, by The New York Times Company.

VOL. LXXXVII....No. 29,211. Entered as Second-Class Matter, Postoffice, New York, N. Y. NEW YORK, SATURDAY, JANUARY 15, 1938. P TWO CENTS in New York City. | THREE CENTS Within 200 Miles. | FOUR CENTS Elsewhere Except in 7th and 8th Postal Zones.

ROOSEVELT INSISTS ON THE DISSOLUTION OF HOLDING COMPANIES, BANKS INCLUDED; HEARS PLEA FOR RECOVERY POLICY SOON

BONNET IS NAMED TO FORM CABINET OF FRENCH CENTER

Socialist Support Necessary, However, if Former Finance Minister Is to Succeed

BLUM THE SECOND CHOICE

Leftist Government With Aid of Communists Is Seen as the Alternative

ELECTIONS A POSSIBILITY

Liberal Capitalist Regime Is Held at Stake in Present Crisis—Strikes Continue

By P. J. PHILIP
Wireless to THE NEW YORK TIMES.

PARIS, Jan. 14.—Facing the fact that as a result of this morning's resignation of the Chautemps Cabinet the choice must be made between Finance Minister Georges Bonnet and Vice Premier Leon Blum for Premier, President Albert Lebrun today turned first to the former.

It was M. Bonnet, with his insistence on the liberty of the franc from exchange control, on moderation in expenditures so as to keep the budget balanced and on the maintenance of confidence in the future among employers, labor, holders of capital and pensioners, who in reality was responsible for the situation which arose yesterday. It was not until this morning that the long torment ended in the rejection of Communist support by Premier Camille Chautemps, the resignation of the Socialist Ministers and finally the resignation of the whole Cabinet.

In asking M. Bonnet to form a new government, the President has responded to what seems to be the general wish of the country for a sound and moderate liberalism in the direction of its affairs. But if M. Bonnet does not succeed, the President's second choice must be M. Blum, with an extreme Left Cabinet and all the adventures which may follow.

Bonnet Talks to Leaders

Fully realizing the difficulty of the task, but confident that in the Chamber of Deputies and in the country the majority is against exchange control and all that can follow in the way of restriction of liberty, M. Bonnet accepted the President's invitation. He had conversations this evening with Jules Jeanneney, President of the Senate; Edouard Herriot, President of the Chamber, and with M. Chautemps. Tomorrow morning he will see Defense Minister Edouard Daladier, Senator Joseph Caillaux, Albert Sarraut and, above all, M. Blum. It is on his interview with the last mentioned that the possibility of his forming a government depends, and that conversation is likely to be an interesting one.

For the man who just a year ago was sent to Washington by M. Blum as Ambassador will put to his former chief the alternative:

"It is either you or me."

Very seldom in this country of frequent Ministerial changes has there been a more dramatic situation for very seldom have bigger issues been involved. Two totally different conceptions of society and State will be in debate. If M. Bonnet gets M. Blum's support there will be a continuation of the old liberal capitalist system on which the French Republic was founded. If M. Blum refuses his support and M. Bonnet has to abandon his effort, M. Blum will have to take as his associates not only his own Socialists but Communists who, while paying lip service to him as a leader and to liberty, are so bent on domination of their class and interests that the regime that has existed for the last sixty years may be completely changed.

Chautemps Rejects Bid

President Lebrun did not immediately send for M. Bonnet. There were first the traditional consultations and the offer to M. Chautemps to remake his Cabinet. M. Chautemps asked to be excused. So did M. Daladier who pleaded that he was sufficiently occupied in keeping the national defense up to the required pitch of efficiency. So did M. Sarraut who, however, reserved himself for later if others should fail.

Meanwhile the Socialists had met and all had given their opinion that another Popular Front government, "under Socialist direction," that is to say under M. Blum's direction, should be formed. M. Blum himself indicated that if such a course were taken he would want to include Communists in the government. But if he does the Radical Socialists will stay out and probably most of them will refuse their support. A return to the Blum Cabi-

Continued on Page Five

Mae West Script Brings Sharp Rebuke From FCC

NBC Is Censured for 'Vulgar' Broadcast of 'Adam and Eve'—59 Substations Are Criticized—Company's Apology Is Rejected

Special to THE NEW YORK TIMES.

WASHINGTON, Jan. 14.—A severe reprimand was sent today by the Federal Communications Commission to the National Broadcasting Company for its broadcast Dec. 12 of the "Adam and Eve" feature by Mae West and Don Ameche, and another part of the same program in which the ventriloquist's dummy "Charlie McCarthy" played opposite Miss West.

Not only the National Broadcasting Company, but the fifty-nine substations which rebroadcast the dialogue, violated the ethics of decency, the commission held. It refused to accept the National Broadcasting Company's apology that it was only a "human error in judgment."

The commission held that while the program originated over the NBC chain the stations which picked it up and broadcast it to their areas could not be excused for carrying this program on the ground that such program was received over the network under a contract for program service.

The letter was sent to Lenox R. Lohr, president of the National Broadcasting Company, and was signed by Frank R. McNinch, chairman of the commission.

Prefacing a reading of the letter to reporters this afternoon, Mr. McNinch said that the commission had read the transcript and then heard an electrical transcription of the feature before deciding that it was "vulgar," "indecent" and "against all proprieties."

The letter to the National Broadcasting Company read:

"The commission has carefully considered the transcript of the 'Adam and Eve' feature by Don Ameche and Mae West and the dialogue between Mae West and Charlie McCarthy, sponsored by Chase & Sanborn and broadcast by the National Broadcasting Company over fifty-nine stations on Sunday night, Dec. 12. It is our considered opinion that both of these features were far below even

Continued on Page Eighteen

PROTESTS ATTACK BY DODD ON HITLER

German Ambassador Visits Hull, Who Says Free Speech Is Guaranteed to Citizens

NO CONTROL OVER EX-ENVOY

Nazi News Agency in Berlin Limits Reference to Incident to Item of Three Lines

Special to THE NEW YORK TIMES.

WASHINGTON, Jan. 14.—Hans Dieckhoff, the German Ambassador, protested to Secretary Hull today against a speech made by former Ambassador William E. Dodd in New York last night and the Secretary replied that the right of free speech was still guaranteed to citizens of the United States.

The German Ambassador visited the State Department early this morning without awaiting instructions from the Wilhelmstrasse, it is understood, remembering the numerous occasions when the German Ambassador had been formally instructed to protest against some utterance which offended Berlin sensibilities.

One of the most memorable of these was when Dr. Hans Luther, former German Ambassador, was instructed to protest at the State Department against Mayor La Guardia's proposal to enshrine Chancellor Hitler's bust in the Chamber of Horrors at the New York World's Fair.

Mr. Hull indicated today that Mr. Dieckhoff's visit might not be interpreted as a formal protest, but added that the Ambassador certainly referred without approval to some of the remarks Mr. Dodd made last night. As on previous occasions, Mr. Hull could only point out to the envoy that the Federal Government had no control over the utterances, public or private, of individual citizens.

He stated that Mr. Dodd was no longer an Ambassador of the United States, and that Mr. Dodd's views could in no way be taken as representing the official views of the government, since he no longer had any connection with the government.

A reporter asked Mr. Hull whether he meant that Mr. Dodd's views did not "necessarily" represent the views of the government, but the Secretary declined to specify further.

Mr. Dodd, in addressing a testimonial dinner given for him last night, said that the democracies of the world must unite to oppose the growth of totalitarianism, pointing to the German-Italian-Japanese agreement as the specific combination he feared.

He ridiculed Chancellor Hitler's assertions that the Germans constitute an "Aryan" race, pointing to Slavic and Latin blood infiltrations resulting from medieval conquests.

Mr. Dodd resigned as Ambassador to Germany because of his lack of sympathy with the National Socialist regime.

Brief Reference in Berlin

By The Associated Press.

BERLIN, Jan. 14.—A three-line reference to the protest of the German Ambassador Hans Heinrich

Continued on Page Six

ACTOR'S 'PROTEGE' SEIZED IN 4 CRIMES

Accused of Holding Up Office, Stealing Cab to Flee and Trying to Kill Policeman

INJURES 2 IN WILD FLIGHT

A Sidewalk Clogger as a Boy —Julius Tannen Sought to Adopt Him 11 Years Ago

About eleven years ago Martin (Red) Ritter, ragged but likable, clogged on the sidewalks for theatregoers' pennies. One night Julius Tannen, master of ceremonies in the "Vanities," saw Ritter and led him into the Earl Carrol Theatre. There the boy made an impromptu "hit" and was showered with coins.

Tannen, who was brought up in an orphan asylum, developed a paternal interest and took the urchin into his home with his two sons. He wished to adopt the boy, but the Children's Court found a barrier. The actor was a Jew and the boy a Catholic.

Yesterday, at 22 years of age, and a little battered, Ritter was under arrest in the West Forty-seventh Street station. The police accused him, chronologically, of holding up a steamship agency, stealing a taxicab, running down two youths with the cab, and trying to kill a policeman. Ritter was with another armed youth who escaped.

Hold Up Three in Office

The two hold-up men walked into the Atlantic Steamship Supply Company at 564 West Fifty-second Street and pointed .38-caliber automatics at Vincenzo Tisbo, the proprietor; Ralph Adramis, a bookkeeper, and Pasquale Detrani, a tenant in the building. They left with $106, 14,000 Italian lire, valued at $580, and $10 taken from the tenant.

Outside the robbers hailed a taxicab and told Arthur Johnson, the driver, of 48 West Seventy-third Street, to go south. In Forty-sixth Street, between Eighth and Ninth Avenues, the driver was ordered to stop. He tried to turn his head, but there was a pistol near each ear.

"Get out!" commanded one man. "Don't turn your head. Look straight ahead and go in the hallway or I'll blow your head off your shoulders."

With both gunmen following, Johnson walked into a hallway. He pleaded for his cab. He said: "Have a heart. All I have is three bucks to my name."

"Give him a five spot," said one of the men. The other man slipped a $5 bill into Johnson's hand.

From an upper hallway window Johnson saw one of the gunmen take the wheel of the cab. At Eighth Avenue and Forty-fifth Street Patrolman Joseph Hulsman was crossing when the taxicab made a right turn west into Forty-fifth Street.

The cab headed straight for the patrolman. He jumped aside but was struck on the left hand, which was temporarily paralyzed. Next the cab knocked down Jack Heyman, 18, of 107-16 120th Street, Richmond Hill, L. I., and Milton Clott, also 18, of 2,815 Brighton Sixth Street, Brooklyn.

Ritter jumped out of the cab and his hand dived into his overcoat pocket, Hulsman said. The patrol-

Continued on Page Sixteen

CHINESE UNBROKEN, WANT WAR PUSHED; FOES TAKE TSINING

Prolonged Hostilities Appear Likely as Defenders Gird Forces to Harry Foe

AIR STRENGTH INCREASED

Three More Generals Said to Have Been Ousted From Defenses in the North

The Chinese, unwilling to yield despite the military reverses they have suffered, want the war pushed and plan to wage savage guerrilla warfare along the Japanese lines of communication, a survey of opinion in Hankow, China's de facto capital, indicated. Observers believed prolonged hostilities were likely. [Page 1.]

Tsining, city in Southern Shantung, was recaptured by the Japanese after a reinforced Chinese army was reported to have taken it. Chinese press reports admitted that the city, badly damaged, had been evacuated by the Chinese, who retreated southward before their advancing foes. [Page 6.]

Generals Yen Hsi-shan, Han Fu-chu and Feng Yu-hsiang, formerly three of China's most important war lords, were reported to have been retired from their army commands. [Page 6.]

Chinese Want to Fight On

By F. TILLMAN DURDIN
Wireless to THE NEW YORK TIMES.

HANKOW, Jan. 14.—The preponderance of evidence in this de facto capital of the Chinese Government points to prolonged continuation of the Sino-Japanese hostilities if the Japanese persist in their campaign of conquest. There is little indication that the Chinese people and the government have been wearied to the point where they are willing to surrender on the basis of any terms likely to be advanced by the Japanese.

Such a situation puts matters squarely up to Japan. There is this alternative for Japan to bring the war to an early termination—either by an early aboutface and withdrawal of her troops, or by delivering an immediate and crushing blow to China. All indications appear to rule out the first, and military experts, Chinese and foreign, see little chance of success for the second.

The ability of the Japanese Army to defeat the Chinese in separate engagements is granted, but observers here believe the Chinese, nevertheless, can offer sufficient frontal resistance, combined with savage guerrilla warfare along the Japanese lines of communications, to make Japanese advance a slow and costly business. A land threat to Hankow within two months is considered highly unlikely; six months is thought more probable.

On Occupation of Railroads

Foreign military observers here believe the most logical Japanese tactics now would be to push occupation of the railroads. This would involve the capture of Hankow and would force the government back into Szechwan, Yunnan and Kansu Provinces, where only straitened and ineffectual resistance would be possible.

However, it is realized that even taking rail lines will be difficult,

Continued on Page Six

Budget Snarl Delays City Salary Checks; Many Workers Won't Get Pay Till Monday

While employes in three departments worked last night to speed through the payrolls, it became apparent that for many city employes today will be a payless payday, in that their checks will be deferred until Monday.

Most of the payrolls will have been cleared through the Controller's office, the Municipal Civil Service Commission and the City Treasurer by today, but as Saturday is a half day and some departments have only a skeleton staff, it was estimated that about one-quarter of the employes will not receive checks until Monday.

Many salary checks were distributed late yesterday, including those in the Mayor's office. It was said at the City Treasurer's office that the police, firemen and sanitation employes had been taken care of. The Controller's office reported, on the other hand, that some payrolls had not yet been received from departments.

Uncertainties arising from the delayed passage of the budget last Tuesday, the shifting of many employes between new and old departments under the new Charter, and the filing of payrolls by county officers which ignored reductions and eliminations made in the disputed budget were held responsible for the fact that all salary checks will not be in the hands of employes today.

One of the payrolls missing last night was that of the City Clerk's office. It was awaited with interest to see who certified it, Robert Lee Tudor, whose election as City Clerk by the City Council is disputed by the Labor-Fusion-Republican bloc, or Michael J. Cruise, who was former City Clerk and is considered by some as a holdover.

Mayor La Guardia, Controller McGoldrick and Mr. Tudor and Mr. Cruise are due to sign the budget at 8:45 this morning in City Hall. Originally set for immediately after midnight last night, the Controller informed the Mayor the action could just as well take place today.

Controller McGoldrick reported that his offering of $15,000,000 in ninety-day revenue bills at the record low rate of interest of ½ of 1 per cent was quickly taken up by the twenty-six banks to which it had been offered.

TOLD OF CONFUSION

Lamont, Lewis, Young and Others Say Aims Need Clarifying

BUSINESS 'NERVES' CITED

Visitors' Purpose Is to Unite Business, Government and Labor, Lewis Announces

Special to THE NEW YORK TIMES.

WASHINGTON, Jan. 14.—President Roosevelt today received a frank appeal from a group representing industry, labor and finance that he enunciate as soon as practicable a "policy of government" and, in the interest of speedy economic recovery, put an end to apparently conflicting statements of some administration spokesmen on questions affecting the national welfare.

The President was told during an hour's conference with the group that the nation seeks reassurance from him as to what his administration intends to do on such questions as prices, taxation, the public utilities, aid to the durable goods industry and monetary policy, and that he must soon "do something" to steady the nerves of the business community, which had been disturbed by a series of attacks.

Those who conferred with the President in the White House soon after noon were Owen D. Young, chairman of the board of the General Electric Corporation; John L. Lewis, chairman of the Committee for Industrial Organization; Phillip Murray, vice president of United Mine Workers of America; Thomas W. Lamont, senior partner of J. P. Morgan & Co.; Charles Taussig, president of American Molasses Company, and A. A. Berle Jr., former City Chamberlain of New York.

Lewis Talks to Reporters

Acting as spokesman for the group, and flanked on either side by the other participants in the conference, Mr. Lewis stood on the porch at the front of the White House and made this statement to newspaper men:

"We attended this conference with the President and discussed the seriousness of the economic and industrial situation in the country. This group had had some preliminary discussion and was impressed with the desirability, if at all possible, of working out with the Administration a definite program of action by business, government and labor.

"The discussions will be continued at the President's discretion. The discussions took a course of wide range in an effort to deal with the situation."

Pressed for further information, particularly as to whether any definite "plan of action" had been proposed, Mr. Lewis stated that there was nothing more that could be said at this time. He turned to the others to ask if they had anything to add to his statement, but all agreed that he had covered the ground adequately.

Later it was learned that neither

Continued on Page Three

Sweeping Tax Revision Proposed In Report by House Subcommittee

Stimulus to Business Is Objective in Urging Changes in Profits, Corporation and Capital Gains Levies

Special to THE NEW YORK TIMES.

WASHINGTON, Jan. 14.—A report recommending the complete revision and codification of the internal revenue laws, with special emphasis on changes in the present method of taxing corporations and investment profits, was presented today to the Ways and Means Committee by its subcommittee on taxation.

The subcommittee predicted that if its program were adopted it would provide a "very substantial stimulation to business."

The report contains sixty-three specific recommendations, among them the retention but liberalization of the undistributed profits tax; a broadening of the restrictions in the capital gains tax and the inclusion of a new title (the "third basket"), to apply to closely held corporations, which would make their taxes as heavy as they are now under the present undistributed profits tax.

Few other basic changes were suggested in the report, hearings on which will start tomorrow morning before the full committee, with the prospect that the new tax bill will be ready for presentation to the House in the week of Jan. 24.

It is believed in the House that the measure, closely following today's 100-page report, will be passed without much delay and turned over to the Senate in the first week in February.

Leaders in both chambers have said that they would send the legislation to the President by March 15.

In its discussion of the undistributed profits tax and the criticisms of it, the report said:

"Your subcommittee has examined these complaints and believes there has been much exaggeration as to hardships in the great majority of cases.

"It is believed, however, that a substantial number of cases of hardship exist, and that in such cases there is a merit in these complaints.

"The severity of the present normal and undistributed profits tax upon corporations has often been overstated," the report continued.

It contained a table showing that the highest effective rates, even with the complete retention of earnings, was only 14.4 per cent on a corporation with a net of $2,000 and 32.2 per cent on very large net incomes, even with complete retention of profits.

The proposed changes in the tax structure, the committee stated,

Continued on Page Two

STATE BILL WIDENS WORK INSURANCE

Would Extend Unemployment Benefits to 150,000 to 200,000 Earning Over $3,000

NO COST TO EMPLOYERS

Measure Aims at Diverting to Albany $7,000,000 a Year Going to Washington

Special to THE NEW YORK TIMES.

ALBANY, Jan. 14.—Extension of the State Unemployment Insurance Law to include within its coverage between 150,000 and 200,000 persons whose salaries of more than $3,000 have heretofore prohibited them from receiving any benefits was advocated in a bill introduced today by Senator Dunnigan of the Bronx, majority leader. A companion measure was submitted in the lower house by Assemblyman Killgrew, Manhattan Democrat.

It is estimated that the measure, suggested by Governor Lehman in his annual message to the Legislature, would add an additional $7,000,000 annually to the State's receipts under the law. It would not, it was pointed out, in any way increase the fees now paid by employers, since the benefits accruing to the higher salaried persons would only be based on their first $3,000.

At present employers within the State are paying a tax on their entire payroll to the Federal Government under the Federal Social Security Act. The State, however, is limited to claiming a fee on the salary of employes now making less than $3,000 annually. If the proposed measure is passed the State would be able to claim additional fees on the first $3,000 of higher salaried persons.

State Entitled to 90 Per Cent

Under the Federal law the State is entitled to receive up to 90 per cent of the tax money paid by employers, but in cases like those involving workers in the over-$3,000 group, where persons are included in the Federal act but not in the State act, the full tax goes to the Bureau of Internal Revenue in Washington.

Governor Lehman and the State Advisory Council on Unemployment Insurance, which is backing the proposal, found after investigation that many employers were not paying to the State anywhere near the 90 per cent to which the State was entitled. The average payment to the State, it was said, was in the neighborhood of 70 to 75 per cent.

It is believed that extending the act would retain $7,000,000 which would otherwise go to the Federal Government, and would result in an increase of the yearly fund of

Continued on Page Sixteen

ALDRICH FOR EASING OF FEDERAL CURBS

Government Policies Helped Bring On Recession, Banker Tells Relief Hearing

HITS 'INFLAMMATORY' TALK

Would Have Both Sides Stop It —Urges Reassurance to Utilities and Tax Relief

By LOUIS STARK
Special to THE NEW YORK TIMES.

WASHINGTON, Jan. 14.—Winthrop W. Aldrich, chairman of the board of the Chase National Bank, an unexpected witness before the Senate Committee on Relief and Unemployment today, declared that government policies had contributed to bring the business recession, "which was a great surprise to many people."

He asserted that the public utilities were "bursting to go ahead" if assured against government competition in their field and that "the one thing that has caused more concern than anything else is the continued unbalanced budget."

If there were some indication that the budget would be balanced and if sincere and mutual trust between government and business could be arranged so that the investing public would have confidence, he said, business would go ahead "in the greatest possible way."

"Inflammatory statements made by members of the government," according to Mr. Aldrich, were "most unfortunate," and, in agreeing with Senator Murray that there also had been "inflammatory statements by business men," he called for an end of such "propaganda" and for cooperation between all citizens and the government in the present situation as a patriotic duty.

Would Restudy Exchange Curbs

While he agreed that the stock exchanges should be regulated, Mr. Aldrich proposed that some provisions of the laws regulating them be "restudied." He maintained that high income taxes, and particularly the capital gains tax and the undivided profits tax, had slowed down the capital market. He was not against taxing capital gains, but felt that this tax should be taken out of the income tax category "and that capital gains be taxed as a separate matter and at a flat rate, or a rate graduated downward.

Mr. Aldrich followed on the stand John D. A. Morrow, president of the Pittsburgh Coal Company, who asserted that in his view "the depression was created here in Washington" and "it will have to be cured here in Washington by a frank acknowledgement of some

Continued on Page Sixteen

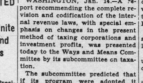

UTILITY RULE IS HIT

President Holds 'Remote Control' of Billions Is 'Intolerable'

'DEATH SENTENCE' STAYS

Administration for Abolishing Holding Concerns in All Fields, He Says

By FELIX BELAIR Jr.
Special to THE NEW YORK TIMES.

WASHINGTON, Jan. 14.—President Roosevelt indicated today that abolition of all holding companies was his ultimate objective, adding that it mattered not whether they existed in the public utility or other fields or whether they were top or intermediate concerns. He particularly specified holding company control of banks and operating utility companies.

In reply to a question asked at a press conference whether he planned to eliminate all holding companies, Mr. Roosevelt replied that he did, and added the question, Why have any?

Meanwhile, the President indicated that the Administration had no intention of modifying its power policy as applied to municipally-owned projects. He said that funds already appropriated would continue to be used for loans and grants for municipal projects with the understanding that the municipalities would first try to buy out existing privately owned facilities at a fair price.

After giving his views about holding companies, President Roosevelt left his office and went to the White House for further conferences with leaders of finance, industry and labor.

Discussion Begun by President

The discussion of holding companies was started by the President himself. He had been asked during a recent press conference to comment on a memorandum left with him by Wendell L. Willkie, president of the Commonwealth and Southern Corporation, in which the utility executive outlined a proposed basis of reconciliation between the utilities and the Administration.

The memorandum was on the President's desk when he opened his press conference today. Taking up the proposals one after another, Mr. Roosevelt replied to each.

In his discussion of the Willkie memorandum, which was left with him in the latter part of November, the President made the following observations:

1. The Administration can never agree to a modification of the "death sentence" requiring dissolution of all but first-degree utility holding companies except under certain conditions.

2. The situation is not to be tolerated wherein utility holding companies with $600,000,000 of assets can control $13,000,000,000 of utility capital. That amounts to a four-inch tail wagging a ninety-six-inch dog and the Administration's plan is to cut the muscle out of the tail.

3. There is very little wind and water in the stock of utility operating companies and what there is of it can be squeezed out without harming such companies or their assets. Utility holding companies present a different picture.

Extent of Power Competition

4. Government competition with privately owned power companies comprises only about 15 per cent of the area, population and power production of the country and there is no intention to ask new funds of Congress to increase this competition in the near future.

5. Why should there be any holding companies? This applies to all fields, but particularly to banking. Why cannot a bank run itself in a community able to support it?

Taking up the Willkie memorandum, President Roosevelt said a lot of water had passed over the dam since its submission. He later indicated that recent conferences with utility operating company executives had increased his determination to abolish holding company control. He had been told, he said, of holding company insistence on the right to finance affairs of operating companies despite the availability of local funds.

The President first criticized what he regarded as an attempt by Mr. Willkie to have the public utility industry considered as a unit, with the good and not so good together. It was the same old story of lumping all business together, he said, add-

Continued on Page Four

Street Scenes in New York City

Museum of the City of New York

Museum of the City of New York

"All the News That's Fit to Print."

The New York Times.

LATE CITY EDITION
Snow or rain today and tomorrow, little change in temperature.
Temperatures Yesterday—Max., 41; Min., 29

Copyright, 1938, by The New York Times Company.

VOL. LXXXVII....No. 29,218. Entered as Second-Class Matter, Postoffice, New York, N. Y. NEW YORK, SATURDAY, JANUARY 22, 1938. P TWO CENTS in New York City. | THREE CENTS Within 200 Miles. | FOUR CENTS Elsewhere Except in 7th and 8th Postal Zones.

CHAUTEMPS BACKED BY CHAMBER, 502-1; FRANC AGAIN DROPS

Extreme Right Abstains From Voting as Moderates Join Left Support of Regime

BERGERY ONLY DISSENTER

Poll and Statement on Policy Do Little to Clear French Political Muddle

CURRENCY CRISIS TO FORE

Government Opposes Exchange Control—Defense Ministries Coordinated Under Daladier

By P. J. PHILIP
Wireless to THE NEW YORK TIMES.

PARIS, Jan. 21.—With one of those votes of 502 to 1, which mean nothing except general approval of the courage of those who have taken upon themselves the government of the country, the Chamber of Deputies this evening voted confidence in Premier Camille Chautemps and his colleagues. Neither the vote nor the Ministerial statement and debate which preceded it are likely to clear the situation greatly.

The Communists and the moderates joined the Radical Socialists and Socialists in supporting the government. Only Gaston Bergery, for reasons of his own, voted against it and the extreme Right abstained.

In debate, what criticism was made came from the Left. In the Ministerial declaration almost every point of policy enumerated was satisfactory to the Right, and at times—notably the passage referring to freedom of exchange—it was the Right which cheered and the Left which sat silent.

But when M. Chautemps replied to his critics, his speech was so "Left" that had he made it a week ago yesterday in the Chamber the present crisis would never have developed.

Franc Again Drops

It is not by any means the first time that the French Government has pursued a conservative policy with the support of the Left, but rarely has Parliament been offered such a variety of political sauces in an effort to make the cold realities of the situation palatable.

Today the franc dropped to 30 francs, 22 centimes to the dollar, and that fact dominated everybody's outlook. Unfortunately also, as always, patriotic and other passions have come quickly into play in the discussion of what is to be done to remedy that situation.

There are those who are advising the new Minister of Finance to use his gold reserves freely to prevent further decline. There are those who urge that the gold reserve is the essential bulwark of national defense and it is preferable to let the franc find a new level than reduce that reserve.

It was notable that enthusiasm was distinctly waning for any of these theoretic cures for sick money which used to find such passionate support. M. Bergery got more applause for his statement that freedom of the franc from exchange control was simply freedom for speculators than M. Chautemps did for his declaration that the government would remain loyal to the tri-partite monetary agreement.

Where the Premier had his biggest success was when he praised Léon Blum's attempt to form a government and majority of wide union and declared that what he was seeking to create was sentiment of unanimity among Frenchmen. But it was evident from the fact that the Socialists were the warmest in their applause that that idea and desire were not yet realizable.

Strong Action Promised

In itself the declaration of Ministerial policy was such as all could easily subscribe to. It promised strong action against any attempted disorder and firm application of the laws of the Republic. It promised to safeguard the social advantages obtained by the workers and the introduction next week of a new social harmony bill and, shortly, of an old age pension bill. It made an energetic defense of the franc and rejection of exchange control one of the principal planks of the government's program, proclaimed the maintenance at full efficiency of national defense, to which end closer coordination was being sought between the three defense Ministries by placing them under a single head. Edouard Daladier has been chosen for the task.

Close cooperation with Britain, fidelity to the League of Nations, continuation of the non-intervention policy in Spain and the maintenance of existing friendships and

Continued on Page Two

Italian Forces in Libya Doubled, Decree Reveals

By The Associated Press.

ROME, Jan. 21.—Details of Premier Mussolini's North African war machine were disclosed today with the publication of a decree of last July that doubled the military forces in Libya by creating an additional army corps for service there.

The new corps, it was revealed, includes six regiments of infantry, four regiments of artillery, one regiment of engineers, one sanitary company, one commissary company and one automotive center.

Early in the Fall Mussolini began moving the Twentieth and Twenty-first Army Corps to Libya. An official explanation gave "the international situation" as the reason. War supplies have been concentrated in Libya in sufficient quantities, reports said, to enable the colonial army to subsist for many weeks without replenishment.

PROTESTANTS PLAN UNION IN ENGLAND

Anglican and Nonconformist Leaders Issue Proposal for One Great Church

VARIETY OF WORSHIP KEPT

People Would Have Voice in Selection of Their Clergy—Keen Controversy Likely

Special Cable to THE NEW YORK TIMES.

LONDON, Jan. 21.—Plans for one great united Protestant Church of England in which Anglicans and Nonconformists would become members of one "visible society" were issued by religious leaders tonight.

Many years of discussion have gone into the formulation of the proposals, which concern the Anglicans, the Methodists, the Baptists, the Congregationalists, the Presbyterians and the Society of Friends.

The final draft was the work of a joint conference under the chairmanship of the Archbishop of Canterbury that included the Archbishop of York with eleven Bishops on the Anglican side and Dr. A. E. Garvie, the Rev. M. E. Aubrey, Dr. Sidney M. Berry and Dr. J. Scott Lidgett from the free churches.

The plan, which was commended for the attention of the Anglican Church by both houses of the Convocations of York and Canterbury and similarly by the Free Church Council, is expected to arouse the keenest controversy.

Proposed Governing Bodies

The proposed new church, it is suggested, would be governed by a general assembly, diocesan synods and congregational councils. Through these councils the people would have an effecitve voice in the selection of their "presbyter in charge," as the ministers or priests in chief charge of congregations would be known.

The report is emphatic in declaring that the proposed unity would mean small change in modes of worship.

"Reunion," it says, "does not mean absorption by any existing body, nor would it involve a flat and meagre uniformity. Rather it would conserve and make more widely available the spiritual treasures presently cherished in separation."

Bishops of the Church of England would be accepted as bishops of the united church if they assented to the basis of union and accepted its constitution. New bishops would be chosen from among the ranks of the "presbyters" of the uniting churches in a number proportion-

Continued on Page Three

3,000 OF LEFT SLAIN IN TERUEL TERROR, RESIDENTS TESTIFY

Witnesses Charge Insurgents Held Execution 'Fetes' With Bands and Feasts

2 AIR FORCES BOMB CITIES

Salamanca and Castellon Are Targets—Rebels' Circling Move at Teruel Gains

By LAWRENCE A. FERNSWORTH
Wireless to THE NEW YORK TIMES.

BARCELONA, Spain, Jan. 21.—Investigating magistrates who have been interrogating residents of Teruel one by one during the last fortnight have accumulated evidence pointing to the assassination or execution of at least 3,000 persons because of their Leftist or labor sympathies during the eighteen months that that town of about 12,000 inhabitants was under Generalissimo Francisco Franco's rule.

The Governor General of Aragon, Ignacio Mantecon, affirms the number to be at least 3,000. At Teruel this correspondent talked with some inhabitants who placed the number as high as 4,000.

Leaders of the Falange Espanola [Fascists] together with members of the Civil Guard and secret police, are accused of maintaining a "brigade of death" which spread terror in Teruel and surrounding towns.

On Sunday, Aug. 23, 1936, the execution of thirteen persons, including a woman, was reportedly turned into a spectacle in a public plaza. Among the victims were listed a university professor, a doctor, a chemist and others known for their Leftist republican sympathies. The spectacle presumably was intended to serve as an example to all others of similar leanings.

Execution "Fetes" Described

The plaza was decorated for the occasion according to witnesses' accounts and victims were shot down at intervals of several minutes by a Falange leader known as "the Cripple of Cella." Crowds in the square and balconies, it is testified, applauded each execution, and when the spectacle was over a band marched past the bodies playing, and at night there were feasts in the plaza with dancing.

After Teruel's fall "the Cripple of Cella" was captured as he attempted to flee among departing refugees.

The republican Mayor of Teruel, Angel Sanchez, was among those slated for execution in the plaza, he testified; but he escaped, and in revenge his wife and 16-year-old daughter were executed.

Carmen Martinez Piedra, a working class woman who said she would not speak of anything except what she had actually seen or experienced, gave one account. Asked whether she knew anything of the execution in the plaza and whether she had any relative among the victims, she told me: "Yes. It was on Sunday, Aug. 23, and my brother was among those killed. He had an insurance office and had gone to work there that morning.

"When I was cooking dinner, I sent my litle girl to the store to buy chocolate. She came back in a little while and said:

"'I can't go to the store because they won't let any one through the plaza.'

"I went down and saw my brother, Manuel Martinez Piedra, with his hands manacled. He had been arrested that morning and never had a trial.

"The plaza was decorated, and there were many people around, but I couldn't see more because they arrested me and took me into a building near by. But I heard a shot, and then people applauded;

Continued on Page Two

Students Set Up Plan For Insurance on Exams

By The Associated Press.

PROVIDENCE, R. I., Jan. 21.—A novel system of examination insurance with the added inducement of scholastic "hot tips" was the hope held out today to Providence College students as they racked their brains at their mid-year tests.

The new plan has been evolved by a group of seniors who have formed the "Students' Protective Insurance Company" and plan to start writing policies during the second semester.

For a premium ranging from 50 cents for freshmen to 35 cents for seniors, the company will guarantee an undergraduate's complete scholastic program for a semester. If he fails to attain the passing mark of 60, the student insurance company will assume the payment of all conditional examination fees to the college, amounting to $2 for the first try and $5 for the next two attempts afforded by the college.

HUGHES GIVES STAY IN B.M.T. UNION ROW

Chief Justice Paves Way for Highest Court to Pass on Legality of Closed Shop

APPEAL BEING PREPARED

Ousting of Six Workers Under Contract Held a Violation of the Basic Law

The United States Supreme Court will soon have an opportunity to decide for the first time whether a worker can be discharged if he refuses to join a labor union with which his employer has signed a closed shop contract.

Counsel for the six New York City subway employes who do not want to belong to a labor union and who lost their case in the Court of Appeals of New York State last Tuesday announced yesterday that Chief Justice Charles Evans Hughes had signed an order granting a stay in the dispute involving the right of the men's employers to sign a closed shop contract.

The suit was brought in behalf of Charles Williams and others to decide whether the New York Rapid Transit Corporation and three other subsidiaries of the B. M. T. system could enter into a closed-shop contract with the Transport Workers Union of America. The stay, signed by Chief Justice Hughes in his home in Washington Thursday, will open the way for counsel for the six men to appeal the case to the highest court.

Appeal to Be Taken

At the offices of Math & Glassman, counsel for the six men, at 275 Fifth Avenue, it was said yesterday that an appeal to the Supreme Court would be taken at once on the grounds that the rights of the six workers as guaranteed by Article XIV of the United States Constitution had been violated.

Article XIV provides, among other things, that "no State shall make or enforce any law which shall abridge the privileges or immunities of the citizens of the United States, nor shall any State deprive any person of life, liberty or property without due process of the law. * * *"

Through a secretary, Chief Justice Hughes said yesterday:

"The parties have had a stay all through the litigation and the present stay is simply pending the beginning of the appeal which will be in the near future."

The signature of Chief Justice Hughes to the stay was obtained Thursday by Nathan W. Math of counsel for the workers who do not want to be compelled to join the Transport union. Mr. Math also obtained the signature of Frederick E. Crane, Chief Judge of the Court of Appeals, to an order of appeal.

Stone Declines to Act

In ordinary process an application for a stay would have been considered in this instance by Harlan F. Stone, associate justice of the Supreme Court, because of the judicial circuit with which Justice Stone is associated. Justice Stone, however, declined to consider the matter because a relative owned stock in one of the companies involved. He gave Mr. Math a note to Chief Justice Hughes, who signed the stay.

It is expected the Supreme Court will decide within two weeks whether it will accept jurisdiction in the case. If it does accept jurisdiction, it is possible that the case may come before the body within forty days.

The issue of the validity of a closed-shop contract has never come before the country's highest court, nor has that body ever been called upon to decide the legality of compelling a worker to join a labor union to keep his job.

JACKSON TO BECOME SOLICITOR GENERAL AS REED QUITS POST

Assistant Attorney General's Acceptance in Conference With President Reported

MAY SHELVE 'TRUST' DRIVE

Roosevelt Feels Promotion Will Help Aide to Governorship Here, Washington Hears

By FELIX BELAIR Jr.
Special to THE NEW YORK TIMES.

WASHINGTON, Jan. 21.—Selection of Robert H. Jackson as Solicitor General of the United States, which was tentatively agreed upon when Stanley Reed was nominated to the Supreme Court, was formally ratified, so far as the Administration is concerned, at a White House conference yesterday between Mr. Jackson and President Roosevelt.

The nomination is expected to go to the Senate early next week immediately after the appointment of Mr. Reed to the Supreme Court has been approved. Mr. Jackson, as assistant attorney general, is now head of the Justice Department's Anti-Trust Division.

In deciding to promote the 45-year-old New Yorker to the post of chief trial lawyer for the Federal Government, President Roosevelt is said to feel that he is giving him a more dignified position in which to run for Governor of New York State in the near future and, eventually, for the Presidential nomination.

Faces Attacks by Conservatives

The President's choice of Mr. Jackson is considered certain to precipitate a lively debate in the Senate, where Democratic conservatives are expected to seize the opportunity presented by his nomination to denounce him for the attacks he recently made against certain elements of so-called big business which he charged with monopolistic practice to the detriment of economic recovery.

In speeches made before and after the convening of the regular Congressional session, Mr. Jackson and Secretary Ickes attacked corporate monopoly in a manner which some construed at the time as a condemnation of corporate bigness per se. With the Democratic opponents of the Jackson appointment will be several Republicans. While approving the nomination, Senator Borah is expected to unloose an attack on the Administration for its apparent about-face on its anti-trust crusade.

In this connection the choice of Mr. Jackson for Solicitor General has been interpreted by some observers as meaning the Administration intends to postpone for a time its anti-monopoly drive as a part of the broad program being mapped by President Roosevelt to reverse the business recession.

Solicitor's Post Exacting

As Solicitor General Mr. Jackson is expected by some to be too busy preparing the government's defense against legal attacks on Administration measures to have much time left either for "trust busting" or for furthering his prospects as a New York Gubernatorial candidate. Aside from the preparation of the government's cases, it is expected that Mr. Jackson will be called upon to spend considerable time in court.

Nevertheless, it is understood in New Deal circles that Mr. Jackson accepted the President's offer of the new post on condition that he would have a hand in the conduct of the anti-trust division he now heads.

Word of Mr. Jackson's selection

Continued on Page Seven

WHOLE TVA IS RULED VALID, ITS POWER PROGRAM UPHELD; AUTO MEN PLEDGE CHANGES

ROOSEVELT PARLEY

Edsel Ford Is in Group Accepting the Idea of Self-Regulation

THEY UPHOLD TIME SALES

President Sees Real Gains in His Conferences as Mutually Clarifying Atmosphere

Special to THE NEW YORK TIMES.

WASHINGTON, Jan. 21.—President Roosevelt's objective of industrial self-regulation for national recovery won apparent acceptance by the automotive industry during a prolonged White House conference today in which manufacturers and sales financing company representatives agreed on the existence of some maladjustments and abuses in the industry, and pledged themselves to work for a correction.

For more than an hour the President conferred with the group in a frank discussion of the industry's problems, their relation to government and the economic welfare of the nation. It was agreed between Mr. Roosevelt and his visitors that they would examine practices in the industry and report back to him on proposed corrections within two weeks.

Those attending the conference were:

Edsel Ford, president, Ford Motor Company.

William S. Knudsen, president, General Motors Corporation.

K. T. Keller, president, Chrysler Motor Corporation.

B. E. Hutchinson, chairman, finance committee, Chrysler Motor Corporation.

Alvan Macauley, president, Packard Motor Car Company and the Automobile Manufacturers Association.

A. E. Duncan, president, Commercial Credit Company.

Henry Ittleson, president, Commercial Investment Trust.

Ernest Kanzler, president, Universal Credit Company.

John J. Schumann Jr., president, General Motors Acceptance Corporation.

Points of Agreement Reported

From sources close to the industry it was reported that the President's visitors agreed:

1. To place limitations on installment selling methods and, possibly, propose restriction of prevailing credit terms.

2. To re-examine high-pressure salesmanship practices which, Mr. Roosevelt contends, have resulted in "overselling" the market for automobiles and brought about production slumps that might easily be avoided.

As the group left the President's office Mr. Macauley issued the following statement:

"We had a broad discussion of the factors affecting business and government and we believe it was very helpful. We reported to the President that we are hopeful a seasonal increase in sales in the Spring will bring an improvement in business.

"We found ourselves in hearty agreement with the President's principles on the subject of installment selling. Properly used, installment buying will continue to help

Continued on Page Five

Farm Bill Compromise Reached by Conferees

By The Associated Press.

WASHINGTON, Jan. 21.—A compromise "ever normal granary" farm program will be ready for final Congressional action next week, House and Senate conferees predicted today.

They said that they had compromised all major differences between farm bills passed by the House and Senate during the special session and that they would agree on remaining minor details early next week.

Chairman Smith of the Senate Agriculture Committee said that they would recess over the week-end to "catch up with what we've agreed upon."

The legislation agreed upon thus far would set up vast machinery for controlling acreage and marketing of five major crops, cotton, wheat, corn, tobacco and rice.

HOUSE VOTES NAVY $553,266,494 FUND

Fiscal Year Appropriation Bill Is Passed, 283 to 15, as Committee Wrote It

ALL AMENDMENTS BEATEN

But Opposition to Two New Battleships Indicates Fight Over Any Big Expansion

Special to THE NEW YORK TIMES.

WASHINGTON, Jan. 21.—The Naval Appropriation Bill carrying $553,266,494 for the fiscal year ended June 30, 1939, and provisions for beginning the construction of twenty-vessels, including two battleships, was passed by the House today and sent to the Senate without change as received from the Appropriations Committee. But mutterings during consideration of the measure pointed to a vigorous debate on any large construction program that President Roosevelt may submit to Congress in his projected special naval message. The bill was passed 283 to 15.

Opposition to a greatly expanded building program concentrated today on the provision for two more battleships in the coming fiscal year. This was due, however, more to apprehensions over the forthcoming message. The opposition was overwhelmed and all other amendments offered were likewise struck down.

The fight over battleships was made on two amendments offered by Representative Gerald J. Boileau of Wisconsin. One would have increased the provision for new airplanes by $3,100,000, the amount stipulated for beginning construction in the fiscal year 1939 of two battleships. It was defeated 25 to 93. The other would have eliminated the appropriation for the two battleships. It was rejected 27 to 101.

Promotion Halt Is Rejected

The House also defeated, 110 to 83, the amendment passed in Committee of the Whole yesterday stopping operation of the navy selection and promotion system for one year. It did this at the suggestion of Representative Byron N. Scott of California, who offered the amendment originally and who explained today that he had received satisfactory assurances from Representative Carl Vinson of Georgia, chairman of the Naval Committee, that that committee early next month would begin hearings on measures long pending before it to improve the selection system.

The purpose of his amendment, Mr. Scott explained, was to obtain just such a promise.

Another amendment, offered by Representative Chester Thompson of Illinois, to relieve the Secretary of the Navy of any discretion, other than represented in differences of costs, in placing contracts for construction and repair in private plants rather than in navy yards was defeated, 33 to 64. Representative William B. Umstead of North Carolina, chairman of the navy subcommittee of the Appropriations Committee, who was in charge of the bill, explained that some discretion was desired with repair and construction work approaching peak loads in navy yards.

The debate on the proposals to use funds for additional planes rather than battleships, while it produced once more extended debate

Continued on Page Four

18 SUITS DISMISSED

Federal Court Denies Every Claim Made by Utilities

FINDS POWER IS INCIDENTAL

Government Officials Hail Decision—Case Going to Supreme Court

Text of the court's decision upholding the TVA is on Page 6.

By The Associated Press.

CHATTANOOGA, Tenn., Jan. 21.—Tennessee Valley Authority competition with private power companies was upheld as "lawful" by a three-judge Federal court here today.

The court dismissed an injunction suit by eighteen utilities which challenged the constitutionality of the TVA Act on grounds that the Authority's low rates would destroy them, rendering property worthless without just compensation.

"These complainants have no immunity from lawful competition," said the ruling, "even if their business be curtailed or destroyed."

Presiding Judge Florence Allen of the Sixth Circuit Court of Appeals, read the 8,000-word decision which closed a hearing begun last Nov. 15. Other members of the court were District Federal Judges John J. Gore and John D. Martin of Tennessee.

"A decree will be entered denying the injunction sought," the court said, "dismissing the bill of complaint and taxing costs against the complainants."

All Charges Are Denied

Most of them are subsidiaries of the Commonwealth and Southern Corporation and Electric Bond and Share Company, operating within 250 miles of TVA dams on the Tennessee River and its tributaries. The court summarized:

"We conclude that, since none of the complainants claims to operate under an exclusive franchise, no fraud, malice, coercion, or conspiracy exists: since the Authority is not exceeding its statutory powers and since the statute is constitutional, the competition with these complainants is lawful.

"It follows that the holding in Alabama Power Company v. Ickes, (recently decided in the United States Supreme Court) squarely applies."

James Lawrence Fly, chief counsel of the TVA, said the decision was "a milestone in the conservation movement."

Utility attorneys announced that a direct appeal would be taken to the Supreme Court.

Conspiracy Plea Denied

The court ruled that the TVA did not conspire to destroy the utilities, to compete illegally or coerce the power companies to sell their properties at distress figures. It also held that municipalities were not coerced into buying TVA power.

Concerning the Federal Agency's competition with private utilities, the decision said:

"The attempt to show that the Authority has endeavored to persuade complainants' customers to breach their existing contracts for purchase of power from complainants has totally failed. In every case where a customer of the complainants has been lost to the Authority, the cause has been not unlawful competition but the lawful allurement of substantially lower prices.

"No fraudulent attempt has been made to secure complainants' markets. Whatever compulsion exists is the inevitable compulsion exercised by the fact that a competitor sells at lower rates than complainants."

TVA-PWA Conspiracy Denied

The decision continued: "Facts do not establish a conspiracy between the TVA and PWA," and added:

"The acts done by the officials of the PWA, in cooperation with the officials of the TVA, as shown by this record, were done with the intent to carry out provisions of the PWA statute; the acts done by the TVA were done with the intent to carry out the TVA statute."

As to coercion of municipalities and cooperatives, the opinion asserted:

"These cities and cooperatives were free to obtain information and counsel from any source. In each case the decision of the municipal-

Continued on Page Seven

City Flounders in Slush as Rain Ends Snow; Storm Due to Continue; Suburbs Blanketed

A damp slushy snow mixed with rain, which later turned completely to rain, yesterday gave New York one of its most dismal days this Winter. Even the Weather Bureau—unofficially—admitted that it was dismal and discouragingly announced that rain or snow would probably continue throughout today and tomorrow.

The snow, which blanketed many sections of Long Island, Westchester County and Northern New Jersey, turned quickly into a heavy slush in New York City. It delayed traffic, particularly during the evening rush hour.

At Floyd Bennett Field the slush was considered a weak enemy by fifty or more employes of the Sanitation Department who took their pre-graduation tests in snow removal. The fifty men, using new equipment, were members of a specially trained squad of more than 200 who began their instruction at Lake Placid. At the flying field, however, they proved the ability of their equipment to remove even small patches of ice on the runways.

The snow, which began to fall heavily early in the afternoon, turned to rain shortly before 8 P. M.

The snowfall was blamed by the police for the death of Mrs. May Davis, 58 years old, of 790 Cromwell Avenue, Dongan Hills, S. I., and the injury of her son Thomas, 38, of the same address. They were riding in a car which was in collision with a bus carrying thirty-nine WPA workers at Hylan Boulevard and Donnelly Avenue, Grassmere, S. I., about 5 P. M.

At about the same time sixteen persons were injured when a bus of the Queens-Nassau Bus Company was in collision with an oil truck at Northern Boulevard and Grand Central Parkway Extension in Corona.

Short Wave Rays a Remedy for Colds And Sinus Ills, Boston Doctors Report

By The Associated Press.

BOSTON, Jan. 21.—A treatment for the common cold and sinus infections, said to be swift and efficient, was announced tonight by the New England Medical Center.

This treatment is by a new type of short wave machine which concentrates and directs the rays onto infected areas, and, through heat, destroys the infection.

In treating a head cold the rays are applied to the nasal region of the face. Doctors at the Boston Dispensary, a unit of the Medical Center, said the treatment gave no pain and no unpleasant sensation.

Six hundred patients were treated at the dispensary before physicians revealed their findings.

The value of the new machine over those previously in use, the center said, lay in its ability to concentrate and focus the rays. Until its perfection these rays had been dispersed by bone and body tissue.

The 600 patients were treated for deep-seated abscesses, such as sometimes form in the lung, carbuncles and certain types of joint diseases, besides colds and sinusitis.

The machine appears rather like a large ice box with a long arm projecting from it. The patient does not come in contact with any current but is placed in an electromagnetic field which is tuned to the wave length desired.

Wider uses for the machine, perfected by Dr. E. Schliephake of Germany, are visioned by doctors, possibly even the destruction of tumors. But at the moment the evidence to substantiate such hopes has not been accumulated.

Only four of these machines are in use in the United States, the dispensary said. Three are in the offices of private physicians.

The New England Medical Center is an organization for furnishing joint services to medical units in Boston.

Tyrone Power receives a ring from Norma Shearer who played the title role in *Marie Antoinette*.

Groucho Marx

Humphrey Bogart, Edward G. Robinson and Maxie Rosenbloom, jewel thieves at work, in *The Amazing Dr. Clitterhouse*.

Harpo Marx

Lucille Ball appeared with the Marx Brothers in *Room Service*.

Chico Marx

"All the News That's Fit to Print."

The New York Times.

LATE CITY EDITION
Rain, mild temperatures, colder in the afternoon and tonight. To-morrow fair and much colder.
Temperatures Yesterday—Max., 50; Min., 37

Copyright, 1938, by The New York Times Company.

VOL. LXXXVII....No. 29,221. Entered as Second-Class Matter, Postoffice, New York, N. Y. NEW YORK, TUESDAY, JANUARY 25, 1938. PPP TWO CENTS in New York City. | THREE CENTS Within 200 Miles. | FOUR CENTS Elsewhere Except in 7th and 8th Postal Zones.

REIGN OF DISORDER GOES ON IN NANKING; SUGGESTS A MUTINY

Looting and Other Scandalous Behavior of the Japanese Unchecked by Officers

FOREIGNERS ARE BARRED

Only Diplomats and Refugee Aides Allowed—Spokesmen Embarrassed by Acts

ROOSEVELT MAKES APPEAL

Urges Red Cross to Collect $1,000,000 in United States for Civilians in China

Conditions in Nanking under Japanese rule remain lawless and scandalous, according to advices reaching Shanghai yesterday, and foreigners, except diplomats, are still barred from the city. Despite Japanese assurances that offending troops would be removed, attacks on women and other offenses have continued. Shanghai observers speculated whether a condition of mutiny existed among the soldiery. Tokyo gave assurance that steps had been taken, and more would be taken, to meet the situation. [Page 1.]

London heard the Japanese were halting the anti-British campaign in the hope that Britain might move for peace in China. Admiral Suetsugu was rebuked in the House of Peers at Tokyo for his recent interview assailing democracies. [Page 8.]

Han Fu-chu, former Governor of Shantung, was shot yesterday because of his retreat before the Japanese. [Page 9.]

President Roosevelt asked the Red Cross to appeal to the American people for a "good-will offering of as much as perhaps one million dollars" to aid the suffering civilians in China. [Page 8.]

Lawlessness at Nanking

By HALLETT ABEND

Wireless to THE NEW YORK TIMES.

SHANGHAI, Jan. 24.—Stripping away all the Japanese excuses about military necessity and similar pleas, the stark fact remains that the conditions in Nanking one month and ten days after the victorious Japanese Army crashed the gates of China's former capital are so lawless and so scandalous that Japanese authorities continue to refuse permission to any foreigners except diplomatic officials to visit the city.

On Dec. 26 high Japanese authorities in Shanghai, while shamefacedly admitting looting and raping were proceeding in Nanking, assured the writer that the undisciplined and defiant Japanese troops in the former capital were being removed to the north bank of the Yangtze River in small contingents and that their places were being taken by picked forces of unimpeachable discipline and good behavior.

Again on Jan. 7 Japanese authorities apologetically admitted to the writer that conditions in Nanking were still deplorable but gave assurances that the division of troops then out of hand and daily criminally assaulting hundreds of women and very young girls would be removed from Nanking within two or three days.

Lawless Reign Goes On

Yet as late as Jan. 20 the reign of lawlessness was still continuing unchecked, and if the promised shift in troops was actually achieved the new arrivals were equally undisciplined with those formerly garrisoning the city and supposedly acting as the guardians of law and order.

Japanese authorities in Shanghai last Friday evening announced frankly that cable messages concerning this situation would not be passed by the censors, declaring in effect that "malicious" reports tending to discredit the Japanese Army would not be permitted to circulate abroad.

The summary of conditions in Nanking, arriving in Shanghai from missionaries and welfare workers who risked their lives to administer refugee camps during the siege, and other reports from consular and other foreign officials now residing in Nanking can scarcely all be malicious. Yet all these reports agree and all contain eye-witness accounts of brutality and unrestrained license on the part of Japanese forces.

These reports, the major part of which are unprintable, are arousing the gravest speculation here. Some observers are asking whether a virtual state of mutiny exists in the

Continued on Page Eight

Hirohito in Poem Hopes For Peaceful Conditions

By The Associated Press.

TOKYO, Jan. 24.—Hopes for peaceful "world conditions" were expressed in verse by Emperor Hirohito in his contribution to the annual imperial New Year poetry contest, published today. The theme was "Morning in a Shrine Garden," and the Emperor's poem was:

"Peaceful is morning in the shrine garden;

"World conditions, it is hoped, also will be peaceful."

The New Year poetry contest has been an annual court function for centuries and is the only occasion when subjects can communicate directly with the throne, for all are permitted to enter poems addressed to the sovereign. The best are chosen for reading at a palace function.

This year 38,000 poems were submitted. Many came from soldiers and sailors in China.

SEABOARD LASHED BY A 48-MILE WIND

Ships Delayed and Fishermen Imperiled by the Storm—Rescues by Coast Guard

SIGNS WRECKED IN CITY

Airplane Lost on a Flight to Washington Lands After 6 Hours in Hartford

A gale, which in New York reached a velocity of 48 miles an hour at times, last night lashed the northeast coast of the United States endangering fishermen, delaying vessels and causing considerable damage to signs, buildings and piers. In this city many signs were loosened or blown down.

During the worst of the storm a fourteen-passenger Eastern Airlines plane was lost for more than six hours with two passengers and a crew of three. After traveling approximately 1,000 miles the plane landed at 3:05 this morning at Hartford, Conn.

At Atlantic City, N. J., four fishermen were rescued by the Coast Guard.

In Boston the arrival of the gale was preceded by fog, The Associated Press said, which delayed steamers and caused the death of at least one man in a collision involving fifteen motor vehicles. Another storm, which roared over Lake Erie, resulted in the death of one man, damaged a number of lakeside buildings and blew three fishermen into the lake from an ice floe.

In New York City the storm, which began late in the day and was expected to last throughout today, was preceded by abnormally high temperatures. At 6:15 P. M. the official temperature was 49 degrees, only eight degrees lower than the all-time high for the date of 57.6 degrees in 1894. The average for the day was 43, 13 degrees above normal. At 10 P. M. the thermometer had reached 50 degrees.

Barometer Falls Rapidly

The barometer fell rapidly throughout the day and at 8:30 P. M. the Weather Bureau reported a southeast gale with an average velocity of forty-two miles an hour.

The twenty-eight-foot motor boat Amanda W. was caught off Atlantic City with the motor stalled as the storm began. Captain Milton Weaver and a fishing crew of three were rescued by the Coast Guard just as the boat was being blown through high seas toward the Million Dollar Pier.

Southeast storm warnings were raised from Eastport, Me., to Cape Hatteras and all fishing operations in that area ceased. Shipping was reported paralyzed all along the New England Coast and many automobile accidents were reported. Pedestrians in Boston were forced to cross streets by "ear," unable to see more than fifty feet.

At Newark Airport the flights of several commercial planes bound for Chicago and the West were canceled. A number of vessels at sea, including the Rex, Aquitania and Carinthia, were reported battling high seas and the Manhattan and American Trader were to dock this morning many hours late.

Plane Fought 75-Mile Wind

The plane which was lost, left Newark Airport for Washington at 8:36 P. M. last night. The flight usually takes about one hour and twenty minutes. An hour after it left Newark the pilot, Captain Fred Jones, reported by radio that winds—at times reaching a strength of 75 miles an hour—had blown him off the course and that he was lost.

Shortly after midnight he again reported that he could see a town below him but that he did not know what it was. Captain E. V. (Eddie) Rickenbacker, general manager of Eastern Airlines, then appealed to radio Station WOR which broadcast a general appeal asking that all listeners in the metropolitan

Continued on Page Ten

INSURGENTS REPORT TERUEL EVACUATED BY FOE UNDER FIRE

Loyalists Driven Out by Heavy Artillery Attacks, Advices Say—All Quiet, Barcelona Holds

AIR RAIDS ON CITIES GO ON

French Shoot at War Planes of Both Sides—Paris Drafts Note to Franco on Bombing

By The Associated Press.

PERPIGNAN, France (At the Spanish Frontier), Jan. 24.—Teruel, center of a month-long battle, was reported tonight to have been evacuated by Spanish Government forces in the face of unceasing Insurgent artillery fire.

Insurgent advices said Generalissimo Francisco Franco's troops held strong positions on three sides of the abandoned city and were seeking to extend their arc to the east. The desperate battle resolved itself into a fight for the surrounding heights, complete possession of which would bring automatic control of the city.

An Insurgent communiqué said observers had reported no signs of life in Teruel since General Miguel Aranda's troops drove down the Alfambra Valley, north of the city, making the provincial capital untenable.

Government troops, however, were still holding two strong positions to the northwest, making it impossible for the Insurgents to enter the city. Should they do so, the government troops could subject them to the same severe punishment they have been receiving.

2 Positions Taken, Rebels Say

The Insurgents reported they had occupied Villalba Baja and Tortajada, north of Teruel, without encountering resistance, and were planning to drive on against Mansueto and Santa Barbara, the strongest of the government positions.

The Insurgents' lines were consolidated roughly several hundred yards south of Teruel, one mile west and four miles north. It was their farthest advance in their erstwhile spearhead salient, 135 miles east of Madrid, since the surprise government offensive wrested it from them in December.

Air raids on government-held cities continued, bringing the total of such attacks within the last few weeks to seventy-seven. A Barcelona communiqué announced that a total of 273 persons had been killed and 456 wounded in the raids. At least eighty persons were killed in the week-end raids of reprisal and counter-reprisal, and hundreds were wounded.

Worst to Come, Loyalists Believe

Wireless to THE NEW YORK TIMES.

BARCELONA, Spain, Jan. 24.—All was quiet on the Teruel front today for the second day in succession, according to Loyalist advices, but this time no one is being deceived into a belief that the worst is over. Every authority here feels that the Teruel battle has a long way to run yet, and as far as the government is concerned the longer the better.

According to the best estimates available at the front, the Rebels have concentrated about nine divisions there—90,000 men. Loyalists say Generalisimo Francisco Franco has suffered appalling casualties,

Continued on Page Twelve

Berle Is Likely Choice For Assistant to Hull

Special to THE NEW YORK TIMES.

WASHINGTON, Jan. 24.—A. A. Berle Jr., former City Chamberlain of New York and a leading member of President Roosevelt's original Brain Trust, was prominently mentioned today as the probable selection for assistant secretary of state to succeed Hugh R. Wilson, recently appointed Ambassador to Germany. Mr. Berle is now a director of the American Molasses Company in New York.

Reports of his selection to the State Department post lacked official confirmation. Secretary Hull referred all inquiries to the White House, and officials there were silent on the subject.

Mr. Berle was formerly head of the railroad division of the Reconstruction Finance Corporation. As assistant secretary of state he would again be an official adviser of the President on general policies.

ROSAMOND PINCHOT ENDS LIFE IN GARAGE

Actress of 'The Miracle' Fame Dies of Fumes in Auto at Long Island Home

SEPARATED FROM HUSBAND

Deeply Affected by Rift Two Years Ago—Lived With Two Sons, 9 and 6

From a Staff Correspondent

OLD BROOKVILLE, L. I., Jan. 24.—Thirty-three-year-old Rosamond Pinchot Gaston, who left a fashionable school fifteen years ago for a career on the stage, was found dead at 7:50 A. M. today in the front seat of her car, the engine of which she had started in the closed garage on her rented estate to asphyxiate herself.

A length of garden hose attached to the exhaust and pushed through a rear window chinked with a burlap bag carried the deadly carbon monoxide gas inside the auto. Servants who found the body discovered a farewell note to her parents and her friends. The note was not made public and the motive that led Mrs. Gaston to take her life was not revealed.

The daughter of Amos Pinchot and his first wife, Mrs. Gertrude Minturn Pinchot, and the niece of Gifford Pinchot, former Governor of Pennsylvania, Mrs. Gaston had been estranged from her husband, William Gaston, grandson of a former Governor of Massachusetts, for the last two or three years. The failure of her marriage, it was said, was a cause of deep and lasting sorrow to Mrs. Gaston.

Rented House Last Fall

Soon after the body was found by Ida Hannenen, a cook in the household, her father and Dr. Lewis Frissell of 772 Park Avenue, his physician, arrived at the long, low, rambling farmhouse on Valentine Lane and Simondton Road, which Mrs. Gaston rented last October from J. Henry Alexandre to be near the Greenvale School, which her two sons, William, 9, and James, 6, attended.

Mathew J. Kramer, a local undertaker, was called and the body removed to Mrs. Gaston's mother's home at 9 East Eighty-first Street. Her mother, who has a Winter

Continued on Page Seven

Lloyd George and Wife Honored by Hundreds On Their Golden Wedding Anniversary

Wireless to THE NEW YORK TIMES.

CANNES, France, Jan. 24.—The fiftieth wedding anniversary of David Lloyd George, Britain's war-time Prime Minister, was celebrated today in glorious weather. With Mrs. Lloyd George he spent the morning in a garden in Cap d'Antibes surrounded by his family.

From every part of the world thousands of messages of congratulations came from all classes of people, from the heads of nations to humble men and women. Mr. Lloyd George was most touched by postcards he received from Wales and from Pennsylvania coal fields from men who, before migrating to America, had been his friends and constituents and had not forgotten the days when he, as a young lawyer, had helped several in law-suits free of charge.

For several days the local postman has been unable to handle the heavy mailbag and a hotel omnibus had to be requisitioned to carry the hundreds of presents to his hotel.

Winston Churchill, former Cabinet colleague of Mr. Lloyd George, gave a luncheon today in the Hotel Carlton for the entire Lloyd George family. Maxine Elliott, American actress, and the Hon. Reginald and Mrs. Fellowes were guests.

"My good friend Joseph Choate celebrated his golden wedding anniversary when he was the American Ambassador to London and then he said to me: 'If I had to do this over again I would want to be Mrs. Choate's second husband.' I certainly echo his sentiments today," Mr. Lloyd George said.

King George and Queen Mary sent a message of congratulation, as did also the Duke and Duchess of Windsor. Liberal Members of the House of Commons sent a gold loving cup engraved with the names of the thirty-eight members.

Mr. Lloyd George played golf early this morning, and during his absence photographers, who had been admitted to make a picture, occupied themselves by preparing an elaborate background. They arranged banks of flowers in gardens and displayed the gifts on a table before which the family was to be posed.

"This is too spectacular," declared Mr. Lloyd George on seeing what had been done. "If you want a picture it must be plain without any fancy trimmings."

RULING PAVES WAY TO OUST CASHMORE FROM COUNCIL POST

McGeehan Upholds Election as Vice Chairman, but Says Tenure Is Not Fixed

COALITION PLANS NEW VOTE

Happy at Decision and Hopes to Use It to Put Burke in the Office Today

Immediately after Supreme Court Justice John E. McGeehan had rendered a decision yesterday upholding Councilman John Cashmore as Vice Chairman of the City Council, members of Mayor La Guardia's bloc drew a plan under which they hope to use the decision to unseat Mr. Cashmore from his position at today's meeting and replace him with Councilman James A. Burke of Queens.

While the Democrats were crying, "We won, we won," up and down the old corridors of the City Hall, President Newbold Morris and his supporters on the anti-Democratic side were equally jubilant. To them, the McGeehan decision cleared the way for the displacement of Mr. Cashmore today and the immediate substitution of Mr. Burke.

Justice McGeehan held that the Vice Chairman was not elected for any fixed term. He also held that thirteen votes constituted a majority sufficient to elect Mr. Cashmore on Jan. 3, when only twenty-five of the twenty-six council members were present. Councilman Michael J. Quill has since returned from his wedding in Ireland.

Now Concede Election

The Mayor's supporters are prepared to concede now that Mr. Cashmore was vice chairman from Jan. 3 to today. Since the election was not for a fixed term, they feel free to have the office declared vacant at today's meeting. Assuming that the party lines hold on such a motion, the Council will divide with thirteen Democrats opposing the thirteen voter of the Mayor's coalition. In that event, President Morris could cast the deciding vote, the fourteenth, to have the office declared vacant.

Proceeding to the election of a new Vice Chairman, the coalition could then name Mr. Burke for the office. Backed by the coalition's thirteen votes, he could expect an equal number in opposition which would again create the tie permitting Mr. Morris to vote. Should the Democrats refrain from voting in a body, Mr. Morris might declare that a tie existed anyhow, and proceed to cast his ballot. When that situation arose last week he declined to call the tie, though he said that he believed a tie existed. Finally, if one or more of the Democrats refrains from voting, the coalition would still have its thirteen votes which would then become even a clearer majority.

To the Mayor's adherents, the beauty of Justice McGeehan's decision lies in the fact that there is no escape from it. Mr. Cashmore brought the action to have himself upheld as Vice Chairman. If Justice McGeehan's decision proves to be the vehicle that removes him today, he cannot well appeal from a ruling that recognized him as victor. Consequently, the anti-Tammany Councilmen feel that the Democrats have been neatly imprisoned in a trap of their own manufacture.

Cashmore Voices Gratitude

Mr. Cashmore, on hearing of the decision at 5 o'clock last evening at City Hall, said he was "gratified" that the Supreme Court had confirmed his contention and expressed the hope that President Morris would now proceed with the work before the Council. Councilman Joseph E. Kinsley, Bronx Democrat, who had kept the telephone between City Hall and the Supreme Court busy all afternoon, was equally jubilant. He burst out of a telephone booth in the press room shouting: "We won, we won."

Reporters who asked Mr. Morris for his comment on the decision were puzzled by his first reaction, which was a loud "Hooray." He said he would recognize Mr. Cashmore as Vice Chairman for current purposes, and that the question of an appeal from the decision would await his study of the twelve-page ruling. Earlier, however, Corporation Counsel William C. Chanler had anuounced that he would take an immediate appeal from Justice McGeehan's ruling. Mr. Chanler represented Mayor La Guardia's side in the controversy. As the situation later developed it became unlikely that any appeal would be taken from the ruling.

In his decision Justice McGeehan reviewed the steps which led up to the court action. On Jan. 3 he found that Mr. Cashmore had received thirteen votes for Vice

Continued on Page Seven

SEC BANS SHORT SELLING; SAYS 11 EXCHANGE MEN LED SHORTS IN FALLING MARKET

Glass Drafts Bill to Liquidate All Bank Holding Companies

Senator's Plan Would Allow Five Years for Process—Program Differs From Patman Measure Chiefly in Time Element

Special to THE NEW YORK TIMES.

WASHINGTON, Jan. 24.—The Administration is preparing a bill for the liquidation of bank holding companies, to be introduced by Senator Glass of Virginia.

This fact developed from announcements by Senator Glass that he was preparing a bill for the "orderly liquidation" of bank holding companies over a five-year period, and by Secretary Morgenthau at a press conference that he and Senator Glass "agreed in principle" on what should be done about the bank holding companies.

President Roosevelt during the past two weeks at least twice stated his disapproval of bank holding companies.

The Glass legislation would appear to differ from a bill already introduced in the House by Representative Wright Patman principally in the length of time required for such liquidation. It was learned that some groups of independent bankers have already shown great interest in the Patman bill.

That Administration officials have been carefully studying the abolition of bank holding companies was disclosed by Secretary Morgenthau's statement that a subcommittee of the Inter-Departmental Banking Committee would present late this week its recommendation for bank holding company legislation to the whole committee.

"The only question, I think," said Secretary Morgenthau, "is whether a holding company should or should not hold bank stock."

He said he was not sure the work of his committee would result in legislation because "some of the committee might disagree."

The Patman bill would prohibit holding companies from holding any stock in the 14,000 banks insured by the F. D. I. C. and would allow three years for liquidation of the holdings of this character now existent.

Facts assembled by members of the Interdepartmental Committee show that there are in all sixty-three bank holding companies, controling some 560 banks.

PRICE RULE IS SET

Stock Can't Be Offered 'at or Below' Level of Last Preceding Sale

EDICT EFFECTIVE FEB. 8

Wall Street Views the Step as Making Public Responsible as Brokers Themselves

Text of SEC rules and statement by the commission, Page 31.

Special to THE NEW YORK TIMES.

WASHINGTON, Jan. 24.—Taking the initiative to prevent speculative short selling of securities on the Stock Exchanges in a declining market, the Securities and Exchange Commission today ruled that beginning Feb. 8, no person, for his own account or for the account of a customer, shall effect a short sale of any security on the Exchanges at or below the price at which the last sale of the same security was effected. Some exceptions were provided, the most important being odd lot transactions.

Under the rule, the short-seller would have to make his offer to sell at a price above the market price, where the chances of execution would be negligible. The term short sale was defined by the commission as any sale of a security which the seller does not own, or which is consummated by the delivery of a security borrowed by or for the account of the seller.

The regulation is the first floor trading rule to be made the subject of a commission decree, those now in force on the New York Stock and other exchanges having been adopted voluntarily by the exchanges after consultation with the commission.

Climax to a Long Argument

The virtual ban on short selling in a declining market climaxes a long and at times heated controversy as to the part that speculative short selling has played in promoting and accentuating breaks in values on the securities Exchanges. At present, the Stock Exchange rule in effect is that a short sale shall not be made below the last sale price. In making public its ruling, the commission said it thought the present Exchange rules "have not proven effective."

Severe breaks in market values on the New York Stock Exchange in the weeks ended Sept. 13 and Oct. 23, respectively, and the sharp controversies that followed as to fundamental causes for the severity of these declines contributed to the commission's action. The position that short selling was responsible for the breaks was not taken, but the commission did state that "the preponderance of available evidence points to the conclusion that in a declining market certain types of short sales are seriously destructive of stability."

This the commission sought to establish in data made public from a study of short selling in twenty securities which are so-called market leaders, including the common stocks of United States Steel, General Motors and Chrysler.

Notes Concentration of Sales

To show that short selling in the week ended Sept. 13 was carried on by a relatively few members of the New York Stock Exchange, the commission broke down its data to establish that the majority of short selling by members in United States Steel, General Motors and Chrysler "was concentrated in only eleven members."

Among the five leading short sellers in the three stocks, the commission also found that one floor trader was a leading short seller in all three stocks and two other floor traders were leading short sellers in two of the three stocks. The commission did not identify the so-called leading short sellers, nor make a definite charge that such member short selling was speculation to accentuate the decline.

Among the findings of the commission in its study of trading in twenty stocks for the weeks ended Sept. 13 and Oct. 23, was that members sold over 920,000 shares and that 30 per cent were short sales. Taking only three stocks, United States Steel, General Motors and Chrysler, this percentage rose to 33 per cent.

Thus while there was heavy liquidation of about 650,000 shares by members in the twenty securities which did not represent short sales,

Continued on Page Thirty-one

BROADWAY SHOWS PICKETED IN STRIKE

Boxoffice Men Called Out In Dispute With Producers and Press Agents' Union

DRIVE AGAINST SHUBERTS

3 Houses Now Open Give Usual Performances — Premieres Due at 2 Others This Week

For the first time in many years, strike conditions existed in five theatres in the Broadway amusement area yesterday as the Theatrical Managers, Agents and Treasurers Union continued its battle with theatrical producers and the New York Theatrical Press Agents.

While no scheduled performances were abandoned, the managers' union, an American Federation of Labor affiliate, ordered its members out of the box-offices of the Imperial, Winter Garden, Broadhurst, Morosco and Golden Theatres. Of the five houses, all controlled by the Shuberts, the first three have shows and the latter two are expecting new plays tonight and tomorrow night.

Employes in other theatres, which union officials would not name last night, will be ordered out today. It was reported that these houses would be the Booth, Music Box and Alvin.

Acting swiftly, the union sent its strike orders and pickets to the theatres so suddenly that accountants last night were still making the inventory necessary before the bonded box-office men would leave. Girl clerks on the Shubert staff were sent into the box-offices to sell tickets.

Guild Dispute Settled

At the same time that it concentrated on the Shubert theatres, the T. M. A. T. adjusted its difficulties with the Theatre Guild, which it had been picketing for some weeks in its campaign for recognition as sole bargaining agent for house and company managers, treasurers and press agents. An agreement signed by Theodore Mitchell, president of the union, and Warren P. Munsell, business manager for the Guild, specified that all Guild treasurers should join the T. M. A. T. The Guild, however, reserves the right to send its own treasurers into whatever theatre a Guild attraction happens to be playing.

T. M. A. T. box-office conditions were also recognized by the Lyceum Theatre, whose house manager, Allan J. Schnebbe, is a member of the union's board of directors. The Plymouth Theatre, which earlier in the day had been on the strike list, was exempted when the general manager of the show now playing there promised that its press agents would join the union or resign their jobs, according to a union official.

A representative of the manage-

Continued on Page Twenty-five

BANKERS OPPOSE BUSINESS TONICS

Warn Against More Artificial Stimulation and Further Attempts at Reform

CONFIDENCE HELD NEED

State Association Is Told the Majority of Youth Is 'Ripe for Rabble-Rousers'

Opposition to further artificial stimulation of business, a plea for postponement of further reforms of business and confidence that, given the right conditions, recovery from the current depression can come quickly were voiced yesterday by speakers before the tenth annual midwinter meeting of the New York State Bankers Association, held in the auditorium of the Federal Reserve Bank, 33 Liberty Street.

At a morning session, attended by several hundred bankers from all sections of the State, Frank K. Houston, president of the Chemical Bank and Trust Company and president of the association, declared the greatest need of business now was restoration of confidence.

"Now, least of all, does it need further artificial stimulation," Mr. Houston said. "To gain that confidence it needs to be assured that the government does not propose to continue its policy of competition with private enterprise or impose such restrictions that private enterprise cannot cooperate with a profit and be able to retain some of said profit when made.

"I believe that business will go forward in a big way when it can look forward with confidence and know the rules by which it will be governed. Whatever the causes of the depression, and history can take care of that, we are now in it, and it behooves us, as business men and bankers, to do everything we can to help get the country out of it and to get the wheels of industry turning again. If further reform of business is desired or needed, let it wait until the patient gets well, or, at least, until it gets over this attack."

Says Slump Can Be Checked

Dr. John H. Williams, vice president of the Federal Reserve Bank of New York, analyzed the causes and characteristics of the current business depression and declared that there were reasons for hoping that it need not go very much farther. Much could be done to shorten it, he said, by the cooperation of business, labor and government.

"It is especially important," he said, "that we should get clear in our thinking as to the difference between reform and recovery. None of this means, however, that I feel the Administration has to go back on its long-range objectives, such as regulation of the security markets, encouragement of collective bargaining and social security, all of

Continued on Page Six

"All the News That's Fit to Print."

The New York Times.

LATE CITY EDITION
Partly cloudy and slightly warmer today. Tomorrow cloudy, warmer, probably occasional rain.
Temperatures Yesterday—Max., 47; Min., 36

VOL. LXXXVII....No. 29,232. Entered as Second-Class Matter, Postoffice, New York, N. Y. NEW YORK, SATURDAY, FEBRUARY 5, 1938. PP TWO CENTS in New York City. | THREE CENTS Within 200 Miles. | FOUR CENTS Elsewhere Except in 7th and 8th Postal Zones.

LITTLE MEN MEET ROOSEVELT REBUFF ON LABOR DEMANDS

TAX PLEA SHUNNED

Delegation Tones Down Small Business Ire in White House Call

PRESIDENT FOR MANY AIMS

Some of Recommendations Are Possible of Fulfillment and Some Are Not, He Says

Text of small business men's suggestions on Page 4.

By FELIX BELAIR Jr.
Special to THE NEW YORK TIMES.

WASHINGTON, Feb. 4.—With its temper cooled, the "conservative manifesto" by which the small business men brought their two-day conference to a rip-roaring finale yesterday was formally presented today to President Roosevelt by the twelve conference chairmen in the presence of Secretary of Commerce Roper and Assistant Secretary Draper.

The resolutions presented to the President omitted some declarations and sharply toned down others to such a degree that they were hardly recognizable from the more caustic form in which they were rushed to adoption amid wild cheering.

A resolution that "unwarranted and malicious attacks on business by Administration representatives should be permanently stopped" in the final draft became a suggestion "that the government continue to cooperate with business."

An adopted resolution from the wage and hours committee representing the conference as "opposed to all form of Federal wage, hour regulations and legislation" was revised to read:

"We question the merit of a standard wage and hour bill because of geographical differentials."

Instead of repeal of the Wagner Labor Relations Act, as advocated in the adopted resolution, the draft presented to Mr. Roosevelt called for an investigation of the administration of the act.

Chairmen Meet With Draper

The metamorphosis was completed yesterday afternoon in Secretary Roper's conference room at a meeting of the twelve conference chairmen with Assistant Secretary Draper. The announced purpose was to eliminate the overlapping and duplication in the separate committee reports and to redraft them into more presentable form.

President Roosevelt listened attentively while Fred Roth of Cleveland, permanent chairman of the conference, read the twenty-three recommendations which made up the "boiled-down" version of the eleven reports adopted.

There were a few questions calculated to draw out the President's reaction to the contribution of the little business men toward a recovery formula. But, according to first-hand accounts, after the reading of the recommendations and the few questions from the visitors, Mr. Roosevelt did practically all of the talking.

Roosevelt's Views Reported

From some of the participants came the information that the White House conference served to bring from President Roosevelt the following observations:

1. He is flatly opposed to the request made by big business men recently and the little business men today that the Wagner Labor Relations Act be so modified as to provide "that employer and employe alike be held responsible for the faithful observance of mutual labor agreements." The President is not yet persuaded that labor unions should be made responsible by legislation.

2. The Administration will not give up the fight for wage-hour legislation. The President is amenable to incorporating in such legislation, however, the North-South differential principle for wage minimums.

3. Substantial modification of tax laws cannot be endorsed by the Administration while the Federal budget remains unbalanced. There was no discussion of the little business men's recommendation that the undistributed profits tax be repealed and the capital gains tax modified.

4. The "small business men" should create a permanent organization as a liaison agency between themselves and the Federal Government, but the President is extremely reluctant to issue a formal

Continued on Page Four

Sons Follow Footsteps Of Fathers in Assembly

Special to THE NEW YORK TIMES.

ALBANY, Feb. 4.—The perfunctory five-minute session of the Assembly today brought two younger members of that body into positions of prominence, similar to those once held by their respective fathers.

With only a scattering of members present, James J. Wadsworth of Livingston County acted as Republican majority leader and Robert F. Wagner Jr. of New York as Democratic minority leader.

Young Wadsworth's father, James W., was Speaker of the Assembly from 1906 through 1910, before he was elected to the United States Senate.

Mr. Wagner's father was Democratic leader in the State Senate from 1911 to 1913. He later succeeded Wadsworth Sr. as United States Senator. James J. Wadsworth has been in the Assembly since 1932, but Mr. Wagner is serving his first term.

NEW HOUSING ACT GOES INTO EFFECT

Roosevelt Signs Bill Intended to Spur Recovery and Increase Employment

AIDS SMALL HOME BUYERS

Law Permits Insurance of Mortgages Up to 90% on Dwellings Up to $6,000

Text of the National Housing Act is printed on Pages 6 and 7.

Special to THE NEW YORK TIMES.

WASHINGTON, Feb. 4.—President Roosevelt opened the way today for what is expected to be the biggest small homes building movement in the history of the country when the White House announced that he had signed the new Housing Bill.

An immediate spur to recovery is expected by government officials through a general increase in the demand for durable goods and the products of allied industries and a wide gain in employment in the building trades.

The law went into effect when it was signed last night and permits the insurance of mortgages on small residences up to 90 per cent of their maximum appraised valuation of $6,000, and up to 80 per cent on more costly homes, at lower interest rates.

Construction of 600,000 to 800,000 small dwellings a year for the next five years was predicted as a result of the easing of the buying burden on the general public.

The bill provides for the insurance of housing mortgages to the extent of $2,000,000,000 and authorizes the President to raise this maximum to $3,000,000,000 if demand warrants the increase.

New Building Field Opened

Should the maximum goal be reached, it would represent triple the amount of housing mortgage insurance done under the old act, which provided mortgage guarantees in a more limited field for housing construction at an annual cost ranging from ¾ to 1 per cent greater than the permitted interest and premium charges under the new act.

This amended version of the housing act opens up a completely new field in the encouragement of heavy building by extending mortgage insurance to rental projects constructed by private persons or corporations to a value as high as $200,000, and on projects by limited dividend corporations to as great a value of $5,000,000.

The operation of the intricate regulations regarding interest and premium payments, as well as other regulations, and the manner in which these contrast with former regulations, were explained officially today in an announcement by Stewart McDonald, Federal Housing Administrator, which read in part as follows:

"The total maximum annual carrying charge for an FHA insured mortgage on which a commitment is hereafter issued will be 5½ per cent.

"This will include 5 per cent interest and one-half of 1 per cent mortgage insurance premium. In the case of newly constructed

Continued on Page Seven

100,000 IN DETROIT PROTEST LAYOFFS, ASK MORE RELIEF

Mass Meeting in Heart of City Demands Debt Moratorium and Cut in Rents

KEYNOTE GIVEN BY MARTIN

Workers 'Not Going to Starve,' He Says, and Asks Slash for While in 'Big Salaries'

Detroit automobile workers at a mass meeting 100,000 strong protested layoffs, demanded "adequate relief," a debt moratorium and reductions in rent, and heard Homer Martin, head of the C. I. O. automobile union, declare that "the workers are not going to starve." [Page 1.]

Renewed effort for labor unity was indicated when the A. F. of L. council at Miami put off action against the C. I. O. unions. [Page 5.]

In Washington, Senator Wagner offered a bill to amend the Wagner act by extending collective-bargaining requirements to companies with Federal contracts or loans. [Page 5.]

Workers Make Demands

By RUSSELL B. PORTER
Special to THE NEW YORK TIMES.

DETROIT, Feb. 4.—Filling Cadillac Square in the heart of the city in a densely packed throng, workers and unemployed staged a mass demonstration this afternoon in protest against the lay-offs in this automobile center and against "inadequate" relief.

Homer Martin, president of the C. I. O. United Automobile Workers of America, the principal speaker, told the crowd that its size was 250,000. City officials and police estimated it at from 80,000 to 100,000. To an unbiased observer it appeared certain that 100,000 would be a conservative figure.

The crowd was vociferous but orderly. It roared out cheers for President Roosevelt, Governor Frank Murphy of Michigan, John L. Lewis and others. It booed and hooted Mayor Richard Reading of Detroit, who defeated the U. A. W. candidate at last year's election and recently has been embroiled in a relief controversy with the union. It also booed and hooted Henry Ford and other individuals and "big business" in general.

With lusty shouts of "Aye" and no dissenting voices the throng adopted resolutions calling for a debt moratorium for the unemployed, 50 per cent rent reductions and a city-wide rent strike if necessary, 100 per cent increase in welfare allotments, larger Federal work relief funds and a "labor government" at City Hall.

2,500 Police on Duty

Although the meeting was promoted chiefly by the U. A. W. A., which says 200,000 of its 300,000 members are now out of work because of the closing or slowing down of automobile factories, other unions, both C. I. O. and A. F. of L., joined in it under the auspices of the General Welfare Committee.

The auto workers marched into the long square from both ends, passing City Hall at one end and the County Building at the other. Both buildings were heavily guard-

Continued on Page Five

NEW PIRACY CURBS ACCEPTED BY ROME; BRITISH SHIP SUNK

Italy Acts a Few Hours After London Hears of Bombing of Vessel by Rebel Planes

CRAFT GETS SHORT NOTICE

Alcira Hit Near Barcelona by Two Bombers From Majorca —All of Crew Rescued

Rome accepted the new anti-piracy proposals for the Mediterranean, the announcement becoming known in London a few hours after receipt of the account of the sinking of another British ship, this time by two Rebel planes from Majorca. The ship, carrying a cargo of coal, was nearing Barcelona when attacked. All the crew was saved. [Page 1.]

The Rebels reported beating off Loyalist thrusts to recapture the rich Santa Barbara lead mines in Southern Spain. [Page 3.]

Italy to Support Patrol

Wireless to THE NEW YORK TIMES.

LONDON, Feb. 4.—Italy tonight announced her complete acceptance of new anti-piracy measures proposed by Foreign Secretary Anthony Eden on Wednesday.

By bitter irony the notification from Rome reached the British Government only a few hours after the deliberate bombing and sinking of the British freighter Alcira by two seaplanes, believed to be Italian Savoia-Marchetti machines operating from the Spanish Insurgents' Italian air base at Palma, Majorca.

Moreover, the Italian answer did not come until both the British and French governments had announced that they would go ahead without Italy if necessary. In this respect the history of the Nyon agreement is being repeated, for Italy last September refused to join the anti-piracy patrol until the others had acted without her.

Cynical observers remark tonight that Italy has promised to sink any of her own submarines seen or detected in the Italian patrol area off Spain. As far as is known here the Italian reply contained no denial of the Spanish Government's charges that Italy had given submarines and destroyers to the Insurgent navy.

To Reveal New Plans

In the House of Commons on Monday Mr. Eden will reveal the details of the new anti-piracy proposals now accepted by the British, French and Italian Governments. Meanwhile the air attack on the Alcira may necessitate still further measures to fight piracy in the air and may require further approaches to the French and Italians.

The British are thoroughly angry over the latest example of "frightfulness" against their shipping and are determined to take stern measures to prevent a repetition.

Three flying boat squadrons are expected to be rushed to Malta from England as a direct consequence of today's sinking. Three squadrons were sent to the Mediterranean last Autumn at the beginning of the Nyon patrol but were withdrawn at the beginning of De-

Continued on Page Two

Two Killed, Five Wounded in Gun Battle At Columbus Hideout of Bank Bandits

By The Associated Press.

COLUMBUS, Ohio, Feb. 4.—Two bank robber suspects were killed and three detectives and two other persons were wounded in a fierce twenty-minute gun battle as police raided a gang hide-out here today in search of bandits.

Police identified the dead as Vincent Grinkowicz of Cleveland and another man known only as "Mac." The latter's fingerprints were sent to Washington.

Ohio highway patrol officers at first believed that one of the slain men was Charles Bird, called "Public Enemy No. 2" by Federal agents.

But Glenn Hoffman, assistant detective chief, who made the identifications, said that Bird was not in the raided house when the detective squad arrived.

The wounded were Detectives Robert Cline, William Danner and Leo Phillips; Carl Boettcher, 24 years old, of Cleveland and Mrs. Eva Watring, 38, of Columbus, a roomer at the house.

Hoffman said that Boettcher and Stephen Figuli, 20, also of Cleveland, were the suspects captured.

Physicians said that Cline's chances to recover were slight. Danner and Boettcher were in serious condition. All were shot in the abdomen. Phillips's eyelid was grazed by a bullet and Mrs. Watring was wounded in the leg.

The detectives sought four men who had robbed the Hilltop office of the Ohio National Bank here of $3,500 five hours earlier and who had also been suspected of looting the Hilltop branch of the Federal Loan Association of $2,200 two days ago.

The raid followed the trailing of the automobile of the suspects by Motor Cycle Patrolman Lawrence Tucker to a yellow, two-story rooming house.

"All hell broke loose in a moment," said Detective Phillips. "A man plunged through a window with a gun in his hand. Another dashed through the front door.

"I ran after them. Everybody was shooting. I felt a stinging sensation under my eye and blood began to trickle down my face. Then I hit one of those fellows."

Detective Danner pursued one of the men and they ran two blocks to a railroad embankment, where the suspect turned and they emptied their pistols at each other. Other policemen found them lying twelve feet apart. This suspect died later in the hospital.

HITLER ASSUMES CONTROL OF ARMY; RETIRES 15 GENERALS AND SHIFTS 25; RIBBENTROP MADE FOREIGN MINISTER

BRITISH PERTURBED

See 'Moderate' Influence of Army Weakened—Ribbentrop Feared

PUTSCH RUMORS ACTIVE

Nazi Drive in Austria Deemed Possible—French View Steps in Berlin as Reply to Them

By FERDINAND KUHN Jr.
Special Cable to THE NEW YORK TIMES.

LONDON, Saturday, Feb. 5.—A sense of foreboding ran through the first astounded comments in London today on the sensational "bloodless purge" in Germany.

The British Government has long dreaded the weakening of what it regarded as the "moderate" influence of the army on German foreign policy. Repeatedly the British have hoped that if a showdown should come the army could successfully assert its authority against the Nazi chieftains.

Now some of the "moderate" army leaders have gone and the British see in the German Foreign Office former Ambassador Joachim von Ribbentrop, chief author of the anti-Comintern pact and one whom even pro-Germans here distrust as an anti-British force in Berlin.

"New Situation" Is Seen

"The effect of the new appointments," says The Daily Telegraph editorially, "is to confirm the dominance of the Nazi party as against the higher command of the army and against moderating influences. Hitler has taken the short way with those who he feared were unsympathetic to his foreign policy. It creates for Germany a new situation. What it may portend must be a matter of keenest interest to the whole of Europe, for on German actions so much in international relationships depends."

The Times of London agrees that "the party's control over the army has been substantially increased." The News-Chronicle expresses the belief, however, that the battle is not over and that "the extent and duration of the increased tension in Europe will depend on how far and how long the proud Reichswehr is content to swallow its snub."

Amid the new anxiety so suddenly created by Berlin, particular attention is being paid here to a speech by Prime Minister Neville Chamberlain at Birmingham yesterday. He gave assurance that "there need be no anxiety that rearmament is not going fast enough or far enough." Today editors are significantly placing excerpts from this speech side by side with their accounts of the sudden overturn in Germany.

Nazi Putsch in Austria Feared

LONDON, Saturday, Feb. 5 (AP).—Fears that Germany would embark on a new adventurous course in Europe, possibly starting with a Putsch in Austria, as a result of her army crisis swept diplomatic quarters here today.

Diplomats took a grave view of what they considered the success of the radical wing of the Nazi party over the moderate element. The elevation of Joachim von Ribbentrop to Foreign Minister and the expected disappearance of Baron Constantin von Neurath's influence in the government were held in informed circles to be an ill omen.

It had been rumored for some time in London that Herr von Ribbentrop would replace Baron von Neurath, but the announcement came as a surprise, nevertheless, to some diplomats, who were apprehensive over what they termed Herr von Ribbentrop's recent anti-British tendencies.

Diplomatic sources predicted that Ulrich von Hassell, retiring Ambassador to Rome, would replace Herr von Ribbentrop in London and that Franz von Papen, recalled from Vienna, would go to Rome.

Some forecast that a "violent" Nazi would be sent to Vienna to carry forward the nazification of Austria. Some quarters reported that a Nazi Putsch in Austria had been planned to coincide with last Sunday's scheduled meeting of the Reichstag, which was canceled. Austrian police activity was credited with forestalling such a move then.

Czechoslovakia and the Free City of Danzig did not figure so prominently in the speculation upon Germany's future plans because, it was pointed out, Czechoslovakia now is

Continued on Page Three

London Hears Hitler Feared Coup By Army and Arrested von Fritsch

Chancellor Is Said to Have Acted After Group of Generals Protested Policy in Spain and Link to Italy

Special Cable to THE NEW YORK TIMES.

LONDON, Saturday, Feb. 5.—The Daily Telegraph publishes the following from its well-informed diplomatic correspondent:

"I have received from a source which I regard as entirely trustworthy the following account of the German crisis. At one moment during the past ten days Chancellor Hitler regarded the situation as so grave that he believed himself threatened by a military coup d'état and acted accordingly. He ordered the arrest of General Werner von Fritsch, Commander in Chief of the army, which was carried out by Heinrich Himmler, commander of all German police.

"For forty-eight hours General von Fritsch was kept in a place of confinement specially designated by the secret police. Later he was allowed to return home, where yesterday he was still under 'house arrest,' guarded by two army officers. This confinement will probably be relaxed and denied when an official statement is issued.

"A General von Fritsch was arrested Tuesday, the day when he was scheduled to give a dinner, to which the British and French Ambassadors had been invited and which was hurriedly postponed on the grounds of his 'ill health.'

"It is now possible to reconstruct the course of this crisis with a fair decree of accuracy. General von Fritsch, it appears, discovered those aspects of General Werner von Blomberg's marriage, which were subsequently to form the subject of representations to Hitler ten days after the marriage.

"General von Fritsch himself did not act as spokesman on that occasion, and Hitler received a deputation of six generals in mufti, headed by General Ludwig Beck, chief of the general staff. This was in the middle of last week. It was the allegations then made that shook Hitler's composure to the extent of forcing him to change his original intention of delivering a speech Jan. 30 and to revoke the prepara-

Continued on Page Three

NAVY CHIEF'S TALK TO BRITISH 'SECRET'

'Vital to Interest and Defense of United States,' Leahy Warns House Group

AVOIDS LINK TO SHIP BILL

Question if President Held Up Plans Pending Report From London Stirs Hearing

By LELAND C. SPEERS
Special to THE NEW YORK TIMES.

WASHINGTON, Feb. 4.—Recent consultations by Captain Royal E. Ingersoll, chief of the navy's War Plans Division, with British officials in London went unexplained today when Admiral William D. Leahy, Chief of Naval Operations, refused a reply to a direct question during testimony on the Administration's Naval Construction Bill.

Admiral Leahy was just completing his fifth day before the House Naval Affairs Committee when Representative Church, Republican, of Illinois, demanded to know what matters involving the American and British navies were discussed by Captain Ingersoll in London.

"I will not answer that question here," said Admiral Leahy, "but I will make a statement in executive session, of course, on the basis that it is absolutely secret, because it is of vital importance to the interests and defense of the United States."

Mr. Church had said he would like to know if it were true that President Roosevelt delayed for about two weeks the submission of the $800,000,000 proposals to Congress because he wanted to confer first with Captain Ingersoll. Admiral Leahy said he had no such information.

"Who is Captain Ingersoll?" asked Representative Brewster, Republican, of Maine.

"He is the chief of the War Plans Division in my office," said Admiral Leahy.

Chairman Vinson banged his gavel. Representative A. N. Phillips, Democrat, of Connecticut, shouted a point of order in effort to stop Mr. Church.

"No, let him ask his question," said Mr. Vinson.

The question was long and involved, so long in fact that Admiral Leahy said he was unable to understand what Mr. Church had in mind. The question was reframed and the fact of Captain Ingersoll's visit at London came into the picture.

Mr. Church said afterward that he would continue his effort to get the information he sought. Whether in open or executive session he did not say.

Previously, Admiral Leahy said in reply to questions that with the fleet based in the Pacific, the Atlantic and Gulf coasts were practically without defense from the navy. In the event of a war in both oceans, he rather reluctantly

Continued on Page Two

UPRISING IN CANTON IS QUICKLY CRUSHED

Japanese Are Believed to Have Inspired Effort to Create an Ally of North China

HANKOW CLASH EXPECTED

Rightists in Kuomintang Are Opposing Communist Demand for Prolonged Warfare

Japanese airplane bombers and warships increased their activity near Canton yesterday, while the officials of the Kwangtung Province port were crushing a revolt believed to have been inspired by Tokyo. Clashes at Hankow are expected because the Right Wing of the government opposes the policies of the Communists, whose power is steadily increasing. [Page 1.]

Chinese troops, from new positions on the north bank of the Hwai River, battled Japanese forces, supported by airplanes. Money and supplies were sent from Hankow to Chinese guerrilla forces in Shansi. [Page 2.]

Washington ordered the Fifteenth Infantry, U. S. A., to leave Tientsin, China, where it has been guarding the railway to Peiping since 1912. Marines from the embassy guard in Peiping will be stationed in Tientsin. [Page 2.]

Japanese Aid Canton Plot

Wireless to THE NEW YORK TIMES.

HONG KONG, Saturday, Feb. 5.—Canton has been in the throes of a serious plot and a coup has been narrowly averted. Despite official denials the facts that have emerged show there was a plot, apparently sponsored by malcontents and fostered by the Japanese, to overthrow some Cantonese officials.

The Cantonese authorities learned of the plot Thursday and immediately prepared for a clash, warning foreign shipping Thursday night to go out to sea. The ships were unable to depart until yesterday morning, when they found the barrier in the Pearl River had been rebuilt and they had to remain in the river.

Since Thursday night virtual martial law has existed in Canton, with wholesale searchings in the streets by soldiers. There was at least one clash in Tungshan, a suburb, where many shots were said to have been fired last night.

It was rumored an attempt was made to assassinate Mayor Tseng Yang-fu. It was reliably reported that at least 100 persons were arrested on charges of being in the pay of the Japanese. It was also rumored that the Governor of Kwangtung Province, General Wu Te-cheng, had been detained, but he denied this and the Mayor denied there had been an attempt to

Continued on Page Two

AIDE TO RULE ARMY

Blomberg, Fritsch Are Retired—Goering Is Made Marshal

PAPEN, OTHERS RECALLED

Neurath Heads Secret Foreign Affairs Board—Reichstag Summoned for Feb. 20

By OTTO D. TOLISCHUS
Wireless to THE NEW YORK TIMES.

BERLIN, Feb. 4.—The National Socialist Cabinet crisis that has been smoldering for a week behind walls of silence came to an end tonight when with a Napoleonic gesture Chancellor Adolf Hitler assumed personal charge both of the armed forces and the Third Reich's foreign policy.

He reorganized both his Cabinet and the high army command along lines that not only further consolidate his own power but also make him the central authority for a military and economic mobilization of Germany analogous to the recent French example.

The principal changes involved in this reorganization are as follows:

I. In the Army Command

Both Field Marshal Werner von Blomberg, the War Minister, and Colonel General Werner von Fritsch, Commander in Chief of the army, are relieved of their posts on grounds of "ill health," and, in the words of a decree issued tonight, Hitler assumes "personal and direct command over all the armed forces."

This command will be exercised through a "supreme command of the armed forces," headed by General Wilhelm Keitel, hitherto chief of the Wehrmachtsamt or administrative department in the War Ministry, who becomes the technical successor of Marshal von Blomberg, equal in rank to a Cabinet Minister and Hitler's personal chief of staff.

He also takes over the War Ministry, and "in peace takes charge," according to Hitler's orders, "of the unitary preparations for national defense in all fields."

Col. Gen. Walther von Brauchitsch, commander of the First Army Corps, is appointed Commander in Chief of the army, succeeding General von Fritsch.

Col. Gen. Hermann Goering, in his capacity as Commander in Chief of the air force, is promoted to field marshal, which puts him in rank above all the generals in the army and may or may not be compensation for his failure to get the War portfolio.

Hitler immediately ordered a complete shake-up of the foremost commanding generals, involving the retirement of seven army and six air force generals in addition to Marshal von Blomberg and General von Fritsch, new commands for twenty-two generals and eight colonels and the placing of three generals at the disposal of the supreme army command and the army's Commander in Chief. The retirements include most of General von Fritsch's liaison officers.

II. In the Cabinet

Baron Constantin von Neurath has been relieved of his post as Foreign Minister and Joachim von Ribbentrop, Ambassador to London, has been appointed his successor.

Simultaneously, however, Hitler has created a "Secret Cabinet Council" for the purpose, it is stated in the decree, of "advising him in the conduct of foreign policy," and Baron von Neurath has been made its president, in which capacity he stays in the Cabinet.

The other members of the Council are Herr von Ribbentrop, Field Marshal Goering, Rudolf Hess, deputy leader of the Nazi party and Minister Without Portfolio; Dr. Joseph Goebbels, Minister of Propaganda; General von Brauchitsch, Admiral-General Erich Raeder, Naval Chief of Staff; General Keitel and Dr. Hans Heinrich Lammers, Minister Without Portfolio and Chief of the Reich Chancellery.

Walther Funk, it is officially announced, has assumed office as Economic Minister as of Feb. 1 and will be formally inducted by Marshal Goering as Commissioner for the Four-Year Plan next Tuesday.

Finally Franz von Papen, Ambassador to Vienna; Ulrich von Hassell, Ambassador to Rome, and Dr. Herbert von Dirksen, Ambassador to Tokyo, have been recalled from their posts. With Herr von Ribbentrop that means a change in four

Continued on Page Three

"All the News That's Fit to Print."

The New York Times.

Copyright, 1938, by The New York Times Company.

LATE CITY EDITION
Fair and moderately cold today. Tomorrow fair, with slowly rising temperature.
Temperatures Yesterday—Max., 38; Min., 29

VOL. LXXXVII....No. 29,248. Entered as Second-Class Matter, Postoffice, New York, N. Y. NEW YORK, MONDAY, FEBRUARY 21, 1938. PP TWO CENTS in New York City. | THREE CENTS Within 200 Miles. | FOUR CENTS Elsewhere Except in 7th and 8th Postal Zones.

HITLER DEMANDS RIGHT OF SELF-DETERMINATION FOR GERMANS IN AUSTRIA AND CZECHOSLOVAKIA; EDEN RESIGNS IN CRISIS OVER BRITAIN'S POLICY

FEDERAL AGENCIES CONSIDER FORCING RAILROAD MERGERS

Groups Shaping Rehabilitation Plans Believe Plight Inclines Congress to Idea

FAVOR THREE YEARS' GRACE

Would Allow Time for Voluntary Consolidations, With Federal Action Afterward

FOR TEMPORARY POOLING

Some Officials Hold This a Need Until a Long-Range Plan Becomes Effective

By JOHN H. CRIDER
Special to THE NEW YORK TIMES.

WASHINGTON, Feb. 20.—Legislation for forced consolidations of railroads is being considered seriously in at least three of the government offices now preparing plans to be laid before President Roosevelt at his rail conference scheduled for the coming week.

It was learned that some officials are advancing a plan which would apply the "death sentence" technique of the Holding Company Act to railroad consolidations. Under this procedure the railroads would have a certain period of years in which to submit voluntary unification plans, after which a government agency would prepare a plan for them.

Like most remedies for the nation's rail problems, the idea of forced or compulsory consolidation has been considered for years, with little favorable response from Congress, even for milder remedies than the one now gaining ground. Rail reformers are hopeful that this time Congress will relent in view of the unusually sad plight of the railroads.

"Wasteful" Competition a Factor

President Roosevelt, Senator Burton K. Wheeler, in charge of the Senate investigation of railroad finances, and the Interstate Commerce Commission in its annual report have stated that "wasteful" competition is one of the fundamental railroad ills.

The I. C. C. went so far in its annual report as to state that "no competitive industry can work out its salvation through a price-increasing policy alone." The best expert opinion in official Washington seems to be that a rate increase, such as the $517,000,000 rate rise which the I. C. C. is expected to grant to the railroads can be at most only a temporary remedy.

It is felt that compulsory consolidations cannot solve the immediate economic emergency faced by the railroads and that rate increases and perhaps some form of pooling may have to be employed until a long-range plan can be effected. Pooling is condemned by some as an incentive to inefficiency since the weak railroads are carried along by the strong.

Senator Wheeler's investigating committee, the I. C. C., the Securities and Exchange Commission, and the Reconstruction Finance Corporation are among the government agencies now formulating plans to be considered at the White House conference.

Financial Position Weak

The current efforts in official circles to work out a permanent solution to the railroad problem arises from the unusually weak financial position of the country's railroads, due partly to increased operating costs, the decline in general business activity, and competition from other forms of transportation, but the real work was started when the President discussed the problem at a press conference on Dec. 10. He questioned the necessity for maintaining parallel lines of railroad with inadequate traffic.

He also referred to the reports of Commissioner Joseph B. Eastman of the Interstate Commerce Commission as Federal Coordinator of Transportation in 1933 and 1934 which discussed the problems of consolidation at some length. As a consequence there has been a considerable demand for these reports, particularly for the first one, which contained in the appendix a report by Leslie Craven, counsel to the coordinator, upholding the constitutionality of compulsory consolidations and recommending a modification of the method employed in England.

Some of those now preparing plans to lay before the President feel with Mr. Craven that under "any consolidation program which is non-compulsory and not fully comprehensive, it is almost certain that uneconomic and inefficient groupings will result due to the inevitable inclination of the carriers which initiate consolidations to grab favorable lines in the effort

Continued on Page Eight

Swiss Make Romansh Fourth Official Tongue

By The Associated Press.

BERNE, Switzerland, Feb. 20.—Swiss voted by an overwhelming majority today to establish Romansh as the fourth official language of Switzerland.

The vote was considered by some observers as a slap at Italy, where Fascisti say Romansh, an obscure language that is spoken only in part of Grisons canton, is an Italian dialect.

German is spoken by about 71 per cent of the Swiss, French by 22 per cent, Italian by 6 per cent and Romansh by 1 per cent.

A resolution giving the Federal Council power to prevent arms shipments to warring nations and providing for partial control of armament industries also was approved.

TENEMENT BLAZE KILLS 3, INJURES 9

Families Routed in 165th St. Fire, Third in Building Unit in Less Than Two Years

DARING RESCUES CUT TOLL

Cripple Is Carried to Safety—Man Leaps to Death, Wife Is Killed Shielding Baby

The third fire since June, 1936, in adjoining three-story buildings at 761-63 East 165th Street, between Forest and Tinton Avenues, the Bronx, killed three persons early yesterday morning and caused injuries to nine others, including an infant orphaned by the blaze.

Hampered by the collapse of a stairway under which the flames were believed to have started, firemen of seven engine companies and two hook-and-ladder units made a series of dangerous rescues from the second and third floors of No. 763, virtually all of which was destroyed except its yellow-brick front.

One of the firemen, exhausted by the struggle in the building, which had no fire escape, was among those treated later by Dr. Harry M. Archer, honorary departmental surgeon.

Fire Not Incendiary

At first it was believed that the fire was incendiary, but after an all-day investigation Assistant District Attorney George Pilzer and Assistant Fire Marshal Martin Scott announced at 9:30 o'clock last night that the fire was not of suspicious origin. They had spent hours questioning tenants of the building and others living near by.

One of those hurt was a passer-by who aided in the rescue work. Another volunteer, boosted on the shoulders of friends before the apparatus arrived, cut his hand in smashing a second-floor window to warn tenants. The two were Thomas Smith, 38, of 1,009 Union Avenue, who suffered a sprained knee and cut thumb, and Joseph Barrett, 27, of 486 East 165th Street, whose left hand was injured.

Francis Dunn, 38, of 857 Fox Street, who was later cut on the head by falling glass, turned in the alarm at 3:04. He was on his way home when he noticed curling flames in the building. By the time the first fire apparatus arrived, Smith, Dunn and others had awakened all the tenants in No. 761 and the building had been cleared.

Flames Burst Through Roof

The blaze centered, however, beneath the stairway of No. 763 and spread rapidly to the top, where it divided and ate its way into the top floor of both units of the building. One witness said it suddenly burst through the roof like a great torch.

Smoke in the hallway thickened, but members of Engine Company 50 tried to get up the stairs anyway. Fireman Terence A. Nugent, who subsequently needed medical aid, was one of those nearly trapped when the stairs crumbled.

While his colleagues swung their ladders toward the building, a man appeared at the third floor window over the entrance, clambered to the sill and stared down, terrified.

A confusion of shouts rose from the street. Some cried "Jump!" and others yelled "Back! Back!" The man jumped. But while would-be rescuers extended their arms, his body struck the broad, jutting cornice between the second and ground floors. The deflection catapulted him beyond them to the street, and he was fatally injured. He was William Theofanna, 42, whose wife, Armione, 41, was burned in the bedroom while shielding their baby, 5-month-old Betsy.

With the fire-fighting crew augmented by men summoned by a second alarm, rescues by ladder were accomplished with comparatively little difficulty. But in the case of William Sculla, 65-year-old paralytic, Firemen John Mullen and Vincent Howard risked their lives to fight their way to his bed,

Continued on Page Twenty

ORTIZ INAUGURATED AMID WIDE ACCLAIM BY THE ARGENTINES

Nation Greets Six American Airplanes as a Major Part of Colorful Ceremony

PRESIDENT IS A CIVILIAN

Public Reaffirms Its Faith in Free Rule, Regarding U. S. as Example and Friend

By JOHN W. WHITE
Special Cable to THE NEW YORK TIMES.

BUENOS AIRES, Argentina, Feb. 20.—Dr. Roberto M. Ortiz was inaugurated the twenty-first constitutional President of the Argentine Republic this afternoon in a colorful ceremony amid widespread popular acclaim. In Argentina lawyers have the title of Doctor and this puts the Presidency again under a civilian title; the last two Presidents were generals.

The presence of six giant U. S. Army bombers of the type known as "flying fortresses" associated the United States with Argentina on this occasion in a manner in which no foreign country has participated at any inauguration in recent years. The planes arrived on Friday after a record-smashing flight from Miami, bearing a letter from President Roosevelt to President Ortiz, expressing the best wishes of the American Government and the American people for his forthcoming government.

Nothing that the United States has done in Latin America, with the possible exception of President Roosevelt's visit a year ago, has ever aroused such an enthusiastic response on the part of the Argentine people. The newspapers have published the most laudatory editorials extending a hearty welcome to the American fliers and expressing their appreciation of the good-will of the government that sent them.

Faith in Democracy

People here have seized upon the visit of the United States fliers as an opportunity to reaffirm their faith in democracy and express their disapproval of totalitarian regimes. South America, including Argentina, has been subjected to such intense propaganda from European totalitarian countries, especially Italy, during the last year that this propaganda has now reached the state expressed in the Spanish words "contra producente"—working to defeat its own aims.

The people have become resentful of this high-pressure propaganda. They have enthusiastically greeted the big American fighting planes as messengers of peace and good-will from the country to which the South Americans have always looked as their model democracy.

Public opinion in Argentina was very cold to the intimation that the Italian planes that recently visited Brazil might come to Buenos Aires for the inauguration. The Italians changed their minds and did not come. No foreign mission has ever been more enthusiastically received than the American aviators whose flight was not announced until two days before they started.

Italian newspapers both here and in Italy have not mentioned the American flight. German papers here gave it a paragraph hidden away on an inside page. Both devoted pages to two recent Italian flights.

This was an ideally beautiful Summer day with the bright blue sky and blazing sun that are featured in the Argentine flag. The Argentine Army and Navy Flying

Continued on Page Seven

Roosevelt Silent on Hitler, But May Give Views Soon

Special to THE NEW YORK TIMES.

HYDE PARK, N. Y., Feb. 20.—The temporary White House was completely silent today on President Roosevelt's reaction to the address of Chancellor Hitler to the German Reichstag. But there were suggestions that he might soon make known in an informal way the views of his Administration toward the political situation abroad.

Marvin H. McIntyre, the President's secretary, insisted that Mr. Roosevelt passed the day resting from the cares of his office, and that he had talked only with members of his immediate family and the vestrymen of St. James Episcopal Church here.

Despite the official reticence, however, there was no doubt that the President was in close touch with the State Department.

EDEN'S RESIGNATION DISTRESSES FRANCE

Belief Prevails That British Capitulation' Must Reduce Leadership of Paris

SMALL ALLIES FEARED FOR

Chautemps and Delbos Confer With Ambassador Phipps, Calling Him Urgently

By P. J. PHILIP
Wireless to THE NEW YORK TIMES.

PARIS, Feb. 20.—The resignation of British Foreign Secretary Anthony Eden has caused much more concern in France than anything that Chancellor Adolf Hitler said today. Immediately after the announcement was made, Ambassador Sir Eric Phipps hurried over to see Premier Camille Chautemps and Foreign Minister Yvon Delbos, presumably to assure them that British friendship for France and Anglo-French cooperation would remain as close as ever.

But such assurances are not likely to alter the conclusion that what is called here the Germanophile clique in Great Britain has won, and that henceforth France will be reduced to a very different role in European affairs from that which she has been accustomed to play.

It is a poor consolation to be told by Hitler that she has nothing to fear from Germany "if she minds her own business." And it will be meat for much criticism of M. Delbos and his aids that this abandonment should be the reward of their steady support of British policy during the past two years, or rather, as it will be called, their constant subservient agreement.

Bitter Clash Forthcoming

It is too early to forecast what the effects will be here. What is clear, however, is that there will be a bitter fight between those who clamor for complete abandonment of the non-intervention policy in Spain and a frank espousal of the republican cause, and those who will counsel prudence and that France

Continued on Page Three

King Issues Fascist Charter for Rumania; Constitution Sets Up a Corporative State

Wireless to THE NEW YORK TIMES.

VIENNA, Feb. 20.—A dictatorial Constitution was given to Rumania tonight by a proclamation signed by King Carol. It was not countersigned by any of his Ministers.

The democratic parliamentary system is abolished and replaced by a Fascist corporative Chamber and Senate, where various trades and occupations will be represented. The distribution of land under the land reform scheme stands, but increased compensation will be given for mineral rights taken over by the State. Special measures will be taken against corruption. Trial by jury is abolished.

In the proclamation Carol says: "I have been moved by one idea only—the love of my people and the need to rescue the fatherland."

The Constitution promises to peoples that have lived for centuries on the soil of present-day Rumania the same treatment as the "Rumanian race" will receive, but it indicates that State jobs will go mostly to ethnical Rumanians.

There are rumors that on Thursday Rumania will go through the form of taking a plebiscite of the people's views on this dictated Constitution.

King Carol assumed direct control of the Rumanian Government early this month, when he forced the pro-Fascist Premier Octavian Goga out of office to make way for a national Cabinet headed by Dr. Miron Cristea, Patriarch of the Rumanian Orthodox Church.

The King suspended the Constitution, promising to replace it as soon as the situation created by M. Goga's leanings toward Germany and Italy and his anti-Semitism had calmed.

The new Constitution had been generally expected to provide for a dual administration: a Crown Council, composed of distinguished Rumanians, that would lay down general principles of policy, and a Cabinet to frame legislation that would be submitted to the King and the Crown Council.

Under a corporative State, such a dual system would resemble that of Italy, with her Fascist Grand Council and Cabinet.

BRITAIN IS SHOCKED

Foreign Secretary Quits Over Issue of Seeking Deals With Dictators

CRANBORNE GOES OUT, TOO

Two Other Ministers Waver—Outburst Is Expected in Commons Today

By FERDINAND KUHN Jr.
Special Cable to THE NEW YORK TIMES.

LONDON, Feb. 20.—Foreign Secretary Anthony Eden resigned from the British Cabinet tonight, no longer willing to approve or support the methods of Prime Minister Neville Chamberlain and a majority of his colleagues in seeking settlements with Italy and Germany.

He took with him into retirement Viscount Cranborne, Under-Secretary for Foreign Affairs. At least two other Ministers—Walter E. Elliot, Secretary of State for Scotland, and William S. Morrison, Minister of Agriculture—had contemplated resigning with Mr. Eden, but late tonight they had not carried their intentions to the point of action.

Viscount Halifax, Lord President of the Council, will direct the Foreign Office temporarily, with Mr. Chamberlain himself probably taking charge of foreign affairs for a time in the House of Commons.

Eden Is Determined

The Cabinet had tried for more than three hours in the afternoon to persuade Mr. Eden to change his mind, but this time nothing could shake his determination.

As a last resort the Ministers begged Mr. Eden to accept some other office or to say he was resigning on grounds of ill health. But he refused all such suggestions. A break had come on a question of policy and he saw no reason why he should conceal it.

Tonight, pale and haggard, Mr. Eden walked dejectedly across Downing Street, where a crowd was waiting to cheer him, and called at No. 10. Inside the historic Prime Minister's house Mr. Chamberlain was in anxious consultation with his Ministers.

But Mr. Eden stayed only long enough to hand in a formal letter of resignation. After four minutes he strode back to the Foreign Office in the darkness with his two years and two months of incessant responsibilities at an end.

The Foreign Secretary's letter and Mr. Chamberlain's reply threw light on what had been known abroad and at home but persistently denied in official quarters and in pro-Government newspapers here. They showed that the resignation had been precipitated by the interview with the Italian Ambassador, Count Dino Grandi, on Friday, but also that disagreements between Mr. Eden and Mr. Chamberlain had been going on for months.

Refers to 'Difference'

"The events of the last few days," wrote Mr. Eden, "have made plain a difference between us on a decision of great importance in itself and far-reaching in its consequences. I cannot recommend to Parliament a policy with which I am not in agreement."

Mr. Eden went on to admit a "difference of outlook between us in respect to international problems of the day and also as to the methods whereby we should seek to resolve them." He reminded Mr. Chamberlain that it was not in the interests of the nation that Ministers should work "in uneasy partnership," especially the Foreign Secretary and the Prime Minister.

The letter ended with a note of thanks for "help and counsel" and a polite and doubtless sincere assurance that "our differences, whatever they may be, cannot efface that memory or influence our friendship."

The stilted wording of Mr. Chamberlain's reply showed what a shock to him and his Cabinet this resignation had been. The Prime Minister wrote of his "most profound regret" and of the "distinction" with which Mr. Eden had administered the Foreign Office. His regret was all the greater, said Mr. Chamberlain, "because such differences as have arisen between us in no way concern the ultimate aims or fundamentals of our policy."

"The decision you find yourself unable to accept," wrote the Prime Minister, "is whether the present

Continued on Page Two

Eden-Chamberlain Letters

By The Associated Press.

LONDON, Feb. 20.—The texts of Foreign Secretary Anthony Eden's letter of resignation to Prime Minister Neville Chamberlain and the Prime Minister's reply follow:

My Dear Prime Minister:

The events of the last few days have made plain a difference between us on a decision of great importance in itself and far-reaching in its consequences.

I cannot recommend to Parliament a policy with which I am not in agreement.

Apart from this, I have become increasingly conscious, as I know you have also, of the difference in outlook between us in respect to the international problems of the day and also as to the methods whereby we should seek to resolve them.

It cannot be in the country's interest that those who are called upon to direct its affairs should work in uneasy partnership, fully conscious of differences in outlook yet hoping they will not recur.

This applies with special force to the relationship between the Prime Minister and the Foreign Secretary.

It is for these reasons that with very deep regret I have decided I must leave you and your colleagues with whom I have been associated during years of great difficulty and stress.

May I end on a personal note?

I can never forget the help and counsel you have always so readily given me, both before and since you became Prime Minister.

Our differences, whatever they may be, cannot efface that memory nor influence our friendship.

Yours ever,
ANTHONY EDEN.

Mr. Chamberlain's Reply

My Dear Anthony:

It is with the most profound regret, shared by all our colleagues, that I have received your intimation of your decision

Continued on Page Three

ITALY IS JUBILANT AS EDEN QUITS POST

Sees Relations With Britain Improved With Change in the Foreign Office

HITLER SPEECH IS HAILED

But Strain on Friendship Is Seen if Reich Interferes Actively in Austria

By ARNALDO CORTESI
Wireless to THE NEW YORK TIMES.

ROME, Feb. 20.—The news of the resignation of Anthony Eden, British Foreign Secretary, reached Rome late this evening and quickly spread throughout the city, causing great satisfaction everywhere, as was to be expected. In the Foreign Office Mr. Eden's resignation is believed to remove one of the great obstacles to the conclusion of an Italian-British understanding and, as this is still one of the main objectives of the present foreign policy, it is thought that official negotiations soon will be opened with better chances of success than in the past.

Italians have, whether rightly or wrongly, been convinced that for a long time there has been a conflict of opinion in the British Cabinet between one school of thought, headed by Prime Minister Neville Chamberlain, that was in favor of an agreement with Italy, and another, headed by Mr. Eden, that made an agreement dependent on conditions, such as the withdrawal of Italians from Spain, that Italy could not accept or was not willing to accept.

Mr. Eden's resignation is regarded as a victory for Mr. Chamberlain's faction and, therefore, likely to bring an Italian-British understanding nearer by insuring that Italy's desire to make friends with Britain is met by an equal desire on Britain's part to make friends with Italy.

Claim Personal Defeat

It is thought in Italy that Mr. Eden is more or less smarting under the failure of his scheme to upset Premier Benito Mussolini's plans in Ethiopia by means of sanctions which it is believed were actuated by personal animosity against Italy.

Mr. Eden has, therefore, always been the target of strong attacks by the Italian press which, sometimes openly and sometimes by innuendo, accused him of allowing his private grudges to play too large a part in his handling of his country's foreign affairs. Italians feel, in other words, that Mr. Eden's fall has caused a personal enemy to disappear as head of the British Foreign Office.

It cannot be doubted that Italy will take advantage of the new sit-

Continued on Page Five

NAZIS CELEBRATE IN AUSTRIAN FETES

Great Strength Is Shown in the Provinces, but Numbers Are Small in Vienna

HITLER THREAT IS FEARED

Patriots Are Bitter, Hearing No Pledge of Independence in Chancellor's Talk

By G. E. R. GEDYE
Wireless to THE NEW YORK TIMES.

VIENNA, Feb. 20. — Throughout Chancellor Adolf Hitler's speech Vienna's streets were like those of a dead city. Patriots and Nazis alike were indoors, patiently listening, the former hoping to hear the promises made at the Berchtesgaden meeting with the Austrian Chancellor fulfilled, the latter to learn whether there would be flaming words with which to light the torch of a Nazi uprising.

Instructions had come from Munich for small but peaceful Nazi demonstrations today. A Nazi journalist told me today, however, that three or four days hence there would be large-scale demonstrations. He would not give the date. Presumably it is Thursday, when Chancellor Kurt Schuschnigg speaks.

It has become fairly common knowledge here that Hitler solemnly promised Dr. Schuschnigg that if he accepted the terms dictated under the threat of invasion Germany would today recognize Austria's independence, the political monopoly of the Fatherland Front and guarantee suspension of the support of the Austrian Nazis with money and propaganda material from Germany.

Newspapers had promised the Austrian population that Hitler's speech would carry out his side of the bargain and repay Austria for the heavy sacrifices she made to avoid invasion.

Threat to Austria Seen

When the speech ended without the least effort by Hitler to fulfill his part of the bargain, there was great indignation. But more serious than this was the bitterness caused by Hitler's silence on the question of Austrian independence, which was taken as equivalent to a threat that will soon be put into execution.

During the broadcast Vienna Nazis listened quietly in their favorite cafes. Immediately afterward street demonstrations began, but not on any serious scale. Three hundred Nazis marched past the German Legation singing the "Horst Wessel Song" and shouting "Heil Hitler." The police allowed the demonstrators to parade but did not allow them to stand outside the legation.

Soon afterward similar small

Continued on Page Three

NAZI POWER CITED

Status Quo Repudiated by Fuehrer—Restates Colonial Demands

TONE OF TALK ANTI-BRITISH

Resignation of Eden Is Hailed as Greatest Victory of German Diplomacy

Chancellor Hitler in a militant speech to the Reichstag yesterday made a strong point of the right of "self-determination" for the 10,000,000 Germans in Austria and Czechoslovakia. He indicated force must be used in the end to break the status quo. He promised to go ahead with plans to enlarge the army. He assailed British policy, making a direct attack on Mr. Eden, and demanded colonies.

Disputes in the British Cabinet over proposed negotiations for a settlement with Italy and Germany led to the resignation of Foreign Secretary Eden. Viscount Halifax took temporary control of the Foreign Office, but Prime Minister Chamberlain will direct its policies.

France was fearful of losing her position as leader on the European Continent as a result of Mr. Eden's retirement. Italians, on the other hand, were jubilant over the passing of the Secretary, long regarded as a foe of their country.

Nazis held large demonstrations in Austrian provinces, but made a poor showing in Vienna.

[All stories on Page 1.]

Main Points of Hitler's Speech to the Reichstag on Page 4.

Hitler Shows Militancy

By OTTO D. TOLISCHUS
Wireless to THE NEW YORK TIMES.

BERLIN, Feb. 20.—In the most militant speech of his career, which is already hailed here as the final cause for the overthrow of British Foreign Secretary Anthony Eden, Chancellor Hitler outlined today before the Reichstag those principles and conditions through which National Socialist Germany proposes to retain her place in the sun and which, in her view, are alone able to preserve peace.

In some respects this most anxiously awaited speech was sufficiently vague to allay some of the worst fears in certain capitals, already primed for sensational extras. In respect to the two events which have most alarmed the world recently, namely the reorganization of the government and the army command and Austria's "cold Anschluss" with the Third Reich, it was even disappointing in its paucity of new revelations.

In both of these cases Hitler has stuck entirely to the understatements of the official communiqués previously published.

Right of Self-Determination

The speech's real keynote was the proposition that by virtue of their efficiency and accomplishments the German people, organized in and represented by the National Socialist Third Reich, constituted a great power therefore entitled to equal rights with all other great powers, including the right of self-determination. This right of self-determination, according to Wilson's fourteen points, was specifically proclaimed by Hitler for the "10,000,000 Germans" living in the two states adjacent to German borders.

These States are Austria, with nearly 7,000,000 inhabitants, and Czechoslovakia, with a German minority of more than 3,000,000.

Despite its occasional vagueness there was no possibility of mistaking the final implications of this speech, with which the world will have to reckon henceforth. It was a frank repudiation of the status quo and any mere legalistic conception of world politics and an equally frank avowal of power politics based on the vital, if egotistic, interests of nations—a dedication to the proposition that might creates new right.

League Policies Repudiated

It is in this sense that the whole speech was also an outspoken repudiation of the legalistic League of Nations policy of Mr. Eden. It was further underlined by the open if ironic attacks on Mr. Eden per-

Continued on Page Three

"All the News That's Fit to Print."

The New York Times.

THE WEATHER
Fair and cool today; Sunday fair and warmer.
Temperature yesterday—Max., 63; min., 54.
For weather report see next to last page.

VOL. LXXXVII....No. 29,268. Entered as Second-Class Matter, Postoffice, New York, N. Y. NEW YORK, SUNDAY, MARCH 13, 1938. Including Rotogravure Picture, Magazine and Book Review. PP TEN CENTS | TWELVE CENTS Beyond 200 Miles Except in 7th and 8th Postal Zones.

HITLER ENTERS AUSTRIA IN TRIUMPHAL PARADE; VIENNA PREPARES FOR UNION, VOIDS TREATY BAN; FRANCE MANS BORDER; BRITAIN STUDIES MOVES

HARRISON DEMANDS END OF PROFITS TAX TO HELP BUSINESS

Levy on Undistributed Gains, Modified by House, Should Be Killed Entirely, He Says

SENATOR ASKS FLAT RATE

He Would Revamp Excise on Capital Increases Also Under the Same Principle

CHAMBER IS 'ENCOURAGED'

It Asserts Federal Attitude to Business Is Improving, but Manufacturers Disagree

By The Associated Press.

WASHINGTON, March 12.—Chairman Harrison of the Senate Finance Committee proposed today that tax relief to "encourage new investments and melt much frozen credit" go far beyond the administration-approved provisions of the House tax bill.

In a statement issued while his committee arranged to begin study of the House measure on Monday, Mr. Harrison declared that the undistributed profits tax should be killed in its entirety.

"While the House retained only the skeleton of the undistributed profits tax," he said, "the remains will haunt business, and its complete removal and return to a sufficient flat corporation tax is preferable. It is simpler and more understandable."

Mr. Harrison declared also that the capital gains provisions of the bill which the House approved yesterday should be revamped to substitute a flat rate for the present sliding scale.

Administration leaders were expected generally to fight abandonment of the principle of the undistributed profits tax, which many business spokesmen have blamed for the current economic slump. The House bill, which must be acted upon by the Senate before it can become law, would modify this levy substantially but retain its principle.

Hints at Broader Tax Base

Mr. Harrison also mentioned the possibility of broadening the tax base to bring new taxpayers under the income levy, and of cutting some of the surtax rates on higher bracket individual incomes.

"If I interpret the sentiment of the Senate correctly, it desires to do justice and give encouragement to business in every provision of the pending tax bill, within government revenue requirements. I know that is the sentiment of the Finance Committee. So far as I am concerned, whatever influence I may possess, as chairman of the committee, I shall exert toward raising the required revenue, removing some complicated provisions, and, as far as possible, restoring confidence to business.

"If we can improve the capital gains provisions of the House bill, by taking capital gains out of the general income provisions and applying a flat rate of about 15 per cent on all capital gains from sales of property held over one or two years, it will, in my opinion, encourage new investment and melt much frozen credit.

"The undistributed profits tax, beautiful in theory, has not worked. Business does not like it, and would prefer a flat rate.

Wants Cut in High Surtax Rates

"I shall make an effort to strengthen Section 102 of the present law, imposing a penalty upon the unreasonable accumulation of reserves for the purpose of evading taxation.

"I do not know whether it is possible to be done, and I can give no one any encouragement that it will be done; but if I could write the tax bill at this time, I would reduce some of the high surtax rates. Tax laws should be written for revenue purposes; and when the surtaxes are as high as they are now, the Treasury observes diminishing returns and realizes less revenue. I have come to the conclusion that, if we are forced to continue an exceptional spending policy, the income tax base should be broader, resulting in an increased tax consciousness upon the part of the people.

"I have a conviction, if there is a sit-down strike upon the part of capital because of fear or the uncertainties of investment, that we should break it up, if possible, and that effective work should be done toward removing some of the barriers that are checking the flow of capital and credit into new investments and new industries."

Special to THE NEW YORK TIMES.

WASHINGTON, March 12.—The United States Chamber of Com

Continued on Page Two

California Senate Kills Pardon for Tom Mooney

By The Associated Press.

SACRAMENTO, Calif., March 12.—The California Senate tonight killed by an almost unanimous voice vote an Assembly-approved resolution "pardoning" Tom Mooney, convicted of the 1916 San Francisco Preparedness Day parade bombing.

The Senate debated the measure only a few minutes. Chairman W. P. Rich of the Rules Committee, which reported the resolution unfavorably, then moved that it be tabled. Only a few "nays" were heard.

The action at least temporarily disposed of the question as to whether the Legislature had the power to pardon. Senate concurrence was necessary to technical enactment.

Remaining before the Assembly, however, was a resolution asking Governor Merriam to pardon Mooney. The Assembly also passed a resolution of that nature a year ago, but the Senate likewise voted not to concur.

5 JERSEY FIREMEN DIE AS WALL FALLS

Deputy Chief in Paterson and Four Others Crushed After Quelling Warehouse Blaze

MANY SHOPPERS ROUTED

Damage of $250,000 Reported as Smoke Fills Store in Heart of Business District

Special to THE NEW YORK TIMES.

PATERSON, N. J., March 12.—A deputy fire chief and four other firemen were killed instantly and another was slightly hurt tonight when a three-story brick wall toppled on them while they were wetting down the smoldering ruins of the Quackenbush Company department store's warehouse, which was ruined by a spectacular fire of undetermined origin this afternoon.

The dead:

Deputy Chief James Sweeny, 58 years old, of 95 Lexington Avenue.

Captain John Davenport, 44, of 132 Franklin Street.

Fireman Louis Rodesky, 49, of 404 East Twenty-sixth Street.

Fireman Mathew O'Neill, 45, of 931 Ward Street.

Fireman John Lynch, 37, of 330 Buffalo Avenue.

Captain Paul Schaub, 44, of 72 Eighteenth Avenue, who was with the group at the time, escaped miraculously with bruises, the debris falling in such a manner as to knock him out of the way.

Fire Chief Collapses

Fire Chief Thomas L. Coyle collapsed when he saw his men buried under the avalanche of stone and had to be taken away from the scene.

Tonight's casualties brought the total to eleven. About 2 P. M., soon after the fire started, an employe trapped in the building suffered a broken leg when he jumped from a second floor window. A fireman was felled by smoke. Both were taken to the hospital.

Only two or three fire crews were at the scene when tonight's tragedy occurred, their job being not only to wet down the ruins but also to remove debris that might endanger public safety. At the time the wall collapsed, the firemen were devising a means to pull it down because they knew it was in danger of falling.

When the blaze was at its height this afternoon, dense clouds of smoke forced fifty families in the vicinity to leave their homes, shoppers to flee from the department store and a motion picture theatre audience to disperse, and damaged the store.

Damage $250,000

Chief Coyle estimated the damage at $250,000 but Robert W. Pyke, president of the Quackenbush Company, said that figure was a conservative one and added that in addition to the loss of the warehouse and its contents the smoke damage to the store proper might be "almost 100 per cent."

Mr. Pyke said he doubted that the store, one of the largest in Paterson, would be open for business on Monday. The concern was celebrating its fifty-third anniversary with a sale that attracted several hundred shoppers, all of whom were forced to leave as well as the 500 employes in the store, situated at Main and Ellison Streets.

The fire was in progress from a little before 2 P. M. until 4:30 P. M., when it was put under control by the city's entire Fire Department force of 125 men summoned on a general alarm, assisted by fifty volunteer firemen from Prospect Park, Haledon and Little Falls.

John Turri of 224 Hamilton Avenue, an employe in the warehouse, received a broken leg when he

Continued on Page Four

18 RUSSIANS TO DIE FOR TREASON PLOT; RAKOVSKY SPARED

Escapes With a Sentence of 20 Years—Bessonoff Gets 15, Physician 25 Years

HEART SPECIALIST SAVED

Dr. Pletneff Alone Among Three Doctors Wins Mercy—Bukharin Shows Fight

By HAROLD DENNY

Special Cable to THE NEW YORK TIMES.

MOSCOW, Sunday, March 13.—Eighteen of the twenty-one defendants in Moscow's third great public treason trial within two years were sentenced to be shot at the final session of the military court at 4:30 this morning.

The only defendants in this most dramatic of all Soviet trials whose lives are to be spared are S. A. Bessonoff and Christian G. Rakovsky, for both of whom mercy was recommended by Prosecutor Andrey Y. Vishinsky in his closing address, and Professor D. H. Pletneff, renowned as one of the foremost heart specialists in Europe, who confessed having helped to kill Maxim Gorky and others under coercion from Henry G. Yagoda, one-time terror of the Ogpu.

Mr. Rakovsky received a sentence of twenty years in prison, Professor Pletneff, twenty-five; Mr. Bessonoff, fifteen. Professor Pletneff and Mr. Rakovsky, who are elderly men, are unlikely to survive such terms.

Those Sentenced to Die

Nikolai Bukharin, Alexis I. Rykoff, Mr. Yagoda and Gregory T. Grinko, whose names have loomed so large in Soviet history, will die probably within the next twenty-four hours. The others sentenced to death are:

Nikolai N. Krestinsky, former First Assistant Foreign Commissar.

A. P. Rosengoltz, once Commissar of Foreign Trade.

Vladimir I. Ivanoff, former chief of the Soviet timber industry.

Akmal Ikramoff, a former leader of the Uzbek Soviet Republic.

Faysulla Khodjaieff, former President of Uzbek.

Mikhail A. Chernoff, former Commissar of Agriculture.

I. A. Zelensky, former head of Consumers Cooperatives.

Dr. I. N. Kazakoff, noted endocrinologist.

Dr. L. G. Levin, former chief of the Kremlin Hospital.

P. P. Kruchkoff, who was Gorky's secretary.

V. F. Sharangovitch, P. T. Zubareff, P. P. Bulanoff and V. A. Maximoff-Dikovsky.

Under the terms of the law governing terrorist cases, decreed after the assassination of Sergei M. Kiroff in 1934, there is no appeal except to the Presidium of the Supreme Soviet, which must act within three days, but which in preceding treason cases has acted much more swiftly.

There were no outcries, no faintings, no demonstrations of any sort on the part of the defendants as Judge Vassidy V. Ulrich finished his dreadful words. Most of the

Continued on Page Thirty

Graz Crowds Pull Down Memorial to Dollfuss

By The Associated Press.

GRAZ, Austria, March 12.—Yelling throngs pulled down the memorial statue to the late Chancellor Engelbert Dollfuss in the main street of Graz tonight.

As the populace, soldiers and police shouted the Nazi greeting of "Heil, Hitler!" a crowd gathered around the Dollfuss memorial and brought the figure of the little Austrian Chancellor, who was murdered in the abortive Nazi putsch of 1934, crashing to the street.

Uninterrupted demonstrations and jubilation swept through the town, with 6,000 persons awaiting the arrival of German troops. The burgomaster of Graz telegraphed an invitation to Chancellor Adolf Hitler to visit the city.

FOREIGN EXCHANGE TUMBLES IN CRISIS

Chief World Currencies Break Sharply in the Flight of Capital to Safer Centers

FRANC IS ONLY EXCEPTION

Rush to Buy Dollars Brings New Lows for Year—Rise in Gold Shipments Due

Conditions bordering on near panic swept the money markets of the world yesterday as Europeans rushed to purchase American dollars and gold after Germany's conquest of Austria. The flight of capital, particularly from the smaller Continental nations, assumed gigantic proportions and brought an unprecedented volume of trading in the foreign exchange markets, both here and abroad.

Coincident with these conditions in the money markets, all the principal foreign currencies broke sharply in relation to the dollar with the exception of the French franc.

Guilders were dumped overboard in such heavy amounts that the price of the unit was forced down 14 points to a new low for the year. All other Continental currencies except the franc likewise touched new low levels for 1938, while the pound sterling dipped to its lowest quotations since last Dec. 1.

Despite the political tangle in France the franc moved forward as a result of the heavy influx of capital from Switzerland, Holland and Belgium. At the close of the market the French unit registered a net gain for the day of 2¾ points to 3.19¾ cents. The pound sterling fell ⅛ cent to $4.99⅞ after dipping at one time to $4.98⅛, which re-

Continued on Page Thirty-five

Mrs. H. D. Gibson Hurt in Long Island Hunt; Wife of Banker Crushed by Falling Horse

Special to THE NEW YORK TIMES.

GLEN COVE, L. I., March 12.—Mrs. Harvey D. Gibson, wife of the banker, received five broken ribs and back injuries when she was thrown from her dappled gray gelding Coq d'Argent during the Meadow Brook Hunt near Syosset this morning.

She was taken to the North Country Community Hospital here for X-ray examination by Dr. Garrett Duryea. Dr. John Morris of the surgical staff of Bellevue Hospital and Dr. H. C. Fleming of 535 Park Avenue came from New York for a consultation with Dr. Duryea and Dr. Opho Hudson of the Meadowbrook Hospital, Hempstead. Though no diagnosis was announced, it was learned she was "injured badly but not critically."

The accident occurred while the field was moving slowly in single line through a narrow and muddy path on the estate of George P. Mann. Mrs. Gibson's mount fell heavily without warning, pinning her before she had any chance to leap aside, according to riders near her.

It was assumed the animal stepped in a hole or tripped on a hidden root. Coq d'Argent, a thoroughbred hunter, won the lightweight division championship at Piping Rock last October. Mrs. Gibson rode sidesaddle as usual.

Mr. Gibson, co-master with Harry Peters of Islip, summoned his chauffeur, who had kept track of the riders from near-by roads. He remounted, unaware of her condition, after she left for the hospital four miles away.

The hunt started auspiciously with fifty riders meeting at the Thistleton Kennels on the Robert E. Tod estate in Syosset. Several jumps were taken without mishap as the riders swung across property owned by Louis J. Horowitz. Then they turned into the lane.

Three foxes were run to ground by the pack of forty hounds. Mr. Gibson dropped out a half hour after the accident. None of the field believed Mrs. Gibson, a veteran horsewoman, had been hurt seriously.

She was married to Mr. Gibson, president and chairman of the board of the Manufacturers Trust Company, in Bern, Switzerland, thirteen years ago. She had been married to George Galt Bourne in 1913. They were divorced eleven years later. She has a daughter, Whitney Bourne, the actress.

Mrs. Gibson's parents were Mr. and Mrs. Charles E. Whitney of Boston. She assisted her husband by radio appeals in 1932 when he was directing the Emergency Unemployment Relief Committee. The Lenox Hill Settlement House has been among her steadfast interests. A benefit entertainment for it attracted 2,000 persons to Land's End, the Gibson summer home, Fox Point, L. I., on July 4, 1936. The affair was described as the most elaborate ever attempted on the North Shore.

PRAGUE NOW CRUX

London Considers Aid to Czechoslovakia if She Is Put Under Threat

EMPTY MOVES SHUNNED

Stunned Britons See End of Anglo-German Talks and Blow to Rome Accord

By FERDINAND KUHN Jr.

Special Cable to THE NEW YORK TIMES.

LONDON, March 12.—Under the pressure of Germany's shock tactics against Austria the British Government began seriously and anxiously today to consider what it would do if the German mailed fist descended soon upon Czechoslovakia.

There is little doubt among British Ministers now that Germany intends to go farther in Central Europe. Prime Minister Neville Chamberlain and his colleagues today found many of their illusions gone and their hopes destroyed, but their awareness of German aims and methods suddenly was made brutally clear.

The spectacle of "coercion backed by force," as it was described in the British protest to Berlin yesterday, appears to have shocked even those British Conservatives who have trusted until now in Germany's underlying peacefulness and good intentions. It remains to be seen how this changed outlook will be reflected in British policy.

Halifax Is Astonished

The story is told that last night when German troops had crossed the frontier, Viscount Halifax, British Foreign Secretary, paced up and down his huge room at the Foreign Office, holding his forehead like a man distracted and exclaiming:

"Horrible! Horrible! I never thought they would do it!"

This was the room where Sir Edward Grey one fateful Summer day in 1914 looked out of the window at lamplighters in the street below and said:

"The lamps are going out all over Europe; we shall not see them lit again in our lifetimes."

The leaders of the British Government wonder now whether other lamps may be extinguished in Prague, Czechoslovakia, as in Vienna unless something can be done. The British Cabinet met for two hours in emergency session this morning, listening to reports and reviewing the Austrian situation, but it was significant that the Ministers talked more of the immediate future than of the past, which neither they nor any one can revoke.

The German conquest of Austria was accepted as an accomplished fact. There was no talk in London today of a spectacular post mortem, such as the session of the League of Nations Council, which met in London after the German re-occupation of the Rhineland and which arraigned Germany as a violator of solemn pledges.

Perhaps if Italy had been willing to join there might have been a concerted protest, but in the present circumstances the British feel that empty gestures would be humiliating and futile.

Naturally the Ministers were indignant. A photographer stopped Leslie Hore-Belisha, War Secretary, on the doorstep of 10 Downing Street and asked him to smile.

"Why should I smile?" was his grim reply.

Shortly after the Cabinet meeting Clement R. Attlee, leader of the Labor party, and Sir Archibald Sinclair, leader of the opposition Liberals, called at Mr. Chamberlain's invitation to discuss the situation with him.

Ministers to Be on Call

The sense of a crisis was deepened by the announcement that the Ministers were staying within reach of London over the week-end and that the Cabinet would meet again Monday morning in any case to approve a statement to be made before the House of Commons later in the day.

A communiqué issued after the Cabinet meeting said the British Government was keeping in closest touch with the French Government and was "giving continuous consideration to the situation."

"It was felt," said the communiqué, "that the action of the German Government was bound to have the most disturbing effect on Anglo-German relations and upon

Continued on Page Thirty-five

The Austrian Situation

Adolf Hitler entered Austria yesterday and in a speech before a great throng at Linz proclaimed the unity of that country with Germany. He will enter Vienna in triumph today. He was preceded by large forces of troops, which occupied important cities, a detachment going to the capital and another to Brenner Pass on the Italian frontier. Many bombing planes also appeared at Vienna. Heinrich Himmler organized the police of that city and many arrests were made. Ex-Chancellor Schuschnigg was under guard. Anti-Nazi newspapers were suppressed. Exodus attempts were balked by closing of neighboring frontiers.

Munich reported that at least 65,000 troops had gone into Austria, with much artillery, including heavy guns and tanks. Some 40,000 more moved toward the frontier and reinforcements were brought up. Men up to 38 were mobilized.

France suspended leaves of absence in the forces guarding the Maginot line and a high military council was held in Paris. Leon Blum again failed to gather a National Union Cabinet, but sought one of the Left. In London the Cabinet met and, while accepting the Austrian situation, considered what would be done in case Czechoslovakia was endangered. [The above dispatches on Page 1.]

The Fascist Grand Council at Rome, after a meeting on Austria, issued a vague communiqué neither approving nor disapproving of Germany's action, but conceding it was "an open expression of the sentiment and will of the Austrian people." It had before it a letter from Hitler to Mussolini explaining the former's course and pledging that the German troops would not go south of Brenner Pass. [Page 36.]

In Berlin Propaganda Minister Goebbels broadcast a proclamation by Hitler declaring the unity of the two German countries and warning that no nations could drive them apart. There were indications that a new Danubian settlement would be sought with Rome. [Page 34.]

PARIS ENDS LEAVES OF BORDER TROOPS

Defenders of the Maginot Line of Forts Opposite Germany Are Ordered to Stand By

BLUM'S EFFORTS BLOCKED

Unable to Get Consent for a National Union Cabinet, He Tries a New Popular Front

By The Associated Press.

PARIS, March 12.—Troops manning the powerful Maginot Line defenses facing the German border were held to their posts tonight as France took an increasingly grave view of the European crisis.

French officials meanwhile sought to convince Great Britain it was necessary for mutual safety to take a joint stand to discourage any German encroachment on Czechoslovakia. They considered the war-created democracy on the Reich's border the real powder barrel, because of its alliances with France and Soviet Russia.

Premier-designate Leon Blum at the same time gave up attempts to form a national union government of all parties and sought desperately to set up another Popular Front Cabinet to give the country a Ministry. His proposal to include Communists in a Cabinet had brought almost united disapproval from Center and Right groups in the Chamber of Deputies.

Ministers Stay at Posts

The Ministers of Camille Chautemps's government, which resigned Thursday, remained at their posts immersed in the international developments.

Edouard Daladier, Minister of National Defense and War in that Cabinet, ordered the troops in the Maginot Line to remain at their posts without leave until further notice after he had conferred with military chiefs. The line is the famous barrier of steel and concrete and heavy guns that was constructed after the World War to halt any new German invasion. It is a vast underground system stretching virtually from Switzerland to Belgium.

The full import of the order canceling leave was not disclosed, but it was agreed generally that it was a sign of grave apprehensions. M. Daladier conferred at length with army and air commanders.

France definitely is committed by treaty to aid Czechoslovakia in the event of aggression; Britain's hands are free.

The Foreign Office pointed out, however, that there were no juridical grounds on which to base a charge of violation of a neutral State's territory in the case of Germany's Nazification of Austria. The Franco-Czechoslovak treaty, it was said, was not intended to cover a similar situation.

By this it was meant that Austria's new Chancellor, Dr. Arthur

Continued on Page Thirty-six

65,000 REICH TROOPS MOVE INTO AUSTRIA

40,000 More Mass Near Border as Planes and Artillery Join the Forces Driving Across

FRONTIER ROADS CLOGGED

Effort Made to Disguise the Movements as Anxiety of the People Persists

By STANLEY SIMPSON

Wireless to THE NEW YORK TIMES.

MUNICH, Germany, March 12.—With troops moving throughout the countryside, with innumerable planes roaring overhead and with men called as reservists taking hurried farewell of their families, Bavaria presented today an even more war-like atmosphere than yesterday.

It became obvious that many more troops than the Seventh Army Corps had been mobilized and equipped for possible war duty. In well-informed quarters it was estimated that about 65,000 German soldiers were on the way into Austria today—30,000 bound for Vienna and 35,000 for the Austrian provinces.

In place of the Bavarian troops thrown into Austria, reinforcements came into Bavaria from other parts of Germany. About 40,000 were transported today to Rosenheim, Traunstein and other points between Munich and the Austrian frontier.

Stream Into Austria

All day troops continued to march into Austria. Heavy artillery and tanks from Ingolstadt and Coburg were observed as late as 3 o'clock this afternoon moving out on the road to Kufstein, while light artillery was being brought up from Bamberg and Regensburg. In fact, local residents insist that Southern Bavaria is seeing more troops on the move than ever it saw during the World War.

Extraordinary activity was seen all along the road to Simbach, Bavarian frontier town separated from Braunau, Chancellor Hitler's Austrian birthplace, by a river bridge, and on roads to every other point on the Austrian frontier. Every small town within thirty miles of the frontier has the appearance of a garrison city.

In Mushldorf, about twenty miles from Braunau, large numbers of recruits were leaving in motor buses to join their units at the frontier. Some districts have been denuded of all able-bodied men. In some cases 38-year-old men—of the 1900 class—have been mobilized.

Some of the planes flying overhead, it was learned, carried loads of leaflets to Vienna and other Austrian cities.

Germans' Anxiety Persists

Residents of villages and towns in the frontier district have recovered from the acute alarm of yesterday morning, but there is still considerable anxiety. Although reassuring broadcasts were sent all day from the Munich station, the anxiety is subsiding only gradually. Classes in schools were interrupted by

Continued on Page Thirty-six

LINZ HAILS HITLER

He Defies World to Part Two Peoples—Will Go to Capital Today

GERMAN TROOPS POUR IN

Reach Vienna and Brenner Pass—Himmler Rounds Up Nazis' Foes—Border Shut

Hitler Proclamation, Page 35; his speech at Linz, Page 33.

By G. E. R. GEDYE

Wireless to THE NEW YORK TIMES.

VIENNA, Sunday, March 13.—For the first time in twenty-four years, save for one or two fleeting visits, Chancellor Adolf Hitler of Germany at 4 o'clock yesterday afternoon set foot in Austria, his native land, as the victor at the head of a triumphal procession of jubilant Nazis.

He crossed the frontier, the River Inn, at Braunau, his birthplace, followed by a long motor column.

Both the German and Austrian banks were lined with enormous crowds to witness the historic moment when the Nazi leader should enter into possession—for it is clear that after the formality of a plebiscite under Nazi control Austria will become part of a new, great Germany—of the country where he was born and raised and where he acquired the political philosophy that has brought him greater power than any German has had in history.

It is the country that ever since his accession to power had formally rejected his doctrines and where his followers until a few weeks ago had been outlawed as members of an illegal movement.

Goes From Braunau to Linz

Amid the deafening cheers of the Nazis both in Germany and in Austria and the pealing of church bells, the Fuehrer's car slowly crossed the bridge over the Inn into Braunau, which was a mass of swastika banners. Then he proceeded to Linz, his first extended halt.

There, amid scenes of the wildest enthusiasm, he made a speech from the balcony of the City Hall in which he proclaimed the unity of Germany and Austria and warned the world that any effort to part the two peoples would be in vain.

In greeting Hitler at Linz, Dr. Arthur Seyss-Inquart, the new Austrian Chancellor, proclaimed the annulment of the peace treaty of St. Germain, which stipulated that the Austrian republic must remain independent and forbade union with Germany except with the consent of the League of Nations.

Hitler spent the night at the Weinzingerhof Hotel in Linz and will make a triumphal entry into Vienna at about 11 o'clock this morning [5 A. M. Eastern standard time].

Meanwhile large forces of German troops had moved into Austria. According to German statements, the first of them did not cross the frontier until 5:30 yesterday morning and the movement was made simultaneously at all the main points of entry.

At Salzburg the troops were preceded by 100 tanks and marched in with bands playing and two men singing Nazi songs. Immediately after their arrival the commandant at the Salzburg garrison was ordered to report at the prefecture to the German commanding officer, General Kiebler.

The Austrian officer was told that he and his troops—including the 1915 class called to the colors by former Chancellor Kurt Schuschnigg in defense of Austrian independence—would henceforth be under General Kiebler's orders and ranked as German troops.

Advance Proceeds Smoothly

The whole German advance proceeded according to an obviously prearranged and well-coordinated plan. A procedure similar to that at Salzburg was followed wherever the Germans crossed the frontier.

Early yesterday afternoon the Italian frontier guards at Brenner Pass had the pleasure of seeing armed forces of the other end of the Berlin-Rome axis arrive at their border.

Formal greetings were exchanged between the German and Italian commanders. At the head of the German troops was a column of machine gunners and motor cycle scouts with anti-tank guns. Here the

Continued on Page Thirty-one

"All the News That's Fit to Print."

The New York Times.

LATE CITY EDITION
Partly cloudy, with moderate temperatures today. Tomorrow cloudy, with little change in temperature.
Temperatures Yesterday—Max., 78; Min., 53

VOL. LXXXVII....No. 29,301. Entered as Second-Class Matter, Postoffice New York, N. Y. NEW YORK, FRIDAY, APRIL 15, 1938. P TWO CENTS in New York City. | THREE CENTS Within 200 Miles. | FOUR CENTS Elsewhere Except in 7th and 8th Postal Zones.

ROOSEVELT ASKS EXPENDITURE OF $5,000,000,000; ON RADIO, HE URGES 'UNITED NATIONAL WILL'; CONGRESS EXPECTED TO ACCEPT HIS PROGRAM

JAPANESE DEFEAT A MAJOR DISASTER; CRISIS IN CABINET

TOLL OF SLAIN HUGE

Only 20,000 of 62,000 in Taierhchwang Area Believed Still Alive

TOKYO PLANS NEW DRIVE

Ministers Reported Divided on Issue of Mobilizing the Nation's Full Strength

Japan met with her first great military reverse in modern times in the recent fighting around Taierhchwang, it became known yesterday. Military experts in Shanghai believe 42,000 men out of an army of 62,000 were killed when the Chinese cut the Japanese supply lines and struck a smashing blow at the trapped forces. [Page 1.]

Stung by their setbacks, the Japanese were reported moving eight divisions in preparation for a smashing counter-offensive, with Suchow as its objective. The Chinese, however, tightened their siege of Yihsien and hoped to capture the Southern Shantung town within two days. [Follows the above.]

But meanwhile the defeat has had its repercussions in Tokyo, where Prince Konoye's Cabinet was said to be facing a crisis on the issue of mobilizing the nation's full strength for the China warfare. [Page 3.]

In Washington it was learned that the Japanese reverses had caused a number of army and navy officers to modify their opinion of Japan's military might. [Page 3.]

Debacle at Taierhchwang

By HALLETT ABEND

Special Cable to THE NEW YORK TIMES.

SHANGHAI, via Hong Kong, April 14.—Japan, despite the official derisive denials concerning the Hankow Government's claims of victories in Southern Shantung, has met with the first great military disaster in her modern history—and this disaster has been one of the first magnitude.

Late in March the Japanese Army along the Hanchwang-Taierhchwang sector numbered about 62,000 men, including the crack divisions of Major Gen. Rensuke Isogai, Japan's military attaché in China just before the outbreak of the war, and Lieut. Gen. Seishiro Itagaki, who was chief of staff of the Japanese Army in Manchukuo.

If today there are 20,000 of those men alive, all the foreign military experts in Shanghai and Hankow will be amazed.

So great has been the débâcle that when the Japanese retreated they even abandoned their dead and wounded, a thing hitherto unknown in modern Japanese military history.

Overconfidence a Factor

Overconfidence and surprise Chinese strategy, largely devised by foreign advisers, are responsible for this amazing overturn.

The Chinese positions along the Taierhchwang-Suchow sector have been in preparation since 1933, their coordinated lines there having required enough concrete to erect several Empire State buildings.

Driving southward along the Tientsin-Pukow Railway, 60,000-odd Japanese began pounding against these positions, but they did not yield.

Then the countryside became filled with innocent-looking Chinese farmers who were really disguised soldiers and who began infiltrating along the Japanese lines of communications, cutting the railway and diverting canals and streams across the right of way. Soon communications with the Japanese bases ceased, whereupon airplanes attempted dropping food and munitions, but this proved insufficient.

Then the Japanese began experiencing a shortage of gasoline, necessitating abandoning tanks, trucks and ambulances. This shortage soon extended to artillery supplies, and ten days ago exhausted shells for six-inch and nine-inch howitzers.

The desperate Japanese soldiers might have dismembered the guns and flung the pieces at their foes, but otherwise their artillery was useless. They found themselves facing about 250,000 infuriated Chi-

Continued on Page Three

Garner Buys Big Ranch, But Plans Vacations Home

By The Associated Press.

WASHINGTON, April 14.—Vice President Garner has bought a big Texas cattle ranch.

The ranch, 23,436 acres, is situated in the northern part of Webb County, about 100 miles southeast of Uvalde, Mr. Garner's home.

It was bought at an unstated price from J. F. Sinclair. The transaction was completed yesterday.

Attractive as the ranch may prove, however, apparently it will not lure the Vice President from his home. Mr. Garner said today he would spend his vacations between sessions of Congress at Uvalde, as usual.

"I don't suppose there is anything in the world as good as your home," he commented.

When Mr. Garner's negotiations for a ranch first became known there was speculation that he might be planning to retire when his current term ends. There has been no substantiation of this, however.

BRITISH SIGN PACT IN ROME TOMORROW

Main Protocol of Agreement Deals With Political Issues Between Two Countries

Britain and Italy agreed yesterday to the signature of their accord in Rome tomorrow afternoon. The various documents will total about 7,000 words, going to the bottom of all outstanding issues. Mussolini showed he was extremely pleased, and the cordial spirit in which the negotiations ended was regarded as most important. Italians now expect an accord with France will be reached. [Page 1.]

Many departures in French foreign policy were expected by Paris under Foreign Minister Georges Bonnet. More rigid impartiality in the Spanish affair and possible sending of an envoy to Franco were forecast. A new Ambassador may be sent to Rome. New harmony between Paris and London was predicted. [Page 4.]

The drive of the Insurgents in Eastern Spain was reported reaching its peak and it was expected the next day or two would determine whether they could reach the seacoast. [Page 2.]

Anglo-Italian Agreement

By ARNALDO CORTESI

Wireless to THE NEW YORK TIMES.

ROME, April 14.—The Anglo-Italian agreement, negotiations for which started March 8, will be signed at the Palazzo Chigi Saturday afternoon, it was decided today by Premier Mussolini and the Earl of Perth, the British envoy, at a meeting in Palazzo Venezia at which Foreign Minister Galeazzo Ciano also was present. Today's meeting definitely closes the negotiations, the Italian and English texts of the document to be signed Saturday having been read, compared and approved.

The various protocols and annexes composing the agreement are to be signed by Count Ciano for Italy and Lord Perth for Britain in the presence of many Italian and British officials who took part in the negotiations.

The Egyptian Minister probably also will be present to sign a further document dealing with some of the aspects of Anglo-Italian relations to which his country is a party.

The text of the agreement signed or, at least, a very full summary will be published immediately afterward.

All Issues Are Included

The agreement will comprise a main protocol consisting of a preamble and nine paragraphs, a number of annexes and an exchange of letters between the two negotiators. The main protocol deals with fundamental political issues between Italy and Britain, while the annexes deal with particular problems, such as Palestine, the Nile waters and the like.

The letters, believed to have been exchanged some days ago, deal with the main points contemplated in the agreement and contain reciprocal assurances that rendered possible Britain's step at Geneva a few days ago in asking a discussion of the situation resulting

Continued on Page Four

CASHMORE RULING GIVES DEMOCRATS COUNCIL DOMINANCE

Appellate Court Upholds His Election as Vice Chairman for Two-Year Term

APPEAL MOVE IS LIKELY

La Guardia Coalition Foes Win Control of Committees and of Patronage

In a unanimous decision the Appellate Division held yesterday that Councilman John Cashmore, Brooklyn Democrat, had been legally elected vice chairman of the City Council on Jan. 3 for a two-year term and that he could not be unseated until that term expired. The court also held that the Democrats had legally organized the Council.

The decision was a sweeping victory for the Democratic forces in the Council. It assures them of control of the committees of the Council and thereby of control over legislation coming before the Council until 1940. It also places at their disposal the patronage of the Council for the same period.

An appeal from the ruling to the Court of Appeals seemed likely last night, although Corporation Counsel William C. Chanler and Councilman B. Charney Vladeck, spokesman for the La Guardia coalition group, were not definite on the subject. Council President Newbold Morris said he thought an appeal should be taken.

Cashmore Is "Gratified"

Mr. Cashmore, when informed of the decision at City Hall, said:

"I am gratified that the Appellate Division has unanimously sustained my election as vice chairman and has approved our contention that I was elected for the term of the Council and my position cannot be vacated. We should now get down to business and endeavor to devote the rest of our term to the consideration of legislation promoting the welfare of our citizens, to which object I pledge myself without prejudice. The delay, to this time, has been due to the rulings of the chair.

"The people of this city elected fourteen Democrats to this Council, a clean majority. It was, therefore, the wish of the electorate that the Democrats should organize and direct the activities of this Council."

The coalition group had gone through the motions of electing James A. Burke, Queens Independent, vice chairman after a motion holding that office vacant had been declared carried by Mr. Morris.

The court's ruling was based on an agreed set of facts accepted by all the members of the Council. Two basic questions were involved: whether a majority of the Councilmen attending the organization meeting could legally elect a vice chairman and whether a majority of the Council at any subsequent meeting could declare the office vacant. Both questions arose through the failure of Councilman Michael J. Quill, Bronx Labor party member, to attend the first meeting, which was held while he was re-

Continued on Page Fifteen

What Congress Has Done With Roosevelt Program

By The Associated Press.

WASHINGTON, April 14.—Here is the status of the Administration's legislative program, three and a half months after Congress began its session:

Crop Control—Enacted into law.

Housing—Enacted into law.

Tax Revision—Passed by Senate and House; now in conference.

Regional Planning—Approved by House Committee.

Naval Expansion—Passed by House; Senate debates it next week.

Wage-Hour—New bill approved by House Labor Committee.

Government Reorganization—Passed by Senate, rejected by House.

Anti-Trust—Presidential message expected soon.

Relief—President requested new funds today.

RFC Loans—Enacted into law.

BANKERS QUESTION EXPANSION WISDOM

Wall Street Doubts Monetary Devices Will Restore Needed Business Confidence

The sweeping character of President Roosevelt's plans for expanding the credit base of the country and "priming the pump" by government spending took the financial community by surprise yesterday in spite of the advance intimations that such a plan was being laid. Among bankers and brokers it was felt that the President was firing the heaviest guns remaining in the monetary arsenal, but that there was good reason to doubt the efficacy of the broadside.

The combined effects of the desterilization of $1,400,000,000 of gold and the reduction of bank reserve requirements, as announced by the President, are calculated to raise excess bank reserves by $2,150,000,000, which would lift the current volume of $1,730,000,000 of excess reserves to a record high of over $3,800,000,000. Such a total would far exceed the highest level to which excess bank reserves rose in late 1935 and early 1936, when their size gave rise of fears of inflation in government as well as in private financial circles. It would provide a potential basis for an expansion of possibly $23,000,000,000 in bank credit. As such, bankers saw in the move the most inflationary step yet made by this Administration. Nevertheless, there was no certainty among them that the immediate results would be inflationary.

The financial markets expressed a varying judgment on the news. United States Government bonds went sharply higher as bankers sought to buy in anticipation of the

Continued on Page Thirteen

Jacob (Gurrah Jake) Shapiro Gives Up Here After Eluding World-Wide Hunt for a Year

Jacob (Gurrah Jake) Shapiro, a poor immigrant boy who made his way to the top of a racketeering empire, gave himself up to Federal authorities yesterday after nearly a year of dodging a world-wide man-hunt in which rewards totaling $7,500 were offered for his arrest.

He said he was tired of being chased by the law.

Still among the fugitives from Federal prosecution in New York, and from District Attorney Thomas E. Dewey was Louis (Lepke) Buchalter, who shared the racketeering command with Shapiro. The two controlled at least a half dozen industrial rackets, maintained an organization of about 200 hired thugs and gunmen, and levied toll on garment makers, fur merchants, flour truckers and other segments of industry.

On Nov. 8, 1936, Shapiro and Buchalter were convicted of anti-trust violations in Federal Court by John Harlan Amen, Special Deputy Attorney General, and received two-year sentences. They appealed, were freed in bail of $10,000 and when, on June 14, 1937, the conviction was upheld as to Shapiro and reversed as to Buchalter, neither could be found.

That was the beginning of the chase. Subsequently another Federal indictment was returned. On Nov. 8, 1937, the Federal Government offered a reward of $2,500 for the arrest of each. Two indictments, one based on racketeering in the garment industry, and another in the flour trucking industry, were returned by the Special Grand Jury under Mr. Dewey, then Special Rackets Prosecutor. The city added $5,000 to the rewards.

The two were then variously reported as being in different parts of the world. Many times they were said to have fled the country. Information from various sources filtered back to the Federal Bureau of Investigation and the search continued unabated.

Against this background, then, Gurrah Jake walked into the Federal House of Detention at Eleventh and West Streets yesterday afternoon at about 3:30 o'clock.

"I want to surrender," he told George Seiss, the guard on duty at the door. He was led to Warden Humphries.

"I'm Jacob Shapiro," he said. "I want to give up."

The warden called Reed Vetterli, local agent in charge of the Federal Bureau of Investigation, and said:

"There's a man named Shapiro down here who says you want him. Do you?"

Shapiro was taken to the Federal Court House for questioning. What happened after that showed the operations of the recently imposed rule that all information concerning the Federal bureau must come through the office of Attorney General Cummings in Washington. Rumors flew through the building and through official quarters about the

Continued on Page Eleven

CONGRESS DIVIDED

Some Members of Each Party Approve the Program in Its Entirety

OTHERS FAVOR PART OF IT

O'Connor Attacks 'Pump-Priming' 'Where There's No Water in Well'

Special to THE NEW YORK TIMES.

WASHINGTON, April 14.—First Congressional response to President Roosevelt's new recovery program today indicated fairly broad support by Democratic members of the House and Senate, who for the most part also said they understood very little about the program. They were particularly hazy about the plan to "desterilize" gold reserves heretofore held in a separate Treasury account.

The one important fact generally grasped was that billions of dollars more were to be added to Federal expenditures, and the principal division of opinion centered around whether the government should obligate itself for further indebtedness to carry out this program.

Most of the House and Senate leaders joined in commending the program, but two of the foremost figures in the recent revolt against the Reorganization Bill, Senator Byrd and Chairman O'Connor of the House Rules Committee, were outspoken in their opposition.

Byrd Warns of New Deficit

Senator Byrd termed the program in effect useless and wasteful, and argued that it would create a total deficit of $5,000,000,000, the greatest in peace-time history, in the fiscal year 1939.

Representative O'Connor observed that "priming the pump won't do any good if there's no water in the well."

Against this opposition, Senator Barkley and Representative Rayburn, majority leaders of their respective Congressional bodies, gave support to the bill, with public backing, among others, by Senator Byrnes and Pittman and Representatives Woodrum and Boland.

Vice President Garner refrained from comment.

The Republicans gave more support to the bill than might ordinarily be expected, although it was generally qualified. Senator Borah, for instance, endorsed the relief part of the program, but opposed "pump-priming" expenditures.

Comment of Individuals

Comment by Senate and House members was as follows:

SENATE

Republicans

VANDENBERG (Mich.)—I applaud the President's recognition of the new depression and his purpose finally to attack it. But, when I take his advice "to avoid the pitfalls of the past," I must reject his renewal of a profligate spending program with its deficits and debt because that is the route, in part, which has brought us where we unhappily are.

NYE (N. D.)—It involves alone the question whether we can hope to accomplish recovery by repeating the effort of the last five years. I am at a loss to see what other program can be pursued. In the absence of any other program I cannot see how we can escape complying in large measure with the request the President has made.

BORAH (Idaho)—I shall vote for any reasonable amount to take care of the unemployed and those who through no fault of their own cannot find work. Beyond that, I will have to be convinced and I don't see much chance of being convinced.

McNARY (Ore.)—The measure proposes a complicated plan for spending additional Federal funds to lift the country out of the depression. It has been tried before without success. I approach the plans with fear.

Democrats

BARKLEY (Ky.)—I think that it is a very reasonable and constructive program. A big part of it is to retain the program that is now in effect. The only thing really new is the $1,500,000,000 for the Public Works Program.

BYRD (Va.)—I'm unalterably opposed to any further pump-priming. It is not correct that the Federal Government is spending less this fiscal year; it is spending more this fiscal year than the previous fiscal year, as the

Continued on Page Thirteen

Text of Roosevelt 'Chat'

Special to THE NEW YORK TIMES.

WASHINGTON, April 14.—The text of President Roosevelt's "fireside chat" by radio tonight on problems of recovery and relief was as follows:

Five months have gone by since I last spoke to the people of the nation about the state of the nation.

I had hoped to be able to defer this talk until next week because, as we all know, this is Holy Week. But what I want to say to you, the people of the country, is of such immediate need and relates so closely to the lives of human beings and the prevention of human suffering that I have felt that there should be no delay.

In this decision I have been strengthened by the thought that by speaking tonight there may be greater peace of mind and the hope of Easter may be real at firesides everywhere, and that it is not inappropriate to encourage peace when so many of us are thinking of the Prince of Peace.

Five years ago we faced a very serious problem of economic and social recovery. For four and a half years that recovery proceeded apace. It is only in the past seven months that it has received a visible setback.

And it is only within the past two months, as we have waited patiently to see whether the forces of business itself would counteract it, that it has become apparent that government itself can no longer safely fail to take aggressive government steps to meet it.

This recession has not returned us to the disasters and suffering of the beginning of 1933. Your money in the bank is safe; farmers are no longer in deep distress and have greater purchasing power; dangers of security speculation have been minimized; national income is almost 50 per cent higher than in 1932, and government has an established and accepted responsibility for relief.

But I know that many of you have lost your jobs or have seen your friends or members of your families lose their jobs, and I do not propose that the government shall pretend not to see these things.

I know that the effect of our present difficulties has been uneven; that they have affected some groups and some localities seriously, but that they have been scarcely felt in others. But I conceive the first duty of government is to protect the economic welfare of all the people in all sections and in all groups.

I said in my message opening the last session of Congress that if private enterprise did not provide jobs this Spring, government would take up the slack—that I would not let the people down. We have all

Continued on Page Fourteen

FEDERAL RESERVE REVERSES POLICY

Roosevelt Move to Ease Loans by Raising Excess Reserves Drops Two-Year Drive

Special to THE NEW YORK TIMES.

WASHINGTON, April 14.—The statement by President Roosevelt that the Federal Reserve Board had agreed to liberalize reserve requirements of the members banks so as to add an additional $750,000,000 to the excess reserves which on April 13 were already about $1,723,000,000 was interpreted to mean that the board would in effect restore the reserve requirements which were applicable before May 1, 1937.

The action then, which raised reserve requirements by one-seventh and completed the program of doubling the requirements begun on Aug. 15, 1936, was intended to decrease the excess reserves by about the figure of $750,000,000 mentioned by President Roosevelt. The actual effect was to cut them by $700,000,000, leaving the total as of May 1 at about $890,000,000.

Just prior to May 1 the Reserve requirements by percentages on classes of deposits were as follows:

Net demand deposits—central Reserve city banks, 23¾; Reserve city banks, 17½; country banks, 12¼. Time deposits, all member banks, 5¼. The increase made May 1 raised these rates to the following, which now are in effect, 26, 20, 14 and 6.

Details Wait Discussion

If the Federal Reserve Board, as expected, restores the rates effective just prior to May 1 and adds about $750,000,000 to the excess reserves this would be added to the $1,703,000,000 as of April 14 for a total of $2,473,000,000.

The latter agreement would further be increased as the $1,392,000,000 of inactive gold was made the base for expenditures and if all the desterilized gold was used the aggregate of the excess reserves would go to $3,873,000,000, a high record. On Dec. 11, 1935, the earlier high mark, excess reserves were $3,304,000,000 and on Aug. 11, 1936, just before the Federal Reserve made its initial raise in reserve requirements, the excess reserves were $3,167,000,000.

At the offices of the Federal Reserve Board it was stated today that formal action had not yet been taken by the board and that exact details of what was to be done would await discussion by the board. But the intimation was that the status as to reserve requirements which existed just prior to May 1 would be restored.

Whatever may be the exact policy adopted, the step will mark a direct reversal of Reserve Board policy which was initiated on Aug. 15, 1936, when excess reserves were approximately $3,000,000,000. Then the board increased the reserve requirements by 50 per cent, stating that this action eliminated "as a

Continued on Page Twelve

$1,392,065,461 GOLD FREED FOR SPENDING

Treasury Shifts to Reserve Banks 'Sterilized' Fund Used as Money Stabilizer

Special to THE NEW YORK TIMES.

WASHINGTON, April 14.—The $1,392,065,461 of gold which has accumulated in the Treasury's inactive gold fund since it was decided in December, 1936, to "sterilize" the incoming deluge of gold from abroad to keep it from inflating the credit structure of the nation was converted into spendable form this afternoon in accordance with President Roosevelt's recovery program.

The announcement of "desterilization" came after the closing of the market in New York. Secretary Morgenthau made the announcement after conferring with members of the Board of Governors of the Federal Reserve System on the mechanics of carrying out the President's proposals.

The effect of the desterilization will be to transfer the fund to the nation's credit structure.

Fund Long Criticized

Attacked on many sides as an extravagance because of the necessity of borrowing to pay for the gold, thus swelling the national debt, the Treasury officials have stated repeatedly that the fund formed a cushion against inflation of the credit structure, on the one hand, and against deflation in the event that a sudden outward movement of gold should threaten to drain the nation's gold reserves. They defended it as a guard against heavy inward or outward movements of gold.

Other steps announced by the Treasury included a decision not to "call" $60,000,000 from special depositories, which had been planned as a means of meeting extraordinary expenses; continuance for the present, at least, of issuance of weekly bills in an amount corresponding to maturing bill issues; and calling of a meeting Wednesday of Secretary Morgenthau with the executive committee of the Federal Reserve Board's Open Market Committee to discuss future financing.

Sterilization Policy Retained

The absence of any statement from the Treasury regarding abandonment of the present sterilization program left the impression, verified by officials, that the present action involves nothing more than use of the present amount of inactive gold for spending purposes.

Thus, the present policy of sterilizing all gold imported in a quarter over the amount of $100,000,000 will be continued unless announcement is made to the contrary. Prior to Jan. 1 all incoming gold was sterilized, but under a Treasury announcement of Feb. 14, made retroactive to Jan. 1, only gold over and above $100,000,000 entering the

Continued on Page Thirteen

WAR ON RECESSION

Spending Drive Linked to Huge Expansion of Bank Credit Base

80 BILLION INCOME GOAL

Crisis Demands Quick Action President Says in Message and in His Radio Chat

By TURNER CATLEDGE

Special to THE NEW YORK TIMES.

WASHINGTON, April 14.—President Roosevelt today struck boldly at the business recession with an emergency program of spending, lending and credit expansion calling for an early Federal outlay which may be $5,000,000,000, but contemplating the eventual addition of less than one-third of that amount to the national debt.

The plan was disclosed in a message to Congress at noon and explained to the country as a whole in a "fireside" chat by radio tonight. Emphasizing a reassuring note, the President called for unity of management, labor, government and the public in ending a condition which, he said, "if allowed to run undisturbed, will continue to threaten the security of our people and the stability of our economic life."

The specific proposals made to Congress entailed the disbursement of $3,012,000,000 within the next few months in appropriations for relief, public works, housing, flood control and other recovery efforts, and loans to States, cities and other public agencies for similar activities. Mr. Roosevelt expected that $950,000,000 of this would be returned eventually in repayments of loans.

To help finance the program and to expand banking credit, he recommended desterilization of the Treasury's nest egg of nearly $1,400,000,000 in idle gold. This proposal was put into effect by the Treasury Department a few hours after the message had been read to Congress, as plans also were begun to reduce the reserve requirements of member banks of the Federal Reserve System, another step recommended by the President as a means for bringing "psychological" recovery.

Later Relief Request Looms

In his request for new relief funds, the President recommended $1,250,000,000 for the first seven months of the new fiscal year, but observers were virtually unanimous in the estimate that it would have to be raised to an eventual $2,000,000,000.

Also added to the recovery weapons and calculated in making up the grand total of Federal funds to be made available if necessary to break the back of the recession was the $1,500,000,000 which the Reconstruction Finance Corporation is now empowered to lend to business under the terms of a bill signed by the President yesterday.

The program was strikingly reminiscent to many of the dark days of 1933, when Mr. Roosevelt first came into power and in rapid-fire fashion set in motion a series of governmental actions to halt the economic depression which started in 1929.

There was one hurdle to clear—Congress. That was easy in 1933; but not so certain today. The first reactions were favorable to the proposals, however, when they were disclosed in the noonday message. There was also in many minds the memory of the favorable fate of former spending bills in election years.

There was something about the demeanor on Capitol Hill, nevertheless, which led observers to predict trouble ahead. That may be represented in a vigorous attempt on the part of substantial blocs to go further with the "earmarking" of funds than the President was willing to go in the program as it was disclosed today. Chances for blocking it altogether were considered meager.

President Ready to Fight

The President intimated, however, particularly in his radio chat, that he was ready for whatever fight may be necessary to put his program through. "I must never give up," he said at one point, and again: "I believe we have been right in the course we have charted."

"I propose to sail ahead," he said. "I feel sure that your hopes and your help are with me. For, to

Continued on Page Twelve

Douglas Corrigan poses with his 9-year-old $900 airplane. When federal officials refused to grant him permission for a non-stop flight across the Atlantic, he took off from New York to California, but went the "wrong way" and landed in Dublin.

In March, eighteen of twenty-one defendants were sentenced to be shot in Stalin's third public treason trial in two years.

Corrigan receives the greetings of an official of the Baldonnel Airdrome, having made the transatlantic flight in 28 hours and 13 minutes.

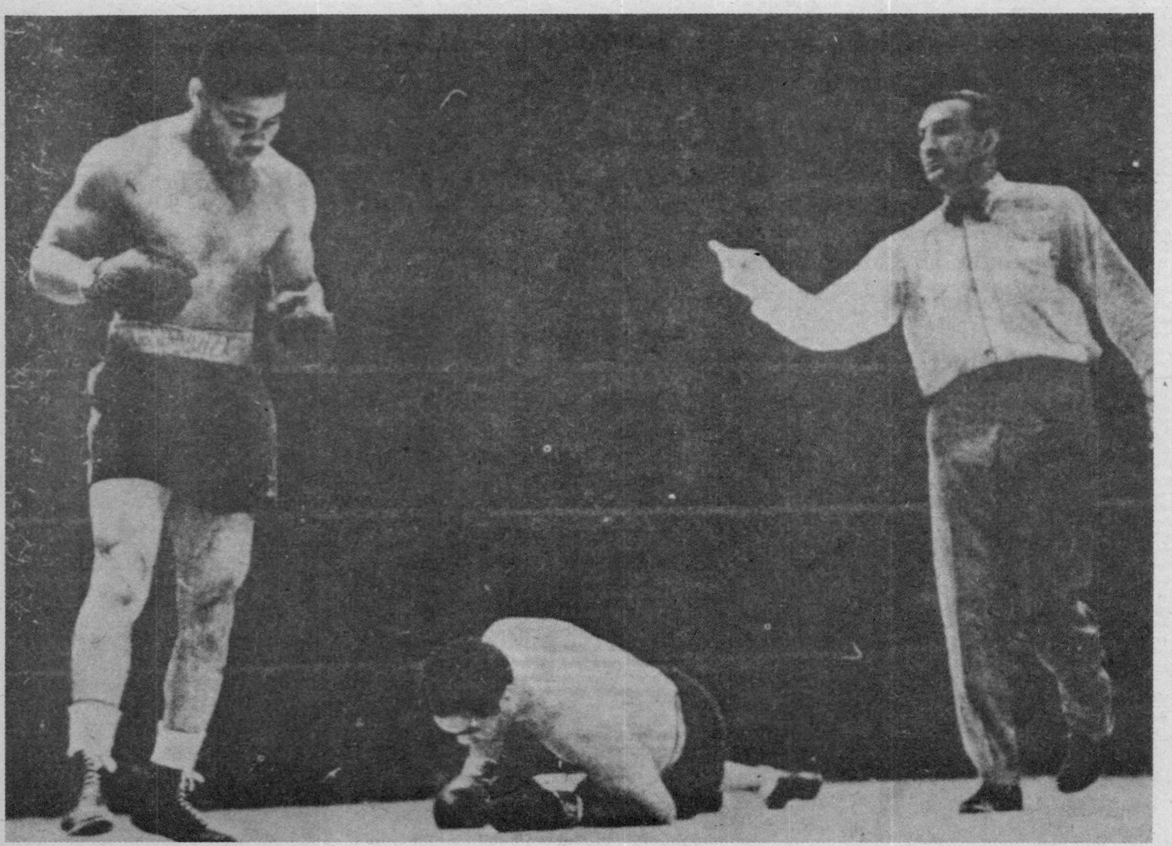

Joe Louis defeated Max Schmeling by a knockout in their famous rematch on June 22.

"All the News That's Fit to Print."

The New York Times.

LATE CITY EDITION
Partly cloudy, possibly scattered showers today and tomorrow; little change in temperature.
Temperatures Yesterday—Max., 80; Min., 66

Copyright, 1938, by The New York Times Company.

VOL. LXXXVII....No. 29,370. Entered as Second-Class Matter, Postoffice, New York, N. Y. NEW YORK, THURSDAY, JUNE 23, 1938. P THREE CENTS NEW YORK CITY and Vicinity | FOUR CENTS Elsewhere Except in 7th and 8th Postal Zones.

LOUIS DEFEATS SCHMELING BY A KNOCKOUT IN FIRST; 80,000 SEE TITLE BATTLE

FIGHT ENDS IN 2:04

Rights Drop the Loser Thrice and Trainer Tosses In Towel

1936 SETBACK AVENGED

Challenger Says He Was Fouled With a Kidney Punch —The Gate Tops $900,000

By JAMES P. DAWSON

The exploding fists of Joe Louis crushed Max Schmeling last night in the ring at the Yankee Stadium and kept sacred that time-worn legend of boxing that no former heavyweight champion has ever regained the title.

The Brown Bomber from Detroit, with the most furious early assault he has ever exhibited here, knocked out Schmeling in the first round of what was to have been a fifteen-round battle to retain the title he won last year from James J. Braddock. He has now defended it successfully four times.

In exactly 2 minutes and 4 seconds of fighting Louis polished off the Black Uhlan from the Rhine, but, though the battle was short, it was furious and savage while it lasted, packed with thrills that held three knockdowns of the ambitious ex-champion, every moment tense for a crowd of about 80,000.

A Representative Gathering

This gathering, truly representative and comparing favorably with the largest crowds in boxing's history, paid receipts estimated at between $900,000 and $1,000,000 to see whether Schmeling could repeat the knockout he administered to Louis just two years ago here and be the first ex-heavyweight champion to come back into the title, or whether the Bomber could avenge this defeat as he promised.

As far as the length of the battle was concerned, the investment in seats, which ran to $30 each, was a poor one. But for excitement, for drama, for pulse-throbs, those who came from near and far felt themselves well repaid because they saw a fight that, though it was one of the shortest heavyweight championships on record, was surpassed by few for thrills.

With the right hand that Schmeling held in contempt Louis knocked out his foe. Three times under its impact the German fighter hit the ring floor. The first time Schmeling regained his feet laboriously at the count of three. From the second knockdown Schmeling, dazed but game, bounced up instinctively before the count had gone beyond one.

On the third knockdown Schmeling's trainer and closest friend, Max Machon, hurled a towel into the ring, European fashion, admitting defeat for his man. The towel sailed through the air when the count on the prostrate Max had reached three.

Ignored in Boxing Here

The signal is ignored in American boxing, has been for years, and Referee Arthur Donovan, before he had a chance to pick up the count in unison with knockdown timekeeper Eddie Josephs, who was outside the ring, gathered the white emblem in a ball and hurled it through the ropes.

Returning to Schmeling's crumpled figure, Donovan took one look and signaled an end of the battle. The count at that time was five on the third knockdown. Further counting was useless. Donovan could have counted off a century and Max could not have regained his feet. The German was thoroughly "out."

It was as if he had been pole-axed. His brain was awhirl, his body, his head, his jaws ached and pained, his senses were numbed from that furious, paralyzing punching he had taken even in the short space of time the battle consumed.

Claims Blurred Vision

Following the bout, Schmeling claimed he was fouled. He said that he was hit a kidney punch, a devastating right, which so shocked his nervous system that he was dazed and his vision was blurred. To observers at the ringside, however, with all due respect to Schmeling's thoughts on the subject, the punches which dazed him were thundering blows to the head, jaw and body in bewildering succession, blows of the old Alabama Assassin reincarnate last night for a special occasion.

Louis wanted to erase the mem-

Continued on Page Fourteen

Bill Introduced in Cuba To Make July 4 a Holiday

Special Cable to THE NEW YORK TIMES.

HAVANA, June 22.—A bill declaring the coming Fourth of July a national holiday was introduced in the House of Representatives last night by Paul de Cardenas, Representative from Havana Province.

The bill is designed to suspend all commercial, industrial and governmental activities to permit attendance at a demonstration being organized for the Fourth of July as homage to the United States.

Plans for the demonstration, which will be held under the auspices of the cultural, social, economic and patriotic groups of the island, were launched last week.

The committee has asserted that homage is being paid to the United States "solely to cultivate and strengthen the sentiment of friendship and close relations that have always existed between the two peoples."

HAUGWITZ DISPUTE RISES OVER CHILD

Former Barbara Hutton Gets Police Guard for Son, 2, but Count Denies Kidnap Threat

Special Cable to THE NEW YORK TIMES.

LONDON, June 22. — Countess Haugwitz-Reventlow, the former Barbara Hutton, Woolworth heiress, broke into the news again today as London buzzed with rumors that her 2-year-old son Lance was under guard against kidnapping.

Late tonight Count Court Haugwitz-Reventlow, who is in Paris, acknowledged in a telephone talk with The Daily Mail that a sharp difference of opinion had arisen between him and the Countess over the future education of their son. According to The Daily Mail, the Danish nobleman also disclosed that the police were anxious to interrogate him should he land in Britain, but he strenuously denied any attempt or threat to kidnap his son.

The gates of Winfield House, the huge Haugwitz-Reventlow mansion, which stands in its own park within Regent's Park, were locked against all comers and policemen patrolled the grounds. Inquirers were referred to a statement issued by W. M. Mitchell, solicitor for the Countess.

Silent for "Legal Reasons"

"I am sure that the press will appreciate that for legal reasons it is impossible for the Countess to make any statement at the present time," he said. "If at a later stage she has anything to say, you may be sure that the press will be informed."

Mr. Mitchell made the statement at the gates of Winfield House, which was a center for reporters and photographers all day. Interest in the statement was heightened by a memorandum from Scotland Yard to the effect that the police had no information about any plot to kidnap the child, although the Countess acknowledged that she had "taken certain precautions."

Later, while Lance was being taken for an airing in the twelve-and-a-half-acre park, the Countess was driven rapidly with Sir Patrick

Continued on Page Ten

REPUBLICANS PLAN CONFERENCE RULE ON CONVENTION VOTE

Party Delegates Agree on a Program to Assure Unity on All Proposals

FIRST SESSION ON MONDAY

Leaders Indicate They Will Welcome Wiretapping as Campaign Issue

By W. A. WARN

Special to THE NEW YORK TIMES.

ALBANY, June 22.—Before the Constitutional Convention adjourned today for the week-end the Republicans took action to insure a firmer control over decisions reached in that body. There will be frequent conferences of all Republican delegates on important pending proposals.

The decision to assure cohesive party action and a united Republican front against the Democratic minority was reached after a discussion held last night at a private dinner given to Chief Judge Frederick F. Crane of the Court of Appeals, president of the convention, by the chairmen of standing committees. All Republican delegates had been invited and all but two or three attended. The conference plan, it was said today, was unanimously approved by all present.

The proposed creation of a steering committee, after having been discussed by Republican delegates for many days, has been definitely dropped.

The conferences, under the plan decided upon, will be held on call from State Senator Perley A. Pitcher, Republican floor leader in the convention. In the event that Senator Pitcher should fail to call a party conference on some important measure, a petition signed by ten of the ninety-two Republican members would compel him to issue the call.

Use of Caucus Barred

Mr. Pitcher stressed the distinction between conferences and caucus action. Where caucus action would bind all participants, conference action would leave a delegate free to vote according to his own convictions, even where that would be in conflict with a decision reached at a conference.

The practice resorted to sometimes at legislative conferences to turn them into a caucus at some critical stage was pronounced taboo by him.

The new plan will have its first application when the convention resumes next week. Senator Pitcher has already issued a call for the first conference, to be held at 4 P. M. Monday. The subject to be discussed is the Dunnigan search and seizure proposal, with its clause forbidding the use in court of evidence obtained through wiretapping or through search and seizure without a court warrant.

The party convention leaders oppose this clause and hope to bring enough persuasive arguments to bear to insure a solid front against the proposal.

Plan Used in the Senate

In establishing its conference plan and its taboo on the caucus, the party has virtually adopted a method which it has followed in the State Senate for fifteen years. It was recalled today that such conferences have demonstrated their effectiveness in keeping party members in line, even though on occasion a Senate leader has had at his command not more than twenty-six Senators, a bare majority.

The Dunnigan search and seizure proposal, and the one favorably re-

Continued on Page Six

Labor Board Gives C. I. O. Control Of All West Coast Longshoremen

A. F. L. Loses to Bridges Union in Sweeping Decision Setting Up Nation's First Major Geographical Bargaining Agency

By LOUIS STARK

Special to THE NEW YORK TIMES.

WASHINGTON, June 22.—The C. I. O. won a major victory over the A. F. of L. today when its affiliate the International Longshoremen's and Warehousemen's Union, District No. 1, was certified by the National Labor Relations Board as the exclusive bargaining agency for all longshoremen in thirty-one Pacific Coast ports.

The Pacific Coast longshoremen led by Harry Bridges, Australian-born radical leader against whom deportation proceedings have been started on a charge of membership in the Communist party, seceded from the A. F. of L.'s International Longshoremen's Union last year and set up the organization.

In certifying the Bridges union the NLRB made an unprecedented decision in establishing the first major geographical bargaining unit in the marine industry.

The board found that 9,557 of the 12,860 longshoremen on the Pacific Coast had designated the Bridges union as their representative for purposes of collective bargaining.

The decision will affect all longshoremen and warehousemen employed by the Ship Owners Association of the Pacific Coast, Waterfront Employers Association of the Pacific Coast, the Waterfront Employers of Seattle, the Waterfront Employers of Portland, the Waterfront Employers Association of San Francisco and the Waterfront Employers Association of Southern California.

In the course of the hearings, the A. F. of L. protested against the request by Mr. Bridges that his union be designated as the exclusive bargaining agency on the ground that the board had no power to designate a bargaining unit larger than employes of one company.

The board's jurisdiction was protested by the A. F. of L. and its affiliate, the International Longshoremen's Union, because the contract between the employer and the Pacific Coast longshoremen was still in the name of the A. F. of L. organization on behalf of the employes.

The companies also argued that the appropriate bargaining unit for longshoremen must be one restricted to those working for a particular employer at a particular port.

Overruling these objections, the board held that, under the Labor Relations Act, it expressly received authority to decide that the "employer" unit shall be that most appropriate unit for purposes of collective bargaining. The act includes within the term employer "any person acting in the interest of an employer, directly or indirectly," and the term person "includes one or more associations."

The present contract between the employers' associations and the longshoremen is held by the A. F. of L. union, and the board ruled that it was not necessary for it to decide whether the contract now passes to the Bridges organization, because a majority of members had voted to leave the A. F. of L. and to join the C. I. O.

The board declared, however, that

Continued on Page Four

TURROU SPY STORY BARRED IN PRESS

Hardy Gets Writ Halting First Installment—Show-Cause Order Up Today

United States Attorney Lamar Hardy obtained yesterday a court order preventing The New York Post from publishing the revelations of Leon G. Turrou, special agent of the Department of Justice, chief investigator in the German espionage inquiry.

The action was taken about 4:30 P. M., but was not verified in New York City until shortly before 8 P. M. The news had been flashed from Washington about 6:30 P. M., however, which indicated that Mr. Hardy's unusual move had the approval of his chief, Attorney General Homer Cummings.

The effect of the order was to halt scheduled publication today of Mr. Turrou's first installment of a series of articles which were intended to run for about twenty-one days. The show cause order served upon J. David Stern, publisher of The Post, and Mr. Turrou, will be argued this morning before Judge Murray Hulbert at 10:30 A. M., in Room 506 of the Federal Court House in Foley Square.

Seeks to Wait on Inquiry

It was understood that Mr. Hardy's chief objection to the projected articles was that agents have not yet completed investigation of incidents listed in the advertisements and which later must be presented to the grand jury, whose proceedings are secret.

Several items listed for publication, it was learned, for a long time have been a source of grave concern to the War and Navy Departments. If proved true they would overshadow in importance any defense secret thus far known to have been obtained by the spy ring. Officials of the two services had nothing to do with Mr. Hardy's action, but early in the investigation they requested secrecy until the truth was established.

The aim of Mr. Hardy's proceeding is to obtain an injunction which would prevent publication of anything by Mr. Turrou concerning the case until the grand jury, which will be reconvened on Monday, has completed its work.

From Mr. Stern the proceeding drew a challenge to fight for the right to publish the series under sanction of constitutional principles.

"By endeavoring to enjoin this paper from printing the news," declared Mr. Stern, "the government is making an unprecedented attempt to erase the freedom of the press from the Constitution.

"The law places responsibility upon the publisher for news which does any injury. The Constitution protects against the restraint in anticipation of such injury because the exercise of such anticipatory

Continued on Page Two

PRESIDENT NAMES 9 FOR BRITISH SURVEY

He Also Includes Sweden in Investigation of Employer-Employe Conditions

By FELIX BELAIR Jr.

Special to THE NEW YORK TIMES.

HYDE PARK, N. Y., June 22.—President Roosevelt today completed the selection of a study group of nine members representing business, industry, labor, the general public and the law to investigate industrial-labor conditions in Great Britain, and added employer-employe relationships in Sweden to the group's field of inquiry.

The reason for including Sweden in the agenda of the investigation was not explained in the announcement of the personnel of the study group, and suggestions that the President might have in mind a legislative redefinition of labor's responsibility to the public and to management in this country were met with a flat denial by Presidential aides.

Mr. Roosevelt has not the slightest intention of attempting to duplicate in this country the well-defined methods of adjusting industrial disputes practiced in either Great Britain or Sweden, nor does he contemplate a combination of the methods of the two as a means of lessening interruptions to business and industrial operations here, it was explained.

Personnel of the Group

To conduct the inquiry, the President named the following group, for which no chairman was chosen, with each member having an equal voice in the preparation of a final report to the Secretary of Labor:

Lloyd K. Garrison, dean of the University of Wisconsin Law School and former head of the Labor Relations Board.

Robert Watt, representing the American Federation of Labor.

Gerard Swope, president of the General Electric Company.

Henry I. Harriman, former president of the Chamber of Commerce of the United States.

William H. Davis, New York attorney and former NRA deputy administrator.

Mrs. Anna M. Rosenberg, regional director of Social Security for New York.

Charles R. Hook, president of the American Rolling Mills Company.

Marion Dickerman, principal of the Todhunter School for Girls, New York City.

William Ellison Chalmers, assistant United States Labor Commissioner at Geneva, who is to act as general secretary and liaison officer of the group.

Conspicuously absent from the personnel list was a representative for the Committee for Industrial Organization. John L. Lewis, its head, had refused to designate such a representative on invitation of Secretary Perkins. He had agreed to do so but withdrew his agreement when it was hinted several weeks ago that one of the purposes of the inquiry was to pave the way

Continued on Page Three

CUT IN STEEL WAGE BROACHED TO LEWIS AS RECOVERY SPUR

U. S. Corporation Opens Talks on Plan to Make Jobs and Aid Trade by Reducing Pay

PRICE DROP IS EXPECTED

C. I. O. Likely to Face Choice Between Granting Request and Losing Contract

Tentative discussions have been held recently between officials of the United States Steel Corporation and of the Steel Workers Organizing Committee, C. I. O. affiliate, on the possibility of a readjustment of wages that would promote increased production and employment in the steel industry.

These discussions, which thus far have been informal and exploratory, involve the complicated relationships of prices, labor costs and operating volume. Officials of the United States Steel Corporation declined yesterday to comment on the situation beyond saying that conferences had been held at frequent intervals, usually in Pittsburgh, ever since a contract was signed with the C. I. O. affiliate early last year.

John L. Lewis, head of the Committee for Industrial Organization, who personally negotiated the union's contract with Myron C. Taylor, former chairman of the Steel Corporation, declined to comment on the reports that a wage reduction was being discussed.

Corporation Losing Money

United States Steel is operating at about 28 per cent of capacity and is losing money rapidly. Although it has officially maintained its published scale of prices unchanged, price-slashing is rampant in the steel industry and Big Steel is reported in financial circles to be giving serious consideration to the advisability of reducing its published price schedules.

According to the belief in well-informed Wall Street quarters, the corporation has suggested or is about to put up to Mr. Lewis and other C. I. O. officials the proposal that the organized workers and the company should agree to take a cut —one in basic wage rates, the other in prices—in the expectation that this adjustment would lead to larger orders, increased production and employment and a gain in total income for both the workers and the corporation.

The alternative, according to steel experts in the financial district, is likely to be a further diminution of the corporation's business and a further reduction in the amount of employment it can provide.

Should the Steel Workers Organizing Committee agree to a reduction in the basic wage rates, it is probable that some understanding would be reached simultaneously providing that the original wage rates would be restored after a substantial recovery in the corporation's business.

Lewis Faces Dilemma

It is recognized in financial circles that Mr. Lewis and other C. I. O. officials would find it peculiarly difficult to agree to a wage reduction. Organized labor in general has taken the stand that reduction of wages cannot contribute to prosperity.

Philip Murray, chairman of the S. W. O. C., in a speech delivered in Cleveland on Feb. 20, described how the committee in renewing its contract with United States Steel had turned back an effort to link wage rates with operating rates, and he declared that, as a result of the contract, the committee had

Continued on Page Four

LABOR PARTY THREATENS 3-CORNERED STATE RACE UNLESS TERMS ARE MET

Yield of Cigarette Tax Likely to Be $9,000,000

New York City's one-cent tax on each package of cigarettes appeared likely to bring in $9,000,000 a year, three times the estimate of the original yield, when collection figures made public yesterday showed that $1,525.305 had been collected since the tax went into effect on May 1.

City Treasurer Almerindo Portfolio said the city had collected $1,369,224 on the sale of penny stamps, $23,745 on the sale of three-cent stamps, $132,200 from the certification of stamping machines and $135 from various penalties.

The City Council will vote on continuance of this tax, along with others in Mayor La Guardia's program, at its meeting in City Hall tomorrow.

LEHMAN DECLINES TO NAME SENATOR

Says He Will Act on Copeland Vacancy Only If Extra Session Is Called

Special to THE NEW YORK TIMES.

ALBANY, June 22.—Governor Lehman will not appoint a United States Senator to succeed Royal S. Copeland, who died last week, unless President Roosevelt should call a special session of Congress before the vacancy can be filled by election.

The Governor, who yesterday announced his willingness to accept the Democratic nomination for the "short" term of two years which remains of Senator Copeland's six-year term, made this announcement soon after his return to his desk early this evening.

In response to questions by the news correspondents Governor Lehman said he had received a number of messages approving his decision and wishing him well in his venture as a Senate candidate. He said also that he had received no word from President Roosevelt, nor had he an appointment to see the President in the near future.

Mr. Lehman, who, in his capacity as Lieutenant Governor while Mr. Roosevelt was Governor, was looked upon as Mr. Roosevelt's right hand man in the State administration, broke with the President over the latter's proposal to enlarge the Supreme Court.

Denies Talk With Roosevelt

The Governor in reply to questions said he had not discussed with President Roosevelt his proposal to become a Senate candidate. He disclosed his intention to Postmaster General Farley who is State as well as National Democratic chairman, and some other party leaders whom he failed to name.

"What did Mr. Farley say when you told him?" the Governor was asked.

"I am not going to say anything about that; in fact, I have nothing to add to the statement I made yesterday."

"Was former Governor Smith one of the party leaders you told that you were going to run for the Senate?" he was asked.

"No comment," was his reply. Then he added: "I am not going to say with whom I did discuss my plans."

Asked if he had discussed the matter with leaders of the Amer-

Continued on Page Six

ASKS TWO OFFICES

Would Pick Senator and Lieutenant Governor in Coalition

REPUBLICAN TIE POSSIBLE

Copeland Post for Hillman Is Proposed by Critics of the Democratic Slate

By JOHN L. UNDERHILL

Unless the American Labor party is permitted to name its candidates for the rest of the term of the late Royal S. Copeland in the United States Senate and for Lieutenant Governor in coalition with one of the two major parties, the Labor party will go it alone and name its own slate this Fall.

This was decided yesterday, it was learned, by the board of strategy of the Labor party, meeting to consider the political developments brought about by the announced candidacies of Governor Herbert H. Lehman for the Senate and Attorney General John J. Bennett Jr. for the Governorship.

The Labor party leaders, it was said, are far from satisfied with the tentative Democratic slate of Senator Robert F. Wagner and Governor Lehman for the Senate and Mr. Bennett for Governor. It was indicated that the Labor party leaders feel that Sidney Hillman, president of the Amalgamated Clothing Workers of America, is eminently fitted for the short-term Senate nomination.

Republicans Are Interested

There is a possibility, it was indicated, that if the Democrats fail to come to terms with the Labor party the Republican will. Republican leaders, it was learned, have been in close touch with Labor party heads within the last few days. As yet, however, there has been no formal conference.

Should the Labor party fail to win either major party to a coalition ticket it can support—and the party insists that the whole ticket must be acceptable, even if it wins its two places — consideration will be given to the naming of a separate slate. In any event the party leaders insist that party independence must be maintained on a stronger basis than ever.

Just where Mayor La Guardia, who is dissatisfied with the Lehman candidacy, stands in the Labor party situation was not clear. He did not take part in yesterday's conference of the Labor party leaders and they have, it was learned, heard nothing directly as to his plans. Whether they would be willing to name him as their candidate for the Senate to run against the major party nominee, leaders were not prepared to say. In any event, he is not considered to be in the inner circles of the party.

In connection with the revelation of the Labor party stand, it was recalled that Alex Rose, executive secretary of the Labor party and its official spokesman, announced earlier in the week that the party would insist on representation before a coalition could be effected. The party choices for Lieutenant Governor, it was learned, are Langdon W. Post, former Tenement House Commissioner, and Frederick F. Umhey, executive secretary of the International Ladies Garment Workers Union.

Mayor Defers Comment

Mayor La Guardia, obviously displeased with the tentative Democratic slate, commented cryptically at City Hall that he would have something to say soon.

"The essential need is for persons who will support good, sound, progressive policies in Washington, Albany and New York," the Mayor said. "I will have something to say on the subject within a few days."

David Dubinsky, president of the International Ladies Garment Workers Union, who had been mentioned as a possible Senate choice, withdrew his name from consideration.

"I am not a candidate for any political office," he said. "I do not believe that the American Labor party will or should make blanket commitments for the support of a slate of candidates of any other political party, Democratic or Republican. The American Labor party is in sympathy with the New Deal and is ready to support outspoken New Dealers, but this is as

Continued on Page Six

Walker Calls on La Guardia at City Hall; Dapper Ex-Mayor Says Visit Is for Clients

Debonair and dapper as ever, former Mayor James J. Walker visited Mayor La Guardia at City Hall yesterday. He said his call was in the interest of several clients who have business dealings with the city.

Tanned and looking healthier than he has in years, Mr. Walker emerged from the Mayor's office after a half-hour chat. Cornered by the City Hall reporters, many of whom he knew, he was asked the nature of his call.

"I could tell you," he smiled, "but why should I? It wasn't anything much—just that I wanted to see the Mayor in the interest of a few clients of mine. Amicus curiae, you might call it—a friend of the court."

The former Mayor hotly denied a hint that he was late for his 2:45 appointment. He swore that he had been in City Hall at 2:40, and had spent the time chatting with Stanley Howe, the Mayor's secretary, until 3 o'clock when Mayor La Guardia was ready to see him. He wore a dark blue suit, a white shirt with a blue tie, Panama hat with the brim turned down, and cornflowers in his buttonhole.

Because there was a hearing going on upstairs on a proposed tax on bookmakers, Mr. Walker was asked if he had any clients who were bookmakers.

"Unfortunately, no," he said with the same eye-crinkling smile. "Taxation," he went on with mock seriousness in his tone, "is a very, very comprehensive subject."

A photographer broke in to ask him to pose "coming through the gate" and shaking hands with Patrolman Charles Stoffers, a veteran police aide in the building.

"Uh-uh," he demurred. "I don't like that coming-through-the-gate business. That picture has been made too many times."

Nevertheless he assumed the pose to satisfy the photographer. Asked if he had discussed a possible successor to the late Senator Copeland with the Mayor, Mr. Walker said:

"Politics? Now what would I know about politics?"

Relief Pickets Ride to WPA Office in Autos; Somervell Wonders How They Can Afford It

Lieut. Col. Brehon B. Somervell, local Works Progress Administrator, has watched scores of picketing demonstrations without comment, but when he saw relief workers driving up to his office in automobiles yesterday to picket against wage cuts he decided it was time to do a little protesting on his own account.

"This is the first time I ever saw relief people come up here with automobiles loaded with banners to protest a wage cut," Colonel Somervell told reporters. "If there is anything that would justify a wage cut, it is that."

It all started when the administrator, returning to the WPA building at 70 Columbus Avenue late in the afternoon, found the WPA Teachers Union, Local 453, an A. F. of L. affiliate, organizing a picket line on the block between Sixty-second and Sixty-third Streets.

As he watched, two cars full of signs and pickets appeared. Asked later whether they were WPA cars, Colonel Somervell replied laughingly that he hoped they were not.

The demonstration brought out 610 persons, but most arrived under their own power, according to the police. Most of them were from WPA educational projects, but a sizable delegation represented the five Federal arts projects, which are outside Colonel Somervell's jurisdiction.

Signs carried by the marchers denounced the wage reductions, which range from $4.70 to $14.95 a month. "Up With Recovery—Down With Wage Cuts," one placard said. More than 26,000 clerical and professional workers are included in the groups affected by the cuts.

Deputy Inspector John Challan and thirty patrolmen watched the picket line for two hours. At one point a bag of water came hurtling from an upper window of the WPA building. There was no other incident.

The New York World's Fair 1939 monoplane of Howard Hughes landing at Floyd Bennett Field after its trip of 3 days 19 hours and 17 minutes in which it covered 14,824 miles.

Times Wide World Photo

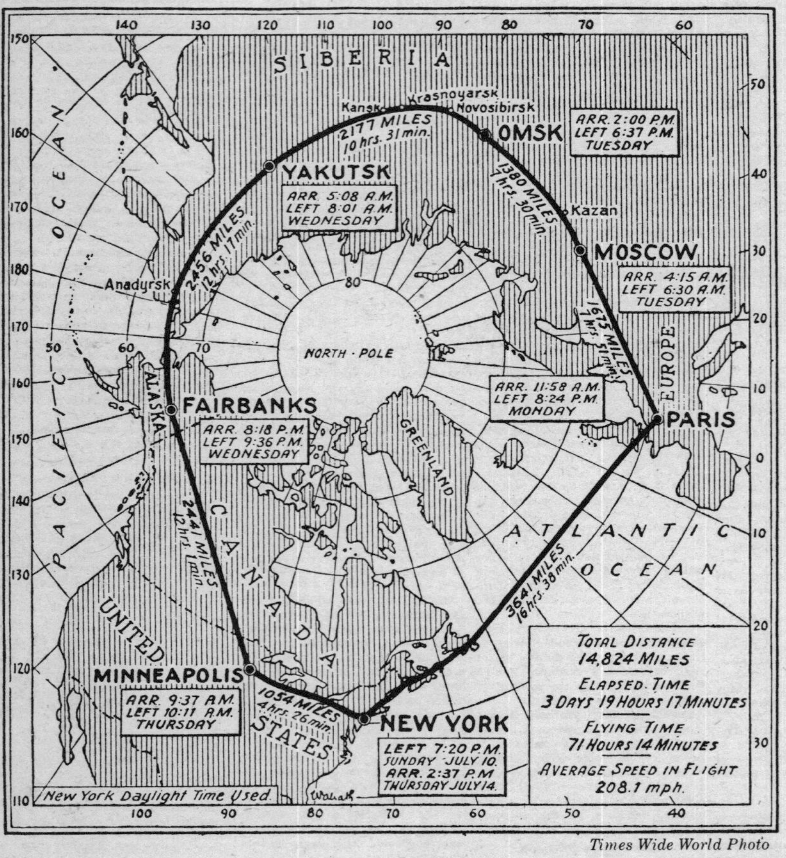

Times Wide World Photo

After circling the top of the globe over three continents in less than four days, Howard Hughes landed at his starting point, halving the previous record for the flight. The black line shows his course.

World Flights Compared

Following are the comparative logs of Howard Hughes and Wiley Post:

Eastern Daylight Time

HOWARD R. HUGHES

Sunday, July 10, 1938

7:20 P. M.—Took off from Floyd Bennett Field.

Monday, July 11

11:58 A. M.—Landed Le Bourget Aerodrome, Paris; 3,641 miles, 16 hours 38 minutes.

8:24 P. M.—Left for Moscow.

Tuesday, July 12

4:15 A. M.—Landed at Moscow; 1,675 miles, 7 hours 51 minutes.

6:30 A. M.—Left Moscow for Omsk, Siberia.

2:00 P. M.—Landed at Omsk; 1,380 miles, 7 hours 30 minutes.

6:37 P. M.—Left Omsk for Yakutsk, Siberia.

Wednesday, July 13

5:08 A. M.—Landed at Yakutsk; 2,177 miles, 10 hours 31 minutes.

8:01 A. M.—Left Yakutsk for Fairbanks, Alaska.

8:18 P. M.—Landed at Fairbanks; 2,456 miles, 12 hours 17 minutes.

9:36 P. M.—Left Fairbanks for Minneapolis, Minn.

Thursday, July 14

9:37 A. M.—Landed at Minneapolis; 2,441 miles, 12 hours 1 minute.

10:11 A. M.—Left for New York.

2:37 P. M.—Landed at Floyd Bennett Field; 1,054 miles, 4 hours 26 minutes.

Total distance flown—14,824 miles.

Total elapsed time—3 days 19 hours 17 minutes (91 hours 17 minutes).

Total flying time—71 hours 14 minutes.

Total time on the ground—20 hours 3 minutes.

Average speed in flight—208.1 miles per hour.

WILEY POST

Saturday, July 15, 1933

5:10 A. M.—Took off from Floyd Bennett Field.

Sunday, July 16

6:55 A. M.—Landed Tempelhof Aerodrome, Berlin; 3,942 miles, 25 hours 45 minutes.

9:10 A. M.—Left Berlin.

1:40 P. M.—Forced down at Koenigsberg, Germany; 340 miles, 4 hours 30 minutes.

Monday, July 17

1:45 A. M.—Left Koenigsberg.

7:20 A. M.—Landed at Moscow; 650 miles, 5 hours 15 minutes.

10:12 A. M.—Left Moscow.

11:27 P. M.—Landed Novo Sibirsk, Siberia; 1,579 miles, 13 hours 15 minutes.

Tuesday, July 18

2:02 A. M.—Left Novo Sibirsk.

8:35 A. M.—Landed at Irkutsk, Siberia; 1,055 miles, 6 hours 33 minutes.

12:00 Midnight—Left Irkutsk.

Wednesday, July 19

7:32 A. M.—Landed at Rukhlovo, Siberia; 750 miles, 7 hours 32 minutes.

4:25 P. M.—Left Rukhlovo.

8:45 P. M.—Landed at Khabarovsk, Siberia; 650 miles, 4 hours 20 minutes.

10:58 P. M.—Left Khabarovsk.

Thursday, July 20

9:30 P. M.—Landed at Flat, Alaska; 2,800 miles; 22 hours 32 minutes.

Friday, July 21

1:28 P. M.—Left Flat.

4:42 P. M.—Landed at Fairbanks, Alaska; 375 miles, 3 hours 14 minutes.

11:45 P. M.—Left Fairbanks.

Saturday, July 22

9:07 A. M.—Landed at Edmonton, Alberta; 1,450 miles, 9 hours 22 minutes.

10:41 A. M.—Left Edmonton.

11:59½ P. M.—Landed Floyd Bennett Field; 2,004 miles, 13 hours 18½ minutes.

Total distance flown—15,596 miles.

Total elapsed time—7 days 18 hours 49½ minutes (186 hours, 49½ minutes).

Total flying time—115 hours 36½ minutes.

Total time on the ground—71 hours 13 minutes.

Average speed in flight—127.43 miles per hour.

Times Wide World Photo

The scene at the airport as Hughes' plane (surrounded by police) landed on the concrete apron in front of the Administration building at Floyd Bennett Field.

"All the News That's Fit to Print."

The New York Times.

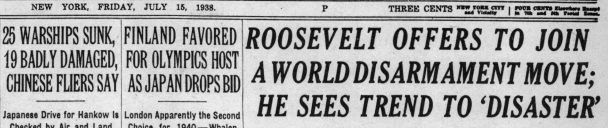

LATE CITY EDITION
Generally fair, moderate temperature today; somewhat cooler tonight. Tomorrow fair, warmer.
Temperatures Yesterday—Max., 80; Min., 71

VOL. LXXXVII....No. 29,392. Entered as Second-Class Matter, Postoffice, New York, N. Y. NEW YORK, FRIDAY, JULY 15, 1938. P THREE CENTS NEW YORK CITY and Vicinity | FOUR CENTS Elsewhere Except in 7th and 8th Postal Zones.

HUGHES ENDS WORLD FLIGHT, SETTING 3-DAY, 19-HOUR MARK; 20,000 CHEER ARRIVAL HERE

POST'S TIME HALVED

Huge Plane Lands at 2:37 P. M. After Hop From Minneapolis

BROADWAY PARADE TODAY

Fliers Will Be Taken to City Hall—La Guardia Greets Them at Floyd Bennett

By F. RAYMOND DANIELL

Five weary-eyed men with bearded faces and clothing that was soiled and wrinkled stepped from an airplane of unblemished sheen into a bedlam of noise and confusion at Floyd Bennett Field in Brooklyn yesterday afternoon, completing the fastest journey that man has yet made around this ever-contracting planet.

Mobbed and hemmed in by well-wishers, Howard Hughes and his four companions gaped and stammered, as inarticulate as men from Mars and as helpless as robots in the hands of the crowd and the police who propelled them from one spot to another to broadcast, be photographed, interviewed and welcomed and finally to escape to the privacy of hotels.

The historic flight of the five men around the world came to an official end when the big silver-winged New York World's Fair 1939 raced out of the murky western sky and shot like an arrow to earth at 2:37 P. M.

Hughes at the Controls

With Hughes, young millionaire sportsman and motion picture producer at the controls, it taxied up to the administration building and stopped almost on the spot from which it took off at 7:20 o'clock Sunday night. Only three days, 19 hours and 17 minutes had elapsed, yet the big plane had touched wheels at Le Bourget in Paris, heard the cheers of Soviet citizens in Moscow, rolled through Siberian mud at Omsk and Yakutsk and raced across Arctic wastes to touch American soil again in Alaska and at Minneapolis before competing its epochal flight.

The plane's average speed while in the air was 208.1 miles an hour.

After one riotous interview at the field and a more decorous one in the home of Grover A. Whalen, the four members of the crew of Hughes's plane fled to Hampshire House on Central Park South, where rooms were ready for them. There they found seclusion and rest.

Hughes, however, managed to escape without being followed. Some time later he arrived in a taxicab at the home of Katharine Hepburn, at 244 East Forty-ninth Street. Earlier in the day a woman who said she was the motion picture actress telephoned Floyd Bennett Field and left a telephone number to be given only to Hughes. When the aviator saw men with cameras around the steps of the Hepburn home, he motioned to his chauffeur to drive on and disappeared.

Later he went to the Drake Hotel, at Fifty-sixth Street and Park Avenue. He was carrying two sweaters under his arm. He nodded to an official and said, "I'm awfully tired—I can't wait to get to bed" and was taken to a room. Hotel officials said later that he had gone to bed and had left orders that he be not disturbed by any one.

Less Than Half Post's Time

Hughes, the careful planner and scientific aviator, with his carefully selected navigators, radio operator and mechanic, more than halved the time it took the late Wiley Post to circumnavigate the earth in the Winnie Mae a little less than five years ago.

Post, flying alone, took seven days, 18 hours and 49½ minutes to complete a slightly longer course at an average speed in the air of 127.43 miles per hour. With his assistants and his mechanical aids to flying, Hughes spent only 20 hours and 3 minutes on the ground, while Post, who damaged his landing gear at Flat, Alaska, was earthbound for 71 hours and 13 minutes.

For the precision and speed with which they carried out their flight, which Hughes said was as much to test new radio and flying apparatus as to advertise the World's Fair, the fliers received the official greeting of Mayor La Guardia and Mr. Whalen and were invited to participate in a parade up lower Broadway and a City Hall reception today at noon.

For the sheer thrill of seeing the

Continued on Page Two

Throng Breaks Down Barriers In Its Wild Acclaim to Airmen

Whalen's Elaborate Plans Fail as Frenzied Admirers Rush to Plane—Even Police Traffic Whistles Join in Din of Welcome

For a two-minute thrill more than 20,000 persons braved threatening skies and waited, crushed against wire fences, to watch Howard Hughes and his crew land at Floyd Bennett Field yesterday.

Although the crowd began to assemble shortly after 9 A. M. it did not assume appreciable proportions until nearly noon. Most of the best places of vantage were taken early by boys on bicycles or scooters. Then 1,000 policemen, with five captains and as many officers of higher rank, arrived to take charge.

The apron, or tarmac as it is known at an airport, was quickly cleared. Groups of workmen hastily set up barriers, captains held conferences with inspectors, lieutenants conferred with captains, sergeants finally got final orders from the lieutenants and snapped them to the men.

The crowd then assembled was moved outside the stout wire fence and all gates leading to the field were locked except one. Picked patrolmen were stationed at that gate.

Shortly before 1 o'clock, as the evicted boys were pressing their noses in the wire mesh of the fences, the earlier groups of celebrities began arriving. Leaders in aviation, members of official parties from the World's Fair of 1939, civic leaders and others made up the group. Some had tickets, some did not.

Among them were Major Gen. Oscar W. Westover, Chief of Air Corps, U. S. A.; Commander John H. Towers, assistant chief of the Bureau of Aeronautics, U. S. N.; Lieut. Comdr. R. P. Kaufman, commandant of the Aviation Unit, U. S. N. R., at Floyd Bennett Field; Kenneth Behr, assistant to Dock Commissioner John McKenzie, in charge of the airport; Inspector Edward M. Shelvey, in charge of the police detail, and the nine men who had spent the week in the radio shack at the fair site in Flushing Meadows, guiding the five record breakers home.

The nine were Glenn Oderkirk, Charles Perrine, W. C. Rockefeller, Albert I. Lodwick and their assist-

Continued on Page Three

HUGHES DESCRIBES TENSE TIMES IN HOP

Flight to Paris Was the Most Perilous, He Says—Barely Missed Siberian Crags

Relaxing in an easy chair that "felt good" to him after four days in a cramped cabin cockpit, Howard Hughes, after satisfying his desire for a shower and a clean shirt, said yesterday afternoon that he had been attended by "great luck" on his record-breaking world flight, but expressed doubt that he ever would attempt the feat again.

Idly fingering his four-day growth of beard, the wealthy young sportsman-pilot, speaking in tones that, through their flatness, betrayed his fatigue, discussed in careful detail the technical features of his flight.

He also found words of praise for the late Wiley Post, whose solo flight around the world Hughes bettered by almost half. Post's feat of flying around the world single-handed in 7 days 18 hours and 49½ minutes is still, to him, "the most impossible bit of flying ever accomplished," Hughes declared.

He Goes to Whalen's Home

Efforts to interview Hughes shortly after he landed at Floyd Bennett Field, Brooklyn, broke up in a bedlam of noise and confusion, with the aviator able to express almost no coherent answers over the general shouting. He discussed his flight and its significance in a more satisfactory manner after being taken to the home of Grover A. Whalen, president of the New York World's Fair, at 48 Washington Mews.

There he revealed that the most perilous part of his trip was the hop from New York to Paris, as he arrived there with "barely enough" fuel. There also were a few anxious moments flying over the Siberian wastes, as existing maps of that bleak section are inaccurate and Hughes had to make up his own maps as he went along.

On the hop to Paris, Hughes said, he made no "special endeavor" to break any speed records.

"I was mainly concerned with getting there, because there was too much early fuel consumption," he said.

"My plane was too small for the purpose because of the amount of gasoline which had to be carried. We had a wing load of forty-seven pounds to the square foot—the greatest wing load I ever have heard of, including the Schneider Cup races—and I took off with a 25,600-pound load, while the most I ever tested the plane at, with water ballast in California, was 24,000 pounds."

Forced to Increase Speed

Because of this great load, he had to travel 125 miles an hour in order to leave Bennett Field, and, once up, he was forced to increase the speed to 175 miles an hour "to keep from 'mushing,'" Hughes said. But the gasoline consumption was reduced from ninety gallons an hour to sixty-five as the trip wore on,

Continued on Page Three

ITALY NOW PLANS 'ARYAN' RACE POLICY

Group of Professors Advocates Measure That Would Preclude Intermarriage With Jews

By ARNALDO CORTESI
Wireless to THE NEW YORK TIMES.

ROME, July 14.—A vigorous racial policy aimed at preserving the "Aryan" and "purely European character of the Italians" from contamination by "any extra-European race" is being advocated by a group of anonymous Fascist scientists. Of these advocates nothing is known except that they are all teachers in Italian universities and have examined the "race problem" under the aegis of the Ministry of Popular Culture.

The official nature of their study of the racial problem and the great publicity the press gives to their findings leave small doubt that their conclusions are about to be adopted as a Fascist Government policy.

In their report the professors disclaim any intention of introducing into Italy German racial theories in their present form, but they make it abundantly clear that in Italy as in Germany Jews are considered an enemy against whom the purity of Italian stock needs defending.

Italians "Homogeneous"

They point out that no noteworthy immigrations of foreign peoples to Italy have taken place for about a thousand years, and therefore, they assert, the Italian population may be considered completely homogeneous except for the Jews, who are the "only population that has never been assimilated because it is made up of non-European racial elements, differing absolutely from the elements that have given origin to the Italians."

The report contains no indication that the professors have the Italian colonies in mind when they urge the necessity of defending Italian blood from any admixture of non-European blood. In the colonies, in fact, Italians are in contact with Negro races and the problem of keeping the Italian population pure is one of color more than of race.

The report contains no hint of what measures in the professors' opinion should be adopted to save the Italian people from pollution, but it is obvious that what is intended is a restriction of marriages between "Aryans" and Jews similar to that applied in Germany. Nor do the professors make any attempt to explain how it is that, although the presence of a tiny, unassimilated Jewish minority has not prevented the Italian people from attaining complete homogeneity, the need for defense measures should be felt only now.

How insignificant is the Jewish minority may be ascertained by a glance at the figures of the last census, April 21, 1931. Jews in Italy at that time totaled 47,825, or 1.2 per 1,000 population, as compared with 41,014,000 Catholics, or 996.1 per 1,000 population.

The Jewish population, moreover,

Continued on Page Six

25 WARSHIPS SUNK, 19 BADLY DAMAGED, CHINESE FLIERS SAY

Japanese Drive for Hankow Is Checked by Air and Land Forces, Defenders Claim

BATTLES RAGE ON YANGTZE

Invaders Reported to Have Failed in Their Efforts to Regain Shansi Province

By F. TILLMAN DURDIN
Wireless to THE NEW YORK TIMES.

HANKOW, China, Friday, July 15.—Twenty-five Japanese warships have been sunk and nineteen have been disabled in the past two weeks by Chinese bombing planes in raids along the Yangtze River, the military spokesman claimed yesterday.

The spokesman announced the total after asserting that yesterday's raids had resulted in the sinking of one large warship and three small ones below Kiukiang, 135 miles downriver from Hankow.

The Japanese have made little headway in their attack on Kiukiang. Chinese reports say Japanese warships in the Yangtze continue shelling Chinese positions east of the city and that land forces have not yet reached this port.

The United States gunboat Monocacy anchored yesterday a mile off the Standard Oil docks at Kiukiang and maintained close contact with the shore.

A dispatch to the Wuhan Daily News said that on Tuesday the Japanese sent troops across the mouth of Poyang Lake under cover of an artillery barrage. The invaders were said to have been met by a large Chinese force about ten miles east of Kiukiang, and after an all-night engagement the advance was halted. The Japanese were said to be surrounded and facing "sure annihilation."

Fire Across Lake's Outlet

The Japanese continue to shell Kutang from the east shore of Poyang Lake's outlet, according to official Chinese reports.

Heavy fighting is still going on between Hukow and Pengtseh on the Yangtze below Kiukiang. The Japanese hold only a narrow strip along the Yangtze in this sector.

Severe fighting also continues a few miles downriver at Hwangshan and Siangshan, held by Chinese who are repulsing Japanese assaults.

The Chinese military spokesman said yesterday that the Japanese strength in the Tsienshan sector, thirty miles west of Anking, had been increased to a full division. Further north the Japanese have withdrawn completely from Showhsien, Chengyangkwan and Fengtai.

The boom across the Yangtze at Matang was said to have been almost completely removed, permitting passage of the biggest Japanese warships.

The military spokesman said the new Japanese offensive in South Shansi had failed. He stressed that it had made little progress in ten days.

The Japanese attack on Yuanchu, Chinese headquarters in South Shansi, was said to have been repulsed. The Chinese were reported to have retaken part of Tsiyuan.

Air Force Victories Listed

HANKOW, China, July 14 (AP).—The Chinese high command announced tonight that during the past two weeks the Chinese air force had put out of commission one aircraft carrier, one light

Continued on Page Seven

FINLAND FAVORED FOR OLYMPICS HOST AS JAPAN DROPS BID

London Apparently the Second Choice for 1940—Whalen Seeks Games for New York

CABINET ACTS IN TOKYO

Public Bitterly Disappointed as Army's Hostility and War Cost Bar Meet

Helsingfors, the capital of Finland, moved into the picture yesterday as a likely site for the 1940 Olympic Games as a result of news from Tokyo that the Japanese Government had withdrawn its invitation for the games.

This move by Japan, which was reported in the final edition of THE NEW YORK TIMES yesterday, was formally approved by the Cabinet today.

While New York, through Grover Whalen, president of the New York World's Fair, Philadelphia and other American cities expressed willingness to conduct the games, Helsingfors will receive primary consideration, according to an Associated Press dispatch from London quoting Count Henri de Baillet-Latour, president of the International Olympic Committee.

Since Helsingfors bid against Tokyo for the 1940 games at the committee's meeting in Berlin prior to the 1936 Olympics and lost the nomination only by a 36 to 27 vote, the Finnish city, which has never held the Games, is deemed to have first call on them, should they have to be reassigned.

London Second Choice

London, which also put in a bid for the 1940 games but withdrew it before the balloting while serving notice of its desire to stage the 1944 meet, is regarded as second choice to Helsingfors, though not overeager to hold the 1940 competition.

The Winter games, which had been awarded to Sapporo, Japan, most likely will be transferred to Oslo, Norway, with Canada a remote possibility. All these matters, however, cannot be decided until official notice of Japan's withdrawal is received by the International Olympic Committee and its executive committee takes action.

At any rate, little chance is seen for so early a return of the Olympics to the United States, which played host at St. Louis in 1904 and again at Los Angeles in 1932.

However, on receipt of the news from Tokyo, Mr. Whalen yesterday issued the following statement:

"As president of the New York World's Fair 1939, I shall be very glad indeed to cooperate in any movement and do everything possible to bring the Olympics to New York in 1940.

"I expect to consult with officials of the American Olympic Committee, the A. A. U. and other organizations interested. We of the fair feel that it would be a great thing to have the Olympics in New York. We are sure that proper arrangements could be made. In the meantime, we extend every welcome."

Officials Voice Relief

The news of Japan's withdrawal evoked mingled sighs of relief, renewed affirmations of faith in the Olympic ideal and assurances that the United States would participate wherever the games are held from leading amateur athletic officials here.

It was generally agreed that if the Olympics had to be shifted, the

Continued on Page Five

WPA Orders $3,000,000 Women's Coats; Plan Will Ease Clothing Field, Says Hopkins

Special to THE NEW YORK TIMES.

WASHINGTON, July 14.—The Works Progress Administration announced today its purpose to buy $3,000,000 worth of women's Winter coats, for distribution in the Autumn.

Harry L. Hopkins, administrator, stated that the program was decided upon after conferences with David Dubinsky, representing the International Ladies Garment Workers Union.

This buying program will supplement orders already given for about $10,000,000 worth of men's Winter-weight suits and overcoats.

All of the clothing is to be bought directly from manufacturers and distributed through State relief organizations. Mr. Hopkins was not certain how much further this program of direct buying and distribution, which has brought numerous complaints from distributive industries, would be carried, but he said that the WPA had used about $13,000,000 of a total of $15,000,000 allocated to this purpose by order of President Roosevelt.

The clothing purchases supplement buying of food by the Federal Surplus Commodity Corporation, which is going forward at the rate of about $500,000 per day.

The coats will be purchased at an average price of about $5 or $6, it is expected, and will come entirely from stocks on hand. No new manufactured goods will be ordered.

"Won't this increase the price of coats of that quality which are sold to the public?" Mr. Hopkins was asked.

"It might," he said.

The WPA administrator argued, however, that the clothing purchase would make no difference to normal business generally as the clothes were to be distributed only to persons who could not possibly buy them. He said that the government had obtained men's clothing at generally low prices, possibly "in some cases too low."

All buying of this type, he said, was handled by experts from mail-order and department stores who were working for one dollar a year.

Mr. Hopkins said that the purchase program would about clear the congestion in the men's and women's cheaper-clothing field and supply work for "thousands of additional people."

ROOSEVELT OFFERS TO JOIN A WORLD DISARMAMENT MOVE; HE SEES TREND TO 'DISASTER'

45,000-Ton Battleship Designs Now Being Drafted by the Navy

Building of Huge Craft Waits on Completion Of Plans Next Year—Bids Are Asked On Four 35,000-Ton Vessels

By HANSON W. BALDWIN
Special to THE NEW YORK TIMES.

WASHINGTON, July 14.—The navy's plans to build 45,000-ton "super-ships" have not been abandoned, but only postponed.

Tentative designs for the battleships which would be the most powerful fighting ships the world has ever seen, are now being developed in the Navy Department and should be ready in about a year.

If the President decides to invoke the authorization given him by Congress to exceed the present 35,000-ton limitation, funds for the construction of two of the new battleships may be asked at the next session of Congress.

This is considered likely because it is understood here that the two new British battleships to be laid down this year, which will increase British capital ships under construction to a total of seven, will displace 40,000 tons.

Although the design of the proposed 45,000-ton ships is still under discussion, it is considered probable that the ideas of the "high-speed school" rather than those of the "greater-gun-power school" will prevail.

The ships may displace about 45,000 tons standard and may have a speed of 32 to 33 knots or more, from 4½ to 5½ knots faster than this country's 35,000-ton battleships now under construction.

They may mount the same number of guns—nine 16-inch rifles in three turrets—and have about the same or a slightly increased thickness of armor—a belt of sixteen inches, and conning tower and turret faces of eighteen inches.

One of the main reasons of the Navy Department for postponing actual work on the 45,000-ton vessels is that the plans will not be available for some time, whereas designs for 35,000-ton vessels, of the same basic type as the Washington and North Carolina, now building, are being carried out.

Consequently the four ships provided at the last session of Congress will be 35,000-ton vessels,

Continued on Page Six

WAITS STEP ABROAD

President, in San Francisco, Says Most of World Wants Peace

A TUMULTUOUS WELCOME

Street Throngs Cheer, Guns Boom, Whistles Shriek—Executive Reviews Fleet

The text of the President's speech is printed on Page 11.

By FELIX BELAIR Jr.
Special to THE NEW YORK TIMES.

SAN FRANCISCO, July 14.—Standing within sight of sixty-three gray-hulled men o' war at anchor in the bay today, President Roosevelt declared that 1939 would be a year of "world-wide rejoicing" if it saw "definite steps toward permanent world peace." He expressed the "fervent hope" that the costly and dangerous world armaments race would be halted and stated that the United States was ready to help in this direction.

"We fervently hope for the day when the other leading nations of the world will realize that their present course must inevitably lead them to disaster," the President said. "We stand ready to meet them and encourage them in any efforts they make toward a definite reduction in world armament."

The President spoke at a luncheon held in the Administration Building of the San Francisco International Exposition on Treasure Island before boarding the cruiser Houston to review the fleet in the bay.

Calls Navy a "Potent Fact"

On orders from President Roosevelt navy authorities revised their original welcoming plans, which included a twenty-one-gun salute from each of the vessels he passed on the review, and the formal recognition was carried out only by the flagship Houston as the President went aboard.

The President's visit was met with marked enthusiasm as many thousands of people, let off from work for a holiday proclaimed officially by Mayor Angelo J. Rossi, lined every street through which the Presidential party was routed. Estimates of the sidewalk crowd ranged fom 250,000 to 500,000.

"The year 1939," Mr. Roosevelt said in his luncheon address, "would go down in history not only as the year of the two great American world's fairs, but would be a year of world-wide rejoicing if it could also mark definite steps toward permanent world peace. That is the hope and the prayer of the overwhelming number of men and women and children in all the earth today."

After mentioning the two world's fairs of New York and San Francisco, Mr. Roosevelt spoke of the fleet which had been resting at anchor off Treasure Island, where the exposition buildings are gradually taking form. He called it "not merely a symbol," but "a potent ever-ready fact in the national defense of the United States."

A Condition Not of Our Choosing

"Every right-thinking man and woman in the United States," he added, "wishes that it were safe for the nation to spend less of our national budget on our armed forces. All know that we are faced with a condition, not a theory—and that the condition is not of our choosing.

"Money spent on armaments does not create permanent income producing wealth, and about the only satisfaction we can take out of the present world situation is that the proportion of our national income that we spend on armaments is only a quarter or a third of the proportion that most of the other great nations of the world are spending at this time."

Although Mr. Roosevelt has contemplated the necessity of some move toward halting the continual piling up of world armaments, his observations today were interpreted by some observers as meaning that this country would expect one or more other world powers to take the initiative independently of the United States.

The President cited the two American international expositions as evidence of confidence by Americans that the United States "and all the Western Hemisphere" would be at peace in 1939.

"It is our hope and our expectation," he said, "that that confidence

Continued on Page Eleven

CONTRACTOR HELD IN RACKET INQUIRY

J. G. Livingston, a Member of Many Clubs, Seized in Dewey Electrical Investigation

John Griswold Livingston, 65 years old, wealthy electrical contractor and club member, was arrested in the office of District Attorney Thomas E. Dewey yesterday as one more victim of the long-continued effort to get at the heart of the electrical racket in New York.

Mr. Livingston, the president and treasurer of J. Livingston & Co., the largest electrical contracting firm in New York and perhaps in the country, was held with Frank W. Cooper, 60, secretary of the firm, on charges of having failed to make material entries on the books of the corporation. The section invoked was 665 of the Penal Code, seldom used in such cases, and it carries a maximum penalty of three years' imprisonment.

Behind the arrest of Mr. Livingston was the drive to break open the racket that has been described as one of the most complex and ramified ever developed in the city. Involved are charges that the electrical contractors made collusive bids on municipal and private jobs, and policed the industry through the power of building trades unions.

Hines Firm Also Involved

Involved also, in the inquiry, is the firm of Emerson & Hines, of which James J. Hines Jr., son of the Tammany leader under indictment as a member of the Arthur (Dutch Schultz) Flegenheimer policy racket, is an official.

Investigation has been under way for months by the special grand jury inquiring into rackets. Thus far the officials of several contracting firms have been charged with making false income-tax returns on the basis of entries on their books for which their explanations have been held unsatisfactory, and one man, Horace Watts, of the firm of McNutt, Watts & Tanker, was cited for contempt for failure to answer grand jury questions.

A complete denial of the charge and of any contact or acquaintance with James J. Hines was entered on behalf of Mr. Livingston and Mr. Cooper yesterday by Kenneth M. Spence, their attorney.

"There has not been even a technical violation of the statute in this case," Mr. Spence said, "and in my opinion the charge is utterly without merit. Neither Mr. Livingston nor Mr. Cooper has ever had any dealings directly or indirectly with James J. Hines. They do not know Mr. Hines."

Are Sole Stockholders

Mr. Livingston, whose home is at 175 Causeway, Lawrence, L. I., and Mr. Cooper, who lives at 116 East Sixty-eighth Street, are the sole stockholders in the contracting firm. The grand jury ordered that an information charging them with omission of entries on their books be filed, and it was drawn up by

Continued on Page Eighteen

LEGISLATURE PLAN CUTS RATIO OF CITY

New Districting Draft Would Give It 64 to 95 for Up-State Areas

By WARREN MOSCOW
Special to THE NEW YORK TIMES.

ALBANY, July 14.—A revised reapportionment plan, designed to remove objections of some up-State Republicans to the draft previously made public, was considered today by the Constitutional Convention's Committee on Legislature. The plan, which, it is expected, will be adopted by the committee on Monday, would increase up-State representation in both Senate and Assembly, and would take away down-State representation, as contrasted with the previous draft.

Both the city and up-State areas would gain in representation, when compared with their present number of legislators, because the size of the Legislature would be increased—the Senate from 51 to 53 members and the Assembly from 150 to 159.

Under the draft before the committee today, New York City would have 64 Assemblymen, as compared with 66 proposed for the city in the first draft, and with the 62 it has at present.

The draft includes a further cut in the New York County representation, from 17 to 16, and Queens would gain one less than it figured to do under the first draft.

The Assembly districting, so far as it affects New York City, would be as follows:

County.	Pres. Number.	Final Draft.	First Draft.
New York	23	16	17
Kings	23	23	23
Bronx	8	12	12
Queens	6	11	12
Richmond	2	2	2
Totals	62	64	66

Of the Assemblymen taken away from New York City under the final draft, one would go to Onondaga County (Syracuse), increasing its number from three to four, and another would go to Suffolk, which would get three instead of two.

Down-State Senate List Is Cut

In the division of the seats between New York City and up-State the final draft would give 64 to the city and 95 to up-State areas. The first draft made it 66 and 93. The present division is 62 and 88.

In dealing with the Senate, the division of seats for New York City would remain unchanged from the first draft, but down-State areas as a whole would lose a seat because Nassau County, to which were given two Senate seats in the first draft, would be cut to one.

At present Nassau shares a seat with Suffolk. The seat to be taken away from Nassau would be given to Renssalaer, which, in the first draft, had been joined with Washington.

Under the new plan, New York City would have 24 Senate seats, instead of 22½ as at present.

The up-State Senate lines would

Continued on Page Ten

Times Wide World

The speed pilot and his four flight companions following their return to New York. Left to right: Lieutenant Thomas Thurlow, Edward Lund, Hughes, Richard Stoddart and Harry P. Connor.

President Roosevelt presented Hughes with the Harmon International Trophy for his record flight.

Times Wide World

Mayor La Guardia welcoming Howard Hughes and Richard Stoddart, left, radio operator, as they stepped out of the cockpit of the plane.

Wives of three of the fliers, Mrs. Harry Connor, Mrs. Richard Stoddart and Mrs. Thomas Thurlow watching the plane as it prepared to land. With them are Mayor La Guardia and Grover Whalen.

Times Wide World

"All the News That's Fit to Print."

The New York Times.

LATE CITY EDITION
Partly cloudy, continued warm today, showers in morning. Tomorrow showers, temperature unchanged.
Temperatures Yesterday—Max., 86; Min., 71

VOL. LXXXVII....No. 29,396. Entered as Second-Class Matter, Postoffice, New York, N. Y. NEW YORK, TUESDAY, JULY 19, 1938. P THREE CENTS NEW YORK CITY and Vicinity | FOUR CENTS Elsewhere Except in 7th and 8th Postal Zones.

REICH STOCKS FALL IN WORST COLLAPSE SINCE NAZIS' ADVENT

Despite Rigid Control, Prices Drop From 4 to 9 Points on 'Black Monday'

FOREIGN TRADE DECLINING

Economic Law Held Beginning to Assert Itself as Nation Feels Results of Tension

By OTTO D. TOLISCHUS
Wireless to THE NEW YORK TIMES.

BERLIN, July 18.—German Stock Exchanges suffered today their worst day since Chancellor Hitler came to power. Despite rigid control prices tumbled four, five, six and in individual cases up to nine points in what some German newspapers themselves call a sensational collapse.

And to some financial circles today, "black Monday" began to look very much like the "black Friday" of May 13, 1927. And this officially recorded slump tells only part of the tale because the real trading in securities no longer is done on the Boerse but privately between banks and at their own price.

Simultaneously, as one contributing factor to that collapse it was revealed that Germany's foreign trade continues to shrink steadily at a quickening pace and exports from Great Germany, including Austria, are now far less than the exports from the old part of the Reich alone just preceding annexation, while Great Germany's total foreign trade deficit for the first half of this year amounts to about 175,000,000 marks compared with a surplus of 194,100,000 for the corresponding period last year.

These new developments are taken to indicate that although German economy is still running at capacity production and although National Socialist spokesmen declare that Germany is crisis-proof because she has made herself independent of world economy, economic law nevertheless is beginning to assert itself in Germany as well.

Tension Having Its Effect

The tense political situation created by the Sudeten German issue undoubtedly contributed to today's slump, but the Stock Exchange survived previous more serious war scares in good shape and the decline has been steady for several weeks. It is necessary, therefore, to look for deeper causes.

The fact is that the tension that first became evident in the Spring, when the National Socialist new deal, like the Roosevelt New Deal in the Spring of 1937, threatened to run away into inflated wage and price levels and was therefore subjected to a dose of deflation, is now having its effect.

In the first place, as outlined in previous dispatches and confirmed by all recent economic reviews in Germany, rising labor costs, rising taxes and growing governmental control have seriously impaired industry's profitableness, making stock values doubtful. In the second place, as frankly stated by the German press, industry itself has been forced to liquidate security holdings in order to raise money for its own replacements, especially for "national tasks" imposed on it under the Four-Year Plan, which involves considerable new plant construction.

It has had to take recourse to this method because the government is no longer pumping into German economy special bills that can be used as "check money," but is financing "public works" with taxes and long-term loans, and at the most with Treasury notes that can neither be discounted with the Reichsbank nor used as collateral for loans and must be redeemed within six months.

Further Aggravation Cited

And since the government still preempts all capital markets for its own purposes there are no buyers to absorb the offerings. This domestic situation, as well as the foreign-trade situation, is further aggravated, first, by the drastic measures taken against Jews; second, by the general decline of world economy from which Germany is unable to escape entirely; third, by her forceful political methods, which on the one hand make other nations wary, even in their trade with Germany, and on the other hand entail counter-measures.

Heavy Jewish liquidations caused by enforced "Aryanizations" and the numerous restrictions imposed on Jewish businesses, together with the sudden exclusion of Jewish brokers from Stock Exchanges, have greatly contributed to the slump in stocks, but anti-Jewish excesses in Vienna have also contributed to the slump in foreign trade. They severed many commercial ties with the Balkans at a time when France and Britain were utilizing Balkan apprehensions of German aims for a trade drive

Continued on Page Ten

City Sales Tax Receipts Drop in Second Quarter

Sales-tax receipts from 140,934 taxpayers amounted to $11,012,606 for the period from April 1 to June 30, it was announced yesterday from the office of City Treasurer Almerindo Portfolio. Payments received included amounts collected during the second quarter of 1938 by retailers, which amounts were payable to the city on or before July 15. The amount collected during the corresponding period last year was $11,990,636, which was received from 117,966 taxpayers.

Mr. Portfolio said that he was gratified with the amount received in view of the fact that department store and other sales this year, according to report, were below last year. He pointed to the efficiency of the cigarette stamp tax, which replaces the sales tax on cigarettes and which proved a fruitful source of revenue.

JONES AGAIN WARNS BANKS TO AID TRADE

RFC Head Says, Otherwise, Government May Lend More —'Overcaution Harmful'

Special to THE NEW YORK TIMES.

WASHINGTON, July 18.—If the banks of the United States hope to preserve their place in the national scene they must "cease frightening potential borrowers away" and seek new lending business on terms which are suitable to the needs of business men, Jesse H. Jones, chairman of the Reconstruction Finance Corporation, told all directors and managing officers of State and national banks in a circular letter today.

Calling attention to the failure of the banks to take a desirable share of participation in the $85,344,788 business and industrial loans made by the RFC since the end of February, the RFC chairman warned the bankers that unless they "did their part" in aiding business and the government through an effective lending policy it might be necessary for "the government to go further into the banking business."

Sends Copy of New Rules

Mr. Jones attached a copy of the new uniform bank examination rules recently announced by the Controller of the Currency in cooperation with the Federal Reserve Board and the Federal Deposit Insurance Corporation, pointing out that these regulations for investment securities "provide a convenient method for making time loans in bond or serial note form to business and industry," and that they also provide "a convenient method of making loans that may be participated in by correspondent banks or the RFC."

He urged the bankers to go out and get some of the business that the finance companies have been taking away from the banks.

"Banks lend to these finance companies at absurdly low interest rates instead of going after the business directly," he said.

With a strong implication that the bankers should do for themselves what they expect of their borrowers, the RFC chairman declared that "when the business man lets his competitor get ahead of him, the bank is quick to notice and take it into account in considering his credit rating."

Points to 17 Per Cent Profit

"Twenty-five finance companies on which data is available," he wrote, "loaned $4,360,000,000 in 1937 on an invested capital of $391,000,000 and borrowings of $1,224,000,000. They reported net profits aggregating $65,785,000, or approximately 17 per cent on the capital invested. While six of our largest banks, with capital funds of a billion dollars and deposits of eight and one-half billion dollars, reported $63,000,000 profit, or 6 1-3 per cent on the invested capital.

"The three largest finance companies loaned $3,620,000,000 of the total sum on an invested capital of $266,000,000, and reported net profits of $47,575,000, 18 per cent on the invested capital.

"The finance companies have proven that installment credit, efficiently handled, can be sold very profitably, while the security they require, as well as their maturities, are well within good banking practice.

"Banks could render this service at much lower interest rates to the borrower and at a good profit to themselves. They would be lending deposits on which they pay little or no interest, while the finance companies borrow most of the money they lend.

Means to Cover Extra Risk Cited

"Many loans to businesses which do not enjoy top credit ratings may be safely and profitably made by adding a small interest charge to cover the extra risk.

"An amortized loan is an installment loan. If from one to three years are required to pay for an electric stove, a refrigerator, a

Continued on Page Four

A. E. MORGAN LAYS IDEAS TO PRESIDENT AS HE TAKES STAND

Many Policies Criticized by Foes Were Roosevelt's, He Testifies in TVA Inquiry

ASSAILS LILIENTHAL ANEW

Plot to Oust Him Was Begun in 1933, Says Ex-Chairman —Hits Panter Appointment

By RUSSELL B. PORTER
Special to THE NEW YORK TIMES.

KNOXVILLE, Tenn., July 18.—Dr. Arthur E. Morgan, deposed by President Roosevelt as member and chairman of the Tennessee Valley Authority this year, testified before the Congressional investigating committee today that many of the policies for which his fellow-directors on the TVA board are now criticizing him were the ideas of President Roosevelt, expressed to him in the early days of TVA or before it came into existence.

The former chairman charged that David E. Lilienthal, director in charge of the power program, had been engaged since soon after TVA was started in 1933 in an attempt to have him removed as chairman to make room for some one in accord with Mr. Lilienthal's ideas on public power.

He accused Mr. Lilienthal or Dr. Harcourt A. Morgan, now chairman of the TVA board, of having instigated a newspaper campaign of detraction against him in order to bring about his downfall. According to the witness, newspaper columnists for several years here repeatedly "made sport" of his "vagaries" in such an intimate way as to make it obvious that they had access to "inside information" available only to the board.

Renews Attack on Engineer

Arthur Morgan repeated before the committee his protest against the committee's appointment of Thomas A. Panter of Los Angeles as its chief engineer. The protest was made recently in a letter to Senator Vic Donahey, chairman of the committee. He charged today that the appointment was of questionable propriety because Mr. Panter was an assistant, in the Los Angeles Municipal Power System, to E. F. Scattergood, whom the witness accused of having tried in 1933 to get President Roosevelt to appoint him (Mr. Scattergood) over the heads of the regular directors as a special agent of the President to direct the TVA power program.

According to the witness, Mr. Scattergood was assisted by Mr. Lilienthal in this scheme. When it failed, according to Arthur Morgan, Mr. Scattergood was appointed as a consultant on power over his (Arthur Morgan's) protests.

Mr. Scattergood and his staff wrote a report in which they sided definitely with Mr. Lilienthal against Arthur Morgan, and later carried on a campaign for several years of attack on Arthur Morgan and support for Mr. Lilenthal, the witness alleged.

The witness asserted that Mr. Panter was a member of the Los Angles staff dominated by Mr. Scattergood, which had taken a positive stand on controversial power issues coming before the committee, and therefore ought not to be the engineering "eyes" through which the committee would see the power controversy.

Panter Denies He Is a "Yes Man"

Committee members questioned the witness at length about Mr. Panter. Although he insisted that he did not think the appointment proper, the witness stated that he knew nothing derogatory to Mr. Panter personally.

Mr. Panter, sworn as a witness, later testified that there was no

Continued on Page Thirteen

225,809 Persons Missing In This Country Last Year

Special to THE NEW YORK TIMES.

WASHINGTON, July 18.—Persons reported missing last year throughout the United States numbered 225,809, of whom the whereabouts of 16,141 remains unknown, according to estimates based on a Federal Bureau of Investigation survey as announced today by the Department of Justice.

The survey disclosed that there were 2,158 amnesia victims, all but 118 of whom were subsequently identified either through medical treatment or a hunt for their fingerprints through FBI files, which last week received their nine-millionth set of fingerprint records.

The estimated number of individuals unidentified at the time of their death last year was characterized as "astounding." This total reached 11,202, of whom 2,603 still remained unidentified at burial.

QUEEN MARIE DIES IN RUMANIA AT 62

Dowager Succumbs to a Rare Liver Ailment After Return From German Sanatorium

Wireless to THE NEW YORK TIMES.

BUCHAREST, Rumania, July 18.—Two days before the eleventh anniversary of the death of her husband, King Ferdinand, the Dowager Queen Marie died at 5:38 P. M. today in the royal castle at Sinaia, where her husband also died. She was 62 years old.

King Carol, Crown Prince Michael, former Queen Elizabeth of Greece, a daughter, and Prime Minister Miron Cristea, who is also Patriarch of the Rumanian Orthodox Church, were present at the death-bed. King Carol, Michael and Elizabeth sat at the bedside for the last half hour of the Dowager Queen's life. Up to twenty minutes before her death she was fully conscious.

On the arrival of Queen Marie's train at Cernauti Saturday from Germany it was obvious that she had not long to live. She was obliged to delay the journey on to Sinaia—which the doctors even in Dresden had stated would be fatal—to recover a little strength and she spent the night at the palace of the Metropolitan. Oxygen was constantly administered. It was her own decision to leave Dresden in order to come home to die, and at Cernauti she insisted again, against the advice of doctors, on doing so.

Doctors Issue Bulletins

A bulletin issued by the doctors at 11 A. M. today showed that the end was near. It stated that the hemorrhage of the liver had become severe and that the Queen's condition was grave. She was extremely weak from the constant loss of blood. At 3 P. M. another bulletin stated that her strength was failing every hour.

When the news of her death reached Bucharest bells began to toll and all public buildings, as well as many private houses, lowered their flags to half staff, draping them in crêpe. Despite the years elapsing since the Dowager Queen played any striking part in the life of the State, she had lost none of her earlier popularity.

Her body will be brought to Bucharest tomorrow on the royal train. Throughout the journey adjutants of the court will act as coffin bearers. Starting at 4 P. M. tomorrow, her body will lie in state in the golden hall of Cotraceni Palace on the same spot Ferdinand's body lay in state. After the Rumanian people have paid their last respects funeral ceremonies will start at 9 A. M. Thursday, when the coffin will be taken to North Station and put on the train for Curtea di Arges. There the Dowager

Continued on Page Twenty-one

Catholic Bus Bill Nears Final Passage; Convention Advances It to Third Reading

Special to THE NEW YORK TIMES.

ALBANY, July 18.—The Constitutional Convention tonight informally put its stamp of approval on the free transportation by the State of parochial school pupils from their homes to the schools and back again. It did so by advancing to third reading, without opposition, an amendment to the present constitutional ban against the State lending financial support in any way to denominational schools.

If the amendment is finally adopted, as it is scheduled to be, and is approved by the people, it will end a long controversy which has agitated members of the Legislature, figured in a recent political campaign, and was the cause of litigation through the Court of Appeals.

The fight started when the Legislature several years ago passed a bill authorizing the transportation of pupils attending denominational schools. The intent was to affect Catholic schools, and it became known as the Catholic Bus Bill. It was vetoed by Governor Lehman, was repassed subsequently, and then signed by the Governor.

However, the Governor's veto of the first bill became an important though not publicized campaign issue in 1936. And it was credited with having cost him more than a hundred thousand votes in New York City alone.

The bill he signed was tested in a taxpayers' action and decided by the Court of Appeals this Spring. The court's decision was that the State could not legally spend money on the transportation of pupils to other than public schools.

LEHMAN DEMANDS CONVENTION DROP CURB ON AUTO FUND

Special Message Warns Earmarking for Roads Would Upset Finances

HINTS TAX RISE AS RESULT

Grade-Crossing Plan Adopted, With Roads to Pay 15 Per Cent of Cost

Governor Lehman's message to the convention is on Page 7.

By WARREN MOSCOW
Special to THE NEW YORK TIMES.

ALBANY, July 18.—Governor Lehman, in a special message read to the Constitutional Convention tonight, announced his unequivocal opposition to the Feinberg proposal which would bar, for the next twenty years, the diversion of gasoline tax revenues from highway purposes into the State's general fund.

After the debate on the Governor's message the convention adopted unanimously an amendment for the elimination of all grade crossings, fixing the maximum cost to the railroads at 15 per cent of the total. The railroad groups, including the Long Island road, previously had agreed to the plan.

Adoption of the auto tax amendment would so seriously affect the finances of the State that the Governor deemed it his duty to state the facts to the convention, he declared in his message.

"A constitutional mandate such as is now proposed would inevitably cause trouble in the future," the Governor declared. "It would unquestionably force imposition of new taxes whenever there was a falling off in State revenues due to business recessions. That is just the time when taxes are most burdensome."

The Governor, in addition, attacked the singling out of highway users as a special group, and hit the whole theory of earmarking of State revenues, declaring that if gasoline-tax revenues were earmarked, other groups of taxpayers could similarly claim the right of aggregation of revenues for their own particular benefit.

Warns of Financing Difficulties

In conclusion the Governor declared:

"At best the financing of government in the future will be an extremely difficult problem. I earnestly urge that your honorable body do not add to that problem by writing into our Constitution a mandate which cannot be carried out over a long period of years without serious threat to the credit of our State and to the well-being of our people."

The Feinberg proposal, which was reported out by Robert Moses's Committee on Highways, Parkways and Grade Crossings, called for the earmarking of two cents, or the first half of the gasoline and motor vehicle tax receipts.

The reading of the message brought from the floor a bitter attack on the Governor, and an equally spirited defense of him from the Democratic side.

Benjamin F. Feinberg, author of the gas tax amendment, declared that while he was always glad to hear from the Governor, "it is getting to be humorous for the Governor to be trying to run this convention by correspondence. He had his chance to be a delegate, and he would undoubtedly have been elected, and he refused it. Why didn't he come, and sit here, and take the same responsibility that all of the other delegates have assumed?"

1929 Roosevelt Message Quoted

He then read from a message by Governor Roosevelt in 1929, pledging the complete revenues from gasoline taxes for highway construction, and accused Mr. Roosevelt and Mr. Lehman of having short memories.

Robert F. Wagner, Democratic leader, was quick to rise to Mr. Lehman's defense.

"I am sure no other delegate in the convention would attack the Governor as Senator Feinberg did," he declared. He then read the section of the rules authorizing addresses from the Governor, and added:

"I should think we would welcome advice on the conduct of the affairs of this State from so outstanding a public servant as the Governor. On three different occasions he submitted himself to the electorate, and three different times he was elected to office by unprecedented majorities. He has fulfilled in every respect the hopes of the people.

"His record will go down in history as one of the great and outstanding Governors, along with Governor Smith and Governor

Continued on Page Seven

CORRIGAN FLIES TO DUBLIN; U. S. OFFICIALS MAY WINK AT FORBIDDEN HOP IN 'CRATE'

Eyes Twinkle in Capital at Flight; No Punishment of Airman Indicated

'Very Interesting,' Says Hull—Mulligan, Head of Air Commerce Bureau, Sees 'Great Day for Irish,' but Admonishes Corrigan

Special to THE NEW YORK TIMES.

WASHINGTON, July 18. — If Douglas G. Corrigan is to be punished for failure to observe laws and regulations in his unheralded flight to Ireland, it appeared here today his chastisement would be extremely light.

When news of the aviator's feat was made known here, there was a visible raising of official eyebrows, but this served as well to reveal a kindly twinkling official eye, which may be a clue to the extent of Mr. Corrigan's future punishment, if any.

Secretary of State Cordell Hull was informed of the flight just before he received newspaper men for his usual daily press conference. As questions were shot at him as to the government's official attitude, Mr. Hull maintained his usual calm, and observed the news was "very interesting."

But there was a gleam in his eyes that bespoke his secret admiration for the young flier's feat, and he referred the reporters to the Commerce Department for its attitude on regulations that Mr. Corrigan broke when he left without a permit or "so much as a calling card."

Denis Mulligan, director of the Bureau of Air Commerce, seemed pleased also at Corrigan's safe arrival at Dublin, but he confirmed the fact that the flier neither held, nor had applied for, a permit. Mr. Mulligan explained that Corrigan had discussed the matter of the flight with Air Commerce Bureau officials last Fall, but had made no application for the permit after the officials had discouraged the attempt on the theory that his equipment was inadequate.

"It's a great day in the history of the Irish people, and we don't want to spoil their fun by talking about punishment," Mr. Mulligan

Continued on Page Three

LOST WAY, HE SAYS

Set Out for California, but Compass 'Got Stuck,' He Asserts

WINS IRISH ADMIRATION

Airman Is Greeted by U. S. Minister—Promises Not to Make Return Flight

By HUGH SMITH
Special Cable to THE NEW YORK TIMES.

DUBLIN, July 18.—Douglas Gorce Corrigan, 31-year-old Californian, added a unique chapter in the history of lone Atlantic fliers today when he completed a trip from New York to Baldonnel Airfield, Dublin, in his 9-year-old Curtiss Robin plane in 28 hours 13 minutes.

At 2:25 o'clock this afternoon [9:25 A. M. yesterday in New York] he made a perfect landing at Baldonnel Field with gasoline to spare out of the 320 gallons with which he took off from Floyd Bennett Field. His whole flight was illegal from beginning to end, but this did not appear to cost the flier a thought as he stepped out of his rather ancient machine. He was more concerned with the performance of his plane, of which he was proud.

He broke American regulations by taking off on the long-distance flight and he broke Irish regulations by landing at Baldonnel field without a permit, but as for himself and the people who greeted him in Dublin this evening this disregard of international air conventions was only a minor detail against his remarkable achievement.

Brave and Unassuming

Among transatlantic fliers this adventurous and brave American must surely rank as one of the most modest and unassuming. Surrounded by a battery of cameramen and journalists at the United States Legation here this evening, this slim and small-set young man in his oil-stained gray pants, leather jacket and open-necked gray shirt had no idea of posing as a figure of world importance in the news. He regarded his hop from New York to Ireland as just another flight.

"I think my trip from California to New York was a bigger thing; it was much more dangerous," he commented, minimizing by comparison his long, lone flight over the wastes of the Atlantic. [Corrigan flew nonstop from California to Roosevelt Field, L. I., on July 10, covering the 2,700 miles in 27 hours 50 minutes.]

He accounted for his presence in Dublin tonight by casually explaining that he had taken a wrong turning and had headed east instead of west because his compass played him false.

Some newspaper folk smiled dubiously, but Corrigan explained in detail how the pivot of one of his compasses stuck and did not come loose until near the end of the flight. He said this was the cause of his landing here instead of in California.

Describes the Flight

Describing his experience, this latest Atlantic hero, who said he was a part-time flying instructor and a part-time aircraft mechanic, explained:

"I left the flying field in New York at 5:15 yesterday morning with 320 gallons of gasoline in the tanks. The machine was heavy and I had to run about 2,500 feet to take off. It was a slow business, but I got off without a hitch. Then, flying by compass, I headed, as I thought, for California.

"I had no intention of flying to Ireland, although I had thought of a flight to this country and had studied maps. When up about 5,000 feet I came into a bank of clouds. For almost twenty-six hours I was in clouds all the time at an altitude of 5,000 to 6,000 feet and reckoned I must be well down toward California.

"It was impossible to try to get my bearings from anything around me, so I just flew by compass and only came down to 1,500 feet when I ran into rain. I caught a glimpse of the water then, but I rose back to 5,000 feet.

"The light was good when I came down again, and the first things I saw were fishing boats, but even then I thought I was off the Pacific Coast. About a half hour later I sighted the first land.

"Then, when I saw the layout of the country and the little white

Continued on Page Two

VALENCIA OUTPOST REBELS' NEXT GOAL

Loyalists Fortify Ragudo Pass, Defending Viver 25 Miles Northwest of Sagunte

By HERBERT L. MATTHEWS
Wireless to THE NEW YORK TIMES.

VALENCIA, Spain, July 18.—The third year of the Spanish civil war dawned today with Valencia in great peril, a peril which, however, is not immediate, since the Rebels are still far distant, but which is none the less real for the coming days.

A special newspaper called the Frente Popular came out here today, published by all journals in Valencia. Its banner line in red ink read:

"Valencia soldier, peasant and worker: Our beloved province is endangered. Resist! Fight! Work without cease in this third year of our struggle."

Colonel Leopoldo Mendez, commander of the Levant army, addressed a stirring appeal to his troops to hold on and to the people in the rear to support them.

Foreign Minister Julio Alvarez Del Vayo opened a proclamation from Barcelona thus:

"Republican Spain enters the third year of the war with more than confidence in victory, with a determination to struggle to the end until the last man for the last piece of Spanish soil."

Everywhere in Loyalist Spain in proclamations, speeches, messages and pledges is to be found that keynote of all Loyalist thought these days, "We are fighting for the independence of Spain against a foreign invader."

Losses Are Admitted

For the first time last night's war communiqué referred to Italian troops as leading the Rebel drive in the Teruel sector. That communiqué admits that on Saturday evening Barracas, Villanueva de la Reina and Pina in the sector about thirty miles southeast of Teruel were lost and the Insurgents continued pressing eastward.

Since then no correspondent has been able to go to the front because of lack of transportation. Presumably, however, the Insurgents will try to press on toward Viver, about eight miles farther southeast, where they will find strong fortifications and doubtless much stiffer resistance. Perhaps it will be so strong that they will try to turn the position instead of attacking directly.

At any rate this week threatens to be a critical one. It is obvious that the Loyalists cannot continue to lose ground as they did last week without placing Valencia in the utmost peril. However, there is every reason to hope a good stand can be made soon.

Already the axis of the Rebel drive has apparently been diverted from a southeasterly to an easterly direction, with the heaviest pressure down the Mijares River Valley. The Rebels have not dared yet to attack the Ragudo Pass defenses, about two miles northwest of Viver. At least that is what we hear here, where one must rely on

Continued on Page Ten

VAST HEALTH PLAN URGED FOR COUNTRY

$850,000,000 a Year for Ten Years Cited at National Session—A.M.A. Objects

By WILLIAM L. LAURENCE
Special to THE NEW YORK TIMES.

WASHINGTON, July 18.—A comprehensive and far-reaching national health program for providing more adequate distribution of medical care to the American people, calling for the expenditure of $850,000,000 a year for a ten-year period, was submitted in outline here today before the National Health Conference.

The conference, called at the suggestion of President Roosevelt by the President's Interdepartmental Committee to Coordinate Health and Welfare Activities, is the first of its kind ever held. It brings together representatives of the various important medical bodies and leaders of organized labor, agriculture and other important lay groups who have a direct interest in bringing the present high cost of medical care within the means of the majority of the population.

The $850,000,000-a-year program was submitted to the Interdepartmental Committee by its technical committee on medical care and was presented to President Roosevelt last February, it was revealed.

The President thereupon, it was stated by Miss Josephine Roche, former assistant secretary of the Treasury and chairman of the conference, suggested calling this conference for the purpose of submitting the various recommendations of the program for discussion by the representatives of the groups most vitally concerned, before taking final action.

Cabot and A. M. A. Heads Clash

The national public health plan brought from Dr. Irvin Abell of Louisville, president of the American Medical Association, the criticism that it was impractical.

Dr. Hugh Cabot of the Mayo Clinic in turn assailed the attitude of organized medicine toward public health services. Dr. Cabot, a member of the Committee of Physicians, who are "rebels" against the policy of the American Medical Association, exchanged caustic words with Dr. Olin West, secretary of the A. M. A.

Dr. Abell told the conference that no practical health administrator could possibly approve a centrally controlled medical service plan which failed to take into account "varying conditions of the States, counties and cities of this country."

"The medical profession and the allied health agencies throughout the country are exerting every effort to determine the needs and the demands for medical care," said Dr. Abell. "Changes to meet health needs must be consistent with local conditions and requirements and must be judged by the effect which such changes will have on the quality of the medical care for the individual sick person."

Dr. Cabot charged that, "as at present organized," medicine was a "competitive business."

"The maintenance of standards of

Continued on Page Nine

"All the News That's Fit to Print."

The New York Times.

LATE CITY EDITION
Showers, little change in temperatures today. Tomorrow generally fair and cooler.
Temperatures Yesterday—Max., 66; Min., 60

Copyright, 1938, by The New York Times Company.

VOL. LXXXVIII...No. 29,458. Entered as Second-Class Matter, Postoffice, New York, N. Y. NEW YORK, MONDAY, SEPTEMBER 19, 1938. PP THREE CENTS NEW YORK CITY and Vicinity | FOUR CENTS Elsewhere Except in 7th and 8th Postal Zones.

BRITAIN AND FRANCE ACCEPT HITLER DEMANDS ON CZECHS; WILL ASK BENES TODAY TO SURRENDER GERMAN AREAS; PRAGUE, INCREDULOUS, REGARDS ACTION AS A BETRAYAL

TRUCK STRIKE'S END TO BE ASKED TODAY; RELIEF FOOD MOVED

Morris to Seek Settlement as Union Weighs Backing for 'Outlaw' Tie-Up

PRIMARY BALLOTS GO OUT

Police Guard Poll Supplies—Morgan Is Not Alarmed Over City's Provisions

Acting Mayor Newbold Morris induced leaders of the "outlaw" truck drivers' strike yesterday to distribute food supplies to home relief families and ballots for tomorrow's primary election, as well as to expedite the movement of newsprint previously conceded.

Meanwhile the strike is expected to enter its crucial stage today with the beginning of the new work week and the holding of a settlement conference and union meetings to take up an authorised strike vote.

The Merchant Truckmen's Bureau of New York and the Highway Transport Association jointly announced yesterday afternoon that they had accepted the invitation to the City Hall settlement negotiation conference arranged from San Francisco by Mayor La Guardia on Saturday.

Michael J. Cashal, vice president of the International Brotherhood of Teamsters, disclosed that a general membership meeting in St. John's Park at 8 A. M. today, originally called to take a strike vote, would merely be preliminary to a second meeting at which the members of the three locals involved would decide whether to take a strike vote.

It is expected that this second meeting will be under way while Mr. Morris is conferring at City Hall with union leaders and representatives of the trucking companies.

Morris Strives for Peace

Although William Fellowes Morgan Jr., Markets Commissioner, was not alarmed by the food situation, Mr. Morris was at City Hall early to confer with strike leaders on the movement of home relief food supplies, primary ballots and newsprint.

Mr. Morris had breakfast at City Hall, which was active on Sunday for the first time in many months. After he had obtained notable concessions from the strike spokesmen, he communicated by telephone with Mayor La Guardia, who is keeping closely in touch with the situation. The Mayor expressed himself as "highly pleased" with the progress made, according to Mr. Morris.

After remaining at City Hall from 8 A. M. until 4 P. M., Mr. Morris was optimistic when he started home. He declared the developments of the day promised a quick settlement of the strike.

Mr. Morris expressed hope that the strikers would capitulate to the union at the St. John's Park meeting, that the strike would have official sanction of the union and that under orderly conditions negotiations between the unions and trucking organizations could be started.

The strikers are demanding a reduction of working hours from 47 to 40 a week without reduction in the base pay of $56.50 a week. They also ask for elimination of "abuses."

Orderly Action Urged

Referring to the conference to be held at City Hall at 9 A. M., Mr. Morris expressed belief that the teamsters would be represented by officers of the union, inasmuch as he expecteed formal sanction of the strike by Locals 807, 816 and 282.

Others at the conference will be Arthur S. Meyer of the State Board of Mediation and Mrs. Anna M. Rosenberg, Regional Director of the Social Security Board, attending in unofficial capacity.

"I am very hopeful that by tomorrow afternoon negotiations for a new contract will have been started," Mr. Morris said. "This could not be done with an outlaw strike. The strikers would have no official representative with whom the corporations could negotiate. If, at tomorrow's meeting at St. John's Park, the situation is turned over to the union, I will meet the union officials at City Hall, and I feel confident that the strike will be suspended pending negotiations for a new contract."

Yesterday's conference of Mr. Morris and strike leaders, headed by Willie May of Local 807, lasted from 1:30 to 2 P. M. The committee agreed to cooperate with Mr. Morris throughout the day. They consented to the delivery of twenty-five truckloads of supplies of the Emergency Relief Bureau. The supplies went to some seventy home relief depots throughout the five boroughs.

Strike spokesmen contended their agreement on Saturday to move perishable supplies did not include all foodstuffs consigned to home

Continued on Page Ten

Hurricane in Atlantic Heads Toward Florida

By The Associated Press.

JACKSONVILLE, Fla., Sept. 18.—A tropical disturbance of "dangerous proportions" roared westward over the Atlantic Ocean tonight, its center at 7 P. M. being about 450 miles north of San Juan, Puerto Rico, and about 900 miles east-southeast of Miami It was moving west-northwest at about 20 miles an hour.

The storm was attended by hurricane winds near the center and by strong shifting gales and squalls over a large area, the Weather Bureau here reported, adding that it would begin to affect the extreme Eastern Bahamas by mid-Monday and Central Bahamas by Monday night.

A bulletin said:

"Caution advised all vessels in path and all small craft, Cape Hatteras to Florida Straits, should remain in port until storm danger passes."

A. F. L. UNION OPENS DRIVE IN THE WPA

Sets Up Rival to the Workers Alliance, but Denies Intent to Fight It or the Reds

A move by the American Federation of Labor to organize workers on WPA white-collar and arts projects, where the Workers Alliance has its greatest strength, was disclosed here yesterday.

Hubert Malkus, chairman of the Federal Project Workers, announced last night that his group had been established as a separate section for WPA employes in the American Federation of Bookkeepers, Stenographers and Accountants Union, Local 20940. Confirmation of this action was given in Washington by Frank Morrison, secretary of the A. F. of L.

The jurisdiction of the new group is still indefinite. It has no independent charter from the A. F. of L. and Mr. Morrison, who was reached at home and was therefore unable to consult his correspondence files, expressed the belief that the organizational rights of the WPA section would extend only to workers in the white-collar field.

Leader Formerly in Alliance

Mr. Malkus, an employe of the Federal Art Project and a former member of the Workers Alliance, said the founders of his organization were all from the five arts projects but that the group had been authorized to accept members from any division of the WPA. The only restriction, he said, was that workers coming within the jurisdiction of established A. F. of L. unions could not be enrolled without the consent of the unions affected.

The aim of the Federal Project Workers, as set forth by its executive committee, is "to unite the unorganized WPA employes and the many groups and branches that have recently split off from the Workers Alliance."

"The Workers Alliance does not represent the ideals of many project workers," said a statement issued by Mr. Malkus in the name of the executive committee. "In the face of widespread accusations that the Workers Alliance is under the domination of Communist leaders and has confused functions of a trade union with political activities, the need has been emphasized for a labor organization that will concentrate on the matters of wages and working conditions on WPA projects."

The Federal Project Workers was not set up to fight communism or the Workers Alliance, the executive committee declared. The group's sole concern was with conditions on WPA and it was willing to cooperate with any other organization "on any action that is concerned with fair dealing, elimination of abuses and discriminations and improvement of wages and working conditions on WPA jobs," according to the statement.

Alliance Leader Sees "Bluff"

Formation of the new body to organize relief workers was described by Willis R. Morgan, president of the Workers Alliance of Greater New York, as "another bluff on the part of the A. F. of L."

"This is all in line with the policy of the federation's executive council to try to split labor at every opportunity," Mr. Morgan said. "They have never shown any interest in the WPA. In fact, the building trades department of the A. F. of L. was in Washington earlier this year lobbying against the Federal Relief Appropriations Act because they wanted work done under contract labor. It seems a little bit ironic for them to turn around now and talk about organizing the WPA."

The national officers of the Workers Alliance have been negotiating with the Committee for Industrial Organization for nearly a year on the possibility of establishing some link between the two

Continued on Page Nine

HITLER ASKS HASTE

Says Sudeten 'Tumor' Must Be Removed 'Once and for All'

LAMENTS RACE IN ARMING

Asserts Czechoslovakia Was Cause of Increases in Air and Other Forces

By The Associated Press.

LONDON, Monday, Sept. 19.—The Daily Mail today quoted Chancellor Adolf Hitler as telling an interviewer that "this Czech trouble has got to be ended once and for all and ended now."

The interview, by G. Ward Price, was published under a Berchtesgaden, Germany, date line. Mr. Price has had access frequently to Herr Hitler and Premier Benito Mussolini for interviews.

"The Czechs say they cannot hold a plebescite because such a measure is not provided for in their Constitution," The Daily Mail quoted Herr Hitler. "To me their Constitution seems to provide for one thing only, which is that 7,000,000 Czechs shall oppress 8,000,000 of minority peoples."

When asked his impression of Prime Minister Neville Chamberlain's flying visit to Berchtesgaden last Thursday, Herr Hitler, according to The Daily Mail, replied: "I am convinced of Mr. Chamberlain's sincerity and good-will."

Wants "Tumor" Removed

The newspaper said the Chancellor described the Czechoslovak-Sudeten German situation as "a tumor which has got to be ended once and for all and ended now."

"It is a tumor which is poisoning the whole European organism," he was quoted as saying. "If it were allowed to go on it would infect international relations until they broke down in fatal collapse.

"This condition has lasted for twenty years. No one can calculate what it has cost the peoples of Europe in that time.

"It was the existence of Czechoslovakia as an ally of Soviet Russia, thrust forward into the very heart of Germany, that forced me to create a great German air force. That in turn led to France and Britain increasing their own air fleets.

"I have doubled the German air fleet once already because of the situation now prevailing in Czechoslovakia. If we fail to settle the crisis now Field Marshal Goering would be asking me to order it doubled again and the British and French would redouble and so the mad race would go on.

"Do you think I like being obliged to stop with my great building and development schemes all over the country in order to send 500,000

Continued on Page Three

Poles and Hungarians Agitate for Territory

By The Associated Press.

WARSAW, Poland, Sept. 18.—The Gazeta Polska, organ of the government party, published a front page editorial today which, in effect, demanded that Czech Silesia be ceded to Poland. It declared other minority problems besides the Sudeten German issue must be adjusted in Czechoslovakia.

In Kattowice, the principal city of Silesia, a committee for the protection of Poles in Czechoslovakia posted an appeal to the population to attend a mass meeting tomorrow at which demands were to be raised that Poles in Czechoslovakia obtain the same rights as other minorities.

BUDAPEST, Sept. 18 (AP).—A demonstration against Czechoslovakia was staged tonight by 500 Hungarian Nazis who marched through the downtown districts of Budapest shouting "Down with the Czechs!" and "Down with the Trianon Treaty!"—which ceded Hungarian territory to Czechoslovakia.

ROOSEVELT URGED TO ACT IN EUROPE

Toronto Newspaper Says Only He Can Avert War—Similar Pleas Are Made in France

Special to The New York Times

TORONTO, Ont., Sept. 18.—An appeal to President Roosevelt to provide "fresh leadership" to stave off war in Europe is made in a front-page editorial to be published tomorrow in The Globe and Mail. The editorial expresses the belief that Mr. Roosevelt could forestall a conflict "without committing his people to anything."

The text of the editorial follows:

"Europe still waits in the shadows of Armageddon. The frantic efforts which British and French statesmen made over the week-end produced only hope. Their struggle reveals more clearly than ever how completely peace and the fate of tens of millions of people depend on the will of Adolf Hitler.

"That struggle suggests, too, that what is needed is not a plan but fresh leadership, free of the national and political entanglements in which the crisis has developed. There is but one man whom the world, if it could speak, would elect for the task: A man universally known for his deep humanitarianism through his concern for the ill-fed, ill-clad masses of his nation—President Franklin D. Roosevelt.

"We in Canada might be excused for seeking to thrust responsibility on him. Our similarity of interests allows us to look upon the issue from the view of North Americans. If it is in the mind of the people of the United States that they can escape physical involvement in another European conflict,

Continued on Page Six

Montreal-New York Bus Hits Parked Truck; Woman Killed, 24 Injured, Driver Jailed

Special to The New York Times.

POUGHKEEPSIE, Sept. 18.—Mrs. Margaret Craine, 58, of New York City was killed and twenty-four other persons were injured early today when a Montreal-New York bus owned by the Champlain Bus Lines, Inc., crashed into the rear of a parked truck on Route 9 about a mile north of Red Hook.

Mrs. Craine was a passenger and resided at 601 West 185th Street, New York City. Her chest was crushed and her skull fractured.

Others seriously hurt, taken to the Northern Dutchess Health Center Hospital at Rhinebeck, were:

BROWN, Mrs. EMMA, 55, of Ottawa.
DRAESKE, CECILE, of Montreal.
DRAESKE, ENA, of Ottawa.
HAMILTON, Mrs. ALICE, of 204 Manhattan Avenue, New York City.
RESNICK, Mrs. GERTRUDE, of Montreal.
SCHLEIDER, HENRY, of Montreal.

Eighteen other persons, including sixteen passengers in the bus, were treated at the hospital. Most of the passengers were asleep just before the crash.

Albert Truax, 36, of 573 West 192d Street, New York City, and Glens Falls, operator of the bus, was arrested by Sergeant William Hamblin of the State police, charged with culpable negligence in the operation of a motor vehicle resulting in death.

Arraigned before Justice of the Peace Frank Jacoby at Red Hook, Truax was remanded to Dutchess County jail in default of $5,000 bail pending further investigation.

District Attorney John R. Schwartz said that the bus crashed into the rear of a produce-loaded truck in charge of Leon J. Keel, 21, of 609 John Street, Utica. Keel and his helper, Grover C. Gaillard, also of Utica, were repairing a flat tire on the left-rear wheel. Both were injured.

"The bus driver said he didn't see the truck until he was almost on top of it," Mr. Schwartz said. "Then he turned the bus to the left, but not in time to avoid the crash. Some of the passengers of the bus told me the bus was proceeding south at a fast rate of speed."

Truax said that he left Glens Falls at 2 A. M., standard time, and the accident occurred at 4:20 A. M.

By The Associated Press.

ELKTON, Md., Sept. 18.—Nine passengers and the driver of a bus bound north over Route 40 were injured today when the bus went off the road and struck a tree near Circus Park, about three miles east of here.

The bus did not overturn, but the impact with the tree threw passengers out of the seats. Harold Slivens, 25, of Philadelphia, bus driver, the most seriously injured, had two ribs fractured.

CZECHS ASTOUNDED

Say No French Cabinet Can Agree to Such a 'Surrender'

HODZA BARS A PLEBISCITE

Premier Asserts It Would Not End Issue—War Viewed as Inevitable, but Calm Reigns

Premier Hodza's speech on the Sudeten crisis is on Page 5.

By G. E. R. GEDYE

Special Cable to The New York Times.

PRAGUE, Czechoslovakia, Monday, Sept. 19.—The terms to which the British are reported to have persuaded the French to agree to present to Czechoslovakia today are felt to represent such a betrayal of this country and such abject surrender to Nazism that the first reaction here is one of sheer incredulity.

This correspondent got into touch early today with persons who are close to government quarters to tell them that the British and French Ministers here were expected to recommend today the surrender, without even a plebiscite, of the Sudeten areas to Germany and to the restrictions of the powers of self-defense of the "rump Czechoslovakia" through cancellation of her French and Russian alliances, coupled with a guarantee of her remaining frontiers.

The story was first met with emphatic expressions of disbelief. One highly placed person said:

"It is not true. Whatever Prime Minister Chamberlain, in whom we have little confidence, recommended in the interests of the international Fascist demands, it just is not possible for any French Cabinet to agree to such a surrender of the Czechoslovak bastion to the enemy."

Prepared to Fight

Earlier the writer had obtained an expression of opinion by an official that certainly was not intended for publication, but that under the circumstances may perhaps be summarized as follows:

"For Czechoslovakia the die is cast. We have prepared and are resolved to defend our country to the very last. The silence from London is disturbing, but despite Bonnet [Foreign Minister Georges Bonnet of France], the French cannot betray us. The day for the piecemeal reduction of our powers of self-defense that the Runciman mission has practiced since its arrival is over. President Benes has always been as firm as a rock.

"We do not yield another millimeter, whatever the outside pressure. We note without great regret that not only Viscount Runciman but also his respected wife has left. We have no further obligations toward this mission. We are reduced to the elementary position of a man faced by a burglar, pistol in hand, and must fight or be robbed."

Rejection Is Held Sure

Unless this position is to be fully abandoned in the face of the reported Anglo-French decision, it would seem that the reported terms must inevitably be rejected. The alternative to rejection would seem to be an immediate revolution against President Eduard Benes and the government in view of the temper of the population generally.

So far both the President and the government are in complete ignorance of the proposed terms. Jan Masaryk, the Czech Minister to London, of late has been regularly ignored by the Chamberlain government in all its projects concerning Czechoslovakia.

The Czechoslovak press is to publish a communique from the Press Bureau today urging the public not to believe any reports suggesting an attempt to impose humiliating terms on this country, to keep calm and to give full confidence to the government, which, it asserted, will not recede from the latest declarations of President Benes and Premier Milan Hodza.

Plebiscite Idea Ruled Out

In a radio speech delivered yesterday the Premier rejected as out of the question any acceptance of a plebiscite and he called for resolution and calm.

Premier Hodza firmly voiced the nation's unalterable will to defend the State's integrity at whatever human sacrifice. He emphasized the far-reaching proofs Czechoslo-

Continued on Page Four

Czech Attitude on Partition Is Seen In Reich as Key to Peace or War

Doubt Is Expressed That Prague Will Accept Dismemberment—Hitler and Chamberlain Are Expected to Discuss the Details

By FREDERICK T. BIRCHALL

Wireless to The New York Times.

COLOGNE, Germany, Sept. 18.—In the pleasant spa of Godesberg, a few miles south of this city, the issue of peace or war over Czechoslovakia is likely to be decided before the present week is out.

The prospect is for peace, with the partition of Czechoslovakia by the consent of all concerned except herself; but the chances of a slip, upsetting what may be arranged between Prime Minister Neville Chamberlain of Britain and Chancellor Adolf Hitler, are heavy nevertheless.

There are the Czechs themselves to consider, although they will not be present at Godesberg while their future is being disposed of. The outcome now in prospect, however good it may be for peace in Europe, is very bad—practically fatal, in fact—for Czechoslovakia. But the Czechs are a stiff-necked and obstinate people, with a profound aversion to national suicide. Can they be persuaded to accept it?

Their choice has been circumscribed by events. In the minds of her powerful friends there is apparently no longer any doubt about Czechoslovakia's having to relinquish the Sudeten region, no matter how necessary to herself she may regard it.

The only question they are considering seems to be whether there shall be amputations for the Hungarians and the Poles, which must logically follow the major operation if they do not form part of it. An anesthetic operation is greatly preferred. Forcible amputation entails the risk of getting other democratic peoples stirred up and bringing in their governments. An important part of the preparations now proceeding concerns, therefore, how the Czechs are to be persuaded to line up for the surgeons.

This involves a further question: What should be done with the remains? There would be left after the amputation a smaller, strictly Czech or Czechoslovak territory, confined to Eastern Bohemia, Central Moravia and Western Slovakia. It would be shorn not only of defenses but of industrial outlets and a large part of its industries. If Czechoslovakia is to make so overwhelming a contribution to European peace, what compensation can be offered to her in return and what guarantees of future security will she have?

In other words, after the amputation, how is the helpless trunk to

Continued on Page Six

SUDETENS ATTACK CZECH BORDER POST

2 Guards Are Wounded When 100 Members of 'Free Corps' Fire on Customs House

By The Associated Press.

SELB, Germany, Sept. 18.—The Sudeten German "free corps," now numbering 10,000, early today attacked and badly damaged a Czechslovakia customs house at Neuhausen and seriously injured two Czech guards.

Neuhausen lies directly on the frontier about one and a fourth miles from Asch, Czechoslovakia, the home of Konrad Henlein, fugitive Sudeten German leader, and on the road to Behan, Germany.

Witnesses said the customs post was badly ripped by hand grenades and bullets.

Sudeten party headquarters, established here five miles from the frontier after having been routed from Eger, Czechoslovakia, put a serious face on the affair.

An authorized spokesman for Herr Henlein said the corps members ambushed two customs guards in the woods.

Troops Come to Rescue

Czechoslovak gendarmes and then troops came to the rescue, the spokesman said, and the Sudeten Germans retired, having "obtained our object, which was to announce our existence along the entire Czechoslovak border."

He declared similar forays would continue and intimated that one of their aims would be forcibly to re-establish Sudeten German party headquarters on Czech soil.

A spokesman for Herr Henlein said tonight that 10,000 Sudeten Germans had enrolled in the "Free Corps" within a few hours after the proclamation and "we expect a force of 30,000."

"Our object," he declared, "is the same as that of any legion that has to free its country. We will be like the old Irish Republican Army—everywhere and nowhere."

Henlein Makes Appeal

Asked whether it was true that the equipment came from the German Government, the spokesman said, "If we had sufficient funds we could buy anywhere we wished."

At the same time Herr Henlein, through the official German news agency, D. N. B., issued an appeal to his followers in Czechoslovakia to continue to be patient because the "hour of liberation is near."

"Sudeten Germans, you still have to bear a reign of terror of Hussite-Bolshevik criminals in Prague. With machine guns, tanks and cannon the Czech rulers are attempting to suppress freedom of the Sudeten Germans," the appeal said.

"Untold misery is the result. Yet

Continued on Page Three

MUSSOLINI BACKS HITLER'S DEMANDS

Says at Trieste That if War Involves All Europe Italy's Place Has Been Chosen

Text of Mussolini's address is printed on Page 2.

Wireless to The New York Times.

TRIESTE, Italy, Sept. 18.—"If a line-up of universal character is brought on for or against Prague, let it be known that Italy's place is already chosen."

With these words, which impressed all hearers, not only because of their import but also because of the vehemence with which they were uttered, Premier Benito Mussolini was believed today to have pledged the Italian nation and all its military resources to support Chancellor Adolf Hitler if the Czechoslovak crisis leads to a European war.

More than 100,000 citizens of Trieste, which Premier Mussolini was visiting for the first time since his accession to power, raised their voices in tumultuous approval while millions of Italians, listening to the radio broadcast, realized, perhaps for the first time, that the hour of supreme decision was at hand.

Despite the frankness with which he referred to the possibility of war Signor Mussolini, however, does not yet despair of peace. He spoke of Prime Minister Neville Chamberlain as "a flying messenger of peace," and expressed the hope that a solution of the Czechoslovak minorities problem might be reached peacefully or at least without bringing about war between nations not directly concerned.

Only in the event of a general conflict growing out of the Czechoslovak crisis would Italy, he intimated, feel called on to intervene actively in support of Germany.

Sees Quick Solution Vital

As to what the solution of the problem should be Signor Mussolini again stated what has been the official Italian view ever since Herr Hitler's Nuremberg speech last Monday, that the solution must be totalitarian and, above all, rapid because "any delay does not hasten the solution but brings on a fatal collision."

"The solution to the problem which at this moment agitates Europe has only one name: plebiscites," he went on. "Plebiscites for all nationalities that demand them, for all nationalities that were forced into what wished to be great Czechoslovakia and which today reveals its organic inconsistency."

This Italian view, he said, is dictated not only by the policy of the Rome-Berlin axis, not only by Italy's friendship for Hungary and other nations that have sections of their peoples included in "mosaic

Continued on Page Two

POWERS DRAW PLAN

Propose End of Czechs' Alliances, With New Border Guaranteed

PEOPLE WOULD BE TRADED

Ministers Hint at Four-Power Parley for Wide Settlement—Benes Attitude Crucial

By FERDINAND KUHN Jr.

Special Cable to The New York Times.

LONDON, Monday, Sept. 19.—Chancellor Hitler won the greatest diplomatic victory of his career just after last midnight when the heads of the British and French Governments agreed to support his full demands against Czechoslovakia to avoid another world war.

After thirteen hours of almost continuous discussion Prime Minister Neville Chamberlain of Britain and Premier Edouard Daladier of France instructed their respective ministers in Prague to see President Eduard Benes of Czechoslovakia this morning and "recommend" to him the following:

First—Outright surrender to Germany without a plebiscite of all predominantly German areas of the Czechoslovak Republic. This would be preceded by an exchange of populations to protect the Czech and anti-Nazi German minorities in the border areas and the Germans who now live in the interior of Czechoslovakia.

Second—Creation of a cantonal system of government transforming the remainder of Czechoslovakia into something like another Switzerland.

Third—Neutralization of Czechoslovakia's foreign policy and abandonment of her present alliances in return for a military guarantee of her new frontiers by Britain, France and possibly other great powers.

Victory for Germans

These staggering "recommendations" will be variously described in the next few days as "peaceful revision of frontiers" or as capitulation by Britain and France or as a sheer "betrayal" of the last democratic State in Germany's path toward the east. But the Germans at least can regard them as a triumphant justification of all Herr Hitler's tactics of the past three months.

Mobilization of the German Army, the press campaign against the Czechs and the disorder in the Sudeten areas have at last shaken British and French nerves to the point of trying to give Herr Hitler what he wants. The Western Powers have recoiled violently from the prospect of war, which came closer to them last week than at any time since 1914.

No doubt Britain and France will still take up arms against Herr Hitler if he chooses to invade Czechoslovakia during the coming period of negotiations. But the incentive to the use of force has been removed unless Czechoslovakia refuses to let herself be carved up at the "recommendation" of her British friend and her French ally.

Details of the Anglo-French agreement were not settled, nor will they be submitted to President Benes this morning. There is some talk of accomplishing the surrender of the Sudeten areas by means of an international commission and of urging Dr. Benes to make an economic pact with Germany, but such details can wait.

Benes's Stand Crucial

The first thing to be discovered is whether the hard-pressed Dr. Benes will accept even the principle of a territorial surrender.

If he refuses there is no telling how dangerous the present crisis may again become, in spite of all British and French efforts to settle it without war. If, on the other hand, Dr. Benes accepts in principle, Mr. Chamberlain will be able to go to Godesberg, on the Rhine, some time this week for another meeting with the German dictator.

A non-committal communiqué issued early this morning hinted that four-power negotiations for "a general settlement" in Europe might follow the Anglo-French de-

Continued on Page Three

Hitler, speaking in Vienna, announces that Germany and Austria "are one — once and forever indivisible."

Times Wide World

The goose step is introduced in Italy. *Il Duce* is seen marching at a demonstration.

The Austrians rejoice in Salzburg when Germany annexed their country.

Neville Chamberlain returns from Munich with a piece of paper which he thought would guarantee "peace in our time."

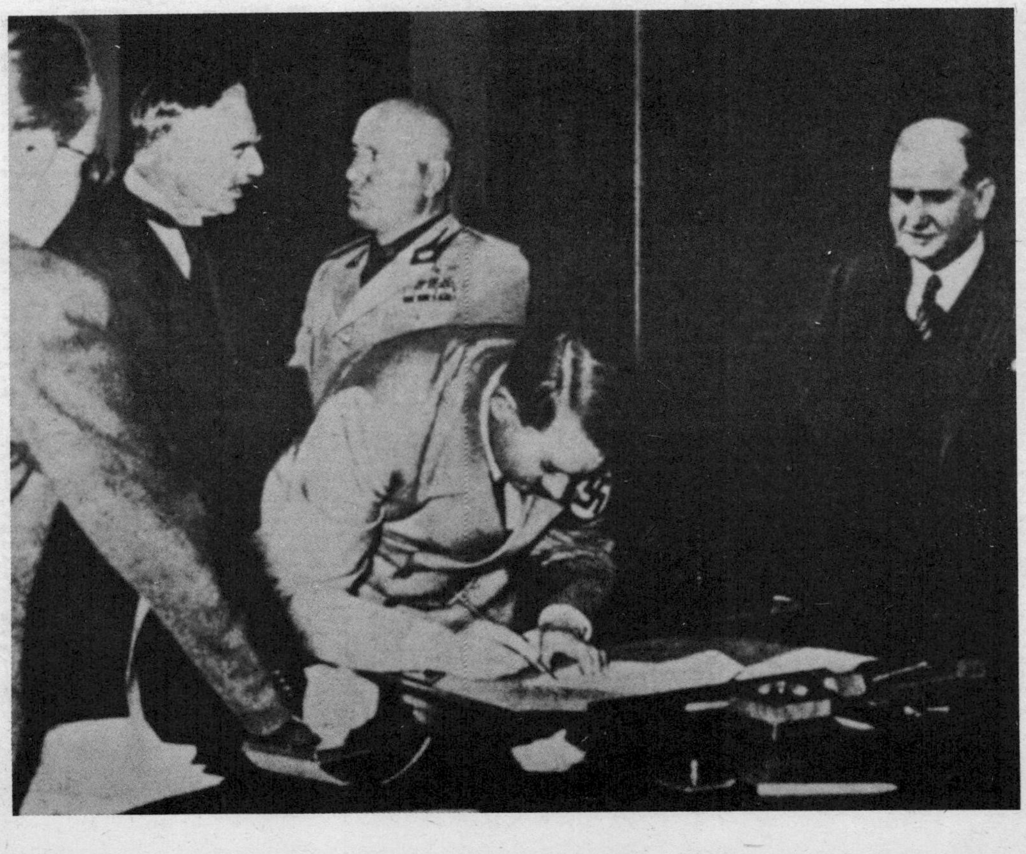

Hitler signs the Munich Pact which sealed the fate of Czechoslovakia. Behind him (from left to right) are Chamberlain, Mussolini and Daladier of France.

"All the News That's Fit to Print."

The New York Times.

LATE CITY EDITION
Rain and cooler today. Tomorrow generally fair with little change in temperature.
Temperatures Yesterday—Max., 72; Min., 56

Copyright, 1938, by The New York Times Company.

VOL. LXXXVIII...No. 29,469. Entered as Second-Class Matter, Postoffice, New York, N. Y. NEW YORK, FRIDAY, SEPTEMBER 30, 1938. PP THREE CENTS NEW YORK CITY and Vicinity | FOUR CENTS Elsewhere Except in 7th and 8th Postal Zones.

FOUR POWERS REACH A PEACEABLE AGREEMENT; GERMANS TO ENTER SUDETEN AREA TOMORROW AND WILL COMPLETE OCCUPATION IN TEN DAYS

DEWEY NOMINATED BY REPUBLICANS; ATTACKS TAMMANY

HAILED IN OVATION

Prosecutor Promises to Rid State of 'Corruption' in 'Bigger Job'

CHOICE BY ACCLAMATION

O'Brian and Corsi Nominated for Senate—A. V. McDermott for Attorney General

Mr. Dewey's acceptance, Page 14; Republican platform Page 15

By JAMES A. HAGERTY
Special to THE NEW YORK TIMES.

SARATOGA SPRINGS, Friday, Sept. 30.—Asserting that the time had come to remove the influence of the "corrupt" Tammany machine from the State government, District Attorney Thomas E. Dewey of New York County last night accepted the Republican nomination for Governor.

Received with wild enthusiasm by the delegates and alternates to the Republican State Convention, Mr. Dewey promised that the fight against organized crime would continue on a wider front than ever before if he were elected Governor. He declared that it was the duty of the State to protect its citizens from economic catastrophe, see that every worker had a job and provide necessary relief and adequate housing. He promised to discuss these and other issues in detail during the campaign.

Mr. Dewey was nominated by acclamation at the morning session yesterday, and the choice was genuinely unanimous.

At an early hour this morning the convention nominated John Lord O'Brian of Buffalo for United States Senator for the full six-year term.

The nomination of Mr. O'Brian, after a three days' search for a candidate, completed the ticket headed by Mr. Dewey. Edward Corsi of Manhattan was chosen as candidate for United States Senator for the two-year balance of the term of the late Senator Royal S. Copeland.

Other nominations were:

Lieutenant Governor—State Senator Frederic H. Bontecou of Dutchess County.

Attorney General—Colonel Arthur V. McDermott of Brooklyn.

Controller—Julius Rothstein of Utica.

Representatives at Large—Mrs. Helen Rogers of Buffalo and Richard B. Scandrett Jr. of Orange County.

Dewey Defends Decision to Run

Mr. Dewey's first words, after he had been cheered intermittently for a quarter of an hour after his entrance into the hall last evening, were:

"I accept your nomination."

This brought another storm of applause, the delegates and alternates seeing in him a candidate who had a chance to end the long series of Republican defeats in State elections and win the first Republican State campaign since the election of Nathan L. Miller.

Mr. Dewey first met the argument, advanced even by some of his friends, that he should not leave the office of District Attorney with his work unfinished. He had been told, he said, that it was too risky to venture into a State campaign and urged to play safe.

"Had I taken that advice, I should have been shirking the bigger job, the harder fight," he said. "I shall not shirk that fight."

The audience seemed to feel that in Mr. Dewey they had a fighting candidate and roared its approval.

Friends also urged him to stay as District Attorney on the assumption that he was the only man in New York City who could run a large law office, investigate rackets and prosecute crime.

"Well, the trouble with that is: It just is not true," he declared.

Points to Prosecuting Staff

Mr. Dewey added that as a candidate for District Attorney he had made a single promise, that the people would be represented by an office of competent, hard-working lawyers.

"And I specifically promised that my assistants would not be chosen by Al Marinelli, Charlie Schneider or any other of the Tammany district leaders who are now selecting my opponent at the Democratic State Convention," he continued, ringing laughter and cheers.

Mr. Dewey said that he had a staff of seventy-two energetic, high-principled lawyers who knew how

Continued on Page Fifteen

Rainstorm and Winds Due to Hit City Today

A rainstorm accompanied by fresh to strong winds, possibly reaching gale force, will strike New York some time today but there is virtually no possibility of tornado conditions similar to those which yesterday damaged Charleston, S. C., it was said at the Weather Bureau here last night.

Bureau officials said the tornado that struck Charleston was probably of "purely local origin." It resulted, however, from a low pressure area that was moving northeastward and was expected to be centered around New York today. Clearing weather is forecast for New York tomorrow.

The following additional advisory report from Washington was received last night at the local office of the Weather Bureau:

"Northeast storm warnings ordered at 9 P. M. from the Virginia Capes to Eastport, Me.; disturbance of moderate but increasing intensity central over Eastern North Carolina, moving northeastward in conjunction with area of high pressure over New England and Eastern Canada, will be attended by increasing northeast or east winds becoming strong and probably reaching gale force from Virginia Capes to the New Jersey coast tonight and north from New Jersey to Eastport on Friday."

DEMOCRATS AWAIT LEHMAN'S REPLY

Draft of Governor Dominates Convention Opening—Labor Party Alignment Sought

The Democratic keynote and Mr. Farley's speech, Page 16.

By WARREN MOSCOW
Special to THE NEW YORK TIMES.

ROCHESTER, N. Y., Sept. 29.—Governor Herbert H. Lehman, faced all day today with a relentless draft movement from the leaders of the Democratic party, failed at a conference tonight to announce his willingness to run again. Despite this, the party leaders indicated that they expected he would be nominated tomorrow to oppose Thomas E. Dewey.

Whatever hints came from the closed-mouthed group of leaders who filed from the Governor's suite at the Hotel Seneca just before midnight were to the effect that it was a question of ironing out the rest of the places on the ticket which was holding up a formal announcement, rather than a declination by the Governor.

They named State Chairman James A. Farley as the spokesman, and his only comment was that there would be another conference at 9 A. M., just five hours before the nominations are to be made on the second day of the party's State convention.

The leaders went into the night conference fully prepared to let the Governor name the rest of the ticket, revise the platform and arrange with the American Labor party for united support of the Democratic nominees.

Tactics of Persuasion

During the day they sent to him a long list of personal friends and social welfare advocates who argued that he owed it to the State to accept the nomination. They contended that Mr. Dewey would have to take a social point of view differing from that held by Mr. Lehman.

Another group concentrated on Mrs. Lehman to overcome her objections to spending four years more in Albany. She has spent ten years there, four as the wife of the Lieutenant Governor and six as the wife of the Governor, and her husband accepted a third nomination in 1936 over her protest.

The Democrats built their entire case against Mr. Dewey around Governor Lehman and the New Deal, despite the fact that the Governor and the New Deal recently have not been so closely associated as in the past.

The Governor went over the platform this afternoon with David F. Lee of Binghamton, the chairman of the resolutions committee, and made changes in a text that had already been approved by high party leaders.

Later he listened over the radio as Robert F. Wagner and James A. Farley went the limit for the New

Continued on Page Seventeen

TORNADOES KILL 26 IN CHARLESTON; HUNDREDS INJURED

Storms Strike City Without Warning, Causing Loss Estimated Up to $5,000,000

OLD LANDMARKS DAMAGED

City in Darkness, With Troops Guarding Streets—Roosevelt, Red Cross Rush Help

From a Staff Correspondent

CHARLESTON, S. C., Sept. 29.—Two tornadoes dipped down into this city at about 8:05 o'clock this morning and brought death to at least twenty-six persons, injuries to hundreds and damage to property estimated at between $2,000,000 and $5,000,000.

Before the storm passed on, the freak winds, which reached a velocity of 72 miles an hour, raged over the old parts of Charleston, damaging many of the landmarks which make this historic city one of the most colorful in the South. Dwellings were razed by the twisters which left their occupants among the dead and injured.

Power and telephone lines were cut by falling walls, trees and poles in the affected areas. Tonight, however, although the city was in darkness and with only meager communications, the residents were taking the situation without panic, cleaning up the debris and putting the streets in order.

Major Gen. Charles P. Summerall, U. S. A., retired, now president of Citadel College and head of the local chapter of the American Red Cross, announced that the Red Cross had provided cots for 1,100 persons tonight. This afforded the first official information about the number rendered homeless by the collapse of their dwellings or by damage to their homes which made them uninhabitable.

Cots Are Set Up for Homeless

Cots were placed in the Y.M.C.A., the Y.W.C.A., the Murray Vocational School, Sumter Guard Armory and the County Agricultural Building. Additional buildings were held in reserve and were being put in order for possible use by the homeless.

In arriving in Charleston by one of the Eastern Air Lines planes, this correspondent and a Times Wide World photographer were afforded a survey of the debris-laden streets in the affected areas by the pilot, J. W. Williams, who circled the city three times.

Flying southward and coming over the northwest section of the city along the Ashley River, observers first noticed a clump of dwellings which had been razed. In these lived several Negroes, who were numbered among the dead or missing. This mass of debris seemingly was separated by at least two miles from any other visible evidence of destruction.

As the plane flew south along the Battery, observers could see the damaged roof of St. Michael's Episcopal Church at Broad and Meeting Streets, the debris about St. Philip's Church, near by, both of which are pre-Revolutionary structures, and the Huguenot church.

The worst destruction was observed as the plane flew up the Cooper River. Gone was most of the roof of the City Market, a row

Continued on Page Three

4 Conferees Said to Plan A Non-Aggression Pact

By The Associated Press.

LONDON, Friday, Sept. 30.—Informed sources said today they understood Prime Minister Neville Chamberlain had obtained from Chancellor Adolf Hitler and Premier Benito Mussolini an agreement to negotiate a four-power non-aggression pact as soon as the Czechoslovak problem was solved.

He was said to have obtained the agreement, envisaging a pact with Great Britain, Italy, France and Germany as its signers, at the Munich four-power conference.

Responsible political circles said that Mr. Chamberlain, through his insistence on negotiations in the Czechoslovak crisis, had brought the three other nations to the stage where negotiation of a four-power pact was possible.

Such a settlement, it was believed, would not only lead to a non-aggression pact but might bring about withdrawal of Italian soldiers from Spain.

LITVINOFF URGES RIGHTS FOR SPAIN

Condemns Roles of Italy and Reich and Asks League to Speed Troop Withdrawals

By CLARENCE K. STREIT
Wireless to THE NEW YORK TIMES.

GENEVA, Sept. 29.—While the four statesmen talked in private at Munich today of Czechoslovakia, and perhaps Spain, Maxim M. Litvinoff of Russia, representing Europe's great outsider, talked in public to the League Assembly's political commission about the Spanish and Czechoslovak situations.

Supporting the request of Premier Juan Negrin of Loyalist Spain for a League commission to guarantee to the world that its voluntary withdrawal of non-Spanish combatants was loyally executed, the Soviet Foreign Commissar said it "cannot even bring down upon us the wrath of the present dictators of Europe, before whom some members of the League have now become accustomed to tremble."

Mr. Litvinoff, in a scathing attack on German and Italian intervention in Spain, found Spain too entitled to the benefit of the principle of self-determination.

"It is a democratic principle," he said, "if I may so, from among the watchwords of the Russian revolution of 1917 but by no means despised (when it serves their purpose) by those who at this very moment perhaps are imposing their will upon Europe's democracies.

"The Spanish people too is fighting for its right to self-determination. For its right to set up the internal regime it pleases and dispose of its natural resources and foreign trade."

He reminded the committee then

Continued on Page Ten

Economic Collapse of Czechoslovakia Seen; Reich Gets the Basic Industrial Resources

By ROBERT CROZIER LONG
Wireless to THE NEW YORK TIMES.

BERLIN, Sept. 29.—Pending the definitive fixing of Czechoslovakia's new frontiers it is impossible to assess precisely Germany's gain in raw materials and manufacturing resources.

But even assuming a conservative delimitation, Germany will acquire valuable material assets and will, indeed, leave to the shrunken republic little but the munitions works of Pilsen and Bruenn, for which, as if in irony, a State with indefensible frontiers will have no use.

Czechoslovakia is primarily an industrial country. Of nearly 15,000,000 inhabitants returned by the last occupation census eight years back, more than 5,000,000 were engaged in industry and a little fewer in agriculture. But as inner Bohemia and Moravia are largely flatlands suitable for farming, it is in the peripheral districts claimed by Germany and, it seems, by Poland that most of the industries and their raw materials are located. All this frontier district with, perhaps, the exception of a few small areas the Czechoslovak population will lose.

Czechoslovakia's industry is largely based on lignite, or brown coal. Germany will acquire this main thermic resource, which occurs in two large fields, one in the Western Egerland salient and the other some distance northeast between Komotau and Aussig. The republic's bituminous coal mines, with associated smelting and engineering plants, lie in the neighborhood of Teschen, Bohumin and Karvina, just west of the Slovak frontier, to which Polish irredentists lay claim.

Between Teschen in the extreme east and Asch in the extreme west of the Bohemian-Moravian complex lies much of the greatest part of Czechoslovakia's manufacturing industry, nearly all in German-speaking territory. The big Germanic identation south of Freiwaldau, on the Silesian frontier, contains textile and glass works, with some chemical plants.

Farther west, after a break in the German frontier population, stretches the Trautenau-Gablonz district with some bituminous coal and important textiles and paper concerns, and still farther west is the Reichenberg center with textile mills, important mechanical and light industries and automotive works.

Farther to the west are the sugar mills of Boesmisch Leipa, which draw raw material from the agricultural south, and next comes Aussig, center of the republic's most important chemical concern. Far-

Continued on Page Eight

CZECHS DEPRESSED

Expected Any Agreement to Be at the Expense of Their Nation

RUNCIMAN VIEW ASSAILED

Prague Fears Difficulties in Withdrawing Army From Its Present Border Positions

By EMIL VADNAY
Wireless to THE NEW YORK TIMES.

PRAGUE, Czechoslovakia, Sept. 29.—The Czech Government contributed its share today toward the success of the Munich conference. A communique issued this afternoon reads:

"A conference of the government Wednesday was devoted to the examination of the British note containing proposals for the step-by-step realization of the Franco-British plan, which was accepted Sept. 21 as the basis for the settlement of the Sudeten German question.

"The answer to the note takes a positive stand—with certain reservations concerning the British proposals, the gradual execution of the various transfers and the drawing of new frontiers. The answer was transmitted to the British Government before the opening of the four power conference at Munich."

The Czech Minister in Berlin, Dr. V. Mastny, left Prague by airplane this afternoon after a conference with President Eduard Benes to act as an observer in Munich. In the event Czechoslovakia should officially be invited to participate, former Premier Milan Hodza would join him as chief representative.

[In Munich early this morning it was said there was no word of Czechoslovak action on the four-power agreement, according to The Associated Press.]

Public Opinion Depressed

Public opinion here is deeply depressed. Every one complains that the agreement that will probably be reached at Munich will be almost entirely at Czechoslovakia's expense. The relief throughout the world that apparently at the last moment Prime Minister Neville Chamberlain's endeavors succeeded in saving the peace of Europe is shared by the Czechs, but the fact that they must foot the bill causes much discontent.

Viscount Runciman's letter to Mr. Chamberlain, published in the British White Paper, advocating the cession of the Sudetenland, caused indignation here and was the subject of sharp criticism. It was recalled that Lord Runciman consulted with Sudeten politicians only when he tried to test the feelings of Sudeten Germans. Whenever he visited the border zone, it was said, he seemed mostly impressed by the Henleinist demonstrations. He never paid a visit to the regions where, according to Czech contentions, he would have had the opportunity of examining the ordinary life of the population and hear the other side of the story.

President Benes and the government are complete masters of the domestic situation. It will not be easy, however, to withdraw a mobilized army from the present frontier and order them to abandon various lines of fortifications built by them at tremendous sacrifice and demobilize men who a week ago went out singing with enthusiasm to the defense of the border. Tens of thousands of anti-Nazis would have to quit their homes in the defense of which they volunteered to fight after having sent their wives and children into the interior.

These grave problems can only be solved if the people are fully convinced that there is no other possibility.

Troops March to Border

In the meantime troops are marching along roads toward the borders, streets in the cities are pitch dark and telegraph traffic remains cut as well as the long distance telephone service. Interurban telephone service has been restored today for urgent calls. Railroad travel is under the control of the army as well as is practically the whole industry of the country. The population endures various inconveniences with good humor. German propaganda is making attempts to sap morale. Rumors about the flight of Cabinet Ministers and their arrests for embezzlement of public funds have been printed and the Germans even succeeded in printing editions of faked Czech news-

Continued on Page Four

Text of 4-Power Accord

By The Associated Press.

MUNICH, Germany, Friday, Sept. 30.—The official communiqué issued at the end of the four-power conference here this morning follows:

Germany, the United Kingdom, France and Italy, taking into consideration the agreement which has already been reached in principle for cession to Germany of the Sudeten German territory, have agreed on the following terms and conditions governing the said cession and the measures consequent thereon and by this agreement they each hold themselves responsible for the steps necessary to secure its fulfillment:

I

The evacuation will begin on Oct. 1.

II

The United Kingdom, France and Italy agree that the evacuation of the territory shall be completed by Oct. 10 without any existing installations having been destroyed and that the Czechoslovak Government will be held responsible for carrying out the evacuation without damage to the said installations.

III

The conditions governing the evacuation will be laid down in detail by an international commission composed of representatives of Germany, the United Kingdom, France, Italy and Czechoslovakia.

Occupation by stages of the predominantly German territories by German troops will begin on Oct. 1. The four territories marked on the attached map will be occupied by German troops in the following order:

Territory marked No. 1 on the 1st and 2d of October; territory marked No. 2 on the 2d and 3d of October; territory marked No. 3 on the 3d, 4th and 5th of October; territory marked No. 4 on the 6th and 7th of October.

The remaining territory of preponderantly German character will be ascertained by the aforesaid international commission forthwith and be occupied by German troops by the 10th of October.

The international commission referred to in Paragraph III will determine the territories in which a plebiscite is to be held. These

Continued on Page Five

ITALIANS SHOUT JOY ON NEWS OF ACCORD

Rome's Streets Echo as People Greet Solution—Victory for Dictatorships Is Seen

By ARNALDO CORTESI
Wireless to THE NEW YORK TIMES.

ROME, Friday, Sept. 30.—The news that an agreement had been reached in Munich caused an explosion of joy in Rome and everywhere in Italy.

Italy had remained calm throughout the crisis, having always been sustained by a secret hope that the Czechoslovak question would not be made a pretext for a general conflagration, but the knowledge that the danger of war had been definitely removed was learned with intense relief and caused every one to exult.

Many streets in Rome echoed with cheers when special editions of newspapers gave the announcement for which every Italian had been waiting anxiously, that the conference in Munich had reached an understanding.

See Victory for Dictatorships

Italians believe that the solution represents a victory for the dictatorships as against the democracies.

Chancellor Adolf Hitler, they point out, obtained without war what he wanted—namely, the dismemberment of Czechoslovakia and annexation to Germany of the Sudeten territories—whereas the democracies, which were bound by treaties to protect Czechoslovakia, were unable or unwilling to take the steps necessary to safeguard the territorial integrity of their ward. Italians, therefore, feel that the balance leans in Herr Hitler's favor.

Great curiosity exists on how the questions of Hungarian and Polish minorities have been dealt with. All Italians feel sure that, owing to the presence of Premier Benito Mussolini, this problem also came up for discussion, and they will be very disappointed if he did not succeed in doing something for his protégés.

All Italians are equally sure that Signor Mussolini would not overlook the opportunity offered by his contacts with Prime Minister Neville Chamberlain of Great Britain and Premier Edouard Daladier of France to broach other subjects that, although not connected directly with the Czechoslovak problem, are of great importance to Italy.

The Spanish civil war, Italo-French and Italo-British relations and an understanding on the lines of the four-power pact of 1933 are among the subjects included under this head. It is generally conceded, however, that the success or failure of Signor Mussolini's efforts in these fields will be visible only in the subsequent development of the European situation.

Yesterday was a day of alternate

Continued on Page Five

CHAMBERLAIN HERO OF MUNICH CROWDS

People Stand Outside Hotel for Hours to Get Glimpse of Him and Cheer Him

By The Associated Press.

MUNICH, Germany, Sept. 29.—Men and women of Munich stood cheerfully for hours today for a glimpse of the 69-year-old man who started this business of man-to-man talks for peace.

That man was Britain's Prime Minister, Neville Chamberlain, a strange figure in black amid the patriotic panorama of this cradle of Nazism.

Every second man who stood and waited and cheered wore a swastika lapel button. Every second woman was of the handsome, well-turned-out sort of which Munich is proud.

They packed lawns in front of the old-fashioned Regina Palace Hotel, headquarters of the British delegation to the four-power conference. The crowd was packed eight and ten feet deep around a square formed by brown-shirted Storm Troopers before the hotel entrance.

Inside additional dozens were camped on the hotel's twin stairways and in every conceivable spot in the tiny red, white and gold lobby.

Little to See Most of Time

Most of the time there wasn't anything to see.

Every half-hour two steel-helmeted, black-coated honor guards with bayonets on shoulders snapped through the manual of arms on a hasty signal. Every now and then new black-shirted guards stamped to posts in front of the hotel's baroque marble pillars and the preceding guard goose-stepped away.

There were exciting intervals when Brownshirts filed in and out and the crowd held its breath in anticipation.

There were real cheers, like the kind one hears in an American football stadium, when the slim, black-coated Chamberlain, with a smile and a careful walk, came out. There were Hitler salutes, it is true, but many of the throng kept their hands at their sides and there was lots of noise of the kind one might hear anywhere where people are glad.

After Mr. Chamberlain had driven away in the sticky Munich afternoon for the conference of the statesmen beneath the gorgeous pagan panels of the Fuehrerhaus, the palace Herr Hitler built to glorify the birth here of the Nazi movement, the same people stood into the night, joking and waiting.

They were still waiting when the British Prime Minister came downstairs again for the third meeting with Chancellor Adolf Hitler, Premier Benito Mussolini of Italy and Premier Edouard Daladier of France. Then there was a thunder

Continued on Page Five

NAZI DEMANDS MET

Hitler Gets Almost All He Asked as Munich Conferees Agree

GUARANTEE FOR PRAGUE

Polish and Hungarian Claims Are to Be Satisfied—Vote in Doubtful Areas Provided

The war for which Europe had been feverishly preparing was averted early this morning when the leading statesmen of Britain, France, Germany and Italy, meeting in Munich, reached an agreement to allow Reich troops to occupy predominantly German portions of Czechoslovakia's Sudetenland progressively over a ten-day period beginning tomorrow. Most of Chancellor Hitler's demands were met. Prime Minister Chamberlain, whose peace efforts were finally crowned with success, received the loudest applause of Munich's crowds.

Before the start of the conference the Czech Government sent to the British Government a memorandum on its position with regard to the Anglo-French proposals. The Czechs felt that whatever agreement was reached would be at their expense and public opinion was deeply depressed.

Italians shouted their joy in Rome and elsewhere at the announcement of the Munich agreement. They regarded the solution as a victory for the dictatorships over the democracies.

Meanwhile, in Geneva, Foreign Commissar Litvinoff denounced Italian and German intervention in Spain and demanded that the principle of self-determination be recognized for the Loyalist government.

[All the above dispatches are on Page 1.]

Paris was relieved at the Munich agreement, but continued its war preparations. [Page 4.] Likewise in London, where the tension was relaxed, precautions went forward. [Page 5.]

Pope Pius broke down and sobbed as he appealed in a world radio broadcast for prayers for peace. [Page 6.] President Roosevelt urged the people of this country to offer such prayers. [Page 6.]

Powers Make Accord

By FREDERICK T. BIRCHALL
Wireless to THE NEW YORK TIMES.

MUNICH, Germany, Friday, Sept. 30.—The four-power conference to decide the fate of Czechoslovakia and avert a general European war by bringing pressure to bear on her to accept its decisions has met here, reached an agreement and adjourned.

In something less than nine hours of actual conversation time it has settled everything to the satisfaction—more or less—of the conferees.

It may be said at once that the decisions give Germany just about all she has demanded except the total extinction of Czechoslovakia as an independent State, which has never in fact been among her formulated demands, although that has been implied.

The decisions indicate, moreover, that the Poles and Hungarians will receive their shares of the spoils of Czechoslovak dismemberment.

The only change discernible from Chancellor Adolf Hitler's Godesberg memorandum is in the period allowed for the fulfillment of the demand. That has been slightly extended and beginning tomorrow the predominantly German territories are to be evacuated and occupied progressively until Oct. 10.

Property Must Be Left

The four governments—Britain, France, Germany and Italy—agree that the evacuation must be completed "without any existing installations being destroyed." This covers the German demand, previously objected to by the British, that Czech farmers in Sudeten territory must leave their farms, stock and crops intact behind them when they evacuate, without compensation for them.

The territories to be evacuated are divided into four categories designated on maps appended to the agreement. The first category will be occupied on Oct. 1 and 2, the second category on Oct. 3 and 3,

Continued on Page Five

"All the News That's Fit to Print."

The New York Times.

LATE CITY EDITION
Fair today, little change in temperatures. Tomorrow partly cloudy and warmer.
Temperatures Yesterday—Max., 56; Min., 47

VOL. LXXXVIII...No. 29,500. Entered as Second-Class Matter, Postoffice, New York, N. Y. NEW YORK, MONDAY, OCTOBER 31, 1938. PP THREE CENTS NEW YORK CITY and Vicinity | FOUR CENTS Elsewhere Except in 7th and 8th Postal Zones.

BOTH PARTIES SEE VICTORY IN FIGHT FOR GOVERNORSHIP

Democrats' Predictions of 865,000 Plurality in the City Viewed as Overoptimistic

REPUBLICAN HOPES GROW

Tremaine and Bennett Face Defeat if Lehman Wins by Only a Small Margin

By JAMES A. HAGERTY

With eight days left before the election, Democratic leaders are confident, probably overconfident, of the re-election of Governor Herbert H. Lehman, and Republican leaders are hopeful, increasingly hopeful, of the election of District Attorney Thomas E. Dewey to the Governorship.

The main interest of the party leaders has been in the contest for the Governorship and no definite estimates have been made of the probable vote for other State-wide candidates.

It is generally admitted that a close vote on the Governorship may result in defeat of Controller Morris S. Tremaine and Attorney General John J. Bennett Jr., who lack the American Labor party endorsement that their running mates on the Democratic State-wide ticket have, and the election of Julius Rothstein and Colonel Arthur V. McDermott, their Republican opponents. Informed Democratic leaders have estimated that Governor Lehman must have about 250,000 plurality to insure the re-election of Messrs. Tremaine and Bennett.

Chances of Poletti

Governor Lehman's re-election by a very small plurality, one not in excess of 100,000, might also result in the defeat of former Supreme Court Justice Charles Poletti, Democratic nominee for Lieutenant Governor, against whom a campaign has been waged by disgruntled Democrats, and the election of State Senator Frederic H. Bontecou, Republican.

There have been few guides to probable results of the contests for United States Senators and Representatives-at-Large. Because of the widespread and favorable publicity that Mr. Dewey has received from his work as a prosecutor, it has been assumed, without definite information to that effect, that he will get a larger vote than the Republican Congressional candidates, although Edward Corsi, candidate for the short Senatorial term, has undoubted strength in New York City, and John Lord O'Brian, candidate for the full Senatorial term, has general strength throughout the State.

Leaders of both major parties agree that it will take a Dewey victory to elect Mr. O'Brian, Mr. Corsi and Mrs. Helen Z. M. Rodgers and Richard B. Scandrett Jr., Republican candidates for Representatives-at-Large, and that Governor Lehman, if re-elected, will carry with him Senator Robert F. Wagner, Representative James M. Mead, candidate for the short Senatorial term, and Mrs. Caroline O'Day and Matthew J. Merritt, Democratic candidates for re-election as Representatives-at-Large.

Farley Estimates the Vote

Postmaster General James A. Farley, Democratic State chairman, bases his expectation of Governor Lehman's re-election on reports from up-State county chairmen that indicate that Mr Dewey's plurality outside of New York City will be held to 350,000 and reports of the New York City Democratic leaders that Governor Lehman's city plurality will reach 865,000.

William S. Murray, Republican State chairman, has estimated Mr. Dewey's up-State plurality at 600,000. In New York City the local Republican leaders hope to hold Governor Lehman's plurality to 450,000 or even below that figure. The Republicans have been greatly encouraged by polls that show Governor Lehman and Mr. Dewey running neck and neck.

The probability is that Mr. Farley is much too high in his estimate of Governor Lehman's plurality in New York City and Mr. Murray is too high in his estimate of Mr. Dewey's plurality up-State.

In their estimate presented to Mr. Farley, the New York City Democratic county leaders predicted 200,000 plurality for Governor Lehman in Manhattan, 210,000 in the Bronx, 340,000 in Brooklyn, 100,000 in Queens and 15,000 in Richmond. Some of these estimates were regarded as far too high, and a revised Democratic estimate is understood to be as follows:

Manhattan, 150,000; Bronx, 210,000; Brooklyn, 320,000; Queens, 75,000; Richmond, 15,000; total estimated New York City plurality for Lehman, 770,000.

Even these revised estimates seem much too high, particularly in Queens and Manhattan. The Re-

Continued on Page Five

Central American Bloc Likely at Lima Parley

Special Cable to THE NEW YORK TIMES.

SAN SALVADOR, El Salvador, Oct. 30.—A solid Central American bloc at the Pan-American Conference in Lima, Peru, in December was foreshadowed today by the newspaper Diario Nuevo. It declared that "it is very likely that the five Central American delegations will present a solid front in the deliberations and voting."

"On the initiative of our Foreign Office," the newspaper added, "negotiations of such importance have started that their success may be taken for granted. From extra-official sources it is reported that the government of Guatemala is in accord with the plan."

ROOSEVELT LETTER ENDORSES EARLE

President Says He Has Right to Speak in Local Campaigns When Name Is Misused

Special to THE NEW YORK TIMES.

PHILADELPHIA, Oct. 30.—In a letter interpreted as an endorsement of the Democratic candidates in Pennsylvania's State-wide election, President Roosevelt has assailed Republican charges that he had refrained from giving formal support to the party's nominees in this State because he was unwilling "to put his hands in that muddy water."

The letter, addressed to Michael Francis Doyle, Democratic lawyer, under date of Oct. 26 but not made public until today, endorsed the State administration of Governor Earle, the Democratic candidate for United States Senator, as one that had always been eager to help forward a program of social and economic justice.

The President reiterated that he had not been asking voters to support Democrats as against Republicans in State and local contests, but added that he had the right to speak out in cases where his name "had been misused," as in Pennsylvania.

The President's statement was hailed in Democratic circles as evidence of Mr. Roosevelt's full support of Governor Earle for the Senate and of Charles Alvin Jones for Governor. Mr. Jones's name was not mentioned in the letter, but its concluding statement was declared by Democrats to make the President's endorsement of the whole party ticket sufficiently clear.

Criticizes "Reactionaries"

This particular statement read:

"It seems to me that liberals in Pennsylvania, irrespective of party, can scarcely place their trust in the liberalism or desire for social justice of any candidates who are sponsored by such obvious reactionaries as the well-known Messrs. Annenberg, Grundy and Pew. So much for that."

His reference was to Mr. L. Annenberg, publisher of The Philadelphia Inquirer; Joseph N. Pew Jr., oil man, and Joseph R. Grundy, industrialist, all of whom are active in the Republican drive to elect Judge Arthur H. James as Governor and re-elect Senator James J. Davis.

The Roosevelt letter was regarded as the President's answer to repeated pleas made to him by the State Democratic leadership for some action on his part that would serve to convince Pennsylvania voters, who gave him a 600,000 ma-

Continued on Page Eight

MEAD STANDS PAT AS A NEW DEALER IN BID FOR SENATE

Democratic Candidate Opposes Any Except Minor Changes in Labor and Security Laws

UPHOLDS THEORY OF TVA

Wants Budget Balanced, but Not if This Means 'Misery,' He Tells The Times

Text of Representative Mead's reply is printed on Page 6.

From a Staff Correspondent

BUFFALO, N. Y., Oct. 30.—Representatives James M. Mead, Democratic candidate for the short-term Senatorial seat in the election Nov. 8, today answered in a statement the six questions on campaign issues propounded by THE NEW YORK TIMES to the four New York nominees of the two major parties in an editorial Oct. 20.

Mr. Mead's answer, in the main, was a broad and little qualified defense of the New Deal legislation which he, as a member of the House of Representatives, had a part in formulating and passing.

The principles of the Social Security and National Labor Relations Acts he defended stoutly, seeing need only for revisions to extend the benefits of the former, a correction of technical defects and a tightening of administration.

Principal opposition to the Social Security Act he saw inspired by those who fear that it will "become too important a monument to the Democratic party and to men like President Roosevelt and Senator Wagner."

Opposes "Pay-as-You-Go" Policy

He unqualifiedly opposed a revision of the law to make social security payments on a "pay-as-you-go" basis.

"Such policy," he declared, "would destroy the reserve funds which are the protection of the future in so far as future benefits are concerned. The Social Security Act is, in simple language, a form of national insurance designed to provide for the well-being of individuals who meet with economic calamities.

"I will favor strengthening amendments to the law and where weaknesses in its administration may become evident they will be met with remedial legislative action which will likewise command my support. I agree with Senator Wagner that we will never return to the way of the poormaster and to the pauper's home."

The principle of the Labor Relations Act, he said, is one that "must be recognized in a democracy such as ours" and as a union man—he was formerly a railroad worker—he unqualifiedly endorsed that, denying that the law was in any way partisan.

"I wish to make it clear, however," he continued, "that I am not blanketing under complete approval every technical phase of the law. It is new. It can almost be termed to be in its experimental stage. It requires the continued concern and legislative assistance of Congress. My eyes are open to the helpful suggestions of business and of labor in the perfection of this legislation."

The main attacks on the measure,

Continued on Page Six

La Guardia in Detroit Tells Labor to Unite Or Lose by a Fly Ball Between Green, Lewis

Special to THE NEW YORK TIMES.

DETROIT, Oct. 30.—If the fly ball of anti-labor falls between Center Fielder William Green and Right fielder John L. Lewis, then the ball game of progressivism is lost by a home run, Mayor La Guardia of New York told a cheering audience of 6,000 at a rally this afternoon.

The Mayor's imaginary world series was presented, complete with gestures, before a stageful of Democratic and Labor leaders, including Homer Martin, president of the United Automobile Workers of America, and Frank X. Martel, president of the Detroit and Wayne County Federation of Labor.

"Franklin D. Roosevelt is the pitcher and Frank Murphy, Governor of Michigan, is catcher," said Mr. La Guardia. "George Norris is at third base, La Follette at second, and I'm shortstop; Bill Green's in center and John Lewis is right field.

"Anti-labor comes to bat and Frank signals for a fast one. The pitcher shakes his head. Then he lets one go, and anti-labor knocks a fly right between Green and Lewis. Both of them shout, 'It's mine!' The ball falls between them, and anti-labor wins."

"Let's start right now healing the breaks in the ranks of labor," the Mayor urged, "so we can all start cooperating with the heads of government. I'm proud to be at a meeting where Homer Martin and Frank Martel sit side by side.

"I hope the example set by the working people of Detroit today in coming out here to endorse the cause of good government will be followed throughout the country.

"I see the dawn of peace in the labor movement right here. We should have a united front in the ranks and I think there could be no better place to begin than in Detroit right now. Labor must have security and industry must have stability, but industry cannot expect to have stability until the needs of its workers are satisfied.

"Frank Murphy and New York's Senator Wagner are real friends of labor. They will help bring peace in the family."

Attention was drawn to the presence of C. I. O. and A. F. of L. leaders together by Mr. Martel as one to the speakers.

"Homer Martin and I have been putting on this Damon and Pythias act in several places," he said. "We hope we can get through the campaign this way without getting orders from our home offices reminding us that we're supposed to be enemies."

Radio Listeners in Panic, Taking War Drama as Fact

Many Flee Homes to Escape 'Gas Raid From Mars'—Phone Calls Swamp Police at Broadcast of Wells Fantasy

A wave of mass hysteria seized thousands of radio listeners throughout the nation between 8:15 and 9:30 o'clock last night when a broadcast of a dramatization of H. G. Wells's fantasy, "The War of the Worlds," led thousands to believe that an interplanetary conflict had started with invading Martians spreading wide death and destruction in New Jersey and New York.

The broadcast, which disrupted households, interrupted religious services, created traffic jams and clogged communications systems, was made by Orson Welles, who as the radio character, "The Shadow," used to give "the creeps" to countless child listeners. This time at least a score of adults required medical treatment for shock and hysteria.

In Newark, in a single block at Heddon Terrace and Hawthorne Avenue, more than twenty families rushed out of their houses with wet handkerchiefs and towels over their faces to flee from what they believed was to be a gas raid. Some began moving household furniture.

Throughout New York families left their homes, some to flee to near-by parks. Thousands of persons called the police, newspapers and radio stations here and in other cities of the United States and Canada seeking advice on protective measures against the raids.

The program was produced by Mr. Welles and the Mercury Theatre on the Air over station WABC and the Columbia Broadcasting System's coast-to-coast network, from 8 to 9 o'clock.

The radio play, as presented, was to simulate a regular radio program with a "break-in" for the material of the play. The radio listeners, apparently, missed or did not listen to the introduction, which was: "The Columbia Broadcasting System and its affiliated stations present Orson Welles and the Mercury Theatre on the Air in 'The War of the Worlds' by H. G. Wells."

They also failed to associate the program with the newspaper listing of the program, announced as "Today: 8:00-9:00—Play: H. G. Wells's 'War of the Worlds'—WABC." They ignored three additional announcements made during the broadcast emphasizing its fictional nature

Mr. Welles opened the program with a description of the series of

Continued on Page Four

B. C. VLADECK DIES; CITY COUNCILMAN

American Labor Party Chief Here Was Manager of The Jewish Daily Forward

B. Charney Vladeck, American Labor party member of the City Council and general manager of The Jewish Daily Forward, died at Mount Sinai Hospital last night at 8:15. He was 52 years old.

Mr. Vladeck was stricken in his office of The Forward Friday night. Dr. I. W. Held of 2 East Ninety-fifth Street diagnosed his illness as coronary thrombosis and ordered him taken to the hospital that night.

Mr. Vladeck is survived by his widow, Mrs. Clara Richman Vladeck, and three children, May, William and Seymour Vladeck. His home was at 2 Horatio Street, Greenwich Village.

Fled From Russia

Soft-spoken, gray-haired and scholarly, Baruch Charney Vladeck looked neither like one who had been through the Russian revolution nor like one who would aspire to the rough-and-tumble atmosphere of New York City politics. Yet he had spent time in Czarist prisons for his revolutionary utterances and he was a member of the old Board of Aldermen years before he became leader of the labor caucus in the new City Council.

Born in the poverty-stricken town of Dookorah, Minsk, Russia, Mr. Vladeck early became identified with revolutionary groups. Radicalism was in the air then, he said many years later, and he "joined the movement as casually as a boy on the West Side might join the Democratic party—the alternatives for us were to emigrate or fight."

Mr. Vladeck's parents were Wolf and Broche Horowitz Charney and Charney was his family name. But in Russia Vladeck was as popular a name as John is here and he was called that by his early revolutionary associates. They feared that reference to his real name might be overheard by a police spy and his family might suffer.

His only formal education was that which he received at Yeshivah, where his devout Jewish parents sent him. When he was 18 years old he was caught by the police recommending "liberal books" to school children and he was sent to prison.

Barely Escaped Siberia

Mr. Vladeck's first prison term lasted eight months, but he was seized again in 1905, and this time narrowly escaped being sent to Siberia. He was saved only by the amnesties granted in that year of revolt. His father died when he was a young boy and his mother struggled hard to provide for her six children. But young Vladeck stuck to his revolutionary principles in the midst of poverty—because of that poverty—and was hounded by the Czar's police. They pierced through all his pseudonyms. Jailed again, he participated in a hunger strike until released.

In 1908, feeling he was approaching a dead end, he left Russia and landed at Ellis Island. He spent his first days in this country studying the provisions of the United States Constitution and learning American history.

In Russia Mr. Vladeck had achieved considerable reputation as

Continued on Page Fifteen

DALADIER PREPARES TO RULE SEVERELY

Calls Cabinet Meeting to Talk Over Decrees to Promote Recovery in Industry

By P. J. PHILIP

Wireless to THE NEW YORK TIMES.

PARIS, Oct. 30.—With his own Radical Socialist party solidly behind him and with the Communists definitely shaken from his ranks, Premier Edouard Daladier returned to Paris this morning. He will attempt to complete the preparation of what promises to be a long and severe series of decrees for the restoration of industry and national finance.

One of the reassuring features of the situation is that since the crisis of last month the treasury has been able to meet all demands without difficulty. There has been a steady recovery in the purchase of national bonds and there has been little or no need to use the exchange stabilization fund to defend the franc.

Just what will be contained in the decree laws is being kept a close secret. The Cabinet has been called to meet at 5 o'clock tomorrow evening for its first formal discussion of the situation.

The decrees will receive final approval at a full Ministerial Council presided over by President Albert Lebrun later in the week. Both of these meetings will be, in a sense, formal, for the work of preparing the decrees has been carefully done during the past month by Premier Daladier himself in close concert with a selected few of his Ministers.

Especially concerned are Paul Marchandeau, Minister of Finance; Raymond Patenotre, Minister of National Economy; Paul Reynaud, Minister of Justice, and Georges Bonnet, Foreign Minister. The last two are also financial experts.

To Follow Marseille Plans

There is little doubt that what will be proposed will follow the plans that were outlined by the Premier and Minister of Commerce Fernand Gentin in speeches at Marseille. These will deal principally with the restoration of production and commerce. It is France's 18,000,000,000-franc adverse trade balance that is considered a primary weakness and also one that can be most easily remedied.

There are certain to be distinguishable traces of that "steered economy" at which M. Gentin hinted in Marseille. There will also certainly be provisions for the extension of the forty-hour-week with reduced rates for overtime. It is probable that there will be some amendment to the five-day-week schedule since this, even in key industries, results in idleness at great plants for many more hours than they produce.

M. Daladier's argument is that it will be slow work to reduce the burden of national charges, which he set at 102,000,000,000 francs for the next year. The only way to make this burden seem lighter is to increase the national income from its present low figure of 220,000,000,000.

Of that 102,000,000,000, which the Treasury will have to pay out, only about 66,000,000,000 will be recovered by ordinary taxation. The rest must be raised by other means. To increase the present taxation rates would be, it is argued, to put a new handicap on business and fur-

Continued on Page Two

OUSTED JEWS FIND REFUGE IN POLAND AFTER BORDER STAY

Exiles Go to Relatives' Homes or to Camps Maintained by Distribution Committee

REVEAL CRUELTY OF TRIP

Others Sent Back to Germany Pending Parleys on Issue by the Two Governments

Wireless to THE NEW YORK TIMES.

WARSAW, Poland, Oct. 30.—The evacuation from frontier areas of thousands of Polish Jews—8,000 according to official reports and 12,000 according to an estimate by the Jewish Relief Committee—deported from Germany began today after they had been massed at frontier stations up and down the border for twenty-six hours. Their terrible ordeal is nearing its end.

Polish authorities have permitted officials of the Joint Distribution Committee to send the victims to relatives' homes in Poland or to special camps the committee maintains. The refugees spent a sleepless night in barracks, crowded station buildings or empty freight cars; many spent the night in the open in the no man's land between the frontiers.

The Joint Distribution Committee supplied food and will also pay specially reduced railway fares into the interior.

It is believed that the evacuation will last another day or so. Many refugees desire to remain in the frontier area pending the outcome of the Warsaw-Berlin negotiations, which may result in the repeal of the deportation order, enabling them to return to their homes in Germany.

Suffering Is Described

Reports from various points along the frontier describe the terrible suffering. The worst situation existed at the Zbaszym frontier station on the Paris-Berlin-Warsaw-Moscow line. There nearly 3,000 men, women and children arrived yesterday morning and were ordered by the Polish authorities to remain within sight of the station building. A large group—estimated at 1,000—was unloaded by the Germans in the open on the border between German Neu-Bentschen and Zbeszym and was not admitted into Poland until this morning. There were many children without parents in this group. They were taken from schools in Berlin and driven directly to the frontier.

Eight Polish Red Cross doctors are attending the refugees at Zbeszym. All Jewish physicians in the frontier areas have been mobilized to care for many of the sick and aged. Four deaths have been reported.

From Radzionka, near Beuthen, a birth was reported in a refugee camp. Deportees taken there by road were left in the open fields. Three hours passed before a telephone could be found to ask medical assistance for the mother.

In Chojnice, near Danzig, 1,500 arrived yesterday, most of them from Berlin. A long German train suddenly pulled into the Polish station and its German locomotive ran off before Polish authorities had time to inspect the train. The refugees were forbidden to leave the station so they remained inside a small building with many in the open until the evacuation began at noon today.

A group of fifteen children from

Continued on Page Three

Panama Limits Doctors To Citizens of Country

Special Cable to THE NEW YORK TIMES.

PANAMA, Oct. 30.—The nationalistic attitude of the National Assembly is indicated by the recent enactment of a law that prohibits the licensing of physicians and surgeons unless they are citizens of Panama.

The professions of oculist, dentist and pharmacist are also limited to citizens. Foreigners engaged in these professions at the time of the passage of the law are permitted to continue.

COL. FRANCO, FLIER, IS KILLED IN CRASH

Brother of Spanish Insurgent Chief Is Victim of a Storm Mishap Near Palma Base

By The Associated Press.

BURGOS, Spain, Oct. 30.—Lieut. Col. Ramon Franco, brother of the Insurgent Generalissimo, Francisco Franco, and former air attaché at the Spanish Embassy in Washington, was killed Friday in an airplane off Palma, Majorca, an Insurgent airplane base.

A statement issued here at Insurgent headquarters said:

"Lieut. Col. Franco left Majorca piloting a seaplane, with another plane following his. Soon after leaving the base a heavy storm arose and the second plane was obliged to return to its base.

"The bodies of Ramon Franco and three other occupants of the plane were found nine miles northwest of Cape Formentor and were conveyed to Palma, where they are lying in state in the Town Hall.

"The body of one occupant is missing. The watch of one of the officers had stopped at 5 minutes past 6, Oct. 28.

"Lieut. Col. Franco was chief of the Majorca base, which he organized."

Was Spain's Leading Aviator

Colonel Franco's fame was divided between rebellious political activities and heroic airplane flights that made him Spain's leading aviator.

He had a leading part in the revolution that resulted in the overthrow of the Spanish monarchy in 1931.

In January, 1926, he became the first to span the South Atlantic by air, flying from Cadiz, Spain, to Buenos Aires, Argentina.

Another chapter of his career in the air was his attempted flight from Spain to the United States in 1929. His plane was forced down in the vicinity of the Azores and it drifted helplessly with him for a week before he was rescued.

Colonel Franco's political theories were based on the assumption that Spain was not in need of a king as a ruler. He believed that almost any kind of capable government, except that of a monarchy, would be acceptable to the Spanish people. After the outbreak of the present war in Spain he decided that a strong dictatorship would solve the problems of the country.

In 1926, during the dictatorship of Miguel Primo de Rivera, he was thrown into jail for working against the regime. He was jailed again in 1930, this time for "breach of discipline," but he escaped to lead the famous Cuatro Vientos airdrome revolt of 500 aviation officers and enlisted men.

Under his leadership airplanes circled Madrid for two hours, raining handbills proclaiming that a successful republican movement had taken place. The field guns of the

Continued on Page Four

Japan Denies Right of Others to Interfere In 'Sacred War' to Create New East Asia

Wireless to THE NEW YORK TIMES.

TOKYO, Monday, Oct. 31.—An apparently inspired press campaign, which is becoming more violent as it proceeds, is pressing on the Japanese people the idea that Japan is now in a position to pursue her policy in East Asia independently of all other powers. Britain and France are particularly mentioned and they are bitterly attacked in editorials.

It is also asserted that even the United States is no longer in a position to suggest what Japan's conduct should be in this sphere.

The comment has given every indication of a spirit of jingoism running wild. The press, including Domei, the more than semi-official news agency, is becoming tenacious in its assertion that Japan's "sacred war" entitles the empire "to make full headway for the reconstruction of a new East Asia."

Domei asserts that the chief question before the country is how to minimize the frictions with foreign powers which will be a consequence of such a policy.

"It is believed," says the news agency, "that the United States and Britain henceforth will approach the imperial government oftener and more tenaciously than is generally supposed in connection with the Open Door in China."

It adds that Hachiro Arita, who has been made Foreign Minister, is expected to make these nations understand "the real intentions of Japan."

[The new press campaign has followed the revelation by the State Department in Washington that the United States early this month delivered a note to Japan demanding observance of the Open Door and cessation of attacks on American rights in China. The note was not published in Tokyo but its nature became known and indication was given that Japan, in a reply to be delivered soon, would insist that a new situation had been created in the Far East.]

Coincidentally with this campaign it is generallly accepted here that all clauses of the national mobilization bill will soon be invoked and implemented, which would give the government powers closely resembling those of the regimes in Berlin, Rome and Moscow. It is understood the bill will probably be utilized for the forcible colonization of Manchukuo by young Japanese.

RAIL PAY PROBLEM UP TO ROOSEVELT AT PARLEY TODAY

Head of Carrier Executives and Leader of Labor Group to Meet President

HIS WORD TO GUIDE ACTION

Eastman Urges Enactment of I. C. C. Plan—Billion-Dollar Loan Talk Discredited

Special to THE NEW YORK TIMES.

WASHINGTON, Oct. 30.—President Roosevelt will meet tomorrow at the White House with George M. Harrison, head of the Railway Labor Executives Association, and John J. Pelley, president of the Association of American Railroads, in an effort to avert a general strike of the nation's 900,000 railroad employes.

The President's emergency fact-finding board recommended yesterday that the railroads withdraw their demand for a 15 per cent wage reduction and, unless railroad management complies with the board's suggestion or some compromise is reached, the strike will follow in thirty days.

Mr. Pelley said this afternoon that there had been no meeting of railroad executives over the week-end and he had not been in consultation with his colleagues on a program to meet the board's demands.

The carriers' conference committee, headed by H. A. Enochs, which planned the railroads' case before the fact-finding board, will meet tomorrow morning.

Situation Coming to a Head

It is expected that railroad management will not act officially until after Mr. Pelley learns what the President has in mind. After his conference at the White House, it is likely that Mr. Pelley will confer with railroad executives. By that time the Enochs committee may have some recommendations of its own.

The prospect for a strike was regarded here as the most serious since 1916, when President Wilson averted what might have been a general strike by obtaining passage of the Adamson Eight-Hour Law.

It seemed to be the view of Federal transportation experts that the report of the fact-finding board had put the railroad situation right back where it was last Spring when the urgent financial needs of the carriers commanded the attention of the President and of Congress but produced no action.

Blocking of Legislation

It was recalled that the President appointed a special committee of three members of the Interstate Commerce Commission to draft an emergency plan for the railroads, and that when the committee had made its recommendations the President asked Congress to act.

But, instead of recommending a concrete railroad program to Congress, Mr. Roosevelt sent the legislators not only the plan of the I. C. C. commissioners but also a group of other recommendations.

Although the President failed to make specific recommendations, Congress seemed well on the way to adopting the plans for immediate relief proposed by the three commissioners when the railroads announced their intention of asking labor to accept a 15 per cent wage reduction. This announcement resulted in blocking remedial legislation.

Joseph B. Eastman, I. C. C. Commissioner, former Federal Coordinator of Transportation and a member of the President's railroad committee last Spring, said today he believed that one of the most important things to be done regarding the transportation problem would be to carry out the committee's proposal for creation of a Federal Transportation Authority for two years to eliminate waste and aid railroad consolidation and coordination.

Liberal Loan Policy

While Congress failed to adopt the committee's recommendations for immediate action, which consisted, in the main, of extending further government credit to the railroads, both the Reconstruction Finance Corporation and the I. C. C., since last Spring, have followed as lenient a railroad lending policy as the law permits.

The committee's recommendation that during the emergency period the RFC be empowered to make railroad loans without I. C. C. certification that the borrower did not require judicial reorganization was not acted upon by Congress.

Nevertheless the I. C. C. approved a number of such loans without the concurrence of Commissioner Charles D. Mahaffie, who said in several such cases that he believed the railroads in question required reorganization.

Indicating the extent to which the I. C. C. has cooperated to facilitate financing of railroad equip-

Continued on Page Sixteen

The Stars of Radio Comedy

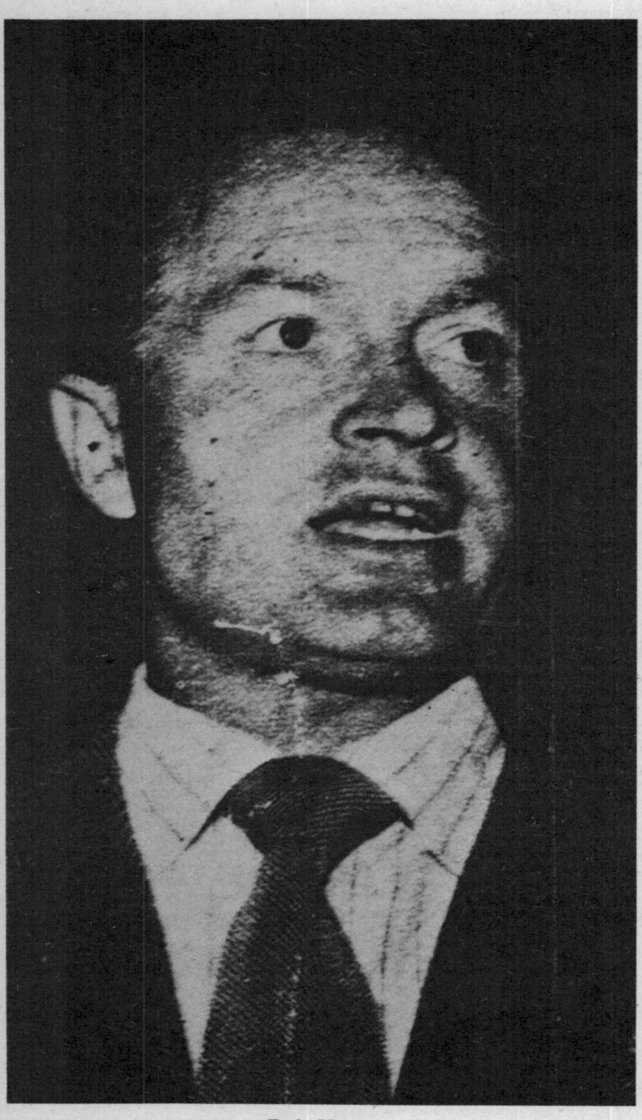

Bob Hope

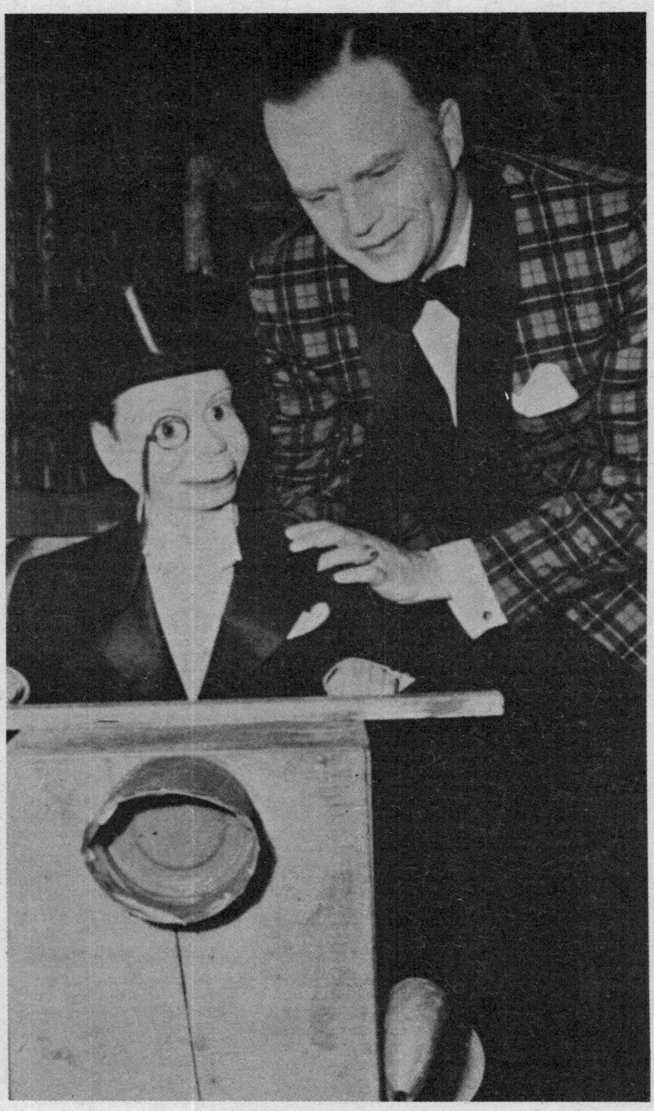

Edgar Bergen and Charlie McCarthy

Fanny Brice as "Baby Snooks"

Milton Berle

Jimmy Durante

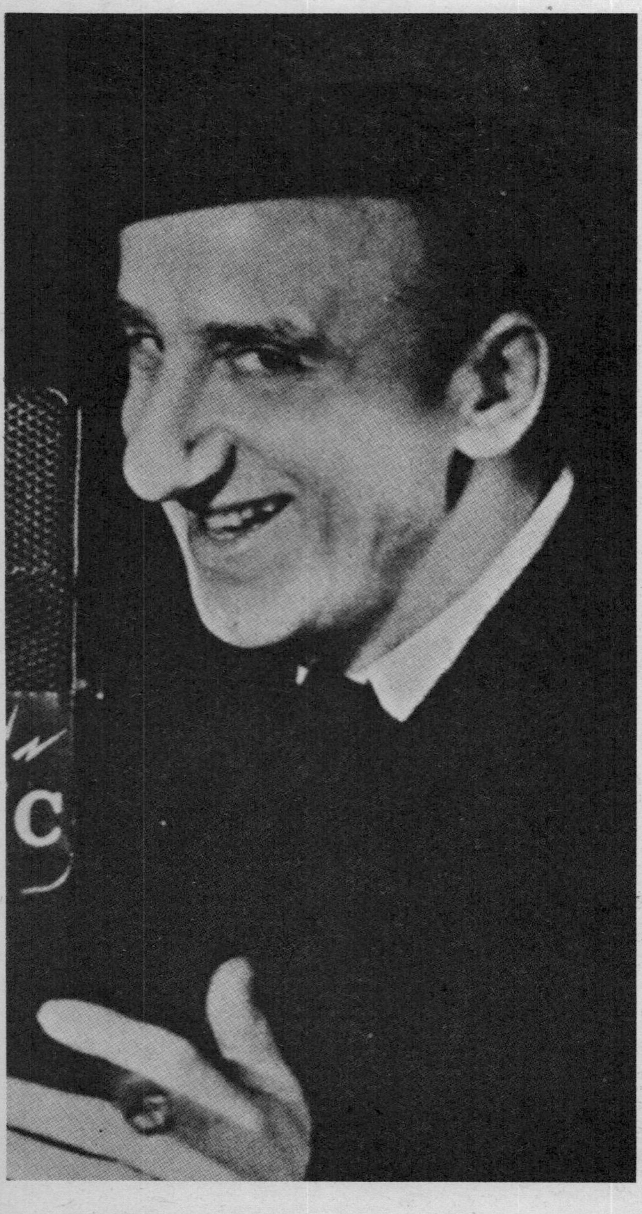

Jack Benny

Fred Allen

"All the News That's Fit to Print."

The New York Times.

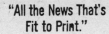

LATE CITY EDITION
Fair, slightly warmer today. Tomorrow cloudy, warmer, probably rain. Sunday much colder.
Temperatures Yesterday—Max., 60; Min., 42

VOL. LXXXVIII...No. 29,511. Entered as Second-Class Matter, Postoffice, New York, N. Y. NEW YORK, FRIDAY, NOVEMBER 11, 1938. P THREE CENTS NEW YORK CITY and Vicinity | FOUR CENTS Elsewhere Except in 7th and 8th Postal Zones.

GAIN OF 81 BY G. O. P. LEAVES HOUSE FATE TO 48 DEMOCRATS

They Can Block Any Roosevelt Measures if Minority Stands Firm in a Coalition

VAN NUYS FINALLY WINS

Contest Possible in Indiana—Gillette, Democrat, Victor on Total Iowa Count

By The Associated Press.

Republican party chieftains, flushed by their party's victories at the polls, expressed confidence last night that by combining with Democrats critical of many Roosevelt policies they could block President Roosevelt if he insisted on following a "leftward" course.

Returns from Tuesday's election showed 81 Republican votes added to that party's roster in the House and 8 in the Senate. The House figure was based on the assumption that the last contest remaining in doubt was won by the incumbent, Representative Knute Hill, Democrat, of the Fourth district in the State of Washington. With several precincts and absentee ballots still not tabulated, Mr. Hill was ahead by 630 votes.

In the Indiana Senatorial race, which was so close that it was decided only yesterday afternoon, Senator Frederick Van Nuys, Democrat, finally defeated Raymond E. Willis, Republican. In Iowa, scene of another nip-and-tuck contest, Senator Guy M. Gillette, Democrat, was the apparent winner over former Senator Lester J. Dickinson, Republican.

How the Two Parties Line Up

On this basis the Republican party held 170 seats in the House out of a total membership of 435 and 23 seats in the Senate out of a total of 96. Thus a coalition of 48 anti-New Deal Democrats with the Republican membership of the House would give such forces a majority. On some past issues many more than 48 Democrats have deserted the Administration. In the Senate the Republicans would have to pick up 26 Democratic votes to assume command.

In the light of this situation, Washington's most popular game was to speculate on what would happen when Congress meets again. To most minds the alternatives were some measure of capitulation to conservative opinion on the part of the President or two years of governmental deadlock.

A Republican member of Congress said that if the President should insist upon following an unchanged course he would be beaten badly in Congress. At the same time, should the Republicans seek to undo major New Deal legislation already enacted, the possibility of a Presidential veto, with the consequent necessity of mustering a two-thirds majority against Mr. Roosevelt in both houses, was regarded as hanging over the conservative forces.

Thus, many observers thought that the result depended upon Mr. Roosevelt's interpretation of what the election meant and his decision as to what course he would follow. According to such opinion he could seek compromise and cooperation or lay down the gauntlet and battle it out for the two years leading up to the 1940 Presidential election.

Van Nuys Ahead by 6,535

Special to The New York Times.

INDIANAPOLIS, Nov. 10.—Senator Frederick Van Nuys, Democrat, held a 6,535 vote lead tonight over his Republican opponent, Raymond E. Willis, on the final returns. The vote stood: Van Nuys, 784,155; Willis, 777,620.

Republicans were watching closely what they called an "unwarranted delay" in counting of the ballots in Terre Haute. Some possibility existed that should Mr. Van Nuys be certified as elected, the Republicans would start a contest.

Should the evidence warrant, Republicans may allege that many votes were cast illegally in Terre Haute, that legal votes were improperly counted, and that an unsuccessful challenge of 5,000 registrations should have been sustained.

Mr. Willis and Senator Van Nuys ran a see-saw race in early returns and then the Republican jumped into a 7,000 vote lead. More than half this margin was sliced abruptly by the count from forty-six of the ninety-three precincts in Vigo County (Terre Haute). Additional Terre Haute returns placed Senator Van Nuys 3,000 votes ahead, and his vote continued upward with each new report. Terre Haute citizens balloted by voting machines.

Republicans were elated over their substantial gains in the Indiana House delegation. In 1936 the lone Republican Representative Indiana sent to Washington was Charles Halleck of Rensselaer. On Tuesday the Republicans elected seven

Continued on Page Nineteen

Ickes Says Roosevelt Won in Vote; Wallace Calls It a New Deal Defeat

Former Asserts Third-Term 'Draft' May Be Necessary—AAA Head Hits Expression as Improper for a Cabinet Member

Special to The New York Times.

WASHINGTON, Nov. 10.—Secretaries Ickes and Wallace discussed the election with the press today but while they started from similar premises they arrived at different conclusions.

Mr. Ickes held that the results were an endorsement of President Roosevelt's policies, and said that the President would have been re-elected if he had been running.

Mr. Wallace accepted the results as a defeat for the New Deal and said that the outcome, displacement of Northeastern Democrats by Republicans in Congress, "would be a hard blow to agriculture."

Both agreed that depression had a good deal to do with the result, Mr. Ickes asserting that what the country had seen was "a reaching out for security," while Mr. Wallace said that the "outstanding conclusion is that people do not like business depression."

They diverged again, however, on the question of a third term for Mr. Roosevelt. Mr. Ickes said that inasmuch as the President was "the liberal leader in the country" he had long thought it might be necessary to "draft" him for a third term.

Informed of this expression, Mr. Wallace, who is believed to have presidential aspirations himself, replied:

"I think it is altogether outside the province of any Cabinet member to express an opinion on that subject."

Elaborating his "victory" views, Mr. Ickes said that "the sentiment of the people of this country is a liberal sentiment and when it has a chance to express itself, the answer will be clear and unmistakable.

"Look at New York, for example. A candidate for Governor was endorsed by the estimable New York Times because he wasn't a rubber stamp, and because he helped save our glorious institutions. And what happened? He just squeaked through and the liberals ran far ahead of him.

"This election means to me that people are interested in individual security. How many Republicans were elected on the strength of promises of support of old-age pensions, even of the Townsend plan? When people become impatient promises are made, and some successful candidates have made promises they can't deliver on."

The Secretary said the Progressive party defeat in Wisconsin was due to a division of the liberal vote in that State. Of Pennsylvania he remarked cryptically:

"They wound up the clock on primary day and it went off on the minute."

Mr. Wallace said that the people

Continued on Page Twenty

LEHMAN RENEWS FULL-TERM PLEDGE

Hopes for Cooperation by the Republicans—Budget Work Already Started

Governor Lehman, in his first general press conference since his re-election on Tuesday, reiterated yesterday his pledge to serve out his full four-year term. The Governor, at the end of that time, will have been in Albany fourteen years, four as Lieutenant Governor under Franklin D. Roosevelt, and ten as Governor.

The question of his serving a full four years which came up immediately after his reluctant acceptance of the nomination at the Rochester Democratic State Convention, was answered by him in his first campaign address, and the new pledge came yesterday in response to a question from newspaper men.

When the question was asked, the Governor, sitting back in an arm chair, smiled, and said,

"Of course I will, there is simply no question about it."

Hopes for Cooperation

Asked if he had any comment on the Republican control of both branches of the Legislature, the Governor said:

"I hope they will cooperate with me as much as possible, and expect that they will."

Later, he was asked if he had any reason for expecting cooperation, beyond the fact that the Republican-controlled Assembly, under Speaker Oswald D. Heck and Ways and Means Chairman Abbot Low Moffat had done so at the last session. The Governor answered:

"They know that whatever legislation I will suggest will be in the interest of the people and I can not conceive that they are going to oppose sound and progressive legislation."

In response to questions as to whether extensive legislative changes would be required as a result of the approval of six of the nine constitutional convention proposals at the polls, the Governor said that he believed most of the changes would be administrative in nature, such as the changes in the budget-making procedure called for in the finance article, incorporated in the omnibus proposal.

Will Suggest Legislation

Asked whether he regarded the task ahead as chiefly administrative or requiring extensive reform legislation, the Governor said:

"I regard it as requiring careful administration. I will have a legislative program to suggest and I will continue to scrutinize all bills passed by the Legislature to make sure that none of them is against the interests of the State."

He reminded his listeners that not the least important part of his tasks in Albany had been the vetoing of some 2,000 of the 7,000 bills that had been presented to him during his tenure thus far.

Asked about the election of Charles Poletti, his personal selection, as Lieutenant Governor, Mr. Lehman said that he was sure that Mr. Poletti "is going to be a great help to me and to the people of the State."

The Governor's only comment on

Continued on Page Twenty-one

BIDS INDUSTRY 'GO' IN PENNSYLVANIA

Judge James Says His Election Was Signal for Forward Movement in Business

Special to The New York Times.

PHILADELPHIA, Nov. 10.—Judge Arthur H. James, Republican Governor-elect, urged Pennsylvania industry today to start its program of rehabilitation "right now" and not wait until he took office.

"The people gave the go-ahead signal at Tuesday's election," he said. "Those industries which had threatened to leave the State if the Democratic organization elected its candidates can unpack their trunks and stay at home."

Judge James came here to confer with James F. Torrance, Republican State chairman, and started tonight for a vacation in Texas with Colonel Carl L. Estes, a newspaper publisher in that State.

In an interview, the Governor-elect, who during the campaign accused Governor Earle's "little New Deal" administration of driving industry from Pennsylvania by levying high taxes on corporations, repeated his charges and defined his own attitude toward industry.

Reports Signs of Upturn

"Although it will be regulated," he asserted, "industry must be given a little more than a breathing spell. It must be given an opportunity to be restored to its feet. We still have the potential possibilities and resources that the State always had and with an eye to the problems of the people, instead of an eye for votes, we can bring Pennsylvania back to its place as a leader in industry."

Judge James asserted that he had had "definite evidence" that confidence was returning to industry.

"Right here in Philadelphia," he added, "I have been advised by a building concern that it plans to build 300 homes at an expenditure of $1,500,000, of which 70 per cent will represent weekly payrolls."

He said that during his vacation he would not consider Cabinet appointments, but would "eat, sleep and rest and do a little fishing and hunting in between."

The plurality by which he defeated Charles A. Jones, Democratic nominee for Governor, was almost 290,000, with the count virtually complete. The plurality of Senator James J. Davis, who won re-election over Governor Earle in the Republican sweep of Pennsylvania, was just short of 400,000.

With the Republicans assured of control of the State House of Representatives by a comfortable margin, interest continued to center on the manoeuvring which is to determine whether Judge James will have support of the State Senate, as well as to put over his legislative program early next year.

Should Senator Weldon B. Heyburn of Delaware County, an Independent Republican holdover elected in 1936 on the Democratic ticket, enter the caucus of Republicans instead of Democrats on the eve of the 1939 legislative session, a deadlock would result over the election of a president pro tem of the State Senate.

If Senator Heyburn stays with the Democrats during the next

Continued on Page Nineteen

ATATURK DIES AT 58; TURKS WILL ELECT A SUCCESSOR TODAY

National Assembly Expected to Name Gen. Inonu, Former Premier, as President

NATION GOES IN MOURNING

Peaceful Transition to New Era Seen—Unity Is Stressed Under Ideal of Founder

Wireless to The New York Times.

ISTANBUL, Turkey, Nov. 10.—Kemal Ataturk, President and creator of modern Turkey, died today at Dolma Baghche Palace at the age of 58. He had survived thirteen wounds received in battle and a number of assassination attempts, but succumbed to cirrhosis of the liver.

It is expected that General Ismet Inonu, former Premier and President Ataturk's comrade-in-arms, will be chosen tomorrow morning by the Republican People's party to succeed the dictator-soldier, hero of the reborn nation.

The bulletin announcing the death of Ataturk and signed by eight doctors read:

"The President's general condition, the gravity of which was announced in a bulletin published last night, grew steadily worse. On Nov. 10, 1938, at 9:05 A. M., our great chief, in a deep coma, breathed his last."

Three minutes after his death Salih Bozuk, former aide and one of the President's closest friends, unsuccessfully attempted suicide by shooting. He was seriously wounded.

Premier Stays at Bedside

Throughout the night Ali Fethi Okyar, Ambassador to London; Ataturk's sister and his adopted daughter, Sabihi Gueukschehn Honoum, the latter a famous airwoman, remained near the bedside. The first indication of the President's death came at 11:30 A. M., when it was noticed that the flags on government buildings were at half-staff. Soon the flags of ships in the harbor were at half-mast, and gradually all shops and houses exhibited similar signs of mourning.

Later, however, the authorities requested the withdrawal of flags except those on government buildings. Although the flags were at half staff the appearance of so much color gave the impression that Istanbul was en fete. All places of public entertainment were closed and no intoxicants will be sold in Turkey until further notice.

The government's communiqué issued this morning states:

"By Ataturk's death Turkey has lost her great creator, a nation its great Chief and humanity a great son. We offer our people deepest condolences in their great loss. Our only consolation in our affliction is our attachment to his great work and our service to our dear country. We declare that before all things his immortal work is the Turkish Republic.

"Your government is at its post at this grave time through which we are passing. The great Turkish nation will, without doubt, work as one body with the government to preserve order.

"In accordance with the Consti-

Continued on Page Eighteen

BRITAIN WILL SPEND HUGE SUM TO PUSH AIR ARMING PLANS

£200,000,000 Will Go to Build Up Force Next Year—5,000 to 6,000 Planes Ordered

EDEN ASKS BIG REFORMS

Plea for Reorganization of National Life Is Viewed as a Bid for Power

By FERDINAND KUHN Jr.

Special Cable to The New York Times.

LONDON, Nov. 10.—The British Government will spend £200,000,000 on its Air Force in the next financial year, Air Minister Sir Kingsley Wood told the House of Commons today. This will be a 75 per cent increase over the budget estimate of £120,000,000 for the present financial year, which ends next March 31.

The new figure does not include a vast additional expenditure upon civilian defenses and anti-aircraft equipment, which the government has already promised without revealing the amount of money needed.

Sir Kingsley also announced that Britain's first-line air strength would be increased by 30 per cent over the present program, which provides for 2,750 first-line planes for home defense, 500 for defense of the empire and an unspecified number of reserves by March, 1940. Without giving away the secret of the reserve strength, Sir Kingsley told the House that fighting planes "now on order or to be ordered" number between five and six thousand.

Intensity Is Indicated

This was at least some indication of the intensity of the British rearmament program six weeks after Prime Minister Neville Chamberlain predicted "peace in our time" as a result of the Munich agreement.

Employment in aircraft factories, said Sir Kingsley, has jumped 15 per cent in two months and many factories are now working double shifts. He surprised the House by disclosing that 3,500 concerns were engaged on sub-contracting work for aircraft production at the present time.

The output of planes in October, he said, was 50 per cent above that in May and by next May would be three times the figure of last Spring. But he did not give a hint as to how British production or British strength at the moment compared with Germany's. Instead, he disclaimed any intention of a race with Germany, and he did not mention Earl Baldwin's famous pledge of an air force equal to that of the strongest power within striking distance of these shores.

"The more I study the matter the more difficulty I find in exactly defining or measuring parity," said Sir Kingsley.

"We cannot just take the number of aircraft one country possesses and compare it with the number in any other country. Each country has its own necessities in reference to its own particular position and responsibilities."

This was oddly like the argument used in German newspapers recently in attempting to justify a continuance of Germany's present enormous superiority over Britain in the

Continued on Page Eleven

Pearl Buck Wins Nobel Literature Prize; Third American to Get the Swedish Award

Wireless to The New York Times.

STOCKHOLM, Sweden, Nov. 10.—The Swedish Academy today awarded the 1938 Nobel prize for literature to Pearl Buck, American, author of "The Good Earth" and other novels about China.

The Academy of Science awarded the Nobel prize for physics to Professor Enrico Fermi of Rome University "for his discovery of new elementary radioactive substances produced by irradiation of neutrons" and for other research on reactions created by neutrons.

Thanks to his discovery of the great explosive power of slow neutrons, Professor Fermi and his associates have been able to produce radio-activity in most elements, including the heaviest ones. Professor Fermi, who is 37 years old, is the discoverer of chemical element 93. Educated at Pisa, Goettingen and Leyden Universities, he was at one time Professor of Physics at the University of Florence.

A member of the Italian Academy since 1929, he is a corresponding member of the Turin and Leningrad academies of science.

The Nobel chemistry prize will probably be reserved until 1939.

Pearl Buck, in private life Mrs. Richard J. Walsh, said yesterday morning, one hour after learning of her triumph, that she was taken aback with the totally unexpected honor. Speaking in the office of her publisher, John Day Company, 40 East Forty-ninth Street, she recalled her first words as follows:

"I said, 'That's ridiculous,' and I suppose a great many others will say the same thing. Did Chinese expressions of gratitude come to mind? Certainly, I thought—though probably not aloud: 'O pu sing sin' (I don't believe it), but 'kung shi-kung shi' (congratulations)."

The author of "The Good Earth" and ten other books, numerous short stories and articles since 1930 was grateful that the Nobel Prize for literature was based on the sum of a writer's work rather than any single product. In a broadcast to Sweden yesterday at noon she defined one successful book as a sign of growth and was hopeful that her development would continue.

Theodore Dreiser merited the honor, the author said over the air, continuing:

"I don't know him and he doesn't know me, but I feel diffident in accepting the award just the same."

She told of having visited Stockholm on a pleasure trip in 1932 and said she would try to be there on Dec. 10 to accept the medal, scroll and check from the hands of King Gustaf. The money will amount to between $40,000 and $50,000, it was learned.

Mrs. Buck, as she prefers to be known publicly, was dressed in a

Continued on Page Five

NAZIS SMASH, LOOT AND BURN JEWISH SHOPS AND TEMPLES UNTIL GOEBBELS CALLS HALT

All Vienna's Synagogues Attacked; Fires and Bombs Wreck 18 of 21

Jews Are Beaten, Furniture and Goods Flung From Homes and Shops — 15,000 Are Jailed During Day—20 Are Suicides

Wireless to The New York Times.

VIENNA, Nov. 10.—In a surge of revenge for the murder of a German diplomat in Paris by a young Polish Jew, all Vienna's twenty-one synagogues were attacked today and eighteen were wholly or partly destroyed by fires and bomb explosions.

Anti-Jewish activities under the direction of Storm Troopers and Nazi party members in uniform began early this morning. In the earlier stages Jews were attacked and beaten. Many Jews awaiting admittance to the British Consulate-General were arrested, and according to reliable reports others who stood in line before the United States Consulate were severely beaten and also arrested.

Apartments were raided and searched and gradually some 15,000 arrested Jews were assembled at police stations. Some were released during the day. Tonight arrests were continuing.

Many of those arrested were sent to prisons or concentration camps in buses. Mobs of raiders penetrated Jewish residences and shops, flinging furniture and merchandise from the windows and destroying wantonly.

In their panic and misery about fifty Jews, men and women, were reported to have attempted suicide; about twenty succeeded.

Scores of bombs were placed in synagogues, blowing out windows and in many cases damaging walls. Floors that had been soaked with kerosene readily caught fire.

Fire brigades were summoned to fight fires in eighteen synagogues, and the fire engines remained in their neighborhood all day. Two of the synagogues were not being used for religious purposes.

Those wholly or partly destroyed were the synagogues in Schiffamtsgasse, Steingasse, Muellnergasse, Neue Welt-Gasse, Tempelgasse, Franz Hochedlinger-Gasse, Stumpergasse, Unter Viadukt-Gasse, Huber-Gasse, Schmalzhofgasse, Siebenbrunnengasse, Kluckegasse, Turnergasse, Neudeggergasse, Palnamitengasse, Schmelzgasse, Schopenhauerstrasse and Humboldtplatz.

At 9 A. M. the first fires broke out in the Hernalser and Hietzinger synagogues. The Hietzinger synagogue, which was in Moorish style and was the largest and finest synagogue in Vienna, was gutted.

At 11:30 A. M. several explosions took place in the Second District, and a number of synagogues were

Continued on Page Two

BATISTA SEES HULL AND TOURS CAPITAL

Tells Press Cuba Will Soon Adopt a Constitution and Elect a President

Special to The New York Times.

WASHINGTON, Nov. 10.—Cuba will shortly proceed with the adoption of a permanent Constitution and the election of a constitutional President "in accordance with the principles of a free people," Colonel Fulgencio Batista, Chief of Staff of the Cuban Army and the leading figure in his country, said here today.

He arrived this morning on a visit to General Malin Craig, Chief of Staff of the United States Army. It is his first visit to this country.

Colonel Batista's statement came in response to a question at the only press interview he gave today. He said that a constitutional convention would be elected as soon as possible, probably next May. He added that the elections might be held on May 20, Cuban Independence Day.

Calls on Hull and Woodring

He paid courtesy calls on Secretary of State Cordell Hull, Secretary of War Harry H. Woodring and Assistant Secretary of War Louis Johnson and devoted the remainder of his day to sight-seeing under the guidance of Dr. Pedro Martinez Fraga, the Cuban Ambassador. Colonel Batista and Señora de Batista are staying at their embassy while they are here.

The Cuban Chief of Staff and former sergeant at Camp Columbia was in an affable and apparently pleased frame of mind today. From the time he arrived at the Union Station at noon through the rest of a tiring day he preserved a friendly and cordial demeanor toward all he saw.

Asked as to the object of his visit here, he said that it was purely a ceremonial visit in response to the invitation of General Craig. However, he said that he would be glad to discuss with interested American officials any problems the solution of which would help the two countries. He made it clear that he had not as yet been asked to take part in any such discussions. By implication, he included among the subjects he would be willing to discuss the American sugar tariff, extension of the existing trade agreement, and arrangements for mutual defense in time of threat from abroad.

General Craig met his guest at the station, and had arranged a fitting military display for him. He was accompanied by Colonel John A. Crane, head of the military attaché and foreign liaison branch of Military Intelligence, and Major Carnes Lee. Sumner Welles, Under-Secretary of State, George T. Summerlin, chief of protocol, and Ellis

Continued on Page Six

ITALY INTENSIFIES CURBS UPON JEWS

Cabinet Decrees Exclude Them From Official Employment, Limit Property Holdings

By ARNALDO CORTESI

Wireless to The New York Times.

ROME, Nov. 10.—The Italian Cabinet met again today under Premier Benito Mussolini's chairmanship and approved two important decrees in which the principles that the Fascist Grand Council laid down Oct. 6 for maintaining the "purity of the Italian race" are codified and promulgated in the form of organic laws.

These decrees closely follow the Grand Council's decisions of last month except that in a number of details they tend to increase the severity of the measures taken against the Jews.

The main points of difference between the decrees and the Grand Council's decisions are:

First, in the definition of a Jew it is added that he is a Jew who has a Jewish mother and an unknown father.

Second, Jews are required to announce that they belong to the "Jewish race" and all personal certificates and papers must mention the fact.

Third, to the disabilities to which Jews are subjected the following are added: They may not be guardians of "Aryan" minors or deficient persons; they may not own or manage industries or interests connected with the national defense, and they may not own land valued at more than 5,000 lire or houses whose taxable value exceeds 20,000 lire, whereas the Grand Council said that they were not to own more than 125 acres of land and made no mention whatever of houses.

Jews who have children not professing the Jewish religion may be deprived of the guardianship of their children if they give them instruction not attuned to the religious principles of the children or to "national ends."

Can't Employ "Aryan" Servants

Fourth, no Jew will be allowed to employ Italian "Aryans" as servants.

Fifth, the Council did not explicitly say that no Jews would be allowed to remain in the employ of the State and State organizations, though it was implicit in the declaration that no Jew could be a member of the Fascist party. The decrees, however, remove all uncertainty on this point, listing the careers closed to Jews.

Henceforth Jews will be excluded from the civil and military administrations of the State, the Fascist party and all the organizations connected with it, provincial and municipal administrations and all dependent organizations, all semi-

Continued on Page Two

BANDS ROVE CITIES

Thousands Arrested for 'Protection' as Gangs Avenge Paris Death

EXPULSIONS ARE IN VIEW

Plunderers Trail Wreckers in Berlin—Police Stand Idle —Two Deaths Reported

By OTTO D. TOLISCHUS

Wireless to The New York Times.

BERLIN, Nov. 10.—A wave of destruction, looting and incendiarism unparalleled in Germany since the Thirty Years War and in Europe generally since the Bolshevist revolution, swept over Great Germany today as National Socialist cohorts took vengeance on Jewish shops, offices and synagogues for the murder by a young Polish Jew of Ernst vom Rath, third secretary of the German Embassy in Paris.

Beginning systematically in the early morning hours in almost every town and city in the country, the wrecking, looting and burning continued all day. Huge but mostly silent crowds looked on and the police confined themselves to regulating traffic and making wholesale arrests of Jews "for their own protection."

All day the main shopping districts as well as the side streets of Berlin and innumerable other places resounded to the shattering of shop windows falling to the pavement, the dull thuds of furniture and fittings being pounded to pieces and the clamor of fire brigades rushing to burning shops and synagogues. Although shop fires were quickly extinguished, synagogue fires were merely kept from spreading to adjoining buildings.

Two Deaths Reported

As far as could be ascertained the violence was mainly confined to property. Although individuals were beaten, reports so far tell of the death of only two persons—a Jew in Polzin, Pomerania, and another in Bunzdorf.

In extent, intensity and total damage, however, the day's outbreaks exceeded even those of the 1918 revolution and by nightfall there was scarcely a Jewish shop, cafe, office or synagogue in the country that was not either wrecked, burned severely or damaged.

Thereupon Propaganda Minister Joseph Goebbels issued the following proclamation:

"The justified and understandable anger of the German people over the cowardly Jewish murder of a German diplomat in Paris found extensive expression during last night. In numerous cities and towns of the Reich retaliatory action has been undertaken against Jewish buildings and businesses.

"Now a strict request is issued to the entire population to cease immediately all further demonstrations and actions against Jewry, no matter what kind. A final answer to the Jewish assassination in Paris will be given to Jewry by way of legislation and ordinance."

What this legal action is going to be remains to be seen. It is known, however, that measures for the extensive expulsion of foreign Jews are already being prepared in the Interior Ministry, and some towns, like Munich, have ordered all Jews to leave within forty-eight hours. All Jewish organizational, cultural and publishing activity has been suspended. It is assumed that the Jews, who have now lost most of their possessions and livelihood, will either be thrown into the streets or put into ghettos and concentration camps, or impressed into labor brigades and put to work for the Third Reich, as the children of Israel were once before for the Pharaohs.

Thousands Are Arrested

In any case, all day in Berlin, as throughout the country, thousands of Jews, mostly men, were being taken from their homes and arrested—in particular prominent Jewish leaders, who in some cases, it is understood, were told they were being held as hostages for the good behavior of Jewry outside Germany.

In Breslau they were hunted out even in the homes of non-Jews where they might have been hiding.

Foreign embassies in Berlin and consulates throughout the country were besieged by frantic telephone calls and by persons, particularly weeping women and children, begging help that could not be given them. Incidentally, in Breslau the United States Consulate had to shut

Continued on Page Four

"All the News That's Fit to Print."

The New York Times.

LATE CITY EDITION
Fair and colder today. Tomorrow cloudy, warmer, probably rain.
Temperatures Yesterday—Max., 48; Min., 36

Copyright, 1938, by The New York Times Company.

VOL. LXXXVIII...No. 29,516. Entered as Second-Class Matter, Postoffice, New York, N. Y. NEW YORK, WEDNESDAY, NOVEMBER 16, 1938. P THREE CENTS NEW YORK CITY and Vicinity | FOUR CENTS Elsewhere Except in 7th and 8th Postal Zones.

ROOSEVELT CONDEMNS NAZI OUTBREAK; 'COULD SCARCELY BELIEVE' IT, HE SAYS; LONDON STUDIES JEWISH COLONIZATION

CUMMINGS TO QUIT HIS POST IN CABINET, ROOSEVELT REVEALS

Attorney General Wants to Resume Private Practice, President States

NEW DEAL CLASH RUMORED

Jackson Is Reported in Line—James Roosevelt Resigns as Father's Secretary

Special to THE NEW YORK TIMES.

WASHINGTON, Nov. 15.—President Roosevelt announced today that Homer Cummings would retire from the post of Attorney General in January. His statement, made at a press conference, was not unexpected. Reports that Mr. Cummings would leave the Cabinet have been current many times in the last two years and they have been accentuated in recent days.

President Roosevelt, in telling of the resignation of the Attorney General, said that the former chairman of the Democratic National Committee had long wished to return to private law practice.

While the President said he had not considered any successor, it is generally agreed that the new Attorney General will be Robert H. Jackson, Solicitor General.

An indication of other Cabinet changes came when the President was asked if more were contemplated. He replied that there were no other resignations and that he had no thought of filling any places. Then he paused and added: "as yet."

Reported Opposed to "Purge"

While President Roosevelt ascribed the departure of Mr. Cummings to a wish to go back to private law practice, it is common belief that that Cabinet member has not been in complete harmony with some leaders in the New Deal. His relations with Mr. Roosevelt are said to be entirely cordial, and it has even been stated that last month the Executive said Mr. Cummings would retire only over the "dead body" of the President.

But Mr. Cummings is said to have opposed the "purge" and to have held that needless antagonisms have been created by some of the President's followers.

Mr. Cummings dislikes, it is understood, the theories of a school of thought in the Department of Justice where some of the staff are demanding that the "technicalities" of the law be thrust aside in favor of the "humanities."

Although he has been a supporter of many of the Administration's proposals, and was the father of the court change bill, he has, it is asserted, not felt that he could go all the way with every ambition of the New Deal.

Roosevelt Praises Record

The President expressed regret over the resignation because, he said, the Department of Justice had accomplished very extraordinary results in the past five years under Mr. Cummings, not only in improved handling of court cases but in tackling serious problems of procedure.

This was a reference to the new system of uniform rules for Federal district courts which now has been pushed into actuality by Mr. Cummings and is regarded by lawyers as an important reform.

Mr. Roosevelt said that, growing out of public demands to cope with kidnapping and interstate crime, the country now has a system of detection and apprehension probably as good as any in the world.

Mr. Cummings made no statement. His friends, however, said that his resignation was not forced, but was of his own volition.

The 68-year-old Attorney General will, it is understood, practice law in Washington, also maintaining offices in Stamford, Conn., his legal residence.

The first intimation of Mr. Cummings's retirement came today when Stephen Early, secretary to the President, told newspaper men that Mr. Roosevelt would discuss reports of Cabinet changes at his press conference.

Mr. Cummings had returned from a golfing trip to Pinehurst and it had been assumed he had been called back to discuss judicial appointments. But his presence in the city, coupled with Mr. Early's statement, seemed to confirm recent reports that his resignation was imminent.

Solicitor General Jackson refused to discuss the possibility that he will become Attorney General.

President Roosevelt's statement that no other Cabinet retirements were expected "as yet" necessarily attracted attention, especially in view of guesses that Mr. Roper might be followed as Secretary of Commerce by Harry L. Hopkins, the WPA Administrator.

Mr. Cummings has been a striking figure in national politics for years and is described in his biog-

Continued on Page Three

First Freezing Weather Is Due Here Tonight

Automobile owners who still have no anti-freeze solution in the radiators of their cars and pedestrians who have not yet got out their overcoats are directed to the forecast of the Weather Bureau, which warns that temperatures will probably be down to freezing tonight.

The first positive sign of coming Winter was brief, light snow flurries between 9 and 9:30 P. M. over lower Manhattan.

Yesterday the mercury dropped to 36 degrees at 6:15 A. M., the lowest this Fall. The highest temperature of the day was 48 at 7:30 P. M. and the average for the preceding twenty-four hours was 42, two degrees below normal for the date. The lowest ever recorded on a Nov. 15 was 19 in 1933, and the highest 70 degrees in 1879.

Weather Bureau officials said that today would be fair and that during the early morning hours temperatures would be in the lower thirties.

MILK FIRMS CITED ON TRUST CHARGES

Chicago Health Chief, Borden, Union Named on Price-Fixing —Ice Cream Industry Hit

Special to THE NEW YORK TIMES.

CHICAGO, Nov. 15.—Thirty-four corporations, scattered from coast to coast, and sixty-three individuals, including business executives, labor leaders and important public officials, were named in two Federal indictments, made public today, on charges of violating the anti-trust laws in the milk and ice cream industries.

Returned before Judge James H. Wilkerson on Nov. 1 but suppressed until today at the request of the government, the indictments were the forerunner of what was expected to be one of the most extensive prosecutions ever undertaken under the anti-trust laws. Hundreds of government investigators have been gathering evidence for more than a year.

One indictment charges conspiracy to fix prices and control the supply of fluid milk in the Chicago area. It names as defendants fourteen corporations and forty-three individuals, including Dr. Herman N. Bundesen, nationally known president of the Chicago Board of Health, and Captain Daniel A. Gilbert, chief investigator for the Cook County State's Attorney's office.

The second indictment, naming twenty individuals and twenty corporations, charges that the defendants entered a conspiracy of nationwide proportions to restrain the sale and use of "counter freezers," with which retailers, small wholesale dealers, hospitals, schools and other institutions could make ice cream.

Various Defendants

Among the defendants in the milk indictment were such major distributors as the Borden Company and Borden-Weiland, Inc., with headquarters in New York, and the Bowman Dairy Company of Chicago. Other defendants were the Associated Milk Dealers, bargaining agency for the major distributors here; the Pure Milk Association, sales and bargaining agency for more than 12,000 member dairy farmers in Illinois, Indiana, Wisconsin and Michigan; the Milk Wagon Drivers Union and L. G. Goudie, head of Joint Council 25 of the International Brotherhood of Teamsters.

The indictment concerning the ice cream industry named the National Dairy Products Corporation, the Borden Company of New York, sixteen other ice cream manufacturing concerns and the International Association of Ice Cream Manufacturers, with about 400 members in forty-seven States.

The companies and individuals will be prosecuted under Section 1 of the Sherman Anti-Trust Law. If convicted, the defendants would be liable to prison terms up to five years and fines up to $1,000 each. However, it has been indicated that the government might be satisfied with only fines or even with a consent decree that would change the conditions complained of. In the latter case, there might be no sentence of any kind.

The defendants had three days to post bond of $1,000 each. District Attorney Michael L. Igoe said he expected all to be arraigned in about three weeks and a date set for trial.

He anticipated an early trial, but said that was largely in the hands of special prosecutors sent here to gather evidence of the alleged milk conspiracy.

Dr. Bundesen, who was the first to appear at the Federal Court House after the indictments were handed up, asked and received from Mayor Edward J. Kelly a leave of absence to fight the case. In granting the request, Mayor Kelly praised Dr. Bundesen as an "efficient health officer."

Dr. Bundesen, who was accompanied to the Federal Court House

Continued on Page Nineteen

LEHMAN ORDERS INQUIRY BY COURT INTO ALBANY VOTE

Designates Justice M'Crate for Special Session to Sift Fraud Allegations

CHARGES MADE BY DEWEY

Governor's Grand Jury Call for Dec. 12 Covers Election Cases of the County

Special to THE NEW YORK TIMES.

ALBANY, N. Y., Nov. 15.—Governor Lehman directed the appointment today of a special term of Supreme Court and a special grand jury to investigate alleged violations of the Election Law in Albany County.

Acting at the request of Attorney General John J. Bennett Jr., he named Supreme Court Justice John MacCrate of Brooklyn, a Republican, to County Court House in the term which will be convened on Dec. 12.

Mr. Lehman's action came less than a week after Senator Thomas C. Desmond, Republican, of Newburgh, announced that he would seek a legislative investigation of the campaign charges of Thomas E. Dewey that thousands of persons had registered illegally for the election in Albany.

Albany County was the only one outside New York City to give Mr. Lehman a majority over Mr. Dewey.

Just before leaving here with Mrs. Lehman for the West Coast on a two-week vacation the Governor, without comment, gave out copies of his executive order and Mr. Bennett's letter requesting it.

Wide Scope Provided

The Governor's order required that the special session should continue "so long as it may be necessary for the purpose of inquiry, trial and/or judgment which may be made, held, conducted or given concerning or relating to any and all alleged violations of the Election Law and the elective franchise section of the Penal Law in Albany County."

Mr. Bennett's letter explained that his assistants, who set up a special bureau to investigate alleged voting frauds, had evidence ready to present to the grand jury in more than 200 cases of false registration and other violations of the Election Law. This volume of work, he said, would seriously interfere with the regular grand jury.

The Attorney General added that presentation of the cases and conduct of any trials which might ensue would be handled by his regular staff.

THE EXECUTIVE ORDER

The text of the Governor's order follows:

"It appearing to my satisfaction that the public interest requires it;

"Therefore in accordance with the statute in such case made and provided, I do hereby appoint an extraordinary special and trial term of the Supreme Court to be held in and for the County of Albany, at the County Court House in the county of Albany, city of Albany, on the 12th day of December, 1938, at 10 o'clock in the forenoon of that day, and to continue so long as it may be necessary, for the purpose of inquiry, trial and/or judgment which may be made, held, conducted or given thereat concerning or relating to any and all alleged violations of the election law

Continued on Page Two

CROP ACREAGE CUT FOR 1939 AAA PLAN; WHEAT TOTAL LOW

Wallace Sets 275,000,000 Out of 365,000,000 as Limit for Benefits

$712,000,000 IS AVAILABLE

Wheat Goal Off 15,000,000 Acres Because of Surplus—Payment Rates Fixed

By The Associated Press.

WASHINGTON, Nov. 15.—American farmers must plant no more than 275,000,000 of their 365,000,000 cultivated acres to cotton, corn, wheat, tobacco, rice and other soil-depleting crops next year if they are to obtain $712,000,000 in subsidy payments authorized by Congress.

Secretary Wallace established this national planting goal today for the 1939 program under the Agricultural Adjustment Act, designed to prevent accumulation of crop surpluses. This year's goal was about 282,500,000 acres.

The Secretary said 275,000,000 acres should produce sufficient crops to supply the nation's domestic requirements and "all possible export markets" and provide an adequate reserve.

The 1939 goal will be divided among various crops and then apportioned to States and allotted to farmers. Growers may comply with, or ignore, their allotments, but in order to be eligible for maximum subsidy payments they must comply. In addition, they must plant land diverted from soil-depleting crops to those classed as soil-building, such as clover, alfalfa, other legumes and pasture crops.

Wheat, Cotton Acreages Affected

Except for wheat, peanuts and certain types of tobacco, the planting goals for major crops will be about the same as this year. The wheat goal was established at 55,000,000 acres, compared with 62,500,000 acres the past year. The large reduction was made because of this year's surplus-producing crop, harvested from a seeded acreage of 80,000,000.

The cotton goal was fixed at between 27,000,000 and 29,000,000 acres, compared with a normal cotton acreage of about 40,000,000. There is a near-record surplus of cotton.

Slight increases in the acreage goals for peanuts and flue-cured tobacco were established.

The department's planting program may be supplemented by marketing regulations under which growers will be assessed penalty taxes if they sell in excess of individual quotas. Cotton, tobacco and rice growers will vote Dec. 10 on a proposal to invoke these regulations. They must be approved by two-thirds of those voting before they can be established. Burley and dark-type tobacco growers will ballot Dec. 17.

From the $712,000,000 in subsidy funds two classes of benefits will be paid, $500,000,000 for soil conservation and $212,000,000 for price adjustments.

Payment Rates on Crops

The minima for soil conservation payment rates will be as follows:

Cotton, 2 cents a pound; corn, 9 cents a bushel; wheat, 17 cents a bushel; rice, 10 cents a hundredweight; flue-cured and burley to-

Continued on Page Fourteen

Lindbergh Said to Plan to Move to Berlin Because of Reich's Aviation Research Fame

Wireless to THE NEW YORK TIMES.

BERLIN, Nov. 15.—According to information from German aviation and American diplomatic quarters, Colonel Charles A. Lindbergh is contemplating transferring his residence from his French island—Illiec, off the coast of Brittany—to Germany and Mrs. Lindbergh is now looking for a furnished apartment in Berlin.

The reason for this reported new transfer of residence is not revealed, but it is assumed that Colonel Lindbergh plans to continue his aviation and other scientific studies in collaboration with German scientific circles.

It is known that Colonel Lindbergh was very favorably impressed with Germany on his recent visit, during which he was well received by the highest German authorities, especially Field Marshal Hermann Goering, and was finally decorated by Chancellor Adolf Hitler with the Service Cross of the Order of the German Eagle with Star—the second highest decoration in Germany.

But the Germans were also favorably impressed by Colonel Lindbergh, especially with his inquiring mind, which was equally interested in city planning and workmen's welfare work and in aviation, and they liked his obvious admiration for the vast scope of German activity.

He prolonged his visit a week beyond his original plans, wherefore it would not surprise German quarters if he desired to settle in Germany either permanently or for some time.

BERLIN, Nov. 15 (AP).—Colonel Charles A. Lindbergh was described today by German friends as finding the Reich such a center for scientific aviation research that he wished to spend the Winter in Berlin, provided he could get suitable living quarters. With this in view he left his plane here when he departed from Berlin Oct. 29.

Ever since then officials of the German air force have been seeking to find accommodations for Colonel Lindbergh and his family.

The Colonel's German friends were particularly anxious to find a house with a garden for him so his two small sons might have a place to play. The big Nazi building program has resulted in the clearing of entire streets and a shortage of suitable dwellings for the moment.

Friends said that the recent abandonment of many Jewish homes might make available apartments for rent.

WOULD AID 700,000

Plan Before Chamberlain Calls for Removing All Jews From Reich

KENNEDY SHARES IN TALKS

Refugees Would Be Helped by U. S.—British Disillusion Over 'Appeasement' Is Spreading

By FERDINAND KUHN Jr.

Special Cable to THE NEW YORK TIMES.

LONDON, Nov. 15.—Prime Minister Neville Chamberlain had before him tonight concrete proposals for the large-scale emigration and resettlement of German Jews under the auspices of Britain, the United States and possibly other interested nations.

The plan was an outcome of another meeting at 10 Downing Street between Joseph P. Kennedy, the United States Ambassador, and the three British Ministers who are trying to grapple with the German Jewish problem—Mr. Chamberlain, Viscount Halifax, the Foreign Secretary, and Malcolm MacDonald, the Dominions and Colonial Secretary. Although details are not yet known, it is understood that the scheme was conceived on a vast scale, with the object of rescuing all the 700,000 Jews in Germany.

It would require enormous financial contributions by private citizens in the United States, Britain and other countries and by the governments as well. It would entail a direct approach to Germany by the British and United States Governments for cooperation and—in spite of recent events—for some financial help in getting the Jews away from Germany.

Finally, it would entail the use of thinly settled colonial areas that are fit for Jewish colonization and that could be developed by the same kind of intensive pioneering effort already so successful on a smaller scale in Palestine.

Northern Rhodesia Cited

What those areas will be can be only conjectured as yet. No single colony could absorb all the hundreds of thousands who now need new homes, but each of a number of colonies could take thousands of settlers if money and agricultural training were available. One example is Northern Rhodesia, where there are only 400 Europeans; another is British Guiana, where the highland areas are said to be healthful and suitable for development.

The British dominions are understood to be willing to receive and train several thousand Jews each for agricultural work—all, that is, except South Africa, which is understood to have refused to admit any more Jewish settlers.

Unexpected help reached Mr. Chamberlain today from Premier Hendryk Colijn of The Netherlands, who proposed "collective relief" for the German Jews by the governments of Britain, France, Switzerland, Belgium, Denmark and The Netherlands. Coming from a small country bordering on Germany, the appeal aroused admiration here.

It is hoped that The Netherlands will be willing not only to rain several thousand refugees in temporary camps, as Premier Colijn offered, but also to allow parts of her rich colonial empire to be used for Jewish settlers.

More Proposals Are Made

Meanwhile, British opinion continued to move with Mr. Chamberlain's along the lines of "deeds, not words," in dealing with the German Jewish tragedy.

Sir Evelyn Wrench, founder of the English-Speaking Union and the Overseas League, suggested in The Times of London today that thousands of Jewish boys between the ages of 14 and 18 years should be prepared in training centers in Britain for subsequent emigration to the dominions.

Another proposal now under consideration is the free admittance of all German Jewish "orphan" children into Britain on the understanding that Jewish organizations here would provide for them in suitable homes. These children would include those whose fathers are dead or in concentration camps.

An appeal for "further large amounts running into the millions" was issued tonight by the British Council for German Jewry, which appeared to be fully cognizant of the gigantic effort that would be needed in the coming months. A Jewish deputation led

Continued on Page Nine

France and Reich Near an Accord; Nazis Would Get Free Hand in East

Paris in Exchange Would Receive Guarantee of Rhineland Border—Basis Reached for Joint Renunciation of Resort to War

By The Associated Press.

PARIS, Nov. 15.—France prepared today to arrange a bargain with Chancellor Hitler that would, in effect, give Germany a free hand in Eastern Europe.

In return France would demand a Nazi guarantee of her Rhineland frontier.

An official spokesman said a preliminary basis had been reached for a joint renunciation of war to insure peaceful cooperation between the traditional enemies, substituting conference tables for war in any future disputes.

It was expected the accord would parallel closely the agreement Herr Hitler and Prime Minister Neville Chamberlain signed at Munich Sept. 30 expressing the desire of their peoples never to fight one another again.

Following that general line, it was forecast the German-French agreement would have these results:

1. If another crisis, such as that over Czechoslovakia's Sudeten regions, should arise France would be pledged to settle her part by conference negotiations, as was done at Munich.

2. Germany, therefore, would be free to pursue her own policies in Eastern Europe without fear of trouble on her western frontier, provided she did not threaten or attempt to attack France either by armed force or propaganda.

Informed sources said negotiations for such a post-Munich agreement were spurred when Herr Hitler shelved at least temporarily the old German imperial policy of westward expansion and of attempting to challenge Britain as a sea power.

Instead he concentrated on another equally well-established policy of spreading German influence eastward to the Black Sea and beyond. During the Czechoslovak crisis Herr Hitler announced Germany did not want Alsace-Lorraine, the provinces France won in the World War, a factor making settlement between the two powers easier.

France was represented by these sources as being willing to abandon thus her twenty-year policy of ringing the Reich with French allies, a policy that received a shattering blow at Munich when France agreed to the dismemberment of her Czechoslovak ally.

It was indicated France was ready now to carry through an accord with Germany in much the same manner as she came to a close agreement with Britain for protection against any possible aggression by Germany in Western Europe.

While French and German diplomats were working out their accord, members of the colonial com-

Continued on Page Six

STATEMENT SHARP

Language Is as Strong as a President Ever Used to a Friendly Nation

OPINION 'DEEPLY SHOCKED'

President Stresses the Word 'Technically' in Terming Wilson's Return No Recall

By BERTRAM D. HULEN

Special to THE NEW YORK TIMES.

WASHINGTON, Nov. 15.—President Roosevelt voiced the condemnation of the American people and their government of Germany's attacks on the Jews today in one of the most vigorous statements that it was possible to make in protest of the events of the past few days.

In a statement that he read at his press conference Mr. Roosevelt denounced the attacks in language as sharp as had ever been employed by a President against the course of a foreign government with which the United States had friendly diplomatic relations.

"I myself could scarcely believe that such things could occur in a twentieth-century civilization," he declared.

It was difficult to conceive of a more forceful expression of this country's displeasure short of severing diplomatic relations. It followed by less than twenty-four hours the summoning from Berlin of Hugh R. Wilson, the United States Ambassador, for the technically phrased purpose of report and consultation here, but for the actual purpose of a dramatically framed method of protest, calculated to be more drastic than any diplomatic note could be.

STATEMENT OF PRESIDENT

The President's statement follows:

The news of the past few days from Germany has deeply shocked public opinion in the United States. Such news from any part of the world would inevitably produce a similar profound reaction among American people in every part of the nation.

I myself could scarcely believe that such things could occur in a twentieth-century civilization.

With a view to gaining a first-hand picture of the situation in Germany I asked the Secretary of State to order our Ambassador in Berlin to return at once for report and consultation.

Because of its unusual character and its vigor the statement immediately posed the question of what would be the reaction of Chancellor Hitler. As to this, President Roosevelt did not appear to be worried.

Instead, after concluding his discussion of the German situation, he turned in response to questions to national defense and made it known that he was discussing adequate measures in collaboration with the twenty other American republics and Canada for defense of this continent—North, Central and South America—against any threat of attack from another continent.

Weighed Attack Thoroughly

The denunciation of Germany was uttered only after thorough consideration. The more than 200 correspondents who crowded the President's office knew it was to be made, for they had had advance notice that he would speak his mind on the subject.

As they entered his office, they found Mr. Roosevelt in high good humor. He leaned back in his chair, puffed at a cigarette from a long holder and exchanged bantering remarks with the front row of correspondents until all had entered. Then he disposed of a few incidental questions that were hastily asked in the realization that otherwise they would be lost in a discussion of more serious matters.

But the President was eager to get to the main business and in a moment he picked up a sheet of paper and announced that he had just finished dictating a statement he had to make on Germany.

He then read it to the correspondents, quoting each sentence rapidly, but pausing once to gaze toward the ceiling, blow a ring of smoke and transpose a sentence from his original draft that he had originally dictated when it was read.

Departing from custom that governs the White House press conferences, he announced as a prelim-

Continued on Page Six

ROOSEVELT TO ARM FOR ALL AMERICAS

Any Overseas Aggressor Gets Warning That Solidarity Is Rule on This Hemisphere

Special to THE NEW YORK TIMES.

WASHINGTON, Nov. 15.—President Roosevelt, conceding frankly the possibility of attempts at foreign aggression in the Western Hemisphere, proclaimed the continental solidarity of all the Americas today and this nation's determination to expand its defenses to the extent required to repel any threat of invasion from any country beyond the seas.

During his press conference Mr. Roosevelt said that the nations of the Western Hemisphere, including North, South and Central America, were as one in their determination to guard their sovereignties against outside aggression.

To this end, the President indicated, it was one of the primary objectives of the Administration's national defense program to make the entire continent impregnable from the air. The possibility of such an attack, he pointed out, was infinitely closer than it had been as recently as five years ago because of the trend of world events and scientific contributions to methods of warfare. It was the business of this nation to prepare for such an eventuality.

President Names No Aggressors

No nation or group of nations was referred to in his discussion of defense plans. In answer to direct questions as to possible sources of aggression, he told the correspondents to read the newspapers of the last five years, thereby leaving the implication that he was thinking of Germany and the ascendancy of Adolf Hitler during the period mentioned.

The President himself chose the topics of discussion. A few minutes before conceding for the first time that some foreign powers might have imperialistic designs on the American Continent, he had referred to the news of the last few days from Germany as having shocked public opinion in the United States. Mr. Roosevelt explained that he had anticipated a request for comment.

Several hours before the conference, White House reporters had been told that Mr. Roosevelt would have something to say on the subject of defense. They were also told that the President probably also would discuss the modernization and expansion of the military and naval establishments, which have been under discussion for several months.

Thus he was quickly asked about the status of defense plans in view

Continued on Page Six

WILSON TO DEPART FROM REICH TODAY

U. S. Envoy Bids Ribbentrop Farewell—Germans Insist His Trip Is 'Normal'

By OTTO D. TOLISCHUS

Wireless to THE NEW YORK TIMES.

BERLIN, Nov. 15.—As a result of Secretary of State Cordell Hull's published instructions to Hugh R. Wilson, the United States Ambassador, to go to Washington for report and consultation in view of the relations between the United States and Germany, Mr. Wilson announced today a change in his original vacation plans and will now leave Berlin tomorrow and sail on the liner Manhattan from Havre Thursday.

Today the Ambassador called on Foreign Minister Joachim von Ribbentrop to say farewell and inform him officially of the order for consultation, while at the same time the Foreign Office received the customary note that Prentiss Gilbert would be Chargé d'Affaires.

The conversation between Herr von Ribbentrop and Mr. Wilson lasted for about twenty minutes.

It is assumed that they went over the points that have beclouded German-American relations, including the anti-Jewish drive, which has not only wrecked American-owned property and imposed disabilities on Americans regarded as contrary to the German-American treaty of friendship and consular relations, but by increasing the stream of Jewish émigrés and refugees will also create a serious international problem.

Trip Held "Perfectly Normal"

On the other hand, it was emphasized in both Embassy and German official quarters that the Ambassador's farewell call on Herr von Ribbentrop preceding his lengthy absence was entirely customary and there was nothing unusual about it. Foreign Office spokesmen especially characterized Mr. Wilson's trip to headquarters as "perfectly normal and without any sensational import."

The German press further underlines this view by denouncing the "brazen attack of the international well-poisoners to draw the strangest conclusions from the Ambassador's homeward trip."

The press declares that Mr. Wilson's earlier is merely beginning a little earlier a trip that he had planned since Summer but had postponed because of the recent European crisis, and the advance of his date of departure is explained by Mr. Hull's desire to consult him before leaving Nov. 25 for the Pan American Conference in Lima, Peru.

Despite this, there is some very interesting speculation both in Ger-

Continued on Page Eight

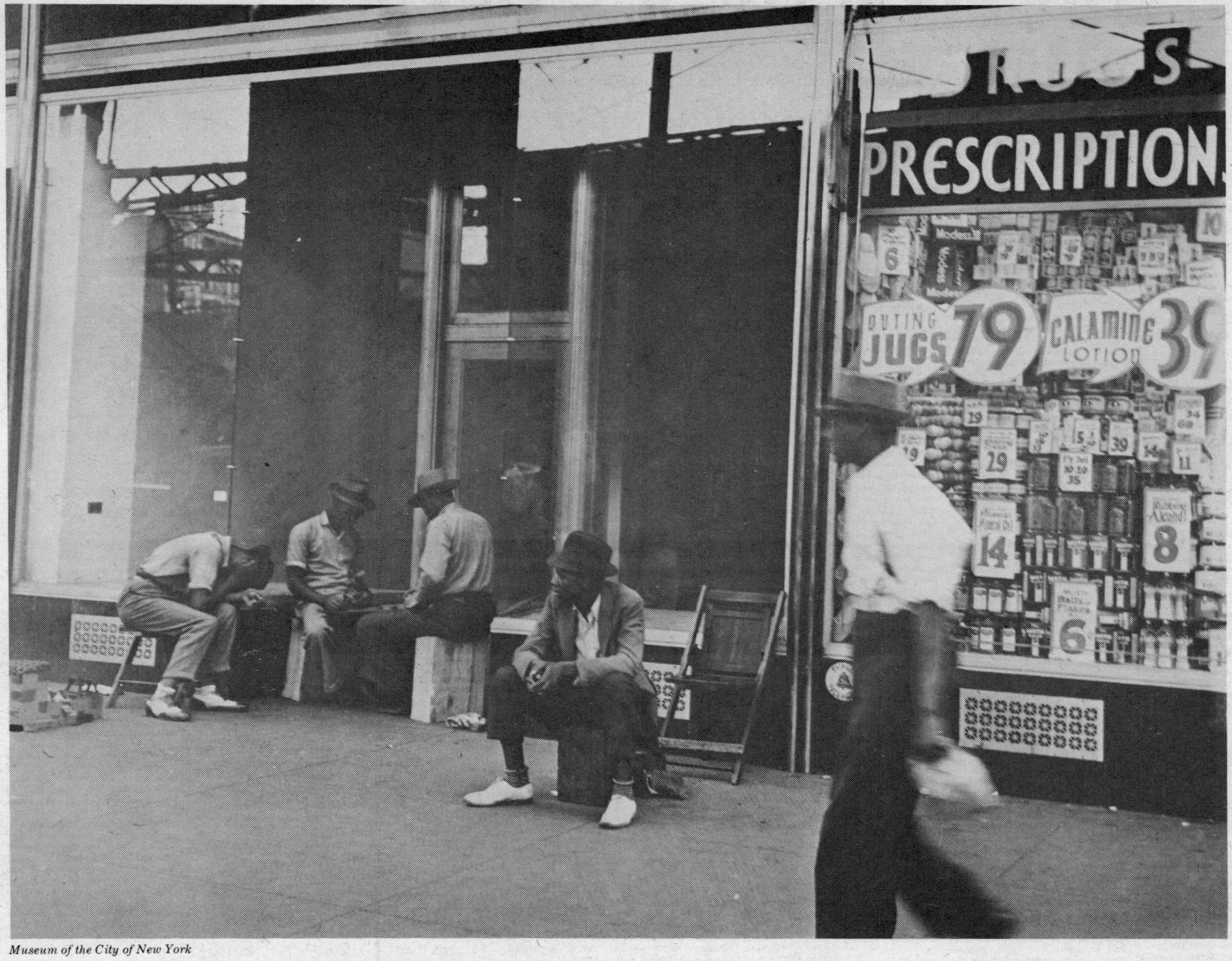

Museum of the City of New York

The unemployed in the streets of Harlem.

Building a public school in Harlem, a Federal Public Works Administration construction project.

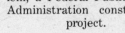

Museum of the City of New York

"All the News That's Fit to Print."

The New York Times.

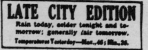

LATE CITY EDITION
Rain today, colder tonight and tomorrow; generally fair tomorrow.
Temperatures Yesterday—Max., 46; Min., 26.

Copyright, 1939, by The New York Times Company.

VOL. LXXXVIII...No. 29,567. Entered as Second-Class Matter, Postoffice, New York, N. Y. NEW YORK, FRIDAY, JANUARY 6, 1939. P THREE CENTS NEW YORK CITY and Vicinity | FOUR CENTS Elsewhere Except in 7th and 8th Postal Zones.

ROOSEVELT OFFERS $9,000,000,000 BUDGET, WITH NEW RECORD TOTALS FOR DEFENSE; ALSO ASKS $875,000,000 FOR RELIEF NOW

LOYALISTS LAUNCH A DRIVE TO RELIEVE PRESSURE ON SEGRE

Report a Rapid Advance in Estremadura Near Mine Center in Southern Spain

CATALAN KEY TOWNS FALL

Rebels Get Borjas Blancas and Artesa de Segre, but Heavy Fighting Goes On

By HERBERT L. MATTHEWS
Wireless to THE NEW YORK TIMES.

BARCELONA, Spain, Jan. 5.—The Loyalist army of the Madrid zone today launched its long-awaited offensive, timed to coincide with the effect of the loss of Borjas Blancas and Artesa de Segre in Catalonia. Tonight's Barcelona War Ministry communiqué gives the following brief account of the action, which it is hoped will in time relieve the pressure on Catalonia as the Ebro drive relieved pressure on the east coast last March.

"In an offensive action begun this morning in the sector of Valsequillo [on the Estremadura front near the south central mining area], Spanish soldiers broke the enemy front, making a deep advance which was continuing victoriously at the time of drawing up this communiqué. All resistance is being rolled back. Among the materials captured, an account of which is being drawn up, is a complete battery of 10.5 centimeter Vickers cannon. The number of prisoners is very high."

Blow Falls At a Weak Spot

[The Government attack in Southwestern Spain hit the Insurgents on one of their weakest fronts, from which it had been reported General Franco had withdrawn large numbers of troops for the offensive against Catalonia, The Associated Press reported from Hendaye, France.

[Madrid and Valencia reports said that the entire Noria chain of mountains had been captured and that the railroad line from Cabeza del Buey, 140 miles southwest of Madrid, to Belmez had been cut. Insurgent resistance in the Noria mountains had collapsed, the Government reported, when militiamen captured Papuido after six hours of hand-to-hand fighting.

[A dispatch to The Associated Press from Valencia said seven Insurgent warships, including the cruisers Canarias and Almirante Cervera, were reported steaming up the east coast, presumably to support the Insurgent land campaign with bombardments from the sea.]

Much depends on the success or failure of this new move in the civil war. However, there is no means of telling yet whether this is the Government's main drive or how large it is going to be, for complete secrecy is being maintained. The Loyalists feel it has come at the psychological moment, for they believe Generalissimo Francisco Franco's troops have to a large extent used themselves up in their Segre offensive.

While bitter fighting continued near Borjas Blancas and Artesa de Segre today, the Loyalists announced, they straightened their lines by retiring to positions that had been fortified in the first few days of the Rebel offensive.

Saw Borjas Blancas Fighting

After first spending some time at Tarragona today to check the gradual destruction of what once was one of the greatest cities of the ancient Roman Empire, this correspondent drove up the Lerida highway beyond Vinaixa [about twenty-five miles northwest in a straight line and more than forty miles by road]. There, from a dominating position we could watch Borjas Blancas [about eight miles away] and much of the disputed territory.

The roads and towns along it are bombed daily, sometimes three or four times a day. Tarragona, however, is apparently left to planes from the Majorca base.

General Enrique Lister's resistance against General Franco's Italian army corps in front of Borjas Blancas for eleven days is spoken of here as one of the outstanding feats of the war. The Insurgents' Moroccan corps also is believed to have paid very heavily for its advance on Artesa de Segre.

For twenty-four hours General Lister's primary objective, aside from inflicting as many casualties as possible, has been to protect the withdrawal of his right [northern] wing to the Urgel Canal. All material and men, we were assured, are coming through safely, since there are many roads in that district and there is no possibility of cutting off any units. Most of the withdrawals are effected at night.

We were close enough to the line to see everything occurring in orderly fashion. There had been heavy artillery fire as we drove up,

Continued on Page Seven

Frankfurter Is Nominated As Supreme Court Justice

Choice of Harvard Professor Is Praised—Dean C. E. Clark of Yale Law Named Appeals Judge—Pope Goes to TVA

Special to THE NEW YORK TIMES.

WASHINGTON, Jan. 5.—Felix Frankfurter, Professor of Law at Harvard University and confidential adviser of President Roosevelt, received from the President today appointment as Associate Justice of the Supreme Court to fill the vacancy created by the death of Justice Cardozo.

Immediate reaction as expressed both in the Senate, which must confirm Mr. Frankfurter's appointment, and by many persons of prominence in outside fields, indicated that this was one of the most popular appointments ever made by the President. While a few Senators declined to comment, confirmation was expected to await only necessary formalities of Senate procedure.

The appointment was not as much a surprise as the timing of it. There was a general assumption that Mr. Frankfurter would receive a place on the Supreme Court some day but there had been indications that this appointment, for geographical reasons, would go to a Western judge.

Coincident with the naming of Mr. Frankfurter President Roosevelt nominated Professor Charles E. Clark, dean of the Yale Law School, to a vacancy on the Court of Appeals in the Second Circuit, which includes New York.

Mr. Clark, incidentally, was the only law dean who appeared in Washington to testify publicly in favor of the bill for the enlargement of the Supreme Court.

The President appointed James P. Pope, former Senator, defeated in the Idaho primaries last Fall when he ran for renomination on a New Deal platform, as a member of the board of directors of the Tennessee Valley Authority. Mr. Pope will succeed Arthur E. Morgan, former chairman, dismissed by the President, serving the unexpired part of a nine-year term dated from May, 1933.

Mr. Frankfurter will sit for a while on the Supreme Court bench beside his fellow Bostonian, Louis D. Brandeis. It is considered possible, however, that Justice Brandeis, now 82 years old, may retire soon to devote his time to the welfare of persecuted Jews.

The appointment of Mr. Frankfurter, who recommended legal assistants for Herbert Hoover before the election of President Roosevelt—he sent Thomas Corcoran to Washington to serve under the Republican President—aroused favorable comment among both proponents and opponents of the President in the fight waged by Mr. Roosevelt in 1937 to change the

Continued on Page Eleven

FIREBUG SUSPECT SEIZED AS FOUR DIE

Accused of Setting Uptown Tenement Blaze, Then Phoning News 'Tip' to a Paper

An unemployed elevator operator, with a checkered police record and a reputation as an amateur tipster, was arrested yesterday afternoon on suspicion of murder for causing the deaths of three women and a man in a spectacular rooming-house fire at 210 West 103d Street shortly before dawn yesterday.

The prisoner is Joseph Malone, 27 years old, of 829 Amsterdam Avenue, who was picked up in front of the blazing five-story old-law tenement while watching the police and firemen rescuing the tenants trapped between two separate fires, one on the ground floor and another on the third.

A familiar figure in the neighborhood and a friend of one of the victims, Malone is said to have admitted to the police that he was in the hallway of the building at the time the fire started, and that his first act was to telephone the news to The Bronx Home News, which conducts a weekly "news tip" contest, with small cash prizes awarded to winners. Although Malone denied setting the fires, the authorities found his story unsatisfactory and he was booked at West 100th Street station under a statute that charges murder where deaths result from an incendiary fire.

Victims of the Fire

The victims of the fire were:

Mrs. Georgette Daugnault, 65, who lived with her son, Robert, 24, on the fifth floor of the building.

Mrs. Anna Le Clair, 52, a third-floor tenant, whose husband suffered slight burns on the face.

Harry Arges, 20, and his wife, Beckie, 18, who lived on the fourth floor.

Scores of other tenants, including several children and two cripples, narrowly escaped being trapped in the fire as the flames, which started in a burning baby carriage on the ground floor, blocked the exit that way, and another fire spread from a discarded Christmas tree on the third floor, preventing egress to the roof.

Radio patrolmen assisted the firemen in making rescues from the fire-escapes and from an eighty-five-foot aerial ladder. The flames lighted the neighborhood for blocks around and hundreds of persons gathered in the streets to watch the fire, which was not entirely under control until nearly 6 A. M.

Mayor Sees Law to Blame

Mayor La Guardia laid the tragedy to a "violation of the law." Addressing the housing committee of the Charity Organization Society at its luncheon at the Hotel Waldorf-Astoria yesterday afternoon, he urged banking institutions that had opposed the Prior Lien Law, recently declared unconstitutional by the Court of Appeals, to join with the city in petitioning the court to reconsider its ruling.

"In this instance," said the Mayor, holding up newspaper headlines of the fire to his audience, "fire-retarding had not been applied and

Continued on Page Two

BRITAIN ASKS HELP FOR SAGGING POUND

Calls on Banks and Bullion Mart to Reimpose Unofficial Embargo on Speculation

Special Cable to THE NEW YORK TIMES.

LONDON, Jan. 5.—The government through the Bank of England today called for the aid of the banks and the bullion market in an effort to ease the continued pressure on sterling by reimposing the system of unofficial embargoes that operated successfully from the financial crisis in the Summer of 1935 until last May.

Under this system the banks and the bullion market refrain from carrying out for customers "undesirable" foreign exchange transactions, refrain from transactions in forward gold and do not facilitate advances against gold.

This move in the banking sphere was foreshadowed by the recent tightening up of restrictions on capital issues and transactions involving the transfer of capital abroad and by the slow but steady drain on sterling that has continued with but slight interruption since mid-July.

In an attempt to check this flow the Exchange Equalization Fund had lost £146,000,000 of gold up to the middle of September and has lost an appreciable amount since. But this did not prevent sterling from falling from $4.85¾ at the beginning of July to $4.63½ tonight.

Bar Gold Declines

Bar gold declined 4d today to 150s 1d from yesterday's all-time record high. It is difficult to estimate the extent of either the forward business in gold or the advances against metal, but the short position thereby created in sterling is known to be appreciable.

Cooperation by the authorities in New York, Paris and other centers will be expected as during the last period of the embargoes, and this is necessary particularly in the case of London branches of foreign banks. The position of these banks is easier when instructions to the managers carry the approval of the respective governments.

"The necessity for these defensive measures for sterling never has been more apparent," says The Times of London in an editorial, "for the fresh outbreak of Continental pessimism toward sterling has come at a moment when, for particular reasons, a weakness of sterling is more than ever undesirable. On one hand the combination of European political anxiety, which has been driving European funds to New York for almost six months, and the revival of domestic confidence in France, which has caused the withdrawal of French funds from London to Paris, has provided fertile soil for spreading pessimistic talk regarding sterling's prospects.

"At the same time a weakness of sterling in terms of the dollar might at the present juncture have unfortunate consequences. It goes without saying that a sharp fall in sterling so soon after the conclusion of the Anglo-American trade agreement would be regrettable in itself."

Further weakness in sterling, it is held, would also strengthen the case of the "school of thought in Paris which favors abandonment of the

Continued on Page Five

ROOSEVELT OPENS FIGHT ON DIES FUND, WASHINGTON HEARS

Urges Aides to Block Inquiry but Is Told It Cannot Be Done, Says Report

FOR HELP TO LA FOLLETTE

Would Have His Committee 'Blanket' Other Hearing, According to Rumor

Special to THE NEW YORK TIMES.

WASHINGTON, Jan. 5.—President Roosevelt has asked his Congressional leaders to block the request of Representative Dies for $150,000 to continue his investigation of un-American activities for two more years, it was reported today. The report states that he was told in response that it could not be done.

According to the same report, the President then suggested that more funds be granted to the Senate's Civil Liberties Committee so that it could blanket the Dies investigation. To this suggestion he got the reply that the Senate was not inclined to give this committee, headed by Senator La Follette, another cent.

Mr. Roosevelt and Secretaries Ickes and Perkins have been sharply critical of the Dies Committee, and Mr. Dies in return has repeatedly assailed the two Cabinet officers and complained that the President's criticisms came from "misinformation."

The Congressional leaders told the President, it is asserted, that returning members report the investigation has attracted widespread interest and approval throughout the country and that they feel it would be politically dangerous for them to vote against the Texas Democrat's proposal to continue it.

Dies Claims Wide Backing

Mr. Dies today voiced the same opinion. He said that a careful check of members at the recent Democratic caucus had brought almost unanimous expressions of approval for going on two years more.

Some members, the chairman said, reported that the only pledges they made in their campaigns were that they would vote for such continuance. Many, he added, wanted approval of his resolution as soon as possible so they would be relieved of the job of answering letters urging such action.

Mr. Dies already has offered a resolution reconstituting the committee as it now stands, with the exception of replacing one member, former Representative Mosier, who was defeated.

To meet administration criticism, he added, he has voiced willingness to have a New Dealer named to this vacant post "so that no charges of political bias can be raised against us."

The original committee, now legally dissolved, had two New Deal members, who criticized the way the inquiry was conducted.

Both were unable to attend more than a few sessions, being busy seeking re-election. Mr. Dies won primary renomination and had no further opposition and so conducted the inquiry practically single-handed.

The chairman said today he had

Continued on Page Eleven

WPA COST AMAZES

Sum Till July 1 Is Third Above Forecasts—Move for Paring Begun

TO DEFER CONTROL ISSUE

President's Plea for No Hasty Changes Is Likely to Put Battle Over to Spring

Text of President's message on relief is printed on Page 14.

By TURNER CATLEDGE
Special to THE NEW YORK TIMES.

WASHINGTON, Jan. 5.—To a Congress already rumbling with complaints against government spending and politics in unemployment relief, President Roosevelt today sent a request for a supplemental appropriation of $875,000,000 with which to carry the Works Progress Administration from Feb. 1 to July 1, the beginning of the new fiscal year.

The amount was at least one-third more than the highest figure hitherto mentioned seriously by any authority outside of the White House.

Although the President did not say as much in the special message, Treasury authorities explained that only $750,000,000 of the amount would be used this fiscal year and that the remaining $125,000,000 would be kept as a cushion against unforeseen emergencies and for commitments beyond June 30.

Rolls Would Be Tapered

The purpose now, according to the President, is to employ 3,000,000 workers on relief projects during February and March and a diminishing number, beginning in April, which would drop to 2,700,000 in June.

Figures published today by the WPA showed a total enrollment of 3,112,322 as of Dec. 24, with a net decline of 62,711 from the previous week.

The extent of the President's request confounded those Congressional leaders who had hoped to hold the additional relief expense for the current year to around $500,000,000.

The President also intimated that he was ready to resist any attempt at this time to change fundamentally the system of relief distribution, regardless of the desires of Congress to return to itself the full measure of the appropriating power or of the agitation for drastic alterations to take the question out of politics.

He requested specifically that consideration of these matters be put off until the policies for the fiscal year 1940 are before Congress for study two months hence.

From the first reactions it was

Continued on Page Fourteen

Machine That Talks and Sings Has Tryout; Electrical Voder Will Speak at Fair Here

By LAWRENCE E. DAVIES
Special to THE NEW YORK TIMES.

PHILADELPHIA, Jan. 5.—Using for raw materials buzzing and hissing sounds produced by two vacuum tubes, the Voder, hailed as the first machine in the world to create speech, made its first public appearance today before an audience of scientists at the Franklin Institute.

With the aid of a dexterous operator who, by means of organ-like keys and a foot pedal, mixed the sounds and controlled the shading in the manner of the human voice, the electrical device exercised its "vocal cords," first by making the individual vowel sounds, then talking in monosyllables and finally, to the amazement of the applauding hearers, speaking in complete sentences. A slight "electrical accent" was observable.

Developed as an exhibit of the Bell Telephone Laboratories for the New York and San Francisco World's Fair, the Voder, so named by combining letters from the words "voice operation demonstrator," was able with ease to transform itself vocally into a man, woman or child. Without much apparent effort by the operator, it exhibited a repertoire which included also the lowing of cattle, bleating of sheep, grunting of pigs and rat-a-tat of the woodpecker.

According to the laboratory workers who built the machine wholly with apparatus used in every-day telephone service, with the exception of the keys, the Voder can do practically anything the human voice can do, from producing the lowest pitch of eighty or ninety cycles to overtones up to almost 10,000 cycles.

It also can sing. The research experts have not seriously considered, however, the matter of developing it into a prima donna capable of attracting the notice of Edward Johnson, manager of the Metropolitan Opera.

It takes a year or more to train an operator to handle the keys and controls enabling Voder to reproduce anything from a Bronx cheer to an oratorical peroration. To develop into a passably good singer would require an operator with a strong sense of musical tones and values.

Mrs. Helen Harper of Jamaica, L. I., one of twenty-four telephone operators chosen from more than 300 applicants to make synthetic speech at the World's Fairs, took her place at the keyboard at the demonstration, while S. S. A. Watkins of the Bell Laboratories posed as "the man with the microphone" to attract the Fair crowds.

Addressing Voder, Mr. Watkins asked it to "take the vowel 'e' and

Continued on Page Ten

Berlin Sees Blow to Trade Hopes In President's Hint of Sanctions

Message Hampers Schacht-Norman Talks Over Release of Jews and Export Drive—Britain and France Expected to Follow Us

By OTTO D. TOLISCHUS
Wireless to THE NEW YORK TIMES.

BERLIN, Jan. 5.—President Roosevelt's message to Congress, which German quarters interpret as a threat of at least economic sanctions against the authoritarian States, cast a dark cloud today over the conferences between Dr. Hjalmar Schacht, president of the Reichsbank, and Montagu Norman, governor of the Bank of England. The German press had anticipated these conferences yesterday with bright hopes for closer economic cooperation between Germany and Britain.

Mr. Norman arrived this morning on a "strictly private visit" to act as godfather to Dr. Schacht's third grandchild, who was christened Norman, at Dr. Schacht's Dahlem villa. Mr. Norman will remain until tomorrow night, when he will leave with Dr. Schacht to attend a meeting of the Bank for International Settlements at Basle, Switzerland.

So far as is known, Mr. Norman did not see and is not scheduled to see any other member of the German Government. But Dr. Schacht, it is understood, visited Chancellor Adolf Hitler at the Berghof Monday, where, presumably, he ascertained the Chancellor's attitude toward such Anglo-German cooperation generally and more particularly toward the Schacht plan for combining Jewish emigration from Germany with expansion of German exports and replenishing Germany's foreign exchange reserves.

Official quarters, of course, maintained complete silence on the subject and trend of the discussions. But informed circles surmised that the topics originally scheduled for discussion included Jewish emigration, export promotion, interstate "cartelization" among export industries, especially Germany's, Britain's and possibly the United States's foreign debts and—an outside chance—currency "alignment."

German hopes have been fed on, first, Germany's need for additional exports; secondly, the apparent willingness of the Evian committee and the powers behind it to consider raising an international loan for putting into effect the Schacht plan for Jewish emigration and export promotion; and, thirdly, the encouraging comment in the Brit-

Continued on Page Four

MUSSOLINI REBUFFS ROOSEVELT ON JEWS

Rejects Plan to Open Ethiopia as Haven—Suggests Russia, Brazil or U. S. Itself

Wireless to THE NEW YORK TIMES.

ROME, Jan. 5.—Premier Mussolini has flatly turned down a proposal by President Roosevelt for throwing Ethiopia open to Jewish immigrants from Italy and other European countries, it was learned today. The proposal had been submitted by United States Ambassador William Phillips Tuesday.

Not only did Premier Mussolini refuse to discuss the question but he also refused to take the matter up with Chancellor Hitler of Germany with a view to exploring the feasibility of the President's plan.

The message that Mr. Phillips delivered consisted merely of a letter from President Roosevelt, who asked the Italian Premier to give the best possible consideration to the proposal, which Mr. Phillips was empowered to submit and discuss in behalf of the President himself. The letter was delivered to Count Galeazzo Ciano, Italian Foreign Minister, soon after the Ambassador's return from the United States, and was a result of the series of conferences that took place in Georgia among the President, Mr. Phillips and Hugh R. Wilson, Ambassador to Germany.

Count Ciano arranged a meeting with Signor Mussolini for Tuesday afternoon and himself attended.

Not a Detailed Plan

The American proposal itself, as explained orally by Mr. Phillips, did not contain a specific solution, but merely submitted certain suggestions, leaving the means to carry them out to Signor Mussolini's discretion. It was purposely phrased vaguely so as to offer an elastic basis of discussion.

In substance the proposal was that Premier Mussolini allow both Italian and foreign Jews—particularly those in Germany, hit by recent drastic measures—to settle in Ethiopia. It urged Signor Mussolini to use his personal influence with Herr Hitler, who, because of the close relations existing between the dictators, would certainly give the plan careful consideration if it were supported by his axis partner.

Mr. Roosevelt's opinion, as it is believed to have been presented to Signor Mussolini by Mr. Phillips, was that Jews should be allowed to take out of countries where they were placed in a position of inferiority sufficient capital to commence life anew. Ethiopia was suggested as a place in which Jews might be welcomed as settlers because it was still largely unexplored and because foreign capital, even if subjected to the Italian Government's control, would therefore materially hasten the process of colonization.

Mr. Phillips is understood to have

Continued on Page Six

CHAMBERLAIN LAUDS ROOSEVELT SPEECH

Statement Is Interpreted as Attempt to Meet American Idea That He Is Fascist

By FERDINAND KUHN Jr.
Special Cable to THE NEW YORK TIMES.

LONDON, Jan. 5.—Prime Minister Neville Chamberlain today took the almost unprecedented course of issuing a personal statement from Downing Street expressing his appreciation of President Roosevelt's message to Congress yesterday.

"Nobody who is charged with the heavy responsibilities of government," said Mr. Chamberlain, "could fail to be impressed by the solemn words with which the President of the United States yesterday greeted the elected representatives of the American people.

"In these islands, where there is so clear a realization that only through freedom and peace can we hope to maintain and develop for ourselves and those that come after us the benefits for which we have labored for generations, the sentiments expressed by the President will be welcomed as yet another indication of the vital role of democracy in world affairs and its devotion to the ideal of ordered human progress."

Such a Statement Rare

From the wording of this carefully drafted statement it was impossible to tell whether Mr. Chamberlain had been most "impressed" by the President's passage about the Neutrality Act, or by the call for a bigger American defense program or by the reaffirmation of democratic ideals against those of the dictatorships.

Yet there is some importance in the fact that Mr. Chamberlain said anything at all on the subject of President Roosevelt's speech. It is extremely rare for such statements to be issued when Parliament is not in session; veteran observers here could not remember any occasion since the war when a Prime Minister had chosen to comment in such circumstances on a speech by an American President.

The question asked everywhere was what had prompted Mr. Chamberlain to do it.

A possible key to the statement could be found at the start of the second sentence in which Mr. Chamberlain spoke of the devotion to "freedom and peace" in this country. For the government here has just begun to realize the extent of the belief in the United States that Mr. Chamberlain is a "Fascist" or at least in sympathy with the Fascist regimes of Europe.

The British Embassy in Washington is known to be perturbed about it; travelers returning from the United States in recent weeks have let Mr. Chamberlain know what is being said of him in the United

Continued on Page Six

DEBT IS NEAR LIMIT

But President Argues Against a Halt Now in 'Recovery' Spending

FOR SOME TAX INCREASES

Tenth Successive Net Deficit Put at $3,326,000,000, and $3,972,000,000 June 30

The text of the budget message will be found on Page 12.

By FELIX BELAIR Jr.
Special to THE NEW YORK TIMES.

WASHINGTON, Jan. 5.—President Roosevelt followed up yesterday's denunciation of dictatorships by a message to Congress today outlining a $9,000,000,000 budget for the fiscal year 1940 to provide for a record peacetime expenditure for the national defense and $2,266,165,000 for recovery and relief. He suggested new taxes to cover part of the cost of both undertakings.

The budget message was followed immediately by another, in which the President asked that $875,000,000 be made available as soon as possible for financing the relief program through the rest of the current fiscal year.

Ignoring the economy consciousness attributed to the incoming Congress, the President, in asking for $2,266,165,000 for recovery and relief for the fiscal year beginning next July, made no estimate for work relief as such, but placed at $1,750,000,000 the probable needs of the Works Progress Administration, the National Youth Administration and the Farm Security Administration.

Another Message on Defense

Under the heading of national defense, Mr. Roosevelt served notice that soon, in a separate message, he would ask Congress to authorize a new $500,000,000 naval and military expansion program, but explained that only $210,000,000 of that extra amount would be spent during the fiscal year 1940.

The President estimated probable expenditures for all national defense purposes during the new fiscal year at $1,319,558,000, an increase of $309,351,000 over the current year's outlay. But scattered throughout the bulky document were lesser items of a semi-military character calculated to carry the total appropriations of a naval or military nature above the $2,000,000,000 mark.

For the new fiscal year, the tenth successive Federal net deficit was forecast—this time $3,326,000,000. It reflected the second highest spending program in New Deal experience, amounting to $8,995,000,000 in a fiscal year when total revenues are not expected to exceed $5,669,000,000.

Adding the projected deficit for the 1940 fiscal year to an already mountainous national debt, the President estimated the gross Federal indebtedness by July, 1940, at $44,456,000,000, or within only about $500,000,000 of the statutory limitation on the public debt. It was disclosed that he was planning to ask Congress for a broadening of the limitation.

1939 Deficit Nearly $4,000,000,000

No less revealing were the new budget estimates for the current fiscal year, which will end with a deficit of $3,972,000,000 if present estimates materialize, despite an increase of $500,000,000 in anticipated receipts over the tentative estimates issued last July.

On the basis of present prospects, total revenue will reach $5,520,000,000 during the fiscal year ending next July, compared with $5,519,000,000 estimated last January and $5,000,270,000 forecast last July.

Total expenditures during the current fiscal year were estimated at $9,492,000,000, against a forecast of $6,869,000,000 last January and $8,985,000,000 in the July forecast. The staggering effect of the business recession, which set in last Spring, upon anticipated receipts and the unexpectedly large public expenditures required to meet the resulting economic situation were held responsible for the heavy deficit.

For the one-sided picture presented by the national balance sheet, however, the President had no apologies to offer. He said the money had been "well spent" and that the greater part of the recurring deficits since 1932 "have gone

Continued on Page Twelve

Buster Crabbe starred in the title role of the serial *Buck Rogers*.

Robert Donat starred in *Goodbye Mr. Chips* with Terry Kilburn.

Judy Garland and Ray Bolger in a scene from *The Wizard of Oz*.

The collapse of the temple in Ranchipur, India, from *The Rains Came*, a special effects extravaganza starring Myrna Loy, Tyrone Power and George Brent.

"All the News That's Fit to Print."

The New York Times.

LATE CITY EDITION
Mostly cloudy and continued cold today; light snow in morning. Tomorrow fair and warmer.
Temperatures Yesterday—Max., 19; Min., 7

VOL. LXXXVIII...No. 29,588. Entered as Second-Class Matter, Postoffice, New York, N. Y. NEW YORK, FRIDAY, JANUARY 27, 1939. P THREE CENTS NEW YORK CITY and Vicinity | FOUR CENTS Elsewhere Except in 7th and 8th Postal Zones.

REBELS IN BARCELONA WITHOUT A FIGHT; HAILED IN STREETS; DISTRIBUTE FOOD; FRENCH WARN ITALY ON HER DEMANDS

SENATE WILL VOTE ON WPA CUT TODAY; CLOSE TEST LOOMS

Leaders Decide Each Faction Has Rallied All Available Strength, So End Delay

'LOBBY' CAUSES A FLURRY

Adams Presents Bulletin Off Relief Headquarters Board, Urging Appeal by Wire

Special to THE NEW YORK TIMES.

WASHINGTON, Jan. 26.—Leaders of the two factions into which the Senate has been divided over the question of how much money the Works Progress Administration shall spend from Feb. 1 to June 30, the end of the fiscal year, agreed late this afternoon to vote at 3 o'clock tomorrow afternoon on whether the appropriation shall be $875,000,000 or $725,000,000.

The Senate looks upon the question of which sum shall prevail as of less importance than the direct test of strength between one group, led by Senator Barkley, the Democratic floor leader, which believes the Congress should follow the President's advice on relief, and another marshaled by Senators Byrnes and Adams, under the direction of Vice President Garner, which insists that some check be made on Federal expenditures as a gesture toward economy.

Few were willing to make a public forecast tonight as to which way the vote would go. Both factions expressed confidence, even though each conceded the margin of victory would be small.

Senator Barkley said he expected to have five or six votes to spare. Senator Byrnes said this was wrong. Mr. Barkley appeared fully confident of his ground, however, since it was he who asked unanimous consent to set a definite time for a vote, after he had placed speaker after speaker on the floor for two days in an open move to hold off a decision.

Gamble on a Few Unpledged Votes

The agreement demonstrated principally the conclusion reached by both sides that whatever strength they hold represents their ultimate vote and both gambled on obtaining the support of a handful of unpledged votes among Democratic members.

A slight advantage may rest with the economy group, however, due to a parliamentary situation arising from the fact that the test will come on an amendment by Senator McKellar to appropriate $875,000,000 instead of the lower figure voted into the bill by the House and approved, 17 to 7, by the Senate Appropriations Committee. The Administration must carry the amendment by a majority to win, as in the case of an amendment a tie vote means defeat.

The agreement to vote after a few hours in which the opposing sides will divide time equally for debate, except for an opening address by Senator Thomas of Oklahoma, came as a surprise to observers who had heard persistent rumors in the Capitol that the Administration forces had lost some of their following.

It came close on the heels of a new threat of extended debate aroused by Senator Adams, who contended that "lobbying" on behalf of the larger appropriation had been undertaken in the WPA headquarters here. That threat evaporated with quick disavowal of knowledge or responsibility for such activities by Colonel F. C. Harrington, WPA Administrator, who ordered them stopped.

Barkley Replies to Charges

Earlier in the day, Senator Barkley had submitted, with the purpose of explaining what the opposition contended were discrepancies in estimates of the funds available to the WPA, letters from Daniel W. Bell, director of the budget, and Colonel Harrington. Senator Adams, who originally charged that there had been misstatements concerning the figures on the WPA carry-over, argued that the correspondence did not clear up his original contention that the WPA was asking for funds to cover one week for which financing already was available.

These questions indicated a field for unlimited debate, but Senators generally appeared to be tired of the controversy, especially as other difficult questions remain to be settled after that, concerning the appropriation itself. A test vote is to be taken on amendments by Senator Hatch which would penalize the use of WPA for political purposes, as well as other controversial points relating to payment of "prevailing wages" for certain types of work.

A quick settlement of those questions was expected, with the possibility that the bill could be sent to the House for a conference on amendments over the week-end. That would make possible final adoption by Feb. 1, when the meas-

Continued on Page Eleven

Chile Rushes Quake Relief; Orders Razed Cities Closed

Entire Population to Be Removed From Chillan and Concepcion—Rigid Curfew Imposed—Death Toll High in Thousands

By CHARLES GRIFFIN
Special Cable to THE NEW YORK TIMES.

SANTIAGO, Chile, Jan. 26.—With martial law in effect, with an inadequate number of relief and medical workers, and with the grave danger of pestilence sweeping through the area in South Central Chile that was devastated by Tuesday's earthquake, the number of dead was estimated high in the thousands today and the injured at many thousands more.

From the welter of confusing reports of the staggering loss of life and property caused by one of the worst disasters in the history of South America, it was impossible to obtain even an approximate reckoning of the number of dead, injured and homeless.

The number of the dead was placed at 10,000 and the injured at 20,000 in Chillan alone, a city of 50,000, fifty miles inland from Concepcion, that was virtually wiped off the map.

Another estimate was that 10,000 had been killed in the area between Talca and Temuco. Many communities in the six Chilean provinces where the earthquake spread havoc have yet to be heard from.

With definite word that both Concepcion and Chillan, two flourishing cities in South Chile, had literally been obliterated, the military authorities ordered the complete evacuation of the two centers and the removal from them, as rapidly as possible, of every man, woman and child via sea routes northward.

The order was issued after a survey showed that 70 per cent of the buildings in Concepcion had been razed and that the remaining structures were in imminent danger of collapse. Fires smoldering in the ruins constituted another menace.

A message received this evening from Concepcion said:

"Drinking water has been completely cut off. We are short of medical supplies and sanitation facilities. We must have serums against tetanus and gangrene, also more nurses, practicing medical students and other medical help. Food is very scarce. More than 15,000 persons are without shelter tonight. We must have tents soon. Already 1,200 dead have been counted but there are many more under ruins and it is impossible so far to get out the bodies."

Doctors, nurses, medical supplies, food and drinking water were being rushed to the stricken area today by airplane, train and boat.

Meanwhile, a pitifully small army of rescue workers, toiling against heavy odds in almost unbearable

Continued on Page Six

MERCURY HITS 7°, LOWEST OF WINTER

Cold Wave Borne Into City on Gales From Canada—Light Snow Flurries Here

A low temperature of 7 degrees combined yesterday with a biting northwest wind rushing in from the Canadian border Provinces to give New York City its coldest day of the Winter. As darkness fell midtown Manhattan had snow flurries, forerunners of a light snowfall forecast by the Weather Bureau, which also promised slowly rising temperatures tomorrow.

Most of the eastern part of the country suffered sub-zero or below-normal temperatures; Northern New York reported temperatures of 40 below zero, New England severe cold and snow-blocked highways, and even in Jacksonville, Fla., the mercury dropped to 36 degrees, four above freezing. A number of deaths and exposure cases were reported as the result of weather conditions.

With the ground snow-covered and lakes and rivers frozen over at near-by resorts, railroads and bus lines expected a large number of Winter sports enthusiasts to leave the city over the week-end.

Accompanied by High Wind

The cold wave was explained by Weather Bureau officials as the result of the storm which struck the coastal area Wednesday. The Canadian cold-air mass moved so rapidly as to be little warmed and the result was an icy blast which tore through New York and the Middle and North Atlantic States from Wednesday night through yesterday. The wind blew at gale force in the early morning hours yesterday and was still strong as the city's workers started for their offices.

The coldest temperature was 7 degrees at 5:45 A. M., and from 8 until 11 A. M., the hours when New Yorkers take to the streets, it remained steadily at 10 above zero. The mercury rose through the day to a high of 19 at 3:30 P. M. The average for the day was 13, 17 degrees below normal for the date. The lowest official temperature ever recorded for the date was four-tenths of a degree below zero in 1905; the highest, 58 in 1916.

The hourly temperatures were as follows:

Midnight	12	2 P. M.	15
1 A. M.	10	3 P. M.	15
2 A. M.	10	3:30 P. M.	19
3 A. M.	9	4 P. M.	18
4 A. M.	9	5 P. M.	17
5 A. M.	10	6 P. M.	17
5:45 A. M.	7	7 P. M.	17
6 A. M.	8	8 P. M.	17
7 A. M.	9	9 P. M.	17
8 A. M.	10	10 P. M.	16
9 A. M.	10	11 P. M.	*17
10 A. M.	10	Midnight	*15
11 A. M.	12	1 A. M.	*15
Noon	13	2 A. M.	*14
1 P. M.	15	3 A. M.	*12

*Unofficial, at Times Square.

Great South Bay Frozen

For the first time in two years Great South Bay was frozen over completely and the Coast Guard icebreaker AB-25 worked throughout the day cutting a channel from Bay Shore to Fire Island Beach to take mail and supplies to the 150-odd residents of the beach colonies along the island. The Coast Guard,

Continued on Page Thirteen

COSTER REVEALED AS SCHULTZ ALLY

McKesson & Robbins Head and Gangster Were Partners in Bootleg Operations

Arthur (Dutch Schultz) Flegenheimer was not only aware that F. Donald Coster was really an ex-convict named Philip Musica, but was associated with him in illegal liquor dealings from 1927 until the gangster's murder eight years later, it was disclosed yesterday at the Federal Building.

Their partnership during the period that Musica was successfully masquerading as Coster and had become president of the drug corporation of McKesson & Robbins was said by persons in touch with the Federal investigation into the case to account for Schultz's frequent visits to Bridgeport, Conn.

In this connection it was recalled that testimony that James J. Hines, Tammany district leader, had visited the gangster at Bridgeport had been given at Hines's first trial last Fall.

Groundwork for Tax Action

The interest of the Federal investigators into the past activities of Schultz and Musica was interpreted by some observers as an indication that they were seeking to lay the groundwork for income tax proceedings against Musica's estate, and also to identify business associates of the pair. It was said that nothing has been discovered to indicate the three other Musica brothers were involved in the liquor deals.

Gregory F. Noonan, United States Attorney, obtained grand jury subpoenas yesterday for three Bridgeport financiers who will be questioned here next Wednesday in an attempt to develop further information about Coster's activities. They were Clinton Barnum Seeley, a grandson of Phineas T. Barnum, the circus proprietor; Egbert Marsh, chairman of the board of directors of the Bridgeport City Trust Company, and Horace B. Merwin, president of the Bridgeport City Trust Company.

Mr. Seeley and Mr. Marsh were at one time stockholders in Girard & Co., the concern through which Coster built up the prestige that enabled him to get control of McKesson & Robbins, and Mr. Merwin was a director of McKesson & Robbins, and McKesson & Robbins, Ltd., of Canada, the investigators said.

Kantor Again Is Questioned

John Kantor, who told the investigators several weeks ago of having attempted to sell 2,000,000 rifles to foreign countries for Coster, was questioned again yesterday. He later said he had also arranged deals for the sale of airplanes, blankets and foodstuffs to the foreign countries, but he insisted his activities were legal.

John H. McGloon, controller of McKesson & Robbins since 1928, completed his testimony yesterday at the inquiry of the Securities and Exchange Commission into the accounting aspects of the case. He testified that any internal accounting system of the drug company was circumvented by collusion with others outside the corporation.

Any employe who had become sus-

Continued on Page Twenty

HAGUE BAN ON C.I.O. BARRED ON APPEAL; COURT SPLIT, 2 TO 1

Mayor and Aides Are Scored in Ruling—Further Curbs Put on Jersey City Officials

EARLIER STAY SUSTAINED

Free Speech and Assembly Held Violated—Way Is Left Open to Change Ordinance

Excerpts from the decision will be found on Page 8.

Special to THE NEW YORK TIMES.

PHILADELPHIA, Jan. 26.—In a sweeping majority decision in which Mayor Frank Hague of Jersey City and his associates were accused of having "troubled the waters in order to fish in them," the Federal Circuit Court of Appeals here today placed even greater restraint upon Jersey City officials in their dealings with the Congress of Industrial Organizations and the American Civil Liberties Union than a broad district court injunction had imposed.

Declaring the evidence to be "uncontrovertible" that Mayor Hague was "the spearhead of the movement to keep the appellee labor groups out of Jersey City" the circuit court upheld every point in Judge William Clark's injunction of last Nov. 2, in which he ordered that the C. I. O. and its affiliates receive the same "free assembly" and "free speech" rights as other groups.

But the majority opinion, written by Judge John Biggs Jr., went even further. It declared unconstitutional the present Jersey City ordinance under which permits for public meetings had been denied to the C. I. O. and its sympathizers and it enlarged Judge Clark's injunction by striking out a clause through which Mayor Hague would have been able to prevent C. I. O. meetings on the streets and in the public parks by denying the same right to other organizations.

Ernst Hails Ruling

The opinion, which was hailed by Morris Ernst, counsel for the Civil Liberties Union, as granting "more than we had hoped for," left the way open for the adoption of a substitute ordinance in Jersey City which would place the granting or withholding of a public meeting permit on the basis of interference or non-interference with traffic rather than on the basis of the belief of city officials that riot was likely or not likely to result from the speeches.

Another ordinance, which had the effect of preventing the C. I. O. from distributing handbills and carrying placards, had been declared unconstitutional by Judge Clark, who now is a member of the Circuit Court but who took no part in the proceedings leading to today's decision.

It is understood that the clause in Judge Clark's decree which was stricken out by the Circuit Court was the language of C. I. O.-Civil Liberties Union counsel in a form of decree as presented by them for

Continued on Page Eight

DALADIER IS FIRM

'Hour of Peril' Nearing, Chamber Is Told—Gets Vote of Confidence

EMPIRE HELD INVIOLATE

France and Britain in Accord on Plan if Italy Refuses to Quit Spain at War's End

The text of Premier Daladier's speech will be found on Page 2.

By P. J. PHILIP
Wireless to THE NEW YORK TIMES.

PARIS, Jan. 26.—Premier Edouard Daladier told a cheering Chamber of Deputies tonight that France "will let no one touch her territorial integrity or her colonial empire or her free communications."

[Speaking earlier in the day before a meeting of his Radical Socialist followers, M. Daladier declared that France and Britain had agreed on the "necessary measures" to counter any Italian refusal to withdraw from Spanish territory at the end of the war, The Associated Press reported.]

"As I have said elsewhere," he continued, "she will not concede a single acre or concede a single right. In saying that I am measuring the full gravity of my words and the gravity of the circumstances.

"But there are times when for a people who are proud of their freedom there can be no question of measuring sacrifice, when sacrifice is necessary, for the maintenance of their integrity and their honor.

"With the hour of peril approaching," M. Daladier said that there was more even than that material empire to defend; there was that ideal that France had defended in other times and was ready to defend again in a world that had enlisted under the banner of force.

Blum Offers Amendment

For a moment it looked as if what M. Daladier wanted would happen and that the House, which had unanimously cheered him, would give him a unanimous vote. But this is a free democracy. Léon Blum, who inaugurated the non-intervention policy in Spain but seems now to regret it, wanted to add an amendment to the motion of confidence, which the government had accepted, inviting it to "regulate the application of the non-intervention agreement in the same way as has been done by other signatory States." In short, to open the Spanish frontier.

Despite M. Daladier's obvious wish for unanimity in the tense situation and the division of opin-

Continued on Page Two

Mussolini Sees Foes 'Biting Dust'; Says Italy Will Go On Conquering

Crowds Celebrating Barcelona's Fall Shout For Corsica and Tunisia—Premier Calls Victory a Step Toward 'New Europe'

By CAMILLE M. CIANFARRA
Wireless to THE NEW YORK TIMES.

ROME, Jan. 26.—Exultantly addressing a cheering crowd of scores of thousands, gathered outside the Palazzo Venezia to celebrate the fall of Barcelona, Premier Benito Mussolini indicated quite clearly this evening that the march of the Italian legionaries would not end in the capital of Catalonia.

He did not say whether the next objective would be Spain or elsewhere, but the crowd's guess, which found expression in shouts of "We want Corsica. We want Tunisia!" showed the direction in which Italian political thought is tending.

"Our enemies are biting the dust," shouted Signor Mussolini and his voice was almost drowned out by applause. "Their motto was 'No paseran,' but we did pass and I tell you we will continue to do so."

This sally was greeted with enormous delight by the crowd, which continued to demonstrate outside the windows for almost a half hour, obliging Signor Mussolini repeatedly to return to the balcony in acknowledgment.

Instructions had been issued early this morning to Fascisti to gather in the Piazza to hear Signor Mussolini speak. Large crowds joined in spontaneously, however, and long before 7 o'clock this evening, when Signor Mussolini appeared, the square and all side streets were filled almost to capacity. Searchlights played and the Victor Emmanuel monument and the buildings surrounding the palazzo were lighted up.

Premier Mussolini, apparently pleased, smilingly contemplated the human sea stretched before him, then motioned the crowd to silence.

"The shout of your exultance, which is fully justified," he said, "blends with that rising in all the cities of Spain, which are now completely liberated from the Reds' infamies, and the shout of joy from all anti-Bolshevists the world over.

"General Franco's magnificent troops and our fearless legionaries not only have beaten [Premier Juan] Negrin's government but many others of our enemies are now biting the dust."

The political allusions contained in the short speech were not lost on the crowd, which frequently in-

Continued on Page Four

BRITAIN INVINCIBLE, HOARE MAINTAINS

Minister Says No Air Attack Can Break Will—Warning to Hitler on Adventure Seen

Excerpts from Sir Samuel Hoare's speech are on Page 4.

By FERDINAND KUHN Jr.
Wireless to THE NEW YORK TIMES.

LONDON, Jan. 26.—The British Empire is invincible and any "blind and foolish people" who think otherwise will have the shock of their lives, Sir Samuel Hoare, Home Secretary and a member of Prime Minister Neville Chamberlain's "Inner Cabinet," told a mass meeting at Swansea tonight.

Sir Samuel declared that British economic power, naval strength and defensive armaments would make it impossible for any one to defeat this country. No air attack, however frightful, would ever destroy the British people's "will to resist," he told his audience.

"Let the world ponder upon these things," he said coolly, "and particularly let those ponder on them who say that we have grown weary with age and feeble in power. So they thought in 1914. They had a rude awakening."

Sir Samuel's speech had been preceded early today by another long meeting—the second this week—of the Cabinet's Subcommittee on Foreign Affairs, of which he is a member. In addition the full Cabinet had devoted most of its three-hour session yesterday to a discussion of the immediate outlook in Europe.

Italy Explains Calling Troops

Italy gave official assurance to the British Government today that the calling up of 60,000 men of the 1901 class had been undertaken purely for "training purposes."

The assurance followed instructions to the British Embassy in Rome to seek an explanation of these military measures, which yesterday had added to public and official uneasiness over the European situation. The calling up of these men was regarded in London as abnormal, coming after the massing of Fascist militiamen around Rome and the concentration of troops at Genoa and Spezia.

No confirmation could be given in Whitehall to a report that Premier Benito Mussolini intended to ask for a four-power conference on Spain—an intention to which the French Foreign Minister, Georges Bonnet, seemed to refer in his speech in Paris today. If Premier Mussolini has such a plan it must have been developed, according to British spokesmen, since his meeting with Mr. Chamberlain. It was said that nothing about such a conference had been mentioned during the recent Anglo-Italian talks in Rome.

Generally, the fall of Barcelona is regarded here as the beginning of

Continued on Page Four

France Rejects Japan's Nominee for Envoy; Political Snub Seen in the Unusual Action

By HUGH BYAS
Wireless to THE NEW YORK TIMES.

TOKYO, Jan. 26.—The French Government has refused to agree to the appointment of Masayuki Tani as Ambassador to Paris, succeeding Yotaro Sugimura, who is at Tokyo seriously ill. The Japanese Government has decided not to appoint an Ambassador in the meantime, leaving the Paris Embassy in charge of Katsutaro Miyakaki, the counselor.

This is the first time that France has declined to approve of a proposed Japanese Ambassador, and only the second time in Japan's history that a Japanese nominee has been rejected by a foreign government. The earlier occasion was the Chinese Government's refusal to accept Tokikichi Obata, who had been active in Peiping as Counselor of Legation at the time the twenty-one demands were presented.

Mr. Tani's name was submitted to Paris fifty days ago. The French Government evidently had wished the Japanese Government to understand by its silence that Mr. Tani was not acceptable, for it delayed giving its answer. Eventually, as Japan pressed for a reply, Foreign Minister Hachiro Arita was informed that France considered that Mr. Tani's attitude toward France had not been cooperative while he was representing Japan as Minister at Large at Shanghai.

It is understood here that the nature of Mr. Tani's non-cooperation was his publication of a statement declaring that France was shipping munitions to Generalissimo Chiang Kai-shek after the French Ambassador had requested him not to make this accusation public. Actually, as everybody except the Japanese public knew, munitions reaching General Chiang were being supplied by many powers and a large proportion by Japan's ideological allies.

The Japanese press professes to believe that France's individual objection to Mr. Tani is camouflage for an intention to administer a political snub. Asahi points out that there has been considerable friction regarding French rights and interests in South China and the transit of munitions through French territory. The Japanese press is astonished by the development, but does not comment editorially.

The French action virtually brings Mr. Tani's career to an end, since after being turned down by France he can hardly be proposed to the other democratic powers or to the totalitarian governments. The affair was discussed yesterday by the conference of five Ministers, which decided to leave the Paris Embassy in the hands of the chargé d'affaires. Mr. Arita will report to the Emperor today.

Baron Michele Scammaca, counselor of the Italian Embassy, visited the Foreign Office yesterday and denied rumors circulating in Tokyo to the effect that Italy still was supplying munitions to General Chiang.

AMERICANS REACH FRANCE IN SAFETY

Cruiser Omaha at Villefranche After Close Calls From Bombers at Caldetas

Wireless to THE NEW YORK TIMES.

VILLEFRANCHE, France, Jan. 26.—The United States cruiser Omaha, after twenty-four hours in the bomb-sprayed harbor of Caldetas, Spain, was lying at anchor again in the harbor of Villefranche tonight, having fulfilled her mission without accident.

Members of the United States Embassy staff who left Barcelona were landed in Marseille at 9 o'clock this morning. Other Americans who wanted to leave had been conveyed ahead aboard the destroyer Badger.

The Omaha's departure from Caldetas was held up last night because in the confusion attendant on the evacuation of Barcelona it was impossible to locate Mr. Harrington, a member of the Embassy staff. Rear Admiral Henry E. Lackey decided to remain until he was heard from, and it was not until 10 o'clock last night that it was learned by radio that Mr. Harrington was safe in Perpignan, France. Then the Omaha weighed anchor and left Caldetas.

Threatened by Bombs

Twice during the short stay there Spanish Insurgent bombers flew over the port and rained bombs which not only threatened the United States cruiser but its boats further inshore and Americans ashore who were trying to come aboard.

The first raid was early yesterday morning, when twelve planes circled over villages and dropped bombs, most of which fell in the water nearer French ships than the Omaha, but close enough. Lieutenant Edward L. Woodyard and Aviation Cadet Frank J. Peterson, who were in the Omaha's whaleboat, said afterward:

"Projectiles and shell fragments were raining about us, and we thought for a while we would bring some of them back in our pockets."

One of the Americans waiting on shore said they had suffered air raids during the night when a house reserved for the French Embassy was destroyed. When Jules Henry, French Ambassador, arrived he had to take refuge with the British Chargé d'Affaires.

"We had had plenty of air raids in Barcelona," said the American refugee, "and the best sight we had seen in weeks was when the Omaha's searchlight played on the Stars and Stripes when she came to anchor at Caldetas."

Even before warning blasts as the bombing planes came into action Commander Harold A. Houser, gunnery officer on the Omaha, had four of his 6-inch guns trained and ready to fire at a second's notice.

"I am inclined to think," he said, "that if any bomb had fallen as close to the Omaha as they did to

Continued on Page Three

DEFENSE COLLAPSES

Loyalists Flee Northward to New Line, With the Rebels in Pursuit

CITY MAY BE CAPITAL AGAIN

Franco Expected to Move His Regime There—His Army Gains in Southwest

Wireless to THE NEW YORK TIMES.

BARCELONA, Spain, Jan. 26 (Dispatch to The Times, London)—Amid scenes of great enthusiasm Generalissimo Francisco Franco's troops entered Barcelona today.

War-stained units of the Army Corps of Morocco and Navarre, weary but triumphant, were met in the streets by huge crowds which unloosed the pent-up emotion of the last three days. Small columns of troops which infiltrated into the center of the city with the red and gold Nationalist [Insurgent] flag at their head were suddenly engulfed by seething, cheering, clapping throngs.

Your correspondent's car, which was the first to cruise down the great "diagonals" and enter the Plaza Catalunya, was surrounded by crowds of madly excited Barcelonians, who, with red and gold bunting in their hands, mounted the mudguards, footboards and bonnet, cheering with arms upraised in the Franco salute. Tears mingled with the shouting and laughter. The people seemed torn between hysterical abandon and unbelief.

Final Push from Two Sides

The final movement against the city was carried out from two sides, the west and the north. On the west General Juan Yague's Moroccan troops, who had been waiting with ill-concealed impatience on the right bank of the Llobregat River, received their orders at dawn. Three divisions pushed across the river and spread over the country toward the industrial suburb of Sans and the grim fortress-crowned hill of Montjuich, which dominates the harbor area.

A few trial rounds fired at Republican [Loyalist] positions brought no reply. It soon became evident that the Republicans had given up all serious hope of defending the city.

The Nationalist advance was methodical, although uneven. In certain parts long stretches of road were covered without difficulty. In others isolated machine-gun nests would hold up whole battalions for an hour.

But the Republican military machine had broken down. Most of these nuclei of resistance consisted of groups of machine gunners, clinging grimly to their weapons long after the country behind them had been evacuated.

Nationalist infantry, carrying their flags before them, moved ahead, preceded by tanks. Gradually they reduced each center of resistance, thus allowing the main body to push on.

Day Is One of Alarms

The day was one of alarms and excursions. Far and wide around Barcelona the countryside was alive with rumors. From the heights west of the city its brilliant white buildings were visible, glinting in a dazzling sunshine. A huge pall of black smoke rising slowly skyward from behind the Hill of Montjuich, where the Campsa petroleum depot had been burning for two days, accentuated the deathly quietude of the doomed city, waiting anxiously for a decision regarding its fate.

The danger of entering a large city whose will to resist was an unknown quantity was obvious. But both the Moroccans and the Navarrese were straining at the leash. Finally bolder counsel prevailed.

Broken bridges obstructed the progress of the Nationalists, although in many cases destruction was averted by brilliant individual initiative. A bridge at the suburb of Esplugas, for instance, was saved by the heroism of an Asturian legionary who, single-handed and in the face of murderous machine-gun fire, cut the cables attached to a dynamite charge.

In the afternoon the final order was given. Troops waiting in the brilliant sunshine in villages surrounding the city broke into a run and, singing marching songs, made off eastward.

The Navarrese, who had been sent again into the mountains and

Continued on Page Two

"All the News That's Fit to Print."

The New York Times.

Copyright, 1939, by The New York Times Company.

LATE CITY EDITION
Cloudy with rain today; warmer tonight. Tomorrow cloudy, preceded by rain; colder at night.
Temperatures Yesterday—Max., 46; Min., 36

VOL. LXXXVIII...No. 29,602. Entered as Second-Class Matter, Postoffice, New York, N. Y. NEW YORK, FRIDAY, FEBRUARY 10, 1939. PPP THREE CENTS NEW YORK CITY and Vicinity | FOUR CENTS Elsewhere Except in 7th and 8th Postal Zones.

POPE PIUS IS DEAD AT THE AGE OF 81; CARDINALS AT BEDSIDE IN THE VATICAN AS END COMES IN SUDDEN SINKING SPELL

ROOSEVELT NAMES JUDGES OPPOSED BY TWO SENATORS

BIDDLE APPOINTED

Not Choice of Guffey—Arant of Ohio Chosen, Upsetting Donahey

BYRD, THOMAS JOIN CRITICS

Cahill Selected Prosecutor Here—Judge Patterson Goes to the Circuit Bench

Senator Byrd's statement is printed in full on Page 14.

Special to THE NEW YORK TIMES.

WASHINGTON, Feb. 9.—To a Senate still smarting under President Roosevelt's charges of attempted individual usurpation of his constitutional prerogative of judicial appointment, the Chief Executive today sent a "blue ribbon" list of judgeship nominations, which, in two important instances, rejected recommendations of as many Senators who had opposed the President's selection.

The appointment list which the President sent to the Senate a short time before its opening hour was headed by Robert P. Patterson for the District Court of the New York Southern District, whose nomination to fill the seat vacated by Circuit Judge Martin Manton was the only one of three which had not been contested by Senators from the States represented.

The President named Francis Biddle of Philadelphia to fill a vacancy on the Third Circuit Court of Appeals and Herschel W. Arant of Ohio to take over the new appellate judgeship in the Sixth Circuit Court. Both appointments were against the wishes of Senators Guffey and Donahey, consistent New Deal supporters, who had made their preferences known to the President.

New Dealer Defends Senate

Although various phases of the verbal warfare which followed the Senate's rejection by a vote of 72 to 9 of the President's nomination of Judge Floyd H. Roberts of Virginia were expected, the sharp difference of opinion between the Senate and the White House was evidenced by a stand against the President taken today by Senator Thomas of Utah.

Quietly a loyal follower of Mr. Roosevelt and his policies, Senator Thomas asserted in a brief unannounced speech that the President had gone too far in personally interpreting the Constitution by attempting to force the confirmation of Judge Roberts over the protest of Senators Glass and Byrd.

"It suggests a spirit that is contrary to much that is good in our American constitutional theory and practice," said the former college professor.

Meanwhile, the junior Virginia Senator, Harry F. Byrd, entered the mounting Senatorial protest against Presidential selections for Federal office not concurred in by Senators representing the States from which the nominees came when he joined Senator Glass with the statement that Mr. Roosevelt's appointment of Judge Roberts was designed "to chastise" both.

Cahill Named District Attorney

As Federal District Attorney for the New York Southern District, President Roosevelt named John T. Cahill, son of a former New York City policeman who worked his way through Columbia and Harvard with a brilliant record to become assistant to the State Attorney General. He would succeed Lamar Hardy, who recently resigned to return to private practice.

The list of judiciary appointments was hailed by Administration officials as proof of the President's determination to elevate the standards of the Federal bench and of the desire of Attorney General Frank Murphy to remove judgeships and similar nominations as far as possible from the field of politics. The high standing of the nominees in their profession was expected in some quarters to strengthen the President's hand should his quarrel with Senators Glass and Byrd lead to Senatorial demands that recommendations from its membership be given greater weight in the selection of candidates for the bench.

In his selection of Mr. Biddle, former chairman of the National Labor Board and now counsel to the Congressional committee investigating the TVA, President Roosevelt overrode the recommendation

Continued on Page Fourteen

Mexico Delays Granting Recognition to Franco

Wireless to THE NEW YORK TIMES.

MEXICO CITY, Feb. 9.—The Cardenas government, it was learned today on the highest authority from sources close to the Foreign Office, has no intention of recognizing the Franco regime in Spain despite economic ties to the totalitarian States resulting from oil seizures and the consequent boycott of the United States and Great Britain.

The Petroleum Administration leans strongly toward the Republican [Loyalist] cause in Spain and Mexico will wait, it was said, until the last possible moment before extending diplomatic recognition to Generalissimo Francisco Franco. The people of Mexico are said to be about equally divided between the Republicans and the Nationalists [Insurgents].

It is believed, however, despite the assertion that as long as the Cardenas regime remained in power it would not recognize General Franco, such action by the United States would be followed here.

JAPANESE OCCUPY ISLAND OF HAINAN

Landing Is a Surprise—French and British See Threat to Colonial Possessions

By HUGH BYAS

Wireless to THE NEW YORK TIMES.

TOKYO, Friday, Feb. 10.—At 3 o'clock this morning the Japanese Army landed forces on Hainan Island, according to a bulletin issued by Imperial Headquarters. The strength of the force landed is not disclosed.

The news is read as a confirmation of fears felt for some time in British and French circles that Japan would seize this island as a preliminary step to the occupation of Pakhoi, with the ultimate intention of advancing into Yunnan Province to cut off supplies and munitions from French ports and from Burma over the new motor road.

Lying across the Gulf of Tongking, Hainan is of vital importance to the safety of French Indo-China and its occupation by Japanese troops is in the strategical sense a menace to the safety of French possessions there.

Recently the Japanese Foreign Office, departing from its usual custom, announced that the French Government had refused to accept Masayuki Tani as Ambassador. The motive for this step, which mystified diplomats at that time is now shown in the occupation of Hainan which must cause the French Government grave anxiety.

Treaty Violation Denied

The Foreign Office spokesman will issue today a statement clarifying the Japanese Government's view of its treaty obligations to France in connection with Hainan Island.

In 1907 Japan and France concluded an agreement pledging mutual support in maintaining peace and security in regions of China adjacent to their possessions. Hainan was such a sphere for France, as Fukien was for Japan.

The Japanese Government's statement will assert that the military occupation of the island does not violate the 1907 agreement because the "present operation is for the purpose of exterminating Chinese military forces and therefore is an affair having nothing to do with the question of assuring peace as envisaged in the Japanese-French agreement."

Party Is Advancing

TOKYO, Friday, Feb. 10 (AP).—The Japanese Admiralty and War Office in a joint announcement today said that a landing had been made on Hainan Island, between the British strongholds of Hong Kong and Singapore and off the coast of French Indo-China.

The announcement said that a naval landing party plus army regulars made a surprise landing "early this morning," and successfully occupied shore positions.

"The landing party and regulars are now advancing," the communiqué said.

Further details were not given in the terse communication.

Observers, however, considered that Japan was making good on her oft-repeated threat to "take necessary measures" against alleged im-

Continued on Page Ten

SPAIN TO FIGHT ON, LOYALISTS DECIDE; NEW PEACE MOVES

General Miaja Announces Stand After Talks With Valencia Popular Front

REBELS OCCUPY MINORCA

Britain and France Still Plan to Recognize Franco as Soon as Struggle Stops

Advices on peace prospects in Spain were confused last night. A meeting of Loyalist leaders in Valencia, under General José Miaja, decided to "fight to the end." Yet at Perpignan, where parleys have been conducted, it was reported General Miaja had been in touch with Generalissimo Franco, and surrender of Central Spain by Feb. 18 was possible. Britain and France were pressing for conclusion of the war, and both were expected to recognize the Franco regime. [Page 1.]

All of Minorca, in the Balearics, was seized by the Insurgents after a British cruiser, which had conveyed an agent to the island to make terms, had taken off 450 persons, including the chief representatives of the Loyalist Government. [Page 6.]

A Franco column reached the French border at Le Perthus, trapping many trucks. Loyalists were still fighting a rear-guard action at the northeast tip of Spain, but were expected to cross the frontier today. [Page 7.]

Italy was suspicious of the British action in taking a Franco emissary to Minorca, holding it was "meddling" intended to keep the Italians away from the island. [Page 6.]

Miaja Declares He Will Fight

By The Associated Press.

VALENCIA, Spain, Friday, Feb. 10.—A decision to "fight on for liberty until the end" was announced early today after an important meeting of General José Miaja, Republican [Loyalist] defense commander and military governor for Central Spain, and representatives of the Popular Front [Left parties].

Taking part in the conference were other military representatives.

The object of the meeting, said General Manuel Matallana, who only tonight was appointed by Premier Juan Negrin to the command of all five armies of the central zone, was "to insure the resistance of both the people and the army, which will eventually bring about the defeat of the invaders."

General Leopoldo Menendez, commander of the Eastern Army; Jesus Hernandez, Political Commissar for the five central armies, and other officers were present.

Madrid Favors Fighting On

MADRID, Feb. 9 (AP).—All Madrid morning newspapers today published a message in which Foreign Minister Julio Alvarez del Vayo stated:

"The Republican government is prepared to fight on until the end, defending the independence of the country. Our means in the central zone [the one-fourth of Spain unconquered by the Insurgents] will

Continued on Page Six

LEHMAN DECLARES DEWEY ARROGANT IN CHARGING LEAK

Governor Calls Statement on Inquiry in Martin Murder an Impertinence

DEFENDS ACTION IN CASE

Warns Prosecutor to Carry Out His Duties—Latter Sticks to His Remarks

Governor Lehman charged Thomas E. Dewey with "inexcusable arrogance" yesterday and gave notice to him that he was expected to "carry out faithfully" his duties as District Attorney of New York County.

The Governor's letter of rebuke was made public in Albany, and in New York Mr. Dewey made a reply. This quarrel between Mr. Lehman, who was re-elected as the Democratic and American Labor party nominee last Fall over Mr. Dewey as the Republican candidate, was centered upon the murder of a gangster in Troy, N. Y., nearly four years ago, but the personalities involved overshadowed the cause.

In his long letter the Governor reviewed his actions, with the comment that it "is quite beyond my understanding" why Mr. Dewey should "presume to object" to his carrying on an "investigation of a murder that has remained unsolved three years."

Events in the Background

There was more in the background, however, than was covered in the Governor's letter. After George Weinberg shot himself on Jan. 29 in White Plains, N. Y., a day or two before he would have taken the witness stand as a star accuser of James J. Hines, the Governor referred to Mr. Dewey an inquiry from a Mineola, L. I., lawyer to the effect that there were no fingerprints on the pistol Weinberg used and asked for an investigation. Mr. Dewey replied that he had already investigated.

Then, on Wednesday, there appeared newspaper reports that two convicts in Atlanta Federal Penitentiary, Hyman Berger and William Dooley, had made affidavits to the effect that Berger saw Weinberg kill Jules Martin, a lieutenant of Arthur (Dutch Schultz) Flegenheimer in Troy in March of 1935.

Mr. Dewey issued a statement which charged that the newspaper accounts appearing under an Atlanta, Ga., date line had really come from a "leak" in Albany and, using the Governor's name, he inferentially laid the leak at the door of the Executive.

The Governor's Letter

The Governor's letter of yesterday was the next step in this sequence, and it follows:

Thomas Edward Dewey,
137 Center Street,
New York City.

My dear Mr. District Attorney:

The press has carried a statement by you in which you criticize my action in investigating the unsolved murder of Jules Martin, which was allegedly committed in Rensselaer County in March, 1935.

The implication which you have

Continued on Page Thirteen

Hope Is Given Up for 37 on Lost Freighter; Rescue Ships Find Only Wreckage at Scene

Mountainous seas and a driving snowstorm whipped by northwest gales hid the fate in mid-Atlantic last night of the crew of thirty-seven men on the British freighter Maria de Larrinaga, after three rescue vessels had plowed through three miles of scattered wreckage all day without finding any sign of life.

Convinced that the 4,988-ton freighter had gone down and that there was virtually no hope that any one on board was still alive, two of the rescue ships abandoned the search as darkness came over a still stormy Atlantic. Two other vessels, the Veendam and the Noordam, both of the Holland-America Line, apparently were continuing the search, although it was not definitely known whether the Noordam had reached the scene.

Three vessels, the Veendam, the Aurania of the Cunard White Star Line and the Scanmail of the American Scantic Line, arrived almost at the same time early yesterday in the vicinity of the last position given by the sinking freighter at 1:39 P. M. Wednesday in a message picked up by the Queen Mary. The sinking ship was about 1,300 miles east of New York and nearly half way on its voyage from Galveston, Texas, to Cobh, Ireland. The Noordam also had turned off its course to head for the position of the distressed ship.

At 7:39 A. M. yesterday the coastal station of the Radiomarine Corporation at Chatham, Mass., received a message from the Scanmail reporting that it was searching for the Maria de Larrinaga in northwest gales, heavy seas and snow that had reduced visibility to half a mile.

Exactly two hours later the Aurania flashed a message that it had sighted wreckage, consisting mainly of hatch covers and oars. Six minutes later the Veendam reported that it also had sighted numerous pieces of wreckage, including ladders and the tops of tables.

After a search of nearly two hours the Aurania sent a message at 11:15 A. M. that it had seen wreckage strewn over the ocean for a distance of a mile and a half on each side. At the same time the Scanmail reported that it would continue the search until dark.

At 3:30 P. M., New York time, as darkness was creeping over the scene, the Scanmail and the Aurania reported that they were abandoning the search. Several hours later an ambiguous message from a passenger on the Noordam indicated that the Veendam had picked up survivors. At 7:53 P. M., however, the Veendam wirelessed that it had not picked up any survivors and did not know of any ship that had.

RITES IN SICKROOM

Holy Water Is Sprinkled as a Preliminary to Extreme Unction

PONTIFF ANOINTED IN OIL

Swiss Guards Surprised by the Arrival of Prelates in Dark and by Tidings of Death

By The Associated Press.

ROME, Friday, Feb. 10.—Vatican City had been quiet all last night before word was sent out to Cardinals and functionaries that the Pope was dying, and the Swiss Guards were surprised as these functionaries began arriving in haste early this morning.

When the Pope was breathing his last St. Peter's Square was dark. The Swiss Guards patrolling at the great bronze door entrance to Vatican City received their first word of their ruler's passing a few minutes after from an Associated Press correspondent on duty at the Vatican.

The guards at first refused to believe the news, since they had had no information from their superiors. At 5:48 the captain of the papal gendarmes came down from the papal palace and confirmed the death. He instructed guards on duty to awaken their sleeping comrades in the barracks. The entire garrison turned out and sleepily donned their brilliant orange, red and blue uniforms while awaiting further orders.

Cardinal Pacelli, Papal Secretary of State, and Cardinal Caccia Dominioni were among the first Cardinals to reach the papal apartment. The latter was for many years the Pontiff's master of ceremonies.

Giving of Extreme Unction

The extreme unction was administered to the Pope by Mgr. Alfonso de Romanis, the Pope's sacristan.

In the room was Cardinal Lauri, Chief Penitentiary, and others of the papal court.

They previously had prepared the articles for the last sacrament. In one corner of the room was a table with a crucifix and lighted wax candles, a vase of holy water and an aspergillum or holy water sprinkler, a plate with small crumbs of bread, a spoon, a towel and seven balls of cotton.

Attendants, watched over by the Papal physicians, had washed the Pontiff's face, hands and feet for his anointing.

Mgr. de Romanis began the ceremony by sprinkling the Pope, the other prelates and dignitaries present and the room itself with holy water, repeating at the same time from the Psalms:

"Thou shalt sprinkle me with hyssop, O Lord, and I shall be cleansed; Thou shalt wash me and I shall be made whiter than snow. Have mercy on me, O God, according to Thy great mercy. Glory be to the Father and to the Son and to the Holy Ghost, as it was in the beginning, is now and ever shall be, world without end. Amen."

Mgr. de Romanis gave the Pope holy communion and recited three prayers.

Prays for "Serene Joy"

The first besought God that "into this house may come eternal happiness, divine prosperity, serene joy, fruitful charity and lasting health; that the devils may flee; that the angels of peace may be present; that all evil discord may disappear."

The second asked for blessing from God on the house and on all who dwelled in it, that God might give them a good angel as their guardian, that He might protect them from all the powers of darkness, from all fear and perturbation.

The third again asked that the angel of God guard, protect, cherish, visit and defend all who dwelt in that abode.

Mgr. de Romanis and the others in the sickroom then recited the confiteor, or confession of faith. The Monsignor concluded with the sign of the cross.

Approaching closer to the dying Pontiff, Mgr. de Romanis made a threefold sign of the cross over him and invoked:

"In the name of the Father and of the Son and of the Holy Ghost, may all the power of the devil be extinguished in thee by the imposition of our hands and by the invocation of all the holy angels, arch-

Continued on Page Five

Times Wide World

POPE PIUS XI

CARDINALS TO NAME POPE AT CONCLAVE

Will Live in Cells in Vatican Before Voting—Candidate Must Get Two-thirds

The election of a new Pope will take place at a gathering of the Sacred College of Cardinals known as a conclave, which dates back in its present form to the end of the thirteenth century and is minutely regulated by the tradition and legislation of the church.

As soon as possible after the death of a Pope the Cardinal Camerlengo, or chamberlain, assumes charge of the Papal household and all the Cardinals are notified of an impending election. Those in Rome join in the obsequies for the dead Pontiff, which last for nine days, and the others proceed there as rapidly as possible.

Meanwhile a large part of the Vatican palace, including two or three floors, is walled off and the space within is divided into apartments of three or four small rooms, or cells, in each of which are a crucifix, a bed, a table and a few chairs. Access to the conclave is through one door only, locked from within by the Cardinal Camerlengo and from without by the Marshal of the Conclave, who since 1721 has always been a member of the Chigi family.

Secretaries Are Taken In

Each Cardinal has a right to take into the conclave an assistant who must be a layman. These assistants are sworn to secrecy and also not to hinder the election.

The Cardinals live with their conclavists within their cells, which are covered with cloth, purple if they are of the last Pope's "creation"; green if they are not.

When a Cardinal wishes to be undisturbed he closes the door of his cell, the framework of which is in the shape of a St. Andrew's cross.

Including Cardinals, prelates and conclavists, there are about 250 persons in the enclosure. They receive their food through four openings communicating with the kitchen of the Vatican, which are carefully guarded both within and without.

Once a conclave begins, the door is opened only to permit the entry of a Cardinal who has been late in arriving, although in case of sickness certified under oath by a physician a Cardinal may leave a conclave and return.

Papal legislation forbids the Cardinals from having discussed the succession among themselves during the lifetime of the Pope, although the Pope may have treated with them concerning the matter. Similar legislation has long since forbidden the once customary "ca-

Continued on Page Four

HEALTH WARNINGS IGNORED BY PONTIFF

He Disregarded the Advice of Doctors in His Determination to Carry On Papal Duties

By The Associated Press

VATICAN CITY, Friday, Feb. 10.—Pope Pius, nearing 82, with two recent grave illnesses behind him, disregarded his doctor's advice to take better care of his health.

Only Tuesday, when he suffered an attack of influenza—his last illness—did he finally cancel his engagements.

Despite his weakened heart and failing strength, he persistently refused to rest, against the warnings of his doctor, Professor Aminta Milani.

"The Pope must not stay in bed," he told Professor Milani, "the Pope must be Pope."

The Pontiff once observed to a prelate that he wanted to die with his boots on. He did not want to die a lingering death, he said, but "sulla brecia" ("in the breach").

He had in mind Leo XIII who lay dying for twenty days.

Neglected Little Routine

And showing his determination not to die in bed, he insisted on neglecting as little as possible the busy routine that falls on the supreme Pontiff of 331,500,000 Catholics throughout the world.

The slightest exertion put a dangerous strain on his taxed strength.

The world marveled at his recovery from an attack of arteriosclerosis which, complicated by other ailments, brought him to the point of death in 1936.

Again in November, 1938, a severe attack of cardiac asthma caused fears for his life, brought Cardinals to his bedside and actually set in motion the ponderous Vatican ceremonial that accompanies the death of a Pope.

He was reported to have had a similar attack while at his Castel Gandolfo country palace last Summer. Ever since the 1938 attack, he had had occasional restless nights.

He sometimes had to get out of bed and sit in an armchair to ease his breathing. The armchair had been in his bedroom for that purpose ever since his 1936 illness.

Once an agile mountaineer and Alpine expert, the Pope more than two years ago gave up all exercise to conserve his strength for his work. In former times, he used to walk daily in the Vatican gardens, even in the rain.

There he would kneel in prayer at a small chapel dedicated to St. Theresa of the Child Jesus, whom he both beatified and canonized.

It was to her care that he entrusted his health.

Then he gave up walking gradu-

Continued on Page Five

DEATH AT 5:31 A. M.

'Let There Be Peace,' He Murmured After He Blessed Gathering

BURIAL TO BE WEDNESDAY

Rally From a Coma Yesterday Had Given Hope That He Would Again Recover

By CAMILLE M. CIANFARRA

Special Cable to THE NEW YORK TIMES.

ROME, Friday, Feb. 10—Pope Pius XI died at 5:31 this morning [11:31 P. M. Thursday, Eastern standard time] serenely slipping from this life almost unconsciously.

He was 81 years old, and had been Pontiff for seventeen years.

His death introduced the so-called regime of the vacant See, which will last until the election of a new Pope, with Eugenio Cardinal Pacelli in his capacity of Cardinal Camerlengo in supreme control.

The Pope's condition became suddenly grave at 4 A. M. when Dr. Filippo Rocchi, who spent the night in the patient's bedroom, suddenly noticed his pulse getting alarmingly weak.

He immediately tried injections of stimulants, but the Pope failed to react to them. Thereupon he called in the secret chamberlains, Mgrs. Venini and Gonfalonieri, who were sleeping in a near-by room. They, in their turn, advised the Papal Secretary of State, Cardinal Pacelli, and other high Vatican dignitaries.

Cardinal Pacelli was among the first to arrive, followed by the Pope's sacristan, by Cardinal Caccia-Dominioni, by the Pope's nephew, Count Franco Ratti, and by the Governor of Vatican City.

Even the Pope's physician, Professor Aminta Milani, though laid low by a high fever, arose from his bed and hurried to the bedside.

Pontiff Sinks Fast

At 5 o'clock it was evident that the Pope was sinking fast. His pulse was getting weaker and he had sunk into a comatose condition.

While the doctors and nurses worked over him trying to give him what relief science has at its command, the Cardinals and other officials sank to their knees at the foot of the bed and intoned prayers for the dying Pope.

About 5:15 the doctors administered a strong stimulant, under the influence of which the Pope rallied somewhat, regaining consciousness. Cardinal Lauri, Chief Penitentiary of the Holy Roman Church, bent over the Pope, who was lying in his bed propped up by pillows, and to him the Pope confessed himself in a whisper. This lasted only a few instants.

The Pope then took holy communion. A few minutes later, it being evident that the effect of the stimulants was evaporating and the end approaching, extreme unction was administered.

Just before the Pontiff lost consciousness again Cardinal Pacelli said, "Holy father, give us your blessing."

While many Cardinals and other officials sobbed openly and there was not a face present unlined by tears, the Pope made a supreme effort to rally his faculties.

With a visible effort he raised his right hand from the bed-covers and went through the motion of giving the apostolic blessing, at the same time mumbling the ritual formula. Then his hand sank heavily onto the bed again and his body relaxed.

Makes a Final Effort

It looked as if the patient had given up the struggle and had again sunk into insensibility, destined soon to be followed by death. But he suddenly made another attempt to regain his hold on life.

He opened his eyes, causing them to travel slowly around the circle of sorrowing faces, at the same time giving a weak imitation of a smile.

Finally, with what evidently was a very great effort, he raised himself in his bed and mumbled a few words that were almost completely incomprehensible to the majority who heard them. Those nearest to him report that he said, "God bless you, my children," followed more weakly by "Let there be peace."

The Pope's condition had taken

Continued on Page Two

"All the News That's Fit to Print."

The New York Times.

LATE CITY EDITION
Cloudy, little change in temperatures today, rain in afternoon and night. Tomorrow clearing.
Temperatures Yesterday—Max., 53; Min., 36

VOL. LXXXVIII...No. 29,620. Entered as Second-Class Matter, Postoffice, New York, N. Y. NEW YORK, TUESDAY, FEBRUARY 28, 1939. PP THREE CENTS NEW YORK CITY and Vicinity | FOUR CENTS Elsewhere Except in 7th and 8th Postal Zones.

SUPREME COURT OUTLAWS SIT-DOWN STRIKES, UPSETS LABOR BOARD RULINGS IN THREE CASES; HOPKINS CONSIDERS WAGNER ACT AMENDMENTS

LONDON AND PARIS RECOGNIZE FRANCO; GET 'ASSURANCES'

M. P.'S CRY 'SHAME'

Chamberlain Refuses to Reveal Guarantees of a Free Spain

BRITONS TO DEBATE TODAY

Censure Motion Is Scheduled—United States Decision Is Left to Roosevelt

By FERDINAND KUHN Jr.
Wireless to THE NEW YORK TIMES.

LONDON, Feb. 27.—Unconditional recognition of the Franco regime in Spain was announced in the House of Commons today by Prime Minister Neville Chamberlain.

Amid shouts of "Shame!" and "Betrayal!" from a handful of Opposition members, Mr. Chamberlain reminded the Commons that Generalissimo Francisco Franco now controlled the greater part of Spain and that any further resistance by the Republicans [Loyalists] "can only result in further suffering and loss of life." It was impossible for the British Government, said Mr. Chamberlain, to regard the scattered Republican government as sovereign over Spain.

Glosses Over "Assurances"

"Certain assurances," he added, had been received from the victorious Franco regime, but apparently they were so vague that he did not think it worth while to disclose them. He simply contented himself with saying:

"His Majesty's government have noted with satisfaction the public statements of General Franco concerning the determination of himself and his government to secure the traditional independence of Spain and to take proceedings only in the case of those against whom criminal charges are laid."

Thus the British Government has finally decided to face realities and take a gambler's chance that the new Spanish Government will not allow Germany or Italy to keep a dominating position on the Iberian Peninsula. As long as resistance continues, the pretense of nonintervention will go on, but henceforth Great Britain will do all she can to be friendly and helpful to the victors. It is taken for granted this will involve a substantial loan for reconstruction in Spain.

Formal announcement is expected this week of the appointment of the Duke of Alba as Spanish Ambassador to London and of Sir George Mounsey, assistant under-secretary of state at the Foreign Office, as the first British Ambassador to Nationalist Spain.

Recognition will be withdrawn from Pablo de Azcarate y Flores, who has represented the Republicans quietly and competently in London. He spent a heartbreaking day today, preparing the palatial embassy building in Belgrave Square for his successor.

Aid Asked for Blacklisted

Meanwhile the British are convinced that the civil war in Spain is ended for all practical purposes and that even the Republicans know surrender is inevitable. It became known here tonight that Señor de Azcarate had asked the British to rescue as many as possible of those on General Franco's blacklist and that the British Government had agreed to do what it could.

It is unlikely that any large number of political fugitives will be admitted to this country. To some of the Republican leaders Britain may offer asylum, just as leading Social Democrats and Communists in the Sudetenland have been rescued from the German Gestapo [secret political police] and brought to Britain in the past few months.

The fate of the Republican leaders will be uppermost in the minds of Members of Parliament tomorrow when the House of Commons devotes the whole day to debating recognition of the Franco regime. The Labor party will move a vote of censure, registering condemnation of Prime Minister Chamberlain's decision today, but a large number of Labor members who are stirred and emotionally shaken by the defeat of the Republican regime now realize that recognition was inevitable.

Clement R. Attlee, the Labor leader, provoked a bitter wrangle with Mr. Chamberlain today, but it had nothing to do with the rightness or wrongness of recognition itself. Mr. Attlee's complaint was

Continued on Page Ten

Nazi Ship Is Reported Filming Our War Game

Wireless to THE NEW YORK TIMES.

CHARLOTTE AMALIE, Virgin Islands, Feb. 27.—Although not officially confirmed, it was reported today that the German shark catcher Equator hovered within reasonable distance from the aircraft carrier Yorktown and several destroyers outside the port of St. Thomas, photographing the United States Navy manoeuvres in the Caribbean Sea.

It was reported that the commanding officer of the Yorktown ordered the shark catcher to lay to in order to receive an armed boarding party which searched the ship for cameras, observed from the Yorktown's crow's nest. The search proved fruitless.

The Equator's captain said the expedition had also been fruitless. The Equator entered St. Thomas Harbor and her papers were inspected by customs officials. She departed soon afterward for Germany.

21 FAIR ADVISERS ON CONSUMER QUIT

Charge Curbing of Powers and Misuse of Their Names to Promote Exhibits

The resignation of twenty-one government officials and consumer experts from the New York World's Fair Advisory Committee on Consumer Interests has been sent to Grover A. Whalen, president of the Fair corporation, it was announced last night by Ruth W. Ayres, acting secretary of the group.

Their letter of resignation says that the purposes of the committee as understood by them have been so altered that the committee has no opportunity to develop a consumer program. The letter further protests that their names are being misused to promote commercial exhibits at the exposition.

Some of the local members resigning from the committee, who preferred not to be quoted otherwise than through their letter, explained that they were not opposed to commercial exhibits that they believed would serve a useful purpose. They declared, however, that they did not propose to have their "names used for window-dressing" for that type of exhibit.

When informed that the letter of resignation had been made public, Mr. Whalen declined to comment. Likewise, Paul S. Willis, chairman of the committee, which originally comprised some 145 members, declined to discuss the controversy inasmuch as the resignations had been sent to Mr. Whalen and he had received no formal notice of them. Mr. Willis, who is president of the Associated Grocery Manufacturers of America, succeeded Mrs. Bert Hendrickson as chairman of the Advisory Committee on Consumer Interests.

Charge Letter Was Ignored

The letter to Mr. Whalen, dated Feb. 10, 1939, said:

"On Dec. 7, 1938, we and other non-commercial members of your Advisory Committee on Consumer Interests addressed a letter to you raising questions as to the purposes to be served by that committee, and offering our cooperation in establishing its work upon a basis which might at the same time command the respect of consumers and be of assistance to the corporation. To that letter we have received no reply nor any acknowledgment of its receipt.

"We accepted membership on the committee with your assurance that it would be empowered to develop plans in good faith to enhance the value of Fair exhibits to consumers. We are forced to the conclusion that the purpose of the committee, as you see it, is solely to advertise the Fair to consumers and others and to promote the commercial interests of persons enjoying the confidence of the corporation.

"We have protested, without effect, the unauthorized use of our names by Mr. Paul S. Willis, acting chairman of the committee, for the purpose of selling space to a prospective exhibitor.

"We now see no opportunity for the committee to promote the interests of consumers in the planning of exhibits or to afford them any safeguard as to the value or reliability of information imparted to them by the Fair.

"The overwhelming preponderance of exhibits at the Fair will be

Continued on Page Twenty-one

PLAN ON PALESTINE REJECTED BY JEWS AT LONDON PARLEY

Delegation Unanimously Rules Out British Proposals for Arab-Dominated State

READY TO QUIT THE TALKS

But a Softening of Terms by MacDonald Is Reported—Scheme Assailed Here

By ROBERT P. POST.
Wireless to THE NEW YORK TIMES.

LONDON, Feb. 27.—The Jewish delegates to the Palestine Conference rejected today the British suggestions for the establishment of an independent Arab State. The rejection was contained in a memorandum submitted at a meeting between British and Jewish delegates after the full conference committee of the delegates and their advisers had agreed that the suggestions in their present form were not even worthy of discussion.

At the same meeting the Jews apparently gave notice of an intention to withdraw from the conference if the British proposals for abrogation of the mandate and for expanding the present Government of Palestine with the appointment of Arabs and of Jews on a population basis were carried out. Presumably, the Jews also informed the British that they would not take part in the proposed round-table conference to draw up a Constitution for Palestine.

Colonial Secretary Malcolm MacDonald said, however, that the British suggestions should be regarded only as a basis for discussion. After a long session, in which Mr. MacDonald is reported to have softened the British proposals in form if not in substance, the Jews agreed to meet him and Richard Austen Butler, Under-Secretary for Foreign Affairs, tomorrow—but only informally, not in an actual session of the conference. It will be decided at that meeting whether further sessions of the British-Jewish section of the conference will be held.

Jewish Action Unanimous

It remains to be seen whether the Jews—who were unanimous in rejecting the British suggestions today, even the non-Zionist and the British Jews agreeing—will decide that Mr. MacDonald's remarks hold out enough hope of a change in the British attitude to justify their remaining at the conference.

Meanwhile, Rabbi Stephen S. Wise, former president of the Zionist Organization of America, and other American representatives on the Jewish delegation have decided to sail for New York on the liner Queen Mary on Saturday.

Ambassador Joseph P. Kennedy of the United States had a discussion on Palestine with Viscount Halifax, the Foreign Secretary, this morning. It was denied later that he had informed Lord Halifax that the British ideas on Palestine would have an unfavorable effect on opinion in the United States. It was said Mr. Kennedy had seen Lord Halifax in the role of a reporter and had merely received a fuller version of the British suggestions than had been revealed.

Extremely irritated over the failure of the British effort to conduct the conference behind a veil of secrecy, Mr. MacDonald in the

Continued on Page Eight

NLRB Suspends Official On Anti-Employer Report

Special to THE NEW YORK TIMES.

WASHINGTON, Feb. 27.—Dr. Towne Nylander, regional director of the National Labor Relations Board at Los Angeles, was suspended today pending the outcome of an investigation to determine whether he was correctly quoted in remarks reported to have been made at a public forum in Inglewood, Calif.

The board stated that The Inglewood News on Feb. 7 carried a report of an address by Dr. Nylander "expressing views which are in no sense the views of the board, and the expression of which by an agent of the board is damaging to its work."

The newspaper quoted Dr. Nylander as saying: "I'll tell you frankly when we go into a hearing the employer hasn't got a chance."

VANDENBERG FIGHTS 'WORLD POLICE' ROLE

In Debate on Army Planes Bill, He Calls for Clarification of Foreign Policy

Special to THE NEW YORK TIMES.

WASHINGTON, Feb. 27.—Senator Vandenberg opened an assault on the Administration's foreign policy today as the $358,000,000 defense bill which would increase the army total of planes to 6,000 was seized upon in the Senate as the basis for an examination of President Roosevelt's ideas and philosophy.

Senator Vandenberg warned that any notion that the United States could pursue a policy involving direct action limited to steps "short of war" was a "deeply dangerous infatuation."

From the debate, in which Senator Connally replied to the Michigan Republican frequently with undisguised sarcasm and largely on the contention that the President's critic had talked an hour without stating his position in clear terms, emerged two leading impressions.

One was that no one on the floor appeared ready to contest the viewpoint that the United States should "keep out of foreign entanglements." The other was that no substantial opposition faces the bill which marks a major step in increasing American armaments.

All of the debate, except an opening statement by Senator Sheppard, chairman of the Military Affairs Committee, its sponsor, disregarded the measure at issue in favor of a discussion of generalities dealing largely with fine points of interpretation concerning the Administration program.

Senator Borah, veteran militant isolationist, took the floor to defend a policy of no foreign entanglements operated in conjunction with the Monroe Doctrine. He spoke in reply to questions addressed to Senator Vandenberg by Senator Logan.

Shortly before the Senate began debating foreign policy the Senate

Continued on Page Four

Mrs. Roosevelt Indicates She Has Resigned From D. A. R. Over Refusal of Hall to Negro

Special to THE NEW YORK TIMES.

WASHINGTON, Feb. 27.—Mrs. Franklin D. Roosevelt indicated today that she had resigned from the Daughters of the American Revolution in disapproval of the national society's refusal to permit the appearance in Constitution Hall of Marian Anderson, Negro contralto, for whom Howard University is seeking to arrange a concert in Washington.

She would "neither affirm nor deny" that the D. A. R. was the organization from which she had announced in her newspaper column she intended to resign rather than by continued membership seem to acquiesce in a policy of which she disapproved. She said she thought it the prerogative of the organization in question to make any announcement on the subject.

Neither would she answer directly a question as to whether the policy in question was the exclusion of Miss Anderson from the society's auditorium, nor comment upon the decision of the society in the matter. However, she said she had joined the society "by request" soon after taking up her residence in the White House.

She said she deplored the fact that Miss Anderson might not be heard in Washington, and so had telegraphed James E. Scott, Negro, treasurer of the Marian Anderson Citizens Committee. Her telegram which she confirmed, was as follows:

"I regret exceedingly that Washington is to be deprived of hearing Marian Anderson, a great artist."

At the D. A. R. offices it was stated that Mrs. Henry M. Robert, president general of the national society, was out of town; her secretary at home, ill, and that if Mrs. Roosevelt's resignation had indeed been submitted, it was yet in the unopened mail accumulating on Mrs. Robert's desk. No such communication thus far has been received by any national officer, according to members of the clerical staff, and the resignation, if submitted, awaits Mrs. Robert's return.

Criticism of the D. A. R. for barring Miss Anderson from Constitution Hall, and of the Public School Board for sustaining the refusal of Dr. Frank G. Ballou, the Superintendent of Schools, to permit the use of the Central High School auditorium for her proposed concert, has crystallized into a petition for protest which will be published

Continued on Page Five

CONTRADICTS NLRB

Court Holds Its Ruling in Sands Case Contrary to the Evidence

JUSTICE ROBERTS CAUSTIC

Finds Facts 'Refute' Charge of Unfairness—Refuses to Reinstate Workers

Special to THE NEW YORK TIMES.

WASHINGTON, Feb. 27.—Conclusions of the National Labor Relations Board from evidence it submitted were flatly contradicted by a majority of the Supreme Court today when five justices refused to uphold a board order charging the Sands Manufacturing Company of Cleveland with refusal to bargain collectively with members of the Mechanics Educational Society of America.

The decision, to which Justices Black and Reed dissented without writing, was one of three by the court rebuffing efforts of the board to sustain its interpretations of the Wagner act, in this instance to force reinstatement of certain workers with back pay. Justice Roberts wrote the finding. Justice Frankfurter did not participate.

The Sixth Circuit Court found, Justice Roberts noted, "that upon the findings of fact and the uncontradicted evidence, the board's conclusions are without support in the record." To this the Supreme Court majority agreed in affirming the lower court.

Contract Signed in 1935

This case originated when Sands signed a contract with M. E. S. A. on June 15, 1935. When work became slack in the following August the concern concluded to keep open only its machine shop, and shut down the rest of the plant. In the middle of August, however, when the company wished to increase the machine-shop workers, a controversy started in the interpretation of the contract. M.E.S.A. argued that Sands could not hire any "new men" as long as "old men" (employes in 1934) were still available. Eventually the plant was closed, but about the last of August the management negotiated with the International Association of Machinists, an A. F. of L. affiliate, and reopened the plant with "practically all" employes members of this union.

M. E. S. A. picketed the plant, and subsequently obtained an order from the Labor Board alleging discrimination, lockouts, coercion, interference with self-organization and failure to bargain collectively.

Criticism of the board's contentions was expressed by Justice Roberts in dealing with the first point in the opinion.

"The petitioner (Labor Board) urges," he said, "the correctness of the ultimate conclusion that the respondent's conduct permits no reasonable inference save that the employes were locked out, discharged and refused employment because they were members of the M. E. S A. and had engaged in concerted activities for the purpose of collective bargaining. We think the conclusion has no support in the evidence and is contrary to the entire and uncontradicted evidence of record.

Evidence of Espionage Denied

"The respondent (Sands) did not attempt to prevent organization of its employes or discourage their affiliation with M. E. S. A. or interfere with their relations with that body. There is no evidence of espionage or coercion by the company."

Discussing meetings between Sands officials and those of M. E. S. A., the justice told how the company manager said he wanted to operate the machine shop with "new men," and when a M. E. S. A. committee refused he requested them to ask the workers whether this could be done or if the plant would have to be shut down.

"On Aug. 21," Justice Roberts said, "the committee brought back a reply to the effect that the company could shut down the plant but could not operate the machine shop on the principle of departmental seniority. The company then closed the plant and did not open it until it had employed new men under a contract with another union which gave it the option to enforce departmental seniority. Save for one item of evidence, this is all the record discloses to indicate that the discharge and the replacement of the men arose from a dis-

Continued on Page Thirteen

Capitol Sees Labor Act Changes As One of Hopkins Recovery Aims

Plan Held Revealed in Request for Data in Senate Committee's Hands—Hearings Put Off Pending Labor Peace Moves

By HENRY N. DORRIS
Special to THE NEW YORK TIMES.

WASHINGTON, Feb. 27.—As a further move in the Administration's program of appeasement to business and industry, Secretary Hopkins is expected by friends on Capitol Hill to make some recommendation concerning the proposed changes in the National Labor Relations Act.

As it became known that the Secretary of Commerce had put in a request for all information on the subject in the hands of the Senate Education and Labor Committee, Senator Thomas, the chairman, today postponed scheduled hearings on the amendments embodying changes in the act until after the American Federation of Labor and the Congress of Industrial Organizations have had a chance to make peace in accordance with the request of President Roosevelt.

Prior to Senator Thomas's announcement, an aide of the Commerce Department had inquired of the Education and Labor Committee whether a limit had been set as to when recommendations concerning the amendments must be filed.

This information seemed to confirm privately expressed opinions in Congress that the Commerce Department would be represented when hearings on the amendments are started, either in the Senate or House committees.

In announcing the postponement of hearings before the committee Senator Thomas said:

"Last week-end the President of the United States wrote letters to President Green of the American Federation of Labor and President John L. Lewis of the Congress of Industrial Organizations. In these letters the President urges the appointment immediately of committees to negotiate peace between the two organizations.

"Almost at the same time that the President sent his letters I set the dates for hearings on amendments to the Labor Relations Act. The Committee on Education and Labor has before it now amendments introduced by Senators Logan, Burke, Holman and Walsh. All of the amendments were to be

Continued on Page Thirteen

HANLEY IS ELECTED TO PITCHER'S POST

Defeats Feinberg as Albany Republicans Choose New Senate Floor Leader

By WARREN MOSCOW
Special to THE NEW YORK TIMES.

ALBANY, Feb. 27.—Joe R. Hanley of Wyoming County was elected majority leader of the State Senate today, after a belated attempt on the part of the Republican State leadership to swing votes to Benjamin F. Feinberg of Plattsburg had failed.

Senator Hanley, who represents the Forty-fourth district, which includes Genesee, Wyoming, Allegany and Livingston counties, succeeds the late Perley A. Pitcher of Watertown, the party "balance-wheel" in the Senate, who died a week ago today. The new floor leader is in his sixty-third year. He is a lawyer, a former Methodist minister, and a Chautauqua lecturer who has a reputation in the party ranks as an excellent orator.

The Republican State leadership, headed by Edwin F. Jaeckel, chairman of the State executive committee, had kept hands off until today, when word was passed around that support should be given to Senator Feinberg.

The result was a series of six ballots, in which Senator Hanley started out with seven votes and slowly forged ahead until he received fourteen on the sixth ballot, a majority of the twenty-six Republican Senators.

The immediate result of the election is to add prestige to the rural bloc of up-State county chairmen who have been on a rampage since the Republican State convention at Saratoga, when they found themselves ignored by the urban leaders in control of the convention. Senator Hanley is from the home county of James E. Nash, the county chairman who is head of the rural block.

Up-State Bloc to Meet

The up-State bloc of which Mr. Nash is leader is scheduled to come into the limelight to an even greater extent next week when it will meet in Albany to be addressed by the Republican national chairman, John D. M. Hamilton.

The understanding here is that the invitation to Chairman Hamilton to speak was made without consultation with the State leadership.

Arthur H. Wicks of Ulster, who had been one of the leading candidates because of seniority, failed to get much of a vote in the balloting, because Senator Wicks and his backers had decided, even before the meeting, that it would be impossible to elect him. They cast their influence toward Senator Hanley and C. Tracy Stagg of Ithaca.

On the third ballot the Stagg strength began to be transferred to Senator Hanley, and this shift continued until Mr. Hanley had a

Continued on Page Four

WALSH-HEALEY PAY ON STEEL ENJOINED

Temporary Writ Bars 62½-Cent Area Minimum on Two Naval Contracts

By The Associated Press.

WASHINGTON, Feb. 27.—Justice Jennings Bailey of the Federal Court for the District of Columbia issued a temporary injunction today enjoining the Secretaries of Labor and Navy from putting into effect the minimum wage rate of 62½ cents an hour on two naval steel contracts to be awarded early in March.

The Secretary of Labor ordered into effect March 1 minimum wage rates she established in January under the Walsh-Healey act for the iron and steel industry.

This act provides that manufacturers bidding on government contracts of more than $10,000 must pay the prevailing minimum wage rate for their localities as determined by the Labor Department.

The temporary injunction was asked by seven small Eastern steel companies and was issued in favor of the Lukens Steel Company, Coatesville, Pa.; the Alan Wood Steel Company, Conshohocken, Pa., and the Central Iron and Steel Company, Harrisburg, Pa., the only companies among the seven which want to bid on the navy steel contracts.

Wages Set for Four Base Areas

After a study of steel wages throughout the country by the Public Contracts Board, the Labor Department promulgated last month minimum steel wages in four areas under the Walsh-Healey act.

In seventeen Northern States, which supply most of the nation's steel, the Labor Department set a minimum of 62.5 cents an hour, the prevailing wage in most of the large companies. In eleven Western States the minimum was set at 60 cents, in seven Middle Western States at 58.5 cents and in thirteen Southern States at 45 cents.

Wage differentials were established for four areas after hearings last December in which the representatives of steel companies objected to an earlier proposal to use two base areas and set wage minimums of 45 cents an hour for the South and 62.5 for the rest of the country.

Several small companies outside of the concentrated industrial areas objected to the 62.5 cents minimum, declaring that it was higher than the prevailing wages of their communities and would prevent them from bidding on government contracts.

The 60 cents minimum in the West benefited the United States Steel Company and several other large companies which have maintained the prevailing 62.5 cents an hour of the East in their Western plants.

BOARD DENOUNCED

Its Order to Re-employ Fansteel Strikers Is Held High-Handed

LABOR DECISIONS BY 5 TO 2

Reed and Black Dissenters—Stone With Majority—Frankfurter Takes No Part

The texts of the Supreme Court opinions are on Page 12.

By LEWIS WOOD
Special to THE NEW YORK TIMES.

WASHINGTON, Feb. 27.—The sit-down strike as a weapon of labor in industrial strife was outlawed by the Supreme Court today in one of three five-to-two decisions through which stunning blows were dealt to the National Labor Relations Board in its administration of the Wagner act.

In a majority opinion by Chief Justice Hughes, the court denied the board the right to compel reinstatement of sit-down strikers in the Fansteel Metallurgical Corporation's plant at North Chicago, denounced the strike, and condemned the board for exceeding its authority.

"It was a high-handed proceeding without shadow of legal right," said the Chief Justice of the Fansteel strike. "To justify such conduct because of the existence of a labor dispute or of an unfair labor practice would be to put a premium on resort to force instead of legal remedies, and to subvert the principles of law and order which lie at the foundations of society."

Justice Stone, for the same majority, rejected a board ruling that the Columbian Enameling and Stamping Company of Terre Haute had declined to bargain collectively with a union the striking members of which the board demanded should be reinstated because of this alleged failure.

The third decision, written by Justice Roberts, defeated a board order against the Sands Manufacturing Company of Cleveland, the majority holding that there had been no discrimination against union members, nor refusal to deal with them. The evidence submitted by the board was contradicted by the authors of both opinions.

How the Justices Lined Up

In each case the dissenters were Justices Black and Reed. Against them were the Chief Justice and Justices McReynolds, Butler, Stone and Roberts. Justice Frankfurter participated in none of the Labor Board cases, although he delivered his first findings from the bench in two other cases. The Labor Board appealed all its cases from Circuit Courts.

Immediately after the court ruling on the Fansteel case, which was brought from the Seventh Circuit Court, Senator Wagner, author of the Labor Act, said:

"I have always stated that the sit-down strike is illegal and should never be resorted to by the workers."

Withholding other comment, Senator Wagner nevertheless indicated general approval of the Fansteel decision. Those close to him said he thought clarification of the law could better be accomplished through interpretative findings than by Congressional amendments now so widely demanded.

Labor Board officials who have swept through so many victories in the court with the exception of the Consolidated Edison and another case would not make official comment on the Fansteel or other decisions. Attachés, however, indicated that what they termed the latitude of the Hughes decision might encourage employers to discharge strikers for various reasons, real or fancied, and that such cases might clog the courts. The employers, it was forecast, might now try to "feel out" how far the courts would go in permitting the discharge of strikers for their tactics during a strike.

New Dealers Not Pleased

The stand taken against the board by the Chief Justice and Justices Stone and Roberts created some dissatisfaction in New Deal quarters, which, on the other hand, greeted the position of Justices Black and Reed with unconcealed pleasure. Roosevelt leaders said they felt that Justice Frankfurter would have stood with Justices

Continued on Page Twelve

"All the News That's Fit to Print."

The New York Times.

LATE CITY EDITION
Generally fair, continued cold today. Tomorrow fair, slowly rising temperatures.
Temperatures Yesterday—Max., 42; Min., 29

VOL. LXXXVIII...No. 29,638. Entered as Second-Class Matter, Postoffice, New York, N. Y. NEW YORK, SATURDAY, MARCH 18, 1939. P THREE CENTS NEW YORK CITY and Vicinity | FOUR CENTS Elsewhere Except in 7th and 8th Postal Zones.

HITLER DEMANDS TRADE CONTROL OF RUMANIA; CHAMBERLAIN BITTER, DROPS APPEASEMENT; WELLES CONDEMNS 'WANTON LAWLESSNESS'

STEPS FOR REMOVAL OF 2 JUDGES HERE BEGUN IN ALBANY

Their Names, the Nature and Source of the Charges Kept Secret by Leaders

COMPLAINT IS AWAITED

Legislature Inquiry May Be Asked After the Bill of Particulars Is Studied

Special to THE NEW YORK TIMES.

ALBANY, March 17.—Steps have been taken toward the removal from office or a legislative investigation of two high-ranking judges on the bench in New York City, it became known at the Capitol today.

Informed legislative leaders said they expected, within a few days, a bill of particulars giving charges against the judges. After this has been studied the decision will be made whether to hold a trial.

The source of the charges remained a mystery tonight, as well as the names of the two judges. Capitol gossip was active in connection with the latter, but the pledge of secrecy remained inviolate so far as the source of the charges was concerned.

Tried to Maintain Secrecy

The leaders had attempted to maintain secrecy about the entire matter, out of deference to those making the charges, but the story leaked out and it was later confirmed that a "responsible individual," not holding political office, had approached a legislative leader and asked whether he would be interested in sponsoring charges on the basis of the material that the individual and a group he represented had collected.

The legislative leader discussed the matter with other leaders, and the decision made was that if the charges were presented they should be made by either the chairman of the Assembly Judiciary Committee, Harry A. Reoux, or by some other member of that committee. The Assembly Judiciary Committee would play an important part if there should be a trial.

Other conversations followed, and the result is that a copy of the complaint is scheduled to be sent here in the next few days. It will be presented to the leaders confidentially, and they will make their decision on the basis of its contents.

John Harlan Amen, special assistant attorney general investigating the conduct of all law enforcement agencies in Brooklyn, declined to comment on the matter. For the last four months Mr. Amen and two extraordinary grand juries have been delving into evidence of alleged official corruption involving the judiciary, Police Department and District Attorney's office in Kings County. On Monday before the Appellate Division in Brooklyn Mr. Amen will prosecute removal charges filed by one of the extraordinary grand juries against Magistrate Mark Rudich of Brooklyn for alleged misconduct on the bench.

A Supreme Court Justice may be removed only by concurrent resolution of both the Assembly and the Senate, with the resolution being approved by a two-thirds vote in each house. A County Court judge, on the other hand, may be removed by a two-thirds vote of the Senate alone, on the recommendation of the Governor, a move that is equivalent to impeachment by the Governor.

Provisions of Constitution

The provisions of the Constitution (unchanged in the new Constitution), dealing with the removal from office of judges, are as follows:

"Judges of the Court of Appeals and Justices of the Supreme Court may be removed by concurrent resolution of both Houses of the Legislature, if two-thirds of all the members elected to each House concur therein.

"All other judicial officers, except justices of the peace, justices of the Municipal Court of the City of New York and judges or justices of inferior courts not of record, may be removed by the Senate, on the recommendation of the Governor, if two-thirds of all the members elected to the Senate concur therein.

"But no officer shall be removed by virtue of this section except for cause, which shall be entered on the journals, nor unless he shall have been served with a statement of the cause alleged, and shall have had an opportunity to be heard. On the question of removal, the yeas and nays shall be entered on the journal."

The office of District Attorney Thomas E. Dewey of New York County authorized the declaration that any statement that Mr. Dewey had anything to do with the charges was "pure fiction."

Printing of the names of the judges would not become privileged until after the charges had been formally recorded. This did not stop

Continued on Page Seven

Ex-Gov. Miller Asks Party In State to Cut Budget

Special to THE NEW YORK TIMES.

ALBANY, March 17.—Republican legislative leaders have received an eight-page handwritten letter from former Governor Nathan L. Miller suggesting drastic cutting of the proposed $415,000,000 budget.

It is understood that Governor Miller's letter was sent from California and declared that economies in State government were much needed at present. He urged that the party take a definite stand on economy to help put the State in the Republican column in the 1940 election.

MEXICAN OIL TALKS END IN A DEADLOCK

Richberg to Leave for Home, but Is Expected to Return Third Week in April

By RAYMOND DANIELL

Wireless to THE NEW YORK TIMES.

MEXICO CITY, March 17.—With organized workers launching a two-day celebration of the first anniversary of the expropriation of foreign oil companies, the news was broken gently to a country uneasy over the loss of gold reserves and depreciation of the currency that the latest effort to break the deadlock between the oil companies and the government had failed.

Donald R. Richberg, who came here representing all seventeen expropriated British and American companies, with the hopes of the Washington State Department, if not its official blessing, behind him, is returning to Washington after a farewell call Wednesday on President Lazaro Cardenas.

Officially, the reason for termination of the conferences is that Mr. Richberg had prior engagements at home. The Mexican Government communiqué says he is returning here the third week in April.

Richberg Issues Statement

Mr. Richberg himself issued a statement outlining the basis of the discussions and his plan for settlement of the oil controversy with mutual benefit, but making it clear that his conversations with the Mexican President did not imply settlement of their differences.

"No agreement on any question is implied or can be assumed until such agreement has been expressly stated by both" parties to the controversy, he said.

Attorneys for the government and the oil companies today presented briefs sustaining and attacking the constitutionality and legality of the seizure of properties representing hundreds of millions of dollars in foreign investment. The court reserved decision.

Meanwhile lottery salesmen in the streets around the court house and the Presidential Palace hawked tickets for a 200,000-peso 'lottery of redemption" tonight which ushers in the expropriation anniversary.

All week teachers in schools have been conducting seminars on the evils and abuses of foreign oil exploitation.

Tomorrow in the bull ring, one of the largest outside Spain, President Cardenas will be the guest of honor at a barbecue given by 2,000 members of the oil workers' syndicate. It was believed he might choose that setting for his promised announcement on the results of his talk with Mr. Richberg.

May Defer Speech to Sunday

However, it is believed more likely that he will reserve that statement until Sunday, when 100,000 workers, peasants and soldiers will gather in the Zocalo, the "Red Square" of Mexico, to hail the man whose supporters say he has freed Mexican economy from foreign imperialism.

While insiders asserted the oil conferences broke down on the question of management, despite the willingness of the companies to yield on restoration of their title to the properties, it was predicted the government would emphasize the month's suspension of the talks to maintain the hope of the Mexican masses, burdened with higher living costs and financial uncertainties, that progress toward a solution has been made.

Mr. Richberg's statement this morning tended to confirm reports that his formula consisted of waiving the issues of law and valuation in favor of discussion of how the companies and the Mexican Government could cooperate for their mutual advantage. Details of his plan are still lacking, however.

Richberg's Statement

Mr. Richberg's statement follows:

In order to aid public understanding and to reduce the harmful effect of rumors and misinformation, I am making a brief statement of my individual opinions regarding some of those basic principles which have been given consideration in discussions of the oil problem.

I have an understanding of the well defined desire and intention of the government of Mexico to exercise that control over the de-

Continued on Page Six

BORDEN MILK PRICE IS CUT 2¼C HERE; STRIKE DEFERRED

Company, in Biggest Single Reduction in 20 Years, Cites Lack of Any Regulation

FARMERS WAIT ON COURT

Syracuse Meeting Heads Pleas Against Violence—Noyes Predicts Law's Return

A two and one-quarter cent reduction in the price of Grade A and Grade B milk delivered to homes, and corresponding reductions in the price of store-bought milk—the biggest single reduction in more than twenty years—were announced last night by the Borden Farm Products Division of the Borden Company, the cut to become effective tomorrow morning.

The price cuts were decided upon as up-State dairymen voted in Syracuse to defer strike action pending a United States Supreme Court review of the recently invalidated price-fixing legislation.

In announcing the reductions, the Borden Company indicated that the chaotic conditions of the now unregulated milk industry made it necessary for the company and all its units to meet the new competitive conditions which had arisen.

Although it is expected that the other large distributors in the metropolitan area will put similar reductions into effect, L. A. Van Bomel, president of the Sheffield Farms Company, said last night that the Sheffield company had not yet determined what action would be taken to meet the new prices of its largest competitor.

Sheffield Officials Meet Today

He said that a meeting of company officials would be held today and that an announcement would be forthcoming then.

There will be a meeting of the larger independents who are members of Milk Industries, Inc., on Monday afternoon. A committee of these independents discussed the situation yesterday but would not comment publicly.

The price of Borden's Grade A milk beginning Sunday will be 14½ cents a quart, and Grade B milk 11½ cents, delivered to the home. Corresponding reduction in wholesale prices, the company indicated, would make it possible for stores to sell Borden's milk at similarly reduced prices.

Although the amount of the cut was the largest in a generation, and a surprise to the industry as a whole, actually it brings the price of milk near the eleven-cent price for Grade B milk which prevailed for a while in 1937 and compares with the twelve-and-one-half-cent milk at this time last year. This is the "flush" season in the milk industry and there is usually a small reduction made in the price to the consumer at this time of the year.

Drop May Be $100,000 Monthly

If Sheffield and the larger independents follow the Borden Company's reductions, it is estimated that consumers of milk in the metropolitan area will be saved about $100,000 a month on their milk bills.

No estimate of the cost to the farmer resulting from these new price levels was made yesterday, as negotiations are still under way between the distributors and the dairymen as to the prices they will receive for their milk.

The present chaos in the industry

Continued on Page Six

'Pilgrimages' to Hitler Are Barred by the Swiss

Wireless to THE NEW YORK TIMES.

GENEVA, March 17.—A warning that Switzerland is prepared to fight, if necessary, to maintain its independence was given today by Federal Councilor Hermann Obrecht, addressing the New Swiss Society.

Stressing the dangers of the international situation, M. Obrecht warned against acts that might create an atmosphere of uncertainty or anxiety and thus be interpreted as indications of fear.

"Let them know abroad," he declared, "that whoever attacks us or threatens our independence or our territorial integrity must be prepared for war. It is not from Switzerland that one goes on pilgrimages to foreign lands."

It was announced tonight that the President would make an appeal tomorrow to the Swiss people in an effort to allay the uneasiness prevalent since the fall of Czecho-Slovakia.

DICTATOR'S POWERS ASKED BY DALADIER

Premier Plans Swift Decrees to Defend France—Trade Envoy Called From Reich

By P. J. PHILIP

Wireless to THE NEW YORK TIMES.

PARIS, March 17.—With the avowed object of turning France into a vast workshop for national defense, Premier Edouard Daladier, in agreement with his Cabinet, today asked Parliament to approve within the next two days a five-line bill giving the government full power to rule by decree in all matters affecting national defense.

This has been the only reply thus far, beyond words of lament, to Chancellor Adolf Hitler's absorption of Czecho-Slovakia in the German Reich.

Former Premier Leon Blum and his colleagues of the Left do not consider it either wise or sufficient.

"Do you think," M. Blum asked, "that you are a man who can now appear before the world as representative of the double will of France to preserve her security and safeguard peace? Do you think these full powers you are demanding are an indication of wisdom and real energy?" He then hinted that the workers might object to this way of acting.

Offers to Resign

M. Daladier offered to resign if, as Deputy Louis-Oscar Frossard had suggested in an earlier speech, it should be found possible to make a government of national union. But he did not believe it possible.

"At least," he said, "I am putting forward a plan of action that I know to be necessary, that I believe to be effective. If you don't approve, turn me out."

This new full powers bill will be discussed in the Chamber of Deputies tomorrow and in the Senate on Sunday. It is very wide in its terms and may lead to a kind of industrial and economic mobilization which will, in effect, suppress the forty-hour law and turn over to

Continued on Page Five

U. S. IN FIRM STAND

Calls 'Extinguishment' of Liberties of Czecho-Slovaks Temporary

WORLD PEACE HELD ISSUE

President Asserts Neutrality Legislation Is Needed at This Session

Text of official statement by the United States, Page 3.

Special to THE NEW YORK TIMES.

WASHINGTON, March 17.—Germany's seizure of Czecho-Slovakia was condemned in strong terms today by the United States through a statement issued by Sumner Welles, Acting Secretary of State, with the approval of President Roosevelt. It was one of the sternest denunciations of another government by the United States in many years, and it received approval in Congress.

This government even refused to regard the partitioning of Czecho-Slovakia as final, much less to recognize it diplomatically. On the contrary, the statement referred to the acts of the past three days as having led only to "the temporary extinguishment of the liberties of a free and independent people." With those people, the statement added, the American people have maintained "specially close and friendly relations" since the "republic of Czecho-Slovakia attained its independence."

Several hours after the statement had been issued the State Department, in response to repeated inquiries, explained the use of the word "temporary." It indicated, the department said, that this government was neither directly nor indirectly recognizing the legitimacy of the acquisition of Czecho-Slovakia.

No Recognition in Sight

This explanation was considered as signifying that there was no intention of recognizing the consolidation of the republic with the Reich.

The statement declared that the United States had every right to speak out. This country, it said, stands for law and order in international relations; it is dedicated to the principles of human liberty and democracy; it has repeatedly contended for observance of treaties and the pledged word; it believes in non-aggression; and it is opposed to military aggression.

"It is manifest," the statement said, "that acts of wanton lawlessness and of arbitrary force are threatening world peace and the very structure of modern civilization."

Of all these things the United States by clear and direct implication accused Chancellor Adolf Hitler. Nor was it any surprise, because from the time that the attack on Czecho-Slovakia was begun it had been evident that all that it represented was condemned here. Furthermore, behind it all stand the broken promises of Chancellor Hitler as given at Munich and on other occasions.

Optimism Is Lacking

There was no indication that officials were optimistic about the immediate effects of the statement on Chancellor Hitler, but it was manifest that they felt it should be made and the position of the United States defined, so that Germany and other nations that might be considering strong-arm tactics to attain territorial ends would know the position and attitude of America. They felt also that the statement could have a long-range effect.

The statement was agreed upon by President Roosevelt and Mr. Welles at an early morning conference in the White House and was read by the Acting Secretary of State at his press conference this noon. Reading slowly and deliberately, and with emphasis, Mr. Welles let the statement speak for itself. He declined to elaborate upon it, but did say that it had the approval of the President. It was not being communicated officially to Germany because that was unnecessary. Press publication was sufficient, he explained.

That the statement was to be made at the State Department was made known by President Roosevelt at his press conference at 11 o'clock. He gave this as the reason for refusing to discuss the European situation himself. However,

Continued on Page Three

Chamberlain Denounces Hitler; Recalls British Envoy to Berlin

Prime Minister Lists Nazi's Broken Pledges —Says Threats Will Be Met by Solidarity With Other Peace-Loving Nations

By FERDINAND KUHN Jr.

Special Cable to THE NEW YORK TIMES.

LONDON, March 17.—In words of bitterness such as no British Prime Minister has ever used toward Nazi Germany, Neville Chamberlain tonight served notice that the British Government would never believe any assurance from Chancellor Adolf Hitler again.

It was the death knell of the policy of "appeasement" based upon trust of the dictator's words, and it was cheered by an audience of 2,500 in the town hall of Mr. Chamberlain's native city, Birmingham. If Britain continues to work for peace, Mr. Chamberlain suggested, it will be on the basis of her armed strength and her solidarity with other peace-loving nations, "perhaps even beyond the confines of Europe."

Mr. Chamberlain charged Herr Hitler had broken solemn pledges and without shadow of justification had extinguished the liberties of "a proud, brave people."

"If it is so easy to discover good reasons for ignoring assurances so solemnly and repeatedly given," he cried in a voice vibrant with anger, "what reliance can we place upon any other assurances that come from the same source?"

All of Mr. Chamberlain's restraint of the past few days had disappeared. He admitted his hopes had been shattered but he did not let himself be discouraged. Replying to a vote of thanks from the audience after his speech he said:

"We need not be downhearted. This is a great and powerful nation—far more powerful than we were even six months ago—and its forces of violence and injustice bring with them, sooner or later, their own reward.

"Every one of these incursions raises up fresh dangers for Germany in the future and I venture the prophecy that in the end she will bitterly regret what her government has done."

While Mr. Chamberlain was speaking the British Ambassador to Berlin, Sir Nevile Henderson, was preparing to return to London tomorrow, ostensibly "to report" but in reality for an indefinite leave of absence. His recall was finally ordered today as a sign of the British Government's indignation at the events of the past few days.

At the same time Robert Hudson, Secretary of the Department of

Continued on Page Four

Text of Prime Minister Chamberlain's address, Page 4.

HITLER IS CHEERED BY VIENNA AS HERO

Throngs Turn Out to See Him After His Tour of Annexed Bohemia and Moravia

By The Associated Press.

VIENNA, March 17.—Adolf Hitler rode into swastika-bedecked Vienna from his new protectorate of Bohemia and Moravia today to the thunderous acclaim of Viennese throngs.

Herr Hitler came here from Bruenn, Moravia, aboard a special train after a two-day swing through his newly acquired territory.

From the railway station he rode to the Hotel Imperial through streets dense with crowds giving the stiff-armed Nazi salute and shouting "Sieg Heil"—hail to victory.

After taking the salute of a guard of honor drawn up in front of the hotel, Herr Hitler went immediately to his first floor suite.

A few minutes later he appeared on the hotel balcony and gave the Nazi salute in response to an unending chant of "We want to see our Fuehrer!" from the crowd below.

All Vienna was decorated with red, white and black swastika banners. They had been displayed for two weeks in celebration of the first anniversary of the Austrian annexation by Germany, which occurred a year ago last Monday.

Tiso May See Hitler

Hours before Herr Hitler reached his hotel details of Nazi storm troopers and black-uniformed Elite Guards, Hitler youth groups and uniformed girls stood in formation awaiting his arrival.

Official and diplomatic circles believed he would return to Berlin tomorrow instead of visiting Bratislava, capital of Slovakia, which only yesterday came under his protection.

There were hopes that fertile Bohemia-Moravia, with a considerable agricultural surplus production, would become a granary for Germany and improve the Reich's food situation.

Experts estimated the new territory would help reduce the present necessity for food imports by one-half.

The wealth of ore gained, they figured, would bring Germany to the point where it would be almost self-sufficient.

The belief prevailed that Premier Joseph Tiso of Slovakia and another member of the Slovak Cabinet might come to Vienna to discuss details of the new regime for their country before Herr Hitler leaves for Berlin.

Bruenn Hails Hitler

BRUENN, Moravia, March 17 (AP). —Adolf Hitler, moving in triumph

Continued on Page Two

HACHA BIDS CZECHS WORK WITH REICH

He Warns Against Opposition —Wave of Suicides in Nazi Terror, Marked Men Seized

By EMIL VADNAY

Wireless to THE NEW YORK TIMES.

PRAGUE, March 17.—The sense of political realism so strongly developed in Czechs was strikingly demonstrated today in an official announcement by former President Emil Hacha and former Premier Rudolf Beran. Dr. Hacha broadcast a description of his historic interview in Berlin. His speech was melancholy in tone but he asked the Czechs to cooperate with the Reich and he warned against opposition to the new regime.

M. Beran, replying to a speech by General Johannes Blaskowitz, Commander in Chief of Bohemia, said that the Czech people were united in their determination to maintain the best relations with the German Army. He assured the general that his (M. Beran's) government would work loyally for the cooperation of Germans and Czechs.

Two Parties Are United

This passage indicated that the "protectorate" government remained in the hands of the Beran Cabinet—only nominally, it is true. Mating the two political parties created after the September events. The Workers party decided on self-dissolution today and joined the National Union movement. Addressing the leaders of that organization today, Dr. Hacha condemned the tactics of General Radula Gajda's Fascists who attempted separate political negotiations with the Germans. He declared that any agreement reached between General Gajda and General von Gablenz, military commander of Prague, was invalid.

The man in the street, however, was somewhat taken aback by such realism. In his newspaper he read that Dr. Hacha accompanied her father on his sad mission to Berlin, how she received a bouquet of beautiful yellow roses tied with a red bow bearing the swastika emblem while State Secretary Otto Meissner was polite enough to send her a box of candy as a farewell gift. He read also the interview between Chancellor Hitler and General Jan Syrovy, hero of the Czech Legionnaries whom the German press only six months ago termed Bolshevist and Hussite.

"Subservience" Assailed

Nationalist organizations are hastening to issue declarations of loyalty to the new regime. The Fascist organ, the Expres, tonight decried such "subservience," adding that the Germans themselves cer-

Continued on Page Two

ASKS INDUSTRY END

Reich Wants Rumania to Be Farm Country and German Supplier

'ULTIMATUM' IS REJECTED

Bucharest Keeps Army in Readiness—Washington Shows No Surprise

Special Cable to THE NEW YORK TIMES.

LONDON, March 17.—The British Government received tonight from its own sources in Bucharest, Rumania, word that a virtual ultimatum had been issued to the Rumanian Government by Dr. Helmuth Wohlthat, head of the German economic mission there. Dr. Wohlthat's "proposals" were said to be as follows:

First, that Rumania should by degrees cease all her efforts to build up her national industry, close down gradually all her existing factories and limit herself to being an agricultural country.

Second, that her entire exports of grain, oil, lumber, cattle and foodstuffs should go exclusively to Germany.

Third, that if Rumania agreed to these terms Germany would be ready to guarantee Rumania's territorial integrity and the independence of the Rumanian people.

The Rumanian Government completely rejected the German proposals.

In view of this German threat, all political leaders, including Dr. Julius Maniu, leader of the powerful Peasant party and a former Premier, have joined together in sacred patriotic union.

Rumanian Army Ready

Wireless to THE NEW YORK TIMES.

BUCHAREST, Rumania, March 17.—The Crown Council met this evening for three hours under the presidency of King Carol and in the presence of a number of army commanders. It is understood that the precautionary measures already taken were approved. No further troop movements have been ordered for the present, but a general state of readiness for any eventuality will be maintained.

Indignant denials were made today in regard to reports circulated abroad that Rumanian troops have made a demonstrative march from Sighet, Rumania, to Huszt, former Carpatho-Ukrainian capital.

Held for Spreading Rumors

BUCHAREST, Rumania, March 17 (AP).—Ion Manolescu-Strunga, former Rumanian Cabinet member and a prominent political leader, was arrested today on a charge of disturbing the public by spreading alarming rumors.

Details of the accusation were withheld, but it was understood the rumors concerned international dangers arising from German penetration to the southeast through former Czecho-Slovakia.

M. Manolescu-Strunga served as Minister of Trade and Industries in 1935 after having previously served as Minister of Communications and Under-Secretary of Finance.

Bulgaria Moves Preparations

Wireless to THE NEW YORK TIMES.

SOFIA, Bulgaria, March 17.—It was announced here today that Bulgaria would soon take measures similar to Rumania's in preparation for any eventuality. Parliament has passed several bills relating to national defense and granting the government special powers in case the country is threatened.

About 1,500 university students demonstrated before the Czecho-Slovak Legation this morning. The Czech Minister, Prokope Maxa, appeared at the window and waved to the cheering crowd.

Extra police were summoned to disperse the demonstrators. The police fired a volley in the air and arrested 150 of the students. Thereupon the students decided upon a strike in protest against Germany's annexation of Czecho-Slovakia, for censorship would have prevented this news from appearing in the press. Anti-German feeling is running high here.

Washington Not Surprised

Special to THE NEW YORK TIMES.

WASHINGTON, March 17.—The news despatch from London reporting the delivery of a German ultimatum to Rumania exacting economic dependence as the price of

Continued on Page Five

Philadelphia Judge Gives Bandit 100 Years And Then Frees Him on His Good Behavior

Special to THE NEW YORK TIMES.

PHILADELPHIA, March 17.—After remarking that his action probably would "shock the community," Judge Harry S. McDevitt today sentenced William (Blackie) Zupkosky, gunman and bandit, to a prison term of 100 days to 100 years and then suspended the sentence.

He told Zupkosky, whose criminal career was cut short in 1929 by arrest, conviction and sentence to the Eastern State Penitentiary for seventy to 140 years, that his debt to society had been paid and that he was "entitled to a receipt 'paid in full.'"

"But if you deviate one inch from decent conduct," the court warned, "I'll sentence you instantly to the penitentiary for the rest of your natural life."

A clamor arose when Zupkosky's original sentence was commuted and he was paroled in December by Governor Earle, on recommendation of the State Board of Pardons. He was arrested soon afterward on order of District Attorney Charles F. Kelley, inasmuch as sixty-three true bills of indictment, upon which he had not been tried, were undisposed of.

In court today, in accordance with his professed determination to "go straight," Zupkosky pleaded guilty to all bills, without exception, on which the prosecutor believed he was able to obtain conviction. Vincent A. Carroll, assistant district attorney, told Judge McDevitt, who has never been inside a penitentiary, that every responsible official was convinced of Zupkosky's rehabilitation.

The court, in imposing the 100-day minimum sentence, pointed out that Zupkosky had spent 105 days in the county prison awaiting trial, so that "the State actually owes him five days."

Judge McDevitt promised to get the 32-year-old former bandit a job and to serve as his parole sponsor if no other was available.

"You won't have to worry about me," Zupkosky replied, with emotion. "I won't betray your confidence. I've learned my lesson after nine years in jail. I want to be respectable. I want to go to work so that my mother won't have to slave any longer."

Times Wide World Photo

Professor and Mrs. Felix Frankfurter pose for reporters at their home in Cambridge, Massachusetts after he was notified that he had been nominated for the Supreme Court.

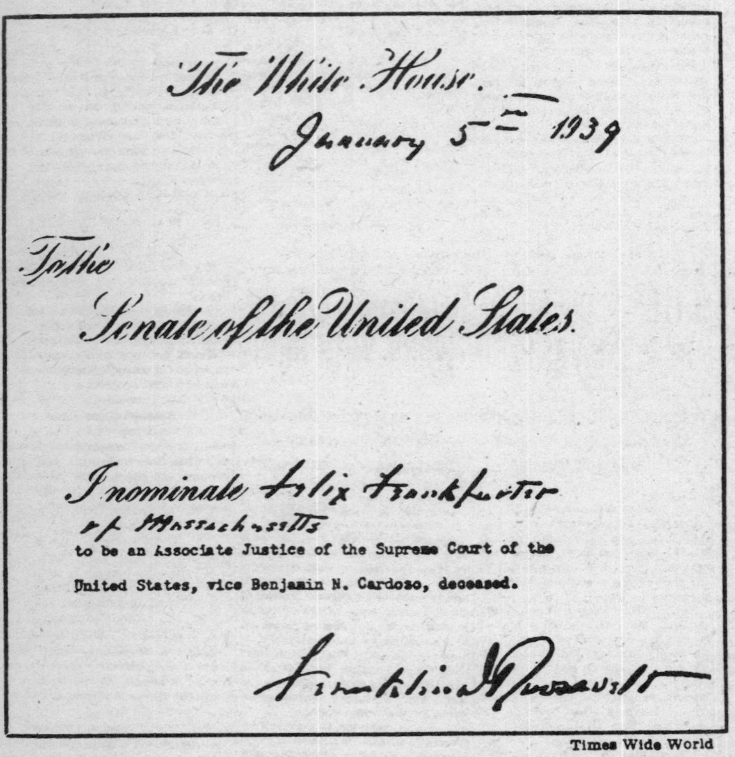

The White House.
January 5th 1939

To the
Senate of the United States.

I nominate Felix Frankfurter
of Massachusetts
to be an Associate Justice of the Supreme Court of the
United States, vice Benjamin N. Cardozo, deceased.

Franklin D. Roosevelt

Times Wide World

A copy of the President's nomination of Professor Frankfurter as an associate justice.

Times Wide World Photo

Supreme Court nominee William O. Douglas.

Mrs. William O. Douglas and their children, Mildred and William O. Jr.

"All the News That's Fit to Print."

The New York Times.

LATE CITY EDITION
Fair and colder today. Tomorrow cloudy, slowly rising temperatures, followed by rain.
Temperatures Yesterday—Max., 46; Min., 31

VOL. LXXXVIII...No. 29,641. Entered as Second-Class Matter, Postoffice, New York, N. Y. NEW YORK, TUESDAY, MARCH 21, 1939. P THREE CENTS NEW YORK CITY and Vicinity | FOUR CENTS Elsewhere Except in 7th and 8th Postal Zones.

BRITAIN SEEKS ANTI-HITLER COMPACT; RUSSIA PROPOSES NINE-POWER PARLEY; U. S. WON'T RECOGNIZE CZECH SEIZURE

PRESIDENT URGES ENDING OF LIMIT ON BONDED DEBT

Asks Congress to Facilitate Borrowing by Eliminating $30,000,000,000 'Ceiling'

STANDS BY TOTAL DEBT TOP

45 Billion All Right for Now, Message Says—Yielding to Economizers Is Seen

Special to THE NEW YORK TIMES.

WASHINGTON, March 20.—President Roosevelt told Congress today that there was no immediate need for raising the $45,000,000,000 limitation on the public debt. He asked, however, that the $30,000,000,000 "ceiling" on Treasury bond issues be removed.

The President's expression of disinterest in increasing the overall debt limit at the present session of Congress was regarded as a reversal of an earlier Administration intention to move immediately for such permission.

The change of plans was interpreted to be the result of a Congressional "revolt" led by Senator Harrison, Finance Committee chairman. Little sympathy for raising the debt limit had been shown on Capitol Hill.

The President's recommendations were based upon a written request from Secretary Morgenthau, a copy of which he enclosed with his own communication to Congress.

Secretary Morgenthau told his press conference a week ago that he would ask for removal of the "partition" on bonded indebtedness, but did not feel it necessary to have the total debt limit raised. He said the present limitation on bonds would block Treasury financing by Sept. 1 if not changed.

TEXT OF PRESIDENT'S LETTER

The text of the President's letter to Congress follows:

I am transmitting herewith a letter dated March 17, 1939, from the Secretary of the Treasury regarding the limitation placed upon the total amount of the public debt obligations which may be issued and outstanding at any one time under authority of the Second Liberty Bond Act, as amended. You will note from this letter that the Secretary of the Treasury feels that there will be no necessity for increasing the present limitation of $45,000,000,000 on the total public debt which may be outstanding at any one time, but does feel very strongly that it will be necessary to increase the present limitation of $30,000,000,000 face amount of bonds which may be outstanding at any one time.

I recommend that the Congress take such action as may be necessary to give the Treasury the authority which will enable it to carry out its financing operations during the next fiscal year as may be for the best interest of the government in line with market conditions at the time of such financing.

THE MORGENTHAU LETTER

The text of Mr. Morgenthau's communication to the President follows:

The Second Liberty Bond Act, as amended, provides that the face amount of bonds, certificates of indebtedness, Treasury bills and notes issued under the authority of that act, and certificates of indebtedness issued under the authority of Section 6 of the First Liberty Bond Act, shall not exceed in the aggregate $45,000,000,000 outstanding at any one time and provides further that the face amount of bonds issued within that limitation shall not exceed in the aggregate $30,000,000,000 outstanding at any one time.

At the present time the Treasury can issue approximately $5,000,000,000 face amount of additional public debt obligations under the Second Liberty Bond Act. On the basis of the current budget estimates this balance will be sufficient to carry the Treasury well into 1940. I do not believe, therefore, that it is necessary to request at this time an increase in the limitation on the total debt that may be issued and outstanding under authority of the Second Liberty Bond Act as amended.

The limitation of $30,000,000,000 on outstanding bonds presents, however, a different problem. The amount of bonds which the Treasury can issue within this limitation, after taking into consideration the March 15 refunding operations, is approximately $1,800,000,000. Taking into consideration our cash requirements between now and Jan. 1, 1940, the monthly issuance of United States savings bonds, and the possible refunding operations which the Treasury may wish to conduct, it seems quite apparent

Continued on Page Fourteen

W. O. Douglas Is Nominated For Seat in Supreme Court

Confirmation of SEC Head, 40, Ardent New Dealer, Is Likely—Born in Minnesota, He Came East as Youth—West Disappointed

By FELIX BELAIR Jr.

Special to THE NEW YORK TIMES.

WASHINGTON, March 20.—William Orville Douglas, 40-year-old chairman of the Securities and Exchange Commission, was nominated by President Roosevelt today to the Supreme Court vacancy recently created by the retirement of Associate Justice Louis D. Brandeis. His confirmation, of which there appeared little question, would make him the youngest man to sit on the tribunal in more than a hundred years.

Born in Minnesota and reared and educated in Washington State before coming East to study law, Mr. Douglas was appointed from Connecticut, his legal residence. Although the President planned originally to name him as coming from the Pacific coast as an answer to demands that a Westerner be appointed, he was dissauded from this course by friendly Senators, who reminded the Executive that Mr. Douglas had been nominated from Connecticut when he joined the SEC.

The Douglas nomination was sent to the Senate a few minutes after it had been announced informally at the White House by Stephen T. Early, Presidential secretary. Indications were that there would be little if any dispute over his selection.

However, Senator Ashurst, chairman of the Senate Judiciary Committee, named a subcommittee on which Westerners predominated to consider the nomination. The subcommittee included Senator Hatch as chairman and Senators King, McCarran, O'Mahoney, Borah and Danaher.

Senator Hatch indicated that Mr. Douglas would be summoned before the group for the customary questioning, but that formal hearings would be dispensed with unless requested by Senators interested. Although several members expressed disappointment both publicly and privately that a man more recently from the West had not been appointed, they showed no disposition to stand in the way of confirmation.

An ardent New Dealer who was Sterling Professor of Law at Yale University before coming to Washington in 1934 to direct the SEC investigation of bondholders' protective committees, Mr. Douglas's name was first brought to the attention of President Roosevelt by Attorney General Murphy. But before that he was the "discovery" of Thomas G. Corcoran, inner-circle White House adviser, and Jerome Frank, SEC member.

Not until after at least half a

Continued on Page Sixteen

COMPROMISE FUND FOR WPA STUDIED

House Group Has $100,000,000 Plan—Cox Slaps Workers Alliance Spokesman

Special to THE NEW YORK TIMES.

WASHINGTON, March 20.—A compromise by which President Roosevelt's request for $150,000,000 for additional relief funds would be cut $50,000,000 was reported today to have been agreed upon by several Democratic members of the House Appropriations subcommittee. They were said to have received assurances that the whole committee would accept the figure of $100,000,000 when it voted on Wednesday.

Republican members were understood to be opposed to any further deficiency funds for the Works Progress Administration, and the compromise was suggested, it was said, because the Democrats wished to avoid an open split in their ranks in the face of next year's elections.

One informed member of the House said that the question of additional relief funds was becoming acute because of the pressure brought upon members of Congress.

Representative Cox of Georgia slapped a lobbyist of the Workers Alliance who allegedly threatened that the votes of the unemployed would go against him if he did not agree to vote for additional funds.

Step Toward Inquiry Seen

Another reason advanced for the compromise was that the economy forces, led by Representative Woodrum of Virginia, could afford to avoid the direct issue of additional funds at this time if they could obtain an investigation of relief looking to a semi-permanent policy that would cut down costs.

In this connection a stiffening of members of the House Rules Committee against Administration pressure was seen.

It was said on good authority that the resolution of Representative Cox, providing for investigation of WPA by the Appropriations subcommittee, of which Mr. Woodrum is a member, would be approved by the Rules Committee and brought to the floor this week. Representative Sabath of Illinois, chairman of the Rules Committee, announced that the committee would consider the Cox resolution Wednesday.

Southern members of Congress, many of whom are opposed to additional relief funds, were besieged by delegates from their States to a Workers Alliance meeting called by David Lasser, president. The delegates demanded approval of the $150,000,000 asked by the Presiednt.

The visit of some of these delegates to the Capitol resulted in the slapping incident which occurred in the corridor outside Speaker Bankhead's office.

As related by an eyewitness and confirmed in major details by Mr. Cox, the circumstances were as follows:

Mr. Cox was called out by the Workers Alliance man, who told him a constituent wanted to talk with him about relief and pointed to a Negro standing a few feet away.

Mr. Cox replied that he was go-

Continued on Page Sixteen

500 IN C. I. O. UNION BOLT TO THE A. F. L.

Members of Office Workers Group Charge Local 16 Is Dominated by Reds

Five hundred office workers, members of the United Office and Professional Workers of America, Local 16, a C. I. O. affiliate, met last night at the Manhattan Center, Thirty-fourth Street near Eighth Avenue, and voted to bolt the organization and affiliate with the American Federation of Labor through its Bookkeepers, Stenographers and Accountants Union.

A resolution adopted at the meeting charged that Local 16 was dominated by Communists who take orders from the Communist party and run the union by "gag rule."

The resolution to join the A. F. of L. was carried by a vote of 474 to 25. Represented at the meeting were office employes of the International Ladies Garment Workers Union, which left the C. I. O. several months ago, League for Industrial Democracy, Union Health Center, Federation of Jewish Philanthropic Societies, Jewish Daily Forward Labor Committee for Palestine, Non-Sectarian Anti-Nazi League, the Sick and Death Benefit Fund, Administrative Board of the Dress Industry and more than sixty other groups.

Most of those who voted last night to join the A. F. of L. union belonged originally to that organization, but left in more than two years ago.

One Dissenter Ejected

A small group said to be Communists who tried to break up the meeting were shouted down and one of them was ejected forcibly for creating disorder when he sought to interfere with the taking of the vote. About 100 who came to the meeting with what the chairman called "forged admission cards" were kept from entering by a committee guarding the doors. For a while the dissenters inside threw the meeting into a bedlam, but order was restored when union ushers intervened.

The resolution to quit Local 16 was presented by Anne Gould, an employe of the Dress Joint Board of the I. L. G. W. U., who was chairman of a committee previously appointed to study the situation in Local 16 and prepare a report.

In adopting the resolution, the meeting rejected the plea of Peter K. Hawley, president of Local 16, who denied the committee's charges as embodied in the resolution and assailed the A. F. of L. as "undemocratic" and "dictatorial."

These were the charges leveled against Local 16 by Miss Gould and her committee and by speakers from the floor. They disclaimed hostility to the C. I. O. but maintained that Communist domination of Local 16 made it impossible for employes interested in trade union organization to remain with it.

The resolution condemned Local 16 as a "sorry failure as a trade union," attributing this to the fact "that the union was 'captured' by an organized machine which violated its oath to serve the membership by placing the interests of the

Continued on Page Eighteen

RUDICH IS ACCUSED BY BURKE OF TRYING TO INFLUENCE HIM

Fellow-Magistrate a Witness as Removal Hearing of Brooklyn Judge Begins

KASSMAN FIRST ON STAND

Bondsman Paints Picture of Partnership on 'Hundreds' of Cases of Judicial 'Fixing'

For six hours yesterday Magistrate Mark Rudich sat in a crowded Appellate Division courtroom in Brooklyn as the hearing of charges seeking his removal got under way. He heard a fellow magistrate, Anthony F. Burke of Manhattan, accuse him of attempting to influence the disposition of a criminal case concerning which Louis Kassman, professional bondsman and self-confessed perjurer, had testified previously that he paid Magistrate Rudich $100 to handle the unsuccessful "fix."

A furor was created in the courtroom when Kassman, in a heated verbal exchange with Magistrate Rudich's attorney, volunteered testimony beyond the scope of the case, declaring that in a fraudulent bail bond transaction he had received $150 for payment to a Supreme Court Justice in Brooklyn along with $50 for payment to another bondsman, both of whom he named.

Irrelevant Remarks Expunged

The court immediately ordered Kassman's remarks expunged from the record. The testimony was deemed irrelevant because it had nothing to do with the charges against Magistrate Rudich and solely concerned a fraudulent transaction to which Kassman recently pleaded guilty and on which he is now awaiting sentence. The other bondsman has been mentioned prominently in connection with the current inquiry by John Harlan Amen, special assistant attorney general, in the Brooklyn bail-bond racket.

The case involving Magistrate Burke was only one of the instances set forth by Kassman in five hours of testimony depicting an almost fantastic picture of Magistrate Rudich and the bondsman with a checkered criminal past as "partners" in bail-bond transactions, fraudulent and otherwise, in which Kassman said he charged his clients an added "fee" to be paid to Rudich for services rendered, with the further understanding that the money would be returned if anything "went wrong." Kassman said he had handled "hundreds" of such cases with Rudich since their first meeting in 1929.

Hearing Halted Abruptly

The hearing halted at 5 P. M. on a note of suspense arising from Mr. Amen's repeated efforts to elicit from Magistrate Burke an answer to questions as to whether Magistrate Rudich had said anything about "making it look right" when he attempted to influence Magistrate Burke's sentencing of a convicted prostitute. The court adjourned abruptly until 10 A. M. today while Magistrate Burke was reading a transcription of his testimony before the grand jury in order to refresh his recollection.

Facing summary removal from the bench and possible professional disbarment if the charges against him are sustained, Magistrate Rudich maintained an imperturbable air throughout the proceedings, conferring constantly with his attor-

Continued on Page Seventeen

Elliott Roosevelt Sees Garner in Lead For Party's 1940 Presidential Nomination

By The Associated Press.

FORT WORTH, Texas, March 20.—Vice President Garner was described as "in the driver's seat right now, well in the lead as a likely Democratic candidate for the Presidency in 1940" by Elliott Roosevelt in his semi-weekly broadcast tonight.

Announcing a "custom" under which he will occasionally discuss Texas citizens who have influenced State, national and world affairs, the son of President Roosevelt selected for the first of the series Mr. Garner and Fred H. Vahlsing, at present of New York City, who operates a 10,000-acre truck garden in the Rio Grande Valley.

Young Roosevelt stressed Mr. Garner's simple home life at Uvalde, his reticence toward public speaking and the power he carries in legislative matters, a power which grew steadily from the time Mr. Garner went to Congress in 1903.

Commenting on differences between President Roosevelt and Mr. Garner, young Roosevelt said:

"There is little room for doubt that Mr. Garner and the President of the United States have traveled separate roads since the Winter of 1937.

"Reports have it that the Vice President became so incensed over the Administration's handling of the sit-down strike situation that he quit Washington and returned to Uvalde for a six-month vacation. Since his return, his opinions have been at variance with the President's as to the path being taken by the Democratic party.

"Mr. Garner is a party man, and, seeing a return to conservatism as evidenced by the election results of last Fall, he is reported to have requested frequently that the Administration sense the trend and bring the Democratic party into a more conservative alignment.

"As to the results thus far and the future attainments of the conservative element as opposed to the New Deal, I do not feel qualified to voice an opinion.

"This much, however, is certain. John Garner is in the driver's seat right now, well in the lead as a likely Democratic candidate for the Presidency in the 1940 elections."

NOTE SCORES COUP

Formal Condemnation of Reich Is Expressed in Welles Document

LEGATION IN PRAGUE SHUT

Pittman Introduces Bill to Sanction Cash-and-Carry Sales of War Materials

By TURNER CATLEDGE

Special to THE NEW YORK TIMES.

WASHINGTON, March 20.—Condemnation by the United States of Chancellor Adolf Hitler's conquest of Czecho-Slovakia, and a flat refusal by this government to recognize the legitimacy of the occupation were made formal and official in a note sent by Acting Secretary of State Sumner Welles to the German Embassy this afternoon.

Details of the communication, a reply to the informative note handed to the State Department Friday evening by Hans Thomsen, German Chargé d'Affaires, were withheld until tomorrow noon to give time for their transmittal to Berlin. However, it was understood to be largely a reiteration of the public statement issued by Mr. Welles soon after the occupation, in which he used so strong a term as "wanton lawlessness" in describing the German action.

To Close Legation at Prague

Earlier in the day the Acting Secretary dispatched instructions to Wilbur J. Carr, American Minister to Czecho-Slovakia, to close the legation at Prague, in view of the realities of the situation. Mr. Welles directed the Minister to turn over the legation property and archives to the consulate-general and to leave Prague at his own convenience. He took occasion, too, to compliment the diplomat for his "highly distinguished service to his country" during the recent critical months in that part of the world.

State Department officials were understood, furthermore, to be drafting an announcement ending officially the trade agreement between the United States and Czecho-Slovakia, at least so long as Germany maintains its so-called "protectorate" over the major constituent parts of the former republic.

While these steps were being taken in the Executive Department apropos the new situation in Central Europe, Chairman Key Pittman of the Senate Foreign Relations Committee introduced his new neutrality bill, designed to permit the United States to sell war materials on a "cash-and-carry" basis to any nations engaged in "declared or undeclared conflict."

A general purpose of the proposed legislation is to give the President a freer hand in steering a course that would keep this country neutral, give him at the same time better legal facilities for aiding nations with wnom the United States sympathizes in case of declared or undeclared war. Senator Pittman explained that the effect of the legislation in the present and pro-

Continued on Page Six

Reich, Lithuania Confer on Memel; 'Decision' Is Expected on Saturday

Urbsys Greatly Perturbed as He Leaves Meeting With Ribbentrop—Berlin Regards Present Situation in Area as Impossible

By OTTO D. TOLISCHUS

Wireless to THE NEW YORK TIMES.

BERLIN, March 20.—With National Socialist organizations in Memel holding mass demonstrations under the slogan, "Home to the Reich," and Saturday set as the deadline for "fundamental decisions," Juozas Urbsys, the Lithuanian Foreign Minister, today called on Foreign Minister Joachim von Ribbentrop to discuss the situation resulting from this open defection of territory still under Lithuania's sovereignty.

The conference lasted three-quarters of an hour, but despite its significance for the next move of the Great German Empire it was treated as a "private visit" about which both sides maintained the utmost reticence.

It is no secret, however, that Mr. Urbsys left the conference in great perturbation and Lithuanian quarters are now convinced that events of the utmost gravity to that little State are now impending.

According to well informed quarters Germany made no specific demands but has let the Lithuanians know that in view of the situation in Memel as developed under National Socialist rule it would be well if Lithuania, of her own accord, made "constructive proposals" to end what is regarded here as an impossible situation.

If the Germans expected Mr. Urbsys to make such proposals immediately they were disappointed; he made none and from that viewpoint the conference ended in a stalemate.

German quarters insist that at the moment Germany wants only a "little solution" in the East affecting Memel alone and there are even hints that a Lithuanian offer for a free State status for Memel, similar to Danzig's, might find sympathetic consideration if made quickly.

Diplomatic quarters, however, keeping in mind the technique employed in the cases of Austria, the Sudetenland and Czecho-Slovakia express open doubts that such an offer would in any way change or delay Germany's predetermined action, and they now look forward to

Continued on Page Two

PSYCHOSIS OF WAR FOMENTED IN ROME

Press and Radio Prepare the Public for Conflict When Claims Are Presented

By CAMILLE M. CIANFARRA

Wireless to THE NEW YORK TIMES.

ROME, March 20.—After waiting to see the reaction caused in Britain and France by Germany's annexation of Czecho-Slovakia, the Italian Government has mobilized all possible means of propaganda to prepare the people for the eventuality of war in the near future.

For the past few days both the radio and the press have been giving an ample account of diplomatic and political events in all European capitals and impressing upon the people the gravity of the situation. Today the press denounces the "policy of encirclement of the totalitarian States on the part of the democracies," and even the more responsible newspapers speak openly of the possibility of war "before long."

The psychological preparation that inevitably precedes the outbreak of war is in full swing. War may or may not come, but the Italians have been told to be ready to face the worst.

Reports circulate in Rome that large numbers of reservists are being recalled to the colors and that troop movements are occurring in various directions. It is difficult to establish the accuracy of these reports, and they find no confirmation in official circles.

Practical Preparations

The newspapers are advising the people to buy gas masks. Electrical crews are replacing the white electric light globes in the streets with blue so as to render inhabited centers invisible from the air. Questionnaires have been sent to the head of every family with the request that he notify the authorities how many persons in his family would have to evacuate the city in case of air raids and how many hold driving licenses.

These preparations, as well as the psychological material, are the more striking because it is the first time they have been taken. One cannot help drawing the comparison with what was done in the most acute period of the Ethiopian war in the Autumn of 1936 and the Czecho-German crisis of last September. The comparison authorizes a pessimistic outlook for the coming months.

Not even when the sanctions were applied against Italy did the people here feel that a European war was inevitable. It is true that there were very violent polemics between Italy and Britain, several thousand men were mobilized, the Italian fleet was placed on a war footing, but the general belief persisted that no serious complications would occur in Europe apart from a great deal of ill feeling.

Last September, despite several speeches by Premier Benito Musso-

Continued on Page Three

REICH HINTS AT END OF BRITISH SEA PACT

Naval and Amity Accords One in Spirit, Says Foreign Office, and May Soon Be Revised

By GUIDO ENDERIS

Wireless to THE NEW YORK TIMES.

BERLIN, March 20.—A communiqué issued by the Foreign Office tonight says that the recall of the German Ambassadors from London and Paris and the rejection of the British and French protest notes did not constitute a mere formality but were intended to express the Reich Government's displeasure with the attitude, especially of Britain, toward the solution of the Czecho-Slovak problem.

This communiqué deals at some length with Anglo-German relations and reaches the conclusion that the Anglo-German naval pact and amity pact concluded between Chancellor Adolf Hitler and Prime Minister Neville Chamberlain in Munich are interlocking commitments in spirit, and if one is no longer valid the other also becomes nullified.

Recent official British utterances, says this communiqué, would seem to suggest that Britain appraises all treaties and problems only from the viewpoint of her position of power, and thus views with antagonism any increase in the strength of the German position. In such circumstances, the official statement adds, Germany would be compelled to subject the orientation of her policy to fundamental and incisive revision.

Ambassador Recalled

It was earlier announced that following the departure of Robert Coulondre, the French Ambassador, last night, Count Johannes von Welczeck, the German Ambassador in Paris, had been ordered home to report.

Further expansion of the diplomatic boycott of the Reich by the Western democracies, it was declared, leaves the German official quarters as emotionless as the threat of a political and economic blockade. A concerted attempt to change the "new order" in Central Europe would necessarily compel Germany to consolidate still more firmly her position there. She would then await a reaction to the question of who is for and who against the Reich.

A significant comment on the seizure of Czech provinces is contained in tonight's Deutsche Allgemeine Zeitung. It observes that in addition to having increased her territory and population it has also vouchsafed to the Reich the needed protection in Central Europe.

"The weak spot in the German defense wall has been wiped out in that our borderline has been shortened by 2,000 kilometers. A defense wall of barely sixty kilometers now guarantees us the accurity that we need in the heart of Europe. How necessary this was is indicated by the nature of the

Continued on Page Two

LONDON'S IRE RISES

Works for a Declaration to Warn Reich Against Further Aggression

HALIFAX CONDEMNS BERLIN

Rejects Its 'Explanations'—Mission to Go to Rumania—German Attack There Seen

Steps were under way in London yesterday toward forming an anti-Hitler coalition. The British proposed a joint declaration and warning by several powers, while the Russians, who hold the key to such a coalition, suggested a nine-power conference. [Page 1.]

Moscow's ultimate attitude, however, was in doubt. The Soviet seemed to be waiting to see what the other nations were ready to do. [Page 2.]

France, operating under the decree powers granted to Premier Daladier, moved nearer to a war footing with the publication of decrees to strengthen the army and lengthen the working time in defense industries. [Page 4.] President Lebrun prepared to go today to London, where, it was reported, he may sign a formal Anglo-French alliance. [Page 6.]

Farther east in Europe a movement got under way in Poland for a national unity government. [Page 2.] Rumania minimized her new trade agreement with Germany, announcing details of the accord showing that the Reich would get oil exploitation rights, but explaining that other nations could make similar deals. Bucharest welcomed news that Britain was going to send a trade mission there. [Page 3.]

In Berlin a Foreign Office communiqué threatened abrogation of the Anglo-German naval agreement. [Page 1.] There, too, officials discounted a note sent yesterday by the United States refusing to recognize the partition of Czecho-Slovakia. [Page 1.] Indeed, the Nazis seemed to be looking ahead to further exploits; Memel was the subject of a conference between the German and Lithuanian Foreign Ministers. [Page 1.]

Meanwhile, in Rome a war psychology was being prepared, presumably to pave the way for the long-expected demands on France. [Page 1.]

Coalition Idea Gains

By FERDINAND KUHN Jr.

Special Cable to THE NEW YORK TIMES.

LONDON, March 20.—A speech in the House of Lords today by Viscount Halifax, British Foreign Secretary, in which he announced that Britain was in direct consultation with other nations, strengthened the general belief—tentative as yet but gathering strength every day—that the British Government was at last seeking to build up a coalition against further fascist aggression.

The consultations of which Lord Halifax spoke went on busily in London and other capitals. Uppermost in these exchanges—because of what is deemed a likelihood of a German attack against Rumania—were diplomatic consultations between London and Moscow.

So far there has been no definite result, but it is realized here that years of Anglo-Russian coolness cannot be wiped out in a day, and there is plenty of satisfaction in London with the way the talks are going.

Russia is still unwilling to pledge her help to the threatened nations of Southeastern Europe without first getting a correspondingly definite pledge from Britain and France. The Russian Government has, however, suggested a conference of representatives of Russia, France, Britain, Poland, Rumania, Yugoslavia, Greece, Bulgaria and Turkey—in other words, a possible nine-power coalition whose shadowy outlines are just beginning to emerge.

The British have answered that they would prefer a continuance of active consultations through diplomatic channels, and to Paris, Warsaw and Moscow they sent a series of alternative suggestions today for

Continued on Page Five

People in Madrid rejoice as Franco's troops enter the city.

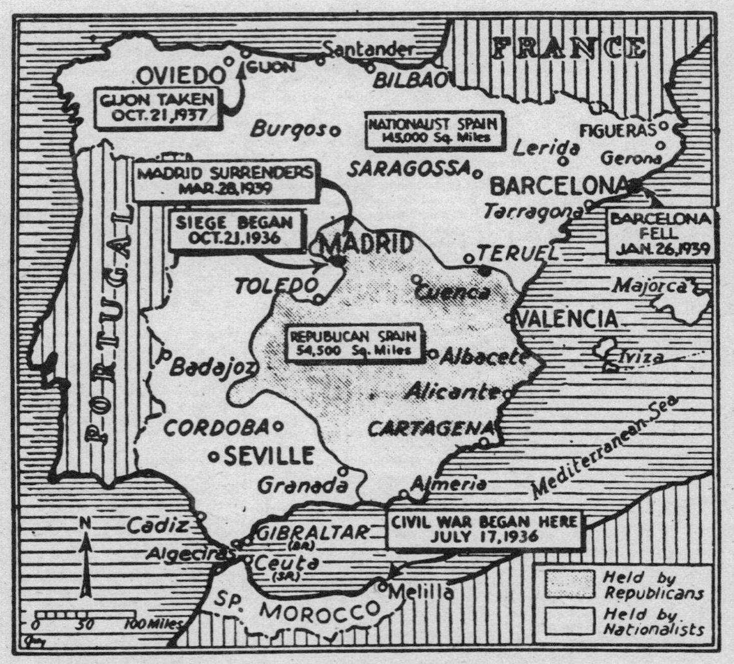

SURRENDER OF CAPITAL ENDS SPAIN'S WAR

Highlights of the civil strife from its outbreak in Morocco in July, 1936, to the capitulation of Madrid yesterday are indicated on the map. Also shown are the areas held by the Nationalists and the Republicans at the time of the surrender.

Ernest Hemingway, who covered the Spanish Civil War for an American newspaper syndicate, left Spain disillusioned just before the final surrender to the fascists.

"All the News That's Fit to Print."

The New York Times.

LATE CITY EDITION
Fair today, increasing cloudiness tonight, followed by rain and warmer tomorrow.
Temperatures Yesterday—Max., 41; Min., 35

VOL. LXXXVIII...No. 29,649. Entered as Second-Class Matter, Postoffice, New York, N. Y. NEW YORK, WEDNESDAY, MARCH 29, 1939. P THREE CENTS NEW YORK CITY and Vicinity | FOUR CENTS Elsewhere Except in 7th and 8th Postal Zones.

MADRID YIELDS, ENDING WAR; VICTORS ENTER UNRESISTED; REPUBLICAN LEADERS FLEE

18,000 LEAVE JAILS

War-Weary Populace Cheers Army Trucks Distributing Food

BURGOS SOUNDS A WARNING

Tells Democracies to Keep Hands Off—Valencia Said to Plan Surrender

Madrid surrendered yesterday, and with reports that Valencia was also negotiating for a capitulation Spain's thirty-two-month-old civil war was believed at an end. [Page 1.]

Franco supporters struck up Nationalist anthems and took over the capital's administration as the conquering troops entered the city to find barricades still standing and the people suffering from hunger. [Page 10.] The long privations of the people in Republican Spain made them welcome peace. [Page 11.]

In jubilant Burgos a spokesman warned the democracies to keep hands off Spain. [Page 12.] Premier Mussolini in a brief speech applauded the defeat of "bolshevism" and ordered flags hung out in honor of the victory [Page 1], and Chancellor Hitler sent a congratulatory telegram to Generalissimo Franco. [Page 12.]

Nationalists Take Capital

By The Associated Press.

MADRID, March 28.—Shell-torn Madrid, symbol of Republican resistance during thirty-two months of civil war, passed today into the hands of Nationalist Generalissimo Francisco Franco.

After holding Nationalist forces at the edge of the war-weary, hungering capital for nearly twenty-nine months, the Central Army withdrew from defense lines and hoisted white flags this morning.

The fall of the city was regarded as the virtual end of the savage, destructive conflict that had unnerved Europe for so long.

A Nationalist spokesman told of sweeping successes in the Madrid, Cordoba and Toledo sectors and said, "We still have a job of work in cleaning up the Red forces in the remainder of Spain, but it will be a walk-over."

He declared that 40,000 prisoners had been taken in those three areas, boosting the total of prisoners taken by the Nationalists since the war started to 492,000.

"The troops are finding resistance hardly anywhere," the spokesman said. "General Gonzalo Queipo de Llano's southern army is smashing through in the Cordoba zone at an unprecedented rate."

People Dance in Madrid

General Franco's triumphant troops marched into Madrid early in the afternoon. Not a shot was fired. The tired populace cheered and danced.

In the early morning hours General José Miaja, head of the National Defense Council and one-time "savior of Madrid," and all Republican leaders except his War Minister, Lieut. Col. Segismundo Casado, and Foreign Minister Julian Besteiro fled the city, going to Valencia.

[A dispasch from Valencia said the National Defense Council was understood to be negotiating there for the early entry of General Franco's troops into Valencia.]

Thousands of Madrid's "Fifth Column"—secret Franco sympathizers—swarmed into the streets then and began taking over public utilities, communications and other vital centers.

Nationalist authorities followed the troops into the capital. They immediately assumed control of the municipal administration. One of their first acts was to free 18,000 political prisoners and Nationalist sympathizers held in Madrid prisons.

Colonel Pio Navarro of the old Civil Guard took charge of the police and an assault guard which maintained order in Madrid in the transition period between the surrender and complete occupation.

As the troops entered, jubilant crowds thronged the streets. They gave the Nationalist salute and shouted "Arriba España!" ["Up Spain!"] and "Viva Franco!" Nationalist flags were flown everywhere.

It was not known when General

Continued on Page Ten

Mussolini Sees 'Bolshevism' Beaten; Predicts Like End for All Enemies

Announces Madrid's Fall to Cheering Crowds in Rome—Press Warns France Anew—Stresses Italian Strength in Air

By CAMILLE M. CIANFARRA

Wireless to THE NEW YORK TIMES.

ROME, March 28.—In a few words addressed to enthusiastic crowds Premier Benito Mussolini late this evening announced Madrid's fall.

"General Franco's infantry and Italian legionaries have entered Madrid," he declared. "Therefore, the Spanish war may be regarded as finished. It has ended with the defeat of Bolshevism. All the enemies of Italy and fascism will come to the same end."

Signor Mussolini spoke to some 10,000 persons who had gathered in the Piazza Venezia as soon as the afternoon newspapers came out with large headlines telling of Madrid's surrender.

The news came too late for the Fascist party to organize a mass demonstration such as the one that greeted the capture of Barcelona. Nevertheless, flags soon appeared in windows and crowds of students singing patriotic songs marched to the Piazza Venezia, where they were joined by thousands of civilians and Fascisti.

Responding to their cries, Signor Mussolini appeared on a balcony to say a few words. However, he was forced to come out several times to acknowledge the insistent applause.

The cold reception that Signor Mussolini's speech Sunday received in Paris, according to Italians today, prompts the press to utter ominous threats warning France that she had better pay the bill overdue to Italy now or it will be much stiffer later.

The intention to apply pressure to France and more specifically to Premier Edouard Daladier, who, it is believed, will reply in his speech tomorrow to Signor Mussolini's offer to negotiate, is seen in the emphasis laid on Italy's military might and the blunt demand that the French should soon decide whether to "take it or leave it" because Italy is not going to wait indefinitely for a reply.

At the same time, in one instance a distinction is made between what Signor Mussolini has asked—concerning Tunisia, Jibuti and the Suez Canal—for reasons of "timeliness and restraint" and what

Continued on Page Eleven

CAREY AND DR. RICE INDICTED IN QUEENS

Accused of Maintaining Five Garbage Dump Nuisances—Trial Set for April 17

William F. Carey, Commissioner of Sanitation, and Dr. John L. Rice, Commissioner of Health, were held yesterday in Queens County Court for trial April 17 on charges of maintaining a nuisance at five city garbage dumps.

Their appearance before Judge Thomas Downs coincided with the revelation that the two officials had been named in an indictment returned by the Queens February grand jury on Monday, but impounded overnight. The grand jurors had been investigating complaints against garbage dumping, made by citizens and civic organizations, and Assistant District Attorney J. Irwin Shapiro, in charge of the inquiry, had indicated that formal charges would be made if the evidence warranted.

Commissioner Carey, together with three of his aides and two Health Department officials, had been indicted in connection with garbage dumping by a Richmond County grand jury on Jan. 10. The Staten Island case has not yet reached trial.

Arrested at Court

With Dr. Rice, Mr. Carey appeared at about 10 A. M. to answer the Queens charges. Detective Lieutenant James Sabbatino, of the Queens District Attorney's office, arrested the two commissioners as they reached court, and afterward booked them at the Hunters Point police station in Long Island City. Both gave the information necessary for the police blotter, but they were not fingerprinted.

Subsequently they appeared in court with Assistant Corporation Counsel Frederick V. P. Bryan as their attorney and pleaded not guilty. In fixing the trial for the middle of next month Judge Downs acceded to a demand for quick disposition of the case on the ground that the indictment described conditions at the garbage dumps named as a menace to public health.

At another point in the proceedings the court returned to the charge that the dumps endangered health. Mr. Shapiro, discussing the release of the prisoners pending trial, had suggested that no bail be fixed, since both defendants were city officials.

"I fail to see any distinction between men in public office and those not in public office where the matter of bail is concerned," Judge Downs said.

A moment later, after other remarks by Mr. Shapiro, the Court added:

"The grand jury indicts these men for endangering the health of people by maintaining a public nuisance. What is the difference between endangering a person's life

Continued on Page Four

MANTON ASSOCIATE ENTERS GUILTY PLEA

Lotsch Admits the Charge He Bribed Ex-Judge—Is Likely to Aid Prosecution

The bribery and corruption case of the government against Martin T. Manton, former senior judge of the Second United States Circuit Court of Appeals, took a surprising turn yesterday when John L. Lotsch, Brooklyn banker and disbarred lawyer, pleaded guilty to an indictment charging him with bribing the judge.

At a hearing before Federal Judge Murray Hulbert, United States Attorney John T. Cahill disclosed that Lotsch, a former business associate of Manton, had been of considerable help to the government. He also indicated that Lotsch would take the witness stand and testify against the former judge. This cooperation contributed to the swift action of the grand jury, which has indicted Manton thrice within the past month.

Manton to Plead Today

Manton will plead this morning to the true bill linking him with Lotsch in an alleged conspiracy to free the latter from an extortion charge in 1936. He has already pleaded not guilty to the two previous indictments involving other circumstances and co-defendants.

Lotsch's decision to plead guilty was announced in the court room by his lawyer, Warren I. Lee.

Judge Hulbert stared down at the defendant for a moment.

"You mean you want to enter a plea of guilty?" Judge Hulbert inquired.

"Yes, Your Honor," responded Lotsch.

"Well, you are a lawyer," remarked Judge Hulbert. "You should know what you're doing."

Paroled in Counsel's Custody

Then Lotsch was paroled in the custody of his attorney with the consent of Mr. Cahill.

"Your Honor, the reason I ask that [parole] is that the defendant has been of material help to the government," explained the United States Attorney. "I would like to suggest the date of May 15 for sentence, for that should follow trial. The date for trial will be set tomorrow. As I have said, the defendant has been of help in preparing the government's case and he can be of material help at the trial."

In 1935 Lotsch was arrested on a charge of accepting a bribe while acting as a Federal court referee. The accusation was dismissed by Federal Judge Edwin S. Thomas, who has been questioned in the judicial inquiry, but Lotsch was rearrested for extortion. The indictment to which he pleaded guilty alleged that he paid former Judge Manton $10,000 in bribes for his unlawful aid and influence in clearing himself in 1936 through a habeas corpus writ, which was granted by the court of which Judge Manton was a member.

CHAMBERLAIN BARS CONSCRIPTION NOW; EDEN LEADS REVOLT

Premier Suggests Compulsory Training Would Upset Harmony With Labor

COALITION REGIME ASKED

Ex-Foreign Secretary Gets 34 Signatures to Motion to Re-Form Cabinet

Prime Minister Chamberlain definitely rejected military conscription last night after having faced in the House of Commons earlier in the day a demand by thirty-four Conservatives led by Anthony Eden for a coalition government "in view of the grave dangers" threatening Britain. Mr. Chamberlain indicated in the House that efforts to form a "stop-Hitler" bloc had not been abandoned. [Page 1.]

Germany in a semi-official statement warned Poland not to heed the calls of "foreign sirens," but Warsaw felt that the tension with Berlin had abated. [Page 13.]

In Berlin the organ of the Elite Guard invited Britain to join with Germany to "dictate the peace of the entire world." [Page 13.]

The frontier negotiations between the Hungarians and the Slovaks were interrupted when Budapest made demands that some observers considered an ultimatum. [Page 14.]

To support her contention that Italy's note of last December 17 did not contain specific demands, France proposes to make the note public. Yet, feeling that Italy is in a perilous situation because of her association with Germany, the French do not wish to close the door to negotiations. It was rumored last night that Foreign Minister Bonnet had offered his resignation. [Page 15.]

British Conscription Rejected

By FERDINAND KUHN Jr.

Special Cable to THE NEW YORK TIMES.

LONDON, March 28.—Prime Minister Neville Chamberlain tonight rejected conscription or any other form of compulsory service at the present time, in a semi-private after-dinner talk to 170 of his most faithful supporters in the House of Commons.

The relations between the government and labor unions were so satisfactory, said Mr. Chamberlain, and the dread of conscription in the labor movement so strong that it would be folly to impose compulsory service until circumstances made it acceptable to the whole nation.

Instead, Mr. Chamberlain hinted, the government was considering a revival of the "Derby scheme" of early World War days, by which volunteers were enlisted in unlimited numbers but were not called up for service until their equipment was ready and their services needed. The scheme bore the name of the present Earl of Derby, who was Director General of Recruiting in 1915, when the "contemptible little army" was already proving hopelessly inadequate for Britain's war effort.

In those days the plan served as

Continued on Page Twelve

Bombs Damage Historic Span Over Thames After 9 Get Prison Terms in Other Blasts

Special Cable to THE NEW YORK TIMES.

LONDON, Wednesday, March 29.—Motorists and pedestrians crossing the famous Hammersmith suspension bridge over the Thames, one of the main exits from Western London, had narrow escapes early today when two time bombs exploded. They were believed to have been dropped from a truck.

As part of the superstructure crashed into the roadway, motorists ran into the wreckage and thus escaped the full force of the second explosion, which occurred a few seconds later.

One side of the bridge is now sagging about a foot below its normal level. Windows in a block of flats 100 yards away, on the north side of the river, were shattered and other property was damaged.

Policemen immediately surrounded the district. No information regarding casualties was reported.

A wave of bombings in various parts of Britain in recent months has been attributed to the outlawed Irish Republican Army.

Michael J. Mason, named by the police as "commanding officer of the Irish Republican Army in Britain" and a leader in recent bombing plots, was sentenced to seventeen years' imprisonment at Old Bailey yesterday.

Mason, a 27-year-old Liverpool mechanic, who said his right name was Cleary, declared from the dock: "I am not a criminal; I am fighting for the freedom of my country." He added:

"After the Easter rising [in 1916] my father suffered imprisonment because he dared take up arms against the British in Ireland. I am bound to follow in his footsteps."

Most of the eight men found guilty with Mason of having conspired to cause explosions and commit arson also received long sentences. One of fifteen years was imposed on Peter Stuart, 25, a poster writer, who on Monday had declared defiantly: "I don't care what sentence I get; I know the fight will go on."

The other defendants were sentenced to a total of fifty-nine and a half years.

Hammersmith Bridge is the farthest up-river of the Thames bridges within the County of London. It is at the western end of the metropolitan bridges, of which the Tower Bridge is the most easterly. The original Hammersmith Bridge was the first suspension bridge erected in or near the city, having been completed in 1827. It was rebuilt in 1887.

BRIDGE AT BATTERY WINS IN COUNCIL; VICTORY FOR MOSES

Way Cleared for Adoption of Albany Bills as Park Head Looks On With Smile

ONLY 6 MEMBERS OPPOSED

Cashmore Quits His Sickbed to Vote for Plan—Relief Fund Plea Blocked by Baldwin

As Park Commissioner Robert Moses watched the proceedings with a happy smile, the City Council approved his plan for a $41,200,000 suspension bridge from the Battery to Brooklyn yesterday by a vote of 19 to 6, with one member absent.

The Council's affirmative action clears the way for adoption of two bills by the Legislature in Albany. One authorizes the Triborough Bridge Authority, of which Mr. Moses is chairman, to finance and build the bridge. The second removes a previous authorization to build a connection between the Battery and Brooklyn from the New York City Tunnel Authority and lodges it in the Triborough Bridge Authority.

Following favorable action at Albany, the bridge plan must be submitted to the Reconstruction Finance Corporation or to private bankers for financing. When the financial set-up is complete, and War Department approval has been obtained, the project goes before the Board of Estimate for final authorization. The estimated construction time is twenty-seven months, which is considered remarkably short.

Cashmore Leaves Sickbed

Soon after the Council meeting began in City Hall, Vice Chairman John Cashmore, who underwent a thyroid operation on Monday night, walked into the chamber on the arm of a physician from Long Island College Hospital, where he has been a patient for a week. His sudden appearance provoked a burst of handclapping and shouts of greeting. As he took his seat in the chamber, his colleagues gathered around to inquire about his health. Mr. Cashmore, after voting for the Moses project, returned to the hospital without delay.

Those who voted against the span included Councilman Joseph E. Kinsley and Charles E. Keegan, Bronx Democrats; Salvatore Ninfo and Michael J. Quill, Bronx Laborites; George Backer, Manhattan Laborite, and Charles Belous, Queens Fusionist. James J. Deering, Democrat, who is the fifth member of the Bronx contingent, was kept away by illness.

Hugh Quinn, chairman of the Council committee on State legislation, said at the outset of the discussion that the committee was reporting the resolution out without recommendation because the members had not had sufficient time to study a project involving $41,200,000. He said he would vote for the bridge because he believed it was necessary for the development of Brooklyn.

"No man in the city or the country could properly analyze the figures, either for the bridge or the alternative tunnel, in the time allotted," he told his colleagues. "I would request the Mayor in the future to allow us more time on matters of this sort. While the pend-

Continued on Page Seven

$250,000,000 PARITY DROPPED AS HOUSE PASSES FARM BILL; ROOSEVELT HAS COTTON PLAN

FOR EXPORT BONUS

President Says Sales Abroad Must Be Made to Cut Surplus

$60,000,000 COST IN YEAR

Manufacturers' Subsidy Also Suggested, First Move of This Kind by New Deal

Text of Roosevelt statement on Cotton Exports is on Page 2.

By TURNER CATLEDGE

Special to THE NEW YORK TIMES.

WASHINGTON, March 28.—President Roosevelt stepped into the cotton surplus problem today with a proposal to employ export bounties to reduce the huge stocks held in this country and reopen the world markets for American-grown fibre.

The immediate objective, the President said, was to build a "spillway" for the 11,000,000 bales of surplus cottton now held under government loans and thereby to circumvent the threatened decline of American cotton exports to the lowest point in more than fifty years.

He offered a two-point program which would cost, he calculated, around $15,000,000 between now and August 1 and would entail between $60,000,000 and $90,000,000 in additional Federal expenditure during the next full year. The estimates were made by the President in discussing his formal statement with newspaper men at his press conference.

Specifically, the plan calls first for a payment of $1.25 a bale to producers who release their loan cotton to the market, and, second, for a "moderate payment," the size of which the President did not fix, on all cotton exported after the plan goes into operation.

As a further refinement he suggested import quotas on cotton materials, such as would "protect both the domestic producers of raw cotton and probably domestic manufacturers as well from foreign importations." The whole plan would require but little new legislation.

Denies Trade Pact Conflict

The President told the newspaper correspondents that what he proposed did not conflict with the reciprocal trade agreement program fathered by Secretary Hull.

He denied emphatically that the plan involved "dumping" in any sense. The purpose, he said, was to provide for the orderly merchandising of our excessive supplies, the maintenance of "our fair share" of the world market, the protection of producer income, and the cheapest possible way out of the surplus problem created by the cotton loan policies.

There was no intention to break the world price, he insisted, or to undersell other countries in the international cotton markets. Most of the extra foreign sales, he said, would be effected through negotiations with other countries.

Although the President virtually conceded in his statement that the loan policy had not lived up to expectations, he dated the present cotton situation to the record crop of 1937, which, he pointed out with emphasis, followed the invalidation by the Supreme Court of the control features of the original Farm Aid Law

Suggests Manufacturers' Bonus

A significant intimation of a policy not hitherto advocated during his administration was noted in the statement. Saying he believed there was "ample authority under existing legislation" for the imposition of import quotas that would protect domestic producers and manufacturers of cotton products from "foreign importations," the President went on:

"A payment could be made on exports of manufactured goods so the program would not put them at a disadvantage in the world markets."

The cotton surplus program aroused speculation in diplomatic circles tonight as to the effect upon a British mission which is due to arrive here in May to discuss methods of stimulating sales of British-made textiles in the United States. The mission, which will be composed largely of Lancashire textile manufacturers, is understood to have been encouraged by the terms of the reciprocal trade treaty with Great Britain to hope that their objective might meet with some degree of success.

Mr. Roosevelt said that his plan

Continued on Page Two

Will Propose Amending Of Wages-Hours Law

Special to THE NEW YORK TIMES.

WASHINGTON, March 28.—Representative Norton, chairman of the Labor Committee, will introduce a bill tomorrow to amend the Wages and Hours Law along the lines discussed recently with the committee by Elmer F. Andrews, the administrator.

Mrs. Norton said the bill would contain these provisions:

1. Exemption of the white-collar worker whose salary is more than a figure to be specified, probably $2,000 a year.

2. A grant of more power to the administrator in making regulations and absolving employers from damages which might be assessed if they conformed to regulations later held invalid by the courts.

3. Exemption of rural telephone exchanges.

4. Modifications of the restrictions placed on Puerto Rican industries to permit more home work and different wage levels.

4. Redefinition of "areas of production," to relax the application of the law in localized industries.

PRESIDENT SPEEDS 45,000-TON SHIPS

Approves Plans for Two Largest Battle Craft in World—Calls Japan One Reason

Special to THE NEW YORK TIMES.

WASHINGTON, March 28.—Construction of the two largest and most powerful battleships in the world was virtually assured today when the White House announced that President Roosevelt had approved the plans of the Navy Department for building of such ships.

Asked at his press conference if the decision could be ascribed to the refusal of Japan last year to divulge her own plans for battleship construction, Mr. Roosevelt replied that that was one of several reasons that led to the decision.

The new ships will be streamlined giants approaching 900 feet in length but of about the same beam as the six 35,000-ton battleships now under construction, thus assuring easy transit of the Panama Canal.

Each of the 45,000-ton ships, which are two of three such vessels provided for in the $1,000,000,000 Naval Authorization Act of 1938, will be about 880 feet long, 108 feet abeam and 36 feet in draught. They are to be 130 feet longer than the Washington, North Carolina, Massachusetts, Indiana, Alabama and South Dakota, the six battleships now under construction.

To Cost $15,000,000 More

Each of the latter is estimated to cost between $70,000,000 and $75,000,000. The cost of the 45,000-ton ships has not been disclosed, but it is said to be between $85,000,000 and $100,000,000, probably nearer the first than the latter figure.

The fact that the President has told the navy to go ahead with its plans for the larger capital units is interpreted in Washington to mean that the government has evidence of the truth of reports that the Japanese are building three battleships, each of more than 40,000 tons' displacement. The Japanese Government has refused to confirm these reports.

To prevent leakage of information, the Japanese have established restricted zones which completely encircle all naval construction yards, no unauthorized person being permitted to approach within fifteen miles of such a yard. Japanese yard workmen must live within these areas. It is said that no white person has entered one of the zones since the restrictions were imposed.

The new Japanese battleships are believed to be of about 42,000 tons' displacement, or about 2,000 more than the 40,000-ton Lion and Temeraire which the British Navy is building. The French, Italian and German navies have no ships under construction of tonnages exceeding 35,000.

Tonnage of 300,000 on Way

The two ships which the President brought nearer to reality today will increase this country's battleship construction to eight vessels, or one less than the British have under way or authorized. They raise the tonnage of the United States' new battleships to an even 300,000 tons, or within 35,000 of the British total. The Italian total is four ships of 35,000 tons each, the German three of 35,000 tons

Continued on Page Eight

FARMS VS. CITIES

Urban Members Balk at Rural Spending Unless Relief Is Voted

DECISIVE VOTE 204 TO 191

Threats of Reprisals Voiced by Defeated—Woodrum Sees Victory for Economy

By HENRY N. DORRIS

Special to THE NEW YORK TIMES.

WASHINGTON, March 28.—The House divided tonight more along farm and urban lines than by political parties, and cut from the Agriculture Department's 1940 supply bill $250,000,000 intended for farm price parity payments. By this action it set the stage for what may prove the deciding battle later in the week over deficiency funds for relief asked by President Roosevelt.

After it had been removed by a point of order, the $250,000,000 appropriation for parity payments was restored in committee of the whole by a teller vote of 175 to 171, but when the House moved to final passage of the bill, it voted by roll call 204 to 191 to remove the item again. Then the House passed the supply bill by a voice vote.

The farm bloc, which had repeatedly spurned the offers of urban colleagues to log-roll, was taken by surprise. But the ending of their hopes, at least temporarily, for parity payments caused many of these members to assert privately tonight that they would square matters with their city friends when the relief deficiency bill comes to a vote, probably next Thursday.

Then, the House is expected to have before it a bill intended to give the Works Progress Administration additional money for this fiscal year. President Roosevelt has asked for $150,000,000, but the House Appropriations Committee is now engaged in a fight over whether to make it $100,000,000 or $125,000,000.

Lines Drawn for a Week

Few observers of the House for the last week or so have failed to see that the fight would resolve itself into a battle between the rural and urban groups. When the House had adjourned tonight after a seven-and-a-half-hour session, member after member from the farm States indicated privately that they would fight any additional relief appropriation.

A comparatively small number of New Dealers furnished the balance of power. They joined with economy-minded Democrats and a large number of Republicans to defeat the parity amendment offered by Representative Cannon of Missouri, who was in charge of the bill as a representative of the Appropriations Committee.

By parties, the roll call revealed that those who supported the amendment included 168 Democrats, 20 Republicans, 2 Progressives and 1 Farmer-Laborite, while 68 Democrats, 135 Republicans and 1 American-Laborite voted against it.

The New Dealers' action was characterized by one farm bloc member as "sticking their noses out to get back nothing but a punch in the nose." What he meant was that the Senate would restore the parity item, and the House eventually would accept it in the form of a conference report. And he meant that if the farm bloc, by voting with the economy Democrats and Republicans, could prevent passage of a relief deficiency bill, the chances of Mr. Roosevelt getting any more money for relief would be dimmed greatly, if not actually ended.

Woodrum Hails Economy

As sent to the Senate, the bill was hailed by Representative Woodrum of Virginia, leader of the House Democratic economy forces, as a victory against Federal spending. He said it represented "one of the most heartening actions of this session."

Probably no greater ovation has been accorded a speech in the House this year than was given to that by Mr. Woodrum, opposing an amendment offered by Representative Jones of Texas, chairman of the House Agriculture Committee, to add $60,000,000 to the funds of the Surplus Commodity Credit Corporation. The amendment was offered after a $60,000,000 fund for cotton farmers had been suggested earlier in the day by President Roosevelt. It was interpreted as a

Continued on Page Three

"All the News That's Fit to Print."

The New York Times.

Copyright, 1939, by The New York Times Company.

LATE CITY EDITION
Generally fair and continued cool today. Tomorrow fair, slowly rising temperatures.
Temperatures Yesterday—Max., 60; Min., 45

VOL. LXXXVIII...No. 29,682. Entered as Second-Class Matter, Postoffice, New York, N. Y. NEW YORK, MONDAY, MAY 1, 1939. PP THREE CENTS NEW YORK CITY and Vicinity | FOUR CENTS Elsewhere Except in 7th and 8th Postal Zones.

PRESIDENT OPENS FAIR AS A SYMBOL OF PEACE; VAST SPECTACLE OF COLOR AND WORLD PROGRESS THRILLS ENTHUSIASTIC CROWDS ON THE FIRST DAY

POLES CONSIDERING COUNTER DEMANDS IN REPLY TO HITLER

Military Circles Say Claim on Danzig Should Be Dropped Before Further Parleys

BALTIC OUTLET STRESSED

Reich Specification of Width of Right of Way in Corridor Said to Be 15.5 Miles

In Warsaw there were indications yesterday that the Polish reply to Germany might call for a dropping of the Nazi demands regarding Danzig and the replacing of the League of Nations link to the Free City by a new Polish one. It was also reported that Chancellor Hitler in a detailed demand had asked a fifteen-and-a-half-mile motor road right-of-way across Pomorze. [Page 1.]

Both Paris and London seemed to be hopeful that a Polish-German compromise on Danzig could be reached. Reports from the two capitals indicated a disinclination to be forced to fight on this issue. [Page 12.]

The question of peace or war, however, was considered by Nazi spokesmen to have been put up to the democracies and their partners. [Page 13.]

With the arrival of the German Army commander in Rome it was believed new pressure was being put on Italy by Germany for a full-fledged military alliance. But it was significant that according to all reports the Brenner Pass between the two countries was being fortified on both sides. [Page 11.]

Poles to Use Hitler Tactics

By JERZY SZAPIRO

Wireless to THE NEW YORK TIMES.

WARSAW, Poland, April 30.—The German memorandum delivered to the Polish Foreign Office on Friday while Chancellor Adolf Hitler was attacking Poland will be answered in the same manner. A Polish memorandum, repudiating the German accusation and rejecting Danzig's incorporation into Germany and a highway across Pomorze [the Polish Corridor], but leaving the door open for further negotiations, will be delivered at the Berlin Foreign Office while Foreign Minister Josef Beck and Premier Felicien Slawoj-Skladkowski are addressing the Sejm [Parliament], probably on Friday.

[It was reported in Poland that Chancellor Hitler had demanded a German motor road right of way across Pomorze 15.5 miles wide, The Associated Press stated.]

Certain influential military circles hold that Warsaw should not enter into new negotiations with the Nazis unless the Germans withdraw their demands regarding Danzig. This view is expressed in the military journal, Polska Zbrojna, which published one of the strongest criticisms of Herr Hitler's speech and of German policy generally.

"Danzig is at the mouth of a great Polish river," it says, "and we cannot give it up. The Polonization of Danzig is notable; wherefore, why should the Germans show so much interest in what to them is but one of their provincial towns?"

Poland to Make Demands

The Gazeta Polska, official organ of the Polish Government, tomorrow will publish a noteworthy statement concerning the position of Danzig.

"Germany," it will say, "has shown her regard for international engagements by her recent occupation of Memel, by her denunciation of solemn treaties. She has demonstrated quite clearly that German policy aims at separating Poland from her outlet on the Baltic Sea, the importance of which to Poland needs no emphasis.

"The policy of Berlin thus creates a situation that forces Poland to go further in her demands concerning the status of Danzig than she did formerly when concluding with Germany the pact of 1934.'"

Although it is not explicitly stated, there is reason to believe that Poland's demands will include the transference of the functions of the League Commissioner to the Polish Government.

Will Close Exchanges

The Polish official answer to the German memorandum, it is believed, will close German-Polish exchanges for the time being. The Poles expect to delay the negotiations until there is a general clarification of the European situation.

No chances are being taken, however. All the military precautions ordered last month are still in force and the army is strengthened by

Continued on Page Twelve

Rider Will Ask Pensions For Congress Members

By The Associated Press.

WASHINGTON, April 30.—A quiet campaign to give pensions to members of Congress has materialized into a legislative proposal.

Chairman Ramspeck of the House Civil Service Committee said today that he intended to add provisions for the pensions to a bill making amendments to the Civil Service Law which has just been passed by the Senate.

Under the proposal, the government and the members would bear about equal shares of the cost. Five per cent of the salary of each member would be deducted monthly and would go toward the purchase of an annuity to be added to the amount to be paid by the government.

Civil service workers receive pensions which increase with length of service. They contribute 3½ per cent of their salaries.

Mr. Ramspeck reported that almost every member he had talked to favored the pension idea.

"They're getting security-minded," he added, laughing.

PARI-MUTUEL VOTE AGAIN UP IN STATE

Republicans Plan Assembly Test on Betting System—Democratic Split Reported

Special to THE NEW YORK TIMES.

ALBANY, April 30.—The question of pari-mutuel betting on horse-racing is returning to plague the 1939 session of the Legislature.

Pressure from pari-mutuel advocates has resulted in a decision on the part of Republican leaders to put the matter to a vote on the Assembly floor. If the proposed constitutional amendment should be passed by both Houses this year, it would be submitted to the people for approval in the Fall, as the 1938 Legislature approved the system.

Despite considerable support on the Republican side, there is no guarantee that the pari-mutuel proposal will pass in either House. The Democrats, who have blown hot and cold on the measure for years, are again reported to be divided on the subject.

In one recent year the proposed amendment was passed by the Senate, and when it came up a second time as is required by the Constitution, its original sponsor voted against it. Last year John J. Dunnigan, the Democratic leader of the Senate, pushed the proposal through the Upper House, and it gained approval in the Republican controlled Assembly as well.

Senate Sponsor Now Lacking

With the intervening elections, the Republicans gained control of the Senate as well and Senator Dunnigan has made no move to introduce the proposal in the Senate. In fact, it has yet to have an official sponsor there. However, John D. Bennett and Norman F. Penny, Nassau County Republican Assemblymen, have introduced in the Assembly resolutions identical with the Dunnigan resolution of the year before, and passage this year by both Houses would constitute the required second action by the Legislature, even if the sponsors are not the same.

In the Assembly the practice of the Republican leadership, under Speaker Heck, is to refuse to throttle in committee any bill of the type of the pari-mutuel proposal, because of rumors always circulated about bookmakers' lobbies. Putting the bill out for a vote leaves it up to the individual membership. The Republicans will seek passage of the measure in the Assembly, but its final fate would appear to rest on the number of Democratic votes it can command.

Whether the matter will be brought to a vote this week, or the following week, was not disclosed today.

Sales Tax Vote Awaited

Tomorrow night the Legislature is expected to adopt the rest of the budget bills, and either then, or the next day, adopt the tax program which will be used to finance the Republican budget. The new taxes on this program are the increase in the liquor tax, effective on May 1, and the two-cent-per-package cigarette tax, effective on July 1.

Later in the week the sales tax probably will come up for a vote, with its eventual fate still depending on the support the Republicans can muster for it in the Senate, where they control by a margin of only two votes. The political aspects of the battle over the budget itself appear to make it unlikely that the Republican sales tax idea can gain any Democratic votes on the Senate side.

Local bills have been cleaned up to a large extent in both houses, and after the enactment of the tax bills, the settling of the sales tax problem, the revision of the unemployment insurance law, and the enactment of a housing measure, the Legislature will be in a position to quit and go home, to await a possible special-session call.

CONGRESS FACING SEVEN BIG ISSUES AS TIME SHORTENS

None Is on Week's Calendars, But All Except Taxes Are in Legislative Process

WAY CLEARED FOR ACTION

Routine Money Bills Passed, Reporting of Vital Measures to Floor Is Expected

By LUTHER A. HUSTON

Special to THE NEW YORK TIMES.

WASHINGTON, April 30.—Congress has been in session nearly four months and has disposed of only two of the major controversial items on its calendar. At least seven important issues remain to be settled in the two months that remain of the session if present plans are followed and a late Summer sitting is avoided by adjournment around July 1.

None of the major measures is on the calendar of either chamber for this week. The most progress that can be expected is that one or more of these measures may come from committees to the floor of the House or Senate.

The two issues that have been settled are the limited authorization for the President to reorganize executive agencies and the expansion of national defense, for which necessary appropriation bills have been passed. The decks also have been cleared of considerable of the routine, most of the important departmental appropriation bills having been disposed of.

Major Questions Outstanding

The following matters remain to be dealt with:

- Amendments to the Social Security Act, the National Labor Relations Act and the Wages and Hours Law.
- Revision or extension of existing neutrality laws.
- The amount of the appropriation and the method of disbursement for relief during the 1940 fiscal year.
- A farm program including the highly controversial question of export and domestic subsidies on farm products.
- Legislation to repeal, modify or continue in effect certain provisions of the tax laws that are estimated to yield an annual revenue of around $2,000,000,000 even if general tax revision is not attempted.

Except for tax proposals, all of these measures are in the legislative mill. On some of them committee hearings are in progress; on others committee action has ended.

There is a possibility that proposed amendments to the Wages and Hours Law may come up in the House tomorrow. Representative Mary Norton, chairman of the Labor Committee, has indicated that she will try to bring up under suspension of the rules the proposals which her committe has approved. If this is not done, the proposals must lie over at least a week.

To Hear Green on C. I. O. Charges

On Capitol Hill tomorrow, however, interest probably will center in the hearing by the Senate Education and Labor Committee on proposed amendments to the National Labor Relations Act, where William Green, president of the American Federation of Labor, will be the witness.

Mr. Green is expected to reply to

Continued on Page Twenty-four

Times Sq. May Be Closed To Autos During Fair

Times Square may be turned over as a playground for World's Fair visitors if their numbers become great enough to warrant special police arrangements in the theatrical area.

Police Commissioner Valentine said yesterday that the Fair crowds may approximate the number of American Legion members who came to New York for their national convention in September, 1937. If that should develop, Mr. Valentine said, it would be advisable to turn over Times Square to the city's guests.

Automobile traffic would be routed north and south on either side of the Square, as it was during the Legion convention. For the last two weeks heavy police details have handled the crowds in Times Square, directing pedestrians to the right to obtain the maximum amount of order.

RUSSIAN AVIATORS, RESCUED, ARRIVE

Two Who Crashed in Canada Here in American Plane—One Fainted During Flight

Brig. Gen. Vladimir Kokkinaki and Major Mikhail Gordienko, the two Soviet airmen who crashed Friday night in a swamp off the coast of New Brunswick were landed in a rescue plane last night at Floyd Bennett Field at 10:31 o'clock.

The two men were brought to New York in the plane of Commodore Harold Vanderbilt, which was chartered by Soviet and American officials for the rescue work, which took more than thirty hours.

They and the rescue party, which left here Friday night after word of the crash of the Moscow-New York non-stop flight came through from Miscou Point, N. B., were "ferried" to the end of the scheduled flight in an American airplane.

Their own craft, in which they sped toward New York from Moscow in 23 hours and 40 minutes, still lay in the frozen morass where Major Gordienko squashed it in an emergency landing. He landed it because General Kokkinaki had fainted at an altitude of more than 27,000 feet, it was learned yesterday when the party first brought the two men as far south as Moncton, N. B.

In recounting last night the events which led up to the forced landing at the field General Kokkinaki said the main difficulty of flying in the substratosphere was at 27,000 feet, where his compass liquids froze and his radio reception was so poor that he could not tune in the directional beams. He offered this explanation as a reason why the ship apparently lost its course, having been reported in the same area for nearly four and a half hours prior to its final landing.

In the plane were the two Russian aces; Russell Thaw, pilot, and his co-pilot, John Revely; V. P. Butosov, Dr. Louis S. Spector and Peter Baranov, all of the Am-

Continued on Page Twenty-four

Hague Ignores Own Plea for Patriotic Rally; Skips Americanization Fete for Ball Game

Special to THE NEW YORK TIMES.

JERSEY CITY, N. J., April 30.—Mayor Frank Hague, who issued a proclamation yesterday calling on residents of Jersey City to "show your Americanism" by attending the city's tenth annual celebration today of Americanization Day, did not appear at that event this afternoon. Instead he attended the double-header baseball game between the Jersey City and Toronto teams of the International League at Roosevelt Stadium.

"As Mayor of Jersey City, I earnestly and respectfully invite all the people of our city to participate actively in the Americanization Day exercises, Sunday, April 30, 2 P. M., at Pershing Field," declared the Mayor's signed proclamation, published yesterday in newspaper advertisements.

"Show your Americanism by parading or being present Sunday afternoon. It is my request that the American flag be displayed on all homes and buildings Sunday. Every citizen should remove his hat as the colors pass by."

The proclamation listed Mayor Frank Hague among the speakers at Pershing Field, from which representative Jerry O'Connell, Montana Democrat and foe of the Jersey City Mayor, was whisked away by police several months ago when he attempted to speak there.

A crowd estimated at 4,000 persons assembled in the field today and 10,000 others marched there. During the parade and speechmaking, however, the Mayor was one of 29,362 baseball fans who did not take part in the Americanization celebration. He occupied a box at the baseball stadium with his nephew and private secretary, former Judge Frank Hague Eggers.

The Jersey City team won both games.

Commissioner Arthur Potterton, who spoke at Pershing Field, declared that "Jersey City takes the lead to show the world that nothing un-American will creep into our lives in this part of the State." Referring to other parts of the State and the nation, he said that "we have given them the courage they did not possess."

Representative Edward J. Hart, Democrat, was another speaker. Governor A. Harry Moore was present, but did not speak.

The Americanization Day celebration is sponsored by Captain Clinton Fisk Post, Veterans of Foreign Wars.

ROOSEVELT SPEAKS

He Sees Nations of This Hemisphere United in Desire for Peace

U. S. DEMOCRACY STRONG

Exposition Here and in West Born of Singleness of the American Ideal, He Says

By FELIX BELAIR JR.

In his first public utterance since Chancellor Hitler's virtual rejection of his plan to assure the peace of Europe for another ten years, President Roosevelt served notice on the world yesterday that the nations of the Western Hemisphere were "united in a desire to encourage peace and good-will among all nations" and voiced their hope that time would break down the barriers to tranquillity on the Continent.

In a brief address dedicating the New York's World's Fair to the cause of international amity and declaring it "open to all mankind," the President said that the American wagon was hitched to the star of peace, and asked that the months ahead "may carry us forward in the rays of that hope."

Avoids Any Direct Reference

For those who had expected a more direct reference by President Roosevelt to the state of affairs in Europe or something that might be interpreted as a reply to the German Chancellor's all but complete throwdown of his peace guarantee proposal there was disappointment, for his attitude regarding that had to be inferred from what he said of the traditional aspirations of the American republics.

Of recent years American historians would write that "sectionalism and regional jealousies diminished and that the people of every part of your land acquired a national solidarity of economic and social thought such as had never been seen before," the President said.

He added that "wise tolerance" almost as much as the American form of government had made possible this unity of sentiment in a nation made up of so many different creeds and national derivations. The President recalled that democratic government had endured unchanged in this country longer than in any other country on the globe at any period of history, a circumstance he attributed to the wisdom of the framers of the Constitution.

He Sees Aim Accomplished

"That this has been accomplished," the President added a little later, "has been due first to our own form of government itself and, secondly, to a spirit of wise tolerance which, with few exceptions, has been the rule.

"We in the United States, and, indeed, in all the Americas, remember that our population stems from many races and kindreds and tongues. Often, I think, we Americans offer up the silent prayer that on the continent of Europe, from which the American hemisphere was principally colonized, the years to come will break down many barriers to intercourse between nations—barriers which may be historic, but which so greatly, through the centuries, have led to strife and hindered friendship and normal intercourse."

From the distant reaches of the Court of Peace, at the head of which he spoke in front of the Federal Building, the President's voice came echoing back. The spectators sat motionless on folding chairs down the long concourse ending with the Trylon and Perisphere as Mr. Roosevelt slowly spoke the principal address of the day.

Not until the completion of his remarks, which carried for at least half a mile through the amplifiers arranged for the occasion, was there a suggestion of applause. The President deliberately had phrased his speech so as not to play upon the emotions and he received none of the clapping that punctuated a preceding address by Mayor La Guardia until he finished what he had to say.

The throng that came to hear him was apparently too much absorbed in his remarks to give any outward demonstration of approval until he was done. But cheering and applause was as spontaneous as it was general when Mr. Roosevelt stepped from the microphones after his concluding pronunciation:

"I hereby dedicate the New York

Continued on Page Four

Crowds Awed by Fair's Vastness And Medley of Sound and Color

Opening Day Has Everything, Including All Kinds of Weather—Spirit of Gayety Wanes When Pelting Rain Menaces Finery

The Fair had everything for its opening yesterday, including all kinds of weather. Early trains rolled to the Flushing Meadows under skies clear and blue, flooded with rich sunlight, carrying thousands come to look upon the miracle wrought by Grover Whalen's armies in the last three years.

Silk-hatted dignitaries, sailors on shore leave, men and women of all ages, dressed for fair weather and a great holiday. They came in hordes down the railroad and subway ramps, forty and fifty abreast, to gaze upon the wonders, to buy guide books from the shouting peddlers and to scramble for the observation cars.

Wealthier fairgoers climbed into motor-driven and man-powered chairs for their first tour of the grounds. Hundreds of thousands preferred to make it on foot, all a little bewildered and puzzled by the tremendous sweep of grounds, by the dazzling color, almost blinding in the bright sun. Guides, ushers, policemen and policewomen were breathless the first hour trying to keep up with the flood of questions.

Men and women, rank amateurs at reading maps, assembled in the walks or took over the benches, to puzzle out the direction of the various exhibits. Thousands were misled by the dazzling sun into thinking that the destinations they had marked off were close at hand. In most cases they learned that this was an illusion. The strong light had something of the effect of a mirage.

Above the grounds, despite notice that aircraft were to be kept from the Fair zone until the President's address, silver ships careened and darted, like gilded gnats. Two lazy blimps, reflecting the sun from their sides, came over the reviewing stand and crossed to the outer borders of the Fair. The crowds craned their necks to watch this activity in the sky, and drivers of observation cars kept sounding their musical horns to warn them to safer spots.

Everywhere, far as the eye could see, men in blue, gray, green and yellow uniforms assembled in military formations and headed toward the parade ground in the Court of Peace. Bugle notes, brassy and thin, sounded and echoed from all corners of the field. Drums rolled and fifes piped sharp marching tunes. The non-military visitors were in a dither, racing from one group to another.

Groups representing the foreign nations caught the eye as they

Continued on Page Two

CITY AND THE FLEET TAKE TURN AS HOST

1,000 Officers and Men Under Admiral Johnson Help Open Fair—Ships Draw Crowds

By HANSON W. BALDWIN

The city played host to the navy yesterday and the navy played host to the city.

It was—all things considered—an even exchange. Some 1,000 officers and men of the thirty-five visiting men-of-war, led by Rear Admiral Alfred W. Johnson, commanding the Atlantic Squadron, took part in the opening ceremonies for the World's Fair, and thousands of others rolled along Broadway and throughout the five boroughs with that walk peculiar to sailors home from the sea.

But the boats that brought the parties ashore took crowds of visitors back to the ships, while other thousands climbed the gangways of ships berthed at piers and stared with absorbing interest at turrets, the burnished muzzles of guns, the ranks of planes aboard the aircraft carrier Ranger, the ominous black hulls of the submarines and the torpedo tubes of the destroyers.

It was the visiting squadron's second day—and first Sunday—in port, and the public took full advantage of it. The men-of-war were a rival attraction, and a stellar one, to the World's Fair, and the crush of visitors was more than the navy could handle.

Estimates of Throng Vary

The crowd estimates varied widely. The police said 23,000 got aboard, while the navy thought 56,000 had crowded onto the battleships, cruisers, destroyers, submarines and auxiliaries in the few hours of the afternoon that the ships received the public. Perhaps 10,000 to 15,000 others were turned away—some of them after several hours in line—when ships' officers and the beach guard said the men-of-war were unable to accommodate any more visitors.

The visiting hours were supposed to have been from 1 to 5 P. M., but at the Ninety-sixth Street landing no more visitors were permitted to leave shore after 3:25 P. M. Naval officials explained that it took some time to clear the ships of visitors, especially when the vessels were lying out in the stream and all visitors had to be transported by small boats.

They explained that it was necessary at times to allow no visitors to leave the shore landing places later than 4 P. M. There was, however, despite the navy's announcement that all ships would be open daily from 1 to 5 P. M., considerable variation on individual ships.

The Ranger, aircraft carrier berthed alongside a pier at Canal

Continued on Page Ten

LIGHT AUTO TRAFFIC SURPRISE TO POLICE

Elaborate System to Cope With Expected Snarls on Roads Goes Unused

Although Police Department traffic experts were ready for the worst, streams of automobiles flowed evenly along principal Queens highways yesterday and not a single accident involving a serious injury was reported.

An elaborate system for emergency communications, worked out to cope with expected road snarls, went unused as 3,300 patrolmen, 523 of the traffic division, and 300 detectives—a total of 4,123—worked overtime to assure a safe and orderly opening to the World's Fair.

By 11 P. M. most of the motorists had either gone home or were on their way there and reports to police centers indicated there was no more congestion than there had been on the way out.

The only mishap on the record—spoiling what otherwise would have been a virtually incredible perfect mark—occurred at 1:10 P. M. just outside the Fair Grounds, at Lawrence and Sanford Avenues.

Louis Hoffman, 70 years old, of 1,266 Spofford Avenue, the Bronx, suffered lacerations of the left leg when struck by a car that the police said was driven by Louis Anzelone of 37-41 108th Street, Corona. Mr. Hoffman went home after treatment by an interne from Flushing Hospital. The driver was not held.

Policeman Is Injured

A patrolman was hurt inside the grounds a little later, when a crush developed outside the French Building. There were seven children lost, a man had an epileptic fit, and fifty peddlers were arrested for operating on the ramp leading from the combined I. R. T.-B. M. T. subway terminal, but otherwise, the first day was as safe as a lawn party.

A false fire alarm was turned in at the box in the R. C. A. building shortly before the opening parade, while the walks near the theme center were cluttered with people. Fire Chief Thomas F. Dougherty said it was "malicious."

Patrolman Bartholomew Nicastro, 35 years old, of 112-02 175th Street, St. Albans, was the man injured. The accident occurred at about 2 P. M. when the resurgent crowd he was trying to keep back threw him against a wooden "horse," which had been used in construction work. He was treated for a cut right leg by one of the Fair surgeons under Dr. Joseph Peter Hoguet, and remained on duty. In general, the Fair's six first aid stations had a dull day.

A checkup by the Fair police at 10 P. M. indicated that the stations,

Continued on Page Four

NATIONS IN PARADE

Mayor and the Governor Voice Welcome to the 'World of Tomorrow'

WEATHER REDUCES THRONG

Attendance Reported Above 600,000—Centers of Religion and Freedom Dedicated

By RUSSELL B. PORTER

The biggest international exposition in history was officially opened at 3:12 o'clock yesterday afternoon when President Roosevelt formally dedicated the New York World's Fair 1939 in an address before a gathering of 60,000 persons in the open-air Court of Peace.

Governor Lehman, Mayor La Guardia, Sir Louis Beale, British Commissioner General to the Fair and spokesman for the nearly sixty foreign nations that have exhibits, and Grover A. Whalen, president of the Fair Corporation, also made speeches at the opening ceremonies. They joined the President in emphasizing the message of peaceful progress that the Fair brings to mankind in an era when the whole world is troubled by war and threats of war.

When the President officially declared the Fair open he brought to a climax ceremonies that included a parade of 20,000 uniformed soldiers, sailors and marines, foreign groups in picturesque native costumes from nearly all the countries of Europe, Asia and the Americas, and the workmen who built the Fair, in their overalls and white caps.

Starting at the Trylon and Perisphere, the Theme Center of the Fair, the parade passed down Constitution Mall to the Court of Peace with flags waving, bands playing and spectators applauding until it ended with a colorful pageant in the Court of Peace.

Spectacle Impresses Visitors

Although the official exercises were the important part of the day from a formal viewpoint, actually the Fair itself made the greatest impression upon the visitors, judging from their comments as they strolled through the 1,216-acre Fair Grounds and as they journeyed homeward last night.

What they saw was a spectacle of surprising beauty and magnificence, especially last night when the whole Fair and the heavens above it were bathed in soft, glowing colors with the most modern lighting effects, and when fireworks combined with flame, water and color displays on the Lagoon of Nations, the pools in Constitution Mall and the surface of Fountain Lake.

In the daytime also the Fair is a beautiful sight, with the whole scene dominated by the 700-foot Trylon and the 200-foot Perisphere, from which radiates a rainbow of many-colored buildings of modernistic, functional architecture, some bizarre in shape and hue, others strikingly handsome and impressive in their suggestion of strength and use.

Green trees, shrubbery and lawns, playing fountains, shady benches and restful spots on all sides make a garden spot of this artificial city within a city which has been constructed within the past three and one-half years on what was formerly the ash dumps of the Flushing Meadows, and will be a great city park after the Fair is over.

See "World of Tomorrow"

In the huge crystal ball of the Perisphere, visitors peered to see what "the World of Tomorrow" would be like, finding it to be a conception of more and more progress in democracy and in the advance of science, industry, commerce, transportation, communication, the arts and the professions to bring peace and happiness to mankind. They found the same ideas expressed in the streamlined, futuristic dimensions of the buildings, statues, murals, dioramas, landscapes and exhibits of the Fair as a whole.

Like the worlds of yesterday and today, and also like the City of New York, which has the reputation of never being finished but of always changing, the "World of Tomorrow" has a great deal of unfinished business before it. The heart of the Fair, the half-mile stretch between the Theme Center and the Court of Peace where the official ceremonies were held, was virtually complete yesterday, but many other sections,

Continued on Page Three

An aerial view of the 1939 World's Fair in New York City.

Times Wide World Photo

Mr. and Mrs. Franklin D. Roosevelt enjoying a joke with Mayor La Guardia and Edward Flynn, United States Commissioner to the Fair, as the President's automobile entered the exposition grounds.

Times Wide World Photo

The re-enactment of the inauguration of George Washington as the first President in front of the huge statue on Constitution Mall.

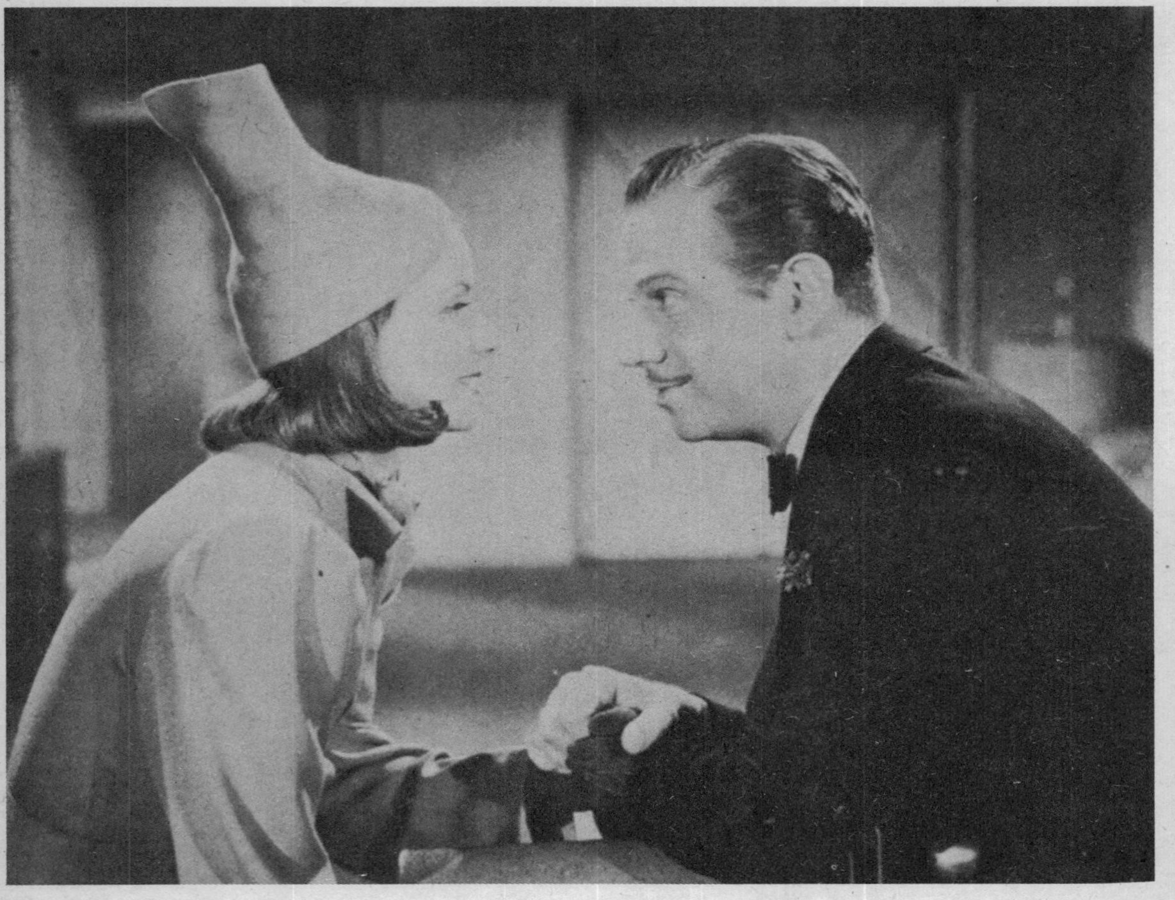

Greta Garbo and Melvyn Douglas in a scene from *Ninotchka*.

Fred Astaire and Ginger Rogers, dancing together again, in *The Story of Vernon and Irene Castle*.

Clark Gable played Rhett Butler and Vivian Leigh was Scarlett O'Hara in *Gone With the Wind*.

Gone With the Wind was produced with an all-star cast, including Olivia de Haviland as Melanie Hamilton and Leslie Howard as Ashley Wilkes.

"All the News That's Fit to Print."

The New York Times.

LATE CITY EDITION
Fair, slightly warmer today. Tomorrow overcast and slightly cooler with showers.
Temperatures Yesterday—Max., 67; Min., 56

VOL. LXXXVIII...No. 29,704. Entered as Second-Class Matter, Postoffice, New York, N. Y. NEW YORK, TUESDAY, MAY 23, 1939. PP THREE CENTS NEW YORK CITY and Vicinity | FOUR CENTS Elsewhere Except in 7th and 8th Postal Zones.

AXIS POWERS SIGN TEN-YEAR ALLIANCE TO REMAKE EUROPE

PACT IS SWEEPING

Automatic Action in War, Regardless of Origin, Is Called For in Treaty

REICH LEADS LAND FORCES

Ribbentrop Warns Democracies at Ceremonies in Berlin—Hitler Shows Delight

The Rome-Berlin Axis was transformed yesterday into an unconditional and automatic military alliance with the ceremonious signing of a ten-year pact in Berlin. According to the accompanying speeches, there was thus created an invincible bloc of 300,000,000 people to obtain a "just peace." In war, it was understood, Germany would have command on land and Italy on the seas. [Page 1; texts of the treaty and of the speeches by Foreign Ministers Ciano and von Ribbentrop, Page 8.]

Interpreted from the Rome point of view, the pact means that the two partners are going to get their "living spaces" and Italy's is asserted to be in Southeastern Europe, in the Mediterranean and in Africa, in which spheres Germany is not to interfere. [Page 8.]

In the Berlin discussions that coincided with the ceremony, it was assumed, there was discussion of a joint attitude toward the latest Danzig flare-up, but this incident was subordinated in the German press. Warsaw received assurances from the Danzig government regarding the safety of Polish customs officers and the Poles were inclined to consider the incident closed. [Page 10.]

Britain's Cabinet was summoned for an extra meeting today to dispose of domestic business and leave tomorrow's session clear for the Anglo-Soviet problem. While there seemed to be a chance that a prompt decision on the proposed accord would be reached, the sense of urgency did not seem so strong as last week. [Page 10.] In Geneva, however, League circles had a definite impression that a British-Russian mutual aid pact would be forthcoming in the next week or so. [Page 10.]

Alliance Sealed in Berlin

By OTTO D. TOLISCHUS
Wireless to THE NEW YORK TIMES.

BERLIN, May 22.—Amid sumptuous ceremonies and an elaborate display of organized popular enthusiasm, Greater Germany and the Italian Empire today signed an unconditional and automatic offensive-defensive alliance. This pact provides for the closest political, economic and military collaboration and support in peace and war, with the declared objective of reorganizing Europe and promoting aggrandizement of the two nations and thereby creating a "just peace" throughout the world.

The alliance converts the Rome-Berlin Axis into a union of "two nations, one will," which, in the words of accompanying speeches, statements and exchanges of congratulatory telegrams, creates an invincible bloc of 150,000,000 people, raised to 300,000,000 by their anti-Comintern friends. Signatures to the pact were affixed at 11 A. M. by Joachim von Ribbentrop, German Foreign Minister, and Count Galeazzo Ciano, Italian Foreign Minister, in the festively decorated Ambassadors Hall of the new Reich Chancellery.

Hitler a Grim Witness

The momentous event was witnessed by Chancellor Adolf Hitler, clad in his simple brown uniform. He looked especially grim and determined as he sat between the two gorgeously uniformed Foreign Ministers.

The equally gorgeously attired assemblage, including Field Marshal Hermann Goering; Col. Gen. Walther von Brauchitsch, Commander in Chief of the German Army; Col. Gen. Wilhelm Keitel, head of the supreme command of the German armed forces; Grand Admiral Erich Raeder, Commander in Chief of the German Navy; Gen-

Continued on Page Eight

Reception to George VI Is Voted in the Senate

Special to THE NEW YORK TIMES.

WASHINGTON, May 22.—Congressional plans for a special reception for King George VI and Queen Elizabeth took form today as the Senate adopted and sent to the House a joint resolution providing for the occasion in the rotunda of the Capitol.

The resolution stipulated that each branch of Congress convene at 10:30 A. M. on June 9 and proceed from the respective chambers to the rotunda at 11 o'clock.

A committee of three Senators and three Representatives will work out details.

The Police Department of Washington was reported to be working out a program for an unprecedented massing of forces around the Capitol to isolate it and the grounds during the ceremonies.

QUINTUPLETS KISS QUEEN AT MEETING

She Hugs All Five—Sisters, With Royal Poise, Dominate Toronto Honors for King

By RAYMOND DANIELL
Special to THE NEW YORK TIMES.

TORONTO, Ont., May 22.—Five little unofficial princesses, the Dionne quintuplets, curtsied today before their King and Queen. This was the big moment of Toronto's welcome to King George VI and Queen Elizabeth, who stopped here today in their royal progress across Canada.

The little girls enjoyed their triumph before the proud eyes of Dr. Allan Roy Dafoe, the country doctor who kept them all alive in the trying hours of their birth nearly five years ago and who has guarded their health ever since.

The meeting of the King and Queen with their five most famous subjects in the New World all but blotted out the other events in the day's crowded program: the great throaty welcome from the city's throngs, the stuffy ceremonies in the City Hall and the legislative buildings and even the colorful show at Woodbine Park, where for the first time in history the King's Plate was run under the eyes of the ruling sovereign.

Sisters Wear Poke Bonnets

After their meeting with the King and Queen the five little girls, in ankle-length white organdie dresses and poke bonnets, walked through the Provincial legislative chamber filled with notables and heroes with as much assurance and aplomb as the Queen herself when she walked out on the arm of Prime Minister Mitchell Hepburn, behind the King.

The King and Queen arrived here at 10:30 A. M. (Eastern standard time) on the blue and silver royal train. The little ladies from Callander preceded them by several hours. They arrived aboard the "Quintland Special," all freshly painted red and equipped with five little cots in a special car called the Dr. Dafoe Nursery Car.

The presentation of the little girls to the King and Queen took place in the music room of the suite of offices in the Provincial Parliament allotted to Lieutenant Governor Albert Mathews. The room has a big bay window, a grand piano, a large sofa and soft chairs. Except for the banked flowers it might have been the living room of a private home.

Flowers Distinguish Them

In the room seated on a sofa were the five little girls, looking like so many fairy princesses in their little frocks and bonnets. While they were dressed exactly alike, individuality found expression in the flowers the quintuplets wore in their hair. There was the cut-up, Marie, with yellow rosebuds, Annette with a spray of green, Cecile with the bluebells of Scotland, Emilie with pink rosebuds and Yvonne with a sprig of heather.

Mr. and Mrs. Oliva Dionne were there in the room, while six of the seven others of their children waited stiffly in the legislative chamber, the boys in Eton jackets and the girls in white organdie.

The quintuplets greeted the King and Queen with hugs and kisses, after presentations by Mr. Hepburn, who acted as master of ceremonies.

"This is Canada's most famous doctor," said Mr. Hepburn, presenting Dr. Dafoe to the King and Queen. Then the proud but slightly puzzled parents were presented and finally each of the little girls

Continued on Page Fourteen

MANTON, ON TRIAL, ACCUSED OF GETTING BRIBE FOR THOMAS

Cahill Declares Defendant Collected $10,000 for Ex-Jurist From Connecticut

TWO MORE ADMIT GUILT

Fallon and Davis Change Pleas—Court Refuses to Isolate Jury—Case Is Rushed

As Martin T. Manton, resigned senior judge of the United States Circuit Court of Appeals, went on trial in Federal court yesterday as a "merchant of justice," United States Attorney John T. Cahill charged that Manton personally collected a $10,000 bribe for Judge Edwin S. Thomas of Connecticut. Thomas, who has also resigned and is in a sanitarium, was one of the judges on whose decisions Manton sat in judgment.

This charge was made by Mr. Cahill in his opening address near the close of a long day in which Judge Calvin W. Chesnut of Baltimore had so pushed the trial that all the usual preliminaries were completed in a single session.

These preliminaries included the selection of a jury of eleven men and three women, including the two alternates, and a flat refusal by Judge Chesnut to order the jurors locked up for the duration of the trial or to deprive them of newspapers. Opening addresses by attorneys for both sides were also completed.

Two More Plead Guilty

A plea of guilty was entered by two more of the co-defendants—William J. Fallon, whom Mr. Cahill described as the "bag-man" for Manton, and Forrest W. Davis, an accountant. Their change of plea—they had previously declared themselves not guilty—brought to three the number of guilty pleas and Mr. Cahill declared that Davis, as well as the third, John L. Lotsch, would testify for the prosecution.

Mr. Cahill took nearly two hours to outline the case the government proposed to prove against its former highest ranking judicial officer next to the nine members of the Supreme Court, and for the defense two attorneys completed their outline in less than half an hour. Benjamin Golder of Philadelphia spoke for the Manton defense, and John T. Dooling, chairman of Tammany Hall's law committee, for the remaining co-defendant, George M. Spector. The first witness will take the stand this morning.

The selection of the jurors followed the Federal system. To the assembled prospective talesmen Judge Chesnut read a list of questions prepared by the attorneys for both sides—these included a question as to whether they were acquainted with William B. Herlands, Commissioner of Accounts, District Attorney Thomas E. Dewey or Murray I. Gurfein, one of his chief assistants, which was taken as suggestive that they might be witnesses—and then twelve persons were called to the jury box.

Judge Chesnut asked each if there was any reason he felt he could not give an impartial trial. A few were excused for opinions, and a few more for acquaintance with persons connected with the

Continued on Page Four

Morgenthau Likens Ideas Of Eccles to Horse Races

By The Associated Press.

WASHINGTON, May 22.—Secretary Morgenthau said today he was looking for a "good" recovery program.

"I hope some one finds a good one and I'll endorse it heartily," he told reporters.

The Treasury head was asked if he had heard of any new spending-lending or other recovery programs being suggested in Administration circles.

He replied that he heard of such plans "every day." Then, limiting his comment to recovery plans as distinguished from spending-lending plans, he commented that he was in search of a "good" one.

He was asked about a speech by Beardsley Ruml, who has served on the President's fiscal policy committee, in which Mr. Ruml endorsed the deficit-spending ideas of Marriner S. Eccles, chairman of the Federal Reserve Board.

"That's what makes horse races," Mr. Morgenthau commented.

CHEERS OF 250,000 GREET ARCHBISHOP

Most Rev. F. J. Spellman Takes Over Archdiocese—Crowds Along Route to City

Acclaimed enthusiastically by crowds estimated at 250,000 persons along the way, New York's new Archbishop, the Most Rev. Francis Joseph Spellman, arrived here late yesterday afternoon from New England, and shortly afterward took formal canonical possession of the Archdiocese of New York.

This morning, at St. Patrick's Cathedral, where he celebrated his first mass in the United States nearly twenty-three years ago, he will be installed as the sixth Archbishop of New York and the immediate successor to the late Cardinal Hayes as spiritual head of 1,000,000 Catholics.

The installing officer will be Archbishop Amleto Giovanni Cicognani, Apostolic Delegate to the United States. In attendance at the installation ceremonies, which will start at 10 A. M., will be fifty other members of the Roman Catholic hierarchy of the United States and Canada and China, hundreds of priests and scores of distinguished laymen.

Greeted at Boundary Line

Archbishop Spellman was escorted from the Connecticut-New York boundary, which also is that of the Archdiocese of New York, to this city yesterday by Bishop Stephen J. Donahue, Auxiliary Bishop and former administrator of the archdiocese; Mgr. Michael J. Lavelle, rector of St. Patrick's Cathedral, and other diocesan officials. The ovation given to him was reminiscent of the warm greeting bestowed on Pope Pius XII when, as Cardinal Pacelli, he visited this country in 1936.

From Port Chester, N. Y., where the new Archbishop first entered the diocese he will now govern, to the end of his journey at the archiepiscopal residence, 452 Madison Avenue, his motor car traversed miles of roads and streets lined with cheering men, women and children. Many of them waited patiently in a drizzling rain for several hours to welcome him.

Constantly during the nearly two

Continued on Page Five

Italy Announces Troops Will Leave Spain, Including Balearics and Morocco, This Month

Wireless to THE NEW YORK TIMES.

ROME, May 22.—Italy's first act today after signing the military alliance with Germany was to announce that all Italian legionaries would be withdrawn from Spain before the end of this month. The following brief communiqué was issued:

"Complete repatriation of Italian legionaries from Spain will occur within the current month. Legionaries will be concentrated at Cadiz and will debark at Naples."

Asked whether Spain included the Balearic Islands and Spanish Morocco, officials here said there was no reason to doubt the withdrawal's "completeness."

There are no authoritative figures on the number of Italian troops remaining in Spain because there has been a steady withdrawal of small groups in the past few months.

[Madrid dispatches last Friday stated that the 10,000 Italians who participated in the victory parade were all that remained in Spain. It was said they would leave for home from Cadiz probably on May 28 and that the Germans would depart from Vigo the same day. The Associated Press reported yesterday, however, that Cadiz was preparing for the departure of about 20,000 Italians on June 5.]

CADIZ, Spain, May 22 (AP).—Several hundred Italian legionaries, with a large quantity of Italian war material, arrived at Puerto Santa Maria and Puerto Real today to embark for home.

The Italians, who fought with the Spanish Nationalists in the civil war, are leaving Cadiz June 5 aboard six Italian troop ships. Large contingents of legionaries also are expected at Jerez and San Fernando, within the Cadiz district.

It was estimated that about 20,000 Italians would be accommodated in Cadiz proper and near-by towns pending their departure. It was reported the bulk of the Italian forces would arrive in Cadiz Wednesday evening.

Wireless to THE NEW YORK TIMES.

HENDAYE, France (at the Spanish Border), May 22.—War material carried into France last February by Spanish Republicans fleeing Catalonia is now being turned over to Generalissimo Francisco Franco by the French Government in accordance with the Bérard-Jordana agreement.

Towed by tractors sent by General Franco for the purpose, military trucks and cars were being hauled in great quantities over the Hendaye and Behobie bridges today. At Perpignan thirteen carloads of munitions were returned to Catalonia.

Spanish military experts are supervising these shipments, which are expected to require a fortnight.

PENDERGAST PLEADS GUILTY IN TAX CASE; GETS PRISON, FINE

Kansas City Boss Admits Evasion as $315,000 Insurance Fund Deal Is Told to Court

RACE BET 'MANIA' BLAMED

$600,000 Losses in Year Bared—15-Month Term Imposed Despite Age and Illness

By JAMES A. HAGERTY
Special to THE NEW YORK TIMES.

KANSAS CITY, May 22.—The amazing career of Thomas J. Pendergast, one of the last of the powerful city bosses, came to an end in United States District Court today when he pleaded guilty to income tax evasion and was sentenced to serve one year and three months in a Federal penitentiary and to pay a fine of $10,000.

The man who rose from a boyhood of poverty to dominate for a quarter of a century the government of this Middle Western metropolis of 400,000, with a suburban population of nearly equal size, received the sentence stoically. He moved not a muscle in his massive, roughly hewn features as Judge Merrill E. Otis read the sentence, but he could not control his eyes.

Without moving his head, his gaze shifted rapidly from his son, Thomas J. Pendergast Jr., who sat on one side of him, to his nephew, James M. Pendergast, who sat on the other side, and then turned to James G. Madden and R. R. Brewster, his counsel.

Only once did Pendergast show any real sign of emotion. That was when Mr. Madden, chairman of the Jackson County Democratic Committee and long a personal friend, urged a suspended sentence because of his age of 67 and his physical condition, declaring that a sentence of imprisonment would be a sentence of death. He said that Pendergast had serious heart and intestinal ailments.

Defendant Lowers Head

When the plea was made Pendergast lowered his head and covered his mouth and chin with his right hand.

The sentence of imprisonment was on the first count of the indictment. This count charged evasion of 1935 income taxes. In imposing the sentence, Judge Otis said that it was his intention that it be served, except as it might be modified by the Federal Board of Parole or by the President. He directed at first that the prison sentence begin immediately, but, at the request of Mr. Madden for time to permit Pendergast to arrange his personal affairs, consented to a week's grace.

In imposing a fine of $10,000 on the second count, charging income tax evasion in 1936, Judge Otis also imposed a three-year prison sentence, but suspended this to place Pendergast on probation for five years, the period to begin on the expiration of his imprisonment on the first count.

As conditions for probation, the judge declared that Pendergast must pay the $10,000 fine, obey all national, State and municipal laws during the period and pay promptly to the Federal Government the full amount, with legal penalties, of income taxes evaded in 1935 and 1936. Judge Otis added that probation would not be revoked if it was found Pendergast was not financially able to pay.

Betting Losses Stressed

In their appeal for clemency Mr. Madden and Mr. Brewster stressed not only Pendergast's age and illness but his fondness for betting on horse racing, which, they declared, amounted to a mania. One reason for his failure to report his entire income, they indicated, was his betting losses.

Maurice M. Milligan, United States Attorney, had opened the racing phase of Pendergast's financial transaction by declaring in his statement to the court that Pendergast was known as one of the biggest plungers on the American turf. The government had been informed, he added, that in 1935 Pendergast wagered $2,000,000 on horse races and lost $600,000.

Mr. Milligan made no recommendation for sentence, but presented a statement of facts. He asserted that Pendergast received $315,000 in insurance company money for his part in bringing about the release of $9,000,000 impounded by the Federal court pending settlement of rate litigation. Pendergast had arranged with R. E. O'Malley, then State Superintendent of Insurance, for the release of this impounded money, Mr. Milligan added, and concealed the receipt of the $315,000 in his income tax report.

Mr. Milligan said that in the eleven years, 1927 to 1937 inclusive, Pendergast had a net income of $1,240,746.56 which he had not re-

Continued on Page Seven

ROOSEVELT MAINTAINS AIMS AND PRINCIPLES OF NEW DEAL AS AID TO SMALL BUSINESS

Relief Refund Asked From City On 'Profits' of Camp La Guardia

Federal Accountant Tells House Inquiry That $54,272 Accrued From 'Illegal' Operations at Refuge for Homeless

Special to THE NEW YORK TIMES.

WASHINGTON, May 22.—A refund of $54,272 has been demanded from the New York City Department of Public Welfare for "profits" made in an alleged illegal manner in the operation of Camp La Guardia with WPA funds, a general Accounting Office investigator today told the House Appropriations subcommittee investigating the administration of relief.

The investigator, Ralph Hale, who is in charge of a staff of eighteen accountants checking WPA affairs in New York, testified that "loose" methods had been conducive to widespread irregularities in the purchase of supplies and rental of equipment, and that in some cases Federal officials there had refused to prosecute.

He detailed many instances of alleged irregularities and put in the record others which he lacked time to present orally.

The operation of Camp La Guardia was halted some time after accountants went into its affairs, Mr. Hale said. The investigation showed that from a deficit of $7,272.15 at the time the project was transferred to the WPA on July 1, 1935, the Camp La Guardia trust fund had been built up to $54,272, which Mr. Hale said was "profit."

The WPA made two allotments, one for $166,500 and another for $671,000, to operate the project. The Treasury drew checks payable to the camp members, who were homeless men from New York City's streets, and these checks in turn were deposited by Harry W. Marsh, first deputy commissioner of the Department of Public Welfare, to the trust fund account.

Mr. Hale testified that the men, upon admittance to camp, were required to sign a power of attorney, an act which he termed a violation of law.

At first, they were charged 50 cents a day for subsistence, and the remainder of their monthly checks for $30.50 was deposited in the fund to the account of the members. Mr. Hale said that out of this credit they could buy cigarettes and other items from the camp-operated store.

Stating that if the WPA had not taken care of the homeless men the

Continued on Page Twenty-one

C. I. O. AUTO STRIKE MAKES 24,000 IDLE

Briggs Local of 15,000 Called Out at Detroit After Hitch on Contract—Chrysler Hit

By The Associated Press.

DETROIT, May 22.—A strike of the United Automobile Workers affiliated with the Congress of Industrial Organizations left more than 24,000 men idle tonight and a government conciliator was reported hastening here to offer his services toward a settlement.

Nine hours after the strike closed seven plants of the Briggs Manufacturing Company and threatened operations in other factories, R. J. Thomas, president of the union, announced that James F. Dewey, Federal mediator, would come here tomorrow from Chester, Pa.

The Briggs strike affected 15,000 employes directly. A few hours after the halt in production of the Briggs car bodies 6,000 day-shift employes of the Plymouth division of Chrysler Corporation became idle. An additional 3,000 Plymouth workers were expected to be laid off.

Shop Stewards Reported Stabbed

The strike was called by Emil Mazey, president of the Briggs local, in five Briggs plants in Detroit proper and one each in Hamtramck and Highland Park. It followed a breakdown in negotiations for renewal of a contract that expired May 16.

One outbreak of violence was reported. Police said that two shop stewards in the Mack Avenue Briggs plant suffered minor knife wounds in a brief fight just before noon as they went through the plant to check on the response to the strike call.

The Briggs plants closed down promptly at 9 A. M. As thousands of workers poured through the gates, company watchmen turned off power and closed windows.

Picket lines were established soon after the exodus. Special details of police were on hand. At the big Meldrum Avenue plant 500 men were reported in the picket line.

Counter-Complaints Issued

Union sources said the U. A. W. had insisted that twenty-six "old grievances" be settled before a new contract should be arranged.

The management said the union had "failed to offer a single concession," and charged that Mr. Mazey was "seeking strife."

The company said an offer to submit the dispute to an arbitrator had been rejected by the union.

Chrysler officials said that other divisions of the corporation would be affected tomorrow if the strike continued. The Ford Motor Company, which obtains bodies from Briggs for its Mercury model, was understood to have a supply of bodies on hand.

HAMILTON DENIES ANY 'WHISPERING'

Tells Dies Committee That He Does Not Know Man Who Warned of a 'Red' Coup

Mr. Hamilton's statement will be found on Page 2.

By HAROLD B. HINTON
Special to THE NEW YORK TIMES.

WASHINGTON, May 22.—John D. M. Hamilton, chairman of the Republican National Committee, took every opportunity today during a hearing before the House Committee on un-American Activities to disassociate himself and his party from anti-Semitic and other whispering campaigns about which the committee has heard.

Mr. Hamilton was on the stand only a few minutes at the end of today's session. His direct testimony was to the effect that he did not personally know James E. Campbell of Owensboro, Ky., author and distributor of "confidential" information about an alleged Communist conspiracy to seize the government by force in August. The committee had found correspondence between Mr. Hamilton and Mr. Campbell which was of a vaguely cordial character on Mr. Hamilton's part and which included the dispatch of a list of the Republican National Committee's members throughout the country.

The Republican chairman was not in a position to say whether or not he had talked with Mr. Campbell, as had been testified, during the "Corn Field rally" of Republicans at Washington, Ind., last Summer. He had not seen nor heard from Mr. Campbell, except for the letters the committee had, since that rally, he stated.

"If a man writes in and says he has met me," Mr. Hamilton said, as the committee laughed with him, "I'm not going to deny it."

Gets Many "Nut Letters"

Mr. Campbell had asked for an appointment to discuss with Mr. Hamilton some information he had on "subversive activities," but the chairman said that his committee gets so many "nut letters" on that subject that little attention is paid to them. They are usually consigned to a special file.

Such would probably have been the fate of Mr. Campbell's letters had not the first one been sent to him by Felix McWhirter, Indianapolis banker, who is treasurer of the Republican State organization in Indiana and finance officer for Indiana for the national committee. Mr. McWhirter, who is under subpoena to appear before the Dies committee, sent Mr. Campbell's first letter to Mr. Hamilton with a warm endorsement in which he called Mr. Campbell "my tried and trusted friend."

Mr. Hamilton read into the record a prepared statement in which he repudiated any inferences that

Continued on Page Two

CRITICS 'RADICALS'

New Dealers Pictured as the Conservatives in Speech to Retailers

PUBLIC SPENDING UPHELD

No Compromise, Says Hopkins—Martin Attack on Policies Received With Applause

Texts of Roosevelt, Hopkins and Martin addresses Page 16.

By TURNER CATLEDGE
Special to THE NEW YORK TIMES.

WASHINGTON, May 22.—Before a friendly forum of the country's leading retailers, President Roosevelt reiterated tonight his determination to press forward with the principles and objectives of the New Deal, and classified as "radicals" and "gamblers" those who are demanding that the government take its hands off the economic system.

The President made it clear that this meant a continuation of all of the major Administration policies, especially that of deficit spending. But he added the assurance that a continuation of deficits was not a permanent part of the Administration's plans. Furthermore, he issued an invitation to the retailers, over whose counters, according to his calculation, more than 50 cents of every Bederally spent dollar passes, to cooperate with him in improving operating methods. His one condition was that they first approve the purposes that lie behind his policies.

The President's speech, delivered at a dinner meeting tonight, marked the first day of a two-day meeting of the Retailers National Forum, under the auspices of the American Retail Federation.

Because of his vigorous defense of his spending policies, many in Washington saw in the President's remarks further evidence to sustain reports that another program of this kind is being considered seriously by the Administration.

Hopkins Follows Same Line

The President's address followed by several hours one delivered by Harry Hopkins, Secretary of Commerce, in which he, too, laid down the proposition that the New Deal's philosophy of social and economic reform must be carried forward at all odds.

In between the two, however, Representative Joseph W. Martin Jr., Minority Leader of the House, had evoked several rounds of applause from the retailers with attacks upon the Administration's spending-lending and labor policies. Another interim speaker, Dr. Beardsley Ruml, treasurer of R. H. Macy & Co., and member of the National Resources Committee, practically prophesied the coming of a permanent compensatory fiscal policy, deliberately operated in the interest of the private, competitive capitalistic system.

The President was greeted with an ovation, lasting the better part of a minute, when he was introduced by Louis E. Kirstein of Boston, chairman of the board of trustees of the American Retail Federation, who presided at the dinner. Frequently the audience interrupted with applause to show its approval of the President's remarks. One of these times was when, during a discussion of taxes, he told his listeners to ask H. Gordon Selfridge, London department store owner, to say what he was "paying to keep England afloat."

Although in the main his address was a defense of the Administration's spending program, the President paused to make public again his stand on the much-agitated question of taxation. Characterizing the current controversy over the undistributed profits tax as "making a mountain out of a mole hill," he reiterated his demand that if the levy were repealed the $20,000,000 it raises annually in revenue must be found, and provision made to prevent tax evasion through the corporate system.

Aims at Larger Corporations

He insisted, too, that the tax yield must come from the 28,000 "bigger corporations" earning more than $25,000 a year, and not from the 175,000 corporations earning less than that sum.

If these conditions were satisfied, the President said, he would be

Continued on Page Fifteen

The *Squalus'* conning tower can be seen above the surface of the water as the ship is towed to Portsmouth Navy Yard.

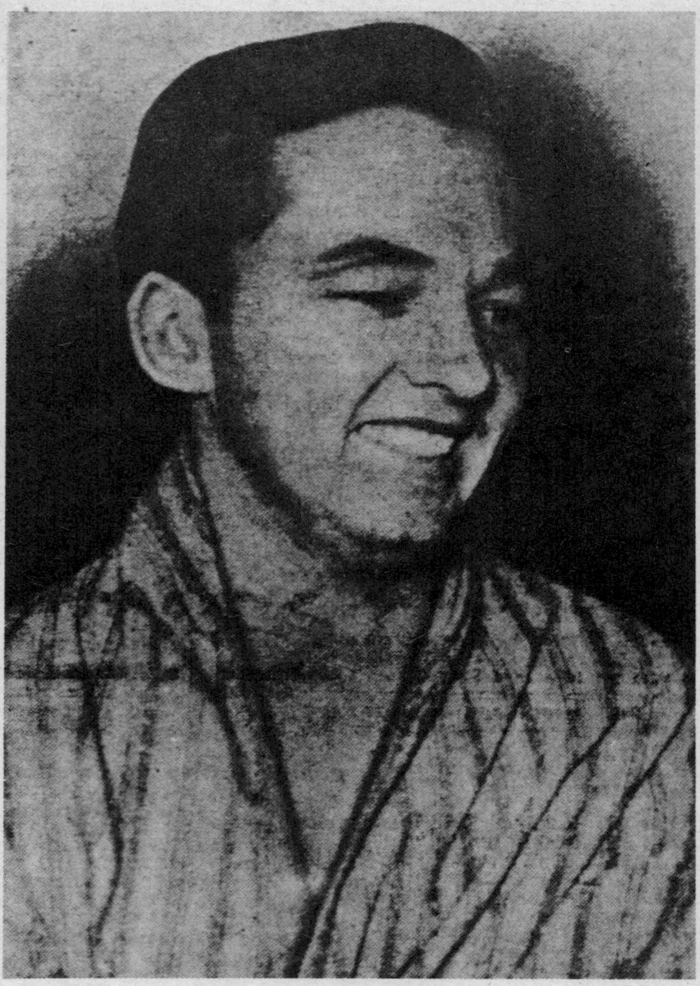

Times Wide World

LAST MAN TO LEAVE SQUALUS, AND HERO OF THE DISASTER

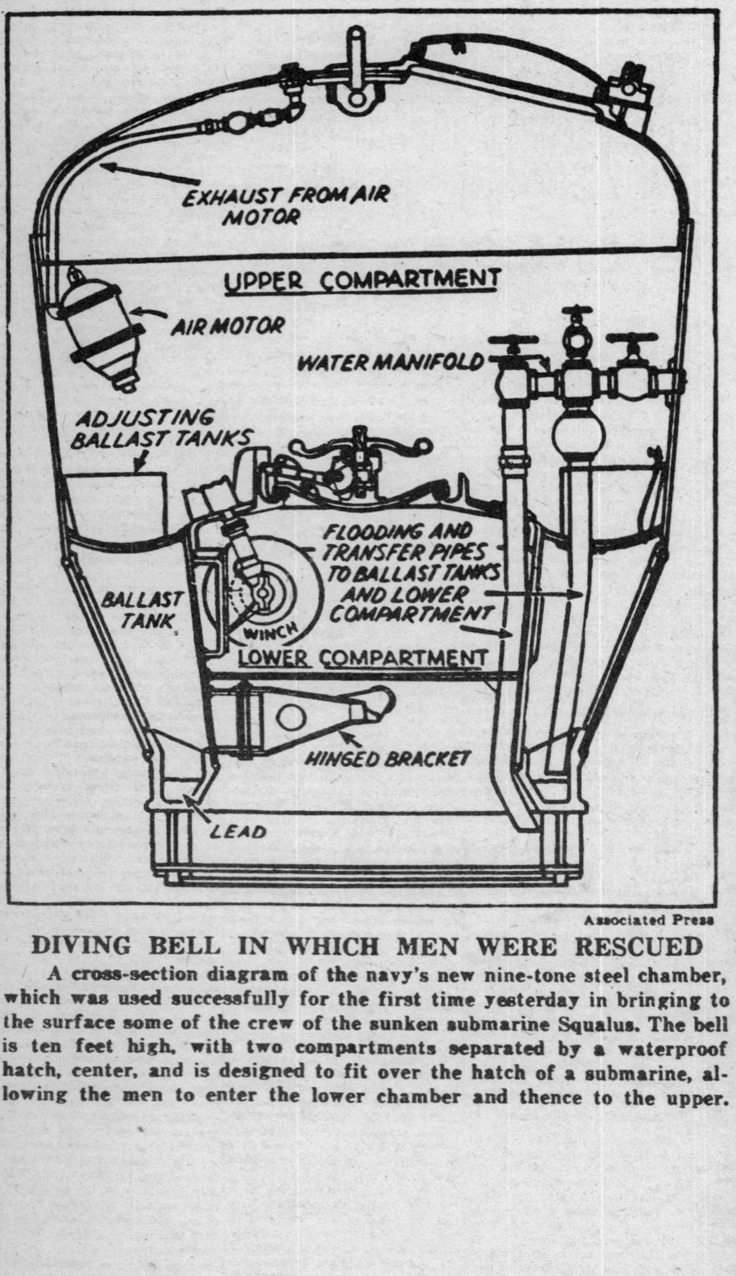

Associated Press

DIVING BELL IN WHICH MEN WERE RESCUED

A cross-section diagram of the navy's new nine-tone steel chamber, which was used successfully for the first time yesterday in bringing to the surface some of the crew of the sunken submarine Squalus. The bell is ten feet high, with two compartments separated by a waterproof hatch, center, and is designed to fit over the hatch of a submarine, allowing the men to enter the lower chamber and thence to the upper.

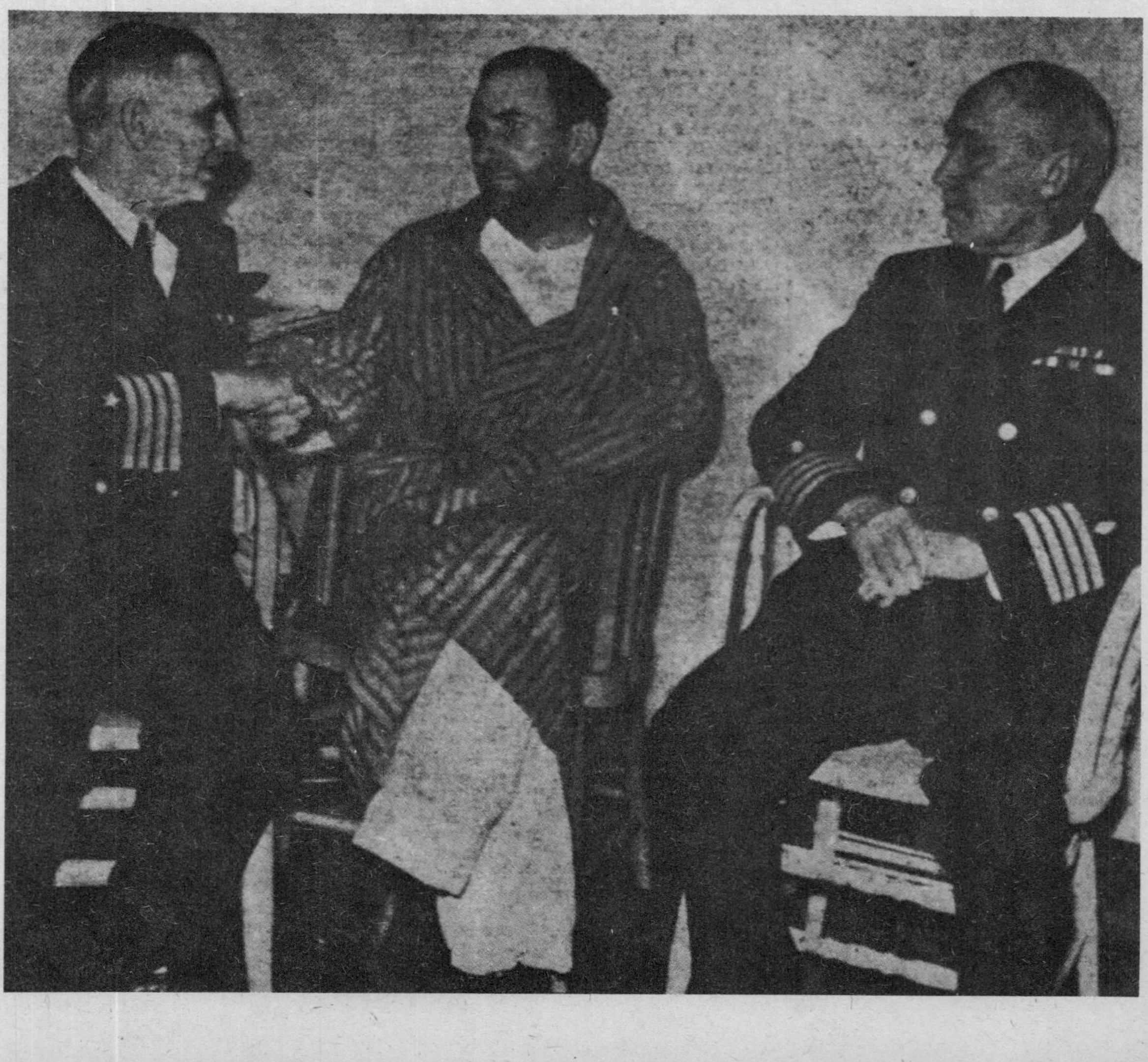

Lieutenant Oliver F. Naquin, the commander of the sunken submarine, being greeted by Captain William Amsden, left, and Captain M.E. Higgins at the Portsmouth Naval Hospital.

"All the News That's Fit to Print."

The New York Times.

LATE CITY EDITION
Fair, little change in temperature today. Tomorrow cloudy, intermittent rains, temperature unchanged.
Temperatures Yesterday—Max., 66; Min., 52

VOL. LXXXVIII...No. 29,706. Entered as Second-Class Matter, Postoffice, New York, N. Y. NEW YORK, THURSDAY, MAY 25, 1939. PP THREE CENTS NEW YORK CITY and Vicinity | FOUR CENTS Elsewhere Except in 7th and 8th Postal Zones.

33 RESCUED FROM SQUALUS BY DIVING BELL; 26 OTHERS FEARED DEAD IN FLOODED CHAMBERS; SURVIVOR TELLS OF COOL, CHEERFUL DISCIPLINE

BRITISH NOW AGREE TO A SOVIET PACT FOR MUTUAL HELP

Cabinet Approves Joint Action to Meet European Attack on Either Power or France

SIGNING BY JUNE 5 LIKELY

Plan Bars Latvia and Estonia —Will Be Linked to League —Staff Talks Are in View

By FERDINAND KUHN Jr.
Special Cable to THE NEW YORK TIMES.

LONDON, May 24.—The British Cabinet brought weeks of hesitation to an end today by agreeing to enter into a mutual-assistance accord with Russia and France against further aggression in Europe.

On good authority it was reported that the Ministers had approved the broad principle of immediate concerted action in the event that any of the three powers were attacked on any European front. In other words, a German onslaught against any one of them would be regarded instantly as an attack upon all and would be met by the combined strength of the powers that formed the Triple Entente in 1914.

Moreover, the plan is said to provide for common action by Britain, France and Russia in the event of an attack upon Poland, Rumania or other smaller powers, although it does not cover the little Baltic republics of Latvia and Estonia. It will also be linked to the League of Nations Covenant by a formula still to be worked out by London, Paris and Moscow.

Decision Reached in Two Hours

It took only two hours of quiet discussion for the Cabinet to reach its momentous decision—a decision more tremendous in some of its implications than any of the other reversals of British foreign policy since the German Army marched into Prague in March.

The Cabinet seems to have given its full approval to a plan brought back by Viscount Halifax, the Foreign Secretary, from his consultations in Geneva. As far as could be discovered tonight the Ministers did not delete or modify any of Lord Halifax's proposals, and instead of having to argue his case before a reluctant Cabinet he found he had to submit to nothing worse than earnest questioning by his colleagues.

The new alliance is not yet signed and sealed and important details have still to be settled, as Prime Minister Neville Chamberlain told the House of Commons today. Nevertheless, the British Ministers seem to realize now that a pact with Russia is the coping-stone of a new defensive structure in Europe and that without it the whole "peace front" might crumble into ineffectiveness and decay.

The British decisions will be embodied in definite proposals to the Soviet Government with the text of a proposed three-power declaration and will be sent without delay to Sir William Seeds, the British Ambassador in Moscow. The question at the moment is whether the Kremlin will be satisfied with the Cabinet's decision in principle or whether it will continue to bargain over details.

Halifax Is Confident

Lord Halifax, at least, believes Moscow will agree. He took the precaution at Geneva of showing his proposals to Ivan M. Maisky, the Soviet Ambassador to London, who answered that as far as he personally was concerned they were satisfactory. The Cabinet here is not sure that it really knows what is in the Kremlin's mind, but Mr. Maisky insists he knows and there is plenty of confidence here that Moscow will accept within a few days.

Certainly Mr. Chamberlain had never been so confident over the Russian negotiations as he was today in making a necessarily guarded statement in the Commons. After having told the House of Lord Halifax's conversations in Paris and Geneva, Mr. Chamberlain said:

"As a result of these conversations all relevant points of view now have been made clear, and I have every reason to hope that as a result of proposals which His Majesty's Government is now in a position to make on the main questions arising it will be found possible to reach a full agreement at an early date.

"There still remain some further points to be cleared up, but I do not anticipate that these are likely to give rise to any serious difficulty."

Clement R. Attlee, the Labor leader, asked whether Mr. Chamberlain could not make a "more definite and fuller statement" before the House adjourned for the Whitsuntide recess on Friday. Mr. Chamberlain replied that he would not rule out the possibility of such

Continued on Page Four

2,500 Police Aspirants Smash Way Into Capitol

Special to THE NEW YORK TIMES.

ALBANY, May 24.—More than 2,500 applicants for thirty-five vacant positions in the State police force, which are to be filled about July 1, crowded into the Capitol today. Despite the activity of State policemen, who had been sent to maintain order, the aspiring guardians of public peace, attempting to get into the Senate chamber to take the examination, crashed through windows, pushed doors off their hinges and crowded the building so much as to give any policeman a headache.

The examination was given in Chancellor's Hall, the Senate and Assembly chambers, the Assembly Parlor and other large rooms. The applicants included many college graduates.

KING POINTS LESSON OF PEACE TO WORLD

In Broadcast He Says Europe Might Find Guidance in Neighborliness Here

By RAYMOND DANIELL
Special to THE NEW YORK TIMES.

WINNIPEG, May 24.—King George VI, in an Empire Day address broadcast to the polyglot peoples all over the world who come under his rule, expressed the wish that the Old World of Europe and Asia might learn a lesson from the New World of North America in the solution of racial aspirations and national differences.

The King was at special pains to emphasize the friendship between the peoples of his empire and those of the United States, and he thanked God that no man in the future would ever again consider a resort to force to resolve differences which might arise between them.

Indeed, he declared, that faith "in reason and fair play" which he said Britons share with the people of the United States "is one of the chief ideals that guide the British Empire in all its ways today."

The royal train left here at 9:10 P. M., Eastern daylight time, carrying the King and Queen into Saskatchewan tomorrow.

The celebration of Empire Day, coinciding with the birthday anniversary of Queen Victoria, the Sovereign's great-grandmother, was in some respects one of the most impressive occasions of the visit of the King and Queen to Canada, the first any rulers of England ever have made to a self-governing Dominion.

Rides Open Car in Rain

Thoroughly soaked in the drizzling rain through which he rode in an open car with his Queen, his hand bandaged from the hundreds of hearty and Western handclasps he has received in the last few days, King George VI and Queen Elizabeth repaired to a study in Government House at noon here to listen to greetings from the great and humble transmitted to them by radio from all parts of the far-flung empire.

Because the King and Queen were visiting here for the day on their way to the West Coast and the United States, this sprawling prairie city of 300,000 was for the time the very center of the empire.

From Nova Scotia, the radio technicians cut in the voice of the skipper of a fishing schooner of Lunenberg sending his King and Queen, who were sitting side by side in their study, a message of loyalty and affection. Other voices from Quebec in French and from Montreal and Toronto, where the royal visitors have been already, chimed in with similar messages.

An airplane pilot from Edmonton, farther along on the route of the King and Queen, spoke up, then from Africa—speaking for the British subjects of the Union of South Africa, Northern and Southern Rhodesia, Basutoland, Swaziland and Bechuanaland, of Uganda, Dararaland and Namaqualand, of Kenya, Tanganyika and Zanzibar, of British Somaliland and the island of Sokotra; Nigeria, Gambia, the Gold Coast and a host of other lands with unfamiliar names—came further greetings in strange tongues.

From Australia and New Zealand, far down under, were heard English voices in expressions of fealty and love, and the voice of a Maori student.

India and Tagore's Words

Next the announcer called in the Indian Empire—the peoples of Bombay, Behar and Orissa, of Coorg, Kashmir and the Punjab, of Baluchistan, Mysore, Assam and Hyderabad and of the Native States of Bengal, Madras and the United Provinces of Agra and Oudh, and finally the Kingdom of Nepal.

And for these peoples the great Indian poet and philosopher Rabindranath Tagore had composed a special poem of greeting which was heard in his native tongue from a recording and afterward in English.

Some listeners read into Tagore's

Continued on Page Ten

MANTON IS ACCUSED OF LETTING LITIGANT HELP WITH OPINION

Lotsch Testifies in One Case Ruling Upheld Concern for Which Draft Was Offered

LOANS DEMANDED, HE SAYS

Declares $50,000 Was Asked From Him and Bank While Suits Were Pending

A tale of judicial intrigue which, in some of its bizarre elements, overshadowed anything ever told in a New York court room, was unfolded in Federal Court yesterday at the trial of Martin T. Manton, resigned senior judge of the United States Circuit Court of Appeals charged with being a "merchant of justice."

The story was told by John L. Lotsch, a patent lawyer and bank chairman who wound up his career by being convicted on a criminal charge, and buttressed from point to point by documents that United States Attorney John T. Cahill put in evidence before Judge Calvin Chesnut of Baltimore and a jury as part of the corroboration without which Lotsch's recital might have seemed fantastic.

The story involved the following allegations:

Two instances in which it was testified that interested parties in cases before Manton took a hand in the preparation of his opinion.

The collection of $10,000 cash "for Judge Thomas" (Edwin S. Thomas of Connecticut), to fix a case in which Lotsch was the defendant and in which Manton found it later necessary to hold Thomas's action in directing a verdict of acquittal in error.

Demands for $50,000 in loans from Lotsch and the Fort Greene National Bank of Brooklyn, of which he was chairman, while cases in which Lotsch was attorney were actually before Manton for consideration.

The promise by Manton that the receivers of two large corporations would make "substantial" deposits in the Fort Greene Bank—and later $100,000 was subsequently deposited—and the delivery to Lotsch by Manton of the government's trial brief, a confidential document, detailing the case against Lotsch, which had been handed to Judge Thomas by an assistant United States Attorney. This was the case in which $10,000, Lotsch said, had been paid.

Story Swiftly Told

The complex account of dealings which began early in 1935 and continued until after the time of Manton's resignation in February of this year when the investigation leading to the present trial had begun, was unfolded swiftly and dramatically.

Occasionally Judge Chesnut fixed his eyes on Manton and then let them rove around the room. At one point Manton's attorney, James M. Noonan of Albany, was on the verge of collapse and hastily asked for a ten-minute recess. He said later that an old stomach ulcer had suddenly become very painful.

Lotsch testified that he first met Manton early in 1935 through William J. Fallon, who has been described in this case as the "bag man" or collector for the former

Continued on Page Two

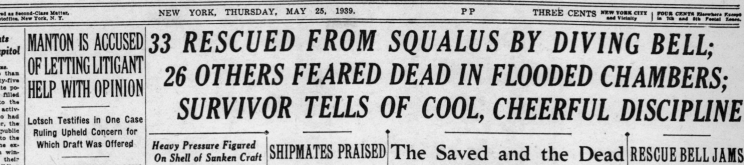

Heavy Pressure Figured On Shell of Sunken Craft

Special to THE NEW YORK TIMES.

PORTSMOUTH, N. H., May 24.—The thirty-two men who were lying in the cold and damp forward compartments of the sunken submarine Squalus were under the same atmospheric pressure of 14.7 pounds a square inch as the men in the bright sunshine on the deck of the rescue ship Falcon.

Yet if they had been forced to use the Momsen lung to leave the cylindrical steel pressure hull, which holds back the weight of water, they would have been under a weight of 105.6 pounds a square inch.

A handkerchief twelve inches square spread out on the shell of the "hog-boat" down under 240 feet of water would bear up on it seven and a half tons pressure. That figure gives an indication of the terrific pressure which the divers had to undergo in their inflexible suits.

FAMILIES ON SHORE WAIT IN SUSPENSE

Bulletins on Rescues Bring Joy to Some, While Others Still Cling to Hope

From a Staff Correspondent

PORTSMOUTH, N. H., May 24.—The navy took its losses today in the manner peculiar to the men who go down to the sea in ships.

Officers and enlisted men of the navy yard here, and the yard workmen who helped to build the Squalus and are now completing two of her sister-ships, the Searaven and Seawolf, took the news of rescue and of death in tight-lipped silence. A yard workman said: "They got some of them, that's good; that's very good"; and a smile lighted his face.

Naval officers crowded close to the radio. Their eyes gleamed with hope at each reassuring bit of news but they said little. It was the navy way.

It was different with the families, for they were bound by ties even stronger than the ties of the service to the men imprisoned in the pressure hull of the Squalus. There were fathers and husbands and brothers forty fathoms below the surface and from noon yesterday—when the news of the sinking of the Squalus became known—until midafternoon today, when a list of those definitely known to be alive was received here, the families and relatives of fifty-seven of the fifty-nine trapped in the Squalus were in suspense.

It was learned in the first telephone conversation yesterday that the captain of the Squalus, Lieutenant Oliver F. Naquin, and the gunnery and torpedo officer, Lieutenant (J. G.) John C. Nichols, were alive; others of the crew were with them; some were thought to be in the flooded compartments, but who was safe, who lost, was not known.

Most of the wives, most of the

Continued on Page Sixteen

SHIPMATES PRAISED

Judson T. Bland Stresses Optimism in Dark as Vessel Settled

SCULPIN'S ENGINES HEARD

Four Men Beat Signals as They Waited—Saving of Air Was a Major Problem

By MARSHALL NEWTON
Special to THE NEW YORK TIMES.

PORTSMOUTH, N. H., May 24.—Judson T. Bland, an electrician's mate on the Squalus, one of the stoic little band that waited on the bottom for mates above to rescue them, was the spokesman selected tonight by the navy to tell the story of their vigil. A stocky, vigorous person, he had come through the ordeal in better condition than any of the others.

He was tired but seemed to be feeling no other ill effects of the long wait for help when he came to the administration office in the navy yard here to tell his story and, by proxy, that of all the men. Speaking deliberately, in low tones, he gave a straightforward account.

Except that he was wrapped in a blanket over his pajamas and was telling of the most dramatic event that can happen to a submarine man, he might have been describing any routine dive.

Navy yard officials were extremely vigilant to see that he was not exhausted, and when one reporter asked insistently that Bland speak louder the marine officer in charge ordered the man ejected from the room by a marine guard. A stenographic transcript of Bland's story was made.

Account of Judson T. Bland

"Mr. Bland, the newspapers would like you to tell them your story in your own words, what happened, how you first knew something was wrong and everything as you saw it," he was asked.

"The first thing I want to say," he replied, "I am very happy to be here and that I was with such a good bunch of shipmates. I never saw men handle a situation any better. The captain was perfectly cool. He gave his orders calmly and the orders were carried out perfectly by each and every man.

"We made a perfectly normal dive. We were making a test dive at fast speed. The navy yard test superintendent was clocking the dive and made the statement as we went down that it would be a good dive. Then something happened—we don't know what it was and we won't know until the boat is brought up. It was something that could not be helped.

"It could happen to any mechanism that requires complicated parts. However, we began taking in water through the ventilation line and we knew something had gone wrong aft. The captain came below just prior to that time. He reported that everything was all right. Men began working fast to shut off the flow of water.

"The instant the diving officer knew the water was coming in he gave word to blow the tanks. This order was carried out immediately and well. We took a terrific up-angle, in my judgment about 45 degrees up by the bow.

"One man closed the door to the affected part of the ship while we were at this angle. It took super-strength to do it. I don't see how he did it. Certain other valves were closed to stop the flow of water and we kept the forward part of the ship pretty dry.

"All men were gotten out of the after part of the ship we could possibly get out. I don't know if all compartments in the afterpart are flooded—I hope they are not. If not, more men may be gotten out. We lost all power and communication aft. Throughout the day no one was excited and every one was living in hopes that we would be found. We fired smoke bombs at intervals.

"We heard the Sculpin's engines—we knew their engines because they are the same type we had. We were very much relieved. We knew we were found and had nothing to worry about. We had no communication with the top side other than beating on the hull. All electric power was gone.

"Two men forward and two men

Continued on Page Seventeen

The Saved and the Dead

From a Staff Correspondent

PORTSMOUTH, N. H., May 24.—Twenty-six of the fifty-nine officers and men who were aboard the Squalus when she sank yesterday were still unaccounted for tonight. Their names and the names of those who have been rescued are listed below.

The Rescued

Officers

Commanding Officer — Lieutenant Oliver F. Naquin of Alexandria, La.
Executive Officer—Lieutenant William T. Doyle Jr. of Baltimore.
Engineering Officer — Lieutenant (J.G.) Robert N. Robertson of Quanah, Texas.
Gunnery and Torpedo Officer—Lieutenant (J. G.) John C. Nichols of Chicago.

Enlisted Men

Blanchard, Roland, fireman, second class, of Hersey, Mich.
Bland, Judson T., electrician's mate, first class, of Norfolk.
Booth, Arthur L., radioman, first class, of Milford, Conn.
Boulton, William D., seaman, first class, of Luton, Iowa.
Bryson, Allen C., machinist mate, second class, R. F. D. 2, Greenville S. C.
Campbell, Roy H., chief torpedoman, of Omaha.
Coyne, Garvin, machinist's mate, second class, of Sacramento, Calif.
Cravens, Eugene D., gunners' mate, second class, of Thayer, Mo.
Elvina, Feliciano, mess attendant, first class, of Malate, Manila.
Fitzpatrick, William J., torpedoman, second class, of Woburn, Mass.
Gainor, Lawrence J., chief electrician's mate, of Honolulu.
Galvan, Basilio, mess attendant, first class, of Ibajay, Capiz, P. I.
Isaacs, William, cook, second class, of Washington.
Jacobs, Theodore, signalman, first class, of Oakwood Heights, S. I., N. Y.
Kuney, Charles S., yeoman, second class, of Tulare, Calif.
Maness, Lloyd B., electrician's mate, third class, of Greensboro, N. C.
McLees, Gerald G., electrician's mate, third class, of Richmond, Kan.
Medeiros, Leonard B., torpedoman, third class, of New Bedford, Mass.
Murphy, Francis, Jr., quartermaster, first class, of Charlestown, Mass.
O'Hara, Raymond F., pharmacist's mate, first class, of Elmira, N. Y.
Persico, Donato, seaman, second class, of Amsterdam, N. Y.
Pierce, Carol N., machinist mate, second class, of Kansas City, Kan.
Powell, Carlton B., machinist's mate, second class, of Cardiff-by-the-Sea, Calif.
Powell, Charles A., radioman, second class, of Leesville, La.
Prien, Alfred G., machinist's mate, second class, of San Francisco.

Continued on Page Eighteen

MEN BROUGHT UP IN FOUR BELL TRIPS

Last Rescue Takes Three Times the Others—Some of the 33 Step Out Dizzily

From a Staff Correspondent

PORTSMOUTH, N. H., May 24.—In a small spot in the open sea, now as busy a traffic intersection as one in Times Square, there were spontaneous cheers at 1:18 o'clock this afternoon (Daylight-saving time) when the first dungaree-clad figure stepped from the hatch of the escape chamber.

Navy and Coast Guardsmen on numerous vessels, as they saw eager hands help the first survivor of the Squalus to the deck of the rescue ship Falcon, began to believe that their hopes for the saving of all in the submarine might be fulfilled. After the first seaman stepped out of the "bell," others followed, including an officer in blue uniform, until seven were out.

They were the first submarine men brought to the surface in a rescue chamber in an actual disaster, recording a new advance in safety measures in which practice had met theory.

Two of the men were laughing as they came out of the hatch. They were stepping into bright sunlight after spending twenty-eight hours in chilling dampness and dark, beset with gnawing uncertainty.

Dizzy From Sudden Fresh Air

One of the men stumbled and faltered as his lungs drew in the sun-warmed air, but there were solicitous arms outstretched to support him. With his mates he went into the decompression chamber for a short period to offset the effect of the ascent in the rescue chamber. Then they were sped to the quiet and peace of the Portsmouth Navy Yard Hospital.

Lieutenant O. F. Naquin, the submarine's commander, sent up Lieutenant J. C. Nichols with the first group of men so that he might tell the story of the tragedy that lay below. There were fifty-nine men aboard the Squalus when it set out from the Portsmouth Navy Yard on a routine diving operation on Tuesday morning. There were thirty-two in the forward compartments which had been reached by the rescue chamber. Their names were sent to the surface by Lieutenant Naquin to end the agonizing suspense among waiting relatives.

For the kinfolk of the men who had been in the after compartments there was no encouraging news. No news was bad news, because the navy assumed that the men unaccounted for had been trapped and drowned.

Besides Lieutenant Nichols of Chicago, in the first group there were: Roland Blanchard, Hersey, Mich., William Isaacs, Bloomfield, N. J.;

Continued on Page Seventeen

RESCUE WATCHED FROM SEA AND SKY

Vessels Silently Open Path for Boat of Survivors—One Feels Like 'Lifting His Hat'

By ROBERT S. BIRD
Wireless to THE NEW YORK TIMES.

ABOARD THE U. S. S. BROOKLYN, OFF PORTSMOUTH, N. H., May 24.—On a sun-dappled blue sea framed in the distance by a long sweep of white beach today a flotilla of vessels ranging from mighty navy craft down to Amesbury fishing dories crowded all day long around the rescue ship Falcon to relay to a waiting world the tragic news from the bottom of the sea.

Into waters usually frequented by only lobstermen's boats there came from ports as far away as New York a variety of craft bringing all the navy's rescue resources and all the devices known to science for speeding to the world each new report that came up from the men trapped below in the frigid depths of the ocean.

The chunky little gray submarine tender Falcon squatted into the sea, her four anchors hooked to the bottom and her after-boom hung out over the water. Every eye was glued to that boom, from which hung the cable that held the bell-shaped rescue chamber on which all hopes were pinned.

Trim Coast Guard cutters hovered about to nose away any non-official vessels that got too near the Falcon. These, cruising around the scene over a three or four mile radius, bore reporters, cameramen, broadcasters and news reel men, who have arrived in such numbers that boats cannot be found to accommodate them.

Largest of all the vessels on the scene was the navy's light cruiser Brooklyn, which arrived early this afternoon after a quick run from New York.

Standing apart from all the other craft, a sinister symbol of the tragedy, lay the Sculpin, a sister ship of the sunken Squalus. She lay with her nose pointed at the Falcon, her jet-black hull sunk so low in the sea that she seemed almost like some evil denizen from the deep.

Overhead there were few moments during the day when a dozen or more planes were not dipping and zooming about over the rescue scene. Most of these bore reporters and photographers, but there were a few navy planes cruising about.

Not for a moment was so much as a single square foot of the sea over the sunken craft left unscrutinized by the rescue crews. All last night huge searchlights from a dozen ships played over the the water just in case some of the men below might attempt to reach the surface by means of the Momsen lung.

When news of the first rescue was given by the Falcon's radio to the other boats waiting so anxiously

Continued on Page Twenty

RESCUE BELL JAMS

Eight on the Last Trip Dangle Three Hours Half Way to Top

DIVERS GET CABLE CLEAR

Naquin Last to Quit His Ship—Navy Orders an Attempt to Bring Up Bodies Next

By HANSON W. BALDWIN
Special to THE NEW YORK TIMES.

PORTSMOUTH N. H., Thursday, May 25.—Man had won a victory against the sea early this morning as new inventions, used for the first time in actual rescue work, brought thirty-three men to safety from the submarine Squalus, sunk in forty fathoms off the New Hampshire coast.

The smooth process of rescue was interrupted, however, for a few hours, when a cable used in hauling up and lowering the great steel rescue chamber jammed while the chamber, on its fourth trip, bringing up the eight remaining survivors in it was about 150 feet below the surface. A diver from the Falcon was sent down immediately to clear the jam.

The release of the chamber was not finally completed until well after midnight. A message from Admiral Cole was received at the navy yard here which said that the chamber had finally been cleared. Lieutenant Naquin, his executive officer, and six of the crew of the Squalus, believed to be the last survivors, had been dangling in the steel shell for more than three hours, adding the final discomfort and suspense to their long hours of suffering within the hull of the imprisoned submarine.

Admiral Cole's message, however, which reached here at 12:45, stated that the eight survivors had at length reached the surface and all were in good condition.

In the same message which reported the final rescue of Lieutenant Naquin and his comrades, Admiral Cole said "this completes the rescue of all known survivors. Investigation of flooded compartments will proceed as expeditiously as possible. Suspending operations for the night due to damage to rescue chamber which must be repaired before further use."

Bell Lowered Over Hatch

Divers, breathing a mixture of helium and oxygen, descended, apparently without difficulty, to the great depths where one of the nation's newest submarines lay in a bed of mud. The ten-ton steel rescue chamber, shaped like a modified diving bell, was lowered over the forward torpedo room escape hatch of the Squalus, and made four trips to bring up the shivering, exhausted survivors of the nation's worst submarine accident since 1927 from the blackness of forty fathoms.

But behind them—in the after compartments of the submarine, most of them flooded when the Squalus dived with an open air induction valve at 8:40 A. M. yesterday—the exhausted living left, it was feared, the bodies of twenty-six of their shipmates, trapped by the swirling waters. A list of the thirty-three known to be alive—was sent to the Navy Yard here from the rescue ship Falcon but it was followed by an ominous note, which read:

"Names omitted from this list probably in flooded compartments, and there is little hope of finding them alive."

The message seemed to doom one officer, Ensign Joseph H. Patterson, a Naval Academy athlete in the class of '36 and a member of the 1936 Olympic Team; Charles M. Woods, a Navy Yard electrician, and Don Smith of the General Motors Corporation, in addition to twenty-three enlisted men.

Will Search Flooded Chambers

They were listed as missing, but the navy prepared immediately to search the silent after compartments of the foundered Squalus. There was still a faint hope that some men might have been able to close the watertight door sealing off the after torpedo room against the pressure of the inpouring sea, and thus might still be alive. It was only a faint flicker of hope, admittedly, but the navy planned to follow it until it no longer glimmered.

The twenty-eight to thirty-six hours of horror which the survivors endured within the steel pressure

Continued on Page Sixteen

Easing of Taxes on Business in Prospect After Congress Leaders Visit Roosevelt

By TURNER CATLEDGE
Special to THE NEW YORK TIMES.

WASHINGTON, May 24.—Prospects for moderate corporate tax revision at this session of Congress, involving deletion of the remaining stump of the undistributed profits levy and collateral changes to protect the revenue, were heightened still further today with the quick development of a better feeling on the subject between President Roosevelt and revenue leaders at the Capitol.

The easing of nerves over the tax question was the first product of a cooperative drive for adjournment of Congress by mid-July. It was signalized by a luncheon given by the President to Senator Harrison, chairman of the Senate Finance Committee, and Senator Byrnes of South Carolina.

The attitude exhibited both at the White House and at the Capitol was in marked contrast to what it was a week ago Monday, when Senator Harrison, critic of the undistributed corporate profits tax, told the President bluntly that he could expect business-encouraging changes in the revenue laws at this session, with or without White House aid.

The White House luncheon was preceded by a conference between the President and Representative Cooper of Tennessee, chairman of the House Ways and Means subcommittee on taxation. It was followed in the afternoon by an exchange between Mr. Cooper and Representative Doughton, chairman of the Ways and Means Committee, and Secretary Morgenthau and Under-Secretary Hanes at the Treasury.

Arrangements were understood to have been made tentatively for Mr. Morgenthau's and Mr. Hanes's appearance next week before the Cooper subcommittee on the subject of corporation tax revision.

Mr. Doughton said at the end of the day that the subcommittees would meet before the end of this week and would arrange to hear Mr. Morgenthau next week. He added that the full committee was "all set" to speed new tax legislation.

He understood, furthermore, that the Senate Democratic leaders proposed to call a party caucus in an attempt to bind their followers to the revisions, if those adopted by the House were in competition with their own proposals.

The changes talked of most were along the lines of those submitted to the President last week by Senator Harrison.

They entailed a lapse of the un-

Continued on Page Fourteen

The royal couple were taken on a boat trip to Mount Vernon to visit George Washington's home.

The King and Queen of Britain and the Roosevelts in a procession down Pennsylvania Avenue on the way from Union Station to the White House.

Mr. and Mrs. Roosevelt with the British rulers before leaving Union Station. At the President's left is Brigadier General Edwin M. Watson.

Times Wide World Photo

"All the News That's Fit to Print."

The New York Times.

LATE CITY EDITION
Partly cloudy, temperature unchanged today. Tomorrow fair, showers in afternoon or at night.
Temperatures Yesterday—Max., 87; Min., 59

Copyright, 1939, by The New York Times Company.

VOL. LXXXVIII...No. 29,721. Entered as Second-Class Matter, Postoffice, New York, N. Y. NEW YORK, FRIDAY, JUNE 9, 1939. P THREE CENTS NEW YORK CITY and Vicinity | FOUR CENTS Elsewhere Except in 7th and 8th Postal Zones.

KING AND QUEEN GUESTS AT THE WHITE HOUSE AFTER AN IMPRESSIVE WELCOME IN WASHINGTON; GEORGE HOPES WE WILL EVER WALK IN FRIENDSHIP

GERMAN POLICEMAN SLAIN NEAR PRAGUE; NAZIS PUNISH AREA

Seven Decrees Issued Placing Kladno District Under What Amounts to Martial Law

MASS ARRESTS REPORTED

Schools and Theatres Closed —Incident Further Evidence of Anti-Reich Feeling

Anti-German feeling in the Reich's Bohemian-Moravian protectorate flared up Wednesday night in the killing of a German policeman in a town near Prague, which evoked from the Reich protector yesterday measures amounting to martial law for the district, with the threat that unless the slayer were found by tonight sterner measures would follow. [Page 1.]

To the German conquest of Czecho-Slovakia Foreign Secretary Halifax of Britain traced the Anglo-French alliance moves in a speech in the House of Lords. In the speech Viscount Halifax in effect told Chancellor Hitler that aggression could not succeed and that the way was still open for negotiation. [Page 12.]

Meanwhile, conferences that the British Ambassador had in Paris indicated that the proposals a British expert is to take to Moscow would be in reality joint Anglo-French proposals. There were signs that the French public was wearying of the protracted coalition negotiations. [Page 12.]

Curbs in Czech Town

Wireless to THE NEW YORK TIMES.

PRAGUE, June 8.—The first serious incident to occur in the protectorate of Bohemia-Moravia was officially announced by Baron Constantin von Neurath, Reich protector, tonight. It involves the fatal shooting in the town of Kladno, near Prague, of Wilhelm Kniest, a German police officer.

The shooting occurred last night in front of the Kladno public school. The assailant escaped.

Following the incident the protector issued a series of seven edicts that placed the entire police district under what virtually amounts to martial law. By his order, effective immediately and until further notice:

All open gatherings in the Kladno district are prohibited.

All cinemas, theatres, public places will be closed.

All schools will be closed because of the agitation of a large part of the teaching staff.

Doors and windows of all houses must be kept closed from 8 P. M. until 5 A. M.—all open windows immediately will be fired on.

The Mayor and municipal authorities of the Kladno district have been removed.

A governmental commissar will be appointed for the district.

The Czech State police in the district will be taken into temporary arrest and disarmed.

It was further stated that if the assailant was not arrested by 8 P. M. tomorrow "further measures will be taken."

The disarmament of the Kladno State police was effected this evening.

Officer on Sentry Duty

From the German side it was said that Kniest, who had been on night sentry duty outside the school building, was found shot by the guard who was to have relieved him.

This morning Karl Hermann Frank, secretary to Baron von Neurath and former right-hand man of Konrad Henlein, accompanied by General Kamptz, police commander, visited Kladno, about twenty miles from Prague. Soon after their arrival the edicts were issued.

Kladno has been known for many years as "Red Kladno," the description given to it early in the century. It was here that the late Thomas G. Masaryk made his first political speech more than forty years ago, and the fact that he took the side of the workers in one of the most important industrial disputes in the history of the Austro-Hungarian Empire set a tradition that has endured.

Anti-German feeling has been running high in the Kladno district. The workers in the steel factories are reported to have said that when the Germans who had been sent from the Reich to work with them into the furnaces.

Four days after the occupation of Prague, shots were fired at German troops from a window in Hostivice, a Kladno suburb, without causing any injury. As a result the Mayor of the village was held hostage and

Continued on Page Ten

Fair Weather Due Here For Royalty Tomorrow

Fair weather for the visit of the King and Queen here tomorrow, but with the possibility of thunder showers in the afternoon or night, was forecast last night by the Weather Bureau. The royal couple will be at the World's Fair grounds during the afternoon and at the home of President Roosevelt at Hyde Park at night.

Slightly cooler weather brought relief from the heat last night as the temperature dropped to the 70's after remaining in the 80's throughout the afternoon and early evening. The high for the day was 87 at 3:15 P. M. and the average of 73 was six degrees above normal for the date. The record high was 92 in 1933 and the record low was 47 in 1932.

Partly cloudy and continued warm weather was forecast for today.

NEW BRIDGE PLAN IS VOTED BY BOARD

Tentative Contract Accepted as Moses Submits Revised Project for Battery

Action by the Board of Estimate yesterday paved the way for an early start on the proposed toll bridge linking Battery Park with Hamilton Avenue, Brooklyn, which the Triborough Bridge Authority plans to have ready for use by July 1, 1941.

With Borough President Stanley M. Isaacs of Manhattan casting the only negative votes, the board, after a public hearing at which Mayor La Guardia presided, approved a tentative contract between the city and the Authority, covering the construction of the bridge, the connections with the West Side express highway in Manhattan and the express highway in Brooklyn and the improvement of Battery Park.

Prospects of an early start on the bridge were enhanced further when word came from Washington that the Treasury Department would have no objection to the bridge if the city would deed to it about 100 feet of Battery Park land just west of the present Barge Office as a site for a new $1,000,000 structure.

Army Approval Indicated

In announcing the Treasury Department's attitude Secretary Henry Morgenthau indicated that the War Department would favor the revised bridge plans as submitted by Park Commissioner Robert Moses, who also is chairman of the Triborough Bridge Authority.

Mr. Morgenthau's position was made known after a conference in Washington attended by engineers of the Authority, the Treasury Department and the War Department. Harry M. Durning, Collector of the Port of New York, also was present. The Authority delegation, it was reported, gave assurance that it would get the city to deed the land needed for the new Barge Office.

The Treasury Department, in recent communications to Mr. Moses, pointed out that the location of one of the bridge piers would interfere with the use of the present Barge Office piers and slips and cut off the view of the harbor.

Mr. Moses disclosed, during the public hearing on the contract between the city and the Authority, that plans for financing the bridge project were virtually completed, with funds to come from Federal sources, private banking interests or a combination of the two. The Authority, he said, was ready to start the job as soon as the Board of Estimate approved the contract.

Mayor Presides at Session

Mayor La Guardia, presiding for the first time in many months at a business meeting of the Board of Estimate, directed Mr. Moses to explain the proposed contract, as a prelude to the hearing of opposition.

Mr. Moses explained that the contract called on the Authority to construct the bridge, the express highways, various ramps and connections and improve Battery Park at no cost to the city. The city was to condemn the necessary land, grant the necessary leases and easements and otherwise cooperate. When the bonds were paid off, Mr. Moses said, the entire project would become the city's property free and clear.

Mr. Moses emphasized that the contract would not bind the city until the Authority submitted to the Mayor a certificate declaring that the War Department's approval had been obtained and the financing of the project was assured.

Efforts of Mr. Isaacs to defer a vote on the contract for a week proved unavailing. At his insistence Mr. Moses agreed to modifications in the proposed agreement, more specifically defining the route of the connection between the bridge and the West Side express highway and making the plan for improving Battery Park subject to approval of the Board of Estimate. Neither change, Mr. Moses said, was necessary, but he accepted them.

The board voted down Mr. Isaacs's

Continued on Page Twelve

WPA UNION TEACHER OUSTED FOR THREAT; AGITATORS WARNED

Somervell Will Not Tolerate 'Coercion,' He Declares After 'Demand' on Ratings

HITS WORKERS ALLIANCE

Closes Door to Its Grievance Chairman for 'Vulgar' Talk to Woman Secretary

Denouncing Local 453 of the Teachers Union, representing WPA employes, and the Workers Alliance, Lieut. Col. Brehon Somervell, Works Progress Administrator here, declared yesterday that he would not tolerate attempts by any organization to coerce or intimidate WPA officials and supervisors in the execution of their duties.

Colonel Somervell charged both the Teachers Union, which recently was suspended from the Central Trades and Labor Council, and the Workers Alliance with "trying to intimidate our people," and announced the dismissal of Allen J. Loeb, a teacher employed in the field activities program of the WPA and chairman for this program of Local 453, for demanding that supervisors give all teachers in this branch of activity an "excellent" rating in order that they might keep their jobs in the event a cut in personnel was ordered.

Offensive Language Charged

At the same time Colonel Somervell made public a letter addressed to Willis Morgan, president of the Workers Alliance of New York, informing him that henceforth the WPA would disregard any communications from Moe Howard, chairman of the alliance's grievance committee. Colonel Somervell explained that he took this action because Howard had used profane and abusive language in a telephone conversation with a woman secretary of John A. Brann, chief of the guard section of the professional and service division of the WPA.

As explained by Colonel Somervell, Howard called Mr. Brann's secretary on the telephone yesterday and warned that his guards would be beaten up if they did not desist from certain actions which the alliance considered objectionable. According to Colonel Somervell, Mr. Brann's guards have been trying to stop minor thefts on the sewing project and enforcing the order forbidding unionization activity during working hours.

Howard denied yesterday that he had used abusive language or had made the threats in question.

Speaking for Local 453, William Levner, the president, said the union assumed responsibility for a letter addressed by Loeb to all supervisors of the field activity program and took the position that the demand embodied in the letter that all teachers receive the rating "excellent" was justified.

Colonel Somervell, however, warned that any employes guilty of acts or attempts of intimidation or coercion such as he ascribed to Loeb would be dismissed.

"This is the first instance of this kind that has been brought to my attention, although I had heard reports of similar conduct before," Colonel Somervell said.

Threat in Letter Reported

As interpreted by Colonel Somervell, Loeb's letter to supervisors of the field activity program warned them that "life would be made miserable for them" if they did not do as they were told by the Teachers Union.

Loeb's letter was written in connection with the semi-annual check of the qualifications of all WPA employes, which is now in progress. While denying that any cuts in the personnel of the 15,000 WPA teachers were immediately contemplated, Colonel Somervell explained

Continued on Page Fourteen

Tickets to See Royalty Good for Two Persons

Although the city's tickets for admission to the West Side Express Highway to see the King and Queen tomorrow do not say so on their face, each is good for the admission of two persons, Stanley H. Howe executive secretary to the Mayor, said yesterday. He added that Police Commissioner Valentine would issue an order directing the police accordingly.

The first supply of 60,000 tickets was exhausted at 1 P. M. yesterday and Mr. Howe ordered 10,000 more tickets printed. Five thousand of these will be good for vantage points at the Battery and along West Street and 5,000 more for admission to the Fifty-seventh Street ramp to the Express Highway. Distribution of these will begin at 11 o'clock this morning.

War veterans in uniform, who will form a guard of honor for their Majesties, will not require tickets.

CITY TO GREET KING ON GIGANTIC SCALE

Police, Tightening Precautions, Say Crowd May Be Greatest Ever Seen Here

By FRANK S. ADAMS

Gayly bedecked with thousands of British and American flags, and bright with bunting in the colors of the two nations, New York City is expecting one of the greatest crowds in its history—perhaps the largest it has ever known—to cheer King George VI and Queen Elizabeth as they ride through fifty-one miles of its streets tomorrow.

With the hotels anticipating a heavy influx of out-of-town visitors, the supply of tickets for vantage points along the West Side Express Highway quickly exhausted, the Board of Education making elaborate arrangements for the 1,000,000 or more school children who will line the drives of Central Park, and the World's Fair expecting a record crowd to see the royal visitors there, the most important element of doubt concerned the weather.

If it remains fair and warm as was the outlook last night, the turnout may rival or even exceed those which greeted Colonel Lindbergh on his return from his flight to Paris, and the Twenty-seventh Division when it came home in 1919, although the procession marking these two events had the benefit of passing up Broadway and Fifth Avenue with their thousands of lofty buildings, the windows of which were filled on those occasions.

High police officials, busy with last-minute precautions against anything going amiss, and with checking up on an anonymous tip of a bomb plot which proved to be groundless, refused to make any definite estimate of how many millions might be expected to see the first reigning monarch of Great Britain to visit this city, but Chief Inspector Louis F. Costuma said that it would undoubtedly be "tremendous."

Police Commissioner Valentine, who has taken personal charge of the arrangements for safeguarding the city's distinguished guests, will hold a final conference this afternoon at headquarters with Chief Constable Albert Canning of Scotland Yard, Colonel Edward Starling of the United States Secret Service

Continued on Page Eight

Landon Breaks 2 Ribs in Fall on Yacht; 'Strapped Up,' He Continues Fishing Trip

By The Associated Press.

ROCKLAND, Me., June 8.—Alfred M. Landon, Republican Presidential nominee in 1936, slipped and broke two ribs in disembarking here late today from the ketch Blue Moon, on which he has been cruising along the Maine coast.

Although hospitalized briefly for X-ray examinations, which Dr. F. F. Brown said showed fractures of the sixth and seventh ribs, Mr. Landon returned to the ketch and continued the cruise.

Lying in his bunk aboard the craft, which is owned by Arthur B. Smith of Southwest Harbor, Mr. Landon said he had slipped in getting from the ketch into a small boat, and had fallen on the coaming, striking his left side.

The former Governor of Kansas said he hoped to be "all right" in time to give the commencement address at Boston University next Monday.

Mr. Landon passed off the mishap, which he attributed to wetness of the Blue Moon's deck, as "nothing very serious," but said Dr. Brown had advised him to "keep strapped up for a few days."

From here the ketch will proceed to Pulpit Harbor, North Haven and Bucks Harbor, on the opposite side of Penobscot Bay.

The cruise, in which Mr. Smith planned to initiate the Republican leader into the pleasures of deep-sea fishing, began on Tuesday at Southwest Harbor.

Besides Mr. Smith, a retired railroad executive whose Winter home is at Greenwich, Conn., Ralph W. Robey of New York and S. C. Badger of Boston were in the party.

CROWDS LINE ROUTE

Throngs Wait Hours and Then Roar Greetings as Sovereigns Pass

KING SALUTES AT CAPITOL

He and President Chat as Queen and Mrs. Roosevelt Ride in Procession

By FRANK L. KLUCKHOHN

Special to THE NEW YORK TIMES.

WASHINGTON, June 8.—A crowd as enthusiastic and large as ever greeted an American President on inauguration day turned out today to watch and take part in the pomp, ceremony and vivid color with which the national capital greeted King George VI and Queen Elizabeth.

A solid mass of people crowded the streets, filled the roofs and windows of buildings, overflowed into grandstands and hung on statues and every possible vantagepoint on the royal route from the Union Station to the White House as flags, booming salutes, soaring fleets of fighting planes, smartly uniformed troops, rumbling tanks and dashing cavalry took part in one of the most impressive demonstrations ever seen in Washington.

This was a human as well as official greeting, and all down the route of march a waving mass of American and British flags, held in thousands of hands, signaled a welcome to the first British monarchs ever to visit this country.

As the King, riding at the front of the procession with President Roosevelt, smiled and saluted and the Queen, much less formal, waved from her seat beside Mrs. Roosevelt in the second car, the crowd, originally more curious than enthusiastic, shouted and clapped its applause.

Crowd Gathered at 4 A. M.

The flags and applause spread like a rolling wave along Delaware Avenue to the Capitol and on down Constitution and Pennsylvania Avenues as the party proceeded.

The crowd, some of its members from out of town, had started to gather at 4 A. M. At 9 the whole line of march was crowded, and by 11 o'clock many people could not get within a block of the parade. The earlier excitement gave way to a hushed expectancy.

Then the twenty-one-gun artillery salute roared from the battery near the station and excitement mounted.

Next bugles sounded attention. The marines, in their dress uniforms of white-visored caps, dark blue coats and light blue trousers with red facings, lining the streets from the station to Pennsylvania Avenue, and the sailors, in their white tropical uniforms with dark blue collars and knotted scarfs before the Capitol, snapped to "present arms" under orders from their officers.

Up Delaware Avenue the royal entourage moved swiftly. First came a white police car, then some thirty motor cycle police, and behind them and directly in front of the royal couple and their hosts a detachment of cavalry moving at a swift, rhythmic trot.

King Salutes at Capitol

The open car bearing the King, dressed in an admiral's full-dress uniform with heavy gold braid, and the President, in his top hat and morning clothes, came directly behind.

Another open car, in which sat Queen Elizabeth, who held a white parasol over her head, and Mrs. Roosevelt, dressed in smart blue ensemble, followed. Both the King and Queen sat at the right of the hosts. Their cars were followed by two automobiles bearing Secret Service men.

The party slowed its pace to walking speed as it passed in front of the Capitol, and the King smiled and saluted, while Mr. Roosevelt frequently raised his hat and smiled also.

Queen Elizabeth seemed to look directly into the faces of massed people as she waved gracefully with her right hand to the onlookers.

After passing before the Capitol, where two American flags flew, the cars doubled back and continued at a speed of four to six miles an hour down the hill on Constitution Avenue. At the juncture of Constitution and Pennsylvania Avenues some thirty speedy midget tanks swung into three columns in front of the royal party and other tanks moved up alongside the party.

By this time other cars bearing

Continued on Page Two

Times Wide World

THE KING AND THE PRESIDENT
George VI and Mr. Roosevelt en route to the White House

QUEEN CAPTIVATES CAPITAL THRONGS

Dense Crowds Cheer Her at Various Stages of a Busy Day, Despite Hot Sun

By KATHLEEN McLAUGHLIN

Special to THE NEW YORK TIMES.

WASHINGTON, June 8. — The King's tour is the Queen's triumph, all the endorses unreservedly. For George VI watched his wife today recapture in a social sense the capital of those colonies yielded long ago by an earlier George on the military fields. The contemporary monarch has gratitude rather than pique for the skill and success with which England's Queen subtly attracts the spotlight which her diffident young husband will not shun but does not relish.

The conquering Queen in Canada was still invincible in the United States, their first few daylight hours on foreign soil revealed. As one of the correspondents commented when the motorcade swept up Pennsylvania Avenue amid thunderous cheers:

"That's the Queen. Give her a crowd and she mows 'em down."

The Queen was unruffled through one of the most taxing schedules yet faced by the royal party in any one day. Through throngs that rated among the largest she has encountered, in temperature almost unendurable even to natives of this city, with four complete changes of wardrobe, thousands of handshakes and curtsies, she was smiling at the close.

Part of her magnetic appeal for the Washington crowds, as elsewhere, is the fascination which they apparently have for her.

High Expectation Is Remarked

There was the almost juvenile gesture, for instance, of high expectation with which she craned her neck at the Union Station this morning, trying to see the crowds outside.

Again like an eager child, she stood for a moment in the tonneau of the automobile that she shared with Mrs. Roosevelt, seeking a glimpse of the throngs, and incidentally giving them a sight of her.

She was a picture worth remembering. Her hair was blacker, her eyes were bluer, and her figure was slimmer than most of the spectators had anticipated, judging by comments of the bystanders. Her complexion is signalized by a gardenia-white skin with a flush of healthy color.

Tiniest of the four central figures in the historic encounter, she gained height with the high-crowned small hat, which carried a feather plume.

The smart headgear harmonized with an ensemble which delighted the crowd but which must have been a disappointment to American wool growers, who had hoped to see her appear in a sheer wool fabric presented for the visit. Mrs. Roosevelt wore the tailored azure blue dress made for her from

Continued on Page Six

SIMPLICITY MARKS THE GARDEN PARTY

'Sociable English Afternoon' Is Comment of Many of 1,400 Embassy Guests

From a Staff Correspondent

WASHINGTON, June 8.—What the now historic garden party at the British Embassy this afternoon turned out to be depends entirely upon whether you were inside having tea with the King and Queen, or outside.

To the 1,400 elect who received invitations, it was just a "simple, sociable afternoon such as any nice family might have enjoyed in England," on the assurance of emerging guests. But this was not England.

From beyond the gates where the uninvited gathered in hordes to survey what could be seen in the spacious garden beyond, it did not seem too modest a fete. Not, at least, after the King and Queen arrived.

No more immune than other male guests from the sartorial idiocies of formal attire under an equatorial sun, the King sweltered and steamed in cutaway coat and striped trousers, just as all except a few of his American and English colleagues did. He carried a gray top hat and at times forbore even to wipe the drops from his brow and chin.

Queen a Watteau Figure

The Queen, in the thinnest and whitest of fabrics, might have stepped from a Watteau painting, in her traditional formal gown and picture hat. She wore a long and generously full skirted gown of the crinoline type, of white organza tucked from shoulder to hem and inset with panels of white lace.

Tiers of lace flounces and ruffles dropped almost from the waistline to the wide ruffle of lace at the hem. The short sleeves were a continuation of the lace and organza that formed the bodice, with its round neck and slight V at the front.

Her gloves were long and white, her hat a huge picture affair of white lace with a flare at one side. Her pumps matched. An extra touch of glamour and femininity was a ruffled organza and lace-trimmed parasol.

"I haven't seen one of those in Washington," murmured one matron, "since the Taft Administration."

A still older guest commented: "* * * Like a Florodora girl's. Pretty they were, too."

As the King and Queen arrived at the Embassy, a bit tardy because of a slight traffic jam on Massachusetts Avenue, they were greeted at the portico of the red brick building by Sir Ronald Lindsay, the Ambassador, and Lady Lindsay. The uniformed band from the Exeter of the British West Indies fleet struck up "God Save the

Continued on Page Four

KING TOASTS PEACE

At State Dinner, Sovereign Voices Hope for a Warless World

ROOSEVELT TELLS AMITY

President Cites Our Relations as an Example to All— Meeting Is Hearty

By RAYMOND DANIELL

Special to THE NEW YORK TIMES.

WASHINGTON, June 8.—The Union Jack of Great Britain and the Stars and Stripes of the United States flew side by side today in Washington. A President and a reigning King of England shook hands and rode together through great, cheering crowds down Pennsylvania Avenue to the White House, where tonight at a State dinner they toasted one another and the King expressed the hope that "our two great nations may ever in the future walk together along the path of friendship in a world of peace."

It was an historic occasion, the visit of King George VI and Queen Elizabeth to the capital of the United States, and it was surrounded by the sort of pageantry suitable to such times. There was the firing of a twenty-one-gun, ear-shattering royal salute at the Union Station by four 3-inch field guns drawn up in the plaza. The Marine Band played "God Save the King" and "The Star-Spangled Banner."

Planes Roar Welcome

Then there was the royal progress from the railroad station to the Capitol, down the hill on Constitution Avenue and along Pennsylvania Avenue to the White House in a procession which gave just a hint of the military might of the nation playing host. Ten of the new "flying fortresses" flew back and forth over the route of the procession, followed by forty pursuit ships in formation. Theirs was a flight of good-will and friendship, but the roar of their engines was an awesome sound.

Leading the procession, behind a phalanx of motor-cycle police, were sixty baby tanks, their gun business with businesslike looking soldiers standing with folded arms in the turrets. Behind these rumbling, rolling forts, surrounded, flanked and followed by police on motor cycles and secret service men in cars, came the two cars with the King and President Roosevelt and Queen Elizabeth and Mrs. Roosevelt. Behind them rode several troops of cavalry, riding in platoon front formation. More than 5,000 soldiers, sailors and marines lined the mile and a quarter route of the procession from the Capitol to the White House.

Sovereigns in White House

Tonight England's King and Queen slept in the White House, which is painted white to hide the scars which remained after it was rebuilt following the burning of the capital by British troops in the War of 1812. For the first time since the war between the States, soldiers with rifles and fixed bayonets went through the military rite of mounting guard and doing sentry duty on the White House lawns. The sentries were soldiers of companies B and C of the Thirty-Fourth Infantry. Only those with special passes to the White House got past them.

The weather was kind to Lady Lindsay, whose garden party was acclaimed a great success. A little after 1 P. M. a sudden downpour boded ill for the social function which caused no much mental anxiety among the socially ambitious. It soon cleared off, however, and not until the last guest had departed from the embassy grounds did a sudden thunderclap and a dash of lightning herald the next shower. Separating at the party, the Queen with Lady Lindsay shook hands with hundreds while the King with Sir Ronald shook hands with hundreds of others.

King Has Tea with Morgan

The guests represented Lady Lindsay's idea, it was said, of a cross-section of American political, social and business life, and of course, the diplomatic corps. At the party, the King and Queen met J. P. Morgan, with whom the King sipped tea on the embassy porch, John D. Rockefeller, Mrs. Cornelius Vanderbilt, John W. Davis, and a score of others. Dolly Gann,

Continued on Page Three

"All the News That's Fit to Print."

The New York Times.

LATE CITY EDITION
Fair and cooler today. Tomorrow fair with moderate temperatures.
Temperatures Yesterday—Max., 85; Min., 68

VOL. LXXXVIII...No. 29,757. Entered as Second-Class Matter. Postoffice, New York, N. Y. NEW YORK, SATURDAY, JULY 15, 1939. P THREE CENTS NEW YORK CITY and Vicinity | FOUR CENTS Elsewhere Except in 7th and 8th Postal Zones.

CAN'T STRIKE AGAINST U. S., ROOSEVELT WARNS WPA MEN; A. F. L. TO CONTINUE WALKOUT

UNION IS DEFIANT

Building Group Head Here Holds Workers Cannot Be Coerced

COMPROMISE IS WEIGHED

President, Union and Mayors Consider a Proposal for Wage Adjustments

Strikes on WPA or any other type of Federal work were forbidden yesterday by President Roosevelt, but striking WPA employes in New York City and other centers announced their intention of staying away from their jobs until Congress restored union wage scales on Federal relief projects.

"You cannot strike against the government," the President declared at a White House press conference. He emphasized his words by authorizing reporters to quote them directly.

A few hours later Thomas A. Murray, president of the Building and Construction Trades Council, representing 125 American Federation of Labor unions in this city, issued a statement in which he said:

"You cannot force any American workingman to work at his job if, for any reason, he decides that he is unwilling to do so. If the day should ever come when a man who abstains from his job because he is dissatisfied with the terms of employment can be coerced into resuming his job against his will, then our cherished democracy will be dead."

Settlement Plan Weighed

A plan for settling the WPA wage dispute and resuming normal project operations was taken under consideration by the President after conferences with a committee of A. F. of L. executives and later with Mayor La Guardia and other members of the United States Conference of Mayors.

The compromise proposal would permit re-establishment of old hourly wage scales on projects begun before the new law went into effect on July 1. The requirement that all WPA employes work 130 hours a month for their security pay would be retained on projects begun after July 1, according to the plan.

It was reported that Mr. Roosevelt would ask Attorney General Frank Murphy to rule on the legality of the proposal. When the idea was laid before Colonel F. C. Harrington, National Work Projects Commissioner, by Mayor La Guardia and his associates before they saw the President, he said he did not believe it could be carried out.

New outbreaks of violence in Minneapolis led to the death by gunfire of one man in a clash between WPA pickets and the police. Earlier in the day the police used tear gas and riot guns in dispersing a crowd of 4,000 strikers and sympathizers. Six persons, including three policemen, were taken to hospitals after the melee.

Following the riots the WPA ordered all projects in the city shut down effective Monday.

Federal Aid Asked

Charges that men who wanted to work in Rochester were being kept from the job by members of the Workers Alliance led Lester W. Herzog, up-State WPA administrator, to telegraph his superiors in Washington for aid. All WPA construction jobs in Rochester were ordered shut down because of the activities of roving bands of pickets.

Mr. Herzog's request for help in curbing "agitators whose activities have included soliciting funds" from WPA workers was answered with a promise of action by the Federal Bureau of Investigation. The up-State WPA chief complained that some persons were apparently attempting to "make a racket" out of the unrest created by the 130-hour law.

The determination of the WPA to enforce all provisions of the new law was reflected in the continued dismissal of strikers for staying away from work for five days and in an announcement by Colonel Harrington that 300,000 WPA employes would be dropped by Aug. 1 and 350,000 others by Sept. 1, in accordance with the law's stipulation that persons on the rolls for eighteen months be dropped not later than the end of next month.

More than 47,000 persons in this city are slated for discharge under the eighteen-month clause. The overall quota for WPA employment here

Continued on Page Sixteen

Situation in WPA Strike

In the face of a blunt warning by President Roosevelt that "you can't strike against the government," A. F. of L. leaders yesterday laid plans to continue the walkout until Fall; the movement spread to new localities and outbreaks of violence were reported. The President had before him a compromise plan whereby the prevailing wage principle would be restored on projects started before the new law was passed. [Page 1.]

The worst outbreak of violence occurred in Minneapolis, where one man was killed and several injured last night when a group of armed police escorting sewing-project workers from a factory were met by a barrage of missiles. Earlier in the day police hurled tear-gas bombs into the ranks of 4,000 belligerent pickets. In this melee six persons were injured severely enough to be taken to hospitals. A woman was stabbed and another trampled by fellow-demonstrators. Following the two riots all WPA projects in Minneapolis were ordered shut down. [Page 1.]

In Pennsylvania, where WPA workers were called out for the first time, A. F. L. leaders seemed at odds. In Philadelphia they waited hopefully, but vainly, for a request from President William Green to rescind the strike call, while Pittsburgh leaders denounced the Roosevelt warning and prepared for a walkout to last until the law was changed. [Page 1.]

Mounting dismissals throughout the nation indicated the determination of WPA officials to enforce the law. In New York City 646 strikers were dismissed yesterday, bringing the total of those discharged here to 8,543. [Page 1.]

FATAL RIOT CLOSES MINNEAPOLIS WPA

State Administrator Orders Shut-Down After Fights in Which Man Is Killed

By The Associated Press.

MINNEAPOLIS, July 14.—Day-long strife centering around a local WPA sewing project, brought death to one man, injuries to nearly a score of men, women and children and resulted in announcement tonight by State WPA Administrator Linus Glotzbach that all WPA work in Minneapolis would be closed indefinitely.

The most serious outbreak occurred shortly after 7 P. M. when 100 women, comprising the late day shift, were escorted from duty amid gunfire, tear gas bomb explosions and brick and rock throwing.

Emil August Bergstrom of Minneapolis was shot in the head and died a few minutes later. Several policemen were hurt by stones. Three persons, including a 14-year-old boy, a woman and a man, were slightly wounded by gunfire. Three policemen and several others suffered from tear gas.

Bergstrom was struck by a bullet as he stood on a gasoline filling station lot almost directly across the street from the sewing project building.

The first violence, when the first day shift went on duty, brought slight injuries to a policeman and a picket. Shortly after noon, when 120 women were escorted from the place, four other minor casualties occurred.

Administrator Glotzbach's suspension of local WPA projects came after Mayor George E. Leach said the city would not assume further responsibility for operation of WPA projects.

F. B. I. Men Study Reports

Federal Bureau of Investigation men, ordered here by Attorney General Frank Murphy, have been studying reports of intimidation of non-strikin WPA workers but took no part in armed protection of the sewing project employes.

A policeman, John P. Gearty, was slugged at the first outbreak Monday, dying of a heart attack two hours later.

The firing tonight began, according to Sergeant John Albrecht, after persons from a filling station lot across the street and from the roofs of near-by buildings pelted the women with missiles.

Earlier in the day six persons received hospital treatment following two clashes.

The sewing project is in a brick building at Second Avenue North and Second Street, on the edge of the business district.

The night rioting broke out as approximately 100 women began walking from the building. They were greeted by yells of "scab," and "traitor." Almost instantly firing began as gas bombs exploded in the street, driving back the crowds which had been milling about the scene all day.

Several of the police detail directed fire from riot guns at the roofs of buildings across the street. As the shooting continued, officers with drawn pistols guided the women workers along the sidewalk, taking a course opposite to that used earlier in the afternoon when the police used gas bombs to disperse pickets who rushed an ar-

Continued on Page Sixteen

STAGE UNION LOSES ITS A.F.L. CHARTER

Sophie Tucker's Group Found Guilty of Misusing Funds—Cantor Heads New Guild

The American Federation of Actors, of which Sophie Tucker is president, lost its American Federation of Labor charter last night after being found guilty by its parent body, the Associated Actors and Artistes of America, of misusing relief funds and mismanaging its affairs. A new union, the American Guild of Variety Artists, with Eddie Cantor as temporary president, was immediately chartered by the parent body to organize actors in the federation's former jurisdiction of vaudeville houses, night clubs, circuses and carnivals.

Miss Tucker, whose union refused to enter any defense to the parent body's charges on the ground it did not have the power to hold a trial, described the parent body's action as "very funny" and said that the federation would seek relief in the courts on Monday. In the meantime, she said, the federation would continue its affairs as usual.

"Now I can understand why Eddie Cantor was very desirous of having me resign from the federation on the ground I was being misled," Miss Tucker said. "It is all very amusing. It is very funny."

Part of One Charge Dismissed

The parent body exonerated the federation of only a part of one charge. That accused Ralph Whitehead, the union's executive secretary, of devoting a substantial portion of his time to the organization of circus laborers who did not come under the parent body's jurisdiction. By a unanimous vote of the parent body's trial board the federation was found guilty of diverting funds collected for purposes of aiding needy actors to such uses as payment of the salaries of executives and purchase of a $1,700 automobile for Mr. Whitehead.

The American Guild of Variety Artists will launch an organizing drive next week, it was announced. A temporary board of directors, which will serve only until "the emergency and organizational period is over," was selected from the presidents and executive secretaries of other branch unions of the parent body.

The temporary board consists of Mr. Cantor, president of the American Federation of Radio Artists, and Mrs. Emily Holt, executive secretary; Ralph Morgan, president of the Screen Actors Guild, and Kenneth Thomson, executive secretary; Bert Lytell, first vice president of Actors Equity Association, and Paul Dullzell, executive secretary; Mr. Lytell, first vice president of Chorus Equity Association, and Ruth Richmond, executive secretary, and Jean Greenfield, president of the Hebrew Actors Union, and Reuben Guskin, executive secretary. Mr. Lytell is serving in the absence of Arthur Byron, president of Actors and Chorus Equity, who is ill.

Mr. Cantor was a former president of the American Federation of Actors, but supported the parent body in its investigation of the union, which received its A. F. of L. charter on March 22, 1934. The parent body communicated by telephone with Mr. Cantor, who is now in Hollywood. He joined with three other parent body officials in a

Continued on Page Sixteen

DR. SMITH INDICTED ON 23 COUNTS; LOSS IS PUT AT $1,000,000

Grand Jury Accuses Former Head of L. S. U. of Forgery and Falsifying Records

HUEY LONG FRIEND NAMED

State Medical Society Head Is Charged With Receiving Embezzled Goods

By RAYMOND DANIELL.
Special to THE NEW YORK TIMES.

BATON ROUGE, La., July 14.—The grand jury which has been investigating charges of graft at Louisiana State University since the resignation as president of Dr. James Monroe Smith and his flight to Canada, brought in twenty-eight true bills just before 6 o'clock this afternoon. Twenty-three of them were against Dr. Smith and two named one of the close friends of the late Senator Huey P. Long, Dr. Clarence Lorio, State Senator, president of the Louisiana Medical Society, head physician at Louisiana State University and political boss of this parish.

Dr. Smith already is in jail under $50,000 bond on an earlier indictment charging him with the embezzlement of $100,000, which he is accused of borrowing from a local bank with a bogus authorization from the board of supervisors.

The other indictments returned today were against E. N. Jackson, business manager for L. S. U., and George Caldwell, the 300-pound construction superintendent, who received a 2 per cent commission on building costs at the university and is under $10,000 bail on a Federal warrant charging him with diverting to the private use of State politicians, material and workmen of the Federal Work Progress Administration.

Bench Warrants Ordered

Judge Charles A. Holcombe, a pipe clenched between his teeth, ordered bench warrants issued for all the defendants except Dr. Smith.

Two indictments accused Caldwell, who lives in a house with gold-plated bathroom fixtures, of embezzlement. Another accused Caldwell and Dr. Lorio, who was one of the physicians in attendance on Huey Long when he lay dying of an assassin's bullet in September, 1935, of embezzlement. It was reported that university material worth $240 was involved. Dr. Lorio was indicted separately also for "receiving and having embezzled goods" in his possession, while Jackson was accused in separate indictments for embezzlement and receiving embezzled goods.

The indictments against Dr. Smith, whose resignation preceded that of former Governor Richard W. Leche by twenty-four hours, charged him with forgery and the falsification and altering of public records. The sum of money involved in the various forms of forgery attributed to the man who was snatched from obscurity by Huey Long and placed at the head of the State university because he had "a hide as tough as an elephant's," amounts to nearly $1,000,000. Governor Earl K. Long and his Attorney General, David M. Ellison, insist, however, that the State is not out a dime and that the banks

Continued on Page Three

BRITISH EMBASSY IN TOKYO MENACED BY JAPANESE MOB

Press Asks Britain to Alter Policy and Cooperate With Japan in East Asia

TSINGTAO OFFICE BOMBED

Delegation Heads for Parley on Tientsin to Meet Today Amid Hostile Propaganda

By HUGH BYAS
Wireless to THE NEW YORK TIMES.

TOKYO, Saturday, July 15.—The leading morning newspapers carry the following joint manifesto to Britain:

"We are firmly determined to overcome all obstacles to the success of our holy war. We earnestly hope that in the negotiations now opening Britain will rectify her conception of East Asia, look squarely at the new situation there and cooperate with Japan in the construction of a new order with open, unbiased mind, thereby contributing to the peace of the world."

The manifesto was signed by Hochi, Nichi Nichi, Asahi, Chugai-shagyo, Osaka Mainichi, Araka Asahi, Yomiuri, Kokumin, Miyako and Domei, the news agency.

Five thousand Tokyo citizens staged in front of the British Embassy yesterday the worst display of anti-foreign feeling ever witnessed in modern Japan. The broad roadway between the Imperial Palace and the moat of the British Embassy was choked with a milling, sweating crowd, shouting, singing and waving banners. The crowd was not violent and was content to make raucous noises.

The procession then marched to the military shrine, where the leaders ostentatiously worshiped the souls of the dead soldiers enshrined there. A characteristic climax, which betrayed a certain lack of spontaneity, came two hours later when the leaders returned to the British Embassy in municipal trucks. They were accompanied by a battery of camera men and their purpose was to be filmed at the embassy gate beneath forests of anti-British slogans they had brought.

Fight at Embassy Gate

Police resistance when they tried to place banners on the embassy gate led to scrimmages. Stones were thrown and attempts were made by heavily bearded men—this style is affected by members of the Black Dragon Society—to charge the gates. Finally the marchers left, leaving a wreath inscribed, "Britain Is Dead."

Not even during the agitation that followed the passing of the United States immigration law has Tokyo witnessed such a display of feeling against any foreign nation. Its organizers were a group of local politicians of the Tammany type, some of whom are notoriously pro-German.

En route to the British Embassy the procession stopped and cheered the German Embassy. Many of those present were prominent supporters of the Berlin-Rome Axis.

Although the Japanese press gives the number present at 30,000 to 60,000, the nucleus of the procession was a meeting in a hall that

Continued on Page Four

Fair Cuts Parking Fee to 25c at 7 Lots After Moses Reduces Rate at City's Field

By RUSSELL B. PORTER

Following its action earlier in the week in reducing the admission fee from 75 to 50 cents for groups of 500 or more, the World's Fair Corporation yesterday announced a cut from 50 to 25 cents for parking at the seven World's Fair parking fields and the one New York City field adjacent to the Fair Grounds.

The reduction was made by agreement between Grover A. Whalen, president of the Fair Corporation, and Park Commissioner Moses, in charge of the city parking field. The new parking rate will be effective today.

Like the decrease in the group admission rate, the slash of the parking fees in half is expected to increase the attendance at the Fair, which has been dropping badly this month, and is about 100,000 a day less than is needed to make the Fair a success. Yesterday saw the downward trend in attendance figures still in progress, with one of the smallest crowds since the Fair opened on April 30 on hand.

The announcement failed to satisfy a group of disgruntled concessionnaires in the Amusement Area who complained they are still losing money because of the low attendance, although they had expected the tide to turn after July 1. They want the Fair to cut its admission charge to 30 or 25 cents for everybody, at least after 10 o'clock at night, when the main exhibit area closes and only the amusement zone remains open.

After holding three meetings during the week to formulate their grievances and demands, the concessionaires appointed a committee that conferred with Mr. Whalen last night. The committee is understood to have brought a number of suggestions for improving attendance at the Fair and business in the amusement zone, besides the plan for lower admission charges.

Mr. Whalen was understood to be against changing the 75-cent rate any further, but to be more willing to consider plans to liven up the amusement area than he has been in the past.

The meeting between Mr. Whalen and the special committee of the Amusement Concessionaires Association ended on an optimistic note. Harry G. Travers, president of the association, was so impressed with the results that he referred to the Fair president as "the greatest showman in the country."

After a three-hour conference, Mr. Whalen announced that there would be additional transportation facilities in the area, that a conference committee would be appointed by the association to meet regularly

Continued on Page Seven

ROOSEVELT ASKS CONGRESS TO CHANGE NEUTRALITY ACT; OPPONENTS AWAIT REACTION

Senators Ask Hull for His Views On a War Embargo Against Japan

Committee Seeks Answer to Whether Such Action Would Violate Treaty of Amity or Run Counter to Nine-Power Pact

Special to THE NEW YORK TIMES.

WASHINGTON, July 14.—The Senate Foreign Relations Committee decided today to ask Secretary Hull for his opinion on whether an embargo on exports of materials of war to Japan would violate the treaty of amity and commerce, signed by the two nations in 1911. The committee deferred further consideration of pending proposals until Mr. Hull's reply was received.

Like most of the general treaties which the United States signed prior to the World War, the agreement with Japan incorporates the "most-favored-nation" clause. Thus some Senators believe that if an embargo was leveled directly at Japan, the Japanese Government might demand, under the treaty, that they be applied to all nations or lifted from Japan.

The members of the committee exchanged views at length. They likewise discussed whether the United States could unilaterally take the proposed action as retaliation against Japan for alleged violation of the nine-power pact, when that instrument provides for consultaton among all its signatories if any power believes it has been violated.

Senator Vandenberg is one of the principal opponents on the committee of any move of the kind. He contends that the legalistic arguments are well founded, and that the proposed embargoes would prove ineffective.

He and others of like mind started the movement to ask Secretary Hull to appear personally before the committee, as they wanted to know the Administration's opinion of the wisdom of the proposal, as well as its purely legal opinion. This plan was modified by the committee this morning to a point where the invitation to Mr. Hull would permit him to submit a written opinion instead of appearing in person, if he so desired.

Senator Pittman, chairman of the committee, and Senator Schwellenbach have introduced resolutions granting to the President varying amounts of authority to impose embargoes against violators of the Nine Power Treaty. Chairman Pittman said today that they have reconciled the differences between their proposals, and that a new draft will be prepared incorporating parts of each as agreed should the committee decide to go ahead with the question.

Opponents of neutrality revision

Continued on Page Two

AID TO PEACE SEEN

Mandatory Embargo Is Called Threat to Our Security as Nation

HULL'S VIEWS IN MESSAGE

Secretary Says Present Law Fosters a General State of War in Europe and Asia

Roosevelt's neutrality message and Hull's statement, Page 2.

Special to THE NEW YORK TIMES.

WASHINGTON, July 14.—President Roosevelt sent to Congress today a special message asking for immediate amendment of the Neutrality Act to eliminate its compulsory arms embargo. This action was necessary, the Chief Executive declared, so that the United States might be on record on the side of preserving world peace, and so that the country would be in the best position to avoid involvement if a general war should break out despite preventive efforts.

Thus for the first time Mr. Roosevelt formally asked for specific changes in the neutrality law, although he has several times previously stated that he thought the statute was not satisfactory. The message took the form of a brief Presidential introduction indorsing and calling to the attention of Congress a detailed statement on the subject by Secretary Hull.

The net effect seemed to be that the President has transferred the issue of revision from Congress to the country. The message was received in the Senate and in the House largely on that basis, and it was believed that Mr. Roosevelt would have much to say about the neutrality situation on his trip around the country, which he has tentatively scheduled to start four days after the adjournment of Congress.

European Situation Noted

The message pointed to the critical situation likely to prevail in Europe for the next several months, and divided, without naming them, the countries of the world into two categories: those bent on forceful change and those desiring to preserve peace.

Secretary Hull found that proponents and opponents of revision are agreed on four cardinal principles of American foreign policy. These he listed as the conviction that the United States must consider first its own peace and security; that the American Government must avoid being drawn into wars between other nations; that this country must steer clear of entangling alliances or involvements, and that this country must maintain strict neutrality to avoid being drawn into war.

The Administration, he said, believes that an arms embargo is a dangerous departure from the practices of international law, while the opponents of change believe the trade in armaments inevitably tends toward involvement and is "immoral."

After more than four years' experience with the various forms of "neutrality" legislation which have been in effect, Mr. Hull reached the conclusion that "the present embargo encourages a general state of war both in Europe and Asia."

Sees Threat to This Country

The result, the Secretary stated, "is directly prejudicial to the highest interests and to the peace and to the security of the United States," since this country can be at its best only in a peaceful world. The aggressors are "more tempted to try the fortunes of war" if they know their less-prepared opponents "would be shut off from those supplies which, under every rule of international law, they should be able to buy in all neutral countries, including the United States."

The message pointed out that "almost all sales of arms and ammunition made in recent years by our nationals have been made to governments whose policies have been dedicated to the maintenance of peace."

Mr. Hull recalled the many years he spent as a member of both houses of Congress in asking for its cooperation on a non partisan basis, in solving the external problems facing this country.

"A peaceful nation like ours cannot complacently close its eyes and ears in formulating a peace and neutrality policy, as though abnor-

Continued on Page Two

PARIS SHOWS MIGHT IN HOLIDAY PARADE

British Forces Take Part as 30,000 March — Daladier Stresses Hope for Peace

By P. J. PHILIP
Wireless to THE NEW YORK TIMES.

PARIS, July 14.—All those qualities of heart, mind and body that mark a strong, vital nation sure of itself and of its cause entered into today's immense celebration in Paris of the 150th anniversary of the capture of the Bastille and the beginning of the French Revolution.

There was an almost terrifying display of military power. Thirty thousand men, selected from all arms and by proved experience among the finest fighters in the world, marched down the Champs Elysees past President Albert Lebrun with a great rumbling of guns, tanks, machine guns and all the complicated machinery of modern war. Four hundred airplanes whirred overhead like flights of geese.

Lebrun Reads Broadcast

President Lebrun read a radio broadcast message to all Frenchmen in France and in her far-flung possessions, and somberly but with a note of confidence Premier Edouard Daladier told the story of the two first July celebrations and drew a moral for the present.

"A free nation is always a pacific nation," was one of his maxims.

"And today," he added, "we threaten no one. We have no dreams of conquest. We desire peace between all nations and we are going to go on seeking to maintain it, for only so can we assure the safety of civilization. Yet any threat or any effort at domination will find us resolute to defend our frontiers and join our effort to those of all peoples who are resolved to defend their independence."

Among the 30,000 marchers today were Foreign Legionaries, goumiers, spahis and Negro riflemen from Africa, fierce little yellow men from Asia and French colonials from wherever the Tricolor has been planted and taken root.

There were friendship and alliance, for although July 14 is no British festival there were British sailors and British guardsmen in this procession, and among those planes that went roaring over the straight mile that leads from Napoleon's Arc de Triomphe to the Place de la Concorde were fifty British bombers, eagerly watched by Leslie Hore-Belisha, the British Secretary for War, and by British admirals and generals.

There was an approving and confident attachment to the government of the republic in the cheers with which President Lebrun and Premier Daladier were greeted.

There was happiness in these im-

Continued on Page Five

FCC SUSPENDS CURB ON WORLD RADIO

Rule Requiring International Broadcasts Promote 'Good-Will' Is Withdrawn

By The Associated Press.

WASHINGTON, July 14.—The Federal Communications Commission today suspended its rule requiring that international broadcasts "reflect the culture of this country" and "promote international good-will, understanding and cooperation."

Thad H. Brown, acting chairman in the absence of Frank R. McNinch, who is ill, announced suspension of the rule, which critics had said tended toward censorship, as the commission opened hearings on it.

He said the suspension was decreed "pending an opportunity to hear and consider the evidence, views and arguments to be presented on the issues in this hearing."

Mr. Brown read a statement saying the commission "has no desire, purpose or intention of setting itself up as a board of censorship, and that it does not and will not exercise any such jurisdiction."

The rule, Mr. Brown said, was intended to do two things:

"(1) To require international broadcast stations to direct their service to foreign countries rather than the United States;

"(2) To define the public interest to be served through the licensing of these stations."

Broadcasters Oppose Rule

"It has not been the practice of the commission in the past," he added, "nor is it the intention of the commission now, with respect to the rule, ever to require the submission of any program continuity or script for editing, modification or revision, or for any other purpose prior to its use by a station."

The National Association of Broadcasters, through President Neville Miller, led the opposition at the hearing, contending the rule involves censorship. The Rev. Edward Lodge Curran of Brooklyn, N. Y., president of the International Catholic Truth Society, championed the rule, saying it was necessary to promote good-will in South America.

The Civil Liberties Union, first to be heard today, argued that the rule "tends to deprive the American public, including the petitioner, of the right of free speech by means of radio communication."

Father Curran, who is in charge of radio activities in the Brooklyn diocese, criticized both the National Association of Broadcasters and the American Civil Liberties Union, calling them "strange bedfellows."

The commission ordered the hearings on a petition by the Civil Liberties Union, which said enforce-

Continued on Page Three

"All the News That's Fit to Print."

The New York Times.

LATE CITY EDITION
Partly cloudy and warm with scattered showers today and tomorrow.
Temperatures Yesterday—Max., 86; Min., 70

Copyright, 1939, by The New York Times Company.

VOL. LXXXVIII...No. 29,797. Entered as Second-Class Matter. Postoffice, New York, N. Y. NEW YORK, THURSDAY, AUGUST 24, 1939. PP THREE CENTS NEW YORK CITY and Vicinity | FOUR CENTS Elsewhere Except in 7th and 8th Postal Zones.

GERMANY AND RUSSIA SIGN 10-YEAR NON-AGGRESSION PACT; BIND EACH OTHER NOT TO AID OPPONENTS IN WAR ACTS; HITLER REBUFFS LONDON; BRITAIN AND FRANCE MOBILIZE

U.S. AND ARGENTINA PLAN TRADE PACT, WELLES DISCLOSES

Our Commerce Will Get Full Equality With That of All Foreigners, He Asserts

BEEF NOT TO BE INCLUDED

Long Preliminary Talks Ease Difficulties, With Offset Seen to Our Recent Losses

Special to THE NEW YORK TIMES.

WASHINGTON, Aug. 23.—The United States intends to negotiate a reciprocal trade treaty with Argentina as a move to put American commerce with that republic on a footing of equality with that of European competitors, Sumner Welles, Acting Secretary of State, stated today. There have been more than four years of preliminary discussion.

The State Department, making public a list of products upon which this country would make tariff concessions, set Oct. 4 as the closing date for submission of briefs by interested Americans and Oct. 16 for the opening of public hearings.

It was emphasized that fresh, chilled or frozen Argentine meats, the entry of which into this country is banned by the Tariff Act of 1930, and fine wools would not be a subject of discussion in the negotiations. This was expected by officials to remove the most serious objections which might have been advanced to conclusion of a reciprocal agreement. Barring of the entry of Argentine fresh beef here has long been a subject of some friction between the two countries in their commercial relations.

"It may be noted that during the fifteen-year period 1924-38 our exports to Argentina have exceeded our imports from that country by $486,900,000," Mr. Welles said in a statement.

Trade Cut by Foreign Pacts

"Our trade with Argentina has suffered in recent years for lack of a trade agreement. The trade of certain European countries with Argentina has been developing at our expense under the influence of their commercial agreements with Argentina. The placing of American commerce in Argentina on a footing of full equality with that of our European competitors was a subject which was gone into fully in preliminary discussions leading up to the present announcement.

"The agreement will enable us to maintain our competitive position in a market of great present and prospective importance.

"On our side we must, of course, offer reciprocal benefits. The products of interest to Argentina with respect to which consideration will be given in the course of the negotiations, with a view to seeing what concessions could be granted, are listed in connection with the announcement of the proposed negotiations. The concessions, which will in due course be formulated, should, of course, permit an increase in Argentina's exports to this country, but will not have injurious effect upon American production.

"The types of wool included in the list are the coarser types, of which there is only a very small production in this country."

Barter Agreement With Germany

It was presumed that in referring to European competitors Mr. Welles was speaking principally of Germany, which concluded a barter agreement with Argentina after the Pan-American Conference in Lima last December. England has long been a large trader with Argentina, however, and is a heavy buyer of Argentine beef.

Among the products upon which the United States will consider lowering duties in favor of Argentina are:

Tallow, oleo oil and oleo stearin, extract of meat, including fluid, pickled or cured beef packed or not packed in air-tight containers; dead turkeys, dead birds, chicken eggs, corn or maize, including cracked corn; asparagus in its natural state, and some wools.

With the possible exception of that made with Brazil, a reciprocal trade treaty with the Argentine would be the most important yet consummated with a Latin-American country, officials indicated. Be-

Continued on Page Thirty-five

BRITAIN ACTS FAST

Air Force Is Ready for Hostilities—Warships Mass in Skagerrak

EXPORT EMBARGO IS FIXED

Parliament Meets Today in an Emergency Session—King to Convene Privy Council

By FERDINAND KUHN Jr.
Special Cable to THE NEW YORK TIMES.

LONDON, Aug. 23.—The British Government prepared for action today with every indication that it was ready to go to war with Germany whenever a call for help from Poland should come.

Warning notices went out to reservists in all departments of the armed and civilian services; the King was returning to London to hold a meeting of the Privy Council tomorrow; Londoners were ordered to darken their windows until further notice; the air force was poised for instant action, and a concentration of an undisclosed number of British warships was reported in the Skagerrak, between the Norwegian and Danish coasts, as if to remind Germany of the blockade that she had to endure during the World War.

The emergency was underlined by a Board of Trade announcement placing an immediate embargo on unlicensed exports of essential war materials "in order to conserve the stocks in this country." The list included copper, nickel and rubber, which the Germans have been buying in large quantities in the past week or two, and also aluminum, lead, iron and steel scrap and raw cotton.

Parliament Session Today

Tomorrow both houses of Parliament will meet in emergency session to give the government sweeping powers of a sort unknown in democratic England since World War days. The new law will be something like the old Defense of the Realm Act, enabling the government to issue Orders in Council, without prior or subsequent Parliamentary sanction, for any purpose that the national interest may require.

Trade-union leaders were invited to examine the bill today and they came away satisfied that all possible safeguards of individual liberty would be included.

The real business of the Parliamentary session, however, will be to hear a complete review of the international situation by Prime Minister Chamberlain in the House of Commons and by Viscount Halifax, the Foreign Secretary, in the House of Lords. All indications are that the Prime Minister's words and the subsequent debate will be more sombre in tone than anything heard in the Commons chamber since Aug. 3, 1914, when Sir Edward Grey made his famous speech on the eve of the World War.

Everywhere it was agreed that a crisis of the utmost gravity now confronts Britain, a crisis far more serious than that of last Autumn, when this country was not committed as it is now. The British determination to carry out all the pledges to Poland was reaffirmed in the government message handed to Chancellor Hitler today by Sir

Continued on Page Five

The Developments in Europe

The signing of the Russo-German non-aggression pact, which many world capitals feared might be Chancellor Hitler's "go-ahead signal," took place in Moscow early this morning, half a day after German Foreign Minister von Ribbentrop had arrived in the Russian capital. The pact, which runs for ten years, in addition to prohibiting attack by either party against the other, forbids either to join any association of powers aimed at the other. Moreover, it provides that if one party is an "object of warlike acts" the other will not support such acts. [Page 1; text of the treaty, also Page 1.]

Signature of the pact followed a day that seemed to bring Europe closer to the brink. When the British Ambassador to Germany conveyed to Chancellor Hitler a warning that Britain would fight for Poland he was bluntly rebuffed. In Berlin word freely circulated that the German Army would march at 6 P. M. today (noon in New York). [Page 1.]

In the face of Herr Hitler's rebuff Britain went ahead with war preparations, including the sending of notices to reservists, poising of the air force and concentration of warships in the Skagerrak, north of Denmark. Parliament prepared to meet today to grant the government sweeping emergency powers. [Page 1.] Reinforcements were reported being sent to the Mediterranean, where the bases at Gibraltar and Malta were on the alert. [Page 3.] The dominions, led by Canada and Australia, were beginning to swing into line behind Britain. [Page 6.]

France, convinced that Germany intends to invade Poland within a few days, called up further reservists after a meeting of the Permanent Committee on National Defense. [Page 1.]

Poland remained outwardly calm, still doubting that Herr Hitler would risk precipitating a general war. [Page 2.]

In Turkey allegiance to the coalition powers was affirmed, although German Ambassador von Papen was flying to Angora from Germany, presumably to try to break that allegiance. [Page 1.] But in Rumania, another State guaranteed by France and Britain, informed circles said that country would strive to remain neutral [Page 7.]

Only in Rome were signs of war lacking. Although the press continued to attack Poland, no unusual defense preparations were evident. [Page 1.]

In an attempt to head off disaster King Leopold of the Belgians, speaking for the seven Oslo powers, appealed for peace. [With the text of the appeal, Page 5.]

President Roosevelt, disturbed by the outlook, was speeding back to Washington [Page 1], where officials were clearing the decks for action if it became necessary to safeguard United States neutrality and help Americans to escape from danger zones. [Page 3.] The State Department advised citizens not to go to Europe [Page 3] and those who were trying to return home found ships still running normally from foreign ports. [Page 3.]

In the Far East the army and navy leaders in Japan were understood to have shaped a policy to be followed in view of the new situation arising from the Russo-German treaty. [Page 4.] In China some observers believed the treaty would mean increased Soviet aid in resisting Japan. [Page 4.]

FRANCE MOBILIZES; NOW EXPECTS WAR

People Confident of Strength to Meet Aggressor as Hopes of Peace Diminish

By P. J. PHILIP
Wireless to THE NEW YORK TIMES.

PARIS, Thursday, Aug. 24.—Convinced by a report from French Ambassador Robert Coulondre at Berlin and by a reply that Chancellor Adolf Hitler gave yesterday to Prime Minister Neville Chamberlain's message through British Ambassador Sir Nevile Henderson at Berchtesgaden that an invasion of Poland is intended by the German Government within the next few days, the French Government last night decided to call up a further contingent of reservists today.

This decision was communicated to the press in an official statement from Premier Edouard Daladier's office as follows:

"On account of the international situation the French Government has decided to complete military measures already taken by calling up an additional contingent of reserve soldiers."

During last night notices were

Continued on Page Two

TURKEY REAFFIRMS PLEDGES TO ALLIES

Will Honor Pact With France and Britain—German Envoy Flies to Woo Her

Special Cable to THE NEW YORK TIMES.

ISTANBUL, Turkey, Aug. 23.—No official pronouncement has yet been made about the Russo-German non-aggression pact. In official quarters the position of Turkey is said to be unchanged; she has made agreements for mutual assistance against aggression with France and Britain and stands by them.

The Turkish people are still bewildered over yesterday's news, but less alarm about its possibilities is noticeable since last night's official British communiqué was published.

Until the Turkish Government has authentic information about the terms of the pact Turkish newspapers will be reticent. Cumhuriet, only Turkish newspaper with an editorial on the subject today, assumed the Soviet Union would stipulate that if Germany was guilty of aggression against any of her Western neighbors, the pact would become null and void.

In this case, the newspaper said, it should act as a deterrent against war in Europe, for the newspaper could not believe the Soviet Government will remain indifferent to the fate of its neighbors on the Baltic and Black Seas simply because it signed a pact of non-aggression with Germany.

Cumhuriet added that although a pact of non-aggreisson was not an alliance, it implied friendly feelings, and it believed, therefore, that the anti-Comintern pact was political, not ideological, and that the Russo-German pact may be regarded as a truce.

Von Papen Flies to Turkey

BUDAPEST, Hungary, Aug. 23 (AP).—Franz von Papen, Germany's Ambassador to Turkey, passed by plane through Budapest today, en route from Salzburg to Angora.

Diplomatic circles conjectured his mission now was to renew attempts to draw Turkey out of the British-French bloc. They recalled German and Italian claims that Turkey's alliance with Britain and France was dependent upon Russia's not joining the opposition camp.

Wireless to THE NEW YORK TIMES.

BUDAPEST, Hungary, Aug. 23.—The international situation was dis-

Continued on Page Five

Sidney Howard Killed by Tractor on Estate; Playwright Is Crushed in Berkshire Garage

Special to THE NEW YORK TIMES.

TYRINGHAM, Mass., Aug. 23.—Sidney Coe Howard, playwright, was crushed to death today by a two and a half ton tractor in his garage on his 700-acre estate here.

Mr. Howard had put in a morning of hard work on a new play based on Carl Van Doren's "Benjamin Franklin" and, as was his custom, was going to seek relaxation in physical work on his estate, which included one of the most modern dairy farms in this part of the State. The chore he had set for himself was harrowing a twenty-eight-acre field which he had recently bought to extend his property.

Driving alone to the garage a quarter of a mile from his studio in the fields, Mr. Howard entered, turned on the ignition switch of the tractor and cranked it. The machine lurched forward, pinning the playwright against the wall of the structure. The tractor, put in the garage the night before by an employe, was believed to have been left in high gear.

Fred L. Fairbanks, superintendent of the estate, discovered Mr. Howard while on an inspection trip. The garage, a former Shaker schoolroom, is set off by itself on the estate and is seldom visited by any one except by those on business.

Mr. Fairbanks found his employer in, an upright position, his head bent over his chest. He was pinned at the chest by the hood of the tractor, which had stalled after crushing him against the wall.

After starting the tractor and moving Mr. Howard's body, Mr. Fairbanks ran to the nearest telephone on the estate to notify Mrs. Howard and summon aid. Mrs. Howard was shopping in Lee, five miles away. When she returned

Continued on Page Nineteen

QUICK ACTION SEEN

Berlin Talks of 6 P. M. Deadline for Move Against Poland

DICTATOR WARNS BRITISH

Henderson So Wrought Up on Leaving Parley With Hitler That He Is Speechless

By OTTO D. TOLISCHUS
Wireless to THE NEW YORK TIMES.

BERLIN, Thursday, Aug. 24.—While Foreign Minister Joachim von Ribbentrop was in Moscow discussing, in the view of some German quarters, not so much a new non-aggression pact as "Poland's fourth and final partition," Chancellor Hitler yesterday received Sir Nevile Henderson, the British Ambassador, for a fifteen-minute conference.

According to reliable information, the conference ended on a rather blunt note that is interpreted in diplomatic quarters as possibly Herr Hitler's last word. The communiqué, issued last night, reads:

"Complying with the wish of the British Government, the Fuehrer received Sir Nevile Henderson at the Berghof today. The Ambassador delivered a letter from the British Prime Minister addressed to the Fuehrer, which was drawn up in the same sense as yesterday's British communication regarding the Cabinet session.

"The Fuehrer left no doubt in the mind of the British Ambassador that the obligations assumed by the British Government could not induce Germany to renounce the defense of her vital national interest."

Hitler's Tone Reported Blunt

Actually Herr Hitler's tone to Sir Nevile was reported to have been even more blunt than the communiqué indicates. In effect, Herr Hitler told the Ambassador that Britain had no business in Eastern Europe and that her guarantee of Poland merely encouraged Polish resistance to German demands, therefore it was up to Britain to persuade the Poles to yield or face the consequences.

Sir Nevile left the conference so wrought up he was speechless. Not trusting his memory to repeat the exact shadings of Herr Hitler's answer, he asked that it be put in writing and he returned for it a half hour later. He got it couched in the same strong terms that Herr Hitler used to him before.

At the same time there are also well-authenticated reports that, in addition to Prime Minister Chamberlain's letter, Sir Nevile also delivered to Herr Hitler an oral message that if Herr Hitler would give the Poles time Britain would try to induce Poland to come forth with new proposals. In that connection some circles launched—perhaps not unintentionally—the suggestion that Foreign Minister Josef Beck of Poland might after all ask to see Herr von Ribbentrop and even Herr Hitler. A preliminary meeting with the former might be arranged at Riga, Latvia, on Herr von Ribbentrop's return from Moscow. But Polish circles declare the suggestion was "extremely unlikely" because it spelled surrender.

As during the last few days the word in Berlin is that the zero hour, which will set the German Army on the march, will come today, and these rumors are supplemented with the additional detail that the exact hour is 6 P. M. [noon, New York time], which might mean "contact with the enemy" some time tomorrow. Furthermore, orders to postpone action, issued after Herr von Ribbentrop's departure for Moscow, have been canceled again.

Germans Elated by News

How much all that is merely a part of the "war of nerves" and how much is bitter reality remains to be seen. In fact the tension developing in Germany, at least in an atmosphere of fantastic unreality, is made no more real by the delayed Summer heat that lures the populace to the woods and beaches, and, together with the elation over the Russian pact and renewed confidence in Herr Hitler's diplomatic superiority over the democratic statesmen, helps to hide the war clouds.

However, the rebuff to Britain yesterday, which in some quarters is compared with the rebuff administered to the French Ambassador by King William of Prussia just preceding the Franco-Prussian War

Continued on Page Two

Text of the Berlin-Moscow Treaty

By The Associated Press.

MOSCOW, Thursday, Aug. 24.—The text of the German-Russian non-aggression pact announced here today follows:

The German Reich Government and the Union of Soviet Socialist Republics, moved by a desire to strengthen the state of peace between Germany and the U.S.S.R. and in the spirit of the provisions of the neutrality treaty of April, 1926, between Germany and the U.S.S.R., decided the following:

Article I

The two contracting parties obligate themselves to refrain from every act of force, every aggressive action and every attack against one another, including any single action or that taken in conjunction with other powers.

Article II

In case one of the parties of this treaty should become the object of warlike acts by a third power, the other party will in no way support this third power.

Article III

The governments of the two contracting parties in the future will constantly remain in consultation with one another in order to inform each other regarding questions of common interest.

Article IV

Neither of the high contracting parties will associate itself with any other grouping of powers which directly or indirectly is aimed at the other party.

Article V

In the event of a conflict between the contracting parties concerning any question, the two parties will adjust this difference or conflict exclusively by friendly exchange of opinions or, if necessary, by an arbitration commission.

Article VI

The present treaty will extend for a period of ten years with the condition that if neither of the contracting parties announces its abrogation within one year of expiration of this period, it will continue in force automatically for another period of five years.

Article VII

The present treaty shall be ratified within the shortest possible time. The exchange of ratification documents shall take place in Berlin. The treaty becomes effective immediately upon signature.

Drawn up in two languages, German and Russian.
Moscow, 23d *of August*, 1939.

For the German Government:
RIBBENTROP.

In the name of the Government of the U.S.S.R.:
MOLOTOFF.

NO MILITARY MOVES APPARENT IN ITALY

Country Remains Tranquil as Regime Fails to Whip Up Any War Fervor Among People

By HERBERT L. MATTHEWS
Wireless to THE NEW YORK TIMES.

ROME, Aug. 23.—The Italian ship of state sailed tranquilly on the edge of the European tornado today. There have been no conferences, communiqués, evacuation orders, special mobilization or troop movements.

There have been only some diplomatic visits to Count Ciano, the Foreign Minister, including those of the British and French Ambassadors. This is the fourth time since last Thursday that Sir Percy Loraine saw Count Ciano, which shows the degree of pressure the British are bringing to bear as well as their anxiety to make the Italian leaders realize Britain's determination to support Poland. Presumably, Sir Percy delivered a copy of the same note that was presented to Chancellor Hitler, although that has not been admitted.

André François-Poncet's visit was his first since returning to Rome last Friday. He has tried steadily to see the Foreign Minister but hitherto without success. It is believed he also impressed on Count Ciano France's intention to abide by her pledges.

The Hungarian Minister, Baron Frederick Villani, also saw Count Ciano today, reviving reports about Germany's demands on Budapest.

Italian People Are Calm

The Italian people are not being whipped up to the fervor that would be required to enter a war in the next few days. Nowhere do you see air shelters being hastily dug or gas masks being distributed.

Only in the newspapers do the commentators warn their readers that a conflict seems near, while relatively full accounts of the developments in various capitals are given. The British Cabinet's statement last night is published fully in all newspapers here, whereas the German press ignored it. If readers trusted their Italian newspapers this evening they would have a biased but reasonably correct appreciation of the dangers of the present situation.

On the other hand, so far as they know their country is making no last-minute efforts to meet the

Continued on Page Four

PRESIDENT SPEEDS TO ACT ON CRISIS

Disturbed by War Threat, He Will End Cruise Today and Board Train at Red Bank

By FELIX BELAIR Jr.
Special to THE NEW YORK TIMES.

RED BANK, N. J., Aug. 23.—Admittedly disturbed by the European war crisis, President Roosevelt is hurrying here aboard the navy cruiser Tuscaloosa after scrapping plans for a more ceremonious landing at Annapolis in order to be back at the White House in the event of an outbreak of hostilities.

A small White House secretarial staff is awaiting the arrival of the President off Sandy Hook early tomorrow to give him a bundle of official diplomatic reports on the latest developments abroad. Mr. Roosevelt plans to study the reports aboard his special train en route to Washington.

After debarking from the Tuscaloosa about 8 A. M. tomorrow the President will motor here with Brig. Gen. Edwin M. Watson, his secretary, and Rear Admiral Ross T. McIntire, White House physician. He is expected to stop long enough before entraining for the capital to telephone Secretary of State Cordell Hull, as well as to the embassies in London and Paris about overnight developments.

To Get War Supplies Report

Back at the White House in the early afternoon the President will have before him a report of the War Industries Committee on the status of the nation's munitions and other heavy industries. The committee has been canvassing the aviation and other industries in the past few days with a view to American preparedness.

Prior to the departure of the White House staff late today it was understood the War Industries Committee had drafted a report informing the President that the aviation and several other industries were prepared for any emergency that might arise and that aircraft manufacturers were ahead of schedule on orders of military planes from France and Great Britain.

Among Presidential intimates as well as the capital's political observers interest centered during the day on the question of whether Mr. Roosevelt considered the situation abroad sufficiently grave to call a

Continued on Page Three

BARS HOSTILE UNION

Treaty Forbids Either to Join Any Group Aimed at Other

ESCAPE CLAUSE OMITTED

Von Ribbentrop's Car, Flying Swastika, Passes Beneath Red Flag at Kremlin

By The Associated Press.

MOSCOW, Thursday, Aug. 24.—Germany and Soviet Russia early today signed a non-aggression pact binding each of them for ten years not to "associate itself with any other grouping of powers which directly or indirectly is aimed at the other party."

By the pact they also agreed to "constantly remain in consultation with one another" on their common interests and to adjust differences by arbitration.

The non-aggression clauses bound each power to refrain from any act of force against the other and if either party is "the object of warlike acts by a third power" to refrain from supporting that third power.

The pact did not include the usual escape clause providing for its denunciation in case one of the contracting parties attacked a third power. This provision has been written into most non-aggression agreements signed in the past by Moscow.

Arrives by Plane

By G. E. R. GEDYE
Special Cable to THE NEW YORK TIMES.

MOSCOW, Thursday, Aug. 24.—With the meticulous punctuality of a perfectly staged arrival, two huge Focke-Wulf Condor planes conveying Joachim von Ribbentrop, the German Foreign Minister, and his thirty-two assistants, landed at the Moscow airdrome on the stroke of 1 P. M. yesterday.

Adequate but not excessive police precautions were taken at the airdrome. For the first time the Soviet authorities displayed the swastika banner, five of which flew from the front of the airdrome building, but were placed so as not to be visible from the outside.

Vyacheslaff M. Molotoff was not present to welcome Herr von Ribbentrop, probably because he is not only Commissar of Foreign Affairs but also Premier, and therefore higher in rank than Herr von Ribbentrop. Instead the visitor was received by Vladimir P. Potemkin, Vice Commissar of Foreign Affairs; Mr. Barkoff, protocol chief; Mr. Merkuloff, Vice Commissar of Internal Affairs, under whom falls the NKVD, formerly the GPU; Mr. Alexandroff, chief of the Central European Department of the Foreign Office, and General Suvoroff, commander of the Moscow garrison.

Almost the entire staff of the huge German Embassy, headed by the Ambassador, Count Friedrich Werner von der Schulenburg, with the military, naval and air attachés in uniform, was present. The German civilians mostly wore top hats and cutaway coats.

The Italian Ambassador, Augusto Russo, with his military attaché in uniform, also was present. The feature of the reception most commented upon was the absence of any Japanese representative.

The German Embassy staff stood lined up like troops on parade. As each was presented to Herr von Ribbentrop he sprang to attention, clicked his heels, gave the Hitler salute and shook hands, again saluting and heel-clicking.

In Old Austrian Embassy

From the airdrome the party drove to the city through streets where police in their white Summer jackets stood every ten paces. For Herr von Ribbentrop the Soviet Government provided a large American car from the Kremlin car park, flying the swastika flag.

The party drove directly to the former Austrian Embassy, where they are being housed. Subsequently Herr von Ribbentrop and leading members of his mission had luncheon at the embassy with Count von der Schulenburg.

At about 3:30 P. M. Herr von Ribbentrop, accompanied by Count von der Schulenburg and an expert translator whom the Germans brought from Berlin, drove through the gates of the Kremlin with its

Continued on Page Six

German troops advance into Danzig.

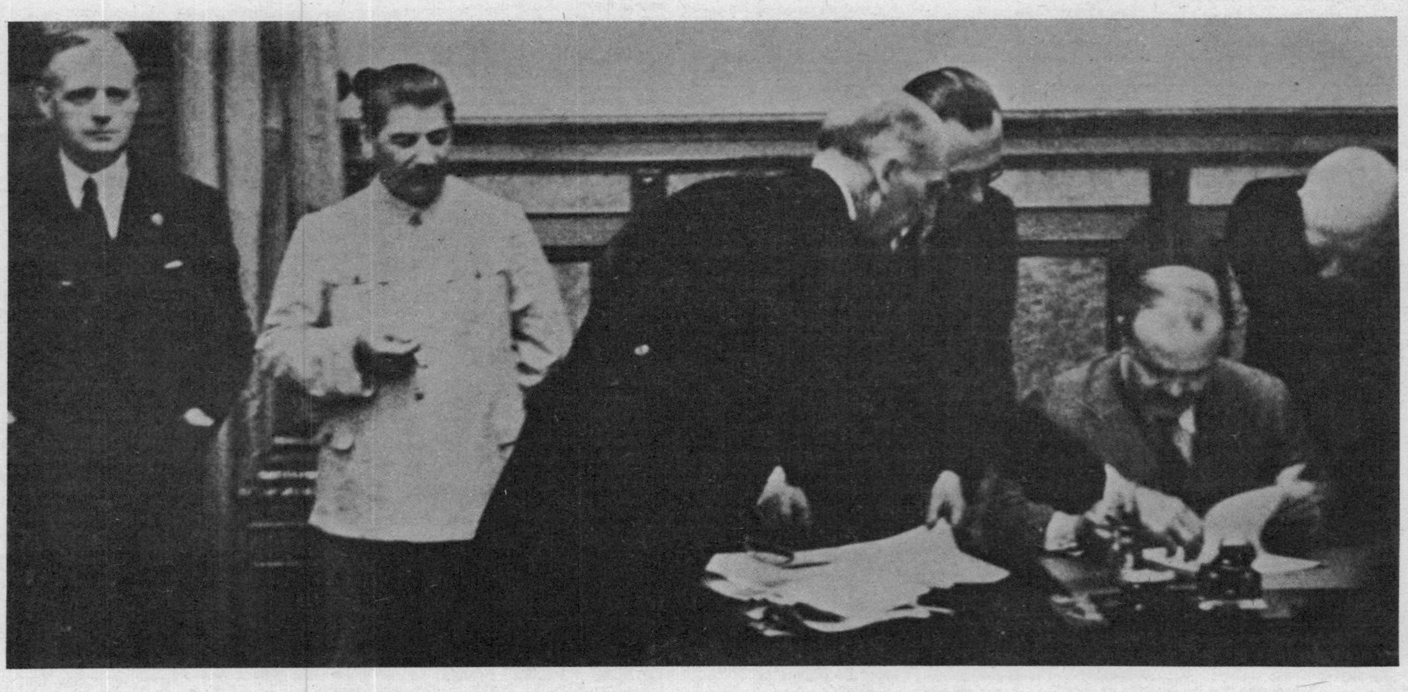

Taking part in the signing of the Nazi-Soviet Pact are (left to right) von Ribbentrop, Stalin, Gaus, Hilger, Molotov and von der Schulenberg.

Victorious German troops parade through the streets of Warsaw, the capital of defeated Poland.

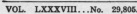

"All the News That's Fit to Print."

The New York Times.

EXTRA

Partly cloudy and somewhat warmer today. Tomorrow generally fair with moderate temperatures.

Temperatures Yesterday—Max., 67; Min., 61

VOL. LXXXVIII...No. 29,805. Entered as Second-Class Matter, Postoffice, New York, N. Y. NEW YORK, FRIDAY, SEPTEMBER 1, 1939. THREE CENTS NEW YORK CITY and Vicinity | FOUR CENTS Elsewhere Except in 7th and 8th Postal Zones.

GERMAN ARMY ATTACKS POLAND; CITIES BOMBED, PORT BLOCKADED; DANZIG IS ACCEPTED INTO REICH

BRITISH MOBILIZING

Navy Raised to Its Full Strength, Army and Air Reserves Called Up

PARLIAMENT IS CONVOKED

Midnight Meeting Is Held by Ministers—Negotiations Admitted Failure

By The Associated Press.

LONDON, Friday, Sept. 1.—The British Parliament was summoned to meet today at 5 P. M. [12 noon in New York].

British Call Up Forces

By FERDINAND KUHN Jr.

Special Cable to THE NEW YORK TIMES.

LONDON, Friday, Sept. 1.—All attempts to bring about direct negotiations between Germany and Poland appeared to have broken down tonight as Great Britain mobilized her fleet to full strength, stretched her other defensive preparations close to the limit and began moving 3,000,000 school children and invalids from the crowded cities into the safety of the countryside.

Censorship was established over cables after London had been cut off for hours from communication with the Continent.

It was the peak of the crisis, but a day of rumors had not shifted the fundamental issue nor given a conclusive answer to the question of peace or war.

At midnight the British Government was not yet convinced that Germany really intended to attack Poland and provoke a world war.

Terms Called Smoke Screen

All that had happened during yesterday, including the sudden broadcasting of Chancellor Hitler's sixteen-point demands, was interpreted here as a smoke screen rather than as the flash of guns.

After hearing Herr Hitler's "terms" officials here quietly announced tonight that "the government primarily interested in the proposals is, of course, the Polish Government."

Until the Polish Government has had time to consider them, it was said in Whitehall that "it would be highly undesirable for any comment to be made."

It was fully expected that Poland would reject them later today; indeed, Polish circles here were describing them tonight as "utterly unacceptable," for they would involve dismemberment of Poland and loss of Poland's capacity to defend her independence. In any event, there was no sign of any intention here to put pressure on Warsaw to accept.

Much might have been said about the German "proposals" here tonight if the government had not been so anxious to leave the first decision to Warsaw without any prompting. That the British regarded them as artful went without saying, since they conveyed a first impression of reasonableness that was not borne out by the terms themselves.

Until the announcement on the German wireless tonight, the British Government had not been told about them officially, and the Polish Government was not informed until Josef Lipski, Polish Ambassador to Berlin, visited Foreign Minister Joachim von Ribbentrop a few minutes before the broadcast took place.

Shortly after midnight last night, Sir Nevile Henderson, the British Ambassador in Berlin, had heard the "points" read to him by Herr von Ribbentrop, but the reading was so fast that the Ambassador could not even take notes of them in detail. In any event, he was told Herr Hitler's "points" were not being given to him or his government officially, on the ground that it was already too late.

Time Limit Expired

On Tuesday Herr Hitler had asked that a Polish negotiator should arrive in Berlin within twenty-four hours; and as nobody had arrived from Warsaw when the time limit expired, Sir Nevile was told that the "points" could not be communicated officially to London.

The German time table with the

Continued on Page Four

Bulletins on Europe's Conflict

London Hears of Warsaw Bombing

LONDON, Friday, Sept. 1 (AP).—Reuters British news agency said it had learned from Polish sources in Paris that Warsaw was bombed today.

French Confirm Beginning of War

PARIS, Friday, Sept. 1 (AP).—The Havas news agency said today that official French dispatches from Germany indicated that "the Reich began hostilities on Poland this morning."

The agency also reported that the Polish Embassy here had announced that "Germany violated the Polish frontier at four points."

"German reports of pretended violation of German territory by Poland are pure invention, as is the fable of 'attack' by Polish insurgents on Gleiwitz," the embassy announcement said.

Attack on Entire Front Reported

LONDON, Friday, Sept. 1 (AP).—A Reuters dispatch from Paris said:

"The following is given with all reserve: According to unconfirmed reports received here, the Germans have begun an offensive with extreme violence on the whole Polish front."

First Wounded Brought Into Gleiwitz

GLEIWITZ, Germany, Friday, Sept. 1 (AP).—An army ambulance carrying wounded soldiers arrived at the emergency hospital here today at 9:10 A. M.

The men, carried in a wagon, were on stretchers. One had on a first-aid field bandage. It could not be ascertained where the ambulance came from.

At about 9:30 a half-mile long truck train manned by the engineering corps drove through the heart of the city with pontoon bridge building material. In the train were caterpillar tread, twenty-passenger motor vans.

Obviously the train had been on the road for a considerable time. All equipment was thickly covered with gray mud.

A scouting plane of the air force was patrolling an area over Gleiwitz.

Early today Gleiwitz residents reported that artillery fire

Continued on Page Four

DALADIER SUMMONS CABINET TO CONFER

News of Attack on Poland Spurs Prompt Action—Military Move Thought Likely

By The Associated Press.

PARIS, Friday, Sept. 1.—Edouard Daladier, Premier and War Minister of France, informed that German troops crossed the Polish frontier today, summoned an urgent meeting of his Cabinet for 10:30 A. M.

It was probable that Parliament would be called tomorrow.

Reports of the German invasion came from Berlin and from the Polish Embassy here. The Ministers were called to the Elysee Palace to meet with President Albert Lebrun.

Upon receipt of word of the German operations M. Daladier rushed to the War Ministry and called General Marie Gustave Gamelin, supreme commander of land, sea and air forces, into consultation.

A little later Daladier summoned Foreign Minister Georges Bonnet.

The Polish Embassy said that Germans violated the Polish frontier at four points and at the same time it characterized German charges that Poles had crossed into Germany as "pure invention."

Havas, Frnch news agency, announced that "a German declaration of war against Poland probably will lead France and Great Britain to take new military measures."

Britain and France are committed to aid Poland in any fight to save her independence.

Ministers Stand Firm

By P. J. PHILIP

Wireless to THE NEW YORK TIMES.

PARIS, Aug. 31.—The Cabinet met with President Albert Lebrun for more than two hours this evening at the Elysée Palace. At the close of the meeting Minister of the Interior Albert Sarraut handed the press the following communiqué:

"MM. Edouard Daladier, President of the Council, and Georges Bonnet, Minister of Foreign Affairs, laid before the Cabinet a detailed account of the international situation as a whole.

"The Cabinet was unanimous in formally maintaining the engagements taken by France."

Later M. Daladier had further conversations with M. Bonnet, Fi-

Continued on Page Four

BRITISH CHILDREN TAKEN FROM CITIES

3,000,000 Persons Are in First Evacuation Group, Which Is to Be Moved Today

By FREDERICK T. BIRCHALL

Special Cable to THE NEW YORK TIMES.

LONDON, Friday, Sept. 1.—The greatest mass movement of population at short notice in the history of Great Britain is under way. It is an evacuation, under government order, of little children, invalids, women and old men from congested areas.

From London, Birmingham, Manchester, Liverpool, Edinburgh, Glasgow and twenty-three other cities the great exodus is going on as this dispatch is being written. The numbers are stupendous. More than 3,000,000 of these helpless human beings are being taken out of danger of German bombs.

Nothing like it has ever been attempted anywhere; yet it is going on without mishap—so far, indeed, without serious confusion.

Scenes everywhere were much the same whether in the aristocratic West End or the proletarian East Side, but one that this correspon-

Continued on Page Three

HOSTILITIES BEGUN

Warsaw Reports German Offensive Moving on Three Objectives

ROOSEVELT WARNS NAVY

Also Notifies Army Leaders of Warfare—Envoys Tell of Bombing of 4 Cities

By JERZY SZAPIRO

Wireless to THE NEW YORK TIMES.

WARSAW, Poland, Friday, Sept. 1.—War began at 5 o'clock this morning with German planes attacking Gdynia, Cracow and Katowice.

At Gdynia three bombs exploded in the sea.

The regular German Army started an offensive in the direction of Dzialdowka—in Upper Silesia and Czestochowa. The German plan apparently is to cut off Western Poland along the line of Dzialdowka-Lodz-Czestochowa.

The offensive is developing, from East Prussia, toward Silesia and northwards from Slovakia.

At 9 o'clock an attempt was made to bombard Warsaw. The planes, however, did not reach even the suburbs.

A military attack on the garrison at Westerplatte in the Danzig area was repulsed.

The Foreign Office at 8:45 A. M. issued a communiqué saying that military action had begun in Westerplatte in the Danzig area as well as in Buschkowa near Gdynia, and in Dzialowka, Chojnice and Lowa.

Hostilities have begun and Poland has been attacked, said the communiqué.

Three cities in Upper Silesia suffered artillery bombardment, particulars of which are lacking, it was said.

While this dispatch was being telephoned, the air-raid sirens sounded in Warsaw.

Danzig Fighting Reported

WARSAW, Poland, Friday, Sept. 1 (AP).—It was reported today that Tczew and Czestochowa were bombed by German airplanes early this morning.

There was no official confirmation of the bombing.

Fighting was reported at Danzig.

It was reported officially that German troops had attacked Polish defenses near Mlawa, bordering the southern part of East Prussia. There was no announcement of the damage resulting from the bombing.

Mist and clouds were overhanging the city. A light drizzle apparently afforded momentary protection against air raids. Warsaw went to work as usual.

Roosevelt Warns Navy

WASHINGTON, Friday, Sept. 1 (AP).—President Roosevelt directed today that all naval ships and army commands be notified at once by radio of German-Polish hostilities.

The White House issued the following announcement:

"The President received word at 2:50 A. M. Eastern standard time

Continued on Page Five

Soviet Ratifies Reich Non-Aggression Pact; Gibes at British and French Amuse Deputies

By G. E. R. GEDYE

Special Cable to THE NEW YORK TIMES.

MOSCOW, Aug. 31.—With Premier and Foreign Commissar Vyacheslaff M. Molotoff, working under high pressure—so suddenly applied without any previous indication and contrasting so sharply with earlier delaying tactics this week as to suggest German insistence that the matter be finally settled—the Supreme Soviet [Parliament] tonight unanimously ratified the Russo-German non-aggression pact.

Ratification, which was first foreshadowed at midday, was preceded by a speech by Mr. Molotoff so precise in its definition of Soviet obligations to refrain from participating on the side of Great Britain and France in any war against Germany, so voluble in its defense against charges of inconsistency against Communist Russia for embracing Fascist Germany, and so insistent on the inevitability of friendship between "not merely the governments but also the peoples" of Germany and Russia as to extinguish the last faint hopes of the western democracies that Moscow might yet find loopholes or excuses for joining them at some subsequent date in resisting German aggression against Poland.

Mr. Molotoff's speech contained nothing to justify constantly repeated suspicions of the existence of a secret German-Soviet pact entitling the latter to participate in a partition of Poland.

The Premier's speech contained much trenchant and seemingly irrefutable evidence of blunders by the British and French Governments in handling the question of Soviet cooperation. It was not diffi-

Continued on Page Eight

FREE CITY IS SEIZED

Forster Notifies Hitler of Order Putting Danzig Into the Reich

ACCEPTED BY CHANCELLOR

Poles Ready, Made Their Preparations After Hostilities Appeared Inevitable

Special Cable to THE NEW YORK TIMES.

DANZIG, Friday, Sept. 1.—By a decree issued early this morning Albert Forster, Nazi Chief of State, proclaimed the annexation of the Free City to the Reich, thus settling by a fell stroke the original point of contention in the international crisis.

In a telegram to Chancellor Hitler Herr Forster explained his action as necessary to remove "the pressing necessity of our people and State." Herr Forster also issued a proclamation to the people of Danzig saying the hour awaited for twenty years had arrived because "our Fuehrer, Adolf Hitler, has freed us."

[A NEW YORK TIMES dispatch from Berlin this morning said Herr Hitler telegraphed Herr Forster today thanking him and all Danzigers, and stating:

"The law for reannexation is in effect immediately."

The Chancellor stated, furthermore, that Herr Forster was appointed head of the civil administration of the Danzig area.]

In a four-article decree Herr Forster declared the Constitution of Danzig no longer valid. He declared himself sole administrator of the Danzig part of the German Reich, and he declared that until the Reich's legal system had been introduced by command of Herr Hitler all laws except the Constitution remained in effect. Then Herr Forster immediately wired Herr Hitler of his action, begged the Chancellor to give his approval of the move and through Reich law complete the annexation.

The German flag is now flying everywhere over Danzig, Herr Forster said, and all church bells resound to the event. "We thank God," he declared, "that He gave the Fuehrer the strength and the possibility to free also us from the evil Versailles treaty."

Hitler Accepts Danzig

By The Associated Press.

BERLIN, Friday, Sept. 1.—The German official news agency, D. N. B., announced today that Albert Forster, Nazi Chief of State in Danzig, had proclaimed the reunion of the Free City with the Reich.

Herr Hitler today accepted the Free City of Danzig into the Reich.

"I acknowledge your proclamation of the return of the Free City of Danzig to the Reich," Herr Hitler's telegram said. "I thank you, Gauleiter Forster, and all Danzig men and women, for your loyalty which you have displayed for so many years.

"Greater Germany welcomes you with joy in her heart.

"The law of reunion will be enacted forthwith. I appoint you, Herr Forster, chief of the civil administration in the Danzig territory."

Forster's telegram to Herr Hitler read:

My Fuehrer.

I have just signed and then put into effect the following basic law, concerning the reunion of Danzig with the German Reich.

The basic State law of the Free State of Danzig and the reunion of Danzig with the German Reich is effective Sept. 1, 1939.

To lift the immediate distress of the people and State of the Free City of Danzig, I decree the following basic State law:

ARTICLE I

The Constitution of the Free City of Danzig has been suspended effective immediately.

ARTICLE II

All legal and administrative power will be executed exclusively by the head of State.

ARTICLE III

The Free City of Danzig with its territory and its peoples forms

Continued on Page Five

Hitler Acts Against Poland

The port of Gdynia, north of Danzig (toward top of map), was blockaded this morning. At Gleiwitz (shown by cross) artillery fire was heard after a Polish-German skirmish had been reported there. Cracow, to the east, was among Polish cities said to have been bombed.

Hitler Tells the Reichstag 'Bomb Will Be Met by Bomb'

Chancellor Vows 'Fight Until Resolution' Against Poland—Gives Order of Succession As Goering, Hess, Then Senate to Choose

Chancellor Adolf Hitler of Germany, in a world broadcast this morning, opened "a fight until the resolution of the situation" against Poland, announcing that "from now on bomb will be met by bomb."

At the same time he announced, to face any eventuality, that if anything "happened" to him, Field Marshal Hermann Goering was to be in charge; if to Marshal Goering, Rudolph Hess; if to Herr Hess, the Senate, which he proposes to appoint, will select a successor.

The Chancellor, after attempting to narrow the conflict with Poland by assuring the Western powers that he had no designs on their frontiers, by assuring the neutrality of the sideline powers and by acknowledging the friendliness of Italy and the new relations with Russia, issued a defy to Poland's allies.

Says He Will Carry on

"I shall carry on this fight regardless of against whom I may come," he declared.

At the same time he held the door open for Poland to capitulate to his demands, declaring that he did not intend to make war against women and children. He said that if a solution did not come from the present Polish Government, it would come from a future Polish Government.

The Chancellor expressed confidence, toward the close of his address, that his decision, which was being broadcast over amplifiers hastily erected by electricians at the last moment in the streets of Berlin and the provincial capitals, would be accepted by the German people.

The scene enacted in the Kroll Opera House in Berlin was carried over sound waves to most of the nations of the world. From Berlin hook-ups had been arranged with the three major networks of the United States, and, according to the announcer for the German broadcasting system, over the Italian, Hungarian, Spanish, Norwegian, Swedish, Danish, Yugoslav, British and French national networks.

The summons to the Reichstag, ordered by Herr Hitler himself, had been sent out only a few hours before the meeting. Most of the members had been awaiting the signal, and when the opera house opened shortly before 10 o'clock [5 o'clock, New York time] this morning, they were dressed in the uniforms of their military formations.

After Herr Hitler finished speaking the deputies enacted a law incorporating Danzig into the Reich, declaring Danzig citizens were now Germans, voiding the Constitution of the Free City and extending to its territory the jurisdiction of German law.

At 5:10 A. M., Marshal Goering opened the meeting and turned the floor over to the Chancellor.

In the early part of his address, Herr Hitler electrified his audience with this declaration:

"We have all been suffering under the tortures that the Versailles treaty has been inflicting upon us."

Then, speaking with measured deliberateness of Germany's claims to the pre-war German areas, he announced, as he had on a previous occasion:

"The Treaty of Versailles is, for us Germans, and has been, for us Germans, not a law."

Anticipating what the announcement's reiteration would lead to, the Deputies roared applause. Then Herr Hitler, his indignation rising as he proceeded, set about building up the German case, asserting that his proposals for a peaceful solution of the problem of Danzig and the Polish Corridor had been rejected, and charging that the Poles had visited atrocities on Germans, especially women and children, "killing many of them."

SUMMARY OF SPEECH

A summary of Herr Hitler's speech was translated as follows:

"For months we have been suffering under the burdens of the Treaty of Versailles. Danzig was and is a German city. All these regions have only Germany to thank for their cultural development.

"Minorities in the Polish Corridor have been shamefully mistreated. Here, as in other respects, I have tried to solve the problems by peaceful means. In the fifteen years of National Socialism we have been

Continued on Page Three

HITLER GIVES WORD

In a Proclamation He Accuses Warsaw of Appeal to Arms

FOREIGNERS ARE WARNED

They Remain in Poland at Own Risk—Nazis to Shoot at Any Planes Flying Over Reich

By OTTO D. TOLISCHUS

Special Cable to THE NEW YORK TIMES.

BERLIN, Friday, Sept. 1.—Charging that Germany had been attacked, Chancellor Hitler at 5:11 o'clock this morning issued a proclamation to the army declaring that from now on force will be met with force and calling on the armed forces "to fulfill their duty to the end."

The text of the proclamation reads:

To the defense forces:

The Polish nation refused my efforts for a peaceful regulation of neighborly relations; instead it has appealed to weapons.

Germans in Poland are persecuted with a bloody terror and are driven from their homes. The series of border violations, which are unbearable to a great power, prove that the Poles no longer are willing to respect the German frontier. In order to put an end to this frantic activity no other means is left to me now than to meet force with force.

"Battle for Honor"

German defense forces will carry on the battle for the honor of the living rights of the reawakened German people with firm determination.

I expect every German soldier, in view of the great tradition of eternal German soldiery, to do his duty until the end.

Remember always in all situations you are the representatives of National Socialist Greater Germany!

Long live our people and our Reich!

Berlin, Sept. 1, 1939.

ADOLF HITLER.

The commander-in-chief of the air force issued a decree effective immediately prohibiting the passage of any airplanes over German territory excepting those of the Reich air force or the government.

This morning the naval authorities ordered all German mercantile ships in the Baltic Sea not to run to Danzig or Polish ports.

Anti-air raid defenses were mobilized throughout the country early this morning.

A formal declaration of war against Poland had not yet been declared up to 8 o'clock [3 A. M. New York time] this morning and the question of whether the two countries are in a state of active belligerency is still open.

Reichstag Will Meet Today

Foreign correspondents at an official conference at the Reich Press Ministry at 8:30 o'clock [3:30 A. M. New York time] were told that they would receive every opportunity to facilitate the transmission of dispatches. Wireless stations have been instructed to speed up communications and the Ministry is installing additional batteries of telephones.

The Reichstag has been summoned to meet at 10 o'clock [5 A. M. New York time] to receive a more formal declaration from Herr Hitler.

The Hitler army order is interpreted as providing, for the time being, armed defense of the German frontiers against aggression. The action is also suspected of forcing international diplomatic action.

The Germans announced that foreigners remain in Polish territory at their own risk.

Flying over Polish territory as well as the maritime areas is forbidden by the German authorities and any violators will be shot down.

When Herr Hitler made his an-

Continued on Page Three

Hitler announces the invasion of Poland during an impassioned speech to the Reichstag.

Polish officer cadets made a futile attempt to defend the Danzig corridor.

German troops readying for action in Poland.

"All the News That's Fit to Print."

The New York Times.

LATE CITY EDITION
POSTSCRIPT
Generally fair with little change in temperature today and tomorrow.
Temperatures Yesterday—Max., 79; Min., 63

VOL. LXXXVIII...No. 29,806. Entered as Second-Class Matter, Postoffice, New York, N. Y. NEW YORK, SATURDAY, SEPTEMBER 2, 1939. THREE CENTS NEW YORK CITY and Vicinity | FOUR CENTS Elsewhere Except in 7th and 8th Postal Zones.

BRITAIN AND FRANCE SEND ULTIMATUMS; WARSAW CALLS ALLIES; ITALY NEUTRAL; GERMANS ATTACK POLES ON 4 FRONTS

ROOSEVELT PLEDGE

He Promises Efforts to Keep U. S. Out of War—Thinks It Can Be Done

WILL ADDRESS NATION

Radio Talk Tomorrow to 'State Our Position'—Congress Call Hinted

By FELIX BELAIR Jr.
Special to THE NEW YORK TIMES.

WASHINGTON, Sept. 1.—President Roosevelt pledged the nation today to make every effort to keep this country out of war. He said he hoped and believed it could be done.

Then he made a final check-up on the machinery already set up for preserving American neutrality, as well as for swinging military, naval and industrial forces into action in event of any unexpected emergency.

The President's promise to do all in his power to keep the nation at peace was given as he gravely faced his regular Friday morning press conference. There was little he could say at this critical period in the world's history, he remarked, except to appeal to the newspaper men present for their full cooperation in adhering as closely as possible to the facts, since this was best not only for this nation but for civilization as a whole.

In this regard, the President set an example for his auditors. He said what he had to say without attempting to minimize or exaggerate the gravity of the European situation. He appeared to be neither exuberant nor depressed by the turn of events that kept him from his bed for all but a few hours last night. Occasionally he was humorous, but throughout his manner was calm.

Would "Allay Anxiety"

Later in the day the President let it be known that he would address the nation over the three major broadcasting networks on Sunday night from 10 to 10:15 o'clock, Eastern daylight time, in an effort "to allay anxiety and relieve suspense." Stephen T. Early, his secretary, who hurried back to Washington from a brief vacation today, said Mr. Roosevelt would speak on international affairs in a manner that would "clearly state our position" and would be of international interest.

The President began his memorable press conference with the explanation that there was little if anything he could say on such anticipated questions as when he would call a special session of Congress and issue a neutrality proclamation. These things, he explained, would have to await developments "over there" during the day, and possibly tomorrow, which would have a direct bearing on any American action.

But if any one had any questions that he was able to answer, Mr. Roosevelt said, he would answer gladly. A reporter observed that the question uppermost in every one's mind just now was: "Can we keep out of it?" The President cast his eyes downward for a moment as he pondered the request for comment. Then he replied:

"Only this—that I not only sincerely hope so, but I believe we can, and that every effort will be made by the Administration to so do."

The President consented readily when permission was asked to quote him directly on his statement.

Mentions Reich Only Once

Only once did Mr. Roosevelt mention Germany by name and then it was unavoidable. He had been asked concerning the nature of the visit to the White House earlier of Hugh R. Wilson, Ambassador to Germany, who returned to this country last February for "consultation and report" and who has remained here ever since.

The President seemed to appear grateful for the rejoinder. He said Mr. Wilson had presented his resignation as Ambassador to Germany and had been assigned to special duty in the State Department. The Ambassador had previously been assigned to special duty in the department, but neither the President nor Secretary of State Cordell Hull, who sat to one side and behind

Continued on Page Eight

The Developments in Europe

The war in Europe was still not a general war last night, but threatened to become so within a matter of hours. Great Britain, joined by France, gave Germany a final warning to cease her aggression on Poland and withdraw her armies. Prime Minister Chamberlain, who addressed the Commons after the Polish Ambassador had invoked the Anglo-Polish mutual aid treaty, obviously held virtually no hope of remaining out of the war, for he said, "Now it remains for us to set our teeth and enter upon this struggle * * * with determination to see it through." British mobilization was being completed. [Page 1; text of Mr. Chamberlain's speech, Page 5; text of the British White Paper containing correspondence with Germany, Page 9.]

France, strengthened by a general mobilization that makes available 8,000,000 trained men, was fully prepared to rush to the side of the Poles. Martial law was established throughout the country. [Page 1.]

Chancellor Hitler was fully expected to reject the ultimatums from London and Paris, and although he was said to be counting on a localized war, hopes of this were greatly weakened by Mr. Chamberlain's speech. The German people seemed to be awakening to the grim reality of the hostilities. [Page 6.]

Germany's ally, Italy, decided to remain neutral unless attacked. The communiqué announcing this decision made no mention of the Axis, nor was there any criticism of Poland. [Page 1.]

On the field of battle the Germans had crossed the Polish border on four fronts, and a principal manoeuvre seemed to be directed at cutting off Pomorze. German fliers, who, according to Berlin, held mastery of the air, unloaded bombs on more than a score of cities. [Page 1.] Warsaw reported early today that its troops were holding fast. The capital was raided four times by bombers in the first day's hostilities. [Page 1.] To the populace of Warsaw the start of strife came almost as a relief after the prolonged crisis. [Page 3.]

The United States will not be dragged into the European maelstrom if President Roosevelt can help it, he declared, adding that he believed he could. [Page 1.] Immediately on receiving news of the outbreak of fighting the President had made an appeal to five nations to abstain from bombing civilian populations. Britain, France and Poland promptly responded favorably. [Page 5.]

Bulletins on European Conflict

Moscow Relieves Ambassador at Berlin

MOSCOW, Sept. 2 (AP).—Soviet Russia has "relieved" her Ambassador to Germany, Alexei T. Merekaloff, of his duties, it was disclosed today.

A. A. Shkvartzeff was appointed to succeed him.

Mr. Merekaloff, who handled much of the important negotiations for the recently signed non-aggression pact between Russia and Germany, was relieved "in connection with his appointment to other work."

President Summons Polish Parliament

WARSAW, Poland, Saturday, Sept. 2 (AP).—President Ignaz Moscicki summoned the Polish Parliament into extraordinary session beginning today. It will enact emergency financial, economic and military measures to run the nation during the war.

Liner Columbus Sails for Germany

HAVANA, Saturday, Sept. 2 (AP).—The German liner Columbus sailed for Germany at 3 A. M. today with all lights out. Last night it landed 775 American tourists who had been making a West Indies cruise, canceling a New York call. The tourists are to sail for home on the P. & O. liner Florida, which was chartered especially for the trip by the North German Lloyd.

French Shipping News Censored

PARIS, Saturday, Sept. 2 (AP).—All shipping news in Paris newspapers was censored today. The papers were reduced to four pages to conserve newsprint.

Polish Air Threat Rumored in Berlin

Special Cable to THE NEW YORK TIMES.

BERLIN, Sept. 1.—There were rumors in Berlin tonight that this afternoon's supposed air raid drill was the real thing. Some sixty Polish bombers are said to have tried to break through the German air defenses in Silesia. One is rumored to have got through but to have been shot down later.

Food Prices Will Be Fixed in Britain

LONDON, Sept. 1 (AP) (Passed by Censor).—The London Provision Exchange announced tonight that by order of the Food Defense Committee prices of all food commodities would be fixed at "standstill" prices until further notice.

The British Press Association said it had learned authoritatively tonight that full plans were ready for the setting up of a war Cabinet, which might include such Opposition leaders as Arthur Greenwood of the Labor party and Sir Archibald Sinclair of the Liberal party, and possibly Winston Churchill, World War First Lord of the Admiralty, and Anthony Eden, former Foreign Secretary.

Danzig Made a Military Region

BERLIN, Sept. 1 (AP).—The commander of the German Army, Col. Gen. Walther von Brauchitsch, tonight declared the former Free City of Danzig to be a region of military operations.

The East Prussian Army was moving in to occupy the region and posters throughout the city informed citizens that Chancellor Hitler had "taken them under his protection."

Danzig's new administration, under Nazi District Leader Albert Forster, took possession of the areas and railways formerly operated by Poland and wharves in the harbor, railway and dock properties.

Germans Say Poles Are Burning Villages

BERLIN, Sept. 1 (AP).—The official German news agency, D. N. B., reported tonight that the glare of burning Polish villages, inhabited by Germans and set afire by Polish

Continued on Page Three

ROME TAKES STAND

Present Military Steps Are Held Adequate by Council of Ministers

AXIS NOT MENTIONED

Italians Receive News of Neutrality With Joy—Press Backs Reich

By HERBERT L. MATTHEWS
Special Cable to THE NEW YORK TIMES.

ROME, Saturday, Sept. 2 (Passed by Censor).—Italy will remain neutral unless attacked, it was decided by the Council of Ministers yesterday, which declared that the country's present military measures were "adequate." No military initiative will be taken nor will any step be made that is not "simply precautionary." Germany fights alone.

The independent character of this move is clearly shown by the fact that the communiqué announcing it contained no mention of the Axis nor of Chancellor Hitler's declaration to the Reichstag that he wanted no help. Herr Hitler repeated that statement in a cordial message addressed to Premier Mussolini thanking him for his political support and adding that there was no need now for Italy's military aid. The text of the letter was given out quite separately from the ministerial statement.

Council Issues Statement

The Council of Ministers met at Palazzo Viminale at 3 o'clock yesterday afternoon and after less than an hour announced its decision as follows:

The Council, having examined the situation brought about in Europe as a consequence of the German-Polish conflict, whose origin lies in the Versailles treaty, took note of all the documents presented by the Foreign Minister showing the work done by the Duce to assure to Europe a peace based on justice;

Gave its full approval to the military measures adopted to date which have and will remain purely precautionary in character and are adequate for that purpose;

Approved dispositions of an economic and social character made necessary by the grave disturbances into which European life has entered;

Declares and announces to the people that Italy will take no initiative whatever toward the military operations;

Paid the highest praise to the Italian people for the example of discipline and calm which it has always given.

It is especially worth noting that there is no criticism of Poland nor any polemics whatever except the reference to the Treaty of Versailles. Three days ago Signor Mussolini's newspaper the Popolo

Continued on Page Two

REICH IS CLOSING IN

Army Command Reports Success in Invasion and Control of Air

CITIES ARE BOMBED

Troops Enter From East Prussia, Pomerania, Slovakia, Silesia

By OTTO D. TOLISCHUS
Special Cable to THE NEW YORK TIMES.

BERLIN, Sept. 1.—In what is still officially characterized as a "German counter-attack with pursuit" and not a technical state of war, German troops estimated at close to 1,000,000 men began an invasion of Poland at 5:45 this morning. After severe fighting they stood deep in Polish territory tonight, while the German air fleet claimed to rule the air over Poland.

The invasion, according to communiqués of the supreme command of the armed forces, took place in a concentric movement over all the German-Polish and Slovak-Polish borders—that is, from the west, north, south and east.

The air fleet immediately raided the flying fields of numerous Polish towns, bombarding military establishments and other important works. A warship of the German Navy bombarded the Polish Westerplatte munition depot in Danzig Harbor.

A communiqué details the first day's fighting, in which German troops are understood to have attained all objectives of the first day, as follows:

"In the course of the German combat action from Silesia, Pomerania and East Prussia, the expected initial successes were attained today on all fronts.

Into Industrial District

"Troops advancing across the mountains from the south have reached the line of Neumarkt [Nowy Targ] and Sucha. South of Maehrisch-Ostrau, troops crossed the Olsa at Teschen. South of the industrial territory our troops are advancing in a line on Kattowitz [Katowice] according to plan. Troops from Silesia are in a fluid advance in the direction of Tschenstochau [Czestochowa] and north of it.

[If the German claim that one of their armies has reached the line Sucha-Neumarkt is true, remarkable progress over some of the most difficult terrain along the German-Polish border has been made. The advance claimed would place their forces along the valley of the Skava River—which farther north flows into the Vistula—and would put the Reich forces less than fifty kilometers from Cracow, strategic rail junction in the southwest of Poland. Such an advance northward from Slovakia could come

Continued on Page Six

'War Industries' Buoy the Markets Here; Stocks and Commodities Up, Bonds Slump

The nation's security and commodity markets heralded yesterday the opening of hostilities in Europe with considerable gains in the "war industry" stocks and staples, declines in bond values and mixed trends in foreign exchange. Sterling and French francs fell sharply and quotations for neutral currencies rose.

Price changes were acute in many instances, with aircraft, mining and steel shares soaring 2 to 7 points for the day. The bond market suffered its worst break in nearly two years, with foreign issues 2 to 10 points lower and domestic bonds down as much as 8 points, while United States Government issues fell fractions to 1¼ points in active trading.

Despite the sharp changes in values in virtually all the markets, the volume of trading was impressive only in contrast to the slow pace of recent years, and business was conducted in a wholly orderly fashion, under the watchful eyes of the heads of the Exchanges and the SEC.

Old-timers, "the boys who knew nothing in 1914 and learned plenty," as one broker put it, ran the markets of the country yesterday. Before the opening of the various Exchanges they were stacking up their orders to buy cocoa, rubber, wheat, corn and hides. When all "war baby" commodities, with the exception of copper and hides, jumped to their limits and left orders for millions of bushels, pounds and tons unexecuted, they switched to the stocks of companies with large inventories.

Commission houses reported scattered and contradictory interest in stocks as the market opened, but their spindles were piled high with commodity orders. Few were executed. Cocoa jumped its permissible limit of 100 points, rubber its 200, hides 150 of their 200, wheat its 5 cents for futures, 8 cents for September; corn its 4 and 8 cents.

Meanwhile the stock market was showing weakness. But investors considered the evidence. Commodities apparently considered a war bullish. So the traders looked at standard copper and found it up 73 points. They bought copper stocks. With hides up 100, they bought United States Leather A and similar issues. Advances in prices of

Continued on Page Eight

Text of Ultimatum to Reich

By The Associated Press.

LONDON, Sept. 1.—Following is the text of the ultimatum handed to the German Government today by the Ambassadors of Britain and France:

Early this morning the German Chancellor issued a proclamation to the German Army which indicated clearly that he was about to attack Poland. Information which has reached His Majesty's Government in the United Kingdom and the French Government indicates that German troops have crossed the Polish frontier and that attacks on Polish towns are proceeding.

In these circumstances it appears to the Governments of the United Kingdom and France that by their action the German Government have created conditions—namely, an aggressive act of force against Poland threatening the independence of Poland—which call for the immediate implementation by the Governments of the United Kingdom and France of the undertaking to Poland to come to her assistance.

I am, accordingly, to inform Your Excellency that unless the German Government are prepared to give His Majesty's Government an assurance that the German Government have suspended all aggressive action against Poland and are prepared promptly to withdraw their forces from Polish territory, His Majesty's Government in the United Kingdom will, without hesitation, fulfill their obligations to Poland.

POLES HOLD FAST, WARSAW REPORTS

Communique Tells of All-Night Fighting and Heavy Toll—Capital Bombed 4 Times

By The Associated Press.

WARSAW, Poland, Saturday, Sept. 2.—Official reports said today that Polish forces were resisting the German invasion on three fronts and were holding fast.

A General Staff communiqué said heavy fighting had raged through the night in the border area, but there were no late reports giving details of land engagements.

The first heavy impact of the undeclared war had come from German planes that bombed more than a score of cities, including Warsaw, in advance of the invading German armies.

A government communiqué admitted "many civilians were killed and wounded" on the first day of hostilities. It was said officially, however, that the air raids had inflicted only slight damage to vital services.

Throughout Poland today's dawn was awaited fearfully, with all cities darkened.

In addition to raids on Warsaw yesterday, a communiqué said, Nazi planes also bombed the following cities: Kutno, Lwow, Cracow, Gdynia, Katowice, Augustow, Brodbica, Tczew, Radomsko, Torun, Tunel, Krosbo, Trzebiba, Jslo, Tomaszew, Misk-Mazowiecki, Grodno, Biale-Podlaska, Radom, Modlin, Pultusk, Kobryn, Pluock and Otwock.

Many Duds Reported

A German plane, the communiqué said, "fired the first shot in the war" by bombing Puck yesterday at 5:20 A. M. An air-defense communiqué said many of the German bombs in the first day's fighting had been duds and failed to explode.

The "most violent fighting," a General Staff communiqué declared, was in Silesia, one of the three main sectors of the German drive.

The main German columns were said to be pointed from East Prussia against Dzialdowo and Mlawa; from Pomerania against Chojnice at the narrowest point of Pomorze (the so-called Polish Corridor), and from Breslau against Katowice.

Marshal Edward Smigly-Rydz, who was made Commander in Chief of all Poland's armed forces yesterday and designated as successor to President Ignaz Moscicki should the Presidency become vacant during the war, broadcast a message of encouragement to Polish soldiers defending the Westerplatte, a munitions base opposite Danzig.

A company of Poles reported it was holding the Westerplatte, despite three German attacks and bombardment by the German naval training ship Schleswig-Holstein. [A German communiqué reported capture of the Westerplatte.]

Gdynia, Polish port near Danzig, was reported being kept under heavy bombardment.

Official reports on air-raid tolls were confined to the terse statement that civilian casualties had

Continued on Page Three

FRANCE MOBILIZES; 8,000,000 ON CALL

Martial Law Declared Over Entire Country—Daladier Meets Deputies Today

By P. J. PHILIP
Wireless to THE NEW YORK TIMES.

PARIS, Saturday, Sept. 2 (Passed by Censor).—France's reply to Germany's violation of Poland was to decree general mobilization for this morning, establish martial law throughout the country and convoke Parliament for 3 P. M. today so as legally to carry out whatever must be done.

These decrees were approved at a Cabinet council held during yesterday morning without midnight secrecy or undue haste.

[Eventually, with general mobilization completed, the French land army could be raised to 8,000,000 well-trained, well-equipped men, says the Associated Press. Their places in the giant military machine have been determined long since.]

Ultimatum Ordered

In the evening the government gave instructions to Ambassador Robert Coulondre in Berlin to hand to the Wilhelmstrasse an ultimatum in terms analagous to and in the same sense as the British note which, Prime Minister Chamberlain announced during the afternoon, had been handed in by the British Ambassador.

Only cessation of hostilities in Poland at this time could enable an international conference such as has been suggested to be set up, and hope of such a happening is frail.

There was much speculation tonight as to whether Premier Daladier will alter and enlarge his Cabinet, but the Premier has taken no one into his confidence. It is not possible now to predict that any "Sacred Union" Cabinet will be formed as was done in 1914.

Relied Upon by Poles

From the Polish Ambassador, Julius Lukasiewicz, Foreign Minister Georges Bonnet learned officially that fire had been opened by German troops along the Polish frontier at 5:45 o'clock yesterday morning, that airplanes had attacked several centers and that Poland, feeling her independence endangered, placed her reliance on France to fulfill her engagements.

This information and request confirmed news that had been pouring out from the German radio since before 8 A. M. when Albert Forster, Danzig's chief of state, handed over the Free City to Germany, an event followed by the Reichstag meeting and Chancellor Hitler's speech.

Formalities Observed

Even as early as that there could be no doubt about the French retort, but formalities must be satisfied in a democratic country, which is not ruled by any personal pronoun. So diplomatic activity continued all during the day and Parliament must have its say simultaneously with the preparations being made by the military command.

General Marie Gustave Gamelin, supreme commander of French de-

Continued on Page Two

LONDON THREATENS

Sends Final Demand to Germany to Cease Her Attack on Poland

WAR FUND IS VOTED

Chamberlain Pins Guilt on Hitler—Railways Are Taken Over

By FREDERICK T. BIRCHALL
Special Cable to THE NEW YORK TIMES.

LONDON, Saturday, Sept. 2 (Passed by Censor).—Twenty-one years after the close of the last war, Europe is again at the beginning of a new one, a war that threatens to be longer and far deadlier than that which began in 1914. For the moment only Germany and Poland are engaged. Last midnight France and Great Britain had not yet intervened by force of arms as their engagements to Poland pledge them to do.

The German Embassy staff is still in London and there is no word that Sir Nevile Henderson, the British Ambassador, has left Berlin. The Italian Council of Ministers, meeting in Rome, announced to the Italian people that their country would not take the initiative in military operations. No intimation as to Russia's course has come from Moscow.

But all this is merely illusory, a brief breathing space before the conflict becomes widespread.

On Threshold of War

Within a day or two, perhaps before twenty-four hours have elapsed, British and French troops will be fighting the Germans. It is a matter only of a short time before a great part of Europe will be involved. Today the two principal allied powers of the last war are on the threshold of war. They merely have not yet crossed it, but they cannot halt.

In the House of Commons yesterday afternoon Prime Minister Chamberlain announced that instructions have been sent to Sir Nevile Henderson to inform the German Government that unless it was prepared to give satisfactory assurances that it would suspend all aggressive action against Poland and was prepared to withdraw its forces from Polish territory, the British obligations to Poland would immediately be fulfilled. If the reply was unfavorable, the Ambassador was to ask for his passport.

[Poland invoked the British-Polish mutual assistance pact, The Associated Press explained, when the Polish Ambassador, Count Edward Raczynski, delivered his country's appeal in a call on Viscount Halifax, British Foreign Secretary.]

As may have done so, for a late message from Berlin, received here by a roundabout route, said Sir Nevile tonight had seen Foreign Minister Joachim von Ribbentrop, who would answer him after communicating with Chancellor Hitler.

[A similar ultimatum—Mr. Chamberlain's speech in the House of Commons yesterday indicated that it was identical—was also dispatched by the French Government.]

Waiting for French

Sir Nevile's departure from Berlin will mean that Great Britain and Germany are at war. All hope of a German backdown has vanished here. If the Ambassador has not left the delay means only that the British are waiting for the French.

From the outset the two governments have acted together, but at the last moment it was found that the French Chamber of Deputies cannot meet before today. It was duly summoned, but railroads and highways alike in France are congested with military traffic, set in motion by the mobilization order, and many Deputies from distant constituencies could not, in consequence, reach Paris until today.

In the meantime the British took further steps of their own when the Commons voted war credits after hearing Mr. Chamberlain's speech and the Transport Ministry took over the railroads.

There is here all the atmosphere of war save only its casualties. Street lamps are all extinguished.

Continued on Page Five

CHAMBERLAIN ANNOUNCES BRITAIN IS AT WAR WITH GERMANY

"All the News That's Fit to Print."

The New York Times.

EXTRA

Generally fair, little change in temperature today. Tomorrow cloudy, showers in afternoon or night.
Temperatures Yesterday—Max., 80; Min., 64

Section 1

NEWS INDEX, PAGE 21, THIS SECTION

Copyright, 1939, by The New York Times Company.

VOL. LXXXVIII....No. 29,807 | Entered as Second-Class Matter, Postoffice, New York, N. Y. | NEW YORK, SUNDAY, SEPTEMBER 3, 1939. | P | Including Rotogravure Picture, Magazine and Book Review. | TEN CENTS | TWELVE CENTS Beyond 200 Miles Except in 7th and 8th Postal Zones.

BRITAIN AND FRANCE IN WAR AT 6 A. M.; HITLER WON'T HALT ATTACK ON POLES; CHAMBERLAIN CALLS EMPIRE TO FIGHT

SOVIET IN WARNING

British-French Action to Bring Western Border Revision, Berlin Hears

NAZIS GREET MISSION

Hitler to Receive New Russian Ambassador and General Today

By OTTO D. TOLISCHUS

Wireless to THE NEW YORK TIMES.

BERLIN, Sunday, Sept. 3.—According to well-informed quarters here Moscow is already supposed to have notified Paris and London that if France and Britain join in the present Reich-Polish conflict Russia will find herself compelled to revise her Western borders.

This is tantamount to the threat that any British and French help to Poland will merely hasten the partition of Poland between Germany and Russia. There are hints that Russia might also seek other "compensation" in regions even less convenient to Britain.

As an impressive demonstration of this new cooperation there arrived today by air from Stockholm a new Russian Ambassador and a new embassy secretary, both of whom were said to be very close to Premier Vyacheslaff Molotoff, and a Russian military mission headed by a commanding general.

Officials Greet the Mission

The new Ambassador is Alexander Shkhartzeff, who, it is pointed out here, collaborated with Mr. Molotoff in the Commissariat of Foreign Affairs in Moscow. The new embassy secretary is Vladimir Perloff, up to now Mr. Molotoff's secretary and interpreter.

The military mission consists of General Maxim Purjakoff, designated as the Military Plenipotentiary of the U. S. S. R., and his staff; Brig. Gen. Michael Beljakoff, Colonel Nikolai Skornjakoff, Major Basanoff and Captain Alexander Seditch.

To show the importance of the occasion the members were met at Tempelhof Airfield by Dr. Ernst Woermann, Under-Secretary of State in the Foreign Office; Baron Alexander von Doernberg, Chief of Protocol, and other Foreign Office officials. Lieut. Gen. Seifert, commander of Berlin, headed the list of army officers greeting the Russians. A guard of honor presented arms.

The Russians received an ovation as their automobiles, flying the hammer-and-sickle flag of the Soviet Union, passed the Reich Chancellery. Those assembled along the street gave the Nazi salute.

Hitler to Receive Envoy

Adding importance to all this is the fact that it was announced at midnight that Herr Hitler would receive the new Ambassador, together with the Military Plenipotentiary, for the submission of credentials later today, which sets a precedent for diplomatic speed.

That such a formidable military mission was sent here to work out close collaboration with the German Army is taken for granted now. But German quarters still hold that the consultative clauses of the German-Russian pact are sufficient to cover all the collaboration necessary and a formal military alliance may be signed only as the last trump card to impress London and Paris.

Ambassador Joseph Lipski and his whole embassy staff left Berlin this morning under safe conduct en route to Sweden, which has also taken over the representation of Polish interests. The German Embassy staff was supposed to have left Warsaw at the same time. German interests in Poland are being represented by the Netherlands. Official quarters hold, however, that this merely represents a "cessation of direct diplomatic relations," not a formal break of relations, just as there is no declared state of war.

Meanwhile, since the German-Polish conflict is now being arbitrated by the roar of cannon the re-

Continued on Page Sixteen

Announcement of Final Ultimatum

By The Associated Press.

LONDON, Sunday, Sept. 3.—Following is the text of today's communique revealing the final ultimatum to Germany:

On Sept. 2 His Majesty's Ambassador in Berlin was instructed to inform the German Government that unless they were prepared to give His Majesty's Government in the United Kingdom satisfactory assurances that the German Government had suspended all aggressive action against Poland and were prepared promptly to withdraw their forces from Polish territory, His Majesty's Government in the United Kingdom would without hesitation fulfill their obligations to Poland.

At 9 A. M. this morning His Majesty's Ambassador in Berlin informed the German Government that unless not later than 11 A. M., British Summer time, today, Sept. 3, satisfactory assurances to the above effect had been given by the German Government and had reached His Majesty's Government in London a state of war would exist between the two countries as from that hour.

His Majesty's Government are now awaiting the receipt of any reply that may be made by the German Government.

The Prime Minister will broadcast to the nation at 11:15 A. M.

21 CIVILIANS KILLED IN RAID ON WARSAW

Women, Children Die as Bomb Hits Workers' Apartment—State of War Decreed

By The Associated Press.

WARSAW, Poland, Sept. 2.—Twenty-one dead and more than thirty wounded were counted tonight after German bombs had struck an apartment house in a Warsaw workingmen's quarter.

The bombs tore off the side of the apartment house as if it had been made of paper. Rescue workers still were clearing away the resultant pile of debris in a search for further casualties when this correspondent inspected it.

One of the bombs had dug a crater fully twenty feet in diameter, and the open ground was piled high with furniture and belongings.

In the center of a large park in the southern section of Warsaw, this writer also saw where a bomb had struck a simple wooden dwelling, killing two persons and wounding one. In an open field near the Vistula River, where ten light bombs apparently had been released simultaneously, they had dug craters in a 100-yard circle.

With the writer on this tour of inspection of damage done by the German air bombings were C. Burke Elbrick, secretary of the American Embassy; Clifford Norton, chargé d'affaires of the British Embassy, and officials of the Polish Foreign Office.

During the tour the party twice was forced to take refuge because of air-raid alarms, five of which in all sounded through the city today. Once the party took cover in a shallow dugout filled with working men, their wives and their crying children.

The worst scene of damage was at Kolo, the workingmen's quarter, where, in addition to wrecking one apartment building, the bombs had smashed windows in several others.

An old man gulped back tears as he said his wife and two children were dead. A woman, still staring blankly into space, said:

"My husband is gone."

An official news service communiqué stated that yesterday German raiders dropped 120 bombs on Warsaw and its vicinity, killing ten and wounding twenty-five in Warsaw proper, with the number of casualties in the suburbs still undetermined.

President Ignaz Moscicki declared that Poland was under a "state of war" today as official reports said that Polish forces were resisting German invasion on three fronts.

The "state of war" supersedes the

Continued on Page Fourteen

News dispatches from Europe are now virtually all subject to censorship

PARIS AUTHORIZED WAR DECLARATION

Chamber Voted Credits After Hearing Daladier—New Ultimatum Being Drawn

By The Associated Press.

PARIS, Sept. 2.—Premier Edouard Daladier today received implied authority from the Chamber of Deputies to declare war on Germany.

With that to support them, he and his Cabinet met at the War Ministry at 7:30 tonight to frame a demand that Chancellor Hitler reply to the British-French "last warning" of yesterday.

The power to declare war was vested in a war budget bill of 69,000,000,000 francs, which the sober Deputies, many wearing army uniforms, adopted unanimously by a show of hands after hearing M. Daladier say the government was still willing to negotiate if Germany would cease hostilities in Poland.

Whether the Premier uses the authority vested in him by adoption of the budget depends upon the possibility—frankly viewed as slight—that Herr Hitler would avail himself of a last-minute loophole for peace.

The Premier told the finance committee after the Chamber session that he planned to call the Chamber to approve an actual declaration of war if that became necessary, but he may simply ask for approval after, rather than before, the action is taken.

"The government will take the same chance as Parisians," M. Daladier told a Deputy who asked whether the government planned to leave Paris immediately.

The session was held in a tense atmosphere from 3 to 3:55 P. M.

Continued on Page Seventeen

ROME ASKED PEACE

Pressed Its Proposal for a 5-Power Parley on Britain and France

WAR MEASURES CUT

Press Expressed the Hope Germany Would Win in Poland

By The Associated Press.

ROME, Sept. 2.—Premier Mussolini tonight sought to prevent Polish-German hostilities from spreading into a general European war by arranging a negotiated settlement.

Conferences that the British and French Ambassadors had with Foreign Minister Count Ciano were believed to be connected directly with an Italian proposal of a five-power conference disclosed in London by Prime Minister Neville Chamberlain and Foreign Secretary Viscount Halifax.

The possibility of halting the German-Polish conflict and arranging a peaceable settlement was believed to have been discussed at the diplomatic conferences, but no official information was forthcoming.

Some foreign observers believed, however, that Signor Mussolini had been asked to use his influence on Adolf Hitler to halt fighting in Poland, call his army back and negotiate a settlement of his demands on the Poles.

For Wide Settlement

Here it was regarded as certain that any five-power conference proposed by Premier Mussolini would not be merely for settling the German-Polish conflict but would be aimed at complete revision of the Treaty of Versailles.

Under such a revision Italy and Germany would seek the political and economic concessions that they consider necessary to end European tension once and for all. This has long been Signor Mussolini's idea and Italian newspapers recently have been stressing it as the only real solution. [Italy has been demanding from France concessions concerning Tunisia, the Suez Canal and Jibuti, French Somaliland port.]

While the Ambassadors of France and Britain conferred with Foreign Minister Ciano Italy continued her policy of watchful waiting and avoidance of any military "initiative".

The important commentator, Virginio Gayda, in the Giornale d'Italia noted uneasily that French and British war preparations made it seem that only a miracle could prevent a "more general explosion." Italy, he said, rested on her arms, confident she had done everything possible to avoid war. He said she was following events

Continued on Page Fifteen

Fuller Breaks Own Bendix Race Records; Crosses Continent in 8 Hours 58 Minutes

Frank Fuller, San Francisco sportsman pilot, broke his own record in the Bendix Trophy Race from Burbank, Calif., to Cleveland yesterday and then kept on to Bendix, N. J., to break his own record for a transcontinental crossing in the event, opening feature of the National Air Races and the country's outstanding air derby.

Flying a stripped-down Seversky military plane equipped with the same twin Wasp engine he had in the 1937 race, when his earlier records were set, Fuller flew the 2,450 miles from Burbank to Bendix in an elapsed time of 8 hours 58 minutes 8.46 seconds. His average speed was 273.14 miles an hour. His elapsed time in 1937 was 9 hours 25 minutes.

The record for a transcontinental flight is 7 hours 28 minutes, established by Howard Hughes in a specially built plane about two years ago.

In crossing the finishing line at Bendix, Fuller, a wealthy paint manufacturer, won three prizes totaling $12,500. For being the first to reach Cleveland he received a prize of $9,000. As the first to fly over the line at Bendix he won another $1,000, and for breaking his 1937 record he won $2,500.

Fuller reached Bendix at 4:24:53 P. M., Eastern daylight time, and proceeded, without landing, to Floyd Bennett Field, where he brought his plane to earth at 4:35 P. M.

Max Constant of Burbank was the second racer to fly over Bendix, reaching there at 6:13:39 P. M. Arthur C. Bussy of Royersford, Pa., appeared at 7:08:15 P. M.

Although Constant arrived at Bendix ahead of Bussy, he took off from Burbank before him and Bussy was declared the second prize winner and received $5,000 for the flight to Cleveland and an additional $800 for continuing to Bendix and Floyd Bennett Field.

Mrs. Arline Davis of Cleveland landed at Newark Airport at 8 P. M., believing that she had crossed the official marker at Bendix and thereby won the $2,500 prize for the first woman to finish

Continued on Page Three

NAZIS REPORT GAINS

Hitler's Aims in Corridor Already Won, They Say, Telling of Big 'Trap'

RESISTANCE IS NOTED

But Armies Drive On and Navy Is in Command of Baltic, Germans Hold

Special Cable to THE NEW YORK TIMES.

BERLIN, Sunday, Sept. 3.—Defying the British and French ultimatums, the German armies reported continued advances into Poland yesterday.

By nightfall, it was asserted, not only had they attained the German war aims in the Polish Corridor as outlined in Chancellor Hitler's "sixteen points" but they were pushing forward in a concentric drive toward Warsaw. According to one report, the German forces stood less than fifty miles north of the Polish capital, and a big battle was believed developing along the Narew River.

According to the latest communiqués of the army command, which apparently have already been overtaken by developments, the German armies operating out of East Prussia and Pomerania had virtually cut the Corridor along the Netze and Vistula Rivers, so that all Polish troops remaining in the bottleneck north of it were hopelessly trapped.

Claim Capture of Teschen

In the South the Germans were reported to have taken the heavily fortified Jablunka Pass, the main strategic highway from Slovakia into Poland; to have captured Teschen and Pless [Pszczyna] and to be breaking through the Polish bunker line approaching Biala. This army group apparently has the task of capturing the Upper Silesian industrial section and the Teschen coal mines, taken by Poland from Czecho-Slovakia, and then of advancing along the Vistula toward Sandomierz, the new Polish armament and industrial center.

At the same time two other German Army groups, operating from the north out of East Prussia and from the southwest out of Silesia, apparently were conducting a pincers movement on Warsaw. The southwestern group was declared to have taken Wielun and to be advancing toward Radomsk and Sieradz.

The Northern army group, according to a communiqué, was advancing on Przasnysz, but, according to private reports, is already beyond that town and approaching a larger Polish army that is supposed to have taken a stand on the Narew, where the first real battle of the undeclared war may take place.

Reich Claims "Air" Domination

The communiqué asserted also that the German air force, after many bombing expeditions against air fields, railroads, military transports, retreating marching columns and other military objectives, in which many planes and the munition factory at Skarzysko-Kamienna were destroyed, now has "unchallenged air domination over the entire Polish territory and so is now free for other tasks in protection of the Reich."

In addition, the Germany Navy, which said it had bombed the fortifications and port of Hela and also Gdynia, reported the sinking of a Polish torpedo boat off Hela. It was said to command the Baltic so completely that the fishing embargo was lifted last night.

A communiqué issued by the high command early today, according to the official German News Bureau, declared:

"The German air force yesterday again proved its absolute superiority. The whole air area over the battle zone and the hinterland is completely controlled by the German air force. Attacks were confined exclusively to military objectives.

"After units of German armored cars had reached the Vistula, approximately at noon, the German

Continued on Page Twelve

Text of Chamberlain Address

The following is the text of the address by Prime Minister Chamberlain from 10 Downing Street this morning:

I am speaking to you from the Cabinet Room from 10 Downing Street. This morning the British Ambassador in Berlin handed the German Government the final note stating unless we heard from them by 11 o'clock [6 o'clock New York time] that they were prepared at once to withdraw their troops from Poland a state of war would exist between us. I have to tell you now that no such undertaking has been received and consequently this country is at war with Germany.

You can imagine what a bitter blow it is to me that all my long struggle to win peace has failed. Up to the very last it should have been quite possible to arrange a peaceful settlement between Germany and Poland.

Hitler has evidently made up his mind to attack Poland whatever may happen. Hitler claims that his proposals were shown to Poland and to us. That is not a true statement. The proposals never were shown to the Poles or to us.

The German Government prepared the proposals in German and the same night the German troops crossed the Polish frontier. Germany will never give up force and can only be stopped by force.

We are prepared to uphold our treaty with Poland and to protect them from the wicked and unprovoked attacks on the Polish people. France is joining Britain in fulfillment of her pledges. We have a clear conscience and the situation has become intolerable. Now that we have determined to finish it I know that you will all play your part.

When I have finished speaking several detailed announcements will be made on behalf of the government giving you plans under which it will be possible to carry on the work of the nation in these days of stress which may be ahead, but these plans need your help. You may be taking part in one of the fighting services or one of the other branches.

It is of vital importance that you carry on with your jobs. May God bless you all and may He defend the right for it is the evil things we shall be fighting against—brute force, broken promises, bad faith. But I am certain that right shall prevail.

Bulletins on European Conflict

Air Raid Warning in London

LONDON, Sept. 3 (Sunday).—Air raid sirens sounded an alarm in London today at 11:32 A. M. (5:32 A. M., E.S.T.).

The whole city was sent to shelters by the wail of the alarm but all clear signals were sounded seventeen minutes later.

Ribbentrop Gives Reply to British Envoy

BERLIN, Sunday, Sept. 3 (AP).—German Foreign Minister Joachim von Ribbentrop received British Ambassador Sir Nevile Henderson at 9 A. M. [4 A. M. in New York] today to hand him Germany's answer to the "final warnings" of Britain and France. Herr von Ribbentrop was expected to see the French Ambassador, Robert Coulondre, shortly before noon.

American Diplomats' Families Leave Reich

BERLIN, Sunday, Sept. 3 (AP).—About fifty women and children of the United States Embassy and consular staffs, as well as several other American families, left Berlin today at 8:50 A. M. [3:50 A. M. in New York] for Copenhagen in compartments reserved for them in a regular train.

They were due in Copenhagen at 5:35 P. M. [12:35 A. M. in New York].

War Announced in France

PARIS, Sunday, Sept. 3 (AP).—The radio announced to the French nation today that British Prime Minister Chamberlain had proclaimed Great Britain at war with Germany.

"No News" at the German Embassy

LONDON, Sunday, Sept. 3 (AP).—At the German Embassy in London at 9:30 A. M. today [5:30 A. M., New York], a half hour before the expiration of the British ultimatum, it was said, "There is no news." A spokesman said, "We are in constant communication with Berlin."

Denies Poles Got Five-Power Parley Offer

LONDON, Sunday, Sept. 3 (AP).—Exchange Telegraph Agency, British news agency, said today that Count Edward Raczynski, Polish Ambassador in London, informed it that "the Italian Government did not approach Poland" concerning a reported five-power conference to settle German-Polish issues.

"Apart from the declarations made yesterday in the British Parliament and apart from contradictory reports in the press," the agency quoted him, "the Polish Government has not knowledge of such a scheme."

Exchange Telegraph said the Ambassador declared that "any talk of such a conference" would be "ludicrous and fantastic" as long as "a single enemy soldier stands on Polish soil."

1,000 Americans Sail on French Liner

PARIS, Sunday, Sept. 3 (AP).—The French Line said today that the Ile de France had sailed from Havre with more than 1,000 Americans on board, bound for home.

Heavy Fighting Is Reported in Silesia

WARSAW, Sept. 2 (AP).—Although official information was lacking, it was reported tonight that severe fighting be-

Continued on Page Twelve

TO END OPPRESSION

Premier Calls It 'Bitter Blow' That Efforts for Peace Have Failed

WARNING UNHEEDED

Demand on Reich to Withdraw Army From Poland Ignored

Prime Minister Neville Chamberlain announced to the world at 6:10 o'clock this morning that Great Britain and France were at war with Germany. He made the announcement over the radio, with short waves carrying the measured tones of his voice throughout all continents, from 10 Downing Street in London.

Mr. Chamberlain disclosed that Great Britain and France had taken concurrent action, announcing that "we and France are, today, in fulfillment of our obligations, going to the aid of Poland."

France, however, had not made any announcement beyond stating that the French Ambassador to Berlin would make a final call upon Foreign Minister Joachim von Ribbentrop at 6 o'clock this morning, and it was assumed the French had proclaimed the existence of the state of war.

Speaks With Solemnity

With the greatest solemnity Mr. Chamberlain began his declaration by reporting that the British Ambassador to Berlin had handed in Great Britain's final ultimatum and that it had not been accepted. Without hesitation he announced Britain's decision and, after touching briefly on the background of the crisis, he expressed the highest confidence that "injustice, oppression and persecution" would be vanquished and that his cause would triumph.

Mr. Chamberlain appealed to his people, schooled during the last year as the crisis deepened in measures of defense and offense, to carry on with their jobs and begged a blessing upon them, warning that "we shall be fighting against brute force."

The declaration came after Great Britain had given Chancellor Adolf Hitler of Germany extended time in which to answer the British Government's final ultimatum of Friday. In the final ultimatum Herr Hitler had been told that unless German aggression in Poland ceased, Britain was prepared to fulfill her obligations to Poland.

Warning Was Sharp

Britain's last warning at 4 o'clock this morning, New York time, left no doubt of her stand, for the phrase, "fulfillment of Britain's obligations to Poland," was replaced by a flat statement that a state of war would exist between the two countries as of the hour of the deadline.

After Mr. Chamberlain had finished his statement, which had been introduced as "an announcement of national importance," the announcer warned the British people not to gather together, broadcast an order that all meeting places for entertainment be closed, and gave precautions to prepare the people against air bombings and poison gas attacks.

Mr. Chamberlain began his

Continued on Page Fifteen

"All the News That's Fit to Print."

The New York Times.

Copyright, 1939, by The New York Times Company.

LATE CITY EDITION
POSTSCRIPT
Generally fair with showers tonight, continued warm.
Temperatures Yesterday—Max., 79; Min., 64

VOL. LXXXVIII...No. 29,808. Entered as Second-Class Matter, Postoffice, New York, N. Y. NEW YORK, MONDAY, SEPTEMBER 4, 1939. P THREE CENTS NEW YORK CITY and Vicinity | FOUR CENTS Elsewhere Except in 7th and 8th Postal Zones.

BRITISH LINER ATHENIA TORPEDOED, SUNK; 1,400 PASSENGERS ABOARD, 292 AMERICANS; ALL EXCEPT A FEW ARE REPORTED SAVED

ROOSEVELT IN PLEA

President, on Air, Asks the Nation to Observe True Neutrality

CALLS ALL TO UNITY

Draws Ring Around Americas—'Even a Neutral' May Judge, He Says

By TURNER CATLEDGE
Special to THE NEW YORK TIMES.

WASHINGTON, Sept. 3.—In an extraordinary message broadcast by radio to "the whole of America," President Roosevelt tonight called for an adjournment of all partisanship and selfishness and substitution of complete national unity in the United States to the end that the newest world war may be kept from the Western Hemisphere.

He declared that, as long as it remained within his power to prevent, "there will be no blackout of peace in the United States."

Linking the present European conflagration to the "invasion of Poland by Germany," the President announced that a proclamation of American neutrality was being prepared for issuance under the present Neutrality Act.

"I trust that in the days to come our neutrality can be made a true neutrality," he added.

Would Seek a "Final Peace"

But it seemed clear to him, he said, "even at the outbreak of this great war," that the influence of America should be consistent "in seeking for humanity a final peace which will eliminate, as far as it is possible to do so, the continued use of force between nations."

In his flat declaration that "this nation will remain a neutral nation," the President said he could not ask that every American remain neutral in thought as well. "Even a neutral has a right to take account of facts," he said. "Even a neutral cannot be asked to close his mind or his conscience."

The President gave no inkling of his intentions about calling Congress into special session to revise the stringent Neutrality Law which places certain mandatory obligations upon him. The universal opinion among observers at the capital was that he would issue a call soon, and that it might come upon the heels of the obligatory neutrality proclamation, placing an embargo on arms and munitions of war to Germany, Poland, France and England. White House sources said the neutrality proclamation could be expected within the next forty-eight hours.

Gives Ideas of Safety

Under the law, the neutrality proclamation, which carries with it the proclamation of an arms embargo, is required as soon as the President makes a finding that a state of war exists between two or more countries. Officials were standing today on the technicality that this government had not been officially notified of Britain's and France's declarations. They conceded, however, that this was a mere technicality.

In the course of his message, the President drew a ring around the Western Hemisphere, saying in substance that this was the area which the United States must and would seek to protect and keep neutral.

This country, he said, had certain ideas and ideals of national safety "and we must act to preserve that safety today and to preserve the safety of our children in future years."

That safety, he continued, is and will be bound up with the safety of the Western Hemisphere "and the seas adjacent thereto."

"We seek to keep war from our firesides by keeping war from coming to the Americas," he said.

Recalls Efforts for Peace

He claimed historic precedent, going back to the days of George Washington, for this country's assuming the responsibility of protecting the whole of the Americas. It is serious enough and tragic enough to every American family in every State in the Union to live in a world torn by wars on other continents, he said. Therefore he considered it our national duty to use

Continued on Page Six

Poles Charge Aerial Gas Attacks on Cities As Germany Agrees to 'Humanize' the War

LONDON, Sept. 3 (AP).—The Polish Ambassador to London, Count Edward Raczynski, tonight declared that new German air attacks in all parts of Poland had disclosed that the civilian population was suffering with the Germans using gas in their raids.

WARSAW, Sept. 3 (Polish Telegraphic Agency).—German bombers threw gas bombs on the unfortified village of Grudisk in the county of Ciechanow.

Wireless to THE NEW YORK TIMES.

BERLIN, Sept. 3.—It was announced today that Germany and the Western Powers had agreed to "humanize" the war by not employing poison gas, not bombing open cities from the air, even when in the zone of war operations, and not taking military measures against civilians as long as both sides observed the agreement.

The reported dropping of gas bombs on Polish towns represents the first use of gas from planes in European warfare.

The inauguration of this form of attack recalls that in 1915 the Germans began the use of poison gas on the battlefields and the Allies followed suit.

In 1917 the German General Staff gave consideration to the use of gas from planes in attacking cities, but after a long debate it was decided not to do so. The reason was that the British and French air forces combined were superior to the air force of the Germans, and the fear of what might happen to German cities deterred the Germans from using gas in air attacks at that time.

ITALY FAILS TO ACT AS HER ALLY FIGHTS

Rome Plans to Stay Neutral Unless Attacked—Fascist Moves Kept Secret

By HERBERT L. MATTHEWS
Special Cable to THE NEW YORK TIMES.

ROME, Monday, Sept. 4.—Although Great Britain and France are at war with Germany, Italy has taken no step to join her Axis partner. She remains friendly to Germany but neutral, and she will make no move against the French and British unless attacked. This was made clear in Premier Mussolini's newspaper, the Popolo d'Italia, this morning, which reaffirmed the declaration of neutrality contained in the Council of Ministers' communiqué Friday.

Whether there is any possibility of Italy going beyond that attitude toward one side or the other cannot be stated yet, for the Italians continue to be completely secret. Since history always repeats itself, one may well suppose that the French and British are doing everything they can to win Italian benevolence, if not aid. That is the normal and natural thing for them to do whether they have hopes for success or not. After all, diplomatic relations between Rome and Paris and London continue on a friendly basis, and none need be surprised if André François-Poncet and Sir Percy Loraine, the French and British Ambassadors, who see Count Ciano, the Foreign Minister, so often these days, should be exerting their greatest efforts to win Italy away from Germany. It is their business to do so.

Attitude Is Not Changing

None can say yet what success, if any, they are having. So far as today is concerned there is that Popolo d'Italia article to go upon, which indicates clearly enough that Italy is not changing her attitude because Britain and France have entered the conflict. Although it was printed before those countries acted it was written at a time when there could be no doubt of what was going to happen.

The editorial begins by saying that the Council of Ministers' communiqué should be "re-read and meditated." Its words were "sculpted in stone," says the editorial, meaning that it was meant to last.

From Premier Mussolini's efforts for "peace with justice," two things are to be deduced it continues:

First, that notwithstanding certain foreign interpretations which are too hasty or ingenuous nothing is changed on the plane of Italo-German friendship.

Second, that Signor Mussolini has worked not only for the solution of the German-Polish problem but for all other problems which like this one now being solved by arms, have their origin in the Versailles Treaty.

"It is therefore natural," the article goes on, "that whatever happens, whether the German-Polish conflict remains localized or spreads to a catastrophe, the Duce's work—that is to say the work that

Continued on Page Seven

HITLER WITH ARMY ON EASTERN FRONT

Leaves Berlin After Placing Blame for War on Britain—Allied Envoys Depart

By OTTO D. TOLISCHUS
Wireless to THE NEW YORK TIMES.

BERLIN, Sept. 3.—At 9 o'clock tonight Chancellor Hitler left Berlin, presumably for the Eastern Front. He had previously sent a message to the Eastern Army stating that he was joining them.

He left the city in a heavily guarded special train that mounted anti-aircraft artillery. He was accompanied by his Foreign Minister, Joachim von Ribbentrop, and by Field Marshal Hermann Goering. It was supposed that their destination was Stolp, Pomerania, where the headquarters of the Eastern Army is believed to be located.

The departure of the Chancellor ended a day of proclamations from the chancellery. There was an appeal to the German people, a proclamation to the Nazi party, a message to the soldiers of the East Army and another to the troops manning the Westwall. There was also given out the text of a German memorandum answering the British ultimatum.

Perhaps the most significant feature of all these proclamations and of the memorandum is that they do not mention France, sidetrack

Continued on Page Two

POLES REPORT GAIN

Tell of Fighting on Foe's Soil After Horsemen Retake 2 Towns

SHELL GERMAN AREA

But Invaders Announce Wide Advances—They Capture Rail Center

By The Associated Press.

LONDON, Monday, Sept. 4.—An Exchange Telegraph dispatch from Warsaw reported early today that Polish troops had crossed the German frontier north of Breslau and were fighting on German soil.

Quoting a Polish short-wave radio broadcast, the news agency said the troops had crossed between Rawicz and Leszno. These towns are on the border about twenty-five miles apart and approximately forty-five miles north of Breslau. The report said Polish cavalry was in the action.

[The Polish Telegraphic Agency reported earlier that Polish cavalry had driven German forces from Rawicz and Leszno, which they had captured in surprise attacks on Friday.]

The agency quoted the following communiqué issued last night by the Polish supreme command:

"During the day the German air force carried out raids on numerous unfortified towns, including Warsaw, Deblin, Radom and Cracow. Near Radom and Cracow twenty-six enemy aircraft were brought down. The total number brought down today was sixty-four. The Polish losses amounted to eleven machines. German raiders did not spare the peasant population working in the fields near their villages.

"Considerable enemy forces launched a strong attack in the direction of Silesia and the region of Podhale. Under the pressure of the enemy, Polish forces were compelled to abandon Czestochowa on the Silesian frontier.

"Our lines were slightly pressed in the Silesia sector. In the north Polish troops recaptured Puck and Orlowo."

In an air encounter over Poznan late yesterday, Exchange Telegraph said, six German bombers were shot down near Wolbrom after they had dropped a number of gas bombs.

The agency said that the German radio had announced that a German Army had crossed the Warta [Warthe] River yesterday east of Wielun in Western Poland.

An attempt by Polish troops cut

Continued on Page Nine

The Developments in Europe

Britain and France plunged into war yesterday morning and soon events began to gather momentum.

The most sensational was the torpedoing and sinking of the British liner Athenia off the Hebrides this morning. She was carrying 1,400 passengers, including 292 Americans, from Liverpool to Montreal. The news shocked the White House. [Page 1].

On top of this came charges by Poles that the Germans had dropped gas bombs on towns. [Page 1.]

Britain, following her tactics of the last war, quickly blockaded Germany and closed the entrances to the Mediterranean Sea as well. The British public was calm and grimly determined after it had heard Prime Minister Chamberlain gravely announce on the radio that "this country is at war with Germany." [Page 1.] He made the same announcement in the House of Commons, where he immediately received the support of such former opponents as Winston Churchill and David Lloyd George. In a new War Cabinet Mr. Churchill resumed the post of First Lord of the Admiralty, which he had held in the last war; Lord Hankey, another veteran statesman of that conflict, became Minister Without Portfolio, and Anthony Eden became Secretary for the Dominions. [Page 8; texts of Mr. Chamberlain's addresses and of addresses in the Commons, Page 8.]

In France Premier Daladier, declaring that the responsibility for bloodshed was Chancellor Hitler's, said that France's cause was the cause of justice. [Page 1; text of Daladier's radio speech, Page 8.]

Herr Hitler in a series of statements during the day put the blame for the strife on the British whom he accused of seeking to encircle Germany. He left for the Polish front. [Page 1; texts of these statements, Page 2.]

On that front the Poles were reported to have carried the fighting to German soil in one sector, but were declared to be giving ground in Silesia and at points in Pomorze [Page 1].

Italy still took no step to join her Axis partner in the conflict and it seemed obvious that the British and the French were doing what they could to win her to their side. [Page 1.]

Russia likewise kept a middle-of-the-road position [Page 6.]

President Roosevelt, in an extraordinary message radioed to "the whole of America," called for national unity as a measure for keeping the Western Hemisphere from becoming embroiled. [Page 1; text of the message, Page 6.]

BRITISH NAVY ACTS

It Cuts Off Entrances to the Baltic, North and Mediterranean Seas

LONDON IS UNSHAKEN

Declaration of War Is Met With Resolve—Air Alarm Orderly

Special to THE NEW YORK TIMES.

WASHINGTON, Sept. 3.—The British Government has ordered a naval blockade of Germany, according to information reaching officials here tonight. This government has not been informed officially by the British Government of this fact, however.

It was understood here that the naval blockade went into effect immediately upon the declaration of war and that British naval vessels were blocking the entrance to the Baltic Sea near Skagerrak and were stretched across the North Sea near the Scandinavian peninsula. It was also understood here that the entrances to the Mediterranean at Gibraltar and Suez were being carefully controlled.

Both Britain and France were cloaking their naval and military moves with greatest secrecy and neither the Navy nor the War Department had specific information about them up to 8 o'clock, Eastern standard time, tonight.

Britain Is Determined

By FREDERICK T. BIRCHALL
Special Cable to THE NEW YORK TIMES.

LONDON, Monday, Sept. 4.—At last midnight Great Britain had been at war with Germany for thirteen hours. France had been at war for seven hours—since 5 o'clock.

A darkened London, in which only hooded red and green crosses at the traffic halts, invisible from above, indicate that there are streets, houses and human life below a clear starry sky, awaits calmly the air attacks that it confidently expects despite Chancellor Hitler's professed desire to avoid bombing open cities. Even these tiny indications will be extinguished the moment that sirens hoot their warnings of approaching raiders.

There are few people in the streets because the authorities have broadcast warnings to every one to stay at home and to go out no more than is necessary. Cinemas, theatres and every other form of entertainment likely to draw a crowd have been shut down by order for the time being, at least. Only the churches have held their customary services.

People Grimly Determined

Thus war has come to Britain, to a people grimly determined to meet it and to see it through. The predominating sentiment, if any, is one of relief that the long period of suspense is over. Throughout the land the watchword now is: "Let's get on with it."

War became a reality yesterday morning just after the church bells had ceased ringing. It came in the shape of a sudden interruption of the regular radio program by an announcer:

"The Prime Minister will broadcast an important announcement to the nation."

Then came Mr. Chamberlain's well-known voice, quiet and sad but clear and firm:

"I am speaking to you from the Cabinet room at 10 Downing Street."

Then followed his terse narration of the course of events. That morning (it was actually at 9 o'clock, two hours earlier) the British Ambassador at Berlin had handed Foreign Minister Joachim von Ribbentrop a final note stating that unless the Germans had agreed by 11 o'clock to withdraw their troops from Poland, a "state of war would exist between us."

"I have to tell you now," continued Mr. Chamberlain in the same level tones, "that no such

Continued on Page Four

FIRST SHIP SUNK IN THE WAR

The Athenia, with 1,400 aboard, torpedoed off the Hebrides

Wired Photo—Times Wide World

List of the American Passengers Aboard the Torpedoed Athenia

Special to THE NEW YORK TIMES.

WASHINGTON, Monday, Sept. 4.—The list of American citizens who embarked on the liner Athenia in Liverpool follows; no addresses were given in the cable received at the State Department from Ambassador Joseph P. Kennedy:

Ralph Ruffieau
Katheryn McGuire
Hasel Casserly
Charles Grant
Florence Malik
Edith Bridge
Harry Bridge
Robert Harris
Gustaf Petersen
Margaret Buchan
Laura Cattle
Mrs. Thomas Kerr
Kate Hinds
Herbert Spierelberg
Mrs. Davis
Margaret McGuire
Elizabeth Wise
William Buchanan
Master Charles Grant
Bernice Jansen
Constance Bridge
Sarah Warenreich
John Hughes
Gertrude Reed
George Cattle
Thomas Kerr
Rhoda Thomas
William Hinds
J. Davis
William Peers
Lillian Peers
Charles Prince
Harold Etherington
Ellen Harrington
Jessie Forle
Francis Cooley
Charles Prince (two Charles Princes)
Geoffrey Etherington
R. Casey
George Keliher
Harry Trehearne
Ella Trehearne
Annie Word
Duncan Wood (Two Duncan Woods)
Ernest Ratcliffe
Faith Ratcliffe
Irene de Munn
Edward O'Connell
Aileen Philipsen
Mary Steinberg
Ralph Child
Peter Birchall
Duncan Wood
Ellin Ratcliffe
Donald Gifford
Jozef Karnowski
Dorris O'Connel
John Youngquist
Donald Edwards
John Lawrence
Tryphene Humphrey
Louise Horte
Mary, Dick and Edward Belton
Elsa Philipsen
Adolph Sadowski
John Harju
Charles Stork
Harold Ruggs
Adolph Leocha
Florence Dery
Wiktor Ponjola
Ethel Russell
William Bohn
Ada Bohn
Montgomery Evans
Franklin Dexter
Cathleen Schurr
Agnes Stappel
Lillian Eilstrap
Rose Churchill
Ellen Howland
Miarine Dexter
Maud Shearer
Alexander Sheshunoff
Cosby Eilstrap
Sarah Burdett
Yvette Pepin
Ena Logan
Herbert Bonn
Thomas Quine
Lulu Sweigard
Romona Allen
Gus Anderson
Eleanor Crowley
Harriet Tolley
Janet Elsen
Annie Quine
Carol Allen
Susan Allen

The following Americans boarded the Athenia at Glasgow, the American Consulate there reports:

James Boyle
Cathryn Brennan
Margaret Campbell
Elva Campbell
Agnes Craig
William Diller
Margaret Diller
Louis Diven
Mary Diven
Mary Dowie
Thomas Fielder
John Bernard
Margaret Ford
Cora Gilroy
Don Gilroy
Helen Hannah
Jar. Hannah
Florence Hargreave
Selena Isaacs
Jeanette Jordan
Margaret Little
Harriet McFadzean
Mary McKellar
Alexander Nichol
Edith Nichol
Marion Nichol
Alice Tocklington
John Pringle
Lottie Tringle
Katherine Scott
Essie Mallery
William Mallery
Helen Stewart
Edgar Wilkes
Margaret Wilkes
Donald Wilkes
William Wilkes
Myrtle Barber
Barbara Bradfield
Joan Outhwaite
Alberta Wood
Lucile Lucas
Elizabeth Martin
Gertrude Martin
Ila Vincent
Michael Flynn
Alice Robinson
Robert Townsend
Bainbridge Hayden
Dirus Ekaube
Doris Elaine Kent
William Ralph Singleton
Margaret Moore
Sarah Bloom
Olive Bloom
Fred Tinney
Madeline Tinney
Charles Cotterman
Bunson Price
Elizabeth Alton (two listed)
Louis Burns
Mary Burns
Harriette Jones
Joan Moffett
Elsie Moffett
Joseph MacDonald
Elmetta MacDonald
Harriet Roney
Wendell Sherk
Nicola Lubitsch
Henry Smith
Ellen Smith
Jeannette Smith
Caroline Stuart
Frieda Windmann
Matthew Brown
Mary Brown
Elizabeth Brown
James Curran
Isobel Bruce
Betsy Brown
Dorothy Fox
W. E. MacBain
Marjorie MacBain
Gus Anderson
Caroline Rice
William Bown
Ada Bown
Elizabeth Lewis
May Lewis
Donald Lewis
William Aitken
Anne Baker
Alma Bloom
Dorothy Feder
Martha Bonnet
William Brown
George Calder (Two listed)
Margaret Calder
Alice Chalmers
William Chalmers
Margaret Doggett
Eileen Duncombe

The names of the Americans who boarded the Athenia at Belfast could not be obtained up to 5 o'clock this morning.

News dispatches from Europe and the Far East are now virtually all subject to censorship.

HIT OFF HEBRIDES

Ship Bound for Canada Carried Some Children Among Americans

CAPITAL IS SHOCKED

President's Aide Notes Liner Had Refugees, Not Munitions

By The Associated Press.

BELFAST, Northern Ireland, Monday, Sept. 4.—All persons aboard the sunken British liner Athenia, except some killed by a German torpedo, were reported saved today.

An agent of the ship's owners here issued the report. He said all survivors had been picked up by other vessels.

By The Associated Press.

LONDON, Monday, Sept. 4.—The British Liner Athenia, with 246 United States citizens among her 1,400 passengers, was torpedoed and sunk 200 miles west of the Hebrides, the British Ministry of Information announced early today. [Washington reports said 292 Americans were aboard the Athenia.]

The United States Embassy, checking on the departures of Americans hurrying home in flight from the European war, said 101 boarded the ship at Liverpool and 145 at Glasgow. [Forty-six more Americans boarded the vessel at Belfast, Washington was informed.]

The Athenia sailed Saturday from Liverpool.

The British Ministry of Information said the 13,581-ton ship reported to the Admiralty she had been torpedoed 200 miles off the Hebrides, west of Northern Scotland.

The Ministry of Information said the last official information received by the Admiralty from the ship was that she was sinking "rapidly." Since there were no further advices, it was then assumed she had gone down.

[Stephen Early, secretary to President Roosevelt, said in Washington that official reports indicated the Athenia was carrying "mostly Canadians and some Americans."

["I'd like to point out," he said, according to The Associated Press, "that, according to official information, the ship had gone from Glasgow to Liverpool and was bound for Canada, bringing refugees.

["I point this out to show that there was no possibility, according to official information, that the ship was carrying any munitions or anything of that kind."]

292 Americans Were Aboard

WASHINGTON, Monday, Sept. 4 (AP).—Dispatches to the State Department indicated today that at least 246 [later news brought the figure to 292] Americans were aboard the liner Athenia, torpedoed in the North Atlantic.

White House Is Informed

Special to THE NEW YORK TIMES.

WASHINGTON, Monday, Sept. 4.—Information received here last night that the Cunard White Star liner Athenia had been torpedoed off the coast of Ireland while en route to the United States brought a prompt statement from the White House acknowledging receipt of the news and information from the State Department that it had received eighteen long-distance calls within a few minutes of a radio broadcast of the news. The calls appealed for information about relatives aboard.

The White House said that the vessel was bound from Glasgow and Liverpool to Montreal with a large group of Canadian passengers and with an undetermined number of Americans among them.

At 6 A. M., British Summer Time [1 A. M. in New York] Ambassador Joseph P. Kennedy cabled the State Department as follows:

"Admiralty unable as yet to indicate whether Athenia has sunk or rescue arrangements; 101 American citizens embarked on her at

Continued on Page Five

"All the News That's Fit to Print."

The New York Times.

LATE CITY EDITION
Mostly cloudy, somewhat warmer, with showers today and tonight. Tomorrow generally fair, cooler.
Temperatures Yesterday—Max., 69; Min., 54

Copyright, 1939, by The New York Times Company.

VOL. LXXXIX...No. 29,824. Entered as Second-Class Matter, Postoffice, New York, N. Y. NEW YORK, WEDNESDAY, SEPTEMBER 20, 1939. PPP THREE CENTS NEW YORK CITY and Vicinity | FOUR CENTS Elsewhere Except in 7th and 8th Postal Zones

HITLER TELLS ALLIES IT IS HIS PEACE OR A FINISH FIGHT; BRITAIN AND FRANCE FOR WAR TILL HITLERISM IS ENDED; RUSSIAN NAVY REPORTED BLOCKADING ESTONIAN COAST

GOLDSTEIN WINNER IN JUDICIAL RACE; SIMPSON IS VICTOR

Schurman Is Behind in Close Contest for Nomination in Democratic Primary

MULLEN AT TOP IN VOTE

Trevor Forces Are Swamped—Kenneally and Keating Defeated as Leaders

Jonah J. Goldstein defeated Chief City Magistrate Jacob Gould Schurman Jr. for a Democratic nomination for Judge of the Court of General Sessions in the primary election yesterday.

By this victory of Mr. Goldstein the enrolled Democratic voters of New York County repudiated the bi-partisan agreement for the nomination of John A. Mullen and Mr. Schurman by both major parties for the two places open on the General Sessions bench. The agreement was approved by the Bar Association of the City of New York and the New York County Lawyers Association and ratified by Representative Christopher D. Sullivan, leader of Tammany, and the New York County Republican Executive Committee. Mr. Mullen, a Democrat, and Mr. Schurman, a Republican, were unopposed for the Republican nomination.

Returns from 1,040 out of 1,055 election districts gave Mullen 48,893, Goldstein 38,525, Schurman 37,443.

This was a lead for Mr. Goldstein of 1,082 over Mr. Schurman, insuring his and Mr. Mullen's nomination on the face of the returns.

Simpson Is Victor

Kenneth F. Simpson, New York County Republican chairman and national committeeman, won an overwhelming victory over a conservative group headed by Bronson Trevor. County committee candidates pledged to support Mr. Simpson for re-election as county chairman swamped the Trevor candidates in Mr. Simpson's home Assembly District, the Fifteenth, and pro-Simpson county committee candidates were elected in virtually all other districts in which there were contests, defeating three district leaders, classed as anti-Simpson, Cornelius M. Shannon in the Fifth District, North; Louis Hopkins in the Twelfth District, North, and Harold Forstenzer in the Twenty-third District, South.

Two veteran Tammany district leaders went down to defeat in sixteen district leadership contests, and the defeat of two or three others was indicated.

Kenneally Is Defeated

The outstanding Tammany contest was that in the Twelfth District, South, where Representative James H. Fay defeated William P. Kenneally, who succeeded the late Charles F. Murphy as leader of the district and who is chairman of the Tammany executive committee.

Mr. Fay, who has been reported to be the man that the New Deal group in Washington would like to see succeed Representative Christopher D. Sullivan as leader of Tammany Hall, last Fall defeated former Representative John J. O'Connor for nomination and election in the one success of the Presidential purge.

It was claimed at the Fay headquarters that his county committee candidates had made a clean sweep of eleven election districts, electing 163 to none for Kenneally. The vote in these districts was 1,948 for Fay and 710 for Kenneally.

"I have definite plans in view concerning the leadership," Mr. Fay said, "but first I must hurry down to Washington to do my bit in keeping this country safely and honorably at peace."

Keating Is Defeated

The other Tammany veteran leader defeated was Andrew B. Keating in the Thirteenth Assembly District. He was overwhelmingly beaten by Assemblyman William J. Sheldrick by a vote of more than two to one, twenty-six election districts out of forty giving Sheldrick 234 committee members to 84 for Keating.

Unofficial returns also indicated the defeat of the two Tammany leaders in the First Assembly District. Dr. Paul E. Santangelo was defeated by former Alderman Paul

Continued on Page Twenty-four

The International Situation

In a speech in reclaimed Danzig Chancellor Hitler yesterday opened his expected peace offensive by declaring that he had no war aims against Britain or France and that Germany desired "lasting peace." But he proclaimed that Poland was doomed and that her fate would be decided by Germany and Russia, and he warned that Nazi Germany would retaliate for whatever kind of war was meted out to her and was prepared to carry through, whether the war lasted three years or seven years. [Page 1; text of the speech, Page 18.]

Britain and France were quick to reply, both indicating that the war would go on until Hitlerism was smashed. An official statement in London said the speech was full of "crass misstatements" [Page 1; text Page 19], while the Paris pronouncement found it full of "lies." [With text, Page 19.]

On his way to Danzig Herr Hitler was within sight and sound of a desperate battle being waged near Gdynia by 6,000 Poles against two German divisions. [Page 5.] Another scene of Polish resistance was Warsaw, where a stubborn fight was still being put up despite aerial bombing and cannonading. But north of Lodz the Germans said they had crushed their foe and taken 50,000 prisoners and much booty. [Page 1.]

From the East the Russians moved steadily forward, penetrating as much as 120 miles and reaching the outskirts of Lwow. [Page 1.] Their chief land action of the day, however, was the occupation of Vilna, former Lithuanian capital, and their subsequent drive to the Lithuanian frontier. [Page 4.]

An even more important Soviet step was the reported blockading of Estonia by the Red Navy following Moscow charges that Estonian authorities had aided in the escape of an interned Polish submarine. This news sent apprehension through the Baltic States. [Page 1.]

Five other States of the North held a conference with a unanimous declaration of determination to stand together in safeguarding their economic rights and in preserving neutrality. [Page 8.]

The Netherlands, through Queen Wilhelmina, explained that the nation was ready to defend its neutrality and expressed the hope that peace could still be obtained. [Page 12.]

Italy felt some uneasiness over Chancellor Hitler's failure to give any assurances regarding the Balkans, but remained determined to continue strengthening her neutral position. [Page 3.]

As London disclosed that the torpedoing of the aircraft carrier Courageous had cost 578 lives of a complement considerably larger than had been thought [Page 8], it was also acknowledged that German submarines had taken a toll of three more British merchant ships. [Page 21.]

PRESIDENT DRAFTS EMBARGO MESSAGE

Will Deliver It in Person to Congress Tomorrow—Meets With Leaders Today

Special to THE NEW YORK TIMES.

WASHINGTON, Sept. 19—President Roosevelt will appear before a joint session of the Senate and House at 2 P. M. (3 P. M., E. D. T.) Thursday to deliver personally his plea for a revamping of the neutrality laws, according to tentative plans announced today by the President himself.

With Senators and members of the House arriving in Washington for the special session, and on the eve of a meeting with titular leaders of both major parties tomorrow, the President guarded carefully the contents of his message. Asked at his press conference if he still planned to hold the session to consideration of neutrality only, the President replied that he would specify only that issue.

In pursuance of a policy of silence pending his meeting with the leaders, the President declined to give any inkling as to whether he would seek substitution of the cash-and-carry plan for the present mandatory arms embargo or whether he would request outright repeal of the Neutrality Act of 1937 and reliance entirely on the traditional principles of international law.

The President as well as other officials withheld comment on the fast changing situation in Europe or Chancellor Hitler's speech in Danzig. Mr. Roosevelt said he was not aware of any new plans for industrial mobilization or expansion of the armed forces beyond recently authorized increases, and said of any future necessary expansion in the army and navy that it was all in the lap of the gods.

Hull Stands by Letter of May 27

Although the President refused to indicate what his recommendations would be on neutrality legislation, Secretary Hull at his press conference several hours earlier made clear that his fundamental views had not changed since May 27, when he outlined them in identic letters to Senator Key Pittman, chairman of the Committee on Foreign Relations, and Representative Sol Bloom, chairman of the Committee on Foreign Affairs.

In his letters, the Secretary of State urged the elimination of the arms embargo provision, but retention of sections in the existing law prohibiting American ships from entering combat areas, restricting travel by Americans in combat areas, providing for a cash-and-carry system for goods destined for belligerents, banning loans and

Continued on Page Sixteen

BRITAIN INSURING ATLANTIC CARGOES

Arranges Underwriting at $2 Per $100, Much Cheaper Than Policies Offered Here

The British Government has arranged to underwrite eastbound cargoes on all ships operating between New York and other Atlantic ports to the United Kingdom, at a rate below that offered by underwriters here, it was disclosed last night.

Regardless of the nationality of the ship carrying cargo to British ports, war risk insurance is available at 2 per cent, and shipping men here said they understood that a similar rate had been placed in effect on westbound cargo out of United Kingdom ports, although they had not actually received verification.

Shippers here have accepted the move of the British Government as assurance of its determination to keep commerce moving at reasonable prices, and many exporters have already sent cargoes abroad in gray-painted freighters and liners carrying the British flag, all of them subject to German submarine warfare on British merchant shipping.

Cunard White Star officials declined last night to say what ships had carried out this cargo, but they declared that a considerable amount of it had been directed to their ships and to other British vessels sailing out of ports along the coast, including Canadian ports.

Insurance Readily Available

The insurance is written by the government war risk insurance scheme, similar to an insurance agency set up abroad during the last war. It has been made readily available in the United States in order to facilitate the movement of cargoes. It can be written by consignees in Britain, or through the American representatives of British insurance companies. Or it can be written here in blanket form by the steamship companies accepting the cargoes.

At a rate of $2 per $100, the foreign plan undersells American protection appreciably. The American rate to United Kingdom ports is $2.50 per $100 on shipments carried in vessels flying the United States flag. On neutral vessels other than Italian it is $5 per $100. On British ships it is $7.50.

The British scheme also offers insurance from ships clear through to warehouses at British points, for an extra 50 cents, whereas American underwriters are not offering

Continued on Page Two

ALLIED CHIEFS MEET

Gort and Gamelin Map Defense—British to Hold Belgian Line

GAINS CONSOLIDATED

Germans Mass Troops Behind Aachen and Invasion Is Feared

By The United Press.

PARIS, Sept. 19—The commanders of the British and French forces on the Western front, meeting in Northern France today with their staffs, were reported to have decided on a strong defense of the Belgian frontier to meet any possible threat of German invasion there.

The Allied commanders, General Maurice Gustave Gamelin and Viscount Gort, commander of the British expeditionary forces, met at Amiens, about sixty-five miles from the Belgian border.

French quarters reported that part of the German forces being diverted from the Polish battlefronts were concentrated "within striking distance" of the Belgian and Netherland frontiers.

There seemed to be a measure of concern among the British and French that the Germans might try to repeat their tactics of 1914 when the German army invaded Belgium at Liége to strike at France.

Paris newspapers reported that the German frontier town of Aachen across from the Belgian border was being evacuated of civilians. Aachen is only a short distance from Eupen, one of the two districts that Germany surrendered to Belgium after the World War.

Troop Placement Discussed

Viscount Gort and General Gamelin in their meeting at Amiens discussed the equitable placing of British and French troops in positions on the Western front.

It was understood that British troops would be assigned chiefly to the French extension of the Maginot Line along the Belgian frontier, westward from the ninety-mile sector between the Rhine and Moselle Rivers where all of the Western fighting thus far has occurred.

The task of the British troops, it was reported, will be to guard the French-Belgian frontier against any surprise German invasion.

French quarters heard tonight that Germany was concentrating large numbers of troops in the Rhineland behind the Belgian frontier, supposedly in the Aachen district.

After conferring with Viscount Gort, General Gamelin returned to Paris and reported to Premier and War Minister Edouard Daladier

Continued on Page Two

BALTIC GRAB SEEN

Soviet Wish for Port Is Thought to Be Behind Action of Fleet

OCCUPATION HINTED

Estonia Aided in Polish Submarine's Escape, Moscow Charges

By The Associated Press.

STOCKHOLM, Sweden, Sept. 19—Reports reaching here from Tallinn, Estonia, tonight said the Soviet Navy had blockaded Estonia's coast.

The reports said the harbor of Tallinn was under particular surveillance and that no ships were allowed to enter or leave.

The action was assumed to be retaliation for the failure of Estonian authorities to prevent the escape of the interned Polish submarine Orzel yesterday from Tallinn.

Tass, the Soviet official news agency, announced early today that "measures" were being taken by the Russian Baltic Fleet on the ground that Polish and other submarines were hiding in neutral Baltic ports.

Particular mention was made in the Tass communiqué of the escape of the Polish submarine from Tallinn. It was charged Estonian authorities had abetted the escape.

Baltic States Worried

By G. E. R. GEDYE

Special Cable to THE NEW YORK TIMES.

MOSCOW, Sept. 19—Perturbation has been caused among the Baltic States, whose representatives in Moscow all conferred throughout the day, by a hostile Tass communiqué directed against Estonia, published in this morning's issue of Pravda. Naturally little value is attached by the Baltic States to the Soviet Union's assurances of neutrality delivered at the moment of the Soviet invasion of Poland.

A Tass report, dated from Leningrad, stated that "one of the Polish submarines interned previously at Tallinn [Estonia] escaped for an unknown destination." The facts concerning the submarine's departure are not in dispute, but natural alarm has been caused in the Baltic States by the Soviet Union's attitude toward the incident.

The Soviet Union's official statement, reported by Tass, alleged that Polish submarines were "hiding in ports of the Baltic States with the covert support of certain government officials." It was alleged in the Tass report that not only Polish submarines but "also submarines of certain other States" were using Baltic ports.

The Baltic States are inclined to regard this communiqué in the light

Continued on Page Six

Thwarting of Hitler by Stalin In Southeast Europe Seen by Gibbs

By SIR PHILIP GIBBS, Famous War Correspondent

Wireless to THE NEW YORK TIMES.

LONDON, Sept. 19—It is not too much to say that the fate of the world depends on what will result from Poland's downfall, hastened and completed by Russia's criminal betrayal and invasion. Poland fighting alone against Germany, cut off from rescue by France and Britain, may have seemed in world opinion no more than a heroic struggle for liberty by a gallant people against overwhelming odds.

Their eventual defeat, however magnificent their courage — and their supreme valor has been proved during twenty days of agony—was foreseen by all military minds. Britain and France knew when they declared war on Germany for this ruthless aggression that before long the main force of Germany's war machine would swing upon them.

We had no illusion about that. But the advance of Russia in Europe alters everything and enlarges everything by increasing the menace and new uncertainties. What Russia does reaches out to problems in the Pacific. It involves the fate of China and Japan.

Australia has new anxieties. For the Russian bear sprawls across the earth from east to west. In Europe this Russian crime which gave the death-blow to Poland terrifies many small nations. Latvia, Lithuania and Estonia stare across their frontiers and await the surging tide of Red soldiers. Their ramparts are not high against that flood.

How far will Stalin, that sinister despot in Moscow, bid his hordes advance; what price has Germany paid for this pact between burglars and murderers? In Downing Street and the Quai d'Orsay, British and French statesmen are trying to read that riddle.

Knowing something of Russia and much of Germany, I believe two things are certain. Germany has opened her gates to the Russian bear who one day will bite her throat. Secondly, Stalin, not Hitler, will dictate terms.

For when German youths have been sacrificed in a blood bath on the Maginot Line, Stalin will laugh and say: "How now, Hitler?" Even now the German leaders have to eat dirt. What pride can they have in the Polish defeat? It was done by

Continued on Page Nine

Hitler Fails to Impress British; 'Crass Misstatements' Charged

Ministry of Information Replies to Speech With Quotations From Previous Tirades Against Bolshevist Menace

By RAYMOND DANIELL

Special Cable to THE NEW YORK TIMES.

LONDON, Sept. 19—Chancellor Hitler's speech in the Danzig market place, replete as usual with protestations of his desire for peace and with reiteration of his satisfaction with the western German boundaries and coupled with new boasts of a close Russo-German understanding and threats to use a new secret weapon, left the British Government and the British people unimpressed tonight with the Chancellor's good faith or his ability to wage a long war.

While a full answer to the Nazi leader's charge that Britain, bent on war, used Poland as a pawn, together with an exposition of the British attitude toward the now obviously prearranged plan to divide the conquered country between two powerful neighbors, is expected from Prime Minister Chamberlain in the House of Commons tomorrow, the Ministry of Information tonight contented itself with an analysis of the contradictions between Herr Hitler's speech today and his earlier utterances.

The most interesting parts of Herr Hitler's speech to his listeners here were his assertions that Russia and Germany, despite their ideological differences, which, he maintained, they still recognized, had decided not to play into the hands of the Western democracies by fighting each other and his declaration that the two totalitarian powers had taken it upon themselves to determine the political and territorial future of the country that together they had erased from the map, at least temporarily. After the first of these statements the British placed a large question mark.

Of special interest, too, was Herr Hitler's statement that the presence of the Red Army in Poland should ease British fears of unlimited German expansion. In that observers here found confirmation for the belief that Joseph Stalin stepped in hurriedly to make sure of getting what Herr Hitler had promised him as the price for the non-aggression treaty. This was also believed to support the suspicion that the Soviet Army's screening movement along the frontier of Southern Poland would guarantee Rumania against German invasion and ease the tension in the Balkans.

Hungary now faces the certainty that her Ruthenian acquisition at the expense of Czecho-Slovakia will give her a common frontier with Russia. South of the Danube, Turkey is the power most vitally

Continued on Page Nineteen

RUSSIANS PUSH ON RAPIDLY IN POLAND

Vilna Taken, They Report Drive to Lwow and Other Gains—Estates Being Liquidated

By The United Press.

MOSCOW, Wednesday, Sept. 20—Cavalry and tank units of the Soviet Army have forced their way into the outskirts of the Polish Ukrainian city of Lwow, already besieged by German troops, a Soviet General Staff communiqué said early today.

The communiqué, telling of penetrations as deep as 120 miles into Poland by Soviet troops advancing along a 500-mile front, also announced the capture of Vilna in the north "after two hours' fighting." [The occupation of Vilna is reported in detail on Page 4.]

Lwow, like Brest-Litovsk, where German and Soviet troops formed a junction Monday and exchanged greetings, lies along a line announced by the Soviet Government newspaper Izvestia as the boundary of Nazi penetration to the east in Poland and Russian penetration to the west. Lwow, a city of 317,000 and chief center of the Polish Ukraine, which the Soviet Army is occupying, is the third largest city in Poland.

[A General Staff communiqué in Berlin yesterday announced that the German Army had served an ultimatum upon Lwow to surrender after taking 10,000 Polish troops prisoners northwest of the city and occupying rich oil fields to the southwest.]

Two Columns in Advance

The Red Army communiqué said that the Soviet cavalry and tank units had entered the northeastern and southern outskirts of Lwow, indicating that one column had moved upon the city from the direction of captured Tarnopol and another from Brody and Ostrog. The communiqué said:

"The general staff of the workers and peasants' Red Army reports on the operations of Sept. 19 that Red Army troops continued pressing Polish troops and by the end of the day occupied:

"In the north, in Western Bye'-Russia [White Russia] the town of Wilno [Vilna], which was taken after two hours' fighting; the towns of Velika, Berestovitsa, Pruzhany [Pruzana] and Kobrin [Kobryn], twenty-five miles northeast of Brest-Litovsk].

"In the south, in Western Ukraine, the towns of Vladimir, Volynski [Wlodzimierz], Sokal [on the Bug River], Brody, Bobrka, Rogatin and Dolina.

"Cavalry and tank units entered

Continued on Page Four

1,000,000 IN WARSAW DEFY NAZI BOMBING

Poles Cling to Capital in Face of Air Threat—Lwow Also Refuses to Surrender

Special Cable to THE NEW YORK TIMES.

BERLIN, Sept. 19—Having apparently reached its desired objective in the East, the German Army concentrated yesterday and today on cleaning-up operations behind the line of its farthest advance while waiting for the Russian troops to complete their advance westward.

The exact course of this German line is not yet determinable and is probably not determined. The purpose of the meeting of the Russian-German military commission yesterday, probably at Brest-Litovsk, was to delineate definitively the line of demarcation between the zones to be occupied by the Germans and the Russians. Whether the commission completed its task or is still in session, however, has not yet been revealed.

Even the maps published in Berlin newspapers differ in details as to the line held by the Germans. Generally, however, it appears to be a broken line running in the north from east of Ossowiec and Bialystok and east of the Bug River southward to Brest-Litovsk. From the latter city it continues east of the Bug in a southeasterly direction through Wlodawa to Wlodzimierz. From there it runs southward to Lwow and Stryj, then westward to Boryslaw.

Furious Fighting Continues

Behind that line, however exactly it may be drawn, furious fighting continues at Warsaw and Lwow. A demand for surrender has been sent to Lwow. Little is known of the fate of Warsaw.

A communiqué issued by the army high command asserts merely that hostilities were renewed before Warsaw when no emissary arrived from the Poles to offer the truce that the Germans had demanded. Emphasis in German official quarters on civilian participation in the defense of the capital makes the city a military objective and therefore a legal object of air bombardment, it is indicated by the communiqué.

"The city is defended by the Poles without consideration for the inhabitants, totaling more than 1,000,000 persons," it adds.

The greatest German success indi-

Continued on Page Six

Dispatches from Europe and the Far East are now subject to censorship.

FUEHRER AT DANZIG

Warns the Allies He Will Unleash Full Air Power if They Resist

'LIBERATOR' IS HAILED

He Tells Free City It Is German Forever—Says Britain Forced War

By OTTO D. TOLISCHUS

Wireless to THE NEW YORK TIMES.

DANZIG, Sept. 19 — Having crushed Poland and partitioned that country between National Socialist Germany and Bolshevist Russia, Chancellor Adolf Hitler today launched his long expected "peace offensive," outlining his war aims.

He spoke for an hour and a quarter in a festively decorated, brightly illuminated Danzig, which he entered today thunderously acclaimed as a "liberator." Even the usual blackout has been waived for his visit, although the guns that Danzig's "liberation" had loosed could still be heard in the region of Gdynia, where a few "death battalions" of Poles were making a last desperate stand.

It was a speech full of pride at Germany's military achievements of the past nineteen days and full of menace for any who dared turn down his peace offer. But, although he asserted that "this Germany will not capitulate," no matter how many years the war may last, and that he would retaliate for every attack with the same method, he made no claim that Germany was able or wanted to deal with France and Great Britain as she had with Poland.

Makes Known His Terms

On the contrary, Herr Hitler re-emphasized his attempt to win the friendship of both France and Britain. He then outlined the terms on which these efforts could be renewed. These terms, which he also laid down as his peace terms, are:

1. The fate of Poland, "which will never rise again in a second Versailles," is to be decided by Germany and Russia within whose spheres of influence it lies.
2. Germany has accepted her western border, despite heavy sacrifices, and has no war aims against either France or Britain.

Any implication that Germany had any further war aims, he denounced as lies.

Whether these terms, involving, as they do, surrender of the proclaimed French and British war aims, are merely designed as a break for actual peace negotiations or a new mediation effort before the war in the West has become general or merely as a propagandistic device to weaken the Allies' will to fight is still not clear. But the political purpose of the speech in launching a peace offensive is also emphasized in German official quarters, and it is pointed out that, except for Poland, Herr Hitler did not make any new demands, not even for colonies. And he expressed how frightful and futile this war was.

Has No Faith in Britain's Word

As for the Allies' charges that they could not have any confidence in the words of a German statesman, he replied that Germany in return had no confidence in the words of those who broke their promises at Versailles.

Poland, Herr Hitler said, was a product of the stupidity of Versailles and was dominated by "a thin, tubercular class," which suppressed both the Germans in Poland and its own people.

Then the Chancellor formulated a principle of international relations which must be considered a fundamental of his foreign policy: There is a difference, he said in effect, whether an inferior people was ruled by a people of high cultural standing, or a culturally high standing people ruled by an inferior people who compensate for their sense of inferiority with brutality. The inference is that the first is right and the second wrong.

Just the same, Herr Hitler said that he had tried to obtain the same measure of security for Germany in the East as in the West and South, and in Marshal Josef Pilsudski, the late Polish dictator, he had found a realist who had tried to create a powerful neighborship. But after Marshal Pilsudski's death, he continued, oppression of

Continued on Page Nineteen

FDR signs the bill which lifted the arms embargo thus opening the European market to American industry.

As protection against an air attack, sandbags are placed on the roofs of London buildings.

July 4, 1939 — Lou Gehrig Day at Yankee Stadium — the day Gehrig retired because of ill health and the baseball world bid him farewell.

"All the News That's Fit to Print."

The New York Times.

LATE CITY EDITION
Fair and slightly colder today. Tomorrow fair with slowly rising temperatures.
Temperatures Yesterday—Max., 57; Min., 45

VOL. LXXXIX...No. 29,868. Entered as Second-Class Matter, Postoffice, New York, N. Y. NEW YORK, FRIDAY, NOVEMBER 3, 1939. P THREE CENTS NEW YORK CITY and Vicinity | FOUR CENTS Elsewhere Except in 7th and 8th Postal Zones.

HOUSE DOOMS ARMS EMBARGO, 243-181; $1,000,000,000 IN WAR ORDERS EXPECTED; BERLIN SEES U. S. TAKING SIDE OF ALLIES

DOCK STRIKE HITS COASTAL SHIPPING; 5,000 CALLED OUT

Longshoremen Act Here After Negotiations on Pay and Hours Break Down

MEDIATION HOPE IS THIN

Nine Lines Affected Ready to 'Close Operations'—Police to Guard Waterfront

A strike of the International Longshoremen's Association in the Port of New York against nine steamship lines in the coastwise trades, following a breakdown of negotiations over a new contract, went into effect last midnight.

Seventy ships and 3,500 men will be affected immediately, and more than 10,000 will be out of work if the strike continues more than a few days, it was estimated.

Early this morning the Bureau of Operations of the Police Department reported that at midnight 300 men went on strike at Pier 25 of the Eastern Steamship Company at the foot of Franklin Street. At the same time police details were assigned to other piers affected by the strike—Pier 11 of the Colonial Line at Cedar Street, Piers 34, 36 and 37 of the Clyde-Mallory Line at Canal, Spring and Charlton Streets and Piers 49 and 51 of the Southern Pacific and Morgan Lines at Bank and Bethune Streets.

The full force of the strike was not due to come, however, until today's normal working day began.

Longshore leaders called the strike during the afternoon after the association's council had declined to accept a proposal from the operators to extend their expired contract for ninety days. The men had asked for a wage increase of 10 cents an hour and a forty-hour week. The old contract called for pay of 95 cents an hour over a forty-four-hour week.

Compromise Turned Down

When the companies, through their labor spokesman, John E. Craig, vice president of the Clyde-Mallory Lines, rejected the demand, the union agreed to compromise on a 5-cent increase, but this also was turned down.

Mr. Craig said last night in behalf of the companies that they did not feel conditions warranted an increase in pay, and other company officials said they could not pay the higher wage.

They said that while freight rates on deep-sea lines had gone up, the coastwise rates remained unchanged. With no additional revenues, they explained, the union demands could not reasonably be met.

The concerns involved in the strike are the Savannah Line, the Pan-Atlantic Line, Clyde-Mallory, Bull Line, United Fruit, Eastern Steamship Lines, Newtex Line, Morgan Line and the Mooremack Gulf Lines of Moore & McCormack.

Only Some Ships Affected

Strike action against the United Fruit Line will be limited to the company's small ships in the coastwise service and will not hamper the movements of the line's Caribbean vessels, it was said. Neither will it involve other services of Moore & McCormack, which operates to Scandinavia and South America.

Shipping officials said there was "only one way to meet a strike—to close down operations."

As soon as the strike action had been taken freight men of the various companies sent out what they term "embargoes" on freight shipments, notifying shippers that they would not be in a position to take merchandise delivery here.

The ships will be tied up in rapid succession as soon as current voyages are terminated, it was expected.

Joseph P. Ryan, president of the longshoremen's organization, said he had exhausted every means in trying to avoid a strike that he indicated might destroy the industry.

"I used every bit of energy to prevail on both sides to be reasonable and not destroy this industry," he said. "But the men felt that their compromise proposal was a reasonable one. I and officers of the New York district council will hold ourselves available for any conferences that may be called toward a speedy settlement of this very unfortunate strike."

The Maritime Labor Board in Washington, it was reported last night, had sent a telegram to Mr. Craig seeking an opportunity to mediate the differences, but the message had not been received last night and ship men would not comment on the possibility of last-minute intervention.

The Labor Board has a mediator in New York at present and if its offer of arbitration is accepted can put him at work on the job immediately.

The Police Department took steps

Continued on Page Fourteen

Justices Sue to Void Pay Slashes; Cuts Made Illegally, They Say

53 in Municipal Court Contend Estimate Board's Salary-Fixing Resolution of 1927 Is Still in Effect

Fifty-three of the sixty-eight justices of the Municipal Court brought suit yesterday in Supreme Court to recover amounts deducted from their salaries between July 1, 1937, and July 1, 1939, as pay cuts and to avoid a further reduction carried in the city's budget for the present fiscal year, which started on the later date.

In their complaint the justices agreed that each was entitled to the full amount of the pay cuts only if he had signed all his pay checks under protest. Those who did not sign all their checks under protest are asking only for the refunds accruing on protested checks.

The justices contend that they are entitled to $12,000 a year under a salary fixation resolution adopted by the Board of Estimate in 1927 which, they allege, was never amended. From July 1, 1937, to July 1, 1939, they were paid at the rate of $10,840 a year and since July 1 have been receiving $9,756.

In order to cut their pay legally, they contend, the Board of Estimate should have amended the 1927 resolution.

An action brought by secretaries to the justices to void pay reductions contained in the new budget for the present fiscal year was recently dismissed by Supreme Court Justice J. Sidney Bernstein and is now on appeal to the Appellate Division. The pay of the secretaries was reduced from $3,240 a year to $1,200.

Commenting on the action, Mayor La Guardia said yesterday as he was leaving City Hall:

"There is no question of law. But if I had the money I would certainly like to pay something more to many of the technical experts in city departments, some of whom are earning as low as $900 and $1,200 a year and doing very fine service."

The justices' suit is scheduled for a hearing next Wednesday.

A second action has been brought by six copyists in the Kings County Register's office to compel the city to provide for them in the current budget. They were receiving from $2,100 to $2,220 annually prior to July 1. Since then, although no provision for them is made in the budget, three have been notified that they will get $1,800 a year, two $1,621, and the sixth has received no notification. Their action will be heard next Thursday.

GERMANS IN TURKEY ARE FACING RECALL

Get Orders to Be Ready to Go at Any Time—Nazis Warn Balkans to Be Neutral

By The United Press.

ISTANBUL, Turkey, Nov. 2—German authorities tonight ordered all German nationals to be ready to leave Turkey "as soon as possible."

The German Ambassador to Turkey, Franz von Papen, is on the way back to Angora from Berlin, where he has been in conferences with Chancellor Hitler and other Nazi leaders for ten days. Herr von Papen was presumed to have been summoned to Berlin to report on Turkey's failure to reach a mutual-aid pact with Russia and her decision to enter into such a treaty with Britain and France.

Hasty preparations for departure were evident among German residents, the number of whom has increased steadily since the World War, in which Turkey was an ally of Germany. After the suspension of the Turkish-Soviet talks and announcement of Turkey's pact with Britain and France considerable apprehension was evident among the German residents.

Some Have Already Gone

Some already have left Turkey and others have sent luggage and belongings to Germany.

[Germany and Russia have been highly critical of Turkey since she signed the pact with Britain and France. The Nazi press has declared that Turkey will regret her decision and has said that the Turkish Government can no longer be considered neutral. Premier-Foreign Commissar Vyacheslaff M. Molotoff of Russia, in his speech Tuesday night outlining Russian foreign policy, took about the same attitude, saying that Turkey's action had put her "in the orbit of war."]

Ismet Inonu, President of Turkey, said in a speech last night opening the Turkish Parliament at Angora that Turkey still was striving for friendship with Russia but relied on her armed forces to guard Turkish independence and integrity. He said the pact with Britain and France was designed to bulwark peace in the Eastern Mediterranean.

Turkish political circles appeared to have been favorably impressed by a friendly gesture on the part of the Rome radio, which, on the occasion of the Turkish republic's recent anniversary, extended congratulations, played the Turkish national anthem and conducted a program in Turkish. It was the first time Italy had made such a friendly gesture toward Turkey in several years.

Nazi Press Warning to Balkans

BERLIN, Friday, Nov. 3 (UP)—The Frankfurter Zeitung published today a warning to the Balkan powers that they would risk the fate of Poland if they should follow Turkey in shifting to the side of the Allies.

"The decision lies primarily with the Balkan States themselves," the newspaper said. "One can be sure that they will not agree to the path that Turkey has chosen. Their wish for neutrality is quite genuine, whether from love of peace or because of the warning example of Poland."

Since the conclusion of the Turk-

Continued on Page Eight

FINNS IN MOSCOW WITH FINAL OFFER

Unyielding on Questions of National Integrity—Soviet Sees 'War Threat'

By G. E. R. GEDYE
Wireless to THE NEW YORK TIMES.

MOSCOW, Nov. 2—The Finnish delegation returned to Moscow this morning—headed by Dr. Juho K. Paasikivi and composed as before, with the addition of R. Hakkarainen, Finnish Chief of Protocol. The members were met at the railroad station at 10:30 A. M. by Vladimir Barkoff, Soviet Chief of Protocol, and the Swedish, Norwegian and Danish Ministers.

It was decided that there would be no meeting with Joseph Stalin and Premier Vyacheslaff Molotoff today as the delegation was busy preparing a translation of final documents. The Finns this evening attended as spectators, accompanied by Mr. Barkoff, the session of the Supreme Soviet, which was devoted to a reception of the White Russian delegation from the former Polish White Russian region.

Information from Helsinki indicates that the Finns are bringing with them their final offer, and apparently they are now willing to meet the Soviet Union to a considerable extent concerning demands for the cession of territory that Moscow claims is essential for the defense of Leningrad.

Finns Not Wholly Yielding

It is believed Finland is willing to cede Hogland and other islands off Kronstadt and further to meet the Soviet Union on the question of the cession of territory in the extreme north of Finland. What the Finns apparently feel unable to do—virtually destroy their independence—is to lease the port of Hangoe to the Soviet Government for the establishment of a Soviet base there. Rather than do this the Finns would prefer to fight.

[A Moscow broadcast intercepted in London this morning said that Finnish Foreign Minister Eljas Erkko in his speech Wednesday had "delivered an open threat of war against the Soviet Union," according to a United Press dispatch. The broadcast also said that comments in Finnish newspapers on Premier Molotoff's address to the Supreme Soviet were of a "hostile nature."]

Despite the alarming character of passages in Premier Molotoff's speech to the Supreme Soviet, in regard to Finland, the Finns seem to believe the Soviet Union will recognize the extent of their concessions as generous and conclude a peaceful agreement rather than proceed to extremes.

There has been constant contact since their arrival between members of the Finnish delegation and the three other Scandinavian Legations. In Scandinavian circles generally every one is looking toward Sweden for an indication of her final attitude, for it is felt unlikely that she has yet said her last word.

Norwegians, Finns and Danes alike feel that Sweden is at a turning point in her history. A definite decision by Sweden to maintain under all circumstances the solidarity of the Scandinavian bloc, it is felt, would stabilize the situation and definitely avert any possibility of a conflict.

Most other Scandinavians and many Swedes feel that Sweden must recognize that cession of Han-

Continued on Page Seven

JAPANESE DECLARE PEACE ASKED BY U.S. IN EAST IMPOSSIBLE

Washington's Aims Also Held Undesirable as Seeking to Perpetuate Inequality

RISK TO TRADE PACT SEEN

Tokyo Is Expected to Abandon Renewal Rather Than Give Up Claims in China

By The Associated Press.

TOKYO, Nov. 2—The Institute of the Pacific, whose membership includes many high-ranking Japanese, issued a statement today declaring that the United States desires a kind of peace which "not only is undesirable but impossible to maintain."

The statement was published as a reply to the Oct. 19 speech in which United States Ambassador Joseph C. Grew said public opinion in the United States deeply resented actions of the Japanese Army in China.

"The first prerequisite to fair and objective understanding must be recognition that hostilities on a large scale now are in progress in China," said the declaration.

It asserted that the United States was attempting to perpetuate a system "which ignores the desire of all peoples of the world to develop by fairly sharing all the fruits and opportunities offered by mother earth." Therefore, it continued, America advocates peace and the maintenance of the status quo.

"Such a peace not only is undesirable but impossible to maintain," the declaration asserted. "We cannot but note the glaring omission of the word 'justice' in the Ambassador's eloquent plea for peace."

Hopes for Better Relations

TOKYO, Nov. 2 (UP)—Former Foreign Minister Kenkichi Yoshizawa, a director, like Premier Nobuyuki Abe, of the Institute of the Pacific, supplemented its declaration in an interview today. He said that he believed the Japanese Government appreciated the seriousness of American problems and expressed confidence that the Foreign Office would do its best to improve relations.

The Cabinet is preoccupied at present with problems concerning China, particularly the proposed establishment of a Japanese-dominated "central Chinese government" under former Premier Wang Ching-wei.

Constantin Smetanin, new Russian Ambassador, was expected to arrive tomorrow from Moscow with detailed instructions bearing on Japanese-Russian relations.

Persons close to Premier Abe said that the government has decided to clarify Japan's program in China by a series of "unmistakable deeds" and believes that after this clarification the empire's broad foreign policy can be determined rapidly. The China program was outlined as follows:

The new Japan-sponsored regime will be launched this month in Nanking and statements will be made to show definitely that this government is to be independent in fact as well as in theory.

No Japanese political advisers will be attached to the new regime, but Japan will be prepared to furnish financial advisers if the Wang administration so desires.

Japan will give immediate diplomatic recognition to the new government and will appoint an Ambassador to Nanking at once.

The informants understood that

Continued on Page Twelve

VOTE ANGERS REICH

Embargo End Held to Mean Direct Support to Foes of Nazis

U-BOAT DRIVE TO WIDEN

Sinking of Many Ships and Dragging Us Into War Is Predicted in Germany

By The United Press.

BERLIN, Nov. 2—Angry Nazis tonight accused the United States of giving "outright support" to Great Britain and France by repeal of the arms embargo.

Official quarters declined to comment for publication until there was time to study the full effects of the legislation, but well-informed individuals left no doubt as to the reaction of the average German to the repeal vote in the House of Representatives.

Nazi quarters, foreseeing heavy British and French orders for American arms and munitions, warned that German U-boats probably will intensify their activities in the Atlantic in an effort to sink as many arms-carrying ships as possible.

Both the Foreign Office and the Propaganda Ministry said that the lifting of the embargo "was no surprise and was to be expected."

Official comment will be withheld, it was explained, until there is time to examine the full significance of the United States Government's move.

But from the tone of Nazi press comment in recent days on the embargo question it is certain that Congress's decision will be assailed bitterly by Nazi spokesmen and newspapers in much the same manner that Vyacheslaff M. Molotoff, Soviet Premier and Foreign Commissar, struck at it in his Tuesday night speech before the Supreme Soviet in Moscow.

The Nazi press has charged that repeal of the mandatory arms embargo would favor only the Allies and threatens to "drag the United States into the war."

News of the repeal of the embargo was received in Berlin by radio at 11 P. M.

Hostility to Roosevelt Renewed

Wireless to THE NEW YORK TIMES.

BERLIN, Nov. 2—Passage by the American Senate of the new Neutrality Law, embracing the cash and carry clause, has revived in the German press the attitude of hostility toward President Roosevelt which had been noticeably lacking in the past several months. Mr. Roosevelt, in the opinion of German editors, is on the same path which President Wilson took and which led America into the World War.

The Senate's action is capable of two commentaries, writes the Boersen Zeitung: The first that echoed in the British and French press that passage of the new neutrality bill in the upper house represents the "first and decisive victory of the Allies" made possible by Mr. Roosevelt; the second is that Mr. Roosevelt's Chautauqua speech—

Continued on Page Three

Allies to Buy 7,800 Planes Here; British Mission Is Expected Soon

Rush of Orders Is Foreseen Within a Few Weeks—Trucks, Clothing, Foodstuffs Are Among Many Needed Products

By The Associated Press.

WASHINGTON, Nov. 2—A flood of European war orders which Administration quarters expect will total $1,000,000,000 in the next few weeks, will be released by repeal of the arms embargo.

Even before the House action today a French purchasing mission contracted for 4,600 aircraft motors from two Eastern manufacturers at a price of about $50,000,000, officials were informed. A British mission, meanwhile, has been negotiating for some 1,600 training planes.

The arms embargo halted delivery on some 600 aircraft early in September. In addition to these, the French contemplate purchases of some 3,800 planes and the British 4,000, it was reported authoritatively. A Swedish mission has been negotiating for upward of 250 aircraft and a Belgian mission for 200.

The British-French allies have stressed their need for war planes of all types, but their purchases are expected to cover a wide range of other products, including:

Motor trucks and motor cycles, clothing, machine tools, field ranges, explosives, foodstuffs, surgical instruments, hospital supplies, searchlights, gas masks, pontoon equipment, water-purifying units, ambulances, tents, saddles, telephones and radio compasses.

An immediate effect of formal repeal of the embargo will be to permit delivery of some 300 war planes for Britain and France which have been completed since the embargo was imposed.

Presumably, it will mean immediate reinstatement of export licenses for planes and other munitions which were canceled. The impounded orders were valued at $14,680,807 for Great Britain and $56,265,739 for France.

Thus far the British and French purchases apparently have not been coordinated as were the allied purchases toward the end of the 1914-18 war, but measures to avoid competition between the two buyers are anticipated shortly.

A British purchasing mission headed by Lieut. Col. J. H. M. Greenly, an official of the British industrial firm of Babcock & Wilcox, Ltd., has been at Montreal, but is expected to transfer its principal activities to New York.

While Congress debated the neu-

Continued on Page Three

BRITISH GRATIFIED, AWAIT OUR ARMS

Repeal of Embargo, However, Means Sharp Cut in Imports of Other American Goods

By The United Press.

LONDON, Nov. 2—Official British quarters tonight received with enthusiasm the word that the American Congress had voted to lift the arms embargo. It was stated that as a result it might be expected that the United States would release "hundreds" of reconnaissance land planes, fighters, light bombers and flying boats awaiting shipment from New York and California.

"It means an unlimited supply of fighting and bombing planes is available to the Allies," an aircraft expert said. "United States manufacturing facilities in this respect never have been actually tested, but are so far beyond anything ever conceived that there is no limit to the supply available."

Referring to German assertions that the British would have trouble in "getting the stuff across," it was said that elaborate arrangements had been made to begin transportation immediately.

It was indicated that the flying boats would be flown to Britain and France direct from the United States.

Among the planes already ordered and understood to be ready for delivery were eighty twin-engined Lockheed reconnaissance bombers for Britain.

There are 100 twin-engined Douglas bombers and 215 Glenn Martin bombers on order for France.

Fund Arrangements Reported

It was stated that future British orders probably would be chiefly for long-range reconnaissance land planes and flying boats, while France would buy fighters and light reconnaissance bombers.

It was reported here that unlimited dollar exchange had been provided to insure immediate and continued shipments.

On the other hand the revision of the United States arms embargo law, while opening the way for arms and munitions purchases, is expected to cause a sharp curtailment of other British imports from the United States.

One source estimated that British imports of some American industrial products and foodstuffs might drop as much as $150,000,000 a year.

The curtailment would be necessary, it was said, to protect exchange and permit unlimited purchases of arms and munitions from the United States.

The importation of many American commodities, including tobacco, automobiles, women's apparel, shoes, hosiery, dried fruits and California barley, already has been reduced since the war began.

The estimated income of the American film industry from the European market, it is understood,

Continued on Page Three

DIES TO TRACE REDS IN SHIPPING UNION

Committee Asks FBI to Produce Man Called Soviet Agent and Power on West Coast

By CHARLES W. HURD
Special to THE NEW YORK TIMES.

WASHINGTON, Nov. 2—A broad investigation of Communist infiltration and control over seamen in the United States merchant marine was voted today by the House Committee to Investigate un-American Activities, coincident with testimony by Frederick C. Phillips, former official of the National Maritime Union, who charged that he was ousted from office because of his opposition to communism.

Phillips, who gave his home as 350 West Fifty-fifth Street, New York City, tended to corroborate William C. McCuistion, another former officer of the N. M. U. Phillips, however, ascribed his difficulties in the union to consistent opposition to Communist control, while McCuistion called himself a former Communist who had turned against the party.

The committee sent Phillips, as it had McCuistion, to the Department of Justice to determine whether his civil liberties had been infringed by the union.

The committee also instructed Rhea Whitley, its counsel, to request the Federal Bureau of Investigation to produce for questioning a man identified as George Mink, whom McCuistion had described as agent in the United States for the GPU of the Soviet Government and "a power in shipping on the West Coast."

These steps by the committee were planned while it still had in its files the names of a long list of other witnesses. At the conclusion of the study of maritime conditions here, Representative Dies plans to go to New Orleans to investigate N. M. U. affairs there.

McCuistion, meanwhile, remained in custody of police here, following his arrest at the request of the police in New Orleans in connection with the slaying there in September of Philip Carey, an official of the N. M. U.

Phillips Tells of Union Rows

Phillips told the committee of conflict within the union and of an attempt on his life after he was ousted by the alleged Communist faction, among which he named Joseph Curran, president of the union.

The attack on him, Phillips said, was made on West Twenty-third Street, in New York City, "with lead pipes," and "probably would

Continued on Page Fourteen

Dispatches from Europe and the Far East are subject to censorship.

OPPONENTS ROUTED

Chamber Rejects Modified and Outright Arms Bans and a Loan Curb

MAJORITY SIZE A SURPRISE

Elated Leaders Send Bill to Conference—It Is Expected to Be Law by Tomorrow

By TURNER CATLEDGE
Special to THE NEW YORK TIMES.

WASHINGTON, Nov. 2—The doom of the embargo against shipment of arms and munitions to warring nations was sealed late today when the House, by majorities surpassing the hopes of Administration leaders, virtually approved the Pittman neutrality resolution as passed by the Senate on Friday. The vote on final passage was 243 to 181, which came in rejection of a motion by Representative Shanley, Democrat of Connecticut, to instruct the House conferees to demand a full arms embargo.

Having withstood three assaults from the House's embargo advocates by favorable margins of 32, 66 and 62 votes, the measure was sent tonight to a conference committee, where the members from the lower body will quickly agree to the basic Senate provisions—repeal of the arms ban and substitution of a modified cash-and-carry plan for future commerce between the United States and belligerents.

Senator Pittman, author of the resolution, called a meeting of the conference tomorrow morning. His purpose was to compose the remaining differences between the versions of the two houses so final action might be taken by each body in time to send the measure to the White House for President Roosevelt's signature tomorrow night or Saturday at the latest.

Little Alteration Expected

The measure as sent to conference, and not expected to be substantially altered, is the same as printed in THE NEW YORK TIMES of Saturday. Technically the House "disagreed" to the measure, in the form of an amendment to the Bloom resolution as passed in the House last June, but this technicality will not stand in the way of an agreement on its essential provisions tomorrow, inasmuch as the House refused today to instruct its conferees to "insist" on its own language.

Administration leaders planned to seek adjournment of the special session as soon as the neutrality resolution has been finally disposed of. They claimed sufficient votes to dissolve the session despite a Republican move to keep Congress in Washington for the duration of the war abroad.

It is expected, however, that the President will renew his request for leaders of the two major parties to remain at the Capital between now and the regular session in January in order that he may consult them frequently "on the course of events in foreign affairs and on the need for future action in this field, whether it be executive or legislative action."

Today's vote in the House, which came after another four and one-half hours of debate, ended, for all intents and purposes, Congress's consideration of a new Neutrality Act, as requested by the President in a message to the special session upon its convening six weeks ago today.

Galleries Are Packed

Although it was a weary, worn body which came to the final stage, these semi-final proceedings were among the high spots of the entire session, both in terms of debate and action. More members were on the floor and answered to their names than at any time in months, while visitors crowded the galleries. A score or more of Senators availed themselves of the floor to witness the finish in the House contest.

The votes came on motions of repeal opponents to instruct the House conferees: First, to insist upon retention of the embargo; second, to seek a compromise that would prohibit the shipment of lethal weapons and poisonous gas to belligerents abroad, and third, to demand further safeguards against the credit being extended for the aid of exports from the United States to any nation at war.

The first roll-call came on the latter proposal—an amendment by Representative Wolcott of Michigan demanding that the House man-

Continued on Page Two

Vatican Reports Lwow Archbishop Killed By Russians, Whose Invasion He Opposed

By Telephone to THE NEW YORK TIMES.

ROME, Nov. 2—The Vatican's Secretariat of State received confirmation today that Mgr. Andreas Szeptycki, the Archbishop of Lwow, had been killed by Russians. As head of the hierarchy of Catholics of the Ruthenian rite, he was hostile to the absorption of Polish Ukraine by the Russians. At the same time, he was leader of the intellectual Ukrainian autonomists.

The Most Rev. Count Andreas Szeptycki, Archbishop of Lwow, was a descendant of a Polish family dating from the fourteenth century. He had held high ecclesiastical office under both the Austro-Hungarian Empire and the Polish Republic.

Leading a flock of mainly Ukrainian origin, Archbishop Szeptycki, before the partition of Poland by the German and Russian invaders, was looked upon by the Polish Government with some hostility because of his connection with the Ukrainian autonomist movement. In 1930, a pastoral letter of his composition was seized by the Polish authorities, who charged that it contained "inflammatory passages" criticizing the government's means of dealing with unrest in Eastern Galicia.

Before the World War Archbishop Szeptycki was a private councilor to Emperor Francis Joseph of Austria, a Vice Marshal of Galicia and a member of the Imperial House of Lords. When the Russians captured Lemberg (Lwow) during the conflict, he was imprisoned in the Suzdal ecclesiastical prison in Russia by order of General Brusiloff. He remained there until he was released by the Bolshevist revolution.

Six feet six and a half inches tall, the Archbishop was a man of vast energy, and at one time was known as the "traveling Archbishop," because of his journeys in all parts of Europe. He was a Doctor of Philosophy, of Law and of Theology of the University of Cracow. A former soldier, he became a monk of the Basilian Order after having completed his military service.

The Archbishop visited the United States in 1910 and again at the end of 1921.